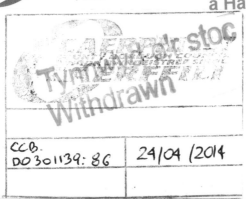

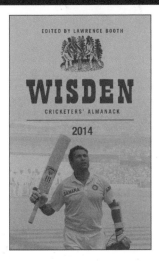

WISDEN

CRICKETERS' ALMANACK

2014

EDITED BY LAWRENCE BOOTH

WISDEN

CRICKETERS' ALMANACK

2014

151st EDITION

John Wisden & Co

An imprint of Bloomsbury Publishing Plc

JOHN WISDEN & CO
An imprint of Bloomsbury Publishing Plc
50 Bedford Square, London WC1B 3DP

WISDEN CRICKETERS' ALMANACK
Editor **Lawrence Booth**
Co-editor **Hugh Chevallier**
Deputy editors **Steven Lynch** and **Harriet Monkhouse**
Assistant editor **James Coyne**
Contributing editor **Richard Whitehead**
Production co-ordinator **Peter Bather**
Chief statistician **Philip Bailey**
Proofreader **Charles Barr**
Database and typesetting **Stephen Cubitt**
Publisher **Charlotte Atyeo**
Consultant publisher **Christopher Lane**

Reader feedback: almanack@wisden.com

www.wisden.com

www.wisdenrecords.com

Follow Wisden on Twitter @WisdenAlmanack
and on Facebook at Wisden Sports

Typeset in Times New Roman and Univers by David Lewis XML Associates, Bungay NR35 1JB
Printed by CPI Group (UK) Ltd, Croydon CR0 4YY

A CIP catalogue record for this book is available from the British Library

"Wisden" and its woodcut device are registered trademarks of John Wisden & Co

© John Wisden & Co 2014
Published by John Wisden & Co, an imprint of Bloomsbury Publishing Plc, 2014

EDITIONS

Cased ISBN 978-1-408175-68-2 £50
Soft cover ISBN 978-1-408175-66-8 £50
Large format ISBN 978-1-408175-67-5 £60
Leatherbound ISBN 978-1-472910-39-4 £275

A Taste of Wisden 2014

"He may have taken 19 wickets in a Test match," said the PC,
"but nobody nicks my changing place." It was generally agreed
that Jim was bang to rights for "taking without consent".
Stars that shone beside the slag heaps, page 76

* * *

Bonus points are awarded for writing one of the very few books
published anywhere in the world in 2013 without a subtitle.
Cricket Books, page 143

* * *

Growing up in Ireland with a passion for cricket is to know
"a love that dare not speak its name".
Cricket People, page 182

* * *

He joined his captain on a tiger shoot and,
alarmed at his inaccuracy, exclaimed:
"Good Lord, you've shot the bloody goat."
Obituaries, page 210

* * *

It was an absurdity, like going back to the same restaurant
a month later just for the pudding.
England v New Zealand, 2013, page 283

* * *

Heard the one about the Englishman, the Irishman and the
Zimbabwean? They all made their first Test appearance in the
same match for the same team.
Australia v England, 2013-14, Fifth Test, page 409

* * *

In 11 seasons of the format, the two most successful batsmen
thus came from Leicester, and the two most successful bowlers
from Rawalpindi.
Friends Life t20, 2013, page 702

* * *

Knight had to be helped off the pitch, but at the end
was wheeled around the ground on an equipment trolley by
her exultant team-mates.
The Women's Ashes, 2013, page 839

6

LIST OF CONTRIBUTORS

Timothy Abraham
Andrew Alderson
Tanya Aldred
David Rayvern Allen
Chris Aspin
James Astill
Mike Atherton
Philip August
Ali Bacher
Stephen Baldwin
Greg Baum
Benedict Bermange
Edward Bevan
Paul Bolton
Richard Boock
Mark Boucher
Stephen Brenkley
Daniel Brettig
Liam Brickhill
Tim Brooks
Colin Bryden
Ian Callender
Aakash Chopra
Giles Clarke
Simon Cleaves
Rex Clementine
David Clough
Paul Coupar
Brydon Coverdale
Tony Cozier
Liam Cromar
Martin Crowe
John Curtis
Shamya Dasgupta
Geoffrey Dean
Tim de Lisle
Ralph Dellor
Norman de Mesquita
William Dick
George Dobell
Philip Eden
Paul Edwards
Vithushan Ehantharajah
Mark Eklid

Matthew Engel
Peter English
John Etheridge
Colin Evans
Melinda Farrell
Andrew Fernando
Warwick Franks
David Frith
Alan Gardner
Mark Geenty
Peter Gibbs
Pat Gibson
Richard Gibson
Haydn Gill
Richard Gillis
Nagraj Gollapudi
Julian Guyer
Gideon Haigh
Duncan Hamilton
Kevin Hand
David Hardy
Douglas Henderson
Paul Hiscock
Richard Hobson
Myles Hodgson
Tristan Holme
David Hopps
Steve James
Paul Jones
David Jordan
R. Kaushik
Abid Ali Kazi
Patrick Kidd
Jarrod Kimber
Paul King
Malcolm Knox
Stephen Lamb
Richard Latham
Jonathan Liew
Andrew McGlashan
Neil Manthorp
Vic Marks
Ali Martin
Alison Mitchell

R. Mohan
Benj Moorehead
Makhaya Ntini
Mark Pennell
Derek Pringle
Qamar Ahmed
Andrew Radd
S. A. Rennie
Andrew Renshaw
Chloe Saltau
Osman Samiuddin
Faraz Sarwat
Neville Scott
Shahid Hashmi
Utpal Shuvro
Mehluli Sibanda
Ed Smith
Giles Smith
Rob Smyth
Richard Spiller
John Stern
Fraser Stewart
Andy Stockhausen
Chris Stocks
Pat Symes
Bruce Talbot
Sa'adi Thawfeeq
John Townsend
Alan Tyers
Sharda Ugra
Tunku Varadarajan
Anand Vasu
Telford Vice
Mike Walters
John Ward
David Warner
Chris Waters
Tim Wellock
John Westerby
Tim Wigmore
Simon Wilde
Martin Williamson
Dean Wilson
Andrew Wu

Photographers are credited as appropriate. Special thanks to Patrick Eagar, Graham Morris, Philip Brown and Roger Mann. **Cartoons** by Nick Newman. Contributors to the **Round the World** section are listed after their articles.

The editor also acknowledges with gratitude assistance from the following: Robin Abrahams, Stephen Anthony, Derek Barnard, Mike Bechley, Trevor Bedells, Abi Carter, Marion Collin, Brian Croudy, Prakash Dahatonde, Tennyson Davey, Nigel Davies, Ted Dexter, Frank Duckworth, Gulu Ezekiel, M. L. Fernando, Ric Finlay, Alan Fordham, Ghulam Mustafa Khan, Richard Holdridge, Julia and John Hunt, David Kendix, Rajesh Kumar, David Lamming, Karen Lee, David Lewis, Tony Lewis, Edward Liddle, Nirav Malavi, Mahendra Mapagunaratne, Mohammad Isam, Anne-Elisabeth Moutet, Dawn Newman, Francis Payne, Joseph Price, Neil Priscott, Andrew Samson, Shahriar Khan, David Sherman, Clare Skinner, Michael Sparrow, Steven Stern, Pete Stonier, Jeremy Tagg, Diane Valli, Chris Walmsley, Charlie Wat, Andrew Wells, Jean Whipps, Beth Wild and Alan Williams.

The production of *Wisden* would not be possible without the support and co-operation of many other cricket officials, county scorers, writers and lovers of the game. To them all, many thanks.

PREFACE

One of the many assumptions Sachin Tendulkar called into question was the first part of historian Greg Dening's claim that "nothing is so fleeting as sporting achievement, and nothing so lasting as the recollection of it". At a time when cricket is in danger of becoming a playground for men in suits, it's a pleasure to point out that the largest chunk of our Comment section is devoted to a man who was more interested in cover-drives. Tendulkar ended up being a reflection of modern India: he had more sponsors than an IPL kit, and his final Test series was hijacked by boardroom wheeler-dealing. Yet precisely because he was anything *but* fleeting, he encouraged cricket lovers to recall gentler times. We hope Dening was right about the second bit.

Five men remembered in Obituaries conjure up gentler times too. Christopher Martin-Jenkins was mentioned here last year, while Frank Keating, Gerald Mortimer (formerly *Wisden's* Derbyshire correspondent), Norman de Mesquita (who died during his 21st summer as our Middlesex man) and Dicky Rutnagur all wrote about the game when the game was the thing to write about. Next year's Almanack will include a section, rather like the one that appeared in *Wisden 1994*, that aims to correct our errors and omissions. Please let us know of possible entries – see page 230 for details.

We are occasionally asked why we run statistics relating to cricketers or matches known or believed to be suspect – and usually plead the can-of-worms defence. But, as of this year, our Records section will be preceded by a list of players who have been banned for corruption or have admitted to some form of on-field corruption. It is the simplest way of allowing readers to reach their own conclusions, without compromising the wider set of statistics: it takes skill to score runs off a no-ball, even if the no-ball is deliberate.

A number of late developments in 2014 placed an additional burden on our editorial team, and I'm grateful as ever for their terrific diligence. Hugh Chevallier was his customary calm, affable self; Harriet Monkhouse remained the last word in sub-editing; Steven Lynch's dedication was remarkable; and James Coyne was the junior member in age only. Christopher Lane oozed good advice.

Thanks also go to our colleagues at Bloomsbury, especially Charlotte Atyeo, Richard Charkin and Lizzy Ewer, who has helped us with our regular online magazine *Wisden EXTRA*. Along with *The Nightwatchman*, the magazine continues to provide a home for quality long-form cricket writing. To our production co-ordinator Peter Bather, our statistician Philip Bailey, our typesetters Stephen Cubitt and Mike Hatt at DLXML, and our contributing editor Richard Whitehead, many thanks.

I am grateful once more to the sports desk of the *Daily Mail*. Head of sport Lee Clayton, sports editor Les Snowdon and cricket correspondent Paul Newman have been typically generous in their support. And special thanks go to Anjali Doshi, for her advice and affection.

LAWRENCE BOOTH
Earlsfield, February 2014

CONTENTS

Part One – Comment

Part Two – The Wisden Review

Contents

Part Three – English International Cricket

Part Four – English Domestic Cricket

STATISTICS

LV= COUNTY CHAMPIONSHIP

ONE-DAY COUNTY COMPETITIONS

Part Five – Overseas Cricket

SYMBOLS AND ABBREVIATIONS

*	In full scorecards and lists of tour parties signifies the captain. In short scorecards, averages and records signifies not out.
†	In full scorecards signifies the designated wicketkeeper. In averages signifies a left-handed batsman.
‡	In short scorecards signifies the team who won the toss.
MoM/PoM	In short scorecards signifies the Man/Player of the Match.
MoS/PoS	In short scorecards signifies the Man/Player of the Series.
D/L	Signifies where a result has been decided under the Duckworth/Lewis method for curtailed matches.

Other uses of symbols are explained in notes where they appear.

FIRST-CLASS MATCHES

Men's matches of three or more days' duration are first-class unless otherwise stated. All other matches are not first-class, including one-day and Twenty20 internationals.

SCORECARDS

Where full scorecards are not provided in this book, they can be found at Cricket Archive (www.cricketarchive.co.uk) or ESPNcricinfo (www.cricinfo.com). Full scorecards from matches played overseas can also be found in the relevant *ACS Overseas First-Class Annuals*.

RECORDS

The entire Records section (pages 1253–1395) can now be found at www.wisdenrecords.com. The online Records database is regularly updated and, in many instances, more detailed than in *Wisden 2014*. Further information on past winners of tournaments covered in this book can be found at www.wisden.com/almanacklinks

PART ONE

Comment

Wisden Honours

THE LEADING CRICKETER IN THE WORLD

Dale Steyn (page 65)

The Leading Cricketer in the World is chosen by the editor of *Wisden* in consultation with some of the world's most experienced cricket writers and commentators. The selection is based on a player's class and form shown in all cricket during the calendar year, and is merely guided by statistics rather than governed by them. There is no limit to how many times a player may be chosen. A notional list of past winners, backdated to 1900, appeared on page 35 of *Wisden 2007*.

FIVE CRICKETERS OF THE YEAR

Shikhar Dhawan (page 97)
Charlotte Edwards (page 99)
Ryan Harris (page 101)
Chris Rogers (page 103)
Joe Root (page 106)

The Five Cricketers of the Year are chosen by the editor of *Wisden*, and represent a tradition that dates back to 1889, making this the oldest individual award in cricket. Excellence in and/or influence on the previous English summer are the major criteria for inclusion as a Cricketer of the Year. No one can be chosen more than once. A list of past winners can be found on page 1508.

WISDEN SCHOOLS CRICKETER OF THE YEAR

Tom Köhler-Cadmore (page 794)

The Schools Cricketer of the Year, based on first-team performances during the previous English summer, is chosen by *Wisden's* schools correspondent in consultation with the editor of *Wisden* and other experienced observers of schools cricket. The winner's school must be in the UK, play cricket to a standard approved by *Wisden's* schools correspondent, and provide reports to this Almanack. A list of past winners can be found on page 796.

WISDEN BOOK OF THE YEAR

Driving Ambition by Andrew Strauss (page 146)

The Book of the Year is selected by *Wisden's* guest reviewer; all cricket books published in the previous calendar year and submitted to *Wisden* for possible review are eligible. A list of past winners can be found on page 150.

WISDEN–MCC CRICKET PHOTOGRAPH OF THE YEAR

was won by Atul Kamble (whose entry appears opposite page 64)

The Wisden–MCC Cricket Photograph of the Year is chosen by a panel of independent experts; all images on a cricket theme photographed in the previous calendar year are eligible.

WISDEN'S WRITING COMPETITION

was won by Liam Cromar (page 119)

Wisden's Writing Competition is open to anyone who has not been commissioned to write for the Almanack. Full details appear on page 120.

Full details of past winners of all these honours can be found at www.wisden.com

NOTES BY THE EDITOR

In *Monty Python's Life of Brian*, Judith is fretting over her lover's impending crucifixion. But her colleagues in the People's Front of Judea – faced with a proper test of their principles after endless procrastination – are too busy watching their own backs. "It's happening, Reg!" she wails. "Something's actually happening!"

The opaque world of cricket politics has long been ripe for satire, but sometimes the facts speak for themselves. And, earlier this year, in another corner of the Middle East, something was definitely happening. The boards of India, England and Australia had quietly crafted a document which claimed to safeguard the game's future, while more obviously safeguarding their own.

In sum, the BCCI wanted an even larger slice of the ICC pie, and the ECB and Cricket Australia happily acquiesced, knowing their portion would grow too. The rest were assured they would be better off. And who could object to a world with more money for everyone?

The politicking that followed, defined by self-interest and short-termism, would have done the People's Front proud. Boards excluded by the Big Three professed outrage in public and jockeyed for position in private, forming alliances that lasted only as long as it took India to seduce them with some trinket or other. Even on February 8, when the thrust of the document was voted through by the ICC Board, Pakistan – who abstained, with Sri Lanka – were accusing South Africa of treachery, having apparently regarded them as allies on February 7. "Nothing in life is perfect," sighed Chris Nenzani, the president of the South African board, almost sounding as if he regretted the fact. Here was colonial-style divide and rule. Here was the realpolitik of modern cricket.

Amid the prognostications of a brave new world, a single sentence, halfway down the ICC's press release (and with our italics), hinted at what lay ahead: "Full Members will gain greater financial recognition based on the contribution they have made to the game, *particularly in terms of finance*, their ICC history and their on-field performances in the three formats."

It was hard to read this any other way: the rich would be getting a whole lot richer. For decades, the rest of world cricket had looked askance at the two phases of the game's imperialism: the veto held until 1993 by England and Australia (based on ancient history), then India's monetary clout (based on a huge population). Now, the also-rans sanctioned a combination of both, knowing they had little choice. Only cricket could move back in time while hailing a revolution.

As the BCCI promised sweeteners to countries who sensed trouble, it was possible to foresee a scenario in which their cricketers actually played more often, though mostly – for the benefit of Indian TV – at home. But the leaking of the document's draft, to journalists at the Abu Dhabi-based *National* newspaper and the ESPNcricinfo website, had already allowed in more light than the Indians – and their English and Australian lapdogs – intended. After all, a draft may reveal the true motivation, before compromise reins it in.

At its heart lay the BCCI's desire not merely to oust the ICC as the game's governing body, but to wean themselves, eventually, off all but the most lucrative international fixtures, and so create more space for domestic Twenty20. It was no coincidence that one of the brains behind the paper was the chief operating officer of the IPL, Sundar Raman, the world game's Cardinal Richelieu. We await the day we are told cricket's pinnacle is Mumbai Indians v Chennai Super Kings.

Once the initial glow subsides and India have honoured their quid pro quos, the consequences for the less lucrative nations could be catastrophic. Already damned as "uneconomic" – contemporary cricket's death sentence – they will risk losing players in even greater numbers to an expanded IPL. Their ability to compete with the richest sides will diminish, further eroding the first principle of any sport: the need for an opposition. What purpose will the proposed Test-match fund serve if fewer teams see the point of Test matches?

There was actually some sense within the document's pages. The draft suggested two divisions of eight teams, which seemed reasonable; Test cricket is indeed in desperate straits; and it's true that the free-marketeers had not found an answer to the conundrum by which India generated four-fifths of the game's income while subsidising Zimbabwe.

But the idea of two divisions was spoiled by the proviso that India, England and Australia could not be relegated – another slap in the face for good governance. And when Bangladesh objected to their presence in the lower tier, the prospect of relegation was shelved anyway. As for enriching the richest, this seemed a strange way of resolving an imperfect situation. (On the plus side, the likes of Ireland and Afghanistan can now qualify for Test status, though not full membership of the ICC: that would mean less money for the rest.)

It's true that many of the poorer boards are basket cases: Pakistan and Sri Lanka remain hopelessly politicised, South Africa are only just recovering from a financial scandal, and Zimbabwe are in tatters. But this is not in itself reason to entrench plutocracy by dressing it up as meritocracy.

Cricket is appallingly administered, and is vulnerable to economic exploitation by the one country powerful enough to exploit it and the two countries prepared to lend their plans credibility. But it will become less of a sport, more of a business. Its future health relies not only on the willingness of the smaller nations to get their own houses in order, but also on some form of benevolent dictatorship. The benevolence could do with some work.

With leaders like these…

According to their website, the ICC are "the international governing body for cricket". It's a lovely thought. But it doesn't quite tally with one of the "key principles" that emerged from the horse-trading: "Recognition of the need for strong leadership of the ICC, involving leading members, which will involve BCCI taking a central leadership responsibility."

At least this had the virtue of coming clean. And it confirmed what David Richardson, the ICC chief executive, told South African journalist Telford

Vice: "The ICC only have as much authority over the members as the members are prepared to give them… At best we can play a facilitating role." What, you may wonder, is the point of a governing body if it can't actually govern?

Part of the answer appeared in October, when the ICC proudly relaunched plans for a World Test Championship in 2017, having failed to implement one in 2013. The marketing blurb came with its own punchline: a consultancy called Bulletproof had created a "WTC icon… designed to be a moving, physical, three-dimensional form that can adapt and reflect its environment". And reflect its environment the icon did: within weeks, the Test Championship was dead. No one had ever explained how it would work, and TV didn't want it anyway.

Even a figurehead such as the Queen has the nominal power to appoint a prime minister or sack a government. But the ICC were losing control of one of their last spheres of influence. And they were losing it to the BCCI, who in 2013 advertised their suitability for power by forcing through the appointment to the ICC's cricket committee of their man Laxman Sivaramakrishnan, making a meal of their own investigations into corruption at the IPL, and bullying Cricket South Africa into submission over the dates for India's tour.

Two days after the February 8 vote, BCCI president N. Srinivasan was being upbraided by India's Supreme Court for misleading the world about the role his son-in-law Gurunath Meiyappan had played at Chennai Super Kings, Srinivasan's IPL franchise. In July, Srinivasan is set to become the chairman of the ICC. As India prepare to take their "central leadership responsibility", international cricket holds its breath.

KP sauce

In early February 2014, four days after the resignation as head coach of Andy Flower, the upper echelons of the ECB let out a sigh of relief. Kevin Pietersen was being thanked for his time, a victim of his tendency to start a fight with his own shadow, and of England's desire to recast what Paul Downton, the new managing director, delicately called their "team ethic and philosophy". It was as much as the lawyers – and sport's *omertà* – would allow. But it was tricky to resist a mischievous simplification: Flower and Pietersen, English cricket's Holmes and Moriarty, had just disappeared together over the Reichenbach Falls.

Some argued that talent should be accommodated at any cost. But without inside knowledge of England's dressing-room, the debate was just an exchange of business-school man-management theories. A few arguments seemed less contentious: it takes a special gift to rile Alastair Cook; with a new MD, a new chief selector (James Whitaker), a would-be replacement for Flower (Ashley Giles), and a captain in urgent need of a pick-me-up, English cricket was hardly likely to hamper itself for the sake of it; and almost no one close to events wanted Pietersen to stay.

England's relationship with him had worked while both parties were flourishing. But in 2013 he averaged 36 in Tests (the worst of his nine years) and 28 in one-day internationals. To point out that he was England's top scorer during the whitewash in Australia was like praising an Olympic sprinter for winning the egg-and-spoon race. He turns 34 in June, and his knees are giving way. In his pomp, he was the most watchable batsman since Brian Lara. But this was no longer the point. And it was no good reciting past heroics as if they guaranteed future glory.

The biggest losers were the public. This was not because they were necessarily owed an explanation for Pietersen's sacking: as any sports team know, full disclosure is legally fraught and ethically unadvisable. It was because they may now be less inclined to watch a team deprived of their main box-office attraction. The months ahead will be filled by cheap shots, especially if Pietersen dazzles in some Twenty20 league while England's Test team are folding in a heap.

Remarkably, Flower was criticised for failing to manage Pietersen. But the acrimony that had surrounded his departures from Natal and Nottinghamshire, and his set-tos with Peter Moores and Andrew Strauss, offered an alternative explanation: Flower, the latest in a long line of decent men to fall out with Pietersen, had in fact accommodated him through to an England-record 13,779 international runs. Both sides had benefited. But the party was over.

The wrong kind of history

A few months earlier, at a time when the cricket mattered more than boardroom bickering or dressing-room disputes, and England were actually beating Australia, Ian Bell's late cut would have sped to the boundary. But on the last afternoon of the Fifth Test at Sydney – a contest in name only – it flew to gully. In July and August, when Bell could do no wrong and England were doing enough, the stroke told of an elegant, almost casual, superiority. Now it smacked of end-of-an-era decadence.

No sporting defeat is a disaster, but 5–0 against a team that had won none of their previous nine Tests came close. England had unexpectedly surrendered the Ashes before, notably in 1958-59 and 1989 – though even then they managed a draw or two. As for the two whitewashes that *had* taken place, England could at least offer excuses: in 1920-21, their game had yet to replenish its post-war stocks; and in 2006-07, the opposition were irresistible.

But Australia's latest vintage were made to look more than the sum of their parts: they had one great (Michael Clarke), two men (Mitchell Johnson and Brad Haddin) at their peak, apparently capable of defying the law of averages, and the previously injury-prone Ryan Harris, who was loving every minute.

If these Australians shared with the class of '06-07 a mongrel's thirst and a bowling attack that combined gold dust with salt of the earth, then they lacked their aura. They had to overcome first-innings wobbles of 132 for six at Brisbane, 143 for five at Perth, 164 for nine at Melbourne, and 97 for five at Sydney. Australia deserved their victory. But it was less resounding than it looked. Drawing on the same XI throughout, they were dubbed the "Unchangeables", which was a polite way of saying they were not the "Invincibles".

This, then, was the worst result in England's history, surpassing the home loss to New Zealand in 1999, which left them bottom of *Wisden's* Test rankings. And it meant their 3–0 victory in the summer vied for another uneasy superlative: the least-remembered Ashes win of all. By January, the bottom line read 5–3 to Australia. It felt like 10–0.

Last year, we argued that ten straight Ashes Tests would dull the magic. We didn't reckon with the half of it. Both sets of players had been asked to scale Everest shortly after conquering K2. Neither side succeeded: only 11 out of the 40 players used across the two series lasted the course. (The miracle was that three of them – Jimmy Anderson, Stuart Broad and Peter Siddle – were seamers.)

But Australia paced themselves more cannily, knowing that victory at home would gloss over defeat away, and that the second series would reverberate beyond the first. Pietersen's assertion in Melbourne – that England had struggled to rouse themselves for the return leg – was not so much a whinge as a cry for help, one that will almost certainly be lost on the administrators, who continue to believe that a good thing can be made better, simply by doing it more often.

For the aching body of the England team, it was all too much. Their spine disappeared with the departure of the exhausted Jonathan Trott, and their heart stopped beating with the retirement of Graeme Swann. The dropping of Matt Prior cost them their eyes and ears. Cook was wondering what had happened to his own nervous system. And then it was off with England's head…

Bloom and bust

Flower's decision to step down confirmed two things. In the fast-changing world of elite sport, where a tactical advantage is no sooner established than it is dissected, and eventually ceded, five years in charge must seem an eternity. And job-shares, while a sensible response to an unmanageable workload, can be fragile. Flower did the right thing.

He should move on with the gratitude of English cricket. Moores, his predecessor, had overseen four defeats in seven Test series. Flower would suffer only four in 19 – and the first of those came in the Caribbean, when he was the caretaker, sweeping up the debris left by the Moores–Pietersen debacle. Under Flower, England won three Ashes series and a World Twenty20, topped the Test rankings, and triumphed in India for the first time in three decades. England had rarely had it so good.

With success came expectation. If the first three years of his reign provided a string of good-news stories, the headlines grew mixed. Three hefty losses (in the UAE against Pakistan, at home to South Africa, and finally in Australia) suggested that the pragmatic modus operandi of Flower's teams fell apart too easily against pace and doosras.

Neither was he – or England – helped by his distance from the one-day set-up. Too often, the 50-over side were sacrificed on the altar of rest and rotation after a long Test series. Between the appointment of Giles as limited-overs coach in late 2012 and the one-day defeat in Australia in January,

England lost four series out of four when the one-dayers followed the Tests. When they did win, in New Zealand, the one-day stuff came first. And when the 50-over side fielded their strongest XI, they nearly lifted the Champions Trophy. But until England play less cricket, the other option – one man in charge of three formats – is not much better.

Pitch imperfect

It was sad that Flower went out on a low. But throughout 2013, England's cricket reeked of attrition – from the defiant draw at Auckland, via the grim go-slow against New Zealand at Headingley, to the pitches left dry and slow and low for the Australians. When the rain came at Old Trafford and The Oval (where the third day brought them a pulse-slowing 215 runs in 98.3 overs), they were disconcertingly grateful.

Australia sensed England could be thrown off a course whose precise and prescribed nature was central to their success. At home, England's run-rate was 2.99 to Australia's 3.37. Away, the gap widened: 2.89 versus 3.75. This was not so much England as Middle England, curtain-twitching and cautious.

Their demise came with a curious twist. In India, during the last of their three Test trips to Asia in 2012, they had finally begun to look comfortable on turning tracks. A few months later, Australia's own visit to India ended in a 4–0 hammering. England resolved to retain the Ashes by mimicking sub-continental conditions. It was a conservative calculation, revealingly so, for English conditions would surely have sufficed.

Swann's 26 wickets were a vindication of sorts, but it was a short-term gain. In his three Tests on Australia's harder, bouncier surfaces – and with his elbow failing him – he managed seven wickets at 80. And England were now batting like Asian stereotypes, at sea against pace. Having failed to be true to themselves in the summer, they seemed unsure what kind of cricket they should be playing.

Another mistake came after the home series. Behind closed doors, the Australians had discussed the importance of flying back with something in the bag. The Tiddlywinks World Cup would probably have sufficed, but England were far more obliging, resting five of their big guns from the one-dayers. At last, Australia remembered what it was like to win.

The selectors had already goofed. The Oval Test had been their chance to find out whether Chris Tremlett – rumoured to be down on pace – could replicate his 2010-11 Ashes form. But they wasted it, picking Chris Woakes and Simon Kerrigan. When Tremlett's lack of zip was exposed at Brisbane, England's three-giants fast-bowling policy looked questionable. When the other two were cut down to size – Boyd Rankin by nerves on Test debut at Sydney, Steven Finn by a technical breakdown – it looked worse than that. Australia ended up outwitting England. But England gave them a helping hand.

Energy efficient

A headline in the satirical *Daily Mash* last summer declared: "People who don't like cricket are wrong, say experts". The *Mash* had a point. But when it came to Mitchell Johnson, so did the experts. Frankly, he was not supposed to have happened. Cricket these days is a batsman's game: sixes are sponsored, boundaries shortened, bats streamlined. Australia had almost washed their hands of him after years of flakiness. And the schedule really ought to prevent a 32-year-old from approaching 95mph throughout a five-Test series. Yet, in taking 37 English wickets, Johnson emitted energy all of his own making – steam, gas *and* electricity.

Whenever he tore in, the mood changed. This was something visceral: a hush followed by a crescendo. John Arlott likened Ian Botham's run-up to a "shire horse cresting the breeze", so perhaps Johnson was Black Beauty – sleek, dark, hair-raising. Egged on by packed houses and giant screens proclaiming his latest triumph over the speedgun, he took wickets in clusters: four brief spells spread across the first four Tests brought 16 at a cost of 63 and an average of 3.95, less than the cost of a thick edge through the slips. He would have demolished better sides than England and, against South Africa at Centurion in February, he did.

Of cricket's two most physical acts – hitting long and bowling fast – one has become devalued: there were a record 65 sixes during the series. But Johnson could now join an Ashes express-pace pantheon that included perhaps only Harold Larwood, Frank Tyson and Jeff Thomson. Whichever side you were cheering for, it was wonderful to watch.

The Cook report

If there was anything more repetitive than England's mishaps, it was the sound of Shane Warne rubbishing Cook's tactics. Warne has become an Aussie amalgam of Botham and Boycott, indignantly sure of his own views and unafraid to repeat them. It was galling to admit he might have had a point.

England's win three years earlier under Strauss had centred on discipline. In India, Cook had led by example rather than ingenuity. Now, he struggled to read the game, to impose himself, to stem the ebb and go with the flow. While Clarke's bowling changes and field-placings assumed a telepathic air, Cook recalled Dorothy Parker's putdown of Katharine Hepburn, running the gamut of emotions from A to B.

The speed with which his job was rubber-stamped by the board after the Sydney loss seemed out of step with the despondency. Some even thought it smug: no crisis here, move along. But there was a crisis, and the pre-series credit generated by 13 Tests without defeat had vanished.

Since there is no obvious candidate to replace Cook, the most pressing question in English cricket right now is this: could he develop as a tactician, given that half his Test upbringing took place in Strauss's school of grind-'em-down? When England's Test summer starts on June 12 against Sri Lanka, he will be watched closely, probably more closely than a sportsman deserves.

England *did* win the Ashes

The Australian women's team who sailed to England in 1963 were issued with a memo that left them in little doubt about their place in the world: act like ladies, don't speak aloud in public, keep cabins tidy and make sure "non-drinkers will not become enticed to drink". Some progress has been made and, when England's women retained the Ashes in January, there were not too many patronising caveats: "Sure, but a shame about the men…"

It was a stirring feat, built on the back of a Test victory at Perth and secured, under the new points system, with a Twenty20 win at Hobart. The temptation was to point out that the men lost their own Perth Test and Hobart Twenty20, but such comparisons are part of the problem – even when they favour the women. The two games are different beasts; less power does not mean less skill.

Despite the ECB's support for women's cricket, it remains the poor relation. Their lone Test of the English summer clashed with the climax of the men's Fourth Test, and their win at the WACA went untelevised. Many continue to refer to adults as "girls". And yet there is only one current captain who has won the Ashes home and away. *Wisden* is delighted to name Charlotte Edwards as a Cricketer of the Year.

The setting of India's son

Sachin Tendulkar's final Test contained all the best bits of Indian cricket – and all its excesses. The nation was on red alert, the hero made a few runs, and the emotion was as thick as the Mumbai air. On the second morning, as he progressed to 74, the Wankhede was in a trance. Don Bradman had once spotted something of himself in Tendulkar's batting. Now, it was as if Tendulkar was righting one of sport's great wrongs – Bradman's farewell duck in 1948 – all by himself.

But it was hard to ignore the whiff of reality TV, with the West Indians the wide-eyed arrivals at the *Big Brother* house, and the in-your-face ads for skin-fairness cream conveying a sinister superficiality. The result of the game seemed neither here nor there.

Tendulkar's 200th Test should actually have been in Cape Town, but politics and money put paid to that: the BCCI wanted to bloody the nose of CSA chief executive Haroon Lorgat, and there were broadcasters to sate. Besides, Tino Best and Darren Sammy were less likely than Dale Steyn and Morne Morkel to embarrass an ageing superstar. Most conveniently, perhaps, the setting allowed Tendulkar's mother to watch him play for the first time. This was touching, but not a policy found in most textbooks on sporting governance.

The hysteria and the machinations detracted from a cracking human story – of an obsessive driven by a passion, yet grounded by the love of parents wary of letting their son be defined by hundreds or ducks. A survey carried out late last year by the Australian Cricketers' Association claimed that a quarter of those who had quit or retired since 2005 went on to suffer "depression or feelings of helplessness". In particular, the ACA flagged up the link between identity and sporting achievement. Ramesh and Rajni Tendulkar had recognised the dangers many years earlier.

Most cricketers decide they have had enough of the goldfish bowl after a decade or so. Tendulkar played Test matches in front of the most demanding fans in the world for 24 years. If further proof was required of just how astonishing this was, it came at Perth in December, when for a few moments one Cook and one Clarke added up to exactly one Tendulkar: 200 Test caps, 15,921 runs and 51 hundreds.

Sport's pleasure resides in meaning so much to so many, while being essentially meaningless itself. Think about this for too long and you'll get a headache. But Tendulkar came closer than anyone to making sense of it.

The bug stops here

Our older readers may nominate 1953. If you're in your fifties, perhaps it was Derek Underwood at The Oval in 1968. A decade younger, and it might be 1981. And for the whippersnappers, 2005. These are summers when, home from school, you might have switched on the TV and caught the bug.

England matches moved to Sky in 2006, and the coverage has almost always justified the cost. But no one below their mid-teens will have any memory of live international cricket on terrestrial TV, and anecdotal evidence is spreading of youngsters unsure how to build an all-round game. It stands to reason that the Channel 5 highlights include precious few forward defensives: Tests are being made to look like Twenty20. The dedication of coaches around the country is not in doubt, and the vast sums brought in by the Sky deal have acted as English cricket's security blanket; the ECB are proud of the number of children now being taught the game. But there is no substitute for watching, absorbing, and falling for the real thing.

Sky are not to blame for the terrestrial broadcasters' loss of interest in cricket, and they deserve praise for making their own winter-Ashes highlights available on Pick, their free-to-air channel. It is a step in the right direction, but only a step. Sky won't give out their viewing figures, but industry estimates suggest around 1.3m tuned in for the final morning of the Trent Bridge Test in 2013, compared with a peak of 8.4m for Channel 4's broadcast of the Ashes Test there eight years earlier.

Universal access to live sport, and its serendipitous discovery – that's what matters above all else. So why not use Pick to broadcast a county game or two, or even the occasional session of a Test? It would hardly cannibalise Sky's paid-for coverage, and might even persuade terrestrial diehards to fork out for a subscription. Sky have little to lose, but English cricket has plenty to gain.

Wakey, wakey!

Matthew Engel once used these pages to stress the importance of the afternoon snooze at Worcester. But, at the start of July, New Road's PA announcer brought mixed news. Spectators were actually being asked to bunch up: the

Australians were in town, and there wasn't enough room. The sun was out, the cricket was on, and the locals were engaging with their team. The snoozers would have to wait.

At Taunton the previous week, Somerset supporters had turned out in their droves to watch the Australians' tour opener. And at Hove, between the Second and Third Tests, fans bowling up on the first morning of their three-day game with Sussex were greeted by a sign proclaiming a sell-out. They had all arrived to watch the kind of game we are often told no longer matters.

There is no prospect of returning to an age when visiting sides played as many of the counties as they could reasonably manage. But the atmosphere at all three games was warm, welcoming and just the right side of competitive; children will have gone home enthused. Sometimes, cricket's headlong dash for cash misses the point.

Holy writ

Our deputy editor Steven Lynch doubles up as ESPNcricinfo's resident agony uncle, furnishing obscure cricket questions with the kind of answers that can make a *Wisden* editor feel rather ignorant. But last year Steven was briefly flummoxed. "Sir," began a correspondent, "I need to know who was the first cricketer born since the beginning of time."

It's possible only one other person alive could have stepped in on his behalf – fellow deputy editor Harriet Monkhouse, who turned for help to Genesis 4:8. "And Cain talked with Abel his brother: and it came to pass, when they were in the field, that Cain rose up against Abel his brother, and slew him." We'll keep doing our best.

MENTAL DISINTEGRATION

Time to smell the roses

MARTIN CROWE

When I first absorbed the idea that cricket was the gentleman's game, I understood it to mean it was played by men who showed a gentle nature to each other – under a hot sun, on a green field, to the sound of soft applause, with breaks for lunch and tea. Call me an idealist if you like. But to me it epitomised the fun sport could be in an often serious society.

Then I began playing professionally. As soon as money and status take over, sport changes for good. A different language permeates the field; and cricket's curse – as well as its charm – is that no game is more suited to conversation. Golf offers scope for chat, yet – unless it's matchplay – the battle is generally with the course, not the man. In tennis, the net gets in the way. In athletics, individuals are too focused on their personal pursuit. In rugby or football, breaks occur in play for the quick quip or throwaway threat. Cycling and long-distance running occasionally free up moments.

But Test-match days contain 540 balls, each with an average lifespan of five seconds or so, from the start of the bowler's run-up to the batsman's retort. That's around 45 minutes of live play per day. In the opportunities cricket provides to speak in the heat of the battle, it rules the lot.

In England, this chatter has always been a mix of wit, whinge and worry; in Australia, slang, sex and sledge. The Australian way under a hot sun is to let rip with colourful language, a release of culture and climate. When the heat gets under an Aussie's collar, when he faces pressure or the prospect of defeat, he releases the pain. Too often, it becomes crudely personal. And that is when cricket's spirit and integrity are lost.

During the second of the two Ashes series, Australia found their voice again. At Brisbane and Adelaide, the verbal combat was appalling and on full display. Jeff Crowe, the match referee, had no hair to pull out; yet, believe me, he tried. His disdain for the sledging that went on – particularly from the Australians – couldn't be conveyed in public. But, behind closed doors, there was a lot of effing and blinding (ironic, I'll grant you). The two captains quietly accepted his point that a repeat of the physical contact between Mitchell Johnson and Ben Stokes at Adelaide would not be tolerated, but it was no coincidence that things calmed down only after Australia had the series in the bag, and England had all but given up. And while Andy Flower was keen on a truce, Darren Lehmann was not.

The pain of three successive Ashes losses had been too much for Australia. Former players, administrators and sections of their media began conjuring up a battle plan to change the course of history. Stung by six Test defeats in a row, Michael Clarke opted for a new approach. Most relevant, he decided, were the stories of Ashes folklore that depicted Australia as tough,

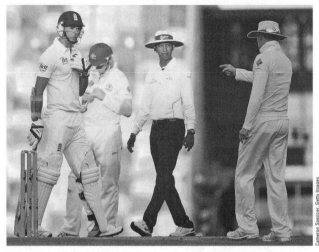

Yes, you! Michael Clarke singles out James Anderson as the Brisbane Test ends in acrimony.

uncompromising and resilient. And chief among these was Allan Border, who had turned Australia around in the mid-1980s. Clarke's search for change included his own game face, his mode of leading a bruised band, as Border himself had done against David Gower's men 24 years earlier. In essence, Clarke (a gentle, misunderstood man) learned that Border (a gentle, humble man) had put on a mask. He felt encouraged to do the same.

The mask hid Border's natural decency, although his fighting qualities were always evident when defending his wicket. In 1989, he didn't need to be cordial any more. Instead he became Captain Grumpy, snarling, snorting and sledging his way to victory. Clarke, too, had had enough of being Mr Nice Guy. On the stroke of winning the First Test at Brisbane, he stormed up to James Anderson and unleashed hell. His face changed colour, his finger jabbed, his mouth screamed an obscenity. It was so unlike Clarke, so well acted, so unnatural. The effect was immediate: Australia hated England. This, the players convinced themselves, was war. It was a vocabulary even the pacific Alastair Cook tapped into.

Too many Ashes Tests in one year, too much greed and overkill – that was part of the problem. Hatred and vengeance built up. (And let's be clear: it wasn't just the Aussies who sledged – Anderson was no angel.) But these two proud nations needed to back off, smell the roses, go back to the family. The tone of the series was wrong. Yes, Australia played superb cricket for most of those live 45 minutes each day, but the other 315 were spent venting and frothing. It was not pleasant to watch. And it reduced England and the spectacle

Bristling: Merv Hughes sends Graeme Hick on his way at Lord's in 1993. Allan Border looks on.

to nothing – unless, of course, you were an Aussie. It was the ultimate in mental disintegration.

When David Warner talked about England's "scared eyes", he did the game a disservice. Rightly, he was pulled into line by Lehmann, who had himself been pulled into line by Cricket Australia for calling on his countrymen to disrespect Stuart Broad. (Broad's crime? He didn't walk. Oh, the hypocrisy!) Both men apologised, but the tactics were clear, and Australia were not going to let up until the Ashes were regained. Yet even Ian Chappell, once a sledger himself – though he drew a distinction between personal abuse and more general, cricket-based observations – called for a truce before the whole thing descended into fisticuffs.

Of course, sledging is all part of the act, the masking of one's doubts about oneself. Don't the psychologists say that what you think about and do to others mirrors only what you think about yourself? Can cricket not be played at the highest level in a quieter environment? Of course it can, and by many teams it is. That Australia chose not to was simply a reflection of their own fears and confusion. The sledging masked that. It was an inglorious disguise.

Take Mitchell Johnson. England had ravaged him in 2009 and – with the exception of Perth – 2010-11. Now he came armed with new-found bullets and an old-style moustache, and he was relentless. Sledging had never come naturally to him, and even here it didn't look quite right. But the mask was convincing enough, and his speed was undeniable. England were spooked. By the end, he was able to laugh in their "scared eyes": fear had been replaced by cockiness.

Does cricket need to get as personal as it did during the Australian summer? Is not the pride of nation against nation enough? Or is patriotism just masking the real purpose – to win at all costs? I experienced very little sledging. In my first Test series, aged 19, Greg Chappell's Australians – Rod Marsh, Dennis Lillee and Jeff Thomson among them – went out of their way to be friendly, and engaged at stumps with a cold beer and warm advice. It was after the 1989 Ashes, with Merv Hughes in tow, that the tune changed. His behaviour, which regularly included spitting, was boorish. I ignored it all, and continued to enjoy the camaraderie of the semi-professional era.

The only other team that bothered to sledge during my time was West Indies, who reserved it for moments when they met with resistance. Yet when they toured New Zealand in 1986-87, it was umpire Fred Goodall who copped it, and not us players. Goodall had famously been barged by Colin Croft during West Indies' ill-tempered visit seven years earlier, and was blamed by them for the hostility that ensued. Now, he was attacked unmercifully. On the fifth day of the Second Test, after the First had been drawn, Viv Richards subjected Goodall to a fearful tirade. It worked, too: the decisions he went on to make were in favour of the sledging skipper. I was the non-striker for much of it, and it was disgusting to observe. It put me off sledging for life; Goodall stood in only one more Test before retiring, a broken man.

The truth is, we have all been guilty of taking cricket too seriously. Instead, we should consider the consequences of winning at any cost. Sport is an athletic activity, not a religion or a ritual. It's not about life or death. It needs to be natural, light, free, healthy and humane. When we add in boring made-up and acted-out elements, we miss the point. Winning becomes not merely everything: it becomes the only thing. It's not. Loving and learning are.

We know cricket was created to express freedom of movement without bodily contact, that it was meant to stimulate the intelligence over long periods, and combine individual character and team culture. It was never meant to be simple or easy. It was a game designed to stretch us. But it was also meant to be played at a faster pace than we see now. The game needs speeding up: it needs less time for banal diatribe.

Are we becoming obsessed with this urge to win, to the point where minds are snapping and the damage is spreading? Or am I not manning up enough? All I know is that I'd like to see less pretending. Let's get back to a shared spirit, which is gentlemanly, absorbing, compelling and fair. Let's get back to a genuine, forgiving and rewarding game. Cricket is already muddied by bookies, mercenaries and politickers.

Too many masks are being worn, and young folk are growing up believing that sledging is winning. Frankly, it's the opposite. Cricket needs to reinvent itself. It could start by calming down.

Martin Crowe captained New Zealand in 16 of his 77 Tests, between 1982 and 1995, and made 5,444 runs at 45.36. He is the younger brother of Jeff Crowe, the ICC match referee.

THE GREATS OF THE WOMEN'S GAME

A formidable quintet

TANYA ALDRED

It has been almost 80 years since two art students, two office workers, a lawyer, an army auxiliary, two ladies of leisure and seven teachers sailed from Tilbury docks to Australia for the first women's Test, starting at Brisbane's Exhibition Ground on December 28, 1934. To celebrate those decades of dedication, bloody-mindedness and no little courage, *Wisden* has picked its five greatest female cricketers.

The process of whittling the candidates down was thorny. How do you compare performances in Test cricket, one-dayers and Twenty20? How do you judge pioneers and semi-professionals, those who are supported by their board, or have largely gone it alone? How do you weigh up performance on the pitch against groundbreaking work off it?

There are many names missing who deserve to be honoured, not least Rachael Heyhoe Flint. You could easily come up with another equally worthy five. And, in ten years' time, with the women's game set to evolve more quickly than ever, the list could look more different still. But those in this one – three Australians, an Englishwoman and an Indian – played mostly for nothing, except enjoyment. They make a formidable quintet.

Betty Wilson

One Thursday evening in 1932, Betty Wilson pottered down to Collingwood Women's Cricket Club in Melbourne with her father. She stood on the boundary for a while, fielding balls and throwing them in. Her arm was so good that she was persuaded to join. Three days later, wearing a borrowed dress shortened especially by one of the players, she made her debut. She was ten. By 16, she was playing for Victoria and, although her ten-year international career was delayed the Second World War, she would became a bona fide superstar, who discarded convention to play the game she loved.

During the 1950s, Wilson was known throughout Australia, drawing crowds of thousands. She was nicknamed the female Bradman, averaging over 57; like him, she preferred to keep the ball safely on the ground. She was able to throw from the boundary of the MCG straight to the wicketkeeper, and for good measure bowled testing spin, turning the ball both ways and taking 68 wickets at under 12. Against England at Melbourne in February 1958, she became the first player of either gender to take ten wickets – her figures were 11 for 16 – and score a century in the same Test.

Wilson was a born sportswoman, athletic and fast. Her dedication was even more special: in an era when female cricketers trained once a week, she trained every day. She would throw stones flat and long, taking the heads off daisies, and bowl for hours in the nets at marks representing different batsmen. And,

Dennis Oulds, Central Press/Getty Images

First love: Betty Wilson, bowling for the Australians against Kent at Sevenoaks, put the 1951 tour of England ahead of her personal life.

in a ritual learned as a girl, she would place a ball in one of her mother's stockings, attach it to the washing line, and hit it repeatedly with a bat, sharpening both her eye and her blissful footwork.

ELIZABETH REBECCA WILSON was born on November 21, 1921, the second of four children. Her father was a bootmaker who would fashion her special lightweight bowling boots, and her mother ran a busy, happy home. Little Betty was a jumping bean, playing in the street for hours. She left school at 13 for a business course, and would do secretarial jobs all her working life.

When at last cricket resumed after the war, she made her debut against New Zealand at Wellington. She hit a speedy 90 and took ten wickets. In her second Test, she became the first Australian woman to score a century against England (there were nine more wickets, too). She seemed unstoppable.

She never married. Her fiancé twice agreed to postpone the wedding because of cricket commitments but, when Wilson decided to tour England in 1951, that was the end of the relationship. There was no contraceptive pill, and she needed more than home-making. "It depended what you wanted out of life," she told the National Library of Australia. "Who was going to knock a chance to go to England and play cricket? No. No way." The team sailed to Southampton; on the way she learned, among other things, how to peel an orange in company.

At the end of that tour, in which she scored 571 runs and took 57 wickets in 14 matches, she stayed on to see the country. She hung around long enough to have a grandstand seat at King George VI's funeral in February, and made friends she wrote to for 50 years. On the boat back she was devastated to learn her father had died. She cared for her mother for many years afterwards.

Her final series was England's tour of 1957-58. In the Second Test, at St Kilda, she scored that century and took those 11 wickets, on a damp pitch, including a hat-trick: "Off-break, leg-break, straight ball." She was so overwhelmed she burst into tears.

She became a champion bowls player in her dotage and continued to support women's cricket, often to be found sitting in the MCG stands, her big white hairdo proud like a huge Mr Whippy. "She was funny," says Cathryn Fitzpatrick. "She didn't hold back. I remember her telling one of the girls to button her shirt up. She'd throw her head back to laugh. Her joy came from watching us play."

When Betty Wilson died, aged 88, on January 22, 2010, she was acclaimed the finest of all female cricketers.

	M	I	NO	R	HS	100	50	Avge	Ct
Tests	11	16	1	862	127	3	3	57.46	10

	Balls	M	R	W	BB	BM	5I	Avge	SR	ER
Tests	2,885	172	803	68	7-7	11-16	4	11.80	42.42	1.67

Enid Bakewell

In the winter of 1968, a vivacious part-time PE teacher was plucked from domesticity and sent to the other side of the world – she returned with 1,031 runs, 118 wickets and a twinkle in her eye. She had found her forte, and England their all-rounder.

In her first Test, against Australia, Enid Bakewell opened the batting and made a century. Against New Zealand, seven weeks later, she made a century and took five wickets. And in the next, it was a century, five wickets, and a fifty that included the winning runs with just four minutes to spare.

She was speedy between the wickets, nimble of footwork and dashing with the bat; her left-arm spinners were patient and had enviable flight. She was small but indomitable, smiling but deadly accurate. On her return, she found herself a minor heroine, and received a civic reception from Nottinghamshire County Council and the Lord Mayor of Nottingham. Thirteen years later, she retired with a Test batting average of nearly 60, as well as 50 wickets at 16, and a stash of records.

Small but indomitable: Enid Bakewell averaged almost 60 in Tests.

ENID BAKEWELL (née Turton) was born on December 16, 1940 in the Nottinghamshire pit village of Newstead. Her Methodist parents were in their forties when she was born, her father a miner who would return home from a shift with coal dust stuck fast about his eyes. The village was patriarchal, but young Enid did as she pleased. She ran about with the boys, had her own pair of football boots, and would play cricket outside until dark on a pitch that she and the other children cut from an unused field using scissors and hedge shears.

Her parents had no real interest in the sport, but Enid loved it. She filled a desk with press cuttings on Tony Lock and Peter May, listened to games on the wireless, and learned the fielding positions from a diagram in the *Radio Times*. At junior school, girls played hockey. Hitting the ball to the right wing used the same action as a cover-drive, so she got lots of practice. By 14 she was playing for Nottinghamshire, mostly as a batsman – it was not until her early twenties that she developed her spin. She went on to train as a PE teacher at Dartford College, where she played alongside Rachael Heyhoe (the Flint would come later).

In 1959, she was picked to play for the Women's Cricket Association against the Netherlands on huge doormat wickets, but had to wait until that winter tour of 1968-69 before winning her full cap. By then she was married to Colin Bakewell, and was desperately torn about leaving her toddler Lorna. In the end, Lorna stayed with Enid's parents, who told her that mummy would be back when the flowers started blooming. Spring came early that year and, when she returned, Lorna had developed a temporary stutter. But modest, bubbly Enid had launched a magnificent career. She was showered with gifts, including a dressing-table set from Kirkby Council, and received them with thanks. It was expensive to play (culottes alone cost seven guineas), and Colin kept a tight grip on the purse strings.

She went on to have two more children, Lynne, named after her opening partner, Glamorgan's Lynne Thomas, and Robert. Enid enjoyed one-day cricket, scoring a century in what effectively became the first World Cup final, in 1973, and 50 in the first women's international at Lord's, in 1976. Her *pièce de résistance* came in her final Test, against a hostile West Indies in 1979, in which she became only the second person, after Betty Wilson, to take ten wickets and score a century in a Test – she carried her bat in England's second innings for 112 out of 164. She was barely off the field all match.

Now in her seventies, she walks, swims and plays bowls, though no longer deliberately makes herself so late for the bus that she has to run. She enjoys a game of Candy Crush on her tablet, stuffs envelopes for the Labour Party and does 4,000-piece jigsaw puzzles: her patience, determination and competitiveness remain undimmed. She continues to turn out for her old team, the Redoubtables, opening the bowling. People, she says, still play her reputation. Cricket has been the love of her life, "a social breaker of barriers" – just as she was, this coal miner's daughter who became England's greatest female all-rounder.

	M	I	NO	R	HS	100	50	Avge	Ct
Tests	12	22	4	1,078	124	4	7	59.88	9
ODIs	23	16	2	500	118	2	2	35.71	7

	Balls	M	R	W	BB	BM	5I	Avge	SR	ER
Tests	2,697	150	831	50	7-61	10-75	3	16.62	53.94	1.84
ODIs	1,313	51	528	25	3-13	–	0	21.12	52.52	2.41

Belinda Clark

Until she was 16, Belinda Clark wanted to win Wimbledon. Thump, thump, thump went the ball against the garage door; thump, thump, thump against the big brick wall at Hamilton South Primary School in New South Wales. Day after day she would be there by 7am, dressed in her brown, yellow and white checked dress, racket in hand, until eventually the worried school phoned home to ensure everything was all right.

She never did get her hands on the Venus Rosewater Dish, but she did achieve almost everything in cricket. She made the Australian team at 20, and became captain at 23, leading them in 11 Tests and 101 one-day internationals, where her win-rate was over 80%. She lifted two World Cups. She was the first player, male or female, to make a double-century in a one-day international. She opened the batting, averaged over 45 in both forms of the game, and was named Cricketer of the Year in the first edition of *Wisden Australia*, in 1998. And all of this while holding down demanding jobs, first as chief executive of Women's Cricket Australia, then as their women's cricket operations manager.

BELINDA JANE CLARK was born on September 10, 1970, the third child of four. The family moved to Newcastle when she was five, and she spent her childhood hitting balls, getting dirty, climbing trees and copying anything that her brother Colin did. It wasn't until she was 12 that she had any idea a woman could play cricket for Australia. From there, things progressed quickly.

At Newcastle High School she played local, state and Australian indoor cricket, and outdoor cricket for the girls' team, and was fast-tracked into New South Wales Under-18. She already had a remarkable work ethic, passed down from her parents, Margaret and Allan: "I expected myself to win. They expected me to do my best, behave properly and give it a good shot."

She trained to be a physiotherapist, but in January 1991 was picked by Australia, scoring a century against India on Test debut. She was a technically brilliant, attacking, classical batter. Within three years, she was made captain. Being a young girl in charge of an experienced team could have been difficult, but she made it work. The side were in flux, and she remoulded them with the coach, John Harmer. She expected discipline, aggression and excellence – and got them.

"I played with a group of people who were very driven," she says. "As captain I wanted to ensure that the Australian team trained with intensity. I always believed my preparation was better than anyone else's. I had confidence in my ability and faith in my technique."

Her greatest experience was winning the World Cup at Eden Gardens in 1997, in front of a fervent 65,000. She considers her best innings the 142 off 130 balls she made against New Zealand in February 1997, after she had accused them of playing boring cricket. It was the sort of forthright opinion she learned to keep to herself.

As she grew older, she became more risk-averse; managing her mind became harder. She retired in 2005, after losing the Ashes in England but winning the one-day series, and landed a job as the first female head of what is now the National Cricket Centre, where she is currently in charge of the whole

Scott Barbour, Getty Images

Flashing blade: Belinda Clark drives Australia to victory over South Africa in the semi-final of the 2000 World Cup.

women's programme and the men's, up to and including Australia A. She enjoys it, although she misses the old freedoms. "I spend a lot of time sitting in a chair, talking to people, sandwiched between layers of management. It is a different challenge."

She has never played cricket again, even though she yearns for the physical sensation of watching the ball, then hitting it. It was time to move on. Instead, she swims and runs, and has completed two marathons. At home she has some memorabilia tucked away – the stumps of her 100th game, some old bats (though one of them sits in the Australian fielding practice bag). Her baggy green is in the Bradman Museum. Her cover-drive should be too.

	M	I	NO	R	HS	100	50	Avge	Ct
Tests	15	25	5	919	136	2	6	45.95	4
ODIs	118	114	12	4,844	229*	5	30	47.49	45
T20Is	1	1	0	4	4	0	0	4.00	1

Clark, an off-spinner, also took one wicket in Tests, and three in ODIs.

Cathryn Fitzpatrick

For 16 years, off a run that was trimmed from 17 steps to 13, Cathryn Fitzpatrick scared people. Her blond mop bothering the air, she bowled spitting outswingers. No woman has taken more international wickets; no woman bowled faster. From just 5ft 6in of solid muscle came 5oz bullets at 75mph. The highest one-day international wicket-taker in the world, with 180, she also

The whirlwind flies in: Cathryn Fitzpatrick bowls against New Zealand in February 2004.

managed 60 in just 13 Tests. She helped Australia to two World Cups, and spearheaded one of the greatest female teams of all time.

CATHRYN LORRAINE FITZPATRICK was born in Dandenong, Melbourne on March 4, 1968. The youngest of three, she grew up kicking around with her brother Gary's friends, messing about with tape on a tennis ball, learning how to control a seam. She was 11 when she played her first competitive game – there were no girls' teams, so it was in an open-age tournament. On Saturday mornings she would pull on her culottes, go to the local milk bar and wait for a lift to the nearest match. She was a whirlwind, "a fast bowler of no use to anyone", she says, but utterly smitten. Her brother grew less keen on facing her in the front yard, but she and her grandfather, Cliff Hill, would constantly talk cricket. By the time she was 16, she realised people were shying away from her in the nets.

She played junior cricket for Victoria, but it was not until she was almost 23 that she made her debut for Australia. It was uneventful, and she was dropped for a couple of years. The man who located her inner sonar was women's coach John Harmer. He wanted the fastest bowlers, and so he wanted Fitzpatrick. He made her action safer and more repeatable. Out went the tangle of arms and legs, in came a smoothness, a more consistent release point, and greater tactical awareness. She became a supreme technician, delivering metronomic crimson crotchets, at a beat, on command. She loved it when the ball was thrown to her in pressure situations. It often was.

Her strategic nous grew, and she built up her fitness, muscle by muscle, with a succession of physical jobs. She ran behind the garbage truck for six years, wrestling with bins, and later delivered letters for Australia Post, first on a bicycle, then on a scooter. These early-morning jobs gave her extra training time in the afternoon. The supreme machine needed constant oiling.

As the clock ticked, her pace dropped a little, but not her guile. And when she at last retired, at 39, after a 16-year international career, she was still one of the fittest in the team. She had spent two years as the scholarship coach at Cricket Australia's Centre of Excellence, ruffling a few feathers, and in June 2007 was appointed coach of the Victorian women's team. She led them to three Twenty20 titles and, when she took over as head coach of the national side in 2012, she helped guide them to 50- and 20-over World Cup triumphs.

She enjoys the different challenges: "Girls want to know why, more than boys." Her self-effacing manner and quietness belie an inner strength – which the team feed off. She ensures they know about their heritage and the battles won. She still bowls sometimes in the nets, off-breaks that don't do anything, and gives plenty of needle.

But the body isn't quite as reliable as it was – sore shoulders where she once hefted bins and parcels, a couple of knee operations, a disc bulge in her back. "I'm 45, and in the morning I bend down to pick up the cat and I can't stand."

There never was, until late in her career, any recompense. She had to pay to tour, a double whammy since this meant unpaid leave. She felt less like a pioneer and "more like a whinger – we were always advocating change, striving to be the best we could. But it meant we changed the game."

	M	I	NO	R	HS	100	50	Avge	Ct
Tests	13	9	0	152	53	0	1	16.88	5
ODIs	109	58	19	651	43	0	0	16.69	25
T20Is	2	–	–	–	–	–	–	–	1

	Balls	M	R	W	BB	BM	5I	Avge	SR	ER
Tests	3,603	216	1,147	60	5-29	9-112	2	19.11	60.05	1.91
ODIs	6,017	188	3,023	180	5-14	–	4	16.79	33.42	3.01
T20Is	48	1	32	0	0-14	–	0	–	–	4.00

Mithali Raj

Great cricketers love what they do. Don't they? Mithali Raj is different. For years, she excelled in something she didn't particularly enjoy. "It took me a really long time to love cricket," she says. "I played it more out of curiosity and to prove to my dad that I was good. I cemented my place and developed a reputation, but it wasn't until really late, 2009, that I actually started loving the game."

By that time she had made what was then the highest score in women's cricket (214) in only her third Test, and led India for five years, including to the World Cup final against Australia in 2005. She is consistently ranked the best one-day batsman, having made more than 4,600 runs; despite limited opportunities she has a wonderful Test record. And all this for a constantly rejigged team and under the gaze of a strangely half-hearted BCCI. In a country where cricket is an obsession, women's cricket is thistledown on the wind: Raj

Double top: Mithali Raj darts towards her record-breaking 214 at Taunton in 2002; the England wicketkeeper is Mandie Godliman.

has a barely-there commercial profile and a tiny social-media following, and is virtually unknown outside cricketing circles.

MITHALI RAJ was born on December 3, 1982, in Rajasthan, where her father, Dorai, was enjoying his last posting in the air force. She was a solitary but happy little girl, whose passion was Indian classical dance, Bharatanatyam. When she grew up she wanted to be a dancer; her mother, Leela, agreed. But Dorai had other ideas. He was a disciplinarian, and disliked Mithali daydreaming and getting up late. When she was nine and a half she was sent to a cricket camp during the summer holiday with her older brother, Mithun. She had never picked up a bat before, but the coach saw something in her, and when she went back to school she joined the girls' team. Along the way, she met her favourite coach, the late Sampath Kumar.

For a while she was able to combine dancing and cricket, but in 1997, aged 14, she was picked as first standby for the World Cup. She had to make a decision. Dance classes had already given way to net sessions and, after much thought, she chose cricket. "It wasn't easy. Dance came naturally to me. Cricket *happened* to me."

The choice went down badly with her extended family, who were upset that she continued to miss family functions. "Perhaps it was hard for them to understand, perhaps they thought that a south Indian girl should be homely, learning cooking and things like that."

She played for Hyderabad age-group teams, as a medium-pace new-ball bowler and opening batsman, and in the domestic competition for Railways, who still employ her off the field. In June 1999, on her one-day international debut against Ireland at Milton Keynes, she made an unbeaten 114. Three years later, she was back in England, in the more bucolic setting of Taunton. The tour had been a shambles, and her double-century became the shining light. She had no idea she had beaten the world record until the twelfth man was sent on to whisper in her ear. Her overriding feeling was exhaustion. She was 19.

Her strengths are her touch and timing, a calmness at the crease, and an awareness of what is going on around her. She loves to grab the game and change its course, though the responsibility of being the middle-order rock leashes her in. She has led the team on and off for ten years, and guided them to their first Test victories over England, in 2006, though she doesn't consider herself a natural captain. Experience has helped, and she enjoys passing on her knowledge to the younger women. Her biggest frustration is the lack of regular cricket. Now in the twilight of her career, she is desperate to guide India back to the top table after their disastrous 2013 World Cup at home.

In a sense she already belongs to a passing generation: she prefers one-day cricket to Twenty20, and wishes she could play more Tests. She is happy in her own company, and in her spare time she reads and sketches. She doesn't watch cricket. She is a woman apart and, in her own way, a trailblazer.

	M	I	NO	R	HS	100	50	Avge	Ct
Tests	8	13	2	572	214	1	3	52.00	7
ODIs	145	132	37	4,622	114*	4	36	48.65	32
T20Is	37	37	10	885	52*	0	3	32.77	8

Raj, a leg-spinner, has also taken eight wickets in ODIs.

THE TAO OF SHORT LEG

Banished to Boothill

JOHN WESTERBY

The landscape around Tombstone, Arizona, is as bleak as the name suggests. These are the barren expanses of cowboy country, an hour's drive north of the Mexican border. On the way out of town, towards the desert, the signs direct you to Boothill Graveyard, home to so many who died "with their boots on", slain in the shootouts of the Wild West.

Boothill is the godforsaken spot where no one chooses to end their days – and the name appropriated by English county cricketers condemned to crouch at short leg. The boots are white and spiked, rather than shin-length and caked in dust, but the implication is the same: the unfortunate shoved into the firing line risks perishing with them on. To borrow from *Gunfight at the OK Corral*: "Good men and women live in Tombstone. But not for long."

Such has been the reluctance to field under the helmet that the job has traditionally gone to the junior pro, chosen for being disposable, not necessarily well-qualified. In the days of the gentlemen–players divide, there was a feeling that the professional was more likely to draw the short straw, especially if the bowling was unreliable. Yet can this convention survive in our more meritocratic times? And is short leg still such an unappealing prospect?

When Alastair Cook became England Test captain in 2012, he enjoyed some predictable perks, including a pay rise and an unofficial say in selection. He could also safeguard his physical safety, having for some time been the team's short leg. Cook moved to first slip, and into his shin pads stepped Ian Bell, who had successfully fielded there earlier in his career. It may be true that, at any level of the game, the cordon tends to be the domain of senior players. But this was not a case of the captain ushering an underling towards the bullets. It now made strategic sense for Cook to take in the broader view from slip. Nor was Bell the junior pro: he was simply the best short leg available.

In modern international cricket, with players' fielding contributions analysed forensically, the position is filled more and more by specialists, rather than by lambs thrown to potential slaughter. The value of a good short leg has also shot up with the advent of DRS: pad-play is less advisable, bringing the inside edge more into the game.

Yet there is still a sense in which the short-leg fielder is the poor relation: more chances go to slip, so the safest catchers are stationed there. The best all-round fielder will probably stand at backward point. But short leg must be chosen with care. Richard Halsall, who was appointed England's first full-time fielding coach in 2007, explains the selection process. "There are positions that take priority, and top of the list are first and second slip," he says. "You're not likely to put a bowler at short leg, because it doesn't make sense for him to be crouching so much. So invariably it's a batsman who isn't fielding at slip. But

Munir uz Zaman, AFP/Getty Images

Catchment area: Ian Bell holds on to another at short leg.

he's got to be good. He's got to be brave, an outstanding catcher and, ideally, a good reader of the batsman."

After taking a reflex short-leg catch to dismiss West Indian tailender Corey Collymore at Old Trafford in 2007, Bell wrote that the key lay in picking up clues from the batsman's body language, while keeping one eye on the ball. Being a batsman helped him decipher the gestures. And so did the bowler's accuracy – Monty Panesar in this case – which Bell said allowed him to stay on his toes; fear of a long-hop would drive him back on to his heels, making him less primed to pounce.

Yajurvindra Singh, the Indian batsman who on his debut against England at Bangalore in 1976-77 equalled Greg Chappell's Test record of seven outfield catches in a match, has spoken of the importance of staying close to narrow the angles, and of taking the ball behind – rather than alongside – you to gain a fraction more time.

There is, then, a high degree of skill involved, yet a move into the slips is still regarded as a promotion – though one based these days as much on ability as seniority. The evidence was there again in Australia, where Graeme Swann's retirement meant that Bell, despite his prowess at short leg, was whisked into the slips. Joe Root had been groomed as Bell's understudy, and remains the most likely regular replacement.

This level of planning has not always been in place. When Andrew Strauss first played Test cricket, in 2004, he found himself performing the new boy's duties under the lid, despite having had no experience there for Middlesex. A couple of fluffed chances meant his short-leg career was short-lived and, while Strauss may not have dropped those chances on purpose, suspicions can arise. "It's like twelfth man," says one county coach. "It's not a job some of them want to do too well in case they get asked again."

Perhaps it will be ever thus. Yet for all the fielders who have served their time at Boothill before graduating to slip, there are plenty who have made the position their own, especially in county cricket. Think of Brian Close's bloody-mindedness, Micky Stewart and Stuart Surridge helping out Jim Laker at Surrey, the vigilance of Peter Walker for Glamorgan, Basharat Hassan's nimbleness for Nottinghamshire – a quality he handed down to Mick Newell – and, more recently, Richard Montgomerie sniffing out catches for Mushtaq Ahmed during Sussex's golden run in the 2000s.

These are the players who perhaps made the mistake of doing too good a job. Either that, or they were happy to trade risks to life and limb for an intense involvement in the game. For some, there is undoubtedly the thrill-seeker's adrenalin rush; for others, the fact that concentration is easier, less optional, when you are one metre from the bat. These are the brave few for whom Boothill is not such a desolate place.

But is it really so dangerous? The answer depends on the quality of the bowling. Watch a short-leg fielder for any length of time, and the perils seem clear enough, especially if the batsman is sweeping. One thing is certain: short leg is a riskier position than silly point. On the off side, there is an extra split second to react, and the ball's trajectory is more predictable.

Yet serious injuries are few and far between. "A lot of people are surprised by this, but you're actually more likely to get injured in the slips, especially breaking a bone," says Halsall. "At short leg, you tend to get glancing blows to soft-tissue areas – as long as you get your evasive action right." The most grisly exception was Raman Lamba, the Indian batsman who died in 1998 after being hit on the temple while fielding at short leg during a club game in Bangladesh.

Protective equipment is more advanced than in the days when Close would, unflinching, take a blow to the forehead, and watch with grim satisfaction as the ball looped to Phil Sharpe at slip, which is how Martin Young was dismissed at Bristol in 1962. Shin pads are now commonplace, while helmets have bigger grilles, throat protectors and an extension to cover the nape of the neck when the fielder turns his back. Close, of course, chuckles at the equipment worn now. "I only remember feeling pain if we lost the game," he says. And he was one captain who made a point of stationing himself, rather than a team-mate, under the batsman's nose.

Even Close, though, recognised the importance of taking the appropriate evasive action. The instinct on seeing a batsman's backlift is to jump up and away. But England's coaches have reasoned that the "down and in" technique is more effective. "You make yourself as small as possible, put your head down and bring your hands into your chest, like the brace position," says Halsall. "That way, your helmet and shin pads are the target. If you jump up

Schweppes. Anything else isn't cricket.

Patrick Eagar

Up close and personal: in the 1976 Test at Trent Bridge, West Indies' Larry Gomes is caught at short leg by Brian Close.

and turn your back, you're exposing quite a few vulnerable areas, like the back of your legs."

Montgomerie remembers a full-blooded pull on to his hip from Shane Watson: "That wasn't pleasant. But the one time my confidence took a knock was fielding against Kevin Pietersen at Horsham. I didn't get hit, but he chose where he wanted to place the ball, and he had the skill to do that, almost irrespective of line or length. That made him really difficult to read."

While Close was the reflex fielder nonpareil, for reasons of bravado as much as skill, Montgomerie knows short leg more intimately than anyone. He learned the ropes at Northamptonshire in 1995, when Anil Kumble took 105 Championship wickets from nearly 900 overs, and Montgomerie's catching accounted for 17 of them. When he moved to Sussex, he played an integral role in the success enjoyed over six seasons by Mushtaq Ahmed. He may well have reached the 10,000 hours that author Malcolm Gladwell argued was a benchmark for mastery of a subject.

"I spent a long time at short leg, and I've got the dodgy hips to prove it," says Montgomerie. "You learn more about the position the longer you spend there. I stood two or three feet squarer at the end of my career than I did at the start, with my right foot on the crease to a right-hander. You learn to come closer if the pitch is dead, to stand back if it's bouncing. You're there for the bat–pad, really. Anything else is a bonus."

The bonus catches, inevitably, are the ones Montgomerie recalls most fondly, especially the three he took from full-blooded sweeps. "The one that really sticks in the mind is Middlesex's Ben Hutton off Mushy at Horsham in 2006. I anticipated the lap-sweep, moved behind square as it was being played, and dived to take the catch." Like most short legs, Montgomerie was originally sent to Boothill because he wasn't good enough in the slips. "I dropped a sitter there with Northants," he says. "So I soon found myself at short leg. I actually enjoyed it."

When Halsall became England's fielding coach, he picked Montgomerie's brains: "He'd been sensational in there for Sussex, muttering under his breath, helping Mushy create that claustrophobic feeling, and taking some incredible catches. He made a difficult job look simple. Most of all, he made it look fun.

"But Ian Bell has been as good as anybody in the world. He loves learning about the game, and reads batsmen brilliantly. There have been some good close fielders: Ponting at silly point to Warne, Jayawardene to Murali. But Belly has been just as good. One catch he took to dismiss Hamish Rutherford off Monty Panesar at Wellington in 2013, diving low to his right at backward short leg when Rutherford turned one off his hip, was as good as it gets."

It remains to be seen whether Bell's move to the white-collar ranks in the slips during the Ashes becomes permanent, or whether he is drawn back to a position in which he has excelled. Perhaps one day he will host a convention for downtrodden, underappreciated short-leg fielders everywhere. If he does, there is a graveyard in Arizona that would make the perfect location.

John Westerby is a sportswriter for The Times.

THE DECISION REVIEW SYSTEM

Let's look at that again

BENJ MOOREHEAD

At times during the Ashes in England last summer, the Decision Review System became a story in itself; even the umpires seemed confused. At other times, the technology worked a treat. But how has it affected the way the game has been officiated, played, covered and watched since its introduction at international level in 2008? Benj Moorehead spoke to ten people covering a cross-section of the sport.

The opening batsman: Chris Rogers

I was new to DRS in the 2013 Ashes, and found it difficult to bat and umpire at the same time, which is effectively what I had to do. The prime example was when, as the non-striker, I told Shane Watson to refer his lbw in the Second Test at Lord's. The umpire was right – he was out. I was bitten by the experience, so I didn't have the courage to refer the decision when Graeme Swann pinned me with a full toss a couple of overs later. In the whole context of the game, with the previous decision weighing on my mind, it was difficult to use DRS, so I didn't. But it was clearly not out. That makes the system not right, if you ask me.

You've got to use it tactically. For instance, if you have two referrals left, you're more likely to do so than if you have one. Also, the better batsmen will tend to use it, not tailenders. The technology is supposed to be there primarily to get the decisions right. That's why I think it should be taken out of the players' hands, and given to the umpires.

We didn't agree with a lot of the decision-making in England. With the umpire's-call element, one ball can be hitting more of the stump than another, but be given not out – whereas the other one ends up as out. That is hard to comprehend. It caused me to make adjustments too. As a left-hander I'd usually move across to off stump when a bowler comes round the wicket. But at Trent Bridge, James Anderson got me with a marginal lbw on the umpire's call – it was clipping leg stump – so I changed my guard and moved towards leg. I ended the year with a few runs, so perhaps I got the measure of it.

Chris Rogers opened the batting for Australia in last year's back-to-back Ashes series, and is one of the Five Cricketers of the Year.

The photographer: Philip Brown

The first DRS picture I got was of Andrew Flintoff looking to the dressing-rooms just above me during the Kingston Test in 2009. His finger was raised as if to say, "Am I getting this decision or not?" The shot was used in *The Times*.

Going upstairs: Philip Brown's first DRS image, from Jamaica in February 2009, before the bright jackets muscled in. This not-out decision was overturned in the bowler's favour.

But as time's gone on, DRS has done my head in. As soon as there's a referral, two blokes with luminous bibs run on with drinks canisters and stand around with the team. If they do get the decision, then celebrate, the picture gets ruined by a pair of bright jackets!

Very occasionally it can work. When Kevin Pietersen was given out on referral at Dubai in 2012, he threw his bat 30ft in the air, which I had never seen before. I was taking a few shots with my remote device and, through a stroke of luck, the bat seemed to be vertically suspended in the air (see *Wisden 2013*, page 275). Even better, Pietersen was right in line with a guy in a bright blue jacket, and hid him from the shot.

Of course cricket photography is not only about celebrations. But Jimmy Anderson taking the last Aussie wicket at Trent Bridge was a magic moment. I didn't get the picture because he ran away from the majority of the photographers. I'm sure the players would have celebrated wildly if there had been no DRS, but then Anderson probably wouldn't have done a 180-degree turn and the team wouldn't have been in a group.

Philip Brown has been a cricket photographer since 1989.

The ICC Elite Panel umpire: Richard Kettleborough

International umpires are now under more scrutiny than ever. There is probably less tolerance for human error than before, because modern technology has redefined marginal decisions as those measured by the millimetre. To assist the TV umpire, the Ashes TV broadcast in Australia, for instance, used 32 cameras, real-time Snickometer, Hot Spot, slow motion, ultra-slow motion, ball-tracking and stump microphones. Over time, DRS has proven just how many decisions we get right, but it also highlights errors of judgment, even if they're only tiny. It is tough that the error is broadcast to all, but if it helps get more correct decisions, it's better for the game.

DRS is not in place for every series, while the type and standard of technology used around the world often differ. For me, it was back to old-fashioned umpiring for Sachin Tendulkar's farewell Test in Mumbai, with no DRS in place. Mumbai has just the sort of conditions where it would be welcome. The ball was turning and bouncing from the word go, and there were fielders around the bat. An exceptionally noisy crowd made hearing a faint edge almost impossible. That is umpiring at its toughest. But it was a great privilege.

When I first started as a TV umpire in 2008 there were adjudications on run-outs, stumpings, bump balls, clean catches and boundary decisions. Since then, the role has become far more demanding. The TV umpire sits next to the ICC match referee and now an ICC technician. There is a high-definition monitor showing all the different tools available. There is also a camera focused on the bowler's front foot, and a feed to the TV director.

As you might expect, when a referral is made your heart-rate goes up: you have to keep your cool and stick to the protocols. We communicate with the TV director to ask for the necessary images, while also relaying what is happening to the on-field umpires. For them, there is nothing worse than the silence while the review is taking place. Clear communication is vital.

Some people have put forward the concept of a specialist TV-umpire panel. This has some merit, but the TV official needs to understand the game and the different roles of an umpire, so on-field experience is also crucial.

Richard Kettleborough won the David Shepherd (ICC Umpire of the Year) award in 2013.

The captain: Andrew Strauss

DRS was first used in an England Test series in the West Indies early in 2009, and it felt like a get-out-of-jail-free card. Referring was an informal process: as captain, I made the decisions – and got quite a few wrong. Ryan Sidebottom had one lbw shout that I reviewed because it looked good from my position at short midwicket. It pitched six inches outside leg stump; I felt like an idiot. We soon realised you needed a strategy: wicketkeeper, bowler and captain had to agree.

You have to start thinking like an umpire. Where does a batsman take guard? Has it hit him in line? Is it going to show up on Hot Spot? So you have to get strategic with the technology rather than simply asking "Is it out?" – which is perhaps an unfortunate by-product. It's easy to get emotional: "We really need a wicket, that looks close, let's review." But these are the high-pressure moments: you've got to be cool. By and large, the bowler would say it was out, and it would be up to me and the wicketkeeper to add a dose of realism.

All for it? In 2010, England had yet to hone their DRS strategy, with Paul Collingwood, Stuart Broad and Andrew Strauss all signalling for a review. Pakistan's Zulqarnain Haider survives.

But it depends on the character. Graeme Swann thought every lbw was plumb, whereas Steven Finn might be unsure, even when it was out.

In the early days I could see a couple of umpires really wilting when decisions were overturned. But they became far more accepting of it, maybe because the best umpires generally have their reputations enhanced by the system. They are more likely to give a batsman out lbw on the front foot now. You have to either get your bat in front of your pad, or your front leg out of the way. We learned this to our cost against Pakistan on the low, skiddy wickets of the UAE in 2011-12.

Life has become more difficult for taller batsmen in particular. Kevin Pietersen has always been an attacking player of spin, but he lost confidence in his defensive technique because he was getting out lbw. So he'd try to keep his leg out of the way, and would then get bowled. Finger-spinners have come far more into the game, possibly at the expense of leg-spin. A good example on that UAE tour was Abdur Rehman, the Pakistani left-arm spinner who bowled quickly – almost as if he was on an old uncovered pitch. Leg-spinners used to have the advantage, because they could turn it both ways. But now it's as if finger-spinners have more modes of dismissal. And the non-turning ball is often more dangerous than the turning one.

Andrew Strauss played 100 Tests for England, captaining in 50 of them.

The spectator: Allan Fairlie-Clarke

The first time I came across DRS was in Barbados in 2009. It drove me nuts that nothing was shown on the big screens. There would be a referral, and the whole ground would look to the dressing-room, where somebody would be desperately trying to watch it on the telly and decide whether they wanted to review. We'd wait for the thumbs up or the thumbs down. At that point I was a DRS naysayer. We were being cut out of a big part of the spectacle. It seemed to prove that the authorities cared more about TV viewers than spectators.

But seeing the review process on the big screens has added a dimension. The time it takes to process reviews doesn't bother me, because you feel involved. At Adelaide in 2010-11, Ryan Harris got a golden duck in the first innings, having referred the decision. In the second, there was a massive shout for lbw against him first ball, and we were all screaming for another review; Harris obliged. The big screen was behind us, so we had to turn our backs to the field. We saw the ball coming down in slow motion, and Hawk-Eye had it hitting the stumps. Everyone turned round again and gave a massive cheer. Harris is the only Aussie to have got a king pair in an Ashes Test; the fact he'd reviewed both added to the hilarity. DRS makes you feel like an umpire – and it's another thing to talk about in the pub.

Allan Fairlie-Clarke has been watching England for more than 30 years.

The spinner-turned-commentator: Phil Tufnell

I'd been saying to umpires for years that my balls were hitting the stumps! In my day, if you couldn't play spin you put your foot down the wicket, hid your bat and were never given out. Things began to change a little in the West Indies in 1997-98, when Robert Croft and I were bowling to Jimmy Adams in Guyana: he had no intention of playing the ball whatsoever. Eventually, Darrell Hair raised the finger, God bless him.

Of my 121 Test wickets, nine were lbw – around 7%. Graeme Swann and Monty Panesar are above 25%. Now that more front-foot lbws are given, batsmen are having to use their bat, which brings in the outside and inside edge. They have to read the spin and the length, instead of just thrusting the pad forward. I always looked to attack just outside the right-hander's off stump, hoping for an edge or a mis-hit, but I would have bowled a lot straighter with DRS.

You probably get fewer No. 11 decisions now. I was once bowling for Middlesex at Lord's, and Ray Julian was umpiring. We needed one wicket to win. Their last man had hung about for a while, and Ray said to me: "Tuffers, hit him on the pad. This bloke's batting me into a traffic jam!" So a couple of overs later I did, and we all got home on time.

Now that I'm a radio commentator, you have to be a tad cautious before you say "He's gone!" I'm a traditionalist – the finger goes up, and that's it – but DRS can add to the drama too. Remember the last wicket at Trent Bridge last summer, when England referred a not-out decision against Brad Haddin? Initially it all came to a disappointing halt. You wallow about for a bit, trying to explain to the listeners what's happening. Then Hot Spot comes up on the screen, and I started shouting: "There's a mark on the bat! He's hit it!"

Phil Tufnell played 42 Tests for England as a left-arm spinner.

Seat of power: Simon Taufel, ICC training and performance manager for umpires, is shown the latest technical possibilities during the Pakistan v Sri Lanka Test in Abu Dhabi, December 2013.

The TV producer: Bryan Henderson

DRS has effectively formalised the technology that was already in place. We had all the toys, and it was used as a tool to enhance the viewers' enjoyment. As broadcasters, we have a duty to the game now that DRS is an official part of the sport. I am a massive fan: generally there are more correct decisions than before.

But there have been issues. The costs to supply DRS are significant, and you can argue that the governing bodies should be financing the process. But the relationship between governing bodies and broadcasters is haphazard. In Bangladesh, the television company might not have the money; in England and Australia, different companies have done the ball-tracking. So there's been no uniformity, and that can make it difficult for the fan to follow.

The other big area of confusion surrounds the umpire's call. Having two possible verdicts for the same scenario strikes me as wrong. That's hard to explain to people new to the sport. One possibility would be to allow viewers to listen in to the decision-making process between the on-field and third umpire. There are concerns over the quality of English spoken by some officials but, as a viewer, it would be good to hear those conversations.

Bryan Henderson is executive producer for cricket at Sky Sports.

The left-arm spinner: Daniel Vettori

Even before DRS, the technology used by broadcasters meant we were realising that a lot of lbw appeals were closer than we thought. Then DRS came in and, because people's eyes had been opened, players were a lot more positive about appealing. Left-arm spinners have always attacked the pads, but with DRS in place it feels like a matter of course. Less talented batsmen know they have to find a way to actually hit the ball, rather than just thrust out their pad.

The flipside is that you're no longer getting those 50–50s against the tailenders. Every decision has become a unique situation, so there tends to be an objective outcome. You used to build up a couple of appeals, and the last two wickets were definitely easier to get decisions for than, say, the first two. But you can't build up pressure on technology – there's no emotion.

I think the creation of a balance between the umpiring decision and the technology has been good for the game. It's important to diminish the umpire's role as little as we can, otherwise it will all become automated and the game will lose something for it. Technology improves cricket, but it would be sad if it replaced the human element altogether.

Daniel Vettori has taken more Test wickets for New Zealand than anyone bar Richard Hadlee.

The club umpire: Terry Burstow

We're never going to have DRS at recreational level, but the fact it's on television does have an impact. There are 72 umpires on the Sussex panel, and we all agree that it has helped players to see how the lbw law works. You'd be surprised how many bowlers still don't fully understand it. If you had a TV programme about cricket's laws, do you think any kids would bother to watch? But if it's in an Ashes Test and they go to Hawk-Eye, they love it. It's been educational.

The thing you do get now when you give a decision is some bugger who will draw a television screen, or ask if you would have referred to that to the third umpire. I'd say that happens four times out of five whenever there's a close decision. I suppose it is a form of dissent, but it's a very mild one. They're only doing that to get in your mind. DRS has just become something else they use to build pressure on us. That's the way life has always been for an umpire. I smile, shrug my shoulders, and tell them I give what I see.

Terry Burstow has been an umpire in Sussex recreational cricket since 1993.

The wicketkeeper-batsman: Kumar Sangakkara

Judging when to review a decision has become an important job for the wicketkeeper, who is normally in a good position to see what's happening. If you are keeping a bit wider than usual, then judging the line of the ball can be difficult; it's a case of appreciating the angles. The more you know about your bowlers, their lines and lengths, and how they look to get batsmen out, the more informed your judgment.

You also need to see how the pitch is behaving. And once you've played against someone for a long time, you know where they are taking guard, how far they go across before the ball is bowled, whether they play on the back or front foot. You can't make a database in your own head, so you need points of reference as you go along.

DRS has not really changed the way I play: I don't think about technology when I go in to bat. But as the non-striker you sometimes have to tell your partner after an lbw appeal: "Don't get too emotional, take a deep breath. I think it's pretty straight." I know some non-strikers who watch the bowler's front foot for no-balls. But do you really dare refer a clear catch because you think the foot was over the line?

It's interesting to think what Muttiah Muralitharan would have achieved with DRS. Umpires were reluctant to give batsmen out on the front foot when he was bowling, and some weren't able to differentiate between a doosra and an off-break. Towards the end of his career, Murali went round the wicket more to convince umpires that the ball was going to straighten and hit the stumps. DRS might have allowed him to be more flexible with his angle. Who knows how many more wickets he would have taken?

Kumar Sangakkara has kept wicket for Sri Lanka in 48 Tests and more than 300 one-day internationals.

TENDULKAR RETIRES (1)

Sachin, the bringer of joy

TUNKU VARADARAJAN

Every Indian fan – and many a non-Indian – has in his head a personal montage of Sachin Tendulkar, the finest sportsman produced by India and, arguably (but not contentiously so), cricket's most complete batsman. This is not to say he was better than Donald Bradman. But Bradman played in an era when there were immensely fewer demands on a cricketer's time, body and mind. And, over a 24-year career, Tendulkar played 200 Tests at 59 different grounds, plus 463 one-day internationals at 96. Bradman's 52 Tests took place at only ten venues, all in Australia or England, allowing him a cosy familiarity with conditions that Tendulkar – except at a few marquee venues in India – never enjoyed. Add to that the pressure of a fanatical, sometimes insane, nation, and one cannot be denied at least this observation: cricket and country asked more of Tendulkar than they ever did of Bradman, or of anyone else.

But back to the montage. My own has five images. The first is from November 1989 when, as a 16-year-old who looked rather younger, Tendulkar was about to make his Test debut, in Karachi. He is flanked in a winsome photograph by Kapil Dev and Mohammad Azharuddin. The veterans are smiling their trademark smiles – Kapil's manly and toothy, Azhar's reliably goofy – and each has a proprietary arm draped around Tendulkar's shoulders. They are proud of their ward, who regards the camera almost bashfully, his hair a lush mop of black curls. A boy among men he was, his callow face yet to be bloodied by a Waqar Younis bouncer; even as he grew older, a vital part of him stayed boyish. It's possible his countrymen kept him from full manhood, their worship freezing him in time.

The second image is from Lord's, eight months later. England are looking for quick second-innings runs to set up a declaration after Graham Gooch's endless 333 and Kapil's cavalier quartet of sixes off Eddie Hemmings to save the follow-on. Allan Lamb skies one back over the head of the bowler, leg-spinner Narendra Hirwani, and a coltish Tendulkar, sprinting in from wide long-off, covers 40 yards and clings on one-handed, low to his right. It is one of the best running catches imaginable, the more so because India could no longer win: Tendulkar was propelled entirely by personal pride. Dazzled by his batting, we tend to overlook the fact that – until M. S. Dhoni – he was the fittest, most naturally athletic cricketer to play for India.

The third is bitter, but defines Tendulkar just as aptly. Chennai, January 1999, and India – with four wickets in hand – are 17 runs away from a rare Test victory over Pakistan. Tendulkar, on 136, has just pulled Saqlain Mushtaq deftly to the fence. And then he throws it all away, caught at deep mid-off. India lose by 12, which confirms what their fans have started to suspect: Tendulkar, for all his gifts and statistical irrefutability, doesn't deliver when it

Leaning on him already: Kapil Dev and Mohammad Azharuddin seek the support of Sachin Tendulkar on his Test debut.

really matters. He is the oak that creaks. In one sense, this matters little to his countrymen, for their gods are never infallible (as a cursory glance at Hindu mythology confirms). Yet even in his moment of fallibility, Tendulkar showed physical courage: his back was in such excruciating pain that he batted with a brace, after three injections.

Image four is seared on the brain. Again, it is Pakistan, this time during the 2003 World Cup in South Africa. Shoaib Akhtar, bulging with muscle and ego, steams in at Centurion like a demented bull for the second over of India's reply to a testing Pakistan total. The ball is short, fast and wide, and Tendulkar scythes it over square third man for six. It is an entirely instinctive stroke, the acme of unorthodoxy. Shoaib's next two balls disappear for four – a silken flick through midwicket, an on-drive of sheer purity. Both are in utter contrast to the six: Tendulkar is butcher and Brahmin. It is this duality, this ability to switch instantly from the brutal to the serene, which made him such an irrepressible one-day player. Not blindly wedded to the straight bat (though he was primarily a purist), he had the eye, strength and flexibility of technique to play shots that would have made Viv Richards proud.

The last image is of Tendulkar being held aloft by team-mates after India beat Sri Lanka in the 2011 World Cup final at Mumbai. His face is ecstatic as he is carried around the ground by Virat Kohli and other young guns. They are unbridled in their affection – no, their *love* – for Tendulkar, an individual

BRAND SACHIN

Giving India a Boost since 1989

Richard Gillis

The story of Sachin Tendulkar is usually told in one currency – runs, and more runs. But there is another: in June 2013, Forbes listed his annual earnings at $US22m. The precise value doesn't really matter: above all, Brand Sachin has been India's confidence index throughout a period of rapid economic liberalisation. As an essentially socialist nation, crippled by the "Hindu rate of growth", gave way to a buoyant capitalism, so Tendulkar's runs enhanced its self-esteem. He was a one-man Sensex – Mumbai's stock exchange – seemingly reflecting the mood of the nation.

Like the IPL, Brand Sachin has been used to project the country as an economic powerhouse; unlike the IPL, its integrity has rarely been questioned. As with the value of traded commodities, the direction of travel is the most important thing. And since 1989, when Tendulkar made his Test debut and endorsed his first brand – Boost, a nutritional drink – his stock price has been going up and up. In all, he is believed to have lent his name to over 50 brands, earning an estimated $80m in endorsements alone.

That wealth is based in particular on his popularity as an endorser of corporate brands, including Coca-Cola, Adidas, Toshiba and BP Castrol oil (alcohol and tobacco are off limits). Tendulkar is often seen as India's answer to David Beckham, or – pre-scandal – Tiger Woods. But there are stronger parallels with the packaging and selling of Arnold Palmer in 1960s USA. Palmer's America prefigured Tendulkar's India, full of economic and social optimism, with sport at its heart.

With the help of his agent Mark McCormack, Palmer defined the role of the brand ambassador, creating the blueprint used by Indian businessman Mark Mascarenhas to build Tendulkar's profile. In 1996, Mascarenhas's WorldTel agency guaranteed his new client $7.5m a year; in 2001, that rose to $18m. Tendulkar introduced commerce to Indian sport. He changed the game.

Palmer's value outlasted his career – 50 years after he last won a major, he remains in the top ten of the world's highest-earning golfers – and Tendulkar's sponsors were keen to plan ahead. "Whether he plays cricket, it will not affect our relationship," said Adidas India brand director Tushar Goculdas. Coca-Cola's Indian representative reckoned Tendulkar was "an icon of happiness, much like Coca-Cola". Property developers Amit Enterprises were planning "Sachin-branded residences"; their managing director described Tendulkar as "an evergreen brand".

His initial post-retirement activity balanced commerce with a strong social agenda: Tendulkar, whose wife Anjali is a paediatrician, became the first UNICEF ambassador for South Asia, with a focus on children's health. Recently, Aviva Life Insurance depicted him as an emblem of reliability, with an advert in which the adult Tendulkar offers advice to his 16-year-old self before his maiden Test innings.

So where next? Harish Krishnamachar, senior vice-president of the Indian branch of World Sport Group, the company that manages Tendulkar's endorsement, says: "Brand Sachin has come to represent respect, consistency, humility and excellence – its stature has grown with Sachin getting the Bharat Ratna and becoming a Rajya Sabha MP. Through the brands he represents, he will be looking to share what it took to become a world-class sportsman, and how he managed to stay there for so long."

India, though, is an increasingly young nation. With half the population aged 30 or under, Tendulkar's legacy may not last for ever. Bollywood star Amitabh Bachchan is one of the most featured faces in Indian advertising, and reinvention has been the hallmark of his 45-year career. But Krishnamachar does not foresee a problem: "Sachin has built up such a stature and reputation over the years that there is no reason why the second phase of his life will not be as successful as the first."

genius who is also a team-player and a player-patriot, a mentor, an elder statesman, and an icon, as much to colleagues and opponents as he is to spectators. A senior Indian cricket writer tells me that the country gained new respect for Kohli – hitherto seen as a brash young man, even a borderline lout – when he said: "Sachin has carried the burden of the nation for 21 years. It is time we carried him." Suddenly, Kohli seemed to have something in common with the whole of India. His quote humanised him.

You will notice that there is no image here from Tendulkar's last, unarguably moving, day in Test cricket, at Mumbai in November. Allan Donald, an old adversary, once said: "I don't think I've seen a hungrier batsman." Sometimes there is an imperceptible line between hunger and greed; and to many who watched Tendulkar linger in Test cricket for his last two years, fused like a cussed tenant to his position at No. 4, there was a sense that he was not being entirely selfless, that he should have announced his retirement after dismounting from Kohli's shoulders in Mumbai, a World Cup in his kit bag. In India, this thought could only be whispered. Nor could it be said too forcefully that Tendulkar had become obsessed with playing 200 Tests, that he had (not for the first time) allowed a personal landmark to cloud his judgment.

Will there ever be another cricketer like him? Given the way the sport is evolving (or possibly disintegrating), it is almost certain no one will play as many Tests. His retirement, then, marks the end of a statistical era, the transition from BT to AT, from Before Tendulkar to After Tendulkar. Even the notion of this shorthand offers a nod to his status as an Indian divinity, a status that those from other countries presumably found disconcerting. For it is unlikely Tendulkar would have received the same obeisance had he been born elsewhere.

An English Tendulkar would have been made to wait for his Test debut until 22 or 23, and retired much earlier, his native self-deprecation having trumped any temptation to linger while younger players awaited their turn; adulation, in any case, isn't an English art. The rugged mateship inherent in the cultures of Australia, New Zealand and South Africa, where there is less of a gulf between player and fan, would have served as an antidote to Tendulkar-worship. West Indies and Sri Lanka have laid-back island cultures, where no man is bigger or prouder than the next, and his popularity depends on his accessibility to fellow citizens. In Pakistan too (for all its reverence of Imran Khan) there is an unwillingness to raise a mortal to superhuman status – a result, no doubt, of Islam.

Tendulkar, then, is an Indian phenomenon: a gifted man born in a land where boys can have adulthood thrust upon them quickly, yet retain a structure of family support well into later life. In fact, Tendulkar is not so much the product of India as of his family: a middle-class boy born to profoundly collaborative parents. His professor father, improbably for a bookish type, was happy for his son to spend more time on cricket than on his studies. And his family arranged for him to live with an uncle and aunt in a different quarter of his native Mumbai to shorten the commute to nets. It mattered not that the boy

Model family man: Sachin Tendulkar with son Arjun, daughter Sara and wife Anjali, in 2009. In the middle is an effigy destined for Mumbai's Madame Tussauds.

wasn't living with his mother and father: young Sachin was saving three hours a day in travel time!

His family's greatest gift was a cricketing cocoon. Sachin entered into it aged 11 (when, cherished and precocious, he was entrusted to his coach, Ramakant Achrekar) and emerged from it only on November 16, 2013, the day of his retirement. For three decades – to the exclusion of all else – he was able to eat, sleep, breathe and play the game. His older brother, Ajit, devoted his life to Sachin's cricket, removing him from the demands of a humdrum world. His wife Anjali, a wealthy and grounded woman six years his senior, took charge of the cocoon when she married him in 1995; he was 22. In contrast to the tumult in the lives of his great batting rival Brian Lara, or his school friend Vinod Kambli, who also played for India but lacked the discipline that can be instilled only at home, Tendulkar never had to worry about anything but cricket.

Did it make him a one-dimensional human being? C. L. R. James's famous question acquires some piquancy when applied to Tendulkar, for it was evident he knew cricket – and knew only cricket. He had no apparent philosophy that was unrelated to the playing and practice of the game. He was a technician, not a thinker. In interviews he was often banal, as if saying to his interlocutors: "Please, just let my bat do the talking." His English and Hindi are imperfect (perhaps because he neglected his schooling), and he reached inevitably for platitudes and diplomatic niceties, as if suspicious of anyone who wasn't hurling a ball at him. There is no big social issue on which he has taken a public stand – this, in a country awash with worthy causes, any one of which would have received a glorious boost had Tendulkar lent his name.

And yet Indian cricket grew gradually stronger for his single-mindedness. Tendulkar was their first player to be held in awe by other sides – and even feared. The awe came early. When, not yet 19, he flayed Australia in a Test at Perth, Merv Hughes told Allan Border: "This little prick's going to get more runs than you, AB." When Border retired two years later, he did so with a Test-record 11,174 runs; and 13 years after that, in November 2007 against Pakistan at Delhi, Tendulkar would prove Hughes right. He would overhaul Lara the following October, since when Tendulkar has always been top of the tree; his Test tally of 15,921 may never be broken.

Every bowler raised his game when charging in at Tendulkar; if only there were some way of factoring that extra effort into the value of his runs. For Indian fans, opposition bowlers became defined by their showdowns with him. James Anderson – who dismissed Tendulkar nine times in Tests, more than anyone – wasn't just James Anderson: he was James-Anderson-when-bowling-to-Tendulkar. And so it was with Courtney Walsh, Glenn McGrath, Muttiah Muralitharan and Dale Steyn. Donald, quoted in Vimal Kumar's *Sachin: Cricketer of the Century*, offered an example of the phenomenon: "My fondest memory of Sachin is bowling him through the gate in the Durban Test. There is no question about the fact that it was the best-ever ball that I bowled in Test cricket." At the spectrum's less rarefied end, Michael Vaughan has dined out on the off-break that once sneaked through Tendulkar in a Test in Nottingham; it was the man who mattered, as much as the delivery.

Despite this, his retirement does not leave Indian cricket noticeably weaker. After all, the batting line-up had been carrying him for two years, the result of Tendulkar being allowed to choose the time of his own retirement. He played on for 23 Tests after the 2011 World Cup final, averaging a downright un-Tendulkarish 32, as against nearly 57 until then. Just as tellingly, he became more susceptible to the straight ball: in that final phase, he was either bowled or lbw in 49% of his innings; until then, the figure had been 34%.

But what Indian cricket – or, more specifically, Indian batting – now has is a fearlessness that was missing in the BT years. Self-belief is Tendulkar's greatest bequest to his country's cricket. To everyone else he gave something of equal consequence: joy, and pleasure – the pleasure that comes from watching a simple, unaffected man perform beautiful feats with the bat, year after year after year.

Tunku Varadarajan is the Virginia Hobbs Carpenter Research Fellow in Journalism at Stanford University's Hoover Institution, and a former editor of Newsweek.

TENDULKAR IN FIGURES (1)

Sachin Tendulkar's 200 Test appearances constitute a record that may never be broken, though the span of his career is only the fifth-longest:

Years	Days	First Test started	Last Test finished		Tests
30	316	1.6.1899	12.4.1930	W. Rhodes (England)............	58
26	357	23.7.1949	13.7.1976	D. B. Close (England)...........	22
25	14	9.8.1909	22.8.1934	F. E. Woolley (England)..........	64
24	11	11.1.1930	21.1.1954	G. A. Headley (West Indies).......	22
24	**2**	**15.11.1989**	**16.11.2013**	**S. R. Tendulkar (India)**..........	**200**
23	41	5.2.1970	17.3.1993	A. J. Traicos (South Africa/Zimbabwe)	7

While Tendulkar was playing in those 200 Tests, there were others going on elsewhere. His first match, against Pakistan at Karachi in November 1989, was the 1,127th Test, and his last, against West Indies in Mumbai last November, the 2,102nd. That span of 976 is comfortably a record, beating Shivnarine Chanderpaul's 856 (though Chanderpaul was yet to retire) and Jacques Kallis's 794.

	Before SRT's Test career	During SRT's Test career
Debutants	1,808	923*
Runs scored.....................	1,067,571	999,645
Wickets taken	34,401	30,052
Centuries......................	1,822	1,836

* *Includes three others making their debut in the same Test.*

In ODIs, Tendulkar's career also overlapped with more matches than anyone else's. His debut, against Pakistan, came at Gujranwala in December 1989, and his last game, against Pakistan once again, at Mirpur in March 2012. His career lasted from ODI No. 593 until No. 3,263, a span of 2,671 – of which 463 involved Tendulkar. In second place is Sanath Jayasuriya (2,569); Kenya's Thomas Odoyo is third (2,415).

	Before SRT's ODI career	During SRT's ODI career
Debutants	595	1,431*
Runs scored	231,441	1,132,790
Wickets taken....................	8,166	38,037
Centuries......................	158	1,033

* *Includes two others making their debut in the same ODI.*

Tendulkar spent more of his life playing international cricket than anyone else:

	Days	Weeks	Months*	Years
Tests	892	127.42	29.73	2.44
ODIs	466	66.57	15.53	1.27
T20Is	1	–	–	–
Total (internationals)	**1,359**	**194.14**	**45.30**	**3.72**
Other senior cricket....................	560	80.00	18.66	1.53
Total (all cricket)....................	**1,919**	**274.14**	**63.96**	**5.25**

* *For this purpose, a month = 30 days*

...and a few other things that happened in India while Tendulkar was playing cricket:

	1989	2013	Increase (%)
Life expectancy at birth	58.1	65.5*	12.73
Indian satellites launched	14	72	414.28
Population.........................	851,400,000	1,237,000,000†	45.29
Gross domestic product ($USbn)	301.2	1,842†	511.55
Fertility rate (births per woman)........	3.99	2.59*	–35.08
Pupils in secondary education	47,022,000	107,687,000	129.01
CO_2 emissions (tonnes)	663,000	1,979,000‡	198.49
Aeroplane departures	156,300	706,500*	352.01

* 2011   † 2012   ‡ 2009

TENDULKAR RETIRES (2)

The god of small things

Aakash Chopra

I was only 12 when Sachin Tendulkar first represented India and left a nation instantly mesmerised. I remember watching him dance down the track to hit Abdul Qadir for three towering sixes, and must have tried to do the same innumerable times, if only in my imagination. While I was still learning how to stand properly at the crease, Tendulkar was earning standing ovations around the globe; while I was still learning how to use my feet to get to the pitch of the ball, Tendulkar was taking giant strides. The more I played the game, the more I admired him, for it was only through playing that one truly understood the scale of what he was doing.

By the end of the 1990s, it was as if he had ceased to be just a player, and now symbolised excellence. It was around this time that I started nurturing the dream of playing for India myself. And yet playing for India and playing alongside Tendulkar seemed two separate things. Playing for India would mean countless hours of toil, something I was prepared for. But nothing had prepared me for sitting in the dressing-room next to my idol.

I was a bundle of nerves when I walked into the conference hall of Ahmedabad's plush Taj hotel for my first India team meeting in October 2003. I had attended many team meetings before, but had little idea of how this one would unfold – and even less idea of how I would react to my first encounter with Tendulkar. Fifteen minutes in, I worried our chat wouldn't go beyond the customary exchange of greetings: words were failing me already.

Our coach, John Wright, divided the team into batsmen and bowlers to discuss the forthcoming Test against New Zealand. I'm glad he did, for that's when Tendulkar and I were introduced properly. I had played a couple of warm-up games against the tourists, so questions were thrown in my direction about how their bowlers were shaping up. To my utter surprise and pleasure, Tendulkar was the most inquisitive. How was Daryl Tuffey bowling? Had Daniel Vettori bowled his arm-ball? He wanted to know everything.

He had played these bowlers many times – and successfully. What need was there for a batsman of his capability to ask such questions of a rookie like me? But he did. And the reason became clear. He wanted to allow me to break the ice, to interact with him, to know him better. I suspect he realised that, as with most Indian debutants, I was overawed, and that this wasn't likely to change unless he made a special effort. I can't thank him enough for the gesture.

A couple of days later, confident from our last interaction, I called his room seeking an audience. Once again, he was happy to oblige. Until then, I'd been to the hotel rooms of many senior and junior cricketers, and had found most of them like any boy's room, strewn with dirty laundry, shoes, cricket gear, laptop and iPod. Tendulkar's was different: meticulous and organised, like his batting.

Aamir Qureshi, AFP/Getty Images

Close to perfection: Aakash Chopra and Sachin Tendulkar at Multan, March 2004.

Gods' idols were on the bedside table, bats neatly arranged in one corner, bed linen without any creases, dirty linen nowhere. He ordered a cup of coffee for us both, and chatted freely, as if we'd known each other for years.

I asked him about his preparation and game plans, and he began to share details. What I saw of Tendulkar in the days that followed left an indelible mark. He was always first to the team bus, because he didn't like rushing. He would plan most of his innings by making mental notes for the bowlers he was likely to face – a habit that meant he wouldn't sleep properly for a fortnight before India's game against Pakistan in the 2003 World Cup. It was during our chat that I realised preparation for every battle was as crucial to success at the top as natural ability. Knowing the opposition is important, but so is knowing your own game. Those 40 minutes I spent with him changed the way I looked at Tendulkar – the player and the man – for ever.

We batted first in the Test, and I made 42. As I walked back to the pavilion, the stadium erupted. Almost everyone in the stands was on their feet. So this was what it was like to play for your country! I was disappointed to have missed a fifty, but that feeling evaporated as I soaked up the ovation. The noise continued even after I was seated in the dressing-room – which was when I realised, to my embarrassment, that the applause might not have been for me.

TENDULKAR IN FIGURES (2)

Just how many records does Sachin Tendulkar hold? The answer depends on the definition of a record – dig deep enough and half this book could be devoted to them. For example, he has hit the highest score in a one-day international at Pietermaritzburg: 152 during the 2003 World Cup (which is also India's highest against Namibia). Neither is likely to rate highly in the definitive Sachin story, but he did annexe several major landmarks in his 24-year international career.

	Tendulkar	Next
Most Test appearances	200	168 (R. T. Ponting, S. R. Waugh)
Most Test runs	15,921	13,378 (R. T. Ponting)
Most Test centuries	51	45 (J. H. Kallis)
Most Test innings	329	287 (R. T. Ponting)
Most ODI appearances	463	445 (S. T. Jayasuriya)
Most ODI runs	18,426	13,704 (R. T. Ponting)
Most ODI centuries	49	30 (R. T. Ponting)
Most ODI scores of 90-99	18	9 (N. J. Astle, P. A. de Silva, G. W. Flower)
Most international runs	34,357	27,483 (R. T. Ponting)
Most international centuries	100	71 (R. T. Ponting)
Most ODI runs in a calendar year	1,894 (1998)	1,767 (S. C. Ganguly, 1999)

Tendulkar in Tests

Opposition	T	I	NO	Runs	HS	100	50	Avge
Australia	39	74	8	3,630	241*	11	16	55.00
Bangladesh	7	9	3	820	248*	5	0	136.66
England	32	53	4	2,535	193	7	13	51.73
New Zealand	24	39	5	1,595	217	4	8	46.91
Pakistan	18	27	2	1,057	194*	2	7	42.28
South Africa	25	45	4	1,741	169	7	5	42.46
Sri Lanka	25	36	3	1,995	203	9	6	60.45
West Indies	21	32	2	1,630	179	3	10	54.33
Zimbabwe	9	14	2	918	201*	3	3	76.50
Total	**200**	**329**	**33**	**15,921**	**248***	**51**	**68**	**53.78**
In India	94	153	16	7,216	217	22	32	52.67
Outside India	106	176	17	8,705	248*	29	36	54.74

Tendulkar also took 46 wickets, at 54.17, and held 115 catches.

Tendulkar in One-Day Internationals

Opposition	M	I	NO	Runs	HS	100	50	Avge	SR
Australia	71	70	1	3,077	175	9	15	44.59	84.74
Bangladesh	12	11	1	496	114	1	2	49.60	85.07
England	37	37	4	1,455	120	2	10	44.09	89.20
New Zealand	42	41	3	1,750	186*	5	8	46.05	95.36
Pakistan	69	67	4	2,526	141	5	16	40.09	87.49
South Africa	57	57	1	2,001	200*	5	8	35.73	76.31
Sri Lanka	84	80	9	3,113	138	8	17	43.84	87.54
West Indies	39	39	9	1,573	141*	4	11	52.43	78.02
Zimbabwe	34	33	5	1,377	146	5	5	49.17	91.55
†Associates	18	17	4	1,058	152	5	4	81.38	96.00
Total	**463**	**452**	**41**	**18,426**	**200***	**49**	**96**	**44.83**	**86.23**

Tendulkar also took 154 wickets, at 44.48, and held 140 catches. He played one Twenty20 international (against South Africa), in which he scored ten, took one wicket for 12 and held a catch.

† Excludes six matches against Bangladesh and one against Zimbabwe before they achieved Full Member status.

Research: Steven Lynch

Needless to say, it had been for the man walking out to bat, not the man walking into the pavilion. Only then did I begin to wonder what it must be like to be Sachin Tendulkar, carrying the burden of so many hopes. And yet he behaved with the utmost humility. In that moment, my respect for him rose several notches.

The real measure of the man lay in the fact that even the most senior members of the team showered him with respect. "I want to protect him. Tendulkar must not come out to bat to play a few balls in the fading light against the raging Aussies – he is our best hope to win the game." Those words, spoken by another great man, Rahul Dravid, to Nayan Mongia during the First Test at Mumbai during the famous 2000-01 series, still ring in my ears. The beauty of the relationship between Tendulkar and the other senior players was their mutual respect; no one behaved like a superstar. All of them encouraged an atmosphere of comfort, in which even a junior could happily pull a prank.

As I spent more time in the dressing-room, I gained a closer look at Tendulkar's quest for excellence. Every net session had a purpose, leading to a discussion about what he was doing right or wrong. And he was quite happy getting feedback from the newcomers, including me. Each time he asked me something, I would remind him that it should be the other way around. But he would have none of it, constantly prodding me for my view. Sachin would ask me about his stance, head position, backlift and downswing. And it wasn't just me: he would ask the net bowlers whether they could see him stepping out, or premeditating his strokes. Greatness isn't just what you know, but what you don't – and the effort you make to bridge that gap. Tendulkar mastered that art.

His gift was to appear in control. And that was so different from how I, or my colleagues, functioned. He didn't always need to score a truckload of runs to spread calm. Sometimes, he just needed to do what felt beyond the rest of us, and put bat to ball. Here was a man who not only timed his moves so well that he looked programmed by computer but, with a twirl of the bat, made the ball kiss the sweet spot.

Criticism is inevitable, and so it was for him. If you've spent your life in the middle, with every move scanned by the peering eyes of a billion people, you are bound to be judged. But he endured all censure without resentment. It was as if greatness went hand in hand with humility. That may have been the greatest lesson of all.

Aakash Chopra played ten Tests between 2003 and 2004, but batted with Tendulkar for only 26 balls.

SACHIN TENDULKAR, WORLD CELEBRITY

How the media loved him

The following are taken from Sachin Tendulkar's many mentions in *Wisden's* Chronicle section. It is safe to assume this is another appearance record.

Wisden 2001
The Russian chess grandmaster Peter Svidler has been nicknamed "Tendulkar" because he became a cricket fan after being introduced to the game by Nigel Short. (*Daily Telegraph*)

Wisden 2002
Tom Gueterbock approached the wisden.com website to help publicise the sale of his £495,000 home in Battersea, south London, which he thought might particularly appeal to Indian cricket fans. The address was 10 Dulka Road. (*Daily Telegraph*)

Wisden 2003
The Sachin Tendulkar lookalike, Balvirchand, who had already co-starred with Tendulkar in an advert for Visa cards, has been chosen to play him in the movie *Kaisi Mohabbat*, in which the heroine fulfils her dream by meeting the great man. (*Gujarat Samachar*, Ahmedabad)

Wisden 2004
Parthiv Patel's uncle, Jagat Patel, has sworn to marry only after the wicketkeeper is performing consistently for India's Test XI, a tactic once tried, successfully, by Sachin Tendulkar's brother, Ajit. (*Rajasthan Patrika*, Ahmedabad)

Wisden 2005
The Indian government waived customs duty and the requirements for a roadworthiness certificate so Sachin Tendulkar could import a £90,000 Ferrari Modena 360. Bharat Petroleum also blended special fuel so the car could run on Indian roads; the 97-octane petrol the car requires is not sold in India. (*Indian Express*)

Sachin Tendulkar is now on the Indian curriculum: children in schools in and around Delhi will study the life and times of the nation's idol. New textbooks for those in the 10–12 age group include an interview with Tendulkar, where he talks about his own childhood and what it takes to be a successful cricketer. Krishna Kumar, an education official, said that the move to include a first-person account of Tendulkar's life was part of an effort to make education "a more pleasurable experience". (Cricinfo)

Indian captain Sourav Ganguly's new Kolkata restaurant – Sourav's, The Food Pavilion – was opened by his team-mate and fellow restaurateur Sachin Tendulkar, who owns two similar establishments in Mumbai. Sourav's is described as "Kolkata's first four-storeyed multiplex restaurant". Ganguly had earlier reportedly been alarmed that Tendulkar was planning to beat him to it by opening a branch in Kolkata. (Sify.com/Press Trust of India)

Rahul Dravid has been voted sexiest Indian sports personality in the 2004 Durex global sex survey. Yuvraj Singh was second with Sachin Tendulkar third. (*Free Press Journal*, Mumbai)

Wisden 2006
The Indian government has reversed a ruling that barred Sachin Tendulkar from displaying the national flag on his helmet. The cabinet said it will amend the Prevention of Insults to National Honour Act, and will allow the flag to be used on sporting uniforms – but not below the belt or on underwear. (*Mid-Day*, Mumbai)

Wisden 2007
Sachin Tendulkar is India's highest earner, according to a new survey, making 1,163 rupees (£13.39) every minute, compared to 361 rupees for film star Amitabh Bachchan and 57 paise (0.6p) for the prime minister, Manmohan Singh. (*The Asian Age*)

Wisden 2008
Sachin Tendulkar is to appear in comic books as the Master-Blaster, a superhero. (*The Asian Age*)

Wisden 2011
A new variety of mango, developed by a horticulturist in Uttar Pradesh, has been named "Sachin" in honour of Sachin Tendulkar. However, the grower claimed he would not be selling the fruit. "Our

Sachin is a world hero and he is priceless," said Hajj Kalimullah. "My attempt will be to send all the mangoes on this tree to Sachin so he can enjoy them with his friends." (*Asian Tribune*)

Sachin Tendulkar was made an honorary Group Captain in the Indian Air Force, complete with uniform and epaulettes, at a ceremony in New Delhi. (*Times of India*)

Wisden 2012

An Indian tax tribunal upheld an appeal from Sachin Tendulkar that he should be classed as an actor for his modelling work. This enabled him to claim tax deductions. "As a model, the assessee brings to his work a degree of imagination, creativity and skill to arrange elements in a manner that would affect human senses and emotions and to have an aesthetic value," the tribunal ruled. (Press Trust of India)

The municipality of Brihanmumbai have given Sachin Tendulkar a final warning after spending 11 years trying to get him to attend a civic felicitation. "We have sent several reminders to Sachin, but he hasn't replied," said a spokesman. "We will now send him a final letter." (*The Asian Age*)

Wisden 2013

Australian Test players were irritated when their prime minister, Julia Gillard, told an official reception for the Indian team that her country's cricket fans were "looking forward to what may be a very special hundred made in Australia" – meaning Sachin Tendulkar's 100th international century. Michael Clarke said his team hoped the century would come somewhere else. His team-mate Mike Hussey called the prime minister's comment "strange". (Sky News)

The Mumbai Cricket Association intends to shower Tendulkar with a hundred gold coins for reaching 100 international centuries. (Press Trust of India)

Ratilal Parmar, 56, whose hobby is collecting banknotes that have special associations with Sachin Tendulkar, has acquired a new prize: a ten-rupee note numbered 240412, the date of Tendulkar's 39th birthday. Parmar wants to present his hero with the notes connected with his milestones, especially 160312, the date of the 100th international hundred. He estimates he has spent a million rupees building his collection, sometimes by pleading with bank clerks for help. (ESPNcricinfo)

British prime minister David Cameron told how he had found his wife Samantha playing French cricket with a bat signed for him by Sachin Tendulkar in the grounds of Chequers and had to warn her: "No, darling, put it down; this is probably the most valuable possession I have." He donated the bat for an auction at Lord's raising £3,400 for the Rwanda Cricket Stadium Foundation. (*Daily Telegraph*)

Sachin Tendulkar has been sworn in as a member of the Indian upper house, the Rajya Sabha. "It has been my dream to be remembered as someone who worked for all sports instead of just cricket statistics," he said after taking the oath. However, he warned that, as an active player, he would continue to focus on his own game. Tendulkar was chosen as one of the 12 members of the parliament the president is allowed to nominate, although some critics claimed that a sportsman did not fulfil the criterion of "special knowledge or practical experience in... literature, science, art and social service" specified for selection under the constitution. (*The Hindu*)

Australian prime minister Julia Gillard made Sachin Tendulkar an honorary member of the Order of Australia on a visit to India, but the award came under fire for not meeting the rule that such awards for non-Australians should reflect "extraordinary service to Australia or humanity at large". Independent MP Rob Oakeshott said: "I love Sachin, I love cricket, but I just have a problem with soft diplomacy. It's about the integrity of the honours list." (*Sydney Morning Herald*)

Wisden 2014

Sachin Tendulkar's waxwork at the new Madame Tussauds museum in Sydney has been given the wrong shirt. It was dressed in an Indian shirt for the World Twenty20, in which Tendulkar never appeared. (*Mid-Day*, Mumbai)

THE WISDEN–MCC CRICKET PHOTOGRAPH OF 2013 Atul Kamble wins the award for his image of Sachin Tendulkar emerging from the Wankhede Stadium dressing-room to resume his final Test innings, Mumbai, November 15.

Atul Kamble

THE WISDEN–MCC CRICKET PHOTOGRAPH OF 2013 For his image of Virat Kohli being struck in the face when failing to hold a catch, Shaun Roy is one of two runners-up. The drop came during the game between Kings XI Punjab and Royal Challengers Bangalore in the IPL, May 6.

The fourth Wisden–MCC Cricket Photograph of the Year, in association with 21SIX, the digitally led marketing experts, attracted more than 500 entries. Any image with a cricket theme taken during 2013 was eligible.

The independent judging panel, chaired by former *Sunday Times* chief photographer Chris Smith, comprised award-winning photographers Patrick Eagar, Eileen Langley and Hugh Routledge, and art director of *The Cricketer* Nigel Davies.

For more details, go to www.lords.org/photooftheyear

THE WISDEN–MCC CRICKET PHOTOGRAPH OF 2013 The other runner-up is Md Khalid Rayhan Shawon's photograph of boys playing cricket beneath the flight path into Shahjalal International Airport, Dhaka, Bangladesh, on April 16.

Md Khalid Rayham Shawon

CRICKET, AFTER A FASHION The Lord's Pavilion is home to a slightly nattier type than usual for a menswear show in June, while in May the inspiration for Karl Lagerfeld's 2013–14 collection is clear. And at Melbourne in January 2014, tennis's Williams sisters are given a crash course in cricket by Australia's Aaron Finch; Serena is batting, Venus at slip.

FACING RETIREMENT A Nagpur school looks to have a strong batting line-up, and in Mumbai artist Ranjit Dahiya paints a mural: two of many signs in November that Sachin Tendulkar was about to play his last game of international cricket.

Charlie Crowhurst, Getty Images

CHAMPAGNE MOMENTS Sarah Taylor holds a breathtaking catch to dismiss Australia's Jodie Fields during a one-day international at Hove as England head towards the Ashes, celebrated in style at Riverside in late August.

Philip Brown

IT'S A DANGEROUS GAME Surrey's Arun Harinath gets closer than intended to Jeetan Patel of Warwickshire during a Championship match at Guildford in June. Meanwhile, at The Oval in July, umpire Trevor Jesty clutches his shoulder after being struck by a straight-drive from Jason Roy; Jesty recovered – and stood for the remainder of the game.

THE LEADING CRICKETER IN THE WORLD Dale Steyn.

THE LEADING CRICKETER IN THE WORLD, 2013

Dale Steyn

NEIL MANTHORP

His return of six for eight against Pakistan at the Wanderers would have looked more at home in an Under-9 fixture than a Test match, but even that mesmerising analysis wasn't Dale Steyn's favourite moment of the year. Instead, he selects the victory over India at Kingsmead in the Boxing Day Test, during which he claimed six for 100 on the least helpful surface the South Africans had encountered anywhere in 2013, including the UAE.

All year, one quality defined Steyn: intensity. It was a quality central to the South African dressing-room. He maintained his characteristic vein-bulging efforts for every over of every spell, no matter how long he had been bowling, nor how hopeless the situation. He even endured the longest barren stint of his career: 416 balls without reward, between the wickets of Shikhar Dhawan in India's first innings at Johannesburg and Cheteshwar Pujara in their first at Durban. Yet his response was simply to try harder.

"Right from the start of my career I was surrounded by people like Jacques Kallis, Mark Boucher and Graeme Smith, who gave 100% in every performance," says Steyn. "They don't look as intense as me, but that's just because they aren't fast bowlers."

The highlight, lowlight and most enduring memories of an unforgettable year all came within a fortnight during that scandalously shortened series against India in December. He claimed only the wicket of Dhawan at the Wanderers, and bowled 51 further overs without success. Then, with three overs remaining, he made the decision to call off the chase, with South Africa requiring only 16 to knock off a Test-record 458. The majority of spectators booed Steyn. Suddenly, he was cast as the villain.

The Second Test followed four days later on a lifeless Kingsmead pitch which horrified South Africa's pace trio – though they had to bite their tongues. India reached 181 for one, a platform for impregnability. Steyn, who after Johannesburg had lost his four-year grip on top spot in the ICC Test rankings to team-mate Vernon Philander, sent down another 18 wicketless overs. On Christmas Day, Kallis had dropped his bombshell: this would be his final Test. It was a shock to everyone, but especially devastating for Steyn.

After the first day's play, he wondered whether his indefatigable spirit was waning. "But Jacques got the bowlers together and asked us how we were going to take 20 wickets, because he was pretty keen to win his last Test," says Steyn, with whimsical understatement. "I said to him: 'Jacques, I won't let you down. I will run through brick walls for you, I promise.'"

Next morning, in the absence of brick walls, Steyn produced a magnificent, late awayswinger to remove Pujara, a short ball which Murali Vijay gloved behind, then an inswinger to bowl Rohit Sharma: three wickets in ten balls without conceding a run. Later, India's recovery was building ominously at 320 for five, but Steyn returned to crush the lower order: 334 all out.

"We have always believed that a wicket is just one ball away," he says. "We have seen teams lose three wickets for nothing and four for 20 against us, more than once, so we know it will happen again. But not if you stop believing and start bowling slower. There have been a few times when I wondered if I was ever going to take a wicket, but you never give up. Once in India, I went from none for 100 to five for 120, so when I was none for 50 after the first day in Durban I wasn't panicking. But six for 100 still felt very special."

Three more wickets in the second innings took his Test haul for the year to 51 in only nine games at an average of 17. The England pair of Stuart Broad (62 wickets) and Jimmy Anderson (52) may have taken more wickets, but Broad averaged 25 and Anderson 31. And both spread their scalps across 14 Tests. Steyn was scarcely less lethal in one-day internationals, claiming 27 wickets at under 16 apiece. Most remarkable, perhaps, for a man of his pace, was his meanness: an economy-rate of 3.65 was comfortably the lowest among bowlers to have sent down 100 one-day international overs in 2013. The next-tightest seamer was Sri Lanka's Angelo Mathews, light years behind on 4.36. Fast, penetrative and parsimonious – it was some combination.

If there are any secrets to his success, they may lie on the dusty streets of Phalaborwa, on the border of the Kruger National Park, where Steyn grew up. Skateboarding was his passion, and he was good enough to have considered a career in it had he not succeeded at cricket. He describes practising a trick on his board many hundreds of times until he got it right, no matter how much it hurt. "There was blood, sometimes a fracture or two, but you keep going. Sounds a bit like fast bowling, doesn't it?"

Another secret is the open-minded naivety about cricket provided by his upbringing. His knowledge of the game was limited, and of its history non-existent. It meant he was underwhelmed by the excellence of his own performances, and undaunted by the expectations that followed. "Allan Donald and Shaun Pollock were my heroes, so I thought averaging 22 or 23 and taking five-wicket hauls was normal," he says. "That was a fast bowler's job."

The third secret lies a long way from his youth – in the video analyst's laptop. What some would call a healthy interest in computers and cameras, others would call an obsession. Ever since Steyn first discovered that what he had regarded as the perfect spell could be disproven by scientific evidence, he has checked his lines, lengths and groupings at every interval, not merely at the end of the day. Time and again he reached his own conclusions about how to dismiss a batsman – and then executed the plan.

Steyn's nine for 147 at Durban took him to 350 wickets in 69 Tests – joint-second-fastest to that mark, alongside Richard Hadlee, and behind Muttiah Muralitharan (66 matches). Among bowlers to have taken 100 wickets, his strike-rate of 42 was bettered only by George Lohmann, Philander and S. F. Barnes – two of whom plied their trade over a century earlier. He shows no signs of slowing down or losing his enthusiasm. "I enjoy taking wickets more than most people can understand," he says. "I'm addicted to that feeling. I live in the moment, but I hope there are many more years of it to come."

DIVIDE AND RULE AT THE ICC

The great carve-up of world cricket

GIDEON HAIGH

During the Second World War, it was Churchill, Stalin and Roosevelt. In the car industry, it used to be General Motors, Ford and Chrysler. But the world of cricket will remember 2014 as the year the game got its own Big Three – even if it was really a Big One (India), with two lesser parties (England and Australia) obediently in step.

In July, cement magnate Narayanaswami Srinivasan is set to become not simply cricket's most powerful figure, but the most powerful figure cricket has ever known. The president of the BCCI and owner of the IPL's Chennai Super Kings has arguably been cricket's Grand Poobah for some time, but his installation as ICC chairman will afford him unexampled pre-eminence in the game's governance – as well as unexampled conflicts of interest.

It says something that this was not even the most extraordinary aspect of the Big Three's campaign to revamp the ICC. That honour went, perhaps, to the notion of distribution of money raised by events such as the World Cup and World Twenty20 according to the size of the "contribution" made by the relevant member – massively enriching the BCCI, and somewhat benefiting the ECB and Cricket Australia. Or to the effective scrapping of the Future Tours Programme in favour of touring arrangements secured bilaterally. Or to a ranking system that ostensibly offered possible admission to Test cricket to the ICC's most advanced Associate Member, be it Ireland or Afghanistan. Take your pick: the so-called position paper, prepared by Srinivasan, the ECB's Giles Clarke and CA's Wally Edwards, made previous revamps look cosmetic.

It's not like there was nothing to fix, of course: the BCCI's economic heft has distorted cricket's finances to breaking point, with the health of other boards basically determined by how often their team played India – entailing, it must be said, an unwonted burden for India's cricketers. It was an environment that lent itself to temporary alliances, tit-for-tat wranglings, and negligible strategic thought.

The ICC's members and other stakeholders had condemned it out of their own mouths in 2011, when they participated in what became "An Independent Governance Review of the International Cricket Council". Its authors, former chief justice Lord Woolf and PricewaterhouseCoopers, found the organisation sunk in squabbles, and divided by financial imbalance, with "those in a strong financial position… using that strength to provide leverage to reach decisions that may be in individual members' interests rather than the interests of the majority of Full Members, or indeed international cricket as a whole".

Tabled before the executive board at the end of January 2012, the review made the case for a more active council, with a fully fledged chairman, independent directors and a funding model "based on need". Woolf and his colleagues argued: "The ICC react as though they are primarily a members' club; their interest in enhancing the global development of the game is secondary… The game is too big and globally important to permit continuation of Full Member boards using the ICC as a 'club'." Sensitive to anything that might curb their influence, the BCCI rejected the review as "not appropriate". ICC chief executive Haroon Lorgat cleared his desk in June.

The atmosphere at meetings grew tense, aggravated by Srinivasan's distaste for Dubai: he was once said to have complained loudly of his inability to find a burger at the airport. By January 2013, relations had broken down irretrievably, as Srinivasan informed other Full Members that he did not feel bound by the ICC's code of ethics to act in the body's fiduciary interests, and that the BCCI reserved the right to exit the FTP if any recommendation of the Woolf Review was even mooted. Further signs of restiveness at the BCCI were the foisting of Srinivasan's protégé, Laxman Sivaramakrishnan, on the ICC cricket committee, and manoeuvrings towards a life ban for his old enemy, Lalit Modi, because of alleged misdeeds in the management of the IPL.

Midway through 2013, Srinivasan experienced pressures of his own, temporarily standing aside from his BCCI and ICC roles when his son-in-law Gurunath Meiyappan was drawn into a new and different IPL corruption crisis. The sight of Srinivasan at bay emboldened both Modi, who plotted a return to the BCCI through his old power base at the Rajasthan Cricket Association, and Lorgat, whom Cricket South Africa, after some hesitation, felt free to appoint as their chief executive. If anything, though, this stiffened Srinivasan's resolve to reshape the ICC – a procedure which the ECB and CA could either collude in or face exclusion from. Pragmatically, they chose collusion. All the while the BCCI were foreshadowing the eclipse of the old FTP by dickering at length over a tour of South Africa to which they had previously committed.

The three-man working group met in London in October, in Mumbai in November, and in Perth in December, co-opting as their scriveners the IPL's chief operating officer Sundar Raman, and CA's legal and business affairs manager Dean Kino. The momentous changes envisioned by the group needed the support of eight of the ten Full Members, so various inducements were devised, from a Test-match fund – to provide grants to boards playing "unviable" Test series – to an understanding that Full Members could "enter into as many or as few FTP agreements as they wish". Lorgat's brainchild, the World Test Championship, was also to be scrapped, with the more lucrative Champions Trophy now restored.

But the Big Three's offer of leadership was mainly a means of entrenching their own position, embodied by a proposed executive committee made up of a representative from each and, a little grudgingly, one other board member: "ExCo would act as the sole recommendation committee… on all constitutional, personnel, integrity, ethics, development and nomination matters."

The Big Three also proposed rotating the chairs among themselves for the executive board, whose importance was now somewhat diminished, and the financial and commercial affairs subcommittee, whose importance was now considerably enhanced by their role in selling broadcast rights to the next

Power brokers: Giles Clarke and N. Srinivasan, October 2013.

eight-year cycle of ICC events (the hosting of which would be shared by the Big Three, with the option of embracing a co-host).

It was on a handsome sale price for these – forecast to be in the region of $US2.5bn, a full $1bn more than in the previous cycle – that the new regime was predicated. The Big Three could then argue that, despite their additional rake-off of hundreds of millions of dollars, no Full Member would be significantly worse off – or not, at any rate, once they had been assured of binding and bankable bilateral tours.

When the paper was tabled at a special meeting of the executive board on January 9, curiosity quickly turned to consternation. In reference to the concentration of executive power among the mighty, the Pakistan Cricket Board's Najam Sethi was said to have asked: "So, are you doing a UN Security Council on us?" It was not denied. Not surprisingly, the paper was quickly leaked to ESPNcricinfo, who led coverage of developments. Other mainstream media, by contrast, veered between partisan and apathetic.

Initial comment, most of it indignant, focused on the Big Three's self-exemption from relegation in two divisions, which they first suggested, then ditched. It was actually a stipulation on which they could give way quite easily; likewise their absolute control of ExCo, now made into a transitional arrangement, and leavened with the addition of a further seat. The new distribution model remained stubbornly impenetrable, with "contribution costs" levied by the Big Three explained as recognising "the role of each Member in contributing to generating the ICC revenues required to sustain the game". There was no clarity as to their calculation, beyond the bland assurance: "The

THE BIG THREE

Our vision for a better game

GILES CLARKE

A huge white elephant sits in the Dubai desert, otherwise known as the purpose-built offices of the ICC. The most bizarre part of this monument to profligacy can be found in the chief executive's office: a private lavatory unavailable to the general staff, but insisted on, at considerable cost, at the time of design.

Combine this with huge travel bills, expensive hotel suites, even golf club memberships that, in the case of one chief executive, amounted to $US57,000 per annum – the equivalent of the annual distribution to six Affiliate Members – and the impression is of a business without adequate controls, run for the management, not for the shareholders. The ICC are a members-owned cooperative, so what exactly have the members been doing?

When Alan Isaac became ICC president in June 2012, he asked me to take over the chairmanship of the finance and commercial affairs committee of IDI, the ICC's commercial arm. I was already chairman of the commercial rights 2015–23 working group, which had produced a first plan in October 2011, drawn up by Campbell Jamieson, the ICC general manager (commercial).

The commercial rights revenues pay all the ICC bills, and provide the key funds for all the Associates and Affiliates, and for important distributions to the ten Full Members. The rights were sold for $500m for 2000–07, and $1.5bn for 2007–15.

Of this vast sum, the ten Full Members each received $52.5m over the eight years – an average of $6.5m per year. From 2007–15 ICC events were budgeted to cost $512m to stage, while ICC administrative costs, squirrelled away in all kinds of accounting places, were $252m. The 96 Associates and Affiliates received $125m in total, from a pool of $314m, which included a $45m payment to the Asian Cricket Council. The remaining amount was swallowed up by their own event costs ($67m), ICC regional expenditure ($40m), subscriptions paid back to ICC ($41m), the High Performance Programme ($8.5m), and other ICC costs.

So much for the numbers. But a disproportionate amount of money was being spent – wasted, some might argue – on costs, rather than being used to develop and promote cricket in the membership.

For the ICC to agree to a media rights contract, all the Full Members must sign a Member Participation Agreement, which sets out the terms under which their teams are available for ICC events. Draft MPAs were sent to all countries in 2012, and it became apparent the BCCI were unhappy.

They believed, correctly, that Indian TV rights had contributed significantly to the two previous ICC deals, and that they were not being adequately compensated for "hiring out their team to the ICC", in the words of Cricket Australia. The BCCI made it clear that, if their concerns were not recognised, they would feel uncomfortable about continuing in the ICC.

For 15 years, India had been paid the same as the other Full Members from the ICC's central fund. Their concerns appeared legitimate. From a purely commercial perspective, it was essential that cricket's position in India remained pre-eminent. The 2011 World Cup, co-hosted by them, Bangladesh and Sri Lanka, was an enormous success. So there were strong reasons to listen to the

BCCI's argument. We advised Alan Isaac of this, and he urged the ECB and CA to work with the BCCI to find an alternative.

An exhaustive series of meetings took place. For the ECB and CA, major changes to the ICC's structure were key to their agreeing with the revised MPA. It was evident that only the members could make the ICC better, and that leadership had to come from the larger, stronger members, who needed to be united, not divided. The three largest boards needed to be willing to sit on, and chair, key committees, to give ICC momentum during this transitional period.

As discussions progressed, we agreed that members had to be encouraged to stand on their own feet economically, and to run the game in their regions in a sustainable and transparent way. Furthermore, the playing system needed to be based on meritocracy, not categories of membership. The glass ceiling had to go: Associates deserved a clear path to both the World Twenty20 and the World Cup – and, most importantly, to Test cricket.

The Test game needed to be nurtured as the primary format, with the World Cup the main generator of finances. Twenty20 was seen as an important driver of domestic revenues, along with a global tournament every four years. Nation-versus-nation cricket required re-energising, with a firm Future Tours Programme. Certainty was crucial.

There is an argument that there was no need for change, that cricket was working fine, that the previous model was fair and sustainable. The finances of the majority of nations suggested otherwise; and most members were dependent on visits by India or England.

There was also a need to financially underpin and encourage Test cricket. Some nations could barely afford even to host Test matches. This had to change. Now, a Test fund will provide $12.5m over eight years to each Full Member – except for the BCCI, the ECB and CA.

The working group obtained vast amounts of information on Full Members' finances, which allowed them to get to grips with the costs of Test cricket, and identify loss-making tours. Finally, a full structural reform of the ICC, acceptable to the three boards, was agreed, along with a complex model that compensated Members for providing their teams for ICC events, the costs of which would now be driven down by a new panel of event experts.

A working draft was produced, intended as a basis for debate. Inevitably it was leaked, causing an absurd furore. The critics did not read it fully, did not ask questions of those involved, and did not realise it was aimed merely at kick-starting meaningful dialogue.

Following much discussion, with two meetings in Dubai and a third in Singapore, agreement was reached, and resolutions were passed on February 8, 2014. As so often in cricket administration, these were widely – perhaps deliberately – misinterpreted. We had to harden ourselves against uninformed and biased comment to deliver our vision for a better and more financially secure cricketing world.

The FTP has not been abolished, but left to individual boards to arrange among themselves. It has been extended to 2023, with the top eight nations playing each other. And India do not get a veto. In fact, they were outvoted during the process, but the key is all major members are actively involved in leadership. India are inside the house now.

The ECB have already reserved a date in the cycle from 2015–23 for a Lord's Test to the Associate who win the Intercontinental Cup and go on to defeat the No. 10 side in the Test rankings. A glittering prize!

Giles Clarke is chairman of the ECB.

agreed principles are sound, and the break-up between categories appropriate." But on January 23, the contribution costs were rendered non-negotiable at a Chennai meeting of the BCCI's working committee, which magisterially pronounced them "in the interests of cricket at large".

Two days later came the first strong voice of opposition, as former ICC president Ehsan Mani went to the lengths of preparing his own paper, charging that the Big Three had "completely undermined the integrity and standing of the ICC… in promoting their own agenda". Mani wrote caustically: "BCCI, ECB and CA say in the paper that they will provide greater leadership and stability to the ICC and their members. They do not demonstrate how they will do this in any meaningful way." The biggest losers, he argued, were the ICC's Associate and Affiliate nations, some hundreds of millions of dollars worse off.

Mani's protest was joined by a variety of old ICC hands: Mani's predecessor Malcolm Gray, and their chief executive Malcolm Speed; former directors Sir John Anderson from New Zealand, Shaharyar Khan and Tauqir Zia from Pakistan, Saber Chowdhury of Bangladesh, and Ali Bacher from South Africa; and former international captains Clive Lloyd, Imran Khan and Martin Crowe.

Their prophecies of strife and division were lent credibility by Paul Marsh, head of the Federation of International Cricketers' Associations: "The result of this will be that the countries who need ICC income the most will receive the least, while the Big Three will get the lion's share, even though they are already financially healthy because of the value of the rights to their bilateral series. The role of ICC events should be to assist in levelling the financial playing field by distributing the proceeds fairly, rather than further widening the gap between the rich and poor."

The house of the other seven Full Members remained divided against itself. Arguably the three closest to their respective governments, the PCB, Sri Lanka Cricket and Cricket South Africa, most acutely felt the position paper's implicit slight on their stature. They gathered for the quarterly executive committee meeting on January 28 full of outward fight, and deferred a vote on the proposals, while further offers and threats were exchanged.

But India hadn't spent so long in the British Empire without learning something about dividing and ruling. Srinivasan, confined to his home for a period of mourning following his mother's death, participated in the meeting by Skype: shot slightly from below, and with the sun behind him, he loomed rather ominously. Pakistan's Zaka Ashraf stood firm, unmoved even by the offer of three series against India in eight years; South Africa's Chris Nenzani, however, settled mainly for a share of proceeds from the Test-match fund, previously denied to CSA. "It is not a perfect world," he mused. When Ashraf returned home, he probably found himself in agreement: he was sacked.

By mid-February 2014, many uncertainties remained about the new regime: how the calendar would look; how teams would be ranked; how what the authors euphemistically called "certain major domestic cricket events", such as the IPL and the Champions League, would be affected (only favourably, one suspected). The position paper's authors and advocates have justified the expedient on the basis of the dysfunctional relations between the BCCI and the

ICC, arguing that, as the BCCI were not amenable to reform, the ICC had to reform instead.

The authors see the "contribution costs" as the price of concord and, even if that doesn't explain why the ECB and CA deserved their enrichments, some justification exists for this view. It's all very well to say that the world must stand up to India; frankly, the finances of world cricket are such that the smaller seven Full Member boards can barely stand up.

In the absence of many checks and any balances, however, a lot depends on the cordiality between ICC members, even the Big Three, and that requires a confluence of self-interests. It may not always be guaranteed. Personalities change; politics and economics are inherently unstable; and cricket, as they say, is a funny game.

Gideon Haigh writes for The Times *and* The Australian. For more details of the ICC's new structure, see page 1528.

THE HEYDAY OF THE NORTHERN LEAGUES

Stars that shone beside the slag heaps

Peter Gibbs

On a Friday evening in August 1959, my anticipation of the cricket match to be played the following day was more intense than usual. I had cleared a corner of the kitchen to prepare my kit. My boots and pads were barely scuffed from their previous outing, but not as pristine as they had to be for my First XI debut alongside F. M. M. Worrell. Frank Mortimer Maglinne Worrell. Sir-to-be Frank Worrell. A spotless turnout was the least he could expect for sharing a changing-room with a 15-year-old. So the match started there and then, in the kitchen, with the whitening.

Worrell had become Norton's professional three years earlier. The North Staffordshire League club had prospered through their association with the National Coal Board, owners of the ground. Like many other northern league venues, its outlook was uncompromisingly industrial. A slag heap on the scale of the Pyramids provided the backdrop, a rattling conveyor belt delivering spoil to its summit day and night.

If Worrell found his surroundings unappealing, he was too gracious to say so. The night before his first appearance, he was introduced to his team-mates at a dinner arranged by the club chairman, Tom Talbot. For a man on a personal political journey that would make him a symbol of the Caribbean drive for independence, Worrell may have been a little startled by a warm but naive Potteries welcome which included a cabaret turn by an Al Jolson impersonator singing "Mammy".

Any discomfort must have dissipated quickly, because he stayed at Norton for three record-breaking seasons, the last of which was also my first. Having performed capably in the Second XI, I had been drafted into a holiday-weakened first team where, overawed and out of my depth, I found myself opening the batting. The Black Prince was at No. 3.

The opposition, Burslem, had a venue in a league of its own for dank inhospitality. A sooty fug invariably clung to that corner of the region and, once a blanket of drizzle was added to the mix of particulates, visibility could be measured in feet. Burslem also had a long tradition of spectator participation. A concrete enclosure was home to a vociferous posse of regulars who came hotfoot from the pub to provide a scathing commentary.

This was the stage on to which I and the most dazzlingly elegant member of the Three Ws stepped that day. A cutting from the late-afternoon edition of *The Sentinel* reveals that, after making a single, I was heading back to the pavilion. As we crossed, it is safe to assume I offered no advice to our No. 3 concerning the nature of the pitch, or how he might counter the swinging ball.

The following Saturday I met much the same fate, out lbw for not very many. Unprotected by my junior-sized pads, I had been hit stingingly on the

The great Pyramid of Norton: the teams for a testimonial match in 1953 for the former West Indian fast bowler Manny Martindale, whose side included four other West Indian Test players. In the back row, next to the bespectacled umpire and Roy Curwen (who fielded for both sides), are Fred Martindale (Manny's elder son), Frank Worrell and Everton Weekes, and also – three to the right of Weekes – Manny's younger son Colin, then Ken Rickards. On the left of the front row are Harold Brewster (later Barbados's deputy High Commissioner in London), Edwin St Hill (two Tests in 1929-30), Martindale himself, and Norton's captain Don Dennis.

inner thigh. Worrell, this time at second wicket down, looked on impassively from the pavilion window. Though a more upholstered frame had superseded his younger profile, he was every bit the imposing figure off the field that he was on it. Sunlight through the part-netted window painted purples and blues on his polished skin, and a sharply trimmed moustache dignified his features. His eyes, sepia-tinged around the iris, were contemplative.

Embarrassingly, my own had welled up. Not only had I been dismissed cheaply, I was still feeling the radiating pain from the blow to the most tender part of my leg. I sat on the dressing-room table to watch the play, and fought back tears. Worrell saved his words of encouragement for later, but his presence alone was enough to convey the message that this was a man's game: I had better shape up. In any case his mind was probably pondering weightier matters. Four thousand miles away in the Caribbean, the campaign to make him the first full-time black captain of West Indies was intensifying under the direction of C. L. R. James.

Worrell's own political views had remained diplomatically restrained, but his support for the People's National Movement was never in doubt. James had suggested in a front-page rant that the non-appointment of Worrell would amount to a "declaration of war". In April 1960, the board finally caved in, and so, with more important things to do, he bowed out of Norton, to be replaced as the professional by Jim Laker.

One could be forgiven for thinking that the club chairman was a Potteries version of Roman Abramovich, especially when, three years later, he signed Garry Sobers. The reality was a little less munificent. Tom Talbot was in fact

One of the people: Jim Laker turns out for Norton CC in 1960.

a local plumbing and heating contractor: no oligarch, then, but just as ambitious. At a time when a player earned perhaps £100 for a Test match, a fee of £60 plus collections for a Saturday afternoon game was no small consideration. A host of world-class cricketers were similarly lured to the northern leagues at a time when county registration rules limited their opportunities to earn a living in the first-class game.

For those who made up the numbers, it was a thrill and a privilege to be stepping on to the field with such stellar players. Before I was out of my teens I would play alongside three of the game's greatest cricketers; and, in Wes Hall and Sonny Ramadhin, bat against two of its most charismatic bowlers.

Laker's written recollections of his 1960 season at Norton reveal a man reasonably satisfied with his contribution. Even so, after his distinguished career with Surrey and England, he must have thought he had fetched up on a different planet. Having arrived early for his first match, he left the dressing-room to turn his arm over on the outfield. Once back in the pavilion, he found his clothes had been replaced on the peg by a policeman's uniform. The officer in question was the club's other off-spinner. "He may have taken 19 wickets in a Test match," said the PC, "but nobody nicks my changing place." It was generally agreed that Jim was bang to rights for "taking without consent".

Perhaps it was an omen: Jim never did find his place that season. The reassuring vastness of The Oval had been replaced by neighbourhood grounds with mean boundaries. Supremely subtle bowler though he was, his flight and guile were wasted on artless batsmen who would swish him unceremoniously over cow corner. Spinners were not automatically second-best to the pace-bowler professionals, but to match them they had to have the bamboozle factor of Ramadhin or the Australian Cec Pepper. Jim was just too classically orthodox to run through a side match after match, and his batting was modest.

For a tall, sturdy man, his studied economy of movement was striking. His short-stepping approach was almost a parody of a bowler's run-up, but the body action, when it came, produced a model of seemingly effortless propulsion. Four seasons before, I had witnessed part of his demolition of the Australian batting in Manchester. Jim smiled sceptically when I told him. "If everyone who claims to have been at the game really was there," he responded, "Old Trafford could have been filled ten times over." Taking his comment as a mild put-down, I was tempted to admit that my most vivid recollection of that game was not of him, but of Neil Harvey who, on being dismissed, sent his bat twirling high into the air like a pipe drum major. That bit of showmanship obviously appealed to my childish mind more than Jim's admirable reticence: "Just doing my job, guv," he seemed to say as he hitched up his high-waisted flannels and took his pullover from the umpire.

Perhaps if Norton had doctored the pitches as Ramadhin's club, Ashcombe Park, routinely did, Laker would have been just as lethal. But a disappointing third in the league was not what the chairman had in mind when he engaged the destroyer of the Aussies. Laker maintained he had only ever intended to play at Norton for one season; the chairman said negotiations had broken down. Whatever the truth, a new contract was not signed. However, even at 40, Jim would make another foray into first-class cricket, with Essex.

By the time Sobers turned up at Norton in 1964, I was at university and acquiring my first taste of the first-class game. His arrival created a buzz, and added excitement to my vacation cricket. Like Worrell, Sobers had spent several seasons with Radcliffe in the Central Lancashire League before arriving in North Staffordshire. Whether or not Worrell had been instrumental in the transfer, he was in a good position to mark Sobers's card.

Just as Worrell had been on the verge of the West Indies captaincy in my club debut season, now Sobers stood to become his successor for the home series against Australia in 1964-65. In the previous ten years, he had performed prodigious feats, including an unbeaten 365 against Pakistan to take the Test batting record from Len Hutton at the age of 21. He had wowed the Australian public in the famous 1960-61 Test series, and returned the following year to play for South Australia and wow them again, before taking a major role in Worrell's triumphant last series, in England in 1963.

Under the steadying hand of Worrell, who knew when to cut his team some slack or rein in any excess, Sobers and company were able to party with the same enthusiasm they displayed on the field. Worrell had banned card-playing among his men. If they wanted to gamble, he preferred them to lose money to bookmakers than team-mates, thereby eliminating potential friction within the dressing-room.

The offer of the captaincy, while not unexpected, threatened to bring the Sobers merry-go-round to a halt. He would not thereafter be one of the boys. Worrell had been eight years older than him when the appointment came, so Sobers's apprehension was unsurprising. With his calm authority, Worrell had

A big draw: in 1967, Garry Sobers picks out the name of an entrant in the Frank Worrell Memorial Cup, a single-wicket competition held at Norton in honour of Worrell, who had died earlier in the year. On the far left is Norton chairman Tom Talbot; second from right is club captain Jim Flannery.

become a father-of-the-nation figure, a mentor who commanded his team's unalloyed love and respect. In C. L. R. James's words, he was a "finished personality". Even though Worrell himself had anointed him as his successor, Sobers was not convinced he wanted the job of controlling a side that contained half a dozen players who considered themselves as senior as he was.

The West Indies board's letter of invitation to captain the team smouldered in Sobers's pocket for five months, his uncertainty easing only on Saturday afternoons, when he wrecked batting line-ups one after the other. In 18 matches, his 97 wickets at 8.38 secured the title for Norton – and a satisfied smile from the chairman.

After dismissing the opposition for a modest total, and with the pro's collection box already doing the rounds, Garry had the disconcerting habit of putting his feet up and inviting our first three batsmen to knock off the runs. So together we would nudge and push our way towards victory in the hope of not bothering our star attraction. The crowd, however, were less than delighted. They may have seen Sobers bowl, but they had paid to see him bat as well. In a matter of a few overs we three stooges had outstayed our welcome: being on the receiving end of impatient heckling became a character-building feature of my Saturday afternoons.

Just as Britons looked upon Nelson and Churchill as national figureheads, so first-generation West Indian immigrants took Worrell and Sobers for their heroes. During his seasons with Norton, Worrell was never short of a fan to help carry his kit from the car park, but when Sobers rolled up, a whole troupe of helpers would greet him. One would carry his bag, another his bat, another his pads – all keen to grab a piece of their idol. Thereby unencumbered, the leading man did his "Stayin' Alive" walk to the pavilion – years before Travolta sashayed along a sidewalk with a tin of paint.

The lively atmosphere engendered by the West Indian professionals became even more boisterous at benefit games, when famous and not-so-famous overseas players came with family and friends. It was at a Frank Worrell benefit match in 1958 that I had first seen Sobers. The standing of the beneficiary meant he had no trouble putting together a team studded with stars. Sobers had not yet announced himself as the pre-eminent cricketer he was to become, and I have no recall of him with bat or ball that day. What I do remember is the moment he fielded a ball in the covers. Glossy red and crisply struck, it described an arc across the turf, heading for what seemed a certain four, when Sobers pounced with such feline grace it took the breath away. The pick-up was clean and, in one silky movement, the arm looped back. With a snap of the wrist he whipped a flat throw smack into the keeper's gloves above the bails.

A more mature observer might have appreciated the liquid engineering required for such apparently fluid motion. Wiser heads could have predicted the wear and tear on muscle and cartilage. But for me, at that moment, ignorance was bliss. And even when his Travolta walk became noticeably stiffer, Sobers still seemed incapable of playing an ugly innings. As Cardus wrote, his batting was "not classical but lyrical".

Inimitable as Garry was, there was no point in me, or anyone else for that matter, trying to adopt him as a role model. He was left-handed for a start, taller than me, quicker of eye and feet, and infinitely more supple. So I copied the only thing I could – I turned up my collar. Sometimes he wore his shirt unbuttoned, à la Elvis in his Vegas days, but I lacked the nerve and the chest to risk further affectation.

Returning to Norton, I discover the pyramid of colliery slag has been levelled, environmentally cleansed, and an estate of mundane houses built in its place. I am sure local residents prefer it, but I confess to a pang of regret at the loss of a landmark. Although they no longer maintain the ground, a residuary body of the NCB remains its owner. To cover day-to-day running costs, the club rely on raffles, curry nights and small-change local sponsorship. The geometry of the ground is much the same, but the tiered seating has been ripped out for want of a crowd, and the few remaining

Staffordshire Sentinel News & Media

Portrait of the author as a young batsman: Peter Gibbs, 1961. Note the collar.

stalwarts know to bring a folding chair. The club is no longer in the premier league, and any match-day hubbub is limited to the on-field exhortations of the players themselves.

Despite the low-octane tenor of the game in progress, the members' welcome is warm, and their joshing as dry as I remember it. "The standard's about the same as our old Second XI," says a team-mate from half a century ago. Nobody dissents. They are hopeful prospects will improve with the arrival of a new overseas professional who has been delayed in a thicket of visa regulations. "There's still value to be had on the subcontinent," one member assures me, "but it's a bind to get the paperwork through the anti-terrorist box-ticking." Something of a reassurance, then, though not especially welcome when league points are at stake.

Worrell, Laker and Sobers – for a cricket-mad youngster to have played alongside such all-time greats seems even now the stuff of make-believe. Although league clubs still enlist professionals, be they unheralded players from abroad or home-grown talent hefted to the local scene, they are unlikely to set the pulse racing like the pros of yesteryear. Today the stars are beamed to us by satellite as they follow a globetrotting schedule far removed from the colliery environs of Norton Cricket Club. And, sadly, no more is heard of the barracker who feigned objection when our star player smacked down divots in the pitch with the back of his bat. "Steady on, Sobers. There's men working under there."

Peter Gibbs is a film and TV screenwriter, and author of the cricket novel Settling the Score *(Methuen). He played for Staffordshire, Oxford University and Derbyshire, hitting 8,885 first-class runs, with 11 hundreds.*

MIDDLESEX AND MCC

A marriage of convenience

JOHN STERN

There is no job too menial for Angus Fraser, the unstinting Middlesex seam bowler who became their managing director of cricket and once volunteered to paint the north London flat given to him by the club, rather than pay a professional decorator. Before each Middlesex match at Lord's, Fraser retrieves a small stack of engraved plastic badges in navy and white – the county's colours – from the dressing-room attendant's office. He slots the badges, which bear the names of the first-team squad, into brass holders next to the coat hooks dotted around the walls of the home dressing-room. When a player leaves the club, his badge is screwed to the inside of his locker, allowing his successors to see its history.

Such a seemingly minor detail is Fraser's way of trying to stamp some of his county's identity on a ground that has been their home since 1877, but over which they have precious little control, and certainly no ownership. His aim is to strike a balance: he wants his cricketers to feel at ease, while retaining respect for their surroundings. "As Middlesex players we've always been aware that it's not our ground," he says. "But that has made people who risk being a bit full of themselves humbler than they might otherwise have been. You're always aware there's something bigger here than you and Middlesex."

This year is the 150th anniversary of Middlesex County Cricket Club, not to be confused with Marylebone Cricket Club, their landlords and owners of Lord's, who are themselves celebrating 200 years at the world's most venerated venue. Whether by design or coincidence, these milestones have prompted the clubs to renegotiate their unique relationship. It is not so much a renewal of vows as a pragmatic reassessment by two organisations who still need each other – even after all this time.

For Middlesex, a county which in administrative terms ceased to exist in 1965, leaving Lord's is inconceivable. "We would be no bigger than Leicester or Derby," is the blunt, not to say condescending, view of one long-standing Middlesex (and MCC) member. Market research is not required to appreciate that, for a large proportion of Middlesex's 8,000 members, the main attraction is watching cricket at Lord's.

For MCC, Middlesex's presence is less about income, as it has sometimes been in the past, than offering first-class cricket to their 18,000 members and retaining a link to the professional game. "It's about reputation, quality of cricket, and community," says Derek Brewer, the MCC secretary and chief executive.

It is a relationship that, according to Fraser, who is also on MCC's main committee, has "ebbed and flowed" and has even been characterised by "childish squabbling". Disputes have arisen over fixture scheduling, pitches

Clare Skinner

Sense of belonging: Middlesex do their best to make the Lord's Pavilion feel like home.

and the leeway given to Middlesex to run their own affairs – and make their own money – at a venue which prefers no blade of grass out of place.

Middlesex came to Lord's in 1877 because MCC needed to bolster a fixture list that, two years earlier, had been publicly derided by one member as "rubbishy". They had twice before resisted MCC's overtures, but finally moved to Lord's after becoming dissatisfied with their own ground, Prince's, near Harrods in Knightsbridge, where the dressing-rooms were considered "hardly fit for gentlemen". The initial agreement was for a year only, but MCC secretary Henry Perkins said: "Provided the rules of Lord's ground were observed, there could be no doubt that MCC would joyfully retain the Middlesex County Cricket Club at Lord's."

As any visitor to Lord's knows, MCC are partial to their rules – not to mention their Laws – and Middlesex's status as high-profile tenants has not afforded them special treatment. "It was clearly understood that MCC ran Lord's, and Middlesex were, so to speak, guests," says Jack Bailey, MCC secretary from 1974 to 1987. Until at least the 1980s, players were required to wear whites in the nets or simply to walk across the grass from Pavilion to Nursery Ground – although, according to Simon Hughes, the former Middlesex seamer, Phil Edmonds and John Emburey used to prefer to drive even when fully padded up.

Bailey's tenure is remembered as "magisterial" by Tim Lamb, a Middlesex seam bowler in the mid-1970s who returned as secretary from 1984 to 1988. "We were always made to feel slightly like second-class citizens," says Lamb, who still recalls a breach of protocol in August 1985. "We were playing the Australians. It was a beautiful, sunny day, but the ground was saturated, and a big crowd were frustrated there was no play. I went out on to the field to encourage the umpires to get the game going. Early the following week I got a letter from Jack along the lines of: 'Dear Tim, I understand that you walked on to the outfield on Saturday to enquire about the prospects of the game starting.' The last line read: 'It must not happen again. Yours sincerely, Jack Bailey.'"

Pitch preparation has been a perpetual area of contention. "At one point the MCC forbade the groundsman from speaking to me," says Mike Brearley, who captained Middlesex from 1971 to 1982. "I am against fixing pitches, except in the broad sense that one should aim for a good balance between batsman and bowler, and give a chance of results. We sometimes felt that pitches were damped down to make sure they didn't break up, which was exactly the worst pitch for us. I used to get a bit annoyed, and no doubt I was a bit arrogant." Brearley's other gripe, shared by captains before and since, was that Middlesex matches were shunted to the edges of the square.

If the county felt disadvantaged, then results – at least during the reigns of Brearley and his successor Mike Gatting (MCC president for 2013–14) – would suggest otherwise. And playing for Middlesex was often seen as a ticket to greater things. "When I considered who to sign for," said Edmonds, "I had in my mind's eye the big press box above the Warner Stand. It would be far easier to play for England by doing well at Lord's than miles away in Glamorgan."

Gatting was known to have had a tetchy relationship with groundsman Mick Hunt, who still prepares the pitches. But Fraser's managerial role has removed some of the heat and opacity. He readily admits to making an annual request for seaming – rather than turning – pitches, but adds: "MCC want to do what's right. I believe that's what most groundsmen around the country would prefer, rather than having to please the head coach."

It inevitably requires a degree of compromise to fit Middlesex's match schedule around the Lord's Tests and one-day internationals. But in previous generations there were different priorities. Middlesex won the Championship in 1947 and shared it two years later, but would have to wait until 1976 for their next triumph. The season often followed a familiar pattern: near the top of the table by the end of June, they would fall away, having typically had to complete around two-thirds of their home games before July, when Lord's was given over to schools and services matches.

At a meeting in 1957, Gubby Allen – the Middlesex and MCC grandee who had his own private entrance to Lord's from his house behind the Pavilion – informed the Middlesex committee that a scheduled home match for the following summer clashed with the annual Clifton v Tonbridge fixture. In 1959, Middlesex played Hampshire at Hornsey in north London but, after making a loss in front of their lowest crowd of the season, they did not repeat the experiment until 1980, when Uxbridge became the first of their regular outgrounds.

The behind-the-scenes, business relationship between MCC and Middlesex has rarely been straightforward or transparent, and has been refashioned often on an informal basis. In 1908 A. J. Webbe, Middlesex's honorary secretary and former captain, felt compelled to provide all the other first-class counties with a detailed breakdown of the business relationship between Middlesex and

Pulling their weight for Middlesex: the 1935 groundstaff mop up for a match next day.

MCC because it was "misunderstood". It was at this point that MCC effectively took over the running of Middlesex, which included paying the professional players' wages. Gate receipts were shared on a sliding scale according to revenue.

It wasn't until 1952 that Middlesex had their own office, a converted tea house at the back of the Pavilion next to the Harris Garden where it remains, alongside the club shop, to this day. Arthur Flower, a Lord's lifer, oversaw Middlesex's affairs from immediately after the Second World War and became the county's first professional secretary in 1964. Mike Murray, who played briefly for Middlesex in the 1950s and was later treasurer and chairman, wrote an obituary of Flower in the club's annual review of 1986: "In those days it was nothing unusual to put one's foot through the floorboards. The heating was the wrong way round – hot in summer, cold in winter. There was no running water and the nearest toilets were in the Pavilion." According to Murray, Flower once described the little road that runs between the Pavilion and the Middlesex office as "wider than the Atlantic Ocean".

In the immediate post-war periods of the 20th century, Middlesex's on-field success (they won outright Championships in 1920, 1921 and 1947) filled MCC's coffers. Gates were closed by 3.15 on the first afternoon of the crucial final match of the 1920 season, also Pelham Warner's last. Crowds poured in for the rest of the game as Middlesex beat Surrey by 55 runs with 40 minutes to spare, to seal their first title since 1903. In 1947, the *annus mirabilis* of Denis Compton and Bill Edrich, around 300,000 people paid to watch Middlesex at Lord's.

As interest and revenue waned in the 1950s, those most closely associated with Middlesex felt unappreciated by their landlords. This resentment boiled over in a letter from a member, John H. Carrow, to the county committee in 1956. Carrow wrote: "Middlesex members are dissatisfied with their subordinate position. MCC members appear to resent the presence of Middlesex members, whom they tend to regard as inferiors." MCC restricted the size of the county's membership, which in turn limited their income; unlike today, members' privileges on Middlesex match days at Lord's were not equivalent to those of MCC members.

By 1958, Middlesex were paying MCC over £4,000 in rent, and fees of 15 shillings per member. In 1960, after a £5,000 loss, Middlesex made it clear to MCC that they considered this arrangement unsustainable. They also grumbled about the quality and cost of the players' lunches and teas: a far cry from the lavish Lord's catering of today.

In November 1963, conveniently just after Gubby Allen had assumed the MCC presidency, a subcommittee was convened to discuss the problems. Middlesex president George Newman complained of "this crippling levy", saying the membership cap made it "impossible to build up capital reserves for the club". At a stroke the levy was scrapped, and Middlesex were allowed to keep all gate receipts as an "incentive to produce better cricket and bring more spectators in".

Allen became MCC treasurer the following year and held the post until 1976. In terms of Middlesex's ongoing relationship with MCC, "Gubby was basically negotiating with himself," according to Bailey. The clubs' agreement remained almost unchanged for more than 30 years: Middlesex kept two-thirds of gate receipts, MCC the rest. It was an arrangement Lamb believes was "very advantageous to Middlesex".

Things changed at the turn of the millennium. Following the arrival from the hospitality industry of David Batts as deputy chief executive, MCC sought to up their commercial game. Now, Middlesex pay MCC a daily fee (thought to be around £3,300), plus the cost of players' catering, for their home Championship and one-day matches, and keep most of the gate receipts. For Twenty20 games, all ground costs are covered before net revenue is distributed. The split is 70–30 in favour of the county, though it had been 80–20 until the roaring success of the first Twenty20 match at Lord's, in 2004, when Middlesex and Surrey produced the highest county crowd outside a one-day final since 1947. All other match revenue, such as from food and drink – around £200,000 for a well-attended Twenty20 game – is retained by MCC.

During the 1970s, as cricket woke up to its commercial possibilities, Middlesex had felt increasingly hamstrung by MCC's inflexibility. The county were given a share of MCC's advertising revenues but, while other grounds have developed myriad ways of earning money, Middlesex still have limited opportunities. "It's swings and roundabouts," says Brewer. "They don't have the overheads and all the hassles of running the place, but nor do they have the opportunity of maximising their revenues from catering, events and conferencing."

Brewer's predecessor, the Australian Keith Bradshaw, tried to bring MCC and Middlesex closer together. "When I first arrived [in 2006], I felt that we as MCC didn't embrace Middlesex as much as we could have," he says.

Bradshaw's proposal was effectively a merger, or perhaps a buyout. "I felt if Middlesex came under our umbrella that we could create a team which, with MCC's resources and infrastructure, could be – as I put it at the time – the Manchester United of cricket."

Bradshaw, now chief executive of the South Australian Cricket Association, foresaw a situation in which MCC might not always be guaranteed, for example, two Tests a summer, and was looking at the domestic game as a revenue generator. His colleagues, however, were wary of closer ties with Middlesex, fearing it would compromise the club's cherished independence. But MCC did underwrite the signing of Adam Gilchrist for Middlesex's home Twenty20 matches in 2010 by offsetting his fees against their ground costs for those games. At MCC's annual general meeting that summer, one member questioned whether other counties might object to "MCC, a national organisation, supporting stars for Middlesex".

And so to the present – and the future. Vinny Codrington, Middlesex's chief executive, says: "The new agreement will be simpler, and based around the need for both clubs to drive revenues on non-major match days [in other words, when Middlesex are playing]. I anticipate it being a closer relationship than has existed for at least 50 years. I see it more as a partnership." Brewer agrees: "Partnership is an important and powerful word." But, after all that has gone before, will it be a civil one?

John Stern, a member of both Middlesex and MCC, is the editor of the commemorative brochure 150 Years of Middlesex County Cricket Club. *With Marcus Williams, he co-edited* The Essential Wisden.

THE INTROVERT–EXTROVERT BALANCE

Character recognition

ED SMITH

"It's like a bloody morgue out there! Make some noise! Especially you youngsters!" All aspiring county cricketers, hoping to make an impact as they begin their journey in professional sport, will have pondered the meaning of this criticism, shouted by a captain or senior player at lunch, tea or stumps.

The assumptions behind it are revealing: that noise is synonymous with purpose, that words lead to deeds, that competitiveness is vocal, that youth is gregarious, that quietness betokens laziness. Put differently, the faith in noise on a cricket pitch is just one manifestation of sport's – indeed society's – love affair with extroversion. It remains the default template for professional sportsmen who play team games. And it is time for a reassessment.

The terms extrovert and introvert were developed by Carl Jung as tools to describe and explore personality types. Over time, their meaning has become coarsened and confused. And it is misleading to see them as mutually exclusive. Some who derive great pleasure from the outer world also crave and cherish the inner world (just as some have a less fulfilling relationship with both modes of experience). Introverts can have a talent for sociability, just as extroverts can have a gift for reflection. The defining issue, in psychological terms, is where people put their attention and gain their energy. Do they like to spend time in the outer world of people and objects (extroversion), or the inner world of ideas and images (introversion)?

On one level it is understandable that sport should naturally celebrate extroversion: it quite obviously takes place in the outer world. Yet it is also true that elite sport revolves around the ability to solve problems. The switch hit and the scoop shot did not just happen: they emerged from reflection and the willingness to look at old problems in new ways.

So sport, like any human activity, is necessarily a mixture of action and reflection. The most famous of all sporting slogans, Nike's "Just do it", should really have been subtitled: "Unless it's time to stop doing it for a while, have a think about things, and come back with a better plan." Perhaps that version didn't sound quite so appealing to the advertising executives.

Questions arise. Is there an optimal balance between introverts and extroverts in the make-up of a cricket team? Is that balance something to which a coach or selector should give thought? And within the personality of a single leader, is there a blend that is innately suited to being captain?

The England team now use psychological profiling, the Myers–Briggs Type Indicator, to assess their players, and tell them where they are on four axes – whether they are introverts or extroverts, prefer concrete facts or intuition, make decisions based on reason or emotion, and like planning ahead or living spontaneously.

Comment

Based on how players respond to an hour of questions, the MBTI will assign them four letters that make up their profile and their relationships with others. The letters derived now even shape how players are briefed before they take the field. Kate Green, head of the ECB's personal development and welfare programme, has argued it is now a central plank of coaching, telling *The Times*: "The more we know about a player, the more support we can give. This includes constructive conflict. When under pressure, how are you going to react?"

During the First Test at Brisbane in November, Stuart Broad revealed, to

Instinctively introvert: Jonathan Trott.

no one's astonishment, that the tests showed he would "thrive" on abuse from the crowd. Booed throughout the tour, he finished as England's leading wicket-taker. There have, though, been some surprises. Kevin Pietersen has claimed that, contrary to his extravagant persona, he emerges from the tests as an introvert. That is not as odd as it first sounds. Many natural showmen, instinctively drawn to the stage, are less expressive in normal life. This discrepancy between persona and person is one reason why players who appear to relish the limelight are often misunderstood.

The balance in any dressing-room between introverts and extroverts is constantly in flux. With the retirement of Graeme Swann, England lost an authentic extrovert. That loss was balanced by the departure – however temporary – of Jonathan Trott, whose instincts are more introverted.

Green's research suggests that cricket contains a higher proportion of introverts than the general population. Perhaps that is due to the isolation of an individual duel within a team context, or because, in the case of batsmen, even very good players must become used to failing more often than they succeed.

And yet it seems to be the case that when teams do address the introvert–extrovert balance, they are more likely to seek to boost the number of extroverts. This in itself probably derives from an *im*balance: introverts recognise, and perhaps admire, the qualities of extroverts more than vice versa. Indeed, sport generally overestimates the loudest voice at the bar, and underestimates the thinkers at ease in their own company.

None of the teams I represented used MBTI-type analysis. However, at the risk of generalising from memory alone, it seemed to me that introverts were more likely to play their own game, independent of the team's momentum and form. As extroverts draw more energy from the social world, they tend to be more affected by the mood of the team. In my experience, highly extroverted players were more likely to be up when the team were up, and down when the team were down. And while an extrovert might express a team's good form with memorable extravagance, introverts were more likely to turn the tide.

Judging from appearances… Matthew Fleming is an extrovert, here publicising the 2004 Village Cup.

The logic follows, from a strategic perspective, that while there may be no such thing as a perfect proportion of extroverts to introverts, some kind of balance helps teams to respond to all situations.

Yet many psychological presumptions about players and temperament can be wide of the mark. A classic example came during the lead-up to England's nomination of captain for the 2006-07 Ashes. The cartoon headlines wrote themselves, presenting a choice between the academic Andrew Strauss and the charismatic Andrew Flintoff. But this missed the truth that on-field persona is not analogous with the man revealed in the dressing-room.

Flintoff, by his own candid admission, oscillated throughout his career between peaks of exuberant self-belief and lows of chronic self-doubt, during which he often retreated into his shell. One of Strauss's great strengths was his steadiness and social versatility: he is assured in most company and not irritated by what introverts might consider to be social impositions.

That can also be said of his predecessor, Michael Vaughan, a natural extrovert. He was England captain in 2003, when I played my three Tests. I sensed he was trying to move his players towards more adventurous, expressive cricket, while nudging the dressing-room towards a more fun-loving mood. He used his own outgoing personality as one of the tools to mould a new team.

What of the other captains I played under in first-class cricket? My first two at Kent were both extroverts, but entirely different kinds. Steve Marsh, our keeper, was an alpha male, always at the centre of the team's collective identity – driving us forward, urging us on. On the field, he put greater faith in competitive juices than reflective analysis. Off it, even in his late thirties, he retained a sociable, playful aura.

Marsh was followed by Matthew Fleming, an aristocratic ex-army officer who had served in Northern Ireland. Fleming was ebulliently extroverted, always leaving his mark on any social occasion. But his extroversion was accompanied by exceptional social self-discipline: he rarely, if ever, let his guard down. Indeed, that sense of invulnerability was both a strength and a weakness. You never worried about him, because he seemed so secure and confident. I greatly admired that self-reliance. But he might have got more out of some players if he had been more prepared to let them in, even if it meant feigning an insecurity or a problem in order to do so.

So far, all extroverts. But the most feted modern captain was an introvert. Mike Brearley, who became a practising psychoanalyst, was aware of the blend of introverts and extroverts within a team – and within a leader. He had retired long before I joined Middlesex, but having spoken to many who played under him, and having got to know him personally, I am confident that Brearley was highly unusual in managing and adapting his own personality to suit the demands of captaincy and the team dynamic.

Many Middlesex players have told me about Brearley's occasional outbursts of genuine anger. They do so with affection, almost reverence, as though it marked Brearley out as flawed and natural, a human being with a breaking point, just like them. His apparent readiness to lose control, paradoxically, was one of the devices Brearley used to neutralise the knee-jerk criticism that he was overly academic and introspective. This seeming loss of control became an agent of control.

The most famous captain I played alongside, though not when he was captain, was also an instinctive introvert: Steve Waugh. Though he didn't relish it, Waugh accepted that being studied and scrutinised, and living at the centre of attention, were bound up with the role. If he wanted to be a great captain of Australia, Waugh had to reach an accommodation with the public demands of the job. He succeeded.

Waugh's example is in stark contrast to another captain I observed at close quarters. He was rightly admired for his intelligence, savvy and tactical nous. Indeed, as a player in the ranks, he routinely criticised other captains for what he regarded as elementary tactical mistakes. As captain, however, the effort of having to manage his introversion weighed heavily on him. In difficult moments on the pitch, his body language conveyed an awkward truth, as if he wanted to shout to the whole ground: "Why don't you all just stop looking at me?" Sadly, that is one privilege a captain is never afforded.

There is now a growing awareness, long overdue, that introverts can suffer from misleading assumptions about effective leadership. Susan Cain's persuasive book *Quiet* is a case in point. Cain ridicules what she terms the "extreme sport" of socialising at Harvard Business School, arguing that these supposed signs of natural leadership are in fact carefully packaged examples of politicking and networking.

But the deck remains more stacked against introverts than ever before. Business has developed an obsession with ultra-sociability: witness the trend for open-plan offices. Politics, thanks to the 24-hour news cycle, has evolved a growing reliance on extroversion. Indeed, the burgeoning influence of the media – in changing the experience of day-to-day leadership, and also in framing the theoretical ideal of a good leader – pushes leaders towards extroversion, whether they like it or not. Whenever I hear Alastair Cook criticised for failing to give a good press conference or on-field interview, I wonder whether the distraction of trying to excel at such things – itself a slippery concept – is worth the psychological energy.

A risk facing all leaders is sacrificing authenticity in pursuit of voguish acceptability. Overarching sentences that begin "Good leaders are always…" are, in fact, nearly always wrong. But one, perhaps, may have some validity. Good leaders are prepared to be themselves. Yes, even the introverts.

Ed Smith played for Kent and Middlesex, where he was captain for two seasons, and in three Tests for England. His latest book is Luck – a Fresh Look at Fortune.

WISDEN AND THE GREAT WAR

Upon another shore

A_NDREW_ R_ENSHAW_

For the historian, contemporary sources provide an immediacy and vitality that the fog of time obscures. Yet in an era of vast social upheaval, it is no surprise that accuracy can be a casualty. Like every other long-running publication, *Wisden* has got many things plain wrong – errors that can have a fascination of their own.

When the Great War stopped play 100 years ago, the Almanack's slim volumes were soon largely devoted to obituaries of the ghostly ranks of soldiers, sailors and pioneering airmen who gave their lives for king and country. Many had just made joyful appearances in the public school averages. One of *Wisden's* own foot soldiers, Ernest Allen, an editorial assistant, rallied to the colours in the first week of the war; his death notice graphically records he was shot through the head at Cuinchy on New Year's Day, 1915. As the casualties mounted, the reduced staff did their best to cope, but errors crept in. A book of record needs to make corrections, even if the best part of a century has elapsed, and a new volume, *Wisden on the Great War: the Lives of Cricket's Fallen 1914–1918*, does just that, casting light on some remarkable characters.

Jack Poole led a full life. He was taken prisoner by the Germans in both world wars, received the DSO from King George V, wrecked a Sopwith Camel in a bravado display of aerobatics – somehow surviving the crash and a subsequent court of inquiry – incurred losses as a Lloyd's underwriter, and served as an administrator in Sudan where, for 35 cows, he bought a bride, with whom he had a son.

He was also a talented schoolboy athlete, enjoyed country-house cricket, and was due to make his first-class debut for MCC against Oxford University at Lord's in July 1922, but had to cry off after being injured in a club game; Patsy Hendren took his place.

"An inspiration to all who knew him, not just behind barbed wire but throughout a life full of friendship and shared laughter," wrote Terence Prittie, a fellow captive during World War Two, in *The Times* after his death in July 1966. So it is remarkable that Poole's obituary appeared in the 1916 *Wisden*:

> 2ND LIEUT. J. S. POOLE (4th King's Royal Rifle Corps) was killed in action in the second week of May [1915], aged 19. He was brilliant in the field and a good slow left-hand bowler. In 1913 and 1914 he was in the Rugby Eleven, and was captain-elect for last year…

Poole must not have seen his premature *Wisden* obituary, or – given his sense of humour – he would surely have used it in his autobiography. Instead, *Undiscovered Ends*, published in 1957, begins on the cricket pitches of Rugby, where his team-mates included C. P. Johnstone, J. L. Bryan and M. D. Lyon, all future first-class players. Poole was stripped of the captaincy in 1914 after a prank involving a fire hydrant, staying on at school only because he was about to take his exams for Sandhurst.

The following May he was captured, one of the few in his battalion to survive 26 continuous days in the Ypres trenches. On May 21, 1915, *The Times* reported him as "missing", so it is unclear how *Wisden* – which relied on the paper for much of its information – got it so wrong. Poole escaped three times and was twice recaptured, eventually making it back to England in late 1916.

Twice he met the King. The first time, in a borrowed uniform, he had a half-hour private audience to recount his exploits. "The King asked me to sit down and offered me a cigarette, thus putting me at my ease immediately. What a shame to smoke it, I thought: I would have preferred to keep it as a souvenir." Six months later he was back at Buckingham Palace to receive the DSO. After service in north Russia, his war was not over until June 1919: "On arriving home, I found an official document awaiting me. It was a certificate from the War Office, informing me that the circumstances of my capture by the Germans in 1915 had been investigated and that no blame attached to my conduct."

Between the wars, Poole worked in Rhodesia and then in the Sudan Political Service, where he had an unofficial marriage to a Sudanese woman named Aneege. In May 1940, Major Poole was captured during a rearguard action at Calais; the rest of his war was spent in POW camps, where he was a valued member of escape committees. He selected a team designed for their ability to cause maximum disruption to their captors; among them were Douglas

Jack Poole, painted by Alistair MacLeod at Eichstätt prison camp.

Bader – "always to be relied upon on a sticky wicket" – Roger Mortimer, the future racing correspondent of *The Sunday Times* who, as wicketkeeper, "would let nothing go by", and Charlie (later Marquess) Linlithgow, who "would bowl fast ones, though sometimes apt to pitch them a bit short – bodyline stuff". Poole died in a London hospital on July 5, 1966, half a century after his *Wisden* obituary.

However, the record for longevity after a premature *Wisden* send-off belongs to Wilfred Shaw. He died 70 years after the 1919 Almanack listed him as "killed March 23. Captain of the XI at Borlase School, Marlow". *The Times* had indeed published an obituary on April 10, 1918, after the regimental diary recorded Shaw as killed during the Bedfordshire Regiment's stand against the German spring offensive. His parents received a letter of condolence from the

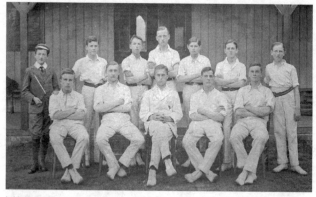

In his element: in 1916, Wilfred Shaw (*seated, hands in lap*) captained Sir William Borlase's Grammar School.

battalion chaplain but, as the *Bucks Free Press* reported on May 17, they later received "splendid news": a War Office telegram explained that their son had been captured. Shaw won many athletics trophies at school, and his fitness may well have helped him survive the rigours of battle and ill-treatment in captivity. After the war, he played for Little Marlow CC. He worked in the furniture trade, and died on November 9, 1989, eight days short of his 92nd birthday, a lifetime after his *Wisden* obituary.

Another survivor had received a sketchy obituary: "Mr George R. Alpen," said *Wisden 1917,* "one of the best-known cricketers of Belgium, has been killed in the War, but no particulars are obtainable." George Alpen was born in Albury, New South Wales, in 1878, and worked in Brussels as the representative of a British firm. Alpen, who had married a Belgian Red Cross sister when he was taken prisoner, was secretary of *La Fédération Belge de Cricket* in the 1930s, and was selected to play for Belgium against France in Brussels in July 1934. However, no details of the game exist, as all Belgian cricket records were destroyed during the Second World War. In 1943 Alpen, who had fled the country with his wife three years earlier, died in Australia.

Wisden did admit some errors. The Rev. Archibald Fargus, "a stout hitter, a good hammer and tongs bowler and a hardworking field" for Cambridge University and Gloucestershire, was given an obituary in 1915. It stated that, as acting-chaplain on HMS *Monmouth*, he went down when the ship sank in the Pacific on November 1, 1914. But it transpired he had missed his train: the ship had sailed without him. The error was corrected two years later, but *Wisden* then missed his actual death in 1963, aged 84 – an oversight itself not remedied until 1994.

Wisden 1916 recorded 2nd Lt R. M. Chadwick as having died of wounds the previous May, which was accurate, though this artillery officer was not the

THE REV. ARCHIBALD HUGH CONWAY FARGUS, who went down in the *Monmouth*, Admiral Cradock's flagship, in the action in the Pacific on November 1, was born at Clifton, Bristol, on December 15, 1878, and was educated at Clifton, Haileybury and Cambridge. He left Clifton too young to be in the Eleven, but played for Haileybury in 1897 and 1898, making 7, 78 and 17 and taking eleven wickets for 123 runs in his two matches v. Cheltenham, and scoring 1, 48, 0, and 1 v. Wellington. He appeared for Cambridge in the drawn games with Oxford in 1900 and 1901, in which he made 8 and 17 not out and obtained six wickets for 260 runs. He assisted Gloucestershire in 1900 and 1901 and Devonshire in 1904, and had been a member of the M.C.C. since 1901. In first-class cricket his highest score was 61 for Cambridge University v. Sussex at Brighton in 1901, and his best performance with the ball to take twelve Middlesex wickets for 87 for Gloucestershire at Lord's in 1900. He was described as a stout hitter, a good hammer and tongs bowler, and a hardworking field. Since 1907 he had been a Chaplain in the Royal Navy, and in 1913 was appointed Vicar of Askham Richard, York. At the beginning of the War he became temporary Acting-Chaplain to the *Monmouth*, on which he went down.

Premature exit: *Wisden's* obituary for Archibald Fargus appeared in 1915.

one who, as a schoolboy, had bowled for Rugby and scored 46 against Marlborough at Lord's in 1904. *Wisden* acknowledged the inaccuracy in 1920: "Mr Chadwick is happily alive and well. The mistake probably arose through some confusion of initials." That was understandable: two men with similar names served in the Royal Garrison Artillery. The officer who died was 20-year-old Richard Markham Chadwick, while the survivor, who became the Rev. Rohan Mackenzie Chadwick, had a second, brief, obituary in 1969, aged 82; there was no mention of the earlier notice.

The Almanack attempted to make amends after publishing an obituary in 1916 for Rifleman Paul Hilleard, "a useful all-round cricketer" who played for Essex Second XI in 1914. He was stated to have died in May 1915 of wounds received near Ypres, but a "correction" in 1917 said he had been reported to be a prisoner. Sadly, the original obituary was not far wrong: he was killed in action on April 24, 1915, and his name is among the 54,400 on the Ypres (Menin Gate) Memorial to the Missing.

A few entries above Hilleard in *Wisden 1916* lies an obituary for Captain C. B. Hayes. But, as the Almanack explained a year later, he "was not the Campbell College cricketer of the same name". In fact, Charles Bianconi Hayes, who died at Gallipoli, was aged 43 and so could not have been the C. B. Hayes who appeared in the batting and bowling averages for the college

THE REV. A. H. C. FARGUS.—He was not lost, as stated in the Press, in Admiral Cradock's flagship, the *Monmouth*, on November 1, 1914. Missing a train, he was prevented from re-joining the ship just before it left for the Pacific and was appointed to another.

Correction: in 1917, *Wisden* chose not to mention that it had been in error two years earlier.

for 1911 and 1912. The college student was Charles Berry Hayes who, after serving as a gunner during the war, became a solicitor and died in 1948, aged 54.

Another case of mistaken identity has remained buried in the pages of *Wisden* for almost 100 years. Lt C. G. Clarke, listed as having died in October 1915, was recorded as being "in the Bradfield Eleven in 1914, when he scored 27 runs in three innings". But the schoolboy Christopher Garrard Clarke continued to appear in the Bradfield averages for 1915 and 1916, when he left to join the navy. In 1925, at the age of 26, he died of illness, unremarked by *Wisden*. Coincidentally, the Cyril George Clarke who had been killed in 1916 was also 26.

The proofreaders did not pick up two similar entries for Lt-Col Frederick Robson in *Wisden 1919*, perhaps because the first entry wrongly gave his name as Frank. In the same volume, Percy Bryden Watt also has two obituaries, while Reginald Gregory appeared in the 1919 and 1920 Almanacks.

A total of 289 first-class cricketers are listed on the Commonwealth War Graves Commission's roll of honour. Of these, 89 did not receive a *Wisden* obituary. Many had played only once or twice, in countries largely beyond *Wisden's* horizons at that time. Among them are Claude Newberry, who appeared in four Tests for South Africa against England in 1913-14; Tony Wilding, a New Zealander better known as a four-time Wimbledon champion; Leonard Sutton, who played 17 matches for Somerset; Norman Callaway, who scored 207 in his only innings, for New South Wales; and Hampshire's Harold Forster, the recipient of more medals for gallantry than any other county cricketer.

Wisden on the Great War, edited by Andrew Renshaw, gives obituaries to the overlooked 89. It also updates and corrects the 1,788 obituaries that appeared in Wisden *from 1915 to 1920.*

WHITE LINES At Auckland in March, New Zealand celebrate the wicket of James Anderson; one more will bring victory, but England survive. In Chennai, a flyover is shut for repairs, and local children take advantage.

Andrew Burton, Reuters

WAR AND PEACE At a military base in Kandahar province, a soldier in the Afghan army lines up the bowler, while Buddhist monks indulge in a spot of recreation at a monastery in Ladakh, India.

Debdatta Chakraborty

HEAVEN OR HIGH WATER After Threlkeld CC's pitch was damaged by floods, they resolved to raise money by making a calendar of extreme cricket. July saw the keeper taking a dip in Derwentwater; August a game on Blencathra. More details from rainstoppedplay.org

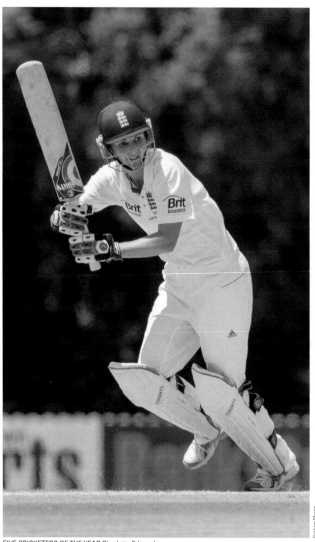

FIVE CRICKETERS OF THE YEAR Charlotte Edwards.

Graham Morris

FIVE CRICKETERS OF THE YEAR Ryan Harris.

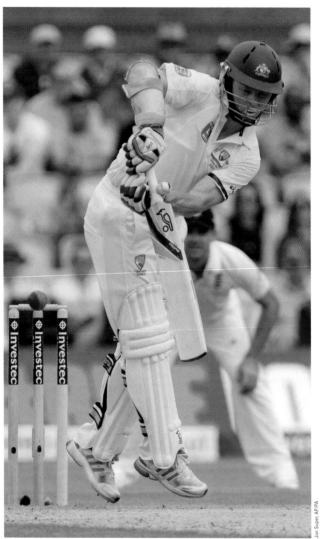

FIVE CRICKETERS OF THE YEAR Chris Rogers.

FIVE CRICKETERS OF THE YEAR Joe Root.

FIVE CRICKETERS OF THE YEAR Shikhar Dhawan.

FIVE CRICKETERS OF THE YEAR

The Five Cricketers of the Year represent a tradition that dates back in Wisden *to 1889, making this the oldest individual award in cricket. The Five are picked by the editor, and the selection is based, primarily but not exclusively, on the players' influence on the previous English season. No one can be chosen more than once. A list of past Cricketers of the Year appears on page 1508.*

Shikhar Dhawan

SHARDA UGRA

Shikhar Dhawan causes a stir well before he picks up his bat. The 'tache, tattoo, earring and rat-tail hairdo mark him out as someone teetering between character and cliché. To an English audience seeing him for the first time in 2013, he might have looked like a stereotype on legs: the 21st-century IPL cricketer, flush with affluence, attitude and a short attention span.

Yet at the crease Dhawan transcends caricature and, with nuanced but bold strokes, creates a memorable portrait of his batsmanship, as he did for a few weeks in the English summer. India's tour of England in 2011 had been miserable. In four Tests, the treats offered by their greatest generation of batsmen ran out quickly. And in the one-day series, their status as World Cup winners was diluted by weather and perverse twists of fortune.

Two years later, under the slate-grey sky of what Cardiff calls summer, Dhawan and Rohit Sharma arrived to open the Champions Trophy, with Dhawan sparkling in a century partnership against South Africa. It was the first time in two years that any opening pair had raised a hundred against their one-day attack. They were without Dale Steyn, but Morne Morkel, Lonwabo Tsotsobe, Rory Kleinveldt and Ryan McLaren bowled under the new rules, with a new ball at each end. They chose to pelt down the short stuff and, after biding his time, Dhawan – a cutlass-wielding, left-handed pirate – broke free, finishing with 114 from 94 balls.

The measured assault became his signature approach throughout the tournament, in which he followed that hundred against South Africa with another against West Indies, then gave India the starts they needed in the semi-final against Sri Lanka and the final against England. The pitches turned out to be drier than the Indians had expected, and Dhawan cashed in.

He shook off a blow on the helmet from McLaren, charged out to the quick bowlers to disturb their length and composure, and sliced and diced portions of the ground by piercing gaps and slapping the ball over deep fielders' heads and flailing arms. It wasn't some reckless hit-and-run: he had prepared well. "Before coming to England, I practised leaving the ball a lot," he says. "I knew that the new rules would make opening in ODIs more of a challenge." They did, but two new balls also helped provide bounce and pace for his favourite cuts and pulls.

Tall, lean, and with an upright, still stance, Dhawan is always looking to create scoring opportunities, either via the conventional route – with creamy cover-drives and a tight follow-through – or through the improvisational approach, stepping out to loft between extra cover and long-off, and leaning back to slash over the slips. In the Champions Trophy, Dhawan's eye-catching 363 runs at 90, with a strike-rate of 101, made him top-scorer and Man of the Tournament. It was the second time he had been named player of an international series, after an Under-19 World Cup. But that was in 2003-04. The promise would not come to fruition for almost a decade.

Born on December 5, 1985, in Delhi, the new millennium's crucible of Indian batting, SHIKHAR DHAWAN scored a century on his club debut at the age of 13 for Sonnet CC. Junior success, however, was followed by a long, bumpy grind in the relative anonymity of first-class cricket. Much of it had to do with his own inconsistency: he would throw his wicket away after good starts, and always verged on indiscretion. Others from that junior World Cup class, such as Suresh Raina, Robin Uthappa, Dinesh Karthik and R. P. Singh, leapt ahead, and it seemed Dhawan had slipped from the selectors' attention. He was given a single one-day international during the run-up to the 2011 World Cup, and four more in the West Indies after it, but could total just 69 in those five.

Yet it was, he says, time spent on the domestic circuit, and a patchy run in 2011-12 following his indifferent showing for India, that gave him the resources and strength to return with his most prolific first-class performance a season later. "This is a race which never ends," Dhawan says. "We never know whose day it is going to be today, whose day it is going to be tomorrow. I always had the belief that I can come back with one good season."

In 2012-13, his ninth season in the first-class game, Dhawan scored 833 domestic runs at 55, with four hundreds. The weight of those runs had him picked for the Third Test against Australia, replacing – of all people – Virender Sehwag, the original 21st-century Delhi swashbuckler. In Mohali, with India 2–0 up, Dhawan scored a startling century off 85 deliveries, the fastest recorded by any debutant. In his sprint to the hundred, he didn't hit a ball in the air. But his race was far from over.

The difference between two seasons, those around him say, is a growing awareness of his game, and maturity after marriage. Dhawan agrees: "I felt bad that my results in 2011-12 had been due to mistakes rather than anything else. God has gifted me talent, and still I had such an average season. So I practised hard and worked on the mental side of my game." It meant keeping notes on every innings, and working through shot selection options with video footage.

Dhawan has remained grateful for the grind that preceded his rather dramatic 2013. "Domestic cricket is very challenging," he says. "We play on every kind of pitch – green seamers, turners, and we'll get maybe two good batting tracks. In seven Ranji games per year, that's a very good mix." It is why, he argues, Delhi has produced all-wicket batsmen over the last decade.

Just before the start of the 2012-13 season, Dhawan took what was considered a radical step in conservative India. He married Aesha Mukherjee, an amateur boxer brought up in Australia, and a mother of two from a previous marriage. He says his wife "has turned my life around. I think she loves cricket more than me, and just wants me to be my best."

Shikhar Dhawan, a quietly spoken 28-year-old, has lived and played his way past the tattoos, the hairdo and the moustache he twirls with pride. In an unpredictable future, the same things could work for him both at the crease and away from it: natural balance and a steady head.

Charlotte Edwards

TIM DE LISLE

Meet the England captain: an all-time great who has lifted the World Cup and the World Twenty20, won the Ashes home and away, and broken the world record for the most international appearances. And yet there are still some cricket lovers who would not recognise her if she sat next to them at Lord's.

It may, alas, be necessary to translate her achievements into the masculine. In terms of success, Charlotte Edwards is Andrew Strauss and M. S. Dhoni rolled into one. In terms of longevity, she is verging on Sachin Tendulkar: after making her Test debut at 16, she remains at the top 18 years later. In terms of talent, she is Mark Waugh, a natural strokemaker, Test No. 4 and one-day opener. In terms of stats, she is Geoff Boycott, averaging 47 in Tests. In terms of history, she is Nasser Hussain, the first England captain to benefit from central contracts.

Edwards has captained England for eight years – longer than the men ever last. The calendar year 2013 was a cross-section of her career. At the World Cup in India, England beat some good teams (India, New Zealand, West Indies), but suffered tantalising defeats – by one wicket to Sri Lanka, and by two runs to Australia, the eventual winners. England's slender chance of making the final evaporated when the Aussies conveniently lost to West Indies. They ended up in the third-place play-off, where Edwards despatched New Zealand with an unbeaten hundred. Back home, it was an Ashes summer, with a difference: all three forms of the game counted. England saved the Test, lost the first one-dayer at Lord's, then won five matches in a row. Under the new points system, they went 2–4 down, before winning 12–4. "It was like playing seven finals," Edwards said. "I loved it."

Five months later, in Australia, England had to do it all again. They won the only Test, shot into an 8–0 lead, then wobbled twice as the Aussies were lifted by Ellyse Perry, the rising superstar of the women's game. Edwards told herself she wasn't going to give up the Ashes without a fight. In a Twenty20 match on a spanking pitch in Hobart, England restricted Australia to 150, then breezed to victory. Edwards made 92 not out off 59 balls, surely the fastest captain's innings in Ashes history.

One Monday in December, she was at the National Cricket Performance Centre in Loughborough, better known as the Academy. We met at 11, an hour after the selection meeting for the Ashes tour (Edwards is not a selector, but "I say my piece"). She had been in the nets at eight after leaving home, in Berkshire, at six. Glamorous life, eh? "Oh yes."

CHARLOTTE MARIE EDWARDS was born in Huntingdon on December 17, 1979. She grew up on a farm in nearby Pidley, playing cricket with her elder brother, Daniel, in their own net. Their father, Clive, a potato farmer, captained Ramsey, and his wife, Yvonne, made the teas. "As soon as I could walk," Charlotte says, "I was on the boundary edge playing cricket with my brother and his friends." She became Ramsey's scorer, and would take her kit along hopefully. "I was a terrible scorer, but I was fascinated by captaincy and would question my dad afterwards – 'Why did you put that bowler on?'" When she was nine or ten, Ramsey were a player short, so she fielded for 50 overs. "I loved every minute. They even gave me one over at the end."

Unlike many of today's England cricketers, she went to a comprehensive school – Ramsey Abbey. "I was lucky," she told the *Daily Telegraph* in 2006. "It was a state school which was heavily into cricket." A batsman and leg-spinner, she captained the First XI and all the Huntingdonshire Boys teams up to Under-17. She was the only girl; the boys didn't object, but some of their parents did. She made her debut for England Women Under-19 at the age of 12. Her first Test, four years later in 1996, was a test of nerve more than skill: "I believed I was good enough. I was incredibly nervous, but I did OK, got a couple of thirties. I felt comfortable and just wanted more."

The next year she proved it by making regular hundreds. Had she been male, she might even have been one of the Five Cricketers of the Year in *Wisden 1998*. But this high was followed by a cruel low: a group-stage exit in the 2000 World Cup, then a snapped cruciate ligament, picked up on the hockey field, which kept her out for a year. "Suddenly it was like, slap bang, oh no, am I ever going to play again? But actually it was a real turning point for me, because I'd taken quite a lot for granted in terms of my natural ability. I look back on it with fond memories. I'm a stronger person for going through it."

When she started, players needed a day job – hers was with Hunts County Bats – and rare was the woman cricketer who went on past 30. She took over as England captain when Clare Connor retired at 29. Edwards's father had died of cancer in March 2006, aged 55, having lived to see her lead England as Connor's understudy. She found her first summer tough as official captain, perhaps because she was grieving. "I was desperate to lead from the front, and I put too much pressure on myself. But I turned it around by the end of the summer. I went down the order and it really helped."

To an outsider, Edwards is friendly, sending quickfire emails with plenty of exclamation marks, and smiling at the end of each spoken answer. But it is the guarded smile of the well-known; she seems polite – endlessly so – rather than curious. With her team, who call her Lottie, the smiles go deeper. "We have an enormous amount of fun. I really try and instil that in the players – and, on the more serious side, honesty and trust, always challenging each other to be better. But underpinning all that is enjoyment."

Once the baby of the team, half as old as Barbara Daniels, she is now the elder stateswoman, twice as old as Tash Farrant. "I see myself as quite a mentor to the younger players. When they're struggling, they just need that comfort of someone else having gone through that process. 'Just hang in there.' I guess it's having a positive mindset, sometimes a bravado. Sometimes you're low in confidence, but you've got to walk out there like you're about to score a hundred."

At Port-of-Spain in November 2013 she became the first person to captain England in 100 one-day internationals – the most by a man is Strauss's 62 – and she has scored more 50-over and Twenty20 international runs than any woman in the history of the game. Although she calls herself "a cricket geek", loves listening to the TV commentators and relishes the titbits the team analyst slips her, she says she leads by instinct, and kicks herself only when she doesn't follow her gut. "But I'm adaptable, I've learned to be more flexible. More aggressive as well – you've got to be in their faces."

The first time she played at Lord's, women were not allowed in the Long Room unless they were players, cleaners, or the Queen. Now Edwards sits on the MCC World Cricket Committee, and England Women have a 12-strong management team, although the players still share rooms on tour (she enjoys deciding who should go with whom). At the start of 2014, the leading players became full-time professionals. Offered the chance to say something militant, she declines. "I don't get too bitter and frustrated. I feel incredibly fortunate to do what I do, and we are starting to get the crowds in to watch us. You always want more, but you've got to be realistic."

Has she had to make sacrifices? "People think I have, but I don't. All I wanted to do was play for England. People say you can't go on a summer holiday, but I don't want to – my holiday is to go and watch the Perth Test. I've chosen to play cricket, I know what comes with that. I've travelled the world doing something I absolutely love. No regrets."

Ryan Harris

MALCOLM KNOX

Ryan Harris finished the 2013 summer as he had started it, and as he has spent too much of his career – in the hands of a physiotherapist. Yet in between, he got through four consecutive Tests for the first time, and asserted himself as Australia's best bowler in England.

Snorting, grunting and barging like a bull let loose in the ring, Harris has one of the international game's more audible approaches to the wicket. His heavy frame and effortful run-up (as much a handicap as a boon) are belied by a smooth, quickish action and a supple wrist. The result – a repeatable ability to box batsmen into their weak areas, and gain natural variation with swing and seam – won universal respect, as did his competitive but genial manner. Harris – "Rhino" to his mates – was more responsible than anyone for England's failure to reach 400.

It was a fine achievement from a 33-year-old who had said his main goal was "just to be on the plane with the rest of the guys when we come home". By the time the second Ashes came around, Harris was part of the furniture: 22 wickets at 19 – making it 46 in his nine back-to-back Ashes Tests – were the perfect foil for Mitchell Johnson. Success has come in its own sweet time.

Born in Nowra, south of Sydney, on October 11, 1979, RYAN JAMES HARRIS once toyed with the idea of playing for England: his Leicester-born father, Jim, had migrated to Australia as a child. In Ryan's words, his parents "did the hard yards". Jim was a manual worker for the Royal Australian Navy and at the Holden car factory in Adelaide's northern suburb of Elizabeth, before becoming a warehouse manager; Ryan's mother, Gai, a travel agent, died of lung cancer in 2006. Ryan has one sibling, Gavin, a Qantas engineer ten years his senior. The only thing Ryan ever dreamed of becoming – other than a cricketer – was a pilot, an ambition quashed by academic under-performance, a fear of heights and, at the age of 19, a contract to play for South Australia.

But it was not the opening of a path to glory. In fact, Harris now sees it almost as a curse. "It came so early," he says. "I probably took it for granted. I thought: 'I have a contract, I'm a full-time cricketer. Great! I can go out and have a lot of late nights with friends.'"

It was another two years before he played first-class cricket, against Tasmania at Hobart in November 2001, when – as if his body was making an early point – he tore his right pec and couldn't complete his tenth over. While Australia's Test team continued to dominate, Harris seemed to have found his level as a useful fast-medium stock bowler in the domestic game. He aspired, at best, to crack the national limited-overs side. But his easy-going nature caught up with him, and his fitness and results were inconsistent. When he was the last South Australian player to be given a contract in 2007, not long after his mother's death, he realised he might be throwing away even a comfortable first-class career: "I thought: 'It's now or never.'"

He had a good season in 2007-08, and Queensland made enquiries. South Australia did not hang on to him. From the outside, it looked like the beginning of a journeyman's end, yet for Harris it was a different kind of start. "I don't think I did anything new with my action, but I just began to work harder and look after myself better. And one day it just sort of clicked."

At Queensland, Harris found a new gear. Six months before his first game for them in 2008, he had appeared briefly for Sussex, but decided against using his British passport to qualify as a non-overseas cricketer, because it would have meant forfeiting his right to play for Australia. It proved an auspicious decision. He made his one-day international debut in early 2009, and won his first Test cap in March 2010, taking six wickets in the thrashing of New Zealand at Wellington. He also appeared in the 2010-11 Ashes, but the frustrations of his early career returned: his body seemed entirely made up of suspect tendons. In total, he would play 12 Tests in the three years between his debut and the 2013 Ashes – but never more than three in a row.

Each time he proved his potential, with a top-of-off-stump relentlessness and subtle sideways movement, effective both on helpful wickets in Western

Australia and sleepy ones in the West Indies. Yet each time his momentum was halted by chronic knee, shoulder, Achilles tendon and hamstring injuries. With Australia beginning to produce a generation of gifted fast bowlers more than a decade Harris's junior, his time seemed to have slipped by again.

Cotton-woolled by Cricket Australia – by the end of last summer, he had played only four one-day internationals since July 2010, and none since February 2012 – Harris missed more than a year of Test cricket, and was eased back through the lead-up to the Ashes. The selectors did not risk him for the First Test at Trent Bridge. But at Lord's he announced himself on the first day, dismissing Joe Root, Kevin Pietersen and Jonathan Trott on his way to a five-wicket haul, providing Australia with a glimmer of joy at a dark time.

"I was just trying to get enough balls in the right spot to create doubt," Harris says. "But I was still frustrated at not getting consistent swing." That came, he reckons, in the second innings at Old Trafford, but was followed by more frustration – rain. At Chester-le-Street, Harris again stood out, taking nine wickets. "We had solid plans for everyone. With Cook, it was not giving him balls to score off. With Trott, when we used the bouncer and put in a leg gully, we forced him to stop pressing forward and he had to change his method. Ian Bell, we gave him too much width, but to his credit he was batting well enough to keep the good balls out."

During the last, tumultuous day of the series, at The Oval, where Harris had bowled through England's long first innings and was back out after less than two hours' rest, his hamstring went again. The Australian physio, Alex Kountouris, ran on to the field to tell Michael Clarke that he should bowl him only if he really needed to. Clarke really needed to. "I was happy to bowl," Harris says. "By that stage I didn't care if I ripped it off the bone."

His series ended with 24 wickets at 19, including Root and Trott four times each, nine caught-behinds, and an award for best Australian player. He appreciated that, "but winning the Ashes would have been a thousand times better" (Australian celebrations on the SCG outfield in January 2014 confirmed that much). But he had achieved his aim of being on the plane home with his team-mates, and hopes to have two or three more years to make up for lost time. "I do feel young at heart, because I started Test cricket late in life," he says. "But one thing's for sure now: I take nothing for granted."

Chris Rogers

John Townsend

Chris Rogers had spent 19 balls and half an hour on 96, his innings in the doldrums and his nerves almost shredded, when he experienced the most magical and fulfilling moment of his life. Feeling like a "cat on a hot tin roof" as Graeme Swann manoeuvred him this way and that on the second evening of the Fourth Test at Chester-le-Street, Rogers had been fearing an imminent demise. The completion of his maiden Test hundred was proving as agonising as it had been long-awaited.

Twice he chipped Swann just short of midwicket. Then he cut at one that skidded a millimetre or so past off stump. Driven by desperation and the instinctive urge to act decisively before his luck frayed for good, Rogers swept firmly at his tormentor. He connected sweetly, and moments later was overwhelmed by emotion as he watched the ball hop over the square-leg rope.

But the emotion was not of the showy kind. The celebration that followed was so subdued it could have been the product of a sepia age. Rogers was drained. And he could barely believe he was living a moment that had been so many years in the making. "There have been a few times when I have stopped to think about it," he says. "It still puts a few shivers up the spine. It was not just the satisfaction of reaching the century, but everything that came with a lifetime of hoping and planning and preparing for it to happen.

"I spent the whole of my career looking upwards and wondering what it would be like to do well at Test level. Then, thinking for so many years that I would never know what it would be like made all that happened so much sweeter."

CHRISTOPHER JOHN LLEWELLYN ROGERS was born in Sydney on August 31, 1977, but soon moved to Perth when his father, John, became the inaugural general manager of the Western Australian Cricket Association. A sports enthusiast who played three Sheffield Shield matches for New South Wales, appeared against the 1968-69 West Indians, and was later a state selector, John returned from watching his son's Ashes debut with his wife, Ros, to buy and operate the Hume and Hovell cricket ground at Strath Creek in country Victoria; it has a slope imitating Lord's. A new start in life at 70…

Rogers was half that age when he had his own epiphany. The second-oldest Australian to score a maiden Test hundred – Arthur Richardson was almost 38 at Headingley in 1926 – Rogers had spent two decades honing his talent and skills to become, paradoxically, an overnight Ashes success. He had long believed his Test record would be limited to a dismal experience as a replacement – and not, he felt, a welcome one – for the injured Matthew Hayden at the WACA against India in 2007-08.

Yet Rogers's arrival as a Test batsman was the product of a long and slow development in first-class cricket in Australia and England, where he had scored almost 20,000 runs and learned how to resist and flourish in virtually all conditions and situations – not bad for a player who is colour-blind and has occasionally had trouble picking up the red ball. Still, it took a chance encounter for the seeds of his Ashes recall to be planted.

That took place in a Perth restaurant nearly a year before the trip to England, when the University of Western Australia Cricket Club's life members were meeting for their annual lunch. Rogers had scored a record ten centuries during his time at the club in the late 1990s, batting alongside new recruit Mark Ramprakash in his first outing, and was invited to attend. He sat next to national selector John Inverarity, who was surprised to learn that Victoria had indicated they would not be offering Rogers a new contract, and that he was contemplating a move to Tasmania. In fact, he wondered if he had a future in Australian cricket at all. A phone call or two later, and Rogers had not only received a contract extension with Victoria but was considering the prospect of a role at the Ashes. He thanked Inverarity on both counts.

"Cricket Australia got criticised for picking the side so far out, but it helped me massively," he says. "It forced me to face my fears – but in a controlled and helpful environment at Middlesex. I knew I was building up to the Ashes and could prepare properly. And guys like [director of cricket] Angus Fraser and sports psych Steve Sylvester and the coaching staff were amazing for me."

As a consequence of his year-round labours in Australia – for Western Australia and Victoria – and England, where he appeared for Derbyshire, Leicestershire and Northamptonshire before finding his best fit at Middlesex, he was the only batsman in the world to have scored 10,000 first-class runs in the five years leading up to the Ashes. Throw in the lack of distractions from limited-overs follies (though he did captain Twenty20 franchise Sydney Thunder when Chris Gayle rejected the post), and Rogers started the 2013 summer with his customary industry. He finished it with 1,536 first-class runs, more than anyone in the country. By the end of Australia's triumphant 5–0 return leg, Rogers's 830 runs – including centuries at Melbourne and Sydney – were more than any player on either side during the ten Ashes Tests.

Runs and hundreds had flowed early for Middlesex, before a composed half-century in the First Test at Trent Bridge appeared to vindicate Inverarity's faith. Then came Lord's. Excited by the opportunity to thrive at his home ground, Rogers twice fell in abysmal fashion. Befuddled by a Swann full toss that sailed above the sightscreen and out of his line of vision before striking him in the midriff, Rogers failed to ask for the review that would have reprieved him. Shouldering arms to a second-innings slider that crashed into off stump was scarcely more palatable.

"You don't get too many chances at 35," he says. "I wasn't a project player: I was expected to perform. To have a bad game at Lord's – not just a bad game, but to get out so poorly in both innings – did not reflect well. The pressure was on. I knew if I didn't get runs in the next game, that was probably it."

He responded with a rollicking 84 at Old Trafford, reaching a half-century off 49 balls, and might have made three figures if his concentration had not been shattered by the constant crowd movement in a pavilion that now stood behind the pitch rather than square of it. Durham beckoned, and Rogers felt his moment had finally come.

"That wicket was completely suited to me," he says. "You need a little bit of luck, but if the Australian management wanted me to do well in any Test, it was that one. My experience and technique and knowledge of seaming English conditions were my tools, and I felt all week leading into the Test that I could have an impact. It was a tough, tough wicket, but it was set up for me."

Foreshadowing his second-innings heroics, Stuart Broad scythed through the Australian top order, only for Rogers to stymie him and the rest of the attack until exactly 24 hours after the innings had started. That epic day included 30 heart-stopping minutes marooned on 96, but also a moment of exhilaration as a veteran finally achieved a life's dream.

Joe Root

Chris Waters

They call him "The Milkybar Kid", and in the summer of 2013 the Milkybars were on Joe Root. A maiden Test hundred at Headingley (the first Yorkshireman to achieve the feat at his home ground), an Ashes century at Lord's, and the first man in England to 1,000 first-class runs – the milestones were sweeter than a slab of white chocolate. It was a season in which the baby-faced Root came of age.

The growing-up process was not confined to the field. Barely had the cheers died down for that landmark in Leeds when Root experienced a less savoury education. In the early hours of a Saturday night out in Birmingham celebrating England's Champions Trophy victory against Australia, he became involved in a bizarre incident with David Warner. As players from both sides relaxed at the Walkabout bar, Warner took exception to Root's deployment of a green and gold wig, threw a punch in his direction, and – once the story emerged a few days later – was banned and fined.

"It was unfortunate, but he apologised and we've moved on, I think," says Root phlegmatically. "A lot was made of it, but these things occur." The shemozzle returned to the spotlight two months later when Warner, in his own good-humoured words, "hooked another one to Rooty" on his comeback in the Third Test at Old Trafford, picking out his nemesis near the square-leg boundary. Thus did Root, who insists he "didn't say much" when Warner had walked out to bat – Warner begged to differ – administer a form of poetic justice.

It was to Root's credit that the rumpus neither derailed nor defined his season. If anything, it made him more ravenous for runs. "It didn't knock me off my stride, and I was adamant I wasn't going to let that happen," he says. "In fact, it just made me want to prove to everyone that it hadn't interrupted me and wasn't going to. In that Champions Trophy, I got 60-odd in the next game against Sri Lanka."

Further confirmation came during the Second Ashes Test, at Lord's in July, when – in only his second game after being promoted to open in place of Nick Compton – he scored 180. Missed on eight on the second evening when he edged Shane Watson between wicketkeeper Brad Haddin and first slip Michael Clarke, Root played regally to become, at 22 years 202 days, England's youngest centurion in a Lord's Ashes Test. "That innings was the pinnacle of my season," he says. "I'd put it above my maiden Test hundred at Headingley." With typical cheek, it ended with a scoop shot into the hands of third man: this was no self-absorbed progress to a double-hundred.

The runs tailed off, and in Australia he was shunted around the order, making a classy 87 in four and a half hours at Adelaide from No. 3, but generally struggling before being left out at Sydney. But it was from No. 5 that he had fashioned that first Test century, 104 against New Zealand in May, when his fifth-wicket stand of 124 with Yorkshire team-mate Jonny Bairstow helped hurry the game away from the tourists.

On a sunlit Saturday, with the West Stand from which he had watched his earliest cricket roaring his every run, Root appeared to be fulfilling his destiny. In its own way, the innings seemed as preordained as Geoffrey Boycott's 100th hundred at Leeds in 1977. "I didn't feel the weight of the occasion," says Root, whose angelic exterior masks devilish determination and a dry wit. "If anything, I just enjoyed the fact it was my home ground. A full house at Headingley and a rowdy West Stand is some atmosphere, especially when you're in the middle of it. It got me going even more."

JOSEPH EDWARD ROOT, born on December 30, 1990, in Sheffield, seemed fated to be a cricketer. His father, Matt, represented Sheffield Collegiate CC and Nottinghamshire age-group teams and, last autumn, led an MCC side to Cyprus. His grandfather, Don, named after Bradman, also encouraged his love for the sport. This was cemented by frequent games in the back garden with brother Billy, 18 months his junior and a talented batsman. Fraternal rivalry sharpened the competitive edge, and it was fitting that Billy – an MCC Young Cricketer – was twelfth man when Joe made history at Lord's. "He abused me all day while bringing drinks out," says Joe, "telling me how slowly I was batting and how he would have smacked it to all parts."

Joe also played for Sheffield Collegiate – the club that nurtured Michael Vaughan, with whom his style has drawn comparison – and worked his way through the Yorkshire system. A little over three years after his first-team debut in a 40-over match against Essex at Headingley, when "I lost us the game by getting 60-odd off about 90 balls", Root made his first Test appearance, against India at Nagpur in December 2012. A calm 73 on a soporific pitch told of a temperament beyond his years and, within a month, he would debut in all three international formats, showing particular inventiveness in the 50-over game. When he finally got to bat in a Twenty20 international, against Australia at Southampton in August, he made 90 not out from 49 balls.

It is often said in Yorkshire that a youngster returns from a winter with England half the player he was when he set off – but not this time. If anything, Root looked twice as good, and started the first-class season with 49, 182, 236 and 179, then 40 and 71 in the First Test. It may have been too much to expect him to accrue the 243 he needed in the Headingley Test to become the first man in a generation to 1,000 runs by the end of May. But he got there in only his 12th innings, 70 runs into his Lord's 180. That Test also provided a reminder that his off-spin was better than occasional. At Trent Bridge, he had removed Ed Cowan; now, in quick succession, he accounted for Clarke and Usman Khawaja.

But it was his precious run-harvesting that most excited observers. "When I was in good form at the start of the season, I just focused on cashing in," says Root. "That's the thing I took from the previous winter more than anything, because when you get an opportunity, you can't just get sixties and seventies, you've got to get really big hundreds." Root says he feels "humbled" to be one of *Wisden's* Five, "particularly when you think of all the great players who've been honoured in the past". Just like the television version, cricket's Milkybar Kid makes for a fine advertisement.

NELSON MANDELA, 1918–2013

It was Madiba who made it happen

Makhaya Ntini

I would never have had the career I did without Madiba – of course not. I wouldn't even have been able to dream about it. There would have been no multiracial cricket, because there would have been no multiracial South Africa. I would have raised goats for the rest of my life. But Dr Ali Bacher was able to start the development programme, which brought cricket to the remotest villages, even mine.

I first met Madiba – his clan name – before the start of the 2003 World Cup, at the team hotel in Cape Town. He walked into the room, and the atmosphere changed immediately, just like so many people have described. Our captain, Shaun Pollock, introduced him to everyone, one by one, and explained what we did. But he knew all of that. He had a special word for every player.

Afterwards, he came back to me and took me aside for another word. He said I must go back to my village and tell the young people that I was a star. But at that stage I was not a regular in the team, and there were so many great players, like Herschelle Gibbs, Lance Klusener and Polly. I did not think I was a star at all. But he said I represented many millions of people, and it was important they knew what I had done.

So every time I wasn't performing at my best after that, I would think of what Tata Madiba had said. Most of the time, I was the only black man in the side, and he made me feel proud of that. He made me aware of my responsibility – that's why he told me to go back to the village and tell people that everything was possible, that they could make their dreams come true.

And that's why I carried the shield next to Shaun at the World Cup opening ceremony: it was an important symbol. Madiba said I should carry the shield for as long as I could, that I should keep myself fit and become an example for many years to come.

A few years later I went to his house in Houghton with a couple of the senior players, and we had a cup of coffee with him. Again, the first thing he said was to remember to go back to the village and encourage everyone else. He said the whole country was looking up to me to set an example. He used words like "leader" and "responsibility", but he said them in a way that made me feel it was an honour, not something daunting.

The rest of the world does not really understand how much our country changed during my lifetime because of Madiba. When I was the age my boys are now, I would run for dear life from a white man, if I ever saw one. Wandering around my village, there was more chance of meeting a hippo.

There were two buses a day into the nearest town, one at six in the morning, one in the afternoon. If you missed them, you had to walk for many hours. I could not speak a word of English when the development clinic arrived one day, but cricket was not strange to us – it had been part of our culture for a hundred years, since the missionaries arrived in the Eastern Cape. But it was nothing like white man's cricket. We had no kit, no boots. There was an annual festival between the villages – Amaghaghahle – at which the winning team would slaughter a sheep and enjoy a feast.

Look at us now: I went to a privileged white school, and my kids go to a white school – or should I say a former white school. These are the things we need to embrace. Many thousands of people gave their lives during the struggle years, and many sacrificed a lot to end apartheid. But it was Madiba who made it happen. He never forgot his own people in Qunu at any stage of his journey, and he asked me not to forget mine.

> **Madiba was not afraid if love challenged our traditional culture**

The kind of racial prejudice I experienced was, obviously, nothing like apartheid. At the start of my career some people thought I was a token player. A few times I was called the k-word, which is the worst insult. I wanted to hit those people, but I remembered what Madiba said, and would try to learn why they said those things, and try to forgive them. Everyone is your brother or your cousin, whether they believe it or not. He taught millions of people about love and peace.

Madiba stands out to me more than my biological father. He did and said things which our fathers could never do or say. Once you were able to walk, you could no longer sit on your father's lap. He would chase you away to go and look after the goats or the cows. Our own fathers taught us what their fathers taught them, what was right and wrong. But Madiba was different. He was not afraid if love challenged our traditional culture or society.

Our fathers taught us what was good for us in the here and now. But Madiba taught us what was good for us in the future – to learn not to take things as hard as we would normally. For example, I would have killed someone for stealing my father's cow, and believed that was the right thing to do.

I was getting ready to drive to Bloemfontein to watch my son play a match when I heard of Madiba's passing. It was like losing a family member – the head of the family, actually. He was sick, and we knew that one day he would leave us, but still… I was in a very emotional state, stunned and shocked. I could not drive. We watched news clips and features that had been filmed about his life years before. There was so much celebration, and I wondered why we could not have celebrated when he was alive. He might have enjoyed some of the tributes.

We have had two presidents after him. Have they followed his lead? What have they done? Madiba said we should take our guns and pangas and throw them into the sea, to stop fighting among ourselves. I owe my career and my life to him. Like millions of other Africans, black and white.

Makhaya Ntini took 390 wickets for South Africa in 101 Tests – more than anyone bar Shaun Pollock. He was talking to Neil Manthorp.

You just couldn't say no

ALI BACHER

South Africa were readmitted to the ICC in London in July 1991, and the World Cup was only seven months away – but there was no discussion about our playing in it. In August, I brought out the former West Indies captain Clive Lloyd to help promote cricket in the townships, and he was terrific. He wanted to meet Mr Mandela, so we went to Shell House – the ANC headquarters, in Johannesburg – where there was a huge contingent of Swedish media (the ANC had enjoyed the support of the Swedish government in the apartheid years).

The door was open, and I saw him for the first time. "Cricket chaps, come in," he said. We all went in, the Swedish media too. He complimented us on the development programme in the townships. Someone asked him: "What about South Africa playing in the World Cup?" He said: "They've got to play." That was it. Lobbying began within 24 hours, and we played in the World Cup. Simple as that. That was his muscle and influence.

He was an extraordinary person – in his capacity to forgive, not forget. When it came to the rugby World Cup in 1995, President Mandela went out publicly to support the springbok emblem – despite it recalling an era when South African international sport was whites-only. It was the main item on the news, and I was asked what I thought. I said: "Look, we have enormous respect for our president, but… we're not going to support it."

Next morning Madiba invited me to lunch, and for 40 minutes he explained to me and two of my board members in simple terms that he knew how important the springbok emblem was to the Afrikaner, and he wanted to thank them for supporting him as the first black president of our country. How can you argue with that?

When he walked on to the field at the final, the crowd was 99% white, mainly Afrikaners. And they were chanting "Nelson! Nelson!" Mind-boggling. But first he had gone into the changing-room wearing his Springbok jersey, which Steve Tshwete – who had been instrumental in South Africa's return to the ICC – had arranged for him that morning. Then he walked unannounced on to the field. There was no way our team weren't going to beat the All Blacks after that.

His touch with kings, prime ministers and the man in the street never changed. When we used to invite him to the cricket, the first thing he'd do was go to the catering area and shake hands with the staff. The administrators, white and black, were all lined up – but we had to wait. And when we introduced everyone in turn, he would use a stock phrase: "You might not remember me."

He phoned me just before South Africa co-hosted the cricket World Cup in February 2003.

"Ali, I just want to wish your team every success."

"Thank you very much, Mr Mandela."

That common touch: Nelson Mandela with Ali Bacher.

"My name is Madiba, Ali."

"Mr Mandela, where I come from, if you respect somebody enormously, you call him Mr."

In a second, he shot back: "Ali, where I come from, if you don't call me Madiba, you're not regarded as a true friend of mine." He had that common touch.

In February 1993, I invited him and Walter Sisulu, who was high up in the ANC, to a triangular one-day competition between South Africa, Pakistan and West Indies. At tea, there was a request for him to come to the changing-room and meet the teams – you can't believe the emotion when these chaps were shaking hands with him.

There were two ways back to the presidential room. Mr Mandela chose to go via the field, and a spectator about five yards away threw an orange at him, like a missile. It missed, and I caught it. Mr Mandela just carried on as though nothing had happened. Later, I asked his main security officer, "Did he see that?"

"Of course he did."

"Why did he stay so calm?"

"He wasn't going to show that person he was ruffled."

He was the greatest fundraiser of all time. Whenever the phone went and it was Mr Mandela, the corporates would say: "I wonder what this call is going to cost me."

Once he said to me, "Ali, you would agree that I've helped you chaps get back into international cricket?"

"Of course, Mr Mandela."

"Look, I've got this school in the Northern Province, and it's in terrible shape. I'm going to need a million Rand to upgrade it… I think it would be a nice gesture if cricket gave a million Rand."

I brought this up at the next board meeting, and someone complained that we weren't a charity organisation, that we were there to administer cricket. So I said, "OK, if your answer's no, that's fine, but *you're* going to tell him, not me."

So Ray White, the chairman, said, "All those who are opposed, put up their hand." Of course, nobody did. Can you imagine if the board had refused? It would have been around the country in a second. Nobody could say no.

Rest in peace. Our beloved Madiba.

Dr Ali Bacher played 12 Tests for South Africa, four as captain. He was the first head of the United Cricket Board of South Africa.

CRICKET ON FILM

A moving record

DAVID FRITH

Death is not absolute so long as there remain photographs or sound recordings or moving images, preferably in colour. For cricket lovers, the camera must feel like man's greatest invention: thanks to celluloid and a crank handle, W. G. Grace, Victor Trumper, Jack Hobbs, Wally Hammond and Don Bradman live on – if only in two-dimensional form and in shades of black and white, though later with audio.

It is frustrating that today's technological wizardry took so long to arrive. The earliest surviving conventional motion film is the little sequence of Ranjitsinhji wielding a wild bat in the Sydney nets late in 1897, although we have Eadweard Muybridge's multi-camera sequences from the 1880s of naked batsmen and bowlers from Pennsylvania University; the processed frames are viewable on his zoopraxiscope. A film clip of Clem Hill batting at Sheffield in 1896 was once listed, but nobody now knows where it is. Nor was proper care taken of shots of A. E. Stoddart's team and Victoria walking on to the field around the time of the Ranji mini-film.

If it's lamentable how little cricket film was taken long ago, then it's true that film was expensive and the reel-length short. Some even believed the novelty would not endure. Blessed, then, are the cameramen who filmed WG and Ranji in the nets, probably at Hastings; Joe Darling and his Australians of 1899 taking the field, probably at Cheltenham; Lord Hawke coming down the steps; and, most captivatingly of all 19th-century cricket film, the procession of the Gentlemen and the Players, taken at Lord's at a leisurely pace by Prestwich Manufacturing on July 18, 1898, to mark WG's 50th birthday. This is the only moving film of many of the great English cricketers of the era. Elsewhere, clips of Bobby Peel, George Hirst and Bobby Abel show them motionless, either perplexed or embarrassed.

So almost 40 years had passed since the first *Wisden* before people paid to see the cricketers magically in motion in Biograph peepshows. As newsreel companies sprang up and picture houses lured audiences, it became a way of life. Topical Budget, Pathé News, British Movietone, Warwick Bioscope, and Gaumont British all devised captivating stories and images, and by the 1920s there were over 20m attendances a week at UK cinemas.

Gems such as the film of Gilbert Jessop, Hirst and Wilfred Rhodes in England's one-wicket victory in the 1902 Ashes Test at The Oval have been lost, but recently two barrels filled with early film shot by Mitchell & Kenyon, the Blackburn-based company, were found; further discoveries should not be impossible. The most exciting of all the M&K material was the 1901 sequence of Arthur Mold trying to demonstrate the purity of his action after being no-balled for throwing. The elderly batsman in the nets is the former England

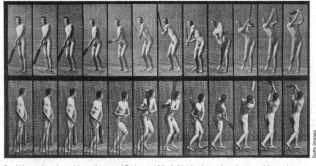

Study in motion: the subject of some of Eadweard Muybridge's pioneering photographic work at Pennsylvania University hints at his Surrey origins.

captain A. N. Hornby, then president of Lancashire. A further bonus is a sweep of the players in that Lancashire v Somerset match leaving the field with the umpires, one of whom is Jim Phillips, the fearless Australian who had just terminated Mold's career.

M&K also served us well with footage of the Accrington v Church league match in 1902, even though – with the telescopic lens years away – the players are unidentifiable. In 1905, however, British Movietone created some of the best early cricket action, filming the Australians clowning around with a ball and in a chaotic team group, then skipping down the steps at Trent Bridge. Further close-up action shots at Lord's do them little justice: Clem Hill and Joe Darling look the part, but Warwick Armstrong and Monty Noble clumsily overbalance, perhaps jittery as they perform for this strange new contraption; Victor Trumper is let down by a ball tossed at his throat. The only other known clip of this deified batsman shows him falling over after being run out in a Sydney Test. Four years later his long funeral cortege was captured on celluloid. At least his spiritual successor, Archie Jackson, was beautifully filmed during a net session in 1929.

Another precious pre-Great War film was shot at Horsham in 1913, when Sussex played Lancashire. The Tyldesley brothers go out to bat, and the only known footage of Albert Trott shows him shuffling out to umpire. The match action is far away, but the elegantly dressed spectators reflect the idyll of pre-war England in summertime.

Topical Budget made newsreels from 1911 to 1931, and were responsible for some significant footage, notably of England's recapture of the Ashes at The Oval in 1926. Jack Gregory blazes away with bat (no gloves) and ball, Hobbs and Herbert Sutcliffe build towards that glorious victory, and young Harold Larwood and the elderly Rhodes prise out the Australians. This major feature set the pattern: newsreels would now give cricket's great events due attention – even if identifications were sometimes adrift. The 1930 Ashes Tests were well covered by the newsreel companies, and some footage is now available on the internet, but the abiding mystery is that there is nothing on Bradman's greatest innings, his 254 at Lord's. In 1948, his famous last-innings duck was recorded clearly enough, although the inserts of leg-spinner Eric Hollies are misleading: he was bowling *over* the wicket.

A substantial silent *Life of Jack Hobbs* is absorbing, and Australian film-maker Ken G. Hall made an enchanting sound documentary called *That's Cricket* in 1931. At Trent Bridge, a Mr Stevens used his 16mm camera to film county and Test matches during the 1930s, invaluable reels now safe with the National Film Archive. From 1946, with television still in its infancy, newsreels remained major attractions. After England won the Ashes at The Oval in 1953, I spent all day in a cinema watching repeat showings, and still treasure indelible images of Len Hutton's running catch to dismiss Neil Harvey off new boy Fred Trueman, Tony Lock's spine-bending ecstasy after taking a wicket, and Denis Compton's sweep to seal the triumph.

A couple of years earlier a landmark feature was *Elusive Victory*, produced by E. W. Swanton and filmed by 24-year-old John Woodcock. This monochrome film of the 1950-51 Ashes, with match footage, player close-ups and informal scenes, might have set a pattern while television was still emerging; but it was not to be, apart from some important tour features shot in colour by Rothmans in the 1960s. Cricket continued to be an ingredient in many a feature film, however, and *The Final Test* (1954, written by Terence Rattigan) centred

And that's a stellar cast...

on a game at The Oval, with current England players taking bit parts. Elsewhere, numerous feature films have included brief cricket scenes, many staged clumsily. From India, though, *Lagaan* (2001) was a highly entertaining musical drama with a cricket match as the central theme.

As *Wisden* reached its century in 1963, newsreels were in decline, and television was becoming the all-powerful medium. With the advent of video recorders, cricket lovers began creating film libraries of their own, collecting highlights, interviews and sometimes even live play. Nostalgia and plain curiosity created a renewed interest in old film. In 1981, I persuaded the British Film Institute to stage annual cricket evenings at London's NFT, showing material from 1897 onwards, fresh discoveries often garnishing the

CRICKET AND TELEVISION IN THE 21ST CENTURY

Impending Armageddon

PAUL KING

When I joined the Sky Sports cricket department in 2001, I was given two pieces of advice by the managing director: "Work hard – and under no circumstances go out drinking with Ian Botham." The first instruction proved easy; the second rather less so.

Producing live cricket is nothing if not unpredictable. No one turning up to the 2007 World Cup final at Bridgetown expected the umpires to forget the tournament regulations. Then there was the sandy outfield in Antigua two years later, which limited a Test match to ten balls.

And I will never forget the *News of the World* front page in 2010, which meant a radical change to our Sunday coverage of the Lord's Test against Pakistan. I had received an early call about the story, and spent a sleepless night wondering how to tackle it. What should our tone be? Could we condemn players who had been found guilty by a newspaper, but not yet in court? What about the future of the game? I recently looked back at tapes of our broadcast that day, and the passion of the likes of Nasser Hussain, Michael Holding and Ramiz Raja stood out. You could see it in their eyes.

Throw in rain, bad light, waterlogged outfields, floodlights endangered by excessive wind, and all the other reasons for not playing cricket, and it was rare when two days were the same. Only one thing was certain: the airtime had to be filled.

The day generally started with the commentators' rota, a screed afforded the scrutiny lavished by the company accountant on a dodgy expenses claim. Too many stints might have given a commentator the impression of being overworked, too few of being unloved. It wasn't long before witty remarks were scrawled over the document when it was pinned to the wall – pointing out that Mike Atherton had been given another early finish, or Hussain had two long hours between appearances.

From then on, it was a series of instant decisions. Dozens of people would constantly be offering ideas for the broadcast: commentators, statisticians, cameramen, graphics wizards, videotape operators, Hawk-Eye and Hot Spot aficionados, as well as a host of engineers and technical staff. If the idea helped tell the story of the game, it got on air. If not, it was politely declined.

There was never time to relax. After many years of covering cricket, we liked to think the machine was pretty well-oiled. But no one was allowed to drift. You needed to be prepared for anything – a clatter of wickets or a dubious umpiring decision or a team refusing to take the field, as happened at The Oval in 2006. Nor, these days, is it all about what appears on the screen. The modern producer needs to think about content for online and various apps, and what to do with Twitter and Facebook. And, if all seems calm, there's always the weather radar to warn of impending Armageddon.

There was no such thing as the perfect broadcast. When the day ended, there were always things you could have done differently. But when you left the ground, you knew you had the chance to do it all again tomorrow – only better. And if Botham was brandishing a bottle of chardonnay? Pretend you've gone teetotal.

Paul King was executive producer for Sky Sports for more than six years.

programmes. Percy Fender's 16mm footage from 1928-29 has been the latest find, containing the earliest film of Don Bradman and Archie Jackson. Jack Badcock's high-quality record of the Australians' tour of England in 1938 has also been shown for the first time in public; so too, at the NFT, Jeff Stollmeyer's film of West Indies' 1951-52 tour of Australasia. Although damaged in storage, it contains some magical sequences.

Probably overshadowed by South Africa's post-apartheid transition, an invaluable 30-part history of that country's Test history from 1888 to 1970 was overseen by Brian Bassano, and is now a video rarity. Something similar was made to mark New Zealand's cricket history, while Jack Egan – utilising Cinesound's newsreel library – produced several videotapes in Australia, including interviews with Bradman and Bill O'Reilly. In 1982, I researched and scripted *Benson & Hedges Golden Greats: Batsmen*, with John Arlott the key presenter (long after he had featured in the charming British Council film *Cricket*, which centred on the 1948 Lord's Test). A companion to that video was one on bowlers, presented by Peter West. Newsreel and privately shot film made up the historical content.

It is a good time now for vintage cricket film. Innumerable clips from the newsreel companies' archives from the past 100 years and more can be watched on the internet, with countless delights on YouTube. With cricket fans wielding mobile phones – mainly to capture grinning players signing things or with arms around fans' shoulders – the game is now awash with images, in stark contrast to those long-ago times when the early marvels of cinematography were scarcely understood by cameramen or cricketers.

Film treasures from the 1930s have been rediscovered. As 16mm cameras became available, cricketers took them on tour. The sight of an old photo of Australian batsman Bill Brown holding a movie camera prompted an enquiry as to the fate of those films: "Oh, I think I lent them some years ago but they weren't returned." Fortunately, others – such as Badcock and Clarrie Grimmett (who filmed the 1930 and 1934 Ashes tours) – were more careful. Fast bowlers H. D. "Hopper" Read and Maurice Allom recorded some fascinating 1930s action around England and on tour, and since the 1950s much important footage has been shot by the Bedser twins, Charles Palmer, Arthur Morris, Alan Oakman, Ken Barrington, Trevor Bailey, Johnny Wardle, Keith Andrew, Frank Tyson and Jack Robertson. Much of this material was shown at the London film nights, while MCC have produced several DVDs.

Oakman's colour sequence of Garry Sobers bowling fast could not be bettered, and his shots of Barrington dressed as WG are another treat. Among Bailey's high-quality films is rare footage of Australia's mystery bowler Jack Iverson, as well as Lindsay Hassett's dismissal by Doug Wright's fast leg-break, the equal of the Warne–Gatting ball of the century over 40 years later. These amateur home movies inevitably contain many scenes around swimming pools, on ships' decks, at airports, and action footage too far away, but there are also some high-quality shots from net practice. One of Wardle's films even features pin-up Sabrina on the pitch with Hutton.

Sid Barnes, the rebel Australian batsman, made a film of the 1948 tour and showed it for the benefit of charity, though the cynics, knowing "Bagga's"

All-rounder: Alan Oakman, Test player, Sussex stalwart and cinematographer.

proclivity for a few quid, felt Sid was his own all-consuming charity. When he was carried into the dressing-room in 1948 after taking a ferocious blow to the kidneys at short leg, he winked at the team-mate holding his camera and said: "Didya get that?" The whereabouts of the complete film are no longer known. Perhaps it simply wore out.

Cricket on early television was seldom recorded and retained. One blissful exception was in 1953, when England won the Ashes. The heroes were interviewed by Brian Johnston on the top deck of the Oval pavilion, with young Trueman displaying a shyness he would later overcome. DVDs have succeeded videotapes, and the Australian television mini-series on Bodyline sold well. This was regrettable in one way, since it contained many ludicrous inaccuracies; some folk, it seems, find the truth dull. The BBC and the ABC have both made admirable documentaries on that most famous of all series. With the archives bulging, future generations should be satisfied.

David Frith is a leading cricket historian.

The play's the thing

LIAM CROMAR

"Why, this is very midsummer madness." The startled spectator Lady Olivia may not have had cricket in mind in *Twelfth Night*, but many unacquainted with the game would echo her. With 2014 marking 450 years since William Shakespeare's debut, and *Wisden's* own 150th birthday, it is clearly the moment to marry the two in a Shakespearean XI.

Setting aside the question of the opposition (Kit Marlowe CC?), let's get to grips with the batting order. Since the survival of aggressive new-ball spells is a priority for any opener, we pick **Macbeth**, who trusts both his back-foot game ("I pull in resolution") and his luck ("I bear a charmed life"). One hopes neither is misplaced. He's joined by **Brutus**, "an honourable man" who can presumably be relied on to uphold the spirit of cricket. But Macbeth should beware his running between the wickets: in Julius Caesar's last appearance, Brutus sold him down the river: "A two, Brute? Then fall, Caesar!"

Prince Hamlet's indecisiveness when facing "slings and arrows" may suggest he lacks the clarity of mind needed against the fastest bowling. However, his warning that "I may sweep to my revenge" hints at a proficiency against spin. He is joined in the middle order by the classy strokemaker **Duke Humphrey of Gloucester**, whose pledge to "drive the back" savours of a penchant for straight-bat shots. With the Flintoff-like physique implied by his name, the all-rounder **Fortinbras** slots in at No. 5.

There can be little quarrel when it comes to wicketkeeper and captain. The boisterous **Petruchio**, just the man to rally his fielders from behind the stumps, is known as the ''keeper'' of "shrewd" skipper **Katharina**, despite their tendency to argue about the light.

To spearhead the bowling attack, we select **Sebastian**: his body blows drove Sir Andrew Aguecheek to retire hurt, calling for the physio: "for the love of God, a surgeon!… He has broke my head across." With his "lean and hungry look", **Cassius**, who "thinks too much", is the perfect new-ball partner: wily and ceding little, he's conspired to topple many an opponent. For slow variation, **Launce's lover** stands out as a professional among amateurs: "she can spin for her living". The curate **Sir Nathaniel** completes the attack. He is, after all, "a very good bowler".

Let's not forget the officials. There's **Lady Macbeth**, who proclaimed "Out, damned spot! Out, I say!", demonstrating her familiarity with thermal-imaging technology. And **Portia**, esteemed in some quarters as a "wise and upright judge!", though not all her decisions prove uncontroversial. As scorer, we have the **Bard** himself: "nor need I tallies… to score".

The trouble, of course, is the weather. Will this motley crew ever make it on to the field? For as Feste, lead singer of the Barmy Army (composed of the rather-less-foolish-than-their-name-implies Fools) warns, "the rain it raineth every day".

The Shakespeare XI

1. Macbeth, King of Scotland (*Macbeth*)
2. M. Brutus (*Julius Caesar*)
3. Hamlet, Prince of Denmark (*Hamlet*)
4. Humphrey, Duke of Gloucester (*Henry IV, Pt II; Henry V; Henry VI, Pts I and II*)
5. Fortinbras, Prince of Norway (*Hamlet*)
6. *Katharina (*The Taming of the Shrew*)
7. †Petruchio (*The Taming of the Shrew*)
8. Sebastian (*Twelfth Night*)
9. C. Cassius (*Julius Caesar*)
10. Launce's lover (*Two Gentlemen of Verona*)
11. Sir Nathaniel (*Love's Labour's Lost*)

Umpires: Lady Macbeth (*Macbeth*) and Portia (*The Merchant of Venice*).
Scorer: W. Shakespeare (*passim*).

Liam Cromar is a cricket geek with a taste for its technology, traditions and teas. Between visits to the homes of MCC and the RSC, he writes @LiamCromar on Twitter and spinnerwebs.co.uk/cricket

THE COMPETITION

Wisden received 108 entries for its second writing competition, up a fraction on 2012. As before, they arrived from all corners of the globe, all ages, and both genders. The standard continued to be exceptionally high, and the business of judging became no easier. In the end, though, the editorial team plumped for this inventive team selection. Liam Cromar is the second winner (after Brian Carpenter) of what is an annual award. The prize is publication, adulation, and an invitation to the launch dinner, held in April.

The rules are unchanged from 2013. Anyone who has never been commissioned for *Wisden* can take part. Entries, which should not have been submitted before (and are restricted to a maximum of two per person), must be:

1. the entrant's own work;
2. unpublished in any medium;
3. received by the end of November 30, 2014;
4. between 480 and 520 words (excluding the title);
5. neither libellous nor offensive;
6. related to cricket, but not a match report.

Articles should be emailed to almanack@wisden.com, with "Writing Competition 2014" as the subject line. Alternatively, they can be posted to: Writing Competition 2014, John Wisden & Co, 13 Old Aylesfield, Golden Pot, Alton, Hampshire GU34 4BY. Please provide your name, address and telephone number. Bloomsbury staff and those who, in the editor's opinion, have a working relationship with *Wisden* are ineligible. The editor's decision is final. Once again, we look forward to receiving your contributions.

THE 2013 ENTRANTS

Richard Allen; Derek Anns; Jeremy Atkinson; Mike Battrum; Phillip Bayliss; Paddy Briggs; Alex Britten; Paul Bullman; Paul Caswell; Vincent Coster; Nigel Cox; Alan Crabtree; Liam Cromar; Ryan Curtis; Somnath Das; Christian Drury; David Early; Giles Falconer; Keith Feaver; Robert Fellows; Rudolph Lambert Fernandez; Paul Filer; Philip Fisher; David Fraser; Venkataraman Ganesan; Allan Garley; Khamchand Goolcharan; Chris Gore; Nick Gormack; Radley Gorringe; Ian Gray; Steve Green; Matthew Hard; Paul Harper; David Haziri; Peter Horne; Icki Iqbal; Michael Jones; Christian Kelly; Tony Kinnear; John Kilkaldy; Joel Lamy; Trevor Lawrence; Ross Lawson; John Austin Locke; Cameron McDill; Carolyn McKay; Anthony McKenna; Ian McMurray; Sean Mahoney; Peter Maiden; Rob Maslin; David Matthews; John Mayes; Tim Mickleburgh; Steve Miller; Rhod Morgan; Peter Morrish; Kieran Mullens; Santokie Nagulendran; Nayeem Islam; Richard Neville-Carlé; Andrew Nixon; Colin Norton; Murrell Osborne; Greg Philp; David Potter; Roberto Rabaiotti; Richard Reardon; David Reavill; Chris Rigby; Timothy Roberts; Mark Sanderson; Robert Selby; Abhijato Sensarma; Isha Shah; Christopher Sharp; David Sherman; Graham Shipstone; Peter Slater; Chris Smith; Stuart Smith; Graham Spiller; Peter Stone; Richard Stone; John Swain; David Taylor; Jack Taylor; Fergal Tobin; John Treeby; Alex Try; James Umpleby; Gordon Veniard; Nicholas Webb; Andrew Welch; John West; Reg White; Zeeshan Mahmud.

JACQUES KALLIS

Three trades, master of all

Neil Manthorp

It's hard to believe, given his physique and the reputation Jacques Kallis commanded in international cricket for almost two decades, but the reason he wasn't selected for Western Province Schools was because he was too small. His headmaster at Wynberg Boys' High, Keith Richardson, had seen beyond his lack of height and breadth, however, and asked him to net with the First XI, aged just 14. Kallis arrived in a helmet, not only a rare luxury in those days, but an apparently futile gesture at protection for one so fragile.

The leader of the attack, Aubrey Martyn, who would be selected by South Africa to tour England in 1994, started gently, but was soon curious – and peeved – enough to be charging in off his full run. Bouncers came and bouncers went, mainly out of the nets: the diminutive Kallis appeared to have an unnatural amount of time. The titters of the watching boys were quickly redirected from the batsman to the bowlers.

A couple of years later, Kallis was playing in a prestigious schools festival. For weeks, his strict but devoted father, Henry, helped him prepare, by throwing him balls in the nets after school. But now Jacques played a loose drive at a wide delivery, and was caught behind for a duck. When the match finished, he couldn't find his father. "I'm afraid he's gone, Jacques," said the master in charge. "He said you can walk home if you're going to play a shot like that." And he did – for seven miles, carrying his kit. Henry explained later that he didn't care about the score; everybody makes nought. Just as long as the bowler earns your wicket! In later years, the rest of the world would understand how seriously Kallis heeded the advice.

And his team-mates loved him for it. This would become the part of his life that was invisible and inaudible to the public, the part between player and captain, player and coach, the dialogue which takes place over a room-service bolognese on the third night of the Second Test halfway through another tour: "The batting is built around you, Jacques. You are the best we have. We need you. Please don't let us down…"

At the beginning of his career, against a background of collapses and brittleness, and with the top and middle order often relying on an endless list of all-rounders to bail them out, Kallis obeyed team orders, adopting as low-risk an approach as possible. It wasn't just team orders, though. When Kallis started his Test career, not one member of South Africa's top six averaged above 40. If that did not immediately concern him and his senior colleagues, then the media's obsession with the stat would eventually drive the players to paranoia. Series against Australia were previewed around South Africa's batting inadequacies and the superiority of the opposition top six, who mostly averaged over 40 – and Steve Waugh over 50.

Alexander Joe, AFP/Getty Images

Unadventurous? Quite the reverse. Jacques Kallis takes on Harbhajan Singh at Newlands in 2011.

It became a duty, more than a desire, to increase his average, and the habit stuck. But with the establishment of Hashim Amla and A. B. de Villiers, and Graeme Smith's encouragement to express himself, Kallis's three quickest Test centuries were all made during the final three years of his career, and two of them converted into his only doubles. Selective criticism that he was unable to dominate an attack receded, as the realisation dawned that he had, in fact, been precluded from doing so. Finally, he was surrounded by players he could trust – and of similar stature. His career strike-rate by the end of 2009, from 133 Tests, was 44. In his final 33 Tests, by which time Smith, Amla and de Villiers were all well entrenched, it was 53. His tally of 97 sixes was bettered only by Adam Gilchrist. Now he can devote himself to one-day cricket.

The observation that Kallis was a great batsman – he averaged 55 – but not a great all-rounder is understandable given the runs he scored. But it is hardly sustainable. Not a single regular bowler in the history of the game has been a fixture at No. 3 or 4. Great all-rounders came in at No. 6 or 7. He led the attack when necessary, taking the new ball and claiming five-wicket hauls when Allan Donald, Shaun Pollock, Makhaya Ntini and Dale Steyn were not. And that is the point: he became labelled as a fill-in fourth seamer because of the bowlers around him, not because he was unwilling or incapable. He accepted the role of bowling maidens because the team needed it, not because he didn't want to take wickets. Like his batting, his bowling genuflected to the greater good.

Granted the rare opportunity to attack, he could still approach 90mph right up until his final Test, and rarely objected to a third slip when the ball was swinging. On plenty of occasions the scorecard would tell of unremarkable analyses – two for 44, or three for 35. But they were often door-opening or innings-changing contributions. One need look only at the role he played with the ball in South Africa's historic series victories in England and Australia in 2008 to grasp his importance. His fielding, too, mainly in the slips, was calm and efficient: his 200 Test catches were bettered only by Rahul Dravid.

He was systematic and clinical in his assessment of everything he did. Kallis had the rare ability to ask himself questions dispassionately, mostly of the risk-versus-reward variety. He pondered the reverse sweep, for example, but believed he had other ways to milk a troublesome spinner. Even so, he played the shot about a dozen times in the nets, just in case. And in January 2011, with South Africa in trouble in a series-deciding Test against India at his beloved Newlands, and Harbhajan Singh – armed with a packed leg-side field – making the ball turn and bounce uncontrollably, he produced the shot. It went for four. Everyone but Kallis was stunned. He played it again soon after: four more. In all, he would reverse-sweep ten times, and only once did he fail to score. Meanwhile, M. S. Dhoni had changed the field: the stranglehold had been broken. Kallis went on to make his second century of the match and save the series.

He also had an ability to switch off. He almost never watched a game on television, and was rarely interested in results or individual performances. When the time came to engage, he was able to tune in instantly, and devoured the information supplied by video analysts.

At the age of 30, Kallis was awarded a benefit year by Western Province, during which he raised over a million Rand. He accepted none of it, preferring instead to start the Jacques Kallis Scholarship Foundation, which allowed promising youngsters from underprivileged backgrounds to finish their high-school education at a traditional cricket-playing school. The emphasis was on education. Since it began in 2005, the foundation has produced over 30 high-school graduates, and put half a dozen through university.

Kallis rarely offered unprompted advice, but was neither reticent nor reluctant when asked. He preferred actions to speak louder than words, and that will apply to his legacy. The debate about his greatness, especially when compared to others, never bothered him during his Test career, and it will not in the future. But the time has come for him to do something he always said he would. "I'll appreciate the records and enjoy what I achieved, but they are not why I played the game," he says. "Winning games and series for my country will always be the best memories, no question."

Neil Manthorp reported on all but four of Jacques Kallis's 166 Tests.

CRICKET IN THE SLUMS

The siren song of the IPL

James Astill

Darkness enveloped Dharavi, a slum in central Mumbai, like a heavy sigh. It was a Sunday eve, the end of a precious day off for most of its hard-working residents, and the week ahead was certain to be a grind. From the tightly packed wood-and-brick shacks came the clanking of cooking pots and the blare of television as the occupants settled in for the evening.

But Sandeep Kunchi Kurve was out celebrating. A small, wiry, 26-year-old, he had hit 49 that afternoon for his club side, MIG Bandra, at the stately Brabourne Stadium down in the affluent Churchgate area of the city. Kurve, a glass stud sparkling in his left ear, is Dharavi's only representative in the A-division of Mumbai's Kanga League. His achievement is remarkable.

A third-generation slum dweller, he learned his cricket in Dharavi, playing street games – *galli* cricket – in its cramped alleys. He did not face a "season ball" until, aged 21, he was referred to a cricket academy belonging to Dilip Vengsarkar, the former Test player. He found it tough. "Playing with a tennis ball gives you some idea of swing, but not of pace or spin," he recalled, sitting on a pitch-dark street corner, a couple of beers to the good. "I found it frightening. I still do."

But he was a quick learner. A trial with a company side, Nirlon, led to regular club cricket and a monthly salary of 8,000 rupees – about £80, more than the boys in the slum's embroidery workshop might earn, less than an auto-rickshaw driver. Kurve had previously worked in one of those tiny workshops – there are hundreds in Dharavi – wearing his eyes out stitching saris. Now he had committed himself to cricket. "It was the only thing I had ever felt passionate about."

To supplement his training with Nirlon, he began practising daily on a patch of gravelly wasteland outside the slum, known as the Sion–Dharavi Sports Club. There, every morning and evening, a loyal childhood friend, Parshu, hurled tennis balls at him from close range. And, amazingly, his efforts paid off: MIG, one of Mumbai's strongest clubs, came calling.

Playing in the Talim Shield contest the previous year, Kurve had hit a dashing 148 for MIG against another famous Mumbai side, Matunga Gymkhana. "No, who knows?" he said. "If I hit a 200 this season I could get picked for Mumbai, and from there, you know, it's only a small step." To the IPL, he meant – that was the ambition driving Kurve. "If I can get a chance, I can do well. I've faced IPL bowlers many times, even this afternoon." I noticed he was wearing an Indian team shirt from the 2013 Women's World Cup, which had been part-held in the city. He had been employed by the team as a net bowler.

This is the facet of the IPL its cheerleaders love to trumpet: the opportunity it has afforded a few dozen journeymen to earn a good living in the game, and

Punit Paranjpe, Reuters

Barely enough room to swing a bat: Dharavi, Mumbai.

the inspiration this has, in turn, provided to many more. Yet India, as Kurve's example suggests, is still far more remarkable for its inability to convert its multitudinous cricket enthusiasm into talent. Dharavi, a mile-square shanty town in the middle of Mumbai, is home to roughly a million cricket-mad people. That Kurve is its most successful player must make it one of the world's least efficient incubators of sporting talent.

The slum has no cricket facilities to speak of, and the Sion–Dharavi patch is one of only three public spaces available to the dwellers for cricket. Yet this paucity has been compounded by galloping socio-economic changes that, in Mumbai and other fast-growing Indian cities, are making it harder for men and boys to spare time for cricket. Both factors have accelerated the demise of India's traditional cricketing culture, nurtured and husbanded in Mumbai, in the face of the television-fuelled IPL onslaught.

For a close-up glimpse of these pressures, I spent a couple of days in Dharavi. I already knew the slum well, having visited it many times; nowhere had taught me so much about the enormous changes afoot in India, in cricket and otherwise. My inquiry had begun in a cobbled clearing, about the size of a squash court, where four slum pathways meet. A well-known *galli* cricket spot, it was – on this and every Sunday afternoon – crowded with men and boys, playing raucously. There were roughly 11 a side; sometimes many more, if you included the passers-by unwittingly entangled in the play.

Pedestrians streamed across the pitch. Then, whenever there was a small break in the flow, the bowler let fly, underarm and fast. He used a hard plastic ball; the players called this sort of *galli* game "T20". The alternative, played with a smaller and bouncier rubber ball, was "ODI".

Comment

Standing before a set of steel stumps, drilled into the cobbles, the batsmen aimed to massacre every delivery for six – by hitting the church below the eaves at the far end of the clearing. In their allotted four overs, the batting side were now chasing a gettable score of 49.

"For six days we work hard, and on the seventh we play cricket. It is our great pleasure," said Abid Ansari, a back-office worker at the opulent Taj Mahal hotel, now waiting to bat. Like all the slum youths crouched eagerly around him, he liked Twenty20 best – to watch as well as play. None was all that interested in Test cricket. "That is not how we play," explained Abid, illustrating an important element in Twenty20's massive appeal: it is the closest approximation to the street games enjoyed by millions of Indians.

Behind the pitch was a biryani restaurant, where Fakhre Alam, a 29-year-old chef, was rushing off to a more serious sort of cricket. His destination, a short walk from the slum, was the Dharavi–Sion Sports Club, the rutted ground where Kurve practised. Above its rusty gateway a banner had been hung to mark the retirement of Sachin Tendulkar the previous day. "With his power and his integrity, he has become a god!" it read in Hindi.

Fakhre's team, Ham Sab Ek Hain – "We Are United" – were about to play their second game of the day, in one of the knockout tournaments held by Dharavi tennis-ball players almost every Sunday outside the monsoon season. The teams are mostly defined by ethnicity, religion or Hindu caste: Fakhre's next opponents, Kunchi Kurve, were named after a Maharashtrian low-caste group (to which Kurve, coincidentally, also belonged). But Ham Sab was a deliberate mishmash: the current line-up boasted five Muslims, four Hindus and two Christians.

It was formed after a bout of communal rioting, in 1992, that left over 200 people dead in Dharavi and its Hindu and Muslim communities bitterly divided. Some of the original team members had lost property in the riots. "It was a way to take the violence out of people's minds," said one of the team's founders, Nigar Khan, as we watched the game against Kunchi Kurve. This was a lesson in how not only sport, but also slum life, can unite. That so many poor people, drawn from almost every region of India, can live crammed together so harmoniously, by and large, is astonishing.

Because of space constraints, batting is only possible from one end of Dharavi–Sion's flattened earth wicket. With the lightning bat speed of the accomplished tennis-ball cricketer, the batsmen aimed straight back over the bowler's head. By hitting the houses opposite above the eaves – about 50 yards away – they scored six. A hit to the first or second storeys fetched four; a boundary in most other directions two. Batting first, Kunchi Kurve reached 31 for four in their four overs. It was a modest score; the Ham Sab players trooped off in a state of nervous excitement.

The rewards for progressing further in the tournament were relatively substantial, with the top three sides standing to divvy up a pot of 12,000 rupees, donated by local patrons. For Fakhre, a beefy all-rounder whose team shirt was speckled with cooking grease, victory would also mean another cherished break from the biryani pot. "This is what I wait all week for," he said, grinning, and promising to hit a string of sixes if he got in.

"It is our great pleasure": boys find space amid the rubbish for a game of cricket.

Dharavi's Sunday cricketers are not all poor. One or two of Ham Sab's players were penniless recent immigrants from the countryside, but most were comfortably middle-class, in Indian terms, and one or two were rich. Babu Khan owned five slum factories and employed over 100 people. Yet when it came to their appreciation of cricket, they were, as their name suggested, all in the same camp. Like the *galli* cricketers, they preferred Twenty20, especially the IPL, to any other form of the game. Hardly any had played pukka cricket on Mumbai's *maidans*. Some could not afford the kit; most said they could not afford the time.

A visit earlier in the day to Shivaji Park, where Tendulkar learned to bat, had also hinted at this. I had expected to see its famous pitches crowded with cricketers. But they were hardly in use: the *maidan* was dominated by a rally for local Hindu nationalists. Storied Mumbai nurseries such as this – the *maidans* in and around Churchgate and Dadar that have produced so many stars – are usually still busy with matches. But they have not felt the explosion in interest witnessed in India's smaller towns, cricketing parvenus, where there is less economic opportunity and more space to play.

These are some features of the ongoing tumult in Indian cricket. What support it will leave for Test and – as the IPL extends its reach – international cricket is unclear. Perhaps the Twenty20 craze will burn out. But there is little sign of that, or reason to think it will otherwise be contained.

Before my visit to the slum ended, I sought to repeat an experiment. Two years previously I had toured Dharavi on the night of a big IPL game – Mumbai Indians against Kolkata Knight Riders – to see who was watching it.

Stepping through its filth and narrow alleys, trying to filter the television sounds that fill the slum by night, I reckoned one in three TV sets was tuned to the cricket. Now, with India playing a one-day international in Durban, I wanted to gauge Dharavi's interest in a more traditional contest.

As South Africa's openers Quinton de Kock and Hashim Amla tore into the Indian attack, I wandered through Dharavi with a local friend, Asghar, peering into the open doorways of hutments, listening for the exhilarating blare of televised cricket. But there was surprisingly little, and it was largely drowned out by the shrieks and beats of Bollywood films. This was only a snapshot, of course; and Dharavi is not India. Yet it is about as close an approximation as there is, and the contrast with my previous tour was dramatic: hardly any of the slum dwellers seemed to be watching the game.

Our walk ended, as it had before, at a tiny third-storey workshop, reachable by a tangle of ladders and ropes. A dozen skinny youths lived and worked here, embroidering saris on the wooden looms they also slept under. Two years ago, they had been avidly watching the IPL match on the small television that was their cell's only comfort. Now, they were watching a game show.

They had started watching the cricket, explained 19-year-old Mohammad Azharuddin (no relation). But India collapsed (they were 95 for six when we arrived), so they had switched off. Indian cricket fans have always been fickle. But for these poor north Indian boys, who had hardly known cricket before the IPL, international contests were a subordinate passion. "Of course IPL is best!" said Mohammad – laughing, because the answer was so obvious. "More runs, less time."

James Astill is the political editor of The Economist, *and author of* The Great Tamasha: Cricket, Corruption and the Turbulent Rise of Modern India.

PART TWO

The Wisden Review

CRICKET BOOKS, 2013

The good, the bad and the unsexy

Jonathan Liew

In November 2013, research by the accountancy firm Wilkins Kennedy found that 98 British publishers had gone out of business in the previous year. This was a rise of 42% on the year before that. There were any number of explanations: the predominance of other media, the hegemony of Amazon, the growth of digital piracy, perhaps even a little thing called the recession. With the industry in retreat, big publishing houses have generally preferred to throw their weight behind proven successes rather than take a punt on an unknown author. "Publishers are more impatient than ever," the novelist Lionel Shriver wrote in *The New Republic* last year, "and they were never patient."

The point is this: unless you are J. K. Rowling or Dan Brown, there has not, financially speaking, been a worse time to write a book since the introduction of the Copyright Act in 1842. And yet far from being the doom-knell this appears, it is underpinned by a deeper truth. To write a book these days, you have to really, really want to write it. Virtually anything that makes it to market has done so through an assault course of publisher scepticism, self-doubt, creative stasis, publisher irritation, time poverty, endless cups of coffee, more self-doubt, unpaid bills, publisher screaming, and vivid, translucent nightmares about misplaced semi-colons. Every book, however big or small, is its own modest triumph.

Which is not to say that every book is a masterpiece. And so we begin this year's round-up with **Ashes, Clashes and Bushy Taches: The talkSPORT Guide to Sport's Greatest Rivalry** by Gershon Portnoi. From the outset of this wide-ranging compendium of Ashes trivia, it is clear that Portnoi has a taste for what might be described as the game's broader brushstrokes. There is the customary section on Barmy Army chants ("We All Shagged Matilda" gives away the dominant theme in its title) and plenty of insightful features, such as "The 10 Greatest England Moustaches".

It's silly, unashamedly lowbrow and about as subtle as a large bucket. But by the same token, it's competently researched and genuinely entertaining in parts. And at its big stupid heart is a big stupid message: we're all cricket-lovers here. You may prefer *Beyond a Boundary* to the beer snake, but there's no reason we can't all share the Peter May Stand on a booze-sozzled Sunday afternoon. *Ashes, Clashes and Bushy Taches* may well be the least distinguished cricket book of the year, and yet here's the thing: it's still not bad. Let's bear that in mind as we go along.

The Ashes inspired a good deal less literature than one might expect, in a year when "the sport's oldest rivalry" ™ went from a rare and enchanting visitor to an unwanted lodger who refused to leave, wash up or tone down his language when ladies were present. A sign, perhaps, that well-worn tropes –

mock obituaries, Bodyline, Bradman and Botham – can be microwaved and reheated only for so long. One book that does manage to breathe a little life into a largely moribund genre is **Cricket's Greatest Rivalry: A History of the Ashes in Ten Matches** by Simon Hughes.

Bookended by English ignominy – it starts at The Oval in 1882 and ends at Adelaide in 2006-07 – Hughes's work weaves a straggly yarn through some of the fixture's greatest encounters. From his earliest days in the Channel 4 analyst's truck, Hughes has had a particular gift for rendering the abstract in arrestingly pithy terms. On post-war rationing, he notes that families were allowed "a piece of meat the size of an iPod once a week".

It was perhaps unfortunate that Hughes released his Ashes paean just as interest in the contest was beginning to wane. An inauspicious sense of timing also afflicts Matt Prior's **The Gloves Are Off: My Life In Cricket**, presumably conceived and written when Prior was one of the best wicketkeeper-batsmen in Test cricket. In much the same way that the *Playfair Cricket Annual* developed a reputation for placing a cruel hex on its cover star, Prior's triumphal tome now jars with the knowledge of the *annus horribilis* that followed. Reading it seems wrong, like leafing through photographs of a missing child.

Those searching for clues as to how Prior might have hauled himself out of his slump are likely to be disappointed. Though there are illuminating passages – his account of the disastrous Stanford Super Series and his observations on playing spin are worth reading – the overall impression is of a book put

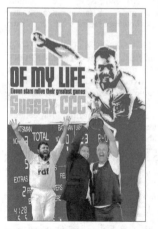

together with undue haste and not nearly enough of its subject's time. Much of it reads like a transcribed interview, padded out with press-conference quotes that were wildly uninteresting first time round and have not improved in the reprinting. Rushed out for last summer's home Ashes, this feels like a book that could have benefited from a little more love.

There is certainly no shortage of love in **Match of My Life**, Bruce Talbot's episodic history of Sussex CCC through interviews with some of their greatest players. Talbot, a long-serving correspondent for *The Argus* in Brighton, brings not just expertise and contacts to his work, but a great deal of affection. Unsurprisingly, given the county's recent success, five of the 11 tales are taken from the last decade. But perhaps the most poignant is a game against Yorkshire, which finished on September 1, 1939, under the most awful of shadows. "War was upon us," Jim Parks senior is quoted as saying. "We knew that this was to be our last taste of freedom for many years, so we enjoyed ourselves while we could." Few enjoyed themselves more than Hedley Verity, who took seven Sussex wickets for nine to win the game. The same day, Germany invaded Poland. Verity never played first-class cricket again.

Sussex proves fertile literary soil. Their former captain John Barclay offers up **Lost in the Long Grass**, a delightful collection of short essays on personalities as diverse as Viv Richards and Barclay's dog, Robert. Such is the richness and warmth of the anecdotes that you can almost hear rain clattering against steamy Arundel windows. Barclay is also responsible for perhaps the single best Ian Botham simile yet. "He has always reminded me of a rainbow trout," he writes. "If something tasty floats past their noses, they are likely to rush at it – impulsive and instinctive. This makes Both a very catchable fish, not too familiar with cunning and guile."

Once again, county cricket is reliably served, with the usual blend of the earnest and the eccentric. A special Austerity Britain mention to **Rose-Tinted Summer: The Dressing Room Diary** by Yorkshire opener Joe Sayers, which spreads its compelling narrative to less than a centimetre of the edge of the page. Mick Pope's **Headingley Ghosts: A Collection of Yorkshire Cricket Tragedies** wins the prize for the year's most depressing book, beginning with

the suicide of David Bairstow and actually managing to get more gloomy as it goes on. **A Year in the Life of Somerset County Cricket Club: Through the Eyes of its Chairman** has a strong claim to be the most unwieldy title in history, but is a strangely readable diary of the club's 2012 season written by Andy Nash. It is a must for the fanatical, die-hard Somerset fan. Having met a few, I can attest there is no other kind.

But back to Sussex, and **Then Came Massacre**, Justin Parkinson's superb biography of the 1920s all-rounder Maurice Tate. It is hard to think of a more unjustly neglected England great – Maurice Leyland, maybe. But Tate has somehow become one of those anomalies of history: perhaps best known for his father, Fred, whose one

England game in 1902 would stand as a monument to his misfortune. Despite claiming more Test wickets than Verity or Wilfred Rhodes, and more runs than W. G. Grace, Maurice Tate lies in a grave that has for years sat neglected and overgrown, his legacy largely forgotten.

Parkinson redresses the balance with gusto. Tate is finally given the credit he deserves for revolutionising the art of seam bowling, being the first to exploit the full potential of the stitching to make the ball deviate. In the

1924-25 Ashes he broke a record by taking 38 wickets. But as if to prove the truism that history is written by the winners, Tate went into sharp decline in the 1930s. A succession of ill-fated business ventures foisted financial difficulties on him for much of his life, and he ended up running a pub in East Sussex until his premature death at the age of 60.

In the final analysis, perhaps Tate was too unfashionable a cricketer to be truly timeless. The fiercely concussive direction that the international game took in the 1930s swept away the dobbers and jobbers – although he was on the Bodyline tour, he played no part in the series. His time had gone.

An interesting companion piece is Harry Pearson's **The Trundlers**. On the surface, it is an idiosyncratic tribute to medium-pacers, the game's thankless foot soldiers, or "the cholesterol of cricket", as Pearson has it. It would appear to be the ideal turf for the Yorkshire-born Pearson's unique brand of childhood tales and gentle whimsy (a term reviewers tend to use to describe any writer who is northern and funny). But really, it is an examination of the very concept of middleness itself. Being medium-pace is a lot like being middle class, Pearson observes, in that it is an unchosen fate that nevertheless carries

> "The Land of the Long White Dobber"

the faintest whiff of apology. It meshes well with middle age, too: a time of life when raising the pulse becomes a vice rather than a virtue.

Pearson argues that, for much of cricket's history, medium-pace has defined the national character, like pace in the Caribbean, or spin in India. Perhaps the greatest English bowler of all time, S. F. Barnes, was not a quick-and-nasty, but a medium-paced conjuror in the true Edwardian tradition (although there is also a case for classifying him as a spinner). But there are also fascinating passages on India and the seamer's paradise of New Zealand, which Pearson redubs "The Land of the Long White Dobber". Not so whimsical, then; but very northern, and very funny.

Just about registering on the humour scale are a number of light-hearted memoirs. In **An Endangered Species**, David Gower produces a second autobiography that is a good deal more carefree than his first, written while he was still playing. In the two decades since he retired, Gower has completed the transition from the elegant prince of the middle order to self-effacing cartoon toff of the Sky commentary box. The artifice of television has given rise to a largely artificial Lord Gower character, and it is Lord Gower who is given mostly free rein here. The gates to Gower's id remain chained shut throughout, but the jolly, champagne-fuelled romp offered in its place is pretty entertaining. You have to admire the spunk of a man who can write the words "So while I got stuck into the Krug…" with what appears to be only the tiniest soupçon of self-awareness.

Beefy's Cricket Tales is by Ian Botham in only the loosest sense. It is, in fact, a collection of anecdotes from people who are not Ian Botham, although the man himself does deign to dictate a couple of introductory sentences at the start of each. Yet the stories themselves, compiled by ghostwriter Dean Wilson of the *Daily Mirror*, are of a consistently high quality. A few are fairly well-known yarns, but some are genuinely uproarious, others genuinely surprising.

Who knew, for instance, that Sourav Ganguly had a gun pulled on him on the London underground during India's 1996 tour of England?

In the same category sits **Squeezing the Orange** by *Test Match Special's* Henry Blofeld, which is unexpectedly good. It is deftly written and very much worthy of your attention, if only to count the impressive number of different phrases Blowers possesses to describe women he fancies: "lovely to look at"; "stunning and elegant"; "extremely attractive"; "incredibly beautiful and never said anything"; "a highly toothsome lady"; "some beautiful young girls from Bollywood"; "a delightful, rather large, Jamaican lady"; "two delicious daughters"; "until I set eyes on her, I had not realised that God made them that good".

Andrew Ramsey's **The Wrong Line** is engaging for different reasons. Ramsey wrote for *The Australian* newspaper for a decade around the turn of the century, covering one of the greatest cricket teams in history. Yet this chronicle of his years on tour drips with world-weary cynicism, as he finds himself caught between the rock of idiot editors and the hard place of wary players who do not mistake proximity for friendship. Never is this predicament more neatly juxtaposed than in early 2002 when, after Australia had lost three consecutive one-day internationals, Ramsey's editor comes up with the idea of a front page calling for both Waugh brothers to be dropped. After Steve Waugh captains Australia to a win over South Africa the next day, a glum Ramsey attempts to maintain the charade.

"Are you disappointed that some commentators questioned your place in the team?" he asks.

"You should know, mate," replies Waugh. "You wrote it."

But by far the best book to come out of Australia last year emerged from Ramsey's counterpart at the *Sydney Morning Herald*. Malcolm Knox's **Bradman's War** is a quite marvellous effort, a mature reassessment of Bradman that manages to veer away from shrill score-settling, and renders a far more accurate history as a consequence.

There was a time, not so long ago, when to tamper with The Don's legacy was tantamount to tampering with Australia's private parts. It just wasn't done – not in polite society, at least. Yet the decade since his death has seen a partial reassessment. In 2002 the sociologist Brett Hutchins created a mini-stir with his agenda-driven polemic *Don Bradman: Challenging the Myth*, which was exactly as impartial as its title suggested. Hutchins's idea of balance was to supplant hagiography with hatchet job. Knox adopts a more nuanced, less

attention-seeking, approach. "When it comes to Bradman," he writes, "we live in revisionist times, when we who were not there have put aside the negative and celebrated his contribution."

The most impressive aspect of *Bradman's War* is its depiction of those airy, fragile post-war years when cricket seemed so simultaneously tangential and essential. Crucial in evoking the mood of the age are Knox's original interviews with the three surviving members of the 1948 Invincibles tour: Neil Harvey, Arthur Morris and Sam Loxton (who died in 2011). Tellingly, none of them described the trip as their favourite. The principal reason for this was the attritional, single-minded determination of Bradman, for whom the idea of an unbeaten tour came to verge on obsession; the definitive swansong that would end his career in a blaze of glory and provide the ultimate rejoinder to his critics. Bradman never forgot his critics.

And yet the sport he re-entered was rather different from the one that had been suspended in 1939. Bradman spent most of the Second World War broking shares in Adelaide, a muscular injury rendering him unfit for active service. The war left him largely unchanged. But for those who had seen battle – men such as Keith Miller and Bill Edrich – those wretched years of fighting and dying could not simply be swept aside so normal service could resume. The Victory Tests of 1945, between English and Australian servicemen, articulated a new, friendlier, more idealistic vision of sport, mirroring the wider spirit of hope felt in the immediate post-war years. "Men who had seen the worst of mankind could play the game in a way that celebrated the best," Knox writes. "Cricket could be a direct antidote and response to warfare."

But Bradman had not yet fought his war. His war was a resentment that had been festering ever since England spinner Jack White had jokingly referred to him as his "bunny" in 1928-29, and nurtured by the naked hostility of Bodyline. As the Australians traipsed unvanquished up and down the country, Bradman's resolve never wavered. Towards the end of the tour, at the Scarborough Festival, he intervened to prevent the home side from fielding a Test-strength line-up. Job done, he went on to select his best XI, just to make doubly sure there was no chance of defeat.

So Bradman got his record. But how to remember him in posterity depends very much on what you want from your sportsmen. As a batsman, and as a competitor, he was unrivalled. But the mistake we so readily make is to conflate a man's talent with his character. Bradman's influence did not just sway the

destiny of the tour; it steered international cricket away from the more recreational, holistic path it might have taken. As Knox skilfully demonstrates, Bradman changed cricket; just not in the way you might think.

An obsession of a different kind consumes Grahame Lloyd, the author and protagonist of **Howzat? The Six Sixes Ball Mystery**. Having already written one book about the over in which Garfield Sobers hit six sixes off Malcolm Nash at Swansea in 1968, he now turns his attention to the ball. In 2006 it resurfaced at auction, having apparently sat behind the bar at Trent Bridge for some years. It sold for £26,400 – a world record for a cricket ball.

> The fake ball had become Lloyd's Maltese Falcon

One problem, though: it wasn't the right ball. What sold at auction was a Duke; only Surridges were used at Swansea. The original, it transpired, was probably lost during the redevelopment of Trent Bridge, or innocently tossed away at some stage. All of which raises some perfectly valid questions. Who had put the Duke up for sale? Why had Sobers signed a certificate guaranteeing its authenticity? And who on earth had spent so much on a forgery?

What follows is a terrifically dotty whodunnit, driven by one man's relentless, borderline-psychotic quest for answers. The fake Sobers ball becomes Lloyd's Maltese Falcon, the humble object that eventually starts to define his existence. Some painstaking detective work leads him down a winding, often duplicitous, trail of rumours and half-truths. The London agent who bought the ball claims to have no idea where it is now. The Indian businessman who tried to sell it on refuses to say how he got it. Most crushingly of all, Channel 4's *Dispatches* programme appears to have virtually no interest in his Sobers-inspired documentary pitch.

Lloyd himself proves a formidable adversary, stoked by the fires of justice and undeterred by the constant trickle of rejection letters from television executives. The story sags a little in the middle third, weighed down by its own excruciating level of detail, but picks up appreciably in time for a dramatic denouement. In it, our hero tracks down and confronts Sir Garfield himself, although to general disappointment fails to throw him over a third-floor balcony to a rocky death, as Sam Spade might have done. Instead, what ensues is a long, spiky telephone conversation that ends up taking most of the weekend to transcribe. Still, the thought was probably there.

Three more books are preoccupied with similarly ambitious vocations. **Masterly Batting: 100 Great Test Centuries** by Patrick Ferriday and Dave Wilson is the most comprehensive attempt yet to rank the finest Test tons. Using a variety of criteria – some objective ("percentage of total"), some partly subjective ("series impact") and some utterly intangible ("intangibles") – numbers have been crunched and a list produced, although such is the nature of the beast that it is ultimately about as definitive as a question mark scrawled on a half-open door. You find yourself shaking your head and nodding firmly on alternate pages.

Each century is accompanied by an essay, most contributed by guest writers, and it is in these that the real value of *Masterly Batting* is to be found. Rob

Smyth's account of a half-fit Graeme Smith's 154 not out against England in 2008 is one of the best pieces of cricket writing of the year, in any medium. Telford Vice runs him close with an ingenious comparison of Jacques Kallis and Ayn Rand.

In **Saving The Test**, Mike Jakeman sets himself the no less onerous task of rescuing the five-day game. Of course, this is a discussion we have all indulged in from time to time, with varying levels of coherence ("Day/night Tests!" "Ban Twenty20!" "Nuke India!") but, as a journalist at *The Economist*, Jakeman brings an analytical nous to the question. His comparison with baseball, illustrating cricket's failure to exploit the digital broadcasting market, is one of several convincing arguments. While the solutions appear over-reliant on the ICC maintaining their robustness, which is a little like hoping ice cream won't melt, bonus points are awarded for writing one of the very few books published anywhere in the world in 2013 without a subtitle.

But perhaps the most outlandish quest of all was undertaken by Oli Broom, a chartered surveyor from London. In 2009, he decided to cycle from Lord's to Brisbane's Gabba in time for the 2010-11 Ashes: a journey that took him through 23 countries over 13 months. He fought depression in India, dengue fever in Thailand, and infernal flies in the Australian outback. Although he tried to set up games of cricket wherever he went, **Cycling to the Ashes: A Cricketing Odyssey from London to Brisbane** is not really a cricket book at all. It is a wacky travel book about a middle-class guy who goes on the world's most epic gap year in an attempt to find himself – occasionally diverting, but a good deal less than the sum of its parts.

Instead, it is **The Great Tamasha** by James Astill that provides the most compelling portrait of cricket beyond our shores, even though it restricts its scope to one country. But what a country! Astill's book is part history, part portrait and part analysis. *Tamasha* is a Hindi word that roughly translates as entertainment, and this is a comprehensive account of how Indian cricket went from being an object of colonial patronage to the ultimate in sporting fun.

Herein lies the first challenge. Bluntly put, Indian cricket is extremely big and extremely complicated, and thus any treatment of it risks descending into anarchy at the planning stage. Astill just about avoids this, although at times it is not quite clear what he is striving to achieve – a comprehensive history, a forensic autopsy, a colourful travelogue, or a mixture of all three? Using cricket as an emblem for India's development as a nation has been a well-

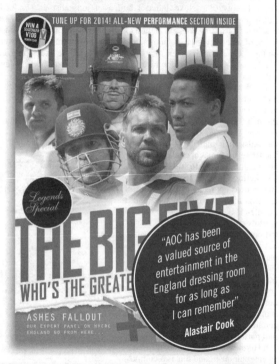

trodden conceit over recent years – start with a base of C. K. Nayudu, add a pinch of Vijay Merchant, throw in some Tiger Pataudi, stir in some Kapil Dev and Sachin Tendulkar, and top the whole thing off with a layer of steaming IPL. But Astill strives for more than this, and so turns a good book into a great one.

The middle chapters, in which Astill steadies himself before plunging into the grimy gutter politics of India's cricket administration, are by far the most engaging. The labyrinth of local and national government, vested interests, entrenched privilege, the caste system and the heady brew of new money have created a world so complex and competitive as to almost qualify as a sport in its own right. Wry and inquisitive, Astill teases out a number of startling frank admissions. Niranjan Shah, the patriarch of cricket in Saurashtra, elucidates at a stroke what outside observers fear most about India's vision for the game: "We should not depend on whether England or South Africa come to India to get money," he says. "Cricket has to go to the level of baseball in America."

> A snapshot of cricket in India – hot, breathless and chaotic

Pataudi told him: "There's great passion for cricket in this country, but little knowledge." Astill gets this across too, breaking up long tracts on history, finance or politics with the sights and sounds of his own travels. He talks to literally hundreds of Indians, from Lalit Modi to Vinod Kambli to a cricket-mad untouchable in a tiny northern village. By filling his account with voices, Astill occasionally sacrifices clarity, but gains far more in atmosphere as a result. What emerges is a snapshot of cricket in India – hot, breathless, chaotic and with only the sketchiest idea of how to harness the vast and sinister winds of change ripping through it – that serves as a perfect analogue for the country itself.

The big event in Indian cricket in 2013 was Tendulkar's retirement after his 200th Test. It is paradoxical that one of the greatest players of all time is yet to inspire a truly great book. In the meantime, we will have to make do with Vimal Kumar's **Sachin: Cricketer of the Century**, which turns the idolatry dial to 11. It is, as one might expect, far too unquestioning, even by the canonically uncontroversial standards of Tendulkar's career. Equally pointless is Unmukt Chand's **The Sky is the Limit**, the autobiography of India's winning captain at the 2012 Under-19 World Cup. It looks like the sort of thing his parents would pay to have printed on his 21st birthday, and reads like a low-budget high-school yearbook, stuffed with tributes from friends and team-mates and anodyne stories about eating nachos. The fact that a teenage cricketer can put out an autobiography before having played a single senior game for his country is perhaps the most arresting thing about this book. It is certainly a good deal more interesting than the content.

But there remains a yawning gap in this year's literature. Of all the books under scrutiny – some fine, some very fine – hardly any makes any sort of privileged attempt to get to grips with the modern game as it is played at the highest level. Never has there been a greater gulf between cricket as we see it and cricket as its protagonists experience it. For all that Twitter and new media have transformed the game, its greatest stars are more remote than they have ever been. Increasingly, the only way to get a feel for modern international cricket – the long nights in lonely hotel rooms, the long days in stuffy dressing-rooms – is through ghostwritten autobiographies, and even these usually have the interest snuffed out of them by the media department. The contemporary dressing-room memoir that is uncompromised by position, yet still current enough to feel relevant, is the rarest of treasures these days. And it is for that reason, and many others, that **Driving Ambition** by Andrew Strauss is *Wisden's* Book of the Year.

The immediate reaction to Strauss's book was as predictable as it was understandable. Cricket journalists scoured it for scurrilous gossip, bitchy score-settling, some dirt on Kevin Pietersen: anything that might make a story for tomorrow's paper. Finding little, and perhaps a touch affronted that he had deigned to touch-type every word himself rather than deploy their reasonably priced ghostwriting skills, they initially wrote off *Driving Ambition* as so much perfumed blandness, the inevitable output of a man predisposed to building bridges, not spilling beans.

A closer analysis exposes the myopia of such snap judgments. Strauss may offer little in the way of tittle-tattle but, over 300 pages, he assembles an X-ray image of the modern game that is mature, insightful and at times breathtakingly intelligent.

Of Strauss's life away from the international treadmill, admittedly, we are given only the most fleeting glimpse. Offspring arrive entirely without warning. By page 16, his mother, father, grandparents and three sisters have already

made their final appearances. So perhaps it is not an autobiography in the strictest sense. In the age of the weepy confessional, Strauss opts for something far rarer: a truly great cricket book. The unique pressures of 21st-century Test leadership are described with a frankness and expertise that no current or recent player has yet managed.

Strauss provides the most convincing refutation to date of the false dichotomy that tends to define modern captains, between the proactive (good) and conservative (bad). Strategy, he argues, is of far greater relevance than tactics – the months of preparation and analysis that help to define a team's innate character. A word that crops up time and again, with just the hint of a Middle England sneer, is "sexy". Strauss uses it to define eye-catching but flawed technique, interesting but ineffective cricket, showy but insubstantial leadership. "Sexy" becomes the quality that Strauss sets himself against.

Not that Strauss's arch-pragmatism should be mistaken for entrenched traditionalism. He enthusiastically supports the use of technology, and encourages the ECB to create a window for the IPL. There is no shortage of anecdotes or humour either, although these are employed in the service of the narrative rather than as an end in themselves. Though the tone is generally dry and reserved, the result is that, when the raw, emotional moments arrive, they hit you like a punch in the stomach.

One such begins the book, on a farm in Orange Free State during the Boer War, when Strauss's Afrikaner great-grandmother is faced with a choice between internment in a British concentration camp, or escaping on foot and trekking for 30 miles across the freezing, pitch-black veldt. This is not, by any stretch of the imagination, your typical opening to a cricket autobiography. Another comes in 2007-08, when Strauss struggles with the humiliation of being dropped. A recurring nightmare stalks his sleep, in which he is unable to get his pads on. "Just when all hope is lost, I wake up," he writes. Then he makes 177 against New Zealand and saves his Test career.

In the final, bittersweet tableau, captain Strauss stands in the England dressing-room for the final time. As he wallows in the dismay of defeat by South Africa, all the strains and tensions of the previous few years – the press, the Australians, the boot camps, the selection dilemmas, Pakistani spinners, Pietersen's text treachery – flood through him at once. He chokes back the tears, just as he had seen Michael Vaughan do four years earlier. Selfless to the end, he does not tell his team-mates that this is his last time.

Does it matter that Strauss wrote the book himself? Of course it does. It lends his text an authenticity and ardour that is sadly lacking from so many ghostwritten accounts. It provides the most accurate portrayal of Strauss, the truest reflection of his hopes and fears. Here is a man with plenty of money, little time and yet a fierce desire that these words should be his own. To write a book these days, you have to really, really want to write it. Fortunately for us, Strauss's pure love of his art drips off every page.

Jonathan Liew is a sportswriter for the Daily Telegraph.

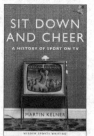

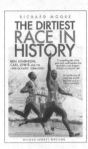

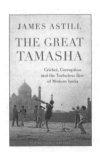

WISDEN BOOK OF THE YEAR

Since 2003, *Wisden's* reviewer has selected a Book of the Year. The winners have been:

2003 *Bodyline Autopsy* by David Frith
2004 *No Coward Soul* by Stephen Chalke and Derek Hodgson
2005 *On and Off the Field* by Ed Smith
2006 *Ashes 2005* by Gideon Haigh
2007 *Brim Full of Passion* by Wasim Khan
2008 *Tom Cartwright: The Flame Still Burns* by Stephen Chalke
2009 *Sweet Summers: The Classic Cricket Writing of JM Kilburn* edited by Duncan Hamilton
2010 *Harold Larwood: The authorized biography of the world's fastest bowler* by Duncan Hamilton
2011 *The Cricketer's Progress: Meadowland to Mumbai* by Eric Midwinter
2012 *Fred Trueman: The Authorised Biography* by Chris Waters
2013 *Bookie Gambler Fixer Spy: A Journey to the Heart of Cricket's Underworld* by Ed Hawkins
2014 ***Driving Ambition* by Andrew Strauss**

THE CRICKET SOCIETY AND MCC BOOK OF THE YEAR AWARD

The Cricket Society Literary Award has been presented since 1970 to the author of the cricket book judged best of the year. The 2013 award, made by the Cricket Society in association with MCC, was won in April by Gideon Haigh for **On Warne** (Simon & Schuster); he received £3,000. A month later, *On Warne* was also named Cricket Book of the Year in the British Sports Book Awards.

BOOKS RECEIVED IN 2013

GENERAL

Allen, Dave and Saunders, Stephen **150 Not Out** Hampshire County Cricket 1863–2013   Preface by Mark Nicholas   Foreword by Jimmy Adams (£20 – more information from Hampshire CCC)

Astill, James **The Great Tamasha** Cricket, Corruption and the Turbulent Rise of Modern India (Wisden Sports Writing, £18.99)

Authors Cricket Club **The Authors XI** A Season of English Cricket from Hackney to Hambledon (Bloomsbury, £16.99)

Barclay, John **Lost in the Long Grass** Foreword by John Woodcock (Fairfield Books, £15)

Botham, Ian, with Wilson, Dean **Beefy's Cricket Tales** My Favourite Stories from On and Off the Field (Simon & Schuster, £18.99)

Carty, Mac **The Vagaries of Swing** Footprints on the Margate Sands of Time (lulu.com, paperback, £6.50)

Fasola, Giacomo, Lombardo, Ilario and Moscatelli, Francesco **Italian Cricket Club** Il gioco dei nuovi italiani (Add Editore, paperback, €14.00)

Ferriday, Patrick and Wilson, Dave, ed **Masterly Batting** 100 Great Test Centuries (Von Krumm Publishing, £15)

Frith, David **Guildford's Cricket Story** Celebrating 75 Years of the Woodbridge Road County Cricket Festival – and much besides (privately published, paperback, £5; also available as a signed, limited-edition hardback, £75 + £5 p&p – more details from secretary@guildfordcc.com)

Furmedge, Bill **What Wisden Means to Me** (privately published; more information from www.wisdenworld.com, paperback, £10.50)

Gibson, Anthony and Chalke, Stephen **Gentlemen, Gypsies and Jesters** The Wonderful World of Wandering Cricket (Fairfield Books, £25 – all proceeds to Chance to Shine)

Gray, Christopher J. **Parsons at Play** The cricketing lives of 65 clergymen (Winsor editions, paperback, £25 inc. p&p to UK; more details from gray.books@bigpond.com)

Hignell, Andrew **The History of Blaina Cricket Club** Little Club – Big Story (St David's Press, paperback, £16.99)

Hughes, Simon **Cricket's Greatest Rivalry** A History of the Ashes in 10 Matches (Cassell Illustrated, £18.99)

Jakeman, Mike **Saving The Test** Foreword by Jon Hotten (Ockley Books, paperback, £9.99)

Knox, Malcolm **Bradman's War** How the 1948 Invincibles Turned the Cricket Pitch into a Battlefield (The Robson Press, £20)

Laughton, Tony **A Guide to Cricket: A Weekly Record of the Game** (Christopher Saunders, paperback, £25 – also available as limited edition hardback, £100)

Lloyd, Grahame **Howzat!** The Six Sixes Ball Mystery   Foreword by Matthew Engel (Celluloid, £14.99)

Nash, Andy **A Year in the Life of Somerset County Cricket Club** Through the Eyes of its Chairman   Foreword by Lord Archer (The History Press, £18.99)

Pearson, Harry **The Trundlers** Underrate them at your peril… The military medium-paced story of cricket's most invaluable breed (Little, Brown, paperback, £13.99)

Pilger, Sam, and Wightman, Rob **The Ashes Match of My Life** Fourteen Ashes Legends Relive Their Greatest Tests (Pitch Publishing, £16.99)

Pope, Mick **Headingley Ghosts** A Collection of Yorkshire Cricket Tragedies (Scratching Shed Publishing, paperback, £14.99)

Portnoi, Gershon **Ashes, Clashes and Bushy Taches** The talkSPORT Guide to Sport's Greatest Rivalry (Simon & Schuster, £9.99)

Potter, David **The Western Union 1893–1997** (privately published; more information from tporteous@executive-benefit.com, paperback, £7.99)

Ramsey, Andrew **The Wrong Line** (ABC Books, paperback, $A27.99)

Sayers, Joe **Rose-Tinted Summer** The Dressing Room Diary In the 150th Anniversary Year of Yorkshire County Cricket Club   Prefaces by Michael Vaughan and Darren Lehmann (Great Northern Books, £17.99)

Scovell, Brian **Our Beloved Cricket** From Village Greens to Lord's (Fonthill, £18.99)

Smith, Martin, ed. **The Promise of Endless Summer** Cricket Lives from The Daily Telegraph (Aurum, £14.99)

Talbot, Bruce **Match of My Life** Sussex CCC Eleven stars relive their greatest games (Pitch Publishing, £16.99)

Walmsley, Keith **Double Headers** (ACS, paperback, £14)

Whiting, Dan and Kenna, Liam **Cricket Banter** Chat, Sledging & Laughs from the Middle Stump   Foreword by Paul Nixon (The History Press, £9.99)

Wilde, Simon **Wisden Cricketers of the Year** A Celebration of Cricket's Greatest Players   Foreword by John Wisden (John Wisden, £40)

Winder, Robert **The Little Wonder** The Remarkable History of Wisden (Bloomsbury, £25)

Wood, Charles **Another Somerset Century** How Somerset County Cricket Club possibly became one of the top four domestic teams in the world and the agonies involved on the journey (Halsgrove, £12.99)

BIOGRAPHY

Bradbury, Anthony **Frank Mitchell** Imperial Cricketer (ACS, paperback, £14)

Fuller, James **Brian Lara** An unauthorised biography (Signal Books, paperback, £9.99)

Garrick, Frank **Willie Watson** A biography of England's most successful double international (SportsBooks, £17.99)

Gibbs, Rowan **W. W. Robinson on the Cricket Field** (Smith's Bookshop, paperback, £12 – more details from esaw@paradise.net.nz

Halford, Brian **The Real Jeeves** The cricketer who gave his life for his country and his name to a legend (Pitch Publishing, £16.99)

Kumar, Vimal **Sachin** Cricketer of the Century (Penguin India, paperback, Rs299)

Miller, Douglas **M. J. K. Smith** No Ordinary Man (ACS, paperback, £12)

Overson, Chris **Jack Robertson and Syd Brown** More Than Just The Warm-Up Act (ACS, paperback, £14)

Parkinson, Justin **Then Came Massacre** The story of Maurice Tate, cricket's smiling destroyer (Pitch Publishing, £17.99)

Rendell, Brian **Walter Robins** Achievements, Affections and Affronts (ACS, paperback, £14)

Smith, Rick **Eric Rowan** The Toughest Springbok (ACS, paperback, £13)

Sweetman, Simon **H. V. Hesketh-Prichard** Amazing Stories (ACS, paperback, £12)

AUTOBIOGRAPHY

Blofeld, Henry **Squeezing the Orange** Life's Great Adventure – and the Cricket too! (Blue Door, £20)

Broom, Oli **Cycling to the Ashes** A Cricketing Odyssey from London to Brisbane (Yellow Jersey, £16.99)

Chand, Unmukt **The Sky is the Limit** My Journey to the World Cup   Foreword by Sir Vivian Richards (Penguin India, paperback, Rs250)

Gower, David, with Wilde, Simon **An Endangered Species** The Autobiography (Simon & Schuster, £18.99)

Prior, Matt **The Gloves Are Off** My Life In Cricket (Simon & Schuster, £20)

Strauss, Andrew **Driving Ambition** My Autobiography (Hodder & Stoughton, £20)

ANTHOLOGY

Agnew, Jonathan, ed. **Cricket** A Modern Anthology (Blue Door, £25)

Stern, John and Williams, Marcus, ed **The Essential Wisden** An Anthology of 150 Years of Wisden Cricketers' Almanack (John Wisden, £50)

ILLUSTRATED

Circosta, Paul **Pinning Down Cricket Badges** A collector's guide to Australian cricket badges, buttons and pins 1897–2011 (Bookkeeper Publishing, paperback, $A49.95)

Powley, Adam **When Cricket Was Cricket: The Ashes** A Nostalgic Look at a Century of the Greatest Rivalry   Photographs from the archives of the *Daily Mirror* (Haynes, £25)

White, John **Those Were the Days** A Yorkshire Boy's Cricket Scrapbook (Christopher Saunders, paperback, £20)

FICTION

Larner, Stuart **Guile and Spin** (FeedARead.com, paperback, £7.99)

Lewis-Foster, H. **Burning Ashes** (Dreamspinner Press, paperback, £19.99)

STATISTICAL

Bailey, Philip comp. **First-Class Cricket Matches 1946** and **1947** (ACS Sales, Blue Bell House, 2–4 Main Street, Scredington, Sleaford, Lincolnshire NG34 0AE, email: sales@acscricket.com, £26 each)

Lawton Smith, Julian ed. **The Minor Counties Championship 1907** (ACS, £16)

Percival, Tony **Devon Cricketers** (ACS, £12)

HANDBOOKS AND ANNUALS

Bailey, Philip ed. **ACS International Cricket Year Book 2013** (ACS, paperback, £30)

Bryant, John ed. **ACS Overseas First-Class Annual 2013** (ACS, paperback, £65)
  Full scorecards for first-class matches outside England in 2012-13.

Bryden, Colin ed. **SA Cricket Annual 2013** (CSA, www.sacricketshop.co.za, R200 plus p&p)

Clayton, Howard ed. **First-Class Counties Second Eleven Annual 2013** (ACS, £11)

Colliver, Lawrie ed. **Australian Cricket Digest** Statistics by Ric Finlay (paperback, $A25 + p&p; more information from lawrie.colliver@gmail.com)

Harman, Jo ed. **The Cricketers' Who's Who 2013** Foreword by Alastair Cook (PCA/All Out Cricket, £19.99)

Lynch, Steven ed. **The Wisden Guide to International Cricket 2014** (Bloomsbury, paperback, £9.99)

Marshall, Ian ed. **Playfair Cricket Annual 2013** (Headline, paperback, £7.99)

Payne, Francis and Smith, Ian ed. **2013 New Zealand Cricket Almanack** (Hodder Moa, $NZ55)

REPRINTS AND UPDATES

Baxter, Peter **Can Anyone Hear Me?** Testing Times with Test Match Special on Tour (Corinthian, paperback, £8.99)

Rodwell, Tom **Third Man in Havana** Finding the heart of cricket in the world's most unlikely places   Foreword by Courtney Walsh (Corinthian, paperback, £8.99)

Williams, Charles **Gentlemen & Players** The Death of Amateurism in Cricket (Phoenix, paperback, £9.99)

PERIODICALS

All Out Cricket ed. Phil Walker (PCA Management/TriNorth, £4.25; £34.15 for 12 issues. Subscriptions: alloutcricket.subscribeonline.co.uk)

The Cricketer (monthly) ed. Andrew Miller (The Cricketer Publishing, £3.95; £39.99 for 12 issues. Subscriptions: www.thecricketer.com or ring 0844 815 0864)

The Cricket Paper (weekly during season) ed. David Emery (Greenways Publishing, £1.50; £20 for ten issues. From www.thecricketpaper.com)

The Cricket Statistician (quarterly) ed. Simon Sweetman (ACS, £3 to non-members)

The Journal of the Cricket Society (twice yearly) (from D. Seymour, 13 Ewhurst Road, Crofton Park, London, SE4 1AG, £5 to non-members)

CRICKET IN THE MEDIA, 2013

Pomnishambolic

GILES SMITH

What with two Ashes series, the retirement of the greatest name in the game, and a pair of entirely discrete public urination controversies, cricket did not exactly struggle for media attention in 2013. The fun lay in deciding which bits of this noisy abundance were the due and necessary soundtrack, and which just the inadvertent racket.

The rivalry between England and Australia has always played well as pantomime, and this time the production was scheduled to be in theatres for the best part of eight months. Moreover the basic storyline would allow the audience to travel quickly between diametrically opposed states of wheezing, hands-on-knees hysteria – from the glory of England's summer ("oh yes they are") through to the winter's Pomnishambles ("oh no they aren't"), when *The Sun's* farewell two-page strapline spoke for many in the stalls: "Thank goodness the agony's over at last."

Additionally, the duty of newspapers nowadays is to heat up events before they happen, as much as to report them once they have, and the preview, in cricket as in all sports, is a growth area. And so the year gave rise to two separate spates of furious preamble ("oh yes they will", "oh no they won't"), bordering in places on pre-fight trash talk and, with hindsight, mercilessly shredding the reputations of many of the game's biggest-name astrologers. (Banner on the BBC News website in October: "England Can Beat Australia 5–0 – Ian Botham".)

England were still warming up in Western Australia when the *Daily Mirror* ran the strangely retrospective headline, "Michael Vaughan Slams Shane Warne". Neither of these greats, of course, would play any part on the pitch, but Warne had accused Alastair Cook's captaincy of lacking imagination, and Vaughan had leapt to the defence. In fairness, you can't have a panto without some squabbling dames.

The rivalry wasn't just reported in the media: it was embedded in it. The Australian papers set a close field for the leaking of England's on-tour dietary requirements – all 82 pages of them: goji-berry breakfast bars, piri-piri breaded tofu, mung-bean curry, lamb-and-pea kofta kebab. "The delicate palate of the touring team goes beyond the traditional fish 'n' chips," noted the *Sydney Morning Herald* tartly, as it were. The English media fought back gamely with a fast-paced assault on the vegan Peter Siddle's alleged banana habit. The *Daily Mail*: "Siddle's going bananas for the Ashes – but isn't eating 15–20 portions of the fruit A DAY a bit too far?"

The phoney war even ran, in August, to a dark tale of subterfuge in the shape of the theory, originated by Australia's Channel Nine, that English batsmen might have been wrapping their bats in "silicone-based tape" to defeat

Hot Spot. As Kevin Pietersen rather irritatedly pointed out, in the case of lbw appeals the batsman is helped, rather than hindered, by the detection of contact, so this would be a uniquely muddle-headed way to seek an underhand advantage. (This, we should be clear, was at a point in the narrative when English batsmen had yet to appear uniquely muddle-headed.) In a double Ashes year, however, simple logic was never going to be enough to stop a story generating steam.

The media temperature was already scaldingly high when Stuart Broad did what Derek Pringle in the *Daily Telegraph* called "that most Australian of things": he edged one so thickly it was obvious even to those watching from the back of the stand, then brazenly stood his ground. The moral debate which ensued threw into relief a division now typical in the press box, between ex-pros, who tend to be sanguine about the foibles of players under pressure, and the non-playing Corinthians, who have less invested in pragmatism and a simple shrug of the shoulder – and also know a story when they see one.

"Most international cricketers don't walk," the ex-pro Pringle coolly added. For Vaughan, too, writing in the same newspaper, Broad was "within his rights". But then there was the *Mail's* Martin Samuel, always ready to bang one in short on behalf of the Corinthian cause: "It is not as if we are at war here," Samuel wrote, with typically caustic lucidity. "These are ball games. If you have edged it to first slip in a game of cricket, just go. It really isn't that important. Indeed, it is remarkable, quite preposterous, that there should even be a debate."

The upshot for Broad was confirmed baddie status on arrival in Australia. Brisbane's *Courier-Mail* took out its own super-injunction, forbidding itself

from naming him directly, and blanking his face in subsequent editions. Thus crushed and neutralised, Broad took five wickets on the first day of the series, and made sure he was carrying a copy of the paper that evening at the press conference. These were heartening scenes for anyone inclined to wonder whether newspapers still have the power to influence events in a digital age. Clearly they do. It might just not be the influence that was intended.

There is, of course, nothing like an Ashes in Australia for making papers look a little steam-powered and cranky, with their quaint late-night deadlines and heritage printing processes, by comparison with the fast-twitch online world. Throughout the year's second Ashes, the British back pages were condemned by time zone to offer the day-before-yesterday's news today. On the plus side, the fact that England were poor on a virtually daily basis meant the papers were largely spared the traditional embarrassment of hostage-to-fortune headlines.

Let's also add that the drawback of reading day-old match reports is lessened if the reporter is someone like Michael Atherton of *The Times*, the Corinthian's ex-pro and the ex-pro's Corinthian. Here he is, digesting the performance of Mitchell Johnson on day three of the Adelaide Test: "The fast men: Harold Larwood, Frank Tyson, Allan Donald, Curtly Ambrose, Malcolm Marshall, Michael Holding, Thomson 'n' Lillee and the rest, and Johnson, a bowler derided as much as celebrated, a bowler scorned by the opposition supporters and by his own selectors only three years ago in this corresponding fixture when he was omitted, believe it or not, in favour of Doug Bollinger."

Ultimately, though, the appeal of two conjoined series appeared to wane even for the writers – and *even* for the Australian ones. For Gideon Haigh of *The Australian*, the Ashes came to be like watching "an over-long reality television series with a cast of characters almost cloyingly familiar. This was always a risk when Cricket Australia and the ECB cooked up this back-to-back, home-and-away, urn-o-max wheeze."

The reality show was brought to us by Sky Sports, whose idea of an urn-o-max wheeze was to devote an entire channel to the summer series, rebranding Sky Sports 2 as Sky Sports Ashes, and filling the gaps when there wasn't any Ashes cricket with recordings of Ashes cricket, thereby creating a kind of perma-Ashes, which not even CA and the ECB have yet had the courage to put forward as a business model.

Sky also gave a debut to The Ashes Zone – a camera-infested, green-walled cricket net to which pundits could retreat as necessary, pick up bat or ball, and deliver in-depth tutorials and practical demonstrations surrounding the finer points of the day's play. This development appeared to be a direct response to the imminent arrival of the voraciously rights-hungry and ominously rich BT Sport, who were due to take up residence in cavernous premises in London's Olympic Park and were promising punditry as a form of battle re-enactment amid life-size scenery. (BT Sport have bought no cricket rights yet, but give them time.)

> A back-to-back, home-and-away, urn-o-max wheeze

Nothing seen in Sky's Ashes Zone would match for stirring, memorable insight the images generated by a simple, static camera in the Long Room at Lord's, capturing the moments when England's opening batsmen made their way through the cheering throng on the Test's first morning. These, surely, were cricket's television images of the year. At the same time, credit is also due to Andrew Strauss – a newcomer to a Sky broadcasting team formed almost exclusively of ex-England captains – who, during a lunchtime seminar on "coping with the bouncer", lodged a racket-served tennis ball in the grille of a stunned Nasser Hussain's helmet.

Strauss has entered punditry at a time of hectic revolution, when analysing cricket is at some remove from simply sitting open-legged at a coffee table and jawing away with Bob Willis. Replays used to appear on our screens magically, by a process invisible to us, but now, in a surprising development of the digital age, gaining access to them is manual labour, with pundits swiping and

Sky Sports

England expects: Alastair Cook and Joe Root prepare to do battle at Lord's.

prodding at increasingly vast and sophisticated touch screens, before doing their stint in the nets in shirtsleeves. The idea of television as a soft post-career option is withering before our eyes. In future, ex-captains hoping to make a living this way will need to be as fit as they were in their playing days – and, in some cases, fitter.

None of this is in any way likely to diminish television's role as cricket's judge and jury. An area yet to be fully explored is how much the exacting scrutiny of TV's skinless eye contributed to the stress which, in November, sent Jonathan Trott home from Australia – with the united sympathy, one should add, of a press more alert to the sensitivities surrounding mental disorder, and less inclined these days to shout "Get on with it!".

During a rare Ashes hiatus, the retirement of Sachin Tendulkar induced a paroxysm of despair in the Indian media. The *Hindustan Times* addressed him personally in their front-page banner headline: "There Will Never Be Another You". Yet how much of the hysteria was reported hysteria, and how much was it newspapers just doing what they do? Raising an eyebrow for *The Guardian*, Ian Jack wrote: "In Mumbai last week it was possible to meet people who never mentioned Tendulkar, who paid more attention to the celebrations marking the end of Muharram, for example… or the price of onions (up 278% in a year), and who were repelled by the Tendulkar affair as a *tamasha*, a great fuss, that had been ordained by the cricket authorities and the media and was now boring them stiff. But none of their distaste made it into any news coverage that I read. Tendulkar had become a monolithic news event, like the grieving for Diana, Princess of Wales, into which any form of sceptical intrusion was forbidden."

In the year's mighty hullaballoo, it was harder than usual for humble county cricket to attract its share of notice, short of setting itself on fire outside auditions for *The X Factor*. It was the year *The Times* reluctantly joined the rest of the world in finding it could no longer fund a reporter at every domestic match. By way of compensation the paper published an exquisite series of features on county grounds by Michael Henderson, who visited Queen's Park, Chesterfield, in glorious July weather, to watch Derbyshire play Yorkshire, and movingly contended, from under the shade of a tree: "You may have been boating last week on Wolfgangsee, surrounded by the mountains of the Salzkammergut. Or measuring a sundowner in the hilltowns of Umbria. Or playing boules in Périgord. Not a patch on Derbyshire, me duck; not in weeks like these. You can't get a cheese-and-beetroot cob there, tha knos. And there's no cricket."

Markedly less pastoral was the scene created, in early August, by Monty Panesar, relieving himself all too close to bouncers from the walkway above a nightclub in Brighton (*Sun* headline: "The Slashes"). Then, later that month, came cricket's very own Watergate, in which England players were spotted casually emptying their bladders during a post-match, late-evening picnic, as anyone might in similar *en plein air* circumstances, behind a bush. Except that this picnic was taking place on the Oval square, where bushes were in short supply and the offending acts of micturition were witnessed by Australian journalists, working late.

This casual desecration seemed primed to cause the game, and indeed the whole country, to choke indignantly on its cheese-and-beetroot cob. The fact that it didn't, that the fuss blew over swiftly, is worth pondering. One can easily imagine the storm of opprobrium that would have been unleashed had,

say, Ashley Cole, of Chelsea and England, been witnessed emptying his bladder in the gloaming at Wembley. The screams for high-level resignations and the overhaul of the nation's education system would have been long and penetrating. Cricketers continue to get off blessedly lightly, and are still more or less free to answer nature's call when it comes – although the lesson would seem to be: avoid the game's historic lawns. And anybody else's lawn.

The year's best headline was in Northumbria's *Journal*: "Gran's disappointment as Swann hangs up bat." The gran in question, Mina Swann (formerly of Blyth, now living in Swindon), was photographed smiling warmly in front of a television. Her claim was that England had not been made welcome by their hosts: "Not all the Australian players – a certain one. There is something nasty happened."

Mrs Swann didn't elaborate, but her grandson was moved to respond via Twitter: "I've heard of some low forms of journalism before but preying on my 90-year-old gran? Hang your head in shame the lowlife responsible." One sympathised with Swann. Yet, with the darker revelations of the Leveson

inquiry still fresh in the mind, it was tricky to feel moral outrage over a local journalist picking up the phone to someone's nan. And, whatever Swann wants to say about the nefarious practices of the media, Nana Swann had the best line on his abrupt retirement – "a damn shame". Swann, we should also note, announced that retirement in his newspaper column.

In 2013, *Strictly Come Dancing* was won by Abbey Clancy, the model and television presenter. One mentions this purely because the victories of Darren Gough and the swivel-hipped Mark Ramprakash awoke hopes that cricket stood at the threshold of an era of glorious domination in the pro–celebrity ballroom arena. But the talent has simply failed to come through, and every year since has been a cricketing bust.

However, eager thoughts now instinctively turn to Swann, who was clearly born for this kind of post-career media limelight, and won't be busy next winter. Redemption on the dance floor could yet be his, and cricket's – although his gran might want to take her phone off the hook.

Mind you, what's the betting the selectors get it wrong again and pick Monty Panesar?

Giles Smith is a columnist for The Times.

JOHN ARLOTT, 1914–1991

The bard of Basingstoke

David Rayvern Allen

John Arlott, born 100 years ago on February 25, 1914, was known to millions for his unmistakeable voice, imitated by after-dinner speakers, on-stage comedians, even the station announcer at Nottingham. That voice, reckoned by one newspaper to be "as much a part of summer as the sound of lawn-mowers", was his passport to fame. But his life outside cricket commentary was even more colourful.

Genes did not immediately suggest a broadcasting career: three ancestors were hanged for violent robbery, and two more deported. And the Arlotts were mostly labourers, not short on temperament. This quality the young John did inherit: at Queen Mary's in Basingstoke, his feud with the "Prussian" headmaster – Arlott had noted his middle name, Wilhelm – led to frequent beatings. On one occasion his rear trouser button was said to have been split in two by the cane, with both parts forming the arc of flighted off-breaks as they flew into the midst of the assembled schoolboys. Had he been in less pain, Arlott might have approved of the imagery.

He went on to take jobs in which education arrived more practically: office boy in the local town hall, where he learned to type; diet clerk in a mental home, where he acquired a sense of order and an insight into the human condition; and policeman on the beat in Southampton, where observation was crucial. On one patrol, he arrested the British fascist leader Oswald Mosley – for his own safety – because his rantings had incited a crowd.

Patrick Eagar

It was as a detective-sergeant screening aliens and questioning conscientious objectors during the Second World War that Arlott learned to write succinct reports. He also picked up a smattering of Norwegian, German and Italian, some of which was useful when delivering Forces lectures in Europe. Hours spent in the public library unleashed a ferocious desire for knowledge, and the sensory deprivation of night duty gave ample opportunity to bring words alive.

"Poetry came to mean more to me than anything else," he remarked. He produced four books of verse – *Landmarks* (in collaboration with Rostrevor Hamilton), *Of Period and Place*, *Clausentum* and *First Time in America*. Then, on the recommendation of John Betjeman, he entered the world of broadcasting.

Succeeding at one remove George Orwell as literary programmes producer in the BBC's Overseas Service, he was now mixing with the *littérateurs* of the day, among them E. M. Forster, Dylan Thomas, Louis MacNeice, Patric Dickinson and Cecil Day-Lewis. At the same time, he began commentating on cricket, and he eventually forsook radio production to take on a job as instructor in BBC staff training, where he advised the legendary tennis commentator Dan Maskell.

For two decades from the late 1940s, Arlott embarked on a phase of incredible productivity. For the *Evening News* alone, he wrote columns entitled Sporting Silhouettes, Table Talk and It Occurs to Me. He went on to write for the *News Chronicle*, *The Observer*, *The Guardian* (where he was wine, as well as cricket, correspondent), and occasionally *The Times*. On the radio, he compered *Twenty Questions*, and did a spot of football commentary, though its pace was generally too fast for his delivery. He was also a founder member of *Any Questions?*

As an actor in one of his first broadcasts, he played John Ball, the Lollard priest of the 1381 peasants' revolt. The part reflected his own unabashed radical liberalism, inherited from his grandfather, who had once walked 30 miles to sit at the feet of Gladstone as he gave an address. When Lloyd George visited Basingstoke, Arlott's mother Nellie – a local Liberal agent – invited him to tea, where Lloyd George symbolically anointed him to the cause with an affectionate pat on the head.

In later years as an aspiring candidate for Epping, Arlott twice increased the Liberal vote. And at a third election, in grave danger of being returned, he chose not to run, as he could not afford to exist solely on the salary of an MP (in those days, nobody mentioned expenses). Meanwhile, an offer of ennoblement to the House of Lords, with the enticement of a marvellous wine cellar, was rejected with the retort: "Maxwell has already sold off all the best plonk!"

Just after the war, Arlott and his first wife, Dawn, took in German Jewish refugees, and his concern for the plight of those ostracised by their own land was again apparent during the D'Oliveira crisis in 1968. Years earlier, he had helped D'Oliveira find employment at Middleton – Arlott looked back on that as his "finest hour" – and said he would refuse to commentate if South Africa's visit in 1970 went ahead.

He produced books on snuff, English cheeses, John Speed maps, and pamphlets on infantile paralysis. He also wrote *Crime and Punishment* and *Death on the Road*, a verse narrative which with savage irony predated by a dozen years the tragic death of his eldest son, Jim, in a car crash. Combined with the loss of a baby daughter and his second wife, Valerie, Arlott's mien was understandably lugubrious in his declining years.

A post-retirement move to Alderney with Patricia, his third wife, in 1980, proved not quite final. A speaking tour of the mainland a few years later encouraged full houses at theatres, with ovations at every venue. On the island he narrated a couple of documentaries, and appeared in two 1920s-style silent films written by Elisabeth Beresford, of *Wombles* fame, as Sir Arlott Johns: in one, an eccentric old gentleman; in the other, an infamous pirate.

He never ceased to be amazed he had got so far. He always retained, according to one who knew him well, "the insecurity of the freelance and a peasant's fear of debt". But it never reached the point of fiscal no-return, despite his diverse collecting enthusiasms: books, pottery, paintings, engraved glass, Gladstoniana; Japanese prints, Himalayan herbs and, as a child, the confetti from bus-ticket stubs.

Arlott could have chosen several disparate careers, but somehow amalgamated them. His friend, the novelist Kingsley Amis, said: "If he had not spread himself so thinly, he would have been an absolutely frontline writer." With over 90 books, booklets, pamphlets and appreciations, plus three hymns for the *English Hymnal* to his name, there is no doubting his work ethic. And he always provided comprehensive coverage of cricket books for *Wisden*.

An abiding memory is Arlott at the head of the long dinner table at home as he regaled his guests with his latest story, then seeing a twinkle in his eye as he stimulated impassioned discussion by introducing a controversial subject. When he felt it was time to move on, he would test the strength of his impressively large Czechoslovakian wine glass by banging it on the wooden surface. Arlott could be mischievous, even wilful, and yet enormously kind, humorous, thoughtful and caring. And, a century on from his birth, he remains the cricket commentator to whom all others aspire.

David Rayvern Allen, an award-winning BBC producer, has also written around 40 books, including an authorised biography of John Arlott.

CRICKET AND BLOGS, 2013

Fans with laptops – and why not?

S. A. RENNIE

At the end of last summer, ECB chairman Giles Clarke emailed across some questions about cricket blogging. Among other things, he was interested in the topics covered by bloggers, the depth of analysis, and the quality of the writing. It was an informal piece of market research prompted by the concern that, against a backdrop of diminishing print coverage, fans were now increasingly turning to the internet for news and opinion. But the tone betrayed a sense of unease, with blogs seemingly characterised as a conduit for uninformed rants, and the blogger as a shadowy, Julian Assange-type maverick with an axe to grind, spreading untruths and misinformation.

Clarke's distrust of the internet isn't new: in 2012 he referred to illegal streaming of live cricket as "the biggest danger" to the sport. And Twitter has also been an object of concern for the ECB, with former managing director Hugh Morris likening players' use of it to "giving a machine gun to a monkey".

For several reasons, Clarke's concerns were unsettling. The first was that bloggers were often more level-headed than many of their print counterparts when it came to some of the controversies of England's Ashes summer. Stuart Broad's refusal to walk at Trent Bridge was, for many chief sportswriters, the death knell for the spirit of the game – a nebulous concept if ever there was one. Bloggers were quick to point this out. Will Atkins, at **theshortmidwicket.blogspot.co.uk**, wrote: "The spirit of cricket is a nice thing to have in the rules... But while the 'unique appeal' of cricket is nice on paper, in reality every team on the planet attempts to push the laws as far as they allow."

Peter Miller, at **thearmchairselector.com**, took a similarly pragmatic view. The fact that Broad is considered such a divisive character, he argued, contributed considerably to the ballyhoo; and the incident would never have occurred had Michael Clarke not wasted an "optimistic" review on an lbw shout against Jonny Bairstow. While arguments raged about Broad's morality, it was DRS – with its implied lack of respect for the umpires and its susceptibility to gamesmanship – that was the real culprit, said Mark Cripps at **goalsandwickets.co.uk**. He wondered whether "results are now to be determined by how participants use a review system to check the degree of human error or otherwise by its umpires," and asked: "How is this in the spirit of the game?"

Fans with laptops they may be, but bloggers also fulfil a crucial role by championing forms of the game that are only now beginning to receive the attention they have long fought for, especially Associate and women's cricket. For some time, Russell Degnan has been flying the flag for the smaller

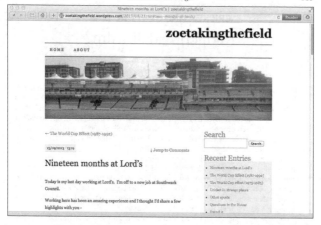

nations at **idlesummers.com**, while increased television coverage of the women's Ashes has led to an upsurge in blogging, notably at **drawingthestumps.blogspot.co.uk**, **womens-cricket.blogspot.co.uk** and **samebat.blogspot.co.uk**. All three challenge the still common misconception that women – writers and players – have less to contribute to the game's culture and history than men. Another terrific example is Zoe English, who spent 19 months helping out as an archivist at the Lord's museum, and blogging about her work in extensive articles illustrated with images from the MCC archives. At **zoetakingthefield.wordpress.com**, she covers women's involvement in the invention of overarm bowling.

What Zoe's blog also demonstrates is the importance of preserving the folk memory of the sport. And what better repository than the internet? Norman Geras, Professor Emeritus of Politics at Manchester University, Marxist philosopher, author and political thinker, died in October (see his obituary on page 200), but his wonderful trove of personal recollections, complemented by quotes from cricket literature, stands as a legacy to his deep love of the game. You can find the collection at **normblog.typepad.com**. And for those who lament there are no more Carduses writing about county cricket, **backwatersman.wordpress.com** may force you to reconsider, with lines such as this description of Leicestershire's Ned Eckersley: "A slightly built, doe-eyed figure who currently sports a scrubby beard, giving him a faintly Rabbinical aspect."

All this was conveyed in the response to Giles Clarke: that bloggers are moved to write about the game – some more eloquently than others – by their love of the sport and their wish to celebrate it.

But corruption, mismanagement and the abuse of power are also powerful motivators when it comes to committing words to screen. The BCCI's dealings

CRICKET AND TWITTER, 2013

Reductio ad absrdm?

ALAN TYERS

Cricket Australia's official Twitter account put on a magnificent all-round display. It provided the statesmanlike observation that a third-umpire decision in favour of Ian Bell "sucked ass. #bullshit". It revealed the Australia A-side to face England in Hobart before the players themselves had been notified, in a nice update to the old "found out on Ceefax I'd been dropped" school of selection. And, at the start of the Adelaide Ashes Test, it gormlessly tweeted a picture of four Sikh men in fancy dress with the caption "Will the real Monty Panesar please stand up?!"

With such shining examples from Australia's governing body, it was hardly surprising that not all their cricketers covered themselves in glory. David Warner took up the cudgels against two journalists, one of whom had questioned his contribution during the tour of India. "All you do is talk shit," he began. "What about encouraging Aus rather than bagging them?" Malcolm Conn replied: "You lose 4–0 in India, don't make a run, and you want to be tickled on the tummy?"

David's brother Steven reckoned Shane Watson had used an Ashes DRS review without thinking of the team: "Fucking selfish Watson the sooner you are out if [sic] the side you great pretender the better." At least Steven's verdict on sacked coach Mickey Arthur – an "escape goat" – coined cricket's Twitter phrase of the year.

Proving that no job is too big, or too small, for the BCCI, they asked Twitter to suspend the account of blogger @AltCricket after he tweeted a link to an illegal website stream of, erm, a Pakistan v Australia one-dayer. If only commentator Sanjay Manjrekar had been such a master of the electronic arts: he tweeted his disgruntlement after being sidelined for the India–Australia series, under the impression he was sending a private message to IPL chief exec Sundar Raman: "Sundar, I have now been kicked off from studio for Ind/Aus by Star TV. Don't you think this is a bit harsh? I have a contract with them." He hurriedly removed the tweet.

Andrew Flintoff took a break from his punishing reality-TV schedule to try his hand at literary criticism: "Enough is enough. 30 pages in of the dullest book ever!" he fumed at Ian Rankin's *The Impossible Dead*. In a crushing swipe at Rankin's mugshot, Flintoff added: "No wonder, look at his picture on the back. #binned."

Perhaps the unlikeliest debate of the year was between Kevin Pietersen and Arsenal footballer Jack Wilshere, on questions of globalisation, identity and the nation state. Wilshere said: "The only people who should play for England are English people." Pietersen took him to task: "Interested to know how you define foreigner? Would that include me, Strauss, Trott, Prior, Justin Rose, Froome, Mo Farah?" Wilshere sought to smooth matters over: "I'm sure most of you agree with me even if some journalist [sic] are trying to make me look bad… again!"

Unmukt Chand of the Delhi Daredevils won the award for creative brevity – and incomprehensibility. "The beauty of dng ntn is d goal of al ur wrk,d fnl acmplshmnt fr wch u r highly cngtltd.Dmre dlghtfly u cn do ntn,d highr ur life's achvmnt." Sorry Unmukt, wht r u on abt?

The best-refreshed cricketer had to be Ryan Harris, who apologised after tweeting: "A tip for all those heading to Perth! Avoid the crown or casino! Shit hole can't get in if you have had a drink #shitplace #dickheads." Imagine how drunk you would have to be to get refused entry to a casino hours after regaining the Ashes…

with Cricket South Africa – in effect holding a series to ransom partly over displeasure at the appointment of Haroon Lorgat as CSA's chief executive – were not only excoriated by bloggers, but seen by many as part of a wider malaise, of self-interest taking precedence over the sport's long-term health. "An act of bastardry artful in its elegance and execution" was how Brett Graham described the temporary sacrifice of Lorgat in exchange for a truncated series at **thatisstumps.wordpress.com**. And Degnan summed up the hell-in-a-handcart scenario that arises when one board wields disproportionate power: "If the BCCI want to control cricket then they have that option. They have the market strength and sufficient control over the major stars of its biggest market to pursue that end. But that comes with a need to actually develop cricket, as a product, not just at grassroots level or by advancing the prospects of their national team."

As the prolific Gideon Haigh writes at **blogs.theaustralian.news.com.au/cutsandglances**, "if you're not spending a fair bit of time writing, thinking and talking about how the game is run, and how it might be done better, then you're part of the problem".

Where there is duplicity and propaganda, instead of honesty and transparency, it is the right – not to say the duty – of the blogger to pass comment. Clarke's concerns call to mind something Andy Flower said in an interview with Sky at The Oval after England wrapped up their 3–0 Ashes win: "We can't control what the media say. Unfortunately."

We must take care that cricket does not follow football's example. At a time when brand protection calls the shots, when football clubs are charging local newspapers for access to press boxes and suggesting that the needs of the fans are best served by the clubs' own in-house media teams, the existence of an independent voice and informed fan base becomes more important than ever.

S. A. Rennie blogs at legsidefilth.com

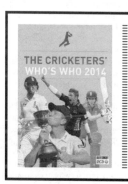

RETIREMENTS

The late developer and the windmill

STEVE JAMES

It was the most controversial of retirements. England had just gone 3–0 down in Australia when **Graeme Swann** decided his time had come. Some considered it treachery, but the truth was that Swann's body, especially his right elbow, operated on twice, had let him down. Swann took 255 wickets in his 60 Tests. Among English slow bowlers, only Derek Underwood has taken more. He was certainly England's finest off-spinner since Jim Laker.

Between his debut in late 2008, when he struck twice in his first over (Gautam Gambhir and Rahul Dravid), and his final game five years later, nobody took more Test wickets. He was a late developer, not making his Test debut until nine years after his first England tour, when he had been exposed as immature, on and off the field. Swann learned his craft on turning pitches at Northampton, but a move to swing-friendly Nottingham rounded his modus operandi, and better harnessed his joker personality. This naturally attacking bowler learned to defend, too, allowing England to play a four-man attack as they rose to the top of the Test rankings.

While the Ashes were being surrendered, it was tempting to glance back to better times – and the summer of 2005. Three members of the four-pronged fast-bowling attack of that year left the first-class game in 2013. Andrew Flintoff had long since departed, but **Steve Harmison, Matthew Hoggard** and **Simon Jones** all followed, though Jones hoped to continue playing Twenty20.

As if to remind us that the perfect farewell is impossible, Harmison did not make a first-class appearance last year. But two details tell his tale: he was the world's No. 1 bowler in 2004; and he sent down that first-ball wide at Brisbane in 2006-07. He possessed wonderful natural gifts of pace and bounce, spectacularly in evidence when taking seven for 12 at Sabina Park, but also an action that could be unreliable, and an attitude that was often misunderstood. He was never the complete package, but he never professed to be. He was not a thinker, or a technician – just a shy lad from Ashington, often uncomfortable in cricket's brightest lights, who could simply bowl fast.

It is easily forgotten that Hoggard was also fast in his younger days, before becoming a genuine swing bowler, tireless but no trundler – though his England captain Michael Vaughan dubbed him his "shop-floor worker". His finest moments were in Barbados in 2003-04, when he took a hat-trick, and the following winter in Johannesburg, where he took 12 wickets to clinch the series. Only seven England bowlers have taken more than his 248 Test wickets.

Jones's career emphasises the cruelty of injury. There was the sickening snap of knee ligaments at Brisbane in 2002-03, but it was the smaller

Glyn Kirk, AFP/Getty Images

Effort ball: Graeme Swann puts his body through it in his last Test in England.

MARK BOUCHER

The best-laid plans…

In July 2012, at the very start of South Africa's tour of England, wicketkeeper Mark Boucher was struck in his left eye by a bail. He has not played again. Here, he reflects on that day in Taunton, and how his life has changed since.

I had thought it was rare for a career to come to such a sudden end. But, since my accident, I've learned that many players experience something similar. They could have been planning their retirement for a while, but there's usually one moment when they think: "Oh my god, this is it. I'm never going to play again."

I had decided about six months before the England tour that it would be my last, but had planned for a season or two of domestic cricket to break my fall into the real world. The level of excitement had been as great as any I experienced in 15 years. I was fitter than ever, and the No. 1 ranking was at stake. I was convinced we would win. And Lord's would have been my 150th Test. There was no bigger stage on which to retire. Yet by the second morning of the trip, I was gone from the game.

It was an awful few days, blurred by strong painkillers, disbelief and shock. The next week, back home, was spent behind closed doors after the first of what became six operations in the 15 months after the accident. There are many more to come.

Dr Jonathon Rossiter – the surgeon in Taunton who saved my eye and hails from my home town of East London – feared the best I could hope for was to save the eyeball cosmetically, but with no sight. Yet Dr Raoul Scholtz, my Cape Town surgeon, realised there was a chance of regaining some sight. He said it would be a painful three-year process, testing my resolve. I had no problem with that. Fifteen months later, I still didn't have my new iris or pupil, but we're getting there.

I followed the Test series on television and spoke to the guys regularly. They had a picture of me on the change-room wall, and it was emotional when Jacques Kallis, my best friend, touched his eye after scoring a hundred at The Oval.

My early problems with depth perception were a source of amusement for friends, who were quick to penalise me two shots for accidentally grounding my sand wedge in a bunker. They enjoyed lobbing objects at me and shouting: "Bouch, catch!" Usually they landed on my head.

Most of my time is now dedicated to South Africa's anti-rhino poaching movement. I am passionate about animals and wildlife conservation: if we conserve our bush and protect our game parks, we can create jobs and improve lives.

Fortunately, I was covered for medical expenses, but there will always be those who assume everything will be fine. I know: for a long time I was one of them. But fairytale endings can't be manufactured – they just happen. I was always worried about people assuming I would play my 150th at Lord's. I kept saying: "I could break a finger." As it happened, I lost an eye.

Mark Boucher's autobiography, Bouch: Through my Eyes, *was published in October 2013. He was speaking to Neil Manthorp.*

ailments that wrecked his career. Here was a talent unfulfilled, his last Test coming at Trent Bridge in 2005, when he took five first-innings Australian wickets before managing just four overs in the follow-on, and limping off, never to wear an England shirt again. His reverse swing was world-class, shocking the Australians with an ability to move the old ball both ways. Jones played just 91 first-class matches following his debut in 1998 and, like Harmison, did not appear at all in 2013, except in 40- and 20-over cricket, finishing at Lord's with a wholehearted spell against Nottinghamshire in the YB40 final.

Owais Shah enjoyed a very good first-class career, making 45 centuries, but the feeling lingered that the promise shown as a teenager was never fully realised. He made 88 on Test debut, in Mumbai, but added only five more caps, the frustration he engendered recalled his former Middlesex colleague, Mark Ramprakash, on whose style he based his game. Shah made a decent fist of one-day international cricket, with some destructive late-innings leg-side hitting, but was dumped suddenly in 2009 because of poor running between the wickets, and a lack of athleticism.

> He had the thighs of a Polynesian rugby player

Ricky Ponting's first-class career ended, rather bizarrely, with Surrey, in only his fourth County Championship match for them. He made 169 not out to save a game against Nottinghamshire, before playing two more Twenty20 matches for the county, then seven for the Antigua Hawksbills in the Caribbean Premier League – a low-key end to a glittering career.

Darren Maddy was English cricket's original Mr Twenty20, becoming the first to pass 1,000 runs in the format and playing a major part in Leicestershire's triumphs in 2004 and 2006. He then won three further titles with Warwickshire, including the 2012 Championship. With the thighs of a Polynesian rugby player, he was a fitness fanatic ahead of his time, a well-liked and hugely respected competitor on the county circuit. It was no disgrace that his international career – three Tests and eight one-day internationals – was not a roaring success. With bustling medium-pace and a bullet arm to add to his sturdy batting, he was a fine cricketer.

So too was Hampshire's **Dimitri Mascarenhas**, who also made a name for himself in Twenty20, and retired as the leading England-qualified wicket-taker in the format, with 147. He was also a groundbreaker, becoming the first English cricketer to play in the IPL. He made his first-class debut in 1996, when Liam Botham was a colleague, and became a highly influential player for Hampshire, whom he captained from 2008 to 2013. He was a stingy seamer, lacking in pace, but not skill: his length was almost always impeccable. He could bat too, and at The Oval in 2007 hit India's Yuvraj Singh for five sixes in an over in one of his 20 one-day internationals.

Michael Powell was a solid middle-order batsman who spent the last two seasons of his career at Kent, after 15 at Glamorgan. His score of 299 against Gloucestershire in 2006 is the second-highest in the club's history. He was called into the England one-day squad in 2004, but did not play.

Mike Hewitt, Getty Images

The tightest of lines: Dimitri Mascarenhas ended his career with 456 limited-overs wickets.

He may have been 38, but **Alan Richardson's** decision to leave Worcestershire to become bowling coach at Warwickshire was still a surprise. On his fourth county, he had just got better and better. Despite an awkward-looking windmill action, he always bowled an immaculate length, regularly hitting the seam. He was a popular choice as one of *Wisden's* Five in 2012.

Claude Henderson was the game's first Kolpak signing, joining Leicestershire in 2004. But Henderson, a left-arm spinner who played seven Tests and four one-dayers for South Africa, was no fleetng mercenary. He stayed at Grace Road for ten seasons, eventually passing 900 first-class wickets.

The career of **Arul Suppiah** was cut short by knee injuries. Born in Malaysia but educated at Millfield, he established himself as an opening batsman with Somerset. He could also bowl some handy left-arm spin, and on a turning pitch at Cardiff in 2011 recorded world-record Twenty20 figures of six for five.

Ben Phillips was a strong and steady seamer when fit, but played only 124 first-class matches in an 18-year career that took in Kent, Northamptonshire, Somerset and Nottinghamshire. Thirty-year-old Yorkshire opener **Joe Sayers** suddenly announced his retirement in January, having written a diary of the club's 2013 season. He was a throwback, a left-handed blocker in an age of blasters, but post-viral fatigue syndrome in 2010 did not help. Left-armer **David Lucas**, 35, had a year of a contract remaining at Worcestershire, but limited opportunities forced his hand. He had also played for Nottinghamshire, Yorkshire and Northamptonshire.

CAREER FIGURES

Players not expected to appear in county cricket in 2014

(minimum 40 first-class appearances)

BATTING

	M	I	NO	R	HS	100	Avge	1,000r/ season
C. D. Collymore	167	223	103	913	23	0	7.60	–
G. D. Cross	62	94	5	2,196	125	3	24.67	–
L. M. Daggett	71	83	35	613	50*	0	12.77	–
Z. de Bruyn	241	406	36	14,239	266*	29	38.48	1+1
S. J. Harmison	211	270	77	1,888	49*	0	9.78	–
C. W. Henderson	273	377	79	5,637	81	0	18.91	–
M. J. Hoggard	239	305	94	1,908	89*	0	9.04	–
S. P. Jones	91	113	37	904	46	0	11.89	–
D. S. Lucas	95	124	27	1,698	60	0	17.50	–
N. D. McKenzie	267	456	58	18,169	237	50	45.65	1
D. L. Maddy	284	460	32	13,796	229*	27	32.23	4
A. D. Mascarenhas	195	291	32	6,495	131	8	25.07	–
B. J. Phillips	124	172	32	2,991	100*	1	21.36	–
M. J. Powell	236	389	40	13,421	299	27	38.45	5
D. J. Redfern	70	116	7	3,213	133	2	29.47	–
A. Richardson	169	194	83	1,176	91	0	10.59	–
J. J. Sayers	108	179	14	5,457	187	11	33.07	1
O. A. Shah	252	428	38	16,357	203	45	41.94	8
G. P. Swann	252	343	37	7,811	183	4	25.52	–
C. D. Thorp	94	127	16	1,664	79*	0	14.99	–

1+1 indicates one season overseas and one in England.

BOWLING AND FIELDING

	R	W	BB	Avge	5I	10M	Ct/St
C. D. Collymore	13,214	492	7-57	26.85	12	2	49
G. D. Cross	–	–	–	–	–	–	155/23
L. M. Daggett	6,300	166	8-94	37.95	2	–	13
Z. de Bruyn	11,175	285	7-67	39.21	4	–	152
S. J. Harmison	20,805	744	7-12	27.96	27	1	31
C. W. Henderson	27,841	905	7-57	30.76	34	2	88
M. J. Hoggard	21,739	786	7-49	27.65	26	1	63
S. P. Jones	8,142	267	6-45	30.49	15	1	18
D. S. Lucas	8,564	264	7-24	32.43	9	1	18
N. D. McKenzie	536	11	2-13	48.72	–	–	233
D. L. Maddy	7,969	253	5-37	31.49	5	–	290
A. D. Mascarenhas	12,701	450	6-25	28.22	17	–	76
B. J. Phillips	8,132	271	6-29	30.00	5	–	38
M. J. Powell	132	2	2-39	66.00	–	–	136
D. J. Redfern	460	10	3-33	46.00	–	–	37
A. Richardson	15,007	569	8-37	26.37	23	4	50
J. J. Sayers	178	6	3-15	29.66	–	–	63
O. A. Shah	1,505	26	3-33	57.88	–	–	200
G. P. Swann	23,741	739	7-33	32.12	32	6	195
C. D. Thorp	6,776	267	7-88	25.37	9	1	53

CRICKETANA IN 2013

We need to talk about Fred

DAVID RAYVERN ALLEN

It looks as though we have reached a tipping point. Over the past 40 or 50 years, the collection of cricketana – be it books, artefacts, ceramics, photographs, autographs or whatever – has grown, roughly in line with the antiques market. But the peak seems to have passed. Indeed prices are ebbing, and the reason is not hard to find.

Many of the great collectors of the 1960s and '70s have died – in 2013 one dealer alone dealt with four major probate valuations – and there are fewer people competing to snap up their possessions. In essence, the number of buyers is tailing off. Tellingly, the supply of *Wisdens* (usually a reliable yardstick) now exceeds demand. With more copies for sale in a smaller market, prices are often 20–30% down from their peaks. The scarce and early volumes still fetch considerable sums, such as the £106,000 paid at a Knight's sale last year for a full set of softbacks. If that sounds like a lot, it is worth remembering that six or seven years ago it could have been as much as a third more.

In the past, someone inheriting a long run of Almanacks might have viewed them as a nest egg. Now they seem to be regarded as a sizeable cheque to be cashed immediately. With many of the younger generation making such extensive use of eBay, the site has no shortage of *Wisdens*. Even though eBay and Amazon are almost 20 years old, some believe the internet has still not come of age as a marketplace for cricketana. Yet far from being worried, some of the old school see cause for optimism, not least because lower prices make it more feasible to start a *Wisden* collection. "I think the process is long-term cyclical," said book-dealer Christopher Saunders. "There will be new collectors coming along, and it's up to the dealers to find them."

In one way, Saunders already has. Thanks in part to an advantageous exchange rate, he has found an increasing number of customers in Australia, especially among the Sri Lankan and Indian communities. Some will already be customers of Roger Page, who has been trading from the Melbourne suburbs for 45 years. But these collectors also look further afield, to Saunders, and to the subcontinent. Last September, Osian's – a Mumbai-based auction house – organised the first substantial sale of Indian cricket memorabilia: 73 of the 100 items were sold, raising nearly £36,000.

Back in July, the week of the Lord's Ashes Test marked the welcome return of a cricket-themed exhibition to the London gallery scene. Nick Potter and Michael Down (of Boundary Books) joined forces to present for sale a range of art, as well as rare books, autograph material and memorabilia. The most expensive items were "A Youth at Cricket" (an 18th-century oil painting by Hugh Barron which sold for £80,000), and one of only three surviving life-size busts of W. G. Grace completed by W. H. Tyler in 1888; at the turn of the

year, this was still available to those with £29,000 to hand. There was also an oil of Ian Botham, dressed in the regalia of Tim Hudson's Hollywood team and dating from around 1985. An attractive, fully illustrated catalogue recorded the merchandise. "The exhibition was a great success, and showed that confidence is beginning to return to the cricketana market," said Down. "The gallery was well attended throughout, with a fair sprinkling of Australian visitors over for the Ashes. This gave us the opportunity to meet collectors in person rather than through the dreaded internet. Everybody seemed to enjoy it, and we will surely do a repeat."

In the 19th century, thousands of indentured labourers were taken by the British from the subcontinent to Mauritius. Whether this hastened the spread of cricket is uncertain, though by the 1860s it must have been flourishing. For auction at Graham Budd's November sale at Sotheby's were three pages of sheet music entitled "The Cricketana Galop" – a hitherto uncatalogued 1865 composition by H. J. Snelling "dedicated to the President & Members of the Mauritius Cricket Club". An albumen photograph of the island club adorned the front, and its estimated price was £200–300. In the event, a phone buyer spent £1,300.

Tim Knight's sales at Leicester in February, June and October included much of the Len Hutton collection; happily several items found their way back to the Broad Acres. What was thought to be the cap from his debut Test (against New Zealand in 1937) fetched £1,500 on the hammer, while Hutton's handwritten account of the Timeless Test at Durban made £800, as did a letter from his mentor George Hirst congratulating him on his record

Scaling the heights: three pages of sheet music fetched £1,300.

364 against Australia in 1938. And £800 was bid a third time for his report of the 1953-54 West Indies tour, in which Hutton conveyed his concerns over the behaviour of Fred Trueman, and said Jim Laker – who, he claimed, had an inferiority complex – was not easy to handle. Exceeding all this was an MCC touring cap, which sold for £1,800. But the sales extended far beyond Huttoniana: Knight's sales usually have as much to offer the collector of unheralded ephemera as of more prominent artefacts.

The surprise of the year arrived in late autumn, when Trevor Vennett-Smith announced that his November auction would be his last. He began in partnership with Neale's of Nottingham, before setting up on his own in the pavilion at Trent Bridge. He then moved to Colwick Racecourse, and finally to the British Legion Hall at Gotham. Vennett-Smith, the "fastest lot-slinger in the West" (or the East Midlands), entertained his clients for a quarter of a century.

"Lot No. 297 at one hundred. A hundred and ten, do I see? Going at a hundred and ten unless you get on. A HUNDRED AND TEN!" The gavel descends. Many a time Vennett-Smith shot through 800–900 lots in around four hours – a staggering speed, though he always had time to share a merry quip with his audience. His last few sales have disposed of much of Anthony Woodhouse's huge cricket library, and the wide-ranging collection of Dr John Turner. He is, however, looking to the future. "I'm not worried about the medium term. There are new collectors coming in – admittedly in their fifties – so the next 20–30 years should be all right. It's after that I worry about. The computer-age kids don't know what a book feels like. They're remote from real things. Will they bother to come along to auctions?"

Finally, a humble suggestion to help the livelihoods of impoverished bookdealers. It is well known that people with deep pockets are prepared to pay well over the odds – perhaps knowingly, perhaps not – at charity auctions. At a recent Lord's Taverners function, photographs of Hobbs and Sutcliffe fetched £2,500 – over ten times their retail price. With the Taverners providing magnificent support for disadvantaged youngsters, this is undeniably a good thing. So maybe booksellers, who worry that frequent auctions harm their trade, should learn from the Taverners and consider holding their own open days. If they lay on some food and booze, and begin the auction of desirable bits and pieces only once the clientele are replete and responsive, they may also do rather well. And as long as a clear amount is given to a stipulated charity, it is, perhaps, a win–win situation. You heard it here first…

CRICKET AND THE WEATHER, 2013

Summer of the century?

PHILIP EDEN

The spring of 2013 was chilly. Indeed, none had been significantly colder since 1892, though several had endured similarly low temperatures. April began with 12 days of frigid weather, with occasional snow. Even in the south Midlands and upland parts of southern England, a few drifts that had arrived in the snowstorm of March 24 lingered until April 13. But the season improved, and there were warm spells during the second half of April and the first week of May; the rest of the month, though, was cold and cloudy.

According to the Wisden Summer Index (see *Wisden 2004*, page 1,597), it was the best summer since 1996, though only July brought lengthy spells of hot, sunny weather. June was a dry month, but distinctly cool. August had a mean temperature slightly above the long-term average, and rainfall slightly below it. Although July had above-average rainfall, there was a long dry spell from the 2nd to the 22nd, before heavy, thundery downpours disrupted the last nine days of the month. Taking the summer as a whole, rainfall was 15% below normal, while sunshine was 9% above, thanks to a particularly bright July.

The season ran from April 5 to September 27, and at 176 days was the longest on record. The county champions were Durham, and it could be argued that the weather played a part in their success. The most northerly of the first-class teams, Durham are frequently bottom of the weather pile, as in 2012. But last year five counties scored lower and, as far as the differences from normal were concerned, there were only three that were more blessed.

The Test series against New Zealand began on May 16. The first match was uninterrupted, but the second, from May 24–28, was less fortunate: the first day was washed out, and the fifth badly interrupted. The Ashes began on July 10, and of the five Tests only two were seriously affected by the weather. The Third, played at Manchester at the beginning of August, lost most of the last day, while the Fifth, at The Oval between August 21–25, lost all of the fourth. They were the only two to end in a draw.

The meteorological statistics, averaged over England and Wales, for the 2013 season, were:

	Average max temperature (°C)	Diff from normal (1981–2010) (°C)	Total rainfall (mm)	% of normal	Total sunshine (hours)	% of normal
April	11.8	−0.6	37	59	181	116
May	14.7	−1.7	74	121	203	100
June	18.4	−0.9	39	57	193	102
July	23.8	+2.7	65	114	289	144
August	21.6	+0.3	63	87	190	97
September	17.8	−0.5	61	74	134	93
2013 season	**18.0**	**−0.1**	**339**	**85**	**1,190**	**109**

Each summer has slightly different regional variations, though in most years northern and western counties are cooler, cloudier and damper than those in the east and south. The Wisden Summer Index compares the summer, county by county. In essence, an index over 650 indicates a good summer, below 500 a poor one. Values for the summer of 2013 against the average for the standard reference period of 1981–2010 were:

	2013	Normal	Difference		2013	Normal	Difference
Derbyshire	594	578	+16	Middlesex	718	668	+50
Durham	606	523	+83	Northamptonshire	672	613	+59
Essex	680	638	+42	Nottinghamshire	602	588	+14
Glamorgan	630	553	+77	Somerset	712	618	+94
Gloucestershire	667	593	+74	Surrey	721	673	+48
Hampshire	752	643	+109	Sussex	718	663	+55
Kent	660	653	+7	Warwickshire	648	553	+95
Lancashire	595	528	+67	Worcestershire	641	613	+28
Leicestershire	600	583	+17	Yorkshire	605	558	+47

Last summer, only Derbyshire and Lancashire were below 600, and every county scored above the long-term average, though for Kent the difference was just +7. Derbyshire, Leicestershire and Nottinghamshire had relatively small excesses. Hampshire, on the other hand, had an index 109 above normal, while Durham, Somerset and Warwickshire were more than 80 above the average.

Taking a national view, last season's index of 657 was 202 points higher than the year before. This is the fifth-greatest improvement between consecutive seasons, behind 1910–11, 1954–55, 1958–59, 1974–75 and 1988–89. It was also the highest result since 1996, beating both 2003 and 2006, previously the best summers of the 21st century. In 2003, there was a significant heatwave in early August that brought Britain's highest temperature, while July 2006 was the warmest and sunniest on record.

2002	506		2005	623		2008	525	
2003	647		2006	633		2009	568	
2004	541		2007	503		2010	610	

2011	582	
2012	455	
2013	657	

Highest: 812 in 1976   Lowest: 309 in 1879

CRICKET PEOPLE, 2013

Lord's nightwatchman

ALI MARTIN

When **Alan Pryer** arrived at Lord's in April 1969 to take up the new role of sales clerk – a position that would become Lord's shop manager and be his until retirement in July 2013 – his first day at work was livelier than most. Pryer had to force his way through a crowd of Peter Hain's "Stop The Tour" campaigners, whose protests were aimed at MCC after a vote in January had ratified South Africa's visit the following summer.

Pryer found his merchandising career on hold, and was instead tasked with guarding the ground overnight. "Myself and MCC curator Stephen Green would sit in the high chairs in the Long Room and keep lookout," he recalls. "The outfield was protected by barbed wire and lit up by temporary floodlights – like a scene from a prisoner of war film. We took it in turns to sleep. I'm not one for the paranormal, but at times it was rather chilling."

The tour's cancellation in May 1970 ruled out any move to sentry duty, allowing Pryer to begin preparations for a summer of retailing. He set up a small concession in the foyer of the museum, and the sale of pens, pencils, mugs and the *Laws of Cricket* during the first day's play between England and West Indies brought in £100 – much to the delight of his employers. The Lord's shop had been created, moving in 1975 to the old East Lodge building, where it was rebuilt in 1996.

Pryer's 44 years at Lord's oversaw the shop's transformation from a one-man operation to a business employing 12, complete with an online arm. One of his most famous employees was MCC Young Cricketer Ian Botham, who would sell seat cushions on major match days. Pryer would net with him and his cohorts during weekday lunch breaks. "The young Botham tried to hit every ball for six," he says.

His most enduring memory was the IRA bomb scare during the 1973 Test against West Indies: "I will never forget the crowd pouring on to the outfield, with umpire Dickie Bird sitting on the covers to protect the wicket. There wasn't the same sense of fear you would get these days. People were in good spirits."

In retirement, Pryer admits he misses the "village-like community" at Lord's. And while he declined the offer of a leaving party for fear of disrupting busy colleagues, an honorary MCC life membership was accepted with surprise and delight. Having worked at all 72 Test matches during his Lord's career, Alan enjoyed his first as a spectator – along with wife Sandra, herself a receptionist at Lord's for 19 years – during England's 347-run victory over Australia. "It was so special to mix with other members and enjoy the beautiful Harris Garden," he says.

According to Neil Hannon, one half of music group **The Duckworth Lewis Method**, growing up in Ireland with a passion for cricket is to know "a love

that dare not speak its name". But the man behind chamber pop act The Divine Comedy was to meet a fellow devotee in Thomas Walsh at the wedding of comedy writer Graham Linehan in 2003. Walsh, of the band Pugwash, subsequently invited Hannon to contribute to his Christmas single that year. En route to the recording studio, a bulletin of cricket scores on the car radio brought to light the duo's secret shared interest.

"The idea followed to write cricket-themed pop songs and so, while imbibing at the Lower Deck pub in Portobello, Dublin, we brainstormed ideas," explains Hannon. "We both love the history of cricket, and its village-green quirkiness lends itself to our style of psychedelic pop." The contents of Hannon's notebook would become the bulk of The Duckworth Lewis Method's eponymous debut album – released in July 2009 – and its 2013 follow-up, *Sticky Wickets*. Their work has been nominated for the prestigious Ivor Novello Awards for songwriting.

The second album featured contributions from broadcaster Stephen Fry, actor Daniel Radcliffe and *Test Match Special* commentator Henry Blofeld, and was promoted with a ten-date UK tour, including a sell-out at Nottingham Playhouse on the eve of the First Ashes Test at Trent Bridge. The set contained such tunes as "Jiggery Pokery" (a homage, from the perspective of Mike Gatting, to Shane Warne's ball of the century in 1993) and "Meeting Mr Miandad" (a cricketing pilgrimage to Pakistan).

"It has been an incredible honour to be taken to the bosom of cricket's following," says Walsh. "We may write more, we may not. The plan is to have no plan going forward."

An American former pro-basketball player was the choice when Durham County Cricket Club used a grant from the Arts Council to commission a writer-in-residence to chronicle their maiden Ashes Test. **Benjamin Markovits**, a novelist and teacher of creative writing at The University of London's Royal Holloway College, attended the Fourth Test and saw stereotypes turned on their heads in a tight contest.

"There is a sense in England that Australians are direct, confident and up for the big moment," he says. "Englishness is in turn seen as dogged and cerebral, but hesitant and unlucky. People see what they want to see, but I'm not sure those traits stood up."

While Markovits insists Americans "would not tolerate outside intervention", such as the bad light which stopped play on day two, he believes his countrymen should be in awe of cricket's mental challenge: "I cannot think of anything that compares with the batsman's test of concentration."

Markovits was taken by Chester-le-Street's backdrop – in particular Lumley Castle – but widened the scope of his essay "Success", later published in the *London Review of Books*, to chart the improvement in British sporting fortunes since the turn of the century. But his conclusions on cricket, which heralded English dominance over an Australian sport in decline, did not foresee the winter series that followed.

CRICKET IN THE COURTS, 2013

Batman – and robbing

FIGHT OVER CLUB'S OUTFIELD CONTINUES

The High Court ruled in favour of Charlton Kings CC, Cheltenham, after an 18-month dispute with a widow over four-tenths of an acre which forms part of the outfield. Jacki Mitchell said the land belonged to the estate of her late husband. The case hinged on the status of a rental agreement signed by the club and the owners in 1947. In a complex ruling, Mr Justice Morgan concluded on July 25 that Mr Mitchell's title was extinguished in 1986 and that the club had "possessory title". He said he would understand if Mrs Mitchell considered his decision "very harsh", and in December she was granted permission to take the case to the Court of Appeal. The club said the case had already cost them at least £80,000 and that defeat could put them out of business.

MAYNARD DEATH "ACCIDENTAL"

A coroner's jury returned a verdict of accidental death on Tom Maynard, 23, the Surrey and England Lions cricketer who was hit by an underground train in south London in 2012. Westminster Coroner's Court heard how Maynard was driving to his girlfriend's house in the early hours after a night's drinking and was stopped by police. He ran off, leaving the engine running, and half an hour later was hit by a train on the District Line. The driver said he thought he saw ballast at the side of the track and realised too late it was a motionless body. The pathologist, Simon Poole, said that marks on Maynard's foot and ankle were consistent with contact with the live electric rail, but that it was not clear whether he had died before being struck.

The inquest also heard that analysis of Maynard's hair showed traces of cocaine and Ecstasy consistent with daily use in the months before his death, and that the level of blood alcohol, combined with cocaine use, would have impaired his judgment. The coroner, Fiona Wilcox, called for compulsory testing of hair samples for sportsmen. After the verdict on February 26, Maynard's family said in a statement: "The results of the inquest do not define our son. He made choices that night that tragically cost him his life, but his devastated family and friends will love and miss him unconditionally, always."

BATMAN TRUMPS BATSMAN

A British Intellectual Property Office adjudicator ruled in favour of DC Comics, American owners of the Batman trademark, against Adelphoi, a London design company, who wanted to establish a range of mainly cricket-related goods under the name Batsman. Oliver Morris decided on February 20 there was a likelihood of confusion, although he accepted there was a "conceptual dissonance" between Batman and Batsman, described as "a type of cricketer or an aircraft safety officer". However, he declined to award costs against Adelphoi, saying DC Comics could have been "more measured", and had no need to submit eight lever-arch files to support their case.

MAN JAILED FOR KILLING ON CLUB TOUR

Thomas Swannell, from Northamptonshire, was jailed for six years on May 29 for killing a man outside a bar in Magaluf on a cricket tour of Majorca in 2011. Two years after the incident occurred, and just before he was due to stand trial in Palma in May, Swannell, 46, admitted the murder of Gary Vigors from Essex with a broken bottle. The court took into account the mitigating factors that Swannell, owner of a scaffolding company, was drunk at the time and would pay €160,000 in compensation to the victim's family. Finedon Dolben CC said Swannell was on the tour as a club sponsor, "one of many".

WICKETKEEPER REVEALED AS BENEFITS CHEAT

A man who said he was so ill he needed help going to the toilet was playing regularly for Boosbeck CC, Yorkshire. Stewart Lorains, 53, was filmed by investigators keeping wicket and opening the batting while claiming more than £22,000 in Disability Living Allowance. He was given a suspended four-month prison sentence at Teesside Crown Court on September 30.

PANESAR FINED FOR URINATING ON BOUNCER

England cricketer Monty Panesar paid a £90 spot-fine on August 12 for being drunk and disorderly after urinating on bouncers at a Brighton nightclub. At about 4am, he had been asked to leave the club, Shoosh, after a group of women complained about his behaviour. He went on to the promenade above the club and relieved himself on the men below. Three weeks later Panesar's ex-wife obtained a "non-molestation order" against him. He left Sussex shortly after the nightclub incident, but was chosen for the England tour of Australia.

PIETERSEN WINS LIBEL DAMAGES

Kevin Pietersen accepted undisclosed but "substantial" libel damages in the High Court on October 8 from the opticians' chain Specsavers after the firm used a photo of him in an advert. It had the caption "Bat tampering in the Ashes? Apparently, Hot Spot should've gone to Specsavers". This followed a claim on Australian TV that England players were using tape on their bats to deceive Hot Spot, for which the broadcasters had already apologised. Specsavers' solicitor, Niri Shan, accepted the allegation was false.

ECB THWART TOUTS

The ECB and three Test-match counties successfully made a civil claim against a Buckinghamshire couple described as ticket touts on an "industrial scale". Nick Hubscher, a pilot, and his wife Judith were said in the High Court in September to have bought hundreds of tickets for Ashes Tests in 2013 using false names and multiple addresses, and resold them on ticketing websites. Although not a crime, this constituted breach of contract, and in September Mr Justice Dingemans upheld a £50,000 action against the Hubschers.

CRICKET AND THE LAWS, 2013

The unappealing truth

Fraser Stewart

In May 2013, MCC submitted a report to the ICC cricket committee about the legality of the switch hit, following consultation with players, umpires, captains, journalists and fans. The key recommendation was that the shot should not be deemed illegal.

Crucially, the umpires stressed the difficulty of discerning exactly what the batsman had done with his hands: for example, had a right-hander briefly transformed himself into a left-hander (a manoeuvre some feel is unfair, since bowlers are not allowed to change hands without informing the umpire first), or had he simply turned the blade, with the right hand still below the left? In fact, the debate becomes rather notional: the shot cannot be ruled illegal if it cannot first be defined. For if the umpires, standing only 20-odd yards away, are uncertain what is happening, any Law to ban the stroke would be unenforceable. The report can be seen on MCC's website (www.lords.org).

A new edition of the Laws came into force on October 1, including a change to Law 2.8. Even the most studious followers of the game might not have known that, until then, a batsman with a runner would have been given run out off a no-ball – in effect stumped – if the batsman was out of his ground (but not attempting a run). The new Law ensures that, when a no-ball is bowled, the batsman cannot be out in that manner. The change means that a batsman with a runner receives the same protection as his uninjured colleagues, who – according to Law 39.1 – cannot be stumped off a no-ball.

As discussed in these pages last year, a no-ball will now be decreed, under Law 24.6, if the bowler breaks the wicket during his delivery stride – partly a response to England fast bowler Steven Finn's habit of doing precisely that. Some at MCC felt a change of Law was not required, but it was decided that a no-ball would make it simpler for everyone: the batsman is protected from dismissal, but can accrue any runs he scores, while the subjective adjudication of whether he has actually been distracted is not required.

MCC decided to relax the Law it created in 2010 concerning practice on the field: players are now allowed to bowl a loosener to a colleague, even if the ball bounces on the ground – as long as it does not waste time or is not being done to damage the ball. This is how the Law had been written prior to the changes. They were well-intentioned, but were being overruled by playing regulations in all professional cricket and at most amateur levels.

The moment at which a batsman can be out handled the ball has now been limited to when he is playing it, or immediately afterwards – in other words, when he is defending his wicket. Consequently, only the striker can be out this way. Any subsequent handling by either batsman will be subject to "obstructing the field". Under Law 34, which governs "hit the ball twice", it is no longer possible for a batsman to score any runs after making a lawful second strike (in defence of his wicket). Previously, runs could be taken from a lawful second strike only after an overthrow had occurred, but this possibility of run-scoring has been removed.

Full explanations of all the changes, and the intention behind them, together with video clips, can be seen on MCC's website. MCC have created a set of animations narrated by Stephen Fry, which aim to simplify some of the Laws in a user-friendly way.

On the field in 2013, games continued to produce scenarios that left players and viewers scratching their heads. During a match in Australia's Big Bash League at the start of the year, Kane Richardson of the Adelaide Strikers accidentally trod on his stumps playing a pull against Perth Scorchers. According to Law 35, he had quite clearly hit his wicket, but nobody noticed – despite the bails being fitted with LED lights which flash when they are out of their groove. And so Richardson set off for a run. A quick replay, however, was enough for the umpires to assess the decision and give Richardson out.

But the drama was not over. Before Richardson reached the edge of the playing area, Perth's captain Simon Katich – after consulting with the umpires – called him back. Katich later explained that his team had not appealed for the dismissal, which is why they offered Richardson a reprieve. It is important to clarify that a batsman may be technically out, without actually being dismissed: the fielding side must appeal, as per Law 27, although the batsman does have the option of giving himself out.

There continues to be confusion over what constitutes obstructing the field when the batsmen are running between the wickets, as there are situations when the ball can be blocked either legally or illegally. Pakistan's Mohammad Hafeez and Anwar Ali were both dismissed this way in international cricket in 2013. In 2011, the ICC had added a clarification in their own playing conditions, which carefully explained what was implied in the Law: "For the avoidance of doubt, if an umpire feels that a batsman, in running between the wickets, has significantly changed his direction without probable cause and thereby obstructed a fielder's attempt to effect a run-out, the batsman should, on appeal, be given out, obstructing the field. It shall not be relevant whether a run-out would have occurred or not."

A batsman must not run on the pitch, and yet will often veer across it to try to get himself between the fielder and the stumps. This is illegal. However, if he happens to be running on a legal path and the ball hits him, there is no offence.

From the amateur game, MCC heard about a stumping after the ball had lodged in the keeper's pads, and he had put down the wicket with his leg, and with the striker out of his ground. The decision should have been not out, as Law 28.1(a)(v) states that the wicket can be put down only "by a fielder with his hand or arm, provided that the ball is held in the hand or hands so used, or in the hand of the arm so used".

Fraser Stewart is Laws manager at MCC. The Laws appear in Wisden 2011, *page 1200, and on the MCC website (lords.org).*

CRICKET EQUIPMENT, 2013

All in the mind

TIM WIGMORE

Worries about the fragile equilibrium between bat and ball are nothing new – from the flat pitches in the era of timeless Tests, to the revenge of the bowlers at the height of the West Indian reign of terror. Australia's one-day series in India last year felt like another staging post, with the six becoming deflatingly matter-of-fact: this was 50-over cricket reincarnated as a Twenty20 highlights show. Even the Ashes in Australia got in on it: a total of 65 sixes was a record for a Test series, smashing the old mark by 14.

When Lance Klusener scythed Shoaib Akhtar over the ropes at the 1999 World Cup, fans gasped because of the rarity of the act. But if the new Klusener emerged now, would we appreciate him in the same way? Without the element of surprise, the six is reduced from cricket's most exhilarating spectacle to one of its most mundane.

It is often remarked that modern bowlers have to contend with flat tracks – "chief executive's wickets", Steve Harmison called them – and a brutal schedule that could be designed with the eradication of quicks in mind. Twenty20 has made six-hitting an essential part of the modern batsman's repertoire. And while anything bowlers do to make the ball more amenable is considered illegal, they also have to contend with improvements in the quality of bats. Bat technology is not a glamorous topic, but it is transforming cricket, rendering the mis-hit a fertile source of runs.

Bats have improved considerably over the past 20 years – but, contrary to the impression created by the hyperinflation of the six, they have actually become lighter. Chris King, master bat-maker at Gray-Nicolls, says: "In the past, a big bat would probably weigh in the region of 3lb or more, whereas now most professional players want between 2lb 8oz and 2lb 10oz."

But that doesn't mean the ball travels less far. While the length and width of bats tightly governed by regulations, their thickness has increased. And modern bats have less moisture, enabling them to weigh less, even as they acquire a chunkier, more imposing look. If this lends itself to bravado, it can come at a price. The image of Michael Carberry's bat folding in half during the Sydney Test in January was more than just a symbol of England's Ashes tour. It was also dramatic proof that the drier bats favoured by modern professionals have a shorter life expectancy.

Batsmen are united by the thrill of the ball meeting the sweet spot. Technology has helped: better pressing techniques have created a bigger sweet spot, giving batsmen more margin for error in their timing. These changes have been pioneered in India, where willow clefts are kept in drier, warmer conditions (and are therefore more prone to damage). "The correct pressing of the blade is what gives the bat its power," says King, "not the bat's size."

It would be easy to blame the proliferation of sixes on skilled bat-makers – too easy, according to King, who believes it is like "saying a modern car is faster than the cars of 20 years ago because of its colour". King says we should be focusing more on the people hitting the sixes, and less on what they use to hit them.

"It's not the bats that are hitting more boundaries," he argues. "It's the modern batsman. At no time before in the history of the game have cricketers been so physically fit. They train to peak performance, and are more powerful, more skilled and more able to dispatch the ball into the stands."

Break in play: Michael Carberry suffers an equipment malfunction at Sydney.

That is certainly all true. Yet bats are clearly providing more help than ever: while most sixes are the result of well-executed shots, there are also more miscued maximums, thanks in part to a modern bat's thicker edges. There may be another factor at play: batsmen are no longer scared. The use of high-quality helmets has liberated them from the fear of serious injury.

If bats look much more formidable than a generation ago, King thinks the main effect is psychological: "If a player believes a big-profiled bat will hit a ball further, it will give him the confident mindset to do just that." In a sport which loves to think of itself as revealing as much about a player's mental strength as his physical prowess, the impact of a bat that looks awe-inspiring – whatever the realities – cannot be overstated.

Yet we may have reached the limits of bat technology. Law 6 controls how bats are made, and from what materials. In recent years, the regulations have been tightened because it was feared that blades made from laminated wood, or handles made of carbon fibre, might give batsmen an unfair advantage.

King says the rules on bats are akin to "the construction of a Formula One racing car: the design and materials are pushed to their absolute limits to create the maximum performance within the sport's restrictions". That means there may not be much scope for bats to improve in the coming decade, though King thinks designers could become "more daring with bat profile shapes".

The next phase is not to make bats bigger, more powerful or lighter: most of what can be done on those fronts has already been achieved. Because cricket is played so much in the mind, bat manufacturers have a different challenge: to "affect the player's confidence with the way the bat is shaped", in the words of King. The Laws will prevent bats from getting much better – but that doesn't mean batsmen won't think their bats are better. Bowlers, beware.

OBITUARIES

ADCOCK, NEIL AMWIN TREHARNE, died on January 6, aged 81. Until Neil Adcock joined forces with Peter Heine in a menacing double act in the mid-1950s, South Africa had never enjoyed the benefits of a great fast-bowling partnership. Even in an era overflowing with world-class pace bowlers, Adcock and Heine stood out, leaving a trail of bruised and traumatised batsmen in their wake. Undisguised aggression and a regular supply of bouncers were key weapons, although Adcock did become an affable figure at close of play.

The hostility was most memorably demonstrated on two occasions. Against New Zealand at Johannesburg's Ellis Park in 1953-54, Adcock put Bert Sutcliffe and Lawrie Miller in hospital, and bowled Murray Chapple and Matt Poore off their chests. Then, at Port Elizabeth in 1957-58, he and Heine launched a ferocious assault as Australia pursued just 68 to win. Trevor Goddard, fielding in the gully, remembered: "I stood two steps further back than normal. Then, after the first ball, I went back two more." Goddard recalled Colin McDonald turning to him when he was dismissed by Adcock for four: "Tell this bastard I've got a family at home." McDonald later called it "virtual bodyline".

Adcock was the first South African fast bowler to take 100 Test wickets, and enjoyed an *annus mirabilis* in England in 1960, when he showed unflagging stamina over a five-month tour to take 26 wickets at 22 in the Tests, and 108 overall at just 14. He was named one of *Wisden's* Cricketers of the Year.

Blond and 6ft 3in, he was a striking figure, although it was not until late in his career that he added muscularity to his speed. His run-up was straight and fluent, and he delivered the ball with a high arm and a perfectly upright body. Batsmen and fellow bowlers were baffled by how much pace and, crucially, lift from a good length he generated from this curious, whippy action – "like a sudden gust turning a light windmill," said *Wisden*.

At school in Port Elizabeth and Johannesburg, Adcock had shown little aptitude for cricket, but while playing for Jeppe Old Boys he improved under the tutelage of Cyril Vincent, the former Test left-arm spinner. However, the first sign that he was capable of serious pace came in a match when he was captained by Eric Rowan: nerves and a desire to impress meant he discovered a speed he did not realise he had.

His first-class debut for Transvaal came in November 1952; just over a year later he was opening the bowling for South Africa against New Zealand at Durban. He played in all five Tests in that series, delivering 24 wickets and plenty of physical and psychological damage. But he failed to live up to expectations in England in 1955, when he was plagued by injury: he missed the Fifth Test after breaking a bone in his foot in the Fourth at Headingley. However, by the time England visited South Africa in 1956-57, he was working superbly in tandem with his permanently snarling new-ball partner, Heine.

Doug Insole, England's vice-captain on that tour, said: "Colin Cowdrey was to open the innings, but on the boat on the way over said he didn't want to. He didn't think his technique was up to coping with Adcock and Heine." Adcock took 21 wickets at under 15 as the series finished 2–2, and rattled most of the England batsmen, notably captain Peter May. "Adcock was undoubtedly very quick," Insole said. "Some thought he was the fastest they played against."

Australia arrived in South Africa the following summer amid dire predictions about the damage Adcock would inflict. "We knew about him," said Richie Benaud. "He was fast, aggressive, didn't like batsmen and hated losing." Instead, Australia won 3–0 and, in that final match, at Port Elizabeth – on a gloomy, chilly evening when the wicket suddenly became lively – Adcock and Heine lost their discipline, bowling repeated bouncers. The captain, Clive van Ryneveld, was forced to withdraw them from the attack. The journalist Charles Fortune described it as "the most terrifying eruption of fast bowling I have ever seen".

Determined to make up for the disappointments of 1955, Adcock put himself through a programme of weight training before the tour of England in 1960, and was rewarded with an injury-free summer of exceptional achievement. "The fastest I ever saw him bowl was in the tour game at Derby," said Goddard. "It was freezing – I think they had to take a layer of ice off the pitch before the start." At Scarborough, as he put his feet up at the end of the final match, Adcock reflected with deep satisfaction that he had left the field only three times all summer – for running repairs to his trousers. His efforts were even more impressive because his young new-ball partner Geoff Griffin did not bowl again on the trip after being no-balled for throwing in the Second Test at Lord's.

Adcock played in just two more Tests, against New Zealand in 1961-62, and ended his international career with 104 wickets at 21 in 26 matches. A year later he played his final game for Natal, whom he had joined from Transvaal in 1960, finishing with an overall record of 405 wickets at 17. In retirement he worked as a travel agent, became a radio commentator and spent some

Popperfoto/Getty Images

Virtual bodyline: Neil Adcock was one of the meanest fast bowlers of his time.

years in Australia, where he coached New South Wales. "Off the field I found him great fun," Benaud recalled. "On the field he was as fast as Fred Trueman and Brian Statham, but not as fast as Frank Tyson. Nor was anyone else."

His significance at home was enormous. "He was the first genuinely great South African fast bowler," said Ali Bacher. "A new era started from that moment because we began to develop our own fast bowlers, and he was one of the best this country has produced."

AHMED MUSTAFA, who died on August 10, would have been only ten years old – and the youngest-ever first-class cricketer – when he made his debut in February 1955, if his stated date of birth (March 7, 1944) was correct. However, Qamar Ahmed – a journalist who played against him in the 1950s – met Mustafa a few months before his death, and was told he was actually about 15 when he appeared for a Pakistan Schools XI against the 1954-55 Indian tourists at Karachi. So he was probably 74 when he died after suffering head injuries in a fall in his bathroom. A stylish batsman good enough to tour England as vice-captain of a Pakistan Eaglets team, Mustafa played on to 1970, and scored 110 for Karachi C against Sind A (and Qamar Ahmed's bowling) in 1957-58. A car accident ended his career, but in 1987 he set up a coaching centre in Karachi, where his charges included Pakistan's Faisal Iqbal and England's Owais Shah.

ALLEN, STANLEY ROWLATT, MBE, who died on December 22, aged 95, was Sussex's secretary for four years from 1976, a period that included the World Series Cricket upheaval – initial details of which emerged during the touring Australians' match at Hove in May 1977. Former Sussex captain John Barclay said: "At the time Stanley arrived at Hove, Sussex cricket was at a bit of a low ebb and he breathed fresh air into the management team." Allen had also done some cricket commentary for Radio Brighton, where he worked with Desmond Lynam; in 1980 he returned to his career as a solicitor.

ALLITT, INEZ, OAM, died on December 10, aged 88. "Mary" Allitt played 11 Tests for Australia, the last three of them as captain of the 1963 side to England. One of 12 children born into a farming family near Deniliquin, on the plains of south-west New South Wales, she learned her cricket playing with her brothers at home and with the other pupils at the one-teacher school at Pretty Pine. This background left her adept at cutting, as she used the pace of the boys' bowling to great effect on a concrete pitch. Four Allitt sisters played for Deniliquin against the touring England women's side in 1948-49, when Mary showed her defensive capabilities with 56 out of a total of 96.

Although she did little in the Tests in England in 1951, Allitt did hit 150 against West Women at Cheltenham, dominating an unfinished opening stand of 218 with Joan Schmidt. On the 1963 tour, she made 76 at Scarborough, the innings of her Test career, putting on 125 with Miriam Knee after they had come together at 51 for five. Australia eventually reached 225, but – mainly thanks to thick fog which swallowed up two hours on the last day – England just managed to avoid defeat, crawling to 93 for nine in 92 overs.

After her retirement, Allitt and her husband, former rodeo horseman Tom Loy, spent over 30 years developing the equestrian skills of local children. She remained active in administering women's cricket, and her work in both arenas was recognised by the Medal of the Order of Australia in 2007. James Sutherland, Cricket Australia's chief executive, paid tribute: "Mary and her team-mates were trailblazers of the game, and she led [them] through a significant period of societal change, helping to pave the way for today's elite players." Norma Whiteman, a fellow tourist in 1951, added: "Mary's cricket reflected her personality: well organised, thoughtful and understated."

AZAD, DESH PREM, who died on August 16, aged 75, played 19 matches in a first-class career that stretched for 19 years – but is best remembered as the coach and mentor of Kapil Dev. "If I achieved anything," said Kapil, "a lot of the credit goes to him." Azad also had a hand in the careers of three other Test cricketers from Haryana: Chetan Sharma, Ashok Malhotra and Yograj Singh (father of Yuvraj). In 1986, not long after Kapil led India to victory in the World Cup, Azad became one of the first recipients of the Indian government's new Dronacharya Award for sports coaching. His highest score was 83, for Southern Punjab against Services in Delhi in 1960-61, made in the follow-on after the whole side had been shot out for 83 in the first innings.

BASHIR AHMED BASTI, who died on January 4, aged 88, was the secretary of the Board of Control for Cricket in Pakistan between 1965 and 1971. He played two first-class matches in India before Partition, opening the bowling and taking eight for 42 in the first innings of his debut, for United Provinces against Bengal at Kanpur in 1945-46.

BELLANY, JOHN, CBE, RA, who died on August 28, aged 71, was an acclaimed Scottish artist, famous for his colourful figurative paintings, many of which featured fishermen from Port Seton, the village in which he grew up. But one, in 1985, depicted Ian Botham, then in the "flower power" stage of his career. The subject was unimpressed: "If an alien landed on the planet with explicit instructions to find Ian Botham and the only thing he had to go on was that picture, he'd never find me in a million years," he grumbled in his 1994 autobiography. "I'm not one who goes in for vandalism, but in this case I'd make an exception." The oil painting is now in the National Portrait Gallery in London. Bellany died in his studio, according to his family, paintbrush in hand.

BREWER, ROBERT, who died on November 9, aged 90, was known as the grandfather of women's cricket in Sydney, pioneering a number of initiatives, such as a night competition. From 1990, he served as a New South Wales selector, and his discerning judgment fostered the talents of Alex and Kate Blackwell, Lisa Sthalekar, Alyssa Healy and Ellyse Perry. The Sydney women's Under-17 grade competition bears his name.

BRUCE, STEPHEN DANIEL, who died on December 12, aged 59, was a useful wicketkeeper-batsman who had a long career in South African domestic cricket, mostly for Western Province. In 1972-73 he had a season with Orange Free State, and made 149 – his first century – against Natal B, sharing a seventh-wicket stand of 155 with Colin Bland. Bruce made four other hundreds, including 176 for Western Province B against Transvaal B in 1982-83.

BULL, CHARLES ARTHUR, died on May 7, aged 91. Intimately associated with the South Perth club as both player and administrator, Charlie Bull became scorer at the

WACA, establishing a reputation for meticulous accuracy. Between 1980-81 and 2003-04 he recorded 76 first-class matches, including ten Tests. Bull delighted in his scoresheet of Matthew Hayden's 380 against Zimbabwe in October 2003, during which he ran out of room to record the new Test-record innings, and had to resort to the space reserved for the twelfth man. Both the scoresheet and Bull's work were mentioned in Hayden's autobiography.

CASHELL, HENRY DESMOND, died on October 6, aged 92. A wicketkeeper and handy club batsman, Des Cashell was better known as an Irish cricket administrator, including several years as a national selector. He was president of the Irish Cricket Union in 1981.

CLARK, DAVID GRAHAM, who died on October 8, aged 94, shared with Lord Harris the distinction of being captain, chairman and president of Kent, and also held a number of high-profile positions with MCC. A gentleman farmer, he maintained Corinthian ideals on the game, yet was caught in a number of controversies. Chief among these was as manager of the England team during the incendiary Ashes tour of 1970-71, when he clashed frequently with the captain, Ray Illingworth, and was on the receiving end of a withering blast from fast bowler John Snow. Clark was also chairman of the ICC at the height of their battle with Kerry Packer, and in the mid-1960s headed an MCC report into the state of the domestic game which was rubbished by the counties.

Clark was educated at Rugby, and during the war served in the 2nd Battalion Parachute Regiment in North Africa and Sicily before being captured and taken prisoner at Arnhem.

He was 27 when he made his Kent debut in 1946, and assumed the captaincy three years later. These were thin times for the county, but his team-mate, wicketkeeper Derek Ufton, said: "He did a tremendous job in the circumstances. He was a Kent gentleman. Before we went up north to play Yorkshire, for instance, he would stress that we had to behave properly – then we would lose in a day and a half." He stood down after Kent came second-bottom in 1951, finishing his playing career with 1,959 runs at just under 16 in 75 matches. His highest score was 78, against Surrey at The Oval, in his final summer.

Clark first served on the MCC committee in 1959, and was manager of the tour of India in 1963-64. The night before the Second Test at Bombay he had to tell Henry Blofeld, covering the trip as a freelance, that he might be required to play, such was England's crisis with injury and illness. When Clark was

Corinthian, and controversial: David Clark at Tonbridge just after the war.

asked to manage the team in Australia in 1970-71, it proved a more bruising experience. His appointment had been made in expectation of Colin Cowdrey's return to the captaincy. Illingworth later took exception to a newspaper article in which Clark criticised England for bowling too many bouncers in the Second Test at Perth, and said it would be better for Australia to win the series than for the Tests to be uninspiring draws. "I didn't mind him as a man at all," said Illingworth, "but we did not get on cricket-wise."

When the Third Test at Melbourne was washed out, Clark agreed to a 40-over match to compensate spectators – unwittingly playing a key role in the creation of the one-day international – and also an additional Test at Sydney at the end of the tour. The players, who were not consulted or initially offered any payment, were furious, and agreed to take part only after a militant meeting in Illingworth's hotel room. In that explosive extra Test, he led his team off the SCG when beer cans were thrown at Snow, only to be met by the manager telling him he had to get back out and play. The captain was not impressed, and neither was the target: "Snowy joined in," Illingworth later wrote, "and got rather a lot off his chest."

In the mid-1960s, Clark chaired an MCC subcommittee with a brief to examine every aspect of the ailing county game. The final report was voluminous, but its main recommendations – a revamped Championship including Sunday play, and a one-day league – were greeted with disdain by many of the counties. "A mountain of labour produced a mouse of achievement," groaned *Wisden*. But the one-day league came into being three years later.

Clark was president of MCC in 1978-79, a role that came with chairmanship of the ICC attached, and was pitched headlong into the Packer affair. His diplomatic skills were fully tested as he tried to persuade national boards to fund the costs of ICC's failed legal action against the players. Clark remained implacably opposed to Packer, and stood down from the Kent committee when the county's four World Series Cricket players were reinstated.

He became MCC treasurer in 1980, but resigned as a gesture of solidarity when his friend Jack Bailey was forced out as secretary seven years later. Clark was chairman of Kent between 1970 and 1974, and president in 1990. Happily, there was no lasting rift with Illingworth, who said: "We always got on well and he was complimentary about my captaincy whenever I went down to Canterbury with Leicestershire."

COMMINS, JOHN EUGENE, was killed by intruders at his home in South Africa on January 2. He was 71, and had played ten matches for Western Province during the 1960s, taking five for 32 with his leg-breaks against Eastern Province at Cape Town in January 1961. His son, Donne, was the agent for several prominent players, including Mark Boucher, who cancelled his farewell parade planned for the New Year Test against New Zealand at Cape Town a few days later; flags at Newlands flew at half mast instead. His nephew, also John Commins, played three Tests for South Africa in 1994-95.

Guy de Alwis: "one of Sri Lanka's best wicketkeepers", according to Arjuna Ranatunga.

DE ALWIS, RONALD GUY, died of cancer on January 12, aged 52. Guy de Alwis was a tall wicketkeeper who played in 11 of Sri Lanka's early Tests in the 1980s, usually vying for a place with Amal Silva, a better batsman but inferior gloveman. "He was one of the best wicketkeepers produced by Sri Lanka," said Arjuna Ranatunga, their long-time captain and a team-mate at the Sinhalese Sports Club. De Alwis was not a rabbit with the bat: his two international fifties came in the space of three days during the 1983 World Cup in England. He became a selector, and also coached the national women's team, later marrying one of his former charges, Rasanjali Chandima Silva, who played one women's Test, in 1998.

DE MESQUITA, SAMUEL NORMAN BUENO, died on July 25, aged 81. Norman de Mesquita, scion of an old Sephardi Jewish family, was a much underrated cricket commentator. In the 1970s and '80s, as sports editor of BBC Radio London, he would take over the station to broadcast single-handed on Sunday League matches. Almost unique among cricket journalists in actually enjoying the 40-over game, he conveyed his relish to the listeners with great skill. His authoritative voice gave him regular work as an announcer at Middlesex outgrounds, tennis tournaments and – a sport he loved – ice hockey. But like a county stalwart whose face doesn't quite fit, he never caught the radio selectors' eye for a crack at the big time. Even after the Sunday coverage was axed, "Mosquito" was a regular at Lord's, and would assiduously keep score in the press box, to the point of sonorously announcing "halfway!" after 27.3 overs of a 55-over Benson and Hedges Cup innings: he was truly a natural broadcaster. His voice was cruelly weakened after illness in 1999, but he continued to write for *The Times* and *Wisden.* He was the Almanack's Middlesex correspondent from 1994 until he died, and his early-season 2013 match reports are in this edition. Norman loved Lord's and, until the 2013 Ashes, was proud to have attended at least a day of every post-war Test there, including the 1945 Victory Tests. A teetotal bachelor, he adored the camaraderie of colleagues.

DENNESS, MICHAEL HENRY, OBE, died on April 19, aged 72. It was Mike Denness's lasting misfortune that his reign as England captain was sandwiched between Ray Illingworth and Tony Greig. He could not match Illingworth's tactical intelligence or Greig's hyperactive charisma – and suffered by inevitable comparison. Instead, Denness was consigned to history as the leader who withdrew from the line of fire during the 1974-75 Ashes, when Dennis Lillee and Jeff Thomson were at their most ferocious.

Yet this overshadowed the fact that, in 19 Tests in charge, he won more games than he lost, and scored four centuries. Denness was also the most successful captain in Kent's history, leading them to six one-day trophies in five seasons. In a glorious era for the county, a team that bristled with box-office names entertained large crowds shoehorned into the St Lawrence Ground. Amid the tension and euphoria, Denness was a leader of cool authority. "He never panicked once," said Alan Knott.

An elegant, fluent batsman, either opening or in the middle order, Denness made almost 26,000 first-class runs at 33, and was a magnificent fielder. He was softly spoken, and uncomfortable in the limelight, but firm, principled and determined – never more so than when, as an ICC match referee, he became embroiled in a huge row after censuring several of India's biggest stars.

He was the first – and so far only – Scottish-born captain of England, and as a boy dreamed of representing Scotland at rugby, an ambition shared with his two closest friends at Ayr Academy, Ian McLauchlan and Ian Ure. They were a precocious trio: McLauchlan captained the national rugby team, while Ure became a football international. Denness himself was an outstanding all-round sportsman – he won nine

Patrick Eagar

Cool authority: Mike Denness heads towards a hundred against India in 1974.

athletics events in one school year – but his focus switched to cricket when his father built a new family home just outside the boundary at Ayr Cricket Club. He made his first-class debut for Scotland, aged 18, against Ireland in Dublin in 1959, scoring 47. Scotland teammate Jimmy Allan, once of Kent, kept his former county abreast of his progress, and Denness set his mind on Canterbury after a chat with E. W. Swanton when he spoke at Ayr CC's centenary dinner.

Denness joined Kent in 1961 and made his Championship debut against Essex at Dover in July 1962, when he was bamboozled by the wiles of Jim Laker. But he made his maiden half-century for them in the next match, and passed 1,000 runs for the first of 14 times the following summer. International recognition came against New Zealand at The Oval in 1969. He took an agonising 43 minutes to get off the mark, before being dismissed for two, but he was called up again for the first match against the Rest of the World in 1970. His most notable contribution to that series, however, came at Headingley where, as an emergency fielder for the World XI, he took the short-leg catch that completed Eddie Barlow's hat-trick.

A more satisfying achievement that year was Kent's first Championship since 1913. Bottom of the table at the end of June, they responded positively to Denness as stand-in captain when Colin Cowdrey was on international duty. In 1972 he took over the leadership full-time, boldly promising the AGM at least one trophy a season. He delivered the John Player League in his first year, and got back into the England team as Tony Lewis's vice-captain in India and Pakistan.

The Welshman and the Scot dubbed themselves the British Lions but, with a top score of 76 in India and 68 in Pakistan, Denness failed to cement a place, and did not feature in the six-Test summer of 1973. However, he continued to polish his CV at Kent with two more trophies and, when Illingworth was sacked after losing heavily to West Indies, the selectors asked Denness to take over for the return series in the winter.

England were beaten by seven wickets in the First Test in Trinidad, and spent the rest of the tour trying to make amends, until magnificent performances from Greig and Geoff Boycott enabled them to win a tense final Test, also at Port-of-Spain, to square the series. It was widely thought that the victory spared Denness the axe. Boycott later wrote: "Keeping Denness in a job was the worst day's work I ever did for England."

India and Pakistan at home proved more straightforward: a lacklustre India lost 3–0, with Denness making centuries at Lord's and Edgbaston, and only a wet late summer prevented an emphatic victory over Pakistan.

The squad to defend the Ashes in 1974-75 was missing Boycott, who had gone into exile, in part because of his lack of respect for the captain. And things got worse for Denness when he fell ill on the outward flight; it took three anxious weeks to diagnose and treat a kidney infection. Poorly prepared for the First Test, he was given a taste of what was to come when his first ball, from Thomson, struck his shoulder. England suffered traumatic defeats at Brisbane and Perth and, although they improved in the Third Test, Denness took the momentous decision to drop himself for the Fourth, at Sydney. He had scored 65 runs in six innings, even if he was not the only England batsman to have struggled. David Lloyd felt he had not properly recovered from his illness: "He played when he was not well enough."

Seizing any opportunity to undermine the captain, the Australians greeted him with the new nickname "Will". Lloyd explained: "It was short for 'wilderness' – because they said that's where he always was." Watching his team go out to field at Sydney was, Denness wrote, "undoubtedly the lowest moment of my life". The match was lost, and so too the Ashes. Though he returned with a half-century in the Fifth Test, it was in another losing cause. Redemption of sorts came in the Sixth, at Melbourne: Thomson was ruled out, Lillee broke down, and Denness made 188.

England gained a consolation victory, and there was another win and a big hundred soon after at Auckland. But Denness arrived home under intense scrutiny. His appointment for only the first match of the four-Test series against Australia in 1975 was hardly a vote of confidence, and he later said he regretted accepting the captaincy under such conditions. He put Australia in beneath grey Edgbaston skies, but his bowlers made little impact. When England replied, it rained after one over: on a damp pitch, they were bowled out cheaply twice.

Denness's fate had been sealed, if not by the result then by a back-page exclusive from Jim Laker in the *Daily Express* on the second morning, which revealed that the selectors had disagreed with his decision to bowl first. Furious at the leak, Denness resigned immediately. His Test career was over after 28 matches, in which he scored 1,667 runs at 39.69. He had struggled to unite the dressing-room but would have been an ideal one-day

Graham Morris

Old haunt: Mike Denness at Canterbury in 1995. He oversaw the most successful period in Kent's history.

leader, said Keith Fletcher: "If the jobs had been divided in those days he would have been excellent."

Welcomed back at Canterbury, he added another Benson and Hedges Cup and John Player League to the groaning trophy cabinet the following summer. While it was true that Kent were able to call on a formidable assembly of talent, Denness's influence was critical. "We did things that are taken for granted now, but were cutting-edge then," said all-rounder Graham Johnson. "We analysed the strengths and weaknesses of the opposition, discussed how to set fields, playing to everyone's strengths." Denness was not a man for extravagant motivational speeches: his most appreciated asset was his serenity. "He never got ruffled," said John Shepherd. Derek Pringle, a future team-mate at Essex, recalled being driven from Colchester to Blackpool by Denness, a trip that lasted seven hours because of a near-religious adherence to the speed limit. "He was the only one in the team who would have stuck to it," said Pringle.

During the summer of 1976, Denness revealed plans for a gradual handover of the captaincy to Johnson, but soon discovered that elements within the club's committee – and some in the dressing-room – wanted him to step down. After several weeks of undignified machinations, he resigned, and then announced he was leaving the club altogether. Johnson said: "Later in life I asked him about what had happened, but even then he would not tell me. He was a deeply honourable man."

Fletcher gave him a warm reception at Essex, where his experience proved important to an emerging team. "We saw him as the final cog in the machine," Fletcher said. "He was absolutely brilliant – an Essex man from the day he arrived." Denness spent four years at Chelmsford, helping the club to a first Championship in 1979.

In 1996 he became an ICC match referee, and in November 2001 was caught up in an ugly dispute during the Second Test between South Africa and India at Port Elizabeth. Denness imposed penalties on six Indian players, including Sachin Tendulkar for interfering with the ball without informing the umpires what he was doing. The punishment prompted outrage in India, and the BCCI threatened to bring their team home if Denness was not withdrawn from the Third Test. The game went ahead, but Denness was denied entry, and the ICC declared the match unofficial.

In the 1990s, to the delight of both sides, there was a rapprochement with Kent and he became cricket chairman in 2001, resigning three years later in protest at an incident at Worcester when Andrew Symonds refused to acknowledge Ed Smith's stand-in captaincy. Denness became club president in 2012 and, though far from well, he attended many county events, touring the tents at Canterbury Week. He died in his final week in office.

DIAS, SYLVESTER ALLAN SOLAMAN, who died on December 1, aged 76, was an opening bowler swift enough to earn the nickname "Typhoon" from admiring team-mates and opponents in Ceylon. He took five wickets – all current or future Test players – on his first-class debut as the Ceylon Board President's XI beat a Pakistan A touring team in August 1964. Dias played only four more first-class matches (opportunities at home were rare), but spent eight years in England, where he appeared in the northern leagues.

DIXON, GRAHAM JOHN, who died on July 27, aged 61, saw Queensland's promise develop into achievement, with seven Sheffield Shield titles and five one-day successes during his tenure as the state cricket association's chief executive from 1996. He supported the appointments as coach of John Buchanan and, later, Darren Lehmann, and drove the development of new headquarters at the Allan Border Field. Queensland Cricket chairman Jim Holding said: "We will miss his counsel, his generosity, his willingness to embrace innovation and think laterally."

DOLLERY, KEITH ROBERT, who died on August 18, aged 88, was an itinerant seamer who played two matches for his native Queensland in 1947-48, two for Auckland in 1949-50, and three for Tasmania in 1950-51, before moving to England to spend two years qualifying for Warwickshire. Once eligible, he took 74 wickets in 1953, including a hat-trick against Gloucestershire at Bristol, which gave him match figures of ten for 60. Dollery was capped the following year, after 72 more wickets, with a career-best eight for 42 against Sussex at Edgbaston – "swinging the ball in the heavy atmosphere," according to *Wisden*. He claimed another hat-trick, against Kent at Coventry in 1956, but that was his final county season. He was not related to Tom Dollery, his captain at Edgbaston.

DRUKER, KALMAN GORDON, died on June 16, aged 78. "Clem" Druker was the first president of the unified Western Province Cricket Association after South Africa's readmission. A lawyer specialising in the entertainment business, Druker had arranged the first floodlit match in Cape Town, in the late 1970s, and later helped found a cricket club – VOB Cavaliers – which welcomed players of all races.

DURITY, LEO ANTHONY, who died on May 13, aged 72, was a stalwart of Irish cricket, a stylish batsman who captained Cork County CC after moving from his native Trinidad. He also represented Munster over some 20 seasons – he was president of the Munster Cricket Union at the time of his death – and served on the board of Cricket Ireland.

ENGLAND, ERNEST JAMES, died on December 7, 2012, aged 85. England's medical studies required him to criss-cross the Nullarbor in order to study at the universities of Western Australia and Adelaide, and his sporting skills earned him selection at cricket and hockey for both states. Short and compact, he was a sound and entertaining batsman, who made a bright 102 for South Australia against Victoria in November 1951. Two years later, in his final first-class match, he made a more sedate 71 for Western Australia against his former team, adding 161 with future Test player John Rutherford.

FELLOWS-SMITH, JONATHAN PAYN, died on September 28, aged 81. Jon "Pom Pom" Fellows-Smith was a well-built all-rounder who played four Tests for South Africa on their 1960 tour of England, an ill-starred venture memorable for Geoff Griffin being no-balled for throwing at Lord's. Fellows-Smith was chosen largely because of his experience in England – he won three Oxford Blues in the 1950s, and also had a season with Northamptonshire – though he was not initially seen as a Test player. But he made a century against Essex in his first innings of the tour, then took six for 37 with his bouncy medium-pacers as Glamorgan were demolished in the last match before the First Test. "He is a most resolute character," wrote the touring South African journalist Charles Fortune. "His burly frame and square protruding jaw are outward evidence of his innate grit and determination." But Fellows-Smith did little of note in the Tests. He soon settled in England, and played only three more, scattered, first-class games – finishing with averages of 29 in batting and bowling. Back in 1957, he had made a sensational start to his brief county career, hitting 109 (with six sixes) and 65 not out against Sussex at Hove on Championship debut, and 90 in his next game, at home to Kent. His efforts helped Northamptonshire to second in the table – equalling what remains their best Championship finish – although they were never really within sight of runaway leaders Surrey. A fine all-round sportsman, Fellows-Smith was also a rugby Blue, and late in life won an age-group tennis championship at Wimbledon. He became unpopular in South Africa by writing, in *The Cricketer* in 1961, in praise of Basil D'Oliveira in a perceptive article, which concluded: "If the game can conceivably be used as a force to unite conflicting racial groups, there seems to be no reason why South African cricket should not recover from its present malaise."

FITZGERALD, JAMES FRANCIS, who died on April 21, aged 67, was a slow left-armer who played 15 matches for Cambridge University in the 1960s, winning a Blue in 1968, his final year. Almost half his career haul of 29 wickets came in his first two games, as a freshman in 1966, when he followed six for 70 on debut against Essex with seven in the match against Middlesex. Fitzgerald played a few non-first-class matches for Warwickshire in 1971, and also represented Cambridgeshire. He taught biology at Eton for 20 years, before qualifying as a solicitor.

FRANCIS, KANDIAH THIRUGNANSAMPANDAPILLAI, died on June 9, aged 73. "KT" Francis umpired in Sri Lanka's inaugural Test, against England in Colombo in

Graham Morris

Implacable: K. T. Francis is unmoved by Alan Mullally, at Harare in 1996-97.

February 1982, and went on to stand in 24 further Test matches and 56 one-day internationals. He became an early member of the ICC's international panel, before bowing out shortly after the 1999 World Cup. Against England in Colombo in March 1993, Francis gave an unamused Neil Fairbrother run out, after the bowler – who had prematurely dislodged the bails – uprooted the stumps. When a spectator remonstrated with him later, Francis took him to the pavilion and calmly showed him a copy of the Laws, which backed up his decision, then asked him to apologise.

FRANKISH, RONALD RICHARD, died on October 17, aged 88. Ron Frankish never quite fulfilled his promise for Western Australia. He made a fine century against Victoria in 1949-50, countering the mystery spin of Jack Iverson, who was creating havoc during his debut season. Frankish was adaptable, either adhesive or attacking as the situation demanded, but the scores dried up as the years passed. He was adaptable with the ball too, bowling either medium-pace or off-breaks, although his quicker one was delivered with a suspicious kink, and he was once called for throwing. He was selected in the All-Australian baseball team of 1948.

FREEMAN, DOUGLAS PERCY, who died on April 3, aged 98, was a long-serving Dorset left-hander – and a cousin of the legendary Kent and England leg-spinner "Tich", who took 304 first-class wickets in 1928. This Freeman – whose father represented Essex – played one first-class match for Kent in 1937, the year after Tich's retirement, but failed to reach double figures in either innings in a thumping defeat by Somerset at Bath, and was never selected again. He was the last surviving Kent player who appeared before the Second World War.

GERAS, NORMAN, died on October 18, aged 70. Norm Geras was an expert in Marxist thought who spent 36 years as an academic at Manchester University, latterly as professor of government. He was also a devoted cricket lover, with a huge library. These two strands of his life came together on the web when he retired in 2003 and began Normblog, an unusually successful and popular representative of the genre, in which he mixed hard-core political argument with a lot of cricket and many other enthusiasms (see Cricket and Blogs, page 165). Politically, Geras was always on the left, but he was a staunch proponent of the Iraq war. He was equally idiosyncratic in his cricket: born in Bulawayo, he spent most of his life in England, yet always supported Australia. He wrote a zestful and very personal book (with Ian Holliday) on the 1997 Ashes, and another on the 2001 series, while one of his last web postings was what he called a "bleg", asking his thousands of followers whether Australia finished the Third Test of 1881-82 on 64 for four or 66 for four (64 was right, he concluded).

GHATAK, ANUP, who died on September 26, aged 72, was a hard-working medium-pacer who played 33 matches for Assam over 13 seasons from 1963-64. He was the first to take 100 wickets for them, finishing with 120 at 22, a sterling performance in a modest team. Ghatak, who also represented East Zone in the Duleep Trophy, never improved on seven for 90 against Bihar in only his second match, at Jamshedpur in December 1963.

GIBSON, ALFRED LEWIS, died on June 28, aged 101. Fred Gibson was born in rural Jamaica, but stayed in England after serving in the RAF during the war. After some useful batting performances for Leicestershire in one-day games in 1945, he joined the staff – on £2 a week – when first-class cricket resumed the following year, but made little impression before badly breaking his arm in a car accident. Gibson was not re-engaged, but continued to play club cricket until his late fifties. An employee of Rolls-Royce, he sometimes surprised opponents by arriving in one of the company's cars – perhaps incongruously, he became a Labour councillor. In 2012 Gibson became the first Leicestershire player known to have reached 100 years of age, and when he died the only older surviving county cricketer was Cyril Perkins – who passed away himself in 2013.

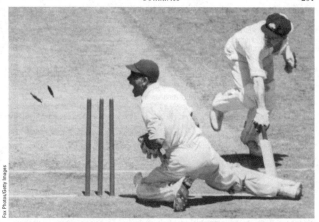

Decent shout: Sam Guillen runs out Lindsay Hassett during the New Year Test of 1951-52, though Australia beat West Indies by one wicket. Later in this game, he walked out without his bat.

GUILLEN, SIMPSON CLAIRMONTE, died on March 2, aged 88. "Sam" Guillen is the only West Indian to win Test caps for two countries. He played three in Australia and two in New Zealand on West Indies' 1951-52 tour, taking over as wicketkeeper after Clyde Walcott injured his back. He liked New Zealand so much that he emigrated there a few months later. His keeping, supplemented by useful runs for Canterbury, earned him three caps for his adopted country, satisfyingly against West Indies on their return visit early in 1956. The West Indies Cricket Board of Control raised no opposition to his selection, as they might have done for reasons of insufficient residential qualification.

"When I came out to bat all the West Indian boys gathered round, raised their caps and raised three cheers," he wrote in his autobiography, *Calypso Kiwi*. "Words can't explain how I felt." It was a rare occasion when Guillen was at a loss for words. All-rounder Gerry Gomez, a team-mate for Queen's Park, Trinidad and West Indies, described him as "a humorous and good-natured man, respected and liked as much for his happy disposition and comedy as for his considerable skill"; to Walter Hadlee, New Zealand's venerated captain who facilitated Guillen's move from Port-of-Spain to Christchurch, he was "an ebullient and ever-cheerful character [with] a fund of stories". An all-round sportsman, he was a cycling champion in Trinidad, and kept goal for Western FC in New Zealand's provincial Chatham Cup final in 1954.

It was Guillen's stumping of Alf Valentine at Auckland in March 1956 which completed New Zealand's first Test victory, after 44 attempts spread over 26 years. Surprisingly, though, this was his last act in international cricket, despite several more successful seasons for Canterbury. He seemed certain to tour England in 1958, but was omitted from the trial matches. In his autobiography he claimed that the chairman of the national selectors had told Canterbury not to select him, an instruction they ignored.

Sir Everton Weekes, team-mate then opponent in the two New Zealand series, described him as "a very good wicketkeeper, but one who thought more of his batting". His 54 at Christchurch in 1952 was his highest Test score; his three first-class hundreds were all for Canterbury. However, sent in as nightwatchman at the MCG in 1951-52, he went out to the middle without his bat, causing much mirth.

Cricket was in the Guillen family's DNA. His father, Victor, played for Trinidad and umpired England's Tests at Port-of-Spain in 1934-35 and 1947-48; his brother Noel and great-nephew Justin also represented Trinidad; and a grandson, Logan van Beek, was in the New Zealand teams for both the Under-19 World Cup and the basketball world championships. Although resident in New Zealand for 60 years, where he and his wife Val (also a wicketkeeper, at provincial level) raised a family of four, Guillen never lost his Trinidadian accent or his affection for his native island. He also belted out calypsos in a rich baritone.

HANUMANTHA RAO, S. N., who died on July 29, aged 83, was an umpire from Bangalore who stood in nine Tests between 1978-79 and 1983-84, as well as two one-day internationals. In the Test at Bombay in February 1980 which marked the golden jubilee of the Indian board, Hanumantha Rao gave Bob Taylor out caught behind – but India's captain, Gundappa Viswanath, was convinced Taylor had not touched it, and persuaded Rao to reverse his decision, a sporting gesture which arguably cost his side victory in a low-scoring game. Later, Rao gave Geoff Boycott out caught behind down the leg side off Kapil Dev, but Boycott turned his back and prepared for the next delivery. To Kapil's chagrin, Rao eventually lowered his finger.

HARRIS, RONALD GEORGE, died on February 1, aged 80. Sydney umpire "Rocky" Harris stood in a solitary international match – but it was a landmark, the first official one-day international under floodlights, between Australia and West Indies at Sydney in November 1979. He also umpired 13 first-class games, later managed New South Wales youth teams, and was in charge of the visitors' dressing-room at the SCG for 15 years until 2012. He kept his own honours board there, logging notable events on the front of a large wooden cupboard: the tradition started in 1999, when South Australia's Mark Harrity was out first ball and kicked it, whereupon Harris wrote his name on the dent.

HASEEB AHSAN, who died on March 8, aged 73, was a big-turning off-spinner with a jerky action who played 12 Tests for Pakistan. After being called for throwing in the First Test against India at Bombay in 1960-61, he took six for 202 from 84 overs in the Fourth, as India amassed 539 at Madras. Haseeb's international career ended after an early departure from Pakistan's 1962 tour of England. This was officially put down to a foot injury, but there were suggestions of a falling-out with the captain, Javed Burki – and unfavourable reports about his action.

Haseeb retired from first-class cricket shortly after, and devoted himself to a business career, in which he rose to become Pakistan International Airlines' general manager in Britain, and cricket administration. After proving an astute selector – Wasim Akram was plucked from obscurity during his tenure – he returned to England as manager of the 1987 team captained by Imran Khan. Haseeb immediately raised eyebrows by publicly demanding that David Constant and Ken Palmer be removed from the umpiring panel for the Tests, after perceived mistakes in previous matches against Pakistan. The English authorities refused, and a prickly relationship developed between them, the manager and the British press. According to Javed Miandad "it was a role he relished".

The result – Pakistan's first series victory in England – arguably vindicated Haseeb's confrontational approach. But many observers were less kind the following winter after an ill-tempered return series marred by disputes about umpiring, most memorably the dust-up between Mike Gatting and Shakoor Rana at Faisalabad. Haseeb was widely thought to be pulling the strings, appointing compliant officials in retaliation for the earlier refusal to sideline Constant and Palmer. Scyld Berry, the long-serving cricket correspondent who later edited *Wisden*, dubbed him the "Grand Vizier", and wrote: "With Byzantine skill he has worked through the complexities of his society to attain day-to-day power over the country's cricket."

Haseeb is recalled rather more fondly at home. "He casts an unexpectedly long and influential shadow over Pakistan cricket," wrote Saad Shafqat. "He will be fondly remembered as a doer, a positive thinker, a patriot, and a man of intelligence and nous who served Pakistan cricket with sincerity and impact."

HEARN, PETER, died on March 25, aged 87. When the elegant, left-handed Peter Hearn made a century on debut for Kent in 1947, he raised premature and unrealistic expectations that the county had unearthed a successor to Frank Woolley. The burden proved too much. It was not that his dream start at Gillingham's Garrison ground, against a Warwickshire attack that included the pace of Tom Pritchard and the spin of Eric Hollies, was a fluke: on his day, Hearn rivalled the most attractive batsmen in the country. But as his career progressed, those days grew infrequent.

Cricket was an inescapable part of Hearn's upbringing in a cottage on the boundary of the Nevill Ground at Tunbridge Wells, where his grandfather was the groundsman, and his father a capable all-rounder; his uncle Sidney had played for Kent in the 1920s. Peter was still in his teens when he appeared alongside Woolley for C. H. Knott's Kent XI in 1942, but any thought of a career in the game was postponed when he joined the Royal Engineers the following year. He was taken prisoner in France and, towards the end of the war he was forced on a 500-mile march as the Germans tried to keep POWs away from the Allied advance.

Hearn was still in the army when he made that century on first-class debut. Not until 1950 did he pass 1,000 runs for the first of three times. "He was a very graceful, good-looking batsman, but he was a nervous starter," said team-mate Bob Wilson. In 1953 Hearn pushed his average up to 30 and scored three hundreds; the following summer he hit 1,413 runs, including a career-best 172 against Worcestershire at Dudley, the last 72 coming in an hour. "It was a magnificent knock," Wilson recalled. "He looked so good. You thought, 'Why can't he do that all the time?'"

Hearn was released after making just three appearances in 1956, and for a time was the professional at Kirkcaldy in Scotland. He also coached at Tonbridge School, and played for Tunbridge Wells into his forties. Kent colleagues cherished the story of the manager Les Ames, furious at a batting collapse, arriving in the dressing-room to administer a lecture without noting that Hearn was not present. Ames was in full tirade when Hearn appeared insouciantly at the door: "Anyone want an ice cream?"

HOLSTROM, JOHN ERIC, who died on October 18, aged 86, was blessed with a mellifluous voice and dry wit which made him a much-loved announcer on BBC Radio Three for a number of years. A lifelong cricket-lover, he regarded a shift while *Test Match Special* was on air with relish – unlike most of his colleagues. His was often the voice listeners heard at the start and end of the day, during technical hiccoughs and, for some years, during extended rain-breaks – before the idea took root that listeners preferred to remain at the ground for the conversation of Arlott, Trueman et al. Holmstrom was also a playwright, theatre critic, translator and shopkeeper. With the writer Timothy d'Arch Smith he developed a cricket game first invented by a pair of Australian POWs in a Japanese camp, which involved two sets of playing cards and a pair of dice. It had, said a friend, rules of "fiendish complexity".

IJAZ HUSSAIN MIRZA, who died on April 7, aged 71, was a batsman and superb cover fielder who played for Karachi and National Bank in a ten-year first-class career from 1962. His only century, 123 for Karachi Blues against Bahawalpur in 1964-65, came during a seventh-wicket partnership of 155 with the future Test wicketkeeper Wasim Bari, who was only 16 at the time.

JACELON, BERTICE, died on August 13, aged 98. An umpire who stood in both Tests at the Queen's Park Oval in his native Trinidad on India's tour in 1961-62, "Bertie" Jacelon was later involved in one of the game's more bizarre fiascos. When the Barbadian Cortez Jordan was chosen to stand in the Test against Australia in Guyana in 1964-65, the local umpires' association directed the other official – Cecil Kippins, one of their members – to withdraw in protest on the eve of the match; until then, each territory had provided both umpires for Tests. Jacelon was hurriedly summoned from Trinidad as a last-minute replacement, but his flight was delayed and he failed to reach Georgetown in time. In a fix, the West Indian board, with the agreement of the Australians, turned to former Test all-rounder Gerry Gomez, by then head of the West Indies Umpires' Association. Gomez was a qualified umpire, but had never officiated in a first-class match, let alone a Test. He was also a board member and a selector and, for good measure, an end-of-play radio summariser. His first task was to order the repainting of the creases, which had been incorrectly marked. In a match West Indies won by 212 runs, the Australians were satisfied with his judgment. Kippins returned for the last two Tests, while Jacelon was never given another.

JACOBSON, Dr LOUIS COLLINS, who died on December 6, aged 95, had been Ireland's oldest surviving cricketer. He was a polished batsman and occasional wicketkeeper, who played most of his club cricket for Clontarf. In 1950 Jacobson saved the annual first-class match against Scotland by scoring 101 not out at Perth, and two years later an unbeaten 41 – out of 68 for six in the follow-on – helped Ireland draw with the Indian tourists in Belfast.

Bob Thomas/Getty Images

No airs and graces: Ted James epitomised the old-fashioned pro.

JAMES, ALBERT EDWARD, died on April 2, aged 88. A dependable seamer, Ted James was an automatic choice for Sussex almost from his debut in 1948 to his retirement a dozen years later: he played 299 first-class matches, all of them for Sussex. He took seven for 12 – from 19.3 overs – against Hampshire at Worthing in 1951, and four years later improved his career-best to nine for 60, against Yorkshire at Hove. "He was the epitome of the good old-fashioned county pro," remembered Ted Dexter, "with a sweet temperament and absolutely no airs and graces." James, who twice took 100 wickets in a season, was always economical, going for little more than two an over throughout his career. "He was one of a breed who maintained metronomic accuracy because they were not rushing through the crease," explained Dexter. "He swung the ball leg to off, starting leg stump – he always bowled with a leg slip for the one that went straight on or came back off the seam." After retirement, James coached at Eastbourne College for many years.

JENKINS, Sir MICHAEL ROMILLY HEALD, KCMG, who died on March 31, aged 77, was a high-ranking diplomat who, after a spell as British Ambassador to the Netherlands, embarked on a successful banking career with Kleinwort Benson. He had also been an influential figure at the European Commission in Brussels, and later became a tireless fundraiser for the Chelsea Royal Hospital. A lifelong cricket fan, he was treasurer of MCC in 1999-2000, and chairman in 2000-01.

JHA, AJAY, who died of a heart attack while playing golf on August 28, aged 57, was a fast-medium bowler who took 159 wickets in a long career in Indian domestic cricket, mainly for Services, after starting with Bihar. His best return was six for 76 for Services against Punjab in 1980-81. A former wing commander in the Indian Air Force, Jha was the chief administrative officer of the National Cricket Academy in Bangalore until shortly before his death, when he was removed from his post after being suspected of involvement in a fraudulent land deal.

KEATING, FRANCIS VINCENT, died on January 25, aged 75. Among the small tribe of star sportswriters who trotted the globe in the late, great days of Fleet Street, Frank Keating was perhaps the most brilliant; he was certainly the most original and the best-loved by his readers. He was a columnist on *The Guardian* for more than 40 years, though his heyday was from the mid-1970s to the mid-'90s. But his unique style – full of wit, wordplay and scintillating observation – helped revolutionise sports journalism in the posher British papers, which were still largely hidebound by public-school formality when he started.

In that sense, he played a similar role to his great *Guardian* predecessor Sir Neville Cardus half a century earlier. Like Cardus, he came to embody his newspaper's approach to sports writing. And, just like him, he took a romantic view of athletes in general and cricketers in particular which, on occasion, led him to make the journalistic pudding a touch too rich for literal-minded tastes. Unlike Cardus, he wrote on every sport, though he had little appetite for modern football, and wrote most often on cricket and rugby. But he painted best on the broad canvas offered by cricket.

Keating was born in Herefordshire, brought up in Gloucestershire (he was steeped in the lore and legends of "Glorse" cricket), and notionally educated at Catholic Douai, where he specialised in leg-spin and scrum-halfing and not much else. He evaded both national service and university, and in the 1950s began an unusually exotic wander round local papers in places as various as Slough and Salisbury in Southern Rhodesia.

He joined *The Guardian* in 1963 for a brief stint as a news sub-editor, before landing a grand-sounding job as editor, outside broadcasts, for the London ITV weekday station Associated-Rediffusion. The title disguised the fact that the channel did little outside broadcasting, an area dominated by the BBC:

Time out in paradise: Frank Keating and David Bairstow (*left*) share a game of tennis in Guyana, February 1981.

much of his work involved covering hockey, schools soccer and the like, designed not to attract audiences but to meet the legal quota for home-grown programming. His seven years in telly gave him enormous pleasure, and a rich fund of anecdotes; but, after the 1970 football World Cup, when ITV were starting to get more serious about sport, he had to retreat to *The Guardian* as a lowly sports sub.

However, an imaginative sports editor, John Samuel, spotted something and, though it took a while for the paper and Keating's penchant for what he himself called "florid flim-flam" to come to terms with each other, his startling skills soon propelled him to journalistic stardom. His descriptive power was matched by an unusual empathy with the performers, which was particularly effective in cricket. In an era when the travails of the England team led to increasing strain between press and players, Keating was adept at straddling the two sides, partly through personal charm, partly because his journalism was almost always supportive. He was able to form lasting relationships with, for instance, both his fellow hellraiser Ian Botham and the stoical Graham Gooch, and wrote books with both. One of Frank's favourite stories was of an epic night's drinking with Botham at Indore that ended with the barman falling asleep at his post. Next day, as Keating and barman recovered, the other man present hit a 50-minute century.

The quotes in Keating's interviews might not always have stood up to a tape-recorder test, but – rather than twisting their opinions – he made his subjects sound more eloquent than they really were, so hardly anyone minded. "Some people would try and force things out of you," said an admiring David Gower. "Frank would just coax it out."

Keating's masterpiece was his book on the 1980-81 England tour of the West Indies, *Another Bloody Day in Paradise!*, when he set out to write a work of semi-fiction, but found that the facts (especially the death of the coach, Ken Barrington, and the team's expulsion from Guyana) were far more dramatic. His touching and affectionate *Guardian* piece the day after Barrington died is one of his best-remembered: "He had been so hale and full of beans. So dynamite chuffed at the end of the West Indians' innings in the morning. His nose crowded out the already jammed pavilion long-room bar. His smile illuminated it…" He covered the following winter's tour of India as acting cricket correspondent. Later, his appearances at major matches would become less frequent.

He did go to Sydney in 1993 and interviewed the aged and blind Harold Larwood, tapping out his pipe on the commemorative ashtray given to him by Douglas Jardine in 1933 "for the Ashes". "I think you've just emptied your ash in my most treasured possession," said Larwood calmly. In later years Keating found more pleasure in his marriage to Jane, his children, dogs and Herefordshire domesticity than in continual travel – eventually ill health made it hard for him to leave home at all.

But he remained a prolific columnist, in magazines as well as the paper, though he ceased being an innovator and became instead a master nostalgist, disguising a sharp memory and a vast library. His huge circle of friends and admirers would trek to Herefordshire or phone, to be greeted always by his customary cheery "M'dear!" His friend and rival columnist Patrick Collins said: "He possessed the priceless knack of finding jewels where nobody had thought to look, and describing them with a brilliance which nobody could hope to rival."

KENYON, JAMES, died on September 3, aged 71. A cricketer good enough to play in the Lancashire League for around 15 years and represent the county's Second XI, Jim Kenyon was better known as a genial sports broadcaster. He was the roving reporter for a long-running BBC Radio Lancashire cricket show. "His enviable list of contacts ensured the station was never short of star guests to fill the airwaves," said his friend and colleague Mike Latham, "all comfortably within the budget, which was nil." Kenyon was also a former secretary of the Lancashire Football Association, a director of Accrington Stanley – and a serious cricket coach. "I owe my career to Jim," said Lancashire's captain Glen Chapple. "He took me to Old Trafford when I was 11."

KHALID HASAN, who died on December 3, aged 76, was only 16 when he played his solitary Test for Pakistan, at Trent Bridge in 1954. His leg-spin did account for Denis Compton, but not before he had made 278. He removed Reg Simpson too – for 101. Hasan had been a surprise choice for the tour, after only two first-class matches: the unrelated Khalid Qureishi had been tipped for selection, but his left-arm spin was similar to A. H. Kardar's, and some felt the autocratic skipper didn't want too much competition. Hasan took only 23 wickets on the tour, at 39; overall, *Wisden* felt he "appeared to bowl a little too fast, and his length and direction suffered". Hasan remains the youngest man to finish his Test career (16 years 352 days). Indeed, he played only one further first-class match, in 1958-59.

KOCH, LLOYD BOWEN, who died on April 16, aged 81, had his greatest success as a batsman for Orange Free State, in between spells for Natal and Rhodesia. In 1952-53 he extended his maiden first-class century to 216 not out for OFS against Natal in Bloemfontein, and two seasons later made 111 against Western Province. He opened for a South African XI against the touring Australians in Johannesburg in 1949-50, but was twice out cheaply in totals of 49 and 90, and was later a reserve for the 1951 South African tour of England. Koch also played hockey for South Africa and Rhodesia, whom he captained at the 1964 Tokyo Olympics, and carried the Rhodesian flag at the opening ceremony.

KRISHNA, SUNDARARAJAN, who died on July 16, aged 75, played eight Ranji Trophy matches for Mysore (now Karnataka). He scored 108 on debut, against Kerala in October 1961, and 122 in his fourth game, against Hyderabad at Bangalore in December 1962.

LAMB, GEORGE CHARLTON, died on March 15, aged 76. Newcastle-born Charlton Lamb was a fine batsman who was a regular member of Durham's Minor Counties side from 1954 to 1971. On moving south, he played for several prominent club sides, including Banstead and Beddington (both in the Surrey Championship) and some notable wandering teams, such as the Nomads and Harold Pinter's Gaieties CC, whose website remembered him as an "ex-captain of enviable experience; stylish batsman, infuriating bowler, seen-it-all-before commentator in the slips".

LANGFORD, BRIAN ANTHONY, who died on February 12, aged 77, appeared in 504 first-class matches for Somerset, more than anyone in their history. He was a patient, probing off-spinner with a placid temperament, unlucky in a golden age of finger-spinners never to play for England. Five times he took 100 wickets in a season, with a best of nine for 26 (and 15 for 54 in the match) against Lancashire at Weston-super-Mare in 1958.

His father died early, forcing him to leave grammar school in Bridgwater at the age of 15. He took work as an errand boy in the accounts department at British Cellophane, and played for the Bridgwater club, showing promise as an opening batsman and medium-pacer. Thanks to a talent competition in a local newspaper, he was taken in 1952 on to the Taunton groundstaff, where the coach Harry Parks turned him into an off-spinner. He stayed through the winter, when duties included cleaning the toilets.

In early June he was summoned to Bath for twelfth-man duties against Lancashire and, to his surprise, found himself making a county debut in a match that turned out to be the most extraordinary of his career. The turfs on the newly relaid square had not knitted together – they could be wobbled about like lumps of jelly – and Lancashire won by an innings and 24 inside a day. It was a calamity, not least for Bath-based Bertie Buse, who had selected the three-day match for his benefit.

Langford's contribution was limited to three overs, but the remaining two games of the Bath Festival made his career. The groundsman rolled bull's blood from the local abattoir into the square, and Air Vice-Marshal Taylor, the Somerset secretary, gave the 17-year-old Langford a few shillings to buy a lighter pair of boots. On a responsive surface, he bowled 131 overs and took 25 wickets for 290 runs. When the national averages next appeared, his name stood above Alec Bedser at the top.

Two years of National Service disrupted his progress, but he re-established himself in 1956, when he again found Bath to his liking, taking 28 wickets in three games. "The only way to enjoy county cricket is to be a regular in the side," he said later in life. "I was too young to know it at the time, but those games at Bath did take the pressure off."

He was a vital member of the Somerset team when, in the 1960s, they shook off their also-ran tag and finished in the top half of the Championship six years running – and as high as third in 1963 and 1966. But key players retired and, by 1969, when he was prevailed upon to take on the captaincy, they were back at rock bottom. "We don't expect you to win a game," he was told. "Try your best." They did manage one win, but finished last.

By this time he was a master craftsman with the ball, and his 88 overs in the first Sunday League season that summer went for only 222 runs. At Yeovil he set an unbeatable record, bowling his eight overs without conceding a run. Forty-over cricket was in its infancy, and Essex's Brian Ward decided Langford was the "danger man", and should be played out.

With the help of some inspired signings – Brian Close from Yorkshire, and Tom Cartwright from Warwickshire – Langford lifted Somerset in the following two summers, passing the captaincy on to Close. He retired at the end of 1972, but reappeared occasionally during the next two seasons, and finished with 1,410 wickets at less than 25 apiece. He could later say with pride that he had played alongside both Harold Gimblett and Viv Richards.

Getting them early: Brian Langford coaches his seven-year-old son Christopher, September 1970.

After retirement he stayed close to Somerset cricket, though his one year as chairman in 1986 ended with the tempestuous departure of Richards and Ian Botham, a schism which proved beyond his conciliatory nature to prevent. The episode damaged the club, but it did not damage Langford's reputation. He was too good a cricketer, and too nice a man.

LEIGH-PEMBERTON, ROBERT (latterly Lord Kingsdown), KG, PC, died on November 24, aged 86. "Robin" Leigh-Pemberton was one of Britain's most high-profile business figures, especially during his decade as Governor of the Bank of England from 1983 to 1993. He was a lifelong cricket enthusiast, and his family home – Torry Hill, a 2,500-acre estate near Sittingbourne – had its own idyllic ground where, every year during Canterbury Week, Leigh-Pemberton assembled a team to play the Old Stagers, an actors' XI. The hospitality was generous, but the host usually ensured there was enough quality in his team – often in the shape of a Cowdrey or two – to secure victory. Leigh-Pemberton played at Eton, and was president of Kent in 2002, having served as a trustee of the county for a number of years. He was chairman of NatWest when the bank succeeded Gillette as sponsors of the 60-over county knockout tournament in 1981.

LELE, JAYWANT YASHWANT, who died on September 19, six days after his 75th birthday, was the secretary of the Board of Control for Cricket in India from 1996 to 2001, after six years as joint-secretary. His tenure included the match-fixing scandal involving Hansie Cronje and the Delhi police, which broke late in 2000. An engineer and a qualified umpire who stood in ten Ranji Trophy matches in the 1980s, Lele had become the secretary of the Baroda Cricket Association in 1969. In 2003 he was expelled from the BCA for alleged financial irregularities, but was planning a return when he died. Malcolm Speed, the former ICC chief executive, called him a "lively and colourful character", and said Lele "would always make sure the relationships between cricket boards remained cordial".

LEWIS, DAVID JOHN, who died on January 19, aged 85, captained Rhodesia for ten seasons in South Africa's Currie Cup, making over 3,000 runs, including eight centuries, the highest 170 not out against North Eastern Transvaal in 1954-55. He was one of the *South African Cricket Annual's* cricketers of the year in 1956. Seasoned observers rank him alongside Duncan Fletcher as the best captain the country ever had. Lewis made his first-class debut in peculiar circumstances in March 1946, when only 18: he and another player were allowed to bat as full substitutes in the second innings against Transvaal, after injuries to others (Rhodesia lost by an innings). He studied law at Oxford, winning a Blue in 1951, before returning home to become a fixture in the national side for more than a dozen years, and later a prominent administrator. The story is still recounted at the Harare Sports Club of a game during the 1960s when, with the home side needing a draw to win the domestic club championship, Lewis was joined by the No. 11. There was plenty of time to go. "Can you count to six?" Lewis asked. "On every sixth ball you run, no matter where the ball is hit." Somehow Lewis manipulated the strike until the last over, when he pushed the final ball back to the bowler and, relieved at saving the match, tucked his bat under his arm. But the No. 11 was still counting, and hurtled down the pitch as instructed. He was run out.

LILIENTHAL, MAURICE, OAM, who died on February 15, aged 95, oversaw the birth of Sydney's Bankstown CC in 1951, and was involved in their administration for 50 years. Among the club's best-known players were Jeff Thomson and the Waugh brothers. Lilienthal managed a number of NSW sides, but his passion was cricket in the bush. In January 2001, he was awarded the Medal of the Order of Australia, for "service to sport, particularly through the New South Wales Country Committee". He pointed proudly to the likes of Mark Taylor, Glenn McGrath, Michael Bevan and Michael Slater as proof of the talent fostered by his committee.

McCORKELL, NEIL THOMAS, who died on February 28, aged 100, was a neat, unobtrusive, highly skilled wicketkeeper for Hampshire between 1932 and 1951. Unlike many of his brethren of the time, he was also a fine batsman, and would have been a strong England candidate had it not been for Les Ames. It was a measure of McCorkell's longevity that, when he made his debut as a 20-year-old at Taunton in May 1932, his captain was Lord Lionel Tennyson, and Phil Mead was at No. 4. In that first summer – "a world of wonder", he said later – opponents included Harold Larwood, Hedley Verity, Patsy Hendren and Walter Hammond.

But he was not wide-eyed for long. Hampshire's 1933 *Cricket Guide* remarked: "McCorkell has already shown that he has the right temperament for county cricket and he has a bright future." By 1935 he was opening the batting regularly, scoring two centuries in a week against Lancashire in July, and passing 1,000 runs for the first time. Next summer, with an Ashes tour approaching and Ames struggling for fitness, he was selected for the Players at Lord's. He kept tidily, but Ames recovered to take his place on the boat.

McCorkell was born near the harbour in Old Portsmouth and, after leaving school, worked at the Navy Officers' Sports Ground and played for his local church team. An impressive performance for a Portsmouth District XI against Hampshire Club and Ground earned him an invitation to join the staff in 1931, although the county's £3,000 overdraft nearly put paid to the offer. George Brown, the former England wicketkeeper, was in his forties, and Walter Livsey, who doubled as Tennyson's butler, had retired, which meant Hampshire had a vacancy behind the stumps: McCorkell swiftly filled it. And though he lost some of his prime years to the war, during which he worked as a firefighter at an aircraft factory, he returned in peacetime for another six seasons. In 1951, aged 39, he made his only double-century, 203 at Gloucester.

He retired at the end of the season, by now a senior professional and quietly passing on his wisdom to such new recruits as Jimmy Gray: "On away trips our captain Desmond

Seizing the moment: in her only Test, Marie McDonough's athleticism is caught for posterity.

Eagar would say, 'Who are you rooming with, Mac?' and he always replied, 'I'll take the nipper.'" McCorkell remained cheerfully uncomplaining when called upon to open the innings at the end of a long stint behind the stumps. Gray remembered: "He'd say, 'Well I've seen it all day, so I'm the ideal chap for the job.'"

McCorkell made 396 first-class appearances, scoring 16,106 runs at 25, including 17 hundreds, and passing 1,000 runs nine times. He took 532 catches and made 185 stumpings (512 and 177 for Hampshire, a county record until it was surpassed by Bobby Parks). Thus a career that began with Mead and Tennyson ended alongside Colin Ingleby-Mackenzie and Derek Shackleton, key figures in Hampshire's first title-winning year, in 1961.

He moved to South Africa, where he lived until he died, and was cricket coach for more than 30 years at Parktown Boys' High School in Johannesburg; the ground there is named after him. At the time of his death he was the second-oldest surviving county cricketer. McCorkell made just one overseas tour, to India with Lord Tennyson's XI in 1937-38. He had no great success on the field, but the trip produced one much-quoted incident when McCorkell joined his captain on a tiger shoot and, alarmed at his inaccuracy, exclaimed: "Good Lord, you've shot the bloody goat."

McDONOUGH, MARIE, who died on October 18, aged 95, captained Western Australia for three seasons in the mid-1950s. In 1957-58, when 40, she played in the first Test staged at the WACA – but Una Paisley, Australia's captain, chose not to use McDonough's left-arm medium-pacers, despite asking six others to plough through more than 220 overs. Later Australia declared before McDonough batted, but her contribution to the match is preserved in a photograph of a spectacular one-handed catch at silly mid-on from the bowling of Betty Wilson. A schoolteacher, she took an active part in developing girls' sport.

McMAHON, NOEL ALBERT, died on June 9, aged 97. A leg-spinner who made two appearances for Auckland in the late 1930s, McMahon played one further first-class match – an unofficial Test against an Australian team, at Dunedin in March 1950. His selection came shortly after he made 102 for Waikato in a two-day game against the tourists. "I hit the greatest six of my life, back over Alan Davidson's head," he recalled. But at Dunedin

McMahon was out cheaply twice – bowled both times by Jack Iverson – and upset his captain Walter Hadlee by arriving only minutes before the start.

MANDELA, NELSON ROLIHLAHLA, who died on December 5, aged 95, fully understood the role sport could play in the new South Africa – especially cricket and rugby, traditionally the games played and watched by whites. After the end of apartheid, South Africa returned to international competition with a one-day series in India in late 1991, the first time the countries had met. But there had been no thought that South Africa would play in the 1992 World Cup in Australia and New Zealand until the question was put to Mandela by a journalist at a meeting with Ali Bacher and the visiting Clive Lloyd. "Of course we must play," Mandela said. And so South Africa did, reaching the semi-finals.

Mandela did not claim to be a cricket lover, but he attended some matches and met visiting teams, most famously when his helicopter landed unannounced on the outfield of the Soweto Cricket Oval, where England were playing an Invitation XI in the third match of their first post-apartheid tour, in 1995-96. Going down the line of players, he stopped at Devon Malcolm. "Ah, I know you," he said. "You are the destroyer," a reference to Malcolm's nine-wicket whirlwind against South Africa at The Oval 14 months earlier.

Malcolm's tour went downhill, with coach Ray Illingworth claiming he had found it hard to cope with the attention. Nor did the furore escape Mandela. When he made his first state visit to Britain, in July 1996, Malcolm was invited to a Downing Street lunch, with

The destroyer, I presume: Nelson Mandela meets Devon Malcolm, October 1995.

Derbyshire granting him permission to miss their NatWest Trophy match against Kent. Malcolm recalled: "When I was introduced to Mr Mandela he said, 'Ah, Devon. If Derbyshire lose today, make sure I get the blame this time.'" They won by two wickets.

MARTIN-JENKINS, CHRISTOPHER DENNIS ALEXANDER, MBE, died in the early hours of January 1, aged 67. In cricket, he was universally just CMJ, initials that became almost as synonymous with the game as lbw or MCC. For someone who never played at first-class level, his list of achievements was unmatchable: editor of *The Cricketer*, cricket correspondent of the BBC (twice), the *Daily Telegraph* and *The Times* and, ultimately, president of MCC – an honour that had eluded even his mentor, E. W. Swanton.

However, he will be best remembered as a radio commentator. Mellifluous, eloquent and with a wonderful eye for the game – though without the individualistic brilliance of John Arlott or Brian Johnston – CMJ was, for 40 of *Test Match Special's* first 57 years, the calm-sounding straight man at the heart of the programme. There has probably never been a more reliable broadcaster on cricket: he could spot the telling detail, and grasp the wider context; he took the game very seriously, but never lost sight of its humour. The calmness was deceptive, since there was a comically chaotic side to his character. It was part of his charm.

Martin-Jenkins was born in Peterborough, the middle of three sons; his father was chairman of the big shipping firm, Ellerman Lines. As a boy, he was engrossed not merely by cricket, but by cricket commentary, and the garden games took place amid the background noise of his descriptions. While at Marlborough College he even wrote to Johnston to tell him of his ambitions. Characteristically, Johnston invited him to lunch, and encouraged him to keep practising. (Later, CMJ would always strive to be just as helpful to aspiring youngsters himself.)

At the heart of the game, with the game at his heart: CMJ at Shenley, 2008.

Philip Brown

As a player he captained Marlborough at Lord's against Rugby, scoring 99 in the second innings as the batting collapsed around him. It was not his last on-field disappointment. Though he captained his Cambridge college, Fitzwilliam, he failed to get a game for the university. But when he graduated he was taken under the Swanton wing, and became his assistant at *The Cricketer*.

The ride to fame was sometimes bumpy. His first major article – "In Defence of Professionalism" – was too radical for Swanton, and printed only with an editorial disclaimer that it did not reflect the magazine's views. He moved on to the BBC sports room, where he crossed swords with both the formidable boss of *Sports Report*, Angus Mackay, who tried to make him change his name to Chris Jenkins, and the equally irascible Don Mosey, who lost out to the 28-year-old whippersnapper when Johnston retired as cricket correspondent in 1973.

CMJ had made his *TMS* debut the previous year and, once established, never looked back. His career followed an unusual path as he tried to balance his love of the game with the need of a growing family for both his presence and a decent income. He left the BBC staff in 1981 (which allowed Mosey a short pre-retirement stint as No. 1) and went back to *The Cricketer* as editor, while continuing his commentaries. Three years later he became BBC correspondent again, and then in 1991 moved into the Swanton role at the *Telegraph*, where he stayed for eight years before – after much prevarication – accepting the blandishments of *The Times*.

In fact (like Arlott) Martin-Jenkins was not a great cricket writer: his match reports were highly competent, even elegant, but he was neither an electrifying phrase-maker nor opinionated enough to be truly Swantonian. However, he was famous enough to make his name an adornment to the sports pages, and had enough connections to turn in a regular supply of medium-level exclusives, especially on stories emanating from Lord's. And his firm but unfusty insistence on the best traditions of the game struck a chord with his readers, as did his insistence that his Test reports should be backed up by full county coverage: on both his newspapers this withered after he left.

He was also not a natural on his excursions into television, which included the 1981 Headingley Test: listeners enchanted by his voice may have been slightly startled by his gangly body and unclassical features. But he was perfect for radio, with an instinct for striking the right tone and – now and again – plucking an arresting phrase, apparently from nowhere. When Graham Onions appeared in the Test team, CMJ described his thin face as "rather medieval", which was not at all unkind, and just so. He was also a hugely popular after-dinner speaker, with a talent for mimicry and jokes that always erred on the side of good taste.

His private life was a happy one: his solid marriage to Judy produced a daughter and two sons, all with the family's exquisite manners and gifted at sport: James won a golfing blue, and his younger son Robin enjoyed a career as an all-rounder with Sussex. Christopher himself played high-standard club cricket whenever work allowed, opening the batting for Sir Paul Getty's XI at Wormsley when he was 61, and was an obsessional golfer. Playing with him on tour, recalled John Woodcock, "he would produce a couple of strokes so good that they would have brought forth roars of applause at a Ryder Cup, only to hit the next, or the next but one, far among the eucalyptus".

He would greet adversity of all kinds with swearwords of his own invention: "Oh, Captain Carruthers!... Fish cakes and buttercup pie!... Bishan Singh Bedi!... Billingsgate Harbour!... Schubert!... Fotherington-Thomas!" Most of his troubles (aside from rabbits on his lawn, which drove him to real bad language) came through his traumatic relationship with technology. His inability to make computers work was a regular source of press-box hilarity. The most famous story, about the time he tried to call the *Telegraph* on a TV remote control, has attained the status of a Fred Trueman yarn, and there are many versions, though the definitive one appears to be Mike Selvey's. It happened in Jamaica, on England's 1997-98 tour, when they were driving from Montego Bay to Kingston; CMJ had left his phone, neatly, on top of his hotel TV. His colleagues called him "The Major", after the absent-minded *Fawlty Towers* character. These misadventures were nearly always regarded fondly, though not necessarily by fellow commentators forced to do unpaid overtime because he was late.

In 2010, John Barclay nominated CMJ to succeed him as MCC president. The role should have crowned his career, especially as it included England's first Ashes triumph in Australia in 24 years. But it turned into a difficult term: he was drawn into the vituperative internal arguments over the redevelopment of Lord's, which gave him far more anxiety than he expected or deserved. It was a year that really needed a more combative president. Perhaps by then he was already ill, though his cancer was not diagnosed until early 2012, after he had commentated on England's series against Pakistan in the Gulf. His last year was a cruel one, though he was sustained by his family and his quiet but profound Anglican faith. And his early death was cruel to the whole game: an enormous database of cricketing knowledge and wisdom had disappeared.

Martin-Jenkins chose the hymns for his own memorial service. What he could not have known was that it would take place in St Paul's Cathedral and certainly not that the following day the cathedral would be the centre of global attention for Margaret Thatcher's funeral. One of the handful who attended both said that the service for CMJ was better-judged and more moving. It was an appropriate tribute to a man who inspired affection from everyone within the cricketing family, and from millions who never met him.

MATTHEWS, BRETT ANTHONY, died on January 31, aged 50, after a car accident earlier in the month. A left-arm seamer who took 120 wickets in a six-year career for three South African provincial sides, Matthews had a best return of five for 32 for Western Province B against Transvaal B in 1985-86. Just before that he had taken seven wickets in the match as South African Universities almost upset the unofficial Australian touring team led by Kim Hughes at Port Elizabeth. His younger brother, Craig Matthews, was a seam bowler for South Africa in the 1990s.

MAYERS, VINCENT, who died on December 5, aged 79, was a diminutive batsman whose appearances for his native Guyana were restricted by a stellar batting order, which often included Roy Fredericks, Steve Camacho, Rohan Kanhai, Clive Lloyd, Basil Butcher and Joe Solomon. When Mayers finally got a chance, against the touring Australians at Bourda in 1964-65, he top-scored with 51. But there were only five other first-class opportunities, and he eventually emigrated to the United States – and represented them in the annual match against Canada in 1976.

MAYES, RICHARD, died on July 10, aged 90. Dicky Mayes was part of a generation of cricketers whose entry into the first-class game was delayed by the war. He joined Kent in 1939 as a leg-spinner, but was not given his debut in that final peacetime summer. By the time he returned to Canterbury from active service in North Africa, he had become a batsman – a result, he explained, of the pitches he encountered in Egypt. He finally made his first appearance in 1947, against Northamptonshire at Gravesend; establishing an unfortunate pattern, he was out for nought. In all, he made 23 ducks, though sometimes his batting came off: in 1952 he made 934 runs, including a career-best 134 against Sussex at Tunbridge Wells. But Mayes was released a year later after 80 appearances in six seasons. "He was a shy chap and not very confident in his own ability," said team-mate Derek Ufton. "He was a bad starter – eventually there were more noughts than bigger scores." Mayes played for Suffolk, and became coach and groundsman at Woolverstone Hall School, where Graham Barlow of Middlesex and England, and the rugby player Martin Offiah, were among his pupils.

MAZHARUL HAQUE, MOHAMMAD CHOWDHURI, died of a suspected heart attack while playing badminton in Dhaka on April 3, aged 32. He was a batsman who played a solitary one-day international, against Australia in the Champions Trophy in Sri Lanka in September 2002, when his dismissal for three reduced Bangladesh to 13 for four. A powerful player, particularly strong square of the wicket, Mazharul hit 171 for Dhaka against Barisal in January 2002. He later worked as the Bangladesh board's tournament manager.

MILLARD, ANTHONY MARIO GLANVILLE, died on August 23, aged 74. Tony Millard was a versatile broadcaster, not only on football – where he was known as the "Voice of the Albion" in Brighton – but speedway, which he covered for Sky Sports, and cricket too. He was a co-founder of the Sussex Cricket League in 1970, and was still umpiring in it when he died.

MILLICAN, JOHN HAROLD, died on September 2, aged 91. Harold Millican was connected to Cumberland cricket for more than 50 years, first as a player in 1951, then as captain, chairman and president (1993–2003). A medium-pacer who could also bowl off-breaks, Millican took 120 wickets in 89 Minor Counties Championship matches. He was also a handy left-handed batsman, good enough to score 56 and 52 against a touring South Australian team on his home ground in Penrith, in 1956.

MITTER, KALYAN, who died on August 16, aged 77, was an all-rounder who had a long career in Indian domestic cricket, mainly for Bengal. He made an undefeated 126, his only century, during a big stand with Test opener Pankaj Roy against Assam at Calcutta in December 1957. His best bowling figures of five for 39 came in his final first-class match, for Bihar against Orissa in 1968-69. Bengal reached the Ranji Trophy final twice during Mitter's playing career, but lost both to Bombay, who won the tournament 15 years running around this time. Later, Mitter coached Bengal to the 1993-94 final, where they lost to Bombay again. His brother Jyotish also played for Bengal.

MOHAN RAI, B. R., who died on November 4, aged 80, was a fast bowler who played 24 first-class matches, mostly for Madras, although he also made two appearances for an Indian XI against Ceylon in 1956-57, his second season. At a time when India's pace resources were thin, Rai was unlucky not to win an official Test cap: some, including captain Polly Umrigar, briefly rated him the quickest bowler in the country. He had a good swinging yorker, but was not a prolific wicket-taker, never managing a first-class five-for.

MORTIMER, JOHN GERALD, died on December 30, aged 77. For those new to cricket writing, the Derbyshire press box was the Becher's Brook of the county circuit. Its regulars were wary of newcomers and suffered fools not at all. One test might involve floating some bizarre piece of misinformation into the air to see if a greenhorn put it into print. Most of those who survived Derby's initiation rites came to love its wit and wisdom. At the heart of it all was a figure with the air of an old-fashioned bachelor housemaster, which is precisely what Gerald Mortimer was before he began his 32 years as cricket and football correspondent of the *Derby Evening Telegraph*. Mortimer was an improbable figure – from an ungrand Derbyshire background, yet educated at Repton and Oxford. He appeared destined for a headship before, aged 34, he left teaching for local journalism.

And so, from 1970 until his retirement in 2002, he was at the heart of Derbyshire sport, for some years as the paper's sports editor as well. He continued writing for it until the year he died, and was *Wisden's* Derbyshire correspondent from 1983 to 2010. For a while Mortimer provided football reports for *The Times* under the name Gerald Richmond. Working for a posh national would have been a more obvious fit, but Derby County were league champions twice in his first five years, under Brian Clough. Even when they were losing, both football and cricket clubs had a glorious penchant for intrigue and ructions. He revelled in it all, as indicated by the title of his well-written memoir *Are the Fixtures Out?* and achieved great respect in Derby: Clough even asked him to type his resignation letter.

He was softer than his sometimes forbidding shell suggested, and cried when Derbyshire won the 1981 NatWest Trophy. It was hard to imagine his tears, and easy to think of him, with his owlish look, sardonic humour and seen-it-all manner, as county cricket's Horace Rumpole. Christopher Martin-Jenkins revealed in his autobiography that Gerald was in fact the brother of Rumpole's creator, John Mortimer, which was an astonishing scoop. Too astonishing, since Mortimer J. was an only child. "Ah," said one journalist, "I think CMJ might have been the unintended victim of a Derby press-box jape."

MUNAWWAR ALI KHAN, who died on October 21, aged 88, was a tall swing bowler who played three unofficial internationals before Pakistan were elevated to Test status in 1952. Against West Indies at Lahore in 1948-49, his four wickets included Clyde Walcott and John Goddard, the captain. But Munawwar's employers, a shipping company, would not allow him leave for long tours, so he missed out on Pakistan's inaugural Test series, in India in 1952-53, and the trip to England in 1954.

MUNIR HOSSAIN, who died on July 29, aged 83, was a journalist and broadcaster on Pakistan cricket, who helped popularise commentary in Urdu, and did much good work for the Karachi City Cricket Association. Munir played one first-class match, captaining Kalat (a smallish town in Balochistan) in their inaugural fixture, against Quetta in Pakistan's Quaid-e-Azam Trophy in August 1969. A handy swing bowler, he took two for 64 in an innings defeat. He missed their next match, a week later: Kalat lost that by an innings and 296, and have not played another first-class game since.

MUNRO, JOHN KNOX EWING, who died on August 16, aged 84, was tall for a wicketkeeper – over six feet – but his athleticism allowed him to make the job look elegantly easy. He kept for Western Australia from the early to mid-1950s, his work drawing an appreciative comment from Alec Bedser, who compared him in build and style to Australia's Don Tallon: "He is tall and slim and able to use his good reach to swoop on low balls and yet fly high for kickers." Munro was also a good enough batsman to open in his first two state matches. And against New South Wales in 1950-51, WA's captain Keith Carmody, a master of lateral thinking, called on Munro to open the bowling in the absence of the injured Harry Price because of what Carmody had seen in the nets. Six overs of respectable medium-pace produced the wicket of Sid Carroll (a batsman who came close to Test selection), before Munro went back behind the stumps. He was also a talented Australian Rules footballer, but his career as a civil engineer caused his retirement from sport by the time he was 30.

NAUMAN SHABBIR, who died on October 22, aged 59, was a batsman and occasional off-spinner who played 34 first-class matches in Pakistan, mainly for Habib Bank. His highest score of 77 came after they had slumped to 50 for six against Muslim Commercial Bank at Rawalpindi in December 1984; Nauman then took a career-best three for ten as MCB slipped to defeat.

Peter O'Toole in 1991.

O'TOOLE, SEAMUS PETER, who died on December 14, aged 81, maintained a long and often eccentric tradition of actors with a passion for cricket. It was a love affair that began during his northern childhood, continued in games for Lazarusians CC (of which he was the founder), and carried on later in life when he coached youngsters at Brondesbury and Cricklewood cricket clubs with unaffected enthusiasm. Thanks to his friendship with MCC head coach Don Wilson, he was a regular visitor to the nets at Lord's, once gleefully facing an over from Imran Khan at full tilt.

Peter O'Toole grew up in Leeds, and recalled sitting in packed pre-war cinemas cheering newsreel footage of Len Hutton's 364 in 1938; Hutton became his first cricket idol. He would seize any opportunity to introduce cricket to film sets, improvising games with Omar Sharif in the desert while filming *Lawrence of Arabia*, and teaching the basics to Katharine Hepburn during the making of *The Lion in Winter*.

He was frank about his own limitations as a batsman and off-spinner: "I have a delivery which is really, really special. It does absolutely nothing." But, when he had a son at the age of 50, he took coaching qualifications. "The only thing I've ever been interested in teaching anyone in life is cricket," he said in his final interview.

PALMER, ANNE, who died on July 9, 2006, aged 91, was a key figure in the inaugural women's Test series in 1934-35, forming an effective spin duo with Peggy Antonio. They practised and played together in Melbourne, and Antonio's leg-spin complemented Palmer's accurate off-breaks so well that they took 22 of the 33 English wickets which fell to bowlers in the three Tests. Palmer showed all her skills in the opening match at Brisbane's Exhibition Ground, with seven for 18 from 13.2 overs. In the Third (and final) Test, at Melbourne, she made an important contribution as Australia forced a draw after two comprehensive defeats. First she made a forthright 39 from No. 10 to limit Australia's deficit to 12, then took three quick wickets which held up England's quest for swift runs. Palmer was unable to raise the fare to make the 1937 tour of England, and played no more cricket. Instead, her appointment as Victoria's first female police officer set her on a lifetime career, although many younger women cricketers in Melbourne benefited from her gentle but perceptive advice. Palmer died in 2006 but, as she had no close relatives, her passing was not immediately noticed by the cricket community.

PANDIT, MADHAVAN BALAN, died on June 5, aged 86. Balan Pandit had a long career in Indian domestic cricket, mainly for Kerala, whom he captained; a stylish batsman, he played his last match in 1969-70, when he was 43. He scored four centuries, all for Kerala and all against Andhra, the highest 262 not out at Palakkad in 1959-60, when he and George Abraham shared a stand of 410.

Pioneer: Anne Palmer was awarded her Test cap in 2004 in Melbourne, almost 70 years after playing in the first women's Test.

Pandit's early first-class matches were for Kathiawar, and he was their wicketkeeper in the 1948-49 match in which Maharashtra's Bhausaheb Nimbalkar was stranded on 443 not out – nine short of the first-class record at the time, held by Don Bradman – when the Kathiawar team refused to continue.

PERKINS, GEORGE CYRIL, who died on November 21, aged 102, was at the time of his death the oldest English first-class cricketer, and one of a diminishing number who played before the Second World War. Perkins, always known as Cyril, was a left-arm spinner who made 56 appearances for Northamptonshire between 1934 and 1937, and achieved the unwanted distinction of never playing on the winning side. It was an English record which he bore with equanimity, and he went on to have a long career with Suffolk.

Perkins arrived at Wantage Road from Wollaston, brought along by coach Ben Bellamy, who also hailed from the village. A right-handed batsman, he initially bowled left-arm seam, but soon switched to spin. He made his debut in a nine-wicket defeat by Middlesex at Lord's, a result which set the tone for his career: Northamptonshire would finish bottom of the Championship in each of his four summers. "We did get a bit despondent at times," he told the *Daily Telegraph* on his 100th birthday. "We had a first-innings lead in quite a few matches and didn't win any of them. But in the end you get so used to not winning you just accept it."

THE LONGEST-LIVED FIRST-CLASS CRICKETERS

Years	Days		Died
103	344	J. M. Hutchinson (Derbyshire)	2000
103	148	S. W. Ward (Wellington)	2010
102	253	R. de Smidt (Western Province)	1986
102	247	E. A. English (Hampshire)	1966
102	**170**	**G. C. Perkins (Northamptonshire)**	**2013**
102	101	J. Wheatley (Canterbury)	1962

Norman Gordon (Transvaal and South Africa), born August 6, 1911, was 102 years 148 days old on January 1, 2014.

One of those squandered positions came at Northampton in July 1935, when Perkins took a career-best six for 54 as Worcestershire were dismissed for 93. Northamptonshire had a first-innings lead of 78 – and lost by 30 runs. That was his best summer, with 63 wickets, but it was followed by two barren seasons. He was released in 1937, and joined Suffolk two years later, taking ten wickets on debut, against Lincolnshire.

He served in the Royal Artillery during the war, then became cricket coach and groundsman at Ipswich School, a position he held until 1977. Perkins resumed his career with Suffolk in 1946, and 46 wickets at seven apiece – the product of accuracy rather than turn – to bowl them to their first Minor Counties Championship. Against Hertfordshire at Felixstowe in 1960, he exploited a damp patch to claim ten for 23 in the second innings.

Perkins retired aged 56 in 1967 after taking 779 wickets, a Suffolk record. He was selected in the Minor Counties team of the century in 1999. When he celebrated his 100th birthday in 2011, there were many tributes, but affectionate letters from former pupils pleased him most. Suffolk's chairman Norman Atkins said: "If anybody wanted a definition of the spirit of cricket, it was Cyril Perkins."

PERTWEE, WILLIAM DESMOND ANTHONY, MBE, died on May 27, aged 86. The comic actor Bill Pertwee did not achieve his schoolboy dream of becoming a professional cricketer, but he did once captain a team that included Fred Trueman. In 1970, Trueman appeared in an episode of *Dad's Army*, the sitcom in which Pertwee earned fame as Hodges, the belligerent air-raid warden. Hodges challenges Captain Mainwaring's Home Guard, his despised rivals, to a cricket match, and covertly recruits "E. C. Egan", played by Trueman, to the wardens' team. With Hodges keeping wicket – and ill-advisedly standing up – Egan marks his full run, bowls one ball which leaves Mainwaring grovelling on the floor, and puts his shoulder out in the process. The Home Guard go on to win and, yet again, Hodges' attempt to get one over on Mainwaring fails. In his autobiography, *A Funny Way to Make a Living*, he detailed his youthful obsession with the game, and his thwarted playing ambitions. But he did inveigle his way into the 1946 Indian touring party as a baggage-handler.

The last laugh? Bill Pertwee (*centre, in cap*) and the cast of *Dad's Army*, with Fred Trueman, 1970.

Evening Standard/Hulton Archive/Getty Images

POCOCK, ANTHONY JOHN, died on February 27, aged 65. Tony Pocock was the head groundsman at Fenner's for 17 years from 1980. He enjoyed his time at Cambridge – "He really loved his job, and worked at it noon and night," said his twin brother Michael – but eventually took early retirement, after a bout of depression caused by criticism of the pitches (which Pocock maintained were difficult to roll). His predecessor, Cyril Coote, did the job for 44 years, and the man before him, Walter Watts, for 48.

PONNADURAI, SELLIAH, who died on August 15, aged 78, was an umpire from Jaffna who stood in three Tests. The first, against India at Colombo's P. Saravanamuttu Stadium in September 1985, resulted in Sri Lanka's first victory, at their 14th attempt. Piyadasa Vidanagamage, the other umpire in that game, died a few days later. Ponnadurai, who also officiated in eight one-day internationals, had a 20-year career as a first-class umpire.

RANDALL, DARRYN, died after being struck while batting during a league game at Alice in South Africa's Eastern Cape on October 27. He was 32. Randall, who was wearing a helmet, was hit on the side of the head after missing a pull. He collapsed, and could not be revived. Late in 2009 he had kept wicket in four first-class matches for Border, scoring 46 against Western Province.

REGE, MADHUSUDAN RAMACHANDRA, who died on December 16, aged 89, was a batsman who won one Test cap for India, against West Indies at Madras in 1948-49. Opening with Mushtaq Ali, Rege made 15 and nought as India lost by an innings, and was never selected again. His first innings lasted 90 minutes, and was ended by fast bowler Prior Jones. Jeff Stollmeyer, West Indies' vice-captain, observed: "Rege, seeking refuge outside the off stump, had his leg peg knocked out of the ground." But Rege remained a heavy scorer in domestic cricket, mainly for Maharashtra: four of his six centuries came for them. That included a valiant performance in the 1948-49 Ranji Trophy semi-final against Bombay at Poona. He scored 133 in Maharashtra's first innings but, already 244 ahead, Bombay batted on and on in a timeless match, eventually declaring at 714 for eight: Rege made a round 100 in the second innings as his side reached 604 – and lost by 354 runs. He was also a useful off-spinner, who once took five for 23 against Baroda.

RICHARDS, GEOFFREY ALAN, died on December 27, aged 91. Alan Richards was a long-serving commentator on many sports, particularly cricket: he covered New Zealand's four Test tours of England between 1973 and 1986, when he worked on *Test Match Special*. He was also on the air for Trevor Chappell's underarm delivery at the end of a one-day international between Australia and New Zealand at Melbourne in February 1981. Richards played five first-class matches in 1955-56, captaining Auckland in all of them, and scored 53 not out against the touring West Indians, for whom Sonny Ramadhin and Alf Valentine shared seven wickets. Later that summer he was behind the microphone when New Zealand won their first Test match, also at Eden Park.

ROBERTS, Sir DENYS TUDOR EMIL, who died on May 19, aged 90, was a left-field choice as president of MCC in 1989-90, since he had not previously served on their committee. But he proved a capable and good-natured figurehead, still fondly remembered at Lord's. He had been a handy schoolboy cricketer – *Wisden 1940* reported that, in a year when Aldenham's batting "was not sound", only Roberts was "anything like reliable" – but missed out on a Blue at Oxford. After university he wrote several novels, and began a legal career from which he retired as the last non-Chinese Chief Justice of Hong Kong.

ROBINS, DONNELL, died on December 8, aged 79. Donn Robins was finally given a chance at first-class level in 1964-65 aged 30, after 13 years of grade cricket in Adelaide. Accurate and able to move the ball in the air and off the pitch at a decent pace, he took five for 60 on debut against Western Australia at Adelaide. Next season he excelled against New South Wales, with six-wicket hauls at Adelaide and Sydney. He took four in four balls in the first of those matches, although the feat went unrecorded for many years: Robins finished NSW's first innings with a hat-trick, then dismissed Bob Simpson with the first ball of the follow-on. The only other instance of this in Australia was by NSW's Hal Hooker in 1928-29. However, one of the scorers had fallen ill shortly before the end of NSW's first innings, and the other, Tom Harry, was left to maintain both scorebooks. In the rush, Simpson's wicket was erroneously entered as falling to the fifth ball of the second innings, not its first. In 1999 Robins raised the issue with the Adelaide cricket historian Bernard Whimpress – through Harry, who admitted the possibility of a mistake. The evidence Whimpress collected – the vivid memories of the bowler, wicketkeeper Barry Jarman (who took the catch) and first slip Ian Chappell, plus a local-paper article mentioning the feat – confirmed the achievement.

ROBINSON, PAUL ANDREW, who died on August 6, aged 57, was a tall fast bowler, nicknamed "Long John", who played 33 first-class matches in his native South Africa – and one for Lancashire, in 1979, when he opened the bowling against Kent at Maidstone, dismissing Paul Downton and Graham Dilley. He also took three wickets in the accompanying Sunday League game. At home, his best figures were six for 46 for Northern Transvaal against Natal at Durban in 1983-84, when his victims included another England Test player, Geoff Miller. Robinson also played for Cheshire, and Cleckheaton in the Bradford League.

RUTHERFORD, JOHN ROBERT FULTON, who died on December 25, aged 78, played 11 matches for Cambridge University in 1957 and 1958 without winning a Blue, at a time when the Varsity sides were strong. A medium-pacer from Kent, he took only ten first-class wickets, five of them in the game against Worcestershire in May 1957; in the next match, against the West Indian tourists, he dismissed Clyde Walcott for 86.

Chat, mischief and guffaws: a press box with Dicky Rutnagur was never dull.

RUTNAGUR, DICKY JAMSHED SOHRAB, who died on June 20, aged 82, was one of the most durable, knowledgeable and travelled of all cricket writers. A Bombay Parsi, Rutnagur began to forge a reputation in India in the 1950s as a writer and commentator on cricket, badminton and squash. Encouraged by the wandering scribe Ron Roberts, he moved to England to join the *Daily Telegraph's* team of county cricket reporters, and between 1966 and 2005 his pieces, under the name D. J. Rutnagur, appeared in the paper thousands of times. Out of season, he would travel the world to freelance on Test matches, disguised under names such as Dilip Rao. His *Telegraph* copy, like his byline, was unadorned, fitting perfectly the paper's old insistence on plain facts. The restrictions largely deprived readers of his excellent cricketing judgment. In person, he was never bland: a press box with Dicky in it was always full of cigarette smoke, chat and mischief, with whisky afterwards. There would be fits of rather comic irritability, directed at "the bloody subs" or the copy-takers – or simply bad cricket. Though the annoyance would soon dissolve into guffaws, he took the game seriously and expected it to be played correctly and well. His son Richard appeared for Oxford in the 1985 and 1986 Varsity matches.

RYAN, MAURICE LLOYD, who died on August 12, 2011, aged 68, was an accomplished batsman, astute captain, handy off-spinner and useful stand-in wicketkeeper who came close to selection for New Zealand. Although he had three seasons with Central Districts

– and made his maiden century for them against Otago in 1968-69, when he shared a big stand with Bevan Congdon – Ryan was more associated with Canterbury. He scored two hundreds in a week in January 1971, including a career-best 129 against Auckland, and made more than 2,000 runs for them in all. His versatility made him a useful one-day performer, and he played for a New Zealand XI that took part in Australia's domestic one-day competition in 1971-72, catching Bill Lawry off the young Richard Hadlee. He was later chairman of the Canterbury Cricket Association, before resigning in 2001 and moving to Sydney, where he died ten years later.

SALIM PERVEZ died on April 24, aged 65, of injuries received in a motorcycle accident in Lahore. He had a successful career in Pakistan, scoring more than 8,000 runs with 16 centuries, the highest 226 not out for National Bank against Quetta in 1978-79. "Paijee" was often tantalisingly close to Pakistan selection, but in fact played just a solitary one-day international, against West Indies at Lahore in 1980-81 – and might have wished he had missed it, as he was sent in first against Sylvester Clarke and Colin Croft, with Joel Garner and Malcolm Marshall to come. Still, he made 18 in an opening stand of 44, and was unlucky not to play again, particularly in 1982-83, when he passed 1,000 runs in the home season. Pervez was later involved in the match-fixing scandals that engulfed Pakistan cricket in the late 1990s. After allegations that he had acted as a go-between for bookies and players, he was summoned to appear before the 1998 Qayyum Inquiry. He testified that he had given money to several cricketers, notably $US100,000 to Salim Malik and Mushtaq Ahmed during a one-day tournament in Sri Lanka in 1994, an allegation both players denied. However, Qayyum concluded, "this commission on the whole believes Salim Pervez".

SANTOSH LAL, who died of pancreatitis on July 17, aged 29, was an all-rounder for Jharkhand (formerly Bihar), scoring 63 against Tripura in December 2006. But his greatest legacy was the whirling helicopter shot later perfected by Mahendra Singh Dhoni, a state team-mate. On hearing of Lal's illness, Dhoni – a friend since childhood – arranged for him to be airlifted from Ranchi to Delhi for specialist treatment, but it was too late.

SHAH, Dr SYED MOHAMMAD ALI, who died on February 4, aged 67, was a Karachi orthopaedic surgeon, and part-time cricket commentator for Pakistan TV and radio, in English and Urdu. He built the Asghar Ali Shah Stadium in the north of Karachi – a fully equipped and floodlit ground, named after his father, which has now staged several first-class matches (Umar Akmal scored 248 there in December 2007). He received awards from the government for his services to sport and medicine, and was Sind's sports minister from 2011 to 2013.

SHAHID ISRAR, who died on April 29, aged 63, was a wicketkeeper who played one Test for Pakistan, against New Zealand in 1976-77, while the long-serving Wasim Bari was temporarily out of favour. Shahid dropped a few in a high-scoring draw, but did catch Richard Hadlee off Intikhab Alam for 87, and Wasim soon returned. Shahid's ten-year career included matches for several teams, most of them based in Karachi. He scored 93 while captaining Sind A against PIA in January 1977.

SHAHID QURESHI, who died on September 2, aged 77, was a batsman who played 20 first-class matches in Pakistan over a decade from 1954-55. His only century, 135, came for Karachi C against Karachi A in October 1957.

SHAMSHER SINGH, who died of a heart attack on March 21, aged 40, was a hard-working medium-pacer who took 55 Ranji Trophy wickets for Rajasthan, with a best of five for 72 against Vidarbha in 1992-93, his first season. He also took five for 26 against them in a one-day game. Shamsher later ran a coaching academy in Jaipur, and was the manager of the Rajasthan Royals team, captained by Shane Warne, which won the inaugural IPL, in 2008.

SHAW, **JOHN**, who died on November 25, aged 56, was a highly regarded journalist and commentator, best known in the Midlands for his reports on music and sport, particularly cricket, for BBC Radio Leicester. "He taught me everything I know in radio," said Charlie Dagnall, the former county player who joined the *Test Match Special* team in 2013. "He'll always be the voice in my head when commentating."

SHEIKH SALAHUDDIN AHMED, who died of a heart attack on October 29, aged 44, was an off-spinner who played six one-day internationals for Bangladesh in pre-Test days. In his second match, against Sri Lanka in Colombo in July 1997, he took two for 48, dismissing Sanath Jayasuriya and Arjuna Ranatunga. First-class cricket did not start in earnest in Bangladesh until Test status was acquired in 2000-01, by which time Salahuddin was bowling less – but he did score 96 on his first-class debut, for Khulna against Biman Airlines in January 2001. After retiring in 2006, he took up coaching.

SIMPSON, **REGINALD THOMAS**, died on November 24, aged 93. In the years between the end of the war and the dawn of the 1960s there were few more eye-catching sights in English cricket than Reg Simpson taking on opposing fast bowlers with a thrilling, nerveless bravado. Tall, tanned and capless, with waves of tight-curled hair, he cut a striking figure, and loved the physical and technical challenges presented by outright pace. England's oldest Test cricketer died just as his modern-day counterparts were in Brisbane, facing the sort of fast-bowling barrage he would have relished.

It was frequently said that Simpson's talent was unfulfilled at Test level, and that he seldom reproduced the uninhibited strokeplay he paraded for his beloved Nottinghamshire.

Tall, tanned and capless: Reg Simpson takes on the South Africans at Lord's, June 1951.

That, though, ignored the fact that – thanks to Len Hutton and Cyril Washbrook – he was never given a chance to establish himself in his preferred role as an opener.

At Melbourne, in the last Test of the 1950-51 Ashes, he played an innings of seminal importance to English post-war cricket. Facing an attack led by Ray Lindwall and Keith Miller, and including the new spin sensation Jack Iverson, England were 4–0 down, and facing a whitewash. Simpson made a magnificent 156 not out – drawing superlatives from Jack Fingleton among others – and reached his hundred on his 31st birthday. He was on 92 and becalmed when joined by last man Roy Tattersall, before making all but ten of a last-wicket stand of 74 in 55 minutes. "The situation really suited me," said Simpson. "I could take some calculated risks and play my shots." It was the foundation for England's first win in an Ashes Test since 1938 and, said Godfrey Evans, "the turning point" at the start of a golden era of success.

Simpson played in all five Tests of the 1950-51 series and, when he made 137 against South Africa in the first match next summer – the first Test century by a Nottinghamshire player at Trent Bridge – he was entitled to feel established in the side. There was, though, a portentous moment, when he advanced to loft Athol Rowan for four. At the end of the over, his partner Hutton warned gravely: "This is a Test match, you know."

Sure enough he did not complete Hutton's first series as captain, against India in 1952, and his second Ashes tour, under Hutton in 1954-55, was an unhappy experience. Dropped

View from the Bridge: Reg Simpson was photographed at Nottingham for *Picture Post* in 1949.

Picture Post/Hutton Archive/Getty Images

along with Alec Bedser after the First Test defeat at Brisbane, he did not feature again in the series. "Hutton didn't want to know me," he said later. Fellow tourist Bob Appleyard said: "He was probably a bit too keen on sunbathing and the beach for Len."

Simpson was more outspoken in an interview with journalist Huw Turbervill two years before his death: "Hutton did me on that tour. I got a hundred in the game before the Test, and he had to pick me, although he didn't want to. In the first innings I got two and then, in the second, he ran me out clean as a whistle. Did he say sorry? Did he bloody hell! He buggered up my career, but there you go. These things happen."

He was born in Sherwood Rise, four miles from Trent Bridge, and attended Nottingham High School, where he made the First XI at 13, and was an outstanding rugby player and one of the leading sprinters in the city. At 15 he was playing for Nottinghamshire Club and Ground, and he joined the special branch of the local police on leaving school. The outbreak of war delayed his entry into first-class cricket, though he provided a reminder of his potential with 134 not out for the county against the RAF in 1940.

Simpson enlisted in the RAF Volunteer Reserve, and flew more than 1,000 hours for Transport Command in India towards the end of the war. His posting to the subcontinent led to a first-class debut, for Sind in the Ranji Trophy, in 1944. He was 26 by the time he first appeared in the Championship for Nottinghamshire, but made up for lost time with a double-hundred against Warwickshire in one of his early matches, and 1,674 runs at 38 in 1947, his first full season.

He had a largely unsuccessful first England tour, to South Africa in 1948-49, but in the next two summers amassed over 5,000 runs and began to open the innings regularly for his county. Against New Zealand at Old Trafford in 1949, his home debut, there was a first Test hundred, his last 53 runs coming in 28 exhilarating minutes. He was a *Wisden* Cricketer of the Year in 1950.

Despite the speed of his scoring, Simpson was no big hitter, and he deserved his reputation as one of the game's most elegant strokemakers. He developed his technique against fast bowling after a wartime match for Nottinghamshire Police, when he was all at sea against Bill Voce. Simpson noted that his partner Frank Shipston was nullifying Voce's threat by going on to the back foot. Thereafter "back and across" became his mantra – one he repeated down the decades whenever his opinion was sought by England teams struggling against pace. It was advice he passed on to Dennis Amiss in 1976, when Amiss was trying to reconfigure his game. On his Test return, he made a double-century against a rampant Michael Holding.

Nottinghamshire team-mate Peter Forman said: "Reg took a leg-stump guard, stood very upright and moved his right leg into middle stump." When bowlers pitched short, Simpson preferred to sway rather than duck, but he was a fine hooker. "He was an amazing player of fast bowling. I watched Frank Tyson against South Africa at Trent Bridge, and he bowled as fast as anyone I have ever seen. I mentioned this to Reg years later, and he raised an eyebrow and said, 'Really? I never had any trouble against Frank.'" One of his most extraordinary innings came against Tyson at Northampton in 1956, when he made 150 before tea on a green wicket, while his team-mates mustered only 128 between them.

Simpson's stop–start international career finally ended after the New Zealand leg of the 1954-55 tour. He played in 27 Tests, making 1,401 runs at 33 with four hundreds. "All the time I had the feeling I was fighting for my place, and it does make you overcautious," he said. Some felt he was susceptible to high-quality spin.

He captained Nottinghamshire between 1951 and 1960, lean years for the county, but always tried to play positively. He could be feisty: when Glamorgan were proceeding at a snail's pace in perfect batting conditions one afternoon, he bowled an over of underarm to an enraged Wilf Wooller. Simpson worked for the Nottingham bat-maker Gunn & Moore, which allowed him to play as an amateur, but it was no sinecure; he rose to become managing director, and an admired businessman.

Simpson scaled back his appearances after giving up the captaincy, and retired in 1963 with over 30,000 runs at 38 in 495 matches, including 64 centuries, ten of them doubles. He bowled occasional off-breaks and was a superb fleet-footed fielder in the covers. He was chairman of the cricket committee at Trent Bridge from 1978 to 1990, weeping openly when Nottinghamshire were crowned champions in 1981.

He spent his final years in Felixstowe, but travelled to Nottingham to watch a day of the Ashes Test in 2013, and gave what turned out to be his final interview, to Brian Scovell for the magazine of the XL Club, six weeks before he died. Sharp as ever, he spent much of it giving a detailed critique of the shortcomings of the present England team against fast bowling. He was not to know how prescient his comments would be.

SMITH, Professor Sir COLIN STANSFIELD, CBE, died on June 18, aged 80. Before he became one of Britain's most famous architects and was knighted for his services to the profession, Colin Smith was an aggressive seam bowler and lower-order batsman, principally for Cambridge University and his native Lancashire. When he ended his first-class career in 1958 aged 25, there were those who thought he might have become a regular new-ball partner for Brian Statham, and some even more than that: "Had Colin played on," said Bob Barber, "he would have made a good replacement for Trevor Bailey in the England team."

Smith was born in Manchester into a cricketing family: his father represented Accrington and Cheshire, and his elder brother, Donald, played three games for Lancashire in the early 1950s. Smith junior was just 18 when he made his Lancashire debut, against Hampshire at Liverpool in 1951, and made occasional appearances during his National Service in the next two summers, before a first season at Cambridge in 1954. When Lancashire visited in May, he bowled Barber and Winston Place, and left Cyril Washbrook bruised and cursing in the dressing-room.

Showing an architect's appreciation of angles, he worked out how to use the back-foot no-ball law to maximum effect, dragging his steel-toecapped right boot some three feet to

The Gentlemen of 1957. *Standing:* Peter Richardson, Esmond Lewis, Colin Smith, Ted Dexter, Colin Cowdrey, Gamini Goonesena; *sitting:* John Warr, Rev. David Sheppard, Peter May, Doug Insole, Robin Marlar.

get closer to the batsman in his delivery stride. Ted Dexter, later a Cambridge team-mate, recalled: "My first meeting with him was in mid-pitch in a trial game at Fenner's. I had walked down the pitch a couple of times and whacked him for four. He said to me. 'I don't know who you are, but if you do that again, I will run through the crease and bowl it straight at your head.' We were never the best of friends thereafter."

Smith played in four Varsity matches, achieving his best figures of four for 42 in his last appearance, in 1957. He also appeared for the Gentlemen that summer, and scored his only first-class century, against Warwickshire at Edgbaston. He was a clean striker of the ball and good enough to be asked to open for Lancashire in emergencies. In all, he made 106 appearances, taking 293 wickets at 24, with a best of six for 35 for Cambridge against Free Foresters in 1955, before architecture claimed him full-time. "In those days the likes of Colin and myself did not think of careers in the game," Barber said. "It was rather a matter of grasping some cricket before you turned 100% to your chosen life pattern or career."

Smith was County Architect for Hampshire County Council from 1974 until 1992, establishing a nationwide reputation for innovative school buildings. In 1991 he won the RIBA Royal Gold Medal, British architecture's highest award. He returned to Fenner's to design the new pavilion, which in 1972 replaced the much-loved but decrepit old building. He improved the facilities but his design did not earn universal acclaim. "Distinctly functional, built of wood and ugly modern brick," wrote George Plumptre in *Homes of Cricket*.

SMITHSON, RALPH, who died on December 26, aged 103, played his first match for Ditchling in Sussex in 1929 – and the last in 2000, when he was 89. He was affectionately known as the club's "run machine". He said, "I was like Jack Hobbs, because I scored more centuries after I was 40"; he was also a good enough bowler to take five hat-tricks for Ditchling as well.

STRAUSS, RAYMOND BERNARD, died on July 28, aged 85. Ray Strauss was one of the most intelligent exponents of swing bowling, but his career is testament to the treasures squandered in Australia as the lust for speed became an obsession. He was able to move the ball appreciably both ways and late, at a peppery fast-medium. His team-mate John Rutherford – Western Australia's first Test player – admiringly remembered the "magnificent control of his bowling" and an ability "to add cut to swing in making himself a complete master of his art". In only his second match for WA, against the 1952-53 South Africans, Strauss exploited the Fremantle Doctor to take seven for 75. But he was not just a home banker: he also prospered at Melbourne (nine for 83 in the match in 1956-57) and Sydney (six for 66 in NSW's first innings that same season).

Strauss never did represent Australia, though: he played in a trial match for the 1957-58 tour of South Africa, but tore a leg muscle on the first day. He did, however, bowl well for an Australian XI against Peter May's 1958-59 MCC tourists, taking four for 77 in the first innings. His batting combined a little study of the textbook with an ability to hit out. A skilled hockey player, he represented Western Australia for six years from 1949, and gained selection for Australia in 1954. Strauss worked as an architect in England while playing league cricket in Lancashire in 1960 and 1961. An urbane and engaging man, he was later a wise mentor to WA's many successful swing bowlers, including Bob Massie.

Strauss had a long friendship with Maurice Foley, who also died in 2013 (see Briefly Noted, below). A bone of good-natured contention between them down the years was that they had worked on a plan to dismiss the fluent state batsman Fred Buttsworth by getting him to hook early on in a Perth grade match. Strauss supplied the ball, Buttsworth supplied the stroke, and Foley dropped the catch.

SURRIDGE, BETTY PATRICIA, died on February 26, aged 91. Betty Surridge succeeded Sir Paul Getty as Surrey's president in 1997, becoming the first (and so far only) woman to hold the position at any county club. She was the widow of Stuart Surridge, who captained Surrey to five successive County Championship titles in the 1950s, and was president himself in 1981. "What I am good at is meeting people," she said. "I know a lot of cricketing people and I shall help entertain." She was also a founder member of the Lady Taverners section. Micky Stewart, who succeeded her as president, said: "Betty was a wonderful lady and was so popular during Stuart's reign as captain – with all the players and throughout the wider club. She will be remembered for her commitment to and love of Surrey CCC, and her amazing personality."

SURTI, RUSI FRAMROZE, who died on January 12, aged 76, played 26 Tests for India in the 1960s. He was a genuine all-rounder: a capable batsman who had extended his maiden century to 246 not out, for Rajasthan against Uttar Pradesh in 1960-61, and a useful bowler who could deliver spin or medium-pace – although he was a little overplayed opening the bowling, which he was forced to do frequently in Tests because of India's shortage of quicks. A left-handed batsman and bowler, he was sometimes, rather unfairly, described as the poor man's Sobers. Farokh Engineer, a fellow Parsi and wicketkeeper in many of Surti's Tests, remembered: "We grew up together and played the game in Dadar's Parsi colony. He was extremely talented, and one of the best fielders I've seen."

Surti was dismissed for 99 (after being dropped twice on the same score) against New Zealand at Auckland in 1967-68. Earlier on that tour he had taken five for 74 against Australia at Adelaide, in between scoring 70 and 53, and his wholehearted efforts led to an offer to join Queensland; he remains the only Indian Test player to appear in the Sheffield Shield. Surti was an immediate hit, taking their first Shield hat-trick, against Western Australia at Perth in January 1969, and adding a century against WA in 1970-71. John Maclean, Queensland's future Test wicketkeeper, said: "Just having someone who had played Tests helped us, because at that stage none of us had." In all, Surti had five productive seasons in Brisbane, but later his time in Australia turned sour: in 1993 he launched legal action against his employers, the Queensland Fire Service, claiming he had been called a "curry eater" and an "Indian bastard". The court ruled that much of the alleged abuse was "mere banter".

TAYLOR, KEEGAN JAMES, died on December 27, aged 29, of complications arising from a diabetic seizure. An off-spinner from Mutare, Taylor took five wickets in three matches for Manicaland, in Zimbabwe's Logan Cup, in 2001-02.

TELANG, VIJAY SHANKAR, who died on June 18, aged 61, was a big-hitting batsman, mainly for the Indian state of Vidarbha, for whom his four hundreds included 155 against Railways at Gorakhpur in 1982-83. He also appeared for Central Zone, scoring half-centuries against both the Australian and Pakistani tourists of 1979-80. Contemporaries recalled a batsman who might have been a Twenty20 star these days.

TOWNSHEND, DERRICK WALTER, who died on June 8, aged 69, was a member of a prominent cricket family in Rhodesia, and played five matches for the national side. When MCC toured southern Africa in 1964-65, he opened Matabeleland's batting in a two-day game, and later dismissed Geoff Boycott with his off-spin. "Dobbo" Townshend – a tall man whose Bulawayo home included a well-stocked cricket museum – became a prominent administrator. His brother Trevor (who died in 2010) and son Matthew also played first-class cricket.

VAN DER MERWE, PETER LAURENCE, who died on January 23, aged 75, captained South Africa in just eight Tests and played only 15 in total, but his place on the list of his country's best leaders remains unquestioned. His CV contains two historic achievements: in 1965 his team won only South Africa's second series victory in England, and they followed that up, in 1966-67, with a first triumph over Australia. With a cool head and shrewd but undemonstrative leadership, he marshalled a precocious collection of talent with such authority that few queried his modest contributions with the bat.

His captaincy credentials were identified early: he was leading Western Province at 23, and chosen as Trevor Goddard's deputy for the tour of Australasia in 1963-64, despite not having played international cricket. He appeared in three Tests during that series, two of them in New Zealand, and two more against Mike Smith's England in 1964-65. Despite a best score in those games of 66, he was chosen as South Africa's first Afrikaner captain for the trip to England in 1965. "The selectors saw him as a man to steer a youthful and talented team in the right direction," said Ali Bacher, one of the tyros on that tour.

South Africa won 1–0, thanks to a famous victory at Trent Bridge remembered for the heroics of the Pollock brothers. They had

Accountant or man about town? Peter van der Merwe flies in to Heathrow, June 1965.

been 80 for five in their first innings when van der Merwe joined Graeme Pollock, and it was the captain's adhesive 38 (at one stage he contributed ten while Pollock plundered 91 off 90 balls) that shored things up. "He was not technically brilliant, but he was gutsy," said Pollock. "If you needed someone to hang around he could do that."

There were other valuable contributions at home against Australia – a pivotal 76 at Johannesburg, his highest Test score, as well as 50 at Cape Town and 42 at Durban – but, after leading South Africa to a 3–1 victory, he retired after one more season with Eastern Province and did not play again in Test cricket.

Van der Merwe was born at Paarl, and educated in Grahamstown and at the University of Cape Town, before taking up a career in accountancy. In 1960 he played a part in supporting Basil D'Oliveira, who had accepted the offer of a contract with Middleton in the Central Lancashire League. Van der Merwe helped organise a team of white cricketers to play a mixed-race XI captained by D'Oliveira at Claremont in Cape Town. While his actions were not illegal, van der Merwe risked official disapproval. With both sets of players taking collecting tins among a large crowd, £150 was added to the fund.

Early in his career he had supplemented his batting and athletic fielding by bowling slow left-arm, but he gave that up in 1963-64 amid doubts over his action. He returned to high-profile roles in cricket in the 1990s: South Africa's first chairman of selectors after readmission, then an early ICC match referee between 1992 and 1999, presiding over the fractious one-day international between England and Sri Lanka at Adelaide in 1998-99, when Arjuna Ranatunga led his team off the field following umpire Ross Emerson's no-balling of Muttiah Muralitharan.

Tall and bespectacled (with England led by Mike Smith, the 1965 series is believed to be the only one in Test history in which both captains wore glasses), van der Merwe looked more suited to his day job in accountancy. But first impressions were misleading: boosted by the emergence of some outstanding individuals, he helped turn the South Africans into a much more attacking unit. "He spent a lot of time thinking about the game, working out how to contain batsmen, and some of his field-placings were a bit different," said Graeme Pollock. "He was not a run-of-the-mill captain."

VERNON, MURRAY TREVOR, died on April 16, aged 76. At its best, Vernon's left-hand batting for Western Australia had charm and class; he stroked the ball rather than struck it. Yet when there were opportunities in the Australian side during the 1960s, Vernon was either absent from the domestic scene or failed to score enough runs to press his case. A confident debut at 18 against New South Wales at Perth in 1955-56 produced an undefeated 69 off an attack including Test players Keith Miller, Pat Crawford, Alan Davidson and Richie Benaud. But after spending the English summers of 1961 and 1962 as Rishton's professional in the Lancashire League, Vernon missed two Sheffield Shield seasons while he established his accountancy practice. In 1965-66, though, he returned in full bloom, beginning with a century against the MCC tourists and ending with his highest score of 173, against NSW. Vernon was a safe slip catcher, and took the occasional wicket with his medium-pace. His single season of state captaincy, 1966-67, was wedged between the more aggressively successful leadership styles of Barry Shepherd and Tony Lock.

VIDANAGAMAGE, PIYADASA WEWA, who died on August 24, aged 79, was the first Sri Lankan to umpire in the World Cup, taking charge of four matches in 1987. In all, "Vida" stood in 23 one-day internationals — and four Tests, including Sri Lanka's maiden victory, over India in Colombo in September 1985. His colleague in that match, Selliah Ponnadurai, died a few days before him.

WATT, WILLIAM BROCKBANK, died on September 11, aged 95. On New Year's Day 1934, the 15-year-old Bill Watt dutifully accompanied his Scottish-born mother to the annual Highland Games at the Sydney Showground. When they climbed to the observation tower of its Grand Stand, an attendant pointed out to Watt that he could look down on the neighbouring Sydney Cricket Ground; better still, he could watch Don Bradman bat. Watt was more interested in the prospects of a job there, despite the grip of the Great Depression: 12 months later, he was on the staff as an assistant groundsman and, after returning from service with the RAAF, was appointed assistant curator in 1947. Following the death of Wally Gorman, Watt became head curator in 1951. Seven years later, he was lured to the Melbourne Cricket Ground, where he remained until 1978. His grounds were flawless, and his pitches provided blandishments for both bowlers and batsmen; the one for the 1977

Centenary Test was a crowning testimony to his skills, and he retired back to Sydney soon after. Sir Robert Menzies, Australia's long-serving prime minister and a knowledgeable cricket lover, had first met Watt on the pitch at the SCG after Tyson's Test in 1954-55. In later years in Melbourne, Sir Robert would invariably greet the curator with "Ah, Watt – the man we pinched from Sydney." Watt was proud of his nickname, which was coined over some beers with the players and SCG groundstaff after a Sheffield Shield match in 1955. The discussion eventually settled on the fact that Watt was the only person present without a nickname, whereupon the future Test wicketkeeper Wally Grout chipped in: "Why don't we call him 'Grassy', after the pitches the bastard prepares for us to cop Lindwall and Miller on each year?"

WATTS, DAVID EARP, died on January 29, the month after his 100th birthday. He was headmaster of Kingsmead School, in Hoylake on the Wirral, for 30 years to 1979. In his youth he kept wicket for Cheshire, and never lost his affection for the game. Birds were another major passion: his two interests clashed one summer when he was forced to cordon off the school's cricket square as skylarks were nesting nearby.

WEEKES, ANDREW EMMANUEL, who died on January 21, aged 72, was the first umpire from the Leeward Islands to stand in Tests, officiating in four between 1983 and 1990. He also stood in three one-day internationals. Julian Hunte, president of the West Indies Cricket Board at the time of Weekes's death, said he had done "some tremendous work" in developing the game in his native St Kitts.

WEEKS, RAYMOND THOMAS, died on December 2, aged 83. Slow left-armer Ray Weeks took 94 wickets in 1951, as Warwickshire won the Championship in his first full season. That included a career-best seven for 70 against Nottinghamshire at Trent Bridge. "His steadiness was of great value," reported *Wisden*, "and at times, particularly when bowling to [Denis] Compton at the top of his form at Lord's, he reached a very high standard." Weeks had claimed five for 42 on his debut the previous year, against Cambridge University, after appearing for his native Cornwall from the age of 17. He played on to 1957, but never quite hit such heights again. "Nobody could have forecast the inexplicable decline in his form," said Jack Bannister, a Warwickshire team-mate. "However, nothing must detract from the part he played in bringing the County Championship title back to Edgbaston after a break of 40 years."

WESTCOTT, RICHARD JOHN, died on January 16, aged 85. Dick Westcott was an attractive batsman, who made four centuries for Western Province, and a superb fielder. Usually an opener, he was strong on the off side, but couldn't claim a regular place in the South African side of the 1950s. He did make 62 in his first Test, against New Zealand at Cape Town in 1953-54, but failed to reach 50 in another two matches in that series, or two more when recalled against Australia at home in 1957-58. He rounded off his Test career with a duck, just a week after a career-best 140 against Eastern Province. Westcott was born in Lisbon, and was the only Portuguese-born Test cricketer – until the month after his death, when Moises Henriques (born in Madeira) made his debut for Australia.

WHITE, JOHN, who died on December 1, aged 74, was a leading authority on the viola; he taught at the Royal Academy of Music for 30 years, and was a founder member of the acclaimed Alberni String Quartet. White grew up in the Yorkshire village of Royston, whose most famous son was Norman Yardley, England's captain in the 1948 Ashes series. White became an assiduous collector of cricket memorabilia, much of it related to Yardley, and shortly before his death published a book, *Those Were The Days: A Yorkshire Boy's Cricket Scrapbook*, illustrated with more than 800 items from his collection.

WHITFIELD, HAROLD VIVIAN LORAINE, who died on May 15, aged 94, played 24 matches, several as captain, for Border in South Africa in a career that stretched from 1936-37 to 1953-54. He made one century, 123 against Western Province at Cape Town in December 1937, and was also a handy leg-spinner. Fortune seemed to smile on Whitfield in the Second World War: he missed one naval posting because of rail delays, only for his ship to go down with all hands shortly afterwards; he served on another vessel with Prince Philip, and opened the batting with him in a regimental game; and, finally, he claimed to have dined out with the stage and screen star Vivien Leigh. Whitfield also represented Border at hockey and golf, and later became president of the South African Golf Union.

WILLARS, IAN WILLIAM WILTON, who died on May 7, aged 75, was a long-standing cricket and football writer in the Midlands, who reported on Warwickshire and Worcestershire for the *Birmingham Post* and its evening sister, the *Mail.* Known to his local colleagues as "The Duke", he exuded a pipe-smoking, rather gentlemanly air which belied his formidable contacts book. He was popular among cricket writers for arranging real-ale nights during Edgbaston Tests. In the office, he had two jackets: one to wear, the other to keep on the back of his chair in case the editor came by when he had nipped out to the Queen's Arms for what he liked to call some "intro juice".

WOSTRACK, JENNIFER GEORGINA (née Worrell), died on August 28, aged 67. Jenny Wostrack, a useful cricketer who played for Surrey Women and the prominent Surrey club Redoubtables, was the niece of the former West Indian captain Frank Worrell. She worked for the London Community Cricket Association, running their centre in Wallington, and was later a director of the Surrey Cricket Board.

ZAFAR MAHMOOD, who died on December 13, aged 65, was a batsman who played 16 first-class matches in Pakistan, scoring one century – 106 for Khairpur against Karachi Whites in March 1972. The previous week he made 94 and 58 against the Pakistan Works Department.

ZAKIR HUSSAIN SYED, who died on March 21, aged 73, was *The Cricketer's* Pakistan correspondent throughout the 1970s, and a radio and TV commentator on cricket and other sports. A prominent badminton player in his youth, "Zak" also played nine first-class matches as a medium-pacer, taking seven wickets for less than 18 each. He was an acclaimed director-general of the Sports Board of Pakistan from 1973 to 1980, becoming the first sporting administrator to be awarded the President's Medal. He was secretary of the Asian Cricket Council from 1999 to 2002.

ZULFIQAR BHATTI collapsed and died after being hit on the chest while batting in a club game in Sukkur in Pakistan on December 18. He was 22. Zulfiqar's team, which was taking part in a local Twenty20 tournament, was captained by his brother. "Doctors made every attempt to revive him," said Ayaz Mehmood, a local official, "but it seems like he breathed his last on the pitch."

The obituaries section includes those who died, or whose deaths were notified, in 2013. Wisden 2015 will include a supplementary obituary section for those whose deaths have been overlooked. Suggestions for this, and information on those who died in 2014, should be sent to almanack@wisden.com, or to John Wisden & Co, 13 Old Aylesfield, Golden Pot, Alton, Hampshire GU34 4BY.

> **"** Russian chess grandmaster Peter Svidler, a frequent visitor to Tests in England, bemused the chess world a few years ago by entering a middle-ranking tournament in Gibraltar just so he could have a net at The Rock's cricket ground."
> Cricket Round the World, page 1237

BRIEFLY NOTED

The following, whose deaths were noted during 2013, played or umpired in a small number of first-class (fc) matches. Further details can be found at www.cricketarchive.co.uk or at www.cricinfo.com

	Died	Age	Main team(s)
BROWN, Alan	23.8.2013	80	Northumberland

Long-serving medium-pacer (1958–79) who took 6-25 against Cheshire in 1979.

CAMPBELL, Margaret Vivian (later Mrs Taylor)   20.8.2013   73   Middlesex Women
Opened the batting when Middlesex won the women's Area Championship in 1981.

DRAPER, James Gordon   10.1.2013   87   Umpire
Durban official who stood in five Tests between 1964-65 and 1969-70.

DRUMMER, Desmond   19.3.2013   72   Western Province
Opening bowler, five fc matches in the 1960s: 4-68 against Eastern Province in 1963-64.

EVANS, William Vincent ("Vin")   14.8.2013   78   Durham
Wicketkeeper in Durham's pre-first-class days: played one Gillette Cup match, in 1964.

FARRELL, Graeme Stanley   25.7.2013   70   South Australia
Left-hander: seven Sheffield Shield games in 1966-67; never improved on debut 66 against Victoria.

FOLEY, Maurice Hinton   1.7.2013   83   Western Australia
Batsman, three fc matches in the 1950s, and was in Australia's hockey team at the 1956 Olympics.

FURNISS, John Brian   19.9.2013   68   Derbyshire
Seamer who took seven wickets in four fc matches in the mid-1950s.

HEFFER, Albert William   3.9.2013   79   N-E Transvaal
Off-spinning all-rounder who played one Currie Cup match, in 1962-63.

JAKEMAN, Ronald Stuart   24.12.2013   70   Northamptonshire
Left-hander, three fc matches in 1962-63; heavy scorer in Yorkshire leagues.

JAQUES, Peter Heath   7.7.2013   93   Leicestershire
Batsman who scored 55 in his only fc match, a non-Championship game against Somerset in 1949.

JENKINS, Huw   21.8.2013   68   Glamorgan
Wicketkeeper, scored 65 in only fc match, against Oxford University in 1970. Later a policeman.

KING, Graham Laird   8.11.2013   69   Administrator
Legendary figure in Border (SA) cricket: administrator, selector (for 23 years) and umpire.

McCORMICK, Ray Vincent   8.6.2013   82   South Australia
Off-spinning all-rounder who made little impression in six Sheffield Shield matches in 1959-60.

McMEEKING, David Peter   29.3.2013   75   Western Province
Leg-spinner who took four wickets in his only fc match, in 1965-66.

MILLS, David Cecil   16.3.2013   75   Glos/Free Foresters
Batsman, two fc matches, both v Cambridge U. Rugby for Cambridge U, Harlequins, Cornwall.

OAK, Shankar Dattatreya   7.9.2013   84   Vidarbha
One fc match in 1963-64 (12 runs, two wickets); later umpired in Ranji Trophy too.

PITTMAN, Brian Harold   26.10.2013   83   South Australia
Left-hander (one fc match 1959-60); prolific scorer for Kensington, Don Bradman's Adelaide club.

RAJ, Des   4.8.2013   69   Umpire
Long-serving Indian umpire who stood in a men's ODI in 1997-98, and a women's Test (and ODIs).

RICE, Christopher Paul Edgar   16.2.2013   64   Suffolk/Norfolk
Left-hand batsman who later played for England Over-60s.

STUART, Ian McGregor   23.2.2013   88   Umpire
Victorian who stood in 14 fc matches, all at the MCG, in the 1960s.

	Died	Age	Main team(s)
SUKIAS, Samuel	2.10.2013	96	Umpire

Auckland official who stood in 17 fc matches – and one game in the 1981-82 Women's World Cup.

| **THRESHER**, Ronald Stanley | 2.5.2013 | 82 | Kent |

Fast bowler and banker: five fc matches, taking eight wickets for Douglas Jardine's XI in one.

| **WATTS**, Colin Arthur | 7.11.2013 | 92 | South Australia |

Leg-spinning all-rounder: 76 v NSW in 1953-54, his final season. Also a noted baseball player.

| **WILLIAMS**, Edward Lovell ("Ted") | 24.12.2013 | 88 | Leicestershire |

Opening bowler who played one fc match in 1949; Tom Graveney was one of his two victims.

| **WILSON**, Ian Barclay Justly | 8.3.2013 | 80 | Ireland |

Munster slow left-armer who played three times for Ireland, taking 3-7 against Scotland in 1957.

A LIFE IN NUMBERS

	Runs	Avge	Wkts	Avge		Runs	Avge	Wkts	Avge
N. A. T. Adcock	451	5.50	405	17.25	Mazharul Haque	1,316	28.60	4	24.75
Ahmed Mustafa	504	24.00	3	14.00	K. Mitter	1,698	26.12	50	31.70
D. P. Azad	658	20.56	8	40.75	B. R. Mohan Rai	373	13.32	52	27.78
Bashir Ahmed	45	15.00	15	13.40	Munawwar Ali Khan	70	5.83	23	32.73
S. D. Bruce	3,113	32.09	2	45.00	Munir Hossain	12	6.00	2	32.00
D. G. Clark	1,959	15.79	1	44.00	J. K. E. Munro	497	11.55	1	18.00
J. E. Commins	110	7.85	27	27.77	Nauman Shabbir	867	19.70	16	43.93
R. G. de Alwis	**673**	**14.63**	–	–	M. B. Pandit	2,317	29.70	5	55.00
M. H. Denness	**25,886**	**33.48**	**2**	**31.00**	G. C. Perkins	589	8.18	93	36.11
S. A. S. Dias	59	16.86	14	24.28	D. Randall	133	19.00	–	–
K. R. Dollery	958	11.97	227	26.51	**M. R. Rege**	**2,348**	**37.26**	**33**	**42.96**
E. J. England	532	33.25	0	–	G. A. Richards	153	21.85	–	–
J. P. Fellows-Smith	**3,999**	**29.40**	**149**	**29.62**	D. Robbins	340	11.72	52	33.59
J. F. Fitzgerald	147	11.30	29	30.82	P. A. Robinson	567	14.92	86	29.48
R. R. Frankish	799	24.21	20	36.25	J. R. F. Rutherford	105	6.56	10	55.50
D. P. Freeman	10	5.00	–	–	M. L. Ryan	3,022	29.05	33	21.39
A. Ghatak	247	6.86	125	22.64	Salim Pervez	8,075	36.21	0	–
A. L. Gibson	17	5.66	–	–	Santosh Lal	280	21.53	9	36.00
S. C. Guillen	**2,672**	**26.98**	**1**	**49.00**	**Shahid Israr**	**868**	**28.00**	–	–
Haseeb Ahsan	242	5.62	142	27.21	Shahid Qureshi	697	27.88	–	–
P. Hearn	8,138	25.81	22	56.59	Shamsher Singh	149	5.73	55	35.45
Ijaz Mirza	985	31.77	2	39.00	Sheikh Salahuddin	881	19.15	5	46.80
L. C. Jacobson	153	30.60	–	–	**R. T. Simpson**	**30,546**	**38.32**	**59**	**37.74**
A. E. James	3,411	12.22	843	27.09	C. S. Smith	2,339	18.71	293	24.50
A. Jha	880	13.33	159	30.18	R. B. Strauss	805	16.42	139	24.29
Khalid Hasan	**113**	**11.30**	**28**	**38.25**	**R. F. Surti**	**8,066**	**30.90**	**284**	**37.07**
L. B. Koch	2,400	29.62	2	43.00	K. J. Taylor	42	10.50	5	27.40
S. Krishna	420	38.18	–	–	V. S. Telang	2,724	29.60	7	49.28
B. A. Langford	7,588	13.59	1,410	24.79	**P. L. van der Merwe**	**4,086**	**29.18**	**82**	**25.70**
D. J. Lewis	3,662	28.16	11	41.54	M. T. Vernon	4,169	34.74	9	25.66
N. T. McCorkell	16,106	25.60	1	117.00	R. T. Weeks	1,051	10.00	236	26.26
N. A. McMahon	13	3.25	3	32.00	**R. J. Westcott**	**3,225**	**36.23**	**10**	**31.40**
B. A. Matthews	158	8.77	120	23.63	H. V. L. Whitfield	726	18.61	31	35.54
V. Mayers	219	19.90	–	–	Zafar Mahmood	729	27.00	5	25.80
R. Mayes	2,689	19.62	0	–	Zakir Hussain Syed	125	10.41	7	17.28

Test players are in bold; their career figures can be found on page 1396. Bruce took 121 catches and made six stumpings; de Alwis 69 and six; Guillen 111 and 34; McCorkell 532 and 185; Munro 56 and four; Pandit 35 and three; Randall six and one; Ryan 87 and 11; and Shahid Israr 66 and 22.

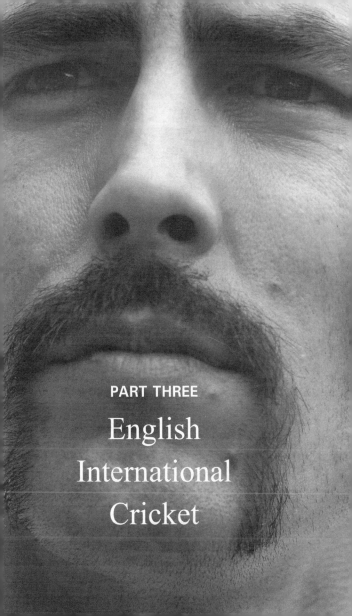

PART THREE

English
International
Cricket

THE ENGLAND TEAM IN 2013

Familiarity breeds discontent

John Etheridge

In the summer, England defeated Australia by three Tests to nil, a margin never bettered in a home Ashes. Yet only a few months later they looked an ageing, fragmented and shell-shocked side. The return leg had been lost 5–0 to opponents hell-bent on revenge – one of the most extraordinary turnarounds in any sport. The whitewash prompted the resignation of team director Andy Flower, and the sacking of Kevin Pietersen, who – it was made clear by the England hierarchy – could no longer be trusted to buy into the team ethos. Captain Alastair Cook kept his job, but was under intense scrutiny.

The hammering confirmed the disintegration of a team who had enjoyed so much success over the previous five years, and had arrived in Australia

ENGLAND IN 2013

	Played	Won	Lost	Drawn/No result
Tests	14	5	4	5
One-day internationals	21	10	10	1
Twenty20 internationals	7	3	3	1

NOVEMBER DECEMBER JANUARY	4 Tests, 5 ODIs and 2 T20Is (a) v India	(see *Wisden 2013*, page 377)
FEBRUARY MARCH	3 Tests, 3 ODIs and 3 T20Is (a) v New Zealand	(page 254)
APRIL		
MAY	2 Tests, 3 ODIs and 2 T20Is (h) v New Zealand	(page 279)
JUNE	Champions Trophy (h)	(page 301)
JULY AUGUST	5 Tests, 5 ODIs and 2 T20Is (h) v Australia	(page 324)
SEPTEMBER	1 ODI (a) v Ireland	(page 845)
OCTOBER		
NOVEMBER DECEMBER JANUARY FEBRUARY	5 Tests, 5 ODIs and 3 T20Is (a) v Australia	(page 372)

unbeaten in 13 Tests. Jonathan Trott flew home after the First Test with a stress-related illness, Graeme Swann retired after the Third, and Matt Prior was dropped for the Fourth. Several other players must have feared they would not play again. By the end of the Fifth Test, in which England's second innings lasted just 31.4 overs, any flicker of fight had been extinguished. Mitchell Johnson's speed and hostility, in particular, crushed their spirit.

Initially, Flower insisted he wanted to continue. But at the end of January, after the limited-overs sides coached by Ashley Giles had also lost heavily to Australia (4–1 in the one-day internationals, 3–0 in the Twenty20s), Flower decided to step aside, citing his dissatisfaction with the split-coaching arrangement; he would, however, remain at the ECB. Cook said he had no intention of stepping down, though at one point hinted he might relinquish the 50-over captaincy – a suggestion he quickly retracted.

Yet there was widespread criticism of his conservative tactics and lack of instinctive thinking, and his endorsement by the ECB – apparently without a moment's hesitation – did not impress everyone. Two key figures of recent years, national selector Geoff Miller and team managing director Hugh Morris, had already chosen to move on, replaced by James Whitaker and former England wicketkeeper Paul Downton respectively; Angus Fraser, the ex-Test seamer and now director of cricket at Middlesex, later joined the selection panel. It all added up to the end of an era.

This was underlined four days after Flower's resignation by the "unanimous" decision to terminate Pietersen's central contract. An ECB press release spoke of the need for a new "team ethos and philosophy", after more rumours had emerged in Australia of his divisive influence on the dressing-room. On February 12, Pietersen was re-signed by his IPL franchise Delhi Daredevils for $1.5m, an international cricketer no longer.

The two Ashes series – ten Tests in which plans were hatched and personal enmities established, some bitterly so – dominated England's landscape. But when the whitewash was completed in 21 days' cricket – a shorter period than their two previous 5–0 defeats by Australia – Cook must have wished no such thing as back-to-back Ashes had ever been dreamed up. In mitigation, few doubted that England had been disadvantaged by being the away team in the second batch of such gruelling, high-pressure games.

Even so, the shift in fortunes was bewildering. At The Oval on August 25, Cook was lifting a replica urn to the accompaniment of champagne corks, "Jerusalem" and ticker tape. Just 133 days later, he cut a desolate figure in Sydney as he watched Michael Clarke and his players revelling in the glory. The pain was in no way assuaged by successes earlier in the year: England reached the Champions Trophy final – and were on course to beat India before a dramatic collapse – and overcame the disappointment of a 0–0 draw in New Zealand by beating them 2–0 at home. No, the Ashes were all that mattered.

England's decline could be traced back to before the home summer. In 13 Tests (and counting) starting in March 2013, they had failed to reach 400. As well as substance, their batting lacked conviction: in the calendar year, only Pakistan and Zimbabwe scored their Test runs more slowly than England's

Messing about: Kevin Pietersen and Alastair Cook after securing a 3–0 Ashes win at The Oval.

2.85 an over. And those frailties came crashing down in Australia, where they were dismissed for under 200 on six occasions out of ten.

The bowlers were able to make inroads, only once failing to capture Australia's fifth wicket in the first innings before the total had passed 150. But they could never close the deal, because of a mixture of thoughtless short-pitched bowling, dropped catches and innate caution. Brad Haddin, counter-attacking brilliantly at No. 7, made a first-innings half-century or more in each of the five Tests. England had no answer.

The reality was they had been flattered by their win at home, where they were able to overcome regular top-order failings, principally thanks to Ian Bell's three centuries, and strike with the ball at key moments. There was certainly plenty of excitement – the thrilling finale at Trent Bridge, and Stuart Broad's irresistible spell at Chester-le-Street – but the overall standard was mediocre. And a number of poor umpiring decisions, despite the use of DRS, did little to improve the flow of the games or reduce tension between the players.

But Australia increased the intensity dramatically on their own turf, with a rejuvenated Johnson the most potent weapon, collecting 37 wickets at less than 14 apiece. England were muted and often intimidated. Australia scored ten centuries to England's one – and that came from 22-year-old Ben Stokes at No. 6, in only his second Test.

Where Flower's desire to improve the one-percenters was once lauded as attention to detail, some now believed his micromanagement of every aspect of the team erred towards control freakery. Unattributed quotes from England players began to emerge, hinting at a suffocating atmosphere in the dressing-room, with Flower and his army of back-room staff said to be watching every move. The England team nutritionist Chris Rosimus produced an 82-page cookbook of recipes and dietary requests for Test days – including such delights as mung-bean curry and goji berries – causing much amusement. It was the sort of thing that looks like sensible preparation when a team win, but comical fussiness when they lose. And there was a clear contrast with Australian coach Darren Lehmann's relaxed, beer-and-fags approach. Crikey, he even asked somebody to tell a joke in the team huddle each morning.

The truth, as ever, lay somewhere in the middle. Flower allowed his players some rope – Broad, Pietersen and others were photographed in an Adelaide bar in the small hours with no repercussions – while Lehmann admitted he sometimes tongue-lashed his players. Flower denied his style was overbearing and, while conceding he would reassess his routines, said he should at times have made his players train with more intensity. Reports that his relationship with Pietersen had reached breaking point once more added to the uncertainty.

The year had begun with England, still glowing from their first Test series win in India for 28 years, losing the one-day matches there 3–2, in Ashley Giles's first extended spell in charge of the team after the start of the job share with Flower. A tour of New Zealand followed. Unusually for a modern series, all three Tests were drawn, though England batted out 170 overs at Dunedin and 143 at Auckland after early examples of their first-innings malaise; in between, rain probably denied them a win at Wellington.

England finished nine down in a thrilling finish at Auckland – their fourth draw with one wicket in hand in four years – and Prior's century clinched his mantle as Player of the Year in May. Yet he hardly made a worthwhile contribution for the rest of 2013. Nick Compton scored two centuries in the series, but would play only two Tests at home before being dropped, apparently because of an intense and self-absorbed attitude, and slow scoring. England won the one-day and Twenty20 series in New Zealand, both 2–1. Swann, who underwent the second elbow operation of his career, did not play a Test there, while Pietersen suffered a knee injury that forced him to miss the final Test, the IPL, and the first half of the English summer; only once, during his Ashes hundred in Manchester, did he approach his fluent best.

Both home Tests against New Zealand were won, but there was further evidence of batting problems, notably when they lost eight for 54 in the first innings at Lord's. At Headingley, Joe Root scored his first Test century, but there was criticism of slow batting from England's top order on the third evening. Thanks to the more scintillating methods of Martin Guptill, New Zealand took the one-day series 2–1.

In the Champions Trophy England were still without Pietersen and Swann. But, after beating Australia and losing to Sri Lanka, they qualified for the semi-final by sneaking past New Zealand in a rain-reduced group match. Next, they thrashed South Africa, then faced an unbeaten Indian side in the final. It became a 20-over affair because of rain – and England should have won. Needing 130, they were 110 for four with 16 balls remaining. But they panicked, fatally, and the next eight deliveries brought three runs and four

An unholy mess: Cook and Pietersen, stony-faced after 5–0 is confirmed at the SCG.

wickets. Still without a global 50-over trophy, England were hurt by the defeat – perhaps more deeply than outsiders realised.

One bizarre incident during the tournament had repercussions for the Ashes. After the win over Australia, Root was struck a glancing blow by David Warner in the Walkabout, an Aussie-themed bar in Birmingham, at around 2.30am. Warner was said to have taken offence at Root sporting a green false beard, apparently thinking he was trying to imitate South African batsman Hashim Amla. While Root was cleared of all blame, Warner was banned, and did not reappear until the Third Test in Manchester.

England won that series because they prevailed when it mattered. They might have lost at Trent Bridge and Chester-le-Street, but magnificent bowling by James Anderson, then Broad proved decisive. Rain probably saved them at Old Trafford, and they had the worse of a weather-interrupted game at The Oval, until a last-day declaration by Clarke presented an opportunity. Eventually, bad light curtailed play with England needing 21 off 24 balls.

Only at Lord's – where they won by 347 runs – did they truly dominate Australia. Dry pitches were prepared for Anderson's reverse swing and Swann's spin, and it worked: Swann's 26 wickets were the most on either side. A watering finally came at around midnight at The Oval after the last day of the series, when several England players decided to pee on the pitch. Some dismissed the gesture as harmless high jinks from young men revelling in the adrenalin of an Ashes victory; others, including Surrey, thought it disrespectful. Eventually, after 48 hours, the team issued an apology; England's public relations and media image were generally poor. After an intervention by ECB chairman Giles Clarke, they were more affable in Australia, though that was rather lost in the debris of defeat.

Bell's technically perfect batting at home earned him a place on the shortlist for the BBC's Sports Personality of the Year. But the voting happened during the Perth Test, in which England lost the Ashes; Bell finished tenth out of ten. Damningly, in 30 innings in the return series, Bell, Cook and Pietersen – England's three most experienced batsmen – managed a top score between them of 72.

England insisted they were expecting aggression from Australia, but were still unable to handle it. Johnson was fast and accurate, there was a torrent of verbal abuse, the local media harassed the visiting Poms, and the home crowd booed Broad incessantly. He had been cast in the role of public enemy No. 1 after refusing to walk at Trent Bridge, where he edged a catch, via Haddin's glove, to Clarke at slip. Later, during an interview with an Australian radio station, Lehmann urged spectators to "get stuck into" Broad for his "blatant cheating". The crowds obeyed the coach's instructions.

Trott's departure damaged England's batting and morale. The management said he had been suffering from the condition – which seemed a mixture of burnout and cricket-induced anxiety – for much of his international career, but had successfully controlled it in the past. In September, Trott had pulled out of the final one-day international of the summer, apparently because of a last-minute back injury. He also avoided a confrontation with Johnson, whose speed and bounce had caused him problems in the earlier games. There had, perhaps, been issues even before the return tour started.

Broad was England's best bowler in Australia, but no other senior player enhanced his reputation, while Swann angered many by not seeing out the series. He claimed his early exit was "selfless" because, with the Ashes lost, he did not want to play in the final two Tests just to bolster his stats. Some, less charitable, spoke of deserting a sinking ship.

The disastrous debut of Lancashire's Simon Kerrigan at The Oval meant England had little alternative but to choose Monty Panesar for the tour, just weeks after he was arrested and fined for urinating over bouncers at a Brighton nightclub. By the Fifth Test at Sydney, even with Swann gone, Panesar was dropped in favour of Scott Borthwick, the wrist-spinning all-rounder from Durham who had been playing grade cricket in Sydney. Others omitted at various times were Chris Tremlett, Tim Bresnan, Prior and even Root, while the out-of-sorts Steven Finn didn't get a game at all, and flew home early in January to rebuild his confidence. Those taking their places made little impression. As English cricket adjusted to a new reality, the worry was it could become a familiar one.

ENGLAND PLAYERS IN 2013

LAWRENCE BOOTH

The following 34 players (there were 31 in 2012 and 33 in 2011) appeared in 2013, when England played 14 Tests, 21 one-day internationals and seven Twenty20 internationals. All statistics refer to the full year, not the 2013 season.

JAMES ANDERSON   Lancashire

Anderson struggled to silence the old prejudice that, to be at his best, he had to glide in under cloudy English skies armed with the Dukes ball. On the tours of New Zealand and Australia that bookended the year, he claimed 21 wickets at 41 apiece; against the same opposition in England, he reaped 31 at 25, overhauling Bob Willis's Test tally of 325. But even that didn't tell the whole story. After winning the Trent Bridge Test almost by himself, Anderson sputtered away. The next four home Ashes matches brought only 12 wickets, and included the worst innings analysis of his Test career – none for 116 – on home turf at Old Trafford. Then came Australia, where he was treated for the most part with respect, but not the fear engendered by Mitchell Johnson; and the swing he had found there in 2010-11 just refused to materialise. Even so, the only serious blot came at Perth, where George Bailey equalled the Test record by whacking him for 28 in an over. His one-day bowling had paved England's way to the Champions Trophy final, but his batting was rabbit-like, and it seemed a retrograde step when their first day of Test cricket in 2014, at Sydney, finished with Anderson on nightwatchman duty.

  14 Tests: 111 runs @ 7.92; 52 wickets @ 31.82.
  10 ODI: 33 runs @ 33.00, SR 132.00; 23 wickets @ 15.26, ER 4.23.

JONNY BAIRSTOW   Yorkshire

Others' lack of faith in his technique may have been shared by Bairstow himself. It was as if he felt obliged to go for his shots before a straight one evaded a crooked bat. Unsurprisingly, the stats did not stack up: 15 innings produced only two half-centuries (21 runs into one of them, against Australia at Lord's, he was bowled by a Peter Siddle no-ball), and he was dropped for Tests 5–8 of the Ashes decathlon. When he returned, at Melbourne, it was only because Prior had lost form, and a shaky performance with the gloves confirmed Bairstow was not ready to keep wicket for England – but then they hadn't thought he would need him to be.

  8 Tests: 379 runs @ 27.07; 6 catches in 1 Test as wicketkeeper.
  3 T20I: 46 runs @ 23.00, SR 148.38.

IAN BELL   Warwickshire

While Bell was scoring hundreds in each of England's three Ashes wins, the year seemed destined to be his. Ultimately, he had to settle for a few baubles: his 20th Test century, first place in England's mediocre set of batting averages, and second in the world to Michael Clarke's tally of 1,093 Test runs. It wasn't bad, but it could have been better – and Bell looked shot by the time he failed twice at Sydney. That was in stark contrast to a honey-sweet summertime, when no England innings was complete until he had rescued it amid a rhapsody of late cuts. Only a big hundred eluded him. His one-day game also purred along. But, in general, a flaw remained: an elegant demise never seemed far away, and sometimes an inelegant one – the first-ball checked drive to mid-off during the meltdown in Melbourne, where he had been made vice-captain after the ditching of Prior, would have been hard to fathom, had it not happened before. It was soft stuff from a player approaching 100 Test caps. But he would always have the summer.

14 Tests: 1,005 runs @ 41.87.
16 ODI: 645 runs @ 43.00, SR 76.87.

RAVI BOPARA   Essex

A 2012-13 winter playing Twenty20 domestic cricket in Bangladesh and South Africa was enough for Bopara to relocate his verve and drive, and his judicious hitting during the Champions Trophy shone brightly. Had he not pulled Ishant Sharma to square leg at a pivotal moment of the final against India, he might have been Man of the Match, having already taken three cheap wickets. Twenty-eight off an over earlier in the tournament against Sri Lanka had been a reminder of his class; so too a 75-ball 101 against Ireland. But the selectors still didn't trust Bopara with the No. 6 Test spot.

11 ODI: 317 runs @ 51.83, SR 108.93; 10 wickets @ 35.00, ER 5.22.
4 T20I: 76 runs @ 76.00, SR 155.10; no wicket for 81 runs, ER 13.50.

TIM BRESNAN   Yorkshire

Two serious injuries drained Bresnan of his zest: in February, he underwent a second elbow operation; in August, he developed a stress fracture of the back. From being a third seamer with pretensions of batting at No. 7, he declined to a fourth seamer who looked a place too high at No. 8 (a two-Test foray in December ended with scores of one and nought in Melbourne). He was unfortunate that his back gave way shortly after the highlight of his year: a rip-snorter to remove David Warner on the fourth afternoon at Chester-le-Street and hasten the Australian collapse that would secure England the series. But the emergence of Stokes made Bresnan look redundant, especially when he couldn't register 80mph at the MCG. After he was dropped for Sydney, observers began referring to his Test career in the past tense once more, even though he would not turn 30 until 2015.

5 Tests: 137 runs @ 17.12; 15 wickets @ 33.46.
11 ODI: 79 runs @ 11.28, SR 73.83; 13 wickets @ 40.07, ER 5.69.

STUART BROAD   Nottinghamshire

The boos that greeted Broad's every deed in Australia obscured a successful year in which he was ten clear of Test cricket's next-highest wicket-taker (Anderson, with 52). Four times he claimed six or more in an innings, equalling George Lohmann's England record for a calendar year, set in 1896. He was never more devastating than during his seven for 44 against New Zealand at Lord's, never more memorable than during his six for 50 to give England a

3–0 Ashes lead in Durham. And, in Australia, he was one of only two English good-news stories, with Stokes. His limited-overs performances were up and down: in successive Twenty20 games in New Zealand, he claimed four for 24, none for 53, then three for 15. His batting took a back seat, except when he failed to walk after edging Ashton Agar at Trent Bridge. The moment was seized upon by Australia's coach Darren Lehmann, who gave an inane radio interview which helped reduce Broad to pantomime-villain status all the way from Brisbane to Sydney. The round of applause he received from the SCG members after an entertaining 42 on the last day of the series better reflected his worth.

14 Tests: 326 runs @ 16.30; 62 wickets @ 25.80.
9 ODI: 15 runs @ 7.50, SR 100.00; 12 wickets @ 35.16, ER 5.80.
5 T20I: 9 runs @ 4.50, SR 112.50; 9 wickets @ 18.44, ER 8.73.

JOS BUTTLER   Somerset

The promise began to bear fruit. After ousting Kieswetter behind the stumps in India at the start of 2013, Buttler shone briefly in New Zealand, then prevented a one-day clean sweep during the return series with a murderous unbeaten 47 from 16 balls at Trent Bridge. His glovework was on the up, too, and he grabbed six chances during the Champions Trophy mauling of South Africa. But the breakthrough innings came six days after a confidence-boosting 75 against Australia at Old Trafford, when he personally took care of a run-chase at Cardiff. After a long search, England appeared to have found their limited-overs keeper.

18 ODI: 298 runs @ 27.09, SR 127.35; 30 catches, 1 stumping.
7 T20I: 130 runs @ 32.50, SR 175.67; 6 catches.

MICHAEL CARBERRY   Hampshire

If Tantalus had been a Test cricketer, this is how it might have been, with the big score always just out of reach. More than three years after his lone cap, at Chittagong, Carberry forced his way in at the Gabba thanks to runs in the warm-up matches. But his outings followed a dispiriting pattern: competent solidity, then fatal inertia. Six of his ten innings got past 30, none past 60. An 81-ball 12 at the MCG summed up the problem: when Australia's seamers went round the wicket, depriving him of his cut,  there was little else to keep the scoreboard moving. Besides, Australia believed he had already made his defining contribution, by dropping Brad Haddin on the first evening in Adelaide. His one-day outings in the summer were characterised by a shaky understanding between the wickets with Pietersen, and one unruffled knock at Cardiff. Aged 33, he did not have time on his side.

4 Tests: 238 runs @ 29.75.
5 ODI: 108 runs @ 21.60, SR 62.79; no wicket for 12 runs, ER 12.00.

Gareth Copley, Getty Images

NICK COMPTON   Somerset

Disaster followed triumph with painful swiftness. Successive hundreds at
Dunedin and Wellington in March had apparently answered questions raised
in India in late 2012, when he had failed to convert several starts. But then
came the second impostor: six innings against New Zealand – at Auckland,
Lord's and Leeds – produced 54 runs, and culminated in a grim 85-minute
seven that sealed his Ashes fate. The selectors feared that the intensity with
which he celebrated those centuries had a flip side: a tendency to analyse
himself into a corner. Others discerned a stiff front leg. Regardless, Compton
went public with his grievance, which did not help. And, when he was passed
over for the trip to Australia, a Test return felt further away than ever.

    5 Tests: 271 runs @ 30.11.

ALASTAIR COOK   Essex

In his first full year in charge, Cook experienced the highs and lows that some
captains take a whole career to accumulate. After a narrow squeak of a draw
in New Zealand, he saw them off at home, then led England to a 3–0 win over
Australia, statistically their most comprehensive Ashes victory since 1978-79.
But there would be no resting on laurels and, by the time England were
slumping to a whitewash in Australia, Cook was answering questions about
his suitability for the job: too nice, said some; tactically naive, said others.
Many felt he was just too rigid, too dependent on prescribed plans, too, well,
English. Cook himself insisted he was the right man for the job, though his
batting fell away: in ten Ashes Tests he scored no hundreds and averaged 26,
as Australia's seamers followed the template established by New Zealand and
kept him on the front foot. His form wasn't a complete disaster: he scored six
half-centuries against Australia, extended his own England record to 25 Test
hundreds, and – at Melbourne – became the youngest man of any nationality
to reach 8,000 Test runs. Yet the pitiless reality was that the Ashes trauma had
the air of a definitive chapter in his life story.

    14 Tests: 916 runs @ 33.92.
    16 ODI: 560 runs @ 35.00, SR 75.16.

JADE DERNBACH   Surrey

A fixture in the Twenty20 side, where he was comfortably England's leading
wicket-taker and – with Wright – their tightest regular bowler, Dernbach was
a liability in 50-over cricket: unpredictability clearly worked better in the
shorter format. But with Broad and Finn absent injured from the first two one-
day internationals at home to New Zealand, Dernbach – ditched in India in
January – was given another chance. The results were dismal: 20 overs leaked
142 runs, making him the most expensive bowler in the history of one-day
cricket among those who had sent down at least 1,000 deliveries.

    6 ODI: 4 runs @ 1.33, SR 30.76; 6 wickets @ 64.66, ER 7.25.
    7 T20I: 0 runs @ 0.00; 13 wickets @ 15.00, ER 8.12.

STEVEN FINN   Middlesex

There may not have been a more cautionary tale of cricketing mechanics all
year. Finn was in incisive one-day form in New Zealand, where a shorter
run-up added focus without blunting his edge. But he was receiving advice

from too many quarters. Back in England, he lengthened his approach once more, and tried to become something he manifestly was not – a pitch-it-up purveyor of outswingers. Any semblance of rhythm disappeared, and his feet appeared to be getting in a curious tangle. At Trent Bridge against Australia, Cook lost faith, treating Finn like a last resort. He bowled accordingly, and was dropped. Taken to Australia as one of three giants in England's seam attack, he could not be trusted with a starting spot even at Perth: England's most promising young quick of 2012 had become unpickable and, in January, he was sent home early to rediscover his zip. Perhaps inevitably, the highlight of his year was with the bat – a nightwatchman's 56 to help save the Dunedin Test. Like his bowling, however, his batting faded: after scoring 24 in the next innings, at Wellington, he could muster only 18 in seven more.

6 Tests: 118 runs @ 13.11; 20 wickets @ 33.50.
14 ODI: 19 runs @ 4.75, SR 50.00; 19 wickets @ 31.63, ER 4.78.
5 T20I: 5 runs without being dismissed, SR 83.33; 5 wickets @ 33.00, ER 8.25.

ALEX HALES   Nottinghamshire
Only one England player could legitimately claim to be the best in the world at his job by the end of 2013: according to the ICC rankings, Hales was cricket's No. 1 Twenty20 batsman. The evidence was small, but pleasingly formed, and two knocks stood out: Hales inspired England's win in New Zealand with 80 not out from 42 balls in Wellington, then squared their home series against Australia with 94 from 61 at Chester-le-Street.

7 T20I: 247 runs @ 49.40, SR 153.41.

MICHAEL LUMB   Nottinghamshire
Lumb set about using England's seven Twenty20 fixtures to advertise his hard-hitting wares – never more explosively than during a 34-ball unbeaten 53 at Wellington in February. His 11 sixes (five in that innings alone) were three clear of his closest team-mate, Hales. The ground lost in the aftermath of the 2010 World Twenty20 success had been regained.

7 T20I: 188 runs @ 31.33, SR 148.03.

EOIN MORGAN   Middlesex
The honour of captaining England in five one-dayers and, with Broad rested, a Twenty20 game against New Zealand was offset by diminishing returns with the bat. In all, 25 innings contained only three scores over 50, including a match-winning hundred at Malahide to bloody the noses of his former Irish colleagues. It was still the case that no game felt beyond England's reach while Morgan was at the crease, and he was their only ever-present in 21 one-day internationals. But, with teams bowling wide of off stump to restrict his scope for sweeps and scoops, he lost a little impact: in eight of his 20 one-day innings, he was out for 15 or fewer. Unsurprisingly, there was no serious talk of a Test recall.

21 ODI: 560 runs @ 35.00, SR 91.20.
6 T20I: 86 runs @ 17.20, SR 119.44.

MONTY PANESAR Sussex/Essex

It was a year to forget, not least because of an ill-fated evening out in Brighton, when Panesar was chased into a fast-food joint by nightclub bouncers after urinating on them. Sussex, already unimpressed by his demeanour, sacked him, and England briefly turned their back, disastrously selecting Kerrigan at The Oval instead. A move to Essex offered redemption, and Panesar was taken to Australia. But a mixture of unhelpful catching by others, unyielding pitches and unsympathetic captaincy limited him to two Tests and three expensive wickets. And he was given only one game, at Melbourne, to cement his new status – following Swann's retirement – as England's first-choice spinner; even there, he was barely handed the ball. It seemed the selectors needed little excuse to look elsewhere, though his card had been marked in New Zealand earlier in the year: without the injured Swann, his five wickets there cost 70 each. Only once did Panesar manage more than one wicket in a Test innings, and not once did he score more than two with the bat (though he was still there with Prior at the end of the draw at Auckland). That, as much as anything, was the problem: the age of the one-dimensional cricketer looked over – unless your one dimension was out of this world. Panesar's left-arm spin was not.

    5 Tests: 7 runs @ 1.40; 8 wickets @ 75.87.

SAMIT PATEL Nottinghamshire

He began the year in clover, but ended it in the long grass, complaining that his treatment by England was, among other things, "wrong", "harsh" and "unfair". While he was hitting an unbeaten 44 from 20 balls to set up England's 2013-opening one-day win at Rajkot, a place in the middle order looked a given. But, following 30 not out amid a collapse in the next match, at Kochi, Patel collapsed too: in four more internationals, including the first two Twenty20s in New Zealand, he managed nine runs and a single wicket. To his evident disgust, the selectors had seen enough.

    5 ODI: 75 runs @ 37.50, SR 119.04; 1 wicket @ 131.00, ER 5.95.
    2 T20I: 8 runs @ 4.00, SR 80.00; no wicket for 37 runs, ER 9.25.

KEVIN PIETERSEN Surrey

An unusually underwhelming year played itself out against a backdrop of niggles and doubts, mainly to do with his knee and his attitude. Then, suddenly, in February 2014, it was all over. Following an Ashes tour in which fresh rumours had circulated about Pietersen's influence over Cook's dressing-room, and his relationship with Andy Flower, an ECB press release spoke of England's desire for a new "team ethic and philosophy". At the age of 33, and after an almost decade-long marriage of convenience with his adopted country, the divorce papers had arrived. The hysterical and, at times, disingenuous debate that followed tended to overlook the fact that, in 2013, he managed only one hundred, helping England avoid the follow-on at Manchester; his Test average of 36 was his lowest in a calendar year. And the manner of his dismissals in Australia – repeatedly caught on the leg side as he tried to hit his way out of trouble, usually against Peter Siddle – drove the pundits to distraction. No matter that he was England's leading scorer in the whitewash:

his average was 29. Pietersen had insisted his goals remained 10,000 Test runs and the 2015 World Cup. But England were unmoved. Barring some miraculous rapprochement, all that remained was Twenty20 freelancing and, possibly, a twinge of regret.

11 Tests: 758 runs @ 36.09.
9 ODI: 256 runs @ 28.44.
1 T20I: did not bat.

MATT PRIOR   Sussex

No sooner had Prior been named England's Cricketer of the Year in May than it all went wrong. In Auckland, he had saved English bacon with a double of 73 and 110 not out. But what followed was horrible: 19 innings yielded 283 runs at 17, nine single-figure dismissals including five ducks, and one half-century, a hit-and-hope affair in a lost cause at Adelaide. His keeping grew scruffy. After the debacle at Perth, where he twice missed chances to stump David Warner, the selectors opted for change, drafting in Bairstow for Melbourne. After 60 successive Tests, five short of Alan Knott's England record for wicketkeepers, Prior had been dropped. It did not have to mean the end – he was only 31. But there would be plenty of catching up to do.

13 Tests: 594 runs @ 31.26; 44 catches.

BOYD RANKIN   Warwickshire

It felt cruel that Rankin's first one-day international for England should be against his native Ireland; all the crueller when he claimed four wickets. But international cricket's realpolitik was England's gain, at least in the one-day arena, where Rankin posed thrifty questions with the new ball in the home series against Australia. That earned him an Ashes tour and, at Sydney in the New Year, a first Test cap. But concerns his body was not up to the workload resurfaced on the opening day, when he limped off twice, and he had to make do with a lone tail-end wicket.

5 ODI: 5 runs @ 5.00, SR 100.00; 9 wickets @ 16.88, ER 3.98.
2 T20I: did not bat; 1 wicket @ 24.00, ER 6.00.

JOE ROOT   Yorkshire

Among team-mates, only Bell scored more runs in all formats than Root's 1,579, but the feeling after a gruelling year, in which he had been asked to bat at every position in the Test team from opener to No. 7, was one of anticlimax. A classy second-innings 87 at Adelaide supported the hunch that Root had it in him to replace Trott at No. 3, but a limited front-foot game was preyed upon by Australia's seamers, and the result was a sequence of go-slows that persuaded the selectors to give him a breather at Sydney. It was all a far cry from the first half of the summer, when a glut of runs for his county was backed up by a heady maiden Test hundred, at Headingley, and 180 against

Australia at Lord's. One-day runs flowed in abundance too, and his adaptability shone through during a 49-ball 90 not out in a Twenty20 game against Australia. His off-breaks could be handy – if only they had been used more often. Like Root himself, they would almost certainly get another chance.

14 Tests: 862 runs @ 34.48; 3 wickets @ 54.66.

20 ODI: 626 runs @ 39.12, SR 82.15; 3 wickets @ 109.33, ER 6.43.

3 T20I: 91 runs without being dismissed, SR 182.00; 2 wickets @ 33.50, ER 11.16.

BEN STOKES   Durham

Given a chance at Adelaide following the departure of Trott – and the decision to play Panesar on a pitch expected to turn – Stokes grabbed it with both hands, raising hopes that England had discovered a new all-rounder to balance the team for years to come. Even at 22, he was instantly the quickest bowler in the side, appeared to relish the fray – while cheerfully admitting he had no idea what the word meant – and scored England's only hundred of the series, a fighting 120 on a cracked deck at Perth. When he pitched the ball up, he looked better than a fourth seamer, and he began 2014 with a bustling six-for at Sydney. Less than a year after being sent home from Australia from a Lions tour for persistent curfew-breaking, Stokes seemed to have learned his lesson – and was itching to expand his education.

3 Tests: 200 runs @ 33.33; 7 wickets @ 47.28.

5 ODI: 57 runs @ 19.00, SR 93.44; 6 wickets @ 36.66, ER 5.64.

2 T20I: 9 runs without being dismissed, SR 180.00; no wicket for 26 runs, ER 8.66.

GRAEME SWANN   Nottinghamshire

The curtain came down in an undignified hurry, as Swann announced his retirement from international and first-class cricket three days before Christmas and five after England had gone 3–0 down at Perth. Amid the struggle to decode a cryptic parting shot aimed at unnamed players said to be "up their own backsides" (Swann later insisted he didn't mean Pietersen), it was easy to overlook the end of an all-too-brief era in which he had established himself as England's best and most effervescent spinner since Derek Underwood. That much had been evident during the summer when, on made-to-order pitches, Swann's 26 wickets – the most he had claimed in a Test series – were at the heart of England's third straight Ashes win. But Australian surfaces have always been less kind to off-spinners, and the batsmen resolved to get after him. In three Tests he harvested only seven wickets at 80 apiece: he would protest that his long-standing elbow injury – which had ruled him out of the Tests in New Zealand – meant he was no longer up to the rigours of the five-day game. If that was the case, the demise had been rapid, for the summer had brought him not only Ashes success – most notably during his nine-wicket match haul at Lord's – but also a bag of ten against New Zealand at Headingley, which had been a graveyard for English spinners since the days of Underwood. Whichever way you looked at it, England had lost their beating heart.

10 Tests: 194 runs @ 16.16; 43 wickets @ 34.09.

6 ODI: 32 runs @ 10.66, SR 106.66; 6 wickets @ 51.50, ER 5.25.

JAMES TREDWELL · Kent

Tredwell's year was the equivalent of haring 30 yards round the boundary, only to tip the ball over the rope for six. The hard part was the one-day series in India in January, when – as stand-in for Swann – his guileful off-breaks earned him 11 wickets. Three more helped dismantle South Africa in the Champions Trophy semi-final. But, during the NatWest Series in September, he became a target for the Australians: an economy-rate that had hovered around 4.60 all year suddenly mushroomed to 7.42. Tredwell remained England's leading one-day wicket-taker in 2013, and he can even tell his grandkids he captained his country for two balls, during the rain-ruined Twenty20 international against New Zealand. But his stock had taken a hit.

15 ODI: 23 runs @ 7.66, SR 50.00; 25 wickets @ 22.36, ER 5.02.
5 T20I: 22 runs @ 22.00, SR 200.00; 2 wickets @ 53.50, ER 10.70.

JONATHAN TROTT · Warwickshire

Trott's year ended abruptly, and poignantly, when he left the Ashes tour in November after the First Test in Brisbane citing a stress-related illness. Team officials explained he had been managing the condition for some time; two cheap dismissals by Mitchell Johnson at the Gabba can have done little for his equanimity. As the cricket community wished him well, England tried to work out how to move forward without their Test-match and one-day rock. For much of the year, he just couldn't fail, at one point topping 25 for a world-record 19 international innings in a row; his one-day strike-rate was answering questions too. But, unusually, he wasn't making his starts count, and during the home Ashes this would come back to haunt him. Five times he reached 40; not once did he get to 60. Australia had worked out that his trigger movement – towards the bowler, no matter what pace – made him vulnerable to the short ball, and Ryan Harris in particular tested out the theory. The seeds for his Brisbane struggles were then sown during the NatWest Series, when Johnson banged it in. But his departure put those technicalities into perspective, and forced cricket, once more, to ask itself uneasy questions about the nature of the modern treadmill.

11 Tests: 793 runs @ 37.76; 2 wickets @ 28.50.
14 ODI: 611 runs @61.10, SR 86.05.

CHRIS WOAKES · Warwickshire

To everyone's frustration – not least his own – Woakes kept falling just short of the cricketer England wanted him to be: a bowling all-rounder capable of troubling one-day batsmen at first change. In four of his seven 50-over internationals, he conceded more than a run a ball, partly because he overdid the short stuff. A surprise Test debut at The Oval confirmed the suspicion that he wasn't quite ready, though he was looking busy with the bat when the light closed in on the final evening.

Neville Williams, Aston Villa FC/Getty Images

1 Test: 42 runs @ 42.00; 1 wicket at 96.00.
7 ODI: 69 runs @ 17.25, SR 72.63; 8 wickets @ 44.12, ER 5.88.
1 T20I: did not bat; no wicket for 19 runs, ER 19.00.

LUKE WRIGHT   Sussex

Wright's brief remained intact: hit the ball out of the park from No. 3 in the
Twenty20 side, and hurry through some in-your-face seam. A strike-rate of
170 and an economy-rate of just over eight ticked both boxes. His two one-
day appearances were the result of squad rotation and a late injury to Trott
against Australia, but he was as much a part of the Twenty20 scene as
cheerleaders and fireworks.

2 ODI: 5 runs @ 2.50, SR 23.80; no wicket for 21 runs, ER 7.00.
7 T20I: 128 runs @ 25.60, SR 170.66; 6 wickets @ 21.66, ER 8.12.

AND THE REST...

For **Simon Kerrigan** (Lancashire; 1 Test) a debut at The Oval on a pitch
expected to turn proved too much: eight erratic overs of left-arm spin cost 53
and prompted some to cite the dreaded yips. Kerrigan said he had lost his
rhythm, not his nerve: "It's what happens to me from time to time. I get out of
sync a bit and drag a few down." **Chris Tremlett** (Surrey; 1 Test) was taken
to Australia in the hope of resurrecting his splice-jarring form there three years
earlier, but one Test in Brisbane was enough to confirm he was not the bowler
of old, mainly because he had lost 6–7mph. **Craig Kieswetter** (Somerset;
3 ODI) was ditched after three one-dayers at the start of the year in India,
culminating in a duck at Ranchi. He was replaced by Buttler, and never got
another look-in. For the second time in three years, **James Taylor**
(Nottinghamshire; 1 ODI) had to settle for a day in Dublin, but could make
only 25. **Gary Ballance** (Yorkshire; 1 ODI) played in the same game, but fell
second ball. An Ashes tour was some compensation, and he didn't look
overawed on Test debut at the SCG at the start of 2014. **Chris Jordan** (Sussex;
1 ODI) made more impact in his only appearance, removing Phil Hughes,
Michael Clarke and James Faulkner as Australia rattled up almost 300 in
Southampton, where **Danny Briggs** (Hampshire; 3 T20I) had been mauled by
Aaron Finch.

ENGLAND TEST AVERAGES IN CALENDAR YEAR 2013

BATTING AND FIELDING

	T	I	NO	R	HS	100	Avge	SR	Ct
C. R. Woakes..................	1	2	1	42	25	0	42.00	50.60	0
I. R. Bell	14	27	3	1,005	113	3	41.87	42.62	13
I. J. L. Trott	11	21	0	793	121	1	37.76	49.93	12
K. P. Pietersen	11	21	0	758	113	1	36.09	51.74	8
J. E. Root.....................	14	27	2	862	180	2	34.48	40.64	8
†A. N. Cook....................	14	27	0	916	130	2	33.92	42.54	18
†B. A. Stokes..................	3	6	0	200	120	1	33.33	46.29	1
M. J. Prior	13	24	5	594	110*	0	31.26	56.14	44
N. R. D. Compton	5	9	0	271	117	2	30.11	35.28	3
†M. A. Carberry................	4	8	0	238	60	0	29.75	38.20	5
J. M. Bairstow	8	15	1	379	67	0	27.07	46.05	7
T. T. Bresnan	5	9	1	137	45	0	17.12	33.33	1
†S. C. J. Broad.................	14	22	2	326	65	0	16.30	58.31	6
G. P. Swann...................	10	16	4	194	34	0	16.16	73.48	10
S. T. Finn	6	10	1	118	56	0	13.11	30.80	2
†J. M. Anderson................	14	22	8	111	23	0	7.92	48.89	11
C. T. Tremlett	1	2	0	15	8	0	7.50	22.05	0
†M. S. Panesar.................	5	8	3	7	2*	0	1.40	9.21	1
S. C. Kerrigan	1	1	1	1	1*	0	–	8.33	0

BOWLING

	Style	O	M	R	W	BB	5I	Avge	SR
S. C. J. Broad	RFM	478.1	87	1,600	62	7-44	5	25.80	46.27
I. J. L. Trott.................	RM	20	3	57	2	1-9	0	28.50	60.00
C. T. Tremlett	RFM	36	5	120	4	3-69	0	30.00	54.00
J. M. Anderson	RFM	531.5	125	1,655	52	5-47	3	31.82	61.36
T. T. Bresnan	RFM	153.3	34	502	15	2-24	0	33.46	61.40
S. T. Finn	RF	179.1	30	670	20	6-125	1	33.50	53.75
G. P. Swann	OB	440	75	1,466	43	6-90	3	34.09	61.39
B. A. Stokes	RFM	87	13	331	7	2-70	0	47.28	74.57
J. E. Root	OB	61	14	164	3	2-9	0	54.66	122.00
M. S. Panesar	SLA	201.1	55	607	8	2-53	0	75.87	150.87
C. R. Woakes	RFM	24	7	96	1	1-96	0	96.00	144.00
S. C. Kerrigan	SLA	8	0	53	0	0-53	0	–	–

> **❝** 'He may have taken 19 wickets in a Test match,' said the PC, 'but nobody nicks my changing place.' It was generally agreed that Jim was bang to rights for 'taking without consent'."
> Stars that shone beside the slag heaps, page 76

ENGLAND ONE-DAY INTERNATIONAL AVERAGES IN CALENDAR YEAR 2013

BATTING AND FIELDING

	M	I	NO	R	HS	100	Avge	SR	Ct/St
I. J. L. Trott	14	14	4	611	109*	1	61.10	86.05	2
R. S. Bopara	11	9	3	317	101*	1	52.83	108.93	2
I. R. Bell	16	16	1	645	113*	1	43.00	76.87	5
J. E. Root	20	19	3	626	79*	0	39.12	82.15	10
S. R. Patel	5	4	2	75	44*	0	37.50	119.04	0
†A. N. Cook	16	16	0	560	78	0	35.00	75.16	7
†E. J. G. Morgan	21	20	4	560	124*	1	35.00	91.20	11
†J. M. Anderson	10	4	3	33	28	0	33.00	132.00	3
K. P. Pietersen	9	9	0	256	76	0	28.44	83.66	1
J. C. Buttler	18	13	2	298	75	0	27.09	127.35	30/1
J. W. A. Taylor	1	1	0	25	25	0	25.00	59.52	0
†M. A. Carberry	5	5	0	108	63	0	21.60	62.79	2
C. Kieswetter	3	3	1	42	24*	0	21.00	68.85	2
†B. A. Stokes	5	3	0	57	27	0	19.00	93.44	1
C. R. Woakes	7	5	1	69	36	0	17.25	72.63	4
C. J. Jordan	1	1	0	14	14	0	14.00	56.00	0
T. T. Bresnan	11	9	2	79	25	0	11.28	73.83	2
G. P. Swann	6	3	0	32	16	0	10.66	106.66	3
†J. C. Tredwell	15	8	5	23	6*	0	7.66	50.00	7
†S. C. J. Broad	9	4	2	15	7*	0	7.50	100.00	1
†W. B. Rankin	5	2	1	5	4	0	5.00	100.00	0
S. T. Finn	14	4	0	19	16	0	4.75	50.00	4
L. J. Wright	2	2	0	5	5	0	2.50	23.80	0
J. W. Dernbach	6	3	0	4	2	0	1.33	30.76	2
†G. S. Ballance	1	1	0	0	0	0	0.00	0.00	1

BOWLING

	Style	O	M	R	W	BB	4I	Avge	SR	ER
J. M. Anderson	RFM	82.5	5	351	23	5-34	1	15.26	21.60	4.23
W. B. Rankin	RFM	38.1	3	152	9	4-46	1	16.88	25.44	3.98
C. J. Jordan	RFM	10	0	51	3	3-51	0	17.00	20.00	5.10
J. C. Tredwell	OB	111.2	4	559	25	4-44	1	22.36	26.72	5.02
S. T. Finn	RF	125.4	11	601	19	3-27	0	31.63	39.68	4.78
R. S. Bopara	RM	67	1	350	10	3-20	0	35.00	40.20	5.22
S. C. J. Broad	RFM	72.4	2	422	12	3-50	0	35.16	36.33	5.80
B. A. Stokes	RFM	39	1	220	6	5-61	1	36.66	39.00	5.64
T. T. Bresnan	RFM	91.3	7	521	13	4-45	1	40.07	42.23	5.69
C. R. Woakes	RFM	60	1	353	8	3-68	0	44.12	45.00	5.88
G. P. Swann	OB	58.5	0	309	6	2-49	0	51.50	58.83	5.25
J. W. Dernbach	RFM	53.3	1	388	6	2-69	0	64.66	53.50	7.25
J. E. Root	OB	51	0	328	3	1-20	0	109.33	102.00	6.43
S. R. Patel	SLA	22	0	131	1	1-46	0	131.00	132.00	5.95
L. J. Wright	RFM	3	0	21	0	0-21	0	–	–	7.00
M. A. Carberry	OB	1	0	12	0	0-12	0	—	—	12.00

> **"** Philander was like a cat in a canary cage, pouncing with every delivery and licking his lips at the discomfort."
> South Africa v Pakistan 2012-13, page 1069

ENGLAND TWENTY20 INTERNATIONAL AVERAGES IN CALENDAR YEAR 2013

BATTING AND FIELDING

	M	I	NO	R	HS	50	Avge	SR	4	6	Ct
†J. C. Tredwell	5	2	1	22	22	0	22.00	**200.00**	3	1	2
J. E. Root	3	2	2	91	90*	1	–	**182.00**	13	1	1
†B. A. Stokes	2	1	1	9	9*	0	–	**180.00**	0	1	0
J. C. Buttler	7	5	1	130	54	1	32.50	**175.67**	13	7	6
L. J. Wright	7	6	1	128	52	1	25.60	**170.66**	13	6	2
R. S. Bopara	4	3	2	76	45	0	76.00	**155.10**	6	2	1
A. D. Hales	7	7	2	247	94	2	49.40	**153.41**	29	8	3
J. M. Bairstow	3	2	0	46	38	0	23.00	**148.38**	5	2	5
*M. J. Lumb	7	7	1	188	53*	1	31.33	**148.03**	16	11	3
†E. J. G. Morgan	6	5	0	86	46	0	17.20	**119.44**	6	5	2
†S. C. J. Broad	5	3	1	9	4*	0	4.50	**112.50**	2	0	2
S. T. Finn	5	1	1	5	5*	0	–	**83.33**	0	0	1
S. R. Patel	2	2	0	8	6	0	4.00	**80.00**	1	0	1
J. W. Dernbach	7	1	0	0	0	0	0.00	**0.00**	0	0	1
D. R. Briggs	3	–	–	–	–	–	–	–	–	–	1
†W. B. Rankin	2	–	–	–	–	–	–	–	–	–	0
K. P. Pietersen	1	–	–	–	–	–	–	–	–	–	0
C. R. Woakes	1	–	–	–	–	–	–	–	–	–	0

BOWLING

	Style	O	M	R	W	BB	4I	Avge	SR	ER
W. B. Rankin	RFM	4	0	24	1	1-24	0	24.00	24.00	**6.00**
J. W. Dernbach	RFM	24	0	195	13	3-23	0	15.00	11.07	**8.12**
L. J. Wright	RFM	16	0	130	6	2-24	0	21.66	16.00	**8.12**
S. T. Finn	RF	20	0	165	5	3-39	0	33.00	24.00	**8.25**
B. A. Stokes	RFM	3	0	26	0	0-26	0	–	–	**8.66**
S. C. J. Broad	RFM	19	0	166	9	4-24	1	18.44	12.66	**8.73**
S. R. Patel	SLA	4	0	37	0	0-17	0	–	–	**9.25**
J. C. Tredwell	OB	10	0	107	2	1-20	0	53.50	30.00	**10.70**
D. R. Briggs	SLA	7	0	76	3	2-25	0	25.33	14.00	**10.85**
J. E. Root	OB	6	0	67	2	1-15	0	33.50	18.00	**11.16**
R. S. Bopara	RM	6	0	81	0	0-15	0	–	–	**13.50**
C. R. Woakes	RFM	1	0	19	0	0-19	0	–	–	**19.00**

> **"** In 11 seasons of the format, the two most successful batsmen thus came from Leicester, and the two most successful bowlers from Rawalpindi."
> Friends Life t20, 2013, page 702

NEW ZEALAND v ENGLAND, 2012-13

REVIEW BY DEREK PRINGLE

Twenty20 internationals (3): New Zealand 1, England 2
One-day internationals (3): New Zealand 1, England 2
Test matches (3): New Zealand 0, England 0

On England's previous visit to New Zealand, in 2007-08, it had been possible to discern the makings of the team that would top the Test rankings a little over three years later. This time, despite a pair of 2–1 wins in the Twenty20 and one-day series, there were few such portents. Instead, the abiding image was of England hanging on for dear life to secure a draw in the Third Test at Auckland, and with it an underwhelming share of a series most onlookers had expected them to win with room to spare.

Such expectations had less to do with arrogance and more with the form book. While England had confirmed their status as the world's second-best Test team behind South Africa with a historic win in India before Christmas, the New Zealanders were languishing in eighth, without a series victory over serious opposition since 2006. They had lost seven of their previous eight Tests – three by an innings, one by ten wickets, one by nine. And their dressing-room looked close to disarray following the Ross Taylor–Mike Hesson debacle. Quite simply, they seemed there for the taking.

Instead, inspired by the innovative captaincy and quicksilver batting of Brendon McCullum, they emerged with their best Test result since brushing aside India's great batting line-up at home a decade earlier. McCullum himself repeatedly confounded England's bowlers, and across the formats made 10, 74, 26, 69 not out, 74, 79, 74, 69, 38 and 67 not out – a total of 580 runs from 496 balls, with 24 sixes. England dropped short too often, but this was still an astonishing performance from a player saddled with the burden of replacing the popular Taylor.

Despite McCullum's excellence, England had been the superior side in the two limited-overs series, even if they were taken to a decider in both; the ten-wicket win in the Twenty20 finale at Wellington's Westpac Stadium was especially brutal. But their Test cricket failed to ignite. With the bat, only the outstanding Matt Prior – whose double of 73 and 110 not out staved off defeat at Auckland – Jonathan Trott and Nick Compton averaged over 40; with the ball, not one member of the frontline attack averaged under 30, though Stuart Broad did return to form during the Second Test at Wellington. A knee injury to Kevin Pietersen, which ruled him out of the Third Test, compounded the sense of frustration.

The time-honoured search for positives did not take long. Having made a steady but unspectacular start to his England career in India as Andrew Strauss's replacement, Compton now scored hundreds in the first two Tests, and earned the priceless commodity of knowing he could perform at the highest level.

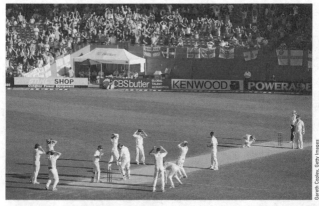

Gareth Copley, Getty Images

Simon says... The New Zealanders can't quite believe it as Monty Panesar clings on at Auckland.

But Alastair Cook fell away after a second-innings hundred at Dunedin, Pietersen flickered briefly, and Ian Bell – as he had done in India – redeemed himself only at the last, paving the way for Prior's last-day heroics at Auckland with a studious 75. For Joe Root, a sparkling performance in the one-day series was followed by a reminder of cricket's capacity to act as a leveller: three Tests brought him a top score of 45.

England could hardly blame the scheduling – an eminently sensible programme comprising three Twenty20s, three one-day internationals and three Tests, all fitted into two months. If there was a flaw, it was that they had only one warm-up match for the Tests, though team director Andy Flower claimed there was simply not enough time to squeeze in a second.

Flower had long advocated the virtues of rest and rotation: Pietersen, James Anderson and Graeme Swann had all missed matches following the Test series in India. But Flower's case was hardly strengthened by what transpired. After bowling shakily in the one-day internationals and the four-day warm-up game at Queenstown, Swann returned home just before the Tests for an operation on his right elbow. A fortnight later, Pietersen followed him, having limped through two Tests with a sore right knee. Anderson, who at least managed to see out his leg of the tour, bowled more Test overs than any of the English seamers but, for reasons nobody could quite pinpoint, lacked his usual threat in conditions most felt would suit him.

Perhaps the truth in Anderson's case applied just as well to the whole team: after the stirring win in India, it was always going to be difficult to produce the same intensity against New Zealand. In the land of the long white cloud, cricket has rarely emerged from rugby's all black shadow. To say the tour was low-key was as readily apparent in Wellington as it was in faraway London. Local interest was mixed: crowds for the limited-overs internationals mostly

Wobble-inducing: New Zealand left-armer Neil Wagner, who often coaxed more swing from the Kookaburra ball than England's bowlers, removes Jonathan Trott at Auckland.

exceeded 10,000 (and nearly 24,000 turned up for the Auckland Twenty20), but the Test attendances were modest, despite a large contingent of English fans.

This was unfortunate, for the New Zealanders needed to impress their own fans after the humiliation in South Africa two months earlier, when they lost both Tests by an innings after totals of 45 and 121 – itself a recovery from 62 for nine.

That drubbing, the unceremonious removal of Taylor as captain in December following the tour of Sri Lanka, and his subsequent replacement by McCullum, made this a pivotal moment for the Test team's public standing. Taylor opted out of that ill-fated tour of South Africa but, after a period of reflection, was now reselected. There was inevitable speculation about the dynamics of a dressing-room containing him, McCullum and Hesson, the coach, but Taylor's return seemed to settle his team-mates. And the warm ovations he received from sympathetic crowds during the limited-overs games were a memorable feature of the early part of the tour. Few innings were better received than his one-day century at Napier.

The pitches during the Twenty20 and 50-over series – especially the drop-ins at Auckland and Wellington – had been quick and bouncy. But the Test strips were toned down to counter what, on paper at least, was England's superior pace attack. In the event, New Zealand's trio of Trent Boult, Tim Southee and Neil Wagner outbowled Anderson, Broad and Steven Finn in two of the three Tests, finding swing where England could find only straight lines.

Monty Panesar toiled for scant reward after being thrust into the First Test at short notice because of Swann's sudden departure. Having sat one of the modules for his Masters degree in international sports management just three days before that game, Panesar may not have been expecting to play. He bowled accordingly, and finished the series with five wickets at 70 – his worst average in a series in which he had played more than one Test.

Finn's new shorter run-up served him well during the one-dayers, but in the Tests he failed to find consistency – or indeed menace. Missing, too, was an ability to take the ball away from the right-hander. His seven wickets in the final Test were consolation rather than compensation, and he may have been distracted by his efforts to cure his habit of striking the stumps with his trailing knee. A marker, placed just behind the back crease, helped him jump wider. But while he knocked into the stumps less often, it was hardly ideal that he was not fully focused on events at the other end. In the event, his main contribution came with the bat: a stoical nightwatchman's 56, compiled with one of Pietersen's spare blades, helped rescue the First Test at Dunedin.

That knock, following hundreds from Cook and Compton, limited the damage done by England's calamitous first-innings 167. Amid a flurry of ill-chosen, sloppily executed shots, they succumbed in 55 overs, gifting four-wicket hauls to Wagner and the debutant left-arm spinner, Bruce Martin. But the warning signs had been there during England's defeat by a New Zealand XI at Queenstown – their first loss in a first-class tour match for seven years. With its adventure sports and heady mountain air, Queenstown is regarded as the adrenalin capital of the world, and England's players were keen to get stuck in, many partaking of the canyon swing – but not the famous bungee jump, from which they were banned. Flower even called a team meeting on top of The Remarkables mountain range – a gathering that, at 7,500 feet, required the use of four helicopters.

The extent of England's first-innings failure at Dunedin was brought into even sharper focus when New Zealand replied with 460 for nine, including 171 from debutant Hamish Rutherford. That served only to heighten the opprobrium aimed at England, with Geoff Boycott sniping at the "holiday camp" atmosphere of the preparations. Flower forcefully rejected the claim, arguing that players could not be expected to spend such long periods away from home without recourse to a spot of recreation. If criticism was to be levelled, he argued, it was at England's habit of making a poor start to overseas Test series. Discounting victory over Bangladesh in 2009-10, they needed to go back to Port Elizabeth in 2004-05 for a win in the First Test of a series abroad.

The Basin Reserve, venue for the Second Test, is a proper cricket ground – it shares its space with no other sport – and Cook's team responded with some proper cricket. Compton scored his second hundred in two games, while Trott consolidated his reputation for quiet reliability with his ninth Test century. Pietersen and Prior also weighed in, and Broad claimed six for 51 as New Zealand – with heavy rain forecast over the final two days – were made to follow on.

But the negativity that occasionally blighted the reign of Strauss now became evident in Cook's captaincy. The most glaring example came when New

Phil Walter, Getty Images

All square: England's Man of the Series Matt Prior keeps New Zealand at bay.

Zealand slumped to 89 for five in the first innings, at which point Cook gave Anderson only two slips and a gully as he bowled to B-J. Watling. Sure enough, an edge soon flew through third slip at catchable height – and Watling proceeded to add a vital 100 with McCullum.

That left the teams with all to play for in Auckland, a quirky venue at which England had already chalked up two victories during the tour. Another fillip came in the knowledge that, when both the Twenty20 and one-day series had come down to a decider, England had twice raised their game.

Instead, it was the New Zealanders who found the players to make inspired interventions amid the toytown dimensions of Eden Park, where the straight boundaries were barely 65 yards long. Of the 17 sixes in the Test, they hit 16. And the lanky Peter Fulton, making a mockery of his average of 23, launched eight of them – one more than he had managed in his previous 12 Tests in total – while compiling a hundred in each innings.

There was a feeling that McCullum had enjoyed a psychological edge over Cook ever since mischievously likening him to Don Bradman in the build-up to the Second Test. Another of his strategies was to tell the media, the day before each Test, what he would do if he won the toss. In Auckland, he said he would bowl, as he had done at Dunedin and Wellington, a decision Cook himself went on to make, with disastrous consequences: at stumps on the first day, New Zealand had reached 250 for one. For England, it was sobering stuff.

From then on, they were fighting to save the series, and eventually entered the last day four wickets down – including Cook and Trott, two of their long-innings specialists. That they escaped with a draw was thanks to some old-fashioned cussedness. Prior's undefeated 110 was monumental, not least in his shepherding of the wide-eyed Panesar. There were 19 balls remaining when England's No. 11 came to the crease; Prior ensured he faced only five of them,

FIVE STATS YOU MAY HAVE MISSED

Benedict Bermange

- Kevin Pietersen's golden duck at Dunedin was his fifth in Tests, putting him equal fifth on this list for England:

8	S. J. Harmison	6	D. L. Underwood	5	R. G. D. Willis
		6	D. E. Malcolm	5	I. T. Botham
		6	D. Gough	**5**	**K. P. Pietersen**

Muttiah Muralitharan (Sri Lanka) holds the overall Test record, with 14.

- New Zealand remained unchanged in a series of three or more Tests for the first time. They had used 12 players on 11 previous occasions, most recently against West Indies at home in 2005-06.

- Nick Compton was the eighth English batsman to follow up a maiden Test century with another in his next innings, after:

E. H. Hendren (132, 142 v SA)	1924
W. R. Hammond (251, 200 v A)	1928-29
K. F. Barrington (128, 121 v WI)	1959-60
P. H. Parfitt (111, 101* v P)	1961-62–1962
M. H. Denness (118, 100 v I)	1974
C. T. Radley (158, 106 v NZ and P)	1978
R. S. Bopara (104, 143, 108 v WI)	2008-09–2009
N. R. D. Compton (117, 100 v NZ)	**2012-13**

Everton Weekes followed his maiden Test century for West Indies, against England in 1947-48, with four more in his next four innings, against India in 1948-49.

- Bruce Martin was 32 years 315 days old when he made his Test debut at Dunedin, New Zealand's oldest debutant since Bert Vance, who was 23 days older when he first appeared, also against England, at Wellington in March 1988.

- Stuart Broad took 102 minutes to get off the mark at Auckland, a Test record. Here are the longest times in minutes (when known) for batsmen to score their first run (a dagger indicates they were dismissed without scoring):

Mins			
102	**S. C. J. Broad**	**England v New Zealand at Auckland**	**2012-13**
101†	G. I. Allott	New Zealand v South Africa at Auckland	1998-99
97	T. G. Evans	England v Australia at Adelaide	1946-47
84	R. K. Chauhan	India v Sri Lanka at Ahmedabad	1993-94
82	P. I. Pocock	England v West Indies at Georgetown	1967-68
74	J. T. Murray	England v Australia at Sydney	1962-63
72	C. G. Rackemann	Australia v England at Sydney	1990-91
72	H. H. Streak	Zimbabwe v Pakistan at Karachi	1993-94
72†	P. M. Such	England v New Zealand at Manchester	1999
72†	Manjural Islam	Bangladesh v Sri Lanka at Colombo (SSC)	2002

Benedict Bermange is the cricket statistician for Sky Sports.

though Panesar did his best to make the experience even more nailbiting when he stumbled taking a quick single to give Prior the strike in the penultimate over. His manic crawl for the crease, like something out of a Looney Tunes cartoon, seemed to capture England's state of mind.

Panesar also had to face the start of the final over from Boult, but took a single third ball before Prior calmly laid the game to rest. If there was tension, he had long absorbed it. Even so, England were left to puzzle over their first 0–0 draw in a series of three games or more for 25 years. The last occurrence had also been in New Zealand – then, as now, a source of English frustration.

ENGLAND TOURING PARTY

*A. N. Cook (Essex; T/50); J. M. Anderson (Lancashire; T/50); J. M. Bairstow (Yorkshire; T/50/20); I. R. Bell (Warwickshire; T/50); S. C. J. Broad (Nottinghamshire; T/50/20); J. C. Buttler (Somerset; 50/20); N. R. D. Compton (Somerset; T); J. W. Dernbach (Surrey; 20); S. T. Finn (Middlesex; T/50/20); A. D. Hales (Nottinghamshire; 20); J. A. R. Harris (Middlesex; 50/20); M. J. Lumb (Nottinghamshire; 20); S. C. Meaker (Surrey; 20); E. J. G. Morgan (Middlesex; 50/20); G. Onions (Durham; T); M. S. Panesar (Sussex; T); S. R. Patel (Nottinghamshire; 50/20); K. P. Pietersen (Surrey; T); M. J. Prior (Sussex; T); J. E. Root (Yorkshire; T/50/20); G. P. Swann (Nottinghamshire; T/50); J. C. Tredwell (Kent; T/50/20); I. J. L. Trott (Warwickshire; T/50); C. R. Woakes (Warwickshire; T/50/20); L. J. Wright (Sussex; 20).

Coach: A. Flower (T), A. F. Giles (50/20). *Assistant coach/fielding coach:* R. G. Halsall. *Batting coach:* G. A. Gooch (T), G. P. Thorpe (50/20). *Fast bowling coach:* D. J. Saker. *Wicketkeeping coach:* B. N. French. *Strength and conditioning coach:* H. R. Bevan. *Team operations manager:* P. A. Neale. *Physiotherapist:* B. T. Langley. *Team doctor:* N. S. Peirce. *Analyst:* G. J. Broad. *Massage therapist:* M. E. S. Saxby. *Sports psychologist:* M. A. K. Bawden (T). *Security manager:* R. C. Dickason. *Media relations manager:* R. C. Evans.

D. R. Briggs (Hampshire) was originally selected for the Twenty20 squad, but injured his ankle and was replaced by Root. Swann was originally named in the Test party, but returned home before the series started with an elbow problem that required an operation, and was replaced by Tredwell. Pietersen flew home after the Second Test with a knee injury, but was not replaced. Broad captained in the Twenty20 matches.

TEST MATCH AVERAGES

NEW ZEALAND – BATTING AND FIELDING

	T	I	NO	R	HS	100	50	Avge	Ct
B. B. McCullum	3	4	1	248	74	0	3	82.66	1
P. G. Fulton	3	5	0	347	136	2	1	69.40	3
K. S. Williamson	3	5	1	213	91	0	2	53.25	1
†H. D. Rutherford	3	5	0	246	171	1	0	49.20	5
B. P. Martin	3	3	1	72	41	0	0	36.00	4
D. G. Brownlie	3	4	0	109	36	0	0	27.25	3
B-J. Watling	3	4	0	99	60	0	1	24.75	9
T. G. Southee	3	3	0	72	44	0	0	24.00	2
L. R. P. L. Taylor	3	5	1	94	41*	0	0	23.50	6
†N. Wagner	3	3	2	6	4*	0	0	6.00	3

Played in three Tests: T. A. Boult 2, 0 (1 ct).

BOWLING

	Style	O	M	R	W	BB	5I	Avge
K. S. Williamson	OB	35.5	11	90	6	4-44	0	15.00
T. A. Boult	LFM	134	42	321	11	6-68	1	29.18
N. Wagner	LFM	127	27	402	12	4-42	0	33.50
B. P. Martin	SLA	171	56	393	9	4-43	0	43.66
T. G. Southee	RFM	136.2	35	337	6	3-44	0	56.16

ENGLAND – BATTING AND FIELDING

	T	I	NO	R	HS	100	50	Avge	Ct
M. J. Prior	3	5	2	311	110*	1	2	103.66	10
I. J. L. Trott	3	5	0	282	121	1	1	56.40	3
N. R. D. Compton	3	5	0	232	117	2	0	46.40	3
I. R. Bell..................	3	5	1	153	75	0	1	38.25	3
†A. N. Cook.................	3	5	0	190	116	1	0	38.00	4
K. P. Pietersen	2	3	0	85	73	0	1	28.33	0
S. T. Finn	3	5	0	100	56	0	1	20.00	0
J. E. Root	3	5	0	88	45	0	0	17.60	1
†J. M. Anderson..............	3	4	1	35	23	0	0	11.66	1
†S. C. J. Broad	3	4	0	38	16	0	0	9.50	2
†M. S. Panesar	3	4	3	3	2*	0	0	3.00	1

Played in one Test: J. M. Bairstow 3, 6.

BOWLING

	Style	O	M	R	W	BB	5I	Avge
S. C. J. Broad	RFM	106.2	22	349	11	6-51	1	31.72
J. M. Anderson..............	RFM	117	26	370	10	4-137	0	37.00
S. T. Finn	RF	108.1	16	392	10	6-125	1	39.20
M. S. Panesar	SLA	130.2	46	350	5	2-53	0	70.00

Also bowled: J. E. Root (OB) 10–2–31–0; I. J. L. Trott (RM) 12–3–27–1.

At Whangarei, February 4, 2013. **No result.** New Zealand XI 70-1 (9.1 overs) v ‡**England XI**. *Rain, which had hampered England's practice sessions, returned to wash out the opening tour match – the first of three Twenty20 games at the New Cobham Oval – after only 41 minutes. Ross Taylor, in his first representative outing since missing New Zealand's tour of South Africa, did not get to bat.*

At Whangarei, February 5, 2013. **England XI won by 46 runs. England XI 186-3** (20 overs) (L. J. Wright 44, E. J. G. Morgan 48*, J. C. Buttler 57*); ‡**New Zealand XI 140** (19.5 overs) (C. Munro 55; S. C. J. Broad 3-22, C. R. Woakes 3-27, J. W. Dernbach 3-24). *After Buttler thwacked 57* from 24 balls to lift England to 186, Broad ensured there would be no late New Zealand fightback with a hat-trick in the 19th over. It was his second for England, but he admitted with a smile that he rated the one in the 2011 Trent Bridge Test against India a notch or two higher: "For a start it didn't have a caught long-on in it."*

At Whangarei, February 6, 2013. **New Zealand XI won by three wickets. England XI 170-5** (20 overs) (M. J. Lumb 45, E. J. G. Morgan 51*, J. C. Buttler 51); ‡**New Zealand XI 171-7** (20 overs) (H. D. Rutherford 30, A. P. Devcich 33, T. W. M. Latham 64; S. C. J. Broad 3-24). *England dipped to 77-4 in the 12th over, the slide started by Matt Henry's brilliant direct hit to run out Hales from fine leg. But Morgan and Buttler added 87 in 50 balls to ensure a competitive total on a sunny Waitangi Day Bank Holiday. Latham then spanked 64 from 38 to keep the New Zealanders abreast of the rate. They needed just five from the final over, bowled by Dernbach; after Bracewell fell to the first ball, skipper Ellis and Henry managed singles from each of the last five to give the New Zealand XI a share of this warm-up series.*

LIMITED-OVERS INTERNATIONAL REPORTS BY DAVID CLOUGH

NEW ZEALAND v ENGLAND

First Twenty20 International

At Auckland, February 9, 2013 (floodlit). England won by 40 runs. Toss: New Zealand. Twenty20 international debuts: T. A. Boult, H. D. Rutherford.

England dominated proceedings in front of a crowd of almost 24,000, who lapped up the spectacle in perfect weather and saw the tourists adapt skilfully to the ground's peculiar layout. Even without the rested Kevin Pietersen, England still had the firepower to clear the ropes 15 times to New Zealand's eight, taking toll of Eden Park's temptingly short straight boundaries. That differential accounted almost exactly for the winning margin, after England – boosted by a fourth-wicket stand of 81 in 43 balls between Morgan and Bairstow – had piled up their best Twenty20 total. New Zealand dropped five catches under troublesome low lights, with Taylor missing two on his return to international cricket. Broad then made sure with career-best Twenty20 figures as England bowled back of a length, successfully forcing the New Zealand batsmen to aim for the less reachable square boundaries. Match awards were not made at any stage of the tour.

Attendance: 23,758.

England

		B	4	6
M. J. Lumb *c 1 b 11*	22	15	1	2
A. D. Hales *st 3 b 9*	21	16	2	1
L. J. Wright *c 9 b 8*	42	20	3	4
E. J. G. Morgan *c 4 b 9*	46	26	4	3
J. M. Bairstow *c 2 b 10*	38	22	3	2
†J. C. Buttler *not out*	32	16	2	3
S. R. Patel *c 3 b 8*	2	3	0	0
*S. C. J. Broad *c 3 b 10*	4	3	1	0
J. C. Tredwell *not out*	0	0	0	0
W 6, n-b 1	7			

6 overs: 62-1   (20 overs) 214-7

1/29 2/89 3/91 4/172 5/194 6/197 7/203

S. T. Finn and J. W. Dernbach did not bat.

McClenaghan 4–0–29–1; Boult 4–0–40–2; Hira 4–0–42–2; N. L. McCullum 4–0–49–0; Ellis 3–0–40–2; Franklin 1–0–14–0.

New Zealand

		B	4	6
H. D. Rutherford *c 9 b 8*	18	11	2	1
M. J. Guptill *c 8 b 3*	44	32	3	2
*†B. B. McCullum *c 4 b 10*	10	5	2	0
L. R. P. L. Taylor *c 5 b 10*	13	14	1	0
C. Munro *b 8*	28	19	0	3
J. E. C. Franklin *c 6 b 8*	8	5	0	1
N. L. McCullum *c 6 b 3*	3	6	0	0
A. M. Ellis *c 3 b 10*	4	5	0	0
R. M. Hira *not out*	20	11	2	1
T. A. Boult *c 7 b 8*	4	6	0	0
M. J. McClenaghan *not out*	6	7	1	0
L-b 8, w 3, n-b 5	16			

6 overs: 54-2   (20 overs) 174-9

1/31 2/46 3/77 4/111 5/127 6/128 7/134 8/135 9/156

Finn 4–0–39–3; Broad 4–0–24–4; Dernbach 4–0–33–0; Wright 4–0–29–2; Patel 2–0–17–0; Tredwell 2–0–24–0.

Umpires: C. B. Gaffaney and D. J. Walker.   Third umpire: G. A. V. Baxter.

NEW ZEALAND v ENGLAND

Second Twenty20 International

At Hamilton, February 12, 2013 (floodlit). New Zealand won by 55 runs. Toss: England.

England had a measure of control after choosing to field first, only for Brendon McCullum to take the game out of their reach with a late onslaught. He helped ensure 38 came from the last two overs, and left Broad nursing his most expensive Twenty20 analysis since India's Yuvraj Singh hit him for six sixes in an over at Durban in September 2007. England needed to pull off their highest successful chase, against a seaming ball under lights, but Mitchell McClenaghan – apparently still fired up after receiving a beamer from Dernbach at Auckland – removed Hales and Wright with successive deliveries in the second over. Only Jos Buttler's maiden international fifty held New Zealand up after that, with England this time losing the six count 10–2. Passed fit despite a jarred back, Morgan could barely lay a bat on the thrifty Ian Butler; earlier, a close shave with a flame-thrower on the boundary had left Morgan shaken and England unhappy at the machine's location.

Attendance: 7,625.

New Zealand

		B	4	6
M. J. Guptill *c 2 b 9*	47	31	4	2
H. D. Rutherford *c 6 b 3*	40	27	1	3
*†B. B. McCullum *c 1 b 11*	74	38	6	5
L. R. P. L. Taylor *c 4 b 3*	4	6	0	0
C. Munro *c 4 b 11*	7	8	1	0
G. D. Elliott *b 11*	4	6	0	0
J. E. C. Franklin *not out*	6	4	1	0
N. L. McCullum *not out*	0	0	0	0
B 1, l-b 3, w 6	10			

6 overs: 54-0   (20 overs) 192-6

1/75 2/105 3/124 4/139 5/154 6/188

I. G. Butler, T. A. Boult and M. J. McClenaghan did not bat.

Tredwell 2–0–20–1; Broad 4–0–53–0; Finn 4–0–33–0; Dernbach 4–0–38–3; Wright 4–0–24–2; Patel 2–0–20–0.

England

		B	4	6
M. J. Lumb *b 8*	17	23	2	0
A. D. Hales *b 11*	5	4	1	0
L. J. Wright *c 1 b 11*	0	1	0	0
J. M. Bairstow *c 11 b 9*	8	9	2	0
E. J. G. Morgan *c 5 b 9*	13	22	2	0
†J. C. Buttler *c 4 b 7*	54	30	9	1
S. R. Patel *run out*	6	7	1	0
*S. C. J. Broad *c 1 b 7*	1	3	0	0
J. C. Tredwell *b 7*	22	11	3	1
S. T. Finn *not out*	5	6	0	0
J. W. Dernbach *c 9 b 7*	0	1	0	0
L-b 3, w 3	6			

6 overs: 31-3   (19.3 overs) 137

1/9 2/9 3/24 4/43 5/47 6/62 7/80 8/115 9/137

Boult 4–0–40–0; McClenaghan 4–0–24–2; Butler 4–0–9–2; N. L. McCullum 3–0–26–1; Franklin 3.3–0–15–4; Elliott 1–0–20–0.

Umpires: G. A. V. Baxter and D. J. Walker.   Third umpire: C. B. Gaffaney.

NEW ZEALAND v ENGLAND

Third Twenty20 International

At Wellington (Westpac Stadium), February 15, 2013 (floodlit). England won by ten wickets. Toss: England.

England made a mockery of their Hamilton defeat in the most one-sided of deciders, as Lumb and Hales hurried them to only their second ten-wicket win in Twenty20 cricket after besting West Indies at The Oval in September 2011. They overhauled New Zealand's below-par total with 44 balls to spare when Lumb helped Butler over backward square leg and out of the stadium. Only once before, when Hales and Ravi Bopara added 159 for the second wicket against West Indies at Trent Bridge in 2012, had an England pair shared a bigger Twenty20 partnership. Their bowlers, though, had done the hard work, and Broad was the key. He had taken the blame for choosing to bowl first in the previous match, but held his nerve to do so again. He and Finn then produced exemplary new-ball spells, and only Guptill hung around.

Attendance: 20,238.

New Zealand

		B	4	6
H. D. Rutherford *c 11 b 8*	11	10	2	0
M. J. Guptill *c and b 8*	59	55	2	1
*†B. B. McCullum *c 5 b 9*	26	20	3	0
L. R. P. L. Taylor *c 5 b 6*	6	4	0	1
G. D. Elliott *c 10 b 11*	15	12	0	1
C. Munro *c 6 b 8*	1	3	0	0
J. E. C. Franklin *c 9 b 11*	15	14	3	0
N. L. McCullum *c 7 b 11*	0	1	0	0
I. G. Butler *not out*	1	1	0	0
B 4, l-b 1	5			

6 overs: 30-1   (20 overs) 139-8

1/17 2/62 3/70 4/95 5/99 6/128 7/130 8/139

T. A. Boult and M. J. McClenaghan did not bat.

Finn 4–0–18–0; Broad 4–0–15–3; Dernbach 4–0–36–3; Wright 2–0–19–0; Tredwell 4–0–31–1; Root 2–0–15–1.

England

		B	4	6
M. J. Lumb *not out*	53	34	1	5
A. D. Hales *not out*	80	42	9	4
L-b 5, w 5	10			

6 overs: 60-0   (12.4 overs) 143-0

L. J. Wright, E. J. G. Morgan, J. M. Bairstow, J. E. Root, †J. C. Buttler, *S. C. J. Broad, J. C. Tredwell, S. T. Finn and J. W. Dernbach did not bat.

Boult 2–0–20–0; McClenaghan 3–1–38–0; Butler 2.4–0–41–0; N. L. McCullum 4–0–32–0; Franklin 1–0–7–0.

Umpires: G. A. V. Baxter and C. B. Gaffaney.   Third umpire: D. J. Walker.
Series referee: R. S. Mahanama.

NEW ZEALAND v ENGLAND

First One-Day International

At Hamilton, February 17, 2013 (day/night). New Zealand won by three wickets. Toss: New Zealand.

A seesaw match culminated in a dramatic – but pyrrhic – victory for New Zealand as Brendon McCullum and a limping Guptill took them over the line. The sting in the tail was that both Guptill, who returned to see them home, having retiring hurt after the sixth over with a hamstring strain, and left-arm seamer McClenaghan – unable to finish his final over because of a side injury – would play no further part in the series. England ought to have made more after reaching 190 for three with ten overs to go, but the onslaught never materialised. In New Zealand's chase, Williamson provided the substance, before McCullum took toll of the previously miserly Anderson, whose ninth over began 644 and proved almost as expensive as his first eight combined. But it was to be Guptill's finale, as – with no runner allowed – he re-emerged in the 46th over, with 41 still needed, and hit 24 from ten balls. For Anderson, there was the consolation of a 529th international victim, which took him past Ian Botham as England's most prolific wicket-taker in all formats.

England

*A. N. Cook b McClenaghan	4	G. P. Swann c Taylor b Franklin	16	
I. R. Bell c B. B. McCullum b Franklin	64	S. T. Finn c Guptill b McClenaghan	0	
I. J. L. Trott b Mills	68	J. M. Anderson not out	0	
J. E. Root b Franklin	56	L-b 4, w 5, n-b 1	10	
E. J. G. Morgan c Guptill b Mills	1			
†J. C. Buttler c Elliott b McClenaghan	21	1/11 (1) 2/95 (2)	(49.3 overs) 258	
C. R. Woakes c B. B. McCullum b Ellis	17	3/184 (3) 4/190 (5) 5/220 (6)		
S. C. J. Broad c B. B. McCullum		6/222 (4) 7/228 (8) 8/247 (7)		
b McClenaghan	1	9/248 (10) 10/258 (9)	10 overs: 33-1	

Mills 10–2–32–2; McClenaghan 9.4–0–56–4; Ellis 10–0–67–1; N. L. McCullum 10–0–42–0; Franklin 6.3–0–38–3; Williamson 2.2–0–12–0; Elliott 1–0–7–0.

New Zealand

B-J. Watling b Anderson	2	N. L. McCullum lbw b Swann	14	
M. J. Guptill not out	27	A. M. Ellis c Finn b Broad	13	
K. S. Williamson run out	74	L-b 7, w 6	13	
L. R. P. L. Taylor c Finn b Woakes	22			
G. D. Elliott c Morgan b Woakes	22	1/2 (1) 2/75 (4)	(7 wkts, 48.5 overs) 259	
*†B. B. McCullum not out	69	3/124 (5) 4/142 (3)		
J. E. C. Franklin c Buttler b Finn	3	5/155 (7) 6/186 (8) 7/218 (9)	10 overs: 32-1	

K. D. Mills and M. J. McClenaghan did not bat.

Guptill, when 3, retired hurt at 18-1 and resumed at 218-7.

Anderson 9–1–36–1; Finn 10–0–54–1; Broad 9.5–0–56–1; Woakes 10–0–52–2; Swann 10–0–54–1.

Umpires: G. A. V. Baxter and S. Ravi.   Third umpire: R. J. Tucker.

NEW ZEALAND v ENGLAND

Second One-Day International

At Napier, February 20, 2013 (day/night). England won by eight wickets. Toss: England. One-day international debut: H. D. Rutherford.

Anderson collected only the second five-wicket haul of his one-day career after he and Finn exerted remarkable control with the new ball. Both got through exemplary six-over spells costing only 11 runs, but from 22 for two New Zealand mustered a worthwhile total through Taylor's return to form and another Brendon McCullum special. The former captain and his successor blitzed a century stand from 53 deliveries, dominated by McCullum's nine fours and four sixes off 36. Taylor, cheered to the wicket in every match since his self-imposed isolation, earned a standing ovation, having made his seventh one-day international hundred. It was not yet vintage Taylor, but it was a start. Even so, England achieved their target with ease, and Root provided another demonstration of his bustle, invention and class. He finished with 79 not out from 56 balls, having shared an unbroken stand of 121 with Trott as England set up a decider at Eden Park.

New Zealand

B-J. Watling c Cook b Anderson	7	
H. D. Rutherford c Cook b Anderson	11	
K. S. Williamson b Woakes	33	
L. R. P. L. Taylor c Buttler b Anderson	100	
G. D. Elliott c sub (J. M. Bairstow) b Finn	23	
*†B. B. McCullum c Woakes b Broad	74	
J. E. C. Franklin c Root b Woakes	1	
N. L. McCullum c Buttler b Anderson	7	
T. G. Southee c Woakes	2	

K. D. Mills not out	3	
T. A. Boult c Woakes b Anderson	1	
L-b 3, w 3, n-b 1	7	

1/12 (1) 2/19 (2) 3/91 (3) (48.5 overs) 269
4/143 (5) 5/243 (6) 6/245 (7)
7/254 (8) 8/261 (9) 9/267 (4)
10/269 (11) 10 overs: 21-2

Anderson 9.5–2–34–5; Finn 10–1–33–1; Woakes 10–0–68–3; Broad 9–0–69–1; Swann 10–0–62–0.

England

*A. N. Cook c and b Southee	78
I. R. Bell c Rutherford b Williamson	44
I. J. L. Trott not out	65
J. E. Root not out	79
L-b 1, w 3	4

1/89 (2) 2/149 (1) (2 wkts, 47.4 overs) 270
10 overs: 45-0

E. J. G. Morgan, †J. C. Buttler, C. R. Woakes, S. C. J. Broad, G. P. Swann, S. T. Finn and J. M. Anderson did not bat.

Mills 6.4–0–43–0; Boult 9–1–55–0; Franklin 5–0–32–0; Southee 9–0–54–1; N. L. McCullum 10–0–46–0; Williamson 8–0–39–1.

Umpires: C. B. Gaffaney and R. J. Tucker.   Third umpire: S. Ravi.

NEW ZEALAND v ENGLAND

Third One-Day International

At Auckland, February 23, 2013 (day/night). England won by five wickets. Toss: England.

After a string of alternating wins and losses, England broke serve at last to seal their second 2–1 victory of the tour, and their first one-day series win in New Zealand since 1991-92. Finn and Anderson were again central, with Finn especially impressive off his economical new 12-stride approach, designed to curb his costly habit of bashing into the stumps. Two days earlier, MCC had announced that any future transgression would be called a no-ball, and not – as previously – a dead ball; the new regulation would take effect from the start of May in internationals. McCullum did his manful best again, thrashing five sixes in 68 balls, but even he could not conjure up a competitive total once Taylor had got the wrong end of a DRS verdict. England's reply was never discomfited, despite the absence of an individual half-century, and Morgan's flourish – 39 from 24 balls – secured a series triumph with more than 12 overs to spare.

New Zealand

B-J. Watling c Swann b Finn	1		K. D. Mills lbw b Woakes	2
H. D. Rutherford c Buttler b Finn	2		T. G. Southee not out	5
K. S. Williamson c Buttler b Anderson	7			
L. R. P. L. Taylor c Buttler b Broad	28		L-b 3, w 8	11
G. D. Elliott run out	24			
*†B. B. McCullum c Anderson b Swann	79		1/2 (1) 2/11 (3) 3/11 (2) (43.5 overs)	185
J. E. C. Franklin c and b Swann	13		4/64 (5) 5/67 (4) 6/99 (7)	
N. L. McCullum c Cook b Finn	4		7/109 (8) 8/146 (9) 9/150 (10)	
A. M. Ellis c Woakes b Broad	9		10/185 (6) 10 overs: 18-3	

Anderson 8–1–34–1; Finn 9–3–27–3; Woakes 9–0–34–1; Broad 9–0–38–2; Swann 8.5–0–49–2.

England

*A. N. Cook c Watling b Southee	46		C. R. Woakes not out	3
I. R. Bell c Rutherford b Ellis	24		L-b 1, w 4	5
I. J. L. Trott c Watling b Southee	38			
J. E. Root not out	28		1/42 (2) 2/109 (3) (5 wkts, 37.3 overs)	186
E. J. G. Morgan c Mills b Ellis	39		3/112 (1) 4/168 (5)	
†J. C. Buttler c Watling b Southee	3		5/171 (6) 10 overs: 50-1	

S. C. J. Broad, G. P. Swann, S. T. Finn and J. M. Anderson did not bat.

Mills 7.3–0–34–0; Southee 10–1–48–3; Ellis 8–0–35–2; N. L. McCullum 7–0–39–0; Williamson 1–0–9–0; Franklin 4–0–20–0.

Umpires: C. B. Gaffaney and S. Ravi. Third umpire: R. J. Tucker.
Series referee: R. S. Mahanama.

NEW ZEALAND XI v ENGLAND XI

At Queenstown, February 27–March 2, 2013. New Zealand XI won by three wickets. Toss: New Zealand XI.

England were left digesting their first defeat in a first-class tour match since going down to the Indian Board President's XI at Vadodara in February 2006. This setback had seemed unlikely after Bell's serene 158 set up England's big total. Rutherford cemented his Test place with 90 in the reply, in which a late flourish from Corey Anderson restricted the deficit to 77. Gillespie and Wagner, who shared 11 wickets in the match, made regular inroads in the second innings, but the New Zealanders' target of 334 from 90 overs still looked far off at 154 for five after 51. Watling, however, inked in as the Test wicketkeeper, busied himself, putting on 82 in 18 overs with Anderson, then 46 in ten with Neesham. With Wagner forthright at the other end, Watling hauled the hosts over the line with eight balls to spare. Onions had match figures of one for 213 as England's bowlers gave an undistinguished performance. The exception was Swann – and he was soon on the plane home after his long-standing elbow problem flared up again.

Close of play: first day, England XI 357-7 (Bell 127, Broad 6); second day, New Zealand XI 224-6 (Watling 26); third day, England XI 256-9 (Swann 41, Onions 2).

England XI

*A. N. Cook c Watling b Wagner	60	– run out	24
N. R. D. Compton c Watling b Neesham	21	– c Watling b Gillespie	1
I. J. L. Trott c Watling b Neesham	1	– c Watling b Gillespie	20
K. P. Pietersen c Rutherford b Neesham	14	– c Watling b Wagner	8
I. R. Bell c sub (M. D. Rae) b Wagner	158	– (8) c and b Cachopa	38
J. E. Root b Cachopa	49	– c Latham b Cachopa	17
†M. J. Prior c Patel b Neesham	41	– (5) c Watling b Wagner	68
C. R. Woakes c sub (M. D. Rae) b Wagner	16	– (7) c Rutherford b Gillespie	9
S. C. J. Broad c Latham b Gillespie	14	– c Brownlie b Gillespie	10
G. P. Swann c sub (M. D. Rae) b Wagner	27	– not out	41
G. Onions not out	3	– not out	2
L-b 6, w 4, n-b 12	22	L-b 3, w 3, n-b 12	18

1/45 (2) 2/65 (3) 3/81 (4)   (103.2 overs) 426   1/19 (2)   (9 wkts dec, 62 overs) 256
4/124 (1) 5/221 (6) 6/281 (7)   2/34 (1) 3/44 (4)
7/318 (8) 8/384 (9) 9/415 (10) 10/426 (5)   4/67 (3) 5/145 (6) 6/147 (5)
                                                       7/167 (7) 8/194 (9) 9/254 (8)

Gillespie 23–2–112–1; Wagner 26.2–5–98–4; Neesham 20–2–73–4; Anderson 8–4–16–0; Patel 14–1–81–0; Cachopa 12–1–40–1. *Second innings*—Gillespie 16–2–87–4; Wagner 19–5–56–2; Neesham 6–0–33–0; Cachopa 14–3–36–2; Patel 7–0–41–0.

New Zealand XI

*T. W. M. Latham lbw b Swann	16	– c Prior b Swann	48
H. D. Rutherford b Woakes	90	– c Compton b Woakes	33
C. Cachopa c Swann b Broad	6	– b Broad	0
N. T. Broom run out	14	– lbw b Broad	41
D. G. Brownlie c Prior b Trott	63	– c Swann b Woakes	17
†B-J. Watling not out	66	– not out	89
J. D. S. Neesham lbw b Swann	0	– (8) c Broad b Root	20
C. J. Anderson c Broad b Onions	67	– (7) b Root	44
N. Wagner not out	11	– not out	28
L-b 8, w 2, n-b 6	16	B 4, l-b 5, n-b 5	14

1/56 (1) 2/63 (3)   (7 wkts dec, 95 overs) 349   1/56 (2)   (7 wkts, 88.4 overs) 334
3/94 (4) 4/175 (2)   2/57 (3) 3/121 (1)
5/223 (5) 6/224 (7) 7/329 (8)   4/129 (4) 5/154 (5) 6/236 (7) 7/282 (8)

J. S. Patel and M. R. Gillespie did not bat.

Broad 21–4–68–1; Onions 22–1–131–1; Woakes 19–5–64–1; Swann 22–7–53–2; Trott 7–2–17–1; Root 4–2–8–0. *Second innings*—Broad 21.4–3–90–2; Onions 16–2–82–0; Woakes 22–6–67–2; Swann 20–7–44–1; Root 9–1–42–2.

Umpires: C. B. Gaffaney and D. J. Walker.

NEW ZEALAND v ENGLAND

First Test Match

RICHARD BOOCK

At Dunedin (University Oval), March 6–10, 2013. Drawn. Toss: New Zealand. Test debuts: B. P. Martin, H. D. Rutherford.

To suggest New Zealand had never started a Test match amid such turmoil might have been stretching a point. But, even by their standards, this wasn't a bad effort. Miffed at

Bungle ahoy: Ian Bell chips to a sprawling Hamish Rutherford as England implode.

losing the captaincy, Taylor was still feeling his way back into the squad after his self-imposed exile, with coach Mike Hesson – the man responsible for his demotion – now cast as public enemy No. 1, and New Zealand's board close behind. Throw in the withdrawal of seamer Doug Bracewell, forced out of the build-up with a cut foot – suffered while cleaning up after a party – and the portents could hardly have been gloomier.

Five days later, it was hard to recall what all the fuss had been about. Not only had New Zealand secured a draw against the team ranked second in the world, but they should have gone one up, as they had on England's previous visit, in 2007-08. It said something, too, that the main emotion of both captains at the end of the game was one of relief: Cook because England had been able to stave off a chastening defeat; McCullum because New Zealand had finally put together a competitive performance. Suddenly, the series felt alive.

England's defeat in the warm-up game at Queenstown had been blithely depicted as a blip, not an omen. And while it would be unfair to say they headed into this match with a swagger, they nevertheless gave off the air of a team who expected to dictate terms. Their first innings was a case in point. After England had been forced to sit out the first day as the drought affecting the region broke in untimely fashion, their batsmen were architects of their own misfortune on the second. Inserted on a slow pitch holding no fears, and against an attack deemed largely harmless, England collapsed for 167.

If Compton and Pietersen could be absolved of some blame, the same could scarcely be said for the rest. After Compton had played on in the game's third over, Cook slapped a long-hop from Wagner to point, Bell drove airily to short extra, and Root jabbed a widish ball from Boult to third slip. Prior was out cutting, Trott sweeping; Broad, back in the side in place of the injured Tim Bresnan, after being dropped in India, and Finn both holed out in the deep. It was as if England's previous Test innings – a 154-over monument to self-denial at Nagpur in December – had never happened.

New Zealand's bowlers deserved credit for their discipline, though even they must have been surprised by England's approach. Wagner's inswinger to undo Pietersen first ball was the delivery of the match, but his other three wickets were free gifts. The 32-year-old debutant slow left-armer Bruce Martin was another beneficiary of England's largesse: his four-wicket bag included three heaves across the line and Prior's miscued cut.

By stumps, Hesson may have been feeling better about life: the selections of Martin and Wagner had paid off, as had his new opening batting partnership, which eased to 131 by the close. Picked for his first Test since December 2009 after a stellar domestic season with Canterbury, Fulton was unbeaten on 46, and the following morning would complete his first Test fifty in nearly seven years. And on his home ground Hamish Rutherford – another debutant – was 77 not out and quietly restoring a measure of family pride: in the Caribbean in 1984-85 his father, Ken, had begun his own Test career with a pair, kicking off a horror series that brought him 12 runs in seven innings.

The third day belonged to Rutherford. Carving powerfully through the off side, and twice in an over lifting Panesar for six, he overhauled England's total all by himself, after putting on 158 with Fulton, New Zealand's best for the first wicket in nine years. He finished with the highest score by a Test debutant for almost a decade, and he beat a record that had stood since the dawn of cricketing time, passing Charles Bannerman's undefeated 165 in the very first Test, at Melbourne in 1876-77, to make the highest score against England in the first innings on debut. In all, he faced only 217 deliveries. It needed Anderson's first offering with the second new ball to see the back of him.

HIGHEST SCORE IN FIRST TEST INNINGS

287	R. E. Foster	England v Australia at Sydney	1903-04
222*	J. A. Rudolph.	South Africa v Bangladesh at Chittagong	2002-03
214	L. G. Rowe	West Indies v New Zealand at Kingston	1971-72
214	M. S. Sinclair.	New Zealand v West Indies at Wellington	1999-2000
201*	D. S. B. P. Kuruppu. . . .	Sri Lanka v Bangladesh at Colombo (CCC).	1986-87
187	**S. Dhawan**	**India v Australia at Mohali**	**2012-13**
171	**H. D. Rutherford**	**New Zealand v England at Dunedin**	**2012-13**
170	Yasir Hameed	Pakistan v Bangladesh at Karachi	2003-04
166	Khalid Ibadulla	Pakistan v Australia at Karachi	1964-65
165*	C. Bannerman	Australia v England at Melbourne.	1876-77

England had their moments but, on a docile surface, disappointingly few. Panesar slipped an arm-ball through Williamson's attempted cut, and Anderson snuffed out promising starts from Taylor and Brownlie. But this merely hastened the arrival of the in-form McCullum, who looked in the mood before the rain returned, with New Zealand in complete control at 402 for seven. Armed with a lead of 235 on the fourth morning, McCullum cracked three sixes before departing for 74 from 59 balls and, after the dismissal of Martin, enjoyed the rare luxury of a declaration. To widespread disbelief, New Zealand led by 293. England were batting to save the game.

In two series already on the tour, they had bounced back successfully. Now their resolve stiffened once more. Cook and Compton defied New Zealand's attack until shortly before the fourth-day close in a stand of 231 – England's highest opening partnership since Andrew Strauss and Marcus Trescothick put on 273 at Durban in 2004-05, and their eighth-highest in all. Cook nicked Boult just before stumps, having completed his 24th Test century and his sixth in seven as captain; two balls after his departure, Compton worked Southee to midwicket for the single that brought up his first. Watched by his father, Richard, he celebrated with gusto, and later admitted: "Reaching the century was the biggest relief of my life." Denis and Nick Compton now joined Vic Richardson and the Chappells, Ian and Greg, as the only grandfathers and grandsons to score Test hundreds.

England began the final day still trailing by 59. But the wicket was playing few tricks, New Zealand's bowlers had been blunted, and the skies were clear. After nearly seven hours, Compton's resistance was ended by Wagner, but Finn was busy knuckling down for one of Test cricket's more unlikely rearguards. Assuming the nightwatchman's role from Anderson, he used his long reach and a newly honed defensive technique to demoralise the bowling.

Begged, borrowed and blocked: nightwatchman Steven Finn used one of Kevin Pietersen's cast-off bats to help England to a draw.

Finn had made a Test-best 20 in the first innings, batting almost an hour – another personal best. Now he lasted for four and three-quarter hours while compiling a maiden first-class fifty, at one stage playing out 49 dot-balls in succession. With Trott resolute at the other end, England's only wobble came when Finn fell in the second over after tea and Root was run out moments later by Southee's direct hit from cover.

But Bell and Prior batted out the last 16 overs to ensure Finn's work would not be wasted. And McCullum, once Finn's team-mate at Otago, wryly observed: "I've seen his batting before. He's certainly worked on it." England were simply grateful, and Finn finished the game with a promise of four crates of wine – two each from Cook and Anderson. Not for the last time in the series, England were toasting a great escape.

Close of play: first day, no play; second day, New Zealand 131-0 (Fulton 46, Rutherford 77); third day, New Zealand 402-7 (McCullum 44, Martin 17); fourth day, England 234-1 (Compton 102, Finn 0).

England

*A. N. Cook c Rutherford b Wagner	10	– c Watling b Boult 116
N. R. D. Compton b Southee	0	– lbw b Wagner 117
I. J. L. Trott c Boult b Martin	45	– (4) c and b Wagner 52
K. P. Pietersen lbw b Wagner	0	– (5) c Watling b Wagner 12
I. R. Bell c Rutherford b Wagner	24	– (6) not out 26
J. E. Root c Brownlie b Boult	4	– (7) run out 0
†M. J. Prior c Williamson b Martin	23	– (8) not out 23
S. C. J. Broad c Brownlie b Martin	10	
S. T. Finn c Rutherford b Wagner	20	– (3) lbw b Martin 56
J. M. Anderson c Wagner b Martin	23	
M. S. Panesar not out	1	
B 4, l-b 1, w 2	7	B 6, l-b 11, w 1, n-b 1 19

1/5 (2) 2/18 (1) 3/18 (4) 4/64 (5) (55 overs) 167
5/71 (6) 6/108 (7) 7/109 (3) 8/119 (8)
9/166 (9) 10/167 (10)

1/231 (1) (6 wkts, 170 overs) 421
2/265 (2) 3/355 (4)
4/367 (5) 5/386 (3) 6/390 (7)

Southee 15–3–45–1; Boult 15–4–32–1; Wagner 11–2–42–4; Martin 14–4–43–4. *Second innings*— Southee 36–8–94–0; Boult 35–12–49–1; Wagner 43–9–141–3; Martin 44–13–90–1; Williamson 12–3–30–0.

New Zealand

P. G. Fulton c Prior b Anderson	55
H. D. Rutherford c sub (C. R. Woakes) b Anderson	171
K. S. Williamson b Panesar	24
L. R. P. L. Taylor c Trott b Anderson	31
D. G. Brownlie b Anderson	27
*B. B. McCullum c Anderson b Broad	74
†B-J. Watling b Broad	0
T. G. Southee b Broad	25
B. P. Martin c Prior b Finn	41
N. Wagner not out	4
L-b 8	8

T. A. Boult did not bat.

1/158 (1) 2/249 (3) 3/267 (2) 4/310 (4) 5/321 (5) 6/326 (7) 7/370 (8) 8/447 (6) 9/460 (9) (9 wkts dec, 116.4 overs) 460

Anderson 33–2–137–4; Finn 26.4–3–102–1; Broad 28–3–118–3; Panesar 22–2–83–1; Trott 2–0–4–0; Root 5–1–8–0.

Umpires: Asad Rauf and P. R. Reiffel.   Third umpire: R. J. Tucker.

NEW ZEALAND v ENGLAND

Second Test Match

MIKE WALTERS

At Wellington (Basin Reserve), March 14–18, 2013. Drawn. Toss: New Zealand.

Bang on cue, after drought had left Wellington within three weeks of the taps running dry, Cyclone Sandra had the final say. It may have been immaterial: as eco-warriors and cricket lovers objected to a planned flyover, which threatened to compromise views around the eastern side of New Zealand's oldest Test ground, curator Brett Sipthorpe's own strip of tarmac would probably have refused to yield a result – even if he had detonated half a dozen sticks of dynamite on a good length. At a venue where England had a fine record of only one defeat in ten previous Tests, they had to settle for soggy anticlimax. The teams would head for Auckland neck and neck once more.

The game began hours after puffs of white smoke at the Vatican had heralded the election of Pope Francis – only for McCullum to commit the cardinal sin of inserting England with neither the conditions nor the fresh attack to back him up. His bowlers had been detained in the field for 170 overs at Dunedin the previous weekend, and were now condemned to another 147 of footslog, spanning ten and a quarter hours. On the first afternoon, one spectator had come dressed as the Pope; it is not known whether McCullum received his forgiveness.

Sipthorpe's tribute to Wellington's highways department proved an ideal surface for Compton – still reassuringly stodgy but playing with more conviction off the front foot – to unfurl a second consecutive hundred. At Dunedin, his father Richard had been an ever-present cheerleader on the boundary, and Compton appreciatively compared his support to the eye contact maintained by tennis stars Novak Djokovic and Rafael Nadal with their coaches. This time, Compton senior tried to stay hidden under the Basin Reserve's line of crimson pohutukawa trees, away from the all-seeing TV cameras. But, as if by magic, he reappeared on the picket fence, a portrait of paternal joy, when Compton's 15th four, a cover-drive off Wagner, took him to three figures. Dad celebrated with a cone of French fries from the catering stall next to the scoreboard – confirming, perhaps, the adage about chips off the old block.

Making a fist of it: Nick Compton's mission to prove his doubters wrong peaked with back-to-back Test hundreds at Dunedin and Wellington.

By the time Compton fell, driving wearily at Martin, he had added 210 in 63 overs with Trott, an England record for the second wicket in New Zealand. For Trott, remorseless off his pads, a ninth Test hundred was steady, chanceless and almost inevitable. Moving through the gears – from neutral to first – he reached his half-century off 106 deliveries, completed his hundred in a further 68, then forensically chiselled his way to 121 from the next 60 before stumps. It was a let-down when he was caught behind off Boult from the first ball he faced next morning.

Pietersen, his movement clearly restricted by his knee injury – despite being passed fit – hit his only six of the tour, a straight blow off Martin. But it felt like a token act of aggression amid three and a half hours of what, by his standards, resembled near-pacifism. Instead, New Zealand spirits were suppressed by Prior, carving through the off side like a chef mutilating the Sunday roast with a chainsaw. His 82 from 99 balls gave England their highest total at Wellington, and their bowlers a licence to attack fuller lengths than they had explored on the doormat of Dunedin.

Broad picked up the gauntlet superbly. Fast, straight and working up a locomotive's head of steam, he partly attributed his six for 51 – figures he had bettered only twice in Tests – to his sister Gemma, England's video analyst. She had compiled a DVD of his greatest hits, and spotted an optimum angle of delivery on the return crease (wider of the stumps, essentially) as a common denominator in his best spells.

When Broad dismissed Rutherford, then castled Taylor next ball, New Zealand were in trouble; when they were reduced to 89 for five in the opening half-hour of the third morning, they were flirting with a rout. But a stand of 100 between McCullum and Watling occupied 31 overs, and bought valuable time as Cyclone Sandra spun like a tumble-dryer towards the Cook Strait. New Zealand ultimately missed their follow-on target by 12, and England's only hope was to hustle them out a second time. Not since Durban in 1999-2000 had they enforced the follow-on in an overseas Test. On that occasion, South Africa's Gary Kirsten responded with 275; a different kind of obstacle awaited England now.

There was brief hope as Panesar, bowling selflessly into a stiff wind, snared Rutherford in the leg trap. But once Williamson – compact and technically assured, especially off the back foot – and Taylor had negotiated 31 overs on the fourth day, steady drizzle and pulses of more organised rain confirmed England's worst fears. In all, 145 overs were lost.

In truth, it would have taken a Herculean effort from Cook's tiring bowlers to dislodge the New Zealanders again on such a true surface. England's fast bowling coach David Saker made some unflattering remarks about how the local pitches were turning the series into a monument to attrition. But his comments were not intended as sour grapes, more a tacit admission that his much-fancied seam attack was struggling to make the predicted impact.

McCullum insisted he had no pangs of guilt about bowling first, and was never fearful he had made the wrong call, or he would "never get out of bed in the morning". He blamed his bowlers' innocuous efforts on the first day on flawed execution of plans rather than fatigue.

On the eve of the Test, McCullum had raised eyebrows by claiming Cook was a "genius", adding that, on recent form, his batting was "as good as anyone who has played the game, barring probably Bradman". As if to prove that flattery gets you everywhere, Cook had tamely chipped Wagner to mid-on for 17. But, as the England captain later spoke of the "cup final" awaiting both sides at Eden Park, any fever pitch – amid a deluge that ended 32 days without rain in Wellington – seemed closer to the Boat Race.

Close of play: first day, England 267-2 (Trott 121, Pietersen 18); second day, New Zealand 66-3 (Williamson 32, Brownlie 8); third day, New Zealand 77-1 (Fulton 41, Williamson 16); fourth day, New Zealand 162-2 (Williamson 55, Taylor 41).

England

*A. N. Cook c Fulton b Wagner	17	J. M. Anderson not out		8
N. R. D. Compton c Taylor b Martin	100	M. S. Panesar c Taylor b Williamson		0
I. J. L. Trott c Watling b Boult	121			
K. P. Pietersen c Fulton b Martin	73	L-b 3, w 7, n-b 3		13
I. R. Bell c Fulton b Martin	11			
J. E. Root c Watling b Martin	10	1/26 (1) 2/236 (2) (146.5 overs)		465
†M. J. Prior c Wagner b Williamson	82	3/267 (3) 4/302 (5)		
S. C. J. Broad c Watling b Boult	6	5/325 (6) 6/366 (4) 7/374 (8)		
S. T. Finn c McCullum b Wagner	24	8/457 (9) 9/465 (7) 10/465 (11)		

Southee 32–9–77–0; Boult 30–4–117–2; Wagner 33–5–122–2; Martin 48–11–130–4; Williamson 3.5–0–16–2.

New Zealand

P. G. Fulton c Cook b Anderson	1	– c Cook b Anderson	45
H. D. Rutherford c Cook b Broad	23	– c Bell b Panesar	15
K. S. Williamson c and b Broad	42	– not out	55
L. R. P. L. Taylor b Broad	0	– not out	41
D. G. Brownlie lbw b Anderson	18		
*B. B. McCullum c Trott b Finn	69		
†B-J. Watling c Prior b Broad	60		
T. G. Southee c Broad b Finn	3		
B. P. Martin not out	21		
N. Wagner c Prior b Broad	0		
T. A. Boult c Prior b Broad	2		
L-b 10, w 2, n-b 3	15	L-b 1, w 5	6

1/6 (1) 2/48 (2) 3/48 (3)	(89.2 overs) 254	1/25 (1)	(2 wkts, 68 overs) 162
4/85 (3) 5/89 (5) 6/189 (6)		2/81 (1)	
7/197 (8) 8/239 (7) 9/252 (10) 10/254 (11)			

Anderson 25–6–68–2; Finn 20–2–72–2; Broad 17.2–2–51–6; Panesar 26–11–47–0; Root 1–0–6–0. *Second innings*—Anderson 12–4–27–1; Broad 14–6–32–0; Finn 11–2–36–0; Panesar 26–12–44–1; Trott 3–0–10–0; Root 2–0–12–0.

Umpires: Asad Rauf and R. J. Tucker. Third umpire: P. R. Reiffel.

NEW ZEALAND v ENGLAND

Third Test Match

MIKE ATHERTON

At Auckland, March 22–26, 2013. Drawn. Toss: England.

And so a three-Test series boiled down to a simple equation: six balls from Boult, to be faced, initially at least, by Panesar, England's often hapless No. 11. New Zealand had beaten England in a series on home soil only once, in 1983-84. It was hard to imagine they would get a better chance to double their tally.

This was now New Zealand's 143rd over in the field, but every evidence of the zeal with which his side had played throughout a series they had begun in discord and disharmony. Panesar, who had joined Prior with 19 balls to go on an increasingly pulsating final evening, played and missed at the first delivery; left the second, which passed harmlessly wide of off stump; and, from the third, a full toss driven down the ground, ran for his life.

Most No. 11s would now have stood motionless at the non-striker's end. But Panesar, perhaps caught up in the panic that had enveloped England four overs from the close – when they had lost Broad and Anderson in three balls to Williamson's off-spin – inexplicably continued to back up, as if he fancied the responsibility of saving the game all by himself.

Prior sent him back and, after four and a half hours of batting which had expertly balanced the demands of defence with his own attacking instincts, nonchalantly defended the final three balls, before turning to the England dressing-room, arms raised in triumph.

THERE AT LAST

The oldest New Zealanders to score a maiden Test hundred:

Yrs	Days			
34	168	P. G. Z. Harris	101 v South Africa at Cape Town	1961-62
34	**49**	**P. G. Fulton**	**136 v England at Auckland**	**2012-13**
32	38	G. O. Rabone	107 v South Africa at Durban	1953-54
31	290	W. A. Hadlee	116 v England at Christchurch	1946-47
31	253	M. P. Donnelly	206 v England at Lord's	1949
31	217	J. V. Coney	174* v England at Wellington	1983-84
31	143	R. T. Latham	119 v Zimbabwe at Bulawayo	1992-93

Unlikely as it had seemed from the third day onwards, when England had conceded a first-innings deficit of 239, the match had been saved – and with it the series. Prior's own hundred, his seventh in Tests, felt almost incidental.

His triumphalism was understandable, although those new to cricket might have found it curious, since New Zealand had outplayed England for most of the match. Ultimately, though, they had not been quite good enough. They dropped crucial catches: two by Brownlie at slip – Prior in the first innings, Bell in the second – cost vital swathes of time. And Martin's inability to locate a consistent length with his left-arm spin on the final day disadvantaged them. As the part-timer Williamson showed, a slow bowler on top of his game ought to have caused more problems.

They also came up against a side that, while well below their best, were prepared to scrap and fight in the best traditions of England teams. Prior's resistance took the headlines, but Bell's skill and determination in a little under six hours, until he was dismissed on the stroke of tea, were equally valuable. Broad, too, played a crucial part: his first run did not come until 102 minutes into a 137-minute stay. It was the longest anyone had ever spent on nought in a Test, edging Geoff Allott's 101 minutes for New Zealand against South Africa on the same ground in 1998-99. Allott, who was out without scoring, faced 77 balls (Broad got off the mark from his 62nd delivery), but the England wicketkeeper John Murray, incommoded by a shoulder injury, spent 79 balls on nought at Sydney in 1962-63, eventually making three not out.

There are those who criticised both McCullum's decision not to enforce the follow-on, and the timing of his declaration. But if the closure, setting England 481 in a minimum of 143 overs, was on the conservative side, then Eden Park's drop-in pitch remained good;

Anthony Devlin, PA Photos

Tough at the top: Trent Boult has Alastair Cook caught behind, starting England's slide.

as for the follow-on, there were sound cricketing reasons either way. In the end, New Zealand had their chances and did not take them. It would be churlish to place the blame for that at McCullum's door, especially as his inspirational leadership had been a principal reason behind their renaissance.

Both captains had difficult decisions. Cook had won the toss and, under clear blue skies and on a pristine strip, chose to bowl – a move that looked bad as New Zealand eased to 250 for one at stumps. But their own failure to bowl England out in the fourth innings applied some retrospective wisdom to Cook's call: the pitch might not have done as much, or been as quick, as England had expected, but nor did it deteriorate. And McCullum would have bowled first too.

But when it transpired that there was little of anything for England's bowlers on the first day – no swing, no seam movement, no spin for Panesar – all that was left was perseverance, and plenty of it. It was the perfect opportunity for Fulton to book a ticket for the return series in England, which he did with a doughty 136, his maiden Test hundred, celebrated with old-fashioned decorum.

No one minded much that he clearly favoured the leg side – and it ought to have been within England's scope to limit his options.

Williamson fell for a pleasant 91 on the second morning, when England fought back, but Southee's late swiping zoomed New Zealand past 400. Finn's six wickets equalled his Test best, but also flattered him a little as he cleaned up the lower order with four in 14 balls. More representative were Prior's five catches. Two of them – a flying horizontal effort off Fulton down the leg side, and one up to the stumps to end McCullum's stay, off Trott of all people – were outstanding.

Crucially, New Zealand then found the swing on the second evening that had eluded England. This was puzzling, since Anderson was by reputation and record the best swing bowler on either side. But it was Boult who now showed him the way. Stocky, lively and indefatigable, he sent back Cook, caught behind, and Trott, leg-before in the classic manner, to underline New Zealand's control. Trott's decision to review a plumb appeal hinted at desperation.

Boult finished England's first innings with a career-best six for 68, although Southee had been equally dangerous, starting the rot on the third morning with an immaculate line to win leg-before decisions against Compton and Bell. The absence of Kevin Pietersen with a knee problem meant Bairstow's return to the middle order – and an unusually callow look to England's top six. And without a sixth-wicket stand of 101 between Root and the ever-resourceful Prior, England would not have managed even 204.

McCullum's captaincy was typically busy, and his decision to bat again instead of enforcing the follow-on based on a desire to ensure England would go in last on a pitch that had yielded only one wicket on the first day, but 22 on the second and third. It was not unreasonable to assume the trend would continue. But it was now England who – belatedly and briefly – found their cutting edge. In eight overs, New Zealand were eight for three, as Broad and Anderson ran amok. Had Fulton and Brownlie not steered New Zealand to the close, England might even have sniffed an unlikely win.

MOST SIXES IN A TEST FOR NEW ZEALAND

11	N. J. Astle (10, 222)	v England at Christchurch	2001-02
9	C. L. Cairns (57, 120)	v Zimbabwe at Auckland	1995-96
9	†T. G. Southee (5, 77*)	v England at Napier	2007-08
8	C. L. Cairns (109, 69)	v Australia at Wellington	1999-2000
8	**P. G. Fulton (136, 110)**	**v England at Auckland**	**2012-13**
7	B. Sutcliffe (80*, 10)	v South Africa at Johannesburg	1953-54
7	C. L. Cairns (158)	v South Africa at Auckland	2003-04
6	C. D. McMillan (0, 142)	v Sri Lanka at Colombo (RPS)	1997-98
6	T. G. Southee (38, 31)	v India at Nagpur	2010-11

† *On Test debut.*

On the fourth morning Fulton showed he was more than the plodding journeyman of general description. A remarkable transformation ensued, as he despatched England's bowlers to all parts of this curiously shaped ground, driving the quicker bowlers with venom, and taking advantage of the short straight boundaries to hit Panesar out of the attack. His first four overs had been maidens; his next five cost 52.

McCullum, having initially played second fiddle, joined in the fun soon enough, scoring 67 in 53 balls to push his team to a mid-afternoon declaration. But it was Fulton, dropped by Anderson at short midwicket on 31, who earned the spotlight: only three New Zealanders – Glenn Turner, Geoff Howarth and Andrew Jones – had previously scored twin hundreds in a Test. When Fulton drove Broad back over his head for six to bring up his second century of the match (and his Test career), it was a moment to treasure for a player who had been wondering whether he would ever make it at the highest level. He was almost two months past his 34th birthday; only Zin Harris, in 1961-62, had scored a maiden hundred for New Zealand at a greater age.

As Fulton and McCullum crashed 117 together in 17 overs, English tempers frayed, although the fielding held up under pressure, with good outfield catches from Bell and Compton. At one point Cook had nine fielders on the boundary. Later in the day, as if to underline the difference between the sides, New Zealand could post eight fielders around the bat.

After all that, and with England embarking on their nominal run-chase, Cook did well to make 43 as the fourth evening drew to a close. But when he joined Compton and Trott in the pavilion, brilliantly caught in the gully off Williamson, and was followed shortly afterwards by the nightwatchman Finn, snared off the final ball of the day, England looked done for.

Among all the cricketing reasons for their eventual survival 24 hours later was another which should not be ignored. Three hours into the final day, Wagner sent a bouncer rearing towards Prior's throat. He attempted to protect himself, but the ball hit bat handle, then helmet, before arcing towards the stumps. It landed behind Prior, and bounced, hard, on to middle stump. After hitting the ground, the ball then rolled back into the stumps once more. Miraculously, the bails remained in their grooves throughout. Prior, who had 28 at the time, shrugged his shoulders: pure, dumb luck.

Close of play: first day, New Zealand 250-1 (Fulton 124, Williamson 83); second day, England 50-2 (Compton 12, Bell 6); third day, New Zealand 35-3 (Fulton 14, Brownlie 13); fourth day, England 90-4 (Bell 8).

New Zealand

P. G. Fulton c Prior b Finn	136	– c Root b Finn	110
H. D. Rutherford c Cook b Finn	37	– c Bell b Broad	0
K. S. Williamson c Prior b Anderson	91	– b Anderson	1
L. R. P. L. Taylor c and b Panesar	19	– lbw b Broad	3
D. G. Brownlie c Compton b Anderson	36	– c Bell b Panesar	28
*B. B. McCullum c Prior b Trott	38	– not out	67
†B-J. Watling c Prior b Finn	21	– c Compton b Panesar	18
T. G. Southee c Prior b Finn	44		
B. P. Martin c Trott b Finn	10		
N. Wagner not out	2		
T. A. Boult c Compton b Finn	0		
B 4, l-b 4, n-b 1	9	B 4, l-b 10	14

1/79 (2)   2/260 (3)   3/289 (4)   (152.3 overs) 443   1/4 (2)   (6 wkts dec, 57.2 overs) 241
4/297 (1) 5/365 (6)   6/373 (5)   2/5 (3)   3/8 (4)
7/424 (8) 8/436 (9)   9/443 (10) 10/443 (11)   4/82 (5) 5/199 (1) 6/241 (7)

Anderson 30–8–79–2; Broad 30–6–94–0; Finn 37.3–8–125–6; Panesar 47–17–123–1; Trott 6–3–9–1; Root 2–1–5–0. *Second innings*—Anderson 17–6–59–1; Broad 17–5–54–2; Finn 13–1–57–1; Panesar 9.2–4–53–2; Trott 1–0–4–0.

England

*A. N. Cook c Watling b Boult	4	– c Brownlie b Williamson	43
N. R. D. Compton lbw b Southee	13	– c Watling b Southee	2
I. J. L. Trott lbw b Boult	27	– c Watling b Wagner	37
I. R. Bell lbw b Southee	17	– c Southee b Wagner	75
J. E. Root b Southee	45	– (6) lbw b Boult	29
J. M. Bairstow lbw b Boult	3	– (7) c Taylor b Southee	6
†M. J. Prior c Rutherford b Wagner	73	– (8) not out	110
S. C. J. Broad c Rutherford b Boult	16	– (9) c Taylor b Williamson	6
S. T. Finn c Taylor b Boult	0	– (5) c Southee b Williamson	0
J. M. Anderson c Watling b Boult	4	– c Taylor b Williamson	0
M. S. Panesar not out	0	– not out	2
W 2	2	L-b 4, n-b 1	5

1/8 (1)   2/44 (3)   3/61 (2)   (89.2 overs) 204   1/2 (2)   (9 wkts, 143 overs) 315
4/65 (4) 5/72 (6)   6/173 (7)   2/60 (3) 3/90 (1)
7/200 (8) 8/200 (9) 9/204 (10) 10/204 (5)   4/90 (5) 5/150 (6) 6/159 (7)
                                                             7/237 (4) 8/304 (9) 9/304 (10)

Boult 25–9–68–6; Southee 23.2–9–44–3; Wagner 15–3–36–1; Martin 26–10–56–0. *Second innings*—Boult 29–13–55–1; Southee 30–6–77–2; Martin 39–18–74–0; Wagner 25–8–61–2; Williamson 20–8–44–4.

Umpires: P. R. Reiffel and R. J. Tucker.   Third umpire: S. J. Davis.
Series referee: R. S. Mahanama.

ENGLAND v NEW ZEALAND, 2013

Review by Julian Guyer

Test matches (2): England 2, New Zealand 0
One-day internationals (3): England 1, New Zealand 2
Twenty20 internationals (2): England 0, New Zealand 1

New Zealand arrived for what was widely billed as an appetite-whetter ahead of the Ashes with genuine hope of winning a Test in England for the first time in 14 years. Five weeks earlier at Auckland they had been one wicket away from a rare series triumph, only to be denied by Matt Prior and Monty Panesar. And the first three days at Lord's maintained the pattern of nip-and-tuck, tooth-and-nail scraps. Yet everything changed in what their captain Brendon McCullum described as "one hour of madness" on the fourth morning. New Zealand slipped to 29 for six, and soon after lunch were all out for 68. It would take them until the limited-overs matches to recover.

Their destroyer was Stuart Broad, who produced the kind of spell – hostile, accurate, full of length – which has sporadically illuminated his career. As his pre-lunch burst of five for 22 turned into Test-best figures of seven for 44, many onlookers felt England were finally fulfilling the script that had apparently been written for them before the First Test at Dunedin in March: self-assertion over the team ranked No. 8 in the world.

For the New Zealanders, the collapse stirred memories of their 45 all out against South Africa at Cape Town in January. And though they avoided another double-figure total in the Second Test at Headingley, scores of 174 and 220 hardly suggested solidity. In all, they managed just 669 runs across their four innings. The inevitable consequence was a 2–0 defeat, their 13th series loss in England to go with a draw in 1949 – when all four Tests were three-day affairs – and wins in 1986 and 1999.

Ross Taylor did provide a hint of his talent with a charming 70 at Leeds, but it was the highest of only three fifties New Zealand managed in both Tests – and Taylor made one of the other two, a fierce 66 at Lord's. He alone ended up averaging over 25. Kane Williamson scored a good-looking 60, but little else, while Hamish Rutherford – flayer of England on debut at Dunedin – failed to pass 42. His opening partner Peter Fulton, who had taken the English bowlers by surprise with twin hundreds at Auckland, totalled a feeble 36. Most crucial of all, perhaps, was the anonymity of McCullum, who was undone by early seam movement, and failed to adapt a game based on fast hands and sharp hand–eye co-ordination; he averaged less than eight.

It was a pity, because New Zealand's bowlers, even in the absence of the injured Daniel Vettori, caused problems to an England top order that struggled to move into a higher gear. At Lord's, the admirable Tim Southee took ten for 108, and he was well supported by Trent Boult, the lively left-arm seamer who finished with eight wickets at 20 apiece and developed something of a hold over Alastair Cook, until a torn side muscle limited him to two overs in the

Philip Brown

Revolving doors: the careers of Nick Compton (*above*), who had a gruesome series, and Joe Root, full of strokes and smiles at Headingley, were heading in opposite directions. Root's Yorkshire team-mate Jonny Bairstow shares his pleasure.

Gareth Copley, Getty Images

second innings at Headingley and ruled him out of the rest of the tour. With Kevin Pietersen continuing to nurse a knee injury, the New Zealanders could operate in the knowledge that no one was going to take them apart.

But while their support bowling lacked depth – slow left-armer Bruce Martin and seamer Doug Bracewell were especially disappointing – the England attack took it in turns to make waves. At Lord's, Jimmy Anderson began with five wickets to become only the fourth England bowler, after Fred Trueman, Bob Willis and Ian Botham, to take 300 in Tests; Broad then weighed in with his seven. And at Leeds an early burst from Steven Finn was followed by ten wickets for Graeme Swann. Between them, the quartet took 39 wickets at an average of 16. There was no weak link.

If New Zealand were chastened, and England a little flattered, by the 170-run margin in the First Test, worse was to follow at Leeds, where the shortfall was 247 – a record between the sides – and that after rain had washed out the first day and almost obliterated the fifth. Honest as ever, McCullum conceded that England had "flexed their muscles". They also had the satisfaction of seeing Joe Root become the first Yorkshireman to score his maiden Test century at Headingley – and in the county's 150th anniversary year, too.

It was just a shame the crowds were disappointing, leaving Yorkshire's new chief executive Mark Arthur to lament the number of international venues in England. With the seven non-London grounds left to fight it out for four Tests a summer – and occasionally three – Arthur regretted that ticket prices had been inflated for the less attractive fixtures in an attempt to recoup staging fees. The bad spring weather did not help.

Root's composed hundred would prove significant not only for him, but also for Nick Compton. Having performed so well in New Zealand, Compton seemed on the verge of establishing an England career in which the phrase "grandson of Denis" would have to wait until at least the second paragraph. He had spoken of wanting to give the bowlers nothing, which was sensible enough. Yet in the second innings at Headingley a combination of New Zealand's accuracy and the tantalising prize of a maiden Ashes series rendered him all but strokeless. He later denied the pressure had got to him, but seven runs in 85 minutes gave him a total of 54 in six innings since back-to-back hundreds at Dunedin and Wellington. Not long after, Root was announced as Cook's opening partner for the Ashes.

Jonathan Trott's laboured progress towards 11 in 69 balls on the third evening at Leeds was symptomatic of England's excessive caution, though he did speed next morning. And so was Cook's decision not to enforce the follow-on, though he did at least lead well with the bat in scoring his 25th Test hundred, thus extending his own England record.

But the fact that he eventually set New Zealand a target of 468 – a full 50 more than any side had made to win in the fourth innings of a Test – took the philosophy of grinding the opposition into the dust to almost absurd lengths, particularly given the uncertain nature of the weather. Cook's rationale was that England had worked hard to establish the ascendancy in what effectively amounted to a five-Test series. They were not, he reasoned, about to give New Zealand a sniff now.

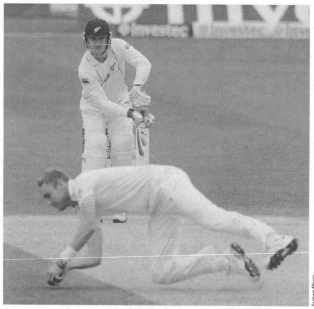

Graham Morris

Not so easy over here: Brendon McCullum, scourge of England back in New Zealand, is out cheaply to Stuart Broad for the fourth time in four innings.

It was just as well, then, that England eventually managed to dodge the showers, with Swann starring on a pitch worn by left-armers' footmarks. Yet there was a revealing moment before play on the final day when team director Andy Flower was seen haranguing the groundstaff over the time they were taking to remove the covers. "I don't think I should be out there doing the officials' job," Flower tetchily told BBC Radio's *Test Match Special*. The party line was that the ends justified the means: England had won. And Cook could now boast three victories and a draw in his first four series in charge, including his stint as stand-in for Andrew Strauss in Bangladesh early in 2010.

Thereafter, things picked up for the New Zealanders, and one of the most glorious sights of the ensuing one-day series, which they deservedly won 2–1, was the batting of Martin Guptill. His unbeaten 27 at Hamilton in February, where he had inspired New Zealand to victory in a one-dayer after returning to the middle with a hamstring injury, had demonstrated his guts. Now he showed his class. Guptill's undefeated 103 at Lord's was a model in how to pace a run-chase and, remarkably in view of what followed, only his third century in 70 one-day internationals. Two days later at Southampton, Guptill

A FAMILY AFFAIR

Steven Lynch

The Headingley Test featured four sons of former Test players – Jonny Bairstow and Stuart Broad for England, and Doug Bracewell and Hamish Rutherford for New Zealand. There was also Nick Compton who, as he is probably tired of hearing, is Denis Compton's grandson. This was not quite a record: a previous Test between these countries, at Old Trafford in 1999, included five sons of former Test players: Mark Butcher, Dean Headley and Alec Stewart for England; Chris Cairns and Chris Harris for New Zealand.

In 1975-76, New Zealand's Third Test against India at Wellington featured four sons of Test players (Dayle and Richard Hadlee, and Mohinder and Surinder Amarnath), Chris Cairns's father (Lance), one with a Test-playing brother (John Parker) and two brothers-in-law (Sunil Gavaskar and Gundappa Viswanath). Hedley Howarth, the brother of Test player Geoff, had appeared in the previous Test at Christchurch, but Cairns missed that.

The record for family involvement on one side was set at Harare in September 1997, when Zimbabwe's XI against New Zealand included three pairs of brothers – Andy and Grant Flower, Gavin and John Rennie, and Bryan and Paul Strang. There was also a place for Guy Whittall, whose cousin Andy was the twelfth man. New Zealand's team included Cairns and Harris.

added a fourth – a stunning 189 – after England had dropped him on 13 for the second match in a row. It equalled Viv Richards's celebrated effort at Old Trafford in 1984 as the highest individual one-day score against England.

That the teams then played two Twenty20 games after the Champions Trophy – in which the New Zealanders were disappointed not to have reached the semi-finals – was an absurdity, like going back to the same restaurant a month later just for the pudding. In the circumstances, Surrey were to be congratulated on attracting a sellout crowd to The Oval for the first of two matches in three days (the second was rained off), and they were rewarded with a textbook Twenty20 as England narrowly failed to chase down 202.

But victory in the two limited-overs series told us little we didn't already know about the New Zealand team. And for the umpteenth time in recent years, they were left bemoaning their lack of quality in the five-day game.

NEW ZEALAND TOURING PARTY

*B. B. McCullum (T/50/20), C. J. Anderson (20), T. A. Boult (T), D. A. J. Bracewell (T/50/20), D. G. Brownlie (T), I. G. Butler (50/20), G. D. Elliott (50), J. E. C. Franklin (50/20), P. G. Fulton (T), M. R. Gillespie (T), M. J. Guptill (T/50/20), R. M. Hira (20), T. W. M. Latham (T/20), M. J. McClenaghan (50/20), N. L. McCullum (50/20), B. P. Martin (T), K. D. Mills (50/20), C. Munro (50/20), L. Ronchi (50), H. D. Rutherford (T/20), T. G. Southee (T/50), L. R. P. L. Taylor (T/50/20), D. L. Vettori (50), N. Wagner (T), B-J. Watling (T), K. S. Williamson (T/50). *Coach:* M. J. Hesson.

Vettori was called up early to reinforce the Test squad after Martin was injured in the First Test – but was not fit enough to play himself. Boult and A. M. Ellis were originally selected for the 50-over squad, but Boult injured his side during the Tests and Ellis broke a rib in training; they were replaced by Butler and Bracewell. New Zealand's squad for the ICC Champions Trophy, which was played between the 50- and 20-over series, can be found in that section (see page 301).

FIVE STATS YOU MAY HAVE MISSED

BENEDICT BERMANGE

- England's two Tests against New Zealand were their 28th and 29th at home starting in May. Of those, England have won 21, drawn six and lost only two (by ten wickets to Australia at Nottingham, 1921; and by 108 runs to Pakistan at Manchester, 2001).

- England's total of 232 at Lord's is the sixth-highest in Tests not to contain an individual fifty or a fifty partnership:

	Top scorer	*Highest partnership*		
284	Tapash Baisya (48)	48 for 6th wkt	B v WI at Kingston	2003-04
252	M. J. Prior (49*), A. N. Cook (49)	48 for 1st	E v P at Dubai	2011-12
240	B. L. D'Oliveira (39)	45 for 6th	E v WI at Leeds	1969
238	Mashrafe bin Mortaza (39)	45 for 1st	B v WI at Arnos Vale	2009
236	T. J. Friend (44)	40 for 1st	Z v SL at Colombo (SSC)	2001-02
232	**J. M. Bairstow (41)**	**45 for 3rd & 4th**	**E v NZ at Lord's**	**2013**

- In New Zealand's second innings at Lord's, Stuart Broad took his first five wickets in 34 balls, making his third-fastest five-wicket haul for England:

Balls			
32	J. Briggs	v South Africa at Cape Town	1888-89
32	B. J. T. Bosanquet	v Australia at Sydney	1903-04
34	**S. C. J. Broad**	**v New Zealand at Lord's**	**2013**
37	G. A. Lohmann	v South Africa at Port Elizabeth	1895-96
40	A. E. R. Gilligan	v South Africa at Birmingham	1924

  The record for all countries is held by Ernie Toshack, who took five in his first 19 balls for Australia against India at Brisbane in 1947-48.

- Broad provided the fourth instance of a Test bowler taking seven or more wickets in an innings without bowling a maiden:

15–0–68–8	W. Rhodes	England v Australia at Melbourne (Second Test).	1903-04
8.3–0–23–7	R. J. Hadlee	New Zealand v India at Wellington	1975-76
6.5–0–28–7	H. Trumble	Australia v England at Melbourne (Fifth Test)...	1903-04
11–0–44–7	**S. C. J. Broad**	**England v New Zealand at Lord's.**	**2013**

- At Leeds, the New Zealand tailenders failed to score a run off the bat for the last 68 balls of the match. This is the longest-known spell since 1964-65, when Australia played out 78 dot-balls in a row against India at Calcutta.

DERBYSHIRE v NEW ZEALANDERS

At Derby, May 4–6. New Zealanders won by 107 runs. Toss: Derbyshire.

New Zealand's back-up bowlers gave their selectors something to think about: in the absence of Trent Boult and Tim Southee, who were rested, the bustling left-armer Wagner took eight wickets in the match, and Bracewell seven. Their batsmen were rather less impressive, although Watling produced two adhesive knocks, and Brownlie played attractively in the first innings. For Derbyshire, left-armer Footitt troubled the top order with his pace, and took six wickets in his first match of the season to boost his chances of a regular place.

Close of play: first day, Derbyshire 24-1 (Godleman 9); second day, New Zealanders 199-5 (Watling 61, Latham 47).

New Zealanders

P. G. Fulton lbw b Footitt	21	– b Evans	3
H. D. Rutherford b Evans	13	– b Footitt	0
*K. S. Williamson c Johnson b Footitt	43	– b Burgoyne	49
M. J. Guptill c Johnson b Footitt	25	– b Higginbottom	8
D. G. Brownlie c Johnson b Footitt	71	– b Footitt	8
†B-J. Watling not out	77	– not out	61
T. W. M. Latham not out	21	– not out	47
B 5, l-b 2, w 2, n-b 9	18	B 3, l-b 8, w 5, n-b 7	23

1/27 (2) 2/50 (1)   (5 wkts dec, 76 overs) 289
3/94 (4) 4/126 (3) 5/242 (5)

1/9 (2)   (5 wkts dec, 48 overs) 199
2/9 (1) 3/31 (4)
4/60 (5) 5/94 (3)

D. A. J. Bracewell, B. P. Martin, N. Wagner and M. R. Gillespie did not bat.

Footitt 18–1–65–4; Evans 14–3–52–1; Higginbottom 11–1–55–0; Whiteley 10–0–43–0; Burgoyne 14–1–40–0; Durston 9–2–27–0. *Second innings*—Footitt 10–2–19–2; Evans 9–1–30–1; Higginbottom 4–0–26–1; Burgoyne 13–0–59–1; Whiteley 7–0–33–0; Durston 5–0–21–0.

Derbyshire

B. A. Godleman c Watling b Wagner	14	– lbw b Wagner	25
C. F. Hughes b Wagner	9	– c Latham b Wagner	15
*W. L. Madsen c Watling b Wagner	12	– b Martin	6
W. J. Durston st Latham b Martin	46	– c Guptill b Bracewell	26
D. J. Redfern c Fulton b Bracewell	10	– c Watling b Wagner	58
R. A. Whiteley c Brownlie b Bracewell	0	– c Brownlie b Bracewell	1
†R. M. Johnson c Williamson b Martin	16	– c Watling b Wagner	14
P. I. Burgoyne b Bracewell	6	– c Watling b Wagner	30
M. Higginbottom c Watling b Martin	2	– b Bracewell	9
A. C. Evans not out	2	– not out	5
M. H. A. Footitt b Bracewell	0	– c Gillespie b Martin	22
B 18, l-b 14, w 1, n-b 4	37	B 9, l-b 5, n-b 2	16

1/24 (2) 2/35 (1) 3/52 (3)   (52 overs) 154
4/89 (5) 5/89 (6) 6/121 (4)
7/139 (7) 8/152 (9) 9/152 (8) 10/154 (11)

1/42 (2) 2/47 (1)   (67.4 overs) 227
3/80 (3) 4/84 (4)
5/98 (6) 6/156 (7) 7/165 (5)
8/195 (9) 9/199 (8) 10/227 (11)

Bracewell 15–6–28–4; Gillespie 17–3–48–0; Wagner 9–1–33–3; Martin 11–6–13–3. *Second innings*—Gillespie 12–2–59–0; Bracewell 19–7–56–3; Wagner 18–8–45–5; Martin 11.4–3–35–2; Williamson 7–2–18–0.

Umpires: N. L. Bainton and N. G. C. Cowley.

ENGLAND LIONS v NEW ZEALANDERS

At Leicester, May 9–12. Drawn. Toss: England Lions.

Any chance of a result was ruined by the weather, which cut the first day in half and allowed only 55 overs in total on the last two. Rutherford compiled an entertaining century, hitting four sixes as well as 18 fours. But after he was run out by Woakes the lower order caved in, with No. 5 Brownlie left high and dry after 162 minutes. Roland-Jones, the uncapped Middlesex seamer, was the pick of the Lions bowlers. Root, who shared hundred stands with Carberry and Bairstow, then batted for more than six hours for 179, his third successive score of 175 or more, following 182 for Yorkshire against Durham, and 236 against Derbyshire. He was only the fourth batsman to achieve this in first-class cricket, after W. G. Grace (1876), Clem Hill (1909–10) and Cheteshwar Pujara (2008-09).

Close of play: first day, New Zealanders 184-3 (Rutherford 116, Brownlie 4); second day, England Lions 219-2 (Root 105, Wright 0); third day, England Lions 315-4 (Root 143, Bairstow 45).

New Zealanders

P. G. Fulton lbw b Onions	7	B. P. Martin lbw b Kerrigan	6
H. D. Rutherford run out	126	D. A. J. Bracewell c Chopra b Roland-Jones	4
K. S. Williamson c Kerrigan b Roland-Jones	7	T. A. Boult b Roland-Jones	4
L. R. P. L. Taylor lbw b Roland-Jones	35	B 2, l-b 8, n-b 9	19
D. G. Brownlie not out	42		
*B. B. McCullum c Carberry b Onions	1	1/16 (1) 2/41 (3) 3/168 (4) (74.5 overs) 285	
†B-J. Watling b Woakes	23	4/211 (2) 5/212 (6) 6/245 (7)	
T. G. Southee lbw b Bopara	11	7/258 (8) 8/274 (9) 9/279 (10) 10/285 (11)	

Onions 15–2–46–2; Woakes 18–5–56–1; Roland-Jones 12.5–3–54–4; Wright 15–1–59–0; Bopara 9–0–29–1; Kerrigan 5–0–31–1.

England Lions

M. A. Carberry c Brownlie b Martin	77	C. R. Woakes b Bracewell	1
V. Chopra c McCullum b Southee	4	T. S. Roland-Jones not out	22
*J. E. Root b Bracewell	179	B 8, l-b 11, w 5, n-b 20	44
C. J. C. Wright b Southee b Boult	5		
J. W. A. Taylor c Watling b Boult	2	1/19 (2) 2/201 (1) (7 wkts, 114 overs) 444	
†J. M. Bairstow lbw b Boult	68	3/228 (4) 4/234 (5)	
R. S. Bopara not out	42	5/369 (6) 6/400 (3) 7/402 (8)	

G. Onions and S. C. Kerrigan did not bat.

Boult 25–5–86–3; Southee 19–3–65–1; Bracewell 27–7–95–2; Martin 25–4–117–1; Williamson 18–2–62–0.

Umpires: J. W. Lloyds and P. R. Pollard.

ENGLAND v NEW ZEALAND

First Investec Test

Hugh Chevallier

At Lord's, May 16–19. England won by 170 runs. Toss: England.

An England victory by plenty. Plain and simple, then: this was a one-sided Test. Except it wasn't. All the margin proved was the adage about lies, damned lies and statistics. For three of the four innings – for 250 of the match's 272 overs – neither side jockeyed ahead of the other. Indeed on the fourth morning, after Southee laid waste the modest reaches of the England batting, it was plausible to imagine New Zealand's momentum carrying them to their target of 239. After all, 61 Tests had been won by making as many or more in the last innings. And in Taylor and McCullum, they arguably possessed the match's most destructive batsmen. England's attack, on the other hand – Anderson excepted – had been short on bite.

Plausible, perhaps, but utterly wrong. Batsman after batsman traipsed out, and writhed in agony for a while before Broad, now butcher-in-chief, despatched them with an ease so contemptuous it seemed cruel to watch – a case of New Zealand lambs to the swiftest of slaughter. Batting was never straightforward on an uncharacteristically slow Lord's pitch, but nothing that had gone before, not even England's surrender to Southee, hinted at the speed of the disintegration.

New Zealand began their second innings an hour before lunch. Within nine balls, Fulton had flirted with a Broad delivery better ignored, gifting Prior his 200th Test dismissal. Next came a corker to remove the left-handed Rutherford: charging in with renewed oomph, Broad got one to pitch on leg, jag up the slope and uproot off. Nirvana for the bowler – and 16 for two. Anderson was making the ball sing, dance and recite poetry from the other end; perhaps the concentration required to withstand him left the batsmen

ONLY TWO BOWLERS IN COMPLETED TEST INNINGS (SINCE 1900)

S. F. Barnes (6-42) and C. Blythe (4-64)	England v Australia at Melbourne.....	1901-02
H. Trumble (3-38) and M. A. Noble (7-17)	Australia v England at Melbourne.....	1901-02
J. V. Saunders (5-43) and M. A. Noble (5-54)	Australia v England at Sydney........	1901-02
G. H. Hirst (4-28) and C. Blythe (6-44)	England v Australia at Birmingham ...	1909
F. R. Foster (5-16) and S. F. Barnes (5-25)	England v South Africa at Lord's	1912
A. E. R. Gilligan (6-7) and M. W. Tate (4-12)	England v South Africa at Birmingham	1924
W. Voce (4-16) and G. O. B. Allen (5-36)	England v Australia at Brisbane	1936-37
Fazal Mahmood (6-34) and Khan Mohammad (4-43)	Pakistan v Australia at Karachi	1956-57
C. E. L. Ambrose (6-24) and C. A. Walsh (3-16)	West Indies v England at Port-of-Spain	1993-94
Wasim Akram (4-32) and Waqar Younis (6-34)	Pakistan v Sri Lanka at Kandy	1994-95
G. D. McGrath (5-28) and J. N. Gillespie (4-18)	Australia v West Indies at Port-of-Spain	1998-99
J. M. Anderson (2-23) and S. C. J. Broad (7-44)	**England v New Zealand at Lord's ...**	**2013**

There are 13 instances from the 19th century.

exposed, since they had no answer to the rampant Broad, whose third victim came in just his third over as Taylor nibbled at an outswinger.

Williamson drove loosely to mid-off, making it 21 for four – yet the rout picked up pace. After Brownlie was undone by trademark Andersonian genius – a big inswinger followed by one that zipped up the hill – McCullum went walkabout in front of his stumps, giving Broad a five-for from 34 balls. In desperation, McCullum reviewed the decision. Hawk-Eye simply laughed in his face.

If lunch at 29 for six brought respite, it also allowed Anderson and Broad to catch their breath and reload. The England snipers regained their range, and the bloodshed resumed. Watling, lame after injuring his knee earlier in the match, and Wagner did rally briefly, before the end came in tragi-comic fashion. Wagner edged skyscraper-high to long leg, where substitute fielder Adam Dobb overran the chance, losing the ball, his balance – and some dignity. But Bairstow spied hesitation over a second run, hurled the ball in, and Anderson did the rest. In fact, Anderson and Broad (who claimed a career-best seven for 44) had done the lot: for the first time in a Test since 1998-99 – and for England since the 1936-37 Ashes – just two bowlers were used in a completed innings. New Zealand's humbling took only 135 balls.

In late March, England's team of Houdinis had escaped Auckland with a draw. They made one change for Lord's, Monty Panesar moving aside for the fit-again Swann, while New Zealand, for the first time, chose the same team for a fourth successive Test. Several factors then combined to ensure a ponderous day: the pitch was grudging, and the outfield – relaid after the Olympic archery – stodgier still; England's batsmen were keen to knuckle down after feeble displays in New Zealand; while their opponents' main stratagem was frustration. Indeed, had the mercury crawled higher up the thermometer – snow had settled in Devon the day before – the familiar Lord's buzz might have become a torpid zzz.

England's top order made starts, but none passed 41 as runs seeped out at two an over. With maidens totting up, Compton betrayed a short fuse with an intemperate slog-slice off Martin's left-arm spin. That put paid to any further thoughts of aggression: the fact that the briskest scorer was Trott, superbly caught by Brownlie at third slip, spoke volumes. When bad light ended the first day after 80 overs – 30 of them maidens – England, with the Yorkshire pair of Bairstow and Root at the crease, were 160 for four.

Root, unusually, was making his Lord's debut in a Test – only the fourth to do so for England after Johnny Arnold (1931), Chris Schofield (2000) and Simon Jones (2002). He was also in Bradmanesque form after hitting three successive first-class scores of 175 or more (not that Bradman had actually managed that feat). Confidence oozed from Root's bat, but he nicked an unthreatening leg-side delivery from Southee, while Prior, just named England's Player of the Year, made a deflating golden duck. The tail contributed little, and a promising 192 for four had dribbled away to a forgettable 232. England's batting frailties would not disappear.

Gareth Copley, Getty Images

Jimmy, Jimmy! Ross Taylor becomes Anderson's 301st Test victim.

Nor would New Zealand's. They were seven for two in the blink of an eye as Anderson struck. Both were smart catches, and the second brought a standing ovation. Fulton edged low to Swann at second slip, making Anderson the 26th bowler, and the fourth from England, to claim 300 Test wickets. Aged 30 and largely untroubled by injury, he looked capable of 400 and more. The problem for England was that, with the swinging conditions crying out for a full length, Broad and Finn would keep feeding Taylor's love of rasping cuts by pitching short; for Broad in particular it was an itch he couldn't stop scratching. When New Zealand reached 100 with just two wickets down and Taylor speeding along at a run a ball, Cook had every right to fret.

But if this game had a defining characteristic it was that the advantage rocked back and forth like Newton's cradle. So when Anderson undid Taylor for a crisp 66, the match situation – 100 for three in reply to 232 – was almost back to square one. England would have grabbed the game by the scruff of the neck soon afterwards had Prior not dropped Williamson on 23. But they did make good use of the DRS to overturn a not-out verdict against Brownlie. One step back; one step forward. All of which meant that the score at the end of the second day – New Zealand 153 for four – was much as it had been at the start, only with the other team batting.

The similarities continued next morning. New Zealand's tailspin began from the fourth legitimate ball of the day, when McCullum flashed at Broad. As he would in the second-innings rout, McCullum asked for a review, but Hot Spot revealed an ugly white mark on his bat. The Test's most magical moment came when Anderson utterly discombobulated Martin. Two nip-backers and a sumptuous outswinger that clipped the top of off had older spectators summoning the ghost of Fred Trueman, who famously said: "It were wasted on thee, lad." With Finn rediscovering menace, the innings unravelled much as England's had 24 hours earlier: six for 72 on the second day; six for 54 on the third.

England gained a lead of 25 – and a shade more urgency as they began to build on it. Both openers fell with the score 36, but Root and Trott consolidated. They looked the

SHORTEST COMPLETED TEST INNINGS AT LORD'S

Balls	Total	Inns		
102	42†	3rd	India v England....................	1974
113	53	1st	Australia v England	1896
118	60	3rd	Australia v England	1888
135	**68**	**4th**	**New Zealand v England**..............	**2013**
157	58	1st	South Africa v England	1912
160	54	3rd	West Indies v England	2000

† *One man absent.*

business when using their bats, but between the wickets they revealed themselves as graduates of the Inzamam School of Advanced Running Cock-ups. Somehow, the only victim of at least three farcical misunderstandings was Watling, who damaged his knee diving for the stumps after gathering a wayward throw. McCullum, once the regular keeper, took over, though he disconcertingly used shin-guards beneath his flannels rather than pads. Eventually, Root's concentration snapped, and he was bowled by Southee via an inside edge. The breakthrough kept New Zealand, 184 behind and seven wickets to capture, in with a shout.

By the third-day close, the shout had become a roar. Southee wrenched the initiative by dismissing Bairstow and, for his first pair in 226 first-class matches, Prior. With Trott spun out by Williamson – bowling in place of Martin, who had injured his calf – and Bell batting at No. 8 because of tonsillitis, a wobblesome England were desperate to leave the field.

England's plight should have been no surprise, as this was a Test memorable for a farrago of middle- and lower-order collapses. Indeed the fourth day, which comprised 101 runs and 14 wickets, was essentially one long collapse. Southee found just enough movement to snaffle three more wickets, becoming only the second New Zealander after Dion Nash in 1994 to take a ten-for at Lord's. England had eyed a huge, defeat-proof lead, but in the end set a flimsy 239. Without Broad, who rode his luck before lumberjacking his way to an unbeaten 26, it would have been worse. As it happened, though, he was just sharpening his axe before the real tree-felling began.

Man of the Match: S. C. J. Broad.   *Attendance:* 106,135.

Close of play: first day, England 160-4 (Root 25, Bairstow 3); second day, New Zealand 153-4 (Williamson 44, McCullum 1); third day, England 180-6 (Finn 6, Bell 0).

England

*A. N. Cook c Watling b Boult	32	– c Brownlie b Boult	21
N. R. D. Compton c Southee b Martin	16	– b Wagner	15
I. J. L. Trott c Brownlie b Boult	39	– b Williamson	56
I. R. Bell c Watling b Wagner	31	– (8) c Brownlie b Southee	6
J. E. Root c Watling b Southee	40	– (4) b Southee	71
J. M. Bairstow c and b Southee	41	– (5) b Southee	5
†M. J. Prior lbw b Southee....................	0	– (6) c sub (M. J. Guptill) b Southee...	0
S. C. J. Broad lbw b Wagner	0	– (9) not out...................	26
G. P. Swann c Watling b Wagner	5	– (10) c McCullum b Southee........	1
S. T. Finn lbw b Southee	4	– (7) c sub (M. J. Guptill) b Southee...	6
J. M. Anderson not out......................	7	– c Southee b Williamson	0
B 1, l-b 9, w 2, n-b 5	17	B 3, w 1, n-b 2	6

1/43 (2)   2/67 (1)   3/112 (3)   (112.2 overs)   232   1/36 (1)   2/36 (2)   (68.3 overs)   213
4/157 (4)   5/192 (5)   6/192 (7)   3/159 (4)   4/167 (5)
7/195 (8)   8/201 (9)   9/221 (10)   10/232 (6)   5/171 (6)   6/171 (3)   7/183 (7)
                                               8/200 (8)   9/210 (10)   10/213 (11)

Boult 27–10–48–2; Southee 28.2–8–58–4; Wagner 28–8–70–3; Martin 26–12–38–1; Williamson 3–1–8–0. *Second innings*—Boult 15–3–56–1; Southee 19–4–50–6; Wagner 13–2–44–1; Martin 13–2–40–0; Williamson 8.3–2–20–2.

New Zealand

P. G. Fulton c Swann b Anderson	2	– c Prior b Broad	1
H. D. Rutherford c Cook b Anderson	4	– b Broad	9
K. S. Williamson c Prior b Anderson	60	– c Finn b Broad	6
L. R. P. L. Taylor lbw b Anderson	66	– c Cook b Broad	0
D. G. Brownlie lbw b Finn	23	– c Cook b Anderson	5
*B. B. McCullum c Prior b Broad	2	– lbw b Broad	8
†B-J. Watling c Prior b Finn	17	– c Trott b Anderson	13
T. G. Southee c Root b Finn	12	– c Root b Broad	7
B. P. Martin b Anderson	0	– (10) b Broad	1
N. Wagner not out	6	– (9) run out	17
T. A. Boult c Anderson b Finn	0	– not out	0
B 4, l-b 8, n-b 3	15	L-b 1	1

1/5 (2) 2/7 (1) 3/100 (4)	(69 overs)	207
4/147 (5) 5/155 (6) 6/177 (3)		
7/194 (8) 8/195 (9) 9/207 (7) 10/207 (11)		

1/1 (1) 2/16 (2)	(22.3 overs)	68
3/16 (4) 4/21 (3)		
5/25 (5) 6/29 (6) 7/41 (8)		
8/54 (7) 9/67 (10) 10/68 (9)		

Anderson 24–11–47–5; Broad 21–4–64–1; Finn 15–3–63–4; Swann 8–0–19–0; Trott 1–0–2–0. *Second innings*—Anderson 11.3–5–23–2; Broad 11–0–44–7.

Umpires: Aleem Dar and S. J. Davis.   Third umpire: M. Erasmus.

ENGLAND v NEW ZEALAND

Second Investec Test

DUNCAN HAMILTON

At Leeds, May 24–28. England won by 247 runs. Toss: England.

Sir Pelham Warner once described an England captain in a way that nowadays requires context to avoid misinterpretation. Of the Honourable Sir Stanley Jackson, who ranked among life's authentic all-rounders, Warner announced: "He was a good tosser."

The patrician world in which Warner lived preserved his general state of ignorance about the real one, which meant he often sounded naïve or came across as a bit buffoonish, like a cricketing Bertie Wooster. The short quotation reinforces that notion; though, of course, Warner meant it as a compliment – commemorating Jackson's feat of winning every coin-flip during the 1905 Ashes – and only a profound shift in common usage has turned it into a pejorative. Warner was tacitly making the broader point that successful leadership frequently depends on luck as much as strategy. On this basis – and if the dead harbour curiosity about the living – you can be sure that the conversation in the celestial pavilion between old Plum and Jacker fairly crackled along throughout this Test.

Headingley doesn't earn high marks for aesthetic charm. There is no grand sweep to architecture assembled piecemeal. But things tend to spark in the Yorkshire air, which makes a largely ugly ground a beautiful venue for a Test. Nearly always as an oddity, a quirk, an exemplary performance or a controversy significantly colours what happens here and leaves a mark on the memory.

THE LAXMAN EFFECT

STEVEN LYNCH

Alastair Cook decided not to make New Zealand follow on at Headingley, despite a lead of 180 (the loss of the first day meant the target was reduced to 150). This continued a trend which, unusually for cricket, can be ascribed to a precise game: Kolkata, March 2001. In that famous Test at Eden Gardens, Australia seemed to be cruising to a record 17th straight victory. "I had enforced the follow-on after bowling India out in only 58 overs for 171, leaving them with a deficit of 274," said Steve Waugh. "It was a decision we discussed as a team, but I was extra-keen to keep them pinned down and keep the momentum going."

It didn't quite work out like that. V. V. S. Laxman made 281 and Rahul Dravid 180 as India amassed 657; they then bowled Australia out for 212 to win handsomely, before going on to claim the series 2–1. Waugh was chary of enforcing the follow-on after that – and the feeling spread.

Prior to that game, there had been 178 occasions in all Tests since the Second World War when the follow-on was possible: it was enforced 155 times (87%). Since Kolkata, this Headingley Test was the 102nd opportunity for a captain to invite the opposition to bat again – and this was the 35th occasion (34%) it had been spurned.

What should perhaps be called the Laxman Effect was most obvious in the immediate aftermath of India's Kolkata heroics, only the third time a Test had been won by the side following on. In the six preceding years there had been only four waived follow-ons; in the next 18 months alone there were five.

There was the washout of the wind-whipped opening day, blanketed beneath the kind of lowering, black-angry sky that the sisters of Haworth put into their novels. There was a maiden Test century for Root, looking like one of Botticelli's cherubs and batting like a steely combination of Hutton and Sutcliffe. There was the stand of 124 between Root and Bairstow to swell the pride of White Rose partisans during England's first-innings 354. There was Swann, consummate in the execution of his thoughtful craft, and on the honours board because of it. There was Anderson finally attaining wicket-parity with Fred Trueman – and doing so from the Kirkstall Lane End, which was Trueman's turf during his faraway pomp. There was the curiosity value early on of seeing Geoffrey Boycott, the Yorkshire president – and The Greatest Living Yorkshireman to boot – striding around with a small, rectangular name badge clipped, slightly askew, to the breast pocket of his jacket, as if among his own he might walk unrecognised. Well, as the locals often remark, there's nowt so strange as folk. There was also nowt so strange as England's tactics, a fact that defined the Test.

What the dry ink of the scorebook records as a whopping win – England beating New Zealand by 247 runs to seal the series 2–0 – was actually much more of a narrow squeak because of timidity, muddled thought, and anxious hand-wringing about three basic decisions: the question of the follow-on, the timing of the second-innings declaration, and the set of the field to make New Zealand's suffering as brief as possible.

Brightly imaginative or innovative captaincy from Cook wasn't necessary. All he needed to show was a modicum of brio and a moderate level of ruthlessness. We saw instead an approach so tentative and over-cautious that you wondered how Cook reacts whenever his own shadow surprises him. As a consequence, he was a dark cloud and a spit of rain away from looking a darned fool.

The complete loss of the first day reduced the follow-on target to 150. New Zealand, bowled out for a pitiful 174, were 180 in arrears when Cook chose instead to bat again. Without the last-wicket stand of 52 between Wagner and Boult, who had the audacity to

Home runs: Yorkshire's Joe Root (born in Sheffield) glides towards his first Test century…

biff Swann for three sixes, New Zealand might as well have run up the white flag there and then.

Modern thinking tends to discriminate against enforcing the follow-on. Fair enough. Cook could argue his corner cogently. Bowlers do benefit from recuperation, especially in an era of back-to-back Tests. The pitch will scuff and deteriorate further. The opposition's spirit can be snuffed out, making everything, especially resistance, appear futile. But you still need to navigate the route you've picked; Cook, alas, allowed England to meander and drift. The plan should have been straightforward: rattle up a lead of just over 400 – no sense in being greedy about it – before cavalry-charging a top order already psychologically bruised and tender. In any case, no team at Headingley have surpassed Bradman's 1948 Invincibles in chasing down 404; and New Zealand's three previous innings had totalled a miserable 449 runs in 135.1 overs. Really, this was about as easy as it gets.

Faffing about was the first mistake. Compton's scratching for a decent score was understandable. His touch and timing had withered, and his place was in jeopardy. Trott's go-slow, however, was emphatically not. England were rolling along serenely – 72 inside 20 overs – when Compton went back to the dressing-room, wearing the expression of a hound on its last visit to the vet. What came next, a paltry 44 runs in 21 overs before the close, was tedious to watch, and almost impossible to rationalise. Trott, as if thinking either the Test was timeless or he was Barnacle Bailey, eked 11 off 69 deliveries. Thinking about that makes you yawn. Thinking about his response to it makes you wince.

Even with satellite technology, the Met Office never seems much more reliable than those meteorologists from ancient times who swore it was possible to soothsay an entire summer's rainfall by examining the entrails of a chicken. But in this case every forecast for Headingley – from whizzy computers and deceased farm-fowl alike – was pretty dismal. The obvious conclusion was that England had to beat New Zealand before the weather beat them.

In a prickly reply to a question about this – he seemed to believe asking it in the first place counted as a breach of protocol – Trott said England shouldn't pay too much attention to the prospect of rain or allow it to dictate their actions. As an example of loyalty towards the captain, as well as an espousal of collective responsibility, it was laudable. As an example of logical thought, it was laughable. He was talking about Leeds in May, for goodness' sake.

Philip Brown

… while Jonny Bairstow (Bradford) was a perfect – and occasionally inventive – foil.

At the beginning of day four, as though the switch working him had been flicked at last, Trott hit another 65 runs, and did so stylishly. Cook reached his 25th Test century – his seventh in 11 matches as captain, and the 100th in all Headingley Tests – compiled in imperious bursts, against an attack shorn of Boult, who bowled only two overs because of a strain in his right side. To see him go was surely a mighty relief to Cook, like waving goodbye to a troublesome house guest: Boult had claimed him twice on England's winter tour and twice more at Lord's barely a week earlier.

The England innings dragged on inexplicably after lunch, and the middle order were obliged to sacrifice themselves for superfluous runs. New Zealand were left hunting 468, a wild goose chase of a score. Even Bradman might have baulked at that – unless he was partnering Trumper. Cook seemed to believe both were padding up. New Zealand had only Rutherford, who made 42, and Taylor, who handled the cunning Swann and the uneven bounce as ably as possible, opting to play well back and across. He did it in some pain too. A first-innings snorter from Finn had thumped into his right shoulder. An ice-pack was pressed against the welt midway through his second innings; Taylor grimaced hard, the way you would if table salt was rubbed into a fresh cut. He got 70 nonetheless, before Swann (as we all knew he would eventually) made the kill.

Cook's meekness still remained the issue. A Yorkshireman invented the guillotine. A Yorkshire crowd expect to see it drop. They want leaders to be mean, like Shylock, rather than cerebral, like Sherlock. Cook was neither. With a mountainous heap of runs, there was no need to have more cover fielders than you had slips. Or a deep point. Or to isolate someone on the square-leg boundary. It was belt-and-braces defence, when the circumstances demanded attack and offered absolute protection from defeat. In achieving match figures of ten for 132 – the best by a spinner at Headingley since 1972, when Derek Underwood took ten for 82 against Australia on a pitch affected by the fusarium fungus – Swann bowled a majestically accurate line, ripping the ball in to the footmarks created by New Zealand's two left-armers. His field ought to have looked a bit like Underwood's did at The Oval in 1968, when a famous close-up photograph showed all 11 England players. But Cook crowded the bat only after the sixth wicket went down, which was shortly before bad light carried the game into the final day. Sages on the old Western Terrace went home grumpy with Cook – and fearing the worst.

He got away with it because the bad weather broke long enough to allow him sufficient time to take out the tail during two truncated sessions, stretching in total to an hour and 26 minutes and ending at 3.36pm in front of a few hundred hardy souls with Thermos flasks. Cook was a lucky lad indeed. Perhaps, like Jackson, he's one of those chaps of infinite good fortune who is able to regularly second-guess the Fates, and feels safe gambling on his instincts. He even won the toss. No doubt Sir Pelham has a phrase he'd like to offer in congratulation about that particular triumph.

Man of the Match: G. P. Swann. *Attendance:* 29,465.

Men of the Series: England – J. E. Root. New Zealand – T. G. Southee.

Close of play: first day, no play; second day, England 337-7 (Prior 38, Swann 21); third day, England 116-1 (Cook 88, Trott 11); fourth day, New Zealand 158-6 (McCullum 0, Southee 4).

England

*A. N. Cook c Brownlie b Bracewell	34	– c Southee b Williamson 130
N. R. D. Compton c Brownlie b Southee	1	– c Rutherford b Williamson 7
I. J. L. Trott c McCullum b Wagner	28	– c McCullum b Wagner 76
I. R. Bell c McCullum b Williamson	30	– c Guptill b Williamson 6
J. E. Root c McCullum b Boult	104	– c Guptill b Wagner 28
J. M. Bairstow c McCullum b Boult	64	– not out 26
†M. J. Prior c Taylor b Southee	39	– not out 4
S. C. J. Broad c McCullum b Boult	0	
G. P. Swann not out	26	
S. T. Finn b Boult	6	
J. M. Anderson c and b Boult	0	
B 9, l-b 7, w 5, n-b 1	22	B 8, l-b 1, w 1 10

1/11 (2) 2/67 (3) 3/67 (1) (99 overs) 354	1/72 (2) (5 wkts dec, 76 overs) 287
4/146 (4) 5/270 (5) 6/279 (6)	2/206 (1) 3/214 (4)
7/286 (8) 8/345 (7) 9/354 (10) 10/354 (11)	4/249 (3) 5/268 (5)

Boult 22–4–57–5; Southee 26–6–76–2; Wagner 23–4–73–1; Bracewell 19–3–83–1; Williamson 9–0–49–1. *Second innings*—Boult 2–1–2–0; Southee 15–4–51–0; Wagner 17–3–67–2; Williamson 24–4–68–3; Bracewell 13–3–49–0; Guptill 5–0–41–0.

New Zealand

P. G. Fulton c and b Finn	28	– c Bell b Broad 5
H. D. Rutherford c Bell b Finn	27	– c Root b Swann 42
K. S. Williamson lbw b Swann	13	– lbw b Swann 3
L. R. P. L. Taylor b Finn	6	– b Swann 70
D. G. Brownlie b Swann	2	– c Bell b Finn 25
M. J. Guptill b Swann	1	– c Trott b Swann 3
*†B. B. McCullum c Prior b Broad	20	– c and b Broad 1
T. G. Southee lbw b Broad	19	– c Trott b Swann 38
D. A. J. Bracewell c Bell b Swann	1	– c Bell b Swann 19
N. Wagner b Anderson	27	– not out 0
T. A. Boult not out	24	– c Prior b Anderson 0
L-b 5, w 1	6	B 2, l-b 11, w 1 14

1/55 (1) 2/62 (2) 3/72 (4) (43.4 overs) 174	1/21 (1) 2/40 (3) (76.3 overs) 220
4/79 (5) 5/81 (6) 6/82 (3)	3/65 (2) 4/144 (5)
7/119 (8) 8/122 (9) 9/122 (7) 10/174 (10)	5/153 (6) 6/154 (4) 7/162 (7)
	8/218 (8) 9/220 (9) 10/220 (11)

Anderson 7.4–2–34–1; Broad 15–2–57–2; Finn 12–3–36–3; Swann 9–1–42–4. *Second innings*—Anderson 11.3–4–28–1; Broad 11–3–26–2; Swann 32–12–90–6; Finn 19–5–62–1; Root 3–2–1–0.

Umpires: S. J. Davis and M. Erasmus. Third umpire: Aleem Dar.

Series referee: D. C. Boon.

LIMITED-OVERS INTERNATIONAL REPORTS
BY ANDREW ALDERSON

ENGLAND v NEW ZEALAND

First NatWest One-Day International

At Lord's, May 31. New Zealand won by five wickets. Toss: New Zealand.

Guptill made the first one-day international century by a New Zealander at Lord's, to secure victory with 19 balls to spare against an attack missing Stuart Broad and Steven Finn, both injured. Anderson had struck twice in his first over as New Zealand began their pursuit of a modest 228, but then Guptill added 120 with the fluent Taylor, cashing in against the inconsistent Woakes. He might have gone on 13, but Bresnan – a few yards in from the fine-leg boundary – could only palm a top-edged hook over the rope for six. A pull for four sealed the win and made Guptill only the second New Zealander to score a one-day international hundred away to England (Mark Greatbatch hit two in 1990). Earlier, England's batsmen – adorned in a new red strip – resembled a procession of out-of-season Santa Clauses bearing gifts amid overcast skies. The most generous donation came from Root, bowled attempting a reverse sweep. Trott top-scored with 37, one of eight double-figure contributions, but Southee continued the form that had brought him ten wickets in the Test here a fortnight earlier. Luke Ronchi, who had played four one-day internationals for Australia in 2008, made his debut for his native New Zealand. His wicketkeeping was adept, but Anderson soon inflicted a third-ball duck.

Man of the Match: M. J. Guptill.   *Attendance:* 27,249.

England

*A. N. Cook c Ronchi b Southee	30	J. M. Anderson not out	5		
I. R. Bell c Ronchi b Southee	18				
I. J. L. Trott c Taylor b N. L. McCullum.	37				
J. E. Root b N. L. McCullum	30	L-b 4, w 6, n-b 1	11		
E. J. G. Morgan c Ronchi b McClenaghan	6				
†J. C. Buttler c McClenaghan b Williamson	14	1/45 (2) 2/50 (1)	(9 wkts, 50 overs)	227	
C. R. Woakes c Guptill b Mills	36	3/117 (4) 4/124 (3)			
T. T. Bresnan b Southee	25	5/126 (5) 6/159 (6)			
G. P. Swann c N. L. McCullum		7/182 (7) 8/216 (8)			
b McClenaghan	15	9/227 (9)	10 overs: 45-0		

J. W. Dernbach did not bat.

McClenaghan 10–0–49–2; Mills 10–0–36–1; Southee 10–2–37–3; N. L. McCullum 10–0–34–2; Franklin 4–0–29–0; Williamson 6–0–38–1.

New Zealand

†L. Ronchi c Swann b Anderson	0	J. E. C. Franklin not out	16		
M. J. Guptill not out	103	B 4, l-b 12, w 10	26		
K. S. Williamson c Buttler b Anderson	0				
L. R. P. L. Taylor c Buttler b Anderson	54	1/1 (1) 2/1 (3)	(5 wkts, 46.5 overs)	231	
G. D. Elliott b Swann	27	3/121 (4) 4/168 (5)			
*B. B. McCullum c Morgan b Dernbach	5	5/185 (6)	10 overs: 52-2		

N. L. McCullum, T. G. Southee, K. D. Mills and M. J. McClenaghan did not bat.

Anderson 9–0–31–3; Dernbach 10–1–55–1; Woakes 6–0–45–0; Bresnan 9.5–1–36–0; Swann 10–0–33–1; Root 2–0–15–0.

Umpires: Aleem Dar and R. K. Illingworth.   Third umpire: S. J. Davis.

66
In Ireland, a passion for cricket is to know 'a love that dare not speak its name'."
Cricket People, page 183

Mike Hewitt, Getty Images

Driving force: Martin Guptill shows no mercy to Chris Woakes as he motors on to back-to-back hundreds.

ENGLAND v NEW ZEALAND

Second NatWest One-Day International

At Southampton, June 2. New Zealand won by 86 runs. Toss: New Zealand.

A majestic unbeaten 189 from Guptill, the highest score for New Zealand in one-day internationals (previously Lou Vincent's 172 against Zimbabwe in 2005-06), condemned England to their first home series defeat in the format for four years. His 155-ball innings, studded with 19 fours and two sixes, equalled the highest against England, set by Viv Richards at Old Trafford in 1984. New Zealand's highest total against England – indeed their highest against any major nation – was also the most conceded by England at home, surpassing 329 for seven by India at Bristol in 2007; and only once before, when India made 387 for five at Rajkot in 2008-09, had England leaked more in any one-day game. But Guptill, who became the second New Zealander to score back-to-back hundreds in the same one-day series, after Greatbatch 23 years earlier, deserved better than to be lost under a pile of stats. Dropped on 13 for the second match running – this time pulling Woakes hard to Trott at short midwicket – he made England pay in style, not least Dernbach, whose 28 deliveries

WORST ECONOMY-RATE IN ONE-DAY INTERNATIONALS

ER		M	Balls	R	W	Avge
6.35	**J. W. Dernbach (England)**	**24**	**1,234**	**1,308**	**31**	**42.19**
6.07	S. Sreesanth (India).	53	2,476	2,508	75	33.44
6.07	**U. T. Yadav (India)**	**28**	**1,292**	**1,308**	**30**	**43.60**
6.01	**K. M. Jarvis (Zimbabwe)**	**24**	**1,217**	**1,221**	**27**	**45.22**
5.95	M. L. Nkala (Zimbabwe)	50	1,582	1,570	22	71.36
5.94	R. Vinay Kumar (India)	31	1,436	1,423	38	37.44
5.88	E. Chigumbura (Zimbabwe/Africa XI)	153	3,955	3,879	95	40.83
5.86	J. P. Faulkner (Australia)	22	1,000	977	30	32.56
5.85	S. I. Mahmood (England)	26	1,197	1,169	30	38.96
5.84	Shahadat Hossain (Bangladesh)	51	2,198	2,143	47	45.59

Qualification: 1,000 balls.

to him yielded 45. As the bowling fell to pieces, Guptill put on 120 with Williamson, 109 with Taylor and an unbroken 118 with Brendon McCullum – only the second time, after South Africa against the Netherlands in the 2007 World Cup, that a one-day international innings had contained three century partnerships. After the final ten overs produced 132 runs, Guptill walked off to a standing ovation, and England were left needing a miracle. Trott made an unbeaten 109 from 104 balls, his fourth one-day hundred, but no one else managed more than 34, as McClenaghan, the pick of the bowlers on either side throughout the series, wrapped things up. The *Jaws* theme that echoed around the ground awaiting decisions by the third umpire doubled as a comment on England's plight.

Man of the Match: M. J. Guptill.   *Attendance:* 11,903.

New Zealand

M. J. Guptill not out	. . . .	189
†L. Ronchi b Anderson	. . . .	2
K. S. Williamson b Swann	. . . .	55
L. R. P. L. Taylor c Woakes b Anderson	.	60
*B. B. McCullum not out	. . . .	40
B 4, l-b 4, w 5	. . . .	13

1/12 (2) 2/132 (3)   (3 wkts, 50 overs) 359
3/241 (4)   10 overs: 36-1

G. D. Elliott, J. E. C. Franklin, N. L. McCullum, D. A. J. Bracewell, K. D. Mills and M. J. McClenaghan did not bat.

Anderson 10–0–65–2; Bresnan 10–1–73–0; Woakes 7–0–49–0; Dernbach 10–0–87–0; Root 3–0–16–0; Swann 10–0–61–1.

England

*A. N. Cook b Mills	. . . .	34
I. R. Bell c Franklin b Bracewell	. . . .	25
I. J. L. Trott not out	. . . .	109
J. E. Root c Bracewell b N. L. McCullum	.	28
E. J. G. Morgan c Ronchi b Elliott	. . . .	21
†J. C. Buttler c Guptill b McClenaghan	. . . .	2
C. R. Woakes st Ronchi b Williamson	. . . .	13
T. T. Bresnan run out	. . . .	0
G. P. Swann b Williamson	. . . .	1
J. M. Anderson b McClenaghan	. . . .	28
J. W. Dernbach c Mills b McClenaghan	. . .	2
L-b 3, w 6, n-b 1	. . . .	10

1/50 (1) 2/64 (2)   (44.1 overs) 273
3/122 (4) 4/166 (5) 5/169 (6)
6/212 (7) 7/213 (8) 8/218 (9)
9/265 (10) 10/273 (11)   10 overs: 64-1

McClenaghan 8.1–0–35–3; Mills 9–0–55–1; Bracewell 8–1–55–1; N. L. McCullum 8–0–47–1; Franklin 5–0–40–0; Elliott 2–0–13–1; Williamson 4–0–25–2.

Umpires: R. J. Bailey and S. J. Davis.   Third umpire: Aleem Dar.

ENGLAND v NEW ZEALAND

Third NatWest One-Day International

At Nottingham, June 5 (day/night). England won by 34 runs. Toss: New Zealand.

After containing England to 211 for five from 46 overs, New Zealand had high hopes of a clean sweep. But 76 were clobbered from the last four to change the picture. Buttler obliterated the death bowling with some brutal straight hits and subtle scoops; his 16-ball innings, which included six fours and three sixes, was enough to earn the match award, and his stand with Morgan raised 62

MOST ONE-DAY INTERNATIONAL RUNS BETWEEN DISMISSALS

405	Mohammad Yousuf (P)..	141*, 76*, 100*, 88	2002-03
400	L. Klusener (SA)......	103*, 35*, 13*, 35*, 12*, 52*, 48*, 52*, 46*, 4	1998-99 to 1999
398	Javed Miandad (P)	31*, 61*, 106*, 3*, 119*, 6*, 72	1982-83 to 1983
389	P. A. de Silva (SL)	49*, 83*, 127*, 75*, 55	1996-97
369	M. S. Dhoni (I)	78*, 50*, 87*, 35*, 15*, 75*, 29	2011 to 2011-12
357	**M. J. Guptill (NZ)....**	**27*, 103*, 189*, 38**	**2012-13 to 2013**
354	A. Jadeja (I)...........	105*, 79*, 6*, 116*, 48	1997-98
346	D. L. Haynes (WI)	145*, 85*, 116	1984-85
320	C. Z. Harris (NZ)	26*, 77*, 29*, 18*, 52*, 9*, 37*, 62*, 10	1996-97 to 1997-98
318	A. B. de Villiers (SA)...	114*, 102*, 102	2009-10 to 2010
310	B. R. M. Taylor (Z)....	128*, 107*, 75	2011-12
301	G. A. Hick (E)........	66*, 126*, 109	1998-99

from just 22 deliveries. Had Buttler hit Southee's final ball for six, he would have broken Sanath Jayasuriya's record for the fastest one-day international fifty – 17 balls, for Sri Lanka against Pakistan at Singapore in 1995-96. But he could manage only two. Amid the destruction, Bell's steady 82 seemed long forgotten. Tredwell led the bowling, offering limited width, but England did not feel safe until he disposed of Taylor, slog-sweeping to deep midwicket, where Finn held on, then lobbed the ball back to Bresnan as he toppled over the boundary. England did at last manage to get rid of Guptill, but not before he had scored 330 runs, breaking Brendan Taylor's record of 310 in a three-match bilateral one-day series (for Zimbabwe at home to New Zealand in 2011-12). During the break between innings, spectator Chris Newell won £50,000 after completing the challenge of hitting three stumps, then two, then one, with successive balls.

Man of the Match: J. C. Buttler.   *Attendance:* 16,157.

Man of the Series: M. J. Guptill.

England

*A. N. Cook lbw b McClenaghan	0	T. T. Bresnan not out................		0
I. R. Bell c N. L. McCullum b McClenaghan	82			
I. J. L. Trott lbw b McClenaghan	37	L-b 2, w 7, n-b 2		11
J. E. Root run out....................	33			
E. J. G. Morgan run out...............	49	1/3 (1) 2/69 (3)	(6 wkts, 50 overs)	287
R. S. Bopara c Taylor b Williamson	28	3/149 (4) 4/153 (2)		
†J. C. Buttler not out	47	5/210 (6) 6/272 (5)	10 overs: 31-1	

S. C. J. Broad, J. C. Tredwell and S. T. Finn did not bat.

McClenaghan 10–1–54–3; Mills 9–1–55–0; Southee 9–0–65–0; Franklin 4–0–24–0; N. L. McCullum 8–0–35–0; Williamson 9–0–42–1; Munro 1–0–10–0.

New Zealand

†L. Ronchi c Trott b Broad	22	K. D. Mills not out.................		28
M. J. Guptill b Tredwell	38	M. J. McClenaghan c Root b Finn........		4
K. S. Williamson lbw b Root	19			
L. R. P. L. Taylor c Bresnan b Tredwell ...	71	B 2, l-b 5, w 6, n-b 2		15
C. Munro c Buttler b Bresnan	0			
*B. B. McCullum c Buttler b Tredwell	6	1/39 (1) 2/70 (2) 3/96 (3)	(46.3 overs)	253
J. E. C. Franklin c Cook b Broad.........	7	4/97 (5) 5/111 (6) 6/122 (7)		
N. L. McCullum c Broad b Bresnan	28	7/175 (8) 8/196 (9) 9/235 (4)		
T. G. Southee c Cook b Finn............	15	10/253 (11)	10 overs: 70-2	

Finn 9.3–0–57–2; Broad 9–0–56–2; Bresnan 8–0–27–2; Tredwell 9–0–51–3; Root 5–0–34–1; Bopara 6–0–21–0.

Umpires: Aleem Dar and R. T. Robinson.   Third umpire: S. J. Davis.

Series referee: D. C. Boon.

For New Zealand's matches in the ICC Champions Trophy, see page 301.

At Canterbury, June 22 (floodlit). **New Zealanders won by 42 runs. New Zealanders 185-7** (20 overs) (M. J. Guptill 56, L. R. P. L. Taylor 52, T. W. M. Latham 38; M. E. Claydon 5-31); ‡**Kent 143-7** (20 overs) (D. J. Bell-Drummond 31, D. I. Stevens 41). *The New Zealanders made a poor start, losing Hamish Rutherford in the first over and Brendon McCullum in the second. But Martin Guptill (44 balls) and Ross Taylor (37) put on 98, before Tom Latham cracked 38 from 18 balls. Mitch Claydon, the Durham seamer on loan to Kent, then cleaned up. Kent made a sluggish start, and were always adrift of the required rate.*

ENGLAND v NEW ZEALAND

First NatWest Twenty20 International

At The Oval, June 25 (floodlit). New Zealand won by five runs. Toss: England.

Three of New Zealand's younger brigade set up their victory, although old hands Brendon McCullum thumped an important 68 and Taylor pulled off a match-changing catch. Rutherford got the innings off to a rollicking start, batting as if he were playing rounders and peppering the fence between mid-on and backward square. Then, as New Zealand defended their highest Twenty20 total away from home, Corey Anderson sent down a tight final over. It started with 16 required, which shrank when Stokes hit the first ball for six — but the last five deliveries produced only four runs. The third relative newcomer, Latham, was all action behind the stumps, catching Wright and running out Buttler to atone for a missed stumping off Hira when Hales hit 31. England had begun quickly, reaching 50 in 3.3 overs, but then Nathan McCullum yorked Lumb and the rate slowed. Still, at 134 for two in the 14th over England seemed on course, but Taylor's one-handed leap disposed of Morgan and justified the brave decision to keep a slip in. The Barmy Army serenaded the new batsman with a chant of "Oh, Ra-vi Bo-pa-ra", to the tune of the White Stripes' "Seven Nation Army", but he couldn't quite repay them with a victory. Earlier, Boyd Rankin had taken a wicket with the fourth ball in his first international for England, after 52 caps for Ireland.

Man of the Match: H. D. Rutherford.   *Attendance:* 19,844.

New Zealand

		B	4	6
H. D. Rutherford *c 2 b 3*		62	35	6	4
J. E. C. Franklin *c 6 b 11*		0	1	0	0
*B. B. McCullum *b 3*		68	48	7	2
L. R. P. L. Taylor *not out*		32	19	2	1
†T. W. M. Latham *c 5 b 10*		22	17	1	1
C. Munro *not out*		0	0	0	0
L-b 6, w 11		17			

6 overs: 54-1   (20 overs) 201-4

1/1 2/115 3/161 4/200

N. L. McCullum, I. G. Butler, C. J. Anderson, M. J. McClenaghan and R. M. Hira did not bat.

Rankin 4–0–24–1; Woakes 1–0–19–0; Dernbach 4–0–31–1; Stokes 3–0–26–0; Tredwell 2–0–32–0; Bopara 2–0–32–0; Wright 4–0–31–2.

England

		B	4	6
M. J. Lumb *b 7*		29	15	3	2
A. D. Hales *c 2 b 11*		39	29	5	1
L. J. Wright *c 5 b 10*		52	34	6	1
*E. J. G. Morgan *c 4 b 8*		7	10	0	0
R. S. Bopara *not out*		30	18	2	1
†J. C. Buttler *run out*		17	10	1	1
B. A. Stokes *not out*		9	5	0	1
L-b 8, w 4, n-b 1		13			

6 overs: 67-1   (20 overs) 196-5

1/50 2/105 3/134 4/139 5/184

C. R. Woakes, J. C. Tredwell, J. W. Dernbach and W. B. Rankin did not bat.

McClenaghan 4–0–37–1; Butler 4–0–35–1; N. L. McCullum 3–0–37–1; Hira 4–0–34–1; Anderson 4–0–40–0; Franklin 1–0–5–0.

Umpires: R. J. Bailey and R. K. Illingworth.   Third umpire: R. T. Robinson.

ENGLAND v NEW ZEALAND

Second NatWest Twenty20 International

At The Oval, June 27 (floodlit). No result. Toss: New Zealand.

Rain set in for good after just two deliveries, the second of which Lumb edged to second slip. The weather derailed Pietersen's England comeback from a knee injury, and meant a brief introduction to international captaincy for Tredwell, the replacement for Morgan (himself a stand-in for the rested Broad), who had injured his hand in the first game. Tredwell's only act was to lose the toss. The match equalled the record for the shortest international in which any play was possible, after the India–Sri Lanka group game in the 1992 World Cup, at Mackay in Queensland.

England

		B	*4*	*6*
M. J. Lumb *c 3 b 10*	2	2	0	0
A. D. Hales *not out*	0	0	0	0
L. J. Wright *not out*	0	0	0	0
(0.2 overs)	2-1			

1/2

K. P. Pietersen, R. S. Bopara, †J. C. Buttler, B. A. Stokes, *J. C. Tredwell, J. W. Dernbach, W. B. Rankin and D. R. Briggs did not bat.

McClenaghan 0.2–0–2–1.

New Zealand

H. D. Rutherford, J. E. C. Franklin, *B. B. McCullum, L. R. P. L. Taylor, †T. W. M. Latham, C. Munro, N. L. McCullum, I. G. Butler, C. J. Anderson, M. J. McClenaghan and R. M. Hira.

Umpires: R. K. Illingworth and R. T. Robinson.   Third umpire: M. A. Gough.
Series referee: J. Srinath.

ICC CHAMPIONS TROPHY, 2013

REVIEW BY HUGH CHEVALLIER

1. India   2. England   3= South Africa and Sri Lanka

An old joke claims there's more craic to be had at a Glasgow funeral than an Edinburgh wedding. Long before the eight teams assembled for the 2013 Champions Trophy, the ICC announced the competition's grave had been dug, and that its seventh incarnation would be its death throe. Defunct tournaments aren't always the cheeriest, but it soon became clear this would be a thoroughly Glaswegian wake. (Several months later, in fact, it emerged that this hadn't been a wake at all.)

None had a better time than India, whose batsmen took barely a false step until the final, where they met an England side eyeing their first global 50-over prize (even if it had shrunk in the wash to 20). But then the Indian bowlers, aided by a dire case of English jitters, proved their own sure-footedness, scoffing at those who had seen the attack as a weak link. No other semi-finalist took eight wickets or more in every match; no other team could boast a *pair* of spinners offering penetration and parsimony.

The tournament was not perfect – poor weather and two one-sided semis precluded that – but by golly it packed a lot of punch (literally, in one instance) into two and a half weeks. It thrived on the UK's manifold diasporas, and an enlightened ticketing scheme. Children paid £5 for each match, adults between £20 for the cheapest seats at group matches and £60 for the best at the final. Crowds flocked in, and 11 of the 14 completed games enjoyed attendance of 89% or higher. The atmosphere was charged throughout: a ban for breaching the spirit of the game, accusations of ball-tampering, scintillating performances from at least two Asian batsmen, a drunken blow aimed by one cricketer at another, and a near-miss from the valiant hosts – no, this competition was not short of action.

Indeed it was so popular that a head of steam built up to raise it, Lazarus-like, from the dead. At first, this seemed improbable. But rumours began to spread that its replacement on the calendar – the World Test Championship – had failed to gather support. In early 2014, it was confirmed that the Champions Trophy had been spared, to reconvene in 2017.

There were signs, too, that the ICC had recognised the virtues of keeping things simple. When the Champions Trophy had last come to Britain, in September 2004, *Wisden* called it "ill-conceived and ill-executed in almost every particular. For sheer dreadfulness, the fourth Champions Trophy surpassed the third, which in Sri Lanka two years earlier had failed to produce a winner at all." Back then, the United States and Kenya had joined the ten Test nations in a tournament pinched by West Indies from under England's noses in autumnal gloom. In June 2013, participation was limited to the eight top-ranked teams, in theory eliminating mismatches.

The structure was as pleasingly straightforward as the midsummer days were long: groups of four in which all played all, with two teams in each

Leaps and boundaries: Shikhar Dhawan gave India a flying start throughout the tournament.

progressing to semi-finals. But in the beauty of a short, sharp contest lay the seeds of its undoing. And all the seeds needed to germinate was a watering.

The ICC made several sound decisions, but they courted disaster by discarding all reserve days. Broadcasters and spectators may dislike play spilling on to a second day, but it shows utter disregard for the integrity of a tournament if the result of a semi-final is decided by position in the group tables – as so nearly happened – or if there is no outright winner. As the competition began, though, a dreich spring gave way to warm summer sun, and the administrators breathed again. (Not that they were optimistic about the British climate: the journalists' welcome pack contained a puffer jacket and an insulated mug…) But then, as sure as night follows day, the weather turned.

Would the whole shebang unravel? Almost. Had rain lasted another half-hour on the afternoon of the final, the trophy would have been shared, as it had been in 2002-03 by India and hosts Sri Lanka. In the event, a 50-over match was decided by a 20-over final (despite the next day being dry). Remarkably, just one group game failed to reach a result, though the weather bit deep into several, including a crunch match between South Africa and West Indies that ended in a Duckworth/Lewis tie.

India were worthy champions, despite a nervy win over a nervier England at a dank Birmingham, after both teams had come through anticlimactic semi-finals largely decided by the toss. The Indians seemed at ease everywhere, even in the wateriness of a British June. Their support had a home-from-home feel, too. The moment M. S. Dhoni's team were involved, flags waved furiously, and the roar grew deafening, especially in the presence of the moustachioed Man of the Tournament, Shikhar Dhawan. With flamboyance and power, but no fear, he made the world listen to his tune. Given his head at the top of the order at the age of 27, the left-handed Dhawan hit two centuries and a fifty in his 363 runs – 134 more than anyone else, and at a strike-rate of 101 – as the ball sang sweetly from his bat. He and Rohit Sharma shared opening stands of 127, 101, 58, 77 and 19. (Sehwag and Gambhir – who they?) The openers epitomised the new athletic India. Fielding was fun, not a fag.

Another hero of the young brigade was slow left-armer Ravindra Jadeja, who stifled the South Africans in a high-scoring first game, and demolished the West Indians in the second, which guaranteed India passage into the semis. He ended with 12 wickets at under 13, conceded just 3.75 an over, and lent clout to the middle order. And Dhoni could call on the variations of unorthodox off-spinner Ravichandran Ashwin. India, who were unchanged throughout the tournament, overcame Pakistan in what was nominally a dead match, though more than a billion subcontinental eyes render that notion absurd. India won on Duckworth/Lewis – and on decibels – to top Group B.

Injuries hampered **South Africa** before and during the competition. Graeme Smith was nursing his ankle, Dale Steyn was risked for just one game, Morne Morkel limped out of the opening defeat by India, while Jacques Kallis opted to stay at home. South Africa shuffled their order, playing a different No. 3 in each group game, while the depleted attack looked largely anodyne. Into the breach stepped Ryan McLaren, who swatted a brisk unbeaten 71 against the Indians to pep up the run-rate, before grabbing four for 19 against Pakistan to set up a do-or-die clash with West Indies.

Trouble was, rain just wouldn't leave Cardiff alone – and those seeds of undoing started to swell. South Africa made 230 in 31 overs, but as the weather deteriorated first Marlon Samuels and then Kieron Pollard walloped West Indies back into contention. After 26 overs, they were four to the good on Duckworth/Lewis – and with one West Indian foot in the semis. But Pollard kitchen-sinked the next ball, from McLaren, and Steyn held a spiralling catch at third man. It proved the last, dramatic, action of a tense match. The maths said there was no longer anything between the sides, and for once the tie suited South Africa, previously specialists at losing out in tussles with the tables.

That result eliminated the quietly fancied **West Indies**. Their first game, a thrilling, low-scoring victory over Pakistan, contained a vicious opening spell from Kemar Roach, who seized his fourth wicket when Misbah-ul-Haq was caught behind. Or so we thought. Square-leg umpire Nigel Llong harboured doubts about the validity of the catch. The evidence, writ large on the giant screen, was damning: the ball squirted from Denesh Ramdin's gloves as he landed on the turf and, as if trying to dispel the notion that the ball was never under full control, he nonchalantly threw it away. Match referee Chris Broad saw the move as calculated, and found Ramdin guilty of conduct contrary to the spirit of the game; he was docked his match fee and banned for two one-day internationals. Roach never did take a fourth wicket, either in the match or the tournament.

The last team in the group was **Pakistan**. They too enjoyed impassioned support, their flags transforming The Oval and Edgbaston into seas of rippling green. But they enjoyed little else, because an exhilarating bowling unit was

No frills, plenty of thrills. The competition zipped along at a cracking rate. Here, Australia's Mitchell Johnson just makes his ground, despite acrobatics from England wicketkeeper Jos Buttler.

neutralised by the weakest of batting line-ups. Without Misbah, who scored an unbeaten 96 against West Indies, and the talented opener Nasir Jamshed, Pakistan would have faced total humiliation: those two accounted for 56% of their team's runs from the bat. In one sense, though, Pakistan were consistency itself, dismissed for 170, 167 and 165. It meant that arguably the tournament's best attack – and unarguably its best trio of left-arm seamers – departed with three defeats. Most eye-catching was the 7ft 1in Mohammad Irfan; when he toured England in 2010 he seemed something of a passing novelty, but now he had added pace and control to his unnerving bounce. He had the potential to trouble the world's best.

For **England**, the tournament represented a real opportunity to end their 38-year wait for a global one-day international trophy. Twice on the day of the final it seemed they would succeed: first when the rain looked set to bring an anticlimactic share of the spoils, then when Eoin Morgan and Ravi Bopara broke the back of the chase. But their eventual five-run defeat followed failure in three World Cup finals and the 2004 edition of this competition.

England's approach was thorough and logical, and for the most part it worked. They reasoned that the use of separate balls at each end tipped the balance towards the seamer, so the need to conserve wickets was greater than ever. When setting a target, England's 20-over score was almost inscribed in stone: against Australia, it was 87 for one, and against Sri Lanka, 85 for one; in the one-day series with New Zealand just before this tournament, they had reached 81 for two and 74 for two. And if that sounded like batting by numbers, there was some truth to it: England were in danger of sticking to their preordained targets come what may. On an Oval featherbed, they should have been quicker at making hay, and an innings of utter genius from Sri Lanka's Kumar Sangakkara inflicted resounding defeat. Jonathan Trott drew flak, as he often does, yet his 229 runs – only Dhawan hit more – came at a jaunty 91 per

THE STORY OF THE CHAMPIONS TROPHY

Season	Winners	Runners-up	Host nation	Teams/matches
1998-99	**South Africa**	**West Indies**	**Bangladesh**	**9/8**

Staged to raise funds for cricket development, the tournament featured all nine Test-playing countries at the time: New Zealand beat Zimbabwe in a "pre-quarter-final". Dhaka was the third-choice venue, after Sharjah and DisneyWorld.

2000-01	**New Zealand**	**India**	**Kenya**	**11/10**

The "ICC Knockout" involved the Test nations – their ranks now swelled to ten by Bangladesh – and the hosts, who were eliminated by India on the opening day. Chris Cairns hit 102* in the final, to win what remains New Zealand's only global trophy.

2002-03	**India/Sri Lanka**	**–**	**Sri Lanka**	**12/15**

The first tournament actually called the ICC Champions Trophy failed to produce a champion: the final in Colombo started twice, on successive days, but was rained off both times. The ten Test teams were joined by Kenya and the Netherlands, playing in four groups of three.

2004	**West Indies**	**England**	**England**	**12/15**

Kenya and the United States joined the ten Test nations, in the same format. West Indies triumphed in the dark of a late-September evening at The Oval.

2006-07	**Australia**	**West Indies**	**India**	**10/21**

Sri Lanka and West Indies eliminated Bangladesh and Zimbabwe in a preliminary group, before joining the six top-ranked nations in two groups of four. Australia won for the first time, despite Chris Gayle's 474 runs (and three centuries).

2009-10	**Australia**	**New Zealand**	**South Africa**	**8/15**

Only the eight top-ranked teams took part (so no place for Bangladesh or Zimbabwe). Australia retained their title, with Shane Watson hitting centuries in the semi and final.

2013	**India**	**England**	**England**	**8/15**

The 2009-10 format was retained. For the second time England lost in the final. Kyle Mills of New Zealand took six wickets in the tournament to lift his overall tally in the Champions Trophy to a record 28. Gayle was the leading run-scorer in the history of the competition, with 791; he, Herschelle Gibbs and Sourav Ganguly scored three hundreds.

---

100 balls; neither of the openers, Alastair Cook and Ian Bell, could manage 80. The bowling, so strong when the ball obliged with swing or spin, looked clueless when it didn't.

The system had, however, delivered victory over Australia at Edgbaston and, with the next fixture five days away, the team were allowed to celebrate. Joe Root was one of a handful of players from both sides who in the small hours fetched up in the Walkabout, an Aussie-themed bar in the centre of Birmingham. The precise events remain unclear, but Root was apparently sporting a wig on his chin when David Warner swung a punch in what an ECB statement described as an "unprovoked" attack. Warner was banned from all matches until the Ashes and fined £7,000. A fortnight later Cricket Australia sacked coach Mickey Arthur; the Walkabout altercation was seen as the last straw.

England were involved in another controversy. George Bailey, Australia's captain, remarked (admiringly) how quickly their bowlers had found reverse swing; then, as the England attack floundered against Sri Lanka, the umpires replaced the ball. There was no five-run penalty, and the incident might have faded away had Bob Willis not waded in. "Let's not beat about the bush," he said on Sky Sports. "Aleem Dar… knows that one individual is scratching the ball for England… and that's why the ball was changed." All eyes were now on English hands, especially Bopara's, who was widely identified as Willis's "individual". A furious England despatched New Zealand in a rain-affected game to guarantee progress – and without exciting any more ball-tampering fervour. South Africa's captain, A. B. de Villiers, couldn't resist referring to the rumpus in the lead-up to the semis, though it was already feeling like a storm in yesterday's teacup before his side conked out, and Willis later wrote to Cook to apologise.

Sri Lanka negotiated a topsy-turvy path to the last four. They came within one New Zealand wicket of defending a meagre 138 at Cardiff, before sauntering past England's daunting 293 at The Oval. On both occasions, Sangakkara led the way. When they met Australia in the last group match, there were enough mathematical permutations to make the heads of even Messrs Duckworth and Lewis spin. The fact that all four teams had an interest in the outcome kept the spectacle compelling. Mahela Jayawardene ensured an adequate total, though Sri Lanka were fortunate to be playing a team desperate to inflate their run-rate.

The Birmingham weather had prevented the Antipodean clash reaching a result: had **New Zealand** won, their run-rate would probably have meant they finished above Sri Lanka, whom they had dismissed inside 38 overs; had it been Australia, any sort of victory in that last group game at The Oval would have seen them qualify. For New Zealand, Mitchell McClenaghan was even more incisive than in the NatWest Series, striking once every 13 balls, while Daniel Vettori put long-term injury behind him to bowl 21 overs for only 66.

Bottom of the heap came the defending champions, **Australia**. How they missed Michael Clarke, struggling to overcome a persistent back injury. Bowled out for 65 by India in a warm-up game, they rather matched the fireworks (think damp squib rather than pyrotechnics) that plopped and dolloped around the grounds in sheepish recognition of a six or wicket. The Australians had their moments – Adam Voges held a steady bat – but not many. Yet by early 2014, both they and the Champions Trophy itself had undergone astonishing revivals.

NATIONAL SQUADS

* Captain. ‡ Did not play.

Australia *‡M. J. Clarke, G. J. Bailey, ‡N. M. Coulter-Nile, X. J. Doherty, J. P. Faulkner, P. J. Hughes, M. G. Johnson, C. J. McKay, M. R. Marsh, G. J. Maxwell, M. A. Starc, A. C. Voges, M. S. Wade, D. A. Warner, S. R. Watson. *Coach:* J. M. Arthur.
  Clarke was unable to play owing to a back problem, and Bailey captained instead.

England *A. N. Cook, J. M. Anderson, ‡J. M. Bairstow, I. R. Bell, R. S. Bopara, T. T. Bresnan, S. C. J. Broad, J. C. Buttler, S. T. Finn, E. J. G. Morgan, J. E. Root, G. P. Swann, J. C. Tredwell, I. J. L. Trott, ‡C. R. Woakes. *Coach:* A. F. Giles.

India *M. S. Dhoni, R. Ashwin, Bhuvneshwar Kumar, S. Dhawan, R. A. Jadeja, K. D. Karthik, V. Kohli, ‡A. Mishra, ‡I. K. Pathan, S. K. Raina, I. Sharma, R. G. Sharma, ‡M. Vijay, ‡R. Vinay Kumar, U. T. Yadav. *Coach:* D. A. G. Fletcher.

New Zealand *B. B. McCullum, ‡D. A. J. Bracewell, ‡I. G. Butler, ‡G. D. Elliott, J. E. C. Franklin, M. J. Guptill, M. J. McClenaghan, N. L. McCullum, K. D. Mills, ‡C. Munro, L. Ronchi, T. G. Southee, L. R. P. L. Taylor, D. L. Vettori, K. S. Williamson. *Coach:* M. J. Hesson.

T. A. Boult and A. M. Ellis were originally selected, but withdrew with injuries to side and rib respectively, and were replaced by Butler and Bracewell. Elliott injured his calf during the tournament, and was replaced by C. J. Anderson.

Pakistan *Misbah-ul-Haq, ‡Abdur Rehman, ‡Asad Ali, Asad Shafiq, ‡Ehsan Adil, Imran Farhat, Junaid Khan, Kamran Akmal, Mohammad Hafeez, Mohammad Irfan, Nasir Jamshed, Saeed Ajmal, Shoaib Malik, Umar Amin, Wahab Riaz. *Coach:* D. F. Whatmore.

South Africa *A. B. de Villiers, H. M. Amla, ‡F. Behardien, J-P. Duminy, F. du Plessis, C. A. Ingram, R. K. Kleinveldt, R. McLaren, D. A. Miller, M. Morkel, ‡A. N. Petersen, R. J. Peterson, A. M. Phangiso, D. W. Steyn, L. L. Tsotsobe. *Coach:* R. C. Domingo.

G. C. Smith was originally selected, but withdrew to undergo an ankle operation and was replaced by Petersen. Morkel injured his thigh during the tournament, and was replaced by C. H. Morris.

Sri Lanka *A. D. Mathews, L. D. Chandimal, ‡L. H. D. Dilhara, T. M. Dilshan, R. M. S. Eranga, H. M. R. K. B. Herath, D. P. M. D. Jayawardene, K. M. D. N. Kulasekara, S. L. Malinga, B. M. A. J. Mendis, M. D. K. J. Perera, N. L. T. C. Perera, K. C. Sangakkara, ‡S. M. S. M. Senanayake, H. D. R. L. Thirimanne. *Coach:* G. X. Ford.

U. W. M. B. C. A. Welagedara was originally selected, but withdrew with an ankle injury and was replaced by Dilhara.

West Indies *D. J. Bravo, T. L. Best, D. M. Bravo, J. Charles, C. H. Gayle, ‡J. O. Holder, S. P. Narine, K. A. Pollard, D. Ramdin, R. Rampaul, K. A. J. Roach, D. J. G. Sammy, M. N. Samuels, R. R. Sarwan, D. S. Smith. *Coach:* O. D. Gibson.

Match reports by Lawrence Booth, Hugh Chevallier, Richard Hobson, Patrick Kidd and Neil Manthorp

GROUP A

ENGLAND v AUSTRALIA

At Birmingham, June 8. England won by 48 runs. Toss: England.

From the first ball, clipped neatly for four through the leg side by Cook, England rarely ceded control of the first of 26 scheduled meetings with their oldest rivals in eight months. Cook's bowlers then made a par target of 270 appear formidable with an outstanding demonstration of reverse swing on a dry surface. Bailey, deputising as Australia's captain for the injured Clarke, was surprised how quickly England generated unorthodox movement: the ball began to shape as early as the eighth over, and the control of Anderson in particular made for an almighty challenge. When Marsh carved to backward point, Anderson overtook Darren Gough's record of 234 one-day wickets for England. Bailey tried to consolidate but eventually holed out, while Faulkner's powerful half-century merely limited the damage to the net run-rate. Earlier, England had faltered during the batting powerplay, but the foundation laid by the top three balanced that. Bell should have been run out before he scored, but looked set for a hundred until he played around a straight one from Faulkner. McKay helped check the scoring-rate, only for Bopara – justifying his inclusion ahead of Finn, No. 3 in the ICC's one-day bowling rankings at the time – and Bresnan to strike 56 from the last 41 balls. As if defeat was not bad enough, Australia were also fined for a slow over-rate.

Man of the Match: I. R. Bell.   *Attendance:* 22,005.

England

*A. N. Cook c Wade b Watson	30	T. T. Bresnan not out	19
I. R. Bell b Faulkner	91		
I. J. L. Trott c Wade b Starc	43	L-b 12, w 6, n-b 1	19
J. E. Root c Bailey b McKay	12		
E. J. G. Morgan b McKay	8	1/57 (1) 2/168 (3)	(6 wkts, 50 overs) 269
R. S. Bopara not out	46	3/189 (2) 4/189 (4)	
†J. C. Buttler b Faulkner	1	5/212 (5) 6/213 (7)	10 overs: 54-0

S. C. J. Broad, J. C. Tredwell and J. M. Anderson did not bat.

Starc 10–0–75–1; Johnson 8–0–44–0; McKay 10–0–38–2; Watson 7–0–26–1; Faulkner 10–0–48–2; Voges 3–0–13–0; Marsh 2–0–13–0.

Australia

D. A. Warner c Buttler b Broad	9	M. A. Starc b Anderson		5
S. R. Watson c Cook b Bresnan	24	C. J. McKay not out		7
P. J. Hughes lbw b Root	30			
*G. J. Bailey c Root b Tredwell	55	L-b 6, w 1, n-b 1		8
A. C. Voges b Bresnan	15			
M. R. Marsh c Morgan b Anderson	5	1/17 (1) 2/47 (2) (9 wkts, 50 overs)		221
†M. S. Wade c Buttler b Anderson	1	3/94 (3) 4/127 (5)		
J. P. Faulkner not out	54	5/134 (6) 6/136 (7) 7/151 (4)		
M. G. Johnson c Morgan b Bopara	8	8/175 (9) 9/190 (10) 10 overs: 35-1		

Anderson 10–0–30–3; Broad 10–2–35–1; Bresnan 10–1–45–2; Tredwell 10–1–51–1; Root 5–0–20–1; Bopara 5–0–34–1.

Umpires: H. D. P. K. Dharmasena and M. Erasmus.   Third umpire: B. F. Bowden.
Referee: J. Srinath.

NEW ZEALAND v SRI LANKA

At Cardiff, June 9. New Zealand won by one wicket. Toss: Sri Lanka.

But for one sliver of luck, it might have been Sri Lanka who earned victory from this low-scoring thriller. Malinga had already removed Williamson and Vettori when he returned to account for the McCullum brothers in three balls and reduce New Zealand to 122 for eight, with 17 still needed. He then struck Southee on the boot with yet another lightning-bolt yorker, only for Bruce Oxenford to rule that the ball had ricocheted to the third-man boundary via the bat; crucially, Sri Lanka had already wasted their review. New Zealand's tailenders somehow survived the rest of that over, as well as Malinga's tenth. But in between, they lost Mills to a freakish direct hit from Tissara Perera, coming round from mid-on. Aiming to throw down the non-striker's stumps and run out Southee, Perera missed – then watched the ball hit the stumps at the other end instead, with an unsuspecting Mills short of his ground. But last pair Southee and McClenaghan scrambled the five New Zealand required, concluding with a leg-side wide from Dilshan, off which they also stole the winning run. The match had begun dramatically, too: off the first ball, Mills found Kushal Perera's edge, and Brendon McCullum clung on in the slip cordon, leaping like a goalkeeper high to his left. McClenaghan then took four wickets, and Vettori picked up one in his first one-day international over after more than two years – Jayawardene lbw, the same batsman and method of dismissal as his previous 50-over wicket, in the 2011 World Cup semi-final. Sangakkara's 68 just about gave his team something to defend, and when New Zealand lost three wickets in eight balls to lurch to 49 for four, it was game on. Vettori was unlucky to be adjudged leg-before to a ball he had edged, but Williamson had used up New Zealand's review, incorrectly challenging his own lbw decision. Then came Malinga, for one final twist.

Man of the Match: N. L. McCullum.   *Attendance:* 4,834.

Sri Lanka

M. D. K. J. Perera c B. B. McCullum b Mills	0	H. M. R. K. B. Herath not out		8
T. M. Dilshan b McClenaghan	20	R. M. S. Eranga c Mills b N. L. McCullum		0
†K. C. Sangakkara c Williamson		S. L. Malinga c Taylor b McClenaghan		2
b N. L. McCullum	68	L-b 1, w 2		3
D. P. M. D. Jayawardene lbw b Vettori	4			
L. D. Chandimal c Ronchi b Mills	0	1/0 (1) 2/27 (2) 3/33 (4) (37.5 overs)		138
*A. D. Mathews b McClenaghan	9	4/34 (5) 5/65 (6) 6/82 (7)		
H. D. R. L. Thirimanne run out	9	7/118 (8) 8/135 (3) 9/135 (10)		
N. L. T. C. Perera c Vettori b McClenaghan	15	10/138 (11) 10 overs: 38-4		

Mills 6–0–14–2; McClenaghan 8.5–0–43–4; Vettori 6–1–16–1; Southee 7–1–25–0; N. L. McCullum 8–0–23–2; Williamson 2–0–16–0.

New Zealand

M. J. Guptill c Jayawardene b Eranga	25	K. D. Mills run out	3
†L. Ronchi c Sangakkara b Eranga	7	M. J. McClenaghan not out	1
K. S. Williamson lbw b Malinga	16		
L. R. P. L. Taylor lbw b Herath	0	L-b 8, w 5	13
J. E. C. Franklin lbw b Dilshan	6		
*B. B. McCullum b Malinga	18	(9 wkts, 36.3 overs)	139
D. L. Vettori lbw b Malinga	5		
N. L. McCullum lbw b Malinga	32		
T. G. Southee run out	13		

1/14 (2) 2/48 (3)   3/49 (4) 4/49 (1)   5/70 (5) 6/80 (7) 7/115 (6)   8/122 (8) 9/134 (10)   10 overs: 49-3

Malinga 10–2–34–4; Eranga 8–0–45–2; Herath 10–0–36–1; Dilshan 6.3–1–12–1; N. L. T. C. Perera 2–0–4–0.

Umpires: B. N. J. Oxenford and R. J. Tucker.   Third umpire: I. J. Gould.
Referee: A. J. Pycroft.

AUSTRALIA v NEW ZEALAND

At Birmingham, June 12. No result. Toss: Australia.

The game was overshadowed by the suspension of David Warner, who had assaulted Joe Root in a Birmingham bar in the early hours of June 9, following Australia's opening-game defeat by England. Warner took his place in the line-up for the national anthems, carried the drinks, and helped with slip-catching practice during the break between innings, but his misdemeanour cast a pall over a day that was every bit as grey as the local weather. Australia slipped to ten for two, including the senseless run-out of Hughes for a duck, but recovered through Bailey and Voges. McClenaghan again grabbed four wickets, but the pick of New Zealand's attack was Vettori, who got through his most economical ten-over analysis for more than four years. McKay then found extra bounce to remove both openers in quick succession, and Australia were in control when heavy rain arrived from the south-west around 3.30pm. Three hours later, the game was called off, five overs short of the 20 needed to constitute a match. The abandonment left Australia reliant on other results to have any chance of making the last four – and awaiting the outcome of Warner's disciplinary hearing the following day in Melbourne.

Attendance: 8,926.

Australia

S. R. Watson c Ronchi b McClenaghan	5	M. G. Johnson c B. B. McCullum	
†M. S. Wade lbw b N. L. McCullum	29	b McClenaghan	8
P. J. Hughes run out	0	C. J. McKay not out	2
*G. J. Bailey b N. L. McCullum	55	B 1, l-b 7, w 4, n-b 4	16
A. C. Voges c B. B. McCullum			
b McClenaghan	71	(8 wkts, 50 overs)	243
M. R. Marsh c Ronchi b McClenaghan	22		
G. J. Maxwell not out	29		
J. P. Faulkner c McClenaghan b Williamson	6		

1/5 (1) 2/10 (3)   3/74 (2) 4/151 (4)   5/193 (6) 6/196 (5)   7/210 (8) 8/219 (9)   10 overs: 32-2

X. J. Doherty did not bat.

Mills 6–1–19–0; McClenaghan 10–0–65–4; Vettori 10–1–23–0; Southee 4–1–26–0; N. L. McCullum 10–0–46–2; Williamson 10–0–56–1.

New Zealand

†L. Ronchi c Watson b McKay 14
M. J. Guptill c Maxwell b McKay 8
K. S. Williamson not out 18
L. R. P. L. Taylor not out 9
    L-b 1, w 1 2
                                               ———

1/18 (2)   (2 wkts, 15 overs)   51
2/26 (1)   10 overs: 38-2

*B. B. McCullum, J. E. C. Franklin, N. L. McCullum, D. L. Vettori, T. G. Southee, K. D. Mills and M. J. McClenaghan did not bat.

Johnson 4–0–18–0; McKay 4–0–10–2; Watson 3–1–11–0; Faulkner 3–0–7–0; Doherty 1–0–4–0.

Umpires: H. D. P. K. Dharmasena and N. J. Llong.   Third umpire: R. A. Kettleborough.
Referee: B. C. Broad.

ENGLAND v SRI LANKA

At The Oval, June 13 (day/night). Sri Lanka won by seven wickets. Toss: Sri Lanka.

At the heart of Sri Lanka's near-faultless run-chase was an innings from Sangakkara as elegant as it was ruthless. Surprisingly, given such dominance, this was his first one-day international hundred in or against England. He arrived in the third over, and gave not a single chance in 135 balls. Dilshan helped him add 92 for the second wicket, but betrayed unnecessary jitters by holing out to long-on in the 21st over. However, Jayawardene realised he had time to play himself in, and made just five from 17 deliveries before hitting his first boundary – a six over long-on off Broad. The old masters played classically, driving in the V when the ball was full, pulling or cutting when short. If panache came from the batsmen, panic came from England's bowlers, who looked toothless in the absence of swing. Some observers wondered whether they had tampered with the ball when umpire Aleem Dar changed it in the 26th over, but not one ball – new, old or replacement – would dance to England's

Right angles: Kumar Sangakkara gives a lesson in technical perfection as England are thwarted at The Oval.

Philip Brown

tune. Sri Lanka promoted Kulasekara to No. 5, a move he took in his stride. He smoked 58 from 38 deliveries as Sri Lanka romped home, dented England's net run-rate and blew the group wide open. England's innings had largely adhered to the master plan: jog along at four or five an over, conserve wickets, pick up speed in the last ten or 15, and give it welly in the late thrash. Root provided the most watchable of the top order's three fifties, and a platform of 218 for two in the 42nd over promised riches. Instead, England's middle order floundered, and only a barnstorming effort from Bopara, who crashed 28 off the last over, from Eranga, restored confidence. It didn't last long.

Man of the Match: K. C. Sangakkara. *Attendance:* 20,944.

England

*A. N. Cook lbw b Herath	59	T. T. Bresnan b Eranga		4
I. R. Bell c Perera b Eranga	20	S. C. J. Broad not out		7
I. J. L. Trott lbw b Herath	76	L-b 10, w 3		13
J. E. Root c Jayawardene b Malinga	68			
E. J. G. Morgan lbw b Malinga	13	1/48 (2) 2/131 (1)	(7 wkts, 50 overs)	293
†J. C. Buttler c Sangakkara b Kulasekara	0	3/218 (3) 4/249 (4)		
R. S. Bopara not out	33	5/249 (5) 6/249 (6) 7/254 (8)	10 overs: 38-0	

G. P. Swann and J. M. Anderson did not bat.

Kulasekara 10–0–42–1; Malinga 10–2–58–2; Eranga 10–0–80–2; Mathews 6–0–28–0; Herath 10–0–46–2; Dilshan 4–0–29–0.

Sri Lanka

M. D. K. J. Perera c Bopara b Anderson	6	K. M. D. N. Kulasekara not out		58
T. M. Dilshan c Root b Swann	44	L-b 6, w 7		13
†K. C. Sangakkara not out	134			
D. P. M. D. Jayawardene		1/10 (1) 2/102 (2)	(3 wkts, 47.1 overs)	297
c sub (J. M. Bairstow) b Anderson	42	3/187 (4)	10 overs: 48-1	

L. D. Chandimal, *A. D. Mathews, H. D. R. L. Thirimanne, H. M. R. K. B. Herath, R. M. S. Eranga and S. L. Malinga did not bat.

Anderson 10–0–51–2; Broad 8.1–0–67–0; Bresnan 10–0–63–0; Root 3–0–27–0; Swann 10–0–50–1; Bopara 6–0–33–0.

Umpires: Aleem Dar and B. F. Bowden. Third umpire: M. Erasmus.
Referee: J. Srinath.

ENGLAND v NEW ZEALAND

At Cardiff, June 16. England won by ten runs. Toss: New Zealand. One-day international debut: C. J. Anderson.

England pipped New Zealand to a semi-final place, having enjoyed the benefit of a desperately tight call during the denouement. With New Zealand needing 35 from 17 balls, Williamson swung Broad to Jimmy Anderson at extra cover, only for the umpires to ask for confirmation that Broad had not overstepped. Replays showed how close he had come: his heel barely kissed the back of the line. Instead of surviving to enjoy a free hit, the increasingly aggressive Williamson departed for 67 from 54 balls, Broad conceded five from the over, and England breathed again; Cook admitted he would not have complained had the decision gone the other way. Earlier, he had risen to the challenge of a match shortened to 24 overs a side by hitting two sixes in a one-day international innings for the first time. Cook's 64 occupied 47 balls, but his departure sprang the loss of seven for 28 in 31 deliveries as Mills wrought late damage. However, Anderson immediately led the England pace attack in snatching back the impetus. With Bopara bustling through, New Zealand struggled to reach four an over, and left themselves chasing 104 from the last ten. Corey Anderson, a strong left-hander making his debut after a late call-up to replace the injured Grant Elliott, helped Williamson yank things forward, despite lengthy treatment for a calf strain; and the 21st over, from Bresnan, brought 19 runs. Broad's moment of fortune settled the matter.

Man of the Match: A. N. Cook. *Attendance:* 13,676.

England

*A. N. Cook c and b N. L. McCullum	64	J. C. Tredwell c McClenaghan b Mills	0
I. R. Bell c B. B. McCullum b McClenaghan	10	J. M. Anderson not out	0
I. J. L. Trott c N. L. McCullum b Mills	8		
J. E. Root c Ronchi b McClenaghan	38	L-b 2, w 4, n-b 1	7
E. J. G. Morgan lbw b Vettori	15		
†J. C. Buttler c N. L. McCullum b Mills	14	1/16 (2) 2/25 (3) (23.3 overs) 169
R. S. Bopara c Williamson b McClenaghan	9	3/100 (4) 4/141 (1) 5/143 (5)
T. T. Bresnan run out	4	6/159 (6) 7/166 (7) 8/169 (8)
S. C. J. Broad c N. L. McCullum b Mills	0	9/169 (10) 10/169 (10) 5 overs: 33-2

McClenaghan 5–0–36–3; Mills 4.3–0–30–4; Anderson 1–0–4–0; Vettori 5–0–27–1; Franklin 2–0–20–0; N. L. McCullum 4–0–30–1; Williamson 2–0–20–0.

New Zealand

M. J. Guptill b Anderson	9	N. L. McCullum c Buttler b Anderson	13
†L. Ronchi c Trott b Anderson	2	K. D. Mills not out	5
K. S. Williamson c Anderson b Broad	67	L-b 8, w 8	16
L. R. P. L. Taylor lbw b Bresnan	3		
*B. B. McCullum c Root b Bopara	8	1/14 (2) 2/14 (1) (8 wkts, 24 overs) 159
J. E. C. Franklin c Morgan b Bopara	6	3/27 (4) 4/48 (5) 5/62 (6)
C. J. Anderson c Anderson b Bresnan	30	6/135 (3) 7/140 (7) 8/159 (8) 5 overs: 17-2

D. L. Vettori and M. J. McClenaghan did not bat.

Broad 5–0–25–1; Anderson 5–0–32–3; Bresnan 5–0–41–2; Bopara 5–0–26–2; Tredwell 4–0–27–0.

Umpires: B. N. J. Oxenford and R. J. Tucker.   Third umpire: S. J. Davis.
Referee: A. J. Pycroft.

AUSTRALIA v SRI LANKA

At The Oval, June 17 (day/night). Sri Lanka won by 20 runs. Toss: Australia.

All four teams in the group had an interest in the outcome of this game. England, assured of a semi-final, would be knocked into second place (and a match against India) if Sri Lanka prevailed by a wide margin. New Zealand would progress if Australia came out on top, but not too convincingly. A win of any sort was enough for Sri Lanka, while Australia's hopes of qualification rested on a crushing victory. The complexities lent the contest a paradoxical air: only when Australia threw in the semi-final towel and throttled back did they glimpse success – while, not for the last time during the summer, their most accomplished partnership was the tenth-wicket pair. Bailey put Sri Lanka in so his team would know precisely how many overs they had in which to squeeze past New Zealand on net run-rate. They were buoyed when an uncharacteristically lazy drive from Sangakkara, the Oval master of four days before, lollipopped to point and, on a pitch offering bounce and gentle turn, the Sri Lankans never quite hit cruising speed. Jayawardene was a nerveless presence, threading cut after glide after clip through the infield to ensure a half-decent total. The crucial number for Australia was not really 254 but 29.1 – if they managed to win by the first ball of the 30th over, they would live on. They gave it leather, Maxwell in particular, but the helter-skelter runs came at too high a cost and, at 127 for six in the 20th over, the game was up. Voges, though, clung on, if forlornly. And had Johnson appreciated the situation – he had neither scoreboard pressure nor demons in the pitch to worry about – rather than adopting brainless-slog mode, the defending

Philip Brown

Going down fighting: Shane Watson holds a fine catch to dismiss Tillekeratne Dilshan, but defeat for Australia knocked them out of the tournament.

champions might have gained a consolation victory. Without fuss or bother, the last pair added 41, and the celebrations that greeted Dilshan's sharp return catch betrayed the rising panic in the Sri Lankan ranks.

Man of the Match: D. P. M. D. Jayawardene.　　*Attendance:* 17,915.

Sri Lanka

M. D. K. J. Perera lbw b Johnson		4
T. M. Dilshan c Watson b Doherty		34
†K. C. Sangakkara c Maxwell b McKay		3
H. D. R. L. Thirimanne c Watson b Johnson		57
D. P. M. D. Jayawardene not out		84
*A. D. Mathews b Faulkner		12
L. D. Chandimal c Hughes b Johnson		31
K. M. D. N. Kulasekara run out		6
H. M. R. K. B. Herath run out		2
S. L. Malinga not out		2
B 5, l-b 7, w 4, n-b 2		18

R. M. S. Eranga did not bat.

1/8 (1)　2/20 (3)　(8 wkts, 50 overs) 253
3/92 (2)　4/128 (4)
5/159 (6)　6/224 (7)
7/234 (8)　8/244 (9)　　　　　10 overs: 40-2

Johnson 10–0–48–3; McKay 10–1–51–1; Faulkner 9–0–60–1; Watson 4–0–14–0; Doherty 10–1–30–1; Marsh 2–0–12–0; Maxwell 5–0–26–0.

Australia

S. R. Watson b Kulasekara		5
P. J. Hughes c Sangakkara b Kulasekara		13
G. J. Maxwell b Malinga		32
*G. J. Bailey run out		4
A. C. Voges c Eranga b Herath		49
M. R. Marsh b Mathews		4
†M. S. Wade c Dilshan b Kulasekara		31
J. P. Faulkner c Sangakkara b Herath		17
M. G. Johnson c Kulasekara b Eranga		4
C. J. McKay c and b Dilshan		30
X. J. Doherty not out		15
L-b 11, w 17, n-b 1		29

1/9 (1)　2/45 (2)　3/59 (3)　　(42.3 overs) 233
4/69 (4)　5/80 (6)　6/127 (7)
7/163 (8)　8/168 (9)　9/192 (5)
10/233 (10)　　　　　　10 overs: 71-4

Eranga 8–1–40–1; Kulasekara 9–0–42–3; Malinga 9–0–60–1; Herath 10–0–48–2; Mathews 3–0–21–1; Dilshan 3.3–0–11–1.

Umpires: M. Erasmus and A. L. Hill.　　Third umpire: Aleem Dar.
Referee: J. Srinath.

GROUP B

INDIA v SOUTH AFRICA

At Cardiff, June 6. India won by 26 runs. Toss: South Africa.

Shikhar Dhawan set the tournament alight with his maiden one-day international century – less than three months after an incandescent Test debut against Australia at Mohali. Cardiff was overcast when de Villiers won the toss and chose to bowl, but the sun quickly poked through, and the ball refused to do the bidding of a South African attack missing the injured Dale Steyn. Dhawan took advantage to put on 127 inside 22 overs with Sharma, then 83 in 13 with Kohli. By then, he had moved to three figures, from 80 balls, with successive fours off the costly Kleinveldt. And though India lost momentum after Dhawan's sweep picked out short backward square, Jadeja's unbeaten 47 in 29 balls reclaimed the ascendancy. A total of 331 for seven was the highest South Africa had conceded since Sachin Tendulkar made a double-century at Gwalior in February 2010. Ingram and Amla fell early, but Peterson – promoted to No. 3 – and de Villiers now gave the South Africans a sniff with an energetic run-a-ball stand of 124. India looked spooked until Peterson, having completed his maiden one-day international fifty, was stranded mid-pitch following a misunderstanding. Jadeja bowled tightly, wickets fell regularly, and McLaren's 61-ball 71 was mere gloss. There was worse news for South Africa when Morkel, who hobbled off with a quad strain in his seventh over, was ruled out of the tournament the following day.

Man of the Match: S. Dhawan.   *Attendance:* 14,377.

India

R. G. Sharma c Peterson b McLaren	65	R. Ashwin run out	10
S. Dhawan c sub (A. M. Phangiso) b Duminy	114	Bhuvneshwar Kumar not out	0
V. Kohli c Amla b Tsotsobe	31	L-b 4, w 8, n-b 2	14
K. D. Karthik c de Villiers b McLaren	14		
*†M. S. Dhoni c du Plessis b Tsotsobe	27	1/127 (1) 2/210 (3) (7 wkts, 50 overs)	331
S. K. Raina c Duminy b McLaren	9	3/227 (2) 4/240 (4)	
R. A. Jadeja not out	47	5/260 (6) 6/291 (5) 7/323 (8) 10 overs: 53-0	

I. Sharma and U. T. Yadav did not bat.

Morkel 6.5–0–27–0; Tsotsobe 10–0–83–2; Kleinveldt 10–0–81–0; McLaren 10–0–70–3; Peterson 3.1–0–24–0; Duminy 10–0–42–1.

South Africa

H. M. Amla c Dhoni b Yadav	22	L. L. Tsotsobe b Jadeja	3
C. A. Ingram c Raina b Bhuvneshwar Kumar	6	M. Morkel b Bhuvneshwar Kumar	8
R. J. Peterson run out	68		
*†A. B. de Villiers c Jadeja b Yadav	70	L-b 1, w 7, n-b 1	9
J-P. Duminy lbw b Jadeja	14		
F. du Plessis c Raina b I. Sharma	30	1/13 (2) 2/31 (1) 3/155 (3) (50 overs)	305
D. A. Miller run out	0	4/182 (5) 5/184 (4) 6/188 (7)	
R. McLaren not out	71	7/238 (6) 8/251 (9) 9/257 (10)	
R. K. Kleinveldt c Dhoni b I. Sharma	4	10/305 (11) 10 overs: 77-2	

Bhuvneshwar Kumar 7–0–49–2; Yadav 10–0–75–2; I. Sharma 8–0–66–2; Ashwin 10–0–47–0; Jadeja 9–1–31–2; Raina 6–0–36–0.

Umpires: I. J. Gould and B. N. J. Oxenford.   Third umpire: R. J. Tucker.
Referee: A. J. Pycroft.

PAKISTAN v WEST INDIES

At The Oval, June 7. West Indies won by two wickets. Toss: West Indies.

A fraught, low-scoring contest ended in a tight West Indies victory. On a greenish Oval pitch with true bounce and only slight lateral movement, it would have needed a superhuman effort to defend 170. Yet Pakistan so nearly did. Roach had earlier reaped the rewards for hostile, accurate fast bowling, and left Pakistan quaking at 15 for three, which fleetingly became 17 for four: but as

Misbah-ul-Haq traipsed off for a duck after under-edging Roach to the keeper, square-leg umpire Nigel Llong asked for confirmation that Ramdin had got the ball under control. He hadn't – indeed he picked it up off the grass before tossing it away in premature celebration – yet his appeal betrayed no doubt whatsoever. In the press conference, Misbah accused him of breaching the game's spirit, a charge formally brought that evening by the umpires. Three days later, Ramdin, who maintained he had made an innocent mistake, was docked his match fee and banned for two one-day internationals. Misbah rebuilt with Nasir Jamshed, who reached an intelligent fifty only to throw away his hard work with a witless smear that sparked a clatter of wickets. No one else passed six as Misbah came within one blow of a maiden one-day hundred before he ran out of partners. Against a posse of left-armers – the tall (Mohammad Irfan), the fast (Wahab Riaz) and the whippy (Junaid Khan) – West Indies never settled. The pressure did not ease: Saeed Ajmal matched his fellow unorthodox spinner, Narine, by reining in the runs and removing a dangerous opener, and when the eighth wicket fell it was anyone's game. But Ramdin managed some form of redemption by seeing West Indies over the line. The match included the first instance in over 3,300 one-day internationals of an innings (extras included) comprising 12 even scores.

Man of the Match: K. A. J. Roach. Attendance: 20,492.

Pakistan

Imran Farhat c D. J. Bravo b Roach	2		Junaid Khan c Gayle b D. J. Bravo		0
Nasir Jamshed c Rampaul b Narine	50		Mohammad Irfan c D. J. Bravo b Rampaul		2
Mohammad Hafeez b Roach	4				
Asad Shafiq c Rampaul b Roach	0		L-b 1, w 5		6
*Misbah-ul-Haq not out	96				
Shoaib Malik c D. J. Bravo b Narine	0		1/2 (1) 2/14 (3) 3/15 (4) (48 overs)		170
†Kamran Akmal c Ramdin b Narine	2		4/105 (2) 5/106 (6) 6/110 (7)		
Wahab Riaz run out	6		7/128 (8) 8/136 (9) 9/138 (10)		
Saeed Ajmal run out	2		10/170 (11)	10 overs: 23-3	

Roach 10–4–28–3; Rampaul 10–0–39–1; D. J. Bravo 9–0–29–1; Samuels 5–0–17–0; Narine 10–1–34–3; Pollard 4–0–22–0.

West Indies

C. H. Gayle b Saeed Ajmal	39		*D. J. Bravo lbw b Saeed Ajmal		19
J. Charles c Wahab Riaz b Mohammad Irfan	9		†D. Ramdin not out		11
D. M. Bravo c Kamran Akmal			S. P. Narine c Kamran Akmal		
b Mohammad Irfan	0		b Mohammad Irfan		11
M. N. Samuels st Kamran Akmal			K. A. J. Roach not out		5
b Mohammad Hafeez	30		L-b 10, w 5, n-b 2		17
R. R. Sarwan c Kamran Akmal					
b Wahab Riaz	1		1/11 (2) 2/15 (3) (8 wkts, 40.4 overs)		172
K. A. Pollard c Kamran Akmal			3/78 (1) 4/81 (5) 5/94 (4)		
b Wahab Riaz	30		6/137 (6) 7/143 (7) 8/165 (9)	10 overs: 49-2	

R. Rampaul did not bat.

Mohammad Irfan 9–0–32–3; Junaid Khan 7.4–0–36–0; Saeed Ajmal 10–1–38–2; Wahab Riaz 10–1–42–2; Mohammad Hafeez 4–0–14–1.

Umpires: S. J. Davis and N. J. Llong. Third umpire: A. L. Hill.
Referee: B. C. Broad.

PAKISTAN v SOUTH AFRICA

At Birmingham, June 10 (day/night). South Africa won by 67 runs. Toss: South Africa. One-day international debut: C. H. Morris.

Both sides bowled well, but South Africa bowled better. And though both sides batted less well, South Africa were merely off-colour, while Pakistan were dreadful. Amla – dropped by Umar Amin at point off Mohammad Irfan when seven – employed every one of his considerable skills to deflect, work and manoeuvre the ball into gaps, but the Pakistan top order appeared to accept that the pitch was an awkward one, and resigned themselves to being tied down. A capacity crowd of fanatical Pakistan supporters became steadily less animated; others might have been screaming "Do something!" South Africa's innings had promised significantly more but was undermined by two run-outs instigated by the 39-year-old Misbah-ul-Haq. He provided urgency with the bat, too, after a slow start. But the rest scratched and blocked as the run-rate climbed in the face of disciplined seam bowling from Tsotsobe, the debutant Chris Morris (drafted in as a replacement for the injured Morne Morkel) and McLaren, who took a career-best four for 19. The last six fell for 38, and Pakistan – dismissed with five overs unused – were left on the brink of elimination. "At the moment," said a mournful Misbah afterwards, "no one is justifying their place in the team."

Man of the Match: H. M. Amla.   *Attendance:* 21,422.

South Africa

C. A. Ingram lbw b Mohammad Hafeez	20	R. J. Peterson not out	16	
H. M. Amla c Mohammad Hafeez b Saeed Ajmal	81	C. H. Morris run out	1	
F. du Plessis c Shoaib Malik b Mohammad Irfan	28	A. M. Phangiso run out	0	
		L-b 5, w 4, n-b 1	10	
*†A. B. de Villiers run out	31			
J-P. Duminy run out	24	1/53 (1) 2/122 (3) (9 wkts, 50 overs) 234		
D. A. Miller c Misbah-ul-Haq b Junaid Khan	19	3/145 (2) 4/186 (4)		
R. McLaren lbw b Shoaib Malik	4	5/195 (5) 6/203 (7) 7/231 (6)		
		8/234 (9) 9/234 (10) 10 overs: 36-0		
L. L. Tsotsobe did not bat.				

Mohammad Irfan 7–1–27–1; Junaid Khan 8–0–45–1; Mohammad Hafeez 10–0–38–1; Wahab Riaz 9–0–50–0; Saeed Ajmal 10–0–42–1; Shoaib Malik 6–0–27–1.

Pakistan

Imran Farhat b Morris	2	Junaid Khan b McLaren	4	
Nasir Jamshed c and b Tsotsobe	42	Mohammad Irfan not out	0	
Mohammad Hafeez c Miller b Morris	7			
Shoaib Malik b Duminy	8	L-b 7, w 8	15	
*Misbah-ul-Haq c Amla b Tsotsobe	55			
Umar Amin c Ingram b McLaren	16	1/4 (1) 2/18 (3) 3/48 (4) (45 overs) 167		
†Kamran Akmal c du Plessis b McLaren	0	4/86 (2) 5/129 (6) 6/134 (7)		
Wahab Riaz b Phangiso	13	7/148 (5) 8/162 (8) 9/167 (9)		
Saeed Ajmal c Ingram b McLaren	5	10/167 (10) 10 overs: 18-2		

Tsotsobe 9–1–23–2; Morris 7–0–25–2; McLaren 8–3–19–4; Phangiso 10–0–50–1; Duminy 7–0–26–1; Peterson 4–0–17–0.

Umpires: B. F. Bowden and R. A. Kettleborough.   Third umpire: N. J. Llong.
Referee: J. Srinath.

INDIA v WEST INDIES

At The Oval, June 11. India won by eight wickets. Toss: India.

India coasted into the semi-finals, in the process condemning Pakistan to an early exit. As in Cardiff the previous week, their batting hero was Dhawan, who survived drops when 23 and 41 to reach a run-a-ball hundred and help overhaul a modest West Indian total with nearly 11 overs to spare. But the damage had already been done by India's bowlers. West Indies had advanced to 103 for one in the 20th over thanks to some rustic blows from Charles, who later doubled up as wicketkeeper following Denesh Ramdin's two-match suspension. But they then came a cropper against India's spinners, with Jadeja taking his first one-day five-for: straight and accurate, he turned the occasional ball just enough to keep the batsmen guessing. Generally, they guessed wrong: eight wickets fell for 79, and it needed Sammy's frolicky 56 from 35 balls to attain respectability. He put on 51 for the last wicket with Roach, whose share was nought. West Indies needed early wickets, but instead ran into an opening stand of 101 in 15.3 overs between Sharma and Dhawan, who also added 109 with Karthik. Strong all round the wicket, Dhawan reached his second hundred in six days with an upper-cut six off Dwayne Bravo. By now, the Indian fans' sadistic chants of "Are you watching, Pakistan?" had given way to admiration.

Man of the Match: R. A. Jadeja.   *Attendance:* 20,757.

West Indies

C. H. Gayle c Ashwin b Bhuvneshwar Kumar .	21
†J. Charles lbw b Jadeja	60
D. M. Bravo st Dhoni b Ashwin	35
M. N. Samuels lbw b Jadeja	1
R. R. Sarwan c Dhoni b Jadeja	1
*D. J. Bravo c Jadeja b Yadav.	25
K. A. Pollard c Bhuvneshwar Kumar b I. Sharma .	22
D. J. G. Sammy not out	56

S. P. Narine c Karthik b Jadeja	2
R. Rampaul b Jadeja	2
K. A. J. Roach not out	0
B 4, l-b 2, w 2	8

1/25 (1) 2/103 (2) (9 wkts, 50 overs) 233
3/105 (4) 4/109 (5)
5/140 (3) 6/163 (6) 7/171 (7)
8/179 (9) 9/182 (10) 10 overs: 55-1

Bhuvneshwar Kumar 8–0–32–1; Yadav 9–0–54–1; I. Sharma 10–1–43–1; Ashwin 9–2–36–1; Kohli 4–0–26–0; Jadeja 10–2–36–5.

India

R. G. Sharma c Charles b Narine	52
S. Dhawan not out	102
V. Kohli b Narine	22
K. D. Karthik not out.	51
B 4, w 5	9

1/101 (1) (2 wkts, 39.1 overs) 236
2/127 (3) 10 overs: 66-0

S. K. Raina, *†M. S. Dhoni, R. A. Jadeja, R. Ashwin, Bhuvneshwar Kumar, I. Sharma and U. T. Yadav did not bat.

Roach 6–0–47–0; Rampaul 6–0–28–0; Narine 10–0–49–2; Sammy 4–0–23–0; D. J. Bravo 5–0–36–0; Samuels 4–0–17–0; Gayle 1–0–11–0; Pollard 3.1–0–21–0.

Umpires: Aleem Dar and A. L. Hill.   Third umpire: S. J. Davis.
Referee: B. C. Broad.

SOUTH AFRICA v WEST INDIES

At Cardiff, June 14. Tied (D/L). Toss: West Indies.

For once, South Africa were left thanking Duckworth/Lewis rather than cursing it. When West Indies began the 27th over of a game reduced to 31 a side by rain, they were four ahead on the D/L charts, thanks to a savage counter-attack from Samuels and some sensible hitting from Pollard. They needed 41 from 30 balls, and drizzle was in the air. But instead of opting to keep his side's nose in front, Pollard now launched himself at McLaren and top-edged to third man, where Steyn – in his only match of the tournament – judged a swirling, slippery catch to perfection. The moment decided the match. In the two minutes it took for Sammy to arrive in the middle, proper rain began to fall. Still, the umpires took their positions: it seemed another ball would be bowled. Then Sammy ran down the wicket to have a word with skipper Dwayne Bravo – at which point umpire Steve Davis called on the groundstaff. And that was that. The electronic scoreboard said it all, though it took a while for the ramifications to sink in. The D/L par score was 190 – and West Indies were 190 for six, which meant a tie, so ensuring South Africa would finish above their opponents on net run-rate. With India already assured of topping the group, West Indies were out. Ingram's 63-ball 73 was worthy of the match award, while de Villiers and Miller, who hit three sixes, provided the boost towards a total thought to be above par, though nobody said it was safe. It had looked anything but while Gayle was stroking an effortless 36 from 27 balls, but a casual waft to cover gave South Africa a sniff – and they hung on tenaciously, despite often looking outgunned.

Man of the Match: C. A. Ingram.   *Attendance:* 6,470.

Lovely weather for Duckworth/Lewis: West Indies captain Dwayne Bravo knows the game is up.

Philip Brown

South Africa

C. A. Ingram c D. M. Bravo b Pollard	73	R. J. Peterson not out	0
H. M. Amla c Gayle b Samuels	23		
*†A. B. de Villiers c D. M. Bravo b Rampaul	37	B 2, l-b 4, w 9	15
J-P. Duminy c Charles b D. J. Bravo	2		
F. du Plessis run out	35	1/80 (2) 2/124 (1) (6 wkts, 31 overs) 230
D. A. Miller c Sammy b D. J. Bravo	38	3/128 (4) 4/153 (3)
R. McLaren not out	7	5/221 (5) 6/229 (6) 6 overs: 32-0

C. H. Morris, D. W. Steyn and L. L. Tsotsobe did not bat.

Rampaul 6–0–37–1; Best 5–0–35–0; Narine 7–0–47–0; Sammy 2–0–18–0; D. J. Bravo 5–0–43–2; Samuels 2–0–14–1; Pollard 4–0–30–1.

West Indies

C. H. Gayle c du Plessis b Morris	36	D. J. G. Sammy not out	0
†J. Charles c de Villiers b Steyn	16		
D. S. Smith lbw b Peterson	30	L-b 5, w 7	12
M. N. Samuels b Steyn	48		
D. M. Bravo run out	12	1/35 (2) 2/75 (1) (6 wkts, 26.1 overs) 190
K. A. Pollard c Steyn b McLaren	28	3/87 (3) 4/104 (5)
*D. J. Bravo not out	8	5/162 (4) 6/190 (6) 6 overs: 31-0

S. P. Narine, T. L. Best and R. Rampaul did not bat.

Duminy 3–0–29–0; Tsotsobe 6–0–37–0; Steyn 6–0–33–2; Morris 4–0–30–1; Peterson 4–0–22–1; McLaren 3.1–0–34–1.

Umpires: S. J. Davis and R. J. Tucker.   Third umpire: B. N. J. Oxenford.
Referee: A. J. Pycroft.

INDIA v PAKISTAN

At Birmingham, June 15. India won by eight wickets (D/L). Toss: India.

With the fate of both teams already sealed, events in the middle rarely matched the excitement in the stands. Rain forced four interruptions, and seemed more likely than an out-of-form Pakistan to end India's 100% record, but the group winners eventually reached their adjusted target of 102 from

22 overs with 17 balls to spare. Indian supporters outnumbered their counterparts by roughly four to one, and their cheers when Dhoni won the toss reflected its importance. For the third game in a row, Pakistan fell well short of 200. Their coach Dav Whatmore described the batting as "a bit naughty", although Bhuvneshwar Kumar in particular made good use of damp, overcast conditions, and there was appreciable turn for Ashwin. Pakistan had been doing reasonably until the first delay after 12 overs. But Jadeja outsmarted Misbah-ul-Haq, and an Indian review against Asad Shafiq revealed a thin edge en route to Dhoni down the leg side. Six wickets fell for 34, the last two to run-outs: one stemming from Kohli's athleticism, the other from Pakistan's confusion. Sharma and Dhawan then continued their productive opening partnership, though Dhawan's 48 from 41 balls, which ended with a misjudged cut off Wahab Riaz, felt like a failure after back-to-back hundreds.

Man of the Match: Bhuvneshwar Kumar.   *Attendance:* 22,832.

Pakistan

Nasir Jamshed c Raina b Bhuvneshwar Kumar.	2	Saeed Ajmal c R. G. Sharma b I. Sharma ..	5
†Kamran Akmal c Kohli b Ashwin	21	Junaid Khan run out	0
Mohammad Hafeez c Dhoni b Bhuvneshwar Kumar.	27	Mohammad Irfan run out.	0
Asad Shafiq c Dhoni b I. Sharma	41	L-b 1, w 2	3
*Misbah-ul-Haq b Jadeja.	22		
Shoaib Malik lbw b Jadeja	17	1/4 (1) 2/50 (3) (39.4 overs) 165
Umar Amin not out	27	3/56 (2) 4/110 (5) 5/131 (4)
Wahab Riaz b Ashwin	0	6/139 (6) 7/140 (8) 8/159 (9)
		9/159 (10) 10/165 (11) 10 overs: 43-1

Bhuvneshwar Kumar 8–2–19–2; Yadav 6.4–0–29–0; I. Sharma 7–0–40–2; Ashwin 8–0–35–2; Kohli 2–0–11–0; Jadeja 8–1–30–2.

India

R. G. Sharma c Misbah-ul-Haq b Saeed Ajmal . 18
S. Dhawan c Nasir Jamshed b Wahab Riaz 48
V. Kohli not out. 22
K. D. Karthik not out. 11
    W 3 3

1/58 (1)   (2 wkts, 19.1 overs) 102
2/78 (2)   8 overs: 45-0

S. K. Raina, *†M. S. Dhoni, R. A. Jadeja, R. Ashwin, Bhuvneshwar Kumar, I. Sharma and U. T. Yadav did not bat.

Mohammad Irfan 4–0–24–0; Junaid Khan 4–0–21–0; Saeed Ajmal 5–0–29–1; Mohammad Hafeez 2.1–0–8–0; Wahab Riaz 4–0–20–1.

Umpires: I. J. Gould and R. A. Kettleborough.   Third umpire: H. D. P. K. Dharmasena.
Referee: B. C. Broad.

FINAL GROUP TABLES

Group A	P	W	L	T	NR	Pts	Net run-rate
ENGLAND.	3	2	1	0	0	4	0.30
SRI LANKA.	3	2	1	0	0	4	−0.19
New Zealand.	3	1	1	0	1	3	0.77
Australia	3	0	2	0	1	1	−0.68

Group B	P	W	L	T	NR	Pts	Net run-rate
INDIA.	3	3	0	0	0	6	0.93
SOUTH AFRICA.	3	1	1	1	0	3	0.32
West Indies	3	1	1	1	0	3	−0.07
Pakistan	3	0	3	0	0	0	−1.03

SEMI-FINALS

ENGLAND v SOUTH AFRICA

At The Oval, June 19. England won by seven wickets. Toss: England.

England bossed this match from the moment Cook chose to bowl in muggy conditions tailor-made for swing. In 601 previous one-day internationals, England had rarely enjoyed such a dream start:

Gently does it: James Tredwell's three wickets helped England into the final.

inside two overs Anderson removed Ingram, while Finn claimed the dangerous Amla, athletically caught by Buttler, who later became the seventh wicketkeeper in one-day internationals to make six dismissals in a match. The promoted Peterson rallied briefly, but the South African innings fell into a clear pattern: batsmen were either at sea against Anderson and Tredwell, or at ease against Finn and Broad (Tim Bresnan was attending the birth of his son). The undemonstrative Tredwell gave the ball air, yet retained control – and a rash of nervy strokes encouraged Cook to go for all-out attack in the hope he would have no need of a weaker fifth bowler. It almost worked. At 80 for eight in the 23rd over, it was a legitimate move, but as the ball stopped swinging, Miller and Kleinveldt counter-attacked against some insipid bowling to add 95, a record for South Africa's ninth wicket. England were not immune to nerves themselves, sliding to 41 for two before Trott – conditions perfect for his steady if slightly dour approach – and the jollier Root bustled England to within touching distance of an emphatic victory.

Man of the Match: J. C. Tredwell.
Attendance: 19,238.

South Africa

C. A. Ingram lbw b Anderson	0	R. K. Kleinveldt c Buttler b Broad	43
H. M. Amla c Buttler b Finn	1	L. L. Tsotsobe c Buttler b Broad	0
R. J. Peterson lbw b Anderson	30		
F. du Plessis c Buttler b Tredwell	26	L-b 6, w 6	12
*†A. B. de Villiers c Buttler b Broad	0		
J-P. Duminy b Tredwell	3	1/1 (1) 2/4 (2) 3/45 (3) (38.4 overs)	175
D. A. Miller not out	56	4/50 (5) 5/63 (6) 6/70 (4)	
R. McLaren run out	1	7/76 (8) 8/80 (9) 9/175 (10)	
C. H. Morris c Buttler b Tredwell	3	10/175 (11)	

10 overs: 45-2

Anderson 8–1–14–2; Finn 8–1–45–1; Broad 8.4–0–50–3; Tredwell 7–1–19–3; Root 3–0–22–0; Bopara 4–0–19–0.

England

*A. N. Cook c de Villiers b Morris	6
I. R. Bell c de Villiers b Kleinveldt	20
I. J. L. Trott not out	82
J. E. Root b Duminy	48
E. J. G. Morgan not out	15
L-b 4, w 4	8

1/22 (1) 2/41 (2)   (3 wkts, 37.3 overs) 179
3/146 (4)   10 overs: 39-1

†J. C. Buttler, R. S. Bopara, S. C. J. Broad, J. C. Tredwell, J. M. Anderson and S. T. Finn did not bat.

Morris 8–1–38–1; Peterson 9.3–1–49–0; Duminy 5–0–27–1; Tsotsobe 5–0–26–0; Kleinveldt 4–0–10–1; McLaren 6–0–25–0.

Umpires: H. D. P. K. Dharmasena and R. J. Tucker.   Third umpire: B. N. J. Oxenford.
Referee: J. Srinath.

INDIA v SRI LANKA

At Cardiff, June 20. India won by eight wickets. Toss: India.

Sri Lanka never found a way into the second semi-final, and departed with 15 overs to spare after the Indian pace attack responded to a gloomy morning as if their whole lives had been spent exploiting damp conditions. Such was the assistance for seam and swing that even Dhoni unstrapped his pads to bowl four overs of 75mph wobble; he was denied a second-ball wicket only when Jayawardene successfully overturned an lbw decision thanks to an inside edge. Sri Lanka's cause was not helped when Dilshan limped off in the fifth over having torn a calf muscle while running, and a combination of Bhuvneshwar Kumar's accuracy, Umesh Yadav's skiddy pace and Ishant Sharma's height and nip denied them any momentum. Raina held three smart catches at second slip, and Sri Lanka did not reach 50 until the 21st over. Dhoni held back his spinners for longer than usual, and Mathews took 85 balls over his half-century, only to fall soon afterwards in a late attempt to take on Ashwin. Defending a modest target of 182, Sri Lanka could afford no errors, but they dropped Dhawan, India's form batsman, on 18 (twice) and 62. Armed with the luxury of time, Kohli waited 42 balls to hit his first boundary, then accelerated to 50 with a six back over Mendis's head. Protesters waving Tamil flags twice held up play. In the second stoppage, one of them managed to run across the pitch before being apprehended.

Man of the Match: I. Sharma.   *Attendance:* 14,221.

Sri Lanka

M. D. K. J. Perera c Raina		N. L. T. C. Perera c Dhawan b I. Sharma ..	0
b Bhuvneshwar Kumar .	4	K. M. D. N. Kulasekara b Ashwin	1
T. M. Dilshan not out	18	S. L. Malinga not out	7
†K. C. Sangakkara c Raina b I. Sharma	17	L-b 2, w 11	13
H. D. R. L. Thirimanne c Raina b I. Sharma	7		
D. P. M. D. Jayawardene b Jadeja........	38	1/6 (1) 2/36 (4) (8 wkts, 50 overs)	181
*A. D. Mathews c Bhuvneshwar Kumar		3/41 (3) 4/119 (5)	
b Ashwin .	51	5/158 (6) 6/160 (8)	
B. M. A. J. Mendis st Dhoni b Ashwin	25	7/164 (9) 8/171 (7) 10 overs: 26-1	

H. M. R. K. B. Herath did not bat.

Dilshan, when 12, retired hurt at 17-1 and resumed at 164-7.

Bhuvneshwar Kumar 9–2–18–1; Yadav 8–2–30–0; I. Sharma 9–1–33–3; Jadeja 10–1–33–1; Dhoni 4–0–17–0; Ashwin 10–1–48–3.

India

R. G. Sharma b Mathews..............	33
S. Dhawan st Sangakkara b Mendis	68
V. Kohli not out....................	58
S. K. Raina not out	7
B 1, l-b 5, w 10	16
1/77 (1) (2 wkts, 35 overs)	182
2/142 (2) 10 overs: 40-0	

K. D. Karthik, *†M. S. Dhoni, R. A. Jadeja, R. Ashwin, Bhuvneshwar Kumar, I. Sharma and U. T. Yadav did not bat.

Kulasekara 10–0–45–0; Malinga 8–0–54–0; N. L. T. C. Perera 6–0–25–0; Mathews 4–0–10–1; Herath 4–0–14–0; Mendis 3–0–28–1.

Umpires: Aleem Dar and R. A. Kettleborough.   Third umpire: N. J. Llong.
Referee: B. C. Broad.

FINAL

ENGLAND v INDIA

LAWRENCE BOOTH

At Birmingham, June 23. India won by five runs. Toss: England.

As rain battered Birmingham and spectators cursed the absence of a reserve day, it seemed England would finally be able to lay some sort of claim to their first global one-day silverware – even if it meant sharing the Champions Trophy with India. Eventually, though, the weather relented, allowing a 20-over-a-side match to start at 4.20, with the close extended by an hour until 8.30. And in the 18th over of their chase, England found themselves staring at outright victory. With 16 balls to go, six wickets in hand, and Morgan and Bopara getting to grips with a slow turner apparently designed for Indian needs, they required 20 runs. Ishant Sharma, meanwhile, had lost his radar. Pulled over fine leg for six by Morgan, he responded with successive off-side wides, the second of them barely locating the cut strip. Kohli later admitted India had very nearly given up.

But now England lost their heads. Morgan failed to clear the leg-side infield after half-connecting with an ugly smear, and Bopara pulled the next ball to square leg, prompting an even uglier send-off from a pumped-up Sharma. Stunned, England now wanted 19 off two overs, but the new batsmen had no time to gauge the pace of the pitch – or rather the lack of it. Buttler was bowled trying to hit Jadeja back over his head, and Bresnan run out as panic took hold. In eight balls, England surrendered four to three.

Broad swung Ashwin to the square-leg fence to reduce the equation to 11 off four deliveries, but Tredwell never looked likely to hit the six demanded from the final ball. For the fifth time out of five – following the World Cups of 1979, 1987 and 1992, and the 2004 Champions Trophy – England had fallen at the last. By contrast India's fans – who so comfortably outnumbered their English counterparts that the home players were booed when the teams were read out – could now celebrate a hat-trick of triumphs under the calm leadership of Dhoni, following the 2007 World Twenty20 and the 2011 World Cup.

Losing it: Tim Bresnan departs, run out for two, as England get in a flap.

Gareth Copley, Getty Images

When Dhoni carved Bopara into the hands of Tredwell at third man – part of an unlikely double-wicket maiden that also accounted for Raina – India were 66 for five after 13 overs, and going nowhere. But Kohli and the utility man Jadeja added 47 in 33 balls, and Jadeja further boosted Indian spirits by taking eight off the last two deliveries of the innings, from Bresnan.

That meant England were chasing 130, a modest total in theory but – on a quickly drying pitch and with the record books there for the rewriting – rather tougher in practice. Cook went early, steering Yadav to first slip, before the in-form Trott overbalanced and was smartly stumped off Ashwin's leg-side wide. Then, after Root had skied to fine leg, a moment of controversy: Dhoni appealed for another stumping, this time against Bell, and third umpire Bruce Oxenford pored over replays. He eventually concluded Bell had to go, though how he divined this from the evidence available was not immediately clear. An incensed Cook later criticised the decision.

From 46 for four, Morgan rebuilt with Bopara. They were careful at first against the turning ball, before hitting out when Dhoni returned to Sharma with 59 required off six overs. He went for 11, and was removed from the attack, before improbably returning with three overs to go and 28 wanted. Briefly, it looked like a move that would cost India the match. But Sharma pulled himself together – and England, as if frozen in history's headlights, disintegrated.

Man of the Match: R. A. Jadeja. *Attendance:* 22,824.

Man of the Tournament: S. Dhawan.

India

R. G. Sharma b Broad	9	R. Ashwin run out		1
S. Dhawan c Tredwell b Bopara	31	Bhuvneshwar Kumar not out.		1
V. Kohli c Bopara b Anderson	43	W 4		4
K. D. Karthik c Morgan b Tredwell	6			
S. K. Raina c Cook b Bopara	1	1/19 (1) 2/50 (2)	(7 wkts, 20 overs)	129
*†M. S. Dhoni c Tredwell b Bopara	0	3/64 (4) 4/66 (5)		
R. A. Jadeja not out	33	5/66 (6) 6/113 (3) 7/119 (8)	4 overs: 19-1	

I. Sharma and U. T. Yadav did not bat.

Anderson 4–0–24–1; Broad 4–0–26–1; Bresnan 4–0–34–0; Tredwell 4–0–25–1; Bopara 4–1–20–3.

England

*A. N. Cook c Ashwin b Yadav	2	S. C. J. Broad not out		7
I. R. Bell st Dhoni b Jadeja	13	J. C. Tredwell not out		5
I. J. L. Trott st Dhoni b Ashwin	20	L-b 1, w 4		5
J. E. Root c I. Sharma b Ashwin	7			
E. J. G. Morgan c Ashwin b I. Sharma	33	1/3 (1) 2/28 (3)	(8 wkts, 20 overs)	124
R. S. Bopara c Ashwin b I. Sharma	30	3/40 (4) 4/46 (2)		
†J. C. Buttler b Jadeja	0	5/110 (5) 6/110 (6)		
T. T. Bresnan run out	2	7/112 (7) 8/113 (8)	4 overs: 24-1	

J. M. Anderson did not bat.

Bhuvneshwar Kumar 3–0–19–0; Yadav 2–0–10–1; Jadeja 4–0–24–2; Ashwin 4–1–15–2; I. Sharma 4–0–36–2; Raina 3–0–19–0.

Umpires: H. D. P. K. Dharmasena and R. J. Tucker. Third umpire: B. N. J. Oxenford.
Referee: R. S. Madugalle.

ENGLAND v AUSTRALIA, 2013

REVIEW BY GIDEON HAIGH

Test matches (5): England 3, Australia 0
Twenty20 internationals (2): England 1, Australia 1
One-day internationals (5): England 1, Australia 2

Ashes series are notorious for defying forecasts. But the 2013 edition made the pundits look pretty good: the eventual margin of 3–0 to England – the first time Australia had failed to win a Test in an Ashes series since 1977 – would probably have been the median prophecy. Even Australians seemed unsurprised, though they were hopeful of better during the imminent sequel Down Under.

England were actually less emphatic than they had been while winning 3–1 in 2010-11. In particular, their top three of Alastair Cook, Joe Root and Jonathan Trott had a far poorer time than Andrew Strauss, Cook and Trott had enjoyed on that tour of Australia, totalling 609 runs fewer; Cook alone regressed by 489, and his average by almost exactly 100. Not once did England make 400; on four occasions they trailed on first innings. Yet they played with the maturity and composure of a side that knew not only how to win, but also how not to lose. Australian grumbles that, given a fairer wind, the series could have turned out differently rather missed the point.

A succession of dry, hard and slow pitches most obviously benefited Graeme Swann, who was the leading wicket-taker on either side, with 26 – his most prolific Test series. But they also made for some dry, hard and slow batting, of which Man of the Series Ian Bell became the foremost exponent. Time and again, more often than not following the fall of three early wickets, he planted himself elegantly in Australia's path; he faced nearly 400 deliveries from their best two bowlers, Ryan Harris and Peter Siddle, and fell to them only three times; and he lost nothing by comparison with the vivid Kevin Pietersen. Bell would have been disappointed only that none of his three centuries became what batting coach Graham Gooch calls a "daddy hundred". In fact, the average of England's five centuries – Root and Pietersen completed the hand – was 124, compared to nearly twice that in 2010-11.

Overall, the series offered confirmation of the old verity about bowlers winning matches. Each of England's victories was underwritten by a great solo performance: by James Anderson at Trent Bridge (ten for 158), by Swann at Lord's (nine for 122), and by Stuart Broad, after a quiet series, at Chester-le-Street (11 for 121). England were occasionally dilatory, and even cynical: Broad is a bigger time-waster than Angry Birds.

But they did not only bore Australia into submission, as some liked to imagine: when they "spiced it up", as Cook put it, they showed bristling purpose and conviction. It scarcely mattered that Anderson faded after Nottingham, adding only 12 wickets in four Tests at 41 apiece, and returning the worst innings analysis of his career, on home turf in Manchester. Someone always stepped in when it mattered.

Mike Hewitt, Getty Images

All the right angles: the series was dominated by Ian Bell, who scored a hundred in each of England's three victories.

Michael Clarke's Australians had good days, and even strung them together. Thanks in part to the captain's gutsy 187 at Old Trafford, they had much the better of a Third Test ultimately ruined by rain, and were ahead after three days at The Oval when the clouds opened again. In both cases, however, they had enjoyed the favour of the toss and first innings. And where England were skilled at soaking up pressure, Australia tended to brittleness: their collapses almost registered on the Richter Scale. The tight moments, including the last-day thriller at Trent Bridge and the fourth evening in Durham, were claimed by England.

Australia's on-field disarray was the counterpart to off-field incohesion, a carry-over from their ruinous visit to India, where coach Mickey Arthur had suspended four players in what became known, in the modern media vernacular, as "Homeworkgate". Certainly, the summer had begun in confusing circumstances, when two Australian teams arrived: a squad for the Champions Trophy, led in name only by Clarke; and an Australia A party led by Brad Haddin. Clarke, in discomfort from his volatile back, was little in evidence and missed the one-day tournament, leaving nobody in obvious charge: there was lots of management but no leadership. Australian players out drinking after their Champions Trophy defeat by England were then witness to a bizarre incident: in Birmingham's Walkabout, an Australian-themed bar where a handful of England players had also gathered, David Warner threw a punch at Root, and was drawn away by team-mate Clint McKay.

The story remained a well-kept secret for three days, when Cricket Australia abruptly issued a statement explaining that Warner had been reported for "unbecoming behaviour" after being "allegedly involved in a physical altercation with an England player". The ECB upped the ante, saying Warner had "initiated an unprovoked physical attack" and apologised. And when Clarke's locum George Bailey described the episode as "a very minor incident" which had been dealt with in-house, that house was revealed to be in a different street from the one belonging to CA's chief executive, James Sutherland.

FIRING BLANKS

Ashes series in which Australia failed to win a match:

	Tests			Tests	
1884	3	England 1, Australia 0	1926	5	England 1, Australia 0
1886	3	England 3, Australia 0	1953	5	England 1, Australia 0
1893	3	England 1, Australia 0	1970-71	6	England 2, Australia 0
1905	5	England 2, Australia 0	1977	5	England 3, Australia 0
1912	3	England 1, Australia 0	**2013**	**5**	**England 3, Australia 0**

Only series of three or more Tests are included. England have similarly failed in 12 Ashes series, including 2013-14 in Australia.

"David Warner has done a despicable thing," he said. "I don't care what explanations people might want to put up. There is no place for violence in society, and there is no place for Australian cricketers to be finding themselves in that position."

The gulf between the team and officialdom was emphasised when Warner was suspended until the First Test, which – being immediately followed by the Second – essentially ruled him out until the Third. He was briefly exiled to Australia A's trip to southern Africa; by the time he returned, he was the tour's official pantomime villain, ripe for the booing by English crowds. Meanwhile, Arthur gave an interview in which he played down the incident: "We are going to get a bit of ill-judgment, and some players are going to learn the hard way, but those are our best players. We've got to back them."

A few days later, with Australia about to play a warm-up match at Taunton, Arthur was called in to meet Sutherland and Pat Howard, CA's general manager of team performance – and emerged 15 minutes later without a job. With just 16 days until the First Test, his replacement was Australia A's coach Darren Lehmann; in another change, Clarke stood down from the selection panel.

The popular Lehmann was welcomed, and enjoyed a honeymoon period, shrewdly courting the electronic media. But CA's left hand continued to experience difficulty in ascertaining the movement of their right. Nobody, for example, seemed to have tidied up after Arthur's departure, so that claims he made in a suit for wrongful dismissal – later settled confidentially – became public. These included the damaging comment that he had been "the meat in the sandwich" between Clarke and Shane Watson, and that Clarke had referred to Watson as a "cancer" – which resonated with remarks made by Howard a few months earlier that he was a team player "sometimes".

Public-affairs professionals produced a constant stream of announcements and clarifications, some of them adding to the confusion. During the Lord's

FIVE STATS YOU MAY HAVE MISSED

BENEDICT BERMANGE

- In the First Test, Ashton Agar became only the ninth No. 11 to top-score in a Test innings:

F. R. Spofforth (50)	Australia (163) v England at Melbourne.	1884-85
T. R. McKibbin (16)	Australia (44) v England at The Oval.	1896
A. E. E. Vogler (62*).	South Africa (333) v England at Cape Town . .	1905-06
Asif Masood (30*).	Pakistan (199) v West Indies at Lahore	1974-75
A. M. J. G. Amerasinghe (34) . .	Sri Lanka (215) v New Zealand at Kandy	1983-84
Talha Jubair (31)	Bangladesh (124) v India at Chittagong	2004-05
S. J. Harmison (42)	England (304) v South Africa at Cape Town . .	2004-05
N. M. Lyon (14).	Australia (47) v South Africa at Cape Town. . .	2011-12
A. C. Agar (98).	**Australia (280) v England at Nottingham**. . .	**2013**

- In the same game, nearly 40% of Australia's runs came from the last wicket, the highest in Tests in which a team had two tenth-wicket partnerships:

    39.58%   Australia (280 and 296) v England at Nottingham. **2013**
    163 by P. J. Hughes and A. C. Agar; 65 by B. J. Haddin and J. L. Pattinson

    29.68%   Australia (112 and 353) v England at Melbourne   1901-02
    18 by W. W. Armstrong and E. Jones; 120 by R. A. Duff and Armstrong

    28.13%   Australia (163 and 125) v England at Melbourne   1884-85
    64 by J. W. Trumble and F. R. Spofforth; 17 by W. Bruce and P. G. McShane

    26.58%   Zimbabwe (199 and 102) v Sri Lanka at Harare   2003-04
    50 and 30 by D. T. Hondo and T. Panyangara

    26.13%   New Zealand (293 and 193) v Australia at Sydney   1985-86
    124 and 3 by J. G. Bracewell and S. L. Boock

- Before the Second Test, England had won only two Tests in which they lost three wickets for 30 runs or fewer in both innings:

16-3 and 28-3	beat Australia by two wickets at The Oval	1890
28-3 and 25-3	beat West Indies by four wickets at Bridgetown.	1934-35
28-3 and 30-3	**beat Australia by 347 runs at Lord's**	**2013**

- By the end of the Fourth Test the England side boasted a total of 866 Test wickets, surpassing their previous record of 853, shared by the side which played at Kanpur in 1981-82. The current side also had an England-record 650 caps between them.

- In the Fifth Test, Chris Woakes became only the 11th England player known to have hit his first ball in Test cricket for four:

Batsman	*Bowler*		
J. Lillywhite	W. E. Midwinter	v Australia at Melbourne	1876-77
P. B. H. May	A. M. B. Rowan	v South Africa at Leeds	1951
D. B. Carr	S. G. Shinde	v India at Delhi.	1951-52
J. T. Murray	K. D. Mackay	v Australia at Birmingham.	1961
J. B. Bolus	W. W. Hall	v West Indies at Leeds	1963
D. I. Gower	Liaqat Ali	v Pakistan at Birmingham	1978
A. J. Lamb	Kapil Dev	v India at Lord's.	1982
A. J. Stewart	B. P. Patterson	v West Indies at Kingston.	1989-90
D. G. Cork	C. L. Hooper	v West Indies at Lord's.	1995
R. L. Johnson	A. M. Blignaut	v Zimbabwe at Chester-le-Street	2003
C. R. Woakes	**M. A. Starc**	**v Australia at The Oval**	**2013**

Full details are not available for many early Tests.

Test, they were simultaneously issuing statements distancing Warner from tweets by his brother Steve about Watson ("Fucking selfish Watson sooner your out if the side you great pretender the better") and Arthur ("Good on Mickey Arthur finally letting the truth be known and proving he was just an escape goat #awesomebloke #Gentleman"); and themselves from their own tweet condemning a decision for a low catch ("That decision sucked ass #bullshit"). This "inappropriate" last one, whose author never came to light, was explained away as not emanating "from CA's official Twitter presence at Lord's".

England and the ECB, themselves entangled by modern communications a year earlier during the Pietersen affair, kept their counsel, staving off their only media misfire until the series was over, when some puerile post-match behaviour by the players at The Oval showed an uncharacteristic lack of judgment. For Australians in need of light relief, England's late-night urination out in the middle was a welcome distraction; for England, it echoed an incident earlier in the month, when Monty Panesar – who was part of the squad for Old Trafford, but got no closer to a final XI – peed on bouncers at a Brighton nightclub. It was almost as silly as the boos which greeted Clarke at the end of the Oval Test, when the umpires aborted England's run-chase because of the light, yet locals blamed Clarke for time-wasting.

In placing an imprint on his charges, meanwhile, Lehmann seemed uncommonly intent on experimentation: only once, almost 30 years previously, had Australia chosen as many as 17 men in an away series. At Trent Bridge, only two batsmen were in the positions they had filled in their previous Test, at Delhi in March: at No. 5 Steve Smith, himself a late addition to the party as cover for Clarke, and James Pattinson at No. 10. By the end of the series, Australia had used three different opening combinations, and four different players at No. 3, none of whom was Phil Hughes, who had occupied the role in Australia's two preceding series. The captain batted at No. 4 on six occasions, and at No. 5 on four. Four different batsmen (plus a nightwatchman) occupied No. 6. Again, by contrast, England altered their top six once – and only after winning the series.

Lehmann's first hunch paid off handsomely, if not predictably, when the teenage left-arm spinner Ashton Agar was included at Nottingham, after Nathan Lyon had played 20 of Australia's previous 24 Tests. Coming in last at 117 for nine, Agar played the innings of his young life, a free-spirited 98 from 101 balls, and with Hughes added a tenth-wicket record of 163. By Old Trafford, however, both Agar and Hughes were gone – as was Ed Cowan, for 18 months a fixture at the top of the order, but now displaced by an abortive experiment to turn Watson back into an opener.

Australia could argue progress was made, The Oval proving their best day of all (though even there they came within a few overs of a 4–0 defeat following Clarke's slightly desperate last-day declaration). But they were lucky: Watson, whose front-foot travails had risked turning him into a laughing stock, made his first Test hundred in three years, batting at No. 3 because it was the only slot in the order left after Australia had selected a fifth bowler; and Smith hit a maiden Test century, having survived only because of his good fortune with umpiring technology at Old Trafford.

HYPER MARKETING

And then there's the cricket

RICHARD WHITEHEAD

If there is one thing that can be guaranteed in a 21st-century Ashes series it is – to misquote the John Lewis boast – that it will never be knowingly under-hyped. Take the opening day at Trent Bridge, which gave us the sensory overload of a firework display (on a sunny July morning), a fly-past by the Red Arrows, Lesley Garrett's rendition of the national anthems accompanied by the band of the Coldstream Guards, and what became the inevitable sight of Sean Ruane belting out "Jerusalem". And all before James Pattinson kicked things off with a loopy, bathetic wide over the head of Alastair Cook.

As the smoke cleared and England supporters wondered if Pattinson had just done a Harmison (see Brisbane 2006-07), it was tempting to ask whether such enthusiasm

Lesley Garrett and the Coldstream Guards band open the Ashes.

Gareth Copley, Getty Images

could possibly survive back-to-back series, to say nothing of the swift return of the Australians in 2015. And for those who sat through 14 years of routine Ashes defeats, an extraordinary thought was taking shape: was it really possible to get tired of beating Australia?

The questions seemed worth posing after England went 2–0 up at Lord's, and all but guaranteed retention of the urn. Perhaps it was the broiling heat but, as they inched towards a crushing four-day victory on the Sunday, a soporific mood descended on St John's Wood. And, with England not securing the win until the day's last over, and the sun threatening to set, some spectators had already headed for home before Graeme Swann trapped Pattinson. This was hardly the behaviour of a nation enchanted by the prospect of beating the Aussies.

That said, there had been little such equivocation in Nottingham, and only sporadic examples of it as the series headed north before returning to London. The crowd at Trent Bridge had been absorbed by the fluctuations of a classic, while at Old Trafford not even the weather could dampen the sense of exultation over the return of Ashes cricket. For the

locals, there was also the bonus of the returning villain David Warner, who cheerfully assumed the role of Australian punchbag filled by Jason Gillespie in 2005 and Ricky Ponting four years later. It was the closest an English crowd came all summer to gloating.

Civic pride was also prominent in the North-East, where the staging of an Ashes Test was just about the only story deemed worthy of the local news bulletins. The Riverside also produced the most febrile atmosphere of the summer, when – on the fourth evening – Stuart Broad clinched the series.

Briefly, Ashes ennui risked taking hold at The Oval, especially when England's pedestrian progress on the Friday, and the Saturday washout, looked to have consigned the match to a draw. But as the last-day crowd stamped, hollered and willed them towards the finishing line in the gathering gloom, old allegiances kicked in.

Perhaps the answer will only truly be provided next summer. But on August 20, the day before the Oval Test, an email arrived from Glamorgan, frantically underlining the importance of registering now for the 2015 ticket ballot. The hype of 2013 was not yet over. But the next round had already begun.

One wondered at times whether Australia entered the series not to win it, but to work out their best XI. Arthur hinted at this in an interview late in the series: "We wanted to try and push England really hard in England, but we wanted to win in Australia." But Clarke, of whom so much had been expected, rather waned as Lehmann waxed. Only at Old Trafford, after enduring an anxious first hour, did he make runs in the quantities he would have liked. He was troubled by the bounce of Broad – who dismissed him five times – cramped in his cross-bat shots, and limited in his freedom of evasive action.

In the field, he was, as ever, an impressively intuitive leader, although – as his predecessor Ricky Ponting observed – "funky" field placing is part and parcel of captaining a middling team and needing to make things happen. Off the field, Clarke seemed more than usually burdened, even though his workload had in theory been lightened. He referred constantly in press conferences to the fact that he was no longer a selector, as if trying to make a point that was not completely clear; his shows of solidarity with Watson had a cloying quality; and he was closest of all, in outward appearance at least, to Shane Warne, who became something of a media apologist for his confrere, in addition to acting as a consultant to Lehmann and duty selector Rod Marsh.

> Warne became a media apologist for his confrere

The chief success of the batting was Chris Rogers, who fulfilled all the selectors' hopes with deep wells of concentration and, on occasion, disarming fluency of strokeplay. He found difficulties only with Swann, who regularly becalmed him and removed him six times. Otherwise he looked, as he was, a mature student, determined to make the best use of his time. "I set myself high standards," he said after his maiden century, at Chester-le-Street. Indeed he said it several times, and from his mouth it sounded like a meaningful statement rather than a self-help cliché.

Otherwise the batting was a thing of rags and patches – some eye-catching patches, but patches all the same. When restored to the team, Warner became Rogers's partner, without quite making the position his own; the relative buoyancy of the end-of-series averages of Watson and Smith obscured the untimeliness of their failures. What Australia would have done for Mike Hussey's *esprit de corps* and counterpunching power.

The bowling was far more disciplined and resilient than in 2010-11. Haddin's 29 catches – a world record for a Test series – were a reflection of the tightness of bowlers' lines and their strivings for sideways movement. And the marauding Harris was a tribute to the surgeons who had rebuilt him over the previous few years. He saved his only injury for the last day of the last Test; until then, he had never been less than excellent, and England may have ended the series quietly grateful that he hadn't been deemed match-fit for Trent Bridge. In his pace, seam and physical presence, Australia had a genuine attack leader; his roughing-up of Trott became one of the subplots of the series. He chipped in with useful runs, too, and threw himself around in the field.

Harris's support varied. Pattinson showed spirit until he was invalided out of the tour with a stress fracture after the Second Test. And while the tireless Siddle started well, and always did his damnedest, only nine of his 17 wickets

Graham Morris

Bit of a dampener: Manchester rain falls on Michael Clarke, denying Australia a chance of victory in the Third Test.

were top-order batsmen, and he did not strike in his last 51 overs. Watson bowled economically but without luck. Mitchell Starc, dropped twice, and Jackson Bird, picked once, suffered from the vagaries of selection and the onset of injury. Lyon, once he had been reselected, bowled steadily, and acquitted himself gamely against the menacing Pietersen. Other pluses were the spirit in which James Faulkner approached his only outing, at The Oval, and the pace Mitchell Johnson worked up in the NatWest one-day series – a miserable, rain-ruined affair further emaciated by a below-strength England side, but which Australia nevertheless deserved to win. Aaron Finch's brutal 156 in the drawn Twenty20 series was an entertaining distraction.

Of England it was harder to obtain an absolute, as distinct from a relative, impression. And they tended to go slightly under-reported, if only because their taciturn leadership, unsentimental proficiency and occasional insouciant gamesmanship made them a less alluring subject than Australia's decline and flux. It is possible that, at times, they overestimated Australia, and that Cook and team director Andy Flower threw their defensive switch prematurely. But, at the centre of a web of tight personal relations, they could take credit for an obviously united dressing-room.

What they tried out was only a qualified success. If he exhibited an immediate pedigree, Root – chosen as Cook's new opening partner in place of Nick Compton, who publicly expressed his displeasure – achieved little more than one big second-innings hundred; his Yorkshire team-mate Jonny Bairstow was impressive mainly in the field; and of two new caps at The Oval, all-

Our friends in the north: Alastair Cook enjoys Chester-le-Street's memorable Ashes debut.

rounder Chris Woakes made but a small contribution, and left-arm spinner Simon Kerrigan a negative one.

But one tough call was dead right: the supplanting of Steven Finn, after a shaky show in Nottingham, with Tim Bresnan, nine of whose ten wickets were in the top six. One of them was perhaps the biggest of the series – a searing lifter which dismissed Warner at the Riverside, precipitating Australia's final subsidence. And though Matt Prior had a mediocre time of it, the lower order of Bresnan, Broad and Swann all helped out. It was with the bat, too, that Broad made arguably his most telling contribution to Ashes folklore, when he nicked Agar to Clarke at slip via Haddin's glove at Nottingham, did not budge and was given not out by Aleem Dar – the error compounded by the fact that Australia had no reviews left. Lehmann was later lured into telling an Australian radio station that Broad had been guilty of "blatant cheating", and urged fans to "give it to him right from the word go" during the return leg in the Australian summer; for his rabble-rousing, Lehmann was fined 20% of his Oval match fee.

At times, the DRS became almost a third participant in the series, without an obvious improvement in the accuracy of the adjudication; the fact that only four of the ICC's 12 elite umpires were eligible to stand (the other eight were English or Australian) did not help matters. Some decisions flew in the face of logic, the umpires being unable to work out the scope for their intervention. Obviously wrong decisions were upheld; a few perfectly fair verdicts were overturned; and the patent unreliability of Hot Spot occasioned a self-serving complaint from its inventor, Warren Brennan, about players using silicone tape on the outside of their bats to defeat the infrared technology. It all meant that the hall outside the third umpire's room might well have been renamed the corridor of uncertainty.

Players sometimes looked entirely mystified by their dismissals, and the sight of a batsman actually walking off after the umpire raised his finger, one of cricket's glories, was turned into a weird archaism. Given how slavishly people are inclined to ape behaviour they see on television, one wonders about the repercussions. Cricket used to worry about dissent; dissent is now respected, even enshrined.

AUSTRALIAN TOURING PARTY

*M. J. Clarke (T/50/20), A. C. Agar (T), G. J. Bailey (50/20), J. M. Bird (T), N. M. Coulter-Nile (50/20), E. J. M. Cowan (T), J. P. Faulkner (T/50/20), Fawad Ahmed (50/20), A. J. Finch (50/20), B. J. Haddin (T), R. J. Harris (T), J. R. Hazlewood (50/20), P. J. Hughes (T/50/20), M. G. Johnson (50/20), U. T. Khawaja (T), N. M. Lyon (T), C. J. McKay (50/20), S. E. Marsh (50/20), G. J. Maxwell (50/20), J. L. Pattinson (T), C. J. L. Rogers (T), P. M. Siddle (T/20), S. P. D. Smith (T/20), M. A. Starc (T/20), A. C. Voges (50/20), M. S. Wade (T/50/20), D. A. Warner (T/20), S. R. Watson (T/50/20).

Coach: D. S. Lehmann. *Assistant coach:* S. J. Rixon. *Manager:* G. Dovey. *Batting coach:* M. J. Di Venuto. *Bowling coach:* A. J. de Winter. *Analyst:* D. F. Hills. *Physiotherapist:* A. Kountouris. *Doctor:* P. Brukner. *Strength and conditioning coach:* D. Bailey. *Logistics/Massage therapist:* G. Baldwin. *Security manager:* F. A. Dimasi. *Media manager:* M. Cenin.

Smith was not originally selected for the Test squad, but was called up as cover for Clarke (chronic back problem). When several players were rested for the tour match against Sussex, A. J. Turner (playing club cricket in southern England) was added as cover. Pattinson left the tour after the Second Test with a stress fracture of the back; Bird left during the Fifth Test with pain in his lower back. Bailey captained in the Twenty20 internationals, from which Smith withdrew with a hamstring injury. Warner was originally named in the one-day squad, but later dropped.

TEST MATCH AVERAGES

ENGLAND – BATTING AND FIELDING

	T	I	NO	R	HS	100	50	Avge	Ct
I. R. Bell	5	10	1	562	113	3	2	62.44	2
K. P. Pietersen	5	10	0	388	113	1	3	38.80	5
J. E. Root	5	10	1	339	180	1	1	37.66	2
I. J. L. Trott	5	10	0	293	59	0	2	29.30	6
J. M. Bairstow	4	7	0	203	67	0	1	29.00	1
†A. N. Cook	5	10	0	277	62	0	3	27.70	7
T. T. Bresnan	3	5	1	103	45	0	0	25.75	0
†S. C. J. Broad	5	7	0	179	65	0	1	25.57	1
G. P. Swann	5	7	2	126	34	0	0	25.20	5
M. J. Prior	5	9	2	133	47	0	0	19.00	18
†J. M. Anderson	5	7	2	36	16	0	0	7.20	4

Played in one Test: S. T. Finn 0, 2*; S. C. Kerrigan 1*; C. R. Woakes 25, 17*.

BOWLING

	Style	O	M	R	W	BB	5I	Avge
J. E. Root	OB	16	5	34	3	2-9	0	11.33
S. C. J. Broad	RFM	185.5	38	604	22	6-50	2	27.45
G. P. Swann	OB	249	41	755	26	5-44	2	29.03
J. M. Anderson	RFM	205.4	43	651	22	5-73	2	29.59
T. T. Bresnan	RFM	91	20	296	10	2-25	0	29.60

Also bowled: S. T. Finn (RF) 25–3–117–2; S. C. Kerrigan (SLA) 8–0–53–0; I. J. L. Trott (RM) 7–0–28–1; C. R. Woakes (RFM) 24–7–96–1.

AUSTRALIA – BATTING AND FIELDING

	T	I	NO	R	HS	100	50	Avge	Ct
M. J. Clarke	5	10	2	381	187	1	1	47.62	6
S. R. Watson	5	10	0	418	176	1	1	41.80	4
†C. J. L. Rogers	5	9	0	367	110	1	2	40.77	4
S. P. D. Smith	5	10	1	345	138*	1	2	38.33	3
†J. L. Pattinson	2	4	2	72	35	0	0	36.00	1
†A. C. Agar	2	4	0	130	98	0	1	32.50	0
†P. J. Hughes	2	4	1	83	81*	0	1	27.66	3
†M. A. Starc	3	6	2	104	66*	0	1	26.00	1
†D. A. Warner	3	6	0	138	71	0	1	23.00	3
B. J. Haddin	5	10	1	206	71	0	2	22.88	29
R. J. Harris	4	7	2	99	33	0	0	19.80	2
†U. T. Khawaja	3	6	0	114	54	0	1	19.00	2
P. M. Siddle	5	8	0	84	23	0	0	10.50	2
N. M. Lyon	3	3	1	12	8	0	0	6.00	1

Played in one Test: J. M. Bird 0*, 1*; †E. J. M. Cowan 0, 14 (1 ct); J. P. Faulkner 23, 22.

BOWLING

	Style	O	M	R	W	BB	5I	Avge
J. P. Faulkner	LFM	27.4	4	98	6	4-51	0	16.33
R. J. Harris	RFM	162.1	37	470	24	7-117	2	19.58
S. P. D. Smith	LB	31	4	106	4	3-18	0	26.50
P. M. Siddle	RFM	189.5	52	537	17	5-50	1	31.58
M. A. Starc	LFM	120	24	357	11	3-76	0	32.45
N. M. Lyon	OB	118.1	30	303	9	4-42	0	33.66
J. L. Pattinson	RFM	91.1	21	307	7	3-69	0	43.85

Also bowled: A. C. Agar (SLA) 84–17–248–2; J. M. Bird (RFM) 42.3–15–125–2; M. J. Clarke (SLA) 3–0–6–0; S. R. Watson (RFM) 85.3–38–179–2.

For Australia's matches in the ICC Champions Trophy, see page 301.

SOMERSET v AUSTRALIANS

At Taunton, June 26–29. Australians won by six wickets. Toss: Somerset.

Chris Jones, a 22-year-old student, was supposed to be at Durham Cathedral to attend his graduation ceremony after gaining a first-class degree in economics. Instead he was drafted in to replace the injured Alviro Petersen, and celebrated with his maiden century as Somerset raced past 300 for the loss of two wickets. But they then lost six with the score stuck on 310, as Starc and Pattinson made the second new ball talk. It was the 17th instance of six wickets falling on the same score in a first-class match, but easily the highest total involved (previously 148 by Wellington, who lost six on 136 against Otago at Queenstown in 2010-11; there are also two cases of seven falling for no runs). Jones had put on 170 with Compton, who hit 81 despite his upset at being dropped by England. Several of the Australians – notably Watson, whose 90 included 20 fours, and Hughes – spent some useful time in the middle, before Clarke declared one run ahead. Hildreth and Trego had some fun, hitting 21 fours and two sixes between them as Somerset left a target of 260, but the Australians sailed home.

Close of play: first day, Australians 2-0 (Watson 0, Cowan 1); second day, Australians 266-4 (Hughes 44, Haddin 38); third day, Australians 36-0 (Cowan 14, Khawaja 18).

Somerset

*M. E. Trescothick c Starc b Pattinson	7	– c Haddin b Pattinson	32
N. R. D. Compton c Clarke b Lyon	81	– lbw b Lyon	34
C. R. Jones c Watson b Faulkner	130	– lbw b Pattinson	1
J. C. Hildreth lbw b Pattinson	66	– c Hughes b Lyon	75
C. Kieswetter b Starc	4	– b Pattinson	18
†A. W. R. Barrow lbw b Starc	0	– b Starc	8
P. D. Trego lbw b Pattinson	0	– c Khawaja b Faulkner	60
C. A. J. Meschede b Starc	0	– b Lyon	0
G. H. Dockrell lbw b Starc	0	– b Starc	0
J. Overton b Pattinson	0	– c Haddin b Siddle	6
G. M. Hussain not out	6	– not out	12
B 4, l-b 13, n-b 9	26	B 4, l-b 2, w 3, n-b 5	14

1/15 (1) 2/185 (2) 3/304 (3)   (86.1 overs) 320
4/310 (5) 5/310 (4) 6/310 (6)
7/310 (8) 8/310 (7) 9/310 (10) 10/320 (9)

1/68 (1) 2/72 (3)   (68 overs) 260
3/87 (2) 4/141 (5)
5/180 (6) 6/180 (4) 7/182 (8)
8/183 (9) 9/204 (10) 10/260 (7)

Starc 16.1–8–33–4; Pattinson 16–4–56–4; Siddle 13–0–62–0; Faulkner 17–3–70–1; Lyon 23–5–75–1; Khawaja 1–0–7–0. *Second innings*—Siddle 14–3–55–1; Faulkner 9–2–24–1; Starc 13–3–41–2; Pattinson 13–2–61–3; Lyon 19–6–73–3.

Australians

S. R. Watson c Trego b Overton	90		
E. J. M. Cowan c Barrow b Hussain	3	– (1) c Barrow b Hussain	46
U. T. Khawaja c Hildreth b Meschede	27	– (2) c Trescothick b Dockrell	73
*M. J. Clarke c Barrow b Meschede	45	– b Dockrell	26
P. J. Hughes not out	76	– (3) b Dockrell	50
†B. J. Haddin lbw b Overton	38	– (5) not out	52
J. P. Faulkner not out	22	– (6) not out	5
B 1, l-b 12, w 1, n-b 6	20	L-b 11	11

1/4 (2) 2/78 (3)   (5 wkts dec, 75.1 overs) 321
3/147 (1) 4/212 (4)
5/266 (6)

1/86 (1)   (4 wkts, 63.5 overs) 263
2/162 (2) 3/201 (3)
4/204 (4)

P. M. Siddle, M. A. Starc, J. L. Pattinson and N. M. Lyon did not bat.

Overton 16–0–89–2; Hussain 13–1–55–1; Meschede 17–4–67–2; Trego 7–2–21–0; Dockrell 22.1–3–76–0. *Second innings*—Overton 4–0–11–0; Meschede 10–1–32–0; Dockrell 21.5–3–78–3; Hussain 21–2–110–1; Trego 7–1–21–0.

Umpires: M. A. Eggleston and D. J. Millns.

WORCESTERSHIRE v AUSTRALIANS

At Worcester, July 2–5. Drawn. Toss: Australians. County debuts: N. R. D. Compton, C. A. J. Morris.

The Australians had the better of the draw, with several of their batsmen showing good form, although in the end Worcestershire had little difficulty in batting out the final day. Watson, whose 109 came at almost a run a ball, put on 170 with Rogers, then Cowan and Clarke applied themselves. When Worcestershire batted, Bird single-handedly engineered a mid-innings collapse of four for seven, but the tail restricted the deficit to 112. Clarke lit up the third day with a classical century, his 124 occupying only 98 balls, and his second declaration set a lofty target of 457 in almost four sessions. Mitchell took his crease-occupation in the match past five hours, and Tom Fell, in only his fourth first-class game, resisted for 150 minutes and reached his maiden fifty. Compton, playing as a guest at the suggestion of the England selectors, made 79 from 181 balls in the first innings, but his omission from the squad for the First Test was confirmed the day after this match.

Close of play: first day, Australians 340-4 (Smith 21, Hughes 10); second day, Worcestershire 246-7 (Andrew 24, Shantry 6); third day, Worcestershire 64-1 (Pardoe 34, Ali 2).

Australians

S. R. Watson c Shantry b Ali	109		
C. J. L. Rogers c Kervezee b Shantry	75	– (1) lbw b Ali	26
E. J. M. Cowan run out	58	– (2) lbw b Shantry	34
*M. J. Clarke run out	62	– c Andrew b Shantry	124
S. P. D. Smith not out	68	– c Kervezee b Ali	43
P. J. Hughes not out	19	– (3) b Russell	86
J. P. Faulkner (did not bat)		– (6) not out	7
A. C. Agar (did not bat)		– (7) not out	10
B 4, l-b 1	5	B 12, l-b 2	14

1/170 (1) 2/207 (2)   (4 wkts dec, 97.3 overs) 396   1/46 (1)   (5 wkts dec, 55 overs) 344
3/303 (4) 4/322 (3)   2/74 (2) 3/206 (3)
4/321 (4) 5/327 (5)

†B. J. Haddin, R. J. Harris and J. M. Bird did not bat.

Russell 11–1–68–0; Morris 23–6–74–0; Andrew 20.3–2–93–0; Shantry 18–4–71–1; Ali 23–2–82–1; Mitchell 2–1–3–0. *Second innings*—Russell 12–0–63–1; Morris 7–1–46–0; Shantry 13–2–62–2; Ali 17–1–101–2; Andrew 3–0–27–0; Mitchell 3–0–31–0.

Worcestershire

M. G. Pardoe c Hughes b Faulkner	16	– c Clarke b Faulkner	57
N. R. D. Compton c Watson b Bird	79	– st Haddin b Agar	26
M. M. Ali c Clarke b Agar	10	– lbw b Faulkner	35
*D. K. H. Mitchell c Haddin b Bird	65	– c Faulkner b Harris	54
A. N. Kervezee lbw b Bird	4	– b Harris	2
T. C. Fell c Watson b Bird	1	– not out	62
†O. B. Cox c Clarke b Agar	25	– not out	25
G. M. Andrew c Haddin b Harris	24		
J. D. Shantry b Harris	13		
C. A. J. Morris not out	25		
C. J. Russell b Faulkner	4		
B 8, l-b 7, n-b 3	18	B 7, l-b 5, n-b 1	13

1/48 (1) 2/88 (3) 3/180 (2)   (92.1 overs) 284   1/57 (2)   (5 wkts, 96 overs) 274
4/184 (5) 5/186 (6) 6/187 (4)   2/114 (1) 3/135 (3)
7/225 (7) 8/248 (8) 9/265 (9) 10/284 (11)   4/144 (5) 5/221 (4)

Harris 21–5–65–2; Bird 25–9–48–4; Agar 23–4–79–2; Faulkner 14.1–2–57–2; Watson 6–4–13–0; Smith 3–0–7–0. *Second innings*—Harris 19–3–60–2; Bird 18.5–5–53–0; Agar 27–6–86–1; Watson 9–3–13–0; Faulkner 17–8–21–2; Smith 5–0–24–0; Hughes 1–0–5–0.

Umpires: I. Dawood and P. J. Hartley.

ENGLAND v AUSTRALIA

First Investec Ashes Test

JAMES COYNE

At Nottingham, July 10–14. England won by 14 runs. Toss: England. Test debut: A. C. Agar.

When a heatwave swept through the country, answering England's prayer for dry pitches, a wag asked whether posterity might record this as the first Ashes Test played in India. Sending a few nudges and winks the way of county groundsmen may not have sat

Philip Brown

Points made: James Anderson wins round one of the battle with Michael Clarke with a sublime outswinger on the opening day of the series.

well with everyone, but the First Test was an instant, and very modern, Ashes classic. Australia were bowled into contention by a vegan fast bowler, revived by the joyous strokeplay of a teenage No. 11 on debut, and finally suppressed by an Englishman with complete command of reverse swing. Improbably, Australia's last-wicket pairs scored 228 runs in the match – 15 more at the end and they would have been celebrating an even more improbable win.

England had grown accustomed to Anderson's brilliance. But they leaned on him a little too uncomfortably here. Cramp ended his 13-over spell on the last morning, and he was patched together during the lunch break to winkle out the final wicket, and his tenth of the match, just in time – even if he had to be persuaded that Haddin had actually edged to Prior, after Aleem Dar turned down the appeal. Having seen the crucial thermal spot up on the replay screen, England celebrated for over a minute before victory was officially confirmed by third umpire Marais Erasmus. Mercifully, he reached the correct decision, because the technology had exhausted just about everyone. Anderson rolled on to the physio's table and went to sleep.

Regardless of where you stood on DRS, there was one undeniable fact: Australia had used it dreadfully. In both second innings, they frittered away their reviews before the fall of the fifth wicket. So when, at six down, Broad edged one not seen by Dar, Australia had no room for manoeuvre, other than perhaps to invoke the Spirit of Cricket – which they didn't bother to do. Stung by criticism directed towards their officials and the technology, the ICC took the rare step of revealing their umpire assessment for the match, adamant that DRS had improved the accuracy of decision-making.

Nervous tension was everywhere on a muggy first day. From some of the world's finest technicians there were madcap swishes at good balls, and a lot of bowling that asked to be hit. Cook probably expected the haze to burn off when he walked out with Root, his seventh opening partner at Test level, after the dropping of Nick Compton. But the captain inadvertently set the tone, edging a full-blooded drive off Pattinson.

No Australian seamer in the post-McGrath era had caused England more grief than Siddle. He began the series as the highest-ranked bowler on either side, yet still some saw

Graham Morris

Twist and clout: Ashton Agar did not stay at No. 11 for long after swatting England everywhere on debut.

fit to patronise him; there was even talk of leaving him out. He then disappeared for 27 in his first four overs here. But when Clarke switched him to the Radcliffe Road End, he immediately tore a late-swinging yorker through Root. Clarke whipped him straight off again to give left-armer Starc a crack at Pietersen, but Siddle returned after a veggie lunch to carve the meat off the bone: a smidgen of swing drew Pietersen and Bell into nicks, and he picked up the bonus wicket of Trott, chopping on a wide ball after he had been striding out imperiously to the fast bowlers. Soon, Siddle had the first five-for of the series, as he had at Brisbane in the previous Ashes opener. There was a peskier technical gremlin lurking in Bairstow, who closed the face on a Starc yorker he should have blocked.

England's batting, like the summer's fashions, had a whiff of 1990s revivalism, capped off when the last four wickets caved in for two runs: their tail had not folded so pliably since November 1998 at Perth. And in all the excitement they had forgotten the value of rotating the strike: of their 215, only 18 had come in singles.

Broad's right shoulder had been softened by a Pattinson bouncer, so Finn took the new ball, having held off Tim Bresnan's claims for the third seamer's spot. Finn and Watson were both in a hurry: the bowler won. Cowan, on notice at No. 3 after losing his opening position, spent much of the day throwing up, then came out and guided a half-hearted drive to slip. It dragged Clarke into the mayhem at No. 4 – a place higher than his liking. He attempted a booming drive at the hat-trick ball, and was millimetres from connecting. But he was nowhere near his sixth, which Anderson darted in, then curved away deliciously to kiss the outside of off. Under the floodlights, Rogers became the 14th and final wicket of the opening day – losing his DRS virginity to a ball that umpires of yore would have imagined slanting down.

Australia badly needed some grit, and found it in two of their most derided cricketers, Smith and Hughes. Smith's fifty was a minor gem, full of livewire footwork. But on the sunny second morning, with the ball barely 20 overs old, it began hooping around. Smith seemed to have adjusted when he was surprised by one that held its line – giving Anderson a record 42nd Test wicket on this ground, passing Alec Bedser. It was the first of five wickets in six overs for him and Swann. Australia were buckling.

TRENT BRIDGE NOTES AND QUOTES

An eleventh-hour plea from Graeme Swann was not enough for the Barmy Army's classically trained trumpeter Billy Cooper to receive special dispensation to play inside Trent Bridge. "Personally, I think it's a shame," said Swann. "I know the whole team are behind Billy, and the Barmy Army are a massive part of the English team." Nottinghamshire chief executive Lisa Pursehouse said: "We just don't let musical instruments into Trent Bridge."

When news reached Melbourne of Ashton Agar's shock selection, his family – parents John and Sonia, and younger brothers William and Wesley – dropped everything to make the 10,500-mile journey to Nottingham. After Agar fell two runs short of becoming Test cricket's first No. 11 centurion, John said: "When they came out to field, he walked over to us and said, 'I'm sorry,' but he didn't have to apologise at all." On Twitter, Agar became an instant hit, not least in the hashtag department – #Agarthehorrible and #Agarmeister both proved popular, as did (inevitably) #Ashtag.

Stuart Broad's refusal to walk during his second-innings 65 prompted a strong response from Michael Holding. Speaking on Sky Sports, Holding insisted the two-match ban handed to West Indies wicketkeeper Denesh Ramdin by Stuart's father, Chris, after claiming a dropped catch during the Champions Trophy should have applied to Broad too. "What Stuart Broad did is contrary to the spirit of the game," he said. "I'm not saying that Broad should have walked in this instance. But what Ramdin did when he was suspended and fined is no different from what Broad has done here."

All Notes and Quotes compiled by Ali Martin

They were right down to Ashton Agar, a 19-year-old slow left-armer picked in the hope he might unsettle Pietersen and the other right-handers more than Nathan Lyon, who was used to being jilted. Word was the youngster could give it a whack too. But there's a difference between a whack, à la Tino Best at Edgbaston the previous year, and the ability to straight-drive Anderson and shimmy down to Swann. A rabbit-out-of-the-hat selection, this was no rabbit. Yet England treated him like one, pushing the field back to give Hughes the single, and trying to bounce Agar out. The approach looked downright foolish when he kept pulling Finn for four. England had little footage to go on, but the virtue of pitching the ball up had been plain to see in reducing Australia to 117 for nine. The yorker had fallen out of vogue altogether.

The ingénu had luck on his side too. Only 14 runs into the partnership, Prior appeared to stump Agar, but Erasmus disagreed. So on he went, and Test records began to tumble: highest score by a No. 11 on debut, highest partnership for the tenth wicket, highest score by any No. 11, beating Best's 95. Lunch was delayed, and Broad – expected to sit out the innings – was forced into the attack. For only the third time in Test history, the last pair doubled the score. When Agar was finally caught by Swann in the leg-side trap to end the stand at 163 and his innings at 98, Tino tweeted: "I'm feeling your pain, lad."

Australia emerged from it all with a lead of 65, then got a little fortunate in reducing England to 11 for two. Root was surprised to be given out caught down the leg side off Starc; replays suggested he might have survived had he not followed his captain's advice to walk off. The next ball was a toe-crunching yorker to Trott, which Dar gave not out, suspecting a tiny nick; Clarke reviewed, and was elated to see no mark on the bat, but that was only because the Hot Spot technicians – still mulling over Root's dismissal – had not reconfigured their side-on camera. Despite lacking this crucial piece of evidence, Erasmus overturned the decision. Dar looked incredulous; for Trott, it was a first golden duck in Test cricket.

In the evening, the game finally calmed down – which had to favour the better side. Cook and Pietersen were opposites in style, but with matching career records (bar the strike-rate). Clarke tried everything to separate them: two midwickets to Pietersen, a short mid-on to Cook, and the driest of bowling from Watson, who did not concede a run until

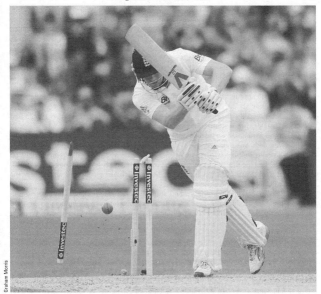

Not quite out of the V: Jonny Bairstow plays across the line to Mitchell Starc – and pays the price.

his 34th ball. On this barren pitch, they soaked it all up, until Pietersen chopped on, ending a stand of 110 in 49 overs. Cook reached his fifty from 164 deliveries – his joint-slowest in Tests and his first at Trent Bridge – but Agar then landed a straightish one in the rough and took Cook's leading edge for a distinguished first Test wicket. (His hat-trick in the Home Counties Premier League for Henley against North Mymms a few weeks earlier had come with arm-balls too.) But as England dug themselves free, with Agar declining to go round the wicket, the suspicion grew that he was no Test-winning spinner just yet. Bell and Prior lapped up the second new ball like thirsty pilgrims, romping along at four an over.

Clarke had exhausted Australia's final review trying to get rid of Bairstow. How he could have done with it later that evening. England's lead was 232 when Broad, cutting Agar off the back foot, edged to Clarke at slip via Haddin's left mitt. Broad's demeanour gave away nothing – and Dar never raised his finger, perhaps confused by the deflection. The romantics cried foul; the professionals shrugged their shoulders. A Broadwalk? Against the Australians? There was more chance of Korean unification. Broad, already dropped by Cowan, rode the ear-bashing to add 138 with Bell. After this masterpiece, Bell had no more breakthrough innings to play; perhaps only at Cape Town in 2009-10 had he assessed the conditions as perfectly. Now he evoked Dravid and Jayawardene, dropping his hands to steer dozens of runs through an unpatrolled third man, but scoring nothing in the erogenous zone between extra cover and mid-on. It was an exquisite show of denial.

Bell's fortitude meant Australia had just over five sessions to attempt 311. In this country, that had been the domain only of Bradman's 1948 Invincibles, Lloyd's 1984

West Indians and Butcher's 2001 odyssey. When they set out on the hottest day of the year so far, on a pitch more Nagpur than Nottingham, they had only an outside sniff. The first 84 came steadily enough. Then, to the first ball after a drinks break, Watson planted his pad, was struck in front by Broad, and reviewed hastily, but it was clipping leg. Cowan drove rashly out of the rough just before tea to give Root a maiden Test wicket, before Rogers – having carefully assembled his first Test fifty – carelessly clipped an off-cutter to short midwicket. It was a plan conceived in India: a grinning Anderson saluted England's bowling coach, David Saker, up on the balcony.

Australia needed Clarke more than ever, but he completed a poor match by feathering behind on 23. He used up the last review anyway, later insisting his batsmen should stand by their gut feeling about edges. If, on the other hand, Clarke was gambling on a Hot Spot blooper, then it was the height of selfishness with his team still 150 short. Australia lost wickets in a cluster for the third time in the match.

A full house assembled on the fifth morning expecting England to mop up the last four by lunch, yet, with Australia needing 137, all too aware of Edgbaston '05. With Haddin, a centurion in both the last two Ashes openers, to guide a strong tail, nothing could be discounted. When the first 35 minutes passed without incident, England took the new ball, and made it work: Agar (promoted to No. 8), Starc and Siddle all edged sharp chances off Anderson to Cook, standing close at slip.

Australia were 80 short when last man Pattinson joined Haddin, and with Anderson in need of a breather. Haddin, sensing Finn was still scarred by the Agar hullaboloo, brought out his Twenty20 shots, while Pattinson blocked securely, but showed enough adventure to swipe Swann – bowling a touch too full – for six. As if Finn's day could get no worse, a tough chance slipped through his hands in the deep with 26 needed. By now, England were desperate to regroup over lunch, and Broad resorted to shameless delaying tactics, manufacturing a problem with his boot; the umpires were having none of it.

A hush descended during the break as the thought dawned that Australia, now just 20 away, might pull this off. Perhaps sensing as much, the ECB wheeled out tenor Sean Ruane to rouse the crowd with some patriotic numbers. It was impossible to say if the mood music worked, but in the third over back an Anderson off-cutter stayed low on Haddin. Prior and Cook heard a noise, and asked for a review. Haddin nodded forlornly at his fellow wicketkeeper, then grimaced as a white spot showed up on the screen, possibly suspecting, deep down, that Australia might not get another chance like this.

Man of the Match: J. M. Anderson. *Attendance:* 85,035.

Close of play: first day, Australia 75-4 (Smith 38, Hughes 7); second day, England 80-2 (Cook 37, Pietersen 35); third day, England 326-6 (Bell 95, Broad 47); fourth day, Australia 174-6 (Haddin 11, Agar 1).

England

*A. N. Cook c Haddin b Pattinson	13	– c Clarke b Agar	50
J. E. Root b Siddle	30	– c Haddin b Starc	5
I. J. L. Trott b Siddle	48	– lbw b Starc	0
K. P. Pietersen c Clarke b Siddle	14	– b Pattinson	64
I. R. Bell c Watson b Siddle	25	– c Haddin b Starc	109
J. M. Bairstow b Starc	37	– c Haddin b Agar	15
†M. J. Prior c Hughes b Siddle	1	– c Cowan b Siddle	31
S. C. J. Broad c and b Pattinson	24	– c Haddin b Pattinson	65
G. P. Swann c Hughes b Pattinson	1	– c Clarke b Siddle	9
S. T. Finn c Haddin b Starc	0	– not out	2
J. M. Anderson not out	1	– c Hughes b Siddle	0
B 6, l-b 5, w 8, n-b 2	21	B 2, l-b 13, w 1, n-b 9	25

1/27 (1) 2/78 (2) 3/102 (4)   (59 overs) 215   1/11 (2) 2/11 (3)   (149.5 overs) 375
4/124 (3) 5/178 (5) 6/180 (7)   3/121 (4) 4/131 (1)
7/213 (8) 8/213 (6) 9/213 (10) 10/215 (9)   5/174 (6) 6/218 (7) 7/356 (8)
                                            8/371 (5) 9/375 (9) 10/375 (11)

Pattinson 17–2–69–3; Starc 17–5–54–2; Siddle 14–4–50–5; Agar 7–1–24–0; Watson 4–2–7–0. *Second innings*—Pattinson 34–8–101–2; Starc 32–7–81–3; Agar 35–9–82–2; Siddle 33.5–12–85–3; Watson 15–11–11–0.

Australia

S. R. Watson c Root b Finn	13	– lbw b Broad	46
C. J. L. Rogers lbw b Anderson	16	– c Bell b Anderson	52
E. J. M. Cowan c Swann b Finn	0	– c Trott b Root	14
*M. J. Clarke b Anderson	0	– c Prior b Broad	23
S. P. D. Smith c Prior b Anderson	53	– lbw b Swann	17
P. J. Hughes not out	81	– lbw b Swann	0
†B. J. Haddin b Swann	1	– c Prior b Anderson	71
P. M. Siddle c Prior b Anderson	1	– (10) c Cook b Anderson	11
M. A. Starc c Prior b Anderson	0	– c Cook b Anderson	1
J. L. Pattinson lbw b Swann	2	– (11) not out	25
A. C. Agar c Swann b Broad	98	– (8) c Cook b Anderson	14
L-b 15	15	B 11, l-b 10, n-b 1	22

1/19 (1) 2/19 (3) 3/22 (4)   (64.5 overs) 280   1/84 (1) 2/111 (3)   (110.5 overs) 296
4/53 (2) 5/108 (5) 6/113 (7)   3/124 (2) 4/161 (4)
7/114 (8) 8/114 (9) 9/117 (10) 10/280 (11)   5/161 (5) 6/164 (6) 7/207 (8)
                                           8/211 (9) 9/231 (10) 10/296 (7)

Anderson 24–2–85–5; Finn 15–0–80–2; Swann 19–4–60–2; Broad 6.5–0–40–1. *Second innings*—Anderson 31.5–11–73–5; Broad 23–7–54–2; Swann 44–10–105–2; Finn 10–3–37–0; Root 2–0–6–1.

Umpires: Aleem Dar and H. D. P. K. Dharmasena.   Third umpire: M. Erasmus.
Referee: R. S. Madugalle.

ENGLAND v AUSTRALIA

Second Investec Ashes Test

Greg Baum

At Lord's, July 18–21. England won by 347 runs. Toss: England.

This game consisted of three typical Test-match totals, reflecting the relative strengths of the teams – and one brief and bizarre interlude of almost comical ineptitude. That was Australia's first innings. In the nature of Test cricket, for all the good and stout-hearted combat elsewhere in the match, it was this capitulation and its consequences, compounding over days, that decided the result, all but settled the fate of the Ashes, and gave rise to fears of a year-long, eight-match dead rubber. Best-laid plans sometimes lead to decisive outcomes; cock-ups always do.

There were so many ways to slice and dice the carnage, but here are a few that leapt out: Cook and Pietersen contributed negligibly, making 27 runs between them; before the end of the second day, England were twice 30 for three or worse; and Anderson took just one top-order wicket. Yet England won the match by a country mile – their second-greatest victory over Australia in terms of runs. Without a contest to thrill to, the packed houses at Lord's settled amiably for a celebration of the United Kingdom's newly rediscovered sporting virtuosity – worn more lightly, it must be said, than by Australia during their halcyon era.

Really, this was only what was foreseen before the series, but suddenly had been obscured by events at Nottingham. The rousing course of that encounter had camouflaged Australia's batting frailty, and inspired hope on their part – and apprehension on England's – that this Ashes series could yet confound the formbook.

The Bicentenary of the present Lord's Ground.

Join in the celebrations and be part of 200 years of history.

Throughout 2014 M.C.C. will host a number of celebrations - on and off the field - which aim to bring the very best of Lord's to everyone.

These include two M.C.C. v. Rest of the World matches, a digital model of Lord's and a series of events in a marquee on the outfield of the Main Ground, amongst many others.

For more information on all the year's events visit:

lords.org/lords200

@homeofcricket #lords200

facebook.com/lordscricket

youtube.com/lordscricketground

WHEN YOU'RE IN A RUT

Australia's longest losing sequences in Test cricket:

7	Melbourne 1884-85 to Sydney 1887-88 (all to England)
6	Bridgetown 1983-84 to Adelaide 1984-85 (all to West Indies)
6	**Chennai 2012-13 to Lord's 2013 (4 to India, 2 to England)**
5	The Oval 1926 to Adelaide 1928-29 (all to England)
4	The Oval 1888 to The Oval 1890 (all to England)
4	Melbourne 1911-12 to Sydney 1911-12 (all to England)
4	Cape Town 1969-70 to Port Elizabeth 1969-70 (all to South Africa)
4	Sydney 1978-79 to Melbourne 1978-79 (3 to England, 1 to Pakistan)

England's biggest victories over Australia by runs:

675	at Brisbane (Exhibition Ground) 1928-29	322 at Brisbane (Gabba)	1936-37
347	**at Lord's 2013**	299 at Sydney	1970-71
338	at Adelaide 1932-33	289 at The Oval	1926

At The Oval in 1938 England won by an innings and 579 runs.

The pre-match headlines blared news of Mickey Arthur's lawsuit against Cricket Australia. Yet the very majesty of the Lord's Test extinguished any but the most noble contemplations. The weather was set fair; a host of former greats from both countries sauntered about; stirring deeds were relived. And the frisson was palpable. The spirit was of a feast day, celebrated by the two remaining countries who can be relied upon to fill a Test ground. The rites concluded with a visit from the Queen, regally delaying the start by 15 minutes.

What followed was a Test classic. Its centrepiece was Bell's third hundred in three Tests against Australia, equalling Jack Hobbs, Wally Hammond and Chris Broad among Englishmen. This was a sleek and streamlined innings, in which the working parts were not visible, yet the ball seemed aimed at the middle of his bat, and every plan to pass it doomed. Bell's second successive 109 was augmented by dedicated half-centuries from Trott and Bairstow, who took advantage of his fortune when, on 21, he was castled by a no-ball from Siddle.

But this heft of runs was offset by three early wickets, and three more in the shadow of stumps. The three at the start – including Cook's to Watson, introduced early – must have struck the Queen as so many baubles presented to her in the colonies: handsome things, but what on earth would she do with them? The three at the end, including the gobsmacked Bairstow – caught and bowled from a low full toss – were the work of mock leg-spinner Steve Smith, not a regular in Australia's plans and brought on so late as to almost represent an addendum. But they squared the honours, further insulating aficionados against the collapse to come.

Bresnan faced the first and last balls of the second day, in separate innings – doughty brackets to mayhem. The first dismissed him but, after a vigorous swish of the tail, England settled on 361, thought to be no more than competitive. Brave, brittle Harris, bowling fast, full and straight, collected five for 72. Historically, he had been like an old bus whose engine causes its frame to rattle and fall apart. But when, as now, his body kept up with his heart, Australia looked a different team. Pattinson struggled with his line, perhaps because of the Lord's slope, but more probably because of what emerged later: he was incubating stress fractures, and would take no further part in the series.

Australia saw off Anderson's mazy new-ball swing and, two deliveries before lunch, were 42 without loss when the red mist descended. The slapstick is worth itemising. Watson again played across a ball angled into his pads, and missed it, and was ruled lbw, and reviewed the decision, and was still out. It had become his groundhog minute. It was also the fluttering of the butterfly's wings. Rogers heaved in ungainly manner at a waist-high full toss from Swann, was given out lbw and – conscious of Australia's DRS prodigality, and

Graham Morris

Slapstick cricket: Shane Watson is lbw to Tim Bresnan – and reviewing it doesn't help. But DRS would have saved Chris Rogers from his "box before wicket" dismissal, which replays showed was sailing past and over leg stump.

Anthony Devlin, PA Photos

LORD'S NOTES AND QUOTES

Former Ashes adversaries Michael Vaughan and Damien Martyn were among eight passengers who spent 35 minutes trapped in one of the Lord's media-centre lifts on the second afternoon. "It was traumatic," Vaughan joked. "It was hot and we were thinking the worst at one point."

England briefly deployed 36-year-old fielding coach Chris Taylor as a substitute on the fourth day, with his one noteworthy contribution coming in the form of a sharp stop at cover off the batting of Siddle. Taylor, a former Gloucestershire batsman, missed with his shy at the stumps – to wry smiles from a number of his pupils.

Australia's two collapses did not go down well with former captain Allan Border, who used his official Cricket Australia column to declare: "Our major concern right now is the performance of the top six. I could honestly say the nine, ten and jack looked more competent than our one, two and three. If that was me in the top three I'd be embarrassed."

By the time Australia last lost six Tests in a row – to West Indies in 1984 – captain Kim Hughes had resigned in tears. After this defeat equalled that sequence, one Australian journalist said to Michael Clarke: "I presume that won't happen this time." Clarke replied, with a weary smile: "Presume nothing."

his own part in persuading Watson to review – chose not to make the referral that would have spared him. The ball was high and wide of leg. Every part of this dismissal was a mistake: the delivery, the shot, the decision, the failure to refer. Swann later wondered whether it was the worst piece of cricket in Test history; for once, he wasn't joking.

As if forgetting his patient deeds in Nottingham, Hughes wafted at Bresnan, and used up Australia's last referral. Khawaja, picked instead of Ed Cowan and with a career to rebuild, slogged intemperately across Swann's line and was caught at mid-off; Smith prodded Swann to short leg, Clarke missed a late-dipping inswinger from Broad, and Agar ran himself out. The tail scarcely twitched. When the sorry procession ended, Australia had lost ten for 86.

England's part was to put the ball into play; for this artistry, Swann became the first English spinner to take an Ashes five-for at Lord's since Hedley Verity in 1934, which not so long ago was known as the last time Australia had lost here. Anderson was left with only a tail-end picking. It is hard to conceive of a more reckless, feckless display than Australia's. By Darren Lehmann's estimate, eight of the wickets were self-inflicted. Back home, viewers turned off their televisions in droves, and many would hardly turn them on again for the rest of the series. Less than two days had gone, and only the formalities remained.

One other accident befell Australia on the second day, though it seemed harmless in its moment. A fever remained upon the match as England batted again, and Siddle quickly bowled Cook and Trott, then had Pietersen caught at point from a grandiose drive. Before any of that, Root tickled a Watson seamer on four. Keeper Haddin and first slip Clarke found themselves staring at each other – and at the catch that either might have taken, but neither did.

Not even Root could have guessed that he would still be there at stumps both that evening and the next, as he pieced together his maiden Ashes century – and then nearly doubled it. Root is, you might say, classically trained. Resolutely he plays back, until at last the bowler pitches so far up that he can drive as handsomely as his Yorkshire predecessor and tireless advocate, Michael Vaughan. Now, he became the first Yorkshireman to score a century in an Ashes Test at Lord's since Willie Watson followed Len Hutton to three figures in 1953, and at 22 the youngest Englishman to score one here against Australia. And didn't he look it? Among the many to acclaim him was his brother, Billy, who was pitch-side as a member of the groundstaff or – as he was described on radio – "part of the twelfth-man team".

The third day was bloodless sport, more like a negotiation of terms of surrender than a contest. England's need for hurry or risk was obviated, and so they tootled along at two an over until the last session, when they could not help expand against a tired and dispirited attack. Though the ball sometimes turned straight to slip, the callow Agar was not the man to make anything of it; Trent Bridge seemed long ago. Bresnan, the nightwatchman, accompanied Root for half the day, Bell and Bairstow for the rest. On 70, Root reached 1,000 first-class runs in the season.

Injustice piled upon insult upon injury for Australia when Smith appeared to catch the newly arrived Bell low in the gully from a Harris lifter, only for the third umpire to reprieve the batsman, counter-intuitively. In dreamy sunshine, yet another Bell century appeared predestined until he swatted a catch from a Smith long-hop; in truth, England did some frittering of their own in this match.

Sunday morning was anything but solemn. Nine Australians dotted the boundary rope when Root, on 180, played a ramp shot at Harris and was caught at fine third man. England declared, a forbidding 582 ahead. As tonic follows gin, Watson was swiftly lbw to Anderson, and Rogers and Hughes both fell to Swann, one leaving, the other missing. As was their wont, Australia were 36 for three. Clarke and Khawaja spared immediate blushes with an attractive stand of 98, but both fell within 11 balls of Root's mild off-spin. There was nothing he could not do.

Khawaja had struck for Australia, in a manner of speaking, when he collided with Swann, forcing him to take tablets that dulled both his pain and his edge. For a while, it seemed there would be a token last day. But the tide was with England. DRS would have spared Haddin if Australia had not already squandered all their referrals again and, although their bottom three resisted stoutly in lengthening shadow, the sun would not set on this new English empire. Swann, with his ninth wicket, finished the job in the final over of the extra half-hour.

This was Australia's sixth Test defeat in succession, and England's fourth Ashes win in a row, sequences barely known in living memory. It was also the first time England had won back-to-back Lord's Tests against Australia since the 1880s. Not since 1978-79 had they won the first two Tests of an Ashes series. Ascendant again in the dominions, they now had reclaimed and fortified their ancient seat of power.

Chris Froome also formalised victory in the Tour de France this day, making with Andy Murray's Wimbledon a trio of British mastery. On the other side of the world, Cricket Australia issued a triumphal press release, replete with statistical proof of the success of the Big Bash League. "Cricket Australia's strategy for the BBL is working," honked the league chief Mike McKenna. Lord's certainly gave Twenty20 in Australia a kick-along.

Man of the Match: J. E. Root.   *Attendance:* 120,056.

Close of play: first day, England 289-7 (Bresnan 7, Anderson 4); second day, England 31-3 (Root 18, Bresnan 0); third day, England 333-5 (Root 178, Bairstow 11).

England

*A. N. Cook lbw b Watson	12	– b Siddle	8
J. E. Root lbw b Harris	6	– c Smith b Harris	180
I. J. L. Trott c Khawaja b Harris	58	– b Siddle	0
K. P. Pietersen c Haddin b Harris	2	– c Rogers b Siddle	5
I. R. Bell c Clarke b Smith	109	– (6) c Rogers b Smith	74
J. M. Bairstow c and b Smith	67	– (7) c Haddin b Harris	20
†M. J. Prior c Haddin b Smith	6	– (8) not out	1
T. T. Bresnan c Haddin b Harris	7	– (5) c Rogers b Pattinson	38
J. M. Anderson c Haddin b Harris	12		
S. C. J. Broad c Haddin b Pattinson	33		
G. P. Swann not out	28		
L-b 11, w 4, n-b 6	21	B 15, l-b 8	23

1/18 (1) 2/26 (2) 3/28 (4)   (100.1 overs) 361
4/127 (3) 5/271 (5) 6/274 (6)
7/283 (7) 8/289 (8) 9/313 (9) 10/361 (10)

1/22 (1) (7 wkts dec, 114.1 overs) 349
2/22 (3) 3/30 (4)
4/129 (5) 5/282 (6) 6/344 (7) 7/349 (2)

Pattinson 20.1–3–95–1; Harris 26–6–72–5; Watson 13–4–45–1; Siddle 22–6–76–0; Agar 13–2–44–0; Smith 6–1–18–3. *Second innings*—Harris 18.1–4–31–2; Watson 12–5–25–0; Siddle 21–6–65–3; Pattinson 20–8–42–1; Smith 14–0–65–1; Agar 29–5–98–0.

Australia

S. R. Watson lbw b Bresnan	30	– lbw b Anderson 20
C. J. L. Rogers lbw b Swann	15	– b Swann 6
U. T. Khawaja c Pietersen b Swann	14	– c Anderson b Root 54
P. J. Hughes c Prior b Bresnan	1	– lbw b Swann 1
*M. J. Clarke lbw b Broad	28	– c Cook b Root 51
S. P. D. Smith c Bell b Swann	2	– c Prior b Bresnan 1
†B. J. Haddin c Trott b Swann	7	– lbw b Swann 7
A. C. Agar run out	2	– c Prior b Bresnan 16
P. M. Siddle c Swann b Anderson	2	– b Anderson 18
J. L. Pattinson not out	10	– lbw b Swann 35
R. J. Harris c Pietersen b Swann	10	– not out 16
B 4, l-b 1, w 2	7	B 4, l-b 5, w 1 10

1/42 (1) 2/50 (2) 3/53 (4)   (53.3 overs) 128   1/24 (1) 2/32 (2)   (90.3 overs) 235
4/69 (3) 5/86 (6) 6/91 (5)   3/36 (4) 4/134 (5)
7/96 (8) 8/104 (9) 9/104 (7) 10/128 (11)   5/135 (3) 6/136 (6) 7/154 (8)
                                                            8/162 (7) 9/192 (9) 10/235 (10)

Anderson 14–8–25–1; Broad 11–3–26–1; Bresnan 7–1–28–2; Swann 21.3–5–44–5. *Second innings*—Anderson 18–2–55–2; Broad 21–4–54–0; Swann 30.3–5–78–4; Bresnan 14–8–30–2; Root 7–3–9–2.

Umpires: H. D. P. K. Dharmasena and M. Erasmus.   Third umpire: A. L. Hill.
Referee: R. S. Madugalle.

SUSSEX v AUSTRALIANS

At Hove, July 26–28. Drawn. Toss: Australians. First-class debuts: C. F. Jackson; A. J. Turner. County debut: J. W. A. Taylor.

This was the most eagerly anticipated fixture of Sussex's summer, but the reality did not match the build-up. The first two days were watched by sell-out crowds of 6,500, but most were left bemused when neither side made any attempt to set up a decent finish. Instead, spectators started drifting home long before the end of the final day as the Australians enjoyed another extended net. Just four of the team beaten in the Second Test at Lord's played here, and none of those auditioning for a place at Old Trafford did much, apart from Bird, who bowled aggressively on a flat pitch. With both first innings limited to 100 overs, James Taylor of Nottinghamshire, playing as a guest, batted for nearly six hours for a prosaic century after being placed on standby for Kevin Pietersen (who was an injury doubt, but ended up playing at Old Trafford anyway). Hamilton-Brown's predetermined attack did little for Lyon's confidence ahead of his expected Test recall, but Smith did manage only the Australians' third hundred of the tour. The locals, though, left feeling short-changed.

Close of play: first day, Australians 354-5 (Smith 98, Agar 0); second day, Sussex 228-5 (Taylor 64, Jordan 23).

Australians

*E. J. M. Cowan c Taylor b Hatchett	66	– not out 77
P. J. Hughes c Jackson b Hatchett	84	– (3) lbw b Hatchett 38
U. T. Khawaja c Jordan b Panesar	40	– (2) c Jordan b Hatchett 1
S. P. D. Smith not out	102	
†M. S. Wade c Liddle b Panesar	0	– (4) not out 30
J. P. Faulkner b Panesar	48	
A. C. Agar not out	8	
B 12, n-b 6	18	L-b 1, w 1, n-b 4 6

1/150 (1) 2/167 (2)   (5 wkts dec, 94.4 overs) 366   1/6 (2)   (2 wkts dec, 44 overs) 152
3/218 (3) 4/218 (5) 5/349 (6)   2/91 (3)

A. J. Turner, M. A. Starc, N. M. Lyon and J. M. Bird did not bat.

Jordan 14–2–80–0; Hatchett 14.4–5–38–2; Panesar 24.4–8–70–3; Liddle 22.2–3–93–0; Nash 9–1–25–0; Wells 7–0–34–0; Yardy 3–0–14–0. *Second innings*—Jordan 8–3–34–0; Hatchett 11–3–28–2; Liddle 5–0–15–0; Panesar 14–1–40–0; Nash 2–0–10–0; Hamilton-Brown 4–0–24–0.

Sussex

*C. D. Nash c Smith b Bird	27	†C. F. Jackson lbw b Lyon	26
L. W. P. Wells b Bird	4	L. J. Hatchett not out	15
M. H. Yardy c Agar b Starc	0	B 16, l-b 11, w 2, n-b 10	39
J. W. A. Taylor not out	121		
R. J. Hamilton-Brown c Wade b Agar	73	1/13 (2) 2/24 (3) (7 wkts, 100 overs) 368	
M. W. Machan c Lyon b Faulkner	16	3/33 (1) 4/139 (5)	
C. J. Jordan b Starc	47	5/185 (6) 6/267 (7) 7/322 (8)	

C. J. Liddle and M. S. Panesar did not bat.

Starc 18–4–43–2; Bird 20–6–62–2; Faulkner 18–4–55–1; Lyon 26–4–99–1; Agar 14–1–66–1; Turner 4–0–16–0.

Umpires: J. H. Evans and G. Sharp.

ENGLAND v AUSTRALIA

Third Investec Ashes Test

JARROD KIMBER

At Manchester, August 1–5. Drawn. Toss: Australia.

The human back is complicated. It doesn't always work. In Michael Clarke's, three discs have been degenerating for some time. On certain days, he has been able to perform his duties exactly as he has wished. On others, he struggles to sit, bend, lift or twist. But, as Australia sought to put their Lord's nightmare behind them, Clarke overcame his back. England, it's true, retained the Ashes in only a fortnight's cricket after rain on the last day ensured a tame draw – only the second time (after 1928-29) they had clinched the Ashes in the Third Test of a full-length series. But Clarke overcame his back. It was a tour on which Australia settled for small mercies.

First, though, Clarke won the toss. Watson went early, poking Bresnan to slip as if to prove he needn't always fall leg-before, before Rogers showed that all those years punishing poor first-class bowling had been time well spent – even if it helped that England seemed to think the best way to dismiss him was with half-volleys. He raced past 50, found the gaps as if he was driving past traffic cones, and scored at a rate that embarrassed anyone who had called him a plodder. And, having hit two-thirds of Australia's total, he was approaching a hundred less than an hour after lunch.

Rogers had spent years in the UK on a paid spying mission. He had faced all their bowlers, played on most of their grounds, and been nicely remunerated for the pleasure. But the one thing county cricket could never truly give him was a crowd. For Rogers, at a venue where a smart refurbishment had increased capacity to 25,750, a small section of

Graham Morris

Copping it: there was little respite for David Warner from the crowd, or England's bowlers, in his first match of the series.

spectators began, inadvertently, to put him off. In a stop–start over from Swann, Rogers was distracted by movement up in the pavilion, which for the first time in a Manchester Test was behind the bowler's arm, not square-on. He advanced down the track, played across the line, and missed: plumb lbw for 84.

Swann had already benefited from outside assistance, ragging one from round the wicket as Khawaja played one of his trademark semi-interested drives. He missed it by a distance, but there was a noise. England roared, umpire Tony Hill agreed, and Khawaja – confused at first – decided on a review. It seemed like a straightforward not-out call: the noise had come from bat clipping pad. Even people watching on pixellated illegal internet streams could see a gap between bat and ball. There was no Hot Spot mark. But, after nearly three minutes of deliberation, Kumar Dharmasena – the ICC's Umpire of the Year – upheld Hill's decision. Understandably, Australia were furious.

The day before the Test, Clarke had reportedly been limping around the nets. At Lord's, Broad had smacked him on the badge of his helmet, and Clarke – as if hypnotised – had barely moved. Before the back became really bad, he had not played the short ball that way. Now he was at No. 4, a position he had spent time avoiding. And the early part of his innings was a struggle. But he was also committing the worst crime in batting: his back foot was inching to square leg. And Clarke was no flincher. This was a worrying sign.

Clarke's first 20 runs were his ugliest in living memory. Had England posted a leg slip, as at Lord's, he might not have got even that far. But from then on he became the painting of himself everyone admires. He pulled short balls from the pacemen, used his feet to Swann, and upper-cut over the slips; he hit Bresnan over mid-off, and slashed at wide ones when he felt like it. If Steve Waugh had played this innings in his more military style, people would have called it a fighting captain's knock. Clarke just batted until he was stopped on 187, by Broad, who had developed a knack against him with a troubling line and length. This time a short ball had Clarke hopping hurriedly in defence: the resultant ricochet disturbed the stumps. It was his 24th Test hundred, and fifth against England.

Broad had been made to wait 326 balls for his 200th Test wicket. But the wicket was more than just a personal milestone: it was a team achievement. For the first time since Derek Underwood, Bob Willis and Ian Botham all toured Sri Lanka in 1981-82, England fielded three bowlers with 200 Test wickets apiece (the other two were Swann, who went on to claim his 17th Test five-for, and the strangely subdued Anderson).

But Clarke had batted Australia into a position of dominance with the help of Smith, who did not depart until the second morning after a stand of 214, a Test record for the fourth wicket at Old Trafford, beating 189 by Sanjay Manjrekar and Mohammad Azharuddin for India in 1990. He had been booed to the crease the previous afternoon as the crowd mistook him for Warner, and could have been lbw before he had scored to a huge off-break from Swann that wasn't hitting quite enough leg stump to support England's review. Then, on 18, he appeared to nick Anderson. Erasmus disagreed, and England reviewed again – to no avail, and their evident consternation. On 24, he ought to have been given out lbw to Broad by Hill; unaccountably, the umpire said no. England had no reviews left. In the circumstances, Smith really should have completed a century.

When he skyed a slog-sweep, in came the real Warner, back from his southern African detour, to a cacophony of jeers. This was how the Colosseum must have been. The situation cried out for Cook to toss the ball to Root, Warner's victim in Birmingham's Walkabout two months earlier. But he kept Swann on – and it worked, as Warner nicked to slip. Confused by the fact that his bat had hit his pad at the same time as the ball, Warner reviewed, having somehow persuaded Clarke to back him up. As the replay showed up on the giant screen, jeers gave way to laughter.

Clarke and Siddle fell in quick succession after lunch, but Starc, back in place of the injured James Pattinson after being left out at Lord's, and Haddin – dropped by Prior on ten – smashed it around in an unbroken stand of 97. Clarke decided 527 for seven was enough. It was comfortably their highest Ashes total in 22 innings since they began the 2009 series with 674 for six at Cardiff, scene of another frustrating draw.

England began their reply like a team playing to avoid defeat, which would be good enough to retain the urn. Root mislaid his Lord's form, and scored eight off 57 balls before he was caught behind off Siddle, who then removed nightwatchman Bresnan. In a game where it seemed no one trusted the technology, Bresnan was oblivious to the fact that he hadn't touched the ball, a review, had he opted for it, would have saved him. England closed on a jittery 52 for two.

The third day, though, belonged to Pietersen. From the moment he walked out following the early demise of Trott, it was hard to tell if he was an international batsman or a strutting peacock. He soon turned his attention to Lyon, back in the side in place of Ashton Agar, whose two wickets had cost 124 each.

There is no way Lyon wouldn't have known what was coming. At first, Pietersen batted as if he was bored with him; then, as if he wanted to eat him. An optimistic lbw shout seemed to upset Pietersen, so he smashed a pair of sixes. Next over, Bell hit Lyon for a six as well. Pietersen was 55 when Clarke took Lyon off; he would finish with 113, and face only another ten balls from him. Between the 66th and the 78th overs, when the spinner pays his way by allowing the seamers to rest for the new ball, he did not bowl a single over. In a series where, no matter how badly Australia fared, Clarke was praised for his attacking instincts, he hid Lyon as if ashamed of him. On his way to his 23rd Test hundred, Pietersen overtook Graham Gooch's England record of 13,190 runs in all international cricket. Lyon stood motionless.

Pietersen, who would have been out on 62 had Australia bothered to refer an lbw shout from Watson, fell to Starc late on the third day, and England resumed next morning on 294 for seven, still 34 adrift of the follow-on mark. But Prior and Broad carved and caroused them to safety within eight overs, and England eventually had to settle for 368

Michael Steele, Getty Images

Inclined to attack: Kevin Pietersen takes the attack to Nathan Lyon in the scintillating hundred the Australians hoped wouldn't come.

and a deficit of 159. There was no shining star for Australia, though Siddle finished with four wickets from third change, again combining doggedness with a curious invisibility. And to think Australia began the series wondering whether to leave him out.

With just over five sessions left and the last-day forecast verging on the apocalyptic, Australia had to score quickly. England's careful run-rate (2.63 to Australia's 3.60) had taken time out of the game, and Clarke decided to open with Warner, who sprinted out to the sound of more boos and the theme tune from *Rocky*, played by the Barmy Army's trumpeter. Rogers went cheaply, but Warner looked far more at home at the top of the order. Then, on 41, he pulled a short ball from Bresnan towards deep square leg. "Is that Root?" people asked. The catch was held. "That *is* Root!"

One path to swift runs had thus been removed, but Cook was keen to quell another. And that meant wasting time. In almost three hours, England sent down 36 overs, despite Swann bowling 15 of them; one over from Broad may have begun before time itself. The tactic worked quite well, and when bad light intervened at 4.26 – much to Clarke's irritation – Australia had stumbled their way to 172 for seven.

Play began half an hour late on the final morning, and Clarke declared immediately, setting England 332 in 98 overs – which, with satellite images showing the rain closing in, felt notional. But Harris charged in all the same. In the third over, he trapped Cook with a beauty that swung in, and soon added Trott via a leg-side strangle. Clarke dropped Root at second slip off Siddle, who then made up for his disappointment by having Pietersen caught behind to leave England 27 for three. Pietersen reviewed, and nothing showed up on Hot Spot. But there was a noise, and the initial decision had been out; Pietersen stomped off.

Rain began falling at lunch, and barely relented, depriving everyone of the chance to see Harris charge in at Bell, and Australia attempt to take the final seven wickets. The contest might have been amazing. Instead, a draw was declared at 4.39, and the Ashes were safe in England's grasp.

For Australia, it was no sort of reward after all their damaged and poorly crafted parts had come together to form a unit that had proved they could win an Ashes Test. And those who thought Clarke was too mild-mannered to be the Australian captain should have seen

OLD TRAFFORD NOTES AND QUOTES

Political fluctuations back home meant Australia's tour spanned the tenures of three prime ministers. Kevin Rudd, whose 84-day premiership was sandwiched between fellow Labor MP Julia Gillard and the Liberal Party's Tony Abbott, took to online punditry before lunch on the first day. Reacting to the wicket of Usman Khawaja, Rudd tweeted: "That was one of the worst cricket umpiring decisions I have ever seen."

Chris Rogers looked set for his maiden Test century when, on 84, his concentration was broken by movement in the pavilion. He pulled away when Daniel Salpietro, a former team-mate at the Prahran club in Melbourne, moved in the seating area above the sightscreen – and Rogers was lbw to Swann next ball. "I know who the guy was and I will make a phone call," joked Rogers. "But I am not going to blame him. I think. Much." A chastened Salpietro insisted he had been trying to persuade a steward to stop spectators walking in and out of a door.

David Warner opted for humour as he faced the media during his first Test back after a ban for punching Joe Root. "Hooked another one to Rooty," he said, after Root had caught him. "Out of all the people on the field, it was quite comical. I can't wait to read Twitter later." Asked what Root had said to him when he came out to bat, Warner replied: "Yeah, Joey... He said it's been a long couple of months, hasn't it? I turned around and had a smile. But I've got a long memory, so that's all right."

Shane Warne used his post-match column in the *Daily Telegraph* to criticise the attitude of England's players. "A lot of us reporting and commentating on the game were really taken aback by the way the England players were interviewing," he wrote. "To me there were a few moments at Old Trafford when I thought, 'Hang on, who do you think you are?' I saw an interview with Ian Ward after day two and he said it had been a tough couple of days for England, which it had been, but Graeme Swann replied, 'No, not really. We will just go out and bat now on this flat Old Trafford wicket.' Matt Prior was also very smug in his comments, which leads me to think perhaps it is a conscious effort or direction from Andy Flower to be arrogant and dismissive of the opposition."

the look in his eyes when the umpires took the players off on the fourth evening. Clarke could overcome his back. He could overcome rifts in the Australian dressing-room. He could bat for an entire team when he needed to. But he couldn't make the sun shine on Australian cricket. No hero could.

Man of the Match: M. J. Clarke.   *Attendance:* 121,137.

Close of play: first day, Australia 303-3 (Clarke 125, Smith 70); second day, England 52-2 (Cook 36, Trott 2); third day, England 294-7 (Prior 6, Broad 9); fourth day, Australia 172-7 (Clarke 30, Harris 0).

Australia

S. R. Watson c Cook b Bresnan	19	– (4) c Pietersen b Bresnan 18
C. J. L. Rogers lbw b Swann	84	– (1) c Prior b Broad 12
U. T. Khawaja c Prior b Swann	1	– b Swann 24
*M. J. Clarke b Broad	187	– (5) not out 30
S. P. D. Smith c Bairstow b Swann	89	– (6) run out 19
D. A. Warner c Trott b Swann	5	– (2) c Root b Bresnan 41
†B. J. Haddin not out	65	– c Broad b Anderson 8
P. M. Siddle b Swann	1	
M. A. Starc not out	66	– (8) c Swann b Anderson 11
R. J. Harris (did not bat)		– (9) not out 0
L-b 6, w 2, n-b 2	10	B 4, l-b 2, w 3 9

1/76 (1) 2/82 (3)   (7 wkts dec, 146 overs) 527
3/129 (2) 4/343 (5)
5/365 (6) 6/427 (4) 7/430 (8)

1/23 (1)   (7 wkts dec, 36 overs) 172
2/74 (2) 3/99 (3)
4/103 (4) 5/133 (6) 6/152 (7) 7/172 (8)

N. M. Lyon did not bat.

Anderson 33–6–116–0; Broad 33–6–108–1; Bresnan 32–6–114–1; Swann 43–2–159–5; Root 4–0–18–0; Trott 1–0–6–0. *Second innings*—Anderson 8–0–37–2; Broad 7–2–30–1; Swann 15–0–74–1; Bresnan 6–0–25–2.

England

*A. N. Cook c Haddin b Starc	62	– lbw b Harris	0
J. E. Root c Haddin b Siddle	8	– not out	13
T. T. Bresnan c Haddin b Siddle	1		
I. J. L. Trott c Clarke b Harris	5	– (3) c Haddin b Harris	11
K. P. Pietersen lbw b Starc	113	– (4) c Haddin b Siddle	8
I. R. Bell b Harris	60	– (5) not out	4
J. M. Bairstow c Watson b Starc	22		
†M. J. Prior c Warner b Siddle	30		
S. C. J. Broad c Haddin b Lyon	32		
G. P. Swann c Haddin b Siddle	11		
J. M. Anderson not out	3		
B 3, l-b 17, n-b 1	21	W 1	1

1/47 (2) 2/49 (3) 3/64 (4)   (139.3 overs) 368   1/0 (1)   (3 wkts, 20.3 overs) 37
4/110 (1) 5/225 (6) 6/277 (7)   2/15 (3) 3/27 (4)
7/280 (5) 8/338 (9) 9/353 (10) 10/368 (8)

Harris 31–9–82–2; Starc 27–5–76–3; Lyon 35–12–95–1; Watson 15–7–26–0; Siddle 29.3–7–63–4; Smith 2–0–6–0. *Second innings*—Harris 7–3–13–2; Starc 4–2–6–0; Watson 2–2–0–0; Lyon 3–0–8–0; Siddle 3.3–0–8–1; Clarke 1–0–2–0.

Umpires: M. Erasmus and A. L. Hill. Third umpire: H. D. P. K. Dharmasena.
Referee: R. S. Madugalle.

ENGLAND v AUSTRALIA

Fourth Investec Ashes Test

LAWRENCE BOOTH

At Chester-le-Street, August 9–12. England won by 74 runs. Toss: England.

As rallying cries go, "let's spice it up a bit" was not quite Henry V at Agincourt, or Churchill and his beaches. But for a group of English cricketers in search of their own tilt at history, it did the job well enough. On the fourth evening of a fluctuating Test, Australia were chasing 299 for a victory that would have turned the series finale into an unexpected crack at redemption, if not the urn. They had just lost Warner to a Bresnan snorter, but even at 168 for three they knew one more decent partnership would break the back of it. Then Cook replaced Anderson with Broad – and issued his instructions.

Nearly two hours later, Broad had penned a piece of Ashes lore to match his burst at The Oval four years earlier, sweeping through Australia with six for 20 in 45 balls. In all, nine wickets had fallen in an elongated session. And, for the first time in 36 years, England had a 3–0 lead over Australia. Spice it up? Broad obviously preferred something with a little more kick than table salt.

Ryan Pierse, Getty Images

Taking the bait: Jonathan Trott has his technique picked apart by Ryan Harris.

This climax-with-a-twist was played out under suitably ominous skies. Rain that had first appeared during the lunch break, with Australia 11 without loss, delayed the restart until 2.50. And throughout a final session that began at 5.05 – and 120 for one – black clouds scudded across the northern horizon and shed their load somewhere around Newcastle. At 7.20, with Broad rampant, Australia nine down, and the umpires fussing over the light, Cook brought on Root's off-breaks. All the while, up on the hill, Lumley Castle surveyed its first Ashes Test with a detachment that felt out of place. This was Test cricket as only northern England knows it: dark, brooding, elemental.

Then a chink in the clouds. Sunshine meant the seamers could return, with play now deep into the extra half-hour claimed by Cook. Anderson, an increasingly listless presence ever since his First Test exertions, sent down a tired over, before Broad – it had to be Broad – persuaded Siddle to chip to mid-off. Not even an exhausted Anderson was going to drop that. He thought briefly about hurling the ball into the crowd, but decided his team-mate might like a keepsake. Modern pros can be softies too.

And so, at 7.40, it was all over. England had secured a victory that brought them three series wins in a row against Australia for the first time since the 1950s. It was also their 48th win at home against Australia, to set against 47 defeats; the last time England had moved ahead on this equation was after winning the First Test of 1997 (39–38). Their players jumped up and down in a huddle, like teenage students celebrating a full house of A* grades.

Top of the class was Broad, whose haul of six for 50 brought him 11 for 121 in the match, the best for England against Australia since Phil Tufnell's 11 for 93 at The Oval in 1997. That game, though, had simply provided England with one of their then-familiar consolation wins. This one felt meaningful, as much as sport can be, for it confirmed a superiority over the Australians that had first been sensed at The Oval four years earlier, then cemented during the 3–1 victory in 2010-11.

Broad was superb, even if it had taken him a while. Like the rest of the England attack, he dropped too short as Australia advanced menacingly to 147 for one. At tea, the bowlers

Right on time: England wrap up their third successive series victory over Australia, after Stuart Broad summons one of his special spells.

resolved to sort out their lengths; Broad himself had described the pitch as one on which it was "a crime to be back-foot-punched". Soon after, Swann – one of the main culprits – removed Khawaja, whose bat became tangled with his front pad as he played forward, and Bresnan returned to unseat the dangerous Warner. It was the incision England needed. Broad barged through.

He began with a ball that was more of a peach, straightening off the seam and hitting the top of Clarke's off stump, as Anderson had done at Trent Bridge. In Broad's next over, Smith tried to pull a short one, but the speedometer was regularly over 90mph now: amid a flurry of just-too-late bat and gloves, the ball ricocheted on to the stumps. Six deliveries later, Bresnan – like Broad, getting it to reverse – pinned Watson leg-before as he moved too far across his stumps, perhaps unsettled by the tension. (Naturally he reviewed it.) And eight balls after that, Broad wrung another lbw verdict out of Tony Hill to see off Haddin. The inevitable review did little to ease Hill's discomfort in what had been an awful match for his reputation: the ball was *just* clipping leg stump, according to Hawk-Eye. "Not again," muttered Haddin, conspiratorially, if a touch unfairly.

But if Hill's decision felt like guesswork, England were not complaining. Broad trapped Harris plumb in front, bowled the swishing Lyon, then completed his best figures against Australia by ousting Siddle. As at Lord's against New Zealand three months earlier, he had ambushed the opposition almost by himself.

The jubilation meant it was easy to forget the batting of Bell. At 49 for three in their second innings, England led by only 17 when he walked out to join Pietersen. It was the kind of moment on which matches, and entire series, can hinge. But Harris concluded a bull-like ten-over burst that had china-shopped the top order, and Bell – as if to redress the balance – got going with a couple of late cuts as delicate as a Ming vase. For once, he was overshadowing Pietersen, but then Bell had been overshadowing pretty well the whole series – the only England batsman for whom the Australians seemed not to have a game

CHESTER-LE-STREET NOTES AND QUOTES

Alastair Cook was on the back foot in his pre-Test press conference, following Shane Warne's criticism of his team's attitude in Manchester. "I've got no qualms with the way we've gone about our business in this series," he said. "The way we've conducted ourselves has been very good."

Warne kept up his Twitter assault on Cook's captaincy throughout this Test, calling it "very defensive and negative" – at least until Australia's fatal collapse. He also questioned Cook's decision to bring on Tim Bresnan ahead of Stuart Broad after tea on the fourth day. Moments later, Bresnan removed David Warner, and the slide was on.

The inventor of Hot Spot reacted to growing doubts over the effectiveness of his technology by issuing a statement after the first day's play. "The type and thickness of the protective coating unquestionably affects the thermal signature of the Hot Spot system," wrote Warren Brennan.

Broad shrugged off growing resentment of him among Australian supporters when he spoke publicly for the first time since standing his ground at Trent Bridge. "I don't think you want Australians to love you because that means you're not doing well," he said. "There are a few England players from the 1990s and early 2000s who would like to have been seen as villains."

plan. A stand of 106 ended when Lyon outmanoeuvred Pietersen for the second time in the match, dragging him to the off side as he aimed repeatedly to leg; a leading edge to cover was the almost inevitable result. And Bell was 96 when Lyon prised out the vulnerable Bairstow.

An involuntary cut just out of Clarke's reach at slip took Bell to 99, before an uppish leg-side single next ball brought up his 20th Test century, placing him alongside England's batting coach Graham Gooch, and Gooch's mentor Ken Barrington. Only Maurice Leyland in 1934, and David Gower in 1985, had scored three hundreds in a home Ashes for England. Throw in Sydney 2010-11, and Bell had four centuries in five Tests against Australia – with barely a moment's inelegance that anyone could remember.

On what turned out to be the final morning, Harris thundered in once more with the new ball, hitting the stumps twice in two deliveries: Bell went to one that kept low, the out-of-nick Prior to one that bounced, then flew down off a defensive poke. England were 251 for seven, a lead of 219. But, not for the first time, they seized the moment. Bresnan – nightwatchman again – went on the attack, and Swann followed suit. Sixty-three runs flowed in the first eight overs after Prior was out. Harris finished with seven for 117, the best by an Australian against England since Glenn McGrath's seven for 76 at Headingley in 2001, but the tourists needed 299, a total they had bettered only once in seven innings in the series.

Australia ought to have been chasing fewer after again having the better of the first-innings exchanges. England had begun solidly after resisting the temptation to replace Bresnan with Graham Onions, born a few miles away in Gateshead. Root fell in a cagey opening session to the parsimonious Watson, after Hill missed the outside edge but Australia successfully reviewed; and Trott had to drag himself off, having moved sweetly to 49 before nudging Lyon to backward short leg. Even so, at 149 for two on the first afternoon, with the sun out, they had Australia at their mercy.

After being hit out of the attack by a frenetic Pietersen, Lyon returned and, staying round the wicket, hustled an arm-ball – or possibly a non-turning off-break – past his grope; Haddin pocketed the edge. Cook shouldered arms to a delivery that jagged back alarmingly to give Jackson Bird, picked ahead of Mitchell Starc, his first Ashes wicket. Then, in the first over after tea, Bell relived his horror-movie moment from Ahmedabad nine months earlier and lofted Lyon to mid-off.

Chastened, England went into their shells. A subdued Prior fell for the ninth time in Tests to Siddle, and Bairstow lingered for over an hour on 12. Two balls after breaking the drought, he tried to sweep Lyon and was given out leg-before. Broad swiped to cover,

Swann hooked to deep backward square. It was headless stuff. A last-wicket stand between Bresnan and Anderson of 24, ended almost immediately on the second morning, gave England something to defend – but not a lot.

Broad supplied early hope. With the score on 12, he bowled Warner and had Khawaja caught behind as he tried to get his bat out of the way; it was Prior's 200th Test catch. When Clarke's hard hands and concrete feet gave Cook a head-high chance at first slip, Australia were 49 for three. And it was 76 for four when Smith lunged at Bresnan in the second over after lunch.

But they began to ride their luck. Bresnan dropped a tough, instinctive, return catch with Watson on five. Next over, Rogers – on 49 – edged Broad into the slips, where Swann at second dived low to his right, grassing a chance that was heading straight to Cook at first. As the clouds rolled in from the west, Broad rumbled in from the south, time and again passing the outside edge of the left-handed Rogers. Watson, meanwhile, was looking more at ease away from the new-ball limelight. Australia were dragging things round.

The stand was worth 129 when Watson was caught down the leg side off Broad. At the other end, Rogers was stuck on 96, as if in some recurring nightmare. For 19 balls, all

WORTH THE WAIT

Most first-class hundreds before first in Tests:

		First Test 100				First Test 100
70	A. Sandham (England)	1929-30		61	D. S. Lehmann (Australia)	2002-03
68	C. B. Fry (England)	1905		**60**	**C. J. L. Rogers (Australia)**	**2013**
67	G. A. Hick (England)	1992-93		54	E. Tyldesley (England)	1927-28
64	W. G. Grace (England)	1880		52	P. N. Kirsten (South Africa)	1994

from Swann, he stayed put – and he might have been out to three of them. Then, after half an hour of torment, a meaty sweep disappeared through square leg, and Rogers could celebrate a first Test hundred at the age of 35, though his reaction was calmness itself. Only one older Australian had made a maiden Test century: Arthur Richardson was 12 days short of his 38th birthday when he scored a round 100 at Headingley in 1926. Not even the England fielders, who had teased Rogers that he would never get another chance, could begrudge him. "I didn't have a care in the world," he joked.

When the Australians began the third morning on 222 for five, England knew that only five quick wickets would keep them in touch. They got precisely that, though not before Hill was made to swallow his pride once more. When Broad appealed for leg-before against Harris, Hill somehow remained unmoved, so England asked for a review. One replay on the giant screen was enough to persuade all 13 players to troop off, even before the DRS had cranked into gear – leaving Hill to observe the protocol and raise his finger to a field that was virtually empty, before racing off for his loyal colleague, Aleem Dar. Broad, already halfway back to the pavilion, had his five-for.

Australia led by 32, which didn't feel like quite enough on a pitch that had begun as a motley collection of loose plates and incipient cracks. But that reckoned without the dynamic between their bowlers and England's top three. Either side of lunch, Harris bowled Root with a gem, induced an awful drive from Cook, then bounced out Trott.

Clarke chose not to post a third man to Bell until he was into the twenties, by which time the ball had lost its hardness and – as per the pattern of the series – blunted the Australian bowlers their threat. While their openers were easing their way to 109 before tea on the fourth day, none of that seemed to matter. But Broad was in one of those moods.

Man of the Match: S. C. J. Broad.   *Attendance:* 62,958.

Close of play: first day, England 238-9 (Bresnan 12, Anderson 16); second day, Australia 222-5 (Rogers 101, Haddin 12); third day, England 234-5 (Bell 105, Bresnan 4).

England

*A. N. Cook lbw b Bird	51	– c Haddin b Harris	22
J. E. Root c Haddin b Watson	16	– b Harris	2
I. J. L. Trott c Khawaja b Lyon	49	– c Haddin b Harris	23
K. P. Pietersen c Haddin b Lyon	26	– c Rogers b Lyon	44
I. R. Bell c Harris b Lyon	6	– b Harris	113
J. M. Bairstow lbw b Lyon	14	– c Haddin b Lyon	28
†M. J. Prior lbw b Siddle	17	– (8) b Harris	0
T. T. Bresnan not out	12	– (7) c and b Harris	45
S. C. J. Broad c Warner b Harris	3	– c Smith b Harris	13
G. P. Swann c Lyon b Harris	13	– not out	30
J. M. Anderson b Bird	16	– c Haddin b Lyon	0
B 5, l-b 1, w 3, n-b 6	15	B 4, l-b 5, w 1	10

1/34 (2) 2/107 (3) 3/149 (4) (92 overs) 238
4/153 (5) 5/155 (5) 6/189 (7)
7/193 (6) 8/198 (9) 9/214 (10) 10/238 (11)

1/17 (2) 2/42 (1) (95.1 overs) 330
3/49 (3) 4/155 (4)
5/221 (6) 6/251 (5) 7/251 (8)
8/275 (9) 9/317 (7) 10/330 (11)

Harris 19–3–70–2; Bird 22–9–58–2; Watson 13–6–21–1; Siddle 18–6–41–1; Lyon 20–7–42–4. *Second innings*—Harris 28–2–117–7; Bird 20.3–6–67–0; Watson 6.3–1–22–0; Siddle 17–4–59–0; Lyon 22.1–3–55–3; Smith 1–0–1–0.

Australia

C. J. L. Rogers c Prior b Swann	110	– c Trott b Swann	49
D. A. Warner b Broad	3	– c Prior b Bresnan	71
U. T. Khawaja c Prior b Broad	0	– lbw b Swann	21
*M. J. Clarke c Cook b Broad	6	– b Broad	21
S. P. D. Smith c Prior b Bresnan	17	– b Broad	2
S. R. Watson c Prior b Broad	68	– lbw b Bresnan	2
†B. J. Haddin lbw b Swann	13	– lbw b Broad	4
P. M. Siddle c Cook b Anderson	5	– c Anderson b Broad	23
R. J. Harris lbw b Broad	28	– lbw b Broad	11
N. M. Lyon lbw b Anderson	4	– b Broad	8
J. M. Bird not out	0	– not out	1
B 2, l-b 11, w 1, n-b 2	16	B 6, l-b 5	11

1/12 (2) 2/12 (3) 3/49 (4) (89.3 overs) 270
4/76 (5) 5/205 (6) 6/224 (7)
7/233 (1) 8/245 (8) 9/258 (10) 10/270 (9)

1/109 (1) 2/147 (3) (68.3 overs) 224
3/168 (2) 4/174 (4)
5/175 (5) 6/179 (6) 7/181 (7)
8/199 (9) 9/211 (10) 10/224 (8)

Anderson 25–8–65–2; Broad 24.3–7–71–5; Bresnan 19–3–63–1; Swann 18–5–48–2; Trott 3–0–10–0. *Second innings*—Anderson 16–1–73–0; Broad 18.3–3–50–6; Bresnan 13–2–36–2; Swann 18–6–53–2; Root 3–2–1–0.

Umpires: Aleem Dar and A. L. Hill.   Third umpire: M. Erasmus.
Referee: R. S. Mahanama.

At Northampton, August 16–17 (not first-class). **Drawn. ‡England Lions 269-7 dec** (M. M. Ali 61, G. S. Ballance 104; N. M. Lyon 3-80). **Australians 227-6.** *This match should have featured Northamptonshire, but they were busy winning the domestic Twenty20 competition at Edgbaston. Instead, Eoin Morgan led England Lions in a low-key two-day game. Gary Ballance brightened up a first day in which the opening session was lost to rain, making a case for selection for the Ashes tour. On the second, the Australians' stand-in captain Shane Watson hit 45 from 44 balls, including a six and seven fours off Simon Kerrigan, which proved to be a warm-up for the Oval Test.*

ENGLAND v AUSTRALIA

Fifth Investec Ashes Test

Steven Lynch

At The Oval, August 21–25. Drawn. Toss: Australia. Test debuts: S. C. Kerrigan, C. R. Woakes; J. P. Faulkner.

A series beset by umpiring controversy ended with one more, when Aleem Dar and Kumar Dharmasena called off play for bad light with England needing 21 from four overs to complete an unprecedented 4–0 Ashes triumph. A draw was probably the right outcome: Australia scarcely deserved to lose after making all the running. But the strict adherence to the rulebook was bad news for the crowd after a boring third day and a pouring fourth – and it didn't feel like much better news for cricket, either.

With the Ashes decided, the match had little riding on it – although a draw put England second in the world rankings, above India – but there was still the subplot of the imminent return series in Australia. That, and some provocative pronouncements from the Australian camp about England's tactics, all but obliged Clarke to make a game of it, and his teatime declaration left a tempting target of 227 in 44 overs. No Test team had ever been bowled out so quickly after such a late declaration and, as Pietersen led the charge, England regained momentum – and some of the moral high ground as Clarke slowed things down – before hostilities were resumed at Brisbane in November.

At 7.35, after Bell was athletically run out by Starc off his own bowling, the umpires conferred for the final time. Oddly, their light meters had only just been sent out, even though the floodlights were increasingly taking over from the setting sun. Dar gently pushed Clarke away, who was trying to see the reading. "I asked him politely not to touch me," Clarke complained. "If I'd touched him I'd have been suspended for three games." Bad light had forced a suspension on the second evening, and the regulations stipulated that play had to cease if the same level was reached later. The batting side no longer had the option of continuing

Not according to plan: Simon Kerrigan endured a tough debut.

– but there was no common-sense option either. It was just unfortunate that the day's 98 overs had started half an hour late after overnight rain, and that the over-rate of both sides was so poor.

The crowd – happy enough with the 3–0 scoreline, as were England's players after some fleeting disappointment – behaved reasonably well, apart from some inevitable booing. (Clarke, the orchestrator of the exciting finish, was a particularly inappropriate target.) But a similarly inflexible approach in different circumstances might have led to serious problems – what if the Ashes had still been alive, or India were about to beat Pakistan at Kolkata? "It's totally unsatisfactory the way the game ended," fumed the ECB's chairman Giles Clarke. "The rules are clearly unacceptable and I expect [the ICC] to change them."

England were up against it once they lost the toss, having abandoned their four-bowler policy to accommodate a second spinner, the Lancashire slow left-armer Simon Kerrigan. He might not have played had Monty Panesar not blotted his copybook shortly after being left out of the Third Test. Even Kerrigan, after being mauled by Watson, might have wished Panesar had not adapted England's old "sprinkler" celebration by urinating over nightclub bouncers in Brighton. Kerrigan's inclusion also meant a first cap for Warwickshire's Chris Woakes, a far better batsman than Steven Finn or Chris Tremlett, and chosen now to avoid an attack light on seam options; Woakes batted coolly, but his bowling made little impression. The changes had been sparked by a back injury to Tim Bresnan, while Jonny Bairstow was also dropped after a modest run; Tremlett, meanwhile, responded to his omission with a career-best eight for 96 for Surrey against Durham. The selectors denied experimenting, but the same side would never have been chosen had the Ashes still been up for grabs.

Australia shuffled their pack again, dropping Usman Khawaja and Jackson Bird, recalling Starc for the second time in the series, and introducing James Faulkner, a strapping all-rounder from Tasmania. He was their 17th player of the summer, equalling the Australian record for any Test series overseas, set in the West Indies in 1983-84. Faulkner batted forthrightly, bowled with variation, and enlivened the wet fourth day by suggesting spectators should also get refunds for the third, when England had scored so slowly; it was mischievous stuff from a debutant in a team trailing 3–0.

The changes meant Watson continued to be zapped around the order like a pinball. After apparently nailing down the No. 6 spot in the previous Test, he now moved up to first drop – and responded with a career-best which doubled as a last laugh during a summer in which his stiff-legged technique had often been the punchline. On a hot and sunny opening day, Watson had strutted in after Warner edged behind, set sail with a beefy square-drive off Anderson, then faced the sort of lbw appeal that had often been his downfall. But it was not given, and England correctly decided against a review. Watson was launched: he enjoyed the debut of Woakes, flicking three fours in his third over, hammered Swann for a sweet straight six and positively revelled in the introduction of Kerrigan, swatting away some undistinguished deliveries as 28 came from his first two overs. Watson had also savaged him in the previous week's England Lions game, and Kerrigan's nerves, plus lack of a solid basic action – a run-up of three paces, then almost no front-arm movement – meant he was a peripheral figure for the rest of the match. One or two even diagnosed an untimely case of the yips.

Playing straighter after inching his guard to leg, Watson surged on. By lunch he had 80, the third-highest score by a No. 3 in the first session of a Test, behind two famous Australians, Charles Macartney and Don Bradman. The departure of the adhesive Rogers slowed things down, then Anderson moved past Bob Willis's 325 Test wickets by nipping one back into Clarke's off stump. Watson soon reached his third Test century – his first for 48 innings – but was badly dropped on 104 by Cook at slip, diving to his right off Anderson. Smith, who survived an airy waft at his first ball, celebrated by smacking Swann for six, and the pair defied their many doubters by doubling the total.

Woakes thought he had his first Test scalp when Watson was given out by Dharmasena on 166, but this time the review was successful (only the second time Watson had successfully overturned an lbw decision in nine attempts). But in the third-last over he skimmed a pull low to deep square, where Pietersen swooped for a fine catch.

The weather changed next day, wiping out the morning session, but England's fortunes remained the same. Smith made up for his swishy start by batting sensibly, although he occasionally broke free, unfurling one superb back-foot square-drive off Broad. He reached his maiden Test century by clouting Trott back over his head for six; the bowler had some revenge when Haddin chopped on later in the same over after a perky partnership of 65. With a declaration imminent, Faulkner collected three fours in a Broad over, then Harris slapped Swann for two sixes. Smith was unbeaten, his six-and-a-half-hour innings ensuring a run in a side whose batting order suddenly – almost accidentally – seemed settled. He was the eighth Smith to score a Test century, edging seven Taylors for clan honours.

Graham Morris

Oval fruits: Shane Watson cashes in against England's two makeweight debutants.

England's openers had little trouble surviving before a slightly early close, when the umpires made what later became an important call on the light: if they had stayed on for the remaining three minutes there would have been no benchmark for the final day.

The third morning dawned fine but, with 261 still needed to avoid the follow-on, England's batsmen eschewed risks against some disciplined bowling, especially from Harris and Lyon. The only morning casualty was Cook, whose indifferent series continued when he poked outside off shortly after drinks. The opening session brought 65 runs from 26.3 overs – sadly for the crowd, the sprightliest scoring of a day straight out of those black-and-white Ashes Tests of the 1950s. England needed to conserve wickets, but Root batted nearly four hours for 68, then Trott fell to the first delivery with the second new ball for 40 in 193 minutes. Even Pietersen seemed unable to come to terms with a slow, bland pitch: after grafting to a three-hour fifty he toe-ended Starc to first slip.

Woakes cracked his first ball square for four, and was still there at stumps, by which time England had scored only 215 runs in 98.3 overs. It wasn't pretty, but as an insurance against defeat it was effective. In mid-afternoon the scoreboard had got stuck at 181 for four: such was the scoring-rate that it was some time before anyone noticed. Defeat – or indeed a result of any kind – seemed even less likely when the fourth day was washed away by almost incessant rain (a football match at nearby Charlton Athletic was abandoned at half-time because of a waterlogged pitch).

Expectations for an exciting conclusion were therefore not high, although England's batsmen did show more enterprise, especially after saving the follow-on. Bell was strangled down the leg side, a maiden Test wicket for left-arm Faulkner, but Prior showed signs

THE OVAL NOTES AND QUOTES

Darren Lehmann was relieved of 20% of his match fee – about £2,000 – by the ICC after an injudicious late-night interview given to Australian rock music radio network Triple M on the eve of the Fifth Test. Lehmann called Stuart Broad's refusal to walk at Trent Bridge "blatant cheating", and incited Australian crowds to abuse him during the Ashes tour. "Certainly our players haven't forgotten, they're calling him everything under the sun as they go past," Lehmann said. "I hope the Australian public just give it to him right from the word go for the whole summer and I hope he cries and he goes home." Lehmann was punished for a Level 1 offence under the ICC Code of Conduct.

Australian captain Michael Clarke was met with some stern verbal defence from Kevin Pietersen when looking to inject some heat into a slow-scoring third day. "No one in your team likes you," proffered Clarke, only to be met with a shrug and smile. "You're captain," Pietersen was said to have replied. "And no one likes you."

England's watchful batting on that third day, when they scored 215 runs in 98.3 overs, prompted a feisty broadside from Australian debutant James Faulkner. "I know the fans get a refund for their tickets today but maybe they should have for yesterday," said Faulkner, whose left-arm seam had then yet to collect a Test wicket. "It didn't surprise me. I suppose any time [England] feel threatened they go into their shell and play pretty defensive cricket."

of a return to form before skying to Starc at mid-on. Swann hit out cheerfully, then provided Faulkner with another wicket in a spell of four for 19.

Watson was promoted to open again as Australia looked to build quickly on their lead of 115. He drilled a catch straight to Broad at mid-off before scoring, but down it went. However, he soon launched Swann to Pietersen at long-off, and wickets continued to tumble – including Haddin first ball – as Clarke tried to set up his last-throw declaration.

It came at tea, and soon looked optimistic when Cook and Root collected boundaries in the first two overs. Root then pushed, firm-footed, at Harris, providing Haddin with his 29th dismissal of the series – a Test record, beating Rod Marsh's 28 in the 1982-83 Ashes – but Cook and Trott kept the score moving until the 20th over. Then Cook, falling over a little, was lbw to Faulkner. In came Pietersen. According to Mike Atherton, you can tell when Pietersen is up for the fight, as his flourishing follow-through hits his own backside – and it was receiving regular slaps now. Faulkner was punished with a four off the legs and a rasping cover-drive; Starc's return was greeted with a stinging straight-drive, and later he was driven, pulled and flicked for three fours in an over as Pietersen motored to a 36-ball fifty, England's quickest in an Ashes Test.

The last 15 overs started with 85 needed. Pietersen's ebullient 62 ended with a well-judged catch by Warner on the longest of long-on boundaries. Trott soon followed, but England were still in the driving seat. But the light was fading fast, field-placings started taking longer as the Australians contemplated that 4–0 scoreline, and eventually the light meters were consulted. That was that. It was a sad end to a stirring Sunday which produced 447 runs in all.

After the presentations and the fireworks, there was time for one more story of the wrong kind. England's celebrations concluded, late in the evening, when several players urinated on the pitch. Australians still in the press box gleefully reported the ceremony, and the team later apologised for an act seen in some quarters as a comment on the lifeless tracks which had hamstrung the series – and in others as an act of solidarity with the absent Panesar.

Man of the Match: S. R. Watson.   *Attendance:* 113,145.
Men of the Series: England – I. R. Bell; Australia – R. J. Harris.
Compton–Miller medal: I. R. Bell.
Close of play: first day, Australia 307-4 (Smith 66, Siddle 18); second day, England 32-0 (Cook 17, Root 13); third day, England 247-4 (Bell 29, Woakes 15); fourth day, no play.

Australia

C. J. L. Rogers c Trott b Swann	23			
D. A. Warner c Prior b Anderson	6	– (1) c and b Anderson	12
S. R. Watson c Pietersen b Broad	176	– (2) c Pietersen b Swann	26
*M. J. Clarke b Anderson	7	– (5) not out	28
S. P. D. Smith not out	138	– (6) c Swann b Broad	7
P. M. Siddle b Anderson	23			
†B. J. Haddin b Trott	30	– (4) c Prior b Broad	0
J. P. Faulkner c Trott b Woakes	23	– (3) c Prior b Broad	22
M. A. Starc b Swann	13	– (8) not out	13
R. J. Harris c and b Anderson	33	– (7) b Broad	1
N. M. Lyon not out	0			
B 1, l-b 12, w 2, n-b 5	20	L-b 2	2

1/11 (2) 2/118 (1)   (9 wkts dec, 128.5 overs) 492   1/34 (1)   (6 wkts dec, 23 overs) 111
3/144 (4) 4/289 (3) 5/320 (6)   2/44 (2) 3/50 (4)
6/385 (7) 7/422 (8) 8/446 (9) 9/491 (10)   4/67 (3) 5/83 (6) 6/85 (7)

Anderson 29.5–4–95–4; Broad 31–4–128–1; Swann 33–4–95–2; Woakes 24–7–96–1; Kerrigan 8–0–53–0; Trott 3–0–12–1. *Second innings*—Anderson 6–1–27–1; Broad 10–2–43–4; Swann 7–0–39–1.

England

*A. N. Cook c Haddin b Harris	25	– lbw b Faulkner	34
J. E. Root c Watson b Lyon	68	– c Haddin b Harris	11
I. J. L. Trott lbw b Starc	40	– lbw b Faulkner	59
K. P. Pietersen c Watson b Starc	50	– c Warner b Harris	62
I. R. Bell c Haddin b Faulkner	45	– run out	17
C. R. Woakes c Clarke b Harris	25	– not out	17
†M. J. Prior c Starc b Faulkner	47	– not out	0
S. C. J. Broad b Starc	9			
G. P. Swann b Faulkner	34			
J. M. Anderson c Haddin b Faulkner	4			
S. C. Kerrigan not out	1			
B 11, l-b 10, w 5, n-b 3	29	L-b 4, n-b 2	6

1/68 (1) 2/118 (2) 3/176 (3)   (144.4 overs) 377   1/22 (2)   (5 wkts, 40 overs) 206
4/217 (4) 5/269 (6) 6/299 (5)   2/86 (1) 3/163 (4)
7/315 (8) 8/363 (9) 9/368 (10) 10/377 (9)   4/170 (3) 5/206 (5)

Starc 33–5–92–3; Harris 28–10–64–2; Faulkner 19.4–3–51–4; Siddle 28–7–74–0; Lyon 28–8–59–1; Smith 8–3–16–0. *Second innings*—Harris 5–0–21–2; Starc 7–0–48–0; Siddle 3–0–16–0; Lyon 10–0–44–0; Clarke 2–0–4–0; Faulkner 8–1–47–2; Watson 5–0–22–0.

Umpires: Aleem Dar and H. D. P. K. Dharmasena.   Third umpire: A. L. Hill.
Referee: R. S. Mahanama.

LIMITED-OVERS MATCH REPORTS BY DEAN WILSON

ENGLAND v AUSTRALIA

First NatWest Twenty20 International

At Southampton, August 29 (floodlit). Australia won by 39 runs. Toss: England. Twenty20 international debut: Fawad Ahmed.

It might have taken them 12 weeks, but Australia could finally celebrate their first international win of the tour – thanks to a record-breaking piece of brutality from the chunky Aaron Finch. In

Stu Forster, Getty Images

Getting it off his chest: Fawad Ahmed, Australia's Pakistan-born Muslim, celebrates a wicket – after taking a principled stand against Victoria Bitter branding.

63 balls of utter mayhem, Finch smashed 156 (the highest score in Twenty20 internationals, beating Brendon McCullum's 123 for New Zealand against Bangladesh at Pallekele in 2012-13). He peppered the leg side, launching 14 sixes, one more than South Africa's Richard Levi had managed against New Zealand at Hamilton in 2011-12. Only Levi had reached three figures faster, by 45 balls to Finch's 47, and Australia's final tally of 18 sixes beat the 17 that South Africa managed, also against England, at Centurion in 2009-10. No bowler was spared Finch's wrath, as Australia racked up their highest score in the format. England were no slouches in reply. The long-awaited international debut of leg-spinner Fawad Ahmed, a former asylum-seeker from Pakistan, produced no wickets, while Root's unbeaten 90 from 49 balls once again highlighted his adaptability, and took them to their second-highest total in Twenty20 cricket. But Finch had left them with far too much to do.

Man of the Match: A. J. Finch.   *Attendance:* 19,059.

Australia

		B	4	6
D. A. Warner *c 7 b 8*	1	5	0	0
A. J. Finch *b 11*	156	63	11	14
S. E. Marsh *c 1 b 10*	28	21	2	1
S. R. Watson *b 11*	37	16	4	2
G. J. Maxwell *b 11*	1	3	0	0
*G. J. Bailey *lbw b 9*	1	2	0	0
†M. S. Wade *not out*	15	7	2	1
J. P. Faulkner *not out*	5	3	0	0
L-b 2, w 2	4			

6 overs: 58-1   (20 overs)   248-6

1/11 2/125 3/226 4/227 5/228 6/242

M. G. Johnson, J. R. Hazlewood and Fawad Ahmed did not bat.

England

		B	4	6
M. J. Lumb *lbw b 9*	22	11	3	1
A. D. Hales *c 7 b 10*	8	9	1	0
L. J. Wright *c 7 b 10*	4	2	1	0
E. J. G. Morgan *c 5 b 9*	0	3	0	0
J. E. Root *not out*	90	49	13	1
R. S. Bopara *c 1 b 4*	45	29	4	1
†J. C. Buttler *b 8*	27	17	1	2
*S. C. J. Broad *not out*	4	2	1	0
B 1, w 6, n-b 2	9			

6 overs: 54-4   (20 overs)   209-6

1/33 2/33 3/37 4/42 5/137 6/203

S. T. Finn, D. R. Briggs and J. W. Dernbach did not bat.

Finn 4–0–45–1; Broad 4–0–47–1; Dernbach 4–0–34–3; Briggs 4–0–51–1; Bopara 1–0–15–0; Root 1–0–27–0; Wright 2–0–27–0.

Johnson 4–1–41–2; Hazlewood 4–0–43–2; Fawad Ahmed 4–0–43–0; Watson 4–0–42–1; Faulkner 4–0–39–1.

Umpires: R. J. Bailey and R. T. Robinson.   Third umpire: M. A. Gough.

ENGLAND v AUSTRALIA

Second NatWest Twenty20 International

At Chester-le-Street, August 31. England won by 27 runs. Toss: Australia.

In his last international match of the summer before being rested, Broad led his team to a series-squaring victory on the ground where he had played a starring role in the Fourth Ashes Test a couple of weeks earlier. This time, he could look on as his Nottinghamshire team-mate Alex Hales narrowly missed out – again – on England's first Twenty20 hundred. But Hales's 61-ball 94, in which all but two of his 13 boundaries came on the leg side, would be enough to take him to the top of ICC world rankings in the format – in a summer where he could barely buy a run in first-class cricket. England grew in confidence once Broad removed Finch in the second over. And, though Warner hit an aggressive 53, four high-quality overs from Dernbach meant Australia never got close.

Man of the Match: A. D. Hales.   *Attendance:* 14,129.

England		B	4	6
M. J. Lumb *c 7 b 11*	43	27	6	1
A. D. Hales *c 1 b 8*	94	61	11	2
L. J. Wright *c 9 b 8*	30	18	3	1
E. J. G. Morgan *c 10 b 11*	20	11	0	2
†J. C. Buttler *b 11*	0	1	0	0
R. S. Bopara *not out*	1	2	0	0
J. E. Root *not out*	1	1	0	0
L-b 5, n-b 1	6			

6 overs: 61-0   (20 overs) 195-5

1/111 2/157 3/187 4/187 5/194

*S. C. J. Broad, S. T. Finn, D. R. Briggs and J. W. Dernbach did not bat.

Johnson 4–0–32–0; Watson 2–0–24–0; Coulter-Nile 4–0–47–0; Faulkner 4–0–37–2; Fawad Ahmed 4–0–25–3; Maxwell 2–0–25–0.

Australia		B	4	6
D. A. Warner *c 2 b 11*	53	42	5	3
A. J. Finch *c 3 b 8*	5	5	1	0
S. R. Watson *run out*	7	6	1	0
S. E. Marsh *b 7*	13	14	0	1
*G. J. Bailey *lbw b 10*	23	13	1	1
G. J. Maxwell *c 1 b 11*	27	16	2	1
†M. S. Wade *b 10*	4	4	0	0
J. P. Faulkner *c 4 b 11*	5	5	1	0
M. G. Johnson *not out*	3	5	0	0
N. M. Coulter-Nile *c 10 b 9* ...	13	6	0	2
Fawad Ahmed *not out*	3	5	0	0
L-b 4, w 7, n-b 1	12			

6 overs: 42-2   (20 overs) 168-9

1/8 2/15 3/82 4/111 5/113 6/123 7/148 8/148 9/162

Finn 4–0–30–1; Broad 3–0–27–1; Dernbach 4–0–23–3; Briggs 3–0–25–2; Root 3–0–25–1; Bopara 3–0–34–0.

Umpires: R. J. Bailey and M. A. Gough.   Third umpire: R. T. Robinson.
Series referee: R. S. Mahanama.

At Edinburgh, September 3. AUSTRALIA beat SCOTLAND by 200 runs (see Cricket in Scotland, page 849).

ENGLAND v AUSTRALIA

First NatWest One-Day International

At Leeds, September 6. Abandoned.

Steady rain forced an abandonment just after 1.30. The sight of a few hardy souls in the stands added to the feeling of sympathy as Headingley suffered its third washout in five one-day internationals, following fixtures against West Indies in 2009 and 2012.

ENGLAND v AUSTRALIA

Second NatWest One-Day International

At Manchester, September 8. Australia won by 88 runs. Toss: England.

In the aftermath of one Ashes tussle and ahead of another, England chose to rest five first-choice players from this series, while a sixth – Tim Bresnan – was missing through injury. It prompted the former England captain Michael Vaughan to suggest that spectators who had paid good money to see the best talent should receive a rebate. Any grumbles would not have been alleviated by the result, as Clarke's eighth one-day hundred – and first against England – set up a comfortable win for Australia. The use of Stokes, a batting all-rounder, as third seamer behind Finn and Rankin left England light on bowling firepower, while a premeditated assault on Tredwell's off-spin allowed Clarke and Bailey, who made 82 off 67 balls, to canter through a fourth-wicket stand of 155 in 22 overs. England's pursuit of 316 hit trouble at 38 for three, and was derailed at 103 for five. Neither Pietersen's 60 nor Buttler's format-best 75 threatened Australia, especially with Johnson – who had removed Carberry and Trott in his second over – seemingly back to his best.

Man of the Match: M. J. Clarke. *Attendance:* 24,450.

Australia

S. E. Marsh c Buttler b Finn	0
A. J. Finch c Root b Tredwell	45
S. R. Watson c Buttler b Bopara	38
*M. J. Clarke c Buttler b Rankin	105
G. J. Bailey c Tredwell b Bopara	82
A. C. Voges not out	16
†M. S. Wade b Rankin	0
J. P. Faulkner c Morgan b Finn	18
M. G. Johnson not out	6
B 1, l-b 1, w 2, n-b 1	5

C. J. McKay and Fawad Ahmed did not bat.

1/0 (1)　2/60 (3)　　(7 wkts, 50 overs) 315
3/116 (2)　4/271 (5)
5/283 (4)　6/283 (7)　7/308 (8)　10 overs: 49-1

Finn 10–1–68–2; Rankin 10–0–49–2; Stokes 10–0–66–0; Bopara 10–0–57–2; Tredwell 8–0–60–1; Root 2–0–13–0.

England

K. P. Pietersen c Faulkner b Watson	60
M. A. Carberry c Clarke b Johnson	4
I. J. L. Trott c Wade b Johnson	0
J. E. Root b Faulkner	3
*E. J. G. Morgan c Clarke b McKay	54
R. S. Bopara c and b Voges	1
†J. C. Buttler c Johnson b Fawad Ahmed	75
B. A. Stokes c Bailey b McKay	5
J. C. Tredwell run out	1
S. T. Finn c Voges b McKay	16
W. B. Rankin not out	1
L-b 1, w 6	7

1/8 (2)　2/9 (3)　　　(44.2 overs) 227
3/38 (4)　4/97 (1)　5/103 (6)
6/154 (5)　7/167 (8)　8/169 (9)
9/216 (7)　10/227 (10)　10 overs: 38-2

McKay 9.2–1–47–3; Johnson 10–2–36–2; Faulkner 8–1–39–1; Voges 6–0–32–1; Fawad Ahmed 7–0–55–1; Watson 4–1–17–1.

Umpires: R. A. Kettleborough and S. Ravi.　Third umpire: Aleem Dar.

ENGLAND v AUSTRALIA

Third NatWest One-Day International

At Birmingham, September 11 (day/night). No result. Toss: Australia.

In scenes that were becoming all too familiar in Birmingham, only 15.1 overs were possible before the rain that had initially delayed the start returned, with a vengeance. Still, there was enough time for Pietersen to run out his opening partner Carberry, then be caught at square leg after Johnson's short ball beat his pull shot for pace.

England

M. A. Carberry run out	....	1
K. P. Pietersen c Bailey b Johnson	....	6
I. J. L. Trott not out	....	28
J. E. Root c and b Voges	....	12
*E. J. G. Morgan not out	....	5
W 7	....	7

1/5 (1) 2/26 (2) (3 wkts, 15.1 overs) 59
3/52 (4) 10 overs: 43-2

R. S. Bopara, †J. C. Buttler, B. A. Stokes, J. C. Tredwell, S. T. Finn and W. B. Rankin did not bat.

McKay 5–0–23–0; Johnson 5–0–20–1; Hazlewood 2–0–6–0; Faulkner 1–0–3–0; Voges 1.1–0–3–1; Clarke 1–0–4–0.

Australia

A. J. Finch, S. E. Marsh, S. R. Watson, *M. J. Clarke, G. J. Bailey, A. C. Voges, †M. S. Wade, J. P. Faulkner, M. G. Johnson, C. J. McKay, J. R. Hazlewood.

Umpires: Aleem Dar and M. A. Gough.   Third umpire: S. Ravi.

ENGLAND v AUSTRALIA

Fourth NatWest One-Day International

At Cardiff, September 14. England won by three wickets. Toss: England. One-day international debut: N. M. Coulter-Nile.

One–nil down with two to play, England navigated their way through a classic to set up a decider. Their star was Buttler, whose unbeaten 65 off 48 balls was his most mature international innings yet, and maintained England's undefeated record from 12 official internationals in Wales. He put on a crucial 75 for the seventh wicket with Stokes, after McKay's hat-trick – the fifth by an Australian in one-day internationals – had reduced England to eight for three in the third over. Carberry and Morgan responded with careful fifties but, when Bopara was sixth out at 144, Australia sensed a series win. Earlier, they were reduced to 57 for four, only for Bailey to ensure a competitive total with 87, which included three sixes from Tredwell's off-spin. But Tredwell held his nerve to take three late wickets as Australia's last five tumbled for 18, leaving ten deliveries unused. Buttler – given lbw to Watson when eight, but reprieved on review – ensured their carelessness would be punished and, with England needing seven off the last over, launched Johnson's first ball high over midwicket for six.

Man of the Match: J. C. Buttler.   *Attendance:* 13,759.

Australia

A. J. Finch lbw b Finn	0	N. M. Coulter-Nile not out	7
S. E. Marsh c Buttler b Stokes	25	C. J. McKay b Tredwell	2
S. R. Watson c Buttler b Rankin	6		
*M. J. Clarke lbw b Finn	22	B 1, l-b 3, w 3	7
G. J. Bailey c Buttler b Rankin	87		
A. C. Voges b Bopara	30	1/1 (1) 2/11 (3) (48.2 overs) 227	
†M. S. Wade c Carberry b Tredwell	36	3/51 (2) 4/57 (4) 5/124 (6)	
J. P. Faulkner run out	1	6/209 (7) 7/210 (8) 8/218 (9)	
M. G. Johnson b Tredwell	4	9/218 (5) 10/227 (11) 10 overs: 31-2	

Finn 10–0–43–2; Rankin 10–1–31–2; Stokes 9–1–42–1; Bopara 10–0–45–1; Tredwell 8.2–0–53–3; Root 1–0–9–0.

England

M. A. Carberry b Coulter-Nile	63	B. A. Stokes b McKay	25
K. P. Pietersen lbw b McKay	5	J. C. Tredwell not out	1
I. J. L. Trott c Finch b McKay	0	L-b 8, w 4	12
J. E. Root c Watson b McKay	0		
*E. J. G. Morgan b Watson	53	1/8 (2) 2/8 (3) (7 wkts, 49.3 overs) 231	
R. S. Bopara lbw b Faulkner	7	3/8 (4) 4/112 (5)	
†J. C. Buttler not out	65	5/126 (1) 6/144 (6) 7/219 (8) 10 overs: 26-3	

S. T. Finn and W. B. Rankin did not bat.

McKay 10–3–39–4; Johnson 9.3–0–64–0; Faulkner 10–1–43–1; Watson 10–0–43–1; Coulter-Nile 10–0–34–1.

Umpires: R. J. Bailey and S. Ravi.   Third umpire: Aleem Dar.

ENGLAND v AUSTRALIA

Fifth NatWest One-Day International

At Southampton, September 16 (day/night). Australia won by 49 runs. Toss: Australia. One-day international debut: C. J. Jordan.

Watson's blunderbuss 143 from 107 balls on a cold autumn evening, with 12 fours and six sixes, ensured Australia would head home with at least some silverware tucked under Clarke's arm. Both men had enjoyed stints with Hampshire – as had Hughes – and they put their local knowledge to good use in a series-clinching fourth-wicket stand of 163. That rescued Australia from 48 for three, at which point Stokes – en route to a hard-working, if expensive, maiden international five-for – had been on a hat-trick. But Clarke eased his way to a run-a-ball 75, while Watson butchered 47 off 19 deliveries from Root's off-breaks alone – his sixth over cost 28, the most expensive for England in one-day internationals. Chris Jordan marked a vigorous debut with three wickets but, even though Australia lost their last seven for 87, England still needed a run shy of 300. Pietersen was run out from the fourth ball of the innings (Carberry had been run out from the sixth in Birmingham). And Wright – a late replacement for Jonathan Trott, who had suffered a back spasm – lasted one ball before failing to run in his bat attempting a quick single and being beaten by Bailey's direct hit from cover. Bopara and Buttler added an entertaining 92 in 13 overs, but the impressive Johnson returned to remove Bopara – his 200th one-day wicket – with the help of a stunning leaping catch in the covers by Voges.

Man of the Match: S. R. Watson.   *Attendance:* 13,042.
Man of the Series: M. J. Clarke.

Australia

P. J. Hughes c Carberry b Jordan	2	C. J. McKay c Root b Rankin	5	
A. J. Finch c Morgan b Stokes	26	Fawad Ahmed not out	4	
S. R. Watson c Buttler b Stokes	143			
†M. S. Wade c Buttler b Stokes	0	L-b 10, w 9	19	
*M. J. Clarke c Pietersen b Jordan	75			
G. J. Bailey st Buttler b Root	4	1/13 (1) 2/48 (2)	(49.1 overs)	298
A. C. Voges c Buttler b Stokes	8	3/48 (4) 4/211 (5) 5/221 (6)		
J. P. Faulkner c Buttler b Jordan	10	6/244 (7) 7/282 (3) 8/284 (9)		
M. G. Johnson c and b Stokes	2	9/294 (8) 10/298 (10)	10 overs: 48-3	

Rankin 9.1–1–26–1; Jordan 10–0–51–3; Stokes 10–0–61–5; Bopara 10–0–54–0; Tredwell 4–0–38–0; Root 6–0–58–1.

England

M. A. Carberry lbw b Faulkner	30	J. C. Tredwell not out	5	
K. P. Pietersen run out	0	W. B. Rankin b Fawad Ahmed	4	
J. E. Root b Johnson	21			
*E. J. G. Morgan st Wade b Voges	30	B 3, l-b 5, w 6	14	
L. J. Wright run out	0			
R. S. Bopara c Voges b Johnson	62	1/1 (2) 2/50 (1) 3/64 (3)	(48 overs)	249
†J. C. Buttler b Faulkner	42	4/68 (5) 5/103 (4) 6/195 (7)		
B. A. Stokes c Clarke b Faulkner	27	7/197 (6) 8/236 (9) 9/240 (8)		
C. J. Jordan c Bailey b Watson	14	10/249 (11)	10 overs: 37-1	

McKay 9–1–54–0; Johnson 10–1–21–2; Faulkner 9–0–38–3; Fawad Ahmed 7–0–51–1; Voges 4–0–25–1; Watson 9–0–52–1.

Umpires: Aleem Dar and R. J. Bailey. Third umpire: S. Ravi.
Series referee: J. J. Crowe.

Wisden EXTRA is a free online magazine, published at key points in the cricket year to complement the Almanack. It is an authoritative and high-class take on the major cricket issues from around the world.

Sign up today at wisden.com/signup to be alerted to each new issue.

Visit the Wisden EXTRA page on our site to read previous issues.

www.wisden.com

AUSTRALIA v ENGLAND, 2013-14

Review by George Dobell

Test matches (5): Australia 5, England 0
One-day internationals (5): Australia 4, England 1
Twenty20 internationals (3): Australia 3, England 0

Rarely can expectation have turned to dejection so quickly and so resoundingly. Alastair Cook's England team arrived in Australia with realistic hopes of winning a fourth straight Ashes series for the first time since 1890, but left nursing only the third 5–0 whitewash in Ashes history, following the defeats for Johnny Douglas's side in 1920-21 and Andrew Flintoff's in 2006-07.

As the series progressed and the margin between the sides grew, so questions mounted about the people, structures and systems that had previously been thought to underpin England's success. By the end, players fundamental to both that success and future plans – Jonathan Trott, Graeme Swann, Matt Prior, Joe Root and Steven Finn – had, for one reason or another, fallen by the wayside. And the position of team director Andy Flower looked as insecure as at any time in his tenure.

Less than a month after the series was over, Flower quit; four days after that, Kevin Pietersen – whose behaviour had once again been the subject of whispers – was dumped, with England's new managing director, Paul Downton, emphasising the need for a fresh "team ethic and philosophy". In the unforgiving heat of an Australian summer, England's foundations had turned to mush.

Not even Glenn McGrath could have predicted the one-sided nature of the contest. England had won five of the previous seven Ashes Tests, and lost only two of the previous 15. They had just beaten Australia 3–0 at home, extending their own unbeaten sequence in all Tests to 13 and Australia's winless run to nine, their worst since 1986. And if that result had been a touch flattering, it hardly hinted at a complete role reversal. England, after all, were at full strength, while three of Australia's most exciting young fast bowlers – Pat Cummins, James Pattinson and Mitchell Starc – would miss the entire series through injury.

But Australia turned that weakness into a strength. Their pace attack, consisting of three experienced seamers, was outstanding. Inspired by Mitchell Johnson, who in his 33rd year had finally found the accuracy to complete an armoury already blessed with sharp pace and left-arm awkwardness, they shocked England with their aggression, and suffocated them with unrelenting consistency and astute lines of attack.

Johnson was as brutal as he was influential. When the series began, some regarded him as a pantomime villain – complete with handlebar moustache – but he finished it doing a passable impression of a great fast bowler. Generating a pace rarely sustained in modern Test cricket, his slingy action, raw hostility and fitness – only James Anderson bowled more deliveries in the series, and some at a reduced pace after his rib was broken by Peter Siddle at Adelaide – gave him 37 wickets at 13.97, surpassing Frank Foster's record of 32, in 1911-12, for a left-arm fast bowler in an Ashes series. Johnson left several England batsmen shell-shocked and questioning their temperament and technique. No Australian seamer had taken more wickets in a five-Test series. It was a performance of which Ray Lindwall, Dennis Lillee (Johnson's mentor) or McGrath would have been proud.

Ryan Harris, fast and wonderfully skilled, lost little by comparison, and the frugal Siddle completed a trio that claimed 75 wickets at a cost of under 18. It seemed they could hardly deliver a poor ball, let alone a poor spell. Supported

---

JOHNSON v XVIII OF ENGLAND

Mitchell Johnson's head-to-head record against the England batsmen:

Wkts		*Runs*	*Balls*	*Avge*	*4*	*6*
4	J. M. Anderson	12	32	3.00	1	0
4	S. C. J. Broad.	25	56	6.25	2	0
4	A. N. Cook	73	128	18.25	9	0
3	G. P. Swann.	15	28	5.00	2	0
3	B. A. Stokes.	61	122	20.33	6	0
3	M. A. Carberry	66	146	22.00	12	0
2	M. S. Panesar.	0	13	0.00	0	0
2	T. T. Bresnan.	7	34	3.50	0	0
2	I. J. L. Trott	10	13	5.00	1	0
2	J. M. Bairstow	14	29	7.00	1	1
2	M. J. Prior	39	69	19.50	8	0
2	K. P. Pietersen	55	104	27.50	6	0
2	J. E. Root.	59	226	29.50	5	0
1	W. B. Rankin.	0	5	0.00	0	0
1	G. S. Ballance	5	19	5.00	1	0
0	C. T. Tremlett	6	17	–	1	0
0	I. R. Bell	48	98	–	5	1

S. G. Borthwick did not face Johnson.

---

by the mean Shane Watson and the improving off-spin of Nathan Lyon, they applied such pressure that England's batting simply cracked.

Johnson was Man of the Series, but a more imaginative choice might have been a joint award with Brad Haddin. He came into the series as a 36-year-old with a reputation as a Test journeyman, and ended it with 493 runs, having recorded at least a half-century in every first innings, and rescued Australia from a succession of challenging positions. No Australian wicketkeeper nor any No. 7 had scored as many runs in a series, or passed 50 as many as six times.

Others chipped in. David Warner was adept at bullying quick second-innings runs and, like his opening partner Chris Rogers, who looked a freer batsman at Melbourne and Sydney following the retirement of Swann, made two hundreds (though it's fair to say that Rogers was a more popular opponent than Warner, whose snide sledging appalled England). Steve Smith made perhaps the greatest strides among Australia's batsmen, casting aside the court-jester persona that had invited mockery in 2010-11 to score centuries of skill and guts at Perth and Sydney.

Fearless firefighter: Brad Haddin revived all five of Australia's first innings.

Michael Clarke made clear his determination with hundreds in the first two Tests, to say nothing of a verbal blast at Anderson during the dying moments at Brisbane. At last, it seemed, Australia had clasped their captain to their bosom; his tactical nous was on a different plane from Cook's. Watson was as infuriating as ever, scoring runs only when the pressure was off; George Bailey looked out of his depth, and was dropped for the tour of South Africa.

England's bowlers – in particular the admirable Stuart Broad – earned them a foothold in every game. In four of the five Tests, Australia were teetering when their fifth wicket fell, but each time Haddin engineered a fightback. Australia's first five first-innings wickets contributed only 90 more runs than England's (709 v 619), but their last five an extra 721 (1,071 v 350). And, while England's lower order were helpless against Johnson, Australia's counter-attacked against a bowling unit that grew weary, partly because they were getting no respite between innings. Just as importantly, Anderson couldn't find the swing and seam that had made him such a handful three years earlier: 24 wickets at 26 in 2010-11 became 14 at nearly 44. Though hard-working and generally tight, he was being made to wait 81 balls for each wicket.

Maybe the tour was simply a bridge too far for this England side. The squad contained the bulk of the team that had won the previous three Ashes series, taken England to the top of the Test rankings in 2011, and won in India a year earlier. Several had been involved in the World Twenty20 triumph of 2010, and come within an ace of winning the Champions Trophy in June 2013. No one in the world had faced as many deliveries in international cricket since the start of the 2010-11 Ashes as Cook (Ian Bell and Trott also featured in the top five); no seamers had bowled as many balls as Anderson and Broad, and among spinners, only Pakistan's Saeed Ajmal had bowled more than Swann. At times it showed.

THE RESCUE ACT

Brad Haddin was the first No. 7 to reach 50 in the first innings of every match of a five-Test series:

	Total on arrival	Haddin's score	Total on dismissal	Final total
Brisbane	100-5	94	295	295
Adelaide	257-5	118	529-9	570-9
Perth	143-5	55	267-6	385
Melbourne	112-5	65	204	204
Sydney	97-5	75	225-6	326

Pietersen, talking before the final Test, speculated that the demands – emotional rather than physical – of back-to-back Ashes might have been a factor in England's decline. He compared their state of mind ("mentally, you are a bit fragile") after beating Australia at home with post-Olympic Games athletes: "To play an Ashes and then another Ashes, and for us being away from home, it's a tough gig."

The flaw in his argument was that the schedule was the same for both sides. But the sense was that, while England were clinging on to the vestiges of former glories, Australia were the coming force: more motivated, more hungry, more energised. It felt as if England were up against not just a team but an entire nation.

Their selection did them few favours. It's true that there was some excitement at the prospect of a squad containing three giant fast bowlers. But Chris Tremlett was dropped after the First Test, Boyd Rankin played only a peripheral part in the Fifth, and Finn lost form and confidence to the extent that, having been ignored during the Tests, he flew home during the equally dispiriting one-day leg, when he was ordered to take a break from the game.

Many of these problems could have been predicted. At Brisbane, Tremlett bowled exactly as he had for Surrey in the 2013 season: tidily, but without any of the menace that had made him so dangerous in 2010-11. Finn had never fully recovered his rhythm since the England coaches recommended he shorten his run-up to counter his problem of knocking over the stumps in his delivery stride. It should have been no surprise that the intensity of an Ashes series did not elicit a miracle cure. It was debatable whether Graham Onions, the best bowler in county cricket over the previous couple of years, would have fared any better, but his omission suggested an unhealthy predilection among the coaches and selectors for height above all else.

Other issues were less predictable. Trott went home suffering from what was described as "a stress-related illness", after a frenetic performance at the Gabba betrayed his mental anguish. His problems against Johnson may have been a catalyst, but Trott's issues were caused as much by long-term mental exhaustion – born largely of an unrelenting schedule – and his refusal to accept a dip in form that jarred with his perfectionist streak. It was not just that England missed his runs (in the summer he had fallen short of his own high standards, though he still reached 40 in five of his ten Ashes innings). But his dressing-room breakdown shocked and disturbed team-mates who had come to rely on his solidity. They never rediscovered their equilibrium.

LESS IS MORE

Lowest bowling averages in an Ashes series (minimum 900 balls):

		T	Balls	Runs	Wkts	BB	5I	10M	Season
9.60	J. C. Laker (E)	5	1,703	442	46	10-53	4	2	1956
12.85	R. M. Hogg (A)	6	1,740	527	41	6-74	5	2	1978-79
13.97	**M. G. Johnson (A)**	**5**	**1,132**	**517**	**37**	**7-40**	**3**	**0**	**2013-14**
14.26	H. Trumble (A)	3	1,036	371	26	8-65	2	2	1902
15.04	G. Miller (E)	6	1,417	346	23	5-44	1	0	1978-79
15.10	D. L. Underwood (E)	4	1,259	302	20	7-50	1	0	1968
15.23	J. B. Iverson (A)	5	1,108	320	21	6-27	1	0	1950-51
15.73	M. Hendrick (E)	5	1,160	299	19	3-19	0	0	1978-79
15.74	W. Rhodes (E)	5	1,032	488	31	8-68	3	1	1903-04
16.00	B. A. Reid (A)	4	1,081	432	27	7-51	2	1	1990-91
16.06	A. V. Bedser (E)	5	1,560	482	30	5-46	2	1	1950-51
16.58	H. Trumble (A)	4	1,198	398	24	7-28	2	0	1903-04

LESS IS LESS

England's lowest average runs per wicket (series of three Tests or more):

15.10	v Australia, 1888 (3 Tests)	
19.06	v Pakistan in UAE, 2011-12 (3)	
19.11	v West Indies, 1934-35 (4)	
19.25	v South Africa, 1905-06 (5)	
20.20	v West Indies, 1985-86 (5)	
21.00	v Australia, 1882-83 (4)	

21.18	v Australia, 1909 (5)
21.43	v Australia, 1950-51 (5)
21.58	**v Australia, 2013-14 (5)**
21.62	v Australia, 1896 (3)
21.65	v West Indies, 1988 (5)
21.78	v Australia, 1958-59 (5)

They never replaced Swann, either. For so long the man who had made England's four-man attack work, he retired with immediate effect a few days after the Third Test, at Perth, and admitted that, after two elbow operations and numerous other aches and pains, he was no longer able to do what he once could. It was telling that, while his first over in Test cricket had produced two prize wickets, his last was clobbered for 22. England had built much of their summer success on the superiority of Swann over Lyon, but now Australia's off-spinner gained more bounce (which proved especially effective from round the wicket), drift and dip, and was more potent.

The timing of Swann's departure provoked murmurs about his commitment – Flower admitted he had wanted him to finish the tour – and highlighted both England's reliance on a few individuals and the hollowness of talk about succession planning. With Monty Panesar losing his way so badly that he was almost unrecognisable from the bowler who once drew comparison with Bishan Bedi, England were obliged to call up two extra spinners – James Tredwell and all-rounder Scott Borthwick, both of whom had just returned modest county figures – to replace Swann. A fading force he may have been, but he remained head and shoulders above anything else England had to offer.

Their main weakness, though, was batting: the line-up that looked so strong on paper folded as if made of the stuff. Prior, for so long a pillar, was dropped after three Tests which produced only two scores above eight (and some increasingly inept glovework); Root, supposedly the future of English batting, was omitted after four, with one score over 26. Even Cook, who became the youngest man in history to 8,000 Test runs, finished the series with questions

THE LEHMANN INFLUENCE

Two nuffies, united by love

GREG BAUM

Whatever else Darren Lehmann brought to the dressing-room, perhaps his most important quality was being a quintessential Australian. At worst it is chauvinism, at best the sense of self-sufficiency that comes from isolation, but Australian sporting teams work best in the hands of one of their own. A fortnight after Lehmann's appointment, the rugby union Wallabies abandoned their five-year experiment with a New Zealander as coach. The brief exceptions were the Socceroos, led out of the wilderness in 2006 by Dutchman Guus Hiddink. But subsequent hirings of other Europeans proved less fruitful and, for the 2014 football World Cup, they also reverted to Australian management.

The recurring word in contemplations of Lehmann is "relaxed". Under Mickey Arthur, the dressing-room was unhappy. Whether it was unhappy because it was losing, or losing because it was unhappy, is the age-old question without answer. But tensions ran high, particularly between captain Michael Clarke and vice-captain Shane Watson. The South African Arthur was, by Cricket Australia's own admission, the scapegoat.

Lehmann was an immediate contrast. He was not a career coach – he fell into jobs in the IPL and with Queensland – nor a technocrat. His strength was his knowingness. The best classroom was the dressing-room after 6pm, he always said. At times he was too much one of the boys, inciting crowds to bait Stuart Broad. But he felt he could stamp his authority when needed. In the new-old idiom, he was not a soft cock.

In the two hours he had to consider the job when it was offered in Bristol, his wife asked him if he thought he could make a difference. He was sure he could. He set the players the tripartite task of playing for their own enjoyment, for the crowd's entertainment and in an identifiably Australian manner. He did not expect it to be easy, and he knew it was not safe. The board had just sacked one coach, and could sack another.

Lehmann abandoned rotation, brought back Craig McDermott as bowling coach and American Mike Young to sharpen the fielding. Instead of charts and diagrams, he opted for simple verities. He wanted at least one Australian hundred in every Test: from the third of the ten in the double Ashes, he got it. It was the bowlers who slowly turned round this *Queen Mary*, but the batsmen played their part, if unevenly. Confronted by CA chief executive James Sutherland after the Lord's debacle, Lehmann reassured him there were already subtle signs of a turning of the tide. Back then, it seemed ludicrous.

The mood lightened. Reflexively, the old boys' club of ex-players in the media also came onside. The public did too: the "Boof" persona proved endearing. Clarke joined them. In rugby or football, the coach is in charge. But in cricket, he has as little or as much control as the captain grants him. It is anecdotally clear that Clarke calls the shots. He is careful never to speak ill of Arthur, whose demise he felt keenly. But despite their different styles, he and Lehmann have developed a fraternal relationship. Both are what Lehmann would call cricket "nuffies". Love (of the game) conquers all.

Oddly enough, in this nascent Lehmann era, Australia weaned themselves off their Clarke dependency. He made three telling hundreds against England, but his average was 43 – modest for him – and in the last three Tests he totalled 79 runs. That was no more than incidental as the last wicket fell at Sydney, and Clarke and Watson walked off arm in arm. Happy because they were winning, winning because they were happy – who can say?

Payback: Steve Smith, written off as a picaresque figure three years earlier, weighed in with two centuries.

about his technique against the quickest bowling and his sometimes passive captaincy. His poor return meant he had averaged more than 28 only once in five series against Australia; his series-defining average of 127 three years earlier felt like a distant memory. His new opening partner, Michael Carberry, kept undoing the good work by retreating into his shell.

It was a statistical horror show. While Australia managed ten centuries – equalling the record for an Ashes series – England managed only Ben Stokes's courageous 120 at Perth. While Australia recorded the four highest totals of the series, England were dismissed for under 180 on six occasions; only twice did they pass 260, and never in the first innings. While six Australians exceeded 300 runs, no England batsman did. And while five Australians averaged over 40, Stokes alone reached 30 for England. By the end of the series, England had gone 26 innings and ten months without reaching 400. It was telling that, the last time they did so, at Wellington in March 2013, Nick Compton had scored a century. But Compton was jettisoned after three bad games a few months earlier. Increasingly, it seemed your face had to fit to win the same continuity of selection as the favoured few.

Pietersen was England's top scorer (which wasn't saying a great deal), yet attracted more questions over his future. He insisted he wanted to continue, but there were rumours of further strains in his uneasy relationship with Flower. The manner of Pietersen's dismissals – one leg-side catch following another – scarcely helped, though it was hard to come by concrete evidence that his presence really was destabilising the dressing-room. Indeed, he often gave the contrary impression, encouraging younger players and helping colleagues in the nets.

FIVE STATS YOU MAY HAVE MISSED

BENEDICT BERMANGE

- At Perth, Matt Prior took his 60th catch off James Anderson, equalling England's previous record for a keeper–bowler combination.

Dismissals		Tests
60	c R. W. Taylor b I. T. Botham........................	51
60	c M. J. Prior b J. M. Anderson........................	64
48	c M. J. Prior b S. C. J. Broad........................	56

- At Perth, Alastair Cook became the first man to suffer a first-ball duck in his 100th Test. The others to make ducks in their 100th Tests were Allan Border, Stephen Fleming, Mark Taylor, Dilip Vengsarkar and Courtney Walsh.

- When David Warner launched Graeme Swann over midwicket at Perth, he became the first England bowler to concede 100 Test sixes. This was the table by the end of the series:

Sixes		Sixes	
195	M. Muralitharan (SL/World)	121	Danish Kaneria (Pakistan)
183	D. L. Vettori (NZ/World)	120	A. Kumble (India)
174	S. K. Warne (Australia)	105	G. P. Swann (England)
157	Harbhajan Singh (India)		

- Nathan Lyon became only the second player to go an entire five-Test series without being dismissed. Bill Johnston managed it for Australia against South Africa in 1949-50, but batted only twice.

- Swann went for 22 runs in the final over of his Test career. The only bowler to concede more in his last Test over was New Zealand's Derek Stirling, with 24 at The Oval in 1986, courtesy of Ian Botham (464604).

But the management had other ideas. After Flower told Downton at the end of January that the split-coaching arrangement with Ashley Giles would hamper efforts to rebuild the England team, Pietersen met with Downton, the new national selector James Whitaker and Cook to discuss his own future. The discussion was brief and to the point: England would be moving on without him. In the blood-letting that followed, explanations were sought, and only partially provided: in a team meeting after Melbourne involving the players alone, Pietersen was said to have been overly critical of Flower's coaching methods; on another occasion, after his final Test innings at Sydney, he stood accused of whistling merrily in a despondent dressing-room. But the anecdotes missed the point: England simply felt he was no longer worth the hassle.

In Australia, many of the tenets of England's recent success – continuity of selection, calmness in victory or defeat – had been abandoned in the storm. By the time Rankin, Gary Ballance and Borthwick, whose leg-breaks had left him 14th in Durham's Championship bowling averages in 2013, were selected at Sydney, England had used 18 men in the series – some feat for a squad that had originally numbered 17. Australia, by contrast, retained faith with the same XI. And while the Australians caught almost everything, England's fielding slipped alarmingly, reflecting their morale. If their mistakes at Adelaide, where they squandered an opportunity to seize the initiative, were the most costly, the errors at Perth, where they missed chances a well-trained Labrador might have taken, were just embarrassing.

Darren Lehmann fully vindicated the decision by Cricket Australia to appoint him in place of Mickey Arthur a fortnight before the First Test at Nottingham in July. He created a relaxed environment for his players, and gelled surprisingly well with the image-conscious Clarke. But the England camp, under the intense leadership of Flower, appeared a joyless place. Instead of relishing the challenge, England seemed cowed by it. Unlike 2006-07, when they were whitewashed by a great Australian team, they now failed to do themselves justice against a decent but far from unbeatable side. The timid debut of Rankin spoke volumes for the tension inside the England bubble. Like Simon Kerrigan before him, Rankin found the step up to Test cricket uncomfortably large.

Such incidents raised questions about the system providing the players. The team that had taken England to No. 1 contained four men who scored hundreds on Test debut, two more who made half-centuries, and one who claimed a five-wicket haul – all developed in the early years of promotion and relegation in the County Championship. But the domestic game had lost its competitive edge – weakened by young-player incentives, the growth of Twenty20 leagues, tougher work-permit criteria (which had reduced the quality and quantity of non-England-qualified players), and the withdrawal of the top players on England (or Lions) duty or even for reasons of strength and conditioning. The divide between county and international level had grown.

There were exceptions. The emergence of Stokes promised much, and suggested England might have found an all-rounder who could balance the side for a decade; he turned out to be the quickest bowler. Broad, too, shrugged off the charmless abuse of the crowds to produce a bowling performance that, in other circumstances, might have helped his side to the Ashes.

It was not always an attractive series. At times, with thousands of spectators answering the call from Lehmann and sections of the Australian media to chant abuse, and with players posturing and bickering on the pitch, it was downright ugly. There were faults on both sides, though it was noticeable that, once Aleem Dar was involved as an on-pitch umpire, the worst excesses were curbed. But there was nothing to curb the pain of an England team in freefall.

Vithushan Ehantharajah writes: For England, the two limited-overs series were a depressing continuation of the Tests. By the time they registered their only international win of the tour, in the fourth one-dayer at Perth, the trip was three months old and the series already gone. Australia's subsequent 3–0 triumph in the Twenty20 matches meant they had won 12–1 across the three formats; it also meant five of those games had in effect been dead, with England playing for little more than pride. They could barely manage even that.

For coach Ashley Giles, the 4–1 loss in the one-day series was especially hard to take. England should have won the second game, at the Gabba, where James Faulkner's late hitting in a last-wicket stand of 57 allowed Australia to chase down 301. And they also blew a winning position in the fifth, at Adelaide,

TWIN PEAKS

The leading performers across the back-to-back Ashes series:

Most runs

		T	Avge				T	Avge
830	C. J. L. Rogers (A)	10	43.68		682	K. P. Pietersen (E)	10	34.10
797	I. R. Bell (E)	10	44.27		672	S. P. D. Smith (A)	10	39.52
763	S. R. Watson (A)	10	40.15		661	D. A. Warner (A)	8	44.06
744	M. J. Clarke (A)	10	43.76		531	J. E. Root (E)	9	33.18
699	B. J. Haddin (A)	10	41.11		523	A. N. Cook (E)	10	26.15

Most wickets

		T	Avge				T	Avge
46	R. J. Harris (A)	9	19.45		33	G. P. Swann (E)	8	39.84
43	S. C. J. Broad (E)	10	27.48		28	N. M. Lyon (A)	10	30.75
37	M. G. Johnson (A)	5	13.97		15	B. A. Stokes (E)	4	32.80
36	J. M. Anderson (E)	10	35.16		15	T. T. Bresnan (E)	5	33.46
33	P. M. Siddle (A)	10	27.96		11	M. A. Starc (A)	3	32.45

Most catches

		T					T
51	B. J. Haddin (A)	10		11	J. M. Bairstow (E)	6
28	M. J. Prior (E)	8		10	G. J. Bailey (A)	5
14	M. J. Clarke (E)	10		10	J. M. Anderson (E)	10
14	A. N. Cook (E)	10		10	S. P. D. Smith (A)	10

There were no stumpings in either series. Ten of Bairstow's catches came while keeping wicket.

Most matches

Forty players appeared at some stage during the two series, but only 11 appeared in all ten Tests: Clarke, Haddin, Rogers, Siddle, Smith and Watson for Australia, and Anderson, Bell, Broad, Cook and Pietersen for England.

Highest partnerships

214	4th	M. J. Clarke/S. P. D. Smith (A)	at Manchester
200	6th	M. J. Clarke/B. J. Haddin (A)	at Adelaide
163	10th	P. J. Hughes/A. C. Agar (A)	at Nottingham
158	3rd	D. A. Warner/M. J. Clarke (A)	at Brisbane
157	1st	C. J. L. Rogers/D. A. Warner (A)	at Perth
153	5th	J. E. Root/I. R. Bell (E)	at Lord's

Highest totals

570-9	Australia	at Adelaide		375	England	at Nottingham
527-7	Australia	at Manchester		369-6	Australia	at Perth
492-9	Australia	at The Oval		368	England	at Manchester
401-7	Australia	at Brisbane		361	England	at Lord's
385	Australia	at Perth		353	England	at Perth
377	England	at The Oval				

Lowest totals

128	Australia	at Lord's		172	England	at Adelaide
136	England	at Brisbane		179	England	at Brisbane
155	England	at Sydney		179	England	at Melbourne
166	England	at Sydney		204	Australia	at Melbourne

losing seven for 58 to fall five runs short. "We could have won 3–2," reflected Giles, who suddenly found himself being touted for the role of England team director after news that Flower had quit reached Australia towards the end of the second Twenty20 international. This was hardly the most timely job interview but, with England missing several of their biggest names, it would have been unreasonable to judge Giles on these performances alone.

There was little to shout about. Eoin Morgan's one-day haul of 282 runs – more than anyone on either side, including Australian opener Aaron Finch, who butchered hundreds at Melbourne and Perth – contained England's only century, at Brisbane. Jos Buttler, who began the series at No. 8 but seemed wasted even when he moved up a place, blasted 71 from 43 balls during the win at Perth, where Stokes's promotion to No. 3 produced an aggressive 70. Bell rarely failed as Cook's opening partner, but fell in wasteful ways, and was run out twice.

Chris Jordan bowled throughout with good pace, and was willing to take on the responsibilities of powerplay and death overs. But too many of the frontline bowlers conceded between five and six an over, and there were times – as during the Ashes – when Cook looked lost in the field. After the Sydney defeat, he hinted he might step down as one-day skipper, only to retract the idea soon after. As Giles pointed out, defeat was "not all down to the captain".

The 50-over series seemed to knock whatever wind remained out of the tourists' sails ahead of the three Twenty20 matches. In those, Australia's batsmen hit 27 sixes to England's 14, and the home bowlers – a motley collection of back-up seamers, and spinners who were either green-raw or part-time – never ceded control. Not for the first time, England's plight was encapsulated by the bowling of Jade Dernbach, who leaked nearly 13 an over, while feeling emboldened to sledge Australia's batsmen. His chuntering provided a bathetic conclusion to a pathetic tour.

ENGLAND TOURING PARTY

*A. N. Cook (Essex; T/50), J. M. Anderson (Lancashire; T), J. M. Bairstow (Yorkshire; T), G. S. Ballance (Yorkshire; T/50), I. R. Bell (Warwickshire; T/50), R. S. Bopara (Essex; 50/20), S. G. Borthwick (Durham; T), T. T. Bresnan (Yorkshire; T/50/20), D. R. Briggs (Hampshire; 50/20), S. C. J. Broad (Nottinghamshire; T/50/20), J. C. Buttler (Somerset; 50/20), M. A. Carberry (Hampshire; T/50), J. W. Dernbach (Surrey; 20), S. T. Finn (Middlesex; T/50), A. D. Hales (Nottinghamshire; 20), C. J. Jordan (Sussex; 50/20), M. J. Lumb (Nottinghamshire; 20), E. J. G. Morgan (Middlesex; 50/20), M. S. Panesar (Essex; T), K. P. Pietersen (Surrey; T), M. J. Prior (Sussex; T), W. B. Rankin (Warwickshire; T/50/20), J. E. Root (Yorkshire; T/50/20), B. A. Stokes (Durham; T/50/20), G. P. Swann (Nottinghamshire; T), J. C. Tredwell (Kent; T/50/20), C. T. Tremlett (Surrey; T), I. J. L. Trott (Warwickshire; T), C. R. Woakes (Warwickshire; 50), L. J. Wright (Sussex; 20).

Trott returned home after the First Test, suffering from a stress-related illness, but was not replaced. Bresnan joined the squad before the Second Test after recovering from a back injury. Swann retired with immediate effect after the Third Test; Borthwick and Tredwell were added to the squad. Finn returned home during the one-day series. Broad captained in the Twenty20 matches.

Coach: A. Flower (T), A. F. Giles (50/20). *Assistant coach/fielding coach:* R. G. Halsall. *Batting coach:* G. A. Gooch (T), G. P. Thorpe (50/20). *Fast-bowling coach:* D. J. Saker. *Spin-bowling coach:* Mushtaq Ahmed (T). *Wicketkeeping coach:* B. N. French (T). *Strength and conditioning coach:* H. R. Bevan. *Team operations manager:* P. A. Neale. *Physiotherapist:* C. A. de Weymarn. *Team doctor:* M. G. Wotherspoon (T), N. S. Peirce (50/20). *Analyst:* N. A. Leamon (T), G. J. Broad (50/20). *Massage therapist:* M. E. S. Saxby. *Sports psychologist:* M. A. K. Bawden. *Security manager:* R. C. Dickason. *Media relations manager:* R. C. Evans.

TEST MATCH AVERAGES

AUSTRALIA – BATTING AND FIELDING

	T	I	NO	R	HS	100	50	Avge	Ct
B. J. Haddin	5	8	0	493	118	1	5	61.62	22
†D. A. Warner	5	10	1	523	124	2	2	58.11	4
†C. J. L. Rogers	5	10	0	463	119	2	3	46.30	4
S. P. D. Smith	5	9	1	327	115	2	0	40.87	7
M. J. Clarke	5	10	1	363	148	2	0	40.33	8
S. R. Watson	5	10	1	345	103	1	2	38.33	3
†M. G. Johnson	5	8	2	165	64	0	1	27.50	4
G. J. Bailey	5	8	1	183	53	0	1	26.14	10
R. J. Harris	5	6	1	117	55*	0	1	23.40	4
P. M. Siddle	5	7	1	38	21	0	0	6.33	0
N. M. Lyon	5	6	6	60	18*	0	0	–	5

BOWLING

	Style	O	M	R	W	BB	5I	Avge
M. G. Johnson	LF	188.4	51	517	37	7-40	3	13.97
R. J. Harris	RFM	166.2	50	425	22	5-25	1	19.31
P. M. Siddle	RFM	156.4	48	386	16	4-57	0	24.12
N. M. Lyon	OB	176.2	42	558	19	5-50	1	29.36
S. R. Watson	RFM	47.4	17	122	4	1-0	0	30.50

Also bowled: S. P. D. Smith (LBG) 11–1–58–1.

ENGLAND – BATTING AND FIELDING

	T	I	NO	R	HS	100	50	Avge	Ct
†B. A. Stokes	4	8	0	279	120	1	0	34.87	1
K. P. Pietersen	5	10	0	294	71	0	2	29.40	3
†M. A. Carberry	5	10	0	281	60	0	1	28.10	6
J. E. Root	4	8	1	192	87	0	1	27.42	2
I. R. Bell	5	10	1	235	72*	0	2	26.11	4
†A. N. Cook	5	10	0	246	72	0	3	24.60	7
†S. C. J. Broad	5	10	2	155	42	0	0	19.37	2
M. J. Prior	3	6	0	107	69	0	1	17.83	10
J. M. Bairstow	2	4	0	49	21	0	0	12.25	10
T. T. Bresnan	2	4	0	34	21	0	0	8.50	1
†J. M. Anderson	5	10	5	41	13*	0	0	8.20	6
G. P. Swann	3	6	1	36	19*	0	0	7.20	4
†M. S. Panesar	2	4	0	4	2	0	0	1.00	0

Played in one Test: †G. S. Ballance 18, 7; †S. G. Borthwick 1, 4 (2 ct); †W. B. Rankin 13, 0; C. T. Tremlett 8, 7; I. J. L. Trott 10, 9.

BOWLING

	Style	O	M	R	W	BB	5I	Avge
S. G. Borthwick	LBG	13	0	82	4	3-33	0	20.50
S. C. J. Broad	RFM	161.5	24	578	21	6-81	1	27.52
C. T. Tremlett	RFM	36	5	120	4	3-69	0	30.00
B. A. Stokes	RFM	116.5	14	492	15	6-99	1	32.80
T. T. Bresnan	RFM	62.3	14	206	5	2-24	0	41.20
J. M. Anderson	RFM	190.3	43	615	14	4-67	0	43.92
G. P. Swann	OB	142	21	560	7	2-71	0	80.00
M. S. Panesar	SLA	70.5	9	257	3	1-41	0	85.66

Also bowled: K. P. Pietersen (OB) 4–1–17–0; W. B. Rankin (RFM) 20.5–0–81–1; J. E. Root (OB) 32–5–98–0.

INCREDULOUS... AND INCREDIBLE Australia's fielders can't believe it after umpire Aleem Dar fails to spot Stuart Broad's edge in the First Test at Trent Bridge. Even worse, they have used up both their reviews. England used theirs more skilfully, and are finally able to rejoice in a 14-run win after technology confirms Brad Haddin *did* edge Jimmy Anderson.

COUNTER-PUNCHES Joe Root hits out during his 180 in the Second Test at Lord's, then celebrates catching David Warner at Manchester. Warner had recently completed a ban for taking a swing at Root on a night out during the Champions Trophy in June.

Graham Morris

Graham Morris

Gareth Copley, Getty Images

FOR WHOM BELL TOLLS On the first morning of the Fourth Test at Chester-le-Street, Ian Bell shows off his back cut, the summer's signature stroke. And on the fourth evening it's all over, as Jimmy Anderson catches Peter Siddle off Stuart Broad to give England a 3–0 lead.

Tom Jenkins, *The Guardian*

A TALE OF TWO CAPTAINS On the final evening of the series, at The Oval, Michael Clarke is kept at arm's length by Aleem Dar during an angry discussion about the light. After a tense draw, Alastair Cook leads England's festivities.

Ryan Pierse, Getty Images

Graham Morris

LOW POINTS Jonathan Trott falls to Mitchell Johnson on the third evening at Brisbane, before shaking hands with David Warner as Australia win the First Test by 381 runs. Warner had described Trott's dismissal as "pretty poor and weak". Soon after, Trott dropped out of the tour. In the Second Test at Adelaide, Michael Carberry puts down Brad Haddin on five; he goes on to make 118 as Australia win again.

LETTING RIP Mitchell Johnson blew England away time and again en route to 37 wickets. A show of resistance came from Ben Stokes, who made a century at Perth, in only his second Test.

DOWN – AND OUT Brad Haddin swoops to catch Joe Root at Perth, one of 51 he held in the ten Ashes Tests. On the second morning at Melbourne, Kevin Pietersen takes leave of his senses against Mitchell Johnson. Nine days later, he walks off at Sydney; a month after that, England sacked him.

THE ARMS HAVE IT Michael Clarke takes the slip catch that seals Australia's 5–0 whitewash at Sydney, while Alastair Cook can't bring himself to watch the post-series formalities.

WESTERN AUSTRALIA CA CHAIRMAN'S XI v ENGLAND XI

At Perth, October 31–November 2, 2013. Drawn. Toss: Western Australia CA Chairman's XI.

England's cunning plan to bombard Australian batsmen with their tall fast bowlers looked misguided after the first innings of the tour, in which all the opposition top six reached 50 and rattled along at better than four an over. Chris Lynn, a tall Queenslander, went on to a century, as Finn, Rankin and Tremlett collected combined figures of two for 303. "The pitch wasn't quite what we expected," Tremlett admitted. "We were a little bit too short and a bit too full at times." The tourists' batsmen showed better form at first, before a worrying precursor of the lower-order collapses to come. The openers shared a century stand, with Carberry cracking a dozen fours in a composed innings, then Trott and Bell put on 193. England looked set for a lead but, following Bell's voluntary departure, the remaining seven wickets went down for 57. Trott soldiered on, eventually facing 236 balls. There was time for some more forthright batting from Lynn and Marsh before the end.

Close of play: first day, Western Australia CA Chairman's XI 369-4 (Allenby 34, Turner 17); second day, England XI 270-2 (Trott 64, Bell 77).

Western Australia CA Chairman's XI

L. J. C. Towers c Prior b Root	77	– c Anderson b Rankin 1
M. S. Harris c Bell b Anderson	69	– lbw b Rankin 22
C. A. Lynn c Carberry b Rankin	104	– not out 61
M. R. Marsh c Prior b Stokes	58	– lbw b Finn 62
J. Allenby lbw b Finn	53	– (7) not out 7
A. J. Turner not out	62	– lbw b Tremlett 12
†T. I. F. Triffitt not out	18	– (5) c Prior b Finn 0
B 5, w 1, n-b 4	10	B 2, n-b 1 3

1/115 (2) 2/225 (1)   (5 wkts dec, 108 overs) 451   1/9 (1) 2/24 (2)   (5 wkts, 39 overs) 168
3/288 (3) 4/326 (4)   3/124 (4) 4/126 (5)
5/405 (5)   5/149 (6)

B. T. Cockley, M. W. Dixon, R. M. Duffield and *M. A. Beer did not bat.

Anderson 23–9–55–1; Tremlett 21–5–88–0; Rankin 20–1–92–1; Finn 23–0–123–1; Root 11–2–32–1; Stokes 10–0–56–1. *Second innings*—Tremlett 8–1–35–1; Rankin 9–2–34–2; Stokes 4–1–18–0; Finn 10–1–53–2; Root 8–1–26–0.

England XI

M. A. Carberry c Allenby b Turner	78	J. M. Anderson c Triffitt b Allenby	8
J. E. Root lbw b Allenby	36	W. B. Rankin c Triffitt b Allenby	0
I. J. L. Trott not out	113		
I. R. Bell retired out	115	L-b 2, w 2, n-b 14	18
G. S. Ballance c Triffitt b Duffield	0		
*†M. J. Prior c Triffitt b Duffield	4	1/100 (2) 2/137 (1) (101.5 overs) 391
B. A. Stokes c Triffitt b Allenby	4	3/330 (4) 4/334 (5)
S. T. Finn b Beer	15	5/338 (6) 6/347 (7) 7/382 (8)
C. T. Tremlett lbw b Beer	0	8/382 (9) 9/391 (10) 10/391 (11)

Cockley 3–0–7–0; Duffield 23.3–3–96–2; Dixon 18.3–1–107–0; Beer 28–6–87–2; Allenby 22.5–6–58–4; Turner 6–0–34–1.

Umpires: M. D. Martell and P. Wilson.   Referee: S. T. Easey.

AUSTRALIA A v ENGLAND XI

At Hobart, November 6–9, 2013. Drawn. Toss: England XI.

Rain washed out the middle two days of a match dominated by England's openers. Cook and Carberry batted throughout the first day, both passing 150 in a stand of 318. Carberry's knock confirmed his call-up for the First Test. Both centurions retired after the rain, and there was time on the fourth day for Root to make an attractive half-century and Anderson to take two wickets, the second of which probably scuppered Khawaja's chances of a Test recall. Pietersen complained of discomfort from his old knee problem during the match, and flew to Melbourne for a cortisone injection. Prior, suffering from a calf injury, did not take the field when England bowled; Root wore the gloves instead, after the umpires overruled an agreement between the captains that Jonny Bairstow could do so, saying the Laws prevented someone not playing in the match from keeping wicket.

Close of play: first day, England XI 318-0 (Cook 154, Carberry 153); second day, no play; third day, no play.

England XI

*A. N. Cook retired out	154	S. C. J. Broad c Khawaja b Holland	8
M. A. Carberry retired out	153		
I. J. L. Trott c Paine b Cutting	4	B 8, l-b 4, w 1, n-b 2	15
K. P. Pietersen lbw b Copeland	8		
J. E. Root not out	58	1/318 (1) (7 wkts dec, 128 overs) 430	
G. S. Ballance lbw b Cutting	4	2/318 (2) 3/329 (4)	
†M. J. Prior lbw b Holland	26	4/345 (3) 5/363 (6) 6/414 (7) 7/430 (8)	

G. P. Swann, C. T. Tremlett and J. M. Anderson did not bat.

Cutting 30–7–75–2; Copeland 33–7–99–1; Henriques 12–2–44–0; Holland 24–1–105–2; Maxwell 27–3–89–0; Khawaja 2–0–6–0.

Australia A

A. J. Doolan b Anderson	31
M. Klinger lbw b Swann	29
U. T. Khawaja c Root b Anderson	3
S. E. Marsh not out	27
C. J. Ferguson not out	15
L-b 2, w 5, n-b 7	14
1/40 (1) 2/48 (3) (3 wkts, 31 overs) 119	
3/80 (2)	

G. J. Maxwell, *M. C. Henriques, †T. D. Paine, B. C. J. Cutting, T. A. Copeland and J. M. Holland did not bat.

Anderson 7–2–20–2; Broad 10–1–47–0; Tremlett 8–2–23–0; Swann 6–0–27–1.

Umpires: S. D. Fry and P. Wilson.   Third umpire: G. C. Joshua.
Referee: R. W. Stratford.

CRICKET AUSTRALIA INVITATION XI v ENGLAND XI

At Sydney, November 13–16, 2013. England XI won by seven wickets. Toss: England XI.

An encouraging all-round performance sent England into the First Test in a positive state of mind. Broad and Finn showed good form with the ball, although Finn's eight wickets were not enough to earn him a place at the Gabba, and all the leading batsmen made runs. It was Broad who made the major inroads on the first day, and he finished with four for 37 from 24 overs. The Invitation XI were up against it at 93 for five when Cowan departed for a workmanlike 51, but Ryan Carters and wicketkeeper Peter Nevill put on 178. Carters looked set for his maiden first-class hundred, ending the first day on 94, but was out first ball next morning; he made up for the near miss with 154 for New South Wales the following week. Solid contributions down the order took England to a lead of 114, then another disciplined bowling display, again led by the parsimonious Broad, left a target which was knocked off midway through the fourth afternoon. It all looked rosy for England: little did they know they would not taste victory again for two months.

Close of play: first day, Cricket Australia Invitation XI 271-5 (Carters 94, Nevill 76); second day, England XI 302-5 (Root 26, Bairstow 11); third day, Cricket Australia Invitation XI 153-4 (Patterson 8, Carters 1).

Cricket Australia Invitation XI

A. J. Finch c Bairstow b Broad	4	– (2) c Carberry b Swann	59
E. J. M. Cowan c Trott b Finn	51	– (1) b Broad	42
C. J. Ferguson lbw b Broad	8	– b Finn	26
K. R. Patterson c Cook b Finn	5	– b Broad	22
B. J. Rohrer c Carberry b Broad	19	– c Bairstow b Rankin	13
R. G. L. Carters c Bairstow b Broad	94	– c Bairstow b Swann	40
*†P. M. Nevill c Bairstow b Finn	83	– c Bairstow b Finn	11
J. K. Lalor c Swann b Finn	0	– c Bell b Rankin	8
C. P. Tremain c Carberry b Rankin	1	– c Pietersen b Finn	20
J. M. Muirhead not out	14	– c Bairstow b Rankin	4
N. D. Bills c Carberry b Finn	6	– not out	7
L-b 12, w 2, n-b 5	19	B 4, l-b 3, n-b 2	9

1/4 (1) 2/27 (3) 3/37 (4)   (103.4 overs) 304   1/81 (2) 2/120 (1)   (88.5 overs) 261
4/90 (5) 5/93 (2) 6/271 (6)   3/135 (3) 4/152 (5)
7/276 (8) 8/279 (7) 9/289 (9) 10/304 (11)   5/180 (4) 6/222 (7) 7/224 (6)
                                         8/241 (8) 9/245 (10) 10/261 (9)

Broad 24–10–37–4; Rankin 23–5–63–1; Finn 28.4–4–103–5; Swann 22–5–66–0; Trott 5–1–22–0; Root 1–0–1–0. *Second innings*—Broad 16–8–32–2; Finn 20.5–6–88–3; Rankin 21–7–46–3; Swann 27–10–69–2; Trott 1–0–3–0; Root 3–0–16–0.

England XI

*A. N. Cook c Nevill b Bills	81	– b Muirhead	21
M. A. Carberry c Nevill b Lalor	4	– c sub (D. P. Hughes) b Muirhead	50
I. J. L. Trott c Nevill b Lalor	83	– not out	38
K. P. Pietersen c sub (D. P. Hughes) b Muirhead	57	– b Tremain	6
I. R. Bell c Rohrer b Muirhead	35	– not out	33
J. E. Root b Bills	75		
†J. M. Bairstow c Nevill b Tremain	48		
S. C. J. Broad c Carters b Bills	16		
G. P. Swann c Cowan b Muirhead	11		
S. T. Finn c Finch b Muirhead	0		
W. B. Rankin not out	3		
B 1, w 1, n-b 3	5	W 1, n-b 2	3

1/19 (2) 2/162 (3) 3/182 (1)   (102.5 overs) 418   1/40 (1)   (3 wkts, 38.4 overs) 151
4/253 (5) 5/266 (4) 6/372 (7)   2/91 (2) 3/99 (4)
7/397 (8) 8/408 (9) 9/409 (10) 10/418 (9)

Tremain 25–5–101–1; Lalor 26–7–99–2; Bills 22–2–76–3; Muirhead 22.5–1–115–4; Rohrer 2–0–4–0; Finch 5–1–22–0. *Second innings*—Tremain 12.4–1–49–1; Lalor 5–1–9–0; Bills 7–0–27–0; Muirhead 14–0–66–2.

Umpires: S. D. Fry and M. D. Martell.   Referee: S. T. Easey.

AUSTRALIA v ENGLAND

First Ashes Test

MALCOLM KNOX

At Brisbane, November 21–24, 2013. Australia won by 381 runs. Toss: Australia. Test debut: G. J. Bailey.

As overwhelming as it was unexpected, Australia's victory in the First Test was only three runs shy of the slaughter of England here 11 years earlier. Paradoxically, however, the similarity of the result only served to underline the contrast between the two series.

In 2002-03, Australia had fielded their most dominant side of the modern era, led by Steve Waugh. England, on the way to a dispiriting eighth straight Ashes defeat, had lost Simon Jones to a long-term injury on an opening-day disaster that began with Nasser Hussain's decision to field. Those were the days when, so complete was Australia's command, some questioned whether Ashes series should be shortened to three Tests.

Fast forward to 2013-14 and Australia, having just lost their third consecutive Ashes, were racked by injury and division. Their new generation of fast bowlers was sidelined and, in seeming desperation, the selectors had returned to Mitchell Johnson, more or less a Test discard in recent years after some poor outings against England. George Bailey, the 31-year-old captain of Tasmania who had excelled in one-day internationals but under-delivered in first-class cricket, was given a Test debut, leaving Australia with seven players over the age of 30. They appeared to have the worst of both worlds: aged, yet also inexperienced.

The character of Clarke, meanwhile, was taking its customary battering from former players. The only voices who held any conviction in their statements that Australia had improved markedly during the 2013 English summer were those emanating from within the camp. But even those claims were carrying a hint of bravado: Australia's batting collapses at Trent Bridge, Lord's and Chester-le-Street had borne the outward signs of inner crisis.

England's lead-up to this match had not been perfect, with the warm-up game in Hobart badly disrupted by rain, and Prior in doubt until shortly before the Test with a calf injury. There was every expectation, nonetheless, that their experience and psychological edge over the Australians would set them right.

The first day reinforced this, as Australia's top-order batting capitulated again. Some of England's team, notably Broad and Pietersen, had been targeted by a Brisbane newspaper with a campaign that had the odour of a joke told against an outsider in a country pub, funny only to the teller. Broad, with five wickets on the opening day, was able to respond with a smile, and Pietersen would surely produce a big innings in his 100th Test. A sobering headline came from *The Australian*, which next morning pronounced: "New Location, Same Old Story".

THE FORTRESSES

Most successive matches without defeat at a single Test venue:

34	Pakistan at Karachi	1954-55–1999-2000
27	West Indies at Bridgetown	1947-48–1992-93
25	England at Manchester	1905–1954
25	**Australia at Brisbane**	**1989-90–**
19	West Indies at Kingston	1957-58–1988-89
18	England at The Oval	1884–1929
18	Australia at Lord's	1938–2005
18	New Zealand at Wellington	1968-69–1992-93

But England's success also gave notice of coming danger. Broad's wickets were achieved through his ability to extract steep bounce from a compliant Brisbane surface. A counter-attack in the last session from Haddin and Johnson, however, threw up another alert, as Swann was unable to get the turn or the variable bounce he had exploited so well back home.

Still, England's upper hand extended into the second morning, as Australia lost their last two wickets cheaply, before Johnson and Harris produced fast but wayward opening spells. Even the dismissal of Cook, driving and edging a full-length ball from Harris, as if it was the English summer all over again, seemed merely to inconvenience them. Then, in the last over before lunch, came the turning point: Trott was at sea against a predictable

Mark Kolbe, Getty Images

Not again: Matt Prior falls cheaply in the leg trap to Nathan Lyon for the second time in the match.

short-pitched attack from Johnson and, flapping away from his body at a ball he should have left alone, was caught down the leg side by Haddin, who in his 50th Test became the second-fastest wicketkeeper to 200 dismissals, after Adam Gilchrist (47). The mood changed entirely.

Carberry, playing his second Test more than three years after his first, and Pietersen looked to consolidate after the break, before Pietersen – dropped by Siddle off his own bowling when eight – carelessly drove Harris to short midwicket. Johnson now mounted a round-the-wicket assault on Carberry, who had been becalmed by the introduction of Lyon and his top-spinning flight, better suited to the conditions than Swann's futile search for more conventional side-spin. The onslaught ended gingerly, with a poke to slip.

Lyon quickly removed Bell and Prior with successive balls, deceiving them with bounce and obtaining near-identical catches by Smith at short leg. By the time Root – squirting to gully and providing Smith with his third catch in nine balls – and Swann were dismissed by Johnson, England had lost six for nine. In one humid Brisbane half-hour, the balance between the teams had been turned upside-down.

England's Black Friday did not improve when the Australians returned to bat with a 159-run lead. Warner, the most positive of the home batsmen on the first morning, opened up with a blazing back-foot square-drive off Anderson, and Rogers – unsteady in the first innings – settled into a supporting role. They added 65 to Australia's lead before stumps, confirming their best day of Test cricket in two years since the visit of India. Recent history, though, suggested they would struggle to string such days together, and the early exchanges on the third morning confirmed the hunch. Rogers and Watson succumbed to the bounce of Broad and Tremlett – playing his first Test since January 2012 – and the atmosphere was thickening, along with the rain clouds, when Clarke joined Warner.

Broad had often attacked Clarke early with short-pitched bowling in England. By the Fifth Test at The Oval, the tactic appeared to be grinding Australia's captain down, and in the first innings here he had been caught out of position by the first bouncer Broad gave him. Now, England treated Clarke with contempt, dropping the field to gift him a single off Anderson so that he would be on strike to Broad.

BRISBANE NOTES AND QUOTES

Brisbane's *Courier-Mail* targeted Kevin Pietersen ahead of his 100th Test. "He's so arrogant not even his own team likes him," screamed their front page. Pietersen tweeted: "Putting me on the front page does wonders for my ego! You've done me proud. Thank you x." He added: "I would have preferred a Sydney front page tbh… No one has heard of Brisbane outside Oz!"

Next day, the paper mocked up a picture of Pietersen in a purple wig and full Queensland regalia: "KP loves himself but not this 'boring' city." At a rare press conference, a jovial Pietersen flirted with a local female TV reporter: "Just for you," he said when asked if he would take back his criticism of Brisbane.

The KP spat was merely a warm-up for the *Courier-Mail's* main event – their "Broad Ban". "Our newspaper coverage will simply refer to 'a 27-year-old English medium-pace bowler', and we will de-identify any images of him," announced the paper, alongside an image of the "smug Pommie cheat" – a reference to his refusal to walk at Trent Bridge in July. Broad responded with five wickets on the first day, and entered the press conference carrying a copy of the paper.

David Warner raised eyebrows when he said England's batsmen had "scared eyes" at the end of the third day. Singling out Jonathan Trott, Warner added: "The way Trotty got out was pretty poor and weak. Obviously there is a weakness there and we are on top of it. He needs to get new sledges because it is not working for him at the moment." Unknown to Warner, Trott was struggling with a stress-related illness, and left the tour within 48 hours.

Resumption after a second rain delay on the final day was held up so Channel Nine could finish broadcasting an episode of *The Fresh Prince of Bel Air*, the American sitcom starring Will Smith (not the county batsman). Nine were forced to apologise to Michael Clarke after he was fined 20% of his match fee when a stump mike picked him up telling James Anderson to "get ready for a broken fucken' arm" in the closing stages.

All Notes and Quotes compiled by Chris Stocks

England's hopes proved short-lived. Broad gave Clarke three full balls, which he defended, and two bouncers, which he swatted for four. Some more short stuff was attempted, but Clarke was in an aggressive mood and blunted the tactic; England's seamers, after being given only four hours' respite by their batsmen, lacked their first-innings edge. Perhaps saving it for another day, they reverted to more conventional fare. Clarke and Warner added 158 in 29 overs either side of lunch, taking the game away from England and reserving their most belligerent batting for Swann, who was hit out of the attack twice within half an hour.

Warner and Clarke both recorded rapid centuries. For Warner, it was the first for a year and a day; for Clarke, it was his 25th in Test cricket, and a return to the confidence he had shown in his previous two, record-breaking, home summers. By the time both were out, the match was beyond England. Smith and Bailey – Swann's 250th Test victim, achieved uniquely within five years of his debut – failed fully to capitalise, but more attacking batting from Haddin and Johnson, a reprise of their first innings, allowed Clarke to choose his time to declare. Haddin took the lead past 500, and stole a glance at the dressing-room. The captain did not appear, and Haddin proceeded to play like a child whose parents had forgotten his bedtime. Clarke was concerned not about the size of the lead, but about the number of overs he wanted to give his bowlers that night. In the hope of keeping them fresh, and the ball new, for Sunday morning, he declared with an hour to go.

Johnson and Harris were as hostile as ever and, to England's dismay, the pitch was not flattening out. Backed by a noisy Brisbane crowd, Harris dismissed Carberry with a short ball that bounced down off the bat, between the pads, and on to the wicket. The small things were going Australia's way. Trott batted in uncharacteristic fashion again, trying to respond positively to Johnson's barrage, but only spooning a catch to backward square leg. Some stout defending from Cook and Pietersen saw England to stumps, but Australia had been dominant for a second day in a row.

Spectacular thunderstorms drenched Brisbane that night, and England's best hope seemed to be more early-summer rain. However, the Sunday downpour would be a false friend. Cook and Pietersen batted with resolve through the first hour, but then came a break for drinks – and in Pietersen's concentration: a top-edged flick off Johnson flew to fine leg, where substitute fielder Chris Sabburg, a 23-year-old Queenslander and former fruit-picker whose senior cricket had been limited to half a dozen games for Brisbane Heat, held on.

England's aspirations for one long partnership rested with Cook and Bell. As their alliance began to blossom on the fourth afternoon, the thunderclouds moved in, and the groundstaff brought their tractors and covers to the edge of the field. Shortly before the storm hit, Siddle cramped Bell, who couldn't pull his bat away before edging to Haddin. So when the rain – which quickly turned into hail – intervened, Cook was the only senior batsman left.

When play resumed 90 minutes later, Australia looked refreshed, England wary. Cook was undone by Lyon's bounce, and edged a cut, before three more wickets fell as Lyon and Johnson homed in on a weakness against the rising ball, whether slow or fast. Another short rain-break hardly held Australia up. England, who had lost their last eight wickets for 54 runs on Friday, now lost their last seven for 49.

FALLING AT THE FIRST

England's results in the opening Tests of overseas series since 2004-05:

Opponent		
South Africa	Won by seven wickets at Port Elizabeth	December 2004
Pakistan	Lost by 22 runs at Multan	November 2005
India	Drawn at Nagpur	March 2006
Australia	Lost by 277 runs at Brisbane	November 2006
Sri Lanka	Lost by 88 runs at Kandy	December 2007
New Zealand	Lost by 189 runs at Hamilton	March 2008
India	Lost by six wickets at Chennai	December 2008
West Indies	Lost by an innings and 23 runs at Kingston	February 2009
South Africa	Drawn at Centurion	December 2009
Bangladesh	Won by 181 runs at Chittagong	March 2010
Australia	Drawn at Brisbane	November 2010
Pakistan	Lost by ten wickets at Dubai	January 2012
Sri Lanka	Lost by 75 runs at Galle	March 2012
India	Lost by nine wickets at Ahmedabad	November 2012
New Zealand	**Drawn at Dunedin**	**March 2013**
Australia	**Lost by 381 runs at Brisbane**	**November 2013**

Like many teams who have been short on swagger, Australia now played with an excess of it. This boiled over in the last minutes of England's second innings, when Clarke and Anderson exchanged words, which resulted in Clarke, whose expletive was broadcast via the stump mike, being docked 20% of his match fee by referee Jeff Crowe. More seriously, it emerged that Trott had been suffering with a stress-related disorder and, after consultation with the team management, left the tour. His departure put into perspective the fractious on-field atmosphere, and sent an implicit warning to all.

In cricketing terms, England were left with not only a 1–0 deficit, but a hole at the top of their order. They had ten days between Tests to restore their self-belief and come to terms with the conditions. Australia's task was to manage their exuberance. This, as a prelude to the Adelaide Test, was the most unexpected outcome of all.

Man of the Match: M. G. Johnson. *Attendance:* 122,910.

Close of play: first day, Australia 273-8 (Haddin 78, Harris 4); second day, Australia 65-0 (Rogers 15, Warner 45); third day, England 24-2 (Cook 11, Pietersen 3).

Australia

C. J. L. Rogers c Bell b Broad	1	– c Carberry b Broad	16
D. A. Warner c Pietersen b Broad	49	– c Prior b Broad	124
S. R. Watson c Swann b Broad	22	– c Broad b Tremlett	6
*M. J. Clarke c Bell b Broad	1	– b Swann	113
S. P. D. Smith c Cook b Tremlett	31	– c Prior b Tremlett	0
G. J. Bailey c Cook b Anderson	3	– b Swann	34
†B. J. Haddin run out	94	– c Anderson b Tremlett	53
M. G. Johnson b Broad	64	– not out	39
P. M. Siddle c Cook b Anderson	7	– not out	4
R. J. Harris c Prior b Broad	9		
N. M. Lyon not out	1		
L-b 11, w 1, n-b 1	13	B 4, l-b 8	12

1/12 (1) 2/71 (3) 3/73 (4)   (97.1 overs) 295   1/67 (1)   (7 wkts dec, 94 overs) 401
4/83 (2) 5/100 (6) 6/132 (5)   2/75 (3) 3/233 (2)
7/246 (8) 8/265 (9) 9/282 (10) 10/295 (7)   4/242 (5) 5/294 (4) 6/305 (6) 7/395 (7)

Anderson 25.1–5–67–2; Broad 24–3–81–6; Tremlett 19–3–51–1; Swann 26–4–80–0; Root 3–1–5–0. *Second innings*—Anderson 19–2–73–0; Broad 16–4–55–2; Tremlett 17–2–69–3; Swann 27–2–135–2; Root 15–2–57–0.

England

*A. N. Cook c Haddin b Harris	13	– c Haddin b Lyon	65
M. A. Carberry c Watson b Johnson	40	– b Harris	0
I. J. L. Trott c Haddin b Johnson	10	– c Lyon b Johnson	9
K. P. Pietersen c Bailey b Harris	18	– c sub (C. J. M. Sabburg) b Johnson	26
I. R. Bell c Smith b Lyon	5	– c Haddin b Siddle	32
J. E. Root c Smith b Johnson	2	– not out	26
†M. J. Prior c Smith b Lyon	0	– c Warner b Lyon	4
S. C. J. Broad c Rogers b Siddle	32	– c Haddin b Johnson	4
G. P. Swann c Bailey b Johnson	0	– c Smith b Johnson	0
C. T. Tremlett c Lyon b Harris	8	– c Bailey b Harris	7
J. M. Anderson not out	2	– c and b Johnson	2
B 4, l-b 2	6	L-b 2, w 1, n-b 1	4

1/28 (1) 2/55 (3) 3/82 (4)   (52.4 overs) 136   1/1 (2) 2/10 (3)   (81.1 overs) 179
4/87 (2) 5/87 (5) 6/87 (7)   3/72 (4) 4/130 (5)
7/89 (6) 8/91 (9) 9/110 (10) 10/136 (8)   5/142 (1) 6/146 (7) 7/151 (8)
                                                8/151 (9) 9/172 (10) 10/179 (11)

Harris 15–5–28–3; Johnson 17–2–61–4; Siddle 11.4–3–24–1; Lyon 9–4–17–2. *Second innings*—Harris 19–4–49–2; Johnson 21.1–7–42–5; Siddle 15–3–25–1; Lyon 20–6–46–2; Smith 4–1–15–0; Watson 2–2–0–0.

Umpires: Aleem Dar and H. D. P. K. Dharmasena.   Third umpire: M. Erasmus.
Referee: J. J. Crowe.

At Alice Springs, November 29–30, 2013. **Drawn. England XI 212-7 dec** (G. S. Ballance 55) **and 47-1**; ‡**Cricket Australia Chairman's XI 254-8 dec** (G. P. Swann 4-56, M. S. Panesar 3-41). *The Chairman's XI chose from 12 players. This two-day fixture at Traegar Park assumed greater importance after England's stunning reverse, and Jonathan Trott's departure, in Brisbane, but few reputations were enhanced in the final audition for the rest of the series. Ballance grafted well, surviving 134 balls for 55, but the big fast bowlers misfired again: Finn, in his last competitive bowl of the tour, finished with 0-61 from 15 overs, and Rankin (14.5–5–52–1) was scarcely more impressive. Panesar did take his chance with three wickets, and his reward was a recall for Adelaide.*

AUSTRALIA v ENGLAND

Second Ashes Test

DAVID HOPPS

At Adelaide, December 5–9, 2013. Australia won by 218 runs. Toss: Australia. Test debut: B. A. Stokes.

If the First Test had been a rude awakening for England, what followed was even harder for them to bear. Australia's most docile surface, much in keeping with the lifeless pitches on which England had won at home a few months earlier, offered the tourists an opportunity to restate their qualities after their hounding at the Gabba. Instead, they lost heavily once more, with the fearsome pace of Johnson again the decisive factor. As they succumbed to a 218-run defeat early on the fifth day, they looked weary and short of answers. They left South Australia to cocksure predictions that Australia's regaining of the Ashes would be a formality in Perth, and with the assumption growing that England faced an awkward period of transition.

They had drawn much comfort in the hiatus between Tests from memories of recovering from 1–0 down in India a year earlier. There were many textbook pronouncements about how dressing-room pride, experience and honesty would sustain them. But none of that mattered when they were sandblasted by Johnson on a sunny Adelaide Saturday. His vaudeville moustache adding to the melodrama, Johnson was simply too quick for England's lower order as he helped himself to six wickets for 16 runs in 26 balls. His eventual analysis of seven for 40 was the best return by an Ashes fast bowler in Adelaide, and gave him 16 wickets in the series at nine runs apiece. Derided by England supporters, he had suddenly justified the assertion of Dennis Lillee that he was a once-in-a-generation bowler. Johnson, who in the modern trend had grown his facial hair for "Movember" to publicise the threat of prostate cancer, certainly had mo-mentum. And, while nobody could be sure it would last the series, it was lasting long enough to swing it in Australia's favour.

Adelaide Oval had become a multi-sports stadium. It was difficult to take for those who cherished the glorious red roofs of old, but it was enlightened enough as stadium builds go, with the protected Moreton Bay figs still visible behind the old scoreboard; you could even see St Peter's Cathedral from the right seat. But England's gaze was locked upon 22 yards of South Australian soil.

MOST SIXES IN AN ASHES INNINGS

Sixes	Score			
7	158	K. P. Pietersen (England)	at The Oval	2005
6	118	I. T. Botham (England)	at Manchester.........................	1981
5	93	S. J. E. Loxton (Australia)	at Leeds	1948
5	152	A. C. Gilchrist (Australia)	at Birmingham.........................	2001
5	68	†A. Flintoff (England)	at Birmingham.........................	2005
5	**118**	**B. J. Haddin (Australia)**	**at Adelaide**	**2013-14**
5	**103**	**S. R. Watson (Australia)**	**at Perth**.............................	**2013-14**
4	91	R. W. Marsh (Australia)	at Manchester.........................	1972
4	138	I. T. Botham (England)	at Brisbane.........................	1986-87
4	73	†A. Flintoff (England)	at Birmingham.........................	2005
4	102*	A. C. Gilchrist (Australia)	at Perth.............................	2006-07
4	**72***	**I. R. Bell (England)**	**at Adelaide**	**2013-14**
4	**42**	**S. C. J. Broad (England)**	**at Sydney**	**2013-14**

At Melbourne in 1882-83, G. J. Bonnor (A; 85) made four hits over the boundary, each worth only five runs at the time.

† *Flintoff hit nine sixes in the match, the Ashes record.*

Anthony Devlin, AP/PA

Gentlemen, please! Kumar Dharmasena separates England debutant Ben Stokes and Mitchell Johnson, wearing a black armband after the death of Nelson Mandela.

A groundshare with the Australian Football League had come hand in hand with Adelaide's first drop-in Test pitch, and two recent stalemates in the Sheffield Shield persuaded curator Damian Hough to keep the surface markedly dry. It encouraged England to field two spinners – Swann and Panesar, who replaced Chris Tremlett – for the first time in a Test in Australia since 1990-91, when Phil Tufnell and Eddie Hemmings combined at Sydney. Ben Stokes, the Durham all-rounder, won a Test debut at No. 6 to fulfil the third seamer's role and become only the fifth New Zealand-born cricketer to play Tests for another country, after Tom Groube, Clarrie Grimmett, Brendon Julian (all Australia) and Andrew Caddick (England). With Jonathan Trott back home, Root moved to No. 3, his third different position in three Tests.

Hough's courage was rewarded, as an otherwise lifeless pitch deteriorated in characteristic Adelaide fashion – but not quite as quickly as England. The choice of two spinners was a logical call, but England lost an important toss, and Australia met Panesar and Swann with a conviction India had never mustered. They declared late on the second day at 570 for nine, guided by hundreds from Clarke, his second in a row, and Haddin, who had narrowly missed out at the Gabba. From then on, the match bowed to Johnson.

And yet England had achieved parity on a keenly contested opening day as Australia closed at 273 for five. They made good use of an on–off morning – restricted to 14.2 overs as squally showers forced three stoppages – by dismissing Warner, who looked eager to repeat his rapid hundred here against South Africa a year earlier before he mis-hit Broad to Carberry at backward point. An obdurate stand of 121 between Rogers and Watson

What have I done? Joe Root can't quite believe it when Brad Haddin cuts short his 87 with a reaction catch.

edged Australia towards supremacy at 155 for one, but the afternoon session finished with England back in it.

Watson fell for a typically unfulfilled 51 to a lithe return catch by Anderson; Rogers followed in the next over, out to Swann for the seventh time in Tests; and Smith succumbed to the last ball before tea, as Panesar got one to straighten. Three wickets had been lost for 19, with English hope abounding that their selection would bear fruit.

But Australia recovered as Bailey achieved his first Test fifty, attacking the spinners with verve, before Broad dismissed him with the second new ball. Swann's wonderful diving grab at square leg, however, could not entirely offset three dropped catches in the final session. The most culpable was a simple miss at backward point when Haddin, on five, cut Panesar – the culprit, Carberry, again evincing a strange mix of athletic fielder but unreliable catcher. Tougher opportunities with the old ball also went astray: Panesar spilled a quick return catch from Bailey, on ten; and Root sprang to his right at short midwicket, with Clarke on 18, but a demanding chance off Swann went to ground.

How England rued those drops, as both Clarke and Haddin reached centuries on the second day, batting until almost an hour after lunch to extend their stand to 200 in 50 overs, a Test record for the sixth wicket at Adelaide. Captain and vice-captain stood side by side: an image to warm Australia. Clarke might have fallen to his first ball of the day, but a sliced drive against Panesar dropped safely. He was otherwise unflustered as he made 148, his sixth hundred in nine Adelaide Tests, before becoming Stokes's first Test victim, chipping to short midwicket.

Haddin's punchy 118 was another forceful intervention, although a fielder better than Panesar might have intervened at long leg when Haddin, on 30, hooked Anderson. He was also caught behind off Stokes when 51, only for replays to reveal a no-ball. Haddin's thoughts on the matter were not well received, and the umpires had to step in. Some praised Stokes's obvious affection for a scrap; others discerned fraying English tempers.

Johnson laid down a marker on the second evening, with his first ten balls all clocked at 148kph (nearly 92mph) or more. The tenth ripped out Cook, his off stump removed by one that shaped to swing towards leg but straightened late. Johnson's post-lunch spell on the third day bore comparison with the great fast-bowling spells of the modern age; in no

---

ADELAIDE NOTES AND QUOTES

The *Adelaide Advertiser* attempts to pick up the *Courier-Mail's* gauntlet with a front-page story about a night out for Kevin Pietersen and Stuart Broad on the day they arrived in the city: "Poms' first drinks break – it's stumps at 3.30am." But neither player was drinking, they were "extremely friendly", according to a spokesperson for the bar they frequented, and it all happened a full three days before the start of the Second Test.

A tweet on the first morning from Cricket Australia's official feed ("Will the real Monty Panesar please stand up?"), is accompanied by a picture of four Sikh men wearing Teletubby outfits. CA later apologised and deleted the tweet. It came a few days after the board had stood down PA announcer David Nixon during England's tour match in Alice Springs. Nixon was accused of introducing Panesar in a mock Indian accent, a claim he angrily denied.

James Anderson had a rib broken by Peter Siddle during England's second innings, but the news wasn't revealed until February. An X-ray before the Melbourne Test confirmed the fracture, but England kept it quiet. He took painkillers for the rest of the series.

---

time at all, a bewildered England had conceded a first-innings lead of 398. He was twice on a hat-trick – a feat not achieved in an Ashes innings since Keith Miller at Brisbane in 1946-47 – with the lower order utterly unable to cope with his potent slingers.

His second over after lunch did the most damage. Stokes had time to steal his first Test run before the ball thundered tellingly into his pad, and Prior was caught at the wicket after enduring a horrific three deliveries. But the real theatre involved Broad, who spent seven minutes fussing about glare from the sightscreen. Boos rained down and, when Johnson ripped out his leg stump, first ball, they became even more resounding. Amid the carnage, Bell's unbeaten 72 was assembled with not a hair out of place.

But if Johnson had created havoc, it was the errors of England's top order which had invited the opportunity. Root, eagerly slog-sweeping his first ball of the day from Lyon, and falling well short of a boundary restricted by building works to 53 metres, and Pietersen, nonsensically manufacturing a leg-side shot against his nemesis Siddle with two short midwickets lying in wait, both gave it away. Pietersen's machismo was justifiable if the statistics supported him; thanks largely to the nagging Siddle, they no longer did. Carberry's maiden Test fifty, crisply assembled, was long forgotten.

Australia did not enforce the follow-on and, by the close of the third day, Warner's untroubled 83 not out had extended their advantage to 530. Their determination to allow England no leeway was emphasised when they did not declare until 15 minutes before play was due to begin next morning. There was some unsettled weather about – Adelaide had been unusually cool, another factor which might have favoured England – but the timing had more to do with unsettling their opponents.

A year earlier, South Africa had batted on 148 overs here to salvage a draw. England would have had to surpass even that. As they had not amassed 531 in three goes, let alone one, defeat looked inevitable. But there was good reason to keep Australia's bowling in the field as long as possible, especially with the Third Test following on only a few days later. If they could knock the edge off Johnson, at least the game would become 11-a-side again.

As it was, only Root and Pietersen managed any sort of response. Both, in their own way, were hair-shirt performances. Root had been strangely skittish in the first innings. But, second time round, he did much to justify his promotion to No. 3, playing Johnson with equilibrium until Lyon dismissed him for the second time in the match, for 87, via an unlucky deflection off bat and thigh which Haddin ran round to grab. Pietersen, who can make even self-restraint look indulgent, reached 53 before Siddle got him again, bowled off an inside edge. Stokes resisted for two hours, although his combative nature almost got the better of him after a mid-pitch collision with Johnson led to an eyeball-to-eyeball discussion. Both were fortunate that referee Jeff Crowe ruled the contact was not deliberate, and decided against a possible one-Test ban.

Elsewhere, England's bad dismissals kept coming. Cook, a captain attempting to set an example by imposing himself on Johnson, hooked to long leg in his first over; Bell contrived to toe-end a low full toss from Smith's leg-spin to mid-on. On a demoralising final morning, the last four wickets then fell within 12 overs against short-pitched bowling, Prior seeking redemption of sorts with a desperate counter-attack. This was not the England – of carefully planned, percentage cricket – to which we had become accustomed.

Man of the Match: M. G. Johnson. *Attendance:* 153,530.

Close of play: first day, Australia 273-5 (Clarke 48, Haddin 7); second day, England 35-1 (Carberry 20, Root 9); third day, Australia 132-3 (Warner 83, Smith 23); fourth day, England 247-6 (Prior 31, Broad 22).

Australia

C. J. L. Rogers c Prior b Swann		72	– c Prior b Anderson	2
D. A. Warner c Carberry b Broad		29	– not out	83
S. R. Watson c and b Anderson		51	– c Carberry b Anderson	0
*M. J. Clarke c Anderson b Stokes		148	– b Panesar	22
S. P. D. Smith b Panesar		6	– not out	23
G. J. Bailey c Swann b Broad		53		
†B. J. Haddin c Prior b Broad		118		
M. G. Johnson c Broad b Swann		5		
P. M. Siddle c Prior b Stokes		2		
R. J. Harris not out		55		
N. M. Lyon not out		17		
B 8, l-b 1, w 1, n-b 4		14	B 1, l-b 1	2

1/34 (2) 2/155 (3)   (9 wkts dec, 158 overs) 570   1/4 (1)   (3 wkts dec, 39 overs) 132
3/155 (1) 4/174 (5) 5/257 (6)   2/4 (3) 3/65 (4)
6/457 (4) 7/474 (8) 8/483 (9) 9/529 (7)

Anderson 30–10–85–1; Broad 30–3–98–3; Swann 36–4–151–2; Panesar 44–7–157–1; Stokes 18–2–70–2. *Second innings*—Anderson 7–1–19–2; Broad 6–0–19–0; Swann 9–3–31–0; Stokes 7–3–20–0; Panesar 10–0–41–1.

England

*A. N. Cook b Johnson		3	– c Harris b Johnson	1
M. A. Carberry c Warner b Watson		60	– c Lyon b Siddle	14
J. E. Root c Rogers b Lyon		15	– c Haddin b Lyon	87
K. P. Pietersen c Bailey b Siddle		4	– b Siddle	53
I. R. Bell not out		72	– c Johnson b Smith	6
B. A. Stokes lbw b Johnson		1	– c Clarke b Harris	28
†M. J. Prior c Haddin b Johnson		0	– c Harris b Siddle	69
S. C. J. Broad b Johnson		0	– c Lyon b Siddle	29
G. P. Swann c Clarke b Johnson		7	– c Clarke b Harris	6
J. M. Anderson b Johnson		0	– not out	13
M. S. Panesar b Johnson		2	– c Rogers b Harris	0
L-b 3, w 2, n-b 3		8	L-b 1, w 4, n-b 1	6

1/9 (1) 2/57 (3) 3/66 (4)   (68.2 overs) 172   1/1 (1) 2/20 (2)   (101.4 overs) 312
4/111 (2) 5/117 (6) 6/117 (7)   3/131 (4) 4/143 (5)
7/117 (8) 8/135 (9) 9/135 (10) 10/172 (11)   5/171 (3) 6/210 (6) 7/255 (8)
                                            8/293 (9) 9/301 (7) 10/312 (11)

Johnson 17.2–8–40–7; Harris 14–8–31–0; Lyon 20–5–64–1; Siddle 14–4–34–1; Watson 3–3–0–1. *Second innings*—Harris 19.4–5–54–3; Johnson 24–8–73–1; Siddle 19–4–57–4; Lyon 26–7–78–1; Watson 6–3–6–0; Smith 7–0–43–1.

Umpires: H. D. P. K. Dharmasena and M. Erasmus. Third umpire: A. L. Hill.
Referee: J. J. Crowe.

AUSTRALIA v ENGLAND

Third Ashes Test

JOHN TOWNSEND

At Perth, December 13–17, 2013. Australia won by 150 runs. Toss: Australia.

Shane Warne's ball of the century seemed just so 20th century. Now, as Australia's first series win over England in seven years moved to within touching distance, Harris lodged a claim for the ball of the 21st. The delivery to Cook which began England's second innings possessed everything a ball of the century should: almost supernatural physical properties, exquisite timing, and an impact beyond the sum of its parts. "It swung in a bit, moved away off the pitch, then flicked the top of off stump," ran the Harris understatement. "Without sounding like I'm pumping up my own tyres, when you're teaching kids, that's what you're trying to show them." When you are bowling to the England captain, in his 100th Test, with a lead of 503 in the bank and nearly two days to go to work on a moonscape featuring cracks two inches wide, that's what you are trying to show *him*.

Harris had begun the Test with doubts growing over his durability, and his 34-year-old knees creaking dangerously. The ordeal of getting though the first two Tests, even with England wickets falling like confetti, had taken a toll. But Harris is nothing if not a man for the moment. With Australia two Tests up, and the third taking place on the bounciest, most evocative 22 yards of clay in world cricket, this was a moment no red-blooded fast bowler was going to miss.

He took the new ball at high noon on the fourth day, with England needing to bat for 161 overs to save the match and keep the series alive. One ball later, and the merest zephyr in England's sails had vanished. That moment, even more than the Test-record-equalling

Ball of this century? Alastair Cook is castled by a perfect opening delivery from Ryan Harris in the second innings.

ENGLAND'S LEAST SUCCESSFUL TEST GROUNDS

	P	W	L	D	%Win
WACA Ground, Perth	13	1	9	3	7.69
Woolloongabba, Brisbane	20	4	11	5	20.00
Sabina Park, Kingston	15	3	6	6	20.00
Eden Gardens, Kolkata	10	2	3	5	20.00
Kensington Oval, Bridgetown	14	3	4	7	21.42
Eden Park, Auckland	16	4	1	11	25.00
Adelaide Oval	31	9	17	5	29.03
Queen's Park Oval, Port-of-Spain	19	6	7	6	31.57
Kingsmead, Durban	15	5	1	9	33.33
Old Trafford, Manchester	74	25	14	35	33.78

Qualification: ten Tests.

28 runs Bailey had just taken from Anderson's final over of the Australian second innings, or the 22 Watson had hammered in what would prove the final over of Swann's lustrous career, announced that the Ashes were about to change hands.

The retention of Harris meant Australia entered a third consecutive Test with an unchanged team, a feat unmatched in seven years of almost equal success and turmoil. Bresnan finally returned for England in place of Monty Panesar. Among all the factors responsible for Australia's resurgence, Clarke's luck at the toss had gone almost unnoticed. The Western Australian Cricket Association had just appointed a new curator, Matt Page, and his fresh approach was evident several days before the match, when the pitch was already baked hard and devoid of much of the grass that had been retained for recent Perth Tests. The forecast promised 46°C, which meant the WACA clay was likely to split and shrink in a fashion not seen since the mid-1990s. Batting first would be a challenge; batting last a potential nightmare.

Rumbled: Harris's change of angle exposes a chink in Michael Carberry's technique.

Philip Brown

Australia started as though their first-innings goal of 400 had to be achieved in a day. Perhaps Rogers was unaccustomed to the frenetic pace: a split-second hesitation midway through an adrenalin-charged single provided Anderson with time for an athletic pick-up and direct hit.

In keeping with one of the themes of the series, Australia's top order continued to misfire. And it was not until Smith was joined by the evergreen Haddin that momentum finally shifted their way. It would remain there for the rest of the match.

Haddin had counterpunched to great effect at Brisbane and Adelaide; here, he was able to extend the onslaught, while simultaneously ushering Smith towards his second Ashes century and the most significant innings of his fledgling career.

Swann indulged his most uncanny habit – an ability to strike at the start of a spell – but his dismissal of Clarke (like Cook, winning his 100th Test cap) proved the falsest of dawns. In a reminder of the weapons at his disposal, Swann's second delivery had the

PERTH NOTES AND QUOTES

England's journalists retrieved some national pride when a team managed by former coach David Lloyd and including Michael Vaughan beat the Western Australian media in the traditional football match. In what failed to be an omen for the Test series, the visitors came back from 2–0 down to win 3–2, despite a missed penalty from Vaughan.

Western Australia's communications manager, Glen Foreman, proved sledging wasn't just confined to the field. In a chirpy sign-off to his introductory email to journalists, he said: "Cheers all and look forward to seeing you here throughout the week, but particularly Friday, when the only thing hotter than the weather will be the bowling of our WACA boy Mitch Johnson."

Temperatures on the first day turned the media tent into a sauna, and forced journalists to place their overheating laptops in the drinks fridge.

"Catches win matches. Me and Shane [Watson] let Michael Carberry know it." Speaking at a corporate breakfast in Perth, David Warner revealed how he told Carberry he had "dropped the Ashes" when he reprieved Brad Haddin at Adelaide. Carberry later caught Warner during Australia's first innings at the WACA.

"It's ours (almost)" – Perth's *Sunday Times* was so confident of victory after the third day that they produced a giant cut-out-and-keep urn on their back page. "You can get your hands on the sacred trophy early with our cut-out memento. Stick it on the TV, take it to the game or post it to a mate in the UK."

hallmarks of a textbook off-spinner's wicket. The ball swerved away from the right-handed Clarke, dropped like a stone, jagged back from the tacky first-session surface and spat, as if from a trampoline. And so it arrived several centimetres higher and straighter, and a moment or two later, than Clarke anticipated. His firm push hovered just long enough for Cook, stationed at short midwicket, to get his hands under the ball.

Steep bounce and turn also accounted for Warner, whose ambitious cut ballooned to point where Carberry held on. Bailey top-edged the third of three successive bouncers from Broad to deep backward square to leave Australia 143 for five. But England lost their discipline, repeatedly dropping short – to the public irritation of bowling coach David Saker – and feeding the cross-bat strengths of Smith and Haddin. In 36 overs, they added 134. Johnson chipped in and, though England's seamers belatedly found their length on the second morning, Australia scrambled to 385.

Moulding his talent and will into a semblance of the cast-iron epics he had delivered so devastatingly three years earlier, Cook fabricated the early stages of a capable English response with a watchful 72. That followed a forthright opening stand of 85 with Carberry – the tourists' best for the first wicket in the series – and the controversial departure of Root, aghast when the third umpire, Tony Hill, turned down his review against a caught-behind decision off Watson. But anything more substantial proved elusive.

Those stalwarts of previous Ashes successes – Pietersen, Bell and Prior – were unable to make meaningful contributions, though Bell was a victim of Hawk-Eye after Harris reviewed an lbw appeal. The midwicket position of the media tent enabled the press to observe how many no-balls were being allowed by umpires Bowden and Erasmus, and confirmed the extreme bounce. Forget technology: this one looked to be going over.

Australia began their second innings with a lead of 134, which was nearly enough to be comfortable. Warner, who should have been stumped twice by Prior off Swann, on 13 and 89, en route to his second century of the series, and Watson, in the fourth of his stuttering and vexed career, made certain. He finally batted with the freedom and verve he has displayed in cricket's more lucrative short forms.

Swann was taken for 14 from the first over of the fourth day, and runs continued to flow at such a torrent – 134 runs came in 17 overs that morning – that Clarke's declaration target of 500 ahead was achieved well before lunch. The absence of Broad helped. Disconcerted by the ferocity of Australia's attack whenever he came out to bat, he went

GRAEME SWANN

No mystery, just magic

VIC MARKS

Graeme Swann's international career was messy at the start and the finish, but in between it was magical. On the 1999-2000 tour of South Africa, where he played a solitary one-day international, he was – by his own admission – an irritant, a bumptious first-time tourist soon ostracised by England for the best part of a decade. In 2013, not long before the Boxing Day Test, he announced his retirement. It was, he said, "a selfless act", before referring enigmatically to current international cricketers "with heads up their own backsides". Another fine mess.

But during the five years in which Swann played Test cricket, he was a revelation. Old-fashioned, conventional finger-spin was reckoned to be as outdated as the hula hoop. Mystery was mandatory, a doosra de rigueur. Yet between Decembers 2008 and 2013 Swann, devoid of a doosra, captured more Test wickets than anyone, spinning himself rapidly into the pantheon of English slow bowlers.

His figures give us a hint of his achievement. In 60 Tests, he took 255 wickets. Of other England off-spinners, Raymond Illingworth snared 122 in 61; John Emburey had 147 in 64; Fred Titmus had 153 in 53. By these standards Swann was incredibly prolific. Since the war, only Jim Laker (193 in 46) approaches his rate of wicket-taking.

Not that it's a like-for-like comparison. Swann may not have had the benefit of bowling on uncovered pitches, but his predecessors were not blessed with Hawk-Eye or DRS, which helped him take 70 lbws. (Illingworth, who took 12, once told me, after due contemplation, that he would have taken 520 more first-class wickets with the modern interpretation of the lbw law.) Then again, bats in Illy's day were not capable of mis-hitting sixes.

Technically, Swann bowled in a similar manner to his predecessors, but his outlook was very different. For Illy and Co, parsimony ruled. Swann was more ambitious, braver even, since he aimed for a more attacking line to right-handers, wider of off stump. This allowed more run-scoring opportunities, but also a greater chance of wickets.

Against left-handers, by contrast, Swann bowled straight, which produced a haul of lbws that Illy's ilk could enjoy only in their dreams. Swann soon became an excellent judge of when to use DRS, though the chances of him exploiting this in retirement by becoming a first-class umpire remain slim. Moreover, Swann spun the ball more vigorously than most. This might result in more turn, but also a steeper dip at the end of the ball's flight path, which was more likely to lead the batsman to misjudge its length.

Beyond all these skills Swann became a wonderfully streetwise cricketer. He was always joking off the field; no one-liner – and he always had some good 'uns to hand – could be resisted. But out in the middle he was a pragmatist and an exceptional reader of the game. He could impose himself on batsmen, infiltrate their heads and sow doubt (though this would prove more difficult against Australians and South Africans). Unlike Monty Panesar, he engaged in a duel with the man at the other end.

He was a match-winner. England won 30 of the 60 Tests Swann played (about the same ratio as Illingworth, who won 29 times, and rather better than Emburey's 15). One more stat: only Derek Underwood among spinners took more wickets for England. Swann would have settled for that at the beginning of December 2008 when, in his 30th year, he had yet to play a Test. No wonder he enjoyed the ride.

back to a Johnson yorker which speared into his right foot and sent him to hospital for scans. "You're still not walking when you're out," one wag informed him as he hobbled through the WACA members' area; Broad soon discovered he would not bowl again in the match and would bat only if absolutely required. He attended the press conference that night on crutches.

Broad's absence left England bereft of defensive options. With Anderson and Swann singled out for harsh treatment, Watson raced from 50 to 102 in 28 balls. He did provide a touch of humour when Bell dropped a sitter, only for Bresnan, the frustrated bowler, to pick the ball up and hurl down the stumps with Watson stationary midway down the pitch. Clarke closed the innings at 369 for six.

GOING DOWN AGAIN

Most consecutive Test victories by one team over another at the same venue:

7	Australia v West Indies at Melbourne	1930-31 to 1975-76
7	**Australia v England at Perth**	**1990-91 to 2013-14**
6	Australia v South Africa at Cape Town	1902-03 to 1966-67
6	England v India at Lord's	1932 to 1967
5	England v Australia at The Oval	1886 to 1896
5	England v South Africa at Cape Town	1888-89 to 1905-06
5	Australia v England at Adelaide	1894-95 to 1907-08
5	West Indies v Australia at Perth	1975-76 to 1996-97
5	West Indies v India at Bridgetown	1975-76 to 2001-02
5	Australia v Pakistan at Perth	1978-79 to 2004-05
5	Australia v India at Melbourne	1991-92 to 2011-12
5	Australia v South Africa at Johannesburg	1996-97 to 2011-12

Harris had the new ball before lunch. Cook had been undone by a Johnson peach in the Second Test, yet even that searing blow could not match the stunning impact of this preemptive strike. Pietersen threatened briefly to harness ambition to ability. But, not for the first time, one exceeded the other: his bid to clear the man at long-on, hitting Lyon into the wind, fell a few fatal yards short. Still, he demonstrated that a cavalry charge may not be any less effective than dogged defence on a shifting and unstable surface from which missiles were jagging in unpredictable fashion.

Stokes, who added 99 at almost five an over with the pugnacious Bell, adapted the Pietersen approach soundly enough to ease to 120, a century in only his second Test that provided England with a rare shining moment. Johnson collected another four wickets to make it 23 in the series, including the last two in a hurry after lunch. That ignited much Australian rejoicing and a rendition of the team song on a pitch soon drenched in a celebratory reprisal of England's sprinkling at The Oval four months earlier – this time of the alcoholic variety.

Man of the Match: S. P. D. Smith. *Attendance:* 83,760.

Close of play: first day, Australia 326-6 (Smith 103, Johnson 39); second day, England 180-4 (Bell 9, Stokes 14); third day, Australia 235-3 (Watson 29, Smith 5); fourth day, England 251-5 (Stokes 72, Prior 7).

> **"** He leaked only 13 but, in a phone conversation with a bookmaker taped by Delhi police, complained that a deliberate no-ball had been missed by the umpire: 'What's my fault if the umpire didn't notice?'"
> The Indian Premier League, 2012-13, page 968

Australia

C. J. L. Rogers run out	11	– c Carberry b Bresnan	54
D. A. Warner c Carberry b Swann	60	– c Stokes b Swann	112
S. R. Watson c Swann b Broad	18	– run out	103
*M. J. Clarke c Cook b Swann	24	– b Stokes	23
S. P. D. Smith c Prior b Anderson	111	– c sub (J. M. Bairstow) b Stokes	15
G. J. Bailey c Pietersen b Broad	7	– not out	39
†B. J. Haddin c Anderson b Stokes	55	– c Swann b Bresnan	5
M. G. Johnson c Prior b Broad	39	– not out	0
P. M. Siddle c Prior b Bresnan	21		
R. J. Harris c Root b Anderson	12		
N. M. Lyon not out	17		
L-b 6, w 3, n-b 1	10	B 8, l-b 5, w 5	18

1/13 (1) 2/52 (3) 3/106 (4) (103.3 overs) 385 1/157 (1) (6 wkts dec, 87 overs) 369
4/129 (2) 5/143 (6) 6/267 (7)   2/183 (2) 3/223 (4)
7/326 (8) 8/338 (5) 9/354 (10) 10/385 (9)   4/301 (5) 5/331 (3) 6/340 (7)

Anderson 23–5–60–2; Broad 22–2–100–3; Bresnan 23.3–4–81–1; Stokes 17–3–63–1; Swann 17–0–71–2; Root 1–0–4–0. *Second innings*—Anderson 19–5–105–0; Bresnan 14–3–53–2; Stokes 18–1–82–2; Swann 27–8–92–1; Root 9–1–24–0.

England

*A. N. Cook c Warner b Lyon	72	– b Harris	0
M. A. Carberry b Harris	43	– lbw b Watson	31
J. E. Root c Haddin b Watson	4	– c Haddin b Johnson	19
K. P. Pietersen c Johnson b Siddle	19	– c Harris b Lyon	45
I. R. Bell lbw b Harris	15	– c Haddin b Siddle	60
B. A. Stokes c Haddin b Johnson	18	– c Haddin b Lyon	120
†M. J. Prior c Haddin b Siddle	8	– c Haddin b Johnson	26
T. T. Bresnan c Haddin b Harris	21	– c Rogers b Johnson	12
S. C. J. Broad lbw b Johnson	5	– (10) not out	2
G. P. Swann not out	19	– (9) c Smith b Lyon	4
J. M. Anderson c Bailey b Siddle	2	– c Bailey b Swann	2
B 11, l-b 7, w 5, n-b 2	25	B 13, l-b 13, w 6	32

1/85 (2) 2/90 (3) 3/136 (1) (88 overs) 251 1/0 (1) 2/62 (2) (103.2 overs) 353
4/146 (4) 5/190 (5) 6/198 (6)   3/76 (3) 4/121 (4)
7/207 (7) 8/229 (8) 9/233 (8) 10/251 (11)   5/220 (5) 6/296 (7) 7/336 (6)
                 8/347 (9) 9/349 (8) 10/353 (11)

Harris 22–10–48–3; Johnson 22–7–62–2; Watson 12–3–48–1; Siddle 16–5–36–3; Lyon 16–6–39–1. *Second innings*—Harris 19–2–73–1; Johnson 25.2–6–78–4; Lyon 22–5–70–3; Siddle 26–11–67–1; Watson 11–1–39–1.

Umpires: B. F. Bowden and M. Erasmus. Third umpire: A. L. Hill.
Referee: J. J. Crowe.

AUSTRALIA v ENGLAND

Fourth Ashes Test

CHLOE SALTAU

At Melbourne, December 26–29, 2013. Australia won by eight wickets. Toss: Australia.
 Much of the Boxing Day Test was played on England's terms, in an attritional style. But at the end, the Australian players and their families gathered for a celebration, every bit as satisfied as when they raucously welcomed the return of the Ashes in Perth. While

Bit of a downer: Jonny Bairstow declines to go, Alastair Cook can't cling on; Chris Rogers survives to wrap up the match with 116.

Johnson received the official accolade for his malevolent spell with the second new ball in the first innings, and for triggering another round of England panic in the second, it was Rogers who took the team's own match award, a tradition – marked by a private presentation – that had begun a few months earlier in England.

Rogers's team-mates could think of no one more deserving, not just because of his contrasting innings of 61 and 116 in the tightest contest of the series, but for the 20,000-odd first-class runs he had on the board before he was granted a second chance in Tests. To make a match-winning century at the grand stadium he called home was, for this adopted Victorian, "what dreams are made of". And perhaps only in his dreams had the 36-year-old Rogers, described before the series by Warner, his opening partner, as a "nudger", played sparkling square-drives like the one carved off Bresnan as Australia motored towards a potentially tricky target of 231 after lunch on the fourth day.

Rogers and Australia felt the love of the biggest crowd ever recorded for a Test completed in four days. Their insurmountable series lead had clearly not diminished public enthusiasm: the attendance of 271,865 at the MCG included 91,112 on Boxing Day, also an official world record, eclipsing the 90,800 who turned out to see Richie Benaud's Australians play Frank Worrell's West Indies here in 1960-61.

The Australians cherished this victory more than most because, for only the second time during Clarke's reign as captain, they had overcome a first-innings deficit to win. For England, this was a game of fluffed chances, both with the bat and, on a forgettable fourth morning for Cook, in the field. The sense that England were in disarray had deepened four days before the Test, when Graeme Swann retired, resulting in a recall for Panesar and further insinuations about a joyless atmosphere in the dressing-room. The decline of another senior player, Matt Prior, led to a change behind the stumps for the first time in 60 Tests dating back to March 2009: Bairstow took the gloves.

Clarke walked out for the toss intending to bat first, only to change his mind when he got there. "I can't believe I'm saying this," he half-winced under cloudy skies. "We're going to have a bowl." For much of the day he wondered if he had made the right decision, as England reached lunch one wicket down, and tea at a painstaking 135 for three.

Watson had bowled Carberry, shouldering arms for 38, with a lovely inswinger from round the wicket, but pulled up during his seventh over, and had to leave the field with a groin niggle. Pietersen then suppressed his aggressive urges against disciplined Australian bowling for four hours, getting to stumps on 67, and moving past Geoffrey Boycott's tally of 8,114 runs into fourth place on England's Test run-scoring list. He had received a let-off on six, when substitute fielder Nathan Coulter-Nile, on for Watson, made a comical mess of a catch at fine leg. Clutching a careless pull off Harris after Pietersen had inched to six from 44 deliveries, he staggered backwards towards the boundary, and tried to toss the ball inside the field of play. Instead, he threw it over his head and into the crowd. It would be Pietersen's only outlandish shot of an ascetic afternoon.

The game changed when Johnson took the second new ball, heralding a vicious spell of nine overs, split across the first evening and second morning, that yielded five for 18. His first ball on the second day reared up at the throat of Bresnan, who could only fend to short leg. Pietersen, no longer a picture of self-denial, seemed to be unsettled by a nasty bouncer two deliveries later; two balls after that, he was bowled for 71, attempting a wild slog. Having resumed at 226 for six, England crumpled to 255 – damningly, their highest first-innings score of the series. Johnson would finish with the tenth five-wicket haul of his Test career – and an unshakeable hold over the batsmen.

Australia's first innings had followed a familiar pattern, as they slumped to 122 for six before Haddin once more rode to the rescue. Anderson had finally found his spark, and Clarke scratched out ten before losing his off stump when he left one that nipped back.

YOUNGEST TO 8,000 TEST RUNS

Yrs	Days		T	I
29	**3**	**A. N. Cook (England)**	**101**	**181**
29	27	S. R. Tendulkar (India)	96	154
30	196	J. H. Kallis (South Africa/World XI)	101	170
31	15	R. T. Ponting (Australia)	100	165
31	51	G. C. Smith (South Africa/World XI)	99	173
31	270	D. P. M. D. Jayawardene (Sri Lanka)	101	165
32	**271**	**M. J. Clarke (Australia)**	**101**	**172**
32	282	K. C. Sangakkara (Sri Lanka)	91	152
32	335	R. Dravid (India/World XI)	94	158
33	68	V. Sehwag (India/World XI)	93	160
33	139	Javed Miandad (Pakistan)	107	162
33	**170**	**K. P. Pietersen (England)**	**102**	**176**

Generally, the Australians lost patience. Rogers was struck a fierce blow on the helmet by Broad, causing blood to trickle from his temple. A replacement helmet did not fit properly, and neither did the one after that, so Rogers wore four different helmets during the innings. When he looped a drive to mid-off, Haddin marched in and pounded the old ball. When he was joined by No. 11, Lyon he told him to swing. With Cook setting obligingly defensive fields, they put on 40 to ensure Australia trailed by only 51 – still sizeable on a grudging track, but hardly insurmountable in a series where England kept finding ways to stuff it up.

With a buffer of 116 and nine wickets by the time Cook departed on the third afternoon for a fluent half-century – his strike-rate of nearly 80 was the highest for any of the 60 Test innings in which he had made 50 – England should have set Australia more than 300. Instead, they lost wickets in two grisly clumps: three for one, then five for six. Suddenly Australia were chasing a more manageable 231. Johnson had again played like a superhero, dismissing Cook with reverse swing, and throwing down the stumps to run out Root, who had thoughtlessly chanced a single to his left hand at mid-off. But the afternoon belonged to a more understated figure.

Lyon used flight and drop, rather than turn, to remove five England batsmen for 50, but those figures didn't begin to sum up the significance of his achievement. When Broad

MELBOURNE NOTES AND QUOTES

An unprompted comment made by Graeme Swann at his retirement press conference was interpreted as a parting shot at Kevin Pietersen: "Some people playing the game at the minute have no idea how far up their own backsides they are." Swann later insisted he was talking about an opposition player: "I've spoken to Kev and assured him there was nothing in it aimed towards him. He said, 'I know exactly who you were talking about.'"

Asked later about Swann's remarks, Pietersen proved less than forthcoming: "My interest levels in yesterday are less than zero. I've got no interest, no interest."

Cricket Australia launched an energetic Twitter campaign to entice a record Boxing Day crowd into the MCG. But it took until the evening session to beat the 90,800 who watched Australia against West Indies there in 1960-61. There were 62,000 in attendance at the start, 85,000 by lunch, and 91,112 after tea. But the figure was still less than the 95,446 who watched the exhibition football match between Melbourne Victory and Liverpool, and the 100,007 at the AFL Grand Final between Hawthorn and Fremantle, both earlier in the year.

A toddler caused a confrontation between Pietersen and Mitchell Johnson on the third day. Pietersen pulled away as Johnson steamed in, leading to a playground tiff which ended with Johnson hurling the ball in his direction. Pietersen had been distracted by a roaming infant coming into his line of vision. But Johnson was unimpressed: "I did find out later there was a little kid crawling across the sightscreen. But if you look at the size of the sightscreen, they're pretty big here."

Monty Panesar could not catch a break on or off the field. He attempted to get round the team's curfew following defeat at the MCG by using a mobile-phone dating app to invite an American backpacker to his hotel room. She declined. "The only maidens on Panesar's mind were on matchmaking phone app Tinder," reported the *Sunday Mirror*.

---

edged him lustily to slip, Lyon became only the sixth Australian off-spinner to reach 100 Test wickets. A laconic lad who looked as if he could be swept off his feet by the blustery wind, he could not contain his glee as he held up the ball to celebrate his first five-for in Australia after Pietersen, running out of partners for the second time in the match, tried to launch him over long-off.

Underrated for much of his career by opponents such as Pietersen, and by selectors who at various stages in India and England had preferred Xavier Doherty, Glenn Maxwell and Ashton Agar, Lyon knew he had the appreciation of his team-mates. After Bell had one of his aberrations against spin and bunted a tame catch first ball to mid-off, Lyon was scooped up in a hug by Johnson. There were signs of wear and tear among the Australians; Watson, back on the field now, bowled four laborious overs, and Harris managed only ten because of a red-raw blister on the back of his heel. England still folded hopelessly for 179.

Australia were 30 without loss overnight, and England needed to strike early on the fourth day to have any hope of derailing a whitewash. That hope was dashed within half an hour. With Rogers on 19, an edge off Broad flew within reach of Bairstow, who didn't move a muscle; diving belatedly to his right at slip, Cook couldn't hang on. From that moment on, Rogers performed an admirable impersonation of his more audacious opening partner, slapping the next ball over the slips. Two overs later, Cook dropped the simplest of chances, with Warner on 22, this time off Stokes. Warner added only three more, but the emboldened Australians knew they were on their way to victory – and England knew it too.

Cook looked all alone as he stood at first slip contemplating life. He was asked whether he felt he was the right man to captain England after such a spectacular unravelling – "100%," he insisted, but he found it hard to explain why he had waited until the 30th over to bowl Panesar, by which time Root had already sent down four overs of gentle off-breaks. Cook said he had been expecting the ball to reverse, though his assertion that he wanted the off-spinner bowling to the two left-handed openers did not necessarily tally with that.

Regardless, Rogers – unshackled by the retirement of Swann, who had accounted for seven of his first 17 Test dismissals – played with such freedom that team-mates poked fun at Warner for being outpaced. Rogers was typically modest: "Congratulations to Swanny for such a great career, but I was probably the biggest winner out of it all." At 36 years 120 days, he became the oldest Australian opener to hit a Test century since 39-year-old Lindsay Hassett at Lord's in 1953.

Rogers eventually fell to Panesar after a partnership of 136 in just 28 overs with Watson, who whipped the winning runs though the leg side, clenched his fist and gathered Clarke – who had followed Cook to 8,000 Test runs – in a mid-pitch embrace. Not since the captain declared behind in Barbados in April 2012 had his side triumphed after trailing on first innings. That sweetened the victory for the Australians, who marched to Sydney determined to finish the job.

Man of the Match: M. G. Johnson.   *Attendance:* 271,865.

Close of play: first day, England 226-6 (Pietersen 67, Bresnan 1); second day, Australia 164-9 (Haddin 43); third day, Australia 30-0 (Rogers 18, Warner 12).

England

*A. N. Cook c Clarke b Siddle	27	– lbw b Johnson	51
M. A. Carberry b Watson	38	– lbw b Siddle	12
J. E. Root c Haddin b Harris	24	– run out	15
K. P. Pietersen b Johnson	71	– c Harris b Lyon	49
I. R. Bell c Haddin b Harris	27	– c Johnson b Lyon	0
B. A. Stokes c Watson b Johnson	14	– c Smith b Lyon	19
†J. M. Bairstow b Johnson	10	– c Haddin b Johnson	21
T. T. Bresnan c Bailey b Johnson	1	– b Lyon	0
S. C. J. Broad lbw b Johnson	11	– c Clarke b Lyon	0
J. M. Anderson not out	11	– not out	1
M. S. Panesar b Lyon	2	– lbw b Johnson	0
B 10, l-b 7, w 1, n-b 1	19	B 5, l-b 6	11

1/48 (1) 2/96 (2) 3/106 (3)   (100 overs) 255   1/65 (1) 2/86 (2)   (61 overs) 179
4/173 (5) 5/202 (6) 6/216 (7)   3/86 (3) 4/87 (5)
7/230 (8) 8/231 (4) 9/242 (9) 10/255 (11)   5/131 (6) 6/173 (7) 7/174 (8)
8/174 (9) 9/179 (4) 10/179 (11)

Harris 24–8–47–2; Johnson 24–4–63–5; Siddle 23–7–50–1; Lyon 22.2–3–67–1; Watson 6.4–2–11–1. *Second innings*—Harris 10–1–34–0; Johnson 15–5–25–3; Lyon 17–3–50–5; Siddle 15–6–46–1; Watson 4–2–13–0.

Australia

C. J. L. Rogers c Pietersen b Bresnan	61	– c Bairstow b Panesar	116
D. A. Warner c Bairstow b Anderson	9	– c Bairstow b Stokes	25
S. R. Watson c Bairstow b Stokes	10	– not out	83
*M. J. Clarke b Anderson	10	– not out	6
S. P. D. Smith c Bell b Broad	19		
G. J. Bailey c Bairstow b Anderson	0		
†B. J. Haddin c Bairstow b Anderson	65		
M. G. Johnson c Anderson b Bresnan	2		
R. J. Harris c Root b Broad	6		
P. M. Siddle c Bresnan b Broad	0		
N. M. Lyon not out	18		
L-b 4	4	N-b 1	1

1/19 (2) 2/36 (4) 3/62 (4)   (82.2 overs) 204   1/64 (2)   (2 wkts, 51.5 overs) 231
4/110 (5) 5/112 (6) 6/122 (6)   2/200 (1)
7/151 (8) 8/162 (9) 9/164 (10) 10/204 (7)

Anderson 20.2–4–67–4; Broad 20–6–45–3; Stokes 15–4–46–1; Bresnan 18–6–24–2; Panesar 9–2–18–0. *Second innings*—Anderson 11–2–26–0; Broad 10–0–58–0; Panesar 7.5–0–41–1; Stokes 12–0–50–1; Root 4–1–8–0; Bresnan 7–1–48–0.

Umpires: Aleem Dar and H. D. P. K. Dharmasena.   Third umpire: B. F. Bowden.
Referee: R. S. Madugalle.

AUSTRALIA v ENGLAND

Fifth Ashes Test

STEPHEN BRENKLEY

At Sydney, January 3–5, 2014. Australia won by 281 runs. Toss: England. Test debuts: G. S. Ballance, S. G. Borthwick, W. B. Rankin.

The film *Groundhog Day* tells the story of a man who is forced to relive the same routine until he finally learns the error of his ways. This series was cricket's own version – but for England there was no atonement. To the end, Cook's team kept repeating the same mistakes; Australia seized on them, and burst through like stampeding kangaroos. And so, once more, England created opportunities which might have put them on the road to victory; once more, through a combination of their own negligence and meekness, and Australia's powerhouse strategy, they were repelled and crushed.

There had been many disappointments for England in the preceding seven weeks, but nothing was quite as weak and woeful as the conclusion to the Fifth Test. More than an hour before the scheduled close on the third day, they had been bowled out in their second innings inside 32 overs, losing their last seven wickets in 64 balls after tea while, bizarrely, adding 79 runs. It was their second-shortest completed Ashes innings since 1903-04.

The game was a triumph for an array of Australia players. Rogers scored his second century in two games, while Harris took the match award for some enviably intelligent and controlled fast bowling. As at Perth, Smith made a crucial and jaunty century after his team had been up against it. And, inevitably, two men whose career had been down the drain a year earlier rallied to the cause, as they had throughout.

Haddin scored the kind of belligerent half-century, his fifth in five Tests to go with a hundred at Adelaide, which was designed to squeeze the will out of opponents. Johnson, Man of the Series and the embodiment of redemption, was yet again irresistible in patches, and provided his own sense of theatre. Six wickets brought his total for the Ashes to 37, the most by an Australian fast bowler in a five-match series, equalling fellow left-arm seamer Bill Whitty at home to South Africa in 1910-11.

Bestriding it all was Clarke. Three years earlier he had been jeered by home fans in Brisbane when he walked out to bat in a one-day international. Now he was king of all he surveyed. It was entirely appropriate that he performed the last act, a bobby-dazzler of a slip catch high above his head to end England's non-resistance.

It had looked so different on the first afternoon – but then it usually did. England won the toss for the first time in the series. They picked three debutants: Gary Ballance, Boyd Rankin and, perhaps most surprisingly, Scott Borthwick, the leg-spinning all-rounder from Sunderland who had been called into the party only after Graeme Swann's retirement. Heard the one about the Englishman, the Irishman and the Zimbabwean? They all made their first Test appearance in the same match for the same team.

SYDNEY NOTES AND QUOTES

Dress codes are strict in the members areas of most grounds. However, SCG stewards took things to another level on the second day, when they barred 35-year-old solicitor Lynda Reid from entry. Dresses must be knee-length to enter the Members Pavilion, but Ms Reid, who hoped to sit in the Ladies Stand, was wearing one with a hemline above the knee. That was enough for stewards to deem she had breached the protocol that decrees all dresses should be "of a respectable length". "I am a corporate solicitor," she said. "I know what is appropriate and not. I am not some hick from wherever. They absolutely ruined my day."

At Australia's post-series party in front of the Opera House, David Warner protested: "Apparently I said some rude things that were picked up on stump mike that you can't say – but I don't recall any of them. You don't cross that line. Probably we got close to it a couple of times, but I think we really got into their heads."

With the game done, Matt Prior, Stuart Broad and team security officer Terry Minish talked down a suicidal British tourist from a bridge in Sydney's Darling Harbour. The trio, on their way back from a charity event, kept the man talking until police arrived. "We just did what anybody would do in that situation," said Prior. "We were trying to help a bloke who was struggling and in a bad way."

The final word goes to Sydney's *Daily Telegraph* and their Truck of Triumph. The paper had been inviting people to apply white paint to a picture of the England team on a truck stationed outside the SCG. The whitewash was completed when the former Australian batsman Doug Walters painted over the faces of Kevin Pietersen and Graeme Swann.

Ballance replaced the out-of-touch Joe Root, who was dropped for the first time, while Rankin came in for Tim Bresnan, and Borthwick for Monty Panesar, who had been revealingly underbowled at Melbourne. It meant England had used 18 players in the series, more than in any away from home, and matched as a touring side only by West Indies in South Africa 15 years previously. Perhaps it was also further evidence of a globalised world: Borthwick had been playing for Haddin's Sydney club side, Northern District, before his unexpected summons. Their line-up contained eight left-handed batsmen, including the three newcomers – to equal the Test record, set by West Indies against Pakistan at Georgetown in 1999-2000.

By contrast, Australia were unchanged for the fifth consecutive match, for the first time in a full series. It said much about the state of the sides. Harris was in doubt because his much put-upon body was feeling the strain, and Bailey's place was in jeopardy because of poor form. But it mattered a great deal to Clarke and Darren Lehmann that Australia saw it through with the same men – their men.

England's decision to field looked to have paid off handsomely just after lunch, when Australia subsided to 97 for five. If it was a slightly fortunate advantage – England still bowled too many four-balls – it seemed to justify Cook's call on a pitch with a green tinge under overcast skies. The fall of Bailey brought Haddin to the wicket. He seemed to cast a spell over England's seam bowlers which compelled them to bowl short and wide, and he took full toll. In both the circumstances and the conditions, it was breathtaking indiscipline. Smith, at least respectfully defending the better balls, played good cop to Haddin's nasty one, but his contribution was significant, and their sixth-wicket partnership was worth 128 by the time Haddin, after clattering 75 from 90 balls, drove to slip to give Stokes the third of his six wickets. Not since Botham or Flintoff had an England all-rounder scored a century and taken a five-for in the same series – and Stokes had done it at the first time of asking.

But it seemed scant consolation, especially with Rankin pulling up with cramp after the first ball of two new spells. Australia's last four wickets now added 101, with Smith enjoying himself hugely. He always seemed to give the bowler a chance, but his assertive strokeplay offered a striking counterpoint. This was his third hundred against England in six matches. He was last out, again to Stokes, after an innings spanning only 154 balls.

England's response was all that it should not have been: insipid and error-strewn. By the close of the first day, with Johnson in his rapid pomp, they had lost Carberry, who played and missed repeatedly before flicking to leg slip, the equivalent of falling for the three-card trick. By lunch on the second, four more wickets had gone, the most poignant that of Cook to the day's second ball, when he inexplicably padded up to Harris. It was the reaction of a mind scrambled by weeks of torment. Only Stokes, once more refusing to take a step back, offered a modicum of resistance. Broad, too, while still the man the Aussies loved to hate, provided some desperate aggression at the end to ensure that the follow-on target of 127 was passed, but with only No. 11 Rankin at the crease.

ENGLAND'S SHORTEST TEST INNINGS SINCE 1910

Overs	Total		
19.1	46	v West Indies at Port-of-Spain	1993-94
26.2	102	v India at Bombay	1981-82
28.2	79	v Australia at Brisbane	2002-03
30.0	89	v West Indies at Birmingham	1995
30.5	81	v Sri Lanka at Galle	2007-08
31.4	**166**	**v Australia at Sydney**	**2013-14**
32.5	71	v West Indies at Manchester	1976
33.2	51	v West Indies at Kingston	2008-09
33.5	102	v Australia at Leeds	2009
36.1	72	v Pakistan at Abu Dhabi	2011-12

Before 1910, England were bowled out in the equivalent of 36 six-ball overs or fewer on 11 further occasions, including their shortest completed innings of all – 15.4 overs (total 61) against Australia at Melbourne in 1901-02.

With a lead of 171, and more than three days remaining, Australia could do pretty much as they wished. There was no fight left in England and, though Anderson took two early wickets as a reminder that he could still be potent with the new ball, it was too little, too late. On the previous Ashes tour, Anderson had taken 24 wickets and been the master of reverse swing; now he was struggling to move the ball off the straight, and picking up wickets at nearly 44 each.

Rogers assembled a craftsman's century. He had gone into the Fourth Test unsure of his place, but a second-innings hundred there had kept the selectors at bay. His 119, containing its full share of cuts and pulls, but also showing an increasing willingness to drive, made him the leading scorer across the two Ashes series of 2013-14.

Drifting in the field, their spirits wilting, England were left a nominal 448 to win. With 236 overs remaining, time was both on their side and against them: there was plenty in which to make the runs – but no way they were capable of batting that long. Cook lasted 12 balls, and for the seventh time in the series was the first England wicket to fall. Johnson and his partner-in-chief Harris were rampant again, and the suspicion when Johnson was steaming in that an England batsman or two were running for cover – or rather square leg – could not be confidently dispelled. Harris completed his fourth five-for against England in only 12 Tests.

The end was as merciful as it was abject. Batsman after batsman surrendered, none more lamely than the senior men: Bell cut loosely to gully, Pietersen prodded casually to short leg (a month later England decided they could do without him). Only Stokes, who took 20 off a Lyon over amid the mayhem, and Broad stood up with their jaws jutting; Broad's four sixes took the series tally from both sides to 65, a full 14 clear of the previous Test record, set during the 2005 Ashes. At 4.23 on the third afternoon, England had lost 5–0 in an Ashes for the third time – but the second in the last three contests away from home. The great victory in 2010-11 was, in this moment, forgotten.

Australia broke with tradition by delivering their match-winning rendition of *Under the Southern Cross* out in the middle, rather than in the confines of the dressing-room. This was orchestrated by Lyon, the eighth and perhaps least illustrious cricketer to lead them in its singing. After he took over the role from Mike Hussey, Australia had gone nine matches without winning (in three of which he did not play), and Lyon must have thought he would never start. As the strains belted out of the team huddle on the SCG, he might have felt as if he would never stop.

Man of the Match: R. J. Harris. *Attendance:* 131,713.

Man of the Series (Compton–Miller Medal): M. G. Johnson.

Close of play: first day, England 8-1 (Cook 7, Anderson 1); second day, Australia 140-4 (Rogers 73, Bailey 20).

Australia

C. J. L. Rogers b Stokes	11	– c and b Borthwick	119
D. A. Warner b Broad	16	– lbw b Anderson	16
S. R. Watson lbw b Anderson	43	– c Bairstow b Anderson	9
*M. J. Clarke c Bell b Stokes	10	– c Bairstow b Broad	6
S. P. D. Smith c sub (J. E. Root) b Stokes	115	– c Cook b Stokes	7
G. J. Bailey c Cook b Broad	1	– c Borthwick b Broad	46
†B. J. Haddin c Cook b Stokes	75	– b Borthwick	28
M. G. Johnson c sub (J. E. Root) b Borthwick	12	– b Stokes	4
R. J. Harris c Anderson b Stokes	22	– c Carberry b Borthwick	13
P. M. Siddle c Bairstow b Stokes	0	– c Bairstow b Rankin	4
N. M. Lyon not out	1	– not out	6
B 10, l-b 2, w 2, n-b 6	20	L-b 14, w 2, n-b 2	18

1/22 (2) 2/51 (1) 3/78 (4) (76 overs) 326   1/27 (2) 2/47 (3) (61.3 overs) 276
4/94 (3) 5/97 (6) 6/225 (7)   3/72 (4) 4/91 (5)
7/269 (8) 8/325 (9) 9/325 (10) 10/326 (5)   5/200 (6) 6/239 (7) 7/244 (8)
8/255 (1) 9/266 (9) 10/276 (10)

Anderson 21–3–67–1; Broad 19.5–5–65–2; Stokes 19.5–1–99–6; Rankin 8.2–0–34–0; Borthwick 7–0–49–1. *Second innings*—Anderson 15–6–46–2; Broad 14–1–57–2; Rankin 12.3–0–47–1; Stokes 10–0–62–2; Borthwick 6–0–33–3; Pietersen 4–1–17–0.

England

*A. N. Cook lbw b Harris	7	– c Haddin b Johnson	7
M. A. Carberry c Lyon b Johnson	0	– c Haddin b Johnson	43
J. M. Anderson c Clarke b Johnson	7	– (10) not out	1
I. R. Bell c Haddin b Siddle	2	– (3) c Warner b Harris	16
K. P. Pietersen c Watson b Harris	3	– (4) c Bailey b Harris	6
G. S. Ballance c Haddin b Lyon	18	– (5) lbw b Johnson	7
B. A. Stokes b Siddle	47	– (6) b Harris	32
†J. M. Bairstow c Bailey b Siddle	18	– (7) c Bailey b Lyon	0
S. G. Borthwick c Smith b Harris	1	– (8) c Clarke b Lyon	4
S. C. J. Broad not out	30	– (9) b Harris	42
W. B. Rankin b Johnson	13	– c Clarke b Harris	0
L-b 1, w 5, n-b 3	9	B 5, l-b 2, n-b 1	8

1/6 (2) 2/8 (1) 3/14 (3) (58.5 overs) 155   1/7 (1) 2/37 (3) (31.4 overs) 166
4/17 (5) 5/23 (4) 6/62 (6)   3/57 (4) 4/87 (2)
7/111 (8) 8/112 (7) 9/125 (9) 10/155 (11)   5/90 (5) 6/91 (7) 7/95 (8)
8/139 (6) 9/166 (9) 10/166 (11)

Harris 14–5–36–3; Johnson 13.5–3–33–3; Siddle 13–4–23–3; Watson 3–1–5–0; Lyon 15–3–57–1. *Second innings*—Harris 9.4–4–25–5; Johnson 9–1–40–3; Siddle 4–1–24–0; Lyon 9–0–70–2.

Umpires: Aleem Dar and M. Erasmus. Third umpire: A. L. Hill.
Referee: R. S. Madugalle.

LIMITED-OVERS MATCH REPORTS BY VITHUSHAN EHANTHARAJAH

AUSTRALIA v ENGLAND

First One-Day International

At Melbourne, January 12, 2014 (day/night). Australia won by six wickets. Toss: England. Finch's first one-day international hundred against a Test nation – and the first by a Victorian at Melbourne – bulldozed Australia to a convincing win with more than four overs to spare. Things might have turned out differently had Ballance, who earlier top-scored for England with a fine 79, his maiden international fifty, caught Finch at mid-off on eight off Jordan. But it was a day when little went right for the tourists. Warner had been happy to walk on 22 after edging Stokes into the gloves of Buttler, diving forward, only for the umpires to intervene, with TV official Dharmasena somehow ruling that the ball had bounced first; Cook described the decision as "wrong". Later Clarke edged the luckless Jordan between keeper and slip. England had made what looked to be an above-par score on a slow track, with Bell and Morgan, who reached his half-century in 46 balls, keeping Ballance company, and Buttler providing a late burst. But Finch and Warner rode their luck against an inexperienced attack to put on 163 inside 28 overs, a one-day record for Australia's first wicket against England, beating the unbroken 118 of Matthew Hayden and Adam Gilchrist at Sydney in 2002-03.

Man of the Match: A. J. Finch.   *Attendance:* 38,068.

England

*A. N. Cook c Haddin b McKay	4	†J. C. Buttler not out	34
I. R. Bell b Doherty	41	T. T. Bresnan not out	16
J. E. Root lbw b McKay	3	L-b 1, w 3	4
G. S. Ballance c Doherty b McKay	79		
E. J. G. Morgan c Coulter-Nile b Maxwell	50	1/4 (1) 2/22 (3) (7 wkts, 50 overs)	269
R. S. Bopara c Haddin b Coulter-Nile	17	3/62 (2) 4/145 (5)	
B. A. Stokes b Faulkner	21	5/173 (6) 6/206 (7) 7/228 (4) 10 overs: 28-2	

C. J. Jordan and W. B. Rankin did not bat.

McKay 10–0–44–3; Coulter-Nile 10–0–51–1; Maxwell 8–0–40–1; Doherty 7–0–29–1; Faulkner 10–0–68–1; Watson 5–0–36–0.

Australia

A. J. Finch c Ballance b Stokes	121	G. J. Maxwell not out	8
D. A. Warner c Stokes b Root	65	L-b 6, w 10	16
S. R. Watson b Jordan	0		
*M. J. Clarke c Cook b Bresnan	43	1/163 (2) 2/165 (3) (4 wkts, 45.4 overs)	270
G. J. Bailey not out	17	3/237 (1) 4/247 (4) 10 overs: 64-0	

†B. J. Haddin, J. P. Faulkner, N. M. Coulter-Nile, C. J. McKay and X. J. Doherty did not bat.

Rankin 8–0–53–0; Jordan 10–0–50–1; Bresnan 9.4–0–56–1; Stokes 10–0–64–1; Bopara 6–0–30–0; Root 2–0–11–1.

Umpires: S. D. Fry and R. E. J. Martinesz.   Third umpire: H. D. P. K. Dharmasena.
Referee: R. S. Madugalle.

At Canberra, January 14, 2014 (day/night). **England XI won by 172 runs.** ‡**England XI** 264-8 (50 overs) (G. S. Ballance 56, J. C. Buttler 61; J. M. Muirhead 3-52); **Prime Minister's XI** 92 (26 overs) (R. S. Bopara 4-3). *England achieved their first win since beating the Cricket Australia Invitation XI at Sydney in mid-November. But there was no respite for Cook and Root, who both fell for a single to the PM's XI captain Brett Lee. From 12-2, Ballance helped stabilise the innings, before Buttler rescued his side after a second stutter to 149-6. England's bowlers then defended a competitive total with ease. Rankin and Jordan reduced the opposition – made up of players not required by the Big Bash League – to 24-3, before Bopara mopped up with four cheap wickets and a run-out.*

AUSTRALIA v ENGLAND

Second One-Day International

At Brisbane, January 17, 2014 (day/night). Australia won by one wicket. Toss: England.

Faulkner's stunning unbeaten 69 off 47 balls from No. 9 lifted Australia to their highest run-chase at the Gabba, and thoroughly deflated England. They had been set for their first international win of the tour when Australia slipped to 244 for nine in pursuit of 301, with only six overs to go. But Faulkner, who had shone with the bat during Australia's high-scoring one-day series in India a couple of months previously, went after Stokes, mowing him for five sixes over midwicket in 12 deliveries spread across three overs; the third was caught by Root, but his momentum carried him over the boundary. With 12 needed off the last over, Faulkner hit Bresnan's first three balls for four to give Australia a 2–0 lead, and start talk of another whitewash. Only one higher tenth-wicket partnership had won a one-day international: the 64 added by Deryck Murray and Andy Roberts for West Indies against Pakistan at Edgbaston in the 1975 World Cup. The result was especially hard on Morgan, whose sixth one-day hundred had lifted England, with the help of Bell and Buttler, to 300. Their total had been boosted by four runs during the interval after a drive to long-off by Buttler in the 48th over, bowled by Johnson, was upgraded from a two to a six: replays confirmed that Marsh, who had caught the ball while in mid-air, then thrown it back into play before he touched the ground, had already stepped over the rope and off the field. Ballance and Jordan held on to smart one-handed catches to send back Australia's openers cheaply, Root struck twice and, when Bresnan removed Haddin and Maxwell – who had reverse-swept his way to 54 off 39 balls – England were in charge. But Faulkner had other ideas.

Man of the Match: J. P. Faulkner.   *Attendance:* 32,232.

England

*A. N. Cook c and b Maxwell	22	T. T. Bresnan not out	1
I. R. Bell run out	68	C. J. Jordan not out	2
J. E. Root lbw b Johnson	2	L-b 4, w 12, n-b 1	17
G. S. Ballance st Haddin b Maxwell	9		
E. J. G. Morgan c Clarke b Faulkner	106	1/57 (1) 2/60 (3) (8 wkts, 50 overs) 300	
R. S. Bopara c Bailey b Faulkner	24	3/78 (4) 4/139 (2)	
†J. C. Buttler c Clarke b Coulter-Nile	49	5/178 (6) 6/295 (7)	
B. A. Stokes c Maxwell b Coulter-Nile	0	7/296 (8) 8/297 (5) 10 overs: 52-0	

W. B. Rankin did not bat.

McKay 9–0–61–0; Johnson 10–0–59–1; Coulter-Nile 9–0–55–2; Faulkner 10–0–73–2; Maxwell 8–0–31–2; Clarke 4–0–17–0.

Australia

D. A. Warner c and b Jordan	18	M. G. Johnson c Buttler b Bopara	1
A. J. Finch c Ballance b Jordan	0	C. J. McKay not out	2
S. E. Marsh b Root	55		
*M. J. Clarke c Ballance b Root	17	L-b 9, w 10	19
G. J. Bailey lbw b Rankin	24		
G. J. Maxwell c Bopara b Bresnan	54	1/6 (2) 2/32 (1) (9 wkts, 49.3 overs) 301	
†B. J. Haddin c Cook b Bresnan	26	3/70 (4) 4/114 (3)	
N. M. Coulter-Nile lbw b Stokes	16	5/120 (5) 6/200 (7) 7/206 (6)	
J. P. Faulkner not out	69	8/235 (8) 9/244 (10) 10 overs: 57-2	

Rankin 7–0–36–1; Jordan 9–0–53–2; Bresnan 9.3–0–64–2; Stokes 10–0–74–1; Root 9–0–46–2; Bopara 5–0–19–1.

Umpires: H. D. P. K. Dharmasena and J. D. Ward.   Third umpire: R. E. J. Martinesz.
Referee: R. S. Madugalle.

AUSTRALIA v ENGLAND

Third One-Day International

At Sydney, January 19, 2014 (day/night). Australia won by seven wickets. Toss: England.

Australia secured the series with two games to go, passing England's lacklustre 243 with seven wickets and ten overs to spare, and prompting Cook to question his own credentials as one-day captain. He had batted fluently after winning his third toss of the series but, among England's other frontline batsmen, only Morgan, with 54 from 58 balls, was able to match him. Morgan's dismissal, to a low return catch by Christian – in his first international since September 2012 – provoked angry scenes: Morgan initially stood his ground, and his partner Buttler exchanged views with Clarke before the umpires stepped in. Bell had been run out for the second match in a row, this time by a superb direct hit by Warner from deep point. From 177 for four, England slipped to 198 for eight, and were kept in it only by some lusty late-order blows from Bresnan. Bopara could have run out Warner off the second ball of Australia's reply, after Finch had set off for a risky single – but Warner went on to 71 from 70 balls, while Marsh's unbeaten 71 occupied 89. He finished the job with Haddin, who entertained the crowd by taking 19 runs off the eight deliveries he faced from Broad, rested from the first two games but still jeered heartily on his return.

Man of the Match: D. A. Warner. Attendance: 37,823.

England

*A. N. Cook c Maxwell b Coulter-Nile	35	C. J. Jordan c Finch b Faulkner		10
I. R. Bell run out	29	J. C. Tredwell not out		2
B. A. Stokes c Clarke b Doherty	15			
G. S. Ballance c Christian b Coulter-Nile	26	L-b 2, w 2, n-b 1		5
E. J. G. Morgan c and b Christian	54			
R. S. Bopara c Haddin b Faulkner	21	1/50 (1) 2/70 (2)	(9 wkts, 50 overs)	243
†J. C. Buttler b Christian	4	3/91 (3) 4/121 (4)		
T. T. Bresnan not out	41	5/177 (6) 6/186 (5) 7/195 (7)		
S. C. J. Broad c Haddin b Coulter-Nile	1	8/198 (9) 9/225 (10)	10 overs: 53-1	

Faulkner 6–0–35–2; Pattinson 6–0–41–0; Coulter-Nile 10–0–47–3; Doherty 10–2–28–1; Maxwell 9–0–38–0; Christian 9–0–52–2.

Australia

A. J. Finch c Bopara b Jordan	22
D. A. Warner c Bell b Stokes	71
S. E. Marsh not out	71
*M. J. Clarke b Bopara	34
†B. J. Haddin not out	35
B 2, l-b 4, w 5	11

1/43 (1) 2/121 (2) (3 wkts, 40 overs) 244
3/172 (4) 10 overs: 67-1

G. J. Maxwell, D. T. Christian, J. P. Faulkner, N. M. Coulter-Nile, J. L. Pattinson and X. J. Doherty did not bat.

Jordan 9–0–56–1; Broad 8–0–61–0; Bresnan 6–0–42–0; Tredwell 9–0–42–0; Bopara 5–0–14–1; Stokes 3–0–23–1.

Umpires: S. D. Fry and R. E. J. Martinesz.   Third umpire: H. D. P. K. Dharmasena.
Referee: R. S. Madugalle.

❝Reading it seems wrong, like leafing through photographs of a missing child."
Cricket Books, 2013, page 132

AUSTRALIA v ENGLAND

Fourth One-Day International

At Perth, January 24, 2014. England won by 57 runs. Toss: Australia.

England's first international win on this tour – at the ninth time of asking – was inspired by Stokes, who followed a feisty 70 with four wickets, at the venue where he had made his maiden Test hundred the previous month. But even his efforts with the bat were outshone by Buttler, who produced a spectacular display of crisp hitting, launching four sixes in a 43-ball 71 to lift England to their second-highest total in Australia, behind 333 for six at Sydney three years earlier (a game they went on to lose). The highlight of Buttler's innings was a flick over square leg for six from a full-length ball from the expensive Johnson. Locals dubbed England's victory a hollow one, with Australia resting Clarke, Warner, Haddin and Watson. That left them overly reliant on Finch: he made a combative 108 in 111 balls, his second century of the series, but none of his team-mates passed 26 as England produced a professional display in the field. Broad and Stokes shared the wickets in the middle of the innings to curtail any momentum, although Stokes earned a ticking-off from umpire Dharmasena for sending Faulkner on his way with a touch too much gusto; he was later fined 15% of his match fee. With Australia nine down, Stokes dropped a sitter at deep square leg to reprieve Coulter-Nile, but England's long-awaited win finally came when Pattinson top-edged Bresnan, and Buttler claimed his fifth catch. The result meant England avoided equalling their worst sequence of international defeats, set in 1993 and repeated in 2001 – and persuaded Cook to state his desire to remain in the job. Referring to the doubts he had aired after the Sydney defeat, he said: "I spoke what I was feeling, and sometimes you probably shouldn't do that – but I did."

Man of the Match: B. A. Stokes.   *Attendance:* 18,271.

England

*A. N. Cook b Maxwell	44	S. C. J. Broad not out	4
I. R. Bell c Faulkner b Christian	55	C. J. Jordan not out	0
B. A. Stokes c Wade b Faulkner	70		
G. S. Ballance c Smith b Pattinson	18	W 16	16
E. J. G. Morgan c Christian b Faulkner	33		
R. S. Bopara c sub (X. J. Doherty)		1/87 (1) 2/138 (2)	(8 wkts, 50 overs) 316
b Coulter-Nile	3	3/190 (4) 4/206 (3)	
†J. C. Buttler c Johnson b Faulkner	71	5/216 (6) 6/287 (5)	
T. T. Bresnan c Johnson b Faulkner	2	7/312 (7) 8/312 (8)	10 overs: 73-0

J. C. Tredwell did not bat.

Johnson 10–0–72–0; Pattinson 8–0–63–1; Faulkner 10–0–67–4; Coulter-Nile 10–0–62–1; Maxwell 9–0–37–1; Christian 3–0–15–1.

Australia

S. E. Marsh c Bell b Bresnan	15	N. M. Coulter-Nile not out	8
A. J. Finch c Broad b Bresnan	108	J. L. Pattinson c Buttler b Bresnan	4
†M. S. Wade c Cook b Bopara	23		
*G. J. Bailey c Buttler b Stokes	11	L-b 5, w 9	14
S. P. D. Smith c Buttler b Broad	19		
G. J. Maxwell c Buttler b Stokes	26	1/46 (1) 2/110 (3)	(47.4 overs) 259
D. T. Christian c Ballance b Broad	23	3/132 (4) 4/174 (5) 5/189 (2)	
J. P. Faulkner c Buttler b Stokes	2	6/222 (6) 7/230 (8) 8/239 (9)	
M. G. Johnson b Stokes	6	9/247 (7) 10/259 (11)	10 overs: 56-1

Jordan 9–0–57–0; Broad 10–0–56–2; Bresnan 8.4–0–45–3; Tredwell 5–0–26–0; Bopara 6–1–32–1; Stokes 9–1–38–4.

Umpires: H. D. P. K. Dharmasena and J. D. Ward.   Third umpire: R. E. J. Martinesz.
Referee: A. J. Pycroft.

AUSTRALIA v ENGLAND

Fifth One-Day International

At Adelaide, January 26, 2014 (day/night). Australia won by five runs. Toss: Australia.

England capitulated to lose their last seven wickets for 58 runs and gift-wrap Australia a 4–1 series win. On a stopping pitch – the most sluggish of the series – they were in control at 154 for three in the 36th over, only for both set batsmen to fall to needless shots: following a run-a-ball 39, Morgan failed to clear mid-off, and two overs later Root – who made his first half-century in seven international innings since the Test here in December after being recalled in place of Gary Ballance – ramped Faulkner to short fine leg. Despite a long batting line-up, and overs in hand, panic set in. Buttler pulled to deep square, Bresnan was run out after a muddle with Bopara, and Broad was bowled, eighth out with only 14 needed off 19 balls. Bopara's laboured innings then ended with a freakish stumping, as the ball ricocheted off Wade – standing up to McKay – and back on to the wicket, before dislodging a bail. Replays struggled to confirm whether Bopara's back foot was raised before the bail came out of its groove, but third umpire Dharmasena had no doubt. With six needed off three balls, Tredwell could only edge Watson to the keeper, to seal a dramatic win for the hosts on Australia Day. Their innings had been revived from 112 for five by Bailey, although rapid spells from Broad and Jordan, who took two wickets in the last over, kept things in check. Bell and Stokes went early in the England reply, but Cook steadied matters before Root and Morgan almost broke the back of the chase. Almost – but not quite.

Man of the Match: J. P. Faulkner.   *Attendance:* 27,071.
Man of the Series: A. J. Finch.

Australia

A. J. Finch b Broad	7	C. J. McKay not out	1
S. E. Marsh c Cook b Stokes	36	X. J. Doherty not out	1
S. R. Watson c Buttler b Broad	0		
*M. J. Clarke b Bresnan	8	L-b 9, w 4	13
G. J. Bailey c Broad b Stokes	56		
G. J. Maxwell c Buttler b Stokes	22	1/14 (1) 2/22 (3) (9 wkts, 50 overs) 217	
†M. S. Wade b Broad	31	3/43 (4) 4/64 (2)	
J. P. Faulkner c Morgan b Jordan	27	5/112 (6) 6/167 (5) 7/176 (7)	
N. M. Coulter-Nile lbw b Jordan	15	8/215 (8) 9/215 (9) 10 overs: 30-2	

Broad 10–2–31–3; Jordan 10–0–37–2; Bresnan 10–0–51–1; Tredwell 7–0–28–0; Stokes 10–0–43–3; Bopara 3–0–18–0.

England

*A. N. Cook c Bailey b Coulter-Nile	39	C. J. Jordan not out	4
I. R. Bell c Finch b Coulter-Nile	14	J. C. Tredwell c Wade b Watson	0
B. A. Stokes c Marsh b McKay	0		
J. E. Root c Doherty b Faulkner	55	B 1, l-b 4, w 6	11
E. J. G. Morgan c Watson b Faulkner	39		
R. S. Bopara st Wade b McKay	25	1/23 (2) 2/29 (3) 3/90 (1) (49.4 overs) 212	
†J. C. Buttler c McKay b Coulter-Nile	5	4/154 (5) 5/157 (4) 6/174 (7)	
T. T. Bresnan run out	13	7/194 (8) 8/204 (9) 9/209 (6)	
S. C. J. Broad b McKay	7	10/212 (11) 10 overs: 31-2	

McKay 10–1–36–3; Coulter-Nile 10–1–34–3; Faulkner 10–0–37–2; Doherty 10–1–40–0; Watson 6.4–0–35–1; Maxwell 3–0–25–0.

Umpires: S. D. Fry and R. E. J. Martinesz.   Third umpire: H. D. P. K. Dharmasena.
Referee: A. J. Pycroft.

AUSTRALIA v ENGLAND

First Twenty20 International

At Hobart, January 29, 2014 (floodlit). Australia won by 13 runs. Toss: Australia. Twenty20 international debuts: C. A. Lynn, J. M. Muirhead.

Australia claimed a win that would have been more emphatic had it not been for the late hitting of Bopara, who smashed a 27-ball 65. With one square boundary barely more than 50 metres away, White – recalled by Australia after good form in the Big Bash and Ryobi Cup, and badly dropped by Root at slip on 11 – and Finch opened with 106 inside 11 overs. Three sixes from the debutant Chris Lynn then helped Australia to 213, their second-highest total in the format at home. Broad bowled with control but, Bopara aside, no one else went for less than ten an over. Australia's bowlers proved expensive too, but took important wickets at crucial moments to stall England's charge; Coulter-Nile was the pick, with four. James Muirhead, a 20-year-old leg-spinner from Victoria with only two first-class matches under his belt, claimed a maiden international victim in Bresnan, before Bopara's fireworks closed the game with a futile flourish. His seven sixes were a Twenty20 record for England, beating Wright's six against Afghanistan in Colombo in September 2012.

Man of the Match: C. L. White.   Attendance: 10,939.

Australia		B	4	6
C. L. White *lbw b 3*	75	43	6	4
A. J. Finch *c 1 b 9*	52	31	5	3
G. J. Maxwell *c 8 b 7*	20	13	2	1
*G. J. Bailey *c 8 b 10*	14	14	1	0
C. A. Lynn *not out*	33	19	1	3
D. T. Christian *not out*	6	2	1	0
B 1, w 6, n-b 6	13			
6 overs: 52-0 (20 overs) 213-4				

1/106 2/134 3/157 4/200

M. C. Henriques, †M. S. Wade, N. M. Coulter-Nile, J. R. Hazlewood and J. M. Muirhead did not bat.

Broad 4–0–25–1; Dernbach 4–0–50–1; Bresnan 4–0–40–0; Bopara 3–0–26–1; Briggs 4–0–53–0; Wright 1–0–18–1.

England		B	4	6
A. D. Hales *lbw b 7*	22	12	5	0
M. J. Lumb *c 5 b 9*	9	6	2	0
L. J. Wright *b 7*	9	10	2	0
J. E. Root *c 2 b 9*	32	24	3	1
E. J. G. Morgan *b 3*	4	4	1	0
†J. C. Buttler *c 11 b 9*	20	14	1	1
R. S. Bopara *not out*	65	27	2	7
T. T. Bresnan *b 11*	11	14	0	0
*S. C. J. Broad *b 9*	13	5	0	2
J. W. Dernbach *run out*	5	4	1	0
D. R. Briggs *not out*	0	0	0	0
L-b 3, w 7	10			
6 overs: 46-3 (20 overs) 200-9				

1/14 2/44 3/45 4/51 5/98 6/100 7/147 8/162 9/176

Maxwell 3–0–30–1; Coulter-Nile 4–0–31–4; Hazlewood 4–0–46–0; Henriques 3–0–35–2; Muirhead 4–0–34–1; Christian 2–0–21–0.

Umpires: S. D. Fry and J. D. Ward.   Third umpire: P. Wilson.

AUSTRALIA v ENGLAND

Second Twenty20 International

At Melbourne, January 31, 2014 (floodlit). Australia won by eight wickets. Toss: England.

Australia sealed their third series win in three formats over a demoralised England, this time thanks to an emphatic victory with more than five overs to spare. The tourists' mood did not improve when reports filtered through from the UK that Andy Flower had resigned as team director. With the cricket itself following a predictable path, almost as much interest focused on the selection of the 39-year-old local favourite Brad Hodge, whose last taste of international cricket had come in a Test at Kingston in May 2008. Hodge was not required to bat, but did open the bowling with his occasional off-breaks, took a stunning catch at cover to remove Wright, then ran out Morgan with a direct hit as England fumbled to 55 for four. Morgan's entire bat was over the line – but it was in the air, having bounced up as he dived for the crease. Australia's ability to build pressure proved the difference, with Hazlewood reaping four wickets. England failed to hit a six in an innings which finished comfortably below par, on 130 for nine. White cracked another half-century – and became involved in a slanging match with Dernbach, whose three overs cost 42 – and Bailey made light work of the target.

Man of the Match: J. R. Hazlewood.   *Attendance:* 64,385.

England

		B	*4*	*6*
A. D. Hales *c 8 b 10*	16	13	3	0
M. J. Lumb *c 9 b 10*	18	15	4	0
L. J. Wright *c 5 b 8*	0	2	0	0
J. E. Root *run out*	18	14	3	0
E. J. G. Morgan *run out*	6	3	1	0
†J. C. Buttler *lbw b 9*	22	27	2	0
R. S. Bopara *c 3 b 11*	6	11	0	0
T. T. Bresnan *b 10*	18	19	1	0
*S. C. J. Broad *not out*	18	15	1	0
J. C. Tredwell *b 10*	0	1	0	0
L-b 4, w 4	8			

6 overs: 48-3   (20 overs) 130-9

1/24 2/30 3/42 4/55 5/63 6/87 7/96 8/130 9/130

J. W. Dernbach did not bat.

Hodge 1–0–10–0; Coulter-Nile 4–0–29–1; Starc 4–0–19–1; Hazlewood 4–0–30–4; Maxwell 1–0–7–0; Muirhead 4–0–17–1; White 2–0–14–0.

Australia

		B	*4*	*6*
C. L. White *not out*	58	45	9	0
A. J. Finch *lbw b 8*	10	11	2	0
G. J. Maxwell *c 8 b 10*	2	5	0	0
*G. J. Bailey *not out*	60	28	7	3
W 1	1			

6 overs: 50-1   (14.5 overs) 131-2

1/48 2/53

B. J. Hodge, C. A. Lynn, †M. S. Wade, M. A. Starc, N. M. Coulter-Nile, J. R. Hazlewood and J. M. Muirhead did not bat.

Broad 3–0–29–0; Dernbach 3–0–42–0; Bresnan 3–0–11–1; Tredwell 3.5–0–37–1; Bopara 2–0–12–0.

Umpires: J. D. Ward and P. Wilson.   Third umpire: S. D. Fry.

AUSTRALIA v ENGLAND

Third Twenty20 International

At Sydney (Stadium Australia), February 2, 2014 (floodlit). Australia won by 84 runs. Toss: Australia. Twenty20 international debut: C. J. Jordan.

England's tour of despair finally came to an end as Australia secured their second whitewash of the summer. The tourists had worked themselves into a reasonable position with the ball: when Broad removed Hodge and Christian in the space of three deliveries in his final over, Australia were 139 for six with four overs to go. But powerful hitting from Bailey, who tucked into some dreadful fare from Dernbach – his final figures for the series were 11–0–141–1 – lifted Australia to an imposing 195. England's revamped top three – Michael Lumb was dropped, with Wright moved up to open and Stokes at No. 3 – all failed, and only Morgan passed 14. England were all out for 111; only twice before had they been dismissed for fewer in Twenty20s. Still, at least the misery was over.

Man of the Match: G. J. Bailey.   *Attendance:* 46,782.

Australia

		B	4	6
C. L. White c 6 b 9	41	37	4	1
A. J. Finch c 10 b 8	30	21	1	3
G. J. Maxwell c 2 b 10	14	7	0	2
B. C. J. Cutting c and b 4	29	16	1	3
*G. J. Bailey not out	49	20	4	3
B. J. Hodge c 11 b 10	7	7	1	0
D. T. Christian b 10	0	2	0	0
†M. S. Wade not out	19	10	1	1
L-b 2, w 4	6			

6 overs: 41-0   (20 overs) 195-6

1/48 2/65 3/118 4/130 5/139 6/139

M. A. Starc, N. M. Coulter-Nile and J. M. Muirhead did not bat.

Broad 4–0–30–3; Jordan 4–0–23–1; Bresnan 4–0–42–1; Stokes 3–0–36–0; Dernbach 4–0–49–0; Root 1–0–13–1.

England

		B	4	6
L. J. Wright c 4 b 9	8	12	1	0
A. D. Hales c 11 b 10	6	8	1	0
B. A. Stokes c 4 b 3	5	4	1	0
J. E. Root c 4 b 3	11	21	1	0
E. J. G. Morgan c 9 b 4	34	20	2	2
†J. C. Buttler c 3 b 7	8	9	1	0
R. S. Bopara b 10	4	5	0	0
T. T. Bresnan st 8 b 11	14	7	1	1
C. J. Jordan not out	10	12	2	0
*S. C. J. Broad b 11	2	4	0	0
J. W. Dernbach run out	1	2	0	0
B 2, l-b 4, w 2	8			

6 overs: 31-3   (17.2 overs) 111

1/11 2/19 3/25 4/60 5/79 6/82 7/92 8/98 9/104

Starc 2.2–0–8–1; Coulter-Nile 4–0–21–2; Maxwell 4–0–31–2; Cutting 3–0–18–1; Christian 2–0–14–1; Muirhead 2–0–13–2.

Umpires: S. D. Fry and P. Wilson.   Third umpire: J. D. Ward.
Series referee: A. J. Pycroft.

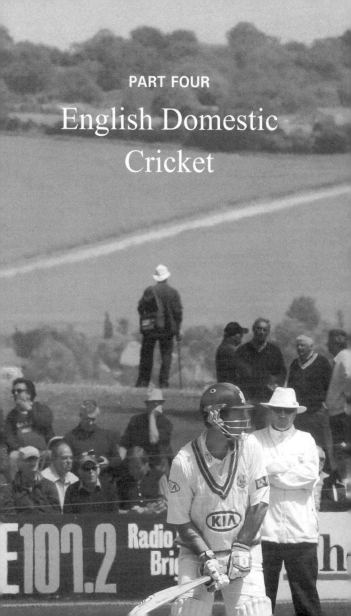

PART FOUR

English Domestic
Cricket

FIRST-CLASS AVERAGES, 2013

Note: These averages include MCC v Warwickshire at Abu Dhabi but exclude Australia A v Scotland and Ireland.

BATTING AND FIELDING

(Qualification: 10 innings)

		M	I	NO	R	HS	100	50	Avge	Ct/St
1	†S. M. Katich (*Lancs*)	12	16	1	1,097	200	4	6	73.13	7
2	J. E. Root (*Yorks, England Lions & England*)	10	18	1	1,228	236	5	2	72.23	8
3	†G. S. Ballance (*Yorks*)	15	22	1	1,363	148	6	6	64.90	13
4	†E. C. Joyce (*Sussex*)	15	23	5	1,152	204*	2	6	64.00	15
5	J. M. Vince (*Hants*)	16	23	4	1,215	148	5	6	63.94	17
6	D. I. Stevens (*Kent*)	16	22	1	1,304	205*	4	7	62.09	13
7	J. Allenby (*Glam*)	16	25	5	1,202	138*	2	8	60.10	28
8	†M. M. Ali (*Worcs*)	17	29	5	1,420	250	4	8	59.16	22
9	M. W. Goodwin (*Glam*)	16	26	4	1,263	194	4	7	57.40	7
10	K. P. Pietersen (*Surrey & England*)	6	11	1	565	177*	2	3	56.50	6
11	L. J. Wright (*Sussex*)	7	12	0	676	187	2	2	56.33	1
12	A. J. Hall (*Northants*)	16	21	4	936	130*	3	5	55.05	13
13	†P. J. Hughes (*Australia A & Australians*)	6	12	3	494	86	0	5	54.88	5
14	†L. M. Reece (*Leeds/Brad MCCU & Lancs*)	12	20	4	877	114*	1	8	54.81	10
15	H. M. Amla (*Surrey*)	6	10	0	545	151	1	4	54.50	1
16	M. J. Clarke (*Australians*)	7	14	2	638	187	2	2	53.16	10
17	C. R. Woakes (*Warwicks, Eng. Lions & Eng.*)	12	19	6	683	152*	1	4	52.53	2
18	S. D. Peters (*Northants*)	10	15	1	735	106	2	5	52.50	4
19	A. U. Rashid (*Yorks*)	15	22	6	825	180	3	3	51.56	7
20	S. R. Watson (*Australians*)	7	12	0	617	176	2	3	51.41	7
21	†C. J. L. Rogers (*Middx & Australians*)	18	33	3	1,536	214	4	9	51.20	15
22	A. P. R. Gidman (*Glos*)	16	22	0	1,125	211	3	5	51.13	12
23	L. J. Evans (*Warwicks*)	15	22	2	1,022	178	3	5	51.10	8
24	V. Chopra (*Warwicks & England Lions*)	18	29	4	1,262	228*	4	5	50.48	31
25	H. J. H. Marshall (*Glos*)	16	21	1	1,007	149	4	2	50.35	5
26	I. R. Bell (*Warwicks & England*)	9	16	1	753	113	3	4	50.20	7
27	G. R. Napier (*Essex*)	17	23	7	796	102*	1	7	49.75	5
28	M. Klinger (*Glos*)	16	26	3	1,140	163	4	4	49.56	16
29	J. W. A. Taylor (*Notts, Eng. Lions & Sussex*)	18	25	3	1,079	204*	3	5	49.04	9
30	†A. G. Prince (*Lancs*)	16	26	2	1,169	134	3	7	48.70	16
31	†M. J. Lumb (*Notts*)	16	26	3	1,120	221*	4	3	48.69	4
32	†B. P. Nash (*Kent*)	17	27	4	1,110	199*	5	5	48.26	4
33	L. A. Dawson (*Hants*)	17	26	4	1,060	136*	1	8	48.18	24
34	N. D. McKenzie (*Hants*)	6	10	1	433	146	1	2	48.11	1
35	†A. Z. Lees (*Yorks*)	9	16	3	621	275*	3	1	47.76	2
36	S. P. D. Smith (*Australia A & Australians*)	8	15	2	568	138*	2	3	47.33	7
37	S. D. Robson (*Middx*)	16	29	4	1,180	215*	3	4	47.20	22
38	A. N. Petersen (*Somerset*)	6	12	0	562	167	2	2	46.83	3
39	†M. A. Carberry (*Hants & England Lions*)	13	19	0	889	154	2	6	46.78	6
40	R. W. T. Key (*Kent*)	17	28	3	1,169	180	5	3	46.76	3
41	E. J. H. Eckersley (*MCC & Leics*)	18	31	3	1,309	147	4	4	46.75	9
42	C. D. Nash (*Sussex*)	18	30	4	1,211	167*	3	5	46.57	11
43	A. Javid (*Warwicks*)	12	18	4	644	133	2	2	46.00	5
44	D. J. Sales (*Northants*)	16	23	3	919	255*	3	1	45.95	11
45	R. I. Keogh (*Northants*)	8	12	2	458	221	1	1	45.80	1
46	†S. M. Davies (*Surrey*)	15	23	4	867	147	2	3	45.63	24/3
47	†J. P. Dent (*Glos*)	16	27	2	1,128	153	2	7	45.12	20
48	N. R. D. Compton (*Somerset, Eng. & Worcs*)	16	31	3	1,260	166	2	9	45.00	6
	J. Leach (*Worcs*)	7	10	3	315	114	1	2	45.00	1

	M	I	NO	R	HS	100	50	Avge	Ct/St
50 †B. W. Harmison (*Kent*)	13	19	3	712	106	2	5	44.50	8
51 †J. H. K. Roderick (*Glos*)	13	19	4	665	152*	2	2	44.33	43
52 †E. J. M. Cowan (*Notts & Australians*)	11	21	3	776	81	0	7	43.11	5
53 †A. W. Gale (*Yorks*)	17	26	1	1,076	272	3	2	43.04	5
54 A. J. Wheater (*Hants*)	16	19	3	687	140	3	1	42.93	19/2
55 G. M. Smith (*Essex*)	11	16	3	555	177	1	2	42.69	2
56 S. R. Patel (*Notts*)	17	26	0	1,104	256	4	0	42.46	17
57 †J. H. K. Adams (*MCC & Hants*)	18	28	4	1,014	219*	3	3	42.25	7
58 S. J. Mullaney (*Notts*)	15	23	0	965	125	3	6	41.95	8
59 †S. G. Borthwick (*Durham*)	17	29	2	1,121	135	3	6	41.51	29
60 B. C. Brown (*Sussex*)	16	23	6	705	93	0	6	41.47	61/3
61 J. C. Mickleburgh (*Essex*)	13	21	1	829	243	2	4	41.45	3
62 W. L. Madsen (*Derbys*)	17	32	2	1,239	152	3	8	41.30	11
63 I. J. L. Trott (*Warwicks & England*)	9	16	0	653	96	0	6	40.81	10
64 P. J. Horton (*Lancs*)	10	16	0	645	156	3	3	40.31	1
65 S. P. Crook (*Northants*)	14	15	3	482	88*	0	5	40.16	3
66 V. S. Solanki (*Surrey*)	16	25	0	995	162	2	5	39.80	18
67 C. B. Cooke (*Glam*)	7	11	1	394	92	0	3	39.40	2
68 T. T. Samaraweera (*Worcs*)	15	22	4	702	144*	2	4	39.00	6
69 K. S. Williamson (*N. Zealanders & Yorks*)	9	16	1	584	97	0	6	38.93	5
70 T. Westley (*Essex*)	11	20	0	774	163	2	3	38.70	7
71 †S. Chanderpaul (*Derbys*)	15	27	4	884	129	1	7	38.43	8
72 J. S. Foster (*Essex*)	17	26	3	883	143	1	6	38.39	49/1
73 J. M. Bairstow (*Yorks, Eng. Lions & England*)	16	26	1	955	186	1	5	38.20	34
74 M. L. Pettini (*Essex*)	9	15	4	419	100*	1	1	38.09	10
75 S. J. Croft (*Lancs*)	8	13	3	379	101*	1	2	37.90	4
76 D. K. H. Mitchell (*Worcs*)	18	32	4	1,061	156	2	7	37.89	21
77 M. J. Powell (*Kent*)	7	10	3	265	70	0	3	37.85	0
78 K. J. Coetzer (*Northants*)	10	15	1	527	219	2	1	37.64	3
79 †G. P. Rees (*Glam*)	9	16	1	564	112	2	3	37.60	5
80 T. R. Ambrose (*Warwicks*)	15	23	2	778	105	1	6	37.04	42/1
81 D. J. Hussey (*Notts*)	9	13	0	478	125	1	3	36.76	2
82 †P. A. Jaques (*Yorks*)	14	21	0	770	152	2	3	36.66	5
83 J. C. Buttler (*Somerset*)	9	15	1	508	119*	1	2	36.28	16
84 †A. N. Cook (*Essex & England*)	9	18	0	651	130	1	5	36.16	12
85 J. D. Middlebrook (*MCC & Northants*)	17	23	2	757	109	1	6	36.04	5
86 O. B. Cox (*Worcs*)	8	13	5	287	65	0	2	35.87	25/1
87 †P. Mustard (*Durham*)	17	27	4	823	77	0	5	35.78	67/1
88 †C. J. Haggett (*Kent*)	12	14	7	249	44*	0	0	35.57	3
89 R. N. ten Doeschate (*Essex*)	9	13	2	391	103	1	1	35.54	3
90 { B. T. Foakes (*Essex*)	15	20	2	639	120	2	3	35.50	11
{ A. P. Agathangelou (*Lancs*)	11	16	2	497	121	1	2	35.50	24
92 T. A. Copeland (*Northants*)	10	10	3	247	70	0	2	35.28	11
93 †R. J. Burns (*Surrey*)	16	27	1	917	115	2	4	35.26	13
94 †J. O. Troughton (*Warwicks*)	9	14	1	458	84	0	4	35.23	6
95 J. C. Hildreth (*Somerset*)	17	31	2	1,008	161	2	4	34.75	17
96 †M. D. Stoneman (*Durham*)	17	32	1	1,068	122	3	6	34.45	6
97 G. C. Wilson (*Surrey*)	12	17	4	447	124	1	1	34.38	12
98 †L. W. P. Wells (*Sussex*)	18	30	1	994	208	2	5	34.27	7
99 †L. A. Procter (*Lancs*)	15	21	0	718	106	1	7	34.19	5
100 R. J. Hamilton-Brown (*Sussex*)	15	21	1	683	126*	2	3	34.15	3
101 R. S. Bopara (*Essex & England Lions*)	9	14	1	443	145	1	2	34.07	6
102 T. C. Fell (*Oxford MCCU & Worcs*)	10	16	2	477	94*	0	3	34.07	3
103 †A. Lyth (*Yorks*)	17	29	4	850	111	2	4	34.00	27
104 R. Clarke (*Warwicks*)	14	19	5	473	92	0	4	33.78	20
105 †W. R. S. Gidman (*Glos*)	14	17	4	439	143	1	1	33.76	3
106 M. J. Richardson (*Durham*)	11	16	0	530	129	2	2	33.12	13
107 D. M. Housego (*Glos*)	10	16	2	463	150	1	3	33.07	6
108 †M. G. Pardoe (*Worcs*)	18	32	3	956	102	1	7	32.96	4
109 W. R. Smith (*Durham*)	17	30	3	889	153	2	2	32.92	15

		M	I	NO	R	HS	100	50	Avge	Ct/St
110	S. J. Thakor (*Leics*)	15	24	3	671	114	1	5	31.95	4
111	C. Kieswetter (*Somerset*)	12	21	2	606	148	1	3	31.89	41/3
112	†K. H. D. Barker (*Warwicks*)	11	12	1	350	125	1	0	31.81	4
113	†K. K. Jennings (*Durham*)	15	28	2	822	127	3	1	31.61	8
114	†B. A. Stokes (*Durham*)	14	25	2	726	127	2	3	31.56	11
115	J. S. Patel (*Warwicks*)	16	18	4	438	78*	0	5	31.28	14
116	N. J. Dexter (*Middx*)	17	28	2	807	104	1	4	31.03	12
117	†M. H. Yardy (*Sussex*)	18	29	2	834	156	2	1	30.88	9
118	†J. A. Simpson (*Middx*)	16	25	4	648	97*	0	5	30.85	55/5
119	†M. A. G. Boyce (*Leics*)	12	23	1	677	135	1	2	30.77	8
120	†A. Harinath (*Surrey*)	12	21	2	584	154	1	4	30.73	4
121	O. A. Shah (*Essex*)	7	11	1	307	120	1	1	30.70	10
122	†C. F. Hughes (*Derbys*)	12	22	1	636	270*	1	2	30.28	7
123	†N. J. O'Brien (*Leics*)	14	23	0	695	67	0	6	30.21	25/3
124	B. A. C. Howell (*Glos*)	17	24	4	596	60	0	4	29.80	8
125	B. J. Haddin (*Australians*)	7	12	2	296	71	0	3	29.60	33/1
126	J. L. Denly (*MCC & Middx*)	18	32	3	855	146	1	4	29.48	6
127	P. D. Collingwood (*Durham*)	15	25	3	646	88*	0	5	29.36	20
128	†D. J. Malan (*MCC & Middx*)	14	22	2	571	156*	1	2	28.55	20
129	D. J. Bell-Drummond (*Kent*)	14	21	1	568	102*	1	4	28.40	7
130	G. G. Wagg (*Glam*)	10	12	1	308	58	0	2	28.00	1
131	G. P. Swann (*Notts & England*)	8	12	4	223	57	0	1	27.87	6
132	†W. D. Bragg (*Glam*)	15	26	2	660	71*	0	4	27.50	4
133	B. J. Wright (*Glam*)	14	25	3	604	68*	0	3	27.45	10
134	†M. A. Wallace (*Glam*)	17	24	0	656	101	1	2	27.33	44/3
135	A. R. Adams (*Notts*)	11	15	2	354	80	0	2	27.23	3
136	†M. E. Trescothick (*Somerset*)	17	32	1	843	74	0	6	27.19	31
137	S. A. Northeast (*MCC & Kent*)	17	29	1	760	94	0	7	27.14	11
138	D. R. Briggs (*Hants*)	13	12	3	244	54	0	1	27.11	6
139	†P. J. Franks (*Notts*)	9	12	0	323	78	0	3	26.91	3
140	K. R. Brown (*Lancs*)	10	16	0	428	87	0	3	26.75	8
141	D. Murphy (*Northants*)	14	14	3	293	81	0	1	26.63	51/4
142	†U. T. Khawaja (*Australia A & Australians*)	6	12	1	290	73	0	2	26.36	5
143	†T. M. J. Smith (*Middx & Glos*)	11	13	4	234	50	0	1	26.00	3
144	†I. J. Westwood (*Warwicks*)	14	23	2	543	71	0	4	25.85	10
145	†S. M. Ervine (*Hants*)	15	19	1	458	86	0	4	25.44	20
146	C. M. W. Read (*Notts*)	16	23	2	532	80	0	3	25.33	59/2
147	M. H. Johnson (*Derbys*)	13	23	1	556	72	0	4	25.27	12
148	†S. C. J. Broad (*Notts & England*)	9	13	1	302	65	0	1	25.16	4
149	†H. D. Rutherford (*New Zealanders & Essex*)	6	10	0	250	126	1	0	25.00	2
150	C. J. Jordan (*Sussex*)	16	20	1	472	92	0	2	24.84	24
151	Z. de Bruyn (*Surrey*)	14	23	0	571	111	1	1	24.82	16
152	D. M. Benkenstein (*MCC & Durham*)	7	13	2	272	74*	0	2	24.72	5
153	†D. J. Willey (*Northants*)	13	15	1	346	81	0	3	24.71	3
154	†Z. S. Ansari (*Cambridge MCCU & Surrey*)	8	12	3	222	72	0	1	24.66	3
155	C. R. Jones (*Durham MCCU & Somerset*)	9	17	1	394	130	1	2	24.62	4
	L. E. Plunkett (*Yorks*)	13	18	2	394	68	0	2	24.62	9
157	N. D. Pinner (*Worcs*)	8	11	0	265	80	0	2	24.09	10
158	G. D. Cross (*Lancs*)	13	17	0	409	100	1	2	24.05	35/2
159	G. K. Berg (*Middx*)	15	23	2	501	71	0	2	23.85	8
	S. H. Choudhry (*Worcs*)	7	10	3	167	61*	0	1	23.85	1
161	G. Chapple (*Lancs*)	14	16	3	308	63	0	3	23.69	9
162	A. Shahzad (*Notts*)	12	18	2	379	77	0	2	23.68	1
163	†W. T. S. Porterfield (*Warwicks*)	13	19	0	450	162	1	0	23.68	9
164	A. W. R. Barrow (*Somerset*)	10	17	1	378	83*	0	2	23.62	12
165	S. J. Walters (*Glam*)	10	17	0	398	98	0	2	23.41	13
166	C. P. Wood (*Hants*)	9	12	1	256	69	0	2	23.27	6
167	†M. J. North (*Glam*)	11	18	1	392	68	0	1	23.05	7
168	A. G. Wakely (*Northants*)	15	21	1	457	88	0	2	22.85	5
169	G. P. Smith (*Leics*)	13	23	1	500	70	0	4	22.72	13

		M	I	NO	R	HS	100	50	Avge	Ct/St
170	G. O. Jones (*Kent*)	15	20	2	404	67	0	2	22.44	40/1
171	M. J. Prior (*Sussex & England*)	14	22	3	421	62	0	1	22.15	39
172	T. Poynton (*Derbys*)	12	22	2	443	63*	0	3	22.15	27/3
173	†J. D. Shantry (*Worcs*)	14	15	1	307	55*	0	2	21.92	4
174	†K. W. Hogg (*Lancs*)	15	16	5	241	58	0	1	21.90	2
175	†M. T. Coles (*Kent & Hants*)	12	14	2	254	68	0	3	21.16	7
176	T. T. Bresnan (*Yorks & England*)	7	10	2	169	45	0	0	21.12	1
177	M. H. Wessels (*Notts*)	11	16	1	316	77	0	1	21.06	13/1
178	J. A. R. Harris (*Middx*)	10	13	4	189	43*	0	0	21.00	2
179	†G. M. Andrew (*Worcs*)	11	15	0	311	66	0	3	20.73	6
180	†D. J. Wainwright (*Derbys*)	9	16	4	241	54*	0	1	20.08	0
181	P. D. Trego (*MCC & Somerset*)	16	27	1	521	87	0	3	20.03	5
182	M. G. Hogan (*Glam*)	14	18	3	297	51	0	1	19.80	5
183	S. C. Kerrigan (*MCC, Lancs, Eng. Ls & Eng.*)	16	14	6	158	62*	0	1	19.75	7
184	†B. T. Slater (*Derbys*)	10	18	1	335	66*	0	3	19.70	3
185	G. J. Batty (*Surrey*)	13	18	2	313	41	0	0	19.56	6
186	L. J. Fletcher (*Notts*)	15	22	3	368	64	0	2	19.36	5
187	M. A. Wood (*Durham*)	8	10	2	153	58*	0	1	19.12	1
188	D. A. Cosker (*Glam*)	16	22	7	286	44*	0	0	19.06	7
189	O. P. Rayner (*Middx*)	14	19	3	303	52*	0	1	18.93	20
190	W. J. Durston (*Derbys*)	10	18	1	317	50	0	1	18.64	8
191	A. P. Palladino (*Derbys*)	8	14	1	233	68	0	1	17.92	1
192	†B. A. Godleman (*Derbys*)	9	16	0	275	55	0	1	17.18	3
193	†J. C. Tredwell (*Kent*)	12	15	1	238	48	0	0	17.00	9
194	†D. J. Redfern (*Derbys*)	8	15	0	252	61	0	2	16.80	6
195	M. A. Thornely (*Leics*)	11	17	0	282	53	0	1	16.58	10
196	J. C. Glover (*Glam*)	8	10	2	127	51*	0	1	15.87	1
197	C. D. Thorp (*Durham*)	8	12	2	157	27	0	0	15.70	2
198	A. C. Thomas (*Somerset*)	13	21	5	239	54*	0	0	14.93	4
199	S. A. Patterson (*Yorks*)	17	18	8	147	40	0	0	14.70	2
200	†J. E. Anyon (*Sussex*)	14	17	6	159	25	0	0	14.45	1
201	M. Davies (*Kent*)	11	15	4	158	41	0	0	14.36	0
202	J. J. Cobb (*Leics*)	12	20	2	258	46*	0	0	14.33	6
203	J. A. Brooks (*Yorks*)	12	14	7	100	33*	0	0	14.28	6
204	M. A. Johnson (*Worcs*)	10	14	1	184	44	0	0	14.15	14
205	G. Onions (*Durham & England Lions*)	14	18	6	169	27	0	0	14.08	3
206	A. D. Hales (*Notts*)	10	18	0	251	58	0	2	13.94	10
207	†J. S. Sykes (*Leics*)	7	12	2	139	34	0	0	13.90	3
208	C. A. J. Meschede (*Somerset*)	10	15	1	192	59	0	1	13.71	6
209	A. Richardson (*Worcs*)	16	18	10	109	21	0	0	13.62	4
210	†R. A. Whiteley (*Derbys & Worcs*)	8	14	0	189	56	0	1	13.50	5
211	C. N. Miles (*Glos*)	13	13	1	161	50*	0	1	13.41	1
212	†M. N. W. Spriegel (*Northants*)	8	12	2	134	76	0	1	13.40	2
213	T. S. Roland-Jones (*Middx & England Lions*)	9	12	2	133	22*	0	0	13.30	4
214	A. L. Hughes (*Derbys*)	6	11	0	136	33	0	0	12.36	3
215	A. V. Suppiah (*Somerset*)	6	11	0	130	36	0	0	11.81	2
	J. L. Clare (*Derbys*)	6	11	0	130	49	0	0	11.81	8
217	C. E. Shreck (*Kent*)	15	15	8	82	19*	0	0	11.71	1
218	A. C. F. Wyatt (*Leics*)	11	17	7	117	28	0	0	11.70	1
219	J. K. H. Naik (*Leics*)	10	13	2	127	47*	0	0	11.54	8
220	†R. J. Sidebottom (*Yorks*)	15	17	0	195	48	0	0	11.47	4
221	S. C. Meaker (*Surrey*)	8	11	4	80	30*	0	0	11.42	0
222	A. N. Kervezee (*Worcs*)	12	18	0	204	47	0	0	11.33	5
223	T. D. Groenewald (*Derbys*)	15	26	5	231	49	0	0	11.00	7
224	O. H. Freckingham (*Leics*)	15	21	2	204	30	0	0	10.73	4
225	†S. J. Magoffin (*Sussex*)	16	20	2	192	32	0	0	10.66	4
226	G. H. Dockrell (*Somerset*)	8	12	2	106	31	0	0	10.60	2
227	D. D. Masters (*Essex*)	14	12	3	95	37*	0	0	10.55	3
228	†J. A. Tomlinson (*Hants*)	15	15	8	72	30*	0	0	10.28	1
229	†T. J. Murtagh (*Middx*)	13	15	4	112	29	0	0	10.18	4

		M	I	NO	R	HS	100	50	Avge	Ct/St
230	C. T. Tremlett (*Surrey*)	11	12	1	110	54	0	1	10.00	3
231	D. J. Balcombe (*Hants*)	12	13	2	106	30*	0	0	9.63	1
232	†M. S. Panesar (*Sussex & Essex*)	18	17	7	95	22	0	0	9.50	2
233	M. J. Hoggard (*Leics*)	7	11	3	75	24	0	0	9.37	1
234	J. Overton (*Somerset*)	13	20	6	131	24	0	0	9.35	0
235	M. H. A. Footitt (*Derbys*)	13	22	5	153	24	0	0	9.00	3
236	†J. M. Anderson (*Lancs & England*)	9	13	4	80	26	0	0	8.88	6
237	M. T. Reed (*Glam*)	12	15	7	71	27	0	0	8.87	2
238	C. Rushworth (*MCC & Durham*)	16	22	9	111	18*	0	0	8.53	4
239	S. P. Kirby (*MCC & Somerset*)	11	17	6	88	15	0	0	8.00	4
240	H. F. Gurney (*Notts*)	15	19	11	62	22*	0	0	7.75	4
241	T. E. Linley (*Surrey*)	12	14	1	84	22*	0	0	6.46	6
242	J. W. Dernbach (*Surrey*)	10	14	5	58	22	0	0	6.44	0
243	C. J. Russell (*Worcs*)	11	12	2	46	10	0	0	4.60	2
244	C. D. Collymore (*Middx*)	10	11	5	22	6*	0	0	3.66	3
245	S. T. Finn (*Middx & England*)	11	12	2	33	8	0	0	3.30	4
246	Azharullah (*Northants*)	9	10	6	12	8	0	0	3.00	3
247	R. J. W. Topley (*Essex*)	13	14	7	12	8*	0	0	1.71	6

BOWLING (Qualification: 10 wickets in 5 innings)

		Style	O	M	R	W	BB	5I	Avge
1	U. Arshad (*Durham*)	RFM	73.1	16	249	16	3-16	0	15.56
2	T. A. Copeland (*Northants*)	RFM	394.4	139	882	48	7-63	4	18.37
3	K. W. Hogg (*Lancs*)	RFM	436	105	1,105	60	7-27	3	18.41
4	G. Onions (*Durham & England Lions*)	RFM	452.1	94	1,382	73	7-62	5	18.93
5	R. J. Sidebottom (*Yorks*)	LFM	385.1	107	1,012	53	4-27	0	19.09
6	A. Richardson (*Worcs*)	RFM	541.4	157	1,368	69	8-37	5	19.82
7	T. J. Murtagh (*Middx*)	RFM	444.1	113	1,224	60	6-93	3	20.40
8	R. J. Harris (*Australia A & Australians*)	RFM	235.1	60	676	33	7-117	2	20.48
9	M. G. Hogan (*Glam*)	RFM	512	133	1,376	67	7-92	4	20.53
10	G. Chapple (*Lancs*)	RFM	430.4	110	1,099	53	5-9	2	20.73
11	C. D. Thorp (*Durham*)	RFM	190.5	68	378	18	3-29	0	21.00
12	S. J. Magoffin (*Sussex*)	RFM	512	134	1,379	65	8-20	3	21.21
13	G. M. Smith (*Essex*)	OB/RFM	114.5	23	365	17	5-42	2	21.47
14	S. C. J. Broad (*Notts & England*)	RFM	323.5	68	1,008	46	7-44	3	21.91
15	W. R. S. Gidman (*Glos*)	RFM	407.2	88	1,209	55	6-15	2	21.98
16	O. P. Rayner (*Middx*)	OB	376.3	78	1,014	46	8-46	4	22.04
17	N. Wagner (*New Zealanders*)	LFM	108	26	332	15	5-45	1	22.13
18	T. C. Smith (*Lancs*)	RFM	150.5	35	498	22	4-49	0	22.63
	T. A. Boult (*New Zealanders*)	LFM	91	23	249	11	5-57	1	22.63
20	W. B. Rankin (*Warwicks*)	RFM	216.4	20	709	31	4-29	0	22.87
21	K. H. D. Barker (*Warwicks*)	LFM	345	83	1,055	46	5-55	1	22.93
22	C. Rushworth (*MCC & Durham*)	RFM	451.2	110	1,333	58	6-58	3	22.98
23	T. G. Southee (*New Zealanders*)	RFM	107.2	25	300	13	6-50	1	23.07
24	S. A. Patterson (*Yorks*)	RFM	435.5	130	1,197	51	5-43	1	23.47
25	S. C. Kerrigan (*MCC, Lancs, Eng. L & Eng.*)	SLA	510.2	111	1,412	60	7-63	5	23.53
26	D. D. Masters (*Essex*)	RFM	489.4	129	1,209	51	6-41	4	23.70
27	J. Harrison (*Durham*)	LFM	96.1	20	336	14	5-31	1	24.00
28	M. A. Wood (*Durham*)	RFM	209.4	38	650	27	5-44	1	24.07
29	J. A. Tomlinson (*Hants*)	LFM	454.5	126	1,281	53	5-44	1	24.16
30	J. A. Brooks (*Yorks*)	RFM	261.2	55	908	37	5-40	1	24.54
31	M. Davies (*Kent*)	RFM	272.3	76	629	26	4-36	0	24.57
32	J. M. Anderson (*Lancs & England*)	RFM	332.3	85	963	39	5-47	3	24.69
33	N. J. Dexter (*Middx*)	RM	176.2	40	445	18	5-27	1	24.72
34	M. J. Leach (*Somerset*)	SLA	149.4	51	324	13	5-63	1	24.92
35	D. J. Willey (*Northants*)	LFM	361.3	66	1,122	45	5-67	2	24.93
36	M. A. Starc (*Australians*)	LFM	167.1	39	474	19	4-33	0	24.94
37	J. P. Faulkner (*Australians*)	LFM	102.5	23	325	13	4-51	0	25.00
38	A. J. Hall (*Northants*)	RM	325.3	85	937	37	5-30	1	25.32

		Style	O	M	R	W	BB	5I	Avge
39	L. E. Plunkett (*Yorks*)	RFM	278.4	49	1,065	42	6-33	2	25.35
40	L. Gregory (*Somerset*)	RFM	119.4	25	358	14	5-38	1	25.57
41	A. C. Thomas (*Somerset*)	RFM	386.4	108	1,077	42	5-69	1	25.64
42	C. D. Collymore (*Middx*)	RFM	247.2	53	668	26	4-61	0	25.69
43	A. E. N. Riley (*Lough MCCU & Kent*)	OB	130.4	12	489	19	7-150	1	25.73
44	C. R. Woakes (*Warwicks, Eng. Ls & Eng.*)	RFM	287.4	58	863	33	5-42	1	26.15
45	J. D. Shantry (*Worcs*)	LFM	396.2	106	1,183	45	7-60	2	26.28
46	G. P. Swann (*Notts & England*)	OB	339	61	1,052	40	6-90	3	26.30
47	S. P. Crook (*Northants*)	RFM	326	46	1,139	43	4-30	0	26.48
48	T. T. Bresnan (*Yorks & England*)	RFM	221.2	51	689	26	4-41	0	26.50
49	B. A. Stokes (*Durham*)	RFM	351.4	59	1,171	44	4-49	0	26.61
50	P. P. Chawla (*Somerset*)	LBG	122.4	13	453	17	5-97	2	26.64
51	R. S. Bopara (*Essex & England Lions*)	RM	148	26	427	16	3-41	0	26.68
52	R. A. J. Smith (*Glam*)	RM	61	6	274	10	3-50	0	27.40
53	J. E. Anyon (*Sussex*)	RFM	399.4	77	1,454	52	5-44	1	27.96
54	A. P. Palladino (*Derbys*)	RFM	214.5	43	644	23	6-90	2	28.00
55	C. J. Jordan (*Sussex*)	RFM	471.3	88	1,719	61	6-48	4	28.18
56	M. E. Claydon (*Kent & Durham*)	RFM	83.3	14	282	10	3-25	0	28.20
57	R. H. Patel (*Middx*)	SLA	134.5	30	395	14	5-69	1	28.21
58	C. A. J. Meschede (*Somerset*)	RM	204.1	38	738	26	4-43	0	28.38
59	R. J. W. Topley (*Essex*)	LFM	411.4	78	1,364	48	6-29	3	28.41
60	H. F. Gurney (*Notts*)	LFM	412.3	70	1,376	48	5-81	1	28.66
61	Azharullah (*Northants*)	RFM	225.4	51	717	25	4-42	0	28.68
62	S. T. Finn (*Middx & England*)	RF	231.5	52	781	27	4-46	0	28.92
63	R. Clarke (*Warwicks*)	RFM	254.3	66	698	24	4-33	0	29.08
64	M. T. Reed (*Glam*)	RFM	330.3	63	1,120	38	6-34	2	29.47
65	T. S. Roland-Jones (*Middx & Eng. Lions*)	RFM	232.1	42	748	25	6-63	1	29.92
66	L. J. Fletcher (*Notts*)	RFM	460.1	133	1,288	43	5-52	2	29.95
67	A. R. Adams (*Notts*)	RFM	302.5	55	929	31	4-69	0	29.96
68	J. S. Patel (*Warwicks*)	OB	576.1	139	1,561	52	5-56	2	30.01
69	J. M. Vince (*Hants*)	RM	119.4	17	452	15	5-41	1	30.13
70	J. L. Pattinson (*Australians*)	RFM	120.1	27	424	14	4-56	0	30.28
71	C. N. Miles (*Glos*)	RFM	358	69	1,315	43	6-88	3	30.58
72	J. W. Dernbach (*Surrey*)	RFM	315	57	1,043	34	5-57	1	30.67
73	G. R. Napier (*Essex*)	RFM	479.1	86	1,572	51	7-90	3	30.82
74	M. T. Coles (*Kent & Hants*)	RFM	289	55	1,053	34	6-71	3	30.97
75	D. A. J. Bracewell (*New Zealanders*)	RFM	93	26	311	10	4-28	0	31.10
76	T. D. Groenewald (*Derbys*)	RFM	437.5	86	1,404	45	5-30	3	31.20
77	J. Allenby (*Glam*)	RM	391.5	109	951	30	4-16	0	31.70
78	C. J. C. Wright (*Warwicks & Eng. Lions*)	RFM	261.5	56	858	27	6-31	2	31.77
79	M. A. Chambers (*Essex & Warwicks*)	RFM	157.2	25	581	18	5-68	1	32.27
80	O. J. Hannon-Dalby (*Warwicks*)	RFM	110.4	18	390	12	4-50	0	32.50
81	J. L. Clare (*Derbys*)	RFM	124	7	554	17	5-29	1	32.58
82	M. H. A. Footitt (*Derbys*)	LFM	380.5	57	1,377	42	6-53	2	32.78
83	D. I. Stevens (*Kent*)	RM	403.4	111	1,051	32	5-39	1	32.84
84	D. A. Griffiths (*Hants*)	RFM	85.3	11	362	11	5-68	1	32.90
85	C. T. Tremlett (*Surrey*)	RFM	349.1	66	1,057	32	8-96	2	33.03
86	S. G. Borthwick (*Durham*)	LBG	297.4	43	1,140	34	6-70	1	33.52
87	J. M. Bird (*Australia A & Australians*)	RFM	127.3	42	370	11	4-48	0	33.63
88	S. M. Ervine (*Hants*)	RFM	179.1	39	577	17	2-17	0	33.94
89	M. J. Hoggard (*Leics*)	RFM	171	35	545	16	6-66	1	34.06
90	J. A. R. Harris (*Middx*)	RFM	251.4	37	854	25	3-46	0	34.16
91	T. E. Linley (*Surrey*)	RFM	438.1	106	1,268	37	4-59	0	34.27
92	D. R. Briggs (*Hants*)	SLA	300.4	76	857	25	3-33	0	34.28
93	B. A. C. Howell (*Glos*)	RM	355	85	1,029	30	5-57	1	34.30
94	G. Cessford (*Worcs*)	RFM	145.4	26	591	17	4-73	0	34.76
95	Sohail Tanvir (*Hants*)	LFM	107.2	19	348	10	3-62	0	34.80
96	C. J. Haggett (*Kent*)	RM	298	72	907	26	4-94	0	34.88
97	J. Overton (*Somerset*)	RFM	304.5	48	1,221	35	6-95	1	34.88
98	P. D. Trego (*MCC & Somerset*)	RFM	374.2	92	1,120	32	4-69	0	35.00
	S. C. Meaker (*Surrey*)	RF	195.4	33	840	24	5-60	1	35.00

	Style	O	M	R	W	BB	5I	Avge
100 Z. S. Ansari (*Camb. MCCU & Surrey*) ..	SLA	204.1	32	602	17	4-70	0	35.41
101 D. A. Cosker (*Glam*)	SLA	462.2	93	1,318	37	5-120	1	35.62
102 J. K. H. Naik (*Leics*)	OB	326.3	67	934	26	5-70	2	35.92
103 G. Keedy (*Surrey*)	SLA	269	51	796	22	7-99	2	36.18
104 P. M. Siddle (*Australians*)	RFM	216.5	55	654	18	5-50	1	36.33
105 M. M. Ali (*Worcs*)	OB	324.4	41	1,127	31	6-77	1	36.35
106 M. Higginbottom (*Derbys*)	RFM	92.5	20	364	10	3-59	0	36.40
107 T. P. Milnes (*Warwicks*)	RFM	128.1	21	476	13	7-39	1	36.61
108 S. H. Choudhry (*Worcs*)	SLA	173.4	26	484	13	4-111	0	37.23
109 G. K. Berg (*Middx*)	RFM	324.4	71	942	25	3-49	0	37.68
110 S. P. Kirby (*MCC & Somerset*)	RFM	300.3	58	998	26	4-18	0	38.38
111 M. S. Panesar (*Sussex & Essex*)	SLA	558	131	1,543	40	5-95	2	38.57
112 G. M. Andrew (*Worcs*)	RFM	242.3	59	818	21	4-79	0	38.95
113 N. M. Lyon (*Australians*)	OB	186.1	45	550	14	4-42	0	39.28
114 J. C. Glover (*Glam*)	RM	174.1	35	558	14	4-51	0	39.85
115 C. E. Shreck (*Kent*)	RFM	435.2	98	1,316	33	4-65	0	39.87
116 A. C. F. Wyatt (*Leics*)	RFM	312.1	74	974	24	3-35	0	40.58
117 P. J. Franks (*Notts*)	RFM	149	34	494	12	3-16	0	41.16
118 J. D. Middlebrook (*MCC & Northants*) .	OB	278.1	55	872	21	6-78	1	41.52
119 L. A. Procter (*Lancs*)	RFM	194	31	633	15	4-39	0	42.20
120 G. J. Batty (*Surrey*)	OB	395.4	68	1,141	27	5-71	2	42.25
121 G. H. Dockrell (*Somerset*)	SLA	254.4	60	722	17	6-96	1	42.47
122 L. C. Norwell (*Glos*)	RFM	139	16	599	14	3-80	0	42.78
123 A. Shahzad (*Notts*)	RFM	343.4	66	1,125	26	3-21	0	43.26
124 T. S. Mills (*Essex*)	LFM	120.4	21	477	11	3-42	0	43.36
125 C. P. Wood (*Hants*)	LFM	231.3	65	659	15	3-30	0	43.93
126 O. H. Freckingham (*Leics*)	RFM	399	61	1,584	36	6-125	1	44.00
127 A. U. Rashid (*Yorks*)	LBG	359.5	39	1,358	29	5-78	1	46.82
128 S. R. Patel (*Notts*)	SLA	460.2	126	1,316	28	3-40	0	47.00
129 K. S. Williamson (*N. Zealanders & Yorks*)	OB	135.1	24	472	10	3-68	0	47.20
130 L. J. Hatchett (*Sussex*)	LFM	141.4	23	489	10	3-56	0	48.90
131 C. J. Russell (*Worcs*)	RFM	235.4	40	930	19	3-47	0	48.94
132 T. M. J. Smith (*Middx & Glos*)	SLA	263.5	38	840	17	4-91	0	49.41
133 J. K. Fuller (*Glos*)	RFM	228.4	44	793	16	5-43	1	49.56
134 D. J. Balcombe (*Hants*)	RFM	349	80	1,101	22	5-104	1	50.04
135 D. A. Payne (*Glos*)	LFM	275.4	59	917	18	3-75	0	50.94
136 R. E. M. Williams (*Leics*)	RFM	145.1	22	521	10	4-69	0	52.10
137 G. G. Wagg (*Glam*)	LM/SLA	295.2	63	971	18	3-78	0	53.94
138 D. J. Wainwright (*Derbys*)	SLA	296	42	924	17	3-64	0	54.35
139 C. D. Nash (*Sussex*)	OB	209.2	35	613	11	2-27	0	55.72
140 J. C. Tredwell (*Kent*)	OB	331.3	67	965	17	5-51	1	56.76
141 W. J. Durston (*Derbys*)	OB	180	23	586	10	2-29	0	58.60
142 L. A. Dawson (*Hants*)	SLA	216.2	55	647	11	2-36	0	58.81
143 J. S. Sykes (*Leics*)	SLA	199.3	30	733	12	4-176	0	61.08
144 Z. de Bruyn (*Surrey*)	RM	253.2	52	824	13	3-28	0	63.38

The following bowlers took ten wickets in fewer than five innings:

	Style	O	M	R	W	BB	5I	Avge
J. E. Lee (*Leeds/Bradford MCCU*)	RFM	52	9	165	15	7-45	2	11.00
O. J. Newby (*Lancs*)	RFM	68.2	12	264	12	4-71	0	22.00
R. S. Buckley (*Durham*)	OB	114.2	21	344	10	5-86	1	34.40

BOWLING STYLES

LBG	Leg-breaks and googlies (3)	**RF**	Right-arm fast (2)
LFM	Left-arm fast medium (18)	**RFM**	Right-arm fast medium (82)
LM	Left-arm medium (1)	**RM**	Right-arm medium (12)
OB	Off-breaks (15)	**SLA**	Slow left-arm (16)

Note: The total comes to 149 because G. M. Smith and G. G. Wagg have two styles of bowling.

INDIVIDUAL SCORES OF 100 AND OVER

There were **255** three-figure innings in 171 first-class matches in 2013, which was 51 more than in 169 matches in 2012. Of these, 24 were double-hundreds, compared with eight in 2012. The list includes 210 hundreds in the County Championship, compared with 169 in 2012.

G. S. Ballance (6)
112 Yorks v Leeds/Brad MCCU, Leeds
107 Yorks v Somerset, Leeds
141 Yorks v Notts, Scarborough
112 Yorks v Warwicks, Leeds
148 ⎫
108* ⎭ Yorks v Surrey, The Oval

R. W. T. Key (5)
104* Kent v Leics, Leicester
106 Kent v Leics, Tunbridge Wells
180 Kent v Hants, Canterbury
101 Kent v Northants, Northampton
134 Kent v Lancs, Canterbury

B. P. Nash (5)
100* Kent v Lancs, Manchester
128* Kent v Leics, Tunbridge Wells
199* Kent v Glos, Cheltenham
126 Kent v Hants, Canterbury
107 Kent v Northants, Northampton

J. E. Root (5)
182 Yorks v Durham, Chester-le-Street
236 Yorks v Derbys, Leeds
179 Eng. Lions v New Zealanders, Leicester
104 England v New Zealand, Leeds
180 England v Australia, Lord's

J. M. Vince (5)
148 Hants v Leics, Southampton
114 Hants v Lough MCCU, Southampton
106 Hants v Lancs, Southport
106 Hants v Worcs, Worcester
147* Hants v Leics, Leicester

M. M. Ali (4)
123 Worcs v Glos, Worcester
250 Worcs v Glam, Worcester
104 ⎫
109 ⎭ Worcs v Lancs, Worcester

V. Chopra (4)
163 Warwicks v MCC, Abu Dhabi
108 Warwicks v Somerset, Taunton
192 Warwicks v Surrey, Guildford
228* Warwicks v Middx, Uxbridge

E. J. H. Eckersley (4)
122 Leics v Worcs, Worcester
147 Leics v Essex, Chelmsford
106 ⎫
119 ⎭ Leics v Worcs, Leicester

M. W. Goodwin (4)
108 Glam v Glos, Bristol
136 Glam v Kent, Canterbury
194 Glam v Lancs, Manchester
178 Glam v Leics, Swansea

S. M. Katich (4)
122 Lancs v Essex, Chelmsford
200 Lancs v Northants, Northampton
115 Lancs v Glam, Manchester
105 Lancs v Worcs, Worcester

M. Klinger (4)
103* Glos v Leics, Leicester
163 Glos v Hants, Bristol
142 Glos v Glam, Bristol
102* Glos v Kent, Cheltenham

M. J. Lumb (4)
123 Notts v Durham, Nottingham
135 Notts v Yorks, Scarborough
221* Notts v Derbys, Nottingham
107 Notts v Somerset, Nottingham

H. J. H. Marshall (4)
149 Glos v Essex, Chelmsford
114 Glos v Hants, Southampton
106 Glos v Kent, Cheltenham
145 Glos v Northants, Northampton

S. R. Patel (4)
256 Notts v Durham MCCU, Nottingham
157 Notts v Sussex, Hove
110 Notts v Surrey, The Oval
117 Notts v Warwicks, Nottingham

C. J. L. Rogers (4)
214 Middx v Surrey, Lord's
184 Middx v Sussex, Lord's
110 Australia v England, Chester-le-Street
108 Middx v Notts, Lord's

D. I. Stevens (4)
136 Kent v Essex, Chelmsford
119 Kent v Glam, Canterbury
126 Kent v Glos, Canterbury
205* Kent v Lancs, Canterbury

J. H. K. Adams (3)
219* Hants v Worcs, Southampton
138* Hants v Glos, Bristol
218 Hants v Northants, Southampton

I. R. Bell (3)
109 England v Australia, Nottingham
109 England v Australia, Lord's
113 England v Australia, Chester-le-Street

S. G. Borthwick (3)
101 Durham v Warwicks, Birmingham
117 Durham v Derbys, Chester-le-Street
135 Durham v Surrey, Chester-le-Street

L. J. Evans (3)
178 Warwicks v Notts, Birmingham
138 Warwicks v Somerset, Birmingham
137 Warwicks v Sussex, Birmingham

A. W. Gale (3)
272 Yorks v Notts, Scarborough
103 Yorks v Middx, Lord's
148 Yorks v Surrey, Leeds

A. P. R. Gidman (3)
110 Glos v Lancs, Liverpool
113 Glos v Glam, Bristol
211 Glos v Kent, Cheltenham

A. J. Hall (3)
113 Northants v Leics, Northampton
130* Northants v Hants, Northampton
103 Northants v Leics, Leicester

P. J. Horton (3)
111 Lancs v Hants, Southport
156 Lancs v Leics, Manchester
106 Lancs v Kent, Canterbury

K. K. Jennings (3)
102* Durham v Durham MCCU, Chester-le-St
123 Durham v Derbys, Chester-le-Street
127 Durham v Sussex, Hove

A. Z. Lees (3)
121 Yorks v Leeds/Brad MCCU, Leeds
100 Yorks v Middx, Lord's
275* Yorks v Derbys, Chesterfield

W. L. Madsen (3)
152 Derbys v Surrey, Derby
141 Derbys v Yorks, Chesterfield
138* Derbys v Middx, Derby

S. J. Mullaney (3)
103 Notts v Durham MCCU, Nottingham
104 Notts v Surrey, The Oval
125 Notts v Middx, Lord's

C. D. Nash (3)
102* Sussex v Surrey, Arundel
167* Sussex v Yorks, Hove
108 Sussex v Durham, Hove

A. G. Prince (3)
113 Lancs v Glam, Manchester
134 ⎫
108 ⎭ Lancs v Kent, Canterbury

A. U. Rashid (3)
180 Yorks v Somerset, Leeds
110* Yorks v Warwicks, Birmingham
103* Yorks v Somerset, Taunton

S. D. Robson (3)
129 Middx v Surrey, Lord's
215* Middx v Warwicks, Birmingham
166 Middx v Sussex, Hove

D. J. Sales (3)
255* Northants v Glos, Northampton
131 Northants v Essex, Colchester
110 Northants v Kent, Northampton

M. D. Stoneman (3)
109 Durham v Yorks, Chester-le-Street
122 Durham v Somerset, Taunton
122 Durham v Yorks, Scarborough

J. W. A. Taylor (3)
112 Notts v Derbys, Derby
204* Notts v Sussex, Nottingham
121* Sussex v Australians, Hove

A. J. Wheater (3)
102* Hants v Lough MCCU, Southampton
140 Hants v Lancs, Southport
122 Hants v Essex, Southampton

S. S. Agarwal (2)
108 Oxford MCCU v Warwicks, Oxford
313* Oxford U. v Cambridge U., Cambridge

J. Allenby (2)
138* Glam v Leics, Leicester
105 Glam v Glos, Bristol

R. J. Burns (2)
115 Surrey v Somerset, The Oval
114 Surrey v Middx, Lord's

M. A. Carberry (2)
118 Hants v Lough MCCU, Southampton
154 Hants v Kent, Canterbury

M. J. Clarke (2)
124 Australians v Worcs, Worcester
187 Australia v England, Manchester

K. J. Coetzer (2)
219 Northants v Leics, Leicester
122 Northants v Glos, Northampton

N. R. D. Compton (2)
105* Somerset v Warwicks, Taunton
166 Somerset v Durham, Taunton

S. M. Davies (2)
147 Surrey v Somerset, The Oval
103 Surrey v Warwicks, Birmingham

C. D. J. Dent (2)
153 Glos v Kent, Cheltenham
129* Glos v Northants, Northampton

B. T. Foakes (2)
101* Essex v Cambridge MCCU, Cambridge
120 Essex v Leics, Chelmsford

R. J. Hamilton-Brown (2)
113 Sussex v Notts, Nottingham
126* Sussex v Yorks, Hove

B. W. Harmison (2)
101* Kent v Glos, Cheltenham
106 Kent v Glos, Canterbury

J. C. Hildreth (2)
115 Somerset v Yorks, Taunton
161 Somerset v Notts, Nottingham

P. A. Jaques (2)
139 Yorks v Derbys, Chesterfield
152 Yorks v Durham, Scarborough

A. Javid (2)
133 Warwicks v Somerset, Birmingham
119* Warwicks v Surrey, Birmingham

E. C. Joyce (2)
204* Sussex v Notts, Nottingham
101 Sussex v Middx, Hove

A. Lyth (2)
111 Yorks v Leeds/Brad MCCU, Leeds
105 Yorks v Somerset, Taunton

J. C. Mickleburgh (2)
243 Essex v Leics, Chelmsford
129 Essex v Glam, Chelmsford

D. K. H. Mitchell (2)
118 Worcs v Oxford MCCU, Oxford
156 Worcs v Essex, Worcester

S. D. Peters (2)
106 Northants v Kent, Canterbury
101 Northants v Essex, Colchester

A. N. Petersen (2)
167 Somerset v Surrey, The Oval
136 Somerset v Warwicks, Taunton

K. P. Pietersen (2)
177* Surrey v Yorks, Leeds
113 England v Australia, Manchester

R. T. Ponting (2)
192 Surrey v Derbys, Derby
169* Surrey v Notts, The Oval

G. P. Rees (2)
112 Glam v Hants, Cardiff
107* Glam v Lancs, Manchester

M. J. Richardson (2)
102 Durham v Yorks, Scarborough
129 Durham v Sussex, Hove

G. H. Roderick (2)
152* Glos v Kent, Canterbury
136 Glos v Essex, Bristol

T. T. Samaraweera (2)
100* Worcs v Leics, Worcester
144* Worcs v Leics, Leicester

S. P. D. Smith (2)
102* Australians v Sussex, Hove
138* Australia v England, The Oval

W. R. Smith (2)
101* Durham v Durham MCCU, Chester-le-St
153 Durham v Notts, Nottingham

V. S. Solanki (2)
130 Surrey v Sussex, Arundel
162 Surrey v Warwicks, Birmingham

B. A. Stokes (2)
111 Durham v Durham MCCU, Chester-le-St
127 Durham v Yorks, Scarborough

T. Westley (2)
133 Essex v Cambridge MCCU, Cambridge
163 Essex v Glos, Chelmsford

S. R. Watson (2)
109 Australians v Worcs, Worcester
176 Australia v England, The Oval

L. J. Wright (2)
187 Sussex v Middx, Lord's
161 Sussex v Middx, Hove

L. W. P. Wells (2)
208 Sussex v Surrey, The Oval
110 Sussex v Derbys, Hove

M. H. Yardy (2)
153 Sussex v Derbys, Derby
156 Sussex v Somerset, Taunton

The following each played in one three-figure innings:

A. P. Agathangelou, 121, Lancs v Hants, Southampton; T. R. Ambrose, 105, Warwicks v Durham, Birmingham; H. M. Amla, 151, Surrey v Yorks, The Oval.

J. M. Bairstow, 186, Yorks v Derbys, Leeds; K. H. D. Barker, 125, Warwicks v Surrey, Guildford; D. J. Bell-Drummond, 102*, Kent v Cardiff MCCU, Canterbury; R. S. Bopara, 145, Essex v Glam, Cardiff; M. A. G. Boyce, 135, Leics v Kent, Leicester; J. C. Buttler, 119*, Somerset v Warwicks, Taunton.

S. Chanderpaul, 129, Derbys v Surrey, Derby; P. P. Chawla, 112, Somerset v Middx, Lord's; A. N. Cook, 130, England v New Zealand, Leeds; S. J. Croft, 101*, Lancs v Hants, Southampton; G. D. Cross, 100, Lancs v Hants, Southampton.

L. A. Dawson, 136*, Hants v Leics, Leicester; Z. de Bruyn, 111, Surrey v Sussex, Arundel; J. L. Denly, 146, MCC v Warwicks, Abu Dhabi; N. J. Dexter, 104, Middx v Sussex, Lord's.

T. C. Elliott, 101, Cambridge U. v Oxford U., Cambridge.

J. S. Foster, 143, Essex v Leics, Leicester.

G. Gambhir, 106, Essex v Glos, Bristol; W. R. S. Gidman, 143, Glos v Leics, Bristol.

A. Harinath, 154, Surrey v Derbys, Derby; D. M. Housego, 150, Glos v Essex, Chelmsford; C. F. Hughes, 270*, Derbys v Yorks, Leeds; D. J. Hussey, 125, Notts v Somerset, Nottingham.

C. R. Jones, 130, Somerset v Australians, Taunton.

R. I. Keogh, 221, Northants v Hants, Southampton; C. Kieswetter, 148, Somerset v Warwicks, Birmingham.

J. Leach, 114, Worcs v Glos, Cheltenham.

M. W. Machan, 103, Sussex v Somerset, Taunton; N. D. McKenzie, 146, Hants v Kent, Southampton; N. J. Maddinson, 181, Australia A v Glos, Bristol; D. J. Malan, 156*, Middx v Cambridge MCCU, Cambridge; J. D. Middlebrook, 109, Northants v Kent, Northampton.

G. R. Napier, 102*, Essex v Lancs, Manchester.

M. G. Pardoe, 102, Worcs v Glam, Worcester; M. L. Pettini, 100*, Essex v Cambridge MCCU, Cambridge; W. T. S. Porterfield, 162, Warwicks v MCC, Abu Dhabi; L. A. Procter, 106, Lancs v Glos, Bristol.

R. J. Quiney, 112, Essex v Cambridge MCCU, Cambridge.

L. M. Reece, 114*, Leeds/Brad MCCU v Leics, Leicester; A. M. Rossington, 103*, Middx v Cambridge MCCU, Cambridge; H. D. Rutherford, 126, New Zealanders v England Lions, Leicester.

O. A. Shah, 120, Essex v Glam, Chelmsford; D. P. Sibley, 242, Surrey v Yorks, The Oval; G. M. Smith, 177, Essex v Glos, Bristol.

R. N. ten Doeschate, 103, Essex v Northants, Colchester; S. J. Thakor, 114, Leics v Kent, Leicester.

A. C. Voges, 150, Middx v Warwicks, Uxbridge.

M. A. Wallace, 101, Glam v Essex, Cardiff; G. C. Wilson, 124, Surrey v Sussex, The Oval; C. R. Woakes, 152*, Warwicks v Derbys, Derby.

> **"** He joined his captain on a tiger shoot and, alarmed at his inaccuracy, exclaimed: 'Good Lord, you've shot the bloody goat.'"
> Obituaries, page 210

FASTEST HUNDREDS BY BALLS...

Balls	Mins		
55	50	A. M. Rossington	Middx v Cambridge MCCU at Cambridge.
68†	67	R. J. Hamilton-Brown	Sussex v Yorks at Hove.
70	79	A. J. Wheater.	Hants v Loughborough MCCU at Southampton.
75†	94	C. D. Nash.	Sussex v Somerset at Taunton.
83	112	S. J. Mullaney	Notts v Durham MCCU at Nottingham.
86	120	S. M. Katich	Lancs v Worcs at Worcester.
90	122	M. J. Clarke.	Australians v Worcs at Worcester.
94	113	S. R. Watson	Australians v Worcs at Worcester.
99	136	M. H. Yardy	Sussex v Somerset at Taunton.
102	121	J. C. Hildreth.	Somerset v Notts at Nottingham.
106	139	N. J. Maddinson	Australia A v Glos at Bristol.
106	139	K. P. Pietersen.	Surrey v Yorks at Leeds.
107	119	S. R. Patel	Notts v Durham MCCU at Nottingham.
110	161	H. D. Rutherford	New Zealanders v England Lions at Leicester.

† *Scored against declaration bowling.*

...AND THE SLOWEST

Balls	Mins		
301	343	D. P. Sibley	Surrey v Yorks at The Oval.
270	348	W. R. Smith	Durham v Notts at Nottingham.
265	342	J. W. A. Taylor.	Notts v Derbys at Derby.
264	321	M. A. G. Boyce	Leics v Kent at Leicester.
260	320	L. J. Evans	Warwicks v Notts at Birmingham.
251	285	R. J. Burns	Surrey v Middx at Lord's.
247	297	K. K. Jennings	Durham v Derbys at Chester-le-Street.
247	343	J. E. Root	England v Australia at Lord's.
243	282	A. Javid	Warwicks v Surrey at Birmingham.
239	308	M. J. Lumb.	Notts v Somerset at Nottingham.

TEN WICKETS IN A MATCH

There were **16** instances of bowlers taking ten or more wickets in a first-class match in 2013, one fewer than in 2012. Four were in Tests and 12 in the County Championship.

A. Richardson (2)
12-63, Worcs v Kent, Canterbury; 12-107, Worcs v Glos, Worcester.

The following each took ten wickets in a match on one occasion:

J. M. Anderson, 10-158, England v Australia, Nottingham.

S. C. J. Broad, 11-121, England v Australia, Chester-le-Street.

P. P. Chawla, 10-208, Somerset v Derbys, Taunton; M. T. Coles, 10-154, Hants v Essex, Southampton; T. A. Copeland, 10-113, Northants v Kent, Canterbury.

W. R. S. Gidman, 10-43, Glos v Leics, Bristol.

S. C. Kerrigan, 12-252, Lancs v Glam, Manchester.

S. J. Magoffin, 12-31, Sussex v Somerset, Horsham; T. J. Murtagh, 10-77, Middx v Somerset, Taunton.

O. P. Rayner, 15-118, Middx v Surrey, The Oval; C. Rushworth, 10-103, Durham v Derbys, Chester-le-Street.

T. G. Southee, 10-108, New Zealand v England, Lord's; G. P. Swann, 10-132, England v New Zealand, Leeds.

R. J. W. Topley, 11-85, Essex v Worcs, Chelmsford.

LV= COUNTY CHAMPIONSHIP, 2013

ALAN GARDNER

"Nobody knows anything" was the verdict of screenwriter and author William Goldman on whether it was possible to predict success in Hollywood. While parallels between the movie business and county cricket are understandably scarce, there is each summer a delicious sense that everything is once again up for grabs. A competition whose seeds were sown almost 150 years ago, when Tinseltown was a collection of adobe huts outside Los Angeles, continues to provide us with fresh, invigorating material.

Who, in April, had been willing to predict another title for Durham, bottom of the table for so much of the previous season? Or promotion, to go with a first limited-overs trophy since 1992, for Northamptonshire, a county that had won four games in all competitions in 2012? Romantics might have had an eye on Yorkshire challenging for the Championship in their sesquicentenary; the club president, Geoffrey Boycott, had practically demanded it. But most were more cautious about their prospects of winning Division One a year after being promoted. Surrey, meanwhile, were tipped in some quarters, only for their slide towards relegation to develop an inexorable quality almost as soon as their overseas signing and captain, Graeme Smith, departed injured after just three games. They finished last. And if anything summed up the unpredictability

COUNTY CHAMPIONSHIP TABLE

Division One	Matches	Won	Lost	Drawn	Bonus points Batting	Bonus points Bowling	Penalty	Points
1 – Durham (**6**).........	16	10	4	2	36	46	2.5	245.5
2 – Yorkshire (**2**).......	16	7	2	7	49	39	0	221
3 – Sussex (**4**)...........	16	5	3	8	45	39	0	188
4 – Warwickshire (**1**).....	16	5	2	9	37	42	0	186
5 – Middlesex (**3**)........	16	6	5	5	32	39	0	182
6 – Somerset (**2**).........	16	3	5	8	33	41	0	146
7 – Nottinghamshire (**5**)...	16	2	5	9	47	40	0	146
8 – Derbyshire (*1*).......	16	3	10	3	31	34	0	122
9 – Surrey (*7*)...........	16	1	6	9	36	37	0	116

Division Two	Matches	Won	Lost	Drawn	Bonus points Batting	Bonus points Bowling	Penalty	Points
1 – Lancashire (**8**).......	16	8	1	7	45	45	1	238
2 – Northamptonshire (*8*)..	16	5	3	8	55	43	0	202
3 – Essex (*5*)............	16	5	4	7	43	41	3	182
4 – Hampshire (*4*)........	16	4	3	9	45	35	0	171
5 – Worcestershire (**9**)....	16	5	6	5	29	43	0	167
6 – Gloucestershire (*9*)....	16	4	4	8	43	36	0	167
7 – Kent (*3*).............	16	3	2	11	39	31	0	151
8 – Glamorgan (*6*)........	16	3	6	7	41	39	0	149
9 – Leicestershire (*7*).....	16	0	8	8	23	32	0	79

2012 positions are shown in brackets: Division One in bold, Division Two in italic.

Win = 16pts; draw = 3pts. Penalties were deducted for breach of team salary payments in 2012 (Durham) and for slow over-rates (Lancashire and Essex).

Stu Forster, Getty Images

Canny job: Paul Collingwood celebrates Durham's third title in six seasons with (*left to right*) Graham Onions, Chris Rushworth, Phil Mustard (partly obscured) and Ben Stokes.

of it all, it was the anonymous county pro in *The Cricketer* whose pre-season prognosis had Surrey top, and Durham, yep, bottom.

Baseball has always had more silver-screen time than cricket, but Kevin Costner could do worse than enquire after the rights to the story of the 2013 champions. Unable to afford an overseas player, and boasting a youthful squad with only a few old hands, **Durham** had begun with a 2.5-point deduction for breaching the salary cap in 2012. They won their opening game, but lost the next two. Forget *Bull Durham*, Costner's baseball rom-com: this felt more like a case of "Durham? Bull!" And yet, despite the heart attack suffered by head coach Geoff Cook midway through the season, Durham just got stronger. As emotion fuelled their momentum, they set a club record of five Championship wins in a row, and a smiling Cook was well enough to join the celebrations as the pennant was secured in the penultimate round. With a third title in six seasons, Riverside once again became a field of dreams.

Their fate seemed entwined with that of **Yorkshire**, who were in possession of several bright young things of their own, and inflicted Durham's only home defeat. Middlesex, then Sussex, set the early pace, but in terms of points per match it was a tussle between the two most northerly counties from mid-June onwards. The pivotal encounter came at Scarborough at the end of August. Durham's bowlers had marauded up and down the land but, at Yorkshire's festival ground, it was the batsmen who pitched their deckchairs, compiling their highest total of the season. Mark Stoneman and Ben Stokes, two locally sourced stars, scored hundreds – as did Michael Richardson – in a maximum-points victory that dashed Yorkshire's hopes and gave Durham captain Paul Collingwood a measure of atonement for his declaration in April. Back then, a masterful 182 from Joe Root had enabled Yorkshire to chase 336, achieving the highest fourth innings at Chester-le-Street; but Root played only one more Championship game (in which he made a double-hundred), and his involvement with England, along with Jonny Bairstow and Tim Bresnan, contributed to the spiking of Tyke guns.

For Collingwood, the blocker of Shotley Bridge, this was a remarkable new chapter in a well-thumbed career. Taking over from Phil Mustard in July 2012, he had first dispelled the spectre of relegation, then marshalled Durham's assault. He had lost his first game in charge, and Durham finished the 2013 season with defeat at Hove, but in between he oversaw a run of 14 wins from 20 (there was one other victory in his absence). The ancient Greeks would have recognised this as *peripeteia*, a reversal of circumstance worthy of the highest drama; those in the North-East might have called it a canny job.

The vast majority of the 18 players Durham used were either born locally or came through the Academy system: their success was a source of great regional pride. In particular, the assembly line of high-quality fast bowlers reached a level of output that would have made Henry Ford purr in approval. In Graham Onions – the leading wicket-taker in the country – and Chris Rushworth, they had a new-ball attack that seemed to take a sadistic pleasure in torturing batsmen, while Stokes continued to develop as an all-rounder. Yet, when the stakes were raised (or when Onions was being toyed with by England), in came Mark Wood, Jamie Harrison and Usman Arshad. Barely known six months earlier, they now contributed a total of 57 wickets at less than 22 apiece. Truly, a rich seam had been struck. The devastation Durham wrought on their own patch was summed up by the fact that visiting teams left with a single batting point out of a possible 40 (even then, Warwickshire had slipped to 116 for seven before scraping to 209). Incredibly, no team managed a half-century opening stand against Durham, either home or away, until the last innings of the season, when – with the Championship long since won – Luke Wells and Chris Nash put on 163 at Hove.

Defeat in that match meant Durham fell short of becoming the first side to collect 11 wins since two divisions were introduced in 2000, and enabled Sussex to cling on to third place ahead of Warwickshire, the defending champions. **Middlesex** won three of their first five fixtures, but only three more

---

BOWLERS' STRIKE-RATES IN 2013 CHAMPIONSHIP

Division One

SR		Balls	Wkts
45.29	Durham (1)	13,406	296
53.68	Yorkshire (2)	12,295	229
56.34	Middlesex (5)	14,256	253
57.46	Somerset (6)	13,160	229
58.00	Sussex (3)	13,574	234
58.45	Warwickshire (4)	13,562	232
64.25	Derbyshire (8)	12,594	196
67.36	Nottinghamshire (7) . .	14,079	209
68.74	Surrey (9)	15,605	227

Division Two

SR		Balls	Wkts
51.60	Lancashire (1)	13,313	258
53.45	Northamptonshire (2)	12,188	228
56.33	Worcestershire (5) . . .	12,000	213
59.00	Essex (3)	13,158	223
62.11	Glamorgan (8)	14,163	228
65.09	Hampshire (4)	13,345	205
67.12	Gloucestershire (6) . .	13,963	208
77.93	Kent (7)	13,638	175
84.31	Leicestershire (9)	12,563	149

2013 Championship positions are shown in brackets.

thereafter, as a potent attack was left overexposed by a middle order that made papier mâché look robust (openers Sam Robson and Chris Rogers scored a third of their runs). **Sussex** again surpassed modest expectations, but didn't manage a victory for more than two months at the business end of the season, and were not helped when Monty Panesar relieved himself of his duties in August. And **Warwickshire**, who ended up fielding 25 different players because of injuries and England call-ups, accepted early on that retaining their title would be beyond them.

For all it delivered, however, the Championship again lacked a finish to stop the national presses. The final round began with the champions of both divisions already decided, and only the second relegation and promotion spots to be resolved. That **Derbyshire** were still scrapping for survival was almost a miracle in itself after their first ten games produced no victories and seven defeats. Three wins from four followed, with their captain, Wayne Madsen, becoming the first player to 1,000 Championship runs. But, needing a hefty victory over Warwickshire, and for either **Somerset** or **Nottinghamshire** to mess up at Trent Bridge, Derbyshire wandered round the back of the bike sheds to be duffed up one last time. They were cushioned from the bottom only by the generous upholstery of **Surrey**, who – in addition to Smith – fielded Ricky Ponting, Hashim Amla and Kevin Pietersen at various times, but could not avert their trajectory. The dismissal in June of Chris Adams, the director of cricket whose reliance on a cadre of players aged 35 and over had set the template for a summer of decline, came too late to halt the slide.

The first-class season lasted a seemingly eternal 188 days (if you start from the MCC–Champions game in Abu Dhabi), and the September 27 finish was the latest since the 19th century. Snowfall at Lord's in the first week of April provided a bizarre measure of some of the challenges counties now face. Preseason, several had experimented with outdoor net sessions inside transparent plastic marquees; others banked on overseas jaunts to obviate the difficulties of a late-sprung spring. Aside from Durham, who could just about scrape together enough for a trip to Loch Lomond, the prizes went to counties who had made their preparations abroad: Lancashire, who romped back to the top tier by winning Division Two, warmed up literally and figuratively in Dubai; while Northamptonshire and Nottinghamshire – Friends Life t20 and Yorkshire Bank 40 winners respectively – plumped for Barbados.

For those who could afford it, the thinking was sound. But, when rumours surfaced of an ECB proposal to play Championship fixtures abroad, confusion prevailed. One director of cricket asked if it was April 1, while chief executives quickly attempted to mollify members, who follow their teams far and wide but might baulk at having to arrange flights to the Caribbean or the UAE. Making changes to the county schedule is a bit like trying to get everyone to agree on a solution to global warming, but the suggestion was indicative of a desire for radical debate.

This year, at least, climatic concerns were less of an issue, as the UK experienced one of its longest sustained warm spells for years. **Lancashire** have traditionally suffered in that regard, but even two early rain-affected draws at Old Trafford could not thwart them. Fears that the bowling might be ineffectual were dispelled when they spectacularly defended 154 at Colwyn Bay, after which the wins flowed. Success was built on the run-making nous of overseas batsmen Simon Katich and Ashwell Prince, a fine new-ball pairing in the 39-year-old Glen Chapple and Kyle Hogg, and – despite his meltdown in the Oval Test – the most successful spinner in the land in Simon Kerrigan. A four-week period in which Lancashire beat their two main rivals, Essex and Northamptonshire (twice) gave them a lead which was never surrendered.

Having missed out on promotion by two points in both 2009 and 2011, **Northamptonshire** again kept opponents interested and supporters anguished until the last. Indeed, had **Essex** won their final match with a full haul of bonus points, they would have gone up instead. In reality, Northamptonshire's game against Worcestershire was still in the balance when Essex were dismissed for 207 by Hampshire shortly after tea on the second day. Neither should Essex's baffling decision to rest several first-team regulars in Southampton detract from Northamptonshire's success, which was richly deserved and roundly applauded. Although no one made 1,000 runs, a line-up that was at times deeper than the Mariana Trench ensured they collected significantly more batting points than any other team in either division; and a varied and penetrative seam department, boosted by the clever signing of Trent Copeland from Australia, helped them to four crushing victories in their first seven games, and ensured they would not be caught.

The final recalibrations were harshest on **Gloucestershire**. A young team, led intelligently by Michael Klinger – one of a number of redoubtable Australians in the Championship – were in with a theoretical chance of going up well into the latter stages, but slipped below **Hampshire** and **Worcestershire**.

Recent additions to the *Oxford English Dictionary* may have felt pertinent to Leicestershire fans. While some county regulars might have presumed a selfie was an SAE, they could spot an omnishambles when they saw one. **Leicestershire** continued to produce talented youngsters, but still failed to win a Championship game for the first time in their history. A total of 79 points was the lowest since the introduction of bonus points in 1968, and left them well adrift of **Glamorgan**, who had a more encouraging season than eighth place suggested, and **Kent**, where mediocrity was something to aspire to.

In among the millefeuille of statistics, there were a few trends. Those with a beady eye on the return of the heavy roller would have noted an improved lot for batsmen – there were 22 double-hundreds, only five fewer than in the three previous (roller-free) seasons combined. A summer worthy of the name also taxed bowlers a little more: the strike-rate in Division One, ignoring joke bowling, rose above a wicket every 61 balls, almost ten higher than the record low of 2012. The balance between results and draws was thus a little saner, though early finishes still proliferated. In terms of overs, excluding rain-affected declarations, 42 of the 144 fixtures did not require a fourth day. Any expected encouragement for spin was not forthcoming – only five slow bowlers managed more than 30 wickets – and bowling first remained conducive to winning, although Durham demonstrated an underplayed strength by achieving victory batting first on six occasions (three after winning the toss). There were anomalies, too. Essex were dismissed for 20 by Lancashire on a blameless Chelmsford pitch, while Marcus Trescothick made his first first-class pair – at the age of 37.

The indie appeal of the Championship was beautifully illustrated when, in April, Derbyshire's Billy Godleman scored what is thought to be the slowest half-century (from 244 deliveries) in the competition's history. At the IPL six days later, Chris Gayle struck a 30-ball hundred. The contrast was piquant, maybe even worthy of a strapline. County cricket: putting the block in blockbuster since the 19th century.

Pre-season betting (best available prices): *Division One* – 9-2 Warwickshire; 11-2 Nottinghamshire; 6-1 Somerset and Surrey; 7-1 Middlesex; 8-1 DURHAM; 9-1 Sussex; 10-1 Yorkshire; 25-1 Derbyshire. *Division Two* – 11-4 LANCASHIRE; 7-2 Hampshire; 5-1 Kent; 13-2 Essex; 15-2 Worcestershire; 16-1 Glamorgan; 20-1 Northamptonshire; 25-1 Gloucestershire and Leicestershire.

Prize money

Division One
£550,000 for winners: DURHAM.
£235,000 for runners-up: YORKSHIRE.
£115,000 for third: SUSSEX.
£35,000 for fourth: WARWICKSHIRE.

Division Two
£135,000 for winners: LANCASHIRE.
£70,000 for runners-up: NORTHAMPTONSHIRE.

These prizes are divided between players' prize money and a county performance payment. For the winners, players receive £400,000 and the county £150,000; for the runners-up, the split is £185,000/£50,000; for third, £100,000/£15,000; for fourth, £30,000/£5,000. In the second division, the split for the winners is £100,000/£35,000, and for the runners-up £60,000/£10,000.

Leaders: *Division One* – from April 13 Middlesex and Sussex; April 19 Middlesex; May 2 Durham; May 18 Middlesex; May 23 Sussex; June 14 Yorkshire; July 10 Sussex; July 19 Yorkshire; September 5 Durham. Durham became champions on September 19.
Division Two – from April 13 Hampshire; April 19 Northamptonshire; July 11 Lancashire. Lancashire became champions on September 20.

Bottom place: *Division One* – from April 20 Yorkshire; April 27 Derbyshire; August 23 Surrey; September 1 Derbyshire; September 5 Surrey.
Division Two – from April 20 Essex and Worcestershire; April 27 Essex; May 1 Worcestershire; May 18 Kent; June 8 Leicestershire; June 24 Kent; July 13 Leicestershire.

Scoring of Points

(*a*) For a win, 16 points plus any points scored in the first innings.

(*b*) In a tie, each side score eight points, plus any points scored in the first innings.

(*c*) In a drawn match, each side score three points (*from 2014, five points*), plus any points scored in the first innings.

(*d*) If the scores are equal in a drawn match, the side batting in the fourth innings score eight points, plus any points scored in the first innings, and the opposing side score three points (*from 2014, five points*) plus any points scored in the first innings.

(*e*) First-innings points (awarded only for performances in the first 110 overs of each first innings and retained whatever the result of the match).

    (i) A maximum of five batting points to be available: 200 to 249 runs – 1 point; 250 to 299 runs – 2 points; 300 to 349 runs – 3 points; 350 to 399 runs – 4 points; 400 runs or over – 5 points. Penalty runs awarded within the first 110 overs of each first innings count towards the award of bonus points.

    (ii) A maximum of three bowling points to be available: 3 to 5 wickets taken – 1 point; 6 to 8 wickets taken – 2 points; 9 to 10 wickets taken – 3 points.

(*f*) If a match is abandoned without a ball being bowled, each side score three points (*from 2014, five points*).

(g) The side who have the highest aggregate of points shall be the champion county of their respective division. Should any sides in the Championship table be equal on points, the following tie-breakers will be applied in the order stated: most wins, fewest losses, team achieving most points in head-to-head contests between teams level on points, most wickets taken, most runs scored. At the end of the season, the top two teams from the second division will be promoted, and the bottom two teams from the first division will be relegated.

(h) The minimum over-rate to be achieved by counties will be 16 overs per hour. Overs will be calculated at the end of the match and penalties applied on a match-by-match basis. For each over (ignoring fractions) that a side have bowled short of the target number, one point will be deducted from their Championship total.

(i) A county adjudged to have prepared a pitch unfit for four-day first-class cricket will have 24 points deducted. A county adjudged to have prepared a poor pitch will have eight points deducted. This penalty will rise to 12 points if the county has prepared a poor or unfit pitch within the previous 12 months. A county adjudged to have provided a playing area in a condition substantially reducing the possibility of play (subsequent to actions within that county's control) will have eight points deducted.

Under ECB playing conditions, two extras were scored for every no-ball bowled, whether scored off or not, and one for every wide. Any runs scored off the bat were credited to the batsman, while byes and leg-byes were counted as no-balls or wides, as appropriate, in accordance with Law 24.13, in addition to the initial penalty.

CONSTITUTION OF COUNTY CHAMPIONSHIP

At least four possible dates have been given for the start of county cricket in England. The first, patchy, references began in 1825. The earliest mention in any cricket publication is in 1864, and eight counties have come to be regarded as first-class from that date, including Cambridgeshire, who dropped out after 1871. For many years, the County Championship was considered to have started in 1873, when regulations governing qualification first applied; indeed, a special commemorative stamp was issued by the Post Office in 1973. However, the Championship was not formally organised until 1890 and before then champions were proclaimed by the press; sometimes publications differed in their views and no definitive list of champions can start before that date. Eight teams contested the 1890 competition – Gloucestershire, Kent, Lancashire, Middlesex, Nottinghamshire, Surrey, Sussex and Yorkshire. Somerset joined in the following year, and in 1895 the Championship began to acquire something of its modern shape when Derbyshire, Essex, Hampshire, Leicestershire and Warwickshire were added. At that point MCC officially recognised the competition's existence. Worcestershire, Northamptonshire and Glamorgan were admitted to the Championship in 1899, 1905 and 1921 respectively, and are regarded as first-class from these dates. An invitation in 1921 to Buckinghamshire to enter the Championship was declined, owing to the lack of necessary playing facilities, and an application by Devon in 1948 was unsuccessful. Durham were admitted to the Championship in 1992 and were granted first-class status prior to their pre-season tour of Zimbabwe. In 2000, the Championship was split for the first time into two divisions, on the basis of counties' standings in the 1999 competition. From 2000 onwards, the bottom three teams in Division One were relegated at the end of the season, and the top three teams in Division Two promoted. From 2006, this was changed to two teams relegated and two promoted.

COUNTY CHAMPIONS

The title of champion county is unreliable before 1890. In 1963, *Wisden* formally accepted the list of champions "most generally selected" by contemporaries, as researched by the late Rowland Bowen (see *Wisden 1959*, pp 91–98). This appears to be the most accurate available list but has no official status. The county champions from 1864 to 1889 were, according to Bowen: 1864 Surrey; 1865 Nottinghamshire; 1866 Middlesex; 1867 Yorkshire; 1868 Nottinghamshire; 1869 Nottinghamshire and Yorkshire; 1870 Yorkshire; 1871 Nottinghamshire; 1872 Nottinghamshire; 1873 Gloucestershire and Nottinghamshire; 1874 Gloucestershire; 1875 Nottinghamshire; 1876 Gloucestershire; 1877 Gloucestershire; 1878 undecided; 1879 Lancashire and Nottinghamshire; 1880 Nottinghamshire; 1881 Lancashire; 1882 Lancashire and Nottinghamshire; 1883 Nottinghamshire; 1884 Nottinghamshire; 1885 Nottinghamshire; 1886 Nottinghamshire; 1887 Surrey; 1888 Surrey; 1889 Lancashire, Nottinghamshire and Surrey.

1890	Surrey	1933	Yorkshire	1976	Middlesex
1891	Surrey	1934	Lancashire	1977	{ Middlesex
1892	Surrey	1935	Yorkshire		{ Kent
1893	Yorkshire	1936	Derbyshire	1978	Kent
1894	Surrey	1937	Yorkshire	1979	Essex
1895	Surrey	1938	Yorkshire	1980	Middlesex
1896	Yorkshire	1939	Yorkshire	1981	Nottinghamshire
1897	Lancashire	1946	Yorkshire	1982	Middlesex
1898	Yorkshire	1947	Middlesex	1983	Essex
1899	Surrey	1948	Glamorgan	1984	Essex
1900	Yorkshire	1949	{ Middlesex	1985	Middlesex
1901	Yorkshire		{ Yorkshire	1986	Essex
1902	Yorkshire	1950	{ Lancashire	1987	Nottinghamshire
1903	Middlesex		{ Surrey	1988	Worcestershire
1904	Lancashire	1951	Warwickshire	1989	Worcestershire
1905	Yorkshire	1952	Surrey	1990	Middlesex
1906	Kent	1953	Surrey	1991	Essex
1907	Nottinghamshire	1954	Surrey	1992	Essex
1908	Yorkshire	1955	Surrey	1993	Middlesex
1909	Kent	1956	Surrey	1994	Warwickshire
1910	Kent	1957	Surrey	1995	Warwickshire
1911	Warwickshire	1958	Surrey	1996	Leicestershire
1912	Yorkshire	1959	Yorkshire	1997	Glamorgan
1913	Kent	1960	Yorkshire	1998	Leicestershire
1914	Surrey	1961	Hampshire	1999	Surrey
1919	Yorkshire	1962	Yorkshire	2000	Surrey
1920	Middlesex	1963	Yorkshire	2001	Yorkshire
1921	Middlesex	1964	Worcestershire	2002	Surrey
1922	Yorkshire	1965	Worcestershire	2003	Sussex
1923	Yorkshire	1966	Yorkshire	2004	Warwickshire
1924	Yorkshire	1967	Yorkshire	2005	Nottinghamshire
1925	Yorkshire	1968	Yorkshire	2006	Sussex
1926	Lancashire	1969	Glamorgan	2007	Sussex
1927	Lancashire	1970	Kent	2008	Durham
1928	Lancashire	1971	Surrey	2009	Durham
1929	Nottinghamshire	1972	Warwickshire	2010	Nottinghamshire
1930	Lancashire	1973	Hampshire	2011	Lancashire
1931	Yorkshire	1974	Worcestershire	2012	Warwickshire
1932	Yorkshire	1975	Leicestershire	2013	Durham

Notes: Since the Championship was constituted in 1890 it has been won outright as follows: Yorkshire 30 times, Surrey 18, Middlesex 10, Lancashire 8, Warwickshire 7, Essex, Kent and Nottinghamshire 6, Worcestershire 5, Durham, Glamorgan, Leicestershire and Sussex 3, Hampshire 2, Derbyshire 1. Gloucestershire, Northamptonshire and Somerset have never won.

The title has been shared three times since 1890, involving Middlesex twice, Kent, Lancashire, Surrey and Yorkshire.

Wooden spoons: Since the major expansion of the Championship from nine teams to 14 in 1895, the counties have finished outright bottom as follows: Derbyshire 15; Somerset 12; Northamptonshire 11; Glamorgan and Leicestershire 10; Gloucestershire 9; Nottinghamshire and Sussex 8; Worcestershire 6; Durham and Hampshire 5; Warwickshire 3; Essex and Kent 2; Yorkshire 1. Lancashire, Middlesex and Surrey have never finished bottom. Leicestershire have also shared bottom place twice, once with Hampshire and once with Somerset.

From 1977 to 1983 the Championship was sponsored by Schweppes, from 1984 to 1998 by Britannic Assurance, from 1999 to 2000 by PPP healthcare, in 2001 by Cricinfo, from 2002 to 2005 by Frizzell, and from 2006 by Liverpool Victoria (LV).

COUNTY CHAMPIONSHIP – FINAL POSITIONS, 1890–2013

	Derbyshire	Durham	Essex	Glamorgan	Gloucestershire	Hampshire	Kent	Lancashire	Leicestershire	Middlesex	Northamptonshire	Nottinghamshire	Somerset	Surrey	Sussex	Warwickshire	Worcestershire	Yorkshire
1890	–	–	–	–	6	–	3	2	–	7	–	5	–	1	8	–	–	3
1891	–	–	–	–	9	–	5	2	–	3	–	4	5	1	7	–	–	8
1892	–	–	–	–	7	–	7	4	–	5	–	2	3	1	9	–	–	6
1893	–	–	–	–	9	–	4	2	–	3	–	6	8	5	7	–	–	1
1894	–	–	–	–	9	–	4	4	–	3	–	7	6	1	8	–	–	2
1895	5	–	9	–	4	10	14	2	12	6	–	12	8	1	11	6	–	3
1896	7	–	5	–	10	8	9	2	13	3	–	6	11	4	14	12	–	1
1897	14	–	3	–	5	9	12	1	13	8	–	10	11	2	6	7	–	4
1898	9	–	5	–	3	12	7	6	13	2	–	8	13	4	9	9	–	1
1899	15	–	6	–	9	10	8	4	13	2	–	10	13	1	5	7	12	3
1900	13	–	10	–	7	15	3	2	14	7	–	5	11	7	3	6	12	1
1901	15	–	10	–	14	7	7	3	12	2	–	9	12	6	4	5	11	1
1902	10	–	13	–	14	15	7	5	11	12	–	3	7	4	2	6	9	1
1903	12	–	8	–	13	14	8	4	14	1	–	5	10	11	2	7	6	3
1904	10	–	14	–	9	15	3	1	7	4	–	5	12	11	6	7	13	2
1905	14	–	12	–	8	16	6	2	5	11	13	10	5	4	3	7	8	1
1906	16	–	7	–	9	8	1	4	15	11	11	5	11	3	10	6	14	2
1907	16	–	7	–	10	12	8	6	11	5	15	1	14	4	13	9	2	2
1908	14	–	11	–	10	9	2	7	13	4	15	8	16	3	5	12	6	1
1909	15	–	14	–	16	8	1	2	13	6	7	10	11	5	4	12	8	3
1910	15	–	11	–	12	6	1	4	10	3	9	5	16	2	7	14	13	8
1911	14	–	6	–	12	11	2	4	15	3	10	8	16	5	13	1	9	7
1912	12	–	15	–	11	6	3	4	13	5	2	8	14	7	10	9	16	1
1913	13	–	15	–	9	10	1	8	14	6	4	5	16	3	7	11	12	2
1914	12	–	8	–	16	5	3	11	13	2	9	10	15	1	6	7	14	4
1919	9	–	14	–	8	7	2	5	9	13	12	3	5	4	11	15	–	1
1920	16	–	9	–	8	11	5	2	13	1	14	7	10	3	6	12	15	4
1921	12	–	15	17	7	6	4	5	11	1	13	8	10	2	9	16	14	3
1922	11	–	8	16	13	6	4	5	14	7	15	2	10	3	9	12	17	1
1923	10	–	13	16	11	7	5	3	14	8	17	2	9	4	6	12	15	1
1924	17	–	15	13	6	12	5	4	11	2	16	6	8	3	10	9	14	1
1925	14	–	7	17	10	9	5	3	12	6	11	4	15	2	13	8	16	1
1926	11	–	9	8	15	7	3	1	13	6	16	4	14	5	10	12	17	2
1927	5	–	8	15	12	13	4	1	7	9	16	2	14	6	10	11	17	3
1928	10	–	16	15	5	12	2	1	9	8	13	3	14	6	7	11	17	4
1929	7	–	12	17	4	11	8	2	9	6	13	1	15	10	4	14	16	2
1930	9	–	6	11	2	13	5	1	12	16	17	4	13	8	7	15	10	3
1931	7	–	10	15	2	12	3	6	16	11	17	5	13	8	4	9	14	1
1932	10	–	14	15	13	8	3	6	12	10	16	4	7	5	2	9	17	1
1933	6	–	4	16	10	14	3	5	17	12	13	8	11	9	2	7	15	1
1934	3	–	8	13	7	14	5	1	12	10	17	9	15	11	4	7	16	5
1935	2	–	9	13	15	16	10	4	6	3	17	5	14	11	7	8	12	1
1936	1	–	9	16	4	10	8	11	15	2	17	5	7	6	14	13	12	1
1937	3	–	6	7	4	14	12	9	16	2	17	10	13	8	5	11	15	1
1938	5	–	6	16	10	14	9	4	15	2	17	12	7	3	8	13	11	1
1939	9	–	4	13	3	15	5	6	17	2	16	12	14	8	10	11	7	1
1946	15	–	8	6	5	10	6	3	11	2	16	13	4	11	17	14	8	1
1947	5	–	11	9	2	16	4	3	14	1	17	11	11	6	9	15	7	7
1948	6	–	13	1	8	9	15	5	11	3	17	14	12	2	16	7	10	4
1949	15	–	9	8	7	16	13	11	17	1	6	11	9	5	13	4	3	1
1950	5	–	17	11	7	12	9	1	16	14	10	15	7	1	13	4	6	3
1951	11	–	8	5	12	9	16	3	15	7	13	17	14	6	10	1	4	2

	Derbyshire	Durham	Essex	Glamorgan	Gloucestershire	Hampshire	Kent	Lancashire	Leicestershire	Middlesex	Northamptonshire	Nottinghamshire	Somerset	Surrey	Sussex	Warwickshire	Worcestershire	Yorkshire
1952	4	–	10	7	9	12	15	3	6	5	8	16	17	1	13	10	14	2
1953	6	–	12	10	6	14	16	3	3	5	11	8	17	1	2	9	15	12
1954	3	–	15	4	13	14	11	10	16	7	7	5	17	1	9	6	11	2
1955	8	–	14	16	12	3	13	9	6	5	7	11	17	1	4	9	15	2
1956	12	–	11	13	3	6	16	2	17	5	4	8	15	1	9	14	9	7
1957	4	–	5	9	12	13	14	6	17	7	2	15	8	1	9	11	16	3
1958	5	–	6	15	14	2	8	7	12	10	4	17	3	1	13	16	9	11
1959	7	–	9	6	2	8	13	5	16	10	11	17	12	3	15	4	14	1
1960	5	–	6	11	8	12	10	2	17	3	9	16	14	7	4	15	13	1
1961	7	–	6	14	5	1	11	13	9	3	16	17	10	15	8	12	4	2
1962	7	–	9	14	4	10	11	16	17	13	8	15	6	5	12	3	2	1
1963	17	–	12	2	8	10	13	15	16	6	7	9	3	11	4	4	14	1
1964	12	–	10	11	17	12	7	14	16	6	3	15	8	4	9	2	1	5
1965	9	–	15	3	10	12	5	13	14	6	2	17	7	8	16	11	1	4
1966	9	–	16	14	15	11	4	12	8	12	5	17	3	7	10	6	2	1
1967	6	–	15	14	17	12	2	11	2	7	9	15	8	4	13	10	5	1
1968	8	–	14	3	16	5	2	6	10	13	4	12	15	17	11	7	1	1
1969	16	–	6	1	2	5	10	15	14	11	9	8	17	3	7	4	12	13
1970	7	–	12	2	17	10	1	3	15	16	14	11	13	5	9	7	6	4
1971	17	–	10	16	8	9	4	3	5	6	14	12	7	1	11	2	15	13
1972	17	–	5	13	3	9	2	15	6	8	4	14	11	12	16	1	7	10
1973	16	–	8	11	5	1	4	12	9	13	3	17	10	2	15	7	6	14
1974	17	–	12	16	14	2	10	8	4	6	3	15	5	7	13	9	1	11
1975	15	–	7	9	16	3	5	4	1	11	8	13	12	6	17	14	10	2
1976	15	–	6	17	3	12	14	16	4	1	2	13	7	9	10	5	11	8
1977	7	–	6	14	3	11	1	16	5	1	9	17	4	14	8	10	13	12
1978	14	–	2	13	10	8	1	12	6	3	17	7	5	16	9	11	15	4
1979	16	–	1	17	10	12	5	13	6	14	11	9	8	3	4	15	2	7
1980	9	–	8	13	7	17	16	15	10	1	12	3	5	2	4	14	11	6
1981	12	–	5	14	13	7	9	16	8	4	15	1	3	6	2	17	11	10
1982	11	–	7	16	15	3	13	12	2	1	9	4	6	5	8	17	14	10
1983	9	–	1	15	12	3	7	12	4	2	6	14	10	8	11	5	16	17
1984	12	–	1	13	17	15	5	16	4	3	11	2	7	8	6	9	10	14
1985	13	–	12	3	2	9	14	16	1	10	8	17	6	7	15	5	11	
1986	11	–	1	17	2	6	8	15	7	12	9	4	16	3	14	12	5	10
1987	6	–	12	13	10	5	14	2	3	16	7	1	11	4	17	15	9	8
1988	14	–	3	17	10	15	2	9	8	7	12	5	11	4	16	6	1	13
1989	6	–	2	17	9	6	15	4	13	3	5	11	14	12	10	8	1	16
1990	12	–	2	8	13	3	16	6	7	1	11	13	15	9	17	5	4	10
1991	3	–	1	12	13	9	6	8	16	15	10	4	17	5	11	2	6	14
1992	5	18	1	14	10	15	2	12	8	11	3	4	9	13	7	6	17	16
1993	15	18	11	3	17	13	8	13	9	1	4	7	5	6	10	16	2	12
1994	17	16	6	18	12	13	9	10	2	4	5	3	11	7	8	1	15	13
1995	14	17	5	16	6	13	18	4	7	2	3	11	9	12	15	1	10	8
1996	2	18	5	10	13	14	4	15	1	9	16	17	11	3	12	8	7	6
1997	16	17	8	1	7	14	2	11	10	4	15	13	12	8	18	4	3	6
1998	10	14	18	12	4	6	11	2	1	17	15	16	9	5	7	8	13	3
1999	9	8	12	14	18	7	5	2	3	16	13	17	4	1	11	10	15	6
2000	*9*	*8*	*2*	*3*	*4*	*7*	**6**	*2*	*4*	*8*	*1*	*7*	**5**	*1*	*9*	*6*	*5*	**3**
2001	*9*	*8*	**9**	**8**	*4*	*2*	**3**	**6**	**5**	*5*	*7*	*7*	**2**	*4*	*1*	*3*	*6*	*1*
2002	*6*	*9*	*1*	*5*	*8*	*7*	**3**	*4*	*5*	*2*	*7*	*3*	**8**	*1*	*6*	*2*	*4*	*9*
2003	*9*	*6*	**7**	*5*	*3*	*8*	*4*	*2*	**9**	*6*	*2*	*8*	*7*	**3**	**1**	*5*	*1*	*4*
2004	*8*	*9*	*5*	*3*	**6**	*2*	*2*	*8*	*6*	*4*	**9**	*1*	*4*	*3*	*5*	*1*	*7*	*7*
2005	*9*	*2*	*5*	**9**	**8**	*2*	*5*	*1*	*7*	*6*	*4*	*1*	*8*	*7*	**3**	*4*	*6*	*3*

	Derbyshire	Durham	Essex	Glamorgan	Gloucestershire	Hampshire	Kent	Lancashire	Leicestershire	Middlesex	Northamptonshire	Nottinghamshire	Somerset	Surrey	Sussex	Warwickshire	Worcestershire	Yorkshire
2006	*5*	**7**	*3*	*8*	*7*	**3**	**5**	**2**	*4*	**9**	*6*	**8**	*9*	*1*	**1**	**4**	*2*	**6**
2007	*6*	**2**	*4*	*9*	*7*	**5**	**7**	**3**	*8*	*3*	*5*	*2*	*1*	**4**	**1**	**8**	**9**	**6**
2008	*6*	**1**	*5*	*8*	*9*	**3**	**8**	**5**	*7*	*3*	*4*	**2**	**4**	**9**	**6**	*1*	*2*	**7**
2009	*6*	**1**	*2*	*5*	*4*	**6**	*1*	**4**	*9*	*8*	*3*	**2**	**3**	*7*	**8**	**5**	**9**	**7**
2010	*9*	**5**	**9**	*3*	*5*	**7**	**8**	**4**	*4*	*8*	*6*	**1**	**2**	*7*	*1*	**6**	*2*	**3**
2011	*5*	**3**	**7**	*6*	*4*	**9**	*8*	**1**	*9*	*1*	*3*	**6**	**4**	*2*	**5**	**2**	*7*	**8**
2012	*1*	**6**	*5*	*6*	*9*	*4*	*3*	**8**	*7*	**3**	*8*	**5**	**2**	**7**	**4**	**1**	**9**	*2*
2013	**8**	**1**	*3*	*8*	*6*	*4*	*7*	*1*	*9*	**5**	*2*	**7**	**6**	**9**	**3**	**4**	*5*	**2**

For the 2000–2013 Championships, Division One placings are in bold, Division Two in italic.

MATCH RESULTS, 1864–2013

County	Years of Play	Played	Won	Lost	Drawn	Tied	% Won
Derbyshire	1871–87; 1895–2013	2,499	613	920	965	1	24.52
Durham	1992–2013	362	95	154	113	0	26.24
Essex	1895–2013	2,461	712	717	1,026	6	28.93
Glamorgan	1921–2013	1,992	442	683	867	0	22.18
Gloucestershire	1870–2013	2,734	798	1,009	925	2	29.18
Hampshire	1864–85; 1895–2013	2,570	676	867	1,023	4	26.30
Kent	1864–2013	2,858	1,021	854	978	5	35.72
Lancashire	1865–2013	2,932	1,085	606	1,238	3	37.00
Leicestershire	1895–2013	2,427	547	878	1,001	1	22.53
Middlesex	1864–2013	2,638	960	675	998	5	36.39
Northamptonshire	1905–2013	2,196	551	747	895	3	25.09
Nottinghamshire	1864–2013	2,767	838	748	1,180	1	30.28
Somerset	1882–85; 1891–2013	2,469	594	960	912	3	24.05
Surrey	1864–2013	3,012	1,177	671	1,160	4	39.07
Sussex	1864–2013	2,907	827	987	1,087	6	28.44
Warwickshire	1895–2013	2,441	680	692	1,067	2	27.85
Worcestershire	1899–2013	2,380	607	828	943	2	25.50
Yorkshire	1864–2013	3,036	1,311	538	1,185	2	43.18
Cambridgeshire	1864–69; 1871	19	8	8	3	0	42.10
		22,350	13,542	13,542	8,783	25	

Matches abandoned without a ball bowled are wholly excluded.

Counties participated in the years shown, except that there were no matches in 1915–1918 and 1940–1945; Hampshire did not play inter-county matches in 1868–1869, 1871–1874 and 1879; Worcestershire did not take part in the Championship in 1919.

> **“** Now in her seventies, she walks, swims and plays bowls, although no longer deliberately makes herself so late for the bus that she has to run. She enjoys a game of Candy Crush on her tablet, stuffs envelopes for the Labour Party and does 4,000-piece jigsaw puzzles.”
> The Greats of the Women's Game, page 32

COUNTY CHAMPIONSHIP STATISTICS FOR 2013

County	Runs	For Wickets	Avge	Runs scored per 100 balls	Runs	Against Wickets	Avge
Derbyshire (**8**)........	6,882	280	24.57	50.29	7,391	196	37.70
Durham (**1**)..........	7,673	252	30.44	55.31	7,316	296	24.71
Essex (*3*)...........	6,723	213	31.56	56.09	7,186	223	32.22
Glamorgan (*8*)	7,435	228	32.60	54.37	7,464	228	32.73
Gloucestershire (*6*)....	7,575	193	39.24	54.66	7,954	208	38.24
Hampshire (**4**).......	7,238	194	37.30	54.20	7,406	205	36.12
Kent (*7*).............	7,509	212	35.41	57.52	7,141	175	40.80
Lancashire (*1*).......	7,914	199	39.76	56.72	6,632	258	25.70
Leicestershire (*9*)	6,179	235	26.29	48.08	7,639	149	51.26
Middlesex (**5**)........	7,004	232	30.18	56.70	7,198	253	28.45
Northamptonshire (**2**)..	7,211	192	37.55	57.22	6,298	228	27.62
Nottinghamshire (**7**)...	7,660	235	32.59	55.40	7,656	209	36.63
Somerset (**6**).........	7,167	259	27.67	56.26	7,219	229	31.52
Surrey (*9*)...........	7,325	217	33.75	52.41	8,561	227	37.71
Sussex (**3**)...........	7,878	218	36.13	59.84	7,628	234	32.59
Warwickshire (**4**).....	7,499	201	37.30	53.21	7,291	232	31.42
Worcestershire (**5**)....	6,536	221	29.57	50.24	6,600	213	30.98
Yorkshire (**2**)........	8,380	211	39.71	56.49	7,208	229	31.47
	131,788	3,992	33.01	54.71	131,788	3,992	33.01

2013 Championship positions are shown in brackets; Division One in bold, Division Two in italic.

ECB PITCHES TABLE OF MERIT, 2013

	First-class	One-day		First-class	One-day
Derbyshire...........	4.40	4.55	Sussex..............	4.70	5.00
Durham.............	4.55	5.69	Warwickshire	4.69	5.33
Essex...............	5.11	5.42	Worcestershire	4.22	4.58
Glamorgan	4.56	4.95	Yorkshire	5.30	5.67
Gloucestershire.......	5.00	4.91			
Hampshire...........	4.69	5.42	Cambridge MCCU	5.43	
Kent	4.17	5.04	Cardiff MCCU	5.00	
Lancashire...........	5.33	4.85	Durham MCCU	4.67	
Leicestershire	4.60	5.85	Leeds/Bradford MCCU	4.00	
Middlesex	5.00	5.13	Loughborough MCCU .	5.00	
Northamptonshire	4.56	5.00	Oxford MCCU	4.40	
Nottinghamshire	5.10	5.27	Netherlands..........		4.00
Somerset	4.25	5.54	Scotland		4.00
Surrey	4.00	5.46	Unicorns		4.83

Each umpire in a match marks the pitch on the following scale: 6 – Very good; 5 – Good; 4 – Above average; 3 – Below average; 2 – Poor; 1 – Unfit.

The tables, provided by the ECB, cover major matches, including Tests, Under-19 internationals, women's internationals and MCCU games, played on grounds under the county's or MCCU's jurisdiction. Middlesex pitches at Lord's are the responsibility of MCC. The "First-class" column includes Under-19 and women's Tests, and inter-MCCU games.

Essex had the highest marks for first-class cricket, and Yorkshire for one-day cricket, though the ECB point out that the tables of merit are not a direct assessment of the groundsmen's ability. Marks may be affected by many factors, including weather, soil conditions and the resources available.

COUNTY CAPS AWARDED IN 2013

Essex . . . . J. C. Mickleburgh, O. A. Shah, R. J. W. Topley, T. Westley.
Glamorgan* . . . . M. G. Hogan, G. G. Wagg.
Gloucestershire*. . . . . D. T. Christian, M. A. H. Hammond, C. L. Herring, M. Klinger, G. H. Roderick, T. W. Shrewsbury, T. M. J. Smith, M. D. Taylor.
Hampshire . . . . D. J. Balcombe, L. A. Dawson, J. M. Vince.
Kent . . . . B. P. Nash.
Lancashire . . . . S. M. Katich, S. C. Kerrigan.
Leicestershire . . . . M. A. G. Boyce, E. J. H. Eckersley, J. K. H. Naik.
Middlesex. . . . . S. D. Robson.
Northamptonshire. . . . K. J. Coetzer, S. P. Crook, L. M. Daggett, D. J. Willey.
Nottinghamshire. . . . . E. J. M. Cowan, S. J. Mullaney, A. Shahzad.
Somerset. . . . . J. C. Buttler, A. N. Petersen.
Surrey. . . . . W. H. Gordon (former head groundsman), R. T. Ponting.
Warwickshire. . . . . . . K. H. D. Barker, W. B. Rankin, C. J. C. Wright.
Worcestershire* . . . . . G. Cessford, T. C. Fell, M. A. Johnson, T. T. Samaraweera, R. A. Whiteley.
Yorkshire . . . . J. A. Brooks, L. E. Plunkett.

* Glamorgan's capping system is now based on a player's number of appearances; Gloucestershire now award caps to all first-class players; Worcestershire have replaced caps with colours awarded to all Championship players. Durham abolished their capping system after 2005.

    No caps were awarded by Derbyshire or Sussex.

COUNTY BENEFITS AWARDED FOR 2014

Durham . . . . G. R. Breese and
                      G. J. Muchall.
Essex . . . . A. N. Cook.

Sussex . . . . M. H. Yardy.
Warwickshire . . . . . I. J. L. Trott.
Yorkshire . . . . T. T. Bresnan.

None of the other 13 counties awarded a benefit for 2014.

DERBYSHIRE

A glimmer amid the gloom

MARK EKLID

The first four months of Derbyshire's season were so dismal that relegation after just one year back in Division One of the Championship came as no surprise. Indeed it looked certain as early as July 19, when their trouncing by Yorkshire gave them a record of seven defeats and three draws.

Yet out of the gloom came a spark of hope. August began with victory over top-of-the-table Sussex, the first of three wins in four matches. All of a sudden, escape seemed possible, only for defeat in their last game to send Derbyshire back to the second division. Though their stirring revival had proved in vain – they simply had too much ground to make up – it did at least give them the belief that they could compete in the top flight, and that a prompt return was a distinct possibility.

Despite the arrival of Shivnarine Chanderpaul, one of the world's most accomplished Test batsmen, the dressing-room was still light on experience. Derbyshire had needed a solid start, so losing six of the first seven tosses was unwelcome. Too often their callow batting was exposed to high-quality bowling on seaming, early-season pitches – and they took a lead into the second innings only once in those first seven games. Increasingly, their top-order batsmen appeared unsure they belonged in such company.

Even Chanderpaul struggled to stamp his mark, with seven scores of 23 or fewer in his first nine innings. But when he came up against Ricky Ponting, playing for Surrey, he was inspired to hit a sparkling century – even if it remained his only hundred of the season. He was due to return in 2014, when he will reach at least one notable milestone: his 40th birthday.

There were few causes for celebration in those early weeks, though Chesney Hughes's promotion to open against Yorkshire at Headingley played an innings that would have graced any match. In his first outing in his new role, the 22-year-old Hughes, now England-qualified, hit an unbeaten 270 and, had he not run out of partners, might well have broken one of cricket's older records: he was within four of equalling the highest score for Derbyshire, set by George Davidson in 1896. In fact, the deployment of Hughes as an opener was not an overwhelming success: the double-hundred aside, he averaged 19 from his 16 innings – though it did allow captain Wayne Madsen to revert to No. 3. And that *was* an overwhelming success.

The Durban-born Madsen, who during the summer also qualified for England, had never previously passed 1,000 first-class runs. Now he became the first in the country to reach four figures in the Championship, and he contributed three of Derbyshire's five first-class centuries. He went on to win a string of end-of-season awards for his batting and for his leadership of a struggling side. He was named Championship Player of the Year by the Cricket

Mark Footitt

Stu Forster, Getty Images

Writers' Club, and claimed the inaugural Christopher Martin-Jenkins Spirit of Cricket elite award, for his decision to walk when given not out in the match against Yorkshire at Chesterfield in July.

Without Madsen's 1,221 Championship runs, Derbyshire would have been in a far sorrier state – the next collapse was never far away. In particular, they needed more runs from Wes Durston, Dan Redfern and Billy Godleman, their winter recruit from Essex. But they scored just one Championship half-century each, and all averaged under 17. For the left-handed Redfern, who had been judged the brightest talent to emerge from the Academy, there was to be no redemption, and he was jettisoned in November, one year into a three-year contract. Stephen Moore, released by Lancashire, was soon signed to add a wise head to the top order.

There were indications that Derbyshire had unearthed home-grown batting talent, however. Ben Slater, Alex Hughes, Peter Burgoyne and Matt Higginbottom, all Academy graduates, had only five Championship appearances between them when they lined up at Hove in August, but Derbyshire won that game, then beat Middlesex at home. Had they held crucial chances on the final day at The Oval, they might have made it three in a row, though they did bounce back with victory at Taunton.

The bowling was more reliable than the batting, with Tim Groenewald the mainstay and Mark Footitt, who signed a two-year deal in September, enjoying much the best season of his career. Tony Palladino's effectiveness was limited by two spells out through injury, and their main spin option, David Wainwright, struggled for rhythm after a winter of back problems.

Tom Poynton kept wicket for all but four Championship matches, when Richard Johnson, shipped in from Warwickshire to provide competition for the spot, took over. Most of Johnson's season was spent as a specialist batsman once Poynton, impeccable with the gloves, was recalled.

One-day success remained elusive. Hindered by the abandonment of their first three home matches, Derbyshire were off the pace in the YB40. And though they won their three opening group matches in the FLt20, they again failed to make the knockouts. Just one quarter-final appearance in 11 years was the worst Twenty20 record of any county.

To learn from the pain of relegation, a winter overhaul of the coaching structure was ordered. And when head coach Karl Krikken ruled himself out of contention for the new role of elite performance director – ending a 27-year association with the club – Derbyshire turned to their former all-rounder, Graeme Welch, whose reputation as a bowling coach had blossomed with Essex and Warwickshire.

Championship attendance: 18,442.

DERBYSHIRE RESULTS

All first-class matches – Played 17: Won 3, Lost 11, Drawn 3.
County Championship matches – Played 16: Won 3, Lost 10, Drawn 3.

LV= County Championship, 8th in Division 1;
Friends Life t20, 5th in North Division; Yorkshire Bank 40, 6th in Group B.

COUNTY CHAMPIONSHIP AVERAGES, BATTING AND FIELDING

Cap		M	I	NO	R	HS	100	50	Avge	Ct/St
2011	W. L. Madsen	16	30	2	1,221	152	3	8	43.60	11
	S. Chanderpaul§	15	27	4	884	129	1	7	38.43	8
	C. F. Hughes	11	20	1	612	270*	1	2	32.21	7
	R. M. Johnson	12	21	1	526	72	0	4	26.30	9
	P. M. Borrington	4	8	0	209	75	0	1	26.12	2
	T. Poynton	12	22	2	443	63*	0	3	22.15	27/3
	P. I. Burgoyne	4	7	1	132	62*	0	1	22.00	2
2012	D. J. Wainwright	9	16	4	241	54*	0	1	20.08	0
	M. L. Turner	5	7	3	79	23*	0	0	19.75	0
	B. T. Slater†	10	18	1	335	66*	0	3	19.70	3
2012	A. P. Palladino	8	14	1	233	68	0	1	17.92	1
	B. A. Godleman	8	14	0	236	55	0	1	16.85	3
2012	W. J. Durston	9	16	1	245	50	0	1	16.33	8
2012	D. J. Redfern	7	13	0	184	61	0	1	14.15	6
	A. L. Hughes	6	11	0	136	33	0	0	12.36	3
2012	J. L. Clare	6	12	1	130	49	0	0	11.81	8
2011	T. D. Groenewald	15	26	5	231	49	0	0	11.00	7
	M. H. A. Footitt	12	20	5	131	24	0	0	8.73	3
	R. A. Whiteley	3	5	0	26	12	0	0	5.20	2
	M. Higginbottom	3	5	1	18	9	0	0	4.50	0

Also batted: A. C. Evans (1 match) 0, 6*.

† *Born in Derbyshire.* § *Official overseas player.*

BOWLING

	Style	O	M	R	W	BB	5I	Avge
A. P. Palladino	RFM	214.5	43	644	23	6-90	2	28.00
T. D. Groenewald	RFM	437.5	86	1,404	45	5-30	3	31.20
J. L. Clare	RFM	124	7	554	17	5-29	1	32.58
M. H. A. Footitt	LFM	352.5	54	1,293	36	6-53	2	35.91
W. J. Durston	OB	166	21	538	10	2-29	0	53.80
D. J. Wainwright	SLA	296	42	924	17	3-46	0	54.35

Also bowled: P. I. Burgoyne (OB) 138.1–25–388–5; S. Chanderpaul (LBG) 18.4–4–40–3; A. C. Evans (RFM) 15–1–92–0; M. Higginbottom (RFM) 77.5–19–283–9; A. L. Hughes (RM) 71–12–230–6; C. F. Hughes (SLA) 5–1–19–1; W. L. Madsen (OB) 43–10–121–3; D. J. Redfern (OB) 32.1–2–119–4; M. L. Turner (RFM) 91.4–9–407–6; R. A. Whiteley (LM) 15–1–71–1.

LEADING YB40 AVERAGES (100 runs/4 wickets)

Batting	Runs	HS	Avge	SR	Ct	Bowling	W	BB	Avge	ER
S. Chanderpaul	207	85*	51.75	86.25	1	W. L. Madsen	4	3-27	15.75	4.50
W. L. Madsen	225	78	37.50	84.58	7	A. C. Evans	4	2-38	19.00	6.33
C. F. Hughes	345	80	34.50	92.74	3	M. H. A. Footitt	11	5-28	22.54	6.88
P. M. Borrington	237	72	26.33	75.23	1	T. D. Groenewald	6	3-53	26.16	6.82
D. J. Wainwright	103	40	25.75	87.28	2	D. J. Wainwright	10	4-11	28.30	5.47
A. L. Hughes	116	59*	23.20	93.54	2	A. L. Hughes	10	3-56	31.70	7.07

LEADING FLt20 AVERAGES (100 runs/18 overs)

Batting	Runs	HS	Avge	SR	Ct	Bowling	W	BB	Avge	ER
W. J. Durston	254	83	31.75	**145.14**	3	J. A. Morkel	9	4-25	15.44	**6.31**
J. A. Morkel	111	51*	27.75	**119.35**	1	W. J. Durston	5	2-25	30.40	**6.60**
C. F. Hughes	208	46	20.80	**116.85**	7	D. J. Wainwright	7	3-21	21.14	**7.04**
W. L. Madsen	164	36	20.50	**116.31**	2	D. J. Redfern	10	2-17	20.10	**7.30**
S. Chanderpaul	207	87*	34.50	**111.89**	1	T. D. Groenewald	12	4-21	20.66	**7.51**

FIRST-CLASS COUNTY RECORDS

Highest score for	274	G. A. Davidson v Lancashire at Manchester	1896
Highest score against	343*	P. A. Perrin (Essex) at Chesterfield	1904
Leading run-scorer	23,854	K. J. Barnett (avge 41.12)	1979–98
Best bowling for	10-40	W. Bestwick v Glamorgan at Cardiff	1921
Best bowling against	10-45	R. L. Johnson (Middlesex) at Derby	1994
Leading wicket-taker	1,670	H. L. Jackson (avge 17.11)	1947–63
Highest total for	801-8 dec	v Somerset at Taunton	2007
Highest total against	**677-7 dec**	**by Yorkshire at Leeds**	**2013**
Lowest total for	16	v Nottinghamshire at Nottingham	1879
Lowest total against	23	by Hampshire at Burton upon Trent	1958

LIST A COUNTY RECORDS

Highest score for	173*	M. J. Di Venuto v Derbys County Board at Derby	2000
Highest score against	158	R. K. Rao (Sussex) at Derby	1997
Leading run-scorer	12,358	K. J. Barnett (avge 36.67)	1979–98
Best bowling for	8-21	M. A. Holding v Sussex at Hove	1988
Best bowling against	8-66	S. R. G. Francis (Somerset) at Derby	2004
Leading wicket-taker	246	A. E. Warner (avge 27.13)	1985–95
Highest total for	366-4	v Combined Universities at Oxford	1991
Highest total against	369-6	by New Zealanders at Derby	1999
Lowest total for	60	v Kent at Canterbury	2008
Lowest total against	42	by Glamorgan at Swansea	1979

TWENTY20 COUNTY RECORDS

Highest score for	111	W. J. Durston v Nottinghamshire at Nottingham	2010
Highest score against	109	I. J. Harvey (Yorkshire) at Leeds	2005
Leading run-scorer	**1,182**	**W. J. Durston (avge 28.82)**	**2010–13**
Best bowling for	5-27	T. Lungley v Leicestershire at Leicester	2009
Best bowling against	5-14	P. D. Collingwood (Durham) at Chester-le-Street	2008
Leading wicket-taker	**49**	**T. D. Groenewald (avge 26.40)**	**2009–13**
Highest total for	222-5	v Yorkshire at Leeds	2010
Highest total against	220-5	by Lancashire at Derby	2009
Lowest total for	**72**	**v Leicestershire at Derby**	**2013**
Lowest total against	84	by West Indians at Derby	2007

ADDRESS

County Ground, Grandstand Road, Derby DE21 6AF (01332 388101;
email info@derbyshireccc.com). **Website** www.derbyshireccc.com

OFFICIALS

Captain W. L. Madsen
Head coach 2013 K. M. Krikken
Elite performance director 2014 G. Welch
Head of development H. B. Dytham
President W. Tucker

Chairman C. I. Grant
Chief executive S. Storey
Head groundsman N. Godrich
Scorer J. M. Brown

At Birmingham, April 10–13. DERBYSHIRE drew with WARWICKSHIRE.

At Lord's, April 17–19. DERBYSHIRE lost to MIDDLESEX by nine wickets.

DERBYSHIRE v NOTTINGHAMSHIRE

At Derby, April 24–27. Nottinghamshire won by nine wickets. Nottinghamshire 22pts, Derbyshire 3pts. Toss: Nottinghamshire.

Derby's first Division One match for 13 years was not quite worth the wait: Broad drew most of the attention, ensuring to ensure Nottinghamshire's first Championship win since the previous May. To warm the Derbyshire faithful, West Indian batting rock Chanderpaul made a sublime unbeaten 87 on home debut. But only Clare and Palladino down the order supported him for long, even though Adams dropped out of the attack with a calf tear. Nottinghamshire were helped to a first-innings lead of 187 by easing batting conditions, slipshod fielding, and a patient century from Taylor. The run-out of Patel, who finished flat on his bottom in the middle of the pitch, became an instant YouTube hit. They had the match in their grip going into the fourth day, with Derbyshire five down and still trailing by 44. Redfern raised hopes of an unlikely draw, but Broad – playing only his 12th Championship game in six seasons with Nottinghamshire – wrecked them in a burst of four wickets in 17 deliveries (interrupted by a 90-minute rainbreak) with the second new ball. On the second day Greg Cork, 18-year-old son of Dominic, caught Cowan while fielding as a substitute.

Close of play: first day, Nottinghamshire 28-0 (Cowan 18, Hales 10); second day, Nottinghamshire 325-5 (Taylor 67, Read 27); third day, Derbyshire 143-5 (Redfern 15, Wainwright 4).

Derbyshire

B. A. Godleman c Read b Broad	31	– (2) lbw b Fletcher	1
*W. L. Madsen lbw b Broad	9	– (1) lbw b Gurney	47
W. J. Durston lbw b Adams	3	– lbw b Gurney	9
S. Chanderpaul not out	87	– c Read b Fletcher	57
D. J. Redfern c Lumb b Broad	4	– lbw b Broad	61
R. A. Whiteley c Read b Gurney	0	– c Hales b Patel	4
D. J. Wainwright c Patel b Gurney	5	– c Read b Broad	33
J. L. Clare c Hales b Broad	49	– b Gurney	5
†T. Poynton c Read b Gurney	4	– lbw b Broad	0
A. P. Palladino c Read b Gurney	39	– lbw b Broad	4
T. D. Groenewald c Cowan b Fletcher	4	– not out	0
B 7, l-b 8, n-b 6	21	L-b 7, w 1	8

1/23 (2) 2/49 (3) 3/61 (1)   (82.3 overs) 256   1/2 (2) 2/24 (3)   (87.1 overs) 229
4/67 (5) 5/69 (6) 6/75 (7)   3/107 (4) 4/130 (1)
7/171 (8) 8/181 (9) 9/249 (10) 10/256 (11)   5/139 (6) 6/218 (5) 7/223 (7)
    8/223 (9) 9/227 (10) 10/229 (8)

Broad 22–6–57–4; Fletcher 17.4–5–36–1; Adams 7.5–1–21–1; Gurney 17–0–86–4; Patel 18–5–41–0. *Second innings*—Broad 23–11–34–4; Fletcher 20–9–41–2; Gurney 17.1–6–62–3; Patel 24–5–71–1; Wessels 2–0–11–0; Cowan 1–0–3–0.

Nottinghamshire

E. J. M. Cowan c sub (G. T. G. Cork) b Wainwright	59	– (2) not out.	15
A. D. Hales lbw b Palladino.	56	– (1) c Poynton b Groenewald	4
M. J. Lumb c Poynton b Clare	44	– not out	24
J. W. A. Taylor c Redfern b Wainwright	112		
S. R. Patel run out	48		
M. H. Wessels c Poynton b Whiteley	8		
*†C. M. W. Read c Poynton b Groenewald	33		
S. C. J. Broad c Groenewald b Clare	41		
A. R. Adams c Durston b Clare	0		
L. J. Fletcher not out	19		
H. F. Gurney lbw b Groenewald	0		
L-b 8, w 1, n-b 14.	23		

1/95 (1) 2/143 (2) 3/186 (3)   (144.1 overs)   443   1/4 (1)   (1 wkt, 5.4 overs)   43
4/275 (5) 5/286 (6) 6/332 (7) 7/391 (8)
8/391 (9) 9/443 (4) 10/443 (11)   110 overs: 328-5

Palladino 36–8–99–1; Groenewald 37.1–10–82–2; Clare 23–2–109–3; Whiteley 9–0–43–1; Wainwright 30–1–78–2; Durston 9–0–24–0. *Second innings*—Groenewald 3–0–15–1; Clare 2.4–0–28–0.

Umpires: M. J. D. Bodenham and S. J. O'Shaughnessy.

At Leeds, April 29–May 2. DERBYSHIRE lost to YORKSHIRE by an innings and 39 runs. *Chesney Hughes's 270* is the fifth-highest score by a player carrying his bat in all first-class cricket.*

At Derby, May 4–6. DERBYSHIRE lost to NEW ZEALANDERS by 107 runs (see New Zealand tour section).

DERBYSHIRE v SUSSEX

At Derby, May 15–18. Sussex won by nine wickets. Sussex 24pts, Derbyshire 4pts. Toss: Sussex. Championship debut: A. C. Evans.

Derbyshire were put in for the fifth Championship game in a row, but had hopes of a lead when Sussex struggled against a new-ball spell from Footitt, who collected a career-best six in his first appearance in the competition for a year. The contest was turned by a stand of 179 between Yardy, with his first century of the season, and Jordan, narrowly missing the first of his career. Both men were dropped, and Jordan survived chopping the ball on to his off stump without dislodging the bail. By batting into the third day, Sussex enabled their captain, Joyce, to come in at No. 11 after being absent throughout the second because of a family emergency. He and Yardy – who reached 150 for the sixth time – claimed two extra batting points. Madsen had completed 5,000 in his first-innings fifty, but no one else passed 32 in either innings for Derbyshire, who slumped to a fourth successive Championship defeat for the first time since 2003. There were 120 extras in the match.

Close of play: first day, Derbyshire 158-6 (Whiteley 12); second day, Sussex 328-8 (Yardy 121, Panesar 0); third day, Derbyshire 189-7 (Johnson 12, Groenewald 4).

Derbyshire

B. A. Godleman c Wells b Jordan	26	– lbw b Anyon	5
C. F. Hughes c Joyce b Magoffin	15	– c Anyon b Magoffin	32
*W. L. Madsen c Brown b Jordan	63	– b Panesar	32
S. Chanderpaul c sub (A. S. Miller) b Magoffin	20	– c Yardy b Magoffin	23
D. J. Redfern lbw b Anyon	0	– c Brown b Anyon	24
R. A. Whiteley c Gatting b Jordan	12	– c Joyce b Jordan	6
A. C. Evans lbw b Panesar	0	– (10) not out	6
†R. M. Johnson not out	22	– (7) c Magoffin b Anyon	16
J. L. Clare b Anyon	25	– (8) c Gatting b Panesar	12
T. D. Groenewald b Anyon	0	– (9) b Magoffin	7
M. H. A. Footitt c Brown b Panesar	6	– c Brown b Magoffin	15
B 2, l-b 12, w 4, n-b 16	34	B 11, l-b 8, w 20, n-b 2	41

(75 overs) 223   (87.5 overs) 219

1/36 (2) 2/71 (1) 3/113 (4)
4/128 (5) 5/157 (3) 6/158 (7)
7/164 (6) 8/216 (9) 9/216 (10) 10/223 (11)

1/7 (1) 2/80 (3)
3/101 (2) 4/134 (5)
5/153 (6) 6/163 (4) 7/184 (8)
8/197 (7) 9/199 (9) 10/219 (11)

Anyon 22–9–56–3; Magoffin 22–7–48–2; Jordan 22–5–77–3; Panesar 7–3–21–2; Gatting 2–0–7–0. *Second innings*—Anyon 16–3–46–3; Magoffin 24.5–9–44–4; Panesar 20–9–41–2; Jordan 17–4–49–1; Nash 7–2–12–0; Wells 3–0–8–0.

Sussex

C. D. Nash c Clare b Footitt	12	– (2) c Johnson b Groenewald	0
L. W. P. Wells c Hughes b Footitt	23	– (1) not out	23
M. H. Yardy b Groenewald	153	– not out	18
R. J. Hamilton-Brown lbw b Footitt	6		
J. S. Gatting c and b Clare	13		
†B. C. Brown c Footitt b Clare	10		
C. J. Jordan c Whiteley b Groenewald	92		
S. J. Magoffin c Redfern b Footitt	9		
J. E. Anyon b Footitt	5		
M. S. Panesar c Clare b Footitt	10		
*E. C. Joyce not out	25		
B 9, l-b 10, w 2, n-b 22	43	N-b 2	2

(82.3 overs) 401   (1 wkt, 5.5 overs) 43

1/26 (2) 2/35 (1) 3/47 (4)
4/79 (5) 5/109 (6) 6/288 (7)
7/309 (8) 8/317 (9) 9/341 (10) 10/401 (3)

1/7 (2)

Groenewald 26.3–3–93–2; Footitt 24–0–120–6; Evans 15–1–92–0; Clare 10–0–58–2; Redfern 7–0–19–0. *Second innings*—Groenewald 3–0–25–1; Footitt 2.5–1–18–0.

Umpires: N. G. B. Cook and R. K. Illingworth.

DERBYSHIRE v SURREY

At Derby, May 30–June 2. Drawn. Derbyshire 8pts, Surrey 9pts. Toss: Derbyshire. County debut: B. T. Slater.

Two batsmen with 69 Test centuries between them lit up a high-scoring but ultimately tame draw between the division's bottom-placed teams. It was notable chiefly for career landmarks. Former Australian captain Ponting marked his first-class debut for Surrey with his 81st hundred, bringing him level with Sunil Gavaskar, Mark Waugh and Sachin Tendulkar. His 192 was also the highest score on Surrey debut, beating Mark Ramprakash's 146 against Kent in 2001. Chanderpaul's 116-ball century, in more demanding first-day conditions – rain had prevented play until 3.15 – was his

67th, and tenth in the Championship, but the first for Derbyshire, his fourth county. He and Madsen, who had won his first toss in six Championship matches, put on 265, Derbyshire's first double-century stand against Surrey. Ponting was backed up by a career-best 154 from Harinath which helped earn a 101-run first-innings lead. Amid the centuries, Tremlett collected eight wickets, his first haul of five for Surrey taking him to 400 in all first-class cricket. Surrey first-team coach Ian Salisbury took over umpiring duties after lunch on the third day when Nigel Cowley complained of light-headedness, which also affected some of the Derbyshire fielders.

Close of play: first day, Derbyshire 232-2 (Madsen 92, Chanderpaul 112); second day, Surrey 35-1 (Harinath 13, Solanki 10); third day, Surrey 362-4 (Ponting 120, Davies 7).

Derbyshire

B. A. Godleman c de Bruyn b Linley	17	– lbw b Tremlett	28
C. F. Hughes b Tremlett	0	– b Tremlett	68
*W. L. Madsen b Meaker	152	– b Tremlett	8
S. Chanderpaul c Ponting b Meaker	129	– not out	24
W. J. Durston c Davies b Tremlett	6	– not out	29
B. T. Slater c Davies b Tremlett	7		
†R. M. Johnson c Wilson b Tremlett	72		
D. J. Wainwright c sub (J. J. Roy) b Meaker	21		
T. D. Groenewald b Linley	3		
M. L. Turner b Tremlett	8		
M. H. A. Footitt not out	8		
B 21, l-b 4, n-b 4	29	L-b 5, n-b 2	7

1/1 (2) 2/29 (1) 3/294 (4)   (132.1 overs) 452   1/76 (1)   (3 wkts, 39 overs) 164
4/320 (5) 5/336 (6) 6/336 (3) 7/395 (8)   2/104 (3) 3/105 (2)
8/404 (9) 9/415 (10) 10/452 (7)   110 overs: 378-6

Tremlett 30.1–5–95–5; Linley 32–7–99–2; Meaker 25–6–98–3; Batty 26–5–86–0; de Bruyn 19–1–49–0. *Second innings*—Tremlett 12–2–38–3; Linley 8–2–27–0; Batty 8–1–32–0; Meaker 8–2–44–0; de Bruyn 3–0–18–0.

Surrey

R. J. Burns run out	4	C. T. Tremlett run out	0
A. Harinath b Wainwright	154	S. C. Meaker not out	3
V. S. Solanki c Godleman b Durston	35	B 10, l-b 11, w 2, n-b 12	35
R. T. Ponting run out	192		
Z. de Bruyn b Wainwright	11	1/4 (1) (8 wkts dec, 146 overs) 553	
†S. M. Davies c Godleman b Wainwright	59	2/137 (3) 3/317 (2)	
G. C. Wilson c Footitt b Durston	45	4/352 (5) 5/457 (6) 6/514 (4)	
*G. J. Batty not out	15	7/546 (7) 8/546 (9) 110 overs: 352-4	

T. E. Linley did not bat.

Groenewald 24–4–75–0; Footitt 27–5–106–0; Turner 21–3–91–0; Wainwright 45–9–164–3; Durston 29–3–96–2.

Umpires: N. L. Bainton and N. G. C. Cowley. I. D. K. Salisbury replaced Cowley on the third day.

At Derby, June 5–7 (not first-class). **Derbyshire won by 65 runs. Derbyshire 436-7 dec** (B. T. Slater 116, W. J. Durston 117, A. L. Hughes 73) **and 224-4** (D. J. Redfern 91, T. Poynton 77); **†Durham MCCU 229** (F. O. E. van den Bergh 106; A. C. Evans 4-35, P. I. Burgoyne 3-43) **and 366** (R. A. C. Shah 57, C. Bishnoi 68, C. J. Purshouse 53; W. J. Durston 3-47). *Slater and Durston both retired out for hundreds on a fast-scoring first day when Derbyshire made 436 in 94 overs. On the second, Durham MCCU were 69-7 before Freddie van den Bergh's aggressive 106 in 115 balls. His team-mates fought harder next time round, but the students lost late on the final day.*

At Nottingham, June 12–15. DERBYSHIRE drew with NOTTINGHAMSHIRE.

DERBYSHIRE v SOMERSET

At Derby, June 21–24. Somerset won by four wickets. Somerset 20pts, Derbyshire 5pts. Toss: Somerset.

On the day he learned he was almost certainly out of England's Ashes plans, Compton helped Somerset to their first Championship victory of 2013. His 56 was the cornerstone of their progress to a modest target on a pitch that challenged batsmen throughout. Derbyshire had begun the final morning 86 ahead with eight wickets left and hoping for a first win of their own. But they lost those eight for 56, and 145 was too little to defend, even though Clare took five wickets (culminating in Compton). He was the third home bowler to do so: Palladino, after seven weeks out injured, and Groenewald had become the first Derbyshire pair to collect five apiece in the same innings since Andrew Harris and Paul Aldred, also against Somerset at Derby, in 1999. They ensured a first-innings lead of 50, but Derbyshire would later regret three dropped catches that might have made it more.

Close of play: first day, Somerset 16-0 (Trescothick 10, Compton 6); second day, Somerset 180-6 (Trego 14, Meschede 1); third day, Derbyshire 36-2 (Godleman 19, Chanderpaul 0).

Derbyshire

B. A. Godleman c Trescothick b Overton	5	– c Barrow b Meschede	24
C. F. Hughes c Trescothick b Thomas	25	– c Thomas b Kirby	0
*W. L. Madsen lbw b Kirby	50	– c Elgar b Kirby	12
S. Chanderpaul c Barrow b Meschede	5	– c Hildreth b Thomas	1
W. J. Durston b Barrow b Thomas	6	– b Overton	20
B. T. Slater c Trescothick b Kirby	14	– b Meschede	0
†R. M. Johnson c Elgar b Overton	56	– c Barrow b Meschede	4
J. L. Clare c Barrow b Thomas	20	– run out	5
A. P. Palladino c Trescothick b Trego	49	– c Trescothick b Kirby	12
T. D. Groenewald not out	4	– c Hildreth b Kirby	0
M. H. A. Footitt b Overton	0	– not out	0
B 15, l-b 5, n-b 12	32	B 10, l-b 5, w 1	16

1/15 (1) 2/67 (2) 3/82 (4)	(86.2 overs) 266	1/2 (2) 2/34 (3) (30.2 overs) 94
4/99 (5) 5/122 (3) 6/141 (6)		3/38 (4) 4/44 (1)
7/173 (8) 8/255 (9) 9/262 (7) 10/266 (11)		5/44 (6) 6/54 (7) 7/64 (8)
		8/90 (9) 9/90 (10) 10/94 (5)

Kirby 20–3–61–2; Overton 11.2–0–35–3; Trego 14–3–38–1; Thomas 24–5–54–3; Meschede 13–2–44–1; Elgar 4–0–14–0. *Second innings*—Kirby 7–1–18–4; Overton 5.2–0–27–1; Meschede 9–3–17–3; Thomas 9–5–17–1.

Somerset

*M. E. Trescothick c Clare b Groenewald	50	– c Madsen b Clare	21
N. R. D. Compton c Durston b Palladino	15	– c Durston b Clare	56
D. Elgar c Madsen b Palladino	26	– c Durston b Clare	5
J. C. Hildreth lbw b Palladino	36	– lbw b Clare	3
C. Kieswetter c Johnson b Palladino	7	– c Johnson b Clare	4
†A. W. R. Barrow c Johnson b Groenewald	5	– c Johnson b Groenewald	16
P. D. Trego b Groenewald	28	– not out	16
C. A. J. Meschede c Johnson b Groenewald	1	– not out	1
A. C. Thomas not out	19		
S. P. Kirby lbw b Groenewald	0		
J. Overton c Durston b Palladino	3		
B 12, l-b 5, w 1, n-b 8	26	B 4, l-b 12, w 1, n-b 6	23

1/56 (2) 2/101 (1) 3/121 (3)	(71.3 overs) 216	1/60 (1) (6 wkts, 32 overs) 145
4/135 (5) 5/156 (4) 6/166 (6)		2/80 (3) 3/98 (4)
7/180 (8) 8/209 (7) 9/213 (10) 10/216 (11)		4/102 (5) 5/109 (2) 6/137 (6)

Footitt 18–4–53–0; Palladino 28.3–7–97–5; Groenewald 18–7–30–5; Clare 7–1–19–0. *Second innings*—Footitt 8–0–35–0; Palladino 8–0–37–0; Groenewald 8–0–28–1; Clare 8–0–29–5.

Umpires: S. A. Garratt and G. Sharp.

At Chester-le-Street, July 8–11. DERBYSHIRE lost to DURHAM by 279 runs.

DERBYSHIRE v YORKSHIRE

At Chesterfield, July 17–19. Yorkshire won by an innings and 113 runs. Yorkshire 24pts, Derbyshire 1pt. Toss: Yorkshire. Championship debut: P. I. Burgoyne.

Alex Lees became Yorkshire's youngest double-centurion, aged 20 years and 95 days, undercutting Richard Blakey, who was 129 days older when he scored 204 not out against Gloucestershire in 1987. Lees batted nine hours and 15 minutes with sublime assurance; his 311-run stand with Jaques was a second-wicket record, for the ground and for Yorkshire against Derbyshire, in both cases beating 305 by James Rothery and David Denton in 1910. Facing a huge total and baking heat, Derbyshire cracked. They began their reply shortly before tea on day two, and by tea on day three were six down following on, still 262 behind; they eventually went down to their seventh Championship reverse in ten and, for the first time since 1928, had lost two games by an innings to Yorkshire in the same season. Madsen made a gallant century but was last out on the third evening. Two months later, however, he won the inaugural Christopher Martin-Jenkins Spirit of Cricket award: in the first innings, he had feathered a catch to the keeper and, though umpire Jeff Evans reprieved him, Madsen signalled the ball had hit his glove, and walked off.

Close of play: first day, Yorkshire 367-2 (Lees 171, Gale 9); second day, Derbyshire 94-5 (Johnson 5, Turner 4).

Yorkshire

A. Lyth c Poynton b Footitt	10
A. Z. Lees not out	275
P. A. Jaques c Durston b Groenewald	139
*A. W. Gale b Burgoyne	74
G. S. Ballance st Poynton b Durston	66
A. U. Rashid c Poynton b Footitt	7
B 2, l-b 13, w 7, n-b 24	46

1/22 (1)   (5 wkts dec, 152.3 overs) 617
2/333 (3) 3/471 (4)
4/580 (5) 5/617 (6)   110 overs: 429-2

†A. J. Hodd, L. E. Plunkett, R. J. Sidebottom, S. A. Patterson and J. A. Brooks did not bat.

Footitt 22.3–3–110–2; Groenewald 24–4–112–1; Turner 17–0–128–0; Burgoyne 55–8–149–1; Durston 32–5–94–1; Redfern 2–0–9–0.

Derbyshire

B. T. Slater c Hodd b Brooks	28	– c Hodd b Brooks	1
C. F. Hughes lbw b Sidebottom	12	– c Ballance b Brooks	16
*W. L. Madsen c Hodd b Patterson	17	– c and b Plunkett	141
W. J. Durston lbw b Patterson	0	– b Patterson	2
D. J. Redfern c Hodd b Brooks	12	– c Gale b Plunkett	2
R. M. Johnson c Plunkett b Rashid	46	– c Hodd b Patterson	23
M. L. Turner c Gale b Brooks	8	– (10) b Sidebottom	0
P. I. Burgoyne c Hodd b Plunkett	15	– (7) b Sidebottom	18
†T. Poynton not out	63	– (8) c Plunkett b Patterson	29
T. D. Groenewald lbw b Plunkett	10	– (9) lbw b Sidebottom	11
M. H. A. Footitt c Lyth b Rashid	6	– not out	0
B 8, l-b 1, w 1, n-b 8	18	B 16, w 2, n-b 8	26

1/17 (2) 2/52 (3) 3/52 (4)   (67 overs) 235   1/1 (1) 2/30 (2)   (65.2 overs) 269
4/80 (5) 5/83 (1) 6/120 (7)   3/35 (4) 4/38 (5)
7/146 (6) 8/166 (8) 9/202 (10) 10/235 (11)   5/74 (6) 6/120 (7) 7/231 (8)
                                     8/269 (9) 9/269 (10) 10/269 (3)

Sidebottom 13–5–31–1; Brooks 16–5–46–3; Patterson 13–5–35–2; Plunkett 13–6–33–2; Rashid 12–1–81–2. *Second innings*—Sidebottom 12–6–27–3; Brooks 9–2–32–2; Patterson 13–3–63–3; Plunkett 12.2–1–57–2; Rashid 15–2–54–0; Lyth 4–1–20–0.

Umpires: N. G. C. Cowley and J. H. Evans.

At Hove, August 2–4. DERBYSHIRE beat SUSSEX by nine wickets. *Derbyshire complete their first Championship win of the season at the 11th attempt.*

DERBYSHIRE v MIDDLESEX

At Derby, August 20–23. Derbyshire won by 56 runs. Derbyshire 23pts, Middlesex 4pts. Toss: Middlesex.

Not only did Middlesex's decision to bowl hand Derbyshire an initiative they held throughout, it allowed Madsen to become the first batsman to 1,000 Championship runs in the season. He got there on 49 as Robson, needing seven for the landmark, watched from the slips. Madsen advanced to an unbeaten 138, with the last two wickets adding 101 to claim four batting points, whereas Middlesex managed just one. Robson was duly second to the milestone – after Murtagh had been second to 50 Championship wickets (behind Chris Jordan of Sussex). He took two more in the second innings as Derbyshire stumbled to 68 for four, before a fifty from Johnson helped set a target of 297. Middlesex slid to 121 for seven at lunch on the final day; despite another defiant innings from Rayner, Derbyshire clinched a second successive victory, escaping the relegation zone for the first time since April. Finn, left out of the Fifth Ashes Test, replaced Harris in the visiting side but saw action only on the third day, when he bagged a pair – as tailender and nightwatchman – and took a single wicket.

Close of play: first day, Derbyshire 279-6 (Madsen 105, Burgoyne 19); second day, Middlesex 197-6 (Simpson 30, Rayner 22); third day, Middlesex 25-2 (Robson 12, Voges 11).

Derbyshire

B. T. Slater c Simpson b Harris	53	– c Simpson b Murtagh	0
C. F. Hughes c Roland-Jones b Berg	16	– lbw b Finn	3
*W. L. Madsen not out	138	– c Denly b Murtagh	2
S. Chanderpaul c Robson b Rayner	2	– lbw b Roland-Jones	32
R. M. Johnson c Harris b Voges	33	– c Robson b Rayner	59
A. L. Hughes lbw b Murtagh	33	– c Denly b Berg	24
†T. Poynton b Murtagh	9	– c Roland-Jones b Rayner	9
P. I. Burgoyne c Berg b Murtagh	23	– lbw b Rayner	4
M. Higginbottom c Morgan b Harris	4	– not out	4
T. D. Groenewald c Simpson b Rayner	49	– c Robson b Rayner	20
M. H. A. Footitt c Rayner b Roland-Jones	19	– c Morgan b Rayner	0
B 1, l-b 14, w 1, n-b 2	18	B 3	3

1/37 (2) 2/118 (1) 3/123 (4)	(115 overs) 385	1/0 (1) 2/4 (3) (63.3 overs) 160
4/179 (5) 5/245 (6) 6/255 (7)		3/16 (2) 4/68 (4)
7/283 (8) 8/284 (9) 9/350 (10)		5/116 (6) 6/131 (7) 7/133 (5)
10/385 (11)	110 overs: 350-9	8/136 (8) 9/160 (10) 10/160 (11)

Murtagh 23–10–63–3; Roland-Jones 23–2–75–1; Berg 15–3–49–1; Harris 26–3–105–2; Dexter 3–1–8–0; Rayner 19–2–60–2; Voges 6–1–10–1. *Second innings*—Murtagh 8–3–24–2; Finn 18–4–50–1; Roland-Jones 7–3–10–1; Rayner 23.3–5–67–5; Berg 7–2–6–1.

Middlesex

S. D. Robson c Johnson b Groenewald	16	– b Groenewald 29
J. L. Denly c Chanderpaul b Groenewald	4	– lbw b Footitt 2
A. C. Voges lbw b Higginbottom	69	– (4) c C. F. Hughes b Burgoyne 48
E. J. G. Morgan c sub (C. A. J. Brodrick) b Higginbottom	28	– (5) b Footitt 9
*N. J. Dexter b Footitt	21	– (6) b Footitt 2
†J. A. Simpson run out	36	– (7) c Madsen b Burgoyne 9
G. K. Berg b Higginbottom	2	– (8) c C. F. Hughes b Higginbottom .. 71
O. P. Rayner not out	52	– (9) not out 46
T. S. Roland-Jones c C. F. Hughes b Groenewald	5	– (10) c Poynton b Footitt 14
T. J. Murtagh c Poynton b Footitt	10	– (11) c C. F. Hughes b Burgoyne 1
S. T. Finn lbw b Footitt	0	– (3) lbw b Groenewald 0
L-b 4, n-b 2	6	B 6, w 1, n-b 2 9

1/16 (1) 2/25 (2) 3/75 (4)   (93.3 overs) 249
4/128 (5) 5/150 (3) 6/154 (7)
7/208 (6) 8/224 (9) 9/249 (10) 10/249 (11)

1/8 (2) 2/11 (3)   (74.3 overs) 240
3/61 (1) 4/83 (5)
5/85 (6) 6/101 (4) 7/121 (7)
8/206 (8) 9/236 (10) 10/240 (11)

Finn replaced J. A. R. Harris after being released from the England squad.

Groenewald 23–7–54–3; Footitt 25.3–5–69–3; Higginbottom 17–3–59–3; A. L. Hughes 12–4–24–0; Burgoyne 10–1–27–0; Madsen 6–1–12–0. *Second innings*—Groenewald 17–1–47–2; Footitt 18–0–65–4; Burgoyne 23.3–6–66–3; Higginbottom 11–1–40–1; A. L. Hughes 1–0–7–0; Madsen 4–1–9–0.

Umpires: R. T. Robinson and P. Willey.

At The Oval, August 29–September 1. DERBYSHIRE lost to SURREY by four wickets.

At Taunton, September 3–6. DERBYSHIRE beat SOMERSET by two wickets.

DERBYSHIRE v DURHAM

At Derby, September 11–14. Durham won by nine wickets. Durham 22pts, Derbyshire 4pts. Toss: Durham.

With Derbyshire battling to avoid relegation, and Durham closing in on the title, the counties held starkly different ambitions – yet there was little to choose between them for much of the contest. All signs pointed to a draw when Durham began the fourth day still 41 behind in their first innings. But, after only 14 wickets had fallen in the first three days (more like two, thanks to rain), the tumble of 16 in two sessions changed all that. A season's-best six from Palladino restricted Durham's lead to 27, before an inspired spell from Onions tore through Derbyshire: five for four in 41 balls as they wilted for 63. Issues at the top and bottom now seemed much clearer. Durham needed only 37 to tie up a fourth successive victory, which took their lead to 27.5 points with two matches to go. Earlier, Borrington had built a strong position for Derbyshire before they lost their last seven for 56. A third-wicket stand of 159 between Borthwick and Smith kept Durham's interests alive.

Close of play: first day, Derbyshire 99-1 (Borrington 30, Madsen 32); second day, Durham 82-2 (Borthwick 21, Smith 3); third day, Durham 257-4 (Richardson 10, Collingwood 13).

Derbyshire

B. T. Slater b Rushworth	13	– lbw b Rushworth	0
P. M. Borrington c Borthwick b Onions	75	– c Smith b Rushworth	10
*W. L. Madsen lbw b Onions	32	– c Borthwick b Onions	16
S. Chanderpaul c Collingwood b Arshad	53	– lbw b Onions	10
R. M. Johnson c Borthwick b Rushworth	29	– (7) c Richardson b Onions	5
A. L. Hughes c Arshad b Onions	2	– (5) b Onions	4
†T. Poynton c Mustard b Rushworth	0	– (6) b Rushworth	1
D. J. Wainwright c Collingwood b Rushworth	16	– not out	5
A. P. Palladino b Onions	22	– c Mustard b Onions	0
T. D. Groenewald not out	5	– c Richardson b Arshad	0
M. H. A. Footitt c and b Rushworth	1	– c Mustard b Arshad	2
B 10, l-b 10, w 10, n-b 20	50	B 5, l-b 2, w 1, n-b 2	10

1/33 (1) 2/100 (3) 3/206 (4)   (104.1 overs) 298   1/1 (1) 2/26 (2)   (29.1 overs) 63
4/242 (2) 5/248 (5) 6/248 (7)   3/33 (3) 4/39 (5)
7/248 (6) 8/290 (9) 9/290 (8) 10/298 (11)   5/44 (4) 6/44 (6) 7/54 (7)
                                      8/54 (9) 9/55 (10) 10/63 (11)

Onions 31–7–62–4; Rushworth 25.1–12–47–5; Harrison 18–3–87–0; Arshad 19–2–63–1; Collingwood 11–3–19–0. *Second innings*—Onions 15–5–23–5; Rushworth 12–3–31–3; Arshad 2.1–1–2–2.

Durham

M. D. Stoneman c Poynton b Palladino	30	– lbw b Palladino	7
K. K. Jennings b Palladino	25	– not out	18
S. G. Borthwick c Groenewald b Chanderpaul	89	– not out	10
W. R. Smith c sub (T. C. Knight) b Footitt	81		
M. J. Richardson c Poynton b Palladino	23		
*P. D. Collingwood c Poynton b Palladino	25		
†P. Mustard not out	23		
U. Arshad run out	8		
G. Onions run out	2		
J. Harrison b Palladino	7		
C. Rushworth c Chanderpaul b Palladino	0		
B 4, l-b 4, w 1, n-b 12	21	N-b 2	2

1/49 (1) 2/68 (2) 3/227 (3)   (113.3 overs) 325   1/13 (1)   (1 wkt, 7.5 overs) 37
4/236 (4) 5/283 (6) 6/287 (5) 7/311 (8)
8/314 (9) 9/323 (10) 10/325 (11)   110 overs: 314-8

Footitt 22–3–84–1; Groenewald 27–7–82–0; Palladino 34.3–7–90–6; Hughes 6–1–19–0; Wainwright 19–7–35–0; Chanderpaul 5–1–7–1. *Second innings*—Footitt 4–1–19–0; Palladino 3.5–0–18–1.

Umpires: T. E. Jesty and M. J. Saggers.

DERBYSHIRE v WARWICKSHIRE

At Derby, September 24–26. Warwickshire won by an innings and 168 runs. Warwickshire 22pts, Derbyshire 2pts. Toss: Derbyshire. County debut: S. W. Poynter.

Nothing less than victory would do for Derbyshire if they were to avoid an immediate return to Division Two, and even a win would not guarantee their survival: they started 15 points behind Nottinghamshire and 16 behind Somerset, who were meeting a few miles away at Trent Bridge. Derbyshire's hopes rose when Warwickshire were 148 for seven on the first afternoon, but their fortunes declined swiftly and decisively. Woakes, who had just learned he was not in England's winter plans, was dropped on 83 and punished the error by completing his seventh century; next day he went on to a career-best unbeaten 152. His partnership of 166 with Chambers, who scored a maiden fifty, was a ninth-wicket record at Derby, beating 135 by Harry Parks and Tich Cornford of Sussex in 1935, and for Warwickshire against Derbyshire, overhauling George Stephens and Alfred

Croom's 154 at Edgbaston in 1925. It also broke Derbyshire's resolve. They crumbled twice in quick succession, and their brief stay in the top flight ended ignominiously with a day and a half to spare. Stuart Poynter, an MCC Young Cricketer and Ireland international, became Warwickshire's fourth official wicketkeeper in four games because of an injury crisis.

Close of play: first day, Warwickshire 285-8 (Woakes 102, Chambers 14); second day, Derbyshire 44-5 (Chanderpaul 24, Poynton 2).

Warwickshire

*V. Chopra lbw b Footitt	6	M. A. Chambers st Poynton b Wainwright	58
I. J. Westwood c Hughes b Footitt	2	W. B. Rankin not out	0
A. Javid c Poynton b Groenewald	46		
L. J. Evans lbw b Groenewald	11	B 5, l-b 9, n-b 26	40
R. Clarke c Hughes b Palladino	22		
C. R. Woakes not out	152	1/17 (2) (9 wkts dec, 124 overs)	391
†S. W. Poynter c and b Groenewald	0	2/18 (1) 3/50 (4) 4/89 (5)	
K. H. D. Barker c Poynton b Groenewald	14	5/120 (3) 6/120 (7) 7/148 (8)	
J. S. Patel c Footitt b Hughes	40	8/217 (9) 9/383 (10) 110 overs: 325-8	

Footitt 29–5–98–2; Palladino 29–6–60–1; Groenewald 24–2–92–4; Hughes 18–1–58–1; Wainwright 23–1–68–1; Chanderpaul 1–0–1–0.

Derbyshire

B. T. Slater lbw b Barker	2	– c Clarke b Chambers		12
P. M. Borrington c Woakes b Barker	0	– c Clarke b Woakes		11
*W. L. Madsen c Chopra b Chambers	1	– c Evans b Woakes		1
S. Chanderpaul lbw b Barker	52	– c Poynter b Barker		6
R. M. Johnson c Clarke b Chambers	4	– c Patel b Woakes		1
A. L. Hughes c Poynter b Barker	4	– c Poynter b Rankin		2
†T. Poynton c Poynter b Rankin	19	– b Patel		41
D. J. Wainwright c Poynter b Barker	3	– c Evans b Rankin		8
A. P. Palladino retired hurt	7	– absent hurt		
T. D. Groenewald c Poynter b Chambers	4	– (9) b Patel		15
M. H. A. Footitt not out	0	– (10) not out		5
L-b 1, n-b 6	7	B 5, l-b 6, n-b 7		18

1/2 (1) 2/5 (3) 3/9 (2)   (43.2 overs) 103   1/17 (1) 2/22 (3)   (29.1 overs) 120
4/14 (5) 5/33 (6) 6/82 (4)   3/35 (4) 4/35 (2) 5/38 (5)
7/88 (8) 8/92 (7) 9/103 (10)   6/60 (6) 7/76 (8) 8/107 (7) 9/120 (9)

In the first innings Palladino retired hurt at 103-9.

Barker 21–9–55–5; Chambers 9–1–27–3; Woakes 9–4–13–0; Rankin 4.2–1–7–1. *Second innings*— Barker 7–3–19–1; Chambers 7–0–37–1; Woakes 8–0–36–3; Rankin 6–0–16–2; Patel 1.1–0–1–2.

Umpires: N. A. Mallender and R. T. Robinson.

DURHAM

Local lads triumph in test of fire

TIM WELLOCK

Buoyed by a collective spirit and locally forged resilience, Durham found strength in all kinds of adversity, defying forecasts of relegation to win their third Championship in six seasons. It was a triumph for the captaincy of Paul Collingwood, who had halted their decline in 2012. After narrowly losing his first match in charge that year, he won 14 of his next 20.

Collingwood praised the local element when he outlined the many setbacks Durham had overcome, including a hotel fire in Nottingham: "Things just kept happening to test us, and somehow we kept showing the resolve. I don't know what it is, or if we can bottle it. It seems to be inside the North-East people. They just want to fight." On his own role, he said: "I feel I have been a sensible captain. I don't generally make decisions straight off the cuff. If I think a youngster can come in and do a job, I will give him the opportunity. Seeing the youngsters blossom has been absolutely wonderful."

There was a brief stage, a few weeks after head coach Geoff Cook suffered a cardiac arrest while out on a morning jog on June 20, when it seemed Durham's season might fall apart. Going into a Twenty20 quarter-final at Northampton, they were the only team with a chance of the treble; they also topped their Yorkshire Bank 40 group. But a Championship loss at Lord's was followed by another in that quarter-final, and heavy YB40 defeats at Chelmsford and Derby. With the one-day challenge in ruins, Cook returned to share duties with second-team coach Jon Lewis. Durham responded with a club-record five successive Championship wins to secure the title with a game to spare. Lewis was promoted to first-team coach; Cook remained as director of cricket, with a focus on developing young players.

Durham's triumph was all the more remarkable in the face of severe cost-cutting. They began the season on minus 2.5 points, after breaking the ECB's £1.8m salary cap. With the financial situation worsening, they set about getting the wage bill down to £1.2m. After reaching the top in 2008, Durham had handed out too many big contracts in an effort to stay there.

Steve Harmison never made the first team, and retired at the end of the season, while the gaps left by Michael Di Venuto, Ian Blackwell and Liam Plunkett were filled by Mark Stoneman, Scott Borthwick and Mark Wood. The lesser lights shone brightly, with Stoneman and Borthwick completing 1,000 Championship runs within 30 minutes of each other – but eight years after Collingwood had become the only previous home-grown batsman to do so.

Home pitches helped, but Durham won at Trent Bridge, The Oval and Scarborough, and at Derby dismissed their hosts for 63. Visitors to Chester-le-Street nearly always bowled first – Durham batted in seven of eight home games, and invariably scored between 237 and 267, except when they made

Gareth Copley, Getty Images

Scott Borthwick

421 against Surrey, while visiting teams averaged 141 in the first innings and managed a single batting point between them.

There was no money for a pre-season tour, and adverse weather meant Durham had only two days of outdoor practice. They opted for a trip to Loch Lomond, where Collingwood strengthened the bonds by leading his men up Beinn Dubh in difficult conditions. His own batting was on the wane, and he did not expect to play on beyond 2014, but his leadership qualities were noticed by Scotland, who engaged him for coaching duties during the winter. England quickly hired him as assistant coach for the limited-overs tour of the West Indies and the World Twenty20 in Bangladesh. One-day captain Dale Benkenstein's season was ended in early June by a shoulder operation, and Stoneman replaced him. Benkenstein was expected back for his ninth year but, in February at the age of 39, he joined Hampshire as first-team coach.

Borthwick's elevation from No. 8 to the troublesome No. 3 slot was a remarkable success. Fears that his leg-spin would suffer were unfounded: he took 28 Championship wickets. Having another all-rounder, Ben Stokes, in the top five was a major strength. Though he gathered only 615 Championship runs, his bowling continued to improve, and Collingwood often spoke of him as a match-winner. In what proved to be the title decider at Scarborough, Stokes was outstanding, scoring 127 and bowling 33 overs in the second innings. He made victory possible by removing Phil Jaques and Kane Williamson on the final morning after they had put on 264. Stokes was also the country's leading six-hitter in the Twenty20 competition. His availability may be less in 2014 after a successful winter with England.

Phil Mustard, ever-present in all three title-winning seasons, reached 163 first-class appearances, a Durham record. He finished third in the Championship averages, with 763 runs at 34, and was the leading wicketkeeper in the tournament, with 65 dismissals. His 72 off 54 balls at Trent Bridge ensured Durham chased down a target of 183 in 23 overs with 16 deliveries to spare.

Despite missing four games and being ignored by England, Graham Onions was as excellent as ever, collecting 70 Championship wickets, while Chris Rushworth took 50 for the first time. The pacy Wood missed September with a side injury but was named in the England Performance Squad, and there was also encouraging progress from Keaton Jennings, Michael Richardson, Jamie Harrison, Usman Arshad and Ryan Buckley. As well as Harmison, the cost-cutting spelled the end for seamers Ruel Brathwaite, Mitch Claydon and Callum Thorp. More surprisingly, Will Smith was not offered a new contract, and was signed by Hampshire, taking the number of ex-Durham players with other counties into double figures.

Championship attendance: 29,002.

DURHAM RESULTS

All first-class matches – Played 17: Won 10, Lost 4, Drawn 3.
County Championship matches – Played 16: Won 10, Lost 4, Drawn 2.

LV= County Championship, winners in Division 1;
Friends Life t20, quarter-finalists; Yorkshire Bank 40, 4th in Group B.

COUNTY CHAMPIONSHIP AVERAGES, BATTING AND FIELDING

Cap		M	I	NO	R	HS	100	50	Avge	Ct/St
	S. G. Borthwick†	16	28	2	1,022	135	3	5	39.30	29
	M. D. Stoneman	16	30	1	1,011	122	3	6	34.86	6
	P. Mustard†	16	26	4	763	77	0	6	34.68	64/1
	M. J. Richardson	10	15	0	501	129	2	2	33.40	13
	W. R. Smith	16	28	2	786	153	1	2	30.23	13
1998	P. D. Collingwood†	15	25	3	646	88*	0	5	29.36	20
2005	D. M. Benkenstein	5	10	2	233	74*	0	2	29.12	5
	U. Arshad	5	6	0	170	83	0	1	28.33	1
	K. K. Jennings¶	14	26	1	707	127	2	1	28.28	7
	B. A. Stokes	13	24	2	615	127	1	3	27.95	10
	G. R. Breese	3	6	2	110	44	0	0	27.50	7
	M. A. Wood†	8	10	2	153	58*	0	1	19.12	1
	C. D. Thorp	7	11	2	147	27	0	0	16.33	1
	J. Harrison	4	4	0	60	35	0	0	15.00	0
	G. Onions†‡	12	17	5	148	27	0	0	12.33	2
	C. Rushworth†	14	20	8	107	18*	0	0	8.91	4

Also batted: R. S. Buckley† (2 matches) 6, 4 (1 ct); M. E. Claydon (1 match) 18*, 12* (1 ct).

† *Born in Durham.* ‡ *ECB contract.* ¶ *Non-England-qualified player.* *Durham ceased to award caps after 2005.*

BOWLING

	Style	O	M	R	W	BB	5I	Avge
U. Arshad	RFM	73.1	16	249	16	3-16	0	15.56
G. Onions	RFM	419.1	87	1,292	70	7-62	5	18.45
C. Rushworth	RFM	402.2	99	1,202	54	6-58	3	22.25
C. D. Thorp	RFM	169.5	59	341	15	3-29	0	22.73
J. Harrison	LFM	96.1	20	336	14	5-31	1	24.00
M. A. Wood	RFM	209.4	38	650	27	5-44	1	24.07
B. A. Stokes	RFM	327.4	50	1,116	42	4-49	0	26.57
R. S. Buckley	OB	114.2	21	344	10	5-86	1	34.40
S. G. Borthwick	LBG	266.4	35	1,064	28	6-70	1	38.00

Also bowled: D. M. Benkenstein (RM/OB) 1–0–1–0; G. R. Breese (OB) 53–18–117–4; M. E. Claydon (RFM) 18.5–2–56–6; P. D. Collingwood (RM/OB) 35.4–14–73–1; K. K. Jennings (RM) 11.2–0–48–2; P. Mustard (LBG) 1.1–0–9–1; W. R. Smith (OB) 34.2–5–137–4.

LEADING YB40 AVERAGES (100 runs/4 wickets)

Batting	Runs	HS	Avge	SR	Ct/St
W. R. Smith	248	120*	62.00	111.71	1
G. J. Muchall	242	57*	48.40	96.80	2
B. A. Stokes	290	87	32.22	97.31	9
M. D. Stoneman	302	85	30.20	95.87	5
P. Mustard	329	92	29.90	100.61	10/3
P. Collingwood	239	79	29.87	80.20	3
S. G. Borthwick	177	80	22.12	84.68	4

Bowling	W	BB	Avge	ER
W. R. Smith	4	2-19	13.00	5.20
P. D. Collingwood	12	3-5	14.08	5.20
G. Onions	10	4-45	17.90	3.97
C. Rushworth	20	5-42	20.35	5.63
G. R. Breese	6	4-33	25.83	4.58
M. A. Wood	12	3-23	26.16	5.50
B. A. Stokes	11	3-50	30.00	5.48

LEADING FLt20 AVERAGES (100 runs/18 overs)

Batting	Runs	HS	Avge	SR	Ct/St	Bowling	W	BB	Avge	ER
G. R. Breese....	126	32	31.50	**185.29**	2	W. R. Smith	6	2-20	18.00	**5.68**
B. A. Stokes ...	328	72*	46.85	**153.27**	2	G. Onions	4	2-23	30.50	**6.42**
G. J. Muchall ...	274	66*	45.66	**137.00**	4	G. R. Breese	8	2-31	27.62	**7.36**
P. Mustard	379	91	34.45	**123.45**	2/3	C. Rushworth ...	13	3-19	22.84	**7.64**
M. D. Stoneman	185	51	16.81	**110.77**	7	R. D. Pringle....	10	2-13	24.50	**7.65**
S. G. Borthwick .	232	62	21.09	**104.97**	4	B. A. Stokes	6	2-27	43.16	**7.73**

FIRST-CLASS COUNTY RECORDS

Highest score for	273	M. L. Love v Hampshire at Chester-le-Street....	2003
Highest score against	501*	B. C. Lara (Warwickshire) at Birmingham	1994
Leading run-scorer	9,055	D. M. Benkenstein (avge 45.96)	**2005–13**
Best bowling for	10-47	O. D. Gibson v Hampshire at Chester-le-Street ..	2007
Best bowling against	9-36	M. S. Kasprowicz (Glamorgan) at Cardiff	2003
Leading wicket-taker	518	S. J. E. Brown (avge 28.30)	1992–2002
Highest total for	648-5 dec	v Nottinghamshire at Chester-le-Street.........	2009
Highest total against	810-4 dec	by Warwickshire at Birmingham	1994
Lowest total for	67	v Middlesex at Lord's.....................	1996
Lowest total against	18	by Durham MCCU at Chester-le-Street	2012

LIST A COUNTY RECORDS

Highest score for	150*	B. A. Stokes v Warwickshire at Birmingham....	2011
Highest score against	151*	M. P. Maynard (Glamorgan) at Darlington	1991
Leading run-scorer	4,956	P. D. Collingwood (avge 31.56)	**1995–2013**
Best bowling for	7-32	S. P. Davis v Lancashire at Chester-le-Street	1983
Best bowling against	6-22	A. Dale (Glamorgan) at Colwyn Bay	1993
Leading wicket-taker	298	N. Killeen (avge 23.96)	1995–2010
Highest total for	332-4	v Worcestershire at Chester-le-Street	2007
Highest total against	361-7	by Essex at Chelmsford	1996
Lowest total for	72	v Warwickshire at Birmingham	2002
Lowest total against	63	by Hertfordshire at Darlington	1964

TWENTY20 COUNTY RECORDS

Highest score for	91	P. Mustard v Yorkshire at Chester-le-Street	**2013**
Highest score against	100	M. B. Loye (Lancashire) at Manchester	2005
Leading run-scorer	2,317	P. Mustard (avge 25.18)	**2003–13**
Best bowling for	5-6	P. D. Collingwood v Northants at Chester-le-St....	2011
Best bowling against	5-16	R. M. Pyrah (Yorkshire) at Scarborough	2011
Leading wicket-taker	81	G. R. Breese (avge 22.06)	**2004–13**
Highest total for	225-2	v Leicestershire at Chester-le-Street	2010
Highest total against	213-4	by Nottinghamshire at Nottingham..............	2011
Lowest total for	93	v Kent at Canterbury......................	2009
Lowest total against	47	by Northamptonshire at Chester-le-Street	2011

ADDRESS

Emirates Durham International Cricket Ground, Riverside, Chester-le-Street, County Durham DH3 3QR (0191 387 1717; **email** reception@durhamccc.co.uk). **Website** www.durhamccc.co.uk

OFFICIALS

Captain (Championship) P. D. Collingwood　　　　**Chairman** C. W. Leach
　　　　(limited-overs) M. D. Stoneman　　　　**Chief operating officer** R. Dowson
Director of cricket G. Cook　　　　**Chief executive** D. Harker
First-team coach J. J. B. Lewis　　　　**Head groundsman** D. Measor
Academy coach J. B. Windows　　　　**Scorer** B. Hunt

DURHAM v DURHAM MCCU

At Chester-le-Street, April 5–7. Drawn. Toss: Durham. First-class debuts: C. Bishnoi, R. D. Cox, I. H. Hobson, O. J. Steele.

A maiden first-class hundred for Jennings and Stokes's seventh were the highlights of a match which began in temperatures barely above freezing; having had no outdoor practice, the county were just glad of a workout. With little life in the pitch, there was never any danger of the students being bowled out for 18, as they had been the previous year, and they lost only five wickets batting out the last two sessions. Borthwick's leg-spin claimed three in each innings to go with the 99 he scored on the first day, when he was bowled going for a big shot in the final over. Jennings and Will Smith extended Durham's lead to 494, reaching their centuries in the same over.

Close of play: first day, Durham 426-9 (Onions 21); second day, Durham 101-1 (Jennings 35, Smith 27).

Durham

M. D. Stoneman c Watkins b Cox	19	– (2) b Green	38
K. K. Jennings b Green	13	– (1) not out	102
W. R. Smith c Steele b Cox	2	– not out	101
*D. M. Benkenstein b van den Bergh	34		
B. A. Stokes c Hobson b Cox	111		
M. J. Richardson b Wallis	29		
†P. Mustard c Hobson b Green	60		
S. G. Borthwick b Patel	99		
C. D. Thorp b Wallis	10		
G. Onions not out	21		
B 9, l-b 11, w 2, n-b 6	28	B 1, l-b 2	3

1/34 (1) 2/38 (3)   (9 wkts dec, 105.4 overs) 426   1/62 (2)   (1 wkt dec, 58 overs) 244
3/40 (2) 4/126 (4)
5/171 (6) 6/252 (5) 7/331 (7) 8/350 (9) 9/426 (8)

C. Rushworth did not bat.

Wallis 20–1–101–2; Green 25–6–60–2; Cox 13–3–49–3; van den Bergh 19–2–65–1; Watkins 19–1–80–0; Bishnoi 6–0–39–0; Patel 3.4–0–12–1. *Second innings*—Wallis 14–1–61–0; Green 8–2–33–1; van den Bergh 13–1–41–0; Cox 5–1–22–0; Watkins 9–2–33–0; Patel 6–0–34–0; Bishnoi 3–0–17–0.

Durham MCCU

*C. R. Jones lbw b Onions	0	– b Borthwick	43
I. H. Hobson c Onions b Rushworth	1	– lbw b Thorp	13
R. A. C. Shah c Mustard b Thorp	28	– not out	57
R. D. Cox c Mustard b Stokes	5	– c Thorp b Stokes	15
C. Bishnoi lbw b Borthwick	60	– lbw b Borthwick	0
L. A. Patel lbw b Thorp	25	– c Jennings b Borthwick	0
†O. J. Steele c Mustard b Smith	14	– not out	5
N. A. T. Watkins c Smith b Borthwick	15		
F. O. E. van den Bergh c Smith b Borthwick	2		
C. A. Wallis c Stokes b Smith	10		
M. J. E. Green not out	0		
B 1, l-b 9, n-b 6	16	B 5, l-b 5, n-b 8	18

1/0 (1) 2/12 (2) 3/39 (3)   (82.2 overs) 176   1/42 (2)   (5 wkts, 58 overs) 151
4/39 (4) 5/121 (6) 6/140 (5)   2/74 (1) 3/125 (4)
7/154 (7) 8/157 (9) 9/168 (8) 10/176 (10)   4/131 (5) 5/143 (6)

Onions 9–3–14–1; Rushworth 12–3–29–1; Stokes 14–4–28–1; Thorp 12–5–15–2; Borthwick 17–3–50–3; Smith 18.2–7–30–2. *Second innings*—Onions 9–2–30–0; Rushworth 9–3–9–0; Stokes 10–5–27–1; Thorp 9–4–22–1; Borthwick 14–5–26–3; Benkenstein 4–0–18–0; Smith 3–0–9–0.

Umpires: J. H. Evans and R. J. Evans.

DURHAM v SOMERSET

At Chester-le-Street, April 10–13. Durham won by 48 runs. Durham 18.5pts (after 2.5pt penalty), Somerset 3pts. Toss: Somerset.

A game of batting collapses concluded when Somerset – well placed at 130 for two in pursuit of 235 – lost eight for 56, surpassing their first-innings slide of seven for 51, to surrender the match. Durham had fared little better, but at least recovered from 94 for five on the first day thanks to the application of Stokes, who later added a watchful second-innings 22 to partially salvage a scoreboard reading 20 for four; he then added three wickets to undermine Somerset's promising run-chase. A career-best six from Rushworth had dismissed Somerset for 132 on the second day, when 18 wickets fell in 78 overs. Onions took the first three, but Rushworth cleaned up either side of lunch. Despite the chill, each of Durham's three slips held two good catches. Five of their batsmen then edged behind in dreary conditions. It was much more pleasant on the final morning, when Somerset resumed on 96 for two. Kieswetter, who scored the game's only fifty, added 34 with Hildreth in the first half-hour, before Durham's seamers bowled them to victory. The two batting points they had picked up earlier felt like a bonus after collecting only one in their first five games in 2012 – though they were wiped out by a penalty for breaching team payment regulations in that season.

Close of play: first day, Durham 250; second day, Durham 92-8 (Mustard 23, Onions 5); third day, Somerset 96-2 (Kieswetter 39, Hildreth 12).

Durham

M. D. Stoneman b Kirby	24	– (2) c Kieswetter b Trego	2
K. K. Jennings b Thomas	28	– (1) b Trego	5
W. R. Smith c Trescothick b Trego	1	– b Trego	0
D. M. Benkenstein c Kieswetter b Thomas	0	– c Kieswetter b Kirby	8
B. A. Stokes c Kieswetter b Dockrell	49	– c Kieswetter b Thomas	22
*P. D. Collingwood lbw b Trego	11	– lbw b Thomas	11
†P. Mustard c and b Dockrell	39	– run out	25
S. G. Borthwick b Kirby	45	– c Trego b Thomas	3
C. D. Thorp b Trego	23	– c Kieswetter b Overton	6
G. Onions c Kieswetter b Kirby	7	– not out	9
C. Rushworth not out	0	– c Kieswetter b Thomas	18
L-b 16, w 3, n-b 4	23	B 1, l-b 5, w 1	7

1/31 (1) 2/38 (3) 3/43 (4) (93.2 overs) 250
4/68 (2) 5/94 (6) 6/154 (5)
7/173 (8) 8/222 (9) 9/243 (10) 10/250 (8)

1/3 (2) 2/5 (3) (47.4 overs) 116
3/16 (1) 4/20 (4)
5/48 (6) 6/54 (5) 7/68 (8)
8/77 (9) 9/94 (7) 10/116 (11)

Trego 26–6–59–3; Kirby 24.2–8–58–3; Thomas 14–3–38–2; Overton 17–3–57–0; Dockrell 12–3–22–2. *Second innings*—Trego 12–5–24–3; Kirby 9–2–17–1; Thomas 14.4–3–29–4; Overton 12–1–40–1.

Somerset

*M. E. Trescothick c Stokes b Onions	6	– b Stokes	22
A. V. Suppiah c Collingwood b Onions	5	– lbw b Onions	17
†C. Kieswetter c Collingwood b Rushworth	21	– b Stokes	72
J. C. Hildreth c Borthwick b Onions	18	– b Onions	27
J. C. Buttler b Rushworth	35	– lbw b Rushworth	0
A. W. R. Barrow b Rushworth	2	– c Mustard b Onions	2
P. D. Trego c Borthwick b Rushworth	0	– lbw b Thorp	12
A. C. Thomas lbw b Rushworth	0	– lbw b Stokes	1
J. Overton not out	21	– c Borthwick b Thorp	0
G. H. Dockrell b Onions	0	– not out	1
S. P. Kirby c Stokes b Rushworth	0	– b Benkenstein b Rushworth	10
L-b 5, n-b 10	15	B 9, l-b 3, n-b 10	22

1/12 (1) 2/13 (2) 3/39 (4) (37.5 overs) 132
4/81 (3) 5/87 (6) 6/87 (7)
7/103 (8) 8/122 (5) 9/129 (10) 10/132 (11)

1/31 (2) 2/74 (1) (63.5 overs) 186
3/116 (3) 4/131 (5)
5/134 (6) 6/151 (7) 7/152 (8)
8/161 (9) 9/175 (3) 10/186 (11)

Onions 14–3–41–4; Rushworth 13.5–1–58–6; Stokes 5–1–23–0; Thorp 5–1–5–0. *Second innings*—Onions 17–2–65–3; Rushworth 14.5–2–46–2; Thorp 17–7–29–2; Stokes 14–4–34–3; Borthwick 1–1–0–0.

Umpires: D. J. Millns and S. J. O'Shaughnessy.

At Birmingham, April 17–20. DURHAM lost to WARWICKSHIRE by 318 runs.

DURHAM v YORKSHIRE

At Chester-le-Street, April 24–27. Yorkshire won by four wickets. Yorkshire 19pts, Durham 4pts. Toss: Durham.

Root played one of the finest innings seen at Chester-le-Street after Collingwood left Yorkshire a day plus seven overs to score 336. They lost two wickets in the final morning's fifth over, but Root's serene progress to 182 was threatened only by a tight run-out call on 87. The scores were level when he was bowled, after a 101-run stand with Rashid, with 6.2 overs left; Bresnan hit his first ball for four. Yorkshire's total was a fourth-innings record at Riverside, and their fourth-highest successful run-chase. A rainbreak had forced Collingwood's hand the previous day, but he thought it was a safe declaration – especially after Yorkshire had slipped to 177 first time round, when Onions singlehandedly removed their top six, including Root for a classy 49 and the run-out of Jaques. "It surprised me how flat the pitch became," said Collingwood. Durham had been reliant on Mustard and the tail to more than double the score from 112 for seven on the first day, but openers Stoneman and Jennings atoned on the third, raising 123 after their previous three partnerships had registered only five; Stoneman survived a straightforward chance to Bairstow on 11, and went on to reach his century.

Close of play: first day, Yorkshire 57-3 (Root 30); second day, Yorkshire 177; third day, Yorkshire 17-0 (Lyth 9, Root 6).

Durham

M. D. Stoneman c Plunkett b Sidebottom	6	– c Ballance b Plunkett	109
K. K. Jennings b Bresnan	0	– c Bairstow b Bresnan	48
W. R. Smith c Sidebottom b Bresnan	42	– c Root b Bresnan	4
D. M. Benkenstein c Root b Patterson	40	– not out	61
B. A. Stokes c Bairstow b Bresnan	2	– c Bairstow b Plunkett	7
*P. D. Collingwood b Bresnan	0	– not out	36
†P. Mustard b Rashid	70		
S. G. Borthwick lbw b Plunkett	1		
C. D. Thorp b Rashid	21		
G. Onions run out	27		
C. Rushworth not out	7		
B 3, l-b 16, n-b 2	21	B 4, l-b 6	10

1/2 (2) 2/8 (1) 3/94 (3)   (73.4 overs) 237   1/123 (2)   (4 wkts dec, 78 overs) 275
4/96 (5) 5/98 (4) 6/104 (6)   2/127 (3) 3/195 (1)
7/112 (8) 8/153 (9) 9/197 (10) 10/237 (7)   4/207 (5)

Sidebottom 16–6–27–1; Bresnan 20–6–41–4; Plunkett 10–1–67–1; Patterson 21–7–44–1; Rashid 6.4–0–39–2. *Second innings*—Sidebottom 9–2–23–0; Bresnan 16–3–70–2; Patterson 10–1–38–0; Plunkett 16–4–49–2; Rashid 22–1–81–0; Root 5–2–4–0.

Yorkshire

A. Lyth b Onions	0	– c Mustard b Rushworth 9
J. E. Root b Onions	49	– b Thorp 182
P. A. Jaques run out	0	– c Mustard b Rushworth 0
*A. W. Gale lbw b Onions	25	– c Collingwood b Jennings 39
†J. M. Bairstow c Stoneman b Onions	16	– c Rushworth b Stokes 26
G. S. Ballance c Mustard b Onions	5	– c Mustard b Stokes 21
A. U. Rashid lbw b Stokes	25	– not out 50
T. T. Bresnan c Collingwood b Rushworth	10	– not out 4
L. E. Plunkett not out	25	
R. J. Sidebottom c Jennings b Stokes	7	
S. A. Patterson b Stokes	7	
L-b 6, n-b 2	8	N-b 8 8

1/0 (1) 2/13 (3) 3/57 (4)   (55.3 overs) 177   1/23 (1)   (6 wkts, 96.5 overs) 339
4/96 (2) 5/97 (5) 6/107 (6)   2/23 (3) 3/103 (4)
7/132 (7) 8/136 (8) 9/161 (10) 10/177 (11)   4/162 (5) 5/234 (6) 6/335 (2)

Onions 19–3–63–5; Rushworth 15–4–49–1; Thorp 12–3–33–0; Stokes 9.3–2–26–3. *Second innings*—Onions 20–7–59–0; Rushworth 20–7–36–2; Stokes 15.5–4–38–1; Stokes 20–1–99–2; Borthwick 15.4–0–84–0; Jennings 2–0–5–1; Smith 3.2–1–18–0.

Umpires: J. H. Evans and A. G. Wharf.

At Nottingham, April 29–May 2. DURHAM beat NOTTINGHAMSHIRE by six wickets.

At The Oval, May 10–13. DURHAM beat SURREY by five wickets.

DURHAM v MIDDLESEX

At Chester-le-Street, May 22–25. Drawn. Durham 8pts, Middlesex 6pts. Toss: Middlesex.
    Since rain caused him to set a generous target against Yorkshire, Collingwood was more cautious after losing the equivalent of a day here, eventually setting Middlesex 304 in 51 overs. Hopes of a third successive win rose when Onions then had them five down as the final hour began, but Denly held out. With Tim Murtagh on Ireland duty, the Middlesex bowling had lacked purpose on the first morning after Durham were put in. It improved after lunch, as 108 for one became 149 for five, but Mustard's 62 earned him two batting points, whereas five wickets for Onions denied Middlesex even one. Rain and hail peppered the second day, and only 18 overs were bowled on the third, when umpire Sharp wore gloves. It was a glorious morning, however, when Durham resumed, 152 ahead with nine wickets standing. But they added only 88 before lunch and batted on for 13 overs afterwards. Borthwick, promoted to No. 3 in the previous game at The Oval, reached an unbeaten 82, Durham's highest score from that position in 22 Championship matches since September 2011.
    Close of play: first day, Middlesex 11-2 (Denly 4, Smith 2); second day, Durham 37-0 (Stoneman 31, Jennings 6); third day, Durham 89-1 (Jennings 28, Borthwick 11).

Durham

M. D. Stoneman c Simpson b Collymore	5	– lbw b Harris	50
K. K. Jennings lbw b Collymore	38	– c Denly b Berg	35
S. G. Borthwick c Simpson b Berg	52	– not out	82
W. R. Smith c Malan b Berg	37	– c Malan b Roland-Jones	17
B. A. Stokes c Simpson b Harris	19	– lbw b Roland-Jones	4
*P. D. Collingwood c Berg b Harris	1	– c Robson b Harris	18
†P. Mustard c Roland-Jones b Harris	62	– c Collymore b Berg	3
G. R. Breese c Simpson b Dexter	9	– not out	20
C. D. Thorp b Collymore	4		
M. A. Wood lbw b Collymore	0		
G. Onions not out	0		
L-b 13, n-b 14, p 5	32	L-b 9, n-b 2	11

1/7 (1) 2/108 (3) 3/114 (2)   (85.2 overs) 259
4/145 (5) 5/149 (6) 6/204 (4)
7/230 (8) 8/245 (9) 9/245 (10) 10/259 (7)

1/68 (1)   (6 wkts dec, 72 overs) 240
2/98 (3) 3/147 (4)
4/154 (5) 5/194 (6) 6/200 (7)

Harris 18.2–3–46–3; Collymore 19.5–61–4; Berg 18–3–42–2; Roland-Jones 17–5–52–0; Smith 5–0–25–0; Dexter 8–0–15–1. *Second innings*—Collymore 11–3–36–0; Harris 24–2–83–2; Roland-Jones 12–2–46–2; Berg 25–6–66–2.

Middlesex

*C. J. L. Rogers lbw b Thorp	3	– lbw b Wood	54
S. D. Robson b Onions	0	– c Mustard b Thorp	7
J. L. Denly c Borthwick b Onions	9	– not out	73
T. M. J. Smith lbw b Stokes	19		
D. J. Malan lbw b Onions	0	– (4) b Wood	5
N. J. Dexter c Mustard b Stokes	52	– (5) c Mustard b Onions	6
†J. A. Simpson c Thorp b Onions	42	– (6) c Borthwick b Onions	4
G. K. Berg c Collingwood b Onions	6	– (7) c Jennings b Wood	8
J. A. R. Harris c Breese b Borthwick	37	– (8) not out	1
T. S. Roland-Jones c Onions b Wood	19		
C. D. Collymore not out	0		
B 1, l-b 7, w 1	9	B 1, l-b 2, n-b 4	7

1/1 (2) 2/3 (1) 3/25 (3)   (68.2 overs) 196
4/31 (5) 5/35 (4) 6/103 (7)
7/119 (8) 8/151 (6) 9/196 (9) 10/196 (10)

1/12 (2)   (6 wkts, 50.3 overs) 165
2/96 (1) 3/106 (4)
4/115 (5) 5/129 (6) 6/158 (7)

Onions 20–5–39–5; Thorp 17–5–29–1; Stokes 14–1–63–2; Wood 14.2–1–46–1; Borthwick 3–0–11–1. *Second innings*—Onions 16–3–44–2; Thorp 7–4–10–1; Stokes 7–1–28–0; Wood 13.3–2–36–3; Borthwick 7–0–44–0.

Umpires: M. J. D. Bodenham and G. Sharp.

At Taunton, June 6–9. DURHAM drew with SOMERSET.

DURHAM v WARWICKSHIRE

At Chester-le-Street, June 12–14. Durham won by 11 runs. Durham 21pts, Warwickshire 4pts. Toss: Durham.

Durham pulled off a thrilling win on the third evening of a match dominated by two New Zealand-born all-rounders. Stokes, who left Christchurch aged 12, took the final wicket, his seventh in all alongside a first-innings 61. But Patel, the Test player from Wellington, almost stole the game with his second fifty, after five vital wickets. Needing 257 to win, Warwickshire were 146 for seven when he came in and added 86 with Javid, bringing the target down to 25. Then Javid edged to second slip, Patel lofted a slower ball to long-on – giving Onions another five-wicket haul – and Stokes pinned Rankin lbw. There was some variable bounce in a pitch which yielded 17 wickets on a cloudy second day; several Warwickshire batsmen, including Troughton, surrendered carelessly, as though they did not trust it. For Durham, Stoneman rose majestically above the shambles, scoring 83 of the first 127 runs in their second innings, and next morning they were indebted to Richardson, who made 55 and shared a last-wicket stand of 42 with Rushworth.

Close of play: first day, Warwickshire 31-1 (Chopra 24); second day, Durham 152-8 (Richardson 26, Wood 2).

Durham

M. D. Stoneman c Ambrose b Barker	0	– b Rankin	83
K. K. Jennings c Patel b Barker	33	– c Clarke b Patel	11
S. G. Borthwick c Troughton b Clarke	36	– c Chopra b Rankin	2
W. R. Smith c Clarke b Patel	45	– c Westwood b Patel	4
B. A. Stokes b Patel	61	– run out	5
*P. D. Collingwood c Chopra b Patel	1	– lbw b Clarke	7
†P. Mustard c Chopra b Clarke	0	– c Patel b Clarke	0
M. J. Richardson lbw b Clarke	26	– c Javid b Rankin	55
M. A. Wood b Barker	22	– (10) b Wright	3
G. Onions not out	22	– (9) b Rankin	5
C. Rushworth c Ambrose b Barker	0	– not out	13
B 1, l-b 11, w 1, n-b 8	21	L-b 7, w 1, n-b 2	10

1/0 (1) 2/62 (3) 3/98 (2) (86.5 overs) 267
4/163 (4) 5/169 (6) 6/170 (7)
7/198 (5) 8/224 (8) 9/267 (9) 10/267 (11)

1/49 (2) 2/52 (3) (60.2 overs) 198
3/57 (4) 4/90 (5)
5/106 (6) 6/106 (7)
7/127 (1) 8/147 (9)
9/156 (10) 10/198 (8)

Barker 19.5–3–41–4; Wright 17–2–63–0; Clarke 19–7–37–3; Rankin 10–0–42–0; Patel 20–4–68–3; Javid 1–0–4–0. *Second innings*—Barker 12–2–22–0; Wright 12–0–55–1; Clarke 7–2–17–2; Patel 16–4–42–2; Rankin 13.2–0–55–4.

Warwickshire

V. Chopra c Richardson b Rushworth	35	– lbw b Onions	18
I. J. Westwood c Rushworth b Onions	5	– c Mustard b Wood	21
W. T. S. Porterfield c Borthwick b Rushworth	24	– b Onions	0
*J. O. Troughton c Mustard b Stokes	21	– c Stokes b Onions	13
†T. R. Ambrose b Wood	12	– b Stokes	46
A. Javid b Wood	6	– c Borthwick b Onions	44
R. Clarke c Smith b Stokes	8	– b Stokes	4
K. H. D. Barker lbw b Rushworth	31	– c Stoneman b Smith	13
J. S. Patel b Stokes	53	– c Jennings b Onions	50
C. J. C. Wright b Stokes	5	– not out	10
W. B. Rankin not out	1	– lbw b Stokes	1
B 1, l-b 3, n-b 4	8	L-b 6, w 5, n-b 14	25

1/31 (2) 2/59 (1) 3/76 (3) (57 overs) 209
4/102 (5) 5/106 (4) 6/116 (6)
7/116 (7) 8/188 (8) 9/208 (9) 10/209 (10)

1/26 (1) 2/26 (3) (63.2 overs) 245
3/56 (4) 4/74 (2)
5/127 (5) 6/131 (7)
7/146 (8) 8/232 (6)
9/235 (9) 10/245 (11)

Onions 14–2–65–1; Rushworth 17–6–38–3; Stokes 13–1–49–4; Wood 11–3–32–2; Borthwick 2–0–21–0. *Second innings*—Onions 20–2–83–5; Rushworth 9–3–20–0; Wood 8–0–39–1; Stokes 16.2–4–42–3; Smith 8–0–43–1; Borthwick 2–0–12–0.

Umpires: N. G. C. Cowley and M. J. Saggers.

DURHAM v DERBYSHIRE

At Chester-le-Street, July 8–11. Durham won by 279 runs. Durham 21pts, Derbyshire 3pts. Toss: Derbyshire.

Three outstanding performers brought Durham victory. Jennings followed a Championship-best 93 with 123, his highest first-class score; Borthwick recorded a fluent, career-best 117; and Rushworth celebrated his 27th birthday by completing his first ten-wicket haul. Derbyshire's decision to field seemed strange given that Onions might have bowled in the later stages if released from England's Ashes squad in time; in the event, Rushworth, nominated to stand down had Onions returned, claimed six for 64, leading a four-man seam attack which consistently hit the right length and swung the ball in warm conditions. Footitt had recorded his best figures, ending Durham's first innings with four wickets in 12 deliveries, but Derbyshire's batting was feeble as they folded for 113. Second time round, they were 49 for five, still 422 behind; Chanderpaul provided some resistance before Rushworth had him caught behind for the second time. Poynton scored a fifty on recall, but Durham needed only 16 balls on the last day to take the final three wickets. Thorp conceded 21 runs in 22 overs in the two innings.

Close of play: first day, Derbyshire 15-1 (Johnson 2, Madsen 13); second day, Durham 208-2 (Jennings 65, Smith 13); third day, Derbyshire 181-7 (Poynton 56, Clare 2).

Durham

*M. D. Stoneman c Johnson b Footitt	3	– lbw b Groenewald	10
K. K. Jennings lbw b Durston	93	– run out	123
S. G. Borthwick lbw b Footitt	22	– lbw b Redfern	117
W. R. Smith c Redfern b Groenewald	43	– c Poynton b Clare	22
M. J. Richardson c Poynton b Groenewald	5	– (6) c Clare b Wainwright	14
†P. Mustard c Clare b Footitt	52	– (7) b Wainwright	1
B. A. Stokes c Madsen b Durston	0	– (5) c Redfern b Clare	8
G. R. Breese c Clare b Footitt	14	– b Redfern	5
M. A. Wood not out	4	– lbw b Redfern	10
C. D. Thorp lbw b Footitt	0	– not out	11
C. Rushworth b Footitt	4		
B 6, l-b 5, n-b 2	13	B 5, l-b 2, w 3	10

1/4 (1) 2/52 (3) 3/122 (4)   (86 overs) 253   1/22 (1)   (9 wkts dec, 95.1 overs) 331
4/132 (5) 5/222 (2) 6/222 (7)   2/190 (3) 3/238 (4)
7/240 (8) 8/241 (6) 9/241 (10) 10/253 (11)   4/254 (5) 5/287 (6) 6/293 (7)
                                               7/306 (8) 8/310 (2) 9/331 (9)

Footitt 19–3–53–6; Groenewald 19–3–52–2; Clare 17–1–51–0; Wainwright 15–2–47–0; Durston 13–5–29–2; Redfern 3–0–10–0. *Second innings*—Footitt 18–3–58–0; Groenewald 17–3–52–1; Clare 12–1–51–2; Durston 13–3–51–0; Wainwright 22–2–79–2; Redfern 13.1–2–33–3.

Derbyshire

C. F. Hughes lbw b Rushworth	0	– c Richardson b Stokes	10
R. M. Johnson b Rushworth	6	– b Stokes	9
*W. L. Madsen c Mustard b Thorp	13	– c Mustard b Thorp	1
S. Chanderpaul c Mustard b Rushworth	14	– c Mustard b Rushworth	76
W. J. Durston c Mustard b Rushworth	16	– lbw b Rushworth	5
D. J. Redfern c Breese b Thorp	2	– c Breese b Rushworth	4
†T. Poynton c Mustard b Wood	1	– not out	58
D. J. Wainwright not out	18	– lbw b Breese	5
J. L. Clare c Smith b Rushworth	0	– c Mustard b Stokes	2
T. D. Groenewald c Stokes b Wood	17	– c Mustard b Rushworth	7
M. H. A. Footitt b Rushworth	16	– b Stokes	2
B 1, l-b 4, w 1, n-b 4	10	B 1, l-b 9, w 1, n-b 2	13

1/0 (1) 2/19 (2) 3/21 (3)   (41.4 overs) 113   1/19 (2) 2/20 (3)   (60.4 overs) 192
4/44 (5) 5/47 (6) 6/51 (7)   3/20 (1) 4/35 (5)
7/69 (4) 8/69 (9) 9/94 (10) 10/113 (11)   5/49 (6) 6/147 (4) 7/173 (8)
                                               8/182 (9) 9/189 (10) 10/192 (11)

Rushworth 14.4–2–64–6; Thorp 11–5–11–2; Stokes 7–2–15–0; Wood 9–3–18–2. *Second innings—* Rushworth 15–5–39–4; Thorp 11–4–10–1; Stokes 17.4–2–62–4; Wood 8–2–26–0; Breese 5–2–11–1; Borthwick 4–0–34–0.

Umpires: S. C. Gale and J. W. Lloyds.

At Lord's, August 2–4. DURHAM lost to MIDDLESEX by six wickets.

DURHAM v SURREY

At Chester-le-Street, August 22–25. Durham won by an innings and 144 runs. Durham 23pts, Surrey 2pts. Toss: Surrey. First-class debut: U. Arshad. County debut: H. M. Amla.

Just as Durham's season looked in danger of slipping off the rails, with one-day hopes quashed, their Championship challenge was hauled back on track. A resounding innings win, lifting them into second place behind Yorkshire, was a huge tonic for coach Geoff Cook, resuming his role two months after a heart attack. Without Stokes, on Lions duty, and the injured Onions and Thorp, academy products came to the fore. Borthwick's 135, his highest score, was followed by career-best returns for Harrison and Wood, while seamer Usman Arshad made a promising debut. Disappointed at missing the Oval Test, Tremlett responded with eight for 96, a personal best. Weak batting played its part, but Surrey were even more woeful, except when their new recruit Amla appeared to be on a different planet, with 89 off 110 balls, as they followed on; Mustard held six catches in the innings. Earlier, Wood's opening delivery had surprised Amla with its bounce, while left-arm Harrison swung the ball into the right-handers at good pace. After choosing to field, Surrey appeared demoralised when Borthwick added 183 with Will Smith. The stand was Durham's best against them for any wicket, as was the total of 421, which provided four home batting points for the first time in two years. On the second morning, local umpire Phil Raine stood at square leg after Mark Benson left because of a family illness.

Close of play: first day, Durham 309-5 (Collingwood 17, Harrison 1); second day, Surrey 97-6 (Davies 36, Batty 8); third day, Surrey 52-3 (Amla 32, de Bruyn 2).

Durham

M. D. Stoneman b Tremlett	8	M. A. Wood c Wilson b Tremlett	3
K. K. Jennings c de Bruyn b Tremlett	35	C. Rushworth c Wilson b Linley	4
S. G. Borthwick lbw b Tremlett	135		
W. R. Smith lbw b Tremlett	87	B 2, l-b 20, w 2, n-b 12	36
M. J. Richardson c Davies b Tremlett	7		
*P. D. Collingwood b Dernbach	36	1/9 (1) 2/77 (2) 3/260 (4) (131 overs) 421
J. Harrison c de Bruyn b Tremlett	10	4/270 (5) 5/307 (3) 6/331 (7)
†P. Mustard not out	45	7/348 (6) 8/392 (9)
U. Arshad c Davies b Tremlett	15	9/408 (10) 10/421 (11) 110 overs: 352-7

Dernbach 28–9–93–1; Tremlett 33–5–96–8; Linley 33–7–99–1; de Bruyn 25–6–66–0; Batty 11–2–29–0; Burns 1–0–16–0.

Surrey

R. J. Burns c Mustard b Harrison	3	– c Borthwick b Arshad	13
A. Harinath c Richardson b Rushworth	1	– b Harrison	0
H. M. Amla b Wood	14	– c Mustard b Rushworth	89
V. S. Solanki lbw b Harrison	9	– c Mustard b Arshad	0
Z. de Bruyn b Arshad	21	– c Richardson b Wood	12
†S. M. Davies not out	41	– c Mustard b Wood	25
G. C. Wilson c Mustard b Arshad	0	– c Mustard b Wood	7
*G. J. Batty c Stoneman b Rushworth	8	– c Mustard b Wood	0
C. T. Tremlett lbw b Harrison	3	– c Mustard b Harrison	0
T. E. Linley lbw b Harrison	0	– c Smith b Wood	8
J. W. Dernbach b Harrison	0	– not out	0
B 1, l-b 1, n-b 6	8	B 9, l-b 2, n-b 4	15

1/5 (1) 2/5 (2) 3/20 (4)   (31.4 overs) 108
4/36 (3) 5/83 (5) 6/83 (7)
7/103 (8) 8/106 (9) 9/108 (10) 10/108 (11)

1/2 (2) 2/33 (1)   (50.5 overs) 169
3/33 (4) 4/101 (5)
5/137 (3) 6/156 (6) 7/156 (8)
8/159 (7) 9/159 (9) 10/169 (10)

Rushworth 11–2–31–2; Harrison 10.4–3–31–5; Wood 7–1–35–1; Arshad 3–1–9–2. *Second innings—* Rushworth 14–3–41–1; Harrison 13–1–43–2; Wood 13.5–4–44–5; Arshad 8–4–25–2; Collingwood 1–0–4–0; Jennings 1–0–1–0.

Umpires: M. R. Benson and M. A. Gough. P. W. Raine and later P. K. Baldwin replaced Benson on the second day.

At Scarborough, August 28–31. DURHAM beat YORKSHIRE by seven wickets.

DURHAM v SUSSEX

At Chester-le-Street, September 3–5. Durham won by 285 runs. Durham 20pts, Sussex 3pts. Toss: Durham. First-class debut: H. Z. Finch.

A two-and-a-half-day win over third-placed Sussex took Durham top of the table. Both teams were depleted. The Ireland–England international deprived Durham of Stokes, and Sussex of Jordan, Wright and Joyce; the visitors were also missing Machan (playing for Scotland against Australia) and Prior (rested by England), while home seamers Wood, Harrison and Thorp were injured. Onions, though, had recovered, and collected seven wickets, while Claydon, recalled from his loan to Kent, took six in what proved his farewell appearance: Kent signed him full-time for 2014. Arshad seized his opportunity, reaching 30 twice in conditions favouring seam, as well as taking three cheap wickets in each innings. On the first day Stoneman survived some superb bowling by the luckless Magoffin to score a capable 96 on a pitch which would produce only one more fifty – a careful second-innings 73 from Mustard. Sussex managed just 112 and 116: Gatting failed to make the most of his recall, Hamilton-Brown looked out of sorts, and the lower order contributed little.

Close of play: first day, Sussex 60-3 (Wells 13, Anyon 10); second day, Durham 212-6 (Mustard 57, Arshad 16).

Durham

M. D. Stoneman b Hatchett	96	– lbw b Anyon	21
K. K. Jennings lbw b Anyon	2	– c Nash b Magoffin	10
S. G. Borthwick c Brown b Magoffin	9	– c Brown b Anyon	10
W. R. Smith c Yardy b Anyon	32	– c Brown b Hatchett	22
M. J. Richardson lbw b Anyon	31	– c Brown b Magoffin	20
*P. D. Collingwood c b Hatchett	1	– lbw b Nash	45
†P. Mustard c Finch b Hatchett	5	– c Gatting b Anyon	73
U. Arshad lbw b Magoffin	30	– c Beer b Anyon	34
M. E. Claydon not out	18	– not out	12
C. Rushworth b Magoffin	0	– not out	8
G. Onions c Beer b Anyon	3		
B 1, l-b 13, n-b 4	18	B 4, l-b 5, w 2, n-b 2	13

1/16 (2) 2/55 (3) 3/122 (4)	(71.4 overs) 245	1/27 (2) (8 wkts dec, 79.4 overs) 268	
4/154 (1) 5/164 (6) 6/170 (7)		2/31 (1) 3/54 (3)	
7/224 (5) 8/226 (8) 9/226 (10) 10/245 (11)		4/84 (4) 5/90 (5)	
		6/183 (6) 7/244 (7) 8/251 (8)	

Magoffin 23–9–57–3; Anyon 23.4–6–87–4; Hatchett 16–2–56–3; Finch 4–0–15–0; Beer 4–0–14–0; Nash 1–0–2–0. *Second innings*—Magoffin 16–4–42–2; Anyon 20.4–4–79–4; Hatchett 18–0–91–1; Gatting 3–0–7–0; Beer 10–1–19–0; Nash 12–5–21–1.

Sussex

*C. D. Nash c Collingwood b Onions	19	– (2) lbw b Claydon	38
L. W. P. Wells c Mustard b Onions	17	– (1) c Borthwick b Onions	4
M. H. Yardy lbw b Onions	0	– lbw b Claydon	25
J. S. Gatting b Claydon	16	– c Mustard b Arshad	5
J. E. Anyon c and b Claydon	19	– (10) not out	6
R. J. Hamilton-Brown c Mustard b Onions	4	– (5) c Mustard b Claydon	1
H. Z. Finch lbw b Arshad	11	– (6) lbw b Arshad	3
†B. C. Brown not out	21	– (7) lbw b Rushworth	6
W. A. T. Beer c Mustard b Arshad	0	– (8) lbw b Arshad	0
S. J. Magoffin c Mustard b Arshad	0	– (9) c Jennings b Onions	20
L. J. Hatchett b Claydon	0	– c Borthwick b Onions	1
W 1, n-b 4	5	L-b 4, w 1, n-b 2	7

1/28 (1) 2/28 (3) 3/48 (4)	(44.5 overs) 112	1/4 (1) 2/52 (3)	(39.3 overs) 116
4/69 (2) 5/75 (6) 6/81 (5)		3/71 (2) 4/73 (5)	
7/103 (7) 8/111 (9) 9/111 (10) 10/112 (11)		5/77 (4) 6/82 (6) 7/82 (8)	
		8/104 (9) 9/110 (7) 10/116 (11)	

Onions 14–4–50–4; Rushworth 14–5–21–0; Arshad 8–2–16–3; Claydon 8.5–0–25–3. *Second innings*—Onions 10.3–2–38–3; Rushworth 9–5–20–1; Borthwick 2–0–5–0; Claydon 10–2–31–3; Arshad 8–3–18–3.

Umpires: N. G. C. Cowley and S. A. Garratt.

At Derby, September 11–14. DURHAM beat DERBYSHIRE by nine wickets.

DURHAM v NOTTINGHAMSHIRE

At Chester-le-Street, September 17–19. Durham won by eight wickets. Durham 21pts, Nottinghamshire 3pts. Toss: Nottinghamshire.

Durham clinched their third Championship title in six seasons on the third afternoon. Rain delayed play until 1.30, but they needed only an hour to score the 62 still needed for their fifth consecutive victory, and tenth in all. The match had begun with a rush, too. It was due to start at 10.15 each morning, because Nottinghamshire wanted to leave an hour early for the YB40 final at Lord's the day after the scheduled finish. Yet they chose to bat – the first county visiting Chester-le-Street in 2013 to do so – and slumped to 42 for six against Onions and Rushworth, before subsiding for 78 inside two hours. Durham's top order struggled too, with the ball doing just enough to find the edge;

Adams took four for 27 in a 13-over spell. But from 74 for six Collingwood and Mustard launched the recovery in a stand of 121. Mustard played freely for 77, while Collingwood gave a masterclass in survival, shepherding the tail to two batting points during a season's-best 88 not out. Nottinghamshire reached 246 second time around, thanks to half-centuries from Mullaney and Hussey, the last of three victims for Stokes to wrap up the innings. After seizing five wickets in the final one-day international against Australia on the eve of this game, Stokes underwent a hamstring scan at 8am the following morning, drove 310 miles from Southampton to join his team, scored a two-ball duck, then left the field twice with a painful toe – but finally played his part in the title triumph.

Close of play: first day, Durham 207-8 (Collingwood 53, Harrison 0); second day, Durham 7-0 (Stoneman 6, Jennings 1).

Nottinghamshire

S. J. Mullaney c Borthwick b Rushworth	6	– lbw b Onions 72
M. H. Wessels lbw b Onions	17	– c Richardson b Rushworth 11
M. J. Lumb c Mustard b Onions	8	– lbw b Onions 28
J. W. A. Taylor lbw b Rushworth	6	– b Rushworth 12
S. R. Patel c Mustard b Rushworth	0	– c Borthwick b Harrison 4
D. J. Hussey c Mustard b Onions	11	– b Stokes 57
*†C. M. W. Read b Harrison	11	– c Mustard b Onions 0
P. J. Franks c Collingwood b Harrison	9	– b Borthwick 29
A. R. Adams b Arshad	1	– c Jennings b Stokes 0
L. J. Fletcher c Jennings b Harrison	9	– c Rushworth b Stokes 20
H. F. Gurney not out	1	– not out 0
L-b 4, w 1, n-b 2	7	B 4, l-b 4, w 1, n-b 4 13

1/7 (1) 2/22 (3) 3/39 (2)   (26.3 overs) 78   1/24 (2) 2/79 (3)   (79.1 overs) 246
4/39 (4) 5/42 (5) 6/42 (6)   3/112 (4) 4/134 (1)
7/62 (7) 8/63 (9) 9/72 (10) 10/78 (8)   5/134 (5) 6/143 (7) 7/202 (8)
                                     8/203 (9) 9/235 (10) 10/246 (6)

Onions 9–2–30–3; Rushworth 9–3–24–3; Harrison 4.3–2–4–3; Arshad 4–0–16–1. *Second innings—* Onions 20–6–50–3; Rushworth 18–2–64–2; Stokes 16.3–2–55–3; Borthwick 7–3–14–1; Harrison 13–3–46–1; Collingwood 4.4–3–9–0.

Durham

M. D. Stoneman c Wessels b Fletcher	7	– not out 35
K. K. Jennings c Wessels b Adams	9	– lbw b Gurney 21
S. G. Borthwick c Read b Gurney	29	– c Franks b Gurney 0
W. R. Smith c Wessels b Adams	2	– not out 0
M. J. Richardson b Patel b Adams	10	
B. A. Stokes b Patel b Adams	0	
*P. D. Collingwood not out	88	
†P. Mustard b Mullaney	77	
G. Onions c Fletcher b Mullaney	6	
J. Harrison lbw b Mullaney	8	
C. Rushworth c Patel b Fletcher	6	
L-b 10, n-b 4	14	L-b 4, w 5, n-b 4 13

1/16 (2) 2/18 (1) 3/25 (4)   (81.4 overs) 256   1/57 (2)   (2 wkts, 17 overs) 69
4/45 (5) 5/45 (6) 6/74 (3)   2/61 (3)
7/195 (8) 8/207 (9) 9/239 (10) 10/256 (11)

Stokes replaced U. Arshad after returning from England duty.

Fletcher 18.4–6–63–2; Adams 28–5–69–4; Franks 6–1–20–0; Gurney 18–3–64–1; Mullaney 8–2–22–3; Patel 3–1–8–0. *Second innings—*Fletcher 5–0–15–0; Adams 5–0–17–0; Franks 4–0–19–0; Gurney 3–0–14–2.

Umpires: S. C. Gale and N. A. Mallender.

At Hove, September 24–27. DURHAM lost to SUSSEX by six wickets.

ESSEX

They thought it was all over

PAUL HISCOCK

So near, yet so far: that was probably the lament of the Essex administration as they looked back on a season in which the club came third in the second division of the Championship, reached Twenty20 finals day, and finished second in their YB40 group without qualifying for the knockout stage. But for Essex members and fans it went further: disappointment at one more summer of unfulfilled promise – and anger at the way the Championship season ended.

Essex arrived at the last match, against Hampshire, with a slim chance of overhauling Northamptonshire for the second promotion spot. Too slim, thought those in charge – and they fielded a weakened side. Predictably, they lost heavily; less predictably, Northamptonshire were also thrashed, at Worcester. Had Essex taken full points at the Rose Bowl, they would have gone up instead.

And so, after throwing in the towel prematurely, Essex were condemned to another season of second-division cricket. In truth, they were woefully inconsistent: coach Paul Grayson made a public apology early in the season after a miserable performance at Northampton, and might have felt inclined to issue another not long after, when Lancashire demolished them for 20 at Chelmsford. He settled for calling that collapse "a freak".

The star performer was Graham Napier who, at 33, enjoyed his best season. For once, he stayed clear of injury, and produced some magnificent all-round performances. He had long been a key member of the one-day side, but now shone in the Championship too, averaging almost 50 with the bat, including a fine century against Lancashire at Old Trafford – not bad considering he usually came in at No. 8 in a brittle line-up. Napier added 48 wickets, backing up the ever-dependable David Masters and the 19-year-old rising star, left-arm seamer Reece Topley, who claimed 99 between them.

The success of those three should have set up more victories – but the support was patchy. Hampered by a hip injury that prevented him from bowling his medium-pacers, Greg Smith turned to off-spin – and immediately took two five-fors. The promising leg-spinner Tom Craddock injured a finger early on, then missed the second half of the season on compassionate leave. Desperate to beef up the slow bowling, Essex signed Monty Panesar when he fell out of favour at Hove. He hardly proved a match-winner, but did enough to earn another two-year contract.

Left-armer Tymal Mills failed to build on his exciting start in 2012 but, blessed with raw pace, remained an exciting prospect. He shook up England's batsmen in a practice match ahead of the home Ashes, and – as probably the closest thing in the English game to Mitchell Johnson – was taken to Australia to help them prepare for the return series. However, Sajid Mahmood – the former Test fast bowler signed from Lancashire – was a letdown, managing only three wickets in seven Championship matches, at an average over 100.

Ryan ten Doeschate – who in January was made limited-overs captain for 2014 – and Ravi Bopara led a strong batting line-up in the YB40. But home-and-away defeats by Hampshire, the eventual group winners, proved costly: despite winning eight of their other ten matches, Essex did not qualify for the last four. In the FLt20, they

Ben Hoskins, Getty Images

Reece Topley

squeaked into the quarter-finals, after finishing third in their group, but then upset highly fancied Nottinghamshire. But Northamptonshire turned the tables in the semi.

A series of overseas players came and went. The Australian Rob Quiney was just beginning to adjust to English conditions when he dislocated his shoulder in early May, and returned to Melbourne. He was replaced by New Zealander Hamish Rutherford, with only sporadic success, while the Indian opener Gautam Gambhir was recruited for the final run-in, but made little impression beyond a century against Gloucestershire at Bristol. The Australian fast bowler Shaun Tait joined Rutherford for the Twenty20s: he proved useful rather than spectacular, although he did take a hat-trick against Nottinghamshire in that quarter-final.

Instead it was home-grown talent that did best in the shortest form. Topley was the pick of the bowlers with 21 wickets, while former Test batsman Owais Shah proved his class with 311 runs, averaging over 50. Shah, who turned 35 shortly after the season ended, announced his retirement from first-class cricket in September, to concentrate on Twenty20. He showed what the longer game would be missing with 84 and 120 in his last two Championship innings.

In a familiar tale, an Essex player's fortunes improved at another county. This time it was fast bowler Maurice Chambers, who went on loan to Warwickshire, where he joined two other Essex exiles, Varun Chopra and Chris Wright. Chambers joined Northamptonshire for 2014.

Since Essex were relegated in 2010, coach Grayson and James Foster, the captain, have insisted that promotion remains the priority. If that is to become reality, they need to acquire two quality batsmen to augment the young talents of Jaik Mickleburgh, Tom Westley and Ben Foakes. On the bowling side, Craddock's return could prove crucial, while Topley and Mills are, on paper, an exciting and incisive new-ball combination.

In the New Year, Essex revamped their coaching structure: assistant coach Matt Walker moved back to Kent and was replaced by Chris Silverwood, who stepped up from the Second XI.

Championship attendance: 26,548.

ESSEX RESULTS

All first-class matches – Played 17: Won 5, Lost 4, Drawn 8.
County Championship matches – Played 16: Won 5, Lost 4, Drawn 7.

LV= County Championship, 3rd in Division 2;
Friends Life t20, semi-finalists; Yorkshire Bank 40, 2nd in Group B.

COUNTY CHAMPIONSHIP AVERAGES, BATTING AND FIELDING

Cap		M	I	NO	R	HS	100	50	Avge	Ct/St
2003	G. R. Napier†	16	22	6	796	102*	1	7	49.75	5
2013	J. C. Mickleburgh	13	21	1	829	243	2	4	41.45	3
2005	A. N. Cook‡	2	4	0	157	60	0	2	39.25	2
	G. M. Smith¶	10	15	2	498	177	1	1	38.30	2
2001	J. S. Foster†	16	24	3	762	143	1	4	36.28	48/1
2005	R. S. Bopara†‡	7	11	0	397	145	1	2	36.09	5
2006	R. N. ten Doeschate¶	9	13	2	391	103	1	1	35.54	3
	G. Gambhir§	5	7	0	239	106	1	0	34.14	4
2013	T. Westley	10	18	0	583	163	1	2	32.38	5
2013	O. A. Shah	7	11	1	307	120	1	1	30.70	10
	B. T. Foakes†	14	18	1	500	120	1	3	29.41	11
2006	M. L. Pettini	8	14	3	319	72	0	1	29.00	7
	R. J. Quiney§	4	7	0	150	56	0	1	21.42	5
	S. I. Mahmood	4	6	0	112	54	0	1	18.66	3
	T. S. Mills	5	6	3	53	17	0	0	17.66	1
2008	D. D. Masters	13	12	3	95	37*	0	0	10.55	7
	M. S. Panesar	6	6	0	55	22	0	0	9.16	2
	N. L. J. Browne†	3	5	1	26	22*	0	0	6.50	1
2013	R. J. W. Topley	13	14	7	12	8*	0	0	1.71	6

Also batted: M. A. Chambers (2 matches) 1, 3 (1 ct); T. R. Craddock (3 matches) 3, 1, 20; T. J. Phillips (cap 2006) (3 matches) 40*, 7, 0 (1 ct); H. D. Rutherford§ (2 matches) 5, 0, 24 (1 ct); K. S. Velani† (1 match) 13, 9.

† *Born in Essex.* ‡ *ECB contract.* § *Official overseas player.* ¶ *Other non-England-qualified player.*

BOWLING

	Style	O	M	R	W	BB	5I	Avge
D. D. Masters	RFM	467.4	122	1,163	51	6-41	4	22.80
G. M. Smith	OB/RFM	112.5	21	365	15	5-42	2	24.33
R. S. Bopara	RM	129.5	24	378	14	3-41	0	27.00
R. J. W. Topley	LFM	411.4	78	1,364	48	6-29	3	28.41
G. R. Napier	RFM	459.1	80	1,516	48	7-90	3	31.58
M. S. Panesar	SLA	189.4	50	504	14	4-49	0	36.00

Also bowled: N. L. J. Browne (LBG) 16.5–4–59–0; M. A. Chambers (RFM) 32–2–151–1; T. R. Craddock (LBG) 43–9–132–3; S. I. Mahmood (RFM) 66–4–329–3; T. S. Mills (LFM) 102.4–18–398–6; T. J. Phillips (SLA) 39.4–10–98–6; O. A. Shah (OB) 2–0–12–0; R. N. ten Doeschate (RM) 77–9–267–8; K. S. Velani (RM) 2–0–8–0; T. Westley (OB) 41–4–142–1.

LEADING YB40 AVERAGES (100 runs/4 wickets)

Batting

	Runs	HS	Avge	SR	Ct
R. N. ten Doeschate	382	180	63.66	131.72	3
R. S. Bopara	441	130	63.00	99.77	5
R. J. Quiney	121	71	60.50	85.81	0
G. M. Smith	290	78	41.42	87.87	4
T. Westley	227	71	32.42	94.97	0
O. A. Shah	155	68	31.00	88.57	2
H. D. Rutherford	214	110	30.57	114.43	0

Bowling

	W	BB	Avge	ER
T. S. Mills	10	3-23	17.30	5.58
G. R. Napier	21	7-32	21.95	5.71
R. N. ten Doeschate	8	3-38	24.50	5.76
R. J. W. Topley	17	4-26	25.58	5.60
T. J. Phillips	12	5-42	25.91	5.79
D. D. Masters	9	2-27	33.88	4.63
S. I. Mahmood	5	2-48	50.20	7.17

LEADING FLt20 AVERAGES (100 runs/18 overs)

Batting	Runs	HS	Avge	SR	Ct	Bowling	W	BB	Avge	ER
H. D. Rutherford	304	84	27.63	**169.83**	3	S. W. Tait	16	4-26	17.18	**6.93**
R. N. ten Doeschate	288	82	41.14	**150.00**	5	D. D. Masters	7	3-26	24.28	**7.08**
M. L. Pettini	120	37	24.00	**139.53**	0	R. J. W. Topley	21	4-26	13.23	**7.51**
G. M. Smith	189	62	17.18	**119.62**	8	T. J. Phillips	5	2-14	44.40	**7.69**
O. A. Shah	311	68	51.83	**118.25**	1	G. R. Napier	12	4-18	26.16	**8.76**
R. S. Bopara	201	39	25.12	**113.55**	5	R. N. ten Doeschate	3	1-17	57.66	**8.94**

FIRST-CLASS COUNTY RECORDS

Highest score for	343*	P. A. Perrin v Derbyshire at Chesterfield	1904
Highest score against	332	W. H. Ashdown (Kent) at Brentwood	1934
Leading run-scorer	30,701	G. A. Gooch (avge 51.77)	1973–97
Best bowling for	10-32	H. Pickett v Leicestershire at Leyton	1895
Best bowling against	10-40	E. G. Dennett (Gloucestershire) at Bristol	1906
Leading wicket-taker	1,610	T. P. B. Smith (avge 26.68)	1929–51
Highest total for	761-6 dec	v Leicestershire at Chelmsford	1990
Highest total against	803-4 dec	by Kent at Brentwood	1934
Lowest total for	**20**	**v Lancashire at Chelmsford**	**2013**
Lowest total against	14	by Surrey at Chelmsford	1983

LIST A COUNTY RECORDS

Highest score for	201*	R. S. Bopara v Leicestershire at Leicester	2008
Highest score against	158*	M. W. Goodwin (Sussex) at Chelmsford	2006
Leading run-scorer	16,536	G. A. Gooch (avge 40.93)	1973–97
Best bowling for	8-26	K. D. Boyce v Lancashire at Manchester	1971
Best bowling against	7-29	D. A. Payne (Gloucestershire) at Chelmsford	2010
Leading wicket-taker	616	J. K. Lever (avge 19.04)	1968–89
Highest total for	391-5	v Surrey at The Oval	2008
Highest total against	**321-5**	**by Derbyshire at Leek**	**2013**
Lowest total for	57	v Lancashire at Lord's	1996
Lowest total against	{ 41	by Middlesex at Westcliff-on-Sea	1972
	{ 41	by Shropshire at Wellington	1974

TWENTY20 COUNTY RECORDS

Highest score for	152*	G. R. Napier v Sussex at Chelmsford	2008
Highest score against	124*	M. J. Lumb (Hampshire) at Southampton	2009
Leading run-scorer	2,077	**M. L. Pettini (avge 25.64)**	**2003–13**
Best bowling for	6-16	T. G. Southee v Glamorgan at Chelmsford	2011
Best bowling against	5-11	Mushtaq Ahmed (Sussex) at Hove	2005
Leading wicket-taker	77	**G. R. Napier (avge 23.14)**	**2003–13**
Highest total for	242-3	v Sussex at Chelmsford	2008
Highest total against	225-2	by Somerset at Chelmsford	2011
Lowest total for	**74**	**v Middlesex at Chelmsford**	**2013**
Lowest total against	82	by Gloucestershire at Chelmsford	2011

ADDRESS

County Ground, New Writtle Street, Chelmsford CM2 0PG (01245 252420; **email** administration.essex@ecb.co.uk). **Website** www.essexcricket.org.uk

OFFICIALS

Captain (Championship) J. S. Foster
    2014 (limited-overs) R. N. ten Doeschate
First-team coach A. P. Grayson
Academy director J. H. Childs
President D. J. Insole

Chairman N. R. A. Hilliard
Chief executive D. W. Bowden
Chairman, cricket committee G. J. Saville
Head groundsman S. G. Kerrison
Scorer A. E. Choat

At Cambridge, April 5–7. ESSEX drew with CAMBRIDGE MCCU.

ESSEX v GLOUCESTERSHIRE

At Chelmsford, April 10–13. Drawn. Essex 8pts, Gloucestershire 9pts. Toss: Essex. First-class debut: C. L. Herring. County debut: M. Klinger. Championship debut: R. J. Quiney.

The bad weather that blighted much of Essex's season in 2012 returned in the first match of 2013, scrubbing off 156 overs after a full first day. There were still moments to savour: Housego and Marshall added 280 for the fourth wicket – Gloucestershire's highest partnership in 138 meetings with Essex – with Housego striking a number of delightful drives in a vigilant innings spanning more than seven hours. Westley responded with an equally mature performance, batting for more than six hours after two early wickets; moving his feet well, he was quick to punish anything loose. Bopara added a typically stylish half-century on a docile pitch, but the frequent interruptions for rain and bad light ruined any chance of a positive result.

Close of play: first day, Gloucestershire 300-3 (Housego 124, Marshall 120); second day, Essex 30-2 (Westley 19, Bopara 3); third day, Essex 177-3 (Westley 82, Pettini 18).

Gloucestershire

*M. Klinger c Foster b Masters	18	W. R. S. Gidman not out	10		
C. D. J. Dent c Foster b Masters	8	B 8, l-b 7, w 2, n-b 8	25		
D. M. Housego lbw b Bopara	150				
A. P. R. Gidman lbw b Bopara	12	1/17 (2)	(5 wkts dec, 124 overs)	409	
H. J. H. Marshall c Quiney b Mills	149	2/34 (1) 3/71 (4)			
B. A. C. Howell not out	37	4/351 (5) 5/378 (3)	110 overs: 362-4		

†C. L. Herring, J. K. Fuller, D. A. Payne and L. C. Norwell did not bat.

Masters 27–7–65–2; Mills 21–5–63–1; Chambers 22–1–89–0; Napier 25–5–79–0; Bopara 16–2–56–2; Westley 13–2–42–0.

Essex

T. Westley c Herring b W. R. S. Gidman	163	G. R. Napier not out	0		
R. J. Quiney b Fuller	4				
B. T. Foakes c Dent b Fuller	4	B 4, l-b 4, w 1, n-b 4	13		
R. S. Bopara lbw b Howell	64				
M. L. Pettini lbw b Norwell	35	1/11 (2) 2/23 (3)	(6 wkts, 102 overs)	353	
*†J. S. Foster c Fuller b Howell	51	3/139 (4) 4/234 (5)			
G. M. Smith not out	19	5/307 (1) 6/349 (6)			

D. D. Masters, M. A. Chambers and T. S. Mills did not bat.

Fuller 26–4–77–2; W. R. S. Gidman 30–4–88–1; Payne 19–3–79–0; Norwell 11–2–57–1; Howell 15–6–42–2; A. P. R. Gidman 1–0–2–0.

Umpires: R. K. Illingworth and M. J. Saggers.

At Northampton, April 17–19. ESSEX lost to NORTHAMPTONSHIRE by an innings and nine runs.

ESSEX v HAMPSHIRE

At Chelmsford, April 29–May 1. Essex won by four wickets. Essex 21pts, Hampshire 3pts. Toss: Hampshire.

Essex eventually prevailed in an absorbing contest of oscillating fortunes on a pitch that encouraged the bowlers throughout. After Hampshire had fallen three runs short of a batting point, Cook – in his first Championship match for almost a year – contributed a well-crafted half-century. But it was Napier who hogged the headlines. First his ninth-wicket stand of 87 with Phillips helped earn Essex a lead of 57, then he opened up in the second innings after they had got themselves into a terrible muddle chasing 143. Two run-outs – including Westley for the second time in the match – betrayed their nerves, and they plummeted to 31 for six. But Napier mixed watchfulness with controlled aggression, hitting three sixes and ten fours, while the admirable Pettini played a vital support role. They spent 29 overs together, completing victory during the extra half-hour on the third day. Hampshire had hoped to set a more formidable target, but were unhinged by Masters, whose nagging accuracy and movement off the seam brought him match figures of nine for 70. Bopara helped him polish off the second innings with three wickets in ten balls.

Close of play: first day, Essex 72-5 (Cook 25, Foakes 19); second day, Hampshire 77-2 (Dawson 31, Bailey 26).

Hampshire

M. A. Carberry c Foster b Topley	5	– c Foakes b Masters	2
*J. H. K. Adams c Foster b Masters	11	– lbw b Masters	9
L. A. Dawson lbw b Masters	14	– c Foakes b Phillips	52
G. J. Bailey c Pettini b Masters	15	– b Masters	31
J. M. Vince lbw b Bopara	43	– c Foster b Masters	67
S. M. Ervine c and b Topley	60	– b Napier	2
†A. J. Wheater c Napier b Topley	1	– c Foster b Masters	14
C. P. Wood c Foakes b Bopara	2	– lbw b Bopara	2
D. J. Balcombe c Cook b Masters	23	– c Quiney b Bopara	2
D. R. Briggs not out	8	– not out	0
J. A. Tomlinson c Pettini b Napier	0	– c Foster b Bopara	0
L-b 15	15	L-b 17, w 1	18

1/5 (1) 2/31 (3) 3/44 (2)   (65.5 overs) 197
4/47 (4) 5/129 (5) 6/146 (7)
7/148 (8) 8/170 (6) 9/194 (9) 10/197 (11)

1/14 (1) 2/21 (2)   (93.5 overs) 199
3/85 (4) 4/144 (3)
5/153 (6) 6/188 (5) 7/193 (8)
8/195 (7) 9/199 (9) 10/199 (11)

Masters 16–5–29–4; Topley 20–2–66–3; Westley 2–0–7–0; Napier 15.5–1–57–1; Bopara 12–4–23–2. *Second innings*—Masters 22–6–41–5; Topley 18–7–42–0; Napier 17–3–37–1; Bopara 23.5–7–41–3; Phillips 13–5–21–1.

Essex

T. Westley run out	16	– run out	8
A. N. Cook lbw b Tomlinson	59	– b Balcombe	4
R. J. Quiney lbw b Tomlinson	4	– c Wheater b Tomlinson	10
R. S. Bopara lbw b Briggs	7	– c Dawson b Balcombe	0
D. D. Masters c Wheater b Ervine	0		
M. L. Pettini c Vince b Ervine	0	– (5) not out	35
B. T. Foakes c Wheater b Tomlinson	20	– (6) lbw b Tomlinson	0
*†J. S. Foster c and b Briggs	25	– (7) run out	5
G. R. Napier lbw b Wood	74	– (8) not out	78
T. J. Phillips not out	40		
R. J. W. Topley c Ervine b Briggs	0		
B 1, l-b 3, w 1, n-b 4	9	B 1, l-b 2	3

1/26 (1) 2/33 (3) 3/51 (4)   (87.3 overs) 254
4/52 (5) 5/52 (6) 6/73 (7)
7/117 (8) 8/156 (2) 9/243 (9) 10/254 (11)

1/6 (2)   (6 wkts, 40.1 overs) 143
2/16 (1) 3/16 (4)
4/24 (3) 5/24 (6) 6/31 (7)

Wood 20–8–55–1; Balcombe 23.5–5–56–0; Tomlinson 18–7–40–3; Briggs 14.3–3–56–3; Ervine 12–2–43–2. *Second innings*—Tomlinson 12–1–38–2; Balcombe 12–4–32–2; Ervine 4–0–23–0; Wood 3–0–13–0; Briggs 7–2–14–0; Dawson 2.1–0–20–0.

Umpires: M. R. Benson and P. J. Hartley.

At Manchester, May 7–10. ESSEX lost to LANCASHIRE by three wickets.

At Cardiff, May 15–18. ESSEX beat GLAMORGAN by five wickets.

ESSEX v KENT

At Chelmsford, May 22–25. Drawn. Essex 7pts, Kent 8pts. Toss: Kent.

Stevens and Davies took Kent close to their first Championship win of the season, despite the loss of the entire third day to rain. But Foakes and Foster kept them at bay in a partnership spanning three hours and 48 overs, before Tredwell called off the hunt with little still left. Earlier, Stevens had chosen the right ball to hit, reaching the fourth century in his last five Championship visits to Chelmsford, and his useful stands with Harmison and Coles lifted Kent to a lead of 84. Davies then demolished Essex's fragile top order, taking four for four in 11 balls, and inflicting a pair on Bopara when Northeast held a good tumbling catch in the gully. Essex nosedived to 24 for five, but Davies lacked quality support: 20-year-old Foakes and the experienced Foster were able to construct their match-saving stand without too many problems.

Close of play: first day, Kent 20-1 (Northeast 14, Nash 4); second day, Kent 214-5 (Stevens 91, Jones 12); third day, no play.

Essex

T. Westley b Davies	30	– c Jones b Davies		17
J. C. Mickleburgh c Coles b Davies	37	– c Jones b Shreck		3
R. S. Bopara c Stevens b Davies	0	– c Northeast b Davies		0
M. L. Pettini lbw b Stevens	16	– c Coles b Davies		4
R. N. ten Doeschate c Jones b Shreck	1	– c Stevens b Davies		0
B. T. Foakes c Stevens b Shreck	0	– not out		86
*†J. S. Foster c Coles b Shreck	47	– not out		52
G. R. Napier c Nash b Stevens	58			
D. D. Masters c Northeast b Stevens	8			
T. R. Craddock c Northeast b Stevens	3			
R. J. W. Topley not out	1			
B 1, l-b 9, w 1	11	B 4		4

1/67 (1) 2/69 (3) 3/74 (2)   (82 overs) 212
4/77 (5) 5/77 (6) 6/109 (4)
7/197 (7) 8/200 (8) 9/211 (9) 10/212 (10)

1/20 (1)   (5 wkts, 60 overs) 166
2/20 (3) 3/24 (4)
4/24 (5) 5/24 (2)

Davies 18–7–31–3; Shreck 20–4–61–3; Coles 15–1–64–0; Stevens 23–9–36–4; Tredwell 6–2–10–0. *Second innings*—Davies 15–3–36–4; Shreck 15–4–38–1; Tredwell 9–2–23–0; Coles 12–2–45–0; Stevens 9–3–20–0.

Kent

S. A. Northeast c Foster b Bopara	31	M. T. Coles run out		30
R. W. T. Key c Foster b Masters	1	M. Davies not out		0
B. P. Nash b Topley	5	C. E. Shreck c Napier b Topley		0
M. J. Powell c Westley b Topley	1	B 4, l-b 10, w 3, n-b 4		21
B. W. Harmison c Foster b ten Doeschate	55			
D. I. Stevens c Napier b Bopara	136	1/11 (2) 2/25 (3) 3/33 (4)	(103.4 overs)	296
†G. O. Jones b Masters	15	4/43 (1) 5/188 (5) 6/224 (7)		
*J. C. Tredwell run out	1	7/227 (8) 8/296 (6) 9/296 (9) 10/296 (11)		

Masters 36–15–64–2; Topley 29.4–9–81–3; Napier 17–5–45–0; Bopara 14–1–73–2; Westley 2–1–4–0; ten Doeschate 5–0–15–1.

Umpires: M. A. Gough and A. G. Wharf.

At Worcester, May 28–31. ESSEX drew with WORCESTERSHIRE.

ESSEX v LANCASHIRE

At Chelmsford, June 12–14. Lancashire won by an innings and 105 runs. Lancashire 23pts, Essex 5pts. Toss: Lancashire. County debut: L. M. Reece. Championship debut: H. D. Rutherford.

Honours were roughly even by the end of the second day, when Lancashire were seven behind with three first-innings wickets standing. But Hogg and Chapple made spirited half-centuries next day to construct a lead of 125, then combined with the new ball as Essex disintegrated spectacularly. In little more than an hour the match was over, with Essex humbled for 20 – easily their lowest first-class total (previously 30 against Yorkshire at Leyton in 1901), the lowest in the Championship since Essex themselves skittled Surrey for 14 at Chelmsford in 1983, and the lowest by any side against Lancashire. Six batsmen were lbw as a lack of technique against the swinging ball was mercilessly exposed. With the panic rising, Foster was run out by a direct hit from Chapple. There were only

LOWEST CHAMPIONSHIP TOTALS

12	Northamptonshire v Gloucestershire at Gloucester (Spa)	1907
13	Nottinghamshire v Yorkshire at Nottingham	1901
14	Surrey v Essex at Chelmsford	1983
15	Nottinghamshire v Yorkshire at Northampton	1908
15	Hampshire v Warwickshire at Birmingham	1922
16	Warwickshire v Kent at Tonbridge	1913
20	Sussex v Yorkshire at Hull	1922
20	Derbyshire v Yorkshire at Sheffield	1939
20	**Essex v Lancashire at Chelmsford**	**2013**
22	Gloucestershire v Somerset at Bristol	1920
22	Glamorgan v Lancashire at Liverpool	1924

eight scoring shots in the whole innings – four boundaries and four singles – and Mickleburgh, who opened and was ninth out, contributed half of them. Only Wilfred Flowers, with 11 out of 19 for MCC against the Australians at Lord's back in 1878, had made a higher score in a lower total. Earlier, there had been little hint of the carnage to follow, although Essex's top order struggled again on the first morning, losing five wickets before 100 was up for the eighth time in 13 Championship innings. They were rescued by ten Doeschate and Foster, but a vigilant innings from Katich, spanning nearly five hours, put Lancashire in front. "I'm still in a state of shock," said Essex coach Paul Grayson. "Emotions are running very high at the moment. There's not a lot of singing and dancing going on."

Close of play: first day, Essex 268-8 (Mahmood 22, Masters 0); second day, Lancashire 266-7 (Katich 120, Hogg 17).

Essex

T. Westley lbw b Hogg	2	– c Katich b Hogg	4
J. C. Mickleburgh c Prince b Hogg	4	– lbw b Chapple	10
H. D. Rutherford c Cross b Chapple	5	– c Chapple b Hogg	0
O. A. Shah b Procter	30	– lbw b Hogg	0
R. N. ten Doeschate c Katich b Kerrigan	77	– lbw b Chapple	1
B. T. Foakes c Reece b Procter	2	– lbw b Hogg	0
*†J. S. Foster lbw b Kerrigan	82	– run out	4
G. R. Napier lbw b White	28	– lbw b Chapple	0
S. I. Mahmood c Agathangelou b Chapple	23	– b Chapple	0
D. D. Masters not out	3	– not out	1
R. J. W. Topley b Chapple	1	– lbw b Chapple	0
B 4, l-b 8, n-b 4	16		

1/4 (2) 2/11 (1) 3/13 (3)   (84.2 overs) 273   1/5 (1) 2/5 (3)   (14.2 overs) 20
4/62 (4) 5/72 (6) 6/167 (5)   3/5 (4) 4/10 (5)
7/226 (8) 8/268 (7) 9/271 (9) 10/273 (11)   5/11 (6) 6/15 (7) 7/15 (8)
8/15 (9) 9/20 (2) 10/20 (11)

Chapple 19.2–7–47–3; Hogg 19–5–47–2; Procter 6–0–37–2; White 17–1–68–1; Kerrigan 23–2–62–2. *Second innings*—Chapple 7.2–4–9–5; Hogg 7–3–11–4.

Lancashire

L. M. Reece c Westley b Napier	24	*G. Chapple not out	50
L. A. Procter lbw b Masters	8	S. C. Kerrigan c Foster b Topley	31
A. G. Prince c Foster b Masters	56		
S. M. Katich lbw b Masters	122	L-b 14, n-b 4	18
A. P. Agathangelou b Napier	6		—
S. J. Croft c Foster b Napier	0	1/25 (2) 2/41 (1) (118.4 overs) 398
†G. D. Cross c Mahmood b Topley	13	3/151 (3) 4/163 (5) 5/165 (6)
W. A. White c Mahmood b Topley	12	6/190 (7) 7/208 (8) 8/277 (4)
K. W. Hogg b Masters	58	9/346 (9) 10/398 (11) 110 overs: 369-9

Masters 30–7–72–4; Topley 23.4–2–75–3; Napier 33–6–128–3; Mahmood 20–1–69–0; Westley 11–1–31–0; Shah 1–0–9–0.

Umpires: R. J. Bailey and P. K. Baldwin.

At Leicester, June 21–24. ESSEX beat LEICESTERSHIRE by four wickets.

At Chelmsford, June 30–July 3 (not first-class). **England XI won by 228 runs. England XI 413-9 dec** (T. T. Bresnan 105*, G. P. Swann 94; T. R. Craddock 5-69) **and 279-4 dec** (A. N. Cook 82, I. J. L. Trott 79); ‡**Essex 278** (J. C. Mickleburgh 90; J. E. Root 4-72) **and 186** (J. C. Mickleburgh 58; G. Onions 4-43, G. P. Swann 5-68). *This started as a first-class match to help England prepare for the Ashes, but lost that standing on the third afternoon, when Essex were allowed to replace two injured bowlers (David Masters and Tymal Mills) with full substitutes Reece Topley and Warwickshire's Boyd Rankin, who bowled in the England XI's second innings. On the fourth day Greg Smith also replaced the injured Tom Westley. The loss of status was unpopular with the spectators, some of whom asked for their money back, and with leg-spinner Tom Craddock who had earlier dismissed Kevin Pietersen (for 49) and Ian Bell on the way to what he thought was a career-best. Tim Bresnan also had what would have been his fourth first-class century chalked off: he and Graeme Swann put on 187 for England's eighth wicket. Swann had to have an X-ray after being hit on the forearm by Mills, but recovered to take five wickets as England completed victory on the fourth day in front of a disappointing crowd. Just to confuse things further, Masters batted at No. 10 in Essex's second innings after supposedly being substituted out of the match earlier.*

ESSEX v LEICESTERSHIRE

At Chelmsford, July 17–20. Essex won by an innings and 25 runs. Essex 21pts, Leicestershire 5pts. Toss: Leicestershire. First-class debut: J. S. Sykes.

A fine innings from Eckersley, who batted more than five and a half hours for his fourth and highest first-class century, appeared to have laid a solid base for Leicestershire. But they collapsed on the second morning, losing six for six as Napier got the ball to swing both ways; Masters, who did not arrive until 2pm after being stuck in a tailback on the M25, was hardly missed. Then Mickleburgh cashed in against an inexperienced attack, making the most of being dropped either side of three figures to convert his fourth Championship hundred into his first double. He batted for 508 minutes and put on 270 with Foakes, whose own century was his first in the competition. The 21-year-old slow left-armer Jamie Sykes took four wickets on debut, but they were costly. Resuming 156 behind, Leicestershire were soon up against it, losing three quick wickets on the third evening, and there was little resistance next morning as the Essex Greg Smith – bowling off-spin rather than his more usual medium-pace – helped himself to a career-best five for 42.

Close of play: first day, Leicestershire 328-4 (Eckersley 133, Boyce 37); second day, Essex 216-4 (Mickleburgh 121, Foakes 25); third day, Leicestershire 47-3 (Burns 13, Thakor 2).

Leicestershire

G. P. Smith c Masters b Craddock	46	– c Foster b Mills	0
†N. J. O'Brien b Mills	51	– c Foster b Smith	18
E. J. H. Eckersley b Napier	147	– lbw b Smith	13
J. A. Burns b Mills	8	– c Foakes b Mills	21
S. J. Thakor c Shah b Craddock	36	– c Rutherford b Smith	3
*M. A. G. Boyce c Foster b Napier	54	– (7) c Foster b Napier	19
J. J. Cobb c sub (R. J. W. Topley) b Napier	4	– (6) lbw b Craddock	1
A. J. Ireland b Napier	0	– b Smith	13
O. H. Freckingham c Foster b Smith	1	– c Masters b Napier	24
J. S. Sykes not out	0	– not out	1
A. C. F. Wyatt b Napier	0	– st Foster b Smith	10
B 8, l-b 8, w 2	18	B 4, l-b 2, n-b 2	8

1/91 (2) 2/102 (1) 3/115 (4)	(114.3 overs)	365
4/212 (5) 5/359 (6) 6/362 (3)		
7/362 (8) 8/363 (9) 9/365 (7)		
10/365 (11)	110 overs: 362-5	

1/1 (1) 2/31 (3)	(43.3 overs)	131
3/32 (2) 4/62 (5)		
5/62 (4) 6/73 (6) 7/92 (8)		
8/120 (7) 9/121 (9) 10/131 (11)		

Masters 25–5–68–0; Napier 20.3–3–77–5; ten Doeschate 5–0–20–0; Mills 20–3–58–2; Craddock 19–1–77–2; Smith 25–8–49–1. *Second innings*—Masters 5–2–17–0; Mills 9–2–24–2; Smith 17.3–4–42–5; Craddock 9–2–29–1; Napier 3–0–13–2.

Essex

H. D. Rutherford c Wyatt b Ireland	24	D. D. Masters b Sykes	11
J. C. Mickleburgh b Freckingham	243	T. S. Mills not out	7
G. M. Smith b Burns b Sykes	8	T. R. Craddock c Cobb b Freckingham	20
O. A. Shah c O'Brien b Wyatt	15	B 1, l-b 7	8
R. N. ten Doeschate c Thakor			
b Freckingham	23		
B. T. Foakes c Freckingham b Sykes	120		
*†J. S. Foster lbw b Wyatt	1		
G. R. Napier c sub (M. A. Thornely) b Sykes	41		

1/62 (1) 2/75 (3)	(150.1 overs)	521
3/98 (4) 4/151 (5) 5/421 (6)		
6/427 (7) 7/460 (2) 8/492 (8)		
9/494 (9) 10/521 (11)	110 overs: 361-4	

Wyatt 29–6–108–2; Freckingham 27.1–11–60–3; Ireland 31–4–109–1; Sykes 43–6–176–4; Cobb 9–1–24–0; Thakor 11–1–36–0.

Umpires: D. J. Millns and C. Shamshuddin.

ESSEX v NORTHAMPTONSHIRE

At Colchester, August 20–23. Drawn. Essex 8pts, Northamptonshire 10pts. Toss: Northamptonshire. County debuts: G. Gambhir, M. S. Panesar.

Three days after they met in the Twenty20 semi-finals – Northamptonshire won, and went on to lift the trophy – the teams resumed their fight for promotion. Northamptonshire made the early running on a docile pitch at Castle Park, with Peters and Sales putting on 205. Hall and Crook stiffened the middle order with a hundred partnership of their own on the second day, and the eventual total was an imposing 531. At 103 for five, Essex seemed to be staring at defeat, but rain washed out the entire third day. On the fourth, ten Doeschate and Foster extended their sixth-wicket stand to 180, then staunch batting from Napier and Masters helped avert the follow-on, which effectively ended the match. Shortly before the game Essex signed Panesar, who had fallen out with Sussex. He contributed a marathon spell against his first county, but lacked guile as he toiled through 54 overs in the first innings for only two wickets.

Close of play: first day, Northamptonshire 343-5 (Hall 15, Keogh 3); second day, Essex 187-5 (ten Doeschate 47, Foster 39); third day, no play.

Northamptonshire

*S. D. Peters b Masters	101	– not out	19
J. D. Middlebrook b Masters	8	– not out	32
D. J. Sales b Napier	131		
A. G. Wakely c Bopara b Panesar	49		
B. M. Duckett c Gambhir b Topley	25		
A. J. Hall b Smith	63		
R. I. Keogh b Napier	38		
S. P. Crook c Gambhir b Panesar	63		
T. A. Copeland b Smith	2		
†D. Murphy not out	23		
Azharullah c Bopara b Smith	8		
L-b 12, w 6, n-b 2	20	L-b 3	3

1/27 (2) 2/232 (1) 3/269 (3)   (145.5 overs) 531   (no wkt dec, 13.4 overs) 54
4/307 (5) 5/338 (4) 6/395 (7) 7/496 (8)
8/500 (6) 9/501 (9) 10/531 (11)   110 overs: 395-5

Masters 25-4–89–2; Topley 19-0–88–1; Napier 25-2–104–2; Panesar 54–18–133–2; ten Doeschate 3–0–19–0; Smith 19.5–1–86–3. *Second innings*—Topley 4–0–30–0; Napier 4–1–5–0; Smith 3–1–11–0; Panesar 2.4–1–5–0.

Essex

J. C. Mickleburgh c Murphy b Copeland	8	D. D. Masters not out	37
G. Gambhir b Crook	31	M. S. Panesar b Middlebrook	7
G. M. Smith lbw b Azharullah	41	R. J. W. Topley lbw b Azharullah	0
R. S. Bopara lbw b Crook	12		
R. N. ten Doeschate c Duckett b Middlebrook	103	B 8, l-b 2, w 1, n-b 4	15
B. T. Foakes c Murphy b Copeland	2		
*†J. S. Foster c Copeland b Middlebrook	95	1/21 (1) 2/65 (2) 3/87 (4) (109 overs) 396
G. R. Napier c sub (V. V. S. Sohal) b Copeland	45	4/98 (3) 5/103 (6) 6/283 (5)
		7/333 (7) 8/357 (8) 9/379 (10) 10/396 (11)

Azharullah 18–2–102–2; Copeland 33–8–81–3; Crook 20–1–87–2; Middlebrook 24–3–79–3; Hall 10–3–28–0; Keogh 4–1–9–0.

Umpires: N. G. B. Cook and S. A. Garratt.

At Bristol, August 28–31. ESSEX drew with GLOUCESTERSHIRE.

ESSEX v WORCESTERSHIRE

At Chelmsford, September 3–5. Essex won by eight wickets. Essex 23pts, Worcestershire 3pts. Toss: Worcestershire.

Career-best figures for Topley propelled Essex to a comfortable victory that kept their Division One hopes bubbling. Using helpful conditions to swing the ball disconcertingly, and assisted by some rash shots, he took six for 29 as Worcestershire were bundled out for 102 on the first afternoon. In the second innings the Essex attack were held up by an opening stand of 113 but, once that was broken by Panesar, wickets fell regularly; Topley took five to finish with match figures of 11 for 85. In between, the in-form Mickleburgh and Greg Smith put on 158 for Essex's second wicket, before Foakes and Napier swelled their lead towards the eventual 249. It proved almost enough for victory, which in any event was completed before tea on the third day. Panesar landed himself in hot water when, increasingly frustrated by Whiteley's defiance, he kicked the ground furiously not far from the batsman and argued with him. Umpire Willey spoke to the bowler, and Foster removed him from the attack; Panesar was later handed a suspended one-match ban by the ECB for not conducting himself "fairly and properly on the field", and behaving in a manner "potentially threatening and intimidating towards a member of the opposition".

Close of play: first day, Essex 199-4 (ten Doeschate 16, Foakes 11); second day, Worcestershire 163-3 (Pardoe 74, Lucas 0).

Worcestershire

*D. K. H. Mitchell c Browne b Masters	2	– c Shah b Panesar	62
M. G. Pardoe c Shah b Topley	7	– c Mickleburgh b ten Doeschate	88
M. M. Ali c Topley b Napier	6	– c Shah b Panesar	21
T. C. Fell lbw b Topley	15	– lbw b Smith	2
J. Leach c ten Doeschate b Topley	24	– (6) c Foster b Topley	4
R. A. Whiteley c Foster b Topley	14	– (7) c Foster b Topley	38
†M. A. Johnson b Masters	0	– (8) c ten Doeschate b Topley	3
S. H. Choudhry b Topley	1	– (9) c Foster b Masters	34
J. D. Shantry c Foakes b Topley	0	– (10) c Foster b Topley	12
D. S. Lucas c Napier b Masters	11	– (5) lbw b Topley	0
A. Richardson not out	8	– not out	14
L-b 10, n-b 4	14	B 6, l-b 12, w 1, n-b 2	21

1/2 (1) 2/17 (3) 3/31 (2) (45.3 overs) 102
4/52 (4) 5/73 (5) 6/80 (7)
7/81 (8) 8/81 (9) 9/86 (6) 10/102 (10)

1/113 (1) 2/147 (3) (91.2 overs) 299
3/162 (4) 4/169 (5)
5/173 (6) 6/200 (2) 7/203 (8)
8/270 (9) 9/270 (7) 10/299 (10)

Masters 17.3–7–33–3; Topley 18–9–29–6; Napier 8–1–26–1; Panesar 2–1–4–0. *Second innings*—Masters 22–5–70–1; Topley 19.2–7–56–5; Napier 11–2–39–0; Panesar 26–5–74–2; Smith 7–1–20–1; ten Doeschate 6–2–22–1.

Essex

J. C. Mickleburgh c Mitchell b Ali	65	– c Ali b Choudhry	28
N. L. J. Browne b Richardson	0	– not out	22
G. M. Smith c Richardson b Ali	94	– c Ali b Choudhry	2
O. A. Shah lbw b Richardson	4	– not out	0
R. N. ten Doeschate c Johnson b Shantry	21		
B. T. Foakes b Richardson	71		
*†J. S. Foster c Johnson b Lucas	9		
G. R. Napier not out	64		
D. D. Masters c Leach b Richardson	11		
M. S. Panesar b Shantry	1		
R. J. W. Topley lbw b Shantry	0		
L-b 8, w 1, n-b 2	11	L-b 1	1

1/1 (2) 2/159 (1) 3/170 (4) (89.2 overs) 351
4/172 (3) 5/209 (5) 6/238 (7)
7/330 (6) 8/350 (9) 9/351 (10) 10/351 (11)

1/45 (1) (2 wkts, 18.1 overs) 53
2/49 (3)

Richardson 26–5–92–4; Shantry 22.2–6–76–3; Lucas 13–3–60–1; Ali 16–3–45–2; Leach 4–0–28–0; Choudhry 8–1–42–0. *Second innings*—Richardson 4–2–12–0; Shantry 5–0–12–0; Ali 5.1–1–21–0; Choudhry 4–1–7–2.

Umpires: M. J. D. Bodenham and P. Willey.

At Canterbury, September 11–14. ESSEX drew with KENT.

ESSEX v GLAMORGAN

At Chelmsford, September 17–20. Drawn. Essex 11pts, Glamorgan 8pts. Toss: Essex.

The loss of 130 overs to the weather, and a pitch that became increasingly benign, ruined any prospect of a positive outcome and dealt a savage blow to Essex's promotion chances. They had started well, with Masters removing the openers inside three overs, but then the dependable Goodwin bedded down for the rest of a first day on which only 42 overs were possible. Next morning, he soon became Masters's 50th Championship victim of the season, but handy contributions down the order took Glamorgan to 322. Essex prospered against an attack which, Hogan apart, was toothless, and piled on 184 runs in 29 overs on the fourth morning before Foster declared with a lead of 102. There were centuries for Mickleburgh and Shah (his 45th, in what turned out to be his last first-class match before becoming a Twenty20 specialist); these two, and Topley, were awarded their county caps during the match. Glamorgan needed only to avoid an early collapse to force the draw, which they did with ease, enjoying some batting practice ahead of their YB40 final against Nottinghamshire at Lord's the following day.

Close of play: first day, Glamorgan 103-2 (Goodwin 48, Wright 44); second day, Essex 107-1 (Mickleburgh 68, Smith 0); third day, Essex 240-2 (Mickleburgh 124, Shah 59).

Glamorgan

G. P. Rees b Masters	0	– c Foakes b Napier	76
W. D. Bragg c Bopara b Masters	4	– c Foster b Napier	27
M. W. Goodwin c Shah b Masters	65	– not out	46
B. J. Wright lbw b Masters	45	– not out	11
C. B. Cooke lbw b Panesar	67		
*†M. A. Wallace b Bopara	38		
A. G. Salter c Shah b Masters	9		
R. A. J. Smith b Napier	23		
J. C. Glover not out	39		
D. A. Cosker c Foakes b Panesar	10		
M. G. Hogan b Topley	6		
L-b 6, w 2, n-b 8	16	B 12, l-b 7, n-b 2	21

1/0 (1) 2/7 (2) 3/114 (4)   (108.1 overs) 322   1/82 (2)   (2 wkts dec, 44 overs) 181
4/131 (3) 5/226 (6) 6/234 (5)   2/157 (1)
7/261 (8) 8/287 (7) 9/313 (10) 10/322 (11)

Masters 36–12–68–5; Topley 14.1–5–51–1; Napier 23–3–81–1; Bopara 20–3–79–1; Panesar 15–6–37–2. *Second innings*—Masters 10–1–35–0; Topley 10–0–40–0; Panesar 11–2–30–0; Napier 11–1–49–2; Smith 1–0–5–0; Shah 1–0–3–0.

Essex

J. C. Mickleburgh c Rees b Hogan	129	G. R. Napier c Wright b Smith	0
G. Gambhir c Salter b Cosker	37	B 4, l-b 6, w 5, n-b 8	23
G. M. Smith c Cosker b Hogan	16		
O. A. Shah c Rees b Smith	120	1/95 (2) (6 wkts dec, 89 overs) 424	
R. S. Bopara c Goodwin b Smith	89	2/132 (3) 3/256 (1)	
*†J. S. Foster not out	10	4/386 (4) 5/421 (5) 6/424 (7)	

B. T. Foakes, D. D. Masters, M. S. Panesar and R. J. W. Topley did not bat.

Hogan 21–7–48–2; Glover 20–0–94–0; Smith 18–0–106–3; Cosker 16–1–74–1; Salter 6–1–34–0; Bragg 8–0–58–0.

Umpires: J. H. Evans and S. J. O'Shaughnessy.

At Southampton, September 24–26. ESSEX lost to HAMPSHIRE by an innings and 31 runs. *Essex rest several first-team players, despite retaining a chance of promotion.*

GLAMORGAN

Land of hope (but not glory)

Edward Bevan

Glamorgan's disappointment at failing to make any progress in the Championship and the FLt20 was tempered by their first appearance in a Lord's final since 2000. They were well beaten in the YB40 showpiece by Nottinghamshire, but it was a joyful occasion for the hordes of supporters who made the long journey to London.

Glamorgan finished next to bottom in the second division of the Championship, but they were a better side than that. The absence of a ruthless streak cost them, while too often they relied on individuals rather than collective contributions. After they won their first four Twenty20 games, a place in the quarter-finals looked a formality – but following defeat in the fifth, off the last ball at Northampton, they won only once more, and missed out. The former Australian Test batsman Marcus North captained in the one-day competitions but, apart from a YB40 century against Middlesex, he made little impact in any format. North returned home at the end of August, and missed the YB40 semi and final; his contract was not renewed. Mark Wallace, who led shrewdly in the four-day game, took charge.

The start of the Championship season had been encouraging enough. Glamorgan beat Worcestershire in their second game, and should have followed up with another win, against Lancashire at Colwyn Bay. Needing 154, Glamorgan were coasting at 94 for two – but eight tumbled for 45, and the collapse seemed to affect them for a while. Although they made the opposition follow on twice, they did not win again until bottom club Leicestershire were walloped by an innings at Swansea in late August.

The decision to sign the Zimbabwean Murray Goodwin proved a masterstroke. Some had queried the acquisition of a 40-year-old who had been released by Sussex, but the personable Goodwin responded with 1,263 runs at 57; only three batsmen made more in the Championship. Matthew Mott, the head of elite performance, praised his attitude and the help he gave to the younger players. Jim Allenby was the only other batsman to reach 1,000 in the Championship. Significant contributions in one-day cricket took him past 2,000 runs in all competitions, and he was rewarded with a four-year contract.

The opening partnership was neither settled nor reliable, producing not a single century stand all summer. There was a partial fix when Gareth Rees returned after being left out since the previous August; he responded with two centuries and a fifty in his first four innings. But the experiment of opening with Ben Wright – a middle-order batsman – unsurprisingly failed.

Rees averaged 40 but, apart from Chris Cooke, who won a deserved place after some impressive one-day form, the other batsmen failed to score regularly. Wright, Will Bragg and Stewart Walters were all left out at various times,

Clive Gee, PA Photos

Michael Hogan

while Bragg again was unable to convert any of his fifties into hundreds, and had managed only one century in a career that began back in 2007.

The attack was superbly led by Michael Hogan, a new signing for 2013 after some success for Western Australia. A British passport holder, Hogan was easily the county's leading wicket-taker in the Championship with 67, and claimed 103 in all competitions. His old-fashioned work ethic was reminiscent of Michael Kasprowicz, another big-hearted Australian who had prospered at Glamorgan. Unfortunately, Hogan's new-ball partners were either injured or ineffective; only Dean Cosker's spin and Mike Reed's enthusiastic medium-pace produced more than 30 wickets. Reed, a former Cardiff MCCU student, was selected for the England Performance Programme during the winter.

At the end of August, Hugh Morris announced he would be relinquishing his position as managing director of the England team to return to his former county as chief executive and director of cricket. His appointment was widely welcomed. One of his first duties was to appoint the former Middlesex and Sussex batsman Toby Radford as coach. The Caerphilly-born Radford had been West Indies' assistant coach, and previously worked under Morris at the ECB.

Morris succeeded Alan Hamer, who stood down after six years, during which he played a big part in the development of Sophia Gardens into a major Test arena. Mott had confirmed he would be leaving at the end of the season, after three years, to pursue other coaching opportunities – preferably in his native Australia. Following North's departure, Glamorgan signed Jacques Rudolph, the former South African Test batsman, as their overseas player on a two-year contract. Rudolph, who had previously appeared for Yorkshire and Surrey, will open the batting.

Cardiff successfully hosted five games in the Champions Trophy, and one of England's one-dayers against Australia. (Early in 2014, they submitted a bid to host the ICC's new headquarters from 2015.) The profit, which comfortably exceeded the staging fees paid to the ECB, helped reduce the operating loss to £315,000, considerably less than the worrying £2m deficit the previous financial year. And with Morris returning, the team slowly improving, and two young local players – Andrew Salter and Ruaidhri Smith – making promising first-class debuts, everything at Glamorgan points to a resurgence.

Championship attendance: 20,167.

GLAMORGAN RESULTS

All first-class matches – Played 17: Won 3, Lost 6, Drawn 8.
County Championship matches – Played 16: Won 3, Lost 6, Drawn 7.

LV= County Championship, 8th in Division 2;
Friends Life t20, 3rd in Midlands/Wales/West Division; Yorkshire Bank 40, finalists.

COUNTY CHAMPIONSHIP AVERAGES, BATTING AND FIELDING

Cap		M	I	NO	R	HS	100	50	Avge	Ct/St
2010	J. Allenby................	15	23	4	1,116	138*	2	8	58.73	27
	M. W. Goodwin¶...........	16	26	4	1,263	194	4	7	57.40	7
2009	G. P. Rees†...............	8	14	1	524	112	2	3	40.30	5
	C. B. Cooke..............	7	11	1	394	92	0	3	39.40	2
	R. A. J. Smith............	3	4	1	100	39	0	0	33.33	0
2013	G. G. Wagg..............	10	12	1	308	58	0	2	28.00	1
2003	M. A. Wallace†...........	16	23	0	631	101	1	2	27.43	40/3
	W. D. Bragg†............	14	24	2	535	71*	0	2	24.31	3
2011	B. J. Wright.............	13	23	2	499	63	0	2	23.76	10
	M. J. North§.............	10	16	1	354	68	0	1	23.60	5
	S. J. Walters¶............	9	15	0	343	98	0	2	22.86	13
2013	M. G. Hogan¶............	14	18	3	297	51	0	1	19.80	5
2000	D. A. Cosker.............	15	21	6	281	44*	0	0	18.73	7
	J. C. Glover†.............	7	9	2	127	51*	0	1	18.14	1
	M. T. Reed..............	11	15	7	71	27	0	0	8.87	2
	A. G. Salter†.............	3	4	0	29	16	0	0	7.25	1

Also batted: A. J. Jones† (1 match) 5* (1 ct); D. L. Lloyd† (1 match) 16; N. L. McCullum§ (1 match) 14, 35*; W. T. Owen† (2 matches) 5, 40, 0 (2 ct).

† *Born in Wales.* § *Official overseas player.* ¶ *Other non-England-qualified player.*

BOWLING

	Style	O	M	R	W	BB	5I	Avge
M. G. Hogan	RFM	512	133	1,376	67	7-92	4	20.53
R. A. J. Smith...................	RM	61	6	274	10	3-50	0	27.40
D. A. Cosker	SLA	429.2	82	1,261	37	5-120	1	34.08
M. T. Reed	RFM	309.5	58	1,074	31	5-27	1	34.64
J. Allenby......................	RM	371.5	103	909	26	4-16	0	34.96
J. C. Glover	RM	147.1	26	498	13	4-51	0	38.30
G. G. Wagg	SLA/LM	295.2	63	971	18	3-78	0	53.94

Also bowled: W. D. Bragg (SLA) 22–2–111–2; A. J. Jones (LM) 12–0–53–0; N. L. McCullum (OB) 47.4–6–191–5; M. J. North (OB) 48.2–6–143–7; W. T. Owen (RFM) 47–8–170–1; G. P. Rees (LM) 1–0–2–0; A. G. Salter (OB) 55–14–182–7; B. J. Wright (RM) 1–0–7–0.

LEADING YB40 AVERAGES (100 runs/4 wickets)

Batting	Runs	HS	Avge	SR	Ct/St
B. J. Wright....	179	75*	59.66	122.60	4
C. B. Cooke ...	546	98	42.00	101.11	9
J. Allenby	454	85	41.27	113.78	4
M. J. North	381	137*	38.10	98.19	2
M. A. Wallace ..	437	118*	36.41	101.62	8/1
W. D. Bragg ...	203	62	33.83	87.12	0
G. P. Rees	218	83	31.14	67.28	1
M. W. Goodwin	333	49	30.27	122.42	4
G. G. Wagg....	174	54	21.75	121.67	7

Bowling	W	BB	Avge	ER
M. G. Hogan	28	4-34	17.42	5.58
W. T. Owen	5	3-48	29.80	6.77
S. P. Jones......	10	2-17	32.90	5.87
D. A. Cosker ...	15	3-32	33.80	5.39
G. G. Wagg	18	4-51	36.50	7.30
J. Allenby	12	3-37	36.58	5.10

LEADING FLt20 AVERAGES (100 runs/18 overs)

Batting	Runs	HS	Avge	SR	Ct/St
J. Allenby	355	85*	50.71	134.98	1
C. B. Cooke	217	57	24.11	130.72	6
M. W. Goodwin	158	59	19.75	128.45	2
M. A. Wallace	188	69*	23.50	118.23	1/3
M. J. North	145	37	24.16	86.82	1

Bowling	W	BB	Avge	ER
M. G. Hogan	8	3-11	24.62	**5.62**
D. A. Cosker	7	2-18	33.14	**6.62**
G. G. Wagg	15	5-14	16.00	**7.27**
J. Allenby	2	1-27	78.00	**7.42**
N. L. McCullum	10	2-20	25.20	**8.12**

FIRST-CLASS COUNTY RECORDS

Highest score for	309*	S. P. James v Sussex at Colwyn Bay	2000
Highest score against	322*	M. B. Loye (Northamptonshire) at Northampton	1998
Leading run-scorer	34,056	A. Jones (avge 33.03)	1957–83
Best bowling for	10-51	J. Mercer v Worcestershire at Worcester	1936
Best bowling against	10-18	G. Geary (Leicestershire) at Pontypridd	1929
Leading wicket-taker	2,174	D. J. Shepherd (avge 20.95)	1950–72
Highest total for	718-3 dec	v Sussex at Colwyn Bay	2000
Highest total against	712	by Northamptonshire at Northampton	1998
Lowest total for	22	v Lancashire at Liverpool	1924
Lowest total against	33	by Leicestershire at Ebbw Vale	1965

LIST A COUNTY RECORDS

Highest score for	162*	I. V. A. Richards v Oxfordshire at Swansea	1993
Highest score against	268	A. D. Brown (Surrey) at The Oval	2002
Leading run-scorer	12,278	M. P. Maynard (avge 37.66)	1985–2005
Best bowling for	7-16	S. D. Thomas v Surrey at Swansea	1998
Best bowling against	7-30	M. P. Bicknell (Surrey) at The Oval	1999
Leading wicket-taker	356	R. D. B. Croft (avge 31.96)	1989–2012
Highest total for	429	v Surrey at The Oval	2002
Highest total against	438-5	by Surrey at The Oval	2002
Lowest total for	42	v Derbyshire at Swansea	1979
Lowest total against	59	by Combined Universities at Cambridge	1983
	59	by Sussex at Hove	1996

TWENTY20 COUNTY RECORDS

Highest score for	116*	I. J. Thomas v Somerset at Taunton	2004
Highest score against	117	M. J. Prior (Sussex) at Hove	2010
Leading run-scorer	1,061	M. A. Wallace (avge 18.94)	2003–13
Best bowling for	5-14	G. G. Wagg v Worcestershire at Worcester	**2013**
Best bowling against	6-5	A. V. Suppiah (Somerset) at Cardiff	2011
Leading wicket-taker	87	R. D. B. Croft (avge 23.16)	2003–12
Highest total for	206-6	v Somerset at Taunton	2006
Highest total against	239-5	by Sussex at Hove	2010
Lowest total for	94-9	v Essex at Cardiff	2010
Lowest total against	81	by Gloucestershire at Bristol	2011

ADDRESS

Swalec Stadium, Sophia Gardens, Cardiff CF11 9XR (029 2040 9380;
email info@glamorgancricket.co.uk). **Website** www.glamorgancricket.com

OFFICIALS

Captain M. A. Wallace
    2014 (Twenty20) J. Allenby
Head coach T. A. Radford
Player development manager R. V. Almond
President F. D. Morgan

Chairman B. J. O'Brien
Chief executive and
    director of cricket H. Morris
Head groundsman K. W. Exton
Scorer/archivist A. K. Hignell

GLAMORGAN v CARDIFF MCCU

At Cardiff, April 5–7. Drawn. Toss: Cardiff MCCU. First-class debuts: F. K. Cowdrey, J. S. T. Denning, D. S. Phillips.

In a match played in freezing conditions, the Cardiff students happily settled for a draw after being set 348 in 56 overs. Their ranks included Fabian Cowdrey: watched by his father, Chris, he marked his first-class debut with 62 in the second innings after a century against Devon the previous week. Michael Reed, a 6ft 6in seamer playing against his old university, claimed career-best figures in a hostile spell. Wallace injured a finger in the course of his 200th first-class match, and substitute Chris Cooke kept wicket in the second innings.

Close of play: first day, Cardiff MCCU 33-0 (Cowdrey 14, Elkin 15); second day, Glamorgan 113-2 (Walters 1, North 2).

Glamorgan

G. P. Rees c Elkin b Harris	7	– (5) c Balbirnie b Salter	33
W. D. Bragg b Phillips	62	– c Elkin b Harris	63
S. J. Walters c Davies b Phillips	36	– b Hobden	19
M. J. North b Hobden	10	– lbw b Hobden	28
B. J. Wright not out	68	– (1) lbw b Harris	37
J. Allenby c Denning b Salter	48	– not out	38
*†M. A. Wallace c Miles b Denning	25		
J. C. Glover c Davies b Denning	0		
D. A. Cosker not out	5		
B 1, l-b 5, w 2, n-b 6	14	L-b 4, w 5, n-b 14	23

1/16 (1) 2/117 (3) (7 wkts dec, 85 overs) 275
3/117 (2) 4/135 (4)
5/236 (6) 6/269 (7)
7/269 (8)

1/103 (1) (5 wkts dec, 58.2 overs) 241
2/110 (2) 3/156 (3)
4/165 (4) 5/241 (5)

H. T. Waters and M. T. Reed did not bat.

Denning 19–5–46–2; Hobden 17–3–68–1; Harris 11–1–37–1; Phillips 14–1–45–2; Salter 16–1–49–1; Balbirnie 7–1–22–0; Cowdrey 1–0–2–0. *Second innings—*Denning 15–4–54–0; Hobden 17–3–81–2; Phillips 9–1–50–0; Harris 7–0–22–2; Salter 9.2–2–24–1; Balbirnie 1–0–6–0.

Cardiff MCCU

F. K. Cowdrey c Wallace b Reed	15	– lbw b Allenby	62
Z. Elkin c Wallace b Waters	23	– c sub (C. B. Cooke) b Reed	2
U. A. Qureshi c Wallace b Reed	0	– run out	13
A. Balbirnie b Reed	15	– c North b Allenby	4
S. L. Davies lbw b Allenby	31	– c sub (C. B. Cooke) b Allenby	4
*†A. J. Miles b Reed	10	– not out	29
A. G. Salter c Wallace b Waters	16	– c Allenby b Waters	12
P. G. Harris lbw b Reed	0	– not out	11
M. E. Hobden c North b Glover	18		
J. S. T. Denning not out	22		
D. S. Phillips c Bragg b Reed	7		
L-b 12	12	L-b 7	7

1/36 (1) 2/36 (3) 3/54 (4) (82.4 overs) 169
4/71 (2) 5/97 (5) 6/113 (6)
7/113 (8) 8/115 (7)
9/153 (9) 10/169 (11)

1/6 (2) 2/60 (3) (6 wkts, 48 overs) 144
3/81 (4) 4/82 (1)
5/91 (5) 6/127 (7)

Waters 18–8–35–2; Glover 20–8–36–1; Cosker 17–8–23–0; Reed 14.4–3–34–6; Allenby 13–3–29–1. *Second innings—*Waters 12–1–54–1; Reed 6–2–12–1; Glover 7–1–24–0; Cosker 16–3–34–0; Allenby 7–3–13–3.

Umpires: N. G. C. Cowley and A. G. Wharf.

GLAMORGAN v NORTHAMPTONSHIRE

At Cardiff, April 10–13. Drawn. Glamorgan 6pts, Northamptonshire 8pts. Toss: Northamptonshire. County debuts: M. W. Goodwin, M. G. Hogan; T. A. Copeland.

Glamorgan were lucky to escape with a draw when rain washed out the final day; in all, 196 overs were swallowed by the weather. In a feeble batting display, Glamorgan lost their last nine first-innings wickets for 76, with Crook – back with Northamptonshire after two years with Middlesex – the most impressive of the visitors' four seamers. Peters and Middlebrook, who batted at No. 7 for more than three hours, then set up a substantial lead. Glamorgan made a better start to their second innings, only to lose four wickets for nine, and were still some way adrift by the end of the third day – but the rain came to their rescue.

Close of play: first day, Northamptonshire 108-3 (Peters 60, Newton 21); second day, Northamptonshire 145-5 (Hall 4, Middlebrook 3); third day, Glamorgan 96-4 (Goodwin 3, Allenby 16).

Glamorgan

B. J. Wright c Murphy b Willey	0	– c Copeland b Hall	20
W. D. Bragg c Coetzer b Crook	22	– lbw b Willey	39
S. J. Walters lbw b Hall	23	– c Murphy b Hall	8
M. J. North c Hall b Crook	2	– c Murphy b Crook	1
M. W. Goodwin c Murphy b Willey	8	– not out	3
J. Allenby lbw b Copeland	16	– not out	16
*†M. A. Wallace b Crook	18		
G. G. Wagg c Copeland b Crook	26		
D. A. Cosker b Hall	0		
M. G. Hogan c Crook b Hall	0		
M. T. Reed not out	0		
B 4, l-b 12, w 1, n-b 2	19	L-b 7, n-b 2	9

1/7 (1) 2/58 (2) 3/58 (3) 4/60 (4) (50 overs) 134 1/62 (2) (4 wkts, 42 overs) 96
5/87 (5) 6/87 (6) 7/117 (7) 8/134 (9) 2/62 (1) 3/69 (4)
9/134 (8) 10/134 (10) 4/71 (3)

Willey 13–0–47–2; Copeland 15–9–23–1; Crook 12–3–30–4; Hall 10–6–18–3. *Second innings*—Willey 11–0–35–1; Copeland 12–3–19–0; Crook 11–4–19–1; Hall 8–2–16–2.

Northamptonshire

*S. D. Peters c Walters b Allenby	67	D. J. Willey b Wagg	5
K. J. Coetzer b Hogan	5	S. P. Crook lbw b Wagg	8
D. J. Sales c Cosker b Reed	16	T. A. Copeland not out	0
A. G. Wakely lbw b Reed	0	B 4, l-b 13, n-b 6	23
R. I. Newton lbw b Allenby	39		
A. J. Hall c Wright b Reed	32		
J. D. Middlebrook c Allenby b Wagg	70		
†D. Murphy c Allenby b Hogan	27		

1/17 (2) 2/58 (3) 3/58 (4) (90.1 overs) 292
4/137 (5) 5/142 (1) 6/202 (6)
7/266 (8) 8/281 (9) 9/291 (10) 10/292 (7)

Hogan 27–7–77–2; Wagg 22.1–6–78–3; Reed 17–3–53–3; Allenby 18–6–43–2; Cosker 6–1–24–0.

Umpires: S. A. Garratt and T. E. Jesty.

GLAMORGAN v WORCESTERSHIRE

At Cardiff, April 17–20. Glamorgan won by ten wickets. Glamorgan 21pts, Worcestershire 3pts. Toss: Glamorgan.

In 2012 Glamorgan did not win a Championship match until mid-July, but now they atoned for their underwhelming opening game by completing their first victory over Worcestershire in Cardiff since 1971, when Tony Lewis was captain. The two tall fast bowlers, Hogan and Reed, did the damage in the first innings, using their height to gain bounce and movement. Reed had spent the winter in Sydney, and said he had benefited from working with Geoff Lawson, the former Australian

Test fast bowler. Allenby, who batted faultlessly for three and a half hours, then set up a big lead. When Worcestershire went in again on the third day, Wallace's decision to give Bragg the final over before tea proved inspirational: an occasional seamer with only two first-class wickets to his name, he dismissed Ali with his second delivery, and added Kervezee three balls after the interval. Samaraweera held Glamorgan up with a watchful 79 but, once he was out, the tail surrendered to Allenby, who completed an outstanding all-round performance.

Close of play: first day, Glamorgan 0-0 (Wright 0, Bragg 0); second day, Glamorgan 235-7 (Allenby 71, Cosker 8); third day, Worcestershire 186-5 (Samaraweera 71, Johnson 17).

Worcestershire

*D. K. H. Mitchell c Walters b Reed	20	– c Bragg b Allenby	10
M. G. Pardoe c Wright b Hogan	11	– b Wagg	0
M. M. Ali c Wright b Hogan	20	– b Bragg	55
T. T. Samaraweera lbw b Hogan	0	– c and b Hogan	79
A. N. Kervezee lbw b Reed	2	– c Allenby b Bragg	0
N. D. Pinner b Allenby	12	– lbw b Hogan	13
†M. A. Johnson b Reed	5	– c North b Allenby	18
G. M. Andrew b Hogan	9	– c North b Hogan	10
D. S. Lucas c Cosker b Reed	12	– b Allenby	0
C. J. Russell b Reed	10	– lbw b Allenby	2
A. Richardson not out	9	– not out	0
B 1, l-b 10, n-b 2	13	B 6, l-b 3, w 5, n-b 6	20

1/13 (2) 2/55 (1) 3/56 (4)   (63.1 overs) 123   1/1 (2) 2/50 (1)   (84.1 overs) 207
4/59 (3) 5/59 (5) 6/69 (7)   3/97 (3) 4/97 (5)
7/85 (6) 8/102 (8) 9/102 (9) 10/123 (10)   5/138 (6) 6/195 (4) 7/195 (7)
     8/197 (9) 9/199 (10) 10/207 (8)

Hogan 19–10–33–4; Wagg 16–4–22–0; Allenby 13–3–30–1; Reed 15.1–4–27–5. *Second innings*—Wagg 19–4–55–1; Hogan 23.1–6–61–3; Reed 15–4–36–0; Allenby 20–10–27–4; Cosker 4–1–9–0; Bragg 3–1–10–2.

Glamorgan

B. J. Wright c Johnson b Richardson	40	– not out	30
W. D. Bragg b Andrew	17	– not out	3
S. J. Walters lbw b Andrew	11		
M. J. North lbw b Richardson	48		
M. W. Goodwin c Pinner b Lucas	1		
J. Allenby c Mitchell b Andrew	78		
*†M. A. Wallace c Johnson b Andrew	1		
G. G. Wagg c Lucas b Richardson	24		
D. A. Cosker not out	44		
M. G. Hogan b Russell	1		
M. T. Reed b Russell	15		
B 9, l-b 6	15	B 2, l-b 1	3

1/22 (2) 2/44 (3) 3/103 (1)   (108.4 overs) 295   (no wkt, 9.1 overs) 36
4/114 (5) 5/143 (4) 6/152 (7)
7/215 (8) 8/256 (6) 9/259 (10) 10/295 (11)

Richardson 33–11–62–3; Russell 20.4–4–74–2; Andrew 32–12–79–4; Lucas 15–5–40–1; Ali 5–0–15–0; Mitchell 3–0–10–0. *Second innings*—Russell 3–1–13–0; Richardson 3–0–11–0; Ali 2–1–2–0; Lucas 1.1–0–7–0.

Umpires: N. L. Bainton and P. Willey.

> **"** Emotions are running high. There's not a lot of singing and dancing going on."
> Essex v Lancashire, page 483

GLAMORGAN v LANCASHIRE

At Colwyn Bay, May 1–3. Lancashire won by 14 runs. Lancashire 19pts, Glamorgan 4pts. Toss: Lancashire.

Needing 154 to win with time in hand, Glamorgan were cruising to victory at 94 for two – but collapsed against the swing and seam of Chapple and the left-arm spin of Kerrigan. The last eight wickets disappeared for 45 in less than 20 overs to a combination of accurate bowling and poor shot selection. To lose a match they had controlled until the final hour was "gut-wrenching", according to Wallace. Bragg and Wright had made a positive start, with the 39-year-old Chapple struck for 22 in his first two overs. But he returned for the 17th over at the other end, and changed the course of the game. Kerrigan, despite minimal turn, also induced some poor strokes, and when he had Hogan caught by a leaping Prince on the long-off boundary Lancashire celebrated as if they had won the Championship (admittedly, it was their first victory in 11 attempts). Earlier, they had been indebted to Cross and Hogg, who put on 63 for the ninth wicket after Katich's gritty half-century to set up what still seemed a modest target.

Close of play: first day, Glamorgan 110-4 (Goodwin 16, Allenby 10); second day, Lancashire 104-4 (Katich 28, Anderson 0).

Lancashire

P. J. Horton b Hogan	0	– c Wallace b Reed	24
L. A. Procter lbw b Allenby	26	– c Wallace b Hogan	4
K. R. Brown b Hogan	6	– b Hogan	13
A. G. Prince lbw b Reed	17	– lbw b Hogan	25
S. M. Katich c Wallace b Glover	19	– c Wallace b Glover	65
S. J. Croft c Goodwin b Reed	8	– (7) c Wallace b Reed	18
†G. D. Cross lbw b Glover	9	– (8) c Cosker b Glover	30
*G. Chapple c Allenby b Hogan	5	– (9) c Glover b Reed	26
K. W. Hogg lbw b Glover	2	– (10) c Wallace b Glover	47
J. M. Anderson not out	11	– (6) b Allenby	0
S. C. Kerrigan c Allenby b North	7	– not out	0
B 1, l-b 1, w 5, n-b 6	13	B 7, l-b 7, n-b 6	20

1/0 (1) 2/14 (3) 3/54 (2)   (52.2 overs) 123   1/9 (2) 2/43 (1)   (107.1 overs) 272
4/54 (4) 5/66 (6) 6/96 (7)   3/49 (3) 4/101 (4)
7/97 (5) 8/103 (9) 9/103 (8) 10/123 (11)   5/105 (6) 6/154 (7) 7/164 (5)
                                       8/208 (9) 9/271 (8) 10/272 (10)

Hogan 15–6–31–3; Glover 12–2–29–3; Allenby 12–4–17–1; Reed 12–3–37–2; Cosker 1–0–7–0; North 0.2–0–0–1. *Second innings*—Hogan 24–7–78–3; Glover 21.1–4–41–3; Reed 23–6–63–3; Allenby 26–8–46–1; North 1–0–1–0; Cosker 12–2–29–0.

Glamorgan

B. J. Wright c Cross b Anderson	6	– c Brown b Anderson	14
W. D. Bragg lbw b Kerrigan	34	– b Chapple	61
S. J. Walters b Anderson	15	– lbw b Kerrigan	5
M. J. North lbw b Anderson	22	– c Cross b Chapple	9
M. W. Goodwin b Hogg	69	– c Katich b Kerrigan	11
J. Allenby c Croft b Kerrigan	46	– lbw b Chapple	4
*†M. A. Wallace c Brown b Kerrigan	0	– b Chapple	12
J. C. Glover lbw b Kerrigan	9	– lbw b Kerrigan	8
D. A. Cosker lbw b Hogg	10	– c Anderson b Kerrigan	2
M. G. Hogan c Brown b Hogg	10	– c Prince b Kerrigan	7
M. T. Reed not out	1	– not out	0
B 1, l-b 13, n-b 6	20	B 4, l-b 2	6

1/12 (1) 2/36 (3) 3/82 (2)   (83.5 overs) 242   1/38 (1) 2/71 (3)   (37.4 overs) 139
4/89 (4) 5/156 (6) 6/156 (7)   3/94 (4) 4/103 (2)
7/174 (8) 8/203 (9) 9/227 (10) 10/242 (5)   5/109 (6) 6/111 (5) 7/129 (7)
                                       8/131 (8) 9/138 (9) 10/139 (10)

Anderson 25–5–63–3; Chapple 17–6–47–0; Hogg 13.5–1–44–3; Procter 12–3–26–0; Kerrigan 16–4–48–4. *Second innings*—Anderson 8–0–31–1; Chapple 13–1–64–4; Hogg 1–0–6–0; Kerrigan 15.4–5–32–5.

Umpires: R. T. Robinson and M. J. Saggers.

GLAMORGAN v ESSEX

At Cardiff, May 15–18. Essex won by five wickets. Essex 22pts, Glamorgan 4pts. Toss: Essex.

Glamorgan fancied their chances after leaving Essex 275 in 70 overs, but the pitch – which had been seamer-friendly over the first three days – flattened out on the final afternoon, and the visitors paced their run-chase perfectly to win with seven balls remaining. Westley and Mickleburgh laid the foundation with a flourishing opening partnership of 143, before Pettini guided them to their second win of the season. Earlier, Glamorgan's top order had struggled again in the first innings before Allenby ensured a batting point. Then Bopara was the catalyst for Essex: newly restored to England's one-day squad, he entered at ten for two, and batted six hours for a classy 145. His efforts trumped a probing spell from Hogan, whose career-best-equalling figures included a superb left-handed diving slip catch from Walters to send back Pettini; Allenby matched it with another fine grab to dismiss Foakes and give Cosker his first wicket of the season. Glamorgan amassed 388 in their second innings, mainly thanks to Walters and Wallace, who broke his thumb during his 15th first-class century. But it wasn't enough.

Close of play: first day, Essex 10-2 (Mickleburgh 6, Bopara 0); second day, Essex 343-9 (Napier 41, Topley 0); third day, Glamorgan 303-6 (Wallace 61, Wagg 32).

Glamorgan

B. J. Wright c Foakes b Masters	6	– b Masters	0
W. D. Bragg c Foster b Napier	17	– lbw b Bopara	42
S. J. Walters c Smith b Topley	67	– c Foster b Phillips	98
M. J. North c Phillips b Masters	8	– b Masters	2
M. W. Goodwin b Topley	1	– c Foster b Topley	42
J. Allenby lbw b Bopara	77	– b Masters	11
*†M. A. Wallace b Masters	5	– b Bopara	101
G. G. Wagg c Foster b Bopara	13	– c Foster b Topley	55
D. A. Cosker b Bopara b Masters	18	– c Foster b Napier	10
M. G. Hogan c Topley b Masters	9	– b Phillips	5
M. T. Reed not out	2	– not out	1
L-b 8	8	B 1, l-b 10, n-b 10	21

1/6 (1) 2/30 (2) 3/87 (4)   (86.1 overs) 231   1/0 (1) 2/65 (2)   (118.1 overs) 388
4/104 (5) 5/105 (3) 6/114 (7)   3/74 (4) 4/165 (5)
7/142 (8) 8/213 (6) 9/229 (10) 10/231 (9)   5/184 (6) 6/234 (3) 7/343 (8)
                                         8/375 (9) 9/386 (7) 10/388 (10)

Masters 21.1–5–44–5; Topley 21–5–52–2; Napier 18–2–67–1; Bopara 19–3–41–2; Phillips 4–2–9–0; Smith 3–0–10–0. *Second innings*—Masters 33–3–116–3; Topley 27–0–104–2; Napier 19–1–61–1; Bopara 22–4–48–2; Phillips 17.1–2–48–2.

Essex

T. Westley b Hogan	0	– run out	88
J. C. Mickleburgh lbw b Hogan	16	– lbw b Allenby	66
D. D. Masters lbw b Hogan	4		
R. S. Bopara b Wagg	145	– (3) c Walters b Cosker	33
M. L. Pettini c Walters b Hogan	28	– (4) not out	47
B. T. Foakes c Allenby b Cosker	38		
G. M. Smith c Wallace b Reed	7	– not out	7
*†J. S. Foster c Wallace b Hogan	27	– (6) c Allenby b Hogan	20
G. R. Napier c Allenby b Hogan	43	– (5) c Bragg b Cosker	10
T. J. Phillips lbw b Allenby	0		
R. J. W. Topley not out	0		
B 6, l-b 8, w 1, n-b 22	37	L-b 4	4

1/0 (1) 2/10 (3) 3/25 (2)   (103.3 overs) 345   1/143 (2)   (5 wkts, 68.5 overs) 275
4/86 (5) 5/169 (6) 6/182 (7)   2/166 (1) 3/211 (3)
7/273 (8) 8/299 (4) 9/304 (10) 10/345 (9)   4/230 (5) 5/268 (6)

Hogan 25.3–7–70–6; Wagg 23–4–92–1; Allenby 20–6–64–1; Reed 22–3–85–1; Cosker 13–4–20–1. *Second innings*—Hogan 16.4–4–50–1; Wagg 16–2–57–0; Reed 6–0–20–0; Cosker 19–0–90–2; Allenby 10.5–1–47–1; North 1–0–7–0.

Umpires: N. G. C. Cowley and G. Sharp.

At Leicester, May 21–24. GLAMORGAN drew with LEICESTERSHIRE.

At Bristol, June 5–8. GLAMORGAN drew with GLOUCESTERSHIRE.

At Canterbury, June 12–15. GLAMORGAN drew with KENT.

At Worcester, June 20–23. GLAMORGAN lost to WORCESTERSHIRE by eight wickets.

GLAMORGAN v HAMPSHIRE

At Cardiff, July 8–11. Hampshire won by 43 runs. Hampshire 21pts, Glamorgan 5pts. Toss: Hampshire.

Wallace's enterprising declaration – 41 behind on first innings – and five wickets for North's off-spin set up a positive finish, but the top order were again unable to provide a solid start, and Glamorgan eventually fell short. Set 221, they stumbled to 58 for five before Goodwin and Wallace put on 80 in 38 overs. But after Wallace was trapped in front, the tail offered little resistance. A slow pitch had not encouraged positive strokeplay, and Hampshire averaged well under three an over in both innings. Rees, recalled after being discarded the previous August, responded with a chanceless century in Glamorgan's first innings, but Wright failed once more and was subsequently dropped. Returning to the city where he played for Cardiff UCCE ten years earlier, Tomlinson took five wickets in the second innings, including the first four; Briggs added three as Glamorgan slid to their fourth defeat of the season.

Close of play: first day, Hampshire 274-5 (Dawson 69, Wheater 14); second day, Glamorgan 196-3 (Rees 84, Goodwin 57); third day, Hampshire 174-9 (Briggs 10).

Hampshire

M. A. Carberry c Walters b Cosker	31	– c Walters b Reed	0
*J. H. K. Adams c Walters b Owen	47	– st Wallace b North	14
L. A. Dawson c Allenby b Hogan	72	– b North	13
N. D. McKenzie b Hogan	11	– c and b Allenby	67
J. M. Vince lbw b Hogan	80	– run out	9
S. M. Ervine c Walters b Allenby	0	– lbw b Hogan	3
†A. J. Wheater c Owen b Cosker	43	– b Hogan	0
Sohail Tanvir c Wallace b Allenby	4	– c Allenby b North	38
D. R. Briggs not out	26	– c Rees b North	15
D. J. Balcombe c Wallace b Reed	3	– b North	5
J. A. Tomlinson c Allenby b Cosker	0	– not out	0
B 2, l-b 10, n-b 12	24	B 4, l-b 1, n-b 10	15

1/76 (1) 2/93 (2) 3/118 (4)   (122.5 overs) 341
4/250 (5) 5/251 (6) 6/281 (3)
7/286 (8) 8/331 (7) 9/338 (10)
10/341 (11)   110 overs: 301-7

1/11 (1) 2/27 (2)   (67.3 overs) 179
3/28 (3) 4/50 (5)
5/53 (6) 6/53 (7) 7/154 (4)
8/156 (8) 9/174 (10) 10/179 (9)

Hogan 29–13–48–3; Owen 16–3–51–1; Allenby 27–6–82–2; Reed 19–5–53–1; Cosker 29.5–5–82–3; North 2–0–13–0. *Second innings*—Hogan 16–7–26–2; Reed 11.2–2–46–1; North 15.1–3–30–5; Allenby 14–2–41–1; Cosker 11–1–31–0.

Glamorgan

B. J. Wright c Wheater b Tomlinson	20	– c Dawson b Tomlinson	5
G. P. Rees c Dawson b Balcombe	112	– c Dawson b Tomlinson	18
S. J. Walters c Ervine b Sohail Tanvir	0	– c Ervine b Tomlinson	7
M. J. North st Wheater b Briggs	18	– lbw b Tomlinson	15
M. W. Goodwin lbw b Sohail Tanvir	86	– not out	56
J. Allenby not out	29	– c Dawson b Balcombe	0
*†M. A. Wallace lbw b Sohail Tanvir	0	– lbw b Tomlinson	44
D. A. Cosker not out	3	– st Wheater b Briggs	2
M. G. Hogan (did not bat)		– c Tomlinson b Sohail Tanvir	18
W. T. Owen (did not bat)		– b Briggs	0
M. T. Reed (did not bat)		– lbw b Briggs	0
B 8, l-b 16, w 2, n-b 6	32	B 4, l-b 6, n-b 2	12

1/24 (1) 2/35 (3)   (6 wkts dec, 98.5 overs) 300
3/84 (4) 4/266 (2)
5/266 (5) 6/272 (7)

1/11 (1) 2/23 (3)   (68 overs) 177
3/42 (2) 4/55 (4) 5/58 (6)
6/138 (7) 7/151 (8) 8/172 (9)
9/177 (10) 10/177 (11)

Sohail Tanvir 21–3–62–3; Tomlinson 16–6–28–1; Balcombe 23–6–56–1; Vince 14.5–3–46–0; Briggs 17–1–58–1; Dawson 6–0–18–0; Carberry 1–0–8–0. *Second innings*—Sohail Tanvir 15–1–43–1; Tomlinson 18–6–44–5; Balcombe 8–2–23–1; Briggs 19–6–33–3; Dawson 8–0–24–0.

Umpires: R. T. Robinson and C. Shamshuddin.

At Manchester, July 15–18. GLAMORGAN drew with LANCASHIRE.

At Southampton, August 2–5. GLAMORGAN drew with HAMPSHIRE.

GLAMORGAN v LEICESTERSHIRE

At Swansea, August 21–24. Glamorgan won by an innings and 37 runs. Glamorgan 24pts, Leicestershire 3pts. Toss: Leicestershire. County debut: B. A. Raine. Championship debut: A. G. Salter.

A masterclass from Goodwin, who batted 400 minutes for 178, his fourth hundred of the summer and the 71st of his career, set up Glamorgan's first victory in four months, and condemned

Leicestershire to their third successive innings defeat. Goodwin put on 140 with Allenby – both reaching 1,000 runs for the season – then 189 with Wallace, and for the second time in three matches missed out on a double-century, when he misjudged a sweep at Sykes's left-arm spin. Glamorgan scored 409 on the second day alone to take a huge lead in response to Leicestershire's inadequate first innings, in which Hogan claimed his 50th first-class wicket of the summer during a spell of three for four. From his first ball in Championship cricket, Andrew Salter, a 20-year-old off-spinner, had Thakor caught behind. Rain, which wiped out 38 overs on the third day, and another stubborn innings from Eckersley gave Leicestershire hope of survival. But after Thakor fell to the third ball of the final morning – from Cosker, who later removed Eckersley as well – resistance was limited to a last-wicket stand of 50.

Close of play: first day, Glamorgan 36-3 (Goodwin 12, Cooke 5); second day, Glamorgan 445-7 (Wagg 16, Salter 16); third day, Leicestershire 134-2 (Eckersley 54, Thakor 18).

Leicestershire

G. P. Smith lbw b Hogan	40	– lbw b Hogan	18
†N. J. O'Brien c Hogan b Cosker	29	– b Salter	29
E. J. H. Eckersley lbw b Hogan	36	– c Wright b Cosker	76
S. J. Thakor c Wallace b Salter	6	– c Wallace b Cosker	18
*M. A. G. Boyce b Wagg	26	– c Allenby b Cosker	19
T. J. Wells lbw b Hogan	0	– b Hogan	1
J. J. Cobb c Allenby b Hogan	10	– not out	46
B. A. Raine b Salter	37	– c Allenby b Salter	11
O. H. Freckingham lbw b Hogan	5	– b Cosker	1
J. S. Sykes c Goodwin b Cosker	3	– c Hogan b Salter	0
A. C. F. Wyatt not out	4	– c Hogan b Wagg	28
L-b 2, w 1, n-b 4	7	L-b 2, w 11, n-b 8	21

1/67 (1) 2/71 (2) 3/100 (4) (77.5 overs) 203
4/125 (3) 5/125 (6) 6/137 (7)
7/156 (5) 8/181 (9) 9/199 (8) 10/203 (10)

1/24 (1) 2/93 (2) (88.5 overs) 268
3/134 (4) 4/175 (5)
5/178 (3) 6/178 (6) 7/212 (8)
8/213 (9) 9/218 (10) 10/268 (11)

Hogan 19–6–43–5; Wagg 12–2–30–1; Allenby 15–1–55–0; Cosker 13.5–2–39–2; Salter 18–8–34–2. *Second innings*—Wagg 6.5–2–34–1; Hogan 19–5–65–2; Cosker 34–9–88–4; Allenby 9–7–13–0; Salter 20–4–66–3.

Glamorgan

G. P. Rees c O'Brien b Freckingham	6	D. A. Cosker not out	17
W. D. Bragg lbw b Wyatt	7	M. G. Hogan not out	27
M. W. Goodwin b Sykes	178	B 4, l-b 13, w 1, n-b 22	40
B. J. Wright c Smith b Freckingham	1		
C. B. Cooke c O'Brien b Raine	22	1/9 (1) (9 wkts dec, 121.3 overs) 508
J. Allenby c O'Brien b Wyatt	76	2/21 (2) 3/24 (4)
*†M. A. Wallace c O'Brien b Raine	86	4/83 (5) 5/223 (6)
G. G. Wagg c Wells b Raine	32	6/412 (7) 7/412 (3)
A. G. Salter c Smith b Raine	16	8/453 (9) 9/462 (8) 110 overs: 433-7

Wyatt 23–1–86–2; Freckingham 28–8–90–2; Raine 23–3–98–4; Sykes 30.3–6–123–1; Cobb 9–0–54–0; Wells 8–0–40–0.

Umpires: J. H. Evans and N. J. Llong.

At Northampton. August 28–30. GLAMORGAN lost to NORTHAMPTONSHIRE by an innings and 25 runs.

GLAMORGAN v KENT

At Cardiff, September 3–5. Kent won by seven wickets. Kent 19pts, Glamorgan 3pts. Toss: Glamorgan. First-class debut: R. A. J. Smith.

Perhaps distracted by their success in one-day cricket, Glamorgan slid to their sixth Championship defeat of the season – losing inside three days at least gave them an extra 24 hours to prepare for their YB40 semi-final against Hampshire on September 7. Fifteen wickets fell on the first day, more because of injudicious shot selection and a failure to cope with swing than any vagaries in the pitch. As Glamorgan slumped to 158, only Wright showed the necessary application – matched by Bell-Drummond when Kent batted. For the second home game in a row, a Glamorgan newcomer struck instantly: Ruaidhri Smith, a 19-year-old Glasgow-born all-rounder, bowled Nash with his maiden first-class delivery. Glamorgan batted a little better in the second innings, but a target of 242 held few terrors for Kent, with Northeast taking them close to victory in a four-hour stay. His eventual dismissal was a minor consolation for Cosker – his 500th first-class wicket for Glamorgan in a career that began in 1996.

Close of play: first day, Kent 102-5 (Bell-Drummond 41, Riley 6); second day, Glamorgan 237-7 (Smith 20, Cosker 17).

Glamorgan

G. P. Rees b Stevens	18	– c Jones b Haggett	52
W. D. Bragg c Jones b Stevens	22	– lbw b Davies	11
M. W. Goodwin c Northeast b Shreck	12	– c Jones b Davies	0
C. B. Cooke c Harmison b Stevens	6	– c Bell-Drummond b Riley	35
B. J. Wright lbw b Riley	55	– lbw b Haggett	37
J. Allenby c Jones b Davies	17	– c Haggett b Riley	29
*†M. A. Wallace c Harmison b Haggett	6	– c Jones b Shreck	29
R. A. J. Smith c Jones b Haggett	1	– not out	37
D. A. Cosker not out	8	– c Nash b Stevens	17
M. G. Hogan c Stevens b Riley	0	– b Stevens	0
M. T. Reed lbw b Stevens	4	– c Harmison b Riley	3
L-b 2, w 1, n-b 6	9	L-b 5, w 1, n-b 2	8

1/31 (1) 2/46 (2) 3/52 (4) (60 overs) 158
4/73 (3) 5/102 (4) 6/127 (7)
7/128 (8) 8/153 (5) 9/153 (10) 10/158 (11)

1/15 (2) 2/15 (3) (77.5 overs) 258
3/82 (4) 4/122 (1)
5/155 (5) 6/179 (6) 7/204 (7)
8/237 (9) 9/237 (10) 10/258 (11)

Shreck 14–4–35–1; Haggett 13–4–56–2; Davies 15–5–27–1; Stevens 15–5–34–4; Riley 3–1–4–2. *Second innings*—Davies 15–7–34–2; Shreck 15–1–67–1; Stevens 16–6–29–2; Haggett 16–5–54–2; Riley 15.5–0–69–3.

Kent

S. A. Northeast b Hogan	4	– b Cosker	88
R. W. T. Key b Hogan	9	– c Goodwin b Reed	33
D. J. Bell-Drummond lbw b Hogan	78	– c Wallace b Cosker	30
B. P. Nash b Smith	5	– not out	70
B. W. Harmison b Reed	1	– not out	9
D. I. Stevens c Cooke b Hogan	29		
A. E. N. Riley b Reed	18		
*†G. O. Jones c Wright b Smith	11		
C. J. Haggett not out	8		
M. Davies b Hogan	0		
C. E. Shreck c Wallace b Hogan	3		
L-b 3, n-b 6	9	B 2, l-b 4, n-b 6	12

1/4 (1) 2/25 (2) 3/37 (4) (61.3 overs) 175
4/38 (5) 5/94 (6) 6/136 (7)
7/159 (8) 8/171 (9) 9/171 (10) 10/175 (11)

1/57 (2) (3 wkts, 72.2 overs) 242
2/119 (3) 3/211 (1)

Hogan 18.3–3–65–6; Reed 19–5–50–2; Smith 11–2–35–2; Allenby 11–5–18–0; Cosker 2–1–4–0. *Second innings*—Hogan 16–2–59–0; Reed 17.2–2–72–1; Allenby 9–4–21–0; Smith 11–1–46–0; Cosker 17–5–34–2; Bragg 2–0–4–0.

Umpires: N. G. B. Cook and G. Sharp.

At Chelmsford, September 17–20. GLAMORGAN drew with ESSEX.

GLAMORGAN v GLOUCESTERSHIRE

At Cardiff, September 24–27. Glamorgan won by eight wickets. Glamorgan 22pts, Gloucestershire 5pts. Toss: Glamorgan.

A close match seemed to have been spoiled by the loss of the third day to rain – but Wallace, who decided against a contrived finish, had the satisfaction of ending the season on a high with Glamorgan's third Championship victory. That had looked unlikely on the final morning when Gloucestershire reached 73 for one in their second innings, but the departure of Roderick – one of four cheap wickets for Allenby – triggered a collapse of four for five in 14 balls before lunch; in all, the last nine wickets added only 59. Two of them went to the promising Ruaidhri Smith, who had earlier made an important 39 from No. 9 as Glamorgan's tail wagged profitably. They were left 42 overs to chase 102; Will Gidman struck twice, but Goodwin and Cooke calmly took them home.

Close of play: first day, Gloucestershire 228-8 (Smith 5, McCarter 0); second day, Glamorgan 271-9 (Cosker 19, Hogan 16); third day, no play.

Gloucestershire

G. H. Roderick b Hogan	5	– (2) c Wagg b Allenby	26
C. D. J. Dent c Allenby b Cosker	84	– (1) c Wallace b Hogan	13
A. P. R. Gidman b Allenby	31	– lbw b Smith	26
*H. J. H. Marshall c Wallace b Wagg	27	– c Allenby b Wagg	17
I. A. Cockbain c Allenby b Cosker	0	– c Wallace b Smith	2
W. R. S. Gidman c Wallace b Smith	33	– lbw b Allenby	2
†C. L. Herring lbw b Hogan	8	– c Wallace b Smith	17
B. A. C. Howell b Smith	27	– b Hogan	3
T. M. J. Smith not out	31	– c Wallace b Allenby	5
G. J. McCarter lbw b Allenby	14	– c and b Allenby	11
M. D. Taylor c Wright b Allenby	5	– not out	0
L-b 4, n-b 6	10	L-b 6, n-b 4	10

1/12 (1) 2/90 (4) 3/132 (2) (104.3 overs) 275
4/132 (5) 5/156 (4) 6/176 (7)
7/219 (8) 8/226 (6) 9/263 (10) 10/275 (11)

1/35 (1) 2/73 (2) (44.3 overs) 132
3/73 (3) 4/75 (5)
5/78 (6) 6/105 (7) 7/110 (8)
8/118 (9) 9/122 (4) 10/132 (10)

Hogan 28–7–62–2; Allenby 19.3–5–31–3; Wagg 24–6–64–1; Smith 9–2–37–2; Cosker 24–4–77–2. *Second innings*—Wagg 11–3–33–1; Hogan 11–3–27–2; Smith 12–1–50–3; Allenby 10.3–1–16–4.

Glamorgan

G. P. Rees c Dent b McCarter	7	– c Cockbain b W. R. S. Gidman	0
M. W. Goodwin c Dent b Taylor	14	– not out	50
B. J. Wright lbw b W. R. S. Gidman	0	– c Herring b W. R. S. Gidman	17
C. B. Cooke b Taylor	50	– not out	31
J. Allenby c Dent b Taylor	85		
D. L. Lloyd c Dent b W. R. S. Gidman	16		
*†M. A. Wallace c Herring b W. R. S. Gidman	7		
G. G. Wagg lbw b McCarter	10		
R. A. J. Smith c Herring b W. R. S. Gidman	39		
D. A. Cosker lbw b Smith	28		
M. G. Hogan not out	42		
B 2, l-b 2, n-b 4	8	N-b 4	4

1/11 (1) 2/12 (3) 3/47 (2) (77.4 overs) 306
4/103 (4) 5/137 (6) 6/147 (7)
7/171 (8) 8/218 (5) 9/244 (9) 10/306 (10)

1/0 (1) 2/36 (3) (2 wkts, 30.3 overs) 102

W. R. S. Gidman 18–3–64–4; McCarter 14–6–35–2; Taylor 20–0–108–3; Howell 11–2–39–0; Smith 14.4–0–56–1. *Second innings*—W. R. S. Gidman 7–1–9–2; McCarter 9.3–1–50–0; Taylor 6–1–20–0; Smith 8–1–23–0.

Umpires: R. J. Bailey and S. A. Garratt.

GLOUCESTERSHIRE

The end of austerity?

ANDY STOCKHAUSEN

In terms of on-field success, Tom Richardson, Gloucestershire's departing chief executive, may have left the county worse off than he found them more than a decade earlier. But there is no doubting his legacy. After years of wrangling with Bristol City Council, he finally saw his ambitious plan to rebuild the County Ground pavilion come to fruition. An imposing four-storey, glass-fronted, state-of-the-art edifice now stands sentinel over the nearby block of luxury apartments. (It was this residential building that provided the funding for the revamping of the Mound Stand and the instalment of several thousand new seats during the winter.)

Richardson's hope was that the combination of upgraded infrastructure and an enhanced capacity of 17,000 would safeguard Bristol's precarious status as an international venue. His successor, Will Brown, must now exploit the Nevil Road facilities so that income is increased, a period of painful austerity brought to an end, and the club restored to long-term profitability. In the words of director of cricket John Bracewell, Gloucestershire can now consider themselves a "destination club", attractive to players, spectators and sponsors. A long-suffering membership have endured underachievement on a scale few would have foreseen when Gloucestershire ruled the one-day roost at the turn of the millennium: there has been no trophy since 2004. But with expectations heightened by the £6m redevelopment, regulars are prepared to entertain the possibility of more bountiful times ahead.

In the short term, though, Bracewell's youthful team remained a work in progress and – if a 2013 campaign littered with might-have-beens was a reliable yardstick – there was clearly much still to be done before Gloucestershire could be considered competitive in all formats.

Bracewell was insistent his young charges should no longer offer inexperience as an excuse; some rose to the challenge of greater responsibility better than others. Gloucestershire played some excellent cricket, yet could not sustain high standards for long enough to realise their targets. Although sixth in Division Two of the Championship was an improvement on 2012, it nevertheless fell short of pre-season expectations and, without further strengthening of the squad, it was hard to see a concerted push for promotion in the next few years. Gloucestershire played their best cricket in the 40-over competition, but missed out on the knockout stages by two defeats in a fortnight at the hands of arch-rivals Somerset. The county's 20-over campaign, however, was one they will want to forget: three wins from ten meant they finished bottom of their group.

At least the decision to recruit South Australia opening batsman Michael Klinger as captain was inspired: he led by example, top-scoring in all three

Chris Dent

formats and passing 1,000 runs in both first-class and limited-overs cricket. Arguably the signing of the season anywhere on the county circuit, the 33-year-old Klinger has one more year of his contract to run.

Klinger, along with Hamish Marshall, Alex Gidman and Chris Dent, was one of four batsmen to reach 1,000 first-class runs at an average of 45 or more. At the age of 22, the left-handed Dent enjoyed a breakthrough summer, demonstrating maturity in translating good starts into substantial scores, including a career-best 153 against Kent during the Cheltenham Festival. Equally prolific in the shorter forms of the game, he is a genuine contender for England Lions. Another 22-year-old, wicketkeeper-batsman Gareth Roderick from Durban, scored his maiden first-class hundred, and quickly followed it with another to establish himself in the top order during the second half of the season.

Gloucestershire's bowlers struggled for the same consistency, a failing that undermined the club's attempts to keep pace with Lancashire and Northamptonshire. Although not one Northamptonshire batsman managed 1,000 first-class runs, their attack proved adept at bowling teams out twice. Gloucestershire's shortcomings were reflected in a disappointing return of just four wins (and four defeats).

Will Gidman once more took on the mantle of bowling mainstay, claiming 55 first-class wickets at a fraction under 22 apiece – despite struggling with injury in May and missing two matches. He was ably supported by Craig Miles, a 19-year-old pace bowler from Swindon and a product of the Academy. His startling progress was understandably being monitored by the ECB. Already tall, and still growing, he played more than expected because of injuries to Ian Saxelby and Liam Norwell, and took 43 wickets in his first full season. But Gloucestershire struggled to find strength in depth, and seamers David Payne, James Fuller and Norwell shared just 48 first-class wickets between them.

The recruitment of slow left-armer Tom Smith from Middlesex – he played nine Championship matches for Gloucestershire while on loan – should go some way to redressing a long-standing deficiency in spin. That meant the county's main need was for an experienced pace spearhead. A wily old fox, Bracewell explored, in vain, the possibility of Klinger playing as an EU passport holder – his late mother was Hungarian – in order to pursue an overseas fast bowler. Crucially, Gloucestershire persuaded their best young players – Dent and Miles among them – to sign contract extensions. Prospects will be dependent on how successful the county are in deterring wealthier rivals from poaching their emerging players.

Championship attendance: 21,548.

GLOUCESTERSHIRE RESULTS

All first-class matches – Played 17: Won 4, Lost 5, Drawn 8.
County Championship matches – Played 16: Won 4, Lost 4, Drawn 8.

LV= County Championship, 6th in Division 2;
Friends Life t20, 6th in Midlands/Wales/West Division; Yorkshire Bank 40, 3rd in Group C.

COUNTY CHAMPIONSHIP AVERAGES, BATTING AND FIELDING

Cap		M	I	NO	R	HS	100	50	Avge	Ct
2013	M. Klinger§	15	24	3	1,105	163	4	4	52.61	16
2004	A. P. R. Gidman	16	22	0	1,125	211	3	5	51.13	12
2006	H. J. H. Marshall¶	16	21	1	1,007	149	4	2	50.35	5
2013	G. H. Roderick¶	12	17	4	625	152*	2	2	48.07	41
2010	C. D. J. Dent†	15	25	2	1,049	153	2	6	45.60	19
2010	J. M. R. Taylor	4	5	1	178	61*	0	1	44.50	4
2012	D. M. Housego	9	14	2	443	150	1	3	36.91	5
2011	W. R. S. Gidman	13	15	4	401	143	1	1	36.45	3
2012	B. A. C. Howell	16	22	4	561	60	0	4	31.16	7
2013	T. M. J. Smith	8	9	2	181	50	0	1	25.85	1
2013	C. L. Herring	5	5	0	105	43	0	0	21.00	12
2011	J. K. Fuller¶	7	6	0	84	42	0	0	14.00	2
2011	C. N. Miles	13	13	1	161	50*	0	1	13.41	1
2012	G. J. McCarter	4	6	1	51	20	0	0	10.20	0
2011	D. A. Payne	10	9	2	42	16	0	0	6.00	2
2011	L. C. Norwell	5	7	5	9	8*	0	0	4.50	1

Also batted: I. A. Cockbain (cap 2011) (1 match) 0, 2 (1 ct); M. A. H. Hammond† (cap 2013) (2 matches) 0, 4 (1 ct); T. W. Shrewsbury (cap 2013) (1 match) 2*; M. D. Taylor (cap 2013) (3 matches) 26*, 5, 0*; E. G. C. Young (cap 2010) (1 match) 0*, 2*.

† *Born in Gloucestershire.* § *Official overseas player.* ¶ *Other non-England-qualified player. Since 2004, Gloucestershire have awarded caps to all players making their first-class debut.*

BOWLING

	Style	O	M	R	W	BB	5I	Avge
W. R. S. Gidman	RFM	384.1	85	1,127	50	6-15	2	22.54
C. N. Miles	RFM	358	69	1,315	43	6-88	3	30.58
B. A. C. Howell	RM	347	83	992	28	5-57	1	35.42
L. C. Norwell	RFM	119	16	491	13	3-80	0	37.76
J. K. Fuller	RFM	211.4	44	699	15	5-43	1	46.60
T. M. J. Smith	SLA	229.5	37	731	15	4-91	0	48.73
D. A. Payne	LFM	275.4	59	917	18	3-75	0	50.94

Also bowled: C. D. J. Dent (SLA) 19.1–5–60–1; A. P. R. Gidman (RM) 28.3–6–93–1; M. A. H. Hammond (OB) 49–3–196–1; D. M. Housego (LBG) 3–0–15–0; G. J. McCarter (RFM) 110–19–431–9; T. W. Shrewsbury (OB) 23–0–94–1; J. M. R. Taylor (OB) 89.1–17–247–6; M. D. Taylor (LM) 75–19–246–4; E. G. C. Young (SLA) 5–0–25–0.

LEADING YB40 AVERAGES (100 runs/4 wickets)

Batting	Runs	HS	Avge	SR	Ct/St
M. Klinger	702	131*	87.75	90.46	10
C. D. J. Dent . .	384	151*	48.00	111.95	4
I. A. Cockbain .	232	53	33.14	100.00	9
B. A. C. Howell .	246	75*	30.75	112.84	4
G. H. Roderick .	139	63	27.80	89.10	10/1
H. J. H. Marshall .	277	67	25.18	109.48	3
A. P. R. Gidman .	167	41	18.55	84.77	6

Bowling	W	BB	Avge	ER
D. A. Payne	19	4-44	23.63	6.06
C. N. Miles	7	2-49	26.57	6.80
T. M. J. Smith . . .	6	3-46	27.00	5.49
G. J. McCarter . . .	4	2-36	31.75	4.70
J. K. Fuller.	12	3-42	33.41	6.21
B. A. C. Howell .	10	2-59	46.10	5.76
E. G. C. Young . .	4	2-31	54.75	6.25

LEADING FLt20 AVERAGES (100 runs/17 overs)

Batting	Runs	HS	Avge	SR	Ct
A. P. R. Gidman .	140	49	17.50	**138.61**	4
M. Klinger......	366	108*	52.28	**129.32**	2
C. D. J. Dent ...	182	63*	20.22	**115.92**	4
I. A. Cockbain ..	184	63	23.00	**115.00**	5
H. J. H. Marshall .	136	49	17.00	**110.56**	0
D. T. Christian...	113	25*	14.12	**108.65**	3

Bowling	W	BB	Avge	ER
T. M. J. Smith ...	11	2-14	20.27	**6.19**
J. K. Fuller.......	7	3-23	17.00	**7.00**
B. A. C. Howell ...	10	2-15	23.30	**7.24**
D. A. Payne	9	3-17	25.66	**8.25**
D. T. Christian	4	1-15	66.00	**8.60**

FIRST-CLASS COUNTY RECORDS

Highest score for	341	C. M. Spearman v Middlesex at Gloucester	2004
Highest score against	319	C. J. L. Rogers (Northants) at Northampton	2006
Leading run-scorer	33,664	W. R. Hammond (avge 57.05).................	1920–51
Best bowling for	10-40	E. G. Dennett v Essex at Bristol	1906
Best bowling against	{ 10-66	A. A. Mailey (Australians) at Cheltenham	1921
	10-66	K. Smales (Nottinghamshire) at Stroud...........	1956
Leading wicket-taker	3,170	C. W. L. Parker (avge 19.43).................	1903–35
Highest total for	695-9 dec	v Middlesex at Gloucester....................	2004
Highest total against	774-7 dec	by Australians at Bristol	1948
Lowest total for	17	v Australians at Cheltenham	1896
Lowest total against	12	by Northamptonshire at Gloucester.............	1907

LIST A COUNTY RECORDS

Highest score for	177	A. J. Wright v Scotland at Bristol	1997
Highest score against	189*	J. G. E. Benning (Surrey) at Bristol............	2006
Leading run-scorer	7,825	M. W. Alleyne (avge 26.89)	1986–2005
Best bowling for	7-29	D. A. Payne v Essex at Chelmsford.............	2010
Best bowling against	6-16	Shoaib Akhtar (Worcestershire) at Worcester	2005
Leading wicket-taker	393	M. W. Alleyne (avge 29.88)	1986–2005
Highest total for	401-7	v Buckinghamshire at Wing	2003
Highest total against	496-4	by Surrey at The Oval	2007
Lowest total for	49	v Middlesex at Bristol	1978
Lowest total against	48	by Middlesex at Lydney	1973

TWENTY20 COUNTY RECORDS

Highest score for	119	K. J. O'Brien v Middlesex at Uxbridge...........	2011
Highest score against	116*	C. L. White (Somerset) at Taunton	2006
Leading run-scorer	**1,728**	**H. J. H. Marshall (avge 27.42)**	**2006–13**
Best bowling for	{ 4-16	J. M. R. Taylor v Somerset at Bristol............	2011
	4-16	I. D. Saxelby v Northamptonshire at Bristol	2012
Best bowling against	5-16	R. E. Watkins (Glamorgan) at Cardiff............	2009
Leading wicket-taker	49	J. Lewis (avge 30.89).......................	2003–11
Highest total for	254-3	v Middlesex at Uxbridge	2011
Highest total against	250-3	by Somerset at Taunton	2006
Lowest total for	68	v Hampshire at Bristol	2010
Lowest total against	97	by Surrey at The Oval	2010

ADDRESS

County Ground, Nevil Road, Bristol BS7 9EJ (0117 910 8000; **email** info@gloscc.co.uk). **Website**
www.gloscricket.co.uk

OFFICIALS

Captain M. Klinger
Director of cricket J. G. Bracewell
Academy director O. A. Dawkins
President J. Light

Chairman R. M. Cooke
Chief executive W. G. Brown
Head groundsman S. P. Williams
Scorer A. J. Bull

At Chelmsford, April 10–13. GLOUCESTERSHIRE drew with ESSEX.

GLOUCESTERSHIRE v NORTHAMPTONSHIRE

At Bristol, April 24–27. Northamptonshire won by seven wickets. Northamptonshire 24pts, Gloucestershire 3pts. Toss: Gloucestershire.

New Gloucestershire captain Michael Klinger was given an object lesson in early-season conditions at Bristol after unwittingly handing Northamptonshire the initiative. Electing to bat on a green-tinged pitch beneath leaden skies, Klinger was one of five batsmen to fall before lunch to swing bowlers Willey and Crook. It was a setback from which they never recovered. The only resistance came from 18-year-old wicketkeeper Cameron Herring, who top-scored with 43 in his maiden first-class innings to lift Gloucestershire to 192. That total was lent perspective when Northamptonshire, boosted by 121 from their last two wickets, reached 404 in the best of the conditions for a first-innings lead of 212. Gloucestershire, given hope by three half-centuries, fared better second time round, yet no one could go on to the big score needed if they were to mount a serious challenge. Northamptonshire were set a modest 88, and Sales carried them over the line to secure a maximum-points victory.

Close of play: first day, Northamptonshire 107-3 (Wakely 23, Newton 14); second day, Gloucestershire 34-1 (Dent 27, Housego 6); third day, Gloucestershire 280-9 (Taylor 30, Norwell 0).

Gloucestershire

*M. Klinger c Murphy b Crook	23	– (2) c Murphy b Copeland	1
C. D. J. Dent c Sales b Willey	6	– (1) b Willey	50
D. M. Housego b Willey	2	– c Murphy b Copeland	6
A. P. R. Gidman c Hall b Crook	20	– c Copeland b Hall	87
H. J. H. Marshall c Murphy b Willey	8	– c Copeland b Hall	4
B. A. C. Howell b Crook	31	– c Sales b Hall	56
W. R. S. Gidman c Sales b Willey	5	– c Murphy b Crook	6
†C. L. Herring st Murphy b Middlebrook	43	– c Wakely b Crook	32
J. M. R. Taylor c Copeland b Middlebrook	31	– b Crook	48
D. A. Payne st Murphy b Hall	0	– b Crook	2
L. C. Norwell not out	8	– not out	1
B 4, l-b 1, n-b 10	15	L-b 2, n-b 4	6

1/7 (2) 2/9 (3) 3/50 (1) (63.1 overs) 192
4/57 (4) 5/70 (5) 6/90 (7)
7/111 (6) 8/159 (9) 9/159 (10) 10/192 (8)

1/2 (2) 2/34 (3) (117.1 overs) 299
3/90 (1) 4/109 (5)
5/178 (4) 6/186 (7) 7/240 (6)
8/268 (8) 9/272 (10) 10/299 (9)

Willey 18–3–71–4; Copeland 18–7–26–0; Crook 12.2–4–47–3; Hall 12.2–2–39–1; Middlebrook 3.1–2–4–2. *Second innings*—Willey 23–3–74–1; Copeland 31–7–69–2; Hall 21–4–69–3; Crook 26.1–6–48–4; Middlebrook 16–5–37–0.

Northamptonshire

*S. D. Peters c W. R. S. Gidman b Norwell	34	– c sub (G. J. McCarter) b W. R. S. Gidman	7
K. J. Coetzer c Herring b W. R. S. Gidman	24	– c Taylor b Payne	6
D. J. Sales c Housego b Norwell	5	– not out	29
A. G. Wakely lbw b W. R. S. Gidman	88	– c Dent b Taylor	20
R. I. Newton c Taylor b Howell	39	– not out	15
A. J. Hall lbw b W. R. S. Gidman	28		
J. D. Middlebrook c Herring b Taylor	62		
†D. Murphy c Herring b Payne	16		
D. J. Willey b Payne	0		
S. P. Crook c Dent b W. R. S. Gidman	53		
T. A. Copeland not out	27		
B 12, l-b 6, n-b 10	28	B 8, l-b 1, n-b 4	13

1/41 (2) 2/58 (3) 3/75 (1) (111 overs) 404
4/149 (5) 5/227 (6) 6/242 (4) 7/283 (8)
8/283 (9) 9/358 (7) 10/404 (10)
110 overs: 404-9

1/14 (2) (3 wkts, 22.3 overs) 90
2/18 (1) 3/51 (4)

W. R. S. Gidman 28–5–109–4; Payne 22–6–64–2; Norwell 20–1–80–2; Howell 17–6–29–1; A. P. R. Gidman 13–2–55–0; Taylor 11–1–49–1. *Second innings*—W. R. S. Gidman 6–1–21–1; Payne 7–0–29–1; Taylor 6–3–12–1; A. P. R. Gidman 3.3–0–19–0.

Umpires: M. A. Gough and R. A. Kettleborough.

At Leicester, April 30–May 3. GLOUCESTERSHIRE beat LEICESTERSHIRE by nine wickets.

GLOUCESTERSHIRE v HAMPSHIRE

At Bristol, May 8–11. Drawn. Gloucestershire 11pts, Hampshire 6pts. Toss: Hampshire. Championship debut: M. D. T. Roberts.

Gloucestershire dominated a rain-affected contest, but paid the price for failing to curb a tactically brilliant century from Adams. Deep in trouble at 97 for eight on the first day, Hampshire were hugely indebted to their captain, who carried his bat in a defiant innings that lasted until the third morning, and spanned six hours and 269 balls. When he was joined by Briggs, the No. 10, Adams had 33, but they shared a stand of 128, a ninth-wicket record for Hampshire against Gloucestershire. Briggs hit a career-best 54, while last man Tomlinson's contribution to a stand of 49 was a single from 50 balls. Hampshire's eventual 274 was competitive, though Klinger, who made a fluent 163, and Dent soon showed what could be achieved in an opening stand of 119. Housego and Alex Gidman contributed half-centuries, and Klinger declared as soon as maximum batting points had been banked. Trailing by 126, Hampshire lurched to 107 for four, including 44 on Championship debut by Michael Roberts. But rain prevented Gloucestershire, who were forced by injuries to use four substitute fielders, from pressing home their advantage.

Close of play: first day, Hampshire 165-8 (Adams 74, Briggs 25); second day, Hampshire 264-9 (Adams 129, Tomlinson 1); third day, Gloucestershire 284-2 (Klinger 131, A. P. R. Gidman 38).

Hampshire

M. D. T. Roberts c Herring b W. R. S. Gidman....	9	– (2) c sub (P. B. Muchall) b Miles....	44
*J. H. K. Adams not out....................	138	– (1) lbw b Howell	21
L. A. Dawson c Klinger b W. R. S. Gidman	0	– b Howell......................	0
G. J. Bailey b Miles	13	– c Payne b Dent	16
J. M. Vince lbw b Miles....................	9	– not out	30
S. M. Ervine c Housego b Miles	4	– not out	3
†A. J. Wheater lbw b Taylor	8		
C. P. Wood c Howell b Payne	7		
D. J. Balcombe lbw b Taylor	12		
D. R. Briggs c Dent b A. P. R. Gidman..........	54		
J. A. Tomlinson c A. P. R. Gidman b Miles	1		
B 4, l-b 8, w 1, n-b 6	19	L-b 1, w 3, n-b 2...........	6

1/14 (1) 2/16 (3) 3/34 (4)   (95.3 overs) 274   1/55 (1)   (4 wkts, 50 overs) 120
4/44 (5) 5/58 (6) 6/69 (7)   2/59 (3) 3/71 (2)
7/80 (8) 8/97 (9) 9/225 (10) 10/274 (11)   4/107 (4)

W. R. S. Gidman 9–2–14–2; Payne 18–4–57–1; Howell 20–2–64–0; Miles 24.3–6–83–4; Taylor 21–4–39–2; A. P. R. Gidman 3–1–5–1. *Second innings*—W. R. S. Gidman 0.2–0–0–0; Miles 12.4–3–45–1; Payne 9–3–27–0; Howell 13–7–15–2; Dent 6–4–12–1; A. P. R. Gidman 6–3–5–0; Housego 3–0–15–0.

Gloucestershire

*M. Klinger c Wheater b Tomlinson.......163		W. R. S. Gidman not out..............	16
C. D. J. Dent c Wheater b Tomlinson 45		B 6, l-b 7, w 3, n-b 6	22
D. M. Housego b Dawson 56			
A. P. R. Gidman c Briggs b Vince 69		1/119 (2) (4 wkts dec, 98.4 overs)	400
B. A. C. Howell not out................ 29		2/228 (3) 3/337 (1) 4/376 (4)	

H. J. H. Marshall, †C. L. Herring, J. M. R. Taylor, D. A. Payne and C. N. Miles did not bat.

Tomlinson 18–5–74–2; Balcombe 18–2–73–0; Wood 15–4–55–0; Briggs 19–0–85–0; Vince 6.4–0–33–1; Ervine 13–1–33–0; Dawson 9–1–34–1.

Umpires: J. H. Evans and R. K. Illingworth.

At Cambridge, May 15–16. GLOUCESTERSHIRE beat CAMBRIDGE MCCU by an innings and 82 runs.

At Worcester, May 22–25. GLOUCESTERSHIRE lost to WORCESTERSHIRE by ten wickets.

At Liverpool, May 29–June 1. GLOUCESTERSHIRE drew with LANCASHIRE.

GLOUCESTERSHIRE v GLAMORGAN

At Bristol, June 5–8. Drawn. Gloucestershire 8pts, Glamorgan 7pts. Toss: Gloucestershire. First-class debut: M. A. H. Hammond.

Gloucestershire's refusal to declare their first innings in deficit and invite Glamorgan to set a target killed this contest. Although Wallace, the Glamorgan captain, was prepared to negotiate, Klinger opted to bat on and apply scoreboard pressure, a strategy undermined by the loss of 21 overs to rain on day three and a collapse on the final morning. A flat pitch had given batsmen the opportunity to entertain spectators, and hundreds from Goodwin – his first for Glamorgan – and Allenby returned the visitors to health after they had stumbled to 85 for four on the first day. Miles claimed his third five-for in three matches, though Goodwin proved a model of patience: his first century since 2011 came in over five hours, and helped Glamorgan reach 448. Klinger and Gidman responded in kind, but Gloucestershire's prospects of establishing a meaningful lead were scuppered by the elements and a fiery spell from Australian pace bowler Hogan, who added a career-best seven for 92 to his maiden first-class fifty. Hogan had fallen victim to Miles Hammond, a 17-year-old off-spinner from Cheltenham.

Close of play: first day, Glamorgan 318-5 (Goodwin 96, Wallace 31); second day, Gloucestershire 179-1 (Klinger 80, Housego 46); third day, Gloucestershire 456-4 (Marshall 27, Howell 13).

Glamorgan

B. J. Wright c Roderick b Miles	15	– c Roderick b Fuller	33
W. D. Bragg c Housego b Miles	23	– not out	71
S. J. Walters c Roderick b Payne	28	– c Roderick b Howell	14
M. J. North c Roderick b Payne	4	– not out	33
M. W. Goodwin c Gidman b Miles	108		
J. Allenby lbw b Fuller	105		
*†M. A. Wallace c Klinger b Payne	94		
J. C. Glover c Roderick b Miles	0		
D. A. Cosker lbw b Miles	0		
M. G. Hogan c Howell b Hammond	51		
M. T. Reed not out	1		
B 1, l-b 7, w 9, n-b 2	19	B 1, l-b 6, w 2, n-b 16	25

1/36 (1) 2/43 (2) 3/56 (4)   (124.1 overs) 448   1/68 (1)   (2 wkts dec, 62.4 overs) 176
4/85 (3) 5/270 (6) 6/339 (5) 7/343 (8)   2/120 (3)
8/343 (9) 9/411 (10) 10/448 (7)   110 overs: 358-8

Fuller 28–8–84–1; Miles 22–3–83–5; Payne 27.1–6–87–3; McCarter 14–1–67–0; Howell 7–2–23–0; Hammond 26–2–96–1. *Second innings*—Fuller 8–0–28–1; Miles 12–2–29–0; Payne 8–3–17–0; McCarter 9–3–22–0; Hammond 15–1–59–0; Howell 10.4–3–14–1.

Gloucestershire

*M. Klinger c Wallace b Allenby	142	D. A. Payne c Wallace b Hogan	2
†G. H. Roderick lbw b Hogan	41	G. J. McCarter not out	0
D. M. Housego c Goodwin b Hogan	82		
A. P. R. Gidman c and b Cosker	113	B 13, l-b 17, n-b 8	38
H. J. H. Marshall c Wallace b Hogan	27		
B. A. C. Howell lbw b Hogan	23	1/79 (2) 2/259 (3) (152.2 overs)	478
J. K. Fuller c Walters b Hogan	9	3/391 (1) 4/432 (4) 5/456 (5)	
M. A. H. Hammond c Wallace b Hogan	0	6/474 (7) 7/475 (6) 8/476 (8)	
C. N. Miles c Wallace b Cosker	1	9/478 (9) 10/478 (10) 110 overs: 314-2	

Hogan 37.2–7–92–7; Cosker 44–7–146–2; Reed 26–6–105–0; Allenby 32–11–68–1; North 10–1–31–0; Bragg 3–0–6–0.

Umpires: P. K. Baldwin and P. J. Hartley.

At Southampton, June 12–14. GLOUCESTERSHIRE beat HAMPSHIRE by 198 runs.

At Bristol, June 21–23. GLOUCESTERSHIRE lost to AUSTRALIA A by 24 runs (see Australia A tour section).

GLOUCESTERSHIRE v KENT

At Cheltenham, July 10–13. Kent won by two wickets. Kent 21pts, Gloucestershire 6pts. Toss: Gloucestershire.

On a sweltering final day, Nash battled heat exhaustion to steer Kent to the brink of an enthralling victory. He had struck 26 fours and a six from 230 balls in just over five hours when forced to retire ill, one run from a maiden double-hundred in England, and with Kent 21 from their target. No one had previously retired on 199. Gloucestershire's bowlers pressed hard on a flat pitch and, when Miles

---

HIGHEST CHAMPIONSHIP TOTALS BY A LOSING SIDE

642	Essex v Glamorgan at Chelmsford	2004
632	Northamptonshire v Essex at Northampton	2002
597	Essex v Derbyshire at Chesterfield	1904
591	Sussex v Essex at Hove	1993
589	Lancashire v Derbyshire at Blackpool	1994
587-9 dec	Lancashire v Derbyshire at Manchester	1996
584-3 dec	Glamorgan v Middlesex at Southgate	2005
562-3 dec	Glamorgan v Middlesex at Cardiff	1993
562-5 dec	**Gloucestershire v Kent at Cheltenham**	**2013**

All instances are in the first innings of the match apart from Lancashire's 589, which was in their second innings, after following on.

HIGHEST CHAMPIONSHIP AGGREGATES ENDING IN A WIN

Runs	Wkts		
1,808	20	Sussex (591 and 312-3 dec) lost to Essex (493-4 dec and 412-3) at Hove	1993
1,795	34	Northants (463-9 dec and 432-9 dec) lost to Somerset (650 and 250-6) at Taunton	2001
1,683	14	Glam (584-3 dec and 256-3 dec) lost to Middx (435-4 dec and 408-4) at Southgate	2005
1,665	33	Warwicks (601-9 dec and 232-4) beat Yorks (351 and 481) at Birmingham	2002
1,642	29	Kent (533 and 287-3 dec) lost to Notts (491-9 dec and 331-7) at Nottingham	1995
1,617	36	Essex (642 and 165) lost to Glam (587 and 223-6) at Chelmsford	2004
1,606	34	Surrey (452-8 dec and 350) lost to Kent (572 and 232-6) at Guildford	2005
1,606	31	Yorks (438 and 363-5 dec) lost to Somerset (326 and 479-6) at Taunton	2009
1,599	**19**	**Glos (562-5 dec and 237-1 dec) lost to Kent (389-5 dec and 411-8) at Cheltenham**	**2013**

removed Tredwell two balls later, Nos 10 and 11 were at the crease. But they clung on to win with 14 balls to spare. At the ninth attempt, Kent had gained their first victory of the Championship season to drag themselves off the foot of the table; at the time, 411 was their third-highest total to win a game. Short boundaries and a fast outfield produced a batsman's paradise, and Dent and Alex Gidman each made career-best scores before Klinger declared Gloucestershire's first innings on 562 for five. Left-hander Dent contributed a chanceless 153, while Gidman batted seven hours for his maiden double-hundred – Gloucestershire's first at Cheltenham since Shaun Young hit 237 against Derbyshire in 1997. When Tredwell removed Marshall, the third century, his figures for the season read 134.1–22–403–1. Harmison then frustrated Gloucestershire with his first hundred for Kent, after which the captains struck an imaginative deal: Kent forfeited a fifth batting point, while Klinger agreed not to enforce the follow-on. Declaration bowling allowed him to set Kent 411 in a full day. Play was held up for almost ten minutes while the groundstaff erected a cover to prevent the sun glinting off scaffolding at the Chapel End.

Close of play: first day, Gloucestershire 348-3 (A. P. R. Gidman 145, Marshall 2); second day, Kent 165-2 (Northeast 79, Nash 4); third day, Gloucestershire 237-1 dec.

Gloucestershire

*M. Klinger c Stevens b Haggett	20	– (2) not out	102
C. D. J. Dent c Jones b Haggett	153	– (1) c and b Northeast	82
D. M. Housego b Haggett	13	– not out	50
A. P. R. Gidman run out	211		
H. J. H. Marshall c Haggett b Tredwell	106		
B. A. C. Howell not out	34		
B 11, l-b 6, w 6, n-b 2	25	W 1, n-b 2	3

1/46 (1) 2/74 (3) (5 wkts dec, 140.5 overs) 562 1/151 (1) (1 wkt dec, 41.5 overs) 237
3/341 (2) 4/509 (4)
5/562 (5) 110 overs: 409-3

W. R. S. Gidman, †G. H. Roderick, J. K. Fuller, T. M. J. Smith and C. N. Miles did not bat.

Philander 25–5–69–0; Shreck 28–4–116–0; Haggett 22–2–87–3; Stevens 24–2–93–0; Tredwell 31.5–4–134–1; Harmison 10–0–46–0. *Second innings*—Philander 3–0–13–0; Shreck 5–0–17–0; Harmison 6–0–31–0; Northeast 14–0–60–1; Key 4–0–37–0; Bell-Drummond 6.5–0–54–0; Tredwell 3–0–25–0.

Kent

S. A. Northeast c Roderick b Miles	94	– c Klinger b W. R. S. Gidman	0
R. W. T. Key c Roderick b W. R. S. Gidman	57	– c Roderick b Miles	42
D. J. Bell-Drummond b Howell	21	– b Miles	25
B. P. Nash b Smith	9	– retired ill	199
B. W. Harmison not out	101	– c Roderick b Howell	23
D. I. Stevens lbw b Smith	75	– c A. P. R. Gidman b Miles	30
†G. O. Jones not out	21	– c Roderick b W. R. S. Gidman	23
V. D. Philander (did not bat)		– c Roderick b Howell	2
*J. C. Tredwell (did not bat)		– b Miles	26
C. J. Haggett (did not bat)		– not out	5
C. E. Shreck (did not bat)		– not out	16
B 5, l-b 4, w 2	11	B 8, l-b 8, w 2, n-b 2	20

1/105 (2) 2/158 (3) (5 wkts dec, 100.3 overs) 389 1/0 (1) (8 wkts, 93.4 overs) 411
3/174 (4) 4/212 (1) 2/48 (3) 3/131 (2)
5/315 (6) 4/195 (5) 5/270 (6)
 6/325 (7) 7/332 (8) 8/390 (9)

In the second innings Nash retired ill at 390-7.

Fuller 15.3–3–50–0; Miles 15–0–76–1; W. R. S. Gidman 20–2–83–1; Smith 37–3–125–2; Howell 12–2–43–1; Dent 1–0–3–0. *Second innings*—W. R. S. Gidman 20–3–69–2; Fuller 18–1–80–0; Miles 17.4–2–72–4; Smith 18–0–107–0; Howell 20–2–67–2.

Umpires: S. A. Garratt and S. J. O'Shaughnessy.

GLOUCESTERSHIRE v WORCESTERSHIRE

At Cheltenham, July 17–20. Gloucestershire won by six wickets. Gloucestershire 22pts, Worcestershire 3pts. Toss: Worcestershire. Championship debut: G. Cessford.

James Fuller's hat-trick on the opening morning put Gloucestershire on course for their first Championship victory over Worcestershire since 1995. Fuller removed Pardoe with the last ball of the eighth over, then – after Will Gidman dismissed Mitchell – he added Ali and Kervezee with the first two deliveries of the tenth, to become the fourth Gloucestershire player to perform the feat at Cheltenham, following Charles Townsend (1893), Mike Procter (1979) and James Franklin (2009). Leach, who struck a career-best unbeaten 82, and Andrew added 120 to drag Worcestershire from the depths of 22 for six, though a total of 182 was still woefully below par. Gloucestershire sailed into the lead just two wickets down, as Roderick justified his promotion to No. 3 with a steady half-century. Andrew ran through the tail, but Gloucestershire, leading by 144, were again held up by Leach, who this time completed a maiden hundred. Worcestershire were dismissed for 337 on the final morning, setting Gloucestershire 194. Klinger batted superbly to help secure victory with plenty to spare. Graeme Cessford, an RAF corporal given special leave to join Worcestershire for the 2013 season, took four wickets on Championship debut.

Close of play: first day, Gloucestershire 83-0 (Klinger 27, Dent 56); second day, Worcestershire 31-0 (Mitchell 16, Pardoe 13); third day, Worcestershire 296-8 (Leach 103, Cessford 4).

Worcestershire

*D. K. H. Mitchell c Roderick b W. R. S. Gidman . .	7	– c Klinger b Smith	36
M. G. Pardoe c Roderick b Fuller	7	– c Roderick b W. R. S. Gidman.	39
M. M. Ali b Fuller	0	– c Marshall b Smith	4
T. T. Samaraweera c Dent b Miles	4	– lbw b W. R. S. Gidman	63
A. N. Kervezee c Roderick b Fuller	0	– run out	8
J. Leach not out	82	– c Hammond b Smith	114
†O. B. Cox c Dent b Miles	0	– c Roderick b Miles	6
G. M. Andrew c Klinger b Howell	54	– c A. P. R. Gidman b W. R. S. Gidman	14
S. H. Choudhry c Roderick b Fuller	2	– b Fuller	10
G. Cessford c Klinger b Smith	0	– c Klinger b Smith	20
A. Richardson c A. P. R. Gidman b Fuller	16	– not out	13
B 1, l-b 5, n-b 4	10	B 4, w 4, n-b 2	10

1/18 (2) 2/18 (1) 3/18 (3) (71 overs) 182
4/18 (5) 5/22 (4) 6/22 (7)
7/142 (8) 8/154 (9) 9/155 (10) 10/182 (11)

1/71 (1) 2/79 (3) (122.4 overs) 337
3/94 (2) 4/102 (5)
5/211 (4) 6/224 (7) 7/254 (8)
8/282 (9) 9/321 (6) 10/337 (10)

W. R. S. Gidman 13–3–36–1; Fuller 19–7–43–5; Miles 13–4–25–2; Howell 8–3–21–1; Smith 14–6–33–1; Hammond 4–0–18–0. *Second innings*—W. R. S. Gidman 25–7–78–3; Fuller 28–6–59–1; Smith 35.4–9–91–4; Miles 18–6–56–1; Howell 11–2–24–0; Hammond 4–0–23–0; A. P. R. Gidman 1–0–2–0.

Gloucestershire

*M. Klinger c Samaraweera b Richardson	36	– (2) b Cessford	92
C. D. J. Dent st Cox b Ali	79	– (1) lbw b Ali	45
†G. H. Roderick c Mitchell b Ali	71	– b Ali	3
A. P. R. Gidman c Cox b Richardson	62	– lbw b Cessford	25
H. J. H. Marshall b Cessford	20	– not out	20
B. A. C. Howell run out	0	– not out	5
W. R. S. Gidman not out	37		
J. K. Fuller c Cox b Andrew	0		
M. A. H. Hammond c Ali b Andrew	4		
T. M. J. Smith c Mitchell b Andrew	5		
C. N. Miles b Cessford	5		
B 4, l-b 2, w 1	7	B 4, l-b 1	5

1/101 (1) 2/129 (2) 3/234 (4) (99.5 overs) 326
4/262 (3) 5/262 (6) 6/301 (5)
7/302 (8) 8/306 (9) 9/313 (10) 10/326 (11)

1/95 (1) (4 wkts, 46.1 overs) 195
2/111 (3) 3/152 (4)
4/187 (2)

Richardson 17–3–59–2; Cessford 13.5–3–42–2; Andrew 16–4–56–3; Ali 33–3–94–2; Choudhry 17–2–52–0; Leach 3–0–17–0. *Second innings*—Richardson 6–0–34–0; Andrew 3–1–15–0; Ali 18–2–62–2; Cessford 7.1–1–35–2; Choudhry 12–3–44–0.

Umpires: N. L. Bainton and N. A. Mallender.

At Northampton, August 2–5. GLOUCESTERSHIRE drew with NORTHAMPTONSHIRE.

At Canterbury, August 21–24. GLOUCESTERSHIRE drew with KENT.

GLOUCESTERSHIRE v ESSEX

At Bristol, August 28–31. Drawn. Gloucestershire 8pts, Essex 11pts. Toss: Gloucestershire.

Roderick came to Gloucestershire's rescue for the second match in succession, salvaging another backs-to-the-wall draw. After hitting his maiden first-class hundred at Canterbury a week before, he now made 136 as Gloucestershire, set 432 by Essex, closed on 355 for six; the stalemate suited neither promotion-seeking county. Roderick's innings contained a lot of grit and a bit of luck: he was struck on the head by a short-pitched delivery from Mills, and caught off a no-ball on 79. Hundreds from Greg Smith in the first innings and Gambhir in the second had established Essex dominance. Smith batted almost seven hours for his career-best 177 as they banked maximum batting points for the first time in 2013, and only an unlikely maiden fifty from No. 11 Miles, who shared a tenth-wicket stand of 78 with McCarter, saved Gloucestershire from the follow-on. After a first-innings duck, Gambhir made amends with his first century for Essex, as he and Mickleburgh sought quick runs to hasten a declaration.

Close of play: first day, Essex 333-7 (Smith 149); second day, Gloucestershire 211-9 (McCarter 6, Miles 29); third day, Gloucestershire 19-0 (Dent 16, Klinger 2).

Essex

J. C. Mickleburgh c Roderick b McCarter	26	– c Marshall b Smith	86
G. Gambhir b W. R. S. Gidman	0	– c Marshall b Miles	106
G. M. Smith b Miles	177	– c A. P. R. Gidman b Smith	40
O. A. Shah lbw b Miles	34	– lbw b Miles	8
R. N. ten Doeschate c Roderick b Howell	24	– not out	23
B. T. Foakes c Dent b W. R. S. Gidman	32		
*†J. S. Foster c Klinger b Payne	26	– (6) not out	1
G. R. Napier c Dent b Payne	10		
M. S. Panesar c Smith b Payne	22		
T. S. Mills c Klinger b Smith	17		
R. J. W. Topley not out	0		
B 8, l-b 7, w 11, n-b 6	32	B 3, l-b 6, n-b 12	21

1/9 (2) 2/46 (1) 3/126 (4)   (108.2 overs) 400   1/201 (2)   (4 wkts dec, 61 overs) 285
4/171 (5) 5/265 (6) 6/316 (7)   2/215 (1) 3/250 (3)
7/333 (8) 8/375 (9) 9/400 (10) 10/400 (3)   4/266 (4)

W. R. S. Gidman 26–4–92–2; Miles 19.2–2–92–2; Payne 23–5–75–3; McCarter 13–0–74–1; Howell 17–4–33–1; Smith 10–2–19–1. *Second innings*—W. R. S. Gidman 13–3–38–0; Payne 11–2–31–0; Miles 11–0–86–2; McCarter 6–0–13–0; Smith 10–0–61–2; Howell 10–2–47–0.

Gloucestershire

*M. Klinger c Foster b Topley	13	– (2) b Panesar	62
C. D. J. Dent c Foster b Napier	8	– (1) lbw b Topley	27
†G. H. Roderick c Shah b Napier	10	– c Foster b Napier	136
A. P. R. Gidman b ten Doeschate	63	– b Panesar	9
H. J. H. Marshall c Foster b Topley	54	– c Gambhir b Topley	42
B. A. C. Howell run out	8	– lbw b Topley	0
W. R. S. Gidman c Foster b Topley	8	– not out	16
T. M. J. Smith c Shah b Napier	7	– not out	33
D. A. Payne b Napier	0		
G. J. McCarter run out	20		
C. N. Miles not out	50		
L-b 5, n-b 8	13	B 8, l-b 8, w 6, n-b 8	30

1/19 (2) 2/21 (1) 3/41 (3)   (68.2 overs) 254   1/43 (1)   (6 wkts, 104.3 overs) 355
4/142 (5) 5/151 (6) 6/161 (5)   2/180 (2) 3/196 (4)
7/172 (8) 8/176 (7) 9/176 (9) 10/254 (10)   4/304 (5) 5/306 (3) 6/306 (6)

Napier 23.2–5–77–4; Topley 20–3–76–3; Mills 8–3–37–0; ten Doeschate 13–2–51–1; Panesar 4–1–8–0. *Second innings*—Napier 22–6–56–1; Topley 25–6–70–3; Panesar 25–6–56–2; Smith 9.3–2–57–0; ten Doeschate 12–0–50–0; Mills 11–3–50–0.

Umpires: N. G. C. Cowley and P. J. Hartley.

GLOUCESTERSHIRE v LEICESTERSHIRE

At Bristol, September 3–5. Gloucestershire won by an innings and 138 runs. Gloucestershire 24pts, Leicestershire 2pts. Toss: Gloucestershire. First-class debuts: M. D. Taylor; A. J. Robson.

Will Gidman became only the fifth Gloucestershire player to score a century and take ten wickets in the same match. Inspiring his team to a three-day demolition of struggling Leicestershire, who had now suffered six straight defeats – four by an innings – Gidman claimed career-best figures of

A CENTURY AND TEN WICKETS FOR GLOUCESTERSHIRE

150; 8-33, 7-46	W. G. Grace	v Yorkshire at Sheffield	1872
179; 4-76, 7-61	W. G. Grace	v Sussex at Hove	1874
167; 4-57, 7-44	W. G. Grace	v Yorkshire at Sheffield	1874
127; 5-44, 5-77	W. G. Grace	v Yorkshire at Clifton	1874
221*; 6-45, 5-75	W. G. Grace	v Middlesex at Clifton	1885
139; 5-121, 5-83	C. L. Townsend	v Warwickshire at Birmingham	1898
168; 5-63, 6-40	C. J. Barnett	v Lancashire at Manchester	1938
108; 7-35, 6-38	M. J. Procter	v Worcestershire at Cheltenham	1977
143; 6-15, 4-28	**W. R. S. Gidman**	**v Leicestershire at Bristol**	**2013**

six for 15 as he and Howell dismantled Leicestershire for 117; as against Essex the week before, Gloucestershire were held up by a man named Greg Smith. Gidman then cracked 143, another career-best, to help build a lead of 399, before rounding off a magnificent all-round performance with four for 28 – including debutant Angus Robson, brother of Middlesex opener Sam – giving him ten wickets for the first time. Leicestershire did fight a fraction harder in their second innings – Eckersley thumped a swift 84 – but they remained rooted to the foot of the table.

Close of play: first day, Gloucestershire 210-4 (Marshall 12, Howell 14); second day, Leicestershire 60-1 (Robson 19, Eckersley 32).

Leicestershire

G. P. Smith c A. P. R. Gidman b W. R. S. Gidman	54	–	(2) lbw b Payne		9
A. J. Robson c Roderick b W. R. S. Gidman	0	–	(1) c Roderick b W. R. S. Gidman		49
†E. J. H. Eckersley c Dent b W. R. S. Gidman	13	–	b Smith		84
*M. A. G. Boyce lbw b W. R. S. Gidman	0	–	lbw b Smith		19
S. J. Thakor c Roderick b Miles	18	–	run out		17
J. J. Cobb lbw b Howell	5	–	c Roderick b Miles		6
B. A. Raine lbw b W. R. S. Gidman	12	–	c Klinger b W. R. S. Gidman		19
J. S. Sykes c A. P. R. Gidman b W. R. S. Gidman	1	–	c Roderick b Smith		7
O. H. Freckingham b Howell	4	–	b W. R. S. Gidman		30
M. J. Hoggard not out	8	–	b W. R. S. Gidman		0
A. C. F. Wyatt c Klinger b Howell	1	–	not out		5
L-b 1	1		B 1, l-b 10, w 1, n-b 4		16

1/11 (2) 2/37 (3) 3/37 (4)   (41.2 overs) 117   1/13 (2) 2/143 (3)   (86.5 overs) 261
4/71 (5) 5/90 (6) 6/94 (1)   3/155 (1) 4/180 (4)
7/96 (8) 8/103 (7) 9/107 (9) 10/117 (11)   5/192 (6) 6/193 (5) 7/218 (8)
8/238 (7) 9/248 (10) 10/261 (9)

W. R. S. Gidman 14–7–15–6; Payne 5–1–20–0; Miles 6–1–37–1; Taylor 6–2–18–0; Smith 2–0–7–0; Howell 8.2–2–19–3. *Second innings*—W. R. S. Gidman 10.5–3–28–4; Taylor 15–8–28–0; Payne 15.3–3–63–1; Miles 11–3–42–1; Howell 16–6–56–0; Smith 19–8–33–3.

Gloucestershire

*M. Klinger c Eckersley b Thakor	86
C. D. J. Dent c Hoggard b Sykes	77
†G. H. Roderick lbw b Wyatt	6
A. P. R. Gidman b Thakor	4
H. J. H. Marshall lbw b Raine	81
B. A. C. Howell c Sykes b Raine	34
W. R. S. Gidman c Smith b Wyatt	143
T. M. J. Smith c Boyce b Sykes	50
C. N. Miles run out	9
D. A. Payne not out	0
B 3, l-b 5, n-b 18	26
(9 wkts dec, 130.3 overs)	516

M. D. Taylor did not bat.

1/163 (2) 2/178 (1) 3/184 (4)
4/184 (3) 5/253 (6) 6/350 (5) 7/481 (8)
8/516 (9) 9/516 (7)   110 overs: 413-6

Hoggard 17–1–58–0; Freckingham 18–2–91–0; Wyatt 20.3–5–66–2; Sykes 31–2–120–2; Cobb 13–1–46–0; Raine 19–3–78–2; Thakor 12–2–49–2.

Umpires: S. C. Gale and M. A. Gough.

GLOUCESTERSHIRE v LANCASHIRE

At Bristol, September 17–20. Drawn. Gloucestershire 6pts, Lancashire 9pts. Toss: Gloucestershire.

Once rain gobbled swathes of the first and third days, the likeliest means of avoiding a draw was contrivance. Gloucestershire were notionally still capable of pipping Northamptonshire to second place, and keen to negotiate; Lancashire, guaranteed promotion, closing in on the title and jealous of their unbeaten record, were not. So a draw it was. Lancashire enjoyed the better of it, despite Will Gidman extracting movement off the pitch to claim a five-for for the second game in a row. He had Lancashire 38 for three, before Procter, who compiled a maiden hundred, and Tom Smith shared a fifth-wicket stand of 159. Chapple declared on 310 for eight, and Lancashire had Gloucestershire in trouble, nine down and six short of saving the follow-on. A spirited fifty partnership between Payne and Taylor prevented that possibility, and thereafter the game petered out into batting practice. Results elsewhere confirmed that Lancashire were second division champions – and that Gloucestershire would stay put.

Close of play: first day, Lancashire 33-2 (Reece 12, Brown 20); second day, Lancashire 292-7 (Smith 88, Hogg 3); third day, Gloucestershire 90-3 (A. P. R. Gidman 21, Marshall 14).

Lancashire

P. J. Horton c Roderick b W. R. S. Gidman	0	– c Howell b Smith	55
L. M. Reece b Payne	35	– b Payne	97
A. G. Prince b W. R. S. Gidman	0	– not out	40
K. R. Brown c Roderick b W. R. S. Gidman	23		
L. A. Procter lbw b W. R. S. Gidman	106		
T. C. Smith b W. R. S. Gidman	88		
†A. L. Davies c Roderick b Taylor	12		
*G. Chapple c W. R. S. Gidman b Howell	1		
K. W. Hogg not out	12		
O. J. Newby not out	9		
B 13, l-b 9, w 2	24	L-b 3	3

1/0 (1) 2/6 (3) (8 wkts dec, 114 overs) 310 1/107 (1) (2 wkts dec, 46.3 overs) 195
3/38 (4) 4/105 (2) 5/264 (5) 2/195 (2)
6/278 (7) 7/287 (8) 8/293 (6) 110 overs: 302-8

S. C. Kerrigan did not bat.

W. R. S. Gidman 28–10–61–5; Payne 24–6–65–1; Taylor 23–8–52–1; Howell 23–5–61–1; Miles 5–1–16–0; Smith 11–2–33–0. *Second innings*—Payne 11.3–0–53–1; Taylor 5–0–20–0; Howell 12–0–48–0; Smith 16–0–61–1; Dent 2–0–10–0.

Gloucestershire

*M. Klinger c Smith b Chapple	13	C. N. Miles c Hogg b Smith	0
C. D. J. Dent lbw b Newby	19	D. A. Payne c sub (A. P. Agathangelou)	
†G. H. Roderick c Reece b Hogg	12	b Newby	16
A. P. R. Gidman lbw b Smith	45	M. D. Taylor not out	26
H. J. H. Marshall c Kerrigan b Newby	26		
B. A. C. Howell lbw b Smith	6	B 8, l-b 22	30
W. R. S. Gidman			
c sub (A. P. Agathangelou) b Smith	3	1/13 (1) 2/44 (3) 3/48 (2) (54.4 overs) 209	
T. M. J. Smith c sub (A. P. Agathangelou)		4/132 (5) 5/133 (4) 6/140 (6)	
b Newby	13	7/151 (7) 8/155 (8) 9/155 (9) 10/209 (10)	

Hogg 16–6–37–1; Chapple 7–0–22–1; Newby 18.4–3–71–4; Smith 12–3–49–4; Kerrigan 1–1–0–0.

Umpires: M. R. Benson and P. Willey.

At Cardiff, September 24–27. GLOUCESTERSHIRE lost to GLAMORGAN by eight wickets.

HAMPSHIRE

Double disappointment

PAT SYMES

A season that brought semi-final appearances in both limited-overs competitions might have satisfied many counties. But after breezing through the group stages, Hampshire – winners of the 40- and 20-over titles in 2012 – were disappointed to retain neither. As the finals beckoned, their form deserted them. There was frustration in the Championship too, where victories in the last two matches, over struggling Leicestershire and a weakened Essex, lifted them to fourth, a flattering gloss on more underachievement.

Off the field, the ground – officially named the Ageas Bowl until 2022 at least – continued to develop into a magnificent stadium throughout the summer. But in October, the construction firm Denizen went into administration, with the bold project, incorporating a 175-bed hotel, only three-quarters complete. Hampshire were confident a replacement company would be quickly found, and the 2014 season unaffected. However, the new year dawned with no apparent signs of progress.

Ambition has not been in short supply on the south coast, and in May the club's chairman, Rod Bransgrove, told *The Times* that "Lord's own the past, but we are the future". That future had been taking shape in the form of the hotel complex, but the winter's delays cast a shadow over his optimism. Vital to the plan was attracting sufficient international fixtures. In 2013, an England team called in four times: the men played one-day internationals against New Zealand and Australia, while both the men and women took on Australia in Twenty20. In July 2014, the ground is due to host its biggest occasion yet, an India Test. An Ashes match remains the ultimate aim.

But, if Hampshire are to achieve that, the wicket will need to be livelier than in the 2013 sunshine. The heavy roller, now obligatory in Championship games, sapped the life from Nigel Gray's strips, and five of the eight fixtures were drawn. Several, such as September's match against Northamptonshire, when both first innings contained a double-hundred, dripped with runs.

Lacking true pace or spin, Hampshire laboured to break down opponents, and only twice took 20 wickets. The tenacious left-arm seamer James Tomlinson did his best, claiming 53 in the Championship, but no one else passed 22 and, towards the end of the summer, Hampshire signed two pace bowlers whom they had already taken on loan: the Barbadian Ruel Brathwaite, from Durham, and Matt Coles – who collected 21 wickets in five matches – from Kent. The spinners, Danny Briggs and Liam Dawson, so effective in one-day matches, managed only 31 Championship scalps between them.

Several others failed to reach the standards of previous years. Michael Carberry, called to the England squad on the back of some outstanding limited-overs innings, hit just one Championship century, while Jimmy Adams's form

Charlie Crowhurst, Getty Images

James Tomlinson

was either excellent (two double-hundreds) or execrable (seven ducks).

James Vince, however, added consistency to his batting, and offered a medium-pace alternative, growing in stature in all forms. He and Carberry forged a dynamic limited-overs opening partnership; Vince and Dawson both passed 1,000 first-class runs for the first time. Hampshire attracted criticism in the spring for dropping the highly regarded home-produced wicketkeeper, Michael Bates, in favour of Adam Wheater, James Foster's understudy at Essex. Wheater was supposedly the better batsman, though only with two late-summer hundreds did he back that up. Bates was recalled for the last four Championship matches.

What baffled Hampshire supporters was how a team so inconsistent in the Championship could be so destructive elsewhere. They won nine out of 12 group games in the YB40, and eight out of ten in the FLt20, often with effortless superiority. Carberry scored high-class unbeaten hundreds against Lancashire: a sumptuous 150 in the YB40, and 100 in the Twenty20 quarter-final. Vince hit a devastating undefeated 129 against Essex, also in the YB40.

Above all, Hampshire capitalised on the experience of Neil McKenzie and Dimitri Mascarenhas, who both left at the end of the season. Hobbled by injuries and nearing the end of his 17-year career, Mascarenhas showed why he had been among England's finest one-day specialists. It was no coincidence that, while he was in his prime, Hampshire dominated the short forms. His know-how will be hard to replace. It looked as if they might send Mascarenhas on his way with more trophies, but two semi-finals produced unexpected defeats. Surrey surprised them when Hampshire's batting – and their nerve – let them down on Twenty20 finals day; and in the YB40 they lost at home to Glamorgan, who had last beaten them in a one-day competition in 2005.

In the close season, Hampshire brought in two top-order batsmen: Will Smith, a Championship-winner with Nottinghamshire and Durham, and Joe Gatting, released by Sussex. South African seam bowler Kyle Abbott joined as the overseas player, while Australian all-rounder Glenn Maxwell returns for the Twenty20. Among departures were seamers David Griffiths and Hamza Riazuddin, and opening batsman Michael Roberts. Griffiths, citing lack of opportunities, moved to Kent. The Academy remained an important part of the club's ethos, and during 2013 Brad Taylor, a schoolboy from Alton, became the youngest to make a first-team debut for Hampshire since 1867, aged 16 years 145 days. Then in the Championship, he grabbed four second-innings wickets against Lancashire, confirming high hopes for his off-spin.

In December, Hampshire announced they were looking to appoint a first-team coach after Giles White was promoted to director of cricket. In February, the post was filled by former Durham captain Dale Benkenstein.

Championship attendance: 21,808.

HAMPSHIRE RESULTS

All first-class matches – Played 17: Won 5, Lost 3, Drawn 9.
County Championship matches – Played 16: Won 4, Lost 3, Drawn 9.

LV= County Championship, 4th in Division 2;
Friends Life t20, semi-finalists; Yorkshire Bank 40, semi-finalists.

COUNTY CHAMPIONSHIP AVERAGES, BATTING AND FIELDING

Cap		M	I	NO	R	HS	100	50	Avge	Ct/St
2013	J. M. Vince	15	22	4	1,101	148	4	6	61.16	16
2013	L. A. Dawson	16	24	3	1,031	136*	1	8	49.09	23
2010	N. D. McKenzie¶	6	10	1	433	146	1	2	48.11	1
2006	M. A. Carberry	11	16	0	687	154	1	5	42.93	3
2006	J. H. K. Adams†	16	24	3	833	219*	3	1	39.66	7
	G. J. Bailey§	5	7	0	263	93	0	2	37.57	3
	A. J. Wheater	15	18	2	585	140	2	1	36.56	19/2
	M. T. Coles	5	5	1	118	68	0	2	29.50	1
	M. D. Bates	5	4	0	117	71	0	1	29.25	16
2012	D. R. Briggs†	12	12	3	244	54	0	1	27.11	6
	Sohail Tanvir§	4	5	0	133	38	0	0	26.60	0
2005	S. M. Ervine	15	19	1	458	86	0	4	25.44	20
	C. P. Wood†	9	12	1	256	69	0	2	23.27	6
	M. D. T. Roberts	5	8	0	143	44	0	0	17.87	2
2008	J. A. Tomlinson†	15	15	8	72	30*	0	0	10.28	1
2013	D. J. Balcombe	12	13	2	106	30*	0	0	9.63	1

Also batted: R. M. R. Brathwaite (3 matches) 9, 17 (1 ct); D. A. Griffiths† (2 matches) 14, 1; A. D. Mascarenhas (cap 1998) (1 match) 41; A. P. Rouse (1 match) 9; B. J. Taylor† (1 match) 0*, 20 (1 ct); S. P. Terry† (2 matches) 58, 57 (2 ct).

† Born in Hampshire.   § Official overseas player.   ¶ Other non-England-qualified player.

BOWLING

	Style	O	M	R	W	BB	5I	Avge
M. T. Coles	RFM	127	27	504	21	6-71	2	24.00
J. A. Tomlinson	LFM	454.5	126	1,281	53	5-44	1	24.16
S. M. Ervine	RFM	179.1	39	577	17	2-17	0	33.94
Sohail Tanvir	LFM	107.2	19	348	10	3-62	0	34.80
D. R. Briggs	SLA	270	59	798	22	3-33	0	36.27
C. P. Wood	LFM	231.3	65	659	15	3-30	0	43.93
D. J. Balcombe	RFM	349	80	1,101	22	5-104	1	50.04

Also bowled: J. H. K. Adams (LM) 14–1–52–1; R. M. R. Brathwaite (RFM) 58–13–222–6; M. A. Carberry (OB) 19.3–2–87–1; L. A. Dawson (SLA) 196.5–49–602–9; D. A. Griffiths (RFM) 53.3–7–237–5; A. D. Mascarenhas (RM) 25–7–61–4; N. D. McKenzie (RM) 10–4–17–1; M. D. T. Roberts (OB) 3.5–1–19–0; B. J. Taylor (OB) 22–3–106–4; J. M. Vince (RM) 102.4–11–396–9.

LEADING YB40 AVERAGES (100 runs/4 wickets)

Batting	Runs	HS	Avge	SR	Ct/St		**Bowling**	W	BB	Avge	ER
J. H. K. Adams .	519	67	51.90	85.08	7		Sohail Tanvir	17	4-29	12.17	4.38
M. A. Carberry .	471	150*	47.10	114.32	2		A. D. Mascarenhas	13	5-42	24.23	4.56
L. A. Dawson . .	318	69	39.75	108.16	8		C. P. Wood	17	3-23	31.29	5.51
J. M. Vince	396	129*	39.60	101.02	5		D. A. Griffiths . . .	5	3-42	32.80	7.45
S. M. Ervine . .	311	65*	34.55	95.39	4		S. M. Ervine	6	2-20	38.83	5.68
A. J. Wheater . .	195	70	27.85	110.79	6/4		L. A. Dawson . . .	10	2-26	43.00	5.65
N. D. McKenzie .	168	65	24.00	73.04	2		D. R. Briggs	10	2-35	51.00	6.07

LEADING FLt20 AVERAGES (100 runs/18 overs)

Batting	Runs	HS	Avge	SR	Ct	Bowling	W	BB	Avge	ER
M. A. Carberry..	502	100*	55.77	**142.61**	4	D. R. Briggs......	15	3-19	19.06	**6.50**
J. M. Vince.....	269	84	24.45	**138.65**	5	L. A. Dawson	13	4-19	21.30	**7.28**
N. D. McKenzie .	301	71*	100.33	**129.18**	3	A. D. Mascarenhas	12	2-19	25.83	**7.56**
S. M. Ervine....	238	60*	29.75	**127.27**	5	C. P. Wood	12	3-31	28.66	**7.78**
J. H. K. Adams..	210	43	19.09	**118.64**	3	Sohail Tanvir	9	3-29	30.22	**8.68**

FIRST-CLASS COUNTY RECORDS

Highest score for	316	R. H. Moore v Warwickshire at Bournemouth	1937
Highest score against	303*	G. A. Hick (Worcestershire) at Southampton	1997
Leading run-scorer	48,892	C. P. Mead (avge 48.84)	1905–36
Best bowling for	9-25	R. M. H. Cottam v Lancashire at Manchester	1965
Best bowling against	10-46	W. Hickton (Lancashire) at Manchester	1870
Leading wicket-taker	2,669	D. Shackleton (avge 18.23)	1948–69
Highest total for	714-5 dec	v Nottinghamshire at Southampton	2005
Highest total against	742	by Surrey at The Oval	1909
Lowest total for	15	v Warwickshire at Birmingham	1922
Lowest total against	23	by Yorkshire at Middlesbrough	1965

LIST A COUNTY RECORDS

Highest score for	177	C. G. Greenidge v Glamorgan at Southampton ...	1975
Highest score against	203	A. D. Brown (Surrey) at Guildford	1997
Leading run-scorer	12,034	R. A. Smith (avge 42.97)	1983–2003
Best bowling for	7-30	P. J. Sainsbury v Norfolk at Southampton......	1965
Best bowling against	7-22	J. R. Thomson (Middlesex) at Lord's	1981
Leading wicket-taker	411	C. A. Connor (avge 25.07).....................	1984–98
Highest total for	371-4	v Glamorgan at Southampton	1975
Highest total against	358-6	by Surrey at The Oval	2005
Lowest total for	43	v Essex at Basingstoke........................	1972
Lowest total against {	61	by Somerset at Bath	1973
	61	by Derbyshire at Portsmouth	1990

TWENTY20 COUNTY RECORDS

Highest score for	124*	M. J. Lumb v Essex v Southampton	2009
Highest score against	98	L. J. Wright (Sussex) at Hove	2007
Leading run-scorer	**1,864**	**S. M. Ervine (avge 28.24)**..................	**2005–13**
Best bowling for	5-14	A. D. Mascarenhas v Sussex at Hove............	2004
Best bowling against	5-21	A. J. Holioake (Surrey) at Southampton	2003
Leading wicket-taker	**94**	**A. D. Mascarenhas (avge 18.19)**............	**2003–13**
Highest total for	225-2	v Middlesex at Southampton	2006
Highest total against	220-4	by Somerset at Taunton	2010
Lowest total for	85	v Sussex at Southampton	2008
Lowest total against	67	by Sussex at Hove	2004

ADDRESS

The Ageas Bowl, Botley Road, West End, Southampton SO30 3XH (023 8047 2002; **email** enquiries@ageasbowl.com). **Website** www.ageasbowl.com

OFFICIALS

Captain J. H. K. Adams
Cricket secretary T. M. Tremlett
Director of cricket G. W. White
First-team coach D. M. Benkenstein
Academy director R. J. Parks
President N. E. J. Pocock

Chairman R. G. Bransgrove
Chief executive D. Mann
Chairman, members committee T. P. Crump
Head groundsman N. C. R. Gray
Scorer K. R. Baker

HAMPSHIRE v LEICESTERSHIRE

At Southampton, April 10–13. Drawn. Hampshire 11pts, Leicestershire 5pts. Toss: Leicestershire. First-class debut: O. H. Freckingham. County debuts: G. J. Bailey, A. J. Wheater; N. J. O'Brien.

Rain washed out the fourth day, and with it Hampshire's chance of converting dominance into victory. The only time an inexperienced Leicestershire team were on top was after Sarwan opted to bowl in overcast conditions, and Hampshire lost both openers for none. But the middle order fired: Australia's Twenty20 captain Bailey made 93 on his county debut before he lost concentration and was stumped; Vince and Ervine added 158; and Wheater, newly arrived from Essex and ousting Michael Bates behind the stumps, also hit a half-century. There were three wickets on first-class debut for Ollie Freckingham, a seamer from the Loughborough Town club, and one of seven bowlers used by Sarwan in the first 30 overs. Adams declared on the second afternoon at 454 for seven, before Leicestershire struggled, especially against Tomlinson's controlled left-arm swing. Following on 311 behind just before stumps, they were grateful for the loss of 24 overs on the third day, when they at last pieced together some resistance. Most of it involved Eckersley, who faced 170 balls for his unbeaten 99. But with only five wickets to take, Hampshire were well placed – if only it had stayed dry.

Close of play: first day, Hampshire 286-4 (Vince 77, Ervine 57); second day, Leicestershire 0-0 (Thornely 0, O'Brien 0); third day, Leicestershire 182-5 (Eckersley 99, Thakor 5).

Hampshire

M. A. Carberry c O'Brien b Hoggard	0	C. P. Wood b Naik	28
*J. H. K. Adams b Wyatt	0	B 5, l-b 1, n-b 8	14
L. A. Dawson c Naik b Freckingham	46		
G. J. Bailey st O'Brien b Freckingham	93	1/0 (2) 2/0 (1) (7 wkts dec, 110.1 overs)	454
J. M. Vince c Thakor b Freckingham	148	3/141 (3) 4/150 (4)	
S. M. Ervine b Hoggard	69	5/308 (6) 6/412 (5)	
†A. J. Wheater not out	56	7/454 (8) 110 overs: 454-6	

D. J. Balcombe, D. R. Briggs and J. A. Tomlinson did not bat.

Hoggard 27–4–114–2; Wyatt 22–7–78–1; Thakor 18–2–78–0; Freckingham 23–0–100–3; Thornely 8–0–34–0; Naik 11.1–2–38–1; Cobb 1–0–6–0.

Leicestershire

M. A. Thornely b Tomlinson	14	– lbw b Ervine	12
†N. J. O'Brien c Ervine b Wood	14	– c Vince b Wood	17
E. J. H. Eckersley b Tomlinson	10	– not out	99
*R. R. Sarwan b Ervine	25	– c Carberry b Tomlinson	3
J. J. Cobb lbw b Tomlinson	8	– c Vince b Briggs	7
M. A. G. Boyce b Ervine	21	– c Wood b Briggs	30
S. J. Thakor lbw b Hoggard	3	– not out	5
J. K. H. Naik c Wheater b Wood	6		
O. H. Freckingham lbw b Briggs	2		
M. J. Hoggard c Bailey b Tomlinson	18		
A. C. F. Wyatt not out	7		
B 3, l-b 8, n-b 4	15	L-b 3, n-b 6	9

1/31 (2) 2/43 (1) 3/52 (3)	(48.4 overs) 143	1/28 (1) (5 wkts, 74 overs) 182	
4/64 (5) 5/97 (4) 6/108 (7)		2/66 (2) 3/71 (4)	
7/112 (6) 8/118 (9) 9/118 (8) 10/143 (10)		4/95 (5) 5/159 (6)	

Wood 13–4–30–3; Balcombe 12–3–37–0; Tomlinson 11.4–4–23–4; Ervine 7–1–29–2; Briggs 5–1–13–1. *Second innings*—Tomlinson 18–9–34–1; Balcombe 18–5–45–0; Ervine 10–0–48–1; Wood 14–9–18–1; Briggs 14–4–34–2.

Umpires: N. L. Bainton and G. Sharp.

❝ The home batsmen had throwdowns from colleagues perched on cooler boxes."
South Africa v Pakistan 2012-13, page 1064

HAMPSHIRE v LOUGHBOROUGH MCCU

At Southampton (Nursery Ground), April 17–19. Hampshire won by 155 runs. Toss: Hampshire. First-class debut: M. D. T. Roberts. County debut: R. G. Querl.

Set an improbable 404 on a seam-friendly wicket, Loughborough held out for almost all the last day, before losing their final wicket in the 99th over; eight more minutes and they would have saved the match. Hampshire included six players who had started the previous Championship game, and for one it was especially memorable. In his 55th first-class match, Vince followed a brisk century by claiming a maiden wicket with his medium-pace. In Loughborough's second innings, though, he was the chief destroyer, ending with five for 41. They had conceded a 214-run first-innings deficit, despite a tenacious effort from Gavin Baker, who added 68 for the eighth wicket with Will MacVicar. Hampshire preferred to bat again rather than enforce the follow-on. This match marked the first-class debut of the Rose Bowl's Nursery Ground: Adams opened the batting, just as he had for Hampshire Seconds against Sussex Seconds in June 2000, when the venue hosted its inaugural game, also on this ground.

Close of play: first day, Loughborough MCCU 16-2 (Patel 1, Cross 5); second day, Hampshire 189-1 (Adams 61, Dawson 5).

Hampshire

M. A. Carberry c Cross b Lester	7	– c Morris b Riley	118
*J. H. K. Adams lbw b Endersby	96	– not out	61
L. A. Dawson c Cross b Morris	24	– not out	5
J. M. Vince c MacVicar b Ratnayake	114		
A. J. Wheater not out	102		
M. D. T. Roberts not out	16		
L-b 13, w 1, n-b 4	18	B 3, l-b 1, w 1	5

1/13 (1) 2/45 (3) (4 wkts dec, 83 overs) 377 1/170 (1) (1 wkt dec, 44 overs) 189
3/239 (4) 4/292 (2)

†M. D. Bates, H. Riazuddin, R. G. Querl, D. R. Briggs and D. A. Griffiths did not bat.

Baker 13–1–73–0; Lester 15–6–33–1; Endersby 11–1–52–1; Morris 12–1–47–1; MacVicar 17–1–73–0; Riley 11–0–64–0; Ratnayake 4–0–22–1. *Second innings*—Baker 7–0–34–0; Lester 10–2–47–0; Morris 6–0–13–0; Endersby 8–1–33–0; MacVicar 8–1–34–0; Riley 4–0–16–1; Ratnayake 1–0–8–0.

Loughborough MCCU

A. K. Patel c Bates b Riazuddin	1	– b Griffiths	38
D. A. D'Souza b Griffiths	4	– b Vince	23
*A. E. N. Riley c Bates b Griffiths	0	– (10) b Dawson	2
†M. H. Cross c Carberry b Griffiths	24	– c Carberry b Briggs	29
J. P. P. Cornick lbw b Griffiths	10	– (3) lbw b Vince	0
D. M. Endersby c Riazuddin b Griffiths	2	– (5) c Vince b Dawson	12
W. A. MacVicar b Querl	41	– c Dawson b Carberry	10
D. E. M. Ratnayake lbw b Vince	7	– (6) b Vince	46
G. C. Baker c Riazuddin b Briggs	35	– (8) lbw b Vince	52
A. J. Morris not out	18	– (9) b Vince	8
T. J. Lester lbw b Briggs	1	– not out	0
B 4, l-b 4, n-b 12	20	B 4, l-b 3, w 1, n-b 20	28

1/10 (2) 2/10 (3) 3/16 (1) (54.4 overs) 163 1/45 (2) 2/45 (3) (98.3 overs) 248
4/40 (4) 5/54 (6) 6/57 (5) 3/96 (1) 4/120 (5)
7/76 (8) 8/144 (9) 9/148 (7) 10/163 (11) 5/120 (4) 6/142 (7) 7/229 (6)
  8/241 (9) 9/248 (8) 10/248 (10)

Riazuddin 11–7–12–1; Griffiths 15–1–68–5; Vince 5–2–15–1; Querl 10–4–20–1; Briggs 11.4–4–31–2; Dawson 2–0–9–0. *Second innings*—Griffiths 17–3–57–1; Querl 17–4–27–0; Vince 12–4–41–5; Riazuddin 12–3–39–0; Dawson 17.3–6–36–2; Briggs 19–13–28–1; Carberry 4–0–13–1.

Umpires: M. J. D. Bodenham and G. D. Lloyd.

HAMPSHIRE v WORCESTERSHIRE

At Southampton, April 24–27. Hampshire won by an innings and 42 runs. Hampshire 24pts, Worcestershire 3pts. Toss: Hampshire.

As in their previous Championship match, Hampshire ended the third day needing five wickets. Rain had saved Leicestershire – but not Worcestershire, who by lunch had suffered their first innings defeat by Hampshire since 1983. The pitch was missing its usual green tinge, and Carberry and Adams proved its innocuousness by putting on 113 for the first wicket. There was help, though, for

HIGHEST FIRST-CLASS SCORES BY A HAMPSHIRE CAPTAIN

316	R. H. Moore	v Warwickshire at Bournemouth	1937
268	E. G. Wynyard	v Yorkshire at Southampton (Northlands Road)	1896
227	C. P. Mead	v Derbyshire at Ilkeston	1933
225	E. G. Wynyard	v Somerset at Taunton	1899
219*	**J. H. K. Adams**	**v Worcestershire at Southampton (Rose Bowl)**	**2013**
218	**J. H. K. Adams**	**v Northamptonshire at Southampton (Rose Bowl)**	**2013**
217	L. H. Tennyson	v West Indians at Southampton (Northlands Road)	1928
207	J. H. K. Adams	v Somerset at Taunton	2011

the seamers, and modest turn for Ali (and later Briggs), yet Hampshire ran up their biggest total since September 2011. Adams faced 382 balls in his third double-century, and his 219 was more than Worcestershire could manage in response. Adams enforced the follow-on 294 ahead and, if there was more spine this time, the result was not in doubt. Mitchell, dropped at the wicket on one, seemed set for a dogged century until he played across the line.

Close of play: first day, Hampshire 367-6 (Adams 151, Wood 11); second day, Worcestershire 159-5 (Pinner 17, Johnson 9); third day, Worcestershire 153-5 (Mitchell 71, Johnson 6).

Hampshire

M. A. Carberry lbw b Ali	62		D. R. Briggs b Ali	25
*J. H. K. Adams not out	219		J. A. Tomlinson not out	1
L. A. Dawson c Pinner b Russell	26		B 12, l-b 13, w 3, n-b 2	30
G. J. Bailey c Mitchell b Ali	11			
J. M. Vince c Richardson b Ali	52		1/113 (1)	(9 wkts dec, 132 overs) 500
S. M. Ervine b Russell	18		2/168 (3) 3/197 (4)	
†A. J. Wheater lbw b Richardson	15		4/279 (5) 5/319 (6)	
C. P. Wood c Samaraweera b Mitchell	41		6/351 (7) 7/447 (8)	
D. J. Balcombe lbw b Jones	0		8/448 (9) 9/493 (10)	110 overs: 420-6

Richardson 30–8–66–1; Russell 23–1–111–2; Jones 15–3–78–1; Andrew 29–7–95–0; Ali 28–1–103–4; Mitchell 7–2–22–1.

Worcestershire

*D. K. H. Mitchell c Dawson b Balcombe	18	– lbw b Wood	92
M. G. Pardoe c Vince b Tomlinson	29	– c Wheater b Wood	6
M. M. Ali c Dawson b Tomlinson	55	– lbw b Tomlinson	16
T. T. Samaraweera c Ervine b Wood	11	– b Briggs	27
A. N. Kervezee c Briggs b Balcombe	11	– b Vince	5
N. D. Pinner lbw b Tomlinson	29	– lbw b Dawson	3
†M. A. Johnson b Ervine	19	– lbw b Briggs	44
G. M. Andrew lbw b Briggs	5	– c Ervine b Briggs	28
R. A. Jones c Balcombe b Briggs	7	– c Wood b Balcombe	4
C. J. Russell not out	5	– b Briggs	0
A. Richardson c Bailey b Ervine	2	– not out	0
B 6, l-b 3, n-b 6	15	B 10, l-b 17	27

1/40 (1) 2/64 (2) 3/98 (4) (79.1 overs) 206
4/123 (5) 5/143 (3) 6/183 (6)
7/189 (7) 8/189 (8) 9/204 (9) 10/206 (11)

1/19 (1) 2/46 (3) (98.3 overs) 252
3/123 (4) 4/128 (5)
5/143 (6) 6/212 (1) 7/226 (7)
8/248 (9) 9/252 (8) 10/252 (10)

Wood 17–4–56–1; Tomlinson 21–7–52–3; Balcombe 19–8–56–2; Ervine 11.1–5–20–2; Briggs 11–5–13–2. *Second innings*—Wood 22–7–56–2; Balcombe 21–11–47–2; Tomlinson 11–4–24–1; Briggs 14.3–3–38–3; Ervine 10–6–10–0; Vince 12–3–37–1; Dawson 8–4–13–1.

Umpires: S. C. Gale and N. A. Mallender.

At Chelmsford, April 29–May 1. HAMPSHIRE lost to ESSEX by four wickets.

At Bristol, May 8–11. HAMPSHIRE drew with GLOUCESTERSHIRE.

HAMPSHIRE v LANCASHIRE

At Southampton, May 23–26. Drawn. Hampshire 8pts, Lancashire 8pts. Toss: Lancashire.

The match died as a contest once it became clear Lancashire would bat deep into the last day. The weather, which gobbled 88 overs, didn't help, though there were some intriguing personal contributions. Andrea Agathangelou, born in South Africa but the holder of a Cypriot passport, was drafted in after Simon Katich was struck on the head in the nets and taken to hospital. Agathangelou grabbed his chance, reaching a maiden Lancashire century – he had already scored four in South African domestic cricket – during a 70-run last-wicket stand with Kerrigan. Balcombe found lateral movement and bounce to take five wickets, though his start had been atrocious: struggling with no-balls, he had conceded 21 before his fourth legal delivery. Chapple, who gave a masterclass in swing bowling, took four middle-order wickets in six balls before Bailey counter-attacked. On the last day, Cross and Croft took advantage of an unmotivated nine-man Hampshire attack to score centuries. Carberry amused a dwindling crowd with a range of bowling impersonations, including Chapple and umpire Martin Saggers.

Close of play: first day, Lancashire 252-9 (Agathangelou 93, Kerrigan 3); second day, Hampshire 7-1 (Carberry 2, Dawson 2); third day, Lancashire 63-3 (Brown 26, Agathangelou 20).

Lancashire

S. C. Moore c Vince b Tomlinson	30	– c Bates b Balcombe	13
L. A. Procter c Bates b Vince	53	– c Ervine b Tomlinson	2
K. R. Brown c Dawson b Balcombe	3	– c Bates b Ervine	58
A. G. Prince c Dawson b Tomlinson	16	– lbw b Tomlinson	1
A. P. Agathangelou run out	121	– c Bailey b Ervine	49
S. J. Croft c Bates b Balcombe	20	– not out	101
†G. D. Cross c Briggs b Balcombe	3	– c Wood b Vince	100
W. A. White c Dawson b Balcombe	1	– not out	29
K. W. Hogg c Carberry b Balcombe	4		
*G. Chapple c Ervine b Wood	10		
S. C. Kerrigan not out	14		
B 3, l-b 4, n-b 13	20	B 6, l-b 6, n-b 8	20

1/54 (1) 2/63 (3) 3/95 (4)   (98.3 overs) 295   1/13 (1)   (6 wkts dec, 108.2 overs) 373
4/115 (2) 5/164 (6) 6/168 (7)   2/25 (2) 3/27 (4)
7/178 (8) 8/182 (9) 9/225 (10) 10/295 (5)   4/126 (5) 5/137 (3) 6/298 (7)

Tomlinson 26–6–57–2; Balcombe 26–4–104–5; Ervine 7–3–28–0; Wood 19.3–7–36–1; Vince 4–0–21–1; Briggs 16–5–42–0. *Second innings*—Tomlinson 19–6–47–2; Balcombe 20–9–61–1; Wood 13.2–1–47–0; Ervine 9–3–17–2; Dawson 13–6–32–0; Briggs 13–1–60–0; Vince 11–1–52–1; Adams 6–1–21–0; Carberry 4–0–24–0.

Hampshire

M. A. Carberry c Cross b Kerrigan	43	D. J. Balcombe c Brown b Chapple	4
*J. H. K. Adams lbw b Hogg	0	D. R. Briggs c Cross b Hogg	31
L. A. Dawson c Cross b Hogg	55	J. A. Tomlinson not out	4
G. J. Bailey c Procter b Hogg	84	B 4, l-b 12, n-b 6	22
J. M. Vince c Agathangelou b Chapple	15		
S. M. Ervine b Chapple	0	1/0 (2) 2/98 (1) 3/107 (3) (76.5 overs) 258
†M. D. Bates b Chapple	0	4/138 (5) 5/138 (6) 6/144 (7)
C. P. Wood b Chapple	0	7/144 (8) 8/164 (9) 9/221 (10) 10/258 (4)

Chapple 22–6–55–5; Hogg 24.5–5–76–4; Procter 17–5–52–0; White 12–2–54–0; Kerrigan 1–0–5–1.

Umpires: N. G. C. Cowley and M. J. Saggers.

At Northampton, May 29–June 1. HAMPSHIRE drew with NORTHAMPTONSHIRE.

HAMPSHIRE v KENT

At Southampton, June 5–8. Drawn. Hampshire 8pts, Kent 7pts. Toss: Hampshire.

Haggett and Riley, Kent's ninth-wicket pair, held out for nearly 22 overs to deny Hampshire. Set 342 in what became 92 overs, Kent ended 46 short – though a draw suited neither side. McKenzie, arriving from South Africa for his first game of the season, was the mainstay of Hampshire's first-innings 455; he and Ervine shared a fifth-wicket stand of 189. At 156 for five, Kent seemed unlikely to avoid the follow-on, but Stevens injected some aggression on a blameless pitch. Jones's enterprising declaration 134 behind breathed life back into the game and, once a target was agreed, Dawson and Vince were fed easy runs at the start of the last day. Kent then lurched to 41 for four before Stevens again lifted spirits in a stand of 144 in 34 overs with Bell-Drummond. Off-spinner Riley, playing because James Tredwell was needed by England, took a career-best seven wickets in the first innings, before thwarting Hampshire with an unbeaten 21 – another personal best.

Close of play: first day, Hampshire 265-4 (McKenzie 85, Ervine 31); second day, Kent 149-4 (Nash 26, Harmison 0); third day, Hampshire 98-3 (Dawson 35, Vince 23).

Hampshire

M. A. Carberry c Northeast b Stevens	33	– lbw b Shreck	8
*J. H. K. Adams lbw b Riley	65	– c Jones b Coles	0
L. A. Dawson lbw b Riley	36	– not out	87
N. D. McKenzie c Jones b Riley	146	– b Coles	27
J. M. Vince c Jones b Riley	10	– not out	79
S. M. Ervine c Jones b Stevens	86		
†A. J. Wheater lbw b Riley	21		
D. R. Briggs c Stevens b Haggett	25		
D. J. Balcombe b Riley	0		
J. A. Tomlinson not out	9		
D. A. Griffiths b Riley	14		
B 1, l-b 6, w 3	10	B 4, l-b 2	6

1/80 (1) 2/118 (2) 3/155 (3) (145.4 overs) 455   1/8 (2) (3 wkts dec, 34.4 overs) 207
4/183 (5) 5/372 (4) 6/403 (7) 7/403 (6)   2/12 (1) 3/53 (4)
8/408 (9) 9/430 (8) 10/455 (11)   110 overs: 327-4

Shreck 25–6–81–0; Coles 20–3–46–0; Stevens 31–11–72–2; Haggett 25–7–93–1; Riley 43.4–7–150–7; Nash 1–0–6–0. *Second innings*—Shreck 6–0–36–1; Coles 5–0–29–2; Riley 7–0–17–0; Haggett 5–1–9–0; Nash 2–0–2–0; Northeast 5–0–61–0; Key 4.4–0–47–0.

Kent

S. A. Northeast lbw b Ervine	59	– c Carberry b Balcombe	13
R. W. T. Key c Ervine b Griffiths	47	– c Ervine b Balcombe	1
D. J. Bell-Drummond b Griffiths	13	– c Vince b Briggs	66
B. P. Nash c Dawson b Tomlinson	27	– c McKenzie b Tomlinson	15
A. E. N. Riley c Vince b Briggs	0	– (10) not out	21
B. W. Harmison c Briggs b Balcombe	63	– (5) c Wheater b Griffiths	2
D. I. Stevens lbw b Vince	60	– (6) c Wheater b Ervine	96
*†G. O. Jones not out	24	– (7) c Vince b Briggs	22
M. T. Coles not out	7	– (8) run out	8
C. J. Haggett (did not bat)		– (9) not out	32
L-b 6, w 1, n-b 14	21	B 9, l-b 8, w 1, n-b 2	20

1/106 (1) 2/110 (2)	(7 wkts dec, 88.3 overs)	321
3/139 (3) 4/142 (5)		
5/156 (4) 6/258 (7) 7/301 (6)		

1/10 (2)	(8 wkts, 91.5 overs)	296
2/15 (1) 3/38 (4) 4/41 (5)		
5/185 (6) 6/219 (3) 7/222 (7) 8/250 (8)		

C. E. Shreck did not bat.

Tomlinson 21–5–72–1; Balcombe 19–2–64–1; Briggs 15–2–51–1; Griffiths 15.3–3–70–2; Ervine 6–1–24–1; Dawson 6–2–16–0; Vince 6–1–18–1. *Second innings*—Tomlinson 18.5–8–50–1; Balcombe 13–1–35–2; Griffiths 16–2–64–1; Ervine 5–1–11–1; Briggs 24–8–62–2; Vince 4–0–29–0; Dawson 11–3–28–0.

Umpires: S. J. O'Shaughnessy and P. Willey.

HAMPSHIRE v GLOUCESTERSHIRE

At Southampton, June 12–14. Gloucestershire won by 198 runs. Gloucestershire 21pts, Hampshire 3pts. Toss: Hampshire. County debut: Sohail Tanvir.

Both sides began with one win out of seven, so the loss of the first day to the weather encouraged a willingness to fashion a result. After two innings were forfeited, Hampshire were left needing 411. If time was not an issue – there were 169 overs available on a greenish yet increasingly friendly pitch – the scale of the task certainly was. Adams fell in the second over for a fourth duck in five innings and, after a brief rally to 63 for one, the Hampshire innings took a swift turn for the worse. Fuller and Will Gidman ran through the batting to leave them deep in trouble at 88 for six. There was some resistance from Wheater, Sohail Tanvir (on county debut) and Mascarenhas, who was making his last Championship appearance before his end-of-season retirement, but Payne polished off the tail to bring victory inside two playing days. Gloucestershire had slipped to a shaky 123 for four after being inserted in difficult conditions, but Marshall oversaw a recovery, sharing a century stand with Howell, a former Hampshire batsman.

Close of play: first day, no play; second day, Gloucestershire 349-7 (Roderick 24, Fuller 5).

Gloucestershire

*M. Klinger lbw b Sohail Tanvir	4	C. N. Miles c Dawson b Mascarenhas	5
C. D. J. Dent c Dawson b Sohail Tanvir	35	D. A. Payne not out	14
D. M. Housego lbw b Mascarenhas	10		
A. P. R. Gidman c Dawson b Balcombe	11	B 5, l-b 16, n-b 32	53
H. J. H. Marshall c Dawson b Balcombe	114		
B. A. C. Howell b Ervine	54	1/6 (1) (9 wkts dec, 116.4 overs) 410	
W. R. S. Gidman c Wheater b Mascarenhas	42	2/41 (3) 3/56 (4) 4/123 (2)	
†G. H. Roderick not out	45	5/229 (6) 6/289 (5) 7/338 (7)	
J. K. Fuller lbw b Mascarenhas	23	8/368 (9) 9/382 (10) 110 overs: 404-9	

Sohail Tanvir 26–6–95–2; Mascarenhas 25–7–61–4; Balcombe 22–3–85–2; Tomlinson 21–2–69–0; Dawson 15.4–4–50–0; Ervine 4–0–28–1; Carberry 3–2–1–0.

Gloucestershire forfeited their second innings.

Hampshire

Hampshire forfeited their first innings.

M. A. Carberry lbw b Fuller		32
*J. H. K. Adams c Roderick		
b W. R. S. Gidman		0
L. A. Dawson c Howell b Fuller		27
N. D. McKenzie lbw b W. R. S. Gidman		0
J. M. Vince c Roderick b W. R. S. Gidman		6
S. M. Ervine c Roderick b Miles		6
†A. J. Wheater c Fuller b W. R. S. Gidman		38
Sohail Tanvir c Housego b Payne		37

A. D. Mascarenhas b Fuller		41
D. J. Balcombe c Housego b Payne		8
J. A. Tomlinson not out		2
B 5, l-b 8, n-b 2		15

1/0 (2) 2/63 (3) 3/66 (4) (62.1 overs) 212
4/68 (1) 5/74 (5) 6/88 (6)
7/136 (7) 8/170 (8) 9/182 (10) 10/212 (9)

Fuller 15.1–4–54–3; W. R. S. Gidman 14–5–46–4; Miles 16–5–40–1; Payne 17–4–59–2.

Umpires: R. T. Robinson and G. Sharp.

At Cardiff, July 8–11. HAMPSHIRE beat GLAMORGAN by 43 runs.

At Canterbury, July 15–18. HAMPSHIRE drew with KENT.

HAMPSHIRE v GLAMORGAN

At Southampton, August 2–5. Drawn. Hampshire 8pts, Glamorgan 11pts. Toss: Glamorgan.
This match was heading nowhere when rain ended the fourth day after 39 overs. By then Hampshire were 108 ahead with six second-innings wickets left, and any hopes Glamorgan nurtured of a win were receding fast. Wallace had chosen to field when play started an hour late and, although pace bowlers Hogan and Glover managed seven wickets, Hampshire recovered from a poor start to make a useful 349, with Carberry and McKenzie adding 130 for the third wicket. In response, Cooke hit a career-best 92 and Glover, at No. 9, made only his second half-century. Glamorgan declared on the third afternoon with a lead of 129 and needed quick wickets to make their advantage tell. But, on a bland surface, that was never likely. Carberry's 62 nudged him past 10,000 first-class runs, and Wood enjoyed nightwatchman duties.
Close of play: first day, Hampshire 260-6 (Vince 51, Wheater 0); second day, Glamorgan 226-4 (Cooke 73, Allenby 15); third day, Hampshire 115-2 (Dawson 34, Wood 0).

Hampshire

M. A. Carberry c Wallace b Hogan	94	– c Cooke b Wagg	62
*J. H. K. Adams c Wallace b Hogan	1	– c Rees b Cosker	10
L. A. Dawson lbw b Glover	1	– run out	42
N. D. McKenzie c Wallace b Cosker	46	– (5) not out	35
J. M. Vince c Wallace b Wagg	61		
S. M. Ervine c North b Hogan	44		
D. R. Briggs c Wallace b Hogan	11		
†A. J. Wheater c Bragg b Glover	20		
Sohail Tanvir b Glover	22		
C. P. Wood not out	32	– (4) c Hogan b Wagg	69
D. A. Griffiths c North b Cosker	1		
B 1, l-b 9, w 2, n-b 4	16	B 5, l-b 7, w 1, n-b 6	19

1/3 (2) 2/4 (3) 3/134 (4) 4/156 (1) (115 overs) 349
5/246 (6) 6/260 (7) 7/276 (5)
8/305 (8) 9/322 (9) 10/349 (11)
110 overs: 326-9

1/20 (2) (4 wkts, 80.2 overs) 237
2/102 (1) 3/142 (3)
4/237 (4)

Hogan 27–5–90–4; Glover 23–4–90–3; Allenby 18–7–34–0; Wagg 22–5–72–1; Cosker 20–7–41–2; North 5–0–12–0. *Second innings*—Wagg 15.2–6–20–2; Hogan 15–4–34–0; Cosker 19–2–62–1; Glover 10–0–42–0; North 7–1–19–0; Allenby 8–2–14–0; Bragg 5–1–32–0; Rees 1–0–2–0.

Glamorgan

G. P. Rees b Griffiths	12	D. A. Cosker c Adams b Dawson	39
W. D. Bragg b Sohail Tanvir	5	M. G. Hogan not out	12
M. W. Goodwin lbw b Briggs	51	B 17, l-b 13, w 2, n-b 14	46
M. J. North b Wood	36		
C. B. Cooke c Ervine b Wood	92	1/12 (2) (9 wkts dec, 120 overs) 478	
J. Allenby c Dawson b Sohail Tanvir	62	2/45 (1) 3/115 (4)	
*†M. A. Wallace b Wood	39	4/170 (3) 5/297 (6)	
G. G. Wagg c Wheater b Griffiths	33	6/297 (5) 7/355 (8)	
J. C. Glover not out	51	8/385 (7) 9/458 (9) 110 overs: 424-8	

Sohail Tanvir 23–6–66–2; Wood 22–5–61–3; Griffiths 22–2–103–2; Ervine 9–2–33–0; Vince 7–0–47–0; Briggs 20–4–73–1; Dawson 17–4–65–1.

Umpires: N. A. Mallender and P. Willey.

At Southampton, August 6. HAMPSHIRE beat BANGLADESH A by eight runs (see Bangladesh A tour section).

At Southport, August 28–31. HAMPSHIRE lost to LANCASHIRE by 122 runs.

HAMPSHIRE v NORTHAMPTONSHIRE

At Southampton, September 3–6. Drawn. Hampshire 8pts, Northamptonshire 8pts. Toss: Hampshire. County debuts: R. M. R. Brathwaite; J. N. Batty.

Only for the first overcast hour was there any interest for the bowlers. In that time Northamptonshire, put in, tottered to 32 for four. Then the sun came out, the wicket flattened and a high-scoring draw – a familiar tale at Southampton in 2013 – ensued, leaving Northamptonshire supporters anxious about losing ground to promotion rivals. Bates burnished his reputation as a fine gloveman with six catches, and a batsman from each side exploited the conditions to hit a double-hundred. Keogh's six first-class matches had brought 132 runs and an average of 16, but – with the help of Spriegel – he underpinned Northamptonshire's revival with an innings of great concentration that spanned 383 balls across almost eight hours and included 32 fours. Adams batted even longer – 444 balls, nine and a half hours, with 35 fours and a six – in the second double of a curate's-egg season. Not until the rain-affected fourth day were Hampshire eventually dismissed, 107 ahead, but it counted for naught. On the third afternoon, they had been gifted five penalty runs under odd circumstances: 39-year-old Jonathan Batty (plucked from retirement because David Murphy was playing for Scotland and Ben Duckett had injured a knee) discarded a wicketkeeping glove while running to fetch a leg-bye; as he hurled the ball in, Batty yelled at Hall not to put on the glove to receive the throw, but it was too late, and Law 41 had been infringed. On the final day Tony Weld, the Hampshire scorer, was taken ill; without anyone to replace him, the umpires could in theory have asked for the game to be replayed from scratch, but pragmatism ruled, and Tony Kingston, the Northamptonshire scorer, carried on alone.

Close of play: first day, Northamptonshire 323-6 (Keogh 158, Spriegel 61); second day, Hampshire 160-2 (Adams 71, McKenzie 22); third day, Hampshire 515-9 (Balcombe 14).

Northamptonshire

*S. D. Peters c Ervine b Tomlinson	6	– c and b Dawson	40
J. D. Middlebrook b Balcombe	1	– c Dawson b Balcombe	7
D. J. Sales c Bates b Coles	9	– not out	66
A. G. Wakely c Bates b Balcombe	6	– c Dawson b McKenzie	2
R. I. Keogh c and b Dawson	221	– not out	14
A. J. Hall c Roberts b Brathwaite	48		
S. P. Crook c Bates b Brathwaite	6		
M. N. W. Spriegel c Bates b Tomlinson	76		
T. A. Copeland c Bates b Brathwaite	14		
†J. N. Batty c Bates b Coles	12		
Azharullah not out	0		
B 16, l-b 16, w 1, n-b 6	39	L-b 3, w 1, n-b 2	6

1/6 (1) 2/10 (2) 3/24 (4) 4/32 (3)   (129 overs) 438   1/12 (2)   (3 wkts dec, 51.5 overs) 135
5/152 (6) 6/162 (7) 7/349 (8)   2/99 (1) 3/102 (4)
8/387 (9) 9/438 (10) 10/438 (5)   110 overs: 364-7

Tomlinson 26–4–67–2; Balcombe 27–2–103–2; Coles 15–2–53–2; Brathwaite 26–4–112–3; Ervine 15–3–35–0; Dawson 17–7–29–1; McKenzie 3–0–7–0. *Second innings*—Tomlinson 12–3–27–0; Balcombe 7–1–28–1; Brathwaite 8–3–14–0; Coles 6–2–23–0; Dawson 7–5–6–1; McKenzie 7–4–10–1; Roberts 3.5–1–19–0; Adams 1–0–5–0.

Hampshire

M. D. T. Roberts b Crook	8	R. M. R. Brathwaite c and b Middlebrook	9
*J. H. K. Adams c Hall b Spriegel	218	J. A. Tomlinson c Peters b Azharullah	14
L. A. Dawson c Copeland b Spriegel	46		
N. D. McKenzie lbw b Azharullah	52	B 19, l-b 19, w 5, n-b 8, p 5	56
S. M. Ervine b Crook	22		
A. J. Wheater b Copeland	19	1/36 (1) 2/133 (3) (160.4 overs) 545
†M. D. Bates c Copeland b Azharullah	71	3/235 (4) 4/278 (5) 5/331 (6)
M. T. Coles c Hall b Middlebrook	0	6/483 (7) 7/486 (8) 8/494 (2)
D. J. Balcombe not out	30	9/515 (10) 10/545 (11) 110 overs: 340-5

Azharullah 26.4–9–69–3; Copeland 34–12–75–1; Crook 28–5–96–2; Hall 18–3–82–0; Middlebrook 26–2–90–2; Spriegel 28–4–90–2.

Umpires: S. J. O'Shaughnessy and M. J. Saggers.

At Worcester, September 11–14. HAMPSHIRE drew with WORCESTERSHIRE.

At Leicester, September 17–20. HAMPSHIRE beat LEICESTERSHIRE by 180 runs.

HAMPSHIRE v ESSEX

At Southampton, September 24–26. Hampshire won by an innings and 31 runs. Hampshire 24pts, Essex 4pts. Toss: Essex. First-class debut: K. S. Velani.

Extraordinarily, Essex selected a weakened team for this match, despite retaining a chance of promotion. Indeed had the points allocation been reversed, with Essex gaining a full set, they would have ousted Northamptonshire from second place. David Masters and Reece Topley, Essex's two leading wicket-takers, were rested, as were Ravi Bopara and Owais Shah, while Foster handed the gloves to Foakes. A club statement feebly said: "Although promotion is still a mathematical possibility, the likelihood is that Northamptonshire will retain their current second position." Coles was the main destroyer for Hampshire, taking ten wickets in a match for the first time, and clearly enjoying a new lease of life on loan from Kent. Foster had won the toss, but then watched as Hampshire built a daunting total around Carberry, Vince and Wheater, who hit a century against his old county; Dawson passed 1,000 Championship runs for the first time. Then, under cloud cover, Coles and Tomlinson found the bounce and movement that had eluded the Essex attack. Following on 249 behind, Essex offered little more resistance, though Napier's 60-ball innings was an exception.

Close of play: first day, Hampshire 398-8 (Wheater 82, Brathwaite 1); second day, Essex 44-0 (Mickleburgh 18, Gambhir 26).

Hampshire

M. A. Carberry c Mills b Smith	85	D. R. Briggs lbw b Panesar		20
*J. H. K. Adams c Westley b Mahmood	20	R. M. R. Brathwaite c Mahmood b Panesar		17
L. A. Dawson c Foster b Mahmood	40	J. A. Tomlinson not out		0
J. M. Vince lbw b Napier	82	B 8, l-b 9, w 1, n-b 33		51
S. M. Ervine c Foakes b Smith	14			
A. J. Wheater c Westley b Smith	122			456
†M. D. Bates b Smith	5			
M. T. Coles lbw b Smith	0			

1/41 (2) 2/127 (3) 3/227 (1) (106 overs) 456
4/268 (5) 5/290 (4) 6/298 (7)
7/304 (8) 8/392 (9) 9/453 (6) 10/456 (10)

Napier 25–5–80–1; Mills 16–2–75–0; Mahmood 15–0–112–2; Panesar 28–5–100–2; Velani 2–0–8–0; Smith 19–2–58–5; Westley 1–0–6–0.

Essex

J. C. Mickleburgh b Coles	5	– lbw b Coles	22
G. Gambhir c Bates b Coles	3	– c Dawson b Tomlinson	26
T. Westley lbw b Brathwaite	40	– c Bates b Coles	8
G. M. Smith c Adams b Tomlinson	37	– c Bates b Tomlinson	15
*J. S. Foster c Brathwaite b Coles	33	– b Ervine	8
†B. T. Foakes c Vince b Ervine	26	– c Bates b Coles	27
K. S. Velani c Adams b Coles	13	– c Bates b Brathwaite	9
G. R. Napier c Vince b Coles	18	– c sub (S. P. Terry) b Tomlinson	53
S. I. Mahmood c Vince b Tomlinson	19	– c Bates b Tomlinson	6
M. S. Panesar c Adams b Coles	3	– b Coles	16
T. S. Mills not out	0	– not out	16
L-b 10	10	B 4, l-b 4, n-b 4	12

1/5 (1) 2/16 (2) 3/81 (4)   (59.1 overs) 207
4/93 (3) 5/138 (6) 6/166 (5)
7/170 (7) 8/195 (8) 9/207 (10) 10/207 (10)

1/49 (1) 2/49 (2)   (57.5 overs) 218
3/69 (3) 4/73 (4)
5/96 (5) 6/117 (7) 7/156 (6)
8/177 (9) 9/188 (8) 10/218 (10)

Tomlinson 18–4–55–2; Coles 19.1–5–71–6; Briggs 6–2–14–0; Brathwaite 10–3–36–1; Ervine 6–2–21–1. *Second innings*—Tomlinson 19–5–63–4; Coles 17.5–4–83–4; Brathwaite 9–1–40–1; Ervine 7–4–11–1; Briggs 3–0–6–0; Vince 2–1–7–0.

Umpires: T. E. Jesty and R. A. Kettleborough.

KENT

Falling apart at the seam

MARK PENNELL

An outpouring of elation and tears greeted Kent's only home Championship victory of the summer. The emotions were all the more intense because the success had not come until the last day of a long season. In knocking off 418 for a two-wicket win over previously unbeaten Division Two champions Lancashire, Kent achieved their second-highest fourth-innings pursuit, and became the only first-class team to overhaul 400 on five occasions.

The hero of the hour – and much more – was 37-year-old Darren Stevens. He hit a season's-best unbeaten 205, striding past Rob Key to become Kent's highest first-class run-scorer for 2013, and was later named landslide winner of the Player of the Season award. Stevens comfortably topped Kent's Championship batting averages and, across all formats, was the leading run-scorer (1,921), wicket-taker (51) and outfield catcher (25). For good measure, he added the Walter Lawrence Trophy for the summer's fastest century, reaching three figures from 44 balls in the YB40 against Sussex in June.

Yet Stevens's season had a bittersweet quality. In August, the ICC charged him with failing to report an illegal approach as part of the Anti-Corruption and Security Unit investigation into the Bangladesh Premier League, staged in January and February 2013. In late February 2014, Stevens was found not guilty at a tribunal appointed by the Bangladeshi board – much to his relief.

"I've had this hanging over me all season," he had said. "It's been playing on my mind for weeks that, if things don't go my way, this could end up being my last match. Jimmy Adams [Kent's head coach] asked us to say a few words in the dressing-room to end the season. I thanked the boys for supporting me throughout, and then it hit me: this could be the end of what I do for a living, the job I love. I couldn't finish what I wanted to say after that."

Back in April, there had been heartfelt tributes to Mike Denness, the former captain of Kent and England, who died, aged 72, after a lengthy illness. Just weeks earlier, in his role as county president, he had nominated as his successor his long-standing friend, the comedian and raconteur Bob "The Cat" Bevan. And so Denness, one of Kent's most successful captains, ensured his final field placing would prove a shrewd and popular one.

The 2013 captain, James Tredwell, had found life tough, and in December he resigned after one summer in charge. Though he fell short of blaming the burden of leadership, his figures spoke volumes. He waited until July 11 for a first Championship scalp (when Gloucestershire's Hamish Marshall holed out searching for quick runs), and ended his first-class campaign with 17 wickets at 56, and 238 runs at 17. For 2014, the captaincy returned to the safe hands of Key, with Sam Northeast as his deputy.

Darren Stevens

The match that brought Tredwell's first wicket also gave Kent their first Championship win, when in searing Cheltenham heat they reached 411 to overcome Gloucestershire. The hero was Brendan Nash, forced to retire ill on 199, by which time he was out on his feet with heat exhaustion. Not until half an hour afterwards, in a darkened treatment room, did he learn of the victory that lifted Kent from the bottom of the table, where they had languished for most of May and June.

With his brother-in-law Tredwell on international duty, Geraint Jones was at the helm in September for their second success, at Cardiff. That effectively staved off the wooden spoon, but by then the highly rated fast bowler Matt Coles had played his last game for the club. He joined Hampshire on loan – a move later made permanent.

Stevens, Key and Nash all passed 1,000 first-class runs, while Northeast and Ben Harmison improved over the summer. Even though runs from the usually reliable Jones dried up – in September, after 115 successive Championship appearances, he made way for Sam Billings – the batting wasn't the problem.

Veteran seamer Charlie Shreck took most wickets, yet his total of 33 (at almost 40 apiece) was the lowest by Kent's leading first-class wicket-taker since 1875. The mid-season overseas signing should have helped, but South Africa's Vernon Philander, then ranked No. 2 in the world, left without a wicket from 64 Championship overs; Mark Davies was dropped for six first-class fixtures. The upshot was Kent struggled to build on their runs: they lost only twice, but won just three games, finishing a disappointing seventh. (Shreck was released, along with Michael Powell and Ben Kemp.)

Kent's limited-overs fortunes were barely more encouraging: three wins from ten in the FLt20, and a slightly rosier six from 12 in the YB40, where the highlight, again inspired by Stevens, was a record 40-over pursuit of 336 to beat Sussex. Though the Canterbury floodlights failed at an important moment in the YB40 campaign, the mood brightened with the debut of Fabian Cowdrey, son of Chris and grandson of Colin, and news that he, Northeast, Daniel Bell-Drummond and Calum Haggett – the former Somerset seamer who had undergone open-heart surgery in 2010 – all had agreed contract extensions. And after impressive Twenty20 performances, Mitch Claydon converted his loan from Durham into a full-time move.

To boost their bowling resources, Kent signed four seamers: Hampshire's softly spoken firebrand David Griffiths, Charlie Hartley from Millfield School, Suffolk's Matt Hunn (who made his debut in the final game of the season) and, in February, Australian left-armer Doug Bollinger, their new overseas player. Former batsman Matt Walker returned from Essex to become Adams's assistant.

Championship attendance: 26,679.

KENT RESULTS

All first-class matches – Played 17: Won 3, Lost 2, Drawn 12.
County Championship matches – Played 16: Won 3, Lost 2, Drawn 11.

LV= County Championship, 7th in Division 2;
Friends Life t20, 5th in South Division; Yorkshire Bank 40, 4th in Group A.

COUNTY CHAMPIONSHIP AVERAGES, BATTING AND FIELDING

Cap		M	I	NO	R	HS	100	50	Avge	Ct/St
2005	D. I. Stevens...............	15	21	1	1,268	205*	4	7	63.40	13
2001	R. W. T. Key	16	27	3	1,168	180	5	3	48.66	3
2013	B. P. Nash¶...............	16	26	4	1,064	199*	5	5	48.36	4
	B. W. Harmison	13	19	3	712	106	2	5	44.50	8
	C. J. Haggett.................	11	13	7	249	44*	0	0	41.50	3
	M. J. Powell.................	6	9	3	203	70	0	2	33.83	0
2012	S. A. Northeast†..........	15	26	1	650	94	0	6	26.00	11
2003	G. O. Jones...............	14	19	2	403	67	0	2	23.70	40/1
	D. J. Bell-Drummond†........	13	20	0	466	79	0	4	23.30	7
	M. E. Claydon	3	4	0	93	40	0	0	23.25	1
2012	M. T. Coles†	7	9	1	136	59	0	1	17.00	6
2007	J. C. Tredwell†‡.............	11	14	1	197	48	0	0	15.15	9
	A. E. N. Riley†..............	5	6	2	60	21*	0	0	15.00	2
	M. Davies.................	10	14	3	158	41	0	0	14.36	0
	C. E. Shreck	14	15	8	82	19*	0	0	11.71	1

Also batted: A. J. Ball† (2 matches) 32, 7, 69; S. W. Billings† (2 matches) 8, 13, 24 (4 ct, 1 st); M. D. Hunn (1 match) 0 (1 ct); V. D. Philander§ (2 matches) 2, 23.

† *Born in Kent.* ‡ *ECB contract.* § *Official overseas player.* ¶ *Other non-England-qualified player.*

BOWLING

	Style	O	M	R	W	BB	5I	Avge
M. Davies.....................	RFM	266.3	74	629	25	4-36	0	25.16
A. E. N. Riley....................	OB	102.3	11	361	14	7-150	1	25.78
D. I. Stevens...................	RM	403.4	111	1,051	32	5-39	1	32.84
C. J. Haggett...................	RM	298	72	907	26	4-94	0	34.88
C. E. Shreck....................	RFM	429.2	98	1,294	33	4-65	0	39.21
M. T. Coles	RFM	162	28	549	13	5-31	1	42.23
J. C. Tredwell..................	OB	331.3	67	965	17	5-51	1	56.76

Also bowled: A. J. Ball (LFM) 37–4–170–3; D. J. Bell-Drummond (RM) 6.5–0–54–0; M. E. Claydon (RFM) 64.4–12–226–4; B. W. Harmison (RFM) 37–1–161–1; M. D. Hunn (RFM) 31.4–6–118–3; R. W. T. Key (RM/OB) 9.2–0–86–0; B. P. Nash (SLA/LM) 9–0–43–1; S. A. Northeast (OB) 20–0–131–1; V. D. Philander (RFM) 64–9–170–0.

LEADING YB40 AVERAGES (100 runs/4 wickets)

Batting	Runs	HS	Avge	SR	Ct/St
F. K. Cowdrey .	110	52*	55.00	102.80	0
R. W. T. Key...	505	144*	50.50	94.04	2
B. P. Nash...	436	98*	48.44	86.33	3
S. A. Northeast .	382	115	38.20	86.03	3
D. I. Stevens ...	309	118	30.90	108.80	8
G. O. Jones	155	46*	22.14	92.81	8/1

Bowling	W	BB	Avge	ER
J. C. Tredwell ...	13	4-22	23.38	4.34
M. T. Coles	15	4-20	24.46	5.88
D. I. Stevens ...	13	3-19	32.38	5.06
M. Davies	8	2-14	35.00	5.45
A. E. N. Riley ...	10	2-33	37.70	5.89
M. E. Claydon ...	5	2-29	38.60	6.97
C. J. Haggett	4	2-97	40.25	8.05
A. J. Ball	4	3-36	70.50	6.55

LEADING FLt20 AVERAGES (90 runs/18 overs)

Batting	Runs	HS	Avge	SR	Ct
D. I. Stevens	267	67*	38.14	160.84	4
F. K. Cowdrey	152	50	38.00	115.15	0
S. A. Northeast	119	61	23.80	112.26	1
S. W. Billings	189	28	21.00	109.24	8
A. J. Blake	98	37*	14.00	102.08	6

Bowling	W	BB	Avge	ER
J. C. Tredwell	7	3-19	16.42	5.75
A. E. N. Riley	6	2-23	38.33	6.83
V. D. Philander	9	4-8	23.44	8.11
D. I. Stevens	6	2-16	36.00	8.30
M. E. Claydon	13	3-22	22.61	8.36
M. T. Coles	8	3-14	34.00	8.58

FIRST-CLASS COUNTY RECORDS

Highest score for	332	W. H. Ashdown v Essex at Brentwood	1934
Highest score against	344	W. G. Grace (MCC) at Canterbury	1876
Leading run-scorer	47,868	F. E. Woolley (avge 41.77)	1906–38
Best bowling for	10-30	C. Blythe v Northamptonshire at Northampton	1907
Best bowling against	10-48	C. H. G. Bland (Sussex) at Tonbridge	1899
Leading wicket-taker	3,340	A. P. Freeman (avge 17.64)	1914–36
Highest total for	803-4 dec	v Essex at Brentwood	1934
Highest total against	676	by Australians at Canterbury	1921
Lowest total for	18	v Sussex at Gravesend	1867
Lowest total against	16	by Warwickshire at Tonbridge	1913

LIST A COUNTY RECORDS

Highest score for	146	A. Symonds v Lancashire at Tunbridge Wells	2004
Highest score against	167*	P. Johnson (Nottinghamshire) at Nottingham	1993
Leading run-scorer	7,814	M. R. Benson (avge 31.89)	1980–95
Best bowling for	8-31	D. L. Underwood v Scotland at Edinburgh	1987
Best bowling against	6-5	A. G. Wharf (Glamorgan) at Cardiff	2004
Leading wicket-taker	530	D. L. Underwood (avge 18.93)	1963–87
Highest total for	384-6	v Berkshire at Finchampstead	1994
Highest total against	344-5	by Somerset at Taunton	2002
Lowest total for	60	v Somerset at Taunton	1979
Lowest total against	60	by Derbyshire at Canterbury	2008

TWENTY20 COUNTY RECORDS

Highest score for	112	A. Symonds v Middlesex at Maidstone	2004
Highest score against	106	A. C. Gilchrist (Middlesex) at Canterbury	2010
Leading run-scorer	**2,290**	**D. I. Stevens** (avge 33.67)	**2005–13**
Best bowling for	5-17	Wahab Riaz v Gloucestershire at Beckenham	2011
Best bowling against	5-17	G. M. Smith (Essex) at Chelmsford	2012
Leading wicket-taker	**89**	**J. C. Tredwell** (avge 24.73)	**2003–13**
Highest total for	217	v Gloucestershire at Gloucester	2010
Highest total against	217-4	by Surrey at Canterbury	2006
Lowest total for	72	v Hampshire at Southampton	2011
Lowest total against	82	by Somerset at Taunton	2010

ADDRESS

St Lawrence Ground, Old Dover Road, Canterbury CT1 3NZ (01227 456886; **email** kent@ecb.co.uk). **Website** www.kentcricket.co.uk

OFFICIALS

Captain 2013 J. C. Tredwell
    2014 R. W. T. Key
Head coach J. C. Adams
High-performance director S. C. Willis
President G. W. Johnson

Chairman G. M. Kennedy
Chief executive J. A. S. Clifford
Chairman, cricket committee G. W. Johnson
Head groundsman S. Williamson
Scorer L. Hart

KENT v CARDIFF MCCU

At Canterbury, April 10–12. Drawn. Toss: Cardiff MCCU. First-class debut: C. J. Haggett.

Kent welcomed the fourth generation of the Cowdrey family to play first-class cricket, though 20-year-old Fabian (son of Chris, grandson of Colin, and great-grandson of Ernest, whose only game had been for Europeans against Indians at Madras in 1927) was the first to appear at Canterbury *against* the county. He was unbeaten on 23 at the end of a chilly opening day which, thanks to rain, also proved the last. Kent gave a first-class debut to seamer Calum Haggett, who had joined from Somerset over the winter. He made a duck, but fellow Millfield old boy Daniel Bell-Drummond – they both turned out for the school in 2008 and 2009 – hit a maiden first-class century. Comfortably the most successful of the student bowlers was Matt Hobden, who recorded a second five-for in his fourth first-class match.

Close of play: first day, Cardiff MCCU 33-1 (Cowdrey 23, Denning 6); second day, no play.

Kent

S. A. Northeast c Miles b Hobden	14	C. J. Haggett lbw b Hobden	0
R. W. T. Key b Hobden	1	M. Davies not out	0
B. P. Nash b Hobden	46		
M. J. Powell run out	62	B 4, l-b 8, n-b 18	30
D. J. Bell-Drummond not out	102		
D. I. Stevens c Balbirnie b Harris	36	1/9 (2) 2/34 (1) (8 wkts dec, 86 overs)	333
†G. O. Jones c Siddique b Denning	1	3/129 (3) 4/164 (4)	
*J. C. Tredwell b Hobden	41	5/226 (5) 6/235 (7) 7/312 (8) 8/314 (9)	

C. E. Shreck did not bat.

Hobden 22–5–89–5; Denning 22–3–56–1; Harris 14–4–49–1; Salter 11–0–46–0; Cowdrey 15–1–68–0; Balbirnie 2–0–13–0.

Cardiff MCCU

F. K. Cowdrey not out	23
Z. Elkin lbw b Davies	3
J. S. T. Denning not out	6
L-b 1	1

1/21 (2)　　　　　(1 wkt, 12 overs)　33

U. A. Qureshi, H. G. Siddique, A. Balbirnie, S. L. Davies, *†A. J. Miles, A. G. Salter, P. G. Harris and M. E. Hobden did not bat.

Davies 6–2–10–1; Shreck 6–0–22–0.

Umpires: P. K. Baldwin and M. J. D. Bodenham.

At Leicester, April 17–20. KENT drew with LEICESTERSHIRE.

At Manchester, April 24–27. KENT drew with LANCASHIRE.

KENT v NORTHAMPTONSHIRE

At Canterbury, May 1–3. Northamptonshire won by seven wickets. Northamptonshire 22pts, Kent 5pts. Toss: Kent.

After two draws away from home, Kent slipped to a three-day defeat at Canterbury. Tredwell chose to bat, but watched his side subside to 55 for three before Powell and Bell-Drummond, with a maiden Championship fifty, saved face in a stand of 149. Unlike Northamptonshire's three previous opponents, Kent did at least manage a batting point (two, in fact), but they were undermined by a collapse in which seven fell for 67 in 27 overs. Copeland, Northamptonshire's willowy Australian spearhead, led the way with five for 71. Peters batted five hours for his 106 to help clinch a lead of

32, before Kent were once again undone by Copeland's accuracy and bounce; he grabbed another five-for to take ten in a match for the second time in his career. Hall, the former Kent favourite, clipped a boundary through midwicket to bring Northamptonshire their third successive win.

Close of play: first day, Kent 271; second day, Kent 6-0 (Northeast 3, Key 3).

Kent

S. A. Northeast b Willey	10	– lbw b Copeland	3
R. W. T. Key c Hall b Copeland	20	– lbw b Copeland	9
B. P. Nash b Crook	18	– c Murphy b Copeland	14
M. J. Powell c Murphy b Crook	70	– (6) not out	7
D. J. Bell-Drummond c sub (O. P. Stone) b Crook	68	– (4) run out	4
†G. O. Jones c Murphy b Copeland	20	– (5) lbw b Willey	57
*J. C. Tredwell c Copeland b Willey	19	– lbw b Crook	0
M. T. Coles c Wakely b Copeland	0	– b Crook	6
C. J. Haggett not out	5	– c Murphy b Copeland	12
M. Davies c Peters b Copeland	12	– c Hall b Copeland	7
C. E. Shreck b Copeland	0	– b Willey	1
B 3, l-b 6, w 2, n-b 18	29	L-b 3, n-b 12	15

1/22 (1) 2/55 (3) 3/55 (2) (94.2 overs) 271
4/204 (4) 5/213 (5) 6/244 (6)
7/250 (8) 8/250 (7) 9/271 (10) 10/271 (11)

1/12 (1) 2/15 (2) (47.1 overs) 135
3/30 (4) 4/51 (3)
5/56 (7) 6/70 (8) 7/117 (9)
8/121 (5) 9/134 (10) 10/135 (11)

In the second innings Powell, when 1, retired hurt at 54-4 and resumed at 117-7.

Willey 19–4–57–2; Copeland 28.2–9–71–5; Crook 17–1–78–3; Hall 16–4–43–0; Middlebrook 14–5–13–0. *Second innings*—Copeland 21–11–42–5; Willey 13.1–7–29–2; Crook 10–0–54–2; Hall 3–1–7–0.

Northamptonshire

*S. D. Peters c sub (A. J. Blake) b Davies	106	– c and b Haggett	37
K. J. Coetzer lbw b Davies	6	– c Tredwell b Haggett	13
D. J. Sales c Jones b Shreck	16	– c Bell-Drummond b Coles	10
A. G. Wakely c Jones b Shreck	1	– not out	14
A. J. Hall lbw b Shreck	12	– not out	27
J. D. Middlebrook c Jones b Haggett	24		
†D. Murphy b Davies	5		
D. J. Willey c Jones b Coles	25		
S. P. Crook c sub (A. J. Blake) b Coles	62		
T. A. Copeland c sub (A. J. Blake) b Shreck	4		
R. I. Newton not out	21		
B 2, l-b 16, w 1, n-b 2	21	L-b 2, n-b 2	4

1/13 (2) 2/76 (3) 3/82 (4) (90.1 overs) 303
4/102 (5) 5/133 (6) 6/150 (7)
7/186 (8) 8/249 (1) 9/260 (10) 10/303 (9)

1/52 (2) (3 wkts, 28.3 overs) 105
2/63 (1) 3/65 (3)

Davies 20–3–51–3; Shreck 24–3–80–4; Coles 15.1–2–62–2; Haggett 16–4–51–1; Tredwell 15–2–41–0. *Second innings*—Davies 6–4–8–0; Shreck 4–0–34–0; Haggett 10–0–26–2; Coles 5–0–25–1; Tredwell 3.3–0–10–0.

Umpires: R. J. Bailey and G. D. Lloyd.

KENT v WORCESTERSHIRE

At Canterbury, May 17–18. Worcestershire won by ten wickets. Worcestershire 19pts, Kent 3pts. Toss: Worcestershire.

Beaten inside three days in their previous Championship match, Kent were now humbled in two by Worcestershire after being shot out for 63 in their second innings. Though Kent's average age was almost five years greater than their opponents', it was Worcestershire who coped more maturely with seamer-friendly conditions. Under leaden skies on the opening day, the match's oldest player – the 38-year-old Richardson – snared five for 41 as Kent folded inside 52 overs; Northeast was the only one of the top six to make double figures. Worcestershire didn't find batting much easier, although at 171 for five they were eyeing at least one bonus point. Thanks to Coles, who enjoyed a spell of four for ten from 27 balls, that never happened – and the lead was restricted to 35. But then Richardson demolished Kent in two hours to take his match figures to 12 for 63, a career-best. Soon after 5pm on the second evening, Worcestershire were celebrating victory, having doubled their points tally for the season.

Close of play: first day, Worcestershire 105-4 (Kervezee 29, Pinner 0).

Kent

S. A. Northeast c Johnson b Richardson	52	– c Ali b Richardson	0
R. W. T. Key b Richardson	8	– lbw b Andrew	5
B. P. Nash c Mitchell b Richardson	0	– c Mitchell b Richardson	4
M. J. Powell c Mitchell b Richardson	0	– c Johnson b Richardson	2
B. W. Harmison c Richardson b Shantry	5	– lbw b Richardson	19
D. I. Stevens lbw b Andrew	3	– c Mitchell b Richardson	3
†G. O. Jones b Andrew	16	– c Pinner b Andrew	11
*J. C. Tredwell lbw b Andrew	4	– not out	6
M. T. Coles lbw b Shantry	21	– c Pinner b Andrew	1
M. Davies c Ali b Richardson	40	– c Kervezee b Richardson	8
C. E. Shreck not out	0	– lbw b Richardson	0
B 4, l-b 6	10	L-b 4	4
	—		—
	159		63

1/35 (2) 2/43 (3) 3/43 (4)   (51.2 overs) 159
4/61 (5) 5/64 (6) 6/90 (7)
7/94 (8) 8/94 (1) 9/137 (9) 10/159 (10)

1/0 (1) 2/4 (3)   (28.3 overs) 63
3/10 (4) 4/30 (2)
5/35 (6) 6/36 (5) 7/48 (7)
8/52 (9) 9/63 (10) 10/63 (11)

Richardson 17.2–7–41–5; Russell 10–0–49–0; Andrew 10–1–34–3; Shantry 14–5–25–2. *Second innings*—Richardson 14.3–6–22–7; Russell 6–1–13–0; Andrew 8–0–24–3.

Worcestershire

*D. K. H. Mitchell lbw b Davies	8	– not out	13
M. G. Pardoe lbw b Shreck	1	– not out	15
M. M. Ali c Jones b Coles	54		
T. T. Samaraweera b Davies	2		
A. N. Kervezee c Jones b Shreck	29		
N. D. Pinner c Jones b Coles	20		
†M. A. Johnson lbw b Coles	38		
G. M. Andrew lbw b Coles	9		
J. D. Shantry c Jones b Coles	12		
C. J. Russell lbw b Davies	1		
A. Richardson not out	0		
B 7, l-b 11, n-b 2	20	B 1, l-b 2	3
	—		—
	194		31

1/2 (2) 2/32 (1) 3/34 (4)   (69.1 overs) 194
4/104 (3) 5/105 (5) 6/171 (7)
7/172 (6) 8/183 (8) 9/194 (10) 10/194 (9)

(no wkt, 8.5 overs) 31

Davies 21–4–52–3; Shreck 17–8–33–2; Coles 15.1–4–31–5; Stevens 12–2–44–0; Tredwell 4–0–16–0. *Second innings*—Coles 2–1–4–0; Shreck 4–0–15–0; Tredwell 2.5–1–9–0.

Umpires: D. J. Millns and P. Willey.

At Chelmsford, May 22–25. KENT drew with ESSEX.

KENT v LEICESTERSHIRE

At Tunbridge Wells, May 29–June 1. Drawn. Kent 10pts, Leicestershire 4pts. Toss: Leicestershire.

Stevens, who was eight years on Leicestershire's books, did his best to provide some entertainment, but for the second year running at The Nevill the only winner was the weather. A positive result was never likely once 22.3 overs were bowled on the first two days. Stevens's medium-pace had been undervalued at Leicestershire – he managed five Championship wickets in 71 matches – but now he took five in an innings to skittle his old side for 186. By the third-day close, Kent were 27 behind for the loss of only Bell-Drummond. When Key, who passed 15,000 first-class runs for the county, fell for 106 on the last morning, Stevens was promoted to No. 4 to speed things up. He came within three runs of cracking a century before lunch, bowled round his legs by Naik from his 58th ball, having smashed eight fours and seven sixes; he and Nash added 149 in 16 overs. Jones promptly declared 167 ahead – Tredwell was with the England one-day team – in an effort to keep the game alive, but fifties from Greg Smith and Eckersley, who was dropped first ball, ensured a draw.

Close of play: first day, Leicestershire 74-4 (Thakor 8, Boyce 0); second day, no play; third day, Kent 159-1 (Key 81, Nash 65).

Leicestershire

G. P. Smith c Riley b Shreck	6	– not out	65
†N. J. O'Brien b Stevens	22	– c Coles b Stevens	6
E. J. H. Eckersley c Jones b Haggett	32	– not out	65
J. A. Burns lbw b Stevens	4		
S. J. Thakor c Harmison b Stevens	30		
M. A. G. Boyce b Haggett	17		
*J. J. Cobb lbw b Stevens	2		
J. K. H. Naik c Coles b Shreck	23		
O. H. Freckingham c Bell-Drummond b Shreck	15		
N. L. Buck not out	16		
R. E. M. Williams c Coles b Stevens	12		
B 1, l-b 5, w 1	7	L-b 2, w 1	3

1/6 (1) 2/62 (2) 3/62 (3) 4/68 (4) (62.3 overs) 186 1/11 (2) (1 wkt, 54.4 overs) 139
5/111 (5) 6/117 (6) 7/123 (7)
8/155 (9) 9/160 (8) 10/186 (11)

Shreck 19–4–54–3; Coles 11–0–48–0; Haggett 13–2–39–2; Stevens 19.3–4–39–5. *Second innings*—Shreck 12–4–27–0; Stevens 8–3–18–1; Riley 16–2–50–0; Haggett 8–2–18–0; Coles 8.4–0–21–0; Nash 2–0–3–0.

Kent

D. J. Bell-Drummond lbw b Freckingham	8
R. W. T. Key c Freckingham b Naik	106
B. P. Nash not out	128
D. I. Stevens b Naik	97
B 5, l-b 4, w 1, n-b 4	14

1/14 (1) (3 wkts dec, 78.3 overs) 353
2/204 (2) 3/353 (4)

M. J. Powell, B. W. Harmison, *†G. O. Jones, M. T. Coles, C. J. Haggett, A. E. N. Riley and C. E. Shreck did not bat.

Freckingham 19–4–75–1; Williams 16–3–56–0; Buck 13–1–67–0; Naik 21.3–5–95–2; Thakor 9–1–51–0.

Umpires: S. C. Gale and P. J. Hartley.

At Southampton, June 5–8. KENT drew with HAMPSHIRE.

KENT v GLAMORGAN

At Canterbury, June 12–15. Drawn. Kent 5pts, Glamorgan 9pts. Toss: Glamorgan. County debut: M. E. Claydon.

A sixth draw (plus two heavy defeats) left winless Kent languishing just four points above bottom-placed Leicestershire. But they could derive encouragement from saving the game after being made to follow on. At the heart of Glamorgan's first innings was a watchful hundred from Goodwin, who steadied the ship in blustery conditions after Haggett had removed the openers cheaply. The next nine Glamorgan batsmen all made double figures, despite numerous rainbreaks, as Claydon – on loan from Durham – took three wickets on Kent debut. By stumps on the second day, his new side had lurched to 73 for four, and a rash of poor shots meant they were dismissed 243 behind next morning. Then came the fightback: in their first innings no one had passed 23; now six passed 32, with Harmison and Stevens adding 163 for the fifth wicket – a partnership broken by Hogan's direct hit from the deep. On an easing pitch, Cosker's left-arm spin was Glamorgan's most potent weapon. He took five, but Kent's second innings was 142 overs old when the captains shook hands.

Close of play: first day, Glamorgan 155-4 (Goodwin 35, Allenby 19); second day, Kent 73-4 (Harmison 8, Stevens 4); third day, Kent 254-4 (Harmison 23, Stevens 35).

Glamorgan

B. J. Wright b Haggett	5	M. G. Hogan b Haggett		14
W. D. Bragg c Jones b Haggett	6	M. T. Reed lbw b Claydon		27
S. J. Walters c Jones b Shreck	38			
M. J. North c Jones b Haggett	46	L-b 9, n-b 4		13
M. W. Goodwin c Northeast b Shreck	136			
J. Allenby c Jones b Shreck	25	1/10 (2) 2/19 (1)	(119.4 overs)	378
*M. A. Wallace c Harmison b Claydon	34	3/79 (3) 4/123 (4) 5/168 (6)		
G. G. Wagg c Harmison b Claydon	24	6/273 (7) 7/293 (8) 8/315 (5)		
D. A. Cosker not out	20	9/338 (10) 10/378 (11)	110 overs: 336-8	

Shreck 33–8–107–3; Haggett 33–10–94–4; Claydon 25.4–7–85–3; Stevens 25–8–59–0; Riley 3–0–24–0.

Kent

S. A. Northeast c Allenby b Wagg	12	– c Cosker b Reed	33
R. W. T. Key c Wright b Hogan	23	– lbw b Cosker	85
D. J. Bell-Drummond c Wright b Reed	16	– c Allenby b Cosker	14
B. P. Nash b Wallace b Hogan	4	– c Walters b Hogan	50
B. W. Harmison c Wallace b Allenby	12	– run out	64
D. I. Stevens lbw b Allenby	10	– b Cosker	119
*†G. O. Jones b Hogan	12	– b Reed	15
C. J. Haggett b Reed	9	– b Cosker	17
M. E. Claydon c Reed b Wagg	3	– c Allenby b Cosker	40
A. E. N. Riley c Wallace b Cosker	10	– not out	9
C. E. Shreck not out	15	– not out	19
L-b 4, w 1, n-b 4	9	B 2, l-b 10, w 2, n-b 10	24

1/21 (1) 2/50 (3) 3/58 (2)	(46.5 overs) 135	1/75 (1)	(9 wkts dec, 142 overs) 489
4/65 (4) 5/80 (6) 6/91 (5)		2/97 (3) 3/192 (4)	
7/105 (7) 8/110 (9) 9/110 (8) 10/135 (10)		4/192 (2) 5/355 (5) 6/399 (6)	
		7/401 (7) 8/437 (8) 9/468 (9)	

Hogan 16–4–42–3; Wagg 11–2–40–2; Reed 7–2–26–2; Allenby 12–3–22–2; Cosker 0.5–0–1–1. *Second innings*—Wagg 23–5–94–0; Hogan 32–4–96–1; Allenby 16–1–72–0; Reed 21–2–95–2; Cosker 50–12–120–5.

Umpires: S. A. Garratt and N. A. Mallender.

At Canterbury, June 22. KENT lost to NEW ZEALANDERS by 42 runs (see New Zealand tour section).

At Cheltenham, July 10–13. KENT beat GLOUCESTERSHIRE by two wickets. *Kent make 411 to win their first Championship match of the season.*

KENT v HAMPSHIRE

At Canterbury, July 15–18. Drawn. Kent 8pts, Hampshire 7pts. Toss: Hampshire. First-class debut: A. P. Rouse.

A slow-paced Canterbury shirtfront produced plenty of runs, if rather less fun. Carberry's first Championship hundred since 2011 dominated the opening day; generally measured, he also hit successive sixes from Nash's occasional left-arm spin. Hampshire fell away once Carberry was fourth out at 291, though Adams could still declare on the second afternoon. Then it was Kent's turn to make hay. Key reached his 22nd century at the St Lawrence ground, and shared hundred stands with Bell-Drummond and Nash – who hit a second consecutive century – before missing a slog-sweep against Briggs. Kent's innings also tailed off, though they still enjoyed a 108-run lead. Any chance of a result vanished when it became clear the pitch was as true (and turgid) as ever. Tredwell finished the match with six wickets, but Philander, Kent's new overseas player and the world's No. 2-ranked Test bowler, now had Championship figures of none for 170 from his first two games.

Close of play: first day, Hampshire 263-3 (Carberry 137, Ervine 24); second day, Kent 200-1 (Key 105, Bell-Drummond 74); third day, Hampshire 15-0 (Carberry 12, Adams 3).

Hampshire

M. A. Carberry c Jones b Haggett	154	– c Jones b Tredwell	66
*J. H. K. Adams c Bell-Drummond b Shreck	8	– lbw b Tredwell	12
L. A. Dawson lbw b Stevens	75	– not out	78
J. M. Vince lbw b Haggett	8	– c Key b Tredwell	4
S. M. Ervine st Jones b Tredwell	72	– c Stevens b Shreck	12
†A. J. Wheater lbw b Haggett	6	– not out	18
A. P. Rouse c Jones b Stevens	9		
Sohail Tanvir c Stevens b Tredwell	32		
D. R. Briggs c Harmison b Tredwell	19		
D. J. Balcombe not out	2		
B 10, l-b 6, n-b 4	20	B 6, l-b 4	10

1/31 (2) 2/177 (3)   (9 wkts dec, 134.2 overs) 405   1/45 (2)   (4 wkts dec, 87 overs) 200
3/192 (4) 4/291 (1)   2/104 (1) 3/112 (4)
5/305 (6) 6/335 (7) 7/375 (5)   4/157 (5)
8/386 (8) 9/405 (9)   110 overs: 318-5

J. A. Tomlinson did not bat.

Philander 25-2-62-0; Haggett 29-5-100-3; Shreck 25-5-74-1; Stevens 26-8-47-2; Tredwell 27.2-4-83-3; Nash 2-0-23-0. *Second innings*—Shreck 19-5-42-1; Philander 11-2-26-0; Tredwell 35-11-87-3; Haggett 16-7-23-0; Stevens 5-3-2-0; Northeast 1-0-10-0.

Kent

S. A. Northeast b Tomlinson	8	*J. C. Tredwell lbw b Tomlinson	2
R. W. T. Key b Briggs	180	C. J. Haggett c Vince b Sohail Tanvir	22
D. J. Bell-Drummond c Wheater b Tomlinson	79	C. E. Shreck not out	4
B. P. Nash c Wheater b Dawson	126	B 1, l-b 9, n-b 20	30
B. W. Harmison c Ervine b Carberry	24		
D. I. Stevens c and b Vince	2	1/37 (1) 2/228 (3) (141.2 overs) 513	
†G. O. Jones lbw b Ervine	13	3/341 (2) 4/379 (5) 5/384 (6)	
V. D. Philander b Sohail Tanvir	23	6/444 (7) 7/466 (4) 8/475 (9)	
		9/496 (8) 10/513 (10) 110 overs: 384-5	

Sohail Tanvir 22.2-3-82-2; Tomlinson 27-4-72-3; Balcombe 20-1-73-0; Vince 11-1-36-1; Briggs 20-1-88-1; Ervine 12-0-46-1; Dawson 20-5-62-1; Carberry 9-0-44-1.

Umpires: S. C. Gale and I. J. Gould.

At Worcester, August 2–5. KENT drew with WORCESTERSHIRE.

KENT v GLOUCESTERSHIRE

At Canterbury, August 21–24. Drawn. Kent 7pts, Gloucestershire 5pts. Toss: Kent.

A last-day washout robbed Kent of almost certain victory: they had managed only one of the two wickets they needed after taking the extra half-hour on the third evening. Gloucestershire, nine down and 92 short of their target, could thank Roderick, their South African-born wicketkeeper-batsman who was undefeated on 152, and No. 11 Norwell, who kept out 12 balls, for steering them to a draw. Centuries from Stevens and Harmison – his second in succession in this fixture – had given Kent a substantial first innings. But an interrupted second day and a poor forecast for the fourth prompted Tredwell and Klinger to make a game of it. Gloucestershire declared on their overnight score, trailing by 394, before Kent nipped back for an unusual second innings: they added four runs in five minutes, by when Gloucestershire – keen to repair a shoddy over-rate – had begun the fourth over. Set 399 from almost six sessions, Gloucestershire lurched to 41 for four before Roderick arrived to shore things up. His maiden hundred, with the help of the lower order, was enough to thwart Kent.

Close of play: first day, Kent 334-6 (Stevens 98, Tredwell 14); second day, Gloucestershire 80-0 (Klinger 31, Dent 44); third day, Gloucestershire 307-9 (Roderick 152, Norwell 0).

Kent

S. A. Northeast b W. R. S. Gidman	0	– not out	2
R. W. T. Key c Roderick b Howell	53	– not out	2
D. J. Bell-Drummond lbw b Payne	9		
B. P. Nash b Norwell	14		
B. W. Harmison c Roderick b Norwell	106		
D. I. Stevens c Klinger b Howell	126		
†G. O. Jones c Roderick b Payne	27		
*J. C. Tredwell c Dent b Miles	48		
C. J. Haggett not out	44		
M. E. Claydon c Roderick b Norwell	17		
C. E. Shreck b Miles	10		
B 1, l-b 16, w 1, n-b 2	20		

1/0 (1) 2/20 (3) 3/46 (4)   (129.5 overs) **474**   (no wkt dec, 3.1 overs) **4**
4/113 (2) 5/246 (5) 6/315 (7)
7/393 (6) 8/399 (8) 9/439 (10)
10/474 (11)   110 overs: 397-7

W. R. S. Gidman 32–9–78–1; Miles 22.5–4–85–2; Payne 27–2–109–2; Norwell 22–2–104–3; Howell 19–1–66–2; Smith 7–0–15–0. *Second innings*—Smith 2–1–1–0; Dent 1.1–0–3–0.

Gloucestershire

*M. Klinger not out	31	– (2) c Tredwell b Shreck	7
C. D. J. Dent not out	44	– (1) c Jones b Haggett	4
B. A. C. Howell (did not bat)		– c Northeast b Shreck	0
A. P. R. Gidman (did not bat)		– c Tredwell b Haggett	47
H. J. H. Marshall (did not bat)		– c Jones b Claydon	15
†G. H. Roderick (did not bat)		– not out	152
W. R. S. Gidman (did not bat)		– c Jones b Stevens	13
T. M. J. Smith (did not bat)		– c Jones b Shreck	32
D. A. Payne (did not bat)		– c Jones b Shreck	4
C. N. Miles (did not bat)		– b Tredwell	22
L. C. Norwell (did not bat)		– not out	0
L-b 1, n-b 4	5	L-b 1, n-b 10	11

(no wkt dec, 28 overs) **80**   1/11 (2)   (9 wkts, 106 overs) **307**
2/11 (3) 3/13 (1)
4/41 (5) 5/96 (4) 6/138 (7)
7/247 (8) 8/257 (9) 9/299 (10)

Shreck 8–2–26–0; Haggett 7–2–25–0; Claydon 7–2–21–0; Stevens 4–2–4–0; Tredwell 2–0–3–0. *Second innings*—Shreck 25–6–65–4; Haggett 18–8–32–2; Stevens 15–4–44–1; Claydon 17–1–68–1; Tredwell 26–4–73–1; Harmison 5–0–24–0.

Umpires: N. L. Bainton and D. J. Millns.

At Cardiff, September 3–6. KENT beat GLAMORGAN by seven wickets.

KENT v ESSEX

At Canterbury, September 11–14. Drawn. Kent 6pts, Essex 8pts. Toss: Kent.

Denied by rain in their previous home game, Kent were saved by it in this one-sided match. Conditions were never easy, and Jones inserted Essex, whose workmanlike total was built round a watchful 84 from Shah – his first Championship fifty of the summer. There were useful middle-order contributions from Foakes, with a stylish half-century, and Foster, last out to the persevering Davies. Essex had not made quick runs, but they had at least made them. Kent displayed less tenacity: Harmison alone passed 25 as Masters proved a thorn in the side of his former county. Napier chipped in with three wickets, and Kent were skittled for 107. Given the weather – only the second day escaped interruption – Foster had no hesitation in imposing the follow-on. Some 63 overs were lost next day as Kent reached 113 for four; and to Essex's chagrin just two hours were possible on the last. Kent had shown some grit in their second innings but, seven down and leading by only 46, were facing probable defeat. The draw dented Essex's hopes of overhauling Northamptonshire for the second promotion place.

Close of play: first day, Essex 186-4 (Shah 83, Foakes 38); second day, Kent 8-0 (Northeast 4, Key 4); third day, Kent 113-4 (Northeast 70, Stevens 8).

Essex

J. C. Mickleburgh c Bell-Drummond b Davies .	0	D. D. Masters b Riley	4
G. Gambhir c Nash b Shreck	36	M. S. Panesar c Shreck b Davies	6
G. M. Smith c Riley b Stevens	15	R. J. W. Topley not out	1
O. A. Shah lbw b Davies	84	L-b 2, n-b 4	6
R. N. ten Doeschate lbw b Riley	11		
B. T. Foakes c Northeast b Shreck	58	1/0 (1) 2/19 (3) 3/74 (2) (110.3 overs) 276
*†J. S. Foster b Davies	46	4/117 (5) 5/198 (4) 6/214 (6)
G. R. Napier c sub (A. J. Ball) b Stevens . .	9	7/223 (8) 8/233 (9) 9/263 (10)
		10/276 (7) 110 overs: 276-9

Davies 24.3–8–67–4; Shreck 25–11–45–2; Stevens 28–8–65–2; Haggett 19–1–50–0; Riley 14–1–47–2.

Kent

S. A. Northeast c ten Doeschate b Masters	11	– lbw b Topley	70
R. W. T. Key b Masters	25	– b Topley	17
D. J. Bell-Drummond b Masters	1	– c Gambhir b Panesar	9
B. P. Nash c Foster b Napier	1	– c Smith b Panesar	0
B. W. Harmison not out	30	– lbw b Panesar	8
D. I. Stevens lbw b Masters	9	– c Shah b Panesar	67
*†G. O. Jones lbw b Napier	16	– lbw b Topley	12
C. J. Haggett b Napier	6	– not out	15
M. Davies b Topley	1	– not out	10
A. E. N. Riley c Foster b Masters	2		
C. E. Shreck c Foakes b Masters	0		
L-b 3, n-b 2	5	L-b 5, w 2	7

1/22 (1) 2/26 (3) 3/28 (4)   (49 overs) 107 1/36 (2)   (7 wkts, 72 overs) 215
4/44 (2) 5/58 (6) 6/91 (7)   2/82 (3) 3/82 (4)
7/99 (8) 8/100 (9) 9/107 (10) 10/107 (11) 4/94 (5) 5/122 (1) 6/149 (7) 7/195 (6)

Masters 18–5–41–6; Topley 13–6–19–1; Napier 16–3–36–3; Panesar 2–0–8–0. *Second innings*—Masters 23–12–39–0; Panesar 20–5–49–4; Smith 8–2–27–0; Topley 13–1–70–3; Napier 8–1–25–0.

Umpires: J. W. Lloyds and N. A. Mallender.

At Northampton, September 17–20. KENT drew with NORTHAMPTONSHIRE.

KENT v LANCASHIRE

At Canterbury, September 24–27. Kent won by two wickets. Kent 21pts, Lancashire 5pts. Toss: Kent. First-class debut: M. D. Hunn. County debut: K. M. Jarvis.

A game in which little was at stake other than Lancashire's desire to remain undefeated produced an enthralling conclusion to the longest-ever season of first-class cricket in the British Isles. Stevens stole the show with a phenomenal unbeaten last-day double-hundred – spoiling the new Division Two champions' record into the bargain. Lancashire were without their three leading wicket-takers, while Kent gave a debut to 19-year-old Suffolk seamer Matt Hunn. Asked to bat, Lancashire relied on a combative 134 from Prince. Playing the ball agonisingly late, he held up an end for over six

HIGHEST FOURTH-INNINGS TOTALS BY KENT

447-9	drew (needing 485) with Hampshire at Canterbury	2005
429-5	beat Worcestershire by five wickets at Canterbury	2004
418-8	**beat Lancashire by two wickets at Canterbury**	**2013**
416-6	beat Surrey by four wickets at Blackheath	1934
411-8	**beat Gloucestershire by two wickets at Cheltenham**	**2013**
410	lost to Middlesex by 119 runs at Southgate	2004
403-7	beat Leicestershire by three wickets at Leicester	2001
392	lost to Lancashire by 33 runs at Dover	1926
382-5	beat Lancashire by five wickets at Dover	1939

hours enroute to his 35th century, first passing 15,000 career runs, then 1,000 for the season. On the second morning, Stevens wrapped up the innings with his 200th first-class wicket. At seven for three, Kent's reply was in disarray until Key rode to the rescue with an even more combative 134, limiting the deficit to 24. Prince then became the 12th Lancashire batsman – and the first since John Crawley at Colwyn Bay in 1998 – to hit twin hundreds. Acting-captain Horton contributed his third century in four matches, and declared on the third evening, 417 ahead. Once again Kent began inauspiciously. Stevens, though, was undaunted, and his magnificent 218-ball 205 turned the game on its head. Even so, wickets fell, and Lancashire had a sniff when two went at 389. In strode Key, batting at No. 10 with a fractured left thumb, and the two thirty-somethings steered Kent to an improbable victory with an hour to spare.

HIGHEST SCORE IN FOURTH INNINGS OF CHAMPIONSHIP MATCH

260*	C. L. White	Somerset (498) lost to Derbys at Derby	2006
243*	A. I. Kallicharran	Warwicks (417-2) beat Glam at Birmingham.	1983
232	G. Cox, jun.	Sussex (428-5) beat Northants at Kettering	1939
221*	W. E. Alley	Somerset (341) lost to Warwicks at Nuneaton	1961
206*	E. H. Hendren	Middx (502-6) beat Notts at Nottingham	1925
205*	G. Cox, jun.	Sussex (376-5) beat Glam at Hove	1947
205	**D. I. Stevens**	**Kent (418-8) beat Lancs at Canterbury**	**2013**
205	G. A. Gooch	Essex (405-6) beat Worcs at Worcester	1994
201*	C. B. Fry	Sussex (327-6) drew with Notts at Hove	1905
200*	Javed Miandad	Glam (311) lost to Essex at Colchester.	1981

Close of play: first day, Lancashire 269-8 (Prince 134, Parry 10); second day, Lancashire 75-0 (Horton 36, Reece 33); third day, Kent 32-1 (Northeast 21).

Lancashire

*P. J. Horton c Stevens b Davies	0	– c Tredwell b Stevens	106
L. M. Reece b Ball	14	– st Billings b Tredwell	47
A. G. Prince c Stevens b Hunn	134	– c Billings b Hunn	108
K. R. Brown c Billings b Stevens	42	– c Hunn b Tredwell	14
L. A. Procter c Stevens b Tredwell	8	– lbw b Stevens	18
A. P. Agathangelou b Ball	13	– not out	51
T. C. Smith c Stevens b Tredwell	10	– not out	13
†A. L. Davies c Tredwell b Davies	16		
O. J. Newby c Harmison b Hunn	1		
S. D. Parry c Tredwell b Stevens	20		
K. M. Jarvis not out	3		
B 1, l-b 10, n-b 12	23	B 5, l-b 23, w 2, n-b 6	36

1/0 (1) 2/47 (2) 3/118 (4)   (103.1 overs) 284   1/103 (2) (5 wkts dec, 104.4 overs) 393
4/137 (5) 5/166 (6) 6/193 (7)   2/270 (1) 3/291 (4)
7/239 (8) 8/244 (9) 9/269 (3) 10/284 (10)   4/317 (5) 5/348 (3)

Davies 23–8–41–2; Hunn 17–4–51–2; Stevens 24.1–8–58–2; Ball 13–3–42–2; Tredwell 23–6–62–2; Harmison 3–0–19–0. *Second innings*—Davies 11–2–26–0; Stevens 24–2–80–2; Ball 10–0–58–0; Harmison 5–0–20–0; Tredwell 40–12–114–2; Hunn 14.4–2–67–1.

Kent

S. A. Northeast c Procter b Jarvis	0	– lbw b Procter	70
R. W. T. Key c Jarvis b Parry	134	– (10) not out	3
D. J. Bell-Drummond b Newby	1	– (2) lbw b Newby	8
B. P. Nash c Smith b Newby	0	– (3) c Davies b Jarvis	6
B. W. Harmison lbw b Newby	59	– (4) lbw b Smith	7
D. I. Stevens lbw b Jarvis	5	– (5) not out	205
†S. W. Billings c Agathangelou b Jarvis	13	– (6) c Davies b Smith	24
A. J. Ball lbw b Parry	7	– (7) lbw b Smith	69
*J. C. Tredwell b Smith	7	– (8) c Smith b Newby	11
M. D. Hunn b Parry	0		
M. Davies not out	15	– (9) lbw b Newby	0
B 5, l-b 4, n-b 10	19	B 2, l-b 5, n-b 8	15

1/6 (1) 2/7 (3) 3/7 (4)   (62.3 overs) 260   1/32 (2)   (8 wkts, 91.4 overs) 418
4/165 (5) 5/179 (6) 6/219 (7)   2/39 (3) 3/60 (4)
7/236 (8) 8/245 (9) 9/245 (2) 10/260 (10)   4/142 (1) 5/213 (6)
   6/361 (7) 7/389 (8) 8/389 (9)

Jarvis 15–1–72–3; Newby 13–2–57–3; Smith 13–2–36–1; Procter 9–3–32–0; Parry 11.3–0–51–3; Reece 1–0–3–0. *Second innings*—Jarvis 19–0–107–1; Newby 13.4–2–55–3; Smith 18–2–74–3; Parry 22–0–85–0; Procter 9–0–40–1; Reece 6–0–25–0; Agathangelou 4–0–25–0.

Umpires: N. L. Bainton and N. G. B. Cook.

LANCASHIRE

Back in the big time

MYLES HODGSON

After several years of instability on and off the pitch as Old Trafford was redeveloped – years which brought the unexpected euphoria of a long-awaited Championship title, swiftly followed by the shock of relegation – things began to look up again for Lancashire in 2013. Promotion as Division Two champions signified a job well done on the field, while the successful staging of an Ashes Test should ensure a healthier financial future, after a period in which the club's cash flow was stretched to the limit.

A pair of new two-tiered stands had to be rebuilt at the end of the season, to fix problems encountered during the original job, but the ground's £44m makeover was praised after the official opening of the renovated Victorian pavilion. A temporary stand holding 9,000 spectators, erected for the Test and one-day international against Australia, increased the capacity to 25,000, the second-highest in England, after Lord's.

Ticket sales and catering for the international matches helped, as did a ground-sponsorship deal that brought in £10m from Emirates. By the end of the season, cash reserves were high enough to fight off competition from Nottinghamshire and Warwickshire to recruit Jos Buttler, England's one-day wicketkeeper, from Somerset. Lancashire also signed Kyle Jarvis, the 24-year-old Zimbabwean fast bowler, as a Kolpak; he said he hoped to qualify for England.

Those additions continued a turnaround in fortunes from the previous year. Lancashire dominated Division Two for much of the summer; they secured promotion with two rounds to spare, and the title in the penultimate game. They had already strengthened the batting with two former Test cricketers, South Africa's Ashwell Prince, who returned as a Kolpak, and Australia's Simon Katich, the overseas player. Both scored more than 1,000 Championship runs, and Katich was averaging 73 when he left with two matches remaining to captain Perth Scorchers in the Champions League. Three players collected more than 50 Championship wickets: evergreen captain Glen Chapple grabbed 53, Simon Kerrigan 57, and Kyle Hogg 60, the best return by a Lancashire seamer since James Anderson also took 60 eight years earlier.

Several young players were integrated into the team. Luis Reece, a 22-year-old former Academy graduate, formed a prolific opening partnership with Paul Horton and averaged 55 in his first Championship season. Luke Procter, the all-rounder from Oldham, established himself in the middle order, Andrea Agathangelou hit a maiden Championship century, while Arron Lilley, a young off-spinner from Tameside, and Alex Davies, a highly rated teenage wicketkeeper-batsman, were given their chances at Championship level.

The season, however, did not begin smoothly. Weather and stubborn opposition ensured draws against Worcestershire and Kent in the opening

Kyle Hogg

Alex Livesey, Getty Images

fixtures, back at Old Trafford after two seasons based mainly in Liverpool. The turning point was a remarkable victory in their third match, at Colwyn Bay, where Glamorgan disintegrated chasing 154 – they lost eight for 45 in a 14-run defeat. That was followed by another hard-fought triumph, against Essex, who bossed most of a rain-affected game at Old Trafford but declared on the final day: Lancashire chased down 253 in 47 overs.

Those victories gave them the confidence to play an aggressive brand of cricket that simply overpowered most of the teams in Division Two. Spearheaded by Chapple and Hogg, and backed up by the left-arm spin of Kerrigan, they claimed 45 bowling points – more than anyone except Division One champions Durham.

In consecutive innings Essex were dismissed at Chelmsford for 20, the lowest-ever first-class total against Lancashire, and Northamptonshire – then the division leaders – for 62 at Old Trafford. That wicket, cleared by Jack Birkenshaw, the ECB pitch inspector, was heavily criticised by Northamptonshire's chief executive David Smith, who believed "it was akin to an outground and a poor one at that". He later apologised.

On both occasions Chapple and Hogg bowled unchanged, but plenty of other players joined in during the second half of the summer, and Lancashire remained unbeaten until their final match, at Canterbury, when Kent reached a target of 418. Reece's partnership with Horton was an important factor, forging five century opening stands in the final six games; revitalised by loyal Lancastrian support, Kerrigan recovered from a mauling on his Test debut at The Oval, taking seven wickets to help beat Hampshire at Southport in his next Championship outing.

Lancashire had suffered a one-day drought in the 21st century, after nine trophies between 1989 and 1999, but made some progress on that front too. Although they failed to qualify for the latter stages of the YB40, Kabir Ali, recruited from Hampshire, claimed 18 wickets. Bolstered by the temporary signing of New Zealand's left-arm seamer Mitchell McClenaghan, they fared better in the Twenty20, until a one-run defeat in a thrilling quarter-final at the Rose Bowl. Lancashire's chances of one-day success should be improved by Buttler's arrival, which followed the decision to release wicketkeeper Gareth Cross. Stephen Moore was also allowed to join Derbyshire, after playing only two Championship matches during the summer.

In January 2014, Lancashire celebrated the 150th anniversary of the club's foundation, and Chapple his 40th birthday. Both hoped to commemorate the landmarks in style.

Championship attendance: 29,983.

LANCASHIRE AT 150

The cream of Manchester

As someone who provoked howls of protest while writing about Lancashire for three and a half decades, I may be perfectly placed to deal with the waves of criticism which – in the club's 150th year – will inevitably greet my all-time XI, *writes Colin Evans*. I wanted it to be balanced, contain only two overseas players (with long-term commitment to the club), and represent various eras.

1 Archie MacLaren *306 matches for Lancashire (1890–1914): 15,716 runs @ 33.36*
The dashing epitome of cricket's Golden Age, he scored 424 at Taunton. At the height of the Bodyline row he stopped his taxi – and the rest of the traffic – in London's Piccadilly to demonstrate to a friend how he would play England's bowling.

2 *Cyril Washbrook *500 matches (1933–59): 27,863 runs @ 42.15*
I mistakenly called him "Cyril" when I first interviewed him in the early 1970s. Bad mistake: "It's Mr Washbrook to you, sonny." Respected, feared and sometimes unpopular, he played in the 1934 title-winning side; 22 years later, he hit 98 in an Ashes Test at the age of 41.

3 John Thomas ("JT") Tyldesley *507 matches (1895–1923): 31,949 runs @ 41.38*
Considered better than his brother, Ernest, who holds the Lancashire career record of 34,222 runs. He often teamed up in entertaining stands with MacLaren and, as a keen dancer, attributed his quick feet to "whirling buxom Lancashire lasses around a room".

4 Clive Lloyd *219 matches (1968–86): 12,764 runs @ 44.94; 55 wickets @ 32.89*
In his prime, the world's most destructive batsman. The summer of 1975 comes to mind: two Man of the Match displays at Lord's in the World Cup and Gillette Cup finals, four first-class centuries in successive games, and a snowball fight after a freak blizzard on June 2 at Buxton.

5 Neil Fairbrother *337 matches (1982–2002): 19,603 runs @ 42.43*
Scored over 35,000 runs in all cricket, and gets the nod over Ernest Tyldesley. Nerves betrayed his Test career, and he became better known for dictating one-day chases. He had a fervent belief in teamwork and dressing-room loyalty.

6 Andrew Flintoff *80 matches (1995–2009): 4,042 runs @ 35.14; 92 wickets @ 29.16*
Not consistently a great player – but a great all-round talent who, with bat or ball, could bring a packed crowd to their feet. And he may have been the only England player to offer his dad a catch. Colin, sitting high in the Edgbaston stand during a Test against West Indies, dropped it.

7 Wasim Akram *91 matches (1988–1998): 3,168 runs @ 24.36; 374 wickets @ 21.65*
He had tears in his eyes when, after his last game, hundreds of fans gathered under the Old Trafford balcony. A dynamic bowler who could transform a match with a sudden burst of stump-and-toe-splattering reverse swing – as in the 1992 World Cup final against England.

8 Johnny Briggs *391 matches (1879–1900): 10,707 runs @ 19.01; 1,696 wickets @ 15.60*
A much-loved comedian and left-arm spinner who three times ticked off ten wickets and 100 runs in the same match. Asked to prove his sobriety before one game, he gave a display of trick cycling. He suffered from epilepsy and died at 39. Four thousand attended his funeral.

9 †Warren Hegg *337 matches (1986–2005): 11,027 runs @ 28.27; 826 catches, 94 stumpings*
Came within five of George Duckworth's first-class record of 925 victims, but in 87 fewer games. He also starred in the serial one-day successes of the 1990s.

10 Brian Statham *430 matches (1950–68): 4,237 runs @ 10.51; 1,816 wickets @ 15.12*
If there are heroes in sport, he was mine – and he still is. A magnificent bowler who smiled ruefully in the face of a batsman's luck, a dropped catch, a flat pitch. "I knew if I kept going there would be something for me," he said. There always was.

11 James Anderson *57 matches (2002–): 339 runs @ 8.69; 222 wickets @ 24.22*
England's most successful seam bowler of the modern age completes a perfect Red Rose attack. He enjoyed a remarkable rise from league cricket with Burnley to the Test side, has continued to improve, and did what even Statham could not – play in a Championship-winning team.

Colin Evans was Wisden's *Lancashire correspondent for nine years, between 1998 and 2006.*

LANCASHIRE RESULTS

All first-class matches – Played 16: Won 8, Lost 1, Drawn 7.
County Championship matches – Played 16: Won 8, Lost 1, Drawn 7.

LV= County Championship, winners in Division 2;
Friends Life t20, quarter-finalists; Yorkshire Bank 40, 3rd in Group B.

COUNTY CHAMPIONSHIP AVERAGES, BATTING AND FIELDING

Cap		M	I	NO	R	HS	100	50	Avge	Ct/St
2013	S. M. Katich§	12	16	1	1,097	200	4	6	73.13	7
	L. M. Reece	10	16	3	722	97	0	8	55.53	8
2010	A. G. Prince¶	16	26	2	1,169	134	3	7	48.70	16
2010	T. C. Smith†	7	8	2	289	88	0	2	48.16	9
2007	P. J. Horton	10	16	0	645	156	3	3	40.31	1
2010	S. J. Croft†	8	13	3	379	101*	1	2	37.90	4
	A. P. Agathangelou¶	11	16	2	497	121	1	2	35.50	24
	L. A. Procter†	15	21	0	718	106	1	7	34.19	5
	K. R. Brown†	10	16	0	428	87	0	3	26.75	8
2013	S. C. Kerrigan†	13	11	5	146	62*	0	1	24.33	3
2007	G. D. Cross†	13	17	0	409	100	1	2	24.05	35/2
1994	G. Chapple	14	16	3	308	63	0	3	23.69	9
	W. A. White	6	9	3	133	61	0	1	22.16	2
2010	K. W. Hogg	15	16	5	241	58	0	1	21.90	2
2011	S. C. Moore	2	4	0	81	34	0	0	20.25	0

Also batted: J. M. Anderson†‡ (2 matches) 26, 11*, 0 (1 ct); A. L. Davies† (3 matches) 12, 16 (3 ct); K. M. Jarvis¶ (1 match) 3* (1 ct); A. M. Lilley† (2 matches) 35*, 4*; O. J. Newby† (3 matches) 9*, 1; S. D. Parry† (3 matches) 5*, 12, 20.

† *Born in Lancashire.* ‡ *ECB contract.* § *Official overseas player.* ¶ *Other non-England-qualified player.*

BOWLING

	Style	O	M	R	W	BB	5I	Avge
K. W. Hogg	RFM	436	105	1,105	60	7-27	3	18.41
G. Chapple	RFM	430.4	110	1,099	53	5-9	2	20.73
S. C. Kerrigan	SLA	461.2	108	1,191	57	7-63	5	20.89
O. J. Newby	RFM	68.2	12	264	12	4-71	0	22.00
T. C. Smith	RFM	150.5	35	498	22	4-49	0	22.63
L. A. Procter	RFM	194	31	633	15	4-39	0	42.20

Also bowled: A. P. Agathangelou (LBG/OB) 43–12–125–3; J. M. Anderson (RFM) 72.1–20–180–8; S. J. Croft (RFM/OB) 41–6–132–1; K. M. Jarvis (RFM) 34–1–179–4; A. M. Lilley (OB) 69–9–212–2; S. D. Parry (SLA) 65.3–5–197–5; L. M. Reece (LM) 22–2–89–2; W. A. White (RFM) 131–16–452–8.

LEADING YB40 AVERAGES (100 runs/4 wickets)

Batting	Runs	HS	Avge	SR	Ct/St
A. G. Prince	506	100	56.22	101.81	6
T. C. Smith	204	97	51.00	84.64	2
J. Clark	145	72	36.25	100.69	1
K. R. Brown	277	80	34.62	83.68	1
S. C. Moore	296	53	26.90	94.56	2
S. M. Katich	174	60	24.85	95.08	4
G. D. Cross	148	36	21.14	111.27	13/4
S. J. Croft	191	65	19.10	77.32	6

Bowling	W	BB	Avge	ER
S. D. Parry	11	5-17	19.63	4.15
G. Chapple	8	3-33	20.50	4.20
W. A. White	10	4-35	20.90	6.96
Kabir Ali	18	4-37	21.00	6.28
A. M. Lilley	7	4-30	21.14	5.28
T. C. Smith	6	2-22	35.50	5.19
S. J. Croft	5	1-11	47.60	6.26
K. W. Hogg	6	2-54	53.16	5.90

LEADING FLt20 AVERAGES (100 runs/18 overs)

Batting	Runs	HS	Avge	SR	Ct	Bowling	W	BB	Avge	ER
G. D. Cross	139	32*	23.16	**149.46**	6	A. M. Lilley	5	1-21	37.40	**6.92**
S. C. Moore	338	75	33.80	**143.22**	3	S. C. Kerrigan	5	1-20	25.20	**7.00**
S. M. Katich	265	62*	44.16	**140.21**	2	S. J. Croft	2	1-15	78.50	**7.13**
T. C. Smith	200	42	22.22	**133.33**	5	G. Chapple	6	2-22	31.83	**7.34**
K. R. Brown	260	62	32.50	**131.31**	4	S. D. Parry	4	1-21	37.50	**7.89**
S. J. Croft	238	52	29.75	**119.00**	6	M. J. McClenaghan	17	5-29	20.88	**8.25**

FIRST-CLASS COUNTY RECORDS

Highest score for	424	A. C. MacLaren v Somerset at Taunton	1895
Highest score against	315*	T. W. Hayward (Surrey) at The Oval	1898
Leading run-scorer	34,222	E. Tyldesley (avge 45.20)	1909–36
Best bowling for	10-46	W. Hickton v Hampshire at Manchester	1870
Best bowling against	10-40	G. O. B. Allen (Middlesex) at Lord's	1929
Leading wicket-taker	1,816	J. B. Statham (avge 15.12)	1950–68
Highest total for	863	v Surrey at The Oval	1990
Highest total against	707-9 dec	by Surrey at The Oval	1990
Lowest total for	25	v Derbyshire at Manchester	1871
Lowest total against	**20**	**by Essex at Chelmsford**	**2013**

LIST A COUNTY RECORDS

Highest score for	162*	A. R. Crook v Buckinghamshire at Wormsley	2005
Highest score against	186*	C. G. Greenidge (West Indians) at Liverpool	1984
Leading run-scorer	11,969	N. H. Fairbrother (avge 41.84)	1982–2002
Best bowling for	6-10	C. E. H. Croft v Scotland at Manchester	1982
Best bowling against	8-26	K. D. Boyce (Essex) at Manchester	1971
Leading wicket-taker	480	J. Simmons (avge 25.75)	1969–89
Highest total for	381-3	v Hertfordshire at Radlett	1999
Highest total against	350-6	by Middlesex at Lord's	2012
Lowest total for	59	v Worcestershire at Worcester	1963
Lowest total against	52	by Minor Counties at Lakenham	1998

TWENTY20 COUNTY RECORDS

Highest score for	102*	L. Vincent v Derbyshire at Manchester	2008
Highest score against	108*	I. J. Harvey (Yorkshire) at Leeds	2004
Leading run-scorer	1,963	**S. J. Croft** (avge 29.74)	2006–13
Best bowling for	**5-29**	**M. J. McClenaghan v Notts at Manchester**	**2013**
Best bowling against	5-21	J. Allenby (Leicestershire) at Manchester	2008
Leading wicket-taker	72	G. Keedy (avge 21.15)	2004–12
Highest total for	220-5	v Derbyshire at Derby	2009
Highest total against	202-3	**by Hampshire at Southampton**	**2013**
Lowest total for	91	v Derbyshire at Manchester	2003
Lowest total against	81-8	by Derbyshire at Manchester	2011

ADDRESS

Emirates Old Trafford, Talbot Road, Manchester M16 0PX (0161 282 4000; **email** enquiries@lccc.co.uk). **Website** www.lccc.co.uk

OFFICIALS

Captain G. Chapple
Director of cricket M. Watkinson
Head coach P. Moores
Academy director J. Stanworth
President J. Livingstone

Chairman M. A. Cairns
Chief executive D. Gidney
Head groundsman M. Merchant
Scorer A. West

LANCASHIRE v WORCESTERSHIRE

At Manchester, April 10–13. Drawn. Lancashire 9pts, Worcestershire 6pts. Toss: Lancashire. County debuts: W. A. White; M. A. Johnson, T. T. Samaraweera.

It was a frustrating start to the summer: rain deducted more than a day, and the match was unfinished – like the revamped pavilion, which was still under scaffolding, though the players were now in new dressing-rooms on the opposite side of the ground. Worcestershire, relegated with Lancashire the previous season, were 123 for four in seamer-friendly conditions on the first afternoon: Wayne White, an all-rounder recruited from Leicestershire, had dismissed Pardoe with his sixth ball. Mitchell, down at No. 7 after contracting a bug, led the recovery with a spirited 74, forging a 96-run stand with Andrew – before Worcestershire's last four fell in 31 balls as the Old Trafford floodlights, used for the first time in the Championship, appeared to generate extra swing. Prince, the South African returning for a fourth season – but his first as a Kolpak player – and the Australian Katich, back for a second after a stint at Hampshire, accelerated to add 181 in 189 balls. But Chapple extended the first innings for four overs into the final afternoon before declaring with a lead of 114. Theoretically, 60 overs remained; rain allowed 11.

Close of play: first day, Worcestershire 227-6 (Mitchell 36, Andrew 2); second day, Lancashire 42-0 (Horton 16, Procter 24); third day, Lancashire 250-3 (Prince 34, Katich 25).

Worcestershire

M. G. Pardoe c Chapple b White	13	– (2) c Cross b Chapple	11
†M. A. Johnson lbw b Procter	18		
M. M. Ali c Prince b Kerrigan	78	– not out	0
T. T. Samaraweera c Cross b Kerrigan	28		
A. N. Kervezee c Croft b White	6		
N. D. Pinner lbw b Procter	29		
*D. K. H. Mitchell c Cross b Chapple	74	– (1) not out	10
G. M. Andrew c White b Procter	52		
D. S. Lucas c Cross b Procter	11		
C. J. Russell b Chapple	0		
A. Richardson not out	1		
B 6, l-b 13, w 1, n-b 4	24	B 2, l-b 1, n-b 2	5

1/28 (1) 2/36 (2) 3/93 (4) (131.4 overs) 334   1/17 (2) (1 wkt, 11.1 overs) 26
4/123 (5) 5/177 (3) 6/219 (6)
7/315 (7) 8/329 (8) 9/330 (10)
10/334 (9)   110 overs: 270-6

Chapple 33–9–71–2; Hogg 24–5–57–0; White 23–1–69–2; Procter 23.4–4–58–4; Kerrigan 25–4–56–2; Croft 3–0–4–0. *Second innings*—Chapple 6–3–9–1; Hogg 5.1–1–14–0.

Lancashire

P. J. Horton run out	66	*G. Chapple not out	15
L. A. Procter c Andrew b Russell	53		
K. R. Brown c Ali b Richardson	34	B 23, l-b 25, n-b 2	50
A. G. Prince c Mitchell b Richardson	95		
S. M. Katich c Johnson b Ali	84	1/97 (2) (7 wkts dec, 126 overs) 448
S. J. Croft c Mitchell b Lucas	25	2/167 (1) 3/179 (3)
†G. D. Cross run out	10	4/360 (4) 5/383 (5)
W. A. White not out	16	6/406 (7) 7/415 (6) 110 overs: 368-4

K. W. Hogg and S. C. Kerrigan did not bat.

Richardson 39–13–95–2; Russell 23–5–96–1; Lucas 26–5–76–1; Andrew 17–4–47–0; Ali 21–2–86–1.

Umpires: R. J. Bailey and R. J. Evans.

LANCASHIRE v KENT

At Manchester, April 24–27. Drawn. Lancashire 8pts, Kent 5pts. Toss: Kent.

The match reprised the plot of the previous game, with Lancashire taking a large first-innings lead and declaring on the final day before having to settle for a draw. Even with Anderson making a rare Championship appearance, a century from Nash denied them. Anderson's availability prompted Chapple to relinquish new-ball duties in the first innings for the only the second time in 72 Championship matches since June 2007. Hogg claimed three wickets and Anderson four as Kent were dismissed for 244, after bravely deciding to bat first under cloudy skies and reaching 130 for two before tea. Difficult batting conditions meant Lancashire scored at less than three an over, despite clear intent from Katich and Croft, who added 141. Katich passed 20,000 first-class runs but missed his century on the final morning, before Lancashire declared during a rainbreak, 151 ahead with 79 overs left. The Kent openers fell cheaply, but an unbroken stand of 142 between Nash and Powell thwarted hopes of a home win.

Close of play: first day, Kent 216-8 (Tredwell 28, Davies 11); second day, Lancashire 43-2 (Brown 11, Anderson 4); third day, Lancashire 356-5 (Katich 93, Croft 47).

Kent

S. A. Northeast lbw b Hogg	8	– b Kerrigan	11
R. W. T. Key lbw b Hogg	31	– c Cross b Chapple	19
B. P. Nash lbw b Croft	50	– not out	100
M. J. Powell b Anderson	57	– not out	39
D. J. Bell-Drummond lbw b Kerrigan	3		
D. I. Stevens c Cross b Hogg	11		
†G. O. Jones b Chapple	4		
*J. C. Tredwell b Anderson	40		
M. T. Coles c Kerrigan b Anderson	4		
M. Davies b Anderson	11		
C. E. Shreck not out	8		
B 13, l-b 4	17	B 4, l-b 5	9

1/11 (1) 2/60 (2) 3/130 (3)   (100.1 overs) 244   1/22 (1)   (2 wkts, 61.2 overs) 178
4/133 (5) 5/151 (6) 6/156 (7)   2/36 (2)
7/185 (4) 8/203 (9) 9/219 (10) 10/244 (8)

Anderson 25.1–8–57–4; Hogg 20–7–32–3; Chapple 19–6–40–1; Procter 8–0–26–0; Kerrigan 22–7–61–1; Croft 6–1–11–1. *Second innings*—Anderson 14–7–29–0; Hogg 5–0–8–0; Chapple 12–2–36–1; Kerrigan 22–7–57–1; Croft 5–0–21–0; Procter 3.2–0–18–0.

Lancashire

P. J. Horton b Coles	15	*G. Chapple not out	22
L. A. Procter c Tredwell b Stevens	9		
K. R. Brown b Shreck	87	B 10, l-b 9, w 2	21
J. M. Anderson lbw b Shreck	26		
A. G. Prince lbw b Stevens	58	1/20 (2) (7 wkts dec, 135.4 overs)	395
S. M. Katich c Jones b Coles	93	2/36 (1) 3/98 (4)	
S. J. Croft not out	64	4/191 (3) 5/218 (5)	
†G. D. Cross lbw b Coles	0	6/359 (6) 7/359 (8) 110 overs: 275-5	

K. W. Hogg and S. C. Kerrigan did not bat.

Davies 29–6–74–0; Shreck 25.4–8–56–2; Stevens 26–7–73–2; Coles 30–10–84–3; Tredwell 25–2–89–0.

Umpires: T. E. Jesty and G. Sharp.

At Colwyn Bay, May 1–3. LANCASHIRE beat GLAMORGAN by 14 runs.

LANCASHIRE v ESSEX

At Manchester, May 7–10. Lancashire won by three wickets. Lancashire 18pts (after 1pt penalty), Essex 3pts (after 1pt penalty). Toss: Essex.

Lancashire snatched their second thrilling win in a week with a ball to spare, after Essex set up an enterprising run-chase. Mahmood, back at Old Trafford for the first time since his angry departure on being denied a new deal, almost inevitably featured in the climax. With Lancashire needing 32 off four overs, Croft hit him for 15 in five deliveries. He was replaced by Topley, who grabbed three wickets in the penultimate over. Then, with one run required off two balls, Mahmood dropped White at long leg, allowing him to scramble the winning single. On the opening day, Essex were 91 for five on a bouncy pitch when Napier was given a life on nine. He went on to a hundred. Even so, 226 looked modest – until Lancashire, failing to mirror Napier's application, conceded a 49-run lead. Instead of batting out another rain-affected encounter, Foster set them 253 in 51 overs, reduced to 47 by a further shower. It seemed to be paying off when both openers fell at 13, but Brown and Prince added 169 to set up the dramatic conclusion. Both teams lost a point for a slow over-rate.

Close of play: first day, Lancashire 7-1 (Procter 0); second day, Essex 120-2 (Cook 57, Mickleburgh 10); third day, Essex 203-3 (Mickleburgh 53, Pettini 36).

Essex

T. Westley b Hogg	5	– b White	17
A. N. Cook c Cross b Procter	34	– c Cross b Hogg	60
R. J. Quiney lbw b Procter	21	– b Chapple	30
J. C. Mickleburgh c Prince b Procter	10	– not out	53
M. L. Pettini lbw b Procter	0	– not out	36
*†J. S. Foster c Cross b White	24		
G. R. Napier not out	102		
T. J. Phillips lbw b Parry	7		
S. I. Mahmood c Brown b Parry	10		
D. D. Masters run out	3		
R. J. W. Topley lbw b Chapple	0		
B 2, l-b 7, w 1	10	B 4, l-b 3	7

1/11 (1) 2/57 (3) 3/72 (2) (91.5 overs) 226
4/72 (5) 5/77 (4) 6/131 (6)
7/151 (8) 8/173 (9)
9/195 (10) 10/226 (11)

1/44 (1) (3 wkts dec, 71 overs) 203
2/96 (3) 3/132 (2)

Chapple 18.5–5–47–1; Hogg 19–8–38–1; White 16–3–41–1; Procter 22–4–66–4; Parry 15–4–24–2; Croft 1–0–1–0. *Second innings*—Chapple 14–3–35–1; Hogg 16–1–34–1; White 13–0–49–1; Procter 9–1–32–0; Croft 3–1–9–0; Parry 16–0–37–0.

Lancashire

P. J. Horton c Foster b Topley	3	– c Quiney b Topley	8
L. A. Procter c Mickleburgh b Masters	0	– lbw b Masters	4
K. R. Brown c Cook b Topley	0	– b Napier	80
A. G. Prince lbw b Masters	14	– c b Topley	80
S. M. Katich lbw b Mahmood	23	– c and b Topley	26
S. J. Croft c Foster b Napier	31	– c Quiney b Topley	28
†G. D. Cross lbw b Phillips	45	– c Masters b Topley	0
W. A. White c Pettini b Napier	10	– not out	3
K. W. Hogg c Topley b Phillips	25	– not out	1
*G. Chapple c Pettini b Phillips	6		
S. D. Parry not out	5		
B 1, l-b 12, n-b 2	15	B 4, l-b 9, w 4, n-b 6	23

1/7 (1) 2/7 (3) 3/21 (2) (58.3 overs) 177
4/22 (4) 5/60 (5) 6/99 (6)
7/115 (8) 8/159 (7)
9/164 (9) 10/177 (10)

1/13 (2) (7 wkts, 46.5 overs) 253
2/13 (1) 3/182 (4)
4/207 (3) 5/248 (6)
6/248 (7) 7/248 (5)

Masters 15–6–25–2; Topley 14–4–36–2; Napier 12–2–44–2; Mahmood 12–1–39–1; Phillips 5.3–1–20–3. *Second innings*—Masters 12–1–51–1; Topley 14–1–80–5; Napier 8.5–0–41–1; Mahmood 9–2–49–0; Westley 3–0–19–0.

Umpires: S. A. Garratt and P. Willey.

At Southampton, May 23–26. LANCASHIRE drew with HAMPSHIRE.

LANCASHIRE v GLOUCESTERSHIRE

At Liverpool, May 29–June 1. Drawn. Lancashire 9pts, Gloucestershire 7pts. Toss: Lancashire.

When Agathangelou claimed Gloucestershire's ninth wicket with the game's penultimate delivery, Lancashire had a flashback to the euphoric, Championship-enabling victory over Hampshire on this ground in September 2011. But last man Norwell, almost hidden by close fielders, survived the final ball. Gloucestershire had made no attempt to chase 359 in 87 overs – which became 99, thanks to the spinners – and Marshall seemed to have ensured their safety at 150 for four with just over an hour to go. Then four wickets fell in 12 overs; suddenly, Lancashire were confident. But Young, nursing a painful wrist, and McCarter denied them for six overs before the last two dramatic balls. Lancashire had struggled to 90 for four early on the first afternoon. Katich revived them, again just missing his maiden century for the county, and the last two wickets added 88. That included Chapple's 8,000th first-class run, followed the same day by his 900th first-class wicket. A career-best six for 88 from Miles, and Gidman's first hundred of the season, lifted Gloucestershire, but determined lower-order batting gave Lancashire a convincing lead on the third day.

Close of play: first day, Lancashire 175-4 (Katich 73, Croft 43); second day, Gloucestershire 143-4 (Gidman 54, Howell 32); third day, Lancashire 239-7 (White 52, Hogg 8).

Lancashire

A. P. Agathangelou lbw b McCarter	14	– c Dent b Miles	0
S. C. Moore c Klinger b Miles	4	– c Miles b McCarter	34
K. R. Brown c Gidman b McCarter	1	– b Norwell	6
A. G. Prince c Roderick b Norwell	29	– c Norwell b Howell	64
S. M. Katich c Dent b Miles	96	– c Roderick b McCarter	0
S. J. Croft c Roderick b Miles	62	– c Roderick b Norwell	5
†G. D. Cross c sub (J. K. Fuller) b Norwell	1	– c sub (J. K. Fuller) b Norwell	64
W. A. White b Miles	0	– c Klinger b McCarter	61
K. W. Hogg b Miles	45	– not out	26
*G. Chapple c Gidman b Miles	14	– c sub (J. K. Fuller) b Howell	4
S. C. Kerrigan not out	21	– c Howell b McCarter	0
B 8, l-b 6, w 5, n-b 4	23	L-b 2, w 2, n-b 2	6

1/13 (2) 2/19 (1) 3/26 (3)   (84.2 overs) 310
4/90 (4) 5/209 (5) 6/210 (7)
7/211 (8) 8/222 (6) 9/244 (10) 10/310 (9)

1/0 (1) 2/25 (3)   (72.3 overs) 270
3/47 (2) 4/47 (5)
5/62 (6) 6/147 (4) 7/214 (7)
8/254 (8) 9/264 (10) 10/270 (11)

Miles 27.2–7–88–6; McCarter 22–6–75–2; Norwell 19–3–80–2; Howell 10–2–25–0; Young 5–0–25–0; Dent 1–0–3–0. *Second innings*—Miles 15–5–47–1; McCarter 22.3–2–95–4; Norwell 17–3–80–3; Howell 18–5–46–2.

Gloucestershire

*M. Klinger c Agathangelou b Chapple	2	– (2) c Agathangelou b Kerrigan	22
C. D. J. Dent lbw b Chapple	18	– (1) c Cross b Hogg	5
D. M. Housego c Cross b White	29	– c Cross b Hogg	18
A. P. R. Gidman c White b Kerrigan	110	– lbw b Agathangelou	46
H. J. H. Marshall c Cross b Hogg	4	– c Prince b White	44
B. A. C. Howell c Brown b Kerrigan	39	– lbw b Kerrigan	17
†G. H. Roderick b Kerrigan	0	– b Chapple	12
C. N. Miles c Prince b Chapple	9	– c Agathangelou b Chapple	12
G. J. McCarter c Croft b Kerrigan	5	– c Chapple b Agathangelou	1
L. C. Norwell lbw b Kerrigan	0	– (11) not out	0
E. G. C. Young not out	0	– (10) not out	2
L-b 4, n-b 2	6	L-b 4, n-b 2	6

1/4 (1) 2/43 (2) 3/55 (3)	(77.2 overs)	222	1/13 (1)	(9 wkts, 99 overs) 173
4/66 (5) 5/155 (6) 6/155 (7)			2/50 (2) 3/60 (3)	
7/166 (8) 8/195 (9) 9/195 (10) 10/222 (4)			4/114 (4) 5/150 (6) 6/151 (7)	
			7/163 (8) 8/170 (5) 9/173 (9)	

Chapple 24–5–58–3; Hogg 20–2–51–1; White 9–2–41–1; Kerrigan 24.2–2–68–5. *Second innings—* Chapple 18–7–40–2; Hogg 13–6–19–2; Kerrigan 39–16–65–2; White 9–4–11–1; Croft 7–2–16–0; Agathangelou 13–6–18–2.

Umpires: I. Dawood and N. A. Mallender.

At Weetwood, Leeds, June 5–7. LANCASHIRE beat LEEDS/BRADFORD MCCU by eight wickets.

At Chelmsford, June 12–14. LANCASHIRE beat ESSEX by an innings and 105 runs. *Essex are dismissed for 20, their lowest first-class total and the lowest against Lancashire.*

LANCASHIRE v NORTHAMPTONSHIRE

At Manchester, June 20–21. Lancashire won by eight wickets. Lancashire 19pts, Northamptonshire 3pts. Toss: Lancashire.

Eleven months after Lancashire escaped with a warning for a poor pitch – on which Worcestershire dismissed them for 63 – there was controversy about the same strip. This time, Lancashire wrapped up a two-day win against Northamptonshire, the second division leaders, after bowling them out for 62. It was the lowest opposition total at Old Trafford since Somerset's 61 in 1975. A week before, Chapple and Hogg had skittled Essex for 20 at Chelmsford; they bowled unchanged again here, with Hogg reaping a career-best seven for 27 in humid conditions under floodlights. Though Lancashire managed only 159, Northamptonshire slumped to 80 for seven second time around, at which point Lancashire's last 27 Championship wickets had cost just 162. Hall and Murphy responded with the game's only half-centuries, but the eventual target was a comfortable 73. Northamptonshire's chief executive, David Smith, likened the pitch to "an outground and a poor one at that". He added: "It looked underprepared, and the scorecard supports this view." Coach David Ripley was less critical of the surface, and Jack Birkenshaw, the ECB pitch inspector, believed consistent seam bowling was mainly responsible for 32 wickets in two days. Smith was later reprimanded for his comments by the ECB Discipline Commission.

Close of play: first day, Lancashire 121-8 (Smith 14, Parry 9).

Northamptonshire

K. J. Coetzer c Agathangelou b Chapple	0	– c Chapple b Hogg	5
J. D. Middlebrook b Chapple	8	– lbw b Hogg	3
D. J. Sales lbw b Hogg	1	– b Chapple	14
*A. G. Wakely lbw b Hogg	6	– c Prince b Procter	17
R. I. Keogh c Cross b Hogg	6	– b Smith	2
A. J. Hall lbw b Hogg	10	– c Smith b Procter	55
S. P. Crook b Hogg	16	– c Reece b Procter	4
D. J. Willey c Smith b Hogg	8	– c Chapple b Smith	5
†D. Murphy not out	5	– lbw b Kerrigan	50
G. G. White c Prince b Chapple	0	– b Procter	0
Azharullah b Hogg	1	– not out	0
L-b 1	1	B 4, l-b 6, n-b 4	14

1/0 (1) 2/1 (3) 3/9 (4)   (29.5 overs) 62   1/5 (1) 2/22 (3)   (65.2 overs) 169
4/21 (5) 5/21 (2) 6/35 (6)   3/22 (4) 4/35 (5)
7/55 (8) 8/56 (7) 9/57 (10) 10/62 (11)   5/59 (4) 6/67 (7) 7/80 (8)
                                                        8/169 (6) 9/169 (10) 10/169 (9)

Chapple 15–4–34–3; Hogg 14.5–5–27–7. *Second innings*—Chapple 14–5–37–1; Hogg 16–1–46–2; Kerrigan 14.2–4–20–1; Parry 1–1–0–0; Procter 12–1–39–4; Smith 8–2–17–2.

Lancashire

L. M. Reece b Willey	16	– not out	22
L. A. Procter b Azharullah	4	– c Murphy b Willey	0
A. G. Prince lbw b Willey	6	– c Murphy b Middlebrook	38
S. M. Katich c Murphy b Azharullah	30	– not out	1
A. P. Agathangelou b Hall	21		
T. C. Smith not out	35		
†G. D. Cross lbw b Crook	4		
K. W. Hogg c Murphy b Hall	3		
*G. Chapple c Coetzer b Crook	0		
S. D. Parry b Azharullah	12		
S. C. Kerrigan b Azharullah	6		
B 5, l-b 5, w 2, n-b 10	22	L-b 8, n-b 4	12

1/6 (2) 2/22 (3) 3/41 (1)   (58 overs) 159   1/1 (2) 2/71 (3)   (2 wkts, 21 overs) 73
4/85 (5) 5/85 (4) 6/93 (7)
7/96 (8) 8/101 (9) 9/129 (10) 10/159 (11)

Willey 12–4–26–2; Azharullah 17–8–42–4; Crook 12–1–39–2; Hall 17–5–42–2. *Second innings*—Willey 4–0–10–1; Azharullah 4–2–9–0; Crook 3–0–14–0; Hall 3–2–6–0; White 4–1–14–0; Middlebrook 3–1–12–1.

Umpires: P. K. Baldwin and R. K. Illingworth.

At Northampton, July 8–11. LANCASHIRE beat NORTHAMPTONSHIRE by eight wickets.

LANCASHIRE v GLAMORGAN

At Manchester, July 15–18. Drawn. Lancashire 7pts, Glamorgan 8pts. Toss: Glamorgan. First-class debut: A. M. Lilley. Championship debuts: C. B. Cooke, N. L. McCullum.

The contrast with Old Trafford's previous Championship match, which Northamptonshire lost in two days, could not have been greater: four centuries were scored, while Chapple and Hogg took only three wickets between them. Kerrigan collected 12, but could not quite spin a victory. Batting first seemed brave after Northamptonshire's experience, but Glamorgan exploited hot weather and a slow, dry pitch. Goodwin, at 40 the oldest active player on the county circuit since Claude Henderson announced his retirement in May, amassed 194, his 70th first-class century and the second-highest for Glamorgan against Lancashire, after Matthew Maynard's 214 at Cardiff in 1996. His 155-run stand with Allenby provided a good platform, but the last six fell for 66, all but one to Kerrigan. Lancashire responded with hundreds from Prince, his first of the season, and Katich, before debutant Arron Lilley steered them past their previous best against these opponents, 564 for nine here in 1938, to a lead of 93. On the final day, Kerrigan reduced Glamorgan to 98 for five shortly before tea, but Rees's century and an 85-run partnership with New Zealand's Nathan McCullum – making a one-off Championship appearance – salvaged a draw.

Close of play: first day, Glamorgan 315-3 (Goodwin 138, Allenby 68); second day, Lancashire 93-0 (Reece 42, Brown 48); third day, Lancashire 423-5 (Procter 53, Cross 10).

Glamorgan

G. P. Rees c Agathangelou b Hogg	58	– not out	107
W. D. Bragg c Prince b Kerrigan	24	– c Agathangelou b Kerrigan	13
M. W. Goodwin c Agathangelou b Kerrigan	194	– c Prince b Kerrigan	10
C. B. Cooke c Procter b Kerrigan	23	– c Prince b Kerrigan	5
J. Allenby lbw b Chapple	92	– b Kerrigan	0
*†M. A. Wallace c Prince b Kerrigan	37	– c and b Kerrigan	1
N. L. McCullum c Katich b Kerrigan	14	– not out	35
G. G. Wagg c Agathangelou b Kerrigan	0		
J. C. Glover c and b Chapple	7		
D. A. Cosker lbw b Kerrigan	14		
A. J. Jones not out	5		
L-b 2, n-b 4	6	B 9, l-b 3	12

1/43 (2) 2/120 (1) 3/185 (4)   (150.1 overs) 474   1/66 (2)   (5 wkts, 60 overs) 183
4/340 (5) 5/408 (6) 6/438 (7)   2/88 (3) 3/94 (4)
7/441 (8) 8/448 (3) 9/454 (9)   4/94 (5) 5/98 (6)
10/474 (10)   110 overs: 358-4

Chapple 31–3–102–2; Hogg 24–7–64–1; Kerrigan 49.1–5–162–7; Procter 24–2–67–0; Lilley 22–2–77–0. *Second innings*—Chapple 5–0–13–0; Hogg 2–1–7–0; Kerrigan 27–4–90–5; Lilley 24–6–52–0; Agathangelou 2–0–9–0.

Lancashire

L. M. Reece lbw b Cosker	53	A. M. Lilley not out	35
K. R. Brown b Wagg	48	S. C. Kerrigan c Jones b McCullum	0
A. G. Prince c Wallace b McCullum	113		
S. M. Katich c Wallace b Wagg	115		
A. P. Agathangelou c Allenby b McCullum	18	B 8, l-b 3, w 3	14
L. A. Procter b McCullum	75		
†G. D. Cross st Wallace b Cosker	64	1/99 (2) 2/123 (1) (164.4 overs) 567
K. W. Hogg lbw b McCullum	1	3/280 (3) 4/316 (5) 5/406 (4)
*G. Chapple st Wallace b Cosker	31	6/461 (6) 7/463 (8) 8/510 (9)
		9/558 (7) 10/567 (11) 110 overs: 318-4

Wagg 34–7–107–2; Glover 23–7–72–0; McCullum 47.4–6–191–5; Cosker 48–11–133–3; Jones 12–0–53–0.

Umpires: M. R. Benson and A. G. Wharf.

At Leicester, August 2–5. LANCASHIRE beat LEICESTERSHIRE by an innings and 52 runs.

At Manchester, August 11. LANCASHIRE beat BANGLADESH A by seven wickets (see Bangladesh A tour section).

At Worcester, August 22–25. LANCASHIRE beat WORCESTERSHIRE by nine wickets. *Lancashire's first maximum-point Championship victory for six years.*

LANCASHIRE v HAMPSHIRE

At Southport, August 28–31. Lancashire won by 122 runs. Lancashire 23pts, Hampshire 4pts. Toss: Lancashire. First-class debut: B. J. Taylor. County debut: M. T. Coles.

After his harrowing Test debut at The Oval, Kerrigan was cheered on by a partisan Southport crowd as he brought promotion into sight. It started with his maiden fifty: he and Chapple, who passed 8,000 runs for Lancashire, put on 114, their last-wicket record against Hampshire. He then recovered from a nervous opening spell to claim three wickets, reaching 50 in the Championship, along with Hogg and Chapple, as Lancashire secured a 211-run lead. Waiving the follow-on, they enjoyed their biggest opening stand of the season, 166 from Horton and Reece, and added 159 in 30 overs on the third morning before setting a target of 496. That initially seemed over-cautious, even when Chapple hobbled off after his 898th wicket for his county. But a stand of 191 between Wheater and Coles – an eighth-wicket record for Hampshire against Lancashire – made it look canny, and the tail kept on thrashing until Kerrigan ended their fun. Last out was Brad Taylor who, at 16 years 167 days, had become Hampshire's youngest first-class debutant since Charles Young (15 years 131 days) in 1867, and dismissed Lancashire's top four with his off-breaks.

Close of play: first day, Lancashire 296-8 (Procter 65, Chapple 1); second day, Lancashire 39-0 (Horton 23, Reece 7); third day, Hampshire 137-7 (Wheater 31, Coles 0).

Lancashire

P. J. Horton c Vince b Tomlinson	4	– c Wood b Taylor	111
L. M. Reece lbw b Tomlinson	50	– c Wheater b Taylor	65
A. G. Prince c Wheater b Ervine	63	– c and b Taylor	38
A. P. Agathangelou c Vince b Coles	30	– c Wood b Taylor	28
S. J. Croft c Roberts b Dawson	9	– not out	8
L. A. Procter c Dawson b Wood	66	– b Dawson	10
T. C. Smith c Vince b Dawson	28		
†G. D. Cross c Ervine b Tomlinson	26		
K. W. Hogg c Adams b Vince	5		
*G. Chapple c Ervine b Vince	63		
S. C. Kerrigan not out	62		
B 5, l-b 5, w 1, n-b 4	15	L-b 14, w 2, n-b 8	24

1/8 (1) 2/128 (3) 3/133 (2) (120.1 overs) 421 1/166 (2) (5 wkts dec, 56 overs) 284
4/163 (5) 5/171 (4) 6/238 (7) 2/225 (3) 3/256 (1)
7/276 (8) 8/292 (9) 9/307 (6) 4/264 (4) 5/284 (6)
10/421 (10) 110 overs: 354-9

Tomlinson 30–9–91–3; Wood 28–8–76–1; Coles 23–5–89–1; Taylor 8–1–42–0; Ervine 9–1–34–1; Dawson 20–2–77–2; Vince 2.1–0–2–2. *Second innings*—Wood 7–0–37–0; Tomlinson 7–1–34–0; Vince 5–0–28–0; Coles 7–2–20–0; Dawson 12–1–70–1; Taylor 14–2–64–4; Ervine 4–0–17–0.

Hampshire

M. D. T. Roberts c Cross b Hogg	16	– lbw b Hogg	19
*J. H. K. Adams lbw b Hogg	0	– c Agathangelou b Chapple	4
L. A. Dawson lbw b Hogg	29	– lbw b Smith	2
N. D. McKenzie c Croft b Hogg	5	– c Smith b Kerrigan	44
J. M. Vince c Chapple b Kerrigan	106	– b Hogg	20
S. M. Ervine c Prince b Chapple	12	– c Procter b Kerrigan	5
†A. J. Wheater c Horton b Kerrigan	22	– c Cross b Kerrigan	140
C. P. Wood b Kerrigan	1	– run out	6
M. T. Coles c Prince b Hogg	0	– b Reece	68
J. A. Tomlinson c Cross b Chapple	7	– not out	30
B. J. Taylor not out	0	– st Cross b Kerrigan	20
L-b 8, w 2, n-b 2	12	B 5, l-b 6, n-b 4	15

1/9 (2) 2/24 (1) 3/42 (4) (59.5 overs) 210 1/8 (2) 2/16 (3) (108.5 overs) 373
4/51 (3) 5/92 (6) 6/148 (7) 3/26 (1) 4/52 (5)
7/155 (8) 8/156 (9) 9/206 (10) 10/210 (5) 5/63 (6) 6/107 (4) 7/129 (8)
 8/320 (7) 9/320 (9) 10/373 (11)

Hogg 14–2–39–5; Chapple 15–5–35–2; Smith 11–1–56–0; Kerrigan 14.5–3–48–3; Procter 3–0–13–0; Croft 2–0–11–0. *Second innings*—Hogg 26–7–75–2; Chapple 2–0–6–1; Smith 19–3–80–1; Kerrigan 37.5–8–97–4; Croft 14–2–59–0; Agathangelou 5–1–20–0; Procter 1–0–5–0; Reece 4–1–20–1.

Umpires: N. L. Bainton and J. W. Lloyds.

LANCASHIRE v LEICESTERSHIRE

At Manchester, September 11–14. Drawn. Lancashire 11pts, Leicestershire 8pts. Toss: Leicestershire.

Lancashire did not achieve promotion in the style they desired, but a weather-hit draw proved enough once Essex failed to beat Kent. Bad light and rain disrupted every day but the last, when a Leicestershire side ravaged by injuries, and with an average age of 23, avoided a seventh successive defeat. Horton, acting-captain for Chapple, who had an Achilles problem, continued his triumphant return after being sidelined for ten weeks with a dislocated finger: a second consecutive century took his aggregate since then to 368 in six innings. Reece completed his seventh successive fifty – the first man to achieve this for Lancashire since Geoff Pullar in 1959 – as he and Horton piled up 137, their third three-figure opening stand in five starts, and the declaration came at a commanding 453 for seven. Leicestershire were three down on the third evening, but Raine, with a maiden half-century on his 22nd birthday, added 61 with Boyce and 69 with Wells to deny Lancashire any chance of the win required to clinch the Division Two title with two rounds to spare.

Close of play: first day, Lancashire 92-0 (Horton 42, Reece 31); second day, Lancashire 344-4 (Horton 150, Procter 1); third day, Leicestershire 60-3 (Thornely 23, O'Brien 23).

Lancashire

*P. J. Horton b Buck	156	K. W. Hogg not out	2
L. M. Reece c Smith b Freckingham	50		
A. G. Prince c Thornely b Raine	14	B 1, l-b 15, w 2, n-b 14	32
S. M. Katich c Smith b Sykes	56		
A. P. Agathangelou c O'Brien b Sykes	46	1/137 (2) (7 wkts dec, 115 overs)	453
L. A. Procter st O'Brien b Eckersley	44	2/163 (3) 3/236 (4)	
T. C. Smith c Smith b Eckersley	23	4/343 (5) 5/363 (1)	
†A. L. Davies not out	30	6/401 (7) 7/434 (6)	110 overs: 432-6

O. J. Newby and S. C. Kerrigan did not bat.

Freckingham 19–1–100–1; Buck 25–4–115–1; Raine 21–5–59–1; Wells 8–1–22–0; Sykes 32–5–98–2; Thornely 5–1–14–0; Eckersley 5–0–29–2.

Leicestershire

A. J. Robson c Agathangelou b Newby	9	J. S. Sykes c Prince b Smith	34
G. P. Smith b Newby	0	O. H. Freckingham lbw b Smith	8
E. J. H. Eckersley c Davies b Hogg	4	N. L. Buck not out	15
M. A. Thornely c Smith b Hogg	36	L-b 6, w 1	7
†N. J. O'Brien c Smith b Kerrigan	63		
*M. A. G. Boyce c Reece b Kerrigan	38	1/9 (2) 2/10 (1) 3/14 (3) (104.1 overs)	329
B. A. Raine c Reece b Kerrigan	72	4/87 (4) 5/123 (5) 6/184 (6)	
T. J. Wells c Agathangelou b Kerrigan	43	7/253 (8) 8/285 (7) 9/304 (10) 10/329 (9)	

Hogg 23–5–52–3; Newby 23–5–81–2; Kerrigan 31–10–95–3; Smith 14.1–3–58–2; Agathangelou 7–3–23–0; Procter 6–2–14–0.

Umpires: D. J. Millns and G. Sharp.

At Bristol, September 17–20. LANCASHIRE drew with GLOUCESTERSHIRE. *Lancashire become second division champions.*

At Canterbury, September 24–27. LANCASHIRE lost to KENT by two wickets. *Lancashire suffer their only Championship defeat, despite setting Kent a target of 418.*

LEICESTERSHIRE

Plumbing new depths

PAUL JONES

There was no escaping the grim truth that Leicestershire were not up to scratch in first-class cricket in 2013. They were not even remotely close. Bottom of the Championship for the second time in three years, they finished a massive 70 points adrift of eighth-placed Glamorgan. Leicestershire's inability to win a game over the course of a Championship season for the first time in their history meant they beat their own 2011 record for the lowest tally since bonus points were introduced in 1968. They did not win a single game in any format after August 11, and lost five of their last six Championship matches. It's probably best not to mention that they were also beaten at home by Leeds/Bradford MCCU.

Injuries to key players, and the unavailability of captain Ramnaresh Sarwan from mid-May, bit hard into a small, inexperienced squad. The statistics made for unpalatable reading. Leicestershire were unable to build substantial totals, leaving them with just 23 batting points. Their bowlers, without an attack leader for much of the season, struggled to dismiss the opposition, who often seized control during the first innings. An experienced pace bowler became Leicestershire's first priority for 2014 – and they plumped for 36-year-old Charlie Shreck, released by Kent.

Only Ned Eckersley will look back with any fondness. He made the No. 3 slot his own with an outstanding 1,275 runs – the second-most in Division Two after Moeen Ali – and struck four centuries, two in the game against Worcestershire at Grace Road in August, after which he was presented with his county cap. Only two other batsmen reached three figures: Matt Boyce and Shiv Thakor, both in the first home game, a draw against Kent when Leicestershire made a season's-best 495.

The loss of Sarwan, who returned to international cricket following a rapprochement with West Indies head coach Ottis Gibson, proved an insurmountable blow. His wisdom had rubbed off on a number of Leicestershire's younger players in 2012, and the club were hoping for more of the same when he took on the captaincy ahead of the season from Matthew Hoggard. But Sarwan played only five Championship matches before joining up with West Indies for the Champions Trophy, and a wrist injury sustained in the Caribbean Premier League meant he was unable to return late in the summer. Leicestershire drafted in 23-year-old Queensland batsman Joe Burns to replace Sarwan for a short time and, though he showed glimpses of class, he struggled to adapt to English conditions.

Leicestershire's bowling also lacked leadership, after injury restricted the 36-year-old Hoggard to ten games in all competitions. He decided before the season was out that he had little left in the tank, and opted for

Stu Forster, Getty Images

Ned Eckersley

retirement. Claude Henderson played just two matches before he too headed off into the sunset, just before his 41st birthday. He will be remembered as the first Kolpak player – and one of the finest. Jigar Naik was by now installed as the first-choice spinner, and captured 21 Championship wickets in the first half of the summer, in conditions more suited to seam bowling. But Naik's season ended when he dislocated his shoulder at the height of the Twenty20 campaign – a bitter blow for player and team. The burden fell to James Sykes, a 21-year-old slow left-armer, who signed a new two-year contract.

The emergence of 24-year-old local boy Ollie Freckingham was a rare bright spot. He joined the staff in the winter of 2012 and appeared to be one of a number of young seamers who would be fighting for a place. Freckingham grasped his early opportunity and, though he tapered off a little, finished as the leading wicket-taker, with 36 from 15 matches. He too signed a new two-year extension, and should return a more dangerous bowler for the experience.

If the Championship was a write-off, the mood in the shorter formats was, mercifully, a little more upbeat. Leicestershire failed to make the knockout stages of either competition, but could easily have done so with a slice of luck here and there. Josh Cobb captained the side enthusiastically and led from the front, especially in the YB40, where he blazed his way to centuries in the first three games. Niall O'Brien, Greg Smith and Eckersley all added hundreds, but Leicestershire could not maintain the early momentum, and slipped back into the pack.

Their sprightly form in Twenty20, allied with sunny weather, produced bumper crowds at Grace Road for a competition they had won three times. Three victories and a tie in their five home matches gave them a chance of reaching the quarter-finals, but a four-run defeat at Old Trafford proved decisive. Cobb and Smith were a formidable opening pair, and left-arm seamer Rob Taylor, benefiting from time in the Scotland set-up, took 28 wickets across both limited-overs competitions. But the Bangladesh all-rounder Shakib Al Hasan failed to influence games as the club had hoped.

After a period of reflection, Leicestershire decided to shake up the coaching structure. Phil Whitticase moved from head coach to a wider role as director of cricket, while Ben Smith took on responsibility for the first team, and Lloyd Tennant the seconds. That was all well and good for the long-term development of players, an area in which Leicestershire have a proud record. But their immediate task was to right a listing ship by producing some respectable performances on the field.

Championship attendance: 13,346.

LEICESTERSHIRE RESULTS

All first-class matches – Played 17: Lost 9, Drawn 8.
County Championship matches – Played 16: Lost 8, Drawn 8.

LV= County Championship, 9th in Division 2;
Friends Life t20, 4th in North Division; Yorkshire Bank 40, 5th in Group C.

COUNTY CHAMPIONSHIP AVERAGES, BATTING AND FIELDING

Cap		M	I	NO	R	HS	100	50	Avge	Ct/St
2013	E. J. H. Eckersley	16	27	3	1,275	147	4	4	53.12	4
	R. R. Sarwan§	5	8	1	255	79	0	2	36.42	4
2013	M. A. G. Boyce	14	21	1	633	135	1	2	31.65	7
	S. J. Thakor†	14	22	3	583	114	1	4	30.68	4
	J. A. Burns§	5	8	1	214	77	0	1	30.57	4
	N. J. O'Brien	14	23	0	695	67	0	6	30.21	25/3
	B. A. Raine	5	8	1	190	72	0	1	27.14	0
	G. P. Smith†	12	21	1	487	70	0	4	24.35	12
	T. J. Wells	5	8	0	177	82	0	1	22.12	2
	M. A. Thornely	10	15	0	269	53	0	1	17.93	8
	A. J. Robson¶	3	4	0	59	49	0	0	14.75	0
	J. J. Cobb†	11	18	2	234	46*	0	0	14.62	3
	J. S. Sykes	7	12	2	139	34	0	0	13.90	3
2013	J. K. H. Naik†	9	11	2	123	47*	0	0	13.66	7
	A. C. F. Wyatt	10	15	6	107	28	0	0	11.88	1
	O. H. Freckingham	15	21	2	204	30	0	0	10.73	4
2010	M. J. Hoggard	7	11	3	75	24	0	0	9.37	1
	R. E. M. Williams	5	5	1	18	12	0	0	4.50	1

Also batted: N. L. Buck† (cap 2011) (4 matches) 6, 16*, 15*; C. W. Henderson¶ (cap 2004) (1 match) 33, 5*; A. J. Ireland¶ (2 matches) 15*, 0, 13; R. M. L. Taylor (2 matches) 12, 0.

† *Born in Leicestershire.*   § *Official overseas player.*   ¶ *Other non-England-qualified player.*

BOWLING

	Style	O	M	R	W	BB	5I	Avge
M. J. Hoggard	RFM	171	35	545	16	6-66	1	34.06
J. K. H. Naik	OB	286.3	53	844	21	5-98	1	40.19
O. H. Freckingham	RFM	399	61	1,584	36	6-125	1	44.00
A. C. F. Wyatt	RFM	287.4	65	904	20	3-35	0	45.20
J. S. Sykes	SLA	199.3	30	733	12	4-176	0	61.08

Also bowled: N. L. Buck (RFM) 94.3–19–365–6; J. J. Cobb (LBG) 58.1–5–202–0; E. J. H. Eckersley (OB) 8.1–1–42–2; C. W. Henderson (SLA) 30–5–93–1; A. J. Ireland (RFM) 54–7–192–2; B. A. Raine (RFM) 98.3–17–349–9; A. J. Robson (LBG) 1–0–11–0; R. R. Sarwan (LBG) 2–0–11–0; R. M. L. Taylor (LM) 48.1–11–156–2; S. J. Thakor (RM) 133.1–21–537–7; M. A. Thornely (RM) 63.2–13–262–3; T. J. Wells (RFM) 37–5–129–1; R. E. M. Williams (RFM) 122.1–20–436–8.

LEADING YB40 AVERAGES (100 runs/4 wickets)

Batting	Runs	HS	Avge	SR	Ct/St
J. J. Cobb	578	130	52.54	113.77	0
N. J. O'Brien	380	104	38.00	90.26	11/1
G. P. Smith	318	135*	31.80	97.84	3
E. J. H. Eckersley	282	108	31.33	92.15	4
R. M. L. Taylor	150	48*	30.00	108.69	4
M. A. Thornely	245	68	27.22	106.98	3
M. A. G. Boyce	223	53	22.30	85.76	3
S. J. Thakor	151	64*	15.10	74.01	4

Bowling	W	BB	Avge	ER
R. M. L. Taylor	14	3-45	31.71	6.48
N. L. Buck	10	3-25	32.40	7.30
J. K. H. Naik	4	2-34	35.50	5.60
S. J. Thakor	9	3-39	43.33	7.59
J. J. Cobb	7	3-34	45.57	5.59
R. E. M. Williams	6	3-34	52.66	6.29
A. J. Ireland	5	2-41	56.80	6.17
J. S. Sykes	4	2-37	67.50	6.00

LEADING FLt20 AVERAGES (100 runs/13 overs)

Batting	Runs	HS	Avge	SR	Ct/St		Bowling	W	BB	Avge	ER
G. P. Smith	279	84	39.85	130.98	3		Shakib Al Hasan	9	2-7	27.00	6.50
Shakib Al Hasan	146	43*	18.25	130.35	2		J. J. Cobb	9	3-9	20.55	7.07
J. A. Burns	197	81*	28.14	129.60	2		A. J. Ireland	15	4-11	15.73	7.08
J. J. Cobb	232	67*	29.00	122.10	8		R. M. L. Taylor	14	4-11	14.00	7.25
E. J. H. Eckersley	104	42	26.00	114.28	0/1		S. J. Thakor	6	3-30	18.16	8.38
N. J. O'Brien	123	47	20.50	104.23	5						

FIRST-CLASS COUNTY RECORDS

Highest score for	309*	H. D. Ackerman v Glamorgan at Cardiff.	2006
Highest score against	341	G. H. Hirst (Yorkshire) at Leicester.	1905
Leading run-scorer	30,143	L. G. Berry (avge 30.32)	1924–51
Best bowling for	10-18	G. Geary v Glamorgan at Pontypridd	1929
Best bowling against	10-32	H. Pickett (Essex) at Leyton	1895
Leading wicket-taker	2,131	W. E. Astill (avge 23.18)	1906–39
Highest total for	701-4 dec	v Worcestershire at Worcester.	1906
Highest total against	761-6 dec	by Essex at Chelmsford	1990
Lowest total for	25	v Kent at Leicester.	1912
Lowest total against {	24	by Glamorgan at Leicester.	1971
	24	by Oxford University at Oxford.	1985

LIST A COUNTY RECORDS

Highest score for	201	V. J. Wells v Berkshire at Leicester.	1996
Highest score against	201*	R. S. Bopara (Essex) at Leicester.	2008
Leading run-scorer	8,216	N. E. Briers (avge 27.66)	1975–95
Best bowling for	6-16	C. M. Willoughby v Somerset at Leicester	2005
Best bowling against	6-21	S. M. Pollock (Warwickshire) at Birmingham.	1996
Leading wicket-taker	308	K. Higgs (avge 18.80)	1972–82
Highest total for	406-5	v Berkshire at Leicester.	1996
Highest total against	350-5	by Essex at Leicester.	2008
Lowest total for	36	v Sussex at Leicester.	1973
Lowest total against {	62	by Northamptonshire at Leicester	1974
	62	by Middlesex at Leicester.	1998

TWENTY20 COUNTY RECORDS

Highest score for	111	D. L. Maddy v Yorkshire at Leeds	2004
Highest score against	92*	S. G. Law (Lancashire) at Manchester.	2005
Leading run-scorer	1,455	P. A. Nixon (avge 21.71)	2003–*11*
Best bowling for	5-13	A. B. McDonald v Nottinghamshire at Nottingham .	2010
Best bowling against	**5-21**	**J. A. Brooks (Yorkshire) at Leeds**	**2013**
Leading wicket-taker	69	C. W. Henderson (avge 26.95)	2004–12
Highest total for	221-3	v Yorkshire at Leeds	2004
Highest total against	225-2	by Durham at Chester-le-Street	2010
Lowest total for	96	v Nottinghamshire at Leicester	2012
Lowest total against	**72**	**by Derbyshire at Derby**	**2013**

ADDRESS

County Ground, Grace Road, Leicester LE2 8AD (0116 283 2128;
email enquiries@leicestershireccc.co.uk). **Website** www.leicestershireccc.co.uk

OFFICIALS

Captain (Championship) R. R. Sarwan	**Chairman** P. R. Haywood
(limited-overs) J. J. Cobb	**Chief executive** M. J. Siddall
Director of cricket P. Whitticase	**Operations manager** P. Atkinson
First-team coach B. F. Smith	**Head groundsman** A. Ward
President D. W. Wilson	**Scorer** P. J. Rogers

At Southampton, April 10–13. LEICESTERSHIRE drew with HAMPSHIRE.

LEICESTERSHIRE v KENT

At Leicester, April 17–20. Drawn. Leicestershire 9pts, Kent 9pts. Toss: Leicestershire. County debut: R. E. M. Williams. Championship debut: C. J. Haggett.

After hinting at a bright future during the second half of the 2012 season, Thakor wasted little time finding his form in 2013. His pre-season build-up had been hampered by a broken finger sustained on tour in South Africa with England Under-19s, but he showed no ill effects as he compiled his maiden Championship century, picking the gaps with beautiful drives. Thakor shared a sixth-wicket stand of 181 with Boyce, who made a career-best 135, as Leicestershire earned a lead of 89 by noon on the final day. It would have been far more if Kent's last four hadn't added 199 to reach maximum bonus points. Leicestershire required early wickets if they were to exert any pressure, but there was little chance of that without Hoggard, who had limped out of the attack on the first day with a hip injury, joining Nathan Buck, Alex Wyatt and Anthony Ireland on the sidelines. Key's hundred and Nash's second fifty ensured there were no dramas.

Close of play: first day, Kent 406; second day, Leicestershire 250-5 (Boyce 53); third day, Leicestershire 452-7 (Thakor 105, Freckingham 0).

Kent

S. A. Northeast run out	15	– c O'Brien b Thakor	32
R. W. T. Key c Thakor b Williams	41	– not out	104
B. P. Nash lbw b Freckingham	50	– c Cobb b Naik	62
M. J. Powell c Williams b Freckingham	25	– not out	2
D. I. Stevens c O'Brien b Naik	27		
†G. O. Jones lbw b Naik	67		
*J. C. Tredwell run out	13		
M. T. Coles st O'Brien b Naik	59		
C. J. Haggett c Boyce b Naik	40		
M. Davies b Thakor	41		
C. E. Shreck not out	6		
B 7, l-b 4, w 1, n-b 10	22	L-b 5, n-b 8	13

1/39 (1) 2/83 (2) 3/142 (4)   (93.5 overs) 406   1/74 (1)   (2 wkts dec, 62.1 overs) 213
4/147 (3) 5/193 (5) 6/207 (7)   2/198 (3)
7/311 (8) 8/317 (6) 9/385 (10) 10/406 (9)

Hoggard 5–0–27–0; Williams 24–3–80–1; Thakor 16–3–68–1; Freckingham 20–2–82–2; Thornely 6–1–38–0; Naik 21.5–0–97–4. *Second innings*—Freckingham 10–0–36–0; Williams 11–2–30–0; Naik 24–1–70–1; Thakor 10–1–36–1; Cobb 4–1–15–0; Thornely 3–0–21–0; Eckersley 0.1–0–0–0.

Leicestershire

M. A. Thornely c Northeast b Haggett	22	R. E. M. Williams b Shreck	2
†N. J. O'Brien c Tredwell b Haggett	63	M. J. Hoggard c Key b Shreck	4
E. J. H. Eckersley c Jones b Haggett	46		
*R. R. Sarwan c Jones b Stevens	54	B 6, l-b 8, n-b 6	20
J. J. Cobb b Davies	8		
M. A. G. Boyce lbw b Nash	135	1/53 (1) 2/133 (3) (169.4 overs) 495
S. J. Thakor c Nash b Davies	114	3/138 (2) 4/155 (5) 5/250 (4)
J. K. H. Naik run out	3	6/431 (6) 7/452 (8) 8/477 (7)
O. H. Freckingham not out	24	9/491 (10) 10/495 (11) 110 overs: 328-5

Davies 29–9–63–2; Shreck 34.4–8–105–2; Coles 23–5–90–0; Haggett 23–5–79–3; Stevens 21–4–64–1; Tredwell 37–9–71–0; Nash 2–0–9–1.

Umpires: R. K. Illingworth and R. T. Robinson.

LEICESTERSHIRE v LEEDS/BRADFORD MCCU

At Leicester, April 24–26. Leeds/Bradford MCCU won by 102 runs. Toss: Leeds/Bradford MCCU. First-class debut: Z. R. Patel.

Luis Reece inspired Leeds/Bradford to their maiden first-class win at only the fourth attempt, although Leicestershire's batsmen – Thakor apart – fell way short of the standards expected from professionals. They should have assumed control after dismissing the students for 165, with Henderson claiming his 900th first-class wicket. But James Lee struck with the last ball of the day, then his first next morning, as he followed seven wickets against Yorkshire with five for 43. The match was in the balance when Leeds/Bradford led by 92 with five second-innings wickets in hand – but then Reece advanced at the spinners and stepped up the assault when he was joined by last man Ivan Thomas. He contributed eight runs to a partnership of 73 in 16 overs, long enough to see his captain through to his first first-class hundred. Set 238, Leicestershire needed to knuckle down – but wickets fell regularly, and Thakor was out hooking in desperation, unable to emulate Reece's shepherding of the tail. Reece rounded off a fine all-round performance by taking four wickets with his left-arm seam.

Close of play: first day, Leicestershire 156-7 (Thakor 53); second day, Leicestershire 10-0 (Smith 7, Thornely 2).

Leeds/Bradford MCCU

N. R. T. Gubbins c Naik b Williams	7	– (2) c Eckersley b Wyatt	11
H. L. Thompson c Thornely b Taylor	10	– (1) c Boyce b Wyatt	40
J. P. Webb lbw b Thakor	7	– c Cobb b Naik	8
D. R. Young lbw b Williams	14	– c Eckersley b Naik	7
*L. M. Reece c Smith b Thakor	35	– not out	114
W. G. R. Vanderspar b Wyatt	28	– c Eckersley b Henderson	8
†C. A. R. MacLeod lbw b Taylor	9	– c Cobb b Naik	15
A. MacQueen c Taylor b Wyatt	36	– c Eckersley b Naik	1
J. E. Lee c Cobb b Henderson	0	– c Thornely b Naik	9
Z. R. Patel lbw b Henderson	0	– lbw b Henderson	0
I. A. A. Thomas not out	0	– lbw b Henderson	8
B 14, l-b 3, n-b 2	19	B 14, l-b 4, w 8, n-b 2	32

1/19 (2) 2/30 (3) 3/32 (2)   (47.3 overs) 165
4/77 (5) 5/82 (4) 6/112 (7)
7/160 (6) 8/161 (9) 9/161 (10) 10/165 (8)

1/42 (2) 2/75 (3)   (89 overs) 253
3/89 (1) 4/91 (4)
5/108 (6) 6/161 (7) 7/163 (8)
8/179 (9) 9/180 (10) 10/253 (11)

Williams 10–2–24–2; Wyatt 12.3–6–28–2; Taylor 9–1–49–2; Thakor 6–1–26–2; Naik 8–2–20–0; Henderson 2–1–1–2. *Second innings*—Williams 13–0–61–0; Wyatt 12–3–42–2; Taylor 4–2–3–0; Thornely 4–0–15–0; Henderson 24–7–40–3; Naik 32–12–70–5.

Leicestershire

G. P. Smith lbw b Lee	0	– c MacLeod b Lee	13
M. A. Thornely lbw b Thomas	0	– b Lee	13
†E. J. H. Eckersley c Young b Lee	8	– c MacQueen b Patel	19
*J. J. Cobb lbw b Patel	21	– lbw b Thomas	3
M. A. G. Boyce c MacLeod b Reece	27	– lbw b Reece	17
S. J. Thakor c Reece b Patel	53	– (7) c Webb b Lee	35
R. M. L. Taylor c Thomas b Reece	25	– (6) c MacLeod b Reece	0
J. K. H. Naik b Lee	4	– c Lee b Reece	0
C. W. Henderson c Young b Lee	0	– c MacQueen b Reece	10
R. E. M. Williams b Lee	10	– not out	0
A. C. F. Wyatt not out	10	– lbw b Thomas	0
B 3, l-b 5, w 3, n-b 12	23	B 2, w 4, n-b 6	12

1/0 (1) 2/3 (2) 3/20 (3)   (44.3 overs) 181
4/70 (5) 5/80 (4) 6/139 (7)
7/156 (8) 8/156 (6) 9/156 (9) 10/181 (10)

1/28 (1) 2/35 (2)   (42 overs) 135
3/44 (4) 4/61 (3)
5/62 (6) 6/79 (5) 7/83 (8)
8/108 (9) 9/129 (7) 10/135 (11)

Lee 12.3–3–43–5; Thomas 10–2–36–1; Patel 11–5–32–2; Reece 7–0–39–2; MacQueen 4–1–23–0. *Second innings*—Lee 10–2–47–3; Thomas 13–5–37–2; Patel 8–3–21–1; Reece 11–1–28–4.

Umpires: I. Dawood and D. J. Millns.

LEICESTERSHIRE v GLOUCESTERSHIRE

At Leicester, April 30–May 3. Gloucestershire won by nine wickets. Gloucestershire 21pts, Leicestershire 5pts. Toss: Leicestershire.

Gloucestershire's margin of victory suggests they had it mostly their way – but there was no obvious winner until the final morning, when Klinger and Dent seized their chance. Both first innings had followed a similar pattern: Leicestershire's fifth wicket fell at 52, and Gloucestershire's at 46, although the visitors' recovery proved marginally more substantial, with Jack Taylor's unbeaten 61 from 69 balls crucial in a low-scoring game. Will Gidman inflicted a three-ball pair on Thornely with the first delivery of the second innings, and Gloucestershire's seamers kept their discipline on a slow pitch. Howell, rarely thrown the ball at Hampshire, his former county, removed Eckersley, Sarwan and Cobb with his outswingers in both innings, and finished with match figures of eight for 96. Gloucestershire set off in pursuit of 188 on the third evening, and rode their luck against some hostile new-ball bowling. But Klinger asserted his authority next morning, clinching his first Championship century with the winning four through point.

Close of play: first day, Gloucestershire 31-2 (Klinger 9, Payne 4); second day, Leicestershire 32-2 (Eckersley 20, Freckingham 5); third day, Gloucestershire 16-0 (Dent 8, Klinger 8).

Leicestershire

M. A. Thornely b W. R. S. Gidman	0	– c Payne b W. R. S. Gidman	0
†N. J. O'Brien c Herring b Payne	2	– lbw b W. R. S. Gidman	7
E. J. H. Eckersley lbw b Howell	15	– b Howell	45
*R. R. Sarwan c Klinger b Howell	14	– (5) b Howell	44
J. J. Cobb b Howell	9	– (6) c W. R. S. Gidman b Howell	43
M. A. G. Boyce c Dent b Howell	55	– (7) c Herring b W. R. S. Gidman	35
S. J. Thakor c Marshall b Taylor	75	– (8) b Taylor	2
J. K. H. Naik c Dent b Howell	7	– (9) c Herring b Miles	21
C. W. Henderson c Herring b W. R. S. Gidman	33	– (10) not out	5
O. H. Freckingham c Klinger b W. R. S. Gidman	11	– (4) lbw b W. R. S. Gidman	7
R. E. M. Williams not out	0	– c Taylor b Miles	4
B 10, l-b 15, w 2, n-b 2	29	B 1, l-b 1, n-b 2	4

1/0 (1) 2/8 (2) 3/32 (4) (85 overs) 250
4/35 (3) 5/52 (5) 6/177 (6)
7/203 (8) 8/209 (7) 9/249 (10) 10/250 (9)

1/0 (1) 2/17 (2) (96.5 overs) 217
3/35 (4) 4/69 (3)
5/145 (6) 6/150 (5) 7/157 (8)
8/207 (7) 9/213 (9) 10/217 (11)

W. R. S. Gidman 22–2–65–3; Payne 17–5–46–1; Howell 19–4–57–5; Miles 16–5–28–0; Taylor 10–2–24–1; A. P. R. Gidman 1–0–5–0. *Second innings*—W. R. S. Gidman 22–7–39–4; Miles 16.5–2–64–2; Payne 15–6–36–0; Howell 20–9–39–3; Taylor 23–5–37–1.

Gloucestershire

*M. Klinger c O'Brien b Williams	9	– (2) not out	103
C. D. J. Dent lbw b Williams	6	– (1) lbw b Naik	71
D. M. Housego c O'Brien b Freckingham	2	– not out	16
D. A. Payne b Freckingham	4		
A. P. R. Gidman c O'Brien b Freckingham	2		
H. J. H. Marshall lbw b Freckingham	47		
B. A. C. Howell lbw b Henderson	52		
W. R. S. Gidman lbw b Naik	52		
J. M. R. Taylor not out	61		
†C. L. Herring c Naik b Williams	5		
C. N. Miles c Eckersley b Williams	23		
L-b 7, n-b 10	17	B 1	1

1/14 (2) 2/19 (3) 3/31 (1)   (93.4 overs) 280   1/129 (1)   (1 wkt, 58.1 overs) 191
4/31 (4) 5/46 (5) 6/107 (6)
7/174 (8) 8/214 (7) 9/229 (10) 10/280 (11)

Freckingham 22–6–69–4; Williams 20.4–5–69–4; Thakor 7–4–17–0; Naik 26–9–56–1; Henderson 17–4–57–1; Cobb 1–0–5–0. *Second innings*—Freckingham 10–2–35–0; Williams 8–2–25–0; Henderson 13–1–36–0; Thakor 6.1–1–25–0; Naik 16.5–42–1; Thornely 2–0–19–0; Cobb 3–0–8–0.

Umpires: N. G. B. Cook and S. J. O'Shaughnessy.

At Worcester, May 8–11. LEICESTERSHIRE drew with WORCESTERSHIRE.

At Northampton, May 15–18. LEICESTERSHIRE drew with NORTHAMPTONSHIRE.

LEICESTERSHIRE v GLAMORGAN

At Leicester, May 21–24. Drawn. Leicestershire 5pts, Glamorgan 10pts. Toss: Leicestershire. County debuts: J. A. Burns, A. J. Ireland.

Bad weather came to Leicestershire's rescue after they had been dominated for three days. Cobb, adding the four-day captaincy to his one-day role after Ramnaresh Sarwan joined up with West Indies for the Champions Trophy, put Glamorgan in, only to see two chances from Walters go down in the slips, and a more pivotal drop at long leg, where Buck missed Allenby on 20. Buck responded with a testing spell, but Allenby survived to equal his career-best unbeaten 138 – made for Leicestershire in 2008 – before Wallace, mindful of rain, declared at the fall of the ninth wicket. (Over at Kibworth, meanwhile, Matthew Hoggard was continuing his comeback from injury with eight for 21 for Leicestershire Second XI.) The home batsmen then struggled against Hogan and Glover, and were made to follow on 300 behind, with two days remaining. They made a much better fist of it, but Glamorgan would still have been confident of forcing victory given a full final day. In the event, less than 13 overs were possible as rain and high winds whipped across Grace Road. Conditions were so wretched that ten Glamorgan players took to the field wearing beanie hats; Wagg even bowled in his. The odd one out was Goodwin, a southern hemisphere toughie who kept faith with his cap.

Close of play: first day, Glamorgan 256-5 (Allenby 39, Wallace 12); second day, Leicestershire 142; third day, Leicestershire 133-1 (Smith 62, Eckersley 23).

Glamorgan

B. J. Wright c Eckersley b Buck	49
W. D. Bragg lbw b Freckingham	5
S. J. Walters c Thornely b Freckingham ...	14
M. J. North c Boyce b Ireland	68
M. W. Goodwin lbw b Buck	57
J. Allenby not out	138
*†M. A. Wallace c Thornely b Freckingham .	16
G. G. Wagg c Smith b Naik	58

J. C. Glover lbw b Naik	8
M. G. Hogan b Buck	12
B 1, l-b 13, w 1, n-b 2	17

1/15 (2)   (9 wkts dec, 132.3 overs) 442
2/39 (3) 3/98 (1) 4/184 (5)
5/228 (4) 6/278 (7) 7/395 (8)
8/421 (9) 9/442 (10)   110 overs: 354-6

M. T. Reed did not bat.

Freckingham 32–4–119–3; Ireland 23–3–83–1; Buck 31.3–8–83–3; Thornely 14–4–45–0; Naik 32–7–98–2.

Leicestershire

G. P. Smith c Allenby b Hogan	11	– lbw b Hogan	70
M. A. Thornely lbw b Glover	3	– lbw b Reed	43
†E. J. H. Eckersley c Goodwin b Hogan	4	– not out	43
J. A. Burns lbw b Hogan	21	– not out	18
S. J. Thakor c North b Wagg	1		
M. A. G. Boyce c Walters b Glover............	17		
*J. J. Cobb b Reed	29		
J. K. H. Naik b Glover.......................	5		
O. H. Freckingham c Walters b Glover	15		
N. L. Buck c Wallace b Hogan	6		
A. J. Ireland not out	15		
L-b 5, w 2, n-b 8...............	15	L-b 4, n-b 4	8

1/16 (1) 2/18 (2) 3/28 (3)   (44.3 overs) 142
4/41 (5) 5/47 (4) 6/84 (6)
7/98 (7) 8/119 (8) 9/122 (9) 10/142 (10)

1/93 (2)   (2 wkts, 54 overs) 182
2/151 (1)

Hogan 11.3–2–25–4; Glover 15–4–51–4; Allenby 1–1–0–0; Wagg 7–0–30–1; Reed 10–2–31–1. *Second innings*—Hogan 15–3–61–1; Glover 10–3–24–0; Wagg 16–4–57–0; Allenby 4–1–19–0; North 1–0–1–0; Reed 8–2–16–1.

Umpires: R. J. Evans and J. W. Lloyds.

At Tunbridge Wells, May 29–June 1. LEICESTERSHIRE drew with KENT.

LEICESTERSHIRE v NORTHAMPTONSHIRE

At Leicester, June 11–14. Drawn. Leicestershire 5pts, Northamptonshire 9pts. Toss: Leicestershire.

Leicestershire's sloppy fielding allowed the Division Two leaders to dictate matters, although rain again had the final say. There was little chance of Northamptonshire pushing for victory after the best part of two sessions was lost on the third day, then more on the last. Leicestershire had spilled a series of early chances, and also struggled to contain boundaries: Coetzer's first fifty took 120 balls, but still included 11 fours. He went on to hit 36 in all, plus a six, in a career-best 219, while Hall weighed in with his second hundred of the season against Leicestershire, though Northamptonshire narrowly missed maximum batting points. Leicestershire were without the in-form Shiv Thakor, because of a finger injury, but the diligence of Queenslander Joe Burns, who made the first fifty of his overseas spell, and Boyce, standing in as captain after Josh Cobb dropped himself citing exhaustion, steered them away from danger.

Close of play: first day, Northamptonshire 320-4 (Coetzer 150, Hall 65); second day, Leicestershire 47-2 (Eckersley 19, Burns 15); third day, Leicestershire 142-3 (Burns 67, Boyce 6).

Northamptonshire

K. J. Coetzer c O'Brien b Wyatt	219	S. P. Crook not out	47
M. N. W. Spriegel lbw b Wyatt	7	B 9, l-b 21, w 1, n-b 8	39
D. J. Sales b Wyatt	32		
*A. G. Wakely c Burns b Buck	18	1/22 (2) (7 wkts dec, 147.1 overs)	567
R. I. Keogh c Freckingham b Thornely	18	2/87 (3) 3/161 (4)	
A. J. Hall c Naik b Buck	103	4/200 (5) 5/375 (6)	
J. D. Middlebrook c Smith b Taylor	84	6/475 (1) 7/567 (7)	110 overs: 395-5

D. J. Willey, †D. Murphy and L. M. Daggett did not bat.

Freckingham 29–5–122–0; Wyatt 33–8–107–3; Buck 25–6–100–2; Taylor 23.1–3–99–1; Thornely 5–1–21–1; Naik 32–7–88–0.

Leicestershire

G. P. Smith c and b Daggett	9	J. K. H. Naik not out	2
†N. J. O'Brien c Murphy b Willey	0		
E. J. H. Eckersley lbw b Middlebrook	43	L-b 7, n-b 14	21
J. A. Burns b Hall	77		
*M. A. G. Boyce not out	40	1/13 (2) 2/19 (1) (6 wkts, 80.1 overs)	238
M. A. Thornely c Murphy b Crook	46	3/118 (3) 4/159 (4)	
R. M. L. Taylor c Murphy b Crook	0	5/236 (6) 6/236 (7)	

O. H. Freckingham, N. L. Buck and A. C. F. Wyatt did not bat.

Willey 17–3–60–1; Daggett 16–5–34–1; Crook 18.1–6–61–2; Hall 17–4–42–1; Middlebrook 12–5–34–1.

Umpires: M. J. D. Bodenham and S. J. O'Shaughnessy.

LEICESTERSHIRE v ESSEX

At Leicester, June 21–24. Essex won by four wickets. Essex 23pts, Leicestershire 6pts. Toss: Leicestershire.

In their first Championship game since being rolled for 20 by Lancashire, Essex showed character to recover from a pair of top-order collapses and chase down a tricky total on the final evening. Leicestershire had looked likely to reopen recent wounds when, after reaching 302, they reduced Essex to 28 for four. Hoggard, making his first appearance since April, took all of them in a testing 12-over spell of outswing interrupted by four stoppages for showers. But Foster responded with a chanceless hundred, his fifth in 11 innings against Leicestershire, and coaxed a first Championship fifty of the season out of Pettini. Napier, who earlier claimed career-best figures of seven for 90, also weighed in, and Essex were able to secure a vital 54-run lead. They tightened their grip with the ball, despite gutsy work from Naik and the tail, leaving themselves a target of 161 in 40 overs. At 79 for five the game was up for grabs. But Foster helped out with a brisk 42, before ten Doeschate and Napier took Essex home with 22 balls in hand.

Close of play: first day, Leicestershire 268-7 (Thornely 37, Freckingham 8); second day, Essex 196-6 (Foster 45, Napier 4); third day, Leicestershire 91-4 (Thakor 10, Boyce 4).

Leicestershire

G. P. Smith lbw b ten Doeschate	27	– lbw b Topley	11
†N. J. O'Brien lbw b Napier	67	– c Foster b Masters	14
E. J. H. Eckersley c Foster b Masters	21	– lbw b ten Doeschate	11
J. A. Burns b Shah b Napier	26	– b ten Doeschate	39
S. J. Thakor run out	54	– c Foster b Napier	19
*M. A. G. Boyce lbw b Napier	11	– lbw b Topley	13
M. A. Thornely lbw b Napier	53	– c Foster b ten Doeschate	9
J. K. H. Naik c and b Napier	0	– not out	47
O. H. Freckingham lbw b Napier	15	– lbw b ten Doeschate	0
M. J. Hoggard not out	9	– c Foster b Masters	24
A. C. F. Wyatt c Mickleburgh b Napier	2	– lbw b Topley	17
L-b 14, w 1, n-b 2	17	L-b 8, n-b 2	10

1/58 (1) 2/102 (3) 3/148 (2)   (104.4 overs) 302   1/25 (2) 2/27 (1)   (81.5 overs) 214
4/157 (4) 5/189 (6) 6/253 (5)   3/73 (3) 4/86 (4)
7/255 (8) 8/287 (9) 9/296 (7) 10/302 (11)   5/109 (5) 6/109 (6) 7/133 (7)
                                                         8/135 (9) 9/178 (10) 10/214 (11)

Masters 32–5–79–1; Topley 25–6–68–0; Napier 30.4–8–90–7; ten Doeschate 13–3–37–1; Craddock 3–0–13–0; Westley 1–0–1–0. *Second innings*—Masters 20–5–47–2; Topley 17.5–1–51–3; Napier 18–3–67–1; ten Doeschate 14–2–28–4; Craddock 12–6–13–0.

Essex

T. Westley c O'Brien b Hoggard	11	– c O'Brien b Wyatt	16
J. C. Mickleburgh c Naik b Hoggard	10	– lbw b Wyatt	4
N. L. J. Browne lbw b Hoggard	0	– lbw b Hoggard	1
O. A. Shah b Hoggard	1	– c O'Brien b Wyatt	11
M. L. Pettini lbw b Wyatt	72	– c Thornely b Freckingham	25
R. N. ten Doeschate c Burns b Wyatt	40	– not out	37
*†J. S. Foster c Thakor b Hoggard	143	– c Boyce b Thornely	42
G. R. Napier lbw b Freckingham	52	– not out	13
D. D. Masters c Burns b Hoggard	9		
T. R. Craddock b Wyatt	1		
R. J. W. Topley not out	0		
B 1, l-b 14, n-b 2	17	L-b 10, n-b 2	12

1/22 (1) 2/22 (3) 3/23 (2)   (104.1 overs) 356   1/8 (2)   (6 wkts, 36.2 overs) 161
4/28 (4) 5/113 (6) 6/191 (5)   2/13 (3) 3/34 (4)
7/305 (8) 8/320 (9) 9/355 (7) 10/356 (10)   4/47 (1) 5/79 (5) 6/145 (7)

Hoggard 29–8–66–6; Wyatt 26.1–5–80–3; Thakor 3–0–34–0; Freckingham 20–1–109–1; Thornely 8–5–15–0; Naik 18–2–37–0. *Second innings*—Hoggard 11–2–36–1; Wyatt 13–4–35–3; Freckingham 9–1–46–1; Naik 2–0–20–0; Thornely 1.2–0–14–1.

Umpires: T. E. Jesty and M. J. Saggers.

At Chelmsford, July 17–20. LEICESTERSHIRE lost to ESSEX by an innings and 25 runs.

LEICESTERSHIRE v LANCASHIRE

At Leicester, August 2–5. Lancashire won by an innings and 52 runs. Lancashire 23pts, Leicestershire 2pts. Toss: Lancashire. First-class debut: T. J. Wells.

Leicestershire presented only a minor obstacle to Lancashire's promotion juggernaut. The Division Two leaders were sloppy enough to miss out on full batting points, but their bowling was far too potent. Horton could have been out twice to the first ball of the match, his first since May: when Hoggard appealed for lbw, he wandered out of his crease and was almost run out from square leg. But he survived to put on a century opening stand with Reece, who had a happy return to the ground where he had scored his maiden first-class hundred and captained Leeds/Bradford MCCU to victory in April. Chapple and Tom Smith then bowled 45 consecutive dot balls to Leicestershire's top order, and the two highest scorers, Thakor and O'Brien – in a new role at No. 6 – were both punished for lapses in concentration. Lancashire's superiority was underlined when they made Leicestershire follow on 226 behind, and Hogg sent down an outswinging yorker which bamboozled Greg Smith first ball. A string of batsmen threw their wickets away, and Lancashire wrapped up victory not long into the final day.

Close of play: first day, Lancashire 303-5 (Procter 37, Smith 8); second day, Leicestershire 127-7 (Freckingham 0, Sykes 0); third day, Leicestershire 128-5 (O'Brien 35, Wells 10).

Lancashire

P. J. Horton c Freckingham b Wyatt	59	K. W. Hogg not out	4
L. M. Reece c Thornely b Wells	85	*G. Chapple c Boyce b Freckingham	4
A. G. Prince c Sykes b Thornely	33	S. C. Kerrigan c O'Brien b Freckingham	4
S. M. Katich c O'Brien b Hoggard	62	L-b 6, w 1, n-b 2	9
A. P. Agathangelou c O'Brien			
b Freckingham	12	1/104 (1) 2/181 (3) (117 overs) 380
L. A. Procter c Wells b Sykes	67	3/181 (2) 4/219 (5) 5/281 (4)
T. C. Smith c Sykes b Hoggard	8	6/303 (7) 7/367 (6) 8/370 (8)
†G. D. Cross c Smith b Freckingham	33	9/374 (10) 10/380 (11) 110 overs: 370-7

Hoggard 25–7–78–2; Wyatt 27–9–66–1; Freckingham 22–3–85–4; Thakor 3–0–22–0; Sykes 23–7–65–1; Wells 10–2–36–1; Thornely 7–1–22–1.

Leicestershire

G. P. Smith c Agathangelou b Hogg		4 – lbw b Hogg	0
M. A. Thornely c Reece b Smith	8	– c Katich b Hogg	6
E. J. H. Eckersley b Chapple	25	– run out	25
S. J. Thakor c Prince b Kerrigan	34	– c Procter b Chapple	14
*M. A. G. Boyce c Agathangelou b Kerrigan	5	– c Cross b Agathangelou	27
†N. J. O'Brien b Chapple	41	– c Agathangelou b Hogg	50
T. J. Wells lbw b Hogg	9	– c Agathangelou b Smith	17
O. H. Freckingham c Reece b Smith	7	– c Cross b Hogg	0
J. S. Sykes c Cross b Smith	10	– c and b Chapple	13
M. J. Hoggard lbw b Kerrigan	0	– b Hogg	1
A. C. F. Wyatt not out	8	– not out	6
L-b 1, n-b 2	3	B 4, l-b 10, w 1	15

1/9 (1) 2/33 (2) 3/41 (3) (70.1 overs) 154
4/46 (5) 5/111 (6) 6/127 (4)
7/127 (7) 8/143 (9) 9/146 (8) 10/154 (10)

1/0 (1) 2/21 (2) (62.1 overs) 174
3/41 (3) 4/53 (4)
5/108 (5) 6/150 (7) 7/150 (6)
8/151 (8) 9/161 (10) 10/174 (9)

Chapple 18–5–37–2; Hogg 12–5–20–2; Kerrigan 20.1–5–52–3; Smith 17–7–35–3; Procter 2–1–9–0; Agathangelou 1–1–0–0. *Second innings*—Hogg 22–6–77–5; Chapple 14.1–4–26–2; Smith 7–5–5–1; Procter 1–0–3–0; Kerrigan 13–3–31–0; Agathangelou 5–0–18–1.

Umpires: M. Burns and J. H. Evans.

At Swansea, August 21–24. LEICESTERSHIRE lost to GLAMORGAN by an innings and 37 runs.

LEICESTERSHIRE v WORCESTERSHIRE

At Leicester, August 28–31. Worcestershire won by nine wickets. Worcestershire 22pts, Leicestershire 5pts. Toss: Leicestershire.

Eckersley was awarded his county cap after becoming the first Leicestershire batsman since Brad Hodge, in 2004, to score centuries in both innings. His outstanding performance, during which he passed 1,000 runs for the season, was not enough to stave off a heavy defeat, as the greater experience of Richardson and Samaraweera proved the difference. Richardson took his 50th wicket of the summer in his opening spell, confused Eckersley with extra bounce, and claimed the first hat-trick of his long career as he polished off the tail on the second morning. Samaraweera then grafted for six hours to make his second hundred against Leicestershire – the only two of an underwhelming overseas stint – to earn a lead of 64. Sykes's dogged 118-ball stay, containing just one four, came too late for Leicestershire, though he was able to see Eckersley through to his second hundred. Worcestershire's final-day target of 185 was made to look straightforward when Ali, in the midst of a golden patch, joined Pardoe at the fall of the first wicket, and they reeled off the last 123 in 25 overs. Eckersley blotted his copybook when he and Cobb – captain here when Matt Boyce dropped out injured – were arrested for being drunk and disorderly in the early hours of the next morning. The club took no formal action for what they said was "a pretty trivial matter".

Close of play: first day, Leicestershire 270-7 (Raine 16, Freckingham 22); second day, Worcestershire 265-5 (Samaraweera 99, Johnson 12); third day, Leicestershire 190-6 (Eckersley 91, Sykes 22).

Leicestershire

G. P. Smith c Ali b Richardson	1	– b Cessford	7
†N. J. O'Brien c Mitchell b Leach	31	– c Shantry b Cessford	12
E. J. H. Eckersley b Richardson	106	– b Shantry	119
S. J. Thakor lbw b Choudhry	9	– lbw b Shantry	1
T. J. Wells lbw b Shantry	8	– b Shantry	17
*J. J. Cobb c Fell b Ali	44	– c Samaraweera b Cessford	11
B. A. Raine not out	16	– b Choudhry	19
J. S. Sykes c Ali b Shantry	14	– lbw b Richardson	32
O. H. Freckingham c Mitchell b Richardson	26	– c Pardoe b Shantry	4
M. J. Hoggard lbw b Richardson	0	– lbw b Choudhry	8
A. C. F. Wyatt lbw b Richardson	0	– not out	8
B 4, l-b 13, n-b 2	19	B 8, l-b 2	10

1/14 (1) 2/53 (2) 3/63 (4)   (100.2 overs) 274   1/20 (2) 2/23 (1)   (100.2 overs) 248
4/94 (5) 5/186 (6) 6/226 (3)   3/31 (4) 4/63 (5)
7/241 (8) 8/274 (9) 9/274 (10) 10/274 (11)   5/97 (6) 6/120 (7) 7/212 (8)
                                               8/231 (9) 9/232 (3) 10/248 (10)

Richardson 24.2–7–57–5; Cessford 12–0–58–0; Shantry 27–8–62–2; Leach 9–1–29–1; Choudhry 16–4–31–1; Ali 11–1–20–1; Mitchell 1–1–0–0. *Second innings*—Richardson 25–9–47–1; Cessford 18.4–4–56–3; Shantry 24.2–7–53–4; Leach 2–0–16–0; Choudhry 21.2–3–52–2; Ali 9–3–14–0.

Worcestershire

*D. K. H. Mitchell lbw b Hoggard	23	– b Hoggard	35
M. G. Pardoe lbw b Hoggard	2	– not out	76
M. M. Ali lbw b Raine	25	– not out	63
T. T. Samaraweera not out	144		
T. C. Fell c O'Brien b Thakor	84		
J. Leach c Smith b Thakor	0		
†M. A. Johnson lbw b Hoggard	17		
S. H. Choudhry b Hoggard	0		
J. D. Shantry c O'Brien b Sykes	22		
G. Cessford b Sykes	0		
A. Richardson b Freckingham	1		
L-b 14, w 1, p 5	20	L-b 8, w 3	11

1/11 (2) 2/53 (3) 3/55 (1)   (110.5 overs) 338   1/62 (1)   (1 wkt, 45.1 overs) 185
4/236 (5) 5/238 (6) 6/276 (7) 7/284 (8)
8/331 (9) 9/331 (10) 10/338 (11)   110 overs: 336-9

Hoggard 26–7–62–4; Wyatt 25–5–68–0; Freckingham 13.5–1–67–1; Raine 12–3–32–1; Sykes 22–3–62–2; Cobb 3–1–4–0; Thakor 9–0–24–2. *Second innings*—Hoggard 11–4–32–1; Wyatt 8–0–36–0; Freckingham 6–0–25–0; Sykes 7–1–42–0; Raine 5–1–16–0; Cobb 6.1–0–23–0; Eckersley 2–1–3–0.

Umpires: S. A. Garratt and T. E. Jesty.

At Bristol, September 3–5. LEICESTERSHIRE lost to GLOUCESTERSHIRE by an innings and 138 runs. *Leicestershire's sixth defeat in succession.*

At Manchester, September 11–14. LEICESTERSHIRE drew with LANCASHIRE. *Leicestershire finish last for the third time in five seasons.*

LEICESTERSHIRE v HAMPSHIRE

At Leicester, September 17–20. Hampshire won by 180 runs. Hampshire 20pts, Leicestershire 0pts. Toss: Leicestershire.

Leicestershire's aim at the start of their final game was straightforward: to avoid the ignominy of going through a Championship season without a victory for the first time in their history. They also wanted to give Hoggard a happy send-off to his 17-year career. The equation was simplified further by rain: no play was possible on the opening day, and only nine balls on the third. In between, Hoggard had a catch dropped in his first over, when Thornely put down a shoulder-high chance at slip, and Hampshire seized control through dominant centuries from Vince, who on-drove

---

THE WILDERNESS YEARS

Lowest points totals in the Championship since the introduction of two divisions in 2000:

| | | Won | Lost | Drawn | Bonus points | | |
					Batting	Bowling	
79	**Leicestershire (D2)**	0	8	8	23	32	**2013**
88	Leicestershire (D2)	1	11	4	24	36	2011
88.5	Glamorgan (D1)	1	14	1	33	38	2005
90.75	Durham (D2)	1	11	4	21	42	2002
92.25	Derbyshire (D2)	1	9	6	20	37	2001
92.5	Glamorgan (D2)	1	9	6	26	37	2007
94	Worcestershire (D1)	0	10	6	30	40	2009
95	Worcestershire (D1)	1	8	7	18	35	2007
96	Worcestershire (D1)	1	8	7	17	42	2012

sumptuously, and Dawson, who celebrated his with a back-of-the-net swish of his right boot. They both passed 1,000 runs – the only Hampshire batsmen to reach the mark in a forgettable season. Adams declared at the start of the last day, and a forfeit apiece tasked Leicestershire with chasing 365. However, they rapidly crashed to 36 for five; Thakor made four either side of being struck on the head by the hostile Coles. A cleanly struck 82 from Wells, featuring 17 boundaries, suggested he was one to keep an eye on, but the rest were wrecked by Tomlinson and Coles. Leicestershire's defeat meant they were now the only county, since the introduction of bonus points in 1968, to collect none from a Championship match on three separate occasions. Hoggard was unable to add to his 786 first-class wickets, but he was applauded off the pitch at the end, unbeaten on a stoic three.

Close of play: first day, no play; second day, Hampshire 362-2 (Dawson 136, Vince 145); third day, Hampshire 364-2 (Dawson 136, Vince 147).

Hampshire

S. P. Terry lbw b Thakor	57
*J. H. K. Adams c O'Brien b Raine	14
L. A. Dawson not out	136
J. M. Vince not out	147
B 1, l-b 5, w 2, n-b 2	10

1/50 (2)   (2 wkts dec, 97.3 overs) 364
2/114 (1)

S. M. Ervine, A. J. Wheater, †M. D. Bates, M. T. Coles, D. R. Briggs, R. M. R. Brathwaite and J. A. Tomlinson did not bat.

Hoggard 20–2–72–0; Wyatt 21–4–70–0; Wells 11–2–31–0; Raine 18.3–2–66–1; Sykes 11–0–47–0; Thakor 10–1–32–1; Thornely 4–0–19–0; Robson 1–0–11–0; Eckersley 1–0–10–0.

Hampshire forfeited their second innings.

Leicestershire

Leicestershire forfeited their first innings.

G. P. Smith b Tomlinson	9	J. S. Sykes c Terry b Tomlinson	24
A. J. Robson c Ervine b Coles	1	A. C. F. Wyatt c Terry b Tomlinson	10
E. J. H. Eckersley b Coles	4	M. J. Hoggard not out	3
M. A. Thornely lbw b Tomlinson	0	B 5, l-b 4, w 5	14
†N. J. O'Brien c Adams b Brathwaite	25		
S. J. Thakor c Ervine b Coles	8	1/19 (1) 2/19 (2) 3/20 (4) (43.2 overs) 184	
B. A. Raine b Coles	4	4/24 (3) 5/36 (7) 6/105 (5)	
T. J. Wells b Coles	82	7/126 (6) 8/155 (8) 9/173 (9) 10/184 (10)	

Thakor, when 4, retired hurt at 28-4 and resumed at 105-6.

Tomlinson 15.2–5–60–4; Coles 17–3–75–5; Ervine 6–0–20–0; Brathwaite 5–2–20–1.

Umpires: M. J. D. Bodenham and M. A. Gough.

MIDDLESEX

Soft in the middle

Kevin Hand

Middlesex were tipped as title contenders before the season started, and were in the running for the Championship for most of the summer. In the end, though, they had to settle for fifth place – another seven points would have meant third, replicating their 2012 finish – and the familiar feeling of what might have been.

Those pre-season hopes were encouraged by the acquisition of James Harris from Glamorgan to bolster an already strong pace attack. And when Middlesex won their first two matches, expectations rose further. But potential victories tended to peter out into draws, and a sobering defeat by Yorkshire just before the Twenty20 break put things into perspective. Still, the good start meant relegation was never likely, which at least removed some of the pressure.

Harris proved a disappointment. He managed only 21 wickets at 38 in the Championship; the consistent Tim Murtagh's haul of 60 came at almost half the cost. Toby Roland-Jones also did well at the start of the season – his hat-trick helped demolish Derbyshire for 60 in the first Championship match at Lord's – but both he and Harris were restricted by injuries later on.

The batting stars were both born in Sydney. Sam Robson began in superlative form, although he fell away a little, perhaps distracted when his name started cropping up in discussions for an England place; he still amassed more than 1,200 Championship runs. Robson remains qualified for both England and Australia – who introduced a new rule, widely seen as crafted with him specifically in mind, enabling home-born players with dual qualifications to take part in the Sheffield Shield without compromising their eligibility elsewhere. Still, Robson's only matches in Australia in the winter were two for the England Performance Programme; he scored centuries in both. Chris Rogers, meanwhile, reached four figures from only 12 Championship appearances, either side of his successful return to Test cricket in the Ashes.

But while the openers shone, the middle order did not – which is why Middlesex failed to mount a serious bid for the Championship. Neil Dexter showed signs of a return to form, but his century against Sussex was one of only two by a non-opener, along with a tenacious 150 by Adam Voges on his Championship debut for Middlesex in July. Voges had originally been signed only for Twenty20 cricket, but stepped in for a few four-day games while Rogers was with Australia.

Joe Denly had played a large part in Middlesex's promotion in 2011, but managed only 652 runs this time, while Dawid Malan fared even worse, and lost his place for a while – which weakened an already suspect fielding unit.

Wicketkeeper John Simpson had a reasonable time with the bat although, like Robson, he peaked early – his highest score of 97 not out came in the first match, against Nottinghamshire. The other all-rounders, Gareth Berg and Ollie Rayner, were both underwhelming with the bat – although Rayner produced the bowling performance of the season, at The Oval, where Surrey needed victory to stave off relegation. But the pitch, used previously, proved ideal for the lofty Rayner, whose off-breaks regularly leapt off a decent length past the shoulders – and helmets – of startled batsmen. Rayner became the first Middlesex bowler to take 15 wickets in a match since Fred Titmus in 1955. His haul of 46 was the second-highest by an

John Walton, PA Photos

Ollie Rayner

England-qualified spinner, and earned him a call for the Lions tour of Sri Lanka early in 2014, after Lancashire's Simon Kerrigan pulled out.

The batting problems were exposed most starkly in a dispiriting defeat by Somerset at Lord's in August – all out for 106 and 164 in response to a total of 449. That ended any lingering hopes the Championship pennant might soon be flying at Lord's for the first time since 1993. Middlesex had effectively been rolled twice in a day on a good batting pitch. Rayner helped restore some pride the following week against Surrey, but the Championship season ended with another comprehensive defeat by Yorkshire.

Middlesex also showed flashes of form in limited-overs matches. In the FLt20 they looked set to reach the quarter-finals before losing their last two matches, then – as in 2012 – just missed out on a semi-final spot in the YB40. Again, it was a defeat at Headingley that cost them – but this was harder to swallow than the Championship setback, as it was administered by an experimental young side; Yorkshire's early results had been so poor they were already out of contention.

There was, though, one bright note during Middlesex's meetings with Yorkshire: the return YB40 game was the inaugural first-team fixture at Radlett, their new training base and Second XI home (where they prepared for the season in a heated marquee, dubbed "our Eden Project" by managing director of cricket Angus Fraser). The match drew a crowd of around 2,000 at a picturesque venue described by one member as feeling like "more of a cricket club and less like a sports facility" – which betrayed how some felt about Middlesex's other outgrounds. However, Radlett cannot accommodate the crowds expected for Twenty20 games, and the jury was out on whether the pitch was yet suitable for four-day matches.

Overall, however, Middlesex have come a long way since the disarray and discontent of a few years ago. The inspired appointment of Fraser – part of a reshuffle presided over by chief executive Vinny Codrington and chairman Ian Lovett – has helped strengthen the county. Now they just need to beef up the middle order.

Championship attendance: 45,238.

MIDDLESEX RESULTS

All first-class matches – Played 17: Won 7, Lost 5, Drawn 5.
County Championship matches – Played 16: Won 6, Lost 5, Drawn 5.

LV= County Championship, 5th in Division 1;
Friends Life t20, 4th in South Division; Yorkshire Bank 40, 4th in Group C.

COUNTY CHAMPIONSHIP AVERAGES, BATTING AND FIELDING

Cap		M	I	NO	R	HS	100	50	Avge	Ct/St
2011	C. J. L. Rogers§	12	22	3	1,068	214	3	6	56.21	11
	A. C. Voges§	4	7	0	383	150	1	2	54.71	6
2013	S. D. Robson	16	29	4	1,180	215*	3	4	47.20	22
2010	N. J. Dexter	16	26	2	772	104	1	4	32.16	11
2008	E. J. G. Morgan‡	2	4	1	96	39*	0	0	32.00	2
2011	J. A. Simpson	16	25	4	648	97*	0	5	30.85	55/5
2012	J. L. Denly	16	28	3	652	77	0	4	26.08	6
2010	G. K. Berg	15	23	2	501	71	0	2	23.85	8
2010	D. J. Malan	12	19	1	387	61	0	2	21.50	19
	O. P. Rayner	13	18	3	293	52*	0	1	19.53	19
	J. A. R. Harris.	9	12	3	146	37	0	0	16.22	2
	R. H. Patel†	3	6	2	47	26*	0	0	11.75	0
2012	T. S. Roland-Jones†	8	11	1	111	21	0	0	11.10	4
2008	T. J. Murtagh	13	15	4	112	29	0	0	10.18	4
2011	C. D. Collymore¶	9	11	5	22	6*	0	0	3.66	3
2009	S. T. Finn‡	6	7	1	15	8	0	0	2.50	2

Also batted: T. G. Helm (1 match) 4, 18; A. B. London† (2 matches) 18, 28, 3 (1 ct); G. S. Sandhu† (2 matches) did not bat; T. M. J. Smith (2 matches) 17*, 19 (1 ct); P. R. Stirling (1 match) 0, 1.

† *Born in Middlesex.* ‡ *ECB contract.* § *Official overseas player.* ¶ *Other non-England-qualified player.*

BOWLING

	Style	O	M	R	W	BB	5I	Avge
T. J. Murtagh	RFM	444.1	113	1,224	60	6-49	3	20.40
N. J. Dexter	RM	163.2	33	415	18	5-27	1	23.05
O. P. Rayner.	OB	356.1	74	958	41	4-36	0	23.36
C. D. Collymore.	RFM	229.2	49	613	25	4-61	0	24.52
S. T. Finn	RF	160.5	38	503	17	4-46	0	29.58
T. S. Roland-Jones	RFM	219.2	39	694	21	6-63	1	33.04
G. K. Berg	RFM	324.4	71	942	25	3-49	0	37.68
J. A. R. Harris.	RFM	227.4	31	805	21	3-46	0	38.33

Also bowled: J. L. Denly (LBG) 28.4–3–96–2; T. G. Helm (RFM) 18–0–78–5; A. B. London (OB) 1–0–5–0; D. J. Malan (LBG) 15.5–0–58–0; R. H. Patel (SLA) 110–24–321–8; G. S. Sandhu (LFM) 28–5–115–2; T. M. J. Smith (SLA) 22–0–71–1; P. R. Stirling (OB) 18–2–47–2; A. C. Voges (SLC) 9–1–16–1.

LEADING YB40 AVERAGES (100 runs/4 wickets)

Batting

	Runs	HS	Avge	SR	Ct/St
J. A. Simpson . .	149	58*	74.50	120.16	3/1
D. J. Malan	552	113*	69.00	91.84	4
A. M. Rossington	139	79*	46.33	96.52	7/1
J. L. Denly	365	99*	40.55	91.70	5
N. J. Dexter. . . .	215	54	35.83	90.33	7
P. R. Stirling . . .	334	132*	33.40	115.57	9
G. K. Berg.	155	75	25.83	105.44	3
E. J. G. Morgan	124	90	24.80	98.41	7

Bowling

	W	BB	Avge	ER
R. H. Patel	4	2-41	22.50	6.42
T. S. Roland-Jones	18	4-44	22.88	5.92
J. A. R. Harris . . .	15	3-30	24.93	6.35
S. T. Finn	5	2-32	26.40	4.55
P. R. Stirling	4	2-18	29.75	5.95
O. P. Rayner	6	3-31	32.33	4.31
T. J. Murtagh	7	3-35	33.28	5.68
G. K. Berg	5	2-38	48.80	5.50

LEADING FLt20 AVERAGES (100 runs/18 overs)

Batting	Runs	HS	Avge	SR	Ct/St		Bowling	W	BB	Avge	ER
A. M. Rossington	182	74	26.00	155.55	8/3		A. C. Voges	7	2-21	17.00	6.61
N. J. Dexter	108	40	21.60	142.10	5		R. H. Patel	10	4-18	18.60	6.64
P. R. Stirling	118	33	14.75	129.67	2		O. P. Rayner	5	2-24	35.40	7.37
J. L. Denly	261	67	37.28	125.48	2		N. J. Dexter	5	2-18	37.40	8.13
D. J. Malan	351	86	39.00	118.98	5		K. D. Mills	11	3-4	26.45	8.55
							G. K. Berg	8	3-19	31.12	8.58

FIRST-CLASS COUNTY RECORDS

Highest score for	331*	J. D. B. Robertson v Worcestershire at Worcester	1949
Highest score against	341	C. M. Spearman (Gloucestershire) at Gloucester	2004
Leading run-scorer	40,302	E. H. Hendren (avge 48.81)	1907–37
Best bowling for	10-40	G. O. B. Allen v Lancashire at Lord's	1929
Best bowling against	9-38	R. C. Robertson-Glasgow (Somerset) at Lord's	1924
Leading wicket-taker	2,361	F. J. Titmus (avge 21.27)	1949–82
Highest total for	642-3 dec	v Hampshire at Southampton	1923
Highest total against	850-7 dec	by Somerset at Taunton	2007
Lowest total for	20	v MCC at Lord's	1864
Lowest total against {	31	by Gloucestershire at Bristol	1924
	31	by Glamorgan at Cardiff	1997

LIST A COUNTY RECORDS

Highest score for	163	A. J. Strauss v Surrey at The Oval	2008
Highest score against	163	C. J. Adams (Sussex) at Arundel	1999
Leading run-scorer	12,029	M. W. Gatting (avge 34.96)	1975–98
Best bowling for	7-12	W. W. Daniel v Minor Counties East at Ipswich	1978
Best bowling against	6-27	J. C. Tredwell (Kent) at Southgate	2009
Leading wicket-taker	491	J. E. Emburey (avge 24.68)	1975–95
Highest total for	350-6	v Lancashire at Lord's	2012
Highest total against	353-8	by Hampshire at Lord's	2005
Lowest total for	23	v Yorkshire at Leeds	1974
Lowest total against	41	by Northamptonshire at Northampton	1972

TWENTY20 COUNTY RECORDS

Highest score for	106	A. C. Gilchrist v Kent at Canterbury	2010
Highest score against	119	K. J. O'Brien (Gloucestershire) at Uxbridge	2011
Leading run-scorer	**1,568**	**D. J. Malan** (avge 32.00)	**2006–13**
Best bowling for	5-13	M. Kartik v Essex at Lord's	2007
Best bowling against	6-24	T. J. Murtagh (Surrey) at Lord's	2005
Leading wicket-taker {	46	T. Henderson (avge 23.69)	2007–10
	46	**T. J. Murtagh** (avge 30.47)	**2007–13**
Highest total for	213-4	v Glamorgan at Richmond	2010
Highest total against	254-3	by Gloucestershire at Uxbridge	2011
Lowest total for	**92**	**v Surrey at Lord's**	**2013**
Lowest total against	**74**	by Essex at Chelmsford	**2013**

ADDRESS

Lord's Cricket Ground, London NW8 8QN (020 7289 1300; **email** enquiries@middlesexccc.com).
Website www.middlesexccc.com

OFFICIALS

Captain (Championship) C. J. L. Rogers
(limited-overs) E. J. G. Morgan
Managing director of cricket A. R. C. Fraser
Head coach R. J. Scott
Academy director A. J. Coleman

President C. T. Radley
Chairman I. N. Lovett
Secretary/chief executive V. J. Codrington
Head groundsman M. J. Hunt
Scorer D. K. Shelley

At Nottingham, April 10–13. MIDDLESEX beat NOTTINGHAMSHIRE by ten wickets.

MIDDLESEX v DERBYSHIRE

At Lord's, April 17–19. Middlesex won by nine wickets. Middlesex 20pts, Derbyshire 4pts. Toss: Middlesex.

This match was decided on the third afternoon, when Derbyshire – looking to build on a slender first-innings lead – encountered Murtagh at his aggressive and accurate best. His spell either side of lunch brought him five for 12 and, with Finn removing Madsen, Derbyshire were floundering at 26 for six. Roland-Jones polished off the innings with a hat-trick – his first in any cricket, he said, since the age of 12. Middlesex wrapped things up with more than a day to spare to take sole possession of first place. In contrast to the hustle and bustle of the third day, the first two had been relatively mundane. Derbyshire scored at barely two an over after being put in: Godleman seemed particularly anxious to occupy the crease against his former county. His half-century came in 244 balls, the slowest recorded in Championship history, beating Arun Harinath's 233 for Surrey at Hove in 2010. In all, he batted for nearly six hours, faced 265 deliveries and hit only one four. Middlesex were not much quicker, and looked set for a big deficit until Berg and Rayner put on 61 for the seventh wicket.

Close of play: first day, Derbyshire 205-9 (Groenewald 16, Turner 7); second day, Middlesex 180-6 (Berg 27, Rayner 16).

Derbyshire

B. A. Godleman lbw b Murtagh	55	– (2) lbw b Murtagh	3
*W. L. Madsen run out	0	– (1) c Simpson b Finn	15
W. J. Durston c Roland-Jones b Finn	48	– lbw b Murtagh	1
S. Chanderpaul c Denly b Berg	18	– not out	18
D. J. Redfern c Simpson b Finn	15	– lbw b Murtagh	4
C. F. Hughes c Simpson b Finn	4	– b Murtagh	0
J. L. Clare lbw b Finn	6	– c Rayner b Murtagh	0
†T. Poynton c Simpson b Roland-Jones	16	– c Simpson b Finn	10
A. P. Palladino run out	0	– c Simpson b Roland-Jones	2
T. D. Groenewald c Simpson b Murtagh	25	– c Malan b Roland-Jones	0
M. L. Turner not out	22	– b Roland-Jones	0
B 4, l-b 5, w 3, n-b 10	22	L-b 7	7

1/3 (2) 2/86 (3) 3/118 (4)   (104.5 overs) 231 1/3 (2) 2/7 (3) 3/19 (1)   (35 overs) 60
4/136 (5) 5/142 (6) 6/150 (7)   4/26 (5) 5/26 (6) 6/26 (7)
7/180 (8) 8/181 (9) 9/181 (1) 10/231 (10)   7/57 (8) 8/60 (9) 9/60 (10) 10/60 (11)

Murtagh 28.5–5–68–2; Finn 26–10–51–4; Roland-Jones 18–6–47–1; Dexter 11–5–11–0; Berg 11–5–13–1; Rayner 10–2–32–0. *Second innings*—Murtagh 12–7–12–5; Finn 12–4–34–2; Berg 5–3–3–0; Roland-Jones 6–4–4–3.

Middlesex

*C. J. L. Rogers lbw b Groenewald	16	– not out	28
S. D. Robson c Durston b Clare	68	– b Palladino	0
J. L. Denly c Durston b Clare	34	– not out	44
D. J. Malan c Poynton b Turner	4		
N. J. Dexter b Palladino	1		
†J. A. Simpson c Redfern b Durston	12		
G. K. Berg not out	42		
O. P. Rayner lbw b Turner	26		
T. S. Roland-Jones b Turner	5		
T. J. Murtagh c Godleman b Clare	1		
S. T. Finn lbw b Clare	0		
L-b 6	6	B 5, l-b 1, n-b 2	8

1/21 (1) 2/72 (3) 3/81 (4)   (77.4 overs) 215 1/4 (2)   (1 wkt, 21.4 overs) 80
4/90 (5) 5/136 (2) 6/140 (6)
7/201 (8) 8/211 (9) 9/215 (10) 10/215 (11)

Palladino 15–1–66–1; Groenewald 15–6–23–1; Clare 12.4–1–40–4; Turner 19–1–51–3; Durston 16–2–29–1. *Second innings*—Groenewald 6–2–16–0; Palladino 6–2–15–1; Turner 4–1–18–0; Clare 4.4–0–24–0; Durston 1–0–1–0.

Umpires: M. R. Benson and P. J. Hartley.

At Cambridge, April 24–26. MIDDLESEX beat CAMBRIDGE MCCU by 234 runs.

MIDDLESEX v SURREY

At Lord's, May 2–5. Drawn. Middlesex 4pts, Surrey 9pts. Toss: Surrey. Championship debut: P. R. Stirling.

Surrey took full advantage of batting first, but might have scored more quickly – their first innings was not completed until 33 overs into the second day. Burns applied himself diligently for 320 minutes, and it seemed to have paid off when Middlesex's batting was found wanting: eight men reached double figures, but the highest score was Robson's 36. They showed much more fortitude in the follow-on, however. As the pitch eased and the bowling lost its menace, they started with an opening stand of 259 – the highest in the fixture, beating the 244 of Jack Hobbs and Andy Sandham for Surrey at The Oval in 1923. Rogers, named the previous week in Australia's Ashes squad at the age of 35, went on to complete his ninth double-century (but first for Middlesex) speeding to 200 on the final morning with 69 from 53 balls after having 131 from 240 overnight. The comeback meant Rogers was disinclined to give Surrey a sniff of victory, although he did eventually declare after Dexter hoisted Solanki for three sixes in an over. The match ended with part-timers Stirling and Malan trying to boost Middlesex's over-rate. Stirling, the Ireland international, had earlier managed only one run in his first Championship match.

Close of play: first day, Surrey 267-4 (de Bruyn 12, Davies 24); second day, Middlesex 161-9 (Murtagh 17, Collymore 0); third day, Middlesex 283-2 (Rogers 131, Finn 4).

Surrey

R. J. Burns b Murtagh	114	– c Simpson b Murtagh	17
*G. C. Smith c Malan b Murtagh	0	– not out	48
A. Harinath c Simpson b Finn	61	– not out	20
V. S. Solanki c Simpson b Collymore	43		
Z. de Bruyn c Simpson b Roland-Jones	34		
†S. M. Davies lbw b Murtagh	24		
G. C. Wilson not out	30		
G. J. Batty c Rogers b Stirling	4		
C. T. Tremlett c Simpson b Collymore	4		
T. E. Linley lbw b Collymore	1		
J. W. Dernbach c Rogers b Stirling	0		
B 1, l-b 9, w 5, n-b 8	23		

1/5 (2) 2/152 (3) 3/216 (4) (129 overs) 338 1/32 (1) (1 wkt, 25 overs) 85
4/234 (1) 5/274 (6) 6/311 (5) 7/320 (8)
8/333 (9) 9/337 (10) 10/338 (11) 110 overs: 301-5

Murtagh 26–11–54–3; Finn 25–7–69–1; Collymore 23–3–72–3; Roland-Jones 25–2–62–1; Dexter 13–3–27–0; Stirling 16–1–43–2; Malan 1–0–1–0. *Second innings*—Murtagh 7–1–26–1; Finn 9–2–33–0; Roland-Jones 4–0–17–0; Collymore 1–0–1–0; Stirling 2–1–4–0; Malan 2–0–4–0.

Middlesex

*C. J. L. Rogers b de Bruyn	21	– b Batty	214
S. D. Robson c Davies b de Bruyn	36	– c Davies b de Bruyn	129
J. L. Denly lbw b Dernbach	21	– c Solanki b Dernbach	12
D. J. Malan lbw b Batty	13	– (5) c Smith b Tremlett	47
N. J. Dexter c Solanki b Dernbach	16	– (7) c Linley b Burns	59
†J. A. Simpson c Linley b Batty	17	– (8) not out	30
P. R. Stirling lbw b Dernbach	0	– (6) c Solanki b Tremlett	1
T. S. Roland-Jones c and b Tremlett	17	– (9) c Burns b Harinath	2
T. J. Murtagh not out	21	– (10) not out	0
S. T. Finn lbw b Linley	3	– (4) c Solanki b Dernbach	8
C. D. Collymore lbw b de Bruyn	1		
		B 2, l-b 5, w 1, n-b 4	12

1/28 (1) 2/72 (3) 3/90 (4)   (66.2 overs) 166
4/92 (2) 5/121 (5) 6/121 (7)
7/137 (6) 8/141 (8) 9/161 (10) 10/166 (11)

1/259 (2)   (8 wkts dec, 131 overs) 514
2/279 (3) 3/287 (4)
4/417 (1) 5/417 (5)
6/420 (6) 7/510 (7) 8/513 (9)

Dernbach 15–4–59–3; Tremlett 12–4–26–1; de Bruyn 9.2–2–32–3; Linley 15–5–26–1; Batty 15–5–23–2. *Second innings*—Dernbach 26–3–83–2; Linley 24–2–110–0; Tremlett 22–1–96–2; de Bruyn 19–4–73–1; Batty 33–5–91–1; Burns 3–0–18–1; Solanki 3–0–34–0; Harinath 1–0–2–1.

Umpires: M. A. Gough and D. J. Millns.

At Birmingham, May 8–11. MIDDLESEX drew with WARWICKSHIRE.

At Taunton, May 15–17. MIDDLESEX beat SOMERSET by nine wickets.

At Chester-le-Street, May 22–25. MIDDLESEX drew with DURHAM.

MIDDLESEX v SUSSEX

At Lord's, June 5–8. Drawn. Middlesex 10pts, Sussex 5pts. Toss: Sussex.

Dropped catches cost Middlesex the match, although it was one that was taken which captured the attention. On the second afternoon the sprawling Robson claimed a catch at silly point, but Prior was convinced the ball had bounced. After a consultation, Prior was eventually given his marching orders – but continued to remonstrate. Surprisingly, the umpires did not report him, saying they saw nothing wrong. Middlesex had been given an ideal start by Rogers, who compiled his 60th first-class hundred and shared a fourth century opening stand of the season with Robson, and then added 155 with Dexter. His fielders let him down, and the most crucial of those drops came when Murtagh reprieved Wright at deep square leg late on the third day. Had it been held, Sussex would have been five down and still 65 short of making Middlesex bat again. Instead, Wright – 40 at the time – carried on to a career-best 187, and put on 159 for the fifth wicket with Joyce, who fell in the nineties for the third time in the season. Wright then shared another hundred partnership, with Beer, and Middlesex were eventually left to bat out time. Rayner had earlier taken his first five-wicket haul for Middlesex – and his first since 2008, when he was playing for Sussex – but he had less success in the second innings.

Close of play: first day, Middlesex 320-3 (Rogers 161, Dexter 62); second day, Sussex 147-7 (Wright 38, Beer 6); third day, Sussex 228-4 (Joyce 75, Wright 48).

Middlesex

*C. J. L. Rogers c Yardy b Magoffin	184	– not out	27
S. D. Robson lbw b Beer	54		
J. L. Denly b Beer	11	– (2) c Brown b Liddle	14
A. B. London lbw b Nash	18		
N. J. Dexter c Jordan b Beer	104	– (3) c Brown b Magoffin	4
†J. A. Simpson c Joyce b Wright	50		
G. K. Berg c Wells b Wright	39	– (4) lbw b Liddle	5
O. P. Rayner c Brown b Liddle	5		
J. A. R. Harris not out	3		
T. S. Roland-Jones not out	12		
B 3, l-b 5, w 1, n-b 10	19		

1/100 (2) 2/152 (3)   (8 wkts dec, 139 overs) 499   1/24 (2) 2/39 (3)   (3 wkts, 8 overs)   50
3/197 (4) 4/352 (1) 5/420 (5)   3/50 (4)
6/466 (6) 7/483 (8) 8/485 (7)   110 overs: 372-4

T. J. Murtagh did not bat.

Magoffin 22–4–73–1; Jordan 26–6–81–0; Wright 12–2–49–2; Liddle 21–4–74–1; Beer 30–3–89–3; Nash 20–0–89–1; Wells 7–1–30–0; Yardy 1–0–6–0. *Second innings*—Magoffin 4–0–26–1; Liddle 4–0–24–2.

Sussex

C. D. Nash c Robson b Murtagh	13	– (2) run out	36
L. W. P. Wells c Berg b Roland-Jones	19	– (1) lbw b Murtagh	0
M. H. Yardy lbw b Harris	22	– c Rogers b Harris	41
*E. C. Joyce st Simpson b Rayner	20	– c Rayner b Murtagh	98
M. J. Prior c Robson b Rayner	10	– c Murtagh b Harris	18
L. J. Wright c and b Rayner	77	– st Simpson b Denly	187
†B. C. Brown c and b Rayner	11	– c London b Harris	3
C. J. Jordan lbw b Harris	0	– c Simpson b Murtagh	3
W. A. T. Beer c Simpson b Dexter	25	– c Berg b Rayner	39
S. J. Magoffin lbw b Rayner	10	– c Murtagh b Denly	7
C. J. Liddle not out	7	– not out	3
N-b 8	8	B 3, l-b 8, n-b 8	19

1/18 (1) 2/47 (2) 3/68 (4)   (83.2 overs) 222   1/0 (1) 2/67 (2)   (137 overs) 454
4/88 (3) 5/92 (5) 6/108 (7)   3/85 (3) 4/123 (5)
7/117 (8) 8/205 (9) 9/205 (6) 10/222 (10)   5/282 (4) 6/297 (7) 7/304 (8)
                                       8/405 (9) 9/451 (6) 10/454 (10)

Murtagh 17–1–54–1; Harris 16–4–34–2; Berg 3–0–9–0; Roland-Jones 13–3–43–1; Rayner 28.2–5–63–5; London 1–0–5–0; Denly 1–0–1–0; Dexter 4–1–13–1. *Second innings*—Murtagh 26–6–74–3; Roland-Jones 19–1–68–0; Harris 29–2–112–3; Rayner 42–10–118–1; Berg 8–0–23–0; Denly 11–2–47–2; Dexter 2–1–1–0.

Umpires: M. J. Saggers and A. G. Wharf.

MIDDLESEX v YORKSHIRE

At Lord's, June 11–14. Yorkshire won by ten wickets. Yorkshire 22pts, Middlesex 2pts. Toss: Yorkshire.

Yorkshire were without three players on England duty and three others injured, but stayed on top throughout, to beat Middlesex for the first time since 1987. They were helped – as Sussex had been the previous week – by sloppy catching. Middlesex had left out their best slip fielder, Dawid Malan, to give London another opportunity with the bat, a move which did little for the runs column and weakened the close catching. Dexter missed two chances at slip, and eventually found himself in the covers. The promising Lees maintained his concentration well on the first day despite five weather interruptions, completing a maiden Championship century – in only his third match – just before the close. Gale also reached three figures next day, his second successive hundred, and a forthright 72 from Rashid enabled Yorkshire to amass 390. Middlesex were soon up against it, slipping to 19 for two on the third morning. Only Berg made it past the twenties and, 215 to the good, Gale had no hesitation in putting them in again. During the follow-on against Surrey, Rogers had scored a double-century, but now he fell for a duck. And although the others showed more application second time round, Rashid worked his way through the order.

Close of play: first day, Yorkshire 215-2 (Lees 100, Gale 61); second day, Middlesex 16-1 (Rogers 6, Denly 0); third day, Middlesex 137-4 (Dexter 25, Simpson 20).

Yorkshire

A. Lyth c Dexter b Murtagh	11	– not out	4
A. Z. Lees c Simpson b Harris	100	– not out	0
P. A. Jaques c Simpson b Berg	20		
*A. W. Gale lbw b Rayner	103		
J. J. Sayers lbw b Murtagh	1		
A. U. Rashid lbw b Harris	72		
†A. J. Hodd c and b Murtagh	13		
R. M. Pyrah c Robson b Harris	1		
L. E. Plunkett lbw b Rayner	26		
R. J. Sidebottom st Simpson b Rayner	9		
S. A. Patterson not out	2		
B 2, l-b 19, w 1, n-b 10	32	L-b 3	3

1/32 (1) 2/70 (3) 3/215 (2)   (128.1 overs) 390   (no wkt, 3.4 overs) 7
4/220 (5) 5/329 (4) 6/343 (6) 7/345 (8)
8/361 (7) 9/387 (10) 10/390 (9)   110 overs: 345-7

Murtagh 32.3–3–93–3; Collymore 19–6–51–0; Berg 28–5–103–1; Harris 14.3–3–48–3; Dexter 9–2–23–0; Rayner 22.1–4–44–3; Denly 3–0–7–0. *Second innings*—Rayner 2–2–0–0; Denly 1.4–1–4–0.

Middlesex

*C. J. L. Rogers c Hodd b Plunkett	27	– c Hodd b Sidebottom	0
S. D. Robson c Lyth b Patterson	5	– b Rashid	46
J. L. Denly c Sayers b Sidebottom	2	– st Hodd b Rashid	31
A. B. London c Sayers b Plunkett	28	– lbw b Rashid	3
N. J. Dexter lbw b Patterson	11	– b Sidebottom	36
†J. A. Simpson b Plunkett	9	– c Pyrah b Patterson	21
G. K. Berg lbw b Patterson	54	– c Pyrah b Rashid	38
O. P. Rayner lbw b Plunkett	1	– lbw b Plunkett	0
J. A. R. Harris lbw b Sidebottom	5	– lbw b Patterson	14
T. J. Murtagh not out	18	– not out	3
C. D. Collymore c Hodd b Patterson	1	– c and b Rashid	5
B 1, l-b 11, n-b 2	14	B 9, l-b 13	22

1/12 (2) 2/19 (3) 3/46 (1)   (55.2 overs) 175   1/0 (1) 2/69 (3)   (71.4 overs) 219
4/59 (5) 5/84 (6) 6/105 (4)   3/90 (2) 4/93 (4)
7/113 (8) 8/141 (9) 9/169 (7) 10/175 (11)   5/143 (6) 6/155 (5) 7/167 (8)
    8/209 (9) 9/209 (7) 10/219 (11)

Sidebottom 15–4–48–2; Patterson 17.2–5–39–4; Plunkett 15–1–50–4; Pyrah 8–1–26–0. *Second innings*—Sidebottom 11–5–17–2; Patterson 16–6–40–2; Plunkett 13–2–46–1; Rashid 24.4–3–78–5; Pyrah 6–1–15–0; Lyth 1–0–1–0.

Umpires: T. E. Jesty and D. J. Millns.

Middlesex v Yorkshire was the final Championship report filed by Norman de Mesquita in his 21st season as *Wisden's* Middlesex correspondent. He died on July 25. For his obituary, see page 194.

MIDDLESEX v WARWICKSHIRE

At Uxbridge, July 8–11. Warwickshire won by five wickets. Warwickshire 22pts, Middlesex 4pts. Toss: Warwickshire.

Middlesex paid dearly for dropping Chopra twice in the slips before he had scored: he went on to a fine double-century – his fourth, and the highest score at Uxbridge – as the 2012 champions amassed a big total on a benign pitch to set up only their second win of the season. Chopra, standing in as captain because Jim Troughton had back trouble, survived for 569 minutes, and shared century stands with Westwood, Evans and Ambrose, who made a perky 60. Middlesex were soon reduced to 28 for four, the first three all caught by Patel at third slip. However, a stand of 180 between Voges – originally signed only for the Twenty20 interlude, but kept on after Chris Rogers's selection for Australia's Ashes squad – and Simpson staved off embarrassment. But Middlesex still had to follow on and, although nine men reached double figures, only Voges passed 37. Warwickshire's target of 110 was trickier than it looked on a pitch now taking spin, but another determined innings from Ambrose all but settled matters.

Close of play: first day, Warwickshire 269-2 (Chopra 141, Javid 16); second day, Middlesex 177-4 (Voges 81, Simpson 50); third day, Middlesex 147-5 (Voges 15, Roland-Jones 1).

Warwickshire

*V. Chopra not out	228	– c Malan b Rayner	2
I. J. Westwood c Malan b Roland-Jones	65	– c Voges b Collymore	6
L. J. Evans c Simpson b Dexter	37	– c Dexter b Rayner	0
A. Javid c Simpson b Collymore	22	– c Simpson b Berg	19
†T. R. Ambrose c Malan b Rayner	60	– c Robson b Patel	47
C. R. Woakes c and b Rayner	34	– not out	20
R. Clarke c Voges b Collymore	22	– not out	12
K. H. D. Barker not out	6		
B 2, l-b 8, n-b 2	12	L-b 3, n-b 2	5

1/113 (2) 2/226 (3)   (6 wkts dec, 150 overs) 486   1/5 (1)   (5 wkts, 40.5 overs) 111
3/281 (4) 4/381 (5)   2/5 (3) 3/21 (2)
5/447 (6) 6/478 (7)   110 overs: 319-3   4/54 (4) 5/98 (5)

J. S. Patel, C. J. C. Wright and W. B. Rankin did not bat.

Collymore 22–1–63–2; Roland-Jones 19–3–61–1; Berg 29–6–105–0; Patel 42–8–119–0; Dexter 11–2–22–1; Rayner 23–1–96–2; Malan 1–0–4–0; Voges 3–0–6–0. *Second innings*—Collymore 10–3–28–1; Rayner 18–8–33–2; Berg 7–0–23–1; Patel 4–0–10–1; Malan 1.5–0–14–0.

Middlesex

S. D. Robson c Patel b Wright	16	– c Clarke b Rankin	29
D. J. Malan c Patel b Barker	2	– b Woakes	3
J. L. Denly c Patel b Barker	4	– b Barker	37
A. C. Voges c and b Patel	150	– (5) c and b Woakes	51
*N. J. Dexter c Ambrose b Wright	0	– (4) c Ambrose b Barker	36
†J. A. Simpson lbw b Patel	63	– c Ambrose b Rankin	17
G. K. Berg c Ambrose b Barker	12	– (8) c Ambrose b Patel	12
O. P. Rayner c Barker b Patel	10	– (9) c Clarke b Patel	19
T. S. Roland-Jones c Chopra b Barker	0	– (7) c Chopra b Patel	16
R. H. Patel not out	26	– c Ambrose b Woakes	19
C. D. Collymore c Javid b Patel	5	– not out	6
B 7, l-b 12, n-b 14	33	B 18, l-b 13, n-b 10	41

1/24 (2) 2/28 (3) 3/28 (1)   (82.4 overs) 309   1/13 (2) 2/37 (1)   (84.2 overs) 286
4/28 (5) 5/208 (6) 6/209 (7)   3/105 (4) 4/110 (3)
7/224 (8) 8/227 (9) 9/299 (4) 10/309 (11)   5/146 (6) 6/187 (7) 7/211 (8)
                                      8/237 (5) 9/253 (9) 10/286 (10)

Wright 7–0–39–2; Barker 15–4–47–4; Woakes 7–1–27–0; Clarke 10–3–22–0; Patel 30.4–2–119–4; Rankin 13–0–36–0. *Second innings*—Woakes 12.2–2–27–3; Barker 15–3–50–2; Clarke 6–3–5–0; Patel 33–6–111–3; Rankin 16–0–55–2; Javid 2–0–7–0.

Umpires: M. A. Eggleston and G. Sharp.

At Hove, July 17–20. MIDDLESEX beat SUSSEX by ten wickets.

MIDDLESEX v DURHAM

At Lord's, August 2–4. Middlesex won by six wickets. Middlesex 19pts, Durham 3pts. Toss: Middlesex.

Middlesex reignited their Championship hopes – and dented Durham's – with a hard-earned victory in a low-scoring match full of scrappy batting. There were 32 wickets on the first two days, and it was all over in an hour on the third. But no pitch inspector was summoned; instead it was the batting coaches who looked perturbed. The tone for a careless performance was set when Stoneman fell to the second ball of the match. Four wickets went to Finn, who had recently lost his England place. Middlesex's batsmen were equally reckless, managing a lead of only 25 in the face of some fine bowling from Onions, another seamer unwanted by England: he wrapped up the innings with five wickets in 20 balls to finish with seven for 62. Murtagh again removed Stoneman in the first over and, although Stokes dug in for 51, the eventual target was hardly imposing. Onions struck twice more, but Morgan – in his first first-class match for almost a year – denied him a repeat of his ten-wicket haul in this fixture in 2012, knuckling down for more than two hours to make sure of victory.

Close of play: first day, Middlesex 126-5 (Dexter 40, Berg 28); second day, Middlesex 103-2 (Voges 36, Morgan 24).

Durham

M. D. Stoneman c Simpson b Murtagh	2	– lbw b Murtagh	0
K. K. Jennings c Simpson b Murtagh	3	– c Robson b Finn	2
S. G. Borthwick c Simpson b Collymore	4	– b Murtagh	26
W. R. Smith c Rayner b Berg	24	– c Finn b Murtagh	30
B. A. Stokes c Robson b Finn	21	– st Simpson b Rayner	51
*P. D. Collingwood c and b Finn	30	– b Collymore	0
†P. Mustard c Simpson b Berg	14	– not out	30
M. J. Richardson c Simpson b Collymore	9	– c Voges b Rayner	0
C. D. Thorp not out	18	– b Finn	23
G. Onions lbw b Finn	4	– b Finn	0
C. Rushworth c Murtagh b Finn	5	– c Robson b Rayner	2
L-b 7, n-b 2	9	B 1, l-b 3, w 1, n-b 2	7

1/2 (1) 2/9 (3) 3/13 (2) (49.5 overs) 143
4/38 (5) 5/73 (4) 6/93 (7)
7/112 (6) 8/116 (9) 9/135 (10) 10/143 (11)

1/0 (1) 2/10 (2) (54.5 overs) 171
3/32 (3) 4/97 (4)
5/98 (6) 6/129 (5) 7/129 (8)
8/168 (9) 9/168 (10) 10/171 (11)

Murtagh 14–3–38–2; Collymore 10–0–30–2; Finn 13.5–2–46–4; Berg 10–2–13–2; Dexter 2–0–9–0. *Second innings*—Murtagh 12–3–32–3; Finn 17–4–56–3; Collymore 9–4–21–1; Berg 7–1–21–0; Dexter 4–1–12–0; Rayner 5.5–2–25–3.

Middlesex

S. D. Robson b Rushworth		1 – c Richardson b Rushworth	6
J. L. Denly c Borthwick b Onions	0	– c Stokes b Onions	32
A. C. Voges c Stokes b Onions	9	– c Mustard b Onions	36
E. J. G. Morgan lbw b Stokes	20	– not out	39
*N. J. Dexter c Mustard b Onions	48	– b Smith b Stokes	25
†J. A. Simpson c Stoneman b Borthwick	20	– not out	1
G. K. Berg c Mustard b Onions	35		
O. P. Rayner c Mustard b Onions	6		
T. J. Murtagh c Mustard b Onions	11		
S. T. Finn c Richardson b Onions	4		
C. D. Collymore not out	4		
L-b 4, w 2, n-b 4	10	L-b 4, n-b 4	8

1/1 (2) 2/1 (1) 3/15 (3) (56.2 overs) 168
4/46 (4) 5/88 (6) 6/136 (5)
7/142 (8) 8/149 (7) 9/161 (10) 10/168 (9)

1/23 (1) (4 wkts, 40.4 overs) 147
2/41 (2) 3/106 (3)
4/146 (5)

Onions 19.2–4–62–7; Rushworth 16–5–45–1; Thorp 7–3–15–0; Stokes 10–3–28–1; Borthwick 4–1–14–1. *Second innings*—Onions 13–3–40–2; Rushworth 13–0–43–1; Thorp 5–1–15–0; Stokes 6.4–0–29–1; Borthwick 3–0–16–0.

Umpires: R. K. Illingworth and S. J. O'Shaughnessy.

At Derby, August 20–23. MIDDLESEX lost to DERBYSHIRE by 56 runs.

MIDDLESEX v SOMERSET

At Lord's, August 28–30. Somerset won by an innings and 179 runs. Somerset 23pts, Middlesex 2pts. Toss: Somerset.

Somerset's biggest victory at Lord's – and their first since 1983 and the glory days of Botham and Richards – boosted their hopes of survival and all but extinguished Middlesex's title ambitions. The match looked evenly balanced when Somerset stumbled to 211 for seven just after tea on the first day, but the complexion was changed by an onslaught from Chawla, the Indian leg-spinner, who biffed a dozen fours and four sixes – one of which, off Patel, brought up a century in only his third innings for the club. He put on 107 with the determined Barrow, and 99 with Thomas as the total rose to 449 – which soon looked huge when Middlesex collapsed to 55 for seven. Chawla ended a brief recovery with three wickets in six balls, and the follow-on was not much better. The main damage this time was done by the promising Gregory, who took a maiden five-for to complete match figures of seven for 52. It was all over shortly after lunch on the third day.

Close of play: first day, Somerset 332-8 (Chawla 58, Thomas 9); second day, Middlesex 52-2 (Robson 26, Malan 9).

Somerset

*M. E. Trescothick lbw b Murtagh	64	A. C. Thomas not out	54
N. R. D. Compton c Robson b Dexter	31	J. Overton lbw b Patel	18
C. R. Jones c Simpson b Dexter	58		
J. C. Hildreth c Simpson b Dexter	7	B 1, l-b 2, n-b 4	7
†C. Kieswetter b Patel	31		
A. W. R. Barrow lbw b Berg	65	1/79 (2) 2/116 (1) (136 overs) 449
C. A. J. Meschede st Simpson b Patel	0	3/139 (4) 4/178 (3) 5/206 (5)
L. Gregory c Robson b Rayner	2	6/206 (7) 7/211 (8) 8/318 (6)
P. P. Chawla c Rayner b Patel	112	9/417 (9) 10/449 (11) 110 overs: 356-8

Murtagh 26–8–68–1; Harris 25–5–79–0; Berg 22–6–71–1; Rayner 21–1–77–1; Dexter 19–3–57–3; Patel 21–4–89–4; Malan 2–0–5–0.

Middlesex

*C. J. L. Rogers c Compton b Overton	8	– lbw b Gregory	2
S. D. Robson c Kieswetter b Meschede	6	– c Trescothick b Gregory	29
J. L. Denly c Meschede b Gregory	8	– c Trescothick b Meschede	13
D. J. Malan c Kieswetter b Meschede	12	– c Trescothick b Meschede	33
N. J. Dexter b Meschede	0	– not out	35
†J. A. Simpson c Compton b Gregory	2	– run out	9
G. K. Berg lbw b Thomas	9	– b Overton	0
O. P. Rayner not out	34	– c Trescothick b Thomas	1
J. A. R. Harris lbw b Chawla	12	– c and b Gregory	22
T. J. Murtagh b Chawla	0	– c Trescothick b Gregory	7
R. H. Patel c Kieswetter b Chawla	0	– b Gregory	0
B 3, n-b 12	15	B 4, l-b 1, n-b 8	13

1/11 (1) 2/28 (3) 3/36 (2)   (37.5 overs) 106   1/4 (1) 2/19 (3)   (51 overs) 164
4/36 (5) 5/39 (6) 6/47 (4)   3/69 (2) 4/85 (4)
7/55 (7) 8/104 (9) 9/106 (10) 10/106 (11)   5/100 (6) 6/101 (7) 7/116 (8)
   8/156 (9) 9/164 (10) 10/164 (11)

Gregory 7–1–14–2; Overton 8–0–36–1; Meschede 9–1–25–3; Thomas 9–6–20–1; Chawla 4.5–1–8–3. *Second innings*—Gregory 16–4–38–5; Overton 7–0–35–1; Meschede 11–3–41–2; Thomas 10–6–22–1; Chawla 7–1–23–0.

Umpires: J. H. Evans and I. J. Gould.

At The Oval, September 3–5. MIDDLESEX beat SURREY by 146 runs. *Ollie Rayner is involved in 18 of the 20 Surrey wickets.*

MIDDLESEX v NOTTINGHAMSHIRE

At Lord's, September 11–14. Drawn. Middlesex 8pts, Nottinghamshire 9pts. Toss: Middlesex.
Rain, which shortened the first and last days and washed out the third, turned this into a scramble for bonus points. Nottinghamshire were more inconvenienced by the frequent interruptions than the bowling, and ran up 430 before declaring on the second afternoon. Mullaney, in his first appearance at Lord's, batted nearly six hours for 125, then some late impetus was supplied by Hussey and Adams, who smacked eight sixes between them. Middlesex's reply was also a stop-go affair, much of the go being provided by Rogers, who cast off his defensive reputation to score 108 – his fourth first-class hundred of the summer – in an opening stand of 151 with Robson. His 41 in almost three hours was his first score above 29 in ten innings.
Close of play: first day, Nottinghamshire 161-2 (Mullaney 88, Taylor 0); second day, Middlesex 96-0 (Rogers 67, Robson 28); third day, no play.

Nottinghamshire

S. J. Mullaney c Dexter b Berg	125	*†C. M. W. Read not out		27
M. H. Wessels c Robson b Dexter	14	B 1, l-b 5, w 1		7
M. J. Lumb c Dexter b Rayner	54			
J. W. A. Taylor lbw b Murtagh	9	1/43 (2)	(7 wkts dec, 129.5 overs)	430
S. R. Patel c Rayner b Harris	47	2/158 (3) 3/193 (4)		
D. J. Hussey c Simpson b Berg	67	4/237 (1) 5/297 (5)		
A. R. Adams c Rogers b Harris	80	6/357 (6) 7/430 (7)	110 overs: 354-5	

P. J. Franks, L. J. Fletcher and H. F. Gurney did not bat.

Murtagh 26–6–80–1; Harris 18.5–1–88–2; Sandhu 13–2–61–0; Dexter 14–2–37–1; Berg 29–9–78–2; Rayner 29–5–80–1.

Middlesex

*C. J. L. Rogers c Fletcher b Adams	108	O. P. Rayner lbw b Adams		9
S. D. Robson c Read b Adams	41	J. A. R. Harris not out		9
J. L. Denly b Gurney	63	B 2, l-b 11, w 1, n-b 8		22
D. J. Malan b Patel	15			
N. J. Dexter c Lumb b Gurney	9	1/151 (1)	(7 wkts dec, 98.1 overs)	353
†J. A. Simpson not out	51	2/152 (2) 3/211 (4)		
G. K. Berg c and b Adams	26	4/245 (3) 5/252 (5) 6/294 (7) 7/314 (8)		

T. J. Murtagh and G. S. Sandhu did not bat.

Fletcher 20–3–75–0; Adams 29.1–8–98–4; Franks 9–1–45–0; Gurney 25–2–81–2; Patel 15–5–41–1.

Umpires: S. A. Garratt and R. T. Robinson.

At Leeds, September 17–20. MIDDLESEX lost to YORKSHIRE by 80 runs.

NORTHAMPTONSHIRE

Never had it so good?

Andrew Radd

At the end of 2012, Northamptonshire followers were locked in a downbeat debate about whether the season just finished had been the worst in living memory. But members who had wondered if it was worth renewing their subs faced a very different quandary 12 months on: where to station themselves to get the best possible view of the open-top bus parade, as players and staff wended their way from the County Ground to Northampton's Guildhall for a celebratory civic reception.

Not since 1949 – the dawn of the club's modern era under Freddie Brown – have Northamptonshire's fortunes been transformed so extraordinarily from one season to the next. Victories over Essex and Surrey in grand manner at Edgbaston secured the Twenty20 title – Northamptonshire's first major trophy in 21 years – and, despite winning only one of their last nine Championship matches, they clinched promotion to end a nine-year stay in the second division. A YB40 semi-final eluded them only, in all probability, because the group game in the Netherlands in May had been rained off.

Much of the credit for sustaining a lengthy campaign on three fronts with limited resources belonged to the personable and quietly determined head coach, David Ripley, who restored a culture of enjoyment. The players' work ethic was possibly stronger under Ripley than under his two immediate predecessors, David Capel and Kepler Wessels, but many of the internal tensions disappeared. Ripley's contribution was recognised at the county's presentation night, where he picked up the clubman award, and the local print media broke with tradition to name him their "player" of the year.

Before a ball was bowled, Ripley and chief executive David Smith – another key figure in the revival – stressed the need for honesty and realism. Memories of how it felt to take the field for Northamptonshire a year earlier were undoubtedly a powerful motivating force. Alex Wakely, the limited-overs captain, said the players were "just absolutely sick of losing".

Ripley and Smith made some of the canniest signings in the county game. Trent Copeland's unyielding accuracy and seam movement were perfect for Division Two pitches in spring: his haul of 36 wickets in seven matches, plus vital runs down the order, helped record four early victories. He was less prolific when he returned during the run-in, but Northamptonshire did not win a Championship match without Copeland in the side. Another Australian, Cameron White proved – in Smith's words, the "cement" in the Twenty20 team – and the thunderous South African hitter Richard Levi made the county's second century in the format.

Steven Crook returned to Northampton after a couple of seasons with Middlesex, and produced telling all-round performances in every format, most

David Rogers, Getty Images

Azharullah

crucially 46 not out off 24 balls to turn around the Twenty20 semi-final. Most surprising of all, though, was the emergence of 29-year-old Pakistani Azharullah, signed almost unnoticed on a one-year deal. He proved one of the most effective white-ball bowlers in the country – undoing batsmen with skid, reverse-swing and a devastating yorker. The holder of a British passport, he went from playing Huddersfield League cricket for Shelley in August 2012 to a national trophy-winner in August 2013.

Championship ever-presents Andrew Hall, David Sales – who failed by 81 to hit a target of 1,000, but was retained on a one-year contract anyway – and James Middlebrook weighed in with vital runs. But the talismanic heart-and-soul of the new Northamptonshire was unquestionably David Willey. He was catapulted to national prominence by his exploits in the Twenty20 final – 60 spectacular runs at the top of the order, followed by a hat-trick to close out the match – and had the priceless knack of making something happen when his side most needed it, whether pummelling Warwickshire for 167 in a must-win YB40 fixture, or picking up an important wicket with not necessarily his best ball of the day. Willey earned England Lions recognition and (even harder, perhaps) raised a grin or two from his father Peter.

Rob Newton, who prospered in 2012, missed most of the season with a serious ankle injury, but his absence gave opportunities to other batsmen, including 21-year-old Rob Keogh from Dunstable, whose maiden first-class three-figure score turned into 221 at Southampton. David Murphy maintained a high standard behind the stumps and joined Kyle Coetzer in the Scotland set-up; the wholehearted Lee Daggett retired to become a physio at Northampton rugby club with the applause from Edgbaston still ringing in his ears. Ben Duckett occasionally sparkled, but met with little sympathy when he was dropped over the winter by England Under-19 for failing fitness tests.

The management didn't attempt to play down the fact that Northamptonshire's two previous promotions, in 2000 and 2003, had been followed by immediate relegation; staying at the top table may prove tougher than getting there. To that end, Northamptonshire signed Essex fast bowler Maurice Chambers, and brought back left-arm spinner Graeme White from Nottinghamshire (following two loan periods in 2013) to address the obvious weakness in spin bowling. Visa restrictions looked set to stymie a return for Copeland and Cameron White, so the club snapped up another Australian with a point to prove, Jackson Bird, for the first half of the season.

Missing from it all will be Martin Lawrence, who chose a high point in Northamptonshire's fortunes to retire after seven years as chairman. He took over in the wake of Wessels's departure, and helped steer the club through tough times with unfailing personal charm.

Championship attendance: 12,296.

NORTHAMPTONSHIRE RESULTS

All first-class matches – Played 16: Won 5, Lost 3, Drawn 8
County Championship matches – Played 16: Won 5, Lost 3, Drawn 8.

LV= County Championship, 2nd in Division 2;
Friends Life t20, winners; Yorkshire Bank 40, 2nd in Group A.

COUNTY CHAMPIONSHIP AVERAGES, BATTING AND FIELDING

Cap		M	I	NO	R	HS	100	50	Avge	Ct/St
2009	A. J. Hall¶	16	21	4	936	130*	3	5	55.05	13
2007	S. D. Peters	10	15	1	735	106	2	5	52.50	4
1999	D. J. Sales	16	23	3	919	255*	3	1	45.95	11
	R. I. Keogh	8	12	2	458	221	1	1	45.80	1
	R. I. Newton	6	8	2	251	81	0	1	41.83	1
2013	S. P. Crook	14	15	3	482	88*	0	5	40.16	3
2013	K. J. Coetzer	10	15	1	527	219	2	1	37.64	3
2011	J. D. Middlebrook	16	21	1	711	109	1	6	35.55	5
	T. A. Copeland§	10	10	3	247	70	0	2	35.28	11
	B. M. Duckett	4	6	1	145	53*	0	1	29.00	4
	D. Murphy	14	14	3	293	81	0	2	26.63	51/4
2013	D. J. Willey†	13	15	1	346	81	0	3	24.71	3
2012	A. G. Wakely	15	21	1	457	88	0	2	22.85	5
	M. N. W. Spriegel	8	12	2	134	76	0	1	13.40	2
	Azharullah	9	10	6	12	8	0	0	3.00	3

Also batted: J. N. Batty (1 match) 12; L. M. Daggett (cap 2013) (3 matches) 1, 11 (1 ct); C. L. White§ (2 matches) 90, 1, 16; G. G. White (1 match) 0, 0.

† *Born in Northamptonshire.* § *Official overseas player.* ¶ *Other non-England-qualified player.*

BOWLING

	Style	O	M	R	W	BB	5I	Avge
T. A. Copeland	RFM	394.4	139	822	45	7-63	4	18.26
D. J. Willey	LFM	361.3	66	1,122	45	5-67	2	24.93
A. J. Hall	RM	325.3	85	937	37	5-30	1	25.32
S. P. Crook	RFM	326	46	1,139	43	4-30	0	26.48
Azharullah	RFM	225.4	51	717	25	4-42	0	28.68
J. D. Middlebrook	OB	249.1	53	775	21	6-78	1	36.90

Also bowled: K. J. Coetzer (RM) 7–1–16–0; L. M. Daggett (RFM) 59.3–13–203–2; R. I. Keogh (OB) 4–1–9–0; M. N. W. Spriegel (OB) 48–7–183–5; A. G. Wakely (OB) 1–0–3–0; C. L. White (LBG) 25.2–4–99–2; G. G. White (SLA) 4–1–14–0.

LEADING YB40 AVERAGES (100 runs/4 wickets)

Batting	Runs	HS	Avge	SR	Ct		Bowling	W	BB	Avge	ER
R. I. Newton	132	88*	66.00	80.98	1		T. A. Copeland	15	5-32	15.26	5.12
C. L. White	181	65	60.33	70.98	1		Azharullah	15	4-20	17.20	5.60
K. J. Coetzer	361	105*	40.11	79.86	3		S. P. Crook	17	5-36	18.47	5.53
A. G. Wakely	366	102	36.60	96.82	3		D. J. Willey	9	3-28	28.11	5.19
D. J. Willey	246	167	30.75	132.25	4		A. J. Hall	6	2-32	30.50	4.63
J. D. Middlebrook	123	43	30.75	82.00	1		L. M. Daggett	7	2-28	32.14	4.09
S. P. Crook	171	61*	21.37	111.76	2		M. N. W. Spriegel	8	3-29	36.25	5.08
D. J. Sales	156	31	17.33	69.33	0		J. D. Middlebrook	4	1-29	72.50	5.47

LEADING FLt20 AVERAGES (100 runs/18 overs)

Batting	Runs	HS	Avge	SR	Ct	Bowling	W	BB	Avge	ER
D. J. Willey	198	60	33.00	**163.63**	5	D. J. Willey	21	4-9	13.33	**6.58**
S. P. Crook	195	63	32.50	**159.83**	1	L. M. Daggett	6	2-22	50.66	**6.75**
R. E. Levi	360	110*	32.72	**145.74**	3	S. P. Crook	9	2-26	26.44	**7.43**
A. G. Wakely	293	59*	29.30	**134.40**	5	Azharullah	27	4-14	12.62	**7.44**
C. L. White	417	71*	46.33	**125.60**	5	J. D. Middlebrook	7	2-21	27.42	**7.68**
K. J. Coetzer	337	71*	30.63	**107.32**	2	M. N. W. Spriegel	5	2-22	42.60	**8.35**

FIRST-CLASS COUNTY RECORDS

Highest score for	331*	M. E. K. Hussey v Somerset at Taunton	2003
Highest score against	333	K. S. Duleepsinhji (Sussex) at Hove	1930
Leading run-scorer	28,980	D. Brookes (avge 36.13)	1934–59
Best bowling for	10-127	V. W. C. Jupp v Kent at Tunbridge Wells	1932
Best bowling against	10-30	C. Blythe (Kent) at Northampton	1907
Leading wicket-taker	1,102	E. W. Clark (avge 21.26)	1922–47
Highest total for	781-7 dec	v Nottinghamshire at Northampton	1995
Highest total against	673-8 dec	by Yorkshire at Leeds	2003
Lowest total for	12	v Gloucestershire at Gloucester	1907
Lowest total against	33	by Lancashire at Northampton	1977

LIST A COUNTY RECORDS

Highest score for	172*	W. Larkins v Warwickshire at Luton	1983
Highest score against	175*	I. T. Botham (Somerset) at Wellingborough	1986
Leading run-scorer	11,010	R. J. Bailey (avge 39.46)	1983–99
Best bowling for	7-10	C. Pietersen v Denmark at Brøndby	2005
Best bowling against	7-35	D. E. Malcolm (Derbyshire) at Derby	1997
Leading wicket-taker	251	A. L. Penberthy (avge 30.45)	1989–2003
Highest total for	360-2	v Staffordshire at Northampton	1990
Highest total against	344-6	by Gloucestershire at Cheltenham	2001
Lowest total for	41	v Middlesex at Northampton	1972
Lowest total against	56	by Leicestershire at Leicester	1964
	56	by Denmark at Brøndby	2005

TWENTY20 COUNTY RECORDS

Highest score for	111*	L. Klusener v Worcestershire at Kidderminster	2007
Highest score against	116*	G. A. Hick (Worcestershire) at Luton	2004
Leading run-scorer	1,340	R. A. White (avge 21.61)	2003–12
Best bowling for	6-21	A. J. Hall v Worcestershire at Northampton	2008
Best bowling against	5-6	P. D. Collingwood (Durham) at Chester-le-Street	2011
Leading wicket-taker	64	A. J. Hall (avge 19.71)	2008–12
Highest total for	224-5	v Gloucestershire at Milton Keynes	2005
Highest total against	227-6	by Worcestershire at Kidderminster	2007
Lowest total for	47	v Durham at Chester-le-Street	2011
Lowest total against	86	by Worcestershire at Worcester	2006

ADDRESS

County Ground, Abington Avenue, Northampton NN1 4PR (01604 514455; **email** reception@ncc.co.uk). **Website** www.northantscricket.com

OFFICIALS

Captain (Championship) S. D. Peters
    (limited-overs) A. G. Wakely
Head coach D. Ripley
Academy coach P. Rowe
President Lord Naseby

Chairman G. Warren
Chief executive K. D. Smith
Head groundsman P. Marshall
Scorer A. C. Kingston

At Cardiff, April 10–13. NORTHAMPTONSHIRE drew with GLAMORGAN.

NORTHAMPTONSHIRE v ESSEX

At Northampton, April 17–19. Northamptonshire won by an innings and nine runs. Northamptonshire 23pts, Essex 1pt (after 2pt penalty). Toss: Northamptonshire.

Northamptonshire, denied by the weather at Cardiff, made no mistake on home turf and wrapped up their first Championship win since the previous May with a day and a half to spare. So comprehensively were Essex outplayed that their coach Paul Grayson could not bring himself to address the media; three days later he issued an apology for his team's "shambolic" and "totally unacceptable" performance. The match took its decisive turn on the second morning, when Crook joined Willey with Northamptonshire eight wickets down and still 12 behind. The pair flayed wayward bowling from Mills and Chambers to put on 111 in just 15 overs, before Crook added a further 117 with Trent Copeland, the new overseas signing who had hit a hundred in February for New South Wales. He said "it wasn't an easy conversation" when he found out he'd be batting at No. 11. Essex were back in again by the second evening and, when Quiney edged Willey, their fate was effectively sealed; they were also docked two points for a sluggish over-rate. Willey finished with eight for 110, including a superb low return catch off Greg Smith, and bowled far better than Essex's two young left-arm seamers, Topley and Mills. Napier, who had prevented a first-innings rout by thrashing five sixes in ten balls and bowled with heart, deserved better than an unwanted Saturday off.

Close of play: first day, Northamptonshire 156-5 (Newton 35, Middlebrook 14); second day, Essex 94-2 (Quiney 44, Chambers 0).

Essex

T. Westley c Murphy b Copeland	30	– (2) c Peters b Willey	38
R. J. Quiney lbw b Hall	25	– (1) c Murphy b Willey	56
B. T. Foakes c Murphy b Crook	4	– c Murphy b Copeland	10
R. S. Bopara c Murphy b Crook	6	– (5) c Murphy b Willey	41
M. L. Pettini c Copeland b Crook	4	– (6) c Sales b Hall	5
*†J. S. Foster b Crook	0	– (7) c Hall b Willey	11
G. M. Smith c Murphy b Willey	16	– (8) c and b Willey	4
G. R. Napier not out	73	– (9) c Crook b Hall	13
M. A. Chambers b Willey	1	– (4) b Crook	3
R. J. W. Topley b Hall	0	– not out	8
T. S. Mills c Newton b Willey	6	– b Crook	7
L-b 7, w 1, n-b 10	18	B 5, l-b 6	11

1/44 (2) 2/61 (3) 3/70 (1) (52.1 overs) 183 1/77 (2) 2/93 (3) (83.2 overs) 207
4/79 (5) 5/79 (6) 6/87 (4) 3/114 (1) 4/120 (4)
7/115 (7) 8/127 (9) 9/138 (10) 10/183 (11) 5/133 (6) 6/159 (7) 7/179 (8)
  8/180 (5) 9/199 (9) 10/207 (11)

Willey 14.1–5–43–3; Copeland 14–5–42–1; Hall 13–3–52–2; Crook 11–2–39–4. *Second innings—* Willey 22–5–67–5; Copeland 25–9–41–1; Crook 17.2–4–52–2; Hall 19–5–36–2.

Northamptonshire

*S. D. Peters c Pettini b Topley	60	†D. Murphy lbw b Napier	2
K. J. Coetzer c Westley b Napier	12	S. P. Crook not out	88
D. J. Sales c Chambers b Napier	4	T. A. Copeland c Topley b Mills	70
A. G. Wakely c Bopara b Chambers	11	L-b 7, w 3, n-b 4	14
R. I. Newton c Foster b Napier	35		
A. J. Hall c Pettini b Napier	13	1/20 (2) 2/24 (3) 3/73 (4) (89.4 overs) 399
J. D. Middlebrook c Foster b Napier	14	4/109 (1) 5/129 (6) 6/156 (5)
D. J. Willey c Quiney b Topley	76	7/161 (7) 8/171 (9) 9/282 (8) 10/399 (11)

Topley 29–2–104–2; Mills 17.4–0–91–1; Napier 25–6–93–6; Chambers 10–1–62–1; Bopara 3–0–17–0; Westley 5–0–25–0.

Umpires: S. C. Gale and N. J. Llong.

At Bristol, April 24–27. NORTHAMPTONSHIRE beat GLOUCESTERSHIRE by seven wickets.

At Canterbury, May 1–3. NORTHAMPTONSHIRE beat KENT by seven wickets.

NORTHAMPTONSHIRE v LEICESTERSHIRE

At Northampton, May 15–18. Drawn. Northamptonshire 10pts, Leicestershire 7pts. Toss: Leicestershire. First-class debut: B. M. Duckett.

Northamptonshire suffered a serious blow before play when their captain, Stephen Peters, had his right ring finger broken in the nets by coach David Ripley, who was sending him throwdowns with the Sidearm device. And, with a fourth consecutive win at stake, many home supporters felt the reconstituted management team waited too long to declare on the last day. Wakely eventually set Leicestershire 337 from 63 overs, but the pitch hardly deteriorated, and O'Brien kept his former county at bay for two and a half hours to ensure a draw. Northamptonshire had rushed Keogh from a Second XI game at Taunton to replace Peters, and struggled after being put in on an opening day shortened to 34 overs. But they rallied through Newton, Hall – who scored his first century for two years – and Willey, who passed his career-best by one. Copeland probed away relentlessly as Northamptonshire earned a substantial lead, although Thakor limited the damage with his fifth half-century in seven innings. Northamptonshire's victory push was disrupted by Freckingham, who finished with nine wickets, and they carried on batting until after lunch on the final day to allow 18-year-old Ben Duckett to complete a fifty on his first-class debut.

Close of play: first day, Northamptonshire 91-4 (Newton 22, Hall 12); second day, Leicestershire 89-1 (Smith 36, Eckersley 16); third day, Northamptonshire 94-5 (Hall 2).

Northamptonshire

J. D. Middlebrook c Naik b Freckingham	2	– c O'Brien b Freckingham 43
M. N. W. Spriegel c Boyce b Williams	11	– lbw b Freckingham 1
D. J. Sales c Naik b Wyatt	10	– c O'Brien b Wyatt 31
*A. G. Wakely b Freckingham.	18	– c Smith b Wyatt 12
R. I. Newton c Sarwan b Naik	81	– c Eckersley b Freckingham 0
A. J. Hall b Freckingham.	113	– c Smith b Williams................. 7
R. I. Keogh lbw b Naik	8	– c Sarwan b Williams 10
†B. M. Duckett c Sarwan b Freckingham	5	– not out 53
D. J. Willey c Cobb b Freckingham.	77	– c Sarwan b Naik................. 10
S. P. Crook c Naik b Freckingham.	4	– not out 34
T. A. Copeland not out.	2	
B 10, l-b 8, n-b 6	24	B 13, l-b 1 14

1/6 (1) 2/21 (3) 3/45 (2)   (107 overs) 355   1/5 (2)   (8 wkts dec, 53 overs) 215
4/63 (4) 5/206 (5) 6/214 (7)   2/68 (3) 3/92 (1)
7/229 (8) 8/344 (6) 9/348 (10) 10/355 (9)   4/92 (5) 5/94 (4)
                                                        6/109 (7) 7/112 (6) 8/133 (9)

Freckingham 31–6–125–6; Wyatt 21–7–58–1; Williams 16–0–75–1; Thakor 10–3–31–0; Naik 28–7–47–2; Cobb 1–0–1–0. *Second innings*—Freckingham 16–2–63–3; Wyatt 19–4–46–2; Williams 8–0–54–2; Naik 10–0–38–1.

Leicestershire

G. P. Smith c Spriegel b Copeland	51	– c Hall b Crook	49
†N. J. O'Brien c Duckett b Copeland	29	– c Duckett b Copeland	59
E. J. H. Eckersley lbw b Copeland	25	– run out	42
*R. R. Sarwan lbw b Copeland	19	– not out	17
J. J. Cobb b Willey	0	– not out	1
M. A. G. Boyce b Copeland	23		
S. J. Thakor not out	64		
J. K. H. Naik lbw b Copeland	2		
O. H. Freckingham lbw b Willey	5		
R. E. M. Williams c Duckett b Hall	0		
A. C. F. Wyatt lbw b Copeland	1		
B 10, l-b 3, n-b 2	15	L-b 7, w 1, p 5	

1/62 (2) 2/108 (1) 3/115 (3)   (71.2 overs) 234   1/80 (1)   (3 wkts, 42 overs) 168
4/116 (5) 5/134 (4) 6/181 (6)   2/139 (3) 3/165 (2)
7/191 (8) 8/202 (9) 9/203 (10) 10/234 (11)

Willey 19–4–63–2; Copeland 28.2–7–63–7; Crook 12–1–59–0; Hall 10–2–26–1; Middlebrook 2–0–10–0. *Second innings*—Willey 9–0–51–0; Copeland 15–5–41–1; Crook 8–0–43–1; Hall 4–1–10–0; Middlebrook 6–2–23–0.

Umpires: R. T. Robinson and A. G. Wharf.

At Loughborough, May 23–25. NORTHAMPTONSHIRE drew with LOUGHBOROUGH MCCU.

NORTHAMPTONSHIRE v HAMPSHIRE

At Northampton, May 29–June 1. Drawn. Northamptonshire 9pts, Hampshire 6pts. Toss: Northamptonshire. Championship debut: Azharullah.

Rain washed out the first day and bad light cut short the second, leaving only bonus points at stake. Once again, Northamptonshire's lower order proved resilient and skilful: Hall made his second century in consecutive matches, putting on 117 with Copeland and 132 with Murphy – who made a career-best 81 – for the eighth and ninth wickets. Hampshire found the going tough in damp and murky conditions after Wakely chose to bowl, but Dawson kept his concentration through the stoppages until he mishit a pull on the third morning. Copeland sent down 19 maidens, while Azharullah, the skiddy seamer making his Championship debut at the age of 29 after 53 first-class appearances in Pakistan spread over nine seasons, picked up three late wickets. Then it was Northamptonshire's turn to struggle against the seamers, before the apparently rejuvenated Hall masterminded another rescue act.

Close of play: first day, no play; second day, Hampshire 149-5 (Dawson 57, Roberts 2); third day, Northamptonshire 159-5 (Hall 29, Middlebrook 8).

Hampshire

M. A. Carberry c Sales b Copeland	10	D. J. Balcombe c Sales b Azharullah	0	
*J. H. K. Adams c Murphy b Willey	0	D. R. Briggs b Willey	10	
L. A. Dawson c Sales b Hall	76	J. A. Tomlinson not out	4	
J. M. Vince lbw b Copeland	8	L-b 7, w 1, p 5	13	
S. M. Ervine lbw b Copeland	26			
†A. J. Wheater b Copeland	40	1/3 (2) 2/17 (1) 3/35 (4)	(88 overs)	206
M. D. T. Roberts lbw b Azharullah	12	4/80 (5) 5/143 (6) 6/179 (7)		
C. P. Wood c Hall b Azharullah	7	7/179 (3) 8/180 (9) 9/199 (8) 10/206 (10)		

Willey 22–4–47–2; Copeland 37–19–56–4; Hall 10–4–32–1; Azharullah 19–4–59–3.

Northamptonshire

K. J. Coetzer c Wheater b Briggs	59	†D. Murphy c Ervine b Adams	81
M. N. W. Spriegel lbw b Tomlinson	3	Azharullah not out	0
D. J. Sales c Wheater b Ervine	15		
*A. G. Wakely c Ervine b Vince	7	B 14, l-b 13, w 7, n-b 2	36
R. I. Newton c Briggs b Wood	21		
A. J. Hall not out	130	1/21 (2)　　　(9 wkts dec, 144.3 overs) 425	
J. D. Middlebrook b Tomlinson	10	2/59 (3)　 3/80 (4)	
D. J. Willey c Ervine b Tomlinson	0	4/108 (1)　5/132 (5)　6/168 (7)　7/172 (8)	
T. A. Copeland lbw b Briggs	63	8/289 (9)　9/421 (10)　　110 overs: 310-8	

Tomlinson 23–5–75–3; Balcombe 20–7–55–0; Ervine 13–5–46–1; Wood 18–3–64–1; Vince 9–1–17–1; Briggs 32–11–58–2; Dawson 20–5–47–0; Adams 7–0–26–1; Carberry 2.3–0–10–0.

Umpires: M. R. Benson and S. A. Garratt.

NORTHAMPTONSHIRE v WORCESTERSHIRE

At Northampton, June 5–7. Northamptonshire won by ten wickets. Northamptonshire 22pts, Worcestershire 3pts. Toss: Northamptonshire.

Northamptonshire's former players were just arriving at Wantage Road for their annual reunion when Coetzer lofted Shantry over extra cover for six to wrap up victory before lunch on the third day, and ensure the reminiscences would not be interrupted by any cricket. The win sent Northamptonshire 44 points clear of Worcestershire at the top of Division Two, and owed much to Copeland, who signed off from his first spell at the club with another relentless display of line and length. He helped maintain Northamptonshire's perfect record of bowling points, and ran through Worcestershire in the second innings for a parting haul of nine for 92 – giving him 36 wickets in seven Championship games. Richardson lost little in comparison, removing both openers in his first over, and there might have been a different outcome had Kapil not dropped Crook, on six, in the deep with Northamptonshire six down and 56 behind. Crook responded by hoisting the next delivery from Andrew over the Gallone's ice cream van at deep midwicket, and raced to 85 at a run a ball. Throughout, Ali was head and shoulders above his team-mates on a spicy pitch, but he could not see off Copeland and Willey on his own. Murphy's reward for hitting 81 in his previous innings was to be dropped to No. 11 – he was the first wicketkeeper to bat there in a Championship match, barring injury or use of a nightwatchman, since Worcestershire's Tim Edwards in 1994.

Close of play: first day, Northamptonshire 100-4 (Keogh 26); second day, Worcestershire 97-6 (Ali 29, Andrew 16).

Worcestershire

*D. K. H. Mitchell lbw b Copeland	1	– b Crook	8
M. G. Pardoe b Crook	22	– c Murphy b Willey	24
M. M. Ali c Murphy b Willey	79	– not out	44
T. T. Samaraweera b Hall	16	– lbw b Copeland	4
A. N. Kervezee b Hall	19	– lbw b Copeland	1
A. Kapil run out	4	– lbw b Willey	4
†M. A. Johnson b Hall	3	– lbw b Copeland	2
G. M. Andrew lbw b Crook	16	– c Murphy b Copeland	18
J. D. Shantry c Keogh b Copeland	3	– lbw b Copeland	0
C. J. Russell c Willey b Copeland	7	– c Murphy b Copeland	2
A. Richardson not out	11	– c Middlebrook b Willey	4
B 4, l-b 6, w 5	15	L-b 4, n-b 10	14

1/1 (1)　2/44 (2)　3/75 (4)　　(61.2 overs) 196		1/18 (1)　2/45 (2)　　(58.1 overs) 125	
4/107 (5)　5/111 (6)　6/130 (7)		3/52 (4)　4/58 (5)	
7/165 (8)　8/176 (9)　9/178 (3)　10/196 (10)		5/63 (6)　6/66 (7)　7/102 (8)	
		8/102 (9)　9/108 (10)　10/125 (11)	

Willey 18–4–52–1; Copeland 17.2–6–51–3; Crook 13–2–38–2; Hall 13–3–45–3. *Second innings*—Willey 18.1–4–48–3; Copeland 28–11–41–6; Crook 11–3–27–1; Middlebrook 1–0–5–0.

Northamptonshire

K. J. Coetzer c Mitchell b Richardson	1	– not out	7
M. N. W. Spriegel c Ali b Richardson	0	– not out	1
D. J. Sales lbw b Richardson	40		
*A. G. Wakely b Andrew	31		
R. I. Keogh c Ali b Andrew	44		
A. J. Hall c Andrew b Richardson	10		
J. D. Middlebrook c and b Ali	39		
S. P. Crook b Russell	85		
T. A. Copeland c Shantry b Russell	31		
D. J. Willey not out	15		
†D. Murphy lbw b Russell	4		
B 10, l-b 4	14		

1/1 (2) 2/2 (1) 3/54 (4)   (80 overs) 314   (no wkt, 2.2 overs) 8
4/100 (3) 5/124 (6) 6/134 (5)
7/230 (7) 8/287 (8) 9/308 (9) 10/314 (11)

Richardson 23–5–71–4; Russell 16–4–59–3; Shantry 11–2–38–0; Andrew 22–4–80–2; Ali 6–0–38–1; Kapil 2–0–14–0. *Second innings*—Shantry 1.2–1–6–0; Russell 1–0–2–0.

Umpires: I. Dawood and D. J. Millns.

At Leicester, June 11–14. NORTHAMPTONSHIRE drew with LEICESTERSHIRE.

At Manchester, June 20–21. NORTHAMPTONSHIRE lost to LANCASHIRE by eight wickets. *Northamptonshire chief executive complains about the pitch after his side are dismissed for 62.*

NORTHAMPTONSHIRE v LANCASHIRE

At Northampton, July 8–11. Lancashire won by eight wickets. Lancashire 23pts, Northamptonshire 5pts. Toss: Lancashire.

The war of words over the Old Trafford pitch used three weeks earlier left both sides eager to prove a point. But the debate was short-lived: Lancashire won emphatically to supplant Northamptonshire at the top of the table. Chapple's decision to bowl appeared suspect when the sun burned through, and Coetzer and Middlebrook negotiated the morning session. But after that only Cameron White, playing his first Championship match since 2007, could make it count. His countryman Katich – told by the Australian selectors that he would not be recalled for the Ashes, which began at Trent Bridge during this game – then offered a masterclass in concentration during an eight-hour double-hundred, the fifth of his career. He was put down on 115 by Sales at slip early on the third day, and punished Northamptonshire in century partnerships with Procter and Chapple to build a decisive lead on a wearing pitch. Kerrigan found turn and variable bounce to bowl Duckett and White, then had Spriegel and Willey clutched at short leg in successive balls next morning. Hall, barely able to move after straining a buttock muscle, passed 10,000 first-class runs in a typically defiant innings, but was finally bounced out by Chapple, who ran almost the length of the wicket to hold a sprawling return catch.

Close of play: first day, Northamptonshire 275-7 (White 61, Murphy 28); second day, Lancashire 262-4 (Katich 114, Procter 62); third day, Northamptonshire 123-4 (Middlebrook 46, Hall 3).

Northamptonshire

K. J. Coetzer b Hogg	38	– c Brown b Chapple	10
J. D. Middlebrook run out	57	– c Hogg b Kerrigan	75
*D. J. Sales c Cross b Chapple	18	– b Kerrigan	30
B. M. Duckett b Chapple	29	– b Kerrigan	24
C. L. White c Cross b Hogg	90	– b Kerrigan	1
A. J. Hall c Katich b Chapple	0	– c and b Chapple	57
M. N. W. Spriegel c Agathangelou b Kerrigan	20	– c Agathangelou b Kerrigan	4
D. J. Willey c Brown b White	6	– c Agathangelou b Kerrigan	0
†D. Murphy lbw b Hogg	30	– lbw b Kerrigan	6
L. M. Daggett lbw b Hogg	1	– b Chapple	11
Azharullah not out	0	– not out	0
L-b 10, w 5, n-b 6	21	B 10, l-b 10, w 1, n-b 2	23
	310		**241**

1/90 (1) 2/107 (2) 3/148 (3) (111.1 overs) 310
4/159 (4) 5/159 (6) 6/200 (7)
7/211 (8) 8/289 (9) 9/305 (10)
10/310 (5) 110 overs: 305-9

1/16 (1) 2/66 (3) (85 overs) 241
3/106 (4) 4/108 (5)
5/180 (2) 6/184 (7) 7/184 (8)
8/192 (9) 9/236 (10) 10/241 (6)

Chapple 28–8–72–3; Hogg 25.1–7–65–4; Kerrigan 35–10–79–1; Procter 8–1–27–0; White 13–1–52–1; Agathangelou 2–0–5–0. *Second innings*—Chapple 18.5–5–38–3; Hogg 12–0–44–0; White 19–2–67–0; Kerrigan 30–8–63–7; Agathangelou 3–0–7–0; Procter 3–1–2–0.

Lancashire

L. M. Reece c Murphy b Azharullah	9	– not out	40
K. R. Brown b Azharullah	13	– c Middlebrook b Azharullah	0
A. G. Prince c Coetzer b Azharullah	42	– lbw b Middlebrook	12
S. M. Katich c Azharullah b White	200		
A. P. Agathangelou b Willey	17	– (4) not out	57
L. A. Procter c Murphy b Hall	85		
†G. D. Cross lbw b Willey	7		
W. A. White lbw b Willey	1		
K. W. Hogg b Willey	0		
*G. Chapple c Hall b Willey	57		
S. C. Kerrigan not out	1		
B 1, l-b 3, n-b 6	10	L-b 1	1
	442		**110**

1/19 (1) 2/26 (2) 3/102 (3) (137.2 overs) 442
4/146 (5) 5/291 (6) 6/302 (7) 7/308 (8)
8/308 (9) 9/436 (10) 10/442 (4) 110 overs: 354-8

1/0 (2) 2/22 (3) (2 wkts, 30.3 overs) 110

Willey 35–4–108–5; Azharullah 29–4–83–3; Hall 18–6–44–1; Middlebrook 25–4–85–0; Daggett 20–3–82–0; Spriegel 4–0–18–0; White 6.2–1–18–1. *Second innings*—Willey 6–1–16–0; Azharullah 7–2–30–1; Middlebrook 11–5–23–1; White 4–0–27–0; Daggett 2.3–0–13–0.

Umpires: J. H. Evans and T. E. Jesty.

NORTHAMPTONSHIRE v GLOUCESTERSHIRE

At Northampton, August 2–5. Drawn. Northamptonshire 11pts, Gloucestershire 8pts. Toss: Gloucestershire. First-class debut: T. W. Shrewsbury.

Sales, out of contract at the end of the season and facing mounting speculation over his future after only 271 runs in 15 Championship innings, delighted the Northamptonshire faithful with an unbeaten 255 from 279 balls – his eighth double-century and highest score for 13 years. The pitch was lifeless, and the Gloucestershire attack persevering rather than penetrative, but the 35-year-old Sales still revived memories of his best days in a blend of powerful strokeplay and deft touches. With Peters (returning from three months out with a broken finger), Coetzer and Hall also relishing the friendly conditions, Northamptonshire opted to bat only once, build a big lead and try to bowl Gloucestershire out on the fourth day. But the surface helped neither seam nor spin, rain delayed the start on the last two days, and diligent batting from Dent and Klinger ensured the match was saved easily. In the first innings, Marshall's aggressive century, his third in four games, had revived Gloucestershire from 123 for two, only for his wicket to spark a collapse of five for 20.

Close of play: first day, Northamptonshire 13-0 (Peters 12, Coetzer 1); second day, Northamptonshire 369-3 (Sales 126, White 6); third day, Gloucestershire 31-0 (Dent 10, Klinger 21).

Gloucestershire

*M. Klinger c Murphy b Hall	47	– (2) c Hall b White	78
C. D. J. Dent c Murphy b Willey	0	– (1) not out	129
†G. H. Roderick lbw b Willey	2	– not out	11
A. P. R. Gidman c Willey b Hall	59		
H. J. H. Marshall c Murphy b Azharullah	145		
B. A. C. Howell c Sales b Hall	60		
W. R. S. Gidman b Azharullah	15		
J. K. Fuller b Willey	9		
T. M. J. Smith lbw b Crook	5		
C. N. Miles lbw b Azharullah	0		
T. W. Shrewsbury not out	2		
B 5, l-b 1, n-b 8	14	B 5, l-b 1, w 1, n-b 2	9

1/5 (2) 2/9 (3) 3/101 (4)   (91.2 overs) 358   1/190 (2)   (1 wkt, 73 overs) 227
4/123 (1) 5/306 (6) 6/338 (5)
7/347 (8) 8/351 (7) 9/351 (10) 10/358 (9)

Willey 21–2–64–3; Azharullah 19–3–69–3; Crook 14.2–0–69–1; Hall 18–2–59–3; Middlebrook 17–1–73–0; White 2–0–18–0. *Second innings*—Willey 10–2–29–0; Azharullah 12–4–26–0; Middlebrook 18–4–73–0; Hall 7–2–14–0; White 13–3–36–1; Crook 5–0–24–0; Coetzer 7–1–16–0; Wakely 1–0–3–0.

Northamptonshire

*S. D. Peters c Roderick b Shrewsbury	87		
K. J. Coetzer b Dent b Howell	122		
D. J. Sales not out	255		
A. G. Wakely c Roderick b Fuller	13		
C. L. White c Howell b Miles	16		
A. J. Hall not out	55		
B 5, l-b 11, w 1, n-b 2	19		

1/170 (1)   (4 wkts dec, 142.3 overs) 567
2/305 (2) 3/356 (4)
4/397 (5)   110 overs: 407-4

J. D. Middlebrook, S. P. Crook, D. J. Willey, †D. Murphy and Azharullah did not bat.

W. R. S. Gidman 26–4–94–0; Fuller 27–6–117–1; Miles 23–3–109–1; Smith 25.3–5–66–0; Shrewsbury 23–0–94–1; Howell 14–3–53–1; Dent 4–0–18–0.

Umpires: P. K. Baldwin and M. J. Saggers.

At Colchester, August 20–23. NORTHAMPTONSHIRE drew with ESSEX.

NORTHAMPTONSHIRE v GLAMORGAN

At Northampton, August 28–30. Northamptonshire won by an innings and 25 runs. Northamptonshire 24pts, Glamorgan 4pts. Toss: Northamptonshire.

Northamptonshire's first win in six matches gave their promotion prospects a shot in the arm, while Glamorgan were left to reflect that life can be luckless in the doldrums. They were solidly placed on 142 for two, after Northamptonshire's bowlers gave them too much to hit on a well-grassed pitch, when – in the space of three overs – Cooke trod on his stumps, and both Goodwin and the left-handed Wallace feathered Willey down the leg side. With their Australian spearhead Michael

Hogan rested ahead of the YB40 semi-final, Glamorgan regained the initiative only for a brief period on the second day, when Northamptonshire's middle order crumbled against the spinners, leaving them five runs behind with four wickets standing. Willey took that as a cue for another scintillating counter-attack, this time thumping six fours and six sixes in 73 balls, setting Northamptonshire on course for a maximum-point victory. His timing and aggression reminded some of the young Andrew Flintoff. Hall proved the perfect foil, and Northamptonshire's five-man seam attack completed the job with four sessions to spare.

Close of play: first day, Northamptonshire 85-0 (Peters 39, Middlebrook 38); second day, Northamptonshire 453.

Glamorgan

G. P. Rees c Sales b Hall	39	– c Sales b Copeland		19
W. D. Bragg c Murphy b Crook	32	– b Azharullah		44
M. W. Goodwin c Murphy b Willey	47	– lbw b Copeland		5
C. B. Cooke hit wkt b Crook	21	– c Murphy b Azharullah		42
J. Allenby c Murphy b Copeland	41	– lbw b Crook		13
*†M. A. Wallace c Murphy b Willey	0	– c Murphy b Crook		9
G. G. Wagg c Wakely b Willey	13	– not out		34
J. C. Glover c Hall b Crook	4	– c Murphy b Azharullah		1
A. G. Salter c Peters b Crook	1	– c Murphy b Hall		3
D. A. Cosker not out	14	– c Crook b Copeland		4
M. T. Reed c Murphy b Copeland	1	– c Copeland b Hall		8
B 8, l-b 10, w 10	28	L-b 5		5

1/74 (1) 2/84 (2) 3/142 (4)   (72.4 overs) 241   1/27 (1) 2/33 (3)   (61.5 overs) 187
4/158 (3) 5/158 (6) 6/184 (7)   3/103 (2) 4/120 (5)
7/189 (8) 8/197 (9) 9/232 (5) 10/241 (11)   5/134 (4) 6/134 (6) 7/143 (8)
                                          8/170 (9) 9/177 (10) 10/187 (11)

Willey 13–3–54–3; Copeland 18.4–5–40–2; Hall 13–4–24–1; Crook 18–1–66–4; Azharullah 10–2–39–0. *Second innings*—Willey 6–0–28–0; Copeland 19–6–41–3; Hall 11.5–3–36–2; Crook 11–1–33–2; Azharullah 13–2–42–3; Middlebrook 1–0–2–0.

Northamptonshire

*S. D. Peters c Allenby b Reed	61	†D. Murphy c Wallace b Allenby		12
J. D. Middlebrook c Wallace b Reed	59	Azharullah lbw b Cosker		2
D. J. Sales b Salter	48			
A. G. Wakely c Rees b Reed	36	B 11, l-b 4, w 1, n-b 4		20
B. M. Duckett c Wallace b Cosker	9			
A. J. Hall not out	91	1/115 (1) 2/136 (2)	(114.5 overs)	453
S. P. Crook c Wallace b Salter	0	3/215 (4) 4/226 (5) 5/236 (3)		
D. J. Willey c Allenby b Wagg	81	6/236 (7) 7/351 (8) 8/413 (9)		
T. A. Copeland b Reed	34	9/436 (10) 10/453 (11)	110 overs: 436-9	

Wagg 17–1–86–1; Glover 13–2–55–0; Allenby 21–4–58–1; Reed 26–4–109–4; Cosker 26.5–5–82–2; Salter 11–1–48–2.

Umpires: M. R. Benson and N. A. Mallender.

At Southampton, September 3–6. NORTHAMPTONSHIRE drew with HAMPSHIRE.

NORTHAMPTONSHIRE v KENT

At Northampton, September 17–20. Drawn. Northamptonshire 10pts, Kent 9pts. Toss: Northamptonshire. Championship debut: S. W. Billings.

Home supporters followed events at Chelmsford – where promotion rivals Essex were taking on Glamorgan – no less intently than the play unfolding in front of them. The ball swung and seamed so extravagantly in the 17 overs possible on the first day that Northamptonshire donated 22 extras. Their hopes of collecting all three bowling points were then dashed by Key, Nash and Stevens, who each passed 1,000 runs in the Championship. Key blasted Middlebrook out of the ground over

HUNDRED AND FIVE WICKETS FOR NORTHAMPTONSHIRE SINCE 1945

G. E. Tribe	101*; 5-10, 4-41	v Worcestershire at Worcester	1953
G. E. Tribe	107*, 9; 0-85, 5-34	v Warwickshire at Coventry	1958
Mushtaq Mohammad	122, 3; 6-58, 1-8	v Leicestershire at Leicester	1972
D. S. Steele	130; 6-36, 5-39	v Derbyshire at Northampton	1978
R. G. Williams	103, 9; 1-32, 5-34	v Derbyshire at Northampton	1985
L. Klusener	122, 51*; 6-69, 1-46	v Leicestershire at Oakham School	2006
N. Boje	125, 4; 1-30, 6-110	v Leicestershire at Leicester	2007
J. D. Middlebrook	121, 19; 1-47, 5-63	v Gloucestershire at Northampton	2012
J. D. Middlebrook	**109; 6-78**	**v Kent at Northampton**	**2013**

There were nine instances before 1945, including five by S. G. Smith between 1912 and 1914.

---

midwicket – causing the ball to be replaced – and thrashed another six two deliveries later to bring up his hundred. But he swept the next ball to slip via his right boot. When Kent's lower order – missing Geraint Jones for the first time in 116 Championship matches stretching back to 2006, after he was dropped for 22-year-old Sam Billings – tried a similar approach, Middlebrook cleaned up for career-best figures. After the third day was halved by rain, Northamptonshire settled down to the task of making 400 inside 110 overs – and achieved it thanks to reassuring hundreds from Middlebrook and Sales, who now had 619 runs in six innings, and purposeful contributions from Wakely and Hall. That did not stop increasingly jittery updates from the PA announcer of the score at Chelmsford, as the crowd waited nervously to see if Essex could contrive a run-chase, or trigger a Glamorgan collapse. Neither materialised, and Northamptonshire carried a 20-point lead into the last round of matches.

Close of play: first day, Kent 60-1 (Key 17, Bell-Drummond 7); second day, Kent 418; third day, Northamptonshire 183-1 (Middlebrook 87, Sales 25).

Kent

S. A. Northeast c Murphy b Hall	14	*J. C. Tredwell c Sales b Middlebrook	10
R. W. T. Key c Hall b Middlebrook	101	M. Davies c Wakely b Middlebrook	9
D. J. Bell-Drummond c Middlebrook		C. E. Shreck not out	0
b Azharullah	11	B 8, l-b 12, w 3, n-b 12	35
B. P. Nash lbw b Middlebrook	107		
B. W. Harmison st Murphy b Middlebrook	28	1/41 (1) 2/76 (3) (112 overs)	418
D. I. Stevens c Azharullah b Daggett	63	3/210 (2) 4/278 (5) 5/295 (4)	
†S. W. Billings lbw b Hall	8	6/327 (7) 7/383 (6) 8/402 (9)	
A. J. Ball c Spriegel b Middlebrook	32	9/418 (10) 10/418 (8) 110 overs: 416-8	

Azharullah 26–4–75–1; Hall 23–7–92–2; Crook 22–2–79–0; Daggett 21–5–74–1; Middlebrook 20–3–78–6.

Northamptonshire

*S. D. Peters c Bell-Drummond b Davies	68	M. N. W. Spriegel not out	8
J. D. Middlebrook c Billings b Ball	109	B 4, l-b 6, n-b 4	14
D. J. Sales c Billings b Shreck	110		
A. G. Wakely lbw b Shreck	55	1/136 (1) (5 wkts dec, 122.4 overs)	431
R. I. Keogh not out	32	2/233 (2) 3/344 (4)	
A. J. Hall c Key b Harmison	35	4/363 (3) 5/417 (6) 110 overs: 405-4	

S. P. Crook, †D. Murphy, L. M. Daggett and Azharullah did not bat.

Davies 28–4–84–1; Shreck 26–3–80–2; Stevens 26–5–100–0; Ball 14–1–70–1; Tredwell 20–2–64–0; Harmison 8–1–21–1; Key 0.4–0–2–0.

Umpires: N. L. Bainton and N. G. C. Cowley.

At Worcester, September 24–26. NORTHAMPTONSHIRE lost to WORCESTERSHIRE by 115 runs. *Northamptonshire are promoted.*

NOTTINGHAMSHIRE

One-day good, four-day bad

SIMON CLEAVES

It has been easy in recent years to predict the pattern of Nottinghamshire's Championship season: a strong seam line-up delivers a string of victories in April and May, before things tail off as pitches harden and spinners come into play. But in 2013 the impact of Andre Adams, the veteran attack leader, was nullified by injury and the return of the heavy roller, and Nottinghamshire secured only two Championship wins before the Twenty20 break. Relegation clouds hovered over the final match, at home to Somerset. Nottinghamshire survived, but the summer would have been a bitter disappointment had it not been for a YB40 triumph at Lord's a few days earlier.

Such celebrations seemed unlikely in a trying August. Nottinghamshire were denied a possible Championship victory at Taunton by the weather, before a humbling Twenty20 quarter-final loss to Essex in front of a record Trent Bridge crowd. That was followed by two defeats in three YB40 matches, which left them needing to win at Kent to reach the semi-finals. A ten-wicket Championship defeat by Yorkshire hardly boded well, but half-centuries from Alex Hales and Samit Patel did the job at Canterbury and, focus renewed, Nottinghamshire swept past Somerset and Glamorgan to lift their first one-day trophy since the 1991 Sunday League.

It was especially sweet for their captain Chris Read: a Lord's final was one of the last remaining career goals in his 16th season at the club. He cast aside his worst summer with the bat since 2000 to contribute a run-a-ball fifty. He managed that only twice in the Championship, and the strength of Nottinghamshire's top order meant he had few opportunities to play his way out of the slump in the shorter formats. "I've been terrible," he admitted.

At the end of the season, Read and director of cricket Mick Newell agreed the time had come to split the captaincy. Read had delegated Twenty20 leadership to an overseas player for the previous four seasons, so it was an arrangement the team were familiar with. The field of candidates, however, was not vast. James Taylor, in his second season at Nottinghamshire, had briefly stood in when Read was injured in May, and had experience of captaining England Lions, so it was to him that Newell entrusted the defence of their one-day title.

After a quiet first season in Division One, Taylor fared better in 2013, but couldn't convince the England selectors he was their next No. 5 or 6. Of the other batsmen, Michael Lumb stood out: he alone passed 1,000 Championship runs, including four hundreds, and always quickened the pulse in the limited-overs games. This was especially true in Twenty20, where he and Hales justified their position at the top of the England order with some electrifying hitting.

The disconnect between Hales's Championship and limited-overs form went some way to explaining Nottinghamshire's travails in four-day cricket. He passed 50 just twice in 18 innings, and looked devoid of confidence. But when he was given the freedom to attack the white ball in the powerplays, he did so with relish. By September, he was the world's No. 1 batsman in Twenty20 internationals – yet had been dropped by his county for the second time in a few weeks.

Harry Gurney

Hales and Newell spent the autumn negotiating how best to satisfy his Twenty20 aspirations, after the coach barred him from playing in the 2013 IPL. Eventually they agreed on a new three-year contract, with permission to play in the IPL should he fetch more than $400,000 a year. A similar deal applied to Patel; Lumb, though, committed to the county. To cover Hales's possible early-season absence, Newell signed the experienced Australian Phil Jaques (holder of a UK passport) on a short-term basis.

In truth, Nottinghamshire's weak Championship showing had more to do with the bowling. Despite the occasional spectacular collapse, they collected 47 batting points – the second-highest in Division One – but were too often unable to finish off the opposition. With Adams's influence waning, and Ajmal Shahzad often misfiring, the responsibility fell to Harry Gurney and Luke Fletcher, both born in Nottingham. The left-armer Gurney finished as the leading wicket-taker with 48 – and was taken on the Ashes trip to help England prepare for Mitchell Johnson – while the nagging Fletcher never offered easy runs. But Nottinghamshire were missing a genuine match-winner, and Newell was delighted to capture his "No. 1 target" for 2014, Peter Siddle.

Glaring holes remained in the spin department. Graeme White was loaned back to his first county, Northamptonshire, at the start of the FLt20, and was later allowed to return there permanently. The abrupt retirement of Graeme Swann in Australia meant the YB40 final had been his domestic farewell; he endorsed 20-year-old off-spinner Sam Wood as one to watch. He would be working closely with Gary Keedy, who was brought in, aged 39, as a player-coach. Batting coach Paul Johnson was let go after 32 years at the club.

Siddle's signing marked a change in policy, after ten years in which a batsman – usually his Australian compatriot David Hussey – had occupied the overseas role. But Hussey, now 36, decided that 2013 was to be his last season in county cricket. He ended with a valedictory century against Somerset – giving him 23 first-class hundreds and more than 10,000 runs for the county in all competitions. An engaging man and spectacular cricketer, Hussey will be remembered as one of Nottinghamshire's finest imports.

Championship attendance: 33,396.

NOTTINGHAMSHIRE RESULTS

All first-class matches – Played 17: Won 3, Lost 5, Drawn 9.
County Championship matches – Played 16: Won 2, Lost 5, Drawn 9.

LV= County Championship, 7th in Division 1;
Friends Life t20, quarter-finalists; Yorkshire Bank 40, winners.

COUNTY CHAMPIONSHIP AVERAGES, BATTING AND FIELDING

Cap		M	I	NO	R	HS	100	50	Avge	Ct/St
2012	M. J. Lumb	15	25	3	1,037	221*	4	2	47.13	4
2012	J. W. A. Taylor†	15	21	1	925	204*	2	5	46.25	4
2013	E. J. M. Cowan§	7	13	2	478	81	0	4	43.45	4
2013	S. J. Mullaney	14	21	0	834	125	2	6	39.71	8
2004	D. J. Hussey§	9	13	0	478	125	1	3	36.76	2
2008	S. R. Patel‡	16	24	0	830	157	3	0	34.58	17
2007	A. R. Adams¶	11	15	2	354	80	0	2	27.23	3
2013	A. Shahzad	11	17	2	363	77	0	2	24.20	1
1999	P. J. Franks†	8	11	0	257	78	0	2	23.36	3
1999	C. M. W. Read	15	22	2	452	58	0	2	22.60	53/2
	M. H. Wessels	11	16	1	316	77	0	1	21.06	13/1
	L. J. Fletcher†	15	22	3	368	64	0	2	19.36	5
2011	A. D. Hales‡	10	18	0	251	58	0	2	13.94	10
	H. F. Gurney†	14	18	11	61	22*	0	0	8.71	4

Also batted: S. C. J. Broad†‡ (cap 2008) (2 matches) 41, 46, 10 (2 ct); A. Carter (1 match) 0*, 0*; B. A. Hutton (1 match) 20*, 42; G. P. Swann‡ (cap 2005) (1 match) 8*, 57; G. G. White (1 match) 0.

† *Born in Nottinghamshire.*   ‡ *ECB contract.*   § *Official overseas player.*   ¶ *Other non-England-qualified player.*

BOWLING

	Style	O	M	R	W	BB	5I	Avge
S. C. J. Broad	RFM	80	21	213	12	4-34	0	17.75
L. J. Fletcher	RFM	460.1	133	1,288	43	5-52	2	29.95
A. R. Adams	RFM	302.5	55	929	31	4-69	0	29.96
H. F. Gurney	LFM	396.3	65	1,334	44	5-81	1	30.31
P. J. Franks	RFM	128	26	449	11	3-16	0	40.81
A. Shahzad	RFM	324.1	60	1,083	22	3-43	0	49.22
S. R. Patel	SLA	446.2	120	1,293	26	3-40	0	49.73

Also bowled: A. Carter (RFM) 28–5–113–2; E. J. M. Cowan (LBG) 1–0–3–0; D. J. Hussey (OB) 4–1–25–0; B. A. Hutton (RM) 22–4–109–1; S. J. Mullaney (RM) 75.3–12–254–5; G. P. Swann (OB) 41–7–146–4; M. H. Wessels (OB) 2–0–11–0; G. G. White (SLA) 35–7–85–2.

LEADING YB40 AVERAGES (100 runs/4 wickets)

Batting

	Runs	HS	Avge	SR	Ct/St
J. W. A. Taylor	585	108	73.12	85.02	3
D. J. Hussey	187	82*	62.33	103.31	4
S. R. Patel	566	129*	47.16	97.92	11
C. M. W. Read	146	53	36.50	108.14	13/4
A. D. Hales	491	101	35.07	101.65	1
M. H. Wessels	172	37*	28.66	124.63	7
M. J. Lumb	345	57	24.64	113.48	4

Bowling

	W	BB	Avge	ER
A. Shahzad	22	3-26	18.27	5.60
S. J. Mullaney	17	4-29	22.17	4.83
J. T. Ball	19	4-25	22.63	5.69
H. F. Gurney	18	5-48	27.55	5.83
G. G. White	4	2-30	31.75	5.29
S. R. Patel	15	3-21	32.80	5.39

LEADING FLt20 AVERAGES (100 runs/18 overs)

Batting	Runs	HS	Avge	SR	Ct	Bowling	W	BB	Avge	ER
M. J. Lumb	330	96	30.00	**165.00**	3	H. F. Gurney	8	3-26	26.37	**6.39**
A. D. Hales	365	82	33.18	**146.58**	2	G. G. White	10	5-22	14.30	**6.80**
D. J. Hussey	298	61	42.57	**143.96**	2	S. R. Patel	14	3-16	21.21	**7.64**
S. R. Patel	169	50	24.14	**129.00**	5	I. G. Butler	12	3-23	25.08	**8.20**
J. W. A. Taylor	196	54	32.66	**104.81**	5	J. T. Ball	8	2-20	28.00	**8.29**

FIRST-CLASS COUNTY RECORDS

Highest score for	312*	W. W. Keeton v Middlesex at The Oval	1939
Highest score against	345	C. G. Macartney (Australians) at Nottingham	1921
Leading run-scorer	31,592	G. Gunn (avge 35.69)	1902–32
Best bowling for	10-66	K. Smales v Gloucestershire at Stroud	1956
Best bowling against	10-10	H. Verity (Yorkshire) at Leeds	1932
Leading wicket-taker	1,653	T. G. Wass (avge 20.34)	1896–1920
Highest total for	791	v Essex at Chelmsford	2007
Highest total against	781-7 dec	by Northamptonshire at Northampton	1995
Lowest total for	13	v Yorkshire at Nottingham	1901
Lowest total against {	16	by Derbyshire at Nottingham	1879
	16	by Surrey at The Oval	1880

LIST A COUNTY RECORDS

Highest score for	167*	P. Johnson v Kent at Nottingham	1993
Highest score against	191	D. S. Lehmann (Yorkshire) at Scarborough	2001
Leading run-scorer	11,237	R. T. Robinson (avge 35.33)	1978–99
Best bowling for	6-10	K. P. Evans v Northumberland at Jesmond	1994
Best bowling against	7-41	A. N. Jones (Sussex) at Nottingham	1986
Leading wicket-taker	291	C. E. B. Rice (avge 22.60)	1975–87
Highest total for	346-9	v Ireland at Nottingham	2009
Highest total against	361-8	by Surrey at The Oval	2001
Lowest total for	57	v Gloucestershire at Nottingham	2009
Lowest total against	43	by Northamptonshire at Northampton	1977

TWENTY20 COUNTY RECORDS

Highest score for	96	**M. J. Lumb v Durham at Chester-le-Street**	**2013**
Highest score against	111	W. J. Durston (Derbyshire) at Nottingham	2010
Leading run-scorer	1,924	**S. R. Patel (avge 26.00)**	**2003–13**
Best bowling for	5-22	**G. G. White v Lancashire at Nottingham**	**2013**
Best bowling against	5-13	A. B. McDonald (Leicestershire) at Nottingham	2010
Leading wicket-taker	85	**S. R. Patel (avge 29.30)**	**2003–13**
Highest total for	215-6	v Yorkshire at Nottingham	2011
Highest total against	207-7	by Yorkshire at Nottingham	2004
Lowest total for	91	v Lancashire at Manchester	2006
Lowest total against	96	by Leicestershire at Leicester	2012

ADDRESS

County Cricket Ground, Trent Bridge, Nottingham NG2 6AG (0115 982 3000; **email** administration@nottsccc.co.uk). **Website** www.nottsccc.co.uk

OFFICIALS

Captain (Championship) C. M. W. Read (limited-overs) J. W. A. Taylor
Director of cricket M. Newell
Academy director C. M. Tolley
President T. I. Hepburn

Chairman P. G. Wright
Chief executive L. J. Pursehouse
Chairman, cricket committee W. Taylor
Head groundsman S. Birks
Scorer R. Marshall

NOTTINGHAMSHIRE v MIDDLESEX

At Nottingham, April 10–13. Middlesex won by ten wickets. Middlesex 23pts, Nottinghamshire 5pts. Toss: Middlesex. County debuts: E. J. M. Cowan, A. Shahzad; J. A. R. Harris.

Nottinghamshire had won a pre-season event in Barbados, while Middlesex made do with a heated marquee in Radlett. But it was Middlesex who looked sharper as they consigned Nottinghamshire to defeat in their opening Championship fixture for the first time since 2002 (when they lost by an innings at Lord's). Cowan, on debut, hit his first three balls for four, and was proceeding serenely until he clipped Roland-Jones, who had earlier removed Hales and Lumb with successive deliveries and would finish with six wickets, to square leg. Shahzad's first over for Nottinghamshire went for 12, but he returned to have Rogers lbw. The floodlights stayed on through a bitingly cold second day, as Simpson set about securing a 75-run lead, helped by 51 extras. Lumb then completed a pair, before Dexter ran through the middle order with his little swingers, taking three in an over on his way to a maiden five-for; he might not have bowled had Harris not tweaked a hamstring. Adams and Fletcher swiped 89 for the ninth wicket, but the damage had already been done.

Close of play: first day, Middlesex 12-0 (Rogers 0, Robson 12); second day, Middlesex 297-6 (Simpson 77, Rayner 0); third day, Nottinghamshire 182-9 (Adams 50, Carter 0).

Nottinghamshire

A. D. Hales c Malan b Roland-Jones	20	– c Simpson b Berg	32
E. J. M. Cowan c Berg b Roland-Jones	61	– b Murtagh	1
M. J. Lumb lbw b Roland-Jones	0	– lbw b Roland-Jones	0
J. W. A. Taylor c Robson b Dexter	55	– c Simpson b Dexter	22
S. R. Patel c Simpson b Roland-Jones	36	– c sub (H. W. Podmore) b Dexter	4
M. H. Wessels run out	30	– (7) c Rayner b Dexter	0
*†C. M. W. Read c Dexter b Roland-Jones	34	– (6) lbw b Dexter	1
A. Shahzad c Simpson b Roland-Jones	4	– c Malan b Dexter	11
A. R. Adams c Rogers b Murtagh	14	– c Rayner b Roland-Jones	50
L. J. Fletcher c Malan b Murtagh	14	– b Murtagh	47
A. Carter not out	0	– not out	0
L-b 4, n-b 6	10	B 4, l-b 7, w 1, n-b 2	14
	278		182

1/51 (1) 2/51 (3) 3/98 (2)   (91.1 overs) 278
4/158 (5) 5/204 (4) 6/219 (6)
7/240 (8) 8/257 (9) 9/278 (10) 10/278 (7)

1/5 (2) 2/6 (3)   (47.1 overs) 182
3/53 (1) 4/60 (5)
5/67 (4) 6/67 (7) 7/68 (6)
8/93 (8) 9/182 (10) 10/182 (9)

Murtagh 24–6–86–2; Harris 14–3–39–0; Roland-Jones 22.1–4–63–6; Berg 14–5–38–0; Rayner 7–0–28–0; Dexter 10–2–20–1. *Second innings*—Murtagh 15–5–49–2; Roland-Jones 15.1–1–75–2; Berg 5–0–12–1; Dexter 9–1–27–5; Rayner 3–1–8–0.

Middlesex

*C. J. L. Rogers lbw b Shahzad	50	– not out	51
S. D. Robson c Read b Fletcher	76	– not out	55
J. L. Denly lbw b Fletcher	0		
D. J. Malan lbw b Shahzad	6		
N. J. Dexter b Adams	7		
†J. A. Simpson not out	97		
G. K. Berg lbw b Fletcher	43		
O. P. Rayner c Hales b Shahzad	13		
J. A. R. Harris c Read b Carter	8		
T. S. Roland-Jones c Patel b Carter	0		
T. J. Murtagh c Read b Adams	2		
B 7, l-b 16, w 16, n-b 12	51	L-b 1, w 1, n-b 2	4
	353	(no wkt, 25 overs)	110

1/106 (1) 2/107 (3) 3/148 (4)   (111 overs) 353
4/164 (5) 5/175 (2) 6/291 (7)
7/320 (8) 8/348 (9) 9/350 (10)
10/353 (11)
110 overs: 352-9

Fletcher 31–5–76–3; Shahzad 26–9–75–3; Adams 23–7–67–2; Carter 21–4–87–2; Patel 10–4–25–0. *Second innings*—Fletcher 5–1–26–0; Shahzad 3–0–19–0; Adams 5–1–21–0; Carter 7–1–26–0; Patel 5–1–17–0.

Umpires: N. G. B. Cook and N. A. Mallender.

NOTTINGHAMSHIRE v DURHAM MCCU

At Nottingham, April 17–19. Nottinghamshire won by 541 runs. Toss: Nottinghamshire. First-class debut: R. J. D. Willett.

This match, switched from Durham two weeks before the start, was one of the most lop-sided in history. Lumb and Patel had both attracted criticism during the defeat by Middlesex, but their violent hitting racked up 210 inside 47 overs before Lumb picked out France seamer Tom Liddiard (on as a substitute for Rory Cox, who had fractured his thumb). Patel went to his 15th first-class century at 12.59 – the first Nottinghamshire batsman to score a hundred before lunch since Paul Pollard, against

LARGEST WINS BY RUNS IN ENGLISH FIRST-CLASS CRICKET

562	Australia (701 and 327) beat England (321 and 145) at The Oval..............	1934
541	**Notts (396-3 dec and 408-9 dec) beat Durham MCCU (142 and 121) at Nottingham**	**2013**
524	Zimbabweans (568 and 258-2 dec) beat Gloucestershire (167 and 135) at Gloucester..	2000
522	Leicestershire (353-6 dec and 361-3 dec) beat Camb. U (127 and 65) at Cambridge...	1984
483	Surrey (494 and 492-9 dec) beat Leicestershire (361 and 142) at The Oval.........	2002
470	Sussex (309 and 307-5 dec) beat Gloucestershire (66 and 80) at Hove.............	1913

Lancashire on this ground in 1991 – and hit 12 sixes in his maiden double-century. Durham MCCU offered little resistance, and Read chose further batting practice, which he and Mullaney exploited. Nottinghamshire completed their heaviest win by runs on the third afternoon – eclipsing a 330-run victory at Chesterfield in 1904, when they bowled Derbyshire out for 32.

Close of play: first day, Durham MCCU 96-3 (Bishnoi 32, Patel 18); second day, Durham MCCU 4-0 (Jones 4, Hobson 0).

Nottinghamshire

M. J. Lumb c sub (T. K. G. Liddiard) b Willett....	83		
S. R. Patel b van den Bergh	256	– (10) c Patel b van den Bergh	18
S. J. Mullaney c Jones b Watkins..............	28	– c Patel b Watkins	103
J. W. A. Taylor not out	17	– (2) lbw b Wallis	14
*†C. M. W. Read (did not bat)		– (1) c Patel b van den Bergh	80
P. J. Franks (did not bat)		– (4) c Willett b Bishnoi	66
A. Shahzad (did not bat)		– (5) b Wallis	16
G. G. White (did not bat)		– (6) c Jones b van den Bergh......	23
B. J. Phillips (did not bat)		– (7) not out...................	53
J. T. Ball (did not bat)		– (8) c Bishnoi b Watkins	15
H. F. Gurney (did not bat)		– (9) c Bishnoi b van den Bergh	1
B 6, l-b 2, w 2, n-b 2	12	B 6, l-b 9, w 2, n-b 2	19

1/210 (1) 2/339 (3) (3 wkts dec, 73.2 overs) 396   1/55 (2) (9 wkts dec, 80.5 overs) 408
3/396 (2)   2/139 (1) 3/242 (3)
                                                    4/277 (4) 5/284 (5) 6/348 (6)
                                                    7/377 (8) 8/386 (9) 9/408 (10)

Wallis 18–1–92–0; Willett 19–3–80–1; Watkins 10–1–81–1; van den Bergh 13.2–2–61–1; Bishnoi 11–0–44–0; Patel 2–0–30–0. *Second innings*—Wallis 11–1–63–2; Willett 15–2–61–0; Watkins 16–0–76–2; van den Bergh 20.5–5–84–4; Bishnoi 10–1–52–1; Hobson 4–0–27–0; Patel 4–0–30–0.

Durham MCCU

*C. R. Jones c Read b Gurney	6	– c Read b Gurney 16
I. H. Hobson c Read b Shahzad	2	– lbw b Shahzad 1
R. A. C. Shah c Read b Gurney	21	– b Phillips 7
C. Bishnoi b Shahzad	54	– b Ball 25
L. A. Patel c Read b Gurney	28	– c Phillips b Patel 19
†O. J. Steele lbw b Franks	0	– lbw b Ball 3
N. A. T. Watkins run out	10	– lbw b Ball 3
F. O. E. van den Bergh c Read b Patel	1	– b White 34
C. A. Wallis b Shahzad	5	– lbw b Mullaney 0
R. J. D. Willett not out	0	– not out 2
R. D. Cox absent hurt		– absent hurt
B 1, l-b 8, n-b 10	19	B 3, l-b 4, n-b 4 11

1/11 (2) 2/36 (1)   (52.3 overs) 142
3/41 (3) 4/107 (5) 5/108 (6) 6/134 (7)
7/135 (8) 8/141 (9) 9/142 (9)

1/11 (2) 2/24 (3)   (54.4 overs) 121
3/54 (1) 4/70 (4) 5/76 (6)
6/80 (7) 7/96 (5) 8/113 (9) 9/121 (8)

Shahzad 12.3–5–21–3; Phillips 6–0–25–0; Gurney 11–3–25–3; Franks 13–3–34–1; Ball 6–3–21–0; Patel 4–2–7–1. *Second innings*—Ball 8–2–18–3; Phillips 7–3–6–1; Shahzad 7–1–21–1; Franks 8–5–11–0; Gurney 5–2–17–1; Patel 10–4–16–1; Mullaney 5–1–10–1; White 4.4–2–15–1.

Umpires: M. Burns and M. A. Gough.

At Derby, April 24–27. NOTTINGHAMSHIRE beat DERBYSHIRE by nine wickets.

NOTTINGHAMSHIRE v DURHAM

At Nottingham, April 29–May 2. Durham won by six wickets. Durham 22pts, Nottinghamshire 5pts. Toss: Nottinghamshire.

Durham's players were woken by a (false) fire alarm at 1.30 on the last morning, then again an hour later when a blaze did break out in the hotel gym. They had to hang around for two hours until they were let into another hotel just after 4.30. By the end of the day, however, it was Nottinghamshire who had suffered the rudest awakening, as Durham chased down 183 inside the final 23 overs. A shell-shocked attack – featuring Broad and Swann ahead of the New Zealand Test series – had no answer to an assault of 125 in the first 12 from Stoneman, whose 24-ball fifty was the fastest for Durham in first-class cricket, and Mustard, the only player who slept through the fire alarms. Swann, playing his first game since undergoing elbow surgery in March, took all four wickets, but he could not stop Durham going top of the table. On the first day, Taylor followed his century against Derbyshire with 97, becoming Breese's first Championship wicket since September 2008. But Durham forged a healthy lead, inspired by Will Smith's 393-ball marathon against his former county. Broad bowled quicker on the third day, despite having edged a ball into his groin during a breezy 46. Nottinghamshire lost five wickets before clearing their deficit, but Lumb and Swann – who took three blows to the body from Onions, and was given three penalty points for waving his bat after being the last man out, lbw to Borthwick – appeared to have staved off defeat. A sleep-deprived Durham had been kept in the field for 116 overs, but they made spectacular use of the last 90 minutes.

Close of play: first day, Durham 34-1 (Smith 3, Rushworth 0); second day, Durham 297-6 (Smith 119, Mustard 15); third day, Nottinghamshire 145-5 (Lumb 77, Fletcher 3).

Nottinghamshire

E. J. M. Cowan c Smith b Onions	40	– (2) c Mustard b Wood	35
A. D. Hales lbw b Onions	2	– (1) b Rushworth	0
M. J. Lumb lbw b Stokes	9	– c and b Breese	123
J. W. A. Taylor c Mustard b Breese	97	– lbw b Wood	1
S. R. Patel c Borthwick b Stokes	17	– c Breese b Wood	4
S. J. Mullaney c Breese b Wood	80	– c Collingwood b Breese	20
*†C. M. W. Read c Stokes b Wood	2	– (8) c Collingwood b Borthwick	29
S. C. J. Broad c Breese b Stokes	46	– (9) c Stoneman b Borthwick	10
G. P. Swann not out	8	– (10) lbw b Borthwick	57
A. Shahzad c Mustard b Rushworth	2	– (11) not out	17
L. J. Fletcher c Wood b Rushworth	2	– (7) c Mustard b Borthwick	17
B 6, l-b 7, n-b 2	15	B 2, l-b 7, w 1, n-b 10	20

1/33 (2) 2/44 (1) 3/74 (3)   (83.5 overs) 320
4/98 (5) 5/209 (6) 6/223 (7)
7/307 (4) 8/307 (8) 9/316 (10) 10/320 (11)

1/1 (1) 2/77 (2)   (116.2 overs) 333
3/85 (4) 4/93 (5)
5/136 (6) 6/182 (7) 7/236 (8)
8/246 (3) 9/258 (9) 10/333 (10)

Onions 17–3–63–2; Rushworth 15.5–2–62–2; Breese 16–2–66–1; Wood 16.5–5–58–2; Stokes 19–3–58–3. *Second innings*—Onions 20–5–59–0; Rushworth 8–1–36–1; Borthwick 24.2–4–87–4; Stokes 12–1–48–0; Wood 20–4–54–3; Breese 32–14–40–2.

Durham

M. D. Stoneman lbw b Shahzad	30	– c Broad b Swann	69
W. R. Smith c Fletcher b Patel	153		
C. Rushworth c Read b Shahzad	12		
S. G. Borthwick c Read b Fletcher	16		
D. M. Benkenstein lbw b Mullaney	27	– (4) c Read b Swann	9
B. A. Stokes c and b Broad	11	– (3) st Read b Swann	12
*P. D. Collingwood c Read b Broad	64	– (6) not out	0
†P. Mustard c Read b Broad	21	– (2) c Hales b Swann	72
G. R. Breese lbw b Broad	44	– (5) not out	18
M. A. Wood not out	58		
G. Onions c Patel b Mullaney	26		
B 1, l-b 6, n-b 2	9	B 3, l-b 1	4

1/34 (1) 2/46 (3) 3/86 (4)   (157.3 overs) 471
4/124 (5) 5/148 (6) 6/263 (7) 7/313 (8)
8/356 (2) 9/401 (9) 10/471 (11)   110 overs: 309-6

1/125 (1)   (4 wkts, 20.2 overs) 184
2/150 (3) 3/164 (4)
4/177 (2)

Broad 31–4–88–4; Fletcher 30–9–84–1; Shahzad 31–6–90–2; Swann 34–7–90–0; Mullaney 13.3–2–51–2; Patel 18.4–4–61–1. *Second innings*—Broad 4–0–34–0; Fletcher 2–0–25–0; Shahzad 1–0–19–0; Patel 6.2–0–46–0; Swann 7–0–56–4.

Umpires: S. A. Garratt and P. Willey.

NOTTINGHAMSHIRE v SURREY

At Nottingham, May 15–18. Nottinghamshire won by 114 runs. Nottinghamshire 21pts, Surrey 4pts. Toss: Surrey.

After a run of 98 consecutive matches Chris Read missed his first Championship game since 2006, because of a neck injury. Taylor captained instead, while Wessels returned from hamstring trouble to take the gloves. But it was Mullaney and Franks who played the instrumental roles in Nottinghamshire's victory – their first without Andre Adams since May 2010. On a typically seamer-friendly surface, Mullaney secured two batting points, with Shahzad hanging around for 84 balls to contribute eight to their partnership of 66. Surrey requested the use of the heavy roller before their reply, but they were soon 71 for six, and Nottinghamshire's bowlers took on a pack mentality; Patel removed Wilson and Batty just as their seventh-wicket stand began to look dangerous.

Nottinghamshire's first-innings lead of 67 seemed telling on a pitch getting trickier. Surrey set off on a difficult pursuit of 259 on the third evening, but Fletcher nipped out two before the close, and Mullaney executed a brilliant back-handed throw from mid-on to run out Solanki. Burns was the major obstacle but, after Franks had him caught behind, Surrey slumped to defeat.

Close of play: first day, Nottinghamshire 273-9 (Fletcher 5, Gurney 6); second day, Nottinghamshire 24-1 (Cowan 4, Fletcher 0); third day, Surrey 73-3 (Burns 41, de Bruyn 9).

Nottinghamshire

A. D. Hales b Dernbach	4	– (2) b Meaker	17
E. J. M. Cowan b Meaker	15	– (1) b Dernbach	20
M. J. Lumb c Linley b Meaker	44	– (4) lbw b Linley	28
*J. W. A. Taylor b Linley	47	– (5) c Wilson b Dernbach	13
S. R. Patel c Wilson b Linley	35	– (6) c de Bruyn b Meaker	37
†M. H. Wessels b Meaker	1	– (7) c Roy b Dernbach	0
S. J. Mullaney lbw b Linley	68	– (8) c de Bruyn b Linley	8
P. J. Franks c Davies b Meaker	4	– (9) c Davies b Meaker	5
A. Shahzad c Davies b Dernbach	8	– (10) run out	20
L. J. Fletcher not out	6	– (3) c de Bruyn b Meaker	26
H. F. Gurney lbw b Dernbach	6	– not out	9
B 4, l-b 18, n-b 14	36	B 1, l-b 4, w 1, n-b 2	8

1/6 (1) 2/54 (2) 3/83 (3) (96.3 overs) 274 1/22 (2) 2/60 (3) (66.2 overs) 191
4/143 (5) 5/160 (6) 6/168 (4) 3/98 (1) 4/98 (4)
7/181 (8) 8/247 (9) 9/265 (7) 10/274 (11) 5/122 (5) 6/122 (7) 7/153 (6)
  8/159 (9) 9/161 (8) 10/191 (10)

Dernbach 24.3–3–76–3; Linley 28–10–54–3; de Bruyn 16–6–45–0; Meaker 23–6–70–4; Batty 5–1–7–0. *Second innings*—Linley 22.2–7–43–2; Dernbach 18–5–60–3; Meaker 20–6–64–4; de Bruyn 6–3–19–0.

Surrey

R. J. Burns c Wessels b Gurney	4	– c Wessels b Franks	53
J. J. Roy b Fletcher	5	– c Hales b Fletcher	5
A. Harinath c Lumb b Shahzad	24	– c Wessels b Fletcher	4
V. S. Solanki lbw b Fletcher	8	– run out	0
Z. de Bruyn c Patel b Franks	9	– c Wessels b Franks	14
†S. M. Davies c Patel b Franks	0	– b Gurney	28
G. C. Wilson c Wessels b Patel	49	– c and b Gurney	0
*G. J. Batty st Wessels b Patel	41	– c Patel b Gurney	4
S. C. Meaker not out	7	– c Cowan b Patel	7
T. E. Linley b Gurney	11	– c Hales b Franks	6
J. W. Dernbach c Franks b Shahzad	15	– not out	0
B 16, l-b 9, w 1, n-b 8	34	B 8, l-b 9, n-b 6	23

1/5 (1) 2/9 (2) 3/27 (4) (76.2 overs) 207 1/7 (2) 2/21 (3) (52.3 overs) 144
4/47 (5) 5/47 (6) 6/71 (3) 3/29 (4) 4/90 (1)
7/152 (7) 8/161 (8) 9/183 (10) 10/207 (11) 5/107 (5) 6/108 (7) 7/114 (8)
  8/129 (6) 9/144 (10) 10/144 (9)

Fletcher 18–10–40–2; Gurney 20–5–57–2; Shahzad 13.2–4–37–2; Franks 14–6–33–2; Mullaney 3–0–11–0; Patel 8–6–4–2. *Second innings*—Fletcher 16–5–40–2; Gurney 15–3–40–3; Shahzad 4–0–22–0; Franks 12–5–16–3; Patel 4.3–1–6–1; Mullaney 1–0–3–0.

Umpires: M. J. D. Bodenham and S. J. O'Shaughnessy.

At Hove, May 31–June 3. NOTTINGHAMSHIRE drew with SUSSEX.

At Scarborough, June 5–8. NOTTINGHAMSHIRE drew with YORKSHIRE.

NOTTINGHAMSHIRE v DERBYSHIRE

At Nottingham, June 12–15. Drawn. Nottinghamshire 11pts, Derbyshire 9pts. Toss: Nottinghamshire.

Nottinghamshire won the toss on an overcast, damp morning, but claimed only two wickets in the 65 overs possible in the day – although Patel put down chances at slip off Gurney from consecutive balls. Hughes's extravagant half-century set a platform for Madsen and Chanderpaul but, with two more sessions lost next day, the match descended into a hunt for bonus points. Lumb mastered tricky conditions as he scored a career-best unbeaten 221 – his third hundred in eight innings – and was ably supported by Fletcher, who turned an appearance as nightwatchman into his second fifty. Lumb's sparkling form helped gloss over Nottinghamshire's perennial problems with their opening pair: Wessels retired hurt on nine with a bruised hand inflicted by Footitt, Alex Hales had been dropped after mustering 34 in his last nine innings, and Cowan was playing his final Championship game before joining Australia's Ashes squad.

Close of play: first day, Derbyshire 245-2 (Madsen 67, Chanderpaul 78); second day, Derbyshire 306-6 (Johnson 8, Wainwright 6); third day, Nottinghamshire 204-3 (Lumb 115, Fletcher 0).

Derbyshire

B. A. Godleman c Read b Adams	28	M. L. Turner not out		23
C. F. Hughes c Adams b Gurney	59	M. H. A. Footitt c Wessels b Patel		24
*W. L. Madsen lbw b Adams	74			
S. Chanderpaul b Adams	87	B 12, l-b 10, w 1, n-b 12		35
W. J. Durston b Gurney	15			
B. T. Slater c Franks b Gurney	2	1/89 (2) 2/100 (1)	(106.3 overs)	391
†R. M. Johnson c Read b Adams	22	3/265 (3) 4/280 (4)		
D. J. Wainwright c Cowan b Franks	22	5/284 (5) 6/291 (6) 7/331 (7)		
T. D. Groenewald c Wessels b Franks	0	8/336 (9) 9/337 (8) 10/391 (11)		

Fletcher 23–3–67–0; Gurney 30–6–94–3; Adams 24–3–69–4; Franks 18–2–70–2; Patel 9.3–0–57–1; Mullaney 2–0–12–0.

Nottinghamshire

M. H. Wessels retired hurt	9	A. R. Adams c Chanderpaul b Turner		11
E. J. M. Cowan c Hughes b Groenewald	24	H. F. Gurney not out		4
M. J. Lumb not out	221			
J. W. A. Taylor b Groenewald	40	B 7, l-b 5, w 2, n-b 4		18
S. R. Patel c Chanderpaul b Footitt	9			
L. J. Fletcher lbw b Durston	64	1/47 (2)	(8 wkts dec, 101.4 overs)	436
S. J. Mullaney c Hughes b Groenewald	7	2/168 (4) 3/201 (5)		
*†C. M. W. Read b Turner	21	4/324 (6) 5/354 (7) 6/394 (8)		
P. J. Franks b Turner	8	7/406 (9) 8/422 (10)		

Wessels retired hurt at 19-0.

Groenewald 24–5–112–3; Footitt 25–2–104–1; Turner 20.4–1–92–3; Wainwright 12–0–61–0; Durston 20–0–55–1.

Umpires: M. R. Benson and J. H. Evans.

NOTTINGHAMSHIRE v SUSSEX

At Nottingham, June 22–25. Drawn. Nottinghamshire 8pts, Sussex 10pts. Toss: Nottinghamshire.

Hunting a fourth win to return to the top of the Championship, Sussex were repelled by the fortitude of Taylor and Shahzad. Joyce overcame lengthy stoppages on the first two days to compile a carefree fifth hundred against his favourite opponents. Helped by a short leg-side boundary, he tucked into Patel on the third day with three sixes and a four in an over – reaching his double-century, taking Sussex past 500, and prompting him to declare. Meanwhile, Hamilton-Brown, who had been dropped to the Second XI after the reverse fixture in May, scored his first hundred in more than a year. Nottinghamshire were forced to withdraw the in-form Michael Lumb five minutes before the toss, due to his involvement in England's Twenty20 international series against New Zealand, which began on the fourth day of this game; the ECB had turned down the county's request to replace him after two days. Mullaney made 30 filling in as opener, but was part of a four-wicket burst for Jordan and, when Panesar removed Read and Franks, Nottinghamshire were still 307 behind with more than a day remaining. But Taylor was unmoved as he made his first double-hundred for Nottinghamshire and, with Shahzad showing restraint in a 200-run partnership for the seventh wicket, the match petered out.

Close of play: first day, Sussex 91-1 (Nash 45, Yardy 7); second day, Sussex 363-4 (Joyce 129, Hamilton-Brown 77); third day, Nottinghamshire 223-6 (Taylor 81, Shahzad 5).

Sussex

C. D. Nash c Patel b Fletcher	46	M. W. Machan not out	25
L. W. P. Wells c Read b Adams	39	B 4, l-b 3, w 1, n-b 6	14
M. H. Yardy c Gurney b Shahzad	35		—
*E. C. Joyce not out	204	1/69 (2) (5 wkts dec, 110 overs)	506
†M. J. Prior lbw b Fletcher	30	2/95 (1) 3/140 (3)	
R. J. Hamilton-Brown c Read b Fletcher	113	4/205 (5) 5/437 (6)	

C. J. Jordan, S. J. Magoffin, L. J. Hatchett and M. S. Panesar did not bat.

Fletcher 25–6–105–3; Gurney 17.3–1–79–0; Shahzad 23–2–103–1; Adams 22–1–97–1; Franks 10.3–1–51–0; Patel 10–0–56–0; Mullaney 2–0–8–0.

Nottinghamshire

S. J. Mullaney b Jordan	30	L. J. Fletcher c Jordan b Nash	14
M. H. Wessels c Panesar b Jordan	49	A. R. Adams not out	28
J. W. A. Taylor not out	204	B 7, l-b 7, w 1, n-b 6	21
S. R. Patel c Machan b Jordan	3		—
D. J. Hussey c Prior b Jordan	6	1/63 (2) (8 wkts dec, 150 overs)	478
*†C. M. W. Read b Panesar	45	2/90 (1) 3/94 (4)	
P. J. Franks c Jordan b Panesar	1	4/106 (5) 5/197 (6) 6/199 (7)	
A. Shahzad c Machan b Jordan	77	7/399 (8) 8/426 (9) 110 overs: 354-6	

H. F. Gurney did not bat.

Magoffin 28–8–77–0; Hatchett 29–3–98–0; Jordan 32–5–130–5; Panesar 29–7–65–2; Wells 10–1–39–0; Nash 18–2–40–1; Hamilton-Brown 4–1–15–0.

Umpires: N. L. Bainton and P. J. Hartley.

At The Oval, July 8–11. NOTTINGHAMSHIRE drew with SURREY.

At Birmingham, July 15–18. NOTTINGHAMSHIRE lost to WARWICKSHIRE by 216 runs.

At Taunton, August 2–5. NOTTINGHAMSHIRE drew with SOMERSET.

At Nottingham, August 14. NOTTINGHAMSHIRE beat BANGLADESH A by four wickets (see Bangladesh A tour section).

NOTTINGHAMSHIRE v YORKSHIRE

At Nottingham, August 21–23. Yorkshire won by ten wickets. Yorkshire 23pts, Nottinghamshire 2pts. Toss: Nottinghamshire. County debut: K. S. Williamson.

Yorkshire swept Nottinghamshire aside by the third afternoon to take their Championship lead to 25.5 points. They showed resolve to recover from 137 for four, and benefited from Bairstow's late arrival: not required for the Oval Test, he came in at No. 8 and almost earned maximum batting points. Fletcher had removed five of the top six, including New Zealand batsman Kane Williamson first ball, for his best return in two years, but eventually succumbed to cramp. In comparison, Sidebottom and Patterson, whose five for 43 was a personal-best, repeatedly asked questions the Nottinghamshire batsmen could not answer. A feckless performance saw them reduced to 65 for eight, and some lusty blows from Adams – 39 in 17 balls – hardly disguised their inadequacies. They were more dogged following on, without ever threatening to halt Yorkshire. Read reached his first Championship fifty of a wretched season, before his old team-mate Sidebottom had him caught behind to pass his father Arnie's career total of 596 first-class wickets.

Close of play: first day, Yorkshire 327-8 (Bairstow 24, Patterson 8); second day, Nottinghamshire 118-4 (Hussey 22, Wessels 12).

Yorkshire

A. Lyth c Read b Fletcher	95	– not out		12
A. Z. Lees c Read b Gurney	8	– not out		0
P. A. Jaques lbw b Fletcher	19			
*A. W. Gale c Read b Fletcher	33			
K. S. Williamson c Patel b Fletcher	0			
A. U. Rashid lbw b Fletcher	78			
L. E. Plunkett c Read b Gurney	41			
†J. M. Bairstow b Adams	62			
R. J. Sidebottom c Read b Gurney	0			
S. A. Patterson c Read b Adams	40			
J. A. Brooks not out	2			
B 4, l-b 16, w 1, n-b 8	29			

1/20 (2) 2/61 (3) 3/137 (4)   (113.3 overs) 407   (no wkt, 0.5 overs) 12
4/137 (5) 5/202 (1) 6/281 (6) 7/303 (7)
8/305 (9) 9/396 (10) 10/407 (8)   110 overs: 383-8

Bairstow replaced A. J. Hodd after being released from the England squad.

Fletcher 28.4–6–93–5; Gurney 18–3–71–3; Adams 24.5–2–95–2; Mullaney 5–3–14–0; Shahzad 23–4–68–0; Patel 14–3–46–0. *Second innings*—Fletcher 0.5–0–12–0.

Nottinghamshire

S. J. Mullaney c Bairstow b Patterson	13	– lbw b Sidebottom		6
A. D. Hales c Bairstow b Sidebottom	0	– c Bairstow b Brooks		14
M. J. Lumb lbw b Sidebottom	0	– c and b Plunkett		20
S. R. Patel c Jaques b Sidebottom	23	– c sub (R. M. Pyrah) b Plunkett		37
D. J. Hussey lbw b Patterson	13	– c Bairstow b Sidebottom		24
M. H. Wessels c Bairstow b Sidebottom	4	– c Lyth b Brooks		22
*†C. M. W. Read lbw b Patterson	1	– c Bairstow b Sidebottom		58
A. Shahzad not out	41	– c Williamson b Rashid		19
L. J. Fletcher c Rashid b Patterson	0	– c Gale b Rashid		19
A. R. Adams c Sidebottom b Patterson	39	– not out		31
H. F. Gurney c Plunkett b Rashid	4	– c Jaques b Rashid		0
B 5, l-b 5, n-b 2	12	B 11, w 1, n-b 4		16

1/5 (2) 2/9 (3) 3/25 (1)   (35.4 overs) 150   1/22 (2) 2/28 (1)   (71.3 overs) 266
4/41 (4) 5/57 (5) 6/59 (6)   3/73 (3) 4/102 (4)
7/61 (7) 8/65 (9) 9/115 (10) 10/150 (11)   5/120 (5) 6/167 (6) 7/209 (8)
                              8/218 (7) 9/252 (9) 10/266 (11)

Sidebottom 14–2–35–4; Brooks 6–0–16–0; Patterson 11–3–43–5; Plunkett 4–0–46–0; Rashid 0.4–0–0–1. *Second innings*—Sidebottom 17–4–38–3; Brooks 13–2–68–2; Plunkett 13–0–70–2; Williamson 7–1–24–0; Patterson 13–3–33–0; Rashid 8.3–1–22–3.

Umpires: T. E. Jesty and G. Sharp.

NOTTINGHAMSHIRE v WARWICKSHIRE

At Nottingham, September 3–6. Drawn. Nottinghamshire 10pts, Warwickshire 8pts. Toss: Nottinghamshire. Championship debut: P. J. McKay.

Nottinghamshire alarm bells were ringing by the first-day close. The good work of Fletcher and Adams in reducing Warwickshire to 192 for eight had been undone by Jeetan Patel's feisty half-century, before three home wickets fell in the first four overs of their reply; Hales's dismal summer reached its nadir as he left a ball that removed his off stump. But Samit Patel dug in next day for his third Championship century of the season, while Wessels contributed 77 and Adams thumped 46 in 26 balls. Fletcher followed up with his second five-wicket haul in consecutive matches – a career-best five for 52 – and Warwickshire found their scoring options squeezed. But persistent rain prevented Nottinghamshire's pursuit of 211 on the final day, so relegation remained a risk. Warwickshire's bad luck with wicketkeepers continued when Pete McKay, playing because Ambrose had a fractured thumb, twisted his ankle while batting. Nottinghamshire's reserve keeper, Matt Cross, stood in briefly, and Jamie Atkinson took over on the second day. On the third evening, Warwickshire had four batsmen in the middle, with runners for Maddy and McKay. Maddy, who had a calf strain, scored a determined 65 in his final first-class innings.

Close of play: first day, Nottinghamshire 14-3 (Mullaney 8, Patel 1); second day, Warwickshire 27-2 (Javid 7, Evans 4); third day, Warwickshire 271.

Warwickshire

*V. Chopra c Read b Fletcher	76	– lbw b Adams 7
I. J. Westwood c Read b Adams	10	– b Fletcher 2
A. Javid c Mullaney b Gurney	0	– c Read b Shahzad 24
L. J. Evans c Read b Adams	32	– c Taylor b Gurney 63
C. R. Woakes run out	1	– b Patel 23
S. A. Piolet c Read b Fletcher	1	– c Hussey b Fletcher ... 30
D. L. Maddy c Gurney b Adams	47	– lbw b Fletcher 65
K. H. D. Barker c Hales b Adams	13	– c Read b Fletcher 18
J. S. Patel not out	66	– c Hussey b Gurney 16
†P. J. McKay c Mullaney b Fletcher	33	– not out 3
M. A. Chambers c Hales b Fletcher	5	– lbw b Fletcher 4
L-b 3, w 1, n-b 10	14	L-b 6, n-b 10 16

1/35 (2) 2/52 (3) 3/125 (1)　　　(88.2 overs) 298
4/125 (4) 5/126 (6) 6/136 (5)
7/179 (8) 8/192 (7) 9/280 (10) 10/298 (11)

1/9 (2) 2/11 (1)　　　(108.3 overs) 271
3/81 (3) 4/126 (5)
5/135 (4) 6/177 (6) 7/208 (8)
8/237 (9) 9/267 (7) 10/271 (11)

Fletcher 22.2–8–56–4; Shahzad 19–7–49–0; Adams 22–1–77–4; Gurney 13–0–68–1; Mullaney 3–0–13–0; Patel 9–0–32–0. *Second innings*—Fletcher 23.3–7–52–5; Shahzad 17–1–70–1; Adams 30–7–79–1; Gurney 21–6–44–2; Patel 16–7–19–1; Hussey 1–0–1–0.

Nottinghamshire

S. J. Mullaney c Chambers b Piolet	28		A. Shahzad c Barker b Chambers	28
A. D. Hales b Barker	0		A. R. Adams c Westwood b Barker	46
L. J. Fletcher b Chambers	2		H. F. Gurney not out	1
M. J. Lumb c Chopra b Chambers	0		B 4, l-b 12, n-b 16	32
S. R. Patel c Piolet b Maddy	117			
D. J. Hussey c sub (J. J. Atkinson) b Woakes	28		1/1 (2) 2/4 (3) 3/10 (4)　(85 overs)	359
M. H. Wessels run out	77		4/78 (1) 5/136 (6) 6/237 (5)	
*†C. M. W. Read c Maddy b Chambers	0		7/251 (8) 8/291 (7) 9/350 (10) 10/359 (9)	

J. W. A. Taylor replaced Wessels after being released from the England squad.

Barker 19–4–81–2; Chambers 21–4–79–4; Woakes 5–1–13–1; Piolet 12–0–59–1; Patel 16–3–61–0; Maddy 12–2–50–1.

Umpires: J. H. Evans and P. J. Hartley.

At Lord's, September 11–14. NOTTINGHAMSHIRE drew with MIDDLESEX.

At Chester-le-Street, September 17–19. NOTTINGHAMSHIRE lost to DURHAM by eight wickets.

NOTTINGHAMSHIRE v SOMERSET

At Nottingham, September 24–27. Drawn. Nottinghamshire 11pts, Somerset 10pts. Toss: Somerset. Championship debut: B. A. Hutton.

Fresh from winning the YB40 final, Nottinghamshire turned their attention to retaining Division One status. Somerset were similarly placed: given that a high-scoring draw would probably save both sides, the ECB sent Tony Pigott as referee to keep an eye on things. He enjoyed an engrossing first day, with Nottinghamshire reduced to 76 for four in swing-friendly conditions, only for Lumb and Hussey to turn the tide with gritty hundreds. Hussey's was his 23rd first-class century for the county in his farewell appearance. Meanwhile Overton, already warned for bowling a beamer, was removed from the attack by the umpires after two consecutive bouncers – to the obvious annoyance of Trescothick. Nottinghamshire secured maximum batting points on the second morning before Compton and Hildreth, who reached a serene run-a-ball hundred, added 248 for Somerset's third wicket. With Derbyshire spiralling to defeat against Warwickshire, the pressure was released. Gurney's career-best gave Nottinghamshire a slender lead, extended to 173 on the third evening, but the teams batted out time. The only remaining point of interest was Patel's unsuccessful effort to take the one wicket or catch he needed to win the PCA's £10,000 prize for the domestic season's Most Valuable Player, which instead went to Worcestershire's Moeen Ali.

Close of play: first day, Nottinghamshire 378-7 (Franks 15, Hutton 6); second day, Somerset 183-2 (Compton 62, Hildreth 102); third day, Nottinghamshire 139-3 (Taylor 23, Patel 7).

Nottinghamshire

S. J. Mullaney b Gregory	17	– c Mescede b Trego	59
M. H. Wessels c Kieswetter b Overton	7	– c Gregory b Trego	20
M. J. Lumb lbw b Gregory	107	– c Thomas b Mescede	20
J. W. A. Taylor lbw b Gregory	0	– c Kieswetter b Thomas	55
S. R. Patel b Thomas	16	– c Buttler b Gregory	29
D. J. Hussey c Kieswetter b Mescede	125	– c Buttler b Thomas	1
*†C. M. W. Read c Kieswetter b Mescede	39	– not out	52
P. J. Franks lbw b Thomas	15	– c Buttler b Thomas	2
B. A. Hutton not out	20	– b Overton	42
L. J. Fletcher c Compton b Thomas	12	– c Kieswetter b Trego	1
H. F. Gurney c Kieswetter b Thomas	0	– b Trego	0
B 6, l-b 11, w 3, n-b 28	48	L-b 2, w 1, n-b 14	17

1/18 (2) 2/40 (1) 3/42 (4)   (104.5 overs) 406   1/79 (2) 2/96 (1)   (83.4 overs) 298
4/76 (5) 5/290 (6) 6/341 (3)   3/114 (3) 4/200 (5)
7/372 (7) 8/378 (8) 9/406 (10) 10/406 (11)   5/201 (6) 6/202 (4) 7/210 (8)
                                        8/285 (9) 9/298 (10) 10/298 (11)

Gregory 28.2–1–105–3; Overton 10.4–2–52–1; Mescede 21–3–67–2; Thomas 26.5–2–103–4; Trego 18–3–62–0. *Second innings*—Gregory 10–2–37–1; Overton 13–2–63–1; Mescede 17–3–71–1; Thomas 20–6–44–3; Trego 20.4–6–69–4; Kieswetter 3–0–12–0.

Somerset

*M. E. Trescothick lbw b Gurney	2	– c Taylor b Hutton	14
C. R. Jones c Read b Fletcher	4	– not out	55
N. R. D. Compton b Patel	87	– not out	25
J. C. Hildreth c Read b Fletcher	161		
†C. Kieswetter c Mullaney b Franks	14		
J. C. Buttler lbw b Gurney	13		
P. D. Trego c Taylor b Gurney	22		
C. A. J. Mescede c Lumb b Gurney	0		
L. Gregory not out	40		
A. C. Thomas c Wessels b Gurney	2		
J. Overton c Read b Franks	0		
L-b 13, n-b 14	27	L-b 7	7

1/3 (1) 2/11 (2) 3/259 (3)   (103.3 overs) 372   1/38 (1)   (1 wkt, 28 overs) 101
4/276 (5) 5/303 (4) 6/303 (6)
7/303 (8) 8/365 (7) 9/371 (10) 10/372 (11)

Fletcher 27–8–79–2; Gurney 25–4–81–5; Hutton 13–1–78–0; Franks 13.3–2–57–2; Patel 16–8–36–1; Mullaney 9–1–28–0. *Second innings*—Fletcher 3–3–0–0; Gurney 3–1–4–0; Hutton 9–3–31–1; Patel 11–4–49–0; Mullaney 2–0–10–0.

Umpires: M. A. Gough and N. J. Llong.

SOMERSET

Class issue as Buttler departs

RICHARD LATHAM

Perhaps being bridesmaids was not so bad after all. Having caught many a bouquet in recent years, Somerset never made it to the church in 2013. They failed to reach a limited-overs final, and struggled so badly in the Championship that relegation was still a threat going into the last game. An eventual placing of sixth disguised the anxiety of the summer's closing matches.

Marcus Trescothick admitted to thinking "thank God that's over" when his season ended with a pull to midwicket off the meat of the bat, handing Nottinghamshire's Brett Hutton his maiden first-class scalp. Trescothick was plagued by ankle trouble for much of the season, and finished with an average of 27 and a top score of 74 from 32 innings – his first year since 1998 without a century. It was an indication of how much Somerset have relied on him over the years that, when his form dipped, so did the team's. He was bitterly disappointed, but vowed to continue as captain for 2014 and emerge as productive as ever following more ankle surgery.

Of the batsmen, Nick Compton alone had a strong season – testament to his resolve after the hammer blow of losing his England place just before the Ashes – although James Hildreth crept past 1,000 first-class runs with a hundred in the last game. Because of Trescothick's below-par tally of 843, Somerset needed someone else to step up. Alviro Petersen averaged 46 during his spell as overseas player, but appeared in only six Championship games, while his short-term replacement, Dean Elgar, failed to score a fifty in three. Alex Barrow progressed without making a big score, and Chris Jones took 130 off the Australians in the tour match but struggled for the same form in county fixtures.

The bowlers underperformed too, with no one getting close to 50 wickets. Nineteen-year-old Jamie Overton's 35 was a good effort in his breakthrough season, but twin brother Craig did not play a competitive match after May due to a stress fracture of the back. Steve Kirby's return of 26 first-class wickets was insufficient, and the fact that, in just four appearances as overseas spinner, Piyush Chawla took as many (17) as Irishman George Dockrell underlined his difficulties. There were some positives: another left-arm spinner, Jack Leach, enjoyed early-season success, while Craig Meschede and Lewis Gregory took up new-ball duties with gusto. But Gemaal Hussain endured a third frustrating year following his move from Gloucestershire, and was not retained.

Somerset were semi-finalists in the YB40, and reached the last eight of the Twenty20 competition, but were unable to bully opponents as in recent years. The YB40 defeat by Nottinghamshire, when they slumped to 119, was possibly the worst performance by a Somerset side in a knockout contest.

Their progress in both tournaments centred on all-rounder Peter Trego, whose dominance brought him more than 1,000 limited-overs runs, fulfilling a long-held ambition. The fact that he scored almost twice as many YB40 runs as the next man, Trescothick, was an indictment of the specialist batsmen. Craig Kieswetter glistened in the Twenty20, with 517 runs at 64 – more than anyone in the country. Meschede's rise as a frontline bowler was sparked by some assured displays in 40-over cricket, while Yasir Arafat proved a predictably reliable Twenty20 signing.

Craig Meschede

Compton eventually agreed a contract extension, but Jos Buttler departed for Lancashire – a decision motivated primarily by the desire to safeguard his international future by keeping wicket regularly, having lost the position to Kieswetter in all formats. His exit did nothing to lighten the mood among supporters, who saw the Taunton-born 23-year-old Buttler, nurtured through the club's youth set-up from an early age, as one of their own. Somerset had found it impossible to satisfy both him and Kieswetter, and ended up losing potentially the most destructive one-day batsman in the country.

It all added up to a trying first season for director of cricket Dave Nosworthy, the South African handed the tough task of replacing club legend Brian Rose; Trescothick compared it to David Moyes taking over from Sir Alex Ferguson at Manchester United. Nosworthy approached the job with quiet determination as he got used to the way Somerset's dressing-room operated. With a summer behind him, he pledged to be more forceful in implementing his methods. The time to judge Nosworthy will be at the end of the 2014 season, after his first winter of recruitment. At least the club was in decent financial shape: they recorded a pre-tax profit for 2013 of almost £470,000.

Some critics blamed Somerset's problems on a lack of specialist coaches in the two main disciplines. Nosworthy changed that with the recruitment of the highly respected Dave Houghton as batting coach, while Jason Kerr moved up from the Academy to work with the bowlers; Andy Hurry's role altered from first-team coach to director of high performance, where he would concentrate on younger players. Nosworthy re-signed Petersen for 2014 – when he was expected to have fewer international distractions – and also snapped up the South African-born limited-overs specialist Johann Myburgh, who was already based in England.

Championship attendance: 42,715.

SOMERSET RESULTS

All first-class matches – Played 17: Won 3, Lost 6, Drawn 8.
County Championship matches – Played 16: Won 3, Lost 5, Drawn 8.

LV= County Championship, 6th in Division 1;
Friends Life t20, quarter-finalists; Yorkshire Bank 40, semi-finalists.

COUNTY CHAMPIONSHIP AVERAGES, BATTING AND FIELDING

Cap		M	I	NO	R	HS	100	50	Avge	Ct/St
2011	N. R. D. Compton‡	12	23	3	1,001	166	2	7	50.05	6
2013	A. N. Petersen§	6	12	0	562	167	2	2	46.83	3
	P. P. Chawla§	4	6	0	231	112	1	0	38.50	1
2013	J. C. Buttler†‡	9	15	1	508	119*	1	2	36.28	16
2009	C. Kieswetter‡	11	19	2	584	148	1	3	34.35	41/3
2007	J. C. Hildreth	16	29	2	867	161	2	2	32.11	16
1999	M. E. Trescothick†	16	30	1	804	74	0	6	27.72	30
	A. W. R. Barrow†	9	15	1	370	83*	0	2	26.42	9
	D. Elgar§	3	5	0	123	33	0	0	24.60	2
	L. Gregory	6	8	1	141	52	0	1	20.14	3
	C. R. Jones	6	11	1	198	58	0	2	19.80	2
2007	P. D. Trego†	14	23	1	374	82	0	1	17.00	4
	C. A. J. Meschede	9	13	1	192	59	0	1	16.00	6
2008	A. C. Thomas¶	13	21	5	239	54*	0	1	14.93	4
	G. H. Dockrell	7	10	2	106	31	0	0	13.25	2
2009	A. V. Suppiah	6	11	0	130	36	0	0	11.81	2
	J. Overton	12	18	6	125	24	0	0	10.41	0
	M. J. Leach†	5	9	2	66	21	0	0	9.42	0
	S. P. Kirby	10	15	6	75	15	0	0	8.33	3

Also batted: G. M. Hussain (2 matches) 2*, 0* (1 ct); C. Overton (1 match) 8.

† *Born in Somerset.*   ‡ *ECB contract.*   § *Official overseas player.*   ¶ *Other non-England-qualified player.*

BOWLING

	Style	O	M	R	W	BB	5I	Avge
M. J. Leach	SLA	149.4	51	324	13	5-63	1	24.92
L. Gregory	RFM	119.4	25	358	14	5-38	1	25.57
A. C. Thomas	RFM	386.4	108	1,077	42	5-69	1	25.64
C. A. J. Meschede	RM	177.1	33	639	24	4-43	0	26.62
P. P. Chawla	LBG	122.4	13	453	17	5-97	2	26.64
P. D. Trego	RFM	340.2	80	1,029	31	4-69	0	33.19
J. Overton	RFM	284.5	48	1,121	33	6-95	1	33.96
S. P. Kirby	RFM	277.5	54	913	26	4-18	0	35.11
G. H. Dockrell	SLA	210.4	54	568	14	6-96	1	40.57

Also bowled: D. Elgar (SLA) 19–4–55–1; G. M. Hussain (RFM) 55.5–4–224–5; C. Kieswetter (OB) 6–0–26–0; C. Overton (RFM) 23–6–67–1; A. N. Petersen (RM/OB) 14–4–48–1; A. V. Suppiah (SLA) 6–1–19–0.

LEADING YB40 AVERAGES (100 runs/4 wickets)

Batting

	Runs	HS	Avge	SR	Ct
P. D. Trego	745	140*	82.77	124.37	6
J. C. Buttler	301	89	75.25	146.11	10
J. C. Hildreth	294	102*	58.80	97.35	9
C. Kieswetter ...	284	126*	56.80	108.81	6
A. N. Petersen ...	191	63*	38.20	93.62	4
M. E. Trescothick ...	393	87	32.75	127.18	2
N. R. D. Compton	124	50	24.80	76.07	0

Bowling

	W	BB	Avge	ER
A. C. Thomas	16	4-41	18.18	6.25
A. J. Dibble	6	4-52	20.83	5.68
C. A. J. Meschede .	22	4-5	21.72	5.60
S. P. Kirby	17	4-52	29.11	6.01
J. Overton	12	3-45	31.41	6.98
M. T. C. Waller ...	8	3-39	40.62	6.25
P. D. Trego	6	2-22	57.33	5.73

LEADING FLt20 AVERAGES (90 runs/18 overs)

Batting	Runs	HS	Avge	SR	Ct/St
J. C. Buttler ..	185	48	26.42	**160.86**	10
A. N. Petersen ..	91	64*	30.33	**142.18**	0
C. Kieswetter...	517	89*	64.62	**137.13**	10/1
C. A. J. Meschede	99	30	19.80	**132.00**	1
P. D. Trego	289	62	36.12	**117.95**	3
C. R. Jones.....	125	53*	31.25	**108.69**	2

Bowling	W	BB	Avge	ER
P. D. Trego......	4	2-16	33.75	**5.86**
S. P. Kirby	8	2-22	30.62	**7.00**
Yasir Arafat	20	4-5	14.60	**7.09**
M. T. C. Waller ..	11	4-27	25.63	**7.83**
A. C. Thomas....	15	4-35	21.66	**8.12**
C. A. J. Meschede	10	3-36	25.10	**9.07**

FIRST-CLASS COUNTY RECORDS

Highest score for	342	J. L. Langer v Surrey at Guildford..............	2006
Highest score against	424	A. C. MacLaren (Lancashire) at Taunton	1895
Leading run-scorer	21,142	H. Gimblett (avge 36.96)....................	1935–54
Best bowling for	10-49	E. J. Tyler v Surrey at Taunton	1895
Best bowling against	10-35	A. Drake (Yorkshire) at Weston-super-Mare.......	1914
Leading wicket-taker	2,165	J. C. White (avge 18.03)....................	1909–37
Highest total for	850-7 dec	v Middlesex at Taunton	2007
Highest total against	811	by Surrey at The Oval	1899
Lowest total for	25	v Gloucestershire at Bristol	1947
Lowest total against	22	by Gloucestershire at Bristol	1920

LIST A COUNTY RECORDS

Highest score for	184	M. E. Trescothick v Gloucestershire at Taunton	2008
Highest score against	167*	A. J. Stewart (Surrey) at The Oval..............	1994
Leading run-scorer	7,349	I. V. A. Richards (avge 39.94).................	1974–86
Best bowling for	8-66	S. R. G. Francis v Derbyshire at Derby	2004
Best bowling against	7-39	A. Hodgson (Northamptonshire) at Northampton ...	1976
Leading wicket-taker	309	H. R. Moseley (avge 20.03)...................	1971–82
Highest total for	413-4	v Devon at Torquay	1990
Highest total against	357-3	by Warwickshire at Birmingham................	1995
Lowest total for	58	v Essex at Chelmsford	1977
	58	v Middlesex at Southgate......................	2000
Lowest total against	60	by Kent at Taunton	1979

TWENTY20 COUNTY RECORDS

Highest score for	141*	C. L. White v Worcestershire at Worcester	2006
Highest score against	116*	I. J. Thomas (Glamorgan) at Taunton	2004
Leading run-scorer	2,131	**J. C. Hildreth (avge 22.91)**..............	**2004–13**
Best bowling for	6-5	A. V. Suppiah v Glamorgan at Cardiff	2011
Best bowling against	5-18	O. P. Rayner (Sussex) at Hove..................	2011
Leading wicket-taker	**109**	**A. C. Thomas (avge 18.82)**.	**2008–13**
Highest total for	250-3	v Gloucestershire at Taunton	2006
Highest total against	227-4	by Gloucestershire at Bristol	2006
Lowest total for	82	v Kent at Taunton...........................	2010
Lowest total against	**73**	**by Warwickshire at Taunton**	**2013**

ADDRESS

County Ground, St James's Street, Taunton TA1 1JT (0845 337 1875;
email enquiries@somersetcountycc.co.uk). **Website** www.somersetcountycc.co.uk

OFFICIALS

Captain M. E. Trescothick
Director of cricket D. O. Nosworthy
Head coach A. Hurry
Academy director J. I. D. Kerr
President R. C. Kerslake

Chairman A. J. Nash
Chief executive G. W. Lavender
Chairman, cricket committee V. J. Marks
Head groundsman S. Lee
Scorer G. A. Stickley

At Chester-le-Street, April 10–13. SOMERSET lost to DURHAM by 48 runs.

At The Oval, April 17–20. SOMERSET drew with SURREY. *Alviro Petersen scores 167 and 91 on Somerset debut.*

SOMERSET v WARWICKSHIRE

At Taunton, April 25–28. Drawn. Somerset 11pts, Warwickshire 6pts. Toss: Somerset.

Trescothick's decision not to enforce the follow-on with a lead of 248 surprised many. Seeking to keep his bowlers fresh, and expecting the pitch to turn more as the game wore on, he opted instead to extend Somerset's advantage to 514, declaring when Compton completed one of his breezier hundreds with a six. Leach then took three wickets on the third evening with his left-arm spin, but the pitch stayed flat on the last day, and Chopra's four-hour hundred – his third meaty score in three visits to Taunton – plus resistance all the way down allowed the champions to escape. Warwickshire had never scored as many as 427 in the fourth innings, and only once before, at Scarborough in 1939, had they faced more deliveries. Just after coming in, last man Hannon-Dalby had his forearm broken by Thomas, but withstood the final 78 minutes with Clarke. He appeared to nick the hostile Jamie Overton behind to Buttler (standing in as wicketkeeper for Kieswetter, who had fractured his thumb), but Nick Cook turned down the appeal. The umpires were also criticised for allowing play to continue in drizzle and gloom – Woakes gave them a glare after being bowled by Overton – only to take the players off when the skies began to clear; the delay cost Somerset two overs. Their formidable position had been built upon first fifties of the season for Trescothick and Compton on a tricky first morning, Petersen's century on home debut, and a noticeably orthodox hundred from Buttler. Thomas then uprooted Warwickshire's middle order in a rush of three wickets in five overs. But, come the end, it felt like a defeat for Somerset.

Close of play: first day, Somerset 358-6 (Buttler 90, C. Overton 5); second day, Somerset 46-1 (Compton 5, Leach 1); third day, Warwickshire 144-3 (Chopra 81, Evans 1).

Somerset

*M. E. Trescothick lbw b Patel	51	– lbw b Patel	37
N. R. D. Compton lbw b Clarke	52	– not out	105
A. N. Petersen c Clarke b Wright	136	– (4) lbw b Woakes	43
J. C. Hildreth c Javid b Woakes	5	– (5) lbw b Woakes	5
†C. Kieswetter c Clarke b Wright	0	– (6) not out	59
J. C. Buttler not out	119		
P. D. Trego c Ambrose b Woakes	3		
C. Overton lbw b Woakes	8		
A. C. Thomas b Clarke	11		
M. J. Leach b Clarke	0	– (3) lbw b Wright	4
J. Overton c Chopra b Clarke	0		
B 13, l-b 6, n-b 2	21	L-b 7, n-b 6	13

1/103 (1) 2/109 (2) 3/118 (4)   (108.3 overs) 406   1/45 (1)   (4 wkts dec, 60 overs) 266
4/143 (5) 5/336 (6) 6/345 (7)   2/50 (3) 3/118 (4)
7/365 (8) 8/404 (9) 9/406 (10) 10/406 (11)   4/132 (5)

Wright 27–3–96–2; Woakes 30–7–78–3; Clarke 17.3–4–70–4; Hannon-Dalby 16–0–79–0; Patel 15–0–52–1; Javid 3–0–12–0. *Second innings*—Wright 14–2–60–1; Woakes 9–0–50–2; Clarke 6–2–15–0; Patel 25–2–94–1; Javid 2–0–12–0; Hannon-Dalby 4–0–28–0.

Warwickshire

V. Chopra lbw b Trego	13	– b Leach	108
W. T. S. Porterfield c Buttler b J. Overton	0	– c Buttler b Leach	36
*J. O. Troughton c Kieswetter b Thomas	26	– lbw b Leach	17
L. J. Evans c Kieswetter b Thomas	25	– (5) c Hildreth b J. Overton	55
†T. R. Ambrose lbw b Thomas	6	– (6) c Hildreth b J. Overton	65
C. R. Woakes c Compton b J. Overton	21	– (7) b J. Overton	42
R. Clarke run out	31	– (8) not out	61
A. Javid not out	18	– (4) c Hildreth b Leach	0
J. S. Patel b Leach	0	– c Trescothick b Leach	4
C. J. C. Wright c Kieswetter b C. Overton	0	– lbw b Thomas	0
O. J. Hannon-Dalby lbw b Leach	5	– not out	10
L-b 3, n-b 10	13	B 3, l-b 14, w 2, n-b 10	29

1/0 (2) 2/24 (1) 3/65 (3)	(65.4 overs)	158
4/75 (5) 5/86 (4) 6/103 (6)		
7/142 (7) 8/142 (9) 9/143 (10) 10/158 (11)		

1/108 (2)	(9 wkts, 144 overs)	427
2/138 (3) 3/138 (4)		
4/194 (1) 5/296 (6) 6/315 (5)		
7/365 (7) 8/373 (9) 9/376 (10)		

Trego 10–3–29–1; J. Overton 15–6–47–2; Leach 19.4–4–43–2; Thomas 11–2–29–3; C. Overton 10–4–7–1. *Second innings*—Trego 18–3–55–0; J. Overton 32–7–126–3; Leach 44–24–63–5; Thomas 34–10–96–1; C. Overton 13–2–60–0; Petersen 3–0–10–0.

Umpires: N. G. B. Cook and M. J. Saggers.

At Taunton Vale, May 1–2 (not first-class). **Somerset won by nine wickets. ‡Cardiff MCCU 103** (C. A. J. Meschede 3-19, L. Gregory 3-24) **and 139** (A. J. Miles 52*; M. J. Leach 4-26); **Somerset 225** (J. C. Buttler 54; M. E. Hobden 4-59, J. S. T. Denning 4-63) **and 19-1**. *County debuts:* T. B. Abell, C. T. Steel. *Jos Buttler's 54 proved the top score in a match dominated by bowlers. Cardiff captain Adam Miles also bucked the trend, with 52*, as Jack Leach continued his impressive early-season control to return figures of 22.5–13–26–4.*

At Leeds, May 7–10. SOMERSET drew with YORKSHIRE.

SOMERSET v MIDDLESEX

At Taunton, May 15–17. Middlesex won by nine wickets. Middlesex 22pts, Somerset 3pts. Toss: Somerset.

Rogers soon found himself facing Jamie Overton, who was a two-year-old toddler running around the boundary at North Devon CC when Rogers arrived from Australia in 1996 as their overseas professional. Overton, now 19 and a strapping 6ft 5in, won the personal battle, dismissing Rogers in both innings and causing a host of other problems with six for 95. But Rogers had the last laugh, captaining Middlesex to a three-day victory which put them back on top of the Championship. It owed much to Murtagh's accurate seam bowling, which brought him career-best match figures of ten for 77, and Dexter's battling half-century on the first day. Following an 195 behind after being unpicked by Murtagh, Somerset slumped to 35 for five, before Buttler and Trego held things up with a stand of 122. Rogers claimed the extra half-hour to finish the job, and used the spare fourth day to pop down to Instow to see his old friends.

Close of play: first day, Middlesex 293-8 (Dexter 73, Smith 9); second day, Somerset 112-5 (Buttler 20, Trego 58).

Middlesex

*C. J. L. Rogers c Buttler b Overton	57	– b Overton	25
S. D. Robson c Trescothick b Overton	42	– not out	24
J. L. Denly b Leach	55	– not out	14
D. J. Malan c Trescothick b Overton	2		
N. J. Dexter c Thomas b Overton	82		
†J. A. Simpson c Hildreth b Leach	22		
G. K. Berg c Trego b Leach	1		
J. A. R. Harris c Buttler b Gregory	0		
T. S. Roland-Jones c Hildreth b Overton	21		
T. M. J. Smith not out	17		
T. J. Murtagh b Overton	29		
B 3, l-b 6, n-b 10	19	B 4, l-b 1, n-b 4	9

1/76 (2) 2/158 (1) 3/162 (3) (110.5 overs) 347   1/39 (1) (1 wkt, 12.3 overs) 72
4/162 (4) 5/211 (6) 6/221 (7) 7/222 (8)
8/270 (9) 9/309 (5) 10/347 (11) 110 overs: 333-9

Trego 15–5–35–0; Kirby 16–3–70–0; Thomas 24–1–92–0; Overton 28.5–8–95–6; Leach 21–8–36–3; Gregory 6–2–10–1. *Second innings*—Trego 4–0–20–0; Overton 6–1–39–1; Kirby 2.3–0–8–0.

Somerset

*M. E. Trescothick c Simpson b Murtagh	24	– c Berg b Harris	7
A. V. Suppiah b Harris	19	– lbw b Murtagh	0
A. N. Petersen b Simpson b Murtagh	0	– b Murtagh	4
J. C. Hildreth c Robson b Murtagh	23	– c Malan b Murtagh	17
L. Gregory lbw b Murtagh	7	– lbw b Murtagh	5
†J. C. Buttler c Malan b Roland-Jones	15	– c Rogers b Berg	85
P. D. Trego b Dexter	34	– c Dexter b Murtagh	82
A. C. Thomas c Malan b Berg	4	– c Smith b Harris	19
M. J. Leach b Roland-Jones	1	– b Smith	21
S. P. Kirby c Simpson b Dexter	10	– lbw b Murtagh	7
J. Overton not out	0	– not out	9
L-b 9, n-b 4	13	B 1, l-b 5, w 1, n-b 2	9

1/36 (1) 2/36 (3) 3/52 (2) (45.2 overs) 152   1/1 (2) 2/11 (3) (84.5 overs) 265
4/71 (5) 5/84 (4) 6/101 (6)   3/11 (1) 4/20 (5)
7/114 (8) 8/121 (9) 9/149 (7) 10/152 (10)   5/35 (4) 6/157 (7) 7/185 (8)
  8/235 (9) 9/249 (6) 10/265 (10)

Murtagh 12–5–28–4; Roland-Jones 11–1–35–2; Harris 11–1–47–1; Berg 8–1–26–1; Dexter 3.2–0–7–2. *Second innings*—Murtagh 21.5–8–49–6; Harris 19–3–71–2; Berg 12–3–41–1; Roland-Jones 8–2–36–0; Dexter 7–1–16–0; Smith 17–0–46–1.

Umpires: M. R. Benson and N. A. Mallender.

At Horsham, May 22–23. SOMERSET lost to SUSSEX by an innings and 116 runs.

SOMERSET v YORKSHIRE

At Taunton, May 28–31. Drawn. Somerset 7pts, Yorkshire 11pts. Toss: Yorkshire. County debut: D. Elgar.

Somerset produced a traditional Taunton surface, intended to help their fragile batsmen discover some form. But it played into the hands of Yorkshire, especially Rashid, who followed 180 in the corresponding fixture at Headingley and 110 not out at Edgbaston with another fluent century. He was the first Yorkshire batsman since Geoffrey Boycott, in 1978, to score hundreds in three successive innings – a golden run his captain put down to a more consistent training regime and settled personal life. "A good woman puts us all on the straight and narrow," said Gale. Only Trescothick and

Hildreth, who ended a rough trot with 115, could muster anything substantial in reply, though Somerset did at least avoid following on for the third match in four. Yorkshire then slipped to 21 for three, with Kirby briefly snarling in against his former county from the Old Pavilion End. But Lyth added a fifty to his earlier hundred – and Somerset ended up grateful for the first-day washout.

Close of play: first day, no play; second day, Yorkshire 341-5 (Rashid 47, Hodd 24); third day, Somerset 232-6 (Hildreth 76, Meschede 16).

Yorkshire

A. Lyth c Trego b Hussain	105	– not out	57
J. J. Sayers c Trescothick b Kirby	1	– c Trescothick b Kirby	1
P. A. Jaques c Barrow b Hussain	26	– lbw b Kirby	0
*A. W. Gale b Trego	75	– lbw b Trego	4
G. S. Ballance c Barrow b Dockrell	48	– c Kirby b Dockrell	31
A. U. Rashid not out	103	– not out	5
†A. J. Hodd not out	68		
B 2, l-b 13, w 1, n-b 8	24	L-b 4, n-b 2	6

1/2 (2) 2/82 (3) (5 wkts dec, 116.2 overs) 450 1/14 (2) (4 wkts dec, 42 overs) 104
3/185 (1) 4/265 (5) 2/14 (3) 3/21 (4)
5/280 (4) 4/91 (5)
110 overs: 400-5

R. M. Pyrah, R. J. Sidebottom, S. A. Patterson and M. A. Ashraf did not bat.

Trego 26–5–87–1; Kirby 25–2–100–1; Meschede 14–0–75–0; Hussain 25–0–106–2; Dockrell 20.2–5–52–1; Elgar 6–2–15–0. *Second innings*—Trego 8–3–22–1; Kirby 8–2–19–2; Dockrell 13–4–21–1; Hussain 8–2–19–0; Meschede 5–0–19–0.

Somerset

*M. E. Trescothick lbw b Pyrah	74	S. P. Kirby c Ballance b Ashraf	5
A. V. Suppiah lbw b Patterson	5	G. M. Hussain not out	2
L. Gregory lbw b Patterson	3		
D. Elgar c Rashid b Sidebottom	28	B 2, l-b 2, n-b 2	6
J. C. Hildreth b Ashraf	115		
†A. W. R. Barrow b Lyth	26		(104.3 overs) 310
P. D. Trego c and b Lyth	0		
C. A. J. Meschede c Pyrah b Patterson	32		
G. H. Dockrell b Ashraf	14		

1/32 (2) 2/52 (3) 3/103 (1) 4/120 (4) 5/172 (6) 6/172 (7) 7/272 (8) 8/298 (5) 9/303 (9) 10/310 (10)

Sidebottom 23–7–49–1; Patterson 24–6–65–3; Rashid 28–4–72–0; Ashraf 15.3–3–60–3; Pyrah 11–3–45–1; Lyth 3–0–15–2.

Umpires: N. G. B. Cook and M. J. Saggers.

SOMERSET v DURHAM

At Taunton, June 6–9. Drawn. Somerset 9pts, Durham 9pts. Toss: Somerset.

Told by England team director Andy Flower to go away and score "heavy runs" for Somerset if he was to retain his place for the Ashes, Compton batted throughout the opening day. In glorious sunshine and on a plum Taunton strip, he displayed the patience and concentration which had earned him a Test spot in the first place, batting seven hours at a steady tempo before being caught between Mustard's legs. Nine other Somerset players reached double figures, but none went on to a fifty. Durham's strong reply featured a century from Stoneman, and a fascinating duel between the genuinely pacy Jamie Overton and Collingwood, who used all his experience to subdue the youngster and contribute a valuable 70. Somerset were in trouble at 79 for four on the last morning, but were steered to safety by a career-best 83 not out from Barrow, who also performed tidily as wicketkeeper in the absence of both Jos Buttler, on England duty in the Champions Trophy, and the injured Craig Kieswetter.

Close of play: first day, Somerset 336-5 (Compton 139, Trego 14); second day, Durham 163-3 (Stoneman 78); third day, Somerset 7-0 (Trescothick 4, Compton 2).

Somerset

*M. E. Trescothick c Borthwick b Onions	36	– b Borthwick	25
N. R. D. Compton c Mustard b Buckley	166	– c Buckley b Wood	18
A. V. Suppiah b Onions	36	– c Borthwick b Buckley	19
D. Elgar b Smith	33	– c Borthwick b Wood	31
J. C. Hildreth lbw b Buckley	32	– c Smith b Borthwick	1
†A. W. R. Barrow b Wood	25	– not out	83
P. D. Trego c Collingwood b Buckley	42	– lbw b Stokes	38
C. A. J. Meschede c Mustard b Wood	12	– c Mustard b Onions	4
G. H. Dockrell c Smith b Borthwick	31	– b Onions	4
J. Overton c Richardson b Borthwick	24	– not out	12
G. M. Hussain not out	0		
B 2, l-b 17, n-b 2	21	B 9, l-b 9, w 1, n-b 12	31

1/47 (1) 2/132 (3) 3/216 (4)   (132.3 overs) 458   1/43 (2)   (8 wkts dec, 82 overs) 266
4/269 (5) 5/307 (6) 6/390 (2)   2/54 (1) 3/76 (3)
7/395 (7) 8/408 (9) 9/458 (10)   4/79 (5) 5/135 (4) 6/218 (7)
10/458 (9)   110 overs: 379-5   7/234 (8) 8/242 (9)

Onions 24–1–62–2; Wood 29–3–89–2; Stokes 19–5–52–0; Collingwood 7–2–18–0; Buckley 34–4–128–3; Borthwick 18.3–0–86–2; Smith 1–0–4–1. *Second innings*—Onions 13–3–33–2; Buckley 20–4–44–1; Wood 16–2–51–2; Borthwick 27–4–108–2; Stokes 6–3–12–1.

Durham

M. D. Stoneman c Meschede b Trego	122	R. S. Buckley c Meschede b Hussain	4
K. K. Jennings c Hildreth b Overton	15	G. Onions not out	17
S. G. Borthwick c Meschede b Dockrell	56		
W. R. Smith c Hussain b Overton	7	B 4, l-b 2, w 5, n-b 14	25
B. A. Stokes c Suppiah b Elgar	57		
*P. D. Collingwood b Hussain	70	1/38 (2) 2/140 (3) (134.5 overs) 493	
†P. Mustard c Suppiah b Hussain	30	3/163 (4) 4/236 (1) 5/283 (5)	
M. J. Richardson run out	70	6/324 (7) 7/425 (8) 8/451 (9)	
M. A. Wood c Hildreth b Overton	20	9/456 (10) 10/493 (6) 110 overs: 407-6	

Trego 16–1–61–1; Overton 25–7–96–3; Hussain 22.5–2–99–3; Dockrell 48–8–151–1; Meschede 13–3–43–0; Suppiah 1–0–11–0; Elgar 9–2–26–1.

Umpires: N. L. Bainton and T. E. Jesty.

At Derby, June 21–24. SOMERSET beat DERBYSHIRE by four wickets.

At Taunton, June 26–29. SOMERSET lost to AUSTRALIANS by six wickets (see Australian tour section).

SOMERSET v SUSSEX

At Taunton, July 8–10. Sussex won by nine wickets. Sussex 23pts, Somerset 4pts. Toss: Somerset.
    Trescothick removed his helmet and raised his bat as he walked off after recording the first pair of his professional career, to go with ducks in his previous two Twenty20 games. The signal was interpreted by some as a farewell, at least to the Somerset captaincy, and Twitter was soon rife with speculation, forcing an embarrassed Trescothick to explain it was merely an ironic gesture. He gloved a snorter from Anyon in the first innings, and later admitted surprise at the extent of the seam movement after he chose to bat on an olive-green pitch. Somerset's 244 was easily eclipsed by Yardy, who brought up his century in 99 balls, and Machan's maiden hundred – watched by around 1,200 pupils on the second day, who snapped up the club's invitation to schools in the South-West to watch for free. The pair put on 275 for the third wicket and seized upon an attack lacking a recognised spinner, at least until Dockrell arrived from Amsterdam for the third day's play after helping Ireland seal qualification for the 2015 World Cup. By then it was too late. Trescothick and Compton both got out in single figures to Anyon and Magoffin for the second time in the match; Magoffin's eight wickets gave him aggregate figures of 20 for 132 in two Championship games

against Somerset in 2013. Machan made way when Joyce, another Ireland international, returned to captain the side, though he was not required to bat: Nash struck Dockrell for four and six to take Sussex top of the Championship.

Close of play: first day, Sussex 174-2 (Yardy 94, Machan 58); second day, Somerset 197-7 (Trego 9, Thomas 6).

Somerset

*M. E. Trescothick c Brown b Anyon	0	– c Brown b Anyon	0
N. R. D. Compton c Jordan b Magoffin	0	– b Magoffin	7
A. N. Petersen c Brown b Magoffin	16	– c Yardy b Anyon	34
J. C. Hildreth c Brown b Jordan	66	– c Nash b Magoffin	49
†C. Kieswetter run out	55	– (6) b Anyon	37
J. C. Buttler c Brown b Anyon	11	– (7) c Brown b Jordan	35
P. D. Trego c Hamilton-Brown b Anyon	10	– (8) c Brown b Jordan	16
C. A. J. Meschede c Nash b Magoffin	12	– (5) c Brown b Anyon	5
A. C. Thomas c Jordan b Magoffin	33	– c Nash b Magoffin	6
S. P. Kirby not out	2	– not out	0
J. Overton c Brown b Jordan	21	– b Magoffin	1
L-b 8, n-b 10	18	L-b 5, w 8, n-b 6	19

1/0 (1) 2/4 (2) 3/33 (3)   (63 overs) 244   1/0 (1) 2/31 (2)   (51.1 overs) 209
4/95 (4) 5/113 (5) 6/133 (7)   3/87 (3) 4/97 (5)
7/152 (8) 8/204 (5) 9/221 (9) 10/244 (11)   5/118 (4) 6/182 (7) 7/182 (6)
                                            8/198 (9) 9/206 (8) 10/209 (11)

G. H. Dockrell replaced Meschede after returning from playing for Ireland.

Anyon 17–1–61–3; Magoffin 18–2–65–4; Jordan 17–2–82–2; Panesar 11–1–28–0. *Second innings*—Anyon 14–1–56–4; Magoffin 15.1–4–36–4; Jordan 9–0–57–2; Panesar 6–1–25–0; Wright 6–1–13–0; Nash 1–0–17–0.

Sussex

*C. D. Nash c Kieswetter b Kirby	4	– (2) not out	61
L. W. P. Wells c Hildreth b Overton	4	– (1) c Trego b Kirby	19
M. H. Yardy b Overton	156	– not out	11
M. W. Machan c Petersen b Meschede	103		
R. J. Hamilton-Brown c Buttler b Meschede	5		
L. J. Wright c Buttler b Thomas	25		
†B. C. Brown b Kirby	17		
C. J. Jordan c Petersen b Trego	5		
S. J. Magoffin c and b Petersen	3		
J. E. Anyon c Meschede b Thomas	8		
M. S. Panesar not out	0		
B 5, l-b 21, w 1, n-b 6	33	B 1	1

1/4 (2) 2/8 (1) 3/283 (4)   (79.5 overs) 363   1/40 (1)   (1 wkt, 19.4 overs) 92
4/293 (5) 5/301 (3) 6/332 (7)
7/344 (8) 8/345 (6) 9/361 (9) 10/363 (10)

E. C. Joyce replaced Machan after returning from playing for Ireland.

Kirby 19–6–59–2; Overton 17–3–67–2; Meschede 10–0–56–2; Thomas 16.5–3–65–2; Trego 11–2–63–1; Petersen 6–1–27–1. *Second innings*—Kirby 6–1–39–1; Overton 3–0–10–0; Dockrell 6.4–0–33–0; Trego 4–0–9–0.

Umpires: M. R. Benson and M. J. D. Bodenham.

SOMERSET v NOTTINGHAMSHIRE

At Taunton, August 2–5. Drawn. Somerset 6pts, Nottinghamshire 10pts. Toss: Nottinghamshire.

Somerset's batting frailties were exposed again, but rain spared them another home defeat. Only on the first day, when a Hungarian touring side watched Mullaney and Hussey build a commanding position for Nottinghamshire, was a full quota of overs possible. Trescothick, who had just bludgeoned 250 for the Second XI against MCC Universities on his return from an ankle injury, made only two from 27 balls, before Somerset crashed from 73 for one to 81 for six as Fletcher and Adams feasted on a middle order bereft of confidence. The stoppages meant Read had to wait until two balls into the last day to enforce the follow-on, but Compton steered Somerset to safety in the 55 overs possible.

Close of play: first day, Nottinghamshire 327-8 (Shahzad 35, Fletcher 30); second day, Somerset 70-1 (Compton 31, Jones 37); third day, Somerset 188-9 (Kirby 6, Overton 0).

Nottinghamshire

S. J. Mullaney c Kieswetter b Overton	75	A. R. Adams c Jones b Trego	20	
A. D. Hales c Kieswetter b Trego	20	L. J. Fletcher c Kieswetter b Overton	58	
M. J. Lumb c Trescothick b Meschede	19	H. F. Gurney not out	22	
J. W. A. Taylor c Kieswetter b Overton	19	L-b 4, w 1, n-b 8	13	
S. R. Patel c Trescothick b Dockrell	7			
D. J. Hussey c and b Dockrell	68	1/31 (2) 2/65 (3) 3/130 (4) (106 overs)	378	
*†C. M. W. Read c Compton b Dockrell	25	4/137 (1) 5/165 (5) 6/229 (7)		
A. Shahzad b Trego	35	7/240 (6) 8/270 (9) 9/327 (8) 10/378 (10)		

Trego 21–7–61–3; Kirby 25–6–92–0; Overton 15–2–67–3; Meschede 10–1–51–1; Dockrell 35–12–103–3.

Somerset

*M. E. Trescothick c Mullaney b Gurney	2	– c Read b Gurney	39
N. R. D. Compton c Mullaney b Fletcher	34	– not out	70
C. R. Jones b Adams	37	– c Read b Shahzad	6
J. C. Hildreth c Fletcher b Adams	2	– not out	16
†C. Kieswetter c Read b Fletcher	1		
J. C. Buttler c Shahzad b Patel	23		
P. D. Trego c Read b Fletcher	0		
C. A. J. Meschede b Gurney	59		
G. H. Dockrell c Taylor b Patel	23		
S. P. Kirby c Taylor b Patel	6		
J. Overton not out	0		
W 1	1	L-b 6, n-b 4	10

1/9 (1) 2/73 (3) 3/75 (2)	(74.2 overs) 188	1/79 (1)	(2 wkts, 55 overs) 141
4/75 (4) 5/81 (5) 6/81 (7)		2/105 (3)	
7/122 (6) 8/175 (8) 9/187 (9) 10/188 (10)			

Fletcher 17–9–24–3; Gurney 10–2–33–2; Shahzad 12–3–30–0; Adams 17–4–56–2; Patel 15.2–7–40–3; Mullaney 3–0–5–0. *Second innings*—Fletcher 8–5–10–0; Gurney 12–2–44–1; Shahzad 12–4–41–1; Patel 21–9–35–0; Mullaney 2–0–5–0.

Umpires: S. C. Gale and R. T. Robinson.

At Birmingham, August 20–23. SOMERSET drew with WARWICKSHIRE.

At Lord's, August 28–30. SOMERSET beat MIDDLESEX by an innings and 179 runs. *Somerset's biggest win at Lord's.*

SOMERSET v DERBYSHIRE

At Taunton, September 3–6. Derbyshire won by two wickets. Derbyshire 21pts, Somerset 3pts. Toss: Somerset.

At the end of an epic relegation battle, Meschede had earned the sympathy of fellow 21-year-old Alex Hughes, after dropping Chanderpaul at deep mid-on when Derbyshire needed 21 for victory with only two wickets standing. In Derbyshire's previous game against co-strugglers Surrey, Hughes had reprieved Hashim Amla, who went on to settle the match. But Hughes turned hero this time, sharing a vital sixth-wicket stand of 68 with Chanderpaul, as Derbyshire chased down 244 on a Taunton dustbowl. It edged them one point above Somerset and into seventh place. The home side paid the price for another wretched first-innings display, on a green pitch dry at the ends, with Palladino excellent on his recall to the side. The tone of the match, however, was set when Chawla and Leach found turn and bounce on the first afternoon to keep Somerset in it. Derbyshire, who picked only one specialist spinner, Wainwright, asked Chanderpaul to try out his seldom-seen leggies, and were rewarded when Kieswetter played on attempting a cut to the last ball of the day (it was his first wicket in any format since having V. V. S. Laxman stumped in a Test two years earlier). Not even a tremendous fightback, stirred by Compton and sustained as the last six wickets added 207, could save Somerset. They did avoid a points deduction when ECB pitch inspector Bill Hughes left satisfied on the second evening, but the pronounced turn still troubled Kieswetter, who let through 41 byes in all and had such trouble with Chawla during Derbyshire's run-chase that he resorted to setting up outside leg to the left-handers; on more than one occasion he took a full step back from the stumps. Trescothick even brought Kieswetter on for three overs of off-spin to try to separate Chanderpaul and Hughes, but to no avail.

Close of play: first day, Derbyshire 220-5 (Johnson 55, Poynton 53); second day, Somerset 231-4 (Compton 64); third day, Derbyshire 127-4 (Chanderpaul 20, Johnson 0).

Somerset

*M. E. Trescothick c Madsen b Footitt	17	– lbw b Madsen	57
N. R. D. Compton c Johnson b Palladino	4	– (3) b Palladino	95
C. R. Jones c Poynton b Palladino	1	– (2) c Groenewald b Palladino	11
J. C. Hildreth lbw b Palladino	7	– b Wainwright	81
†C. Kieswetter c Slater b Groenewald	9	– b Chanderpaul	16
A. W. R. Barrow b Groenewald	1	– c Madsen b Palladino	36
C. A. J. Meschede c Poynton b Groenewald	6	– (8) run out	33
L. Gregory c Poynton b Groenewald	5	– (9) c Poynton b Chanderpaul	52
P. P. Chawla c Borrington b Groenewald	27	– (7) c Palladino b Wainwright	16
A. C. Thomas b Palladino	5	– c Madsen b Wainwright	0
M. J. Leach not out	6	– not out	19
B 4, l-b 7	11	B 4, l-b 14, n-b 4	22

1/25 (1) 2/25 (2) 3/34 (3)	(33.1 overs) 103	1/40 (2) 2/90 (1)	(121.4 overs) 438
4/43 (5) 5/45 (6) 6/47 (4)		3/206 (4) 4/231 (5)	
7/53 (7) 8/68 (8) 9/75 (10) 10/103 (9)		5/294 (3) 6/305 (6) 7/342 (7)	
		8/384 (8) 9/399 (10) 10/438 (9)	

Groenewald 13.1–4–33–5; Footitt 7–2–25–1; Palladino 13–5–34–4. *Second innings*—Footitt 15–3–68–0; Groenewald 19–3–77–0; Palladino 19–4–57–3; Wainwright 34–4–105–3; Madsen 22–2–81–1; Chanderpaul 12.4–3–32–2.

Derbyshire

B. T. Slater c Hildreth b Chawla	45	– c Barrow b Chawla	59
P. M. Borrington c Trescothick b Chawla	27	– lbw b Leach	16
*W. L. Madsen c Trescothick b Chawla	7	– c Trescothick b Leach	3
S. Chanderpaul lbw b Meschede	4	– not out	74
R. M. Johnson b Chawla	68	– (6) c Kieswetter b Chawla	0
A. L. Hughes lbw b Chawla	6	– (7) lbw b Leach	33
†T. Poynton c Kieswetter b Thomas	57	– (8) lbw b Chawla	7
D. J. Wainwright c Kieswetter b Thomas	2	– (9) st Kieswetter b Chawla	7
A. P. Palladino lbw b Thomas	11	– (5) c Trescothick b Chawla	1
T. D. Groenewald not out	36	– not out	6
M. H. A. Footitt c Gregory b Meschede	11		
B 18, l-b 2, n-b 4	24	B 23, l-b 9, n-b 6	38

1/52 (2) 2/62 (3) 3/67 (4)	(85.1 overs) 298	1/49 (2)	(8 wkts, 83.2 overs) 244
4/121 (1) 5/127 (6) 6/230 (7)		2/53 (3) 3/117 (1)	
7/236 (8) 8/250 (9) 9/256 (11) 10/298 (11)		4/127 (5) 5/127 (6)	
		6/195 (7) 7/206 (8) 8/216 (9)	

Thomas 21–7–52–3; Gregory 19–3–60–0; Meschede 8.1–0–30–2; Chawla 26–2–111–5; Leach 11–3–25–0. *Second innings*—Thomas 12.5–5–27–0; Gregory 5.2–5–0–0; Chawla 29–5–97–5; Leach 29–9–54–3; Meschede 5–1–20–0; Kieswetter 3–0–14–0.

Umpires: N. L. Bainton and D. J. Millns.

SOMERSET v SURREY

At Taunton, September 11–14. Somerset won by seven wickets. Somerset 21pts, Surrey 3pts. Toss: Surrey. First-class debut: D. P. Sibley.

Somerset's first home Championship win of the season, at the final attempt, gave them a fighting chance of survival, and pushed Surrey to the brink of relegation. In a match riddled with tension and interrupted several times by the weather, no visiting batsman passed 40 once Batty – roundly booed on his way to the middle after two bust-ups with Somerset in the past year – chose first use of a seaming pitch. Amla darted down the M4 from Heathrow after being showered with laurels at Cricket South Africa's annual ceremony in Johannesburg, and bumped back to earth with a leg-side tickle, one of three wickets to fall on 31. Surrey never got going: Ansari took 42 balls to score a run, and they missed even a solitary batting point when Thomas swept through the tail. Compton's technique stood up better than most to the testing conditions, but no England selector was present to watch his flawless 66 nudge Somerset towards a precious lead. Their disciplined seam quartet worked together neatly in the second innings, and Gregory completed Amla's pair, only the second of his career. Dernbach struck a couple of early blows, but Hildreth and Kieswetter knocked off a target of 133 to haul Somerset out of the bottom two.

Close of play: first day, Surrey 195-8 (Meaker 30, Tremlett 1); second day, Surrey 13-0 (Burns 5, Sibley 4); third day, Surrey 97-4 (de Bruyn 3, Davies 0).

Surrey

R. J. Burns c Kieswetter b Thomas	21	– c Hildreth b Trego	40
D. P. Sibley lbw b Meschede	10	– c Trescothick b Gregory	12
H. M. Amla c Kieswetter b Meschede	0	– c Kieswetter b Gregory	0
V. S. Solanki lbw b Chawla	14	– c Trescothick b Trego	36
Z. de Bruyn lbw b Meschede	30	– c Kieswetter b Meschede	10
†S. M. Davies c Barrow b Chawla	38	– c Compton b Meschede	11
Z. S. Ansari c Hildreth b Trego	8	– c Kieswetter b Meschede	14
*G. J. Batty c Jones b Thomas	39	– c Hildreth b Meschede	37
S. C. Meaker not out	30	– c Trescothick b Chawla	20
C. T. Tremlett c Kieswetter b Thomas	1	– not out	6
J. W. Dernbach c Trescothick b Thomas	0	– c Thomas b Chawla	0
L-b 1, w 1, n-b 2	4	B 1, l-b 1, w 1, n-b 8	11

1/31 (2) 2/31 (3) 3/31 (1)   (83.2 overs) 195
4/61 (4) 5/81 (5) 6/116 (7)
7/130 (6) 8/194 (8) 9/195 (10) 10/195 (11)

1/21 (2) 2/21 (3)   (58.5 overs) 197
3/84 (4) 4/97 (1)
5/111 (6) 6/116 (5) 7/153 (7)
8/180 (8) 9/197 (9) 10/197 (11)

Trego 16–6–30–1; Gregory 18–4–46–0; Meschede 17–8–37–3; Thomas 16.2–9–23–4; Chawla 16–0–58–2. *Second innings*—Trego 10–2–26–2; Gregory 10–3–48–2; Thomas 18–7–50–0; Chawla 5.5–0–28–2; Meschede 15–5–43–4.

Somerset

*M. E. Trescothick b Dernbach	0	– c Burns b Dernbach	25
C. R. Jones c Davies b Tremlett	0	– b Dernbach	5
N. R. D. Compton b Dernbach	66	– run out	24
J. C. Hildreth lbw b Meaker	12	– not out	36
†C. Kieswetter c Burns b de Bruyn	32	– not out	34
A. W. R. Barrow lbw b Dernbach	13		
P. D. Trego c Sibley b Ansari	38		
C. A. J. Meschede b Ansari	27		
L. Gregory c Tremlett b Ansari	23		
P. P. Chawla lbw b Batty	32		
A. C. Thomas not out	2		
B 4, l-b 7, n-b 4	15	L-b 5, n-b 4	9

1/0 (1) 2/4 (2) 3/46 (4)   (65.4 overs) 260   1/15 (2)   (3 wkts, 23.4 overs) 133
4/108 (5) 5/130 (3) 6/133 (6)   2/44 (1) 3/78 (3)
7/201 (7) 8/201 (8) 9/256 (10) 10/260 (9)

Dernbach 18–1–80–3; Tremlett 16–5–42–1; Meaker 10–1–47–1; de Bruyn 11–2–42–1; Ansari 8.4–0–30–3; Batty 2–0–8–1. *Second innings*—Dernbach 8–1–44–2; Tremlett 6–1–45–0; Ansari 5.4–1–23–0; Meaker 4–0–16–0.

Umpires: P. J. Hartley and P. Willey.

At Nottingham, September 24–27. SOMERSET drew with NOTTINGHAMSHIRE.

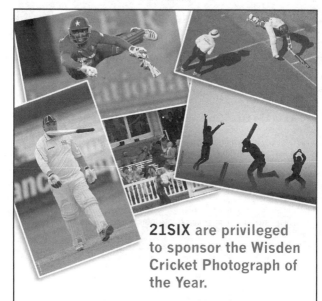

SURREY

Profit and loss

Richard Spiller

It's all very well presenting a shiny new exterior to the public. The Oval looks superb these days, and positively heaved during the Champions Trophy and the Fifth Ashes Test. But there wasn't much beneath the surface. Despite several expensive signings, Surrey finished bottom of the first division.

After the death of Tom Maynard and the on-field struggles of 2012, hopes of a fresh start were fuelled by the capture of Graeme Smith, as captain, and Ricky Ponting, for the duration of the Champions Trophy. But there were no Championship wins before the Twenty20 break, by when Smith had undergone an ankle operation. No wins in the first eight games cost team director Chris Adams his job, after four and a half years high on promises but low on achievement. First-team coach Ian Salisbury was also shown the door.

The 2013 squad was made up of greenhorns and pricey grizzled veterans – with nothing much in between. Surrey often fielded five or six players aged 35 or over, then had to read about the successes elsewhere of Chris Jordan and Laurie Evans, two young talents nurtured at The Oval. Jordan, who first played for Surrey at 18 in 2007, thrived after moving to Sussex, and made his England one-day debut in September.

The CB40 title and promotion from the second division, both in 2011, were all Adams had to show after splashing the cash. Critics eagerly pointed to profit off the field and poverty on it: Surrey recorded a surplus of £805,000 in 2012, but their commercial sharpness only made questions about frittered resources more pointed. Adams had arrived pledging to "build the team of the next decade", but managed only 16 victories from 72 Championship matches. In that time he tried no fewer than 24 opening partnerships, symptomatic of a management style based more on soundbites than common sense.

Alec Stewart, Surrey's executive director, exchanged an advisory role for real power and responsibility. He instantly added urgency and industry, in tandem with bowling coach Stuart Barnes, who took temporary charge of the first team. The new regime had immediate success in the FLt20, which attracted big crowds to The Oval. Surrey reached the quarter-finals for the first time since 2006, but the victory over Somerset was marred by a mid-pitch dust-up involving the captain Gareth Batty, who was banned from finals day as a result. Despite his absence, Surrey overcame defending champions Hampshire in the semi-finals, before losing to unfancied Northamptonshire.

The later stages of a disappointing YB40 campaign were used to blood youngsters. One of them, Tom Curran – the 18-year-old son of former Zimbabwe all-rounder Kevin – took five for 34 against Scotland.

But the Championship spelt misery almost throughout. Rare highlights included Ponting's two classical centuries in his first-class swansong, while

Dominic Sibley

Kevin Pietersen's fine hundred at Headingley, in his only appearance, merely prevented another defeat. Hashim Amla, signed to replace Smith, found it all but impossible to prop up a flaky batting order. Surrey seemed set for a repeat of their winless 2008 before finally overcoming fellow strugglers Derbyshire. But hopes of a revival were snuffed out by three more defeats.

Right at the end, though, came a beacon of hope. Dominic Sibley, only 18 and given leave of absence by Whitgift School, became the youngest double-centurion in County Championship history, compiling 242 against Yorkshire. Sibley was one of ten centurions in the season; though no one managed 1,000 Championship runs, Vikram Solanki (one of the new old boys) finished only five short. Rory Burns, a neat and unflappable left-hander, had a good first full season as an opener, while Arun Harinath also performed well, before fading.

Steve Davies returned to form with the bat, but his keeping was often scratchy; the Irishman Gary Wilson sharpened things up when he took over, and also became an outstanding Twenty20 finisher. Jason Roy's explosive early hitting led the way in limited-overs matches, but his longer game went backwards. Zander de Bruyn and Jon Lewis, both Adams imports, did their bit in the Twenty20 run, but were released. Another golden oldie, Azhar Mahmood, was effective in the limited-overs competitions, hitting hard and bowling shrewdly late on alongside Jade Dernbach.

The batsmen did not adapt to the variable nature of the Oval pitches; nor did the bowlers. No one managed even 40 Championship wickets; Tim Linley took most, but suffered from some strange selection decisions. Chris Tremlett only occasionally looked the force of old, and a knee injury – eventually needing an operation – disrupted Stuart Meaker's summer. His pace was missed.

Saddled with the captaincy again, Batty lost form, not helped by a niggling side strain. Slow left-armer Gary Keedy, another ageing newcomer, had occasional good days, but left to join Nottinghamshire as a player-coach.

Zafar Ansari superseded Keedy during the summer, and is one of the young players who can help revive Surrey's fortunes, along with Sibley and Burns. They will have a new figurehead: Graham Ford, who had been in charge at Kent, Sri Lanka and his native South Africa, was appointed head coach, with Stewart as director of cricket. Everyone should be helped by the decision to skim a centimetre off the top of the Oval square, and dig up four pitches to try to recapture the pace and bounce of old.

Championship attendance: 44,641.

SURREY RESULTS

All first-class matches – Played 16: Won 1, Lost 6, Drawn 9.
County Championship matches – Played 16: Won 1, Lost 6, Drawn 9.

LV= County Championship, 9th in Division 1;
Friends Life t20, finalists; Yorkshire Bank 40, 5th in Group B.

COUNTY CHAMPIONSHIP AVERAGES, BATTING AND FIELDING

Cap		M	I	NO	R	HS	100	50	Avge	Ct/St
2013	R. T. Ponting§	4	6	2	493	192	2	1	123.25	4
	D. P. Sibley†	3	4	0	264	242	1	0	66.00	1
	H. M. Amla§	6	10	0	545	151	1	4	54.50	1
2011	S. M. Davies	15	23	4	867	147	2	3	45.63	24/3
	V. S. Solanki	16	25	0	995	162	2	5	39.80	18
	R. J. Burns†	16	27	1	917	115	2	4	35.26	13
	G. C. Wilson	12	17	4	447	124	1	1	34.38	12
	A. Harinath†	12	21	2	584	154	1	4	30.73	4
2013	G. C. Smith§	3	5	1	120	67	0	1	30.00	4
	Z. de Bruyn¶	14	23	0	571	111	1	1	24.82	16
	Z. S. Ansari	6	8	3	114	27	0	0	22.80	3
2011	G. J. Batty	13	18	2	313	41	0	0	19.56	6
2012	S. C. Meaker	8	11	4	80	30*	0	0	11.42	0
	C. T. Tremlett	11	12	1	110	54	0	1	10.00	3
	J. J. Roy	4	7	1	49	17	0	0	8.16	3
	T. E. Linley	12	14	1	84	22*	0	0	6.46	6
2011	J. W. Dernbach‡	10	14	5	58	22	0	0	6.44	0
	G. Keedy	6	6	4	2	2*	0	0	1.00	2

Also batted: M. P. Dunn† (1 match) did not bat; G. A. Edwards† (1 match) 0; T. M. Jewell (1 match) did not bat; J. Lewis (2 matches) 2*; K. P. Pietersen‡ (1 match) 177* (1 ct).

† *Born in Surrey.* ‡ *ECB contract.* § *Official overseas player.* ¶ *Other non-England-qualified player.*

BOWLING

	Style	O	M	R	W	BB	5I	Avge
J. W. Dernbach	RFM	315	57	1,043	34	5-57	1	30.67
Z. S. Ansari	SLA	164.1	30	468	15	4-70	0	31.20
C. T. Tremlett	RFM	349.1	66	1,057	32	8-96	2	33.03
T. E. Linley	RFM	438.1	106	1,268	37	4-59	0	34.27
S. C. Meaker	RF	195.4	33	840	24	5-60	1	35.00
G. Keedy	SLA	269	51	796	22	7-99	2	36.18
G. J. Batty	OB	395.4	68	1,141	27	5-71	2	42.25
Z. de Bruyn	RM	253.2	52	824	13	3-28	0	63.38

Also bowled: H. M. Amla (RM) 5–0–22–0; R. J. Burns (RM) 15–0–90–1; M. P. Dunn (RFM) 35–2–133–4; G. A. Edwards (RFM) 37–14–80–3; A. Harinath (OB) 3–0–6–1; T. M. Jewell (RFM) 33.5–147–3; J. Lewis (RFM) 60–14–154–3; K. P. Pietersen (OB) 4–1–13–0; J. J. Roy (RM) 5.4–0–35–3; D. P. Sibley (LBG) 1–0–4–0; V. S. Solanki (OB) 15–0–90–2; G. C. Wilson (RM) 7–0–43–0.

LEADING YB40 AVERAGES (100 runs/4 wickets)

Batting	Runs	HS	Avge	SR	Ct/St	**Bowling**	W	BB	Avge	ER
S. M. Davies	387	127*	48.37	130.74	8/2	T. K. Curran	9	5-34	22.44	6.27
J. J. Roy	432	117	43.20	105.62	2	J. Lewis	13	4-59	24.84	5.56
V. S. Solanki	379	109*	42.11	84.03	7	G. J. Batty	6	3-35	25.00	4.54
R. J. Burns	136	49	27.20	106.25	2	Z. S. Ansari	8	4-42	27.25	6.22
G. C. Wilson	217	85	27.12	87.50	4	T. E. Linley	5	2-59	37.40	6.71
Z. S. Ansari	152	62	25.33	85.87	2	C. T. Tremlett	5	2-23	40.20	5.02
Z. de Bruyn	174	60	24.85	70.44	4	Z. de Bruyn	8	4-72	42.62	7.75

LEADING FLt20 AVERAGES (100 runs/18 overs)

Batting	Runs	HS	Avge	SR	Ct/St		Bowling	W	BB	Avge	ER
S. M. Davies ...	280	95*	25.45	**139.30**	7/3		G. J. Batty.......	9	2-14	22.33	**6.48**
Azhar Mahmood	154	47*	15.40	**128.33**	1		J. Lewis.......	8	2-15	28.50	**6.51**
J. J. Roy	290	52	22.30	**125.00**	6		J. W. Dernbach....	18	3-15	16.44	**6.70**
G. J. Maxwell...	142	32	17.75	**124.56**	3		Z. S. Ansari......	5	2-7	41.60	**7.17**
G. C. Wilson ...	240	44*	24.00	**121.82**	6		Azhar Mahmood	16	2-9	21.62	**7.20**
V. S. Solanki ...	147	38	16.33	**114.84**	3		Z. de Bruyn......	13	4-19	18.38	**8.43**

FIRST-CLASS COUNTY RECORDS

Highest score for	357*	R. Abel v Somerset at The Oval	1899
Highest score against	366	N. H. Fairbrother (Lancashire) at The Oval......	1990
Leading run-scorer	43,554	J. B. Hobbs (avge 49.72)	1905–34
Best bowling for	10-43	T. Rushby v Somerset at Taunton	1921
Best bowling against	10-28	W. P. Howell (Australians) at The Oval	1899
Leading wicket-taker	1,775	T. Richardson (avge 17.87)	1892–1904
Highest total for	811	v Somerset at The Oval	1899
Highest total against	863	by Lancashire at The Oval...................	1990
Lowest total for	14	v Essex at Chelmsford	1983
Lowest total against	16	by MCC at Lord's	1872

LIST A COUNTY RECORDS

Highest score for	268	A. D. Brown v Glamorgan at The Oval........	2002
Highest score against	180*	T. M. Moody (Worcestershire) at The Oval	1994
Leading run-scorer	10,358	A. D. Brown (avge 32.16)....................	1990–2008
Best bowling for	7-30	M. P. Bicknell v Glamorgan at The Oval	1999
Best bowling against	7-15	A. L. Dixon (Kent) at The Oval.............	1967
Leading wicket-taker	409	M. P. Bicknell (avge 25.21).................	1986–2005
Highest total for	496-4	v Gloucestershire at The Oval	2007
Highest total against	429	by Glamorgan at The Oval	2002
Lowest total for	64	v Worcestershire at Worcester................	1978
Lowest total against	44	by Glamorgan at The Oval	1999

TWENTY20 COUNTY RECORDS

Highest score for	101*	J. J. Roy v Kent at Beckenham	2010
Highest score against	106*	S. B. Styris (Essex) at Chelmsford..............	2010
Leading run-scorer	1,719	M. R. Ramprakash (avge 32.43)	2003–10
Best bowling for	6-24	T. J. Murtagh v Middlesex at Lord's	2005
Best bowling against	**4-9**	**D. J. Willey (Northants) at Birmingham**	**2013**
Leading wicket-taker	**55**	**J. W. Dernbach (avge 25.12)**..................	**2005–13**
Highest total for	224-5	v Gloucestershire at Bristol	2006
Highest total against	217-4	by Lancashire at The Oval	2005
Lowest total for	88	v Kent at The Oval.........................	2012
Lowest total against	68	by Sussex at Hove	2007

ADDRESS

The Oval, Kennington, London SE11 5SS (0844 375 1845; **email** enquiries@surreycricket.com).
Website www.surreycricket.com

OFFICIALS

Captain G. C. Smith	**Academy director** G. T. J. Townsend
Team director 2013 C. J. Adams	**President** Sir Trevor McDonald
Director of cricket 2014 A. J. Stewart	**Chairman** R. W. Thompson
First-team coach 2013 I. D. K. Salisbury	**Chief executive** R. A. Gould
Head coach 2014 G. X. Ford	**Head groundsman** L. E. Fortis
Assistant head coach S. N. Barnes	**Scorer** K. R. Booth

SURREY v SOMERSET

At The Oval, April 17–20. Drawn. Surrey 8pts, Somerset 9pts. Toss: Somerset. County debuts: G. Keedy, G. C. Smith, V. S. Solanki; A. N. Petersen.

South Africa's Test openers made their first appearances for their new counties, and it was the less-heralded Alviro Petersen who grabbed the limelight from Surrey's high-profile captain Graeme Smith. Petersen's 258 runs in the match broke the record for a Somerset debutant of 208 set by another overseas player, the Australian Cameron White, in 2006. Petersen made the most of a slow early-season pitch with some forceful strokeplay during his first-innings 167, although Dernbach kept Surrey in touch with his first five-for in almost two years, including wickets from the first two deliveries with the second new ball. Their reply owed much to left-handers Burns, who confirmed the fine impression of his first full season with some deft placement off his legs, and Davies, who demonstrated a return to form after the sorrows of the previous summer. Somerset wobbled briefly when Meaker – rusty in the first innings – blasted out Trescothick and Compton, but three dropped catches on the final morning and a lack of seam back-up cost Surrey any chance of forcing victory. Petersen came close to a second century, then Buttler just missed one when he holed out at long-on in the dying moments.

Close of play: first day, Somerset 344-8 (Thomas 18, Dockrell 7); second day, Surrey 98-4 (Burns 43, Davies 9); third day, Somerset 6-0 (Trescothick 6, Compton 0).

Somerset

*M. E. Trescothick lbw b Batty	25	– c Wilson b Meaker		14
N. R. D. Compton b Dernbach	0	– b Meaker		16
A. N. Petersen lbw b de Bruyn	167	– c Burns b Batty		91
J. C. Hildreth b Dernbach	34	– lbw b Batty		21
†C. Kieswetter st Davies b Batty	43	– lbw b de Bruyn		1
J. C. Buttler b Dernbach	19	– c Batty b Keedy		94
P. D. Trego c Solanki b Dernbach	0	– c Solanki b Meaker		4
A. C. Thomas c Burns b Dernbach	32	– b Meaker		0
J. Overton b Meaker	8	– lbw b Meaker		6
G. H. Dockrell c Smith b Meaker	22	– not out		2
S. P. Kirby not out	9			
B 17, l-b 3, w 5	25	W 2		2

1/11 (2) 2/58 (1) 3/117 (4)   (108.4 overs) 384   1/22 (1)   (9 wkts dec, 74.5 overs) 251
4/260 (5) 5/295 (6) 6/295 (7)   2/35 (2) 3/75 (4)
7/319 (3) 8/328 (9)   4/82 (5) 5/193 (3)
9/363 (8) 10/384 (10)   6/198 (7) 7/202 (8)
                                              8/208 (9) 9/251 (6)

Dernbach 27–6–57–5; Meaker 23.4–4–115–2; de Bruyn 13–2–50–1; Batty 21–2–76–2; Keedy 24–6–66–0. *Second innings*—Meaker 13–1–60–5; Dernbach 17–3–49–0; Batty 23–6–53–2; de Bruyn 8–1–39–1; Keedy 13.5–2–50–1.

Surrey

R. J. Burns c Kieswetter b Kirby	115	J. W. Dernbach not out	0
*G. C. Smith c Hildreth b Trego	2		
A. Harinath c Hildreth b Thomas	5	B 6, l-b 4, w 1, n-b 2	13
V. S. Solanki b Overton	30		
Z. de Bruyn b Kirby	1	1/5 (2) (9 wkts dec, 134.4 overs) 366
†S. M. Davies c Kirby b Overton	147	2/30 (3) 3/86 (4)
G. C. Wilson c Kieswetter b Thomas	17	4/87 (5) 5/246 (1)
G. J. Batty lbw b Overton	36	6/284 (7) 7/355 (8)
S. C. Meaker c Kieswetter b Kirby	0	8/356 (9) 9/366 (6) 110 overs: 290-6

G. Keedy did not bat.

Trego 21–5–62–1; Kirby 33–7–89–3; Thomas 26–11–45–2; Dockrell 27–8–74–0; Overton 22.4–3–75–3; Petersen 5–3–11–0.

Umpires: J. H. Evans and R. A. Kettleborough.

SURREY v SUSSEX

At The Oval, April 24–27. Drawn. Surrey 8pts, Sussex 9pts. Toss: Surrey.

Luke Wells reaffirmed his liking for Surrey's bowling, following home-and-away hundreds in 2012 with a maiden double-century, the first for Sussex at The Oval since Ranjitsinhji in 1908. First, however, he had to watch Wilson – one of three wicketkeeper-batsmen in Surrey's ranks – make his second first-class century after a sudden promotion: he was pushed up to No. 3 when Harinath was struck on the hand in the nets by Tremlett, who had been overlooked for the first match. The pitch, though generally docile, was at its liveliest on the first day, and the speedy Jordan shone against the county who had released him the previous year. Another returnee, Hamilton-Brown, batted for an hour against the team he captained for three seasons. The left-handed Wells then used his feet nimbly to spin, and his long reach to punish anything overpitched, dropping anchor for 526 minutes. He was accompanied first by Joyce, who showed similar patience, before Prior injected some urgency: all but 16 of his runs came in boundaries against a tiring attack in which Linley stood out. Overall, though, the slow tempo meant Surrey were never seriously threatened. Smith atoned for two previous failures, while Solanki, another new signing, gracefully found his touch.

Close of play: first day, Surrey 301-7 (Batty 19, Tremlett 9); second day, Sussex 204-2 (Wells 108, Joyce 51); third day, Surrey 66-1 (Smith 43, Wilson 14).

Surrey

R. J. Burns c Brown b Jordan	32	– c Brown b Magoffin	7
*G. C. Smith c Brown b Anyon	3	– b Panesar	67
G. C. Wilson lbw b Jordan	124	– c and b Nash	60
V. S. Solanki c Brown b Anyon	51	– c Jordan b Wells	83
Z. de Bruyn lbw b Anyon	31	– lbw b Wells	26
†S. M. Davies lbw b Magoffin	6	– not out	27
J. J. Roy b Magoffin	0	– not out	16
G. J. Batty c Wells b Jordan	37		
C. T. Tremlett b Jordan	34		
T. E. Linley b Jordan	3		
J. W. Dernbach not out	0		
B 14, l-b 4, w 2, n-b 10	30	B 2, l-b 14, n-b 6	22

1/5 (2) 2/63 (1) 3/181 (4)　　　　(109.2 overs) 351
4/247 (3) 5/260 (6) 6/260 (7)
7/277 (5) 8/338 (8) 9/344 (10) 10/351 (9)

1/9 (1)　　　(5 wkts dec, 87 overs) 308
2/116 (4) 3/182 (3)
4/250 (5) 5/257 (4)

Anyon 20–3–86–3; Magoffin 25–5–74–2; Jordan 23.2–3–92–5; Panesar 28–3–50–0; Nash 11–1–26–0; Hamilton-Brown 2–0–5–0. *Second innings*—Anyon 17–2–63–0; Magoffin 10–1–31–1; Jordan 15–4–63–0; Panesar 17–5–67–1; Nash 14–3–24–1; Wells 14–2–44–2.

Sussex

C. D. Nash lbw b Linley	12	M. S. Panesar c Smith b Tremlett	3
L. W. P. Wells b Solanki	208	S. J. Magoffin not out	3
M. H. Yardy c Burns b Batty	23		
*E. C. Joyce b Batty	98	B 2, l-b 2, n-b 14	18
M. J. Prior c Smith b Dernbach	62		
R. J. Hamilton-Brown c and b Solanki	39	(157 overs) 526
†B. C. Brown b Linley	23	
C. J. Jordan b Linley	23	
J. E. Anyon c Roy b Batty	14	

1/22 (1) 2/100 (3)　　　　(157 overs) 526
3/300 (4) 4/391 (5) 5/451 (2)
6/464 (6) 7/497 (7) 8/520 (8)
9/522 (9) 10/526 (10)　　　110 overs: 316-3

Dernbach 26–3–89–1; Tremlett 28–5–85–1; de Bruyn 15–1–46–0; Linley 32–8–82–3; Batty 47–6–174–3; Solanki 9–0–46–2.

Umpires: N. G. C. Cowley and G. D. Lloyd.

At Lord's, May 2–5. SURREY drew with MIDDLESEX.

SURREY v DURHAM

At The Oval, May 10–13. Durham won by five wickets. Durham 21pts, Surrey 4pts. Toss: Surrey. First-class debut: R. S. Buckley.

Durham's 19-year-old off-spinner Ryan Buckley had never even visited London before a sudden call-up to replace the injured Gareth Breese. His visit started inauspiciously: he headed to the wrong hotel, then found no room at the inn when he reached the right one. But a night on a sofa bed in coach Alan Walker's room did him no harm, as Surrey wilted, having failed to exploit the advantage of batting first on a pitch that turned from the start. Buckley's first spell lasted 22 overs, and he returned to help wrap up a compliant tail with four for four in 16 balls. Stoneman and Benkenstein displayed the graft Surrey had lacked, and eked out a lead despite Batty's determination to keep his side in the match. Surrey showed more grit second time round, although inconsistent bounce was becoming a problem on a surface Collingwood condemned as a "lottery", which he blamed on stud-marks from an Australian Rules football match six months previously. Borthwick chipped away with his leg-breaks, then made sure of Durham's third victory of the season in a stand of 100 with Stoneman.

Close of play: first day, Durham 48-0 (Stoneman 33, Smith 12); second day, Durham 279-9 (Benkenstein 70, Buckley 3); third day, Surrey 164-6 (Wilson 12, Batty 5).

Surrey

R. J. Burns c Mustard b Thorp	1	– lbw b Borthwick		38
J. J. Roy c Benkenstein b Thorp	17	– b Thorp		4
A. Harinath c Collingwood b Thorp	53	– lbw b Wood		11
V. S. Solanki c Smith b Buckley	38	– lbw b Collingwood		20
Z. de Bruyn c Mustard b Buckley	57	– b Borthwick		20
†S. M. Davies b Borthwick	52	– c Stoneman b Borthwick		46
G. C. Wilson b Borthwick b Buckley	6	– c Collingwood b Borthwick		26
*G. J. Batty c Benkenstein b Borthwick	0	– lbw b Buckley		27
S. C. Meaker not out	0	– c and b Borthwick		9
T. E. Linley c Borthwick b Buckley	0	– c and b Borthwick		19
G. Keedy lbw b Buckley	0	– not out		0
B 6, l-b 7	13	B 5, l-b 3, w 1		9

1/3 (1) 2/28 (2) 3/89 (4)   (82.2 overs) 237   1/11 (2) 2/37 (3)   (86.5 overs) 229
4/137 (3) 5/221 (6) 6/232 (7)   3/65 (1) 4/87 (4)
7/237 (8) 8/237 (5) 9/237 (10) 10/237 (11)   5/138 (5) 6/155 (6) 7/201 (8)
                                        8/201 (7) 9/224 (9) 10/229 (10)

Rushworth 12–3–38–0; Thorp 12–2–29–3; Collingwood 4–3–8–0; Wood 14–3–40–0; Buckley 30.2–8–86–5; Borthwick 9–2–22–2; Benkenstein 1–0–1–0. *Second innings*—Thorp 7–3–13–1; Rushworth 4–0–10–0; Buckley 30–5–86–1; Wood 13–2–28–1; Borthwick 27.5–5–70–6; Collingwood 5–1–14–1.

Durham

M. D. Stoneman c Burns b Batty	77	– b Meaker		67
W. R. Smith lbw b Batty	27	– c Davies b Linley		3
S. G. Borthwick c Davies b de Bruyn	14	– lbw b Batty		42
D. M. Benkenstein not out	74	– c Batty b Linley		6
B. A. Stokes b de Bruyn	20	– not out		35
*P. D. Collingwood lbw b de Bruyn	4	– b Keedy		9
†P. Mustard lbw b Batty	35	– not out		6
C. D. Thorp c Roy b Batty	2			
M. A. Wood c Davies b Linley	13			
C. Rushworth c and b Linley	0			
R. S. Buckley lbw b Batty	6			
B 4, l-b 2, w 2, n-b 6	14	B 4, l-b 4, w 1, n-b 4		13

1/88 (2) 2/131 (3) 3/131 (1)   (101 overs) 286   1/7 (2)   (5 wkts, 48.2 overs) 181
4/170 (5) 5/182 (6) 6/236 (7)   2/107 (3) 3/126 (1)
7/246 (8) 8/267 (9) 9/267 (10) 10/286 (11)   4/126 (4) 5/156 (6)

Meaker 10–1–58–0; Linley 18–3–40–2; Keedy 30–8–74–0; Batty 31–6–80–5; de Bruyn 12–4–28–3. *Second innings*—Linley 12–4–38–2; Batty 18–2–57–1; Keedy 13–0–51–1; Meaker 5.2–0–27–1.

Umpires: P. J. Hartley and N. A. Mallender.

At Nottingham, May 15–18. SURREY lost to NOTTINGHAMSHIRE by 114 runs.

At Oxford, May 22–24. SURREY drew with OXFORD MCCU.

At Derby, May 30–June 2. SURREY drew with DERBYSHIRE.

SURREY v WARWICKSHIRE

At Guildford, June 5–8. Drawn. Surrey 7pts, Warwickshire 11pts. Toss: Warwickshire.

This match marked the 75th anniversary of first-class cricket at Woodbridge Road, but the 2012 champions were in no mood for generosity, and batted beyond tea on the second day. Their eventual total was their highest against Surrey, beating 585 for seven at The Oval in 1905. Chopra greedily dominated the opening day, peppering the short boundaries with 29 fours as the bowlers – finding little assistance from an amiable pitch – dropped short and wide. Westwood and the perky Ambrose helped ram home the advantage. Once Dernbach (like Rankin, a late arrival after being released from England's one-day squad) had broken up the party on the second morning, Barker and Javid punished an increasingly irritable attack for career-bests in a seventh-wicket stand of 211. Harinath and Solanki – Surrey's third captain of the season – found life similarly agreeable after 37 overs were lost to rain on the third day, before Rankin initiated a bewildering slide of seven for 12, with three of them in one devastating over towards the close after conjuring up some reverse swing. But there was little sign of it in the follow-on, as Surrey batted out the rest of a quiet final day: there had been more excitement the previous morning, when Kevin Pietersen undertook a fitness test on the outfield.

Close of play: first day, Warwickshire 359-3 (Chopra 187, Ambrose 64); second day, Surrey 49-0 (Burns 21, Harinath 17); third day, Surrey 269-7 (Ponting 50).

Warwickshire

V. Chopra c de Bruyn b Dernbach	192	T. P. Milnes c Wilson b Roy		15
I. J. Westwood b Keedy	71	J. S. Patel not out		2
W. T. S. Porterfield b de Bruyn	11	B 8, l-b 8, w 1, n-b 14		31
*J. O. Troughton b Meaker	9			
†T. R. Ambrose lbw b Dernbach	84	1/153 (2)	(9 wkts dec, 168.4 overs)	631
A. Javid c Wilson b Roy	85	2/178 (3) 3/208 (4)		
R. Clarke c de Bruyn b Dernbach	6	4/369 (1) 5/384 (5) 6/398 (7) 7/609 (6)		
K. H. D. Barker lbw b Roy	125	8/612 (8) 9/631 (9)		110 overs: 401-6

C. J. C. Wright did not bat.

W. B. Rankin replaced Milnes after being released from the England squad.

Lewis 18–5–40–0; Tremlett 28–4–101–0; Meaker 23–0–129–1; de Bruyn 29–6–97–1; Keedy 42–7–141–1; Dernbach 23–4–72–3; Roy 5.4–0–35–3.

Surrey

R. J. Burns c Clarke b Barker	34	– c Ambrose b Clarke	85
A. Harinath c Troughton b Clarke	65	– c Chopra b Patel	26
*V. S. Solanki lbw b Javid	69	– c Ambrose b Rankin	18
R. T. Ponting c Chopra b Barker	52	– not out	38
Z. de Bruyn b Rankin	17	– c Chopra b Patel	19
S. C. Meaker b Rankin	0		
†G. C. Wilson lbw b Rankin	2	– (6) not out	28
J. J. Roy c Troughton b Barker	2		
C. T. Tremlett c Ambrose b Rankin	0		
G. Keedy not out	0		
J. W. Dernbach c Troughton b Barker	2		
L-b 4, w 1, n-b 26	31	B 8, l-b 6, n-b 6	20

1/69 (1) 2/169 (3) 3/232 (2) (85.4 overs) 274 1/46 (2) (4 wkts, 87 overs) 234
4/262 (5) 5/262 (6) 6/264 (7) 2/112 (3) 3/161 (1)
7/269 (8) 8/272 (9) 9/272 (4) 10/274 (11) 4/186 (5)

Dernbach replaced J. Lewis after being released from the England squad.

Barker 18.4–4–45–4; Wright 16–5–49–0; Clarke 13–1–49–1; Patel 16–5–50–0; Rankin 12–3–43–4; Javid 10–0–34–1. *Second innings*—Barker 7–0–21–0; Rankin 16–2–58–1; Patel 40–13–77–2; Javid 15–7–32–0; Clarke 9–1–32–1.

Umpires: M. J. D. Bodenham and N. G. B. Cook.

At Arundel, June 12–15. SURREY drew with SUSSEX.

At Leeds, June 21–24. SURREY drew with YORKSHIRE. *Kevin Pietersen hits 177 not out in his first innings of the season – and his only one of the Championship.*

SURREY v NOTTINGHAMSHIRE

At The Oval, July 8–11. Drawn. Surrey 5pts, Nottinghamshire 10pts. Toss: Surrey.

Ponting, widely feted as Australia's best batsman since Don Bradman, closed his first-class career on the ground where Bradman famously played his final Test, in 1948. The crowd was rather smaller, but – while The Don signed off with a duck – Ponting graced the occasion with his 82nd hundred, including some signature swivel-pulls and on-drives. He ensured that Surrey batted out the final day for a draw, and passed 24,000 runs in the process. In their first innings, they had thrown away the advantage of winning the toss, with only Burns and Davies making headway against a disciplined attack. Nottinghamshire then ran up a big lead. Mullaney had not reached three figures in the Championship since his second match, in May 2010, but warmed to his new role of opener with an adhesive 282-minute innings; Patel added a mature century, his third of the summer. The pitch, which had been used for a Twenty20 game the previous week, was expected to turn – Surrey fielded three spinners – but ended up providing more help for Dernbach and Tremlett. Neither side were willing to risk defeat, so Surrey batted out the match: Harinath knuckled down, but Ponting's seven-hour tour de force put everyone else in the shade.

Close of play: first day, Nottinghamshire 50-0 (Mullaney 22, Wessels 22); second day, Nottinghamshire 360-6 (Patel 87, Shahzad 10); third day, Surrey 186-2 (Harinath 69, Ponting 41).

Surrey

R. J. Burns c Read b Gurney	57	– b Adams	38
A. Harinath c Patel b Shahzad	4	– b Gurney	69
V. S. Solanki lbw b Adams	8	– run out	11
R. T. Ponting c Wessels b Patel	29	– not out	169
Z. de Bruyn c Read b Shahzad	16	– run out	1
†S. M. Davies not out	65	– b Adams	8
Z. S. Ansari c Wessels b White	7	– c sub (A. D. Hales) b Patel	27
*G. J. Batty c Read b Gurney	0	– lbw b Patel	0
C. T. Tremlett run out	0	– lbw b Patel	8
J. W. Dernbach c Read b White	0	– not out	18
G. Keedy b Shahzad	0		
L-b 4, w 2, n-b 6	12	B 8, l-b 18, w 2, n-b 18	46

1/16 (2) 2/42 (3) 3/93 (1)   (75.5 overs) 198   1/70 (1)   (8 wkts dec, 148 overs) 395
4/105 (5) 5/138 (5) 6/173 (7)   2/89 (3) 3/187 (2)
7/175 (8) 8/182 (9) 9/187 (10) 10/198 (11)   4/189 (5) 5/218 (6)
                                            6/316 (7) 7/316 (8) 8/336 (9)

Gurney 17–4–37–2; Shahzad 11.5–1–43–3; Adams 12–3–31–1; Patel 23.5–5–59–1; White 12–1–24–2. *Second innings*—Gurney 20–3–59–1; Shahzad 26–5–60–0; Patel 51–13–109–3; Adams 24–4–68–2; White 23–6–61–0; Hussey 2–1–6–0; Mullaney 2–0–6–0.

Nottinghamshire

S. J. Mullaney c Burns b Ansari	104	A. R. Adams c Ponting b Dernbach	16
M. H. Wessels lbw b Tremlett	47	H. F. Gurney not out	2
M. J. Lumb lbw b Tremlett	22		
J. W. A. Taylor st Davies b Keedy	5	L-b 9, w 2, n-b 8	19
S. R. Patel c Solanki b Dernbach	110		
D. J. Hussey c and b Keedy	37	1/105 (2) 2/155 (3)	(136.3 overs) 410
*†C. M. W. Read b Tremlett	31	3/168 (4) 4/207 (1) 5/265 (6)	
A. Shahzad c and b Ansari	17	6/325 (7) 7/386 (5) 8/386 (9)	
G. G. White c Davies b Dernbach	0	9/392 (8) 10/410 (10)	110 overs: 356-6

Dernbach 30.3–5–84–3; Tremlett 27–7–77–3; de Bruyn 13–1–62–0; Keedy 35–10–80–2; Batty 19–3–63–0; Ansari 12–2–35–2.

Umpires: R. J. Bailey and M. J. Saggers.

At Chester-le-Street, August 22–25. SURREY lost to DURHAM by an innings and 144 runs.

SURREY v DERBYSHIRE

At The Oval, August 29–September 1. Surrey won by four wickets. Surrey 21pts, Derbyshire 4pts. Toss: Derbyshire.

The elegant strokeplay of Amla gave Surrey illusory hopes of avoiding relegation after their first (and, as it turned out, only) win of the season. The pitch, relaid in 2007, was far from the featherbed on which Amla had crafted a Test triple-century against England in 2012: lift from the start, and increasingly variable bounce, tested even his technique. But, after being missed at short cover on 25 by Hughes, he took Surrey close to their target of 217, which they eventually reached with 38 balls to spare. Earlier, Derbyshire had been unsettled by the pace of Edwards, in his first match of the summer, and the swing of Linley. Then it was Footitt's turn to make the batsmen hop around, although Solanki's wristiness guided Surrey to a lead which promised greater heights before the last four wickets crashed for two runs. The fluctuations continued as Derbyshire dipped to 183 for seven, only for Poynton and Wainwright to put on 93. But, just as the lead threatened to become decisive, Batty mopped up on the final morning to finish with his best figures of the season, and the 500th first-class wicket of his career.

Close of play: first day, Surrey 8-0 (Burns 4, Harinath 0); second day, Derbyshire 13-0 (Slater 4, Borrington 5); third day, Derbyshire 231-7 (Poynton 29, Wainwright 22).

Derbyshire

B. T. Slater c Batty b Tremlett	4	– c Ansari b Linley	13
P. M. Borrington c Batty b Edwards	32	– b Linley	38
*W. L. Madsen c Ansari b Edwards	11	– lbw b Tremlett	59
S. Chanderpaul lbw b Edwards	46	– lbw b Batty	14
R. M. Johnson b Linley	23	– b Ansari	27
A. L. Hughes lbw b Ansari	16	– lbw b Tremlett	1
†T. Poynton c Davies b Linley	37	– c Burns b Batty	49
P. I. Burgoyne lbw b Batty	5	– c de Bruyn b Batty	5
D. J. Wainwright not out	17	– not out	54
M. Higginbottom c de Bruyn b Linley	4	– c Tremlett b Batty	1
M. H. A. Footitt c Amla b Linley	9	– c de Bruyn b Batty	1
L-b 6, w 5, n-b 4	15	B 7, l-b 15, n-b 2	24

1/4 (1) 2/39 (3) 3/88 (2) (89.5 overs) 219
4/109 (4) 5/139 (5) 6/151 (6)
7/162 (8) 8/197 (7) 9/205 (10) 10/219 (11)

1/29 (1) 2/80 (2) (123.1 overs) 286
3/120 (4) 4/157 (3)
5/167 (5) 6/167 (6) 7/183 (8)
8/276 (7) 9/280 (10) 10/286 (11)

Tremlett 17–4–37–1; Linley 24.5–8–59–4; Edwards 16–6–29–3; Batty 15–4–33–1; Ansari 12–2–36–1; de Bruyn 5–0–19–0. *Second innings*—Edwards 21–8–51–0; Linley 22–10–33–2; Batty 28.1–5–71–5; Tremlett 23–7–41–2; Ansari 27–7–62–1; de Bruyn 2–0–6–0.

Surrey

R. J. Burns lbw b Burgoyne	24	– c Madsen b Footitt	4
A. Harinath lbw b Footitt	1	– c Chanderpaul b Higginbottom	0
H. M. Amla c Burgoyne b Footitt	16	– c Madsen b Wainwright	88
V. S. Solanki b Wainwright	93	– lbw b Footitt	44
Z. de Bruyn lbw b Wainwright	40	– c Poynton b Hughes	31
†S. M. Davies c Borrington b Wainwright	29	– c Madsen b Wainwright	18
Z. S. Ansari not out	18	– not out	15
*G. J. Batty lbw b Higginbottom	35	– not out	6
C. T. Tremlett c Poynton b Footitt	0		
T. E. Linley b Footitt	0		
G. A. Edwards b Higginbottom	0		
B 17, l-b 3, w 3, n-b 10	33	B 1, l-b 5, n-b 6	12

1/10 (2) 2/41 (3) 3/81 (1) (90.5 overs) 289
4/177 (5) 5/217 (4) 6/240 (6)
7/287 (8) 8/288 (9) 9/288 (10) 10/289 (11)

1/4 (1) (6 wkts, 66.4 overs) 218
2/4 (2) 3/88 (4)
4/146 (5) 5/191 (3) 6/200 (6)

Footitt 19–5–50–4; Higginbottom 13.5–3–66–2; Burgoyne 26–5–73–1; Hughes 8–1–34–0; Wainwright 23–6–46–3; Madsen 1–1–0–0. *Second innings*—Footitt 13–1–52–2; Higginbottom 10–5–25–1; Wainwright 25–4–72–2; Burgoyne 10.4–2–41–0; Madsen 5–2–10–0; Hughes 3–0–12–1.

Umpires: N. G. B. Cook and S. C. Gale.

SURREY v MIDDLESEX

At The Oval, September 3–5. Middlesex won by 146 runs. Middlesex 21pts, Surrey 3pts. Toss: Middlesex.

Batsmen often admit to having nightmares about bowlers, but it's unlikely many would have lost much sleep over Ollie Rayner, the tall off-spinner whose previous ten Championship matches in 2013 had produced 25 wickets at 30 each. But now, on a reused pitch which spun from the start, Rayner returned Middlesex's best match figures since Fred Titmus captured 15 for 95 against Somerset at Bath in 1955. He also had a hand in three other wickets, featuring in 18 in all – second only to Jim Laker. Rayner's tour de force began on the second day, after a fluent half-century from

---

IF YOU WANT SOMETHING DONE...

Players featuring in most separate dismissals on the scorecard:

19	J. C. Laker (19-90)	England v Australia at Manchester	1956
18	W. Mycroft (17-103, 1 ct)	Derbyshire v Hampshire at Southampton (Antelope)	1876
18	F. C. L. Matthews (17-89, 1 ct)	Nottinghamshire v Northamptonshire at Nottingham	1923
18	J. M. Davison (17-137, 1 ct)	Canada v USA at Fort Lauderdale.............	2004
18	**O. P. Rayner (15-118, 3 ct)**	**Surrey v Middlesex at The Oval............**	**2013**

G. Giffen, playing for South Australia v Victoria at Adelaide in 1885-86, took 17 for 201 and also played a part in a run-out. H. Arkwright took 18 for 96, and also took a catch off another bowler, for Gentlemen of MCC v Gentlemen of Kent at Canterbury in 1861, in a match generally regarded as first-class – but it was a 12-a-side game.

Malan – his first of the Championship season – and a gritty innings from Dexter led to a useful total. The first two Surrey wickets fell to Harris and Patel, both to catches by Rayner. Then he took over with the lot, leaving a procession of batsmen bemused by bounce and turn on the way to a career-best eight for 46. All eight came in a frenetic afternoon session; Robson helped with two stunning catches at short leg. Middlesex lost five more themselves on a second day when 18 wickets went down, and their declaration next morning set an unlikely target of 385. Rayner was soon at it again, trapping Burns in front, and, although wickets were harder to come by, he finished with seven, and the best match figures in the Championship since Mohammad Sami's 15 for 114 for Kent against Nottinghamshire at Maidstone in 2003. "I'm very grateful to Rayner," said Rayner. "They've been very patient and stuck with me even when I haven't been able to take any wickets and my batting has been crap." Amla resisted well for 84, but the match was completed in the extra half-hour of the third day.

Close of play: first day, Middlesex 280-7 (Dexter 77, Harris 11); second day, Middlesex 133-5 (Malan 28, Harris 6).

Middlesex

*C. J. L. Rogers run out	55	– c Harinath b Keedy	32
S. D. Robson c Davies b Dernbach	0	– c Solanki b Keedy............	18
J. L. Denly c Solanki b Linley	12	– (8) lbw b Batty	31
D. J. Malan c de Bruyn b Linley	61	– (3) lbw b Batty	50
N. J. Dexter not out	90	– (4) c Solanki b Keedy...........	14
†J. A. Simpson c Harinath b Keedy............	23	– (5) c Burns b Keedy	12
G. K. Berg c Davies b Keedy................	19	– (6) c Solanki b Keedy............	15
O. P. Rayner c de Bruyn b Keedy	4	– (9) lbw b Batty	28
J. A. R. Harris lbw b Dernbach	11	– (7) c Harinath b Keedy............	24
R. H. Patel c Batty b Meaker	1	– not out	1
C. D. Collymore b Dernbach	0		
B 7, l-b 7, n-b 4	18	B 5, l-b 5	10

1/7 (2) 2/24 (3) 3/117 (1)   (101 overs) 294   1/47 (2)   (9 wkts dec, 53.3 overs) 235
4/159 (4) 5/204 (6) 6/240 (7)   2/60 (1) 3/76 (4)
7/248 (8) 8/280 (9) 9/283 (10) 10/294 (11)   4/90 (5) 5/118 (6) 6/170 (3)
                                                 7/204 (8) 8/216 (7) 9/235 (9)

Dernbach 18–3–63–3; Linley 21–5–59–2; de Bruyn 9–4–22–0; Meaker 10–4–28–1; Batty 18–2–47–0; Keedy 25–3–61–3. *Second innings*—Dernbach 2–0–21–0; Linley 5–1–17–0; Keedy 25–6–101–6; Batty 21.3–2–86–3.

Surrey

R. J. Burns c Robson b Rayner	38	– lbw b Rayner ... 24
A. Harinath c Rayner b Harris	0	– lbw b Patel ... 23
H. M. Amla c Rayner b Patel	26	– c Rogers b Rayner ... 84
V. S. Solanki c Dexter b Rayner	24	– c Rogers b Rayner ... 14
Z. de Bruyn c Rogers b Rayner	16	– c Robson b Rayner ... 6
†S. M. Davies c Robson b Rayner	1	– c Rayner b Collymore ... 38
*G. J. Batty lbw b Rayner	13	– c Denly b Rayner ... 11
S. C. Meaker c Dexter b Rayner	3	– c Rogers b Rayner ... 1
T. E. Linley c Rogers b Rayner	2	– c Berg b Patel ... 0
J. W. Dernbach c Harris b Rayner	1	– c Collymore b Rayner ... 22
G. Keedy not out	0	– not out ... 2
B 14, l-b 1, n-b 6	21	B 12, l-b 1 ... 13

1/2 (2) 2/72 (3) 3/74 (1) (54.4 overs) 145 1/44 (2) 2/56 (1) (94.4 overs) 238
4/106 (5) 5/108 (6) 6/117 (4) 3/88 (4) 4/102 (5)
7/135 (8) 8/139 (9) 9/140 (7) 10/145 (10) 5/188 (6) 6/207 (7) 7/209 (8)
  8/212 (7) 9/212 (9) 10/238 (10)

Collymore 9–2–18–0; Harris 7–1–25–1; Berg 4–1–10–0; Rayner 19.4–3–46–8; Patel 15–5–31–0. *Second innings*—Collymore 5–2–10–1; Harris 5–0–28–0; Rayner 37.4–14–72–7; Patel 28–7–72–2; Denly 9–0–28–0; Malan 5–0–10–0; Dexter 5–3–5–0.

Umpires: T. E. Jesty and J. W. Lloyds.

At Taunton, September 11–14. SURREY lost to SOMERSET by seven wickets.

At Birmingham, September 17–20. SURREY lost to WARWICKSHIRE by six wickets. *Surrey are relegated.*

SURREY v YORKSHIRE

At The Oval, September 24–27. Drawn. Surrey 8pts, Yorkshire 7pts. Toss: Yorkshire.
  Surrey were cheered up by a record-breaking innings from Dominic Sibley, who in only his third first-class match was the youngest to score a double-century in the Championship. Earlier on the same day he had become Surrey's most youthful centurion. In all, he batted for a minute shy of ten hours for 242, faced 536 balls and hit 24 fours and two sixes. Just 18, and given special leave of absence by Whitgift School, Sibley – faced by six men in catching positions in front of the bat –

THE PRODIGIES

The youngest batsmen to score a double-century in English first-class cricket:

Years	Days			
18	12	W. G. Grace (224*)	England v Surrey at The Oval	1866
18	**21**	**D. P. Sibley (242)**	**Surrey v Yorkshire at The Oval**	**2013**
18	237	D. J. Sales (210*)	Northamptonshire v Worcestershire at Kidderminster	1996
19	19	G. A. Hick (230)	Zimbabweans v Oxford University at Oxford	1985
19	95	E. J. Craig (208*)	Cambridge University v L. C. Stevens' XI at Eastbourne	1961
19	207	J. W. A. Taylor (207*)	Leicestershire v Surrey at The Oval	2009
19	235	D. N. Moore (206)	Gloucestershire v Oxford University at Oxford	1930
19	250	D. Nicholls (211)	Kent v Derbyshire at Folkestone	1963
19	308	R. A. Young (220)	Sussex v Essex at Leyton	1905

The youngest double-centurion in all first-class cricket is Hasan Raza, who was reputedly 15 years 215 days old when he scored 204* for Karachi Whites v Bahawalpur at Karachi in 1997-98. Grace is 12th and Sibley 13th on the overall list: nine of those above them are from Pakistan or India.

inched nervily to three figures after starting the third day with 81. But he widened his range of shots, off front foot and back, and continued to concentrate fiercely. He put on 236 with Amla, who made his first hundred for Surrey, and was finally yorked by Sidebottom after facing 536 balls, and hitting 24 fours and two sixes. Sibley's performance overshadowed a notable double from Ballance, who was named in England's squad for the Ashes tour the day before the match. He made 148 in the first innings and, after Yorkshire slipped to 84 for four in the second – still 116 adrift – another fine century to save the game, using his feet well as the spinners aimed into the footmarks, but frequently rocking back to force square.

Close of play: first day, Yorkshire 316-6 (Ballance 72, Rashid 14); second day, Surrey 172-1 (Sibley 81, Linley 0); third day, Surrey 572-4 (Sibley 220, Davies 25).

Yorkshire

A. Lyth c Davies b Dunn	24	– c Solanki b Linley	4
A. Z. Lees c Davies b Dunn	8	– c Davies b Linley	11
P. A. Jaques c Batty b Ansari	88	– b Dunn	1
K. S. Williamson b Ansari	23	– c Solanki b Batty	60
†J. M. Bairstow lbw b Jewell	24	– lbw b Linley	35
G. S. Ballance c Wilson b Ansari	148	– not out	108
*A. W. Gale c Solanki b Jewell	29	– c Wilson b Ansari	13
A. U. Rashid lbw b Jewell	43	– not out	8
R. J. Sidebottom c Davies b Dunn	6		
S. A. Patterson not out	5		
J. A. Brooks c Davies b Ansari	0		
B 13, l-b 8, w 7, n-b 8	36	B 13, l-b 8, n-b 4	25

1/22 (2) 2/58 (1) 3/146 (4)   (124.5 overs) 434   1/4 (1) 2/11 (3)   (6 wkts, 71 overs) 265
4/169 (5) 5/227 (5) 6/296 (7) 7/368 (8)   3/21 (2) 4/84 (5)
8/402 (9) 9/434 (6) 10/434 (11)   110 overs: 368-7   5/133 (4) 6/198 (7)

Linley 27–5–100–0; Dunn 25–1–97–3; Jewell 25–4–100–3; Batty 20–4–79–0; Ansari 27.5–7–70–4. *Second innings*—Linley 10–3–33–3; Dunn 10–1–36–1; Jewell 8–1–47–0; Ansari 24–4–79–1; Batty 18–4–45–1; Sibley 1–0–4–0.

Surrey

R. J. Burns c Bairstow b Patterson	82	G. C. Wilson not out	15
D. P. Sibley b Sidebottom	242	B 13, l-b 10, w 2, n-b 10	35
T. E. Linley lbw b Rashid	12		
H. M. Amla c Bairstow b Sidebottom	151	1/171 (1) (5 wkts dec, 173.4 overs) 634
V. S. Solanki c Ballance b Rashid	51	2/190 (3) 3/426 (4)
†S. M. Davies not out	46	4/502 (5) 5/596 (2) 110 overs: 303-2

Z. S. Ansari, T. M. Jewell, *G. J. Batty and M. P. Dunn did not bat.

Sidebottom 26.4–7–69–2; Patterson 27–8–82–1; Brooks 24–4–85–0; Rashid 55–6–227–2; Williamson 28–6–94–0; Lyth 11–0–44–0; Ballance 2–0–10–0.

Umpires: I. J. Gould and M. J. Saggers.

SUSSEX

There for the taking

BRUCE TALBOT

Third place in the Championship was Sussex's best finish since winning the title in 2007, but there was still irritation that they didn't do better. Throw in some disappointing limited-overs form, and the sense was that Sussex never quite did as well as they should.

They were top of Division One after beating Somerset in early July, and unbeaten after ten games. But an atrocious Twenty20 campaign and a punishing schedule affected morale, and Sussex surprisingly lost successive Championship matches, both at home, to Derbyshire and Middlesex. Momentum vanished, though they rallied in the final fixture to beat champions Durham and end a 13-month wait for a Championship victory at Hove. "The table doesn't lie, but it's frustrating," reflected captain Ed Joyce. "I think we deserved third place, but the title was there for the taking at one stage. Those two home defeats really set us back."

On a personal level, at least, Joyce could reflect on a satisfying first summer in charge. Captaincy seemed to help, rather than hinder, his batting, and he finished with 1,152 first-class runs, including a magnificent double-hundred at Trent Bridge; he also fell in the nineties on three occasions. He was a calm leader with a shrewd tactical brain and a phlegmatic attitude, particularly when it came to handling the troubled Monty Panesar.

It was clear long before the county sacked Panesar in August, when police fined him for urinating on two nightclub bouncers, that Joyce had lost confidence in a bowler who ought to have been Sussex's trump card in the second half of the season. It was suggested by those closest to the dressing-room that missing out on the Ashes Tests was the main source of Panesar's unhappiness, which manifested itself in petulance on the field and a discordant attitude off it, much to his captain's exasperation. He clearly didn't enjoy the role of stock bowler on unresponsive, slow wickets, especially at Hove. In truth, a parting was inevitable – even before Panesar put his career in jeopardy on Brighton seafront – and suited both parties.

It meant an unexpected opportunity for 32-year-old left-arm spinner Ashar Zaidi, who was playing in the Championship against Yorkshire within a fortnight of emailing the club for a trial. Zaidi, the holder of a UK passport through marriage, had last appeared in first-class cricket in 2009, in Pakistan, since when he had become a regular for Accrington in the Lancashire League. He took five wickets on debut, and batted aggressively against Durham, despite breaking a finger. Sussex saw enough to give him a two-year contract, likening him to Samit Patel.

His presence will help balance a bowling attack heavily reliant on seamers Steve Magoffin, Chris Jordan and James Anyon. For the first time since 2005,

Chris Jordan

three Sussex bowlers took 50 first-class wickets – and the Magoffin–Jordan axis looked a new-ball pairing to rival any in the land. If Magoffin's success was no great surprise given his achievements in 2012, Jordan was a revelation. His aggressive fast bowling was the perfect foil for Magoffin's accuracy, and his potency earned him an England debut. Just as importantly, Jordan remained fit. Susceptibility to injury had been a concern when Sussex signed him from Surrey, but he hardly missed a game and, not for the first time, coach Mark Robinson seemed to have turned a player of untapped potential into the real deal. Anyon was sometimes expensive, but he was a wicket-taker, and the injured Amjad Khan was scarcely missed.

Chris Nash, Joyce's vice-captain, also passed 1,000 runs, helped by a facile hundred against Yorkshire's declaration bowling. In Joyce's absence on Ireland duties, Nash led the side intelligently, especially enjoying the rout of Somerset in a day and a half on his home ground at Horsham. Luke Wells showed further improvement, narrowly missing his 1,000, and Ben Brown played some crucial innings, while also brushing up his performances with the gloves. On his return to Hove, Rory Hamilton-Brown showed flashes of his talent as he settled back into familiar surroundings after a difficult stay at Surrey. Mike Yardy twice scored over 150, before his form tailed off.

Given that Sussex had been one of the most consistent limited-overs sides of recent years, they were not expected to struggle. But when Australian John Hastings pulled out of the Twenty20 campaign with injury, their lack of an out-and-out strike bowler was exposed in a strong group. They failed to win a home game, although attendances at Hove, particularly the floodlit games, held up. Semi-finalists in the 40-over tournament for the previous two years, they were beaten in their opening game by Worcestershire, while winnable matches against Warwickshire and the Netherlands – the group's weakest teams – were lost to rain. Pluses included the batting of Luke Wright, who scored 502 runs in eight matches, and Matt Machan, who benefited from his exposure to international cricket with Scotland.

With the impressive redevelopment of Hove complete, chief executive Zac Toumazi saw his role as maximising revenue amid continuing economic uncertainty. The three-day game against Australia attracted an aggregate attendance of 17,000 and made around £200,000. While fewer enjoyed the Cliff Richard concert in June, it was still a major source of income. However, at the end of the season the pragmatic Toumazi warned of continuing austerity, despite not having to pay Panesar's salary.

Championship attendance: 31,456.

SUSSEX RESULTS

All first-class matches – Played 18: Won 5, Lost 3, Drawn 10.
County Championship matches – Played 16: Won 5, Lost 3, Drawn 8.

LV= County Championship, 3rd in Division 1;
Friends Life t20, 6th in South Division; Yorkshire Bank 40, 3rd in Group C.

COUNTY CHAMPIONSHIP AVERAGES, BATTING AND FIELDING

Cap		M	I	NO	R	HS	100	50	Avge	Ct/St
2009	E. C. Joyce	14	21	4	1,118	204*	2	6	65.76	14
2007	L. J. Wright‡	7	12	0	676	187	2	2	56.33	1
	M. W. Machan†	4	5	1	193	103	1	0	48.25	4
2008	C. D. Nash†	16	27	3	1,072	167*	3	3	44.66	10
	B. C. Brown†	15	22	6	620	93	0	5	38.75	58/2
	L. W. P. Wells†	16	27	1	982	208	2	5	37.76	7
2005	M. H. Yardy	16	26	2	834	156	2	1	34.75	9
	R. J. Hamilton-Brown	13	19	1	576	126*	2	2	32.00	3
2003	M. J. Prior‡	7	9	0	245	62	0	1	27.22	15
	C. J. Jordan	14	18	1	408	92	0	2	24.00	22
	W. A. T. Beer†	3	6	0	106	39	0	0	17.66	2
2011	J. E. Anyon	13	16	6	134	24*	0	0	13.40	1
	J. S. Gatting†	4	5	0	58	20	0	0	11.60	3
	S. J. Magoffin§	15	19	2	187	32	0	0	11.00	4
2010	M. S. Panesar	11	11	7	40	17*	0	0	10.00	2
	L. J. Hatchett†	4	5	0	27	21	0	0	5.40	0

Also batted: Ashar Zaidi¶ (2 matches) 17, 45 (1 ct); H. Z. Finch† (1 match) 11, 3 (1 ct); C. J. Liddle (1 match) 7*, 3*; A. S. Miller (1 match) did not bat.

† *Born in Sussex.* ‡ *ECB contract.* § *Official overseas player.* ¶ *Other non-England-qualified player.*

BOWLING

	Style	O	M	R	W	BB	5I	Avge
S. J. Magoffin	RFM	496	128	1,354	63	8-20	3	21.49
C. J. Jordan	RFM	435.3	78	1,577	59	6-48	1	26.72
J. E. Anyon	RFM	386.4	71	1,432	50	5-44	1	28.64
M. S. Panesar	SLA	329.4	72	929	23	5-95	2	40.39

Also bowled: Ashar Zaidi (SLA) 39.3–6–129–7; W. A. T. Beer (LBG) 72–8–215–4; H. Z. Finch (RFM) 4–0–15–0; J. S. Gatting (OB) 5–0–14–0; R. J. Hamilton-Brown (OB) 7–1–28–0; L. J. Hatchett (LFM) 116–15–423–6; C. J. Liddle (LFM) 25–4–98–3; A. S. Miller (RFM) 28–6–102–0; C. D. Nash (OB) 188.3–30–551–9; L. W. P. Wells (OB) 45–4–164–2; L. J. Wright (RFM) 77.3–15–256–6; M. H. Yardy (LM/SLA) 7–0–27–0.

LEADING YB40 AVERAGES (100 runs/4 wickets)

Batting	Runs	HS	Avge	SR	Ct
M. W. Machan	257	79	64.25	129.79	1
L. J. Wright	502	115	62.75	148.52	3
E. C. Joyce	403	123*	57.57	95.72	0
M. H. Yardy	248	52	41.33	95.75	1
C. D. Nash	286	95	35.75	98.28	5
R. J. Hamilton-Brown	103	40	12.87	67.32	9

Bowling	W	BB	Avge	ER
C. J. Liddle	19	3-21	20.52	5.70
C. J. Jordan	11	3-20	22.18	6.02
W. A. T. Beer	11	3-49	22.72	5.43
L. J. Hatchett	10	3-65	23.90	5.73
C. D. Nash	8	2-13	27.62	5.02
J. E. Anyon	6	2-14	30.33	6.00
M. H. Yardy	6	1-22	47.66	5.83

LEADING FLt20 AVERAGES (100 runs/18 overs)

Batting	Runs	HS	Avge	SR	Ct	Bowling	W	BB	Avge	ER
M. W. Machan . . .	219	67	31.28	**133.53**	3	C. D. Nash.	5	2-12	28.20	**6.08**
L. J. Wright	130	81	21.66	**130.00**	3	S. B. Styris	2	1-19	90.50	**6.91**
C. D. Nash	244	61*	27.11	**125.12**	1	W. A. T. Beer	6	2-20	37.33	**7.00**
S. B. Styris	209	46	26.12	**122.22**	0	M. H. Yardy	10	3-30	21.90	**7.06**
D. R. Smith	110	26	13.75	**119.56**	6	C. J. Jordan	8	2-28	25.12	**8.43**
R. J. Hamilton-Brown	233	47	23.30	**114.77**	4	C. J. Liddle	11	3-43	26.45	**9.09**

FIRST-CLASS COUNTY RECORDS

Highest score for	344*	M. W. Goodwin v Somerset at Taunton	2009
Highest score against	322	E. Paynter (Lancashire) at Hove	1937
Leading run-scorer	34,150	J. G. Langridge (avge 37.69)	1928–55
Best bowling for	10-48	C. H. G. Bland v Kent at Tonbridge	1899
Best bowling against	9-11	A. P. Freeman (Kent) at Hove	1922
Leading wicket-taker	2,211	M. W. Tate (avge 17.41)	1912–37
Highest total for	742-5 dec	v Somerset at Taunton	2009
Highest total against	726	by Nottinghamshire at Nottingham	1895
Lowest total for	{ 19	v Surrey at Godalming	1830
	19	v Nottinghamshire at Hove	1873
Lowest total against	18	by Kent at Gravesend	1867

LIST A COUNTY RECORDS

Highest score for	163	C. J. Adams v Middlesex at Arundel	1999
Highest score against	198*	G. A. Gooch (Essex) at Hove	1982
Leading run-scorer	7,969	A. P. Wells (avge 31.62)	1981–96
Best bowling for	7-41	A. N. Jones v Nottinghamshire at Nottingham . . .	1986
Best bowling against	8-21	M. A. Holding (Derbyshire) at Hove	1988
Leading wicket-taker	370	R. J. Kirtley (avge 22.35).	1995–2010
Highest total for	399-4	v Worcestershire at Horsham	2011
Highest total against	377-9	by Somerset at Hove	2003
Lowest total for	49	v Derbyshire at Chesterfield	1969
Lowest total against	36	by Leicestershire at Leicester.	1973

TWENTY20 COUNTY RECORDS

Highest score for	117	M. J. Prior v Glamorgan at Hove	2010
Highest score against	152*	G. R. Napier (Essex) at Chelmsford.	2008
Leading run-scorer	2,200	M. W. Goodwin (avge 29.33)	2003–12
Best bowling for	5-11	Mushtaq Ahmed v Essex at Hove	2005
Best bowling against	5-14	A. D. Mascarenhas (Hampshire) at Hove.	2004
Leading wicket-taker	65	M. H. Yardy (avge 25.83)	**2004–13**
Highest total for	239-5	v Glamorgan at Hove	2010
Highest total against	242-3	by Essex at Chelmsford	2008
Lowest total for	67	v Hampshire at Hove	2004
Lowest total against	85	by Hampshire at Southampton	2008

ADDRESS

County Ground, Eaton Road, Hove BN3 3AN (0844 264 0202; **email** info@sussexcricket.co.uk).
Website www.sussexcricket.co.uk

OFFICIALS

Captain E. C. Joyce
Professional cricket manager M. A. Robinson
Cricket performance manager K. Greenfield
President J. M. Parks
Chairman J. R. May

Chief executive Z. Toumazi
Chairman, cricket committee J. R. T. Barclay
Head groundsman A. Mackay
Scorer M. J. Charman

SUSSEX v LOUGHBOROUGH MCCU

At Hove, April 5–7. Drawn. Toss: Sussex. First-class debuts: J. P. P. Cornick, M. H. Cross, W. A. MacVicar, A. K. Patel. County debut: C. J. Jordan.

The loss of the first day to rain meant there was little chance of a result. On a pitch offering good pace and carry so early in the spring, wickets were evenly distributed, including a couple for Chris Jordan, a new arrival after six seasons at Surrey. In between spells at first slip, where he wore five layers and a woollen hat against the bitter cold, he produced some hostile deliveries. Sussex's batting looked assured: Gavin Baker removed Wells and Yardy for ducks in the first innings – Adam Soilleux despatched them cheaply in the second – and it was down to Gatting and Brown, who was given two lives, to oversee a recovery. Adam Riley, an off-spinner on Kent's books, claimed the last four wickets. Baker gave the students' innings a late boost with a combative 44.

Close of play: first day, no play; second day, Loughborough MCCU 54-3 (Patel 21, Endersby 5).

Sussex

C. D. Nash c Patel b MacVicar	52	– (2) not out			60
L. W. P. Wells c Cross b Baker	0	– (1) c Cross b Soilleux			8
M. H. Yardy lbw b Baker	0	– c Cross b Soilleux			0
*E. C. Joyce c MacVicar b Lester	5	– not out			29
R. J. Hamilton-Brown b MacVicar	34				
J. S. Gatting c Ratnayake b Lester	61				
†B. C. Brown lbw b Riley	85				
C. J. Jordan c Endersby b Riley	17				
S. J. Magoffin c Cornick b Riley	5				
J. E. Anyon lbw b Riley	25				
C. J. Liddle not out	2				
B 6, l-b 3, w 2	11	B 5, l-b 1, n-b 2			8

1/3 (2) 2/7 (3) 3/27 (4)   (72.1 overs) 297   1/31 (1)   (2 wkts dec, 24 overs) 105
4/94 (5) 5/99 (1) 6/200 (6)   2/59 (3)
7/225 (8) 8/243 (9) 9/283 (10) 10/297 (7)

Baker 13–3–57–2; Lester 15–1–58–2; Soilleux 10–0–44–0; MacVicar 13–3–46–2; Endersby 8–0–35–0; Riley 13.1–1–48–4. *Second innings*—Baker 5–1–39–0; Soilleux 9–2–36–2; Lester 4–1–9–0; Endersby 6–1–15–0.

Loughborough MCCU

D. A. D'Souza c Brown b Liddle	10	*A. E. N. Riley c Brown b Magoffin	1
J. P. P. Cornick b Magoffin	1	A. C. Soilleux st Brown b Nash	9
A. K. Patel c Brown b Liddle	22	T. J. Lester not out	0
†M. H. Cross b Jordan	8	B 11, l-b 6, n-b 4	21
D. M. Endersby c Nash b Anyon	22		
D. E. M. Ratnayake c Joyce b Anyon	7	1/2 (2) 2/21 (1) 3/34 (4) (70.5 overs) 155
W. A. MacVicar b Jordan	10	4/68 (3) 5/79 (6) 6/88 (5)
G. C. Baker lbw b Nash	44	7/104 (7) 8/127 (9) 9/148 (8) 10/155 (10)

Anyon 13–6–22–2; Magoffin 16–6–25–2; Liddle 14–6–30–2; Jordan 14–5–28–2; Wells 3–2–1–0; Nash 9.5–4–27–2; Gatting 1–0–5–0.

Umpires: M. R. Benson and M. J. Saggers.

At Leeds, April 10–13. SUSSEX beat YORKSHIRE by an innings and 12 runs.

At The Oval, April 24–27. SUSSEX drew with SURREY.

SUSSEX v WARWICKSHIRE

At Hove, May 1–4. Drawn. Sussex 8pts, Warwickshire 8pts. Toss: Warwickshire. County debut: A. S. Miller.

Two well-matched sides were frustrated by an awful pitch long before rain restricted the final day to 20 balls. Groundsman Andy Mackay was re-laying the square, but this was a slow, low, old-school Hove surface on which two strong batting sides struggled to score at three an over. Panesar, meanwhile, was rebuked by his captain for letting his frustration at its lack of pace become clear. The new ball offered some succour, and Jordan produced high-class deliveries that bounced and seamed to remove Bell and Trott, who was in sight of a sixth hundred against Sussex. Rankin, using his 6ft 8in height to good effect, was also threatening, though a string of useful contributions ensured Sussex were not in danger of following on. On the second day, Prior equalled the Sussex record of six dismissals in an innings.

Close of play: first day, Warwickshire 276-4 (Trott 87, Ambrose 0); second day, Sussex 129-1 (Wells 76, Yardy 1); third day, Sussex 416-7 (Brown 82, Anyon 19).

Warwickshire

V. Chopra c Prior b Nash	87	J. S. Patel not out		14
W. T. S. Porterfield c Jordan b Anyon	33	W. B. Rankin c Prior b Anyon		6
I. J. L. Trott c Prior b Jordan	96			
*I. R. Bell c Prior b Jordan	56	B 8, l-b 10, w 3, n-b 4		25
C. J. C. Wright c Prior b Jordan	3			
†T. R. Ambrose c Prior b Jordan	0	1/67 (2) 2/141 (1)	(145 overs)	453
C. R. Woakes b Panesar	72	3/272 (4) 4/276 (5) 5/285 (3)		
L. J. Evans b Panesar	19	6/292 (6) 7/329 (8) 8/432 (9)		
T. P. Milnes b Anyon	42	9/446 (7) 10/453 (11)	110 overs: 328-6	

Anyon 26–5–82–3; Jordan 28–8–73–4; Miller 28–6–102–0; Panesar 41–11–112–2; Hamilton-Brown 1–0–8–0; Nash 18–1–47–1; Wells 3–0–11–0.

Sussex

C. D. Nash c Chopra b Wright	43	J. E. Anyon not out		24
L. W. P. Wells b Rankin	96			
M. H. Yardy c Ambrose b Rankin	32	B 1, l-b 11, w 1, n-b 8, p 5		26
*E. C. Joyce c Chopra b Milnes	42			
†M. J. Prior c Ambrose b Wright	42	1/108 (1)	(7 wkts, 145.2 overs)	421
R. J. Hamilton-Brown lbw b Woakes	18	2/177 (3) 3/186 (2)		
B. C. Brown not out	82	4/252 (5) 5/280 (6)		
C. J. Jordan c Chopra b Rankin	16	6/315 (4) 7/360 (8)	110 overs: 335-6	

A. S. Miller and M. S. Panesar did not bat.

Wright 27–4–81–2; Woakes 24.2–4–40–1; Patel 45–6–127–0; Rankin 22–2–60–3; Milnes 20–1–72–1; Evans 7–0–24–0.

Umpires: N. A. Mallender and G. Sharp.

At Derby, May 15–18. SUSSEX beat DERBYSHIRE by nine wickets.

SUSSEX v SOMERSET

At Horsham, May 22–23. Sussex won by an innings and 116 runs. Sussex 22pts, Somerset 3pts. Toss: Somerset.

A frail Somerset had no answer to the sustained hostility of Magoffin, whose match figures of 12 for 31 were the best by a Sussex seamer since 2001. A pitch that started damp offered seam movement and excellent carry, and once he had settled on an immaculate length the long-striding Magoffin was virtually unplayable. Only six of the runs he conceded came in front of the bat, and at one stage he took four for none in eight balls. He bowled unchanged in Somerset's first innings to

BEST FIRST-CLASS FIGURES AT HORSHAM

9-35	V. Broderick	Northamptonshire v Sussex	1948
†9-50	G. Cox, sen.	Sussex v Warwickshire (second innings)...............	1926
8-18	M. W. Tate	Sussex v Worcestershire.............................	1924
8-20	**S. J. Magoffin**	**Sussex v Somerset**.............................	**2013**
8-30	M. W. Tate	Sussex v Glamorgan.................................	1923
†8-56	G. Cox, sen.	Sussex v Warwickshire (first innings)	1926
8-68	M. W. Tate	Sussex v Kent......................................	1927

† *In the same match, when Cox was 52 years old.*

QUITE A LOT FOR NOT VERY MANY

Bowlers taking 12 or more wickets for fewer than 50 runs in a Championship match since 1945:

15-31	G. E. Tribe	Northamptonshire v Yorkshire at Northampton.........	1958
14-29	D. Shackleton	Hampshire v Somerset at Weston-super-Mare.	1955
13-46	A. V. Bedser	Surrey v Nottinghamshire at The Oval	1952
13-49	D. L. Underwood	Kent v Surrey at The Oval	1978
12-31	**S. J. Magoffin**	**Sussex v Somerset at Horsham**	**2013**
12-34	G. A. R. Lock	Surrey v Glamorgan at The Oval	1957
12-35	A. V. Bedser	Surrey v Warwickshire at The Oval...................	1953
12-43	R. Appleyard	Yorkshire v Essex at Bradford	1951
12-48	B. Dooland	Nottinghamshire v Somerset at Nottingham	1953
12-49	A. L. Dixon	Kent v Essex at Blackheath	1964
12-49	A. B. Jackson	Derbyshire v Warwickshire at Coventry	1966

claim a career-best eight for 20 – allowing Sussex to begin their reply ten minutes before lunch on the first day. The openers gave them the lead before Hamilton-Brown showed that run-scoring with positive intent was feasible. Of the visiting attack, Thomas alone could come close to matching Magoffin's consistency in helpful conditions. Somerset fared only slightly better in their second innings, with Anyon gaining rewards for a lively spell before Magoffin finished things off at 2.35 on the second day. Somerset captain Trescothick said he was "embarrassed" at his side's batting; Sussex went top of the table.

Close of play: first day, Sussex 298-9 (Magoffin 21, Panesar 17).

Somerset

*M. E. Trescothick c Brown b Magoffin	20	– c Brown b Magoffin...............	13
A. V. Suppiah b Magoffin	7	– c Panesar b Anyon	22
A. N. Petersen lbw b Magoffin	12	– c Hamilton-Brown b Anyon.......	1
J. C. Hildreth c Jordan b Magoffin...........	3	– lbw b Anyon.....................	0
A. W. R. Barrow lbw b Jordan...............	0	– lbw b Jordan....................	14
†J. C. Buttler b Magoffin	22	– c Machan b Panesar	29
P. D. Trego c Brown b Magoffin	0	– c Brown b Jordan	2
A. C. Thomas lbw b Magoffin	0	– c Machan b Magoffin............	7
M. J. Leach c Brown b Magoffin	5	– c Jordan b Magoffin	2
S. P. Kirby c Nash b Jordan	3	– not out	2
J. Overton not out...........................	0	– c Brown b Magoffin	0
L-b 2, n-b 2	4	B 4, l-b 8, n-b 4	16

1/12 (2) 2/28 (3) 3/42 (4)   (22.4 overs) 76   1/27 (1) 2/32 (3)   (35.3 overs) 108
4/43 (5) 5/43 (1) 6/43 (7)   3/32 (4) 4/47 (2)
7/43 (8) 8/53 (9) 9/76 (6) 10/76 (10)   5/57 (5) 6/63 (7) 7/103 (6)
                               8/103 (8) 9/108 (9) 10/108 (11)

Anyon 5–0–22–0; Magoffin 11–4–20–8; Jordan 6.4–0–32–2. *Second innings*—Jordan 9–3–36–2; Magoffin 12.3–5–11–4; Anyon 9–2–25–3; Panesar 5–3–24–1.

Sussex

*C. D. Nash b Thomas	46	S. J. Magoffin c Kirby b Thomas	23
L. W. P. Wells c Buttler b Kirby	30	J. E. Anyon c Buttler b Kirby	13
M. H. Yardy b Trego	15	M. S. Panesar not out	17
J. S. Gatting c Trescothick b Thomas	4	B 12, l-b 9, n-b 10	31
R. J. Hamilton-Brown c Hildreth b Thomas	77		
M. W. Machan run out	26	1/83 (2) 2/87 (1) 3/91 (4) (72 overs)	300
†B. C. Brown lbw b Thomas	18	4/116 (3) 5/201 (6) 6/232 (5)	
C. J. Jordan c Trescothick b Trego	0	7/237 (8) 8/241 (7) 9/271 (10) 10/300 (9)	

Trego 12–1–46–2; Kirby 17–1–72–2; Thomas 23–9–69–5; Overton 17–3–65–0; Leach 3–0–27–0.

Umpires: S. A. Garratt and R. T. Robinson.

SUSSEX v NOTTINGHAMSHIRE

At Hove, May 31–June 3. Drawn. Sussex 9pts, Nottinghamshire 10pts. Toss: Sussex.

A superb game on an excellent pitch ended with Brown and Jordan holding out for 23 overs to defy Nottinghamshire, who had recovered from 112 for six on the first day thanks to a commanding century from the increasingly dominant Patel. He received excellent support from Franks, dropped on three, and Shahzad, who hit his first fifty since leaving Yorkshire. Jordan enjoyed a bouncy surface to finish with nine wickets, as he and Magoffin continued their duel at the top of the leading first-class wicket-takers' list: each now had 36. Several Sussex batsmen threatened to play the major innings demanded, though none quite did. Gurney wrapped things up with the first hat-trick for Nottinghamshire since 2006, and his colleagues then built solidly on a lead of 50, before another hostile burst by Jordan checked their progress. Nottinghamshire scented victory with four wickets needed as the last hour began – but Brown and Jordan kept them out.

Close of play: first day, Nottinghamshire 321-8 (Shahzad 35, Fletcher 0); second day, Sussex 290-6 (Brown 29, Jordan 21); third day, Nottinghamshire 304-9 (Franks 56, Gurney 4).

Nottinghamshire

A. D. Hales b Jordan	2	– (2) c Wright b Magoffin	0
E. J. M. Cowan lbw b Jordan	27	– (1) b Nash	81
M. J. Lumb c Jordan b Magoffin	10	– c Brown b Magoffin	8
J. W. A. Taylor c Brown b Jordan	11	– c Brown b Jordan	97
S. R. Patel c Joyce b Jordan	157	– c Brown b Jordan	18
S. J. Mullaney c Brown b Magoffin	5	– c Wells b Jordan	5
*†C. M. W. Read c Brown b Jordan	18	– lbw b Panesar	10
P. J. Franks b Anyon	36	– b Wright	78
A. Shahzad c Brown b Anyon	56	– b Magoffin	3
L. J. Fletcher c Yardy b Jordan	8	– c Joyce b Magoffin	0
H. F. Gurney not out	4	– not out	8
B 5, l-b 6, w 1, n-b 10	22	B 1, l-b 8, w 3, n-b 10	22

1/3 (1) 2/22 (3) 3/50 (4)	(111 overs) 356	1/4 (2) 2/24 (3)	(94.3 overs) 330
4/53 (2) 5/72 (6) 6/112 (7) 7/204 (8)		3/175 (1) 4/205 (4)	
8/318 (5) 9/331 (10) 10/356 (9)	110 overs: 354-9	5/218 (5) 6/233 (6) 7/239 (7)	
		8/288 (9) 9/288 (10) 10/330 (8)	

Magoffin 22–3–87–2; Jordan 30–5–97–6; Anyon 21–0–75–2; Wright 10–3–24–0; Panesar 21–4–49–0; Nash 7–1–13–0. *Second innings*—Anyon 10–2–51–0; Magoffin 17–5–60–4; Panesar 24–7–59–1; Jordan 16–2–58–3; Wright 10.3–1–40–1; Nash 17–3–53–1.

Sussex

C. D. Nash b Shahzad	22	– (2) b Shahzad	46
L. W. P. Wells c Fletcher b Patel	59	– (1) c Read b Fletcher	11
M. H. Yardy b Shahzad	46	– c Read b Franks	14
*E. C. Joyce c Taylor b Gurney	59	– c Read b Gurney	20
R. J. Hamilton-Brown c Hales b Shahzad	10	– b Shahzad	23
L. J. Wright c Read b Patel	14	– c Mullaney b Shahzad	0
†B. C. Brown c Patel b Gurney	35	– not out	51
C. J. Jordan run out	22	– not out	28
S. J. Magoffin not out	7		
J. E. Anyon c Mullaney b Gurney	0		
M. S. Panesar c Patel b Gurney	0		
B 5, l-b 13, w 2, n-b 12	32	B 7, l-b 5, w 2, n-b 16	30

1/72 (1) 2/118 (2) 3/176 (3)   (82.5 overs) 306
4/188 (5) 5/223 (6) 6/249 (4)
7/291 (8) 8/306 (7) 9/306 (10) 10/306 (11)

1/23 (1)   (6 wkts, 88.3 overs) 223
2/55 (3) 3/95 (4)
4/112 (2) 5/112 (6) 6/153 (5)

Fletcher 20–6–59–0; Gurney 17.5–2–69–4; Shahzad 16–1–57–3; Patel 18–2–63–2; Franks 11–3–40–0. *Second innings*—Fletcher 11–3–18–1; Gurney 18–5–41–1; Shahzad 16–1–71–3; Patel 32.3–13–60–0; Franks 11–3–21–1.

Umpires: D. J. Millns and P. Willey.

At Lord's, June 5–8. SUSSEX drew with MIDDLESEX.

SUSSEX v SURREY

At Arundel, June 12–15. Drawn. Sussex 7pts, Surrey 11pts. Toss: Surrey.

A first-day washout and a desperately slow pitch frustrated both teams, although Surrey, who claimed maximum bonus points for the first time since September 2011, could take more encouragement. Acting-captain Solanki played with the greatest fluency, recompensing a third-day crowd of 3,000 – many had come to see Ponting play his first (and probably last) first-class innings at Arundel – with a century including a six that missed a slumbering dog in the press tent by inches. De Bruyn ended a poor run with a more prosaic hundred, before Tremlett, who reached 50 from 29 balls after biffing four sixes off Magoffin, allowed Solanki to declare an hour into the last day with a lead of 161. Panesar, benefiting from some intensive work with England spin coach Peter Such before the game, had looked more like his old self, and claimed five wickets. Sussex, whose first innings had wilted after reaching a healthy 176 for three, had no trouble saving the match: Nash reached his first hundred of the season, while Wells took his aggregate in four matches against Surrey to 528. Sussex had yet to lose, Surrey to win. Chris Adams, their director of cricket, said the match was "comfortably our most complete performance yet, and we feel, had we had four days' play, this would have been our first win". Two days later, he was sacked, along with first-team coach Ian Salisbury.

Close of play: first day, no play; second day, Surrey 1-0 (Burns 1, Harinath 0); third day, Surrey 363-6 (de Bruyn 99, Ansari 9).

Sussex

C. D. Nash c Solanki b Linley	32	– (2) not out	102
L. W. P. Wells lbw b Dernbach	3	– (1) c Wilson b Ansari	50
M. H. Yardy lbw b de Bruyn	69	– c Burns b Ansari	8
*E. C. Joyce c and b Linley	36	– not out	26
M. J. Prior c Wilson b Ansari	38		
L. J. Wright c Ponting b Tremlett	41		
†B. C. Brown b Dernbach	1		
C. J. Jordan b Linley	41		
S. J. Magoffin c Ponting b Linley	11		
J. E. Anyon lbw b Tremlett	0		
M. S. Panesar not out	4		
L-b 7, n-b 12	19	B 8, l-b 2, w 1, n-b 4	15

1/17 (2) 2/68 (1) 3/129 (4)   (89.1 overs) 295   1/107 (1)   (2 wkts dec, 59 overs) 201
4/176 (5) 5/205 (5) 6/206 (7)   2/131 (3)
7/265 (6) 8/280 (9) 9/283 (10) 10/295 (8)

Dernbach 21–3–68–2; Tremlett 21–0–74–2; Linley 21.1–5–68–4; de Bruyn 14–4–40–1; Ansari 12–2–38–1. *Second innings*—Dernbach 13–4–45–0; Tremlett 7–0–34–0; Linley 12–0–48–0; Ansari 20–3–49–2; de Bruyn 4–1–9–0; Harinath 2–0–4–0; Burns 1–0–2–0.

Surrey

R. J. Burns c Jordan b Panesar	36	C. T. Tremlett c Prior b Jordan	54
A. Harinath c Joyce b Jordan	23	T. E. Linley not out	22
*V. S. Solanki c Prior b Panesar	130	B 7, l-b 10, w 3, n-b 8, p 5	33
R. T. Ponting c Jordan b Magoffin	13		
Z. de Bruyn c Joyce b Panesar	111	1/56 (2) (9 wkts dec, 115.3 overs) 456	
†S. M. Davies c Brown b Panesar	11	2/96 (1) 3/113 (4)	
G. C. Wilson c Yardy b Jordan	10	4/290 (3) 5/301 (6) 6/328 (7) 7/372 (8)	
Z. S. Ansari c Prior b Panesar	13	8/382 (5) 9/456 (9) 110 overs: 404-8	

J. W. Dernbach did not bat.

Anyon 24–6–82–0; Magoffin 27–10–89–1; Panesar 38–3–142–5; Jordan 20.3–1–94–3; Nash 6–0–27–0.

Umpires: S. C. Gale and M. A. Gough.

At Nottingham, June 22–25. SUSSEX drew with NOTTINGHAMSHIRE.

At Taunton, July 8–10. SUSSEX beat SOMERSET by nine wickets.

SUSSEX v MIDDLESEX

At Hove, July 17–20. Middlesex won by ten wickets. Middlesex 24pts, Sussex 2pts. Toss: Middlesex. Championship debut: G. S. Sandhu.

On the relaid pitch used when beating Middlesex in 2012, Sussex lost the last undefeated record in Division One. The bounce was occasionally disconcerting, and it was Middlesex, after choosing to bowl, who exploited it better. With one exception, Sussex lacked patience against an accurate attack: the unflustered Joyce batted sublimely for his second hundred of the season. Robson trumped that with his own magnificent century, mixing assured accumulation with diligent defence. Despite a late collapse to Panesar, all the batsmen chipped in – Denly made his highest score of a disappointing summer – to give Middlesex a lead of 267. Finn, released by England on the second day of this game, preferred not to take the new ball, but struck twice in his first seven deliveries to leave Sussex in trouble in their second innings at 45 for four. After a careful start, Wright got off the mark with four successive fours from a now-chastened Finn, took his aggregate in four innings against Middlesex in 2013 to 447 with a combative 161, including 102 in boundaries. Even so, Middlesex strolled to victory on the fourth morning.

Close of play: first day, Middlesex 44-0 (Robson 11, Malan 27); second day, Middlesex 445-5 (Simpson 39, Berg 26); third day, Sussex 288-6 (Wright 151, Jordan 1).

Sussex

C. D. Nash c Robson b Berg	40	– (2) c Voges b Murtagh	0
L. W. P. Wells c Simpson b Sandhu	15	– (1) c Rayner b Finn	19
M. H. Yardy c Simpson b Berg	0	– c Simpson b Collymore	18
*E. C. Joyce b Dexter	101	– c Simpson b Dexter	47
R. J. Hamilton-Brown b Dexter	16	– c Voges b Finn	1
L. J. Wright c Dexter b Rayner	22	– c Dexter b Collymore	161
†B. C. Brown c Berg b Sandhu	7	– c Voges b Berg	38
C. J. Jordan b Murtagh	8	– c Simpson b Murtagh	2
S. J. Magoffin c Simpson b Murtagh	0	– c Simpson b Collymore	0
J. E. Anyon c Robson b Berg	9	– c Simpson b Murtagh	10
M. S. Panesar not out	2	– not out	0
L-b 4, w 1, n-b 4	9	B 5, l-b 3, n-b 6	14

1/48 (2) 2/49 (3) 3/76 (1)   (80.2 overs) 229   1/11 (2) 2/42 (1)   (87.3 overs) 310
4/117 (5) 5/173 (6) 6/180 (7)   3/44 (3) 4/45 (5)
7/196 (8) 8/196 (9) 9/226 (4) 10/229 (10)   5/155 (6) 6/262 (7) 7/292 (8)
8/293 (9) 9/308 (10) 10/310 (6)

Murtagh 19–3–61–2; Collymore 11–3–29–0; Sandhu 15–3–54–2; Berg 16.2–3–49–3; Dexter 6–2–14–2; Rayner 13–3–18–1. *Second innings*—Murtagh 22–5–57–3; Collymore 19.3–1–52–3; Berg 10.2–2–50–1; Finn 18–4–74–2; Rayner 8–0–33–0; Dexter 10.1–1–36–1.

Middlesex

S. D. Robson b Panesar	166	– not out	18
D. J. Malan c Brown b Anyon	32	– not out	19
J. L. Denly c Nash b Magoffin	77		
A. C. Voges c Wells b Anyon	20		
*N. J. Dexter b Magoffin	48		
†J. A. Simpson c Brown b Jordan	59		
G. K. Berg c Magoffin b Panesar	39		
O. P. Rayner lbw b Panesar	0		
T. J. Murtagh st Brown b Panesar	9		
S. T. Finn not out	0		
C. D. Collymore c Brown b Panesar	0		
B 18, l-b 7, w 1, n-b 20	46	B 5, n-b 2	7

1/60 (2) 2/180 (3) 3/230 (4)   (123.4 overs) 496   (no wkt, 9 overs) 44
4/332 (5) 5/394 (1) 6/476 (7)
7/483 (6) 8/485 (8) 9/496 (9)
10/496 (11)   110 overs: 450-5

Finn replaced G. S. Sandhu after being released from the England squad.

Anyon 26–2–108–2; Magoffin 28–3–86–2; Jordan 27–2–128–1; Panesar 31.4–3–95–5; Wright 7–0–25–0; Nash 2–0–24–0; Wells 2–0–5–0. *Second innings*—Magoffin 3–0–16–0; Jordan 2–0–11–0; Wells 2–0–7–0; Yardy 2–0–5–0.

Umpires: N. G. B. Cook and J. W. Lloyds.

At Hove, July 26–28. SUSSEX drew with AUSTRALIANS (see Australian tour section).

SUSSEX v DERBYSHIRE

At Hove, August 2–4. Derbyshire won by nine wickets. Derbyshire 21pts, Sussex 6pts. Toss: Derbyshire. First-class debut: A. L. Hughes. Championship debut: M. Higginbottom.

For the second Championship match in a row Sussex gambled on a relaid wicket and lost. Once again their top-order frailties were exposed, particularly in the second innings, when they never recovered from excellent new-ball spells by Groenewald and Footitt. Derbyshire had hardly been in a winning position all season but, with Slater scoring his maiden Championship half-century, they made light of a target of 174 to secure their first victory in Division One since 2000, and their first at Hove since 1996. Slater was one of five Academy products in the team – four of whom could boast just five previous Championship appearances between them – but they all made a contribution, notably the 21-year-old medium-pace all-rounder Alex Hughes, who claimed a wicket with his fifth delivery in first-class cricket. Wells had held Sussex's first innings together with a dogged 253-ball hundred, and a lead of 40 might have been a platform for victory. Jordan won the race to 50 first-class wickets by removing Chesney Hughes, before Magoffin followed him to the landmark three overs later with the scalp of Slater. But Groenewald's five-for left Sussex contemplating a tenth defeat in their last 12 matches in all formats – and a winless Championship run at Hove stretching back almost 12 months.

Close of play: first day, Sussex 314; second day, Sussex 11-1 (Wells 2, Hatchett 5).

Sussex

C. D. Nash c Chanderpaul b Higginbottom	22	– (2) b Groenewald	2
L. W. P. Wells c Groenewald b Madsen	110	– (1) c Burgoyne b Groenewald	2
M. H. Yardy c Slater b A. L. Hughes	12	– (4) c Poynton b Footitt	11
*E. C. Joyce c Poynton b Footitt	22	– (5) lbw b Higginbottom	17
R. J. Hamilton-Brown b A. L. Hughes	11	– (6) lbw b Footitt	5
L. J. Wright c and b A. L. Hughes	0	– (7) c Poynton b Groenewald	49
†B. C. Brown c Chanderpaul b Madsen	20	– (8) c Chanderpaul b A. L. Hughes	11
C. J. Jordan c Slater b Groenewald	48	– (9) b Groenewald	23
S. J. Magoffin c Poynton b Groenewald	32	– (10) lbw b Footitt	1
M. S. Panesar not out	3	– (11) not out	0
L. J. Hatchett lbw b Groenewald	0	– (3) lbw b Groenewald	5
B 1, l-b 13, n-b 20	34	L-b 3, n-b 4	7

1/40 (1) 2/66 (3) 3/109 (4) (93.2 overs) 314
4/144 (5) 5/144 (6) 6/189 (7)
7/242 (2) 8/301 (9) 9/312 (8) 10/314 (11)

1/4 (2) 2/11 (1) (47.4 overs) 133
3/22 (4) 4/22 (3)
5/29 (6) 6/62 (5) 7/87 (8)
8/124 (7) 9/125 (10) 10/133 (9)

Groenewald 22.2–4–74–3; Footitt 23.5–5–67–1; Higginbottom 15–2–69–1; A. L. Hughes 15–4–49–3; Burgoyne 13–3–32–0; Madsen 5–3–9–2. *Second innings*—Footitt 13–3–39–3; Groenewald 15.4–3–40–5; Higginbottom 11–5–24–1; A. L. Hughes 8–1–27–1.

Derbyshire

B. T. Slater c Brown b Magoffin	16	– not out	66
C. F. Hughes c Brown b Jordan	13	– b Jordan	34
*W. L. Madsen lbw b Panesar	97	– not out	62
S. Chanderpaul c Jordan b Wright	9		
R. M. Johnson c Joyce b Wright	1		
A. L. Hughes c Nash b Jordan	11		
†T. Poynton c Brown b Panesar	13		
P. I. Burgoyne not out	62		
T. D. Groenewald c Yardy b Jordan	0		
M. Higginbottom b Magoffin	9		
M. H. A. Footitt run out	6		
B 13, l-b 8, w 2, n-b 14	37	B 2, l-b 2, n-b 8	12

1/36 (2) 2/40 (1) 3/73 (4) (87 overs) 274
4/75 (5) 5/103 (6) 6/139 (7)
7/217 (3) 8/218 (9) 9/263 (10) 10/274 (11)

1/69 (2) (1 wkt, 42.3 overs) 174

Magoffin 21–5–53–2; Hatchett 19–3–46–0; Jordan 23–4–73–3; Wright 10–1–36–2; Panesar 14–2–45–2. *Second innings*—Magoffin 9–0–36–0; Hatchett 10–1–44–0; Jordan 7–0–33–1; Panesar 11–2–42–0; Nash 5.3–2–15–0.

Umpires: R. J. Evans and P. J. Hartley.

At Birmingham, August 28–31. SUSSEX drew with WARWICKSHIRE.

At Chester-le-Street, September 3–5. SUSSEX lost to DURHAM by 285 runs.

SUSSEX v YORKSHIRE

At Hove, September 11–14. Drawn. Sussex 7pts, Yorkshire 9pts. Toss: Yorkshire. County debut: Ashar Zaidi.

Yorkshire's title challenge effectively vanished in the rain that thwarted their assault on an agreed target of 300 in 64 overs. On the last morning, Nash and Hamilton-Brown were the beneficiaries of 32 overs of joke bowling (which at least gave Jaques his maiden first-class wicket in his 187th match) as they coasted to average-fattening unbeaten hundreds greeted with a sheepish wave of the bat. With Yorkshire committed to the chase, it should have been a tense finale, but a heavy shower ended play before three o'clock, just as Durham were routing Derbyshire to open a 27.5-point lead. In truth, Yorkshire seldom resembled potential champions. After winning a useful toss they let Sussex's last three wickets add 128, and their own run-rate stayed below three an over; Lyth and Williamson were the only batsmen to counter Magoffin's accuracy and occasionally steepling bounce. In his first first-class match since December 2009, Ashar Zaidi, a 32-year-old slow left-armer from Karachi drafted in to replace Monty Panesar and who three days earlier had been playing for new Lancashire League champions Accrington, took five wickets with his flattish spin.

Close of play: first day, Sussex 276-9 (Brown 78, Hatchett 11); second day, Yorkshire 246-4 (Williamson 80, Patterson 2); third day, Sussex 48-2 (Nash 21, Joyce 4).

Sussex

C. D. Nash c Bairstow b Plunkett	35	– (2) not out	167
L. W. P. Wells c Lyth b Brooks	10	– (1) b Sidebottom	0
M. H. Yardy b Plunkett	29	– c Jaques b Plunkett	15
*E. C. Joyce b Sidebottom	3	– c Brooks b Jaques	14
M. J. Prior b Patterson	23		
R. J. Hamilton-Brown b Williamson	20	– (5) not out	126
†B. C. Brown not out	84		
Ashar Zaidi lbw b Sidebottom	17		
S. J. Magoffin c Bairstow b Sidebottom	26		
J. E. Anyon b Williamson	6		
L. J. Hatchett c Lyth b Sidebottom	21		
B 4, l-b 8, n-b 6	18	B 8, l-b 3	11

1/24 (2) 2/58 (1) 3/79 (3) (79.5 overs) 292 1/4 (1) (3 wkts dec, 47 overs) 333
4/83 (4) 5/114 (6) 6/137 (5) 2/33 (3) 3/73 (4)
7/164 (8) 8/238 (9) 9/254 (10) 10/292 (11)

Sidebottom 15.5–5–50–4; Brooks 13–2–42–1; Patterson 14–4–59–1; Plunkett 14–0–54–2; Williamson 9–2–44–2; Rashid 14–0–31–0. *Second innings*—Sidebottom 5–1–11–1; Brooks 4–0–17–0; Plunkett 1–0–1–1; Rashid 3–0–7–0; Williamson 2–0–4–0; Jaques 6–0–75–1; Gale 9–0–94–0; Ballance 12–0–88–0; Lyth 5–0–25–0.

Yorkshire

A. Lyth c Prior b Ashar Zaidi	93	– not out	40
P. A. Jaques lbw b Magoffin	21	– (3) lbw b Ashar Zaidi	23
K. S. Williamson lbw b Anyon	80	– (4) not out	5
*A. W. Gale c Brown b Anyon	28		
†J. M. Bairstow b Anyon	8		
S. A. Patterson c Brown b Magoffin	11		
G. S. Ballance c Prior b Ashar Zaidi	19		
A. U. Rashid c Magoffin b Ashar Zaidi	13		
L. E. Plunkett st Brown b Ashar Zaidi	27	– (2) c Joyce b Hatchett	11
R. J. Sidebottom b Hatchett	5		
J. A. Brooks not out	0		
B 6, l-b 7, n-b 8	21	N-b 2	2

1/25 (2) 2/189 (1) 3/234 (4) (115.2 overs) 326 1/22 (2) (2 wkts, 20 overs) 81
4/243 (5) 5/250 (3) 6/276 (6) 7/284 (7) 2/64 (3)
8/313 (8) 9/320 (10) 10/326 (9) 110 overs: 303-7

Magoffin 37–18–59–2; Hatchett 19–5–71–1; Ashar Zaidi 23.2–3–57–4; Anyon 29–4–107–3; Nash 7–0–19–0. *Second innings*—Magoffin 5–0–22–0; Hatchett 5–1–17–1; Nash 4–0–14–0; Ashar Zaidi 5–0–24–1; Anyon 1–0–4–0.

Umpires: M. R. Benson and S. J. O'Shaughnessy.

SUSSEX v DURHAM

At Hove, September 24–27. Sussex won by six wickets. Sussex 22pts, Durham 3pts. Toss: Durham.
Sussex paced their pursuit of 295 in 75 overs to perfection, ensuring third place, behind Durham – their opponents and new champions – and Yorkshire. On a pitch that became easier for batsmen, the stylish Joyce finished things off after Nash and Wells had put on 163 for the first wicket – and after Mustard had bowled for the first time in all senior cricket. It was his 469th game, and with his fifth ball he befuddled Wright with a flipper. Forced to spend the first two nights at a hotel near Arundel because local accommodation was booked up for the Labour Party conference, Durham started poorly when Collingwood's gamble to bat on a pitch tailor-made for Sussex's pacier attack backfired, with Anyon grabbing a cheap five-for. Sussex then slipped to 90 for five before the aggressive Wright began a recovery. Under dank skies, Durham in turn slumped to 120 for six in their second innings – still 44 behind – and a three-day finish seemed probable. But Jennings, who faced 308 balls, dropped anchor, and Richardson flayed a tiring attack, adding 218 for the seventh wicket, before Arshad helped Jennings put on a further 106. All three had career-bests – though a finger injury restricted Ashar Zaidi to one over on the third day – to set up an enthralling finale.
Close of play: first day, Sussex 186-5 (Wright 74, Brown 18); second day, Durham 2-0 (Stoneman 0, Jennings 0); third day, Durham 380-7 (Jennings 113, Arshad 38).

Durham

M. D. Stoneman c Brown b Anyon	20	– c Wells b Jordan	5
K. K. Jennings c Prior b Jordan	11	– c Brown b Nash	127
S. G. Borthwick c Joyce b Jordan	36	– b Magoffin	1
W. R. Smith c Prior b Jordan	32	– c Nash b Wright	9
B. A. Stokes c Wells b Jordan	7	– b Jordan	45
*P. D. Collingwood c Ashar Zaidi b Anyon	25	– c Nash b Jordan	4
†P. Mustard c Jordan b Anyon	5	– c Jordan b Anyon	5
M. J. Richardson lbw b Anyon	0	– c Magoffin b Anyon	129
U. Arshad b Anyon	0	– c Joyce b Ashar Zaidi	83
G. Onions c Prior b Magoffin	13	– not out	5
C. Rushworth not out	0	– b Ashar Zaidi	9
L-b 1, n-b 14	15	B 11, l-b 3, w 1, n-b 21	36

1/22 (2) 2/38 (1) 3/81 (3) (51.2 overs) 164 1/15 (1) 2/16 (3) (115.1 overs) 458
4/107 (5) 5/114 (4) 6/137 (7) 3/35 (4) 4/105 (5)
7/137 (8) 8/143 (9) 9/162 (10) 10/164 (6) 5/111 (6) 6/120 (7) 7/338 (8)
8/444 (2) 9/444 (9) 10/458 (11)

Magoffin 13–1–41–1; Jordan 18–7–50–4; Anyon 10.2–1–44–5; Wright 8–2–24–0; Ashar Zaidi 2–1–4–0. *Second innings*—Magoffin 22–5–45–1; Jordan 24–3–92–3; Wright 14–5–45–1; Anyon 26–4–154–2; Nash 18–5–55–1; Ashar Zaidi 9.1–2–44–2; Wells 2–0–9–0.

Sussex

C. D. Nash lbw b Onions	0	– (2) c Richardson b Borthwick	108
L. W. P. Wells c Mustard b Stokes	20	– (1) c Collingwood b Onions	88
M. H. Yardy lbw b Onions	0		
*E. C. Joyce b Arshad	45	– (3) not out	65
M. J. Prior c Mustard b Arshad	16	– (4) c Borthwick b Smith	6
L. J. Wright b Rushworth	87	– (5) lbw b Mustard	13
†B. C. Brown c Stokes b Borthwick	64	– (6) not out	5
Ashar Zaidi c Borthwick b Stokes	45		
C. J. Jordan c Collingwood b Borthwick	9		
S. J. Magoffin c Borthwick b Onions	13		
J. E. Anyon not out	5		
L-b 4, w 2, n-b 18	24	B 4, l-b 6, n-b 2	12

1/0 (1) 2/6 (3) 3/64 (4)   (80 overs) 328   1/163 (1)   (4 wkts, 67.1 overs) 297
4/90 (5) 5/90 (2) 6/203 (6)   2/243 (2) 3/263 (4)
7/286 (8) 8/309 (7) 9/314 (9) 10/328 (10)   4/291 (5)

Onions 20–3–103–3; Rushworth 15–6–47–1; Arshad 13–2–73–2; Stokes 21–2–69–2; Borthwick 11–2–32–2. *Second innings*—Onions 11–4–22–1; Rushworth 8–2–36–0; Borthwick 24–2–120–1; Stokes 11–0–54–0; Arshad 8–1–27–0; Smith 4–0–19–1; Mustard 1.1–0–9–1.

Umpires: J. W. Lloyds and S. J. O'Shaughnessy.

WARWICKSHIRE

Mr Brown's boys

PAUL BOLTON

Warwickshire lost ground in a season of transition and treatment tables in which little went right for Dougie Brown, their new director of cricket. It was always going to be daunting for Brown, who stepped up from duties with the Second XI and Academy, to take over when the highly successful Ashley Giles departed to become England's limited-overs coach. But he had to contend first with a lack of preparation time – his appointment was not confirmed until the last day of January 2013 – then with a crippling absentee list that deprived him of most of his senior players at one stage or another.

It was not until July that Warwickshire began to produce the cricket that made them champions in 2012. They beat Middlesex and Nottinghamshire in successive matches, and had reached handy positions against Yorkshire and Somerset before being thwarted by the weather. For Brown, fourth in the Championship and a share of the prize money represented an acceptable start – but no more. "When it came to key moments, we didn't quite manage to get over the line," he admitted.

Even with one of the largest playing staffs on the circuit, Warwickshire's resources were stretched by injuries and international calls. The situation reached farcical levels in the last few weeks of the season, when seamer Richard Jones was signed on loan from Worcestershire, only to injure himself in his first net session. Four wicketkeepers were required for the last four Championship matches, with Brown forced to draft in Hong Kong captain Jamie Atkinson, who hurt a thumb on his debut, and Ireland international Stuart Poynter, who subsequently joined Durham.

The lengthy absences of Chris Wright, with a stress fracture of the back, and Keith Barker, who missed the start of the season with a hamstring injury, then suffered an intercostal strain on his return, hit Warwickshire hardest. It denied them the new-ball pair who had shared 118 Championship wickets in 2012. This time, Wright and Barker combined for 65 from 19 appearances.

Boyd Rankin's early availability was restricted by a foot injury, then by England commitments after his pace, bounce and hostility caught the eye of the selectors. A back problem meant little was seen of Oliver Hannon-Dalby, a winter recruit from Yorkshire; Maurice Chambers did enough on loan from Essex to be offered a contract, but was lured to Northamptonshire.

Warwickshire's seam department was well furnished – and it 2014 it will be tended by Alan Richardson, who arrived from Worcestershire to replace the Derbyshire-bound Graeme Welch. But batting and spin remained problematic. The popular Jeetan Patel managed to stay fit, and completed another outstanding stint as overseas cricketer. He played every match in every competition, which was just as well given that left-arm spinners Paul Best and Chris Metters

Joe Giddens, PA Photos

Ateeq Javid

managed none at all because of long-term injuries. The luckless Metters was released in mid-season after an unsuccessful attempt to return from shoulder surgery.

Best, as Second XI captain, was singled out by an ECB disciplinary panel after Freddie Coleman tampered with the ball with his knowledge during a game at Cardiff. Coleman was spotted by umpire Martin Saggers sucking a Murray Mint, then applying saliva to the ball: he pleaded guilty, earning a suspended two-game ban, while Warwickshire were fined £5,000, deducted five points in the Second XI Championship, and criticised for not providing "sufficient discouragement" of ball-tampering.

Darren Maddy marked the end of a 20-year career with a match-saving innings at Trent Bridge, ten days after he waved farewell in a YB40 game at Edgbaston. He was unexpectedly called up because opener William Porterfield lost form spectacularly, failing to reach 40 in 16 Championship innings, having made his first century for Warwickshire in March against MCC at Abu Dhabi.

Club captain Jim Troughton was hindered by a degenerative back problem, which meant Brown had to work for much of the season with an inexperienced deputy, Varun Chopra. He relished the additional responsibility without losing productivity as an opener. For the third year running, Chopra was the only batsman to top 1,000 Championship runs, although Laurie Evans came close in his breakthrough season, despite missing two months with a fractured hand. Ateeq Javid lived up to Brown's billing as "a streetfighter" with a string of gritty innings, including his maiden first-class hundred, and another which confirmed Surrey's relegation.

Warwickshire remained resilient in the Championship, but were a softer touch in white-ball cricket. A year after reaching the Lord's final, they finished bottom of their YB40 group, and suffered a humiliating home defeat by the Netherlands. They were similarly rusty at the start of the Twenty20, but almost scrambled into the quarter-finals. With the benefit of a full year in charge, Brown was expected to sharpen the limited-overs cricket. "I need to be allowed to put my style and stamp on things," he said. He was also tasked with helping Jonathan Trott, after his withdrawal from England's Ashes tour with a stress-related illness.

The move to rebrand the Twenty20 side as Birmingham Bears for 2014 met with considerable protest from supporters. Warwickshire made little attempt to disguise the hand of Birmingham City Council, the club's major financial backers, in the decision.

Championship attendance: 22,869.

WARWICKSHIRE RESULTS

All first-class matches – Played 18: Won 7, Lost 2, Drawn 9.
County Championship matches – Played 16: Won 5, Lost 2, Drawn 9.

LV= County Championship, 4th in Division 1;
Friends Life t20, 4th in Midlands/Wales/West Division; Yorkshire Bank 40, 7th in Group C.

COUNTY CHAMPIONSHIP AVERAGES, BATTING AND FIELDING

Cap		M	I	NO	R	HS	100	50	Avge	Ct/St
2009	C. R. Woakes†‡	10	16	5	640	152*	1	4	58.18	2
	L. J. Evans	13	19	2	943	178	3	4	55.47	6
2012	V. Chopra	15	25	4	1,069	228*	3	5	50.90	26
	A. Javid†	11	17	3	619	133	2	2	44.21	5
2007	D. L. Maddy	3	5	1	157	65	0	1	39.25	1
2007	T. R. Ambrose	13	20	2	685	105	1	5	38.05	39/1
2002	J. O. Troughton	7	11	1	322	84	0	2	32.20	5
2011	R. Clarke	13	18	4	449	92	0	4	32.07	19
2013	K. H. D. Barker	11	12	1	350	125	1	0	31.81	4
2012	J. S. Patel§	16	18	4	438	78*	0	5	31.28	14
2008	I. J. Westwood†	12	20	2	481	71	0	4	26.72	8
	T. P. Milnes	7	7	0	160	48	0	0	22.85	3
	M. A. Chambers	4	4	0	80	58	0	1	20.00	1
	W. T. S. Porterfield	11	16	0	235	36	0	0	14.68	7
2013	W. B. Rankin	9	9	6	32	12*	0	0	10.66	0
2013	C. J. C. Wright	8	8	1	30	11	0	0	4.28	0

Also batted: T. W. Allin (1 match) 0; J. J. Atkinson¶ (1 match) did not bat; I. R. Bell†‡ (cap 2001) (2 matches) 56, 62; R. O. Gordon (3 matches) 13, 10 (1 ct); O. J. Hannon-Dalby (2 matches) 5, 10*; P. J. McKay (1 match) 33, 3*; S. A. Piolet (1 match) 1, 30 (1 ct); S. W. Poynter (1 match) 0 (6 ct); I. J. L. Trott‡ (cap 2005) (2 matches) 96, 65 (1 ct).

† Born in Warwickshire.   ‡ ECB contract.   § Official overseas player.   ¶ Other non-England-qualified player.

BOWLING

	Style	O	M	R	W	BB	5I	Avge
W. B. Rankin	RFM	216.4	20	709	31	4-29	0	22.87
K. H. D. Barker	LFM	345	83	1,055	46	5-55	1	22.93
C. R. Woakes	RFM	245.4	46	711	31	5-42	1	22.93
M. A. Chambers	RFM	103.2	16	383	14	5-68	1	27.35
J. S. Patel	OB	576.1	139	1,561	52	5-56	2	30.01
R. Clarke	RFM	229.3	61	642	19	4-70	0	33.78
C. J. C. Wright	RFM	209	43	689	19	6-31	1	36.26

Also bowled: T. W. Allin (RFM) 17–3–65–0; V. Chopra (LBG) 2–0–2–0; L. J. Evans (RFM) 14–2–37–0; R. O. Gordon (RFM) 70–9–220–4; O. J. Hannon-Dalby (RFM) 33–4–164–1; A. Javid (RM/OB) 49–10–154–2; D. L. Maddy (RM) 26–5–71–1; T. P. Milnes (RFM) 89.1–9–382–4; S. A. Piolet (RM) 12–0–59–1; I. J. L. Trott (RM) 16–2–47–0; I. J. Westwood (OB) 6.5–1–11–1.

LEADING YB40 AVERAGES (100 runs/4 wickets)

Batting

	Runs	HS	Avge	SR	Ct
A. Javid	194	43	38.80	101.04	3
V. Chopra	352	111	35.20	76.35	2
R. Clarke	208	65	34.66	99.04	1
W. T. S. Porterfield	290	62	32.22	80.55	7
T. R. Ambrose	125	55	25.00	86.80	2
D. L. Maddy	152	56	15.20	103.40	4
J. O. Troughton	111	36	13.87	83.45	3

Bowling

	W	BB	Avge	ER
W. B. Rankin	5	2-45	22.20	4.53
J. S. Patel	16	4-43	22.68	5.41
C. J. C. Wright	7	3-27	28.42	7.37
D. L. Maddy	8	2-27	29.37	5.46
S. A. Piolet	10	3-74	35.20	6.40
A. Javid	5	2-34	58.40	6.48

LEADING FLt20 AVERAGES (90 runs/18 overs)

Batting	Runs	HS	Avge	SR	Ct	Bowling	W	BB	Avge	ER
D. L. Maddy.....	296	84*	42.28	**129.25**	1	J. S. Patel........	10	2-13	19.90	**6.09**
C. R. Woakes....	90	28*	18.00	**121.62**	4	R. Clarke.........	7	2-15	24.85	**6.96**
R. Clarke	216	42	30.85	**118.68**	3	C. R. Woakes	10	3-28	23.30	**7.43**
W. T. S. Porterfield	124	34	15.50	**102.47**	5	A. Javid..........	11	4-17	19.54	**7.67**
V. Chopra.......	282	75*	31.33	**99.29**	3	S. A. Piolet	6	3-24	44.66	**7.76**

FIRST-CLASS COUNTY RECORDS

Highest score for	501*	B. C. Lara v Durham at Birmingham.............	1994
Highest score against	322	I. V. A. Richards (Somerset) at Taunton	1985
Leading run-scorer	35,146	D. L. Amiss (avge 41.64).......................	1960–87
Best bowling for	10-41	J. D. Bannister v Combined Services at Birmingham	1959
Best bowling against	10-36	H. Verity (Yorkshire) at Leeds	1931
Leading wicket-taker	2,201	W. E. Hollies (avge 20.45)	1932–57
Highest total for	810-4 dec	v Durham at Birmingham	1994
Highest total against	887	by Yorkshire at Birmingham....................	1896
Lowest total for	16	v Kent at Tonbridge..........................	1913
Lowest total against	15	by Hampshire at Birmingham	1922

LIST A COUNTY RECORDS

Highest score for	206	A. I. Kallicharran v Oxfordshire at Birmingham....	1984
Highest score against	172*	W. Larkins (Northamptonshire) at Luton	1983
Leading run-scorer	11,254	D. L. Amiss (avge 33.79).......................	1963–87
Best bowling for	7-32	R. G. D. Willis v Yorkshire at Birmingham	1981
Best bowling against	6-27	M. H. Yardy (Sussex) at Birmingham	2005
Leading wicket-taker	396	G. C. Small (avge 25.48)......................	1980–99
Highest total for	392-5	v Oxfordshire at Birmingham	1984
Highest total against	341-6	by Hampshire at Birmingham	2010
Lowest total for	59	v Yorkshire at Leeds	2001
Lowest total against	56	by Yorkshire at Birmingham...................	1995

TWENTY20 COUNTY RECORDS

Highest score for	89	N. V. Knight v Worcestershire at Worcester	2003
Highest score against	100*	I. J. Harvey (Gloucestershire) at Birmingham	2003
Leading run-scorer	1,871	I. J. L. Trott (avge 40.67)......................	2003–11
Best bowling for	5-19	N. M. Carter v Worcestershire at Birmingham	2005
Best bowling against	5-25	D. J. Pattinson (Nottinghamshire) at Birmingham..	2011
Leading wicket-taker	81	N. M. Carter (avge 26.65)	2003–12
Highest total for	{ 205-2 { 205-7	v Northamptonshire at Birmingham............. v Glamorgan at Swansea	2005 2005
Highest total against	215-6	by Durham at Birmingham	2010
Lowest total for	**73**	**v Somerset at Taunton.......................**	**2013**
Lowest total against	{ 96 { **96**	by Northamptonshire at Northampton .... **by Gloucestershire at Cheltenham ....**	2011 **2013**

ADDRESS

County Ground, Edgbaston, Birmingham B5 7QU (0844 635 1902; **email** info@edgbaston.com). **Website** www.edgbaston.com

OFFICIALS

Captain J. O. Troughton
Director of cricket D. R. Brown
Academy director I. G. S. Steer
President Earl of Aylesford
Chairman N. Gascoigne

Chief executive C. Povey
Chairman, cricket committee J. H. Dodge
Head groundsman G. Barwell
Scorer M. D. Smith

At Abu Dhabi, March 24–27. WARWICKSHIRE beat MCC by an innings and 29 runs (see MCC section).

At Oxford, April 5–7. WARWICKSHIRE beat OXFORD MCCU by 21 runs.

WARWICKSHIRE v DERBYSHIRE

At Birmingham, April 10–13. Drawn. Warwickshire 7pts, Derbyshire 5pts. Toss: Warwickshire. County debuts: S. Chanderpaul, B. A. Godleman.

Miserable weather blighted the start of Warwickshire's title defence and Derbyshire's return to the top flight after a 12-season absence. Almost two-thirds of the match was lost to rain or bad light, even though Warwickshire were able to use floodlights in the Championship for the first time, following the relaxation of planning restrictions by the city council. It was so cold that chunks of snow cleared from the field a fortnight earlier had yet to melt from shaded areas in front of the pavilion. Madsen clipped Wright's first ball for four, but otherwise Derbyshire found the going tough: Chanderpaul, their blue-chip overseas signing, scratched around for 78 deliveries before he was lbw in a collapse of four for 12. That was brought about by Patel's diligence and the aggression of Wright, on the day he signed a new four-year contract and received his county cap. Last pair Palladino and Turner put on the highest partnership of the innings to scramble a batting point, but only 55 overs were possible after the opening day.

Close of play: first day, Warwickshire 14-0 (Chopra 6, Westwood 4); second day, no play; third day, Warwickshire 90-0 (Chopra 48, Westwood 31).

Derbyshire

*W. L. Madsen c Chopra b Wright	13	A. P. Palladino c Troughton b Milnes	68
B. A. Godleman c Chopra b Wright	2	T. D. Groenewald c Porterfield b Clarke	3
W. J. Durston lbw b Hannon-Dalby	32	M. L. Turner not out	18
S. Chanderpaul lbw b Patel	15	B 9, l-b 3, n-b 4	16
D. J. Redfern lbw b Patel	34		
R. A. Whiteley run out	4	1/7 (2) 2/18 (1) 3/56 (3) (87.1 overs)	226
C. F. Hughes c Chopra b Wright	20	4/105 (5) 5/110 (4) 6/116 (6)	
†T. Poynton c Clarke b Patel	1	7/117 (8) 8/154 (7) 9/171 (10) 10/226 (9)	

Wright 26–11–48–3; Hannon-Dalby 13–4–57–1; Clarke 19–9–32–1; Milnes 11.1–1–40–1; Patel 18–5–37–3.

Warwickshire

V. Chopra c Poynton b Hughes	76	†T. R. Ambrose not out	14
I. J. Westwood c Whiteley b Groenewald	56	B 8, l-b 2, w 1, n-b 14	25
W. T. S. Porterfield c Whiteley b Durston	6		
*J. O. Troughton st Poynton b Durston	5	1/139 (2) 2/162 (3) (4 wkts, 59 overs)	201
L. J. Evans not out	19	3/164 (1) 4/172 (4)	

R. Clarke, T. P. Milnes, J. S. Patel, C. J. C. Wright and O. J. Hannon-Dalby did not bat.

Groenewald 18–5–48–1; Palladino 12–4–37–0; Whiteley 6–1–28–0; Turner 10–3–27–0; Durston 8–0–32–2; Hughes 5–1–19–1.

Umpires: M. A. Gough and J. W. Lloyds.

WARWICKSHIRE v DURHAM

At Birmingham, April 17–20. Warwickshire won by 318 runs. Warwickshire 22pts, Durham 5pts. Toss: Durham.

A finely balanced contest was tilted in Warwickshire's favour by Ambrose's bustling century. He shared hundred partnerships with Troughton and Clarke to set Durham 413, which Wright put paid to in a burst of three for four on the final morning, on the way to his best figures for the county. Durham's total was their lowest against Warwickshire, and they were left to rue the failure of their top four in both innings, as well as three dropped catches on a first day of swirling winds. Bowlers also struggled for control, especially Borthwick, though he went on to excel with a maiden

Championship century. He and the doughty Collingwood rescued Durham from 50 for six with a partnership of 153, as the home bowlers flagged on the second evening in a session lasting close to four hours after rain caused an early tea.

Close of play: first day, Warwickshire 299-7 (Woakes 19, Barker 39); second day, Warwickshire 6-0 (Chopra 6, Westwood 0); third day, Durham 11-1 (Stoneman 1, Smith 10).

Warwickshire

V. Chopra c Borthwick b Onions	8	– c Mustard b Stokes	24
I. J. Westwood lbw b Rushworth	28	– c Mustard b Rushworth	11
W. T. S. Porterfield c Smith b Rushworth	27	– c Mustard b Thorp	21
*J. O. Troughton c Benkenstein b Stokes	84	– lbw b Stokes	45
L. J. Evans c Collingwood b Thorp	44	– c Benkenstein b Stokes	2
†T. R. Ambrose b Stokes	31	– lbw b Thorp	105
R. Clarke c Mustard b Smith	1	– st Mustard b Borthwick	92
C. R. Woakes not out	52	– not out	38
K. H. D. Barker c Collingwood b Onions	45		
J. S. Patel c Smith b Onions	5	– (9) c Onions b Jennings	1
C. J. C. Wright c Collingwood b Onions	1		
L-b 11, n-b 8	19	B 2, l-b 10	12

1/34 (1) 2/49 (2) 3/111 (3) (108.2 overs) 345
4/188 (5) 5/234 (6) 6/235 (7)
7/237 (4) 8/329 (9) 9/341 (10) 10/345 (11)

1/22 (2) (8 wkts dec, 90.2 overs) 351
2/62 (3) 3/62 (1)
4/64 (5) 5/164 (4)
6/273 (6) 7/346 (7) 8/351 (9)

Onions 26.2–2–86–4; Rushworth 24–5–73–2; Thorp 25–9–61–1; Stokes 18–2–60–2; Smith 9–2–24–1; Borthwick 3–0–16–0; Jennings 3–0–14–0. *Second innings*—Onions 16–6–50–0; Rushworth 17–2–59–1; Thorp 18–8–43–2; Stokes 18–2–70–3; Borthwick 14–0–77–1; Smith 2–0–12–0; Jennings 5.2–0–28–1.

Durham

M. D. Stoneman c Ambrose b Barker	0	– c Ambrose b Wright	1
K. K. Jennings c Clarke b Barker	7	– lbw b Wright	0
W. R. Smith c Ambrose b Barker	0	– c Chopra b Wright	15
D. M. Benkenstein c Ambrose b Wright	5	– c Patel b Wright	3
B. A. Stokes b Woakes	33	– lbw b Barker	8
*P. D. Collingwood c Clarke b Woakes	74	– c Clarke b Woakes	5
†P. Mustard lbw b Woakes	0	– c Evans b Woakes	28
S. G. Borthwick c Chopra b Clarke	101	– c Ambrose b Wright	19
C. D. Thorp run out	27	– c Ambrose b Wright	12
G. Onions c Ambrose b Patel	2	– c Porterfield b Patel	0
C. Rushworth not out	18	– not out	0
B 4, l-b 2, w 1, n-b 10	17	L-b 1, n-b 2	3

1/0 (1) 2/0 (3) 3/5 (4) (77.2 overs) 284
4/38 (2) 5/48 (5) 6/50 (7)
7/203 (6) 8/261 (8) 9/264 (10) 10/284 (9)

1/0 (1) 2/11 (1) 3/16 (3) (55 overs) 94
4/23 (4) 5/29 (5) 6/37 (6)
7/61 (8) 8/77 (9) 9/94 (10) 10/94 (7)

Barker 18–4–53–3; Wright 16–3–65–1; Woakes 16–1–59–3; Clarke 14–2–53–1; Patel 13.2–2–48–1. *Second innings*—Barker 10–6–9–1; Wright 16–7–31–6; Patel 7–2–11–1; Woakes 10–6–13–2; Clarke 11–3–29–0; Evans 1–1–0–2.

Umpires: R. J. Bailey and I. J. Gould.

At Taunton, April 25–28. WARWICKSHIRE drew with SOMERSET. *Warwickshire's last pair hold out for 21 overs.*

At Hove, May 1–4. WARWICKSHIRE drew with SUSSEX.

WARWICKSHIRE v MIDDLESEX

At Birmingham, May 8–11. Drawn. Warwickshire 8pts, Middlesex 10pts. Toss: Middlesex. First-class debut: T. W. Allin.

Robson's career-best 215 dominated a rain-ruined draw on a benign pitch. He was dropped twice, on 73 and 141 – lapses Warwickshire could ill afford with three first-team players out injured, three others on England Lions duty, and Clarke pressed into action despite failing a fitness test. They even considered calling up 38-year-old Neil Carter, who had left the club in 2012, but was staying at Trott's home in Birmingham. Robson came through a tough examination from Rankin, who struck Rogers on the elbow, and bedded in for seven hours until rain forced a declaration. Warwickshire's injury problems worsened when Finn, who had opted for extra match practice ahead of the New Zealand Test series, broke Evans's left hand with a lifter. Otherwise Warwickshire's batsmen prospered, with Trott scoring a half-century in a match marking the tenth anniversary of his county debut. There was just enough time for Rankin to edge Murtagh past second slip for a fourth batting point, then see out what remained of the 110th over to deny Middlesex a full bowling quota.

Close of play: first day, Middlesex 280-3 (Robson 136, Dexter 21); second day, Middlesex 428-5 (Robson 215, Berg 23); third day, Warwickshire 267-5 (Clarke 4, Milnes 0).

Middlesex

*C. J. L. Rogers c Ambrose b Rankin	33	G. K. Berg not out	23
S. D. Robson not out	215	B 9, l-b 6, w 1, n-b 4	20
J. L. Denly st Ambrose b Patel	35		
D. J. Malan lbw b Patel	37	1/85 (1) (5 wkts dec, 112.4 overs)	428
N. J. Dexter c Trott b Rankin	46	2/180 (3) 3/242 (4)	
†J. A. Simpson c Clarke b Patel	19	4/325 (5) 5/373 (6) 110 overs: 401-5	

O. P. Rayner, T. J. Murtagh, S. T. Finn and C. D. Collymore did not bat.

Rankin 27.4–1–87–2; Milnes 13–1–79–0; Allin 17–3–65–0; Trott 16–2–47–0; Patel 31–6–99–3; Clarke 8–0–36–0.

Warwickshire

W. T. S. Porterfield c Rayner b Collymore	20	T. W. Allin c Malan b Murtagh	0
L. J. Evans retired hurt	59	W. B. Rankin not out	9
I. J. L. Trott c Malan b Murtagh	65		
I. R. Bell lbw b Collymore	62	B 1, l-b 3, w 1, n-b 4	9
*J. O. Troughton c Denly b Murtagh	0		
†T. R. Ambrose lbw b Collymore	55	1/45 (1) 2/158 (3) (8 wkts, 114 overs)	374
R. Clarke not out	66	3/162 (5) 4/258 (4)	
T. P. Milnes c Collymore b Murtagh	24	5/267 (6) 6/332 (8)	
J. S. Patel b Murtagh	5	7/338 (9) 8/338 (10) 110 overs: 352-8	

Evans retired hurt at 128-1.

Murtagh 26–3–85–5; Finn 22–1–90–0; Collymore 25–4–78–3; Berg 11–3–20–0; Rayner 19–6–48–0; Dexter 5–0–20–0; Malan 3–0–20–0; Denly 3–0–9–0.

Umpires: R. J. Bailey and S. C. Gale.

WARWICKSHIRE v YORKSHIRE

At Birmingham, May 15–17. Yorkshire won by an innings and 139 runs. Yorkshire 23pts, Warwickshire 2pts. Toss: Yorkshire.

Yorkshire's disciplined performance in helpful bowling conditions consigned Warwickshire to their first Championship defeat at home since August 2011. Warwickshire decided against using the heavy roller after losing the toss, for fear of adding moisture to the pitch from a damp outfield. But their demise for 128 was down to outstanding swing bowling, with Plunkett recording his best Championship figures for four years, and Sidebottom and Patterson hitting a full length. Yorkshire's patient approach wore down the Warwickshire attack, and Rashid – the first right-hander in the order at No. 6 – profited with his second successive hundred, though he had a lucky escape on 68 when Wright bowled him with a no-ball which sped away for four byes. Bresnan, who arrived at lunch on the second day after he was released from England's Test squad at Lord's, helped Rashid stretch the lead, then pinned Chopra lbw with his first ball. Yorkshire supported their seamers with sharp slip catching, and Warwickshire caved in.

Close of play: first day, Yorkshire 11-0 (Lyth 5, Sayers 4); second day, Yorkshire 318-7 (Rashid 68, Plunkett 1).

Warwickshire

V. Chopra c Lyth b Sidebottom	4	– lbw b Bresnan	0
W. T. S. Porterfield c Pyrah b Plunkett	14	– lbw b Sidebottom	0
*J. O. Troughton not out	65	– lbw b Sidebottom	37
D. L. Maddy lbw b Plunkett	0	– c Lyth b Bresnan	5
†T. R. Ambrose c Lyth b Plunkett	0	– c Lyth b Sidebottom	22
C. R. Woakes b Patterson	1	– b Patterson	10
R. Clarke lbw b Sidebottom	13	– lbw b Patterson	15
T. P. Milnes c Lyth b Patterson	11	– c Hodd b Bresnan	18
J. S. Patel c Ballance b Patterson	9	– c Plunkett b Patterson	6
C. J. C. Wright c Ballance b Plunkett	0	– b Plunkett	11
W. B. Rankin c and b Plunkett	0	– not out	12
B 4, l-b 5, n-b 2	11	L-b 4	4

1/12 (1) 2/42 (2) 3/42 (4)   (51.3 overs) 128
4/46 (5) 5/55 (6) 6/71 (7)
7/111 (8) 8/127 (9) 9/128 (10) 10/128 (11)

1/0 (1) 2/4 (2)   (48.2 overs) 140
3/9 (4) 4/40 (5)
5/63 (6) 6/87 (3) 7/89 (7)
8/99 (9) 9/112 (10) 10/140 (8)

Sidebottom 15–5–23–2; Patterson 17–4–46–3; Plunkett 13.3–6–32–5; Pyrah 6–1–18–0. *Second innings*—Bresnan 13.2–4–41–3; Sidebottom 14–6–23–3; Patterson 11–4–19–3; Plunkett 10–1–53–1.

Yorkshire

A. Lyth c Milnes b Rankin	43	R. J. Sidebottom lbw b Patel	20
J. J. Sayers c Ambrose b Rankin	24	S. A. Patterson c Milnes b Patel	11
P. A. Jaques c Ambrose b Patel	25		
*A. W. Gale c Clarke b Patel	40	B 1, l-b 6, w 1, n-b 18	26
G. S. Ballance b Patel	52		
A. U. Rashid not out	110	1/77 (1) 2/80 (2) (123 overs) 407
†A. J. Hodd lbw b Woakes	9	3/122 (3) 4/147 (4) 5/225 (5)
T. T. Bresnan c Ambrose b Rankin	38	6/239 (7) 7/314 (6) 8/354 (9)
L. E. Plunkett c Ambrose b Wright	9	9/389 (10) 10/407 (11) 110 overs: 356-8

Bresnan replaced R. M. Pyrah after being released from the England squad.

Woakes 28–8–76–1; Wright 31–6–102–1; Clarke 13–0–55–0; Patel 24–7–56–5; Rankin 18–2–75–3; Milnes 9–1–36–0.

Umpires: M. A. Gough and T. E. Jesty.

At Guildford, June 5–8. WARWICKSHIRE drew with SURREY.

At Chester-le-Street, June 12–14. WARWICKSHIRE lost to DURHAM by 11 runs.

At Uxbridge, July 8–11. WARWICKSHIRE beat MIDDLESEX by five wickets.

WARWICKSHIRE v NOTTINGHAMSHIRE

At Birmingham, July 15–18. Warwickshire won by 216 runs. Warwickshire 22pts, Nottinghamshire 3pts. Toss: Warwickshire.

Chopra's decision to waive the follow-on, giving his bowlers time to recover from the sweltering heat, paid off handsomely. Warwickshire had been rewarded for their attritional approach on a slow pitch with Evans's maiden Championship hundred, six years after he scored a first-class century for Durham UCCE, and an equally gritty 83 from Javid, who battled heatstroke down at No. 8. Mullaney fell to the first ball of Nottinghamshire's reply, and Barker later took three wickets in 16 deliveries, squaring up Taylor after he had seemed set for a hundred. Barker's habit of flicking out his left hand early in his run-up distracted Shahzad, who twice stepped away, prompting Clarke to weigh in from slip; Chopra had to step in to defuse the argument, and the pair were given a dressing-down by umpire Trevor Jesty. Clarke enjoyed the last word, however, when he had Shahzad caught at short leg. Adams was absent from the attack through illness on his 38th birthday as Woakes and Clarke stretched Warwickshire's lead to 426. Hales came through a tricky passage before the close, and faced 182 balls for his highest score of a miserable Championship season, but Nottinghamshire lost their last seven wickets cheaply for the second time in the match. Their lack of a specialist spinner was exposed by the success of Jeetan Patel, who finished with eight for 128.

Close of play: first day, Warwickshire 254-6 (Evans 85, Javid 8); second day, Nottinghamshire 131-2 (Lumb 50, Taylor 54); third day, Nottinghamshire 38-0 (Mullaney 26, Hales 9).

Warwickshire

*V. Chopra c Patel b Fletcher	10	– lbw b Fletcher		13
I. J. Westwood c Adams b Patel	68	– c Patel b Shahzad		0
W. T. S. Porterfield b Adams	10	– c Read b Gurney		24
L. J. Evans b Patel	178	– b Shahzad		2
†T. R. Ambrose c Read b Adams	39	– c Hales b Patel		21
C. R. Woakes b Patel	14	– st Read b Patel		60
R. Clarke c Taylor b Adams	0	– not out		54
A. Javid c Read b Shahzad	83	– not out		1
K. H. D. Barker c Mullaney b Fletcher	23			
J. S. Patel b Fletcher	6			
W. B. Rankin not out	0			
B 5, l-b 14, w 3, n-b 10	32	W 1, n-b 4		5

1/28 (1) 2/43 (3) 3/132 (2) (154.3 overs) 463 1/0 (2) (6 wkts dec, 44 overs) 180
4/193 (5) 5/208 (6) 6/213 (7) 7/412 (4) 2/27 (1) 3/32 (4)
8/450 (8) 9/458 (10) 10/463 (9) 110 overs: 300-6 4/55 (3) 5/75 (5) 6/179 (6)

Fletcher 21.3–4–57–3; Shahzad 33–9–80–1; Gurney 29–4–83–0; Adams 29–8–64–3; Patel 39–8–123–3; Mullaney 2–0–19–0; Hussey 1–0–18–0. *Second innings*—Fletcher 12–3–50–1; Shahzad 13–0–54–2; Patel 11–2–46–2; Gurney 8–0–30–1.

Nottinghamshire

S. J. Mullaney lbw b Woakes	0	– b Woakes	27
A. D. Hales lbw b Patel	17	– c Porterfield b Patel	58
M. J. Lumb c and b Patel	51	– c Ambrose b Barker	18
J. W. A. Taylor c Ambrose b Barker	80	– lbw b Rankin	2
S. R. Patel c Chopra b Barker	19	– c Porterfield b Clarke	36
D. J. Hussey c Porterfield b Patel	16	– c Chopra b Woakes	33
*†C. M. W. Read c Ambrose b Barker	0	– lbw b Patel	1
A. Shahzad c Westwood b Clarke	8	– b Patel	5
L. J. Fletcher b Patel	4	– (10) c Porterfield b Rankin	1
A. R. Adams b Rankin	7	– (9) c Westwood b Patel	11
H. F. Gurney not out	0	– not out	0
B 4, l-b 1, n-b 10	15	B 5, l-b 6, w 3, n-b 4	18

1/0 (1) 2/47 (2) 3/134 (3) (73.1 overs) 217 1/40 (1) 2/75 (3) (87.2 overs) 210
4/177 (5) 5/182 (4) 6/182 (7) 3/84 (4) 4/154 (2)
7/202 (8) 8/210 (6) 9/217 (9) 10/217 (10) 5/154 (5) 6/155 (7) 7/171 (8)
8/185 (9) 9/210 (6) 10/210 (10)

Woakes 13–1–43–1; Barker 16–6–44–3; Patel 21–3–60–4; Clarke 13–3–27–1; Rankin 9.1–1–38–1; Javid 1–1–0–0. *Second innings*—Woakes 13–5–41–2; Barker 16–3–39–1; Patel 30–12–68–4; Clarke 15–8–13–1; Rankin 13.2–3–38–2.

Umpires: R. K. Illingworth and T. E. Jesty.

At Leeds, August 2–5. WARWICKSHIRE drew with YORKSHIRE.

WARWICKSHIRE v SOMERSET

At Birmingham, August 20–23. Drawn. Warwickshire 9pts, Somerset 7pts. Toss: Somerset. County debut: P. P. Chawla. Championship debut: R. O. Gordon.

Bad light ended play with Warwickshire needing 66 from 18 overs. After consulting for the fourth time, the umpires took the players off because they were worried about the fielders' safety, but – with the floodlights on – Warwickshire director of cricket Dougie Brown felt there was minimal threat. Play had been called off for good by the time a deluge arrived in Edgbaston. Warwickshire would surely have won had they not dropped Kieswetter twice before he reached 75. After Recordo Gordon opened as nightwatchman, on Championship debut, Evans and Javid, who scored his maiden first-class hundred four years on from his debut as a 17-year-old, prospered on a pitch already used for Twenty20 finals day and a YB40 match. Chawla was rusty on arrival from India; Dockrell the model of parsimony as he conceded only nine boundaries in his best return of the Championship season – despite an entertaining cameo from Maddy, who was coaching in Shrewsbury when he received a last-minute call-up following Jim Troughton's withdrawal with a back problem. Patel then teased out Somerset in another exemplary display, but Barrow and Chawla resisted long enough for the gloom to disrupt Warwickshire's chase.

Close of play: first day, Warwickshire 0-0 (Gordon 0, Westwood 0); second day, Warwickshire 283-3 (Javid 103, Evans 130); third day, Somerset 133-2 (Compton 83, Dockrell 0).

Somerset

*M. E. Trescothick	c Clarke b Patel	46	–	c Clarke b Patel	27
N. R. D. Compton	lbw b Barker	6	–	c Ambrose b Barker	91
C. R. Jones	c Patel b Milnes	5	–	run out	16
J. C. Hildreth	c Chopra b Milnes	33	–	(5) b Patel	6
†C. Kieswetter	c Ambrose b Barker	148	–	(6) b Barker	0
A. W. R. Barrow	c Patel b Patel	43	–	(7) c Evans b Patel	39
P. D. Trego	c Barker b Patel	0	–	(8) c Chopra b Patel	16
P. P. Chawla	c Westwood b Clarke	18	–	(9) lbw b Patel	26
A. C. Thomas	c Ambrose b Clarke	4	–	(10) c Patel b Barker	1
G. H. Dockrell	c Patel b Barker	2	–	(4) c Ambrose b Gordon	7
S. P. Kirby	not out	6	–	not out	0
	B 6, l-b 13, w 1, n-b 9	29		B 8, l-b 13, w 1, n-b 4	26

1/23 (2) 2/52 (3) 3/65 (1)   (92.1 overs) 340
4/154 (4) 5/273 (6) 6/273 (7)
7/321 (5) 8/332 (9) 9/333 (8) 10/340 (10)

1/81 (1) 2/133 (3)   (92.3 overs) 255
3/149 (2) 4/158 (5)
5/159 (6) 6/170 (4) 7/193 (8)
8/248 (7) 9/255 (9) 10/255 (10)

Barker 19.1–4–67–3; Clarke 16–4–40–2; Milnes 15–3–64–2; Gordon 14–0–67–0; Patel 23–5–71–3; Maddy 4–0–9–0; Javid 1–0–3–0. *Second innings*—Barker 21.3–5–71–3; Clarke 10–2–34–0; Patel 36–13–67–5; Maddy 10–3–12–0; Milnes 4–0–18–0; Gordon 11–3–32–1.

Warwickshire

R. O. Gordon	lbw b Dockrell	13			
I. J. Westwood	c Kieswetter b Trego	8	–	b Kirby	49
*V. Chopra	c Trescothick b Dockrell	13	–	(1) not out	55
A. Javid	c Kieswetter b Dockrell	133	–	(3) b Kirby	2
L. J. Evans	lbw b Trego	138	–	(4) c Kieswetter b Thomas	0
†T. R. Ambrose	lbw b Thomas	12	–	(5) not out	5
R. Clarke	run out	1			
D. L. Maddy	not out	40			
K. H. D. Barker	st Kieswetter b Dockrell	5			
T. P. Milnes	c Chawla b Dockrell	2			
J. S. Patel	st Kieswetter b Dockrell	20			
	B 2, l-b 7, w 5, n-b 8	22		B 1, l-b 3, n-b 8	12

1/14 (2) 2/33 (1) 3/38 (3)   (142.4 overs) 407
4/307 (5) 5/326 (6) 6/327 (7) 7/354 (4)
8/370 (9) 9/381 (10) 10/407 (11)   110 overs: 315-4

1/101 (2)   (3 wkts, 31 overs) 123
2/103 (3) 3/110 (4)

Dockrell 43.4–14–96–6; Kirby 27–8–55–0; Trego 24–6–64–2; Thomas 20–5–75–1; Chawla 28–3–108–0. *Second innings—*Thomas 11–0–46–1; Kirby 9–0–37–2; Dockrell 5–0–16–0; Chawla 6–1–20–0.

Umpires: R. J. Bailey and S. C. Gale.

WARWICKSHIRE v SUSSEX

At Birmingham, August 28–31. Drawn. Warwickshire 9pts, Sussex 8pts. Toss: Sussex. County debut: M. A. Chambers.

Sussex's decision to bat through the final day all but extinguished Warwickshire's hopes of retaining the Championship. They had won only once in Birmingham since 1961, and their over-cautious approach suggested they lacked the self-belief to win the title themselves; the absence of Monty Panesar, released a week earlier, did not help. Sussex felt they had little chance of restricting the home side a second time on a pitch so close to the edge of the square that Warwickshire had to obtain approval to use it from the ECB: the boundary on the Rea Bank side was shorter than the minimum 50 yards. Seven wickets had gone down for 74 after Chambers, signed on loan from Essex on the morning of the match to bolster a depleted attack, ended a century opening partnership. He finished with his first five-wicket haul in three years, before Evans scored his third century in consecutive home matches. Ambrose helped him add 137 with a broken finger, until Jordan fractured his right thumb with a bouncer that Hamilton-Brown caught on the dive as he ran in from gully; Pete McKay had to deputise as wicketkeeper for the rest of the match. Patel held up the bowlers for more than two and a half hours, then took his 50th wicket of the season when Sussex opted for batting practice.

Close of play: first day, Sussex 278-7 (Jordan 58, Beer 23); second day, Warwickshire 252-6 (Milnes 24, Barker 0); third day, Sussex 148-3 (Joyce 15, Beer 1).

Sussex

C. D. Nash lbw b Chambers	59	– (2) c Westwood b Patel	27
L. W. P. Wells c Gordon b Barker	65	– (1) c Milnes b Patel	46
M. H. Yardy lbw b Barker	21	– run out	46
*E. C. Joyce c Ambrose b Barker	16	– lbw b Barker	68
R. J. Hamilton-Brown c Chopra b Patel	0	– (6) lbw b Patel	75
M. W. Machan c Javid b Chambers	12	– (7) c sub (P. J. McKay) b Gordon	27
†B. C. Brown lbw b Chambers	0	– (8) not out	20
C. J. Jordan b Barker	61	– (9) c Evans b Javid	27
W. A. T. Beer lbw b Chambers	31	– (5) lbw b Gordon	11
S. J. Magoffin b Chambers	11	– lbw b Westwood	0
J. E. Anyon not out	4	– not out	7
B 5, l-b 3, w 1, n-b 22	31	B 10, l-b 11, w 1, n-b 18	40

1/121 (1) 2/156 (3) 3/161 (2) (109.2 overs) 311
4/162 (5) 5/186 (4) 6/188 (6)
7/195 (4) 8/292 (8) 9/292 (9) 10/311 (10)

1/78 (2) (9 wkts dec, 124.5 overs) 394
2/121 (1) 3/143 (3)
4/192 (5) 5/298 (4) 6/334 (6)
7/334 (7) 8/377 (9) 9/378 (10)

Barker 30–7–98–3; Chambers 27.2–7–68–5; Milnes 9–2–38–0; Gordon 19–2–45–1; Patel 23–10–52–1; Javid 1–0–2–0. *Second innings—*Barker 22–4–100–1; Chambers 20–4–74–0; Gordon 17–4–45–2; Patel 36–12–74–3; Javid 9–2–27–1; Milnes 8–0–35–0; Westwood 6.5–1–11–1; Evans 4–1–5–0; Chopra 2–0–2–0.

Warwickshire

*V. Chopra c Jordan b Magoffin	0	M. A. Chambers c Jordan b Magoffin	13
I. J. Westwood b Anyon	16	R. O. Gordon c Brown b Beer	10
A. Javid c Joyce b Magoffin	0		
L. J. Evans c Joyce b Nash	137	B 4, l-b 3, n-b 16	23
W. T. S. Porterfield c Brown b Magoffin	0		
†T. R. Ambrose c Hamilton-Brown b Jordan	61	1/0 (1) 2/0 (3) 3/38 (2) (124 overs) 394
T. P. Milnes c Jordan b Nash	48	4/47 (5) 5/184 (6) 6/250 (4)
K. H. D. Barker c Brown b Magoffin	8	7/268 (8) 8/325 (7) 9/358 (10)
J. S. Patel not out	78	10/394 (11) 110 overs: 339-8

Magoffin 26–8–87–5; Jordan 32–7–79–1; Anyon 18–3–61–1; Beer 28–4–93–1; Nash 16–3–51–2; Yardy 4–0–16–0.

Umpires: S. J. O'Shaughnessy and P. Willey.

At Nottingham, September 3–6. WARWICKSHIRE drew with NOTTINGHAMSHIRE.

WARWICKSHIRE v SURREY

At Birmingham, September 17–20. Warwickshire won by six wickets. Warwickshire 17pts, Surrey 5pts. Toss: Warwickshire. County debut: J. J. Atkinson.

Surrey were relegated after a desperate attempt by Batty to conjure a result from a rain-reduced contest ended in defeat. When play was delayed on the third day until 3pm, Surrey reasoned that only a contrived run-chase could bring the points required to stay in touch with Somerset and Nottinghamshire going into the last round of games. Chopra, with less need to gamble, was able to drive a hard bargain, and Warwickshire made light of their target of 281 in 117 overs. After just 18 overs had been possible on the opening day, Surrey returned to collect maximum batting points for only the second time in the season: Solanki's elegant 162 and a more aggressive 103 from Davies were the county's first centuries since Ricky Ponting's farewell 169 in July. But they had to sacrifice potential bowling points to set up a declaration. When normal cricket resumed on the third evening, Warwickshire slipped to 19 for two. Thereafter, Javid scarcely put a foot wrong and, joined by Woakes, sealed Surrey's fate with an unbroken 155-run stand for the fifth wicket. Warwickshire gave a debut to Hong Kong's captain and wicketkeeper Jamie Atkinson, who had been playing for Dorridge in the Birmingham & District League, but he soon joined Tim Ambrose and Pete McKay on the injured list with a knock to his left thumb in the first innings.

Close of play: first day, Surrey 59-2 (Amla 30, Solanki 20); second day, Surrey 400-5 (Wilson 16, Ansari 12); third day, Warwickshire 55-2 (Javid 16, Evans 20).

Surrey

R. J. Burns lbw b Barker	4	Z. S. Ansari not out	12
D. P. Sibley lbw b Barker	0	B 9, l-b 4, w 1, n-b 12	26
H. M. Amla c Chopra b Barker	77		
V. S. Solanki b Woakes	162	1/5 (2) 2/18 (1) (5 wkts dec, 98 overs) 400	
†S. M. Davies c Javid b Chambers	103	3/184 (3) 4/366 (4)	
G. C. Wilson not out	16	5/374 (5)	

*G. J. Batty, S. C. Meaker, C. T. Tremlett and T. E. Linley did not bat.

Barker 23–5–98–3; Woakes 22–2–90–1; Chambers 19–0–98–1; Gordon 9–0–31–0; Patel 20–6–44–0; Javid 3–0–18–0; Evans 2–0–8–0.

Surrey forfeited their second innings.

Warwickshire

*V. Chopra not out	69	– lbw b Tremlett	0	
I. J. Westwood not out	42	– c Davies b Meaker	14	
A. Javid (did not bat)		– not out	119	
L. J. Evans (did not bat)		– c Burns b Meaker	34	
R. Clarke (did not bat)		– b Linley	17	
C. R. Woakes (did not bat)		– not out	79	
B 1, w 6, n-b 2	9	B 1, l-b 3, n-b 14	18	
(no wkt dec, 22 overs) 120		1/12 (1) (4 wkts, 91.4 overs) 281		
		2/19 (2) 3/98 (4)		
		4/126 (5)		

K. H. D. Barker, J. S. Patel, †J. J. Atkinson, M. A. Chambers and R. O. Gordon did not bat.

Wilson 7–0–43–0; Burns 10–0–54–0; Amla 5–0–22–0. *Second innings*—Tremlett 19–8–43–1; Linley 21–6–70–1; Meaker 20.4–2–84–2; Ansari 15–2–46–0; Batty 16–3–34–0.

Umpires: R. A. Kettleborough and D. J. Millns.

At Derby, September 24–26. WARWICKSHIRE beat DERBYSHIRE by an innings and 168 runs.

WORCESTERSHIRE

Disconcertingly quiet

JOHN CURTIS

For the first time in eight seasons, Worcestershire were embroiled in neither a promotion push nor a relegation battle. Not since 2005, when they finished sixth in Division Two, had there been a climax to the Championship season with nothing at stake – following three promotions, three demotions, and one successful fight to stay up, in 2011. And it may be some time before Worcestershire, who have often made the most of meagre resources, challenge again for a place in the top tier, although promoted Northamptonshire did show what could be achieved with the kind of smaller budget now in operation at New Road. Once more, there was little joy to be had in the shorter formats: a first appearance at Twenty20 finals day, or a first Lord's showpiece since 2004, continued to look distant objectives.

The club calculated that the £10m redevelopment of the River Severn side of the ground, comprising a 120-room hotel and striking new corporate facilities, would produce increased funds to invest in the playing side. For the immediate future, however, Worcestershire made it clear that developing the current crop of young players was the bedrock of their on-field strategy. But with that policy came inevitable fluctuations in performance.

There were isolated signs of progress: the unorthodox left-arm seamer Jack Shantry, the raw but sometimes wayward pace of Graeme Cessford, the solid left-handed opener Matt Pardoe, and the composed middle-order batsman Tom Fell, who quit his course at Oxford Brookes University after one year to try to make the grade. But senior players needed to play a full part if Worcestershire are to make strides.

How director of cricket Steve Rhodes must have been relieved that Moeen Ali signed a new five-year contract at the start of the season. There was amazement in some quarters that an aspirant England player had committed himself for so long to a Division Two club. "Yes, I could have earned more money at another club," he said. "And maybe they would have had better facilities. But Worcestershire have been good to me, I enjoy being one of the main men in the team and I like the people. It's not all about money. But I did get a very good deal."

Ali became a father at 26, and thrived on the greater responsibility after Vikram Solanki's departure for Surrey, scoring a career-best 1,420 first-class runs – the highest tally in the country. He has always been pleasing on the eye, but had now settled on a more compact stance, and resolved to leave everything outside off stump before getting to 20. Ali was rare among English off-spinners in being able to bowl the doosra – a skill learned from former team-mate Saeed Ajmal, who was expected for another stint as overseas player in 2014 – and

Scott Heavey, Getty Images

Jack Shantry

deserved his trip to Australia with the England Performance Squad. For the first time, he was in the running for a Test spot.

Worcestershire possessed no other batsman approaching Ali's class. Captain Daryl Mitchell, who signed an extension until 2016, passed 1,000 runs for the third time, but managed just one half-century in his final 16 Championship innings. Pardoe showed the kind of stickability associated with one of his predecessors as opener, Tim Curtis, although he was not yet of his quality. Fell looked at home after scoring his maiden first-class fifty, against the touring Australians. But Alexei Kervezee, who had abandoned international cricket with the Netherlands, endured another grim first-class season, while the Sri Lankan Test player Thilan Samaraweera rarely produced his best form. Across the two divisions, only bottom side Leicestershire managed fewer batting points than Worcestershire's 29.

Richardson again defied the years with 69 wickets – second only to Durham's Graham Onions – despite suffering from an ankle impingement for much of the summer. He produced a golden spell of 24 wickets in successive matches against Kent and Gloucestershire in May. In the last game, he took his 250th wicket in four seasons at New Road, and there was disappointment when he announced he would be taking up the role of bowling coach at Warwickshire.

So it was a concern that Shantry, who took a Championship-best seven for 69 against Essex, was the only other seamer to improve. Gareth Andrew and Chris Russell endured long injury spells, while David Lucas and Richard Jones slipped so far down the pecking order that they were made available on loan; Lucas was eventually let go, and later retired, while Jones, once viewed as the future leader of the attack, left for Warwickshire. Worcestershire will hope Ross Whiteley can flourish after arriving from Derbyshire on a three-year deal midway through the season, especially as the squad were one all-rounder light following the release of Aneesh Kapil.

Ben Cox still had room for improvement, and was given the chance to make the wicketkeeping spot his own in 2014 after Michael Johnson, an Australian signed before the season, was discarded, having failed to score a fifty in ten Championship games.

Mitchell's hundred inspired Worcestershire to a surprise win at Hove in the opening YB40 game, but the campaign soon fizzled out. It was a similar story in Twenty20, where a rare double over Somerset was the highlight. The West Indian all-rounder Andre Russell made his only significant contribution to help chase down 189 in the televised home game against Somerset. But, by then, qualification had slipped by.

Championship attendance: 20,547.

WORCESTERSHIRE RESULTS

All first-class matches – Played 18: Won 6, Lost 6, Drawn 6.
County Championship matches – Played 16: Won 5, Lost 6, Drawn 5.

LV= County Championship, 5th in Division 2;
Friends Life t20, 5th in Midlands/Wales/West Division; Yorkshire Bank 40, 5th in Group A.

COUNTY CHAMPIONSHIP AVERAGES, BATTING AND FIELDING

Colours		M	I	NO	R	HS	100	50	Avge	Ct/St
2007	M. M. Ali	16	27	5	1,375	250	4	8	62.50	22
2013	T. T. Samaraweera§	15	22	4	702	144*	2	4	39.00	6
2012	J. Leach	6	9	2	260	114	1	1	37.14	1
2013	T. C. Fell	7	10	1	333	94*	0	2	37.00	3
2005	D. K. H. Mitchell†	16	29	4	824	156	1	4	32.96	21
2011	M. G. Pardoe†	16	29	3	794	102	1	5	30.53	3
2009	O. B. Cox†	6	9	2	180	65	0	1	25.71	16/1
2013	R. A. Whiteley	4	7	0	162	56	0	1	23.14	2
2009	J. D. Shantry.	12	14	1	294	55*	0	2	22.61	3
2010	S. H. Choudhry	6	9	2	146	61*	0	1	20.85	0
2008	G. M. Andrew	10	14	0	287	66	0	3	20.50	5
2011	N. D. Pinner†	7	9	0	131	29	0	0	14.55	9
2013	M. A. Johnson¶	10	14	1	184	44	0	0	14.15	14
2010	A. Richardson.	16	18	10	109	21	0	0	13.62	4
2013	G. Cessford.	5	6	2	45	20	0	0	11.25	0
2009	A. N. Kervezee¶.	10	14	0	148	35	0	0	10.57	3
2012	D. S. Lucas.	3	5	0	34	12	0	0	6.80	1
2012	C. J. Russell	9	11	2	42	10	0	0	4.66	2

Also batted: R. A. Jones† (colours 2007) (1 match) 7, 4; A. Kapil (colours 2011) (1 match) 4, 4.

† *Born in Worcestershire.* § *Official overseas player.* ¶ *Other non-England-qualified player.* *Since 2002, Worcestershire have awarded colours to all on Championship debut.*

BOWLING

	Style	O	M	R	W	BB	5I	Avge
A. Richardson.	RFM	541.4	157	1,368	69	8-37	5	19.82
J. D. Shantry.	LFM	323.5	88	949	34	7-69	1	27.91
G. M. Andrew	RFM	219	57	698	21	4-79	0	33.23
M. M. Ali	OB	284.4	38	944	28	6-77	1	33.71
G. Cessford.	RFM	118	13	524	15	4-73	0	34.93
S. H. Choudhry	SLA	156.4	21	443	12	4-111	0	36.91
C. J. Russell	RFM	181.4	32	710	16	3-47	0	44.37

Also bowled: R. A. Jones (RFM) 15–3–78–1; A. Kapil (RFM) 2–0–14–0; J. Leach (RM) 65–6–293–5; D. S. Lucas (LFM) 55.1–13–183–3; D. K. H. Mitchell (RM) 26.2–6–70–2; N. D. Pinner (OB) 3–0–15–0; R. A. Whiteley (LM) 8–0–42–1.

LEADING YB40 AVERAGES (100 runs/4 wickets)

Batting	Runs	HS	Avge	SR	Ct	**Bowling**	W	BB	Avge	ER
D. K. H. Mitchell	530	107	44.16	92.17	5	J. D. Shantry.	16	3-11	24.25	5.50
T. T. Samaraweera	344	78	38.22	90.52	4	C. J. Russell	4	4-32	25.50	5.10
M. M. Ali	368	114	30.66	116.45	3	G. Cessford	5	4-24	25.60	6.45
G. M. Andrew . .	194	62*	27.71	115.47	2	D. K. H. Mitchell . .	11	3-27	26.54	5.03
A. N. Kervezee . .	279	81	23.25	86.37	3	B. L. D'Oliveira . . .	9	3-35	27.44	6.17
B. L. D'Oliveira . .	108	28	18.00	99.08	2	M. M. Ali	8	3-28	28.53	5.62
T. C. Fell.	100	55	16.66	74.62	1	C. A. J. Morris	4	2-25	34.75	5.95
O. B. Cox	139	34*	15.44	102.20	6	G. M. Andrew	5	2-20	44.40	6.28

LEADING FLt20 AVERAGES (100 runs/18 overs)

Batting	Runs	HS	Avge	SR	Ct/St
A. D. Russell ...	240	77*	34.28	**158.94**	5
M. M. Ali......	273	85	27.30	**155.11**	1
T. T. Samaraweera	155	65	19.37	**142.20**	0
O. B. Cox......	139	37	19.85	**124.10**	5/1
A. N. Kervezee .	267	53	29.66	**114.10**	6
D. K. H. Mitchell	139	38*	17.37	**102.20**	5

Bowling	W	BB	Avge	ER
S. H. Choudhry...	4	2-21	46.25	**6.85**
M. M. Ali	9	5-34	22.33	**7.05**
J. D. Shantry.....	12	3-34	25.91	**7.97**
G. M. Andrew....	6	3-27	36.00	**8.47**
A. D. Russell	9	2-26	24.33	**9.12**

FIRST-CLASS COUNTY RECORDS

Highest score for	405*	G. A. Hick v Somerset at Taunton..............	1988
Highest score against	331*	J. D. B. Robertson (Middlesex) at Worcester	1949
Leading run-scorer	34,490	D. Kenyon (avge 34.18)	1946–67
Best bowling for	9-23	C. F. Root v Lancashire at Worcester	1931
Best bowling against	10-51	J. Mercer (Glamorgan) at Worcester	1936
Leading wicket-taker	2,143	R. T. D. Perks (avge 23.73)...................	1930–55
Highest total for	701-6 dec	v Surrey at Worcester	2007
Highest total against	701-4 dec	by Leicestershire at Worcester.................	1906
Lowest total for	24	v Yorkshire at Huddersfield...................	1903
Lowest total against	30	by Hampshire at Worcester	1903

LIST A COUNTY RECORDS

Highest score for	180*	T. M. Moody v Surrey at The Oval............	1994
Highest score against	158	W. Larkins (Northamptonshire) at Luton	1982
	158	R. A. Smith (Hampshire) at Worcester	1996
Leading run-scorer	16,416	G. A. Hick (avge 44.60)	1985–2008
Best bowling for	7-19	N. V. Radford v Bedfordshire at Bedford.......	1991
Best bowling against	7-15	R. A. Hutton (Yorkshire) at Leeds	1969
Leading wicket-taker	370	S. R. Lampitt (avge 24.52)	1987–2002
Highest total for	404-3	v Devon at Worcester	1987
Highest total against	399-4	by Sussex at Horsham	2011
Lowest total for	58	v Ireland v Worcester	2009
Lowest total against	45	by Hampshire at Worcester...................	1988

TWENTY20 COUNTY RECORDS

Highest score for	116*	G. A. Hick v Northamptonshire at Luton..........	2004
Highest score against	141*	C. L. White (Somerset) at Worcester.............	2006
Leading run-scorer	**1,492**	**M. M. Ali (avge 23.68)**	**2007–13**
Best bowling for	**5-34**	**M. M. Ali v Northamptonshire at Northampton..**	**2013**
Best bowling against	6-21	A. J. Hall (Northamptonshire) at Northampton	2008
Leading wicket-taker	**56**	**G. M. Andrew (avge 27.89)**	**2008–13**
Highest total for	227-6	v Northamptonshire at Kidderminster	2007
Highest total against	222-3	by Northamptonshire at Kidderminster	2007
Lowest total for	86	v Northamptonshire at Worcester	2006
Lowest total against	93	by Gloucestershire at Bristol	2008

ADDRESS

County Ground, New Road, Worcester WR2 4QQ (01905 748474; **email** info@wccc.co.uk).
Website www.wccc.co.uk

OFFICIALS

Captain D. K. H. Mitchell
Director of cricket S. J. Rhodes
Academy director D. B. D'Oliveira
President J. W. Elliott

Chairman J. M. Price
Chief executive D. A. Leatherdale
Head groundsman T. R. Packwood
Scorer D. E. Pugh

At Manchester, April 10–13. WORCESTERSHIRE drew with LANCASHIRE.

At Cardiff, April 17–20. WORCESTERSHIRE lost to GLAMORGAN by ten wickets.

At Southampton, April 24–27. WORCESTERSHIRE lost to HAMPSHIRE by an innings and 42 runs.

At Oxford, May 1–3. WORCESTERSHIRE beat OXFORD MCCU by 130 runs.

WORCESTERSHIRE v LEICESTERSHIRE

At Worcester, May 8–11. Drawn. Worcestershire 7pts, Leicestershire 8pts. Toss: Worcestershire.
Worcestershire had played all their games away from New Road for the first month of the season to allow building work on the hotel and five-storey conference block to continue uninterrupted. And the opening fixture – when it came – was instantly forgettable, with nearly 100 overs lost to the weather. After four winter floods, it was no surprise to find a slow-turning pitch, with the occasional ball liable to misbehave; both teams crawled along at under three runs an over. On the first day, Pardoe had ended a sequence of 19 Championship innings without a fifty. Naik's off-spin was on as early as the tenth over, and he thought he had Samaraweera caught at short leg on two, but the umpires decided the ball had deflected off Boyce's helmet before landing in his hands. In a passage of 94 balls without a boundary, Samaraweera went on to reach 15,000 career runs; the clip off his legs that heralded his maiden hundred for Worcestershire – and the declaration – was only his ninth four. Leicestershire were even slower, despite a relatively smooth century from Eckersley.

Close of play: first day, Worcestershire 198-3 (Samaraweera 52, Kervezee 18); second day, Worcestershire 294-7 (Samaraweera 92, Choudhry 15); third day, Leicestershire 229-2 (Eckersley 108, Sarwan 46).

Worcestershire

*D. K. H. Mitchell c Thornely b Freckingham	8	– not out	20
M. G. Pardoe b Naik	59	– lbw b Naik	14
M. M. Ali c Thornely b Taylor	48	– not out	24
T. T. Samaraweera not out	100		
A. N. Kervezee c Boyce b Naik	35		
N. D. Pinner c Thornely b Naik	0		
†M. A. Johnson b Naik	17		
G. M. Andrew c O'Brien b Naik	0		
S. H. Choudhry not out	32		
B 2, l-b 13, w 4, n-b 2	21	B 1, n-b 2	3

1/16 (1) 2/94 (3)   (7 wkts dec, 109.3 overs) 320   1/22 (2)   (1 wkt dec, 20 overs) 61
3/163 (2) 4/227 (5)
5/227 (6) 6/257 (7) 7/257 (8)

J. D. Shantry and A. Richardson did not bat.

Freckingham 21–2–68–1; Williams 18.3–5–47–0; Naik 35–6–98–5; Taylor 24–8–53–1; Cobb 2–0–5–0; Thakor 9–2–34–0. *Second innings*—Freckingham 3–0–17–0; Taylor 1–0–4–0; Naik 9–2–21–1; Cobb 5–1–8–0; Sarwan 2–0–11–0.

Leicestershire

M. A. Thornely b Choudhry	17	J. K. H. Naik c Mitchell b Choudhry	7
†N. J. O'Brien b Ali	46	O. H. Freckingham not out	0
E. J. H. Eckersley c Andrew b Shantry	122	B 7, l-b 5, w 3	15
*R. R. Sarwan c Pinner b Ali	79		
J. J. Cobb c Andrew b Shantry	0	1/51 (1) (8 wkts dec, 138.2 overs) 379
M. A. G. Boyce b Choudhry	29	2/106 (2) 3/245 (3)
S. J. Thakor not out	52	4/247 (5) 5/287 (4) 6/309 (6)
R. M. L. Taylor lbw b Choudhry	12	7/341 (8) 8/379 (9) 110 overs: 303-5

R. E. M. Williams did not bat.

Richardson 20–4–48–0; Shantry 18–6–40–2; Ali 37–8–113–2; Andrew 8–2–21–0; Choudhry 45–5–111–4; Mitchell 7.2–1–19–0; Pinner 3–0–15–0.

Umpires: R. A. Kettleborough and M. J. Saggers.

At Canterbury, May 17–18. WORCESTERSHIRE beat KENT by ten wickets.

WORCESTERSHIRE v GLOUCESTERSHIRE

At Worcester, May 22–25. Worcestershire won by ten wickets. Worcestershire 23pts, Gloucestershire 3pts. Toss: Worcestershire. Championship debut: G. H. Roderick.

Richardson's second 12-wicket haul in a week extended Gloucestershire's winless run at New Road to 17 matches in 27 years – although stubborn last-day resistance ensured the game went down to the final session. Richardson exploited a pitch with a tinge of grass to take a career-best eight for 37, starting with the wicket of Klinger, who had been Worcestershire's overseas player a year earlier. Ali then demonstrated his full repertoire in a delicious hundred, although he was fortunate to be dropped by Norwell at mid-off on 99. Ali dominated a second-wicket stand of 173 with another left-hander, Pardoe, before Andrew piled in to off-spinner Jack Taylor – who was suspended from bowling a few days later by the ECB, having failed to convince analysts at Loughborough that his action was legal. More happily, Miles completed his maiden five-wicket haul in his fourth game. With Richardson again rampant, Gloucestershire trailed by 136 with five wickets left heading into the last day. But the sun came out, and Gareth Roderick – a 21-year-old from Durban with a British passport who had been snapped up after excelling in the West of England Premier League with Cheltenham in 2012 – used up 30 overs alongside Fuller, until Andrew broke through.

Close of play: first day, Worcestershire 65-0 (Mitchell 46, Pardoe 17); second day, Worcestershire 302-3 (Ali 122, Kervezee 13); third day, Gloucestershire 87-5 (Howell 5, Roderick 0).

Gloucestershire

*M. Klinger lbw b Richardson	5	– (2) b Andrew	26
C. D. J. Dent c Johnson b Richardson	29	– (1) lbw b Richardson	12
D. M. Housego lbw b Richardson	9	– c Johnson b Richardson	0
A. P. R. Gidman b Richardson	41	– c Johnson b Richardson	32
H. J. H. Marshall c Mitchell b Russell	45	– c Johnson b Russell	12
B. A. C. Howell c Johnson b Mitchell	36	– lbw b Richardson	10
†G. H. Roderick c Pinner b Richardson	26	– not out	79
J. M. R. Taylor c Johnson b Richardson	29	– b Andrew	9
J. K. Fuller c Johnson b Richardson	1	– c Russell b Andrew	42
C. N. Miles b Richardson	5	– c Pinner b Russell	20
L. C. Norwell not out	0	– b Russell	0
B 6, l-b 2	8	B 5, l-b 5, w 2	12

1/10 (1) 2/28 (3) 3/80 (2)   (70.3 overs) 234   1/24 (1) 2/24 (3)   (104.5 overs) 254
4/99 (4) 5/173 (6) 6/173 (5)   3/49 (2) 4/71 (5)
7/219 (8) 8/221 (9) 9/231 (10) 10/234 (7)   5/87 (4) 6/98 (6) 7/107 (8)
                                                      8/206 (9) 9/254 (10) 10/254 (11)

Richardson 21.3–5–37–8; Russell 12–2–65–1; Shantry 18–8–50–0; Ali 3–0–16–0; Mitchell 2–1–1–1. *Second innings*—Richardson 31–11–70–4; Andrew 31–11–79–3; Shantry 14–5–26–0; Russell 18.5–4–47–3; Ali 9–4–20–0; Mitchell 1–0–2–0.

Worcestershire

*D. K. H. Mitchell c Howell b Norwell	63	– not out	22
M. G. Pardoe b Fuller	89	– not out	9
M. M. Ali c Taylor b Miles	123		
T. T. Samaraweera lbw b Miles	5		
A. N. Kervezee lbw b Miles	22		
N. D. Pinner c Gidman b Norwell	18		
†M. A. Johnson lbw b Miles	0		
G. M. Andrew c Gidman b Miles	66		
J. D. Shantry run out	31		
C. J. Russell not out	9		
A. Richardson c Marshall b Miles	5		
B 7, l-b 14, w 5	26	B 1, l-b 1	2

1/90 (1) 2/263 (2) 3/276 (4)   (124.5 overs) 457   (no wkt, 4.1 overs) 33
4/311 (3) 5/312 (5) 6/312 (7) 7/332 (6)
8/430 (8) 9/443 (9) 10/457 (11)   110 overs: 377-7

Fuller 25–5–93–1; Miles 31.5–5–99–6; Norwell 30–5–90–2; Howell 16–3–61–0; Taylor 18–2–82–0; Dent 4–1–11–0. *Second innings*—Fuller 2–0–14–0; Miles 2–0–13–0; Taylor 0.1–0–4–0.

Umpires: M. R. Benson and T. E. Jesty.

WORCESTERSHIRE v ESSEX

At Worcester, May 28–31. Drawn. Worcestershire 10pts, Essex 6pts. Toss: Worcestershire. First-class debut: N. L. J. Browne.

After 185 overs were lost to rain on the first two days, a confident Worcestershire dominated what remained of the match. Shantry, swinging the ball both ways from round the wicket, had bursts of three wickets in eight balls and three in ten, as he returned a Championship-best seven for 69. It took Westley's gritty effort on a green pitch, plus 11 fours from Mahmood, to get Essex out of a complete mess. Only two balls of the reply were possible on the third day before further rain, but the last was warm and sunny, allowing Worcestershire to rack up four batting points – and umpire Jeremy Lloyds to shed his thermals for the first time in the season. Mitchell compiled a stop-start tenth Championship century: he spent 38 balls in the nineties, but reached 150 in another 53 balls.

Close of play: first day, no play; second day, Essex 9-1 (Westley 4, Browne 0); third day, Worcestershire 0-0 (Mitchell 0, Pardoe 0).

Essex

T. Westley c Russell b Shantry	90	S. I. Mahmood b Shantry	54
J. C. Mickleburgh c Ali b Russell	4	D. D. Masters c Pinner b Shantry	4
N. L. J. Browne lbw b Richardson	3	R. J. W. Topley not out	1
M. L. Pettini b Richardson	12	B 2, l-b 1, w 2	5
R. N. ten Doeschate c Mitchell b Shantry	30		
B. T. Foakes lbw b Shantry	0	1/5 (2) 2/18 (3) 3/36 (4) (63.2 overs) 215
*†J. S. Foster c Pinner b Shantry	0	4/95 (5) 5/95 (6) 6/95 (7)
G. R. Napier c Andrew b Shantry	12	7/115 (8) 8/206 (9) 9/209 (1) 10/215 (10)

Richardson 22–3–84–2; Russell 14–4–29–1; Shantry 18.2–6–69–7; Andrew 9–3–30–0.

Worcestershire

*D. K. H. Mitchell b Masters	156	†M. A. Johnson not out	0
M. G. Pardoe c Foakes b Westley	17		
M. M. Ali c Pettini b Napier	54	B 6, l-b 9, n-b 20	35
T. T. Samaraweera not out	70		
A. N. Kervezee b Masters	7	1/62 (2) (6 wkts dec, 94.5 overs) 351
G. M. Andrew lbw b Napier	5	2/189 (3) 3/296 (1)
N. D. Pinner c Foster b Masters	7	4/324 (5) 5/335 (6) 6/344 (7)

J. D. Shantry, C. J. Russell and A. Richardson did not bat.

Masters 22–4–70–3; Topley 17–3–76–0; Mahmood 10–0–60–0; Westley 3–0–7–1; Napier 20–5–39–2; Browne 16.5–4–59–0; ten Doeschate 6–0–25–0.

Umpires: G. D. Lloyd and J. W. Lloyds.

At Northampton, June 5–7. WORCESTERSHIRE lost to NORTHAMPTONSHIRE by ten wickets.

WORCESTERSHIRE v GLAMORGAN

At Worcester, June 20–23. Worcestershire won by eight wickets. Worcestershire 23pts, Glamorgan 3pts. Toss: Glamorgan. Championship debut: T. C. Fell.

Wallace's decision to bowl first exploded in his face, as Ali became the eighth Worcestershire player to reach 250. His marathon innings spanned four and a half sessions, and installed him ahead of Joe Root as the country's leading run-scorer, on 900. After Hogan nipped one back to remove Mitchell, Glamorgan endured a day of penance, with Pardoe and Ali adding 219 – Worcestershire's first double-century partnership in a Championship match for almost three years. Pardoe struck North for six and four in consecutive deliveries to reach his maiden first-class hundred at the 70th time of asking, before edging Cosker next ball. Cox, recalled as wicketkeeper, prospered too, but another Academy graduate, Tom Fell, was out for a golden duck on Championship debut. With the exception of Allenby and Wallace in a stand of 114, Glamorgan succumbed to a nagging pace attack on a largely unresponsive pitch, and were made to follow on, 228 behind. Allenby was dropped at slip on one, and made it count with his second fifty of the game. But Shantry was a constant menace, and continued his fine form with eight wickets in the match.

Close of play: first day, Worcestershire 322-3 (Ali 155, Shantry 0); second day, Glamorgan 164-5 (Allenby 56, Wallace 18); third day, Glamorgan 200-7 (Allenby 53, Owen 34).

Worcestershire

*D. K. H. Mitchell lbw b Hogan	2	– c Walters b Reed	22
M. G. Pardoe c Allenby b Cosker	102	– c Owen b North	12
M. M. Ali c Reed b Cosker	250	– not out	8
T. T. Samaraweera c Wright b Allenby	38	– not out	1
J. D. Shantry c and b Cosker	32		
A. N. Kervezee c Goodwin b Reed	3		
T. C. Fell lbw b Cosker	0		
†O. B. Cox not out	40		
J. Leach not out	6		
B 5, l-b 9, n-b 18	32	B 4, n-b 4	8

1/12 (1) 2/231 (2)   (7 wkts dec, 138 overs) 505   1/37 (1)   (2 wkts, 9.5 overs) 51
3/321 (4) 4/391 (5)   2/46 (2)
5/396 (6) 6/397 (7) 7/498 (3)   110 overs: 371-3

C. J. Russell and A. Richardson did not bat.

Hogan 29–4–85–1; Owen 28–5–109–0; Reed 31–3–126–1; Allenby 25–4–71–1; Cosker 18–2–68–4; Bragg 1–0–1–0; North 5–1–24–0; Wright 1–0–7–0. *Second innings*—Hogan 2–0–8–0; Reed 4–0–24–1; Owen 3–0–10–0; North 0.5–0–5–1.

Glamorgan

B. J. Wright b Shantry	27	– c Mitchell b Shantry	63
W. D. Bragg c Cox b Richardson	5	– c Kervezee b Russell	1
S. J. Walters c Pardoe b Shantry	6	– lbw b Richardson	9
M. J. North b Russell	36	– c Samaraweera b Ali	6
M. W. Goodwin c Cox b Richardson	11	– c Ali b Shantry	2
J. Allenby lbw b Leach	82	– not out	74
*†M. A. Wallace c Cox b Shantry	43	– lbw b Shantry	11
D. A. Cosker lbw b Richardson	4	– c Kervezee b Shantry	13
W. T. Owen lbw b Leach	5	– b Richardson	40
M. G. Hogan c Mitchell b Shantry	37	– b Leach	46
M. T. Reed not out	4	– c Cox b Russell	4
B 5, l-b 12	17	L-b 8, w 1	9

1/13 (2) 2/25 (3) 3/54 (1)   (74 overs) 277   1/11 (2) 2/31 (3)   (79.1 overs) 278
4/71 (5) 5/98 (4) 6/212 (6)   3/66 (4) 4/84 (5)
7/217 (8) 8/222 (9) 9/268 (7) 10/277 (10)   5/87 (1) 6/109 (7) 7/129 (8)
                                      8/211 (9) 9/268 (10) 10/278 (11)

Richardson 25–7–74–3; Russell 16–4–66–1; Shantry 18–2–65–4; Leach 11–1–36–2; Ali 4–0–19–0. *Second innings*—Richardson 22–9–37–2; Russell 14.1–1–72–2; Shantry 23–5–77–4; Ali 7–0–31–1; Leach 13–1–53–1.

Umpires: M. J. D. Bodenham and M. A. Gough.

At Worcester, July 2–5. WORCESTERSHIRE drew with AUSTRALIANS (see Australian tour section).

At Cheltenham, July 17–20. WORCESTERSHIRE lost to GLOUCESTERSHIRE by six wickets.

WORCESTERSHIRE v KENT

At Worcester, August 2–5. Drawn. Worcestershire 8pts, Kent 8pts. Toss: Worcestershire.

Only 15 overs were possible after the second day, denying 19-year-old Fell the chance of a maiden century. He did his level best, adding 30 in the 39 balls he faced between the stoppages, but rain killed the game on the fourth afternoon. There was just enough time for Tredwell to complete his first five-wicket haul for two years, bowling Shantry after his maiden fifty had helped Worcestershire avoid the follow-on. Andrew's burst of three wickets in 17 balls had left Kent 25 for four after they were put in on a new, green-tinged pitch. Stevens led an emphatic recovery, repeatedly lofting Shantry over the top until he was out in the nineties for the third time in the season; Harmison, who mucked in alongside him, met a similar fate. On 43, Ali reached 1,000 first-class runs. Leach had less joy: he nicked Tredwell behind fourth ball, and had his car windscreen smashed by a shot from a match on the adjacent King's School ground. Screeches from a bird-scarer, designed to stop seagulls pecking at the covers, provided the soundtrack for the last two days.

Close of play: first day, Kent 324; second day, Worcestershire 213-7 (Fell 64, Shantry 20); third day, Worcestershire 241-7 (Fell 75, Shantry 30).

Kent

S. A. Northeast c Ali b Andrew	10	C. J. Haggett not out	34
R. W. T. Key c Cox b Richardson	12	M. E. Claydon c Cox b Richardson	33
D. J. Bell-Drummond lbw b Andrew	2	M. Davies c Ali b Shantry	4
B. P. Nash c Cox b Andrew	0	B 2, l-b 5, n-b 4	11
B. W. Harmison b Shantry	96		
D. I. Stevens c Ali b Leach	95	1/21 (1) 2/25 (3) 3/25 (2) (95.5 overs) 324
†G. O. Jones c Cox b Cessford	17	4/25 (4) 5/199 (6) 6/218 (7)
*J. C. Tredwell lbw b Shantry	10	7/248 (8) 8/257 (5) 9/309 (10) 10/324 (11)

Richardson 23–8–61–2; Andrew 20–5–81–3; Shantry 22.5–5–69–3; Leach 11–3–38–1; Cessford 15–3–53–1; Ali 4–0–15–0.

Worcestershire

*D. K. H. Mitchell c Tredwell b Stevens	...	22	G. M. Andrew c Bell-Drummond b Tredwell	1
M. G. Pardoe c Northeast b Stevens	......	13	J. D. Shantry b Tredwell	54
M. M. Ali c Claydon b Tredwell	....	59	B 2, l-b 3, w 5, n-b 2	12
T. T. Samaraweera c Jones b Haggett	.....	13		
T. C. Fell not out	....	94	1/25 (2) 2/46 (1) (8 wkts, 95 overs)	284
J. Leach c Jones b Tredwell	....	0	3/94 (4) 4/124 (3)	
†O. B. Cox c Stevens b Tredwell	....	16	5/126 (6) 6/154 (7) 7/158 (8) 8/284 (9)	

G. Cessford and A. Richardson did not bat.

Davies 12–4–35–0; Haggett 25–7–71–1; Stevens 22–7–70–2; Claydon 15–2–52–0; Tredwell 21–6–51–5.

Umpires: R. J. Bailey and M. A. Gough.

At Worcester, August 16. WORCESTERSHIRE beat BANGLADESH A by six wickets (see Bangladesh A tour section).

WORCESTERSHIRE v LANCASHIRE

At Worcester, August 22–25. Lancashire won by nine wickets. Lancashire 24pts, Worcestershire 5pts. Toss: Lancashire.

Ali produced jaw-dropping strokeplay while becoming the 14th Worcestershire player to score two hundreds in a match, but there was little else to prevent Lancashire from achieving their first maximum-points victory for six years. Their bowlers had yet to crank into top gear when Worcestershire's careless batsmen came to their aid: Samaraweera wandered out of his ground after leaving an innocuous delivery from Hogg, and was stumped by an underarm throw from Cross; then Fell, who had helped Ali add 91, was run out by Reece to spark a collapse of six for 37. Ali was matched by a dazzling display from Katich, who scored an 86-ball hundred between lunch and tea on the second day, passing 1,000 runs for the season. Rain ruined the evening session, and Lancashire were still 11 behind when Katich was out early next day. But Worcestershire rolled over as Tom Smith, who scored his first fifty of an injury-hit season, and Procter, who hit his fourth in succession, propelled Lancashire to full batting points for the first time since April 2012. Ali deposited off-spinner Lilley for three sixes, and strode on to another century, giving him a double, three hundreds and two fifties in his last seven Championship innings at New Road. But he could add only eight more on the last morning before edging Chapple – and there Worcestershire's resistance ended.

Close of play: first day, Lancashire 0-0 (Chapple 0, Reece 0); second day, Lancashire 271-5 (Katich 104, Procter 3); third day, Worcestershire 166-5 (Ali 101, Shantry 10).

Worcestershire

*D. K. H. Mitchell c Agathangelou b Smith	 22	– lbw b Chapple	 8
M. G. Pardoe c Cross b Reece	 35	– c Cross b Hogg	 0
M. M. Ali c Cross b Hogg	 104	– c Cross b Chapple	 109
T. T. Samaraweera st Cross b Hogg	 6	– lbw b Smith	 17
T. C. Fell run out	 43	– c Smith b Chapple	 11
R. A. Whiteley b Lilley	 0	– c Agathangelou b Lilley	 13
J. Leach lbw b Chapple	 10	– (8) c Cross b Hogg	 20
†O. B. Cox b Reece b Smith	 7	– (9) lbw b Smith	 11
J. D. Shantry c Agathangelou b Hogg	 5	– (7) c Cross b Hogg	 31
G. Cessford not out	 13	– c Cross b Smith	 11
A. Richardson c Katich b Hogg	 21	– not out	 2
B 4, l-b 5, w 8, n-b 4	 21	B 1, l-b 5, w 2	 8

1/38 (1) 2/92 (2) 3/124 (4)   (92.1 overs) 287   1/5 (2) 2/15 (1)   (70.4 overs) 241
4/215 (5) 5/215 (6) 6/234 (7)   3/79 (4) 4/113 (5)
7/246 (3) 8/252 (9) 9/252 (8) 10/287 (11)   5/147 (6) 6/185 (3) 7/214 (8)
                                                      8/216 (7) 9/234 (10) 10/241 (9)

Chapple 22–3–66–1; Hogg 21.1–6–57–4; Smith 19–7–48–2; Procter 9–3–41–0; Reece 8–1–25–1; Lilley 13–0–41–1. *Second innings*—Hogg 20–3–58–3; Chapple 18–4–53–3; Smith 12.4–0–40–3; Procter 6–0–26–0; Lilley 10–1–42–1; Reece 3–0–16–0; Agathangelou 1–1–0–0.

Lancashire

*G. Chapple c Cox b Cessford	0		
L. M. Reece c Ali b Richardson	59	– not out	56
P. J. Horton c Richardson b Ali	30	– (1) c Pardoe b Cessford	8
A. G. Prince c Samaraweera b Cessford	52	– (3) not out	21
S. M. Katich c Samaraweera b Shantry	105		
A. P. Agathangelou lbw b Richardson	14		
L. A. Procter c Shantry b Richardson	76		
T. C. Smith c Cox b Cessford	84		
†G. D. Cross c Cox b Richardson	0		
K. W. Hogg c Cox b Cessford	6		
A. M. Lilley not out	4		
B 4, l-b 3, w 2, n-b 2	11	L-b 5	5

1/1 (1) 2/78 (3) 3/111 (2)   (109.2 overs) 441   1/17 (1)   (1 wkt, 19 overs) 90
4/203 (4) 5/268 (6) 6/276 (5)
7/412 (7) 8/419 (9) 9/426 (10) 10/441 (8)

Richardson 33–6–102–4; Cessford 16.2–0–73–4; Shantry 24–3–97–1; Leach 12–0–76–0; Ali 19–2–66–1; Whiteley 4–0–19–0; Mitchell 1–0–1–0. *Second innings*—Richardson 8–4–20–0; Cessford 7–1–39–1; Ali 2–0–11–0; Shantry 2–0–15–0.

Umpires: N. G. C. Cowley and S. J. O'Shaughnessy.

At Leicester, August 28–31. WORCESTERSHIRE beat LEICESTERSHIRE by nine wickets.

At Chelmsford, September 3–5. WORCESTERSHIRE lost to ESSEX by eight wickets.

WORCESTERSHIRE v HAMPSHIRE

At Worcester, September 11–14. Drawn. Worcestershire 10pts, Hampshire 10pts. Toss: Worcestershire.

Worcestershire opened the turnstiles on the final day so they could show off The View, the new hospitality suite at the heart of New Road's £10m redevelopment. But there was not much to see in the middle. Hampshire rejected three separate approaches to set up a run-chase; Mitchell had his revenge by declaring eight wickets down to deny them a third bowling point. Adams was out to the game's third ball, for his seventh duck of the season, before Vince and Dawson – both dropped by Ali at first slip – prospered thanks to the short boundary on the River Severn side of the ground. Only Richardson posed a threat as Sean Terry chiselled out his first Championship fifty, 21 years after his father Paul had scored a century here for Hampshire, and Coles raced to another from 38 balls. Worcestershire's response straddled three interrupted days, and they were 69 adrift of the follow-on target when the sixth wicket went down. But Cox, who had just found out that his wicketkeeping rival Michael Johnson was being released, responded with a career-best 65.

Close of play: first day, Hampshire 197-3 (Vince 106, Wheater 2); second day, Worcestershire 101-2 (Ali 28, Samaraweera 40); third day, Worcestershire 189-5 (Whiteley 35, Cox 5).

Hampshire

*J. H. K. Adams c Cox b Richardson	0	– not out	22
M. D. T. Roberts c Ali b Richardson	13	– b Ali	22
L. A. Dawson run out	70	– c Whiteley b Cessford	8
J. M. Vince c Ali b Richardson	106	– not out	11
A. J. Wheater run out	2		
S. P. Terry c Ali b Whiteley	58		
†M. D. Bates lbw b Richardson	41		
C. P. Wood lbw b Ali	61		
M. T. Coles not out	50		
D. J. Balcombe b Cessford	17		
J. A. Tomlinson lbw b Shantry	0		
L-b 8, n-b 2	10	B 4, n-b 2	6

1/0 (1) 2/23 (2) 3/181 (3)	(110.4 overs) 428	1/39 (2)	(2 wkts dec, 20.1 overs) 69
4/197 (4) 5/198 (5) 6/275 (7) 7/356 (6)		2/50 (3)	
8/366 (8) 9/421 (10) 10/428 (11)	110 overs: 421-9		

Richardson 34–12–69–4; Shantry 33.4–12–97–1; Cessford 22–1–139–1; Whiteley 4–0–23–1; Choudhry 9–0–40–0; Mitchell 4–1–15–0; Ali 4–0–37–1. *Second innings*—Richardson 4–2–9–0; Shantry 3–2–14–0; Cessford 6–0–29–1; Ali 6.1–3–9–1; Choudhry 1–0–4–0.

Worcestershire

*D. K. H. Mitchell c Dawson b Tomlinson	13	J. D. Shantry b Wood	27
M. G. Pardoe c Adams b Coles	4	G. Cessford not out	1
M. M. Ali lbw b Tomlinson	32	B 9, l-b 10, w 2, n-b 6	27
T. T. Samaraweera c Wood b Tomlinson	51		
T. C. Fell c and b Coles	32	1/6 (2)	(8 wkts dec, 103.4 overs) 351
R. A. Whiteley b Tomlinson	38	2/21 (1) 3/105 (3)	
†O. B. Cox c Wheater b Coles	65	4/122 (4) 5/180 (5)	
S. H. Choudhry not out	61	6/210 (6) 7/288 (7) 8/346 (9)	

A. Richardson did not bat.

Tomlinson 28–10–85–4; Coles 22–4–90–3; Balcombe 21–4–68–0; Wood 19.4–5–55–1; Vince 8–0–23–0; Dawson 5–0–11–0.

Umpires: M. Burns and N. G. C. Cowley.

WORCESTERSHIRE v NORTHAMPTONSHIRE

At Worcester, September 24–26. Worcestershire won by 115 runs. Worcestershire 19pts, Northamptonshire 4pts. Toss: Northamptonshire.

At 4.20 on the second day news filtered to the middle that, after almost a decade of trying, Northamptonshire had been promoted to Division One. Down at Southampton, Essex had been dismissed for 207 in their first innings – well short of the maximum bonus points needed for a chance of pinching second place. Northamptonshire's slip fielders embraced, and applause rippled round the ground. Naturally, much of the intensity drained from their performance – and they went down limply to their third defeat of the season. There was plenty of undistinguished batting from both sides under misty skies on a turning pitch: 18 lbw decisions – 11 by Peter Hartley – equalled the Championship record. He gave two in the first over, when Willey, returning after two matches out with a back injury, made spectacular use of the toss. Three others were bowled shouldering arms, easing Hall's passage to 600 first-class wickets. Northamptonshire needed to score 250 to make absolutely sure of promotion, but lost three wickets in an impeccable 14-over spell from Richardson on the second morning, including his 250th for Worcestershire in only his fourth season with them. And when Keogh, run out in chaotic fashion, and Murphy fell in quick succession, Northamptonshire had to wait for Essex to drop points. Their attack lacked a cutting edge as Ali took his season's tally to 1,420 runs, and Whiteley opened up for his maiden Worcestershire fifty. After an evening celebrating in Worcester, Northamptonshire were not in the best condition to chase 257, and collapsed to the spinners with a rush of carefree strokes; they were back in Northampton in plenty of time for their open-top bus parade the next day. Ali concluded his most successful season with the third-best bowling figures of his career, narrowly beating Nottinghamshire's Samit Patel to the £10,000 prize as the PCA's Most Valuable Player of the season.

Close of play: first day, Northamptonshire 103-4 (Keogh 19, Hall 10); second day, Worcestershire 155-5 (Ali 40, Fell 9).

Worcestershire

*D. K. H. Mitchell lbw b Willey	0	– lbw b Middlebrook	47
M. G. Pardoe st Murphy b Middlebrook	51	– c Murphy b Spriegel	38
M. M. Ali lbw b Willey	0	– c Azharullah b Middlebrook	44
T. T. Samaraweera b Azharullah	6	– b Azharullah	17
T. C. Fell b Hall	12	– lbw b Middlebrook	40
R. A. Whiteley lbw b Crook	3	– lbw b Hall	56
†O. B. Cox lbw b Hall	1	– not out	34
S. H. Choudhry b Hall	6	– lbw b Hall	0
J. D. Shantry not out	55	– lbw b Spriegel	10
C. J. Russell c Middlebrook b Hall	6	– c Wakely b Spriegel	0
A. Richardson c Murphy b Hall	0	– b Middlebrook	2
B 2, l-b 14, w 1, n-b 6	23	B 4, l-b 2, w 1	7

1/0 (1) 2/0 (3) 3/23 (4)   (57.4 overs) 163
4/46 (5) 5/55 (6) 6/64 (7)
7/76 (8) 8/148 (3) 9/163 (10) 10/163 (11)

1/77 (1) 2/117 (2)   (96 overs) 295
3/145 (4) 4/163 (3)
5/232 (5) 6/260 (6) 7/260 (8)
8/288 (9) 9/292 (10) 10/295 (11)

Willey 13–3–32–2; Azharullah 14–1–46–1; Crook 5–1–15–1; Hall 14.4–2–30–5; Middlebrook 11–3–24–1. *Second innings*—Willey 5–1–11–0; Azharullah 11–4–26–1; Hall 16–5–45–2; Middlebrook 39–8–110–4; Spriegel 16–3–75–3; Crook 9–0–22–0.

Northamptonshire

*S. D. Peters lbw b Richardson	23	– lbw b Ali	19
J. D. Middlebrook c Ali b Shantry	4	– c Cox b Richardson	0
D. J. Sales c Whiteley b Richardson	12	– c Mitchell b Ali	17
A. G. Wakely lbw b Ali	35	– lbw b Choudhry	18
R. I. Keogh run out	57	– c Fell b Choudhry	8
A. J. Hall c Ali b Richardson	20	– lbw b Ali	27
M. N. W. Spriegel lbw b Richardson	2	– lbw b Ali	1
S. P. Crook lbw b Richardson	8	– lbw b Ali	4
D. J. Willey b Ali	12	– b Ali	26
†D. Murphy c Mitchell b Ali	18	– not out	14
Azharullah not out	0	– c Fell b Choudhry	1
B 1, l-b 9, w 1	11	B 5, l-b 1	6

1/10 (2) 2/25 (3) 3/46 (1)   (74.2 overs) 202
4/83 (4) 5/116 (6) 6/122 (7)
7/134 (8) 8/157 (9) 9/202 (5) 10/202 (10)

1/1 (2) 2/36 (3)   (48.2 overs) 141
3/49 (1) 4/63 (4)
5/72 (6) 6/73 (7) 7/77 (8)
8/113 (9) 9/140 (6) 10/141 (11)

Richardson 26–7–70–5; Shantry 18–3–46–1; Russell 4–1–14–0; Choudhry 11–1–32–0; Ali 15.2–3–30–3. *Second innings*—Richardson 10–3–18–1; Shantry 6–2–12–0; Ali 20–1–77–6; Choudhry 12.2–1–28–3.

Umpires: P. J. Hartley and G. Sharp.

YORKSHIRE

Everything but the crown

DAVID WARNER

Yorkshire shoved all their eggs into one basket in their 150th anniversary year, but an unexpected late stumble scrambled their hopes of celebrating their sesquicentenary by winning the County Championship straight after promotion. Instead, they had to make do with second place. It was not quite the glory they were seeking, but nobody could question their commitment: Yorkshire won seven matches, enough to have given them the title in many a season.

It reflected well on the club that, despite their disappointment, everyone freely acknowledged it was Durham who deserved the title. The epic Battle of Scarborough at the end of August proved decisive. Yorkshire were a hefty 25.5 points clear going into the match; even though second-placed Durham had a game in hand, a Yorkshire victory would surely have settled the issue. But Durham showed their extra drive, and emerged worthy winners, despite being without the injured Graham Onions, then losing another seamer, Mark Wood, to injury. By the time Yorkshire started their penultimate game, Durham were 27.5 points in front. Middlesex were soundly beaten, but the victory could secure only the runners-up spot.

There was a downside to Yorkshire's season: they were well and truly humbled in the FLt20, ending up bottom of their group just a year after reaching the final. They badly missed the contributions made by their overseas players in 2012, when David Miller scored 390 runs and Mitchell Starc took 21 wickets.

Yorkshire did not turn up for the YB40, either. It had been impressed strongly on coach Jason Gillespie and his squad, by everyone from club president Geoffrey Boycott down, that winning the Championship meant more than anything else – so much so that, after a poor start in the one-dayers, key players (particularly bowlers) were rested to make sure they remained fit for the four-day games. Gillespie duly gave youth its fling in limited-overs matches, and several promising colts made their county debuts, including seamer Matthew Fisher, who at 15 years seven months became the youngest player to appear in a competitive county match.

Durham may have finally ended Yorkshire's Championship ambitions, but it had also been against Durham – back in April – that they really got going, after a slow start which included an innings defeat by Sussex. Durham made most of the running at the Riverside, and declared late on the third evening, setting Yorkshire 336, with rain a constant threat. But it remained dry, and a brilliant 182 from Joe Root cemented his England place for the summer and spirited his county to their fourth-highest successful chase. A second consecutive loss, early in a season of such high expectations, could well have deflated Yorkshire, but Root's classic display energised the whole team.

Michael Steele, Getty Images

Gary Ballance

For the next few months they seemed unbeatable, despite often being without their England trio of Root, Jonny Bairstow and Tim Bresnan. The strength was significantly helped by the shrewd winter decision to spice up the fast-bowling stocks by signing Liam Plunkett from Durham and Jack Brooks from Northamptonshire; they both injected enthusiasm and flair, without pushing the long-serving regulars Ryan Sidebottom and Steven Patterson into the shadows. It was a formidable quartet, and the old warhorse Sidebottom showed he still had plenty of cricket left in him.

It was fortunate that the pace attack was so strong, as the spin reserves lacked depth. Adil Rashid chipped in occasionally without recapturing all his early promise, but Azeem Rafiq hardly featured, never regaining his form after missing a large chunk of the season with a knee injury.

Root followed up his Durham rampage with 236 in the innings victory over Derbyshire, helped by 186 from Bairstow. But they were by no means the only batsmen to shine. Rashid and Andrew Gale both began the summer with question marks over their form, which they answered with an avalanche of runs. Rashid plundered three consecutive centuries for once out, while Gale thundered his way to 272 against Nottinghamshire at Scarborough during a sequence that brought him 676 runs in seven innings. Not to be outdone, Alex Lees – after making his maiden century, at Lord's – hit an unbeaten 275 at Chesterfield. Only Darren Lehmann, with 339 against Durham in 2006, had made more for Yorkshire since Len Hutton hit 280 not out against Hampshire in 1939.

Gary Ballance never quite matched these dazzling performances, but was still the most clinically efficient of the batsmen, often succeeding when it mattered most for the team – and himself: the day before the winter tour was announced, he made 90 against Middlesex. After being named for the trip, Ballance scored a century in each innings to ensure a draw at The Oval. He ended up as Yorkshire's heaviest scorer in the Championship, his 1,251 runs including five centuries. Gale also passed 1,000.

The possibility that Yorkshire might be supplying three batsmen to the England team (which never quite materialised) led to the decision to sign up the young New Zealander Kane Williamson for the second part of the season, and he performed so outstandingly that he was invited back for 2014.

Despite finishing second best, Yorkshire received a standing ovation after their last home match at Headingley – proof, if it were needed, that they hadn't been doing too much wrong.

Championship attendance: 49,788.

YORKSHIRE RESULTS

All first-class matches – Played 17: Won 8, Lost 2, Drawn 7.
County Championship matches – Played 16: Won 7, Lost 2, Drawn 7.

LV= County Championship, 2nd in Division 1;
Friends Life t20, 6th in North Division; Yorkshire Bank 40, 6th in Group C.

COUNTY CHAMPIONSHIP AVERAGES, BATTING AND FIELDING

Cap		M	I	NO	R	HS	100	50	Avge	Ct/St
2012	G. S. Ballance	14	21	1	1,251	148	5	6	62.55	13
2008	A. U. Rashid†	15	22	6	825	180	3	3	51.56	7
	K. S. Williamson§	5	9	1	403	97	0	5	50.37	4
	A. Z. Lees†	8	14	3	500	275*	2	1	45.45	1
2008	A. W. Gale†	16	24	0	1,067	272	3	3	44.45	4
2011	J. M. Bairstow†‡	8	13	0	528	186	1	2	40.61	27
2005	P. A. Jaques¶	14	21	0	770	152	2	3	36.66	5
2010	A. Lyth†	16	27	4	730	105	1	4	31.73	25
	A. J. Hodd	9	9	2	217	68*	0	1	31.00	17/1
2013	L. E. Plunkett†	12	17	2	394	68	0	2	26.26	9
2006	T. T. Bresnan†‡	4	5	1	66	38	0	0	16.50	1
2012	S. A. Patterson†	16	17	8	147	40	0	0	16.33	2
	Azeem Rafiq	2	4	0	55	28	0	0	13.75	0
2013	J. A. Brooks	11	13	6	79	33*	0	0	11.28	5
2000	R. J. Sidebottom†	14	16	0	155	48	0	0	9.68	3
2007	J. J. Sayers†	5	7	0	57	24	0	0	8.14	4

Also batted: M. A. Ashraf† (2 matches) did not bat; J. A. Leaning (1 match) 0; R. M. Pyrah† (cap 2010) (5 matches) 55, 14*, 1 (5 ct); J. E. Root†‡ (cap 2012) (2 matches) 49, 182, 236 (3 ct).

† *Born in Yorkshire.*   ‡ *ECB contract.*   § *Official overseas player.*   ¶ *Other non-England-qualified player.*

BOWLING

	Style	O	M	R	W	BB	5I	Avge
R. J. Sidebottom	LFM	369.1	100	995	49	4-27	0	20.30
T. T. Bresnan	RFM	130.2	31	393	16	4-41	0	24.56
S. A. Patterson	RFM	413.5	119	1,153	46	5-43	1	25.06
J. A. Brooks	RFM	241	49	859	34	5-40	1	25.26
L. E. Plunkett	RFM	258.5	42	1,020	36	5-32	1	28.33
A. U. Rashid	LBG	359.5	39	1,358	29	5-78	1	46.82

Also bowled: M. A. Ashraf (RFM) 38.3–13–119–4; Azeem Rafiq (OB) 16–1–74–1; G. S. Ballance (LBG) 14–0–98–0; A. W. Gale (LBG) 9–0–94–0; P. A. Jaques (SLC) 6–0–75–1; J. A. Leaning (RFM) 4–0–22–0; A. Z. Lees (LBG) 1–0–14–0; A. Lyth (RM) 36–4–155–4; R. M. Pyrah (RM) 77–19–244–2; J. E. Root (OB) 9–4–14–0; K. S. Williamson (OB) 65.4–13–247–4.

LEADING YB40 AVERAGES (100 runs/4 wickets)

Batting	Runs	HS	Avge	SR	Ct
G. S. Ballance . . .	426	139	60.85	97.93	2
A. U. Rashid	183	46*	45.75	116.56	1
A. Lyth	397	58*	44.11	92.75	6
D. M. Hodgson . .	197	90	39.40	103.68	5
A. Z. Lees	155	63	38.75	81.15	1
P. A. Jaques	211	81	35.16	84.06	0
A. W. Gale	272	65	27.20	82.42	2

Bowling	W	BB	Avge	ER
J. A. Leaning	6	5-22	10.00	5.45
I. Wardlaw	14	3-39	23.78	6.32
R. M. Pyrah	15	4-43	29.73	5.94
L. E. Plunkett	7	2-38	31.57	5.81
W. M. H. Rhodes . .	4	2-26	33.25	6.65
S. A. Patterson	4	3-25	36.25	6.04
M. A. Ashraf	10	3-38	36.60	6.63
A. U. Rashid	5	2-27	65.60	5.75

LEADING FLt20 AVERAGES (100 runs/18 overs)

Batting	Runs	HS	Avge	SR	Ct/St
R. M. Pyrah....	104	42	14.85	**119.54**	5
G. S. Ballance..	269	68	29.88	**116.45**	4
A. Lyth	101	32	16.83	**108.60**	2
L. E. Plunkett ..	101	30	12.62	**107.44**	3
D. M. Hodgson .	177	52*	19.66	**102.90**	5/1

Bowling	W	BB	Avge	ER
R. M. Pyrah.....	9	3-15	21.33	**6.00**
R. J. Sidebottom..	3	1-29	66.66	**7.18**
J. A. Brooks.....	13	5-21	14.53	**7.56**
Azeem Rafiq	13	3-22	19.00	**7.96**
A. U. Rashid	1	1-24	156.00	**8.21**
L. E. Plunkett....	8	2-20	34.62	**8.26**

FIRST-CLASS COUNTY RECORDS

Highest score for	341	G. H. Hirst v Leicestershire at Leicester	1905
Highest score against	318*	W. G. Grace (Gloucestershire) at Cheltenham....	1876
Leading run-scorer	38,558	H. Sutcliffe (avge 50.20)	1919–45
Best bowling for	10-10	H. Verity v Nottinghamshire at Leeds..........	1932
Best bowling against	10-37	C. V. Grimmett (Australians) at Sheffield	1932
Leading wicket-taker	3,597	W. Rhodes (avge 16.02)	1898–1930
Highest total for	887	v Warwickshire at Birmingham................	1896
Highest total against	681-7 dec	by Leicestershire at Bradford	1996
Lowest total for	23	v Hampshire at Middlesbrough	1965
Lowest total against	13	by Nottinghamshire at Nottingham	1901

LIST A COUNTY RECORDS

Highest score for	191	D. S. Lehmann v Nottinghamshire at Scarborough ..	2001
Highest score against	177	S. A. Newman (Surrey) at The Oval	2009
Leading run-scorer	8,699	G. Boycott (avge 40.08).......................	1963–86
Best bowling for	7-15	R. A. Hutton v Worcestershire at Leeds	1969
Best bowling against	7-32	R. G. D. Willis (Warwickshire) at Birmingham	1981
Leading wicket-taker	308	C. M. Old (avge 18.96)	1967–85
Highest total for	411-6	v Devon at Exmouth	2004
Highest total against	375-4	by Surrey at Scarborough.....................	1994
Lowest total for	54	v Essex at Leeds...........................	2003
Lowest total against	23	by Middlesex at Leeds.......................	1974

TWENTY20 COUNTY RECORDS

Highest score for	109	I. J. Harvey v Derbyshire at Leeds...............	2005
Highest score against	111	D. L. Maddy (Leicestershire) at Leeds...........	2004
Leading run-scorer	**1,837**	**A. W. Gale (avge 27.01)**	**2004–13**
Best bowling for	5-16	R. M. Pyrah v Durham at Scarborough	2011
Best bowling against	4-9	C. K. Langeveldt (Derbyshire) at Leeds	2008
Leading wicket-taker	**88**	**R. M. Pyrah (avge 20.59)**......................	**2005–13**
Highest total for	213-7	v Worcestershire at Leeds	2010
Highest total against	222-5	by Derbyshire at Leeds	2010
Lowest total for	90-9	v Durham at Chester-le-Street	2009
Lowest total against	98	by Durham at Chester-le-Street	2006

ADDRESS

Headingley Cricket Ground, Leeds LS6 3BU (0871 971 1222; **email** cricket@yorkshireccc.com).
Website www.yorkshireccc.com

OFFICIALS

Captain A. W. Gale
Director of cricket M. D. Moxon
First-team coach J. N. Gillespie
Director of cricket development I. Dews
President H. D. Bird

Chairman C. Graves
Chief executive M. A. Arthur
Head groundsman A. W. Fogarty
Scorer J. T. Potter

YORKSHIRE v LEEDS/BRADFORD MCCU

At Leeds, April 5–7. Yorkshire won by 294 runs. Toss: Leeds/Bradford. First-class debuts: N. R. T. Gubbins, C. A. R. MacLeod, H. P. Rouse, H. L. Thompson, W. G. R. Vanderspar, D. R. Young. County debuts: J. A. Brooks, L. E. Plunkett.

Yorkshire won easily in the end, but they had a fright on the first morning, when James Lee – who had played half a dozen first-team games for them – reduced his former colleagues to 65 for seven en route to figures of seven for 45. They were pulled round by a partnership of 156 between Ballance and Sidebottom. Batting at No. 10, Lee then scored twice as many runs as any of his Leeds/Bradford team-mates as the Yorkshire seamers enforced a lead of 126. Lyth and Lees, who reached a maiden first-class century, had few problems in an opening stand of 221, before Plunkett marked his Yorkshire debut with a career-best six for 33 – concluding with Lee. Top scorer in the students' second innings was Will Vanderspar, *Wisden's* Schools Cricketer of the Year in 2011. Before play on the first day, both teams observed a minute's silence in memory of Leeds/Bradford all-rounder Tom Hardman, who died in his sleep, aged 21, during the winter.

Close of play: first day, Leeds/Bradford MCCU 40-3 (Thompson 14, MacLeod 2); second day, Yorkshire 192-0 (Lyth 93, Lees 86).

Yorkshire

A. Lyth c Young b Thomas	9	– c Vanderspar b MacQueen	111
A. Z. Lees c Reece b Lee	0	– b Rouse	121
J. J. Sayers c Gubbins b Lee	1	– not out	25
*A. W. Gale lbw b Lee	0	– not out	9
†J. M. Bairstow c MacLeod b Reece	20		
G. S. Ballance c MacLeod b Lee	112		
Azeem Rafiq c Webb b Lee	3		
L. E. Plunkett lbw b Lee	0		
R. J. Sidebottom b Vanderspar	40		
J. A. Brooks not out	21		
S. A. Patterson b Lee	0		
B 11, l-b 9, w 8, n-b 10	38	B 10, l-b 3, w 6, n-b 4	23

1/9 (1) 2/9 (2) 3/9 (4)   (84.3 overs) 244   1/221 (1)   (2 wkts dec, 101 overs) 289
4/10 (3) 5/59 (5) 6/65 (7)   2/272 (2)
7/65 (8) 8/221 (9) 9/244 (6) 10/244 (11)

Lee 14.3–1–45–7; Thomas 15–3–52–1; Rouse 12–3–41–0; Reece 16–3–34–1; Vanderspar 7–1–26–1; MacQueen 19–6–26–0; Thompson 1–1–0–0. *Second innings*—Lee 15–3–30–0; Thomas 20–4–52–0; Rouse 18–1–64–1; Reece 24–2–68–0; MacQueen 18–6–45–1; Thompson 2–1–6–0; Vanderspar 3–0–9–0; Young 1–0–2–0.

Leeds/Bradford MCCU

H. L. Thompson lbw b Patterson	15	– c Bairstow b Plunkett	2
N. R. T. Gubbins c Bairstow b Brooks	14	– c Bairstow b Patterson	8
J. P. Webb b Brooks	0	– c Gale b Plunkett	0
D. R. Young c Bairstow b Sidebottom	5	– lbw b Patterson	0
†C. A. R. MacLeod c Lyth b Patterson	3	– (10) c Lees b Plunkett	0
*L. M. Reece c Bairstow b Sidebottom	0	– (5) c Brooks b Plunkett	6
W. G. R. Vanderspar c Bairstow b Patterson	5	– (6) b Plunkett	37
H. P. Rouse c Lyth b Azeem Rafiq	14	– (7) b Azeem Rafiq	15
A. MacQueen lbw b Sidebottom	2	– (8) lbw b Sidebottom	30
J. E. Lee b Brooks	34	– (9) c Sidebottom b Plunkett	20
I. A. A. Thomas not out	10	– not out	1
B 4, l-b 11, w 1	16	L-b 2	2

1/22 (2) 2/22 (3) 3/33 (4)   (54.2 overs) 118   1/7 (1) 2/11 (2)   (47.5 overs) 121
4/41 (5) 5/42 (6) 6/42 (1)   3/11 (3) 4/15 (4)
7/53 (7) 8/60 (9) 9/88 (8) 10/118 (10)   5/17 (5) 6/38 (7) 7/81 (8)
   8/104 (6) 9/104 (10) 10/121 (9)

Patterson 16–7–39–3; Brooks 13.2–5–26–3; Sidebottom 11–5–9–3; Plunkett 8–3–12–0; Azeem Rafiq 6–1–17–1. *Second innings*—Patterson 6–4–5–2; Plunkett 11.5–4–33–6; Azeem Rafiq 18–7–50–1; Brooks 7–1–23–0; Sidebottom 5–2–8–1.

Umpires: P. J. Hartley and P. R. Pollard.

YORKSHIRE v SUSSEX

At Leeds, April 10–13. Sussex won by an innings and 12 runs. Sussex 23pts, Yorkshire 3pts. Toss: Sussex. Championship debut: A. Z. Lees.

Yorkshire made a dreadful start to their 150th anniversary season. On their return to the first division, they were utterly outplayed, suffering their first defeat in 19 Championship matches since August 2011. After Sussex won the toss – with an 1863 penny – their seamers bowled a disciplined length, extracted movement, and rolled over their hosts for 96. Yorkshire's previous low against Sussex at Headingley had been 111 in 1893, when they went on to win the game – and eventually their first Championship. Jordan, a recruit from Surrey, returned his best figures in England, and Magoffin did the damage second time round. In between, Sussex batted with purpose, as well as awareness of the weather, which took out several chunks of play. Nash punished Brooks, signed from Northamptonshire, with five fours in seven balls, while Joyce and Brown got just short of centuries. Sidebottom, the most effective home bowler, also helped stretch the game into a fourth day by adding 81 with Ballance, who was defiant to the end.

Close of play: first day, Sussex 104-3 (Joyce 4, Hamilton-Brown 0); second day, Yorkshire 27-1 (Lyth 8, Jaques 15); third day, Yorkshire 228-8 (Ballance 46, Brooks 2).

Yorkshire

A. Lyth b Anyon	3	– c Brown b Anyon	25
A. Z. Lees c Brown b Jordan	6	– c Jordan b Magoffin	4
P. A. Jaques lbw b Magoffin	2	– c Yardy b Magoffin	57
*A. W. Gale c Brown b Jordan	2	– c Joyce b Anyon	3
†J. M. Bairstow c Brown b Anyon	29	– b Jordan	18
G. S. Ballance c Brown b Magoffin	13	– c Brown b Magoffin	63
Azeem Rafiq c Jordan b Magoffin	23	– b Magoffin	0
L. E. Plunkett c and b Jordan	5	– b Magoffin	5
R. J. Sidebottom b Jordan	2	– c Jordan b Anyon	48
J. A. Brooks b Jordan	2	– c Yardy b Jordan	5
S. A. Patterson not out	0	– not out	0
L-b 5, n-b 4	9	B 16, l-b 4	20

1/4 (1) 2/9 (3) 3/11 (4)   (46.2 overs) 96   1/4 (2) 2/60 (1)   (82.1 overs) 248
4/18 (2) 5/58 (5) 6/70 (6)   3/64 (4) 4/103 (5)
7/82 (8) 8/94 (9) 9/96 (10) 10/96 (7)   5/128 (3) 6/128 (7) 7/140 (8)
                                     8/221 (9) 9/248 (10) 10/248 (6)

Anyon 16–7–24–2; Magoffin 13.2–5–18–2; Jordan 15–3–48–6; Panesar 2–1–1–0. *Second innings*—Anyon 15–6–59–3; Magoffin 21.1–3–51–5; Jordan 16–4–42–2; Panesar 24–7–63–0; Nash 4–2–2–0; Wells 2–0–11–0.

Sussex

C. D. Nash c Bairstow b Sidebottom	80	S. J. Magoffin c Ballance b Brooks	11
L. W. P. Wells lbw b Sidebottom	2	J. E. Anyon not out	4
M. H. Yardy c Bairstow b Sidebottom	14	M. S. Panesar lbw b Sidebottom	1
*E. C. Joyce c Lyth b Brooks	92	L-b 9, n-b 4	13
R. J. Hamilton-Brown lbw b Plunkett	26		
J. S. Gatting c Brooks b Azeem Rafiq	20	1/11 (2) 2/87 (3) 3/104 (1) (80.5 overs) 356
†B. C. Brown b Brooks	93	4/155 (5) 5/198 (6) 6/318 (4)
C. J. Jordan lbw b Brooks	0	7/318 (8) 8/342 (9) 9/355 (7) 10/356 (11)

Sidebottom 21.5–6–72–4; Patterson 19–5–65–0; Brooks 13–1–76–4; Plunkett 11–2–53–1; Azeem Rafiq 15–1–70–1; Lyth 1–0–10–0.

Umpires: N. J. Llong and R. T. Robinson.

At Chester-le-Street, April 24–27. YORKSHIRE beat DURHAM by four wickets. *Yorkshire score 339 to win, their fourth-highest winning total in the fourth innings.*

YORKSHIRE v DERBYSHIRE

At Leeds, April 29–May 2. Yorkshire won by an innings and 39 runs. Yorkshire 21pts, Derbyshire 5pts. Toss: Yorkshire.

With the buds of May still to blossom, records fell like autumn leaves. Derbyshire started with 475, yet Yorkshire won by an innings in a match of 1,315 runs. Root made a faultless 236, but even that was overshadowed by an epic 270 from 22-year-old Chesney Hughes, who batted nine hours and four minutes, and hit 40 fours and three sixes. Hughes had been fighting for his place but – in constant touch by text with his mentor, fellow Anguillan Cardigan Connor – he exhibited new-found powers of concentration between full-blooded strokes of breathtaking quality. Dropped once, on 70, he advanced to the highest score by anyone carrying his bat since Bill Ashdown's 305 for Kent v

HIGHEST TOTALS FOR YORKSHIRE

887	v Warwickshire at Birmingham	1896
704	v Surrey at The Oval	1899
681-5 dec	v Sussex at Sheffield	1897
677-7 dec	v Durham at Leeds	2006
677-7 dec	**v Derbyshire at Leeds**	**2013**
673-8 dec	v Northamptonshire at Leeds	2003
662	v Derbyshire at Chesterfield	1898
660	v Leicestershire at Leicester	1896
617-5 dec	**v Derbyshire at Chesterfield**	**2013**
610-6 dec	v Durham at Leeds	2010

Derbyshire in 1935. It was the second-highest innings for Derbyshire, after George Davidson's 274 at Old Trafford in 1896, and the highest against Yorkshire on their own soil. He and Madsen added 258 for the second wicket. On a benign pitch, however, Yorkshire did even better. A stand of 231 between Root and Bairstow put them on course for 677 for seven, their joint-fourth-biggest total and the most conceded by Derbyshire. Trailing by 202 with a minimum 84 overs left, the visitors suffered a mortal blow when Chanderpaul fell to Plunkett just before lunch. Madsen and Durston resisted, until Brooks ran amok with five for 16 in 44 balls.

Close of play: first day, Derbyshire 302-4 (Hughes 171, Redfern 14); second day, Yorkshire 164-1 (Root 75, Jaques 15); third day, Yorkshire 597-5 (Ballance 50, Rashid 0).

Derbyshire

B. A. Godleman c Root b Bresnan	2	– lbw b Bresnan	9
C. F. Hughes not out	270	– c Ballance b Plunkett	15
*W. L. Madsen c Lyth b Patterson	93	– lbw b Brooks	52
S. Chanderpaul c Lyth b Rashid	4	– c Bairstow b Plunkett	4
W. J. Durston c Bresnan b Plunkett	3	– c Jaques b Brooks	50
D. J. Redfern c Lyth b Bresnan	14	– c Bairstow b Brooks	8
D. J. Wainwright b Rashid	18	– b Rashid	7
J. L. Clare lbw b Patterson	5	– not out	1
†T. Poynton b Plunkett	27	– lbw b Brooks	0
A. P. Palladino b Brooks	18	– (11) lbw b Brooks	0
T. D. Groenewald lbw b Rashid	0	– (10) b Rashid	5
B 16, l-b 5	21	B 8, l-b 4	12

1/10 (1) 2/268 (3) 3/275 (4) (142 overs) 475
4/279 (5) 5/302 (6) 6/383 (7)
7/388 (8) 8/441 (9) 9/474 (10)
10/475 (11)
110 overs: 354-5

1/12 (1) 2/43 (2) (54.4 overs) 163
3/47 (4) 4/139 (5)
5/150 (3) 6/157 (7) 7/157 (6)
8/157 (9) 9/162 (10) 10/163 (11)

Bresnan 30–5–103–2; Brooks 26–10–63–1; Plunkett 28–5–86–2; Patterson 26–6–70–2; Rashid 30–4–122–3; Root 2–0–10–0. *Second innings*—Bresnan 11–3–30–1; Brooks 14.4–5–40–5; Plunkett 7–2–20–2; Rashid 20–6–61–2; Root 2–2–0–0.

Yorkshire

A. Lyth c Redfern b Groenewald	69	L. E. Plunkett not out. 21
J. E. Root b Redfern	236	
P. A. Jaques run out.	39	B 4, l-b 8, w 4, n-b 2 18
*A. W. Gale c Groenewald b Wainwright. . .	5	—
†J. M. Bairstow c Groenewald b Durston . . .	186	1/126 (1) (7 wkts dec, 151 overs) 677
G. S. Ballance c Madsen b Clare.	53	2/218 (3) 3/246 (4)
A. U. Rashid not out	36	4/477 (2) 5/594 (5)
T. T. Bresnan c Clare b Groenewald	14	6/616 (6) 7/643 (8) 110 overs: 381-3

J. A. Brooks and S. A. Patterson did not bat.

Groenewald 34–3–142–2; Palladino 10–1–34–0; Wainwright 48–6–169–1; Durston 25–3–127–1; Clare 27–1–145–1; Redfern 7–0–48–1.

Umpires: S. C. Gale and R. A. Kettleborough.

YORKSHIRE v SOMERSET

At Leeds, May 7–10. Drawn. Yorkshire 10pts, Somerset 7pts. Toss: Yorkshire.
Rather than turning the contest into a damp squib, rain led to a firecracker of a final session in which Yorkshire almost pulled off an astonishing victory. At tea, Somerset were 243 for eight in their first innings (during which Hildreth completed 10,000 first-class runs), still trailing by 262; a further short stoppage suggested the game was dead. But Bresnan took two in two and, though another shower left only 23 overs for the follow-on, Somerset were quickly floored by the energetic Brooks, who grabbed four for 17 in 25 balls before breaking his left thumb stopping a return drive from Buttler. His replacement, Patterson, maintained the momentum with two wickets, and Somerset were 48 for six with 5.1 overs remaining. Yorkshire kept up the attack but Trescothick stayed cool, supported by Thomas. Movement and bounce on the first morning had worried the home side until Ballance and Rashid put on 207, a Yorkshire fifth-wicket record at Headingley. Rashid slowed down next day, but still managed a career-best 180.
Close of play: first day, Yorkshire 332-5 (Rashid 120, Hodd 14); second day, Somerset 92-1 (Compton 33, Leach 2); third day, Somerset 190-5 (Hildreth 31, Buttler 1).

Yorkshire

A. Lyth c Buttler b Trego	0	R. M. Pyrah b Overton 55
J. J. Sayers c Buttler b Trego.	1	J. A. Brooks not out. 33
P. A. Jaques c Trescothick b Kirby	49	B 15, l-b 10, n-b 11 36
*A. W. Gale c Buttler b Thomas	17	—
G. S. Ballance lbw b Kirby	107	1/0 (1) (9 wkts dec, 135.4 overs) 505
A. U. Rashid c Buttler b Trego	180	2/17 (2) 3/71 (4)
†A. J. Hodd c Buttler b Kirby	27	4/75 (3) 5/282 (5) 6/370 (7) 7/371 (8)
T. T. Bresnan lbw b Trego	0	8/450 (9) 9/505 (6) 110 overs: 395-7

S. A. Patterson did not bat.

Trego 33.4–8–107–4; Kirby 30–4–119–3; Thomas 26–3–81–1; Overton 19–0–89–1; Leach 22–3–76–0; Suppiah 5–1–8–0.

Somerset

*M. E. Trescothick lbw b Brooks	53	– not out	33
N. R. D. Compton lbw b Bresnan	33	– c Lyth b Brooks	0
M. J. Leach b Bresnan	8		
A. N. Petersen c Patterson b Rashid	54	– (3) c Lyth b Brooks	4
J. C. Hildreth c Rashid b Pyrah	39	– (4) b Brooks	12
A. V. Suppiah c Sayers b Rashid	0	– (5) b Brooks	0
†J. C. Buttler c Hodd b Patterson	1	– (6) c Ballance b Patterson	7
P. D. Trego c Pyrah b Patterson	10	– (7) lbw b Patterson	1
A. C. Thomas not out	26	– (8) not out	4
S. P. Kirby c Sayers b Bresnan	15		
J. Overton lbw b Bresnan	0		
B 1, l-b 10, n-b 2	13		

1/90 (1) 2/92 (2) 3/123 (3) (96 overs) 252   1/6 (2) (6 wkts, 22.3 overs) 61
4/189 (4) 5/189 (6) 6/190 (7)   2/10 (3) 3/30 (4)
7/200 (5) 8/222 (8) 9/252 (10) 10/252 (11)   4/32 (5) 5/46 (6) 6/48 (7)

Bresnan 29–8–76–4; Brooks 20–6–51–1; Pyrah 17–5–48–1; Patterson 22–5–46–2; Rashid 8–2–20–2. *Second innings*—Bresnan 11–2–32–0; Brooks 5.3–2–22–4; Patterson 4.3–3–4–2; Rashid 1.3–0–3–0.

Umpires: M. J. D. Bodenham and G. Sharp.

At Birmingham, May 15–17. YORKSHIRE beat WARWICKSHIRE by an innings and 139 runs.

At Taunton, May 28–31. YORKSHIRE drew with SOMERSET. *Adil Rashid scores his third century in successive innings.*

YORKSHIRE v NOTTINGHAMSHIRE

At Scarborough, June 5–8. Drawn. Yorkshire 8pts, Nottinghamshire 6pts. Toss: Yorkshire.
Gale had scored only 219 in 11 first-class innings before finding form with a vengeance here. He reached his first century for two years with a six, pushed on to a maiden double, did not give a chance until 250, when his former team-mate Shahzad helped a high catch over the rope at long-on, and finished on 272 – a record for a county game at Scarborough, and at the time the 13th-highest innings in Yorkshire's history and third-largest since the Second World War. Gale finally skied Patel to Read, who had to run to point, after batting 535 minutes, facing 404 balls and hitting 25 fours and four sixes. Despite a virus, Ballance, with a career-best 141, helped him add 297, a county record for any wicket against Nottinghamshire and their third-highest for the fifth against any side. A total of 572 was Yorkshire's biggest against Nottinghamshire. On the opening day, drizzle had prevented a start until 1.10, but Lumb displayed admirable fluency, patience and sumptuous strokes against his old side – in sharp contrast to the struggling Taylor, who spent 148 deliveries over 38 and did not find the boundary until the 110th.
Close of play: first day, Nottinghamshire 177-2 (Lumb 116, Taylor 12); second day, Yorkshire 29-3 (Jaques 19, Gale 0); third day, Yorkshire 358-4 (Gale 159, Ballance 103).

Nottinghamshire

A. D. Hales c Hodd b Sidebottom	0	– lbw b Patterson 5
E. J. M. Cowan c Ballance b Patterson	47	– not out 53
M. J. Lumb c Lyth b Patterson	135	– not out 47
J. W. A. Taylor lbw b Patterson	38	
S. R. Patel c Lyth b Ashraf	17	
S. J. Mullaney c Lees b Rashid	79	
*†C. M. W. Read c Hodd b Sidebottom	14	
P. J. Franks c Ballance b Rashid	70	
A. Shahzad c Sidebottom b Lyth	12	
L. J. Fletcher not out	25	
H. F. Gurney c and b Rashid	0	
B 1, l-b 3, n-b 2	6	

1/0 (1) 2/101 (2) 3/210 (3)   (152.5 overs) 443   1/6 (1)   (1 wkt, 24 overs) 105
4/242 (5) 5/242 (4) 6/275 (7) 7/362 (6)
8/409 (8) 9/437 (9) 10/443 (11)   110 overs: 262-5

Sidebottom 28–4–89–2; Patterson 37–12–74–3; Pyrah 29–8–92–0; Ashraf 23–10–59–1; Rashid 29.5–2–98–3; Lyth 6–0–27–1. *Second innings*—Sidebottom 6–1–19–0; Patterson 9–2–42–1; Rashid 6–0–17–0; Lyth 2–0–13–0; Lees 1–0–14–0.

Yorkshire

A. Lyth c Patel b Gurney	7	R. M. Pyrah not out	14
A. Z. Lees lbw b Fletcher	2		
P. A. Jaques c Taylor b Patel	51	B 8, l-b 24, n-b 12	44
S. A. Patterson c Read b Fletcher	1		
*A. W. Gale c Read b Patel	272	1/7 (1) (8 wkts dec, 155.1 overs)	572
G. S. Ballance c Read b Franks	141	2/17 (2) 3/27 (4)	
A. U. Rashid c Cowan b Fletcher	0	4/121 (3) 5/418 (6) 6/431 (7)	
†A. J. Hodd c Gurney b Patel	40	7/552 (5) 8/572 (8) 110 overs: 361-4	

R. J. Sidebottom and M. A. Ashraf did not bat.

Fletcher 34–9–85–3; Gurney 22–3–93–1; Franks 19–2–77–1; Shahzad 24–3–95–0; Patel 38.1–7–143–3; Mullaney 18–4–47–0.

Umpires: N. G. C. Cowley and J. W. Lloyds.

At Lord's, June 11–14. YORKSHIRE beat MIDDLESEX by ten wickets.

YORKSHIRE v SURREY

At Leeds, June 21–24. Drawn. Yorkshire 8pts, Surrey 9pts. Toss: Surrey. First-class debut: J. A. Leaning.

Pietersen stole the show in his first game after three months nursing a bruised knee. He demonstrated his readiness for the Ashes with a brilliant 177 that brought the Championship leaders up against a brick wall, and held sway for four hours, facing 188 balls and hitting 17 fours and seven sixes with perfect timing; Rashid bore the brunt of the assault. Pietersen could have been run out first ball, or caught behind off his next. A stinging low return to Rashid was technically a third chance and, after reaching his century in 106 deliveries, he was dropped on 120 before substitute James Wainman almost held a running catch. Pietersen replied by smacking Sidebottom for two sixes and a four. He had arrived at 62 for three, with Surrey 222 away from avoiding the follow-on; his onslaught allowed Solanki to press Yorkshire by declaring 80 behind. Earlier, Gale had emulated Rashid with a third century in successive innings. He added 204 with Ballance, who then left for England's Twenty20 squad. His replacement, Jack Leaning, began his career with a duck, one of seven victims for Keedy. Alec Stewart took charge of Surrey, still winless, after the sacking of team director Chris Adams and first-team coach Ian Salisbury, but Ponting dropped out with a sore hand. Patterson could not bowl after breaking his big toe while batting, which was one reason for Yorkshire's failure to set a target; Pietersen was the other.

Close of play: first day, Yorkshire 292-5 (Gale 114, Hodd 5); second day, Surrey 53-1 (Burns 15, Linley 0); third day, Yorkshire 52-1 (Lyth 19, Sayers 5).

Yorkshire

A. Lyth c Solanki b Tremlett	41	– b Keedy 32
A. Z. Lees lbw b de Bruyn	15	– lbw b Keedy 13
J. J. Sayers c de Bruyn b Linley	5	– c Keedy b Tremlett. 24
*A. W. Gale b Keedy	148	– c Harinath b Keedy 0
G. S. Ballance lbw b Lewis	90	
A. U. Rashid c Solanki b Lewis	1	– b Keedy 45
†A. J. Hodd c Burns b Linley	9	– lbw b Linley 16
L. E. Plunkett c Davies b Lewis	51	– st Davies b Keedy 68
R. J. Sidebottom c Pietersen b Linley	26	– c de Bruyn b Keedy 4
S. A. Patterson not out	11	– c and b Linley 7
J. A. Brooks (did not bat)		– not out 1
J. A. Leaning (did not bat)		– (5) c de Bruyn b Keedy 0
B 10, l-b 9, w 1, n-b 16	36	B 4, l-b 3, w 1, n-b 36 44

1/62 (1) 2/64 (2)   (9 wkts dec, 135.5 overs) 433   1/42 (2) 2/76 (1)   (93.1 overs) 254
3/77 (3) 4/281 (5)   3/86 (4) 4/86 (5)
5/283 (6) 6/304 (7) 7/385 (4)   5/114 (3) 6/160 (6) 7/182 (7)
8/391 (8) 9/433 (9)   110 overs: 326-6   8/209 (9) 9/248 (10) 10/254 (8)

Leaning replaced Ballance who left to join England's Twenty20 squad.

Tremlett 28–5–79–1; Lewis 30–6–80–3; Linley 31.5–5–108–3; de Bruyn 18–4–56–1; Keedy 22–1–73–1; Pietersen 4–1–13–0; Solanki 2–0–5–0. *Second innings*—Tremlett 20–3–48–1; Linley 18–3–55–2; Keedy 39.1–8–99–7; Lewis 12–3–34–0; de Bruyn 3–0–6–0; Solanki 1–0–5–0.

Surrey

R. J. Burns lbw b Sidebottom	29	– not out 0
A. Harinath c Hodd b Brooks	36	– not out 4
T. E. Linley c Lyth b Sidebottom	0	
*V. S. Solanki c Gale b Brooks	4	
K. P. Pietersen not out	177	
Z. de Bruyn c sub (J. C. Wainman) b Brooks	38	
†S. M. Davies c Brooks b Plunkett	44	
G. C. Wilson c Plunkett b Lyth	12	
J. Lewis not out	2	
B 6, l-b 3, n-b 2	11	

1/51 (2) 2/53 (3)   (7 wkts dec, 82.5 overs) 353   (no wkt, 2 overs) 4
3/62 (4) 4/76 (1)
5/173 (6) 6/291 (7) 7/329 (8)

C. T. Tremlett and G. Keedy did not bat.

Sidebottom 21.5–6–84–2; Brooks 18–1–64–3; Plunkett 19–2–64–1; Rashid 19–1–114–0; Leaning 3–0–18–0; Lyth 2–2–0–1. *Second innings*—Lyth 1–1–0–0; Leaning 1–0–4–0.

Umpires: N. A. Mallender and S. J. O'Shaughnessy.

At Chesterfield, July 17–19. YORKSHIRE beat DERBYSHIRE by an innings and 113 runs. *Alex Lees scores 275 not out.*

YORKSHIRE v WARWICKSHIRE

At Leeds, August 2–5. Drawn. Yorkshire 9pts, Warwickshire 9pts. Toss: Warwickshire.

Notices warned spectators in the grandstand: "Beware – bees active in this area." Yet it was the Yorkshire players who risked being stung until rain severely curtailed the final day, helping to extend their lead at the top of the table to ten points. They were still 81 ahead on the second evening, but that was quickly erased when Barker and Patel stretched their ninth-wicket stand to 99, clearly rattling the home side. The century was averted when Barker was run out going for a second; Patel, dropped twice, was last out. Woakes dismissed both openers by lunch on the third day, and he grabbed two more before bad light ended play. When the weather allowed a 2.40 start on the fourth, Woakes completed his only five-wicket haul of the season, with Yorkshire finished off in another 13 overs. Warwickshire needed 174 off 36, but only 12 balls were possible. Earlier, Ballance's century, his seventh score of 50-plus in nine innings, gave his team backbone; Evans was equally solid for Warwickshire. Brooks and Plunkett were capped before the game.

Close of play: first day, Yorkshire 294-9 (Patterson 19, Brooks 12); second day, Warwickshire 221-8 (Barker 12, Patel 16); third day, Yorkshire 148-7 (Hodd 6, Sidebottom 0).

Yorkshire

A. Lyth c Clarke b Woakes	11	– lbw b Woakes	15
A. Z. Lees c Chopra b Woakes	56	– c Patel b Woakes	2
*A. W. Gale c Ambrose b Barker	0	– c Porterfield b Rankin	34
G. S. Ballance lbw b Barker	112	– b Woakes	45
A. U. Rashid c Ambrose b Rankin	7	– c Evans b Rankin	0
Azeem Rafiq c Patel b Clarke	28	– c Westwood b Patel	4
†A. J. Hodd b Clarke	21	– not out	14
L. E. Plunkett lbw b Barker	11	– c Ambrose b Woakes	23
R. J. Sidebottom c Ambrose b Woakes	4	– b Woakes	9
S. A. Patterson not out	21	– c Westwood b Rankin	10
J. A. Brooks c Ambrose b Rankin	18	– c Barker b Rankin	0
B 4, l-b 8, w 1	13	B 10, l-b 10, n-b 4	24

1/25 (1) 2/26 (3) 3/100 (2)   (98.4 overs) 302
4/123 (5) 5/173 (6) 6/233 (7)
7/250 (8) 8/257 (4) 9/267 (9) 10/302 (11)

1/14 (2) 2/19 (1)   (71 overs) 180
3/95 (3) 4/95 (5)
5/104 (6) 6/121 (4) 7/148 (8)
8/157 (9) 9/180 (10) 10/180 (11)

Barker 20.5–3–61–3; Woakes 24–0–63–3; Rankin 20.5–1–70–2; Clarke 18–6–51–2; Patel 15–4–45–0. *Second innings*—Barker 14–4–34–0; Woakes 15–4–42–5; Rankin 15–4–29–4; Clarke 5–1–25–0; Patel 21–7–27–1; Javid 1–0–3–0.

Warwickshire

*V. Chopra lbw b Patterson	23	– not out	2
I. J. Westwood lbw b Sidebottom	7	– not out	0
W. T. S. Porterfield c Hodd b Plunkett	9		
L. J. Evans c Lyth b Plunkett	88		
†T. R. Ambrose c Lyth b Patterson	0		
C. R. Woakes c Rashid b Plunkett	21		
R. Clarke lbw b Rashid	24		
A. Javid c Hodd b Plunkett	17		
K. H. D. Barker run out	49		
J. S. Patel c Hodd b Sidebottom	63		
W. B. Rankin not out	3		
L-b 5	5	B 1	1

1/13 (2) 2/36 (3) 3/50 (1)   (110 overs) 309
4/50 (5) 5/95 (6) 6/150 (7) 7/182 (4)
8/196 (8) 9/295 (9) 10/309 (10)

(no wkt, 2 overs) 3

Sidebottom 24–6–66–2; Brooks 13–4–46–0; Plunkett 24–7–74–4; Patterson 24–9–50–2; Azeem Rafiq 1–0–4–0; Rashid 24–3–64–1. *Second innings*—Sidebottom 1–0–2–0; Brooks 1–1–0–0.

Umpires: N. L. Bainton and M. R. Benson.

At Leeds, August 9. YORKSHIRE beat BANGLADESH A by seven runs (see Bangladesh A tour section).

At Nottingham, August 21–23. YORKSHIRE beat NOTTINGHAMSHIRE by ten wickets.

YORKSHIRE v DURHAM

At Scarborough, August 28–31. Durham won by seven wickets. Durham 24pts, Yorkshire 4pts. Toss: Durham.

An epic encounter, rain-free and watched by an aggregate crowd of 18,500, deservedly went Durham's way. Had Yorkshire won, their Championship lead would have been practically unassailable, but maximum points left Durham only five and a half behind with a game in hand. Although the toss was vital, the visitors showed greater resolve, despite missing the injured Onions and – in the second innings – Wood, who had strained his side. Durham's 573 was their highest total against Yorkshire, with hundreds for Stoneman (Sidebottom's 600th first-class wicket), Stokes and a first one for Richardson. Had Collingwood scored 19 more, Yorkshire would have conceded four in an innings for the first time. Stokes looked outstanding, following his 127 with aggressive bowling that brought wickets when it really mattered, and never more so than early on the final morning, when he removed Williamson and Jaques in three deliveries. They had rallied Yorkshire's follow-on by adding 264; only Willie Watson and Vic Wilson, with 302 against Derbyshire in 1948, had shared more for the county's second wicket at North Marine Road. Borthwick wound up the innings, leaving Durham to chase 121 in 37 overs, then his fifty snuffed out any thought of a home win, briefly raised when Sidebottom accounted for Stoneman first ball.

Close of play: first day, Durham 406-6 (Collingwood 74, Richardson 3); second day, Yorkshire 182-3 (Williamson 76, Bairstow 42); third day, Yorkshire 276-1 (Jaques 151, Williamson 90).

Durham

M. D. Stoneman c Bairstow b Sidebottom	122	– c Williamson b Sidebottom	0
K. K. Jennings lbw b Sidebottom	0	– c Jaques b Rashid	17
S. G. Borthwick lbw b Sidebottom	0	– b Rashid	65
W. R. Smith c Williamson b Brooks	20	– not out	27
B. A. Stokes c Bairstow b Rashid	127	– not out	11
*P. D. Collingwood lbw b Sidebottom	81		
†P. Mustard lbw b Williamson	42		
M. J. Richardson c Ballance b Williamson	102		
M. A. Wood c Brooks b Plunkett	20		
J. Harrison run out	35		
C. Rushworth not out	1		
B 4, l-b 15, n-b 4	23	L-b 1, w 1, n-b 2	4

1/5 (2)   2/5 (3)   3/67 (4)   4/195 (1)   (138 overs) 573   1/0 (1)   (3 wkts, 27.4 overs) 124
5/315 (5)   6/403 (7)   7/414 (6)   2/72 (2) 3/103 (3)
8/463 (8)   9/547 (10)   10/573 (8)   110 overs: 454-7

Sidebottom 24–4–85–4; Brooks 27–3–111–1; Patterson 30–8–82–0; Plunkett 17–1–89–1; Williamson 15–2–67–2; Rashid 25–3–120–1. *Second innings*—Sidebottom 8–0–31–1; Brooks 2–1–13–0; Patterson 8–2–19–0; Rashid 7–0–47–2; Williamson 2.4–1–13–0.

Yorkshire

A. Lyth c Stokes b Rushworth	10	– lbw b Rushworth	10
P. A. Jaques c Smith b Borthwick	36	– c Mustard b Stokes	152
K. S. Williamson lbw b Stokes	84	– c Smith b Stokes	97
*A. W. Gale lbw b Harrison	12	– c Richardson b Harrison	5
†J. M. Bairstow c and b Borthwick	82	– c Richardson b Rushworth	34
G. S. Ballance run out	1	– c Mustard b Stokes	26
A. U. Rashid c Mustard b Harrison	1	– c Jennings b Rushworth	1
L. E. Plunkett b Wood	10	– c Stokes b Borthwick	42
R. J. Sidebottom c Mustard b Stokes	5	– c Mustard b Borthwick	9
S. A. Patterson b Wood	0	– not out	4
J. A. Brooks not out	14	– c Collingwood b Borthwick	0
L-b 13, n-b 6	19	B 9, l-b 19, w 1, n-b 10	39
	274		**419**

1/18 (1) 2/72 (2) 3/107 (4) (83 overs) 274
4/211 (3) 5/212 (6) 6/219 (7)
7/253 (5) 8/257 (8) 9/257 (10) 10/274 (9)

1/19 (1) 2/283 (3) (123.2 overs) 419
3/284 (2) 4/313 (4)
5/349 (5) 6/351 (7) 7/357 (6)
8/410 (9) 9/419 (8) 10/419 (11)

Rushworth 14–1–52–1; Harrison 19–6–66–2; Stokes 14–3–32–2; Wood 17–3–54–2; Borthwick 19–4–57–2. *Second innings*—Harrison 18–2–59–1; Rushworth 24–7–72–3; Stokes 33–5–108–3; Borthwick 38.2–7–134–3; Smith 7–2–17–0; Collingwood 3–2–1–0.

Umpires: M. J. D. Bodenham and R. A. Kettleborough.

At Hove, September 11–14. YORKSHIRE drew with SUSSEX.

YORKSHIRE v MIDDLESEX

At Leeds, September 17–20. Yorkshire won by 80 runs. Yorkshire 20pts, Middlesex 3pts. Toss: Middlesex. First-class debut: T. G. Helm.

News from Chester-le-Street ended Yorkshire's title hopes, but neither that nor poor weather deflected them from the job in hand: their seventh win, over close challengers Middlesex, secured second place. Both sides exploited a seamer-friendly pitch with late movement, but the home bowlers had the edge. It was the first time all 40 wickets had fallen in Yorkshire's last 36 Championship matches, since the Roses game at Headingley in July 2011. Williamson's four-and-a-half-hour 52, after they were put in, inched them towards 210, a more challenging total than it appeared. Simpson and Bairstow each held six first-innings catches, one short of their respective county records (Simpson's haul had been bettered only by Fred Price, also against Yorkshire, at Lord's in 1937; Bairstow's by his father David, against Derbyshire at Scarborough in 1982). A fluent 90 from Ballance, witnessed by selector James Whitaker, helped him into the Ashes party three days later; Gale became the first Yorkshire batsman to 1,000 Championship runs in 2013, before being trapped by 19-year-old seamer Tom Helm. Middlesex were never quite out of the reckoning until Rogers was removed.

Close of play: first day, Yorkshire 109-3 (Williamson 34, Bairstow 1); second day, Yorkshire 4-0 (Lyth 0, Jaques 3); third day, Yorkshire 130-5 (Ballance 53, Rashid 0).

Yorkshire

A. Lyth lbw b Collymore	0	– lbw b Collymore	0
P. A. Jaques c Simpson b Murtagh	1	– c Malan b Murtagh	21
K. S. Williamson c Simpson b Helm	52	– b Murtagh	2
*A. W. Gale c Simpson b Collymore	66	– lbw b Helm	40
†J. M. Bairstow c Malan b Murtagh	5	– b Collymore	3
G. S. Ballance c Simpson b Berg	12	– c Malan b Helm	90
A. U. Rashid c Simpson b Helm	19	– c Malan b Murtagh	21
L. E. Plunkett c Rayner b Berg	18	– c Dexter b Helm	1
R. J. Sidebottom c Rayner b Murtagh	1	– c Rayner b Berg	0
S. A. Patterson c Simpson b Collymore	16	– not out	1
J. A. Brooks not out	4	– c Robson b Berg	0
B 4, l-b 8, n-b 4	16	L-b 12, w 1, n-b 2	15

1/1 (1) 2/1 (2) 3/98 (4) (79.5 overs) 210
4/117 (5) 5/142 (6) 6/166 (7)
7/187 (3) 8/189 (8) 9/204 (9) 10/210 (10)

1/4 (1) 2/7 (3) (53.2 overs) 194
3/40 (2) 4/50 (5)
5/129 (4) 6/166 (7) 7/178 (8)
8/179 (9) 9/193 (6) 10/194 (11)

Murtagh 28–9–49–3; Collymore 22.5–8–38–3; Berg 12–2–44–2; Helm 9–0–32–2; Dexter 8–2–35–0. *Second innings*—Murtagh 18–3–74–3; Berg 8.2–0–27–2; Collymore 13–4–25–2; Helm 9–0–46–3; Rayner 5–0–10–0.

Middlesex

*C. J. L. Rogers c Rashid b Patterson	8	– (2) c Bairstow b Plunkett	65
S. D. Robson c Bairstow b Brooks	45	– (1) c Lyth b Patterson	3
J. L. Denly c Lyth b Patterson	2	– b Sidebottom	12
D. J. Malan c Bairstow b Patterson	1	– lbw b Plunkett	31
N. J. Dexter c Bairstow b Sidebottom	12	– c Williamson b Brooks	8
†J. A. Simpson lbw b Brooks	14	– c Lyth b Patterson	9
G. K. Berg c Bairstow b Sidebottom	8	– c Bairstow b Patterson	6
O. P. Rayner c Brooks b Sidebottom	14	– c Patterson b Brooks	25
T. G. Helm c Bairstow b Brooks	4	– lbw b Brooks	18
T. J. Murtagh c Bairstow b Sidebottom	0	– c Ballance b Brooks	0
C. D. Collymore not out	0	– not out	0
B 1, l-b 1, n-b 4	6	L-b 8, w 1, n-b 10	19

1/9 (1) 2/21 (3) 3/45 (4) (41 overs) 128
4/86 (2) 5/92 (5) 6/106 (7)
7/110 (6) 8/114 (9) 9/115 (10) 10/128 (8)

1/9 (1) 2/34 (3) (49.5 overs) 196
3/90 (4) 4/103 (5)
5/134 (2) 6/138 (6) 7/149 (7)
8/185 (9) 9/185 (10) 10/196 (8)

Sidebottom 16–7–27–4; Patterson 12–4–44–3; Plunkett 5–0–21–0; Brooks 8–0–34–3. *Second innings*—Sidebottom 12–1–49–1; Patterson 15–4–50–3; Plunkett 13–1–55–2; Brooks 7.5–0–33–4; Williamson 2–1–1–0.

Umpires: N. J. Llong and M. J. Saggers.

At The Oval, September 24–27. YORKSHIRE drew with SURREY.

FRIENDS LIFE t20, 2013

Review by Neville Scott

In the myriad obituaries of Margaret Thatcher last April it proved all but mandatory to deploy the epitaph "divisive". When it comes to cricket, at least, nothing since the Packer circus has split sentiment so profoundly as Twenty20. As with Thatcher, the issue, dare one say it, almost embraces philosophy. It is hard to speak of Twenty20 without invoking the F-word – is it Frankenstein cricket, a monster begat of marketing men and set to devour the whole game, or the saviour for a new age?

Of the British print journalists who cover a lot of Twenty20, most would plaintively repeat Christopher Martin-Jenkins's uneasy query: "It's more or less rubbish, isn't it?" When a mascot race, breathlessly described by the BBC Radio commentary team, takes centre stage at finals day, many will despair at grown adults succumbing to an infantile disorder. But it was genuinely engrossing to watch a Northamptonshire side under the guidance of coach David Ripley shed their inhibitions to grasp a major trophy for the first time in 21 years. Ripley has always been among the more astute and decent men in the game. Facing pressure, always a fascinating process, his charges revelled.

The defining essence of so-called proper cricket is time. It is through time that the game's wider virtues emerge: stoicism and audacity; analysing when to resist, when to attack; seizing the decisive shifts in a long narrative. In Twenty20, stoicism is a thoughtcrime. Space, not time, dictates the outcome, specifically the batsman's ability to hit – or mishit – into vacant areas that, under the imposed restraints of the form, will be empty of fielders.

Twenty20 is often likened to baseball. At heart, the analogy is false. For in baseball, a far more subtle game, the action – as in real cricket – is initiated, and usually determined, by the bowler (or pitcher), who must dismiss three batters for the match even to proceed. In Twenty20, however, wickets do not necessarily need to fall. Nor, with rare exceptions, do bowlers positively seek them. Rather, they pursue control. And since batsmen, who dictate the real action, have little choice but to attack, wickets may well fall through error.

In 2013, the top five run-scorers up to finals day were all openers, and five of the top dozen were left-handers. Six of the 15 highest wicket-takers were left-arm seamers, followed in the list by three left-arm spinners. There is a crude geometry to Twenty20 and it is one that makes left-handedness a godsend. Since the majority of bowlers are right-handers who come over the wicket, and only two fielders are permitted outside the circle in the first six powerplay overs, the left-handed opener can hit into space on both sides with less risk, because of the angles involved. For his part, the good left-arm bowler has an angle of attack that restricts right-handers to playing to off or hitting across the line. There *are* middle-order right-handers who revive innings after top-order failure: Jim Allenby and Darren Maddy often succeeded, while Ryan ten Doeschate effectively won the quarter-final for Essex. But even the crucial middle-order role played by Ben Stokes in Durham's late surge to the last eight

David slays Goliath: Northamptonshire's uncompromising left-hander David Willey swings hard at Surrey, then wraps up his county's first major title in 21 years with a hat-trick.

left one wondering whether, as a left-hander, he might have been more effective in the top three.

For all the claims made for its excitement, there is a predictability to Twenty20. Ignoring rain-affected matches, first-innings totals produced the following results in 2013:

a) scores of 136 and below: P21 W0 L21.

b) 137–154: P26 W7 L17 T2.

c) 163 and above: P35 W26 L9.

Only in the narrow first-innings range of 155–162 (P9 W4 L5) was a tight game all but assured. For the rest, just as in the first season in 2003, tension was far less likely. If, at the halfway stage, you had bet that all first-innings scores below 155 would bring defeat, and all 163 and above victory, you would have successfully predicted the outcome of around three-quarters of matches.

But the most revealing statistic concerns relative positions at the fall of the second wicket in the group stage. While the first-wicket score has a less marked bearing, the side which had scored more runs by the fall of the second went on to win exactly 3.5 matches for every one lost. The formula held less well for the quarter-finals onwards, when better-resourced teams showed the belief to fight back, but it indicated the extent to which runs in the powerplay overs decided games. If caution followed a second dismissal, loss of momentum in those six overs largely cost the match.

MOST SIXES IN ENGLISH TWENTY20

6	M		6	M	
101	113	D. I. Stevens (*Leics, Kent*)	75	62	S. B. Styris (*Mx, Dham, Ex, Sx*)
87	78	O. A. Shah (*Middx, Essex*)	71	109	Azhar Mahmood (*Surrey, Kent*)
81	92	M. J. Lumb (*Yorks, Hants, Notts*)	71	70	D. J. Hussey (*Notts*)
79	69	M. E. Trescothick (*Somerset*)	67	91	R. N. ten Doeschate (*Essex*)
75	91	D. L. Maddy (*Leics, Warwicks*)	66	79	A. D. Brown (*Surrey, Notts*)

The pattern was hard to ignore. Batsmen hit out in the all-important powerplay against seamers bowling as many variations of pace as possible to a good or very full length; then spinners, taking speed off the ball, took over. Even net bowlers, almost delivering from a standing start, can profit. The endangered spinner has found salvation from a curious mix of Twenty20 and, at Test level, the Decision Review System. Young, even unknown, spinners prosper, and in the competition's first seasons their success misled good observers to predict first-class potential that never materialised.

After a third of the divisional games, the quarter-final chances of most sides already seemed clear. The two real surprises were Glamorgan, sometimes playing six men raised abroad, and Durham. But of their last six games, Glamorgan lost five and Durham won five. In the Midlands/Wales/West group, Somerset advanced at the expense of Warwickshire, who needed 14 from the final over but could manage only three singles off Yasir Arafat. Maddy, unbeaten at the crease but on the losing side, finished his illustrious Twenty20 career in second place among all-time domestic run-scorers, behind his former Leicestershire team-mate Darren Stevens. Arafat, at season's end, was the highest wicket-taker, ahead of Surrey's Azhar Mahmood, surely the outstanding player in English Twenty20. In 11 seasons of the format, the two most successful batsmen thus came from Leicester, and the two most successful bowlers from Rawalpindi.

Northamptonshire's run to first place in their group was sparked by another itinerant Punjabi – Azharullah, plucked from the Bradford League aged 29. Like Arafat, he pitter-pattered in, targeting the base of the stumps with reverse swing, a formula which delivered bagfuls of wickets against unsuspecting opponents in the group stage; on finals day, however, he struggled to hit yorker length, and was easy prey.

In the quarter-finals, Surrey beat Somerset on a low-scoring pitch at The Oval, while Northamptonshire and Essex brushed past Durham and Nottinghamshire, whose defeat was their fourth consecutive home quarter-final, of which they had lost three. Lancashire, already involved in the tournament's only two ties, lost by one run to Hampshire.

It was clear, however, almost from Mahmood's first over in the semi-final – a maiden to Michael Carberry – that Hampshire were not going to win. Appearing at their fourth successive finals day, they excelled at the pub-quiz level of Twenty20, but seemed to find four-day scholarship beyond them. Hampshire had twice beaten Surrey in the group stages, yet did not score a run off them until the tenth ball. They froze, and never overcame Mahmood's figures of 4–1–9–2.

MOST ECONOMICAL BOWLING ON TWENTY20 FINALS DAY

ER				
1.75	R. J. Sidebottom	4–0–7–0	Nottinghamshire v Surrey (semi-final) at Nottingham	2006
2.00	D. Mongia	3–0–6–2	Lancashire v Surrey (SF) at Birmingham	2004
2.25	**Azhar Mahmood**	**4–1–9–2**	**Surrey v Hampshire (SF) at Birmingham**	**2013**
2.50	**L. M. Daggett**	**2–0–5–1**	**Northamptonshire v Surrey (F) at Birmingham** . .	**2013**
2.75	J. Ormond	4–0–11–4	Surrey v Warwickshire (F) at Nottingham	2003
2.75	A. D. Mascarenhas	4–0–11–2	Hampshire v Somerset (SF) at Cardiff	2012
2.75	A. M. Smith	4–0–11–0	Gloucestershire v Surrey (SF) at Nottingham.	2003
2.75	C. W. Henderson	4–0–11–0	Leicestershire v Somerset (F) at Birmingham	2011
3.25	D. I. Stevens	4–0–13–1	Kent v Sussex (SF) at Birmingham	2007
3.50	M. Kartik	4–0–14–0	Somerset v Hampshire (SF) at Birmingham.	2011
3.60	**D. J. Willey**	**2.3–0–9–4**	**Northamptonshire v Surrey (F) at Birmingham** . .	**2013**
3.75	S. D. Parry	4–1–15–1	Lancashire v Leicestershire (SF) at Birmingham	2011

Minimum: 12 balls.

Once the same bowler was assaulted in the final by Northamptonshire, who had strolled past mercurial Essex in the first semi, the trophy was never really in doubt. Northamptonshire had won only three games and lost 18 in the previous two seasons, lacking top-order power, but they solved that with the overseas signings of Richard Levi and Cameron White. In the final, they unleashed their Three Ws: David Willey, whose 19-ball fifty was the fastest of the summer, captain Alex Wakely and the astute White, to soar to 194 for two. It was the highest score on a finals day – though made from just 18 overs, in one of only five rain-reduced games all campaign – and unassailable long before Willey ended things with a hat-trick.

Surrey captain Gareth Batty was banned from playing on the day, after an ECB disciplinary commission deemed his conduct "appalling" in the quarter-final, when he clashed with Somerset's Peter Trego. Jade Dernbach, having had his variations exposed at international level (though Surrey had never met Northamptonshire in Twenty20 before) was savaged by Willey, who with a glorious disregard for ECB-speak gave the quote of the day after his innings: "I don't particularly like the bloke, to be honest."

In Twenty20 across the world there was much to dislike, even fear. Corruption in the Indian and Bangladesh Premier Leagues left the whiff not of sport but of empty spectacle, like American wrestling. In this competition, the ECB confirmed their anti-corruption officers had ejected "runners" from a dozen different county grounds – suspected of relaying the score back to gambling dens in India, so as to fix the odds ahead of the satellite picture. Meanwhile, in baseball, Alex Rodriguez, a master batter and the game's highest-paid star, was banned for taking performance-enhancing drugs. Twenty20 involves a reliance on power hitters never before seen in cricket; the incentive for steroid abuse, long a problem with baseball sluggers, is plain. Neither evil has yet ruined our game. But Frankenstein certainly lurks.

Prize money (unchanged from 2012)

£200,000 for winners: NORTHAMPTONSHIRE.
£84,000 for runners-up: SURREY.
£27,000 for losing semi-finalists: ESSEX, HAMPSHIRE.

£5,000 for losing quarter-finalists: DURHAM, LANCASHIRE, NOTTINGHAMSHIRE, SOMERSET.

Match-award winners received £2,000 in the final, £1,000 in the semi-finals, £500 in the quarter-finals and £250 in the group games.

FINAL GROUP TABLES

Midlands/Wales/West Group

	Played	Won	Lost	Tied	No result	Points	NRR
NORTHAMPTONSHIRE	10	7	3	0	0	14	0.329
SOMERSET	10	6	4	0	0	12	0.841
Glamorgan	10	5	5	0	0	10	-0.168
Warwickshire	10	5	5	0	0	10	-0.410
Worcestershire	10	4	6	0	0	8	-0.327
Gloucestershire	10	3	7	0	0	6	-0.245

North Group

	Played	Won	Lost	Tied	No result	Points	NRR
NOTTINGHAMSHIRE	10	7	3	0	0	14	1.009
LANCASHIRE	10	5	3	2	0	12	0.177
DURHAM	10	6	4	0	0	11.75†	0.317
Leicestershire	10	4	5	1	0	9	0.417
Derbyshire	10	4	6	0	0	8	-0.604
Yorkshire	10	2	7	1	0	5	-1.223

South Group

	Played	Won	Lost	Tied	No result	Points	NRR
HAMPSHIRE	10	8	1	0	1	17	0.810
SURREY	10	7	3	0	0	14	0.915
ESSEX	10	5	4	0	1	11	-0.040
Middlesex	10	5	5	0	0	10	-0.194
Kent	10	3	7	0	0	6	-0.941
Sussex	10	1	9	0	0	2	-0.520

† *Durham's total includes a 0.25-point penalty for breaching salary cap restrictions in 2012.*

Where counties finished with an equal number of points, the positions were decided by (a) net run-rate, (b) most points in head-to-head matches, and (c) drawing lots.

FRIENDS LIFE t20 AVERAGES

BATTING (250 runs, average 30.00)

		M	I	NO	R	HS	100	50	Avge	SR	4	6
1	N. D. McKenzie (*Hants*)	10	8	5	301	71*	0	1	100.33	129.18	33	2
2	C. Kieswetter (*Somerset*)	11	11	3	517	89*	0	5	64.62	137.13	46	19
3	†M. A. Carberry (*Hants*)	12	11	2	502	100*	1	4	55.77	142.61	59	16
4	M. Klinger (*Glos*)	10	10	3	366	108*	1	2	52.28	129.32	33	11
5	O. A. Shah (*Essex*)	9	8	2	311	68	0	2	51.83	118.25	21	16
6	J. Allenby (*Glam*)	9	9	2	355	85*	0	3	50.71	134.98	41	9
7	†B. A. Stokes (*Durham*)	11	11	4	328	72*	0	2	46.85	153.27	15	22
8	C. L. White (*Northants*)	13	13	4	417	71*	0	4	46.33	125.60	29	18
9	G. J. Muchall (*Durham*)	11	11	5	274	66*	0	1	45.66	137.00	23	5
10	†S. M. Katich (*Lancs*)	10	9	3	265	62*	0	1	44.16	140.21	27	6
11	D. J. Hussey (*Notts*)	11	11	4	298	61	0	3	42.57	143.96	24	7
12	D. L. Maddy (*Warwicks*)	10	10	4	296	84*	0	2	42.28	129.25	25	8
13	R. N. ten Doeschate (*Essex*)	12	10	3	288	82	0	2	41.14	150.00	14	14
14	G. P. Smith (*Leics*)	8	8	1	279	84	0	2	39.85	130.98	35	4
15	†D. J. Malan (*Middx*)	10	10	1	351	86	0	3	39.00	118.98	42	6
16	D. I. Stevens (*Kent*)	10	9	2	267	67*	0	1	38.14	160.84	20	15

		M	I	NO	R	HS	100	50	Avge	SR	4	6
17	J. L. Denly (*Middx*)	10	10	3	261	67	0	3	37.28	125.48	22	10
18	P. D. Trego (*Somerset*)	11	10	2	289	62	0	1	36.12	117.95	31	8
19	†P. Mustard (*Durham*)	11	11	0	379	91	0	3	34.45	123.45	41	11
20	S. C. Moore (*Lancs*)	11	11	1	338	75	0	3	33.80	143.22	39	18
21	A. D. Hales (*Notts*)	11	11	0	365	82	0	2	33.18	146.58	32	17
22	R. E. Levi (*Northants*)	12	12	1	360	110*	1	2	32.72	145.74	39	18
23	K. R. Brown (*Lancs*)	11	11	3	260	62	0	2	32.50	131.31	22	9
24	W. J. Durston (*Derbys*)	10	10	2	254	83	0	2	31.75	145.14	23	10
25	V. Chopra (*Warwicks*)	10	10	1	282	75*	0	2	31.33	99.29	22	4
26	K. J. Coetzer (*Northants*) . .	12	12	1	337	71*	0	1	30.63	107.32	46	1
27	†M. J. Lumb (*Notts*)	11	11	0	330	96	0	2	30.00	165.00	40	16

BOWLING (12 wickets at 25.00)

		Style	O	M	R	W	BB	4I	Avge	SR	ER
1	G. G. White (*Northants, Notts*) . .	SLA	32	0	203	17	5-22	2	11.94	11.29	6.34
2	Azharullah (*Northants*)	RFM	45.5	1	341	27	4-14	3	12.62	10.18	7.44
3	R. J. W. Topley (*Essex*)	LFM	37	0	278	21	4-26	2	13.23	10.57	7.51
4	D. J. Willey (*Northants*)	LFM	42.3	1	280	21	4-9	2	13.33	12.14	6.58
5	R. M. L. Taylor (*Leics*)	LFM	27	0	196	14	4-11	2	14.00	11.57	7.25
6	J. A. Brooks (*Yorks*)	RFM	25	1	189	13	5-21	2	14.53	11.53	7.56
7	Yasir Arafat (*Somerset*)	RFM	41.1	1	292	20	4-5	1	14.60	12.35	7.09
8	A. J. Ireland (*Leics*)	RFM	33.2	1	236	15	4-11	2	15.73	13.33	7.08
9	G. G. Wagg (*Glam*)	LM	33	0	240	15	5-14	1	16.00	13.20	7.27
10	J. W. Dernbach (*Surrey*)	RFM	44.1	0	296	18	3-15	0	16.44	14.72	6.70
11	S. W. Tait (*Essex*)	RF	39.4	0	275	16	4-26	2	17.18	14.87	6.93
12	Z. de Bruyn (*Surrey*)	RM	28.2	0	239	13	4-19	1	18.38	13.07	8.43
13	Azeem Rafiq (*Yorks*)	OB	31	0	247	13	3-22	0	19.00	14.30	7.96
14	D. R. Briggs (*Hants*)	SLA	44	0	286	15	3-19	0	19.06	17.60	6.50
15	T. D. Groenewald (*Derbys*)	RFM	33	0	248	12	4-21	1	20.66	16.50	7.51
16	M. J. McClenaghan (*Lancs*)	LFM	43	1	355	17	5-29	1	20.88	15.17	8.25
17	S. R. Patel (*Notts*)	SLA	38.5	0	297	14	3-16	0	21.21	16.64	7.64
18	L. A. Dawson (*Hants*)	SLA	38	0	277	13	4-19	1	21.30	17.53	7.28
19	Azhar Mahmood (*Surrey*)	RFM	48	1	346	16	2-9	0	21.62	18.00	7.20
20	A. C. Thomas (*Somerset*)	RFM	40	1	325	15	4-35	1	21.66	16.00	8.12
21	K. Ali (*Lancs*)	RFM	36.1	0	316	14	3-23	0	22.57	15.50	8.73
22	M. E. Claydon (*Kent*)	RFM	35.1	0	294	13	3-22	0	22.61	16.23	8.36
23	C. Rushworth (*Durham*)	RFM	38.5	0	297	13	3-19	0	22.84	17.92	7.64

LEADING WICKETKEEPERS

Dismissals	M	
11 (8 ct, 3 st)	10	A. M. Rossington (*Middx*)
10 (6 ct, 4 st)	10	T. Poynton (*Derbys*)
10 (7 ct, 3 st)	12	S. M. Davies (*Surrey*)
10 (9 ct, 1 st)	12	J. S. Foster (*Essex*)
9 (8 ct, 1 st)	11	C. Kieswetter (*Somerset*)
9 (6 ct, 3 st)	11	C. M. W. Read (*Notts*)

Dismissals	M	
9 (8 ct, 1 st)	13	D. Murphy (*Northants*)
6 (4 ct, 2 st)	7	B. C. Brown (*Sussex*)
6 (5 ct, 1 st)	10	O. B. Cox (*Worcs*)
6 (4 ct, 2 st)	10	P. J. McKay (*Warwicks*)
6 (6 ct)	11	G. D. Cross (*Lancs*)

LEADING FIELDERS

Ct	M	
9	9	A. G. Prince (*Lancs*)
9	11	J. C. Buttler (*Somerset*)
9	12	L. A. Dawson (*Hants*)
9	13	M. N. W. Spriegel (*Northants*)
8	10	J. J. Cobb (*Leics*)
8	11	G. M. Smith (*Essex*)

Ct	M	
7	10	M. T. Coles (*Kent*)
7	10	J. C. Hildreth (*Somerset*)
7	10	C. F. Hughes (*Derbys*)
7	10	S. J. Mullaney (*Notts*)
7	11	M. D. Stoneman (*Durham*)

MIDLANDS/WALES/WEST GROUP

GLAMORGAN

At Cardiff, July 3 (floodlit). **Glamorgan won by four wickets. Warwickshire 118** (20 overs) (D. L. Maddy 30, R. Clarke 42; G. G. Wagg 3-24); ‡**Glamorgan 121-6** (19.1 overs) (M. J. North 37). *MoM:* N. L. McCullum (Glamorgan). *Attendance:* 2,241. *County debut:* N. L. McCullum. *Nathan McCullum came out to bat on a turning pitch with Glamorgan needing 17 from 11 balls. He struck his fellow New Zealander Jeetan Patel for 13 off his first four, then Chris Wright into the sightscreen to win the game.*

At Cardiff, July 12 (floodlit). **Glamorgan won by nine wickets.** ‡**Somerset 125-6** (20 overs) (P. D. Trego 42*, C. A. J. Meschede 30; G. G. Wagg 3-29); **Glamorgan 126-1** (15.2 overs) (M. A. Wallace 30, J. Allenby 47*, C. B. Cooke 42*). *MoM:* J. Allenby. *Attendance:* 8,719. *Somerset were kept in check after Graham Wagg removed Marcus Trescothick (for seven, ending a sequence of four ducks in all cricket) and Craig Kieswetter in successive balls. Jim Allenby underpinned two fifty partnerships to secure Glamorgan's fourth consecutive win, and their first over Somerset in 11 attempts. Somerset switched wicketkeeping duties from Jos Buttler to Kieswetter – meaning England's limited-overs gloveman was no longer behind the stumps in any format for his county. Kieswetter kept wicket in customised, spiked Converse trainers.*

At Cardiff, July 23 (floodlit). **Glamorgan won by five wickets.** ‡**Worcestershire 157-6** (20 overs) (T. T. Samaraweera 65, A. N. Kervezee 44; G. G. Wagg 3-15); **Glamorgan 161-5** (19.1 overs) (J. Allenby 50, M. W. Goodwin 59; G. M. Andrew 3-27). *MoM:* M. W. Goodwin. *Attendance:* 3,244. *Glamorgan bounced back from three away defeats. Allenby was solid, Murray Goodwin forceful, and Ben Wright (22*) thumped Jack Shantry for 17 in the penultimate over. Two doctors came out of the crowd to treat Andre Russell when he left the field complaining of chest pains and dizziness while bowling; he was given the all-clear in hospital.*

At Cardiff, July 26 (floodlit). **Northamptonshire won by six wickets. Glamorgan 125-9** (20 overs) (C. B. Cooke 50; D. J. Willey 3-17, Azharullah 4-16); ‡**Northamptonshire 129-4** (18.3 overs) (C. L. White 71*). *MoM:* C. L. White. *Attendance:* 7,046. *A large crowd arrived hoping to see Glamorgan take a giant step towards their first quarter-final since 2008; instead, Cameron White's ice-cool 71* from 48 balls sent Northamptonshire through as group winners. David Willey and Azharullah had dovetailed superbly to claim five wickets in the last four overs.*

At Cardiff, July 30 (floodlit). **Gloucestershire won by nine wickets. Glamorgan 141-5** (20 overs) (J. Allenby 85*); ‡**Gloucestershire 145-1** (16.3 overs) (M. Klinger 86*). *MoM:* M. Klinger. *Attendance:* 4,273. *County debut:* T. W. Shrewsbury (Gloucestershire). *The average age of Glamorgan's side – 32 years 118 days – was the oldest in the competition's history, but their wise heads could not prevent a fifth defeat in six that cost them a quarter-final place. Simon Jones was recalled for his first Twenty20 game of the season, but conceded 44 in four overs, including two no-balls that gave Dan Christian (25* from 20 deliveries) and Michael Klinger (86* from 60) free-hits.*

Glamorgan away matches

June 28: beat Worcestershire by 58 runs (D/L).
July 6: beat Warwickshire by eight wickets.
July 14: lost to Northamptonshire by seven wickets.

July 19: lost to Somerset by 64 runs.
July 21: lost to Gloucestershire by ten wickets.

GLOUCESTERSHIRE

At Bristol, June 30. **Gloucestershire won by 48 runs.** ‡**Gloucestershire 184-5** (20 overs) (M. Klinger 108*); **Worcestershire 136** (20 overs) (A. N. Kervezee 39, O. B. Cox 37; J. K. Fuller 3-23). *MoM:* M. Klinger. *Attendance:* 2,029. *Michael Klinger's impeccable career-best 108* from 64 balls against his 2012 team-mates pushed Gloucestershire out of reach. Alex Gidman added 65 with Klinger, and was struck in the chest by Chris Russell's second beamer, forcing the bowler out of the attack. Gareth Andrew was asked to complete the over, and bowled Gidman first ball. Worcestershire were then undone by James Fuller's pace.*

At Cheltenham, July 14. **Warwickshire won by six wickets. Gloucestershire 96** (18.4 overs) (C. D. J. Dent 33; A. Javid 4-17); ‡**Warwickshire 97-4** (17.1 overs) (V. Chopra 33). *MoM:* A. Javid.

Attendance: 4,999. County debut: F. R. J. Coleman (Warwickshire). Only Chris Dent grasped how to bat on a slow turner as Gloucestershire were dismantled by Ateeq Javid's occasional off-spin. The ECB later ruled the pitch guilty of "excessive turn", and handed Gloucestershire a two-point penalty to take effect in 2014.

At Cheltenham, July 16. **Northamptonshire won by 17 runs. Northamptonshire 206-3** (20 overs) (R. E. Levi 110*, A. G. Wakely 35); ‡**Gloucestershire 189-6** (20 overs) (I. A. Cockbain 60, A. P. R. Gidman 49; D. J. Willey 4-32). *MoM:* R. E. Levi. *Attendance:* 3,444. *Stung by the reaction to the pitch used two days earlier, Cheltenham College produced a more docile surface. Richard Levi sized it up before smashing 110 from 62 balls, with 84 in boundaries – and finished one short of Lance Klusener's record Twenty20 score for Northamptonshire. David Willey then ripped out Gloucestershire's top three inside the first four overs.*

At Cheltenham, July 21. **Gloucestershire won by ten wickets.** ‡**Glamorgan 98-9** (20 overs) (M. J. North 35; D. A. Payne 3-17, E. G. C. Young 3-21); **Gloucestershire 99-0** (12.5 overs) (C. D. J. Dent 63*, M. Klinger 35*). *MoM:* D. A. Payne. *Attendance:* 4,999. *Glamorgan's frustration at coming unstuck on a two-paced track was compounded when Dent and Klinger leapt to the modest target with seven overs to spare – giving Gloucestershire their only win of the Cheltenham Festival.*

At Bristol, July 26. **Somerset won by nine wickets. Gloucestershire 125** (20 overs) (H. J. H. Marshall 33; A. C. Thomas 4-35); ‡**Somerset 129-1** (16.1 overs) (C. R. Jones 53*, C. Kieswetter 61). *MoM:* C. Kieswetter. *Attendance:* 4,000. *Gloucestershire were taken aback by a slow surface at their county headquarters, and hustled out by Somerset's seasoned Twenty20 operators. The reply was embarrassingly one-sided: Craig Kieswetter smashed 61 from 43 balls, while Chris Jones – opening in place of the injured Marcus Trescothick – raised his maiden Twenty20 fifty.*

Gloucestershire away matches

June 28: lost to Northamptonshire by 41 runs.
July 5: lost to Somerset by four wickets.
July 7: lost to Worcestershire by five wickets.
July 24: lost to Warwickshire by seven wickets.
July 30: beat Glamorgan by nine wickets.

NORTHAMPTONSHIRE

At Northampton, June 28 (floodlit). **Northamptonshire won by 41 runs.** Reduced to 12 overs a side. **Northamptonshire 124-4** (12 overs) (K. J. Coetzer 39, A. G. Wakely 36); ‡**Gloucestershire 83-9** (12 overs) (Azharullah 3-23, G. G. White 4-14). *MoM:* G. G. White. *Attendance:* 2,429. *County debut:* R. E. Levi (Northamptonshire). *Rain delayed the start and, apart from the early loss of South African Twenty20 specialist Richard Levi, Northamptonshire controlled what remained. Graeme White – returning to his old club on loan from Nottinghamshire – strangled Gloucestershire with four wickets in nine deliveries, and the unknown Azharullah tailed the ball in to bowl three others. It was Northamptonshire's first win in a home Twenty20 match since July 2010.*

At Northampton, July 5 (floodlit). **Northamptonshire won by 27 runs.** ‡**Northamptonshire 161-2** (20 overs) (R. E. Levi 35, K. J. Coetzer 71*); **Warwickshire 134-8** (20 overs) (A. Javid 41; Azharullah 4-25). *MoM:* Azharullah. *Attendance:* 4,108. *Northamptonshire put in another emphatic display. Kyle Coetzer batted through the innings, and received solid support from Levi, Cameron White (28) and Alex Wakely (24*). Azharullah's four wickets – three of them bowled – settled the issue.*

At Northampton, July 14. **Northamptonshire won by seven wickets. Glamorgan 153-7** (20 overs) (J. Allenby 36, M. W. Goodwin 47; Azharullah 4-14); ‡**Northamptonshire 157-3** (20 overs) (C. L. White 68, A. G. Wakely 52*). *MoM:* Azharullah. *Attendance:* 1,850. *Another magnificent spell of reverse swing from Azharullah, who took three late wickets in ten balls, dampened the fine early work of Jim Allenby and Murray Goodwin. A 92-run stand in 11 overs between White and Wakely then ended Glamorgan's winning start. Before the match, former Northamptonshire and Gloucestershire team-mates of Kevin Curran, who had died in October 2012 at the age of 53, contested a 12-over game to raise money for the British Heart Foundation.*

At Northampton, July 17 (floodlit). **Northamptonshire won by ten runs.** ‡**Northamptonshire 150-8** (20 overs) (K. J. Coetzer 34, S. P. Crook 63; Yasir Arafat 3-21, C. A. J. Meschede 3-36); **Somerset 140-8** (20 overs) (C. Kieswetter 38, J. C. Buttler 37; Azharullah 3-16). *MoM:* S. P. Crook. *Attendance:* 3,525. *Victory in a tight battle with one of the country's strongest limited-overs sides* *took Northamptonshire top of the group. They owed much to Steven Crook, who blazed four sixes in 36 balls after Yasir Arafat had removed Levi and Cameron White in the first over. Lee Daggett's run-out of Jos Buttler spoiled Somerset's hopes of scoring the 24 they needed off the final ten balls.*

At Northampton, July 30 (floodlit). **Worcestershire won by 37 runs. ‡Worcestershire 182-6** (20 overs) (M. M. Ali 72); **Northamptonshire 145-6** (20 overs) (R. E. Levi 31; C. L. White 30; M. M. Ali 5-34). *MoM:* M. M. Ali. *Attendance: 3,585. With the group already won, Northamptonshire turned in their worst performance, and were punished by Moeen Ali. He smashed six fours and four sixes – three in an over off Matt Spriegel – then snapped a promising opening stand between Levi and Coetzer (23) on his way to career-best figures. Ali was only the fourth player in the competition's history – after Andrew Hall, Jim Allenby and Andrew McDonald – to score a fifty and take five wickets in the same match.*

Northamptonshire away matches

July 7: lost to Somerset by six wickets.
July 16: beat Gloucestershire by 17 runs.
July 20: lost to Warwickshire by three wickets.

July 21: beat Worcestershire by five runs.
July 26: beat Glamorgan by six wickets.

SOMERSET

At Taunton, July 5. **Somerset won by four wickets. ‡Gloucestershire 190-6** (20 overs) (H. J. H. Marshall 49, I. A. Cockbain 63, A. P. R. Gidman 36); **Somerset 192-6** (19.5 overs) (C. Kieswetter 89*; J. K. Fuller 3-33). *MoM:* C. Kieswetter. *Attendance: 7,954. County debut: Yasir Arafat (Somerset). Yasir Arafat, on debut in his fifth county, came out to bat before a capacity crowd with Somerset needing three off two balls. He sliced his first, from David Payne, over short third man to settle a superb contest graced by 89* from 55 from Craig Kieswetter, who was largely responsible for Dan Christian's figures of 4–0–57–0 – the worst of the season.*

At Taunton, July 7. **Somerset won by six wickets. ‡Northamptonshire 152-7** (20 overs) (K. J. Coetzer 32, D. J. Willey 47; A. C. Thomas 3-33); **Somerset 155-4** (18.5 overs) (P. D. Trego 41, A. N. Petersen 64*). *MoM:* A. N. Petersen. *Attendance: 6,411. Alviro Petersen, supposed to be the rock among Somerset's big hitters, smashed seven fours and two sixes to trump David Willey's electric all-round performance: 47 off 29 balls, 2-19 and a run-out.*

At Taunton, July 14. **Worcestershire won by eight runs. Worcestershire 168-7** (20 overs) (A. N. Kervezee 53; Yasir Arafat 3-29); **‡Somerset 160-8** (20 overs) (M. E. Trescothick 49; J. D. Shantry 3-34, J. Leach 3-20). *MoM:* J. Leach. *Attendance: 6,761. Andre Russell's spectacular fielding was instrumental in Worcestershire's surprise win. Somerset mistimed their run-chase after Marcus Trescothick fell for 49, and not even Jos Buttler's late improvisation could save them.*

At Taunton, July 19. **Somerset won by 64 runs. Somerset 199-6** (20 overs) (C. Kieswetter 37, P. D. Trego 30, J. C. Buttler 48); **‡Glamorgan 135** (18.1 overs) (J. Allenby 69; M. T. C. Waller 4-27). *MoM:* M. T. C. Waller. *Attendance: 7,531. Somerset, missing Trescothick with an ankle injury, ended their three-match losing streak. Buttler's 19-ball 48 supplied the finishing touch to a powerful batting display, before Max Waller claimed four wickets and two stunning catches.*

At Taunton, July 21. **Somerset won by ten wickets. ‡Warwickshire 73** (17 overs) (Yasir Arafat 4-5); **Somerset 78-0** (8.3 overs) (C. R. Jones 30*, C. Kieswetter 39*). *MoM:* Yasir Arafat. *Attendance: 7,190. Yasir Arafat swept up his best figures, 3–0–5–4, in more than 150 Twenty20 matches, as Warwickshire were shot out for their lowest total in the format. At the time it was the joint-cheapest four-for in all Twenty20.*

Somerset away matches

July 12: lost to Glamorgan by nine wickets.
July 17: lost to Northamptonshire by ten runs.
July 26: beat Gloucestershire by nine wickets.

July 27: lost to Worcestershire by five wickets.
July 30: beat Warwickshire by ten runs.

WARWICKSHIRE

At Rugby, July 6. **Glamorgan won by eight wickets.** ‡**Warwickshire 126-8** (20 overs) (V. Chopra 30; M. G. Hogan 3-11); **Glamorgan 132-2** (17.4 overs) (M. A. Wallace 69*). *MoM:* M. A. Wallace. *Attendance:* 2,964. *Warwickshire slumped to their third consecutive defeat on the county's first competitive appearance at Rugby School. It was a fitting venue a few hours after the British & Irish Lions had won their Test series in Australia, although it was a New South Welshman, Michael Hogan, whose accuracy stymied Warwickshire. Glamorgan celebrated the 125th anniversary of their founding with victory, and a dousing of beer by a group of well-oiled Welsh fans.*

At Birmingham, July 20. **Warwickshire won by three wickets.** Northamptonshire 111 (19.2 overs) (K. J. Coetzer 33; S. A. Piolet 3-24); ‡**Warwickshire 115-7** (19.3 overs) (R. Clarke 36; D. J. Willey 3-22). *MoM:* S. A. Piolet. *Attendance:* 4,200. *Rikki Clarke's three sixes in four balls off Matt Spriegel proved decisive. Steffan Piolet, at mid-on brilliantly ran out Cameron White backing up at the non-striker's end, before taking three wickets in ten balls in his competition-best return.*

At Birmingham, July 24 (floodlit). **Warwickshire won by seven wickets.** Gloucestershire 145-7 (20 overs) (M. Klinger 68; A. Javid 3-26); ‡**Warwickshire 149-3** (17.4 overs) (W. T. S. Porterfield 34, V. Chopra 37, R. Clarke 40). *MoM:* R. Clarke. *Attendance:* 3,158. *It was a miserable day for Gloucestershire: the ECB levied a two-point pitch penalty for the home game against Warwickshire, harming their 2014 prospects; then defeat by the same opponents ended interest in this year's competition. Clarke was again pivotal on a slow surface, hitting three sixes in one Ed Young over.*

At Birmingham, July 26 (floodlit). **Warwickshire won by eight wickets.** Worcestershire 146-8 (20 overs) (T. T. Samaraweera 33, M. M. Ali 37; C. R. Woakes 3-28); ‡**Warwickshire 149-2** (17.3 overs) (V. Chopra, D. L. Maddy 44). *MoM:* V. Chopra. *Attendance:* 11,989. *Thilan Samaraweera and Mooen Ali gave Worcestershire a flying start, but they were reined in by Jeetan Patel (2-26). Varun Chopra and Darren Maddy ensured victory with their second century stand against Worcestershire in a fortnight.*

At Birmingham, July 30 (floodlit). **Somerset won by ten runs.** Somerset 175-5 (20 overs) (C. Kieswetter 76, P. D. Trego 32, N. R. D. Compton 32); ‡**Warwickshire 165-3** (20 overs) (W. T. S. Porterfield 34, D. L. Maddy 67*, L. J. Evans 51*). *MoM:* C. Kieswetter. *Attendance:* 4,940. *Maddy's decorated Twenty20 career came to an end when he narrowly failed to haul Warwickshire into the quarter-finals. He put on an unbroken 100 in 11 overs with Laurie Evans – who batted with a dislocated finger – but neither Alfonso Thomas nor Yasir Arafat gave away a boundary in the last two overs. Fingers were pointed at stand-in captain Chopra after Craig Kieswetter battered Maddy for 24 in Somerset's 17th over: at that stage, Boyd Rankin, Warwickshire's best bowler, still had two overs available; he finished with 3–0–9–2.*

Warwickshire away matches

July 3: lost to Glamorgan by four wickets.
July 5: lost to Northamptonshire by 27 runs.
July 12: beat Worcestershire by seven wickets.

July 14: beat Gloucestershire by six wickets.
July 21: lost to Somerset by ten wickets.

WORCESTERSHIRE

At Worcester, June 28. **Glamorgan won by 58 runs** (D/L). Glamorgan 159-4 (14 overs) (J. Allenby 37, M. A. Wallace 33, C. B. Cooke 57); ‡**Worcestershire 102-9** (14 overs) (G. G. Wagg 5-14). *MoM:* G. G. Wagg. *Attendance:* 2,106. *County debut:* A. D. Russell (Worcestershire). *After rain interrupted Glamorgan's innings, Worcestershire were set 161 from 14 overs. Graham Wagg quashed that prospect with three wickets in four balls of the fourth over, on his way to the best Twenty20 figures for Glamorgan. Chris Cooke hit 57 off 27 deliveries either side of the stoppage.*

At Worcester, July 7. **Worcestershire won by five wickets.** ‡Gloucestershire 119-9 (20 overs) (D. K. H. Mitchell 3-21); Worcestershire 120-5 (15 overs) (A. N. Kervezee 42*). *MoM:* M. M. Ali (Worcestershire). *Attendance:* 2,683. *Worcestershire's spin-heavy attack prospered on a dry pitch once Shaaiq Choudhry recovered from shipping 19 in the third over; Gloucestershire managed only 12 boundaries in all. Andre Russell was run out ambling from his crease off a no-ball, but Alexei Kervezee secured Worcestershire's first win of the season.*

At Worcester, July 12. **Warwickshire won by seven wickets.** ‡Worcestershire 188-5 (20 overs) (M. M. Ali 85, A. D. Russell 47*); **Warwickshire 189-3** (19 overs) (V. Chopra 65, D. L. Maddy 84*). *MoM:* D. L. Maddy. *Attendance: 3,705. Moeen Ali's career-best 85* from 42 balls was still not enough for Worcestershire. Varun Chopra and Darren Maddy responded with 119 in 12 overs – Warwickshire's highest partnership in Twenty20 – which left them needing 29 off 16 balls. Chris Woakes (28*) stepped up to hit six fours and round off their highest successful run-chase.*

At Worcester, July 21. **Northamptonshire won by five runs.** ‡Northamptonshire 137-6 (20 overs) (R. E. Levi 70); Worcestershire 132-6 (20 overs) (D. K. H. Mitchell 38*, A. D. Russell 44; D. J. Willey 3-13). *MoM:* R. E. Levi. *Attendance: 2,041. Richard Levi's brutal 70 off 43 balls, including three sixes and a four in succession off Joe Leach, was of a different level to anything else on a slow pitch. Russell brought Worcestershire to within sight, but he holed out off David Willey – splitting the seam as he executed the shot – and the task of scoring 21 from Lee Daggett's final over proved beyond them.*

At Worcester, July 27. **Worcestershire won by five wickets.** Somerset 188-4 (20 overs) (C. Kieswetter 80, P. D. Trego 62); ‡Worcestershire 191-5 (19.4 overs) (A. N. Kervezee 32, A. D. Russell 77*, R. A. Whiteley 43). *MoM:* A. D. Russell. *Attendance: 3,279. County debut: R. A. Whiteley (Worcestershire). Russell ended his spell at Worcestershire with his best Twenty20 score, sprinkled with six sixes, to overhaul a demanding target. Ross Whiteley, signed earlier in the week from Derbyshire on a three-year contract, chipped in to a stand of 88. That made amends for a fielding display littered with elementary errors, and powerful hitting from Craig Kieswetter and Peter Trego.*

Worcestershire away matches

June 30: lost to Gloucestershire by 48 runs.
July 14: beat Somerset by eight runs.
July 23: lost to Glamorgan by five wickets.

July 26: lost to Warwickshire by eight wickets.
July 30: beat Northamptonshire by 37 runs.

NORTH GROUP

DERBYSHIRE

At Derby, July 2 (floodlit). **Derbyshire won by seven wickets.** Lancashire 151-8 (20 overs) (K. R. Brown 50; T. D. Groenewald 4-21); ‡Derbyshire 154-3 (19.3 overs) (S. Chanderpaul 87*). *MoM:* S. Chanderpaul. *Attendance: 1,399. County debut: J. A. Morkel (Derbyshire). For the first time, Derbyshire opened a Twenty20 season with three consecutive wins. Tim Groenewald reduced Lancashire to 19-3, and Shivnarine Chanderpaul put together his best score in Twenty20.*

At Derby, July 5 (floodlit). **Nottinghamshire won by six wickets.** Derbyshire 115-9 (20 overs) (W. L. Madsen 36; S. R. Patel 3-16); ‡Nottinghamshire 116-4 (17.3 overs) (M. J. Lumb 49, J. W. A. Taylor 34; D. J. Wainwright 3-21). *MoM:* M. J. Lumb. *Attendance: 4,804. The full-house signs were out for this meeting between unbeaten neighbours, but Derbyshire could not rise to the occasion: they went 51 balls without finding the boundary.*

At Chesterfield, July 14. **Yorkshire won by six runs.** Yorkshire 142-9 (20 overs) (D. M. Hodgson 31; J. A. Morkel 4-25, M. L. Turner 3-21); ‡Derbyshire 136-5 (20 overs) (J. A. Morkel 51*, Azeem Rafiq 3-22). *MoM:* J. A. Morkel. *Attendance: 4,057. Yorkshire held off a stunning performance from Albie Morkel. He pummelled Liam Plunkett for three fours and two sixes in the last over, but with six needed to tie off the final ball, he missed a full toss outside off stump.*

At Chesterfield, July 21. **Durham won by four wickets.** Derbyshire 136-7 (20 overs) (C. F. Hughes 32, W. L. Madsen 32); ‡Durham 137-6 (18.4 overs) (B. A. Stokes 46, G. J. Muchall 37). *MoM:* B. A. Stokes. *Attendance: 1,611. A fifth-wicket stand of 77 between Ben Stokes and Gordon Muchall revitalised Durham, and condemned Derbyshire to their fourth defeat in a row. Will Smith's off-spin throttled Derbyshire with 3–0–9–1 at the start.*

At Derby, July 26 (floodlit). **Leicestershire won by 79 runs.** ‡Leicestershire 151-6 (20 overs) (G. P. Smith 42, E. J. H. Eckersley 42; A. L. Hughes 3-32); Derbyshire 72 (14.1 overs) (A. J. Ireland 4-11, J. J. Cobb 3-19). *MoM:* A. J. Ireland. *Attendance: 3,569. Four wickets in Anthony Ireland's* *first two overs gave him career-best figures, and sent Derbyshire spiralling to their lowest completed total in Twenty20, and their second-heaviest defeat by runs.*

Derbyshire away matches

June 28: beat Yorkshire by two wickets.
June 29: beat Leicestershire by 24 runs.
July 12: lost to Lancashire by 12 runs.

July 23: beat Nottinghamshire by 16 runs.
July 28: lost to Durham by 37 runs.

DURHAM

At Chester-le-Street, June 28. **Lancashire won by nine runs. Lancashire 165-3** (20 overs) (S. C. Moore 75, A. G. Prince 32, S. M. Katich 43*); ‡**Durham 156-8** (20 overs) (M. D. Stoneman 33, B. A. Stokes 34; M. J. McClenaghan 3-35). *MoM:* S. C. Moore. *Attendance:* 5,843. *County debuts:* M. G. Morley (Durham); M. J. McClenaghan (Lancashire). *On the day New Zealander Mitchell McClenaghan linked up with his new team-mates, he was hit for 21 in his first two overs; when he returned with four overs left, his first ball was driven for six by Ben Stokes. But McClenaghan kept his head to remove Gordon Muchall and Stokes in successive balls, and derail Durham's run-chase.*

At Chester-le-Street, July 6. **Nottinghamshire won by eight wickets. Durham 154-4** (20 overs) (M. D. Stoneman 51, S. G. Borthwick 44); ‡**Nottinghamshire 156-2** (15.3 overs) (A. D. Hales 34, M. J. Lumb 96). *MoM:* M. J. Lumb. *Attendance:* 5,236. *Michael Lumb made the highest Twenty20 score for Nottinghamshire, breaking a record Mark Ealham had held since 2004. Lumb had just driven Scott Borthwick for his third six when he was stumped with four needed for his hundred, and eight for the win.*

At Chester-le-Street, July 12. **Durham won by 76 runs. Durham 215-6** (20 overs) (P. Mustard 91, S. G. Borthwick 35); ‡**Yorkshire 139-8** (20 overs) (G. S. Ballance 68). *MoM:* P. Mustard. *Attendance:* 7,157. *Phil Mustard hammered 91 off 52 balls, a Durham Twenty20 record. Yorkshire, without their England players and injured skipper Andrew Gale, slid to 22-3 before a one-man show from Gary Ballance saved a little face.*

At Chester-le-Street, July 25. **Durham won by five wickets. Leicestershire 119-7** (20 overs) (S. J. Thakor 42; C. Rushworth 3-19); ‡**Durham 120-5** (18 overs) (S. G. Borthwick 30, B. A. Stokes 41*; R. M. L. Taylor 4-11). *MoM:* B. A. Stokes. *Attendance:* 5,253. *After smiting five sixes in each of the previous two games, Stokes added three more to claim his third consecutive match award. Durham laboured to 56-5 against Rob Taylor's nagging left-arm seam, but Gareth Breese (24*) helped Stokes knock off the rest.*

At Chester-le-Street, July 28. **Durham won by 37 runs. Durham 187-3** (20 overs) (M. D. Stoneman 47, S. G. Borthwick 31, G. J. Muchall 66*); ‡**Derbyshire 150** (18.5 overs) (C. F. Hughes 34, D. J. Redfern 43). *MoM:* G. J. Muchall. *Attendance:* 3,678. *Muchall struck three sixes in a 26-ball half-century, and pressed on to his best score. He helped Durham win their fifth game in a row – a county record – but the deduction of a quarter of a point as punishment for breaching the salary cap the previous season cost them second place in the group. But they still reached the quarter-finals when Glamorgan, Warwickshire and Middlesex lost their last games in the other groups.*

Durham away matches

June 30: beat Yorkshire by four wickets.
July 5: lost to Leicestershire by 11 runs.
July 14: lost to Lancashire by 25 runs.

July 19: beat Nottinghamshire by three wickets.
July 21: beat Derbyshire by four wickets.

LANCASHIRE

At Manchester, July 1 (floodlit). **Nottinghamshire won by four wickets. Lancashire 155-6** (20 overs) (S. J. Croft 52, S. M. Katich 48); ‡**Nottinghamshire 159-6** (17.4 overs) (A. D. Hales 49, D. J. Hussey 52; M. J. McClenaghan 5-29). *MoM:* M. J. McClenaghan. *Attendance:* 5,886. *Nottinghamshire had David Hussey – one of only three players in the format with 5,000 runs – to thank for their first Twenty20 win at Old Trafford in seven attempts. They overcame Mitchell McClenaghan's 5-29 on home debut – Lancashire's first five-wicket haul in the format.*

At Manchester, July 7. **Lancashire won by four runs.** ‡**Lancashire 155-4** (20 overs) (S. M. Katich 62*); **Leicestershire 151-7** (20 overs) (G. P. Smith 84; K. Ali 3-26). *MoM*: G. P. Smith. *Attendance: 5,308. Lancashire sneaked a nip-and-tuck affair: Kabir Ali dismissed Greg Smith with 19 needed from nine balls and, though Michael Thornely hit McClenaghan's penultimate delivery for six over midwicket, he was run out off the last.*

At Manchester, July 12 (floodlit). **Lancashire won by 12 runs. Lancashire 165-9** (20 overs) (S. C. Moore 74; T. D. Groenewald 3-32, M. L. Turner 4-35); ‡**Derbyshire 153-6** (20 overs) (W. J. Durston 48, S. Chanderpaul 39, W. L. Madsen 36). *MoM*: M. J. McClenaghan (Lancashire). *Attendance: 5,783. Simon Kerrigan and Arron Lilley, an off-spinner from Tameside playing only his fourth first-team game for Lancashire, recorded identical figures of 4–0–25–1 to strangle Derbyshire.*

At Manchester, July 14. **Lancashire won by 25 runs.** ‡**Lancashire 170-5** (20 overs) (K. R. Brown 62, S. M. Katich 40*); **Durham 145-5** (20 overs) (S. G. Borthwick 62; K. Ali 3-30). *MoM*: K. R. Brown. *Attendance: 5,174. Karl Brown and Scott Borthwick both made career-best scores of 62, but Durham batted too slowly in the middle overs.*

At Manchester, July 24 (floodlit). **Lancashire won by eight wickets.** ‡**Yorkshire 124-8** (20 overs) (A. Lyth 32); **Lancashire 127-2** (11 overs) (S. C. Moore 66*, T. C. Smith 42). *MoM*: T. C. Smith. *Attendance: 12,036. Lancashire tried out the temporary seating installed for the upcoming Ashes Test, and won convincingly over their great rivals, who never recovered from being 23-2 at the end of the powerplay. Stephen Moore and Tom Smith responded with a blaze inside Lancashire's first eight overs. The county's major concern had been a 20-minute power cut before the start, which wiped out electricity to the dressing-rooms and two floodlights at the Statham End. The man who fixed the problem was Jimmy Anderson – Old Trafford's 43-year-old resident electrician, and no relation of the swing bowler from Burnley.*

Lancashire away matches

June 28: beat Durham by nine runs.
July 2: lost to Derbyshire by seven wickets.
July 5: tied with Yorkshire.

July 23: tied with Leicestershire.
July 28: lost to Nottinghamshire by 60 runs.

LEICESTERSHIRE

At Leicester, June 29. **Derbyshire won by 24 runs. Derbyshire 173-3** (20 overs) (C. F. Hughes 34, W. J. Durston 83, S. Chanderpaul 38); ‡**Leicestershire 149** (18.2 overs) (J. J. Cobb 47, J. A. Burns 36; D. J. Wainwright 3-24). *MoM*: W. J. Durston. *Attendance: 2,172. Josh Cobb had hit all but seven of Leicestershire's 54 runs by the time he fell in the sixth over. Dan Redfern's part-time off-spin (2-24) then triggered a collapse of nine for 62.*

At Leicester, July 5. **Leicestershire won by 11 runs. Leicestershire 176-5** (20 overs) (G. P. Smith 67, J. A. Burns 81*); ‡**Durham 165** (19.5 overs) (P. Mustard 69, B. A. Stokes 35; A. J. Ireland 4-22). *MoM*: A. J. Ireland. *Attendance: 2,333. Joe Burns's 81* from 52 balls – his highest score in Twenty20, and the best of his underwhelming stint at Grace Road – was the cornerstone of Leicestershire's emphatic total. Anthony Ireland exploited Durham's charge for quick runs.*

At Leicester, July 12. **Leicestershire won by seven wickets. Nottinghamshire 158-6** (20 overs) (S. R. Patel 50, J. W. A. Taylor 33*; S. J. Thakor 3-30); ‡**Leicestershire 161-3** (17.4 overs) (J. J. Cobb 67*, Shakib Al Hasan 43*). *MoM*: J. J. Cobb. *Attendance: 3,028. Nottinghamshire suffered their first defeat. Cobb used eight bowlers, partly because Jigar Naik dislocated his shoulder trying to stop a run off his bowling; he was ruled out for the season. The constant changes seemed to unsettle Nottinghamshire's batsmen, who made only 69 from their last ten overs. Cobb thrashed Leicestershire over the line with a Twenty20-best 67*, aided by three sixes from Shakib Al Hasan.*

At Leicester, July 23. **Tied. Leicestershire 139-9** (20 overs) (G. P. Smith 45; K. Ali 3-23); ‡**Lancashire 139-9** (20 overs) (R. M. L. Taylor 4-23). *MoM*: R. M. L. Taylor. *Attendance: 1,743. Momentum swung back and forth until the end. Gareth Cross (28) lofted Shakib to long-off from the penultimate ball, and then, with Lancashire needing five to win, last man Mitchell McClenaghan walked across his stumps, and flicked Shakib through a vacant fine leg to seal Lancashire's second tie of the season. Neither side celebrated much: Leicestershire's interest in a competition they had won three times came to an end; Lancashire still needed at least another victory to qualify.*

At Leicester, July 28. **Leicestershire won by ten wickets.** ‡Yorkshire 105 (17.2 overs) (A. Z. Lees 32; J. J. Cobb 3-9); **Leicestershire 106-0** (12.1 overs) (J. J. Cobb 52*, G. P. Smith 39*). MoM: J. J. Cobb. *Attendance: 2,064. Cobb sentenced Yorkshire – 2012's beaten finalists – to bottom in the group. He bowled the first over for only two runs, then took wickets in each of his next three, and brushed Yorkshire's bowling aside in an unbroken stand with Greg Smith that gave Leicestershire their first ten-wicket win in the format. The Yorkshire side had an average age of 23 years 336 days – the youngest in any English Twenty20 match.*

Leicestershire away matches

June 28: lost to Nottinghamshire by seven wickets.
July 7: lost to Lancashire by four runs.
July 9: lost to Yorkshire by seven wickets.

July 25: lost to Durham by five wickets.
July 26: beat Derbyshire by 79 runs.

NOTTINGHAMSHIRE

At Nottingham, June 28. **Nottinghamshire won by seven wickets. Leicestershire 183-8** (20 overs) (N. J. O'Brien 47, Shakib Al Hasan 31; I. G. Butler 3-39); ‡Nottinghamshire 184-3 (17.4 overs) (M. J. Lumb 50, J. W. A. Taylor 37*, D. J. Hussey 49*). MoM: D. J. Hussey. *Attendance: 7,390. County debuts: I. G. Butler (Nottinghamshire); Shakib Al Hasan (Leicestershire). A challenging target was made to look simple by Nottinghamshire's intimidating top five. David Hussey, captain in this format, was imperious in closing out the match.*

At Nottingham, July 19. **Durham won by three wickets. Nottinghamshire 159-7** (20 overs) (A. D. Hales 41, S. R. Patel 33, J. W. A. Taylor 54); ‡Durham 160-7 (20 overs) (B. A. Stokes 72*, G. R. Breese 32; H. F. Gurney 3-26). MoM: B. A. Stokes. *Attendance: 9,873. Durham used four spinners to bowl 14 overs, and kept Nottinghamshire on the leash once Samit Patel was yorked by Graham Onions in the seventh. Durham shed early wickets, but Ben Stokes exploded with 72* from 48 balls – the kind of sustained hitting he had long promised to deliver in Twenty20. Michael Richardson, Durham's specialist No. 8, scrambled the winning run off the last ball.*

At Nottingham, July 23. **Derbyshire won by 16 runs.** Reduced to nine overs a side. **Derbyshire 108-1** (9 overs) (C. F. Hughes 46, W. J. Durston 50*); ‡Nottinghamshire 92-7 (9 overs) (M. J. Lumb 43). MoM: W. J. Durston. *Attendance: 4,655. After a storm cut the match in half, Chesney Hughes and Wes Durston thrashed the home bowlers to all parts, with Hussey's single over going for 20. Nottinghamshire's hopes rested on Michael Lumb, who blazed all their first 43 runs by the fourth over; no other batsman connected so cleanly from the off.*

At Nottingham, July 26. **Nottinghamshire won by six wickets.** ‡Yorkshire 132-7 (20 overs) (G. S. Ballance 30, R. M. Pyrah 42; S. R. Patel 3-17); **Nottinghamshire 133-4** (16.1 overs) (A. D. Hales 62). MoM: A. D. Hales. *Attendance: 10,148. Nottinghamshire left-arm spinners Patel and Graeme White took a combined 4-34 from eight overs, before Alex Hales enjoyed some respite from his awful Championship form, racing to 62 in 38 balls. The attendance was the highest for a Twenty20 group game at Trent Bridge since the corresponding fixture five years earlier.*

At Nottingham, July 28. **Nottinghamshire won by 60 runs. Nottinghamshire 194-6** (20 overs) (A. D. Hales 82, M. J. Lumb 30); ‡Lancashire 134 (16.5 overs) (S. R. Patel 3-34, G. G. White 5-22). MoM: A. D. Hales. *Attendance: 8,219. Nottinghamshire ambled to victory in the fight for a home quarter-final. Their openers smashed 59 in the powerplay, with Hales rolling on to his best score of the campaign. Stephen Moore chipped back to Patel first ball, and White completed the demolition with Nottinghamshire's best Twenty20 figures, having taken 4-14 earlier in the competition on loan at former club Northamptonshire.*

Nottinghamshire away matches

July 1: beat Lancashire by four wickets.
July 5: beat Derbyshire by six wickets.
July 6: beat Durham by eight wickets.

July 12: lost to Leicestershire by seven wickets.
July 21: beat Yorkshire by 25 runs.

YORKSHIRE

At Leeds, June 28. **Derbyshire won by two wickets. Yorkshire 119-8** (20 overs) (G. S. Ballance 44; M. H. A. Footitt 3-22); **‡Derbyshire 120-8** (19.3 overs) (C. F. Hughes 36, J. L. Clare 35*; J. A. Brooks 4-21). *MoM*: J. L. Clare. *Attendance: 3,446. Yorkshire's score was inadequate, but four wickets in nine balls for Jack Brooks helped reduce Derbyshire to 92-8. Jon Clare hit four late boundaries.*

At Scarborough, June 30. **Durham won by four wickets. Yorkshire 146-7** (20 overs) (A. W. Gale 34, L. E. Plunkett 30); **‡Durham 147-6** (19.5 overs) (P. Mustard 59, G. J. Muchall 44*). *MoM*: G. J. Muchall. *Attendance: 3,709. Ryan Pringle, a 21-year-old off-spinner from Sunderland, was the latest to exploit a nervous Yorkshire in the middle overs. Liam Plunkett enjoyed laying into his former county until he was run out by Michael Richardson's direct hit from long-on, but it was Plunkett's disastrous 19th over, containing two leg-side full tosses which Gordon Muchall swung for four, that all but settled the match.*

At Leeds, July 5. **Tied. Yorkshire 152-6** (20 overs) (P. A. Jaques 66*); **‡Lancashire 152-5** (20 overs) (T. C. Smith 35, S. J. Croft 42*; R. M. Pyrah 3-15). *MoM*: R. M. Pyrah. *Attendance: 14,513. Headingley's first capacity crowd for a Twenty20 match in nine seasons watched the first tie in 164 years of Roses history. Tom Smith thrashed 24 off a Brooks over, but Rich Pyrah hit back with three cheap wickets to set up a thrilling climax. Lancashire were aggrieved when Gareth Cross under-edged into his stumps trying to fend off a waist-high delivery from Plunkett which escaped a no-ball call. At the end of an exemplary closing over from Ryan Sidebottom costing nine runs, Steven Croft squeezed the final delivery for two to deep cover.*

At Leeds, July 9. **Yorkshire won by seven wickets. Leicestershire 113-9** (20 overs) (J. A. Brooks 5-21); **‡Yorkshire 117-3** (16.5 overs) (D. M. Hodgson 52*). *MoM*: J. A. Brooks. *Attendance: 3,917. Leicestershire were beaten inside the first eight overs when Brooks knocked over the top five to capture Yorkshire's second-best figures in Twenty20. The overhead, diving, left-handed boundary catch by Gary Ballance to dismiss Josh Cobb was worth the admission price alone.*

At Leeds, July 21. **Nottinghamshire won by 25 runs. Nottinghamshire 155-8** (20 overs) (S. R. Patel 46, D. J. Hussey 52*); **‡Yorkshire 130-6** (20 overs) (J. J. Sayers 38, D. M. Hodgson 32). *MoM*: S. R. Patel. *Attendance: 6,938. Yorkshire needed their highest score of the season to win, but panic set in against spinners Samit Patel (2-19) and Graeme White (2-18).*

Yorkshire away matches

July 12: lost to Durham by 76 runs.
July 14: beat Derbyshire by six runs.
July 24: lost to Lancashire by eight wickets.

July 26: lost to Nottinghamshire by six wickets.
July 28: lost to Leicestershire by ten wickets.

SOUTH GROUP

ESSEX

At Chelmsford, June 28 (floodlit). **No result.** Reduced to 11 overs a side. **Essex 18-1** (2.1 overs) v **‡Hampshire.** *County debut: S. W. Tait (Essex). A deluge ended the match after 13 balls, two of them lifted for six by Hamish Rutherford.*

At Chelmsford, July 8 (floodlit). **Essex won by 62 runs. Essex 180-8** (20 overs) (M. L. Pettini 33, O. A. Shah 39, R. S. Bopara 39; M. E. Claydon 3-29, J. C. Tredwell 3-19); **‡Kent 118** (17.3 overs) (S. A. Northeast 32; R. J. W. Topley 4-26, R. S. Bopara 3-12). *MoM*: R. S. Bopara. *Attendance: 4,554. Essex completed a Twenty20 double over their local rivals; Kent had lost all five games this far. Mark Pettini and Rutherford (27) launched the match with 59 in 4.4 overs, but Rutherford was reported by the umpires for disputing his third lbw dismissal in four days. After Ravi Bopara removed the top three, Kent lost seven wickets in 30 balls; four to Reece Topley in a career-best performance.*

At Chelmsford, July 12 (floodlit). **Middlesex won by eight wickets. ‡Essex 74** (16.5 overs) (O. A. Shah 39; K. D. Mills 3-4); **Middlesex 77-2** (9.5 overs) (J. L. Denly 34*). *MoM*: K. D. Mills. *Attendance: 5,550. Kyle Mills opened with a double-wicket maiden, and Essex were an abject 12-5* *en route to their lowest Twenty20 total. Mills's final analysis was 3–1–4–3. Essex were booed off by a capacity crowd.*

At Chelmsford, July 14. **Essex won by six wickets. Sussex 171-9** (20 overs) (M. W. Machan 57, R. J. Hamilton-Brown 40; S. W. Tait 4-26); ‡**Essex 172-4** (19.2 overs) (O. A. Shah 40, R. S. Bopara 35, R. N. ten Doeschate 42*). *MoM:* S. W. Tait. *Attendance:* 4,861. *Sussex reached 100 only one wicket down, and had their total boosted by 12 due to Essex's tardy over-rate, yet still could not press home the advantage. Shaun Tait slowed Sussex down with 3-3 in his second spell, before Ryan ten Doeschate (42* from 26 balls) and James Foster (27* from 15) took care of the last 57 runs.*

At Chelmsford, July 31 (floodlit). **Surrey won by 61 runs.** ‡**Surrey 165** (20 overs) (S. M. Davies 54, Z. de Bruyn 39, G. C. Wilson 43; G. R. Napier 4-18, R. J. W. Topley 3-40); **Essex 104** (16.2 overs) (R. N. ten Doeschate 60; Z. de Bruyn 4-19). *MoM:* S. M. Davies. *Attendance:* 5,550. *Essex, chasing 166 to make sure of a quarter-final place, collapsed amid a collection of mistimed hoicks. Only ten Doeschate reached double figures: his 60 from 39 balls prevented Essex from rewriting their record lowest total for the second time in a fortnight. They badly missed their leading scorer Owais Shah, sidelined with a torn hamstring. Home players and staff nervously watched on television as Middlesex failed to beat Hampshire, meaning Essex qualified as one of the two best third-placed sides. Surrey snapped up second place and a home tie – it was the first time they had qualified for the knockout stages since 2006. Steve Davies stroked a 26-ball fifty, and Zander de Bruyn put in a canny all-round performance.*

Essex away matches

July 4: lost to Middlesex by seven wickets.
July 5: beat Kent by 47 runs.
July 15: beat Surrey by eight wickets.

July 21: beat Sussex by seven wickets.
July 26: lost to Hampshire by five wickets.

HAMPSHIRE

At Southampton, June 26 (floodlit). **Hampshire won by five wickets.** ‡**Surrey 139-6** (20 overs); **Hampshire 144-5** (19.2 overs) (M. A. Carberry 60, N. D. McKenzie 37*; Z. de Bruyn 3-14). *MoM:* M. A. Carberry. *Attendance:* 5,484. *County debut:* G. J. Maxwell (Surrey). *Garry Sobers was among the spectators as Michael Carberry and Neil McKenzie ensured Hampshire began their title defence with a comfortable win. Danny Briggs drove back from The Oval after being left out of England's Twenty20 international against New Zealand, and bowled Rory Burns and Vikram Solanki in the ninth over. Surrey, missing Ricky Ponting through a hand injury, mustered only 68 in the second half of their innings.*

At Southampton, July 12 (floodlit). **Hampshire won by four wickets.** ‡**Sussex 118-7** (20 overs) (C. D. Nash 40); **Hampshire 122-6** (20 overs) (M. A. Carberry 41). *MoM:* C. D. Nash. *Attendance:* 9,321. *Carberry and James Vince plundered 24 from Dwayne Smith's only over but, when their partnership was halted at 59, Hampshire lost direction in search of a small target. They needed one off the last ball, bowled by Scott Styris; McKenzie calmly clipped it over midwicket for four.*

At Southampton, July 21. **Kent won by eight runs.** ‡**Kent 143-8** (20 overs) (Sohail Tanvir 3-29, D. R. Briggs 3-19); **Hampshire 135-8** (20 overs) (M. A. Carberry 35, N. D. McKenzie 47). *MoM:* M. E. Claydon (Kent). *Attendance:* 6,393. *Kent, who had lost all five previous games, ended Hampshire's run of 13 victories stretching back to the same fixture in June 2012; it was to prove their only slip-up in the group stage. Hampshire needed 20 from three overs with McKenzie and Sean Ervine well set, but Mitch Claydon got them both in a collapse of five for nine.*

At Southampton, July 26 (floodlit). **Hampshire won by five wickets. Essex 182-5** (20 overs) (O. A. Shah 68); ‡**Hampshire 183-5** (19.2 overs) (M. A. Carberry 54, S. M. Ervine 36, Extras 33; R. J. W. Topley 3-30). *MoM:* M. A. Carberry. *Attendance:* 8,759. *The umpires paused play in the game's penultimate over to levy a six-run penalty against Essex for failing to bowl their overs in time. Remarkably, it was their fourth over-rate punishment of the season in all cricket. Fifteen wides and ten leg-byes did not help. Frustratingly for them, Reece Topley then removed Ervine and Adam Wheater – caught behind first ball against his former county – with consecutive deliveries. Hampshire would have needed eight from the last over without the penalty. Owais Shah tore his hamstring early on, forcing him to employ a runner, but still belted 68 off 43 balls.*

At Southampton, July 31 (floodlit). **Hampshire won by eight runs. ‡Hampshire 190-3** (20 overs) (J. H. K. Adams 43, N. D. McKenzie 47*, S. M. Ervine 60*); **Middlesex 182-7** (20 overs) (J. L. Denly 67; C. P. Wood 3-31). *MoM*: S. M. Ervine. *Attendance*: 6,270. *McKenzie and Ervine put on 101* in the second half of the innings to set up Hampshire's eighth win. Middlesex needed ten from the last two balls to join Hampshire in the quarter-finals – because Essex had lost their last match – but Joe Denly was caught behind off Chris Wood.*

Hampshire away matches

June 28: no result v Essex.
July 5: beat Sussex by five wickets.
July 14: beat Middlesex by seven wickets.

July 19: beat Surrey by seven wickets.
July 29: beat Kent by 62 runs.

KENT

At Canterbury, June 28 (floodlit). **Middlesex won by four wickets** (D/L). Kent 129-5 (15 overs); **‡Middlesex 111-6** (11.4 overs) (A. M. Rossington 41*; V. D. Philander 4-8). *MoM*: A. M. Rossington. *Attendance*: 1,962. *County debuts*: V. D. Philander (Kent); K. D. Mills (Middlesex). *Rain arrived in Kent's powerplay to slice five overs off each innings. Vernon Philander then ripped through his former county for 3–1–8–4 on Kent debut, either side of a partial floodlight failure and another shower that tweaked Middlesex's target to 111 from 12 overs. The burly Adam Rossington hit three sixes, the last off Matt Coles with two balls remaining.*

At Canterbury, June 30. **Surrey won by 31 runs. ‡Surrey 176-3** (20 overs) (S. M. Davies 95*, G. J. Maxwell 32); **Kent 145-9** (20 overs) (S. A. Northeast 61, D. I. Stevens 30; J. W. Dernbach 3-22). *MoM*: S. M. Davies. *Attendance*: 3,359. *Sam Northeast and Darren Stevens carried the reply to 97-2 after 11 overs, but a crash of wickets allowed death-bowling specialists Jade Dernbach and Azhar Mahmood – released by Kent the previous season – to mop up the tail. Surrey's innings was underpinned by Steve Davies's stunning 95* from 70 balls, and rounded off by Glenn Maxwell's 32 from 18.*

At Canterbury, July 5 (floodlit). **Essex won by 47 runs. Essex 164-6** (20 overs) (O. A. Shah 59, R. N. ten Doeschate 31); **‡Kent 117** (17.3 overs) (G. R. Napier 3-12, R. J. W. Topley 3-19). *MoM*: O. A. Shah. *Attendance*: 3,752. *A season's-best crowd at St Lawrence watched Kent slide to their third consecutive defeat. Owais Shah was at his bottom-handed best, launching six sixes in 59 from 38 balls. Graham Napier had Northeast lbw with the first ball of the reply, and only Rob Key (26) passed 19.*

At Canterbury, July 24 (floodlit). **Kent won by nine runs. ‡Kent 173-3** (20 overs) (F. K. Cowdrey 40, D. I. Stevens 67*; C. J. Liddle 3-43); **Sussex 164-6** (20 overs) (M. W. Machan 67, C. D. Nash 31). *MoM*: D. I. Stevens. *Attendance*: 3,247. *Sussex required 23 from Mitch Claydon's last over, and were assisted when he conceded a four and a six to Scott Styris – who then holed out off the fourth ball. Stevens held Kent's fragile batting together with a sumptuous 67*, including a last-ball six carved over extra cover off Lewis Hatchett.*

At Canterbury, July 29 (floodlit). **Hampshire won by 62 runs. ‡Hampshire 185-6** (20 overs) (M. A. Carberry 83*, N. D. McKenzie 45); **Kent 123-9** (20 overs) (D. I. Stevens 39; L. A. Dawson 4-19). *MoM*: M. A. Carberry. *Attendance*: 2,922. *Michael Carberry, who had struck 154 and 66 in the recent Championship fixture here, prospered again at his old ground to wrap up the group for Hampshire. He plundered his fourth half-century of the campaign, against an experimental Kent side resigned to missing the knockout stages. When Stevens clubbed Liam Dawson for a second successive six in the 11th over, he became the first player to hit 100 sixes in the English Twenty20 competition.*

Kent away matches

July 7: lost to Middlesex by nine wickets.
July 8: lost to Essex by 62 runs.
July 21: beat Hampshire by eight runs.

July 26: lost to Surrey by five wickets.
July 31: lost to Sussex by eight wickets.

MIDDLESEX

At Lord's, June 30. **Sussex won by 24 runs. ‡Sussex 202-3** (20 overs) (C. D. Nash 45, L. J. Wright 81, R. J. Hamilton-Brown 47); **Middlesex 178-8** (20 overs) (P. R. Stirling 33, D. J. Malan 61; M. H. Yardy 3-30). *MoM:* L. J. Wright. *Attendance:* 13,633. *In glorious sunshine, Sussex's top four all recorded a strike-rate of 150-plus; Luke Wright, who smashed 81 off 49 balls, had scored 602 runs in all cricket during a golden June. With Eoin Morgan sidelined by a hand injury sustained while captaining England, the match felt over when Paul Stirling fell in the seventh over.*

At Lord's, July 4 (floodlit). **Middlesex won by seven wickets. ‡Essex 170-8** (20 overs) (M. L. Pettini 37, H. D. Rutherford 38, R. S. Bopara 32*); **Middlesex 174-3** (19.4 overs) (D. J. Malan 86, J. L. Denly 52*). *MoM:* D. J. Malan. *Attendance:* 20,017. *Middlesex left-arm spinner Ravi Patel conceded only 17 from his first spell in Twenty20, and bowled Mark Pettini after a painful blow to the inside thigh from Toby Roland-Jones had forced him to use a runner. Essex hit no sixes from the fall of Pettini and Hamish Rutherford until the arrival of Graham Napier – ludicrously low at No. 9 – who whacked 24 from eight balls. They could not contain Dawid Malan, who tamed Shaun Tait with a memorable six over extra cover in his second spell.*

At Uxbridge, July 7. **Middlesex won by nine wickets. Kent 140-6** (20 overs) (A. J. Blake 37*); **‡Middlesex 142-1** (15.4 overs) (A. M. Rossington 74, D. J. Malan 31*, J. L. Denly 33*). *MoM:* A. M. Rossington. *Attendance:* 2,270. *Kent's batsmen did little to divert the Uxbridge crowd from their smartphones and tablets, as they nervously followed Andy Murray's progress to his first Wimbledon title. Middlesex did themselves no favours by spilling four catches, three off Kyle Mills's bowling. After a sedate start, Adam Rossington exploded: he hit a six off Vernon Philander and four fours in five balls off Darren Stevens, and sprinted to 74 from 37, his maiden Twenty20 half-century.*

At Richmond, July 14. **Hampshire won by seven wickets. Middlesex 162-5** (20 overs) (D. J. Malan 77); **‡Hampshire 164-3** (15.1 overs) (M. A. Carberry 43, J. M. Vince 84). *MoM:* J. M. Vince. *Attendance:* 3,149. *Malan aside, Middlesex made a slow club pitch look like a minefield. But Hampshire's opening pair knocked off 89 in 6.4 overs: Michael Carberry whacked Mills for 24 in the third; Gurjit Sandhu replaced him, and was hit for five consecutive fours by James Vince.*

At Lord's, July 25 (floodlit). **Surrey won by 86 runs. Surrey 178-7** (20 overs) (V. S. Solanki 37, K. J. O'Brien 54, Azhar Mahmood 35; G. K. Berg 3-37, R. H. Patel 3-28); **‡Middlesex 92** (14 overs) (G. K. Berg 33). *MoM:* K. J. O'Brien. *Attendance:* 26,285. *This pivotal meeting of the two London counties on a balmy evening nudged the attendance up towards the record for a domestic Twenty20 match in England (27,509, for their first match at Lord's, in 2004), thanks to new seating in the Compton and Edrich stands. It was the short distance to the Mound and Tavern stands – barely 45 yards in Kevin O'Brien's estimation – that held the key to victory. O'Brien and Vikram Solanki, restored to the side when Ricky Ponting withdrew with a groin strain, took full advantage in a third-wicket partnership of 90 in 45 balls. A disjointed Middlesex, meanwhile, hit just two sixes, and plunged to their first sub-100 total in Twenty20.*

Middlesex away matches

June 28: beat Kent by four wickets (D/L).
July 5: lost to Surrey by 15 runs.
July 12: beat Essex by eight wickets.

July 16: beat Sussex by six wickets.
July 31: lost to Hampshire by eight runs.

SURREY

At The Oval, July 3 (floodlit). **Surrey won by three runs. ‡Surrey 139-6** (20 overs) (G. C. Wilson 44*); **Sussex 136-8** (20 overs) (S. B. Styris 46). *MoM:* S. B. Styris. *Attendance:* 12,837. *Scott Styris threatened to steal victory when he took Sussex to within 13 of victory with nine balls left. Then Jade Dernbach uprooted his stumps, and Ben Brown failed to connect when trying to ramp Azhar Mahmood for four off the last ball. Umpire Trevor Jesty was flattened by a fearsome blow to the shoulder from Jason Roy (29), but he waved away a stretcher and staggered to square leg for the next over. A lucky spectator clung on to one of Dwayne Smith's two sixes, earning a £1,000 prize from ground sponsors Kia.*

At The Oval, July 5 (floodlit). **Surrey won by 15 runs. Surrey 147-9** (20 overs) (J. J. Roy 52; R. H. Patel 4-18); **‡Middlesex 132-8** (20 overs) (N. J. Dexter 40). *MoM:* J. J. Roy. *Attendance:* 19,747.

Surrey, without a victory in the Championship, won their fourth Twenty20 match in a row. Their innings faded badly after Roy and Ricky Ponting fell in successive balls to Ravi Patel; Roy received a reprimand from the ECB for disputing Richard Kettleborough's lbw decision. Middlesex failed to recover sufficiently from 45-4, despite Neil Dexter's clever harbouring of the tail.

At The Oval, July 15 (floodlit). **Essex won by eight wickets.** ‡Surrey 148-6 (20 overs) (J. J. Roy 30; R. T. Ponting 65); **Essex 149-2** (18.5 overs) (G. M. Smith 62, H. D. Rutherford 30, O. A. Shah 46*). *MoM:* G. M. Smith. *Attendance:* 14,118. *Ponting's silken 65 from 54 balls – his first and only limited-overs fifty for Surrey – stood alone for the home side on a sweltering night. Hamish Rutherford's 30 from 17 set the tone of the Essex reply, and Surrey could not contain the unorthodox pair of Greg Smith and Owais Shah, who sealed the deal with his fifth substantial score in a row.*

At The Oval, July 19 (floodlit). **Hampshire won by seven wickets.** ‡Surrey 126-6 (20 overs); **Hampshire 127-3** (18.2 overs) (J. H. K. Adams 30). *MoM:* S. M. Ervine (Hampshire). *Attendance:* 17,182. *County debut:* K. J. O'Brien (Surrey). *Once Roy was out to his eighth ball for 22, Surrey were imprisoned by a tight bowling display, shedding four wickets in successive overs. Ponting received his Surrey cap before play, but made only three before chipping Chris Wood to extra cover, then tweaked his groin in the field.*

At The Oval, July 26 (floodlit). **Surrey won by five wickets.** ‡Kent 139-4 (20 overs) (F. K. Cowdrey 50); **Surrey 140-5** (19.1 overs) (J. J. Roy 30, Z. S. Ansari 30*, Azhar Mahmood 47*). *MoM:* Azhar Mahmood. *Attendance:* 20,478. *Spectators flocked to The Oval in the hope of seeing Ponting's last appearance for Surrey, but he failed to recover from injury in time, and flew out to prepare for the Caribbean Premier League. The pick of Fabian Cowdrey's strokes in a maiden Kent fifty was an impudent ramp over his right shoulder off Chris Tremlett. Azhar Mahmood's last over cost 20, but he returned with the bat to take toll of his old team-mates. Surrey's collapse from 47-0 to 61-5 in a rain of bewildering shots was put right by Zafar Ansari's sensible approach and Mahmood's muscling of 17 off Matt Coles in the penultimate over.*

Surrey away matches

June 26: lost to Hampshire by five wickets.
June 28: beat Sussex by ten runs.
June 30: beat Kent by 31 runs.

July 25: beat Middlesex by 86 runs.
July 31: beat Essex by 61 runs.

SUSSEX

At Hove, June 28 (floodlit). **Surrey won by ten runs.** ‡Surrey 157-6 (20 overs) (J. J. Roy 42, G. C. Wilson 31); **Sussex 147-7** (20 overs) (R. J. Hamilton-Brown 34, M. H. Yardy 44, S. B. Styris 35; J. W. Dernbach 3-15). *MoM:* J. W. Dernbach. *Attendance:* 6,319. *Sussex looked favourites with 19 needed from two overs, but Azhar Mahmood and Jade Dernbach conceded just four runs each. Mahmood's 23 off 13 balls gave Surrey late momentum, before Mike Yardy found the boundary only three times in 45 deliveries.*

At Hove, July 5 (floodlit). **Hampshire won by five wickets.** ‡Sussex 145-6 (20 overs) (S. B. Styris 39*); **Hampshire 148-5** (19.3 overs) (M. A. Carberry 50, N. D. McKenzie 71*). *MoM:* N. D. McKenzie. *Attendance:* 5,866. *Neil McKenzie's well-paced 71* from 50 balls was the difference between the sides, but he needed a slice of luck. Hampshire needed 12 from the last over, and they got six when Chris Liddle attempted to run out McKenzie as he came back for a second; the ball bounced unkindly for wicketkeeper Ben Brown, deflected off his gloves and flew to the unguarded extra-cover boundary. McKenzie crashed Chris Jordan's next delivery, a low full toss, for the winning four.*

At Hove, July 16 (floodlit). **Middlesex won by six wickets.** Sussex 148-7 (20 overs) (C. D. Nash 61*; G. K. Berg 3-19); ‡**Middlesex 152-4** (19.4 overs) (D. J. Malan 41, J. L. Denly 53). *MoM:* J. L. Denly. *Attendance:* 4,565. *Chris Nash was hit on the collarbone by Gareth Berg early in his innings, but hauled him for six later in the over. Nash threw Lewis Hatchett the ball for the opening over on his Twenty20 debut, but the experience was chastening: the first delivery went for four leg-byes, and the next five were all hit to the boundary by Paul Stirling. Andrew Miller removed Stirling's off stump next over, but Middlesex's more aggressive approach proved telling.*

At Hove, July 21. **Essex won by seven wickets.** ‡Sussex 146-8 (20 overs) (R. J. Hamilton-Brown 31; R. J. W. Topley 4-26); **Essex 147-3** (17.1 overs) (G. M. Smith 42, H. D. Rutherford 84). *MoM:*

H. D. Rutherford. *Attendance: 4,841. The Sussex seamers had no answer to Hamish Rutherford's placement and power, which delivered 84 in 43 balls. Sussex handed 18-year-old wicketkeeper Callum Jackson a competitive debut, as Brown had broken a finger, and he claimed all three Essex wickets with stumpings. Reece Topley was hit out of the ground by Scott Styris, but went over the wicket next ball, and had him held on the boundary; he later added three wickets in the final over.*

At Hove, July 31 (floodlit). **Kent won by eight wickets.** ‡Sussex 113 (20 overs) (M. W. Machan 31; M. E. Claydon 3-22, M. T. Coles 3-14); **Kent 117-2** (13.1 overs) (M. T. Coles 40). MoM: M. T. Coles. *Attendance: 5,117. A large crowd turned up for what proved to be Sussex's ninth defeat of the competition. Kent's bowlers feasted on a side lacking in confidence: Matt Coles picked up the match award in his last Twenty20 appearance for them before moving to Hampshire.*

Sussex away matches

June 30: beat Middlesex by 24 runs.
July 3: lost to Surrey by three runs.
July 12: lost to Hampshire by four wickets.

July 14: lost to Essex by six wickets.
July 24: lost to Kent by nine runs.

QUARTER-FINALS

At The Oval, August 6. **Surrey won by three wickets.** ‡Somerset 148-6 (20 overs) (C. Kieswetter 70*, P. D. Trego 33); **Surrey 151-7** (19 overs) (S. M. Davies 35, V. S. Solanki 38). MoM: V. S. Solanki. *Attendance: 13,305. Surrey reached Twenty20 finals day for the first time in seven years, but that was not the main talking point. When Gareth Batty bowled Peter Trego to end a second-wicket stand of 60, the Surrey captain clapped his hands furiously and let out a roar in the batsman's direction. Trego took exception, removed his helmet, and they collided moments later in a gaggle of Surrey players; Craig Kieswetter, the other batsman, had to be restrained by Jade Dernbach, and was later reprimanded for his angry reaction. Batty was reported by all three umpires for "inappropriate and deliberate physical contact in the course of play", and for "using obscene or insulting language". Gerard Elias QC, chairman of the ECB disciplinary commission, called his behaviour "appalling", and banned him for two matches, invoking a directive which ensured he would miss finals day rather than dead-rubber YB40 fixtures. Surrey expressed their regret at Batty's actions, but were unhappy at the summary nature of the penalty – no formal hearing was convened – and claimed any physical contact was accidental. Surrey had already expressed annoyance at the 4pm Tuesday start foisted upon them by television schedules, which led to a modest crowd, despite special offers and free tickets handed out to local clubs. Kieswetter dealt brutally with the bowling given the chance, but Batty cannily limited him to only 51 balls through the innings. Surrey's openers responded with 62 in 7.3 overs, ended by a superlative catch in the deep by Jos Buttler to remove Jason Roy. Vikram Solanki then tore into George Dockrell to make sure of victory, despite two comical run-outs.*

At Northampton, August 6 (floodlit). **Northamptonshire won by 36 runs.** ‡Northamptonshire 183-4 (20 overs) (K. J. Coetzer 44, D. J. Willey 46, C. L. White 58*); **Durham 147-6** (20 overs) (P. Mustard 46, B. A. Stokes 51*). MoM: C. L. White. *Attendance: 5,200. Northamptonshire drew inspiration from their biggest crowd in the competition since reaching the same stage in 2009; Durham had now lost their last three quarter-finals. Richard Levi was absent on South Africa A duty, but David Willey helped Kyle Coetzer make excellent use of a pacy pitch, before Cameron White muscled 58* from 32 balls, including three sixes off Gareth Breese in the 16th over. "It's scary stuff when the ball is hitting the bottom of the bat, but still going over the ropes," said Paul Collingwood. Stokes thumped three sixes in ten deliveries – but Northamptonshire were not to be denied.*

At Southampton, August 7. **Hampshire won by one run. Hampshire 202-3** (20 overs) (J. M. Vince 60, M. A. Carberry 100*); ‡Lancashire 201-4 (20 overs) (S. C. Moore 44, K. R. Brown 49, S. J. Croft 43*, G. D. Cross 32*). MoM: M. A. Carberry. *Attendance: 8,065. More than 400 runs had been scored by the time Hampshire secured victory off the last ball of an amazing match. In a game of such fine margins, Lancashire could look back with a little frustration at Karl Brown's dismissal, bowled attempting to cut Danny Briggs, when replays suggested that wicketkeeper Adam Wheater had inadvertently knocked the bails off first; Briggs also bowled Simon Katich next ball. Lancashire were 70 away with six overs left when Steven Croft and Gareth Cross joined forces, and they came within an ace of pulling it off, helped by two late no-balls from Sohail Tanvir. Cross needed a boundary off Tanvir's last delivery, but could only punch a low full toss down the ground for two.*

Jan Kruger, Getty Images

No love lost: Peter Trego takes exception to Gareth Batty's piercing celebration.

For Lancashire to get close was a phenomenal achievement, though, after James Vince and Michael Carberry crunched 110 in the first ten overs: Vince sprinted along at two runs a ball, while Carberry's bruising forearm strength allowed him to bring up his maiden Twenty20 century off the last delivery of the innings. England could no longer ignore Carberry, and called him up for the limited-overs matches against Australia. Mitchell McClenaghan's tweet – "Ta ta Hampshire" – when the quarter-final draw was announced, came back to haunt him with figures of 4–0–49–0, as he bore the brunt of Carberry's punishment.

At Nottingham, August 8. **Essex won by 47 runs. Essex 187-6** (20 overs) (R. S. Bopara 38, R. N. ten Doeschate 82; I. G. Butler 3-23); ‡**Nottinghamshire 140** (17.2 overs) (A. D. Hales 31, D. J. Hussey 61; S. W. Tait 4-29, D. D. Masters 3-26). *MoM:* R. N. ten Doeschate. *Attendance:* 12,106. *This was a record crowd for a Twenty20 match at Trent Bridge, but Nottinghamshire were the only home quarter-finalists to lose – they had now been dumped out at this stage three seasons running. Ryan ten Doeschate, unfathomably given not out on six by umpire Nigel Llong to Ian Butler's impassioned lbw appeal, targeted the home spinners, thrashing 47 off the 22 balls he faced from Samit Patel and Graeme White. Essex learned by not bowling slow left-armer Tim Phillips at all. Alex Hales and Michael Lumb thumped 46 from the first 20 balls, but both succumbed to David Masters, and Patel completed a forgettable match with a grim two off 12. David Hussey fought valiantly, but became the first victim of Shaun Tait's hat-trick, in an over which began with the run-out of Chris Read.*

FINALS DAY REPORTS BY JAMES COYNE

SEMI-FINALS

ESSEX v NORTHAMPTONSHIRE

At Birmingham, August 17, 2013. Northamptonshire won by seven wickets. Toss: Northamptonshire.
    Even by the standards of elite fielding, it was no more than a quarter-chance. But it was the only one Essex would get to split Crook and White – and they missed it. Crook, on five, leant back to

crack Tait towards extra cover, where Pettini flung himself to his right and got a hand to the ball as it dipped. The next delivery was a touch quicker and fuller, and Crook rifled it back over Tait's head. Foster persisted with Phillips, whose first three overs had cost only 16, and the batsmen pummelled 62 off the next 20 balls to convert the tallest run-chase on finals day into something of a cakewalk. Cobblers back home were calling Crook "the Northants Botham" – not that Beefy ever fronted an indie band, or took on a gig as his county's in-house DJ when injuries laid him low. Now Crook was blasting Northamptonshire into their first final since the Britpop era. "There are probably a handful of guys in the world that can go out and strike the ball like that," said Foster, who had now lost all four of his Twenty20 semi-finals. This one baffled him, because Essex had punished Northamptonshire's lacklustre fielding: Rutherford thrashed 36 after White got one hand to a sharp chance at slip in the first over, then Napier 23 off his last six balls after Wakely dropped a dolly at mid-off. Although Levi thundered anything on his pads, Topley did for him with a full toss on the legal side of waist-high. His wicket sent the asking-rate spiralling towards 12 an over – but Crook was undaunted.

Man of the Match: S. P. Crook.

Attendance (for all three matches on finals day): 22,508.

Essex

		B	4	6
G. M. Smith *c 10 b 5*	2	5	0	0
H. D. Rutherford *c 4 b 11*	36	19	2	2
M. L. Pettini *c 9 b 7*	27	23	3	0
R. S. Bopara *c 8 b 2*	14	19	1	0
R. N. ten Doeschate *c 1 b 11*	13	15	0	0
*†J. S. Foster *not out*	32	24	3	1
G. R. Napier *not out*	38	15	3	3
B 1, l-b 4, w 1	6			

6 overs: 51-2   (20 overs)   168-5

1/13 2/44 3/79 4/82 5/114

T. J. Phillips, D. D. Masters, S. W. Tait and R. J. W. Topley did not bat.

Willey 4–0–43–0; Crook 4–0–32–1; Azharullah 4–0–38–2; Daggett 4–0–29–0; Middlebrook 2–0–12–1; Coetzer 1–0–4–1; Spriegel 1–0–5–0.

Northamptonshire

		B	4	6
R. E. Levi *c 2 b 11*	57	35	4	4
K. J. Coetzer *c 4 b 11*	18	19	2	0
C. L. White *not out*	36	25	4	1
*A. G. Wakely *c and b 9*	3	7	0	0
S. P. Crook *not out*	46	24	3	4
L-b 7, w 2, n-b 2	11			

6 overs: 51-0   (18.1 overs)   171-3

1/74 2/83 3/93

D. J. Willey, J. D. Middlebrook, M. N. W. Spriegel, †D. Murphy, L. M. Daggett and Azharullah did not bat.

Masters 4–0–30–1; Napier 3–0–45–0; Tait 3.1–0–29–0; Topley 4–0–24–2; Phillips 4–0–36–0.

Umpires: N. A. Mallender and R. T. Robinson.   Third umpire: M. A. Gough.

HAMPSHIRE v SURREY

At Birmingham, August 17, 2013. Surrey won by four wickets. Toss: Surrey.

Hampshire, two wins from a third title in four years, had started to acquire an aura in Twenty20 – but it took only a few balls for Azhar Mahmood to dispel it. Carberry had scored so many runs (496, with only a single failure) getting them to the semi-final that it was perhaps inevitable he would miscue one. He was not the only batsman rattled by the ageless Mahmood, who conceded no runs from his first 11 balls, and one boundary, off his last. The cardinal sin, though, was committed by Dawson and Wheater who, with Ervine playing a blinder to keep the innings afloat, fell to ill-conceived shots. Mascarenhas endured a thoroughly joyless goodbye to English Twenty20: he ran out his partner Wood attempting a single to wicketkeeper Davies, then top-edged the next ball high into the gloom. Hampshire's score was plainly insufficient but, after teasing spots of rain began to fall in the first over of the reply, Surrey were content to inch ahead of Duckworth/Lewis. Wood's death spell represented Hampshire's last throw of the dice: McKenzie held a superb catch running back from point to remove Wilson with its first ball; then Dawson's direct hit beat Mahmood – no longer a spring chicken between the wickets – as he returned for a second. But, with 17 needed off 11 balls, Wood fired in a yorker. Ansari saw it coming, and bunted a sweet straight six to release the tension.

Man of the Match: Azhar Mahmood.

Hampshire

		B	4	6
M. A. Carberry *c 1 b 9*	6	9	1	0
J. M. Vince *b 11*	13	11	1	1
J. H. K. Adams *b 5*	19	20	1	1
N. D. McKenzie *lbw b 11*	5	3	1	0
S. M. Ervine *c 8 b 7*	47	32	2	3
L. A. Dawson *c 4 b 8*	8	12	0	0
†A. J. Wheater *lbw b 3*	2	3	0	0
*A. D. Mascarenhas *c 3 b 7*	15	15	1	0
C. P. Wood *run out*	12	5	1	1
Sohail Tanvir *not out*	7	7	1	0
D. R. Briggs *not out*	5	3	1	0
L-b 1, w 2	3			

6 overs: 39-3   (20 overs)   142-9

1/8 2/32 3/38 4/58 5/85 6/96 7/115 8/130 9/130

Azhar Mahmood 4–1–9–2; Tremlett 2–0–26–0; Lewis 2–0–12–1; Dernbach 4–0–32–2; de Bruyn 3–0–23–1; Ansari 3–0–26–1; Maxwell 2–0–13–1.

Surrey

		B	4	6
J. J. Roy *c 6 b 8*	5	5	1	0
†S. M. Davies *c 8 b 9*	9	8	1	0
G. J. Maxwell *c 5 b 6*	26	21	4	0
*V. S. Solanki *lbw b 11*	19	15	4	0
Z. de Bruyn *not out*	41	40	3	0
G. C. Wilson *c 4 b 9*	15	15	1	0
Azhar Mahmood *run out*	0	0	0	0
Z. S. Ansari *not out*	21	12	2	1
W 9	9			

6 overs: 43-2   (19.2 overs)   145-6

1/9 2/17 3/53 4/71 5/111 6/112

J. Lewis, C. T. Tremlett and J. W. Dernbach did not bat.

Sohail Tanvir 3.2–0–24–0; Mascarenhas 4–0–24–1; Wood 4–0–40–2; Briggs 4–0–28–1; Dawson 4–0–29–1.

Umpires: R. J. Bailey and M. A. Gough.   Third umpire: R. T. Robinson.

FINAL

NORTHAMPTONSHIRE v SURREY

At Birmingham, August 17, 2013 (floodlit). Northamptonshire won by 102 runs (D/L). Toss: Surrey.

Northamptonshire's recent existence, chugging along in the backwaters of the domestic game, had often been dismissed as a life of handouts. The reality was actually far more corrosive. In May, after they had lost 32 of their last 37 limited-overs matches, their overseas player Trent Copeland halted a team meeting to express amazement at his new colleagues' lack of belief.

Three months later, the same county belted runs with a joyful freedom. Players who had never lifted a trophy grinned their way between overs, telling each other to savour the moment. Their young captain Wakely, who first came into a dreary dressing-room dominated by Kolpaks, said the last 20 minutes, when only the margin of victory was in doubt, was his best cricketing experience. The symbolism was lost on no one when their 21-year footslog to a major title – the longest wait of all the counties – was ended by a hat-trick from Willey, their most charismatic home-grown player since Graeme Swann.

Virtually everything went right for them. After Kyle Coetzer hurt his wrist batting in the semifinal, the left-handed Willey was sent up to open. Whereas Hampshire had found Azhar Mahmood impossible to get away, Willey's hitting worked just fine – and Northamptonshire were 37 for one by the time rain began hosing down in the fourth over, cutting the match to 18 a side. Both captains had wanted to bowl first given the grim forecast, but that had complications too. Ansari had conceded only a single in the first over but, when play resumed, Solanki trusted neither of his spinners with another, for fear the skidding ball would be too easy to hit. Tremlett seemed wary about breaking down four days before his mooted Test return at The Oval (which never materialised), while Dernbach was a sitting duck. Willey walloped his length deliveries for 20 in the over after the restart, and raced to a 19-ball fifty – the fastest of the season. Dernbach called him a "filthy slogger"; Willey reasoned that was mostly the point of Twenty20. "I don't particularly like the bloke, to be honest, so it's good to ruin his figures," Willey told Sky's dugout interviewer. He won the argument: Dernbach's analysis was the second-worst in a Twenty20 final, Willey's would be the best.

Northamptonshire's domestic players marvelled at how brilliantly White, who had captained Australia in Twenty20, read the game. Four overs passed with him barely looking for a boundary, during which time Wakely found seven, sometimes streakily. But when White took a step inside and hoisted Mahmood imperiously over the sightscreen, Surrey must have thought Kevin Pietersen – resting between Ashes Tests – had left them for a fourth county. White and Wakely crashed 107 in the second half of the innings; Surrey, like Essex earlier in the day, were frazzled enough to give away a no-ball for letting a sixth fielder slip outside the circle.

By now, Willey was making his own luck. In Surrey's third over, Murphy stood up, dragging Roy back into his crease; he was glued inside, and late on the drive, when Willey seared one through his defences next ball. Soon after, Davies tried to pinch a second run when Willey fumbled at long-on, but he recovered and slung down middle stump. Of Surrey's expensively assembled side, Maxwell was likeliest to do something spectacular. But after he smote three sixes, Crook foxed him with a gem of a slower ball. Willey was then brought back for his second spell and instantly won the match with a hat-trick – only the second in the Twenty20 final, after Ryan McLaren for Kent in 2007 – completed when Tremlett prodded outside off stump, and was clasped one-handed by a tumbling Murphy. Soon Willey was bear-hugging Northamptonshire's long-suffering supporters, and leading his team-mates in their self-deprecating victory song, "Fields of Green", about their unfashionable – and for too long, irrelevant – provincial team.

Man of the Match: D. J. Willey.

Northamptonshire

		B	*4*	*6*
R. E. Levi *b 5*	14	13	1	1
D. J. Willey *c 7 b 9*	60	27	6	4
C. L. White *not out*	54	39	2	2
*A. G. Wakely *not out*	59	30	7	2
L-b 1, w 4, n-b 2	7			

5 overs: 57-1   (18 overs)   194-2

1/37 2/87

S. P. Crook, B. M. Duckett, J. D. Middlebrook, M. N. W. Spriegel, †D. Murphy, L. M. Daggett and Azharullah did not bat.

Ansari 1–0–1–0; Azhar Mahmood 4–0–53–1; Tremlett 3–0–29–0; Dernbach 4–0–55–0; Lewis 3–0–24–1; de Bruyn 3–0–31–0.

Surrey

		B	*4*	*6*
J. J. Roy *b 2*	13	12	2	0
†S. M. Davies *run out*	8	7	1	0
G. J. Maxwell *c 9 b 5*	29	17	2	3
*V. S. Solanki *c 6 b 7*	12	15	1	0
Azhar Mahmood *c 2 b 11*	2	4	0	0
Z. de Bruyn *c 3 b 10*	4	4	0	0
G. C. Wilson *b 5*	14	11	1	1
Z. S. Ansari *c 5 b 2*	6	8	0	0
J. Lewis *c 7 b 2*	0	2	0	0
C. T. Tremlett *c 9 b 2*	0	1	0	0
J. W. Dernbach *not out*	0	0	0	0
L-b 3, w 1	4			

5 overs: 38-1   (13.3 overs)   92

1/17 2/39 3/53 4/59 5/70 6/72 7/92 8/92 9/92

Willey 2.3–0–9–4; Crook 3–0–26–2; Azharullah 3–0–30–1; Daggett 2–0–5–1; Middlebrook 3–0–19–1.

Umpires: M. A. Gough and N. A. Mallender.   Third umpire: R. J. Bailey.

YORKSHIRE BANK 40, 2013

Review by John Westerby

Sunday lunch will not be the same for county supporters this summer. Much else will be new in the restructured English domestic programme, but perhaps the most conspicuous absentee will be a competition that owed its enduring appeal to the fact that spectators could finish their meal, without serious risk of indigestion, and still take their seats in time for a 1.45 start.

This year, for much of the summer, Sunday lunch will have to be squeezed into the interval on the first day of a Championship match. As for the longer of the two county one-day competitions, now called the Royal London One-Day Cup, it's not just the title that has changed.

The main alteration is that innings have swollen to 50 overs, bringing the format into line with one-day internationals. Other revisions include a new structure – two groups of nine, rather than three of seven, so it's farewell to English domestic cricket for Scotland, the Netherlands and the Unicorns – and the concertinaing of the tournament into a late-summer block, starting on July 26. Despite this, there will thankfully be time for quarter-finals, at a stroke greatly reducing the likelihood of dead matches, and the temptations to which they can fall prey.

As a result, the 2013 final, in which Nottinghamshire beat Glamorgan by 87 runs, was the last 40-over game likely to be played for the foreseeable future. There have been summers without 40-over cricket before, but it looks as if a format that began with the International Cavaliers in the mid-1960s, spawned the popular Sunday League, and survived longer than many expected, has finally been consigned to the archives. The death knell came in the report into the county season carried out by David Morgan, the former ECB chairman.

Within the domestic game, the changes were viewed with mixed feelings, because the format had remained popular with players, spectators and administrators alike. The strongest pressure for reform came from those associated with the England team, who argued that the cause of the national side – yet to win either the World Cup or Champions Trophy – was being hindered by the absence of 50-over cricket from the county schedule.

The most ardent opponents of change remained the county chief executives, who saw the 40-over competition as a reliable source of income. The point about spectators enjoying their Sunday roast was not entirely trivial: smaller crowds are probable. "It will be a different Sunday audience for a Championship match, and I'm not sure how many clubs will make up the money they'll lose," said David Smith, the Northamptonshire chief executive. Morgan's report prompted heated discussion, but the interests of the all-powerful national team prevailed.

So perhaps it was appropriate that the final blows of the 40-over game were struck by an England player: in his only appearance in the competition in 2013, Stuart Broad took three wickets in an over to complete Nottinghamshire's demolition of Glamorgan.

Broad and Graeme Swann had been rested from the NatWest Series against Australia that had just finished, but both played their part for Nottinghamshire in front of a Lord's crowd of over 17,000. The satisfaction may have been greater, though, for Samit Patel, who picked up the match award for his left-arm spin and had also been one of the competition's leading batsmen.

Mick Newell, the Nottinghamshire coach, was one of many who lamented the passing of 40-over contests. "I liked the pace of the game, and county cricket needs people coming through the gate," he said. "The biggest challenge in 2014 will be for my top-order batsmen. Longer innings will be needed from them in 50-over cricket; a cameo 30 or 40 in the powerplay won't be enough."

In case this view is seen as peculiarly English, it was echoed by Jason Gillespie, Yorkshire's Australian coach. "I'm not sure the overs difference is as big an issue as some people think," he said. "It's good entertainment, and it challenges players to get their skills right." Their view is perhaps best summed up by Alex Wakely, Northamptonshire's limited-overs captain. He enjoyed the old format, but had an eye on the bigger picture. "A lot of us haven't really played 50 overs, and if we have aspirations of playing for England, that's

HIGHEST TOTALS IN 40-OVER CRICKET

399-4	Sussex v Worcestershire at Horsham	2011
386-3†	Surrey v Glamorgan at The Oval	2010
376-6	Worcestershire v Surrey at The Oval	2010
375-4	Surrey v Yorkshire at Scarborough	1994
368-4	Somerset v Glamorgan at Taunton	2010
368-7	**Essex v Scotland at Chelmsford**	**2013**
360-3	Somerset v Glamorgan at Neath	1990
350-6	Middlesex v Lancashire at Lord's	2012

† *Reduced to 38 overs a side.*

probably not right," he said. Wakely would not be surprised to see scores of between 350 and 400, when conditions allow. "We usually felt 230 to 240 was a good score from 40 overs, but sometimes teams will just keep going."

The highest total in 2013 was 368 for seven, by Essex against Scotland at Chelmsford in June, a game featuring 180 from Ryan ten Doeschate, the largest individual score. The outstanding bowling performance also came at Chelmsford, where Graham Napier took seven for 32 against Surrey. Peter Trego, of Somerset, was the competition's highest scorer, with 745 runs from 12 innings, and Glamorgan's Michael Hogan the leading wicket-taker, with 28.

Perhaps the most remarkable match was Kent's breathless victory over Sussex under floodlights at Canterbury. Luke Wright hit a 54-ball hundred, only to watch Darren Stevens reach three figures from 44 as Kent passed Sussex's 336 for five with nine balls to spare.

Counties whose scope for progression to the semis had been derailed by early defeats used the competition to blood young players, not least Yorkshire, who gave a debut to Matthew Fisher, a 15-year-old seam bowler, in their defeat by Leicestershire at Scarborough in June.

When the new 50-over tournament makes its bow in July, one who will be well placed to judge its success will be Hugh Morris. His return to Glamorgan as chief executive and director of cricket was announced a few weeks before their defeat in the YB40 final at Lord's. In his role as managing director of the England team, he had been an influential advocate of county cricket emulating the international format. In 2014, he sits on the other side of the fence, and will face the challenge of balancing the books at a club without the competition that has kept so many chief executives happy.

Prize money

£150,000 (no change from 2012) for winners: NOTTINGHAMSHIRE.
£75,000 (no change) for runners-up: GLAMORGAN.
£25,000 (no change) for losing semi-finalists: HAMPSHIRE, SOMERSET.
There was no financial reward for winning individual matches.

Attendance figures supplied by the ECB. Approximate figures are given for the home matches of Scotland and the Netherlands.

FINAL GROUP TABLES

Group A

		Played	Won	Lost	No result	Points	NRR
1	NOTTINGHAMSHIRE	12	9	3	0	18	0.45
2	Northamptonshire	12	8	3	1	17	0.39
3	Sussex	12	6	4	2	14	0.46
4	Kent	12	6	6	0	12	0.22
5	Worcestershire	12	5	7	0	10	0.24
6	Netherlands	12	2	7	3	7	−1.15
7	Warwickshire	12	2	8	2	6	−0.92

Group B

		Played	Won	Lost	No result	Points	NRR
1	HAMPSHIRE	12	9	3	0	18	0.73
2	Essex	12	8	4	0	16	0.97
3	Lancashire	12	7	4	1	15	−0.02
4	Durham	12	7	4	1	14.75†	0.65
5	Surrey	12	4	6	2	10	−0.52
6	Derbyshire	12	3	6	3	9	−0.25
7	Scotland	12	0	11	1	1	−1.94

Group C

		Played	Won	Lost	No result	Points	NRR
1	SOMERSET	12	8	3	1	17	1.00
2	GLAMORGAN	12	8	3	1	17	0.57
3	Gloucestershire	12	7	4	1	15	0.16
4	Middlesex	12	7	4	1	15	0.14
5	Leicestershire	12	5	7	0	10	−0.35
6	Yorkshire	12	3	9	0	6	−0.46
7	Unicorns	12	1	9	2	4	−1.19

† *Durham were docked 0.25pts for a salary-cap infringement in 2012.*

Where two or more counties finished with an equal number of points, the positions were decided by (a) most wins (b) net run-rate (c) most points in head-to-head matches (d) drawing lots.

YORKSHIRE BANK 40 AVERAGES

BATTING (300 runs at 42.00)

		M	I	NO	R	HS	100	50	Avge	SR	4	6
1	M. Klinger (*Glos*)	12	11	3	702	131*	1	5	87.75	90.46	62	11
2	P. D. Trego (*Somerset*).....	12	12	3	745	140*	2	5	82.77	124.37	90	17
3	J. C. Buttler (*Somerset*)	8	7	3	301	89	0	4	75.25	146.11	31	10
4	J. W. A. Taylor (*Notts*)	13	13	5	585	108	1	4	73.12	85.02	47	3
5	D. J. Malan (*Middx*)	12	11	3	552	113*	1	4	69.00	91.84	58	6
6	M. S. Lineker (*Unicorns*)...	5	5	0	339	132	2	1	67.80	107.61	38	5
7	R. N. ten Doeschate (*Essex*)	9	9	3	382	180	1	1	63.66	131.72	23	23
8	R. S. Bopara (*Essex*)	8	8	1	441	130	2	2	63.00	99.77	36	11
9	L. J. Wright (*Sussex*)	8	8	0	502	115	3	1	62.75	148.52	55	20
10	G. S. Ballance (*Yorks*)	8	7	0	426	139	1	3	60.85	97.93	40	9
11	E. C. Joyce (*Sussex*).......	10	9	2	403	123*	1	3	57.57	95.72	39	3
12	A. G. Prince (*Lancs*)	12	11	2	506	100	1	3	56.22	101.81	49	7
13	J. J. Cobb (*Leics*)	12	12	1	578	130	3	1	52.54	113.77	68	12
14	J. H. K. Adams (*Hants*)	13	13	3	519	67	0	5	51.90	85.08	41	4
15	R. W. T. Key (*Kent*).......	11	11	1	505	144*	2	2	50.50	94.04	62	2
16	B. P. Nash (*Kent*)	12	12	3	436	98*	0	2	48.44	86.33	38	0
17	S. M. Davies (*Surrey*)	9	9	1	387	127*	1	3	48.37	130.74	47	9
18	C. D. J. Dent (*Glos*)	12	10	2	384	151*	1	1	48.00	111.95	41	10
19	S. R. Patel (*Notts*)	14	14	2	566	129*	1	3	47.16	97.92	59	7
20	M. A. Carberry (*Hants*)	11	11	1	471	150*	1	1	47.10	114.32	57	10
21	D. K. H. Mitchell (*Worcs*)..	12	12	0	530	107	1	5	44.16	92.17	48	2
22	A. Lyth (*Yorks*)	11	11	2	397	58*	0	2	44.11	92.75	35	8
23	J. J. Roy (*Surrey*)	12	11	1	432	117	2	1	43.20	105.62	56	3
24	V. S. Solanki (*Surrey*)	12	11	2	379	109*	1	2	42.11	84.03	32	6
25	C. B. Cooke (*Glam*).......	13	13	0	546	98	0	5	42.00	101.11	54	5

BOWLING (12 wickets at 25.00)

		Style	O	M	R	W	BBI	4I	Avge	SR	ER
1	Sohail Tanvir (*Hants*)........	LFM	47.1	4	207	17	4-29	2	12.17	16.64	4.38
2	P. D. Collingwood (*Durham*)...	RM	32.3	0	169	12	3-5	0	14.08	16.25	5.20
3	T. A. Copeland (*Northants*)	RFM	44.4	0	229	15	5-32	2	15.26	17.86	5.12
4	Azharullah (*Northants*)	RFM	46	0	258	15	4-20	2	17.20	18.40	5.60
5	M. G. Hogan (*Glam*)	RFM	87.2	9	488	28	4-34	2	17.42	18.71	5.58
6	A. C. Thomas (*Somerset*)......	RFM	46.3	0	291	16	4-41	1	18.18	17.43	6.25
7	Shahzad (*Notts*).............	RFM	71.4	3	402	22	3-26	0	18.27	19.54	5.60
8	S. P. Crook (*Northants*)	RFM	57	2	314	17	5-36	2	18.47	20.11	5.50
9	C. Rushworth (*Durham*).......	RFM	72.1	5	407	20	5-42	1	20.35	21.65	5.63
10	C. J. Liddle (*Sussex*).........	LFM	68.2	2	390	19	3-21	0	20.52	21.57	5.70
11	K. Ali (*Lancs*)...............	RFM	60.1	2	378	18	4-37	1	21.00	20.05	6.28
12	C. A. J. Meschede (*Somerset*) ..	RFM	85.2	4	478	22	4-5	2	21.72	23.27	5.60
13	G. R. Napier (*Essex*).........	RFM	80.4	6	461	21	7-32	2	21.95	23.04	5.71
14	S. J. Mullaney (*Notts*)........	RFM	78	3	377	17	4-29	1	22.17	27.52	4.83
15	J. T. Ball (*Notts*)...........	RFM	75.3	0	430	19	4-25	1	22.63	23.84	5.69
16	J. S. Patel (*Warwicks*)........	OB	67	1	363	16	4-43	1	22.68	25.12	5.41
17	T. S. Roland-Jones (*Middx*)	RFM	69.3	2	412	18	4-44	1	22.88	23.16	5.92
18	J. C. Tredwell (*Kent*)	OB	70	2	304	13	4-22	1	23.38	32.30	4.34
19	D. A. Payne (*Glos*)...........	LFM	74	0	449	19	4-44	1	23.63	23.36	6.06
20	I. Wardlaw (*Yorks*)..........	RFM	52.4	1	333	14	3-39	0	23.78	22.57	6.32
21	A. D. Mascarenhas (*Hants*)	RM	69	1	315	13	5-42	1	24.23	31.84	4.56
22	J. D. Shantry (*Worcs*)	LFM	70.3	4	388	16	3-11	0	24.25	26.43	5.50
23	M. T. Coles (*Kent*)	RFM	62.2	2	367	15	4-20	1	24.46	24.93	5.88
24	J. Lewis (*Surrey*)	RFM	58	4	323	13	3-57	0	24.84	26.76	5.56
25	J. A. R. Harris (*Middx*)........	RFM	58.5	2	374	15	3-30	0	24.93	23.53	6.35

GROUP A

KENT

At Canterbury, May 15 (day/night). **Kent won by three wickets.** Reduced to 25 overs a side. **Worcestershire 110-9** (25 overs) (M. T. Coles 4-20); ‡**Kent 111-7** (23.1 overs) (J. C. Tredwell 42*; J. D. Shantry 3-11). *Attendance:* 784. *Kent recovered from 45-6 to scrape home, as new captain James Tredwell more than doubled the score alongside his brother-in-law Geraint Jones (30). Superb catches at full stretch from Sam Billings and Ben Harmison helped contain Worcestershire.*

At Tunbridge Wells, May 27. **Kent won by eight wickets.** ‡**Netherlands 249-5** (40 overs) (W. Barresi 69, T. L. W. Cooper 54, D. P. Michael 51*); **Kent 250-2** (35.4 overs) (R. W. T. Key 144*, B. P. Nash 57). *Attendance:* 1,954. *Rob Key's imperious 144* from 121 balls, his one-day best, eased Kent to an emphatic win on the opening day of the 101st Tunbridge Wells Week. Kent's lack of death-bowling expertise had earlier been exposed by the Queenslander Dom Michael, who struck three sixes.*

At Tunbridge Wells, June 2. **Northamptonshire won by 29 runs. Northamptonshire 263-4** (40 overs) (R. I. Newton 88 retired hurt, A. G. Wakely 102); ‡**Kent 234** (39.4 overs) (S. A. Northeast 41, S. W. Billings 57, A. J. Blake 43; T. A. Copeland 4-46). *Attendance:* 2,584. *Rob Newton, on a career-best 78*, went down on one knee and flipped Adam Ball over his left shoulder for four, but twisted his right ankle in doing so. Newton lofted the next ball for a straight six, but the effort caused so much pain he had to retire hurt, and treatment revealed ruptured ligaments. At the other end, Alex Wakely timed the ball superbly in a 76-ball hundred – his first in one-day cricket and first in any competition for three years. Kent's reply was spirited, but ultimately muzzled by Trent Copeland, who took four wickets in his second spell.*

At Canterbury, June 19 (day/night). **Kent won by three wickets. Sussex 336-5** (40 overs) (C. D. Nash 83, L. J. Wright 115, M. H. Yardy 46, M. W. Machan 41*); ‡**Kent 337-7** (38.3 overs) (S. A. Northeast 115, R. W. T. Key 52, D. I. Stevens 118; W. A. T. Beer 3-59). *Attendance:* 1,755. *Darren Stevens masterminded Kent's world-record 40-over pursuit of 337 with a 44-ball century that won him the Walter Lawrence Trophy. It was the joint-third-fastest in county cricket. For about two hours, it was Luke Wright who had made the season's fastest, taking just 54 deliveries to reach his own hundred as he plundered 115 in an opening stand of 194 with Chris Nash inside 19 overs. Calum Haggett (8–0–97–2) suffered Kent's most expensive one-day figures, but did at least halt the mayhem by having Wright caught at third man; Nash fell to his namesake Brendan, who was bowling left-arm spin. But Stevens, who smashed seven sixes, joined Sam Northeast, who contributed his maiden one-day hundred, to add 159 for the third wicket, and make light of an asking-rate of 8.5.*

At Canterbury, August 15 (day/night). **Warwickshire won by seven runs** (D/L). **Warwickshire 213-7** (40 overs) (W. T. S. Porterfield 57, A. Javid 43, R. Clarke 43); ‡**Kent 113-4** (24.3 overs) (D. I. Stevens 42*). *Attendance:* 2,992. *Floodlight failure 25 overs into Kent's reply killed off their semi-final hopes. The power supply to the PA system and the light nearest the St Lawrence lime tree went out at 8.56, just as Stevens was warming up in a pursuit of 214. Ground officials were unable to fix the problem and, after a 25-minute stoppage, umpires Ian Gould and Tim Robinson had to end the game, giving Warwickshire only their second win of the competition.*

At Canterbury, August 26. **Nottinghamshire won by five wickets.** ‡**Kent 195-6** (40 overs) (R. W. T. Key 41, B. P. Nash 47); **Nottinghamshire 199-5** (38.2 overs) (A. D. Hales 74, S. R. Patel 59). *Attendance:* 3,130. *Alex Hales and Samit Patel strung together a decisive partnership of 107 that earned Nottinghamshire a home semi-final against Somerset.*

Kent away matches

May 6: beat Warwickshire by one run.
May 8: lost to Nottinghamshire by seven wickets (D/L).
May 10: beat Netherlands by seven wickets (D/L).

May 26: lost to Sussex by 20 runs.
August 11: beat Worcestershire by 39 runs.
August 13: lost to Northamptonshire by five wickets.

NETHERLANDS

At Deventer, May 10. **Kent won by seven wickets** (D/L). **Netherlands 101** (32.1 overs) (J. C. Tredwell 4-22, D. I. Stevens 3-19); ‡**Kent 102-3** (22.5 overs) (B. P. Nash 45*; P. A. van Meekeren 3-42). *Attendance:* 150. *Netherlands debut:* D. P. Michael. *The Netherlands never gained any momentum after being 6-3 either side of a shower that trimmed an over off each innings. Matt Coles exploited irregular bounce on a softened pitch to take 2-5 in four overs, before James Tredwell and Darren Stevens swept through the lower order. Paul van Meekeren, a 20-year-old seamer from Amsterdam, also relished the conditions, but was hampered by shin splints towards the end.*

At Schiedam, May 20. **No result. Netherlands 28-2** (10.2 overs) v ‡**Sussex.** *Lewis Hatchett, on List A debut, took both wickets before rain arrived.*

At Schiedam, May 21. **Netherlands v Northamptonshire. Abandoned.**

At Hazelaarweg, Rotterdam, June 3. **Worcestershire won by 44 runs.** ‡**Worcestershire 293-4** (40 overs) (M. M. Ali 48, D. K. H. Mitchell 92, A. N. Kervezee 81); **Netherlands 249** (38 overs) (W. Barresi 65, T. L. W. Cooper 78*; C. J. Russell 4-32). *Attendance:* 150. *Netherlands debuts:* J. F. M. Gruijters, V. J. Kingma. *Six weeks after announcing his retirement from the Netherlands international team aged 23, Alexei Kervezee took their bowlers for a classy 81 from 68 balls. Chris Russell donated seven wides to the Dutch score before delivering a legitimate ball, but he located his radar to bowl four of the last six batsmen; Gareth Andrew bowled the other two. Tom Cooper ran out of partners, finishing on a fine 78* from 59 balls.*

At Truro, June 19. **Nottinghamshire won by four wickets.** ‡**Netherlands 188-7** (40 overs) (T. L. W. Cooper 49); **Nottinghamshire 190-6** (38.5 overs) (J. W. A. Taylor 90*). *Attendance:* 1,100. *Netherlands debut:* Q. W. M. Gunning. *The Dutch played their fifth home fixture as part of the Cornish Cricket Festival in Truro – a long trek for both teams. Their total was never likely to be enough against Nottinghamshire, who made it seven wins from seven, though James Taylor had to bat from the fifth ball to the end on a testing wicket after Alex Hales fell for his third duck in five innings in all cricket. When Riki Wessels pulled out with a finger injury, Ed Cowan cancelled a family holiday in Devon to make his last appearance for Nottinghamshire before joining up with Australia's Test squad.*

At Amstelveen, June 21. **Netherlands v Warwickshire. Abandoned.**

Netherlands away matches

May 26: lost to Nottinghamshire by 89 runs.
May 27: lost to Kent by eight wickets.
June 16: beat Worcestershire by six wickets.

August 11: beat Warwickshire by five runs.
August 13: lost to Sussex by nine wickets.
August 15: lost to Northamptonshire by four wickets.

NORTHAMPTONSHIRE

At Northampton, May 5. **Nottinghamshire won by 83 runs.** ‡**Nottinghamshire 287-4** (40 overs) (A. D. Hales 50, J. W. A. Taylor 108, S. R. Patel 95); **Northamptonshire 204-8** (40 overs) (A. J. Hall 58*, J. D. Middlebrook 43; S. R. Patel 3-30). *Attendance:* 1,350. *County debut:* M. N. W. Spriegel (Northamptonshire). *Nottinghamshire took 15 off Steven Crook's opening over, and batted Northamptonshire out of the game as James Taylor (108 from 102 balls) and Samit Patel (95 from 66) put on 149 in 18 overs. Northamptonshire slumped to 92-7 before Andrew Hall and James Middlebrook salvaged some respectability.*

At Northampton, May 10 (day/night). **Sussex won by 61 runs** (D/L). ‡**Sussex 215-7** (40 overs) (C. D. Nash 95, E. C. Joyce 90; T. A. Copeland 5-32); **Northamptonshire 122-9** (26.3 overs) (C. J. Jordan 3-20, C. J. Liddle 3-31). *Attendance:* 308. *Reduced to 12-3 by David Willey and the outstanding Trent Copeland, Sussex recovered thanks to a superb fourth-wicket stand of 173 between Chris Nash and Ed Joyce. Northamptonshire's rain-interrupted reply was undermined by regular wickets.*

At Northampton, May 27. **Northamptonshire won by 36 runs.** ‡**Northamptonshire 229-9** (40 overs) (S. P. Crook 40; C. J. C. Wright 3-47); **Warwickshire 193** (37.3 overs) (W. T. S. Porterfield 47, R. Clarke 65; S. P. Crook 5-36). *Attendance:* 2,206. *Northamptonshire's innings of fits and starts received a vital injection from Crook, who thumped 40 from 30 balls. He soon had the* *opposition reeling at 12-3 for the second match in a row at Northampton and, once Rikki Clarke perished with 89 needed, Crook stepped in to demolish the tail and claim his first List A five-wicket haul. It was Northamptonshire's first home victory in white-ball cricket since May 2011.*

At Northampton, June 24 (day/night). **Northamptonshire won by seven wickets. Worcestershire 187-8** (40 overs) (T. C. Fell 55; Azharullah 4-38); ‡**Northamptonshire 188-3** (33.5 overs) (K. J. Coetzer 105*, A. G. Wakely 43). *Attendance: 561. Kyle Coetzer batted through the innings to steer Northamptonshire to their fifth consecutive YB40 win heading into the Twenty20 break. Tom Fell resisted with his maiden half-century, but was castled by a beautiful yorker from Azharullah, who bowled his other three victims too.*

At Northampton, August 13 (day/night). **Northamptonshire won by five wickets.** ‡**Kent 188-7** (40 overs) (S. A. Northeast 44, G. O. Jones 46*; S. P. Crook 3-36); **Northamptonshire 189-5** (39.4 overs) (K. J. Coetzer 90, C. L. White 65). *Attendance: 531. Northamptonshire lost three late wickets, but limped over the line with two balls to spare. The hard work was done by Coetzer and Cameron White, who added 142 at a good rate to put their side within striking distance of a modest Kent total.*

At Northampton, August 15 (day/night). **Northamptonshire won by four wickets.** ‡**Netherlands 176-8** (40 overs); **Northamptonshire 178-6** (36.5 overs) (C. L. White 63*). *Attendance: 359. The Netherlands sniffed an upset in their last match in English 40-over cricket when Northamptonshire, perhaps distracted by the forthcoming Twenty20 finals day, slipped to 44-4. But the experience of White, Middlebrook (37) and Hall (21*) pulled them through to sustain hopes of reaching both limited-overs semi-finals. White also picked up two rare wickets with his leg-spin as the home attack kept it tight. Daniel Doram, a left-arm spinner from the Dutch overseas territory of Sint Maarten in the Caribbean, made his List A debut aged 15.*

Northamptonshire away matches

May 21: no result v Netherlands.
May 26: beat Worcestershire by 42 runs.
June 2: beat Kent by 29 runs.

June 16: beat Sussex by 63 runs.
August 11: lost to Nottinghamshire by six wickets.
August 26: beat Warwickshire by 125 runs.

NOTTINGHAMSHIRE

At Nottingham, May 8 (day/night). **Nottinghamshire won by seven wickets** (D/L). **Kent 220-6** (40 overs) (R. W. T. Key 62, B. P. Nash 42; S. J. Mullaney 4-29); ‡**Nottinghamshire 140-3** (16.3 overs) (J. W. A. Taylor 50*). *Attendance: 1,571. Kent were impeded by career-best figures from Steven Mullaney, who benefited from bowling in tandem with Graeme Swann (8–0–24–0). Two spells of rain left Nottinghamshire with a revised target of 140 off 19 overs, and James Taylor marshalled the chase expertly.*

At Nottingham, May 26. **Nottinghamshire won by 89 runs. Nottinghamshire 263-5** (40 overs) (M. J. Lumb 54, J. W. A. Taylor 75, S. R. Patel 61); ‡**Netherlands 174** (38.1 overs) (D. P. Michael 59*; A. Shahzad 3-26). *Attendance: 2,850. Any pretensions the Netherlands had of challenging a target of 264 evaporated when Ajmal Shahzad seized three top-order wickets in ten balls.*

At Nottingham, June 16. **Nottinghamshire won by six wickets.** ‡**Warwickshire 238-7** (40 overs) (T. R. Ambrose 55, D. L. Maddy 56; H. F. Gurney 3-41); **Nottinghamshire 243-4** (39.1 overs) (J. W. A. Taylor 46, S. R. Patel 129*). *Attendance: 3,168. Samit Patel's first List A century in three years led Nottinghamshire to their sixth successive victory – their best start to a one-day season since 1976. Patel had rarely seen a run-chase through to the finish, but he did so in style by launching Oliver Hannon-Dalby for a straight six. Warwickshire were given a solid foundation by Tim Ambrose, whose 55 contained just one four, and Darren Maddy, who rushed to 56 in 33 balls.*

At Nottingham, June 21 (day/night). **Nottinghamshire won by 50 runs.** ‡**Sussex 223-9** (40 overs) (C. D. Nash 40, E. C. Joyce 58, M. W. Machan 68; H. F. Gurney 5-48); **Nottinghamshire 173** (35.5 overs) (J. W. A. Taylor 48, S. R. Patel 45; C. J. Liddle 3-21). *Attendance: 8,181. County debut: M. E. Hobden (Sussex). Nottinghamshire cut ticket prices to £1 for this Friday night match, attracted the biggest gate of the competition bar the final, and gave the proceeds to the club's charitable arm. They were hoping to put one foot in the semi-finals. That prospect was raised by terrific swing bowling from Harry Gurney, who claimed his second List A five-wicket haul. Matt Hobden launched his Sussex career by bowling Michael Lumb in the fourth over, before Taylor and Patel pulled*

Nottinghamshire round to 100-2, only for the last eight wickets to tumble for 73. Rory Hamilton-Brown took four catches in the outfield.

At Nottingham, August 11. **Nottinghamshire won by six wickets.** ‡**Northamptonshire 205-9** (40 overs) (A. G. Wakely 59; A. Shahzad 3-40, J. T. Ball 3-33); **Nottinghamshire 207-4** (32.2 overs) (A. D. Hales 75). *Attendance: 2,805. A typically forthright Alex Hales helped Nottinghamshire overcome the disappointment of their recent Twenty20 quarter-final exit. Alex Wakely was the only Northamptonshire batsman to bed in after he won the toss, and Shahzad produced a double-wicket maiden in the powerplay.*

At Nottingham, August 13 (day/night). **Worcestershire won by 38 runs.** Reduced to 37 overs a side. ‡**Worcestershire 220-8** (37 overs) (D. K. H. Mitchell 56; A. Shahzad 3-54); **Nottinghamshire 182** (33 overs) (J. W. A. Taylor 67*; M. M. Ali 3-28). *Attendance: 2,629. Nottinghamshire, knowing that victory would clinch a semi-final, crumbled chasing 221 off 37 overs, after rain delayed the start. Moeen Ali's removal of Patel, David Hussey and Riki Wessels left Taylor high and dry.*

Nottinghamshire away matches

May 5: beat Northamptonshire by 83 runs.
May 12: beat Worcestershire by five wickets (D/L).
May 23: beat Warwickshire by seven wickets (D/L).

June 19: beat Netherlands by four wickets.
August 15: lost to Sussex by four wickets.
August 26: beat Kent by five wickets.

SUSSEX

At Hove, May 5. **Worcestershire won by 91 runs.** ‡**Worcestershire 245-9** (40 overs) (D. K. H. Mitchell 107, T. T. Samaraweera 41; C. J. Liddle 3-37); **Sussex 154** (31.5 overs) (M. H. Yardy 45; J. D. Shantry 3-29). *Attendance: 4,689. LED Sport Europe, the sponsors of the new electronic screen at Hove, offered free entry, and most in the crowd didn't seem too upset that Sussex were well beaten. Daryl Mitchell's maiden one-day hundred justified his decision to open, and Sussex were never in contention after their powerful top four fell inside 11 overs. That included Matt Prior, who was dropped by Mitchell at slip first ball, but soon stumped off Moeen Ali.*

At Horsham, May 26. **Sussex won by 20 runs.** ‡**Sussex 222-9** (40 overs) (R. J. Hamilton-Brown 40, M. H. Yardy 42; A. J. Ball 3-36); ‡**Kent 202** (39.2 overs) (D. I. Stevens 51, B. W. Harmison 42). *Attendance: 3,577. A bumper crowd was ample compensation for the Horsham festival organisers after a two-day finish to the Championship fixture. It was an excellent game too, not settled until Luke Wright, in his first game back from the IPL, took a sensational one-handed catch on the third-man boundary to oust Ben Harmison. Chris Jordan added the important wicket of Darren Stevens, and pulled a flat six off Adam Ball in an important 37*.*

At Hove, May 30 (day/night). **Warwickshire won by eight runs.** Reduced to 21 overs a side. **Warwickshire 157-7** (21 overs) (T. R. Ambrose 40, D. L. Maddy 49; C. J. Jordan 3-27); ‡**Sussex 149-7** (21 overs) (L. J. Wright 44; C. J. C. Wright 3-27). *Attendance: 2,630. After rain delayed the start until 7.30, Chris Wright undermined Sussex's pursuit of 158 in 21 overs with excellent spells at either end of the chase. He took two wickets in the first five balls, then returned to concede only ten from his last two overs, including the wicket of Sussex's last hope Mike Yardy (25). Darren Maddy's two sixes off Chris Liddle in Warwickshire's final over proved decisive.*

At Arundel, June 16. **Northamptonshire won by 63 runs.** Reduced to 39 overs a side. **Northamptonshire 191-6** (39 overs) (A. G. Wakely 69, B. M. Duckett 47*); ‡**Sussex 128** (34.3 overs) (M. H. Yardy 52, B. C. Brown 40; S. P. Crook 4-26, Azharullah 3-20). *Attendance: 3,593. Sussex slumped to 7-4 on a two-paced pitch, as Steven Crook bemused Luke Wells and Ed Joyce with slower balls. They were briefly revived by Yardy, but the tail caved in to Azharullah. Alex Wakely made the most of being dropped on 28, and 18-year-old Ben Duckett improvised smartly.*

At Hove, August 13 (day/night). **Sussex won by nine wickets.** ‡**Netherlands 185** (35.4 overs) (W. Barresi 64; W. A. T. Beer 3-49); **Sussex 188-1** (21.2 overs) (E. C. Joyce 51*, L. J. Wright 114). *Attendance: 1,824. Luke Wright's 114 from 69 balls rushed Sussex to their first win at Hove in any competition for 363 days – admittedly off an anodyne Dutch attack looking a shadow of the side that upset Warwickshire two days earlier. Wesley Barresi's dismissal sparked a collapse of seven for 60.*

At Hove, August 15 (day/night). **Sussex won by four wickets.** ‡Nottinghamshire 290-5 (40 overs) (A. D. Hales 101, S. R. Patel 43, D. J. Hussey 82*; L. J. Hatchett 3-65); **Sussex 293-6** (38.3 overs) (E. C. Joyce 123*, L. J. Wright 62, M. W. Machan 51; A. Shahzad 3-49). *Attendance:* 2,097. *Ed Joyce's superbly paced hundred – his 13th in List A cricket – completed a Sussex double over Nottinghamshire, inflicted their third defeat in four, and left them still needing one win to sew up the group. Joyce was badly dropped on 108 by Samit Patel at extra cover, but otherwise played hardly a false shot, and Wright and Matt Machan offered vicious support. Together they eclipsed an 87-ball hundred from Alex Hales, and a total embellished by David Hussey's late acceleration.*

Sussex away matches

May 10: beat Northamptonshire by 61 runs (D/L).
May 12: no result v Warwickshire.
May 20: no result v Netherlands.

June 19: lost to Kent by three wickets.
June 21: beat Nottinghamshire by 50 runs.
August 26: beat Worcestershire by seven wickets.

WARWICKSHIRE

At Birmingham, May 6. **Kent won by one run.** Kent 239-8 (40 overs) (R. W. T. Key 44, B. P. Nash 98*); ‡**Warwickshire 238** (40 overs) (V. Chopra 65, W. T. S. Porterfield 47, J. S. Patel 50). *Attendance:* 3,170. *Jeetan Patel's maiden one-day fifty, in 27 balls, narrowly failed to snatch a tie. He was run out by Adam Ball's direct hit as he tried to scramble a last-ball single, meaning Warwickshire – featuring Ian Bell, as captain, and Jonathan Trott in their only YB40 appearances of the season – went down to their first defeat in any competition under new director of cricket Dougie Brown. Brendan Nash had buttressed Kent's innings with his highest one-day score.*

At Birmingham, May 12. **Warwickshire v Sussex. Abandoned.**

At Birmingham, May 23 (day/night). **Nottinghamshire won by seven wickets** (D/L). Warwickshire 186-7 (30 overs) (V. Chopra 42, R. Clarke 59); ‡**Nottinghamshire 133-3** (19.3 overs) (M. J. Lumb 57). *Attendance:* 920. *Rikki Clarke eventually got Warwickshire into gear after the players were twice driven off by hailstorms. Nottinghamshire's target was finally adjusted to 133 in 21 overs, and Michael Lumb's aggressive 57 ensured they were always ahead of the rate.*

At Birmingham, August 11. **Netherlands won by five runs.** ‡Netherlands 248-7 (40 overs) (S. J. Myburgh 76, M. R. Swart 67); **Warwickshire 243-8** (40 overs) (W. T. S. Porterfield 62, V. Chopra 111; P. W. Borren 3-37). *Netherlands debut: B. N. Cooper. Attendance:* 1,551. *Warwickshire, bottom of the group coming out of the Twenty20 recess, decided to rest their frontline seam attack for the Championship campaign – and it cost them their fourth List A defeat against minor opposition. Stephan Myburgh and Michael Swart began with an opening stand of 125 in 21 overs, and the Dutch middle order mustered more than Warwickshire's, after Varun Chopra and William Porterfield had themselves opened with 134. Mudassar Bukhari wobbled in the penultimate over, but the Netherlands held on to claim their 13th – and last – victory in four seasons in the 40-over competition.*

At Birmingham, August 19 (day/night). **Worcestershire won by 140 runs.** ‡**Worcestershire 291-9** (40 overs) (M. M. Ali 114, D. K. H. Mitchell 60, A. N. Kervezee 58; S. A. Piolet 3-74, J. S. Patel 4-43); **Warwickshire 151** (35.5 overs) (L. J. Evans 47*; G. Cessford 4-24, D. K. H. Mitchell 3-35). *Attendance:* 2,224. *Moeen Ali plundered 114 from 85 balls, his seventh one-day century, to set up a rare double for Worcestershire – it was their biggest one-day victory by runs over their closest rivals. Four wickets in 17 balls for Jeetan Patel and three in the last over for Steffan Piolet slowed Worcestershire, but Warwickshire lost their top three to Graeme Cessford.*

At Birmingham, August 26. **Northamptonshire won by 125 runs.** ‡**Northamptonshire 324-6** (40 overs) (D. J. Willey 167, R. I. Keogh 61); **Warwickshire 199** (40 overs) (W. T. S. Porterfield 44; Azharullah 4-20). *Attendance:* 1,912. *David Willey followed his title-winning display in the Twenty20 final at Edgbaston nine days earlier by thrashing his maiden century in any format, but results elsewhere would deny Northamptonshire a semi-final place. "The format isn't great – everyone knows that," said their deflated captain Alex Wakely. Willey's century came from 62 balls, and his eventual 167, which included ten sixes, from 101 in Northamptonshire's record 40-over total. Rob Keogh lent energetic support in a partnership of 101, and Willey was eyeing Wayne Larkins's county-record 172 when he holed out to long-on. Northamptonshire formed a guard of honour for Darren Maddy on his farewell limited-overs appearance, but he managed only a single before he was brilliantly stumped down the leg side by David Murphy off Trent Copeland.*

HIGHEST LIST A SCORES FOR NORTHAMPTONSHIRE

172*	W. Larkins	v Warwickshire at Luton	1983
167	**D. J. Willey**	**v Warwickshire at Birmingham**	**2013**
161	D. J. Sales	v Yorkshire at Northampton	2006
158	W. Larkins	v Worcestershire at Luton	1982
153*	R. J. Bailey	v Pakistan A at Northampton	1997

Warwickshire away matches

May 27: lost to Northamptonshire by 36 runs.
May 30: beat Sussex by eight runs.
June 1: lost to Worcestershire by nine runs.

June 16: lost to Nottinghamshire by six wickets.
June 21: no result v Netherlands.
August 15: beat Kent by seven runs (D/L).

WORCESTERSHIRE

At Worcester, May 12. **Nottinghamshire won by five wickets** (D/L). Reduced to 25 overs a side. **Worcestershire 132-5** (16 overs) (G. M. Andrew 62*); ‡**Nottinghamshire 129-5** (15.2 overs) (A. D. Hales 72). *Attendance: 563. Gareth Andrew helped bludgeon 80 off the last five overs after a rain delay further cut the match to 16 a side. But Twenty20 specialist Alex Hales made light of the adjusted target of 127 with 72 off 41 balls.*

At Worcester, May 26. **Northamptonshire won by 42 runs.** ‡**Northamptonshire 219-6** (40 overs) (S. P. Crook 61*; M. M. Ali 3-40); **Worcestershire 177** (37.4 overs) (T. T. Samaraweera 78; M. N. W. Spriegel 3-29, D. J. Willey 3-28). *Attendance: 1,884. Steven Crook profited from one of four spilled catches by Worcestershire in carving 61* from 42 balls, including two sixes over the longest boundary at midwicket. Thilan Samaraweera showed his class on a sluggish pitch in caressing 78 at a run a ball, but his lbw dismissal – one of two in successive deliveries for Andrew Hall – proved crucial.*

At Worcester, June 1. **Worcestershire won by nine runs.** ‡**Worcestershire 210-9** (40 overs) (M. M. Ali 56, D. K. H. Mitchell 71, A. Kapil 42; J. S. Patel 3-43); **Warwickshire 201** (38.3 overs) (A. Javid 40*; D. K. H. Mitchell 3-27, B. L. D'Oliveira 3-35). *Attendance: 2,841. County debut: S. R. Hain (Warwickshire). Ateeq Javid, coming in at No. 9, and Steffan Piolet (30) looked to have turned the run-chase around with a ninth-wicket stand of 47. But Piolet was bowled by Alan Richardson, playing his first limited-overs match for three years. Javid then hauled Moeen Ali for consecutive sixes but, next ball, last man Chris Wright was overeager to return for a second, and was run out when sent back by his partner. Worcestershire had lost their last six wickets for 26 to undermine Ali's rapid start.*

At Worcester, June 16. **Netherlands won by six wickets.** Reduced to 18 overs a side. **Worcestershire 90-6** (18 overs) (T. T. Samaraweera 47*); ‡**Netherlands 92-4** (15.4 overs). *Attendance: 929. County debut: T. C. Fell (Worcestershire). The light was fading fast when the Netherlands beat Worcestershire away for the third time in succession. Only Samaraweera provided any staying power, but he ran out 19-year-old Tom Fell on debut. Vivian Kingma, only 18, took Ali's edge second ball, and added the prize wicket of former Netherlands batsman Alexei Kervezee, for six.*

At Worcester, August 11. **Kent won by 39 runs.** ‡**Kent 289-6** (40 overs) (S. A. Northeast 93, R. W. T. Key 112, F. K. Cowdrey 92*); **Worcestershire 250** (39.5 overs) (D. K. H. Mitchell 68, G. M. Andrew 43). *Attendance: 1,558. Rob Key picked the gaps masterfully as he and Sam Northeast opened with 182 inside 26 overs. Fabian Cowdrey marked his one-day debut with a 30-ball half-century, reached with a six off the final delivery, from Jack Shantry.*

At Worcester, August 26. **Sussex won by seven wickets.** ‡**Worcestershire 243-6** (40 overs) (M. M. Ali 51, T. T. Samaraweera 72*); **Sussex 246-3** (28.2 overs) (L. J. Wright 112, M. W. Machan 79). *Attendance: 2,254. Luke Wright returned from captaining England Lions to carve his fourth List A century of the season, and the eighth of his career. He smashed 112 from 69 balls, as he and Matt Machan swept Sussex towards victory with 184 in 19 overs for the second wicket. Worcestershire had lost momentum on a plum wicket after Ali was run out risking a single to mid-off.*

Worcestershire away matches

May 5: beat Sussex by 91 runs.
May 15: lost to Kent by three wickets.
June 3: beat Netherlands by 44 runs.

June 24: lost to Northamptonshire by seven wickets.
August 13: beat Nottinghamshire by 38 runs.
August 19: beat Warwickshire by 140 runs.

GROUP B

DERBYSHIRE

At Derby, May 12. **No result. Derbyshire 12-0** (3 overs) v ‡**Lancashire.**

At Derby, May 29 (day/night). **No result. Surrey 100-1** (9 overs) (S. M. Davies 50, J. J. Roy 42*) v ‡**Derbyshire.** *County debut:* R. T. Ponting (Surrey). *More Derby rain prevented Ricky Ponting, Surrey's new overseas signing, from taking any part in a game reduced before the start to 19 overs a side. Surrey openers Steve Davies and Jason Roy put on 97 at breakneck speed, with Davies needing only 21 balls for his fifty.*

At Leek, June 9. **Derbyshire won by 63 runs. Derbyshire 321-5** (40 overs) (W. J. Durston 71, S. Chanderpaul 85*, A. L. Hughes 59*); ‡**Essex 258** (33.1 overs) (M. L. Pettini 88; M. H. A. Footitt 3-40, A. L. Hughes 3-56). *Attendance:* 1,199. *Early hitting from Wes Durston, consistent driving from Shivnarine Chanderpaul and a late flurry from Alex Hughes took Derbyshire to 321, their best from 40 overs, and the largest one-day total conceded by Essex. Even on a small ground, it was too much for the visitors, whose four-match winning streak in the competition came to an abrupt end. Hughes also claimed three wickets.*

At Derby, June 20 (day/night). **No result. Derbyshire 36-2** (9.3 overs) v ‡**Scotland.** *Once again rain greeted Derbyshire at HQ – the third successive no result at the County Ground.*

At Derby, August 15 (day/night). **Derbyshire won by 107 runs. Derbyshire 217-8** (40 overs) (R. M. Johnson 58); ‡**Durham 110** (28.4 overs) (W. L. Madsen 3-27, T. C. Knight 3-36, D. J. Wainwright 4-11). *Attendance:* 1,134. *Three Derbyshire spinners – David Wainwright, Tom Knight and Wayne Madsen – completed career-best figures to dismiss Durham for 110, their lowest total in this fixture. But the pitch was marked "poor", meaning Derbyshire would start the revamped 2014 competition with a two-point penalty. Mark Turner was unable to play after having a medicine ball dropped on his head in the warm-up.*

At Derby, August 26. **Hampshire won by 41 runs.** ‡**Hampshire 219-7** (40 overs) (J. M. Vince 40, J. H. K. Adams 64); **Derbyshire 178** (35.5 overs) (C. F. Hughes 74; C. P. Wood 3-23, M. A. Carberry 3-37). *Attendance:* 1,375. *Jimmy Adams guided Hampshire to a respectable total on a slow pitch. When Chesney Hughes fell at 122-3 in the 23rd over the complexion of the match changed. Michael Carberry took three wickets with his little-used off-spin, and victory brought Hampshire a home semi-final.*

Derbyshire away matches

May 26: beat Scotland by six wickets.
May 27: lost to Durham by 43 runs (D/L).
June 18: lost to Hampshire by 46 runs.

August 11: lost to Surrey by three wickets.
August 13: lost to Lancashire by six wickets.
August 25: lost to Essex by 107 runs.

DURHAM

At Chester-le-Street, May 5. **Essex won by four wickets. Durham 209-5** (40 overs) (B. A. Stokes 51, G. J. Muchall 49*, G. R. Breese 41*); ‡**Essex 212-6** (39 overs) (R. J. Quiney 50, T. Westley 71). *Attendance:* 1,833. *Durham, labouring on a sluggish pitch, suffered a blow when the third umpire ruled Ben Stokes narrowly run out with ten overs remaining. In pursuit of a modest 210, Rob Quiney and Tom Westley shared an opening stand of 103, yet Essex made heavy weather of victory.*

At Chester-le-Street, May 27. **Durham won by 43 runs** (D/L). **Durham 273-6** (40 overs) (S. G. Borthwick 83, P. D. Collingwood 79, B. A. Stokes 40, G. J. Muchall 57*; M. H. A. Footitt 3-55); ‡**Derbyshire 70-3** (16 overs) (G. Onions 3-27). *Attendance:* 1,294. *Paul Collingwood made his best one-day score since late 2011 as almost all the Durham top order fired; Gordon Muchall faced 34*

balls for his 57*. Derbyshire, whose target was revised to 270 in 39 overs, had been derailed by
Graham Onions when the rain arrived.

At Chester-le-Street, June 2. **Durham won by 39 runs. Durham 297-9** (40 overs) (M. D. Stoneman
85, P. Mustard 65, B. A. Stokes 40, G. J. Muchall 48); **‡Lancashire 258** (36.1 overs) (J. Clark 72,
K. Ali 59; G. Onions 4-45, B. A. Stokes 3-50). *Attendance:* 1,930. *County debut: K. Ali. In his first*
game for his third county, Kabir Ali arrived at 162-8, adding 45 in four overs with Jordan Clark –
who made a career-best 72 – and 51 with last man Stephen Parry. Ali thrashed five sixes, four off
Chris Rushworth, as he reached his fifty from 22 balls. But it was not enough. Mark Stoneman,
Durham's acting-captain, and Phil Mustard had put on 126 in 14 overs for the first wicket.

At Chester-le-Street, June 16. **Durham won by seven wickets. ‡Scotland 91** (23.3 overs) (G. Onions
3-26, M. A. Wood 3-23, P. D. Collingwood 3-5); **Durham 93-3** (12.5 overs). *Attendance:* 1,656.
There were five ducks in the Scotland innings, including one that, despite an extra "e", was still a
scorecard entry to savour: "Coleman c Mustard b Onions 0". The chief resistance came from New
Zealander Tom Latham, who made a dogged 30 for Scotland four days after hitting a century for
Durham Second XI in a 20-over game at York.

At Chester-le-Street, June 22. **Durham won by six wickets** (D/L). **Hampshire 224-9** (40 overs)
(L. A. Dawson 69; C. Rushworth 5-42); **‡Durham 218-4** (35.2 overs) (P. Mustard 92, S. G.
Borthwick 80; Sohail Tanvir 4-39). *Attendance:* 1,797. *As coach Geoff Cook recovered in hospital*
two days after a heart attack, Durham won convincingly to replace Hampshire at the top of the table.
Dawson's 46-ball 69 helped the visitors reap 93 from the last ten overs, despite Rushworth's 5-42.
But a second-wicket stand of 163 by Mustard and Scott Borthwick – interrupted by a shower that
revised the target to 218 in 38 overs – was decisive.

At Chester-le-Street, August 26. **Durham won by 133 runs. ‡Durham 275-5** (40 overs) (W. R.
Smith 120*, G. J. Muchall 52*); **Surrey 142** (30.5 overs) (S. G. Borthwick 3-41, G. R. Breese 4-33).
Attendance: 3,007. *Will Smith walloped only his second limited-overs hundred in 12 seasons, from*
79 balls; he hit five sixes and ten fours, swishing 81 from the last five overs with Gordon Muchall.
Surrey lost eight wickets to spin.

Durham away matches

May 6: beat Lancashire by five wickets.   August 11: beat Scotland by eight wickets (D/L).
May 9: no result v Surrey.   August 13: lost to Essex by six wickets.
May 19: lost to Hampshire by five wickets.   August 15: lost to Derbyshire by 107 runs.

ESSEX

At Chelmsford, May 3 (day/night). **Hampshire won by nine wickets. Essex 244-7** (40 overs) (R. J.
Quiney 71, G. M. Smith 47, G. R. Napier 50); **‡Hampshire 245-1** (29.4 overs) (M. A. Carberry 65,
J. M. Vince 129*). *Attendance:* 1,350. *County debut: S. I. Mahmood (Essex). James Vince reached*
a cleanly struck hundred from 71 balls after sharing a lightning stand of 156 with Michael
Carberry. Sajid Mahmood's 0-46 from four overs was an inauspicious debut. Greg Smith and
Graham Napier had given the Essex innings a late boost with 93 in 51 deliveries.

At Chelmsford, June 2. **Essex won by 125 runs. Essex 368-7** (40 overs) (H. D. Rutherford 110,
R. N. ten Doeschate 180; G. D. Drummond 3-60); **‡Scotland 243-8** (40 overs) (P. L. Mommsen 42,
M. H. Cross 54*). *Attendance:* 1,659. *County debut: H. D. Rutherford. Scotland reduced Essex to*
49-3, but thereafter it was one-way traffic: New Zealand opener Hamish Rutherford and Ryan ten

MOST SIXES IN A ONE-DAY INNINGS

23	Essex (368-7, 40 overs) v Scotland at Chelmsford	**2013**
22	Surrey (496-4, 50 overs) v Gloucestershire at The Oval	2007
20	Namibia (358-7, 50 overs) v United Arab Emirates at Windhoek	2007-08
19	Victoria (352-4, 46.4 overs) v New South Wales at Sydney	**2012-13**
19	†India (383-6, 50 overs) v Australia at Bangalore	**2013-14**
19	†Australia (326, 45.1 overs) v India at Bangalore	**2013-14**

† *The same match.*

Doeschate blasted 230 in 22 overs, a fourth-wicket county record. Ten Doeschate's one-day career-best 180 occupied 98 balls, and precisely half his runs came in sixes. At the time, his total of 15 sixes had been exceeded only by Gerrie Snyman, who hit 17 for Namibia against UAE at Windhoek in 2007-08 (see also India v Australia, page 942). The last ten overs produced 159 runs. Essex's highest 40-over total (and their fourth-highest in any limited-overs format) was quite beyond the Scots.

At Chelmsford, June 3 (day/night). **Essex won by 178 runs. Essex 312-7** (40 overs) (M. L. Pettini 43, R. S. Bopara 54, O. A. Shah 68; J. Lewis 3-57); ‡**Surrey 134** (29.5 overs) (G. R. Napier 7-32). *Attendance:* 1,538. *On the pitch used against Scotland the previous day, the Essex batsmen continued to make hay, before Napier scattered Surrey with a career-best 7-32, bettered for Essex only by Keith Boyce's 8-26 at Old Trafford in 1971. Napier became just the sixth player in one-day cricket to take four wickets in four balls – and the second, after Vasbert Drakes for Nottinghamshire in 1999, to do so without assistance, trapping two batsmen lbw and bowling two more – as Surrey nosedived from 113-4 to 113-8. Napier needed the help of a fielder for only one wicket, his seventh.*

At Chelmsford, June 16. **Lancashire won by 64 runs. Lancashire 230-8** (40 overs) (S. M. Katich 60; R. N. ten Doeschate 3-38); ‡**Essex 166** (34.3 overs) (H. D. Rutherford 63, O. A. Shah 42; G. Chapple 3-33, K. Ali 3-30). *Attendance:* 2,253. *Two days after Lancashire routed Essex for 20 in the Championship, they won at Chelmsford again. Simon Katich alone passed 31 as the visitors made a respectable 230; Essex seemed on course at 112-2, but fell apart.*

At Chelmsford, August 13 (day/night). **Essex won by six wickets. ‡Durham 138** (34.1 overs) (W. R. Smith 53; G. R. Napier 5-21, T. S. Mills 3-23); **Essex 139-4** (26.3 overs) (R. N. ten Doeschate 74*). *Attendance:* 3,443. *Durham, top of the table at the start, were reeling at 9-4 in the fifth over, at which point Napier's figures read 2.2–1–1–4. Will Smith oversaw a recovery of sorts, until the last three departed for a single in seven deliveries. Essex were wobbling at 30-3 before ten Doeschate took over.*

At Colchester, August 25. **Essex won by 107 runs. Essex 259-7** (40 overs) (R. S. Bopara 88, J. S. Foster 41; A. L. Hughes 3-63); ‡**Derbyshire 152** (31.1 overs) (B. A. Godleman 60; R. J. W. Topley 4-26). *Attendance:* 2,821. *County debut:* S. L. Elstone (Derbyshire). *All the Essex top order made scores, unlike the Derbyshire batsmen, who contributed neither runs nor entertainment for a sizeable crowd, enduring a sixth consecutive one-sided home game. Essex retained an outside chance of reaching the semis.*

Essex away matches

May 5: beat Durham by four wickets.	August 2: beat Surrey by seven wickets.
May 12: beat Scotland by 59 runs.	August 11: lost to Hampshire by 30 runs.
June 9: lost to Derbyshire by 63 runs.	August 26: beat Lancashire by 70 runs.

HAMPSHIRE

At Southampton, May 5. **Hampshire won by five wickets. Scotland 192-7** (40 overs) (P. L. Mommsen 60*); ‡**Hampshire 194-5** (37.3 overs) (J. H. K. Adams 51, L. A. Dawson 54*). *Attendance:* 2,573. *Scotland captain Preston Mommsen ensured a decent total with what was then a career-best 60*. Hampshire lost openers Michael Carberry and James Vince early, but Jimmy Adams and Liam Dawson steered them towards victory with steady half-centuries.*

At Southampton, May 19. **Hampshire won by five wickets. Durham 241-8** (36 overs) (B. A. Stokes 87, W. R. Smith 50; C. P. Wood 3-37, D. A. Griffiths 3-42); ‡**Hampshire 242-5** (35.1 overs) (M. A. Carberry 96, J. H. K. Adams 67). *Attendance:* 1,670. *Carberry, whose 133-run partnership with Adams began when Vince was stumped off the second ball of the reply, was dismissed for 96 with the scores level. In a match reduced to 36 overs a side, Ben Stokes and Will Smith had helped Durham recover from 45-4. Paul Collingwood passed 10,000 List A runs.*

At Southampton, May 22 (day/night). **Hampshire won by nine wickets. Lancashire 244-6** (40 overs) (A. G. Prince 100, K. R. Brown 44); ‡**Hampshire 250-1** (34 overs) (M. A. Carberry 150*, J. H. K. Adams 66*). *Attendance:* 1,825. *Carberry's fifth six clinched Hampshire's fourth win in* *five, and took him to a career-best 150*. This time, he and Adams shared 173* for the second wicket. For Lancashire, Ashwell Prince's 100 was only his third one-day century in 209 innings.*

At Southampton, June 18 (day/night). **Hampshire won by 46 runs. Hampshire 277-8** (40 overs) (M. A. Carberry 53, A. J. Wheater 70); **‡Derbyshire 231-8** (40 overs) (P. M. Borrington 42, W. L. Madsen 43, D. J. Redfern 53; Sohail Tanvir 3-42). *Attendance: 2,060. Adam Wheater's 70 came from 41 balls as Hampshire worked up a head of steam after stumbling to 137-5; one Mark Turner over cost 21. Derbyshire did not score quickly enough in reply: 194-4 looked healthy, but the required rate was above 12, and the pressure told.*

At Southampton, August 11. **Hampshire won by 30 runs. Hampshire 216** (39.2 overs) (J. M. Vince 68, C. P. Wood 41); **‡Essex 186** (38.1 overs) (G. M. Smith 48, G. R. Napier 48; Sohail Tanvir 4-29). *Attendance: 7,213. Sohail Tanvir struck three times to leave Essex in tatters at 14-3. Greg Smith and Napier each hit 48, but wickets kept falling, and Hampshire's win lifted them above the visitors into second. Earlier, Wheater (38) and Chris Wood put on 64 for the ninth wicket to ensure Hampshire's recovery from 148-8; Essex's James Foster held five catches and made a stumping.*

At Southampton, August 15 (day/night). **Hampshire won by three wickets. Surrey 219-9** (40 overs) (R. J. Burns 49, Z. S. Ansari 62); **‡Hampshire 220-7** (38.4 overs) (S. M. Ervine 65*, L. A. Dawson 40). *Attendance: 3,930. Hampshire lost prolific openers Carberry and Vince eight balls into their chase. After 20 overs, they were a precarious 68-4, needing another 152, and were reliant on the experience of Sean Ervine and Dimitri Mascarenhas, who added 71 for the seventh wicket, to guide them towards victory – and a clean sweep of six home matches. Surrey had been glued together by a career-best 62 from Zafar Ansari.*

Hampshire away matches

May 3: beat Essex by nine wickets.
May 6: lost to Surrey by nine wickets.
June 22: lost to Durham by six wickets (D/L).

August 13: beat Scotland by nine wickets.
August 20: lost to Lancashire by five runs.
August 26: beat Derbyshire by 41 runs.

LANCASHIRE

At Manchester, May 6. **Durham won by five wickets. Lancashire 216-9** (40 overs) (S. C. Moore 46; C. Rushworth 3-44); **‡Durham 218-5** (34.5 overs) (P. Mustard 91). *Attendance: 2,452. Lancashire faltered after the openers put on 73 inside 11 overs, losing five for 65 and ending on a workmanlike 216. Phil Mustard helped secure Durham's success, scoring 91 from 86 balls and sharing stands of 71 with Mark Stoneman and 90 with Paul Collingwood. It was 13th time lucky for Durham: 12 List A games at Old Trafford had previously brought ten defeats, a no-result and an abandonment.*

At Manchester, May 19. **Lancashire won by seven runs. Lancashire 176-9** (40 overs) (K. R. Brown 80; G. J. Batty 3-35); **‡Surrey 169** (40 overs) (W. A. White 4-35, S. D. Parry 5-17). *Attendance: 1,866. A career-best 5-17 from slow left-armer Stephen Parry denied Surrey victory after they reached 60-0 in eight overs. Karl Brown had little help in the Lancashire innings: he hit 80 from 84 balls after they slipped to 59-5, and the only other player to pass 15 was No. 10 Parry, with 23. Surrey's total was boosted by six runs because of Lancashire's slow over-rate.*

At Manchester, June 18 (day/night). **Lancashire won by seven wickets. ‡Scotland 217-9** (40 overs) (F. R. J. Coleman 63, C. S. MacLeod 55, P. L. Mommsen 46; W. A. White 4-38); **Lancashire 218-3** (36.3 overs) (S. C. Moore 53, A. G. Prince 98*). *Attendance: 1,485. Ashwell Prince missed out on a century when Gordon Goudie ended the match with a no-ball that went for four byes. At 190-3 and with five overs remaining, Scotland had looked set for a bigger total, but Wayne White scuppered that, claiming four wickets for the second successive home YB40 game.*

At Manchester, August 13 (day/night). **Lancashire won by six wickets. ‡Derbyshire 190-9** (40 overs) (W. L. Madsen 78, D. J. Wainwright 40; K. Ali 4-37, A. M. Lilley 4-30); **Lancashire 196-4** (35.4 overs) (A. G. Prince 80*). *Attendance: 2,100. Prince passed 75 for the fourth time in the 2013 tournament and guided Lancashire to another comfortable victory. Kabir Ali and off-spinner Arron Lilley (for the first time) picked up four wickets.*

At Manchester, August 20 (day/night). **Lancashire won by five runs. ‡Lancashire 261-9** (40 overs) (S. C. Moore 51, K. R. Brown 66, S. J. Croft 65; A. D. Mascarenhas 5-42); **Hampshire 256-8**

(40 overs) (J. H. K. Adams 41, N. D. McKenzie 65, S. M. Ervine 43; K. Ali 3-63, A. M. Lilley 3-37). *Attendance: 2,753. Lancashire won their sixth match in a row after three half-centuries had set Hampshire – their lead at the top of the table now cut to a point with one to play – too stiff a target on a slow pitch. In a tight denouement, an understrength Hampshire needed 12 off the final over, bowled by Ali, who after seven expensive overs seized two wickets and conceded just six runs. He and Lilley each claimed three-fors.*

At Manchester, August 26. **Essex won by 70 runs.** ‡**Essex 297-4** (40 overs) (G. M. Smith 78, R. S. Bopara 130, R. N. ten Doeschate 46*); **Lancashire 227** (36.4 overs) (T. C. Smith 97, P. J. Horton 45; R. J. W. Topley 3-27, T. J. Phillips 5-42). *Attendance: 4,167. Both teams had hopes of reaching the semis, but Hampshire's victory at Derby meant neither progressed. Essex inflicted a crushing defeat on Lancashire thanks largely to Ravi Bopara's 130, which occupied 102 balls. Tom Smith smashed 97 off 84 in reply, but the end came in a hurry: left-arm spinner Tim Phillips claimed 5-42 as eight men departed for 41.*

Lancashire away matches

May 12: no result v Derbyshire.
May 22: lost to Hampshire by nine wickets.
June 2: lost to Durham by 39 runs.

June 9: beat Surrey by five wickets.
June 16: beat Essex by 64 runs.
August 15: beat Scotland by seven wickets (D/L).

SCOTLAND

At Edinburgh, May 12. **Essex won by 59 runs.** Reduced to 29 overs a side. **Essex 217-7** (29 overs) (T. Westley 63, M. L. Pettini 47); ‡**Scotland 158-4** (29 overs) (F. R. J. Coleman 64, P. L. Mommsen 70*; T. J. Phillips 3-21). *Attendance: 350. In a match reduced by rain to 29 overs, Scotland were never able to keep up with a required rate of almost eight. Three quick wickets put them on the back foot, though Freddie Coleman and Preston Mommsen ensured they went down fighting. Tom Westley had anchored Essex to a healthy total.*

At Edinburgh, May 26. **Derbyshire won by six wickets.** ‡**Scotland 182-9** (40 overs) (P. L. Mommsen 42; M. H. A. Footitt 5-28); **Derbyshire 186-4** (37.4 overs) (C. F. Hughes 74, S. Chanderpaul 54). *Attendance: 300. Mark Footitt claimed one-day best figures of 5-28 to restrict the Scots to 182-9; Mommsen top-scored with 42. Chesney Hughes, who raced to a run-a-ball 74, and Shivnarine Chanderpaul put on 120 for the first wicket.*

At Edinburgh, May 27. **Surrey won by 14 runs.** ‡**Surrey 237-5** (40 overs) (S. M. Davies 54, V. S. Solanki 109*; G. Goudie 3-39); **Scotland 223-8** (40 overs) (C. S. MacLeod 59). *Attendance: 400 After Steve Davies gave Surrey a sure start, Vikram Solanki stroked 109 to help reach a handy total. Yet this game was as near as Scotland came to a win all season: Calum MacLeod struck 59, and some late hitting from Majid Haq and Gordon Goudie took them close – if not close enough.*

At Glasgow, August 11. **Durham won by eight wickets** (D/L). ‡**Scotland 161-6** (37 overs); **Durham 106-2** (16.1 overs) (M. D. Stoneman 54*). *Attendance: 200. The weather threatened to prevent a result, but it relented enough for Durham to canter to a revised target of 104 from 20 overs. Mark Stoneman hit a 49-ball 54*.*

At Glasgow, August 13. **Hampshire won by nine wickets.** Scotland 136 (40 overs); ‡**Hampshire 137-1** (15.1 overs) (M. A. Carberry 45, J. M. Vince 75*). *Attendance: 250. After scratching together a modest 136, Scotland leaked runs at an embarrassing rate. While they had hobbled to 100 in the 35th over, Hampshire flew past three figures in the 12th, roaring to victory with 149 balls in hand. Michael Carberry, an old nemesis, made 45, and James Vince walloped 75* from 52 deliveries.*

At Glasgow, August 15. **Lancashire won by seven wickets** (D/L). Reduced to 39 overs a side. **Scotland 145** (35.4 overs) (K. Ali 3-33); ‡**Lancashire 125-3** (23.2 overs) (T. C. Smith 42*). *Attendance: 300. Lancashire's bowlers exploited helpful conditions to dismiss Scotland cheaply. Rain had knocked an over off each innings before the start, and both teams had to dodge more showers. Lancashire suffered few other alarms in reaching a revised target of 125 in 28 overs.*

Scotland away matches

May 5: lost to Hampshire by five wickets.
June 2: lost to Essex by 125 runs.
June 16: lost to Durham by seven wickets.

June 18: lost to Lancashire by seven wickets.
June 20: no result v Derbyshire.
August 4: lost to Surrey by 100 runs.

SURREY

At The Oval, May 6. **Surrey won by nine wickets.** ‡Hampshire 228 (40 overs) (S. M. Ervine 63; Z. S. Ansari 4-46); **Surrey 229-1** (31.2 overs) (G. C. Smith 74, S. M. Davies 127*). *Attendance: 3,603. Sean Ervine dragged defending champions Hampshire from 89-4 towards respectability. But they had no answer to Steve Davies's career-best 104-ball 127*. In 20 overs, he and Graeme Smith put on 162 for the first wicket, though at a cost: Smith suffered a recurrence of an injury to his left ankle, which ended his season with Surrey.*

At The Oval, May 9 (day/night). **No result. Surrey 216** (37.3 overs) (J. J. Roy 117; C. Rushworth 4-44) v ‡**Durham.** *Attendance: 1,408. Jason Roy cracked his third one-day century, but had little support – the next-best score was 24 – as Chris Rushworth topped and tailed the Surrey innings. Rain spoiled things at the interval.*

At Guildford, June 9. **Lancashire won by five wickets. Surrey 264-8** (40 overs) (J. J. Roy 50, S. M. Davies 53); ‡**Lancashire 265-5** (37.3 overs) (A. G. Prince 76, S. M. Katich 57*). *Attendance: 3,808. Roy and Davies saw Surrey to three figures in 12 overs, but the scoring had started to slow when Ricky Ponting was run out by Stephen Moore's direct hit from midwicket, making it 139-3. Ashwell Prince set the pace of the reply, before Simon Katich took advantage of the short square boundaries.*

At The Oval, August 2 (day/night). **Essex won by seven wickets.** ‡**Surrey 223-7** (40 overs) (V. S. Solanki 86); **Essex 226-3** (35.1 overs) (R. S. Bopara 115*, G. M. Smith 65). *Attendance: 6,094. County debut: T. K. Curran (Surrey). A magnificent 94-ball 115* from Ravi Bopara hastened Essex to victory over a Surrey side missing several first-teamers ahead of their Twenty20 quarter-final. From a hesitant 15-2, he and Greg Smith shared a third-wicket stand of 152 in 25.3 overs. Play was held up for nearly ten minutes when Dominic Sibley, in his first one-day appearance, gashed his knee diving for his ground on two, and was stretchered off; Tom Curran, 18-year-old son of the Zimbabwean all-rounder Kevin, who died the previous October, had a low-key debut.*

At The Oval, August 4. **Surrey won by 100 runs.** ‡**Surrey 303** (39.1 overs) (J. J. Roy 113, V. S. Solanki 63; R. A. J. Smith 3-48); **Scotland 203** (35.1 overs) (H. J. W. Gardiner 48, F. R. J. Coleman 53; Z. S. Ansari 4-42, T. K. Curran 5-34). *Attendance: 1,835. Scotland debut: H. J. W. Gardiner. Against an amiable attack, Roy reached three figures from 77 balls as he and Solanki added 126 for the second wicket at almost nine an over. Hamish Gardiner, born in Queensland, batted fluently on debut, sharing an opening stand of 94 with Freddie Coleman. All Curran's five victims were bowled or lbw – reward for bowling fast and straight.*

At The Oval, August 11. **Surrey won by three wickets.** ‡**Derbyshire 294-9** (40 overs) (C. F. Hughes 80, P. M. Borrington 72; Z. de Bruyn 4-72); **Surrey 297-7** (40 overs) (A. Harinath 52, Z. de Bruyn 60, G. C. Wilson 85; T. D. Groenewald 3-53). *Attendance: 2,513. Surrey won a high-scoring thriller off the last ball of a final over in which the initiative swung back and forth. In the end, Gary Wilson's sizzling 85 from 62 deliveries was enough to wrench the match from Derbyshire, despite 102 being needed from ten overs. Earlier, Chesney Hughes and Paul Borrington had added 123 in 18 overs, while Zander de Bruyn claimed four expensive scalps.*

Surrey away matches

May 19: lost to Lancashire by seven runs.
May 27: beat Scotland by 14 runs.
May 29: no result v Derbyshire.

June 3: lost to Essex by 178 runs.
August 15: lost to Hampshire by three wickets.
August 26: lost to Durham by 133 runs.

GROUP C

GLAMORGAN

At Colwyn Bay, May 5. **Glamorgan won by 28 runs.** ‡Glamorgan 285-7 (40 overs) (W. D. Bragg 50, C. B. Cooke 58, M. J. North 68, M. W. Goodwin 45; R. M. Pyrah 4-43); **Yorkshire** 257 (38.2 overs) (A. W. Gale 65, G. S. Ballance 50, J. M. Bairstow 53, A. U. Rashid 42*; M. G. Hogan 3-29, D. A. Cosker 3-36). *Attendance: 1,814. County debut: W. M. H. Rhodes (Yorkshire). Marcus North, who skippered throughout the YB40 campaign in place of Championship captain Mark Wallace, led Glamorgan to a challenging total. Then Graham Wagg dismissed Phil Jaques and Joe Root in his first over. Andrew Gale and Gary Ballance put on 92, but Yorkshire's fate was sealed when Jonny Bairstow holed out to long-on.*

At Cardiff, May 12. **Glamorgan v Unicorns. Abandoned.**

At Cardiff, May 19. **Gloucestershire won by seven runs.** Gloucestershire 288-5 (40 overs) (M. Klinger 40, C. D. J. Dent 151*); ‡Glamorgan 281-6 (40 overs) (M. A. Wallace 118*, G. G. Wagg 54; J. K. Fuller 3-42). *Attendance: 1,492. Chris Dent's 151* from 113 deliveries was the fifth-highest for Gloucestershire in any one-day game, but Wallace's 98-ball century – after Will Bragg was out to the second delivery of the innings – almost snatched a thrilling victory. Wagg struck 54 from 31 balls, and added 84 quick runs with Wallace – but Glamorgan's hopes died when he was caught on the long-on boundary in the penultimate over.*

At Cardiff, August 12 (day/night). **Glamorgan won by one wicket.** Somerset 222-8 (40 overs) (P. D. Trego 42, N. R. D. Compton 50, J. C. Buttler 67; M. G. Hogan 4-34); ‡Glamorgan 226-9 (39.3 overs) (M. A. Wallace 70, C. B. Cooke 44; S. P. Kirby 3-34). *Attendance: 1,357. After Wallace and Chris Cooke put on 116 for the second wicket in reply to Somerset's modest total, Glamorgan were cruising at 195-4 in the 33rd over. But five wickets clattered for 20 in 26 balls, and it was left to No. 11 Simon Jones to drive Craig Meschede for the winning boundary in the final over.*

At Cardiff, August 14 (day/night). **Glamorgan won by 11 runs.** Reduced to 25 overs a side. **Glamorgan** 153-9 (25 overs) (T. S. Roland-Jones 3-13); ‡Middlesex 142-9 (25 overs) (N. J. Dexter 54; D. A. Cosker 3-32). *Attendance: 780. Glamorgan's total hardly looked imposing, even in a rain-reduced match, but Middlesex never recovered properly after slumping to 32-5. Neil Dexter organised a comeback of sorts, but fell to the second ball of the final over, which started with 20 still required.*

At Swansea, August 25. **Glamorgan won by 68 runs.** ‡Glamorgan 303-6 (40 overs) (G. P. Rees 45, M. A. Wallace 50, C. B. Cooke 85, M. W. Goodwin 48); **Leicestershire** 235-6 (40 overs) (N. J. O'Brien 92, M. A. Thornely 68; J. Allenby 3-37). *Attendance: 1,942. Glamorgan kept their semi-final hopes alive, storming past 300 thanks to Cooke's 76-ball innings and a late onslaught from Murray Goodwin (48 in 19 balls). Leicestershire were never in touch, and there was controversy afterwards concerning Niall O'Brien, whose 121-ball innings ended in the 38th over. Leicestershire's director of cricket, Phil Whitticase, said O'Brien – who had made little effort to accelerate – "had not played in the interests of the team", and dropped him from the final match. Glamorgan's net run-rate, meanwhile, received a boost.*

Glamorgan away matches

May 6: beat Middlesex by 26 runs.
June 2: lost to Somerset by three wickets.
June 9: beat Unicorns by 85 runs.

June 19: beat Leicestershire by 34 runs.
August 18: lost to Gloucestershire by two wickets.
August 26: beat Yorkshire by four wickets.

GLOUCESTERSHIRE

At Bristol, May 12. **Gloucestershire v ‡Middlesex. Abandoned.**

At Bristol, May 26. **Gloucestershire won by 29 runs.** ‡Gloucestershire 260-7 (40 overs) (M. Klinger 61, B. A. C. Howell 75*, I. A. Cockbain 53); **Unicorns** 231-5 (40 overs) (T. J. Lancefield 76, G. T. Park 47). *Attendance: 785. The Unicorns' modest attack struggled on a true pitch: both Benny Howell (75* from 69 balls) and Ian Cockbain (53 from 30) hit three sixes. Tom Lancefield, the* *former Surrey batsman, did his prospects of a county return no harm with a responsible 76, but his side's prospects fizzled out after he was run out in the 29th over.*

At Bristol, June 16. **Gloucestershire won by 36 runs.** Reduced to 27 overs a side. **Gloucestershire 229-6** (27 overs) (M. Klinger 45, C. D. J. Dent 56, I. A. Cockbain 46*; I. Wardlaw 3-44); ‡**Yorkshire 193** (26.3 overs) (D. M. Hodgson 76; D. A. Payne 4-44). *Attendance: 744. Gloucestershire's handy total in a rain-affected match looked under threat as Dan Hodgson biffed 76 from 55 balls before falling to the 17-year-old off-spinner Miles Hammond. But David Payne returned to take three late wickets, and Yorkshire fell short: their last eight tumbled for 64.*

At Bristol, August 13. **Gloucestershire won by seven wickets. Leicestershire 163** (35.2 overs) (N. J. O'Brien 43); ‡**Gloucestershire 164-3** (30.2 overs) (M. Klinger 89*). *Attendance: 1,136. Leicestershire's batsmen succumbed on a two-paced pitch, with only Niall O'Brien surviving for long. Michael Klinger took his side to victory with almost ten overs to spare.*

At Bristol, August 18. **Gloucestershire won by two wickets.** ‡**Glamorgan 247-7** (40 overs) (G. P. Rees 83, M. W. Goodwin 41); **Gloucestershire 251-8** (39.5 overs) (M. Klinger 87, H. J. H. Marshall 55). *Attendance: 1,214. Gloucestershire's tailenders held their nerve to keep their semi-final hopes alive, and damage their opponents'. Gareth Rees had anchored the Glamorgan innings, chiselling 83 from 110 balls to set up a competitive total. Klinger and Hamish Marshall then added 100 for Gloucestershire's first wicket, but 237-5 became 246-8, and it was left to James Fuller and Payne to drag them over the line.*

At Bristol, August 26. **Somerset won by 12 runs. Somerset 258-9** (40 overs) (M. E. Trescothick 50, C. Kieswetter 42, J. C. Buttler 68*; D. A. Payne 3-35, T. M. J. Smith 3-46); ‡**Gloucestershire 246-7** (40 overs) (M. Klinger 40, A. P. R. Gidman 41; A. C. Thomas 3-41). *Attendance: 4,071. Somerset started well as Marcus Trescothick and Craig Kieswetter put on 105, before stumbling, with Nick Compton falling first ball. But Jos Buttler hauled them to a decent total with a responsible 71-ball innings. Slow left-armer Tom Smith's three wickets came in the form of a mid-innings hat-trick split across two overs. All Gloucestershire's batsmen made starts: the top five reached 30, but none made more than 41 as old stagers Steve Kirby and Alfonso Thomas kept Somerset on course for the victory that ensured they topped the group.*

Gloucestershire away matches

May 4: lost to Leicestershire by 115 runs.
May 6: beat Unicorns by nine wickets.
May 19: beat Glamorgan by seven runs.

June 2: beat Yorkshire by five wickets.
August 11: lost to Somerset by seven wickets.
August 15: lost to Middlesex by 19 runs (D/L).

LEICESTERSHIRE

At Leicester, May 4. **Leicestershire won by 115 runs. Leicestershire 289** (40 overs) (J. J. Cobb 107, N. J. O'Brien 104; D. A. Payne 3-45); ‡**Gloucestershire 174** (34.1 overs) (R. E. M. Williams 3-34, J. J. Cobb 3-34). *County debut: G. H. Roderick (Gloucestershire). Attendance: 899. Josh Cobb and Niall O'Brien, in his first one-day match for Leicestershire, helped themselves to rapid centuries in an opening stand of 193 in 26 overs, and set up a total that proved well beyond Gloucestershire, who never recovered from 44-5.*

At Leicester, May 26. **Leicestershire won by six wickets. Somerset 323-3** (40 overs) (M. E. Trescothick 57, P. D. Trego 118, A. N. Petersen 63*, J. C. Buttler 54*); ‡**Leicestershire 324-4** (38.5 overs) (J. J. Cobb 130, G. P. Smith 135*). *Attendance: 3,975. Peter Trego's 90-ball century looked to have put Somerset in control. But for the second home match running both Leicestershire's openers posted hundreds: this time Cobb was joined by Greg Smith in a stand of 235 in 24.5 overs. Smith, whose previous-highest one-day score of 58 dated from September 2008, saw the tall run-chase through to the finish.*

At Leicester, June 2. **Middlesex won by ten wickets. Leicestershire 220** (39.5 overs) (N. J. O'Brien 41); ‡**Middlesex 221-0** (30.2 overs) (P. R. Stirling 132*, D. J. Malan 80*). *Attendance: 876. Batsmen continued to prosper at Grace Road, and this time it was Middlesex's to the fore: Paul Stirling hurtled to 132* from 96 balls during a stand of 221* with Dawid Malan.*

At Leicester, June 19. **Glamorgan won by 34 runs. Glamorgan 265-8** (40 overs) (M. A. Wallace 61, C. B. Cooke 55, M. W. Goodwin 41; R. M. L. Taylor 3-57); ‡**Leicestershire 231** (39.5 overs)

(J. A. Burns 71; M. G. Hogan 3-38). *Attendance: 1,705. Leicestershire seemed set to challenge Glamorgan's sizeable total when their openers kicked off the chase by putting on 60. But Cobb and Smith fell to successive balls from Jim Allenby, O'Brien also went without addition, and Leicestershire were never really on terms after that, despite Joe Burns's 71.*

At Leicester, August 11. **Leicestershire won by three wickets. ‡Yorkshire 228-7** (40 overs) (G. S. Ballance 56); **Leicestershire 232-7** (39.5 overs) (J. J. Cobb 45, E. J. H. Eckersley 108). *Attendance:* 2,353. *County debut:* O. E. Robinson (Yorkshire). *Ned Eckersley's maiden one-day century set up Leicestershire's victory, although there was a nervous finish after he departed in the 38th over with 12 still required: No. 8 Rob Taylor muscled a straight six off the penultimate delivery, from his Scotland team-mate Iain Wardlaw.*

At Leicester, August 18. **Unicorns won by 42 runs. Unicorns 259-5** (40 overs) (M. S. Lineker 132); **‡Leicestershire 217** (39 overs) (J. J. Cobb 53, N. J. O'Brien 44; G. T. Park 4-39). *Attendance:* 403. *After nine defeats and two no-results this season, the Unicorns finally broke their duck in their farewell fixture. Their imposing total owed much to former Derbyshire batsman Matt Lineker's magnificent 132 from 106 balls. Leicestershire's reply began brightly, as Cobb and O'Brien shared an opening stand of 89 in 15 overs, but no one could play the big innings required.*

Leicestershire away matches

May 27: beat Unicorns by six wickets.
June 9: beat Yorkshire by three wickets.
June 16: lost to Somerset by five wickets.

August 13: lost to Gloucestershire by seven wickets.
August 25: lost to Glamorgan by 68 runs.
August 26: lost to Middlesex by four wickets.

MIDDLESEX

At Lord's, May 6. **Glamorgan won by 26 runs. Glamorgan 280-3** (40 overs) (W. D. Bragg 62, M. J. North 137*, J. Allenby 69*); **‡Middlesex 254-9** (40 overs) (M. G. Hogan 3-57, W. T. Owen 3-48). *Attendance:* 3,349. *Neil Dexter chose to bowl first but, after two wickets went down in the eighth over, Marcus North took control, blasting 137* from 98 balls, and putting on 86 with Will Bragg and 156* with Jim Allenby. Middlesex were up against it at 172-6 after 30 overs, and Gareth Berg's 75 from 57 balls wasn't enough.*

At Radlett, May 27. **Middlesex won by six wickets. ‡Yorkshire 236-8** (40 overs) (P. A. Jaques 81, G. S. Ballance 40, A. U. Rashid 46*; T. S. Roland-Jones 4-44, J. A. R. Harris 3-54); **Middlesex 237-4** (35.4 overs) (D. J. Malan 96, A. M. Rossington 79*). *Attendance:* 1,979. *Middlesex celebrated their first match at Radlett by purring to victory with 26 balls to spare on a club ground. Dawid Malan fell just short of a century as Middlesex closed in.*

At Lord's, June 4 (day/night). **Middlesex won by four wickets. Somerset 247-7** (40 overs) (M. E. Trescothick 41, J. C. Hildreth 102*; O. P. Rayner 3-31); **‡Middlesex 250-6** (39.1 overs) (D. J. Malan 99; C. A. J. Meschede 3-53). *Attendance:* 2,330. *Malan was out in the nineties for the second week running, with his dismissal completing a slide from 159-1 to 185-5. But Neil Dexter (39*) made sure of another victory. Somerset's innings had owed much to James Hildreth's 94-ball century.*

At Lord's, August 11. **Middlesex won by one wicket. Unicorns 208-7** (40 overs) (G. T. Park 43, K. A. Parsons 64*; T. S. Roland-Jones 3-33); **‡Middlesex 209-9** (39.1 overs) (P. R. Stirling 42, J. L. Denly 57, J. A. Simpson 50*; J. E. Poysden 3-33, L. E. Beaven 3-43). *Attendance:* 2,894. *The Unicorns came close to their first victory of the season as Middlesex scraped home. It had looked all over at 186-9, but John Simpson got them over the line, bringing up his half-century with the winning hit – despite appearing to be run out when tying the scores just before.*

At Lord's, August 15 (day/night). **Middlesex won by 19 runs** (D/L). **‡Middlesex 206-5** (38 overs) (D. J. Malan 113*); **Gloucestershire 186-9** (38 overs) (M. Klinger 46; J. A. R. Harris 3-30). *Attendance:* 4,091. *A shower after two overs of Middlesex's innings reduced this to a 38-over match, and Gloucestershire's target was later revised to 206. Malan continued his good one-day form with a 111-ball century, and Gloucestershire struggled after losing Hamish Marshall to the first delivery of the reply, then Chris Dent in the second over.*

At Lord's, August 26. **Middlesex won by four wickets. Leicestershire 274-8** (40 overs) (G. P. Smith 56, E. J. H. Eckersley 73, M. A. G. Boyce 53); **‡Middlesex 275-6** (38.2 overs) (E. J. G.

Morgan 90, J. A. Simpson 58*). *Attendance: 3,486. Eoin Morgan, making a rare county appearance and replacing the rested Dexter as captain, cracked 90 from 63 balls to spirit Middlesex past Leicestershire's more-than-useful total.*

Middlesex away matches

May 12: no result v Gloucestershire.
May 19: lost to Somerset by six wickets.
June 2: beat Leicestershire by ten wickets.

June 20: lost to Yorkshire by 17 runs (D/L).
June 23: beat Unicorns by nine wickets.
August 14: lost to Glamorgan by 11 runs.

SOMERSET

At Taunton, May 5. **Somerset won by eight wickets. Unicorns 183-8** (40 overs) (S. L. Elstone 75*); ‡**Somerset 184-2** (15.3 overs) (M. E. Trescothick 87, P. D. Trego 75*). *Attendance: 1,959. Scott Elstone, later to make a county return with Derbyshire, ensured the Unicorns made a respectable score – but it soon looked insignificant. Marcus Trescothick muscled eight sixes and seven fours from 49 balls, while Peter Trego carved ten fours and four sixes from 38 in an opening stand of 159 in 13.3 overs. Leg-spinner Josh Poysden's only over, on his List A debut, went for 24 as Trescothick helped himself to four successive sixes; later Garry Park was smashed for 27 (414666, the last 22 to Trescothick).*

At Taunton, May 19. **Somerset won by six wickets. Middlesex 252-9** (40 overs) (D. J. Malan 49, J. L. Denly 60; S. P. Kirby 4-52, M. T. C. Waller 3-39); ‡**Somerset 257-4** (35.5 overs) (P. D. Trego 81, A. V. Suppiah 60). *Attendance: 2,322. Middlesex's total looked serviceable, but once again Trego put it in perspective, hammering 81 from 67 balls. Neil Dexter tried eight bowlers to stem the flow but, by the time Tom Smith eventually got his man in the 22nd over, the damage was done. Arul Suppiah's 60 was his last major contribution for Somerset before knee problems forced his retirement.*

At Taunton, June 2. **Somerset won by three wickets. Glamorgan 245-9** (40 overs) (M. J. North 46, B. J. Wright 75*; J. Overton 3-45); ‡**Somerset 246-7** (38.2 overs) (P. D. Trego 72, D. Elgar 51, C. A. J. Meschede 40*; D. A. Cosker 3-41). *Attendance: 3,467. Another chase, another onslaught from Trego: his 72 from 66 balls took his tally in the first five games to 401. But Somerset slipped after he fell to Marcus North's straightforward off-spin, and needed an eighth-wicket stand of 43* in 25 balls between Craig Meschede and Max Waller (25*) to get them home.*

At Taunton, June 16. **Somerset won by five wickets.** Reduced to 25 overs a side. **Leicestershire 124** (24.3 overs) (M. A. Thornely 49*; A. C. Thomas 3-33, C. A. J. Meschede 4-5); ‡**Somerset 127-5** (21.3 overs) (C. Kieswetter 50; N. L. Buck 3-25). *Attendance: 1,885. It was a forgettable day for Leicestershire, who slumped to 74-8 before recovering slightly to 124; Anthony Ireland (27*) cheered himself up by hitting Steve Kirby, his former Gloucestershire team-mate, into the River Tone for six. Meschede's second successive four-for briefly made him the competition's leading wicket-taker with 20 (he would finish joint-second).*

At Taunton, August 11. **Somerset won by seven wickets. Gloucestershire 263-8** (40 overs) (M. Klinger 131*); ‡**Somerset 267-3** (33.3 overs) (C. Kieswetter 126*, P. D. Trego 59). *Attendance: 4,820. Michael Klinger batted through Gloucestershire's innings for an unbeaten century, but was outshone by Craig Kieswetter, whose 126* from 97 balls included six sixes.*

At Taunton, August 15. **Somerset won by three wickets. Yorkshire 261-8** (40 overs) (A. Z. Lees 62, A. Lyth 58, J. A. Leaning 60; A. J. Dibble 4-52, A. C. Thomas 3-49); ‡**Somerset 262-7** (39.1 overs) (C. Kieswetter 40, P. D. Trego 140*, A. N. Petersen 51; I. Wardlaw 3-35). *Attendance: 3,566. Somerset made it six wins from their six home games, and topped the group table. They overhauled a good Yorkshire total in the final over, thanks to Trego's 140* from 103 balls. Alviro Petersen added 51 in his final innings for Somerset.*

Somerset away matches

May 11: beat Yorkshire by 131 runs.
May 26: lost to Leicestershire by six wickets.
June 4: lost to Middlesex by four wickets.

June 14: no result v Unicorns.
August 12: lost to Glamorgan by one wicket.
August 26: beat Gloucestershire by 12 runs.

UNICORNS

At Wormsley, May 6. **Gloucestershire won by nine wickets.** ‡**Unicorns 153-9** (40 overs) (M. P. O'Shea 41; D. A. Payne 3-29); **Gloucestershire 156-1** (23.2 overs) (M. Klinger 52*, H. J. H. Marshall 67). *The Unicorns' total looked insufficient on Wormsley's batsman-friendly pitch, and Gloucestershire knocked off the runs with 100 balls to spare.*

At Chesterfield, May 19. **Yorkshire won by five wickets.** ‡**Unicorns 189-9** (40 overs) (R. M. Pyrah 3-34); **Yorkshire 191-5** (38.5 overs) (G. S. Ballance 44, A. Lyth 58*). *Yorkshire needed to dig deep after slipping to 24-2 – both wickets went to Warren Lee, a seamer formerly on Kent's books – and eventually got home with only seven balls to spare.*

At Wormsley, May 27. **Leicestershire won by six wickets.** **Unicorns 253-8** (40 overs) (T. J. Lancefield 58, G. T. Park 54, V. Tripathi 43; R. M. L. Taylor 3-45); ‡**Leicestershire 256-4** (39 overs) (J. J. Cobb 128*, S. J. Thakor 64*). *A competitive total raised the Unicorns' hopes of a first victory of the summer, which were boosted when Leicestershire slipped to 120-4 – but Josh Cobb and Shiv Thakor stopped the rot with a stand of 136* in 15.3 overs.*

At Southend, June 9. **Glamorgan won by 85 runs.** **Glamorgan 300-6** (40 overs) (M. A. Wallace 51, C. B. Cooke 98, J. Allenby 85; D. T. Reed 5-31); ‡**Unicorns 215-9** (40 overs) (S. L. Elstone 48, G. T. Park 74; G. G. Wagg 4-51). *The result was never really in doubt once Glamorgan reached 300 at Garon Park, the major thrust coming in a fourth-wicket stand of 162 between Chris Cooke (98 from 77 balls) and Jim Allenby (85 from 57, with six sixes). Garry Park applied himself for 74, but Graham Wagg haunted the middle order, adding two catches to his four wickets.*

At Truro, June 14. **No result. Unicorns 231-8** (40 overs) (T. J. Lancefield 80; C. A. J. Meschede 4-43); ‡**Somerset 22-0** (2 overs). *Tom Lancefield's 80 from 88 balls lifted the Unicorns to a testing total, and an interesting contest looked on the cards when a shower during the innings break meant Somerset's target was revised to 206 in 32 overs.*

At Southend, June 23. **Middlesex won by nine wickets. Unicorns 170** (36.4 overs) (M. S. Lineker 53; T. J. Murtagh 3-35, T. G. Helm 3-27); ‡**Middlesex 172-1** (27.5 overs) (D. J. Malan 58*, J. L. Denly 99*). *County debut:* A. C. Voges. *Middlesex brushed their amateur opponents aside, losing only one wicket after restricting them to 170. With three wanted for victory, Joe Denly needed six off Michael O'Shea to reach his hundred – but managed only four.*

Unicorns away matches

May 5: lost to Somerset by eight wickets.
May 12: no result v Glamorgan.
May 26: lost to Gloucestershire by 29 runs.

August 11: lost to Middlesex by one wicket.
August 13: lost to Yorkshire by 32 runs.
August 18: beat Leicestershire by 42 runs.

YORKSHIRE

At Leeds, May 11. **Somerset won by 131 runs. Somerset 338-5** (40 overs) (P. D. Trego 58, A. N. Petersen 42, J. C. Hildreth 96*, J. C. Buttler 89); ‡**Yorkshire 207** (30 overs) (G. S. Ballance 60; A. C. Thomas 4-41). *Attendance:* 1,463. *Yorkshire were never in with a shout after Jos Buttler's remarkable 51-ball 89 helped produce the highest one-day total by any visiting side at Headingley. Moin Ashraf took 1-80 in his eight overs, while Ryan Sidebottom managed 2-77.*

At Leeds, June 2. **Gloucestershire won by five wickets.** ‡**Yorkshire 240-6** (40 overs) (P. A. Jaques 70, A. U. Rashid 43*); **Gloucestershire 243-5** (38.1 overs) (H. J. H. Marshall 44, M. Klinger 96, G. H. Roderick 63). *Attendance:* 3,619. *County debut:* B. O. Coad (Yorkshire); M. A. H. Hammond (Gloucestershire). *Phil Jaques seemed to have set up a handy Yorkshire total, but their weakened attack struggled: Michael Klinger put on 74 with Hamish Marshall, and 119 for the second wicket with Gareth Roderick. Four late strikes made the result appear closer than it was.*

At Scarborough, June 9. **Leicestershire won by three wickets.** ‡**Yorkshire 258-9** (40 overs) (A. W. Gale 44, J. J. Sayers 58, L. E. Plunkett 53; S. J. Thakor 3-39); **Leicestershire 260-7** (39.1 overs) (G. P. Smith 58, M. A. G. Boyce 42, R. M. L. Taylor 48*). *Attendance:* 3,078. *County debuts:* M. D. Fisher, R. Gibson (Yorkshire). *At 15 years 212 days, York-born Matthew Fisher became the youngest player to appear for a first-class county in a competitive match (only Peter Wilshaw, who at the age* *of 15 years 45 days played for Nottinghamshire Cricket Board v Cumberland at Keswick in 2002, has played a List A game in England at a younger age). Fisher was one of four teenage pacemen in the Yorkshire ranks: Richard Gibson, 17, from Whitby, was also making his debut, while 19-year-olds Ben Coad had one previous appearance and Will Rhodes five. Spurred on by family and friends from Sheriff Hutton Bridge CC, Fisher began with a tight four-over spell that cost 18, and later trapped Shiv Thakor lbw for a duck. But a return for the penultimate over proved too much: with 14 required, Fisher had Jigar Naik caught – but it was a no-ball on height, and was followed by a wide as the over cost 11. Yorkshire might have won but for an eighth-wicket stand of 71* between Rob Taylor and Naik (22*).*

At Leeds, June 20. **Yorkshire won by 17 runs** (D/L). **Middlesex 217-8** (40 overs) (A. M. Rossington 42, G. K. Berg 43; I. Wardlaw 3-39, R. M. Pyrah 3-33); ‡**Yorkshire 81-0** (17.2 overs). *Attendance:* 1,476. *County debut:* T. G. Helm (Middlesex). *After six defeats by counties, Yorkshire won – and would probably have done so even without the bad weather which eventually ended the match (their target had already been revised to 197 from 35 overs). Paul Stirling (32) got Middlesex off to a flyer, but Iain Wardlaw (with career-best figures) and Rich Pyrah pegged them back. With rain threatening, Andrew Gale (34*) and Adam Lyth (38*) made sure Yorkshire were always on the right side of Duckworth/Lewis.*

At Leeds, August 13. **Yorkshire won by 32 runs. Yorkshire 266-6** (40 overs) (A. Z. Lees 63, G. S. Ballance 139); ‡**Unicorns 234** (38.2 overs) (M. S. Lineker 107; J. A. Leaning 5-22). *Attendance:* 2,131. *The group's bottom two teams played some entertaining cricket, and the result was in doubt until the last few overs when Jack Leaning, the seventh bowler tried, grabbed five wickets with his off-spin, starting with Matt Lineker, whose century was his second of the season. Earlier, Gary Ballance lashed a career-best 139 off 113 balls.*

At Leeds, August 26. **Glamorgan won by four wickets.** ‡**Yorkshire 215-5** (40 overs) (D. M. Hodgson 90, K. S. Williamson 45, A. Lyth 44); **Glamorgan 216-6** (38.5 overs) (C. B. Cooke 84, J. Allenby 40; M. A. Ashraf 3-38). *Attendance:* 2,884. *Pyrah led Yorkshire as Andrew Gale and other key players were rested ahead of the important Championship match against Durham, but his young side were unable to prevent a ninth defeat in the 12 group games. After Dan Hodgson's 90 helped rescue Yorkshire from 7-2, Glamorgan started their chase knowing victory would guarantee them a semi-final place. Chris Cooke set things up with a 91-ball 84, then Graham Wagg virtually ensured success with three sixes in the 37th over, from Pyrah.*

Yorkshire away matches

May 5: lost to Glamorgan by 28 runs.
May 19: beat Unicorns by five wickets.
May 27: lost to Middlesex by six wickets.

June 16: lost to Gloucestershire by 36 runs.
August 11: lost to Leicestershire by three wickets.
August 15: lost to Somerset by three wickets.

SEMI-FINALS

HAMPSHIRE v GLAMORGAN

At Southampton, September 7. Glamorgan won by 31 runs. Toss: Hampshire.

Unfancied Glamorgan knocked out the holders to reach only their third Lord's final, and their first since 2000. Hampshire's strategy – at least at home, where they won all six group games – was to chase, and once again Adams chose to bowl. On a slow pitch, scoring was not straightforward, and for much of the Glamorgan innings Allenby preferred restraint to attack. He and Wright opened up towards the end, though, as 57 runs gushed from the last four overs – including 35 off 12 balls from Wood. In his final match before retirement, Mascarenhas received a warm hand from the crowd, but could not claim a wicket. At the start of the reply, Allenby removed the openers in an eight-over spell that cost just 18. Hogan was more expensive, though he grabbed wickets as the pressure began to tell. At the end, Mascarenhas was eight not out, an anticlimactic conclusion to 18 successful seasons on the south coast.

Man of the Match: J. Allenby. *Attendance:* 3,976.

Glamorgan

G. P. Rees c Wheater b Wood	25	B. J. Wright not out		47
*†M. A. Wallace c Wood b Sohail Tanvir	18	B 1, l-b 4, w 1		6
C. B. Cooke lbw b Briggs	37			
J. Allenby not out	74	1/30 (2) 2/60 (1)	(4 wkts, 40 overs)	234
M. W. Goodwin c Dawson b Sohail Tanvir	27	3/99 (3) 4/150 (5)	8 overs: 33-1	

G. G. Wagg, A. G. Salter, D. A. Cosker, M. G. Hogan and S. P. Jones did not bat.

Sohail Tanvir 8–1–40–2; Mascarenhas 8–0–39–0; Wood 8–0–58–1; Dawson 8–0–35–0; Briggs 8–0–57–1.

Hampshire

J. M. Vince b Allenby	20	A. D. Mascarenhas not out		8
M. D. T. Roberts c Cooke b Allenby	23	C. P. Wood b Hogan		3
*J. H. K. Adams c and b Hogan	59	L-b 3, w 6, n-b 2		11
N. D. McKenzie run out	7			
S. M. Ervine c Wagg b Hogan	54	1/46 (1) 2/49 (2)	(8 wkts, 40 overs)	203
L. A. Dawson c Wright b Hogan	17	3/73 (4) 4/159 (3) 5/177 (5)		
†A. J. Wheater c Cosker b Wagg	1	6/183 (7) 7/195 (6) 8/203 (9)	8 overs: 41-0	

Sohail Tanvir and D. R. Briggs did not bat.

Hogan 8–0–51–4; Allenby 8–1–18–2; Wagg 7–0–38–1; Cosker 8–0–45–0; Salter 6–0–33–0; Jones 3–0–15–0.

Umpires: P. J. Hartley and D. J. Millns. Third umpire: M. A. Gough.

NOTTINGHAMSHIRE v SOMERSET

At Nottingham, September 9. Nottinghamshire won by eight wickets. Toss: Nottinghamshire.

In recent years, Nottinghamshire had repeatedly stumbled in the knockout stages of limited-overs competitions – twice losing to Somerset in Twenty20 – but they gained revenge in emphatic fashion. After a delayed start shaved five overs from each innings, Gurney had Trescothick caught behind off his fourth ball. Somerset also lost Kieswetter in the sixth over, but recovered to 62 for two in the 11th. Thereafter, though, little went right. Jake Ball, whose first two, wicketless, overs had yielded 18, returned to dismantle the visitors. Still to make his Championship debut, he swung his way to four for 25 as the last six Somerset wickets tumbled for 28 in seven overs. With Lumb and Patel in no mood to hang around, Nottinghamshire needed less than 17 overs to romp to a victory that brought them a first Lord's final since 1989.

Man of the Match: J. T. Ball. *Attendance:* 4,571.

Somerset

*M. E. Trescothick c Read b Gurney	0	J. Overton lbw b Ball		0
†C. Kieswetter c Read b Shahzad	22	S. P. Kirby lbw b Shahzad		0
P. D. Trego c and b Mullaney	40			
N. R. D. Compton c Hussey b Mullaney	14	L-b 3, w 1		4
J. C. Hildreth b Ball	5			
L. Gregory c and b Mullaney	12	1/0 (1) 2/37 (2) 3/62 (4)	(25.4 overs)	119
C. A. J. Meschede not out	20	4/73 (5) 5/91 (3) 6/102 (6)		
P. P. Chawla c Read b Ball	1	7/112 (8) 8/116 (9) 9/116 (10)		
A. C. Thomas lbw b Ball	1	10/119 (11)	7 overs: 41-2	

Gurney 4–0–11–1; Ball 5–0–25–4; Shahzad 4.4–0–23–2; Mullaney 7–0–35–3; Patel 5–0–22–0.

Nottinghamshire

M. J. Lumb c Kieswetter b Overton	46
A. D. Hales lbw b Kirby	5
J. W. A. Taylor not out	20
S. R. Patel not out	43
L-b 2, w 4, n-b 2	8

1/11 (2) 2/62 (1)   (2 wkts, 16.2 overs) 122
                         7 overs: 43-1

D. J. Hussey, M. H. Wessels, *†C. M. W. Read, S. J. Mullaney, A. Shahzad, J. T. Ball and H. F. Gurney did not bat.

Trego 2–0–15–0; Kirby 6.2–0–40–1; Thomas 2–0–15–0; Meschede 2–0–15–0; Overton 4–0–35–1.

Umpires: T. E. Jesty and J. W. Lloyds.   Third umpire: R. J. Bailey.

FINAL

GLAMORGAN v NOTTINGHAMSHIRE

Richard Gibson

At Lord's, September 21. Nottinghamshire won by 87 runs. Toss: Glamorgan.

Boosted by the presence of their England players, Swann and Broad, Nottinghamshire doused Glamorgan's fire in late afternoon. Pre-match debate had centred on whether it was right to draft them in from central-contract cold storage – their arrival denied semi-final hero Jake Ball a game – but in the event it was an overlooked international who shifted the contest's equilibrium.

Patel, still smarting at his omission from England's limited-overs squads, outshone his more illustrious colleagues. Twice he hit off stump with balls that turned prodigiously, removing the well-set third-wicket pair of Cooke and Allenby, then outfoxing Goodwin on the sweep. Patel had been unsure if his left-arm spin would even get an airing, but a spell of three for four in nine balls settled the last 40-over final.

Taking off: Samit Patel begins his celebrations after bowling Jim Allenby for 34.

Glamorgan's prospects of at last winning a cup competition (to go with three Championships and two League titles) were enhanced when they won the toss and bowled in the gloom of a late September morning. But as the floodlights took hold, Nottinghamshire's usually expansive openers countered the conditions with uncharacteristic circumspection, and the first boundary took 35 deliveries.

Neither Lumb nor Hales went on to a significant score, but their stand of 52 provided stability. And so, when Jones and Salter, bowlers at opposite ends of the career spectrum, shared four wickets in ten overs, there was no immediate panic. All the same, a score of 90 for four increased excitement among the Welsh contingent, not least Jones, who fanned the embers of an injury-ravaged career with an emotional eight-over spell from the Pavilion End. Now 34, it was not the first time he had excelled at Lord's – scene of five of his 18 Tests – but as his future lay as a Twenty20 specialist, it risked being the last.

Had Rees, at mid-off, held a chance that would have brought the end of Hussey and reduced Nottinghamshire to 94 for five, Lord's might have offered Jones even fonder memories. But Hussey and Read added 99. Read shed his miserable form – his run-a-ball 53 was just his second competitive half-century of the season – and late swiping from Swann and Mullaney set up a demanding total.

At 108 for two in the 20th over, Glamorgan seemed better placed – but Patel yanked the game away from them, and they never recovered. Broad, playing only his second one-day game for Nottinghamshire since arriving in 2008, brought things to a triumphant conclusion with three wickets in an over. It was their first limited-overs trophy since 1991.

Man of the Match: S. R. Patel. *Attendance:* 17,226.

Nottinghamshire

M. J. Lumb c and b Salter	28	S. J. Mullaney b Wagg		21
A. D. Hales c Goodwin b Jones	18	S. C. J. Broad b Hogan		0
J. W. A. Taylor c Wallace b Jones	22	L-b 12, w 9		21
S. R. Patel c Rees b Salter	10			
D. J. Hussey run out	42	1/52 (1) 2/58 (2)	(8 wkts, 40 overs)	244
*†C. M. W. Read c Cooke b Hogan	53	3/80 (4) 4/90 (3) 5/189 (5)		
G. P. Swann not out	29	6/195 (6) 7/237 (8) 8/244 (9)	8 overs: 47-0	

A. Shahzad and H. F. Gurney did not bat.

Hogan 8–0–49–2; Allenby 6–0–38–0; Jones 8–0–36–2; Salter 7–1–41–2; Cosker 7–0–37–0; Wagg 4–0–31–1.

Glamorgan

G. P. Rees b Shahzad	29	M. G. Hogan b Broad		0
*†M. A. Wallace c Taylor b Gurney	2	S. P. Jones not out		0
C. B. Cooke b Patel	46			
J. Allenby b Patel	34	B 2, w 1		3
M. W. Goodwin lbw b Patel	6			
B. J. Wright c Lumb b Shahzad	14	1/4 (2) 2/42 (1) 3/108 (3)	(33 overs)	157
G. G. Wagg c Read b Broad	18	4/115 (4) 5/118 (5) 6/144 (6)		
A. G. Salter lbw b Shahzad	2	7/147 (8) 8/155 (9) 9/157 (7)		
D. A. Cosker c Mullaney b Broad	3	10/157 (10)	8 overs: 40-1	

Broad 7–0–29–3; Gurney 5–0–22–1; Shahzad 6–0–33–3; Swann 6–0–36–0; Mullaney 2–0–14–0; Patel 7–0–21–3.

Umpires: P. J. Hartley and R. A. Kettleborough. Third umpire: N. A. Mallender.

AUSTRALIA A IN THE BRITISH ISLES, 2013

Australia A's three first-class games essentially marked the start of the Ashes campaign – giving their Test specialists the kind of extended limber-up that touring teams once took for granted. Brad Haddin's initial party of 14 included nine members of the Ashes Test squad and, when Australia were dumped out of the Champions Trophy at the group stage, they acquired two more.

It was during the last match of this trip, against Gloucestershire, that Cricket Australia grandees James Sutherland and Pat Howard descended on Bristol, and removed Mickey Arthur as head coach. A few hours later, Darren Lehmann – the A-side's assistant coach – was appearing alongside Michael Clarke in the Radisson Blu hotel as Arthur's replacement. Lehmann was the coming man: adored by many of the current players, and rated highly by the administrators, who had seconded him to the A-tour following a string of titles with Queensland, Brisbane Heat and two IPL franchises.

When the A-squad was announced in April, national selector John Inverarity ascribed the omission of leg-spinner Fawad Ahmed, an asylum seeker from Pakistan, to a desire not to overload the side with slow bowlers. That decision surprised some, because the ICC regulations that prevented Ahmed from representing his country of refuge did not apply to A-team cricket. But late on June 5, the House of Representatives in Canberra passed a bill clearing the way for his citizenship application to be fast-tracked, and he was hastily flown to the UK in time for the last two A-team games. Ahmed arrived, a little nervous, at Stormont, and formed a three-pronged spin attack with Nathan Lyon and Ashton Agar. Ireland's batsmen nominated Lyon as the pick, but Agar's all-round game had clearly made a big impression on the selection panel (now lacking Clarke, who stood down when Arthur was sacked). He – not Ahmed – leapfrogged Lyon to play in the First Test at Trent Bridge, and made an unforgettable 98 on debut.

It was a little surprising, given the appeal of an Australian team in an Ashes summer, that Gloucestershire were the only county to host a match. Certainly, the sporting pitches the Australians encountered at Edinburgh and Belfast were a far cry from the parched wickets produced for the five Tests. The Australians, unsure of their best Test side after the 4–0 drubbing in India, might have been better served by the intensity of an England Lions fixture. In the event, Gloucestershire looked capable of causing an upset, until Ryan Harris and Jackson Bird, each returning from injury, swept through the middle order for some morale-boosting wickets. Nic Maddinson, assumed by many to be a Twenty20 specialist, made his second spectacular century of the tour.

An Australian side played first-class matches in Scotland and Ireland for the first time since 1998 – and won a little too easily for their own good. Scotland were blown away by James Pattinson's pace, and even allowed Peter Siddle, an honest but limited tailender, to score his maiden first-class hundred. Scotland's captain, Preston Mommsen, admitted they were not good enough to face something akin to a Test team.

Ireland, desperate to prove their worth beyond Associate level, were a slightly different case. Their coach Phil Simmons believed this Australian side represented the toughest first-class opposition in Ireland's history – and they were determined to make the most of it. Rain cut the equivalent of a day's play, but the captains agreed at tea on the third to set up a run-chase of 301 for Ireland. That proved beyond them, but a fearless hundred by Paul Stirling in the first innings had already shown Australia that the Irish deserved more opportunities of this kind.

AUSTRALIA A TOURING PARTY

*B. J. Haddin, A. C. Agar, J. M. Bird, A. J. Doolan, R. J. Harris, M. C. Henriques, U. T. Khawaja, N. M. Lyon, N. J. Maddinson, J. L. Pattinson, C. J. Sayers, P. M. Siddle, J. C. Silk, S. P. D. Smith. *Coach:* T. J. Cooley. *Assistant coach:* D. S. Lehmann.

P. J. Cummins accompanied the squad as an unofficial member in a bid to regain fitness. Fawad Ahmed was added in time for the Ireland fixture, after it was announced that his eligibility to play for the full Australia team was likely to be fast-tracked. P. J. Hughes and M. S. Wade, who had played for Australia in the Champions Trophy, were added for the Gloucestershire match.

SCOTLAND v AUSTRALIA A

At Edinburgh, June 7–9. Australia A won by 360 runs. Toss: Scotland. First-class debut: C. G. Burnett.

A month before the Ashes, seven of Australia's Test squad took the field for a gentle introduction to British conditions. But they were so dominant that a four-day match finished halfway through the third. Even Scotland captain Mommsen – standing in for Kyle Coetzer – questioned why the fixture had been organised, such was the lack of first-class experience in his side. Scotland were at their best on the opening morning but, in the absence of injured off-spinner Majid Haq, they were soon deploying occasional bowlers, and the quick men bowled too short at Haddin, who steadied the innings, then cut and pulled ferociously. Siddle thrived in the rarefied air of No. 7, and scored his maiden first-class hundred, complete with a lucky escape on 93, when mid-on and mid-off both converged on a skier. MacLeod put down the catch, but without his fifty, and a stand of 66 with last man Wardlaw, Scotland's total would have been embarrassing. Khawaja and Smith, competing for a Test spot, both missed out when the Australians opted for further batting practice, but Agar's breezy fifty cleared the path for his shock call-up at Nottingham. Scotland were set 454 just before lunch on the third day, and folded in 30 overs to the pace of Pattinson and Sayers.

Close of play: first day, Australia A 335-6 (Siddle 85, Pattinson 9); second day, Australia A 165-4 (Henriques 29, Agar 31).

Australia A

J. C. Silk c Mommsen b Goudie	4	– c Machan b MacLeod	22
A. J. Doolan b Wardlaw	14	– lbw b Burnett	47
U. T. Khawaja c Cross b Wardlaw	51	– c Machan b Goudie	8
S. P. D. Smith c Goudie b MacLeod	22	– lbw b Iqbal	18
*†B. J. Haddin c Mommsen b Iqbal	113		
M. C. Henriques c Goudie b MacLeod	20	– (5) not out	59
P. M. Siddle not out	103		
J. L. Pattinson lbw b Goudie	20		
A. C. Agar c Cross b Wardlaw	5	– (6) c Mommsen b Machan	56
N. M. Lyon (did not bat)		– (7) not out	7
B 4, l-b 11, w 3, n-b 2	20	B 7, l-b 4, w 1, n-b 1	13

1/15 (1) 2/23 (2)   (8 wkts dec, 99 overs) 372   1/37 (1)   (5 wkts dec, 51 overs) 230
3/65 (4) 4/138 (3) 5/171 (6)   2/54 (3) 3/97 (2)
6/289 (5) 7/357 (8) 8/372 (9)   4/115 (4) 5/206 (6)

C. J. Sayers did not bat.

Wardlaw 28–5–101–3; Goudie 25–8–59–2; MacLeod 17–1–70–2; Burnett 15–2–65–0; Berrington 1–0–8–0; Machan 5–1–23–0; Iqbal 8–0–31–1. *Second innings*—Goudie 11–2–34–1; Wardlaw 9–3–22–0; MacLeod 5–0–35–1; Iqbal 9–0–57–1; Burnett 10–2–35–1; Machan 7–0–36–1.

Scotland

J. H. Davey c Doolan b Pattinson	0	– (2) c and b Sayers	14
M. W. Machan st Haddin b Lyon	21	– (1) lbw b Pattinson	7
F. R. J. Coleman run out	2	– c Henriques b Pattinson	0
R. D. Berrington b Pattinson	1	– c Smith b Sayers	3
*P. L. Mommsen c Haddin b Siddle	12	– c Silk b Lyon	12
M. M. Iqbal b Pattinson	0	– lbw b Sayers	0
†M. H. Cross c Doolan b Henriques	17	– c Haddin b Siddle	1
C. S. MacLeod c Agar b Lyon	51	– not out	30
G. Goudie c Haddin b Agar	0	– c Haddin b Pattinson	13
C. G. Burnett b Agar	0	– c Siddle b Lyon	2
I. Wardlaw not out	33	– c Smith b Pattinson	1
W 2, n-b 10	12	B 4, l-b 1, n-b 5	10

1/12 (1) 2/29 (3) 3/29 (2)   (43.5 overs) 149   1/11 (1) 2/17 (3)   (30.2 overs) 93
4/31 (4) 5/41 (6) 6/44 (5)   3/27 (2) 4/34 (4)
7/78 (7) 8/79 (9) 9/83 (10) 10/149 (8)   5/34 (6) 6/39 (7) 7/45 (5)
                                                8/70 (9) 9/75 (10) 10/93 (11)

Pattinson 8–4–16–3; Sayers 4–0–19–0; Lyon 8.5–1–51–2; Agar 11–2–29–2; Siddle 6–2–14–1; Henriques 6–2–20–1. *Second innings*—Pattinson 9.2–3–21–4; Sayers 9–4–16–3; Siddle 6–1–18–1; Lyon 6–0–33–2.

Umpires: A. J. T. Dowdalls and I. N. Ramage.

IRELAND v AUSTRALIA A

At Belfast, June 14–17. Australia A won by 93 runs. Toss: Ireland.

Ireland were missing several of their best players on county duty, but were enthusiastic enough to pull out of their first innings behind the Australians, in order to ensure a competitive last day's cricket. After O'Brien won the toss on a helpful pitch, Sorensen, working up a brisk pace, and Johnston, once of New South Wales, reduced the tourists to 139 for six. As the conditions eased, Australia A were pulled around by Smith's sixth first-class hundred and Pattinson's maiden fifty, before rain trimmed the last hour, and most of the next day. Haddin began the third with the first of three declarations, before Stirling – not required by Middlesex in the County Championship – set off in Twenty20 mode, crashing 26 from his first ten balls, and 50 from 44. A top-edged six apart, there was little fluky about a century bursting with off-side power; it was his eighth for Ireland in all formats, behind only Will Porterfield. Ireland progressed to 186 for four at tea. But, keen to make a game of it, O'Brien persuaded the Australians to go back in, and take whatever time was necessary to reach a lead of 300. Doolan and Maddinson – whose 51-ball hundred made Stirling's look pedestrian – needed barely 20 overs, as the ball refused to swing. It left Ireland more than a day to get the runs, but their hopes of a famous win were hit when Pattinson drew Stirling into an edge before the close. Third-choice wicketkeeper Stuart Poynter, an MCC Young Cricketer from Hammersmith, scored a confident maiden first-class fifty shortly before the Australians wrapped up victory. Fawad Ahmed had a quiet first match for his new country, and was outbowled by Lyon.

Close of play: first day, Australia A 248-6 (Smith 104, Pattinson 42); second day, Australia A 312-9 (Agar 5); third day, Ireland 51-3 (Shannon 11, White 2).

Australia A

N. J. Maddinson b Sorensen	6	– (2) not out	113
A. J. Doolan c Poynter b Johnston	40	– (1) not out	56
U. T. Khawaja b Sorensen	0		
S. P. D. Smith c Poynter b Johnston	133		
*†B. J. Haddin b Johnston	2		
M. C. Henriques c Johnston b Sorensen	47		
P. M. Siddle c Mooney b Sorensen	0		
J. L. Pattinson c Poynter b Sorensen	66		
A. C. Agar not out	5		
N. M. Lyon c Sorensen b Johnston	2		
B 9, n-b 2	11	L-b 4, w 1	5

1/14 (1) 2/22 (3)   (9 wkts dec, 88 overs) 312   (no wkt dec, 20.2 overs) 174
3/61 (2) 4/65 (5) 5/139 (6)
6/139 (7) 7/296 (4) 8/310 (8) 9/312 (10)

Fawad Ahmed did not bat.

Sorensen 16–5–50–5; Johnston 22–4–68–4; Mooney 13–2–45–0; Thompson 11–1–52–0; Cusack 7–2–27–0; Stirling 10–0–24–0; O'Brien 6–0–22–0; White 3–0–15–0. *Second innings*—Sorensen 5–1–42–0; Johnston 3–0–25–0; Thompson 3–0–39–0; Cusack 5–0–37–0; Stirling 3–0–17–0; White 1.2–0–10–0.

Ireland

P. R. Stirling st Haddin b Lyon	115	– c Haddin b Pattinson	6
J. Anderson c Smith b Pattinson	2	– c Haddin b Henriques	8
A. R. Cusack c Haddin b Agar	0	– c Maddinson b Henriques	15
J. N. K. Shannon c and b Agar	0	– c Maddinson b Lyon	35
A. R. White not out	40	– c Maddinson b Lyon	23
*K. J. O'Brien not out	16	– c Haddin b Henriques	10
J. F. Mooney (did not bat)		– c Haddin b Henriques	0
S. R. Thompson (did not bat)		– lbw b Lyon	27
†S. W. Poynter (did not bat)		– c Haddin b Siddle	63
D. T. Johnston (did not bat)		– lbw b Fawad Ahmed	5
M. C. Sorensen (did not bat)		– not out	0
B 3, l-b 5, n-b 5	13	B 1, l-b 2, w 8, n-b 4	15

1/33 (2) 2/55 (3)   (4 wkts dec, 55 overs) 186   1/6 (1) 2/27 (2)   (65.2 overs) 207
3/58 (4) 4/154 (1)   3/38 (3) 4/92 (5)
                                                  5/100 (4) 6/109 (7) 7/112 (6)
                                                  8/182 (8) 9/203 (10) 10/207 (9)

Pattinson 8–1–49–1; Siddle 7–1–23–0; Agar 13–3–32–2; Lyon 16–4–34–1; Fawad Ahmed 11–1–40–0. *Second innings*—Pattinson 14–3–55–1; Siddle 20.2–5–62–1; Henriques 10–1–22–4; Lyon 15–3–40–3; Fawad Ahmed 6–2–25–1.

Umpires: M. Hawthorne and A. J. Neill.

GLOUCESTERSHIRE v AUSTRALIA A

At Bristol, June 21–23. Australia A won by 24 runs. Toss: Australia A. County debuts: D. T. Christian, T. M. J. Smith.

Maddinson treated Nevil Road to an innings of rare power. He took advantage of wayward bowling on a true pitch to hammer nine sixes, and peppered the new pavilion under construction at the Ashley Down Road End, racing from 100 to a career-best 181 in just 34 balls. Sayers then produced late outswing to roll Gloucestershire for 122, but the Australians – with national selectors John Inverarity, Rod Marsh and Mickey Arthur in attendance – again declined to enforce the follow-on, swayed by the need to give out-of-touch Test batsmen practice before the Ashes. That offered Gloucestershire a way back into the match: Maddinson was caught behind first ball, Hughes and Smith failed, and Khawaja and Silk were both run out by Fuller, roaming in the deep. Gidman used the smidgen of seam movement intelligently, and the Australians collapsed to 111. When Gloucestershire closed the day on 162 for three in pursuit of 321, with Christian taking a liking to the leg-spin of his new compatriot Fawad Ahmed, they had an outside chance. But it was snuffed out as Harris and Bird, both in the Ashes squad, continued their return to fitness and form on the final morning. The day after the game, and with the Ashes tour about to start, Arthur was sacked as head coach – and replaced by the A-team's assistant coach, Darren Lehmann.

Close of play: first day, Gloucestershire 104-5 (Howell 27, Gidman 19); second day, Gloucestershire 162-3 (Roderick 21, Christian 40).

Australia A

J. C. Silk b Christian	41	– (6) run out	9
N. J. Maddinson c Christian b Howell	181	– (5) c Roderick b Gidman	0
P. J. Hughes c Herring b Howell	47	– (2) lbw b Gidman	11
U. T. Khawaja not out	29	– (1) run out	6
*S. P. D. Smith c Herring b Gidman	10	– (3) c Dent b Norwell	0
†M. S. Wade not out	3	– (4) c Smith b Christian	28
R. J. Harris (did not bat)		– c Housego b Fuller	3
A. C. Agar (did not bat)		– c Howell b Gidman	27
C. J. Sayers (did not bat)		– b Smith	15
J. M. Bird (did not bat)		– c Roderick b Gidman	6
Fawad Ahmed (did not bat)		– not out	4
B 8, l-b 8, w 2, n-b 2	20	L-b 2	2

1/103 (1) 2/236 (3)   (4 wkts dec, 58 overs) 331   1/14 (1) 2/14 (3)   (35.1 overs) 111
3/295 (2) 4/313 (5)   3/20 (2) 4/20 (5)
                                                   5/55 (4) 6/58 (6) 7/67 (7)
                                                   8/88 (9) 9/106 (8) 10/111 (10)

Fuller 11–0–64–0; Gidman 12–1–57–1; Norwell 13–0–85–0; Christian 8–2–46–1; Smith 6–0–26–0; Howell 8–2–37–2. *Second innings*—Gidman 11.1–2–25–4; Norwell 7–0–23–1; Christian 5–1–19–1; Fuller 6–0–30–1; Smith 6–1–12–1.

Gloucestershire

*M. Klinger c Fawad Ahmed b Sayers	13	– (2) lbw b Bird	22
C. D. J. Dent b Sayers	23	– (1) c Khawaja b Sayers	56
D. M. Housego c Wade b Harris	1	– b Sayers	19
G. H. Roderick b Sayers	7	– c Fawad Ahmed b Agar	33
D. T. Christian c Khawaja b Agar	1	– c Wade b Harris	46
B. A. C. Howell c Smith b Fawad Ahmed	35	– lbw b Harris	0
W. R. S. Gidman c Wade b Harris	19	– b Bird	19
†C. L. Herring run out	8	– c Silk b Bird	9
T. M. J. Smith c Smith b Sayers	0	– (10) not out	17
J. K. Fuller c Wade b Sayers	0	– (9) c Smith b Harris	38
L. C. Norwell not out	0	– c Wade b Sayers	16
B 5, l-b 1, n-b 9	15	B 18, l-b 1, n-b 2	21

1/32 (2) 2/41 (3) 3/49 (1)   (47.2 overs) 122   1/53 (2) 2/89 (1)   (80.3 overs) 296
4/50 (4) 5/57 (5) 6/104 (7)   3/105 (3) 4/169 (5)
7/116 (6) 8/122 (9) 9/122 (10) 10/122 (8)   5/169 (6) 6/211 (7) 7/211 (4)
                                                   8/259 (8) 9/260 (9) 10/296 (11)

Bird 10–3–29–0; Harris 14–6–25–2; Sayers 9–3–24–5; Agar 5–2–18–1; Fawad Ahmed 9.2–5–20–1. *Second innings*—Harris 19–9–56–3; Sayers 21.3–3–68–3; Bird 12–4–53–3; Fawad Ahmed 22–4–80–0; Agar 6–3–20–1.

Umpires: J. H. Evans and P. Willey.

BANGLADESH A IN ENGLAND, 2013

As England retained the Ashes at Old Trafford, a more low-key tour was about to get under way at the other end of the country. Bangladesh A played eight one-day games – and looked set to lose the lot before finally turning the tables in the last of three matches against England Lions. But that hardly made up for two thumping defeats in the other Lions games, and five against county sides, some of which were virtual Second XIs.

The Bangladeshis were an experienced bunch: 11 had already played Test cricket. Of the others, three more – Al-Amin Hossain, Anamul Haque and Shamshur Rahman – would win their first Test caps in the six months following the tour, while the odd man out, Farhad Reza, had made his one-day international debut as long ago as 2006.

The batting was prone to collapse, but had its moments, notably when Ziaur Rahman – after grafting to 32 from 45 balls at Trent Bridge – cracked 68 from the next 22 to reach a rapid century. Anamul, a compact wicketkeeper, and Naeem Islam also made hundreds, Naeem's coming in the consolation win at Taunton that rounded off the trip.

But the bowling was the real problem. No one averaged less than 38, or went for under five an over – not even Sohag Gazi, the off-spinner who had made a promising start to his Test career. Rubel Hossain, the fastest of the seamers, took only two wickets in his four games. "We prepared really well for this tour as we knew what conditions we would likely face," said their Australian coach, Corey Richards, as he contemplated a chastening experience. "Unfortunately we just didn't compete with either bat or ball for the full game."

BANGLADESH A TOURING PARTY

*Jahurul Islam, Al-Amin Hossain, Anamul Haque, Elias Sunny, Farhad Reza, Imrul Kayes, Marshall Ayub, Mominul Haque, Naeem Islam, Raqibul Hasan, Robiul Islam, Rubel Hossain, Shamshur Rahman, Sohag Gazi, Ziaur Rahman. *Coach:* C. J. Richards.

At Southampton, August 6. **Hampshire won by eight runs. Hampshire 223** (49.1 overs) (L. A. Dawson 97); ‡**Bangladesh A 215-9** (50 overs) (Elias Sunny 45*; L. A. Dawson 3-11). *County debuts:* J. H. Davey, M. J. King, A. B. London, D. J. Sheppard, B. J. Taylor. *An unfamiliar Hampshire side looked set for a comfortable victory when the Bangladeshis crashed to 99-7, and later 157-9. But a last-wicket stand of 58* between Elias Sunny and Robiul Islam – whose 34* contained five sixes – made it close, although 22 from Josh Davey's final over proved beyond them. Earlier, Liam Dawson put on 54 for Hampshire's last wicket with 16-year-old Brad Taylor (2*), who faced only four balls.*

At Leeds, August 9. **Yorkshire won by seven runs.** ‡**Yorkshire 198** (47.4 overs) (A. Lyth 45, L. E. Plunkett 47*; Elias Sunny 3-25); **Bangladesh A 191** (44.1 overs) (Anamul Haque 69; Azeem Rafiq 5-30). *Yorkshire were 11-2, and approached 200 thanks only to a ninth-wicket stand of 49 between Liam Plunkett and Iain Wardlaw (18). Bangladesh A were cruising at 116-2 in the 25th over, but then lost three for three, before Azeem Rafiq instigated a final collapse of five for 44.*

At Manchester, August 11. **Lancashire won by seven wickets.** ‡**Bangladesh A 171** (47.3 overs) (Shamshur Rahman 51, Naeem Islam 57; A. M. Lilley 3-24, S. J. Croft 3-16); **Lancashire 175-3** (44.1 overs) (S. C. Moore 61, P. J. Horton 43*). *The Bangladesh batsmen struggled again, with only Shamshur Rahman and Naeem Islam making more than 18. Lancashire avoided early problems, and sailed home with more than five overs to spare.*

At Nottingham, August 14. **Nottinghamshire won by four wickets.** ‡**Bangladesh A 292-7** (50 overs) (Shamshur Rahman 52, Mominul Haque 47, Ziaur Rahman 104*; P. J. Franks 3-56); **Nottinghamshire 293-6** (48.5 overs) (M. H. Cross 47, A. D. Tillcock 97*; P. J. Franks 75). *County debuts:* G. P. W. Bacon, M. H. Cross, T. C. Rowe, A. D. Tillcock. *In a topsy-turvy match, Nottinghamshire looked in charge when Bangladesh slipped to 148-7 in the 32nd over, only for Ziaur Rahman to slap seven sixes in a 67-ball century; he and Elias Sunny (37*) put on 144* for the eighth wicket. Nottinghamshire were in trouble themselves at 48-3, but were rescued by the 19-year-old debutant Adam Tillcock, who put on 170 with Paul Franks for the sixth wicket in 20 overs.*

At Worcester, August 16. **Worcestershire won by six wickets.** ‡**Bangladesh A 274-8** (50 overs) (Anamul Haque 110, Mominul Haque 64, Naeem Islam 47*; S. H. Choudhry 3-35); **Worcestershire 275-4** (47.3 overs) (T. Köhler-Cadmore 47, D. K. H. Mitchell 101, A. N. Kervezee 45, T. C. Fell 42*). *County debut:* T. Köhler-Cadmore. *A patient century from Anamul Haque ensured a respectable total – although, from 232-3 in the 44th over, Bangladesh might have hoped for more. It wasn't enough: Daryl Mitchell shared an opening stand of 97 with the debutant Tom Köhler-Cadmore, the Wisden Schools Cricketer of the Year, then put on 92 with Alexei Kervezee.*

At Bristol, August 20. **England Lions won by 202 runs. England Lions 353-4** (50 overs) (J. W. A. Taylor 40, G. S. Ballance 115, L. J. Wright 143*); **Bangladesh A 151** (47 overs). *When James Taylor departed in the 29th over, the Lions were chugging along at 112-3 – but a whirlwind knock from their captain Luke Wright changed the complexion of the match. He hurtled to a century from only 51 balls, and from 68 in all blitzed 11 fours and ten sixes, including three in a row off Mominul Haque, whose only over cost 24. Wright piled on 225 in 20 overs with Gary Ballance, who was no slouch himself, reaching his own hundred in 82 balls. Bangladesh A lost Anamul Haque to the second ball of the innings, and wickets went down regularly. With five overs left and more than 200 required, Wright gave himself and Michael Carberry a bowl: they both took two wickets to polish things off.*

At Taunton, August 22. **England Lions won by 191 runs.** ‡**England Lions 367-3** (50 overs) (M. A. Carberry 146, J. W. A. Taylor 106*, J. C. Buttler 47); **Bangladesh A 176** (44.4 overs) (Jahurul Islam 53; C. J. Jordan 4-38). *The Lions made sure of the series with another clinical display. The stars this time were Carberry and Taylor, who hit four sixes apiece in a second-wicket stand of 185. Jahurul Islam dropped anchor but, although seven team-mates reached double figures, only Naeem Islam (31) passed 16. Carberry again applied the coup de grâce, and finished with 3-3 in the series.*

At Taunton, August 24. **Bangladesh A won by four wickets.** ‡**England Lions 319-7** (50 overs) (J. M. Vince 63, G. S. Ballance 87, J. W. A. Taylor 44; Al-Amin Hossain 3-70); **Bangladesh A 324-6** (50 overs) (Raqibul Hasan 72, Naeem Islam 121*; B. A. Stokes 3-74). *When Wright won the toss and his side ran up more than 300, it looked as if Bangladesh A would leave without a win. But at last their batting fired: the third-wicket pair added 104 and, after Raqibul was stumped, Naeem carried on, finishing with 15 fours and two sixes from 100 balls. He and Shamshur Rahman (35 from 20 balls, with three sixes) put on 76 in less than seven overs to swing the match Bangladesh's way, and Farhad Reza clinched it with a six off Tymal Mills. England Lions took the brief series 2–1.*

THE UNIVERSITIES, 2013

The season was dominated by Leeds/Bradford MCCU, who won a treble of university titles – all in the space of a fortnight in June. They pipped Cardiff to the two-day MCC Universities Championship, crept home against them in a rain-shortened MCCU one-day Challenge final at Lord's, then ran down 202 at Wormsley to beat Loughborough in the BUCS one-day final.

They were almost Twenty20 champions too. On finals day at the ECB Academy grounds, left-arm spinner David Foster took four for 14 in the semi-final to help overcome Cardiff again, but the batting then malfunctioned against Loughborough, who knocked off 133.

Leeds/Bradford's success followed tragedy, after all-rounder Tom Hardman, 21, died in his sleep in November 2012. He had been earmarked to captain the combined MCC Universities side in 2013. In May, Leeds Metropolitan University – where Hardman had been studying sports science – played the University of Leeds in a Twenty20 match in aid of Cardiac Risk in the Young; his former club, Heywood in Lancashire, also held a match to raise money for the charity.

For the second year in succession, Leeds/Bradford were the only MCCU to beat a county side. They had beaten Sussex in 2012, but in a non-first-class match. Now, though, they gained their maiden first-class victory, over Leicestershire. The triumph owed much to captain Luis Reece, who turned the game with a counter-attacking 114 not out in the second innings. He made 41 and 77 against his parent county Lancashire, who then picked him to open the batting in their next Championship match. The other hero of Leeds/Bradford's season was seamer James Lee, who had made his first-class debut as a 17-year-old for Yorkshire back in 2006, before falling from favour. But on the opening morning of the season at Headingley he ran in to leave Yorkshire ten for four, and finished the innings with seven for 45. He followed up with eight wickets in the match against Leicestershire, and four against Lancashire.

REPORTS BY RALPH DELLOR AND STEPHEN LAMB

CAMBRIDGE MCCU v ESSEX

At Cambridge, April 5–7. Drawn. Toss: Cambridge MCCU. First-class debuts: A. T. A. Allchin, A. G. Hearne, G. F. Nicholson, A. W. Pollock, N. V. S. Senaratne. County debut: R. J. Quiney.

Cambridge did well to escape with a draw after Mills gave them a technical and physical going-over in the first innings. As in the 2012 fixture, the pick of the home attack was Matt Salisbury, whose three wickets on the opening morning included Test batsmen Quiney and Bopara, but Pettini restored order with his first hundred in England since June 2009. Mills then terrorised the batsmen, and Cambridge declined to 35 for seven, before Alasdair Pollock, who have taken several stinging blows, twice struck him into the Fenner's car park. Essex opted for further batting practice: the Australian Quiney scored a century on county debut, Westley followed him to three figures, and Foakes hit his maiden first-class hundred; Bopara, though, bagged a golden duck. Given two and a half sessions to make 650, Cambridge were steered to safety by Nipuna Senaratne and the Ansari brothers.

Close of play: first day, Cambridge MCCU 20-4 (Bell 4, Elliott 0); second day, Essex 335-3 (Foakes 49, Foster 34).

Essex

T. Westley c Bell b Salisbury	58	– (2) st Bell b A. S. Ansari	133
R. J. Quiney c Bell b Salisbury	5	– (1) b Pollock	112
B. T. Foakes c Bell b Allchin	38	– not out	101
R. S. Bopara lbw b Salisbury	4	– lbw b A. S. Ansari	0
M. L. Pettini not out	100		
*†J. S. Foster c Pollock b Z. S. Ansari	54	– (5) c Johnson b Salisbury	67
G. M. Smith not out	57		
G. R. Napier (did not bat)		– (6) not out	0
B 1, l-b 11	12	B 5, l-b 1, w 1	7

1/13 (2) 2/90 (3)   (5 wkts dec, 83 overs) 328   1/209 (1)   (4 wkts dec, 84 overs) 420
3/110 (1) 4/113 (4) 5/215 (6)   2/281 (2) 3/281 (4)
4/412 (5)

D. D. Masters, M. A. Chambers and T. S. Mills did not bat.

Salisbury 20–4–64–3; Nicholson 10–1–47–0; Pollock 10–1–45–0; Allchin 26–1–98–1; Z. S. Ansari 17–0–62–1. *Second innings*—Salisbury 18–2–53–1; Nicholson 22–0–127–0; Allchin 12–0–80–0; Pollock 19–2–68–1; A. S. Ansari 13–0–86–2.

Cambridge MCCU

J. A. M. Johnson c Pettini b Mills	10	– c Westley b Mills	4
*Z. S. Ansari lbw b Mills	2	– b Mills	31
N. V. S. Senaratne c Foster b Chambers	4	– c Quiney b Napier	82
A. S. Ansari c Pettini b Mills	4	– lbw b Chambers	31
†D. W. Bell c Bopara b Napier	4	– not out	6
T. C. Elliott c Westley b Smith	18	– not out	4
A. G. Hearne c Pettini b Napier	6		
M. E. T. Salisbury c Quiney b Chambers	5		
A. W. Pollock not out	44		
A. T. A. Allchin lbw b Smith	0		
G. F. Nicholson lbw b Bopara	1		
L-b 5	5	B 3, l-b 11, w 1, n-b 4	19

1/11 (1) 2/12 (2) 3/14 (4)   (31.1 overs) 99   1/9 (1)   (4 wkts, 69 overs) 177
4/20 (3) 5/20 (5) 6/30 (7)   2/100 (2) 3/150 (3)
7/35 (8) 8/61 (6) 9/73 (10) 10/99 (11)   4/172 (4)

Masters 5–1–10–0; Mills 8–1–42–3; Chambers 8–4–19–2; Napier 7–2–21–2; Smith 2–2–0–2; Bopara 1.1–0–2–1. *Second innings*—Masters 17–6–36–0; Mills 10–2–37–2; Chambers 14–3–28–1; Westley 7–4–9–0; Napier 13–4–35–1; Bopara 8–2–18–0.

Umpires: B. J. Debenham and S. J. O'Shaughnessy.

At Chester-le-Street, April 5–7. DURHAM MCCU drew with DURHAM.

At Cardiff, April 5–7. CARDIFF MCCU drew with GLAMORGAN.

OXFORD MCCU v WARWICKSHIRE

At Oxford, April 5–7. Warwickshire won by 21 runs. Toss: Warwickshire. First-class debuts: C. J. Bodenstein, S. R. Davison, T. C. Fell, L. M. Sabin; S. A. Ali, R. O. Gordon, P. J. McKay.

Oxford were one partnership away from emulating their win at Edgbaston in 1973 – the last time a university side beat the reigning county champions. On a bitterly cold opening day, Warwickshire's seasoned batting line-up got tied down by Sam Agarwal's off-spin and the left-arm seam of Cornelis Bodenstein – born in Pretoria, but arriving at Oxford via Jersey. Troughton declared shortly before the close and was rewarded with two wickets, though Agarwal survived and made a hundred next day with little support. Building on a slender lead of 23, Warwickshire were in command at 92 for two on the last morning, before suffering a collapse of eight for 39 as a slow pitch began to misbehave. Oxford were left needing 155 for their first win over a county since 2000, and looked on course when Lloyd Sabin and former Warwickshire youth player Ben Williams took the score from 13 for four to 108. But Milnes, charging in from the Norham Gardens End, took advantage of low bounce to complete a career-best seven for 39, five of them lbw and one caught behind by Ambrose, who kept wicket in the second innings after 18-year-old Pete McKay broke a finger.

Close of play: first day, Oxford MCCU 2-2 (Agarwal 1); second day, Warwickshire 72-2 (Porterfield 4, Troughton 15).

Warwickshire

V. Chopra lbw b Kemp	1	– c Davison b Kemp	25
I. J. Westwood c Morris b Bodenstein	37	– c Davison b Morris	25
W. T. S. Porterfield lbw b Bodenstein	43	– c Davison b Morris	10
*J. O. Troughton c Davison b Agarwal	52	– c Agarwal b Morris	30
L. J. Evans b Bodenstein	2	– b Kemp	5
T. R. Ambrose c Ellison b Agarwal	59	– b Kemp	3
T. P. Milnes not out	52	– c Kemp b Bodenstein	3
†P. J. McKay lbw b Agarwal	4	– lbw b Ellison	5
S. A. Ali b Morris	8	– c Davison b Bodenstein	2
O. J. Hannon-Dalby run out	13	– not out	9
R. O. Gordon not out	6	– b Ellison	9
B 4, l-b 10, n-b 2	16	L-b 1, w 2, n-b 2	5

1/9 (1) 2/86 (2) (9 wkts dec, 96.1 overs) 293
3/86 (3) 4/92 (5) 5/204 (6)
6/207 (4) 7/215 (8) 8/251 (9) 9/282 (10)

1/50 (2) 2/56 (1) (54.1 overs) 131
3/92 (3) 4/95 (4)
5/98 (6) 6/105 (5) 7/105 (7)
8/111 (9) 9/113 (8) 10/131 (11)

Ellison 21.1–2–76–0; Morris 16–8–39–1; Kemp 18–6–37–1; Jones 11–0–48–0; Bodenstein 18–6–53–3; Agarwal 12–5–26–3. *Second innings*—Ellison 11.1–1–50–2; Morris 15–4–33–3; Kemp 16–7–31–3; Bodenstein 8–4–12–2; Agarwal 4–3–4–0.

Oxford MCCU

S. S. Agarwal b Gordon	108	– lbw b Milnes	0
L. M. Sabin c Evans b Milnes	0	– c Ambrose b Milnes	50
C. J. Bodenstein lbw b Milnes	1	– (8) lbw b Milnes	4
O. J. Jones lbw b Hannon-Dalby	2	– (3) lbw b Milnes	2
F. R. J. Coleman c Gordon b Hannon-Dalby	3	– (4) lbw b Milnes	2
T. C. Fell lbw b Ali	16	– (5) lbw b Hannon-Dalby	4
B. Williams c Porterfield b Hannon-Dalby	36	– (6) c Chopra b Gordon	41
†S. R. Davison c Evans b Gordon	13	– (7) lbw b Milnes	3
*C. A. J. Morris not out	33	– c Ambrose b Hannon-Dalby	11
C. P. Ellison c Ambrose b Ali	36	– c Chopra b Milnes	7
B. W. Kemp b Hannon-Dalby	9	– not out	0
L-b 3, n-b 10	13	L-b 6, w 1, n-b 2	9

1/0 (2) 2/2 (3) 3/5 (4) (86.4 overs) 270
4/31 (5) 5/89 (6) 6/157 (7)
7/186 (8) 8/189 (1) 9/251 (10) 10/270 (11)

1/0 (1) 2/2 (3) (53.2 overs) 133
3/8 (4) 4/13 (5)
5/108 (6) 6/108 (2) 7/112 (8)
8/121 (7) 9/133 (10) 10/133 (9)

Hannon-Dalby 21.4–5–50–4; Milnes 23–7–55–2; Ali 18–4–76–2; Gordon 14–4–50–2; Evans 8–1–26–0; Chopra 2–0–10–0. *Second innings*—Milnes 16–5–39–7; Hannon-Dalby 15.2–4–43–2; Ali 11–1–27–0; Gordon 11–5–18–1.

Umpires: M. A. Eggleston and J. W. Lloyds.

At Hove, April 5–7. LOUGHBOROUGH MCCU drew with SUSSEX.

At Leeds, April 5–7. LEEDS/BRADFORD MCCU lost to YORKSHIRE by 294 runs.

At Canterbury, April 10–12. CARDIFF MCCU drew with KENT.

At Southampton (Nursery Ground), April 17–19. LOUGHBOROUGH MCCU lost to HAMPSHIRE by 155 runs.

At Nottingham, April 17–19. DURHAM MCCU lost to NOTTINGHAMSHIRE by 541 runs. *The second-heaviest defeat by runs in an English first-class match.*

CAMBRIDGE MCCU v MIDDLESEX

At Cambridge, April 24–26. Middlesex won by 234 runs. Toss: Middlesex. First-class debut: B. A. Wylie.

Cambridge were given a promising start by their home-town left-arm seamer James Cowan, who dismissed Dexter and Denly in an impressive 14-over opening spell. But that was as good as it got, and career-best scores from Malan and Rossington allowed Middlesex to rack up 438 in the day. Rossington hoisted Akbar Ansari's leg-breaks for five consecutive sixes in an over, all in the arc between midwicket and long-on, then a sixth in Ansari's next to reach a 55-ball hundred. Middlesex's own left-armer Gurjit Sandhu then ran through the students' lower order on his second first-class appearance. Harris and Rossington were pushed up the card before Middlesex declared overnight for a second time. Cambridge's attempt to see out the last day was boosted by an 80-minute stoppage for rain, and a steady hand from Zafar Ansari, but they floundered against the spinners, with Patel twice on a hat-trick as he recorded his maiden first-class five-for. He and Rayner took on a greater workload after Sandhu's match turned sour: he tore a hamstring in his fifth over and had to be carried off.

Close of play: first day, Middlesex 438-4 (Malan 156, Rossington 103); second day, Middlesex 132-3 (Harris 43, Rossington 57).

Middlesex

A. B. London c A. S. Ansari b Z. S. Ansari	81		
*N. J. Dexter c Bell b Cowan	21	– (1) c Sadler b Cowan	14
J. L. Denly c Johnson b Cowan	2	– (2) c Sadler b Salisbury	8
D. J. Malan not out	156		
P. R. Stirling c Bell b Salisbury	54		
†A. M. Rossington not out	103	– (5) not out	57
O. P. Rayner (did not bat)		– (3) b Cowan	10
J. A. R. Harris (did not bat)		– (4) not out	43
B 2, l-b 9, w 6, n-b 4	21		

1/38 (2) 2/60 (3)   (4 wkts dec, 102 overs) 438   1/13 (2)   (3 wkts dec, 32 overs) 132
3/184 (1) 4/311 (5)   2/23 (1) 3/38 (3)

G. S. Sandhu, R. H. Patel and C. D. Collymore did not bat.

Salisbury 21–4–69–1; Cowan 22–6–73–2; Sadler 16–2–88–0; Z. S. Ansari 20–2–57–1; Poysden 11–0–45–0; Wylie 9–0–52–0; A. S. Ansari 3–0–43–0. *Second innings*—Salisbury 10–1–32–1; Cowan 8–2–29–2; Sadler 8–0–34–0; Z. S. Ansari 3–0–15–0; Wylie 2–0–19–0; Poysden 1–0–3–0.

Cambridge MCCU

J. A. M. Johnson c Rossington b Harris	2	– c London b Rayner	22
*Z. S. Ansari c Rossington b Collymore	3	– lbw b Harris	72
N. V. S. Senaratne c Rossington b Harris	20	– c Stirling b Patel	7
A. S. Ansari lbw b Patel	27	– b Patel	0
†D. W. Bell b Rayner	47	– c London b Rayner	1
T. C. Elliott c Rossington b Sandhu	26	– c Rayner b Patel	24
B. A. Wylie b Sandhu	0	– not out	29
J. E. Poysden c London b Sandhu	0	– c London b Patel	9
M. E. T. Salisbury lbw b Rayner	4	– lbw b Patel	0
J. D. Cowan c Dexter b Sandhu	7	– c Rossington b Harris	1
P. T. Sadler not out	4	– c sub (T. G. Helm) b Rayner	6
L-b 9, n-b 8	17	B 4, l-b 4	8

1/4 (2) 2/12 (1) 3/36 (3) (64.5 overs) 157 1/69 (1) 2/86 (3) (57.2 overs) 179
4/68 (4) 5/126 (6) 6/130 (7) 3/86 (4) 4/89 (5)
7/138 (8) 8/146 (5) 9/153 (9) 10/157 (10) 5/122 (6) 6/141 (2) 7/152 (8)
8/152 (9) 9/157 (10) 10/179 (11)

Harris 13–4–20–2; Collymore 11–3–34–1; Sandhu 17.5–4–49–4; Dexter 11–6–22–0; Patel 5–2–5–1; Rayner 7–1–18–2. *Second innings*—Harris 11–2–29–2; Collymore 7–1–21–0; Sandhu 4.1–1–6–0; Dexter 2–1–8–0; Patel 19.5–4–69–5; Rayner 13.2–3–38–3.

Umpires: S. A. Garratt and B. V. Taylor.

At Leicester, April 24–26. LEEDS/BRADFORD MCCU beat LEICESTERSHIRE by 102 runs. *Leeds/Bradford's maiden first-class victory.*

OXFORD MCCU v WORCESTERSHIRE

At Oxford, May 1–3. Worcestershire won by 130 runs. Toss: Worcestershire. First-class debuts: W. J. Marriott; G. Cessford.

Worcestershire had lost two of their first three Championship games, and were intent on a clinical victory rather than a mere workout. Oxford's bowlers, impressive against Warwickshire a month earlier, were dealt some lessons by Mitchell and Pardoe, who put on 210 for the first wicket. Wilf Marriott was the cornerstone of the reply on his first-class debut, but Richard Jones kept chipping away. All ten wickets went to catches, with wicketkeeper Cox taking seven to equal Hugo Yarnold's Worcestershire record for dismissals in an innings, made against Scotland at Broughty Ferry, near Dundee, in 1951 (although six of his were stumpings). Pinner registered a second fifty before a declaration 20 overs into the last day set the students a theoretical 339. Shantry blew them away with a career-best seven for 60. Leslie Reifer, a 23-year-old cousin of one-time West Indies captain Floyd, stood in his first match as part of the ECB's umpire exchange scheme with the West Indies Cricket Board. He was believed to be the youngest person to have umpired a first-class fixture in England since 1928, when the 21-year-old E. F. Wilson, a Surrey professional, stood in the Royal Navy v Royal Air Force game at The Oval.

Close of play: first day, Oxford MCCU 14-0 (Agarwal 5, Sabin 5); second day, Worcestershire 80-0 (Kervezee 47, Pinner 31).

Worcestershire

*D. K. H. Mitchell c Davison b Jones	118		
M. G. Pardoe c Davison b Morris	89		
A. N. Kervezee c Bodenstein b Agarwal	3	– (1) lbw b Morris	47
N. D. Pinner c Sabin b Kemp	54	– (2) lbw b Kemp	80
J. Leach not out	55		
†O. B. Cox not out	5	– (3) not out	52
S. H. Choudhry (did not bat)		– (4) not out	21
B 10, l-b 8, w 6	24	B 6, l-b 3, w 1	10

1/210 (1) 2/213 (3) (4 wkts dec, 98 overs) 348 1/80 (1) (2 wkts dec, 43.4 overs) 210
3/250 (2) 4/330 (4) 2/158 (2)

G. Cessford, J. D. Shantry, R. A. Jones and C. J. Russell did not bat.

Thompson 12–5–26–0; Morris 21–7–47–1; Kemp 18–3–91–1; Bodenstein 12–2–43–0; Jones 15–2–58–1; Agarwal 20–2–65–1. *Second innings*—Kemp 14–1–55–1; Morris 13–0–50–1; Bodenstein 6.4–1–33–0; Jones 4–0–19–0; Agarwal 5–0–38–0; Marriott 1–0–6–0.

Oxford MCCU

S. S. Agarwal c Cox b Jones	39	– lbw b Shantry	0
L. M. Sabin c Choudhry b Jones	11	– c Pinner b Jones	30
O. J. Jones c Cox b Jones	9	– lbw b Shantry	11
F. R. J. Coleman c Cox b Shantry	11	– c Cox b Cessford	46
T. C. Fell c Cox b Jones	33	– c Cox b Shantry	28
W. J. J. Marriott c and b Cessford	81	– lbw b Shantry	5
C. J. Bodenstein c Cox b Jones	0	– lbw b Shantry	27
†S. R. Davison c Cox b Choudhry	7	– b Shantry	3
J. S. Thompson c Cox b Leach	8	– b Russell	15
*C. A. J. Morris c Pardoe b Russell	0	– not out	2
B. W. Kemp not out	0	– c Jones b Shantry	11
B 5, l-b 9, w 1, n-b 6	21	B 12, l-b 15, w 1, n-b 2	30

1/49 (2) 2/69 (3) 3/76 (1) (80.4 overs) 220 1/0 (1) 2/48 (2) (59.3 overs) 208
4/95 (4) 5/137 (5) 6/139 (7) 3/48 (3) 4/124 (5)
7/175 (8) 8/197 (9) 9/204 (10) 10/220 (6) 5/124 (4) 6/140 (6) 7/166 (8)
  8/195 (7) 9/195 (9) 10/208 (11)

Shantry 19–7–41–1; Cessford 17.4–8–38–1; Choudhry 10–4–20–1; Russell 19–6–49–1; Jones 11–2–45–5; Leach 4–0–13–1. *Second innings*—Shantry 22.3–5–60–7; Cessford 10–5–29–1; Jones 7–2–27–1; Russell 12–1–40–1; Choudhry 7–1–21–0; Pinner 1–0–4–0.

Umpires: T. E. Jesty and L. S. Reifer.

At Taunton Vale, May 1–2. CARDIFF MCCU lost to SOMERSET by nine wickets.

At Cambridge, May 15–16 (not first-class). **Gloucestershire won by an innings and 82 runs. Gloucestershire 342-5 dec** (C. D. J. Dent 53, A. P. R. Gidman 140*, H. J. H. Marshall 98; A. W. Pollock 3-102); ‡**Cambridge MCCU 98** (L. C. Norwell 4-20) **and 162** (A. Gupta 55; L. C. Norwell 5-21). *A fourth-wicket partnership of 228 in 37 overs between Alex Gidman and Hamish Marshall enabled Gloucestershire to declare shortly after tea. Gidman's 140* included 22 in an over from Amit Gupta, who was not seen again, and 20 in one from Alasdair Pollock. Fine bowling from Gloucestershire's young seam attack, led by Liam Norwell – who had match figures of 18–6–41–9 – propelled them to victory inside two days.*

At Oxford, May 22–24 (not first-class). **Drawn.** ‡**Oxford MCCU 212** (T. C. Fell 56; C. T. Tremlett 5-39) **and 20-0; Surrey 233** (A. Harinath 74; O. J. Jones 3-63, B. W. Kemp 4-55). *County debuts:* M. G. K. Burgess, D. P. Sibley, J. R. Winslade. *Oxford ran into Chris Tremlett, on the comeback trail from a succession of injuries. He took five wickets in an innings for the first time since the 2011 Southampton Test against Sri Lanka, including that of Wilf Marriott, who was promoted to open after his 81 against Worcestershire, but fell lbw fourth ball. An inexperienced Surrey batting line-up relied heavily on Arun Harinath's doughty 74 and Tremlett's brisk 36 but, with the final two days hit by rain, a draw was inevitable.*

At Loughborough, May 23–25 (not first-class). **Drawn. Northamptonshire 243-9 dec** (R. I. Keogh 56; T. J. Lester 3-69, S. G. Whittingham 6-79) **and 125-0 dec** (K. J. Coetzer 63*, R. I. Keogh 59*); ‡**Loughborough MCCU 196** (Azharullah 5-65). *County debuts:* Azharullah, R. A. L. Moore, V. V. S. Sohal, J. R. Tolley. *Stuart Whittingham struck twice in his first over and finished with six for 79 to give Loughborough early momentum. But they were reduced to 73-7 by Azharullah, a Pakistani fast bowler with a British passport spotted in the Bradford League, who set the tone for his spell at Northamptonshire with some dangerous reverse swing. No. 9 Adam Riley drew on his experience with Kent to lead Loughborough's recovery with 48. But rain fell on all three days, prompting Northamptonshire's openers to bat out time, with Rob Keogh recording his second half-century of the match.*

At Derby, June 5–7. DURHAM MCCU lost to DERBYSHIRE by 65 runs.

At Weetwood, Leeds, June 5–7 (not first-class). **Lancashire won by eight wickets.** ‡**Lancashire 309** (S. C. Moore 58, A. L. Davies 69; J. E. Lee 4-40) **and 73-2; Leeds/Bradford MCCU 116** (Kabir Ali 3-21, S. D. Parry 3-28) **and 265** (N. R. T. Gubbins 82, L. M. Reece 77; J. Clark 3-40, S. D. Parry 5-70). *County debuts:* G. T. Griffiths, L. S. Livingstone. *Luis Reece, in his first year on the Lancashire staff, captained against his county, and impressed the watching Glen Chapple enough to leapfrog Tom Smith and Karl Brown – the openers in this match – to a place in the Championship team at Chelmsford a week later. As a 17-year-old back in 2006, James Lee had been plucked from Yorkshire's academy to play in the Roses match at Old Trafford; now he took four wickets, to give him 19 in three games against the first-class counties in 2013. The other student bowlers did not pose the same threat. Oliver Newby and Kabir Ali had the Leeds/Bradford response in tatters at 19-4, and Lancashire enforced the follow-on; Newby had limped off with a groin strain in the first innings, and Ali did not bowl on the last day as a precaution. Lancashire were kept in the field for 101.3 overs as Nick Gubbins and Reece, down at No. 5, made patient half-centuries.*

THE UNIVERSITY MATCHES, 2013

At Lord's, June 15. **Oxford University won by seven wickets** (D/L). **Cambridge University 153-8** (46.3 overs) (T. C. Elliott 62); ‡**Oxford University 89-3** (16.2 overs). *Sam Agarwal's decision to bowl in swinging conditions was backed up by a disciplined Oxford performance. The Cambridge innings began with four successive maidens, before Fred Johnson (7–2–10–2) had Alex Hearne lbw. Tom Elliott rebuilt with 62 from 92 balls, but rain cut into the end of the innings. The Duckworth/Lewis recalculation set Oxford only 89 from 20 overs, which Gus Kennedy (43*) brushed aside.*

At Cambridge, June 20. **No result.** Reduced to 17 overs a side. **Cambridge University 149-5** (17 overs) (P. M. Best 51, A. S. Ansari 31); ‡**Oxford University 23-0** (3.2 overs). *Paul Best, playing in the Varsity Twenty20 fixture for the third year running, cleared the pavilion with one of his three sixes as Cambridge posted a formidable total in the 17 overs available. Heavy rain fell early in Oxford's reply.*

CAMBRIDGE UNIVERSITY v OXFORD UNIVERSITY

At Cambridge, July 2–4. Oxford University won by an innings and 186 runs. Toss: Cambridge University. First-class debuts: J. L. Joyce; S. J. Cato, J. Marsden, S. V. S. Mylavarapu, T. J. Williams, M. J. Winter.

Oxford's thumping win, their third-heaviest in the Varsity Match, was dominated by the 22-year-old Sam Agarwal's unbeaten 313. He had just completed his undergraduate degree in materials science at Queen's College, and let off steam by making the first triple-century in the fixture's 186-year history, at a run a ball in just over seven hours. Agarwal hoped the innings would help him pursue a career with Surrey, for whom he had already played Second XI cricket. He carried the game away from Cambridge on the first evening in a fourth-wicket stand of 194 with Matt Winter. By then, the umpires seemed as jaded as the Cambridge bowlers, allowing them to get away with a five-ball and a four-ball over. The Agra-born Agarwal surpassed Salil Oberoi's Varsity record next morning, when Kingsmill Key's overall record for Oxford, which had stood since 1887, before calling time on himself in the afternoon. A shell-shocked Cambridge were blown away for 119, with the wickets shared by fresher Tom Williams and Sachin Mylavarapu, a former Singapore Under-19 left-arm spinner. From seven for three in the follow-on, Phil Hughes and Tom Elliott put up stronger resistance, but Cambridge still failed to take the game into a fourth day. Oxford wicketkeeper Sam Westaway's ten catches in the match were also a record for either university.

HIGHEST INNINGS FOR OXFORD

313*	**S. S. Agarwal**	**v Cambridge University at Cambridge**	**2013**
281	K. J. Key	v Middlesex at Chiswick..........................	1887
264*	G. J. Mordaunt	v Sussex at Hove...............................	1895
247	S. Oberoi	v Cambridge University at Cambridge	2005
238*	Nawab of Pataudi, sen.	v Cambridge University at Lord's..................	1931
236*	J. W. M. Dalrymple	v Cambridge University at Cambridge	2003
236	E. R. T. Holmes	v Free Foresters at Oxford........................	1927
228	T. Bowring	v Gentlemen of England at Oxford	1908
221*	A. A. Baig	v Free Foresters at Oxford........................	1959

The only Oxford player who suffered was Sam Cato, who broke a finger intercepting Elliott's drive off his first ball in the second innings.

Close of play: first day, Oxford University 377-4 (Agarwal 213, Westaway 5); second day, Cambridge University 119.

Oxford University

B. A. Jeffery lbw b Probert	17	S. J. Cato b Pollock	33
A. D. J. Kennedy lbw b Pollock	25	T. J. Williams not out	9
B. Williams lbw b Wylie...............	43		
*S. S. Agarwal not out..................	313	B 6, l-b 13, n-b 8	27
M. J. Winter b Pollock................	51		
†S. A. Westaway c sub (M. E. Carson)		1/45 (2) (7 wkts dec, 135.5 overs)	550
b Sadler..	17	2/69 (1) 3/131 (3)	
T. R. Chadwick c Joyce b Probert.....	15	4/325 (5) 5/423 (6) 6/456 (7) 7/527 (8)	

J. Marsden and S. V. S. Mylavarapu did not bat.

Sadler 34–5–122–1; Pollock 36–8–105–3; Probert 26.5–2–125–2; Wylie 23–5–111–1; Hickey 16–3–68–0.

Cambridge University

P. H. Hughes c Agarwal b T. J. Williams	21	– lbw b Mylavarapu	92
N. V. S. Senaratne lbw b T. J. Williams	5	– c Westaway b T. J. Williams	0
A. G. Hearne lbw b Mylavarapu	39	– c Westaway b T. J. Williams	2
A. S. Ansari c Chadwick b Mylavarapu..........	14	– lbw b T. J. Williams..............	0
T. C. Elliott c Westaway b Mylavarapu..........	10	– lbw b Agarwal	101
M. R. Hickey c Westaway b Mylavarapu	5	– b Marsden...................	0
B. A. Wylie c Westaway b T. J. Williams	2	– c Westaway b Marsden	4
†J. L. Joyce not out	2	– c Westaway b Marsden	25
A. W. Pollock c Westaway b T. J. Williams	0	– c Westaway b Mylavarapu........	0
*P. T. Sadler c Chadwick b T. J. Williams	0	– c Jeffery b Mylavarapu..........	8
T. J. W. Probert c Westaway b Mylavarapu......	3	– not out	0
B 11, l-b 3, w 2, n-b 2	18	B 3, l-b 6, w 2, n-b 2	13

1/23 (2) 2/32 (1) 3/58 (4)	(55.2 overs) 119	1/4 (2) 2/7 (3) (80.2 overs)	245
4/92 (5) 5/110 (6) 6/114 (3)		3/7 (4) 4/169 (5)	
7/114 (7) 8/114 (9) 9/114 (10) 10/119 (11)		5/178 (6) 6/194 (7) 7/223 (1)	
		8/225 (9) 9/233 (10) 10/245 (8)	

Marsden 14–6–32–0; T. J. Williams 15–6–34–5; B. Williams 4–1–13–0; Mylavarapu 19.2–8–23–5; Agarwal 1–0–3–0; Cato 2–2–0–0. *Second innings*—Marsden 11.2–3–32–3; T. J. Williams 12–3–35–3; Mylavarapu 23.5–4–87–3; B. Williams 2–0–17–0; Agarwal 31–8–65–1; Cato 0.1–0–0–0.

Umpires: P. K. Baldwin and B. V. Taylor.

This was the 168th University Match, a first-class fixture dating back to 1827. Cambridge have won 58 and Oxford 55, with 55 drawn.

MCC UNIVERSITIES CHAMPIONSHIP

	Played	Won	Lost	1st-inns wins	1st-inns losses	Drawn/ no result	Bonus points	Points
Leeds/Bradford........	5	0	0	3	0	2	33	73
Cardiff	5	0	0	3	1	1	32	67
Durham..............	5	0	0	3	2	0	30	60
Cambridge	5	0	0	1	3	1	33	48
Oxford	5	0	0	1	3	1	27	42
Loughborough	5	0	0	1	3	1	25	40

Outright win = 17pts; 1st-innings win in a drawn match = 10pts; no result on 1st innings = 5pts; abandoned = 5pts. Up to six bonus points for batting were available (four in 1st innings and two in 2nd).

WINNERS

2001	Loughborough	2006	Oxford	2011	Cardiff
2002	Loughborough	2007	Cardiff/Glamorgan	2012	Cambridge
2003	Loughborough	2008	Loughborough	2013	Leeds/Bradford
2004	Oxford	2009	Leeds/Bradford		
2005	Loughborough	2010	Durham		

MCC UNIVERSITIES ONE-DAY CHALLENGE FINAL

At Lord's, June 21. **Leeds/Bradford MCCU won by three wickets** (D/L). **Cardiff MCCU 143** (47.2 overs) (A. R. Laws 3-37); ‡**Leeds/Bradford MCCU 121-7** (36.3 overs) (P. G. Harris 3-34). *Leeds/Bradford were cruising to the title at 93-3, before a collapse of four for 11 either side of an hour-long stoppage for rain. They needed five from the 37th and last over to reach their adjusted target of 118, and No. 9 Charlie MacLeod (13*) slapped Phil Harris through midwicket for the winning runs. The toss proved crucial, as Cardiff struggled early on against the moving ball.*

MCC IN 2013

Steven Lynch

Following a quieter year in 2012, the subject of the redevelopment of Lord's claimed the attention of MCC's committee and membership again for much of 2013. After the controversial decision to abandon the original plan, which led to a legal case between MCC and the developers, the club's chief executive Derek Brewer unveiled a revised blueprint at the AGM in May.

The new plan is expected to cost £200m, but will be funded from current resources rather than by outside investors. The Warner, Tavern, Allen, Compton and Edrich Stands will be rebuilt by 2017, the Pavilion extended, and a new members' entrance constructed. Later, there will be more redevelopment at the Nursery End. In all, the scheme is expected to last 15 years.

Not everyone was pleased. A group of disaffected members called a special meeting, at which they demanded an independent inquiry into the finances and administration of the redevelopment project – and, by imputation, the way the club was run in general. The committee insisted the plans were necessary to increase ground capacity (by about 2,700), and maintain Lord's as the premier venue for international cricket in England. The meeting took place in October, and the Reform Group's motion was rejected by 6,191 votes to 1,556.

"Few subjects exercise and interest the membership as much as how best to develop this wonderful ground," said Mike Gatting, the former Middlesex and England captain who succeeded Mike Griffith as MCC president for 2013-14. "Lord's is one of the jewels in cricket's crown, and must be looked after for the benefit of everyone who loves the game, not just now, but in the future." However, hopes that the grumbling might cease were premature: unhappy members pored over the plans for the new Warner Stand (the first to be replaced), and complained there was not enough leg-room between each row of seats. Harassed club officials pointed out that increasing the space would reduce the number of seats available, below the amount in the existing stand.

MCC arranged 463 matches in 2013, mainly against schools and clubs, of which 205 were won, 84 drawn, 114 lost, and two tied; 53 were abandoned and five cancelled. There were also 12 regional games. MCC women's teams played 29 matches, winning 19 and losing five, with three abandoned and two cancelled; there was also one regional women's match.

The first game on the current Lord's ground was played on June 22, 1814, between MCC and Hertfordshire. As *Scores and Biographies* put it, "There had been two grounds previously, from both of which the Marylebone Club had to remove. The original turf, as laid down in Dorset Square, was taken up with each removal." The bicentenary of the modern ground will be celebrated with numerous events, the showpiece being a one-day game between MCC (due to be captained by Sachin Tendulkar) and the Rest of the World (led by Shane Warne) on Saturday, July 5. There will also be a women's match between MCC and the Rest of the World on May 19.

MCC v WARWICKSHIRE

At Abu Dhabi, March 24–27, 2013 (day/night). Warwickshire won by an innings and 29 runs. Toss: Warwickshire. County debut: O. J. Hannon-Dalby.

With Edgbaston under six inches of snow, it felt ironic when the second day at the Sheikh Zayed Stadium was briefly held up by thunderous skies and rain. But little else got in Warwickshire's way. Under floodlights, the pink Kookaburra ball had tended to behave like the red ball under cloud cover, but Chopra and Porterfield batted with equal ease during day and night to put on 308 for the second wicket after Westwood fell in the second over. The same could not be said of MCC, whose batting line-up was obliterated under the lights by Wright's masterful swing. After almost two days of fielding in the desert, Northeast was run out backing up, and his misfortune was matched by Denly, who was forced off with a migraine. That was quickly followed by a collapse of seven for 31, including a burst from Wright of four for nought in 14 balls. But both men featured strongly as MCC followed on, a massive 431 behind: Northeast made 89, and put on 156 for the second wicket with Denly, who became one of four victims for Clarke when he was eighth out for 146. Trego's dazzling 87 off 76 balls was good fun, but futile. Pete McKay was allowed to keep wicket after Ambrose was injured on the third day. DAVID JORDAN

Close of play: first day, Warwickshire 370-3 (Evans 15, Troughton 8); second day, MCC 73-7 (Middlebrook 11, Kirby 5); third day, MCC 308-4 (Denly 119, Trego 57).

Warwickshire

V. Chopra c Kirby b Kerrigan	163	A. Javid not out	25
I. J. Westwood c Kerrigan b Trego	0		
W. T. S. Porterfield c Kerrigan b Rushworth	162	B 13, l-b 13, n-b 4	30
L. J. Evans c Malan b Rushworth	72		
*J. O. Troughton c Eckersley b Kerrigan	54	1/0 (2) (6 wkts dec, 150.4 overs)	561
†T. R. Ambrose c Kerrigan b Rushworth	31	2/308 (1) 3/350 (3)	
R. Clarke not out	24	4/461 (5) 5/496 (4) 6/507 (6)	

P. M. Best, C. J. C. Wright and O. J. Hannon-Dalby did not bat.

Kirby 22.4–4–85–0; Trego 20–9–49–1; Rushworth 28–5–93–3; Kerrigan 36–3–137–2; Middlebrook 29–2–97–0; Malan 11–1–48–0; Benkenstein 4–1–26–0.

MCC

S. A. Northeast run out		7 – c Hannon-Dalby b Wright	89
J. H. K. Adams c Chopra b Wright	20	– c Westwood b Best	4
J. L. Denly lbw b Hannon-Dalby	47	– b Clarke	146
*D. M. Benkenstein b Wright	0	– b Clarke	5
D. J. Malan lbw b Wright	0	– c sub (P. J. McKay) b Hannon-Dalby	28
P. D. Trego c Porterfield b Wright	0	– c Chopra b Hannon-Dalby	87
†E. J. H. Eckersley c Westwood b Clarke	6	– c Eckersley b Wright	1
J. D. Middlebrook not out	29	– c sub (P. J. McKay) b Clarke	17
S. C. Kerrigan lbw b Hannon-Dalby	1	– c sub (T. P. Milnes) b Wright	10
S. P. Kirby b Wright	9	– c Troughton b Clarke	4
C. Rushworth b Hannon-Dalby	0	– not out	4
B 3, w 2, n-b 6	11	B 1, l-b 4, n-b 2	7

1/13 (1) 2/47 (4) 3/47 (5)	(56.4 overs)	130
4/49 (6) 5/50 (2) 6/56 (7)		
7/61 (9) 8/78 (10) 9/130 (3) 10/130 (11)		

1/25 (2) 2/181 (1)	(102.5 overs)	402
3/187 (4) 4/229 (5)		
5/350 (6) 6/351 (7) 7/377 (8)		
8/394 (3) 9/398 (10) 10/402 (9)		

In the first innings Denly, when 19, retired ill at 45-1 and resumed at 78-8.

Wright 18–9–35–5; Hannon-Dalby 13.4–1–30–3; Clarke 13–3–23–1; Best 11–2–38–0; Javid 1–0–1–0. *Second innings*—Hannon-Dalby 27–4–103–2; Wright 19.5–3–75–3; Best 8–0–37–1; Evans 25–0–120–0; Clarke 12–2–33–4; Westwood 9–1–25–0; Chopra 2–0–4–0.

Umpires: T. E. Jesty and P. Willey.

THE MINOR COUNTIES, 2013

Philip August

The 2013 season should finally silence those who claim the Minor County game is played by mature club cricketers and former professionals. The requirement to field at least nine players aged under 26 was met in every Championship match; frequently the average age was closer to 20. And with the sole exception of Norfolk, every team complied in all their one-day fixtures, too. Minor County cricket has become a young man's game, and few now have lengthy careers.

Much better weather than in 2012 produced many more results in the Championship, while only one 50-over match was washed out. The three-day table showed positive cricket was played in the Western Division (five draws), but rather less in the East (11 draws), where some pitches were just too flat. The disparity also suggests that some captains – fed a diet of limited-overs cricket in their club games – were failing to appreciate the art of declaring. Points for bowling continued to outstrip batting, with counties often unable to survive the allotted 90 overs in the first innings.

Cheshire won the Championship, and Berkshire the one-day trophy, after each played intelligent cricket in their respective finals. **Cheshire** captain Danny Woods, who totalled 59 wickets with his left-arm spin, took 13 for 178 against Dorset and 13 for 111 in the next game, against Berkshire. Woods managed seven separate five-fors, with 36 of his wickets coming in the second innings. He was the first Cheshire bowler to take more than 50 wickets since 1922. To give Woods the freedom to take risks, Cheshire needed runs – and they flowed from Khalid Sawas, Warren Goodwin and Rick Moore. James Duffy scored 203 in the last division game, against Shropshire.

Tom Huggins of Suffolk enjoyed a magnificent summer: not only did he win the Wilfred Rhodes Trophy for the highest batting average – he hit 751 runs at 83 – but he added 36 wickets at 17 with his off-breaks. The Frank Edwards Trophy for the season's best bowling average went to Aneurin Norman of Wales, whose medium-pace claimed 19 wickets at just 7.42.

Wales were the surprise package, finishing three points behind Cheshire in comfortably their best season since 1997. It might have been even better had rain not washed out the first and last days of their penultimate game, against Wiltshire, who were 28 for six in reply to 128. However, Wales won their last fixture to match Cheshire's record of five wins and a draw. The policy of selecting young players from Welsh clubs and Welsh age-group teams, augmented by Glamorgan Academy players, certainly paid dividends.

Shropshire won their first four games before weather prompted a manufactured finish against Berkshire. Shropshire narrowly lost, and were then batted out of the last match by Cheshire, who set them 394 in 41 overs. For **Devon**, it was a summer of change and development, with 24-year-old Joss Bess replacing Chris Bradley as captain mid-campaign. Eighteen-year-old

Rhys Davies, from Plymouth, played all six Championship games and showed great consistency in his debut season to score 346 runs, including four fifties in ten innings. The experienced Trevor Anning was back to his best, with 24 wickets. James Morris, the new **Berkshire** captain, led from the front with 439 runs, though the key contribution came from the much-travelled Richard Logan, who combined 39 wickets and 365 runs.

Heavy defeats in their first two games put **Herefordshire** on the back foot, but they rallied to overcome Dorset and Wiltshire, and finish sixth. Bradley Wadlan enjoyed a fine season, collecting 375 runs and 31 wickets, while there were useful performances from batsmen Danny Cox, Charlie Walker, Nitesh Patel and the ever-reliable David Exall. With just five batting points, it was clear why **Cornwall** failed to build on their Championship success of 2012. They too lost their opening games, to Devon and Oxfordshire, and also their captain, Tom Sharp, who retired in June. Slow left-armers Neil Ivamy and Shakeel Ahmed twice bowled them to victory.

Despite gaining maximum bowling points, **Oxfordshire** had a poor summer under Luke Ryan, their youngest-ever captain at 24. Their batting was generally frail, but in their one win, against Cornwall, wicketkeeper Jonny Cater scored two unbeaten hundreds. **Wiltshire's** season was perhaps not as bad as five defeats suggest. They gained a full hand of bowling points, plus 18 for batting, and – a seven-wicket defeat by Shropshire aside – their losses were by small margins. Michael Coles returned after a two-year absence and made hay: his unbeaten 227 against Shropshire was the summer's highest score. **Dorset** struggled to cope with the retirement of senior players, and became the first county to lose all six Championship games since the reduction of fixtures in 2001. However, with talented youngsters coming through, the season could be viewed as a learning experience.

For the second time in three years **Cambridgeshire**, who won five of their six games, headed the Eastern Division. Once again, though, they squandered home advantage in the final. Paul McMahon was a key figure, taking 50 Championship wickets and captaining with nous. Fellow off-spinner Lewis Bruce claimed 23, and they made a formidable pair. Nineteen-year-old seamer Joe Dawborn picked up eight for 28 as Bedfordshire were humiliated in five sessions, but he failed to take a wicket in his two other matches. Middle-order batsman James Williams hit 408 runs, while Darren Bicknell was next, with 340.

Suffolk were runners-up for the fourth time in eight seasons, and inflicted the only defeat on Cambridgeshire. An inexperienced side relied heavily on Matt Hunn (who took 25 wickets and later signed for Kent), keeper Simon Guy – a double-century against Lincolnshire – and Minor County Player of the Season Tom Huggins. **Hertfordshire** were possibly the best all-round side in the Division. New-ball bowlers George Scott (aged 17) and Will Jones (21) both took 21 wickets in four games, while Eddie Ballard, Jamie Southgate and Dan Blacktopp all passed 440 runs.

Norfolk lost their opening games by eight wickets, against Cambridgeshire and Cumberland, but then found form. James Spelman (539 runs) and Trevor Ward (548) were the heaviest scorers, with Spelman striking 181 against

Northumberland and 149 against Buckinghamshire in consecutive games. A gap of 29 points separated Norfolk from fifth-placed **Buckinghamshire**, who drew four matches. Against Bedfordshire just 15 wickets fell, and there were only 17 against Northumberland when, in their second innings, Buckinghamshire racked up their highest-ever total, 560 for four: openers Fahim Qureshi and Hamzah Taj ticked off centuries, while Rob White made 211 not out, a county record. The Buckinghamshire bowlers failed to match the batsmen's achievements.

Staffordshire's season was essentially an exercise in rebuilding, but included some successes. Dismissed for 101 on the first morning by Bedfordshire, they scored 571 for four second time around, with Tim Maxfield compiling 221. And their solitary win was convincing: a ten-wicket demolition of Lincolnshire owed much to Greg Willott's match figures of ten for 73. The fragility of **Cumberland's** line-up was reflected by only ten batting points, fewer than anyone else in their division. New wicketkeeper Liam Parkinson had an outstanding season, though, and made 23 dismissals – the most in the competition – including eight against Cambridgeshire.

In their last game, against Bedfordshire, **Lincolnshire** recorded their first win in two years. Matt Lineker was their outstanding batsman, but he has now moved to Australia. **Bedfordshire**, meanwhile, have not won a Championship match since 2010, and their season began dreadfully when the captain, Steve Stubbings, left after the first one-day game to become Second Eleven coach at Derbyshire. Jamie Hewitt assumed the role of captain-cum-coach, and led a young side well. Wickets were few and far between, left-arm seamer Martin Weightman taking most with a modest 17. George Thurstance showed class in accumulating 600 runs in 11 innings. **Northumberland** also went winless, but did reach the semi-finals of the one-day competition. Adam Cragg was invaluable as captain and wicketkeeper-batsman. Nick Phillips was their leading bowler with 24 wickets – but at a cost of almost 36 each. And that tells a story in itself.

MINOR COUNTIES CHAMPIONSHIP, 2013

	Eastern Division	P	W	D	L	Batting	Bowling	Total points
1	CAMBRIDGESHIRE (2) .	6	5	0	1	15	21	116
2	Suffolk (5)	6	4	1	1	14	23	105
3	Hertfordshire (8).	6	3	2	1	20	23	99
4	Norfolk (3).	6	3	1	2	20	22	92
5	Buckinghamshire (1)	6	1	4	1	16	15	63
6	Staffordshire (6).	6	1	3	2	14	21	63
7	Cumberland (4)	6	1	3	2	10	23	61
8	Lincolnshire (10)	6	1	2	3	14	21	59
9	Bedfordshire (9).	6	0	4	2	14	18	48
10	Northumberland (7)	6	0	2	4	16	19	43

	Western Division	P	W	D	L	Bonus points Batting	Bonus points Bowling	Total points
1	CHESHIRE (7).........	6	5	1	0	21	18	123
2	Wales (9)	6	5	1	0	14	22	120
3	Shropshire (4)...........	6	4	1	1	15	23	106
4	Devon (8).............	6	3	1	2	12	23	85‡
5	Berkshire (6)...........	6	3	1	2	12	19	83
6	Herefordshire (10)	6	2	2	2	18	23	81
7	Cornwall (1)............	6	2*	1	3	5	20	57
8	Oxfordshire (2).........	6	1	1	4	9	24	53
9	Wiltshire (3)............	6	0	1	5	18	24	44
10	Dorset (5).............	6	0	0	6†	8	17	29‡

Final Cheshire beat Cambridgeshire by 129 runs.

Win = 16pts; draw = 4pts.

* *Cornwall received 12pts for winning a match reduced to a single innings.*
† *Dorset received 4pts for losing a match reduced to a single innings.*
‡ *2pt penalty for slow over-rate.*

LEADING AVERAGES, 2013

BATTING (300 runs in 6 completed innings, average 50.00)

		M	I	NO	R	HS	100	50	Avge	Ct/St
1	T. B. Huggins (*Suffolk*)	6	12	3	751	154	3	3	83.44	2
2	J. J. Bess (*Devon*)	6	11	3	619	113*	1	5	77.37	7
3	M. S. Coles (*Wiltshire*)	4	8	1	538	227*	2	1	76.85	3
4	S. G. Leach (*Shropshire*).........	5	9	2	453	157*	1	3	64.71	4
5	S. M. Guy (*Suffolk*)	5	9	2	452	216	2	0	64.57	14/1
6	S. D. Thomas (*Wales*)	6	9	3	383	98*	0	3	63.83	2
7	G. R. Thurstance (*Bedfordshire*).....	6	11	1	600	121	2	4	60.00	5
8	E. R. Kilbee (*Wiltshire*)..........	4	8	0	480	125	1	4	60.00	3
9	A. D. Cragg (*Northumberland*).....	6	10	2	456	164	1	3	57.00	11/7
10	T. R. Ward (*Norfolk*)...........	6	11	1	548	123	2	2	54.80	5
11	J. T. Ralph (*Shropshire*)	6	10	2	436	124	1	2	54.50	7
12	D. R. J. Cranfield-Thompson (*Bucks*) ..	5	9	2	381	108	1	2	54.42	3/1
13	M. S. Lineker (*Lincolnshire*).......	4	7	1	323	109*	1	1	53.83	0
14	D. J. M. Cox (*Herefordshire*)	6	10	3	374	80*	0	4	53.42	1
15	O. Ali (*Shropshire*)	5	8	1	371	123*	1	2	53.00	2
16	K. Ali (*Staffordshire*).............	6	12	1	579	148	1	4	52.63	4
17	A. White (*Buckinghamshire*)	6	11	1	522	211*	2	1	52.20	5
18	R. J. Logan (*Berkshire*)	6	10	3	365	67	0	5	52.14	3
19	E. C. Ballard (*Hertfordshire*).......	5	10	0	518	133	2	3	51.80	4
20	T. Maxfield (*Staffordshire*)	6	11	0	563	221	2	2	51.18	7
21	C. A. M. Walker (*Herefordshire*)	6	12	1	557	155	2	2	50.63	4
22	R. F. Evans (*Wales*).............	5	10	2	404	168	1	1	50.50	10
23	N. J. Longhurst (*Cumberland*).......	3	6	0	302	169	1	1	50.33	0
24	N. Patel (*Herefordshire*)..........	5	10	1	452	137*	1	2	50.22	9

BOWLING (20 wickets at 30.00)

		O	M	R	W	BB	Avge	5I
1	D. A. Woods (*Cheshire*)	279.4	74	801	59	8-38	13.57	7
2	N. Ivamy (*Cornwall*).....................	116.2	31	299	20	7-34	14.95	3
3	P. J. McMahon (*Cambridgeshire*)...........	351.2	104	801	50	5-28	16.02	4
4	B. Sanderson (*Shropshire*)	126.1	41	324	20	7-50	16.20	1
5	R. J. Logan (*Berkshire*)	193	35	666	39	7-101	17.07	3
6	G. F. B. Scott (*Hertfordshire*).............	87.4	12	365	21	6-44	17.38	2
7	T. B. Huggins (*Suffolk*)	250.2	80	640	36	8-90	17.77	3
8	W. V. M. Jones (*Hertfordshire*)	138	40	382	21	6-73	18.19	1

		O	M	R	W	BB	Avge	5I
9	M. D. Hunn (*Suffolk*)	153.5	25	505	25	6-29	20.20	2
10	F. W. Vainker (*Oxfordshire*)	178.3	24	591	29	7-65	20.37	2
11	N. H. Davies (*Wales*)	197.1	65	449	22	5-25	20.40	1
12	T. Bulcock (*Cumberland*)	312.5	99	716	35	6-69	20.45	2
13	T. S. Anning (*Devon*)	164.2	41	518	24	6-55	21.58	1
14	J. J. Bess (*Devon*)	126.4	26	479	22	6-25	21.77	1
15	G. Singh (*Berkshire*)	206.4	47	651	29	7-51	22.44	1
16	T. Afridi (*Wiltshire*)	193.1	37	782	34	6-37	23.00	5
17	B. L. Wadlan (*Herefordshire*)	241	58	719	31	7-121	23.19	3
18	S. Ahmed (*Cornwall*)	310.3	80	914	38	7-84	24.05	3
19	L. R. Bruce (*Cambridgeshire*)	173.4	42	569	23	4-40	24.73	0
20	G. R. Willott (*Staffordshire*)	173	32	523	21	5-9	24.90	2
21	L. C. Ryan (*Oxfordshire*)	169.3	26	555	22	5-52	25.22	2
22	C. Brown (*Norfolk*)	220.4	63	616	22	5-74	28.00	1
23	D. L. Bowen (*Shropshire*)	156.3	25	684	24	4-94	28.50	0

A. J. Norman (Wales) took 19 wickets at an average of 7.42.

CHAMPIONSHIP FINAL

At Wisbech, September 8–11. **Cheshire won by 129 runs.** ‡Cheshire **372-9** (90 overs) (R. A. L. Moore 175*, K. Sawas 79; L. R. Bruce 4-101) **and 303-5 dec** (51.5 overs) (W. M. Goodwin 54, J. P. Kettle 143; P. J. McMahon 3-99); **Cambridgeshire 296** (85.5 overs) (B. H. N. Howgego 56; D. A. Woods 5-75, J. J. Williams 3-56) **and 250** (99 overs) (A. G. Burton 52; A. J. Syddall 3-53, J. J. Williams 3-56). *MoM:* R. A. L. Moore. *Cheshire outplayed Cambridgeshire to become Minor County champions for the seventh time, but they cut things fine. The cornerstone of their first innings was a patient 175* from Rick Moore, who shared a fourth-wicket stand of 156 with Khalid Sawas, before the hunt for quick runs saw six wickets tumble in ten overs. Cambridgeshire just about kept in touch thanks to their last pair – Paul McMahon and Sam Rippington – who added 76. Danny Woods, Cheshire's captain, claimed a seventh five-wicket haul in his seventh game of the summer. Then, on an interrupted third day, his batsmen scored at six an over, before Woods set a target next morning of 380 in a minimum of 97 overs. Cambridgeshire didn't threaten to overhaul that, but did threaten to salvage a draw: not until well into the last hour did Adam Syddall – a medium-pacer who had been unable to bowl while autumnal gloom had descended – take the tenth wicket, 16 overs after the ninth had fallen.*

MCCA TROPHY FINAL

At Wormsley, August 28. **Berkshire won by 128 runs.** ‡Berkshire **284-9** (50 overs) (R. K. Morris 112, E. J. Foster 3-42), **Shropshire 156** (39.3 overs) (E. E. Brock 3-38, H. C. Stephens 4-16). *MoM:* R. K. Morris. *A large, sun-bathing crowd at picturesque Wormsley saw Shropshire trounced. Berkshire began steadily, but the runs gushed once Richard Morris – who added 57 for the third wicket with his captain and older brother James – hit his stride. None of the Shropshire attack could rein him in, and Elliot Green's ten overs of leg-spin cost 76. Eventually Morris fell for a 95-ball 112. Shropshire also started promisingly, and the openers put on 65. But it was a different matter when Berkshire took the pace off the ball, and they crashed from 127-3 to 156 all out. Slow left-armer Euan Brock and off-spinner Harry Stephens exploited poor shot selection to share seven wickets.*

SECOND ELEVEN CHAMPIONSHIP, 2013

North Division	P	W	L	D	A	Bonus points Bat	Bowl	Pen	Total points
1 Lancashire (3)	9	6	0	3	0	32	33	0	170
2 Derbyshire (7)	9	5	0	4	0	22	28	0	142
3 Worcestershire (5)	9	4	4	1	0	22	35	0	124
4 Yorkshire (9)	9	3	4	2	0	22	30	0	106
5 *Glamorgan (3)	9	3	2	3	1	17	28	0	105
6 Nottinghamshire (10)	9	2	2	5	0	16	29	0	92
7 *MCC Young Cricketers (8)	9	1	4	4	0	22	26	0	76
8 Warwickshire (8)	9	1	3	5	0	16	27	6.5	67.5
9 Leicestershire (1)	9	0	3	6	0	25	24	0	67
10 Durham (2)	9	1	4	3	1	17	21	0	66

South Division	P	W	L	D	A	Bonus points Bat	Bowl	Pen	Total points
1 Middlesex (4)	9	5	1	3	0	25	35	0	149
2 Essex (6)	9	5	3	1	0	21	34	0	138
3 Gloucestershire (10)	9	4	1	4	0	24	24	0	124
4 Kent (1)	9	3	2	4	0	30	33	0	123
5 Somerset (5)	9	3	2	4	0	25	31	6.5	109.5
6 *Northamptonshire (4)	9	3	1	5	0	24	19	0	106
7 Surrey (2)	9	3	4	2	0	18	30	4.5	97.5
8 Hampshire (5)	9	1	4	4	0	20	29	3	74
9 Sussex (7)	9	0	5	4	0	24	27	0	63
10 *MCC Universities (6)	9	0	4	5	0	23	24	0	62

* In 2012 Glamorgan and MCC Young Cricketers played in the South Division, and Northamptonshire and MCC Universities played in the North Division.

Win = 16pts; draw/abandoned = 3pts.

Warwickshire were deducted 5pts for ball-tampering v Glamorgan, and Hampshire deducted 2pts for fielding an ineligible player v Surrey. All other penalties were for slow over-rates.

LEADING AVERAGES, 2013

BATTING (400 runs)

		M	I	NO	R	HS	100	Avge	Ct/St
1	L. M. Reece (Lancs)	5	7	2	546	201*	2	109.20	3
2	A. W. R. Barrow (Somerset)	5	8	3	540	106	2	108.00	0
3	B. M. Shafayat (Sussex)	3	6	0	498	161	1	83.00	6/2
4	F. K. Cowdrey (Kent)	6	9	2	554	201*	3	79.14	4
5	N. L. J. Browne (Essex)	8	15	3	838	219*	3	69.83	19
6	M. D. Bates (Hants)	9	16	4	683	179*	2	56.91	33/1
7	I. A. Cockbain (Glos)	7	11	0	600	224	2	54.54	10
8	W. A. Tavaré (Glos)	8	15	3	642	179*	3	53.50	8
9	S. P. Terry (Hants)	7	12	1	558	135*	1	50.72	4
10	A. J. Ball (Kent)	5	8	0	402	125	1	50.25	6
11	A. P. Rouse (Hants)	7	12	1	497	113*	1	45.18	7
12	P. M. Borrington (Derbys)	9	13	2	457	107	1	41.54	6
13	T. J. Lancefield (Glam, Glos, Northants)	9	17	5	498	100*	1	41.50	4
14	W. T. Root (Leics, MCCYC)	7	11	0	449	165	1	40.81	4
15	C. D. Piesley (MCCYC)	9	14	0	566	120	2	40.42	8
16	L. S. Livingstone (Lancs)	10	11	0	440	149	2	40.00	3
17	A. Harinath (Surrey)	6	12	1	408	124*	1	37.09	0
18	T. B. Abell (Somerset)	9	15	0	552	174	1	36.80	10
19	C. A. L. Davis (Northants)	8	14	1	473	170*	2	36.38	3

		M	I	NO	R	HS	100	Avge	Ct/St
20	A. Patel (*Kent, Surrey*)...............	7	13	1	435	97	0	36.25	5
21	W. G. R. Vanderspar (*MCCU*)	9	15	0	527	125	2	35.13	1
22	S. W. Poynter (*Durham, MCCYC*)	8	15	0	494	172	2	32.93	12/2
23	A. K. Patel (*MCCU*)	9	16	0	523	108	1	32.68	2
24	N. Singh (*Durham*)	8	16	0	509	94	0	31.81	6
25	A. J. Robson (*Leics*)................	9	14	1	412	82	0	31.69	6
26	S. Kelsall (*Notts*)	9	15	0	438	83	0	29.20	7/1
27	J. A. M. Johnson (*MCCU*)............	9	16	1	425	75	0	28.33	10

BOWLING (18 wickets)

		O	M	R	W	BB	5I	Avge
1	S. H. Choudhry (*Worcs*)	75.1	26	145	19	5-2	1	7.63
2	L. Gregory (*Somerset*).....................	106	35	320	20	5-46	1	16.00
3	M. N. W. Spriegel (*Northants*)	90.2	15	300	18	6-49	3	16.66
4	Enamul Haque, jun. (*Warwicks*)	124.1	35	323	19	8-93	1	17.00
5	O. E. Robinson (*Leics, Yorks*).............	109.3	33	315	18	3-14	0	17.50
6	G. A. Edwards (*Surrey*)....................	135	31	442	24	5-53	1	18.41
7	C. M. Stewart (*Somerset*)	121.2	39	351	18	7-33	1	19.50
8	S. K. W. Wood (*Notts*)	104.5	22	376	19	5-34	1	19.78
9	J. P. Bousfield (*Durham*).................	125.3	29	402	19	5-30	1	21.15
10	A. J. Dibble (*Somerset*).................	195.5	56	554	26	5-47	1	21.30
11	T. M. Jewell (*Surrey*)....................	193.4	49	625	29	4-104	0	21.55
12	M. E. T. Salisbury (*Essex*)...............	159.4	30	519	24	4-24	0	21.62
13	M. A. Chambers (*Essex, Notts*)............	196.5	49	577	26	7-70	2	22.19
14	R. M. R. Brathwaite (*Durham, Hants*)	133.4	35	411	18	5-53	1	22.83
15	G. T. Griffiths (*Lancs*).................	141.5	13	479	20	3-28	0	23.95
16	H. W. Podmore (*MCCYC, Middx*)	191.2	44	571	21	4-14	0	27.19
17	P. B. Muchall (*Glos*)....................	162.0	33	528	19	6-42	1	27.78
18	G. P. W. Bacon (*Notts*)	139.5	18	593	21	4-43	0	28.23
19	G. Keedy (*Surrey*)....................	186.5	41	553	19	5-37	1	29.10
20	A. MacQueen (*Hants, MCCU, Northants, Surrey*)	164.5	40	585	20	6-97	1	29.25
21	C. F. Hartley (*Kent*)....................	180.0	43	566	18	4-46	0	31.44
22	A. O. Morgan (*MCCU*).....................	148.1	18	662	19	4-44	0	34.84
23	T. G. Helm (*Middx*).....................	197.0	38	690	19	4-56	0	36.31
24	Z. R. Patel (*MCCU*).....................	196.0	34	811	19	4-62	0	42.68

CHAMPIONSHIP FINAL

At Radlett, September 16–19. **Drawn. Lancashire 113-2** (22.5 overs) **v ‡Middlesex.** *Each side chose from 12 players. After the first three days were washed out, play began at last on the fourth morning. But the break in the weather was short-lived, and there was no resumption after lunch. The counties shared the Championship title.*

SECOND ELEVEN TROPHY FINAL, 2013

At Nettleworth, September 11–12. **Lancashire won by 76 runs. Lancashire 259-8** (40 overs) (S. C. Moore 85, S. J. Croft 61, J. Clark 60; J. T. Ball 4-36); **‡Nottinghamshire 183** (32.3 overs) (B. A. Hutton 41; G. T. Griffiths 3-37).

SECOND ELEVEN TWENTY20 FINAL, 2013

At Arundel, July 12. **Surrey won by six runs. ‡Surrey 169-8** (20 overs) (G. C. Wilson 57, A. Patel 32, S. S. Agarwal 40; T. G. Helm 5-37); **Middlesex 163-8** (20 overs) (N. R. T. Gubbins 30, A. Balbirnie 81). *Four Middlesex batsmen were run out.*

LEAGUE CRICKET, 2013

Geoffrey Dean

Yorkshire Premier League teams continued to wonder what they had to do to stop York's remarkable domination of the competition. They clinched their seventh successive title when left-arm spinner Dan Woods took nine for 48 in an emphatic victory over Appleby Frodingham in early September, putting them out of reach of second-placed Yorkshire Academy. If Woods's tally of 96 victims at 11 apiece – including all ten for 42 against Castleford – was instrumental in York's success, the top-order batsmen also played a major part. Duncan Snell and Jack Leaning amassed more than 1,400 runs, while Liam McKendry passed 1,000 as well. One weekend in August was especially memorable for Snell, who claimed a career-best six for 32 to help skittle Yorkshire Academy for 65 on the Saturday, following it up next day with 157 not out – another personal-best – against Hull.

Snell, who has turned out for several county Second XIs, recalled how he was not initially regarded as a batsman. "I actually started out as a left-arm seamer, but I always knew I could bat. Luckily York noticed that, and it's gone from there. I never thought when I joined the club that I would get this amount of runs. It's great to be so successful as a side, but with that comes the fact that everyone wants to beat us. But we have learned to cope with it."

So too do Wimbledon, the national club Twenty20 champions, who wrapped up a hat-trick of Surrey Championship titles on the final day of the season, when they beat Banstead by one wicket. Set 198 after Daniel Newton had made 101 not out, they were steered home by an unbeaten 75 from Ben Compton, first cousin of Somerset batsman Nick.

It was a case of winner takes all on the last day of the Essex League. Shenfield soon regretted their decision to bat against leaders Wanstead & Snaresbrook, who shot them out for 95, with Kishen Velani (four for ten) and Rehan Hassan (four for five) causing mayhem. Hassan guided Wanstead to a convincing win with an unbeaten 45.

Thanks to some assistance from the elements, Leyland leapfrogged Barrow to claim the Northern League title on a dramatic day. Leyland secured maximum points after Dale Jones grabbed five for 24 to help bowl Darwen out for 85; Barrow had to beat Blackpool to win the league. In a match reduced to 31 overs a side, Barrow declared early on 158 for two to give themselves more time to dismiss Blackpool, but their chances were sabotaged when rain set in, with Blackpool 17 for one.

Shrewsbury had double cause for celebration. Not only did they run away with the Birmingham League, but they saw John Foster's club-record score beaten by his son. Ed Foster struck 169 out of a colossal 362, which proved 222 runs too many for Kidderminster. Ed's brother Rob was at the crease when he broke the record, with father John watching on.

There was real drama at the foot of the Birmingham League. Relegation-threatened Walmley secured their place in the league after an extraordinary collapse by Wolverhampton. Needing 237 to win, they were cruising at 224 for three. But four wickets by Greg Ricketts turned the game on its head, and Wolverhampton were bowled out for 235 – and relegated instead.

North Mymms also had a narrow escape, in the Home Counties League. On the final Saturday they made just 134, and seemed to be facing defeat. But the bowlers chipped away, eventually dismissing Potters Bar, already doomed to relegation, for 125. North Mymms would still have gone down had Welwyn Garden City beaten Tring Park, but they could not defend a total of 271.

Two 14-year-olds made an encouraging mark on league cricket in July. Finchley's Thomas Powe took six for 42 on his Middlesex League debut to hasten victory over Twickenham. "People are surprised he is 14," said his captain, Jake Milton, "but he has a wise head on young shoulders." And in the North Staffs & South Cheshire League, Liam Banks, a member of the Warwickshire Academy, hit 103 from 126 balls, then took three for 33, for Hem Heath in the draw with Burslem.

At the other end of the age spectrum, the 43-year-old former England batsman Mark Ramprakash, now back playing for Stanmore, made 117, the exact total by Twickenham, who lost by 132 runs.

Chris Aspin writes: The Central Lancashire League began a two-year experiment with a split into two divisions – the premier league and the championship – while the Lancashire League introduced restrictions on bowlers: one was allowed 17 overs, the others a maximum of 14. The CLL format received a mixed response, but there was widespread approval of opening up the bowling.

Accrington, captained by Graham Lloyd, the former Lancashire batsman, ran away with the Lancashire League, notching up 259 points, some 55 ahead of Lowerhouse, and winning 22 games – a total only once exceeded. They were greatly indebted to their Pakistani professional, Ashar Zaidi, who became the second player since the league began in 1892 to score most runs and take most wickets. Zaidi hit 1,446 at 63 and claimed 79 at under 14. (Roger Harper had topped both lists in 1994.)

At the start of the last game, against bottom club Colne, Zaidi needed 90 runs to beat the club record of 1,444, set by the Australian Bobby Simpson in 1959. With 48 still required for victory, he was 40 short of his target, but scored the vital run off the last ball. Zaidi then caused a sensation by saying he was joining neighbouring club Church for 2014. However, that plan was scuppered when Sussex gave him a two-year contract after he had made an encouraging debut in September.

Burnley beat Haslingden by 85 runs to take the Worsley Cup for the seventh time. Chairman Michael Brown, formerly of Middlesex, Hampshire and Surrey, donned his whites to smash a rapid 82 not out – including a six that cleared the clubhouse – and earn the match award.

Daniel Salpietro, the Rishton pro, headed the batting averages with 1,172 runs at 68, and also made the headlines during the Third Ashes Test at Old Trafford, when he moved behind the bowler's arm in the refurbished pavilion and distracted Australian opener Chris Rogers, a former team-mate at

Melbourne club Prahran; charging at Graeme Swann, Rogers was out lbw, 16 short of a maiden Test hundred. Todmorden's Geeth Alwis (1,111 at 58) and Pieter Malan of Ramsbottom (1,013 at 56) were the others to reach four figures. Alwis made an unbeaten 149, the season's highest score, against Colne; his team-mate Simon Newbitt hit 140 not out against Haslingden. Burnley's Qasim Ali was the leading amateur, striking 791 at 39, while Jon Fielding claimed 64 wickets at 15 for Ramsbottom. His colleague Tom Paton contributed 670 runs and 51 dismissals, becoming only the third keeper in the league's history to do the double of 500 runs and 50 dismissals.

The season included some notable milestones. Chris Bleazard of Lowerhouse reached 15,000 runs, spurring the Burnley-based Moorhouses to brew a celebratory beer called Bleazard's Brilliance. (Only two other batsmen had made as many runs in the Lancashire League.) Graham Knowles, the Haslingden captain, scored his 10,000th run, while Rawtenstall's Keith Roscoe took his 1,500th wicket.

Walsden won the Central Lancashire Leagues premier division – they had been full league champions a year before – gaining the vital point when Heywood conceded their fixture in order to play Crosby in the semi-final of the Lancashire Cricket Board knockout competition. The League executive agreed Heywood could arrange another date, but Walsden invoked a rule that league games had priority. Heywood lost a home gate and points; to make matters worse, they also lost the semi. They had earlier beaten Walsden by four wickets to take the Lees Wood Cup for the 11th time, with skipper Bobby Cross named Man of the Match for his unbeaten 88.

Werneth and Royton gained promotion to the premier league – replacing Milnrow and Middleton – and became the first two sides to pass 400. On both occasions, Oldham were the whipping boys. Werneth rattled up 419 for three, with their professional Mohammed Khan undefeated on 221, including 154 in boundaries to set up a 257-run win. Royton made 406 for six, with Australian professional Ben Dunk hammering 196 from 102 balls; Oldham managed 199. Dunk, who had earlier hit 154 against Ashton and 146 against Crompton, finished the season with 1,143 runs at 81, though it was Khan who topped the averages, with 1,429 at 89. In a miserable season, Oldham were bowled out for 31 by Crompton, with Carl Taylor taking eight for 12. He was the leading wicket-taker in the Championship, with 69 at 12.

Other pros to reach four figures were Paul Green (Monton & Weaste), who cracked 1,015 at 56, and Babar Naeem (Milnrow), who made 1,142 at 54. Chris Schofield led the amateurs with 1,191 at 70 for runners-up Littleborough. Chris Williams, Unsworth's pro, claimed 85 wickets at 13, while Clifton's Stephen Cheetham was the most successful amateur with 76, also at 13.

> " Anyone who scores a direct hit on a goose will get to take it home, plucked and trussed – a prize offered in 2013, but won by nobody."
> Cricket Round the World, page 1236.

ECB PREMIER LEAGUE TABLES, 2013

Birmingham & District League

	P	W	L	Pts
Shrewsbury	**22**	**14**	**3**	**377**
Brockhampton	22	10	7	287
Knowle & Dorridge	22	10	7	282
Himley	22	10	7	279
Kidderminster Victoria	22	9	9	264
Walsall	22	8	9	258
Barnt Green	22	8	6	258
Berkswell	22	9	9	257
W. Bromwich Dartmouth	22	9	9	244
Walmley	22	7	9	235
Wolverhampton	22	3	12	203
Wombourne	22	3	13	148*

* *One-point penalty for slow over-rate.*

Cheshire County League

	P	W	L	Pts
Chester Boughton Hall	**22**	**15**	**4**	**436**
Neston	22	15	3	423*
Hyde	22	12	3	383
Alderley Edge	22	11	7	341
Oxton	22	10	10	319
Grappenhall	22	8	10	314
Bowdon	22	8	11	294
Nantwich	22	8	10	294
Toft	22	8	10	294
Marple	22	5	13	232
Didsbury	22	5	15	231
Macclesfield	22	4	13	216

* *Eight-point penalty for slow over-rate.*

Cornwall Premier League

	P	W	L	Pts
Werrington	**18**	**12**	**2**	**284***
Falmouth	18	13	2	277†
St Just	18	8	5	231
Callington	18	9	6	230
Truro	18	7	7	218*
Grampound Road	18	5	8	188
Camborne	18	5	9	180
Paul	18	4	10	169*
St Austell	18	3	10	162*
Redruth	18	4	11	159

* *One-point penalty for slow over-rate.*
† *Two-point penalty for slow over-rate.*

Derbyshire Premier League

	P	W	L	Pts
Swarkestone	**22**	**14**	**0**	**458**
Ticknall	22	6	1	344*
Spondon	22	9	5	340
Denby	22	6	5	317
Sandiacre Town	22	7	7	314
Chesterfield	22	7†	5	304
Dunstall	22	6†	8	301
Ockbrook & Borrowash	22	6	8	294
Lullington Park	22	8	9	290
Alvaston & Boulton	22	7	12	259
Eckington	22	2	8	206
Matlock	22	2	12	194

* *Two-point penalty for slow over-rate.*
† *Plus one tie.*

Devon League

	P	W	L	Pts
Exmouth	**18**	**13**	**3**	**286**
Sidmouth	18	12	4	271*
Bovey Tracey	18	12	4	262†
North Devon	18	9	7	226
Plymouth	18	9	7	208
Exeter	18	8	8	206‡
Torquay	18	6	11	184*
Cornwood	18	5	10	171
Bradninch	18	4	12	152
Budleigh Salterton	18	2	14	138*

* *One-point penalty for slow over-rate.*
† *Five-point penalty for fielding an unregistered player.*
‡ *Five-point penalty for slow over-rate.*

East Anglian Premier League

	P	W	L	Pts
Swardeston	**22**	**14**	**3**	**432**
Cambridge Granta	22	13	3	411
Burwell	22	9	5	341
Saffron Walden	22	7	6	334
Great Witchingham	22	7	5	332
Clacton-on-Sea	22	8	8	298*
Vauxhall Mallards	22	6	8	283
Horsford	22	5	8	257
Woolpit	22	4	7	253
Bury St Edmunds	22	3	10	235
Copdock & Old Ipswichian	22	4	9	231†
Sudbury	22	3	11	203

* *One-point penalty for slow over-rate.*
† *Two-point penalty for slow over-rate.*

Essex Premier League

	P	W	L	Pts
Wanstead & Snaresbrook	**18**	**10**	**4**	**264**
Shenfield	18	10	6	254
Brentwood	18	10	5	252*
South Woodford	18	9	5	246
Chelmsford	18	8†	3	238
Chingford	18	7	6	229
Ilford	18	5†	7	191
Upminster	18	5	8	183
Colchester & East Essex	18	3	12	143‡
Buckhurst Hill	18	2	13	108*

* *One-point penalty for slow over-rate.*
† *Plus one tie.*
‡ *Two-point penalty for slow over-rate.*

Home Counties Premier League

	P	W	L	Pts
Henley	**18**	**12**	**3**	**337**
Slough	18	10	5	310
Banbury	18	9	7	280
Harpenden	18	7	6	261
Tring Park	18	7	6	254
High Wycombe	18	6	7	237
Burnham	18	6	7	226
North Mymms	18	4	8	201
Welwyn Garden City	18	3	8	179*
Potters Bar	18	3	10	158†

* *One-point penalty for slow over-rate.*
† *Five-point penalty for slow over-rate.*

Kent League

	P	W	L	Pts
Hartley Country Club	**18**	**14**	**2**	**292**
Lordswood	18	9*	5	224
Blackheath	18	9	6	217
Bromley	18	8	6	216
Bickley Park	18	9	5	215†
Beckenham	18	7*	7	199
Bexley	18	7	9	180
Sevenoaks Vine	18	5	10	153
Sibton Park	18	5	12	136
Whitstable	18	1	12	101

* *Plus one tie.*
† *One-point penalty for slow over-rate.*

Leicestershire County League

	P	W	L	Pts
Kibworth	**22**	**14**	**3**	**425**
Market Harborough	22	12	2	393
Syston Town	22	10	5	350
Leicester Ivanhoe	22	9	7	344
Kegworth Town	22	11	8	328
Barrow Town	22	6	10	311
Loughborough Town	22	9	6	305
Earl Shilton Town	22	7	10	279
Broomleys	22	5	8	273
Sileby Town	22	6	9	248
Stoughton & Thurnby	22	6	12	220
Ashby Hastings	22	1	16	128

Lincolnshire Cricket Board Premier League

	P	W	L	Pts
Woodhall Spa	**22**	**14**	**4**	**322**
Sleaford	22	14	4	321
Lindum	22	11	6	301
Bracebridge Heath	22	10	5	300
Market Deeping	22	11	7	268
Skegness	22	9	10	239
Grimsby Town	22	6*	8	227
Bourne	22	4*	7	222
Louth	22	4	11	205
Spalding	22	4	8	190
Haxey	22	5	12	164
Hartsholme	22	3	13	133

* *Plus one tie.*

Liverpool & District Competition

	P	W	L	Pts
Northern	**22**	**17**	**2**	**421**
Ormskirk	22	12	3	347
Leigh	22	11	4	332
Lytham	22	12	5	328
Bootle	22	11	8	305
Wallasey	22	9	8	279
Maghull	22	8	7	274
New Brighton	22	4	12	194
Southport & Birkdale	22	5	12	187
Fleetwood Hesketh	22	4	10	183
Highfield	22	3	12	180
Hightown	22	3	16	157

Middlesex County League

	P	W	L	Pts
Hampstead	**18**	**12**	**2**	**130**
Ealing	18	11	5	112
Stanmore	18	7	4	89
Twickenham	18	8	5	88
Richmond	18	7	7	77
Teddington	18	6	8	70
Finchley	18	6	9	66
Hornsey	18	5	8	55
Winchmore Hill	18	4	10	47
Eastcote	18	3	11	17*

* *20-point penalty for fielding two unregistered players.*

Northamptonshire League

	P	W	L	Pts
Peterborough Town	**22**	**17**	**1**	**521**
Finedon Dolben	22	13	3	456
Old Northamptonians	22	12	7	389
Rushton	22	9	5	374
Wollaston	22	11	8	360
Brixworth	22	7	7	327
Northampton Saints	22	8*	9	326
Oundle Town	21	9	9	286
Stony Stratford	22	6	10	236
Burton Latimer	21	3*	13	223
Horton House	22	4	13	214
Wellingborough Town	22	2	16	177

* *Plus one tie.*

North East Premier League

	P	W	L	Pts
Stockton	**22**	**16**	**1**	**486***
South Northumberland	22	10	5	365†
Hetton Lyons	22	9	8	345
Newcastle	22	9	7	332†
Blaydon	22	9	7	326
Chester-le-Street	22	8	4	326
Benwell Hill	22	8	6	305
Tynemouth	22	7	9	271
Sunderland	22	7	8	260
Durham Academy	22	6	8	256
Gateshead Fell	22	3	13	159
South Shields	22	0	16	120

* *One-point penalty for slow over-rate.*
† *Two-point penalty for slow over-rate.*

Northern Premier Cricket League

	P	W	L	Pts
Leyland	**23**	**11**	**3**	**211**
Barrow	23	11	4	202
Lancaster	23	10	6	180*
Morecambe	23	9	5	164
Fleetwood	23	8	8	158
St Annes	23	7	6	151
Chorley	23	9	8	149*
Kendal	23	6	6	145
Netherfield	23	6	7	138
Darwen	23	4	6	136
Blackpool	23	4	9	124*
Lancashire Academy	12	2	5	113†
Preston	23	1	15	56

* *Five-point penalty for failure to submit result.*
† *Played only 12 games; their points were obtained by multiplying by 23 and dividing by 12.*

North Staffs & South Cheshire League

	P	W	L	Pts
Leek	**22**	**10**	**1**	**350**
Stone	22	12	5	343
Checkley	22	10	6	312
Longton	22	10	7	302*
Knypersley	22	9	7	290
Porthill Park	22	8	9	277†
Wood Lane	22	9	8	269‡
Hem Heath	22	8	8	262¶
Whitmore	22	7	9	247
Burslem	22	6	8	229
Audley	22	3§	14	193
Elworth	22	3§	13	184¶

* *Six-point penalty for slow over-rate.*
† *Three-point penalty for slow over-rate.*
‡ *Two-point penalty for slow over-rate.*
¶ *One-point penalty for slow over-rate.*
§ *Plus one tie.*

North Wales Premier League

	P	W	L	Pts
Llandudno	**22**	**16**	**2**	**497**
Menai Bridge	22	16	2	438
Mochdre	22	14	5	404
Pontblyddyn	22	13	8	373
Hawarden Park	22	9	10	296
Mold	22	9	10	283
Connah's Quay	22	6	12	249
Llanrwst	22	7	12	243
Brymbo	22	7	11	236*
St Asaph	22	6	13	231
Northop	22	5	13	209
Denbigh	22	4	14	184

* *One-point penalty for slow over-rate.*

North Yorkshire & South Durham Premier League

	P	W	L	Pts
Richmondshire	**26**	**15**	**2**	**441**
Darlington	26	18	2	420
Marton	26	13	3	378
Great Ayton	26	10	6	347
Guisborough	26	11	6	334*
Middlesbrough	26	9	7	320
Hartlepool	26	10	9	299
Barnard Castle	26	9	11	273
Redcar	26	5	9	264
Saltburn	26	7	13	254
Stokesley	26	6	11	234
Sedgefield	26	5	12	229
Normanby Hall	26	3	12	197
Thornaby	26	1	19	134†

* *Five-point penalty for slow over-rate.*
† *Two-point penalty for slow over-rate.*

Nottinghamshire Cricket Board Premier League

	P	W	L	Pts
West Indian Cavaliers	**22**	**16**	**4**	**359**
Rolls Royce	22	13	3	353
Cuckney	22	11	3	351
Notts Cricket Board	22	8	5	295
Caythorpe	22	6	9	244
Mansfield Hosiery Mills	22	7	7	240
Welbeck Colliery	22	6	9	229
Kimberley Institute	22	4	8	222
Clifton Village	22	6	9	212
Plumtree	22	6	10	212
Farnsfield	22	6	9	203
Papplewick & Linby	22	2	15	123

Southern Premier League

	P	W	L	Pts	Avge pts
South Wilts	18	10	3	277	18.46
Havant	18	12	4	284	16.70
Bashley (Rydal)	18	7	5	226	15.06
Ventnor	18	7	6	220	14.66
Hants Cricket Academy	18	8	6	234	14.62
Lymington	18	8	9	212	12.47
Totton & Eling	18	5	7	177*†	11.06
St Cross Symondians	18	4	9	165	10.31
Alton	18	5	9	152	10.13
Bournemouth	18	3	11	134	8.37

* *Five-point penalty for an administrative error.*

† *One-point penalty for a slow over-rate.*

Surrey Championship

	P	W	L	Pts
Wimbledon	18	12	3	140
Weybridge	18	10	5	128
Sunbury	18	10	5	120
Reigate Priory	18	8	8	90
Spencer	18	7	7	87
Banstead	18	6	7	81
Guildford	18	7	8	72
Sutton	18	4	10	63
East Molesey	18	4	9	55*
Malden Wanderers	18	3	9	46

* *One-point penalty for failure to submit captain's report.*

Sussex League

	P	W	L	Pts
Preston Nomads	19	13	3	449
East Grinstead	19	11	4	402
Horsham	19	9	7	363
Hastings & St Leonards Priory	19	9	6	355
Sussex Development XI	10	4	3	348*
Cuckfield	19	7	6	296
Three Bridges	19	6	7	287
Roffey	19	6	5	283
Brighton & Hove	19	4	11	247
Chichester Priory Park	19	4	11	238
Worthing	19	3	13	225

* *Played ten games; their points total (183) was multiplied by 1.9.*

Swalec Premier League

	P	W	L	Pts	Avge pts
Mumbles	18	8	1	327	19.23
Ynysygerwn	18	11	3	254	16.93
Sully Centurions	18	6	6	204	13.60
Newport	18	7	6	194	12.12
Pontarddulais	18	5*	6	206	12.11
Bridgend Town	18	4	6	190	11.87
Swansea	18	5	6	178	11.12
Port Talbot Town	18	6	6	160	10.66
Cardiff	18	4	7	148	9.86
Ammanford	18	2*	11	137	8.56

* *Plus one tie.*

West of England Premier League

	P	W	L	Pts
Bath	18	15	2	307*
Frocester	18	11	5	264*
Bristol	18	10	5	248*
Taunton St Andrews	18	10	7	237*
Bridgwater	18	10	7	236
Downend	18	7	9	210
Ashcott & Shapwick	18	7†	8	209
Corsham	18	5†	9	187‡
Keynsham	18	5	12	165
Ilminster	18	0	16	82

* *Two-point penalty for a slow over-rate.*

† *Plus one tie.*

‡ *Four-point penalty for a slow over-rate.*

Yorkshire Premier League

	P	W	L	Pts
York	26	20	2	167
Yorkshire Academy	26	17	2	156
Harrogate	26	14	6	130
Scarborough	26	12*	5	106
Doncaster Town	26	12	9	112
Driffield Town	26	13	9	109
Sheffield Collegiate	26	12	12	102
Barnsley	26	9	12	83
Cleethorpes	26	8	13	76
Appleby Frodingham	26	8*	14	75
Rotherham Town	26	6	14	65
Hull	26	5	15	55
Castleford	26	4	15	45
Sheffield United	26	2	14	33

* *Plus one tie.*

The following leagues do not have ECB Premier League status:

LANCASHIRE LEAGUES, 2013

Lancashire League

	P	W	L	Pts
Accrington	**26**	**22**	**3**	**259**
Lowerhouse	26	15	8	204
Burnley	26	15	8	197*
Ramsbottom	26	15	6	194
Church	26	15	7	183
Haslingden	26	12	12	164
Nelson	26	12	11	158
Enfield	26	11	10	157
East Lancashire	26	10	13	143
Todmorden	26	10	13	139
Rawtenstall	26	9	12	135
Rishton	26	8	15	124
Bacup	26	4	19	80
Colne	26	1	22	38†

* *One-point penalty for a slow over-rate.*
† *Two-point penalty for a slow over-rate.*

Central Lancashire League – premier division

	P	W	L	Pts
Walsden	**28**	**18**	**5**	**97**
Littleborough	28	16	7	85
Rochdale	28	14	9	80
Heywood	28	13	10	74
Norden	28	12	11	71
Clifton	28	11	12	67
Middleton	28	4	19	33
Milnrow	28	4	19	31

Central Lancashire League – championship division

	P	W	L	Pts
Werneth	**28**	**18**	**3**	**103**
Royton	**28**	**18**	**4**	**100**
Unsworth	28	12*	9	76
Crompton	28	12	10	73
Monton & Weaste	28	8*	13	61
Radcliffe	28	8	12	59
Ashton-under-Lyne	28	6	16	45
Oldham	28	4	19	31

* *Plus one tie.*

OTHER LEAGUE TABLES, 2013

Airedale & Wharfedale	Beckwithshaw
Bolton Association	Atherton
Bolton League	Little Lever
Bradford	Cleckheaton
Cambridgeshire & Huntingdonshire	Godmanchester Town
Central Yorkshire	Townville
Hertfordshire	Hertford
Huddersfield	Shepley
Lancashire County	Denton West
NEPL Division One	Whitburn
Norfolk Alliance	Norwich
North Essex	Colchester
North Lancs & Cumbria	Furness
Northumberland & Tyneside Senior	Swalwell
Pembrokeshire	Neyland
Quaid-e-Azam	Keighley RZM
Ribblesdale	Briscall
Saddleworth	Heyside
Shropshire	Newport
South Wales Association	Neath
South Yorkshire	Elsecar
Thames Valley	Amersham
Two Counties	Frinton
Warwickshire	Sutton Coldfield
Worcestershire	Astwood Bank
York Senior	Woodhouse Grange

LORD'S TAVERNERS CITY CUP, 2013

It was the driest summer for seven years, and the first in four to feature the heavy roller – yet county pitches still did little for the thoroughbred spin bowler. Things were a little different in the Lord's Taverners City Cup. By its fifth season (and the first under new title sponsors) the City Cup had expanded to eight competitions in North London, South London, Luton, Leicester, Birmingham, Wolverhampton, Bradford and Manchester, followed by an inter-city knockout. The aim remained the same as it was when Scyld Berry, then the *Wisden* editor, and Phil Knappett, Middlesex Academy coach at the time, launched the Wisden City Cup in London in 2009: to provide inner-city cricketers aged between 16 and 22, and playing outside ECB development pathways, a route into elite cricket. Most ECB Premier Leagues are very diverse, but the fact there were only around 20 black and Asian state-educated cricketers in the 18 county squads last year suggested plenty of squandered talent.

The chance of a spin bowler slipping through the net at an early age is presumably greater: they tend to develop variations and strategy as they grow older, and some switch from bowling seam in their mid-to-late teens. Added to that, many inner-city cricketers are still cocooned in obscure leagues played on underprepared park pitches, giving them little chance of being spotted by mainstream coaches. The City Cup has sought to combat this by playing its tournaments on established club grounds, with local league umpires. And with July and August 2013 warm and dry, and groundsmen re-using old wickets from one game to the next, spin bowlers had every opportunity to seize the moment in front of ECB regional development officers.

Following the national quarter-finals, semis and final, the City Cup assembled 16 of its most promising players from the eight regions to play against MCC Young Cricketers at Wardown Park, Luton, on the last Sunday in September. It was surely no coincidence that Monty Panesar learned his cricket here: the pitch was dusty and worn, and the boundaries spread far and wide. For the third year in succession, the YCs head coach Mark Alleyne had the pick of the players to join his professional squad for the following year. He could easily have plumped for leg-spinners Mohammad Akeel, from the Birmingham League, or Mohammad Bhada from East Lancashire CC. Imran Qayyum, Finchley's slow left-armer, had been for trials for Sussex and Northamptonshire, and baffled a couple of the YCs batsmen with his arm-ball. Ultimately, though, Alleyne chose Janak Valand, a 19-year-old off-spinning all-rounder with Leicester Ivanhoe. Alleyne said he was impressed by the turn he generated in the unforgiving Lord's nets during the previous day's indoor trial, and by how hard he clouted the ball – shades of a young Virender Sehwag, he thought. Diyapan Paul, the first City Cup cricketer to win a YCs contract back in 2012, will join Valand, as Paul makes his comeback from knee operations.

Watching from the boundary at Luton was left-arm spinner Mohammad Younis "Shaan" Ahmadzai, a 16-year-old Afghan. He arrived in the UK in early 2012, with a mildly suspect action and cricketing experience based on the tape-ball version in Afghanistan. He was spotted by Panesar's old club,

Luton Town & Indians, who helped smooth out his bowling so he could play in league and age-group cricket. Ahmadzai took more wickets than anyone in the 2013 Luton Taverners competition, then three for eight as the Luton representative side defended a low total against Leicester. He was hampered by a split spinning finger in the national final at Aston Manor, which Luton lost to a polished Birmingham side coached by Kadeer Ali. But here was the cricketer the City Cup was designed for.

In 2014 the LTCC will consolidate its position in the eight cities, with four teams in each, rather than some having three. Paul Bedford, the ECB's head of non-first-class cricket, plans to expand to 16 cities in 2015. Peter Such, the national spin bowling coach, has pledged to get involved, and Clare Connor, ECB head of women's cricket, has responded positively to the idea of a women's competition. For a variety of reasons, ethnic minority female cricketers are under-represented in English cricket even more than their male counterparts. All in all, there should be more opportunities to unearth other Ahmadzais and Valands, and go some way to redressing the English game's reliance on the middle class and privately educated.

LORD'S TAVERNERS CITY CUP NATIONAL KNOCKOUT

Quarter-finals

At Walsall, August 25. **Birmingham won by eight wickets. Wolverhampton 144-6** (20 overs) (N. Cooper 33, Hafeez Khan 35); **Birmingham 145-2** (17.4 overs) (Khalil Ahmed 99*).

At Burnley, August 26. **Bradford won by seven wickets. Manchester 113** (19 overs) (Mohammad Bhada 30; Hamza Hussain 3-15); ‡**Bradford 114-3** (18.5 overs) (Saim Butt 50, Akram Asif 42*).

At Luton, August 26. **Luton won by 27 runs. Luton 107** (19.4 overs) (S. Patel 3-25); **Leicester 80** (18 overs) (Mohammad Younis Ahmadzai 3-8).

At Dulwich Common, August 26. **South London won by seven wickets. North London 120-9** (20 overs) (Vibhor Yadav 36; P. France 4-25); **South London 122-3** (17 overs) (L. O'Neill 39, A. Send 51*).

Semi-finals

At Keighley, September 8. **Birmingham won by 31 runs.** ‡**Birmingham 151-7** (20 overs) (Saqib Akbar 52, Usman Khan 35, Iftikhar Khan 39); **Bradford 120** (18 overs) (Usman Khan 4-21).

At Luton, September 14. **Luton v South London. Abandoned.** *Luton progressed on net run-rate in the regional competitions.*

Final

At Aston Manor, September 22. **Birmingham won by 24 runs. Birmingham 162-8** (20 overs) (A. Shah 3-31); **Luton 138-9** (20 overs) (B. Naik 35; Shirjeel Mir 3-27). *MoM:* Shirjeel Mir. *Birmingham, coached by the former county batsman Kadeer Ali and watched by Warwickshire players Ateeq Javid and Chris Woakes, were slicker in every department. Luton committed a series of blunders in the field, which helped Birmingham up to their commanding score. Luton's response was boosted by some early wides, but their second-wicket pair of Badal Naik and Dhruv Patel waited too long to launch the all-out assault, and Shirjeel Mir triggered the final collapse.*

ECB NATIONAL CLUB CHAMPIONSHIP AND T20, 2013

Paul Edwards

At the end of a summer in which the ECB's major recreational competitions rubbed along on good weather and efficient administration, it was ironic that both finals were affected by rain. At Chester-le-Street, West Indian Cavaliers became the first Nottinghamshire club to win the National Club Championship, after a final which began late and was twice interrupted by the weather. No one could question the strength of Usman Afzaal's side, which featured eight former first-class cricketers, but it was easy to feel a little sorry for Ealing, who had now lost all four of their national knockout finals.

Ealing were unhappy at being penalised 18 runs at the business end of the chase. As Cavaliers had needed 24 from three overs, the sanction essentially handed them the title. "We feel there was more than one umpiring error concerning the regulations," said John Poore, Ealing's president. "We thought the 18-run penalty was harsh; it came out of the blue. The players feel hard done by." Ealing lodged a complaint with the ECB, and asked that the final be replayed – but to no avail.

Two days earlier, rain had wrecked finals day of the Twenty20 competition at The Oval. Only 6.2 overs of the first semi could be played before the weather closed in, and three bowlouts in the indoor school were needed before Wimbledon retained the trophy they had won in altogether more enjoyable circumstances at Edgbaston in 2012. It all added up to "a challenging few days", in the words of the ECB's competitions executive Aaron Campbell.

The response of the board to September's events was to leave the structure of both competitions untouched, except for the addition of a reserve day to the Twenty20 final. The 45-over national knockout final already had such a provision, but the ECB's intention has been to get the match completed on the scheduled day if possible. Certainly a reserve day would have been difficult in 2013 for Durham, who staged the game on the strip furthest from the pavilion, in order to protect the square ahead of the vital County Championship match against Nottinghamshire starting two days later. Besides, clubs that reach the latter stages are familiar with the Duckworth/Lewis method. Twenty20 finals day offers club cricketers their one chance to be on television, so last September's rain was particularly cruel on Banbury and Ormskirk, who were making their first appearances at a showpiece occasion.

In 2014, the two competitions will be branded in line with the ECB's international and county competitions: the Club Championship will be sponsored by Royal London, and the Twenty20 tournament by NatWest.

" Knight had to be helped off the pitch, but at the end was wheeled around the ground on an equipment trolley by her exultant team-mates."
The Women's Ashes, page 839

KINGFISHER BEER NATIONAL CLUB CHAMPIONSHIP FINAL

EALING v WEST INDIAN CAVALIERS

At Chester-le-Street, September 15. **West Indian Cavaliers won by six wickets (D/L).** Toss: West Indian Cavaliers.

Twenty-four hours after winning their ninth Nottinghamshire Premier League title in 15 seasons, West Indian Cavaliers clinched the National Club Championship, having come through rain delays, the issue of penalty runs and constant wrestling with the Duckworth/Lewis method. Wet weather reduced the game to 42 overs, and a long stoppage in Ealing's innings cut it again, to 29. They did well to reach 209: Chris Wakefield held the first half of the innings together, before Leigh Parry took a liking to Usman Afzaal's left-arm spin, hoisting five sixes in 23 balls. Ricky Anderson, the former Essex and Northamptonshire seamer, was the pick of the attack. Cavaliers' slow over-rate meant they were deducted one over in their chase of 210, which was tweaked to 202 off 26 after another shower. Their string of imposing names all made significant contributions, with the former Pakistan No. 11 Ata-ur-Rehman whacking three sixes when his side were lagging behind on D/L. With 24 needed off three overs, the game was set for a tense conclusion, until the umpires suddenly awarded Cavaliers 18 penalty runs because Ealing had slipped three overs behind the rate. Cavaliers began celebrating, but Afzaal and Patrick Gada had to return to the middle to complete the formality of scoring the last six runs before rain swept in again.

Man of the Match: L. J. Parry.

Ealing

Elech Ahmed c Williamson b Anderson	11	R. Haxby not out		19
C. F. Wakefield b Shafayat	41			
L. R. F. Stoughton b Anderson	10	L-b 12, w 11, n-b 3		26
†M. Wilkin c Williamson b Shafayat	23			
C. T. Peploe c Anderson b Afzaal	12	1/22 (1) 2/42 (3)	(6 wkts, 29 overs)	209
*D. R. Holt c Thomas b Afzaal	18	3/100 (2) 4/109 (4)		
L. J. Parry not out	49	5/137 (6) 6/140 (5)		

H. W. Podmore, K. Martin and C. Glasper did not bat.

Anderson 6–0–27–2; Ameer Ahmed 3–0–24–0; Rehman 6–0–27–0; Shafayat 5–0–37–2; Patel 4–0–29–0; Afzaal 5–0–53–2.

West Indian Cavaliers

A. Patel st Wilkin b Parry	32	P. K. Gada not out		20
S. Hassan c Podmore b Glasper	23	B 6, l-b 3, w 14, n-b 3, p 18		44
B. M. Shafayat c Elech Ahmed b Parry	21			
*U. Afzaal not out	37	1/58 (2) 2/63 (1)	(4 wkts, 23.4 overs)	202
Ata-ur-Rehman b Martin	25	3/101 (3) 4/136 (5)		

†A. C. Thomas, D. Williamson, S. Levy, Ameer Ahmed and R. S. G. Anderson did not bat.

Glasper 6–0–37–1; Podmore 3.4–0–38–0; Parry 5–0–25–2; Peploe 5–0–34–0; Elech Ahmed 1–0–17–0; Martin 3–0–24–1.

Umpires: J. Attridge and K. Fergusson.

A full list of winners from the start of the competition in 1969 appears in Wisden 2005, page 941.

ECB CLUB T20 FINALS DAY

At The Oval, September 13. **First semi-final: No result.** Reduced to seven overs a side. **Banbury 27-5** (6.2 overs) v ‡**Wimbledon. Wimbledon won 3–1 on a bowl-out.**

At The Oval, September 13. **Second semi-final: Chester-le-Street v Ormskirk. Abandoned. Ormskirk won 3–2 on a bowl-out.**

At The Oval, September 13. **Final: Ormskirk v Wimbledon. Abandoned. Wimbledon won 5–1 on a bowl-out.**

DAVIDSTOW VILLAGE CUP, 2013

BENJ MOOREHEAD

Few places in Britain can be described as cut off from the rest of the world in the digital age, but Cleator and Rockhampton, whose cricketers produced a thrilling final at Lord's, do better than most to slip the mainstream. Both villages, without a pub between them and with a combined population that might squeeze into the Long Room, lie in largely forgotten sprawls of land: Cleator lost beyond the western lakes of Cumbria; Rockhampton nestled on the floodplains of the River Severn in Gloucestershire.

Their convergence at St John's Wood was gloriously improbable. Rockhampton, who had never passed the second round, were inspired by the arrival of James Williams to captain their Village Cup XI. Williams had caught the scent of Lord's during a cup run with Marshfield, and he carried it into his new dressing-room. Seven emphatic victories preceded a Lord's final Rockhampton might have won. Williams had recast this competition as something to be conquered, not simply a means of whiling away the Sunday ennui. Thus are contenders and pretenders separated in the Village Cup.

Cleator required no such education. The hurt of their semi-final defeat in 1987 had tugged at the strings of the club ever since; now it was expunged in the most dramatic fashion. Their triumph capped the sweetest of summers for Ian Clark, the one survivor from the team of '87. In April his son, Jordan, had hit six sixes in an over for Lancashire Second XI against Yorkshire, while Jordan's elder brother Darren took six for 20 and scored 53 not out in Cleator's semi-final victory over Rolleston. Just as valuable was the unsung veteran spinner David Bell, who had 18 wickets at ten apiece. Perhaps a sense of shared identity, a connection with the village they represent, was Cleator's greatest asset. Most of the team had grown up playing street cricket there; eight work in the nearby Sellafield nuclear plant.

Challenges elsewhere fizzed and fizzled. Scotland were represented by the Dumfries club Kirkwood, who made the national phase of the competition for the first time under the captaincy of Anthony Steel, great-great-nephew of Lancashire and England's A. G. Steel. From Cornwall came Stithians, conquerors of the mighty Troon, but defeated in the last 32 by Hambledon, who briefly threatened to stir some predictable headlines. Others settled for less. Jolly Sailor, the Leicestershire pub XI with a 74-year-old captain, won their first match in four years of trying. Donnington returned to the competition after two decades: their victory over Pinkneys Green in the Berkshire section was their first in the Village Cup for more than 30 years. Wiltshire's Beehive were stung by a heavy loss on their maiden Village outing.

The highest score of the summer was Paul Bennett's unbeaten 200 off 139 balls for Essex debutants Belhus. Behind him was Colwall's Tom Coleman, who followed up 178 not out at Goodrich with 123 at Longdown Lane against Barby. That match, won at the death, was one of many during a period under midsummer's blue skies that lived up to the idyll of village cricket: long shadows, pretty grounds and tense finishes, with a hush as the bowler hits his stride. You had it under the Malvern Hills at Stowe Lane, where 53-year-old Tim Riley made a visibly breathless hundred which nearly snatched victory for Colwall against Rolleston; or below the Mayflower Railway Line which rises above Mistley's ground in Essex, where Dinton's last pair put on 25 to dispose of their hosts in the quarter-finals. The charm of these occasions could not have been lost on anyone.

FINAL

CLEATOR v ROCKHAMPTON

At Lord's, September 8. Cleator won by one wicket. Toss: Cleator.

Where to begin? Perhaps with the first ball received by the old stager Ian Clark, a snorter from William Cartlidge which burst through to the keeper and brought on a huge appeal from the Rockhampton fielders. By now they were like grizzly bears feasting at the salmon run, after Cartlidge had extracted the Cleator top order with a high-class spell of seam and swing. Not out was the verdict. But did it matter when Cleator were already 64 for five chasing 193 in 40 overs? Clark scratched his way to seven runs in the next eight, but a 45-minute rain delay washed away his inhibition, as he swept and pulled the spinners into the near Tavern and Mound stands. He eventually fell to a stunning overhead catch at deep square leg, before the Cleator tail wagged enough for David Rooney, captain and last man, to walk in with 15 wanted. The state of a partisan crowd was like a shaken bottle of bubbly. The cork popped when a dribbled leg-bye brought Cleator's winning run, and a stream of Cumbrians came bursting out of the stands past helpless MCC stewards. It all obscured a dashing knock by the helmetless Rockhampton skipper, James Williams. If Matt Tyler's 50 had grounded the innings, Williams gave it take-off with a 37-ball 57 which balanced deft touch and bludgeon. Off-spinner David Bell beat him in the flight just when Rockhampton were disappearing from range – another tipping point in a match of many.

Man of the Match: I. D. Clark.

Rockhampton

M. Tyler c I. D. Clark b Rooney	50	W. Cartlidge not out	10
W. Tyler c Quin b D. Clark	19	S. Nichols not out	2
*J. Williams b Bell	57	B 3, l-b 6, w 1	10
G. Brothwood lbw b Bell	2		
S. Hore b Blackwell	14	1/46 (2) 2/130 (3)	(7 wkts, 40 overs) 192
†R. Cartlidge b I. D. Clark	23	3/133 (1) 4/134 (4)	
J. Spence run out	5	5/166 (5) 6/178 (6) 7/184 (7)	

J. Hancox and C. Pearce did not bat.

Blackwell 9–2–35–1; D. Clark 7–2–35–1; Rooney 9–0–28–1; Bell 9–2–33–2; I. D. Clark 6–0–52–1.

Cleator

J. Rogers b W. Cartlidge	35	D. Bell not out	16
C. J. Quin b W. Cartlidge	2	D. W. Blackwell lbw b Hancox	13
D. Clark lbw b W. Cartlidge	11	*D. J. Rooney not out	10
R. W. Mason c R. Cartlidge b W. Cartlidge	3	B 2, l-b 6, w 18, n-b 1	27
T. S. Sharpe b Nichols	2		
S. M. Kiggins b Brothwood	26	1/14 (2) 2/26 (3)	(9 wkts, 38.4 overs) 193
I. D. Clark c Spence b Nichols	37	3/42 (4) 4/64 (5) 5/64 (1)	
†G. Lilly c and b Nichols	11	6/99 (6) 7/147 (7) 8/158 (8) 9/178 (10)	

W. Cartlidge 9–2–35–4; Pearce 4–0–17–0; Nichols 9–1–31–3; Hancox 7.4–0–52–1; Brothwood 9–0–50–1.

Umpires: A. P. Hemmings and J. D. Smith.

DISABILITY CRICKET, 2013

Paul Edwards

One of the most significant developments for the long-term growth of the disabled game in England occurred in 2013 when Ian Martin, the ECB's national disability cricket manager, took his place in the England Cricket Department. Chaired by Paul Downton, who succeeded Hugh Morris as England managing director at the start of 2014, the group are responsible for the ECB's elite programmes. Martin now sits in meetings which determine the future strategy of the national game.

"The game is now recognising, at least in England, the commitment and ability of our disabled players," said Martin. "It was one thing to be treated and talked about as England cricketers, another thing entirely to be accepted and managed as such."

A more material development was the establishment of three regional Disability Talent Development Centres in the North, Midlands and South-East. (A fourth, in the South-West, was due to become operational in 2014.) These centres, mirroring as far as possible the structure used for the full national side, are aimed at helping the next generation of disabled cricketers across all impairment groups to refine the skills needed to excel at the highest level, including strength and conditioning support, and nutritional advice.

The leaders of England's disability cricket hope that a greater regimentation will bring about more games. In 2013, the only major series involving England's disabled cricketers was in South Africa, where England Deaf won all seven of their matches. Umesh Valjee and George Greenway were named batsman and bowler of the four-match one-day international series, in the first of which Stephen George scored a century.

England's deaf cricketers would acknowledge that one of the major reasons for their success had been the availability of Bobby Denning to offer astute and sympathetic coaching. So it was a sad day when Denning stepped down from his role with the deaf side, following his appointment as acting-director of the Lancashire Cricket Board. "Bobby has been involved in disability cricket for over a decade," said Martin. "He has coached our learning disability, deaf and blind teams. His legacy is the professionalism that all our teams now demonstrate."

There were honours for those involved in the disabled game. Matt Dean, who plays for England Blind, was named Disabled Cricketer of the Year, and Roger Fuggle – formerly the ECB's disability cricket consultant – was awarded an MBE in the Queen's Birthday Honours. Stefan Pichowski, secretary of the English Cricket Association for the Deaf, won the NatWest OSCA for Outstanding Contribution to Disability Cricket. And there was a pleasing distinction at Arundel in August, when England's Physical Disability side played against a Duke of Norfolk's XI composed of players from the different impairment groups. It was the first time a team of disabled players had represented the Duke.

UNDER-19 TRI-SERIES, 2013

1. Pakistan   2. England   3. Bangladesh

Not so long ago, England would have expected to win the odd game against Pakistan at Under-19 level – certainly at home. But in the first Under-19 triangular series staged by the ECB, both England and Bangladesh found themselves trampled by a ruthless Pakistan side which had all the bases covered. The global cricket family had every right to be concerned when overseas teams were unable to tour one of their Full Members, but Pakistan's problems obviously did not stop them getting the best from their young cricketers. As so often, the Pakistanis played like men two or three years their senior.

Only once, on a disgrace of a pitch at Derby, did England run Pakistan close. On the same strip the previous evening, Derbyshire's spinners had taken all ten wickets in a YB40 match, and the county were later docked two points for "excessive turn". But Sky Sports had already set up their cameras in line with the wicket, and there was no time for the groundstaff to prepare a new one. The new ball leapt off a length, and the old ball turned extravagantly. Pakistan, undefeated in the series and brimming with confidence, pulled themselves around from 16 for three to post 227, though England deserved praise for getting within five of the target. "Our players learned a great deal from the experience," said Tim Boon, the England Development Programme head coach, who chose not to lodge a complaint.

Otherwise, whether on club or first-class wickets, Pakistan held all the aces. Success at Under-19 level remained no guarantee of a healthy professional career, but many back in Pakistan were convinced that those in possession of an opening spot in the senior side were simply keeping it warm for Sami Aslam. A powerful strokemaker, he worked hard in between games too, and was rewarded by passing 50 in five innings out of seven. The bespectacled Imam-ul-Haq, another left-hander, was more of a steady accumulator than uncle Inzamam, but no less assured at his age. Opening bowlers Mohammad Aftab and Zia-ul-Haq were both left-armers who grew up idolising Wasim Akram, and they had two fine left-arm spinners, Zafar Gohar and Kamran Ghulam, to exploit the driest August for a decade.

It was asking a lot for England's (mainly right-handed) batsmen to counter that. Neither were they helped by the withdrawal of two top-order players, Dominic Sibley and Tom Alsop, through injury, on the eve of the series. The captain and wicketkeeper Ben Duckett came in and out of the squad depending on Northamptonshire calls. Still, centuries by Will Rhodes, Harry Finch and Ryan Higgins showed the batsmen had it in them to construct innings. Once again it was spin bowling, a concern at all levels of English cricket, where the hosts conceded most to their opponents – although the problem was magnified in a series containing two Asian sides.

Bangladesh arrived with several players aged 15 and 16, including captain Mehedy Hasan, and managed to beat England at Sleaford through a superb all-round performance from Mosaddek Hossain. The sides' last meeting, at Worcester, effectively became a shootout to face Pakistan in the final, and – to considerable relief at the ECB – Tattersall and Higgins put on an unbroken 183 to get England there.

It is too crude to judge developing cricketers on results alone – as coaches constantly point out. Yet in their Strategic Plan 2014–17, announced last May, the ECB set a target of reaching the 2016 Under-19 World Cup final in Bangladesh; later in the year, chairman Giles Clarke said he wanted to see an improvement in England's results at this level. In today's game, everything is measured.

SQUADS

England *B. M. Duckett (Northamptonshire), T. E. Barber (Hampshire), K. Carver (Yorkshire), H. Z. Finch (Sussex), M. D. Fisher (Yorkshire), H. Hameed (Lancashire), M. A. H. Hammond (Gloucestershire), R. F. Higgins (Middlesex), R. Jones (Lancashire), L. D. McManus (Hampshire), W. M. H. Rhodes (Yorkshire), J. Shaw (Yorkshire), J. A. Tattersall (Yorkshire), J. R. Winslade (Surrey). *Coach:* T. J. Boon. *Manager:* J. Abrahams.

T. P. Alsop (Hampshire) and D. P. Sibley (Surrey) were originally selected, but Alsop withdrew with a knee injury and Sibley with a gashed leg; they were replaced by Hameed and Jones. A. W. Ireland (Durham) and A. Sakande (Sussex) provided cover for the matches at Leicester.

Bangladesh *Mehedy Hasan, Abu Haider, Abu Sayeem, Jashimuddin, Joyraz Sheik, Jubair Hossain, Mehedi Hasan, Mohammad Saifuddin, Mosaddek Hossain, Munim Shahriar, Mustafizur Rahman, Nazmul Hossain, Rahatul Ferdous, Rifat Pradhan, Sadman Islam. *Coach:* R. J. McInnes.

Pakistan *Sami Aslam, Farhan Nazar, Hasan Raza, Hussain Talat, Imam-ul-Haq, Imran Butt, Kamran Ghulam, Mohammad Aftab, Nauman Akram, Rafay Ahmed, Saifullah Bangash, Saud Shakil, Shayan Jahangir, Zafar Gohar, Zia-ul-Haq. *Coach:* Azam Khan.

Awais Munir was originally selected, but replaced before departure by Farhan Nazar.

At Loughborough, August 5. **No result. Bangladesh Under-19 145** (42.1 overs); ‡**Pakistan Under-19 38-4** (17 overs). Bangladesh 1pt, Pakistan 1pt. *Three ducks, three run-outs and 17 wides in Bangladesh's innings made for a scrappy start to the series for both touring sides. Pakistan then tumbled to 20-4 before a downpour killed the game.*

At Sleaford, August 6. **Pakistan Under-19 won by 46 runs. Pakistan Under-19 288-5** (50 overs) (Sami Aslam 60, Imam-ul-Haq 120); ‡**England Under-19 242** (48 overs) (H. Z. Finch 50, W. M. H. Rhodes 102; Mohammad Aftab 4-60). Pakistan 2pts. *MoM:* Imam-ul-Haq. *Pakistan lapped up Sleaford's short boundaries: all six batsmen to face a ball hit at least one of them for six. The innings was dominated by Imam-ul-Haq, who scored 120 from 142 deliveries, but was prepared to cede the main thrust to partners Sami Aslam (60 from 79) and Farhan Nazir, who whacked 46 from 22 at the end. Harry Finch and Will Rhodes hauled England into contention with a fifth-wicket stand of 134, but Rhodes was running out of partners by the time he brought up a century off 81 balls. Jonny Tattersall captained England, with Ben Duckett away on Twenty20 duty with Northamptonshire.*

At Sleaford, August 7. **Bangladesh Under-19 won by 38 runs.** ‡**Bangladesh Under-19 286-4** (50 overs) (Sadman Islam 86, Mosaddek Hossain 110*); **England Under-19 248** (47.1 overs) (H. Hameed 67, B. M. Duckett 56). Bangladesh 2pts. *MoM:* Mosaddek Hossain. *England faced an uphill battle to make their own tournament final after a second defeat. This time they were floored by Mosaddek Hossain, familiar from the 2011-12 tour of Bangladesh, who struck a polished 110* from 113 balls. Haseeb Hameed, a 16-year-old late addition to the England squad from Bolton, then mucked in alongside Duckett, and Rhodes (32) whacked three sixes in 23 balls. But Mosaddek's off-spin (3-38) brought the shutters down.*

At Market Harborough, August 9. **Pakistan Under-19 won by eight wickets. Bangladesh Under-19 192** (49 overs) (Jashimuddin 50); ‡**Pakistan Under-19 196-2** (44.1 overs) (Sami Aslam 120*). Pakistan 2pts. *MoM:* Sami Aslam. *Left-arm spin is a Bangladeshi speciality, but their batsmen still* *found Kamran Ghulam (2-34) and Zafar Gohar (1-29) a tricky proposition. Sami Aslam then stroked 120* from 142 balls.*

At Kibworth, August 11. **Pakistan Under-19 won by seven wickets.** ‡**Bangladesh Under-19 149** (43.4 overs) (Kamran Ghulam 4-18); **Pakistan Under-19 150-3** (31.5 overs) (Sami Aslam 58, Hussain Talat 71*). Pakistan 2pts. *MoM:* Kamran Ghulam. *Ghulam and Gohar combined again to return eye-watering figures of seven for 32 from 17.4 overs. Pakistan's win was a formality by the time Aslam raced to 58 out of an 81-run opening stand with Hussain Talat.*

At Leicester, August 12. **England Under-19 won by five wickets.** ‡**Bangladesh Under-19 170** (42.3 overs) (J. R. Winslade 4-39); **England Under-19 171-5** (49.3 overs) (H. Z. Finch 100*). England 2pts. *MoM:* H. Z. Finch. *Bangladesh snapped up the chance to bat on a county ground for the first time in the series, only to have their top five uprooted by Jack Winslade and 15-year-old Matthew Fisher (3-28) inside the first 12 overs. The bruising Finch buttressed the reply, and tied the scores with a four to reach his hundred, before Miles Hammond scampered a single with three balls remaining to give England a much-needed first win.*

At Leicester, August 13. **Pakistan Under-19 won by 180 runs.** ‡**Pakistan Under-19 369-7** (50 overs) (Sami Aslam 57, Hasan Raza 71, Kamran Ghulam 102*); **England Under-19 189** (35 overs) (R. F. Higgins 65). Pakistan 2pts. *MoM:* Kamran Ghulam. *Aslam rolled on to his fourth consecutive half-century, but the punishment Ghulam meted out was of a different order. He accelerated to 102* from 56 balls, tearing into Josh Shaw with a sequence of 666464664 in the seamer's last two overs – handing him figures of 10–0–92–1, England's most expensive in youth ODIs. Shaw did not help his cause by donating five no-balls and four wides; Tom Barber also bowled eight wides. Ryan Higgins smashed 65 off 46 deliveries but, once he was out in the 16th over, England folded swiftly.*

At Worcester, August 15. **England Under-19 won by nine wickets.** ‡**Bangladesh Under-19 198** (50 overs); **England Under-19 199-1** (40.5 overs) (J. A. Tattersall 73*, R. F. Higgins 112*). England 2pts. *MoM:* R. F. Higgins. *England put their Leicester laceration behind them to sew up a place in the final. Bangladesh did well to recover from 15-3, but Higgins made short work of the target in a terrific century, assisted by an obdurate 128-ball 73* from Tattersall.*

At Derby, August 16 (day/night). **Pakistan Under-19 won by four runs.** ‡**Pakistan Under-19 227-8** (50 overs) (Imam-ul-Haq 64, Hasan Raza 71); **England Under-19 223-6** (50 overs) (J. A. Tattersall 53, H. Z. Finch 53, R. F. Higgins 54). Pakistan 2pts. *MoM:* Zafar Gohar (Pakistan). *The 900th youth one-day international was marred by the playing surface, which had been used for a YB40 game 24 hours earlier. It turned sharply and offered occasional tennis-ball bounce, making this a hard assignment for all players; England found the challenge of batting second under lights just beyond them. Their opening bowlers made a superb start, ending Aslam's run-spree in the first over, and bouncing out Hussain Talat and Rafay Ahmed. Imam and Hasan Raza then rebuilt in a partnership of 124 in 30 overs, peppered with sumptuous sweeps. Tattersall and Finch – who kept his calm when hit flush on the back by bowler Mohammad Aftab's shy at the stumps – gave England a steady start in reply, both getting their heads down to make half-centuries. But Pakistan's added ingredient was the accuracy of their left-arm spinners, whom the right-handers found near-unplayable. Ryan Higgins bucked the trend with a 66-ball fifty, but in his final over Gohar (3-24) had Rhodes stumped on the charge, then bowled Higgins attempting one switch-hit too many. Winslade was sent in to smite Zia-ul-Haq for six off the last ball, but he missed a cutter outside off stump.*

Pakistan 11pts, England 4pts, Bangladesh 3pts.

Final

At Nottingham, August 19. **Pakistan Under-19 won by 192 runs.** ‡**Pakistan Under-19 343-6** (50 overs) (Sami Aslam 110, Shayan Jahangir 85, Kamran Ghulam 61*); **England Under-19 151** (33 overs) (R. F. Higgins 70*; Zafar Gohar 4-25). *MoM:* Sami Aslam. *Pakistan rammed home their supremacy with the heaviest of their four wins over England. They came up with the perfect 50-over innings: Aslam scored another century, Shayan Jahangir grew into a partnership of 163, and Ghulam rounded things off with 61* from 49 balls, including four boundaries in a row off left-arm spinner Karl Carver. Aftab then removed Tattersall and Finch. Higgins once again stood firm, but Gohar and medium-pacer Talat (3-18) ripped through the rest with alarming ease.*

YOUTH CRICKET, 2013

James Coyne

Almost as soon as India, England and Australia pushed through their restructuring of the world game, the ECB were proclaiming it a victory for the grass roots. Should the ICC, as forecast, procure more money from their next rights deal, ECB chairman Giles Clarke promised to plough a greater chunk of their share into inner-city and women's cricket in England and Wales. "Where there are no facilities," he said, "we will work with local authorities and the outstanding Chance to Shine project to build grounds. That way we can build proper inner-city clubs which will attract thousands of new players to the game."

Clarke's pledge was music to the ears of the organisations trying to revive cricket in the state sector, and rebalance the elite game's over-reliance on the privately educated. In February 2014, the Cricket Foundation celebrated the millionth girl to have participated in their decade-long Chance to Shine programme – Lillie Edwards, 12, from Cromer Academy in Norfolk. She was one of 191,700 girls involved in 2013 alone. But that leads to the inevitable question: how many of them go on to play cricket between two teams and with a hard ball? Certainly the cricket was competitive enough in the Chance to Compete girls' national finals at Wormsley, where Ormskirk School beat South Dartmoor Community College 2–1, watched by the England women's team that had just drawn the Ashes Test. At Northampton's County Ground, Vyners School from Ickenham won the boys' Under-13 final, and Prince Henry High School from Evesham the Under-15 title.

In London, hard work has been put in by Capital Kids Cricket volunteers to cement the game in primary schools. And in Tottenham, Tower Hamlets and West Ham, CKC have already established the kind of pilot clubs Clarke has pledged to help expand. Back in 1990, CKC's founders discovered that barely 20 of London's 800 or so primary schools were teaching any form of cricket; in 2013, that figure was up to around 600. Ravi Bopara is the most illustrious beneficiary, having entered – and won – a CKC tournament while at Central Park primary in Newham. And it was kids from just up the road who prevailed in a thrilling finale to CKC's 2012–13 British Land Kids League at Lord's, as Elmhurst (54 all out) tied with the previous season's defeated finalists Belleville, from Wandsworth. Elmhurst's entirely Asian, mixed-gender side won the bowl-out 2–1.

With a fair wind, perhaps the best of these players will one day make it to the ECB's Elite Player Development Programme, whose summer culminated with the visit of three subcontinental teams. England Under-17s lost by four wickets to a formidable Pakistan Under-19 side – who went on to sweep all before them in their one-day triangular series – before escaping defeat against Bangladesh Under-19 through rain. The opening two-day game between England and Sri Lanka Under-17s ended with the tourists' ninth-wicket pair at the crease, needing to hit the last ball for six to win; they could manage only a four. England received expert advice from Andrew Strauss and Michael Vaughan before and during the next three-day fixture, but they lost by an innings and 78 runs, with Sri Lanka's off-spinner Ravin Sayer claiming nine for 91.

These players should get more opportunities for two-innings age-group cricket, after the ECB restored Under-19 Tests to the schedule for the first time in four seasons. Sri Lanka also won the one-day series 2–1, although England came within eight runs of stealing it after an unbeaten 100 from Lancashire's Rob Jones, an innings described as "heroic" by head coach Iain Brunnschweiler.

Winners of county age-group competitions – Under-17 County Championship Durham. **Under-17 County Cup** Kent. **Under-17 B County Cup** Gloucestershire. **Under-17 Women's County Championship** Sussex. **Under-15 County Cup** Surrey. **Under-15 B County Cup** Worcestershire. **Under-15 Bunbury Festival** The Midlands.

SCHOOLS CRICKET, 2013

Review by Douglas Henderson

Similarities between schools cricket and Premier League are not immediately obvious, but both suffer from a few institutions having deeper pockets than others. "Schools cricket," one experienced and influential headmaster recently lamented, "is a world dominated by sports scholarships – a long way from where my school will ever be."

Until 1990, the Headmasters' and Headmistresses' Conference (the body representing most leading independent schools) forbade sports scholarships. At least that was the theory. It was hard, though, to defend a situation in which awards could be made for academic, musical or artistic prowess, but not sporting ability, and so barriers were removed. With the cost of private education so great, it is not unusual for parents to hawk athletic offspring round the circuit in search of the best deal.

The result is a chasm separating schools with a generous budget for sports scholarships from those without. And since a first XI can comprise players from four or even five different years, it's quite possible to have a team made up almost entirely of such scholars. Of course, schools vary greatly in size, and the clichéd level playing field has never existed, but the spread of sporting excellence is being distorted by cash. Then there's the practice of admitting for a couple of terms students who have completed their studies elsewhere, often in South Africa. This happens more than many realise – perhaps unsurprisingly, given the counties' similar tendency to import ready-made players rather than nurture and develop their own.

For many years, it has been far more difficult for bowlers to make a mark in schools cricket than for batsmen. There is in part a good reason for this: to guard against serious long-term injury, the ECB impose restrictions on how much young seamers can bowl. But another factor is the inexorable march of limited-overs cricket. While no one may send down more than a fifth of the overs available, a top-order batsman can hang around for most or all of the innings. A partial solution is for schools to follow the ECB's recommendation and play a mix of all formats – including declaration games.

In fact, 2013 was an exceptional year for bowlers. Or rather it was an exceptional year for spinners. The most impressive performance was by Repton's Nitish Kumar, who took eight for 11 against the Free Foresters. He had already played at the 2011 World Cup for Canada (for whom he has a first-class hundred), and bolstered his off-breaks with 909 runs for his school. Slow left-armer George Furbank of Kimbolton, aged 16, enjoyed a return of eight for 15 against a strong Headmaster's XI. However, since Kimbolton do not play rugby – at which he also excels – Furbank moved to Bedford School for his sixth-form years. Another remarkable analysis came from Uppingham's Otto Esse, an off-spinner who had figures of eight for 19 against Oundle, while leg-spinner Feroz Baig, from St Edward's, Oxford, and Tiffin's 15-year-old slow left-armer, Bashir Bhatti, shared top spot in the table of leading wicket-

Tom Köhler-Cadmore of Malvern College, the seventh *Wisden* Schools Cricketer of the Year.

takers, with 45. All told, 18 bowlers took ten wickets or more at an average of under ten.

Despite the perception that 2013 was a dry season – and few denied it was a great improvement on the year before – several reports, particularly from Scotland and the north of England, mention frustratingly wet campaigns. So it is a great credit to all involved in schools cricket that, despite its huge demands on time, so many choose it as their main summer sport.

In a further hint that the season was a mixed meteorological bag, just two batsmen reached the 1,000-run mark; in 2011, it had been ten. Of those ten, three were still playing for their schools last year. Ben Duckett, one of the most accomplished young cricketers, started 2013 in style, hitting two centuries in a week for Stowe. He later struck 134 (in a total of 302 for one) in the National Schools Twenty20 competition. However, Duckett, who played four Championship matches for Northamptonshire, had already begun to move beyond this level, and he totalled 700 for the schools season. Jack Mynott, another who had reached 1,000 in 2011, signed off from Dauntsey's with 657; he also played with some success for South Wilts CC. The last of the trio was Tom Köhler-Cadmore, from Malvern.

If the other two had respectable seasons, Köhler-Cadmore's was impeccable. There was no doubt he was the outstanding schools cricketer of 2013. His season aggregate of 1,409 runs (at an average of over just over 100) made him the most prolific run-scorer in schools cricket since the new millennium – and the seventh *Wisden* Schools Cricketer of the Year. "Tom is a tall, powerful young batsman with a good technique," said Mark Hardinges, in charge of cricket at Malvern. "Batting is his forte, although he can bowl some decent awayswingers, and catches pigeons in the slip cordon. He has achieved so much because he's a very good player who at schoolboy level hits the ball like a man. He also has an insatiable appetite for practice and batting." Indeed his medium-pace was good enough to take seven for 27 in a National Schools Twenty20 game against Bloxham. Köhler-Cadmore, who has German forebears, was born in Kent and brought up in Yorkshire, but has signed a three-year contract with Worcestershire. He made his county debut in the victory over Bangladesh A, and hit 47 from the top of the order.

Richard O'Grady, from Tonbridge, also reached four figures for the season, but cut it fine: he hit two centuries, was dismissed in successive weeks for 99 and 98, and finished on 1,001. There was just one double-century in intra-schools cricket: Jeremy Lawlor of Monmouth scored 203 not out against Solihull, and averaged a notch over 100. Spare a thought, though, for Clifton's Tom Smith. On 198 facing the last ball of a 50-over match, he could manage only a single. There was in fact one other double-hundred in a schools match, though this one – 212 not out by the South Africa Under-19 international David Bedingham – came for Colston Bassett CC in a 40-over game against Ratcliffe College. Undaunted, the school chased down a target of 298 with seven wickets and 15 balls to spare.

An utter determination to protect one's wicket produced some bulging averages. Tim Moses of Hurstpierpoint, dismissed only once in five innings, ended with 226. He missed much of the season because of an injury picked up while playing for Sussex Seconds. Almost as impossible to dislodge was Sam Redmayne of Alleyn's: only three times in 13 innings did his opponents winkle him out, and he finished with an average of 180. Meanwhile, Dylan Budge, a Year 12 from Woodhouse Grove, managed 135 thanks in part to eight not-outs – including a highest score of 153. Will Macdonagh of Queen's, Taunton, also joined the hundred club after remaining undefeated in two of his four innings. Like Moses, he missed much of the season through injury.

One of the most explosive performances came from Kyle Cunningham of Bedford Modern School (*alma mater* of Monty Panesar). Against Haileybury, Cunningham struck six sixes in an over. He hit his next ball for six too, eventually falling for 99 from his 35th delivery. His side won by one run. What a day!

He wasn't alone in stumbling one shy of a century. A Swedish player, Torsten Wrigley of St George's, Weybridge, was dismissed when a seamer accidentally delivered a ball that bounced twice before hitting the stumps. St George's may have a star in the making in 14-year-old Will Jacks. Playing for various age-group teams, he totalled 1,076 runs from 684 balls, hitting 60 sixes and 121 fours. He scored three centuries – one for the first team – and a double.

Two sides went through the regular season winning every fixture: Bede's and King's, Taunton. Both also featured in the finals day of the National Schools Twenty20 competition at Arundel. While Bede's lost the final (for the second year running) to Shrewsbury, King's failed to reprise the extraordinary power that had seen them crush nearby Wellington School in the first round. Rhys Davies had smashed 13 sixes and 13 fours in his 66-ball 152. Wellingborough went unbeaten, though they tied games against Bloxham and Kimbolton.

Ten schools enjoyed a win ratio of 80% or higher. Malvern, who celebrated a rare victory against old foes Repton, would have remained unbeaten, had not Will Gifford (eight first-class games for Loughborough University) and master-in-charge Hardinges (ten seasons at Gloucestershire) steered the Old Boys to victory.

Electronic scoring was used more and more in 2013. There is little danger of losing the data since all systems save the information after every ball, but a conspicuous hazard is loss or theft of a laptop. After one master had his computer stolen, it took much research to reconstruct the statistics. Moral: as in batting, don't forget to back up!

Douglas Henderson is the current editor of Schools Cricket Online (www.schoolscricketonline.co.uk).

WISDEN SCHOOLS CRICKETERS OF THE YEAR

2007	Jonathan Bairstow	St Peter's School, York
2008	James Taylor	Shrewsbury School
2009	Jos Buttler	King's College, Taunton
2010	Will Vanderspar	Eton College
2011	Daniel Bell-Drummond	Millfield School
2012	Thomas Abell	Taunton School
2013	**Tom Köhler-Cadmore**	**Malvern College**

MCC Schools v ESCA

At Lord's, September 2. **ESCA won by six wickets.** ‡MCC Schools 262-7 (50 overs) (J. M. A. Mynott 55, J. L. Lawlor 119); ESCA 264-4 (45.4 overs) (H. E. Dearden 94, H. I. Hameed 70, M. Hussain 45*, R. P. Jones 41*).

ESCA *R. P. Jones (*Priestley College*), H. E. Dearden (*Tottington HS*), A. H. T. Donald (*Ysgol Gyfun Pontarddulais*), H. I. Hameed (*Bolton*), M. Hussain (*City of Leeds HS*), S. Mahmood (*Matthew Moss HS*), T. J. Moores (*Millfield*), M. J. G. Taylor (*Rugby*), J. A. Thompson (*Benton Park School*), J. D. Warner (*Kettlethorpe HS*), J. J. Weatherley (*King Edward VI, Southampton*).

MCC Schools *J. L. Lawlor (*Monmouth*), H. C. Blofield (*Shrewsbury*), T. J. Dinnis (*Plymouth College*), O. T. H. Esse (*Uppingham*), B. W. M. Graves (*Oundle*), A. J. Jackson (*Cheadle Hulme School*), J. M. A. Mynott (*Dauntsey's*), C. A. Pepper (*Perse*), P. B. Richardson (*Kent College*), S. J. R. Wyatt-Haines (*Blundell's*).

Full coverage of the 2013 Eton v Harrow match can be found at wisden.com

Schools who wish to be considered for inclusion should email *Wisden* on almanack@wisden.com State schools and girls' schools are especially welcome.

Note: The following tables cover only those schools listed in the A–Z section.

BEST BATTING AVERAGE (5 completed innings)

		I	NO	Runs	HS	100s	Avge
1	D. E. Budge (*Woodhouse Grove School*)	15	8	949	153*	4	135.57
2	T. Köhler-Cadmore (*Malvern College*)	15	1	1,409	186	5	100.64
3	J. L. Lawlor (*Monmouth School*)	9	2	703	203*	2	100.42
4	T. J. W. Phillis (*St Edmund's, Canterbury*)	8	3	485	130*	1	97.00
5	T. J. A. Collins (*St Lawrence College*)	8	3	468	111	2	93.60
6	B. A. Morley (*Leeds Grammar School*)	11	4	598	116	2	85.42
7	T. F. Smith (*Clifton College*)	11	4	574	199*	2	82.00
8	R. S. Vasconcelos (*Gordonstoun School*)	10	2	633	110*	2	79.12
9	R. T. Pratt (*Ampleforth College*)	13	3	781	122*	3	78.10
10	C. A. Cash (*George Watson's College*)	13	4	697	132*	2	77.44
11	T. H. R. Norman (*Hymers College*)	13	3	794	177*	3	77.20
12	G. Macdonald (*City of London Freemen's School*)	16	6	745	123*	3	74.50
13	F. P. A. Martin (*Malvern College*)	16	7	670	54*	0	74.44
14	D. S. Buck (*Sherborne School*)	6	0	442	170	2	73.66
15	C. M. Macdonell (*Wellingborough School*)	12	4	583	150*	1	72.87
16	L. W. Hansford (*Christ's Hospital*)	12	2	728	143*	4	72.80
17	T. G. Weston (*Wolverhampton Grammar School*)	12	4	582	92*	0	72.75
18	M. Campopiano (*Hurstpierpoint College*)	9	4	355	99*	0	71.00
19	S. Cott (*Reed's School*)	18	4	980	159*	4	70.00
	B. M. Duckett (*Stowe School*)	11	1	700	140	4	70.00
	M. C. Rose (*Watford Grammar School*)	8	2	420	87*	0	70.00
22	B. Shaw (*Ratcliffe College*)	10	3	484	144	2	69.14
23	S. A. McCullagh (*St Peter's School, York*)	16	9	482	76*	0	68.85
24	A. Gorvin (*Portsmouth Grammar School*)	9	4	343	125*	1	68.60
25	J. A. L. Maunder (*Blundell's School*)	11	6	333	100*	1	66.60
26	L. E. W. Gallichan (*Victoria College, Jersey*)	10	3	465	135	2	66.42
27	J. M. A. Mynott (*Dauntsey's School*)	14	4	657	125*	2	65.70
28	D. N. Warne (*Ratcliffe College*)	10	3	458	102	2	65.42

Three other batsmen averaged over 100, but from fewer than five completed innings: T. H. Moses (Hurstpierpoint College) 226.00; S. R. Redmayne (Alleyn's School) 180.33; and W. P. Macdonagh (Queen's College, Taunton) 105.50.

MOST RUNS

		I	NO	Runs	HS	100s	Avge
1	T. Köhler-Cadmore (*Malvern College*)	15	1	1,409	186	5	100.64
2	R. J. O'Grady (*Tonbridge School*)	22	5	1,001	143*	2	58.88
3	S. Cott (*Reed's School*)	18	4	980	159*	4	70.00
4	T. G. L. Colverd (*Haberdashers' Aske's Boys' School*)	18	2	979	148	3	61.18
5	D. E. Budge (*Woodhouse Grove School*)	15	8	949	153*	4	135.57
6	R. Hussain (*Felsted School*)	19	2	936	181	2	55.05
7	N. R. Kumar (*Repton School*)	16	1	909	154*	3	60.60
8	E. W. R. James (*Eton College*)	19	2	899	144*	3	52.88
9	N. A. Hammond (*King's School, Worcester*)	16	1	874	177	2	58.26
10	C. H. O'Brien (*Hampton School*)	15	1	863	129*	4	61.64
11	D. B. Goodyear (*RGS, Worcester*)	24	4	844	114*	2	42.20
12	J. E. P. Hebron (*Felsted School*)	19	2	838	153*	2	49.29
13	J. A. L. Scriven (*Cranleigh School*)	17	0	810	138	2	47.64
14	T. H. R. Norman (*Hymers College*)	13	3	794	177*	3	77.20
	O. R. Batchelor (*Charterhouse*)	16	1	794	163	2	52.93
16	B. Ringrose (*Cheltenham College*)	16	1	793	136	4	52.86
	W. E. C. Wright (*Haberdashers' Aske's Boys' School*)	17	1	793	146	3	49.56
18	R. T. Pratt (*Ampleforth College*)	13	3	781	122*	3	78.10
19	J. J. C. Smallwood (*Tonbridge School*)	20	3	778	105*	3	45.76
20	A. G. Milton (*Malvern College*)	15	3	776	136*	2	64.66

		I	NO	Runs	HS	100s	Avge
21	J. H. Barrett (*St Edward's School, Oxford*)	19	0	764	129	2	40.21
22	H. Z. Finch (*Eastbourne College*)	17	1	751	132*	3	46.93
23	G. Macdonald (*City of London Freemen's School*)	16	6	745	123*	3	74.50
24	L. W. Hansford (*Christ's Hospital*)	12	2	728	143*	4	72.80
25	J. Hunter-Jordan (*Felsted School*)	18	3	713	103*	2	47.53
26	J. L. Lawlor (*Monmouth School*)	9	2	703	203*	3	100.42
27	B. M. Duckett (*Stowe School*)	11	1	700	140	4	70.00

BEST BOWLING AVERAGE (10 wickets)

		O	M	R	W	BB	Avge
1	C. T. Russell-Vick (*Cranbrook School*)	17	2	47	11	6-4	4.27
2	C. M. Macdonell (*Wellingborough School*)	51.5	7	155	21	5-3	7.38
3	D. P. Jones (*Ellesmere College*)	64	22	153	20	4-16	7.65
4	W. K. Porter (*Glenalmond College*)	23	3	109	14	5-7	7.78
5	L. C. Williams (*Rossall School*)	62	11	187	23	7-9	8.13
6	O. Jump (*Kirkham Grammar School*)	54	14	131	16	5-6	8.18
7	H. Furze (*Colfe's School*)	68	16	194	23	3-23	8.43
8	F. C. Sutton (*Gresham's School*)	56	12	165	19	6-34	8.68
9	K. A. Gibson (*Kingswood School, Bath*)	50	10	140	16	4-26	8.75
10	A. N. Goble (*Eastbourne College*)	69.1	10	237	27	6-11	8.77
11	D. Emanuel-Burns (*Harvey Grammar School*)	42	11	106	12	3-8	8.83
12	P. M. Makin (*Manchester Grammar School*)	27.5	7	98	11	5-14	8.90
13	B. Upton (*Barnard Castle School*)	57.5	15	161	17	5-15	9.47
14	G. T. Cork (*Denstone College*)	42.2	9	105	11	4-22	9.54
15	G. A. Furbank (*Kimbolton School*)	100.1	23	255	26	8-15	9.80
16	T. Groves (*Ryde School with Upper Chine*)	54	14	167	17	5-23	9.82
17	E. O. Hooper (*Bede's School*)	61.1	13	198	20	5-27	9.90
18	J. A. Loft (*Simon Langton GS*)	35.3	7	119	12	3-16	9.91
19	E. G. Barnard (*Shrewsbury School*)	53.4	7	181	18	4-26	10.05
20	S. Packard (*Colfe's School*)	49	16	143	14	2-12	10.21
	A. Walters (*Berkhamsted School*)	39.1	5	143	14	5-10	10.21
22	C. J. K. Till (*Stonyhurst College*)	31	5	113	11	4-24	10.27
23	F. J. C. Wordsworth (*Christ's Hospital*)	24.1	3	105	10	3-7	10.50
24	R. G. Williams (*Denstone College*)	89.3	23	243	23	5-19	10.56
25	P. Scott (*St Albans School*)	55	13	127	12	3-2	10.58
26	B. T. Wall (*Wellingborough School*)	69	10	195	18	5-8	10.83
27	H. A. Douglas (*St Joseph's College, Ipswich*)	63.4	9	218	20	4-22	10.90
	B. J. Butcher (*Chislehurst & Sidcup GS*)	38	7	109	10	5-66	10.90
29	A. S. Crump (*Denstone College*)	88.5	12	275	25	6-21	11.00
	W. K. Doerr (*Ellesmere College*)	84.2	22	231	21	5-39	11.00
	T. B. Nightingale (*Elizabeth College, Guernsey*)	31.2	4	132	12	3-7	11.00
	J. Badawi-Crook (*University College School*)	33	5	110	10	3-22	11.00

MOST WICKETS

		O	M	R	W	BB	Avge
1	F. Baig (*St Edward's School, Oxford*)	189	31	647	45	6-66	14.37
	B. A. Bhatti (*Tiffin School*)	190.5	38	664	45	8-40	14.75
3	M. Mohammad (*Charterhouse*)	195.3	30	648	41	6-85	15.80
	J. E. P. Hebron (*Felsted School*)	213	28	843	41	5-35	20.56
5	N. Brand (*King's College, Taunton*)	143.4	20	529	38	7-18	13.92
	K. M. Corbett (*Reed's School*)	185.2	39	537	38	6-20	14.13
	F. J. H. Foster (*Eltham College*)	201.4	28	662	38	5-18	17.42
8	J. M. Foley (*Felsted School*)	174	16	732	37	5-22	19.78
9	H. M. Selvey (*RGS, Worcester*)	143	15	511	36	4-20	14.19
	A. J. Watkins (*Tiffin School*)	155.3	27	589	36	5-21	16.36
	T. K. M. Eckett (*Eton College*)	180.3	14	787	36	4-24	21.86

		O	M	R	W	BB	Avge
12	D. F. L. Howe (*St Benedict's School, Ealing*)	123.3	16	441	35	5-11	12.60
	D. Williams (*Bromsgrove School*)	154	31	465	35	6-59	13.28
	J. D. Gilder (*Rugby School*)	190	35	641	35	5-38	18.31
15	J. J. Dilley (*Clifton College*)	132	25	421	34	7-13	12.38
	N. R. Kumar (*Repton School*)	125	7	469	34	8-11	13.79
	X. G. Owen (*Berkhamsted School*)	144.4	20	483	34	6-8	14.20
	J. R. Stewart (*Haileybury*)	148.5	19	665	34	5-26	19.55
19	M. W. Karslake (*Rugby School*)	159	38	465	33	5-10	14.09
	M. T. Maciver (*Berkhamsted School*)	149	20	476	33	4-8	14.42
21	H. W. H. Woodward (*Stowe School*)	119.4	16	376	32	6-30	11.75
	J. Patel (*City of London Freemen's School*)	127.4	15	472	32	6-49	14.75
	S. Shah (*RGS, Worcester*)	127.3	7	551	32	5-33	17.21
	N. J. Winder (*Tonbridge School*)	186	22	611	32	5-67	19.09
25	W. J. Hodgson (*King's School, Macclesfield*)	103.5	13	393	31	4-21	12.67
26	J. B. R. Keeping (*Stowe School*)	103.3	14	396	30	5-8	13.20
	W. J. L. Rollings (*Cranleigh School*)	156.1	38	451	30	5-55	15.03
	H. Q. Don (*Charterhouse*)	178	24	583	30	4-58	19.43
	B. W. M. Graves (*Oundle School*)	175.4	33	627	30	5-20	20.90
	E. A. Bartlett (*RGS, Worcester*)	155.1	16	643	30	6-4	21.43
	W. J. E. Bury (*RGS, Worcester*)	159.1	15	664	30	6-8	22.13

OUTSTANDING SEASONS (minimum 7 matches)

	P	W	L	D	A	%W
King's College, Taunton	16	16	0	0	0	100.00
Bede's School	9	9	0	0	3	100.00
Cranbrook School	20	17	2	1	6	85.00
Denstone College	13	11	2	0	0	85.00
Repton School	18	15	1	2	0	83.00
Portsmouth Grammar School	11	9	2	0	0	82.00
Silcoates School	11	9	2	0	0	82.00
Stewart's Melville College	16	13	2	1	2	81.00
St Edward's School, Oxford	20	16	1	3	2	80.00
Cranleigh School	15	12	1	2	0	80.00
Malvern College	19	15	1	3	1	79.00
Berkhamsted School	22	16	4	2	0	73.00
Victoria College, Jersey	15	11	3	1	0	73.00
Reading Blue Coat School	11	8	2	1	5	73.00
Cheadle Hulme School	11	8	3	0	1	73.00
King's College School, Wimbledon	17	12	4	1	0	71.00
Blundell's School	14	10	4	0	1	71.00
Dame Allan's School	7	5	2	0	2	71.00
Rossall School	10	7	3	0	0	70.00

SCHOOLS A–Z

In the results line, A = abandoned without a ball bowled. An asterisk next to a name indicates captain. Schools provide their own reports and averages. The qualification for the averages is 150 runs or ten wickets. Twenty20 games and overseas tours are excluded from results and averages.

Abingdon School
P14 W8 L4 D2

Master i/c D. C. Shirazi   **Coach** C. J. Burnand

An ever-improving side contained only two leavers. Daniel Matthews and Rory Garrett had fine seasons with the bat, while captain Sasha Barras claimed the top bowler prize in his fourth and final year in the senior team.

Batting D. S. Matthews 446 at 44.60; R. Garrett 512 at 39.38; C. J. Russell 277 at 30.77; J. Fitzjohn 318 at 28.90; A. S. Barras* 151 at 18.87.

Bowling A. S. Barras 25 at 14.48; L. Bethell 15 at 14.66; D. S. Matthews 19 at 18.63; J. Fitzjohn 13 at 19.53.

Aldenham School   P22 W10 L9 D3
Master i/c M. I. Yeabsley   **Coaches** D. J. Goodchild/M. S. W. Hughes
This was a very enjoyable and successful season. The leading batsman was Lee Tyrrell, while the captain Jack Gibbins was the leading bowler. Other notable achievements were five-fors from Ben James and Alex Milligan, and Harry Copley scoring 99.
Batting L. H. I. Tyrrell 556 at 39.71; H. A. H. Copley 495 at 29.11; J. S. Gibbins* 434 at 27.12; J. R. F. Bryer 256 at 21.33; J. A. Stowell 162 at 18.00; G. P. Uttley 230 at 17.69.
Bowling L. H. I. Tyrrell 20 at 16.50; A. J. Milligan 16 at 17.25; J. S. Gibbins 27 at 20.55; J. R. F. Bryer 10 at 20.60; B. D. James 22 at 21.00; L. R. W. Paice 10 at 25.30; H. A. H. Copley 11 at 33.18.

Alleyn's School   P14 W5 L5 D4 A1
Master i/c R. N. Ody   **Coach** P. E. Edwards
Well captained by Daniel King, the team enjoyed a successful season, losing only five of 14 games and reaching the London Cup Final. The batting of Sam Redmayne was a real highlight, and he finished with an astonishing average.
Batting S. R. Redmayne 541 at 180.33; F. J. W. Glen 217 at 31.00; F. S. Neve 260 at 23.63.
Bowling F. J. W. Glen 15 at 18.46; D. J. King* 15 at 23.80.

Ampleforth College   P12 W3 L5 D4 A4
Master i/c G. D. Thurman   **Coach** A. Rowsell
An extremely young and inexperienced squad performed valiantly. Ferdinand Rex showed maturity as he helped the youngsters blend into the side and, as captain, developed enormously. Toby Pratt batted beautifully and scored three centuries.
Batting R. T. Pratt 781 at 78.10; M. A. R. Darbishire 379 at 27.07; J. E. Lush 222 at 18.50; M. F. M. Wittmann 203 at 18.45; F. C. Rex* 221 at 18.41; G. P. Hodson 150 at 11.53.
Bowling M. A. R. Darbishire 15 at 24.20; H. C. Blakiston Houston 12 at 25.41; F. C. Rex 13 at 44.15; G. P. Hodson 11 at 45.45.

Bancroft's School   P16 W7 L8 D1
Master i/c J. K. Lever
This proved to be a pleasing season from a young side containing only four sixth-formers. Yusuf Sohoye proved the most penetrating bowler, and the contributions of Samraj Sadra as captain and all-rounder were significant.
Batting S. S. Sadra* 389 at 29.92; M. Tann 248 at 27.55; I. Thankarajah 321 at 24.69; V. Handa 363 at 24.20; F. D. Edwards 153 at 21.85; T. Oliver 175 at 15.90; A. S. Nijjar 203 at 15.61.
Bowling A. S. Nijjar 14 at 21.21; Y. A. Sohoye 19 at 21.52; S. S. Sadra 10 at 36.30.

Barnard Castle School   P8 W5 L2 D1 A5
Master i/c M. T. Pepper   **Coach** J. Lister
This was another encouraging season, with ten players expected to return for 2014. The bowling proved a real threat: captain Bret Upton claimed five for 15 against Edinburgh Academy, and Kit Wilson five for six against Rossall. Tom Sowerby and Guy Coser showed real potential, batting with maturity.
Batting T. Sowerby 235 at 29.37; R. Newman 208 at 23.11; G. Coser 171 at 19.00.
Bowling B. Upton* 17 at 9.47; A. Finkill 12 at 14.00; K. Wilson 18 at 15.22; R. Barrett 13 at 16.30.

Bede's School   P9 W9 A3
Master i/c A. P. Wells   **Coach** R. J. Davies
Once again, Bede's were undefeated in 50-over cricket, securing overwhelming wins against Eton, Whitgift and Charterhouse. The side also prospered in the short form of the game, finishing runners-up in the National Twenty20 competition.
Batting C. J. Guest 191 at 47.75; T. B. Allport 183 at 45.75; F. J. Hudson-Prentice 304 at 43.42; C. F. Jackson* 169 at 28.16; D. A. C. Wells 178 at 25.42; J. A. R. Phelps 152 at 25.33.
Bowling E. O. Hooper 20 at 9.90; F. J. Hudson-Prentice 12 at 11.16; C. D. Hodgson 10 at 14.80; N. A. Persaud 11 at 15.00.

Bedford Modern School   P16 W7 L8 D1
Master i/c P. J. Woodroffe
The highlights of the season were Kyle Cunningham's six sixes in an over against Haileybury, and Nish Narayanan's hat-trick against Stamford. Another notable performer was wicketkeeper Nick Barden, who made 12 stumpings.

Batting H. P. Thurstance* 434 at 31.00; T. H. J. Burman 378 at 25.20; R. J. Baxter 262 at 21.83; K. S. Cunningham 317 at 21.13; S. K. Mahendran 204 at 18.54; N. J. Barden 252 at 15.75.
Bowling N. Narayanan 17 at 18.00; R. T. Kraus 29 at 18.41; S. K. Mahendran 19 at 21.10; K. S. Cunningham 12 at 28.91; B. R. Rodgers 10 at 31.70.

Bedford School
P13 W9 L1 D3 A1

Master i/c P. Sherwin

Vicram Sohal's excellent captaincy helped bring about an outstanding season, with just one defeat and nine wins. Fifteen-year-old off-spinner Ben Slawinski topped the bowling averages in his debut season, while Charlie Thurston, with a year left, headed the batting for a second year.
Batting C. O. Thurston 610 at 40.66; T. J. O. Graham 547 at 39.07; G. W. H. Adams 272 at 38.85; V. V. S. Sohal* 382 at 38.20; T. Bradbeer 342 at 38.00; L. C. Adams 355 at 35.50; P. R. J. McDuell 328 at 27.33.
Bowling B. Slawinski 20 at 14.80; P. R. J. McDuell 14 at 17.71; W. F. P. Wright 29 at 18.55; R. Wright 14 at 21.07; T. J. O. Graham 11 at 26.00; V. V. S. Sohal 11 at 38.45.

Berkhamsted School
P22 W16 L4 D2

Master i/c D. J. Gibson   **Coach** B. R. Mahoney

The team had a fantastic season, winning 16 matches. Wicketkeeper James Hawkes was an excellent captain, while Max Maciver had a superb all-round summer, scoring 568 runs and taking 33 wickets. Xavier Owen was the pick of the bowlers.
Batting H. J. Bartlett 320 at 40.00; S. C. Masters 490 at 35.00; M. T. Maciver 568 at 31.55; A. G. Leighton 516 at 27.15; M. G. Pugh 166 at 20.75; H. D. J. Sambrook 234 at 15.60.
Bowling A. Walters 14 at 10.21; X. G. Owen 34 at 14.20; M. T. Maciver 33 at 14.42; H. J. Robertson 11 at 18.45; H. D. J. Sambrook 10 at 21.10; O. M. Lansdowne 22 at 23.04; J. P. Ryan 15 at 25.26; S. C. Masters 13 at 29.61.

Birkenhead School
P15 W5 L8 D2 A1

Master i/c P. N. Lindberg   **Coach** G. J. Rickman

As expected, this was a challenging year for a young and inexperienced side, though they competed well in most games. Upper Sixth-formers Harry Sturgess, the captain, all-rounder Alex Watkins and opening bowler Olly Mills held things together. Victories against Cheadle and King's Chester were the highlights.
Batting H. D. Sturgess* 441 at 31.50; A. R. Watkins 350 at 29.16; L. E. W. Filer 208 at 20.80; D. I. Smith 184 at 20.66; W. Brewster 188 at 18.80.
Bowling A. R. Watkins 16 at 17.93; O. J. G. Mills 12 at 23.66.

Bishop's Stortford College
P10 W5 L4 D1 A1

Master i/c M. Drury   **Coach** N. D. Hughes

An excellent win against MCC, with Tom Foot taking five for 38, was the most memorable moment of an encouraging season. Taylor Weeks was top run-scorer, and James McGran led the side effectively.
Batting T. J. E. Weeks 256 at 42.66; E. J. S. Goodman 254 at 42.33; O. R. J. Radley 162 at 32.40.
Bowling T. A. Shepherd 10 at 19.60; T. E. Foot 13 at 21.84.

Bloxham School
P13 W7 L4 T1 D1 A2

Master i/c R. S-R. Pyper   **Coach** M. Walton

This was a transitional year for Bloxham, whose team included six regular Year 11 pupils. Tom Falkingham bowled efficiently and was tireless with his encouragement of the younger members of the team.
Batting L. B. Nardone* 358 at 35.80; O. W. B. Tice 285 at 28.50; W. E. S. Gurney 204 at 20.40.
Bowling T. L. Falkingham 18 at 15.33; A. T. Mansfield 16 at 23.37; D. E. N. Craven 10 at 28.90.

Blundell's School
P14 W10 L4 A1

Master i/c R. J. Turner   **Coach** C. L. L. Gabbitass

A most successful summer included ten wins. The captain, Jack Dart, featured in the full Devon squad, while Sam Wyatt-Haines and Jack Maunder are Nottinghamshire Academy members. Numerous strong cricketers will be competing for places in 2014.
Batting J. A. L. Maunder 333 at 66.60; J. F. S. Dart* 507 at 56.33; S. J. Wyatt-Haines 467 at 38.91; B. H. P. Hancock 389 at 38.90; D. T. Penberthy-Hutchings 333 at 33.30; A. E. Chilcott 327 at 27.25.
Bowling J. F. S. Dart 22 at 13.81; W. J. Browne 15 at 23.86.

Bradfield College
P17 W10 L6 D1

Master i/c M. S. Hill   Coach J. R. Wood

With many of the team having returned for a final year of first-team cricket, expectations were high. At times the side were excellent. However, standards occasionally slipped against the strongest schools.

Batting R. F. Higgins* 388 at 43.11; C. N. Gaur 495 at 41.25; A. J. Rishton 630 at 39.37; M. P. N. Covers 250 at 25.00; N. M. G. Farr 192 at 16.00.

Bowling M. P. N. Covers 21 at 14.14; C. M. M'Crystal 10 at 17.40; R. F. Higgins 18 at 20.22; O. W. Smithson 13 at 30.92; O. Birts 11 at 32.09.

Bradford Grammar School
P19 W6 L10 D3 A1

Master i/c A. G. Smith   Coach S. A. Kellett

A competitive – but ultimately slightly disappointing – season saw defeat in several games that could have been won. The batting relied on Navjyot Devesher and Rama Patel, who shared four century stands; Under-14 leg-spinner Kyme Tahirkheli prospered in his first season.

Batting N. Devesher 565 at 40.35; R. Patel 418 at 29.85; G. D. Gill 278 at 19.85; M. Green 153 at 19.12.

Bowling K. Tahirkheli 27 at 18.40; M. P. Celaire 12 at 19.83; D. W. Heslop 11 at 21.81; R. A. Butt* 18 at 24.38; R. Ishtiaq 12 at 26.50; T. P. Mountain 10 at 27.70; G. D. Gill 11 at 29.09.

Brentwood School
P16 W10 L3 D3 A1

Master i/c B. R. Hardie

Brentwood had another consistent season despite the limited availability of top players. Kishen Velani again received England Under-19 recognition, and Harry Levy was part of the Under-16 squad.

Batting K. S. Velani* 412 at 58.85; R. K. Patel 270 at 38.57; K. N. Ali 417 at 37.90; R. C. Horswill 208 at 26.00; M. S. Bell 205 at 25.62; M. K. Baldock 172 at 21.50; S. S. Prabhakar 186 at 20.66; H. J. D. Levy 159 at 19.87; R. F. Syed 162 at 14.72.

Bowling H. J. D. Levy 18 at 12.16; A. K. Minocha 18 at 13.22; K. S. Velani 19 at 13.47; O. Sarkar 11 at 21.18; S. S. Prabhakar 17 at 22.00.

Brighton College
P17 W8 L8 D1 A1

Master i/c Miss A. L. Walker   Coach N. J. Lamb

Brighton College enjoyed some memorable victories, plus a run to the final of the Langdale Cup. Sam Grant's match-winning centuries against Whitgift and the Sussex Martlets were especially impressive.

Batting S. E. Grant 584 at 36.50; T. G. Prideaux de Lacy 383 at 25.53; E. Coombs 402 at 23.64; E. D. Catt 235 at 23.50; C. J. M. Waters 185 at 16.81; K. Rajkumar* 258 at 16.12; O. J. Male 152 at 13.81.

Bowling J. A. Hayward 28 at 13.14; H. J. O. Klus 21 at 27.90; S. E. Grant 13 at 28.38; D. A. Glynne-Jones 13 at 36.73.

Bristol Grammar School
P18 W7 L10 D1 A1

Masters i/c K. R. Blackburn/R. S. Jones

A young team grew up in 2013, finishing strongly and giving some excellent performances; hundreds from Dan Tailor and Ciaran Moran were memorable moments. The spin trio of Cameron Scott, Callum Bluck and Rishi Panchal led the attack. Most will return for 2014.

Batting C. J. Moran 323 at 40.37; D. H. Tailor* 342 at 28.50; C. J. Y. Scott 310 at 28.18; H. M. Thompson 225 at 22.50; T. J. Rowland 256 at 19.69.

Bowling C. M. Bluck 19 at 16.89; R. N. Panchal 13 at 19.76; C. J. Y. Scott 17 at 23.58.

Bromsgrove School
P16 W9 L6 D1 A1

Master i/c D. J. Fallows

The team reached the national semi-final of the Under-17 cup and the quarter-final of the National Twenty20; and they won the Chesterton Cup at New Road – the first time they had entered. Major contributions came from Matt Lamb, Darrel Williams, Will Fraine, Henry Moberley, James Kinder and Tom Banton.

Batting M. Lamb 434 at 62.00; W. A. Fraine 596 at 59.60; D. Williams 434 at 33.38; H. F. Moberley 341 at 31.00; B. Huxley* 369 at 28.38; C. J. Edwards 211 at 17.58.

Bowling D. Williams 35 at 13.28; B. Huxley 14 at 21.14; A. R. Wilkinson 17 at 24.94; C. W. Davies 12 at 28.16; O. E. Strong 10 at 35.30.

Kyle Cunningham, from Bedford Modern, struck six sixes in an over against Haileybury. Cordelia Griffith headed Chigwell's bowling averages, and attended the England Women's Academy.

Bryanston School
P14 W6 L8 A1

Master i/c B. J. Lawes   **Coach** P. J. Norton

Captain Joe Horsham provided the energy and enthusiasm, and was a fantastic fielder. Rebecca D'Erlanger-Bertrand opened the batting for the third straight year, and we hope to see her in the England Women's team soon. Player of the summer was Alex Jones, with 265 runs and 12 wickets.

Batting A. G. Jones 265 at 29.44; E. L. Clements 268 at 20.61; O. L. C. Weld 253 at 18.07; S. A. E. Carter 215 at 17.91.

Bowling A. G. Jones 12 at 19.83; O. L. C. Weld 19 at 19.84; P. C. Oakshott 14 at 23.85.

Canford School
P13 W9 L2 D2

Master i/c B. C. Edgell   **Coach** M. Keech

This was an excellent season for the senior side, who lost only twice in 13 matches. An outstanding group of boys have worked incredibly hard.

Batting B. J. Boon* 366 at 40.66; J. Roberts 389 at 35.36; F. H. Ambrose 366 at 33.27; B. S. Rogers 264 at 26.40; M. W. B. Haines 151 at 15.10.

Bowling F. H. Ambrose 22 at 13.09; E. I. C. Wordsworth 11 at 18.54; J. Manley 16 at 18.81; A. J. Maher 16 at 20.93; G. C. Chippendale 10 at 29.20.

Charterhouse
P18 W9 L6 D3 A2

Master i/c M. P. Bicknell

A very good campaign was nearly an outstanding one. Marwan Mohammad came of age as a left-arm spinner, while Oliver Batchelor's batting went from strength to strength. Even more will be expected of them next year.

Batting O. R. Batchelor 794 at 52.93; T. E. W. Hurley 232 at 46.40; H. G. Clinton 333 at 20.81; M. Mohammad 263 at 20.23; H. Q. Don 202 at 20.20; R. L. Hughes 314 at 19.62; T. P. Gordon-Martin* 263 at 18.78; A. J. Beddows 187 at 14.38.

Bowling M. Mohammad 41 at 15.80; A. G. Gilbert 29 at 18.93; H. Q. Don 30 at 19.43; S. D. T. Brennan 19 at 25.52; T. E. W. Hurley 23 at 26.08.

Cheadle Hulme School
P11 W8 L3 A1

Master i/c S. Burnage

This was a highly successful season, and notable wins came against King's Macclesfield, Denstone College and Bolton School. The highlight of the year was Under-14 James Scott scoring 102 against King's Macclesfield, with ten sixes and six fours.

Batting A. J. Jackson 308 at 51.33; D. Carswell* 315 at 45.00; K. Dafedar 162 at 40.50; J. S. A. Scott 241 at 40.16.

Bowling A. J. Jackson 14 at 11.85; D. Carswell 19 at 11.89; J. M. Ridler 17 at 13.58.

Cheltenham College
P13 W9 L4 A2

Master i/c R. E. T. Moore   **Coach** M. P. Briers

Cheltenham played their best cricket in the John Harvey Cup, recording several impressive wins. Ben Ringrose, in his fourth season opening the batting, proved an astute captain. He was well assisted by all-rounder Alex Duncliffe-Vines, who struck a destructive 103 not out against St Edward's.

Batting B. Ringrose* 793 at 52.86; A. Duncliffe-Vines 413 at 41.30; Jamie Jamieson-Black 404 at 40.40; O. Soames 258 at 36.85; H. Lait 371 at 30.91; J. Sharam 176 at 17.60.

Bowling A. Duncliffe-Vines 18 at 19.11; B. Ringrose 20 at 20.60; Jock Jamieson-Black 16 at 23.37; A. Montagu 17 at 23.70; B. Wyatt 11 at 32.63.

Chigwell School
P13 W5 L8

Master i/c F. A. Griffith   **Coach** V. M. Griffith

The season started with a fantastic win against City of London. Although the squad didn't manage a century, there were encouraging individual performances. The best moment was the three-run victory against Brentwood. Chigwell lost Saf Imtiaz to Essex Seconds for most of the season, where he scored centuries against Derbyshire and Somerset. Cordelia Griffith also missed several matches while with England Under-19s and the England Women's Academy.

Batting S. K. M. Imtiaz 155 at 31.00; H. K. M. Blogg 153 at 21.85.

Bowling C. L. Griffith 11 at 20.09; J. L. N. Banfield 10 at 23.90; A. Shamsudin* 10 at 27.20.

Chislehurst & Sidcup Grammar School
P5 W2 L3

Master i/c R. Wallbridge   **Coach** D. L. Pask

The squad worked extremely hard pre-season but, owing to exams, only five matches were played; the highlight was Ben Butcher's five for 66 against MCC.

Batting W. L. Davy 189 at 47.25.

Bowling B. J. Butcher 10 at 10.90.

Christ College, Brecon
P9 W4 L5

Master i/c T. J. Trumper   **Coach** A. J. Copp

The ongoing tussle for supremacy between the Mitchell brothers, James and Iain, powered an improved season. They formed an effective opening pace attack, well supported by Harrison Kent; Will Trumper made useful runs too. Most pleasing were wins over King's Gloucester and Llandovery College.

Batting I. H. Mitchell 249 at 27.66; J. P. Mitchell* 164 at 18.22; W. J. C. Trumper 163 at 18.11.

Bowling T. H. Kent 12 at 13.33; J. P. Mitchell 13 at 16.07; I. H. Mitchell 11 at 20.72.

Christ's Hospital
P12 W6 L4 D2 A3

Master i/c H. P. Holdsworth   **Coach** T. E. Jesty

The season began and ended poorly, but in between came six wins in seven matches. The team was inspired by the captain, Luke Hansford, who in five innings hit four hundreds – a school record – and a 93. Only two of the young side leave, so prospects are good for the new master-in-charge; Howard Holdsworth stands down after 22 years.

Batting L. W. Hansford* 728 at 72.80; A. G. Elmes 213 at 21.30; A. Walker 186 at 18.60.

Bowling F. J. C. Wordsworth 10 at 10.50; J. S. Heath 16 at 13.93; F. L. Burgess 22 at 14.68; L. S. Barnard-Masterson 11 at 22.27; A. Walker 12 at 25.33.

City of London Freemen's School
P17 W11 L5 T1 A3

Master i/c A. E. Buhagiar   **Coach** N. M. Stewart

The senior players led the way in an unexpectedly rewarding summer. George Macdonald was the epitome of consistency, and recorded three centuries. The school came second in a four-team festival at Bruton, thanks to an entertaining victory against the hosts on the last day; Oscar Coyle struck 104 not out in his final first-team game.

Batting G. Macdonald 745 at 74.50; O. M. Coyle 354 at 29.50; M. Dawes 268 at 24.36; A. F. A. Culhane* 183 at 18.30; J. A. T. Turton 188 at 15.66.
Bowling A. F. A. Culhane 20 at 13.95; J. Patel 32 at 14.75; M. Jackson 13 at 15.07; M. Dawes 27 at 15.59; B. Lumsden 11 at 19.36; T. Rudnai 10 at 28.20.

Claycsmore School
P9 W3 L4 D2

Master i/c R. S. Miller   **Coach** D. C. Conway
Jack Whiteside's thoughtful and inclusive captaincy ensured that this young team had a most enjoyable and rewarding season of development. Lewis McManus, with the Hampshire Academy, produced some high-class performances as we welcomed several hard-working newcomers.
Batting L. D. McManus 188 at 94.00; C. M. Martin 184 at 26.28.
Bowling J. D. Adamson 10 at 14.30.

Clifton College
P14 W9 L3 D2

Master i/c J. C. Bobby   **Coach** P. W. Romaines
An excellent season brought convincing wins over Sherborne, when Tom Smith scored a wonderful 199 not out, and Cheltenham. Hamish Matthews and Ben McGeoch also made centuries. Spearhead of the attack was slow left-armer Jonathan Dilley, son of Graham; he twice took a hat-trick, and ended with 34 wickets.
Batting T. F. Smith 574 at 82.00; B. J. McGeoch 327 at 54.50; H. M. Matthews 438 at 48.66; J. H. Ellison 240 at 30.00; W. J. Higgins 196 at 19.60.
Bowling T. F. Smith 18 at 11.16; J. J. Dilley 34 at 12.38; J. S. Probert 13 at 29.69; D. J. Trenouth 11 at 37.45.

Colfe's School
P16 W4 L9 D3 A2

Master i/c G. S. Clinton
The school often had no option but to field an understrength side, especially during the exam period.
Batting M. Stiddard* 515 at 64.37; H. Furze 398 at 36.18.
Bowling H. Furze 23 at 8.43; S. Packard 14 at 10.21; C. Hill 13 at 12.84.

Cranbrook School
P20 W17 L2 D1 A6

Master i/c C. Pohio
This was a wonderful season, full of thrilling cricket. Skipper Finn Hulbert represented the Sussex Academy, while Charlie Russell-Vick and Dom Thompson, both Year 9s, are genuine prospects. Doug Gordon scored his maiden century, against the Old Boys.
Batting F. W. Hulbert* 491 at 35.07; A. J. C. Smallwood 397 at 30.53; J. Clark 337 at 25.92; D. J. Gordon 326 at 23.28; A. T. Lloyd-Dyke 325 at 23.21; H. M. Cloke 285 at 19.00.
Bowling C. T. Russell-Vick 11 at 4.27; F. W. Hulbert 25 at 11.80; J. Clark 25 at 17.80; T. W. Russell-Vick 18 at 19.22; D. Thompson 12 at 19.91; A. T. Lloyd-Dyke 15 at 20.33.

Cranleigh School
P15 W12 L1 D2

Master i/c J. S. Ross   **Coach** S. D. Welch
Cranleigh had a highly successful season, in which they pulled off several exciting run-chases. The captain Jack Scriven led by example: his aggregate 2,470 runs were a school record.
Batting J. A. Corbishley 158 at 79.00; J. A. L. Scriven* 810 at 47.64; B. M. Broughton 326 at 36.22; O. J. D. Pope 251 at 31.37; W. J. L. Rollings 281 at 28.10; J. E. Trower 431 at 26.93; N. J. Thorpe 319 at 26.58; H. T. Jackson 188 at 17.09.
Bowling W. J. L. Rollings 30 at 15.03; B. M. Broughton 28 at 15.75; N. J. Thorpe 11 at 16.18; S. R. Thomson 14 at 22.57; J. A. L. Scriven 15 at 28.13.

Culford School
P13 W5 L5 D3 A1

Master i/c A. H. Marsh
Culford were a strong bowling and fielding unit. A lack of runs in the early season was a cause for frustration, so it was a relief when the senior batsmen found form after half-term, helping the side finish with four convincing victories.
Batting J. A. Beaumont* 454 at 56.75; E. Smith 188 at 23.50; H. J. Youngson 186 at 23.25; C. Downing 154 at 19.25.
Bowling H. W. Stenton 19 at 15.57; J. A. Beaumont 21 at 17.33; B. T. C. Milner 11 at 22.27; H. J. Youngson 11 at 25.45.

Dame Allan's School

P7 W5 L2 A2

Master i/c J. A. Benn

In a short but encouraging season, Dav Cook and Jack Hearn proved reliable and stylish batsmen, while Ollie Ranken and Jonny Ridley posed a threat with the ball. Five wins out of seven was a fair reflection of the team's strength.

Batting J. Hearn 215 at 43.00; D. Cook 205 at 34.16.

Bowling No one took ten wickets; the leading bowler was O. Ranken, who claimed seven at 18.14.

Dauntsey's School

P16 W10 L4 D2

Master i/c A. J. Palmer   **Coach** J. R. Ayling

After a successful West Indies tour, Dauntsey's home season started well, and progress was made in the Twenty20 Cup. Following some mid-season defeats against strong opponents, the squad recovered well to win eight of the final ten games, retaining the Peak Sports League title and defeating MCC. Jack Mynott ended his first-team career with over 3,200 runs and 80 wickets.

Batting J. M. A. Mynott 657 at 65.70; K. Patrick* 409 at 29.21; A. K. F. Walker 281 at 25.54; W. J. Christofi 218 at 21.80; K. J. Ridley 160 at 20.00; M. H. Romer-Lee 230 at 19.16; L. B. Hannaford 192 at 17.45.

Bowling R. Duckworth 10 at 11.60; L. B. Hannaford 23 at 19.47; K. Patrick 12 at 22.58; M. C. A. Janes 17 at 23.35; J. M. A. Mynott 15 at 27.60.

Denstone College

P13 W11 L2

Master i/c Miss J. R. Morris

This proved a productive season for a young side well captained by Greg Cork, son of former England all-rounder Dominic. Denstone lost only twice, both times in the final over. Off-spinners Austen Crump and Richard Williams took 48 wickets between them; Harvey Hosein topped the batting averages.

Batting H. R. Hosein 196 at 65.33; A. S. Crump 483 at 43.90; R. E. W. Jackson 362 at 36.20; W. G. Burrows 250 at 25.00.

Bowling G. T. Cork* 11 at 9.54; R. G. Williams 23 at 10.56; A. S. Crump 25 at 11.00; C. H. Baynes-Holden 14 at 17.50.

Dr Challoner's Grammar School

P10 W5 L5

Master i/c D. J. Colquhoun

This was a mixed campaign, despite several excellent bowling performances, especially from the leg-spin duo of Robin Collins and Asad Rehman; the problem lay in the inconsistent batting. The captain George Shiel's outstanding 114 against Watford GS was the individual highlight.

Batting G. S. Shiel* 268 at 44.66; M. C. Yeabsley 191 at 23.87.

Bowling R. P. J. Collins 12 at 11.33; A. U. Rehman 11 at 15.36; P. C. A. Rigby 11 at 18.90.

Dollar Academy

P14 W7 L6 T1 A3

Master i/c J. G. A. Frost

Dollar played some excellent cricket at the end of the season to win five of their last six games. They beat Strathallan, Glenalmond and Gordonstoun in the Scottish Twenty20 Cup, and tied with Merchiston.

Batting R. J. Weir* 445 at 34.23; T. I. M. Torrance 223 at 27.87; M. J. M. Mills 246 at 20.50; A. J. Mackie 170 at 18.88.

Bowling A. D. Knapman 19 at 13.26; A. J. Mackie 12 at 22.83.

Dover College

P11 W1 L9 D1 A4

Master i/c G. R. Hill   **Coach** T. L. N. Root

This was a tough season for a very young side. Although the team rarely made enough runs, the prospects for the next few years are encouraging. The opening bowlers in 2013 should still be playing in 2016; Guy Cloake, in Year 9, scored most runs.

Batting G. P. A. A. Cloake 107 at 11.88.

Bowling S. Rai 14 at 20.50; M. J. Walsh* 16 at 23.93.

The Duke of York's Royal Military School

P11 W4 L6 D1

Master i/c S. Cloete

This was a year of rebuilding. Although results were not exceptional, it was a useful season for the development of both current and future players. The young team trained hard, and many made valuable contributions. Nine of the side return for 2014.

Batting J. B. Crawley 323 at 29.36; S. Ghale 285 at 25.90; M. F. Hutchinson 161 at 23.00; N. Gurung 155 at 15.50.
Bowling P. J. Askew 13 at 15.30; S. Ghale 14 at 21.14; F. D. H. Wenham* 14 at 22.64; J. B. Crawley 14 at 23.78.

Dulwich College
P16 W9 L6 D1

Master i/c K. G. Shaw   **Coach** C. W. J. Athey

In a mixed year, the most notable performance was an innings of 175 from Ali Neden during a successful run-chase against Bedford. After that, Dulwich won their last ten matches (in all formats). The team was well captained by Theo Gwyther.
Batting A. G. Neden 468 at 52.00; A. D. Greenidge 395 at 39.50; T. T. Gwyther* 445 at 31.78; P. R. MacCormack 390 at 27.85; D. Chohan 390 at 26.00; A. J. W. Rackow 154 at 22.00; J. S. Orford 171 at 17.10; P. T. W. Stuff 150 at 16.66.
Bowling T. T. Gwyther 19 at 17.36; T. G. Purwar 25 at 19.44; J. M. C. Murray 20 at 27.65; D. Chohan 22 at 27.86; P. T. W. Stuff 13 at 35.15.

Durham School
P17 W11 L4 D2 A1

Master i/c M. B. Fishwick

The highlight of a good season was the win over a Durham Pilgrims side containing four overseas professionals. The bowling award went to Sam Hardy; the fielding and Bell awards to Jordan Grosert; the batting and Hirsch awards to Jacob Bushnell. The emergence of talented youngsters augurs well.
Batting J. M. Bushnell 405 at 40.50; A. A. Arif 428 at 30.57; M. E. Whalley 320 at 26.66; J. W. Durie 223 at 24.77; W. G. A. Proctor 232 at 23.20; S. J. Hardy* 310 at 19.37.
Bowling E. Horner 14 at 12.64; S. J. Hardy 29 at 14.24; J. D. Grosert 21 at 15.52; S. Taylor-Gell 17 at 21.41; R. A. West 16 at 24.56.

Eastbourne College
P18 W11 L6 D1

Master i/c M. J. Banes   **Coach** R. S. Ferley

Having bonded on a pre-season tour to Sri Lanka, the team surpassed expectations. Harry Finch led the side well and represented both Sussex and England Under-19s, though it was team spirit, backed up by contributions from so many, that took the wins into double figures.
Batting H. Z. Finch* 751 at 46.93; S. H. W. Hyne 338 at 28.16; C. R. Hobden 307 at 25.58; J. W. Skinner 327 at 23.35; J. E. Smith 256 at 19.69; T. H. Marriott 352 at 19.55.
Bowling A. N. Goble 27 at 8.77; C. R. Hobden 19 at 17.94; H. J. B. Smith 17 at 18.00; J. E. Smith 23 at 19.26; H. Z. Finch 18 at 22.61.

The Edinburgh Academy
P16 W5 L11 A1

Master i/c M. J. D. Allingham

In terms of results, this was a mixed season, yet the happy squad enjoyed excellent team spirit. They were well led by all-rounder Gair Currie, while good contributions came from vice-captain Rory Simpson and Coinneach Carmichael, another all-rounder.
Batting R. E. A. W. Simpson 386 at 29.69; G. Currie* 312 at 22.28; C. G. D. Carmichael 307 at 21.92; C. P. Huntington 150 at 13.63; B. S. Kinghorn 160 at 12.30.
Bowling J. R. Balfour 16 at 14.25; C. P. Huntington 13 at 19.92; G. Currie 14 at 20.92; C. G. D. Carmichael 10 at 27.40; W. D. Graham 10 at 29.20.

Elizabeth College, Guernsey
P8 W4 L4

Master i/c S. S. Tansey   **Coach** J. D. J. Frith

The individual and team highlights came in the same match, when Oliver Nightingale's 129 helped ensure a magnificent win over MCC. There were also excellent performances against Myerscough, Melbourne Grammar School and Victoria College.
Batting A. E. Le Page 225 at 32.14; A. D. H. Bushell 164 at 27.33; O. W. Nightingale 207 at 25.87.
Bowling T. B. Nightingale 12 at 11.00.

Ellesmere College
P13 W7 L5 D1 A1

Master i/c P. J. Hayes   **Coach** G. Owen

A strong bowling attack ensured a productive and satisfying season. Eight sides were dismissed for under 120, including Worksop for 82 at the Woodard Festival. The only century came from Ayush Prakash in an unbroken eighth-wicket partnership of 135 to secure a draw against Wrekin. The captain Dewi Jones played for Wales Minor Counties.

Batting S. L. Owen 173 at 28.83; J. Thind 216 at 21.60; W. K. Doerr 163 at 14.81.
Bowling D. P. Jones* 20 at 7.65; W. K. Doerr 21 at 11.00; H. J. H. Stow 20 at 14.40; A. Bowyer 22 at 16.59.

Eltham College

P15 W7 L4 D4

Master i/c E. T. Thorogood   **Coach** J. N. Batty

Eltham enjoyed their most successful season in a decade, led by departing captain Alex Tate. The college celebrated notable wins against Reed's, Trinity, Brentwood, Sevenoaks and Sutton Valence. Nine of the team should return next year, and will be expected to carry on the good work.
Batting G. P. R. Haley 487 at 44.27; A. Tate* 540 at 41.53; H. L. Thompson 328 at 32.80; D. G. A. Lawrence 221 at 31.57.
Bowling F. J. H. Foster 38 at 17.42; S. R. Baker 13 at 18.53; N. R. Dasan 14 at 23.00; D. J. F. Norris 20 at 24.65; J. Radhakrishnan 14 at 25.57.

Emanuel School

P7 W4 L2 D1 A3

Master i/c P. A. King   **Coach** M. J. Roberts

After a successful training camp in La Manga, Emanuel enjoyed another winning season, including victories over many local rivals. Will Serocold, the skipper, led the way, finishing with good bowling and batting averages.
Batting No one scored 150 runs. The leading batsman was W. R. Serocold*, who hit 138 at 27.60.
Bowling O. J. Goodwin 11 at 14.36; W. P. R. Davis 10 at 18.60.

Enfield Grammar School

P11 W1 L10

Master i/c T. M. Price

Enfield fielded an extremely youthful team, and their inexperience showed in the results. On several occasions the side managed either good batting or bowling, but rarely both.
Batting A. Mackay 193 at 24.12; B. Garrard 153 at 21.85; G. Garnsworthy 151 at 18.87.
Bowling No one took ten wickets; the leading bowler was H. Norris, who claimed nine at 15.77.

Epsom College

P10 W4 L4 D2

Master i/c N. R. Taylor

A disappointing start to the summer, despite a promising pre-season tour to Dubai, was gradually rectified. A hard-fought draw against MCC and a resounding victory over the Old Epsomians were the highlights. All-rounder Harry Allen, batsman Myles Pittam and bowler Nick Williams were the leading performers.
Batting M. T. Pittam 384 at 54.85; H. A. J. Allen* 337 at 48.14; J. M. Booker 150 at 30.00; T. A. Standen 152 at 19.00.
Bowling N. O. Williams 15 at 15.60; H. A. J. Allen 13 at 21.76.

Eton College

P19 W11 L7 D1

Master i/c R. R. Montgomerie   **Coach** J. M. Rice

Exciting wins over Marlborough and MCC early on allowed the team to gain confidence and fulfil their potential. Teddy James was the mainstay with 899 runs, including three centuries, and Tom Eckett took 36 wickets with his left-arm spin.
Batting E. W. R. James* 899 at 52.88; J. S. D. Gnodde 647 at 49.76; J. F. G. Halstead 513 at 36.64; J. A. Langen 625 at 34.72; M. J. Roy 302 at 27.45; A. D. L. Russell 200 at 15.38.
Bowling T. K. M. Eckett 36 at 21.86; M. H. P. Carleton-Smith 25 at 25.48; C. R. D. Griffin 21 at 27.61; P. H. A. Mould 20 at 33.90; M. J. Roy 13 at 46.00.

Exeter School

P13 W8 L4 D1 A2

Master i/c J. W. Fawkes

A young, improving side was led well by Marcus Hoddinott who, along with Anthony Dibble, batted encouragingly. The new-ball pair, Ben Green and Gillam Crouch, performed with real discipline on batsman-friendly tracks. Green played in the Bunbury Festival.
Batting M. J. Hoddinott* 381 at 63.50; A. S. Dibble 313 at 31.30; T. M. Poustie 227 at 25.22; B. G. F. Green 179 at 22.37; T. C. Thomson 155 at 17.22.
Bowling G. S. Crouch 10 at 22.40; M. J. Hoddinott 11 at 27.36; A. S. Dibble 10 at 38.70.

Tom Smith, from Clifton College, hit 199 not out against Cheltenham. Felsted's captain, Joshua Hunter-Jordan, made 713 runs.

Felsted School
P20 W12 L3 D5

Master i/c J. E. R. Gallian **Coaches** C. S. Knightley/N. J. Lockhart

Felsted had a rewarding season, winning their fair share of games. They set high totals all term; Reece Hussain hit most runs. They were well led by Joshua Hunter-Jordan.

Batting A. A. Cox 177 at 59.00; R. Hussain 936 at 55.05; M. H. Malins 457 at 50.77; J. E. P. Hebron 838 at 49.29; J. Hunter-Jordan* 713 at 47.53; P. D. Kilpatrick 339 at 26.07; J. M. Foley 250 at 25.00; O. J. Grayson 272 at 19.42.

Bowling J. M. Foley 37 at 19.78; A. A. Cox 12 at 20.50; J. E. P. Hebron 41 at 20.56; T. J. Burslem 13 at 28.76; R. W. Burns 11 at 31.81; C. M. Price 20 at 31.90; P. D. Kilpatrick 10 at 42.40.

Fettes College
P14 W6 L6 D2

Master i/c A. B. Russell **Coach** J. D. Pillinger

The side featured only one Year 13 boy, so it was encouraging to win five matches against other schools. Year 10 leg-spinner Matthew Spencer claimed 22 wickets.

Batting H. P. A. MacLeod* 345 at 28.75; W. A. Edwards 169 at 28.16; T. S. Darling 183 at 20.33; R. C. Mather 201 at 18.27; G. A. M. Milne 233 at 17.92; O. M. F. Gray 182 at 14.00.

Bowling M. D. Spencer 22 at 11.81; R. A. Martin 17 at 16.88; H. P. A. MacLeod 16 at 19.25; H. A. M. Dingwall 17 at 22.58.

Forest School
P12 W5 L7 A3

Master i/c S. J. Foulds **Coach** J. J. Kay

Results were mixed, but despite a lack of depth the team were rarely outplayed, and the boys worked hard. Batsmen Peter McDermott and Wiaan Mulder stood out, while Robert Chadwick and captain Ross Ritchie led the attack tirelessly.

Batting P. F. McDermott 492 at 54.66; P. W. A. Mulder 386 at 42.88; R. I. Ritchie* 224 at 20.36; G. R. Coles 159 at 19.87.

Bowling J. E. Bennett 10 at 17.60; A. V. Gandhi 11 at 17.72; P. F. McDermott 12 at 19.25; P. W. A. Mulder 12 at 23.25; R. I. Ritchie 14 at 25.14; R. J. Chadwick 14 at 26.28.

Framlingham College
P16 W4 L6 D6 A1

Master i/c M. J. Marvell   **Coach** B. J. France

Despite the Herculean efforts of captain Tim Alexander, results were disappointing. Kristian Williman, Josh McAvoy and Lewis Gooderham all scored runs, but wickets were harder to come by. Charlie Lewis and Will Hunt did well in what was a very youthful side.

Batting K. N. Williman 592 at 49.33; L. S. Gooderham 495 at 41.25; J. A. McAvoy 403 at 33.58; T. D. Alexander* 313 at 28.45.

Bowling T. D. Alexander 20 at 22.20; A. R. A. Skitch 10 at 31.00; S. R. Keshwani 11 at 43.36.

George Watson's College
P17 W9 L7 D1 A2

Master i/c M. J. Leonard   **Coach** A. D. W. Patterson

Watson's made a slow start, but improved steadily, finishing with four wins in a row. Chris Cash was a terrific skipper, hitting two big centuries and averaging 77; Kathryn Bryce became the first girl to play for the first team.

Batting C. A. Cash* 697 at 77.44; W. Brown 304 at 33.77; A. M. Cockburn 313 at 22.35; R. J. Evans 254 at 21.16; T. R. R. Dryden 238 at 19.83.

Bowling F. J. Hutchison 14 at 16.07; J. W. Bedford 18 at 21.44; A. A. Thomson 18 at 28.72.

The Glasgow Academy
P6 W3 L1 D2 A5

Master i/c G. S. Wood   **Coach** V. Hariharan

Although it was frustrating to see a promising season curtailed by the weather, it was pleasing to see youngsters setting high standards of on-field behaviour and playing in the spirit of the game.

Batting B. Mazzucco 132 at 66.00.

Bowling No one took ten wickets; the leading bowler was M. J. G. Forbes, who claimed seven at 4.71.

The High School of Glasgow
P8 W1 L4 D3 A5

Master i/c D. N. Barrett   **Coaches** N. R. Clarke/K. J. A. Robertson

The weather was again unkind, and most weekend fixtures were cancelled. More games were played in one week than in the rest of the season put together. Creditable draws were achieved on tour against Strathallan and Gordonstoun.

Batting D. N. Satpute* 182 at 36.40.

Bowling No one took ten wickets; the leading bowler was R. N. Isdale, who claimed nine at 18.55.

Glenalmond College
P9 W2 L5 T1 D1 A2

Master i/c M. J. Davies

After an Easter tour of Antigua, Glenalmond played all their matches away from home because of extensive drainage work on the main ground. A very young team found the transition from Under-15 cricket challenging, but made excellent progress.

Batting R. A. M. Davies* 191 at 38.20.

Bowling W. K. Porter 14 at 7.78; R. W. P. Leader 10 at 12.50.

Gordonstoun School
P13 W7 L4 D2 A3

Master i/c C. J. Barton   **Coach** R. Denyer

Gordonstoun's policy of supporting youth cricket benefited the school, with the top four batsmen all aged 15. Archie Houldsworth and Ricardo Vasconcelos batted fantastically, and were superbly supported by Jack Congdon.

Batting R. S. Vasconcelos 633 at 79.12; A. J. I. Houldsworth 406 at 50.75; J. J. Congdon 350 at 35.00.

Bowling M. B. Rind 10 at 12.70; A. J. I. Houldsworth 20 at 15.65; D. J. Marshall* 10 at 26.70; H. J. Knight 16 at 26.87.

Gresham's School
P14 W8 L3 D3 A1

Master i/c D. G. Bailey   **Coaches** A. M. Ponder/C. Brown

After a successful tour to Barbados, Gresham's enjoyed a good summer. Early runs and wickets from all the players helped, and Harry Blackiston led with imagination. In his first season, Matt Barker broke the 500-run barrier.

Batting F. C. Sutton 298 at 49.66; B. E. Stromberg 303 at 43.28; M. Barker 518 at 37.00; H. G. Blackiston* 276 at 23.00; P. Sheridan 159 at 19.87.

Bowling F. C. Sutton 19 at 8.68; P. Sheridan 27 at 12.51; N. Lomax 11 at 12.81; J. Park 13 at 16.92; B. E. Stromberg 21 at 17.85.

The openers for Haberdashers' Aske's – captain Tom Colverd and Will Wright – shared six century partnerships, and scored three hundreds each.

Haberdashers' Aske's Boys' School
P18 W11 L6 D1 A5

Master i/c S. D. Charlwood   **Coaches** D. H. Kerry/D. I. Yeabsley

An inexperienced side endured a torrid start to the season but found their feet after half-term, winning nine of 11 games. Notable victories were registered over Bedford Modern, Bancroft's and a very strong Fraser Bird XI. The captain Tom Colverd and Will Wright shared six hundreds – three each – and six century opening partnerships.

Batting T. G. L. Colverd* 979 at 61.18; W. E. C. Wright 793 at 49.56; J. P. Lawrence 237 at 23.70; R. S. Mandumula 300 at 20.00; I. M. Harris 172 at 19.11; I. D. Patel 164 at 18.22; R. O. Jenkins 204 at 17.00.

Bowling K. A. Osman 26 at 23.80; I. D. Patel 23 at 28.43; W. E. C. Wright 13 at 29.00; C. W. T. Mack 18 at 35.50; J. Purohit 12 at 38.91.

Haileybury
P15 W5 L6 D4

Master i/c H. T. B. Baxendale   **Coaches** M. J. Cawdron/G. P. Howarth

Haileybury often played very good cricket and should perhaps have gained another four wins. Though many will be back in 2014, Ben Spencer, Greg Horwood and Ralph Lane – whose six-hitting was frequent and joyful – will be missed.

Batting H. A. Bexson 383 at 47.87; B. Spencer* 409 at 45.44; R. C. Lane 436 at 33.53; L. T. Dinwoodie 202 at 28.85; J. S. Carter 199 at 28.42; G. N. Horwood 422 at 28.13; J. B. Howe 257 at 19.76; T. Stevens 155 at 17.22; J. R. Stewart 258 at 17.20.

Bowling B. Spencer 23 at 16.30; J. R. Stewart 34 at 19.55; R. C. Lane 17 at 31.70; T. Stevens 13 at 40.07.

Hampton School
P17 W10 L6 D1 A2

Master i/c A. M. Banerjee   **Coach** C. P. Harrison

The season was notable for some excellent victories, many outstanding performances, and Greg King's assured captaincy. Charlie O'Brien batted magnificently throughout to make 863 runs, including four centuries, the highest an undefeated 129 against Dulwich. Elliot Morley, bowling with pace and accuracy, took 26 wickets.

Batting C. H. O'Brien 863 at 61.64; D. J. Campbell 298 at 37.25; G. C. Harper 439 at 33.76; G. T. E. King* 461 at 28.81; R. M. Gardiner 164 at 23.42; D. J. Fryer 229 at 22.90; E. D. Morley 188 at 14.46.
Bowling H. B. Mayes 16 at 13.12; E. D. Morley 26 at 21.26; R. J. Bentley 10 at 33.00; H. W. Comerford 13 at 40.30.

Harrow School
P17 W8 L8 D1
Master i/c S. J. Halliday   **Coach** S. A. Jones
Harrow had mixed fortunes: they lost out in several tight games, but did record good wins against Tonbridge, Radley and MCC. The attack was well led by Arthur Boyd, with strong spin support from Miles Kellock and Max Fosh, while Mikey Cousens, Robbie White and Freddie Ruffell were consistent batsmen.
Batting M. E. Cousens* 534 at 41.07; F. W. A. Ruffell 531 at 40.84; R. G. White 531 at 37.92; A. W. Boyd 339 at 26.07; L. Bose 386 at 25.73; R. S. Wijeratne 173 at 19.22; V. M. Patel 169 at 13.00.
Bowling A. W. Boyd 27 at 21.07; S. J. S. Assani 17 at 22.29; M. G. Kellock 22 at 23.90; M. A. Fosh 22 at 25.68; M. P. Ward 12 at 27.08.

The Harvey Grammar School
P11 W6 L3 D2 A3
Master i/c P. M. Castle   **Coach** M. Green
The school enjoyed more success than for several years; the majority of players will be available for one or two more seasons.
Batting B. R. Goodsell* 278 at 46.33; D. Marsh 241 at 34.42.
Bowling D. Emanuel-Burns 12 at 8.83.

Highgate School
P19 W6 L11 D2
Master i/c A. G. Tapp   **Coach** S. Patel
Highgate enjoyed some pleasing early-season victories, and the summer culminated in a tour to Sri Lanka. Jamie Powe batted purposefully, and Jack Bruce – a Year 9 pupil – showed much promise as an all-rounder.
Batting J. D. Powe* 335 at 25.76; C. T. S. Yorke-Starkey 186 at 23.25; N. Friend 259 at 21.58; J. M. Bruce 213 at 21.30; F. Hunter 224 at 17.23.
Bowling J. M. Bruce 19 at 15.63; N. Friend 26 at 21.46.

Hurstpierpoint College
P15 W10 L5
Master i/c N. J. K. Creed   **Coach** R. S. C. Martin-Jenkins
There were ten wins from 15 in the regular fixtures, and the College finished joint-first at the Woodard Festival. They also lifted the Langdale Twenty20 Cup. Bradley Gayler won the Gordon Grantham award. Tim Moses, Leo Cammish and George Garton all represented Sussex Seconds.
Batting T. H. Moses 226 at 226.00; M. Campopiano 355 at 71.00; B. J. Gayler* 566 at 62.88; L. G. Cammish 302 at 50.33; G. N. Wisdom 464 at 38.66; D. C. Keats 238 at 29.75; J. H. Ludlow 280 at 28.00.
Bowling G. N. Wisdom 16 at 14.18; W. A. Wright 15 at 15.20; D. C. Keats 16 at 16.00; B. D. Cooke 11 at 22.45; G. H. S. Garton 13 at 26.61.

Hymers College
P15 W4 L11 A1
Master i/c M. P. Smethurst
Hymers fared well, considering the inexperience of the squad. Tom Norman, in Year 11, scored 794 runs, including a school-record 177 not out.
Batting T. H. R. Norman 794 at 77.20; H. W. Tyson 451 at 50.11; L. J. Warkup 232 at 25.77; T. B. Jones 261 at 21.75; R. W. Wicks 150 at 12.50.
Bowling L. M. Parker 11 at 22.27; J. A. Nettleton 20 at 24.85; T. H. R. Norman 15 at 31.53.

Ipswich School
P16 W9 L3 D4 A1
Master i/c G. Tipping
The team remained unbeaten after half-term. Skipper Felix Ward was in prime form, scoring 529 runs, including two centuries, and taking 17 wickets. Tom Watson tirelessly led the fast bowlers, claiming 20 wickets – and in the win over St Joseph's he took six for nine.
Batting F. C. R. Ward* 529 at 48.09; R. J. Wilson 320 at 45.71; C. R. Rule 357 at 39.66; J. M. Hodgkinson 403 at 36.63; S. Webb-Snowling 281 at 25.54.

Bowling C. R. Rule 13 at 12.84; F. C. R. Ward 17 at 15.94; T. W. Watson 20 at 17.30; H. W. A. Fiddes 14 at 17.71; O. S. Bocking 11 at 22.72; P. L. Young 18 at 23.05.

The John Fisher School
P18 W7 L10 D1 A1

Master i/c T. L. Vandoros

This was a talented set of individuals who showed belief and ambition. Solid leadership came from Seb Chmielinski and vice-captain Connor Cody. Both had wisdom and experience, and worked hard to keep the team focused.

Batting A. J. Dombrandt 393 at 28.07; C. Cody 268 at 26.80; S. T. D. B. Chmielinski* 219 at 18.25; G. Simpson 181 at 18.10; I. M. Etheridge 175 at 12.50; B. M. Dombrandt 168 at 11.20.

Bowling C. T. Taylor 26 at 12.42; P. Arthur 10 at 14.80; I. M. Etheridge 15 at 18.80; C. Cody 19 at 19.00; A. J. Dombrandt 10 at 26.30.

The John Lyon School
P14 W6 L7 D1 A1

Master i/c A. S. Ling   **Coach** C. T. Peploe

A successful start brought wins in six of the first seven games, including a nailbiting three-run victory against Worth. Scott Wilsher and Seerone Kandasamy prospered with the bat, while Adam Wright took most wickets.

Batting S. M. Wilsher* 227 at 37.83; A. Jamil 209 at 19.00; H. D. Talati 156 at 17.33; T. B. W. Marshall 163 at 16.30.

Bowling S. M. Wilsher 12 at 13.41; A. J. G. Wright 13 at 19.69.

The Judd School
P12 W4 L8

Master i/c D. W. Joseph

Ross Pilkington led well through a period of transition. Encouragingly, the influential Alex Harbourne and Alex Everett, two Year 11 students, are among those who return for 2014.

Batting M. W. Dowding 180 at 22.50; A. D. Harbourne 245 at 22.27; P. A. Everett 159 at 19.87.

Bowling P. A. Everett 12 at 14.66; M. W. Tucker 10 at 16.60; C. S. J. Barkhan 12 at 19.50; N. J. Farr 11 at 21.00.

Kimbolton School
P15 W7 L4 T1 D3

Master i/c M. S. Gilbert   **Coach** W. Kerr-Dineen

This was a solid season for Kimbolton: outstanding fielding gave excellent support to a talented spin quartet led by George Furbank, whose eight for 15 was a record. Charlie Gingell and John Bowers hit maiden hundreds and provided the bulk of the runs.

Batting C. G. Gingell* 478 at 34.14; J. Bowers 453 at 30.20; G. A. Furbank 185 at 15.41.

Bowling G. A. Furbank 26 at 9.80; M. H. Lane 15 at 18.60; J. A. Blindt 14 at 18.78; W. M. J. Tatman 16 at 18.93; C. M. Neeter 17 at 23.47; G. R. J. Napier 11 at 31.27.

King Edward VI School, Southampton
P9 W5 L4 A1

Master i/c M. G. Mixer

Being competitive in most games and reaching a cup final were excellent achievements for a team with just two regular Year 13s. The captain Toby Edwards was supported well by Jack Stanley, while Oscar Birnie and Tom Fay look to have strong futures.

Batting H. E. McGhee 308 at 61.60; J. E. Stanley 353 at 50.42; T. I. Edwards* 296 at 49.33; J. D. Culmer 153 at 25.50.

Bowling T. Fay 19 at 11.21.

King Edward's School, Bath
P14 W4 L8 T1 D1 A1

Master i/c M. H. Hawker   **Coach** G. Brown

A side containing only three Year 13s showed promise for 2014. Highlights were George Simonds's five for 35 in a tied game with Beechen Cliff – which also included 73 from Oscar Travers – and Anthony Dalrymple's chanceless 106 not out against Prior Park.

Batting A. R. Dalrymple 387 at 29.76; J. Smith 266 at 29.55; O. Travers* 314 at 22.42; D. M. Bride 272 at 19.42.

Bowling G. W. Simonds 10 at 24.70; H. G. Taylor 14 at 27.00; K. H. Chapman 11 at 30.16.

King Edward's School, Birmingham

P21 W5 L13 D3 A2

Master i/c L. M. Roll   **Coach** D. Collins

Life was tough for a team who struggled to make enough runs. With all but two boys returning for 2014, there are hopes that harsh lessons will pay dividends.

Batting S. J. Mubarik 340 at 21.25; T. H. Claughton 326 at 19.17; N. O. Porter 306 at 19.12; J. H. Roberts 316 at 17.55; M. T. Galla* 171 at 15.54; S. M. Pabari 194 at 14.92.

Bowling J. H. Roberts 12 at 19.25; S. Rao 23 at 23.34; N. M. H. Kumararatne 17 at 26.76; A. Patel 17 at 27.29; S. J. Mubarik 14 at 29.21.

King's College, Taunton

P16 W16

Master i/c P. D. Lewis   **Coach** R. J. Woodman

King's enjoyed great success, winning all 16 matches during the regular season. The team qualified for the National Twenty20 finals day. Players of the season were Neil Brand, Lawrence May and Rhys Davies.

Batting L. R. May 579 at 64.33; S. J. D. Underdown 395 at 49.37; R. W. Davies 401 at 36.45; M. H. Richards 218 at 36.33; N. Brand 358 at 35.80; R. D. Preston 200 at 28.57.

Bowling N. Brand 38 at 13.92; S. J. G. Venn 19 at 14.57; L. T. Redrup 23 at 16.47; L. R. May 20 at 17.50; C. G. Harrison 16 at 32.18.

King's College School, Wimbledon

P17 W12 L4 D1

Master i/c J. S. Gibson   **Coach** S. G. Davies

A very satisfying season included victories against Dulwich, MCC, St Paul's and Hampton. James Churchman hit 126 not out against St John's Leatherhead, while Ruari Crichard and Alex Hughes both claimed 20 wickets.

Batting J. R. T. Churchman 471 at 58.87; M. C. Clifford* 339 at 42.37; G. M. Thomas 283 at 31.44; J. E. Huxtable 258 at 23.45; H. Goodwin 221 at 22.10.

Bowling M. P. Neat 11 at 13.18; R. J. Crichard 21 at 16.38; M. C. Clifford 11 at 16.90; A. R. Hughes 20 at 17.45; A. Kulukundis 10 at 29.00.

King's School, Bruton

P13 W4 L7 T1 D1

Master i/c B. Dudley

Josh White was the outstanding all-round cricketer in a young and developing side. Lessons learned this summer should bear fruit in years to come.

Batting J. R. C. White 396 at 33.00; E. M. Latham 166 at 23.71; B. W. Pitt-Brown 206 at 17.16; R. A. J. Valentine 152 at 15.20; D. T. Baldwin* 182 at 15.16.

Bowling C. A. V. Plummer 22 at 12.81; D. T. Baldwin 16 at 20.87; J. R. C. White 20 at 22.10.

The King's School, Canterbury

P12 W3 L6 D3 A1

Master i/c R. A. L. Singfield   **Coach** M. A. Ealham

Several of the top five made decent starts, but few scored the big runs needed to challenge opponents. Bowlers Harry Mann and Seb Leggett starred in their final season.

Batting J. H. R. Meddings 304 at 27.63; L. J. Bromfield 177 at 25.28; W. G. J. Baker White 240 at 21.81; B. L. I. Methven 252 at 21.00; J. N. Leggett 164 at 20.50; H. G. Woodward 197 at 17.90.

Bowling S. N. Leggett* 14 at 25.71; H. J. B. Mann 16 at 29.00; J. H. R. Meddings 15 at 31.33; J. M. T. Adams 10 at 34.00.

King's School, Chester

P15 W5 L8 D2 A4

Masters i/c S. Neal/T. R. Hughes   **Coach** N. R. Walker

Off-spinner Jeevan Kurukkal's six for 58 against MCC was the highlight of an indifferent season. Guy Dunbavand made six fifties, while Josh Duckworth and Oliver Moore's medium-pace gained consistent reward. Alastair Andrady's batting promised much for the future.

Batting G. T. Dunbavand 383 at 54.71; A. M. Andrady 186 at 46.50; C. E. P. Evans 216 at 27.00; M. E. R. Williams* 249 at 22.63; H. H. W. Makings 184 at 20.44.

Bowling O. J. Moore 15 at 14.93; J. M. Duckworth 23 at 17.13; J. Kurukkal 23 at 17.30.

The King's School in Macclesfield

P16 W10 L3 D3 A3

Master i/c S. Moores   **Coach** A. Kennedy

Ben Marsden held the batting together in the first half of the season, while consistently good bowling ensured satisfying results. Under-15 leg-spinner Will Hodgson took most wickets; all-rounder Adam Siddall will skipper the side in 2014.

Batting B. J. Marsden* 492 at 44.72; F. J. McCance 316 at 31.60; C. McIlveen 183 at 26.14; W. J. Hodgson 278 at 25.27; A. J. Siddall 290 at 22.30; J. W. Winrow 213 at 21.30.
Bowling W. J. Hodgson 31 at 12.67; A. J. Siddall 21 at 13.38; H. E. C. Holden 14 at 20.64; C. McIlveen 12 at 22.75; B. T. Winrow 13 at 24.07.

King's School, Rochester
P11 W5 L4 D2 A3

Master i/c W. E. Smith
Coach C. H. Page

A young side were intelligently led by Angus Wilson in his third year in the first team. The boys played well all season and enjoyed some success. Jack Baulch was outstanding, and James Carslaw looks a prodigious talent.
Batting D. G. A. Wilson 160 at 40.00; T. F. O'Shea 214 at 23.77; C. T. Medhurst 161 at 17.88; J. A. Baulch 155 at 15.50.
Bowling J. A. Baulch 20 at 14.60; A. J. A. Wilson* 11 at 27.54.

King's School, Tynemouth
P5 W1 L4 A2

Masters i/c W. Ryan/P. J. Nicholson

The school's final season (before merger and conversion to an academy) was anticlimactic, and brought just one win. For the first time we played against MCC, but the cricketing future is uncertain.
Batting A. W. O. Appleby 284 at 94.66.
Bowling No one took ten wickets; the leading bowler was J. W. Brown, who claimed six at 29.83.

King's School, Worcester
P17 W8 L9 A1

Master i/c D. P. Iddon
Coach A. A. D. Gillgrass

A successful tour to Sri Lanka preceded an inconsistent summer. Fifteen-year-old Nick Hammond led the batting, coming within three runs of scoring a second consecutive century against MCC. Ali Hunt, the skipper, and Jack Park proved valuable all-rounders.
Batting N. A. Hammond 874 at 58.26; A. D. J. Hunt* 460 at 32.85; J. G. B. Park 500 at 31.25; W. O. Dovey 304 at 27.63; T. G. Evans 179 at 16.27.
Bowling H. C. Wilde 15 at 17.33; A. D. J. Hunt 25 at 23.12; C. E. Lamb 15 at 24.80; D. J. Lee 14 at 29.07; J. G. B. Park 18 at 29.66; J. L. Salter 12 at 40.00.

Kingswood School, Bath
P15 W10 L4 D1

Master i/c J. O. Brown

A very young team had a rewarding year, winning ten of the 14 completed games. Tim Rouse and Felix Barnard-Weston both scored maiden first-team hundreds; Rouse was Player of the Tournament at the ECB Super Fours festival.
Batting T. D. Rouse 208 at 41.60; H. M. Jones 344 at 34.40; F. P. Barnard-Weston 242 at 24.20; S. J. Morris* 335 at 23.92; M. T. M. Scott 248 at 22.54; O. W. Waters 217 at 15.50.
Bowling K. A. Gibson 16 at 8.75; O. C. Devlin-Cook 19 at 15.84; M. T. M. Scott 15 at 22.33; F. P. Barnard-Weston 11 at 23.00; D. G. J. Mackenzie 15 at 23.40.

Kirkham Grammar School
P8 W2 L2 D4

Master i/c Dr M. A. Whalley
Coach N. S. Passenger

Much of the season was rain-affected, but there were superb performances against Arnold, King Edward's Lytham and MCC. George Brookes captained well, and was ably supported by Oliver Jump and James Seward; both scored centuries.
Batting J. Seward 216 at 36.00; O. Jump 167 at 33.40.
Bowling O. Jump 16 at 8.18.

Lancaster Royal Grammar School
P19 W9 L8 D2 A3

Master i/c I. W. Ledward
Coach I. Perryman

This was a mixed season, and the batting was inconsistent: Joe Atkinson alone came close to 400 runs, though Billy Swarbrick showed promise in the top order. There were notable wins against RGS Worcester and Kent Street High, from Western Australia.
Batting B. S. Swarbrick 293 at 26.63; K. J. Parekh 347 at 24.78; T. R. Williamson 317 at 21.13; J. L. Atkinson 376 at 20.88; T. I. Whitehouse* 303 at 17.82; D. C. Chambers 280 at 16.47; M. J. Rosbottom 151 at 15.10; T. A. Deakin 164 at 12.61.
Bowling T. I. Whitehouse 27 at 18.48; D. I. Chambers 23 at 18.60; M. B. Liver 20 at 20.95; S. A. Letcher 15 at 26.53; T. R. Williamson 14 at 30.78.

Lancing College   P14 W4 L8 D2 A2
Master i/c R. J. Maru

A very young side featuring four Year 10 players won four of their 14 games. Star performers were Mason Crane (29 wickets and a best of five for four) and Nick Ballamy (442 runs and a top score of 135 not out).

Batting N. M. Ballamy 493 at 37.92; W. N. Fazakerley 172 at 28.66; M. S. Crane 343 at 28.58.
Bowling M. S. Crane 29 at 15.24; J. A. I. Allen 18 at 18.61; W. N. Fazakerley 13 at 20.61; N. M. Ballamy 14 at 24.78.

The Grammar School at Leeds   P15 W9 L5 D1 A2
Master i/c S. H. Dunn

Ben Morley led a young side with aplomb on and off the field: the players responded well to his leadership and, despite their inexperience, had a productive summer. Fourteen-year-old Tom Burton took 19 wickets in his debut season and is one for the future.

Batting B. A. Morley* 598 at 85.42; J. Harrison 353 at 44.12; J. E. Haslem 249 at 27.66.
Bowling B. A. Morley 24 at 12.83; T. B. J. Burton 19 at 16.68; E. J. Mason 12 at 18.08; J. E. Haslem 16 at 19.25; C. J. Bridge 13 at 20.53.

Leicester Grammar School   P11 W7 L3 D1
Master i/c L. Potter

This was the most successful season in the school's history. William Hunt and Tom Smith set a school-record opening partnership of 285*. With nine players returning, we look forward to a prosperous 2014.

Batting T. Smith 304 at 43.42; W. O. Hunt 387 at 38.70; R. A. Scudamore 166 at 27.66.
Bowling H. A. Sawers 17 at 15.58; Z. Rizvi* 10 at 21.50; J. D. O'Callaghan 12 at 22.83.

The Leys School   P12 W5 L5 D2 A1
Master i/c R. I. Kaufman   **Coach** R. J. Darkins

The season began with a tour of Sri Lanka, which forged a strong unit who later produced several good performances. Oliver Lawson claimed 20 wickets, and there are some very talented youngsters coming through.

Batting M. A. Mniszko 231 at 38.50; T. A. Wilson 204 at 34.00; J. P. Albery 185 at 26.42; C. J. Tapping 249 at 24.90; W. M. Hales 227 at 20.63; O. H. Lawson* 203 at 16.91.
Bowling T. P. Cox 10 at 14.70; O. H. Lawson 20 at 16.95; T. A. Dunn 14 at 21.21; S. J. Lawson 15 at 22.26; T. A. Wilson 11 at 27.27.

Lord Wandsworth College   P10 W3 L6 D1 A1
Master i/c E. J. Coetzer   **Coach** D. M. Beven

The team enjoyed good wins against Tiffin, St Paul's and The Oratory, but could not prevail in close games with RGS Guildford, Hampton and Reed's. Simon Culmer, only Year 10, missed his maiden century by one run, and the team were shrewdly led by Alex Hammond, who in October captained the England Disability side.

Batting S. H. R. Culmer 230 at 38.33; A. T. S. Hammond* 282 at 35.25.
Bowling W. P. Gee 10 at 22.10; T. L. B. Salmon 12 at 28.08.

Loughborough Grammar School   P17 W10 L6 D1 A1
Master i/c M. I. Gidley

Winning ten out of 17 games constituted a decent return. The side were excellently led by Richard Cartwright. Danny Murty, Eben Kurtz and David Tew all topped 550 runs, while Rishan Chopra took 27 wickets.

Batting D. P. Tew 597 at 49.75; R. P. E. Cartwright* 338 at 48.28; D. Murty 554 at 42.61; E. E. Kurtz 565 at 40.35; R. Chopra 306 at 30.60; W. J. L. Rowell 200 at 18.18.
Bowling R. Chopra 27 at 18.25; S. M. Sharma 14 at 20.21; G. Foster 15 at 29.60.

Magdalen College School, Oxford   P17 W3 L12 T1 D1
Master i/c D. Bebbington   **Coach** P. A. J. DeFreitas

A record of three wins does no justice to the efforts made by this youthful squad, captained with spirit by Chris Nourse. The bowlers often engineered promising positions, but the batsmen struggled to maintain the initiative.

Batting C. J. Nourse* 348 at 26.76; T. R. A. Scriven 227 at 25.22; A. T. Spittles 311 at 20.73; J. T. Earnshaw 284 at 18.93; B. T. Hambidge 253 at 18.07; A. P. Tolson 277 at 17.31.

Bowling A. P. Tolson 21 at 20.42; H. J. H. Stevenson 16 at 21.12; B. T. Hambidge 16 at 23.00; T. R. A. Scriven 16 at 25.87.

Malvern College
P19 W15 L1 D3 A1

Master i/c M. A. Hardinges   **Coach** N. A. Brett

Tom Köhler-Cadmore led with distinction in his final year, steering Malvern to one of their most successful seasons, with 15 wins. Three times Köhler-Cadmore passed 150 as he totalled 1,409 runs at an average of 100 – enough to make him *Wisden* Schools Cricketer of the Year for 2013.

Batting T. Köhler-Cadmore* 1,409 at 100.64; F. P. A. Martin 670 at 74.44; A. G. Milton 776 at 64.66; F. G. F. Wynn 625 at 48.07; B. E. Tegg 163 at 40.75; M. F. Jefferson 202 at 40.40.
Bowling H. T. R. Children 12 at 13.08; F. P. A. Martin 14 at 13.50; F. G. F. Wynn 24 at 14.87; L. J. Smith 19 at 25.52; A. H. Shah 25 at 27.60; O. H. Greensted 15 at 30.73; T. Köhler-Cadmore 10 at 33.10.

The Manchester Grammar School
P17 W11 L4 D2 A2

Master i/c M. J. Chilton

A satisfying season was built around opening partnerships with bat and ball. Ali Qasim and Luke Wolstenholme laid strong foundations at the start of the innings, while the new-ball pair of Alex Gill and Matthew Tully unsettled the opposition with probing line and length.

Batting A. A. Qasim 644 at 58.54; L. R. Wolstenholme 503 at 50.30; J. Dooler 272 at 38.85; J. Hinds 206 at 29.42; M. R. Tully* 265 at 22.08; J. T. Cheetham 279 at 21.46.
Bowling P. M. Makin 11 at 8.90; M. R. Tully 22 at 13.36; R. Vaish 12 at 16.25; A. T. S. Gill 27 at 16.51; J. Hinds 13 at 26.38; E. Y. Dingley 17 at 26.52.

Marlborough College
P13 W5 L7 D1 A2

Master i/c N. E. Briers

Despite an extended injury list, there were emphatic wins against MCC, the Blues, Free Foresters, Winchester and Sherborne; the two-day match with Rugby was drawn. Billy Mead became only the second 14-year-old to play in the side since his uncle Mike Griffith (2013 MCC president) in 1958.

Batting J. C. Sennett* 449 at 37.41; A. J. Turner 311 at 25.91; A. J. Butler 201 at 25.12; A. J. Combe 309 at 23.76; M. J. B. Koe 180 at 22.50; M. G. Cattermull 199 at 22.11; T. N. N. Foot 218 at 21.80.
Bowling M. J. B. Koe 24 at 21.41; T. T. Jones 17 at 23.58; S. W. Mead 10 at 28.40; M. G. Cattermull 18 at 29.22.

Merchant Taylors' School, Crosby
P18 W6 L8 D4

Master i/c S. P. Sutcliffe   **Coach** J. Bell

Results ranged widely, but overall this was a reasonable summer for an inexperienced team. A close draw with MCC, and Nick Knight's unbeaten century in another draw, against Manchester GS, were highlights.

Batting C. A. Bell* 456 at 41.45; M. J. Barton 402 at 28.71; T. S. Sutcliffe 358 at 25.57; J. D. Snaylam 329 at 23.50; N. Knight 259 at 19.92.
Bowling D. Hughes 18 at 19.38; T. S. Sutcliffe 25 at 20.00; M. S. Burridge 16 at 34.75; M. J. Sutcliffe 10 at 38.70.

Merchant Taylors' School, Northwood
P17 W10 L3 D4

Master i/c T. Webley

Ten victories exceeded a young side's expectations, with Ashil Shah recording the highest runs total for 20 years – 658 at nearly 60 – and also heading the bowling averages. Tom Woods was the leading wicket-taker, Armaan Mahmood and Kavir Vedd played some good innings, while Under-15 wicketkeeper-batsman Nikhil Rawal looks a fine prospect.

Batting A. K. Shah* 658 at 59.81; A. Mahmood 263 at 29.22; S. R. B. Gates 174 at 21.75; K. A. Vedd 319 at 21.26; R. S. Wijeratne 256 at 19.69; M. A. Patel 165 at 16.50.
Bowling A. K. Shah 20 at 13.30; K. A. Vedd 10 at 13.60; T. J. Woods 22 at 15.68; S. R. B. Gates 14 at 18.35; M. A. Patel 16 at 19.81; U. A. Khan 15 at 19.86.

Merchiston Castle School
P10 W5 L2 T2 D1 A1

Master i/c S. D. Gilmour

A mixed season brought five wins, two defeats and – extraordinarily – ties in consecutive weeks. Highlights were George Hairs' brisk swing bowling and Tom Sole's blistering 77-ball 110 against Gordonstoun.

Batting T. B. Sole 397 at 44.11; D. D. Balfour 186 at 20.66; H. R. E. Shaw* 153 at 15.30.
Bowling G. P. Hairs 26 at 12.23; H. R. E. Shaw 10 at 24.80.

Mill Hill School
P14 W7 L5 D2

Master i/c I. J. F. Hutchinson
Coach N. R. Hodgson

Another great season saw Benedict Relf play a central role as captain and all-rounder. Retention of the Middlesex Cup was a high point. Thomas Harley led the bowling averages; his brother, William, the batting.

Batting W. G. Harley 429 at 39.00; N. R. Schild 204 at 29.14; B. B. Relf* 370 at 26.42; J. A. Kilbourn 151 at 15.10.
Bowling T. C. M. Harley 28 at 15.17; J. Kilbourn 17 at 21.64; B. B. Relf 15 at 23.06.

Millfield School
P15 W8 L6 D1 A2

Master i/c R. M. Ellison
Coach M. A. Garaway

Results were mixed, although five different players scored hundreds, and Charlie Vickery showed promise as an all-rounder. Success in the Lord's Taverners Under-15 competition inspires optimism for the future.

Batting J. J. Stratton 251 at 50.20; T. M. J. Brock 404 at 44.88; C. B. Vickery 512 at 36.57; G. T. Hankins 265 at 26.50; O. J. Ebsworth-Burland 159 at 26.50; A. J. Easton* 413 at 25.81; W. J. S. Sobczak 314 at 24.15.
Bowling C. P. E. McMorran 15 at 21.73; B. D. Fullard 12 at 23.00; S. D. Weller 14 at 33.71; W. J. S. Sobczak 10 at 34.70.

Monkton Combe School
P17 W4 L11 D2 A1

Master i/c S. P. J. Palmer
Coach M. C. Parfitt

Despite a very slow start, the side made great strides. They were excellently skippered by James Arney, who signed off with an entertaining 107 from 79 balls against Fettes. Only four have left, and three Year 10s made debuts.

Batting J. C. W. Arney* 455 at 35.00; J. C. Jenkins 348 at 29.00; W. D. B. Stoyle 228 at 22.80; D. T. B. Salmon 317 at 22.64; E. D. N. Jameson 163 at 16.30; A. J. Halle 162 at 14.72.
Bowling J. C. Jenkins 18 at 15.66; T. M. G. Wortelhock 20 at 17.10; E. D. N. Jameson 17 at 19.82; G. F. B. Rocke 14 at 22.78; C. T. E. Williams 11 at 28.18; J. C. W. Arney 12 at 31.08.

Monmouth School
P16 W11 L3 D2 A1

Master i/c A. J. Jones
Coach G. I. Burgess

Monmouth had an excellent summer. Jeremy Lawlor batted brilliantly, and scored a magnificent double-hundred against Solihull. He would have threatened his brother Chris's school runs record had he not missed so many games playing for Glamorgan Seconds. Gareth Ansell won the match award against the OMs.

Batting J. L. Lawlor 703 at 100.42; G. D. M. R. Warwick 467 at 46.70; G. A. Ansell 388 at 29.84; J. Aldous-Fountain 294 at 26.72; D. G. Monk 199 at 19.90; T. M. Vickers 217 at 19.72.
Bowling D. G. Monk 24 at 13.45; J. Aldous-Fountain 13 at 16.46; G. O. Weatherall 16 at 19.00; J. L. Lawlor 11 at 19.90; G. D. M. R. Warwick 25 at 20.68.

New Hall School
P12 W6 L5 D1 A1

Master i/c G. D. James
Coach N. Hussain

A young team thoroughly enjoyed their first season together, which included the inaugural MCC fixture. Highlights were victories across all formats, the best of which was a thrilling run-chase against Forest School, in which captain Thomas Styles struck 141 not out.

Batting T. E. A. Styles* 306 at 61.20; G. S. A. Styles 377 at 47.12; M. Jahanfar 192 at 24.00; L. E. Poynter 167 at 23.85.
Bowling H. Munt 16 at 15.62; C. M. Whetstone 15 at 24.00.

Newcastle-under-Lyme School
P12 W6 L5 D1 A2

Master i/c G. M. Breen

Newcastle-under-Lyme's season included six fine victories, culminating in a two-wicket win against MCC – the first for 20 years. Tom Vickers of Year 10 made a remarkable entry into first-team cricket, scoring 55, 8 (run out), 70 and 68 not out in his first four innings.

Batting T. Y. Vickers 201 at 67.00; G. T. P. Mellor* 160 at 26.66; U. Ojha 217 at 21.70.
Bowling U. Ojha 22 at 16.77; G. A. Morley 11 at 19.90; R. J. Bostock 14 at 21.35; G. T. P. Mellor 13 at 22.46.

KCS Wimbledon's James Churchman averaged 58, including an unbeaten century against St John's, Leatherhead. Ben Carr was a "shining example" for Nottingham HS.

Norwich School
P11 W5 L3 D3 A1

Master i/c E. D. Hopkins   **Coach** R. W. Sims

Despite a strong line-up, the batsmen failed to make big individual scores, and Norwich never put the opposition under serious pressure when batting first. Lasith Ranasinghe was the pick of the bowlers, and was unlucky not to have taken more wickets.

Batting M. J. Plater 228 at 45.60; H. L. D. Windridge 295 at 26.81; W. G. Fleming 152 at 25.33; S. S. E. T. Hunt 259 at 23.54; L. W. P. Randle 165 at 16.50.

Bowling L. P. Ranasinghe 14 at 24.50; R. W. Pearson 12 at 25.83.

Nottingham High School
P15 W6 L8 D1 A1

Master i/c M. Baker

A tough season was no surprise for a very young side needing time to bed in to first-team cricket. Ben Carr captained the team most capably, and his batting was a shining example. A few memorable wins and an excellent tour were the main successes in 2013.

Batting B. F. D. Carr* 585 at 53.18; S. S. Kulkarni 332 at 33.20; J. C. McElhone 265 at 26.50; D. R. McCarthy 163 at 23.28; H. D. Llewelyn 210 at 19.09.

Bowling D. R. McCarthy 11 at 22.63; L. J. Dickinson 10 at 24.10; H. Patel 10 at 26.10; J. C. McElhone 10 at 38.50.

Oakham School
P18 W9 L2 D7

Master i/c J. P. Crawley   **Coach** F. C. Hayes

There were fears that batting would not match bowling strength but, as it turned out, runs were less of a problem – the side were never bowled out – than taking wickets. However, the attack eventually found form, and Oakham won the BOWS festival, giving a lift to a pleasing season marked by some fine team and individual performances.

Batting J. Kendall 581 at 52.81; J. E. Crace 382 at 38.20; H. G. Foster* 473 at 36.38; B. K. Lewis 405 at 31.15; C. W. J. Hurley 427 at 30.50; S. G. Williams 177 at 19.66.

Bowling T. J. Juggins 10 at 23.20; H. G. Foster 23 at 24.26; J. Ilott 22 at 26.54; O. J. Elson 17 at 27.23; J. E. Crace 12 at 30.08; C. W. J. Hurley 11 at 32.72.

The Oratory School

P19 W9 L10 A5

Master i/c S. C. B. Tomlinson   **Coach** C. B. Keegan

After a successful tour to Barbados, the team, well guided by Cameron Jacobsen, played some excellent cricket. With the core of the squad returning, not forgetting a healthy crop of colts, 2014 is keenly anticipated.

Batting E. R. Howlett 328 at 20.50; C. E. Jacobsen* 346 at 20.35; A. F. Wilson 268 at 15.76; R. F. Huysinga 184 at 13.14.

Bowling C. Anderson 11 at 12.27; C. E. B. Dunn 11 at 12.72; C. E. Jacobsen 21 at 12.76; C. M. J. Beveridge 17 at 13.17; D. J. Williams 19 at 15.31; A. J. Clifton 12 at 16.00.

Oundle School

P16 W2 L14

Master i/c J. C. Wake   **Coaches** R. Swann/C. J. Wake

Results were disappointing, with only two victories. Nevertheless, Sam Olver, who hit two centuries, was a stoical leader and talented batsman. There was further encouragement in the left-arm spin of Ben Graves, the young captain-elect. He played for MCC Schools against ESCA at Lord's.

Batting S. T. Olver* 416 at 32.00; A. G. Titcomb 242 at 18.61; B. W. M. Graves 265 at 16.56; C. D. F. Field 169 at 14.08; F. P. B. Cundell 162 at 12.46.

Bowling T. Lawes 13 at 20.38; B. W. M. Graves 30 at 20.90; W. C. O. Meredith 14 at 26.14; C. D. F. Field 15 at 38.33.

Pate's Grammar School

P10 W3 L6 D1 A1

Master i/c S. J. Dandy   **Coach** C. Stuart-Smith

Joe Moore, aged 16, proved the most potent bowler, while Mark Morris's 110 not out against Gloucestershire Gipsies was the batting highlight. Festival week, including a draw against MCC and a narrow defeat by Assumption College from Melbourne, was a huge success.

Batting M. D. Morris 306 at 43.71; J. E. Moore 223 at 31.85; H. W. H. Mitchell 173 at 21.62.

Bowling J. E. Moore 17 at 15.17; G. S. Adams 11 at 27.00.

The Perse School, Cambridge

P12 W2 L6 D4

Master i/c D. G. Roots   **Coach** J. C. Read

Alex Jackson was the outstanding player in a season of hard but enjoyable cricket. A young team found some fixtures very challenging, but the experience was invaluable. Results might have been better had rain not twice intervened when the school were in a strong position.

Batting A. T. F. Jackson 422 at 35.16; C. A. Pepper 165 at 27.50; N. P. Taylor 262 at 26.20; P. J. Picton-Turbervill* 236 at 21.45; J. W. L. Howe 199 at 19.90.

Bowling F. J. G. Roebuck 14 at 18.85; C. A. Pepper 12 at 19.58.

Plymouth College

P9 W3 L5 D1 A4

Master i/c J. R. Mears   **Coach** A. Summons

A year of rebuilding – this was a very inexperienced side – culminated in a successful Under-17 development tour to Sri Lanka. The team were thoughtfully led by Callum Cload, though Cornwall Under-15 captain Tom Dinnis skippered later in the season; he seems one for the future.

Batting T. J. Dinnis 307 at 51.16; C. Cload* 163 at 32.60.

Bowling No one took ten wickets; the leading bowler was T. J. Dinnis, who claimed nine at 18.22.

Pocklington School

P17 W7 L9 D1

Master i/c D. Byas

After starting with a terrific game against Ampleforth, form proved elusive until three festival wins – against Stewart's Melville, Strathallan and Hymers – rounded the season off in style. Most runs came from James Hanley, most wickets from Frank Beal.

Batting J. R. Hanley 547 at 42.07; T. Loten 203 at 25.37; T. A. Benthall* 203 at 18.45; S. S. Gopal 236 at 18.15; W. H. Stephenson 238 at 17.00; F. C. H. Beal 219 at 16.84.

Bowling F. C. H. Beal 21 at 22.61; L. J. Hessay 11 at 36.27; T. A. Benthall 10 at 40.70.

Portsmouth Grammar School

P11 W9 L2

Master i/c S. J. Curwood   **Coach** S. Lavery

A strong performance – nine wins from 11 – included a place in the quarter-finals of the National Twenty20 competition. Andy Marston bowled beautifully to take 23 wickets, while Sam Collings-Wells was the leading run-scorer. Many thanks are due to outgoing captain Seth Jackson.

Batting A. Gorvin 343 at 68.60; S. R. Collings-Wells 378 at 63.00; J. R. Marston 343 at 49.00; J. J. Brown 253 at 42.16.
Bowling A. G. Marston 23 at 14.82; R. A. C. Prentice 14 at 17.50; A. Gorvin 11 at 17.54; S. A. Jackson* 10 at 22.50.

Prior Park College   P11 W6 L4 D1 A1
Master i/c S. J. Capon   **Coach** R. D. Staunton
A thoroughly enjoyable summer brought strong individual and group performances against decent opposition. The team were well led by Hamish Pearson; he and Kieran Kelly made fine all-round contributions. Luke Tapsfield and Wilfred Neville are promising batsmen.
Batting J. L. Tapsfield 419 at 41.90; W. W. Neville 262 at 29.11; K. M. Kelly 240 at 21.81; H. Pearson* 172 at 19.11.
Bowling K. M. Kelly 19 at 14.15; H. Pearson 21 at 18.04; J. L. Smith 13 at 18.92; M. J. Mortimer 12 at 19.75; N. G. R. Lees 10 at 20.80.

Queen Elizabeth Grammar School, Wakefield   P12 W5 L7 A1
Master i/c I. A. Wolfenden   **Coach** C. Lawson
Jon Dabbs was an admirable captain of a young side who learned much during the summer. Performances in the field were positive, though discipline and application at the crease perhaps need some improvement.
Batting H. W. Booth 417 at 52.12; T. A. Booth 256 at 32.00; M. J. Brookes 197 at 21.88.
Bowling C. J. Nuttall 18 at 17.50; J. S. Patel 12 at 21.16; D. R. Wills 13 at 23.76.

Queen Elizabeth's Hospital   P10 W6 L4 A1
Master i/c P. E. Joslin   **Coach** D. Forder
For the second year Will Pearce proved an able leader. There were some good Saturday results, and several promising youngsters played a significant part.
Batting A. J. Agar 168 at 24.00; W. M. G. Pearce* 184 at 23.00; G. M. J. Sackett 152 at 19.00.
Bowling A. C. Barnsley 13 at 12.84.

Queen's College, Taunton   P12 W1 L10 D1 A1
Master i/c A. S. Free   **Coach** D. R. Bates
An inexperienced side bowled and fielded with determination and enthusiasm, but struggled to make sufficient runs. Maaz Akhter showed great patience as captain, and was a talented all-rounder. Tor Ziegler-Evans led the attack, gaining control and pace during the summer.
Batting W. P. Macdonagh 211 at 105.50; S. M. Akhter* 242 at 22.00; F. W. G. Spurway 207 at 20.70.
Bowling T. W. Ziegler-Evans 18 at 21.77; S. M. Akhter 11 at 32.81; S. A. Akhter 11 at 37.09.

Radley College   P17 W5 L11 D1
Master i/c J. R. W. Beasley   **Coach** A. R. Wagner
Radley had mixed fortunes on a strong circuit, and often struggled to score enough runs. The captain Freddie Fairhead topped both wicket-taking and run-scoring tables, and he was well supported by a side who never stopped trying.
Batting F. J. B. Fairhead* 589 at 39.26; H. S. Over 393 at 26.20; C. J. E. Hollingworth 398 at 22.11; T. J. A. Swift 300 at 21.42; G. S. Buckley 161 at 16.10; M. L. P. Fawcett 183 at 15.25; M. R. Arkwright 205 at 14.64.
Bowling C. J. E. Hollingworth 18 at 24.50; F. J. B. Fairhead 24 at 24.66; A. M. Oliver 18 at 25.16; M. L. P. Fawcett 13 at 30.38; G. H. M. Bibby 14 at 35.35; C. W. S. Bailey 15 at 37.20.

Ratcliffe College   P12 W5 L2 D5 A2
Master i/c E. O. Woodcock
The gratifying results of the best season for years were largely thanks to excellent batting – especially from Ben Shaw and Dominic Warne – and to good captaincy from Fred Notman.
Batting B. Shaw 484 at 69.14; D. N. Warne 458 at 65.42; S. C. Nightingale 220 at 31.42.
Bowling R. D. Soni 12 at 18.25; F. R. Notman* 14 at 21.28; D. N. Warne 10 at 22.30; S. C. Nightingale 14 at 24.00.

Reading Blue Coat School
P11 W8 L2 D1 A5

Master i/c G. C. Turner   **Coach** P. D. Wise

Strong batting performances, particularly from captain James Halson and Martin Andersson, as well as excellent fielding, provided the backbone of an enjoyable and successful season.

Batting J. J. Halson* 455 at 56.87; M. K. Andersson 391 at 55.85; W. J. Stone 168 at 24.00; J. Pajwani 161 at 20.12.

Bowling O. E. Woodbridge 10 at 12.80; J. Pajwani 16 at 15.43.

Reed's School
P18 W10 L3 D5

Master i/c M. R. Dunn   **Coach** K. T. Medlycott

A young team gained outstanding results. Sonny Cott hit a record 980 runs, and was assisted by Matthew Macpherson, Philip Salt, Sebastian Stewart-Taylor and Oskar Kolk. Kieran Corbett led the attack, and Daniel Douthwaite bowled with pace.

Batting S. Cott 980 at 70.00; M. A. Macpherson* 449 at 64.14; S. S. Stewart-Taylor 492 at 37.84; P. D. Salt 493 at 32.86; O. M. D. Kolk 334 at 27.83; D. Douthwaite 197 at 24.62.

Bowling K. M. Corbett 38 at 14.13; S. Hobson 16 at 25.31; O. M. D. Kolk 12 at 26.83; D. Douthwaite 20 at 28.05; B. M. Sandwith 16 at 30.50; N. H. Spreeth 13 at 31.15; H. J. Thorpe 14 at 31.57.

Reigate Grammar School
P15 W8 L7

Master i/c P. R. Mann   **Coach** J. E. Benjamin

Reigate's developing team took a huge step forward, prompted by Thomas Massey, who captained the team with imagination and respect. All return for another season.

Batting D. M. P. Drage 360 at 40.00; L. H. S. Haughton 356 at 35.60; T. M. O. Massey* 340 at 34.00; M. R. Ellis 193 at 19.30.

Bowling D. M. P. Drage 20 at 16.65; M. D. N. Norman 14 at 22.35; M. R. Ellis 15 at 26.40; L. H. S. Haughton 11 at 26.63.

Repton School
P18 W15 L1 D2

Master i/c I. M. Pollock   **Coaches** H. B. Dytham/J. A. Afford

Repton enjoyed a magnificent season, winning more games than ever before. The performances of all-rounder and captain Nitish Kumar were vital, but the entire bowling unit deserved praise: only three times did they concede 200 runs.

Batting N. R. Kumar* 909 at 60.60; J. W. Gough 248 at 49.60; M. J. I. Goodacre 541 at 38.64; S. P. Cotter 304 at 27.00; J. A. Wilkins 304 at 23.38.

Bowling N. R. Kumar 34 at 13.79; S. P. Cotter 24 at 17.79; L. P. Cosford 10 at 19.60; C. B. Bee 20 at 20.25; P. Blair 10 at 26.50; H. J. White 20 at 26.70; J. A. Wilkins 14 at 28.85.

Rossall School
P10 W7 L3

Master i/c N. P. James

The highlight of a successful term was the crushing defeat of Stonyhurst, who were bowled out for 22 in pursuit of 193. Luke Williams, captain and outstanding all-rounder, had figures of 6–3–9–7.

Batting L. C. Williams* 357 at 39.66; T. Morrison 287 at 35.87; J. Morrison 231 at 28.87; H. Southern 187 at 26.71; F. J. Forster 169 at 18.77.

Bowling L. C. Williams 23 at 8.13; D. T. Robson 17 at 12.58; C. P. Andrews 10 at 24.30.

Royal Grammar School, Guildford
P17 W11 L5 D1

Master i/c C. J. L. Sandbach

Winning the 50/40 South London Schools league was a huge achievement. Charlie Warren managed the side capably and hit most runs; Jonathan French and Alex Sweet provided good support. The mainstays of the attack were Alex Waghorn, Rob Clayden and Sam Jelley.

Batting C. F. Warren* 634 at 48.76; A. R. I. Sweet 331 at 41.37; J. R. G. French 445 at 31.78; M. E. Budd 261 at 29.00; L. R. Jones 252 at 28.00; A. C. Waghorn 248 at 17.71.

Bowling A. C. Waghorn 26 at 19.69; R. J. Clayden 20 at 21.25; S. J. Jelley 19 at 26.89; J. R. G. French 18 at 28.88.

The Royal Grammar School, Worcester
P24 W16 L8

Master i/c M. D. Wilkinson   **Coach** P. J. Newport

As batsman and captain, Dan Goodyear led the side superbly. The pace attack of Huw Selvey and Will Bury gained support from young spinners Elliott Bartlett and Suleyman Shah. Wins over MCC, RGS Guildford and RGS High Wycombe were the highlights of a season that also brought three wins over King's Worcester.

Batting D. B. Goodyear* 844 at 42.20; C. E. J. Lawton 667 at 41.68; J. D. G. Taylor 586 at 29.30; E. A. Bartlett 352 at 19.55; S. Shah 202 at 16.83; J. M. Watts 336 at 16.80; C. D. Tonks 154 at 14.00.
Bowling H. M. Selvey 36 at 14.19; S. Shah 32 at 17.21; E. A. Bartlett 30 at 21.43; J. D. G. Taylor 28 at 21.78; W. J. E. Bury 30 at 22.13.

Royal Hospital School
P11 W5 L5 D1 A1

Master i/c T. D. Topley   **Coach** D. W. Hawkley

Under skipper Ben Allday the team made significant strides and played with resilience. When injury struck, Ben Moore was a fine deputy. Matt Rudston bowled with pace and added important runs. Brendon Tait claimed most wickets, with strong support from keeper Drew Felstead.
Batting M. J. Rudston 266 at 29.50; B. N. Allday* 167 at 27.80; J. E. Allday 270 at 24.50.
Bowling B. Tait 16 at 18.60; B. A. Moore 14 at 21.50; M. J. Rudston 12 at 28.10.

Rugby School
P19 W11 L3 D5

Master i/c M. J. Semmence   **Coach** T. W. Roberts

An excellent summer contained emphatic victories against Oundle, Stowe, Uppingham and MCC. Paul Clarke led a happy and well-balanced team who habitually bowled sides out cheaply. Between them, Jacob Gilder, Matthew Karslake and Bertie Bennett-Jones shared 97 wickets.
Batting J. D. Gilder 594 at 45.69; C. R. D. Goodfellow 567 at 43.61; R. J. Povey 540 at 38.57; P. G. Clarke* 404 at 36.72; W. J. Briggs 408 at 29.14.
Bowling M. W. Karslake 33 at 14.09; P. G. Clarke 22 at 15.50; J. H. Woodhead 14 at 16.14; A. G. Bennett-Jones 29 at 17.10; J. D. Gilder 35 at 18.31; R. J. Povey 11 at 34.45.

Rydal Penrhos
P9 W3 L4 D2

Master i/c M. T. Leach

Captained well by Andrew Welden, the side played some solid cricket. Sean Kitchen and Joe Maguire – who return in 2014 – offered fine support, and some talented players are coming through.
Batting S. T. Kitchen 291 at 48.50; A. M. Welden* 287 at 41.00.
Bowling J. P. Maguire 15 at 20.00; A. M. Welden 12 at 26.33.

Ryde School with Upper Chine
P8 W2 L5 D1 A3

Master i/c M-A. Eysele

Exams and other commitments made selection tricky, but some good individual performances from the bowlers in particular made the team competitive. Left-arm seamer Tom Groves had a fantastic season, and Josh Robinson coped well with his move to the top of the order. The captain, Julion Jayerajah, showed great professionalism and determination.
Batting J. D. Procter 219 at 27.37; J. C. Robinson 214 at 26.75.
Bowling T. A. Groves 17 at 9.82; M. L. Walter 12 at 13.50; J. Jayerajah* 12 at 19.00.

St Albans School
P10 W6 L3 D1 A1

Master i/c C. C. Hudson   **Coach** M. C. Ilott

George Scott scored more than a third of the team's runs, taking his aggregate to a record 2,929. The school played as many Twenty20 contests as traditional matches.
Batting G. Scott* 418 at 52.25; J. E. Killen 151 at 25.16; P. Scott 158 at 19.75; J. Barber 165 at 18.33.
Bowling P. Scott 12 at 10.58; G. Scott 22 at 13.27; G. A. Taylor 15 at 15.86.

St Benedict's School, Ealing
P21 W10 L9 T1 D1

Master i/c J. P. Thisanayagam

A side built on youth showed considerable promise, but never quite hit the heights of 2012. David Howe's left-arm spin earned 35 wickets; he was supported by all-rounder Nabel Shaikh and batsmen Louie Millman and Harry Britt, the skipper.
Batting L. J. Millman 494 at 27.44; H. Britt* 523 at 26.15; N. J. Shaikh 469 at 24.68; M. G. Cassidy 206 at 12.11; D. F. L. Howe 166 at 11.06.
Bowling D. F. L. Howe 35 at 12.60; G. D. Johnson 10 at 15.70; N. J. Shaikh 21 at 21.61; R. J. Oubridge 12 at 22.25; B. D. P. Chippendale 20 at 22.60; G. P. Atkins 16 at 27.50.

Will Jacks, of St George's, Weybridge: he hit 60 sixes and 121 fours, in all formats. Miles Hammond, from St Edward's, Oxford, made his first-class debut for Gloucestershire.

St Edmund's School, Canterbury
P8 W3 L5 A2

Master i/c A. R. Jones   **Coach** S. Buckingham

Reliance on a dominant player put the team under pressure, yet Tom Phillis coped with the responsibility. His form was outstanding, and he is certainly a player to watch.

Batting T. J. W. Phillis 485 at 97.00.

Bowling T. J. W. Phillis 11 at 17.27; Y. K. Kim 10 at 22.30.

St Edward's School, Oxford
P20 W16 L1 D3 A2

Master i/c S. J. O. Roche   **Coaches** R. W. J. Howitt/R. C. Hooton

Ruairi Willis captained St Edward's to a record 16 wins – a fine season. Feroz Baig's 45 wickets were crucial to the team's success, as were Joe Barrett's 764 runs, and all-round contributions from Freddie Simon and Calvin Dickinson. Highlights included winning the John Harvey Cup, and Miles Hammond's first-class debut for Gloucestershire.

Batting C. M. Dickinson 538 at 48.90; M. A. H. Hammond 562 at 46.83; J. H. Barrett 764 at 40.21; H. J. Kennedy 295 at 32.77; F. P. A. Simon 197 at 24.62; R. C. H. Everett 318 at 21.20; F. Baig 379 at 19.94; R. T. L. Willis* 223 at 14.86; O. C. Oakley 153 at 10.92.

Bowling J. M. Morland 17 at 12.41; F. Baig 45 at 14.37; M. A. H. Hammond 24 at 14.62; A. S. Hargreaves 19 at 17.42; F. P. A. Simon 19 at 19.15; R. T. L. Willis 21 at 21.76; J. H. Barrett 11 at 25.45.

St George's, Weybridge
P15 W10 L5 A1

Master i/c M. T. Harrison   **Coach** W. A. Adkin

Only once in 50 years had St George's matched these results; great teamwork achieved nine wins in the last ten matches. Torsten Wrigley hit most runs and topped the bowling averages. Will Jacks, an Under-14, set a college record for one season: in all age-groups and formats he scored 1,076 runs from 684 balls. He struck 60 sixes and 121 fours, and rattled up three hundreds and one double.

Batting J. D. Hart 341 at 56.83; W. G. Jacks 235 at 47.00; T. H. Wrigley* 468 at 39.00; J. G. Dominy 223 at 24.77; F. H. Annandale 319 at 22.78; T. C. Rowland 245 at 20.41.

Bowling T. H. Wrigley 15 at 18.26; A. C. Hackett 20 at 19.60; J. A. Smith 19 at 22.94; W. F. C. Shellard 10 at 24.80.

St John's School, Leatherhead
P10 W4 L5 D1

Master i/c J. M. A. Ashton   **Coach** I. S. Trott

A young side performed well on a competitive circuit. Adrian van der Ploeg and Keiran Hanratty batted responsibly, while bowlers Dimil Patel and Will Mead showed promise.

Batting A. L. van der Ploeg 258 at 64.50; K. J. Hanratty 370 at 52.85; Dhiraj Patel 263 at 37.57; J. J. Stainer 219 at 31.28.

Bowling Dimil Patel 14 at 20.71; W. J. Mead 10 at 28.50; H. Strudwick 10 at 32.40.

St Joseph's College, Ipswich
P16 W8 L7 T1 A2

Master i/c R. Jones   **Coach** M. W. Patterson

Very good performances on the Saturday circuit bolstered a mixed season. The bowlers fared well, though losing wickets in clusters hampered the batting. Hugo Douglas bowled well with the new ball and at the death, while George Isherwood's 128 and five wickets against Framlingham was the first time this double has been achieved in over a decade.

Batting H. A. Douglas 275 at 30.55; G. T. Isherwood 311 at 28.27; E. C. Waddleton 219 at 27.37; R. D. Clark* 199 at 16.58; A. Wilkinson 162 at 16.20; L. R. Brame 156 at 15.60; A. Sayer 165 at 15.00.

Bowling H. A. Douglas 20 at 10.90; G. T. Isherwood 11 at 17.36; A. Kingdon 19 at 18.05; A. Sayer 11 at 23.63; J. De Cosimo 12 at 25.58.

St Lawrence College
P9 W5 L2 D2 A2

Master i/c S. C. Simmons   **Coach** T. Moulton

Big partnerships at the top of the innings from Tim Collins, who hit two centuries, and Ross Keeley made this the most successful season for several years. There was depth in the bowling, and some promising performances by youngsters inspire optimism.

Batting T. J. A. Collins* 468 at 93.60; R. A. Keeley 289 at 48.16.

Bowling S. P. Kenny 11 at 12.09; T. J. A. Collins 14 at 13.42.

St Paul's School
P15 W6 L9 A2

Master i/c W. T. D. Hanson

This was an inexperienced but talented team. The number of victories might have been very different: six fixtures were lost by fewer than 15 runs. Oscar Dewhurst and Tom Powe were the outstanding players.

Batting A. C. H. Dewhurst 415 at 41.50; T. B. Powe 419 at 29.92; S. R. G. Howard 282 at 23.50; M. S. Madhvani 224 at 22.40; T. B. Edmonds* 287 at 17.93; A. C. A. Foster 174 at 17.40; A. J. Meyer 187 at 15.58.

Bowling W. S. Bell 15 at 16.66; T. B. Powe 28 at 18.17; O. R. B. Dewhurst 26 at 20.76; M. J. Lever 12 at 23.08; G. R. T. Essex 12 at 36.25.

St Peter's School, York
P14 W9 L4 D1 A1

Master i/c G. J. Sharp   **Coach** D. A. Woods

The school reached the National Twenty20 North final against Bolton, and were excellently directed by William Booth: his calm confidence reverberated through the team. The boys played with enthusiasm and thoroughly deserved their successes.

Batting S. A. McCullagh 482 at 68.85; C. R. Elliot 576 at 44.30; W. A. Booth* 547 at 42.07; F. J. Adams 340 at 24.28; N. A. Stephen 289 at 19.26.

Bowling H. A. Stothard 12 at 15.58; J. E. A. Eleanor 23 at 20.21; C. R. Elliot 17 at 22.29; F. J. Adams 20 at 24.85; C. J. Burn 14 at 26.92; C. J. Brown 10 at 33.10.

Sedbergh School
P14 W8 L2 D4 A4

Master i/c C. P. Mahon   **Coach** M. P. Speight

With the weather preventing a result in seven games, this was another frustrating season. But a talented side played some exciting cricket, securing excellent victories against Shrewsbury, Bolton and a strong Durham CCC Academy side. Charlie Parker led by example and produced some magnificent all-round performances.

Batting C. R. Parker* 473 at 59.12; D. J. Gomersall 440 at 44.00; J. H. Jessop 437 at 43.70; G. A. M. Francis 249 at 35.57; M. D. Lloyd 158 at 31.60; O. B. Field 177 at 19.66.

Bowling C. R. Parker 26 at 14.69; S. R. Croft 23 at 14.69; T. W. Carlyle 19 at 17.10; A. J. Moon 11 at 27.18.

Sevenoaks School
P16 W7 L9

Master i/c C. J. Tavaré   **Coach** P. J. Hulston/J. C. Emmitt

Although no batsman made a fifty, the team showed resilience and character. We were without our most successful bowler from last season, Tash Farrant, who was called up by England.

Batting L. A. F. Ashe-Jepson 177 at 22.12; J. H. McQuin 285 at 20.35; N. M. Makepeace* 153 at 19.12; R. R. C. Boulter 162 at 14.72.

Bowling J. H. McQuin 17 at 11.94; J. A. Richardson 19 at 12.52; R. W. J. Harris 16 at 17.50; K. G. Davey 15 at 18.73.

Sherborne School
P13 W4 L8 D1

Master i/c T. O. Flowers   **Coach** A. Willows

The season started well, with David Buck smashing 170 and 158 in the first fortnight. However, senior players struggled with injuries, making it hard to achieve consistency. Promising youngsters include Greg Willows and Conrad Fish.

Batting D. S. Buck 442 at 73.66; E. C. Coulsen 333 at 30.27; O. R. T. Sale 259 at 28.77; O. Calcott 281 at 17.56.

Bowling C. Smith 13 at 14.30; B. Weatherhead 14 at 23.21; J. Vitali 16 at 23.87; H. G. C. Barron* 19 at 24.15; F. S. Cave 21 at 25.90.

Shiplake College
P20 W9 L9 D2

Master i/c J. H. Howorth   **Coaches** C. Ellison/A. T. Kersey

A first team with several Year 13 leavers had an enjoyable summer. Skipper Zac Jones batted consistently, and the wickets were shared around, with opener Toby Stevens the pick of the seamers. Fifteen-year-old Harry Ibbitson showed great promise, taking 23 wickets and topping the averages.

Batting Z. D. A. Jones* 646 at 38.00; J. H. Riley 222 at 22.20; T. F. Stevens 238 at 18.30; H. A. S. Ibbitson 206 at 17.16; J. C. Westbrook 254 at 15.87.

Bowling H. A. S. Ibbitson 23 at 14.04; H. N. Wallace 15 at 15.86; T. F. Stevens 25 at 17.56; Z. D. A. Jones 26 at 18.07; O. Maclaurin 16 at 25.93.

Shrewsbury School
P20 W12 L4 D4 A1

Master i/c A. S. Barnard   **Coach** A. P. Pridgeon

Despite losing England Under-19 all-rounder Ed Barnard at half-term through injury, Shrewsbury finished the season strongly by winning the Silk Trophy. They also won the National Twenty20 competition and qualified for the National Under-17 final.

Batting E. J. Pollock 622 at 62.20; E. G. Barnard* 263 at 43.83; J. D. Carrasco 524 at 37.42; G. P. G. Lewis 372 at 28.61; W. G. Cook 249 at 22.63.

Bowling E. G. Barnard 18 at 10.05; C. M. G. White 11 at 13.45; E. J. Pollock 13 at 14.00; M. A. Gregson 18 at 14.88; C. M. J. Kidson 13 at 20.00; H. C. Blofield 12 at 27.58; W. G. Cook 11 at 27.81; C. E. Farquhar 12 at 31.91.

Silcoates School
P11 W9 L2

Master i/c G. M. Roberts   **Coach** J. F. C. Leathley

A rewarding campaign started with an excellent tour to Dubai and finished with a victorious festival at King's Tynemouth. Confident and mature batting from Harvey Jones, Joe Seddon and the captain Charlie Mitchell, selected for Yorkshire Under-19s, provided the backbone for success.

Batting C. H. Mitchell* 647 at 49.76; J. W. H. Seddon 478 at 39.83; W. H. Jones 390 at 35.45.

Bowling M. I. Khan 19 at 18.47; K. P. Hogan 15 at 20.46; C. Hyde 11 at 30.36; L. Hyde 13 at 33.07.

Simon Langton Grammar School
P8 W4 L3 D1 A2

Master i/c R. H. Green

A surprisingly full season with a relatively settled side delivered some competitive cricket. The grand finale was a win against the Old Langtonians – a feat not achieved for many years. Jordan Loft excelled with bat and ball.

Batting J. A. Loft 182 at 36.40; T. G. Guest 162 at 32.40.

Bowling J. A. Loft 12 at 9.91; B. J. Carter 11 at 14.54; B. Rogers 10 at 17.10.

Solihull School
P19 W7 L9 D3 A4

Master i/c D. L. Hemp

A largely disappointing season finished with some entertaining cricket. Darryl Brotherhood shrewdly guided the team in his second year as captain. Jamie Hughes and Oliver Haley batted consistently.

Batting O. J. Haley 591 at 59.10; J. Hughes 610 at 40.66; D. Brotherhood* 380 at 34.54; N. W. Starkey 195 at 27.85; L. T. Turpie 203 at 25.37; J. W. B. Allen 165 at 20.62.

Bowling D. Brotherhood 19 at 27.26; O. J. Haley 14 at 29.42; D. J. Wigley 10 at 33.60; J. Hughes 12 at 37.50.

Stamford School
P13 W8 L2 D3 A2

Master i/c D. N. Jackson   **Coach** D. W. Headley

This was a fine season for a maturing side ably skippered by all-rounder Charlie Page-Morris. Ben Groom hit back-to-back centuries, and the 2014 captain Henry Charlton twice took a five-wicket haul to seal victories.

Batting T. H. Charlton 294 at 49.00; B. E. Groom 374 at 41.55; Z. J. Chappell 363 at 40.33; C. Page-Morris* 289 at 36.12; P. J. Foster 167 at 33.40; J. A. Richardson 198 at 22.00.

Bowling T. H. Charlton 19 at 17.31; C. Page-Morris 22 at 20.18.

Stewart's Melville College
P16 W13 L2 D1 A2

Master i/c A. Ranson

Highlights of a rewarding summer included Scott Docherty's 98-ball 135 against MCC, and the selection of Michael Miller, Cameron Sloman and Matthew Angelini for Scotland Under-18s.

Batting S. Docherty 395 at 43.88; M. Miller 536 at 38.28; M. Angelini 410 at 37.27; R. Turnbull 282 at 31.33; C. Sloman 166 at 23.71.

Bowling C. Sloman 23 at 12.21; M. Miller 15 at 12.86; M. Hancock 19 at 13.10; B. Scott 13 at 14.69; S. Docherty 19 at 16.15; B. McGlinchey 10 at 21.70; J. Pennell 15 at 26.60.

Stonyhurst College
P5 W2 L2 D1 A5

Master i/c G. Thomas

Disappointing weather again curtailed the number of completed fixtures. The bowlers performed well at times, and the fielding was enthusiastic, though the only real batting success was Josh Katz, who top-scored in every game and hit the only half-century.

Batting J. G. Katz 179 at 44.75.

Bowling C. J. K. Till 11 at 10.27.

Stowe School
P17 W11 L3 D3 A2

Master i/c J. A. Knott   **Coach** P. R. Arnold

The most memorable moments were beating Eton – the last such fixture had been 50 years ago – and a record Twenty20 score of 302 for one, against The Oratory. Ben Duckett captained England Under-19, signed a contract with Northamptonshire, and made his first-class debut. Henry Woodward had a fine all-round season and played for the Northamptonshire Academy, along with Russell White. Jack Keeping and Tom Young look fine prospects.

Batting B. M. Duckett* 700 at 70.00; J. A. Olley 558 at 39.85; R. D. R. White 413 at 29.50; G. L. Jackman 336 at 22.40; H. W. H. Woodward 295 at 21.07; H. A. A. Dixon-Smith 168 at 16.80.

Bowling H. W. H. Woodward 32 at 11.75; T. E. Young 14 at 12.42; J. B. R. Keeping 30 at 13.20; R. D. R. White 20 at 15.65.

Strathallan School
P14 W7 L4 D3 A1

Master i/c G. S. R. Robertson   **Coach** I. L. Philip

Sam Culham and fellow opener Max Wallner both passed 400 runs, providing the basis for several fine wins. Victory over MCC was the pinnacle of the season, with opening bowler Jamie Ritchie taking six for 42. All but two players return for 2014.

Batting S. D. Culham 486 at 37.38; M. J. Wallner 427 at 30.50; C. F. Mearns 173 at 28.83; J. S. Waller 345 at 24.64; D. T. Adams 169 at 21.12; G. R. T. Doig* 209 at 20.90.

Bowling J. T. Ritchie 16 at 12.50; M. J. Wallner 11 at 21.00; C. G. Robertson 10 at 27.30; K. McAlister 10 at 34.40.

Sutton Valence School

P14 W3 L7 D4 A1

Master i/c V. J. Wells

Despite the efforts of Rob Sehmi and Will Cook, the main problem was a lack of runs. The Dooley twins, Adam and Robin, were the pick of the bowlers. With seven boys leaving, 2014 will be a period of rebuilding.

Batting R. T. Sehmi 485 at 48.50; W. P. Cook 354 at 29.50; L. J. Burnham 201 at 20.10; A. J. Newport 251 at 19.30; H. J. Wells* 150 at 13.63.

Bowling A. J. Dooley 18 at 20.77; R. E. Dooley 15 at 24.40; G. H. P. Poland 11 at 27.72.

Taunton School

P14 W6 L8

Master i/c D. Jessep

An enjoyable summer brought some impressive results against strong opposition. A youthful team made clear progress, and there were several excellent individual performances. With the majority of the team staying on, prospects are positive.

Batting M. P. Kelly 387 at 38.70; H. J. Gater 352 at 35.20; G. P. Hallas* 370 at 28.46; M. R. Pearce 289 at 26.27; W. R. Abell 223 at 22.30.

Bowling C. A. Smith 13 at 20.30; H. J. Gater 12 at 23.41; W. R. Abell 10 at 35.60; M. P. Kelly 10 at 38.70.

Tiffin School

P22 W9 L12 D1

Master i/c M. J. Williams

The youngest side ever to represent the school played some outstanding cricket. Vinay Samtani hit two centuries just a couple of weeks after his 15th birthday. Another 15-year-old, Bashir Bhatti, claimed an impressive 45 wickets with his left-arm spin.

Batting V. K. Samtani 465 at 35.76; S. P. Krishnan 370 at 26.42; A. Hutcheson 414 at 23.00; C. J. Fulton 329 at 20.56; A. K. Rana 284 at 20.28; P. G. Chamberlain 210 at 17.50; J. B. Graham 202 at 16.83; J. B. Baugh 211 at 16.23.

Bowling B. A. Bhatti 45 at 14.75; A. J. Watkins 36 at 16.36; J. B. Baugh 25 at 23.04; P. K. Patel* 24 at 28.45.

Tonbridge School

P21 W14 L4 D3 A1

Master i/c A. R. Whittall   **Coach** I. Baldock

Another highly rewarding season saw the school win all their matches in the home festival – including a nine-wicket victory against Millfield. Tonbridge reached the South-East final of the National Twenty20 competition, and they also beat Eton, winners of the Cowdrey Cup. The captaincy of Richard O'Grady, who hit 1,001 runs and took 25 wickets, was outstanding. The leading wicket-taker was Nick Winder.

Batting R. J. O'Grady* 1,001 at 58.88; J. J. C. Smallwood 778 at 45.76; M. J. Withers 178 at 44.50; M. O'Riordan 524 at 40.30; A. H. Ward 256 at 36.57; Z. Crawley 511 at 31.93; H. J. FitzGerald 178 at 22.25; D. J. V. Barnes 236 at 15.73.

Bowling H. T. B. Cope 23 at 17.34; N. J. Winder 32 at 19.09; R. J. O'Grady 25 at 20.08; H. J. FitzGerald 25 at 20.12; M. O'Riordan 10 at 31.10; J. E. Monkhouse 14 at 33.00; A. W. Hume 17 at 34.29.

Trent College

P14 W9 L3 D2 A2

Master i/c S. A. J. Boswell   **Coach** D. Hartley

A young team containing three Year 9s and two Year 10s were well led by Ross Carnelley. Three players passed 450 runs, while vice-captain and leading wicket-taker James Fisher seized five for 11 against Loughborough GS.

Batting C. R. Marshall 286 at 47.66; B. T. Trembling 490 at 32.66; R. T. Carnelley* 498 at 31.12; T. J. Hill 472 at 29.50.

Bowling R. T. Carnelley 21 at 17.23; C. P. Proctor 13 at 17.46; C. R. Marshall 11 at 20.54; M. O. Brown 23 at 23.00; J. M. A. Fisher 22 at 24.09; J. P. North 12 at 37.41.

Truro School

P13 W3 L7 T1 D2

Master i/c A. D. Lawrence

In a mixed season there were notable individual performances from several young players, which augurs well. Junior boys and girls achieved county honours.

Batting C. J. P. Conchie 317 at 26.41; R. P. Jelbert* 262 at 26.20.

Bowling J. R. Turpin 19 at 11.89; J. Vanstone 11 at 26.81.

University College School
P9 W3 L6 A1
Master i/c L. J. Greany   **Coach** A. J. Wilkes
After several tight games early in the spring did not go their way, UCS finished on a winning streak. Some excellent bowling and fielding performances brought rewards, notably the two-wicket victory over MCC.
Batting A. Patel 194 at 24.25; J. Bridgland 168 at 21.00.
Bowling J. Badawi-Crook 10 at 11.00; J. Bridgland 10 at 13.10; B. Powell 10 at 13.90.

Uppingham School
P14 W4 L7 D3
Master i/c Q. H. Sayed   **Coaches** T. R. Ward/T. Makhzangi
The batting started to click in the final third of the season – too late to tilt the win-loss ratio in our favour. Otto Esse's off-spin was unplayable at times, and against Oundle he took eight for 19, the best figures in the school's 150-year history. He played for MCC Schools at Lord's.
Batting S. C. R. Snoxall 285 at 31.66; L. S. W. Blakey 251 at 25.10; O. T. H. Esse 241 at 24.10; H. E. J. Preston 232 at 23.20; L. R. Frankel 219 at 19.90.
Bowling O. T. H. Esse 20 at 18.45; C. A. A. Hunter-Jones 11 at 18.54; R. H. M. Clark 14 at 21.21; D. Patel 12 at 27.50; E. J. Prior 11 at 40.00.

Victoria College, Jersey
P15 W11 L3 D1
Master i/c M. D. Smith   **Coach** C. E. Minty
Victoria produced some pleasing performances, especially when they won the Castle Festival at Dean Close. The captain Luke Gallichan hit two good hundreds, and 15-year-old Jonty Jenner made a magnificent 105 not out against Elizabeth College. James Duckett led the bowling with 24 wickets.
Batting L. E. W. Gallichan* 465 at 66.42; D. G. Blampied 321 at 45.85; J. W. Jenner 359 at 44.87; S. Le Maistre 325 at 40.62; E. C. Corbel 242 at 26.88; J. N. Duckett 171 at 24.42; T. E. W. Sutton 222 at 22.20.
Bowling J. N. Duckett 24 at 16.91; W. P. Harris 13 at 18.69; J. F. Ingle 21 at 21.76; L. E. W. Gallichan 11 at 23.54.

Warwick School
P16 W9 L5 D2 A3
Master i/c S. R. G. Francis   **Coach** N. M. K. Smith
The summer contained many moments to savour, among them a historic defeat of Oakham, bowling KES Birmingham out for 34, and several nailbiting victories, including one against MCC. Six players completed three years of service. Once again, Harry Philpot and Tom Pigott were the pre-eminent batsmen.
Batting H. J. Philpot* 639 at 45.64; T. R. Pigott 512 at 42.66; J. Hickman 182 at 36.40; E. L. Pettifer 203 at 33.83; T. J. M. Glanfield 242 at 30.25; J. E. Salmon 446 at 27.87; N. J. Couzens 338 at 26.00; A. Gothoskar 207 at 18.81.
Bowling J. E. Salmon 14 at 25.00; J. R. Jones 17 at 32.23; J. Hickman 13 at 38.07; N. J. Couzens 13 at 45.15.

Watford Grammar School
P10 W5 L3 D2
Master i/c J. P. Shafe   **Coach** A. Needham
Simon Walker hit a century in the opening fixture, against Merchant Taylors', though Matthew Rose was the most consistent batsman, making five half-centuries in eight innings. The bowling lacked penetration – and sometimes luck – leaving the skipper William Gage alone in reaching 15 wickets.
Batting M. C. Rose 420 at 70.00; D. Solanki 201 at 40.20; S. M. Walker 238 at 26.44; M. J. Burgess 188 at 20.88.
Bowling A. J. Ball 10 at 14.60; W. R. Gage* 15 at 20.26; S. M. Walker 12 at 21.16.

Wellingborough School
P14 W9 T2 D3
Master i/c G. E. Houghton   **Coach** M. B. Loye
An unbeaten campaign made it one of the best in Wellingborough's history. Fine leadership from Charlie Macdonell, who topped batting and bowling tables, saw the school dismiss five sides for under 100, while only once did our opponents pass 145 – a testament to the quality of the bowling and fielding.
Batting C. M. Macdonell* 583 at 72.87; M. J. Bell 240 at 24.00; B. T. Wall 249 at 20.75.
Bowling C. M. Macdonell 21 at 7.38; B. T. Wall 18 at 10.83; M. J. Bell 21 at 12.00; J. A. Staughton 13 at 12.07; T. E. Knibbs 14 at 13.14; T. H. B. Reading 12 at 14.33.

Wellington College

P18 W11 L6 D1

Master i/c D. M. Pratt   **Coach** G. D. Franklin

In an otherwise excellent season, Wellington narrowly missed out on the Cowdrey Cup, on net run-rate. The attack was led by the left-arm spin of Jonathan Dewes and Virain Kanwar's swing. The batting performance of the season was a sublime hundred against MCC by Adam Dewes.

Batting A. H. J. Dewes 423 at 30.21; T. K. Curran 347 at 26.69; C. G. J. Leith 209 at 26.12; O. W. Beswick 260 at 26.00; B. J. Curran 221 at 24.55; W. T. G. Membrey 189 at 23.62; C. J. Nurse* 371 at 21.82; J. C. H. Hersh 276 at 21.23.

Bowling W. T. G. Membrey 22 at 14.59; J. J. N. Dewes 27 at 16.70; V. Kanwar 23 at 17.69; T. K. Curran 12 at 25.08; A. H. J. Dewes 11 at 26.81; C. J. Nurse 11 at 27.36.

Wellington School

P13 W7 L6 A1

Master i/c M. H. Richards   **Coach** P. S. Jones

An enthusiastic squad, featuring four Under-14s, were capably guided by all-rounder Josh Horler, himself in Year 11. Regular Twenty20 cricket in triangular competitions enlivened the summer.

Batting J. Horler* 317 at 26.41.

Bowling W. H. Mellor 13 at 15.46.

Wells Cathedral School

P14 W5 L6 D3 A1

Master i/c R. J. Newman   **Coach** C. R. Keast

An inexperienced side improved markedly during the summer. After several heavy early defeats, the squad showed great character to remain undefeated in the cricket festival.

Batting C. P. Cook 207 at 23.00; M. A. Murton* 201 at 22.33; J. W. S. Connock 192 at 19.20; J. Betley 172 at 17.20.

Bowling J. Betley 27 at 17.62; H. O. S. Connock 13 at 22.46; M. A. Strachan-Stephens 10 at 26.20; J. W. S. Connock 14 at 28.85.

West Buckland School

P13 W8 L4 D1 A2

Master i/c D. R. Ford

A balanced team without any superstars lost only once to another school.

Batting R. Clayton 342 at 34.20; G. H. Laing 252 at 28.00; J. C. Brazier 192 at 19.20; H. Platts-Martin* 209 at 19.00.

Bowling J. J. Quinn 12 at 12.16; T. Latham 15 at 17.40; W. H. Brockman 11 at 21.90; S. R. Davies 10 at 26.10.

Westminster School

P19 W13 L3 D3

Master i/c J. D. Kershen   **Coach** S. K. Ranasinghe

A memorable year saw the team win the London Schools' Under-19 Cup and remain unbeaten for the last 15 matches of the season. Leo Nelson-Jones, Kit Winder, Kavi Amin and Eugene Daley were the top all-rounders; Milo Johnson was leading run-scorer, while wicketkeeper-batsman Angus Mylne was the most improved player.

Batting K. D. Amin 176 at 35.20; L. R. Nelson-Jones* 440 at 31.42; K. J. Winder 415 at 27.66; M. A. Johnson 520 at 27.36; Y. D. Diwan 520 at 27.00; J. D. E. Fairhead 241 at 26.77; A. S. A. Mylne 233 at 23.30; E. E. Daley 162 at 23.14; G. D. Bustin 255 at 19.61.

Bowling K. J. Winder 28 at 14.25; L. R. Nelson-Jones 25 at 17.16; K. D. Amin 20 at 18.35; E. E. Daley 13 at 20.38; D. A. Andreyev 16 at 21.81.

Whitgift School

P16 W10 L6 A4

Master i/c D. M. Ward   **Coach** S. J. Woodward

A heartening season contained several excellent individual and team performances. Dominic Sibley shepherded the side with maturity, hit three hundreds, and in late September compiled a first-class double-century for Surrey against Yorkshire. Senior players Harshil Patel and Jack Winslade made key contributions and will be missed.

Batting D. P. Sibley* 441 at 63.00; B. R. Erasmus 233 at 29.12; G. J. Dann 256 at 28.44; J. R. Lloyd 324 at 23.14; T. Walters 175 at 15.90.

Bowling J. R. Winslade 18 at 14.72; B. R. Erasmus 13 at 19.84; D. P. Sibley 11 at 22.36; J. J. Murtagh 13 at 29.23; H. A. Patel 12 at 33.50.

Slow left-armer Bashir Bhatti, of Tiffin, was the country's joint-top wicket-taker, with 45. Dylan Budge was in fine form for Woodhouse Grove, with 949 runs at an average of 135.

Winchester College
P19 W4 L12 D3 A1

Master i/c G. J. Watson   **Coach** P. N. Gover

Victories in the final three games were a deserved reward for a hard-working team who competed in almost every game. All-rounders Edmund Wylde and Daniel Escott made telling contributions, and the younger players pitched in, giving grounds for optimism.

Batting D. A. Escott 624 at 41.60; E. T. A. Wylde 543 at 31.94; M. T. Hargrove 215 at 21.50; H. A. E. B. Portman 277 at 18.46; A. J. Sachak 235 at 13.05; H. A. Sever 178 at 11.86; H. R. Duxfield 151 at 10.06.

Bowling R. J. Richards 11 at 22.00; E. T. A. Wylde 25 at 24.20; H. A. E. B. Portman 18 at 27.16; D. A. Escott 19 at 28.21; A. J. Sachak 21 at 31.71; J. P. Truell* 16 at 41.37.

Wolverhampton Grammar School
P14 W5 L7 D2 A2

Master i/c T. King   **Coach** N. H. Crust

The side played positive cricket in excellent spirit throughout an enjoyable season. While the whole squad deserved credit, the captain, Tom Weston, produced several impressive batting displays.

Batting T. G. Weston* 582 at 72.75; J. P. Caswell 201 at 22.33; A. Patel 224 at 18.66.

Bowling E. G. Farley 14 at 17.28; S. Linney 18 at 18.72; A. Patel 17 at 20.88.

Woodbridge School
P12 W7 L4 D1

Master i/c M. R. Fernley

Woodbridge School fared better than at any time in the past ten years, thanks largely to the team spirit created by the Year 13 leavers. The strength lay in batting, with both Jack Rowett and Monty Scowsill scoring centuries. The attack was led by two younger players, Christopher Elmer and Samuel Stowe.

Batting J. A. Rowett* 607 at 60.70; M. J. Scowsill 358 at 44.75.

Bowling S. J. Stowe 15 at 14.20; C. A. Elmer 12 at 19.33; A. J. Marshall 10 at 20.70.

Woodhouse Grove School
P14 W7 L3 D4 A2

Master i/c R. I. Frost   **Coach** A. Sidebottom

Woodhouse Grove won six of their seven matches on a pre-season tour of Antigua and St Lucia – and then enjoyed their term-time cricket. Dylan Budge hit a record 949 runs, including twin unbeaten hundreds in a two-day game at Warwick. Both Budge and Bailey Worcester played for Yorkshire Schools at Under-19 level.

Batting D. E. Budge 949 at 135.57; P. R. Dixon 381 at 42.33; L. M. Edward 337 at 28.08; B. J. Worcester 200 at 25.00; A. J. Baldwin* 372 at 24.80.
Bowling J. I. Morley 17 at 13.00; A. J. Baldwin 21 at 13.76; D. E. Budge 22 at 13.86; L. M. Edward 19 at 17.00; T. G. Newark 11 at 33.54.

Worth School
P9 W2 L5 D2

Master i/c R. Chaudhuri

The team played well before half-term but failed to fulfil their potential. The two Lukes, Donegan and Cummins, were the key performers.
Batting L. D. P. Donegan* 250 at 27.77.
Bowling L. R. Cummins 11 at 16.36.

Wrekin College
P10 W2 L6 D2 A2

Master i/c N. P. Benwell   **Coach** R. K. Oliver

Wrekin competed well with larger schools despite an absence of Year 13s in the side. James Flynn propped up the batting, and his tactical nous improved during the summer. All return for 2014, providing a better chance of emerging victorious from tight games.
Batting J. M. Flynn* 258 at 25.80; M. Bedson 194 at 24.25; R. Aucott 152 at 19.00; T. G. W. Masters 160 at 16.00.
Bowling J. A. J. Tanser-Harvey 19 at 11.94; R. C. Howells 10 at 12.00.

Wycliffe College
P16 W4 L11 D1

Master i/c M. J. Kimber

In a frustrating season, the failure of batsmen to chase down targets often undid sound bowling, fielding and team spirit. Jack Butler proved an imaginative captain; Tom Shrewsbury represented England Under-19s.
Batting J. Bamber 337 at 37.44; T. W. Shrewsbury 324 at 36.00; H. A. J. Pritchard 176 at 25.14; J. M. Butler* 297 at 22.84; J. B. Osborne 184 at 16.72.
Bowling C. A. Webb 19 at 14.47; T. M. Woods 10 at 15.20; J. P. Meehan 19 at 18.84; G. W. H. Field 15 at 22.73; J. B. Osborne 17 at 23.17.

WOMEN'S CRICKET, 2013

ENGLAND WOMEN v PAKISTAN WOMEN, 2013

One-day internationals (2): England 2, Pakistan 0
Twenty20 internationals (2): England 1, Pakistan 1

England's failure to win either the World Twenty20 or the World Cup over the 2012-13 winter forced the hand of Mark Lane, who resigned as head coach after five years of unprecedented success. The departure of Lane, who had played a major part in revolutionising the women's game, gave the ECB an opportunity to revamp their coaching set-up: Paul Shaw was promoted to become the new head of England women's performance, while extra funding allowed them to add David Capel, the former Northamptonshire player and coach as a second assistant coach alongside Carl Crowe, the ex-Leicestershire spinner. It was hoped they could rejuvenate England ahead of an Ashes summer and a new World Cup cycle.

First up, though, was the visit of Pakistan, who returned with 11 of the players from their tour of England the previous summer. It was a mark of their progress that the ECB felt confident enough to stage the first bilateral one-day series between the countries, although they still lacked the firepower to stretch England across 50 overs. But Twenty20 was a different matter – and Pakistan pipped an experimental England line-up in the second of back-to-back games at Loughborough. They went on to beat Ireland six times in a row heading into the World Twenty20 Qualifier tournament in Dublin, a trophy they shared with Sri Lanka. For England, there were encouraging debuts from Tash Farrant and Natalie Sciver, who were among the uncapped players called in after injuries to Katherine Brunt, Laura Marsh and Holly Colvin.

PAKISTAN TOURING PARTY

Sana Mir, Asmavia Iqbal, Batool Fatima, Bismah Maroof, Iram Javed, Javeria Khan, Javeria Rauf, Nahida Khan, Nain Abidi, Nida Dar, Qanita Jalil, Rabiya Shah, Sadia Yousuf, Sumaiya Siddiqi. Coach: Mohtashim Rashid.

At Loughborough, June 27. **England Academy won by nine wickets. Pakistan XI 100-8** (20 overs); ‡**England Academy 104-1** (19 overs) (T. T. Beaumont 50*, F. C. Wilson 47*). *As in the next game, Pakistan chose from 12 players.*

At Loughborough, June 27. **No result.** ‡**Pakistan XI 85-4** (15 overs) (Nain Abidi 34*) v **England Academy.**

At Loughborough, June 29. **Pakistan XI won by two wickets.** ‡**England Academy 174-7** (50 overs) (H. C. Knight 31, F. C. Wilson 55, S. B. Odedra 37; Sadia Yousuf 4-26); **Pakistan XI 176-8** (46.3 overs) (Nain Abidi 65*, Bismah Maroof 30, Extras 35). *Each side chose from 14 players.*

At Louth, July 1. **First one-day international: England won by 111 runs.** ‡**England 227-7** (50 overs) (C. M. Edwards 83, A. Brindle 55, L. S. Greenway 38*; Sadia Yousuf 3-33); **Pakistan 116** (41.2 overs) (Javeria Khan 39; J. L. Gunn 5-22). *PoM:* J. L. Gunn. *One-day international debuts:* N. R. Sciver, L. Winfield (England). *Charlotte Edwards and Arran Brindle, on her club ground, began with a 112-run opening stand, and England never looked back. Jenny Gunn went wicketless* *with the new ball, but had the dogged opener Javeria Khan caught at mid-on three deliveries into her second spell. It was the start of a painful collapse for Pakistan, who shed their last eight wickets for 15 runs in ten overs. Gunn claimed four more with her in-duckers to finish with career-best figures.*

At Loughborough, July 3. **Second one-day international: England won by six wickets.** ‡Pakistan **156-6** (50 overs) (Bismah Maroof 57*; N. R. Sciver 3-28, A. Brindle 3-38); **England 157-4** (38 overs) (C. M. Edwards 62, S. J. Taylor 34). *PoM:* N. R. Sciver. *Bismah Maroof was forced to play catch-up after three team-mates succumbed to some testing bowling from England's Tokyo-born seamer Natalie Sciver, playing only her second international match. England sauntered home thanks to another half-century from Edwards.*

At Loughborough, July 5. **First Twenty20 international: England won by 70 runs.** ‡England **145-7** (20 overs) (C. M. Edwards 46, S. J. Taylor 57); **Pakistan 75-6** (20 overs) (D. N. Wyatt 3-16). *PoM:* S. J. Taylor. *Twenty20 international debuts:* N. E. Farrant, A. E. Jones, N. R. Sciver, L. Winfield (England). *Edwards was soon into her stride, especially authoritative down the ground as she hit 46 from 33 balls, and Sarah Taylor rounded off a strong total with 57 from 50. Tash Farrant, born in Athens to British parents, became England's second-youngest debutant in Twenty20 internationals, aged 17 years 37 days, after Anya Shrubsole. Bowling left-arm seam, Farrant removed Qanita Jalil and Bismah Maroof in her second over to leave Pakistan 14-4.*

At Loughborough, July 5. **Second Twenty20 international: Pakistan won by one run.** ‡Pakistan **116-8** (20 overs) (Nain Abidi 45, Sana Mir 31*); **England 115** (20 overs) (A. Brindle 39; Sadia Yousuf 3-22). *PoM:* Sana Mir. *Easily beaten in the morning, Pakistan inflicted a shock victory – their first against England, and only their second over one of the traditional powerhouses of women's cricket. As with their win against India at the 2012 World Twenty20, it was sealed off the last ball and by the narrowest margin. England, however, used the game to shake up their batting order – resting Taylor, and holding Edwards back until No. 9, where she made just two and holed out to long-on with 13 needed from seven deliveries. Brindle bashed Bismah Maroof back over her head for six in the last over, but was run out returning for the second that would have tied the match, when wicketkeeper Batool Fatima collected square leg's throw and dived at full stretch to dismiss her by inches. Pakistan's score was no more than decent against a strong attack, but the graft of Nain Abidi and Sana Mir looked priceless come the end.*

THE WOMEN'S ASHES, 2013

MELINDA FARRELL

Test match (1): England 0, Australia 0
One-day internationals (3): England 2, Australia 1
Twenty20 internationals (3): England 3, Australia 0

The first multi-format Ashes was a watershed moment for women's cricket: a single series testing the skill, resolve and adaptability of the world's best two sides. The idea came from Clare Connor, the ECB's head of women's cricket, who thought that by awarding points for every game – six for the winners of the Test, two for each limited-overs match, with the overall victor taking home the Ashes trophy – the main prize could be at stake for longer than the four days set aside for the Test.

If the concept was to be judged by bumper crowds and unprecedented media interest, then Connor succeeded beyond all expectations. The prolonged Ashes narrative persuaded Sky Sports to add live coverage of the third one-day international to the three Twenty20s, while the Lord's match was streamed on the ECB's website; BBC Five Live Sports Extra offered commentary on all four days of the Test at Wormsley. When England won back the Ashes with a game to spare, it was a lead story on that evening's BBC news, and on the front page of early editions of *The Times* next day.

The format would have worked less well in the men's game, partly because of the sanctity of their Ashes, but also because the volume of cricket has meant rest and rotation, and Test sides often bear little resemblance to those sent out in coloured clothing. But while there were some format specialists playing for the women's teams, the personnel stayed largely the same. And the challenge of switching styles led to some surprising performances, none so stark as when Laura Marsh, a frequent Twenty20 opener, scored one of English cricket's slowest Test fifties.

Marsh's innings showed up what many saw as a flaw in the system. A win in the solitary Test, held at the beginning of the series, would have handed one side a huge advantage heading into the limited-overs games, with a maximum of only 12 more points possible. In other words, it was a match neither side could afford to lose, and, once Australia took the upper hand on the second day, England's only ambition was a draw, as Marsh and Heather Knight blocked and parried for an eternity. Of course, many listless draws have been played out in men's cricket with little criticism. This is where the women's game faces a challenge, to prove the play can be entertaining and skilful enough to lure crowds, broadcasters and sponsorship.

Setting the agenda: Charlotte Edwards and Katherine Brunt made the front page of *The Times* when England secured the Ashes.

There were suggestions the Test ought to have been the climax of the tour but, if the games had been staged in a different order, England would have entered the final match with an unassailable 10–2 lead, reducing the showpiece to a dead rubber. And playing it in the middle of the series would not have solved the problem of having too much to lose.

Tinkering with the points system could be the answer: clearly, the Test should be worth more than the shorter formats, but was six too many? Perhaps emulating the Sheffield Shield system of first-innings bonus points would encourage more positive play. The state of the pitches also came under scrutiny: a number were low and slow, and several players suggested a little more spice would have gone a long way.

Anya Shrubsole and Katherine Brunt were outstanding with the new ball for England, and removed at least one opener in single figures in all the limited-overs games. In contrast, the Australian attack struggled, and captain Jodie Fields was frequently forced to alter the new-ball partnership. Ellyse Perry,

Paul Gilham, Getty Images

Timing is everything: Lydia Greenway switches grip, and turns the tables on Australia at Southampton to win back the Ashes for England.

usually the Southern Stars' most incisive seamer, took just two wickets in the entire series, perhaps still suffering the effects of ankle surgery a few months earlier, although she was the only batsman on either side with a strike-rate over 100. The sterling effort of Sarah Elliott, scoring a Test century while breastfeeding her nine-month-old son in the lunch and tea breaks, was the most touching story. Meg Lanning – who led the way with 298 runs – and Jess Cameron were dangerous, but most of the Australians found England's bowlers difficult to put away.

While Knight gritted her teeth in the Test, and Edwards and Lydia Greenway made runs when it mattered, Sarah Taylor was the most exhilarating batsman – with assured footwork, impeccable timing and a knack for piercing a gap. Her wicketkeeping was also top-class, never more so than in the televised match at Hove, when Fields lined up a reverse sweep, Taylor flung herself to her right in anticipation, and pulled off a one-handed catch. That single image (see first colour section) could encourage more youngsters to take up cricket than any other moment in the Ashes summer.

AUSTRALIAN TOURING PARTY

*J. M. Fields, A. J. Blackwell, J. E. Cameron, S. J. Coyte, S. J. Elliott, H. L. Ferling, R. L. Haynes, A. J. Healy, J. L. Hunter, J. L. Jonassen, M. M. Lanning, E. A. Osborne, E. A. Perry, M. L. Schutt, G. L. Triscari, E. J. Villani. *Coach:* C. L. Fitzpatrick.

At Radlett, August 5–6. **Australia XI won by 116 runs.** ‡**Australia XI 340** (M. M. Lanning 104, J. E. Cameron 40, A. J. Blackwell 32, E. A. Osborne 33, E. J. Villani 45; K. L. Cross 4-48, R. L. Grundy 3-29); **England Academy 224** (L. Winfield 74, Extras 32; E. A. Perry 3-49, J. L. Jonassen 4-16). *England Academy chose from 14 players, and the Australians 15.*

ENGLAND v AUSTRALIA

Test Match

Pat Gibson

At Wormsley, August 11–14. Drawn. England 2pts, Australia 2pts. Toss: Australia. Test debuts: T. T. Beaumont, A. Shrubsole; H. L. Ferling, M. M. Lanning, E. A. Osborne, M. L. Schutt.

Times have changed, thankfully, since Len Hutton remarked that watching women's cricket was like watching men trying to knit. But sadly for the women's Test game, now clinging on solely in the form of a single fixture on an Ashes tour, this match never came close to matching its sublime setting in the Chiltern Hills. The six points on offer for victory were simply too much for either side to risk defeat, which ultimately meant that a well-intentioned innovation was snuffed out by pragmatism. Hutton, though, would almost certainly have appreciated the hard-nosed professionalism and solid techniques of two teams desperate not to fall at the first hurdle. England, despite the advantage of playing regularly with a red ball in the women's County Championship and men's club cricket, never looked like winning, and missed Holly Colvin's ability to turn it away from the right-handers. More than 3,000 came to watch on the first day as Sarah Elliott shrugged off sleepless nights with her baby son to make 104 from 276

HIGHEST TEST INNINGS FOR ENGLAND

189	E. A. Snowball	v New Zealand at Christchurch	1934-35
179	R. Heyhoe Flint	v Australia at The Oval	1976
177	S. C. Taylor	v South Africa at Shenley	2003
167	J. A. Brittin	v Australia at Harrogate	1998
160	B. A. Daniels	v New Zealand at Scarborough	1996
158*	C. A. Hodges	v New Zealand at Canterbury	1984
157	**H. C. Knight**	**v Australia at Wormsley**	**2013**
146	J. A. Brittin	v Australia at Guildford	1998
144*	J. A. Brittin	v New Zealand at Leeds	1984
144	K. M. Leng	v New Zealand at Scarborough	1996

---

balls. On 331 for six, Jodie Fields then surprised everyone by declaring before lunch on the second day. It looked like an inspired decision when England lurched to 113 for six, with Holly Ferling bagging two high-profile maiden Test wickets in Sarah Taylor and Charlotte Edwards, although the captain was visibly unhappy at her leg-sidish lbw dismissal. (Ferling was the fourth 17-year-old of either gender to pull on the Baggy Green, after Peggy Antonio, Ian Craig and Ellyse Perry.) But Heather Knight held the innings together with a monumental 157 in almost seven hours, and Laura Marsh supported her stoically in a 291-ball footslog to 50, with only three fours. Their stand ended one short of the seventh-wicket record in women's Tests – by Mithali Raj and Jhulan Goswami for India at Taunton in 2002 – when Knight hit the ball to cover and chanced a single. Australia were further held up by showers on the third afternoon and, by the time Fields felt safe to declare a second time, with a lead of 248, there were only 45 overs left.

Player of the Match: H. C. Knight.

Close of play: first day, Australia 243-3 (Elliott 95, Blackwell 29); second day, England 172-6 (Knight 85, Marsh 13); third day, Australia 64-1 (Lanning 29, Elliott 10).

Australia

R. L. Haynes b Shrubsole	10	– c Beaumont b Gunn	23
M. M. Lanning run out	48	– c Brindle b Shrubsole	36
S. J. Elliott c Greenway b Shrubsole	104	– run out	10
J. E. Cameron lbw b Marsh	50	– c Edwards b Gunn	24
A. J. Blackwell lbw b Marsh	54	– lbw b Marsh	22
*†J. M. Fields b Brunt	6	– not out	78
E. A. Osborne not out	10	– not out	28
E. A. Perry not out	31		
B 8, l-b 7, w 1, n-b 2	18	B 5, l-b 2, w 1, n-b 2	10

1/17 (1) 2/87 (2)   (6 wkts dec, 124 overs) 331   1/40 (1)   (5 wkts dec, 86 overs) 231
3/167 (4) 4/266 (3)   2/72 (2) 3/76 (3)
5/277 (6) 6/287 (5)   4/108 (4) 5/150 (5)

S. J. Coyte, M. L. Schutt and H. L. Ferling did not bat.

Brunt 23–8–48–1; Shrubsole 27–4–57–2; Gunn 26–12–47–0; Brindle 4–0–19–0; Marsh 27–7–74–2; Hazell 17–2–71–0. *Second innings*—Brunt 15–7–28–0; Shrubsole 20–6–48–1; Gunn 9–3–11–2; Marsh 24–7–57–1; Hazell 14–1–51–0; Edwards 1–0–7–0; Brindle 3–0–22–0.

England

H. C. Knight run out	157	– run out	4
A. Brindle lbw b Perry	5	– c and b Elliott	20
†S. J. Taylor c Elliott b Ferling	33	– not out	38
*C. M. Edwards lbw b Ferling	3	– not out	23
L. S. Greenway c and b Osborne	4		
T. T. Beaumont c Blackwell b Osborne	1		
J. L. Gunn lbw b Osborne	6		
L. A. Marsh b Schutt	55		
K. H. Brunt lbw b Coyte	4		
D. Hazell not out	9		
A. Shrubsole c Fields b Osborne	9		
B 5, l-b 13, w 1, n-b 9	28	B 2, l-b 3, n-b 3	8

1/36 (2) 2/80 (3) 3/84 (4)   (139.5 overs) 314   1/11 (1)   (2 wkts, 34 overs) 93
4/97 (5) 5/102 (6) 6/113 (7)   2/48 (2)
7/269 (10) 8/274 (9) 9/303 (8) 10/314 (11)

Perry 29–10–51–1; Schutt 15–3–43–1; Coyte 25–11–39–1; Ferling 17–2–59–2; Osborne 36.5–11–67–4; Elliott 15–4–29–0; Haynes 2–0–8–0. *Second innings*—Perry 5–1–11–0; Schutt 4–1–11–0; Ferling 6–1–11–0; Osborne 5–1–16–0; Coyte 4–1–4–0; Elliott 7–1–28–1; Lanning 3–0–7–0.

Umpires: M. R. Benson and M. Burns.   Referee: D. T. Jukes.

At Wellington College, Crowthorne, August 17. **Australia XI won by 101 runs** (D/L). ‡**Australia XI 306-9** (50 overs) (M. M. Lanning 61, A. J. Healy 41, J. E. Cameron 31, E. A. Perry 38, E. A. Osborne 40); **England Academy 124-9** (30 overs) (D. N. Wyatt 39, J. J. Watson 33). *England Academy chose from 12 players, and the Australians 14. The home side's target was revised to 226 from 30 overs.*

At Lord's, August 20. **First one-day international: Australia won by 27 runs.** ‡**Australia 203-8** (50 overs) (M. M. Lanning 56, J. M. Fields 32; K. H. Brunt 3-29); **England 176** (47.3 overs) (C. M. Edwards 61; E. A. Osborne 3-39, J. L. Jonassen 4-38). *Australia 2pts. PoM: E. A. Osborne. The Wormsley stalemate had left everything to play for, and England fired the opening shot when Rachael Haynes skied a return catch to the speedy Katherine Brunt in the first over. Meg Lanning's range of aerial strokes stood out in an innings of soft dismissals, during which Jenny Gunn passed Clare Taylor to become England's leading wicket-taker in one-day internationals, with 103. Sarah Coyte then took a smart catch, running in from mid-on, to end England's opening stand at 63, but Charlotte Edwards nicked a cut behind to make it 142-4, and the innings swiftly unravelled against spinners Erin Osborne and Jess Jonassen. It was Australia's only international win of the tour.*

At Hove, August 23. **Second one-day international: England won by 51 runs.** ‡**England 256-6** (50 overs) (C. M. Edwards 53, H. C. Knight 31, S. J. Taylor 32, L. S. Greenway 46, A. Brindle 42); **Australia 205** (48.2 overs) (J. E. Cameron 81, J. L. Jonassen 34*). *England 2pts. PoM:* A. Shrubsole (England). *The shift to Hove proved the turning point of the series, as England produced a superb all-round performance. When Jonassen removed Sarah Taylor and Edwards – two balls after the England captain brought up her 50th score of 50-plus in one-day internationals – Australia were banking on a repeat of the Lord's collapse. But this time England's middle order thrived: Lydia Greenway and Arran Brindle both made brisk forties, and Natalie Sciver chimed in with 26* from 20 balls. Australia then lost both openers for ducks, and although Jess Cameron responded with the best innings of the day, Brunt returned for her second spell and knocked over her stumps.*

At Hove, August 25. **Third one-day international: England won by five wickets.** Reduced to 36 overs a side. ‡**Australia 203-4** (36 overs) (M. M. Lanning 64, E. A. Perry 45*, A. J. Blackwell 35*); **England 204-5** (33.2 overs) (H. C. Knight 69, S. J. Taylor 64; E. A. Osborne 3-49). *England 2pts. PoM:* S. J. Taylor. *Australia's attempt to strike back was delayed by a damp outfield, then hampered by their opening-wicket blues. After failing to score in the first two ODIs, Haynes was left out, only for her replacement Alyssa Healy to register a duck too. Taylor then wowed spectators with her nimble wicketkeeping: first she took the ball on the half-volley to stump Cameron with a flick of the left glove; then she sensed the destination of Jodie Fields's reverse sweep and dived one-handed to her right. Ellyse Perry and Alex Blackwell crashed 77 from the last ten overs, momentarily disrupted by two flag-waving male streakers who embarked on an excruciatingly slow lap of the field. Edwards fell early, but Heather Knight and Taylor piled on 126 in 18.4 overs – England's highest second-wicket partnership against Australia – and a tough target was reached with ease.*

At Chelmsford, August 27. **First Twenty20 international: England won by 15 runs.** ‡**England 146-4** (20 overs) (S. J. Taylor 77); **Australia 131-5** (20 overs) (J. E. Cameron 35, E. A. Perry 30*). *England 2pts. PoM:* S. J. Taylor. *In front of a crowd of around 5,000, Taylor tormented Australia with a brazen 77 off 58 balls. She passed England's record score in this format – 76*, jointly held by Edwards and Claire Taylor – just before she was bowled charging at Osborne off the last ball. Brindle ran out Lanning with a direct hit from midwicket, Healy was caught behind four deliveries later, and the chase fell short. Defeat left Australia needing to win the last two games to retain the Ashes.*

At Southampton, August 29. **Second Twenty20 international: England won by five wickets.** ‡**Australia 127-7** (20 overs) (M. M. Lanning 60); **England 128-5** (19 overs) (L. S. Greenway 80*). *England 2pts. PoM:* L. S. Greenway. *Twenty20 international debut:* H. L. Ferling (Australia). *This match and the next were played back to back with a men's Twenty20, and the attendance here had swelled to nearly 10,000 by the time Greenway's superb innings secured the Ashes for England. Lanning belted 60 off 53 balls, but was run out in the unluckiest fashion when bowler Holly Colvin steered Blackwell's drive on to the stumps. Australia's innings sputtered out with a hat-trick of wickets – including a run-out – in the last over. England were 9-3 after Coyte took a superb return catch off Taylor, then nipped an inswinger through Wyatt. But Greenway led a spectacular revival with a high-class display of deft deflections and reverse sweeps, breaking Taylor's two-day-old England record. Edwards called it "the best T20 innings I've seen under the circumstances". England didn't have long to celebrate: they dashed up the motorway to catch a flight from Gatwick to Newcastle for the last game in Durham, where they would receive the trophy.*

At Chester-le-Street, August 31. **Third Twenty20 international: England won by seven wickets.** **Australia 91-7** (20 overs) (M. M. Lanning 32); ‡**England 92-3** (16.2 overs) (L. S. Greenway 35*, N. R. Sciver 37*). *England 2pts. PoM:* K. H. Brunt (England). *PoS:* H. C. Knight (England). *The gap between the sides looked wider than at any stage of the tour in England's fifth consecutive victory. Their superiority was plain to see when Brunt, fielding at deep cover after an opening spell of 4–0–14–1, ran out Healy by firing in a direct hit. Lanning was again the only Australian batsman to put up much resistance, but England soon found themselves in trouble against Coyte at 14-3. Greenway and Sciver came to the rescue, putting on a cool 78* to ensure a clean sweep of the Twenty20 matches. Knight tore her hamstring as she edged behind for a duck and tried to slide her back leg into the crease. She had to be helped off the pitch, but later received the series award for her Test hundred, and was wheeled around the ground on an equipment trolley by her exultant team-mates.*

England won the Ashes by 12pts to Australia's 4.

ENGLISH WOMEN'S CRICKET, 2013

Sussex and Kent continued to dominate the domestic game: Sussex took the County Championship, and Kent the Twenty20 Cup, swapping the previous season's spoils. But Yorkshire – the team of the 1990s, and the last to win the Championship in 2002 before the southern duo took control – beat both of them in Division One, and squeezed Kent out of the final by half a point. Sussex reasserted themselves on the day, thanks to a run-a-ball century from England keeper Sarah Taylor, to claim their sixth Championship in 11 seasons.

It was their third trophy of 2013, as their youngsters had already won two. At the climax of the inaugural Under-17 county Twenty20 tournament, Sussex were declared winners with the scores level after losing seven wickets to Yorkshire's eight, and they also beat Devon, by 88 runs, to clinch the Under-17 Championship. Their only reverse came in the senior Twenty20 final when, missing Taylor, they lost to Kent, led by England captain Charlotte Edwards.

Kent were a little lucky to reach the Twenty20 finals – they joined the three regional winners in the semis as the losing regional finalist with the best net run-rate. Once there, a couple of aggressive innings from Tammy Beaumont helped them beat Midlands/North winners Nottinghamshire, then Sussex.

In 2014, the structure of the Twenty20 Cup was to change. Rather than three regional groups, the teams were assigned to four divisions initially identical to those in the Championship, though they should eventually diverge through promotion and relegation. As it happened, there was no change in the Championship divisions between 2013 and 2014: the promotion–relegation play-offs all ended in favour of the side fighting to stay up. It was disheartening for Lancashire and Somerset, who lost only to each other in Division Two, and the Netherlands, invincible in Division Three.

Heather Knight of Berkshire scored most Championship runs, with 604 at 100, while Edwards made 485 at 97. Somerset leg-spinner Jenny Withers took 20 wickets at ten apiece, and Lancashire seamer Jasmine Titmuss 18 at eight.

Lancashire Under-15 were Twenty20 winners, but lost the Championship final to Middlesex by one wicket. The Under-13 finals were postponed to 2014.

In June, the Super Fours for the leading players departed from tradition by including a male team. The intention was to pick only the best women players – the top 36 rather than 48 – but a meaningful competition required a fourth side. Leicestershire and Rutland Under-16 boys played against the Emeralds, Sapphires and Rubies, but lost all four of their games. Edwards led Sapphires to victory in both their Twenty20 matches, including the final against Knight's Emeralds, who beat them across 50 overs the following weekend, though as usual no overall 50-over winner was declared.

In club cricket, Newport met with astonishing success in their inaugural season. They won the South-West League, then beat New Farnley, winners of the North League, in the national semi-final.

Finally, they defeated Finchley Gunns, the South League champions, to claim the Premier League Cup. Meanwhile, Newport's junior teams reached the Lady Taverners' Club Twenty20 finals. They lost the Under-15 match to Walmley, but beat Ealing to become Under-13 champions.

SUPER FOURS TWENTY20 FINAL, 2013

At Loughborough, June 1. **Sapphires won by five wickets. Emeralds 108-3** (20 overs) (H. C. Knight 31, A. Brindle 44); ‡**Sapphires 112-5** (19.4 overs) (S. E. Rowe 34, N. T. Miles 41).

LV= COUNTY CHAMPIONSHIP, 2013

50-over league

Division One

	Played	Won	Lost	NR	A	Bonus points Batting	Bowling	Points	Avge pts
Sussex	8	6	2	0	0	28	28	116	14.50
Yorkshire	8	6	2	0	0	24	27	111	13.87
Kent	8	6	2	0	0	27	20	107	13.37
Nottinghamshire.......	8	4	4	0	0	27	21	88	11.00
Berkshire	8	4	4	0	0	24	20	84	10.50
Warwickshire..........	8	4	4	0	0	20	22	82	10.25
Middlesex............	8	2	6	0	0	28	17	65	8.12
Essex	8	2	5	0	1	17	15	52	7.42
Surrey...............	8	1	6	0	1	19	18	47	6.71

Division Two

	Played	Won	Lost	NR	A	Bonus points Batting	Bowling	Points	Avge pts
Lancashire	8	8	0	0	0	27	31	138	17.25
Somerset..............	8	7	1	0	0	25	23	118	14.75
Worcestershire	8	4	3	1	0	18	22	80	11.42
Ireland A	8	4	4	0	0	24	26	90	11.25
Staffordshire..........	8	4	4	0	0	21	17	78	9.75
Cheshire	8	3	4	1	0	17	21	68	9.71
Wales	8	1	6	0	1	20	15	45	6.42
Devon...............	8	1	6	0	1	17	15	42	6.00
Durham	8	1	5	0	2	10	16	36	6.00

Division Three

	Played	Won	Lost	NR	A	Bonus points Batting	Bowling	Points	Avge pts
Netherlands	8	8	0	0	0	31	27	138	17.25
Northamptonshire	8	6	2	0	0	24	30	114	14.25
Scotland	8	5	3	0	0	29	25	104	13.00
Leicestershire..........	8	5	3	0	0	26	27	103	12.87
Hertfordshire	8	4	4	0	0	25	23	88	11.00
Derbyshire	8	3	5	0	0	21	19	70	8.75
Gloucestershire	8	2	5	1	0	22	19	61	8.71
Hampshire	8	2	6	0	0	21	21	62	7.75
Oxfordshire	8	0	7	1	0	13	18	31	4.42

Win = 10pts. Up to four batting and four bowling points are available to each team in each match. Final points are divided by the number of matches played (excluding no-results) to calculate the average number of points.

Division Four

North and East: Suffolk avge pts 16.75, Cumbria 13.50, Northumberland 8.33, Cambs & Hunts 8.00, Norfolk 3.75.
South and West: Cornwall avge pts 16.50, Wiltshire 11.25, Shropshire 10.75, Buckinghamshire 9.50, Dorset 2.25.
Division Four Final: Suffolk beat Cornwall by two runs.

Division One Final

At Milton Keynes, September 15. **Sussex won by 95 runs. Sussex 242-4** (50 overs) (S. J. Taylor 128*, I. V. Collis 51*); ‡**Yorkshire 147** (38.5 overs) (K. H. Brunt 46*; H. L. Colvin 3-23). *Sarah Taylor, who hit 128* in 127 balls, and 16-year-old Izzy Collis, with a maiden fifty, shared an unbroken fifth-wicket stand of 143 to carry Sussex to their highest total of the season. Taylor later made two catches and a stumping, while Collis carried out two run-outs, as Sussex regained the county title with 11 overs to spare.*

Division Two Final

At Leigh, September 1. **Somerset won by 13 runs. Somerset 194-9** (50 overs) (E. P. Campbell 79, S. N. Luff 43; J. E. Titmuss 3-31); ‡**Lancashire 181** (48 overs) (N. Brown 70). *Lancashire's first defeat of the season cost them the chance of promotion.*

Division Three Final

At Wellesbourne, September 1. **Netherlands won by 70 runs. Netherlands 205-9** (50 overs) (T. van der Gun 73*; M. Boddington 3-37); ‡**Northamptonshire 135** (45.4 overs) (D. M. Braat 3-18, C. C. Crewdson 3-24). *Marloes Braat and Clare Crewdson reduced Northamptonshire to 48-5.*

Relegation and promotion play-offs

Division One relegation play-off: Surrey beat Essex by five wickets. **Division One/Division Two play-off:** Essex v Somerset abandoned; Essex stayed up. **Division Two relegation play-off:** Devon beat Durham by 108 runs. **Division Two/Division Three play-off:** Durham beat Netherlands by two wickets and stayed up. **Division Three relegation play-off:** Hampshire beat Oxfordshire by five wickets. **Division Three/Division Four play-off:** Oxfordshire beat Suffolk on faster scoring-rate and stayed up.

ECB TWENTY20 CUP, 2013

Semi-finals

At Fulking, September 7. **Kent won by eight runs. Kent 131-4** (20 overs) (T. T. Beaumont 47; D. N. Wyatt 3-28); ‡**Nottinghamshire 123-7** (20 overs) (J. Smit 59; M. S. Belt 3-18).

At Fulking, September 7. **Sussex won by eight wickets.** Reduced to 15 overs a side. **Berkshire 59-7** (15 overs); ‡**Sussex 63-2** (13.2 overs). *Poor batting from Berkshire ended their hopes of a fourth successive Twenty20 final.*

Third-place play-off

At Fulking, September 7. **Berkshire won by five wickets. Nottinghamshire 113-8** (20 overs); ‡**Berkshire 114-5** (18.4 overs) (A. M. Rogers 46; R. Sprawson 3-15).

Final

At Fulking, September 7. **Kent won by eight wickets.** ‡**Sussex 107-5** (20 overs); **Kent 108-2** (18.2 overs) (C. M. Edwards 49, T. T. Beaumont 35*). *England captain Charlotte Edwards fell one run short of her fifty, but five runs short of Kent's victory, but Tammy Beaumont finished the job.*

PREMIER LEAGUE CUP FINAL

At Dunstable, September 29. **Newport won by five wickets.** ‡**Finchley Gunns 62** (26.4 overs) (N. Reid 5-9); **Newport 64-5** (19.2 overs) (D. L. Warren 4-25). *Fifteen-year-old leg-spinner Nicole Reid devastated favourites Finchley with a spell of 6.4–1–9–5.*

CRICKET IN IRELAND, 2013

Bashing the door down

IAN CALLENDER

If this was not Ireland's most memorable year, it was certainly their most ruthlessly successful. Only three matches were played against Full Member nations, but their demand for more fixtures against the elite was amplified by dominant performances at Associate level: they became the first team to hold trophies in all three formats simultaneously. Ireland secured the World Cricket League Championship with two games to spare, confirming their place at the 2015 World Cup; they won the World Twenty20 Qualifier in the UAE with eight wins from eight; and they regained the first-class Intercontinental Cup from Afghanistan's grasp.

Ireland's margins of victory against Afghanistan – their closest rivals – were 122 runs in the five-day final, and 68 in the Twenty20 final, which underlined just how far ahead of their peers they were. The long-term vision of Cricket Ireland remained Test status by 2020, although the restructuring of the world game now offers the leading Associate Member nation the tantalising prospect in 2019 of a Test at Lord's. In the meantime, Ireland snapped up West Indies' invitation to take part in their 2013-14 regional 50-over tournament.

Ireland failed to win any of their three summer one-day internationals against Pakistan and England, but they were in a strong position each time, and only a lack of big-match experience cost them. The first game against Pakistan, at Clontarf, ended in a tie, when Kevin O'Brien hit the last ball for four; Paul Stirling's century nudged him into the top ten of the ICC's batting rankings. Three days later, Ed Joyce made his first one-day hundred for Ireland, as they compiled 229 for nine. Pakistan were reduced to 133 for seven, but the Irish bowlers lost their composure, and Kamran Akmal and Wahab Riaz fashioned a two-wicket win with eight balls to spare. Both games were live-streamed on YouTube.

England's visit was the highlight of the summer, watched in wonderful weather by the biggest crowd in Ireland's history. Almost 10,000 people, including the Irish president Michael D. Higgins and 650 in hospitality, packed into the freshly extended Malahide venue, the new home of Irish cricket. For the second successive visit, Eoin Morgan captained England, this time at the ground where he learned his cricket from the age of 13. He made no new friends the day before when, at a press conference with the Irish media, he brazenly announced that he was trying to persuade Middlesex team-mate Stirling to be the next Ireland player to declare for England. Coming less than a year after Boyd Rankin switched allegiance, it seemed a step too far.

Fate dictated that Rankin made his one-day international debut for England in the match, and took four wickets in Ireland's 269 for seven. When Tim Murtagh replied with three in a ten-over spell, England were struggling, but

Morgan and Ravi Bopara each scored centuries, and put on a world-record fifth-wicket stand of 226. England's win, however, could not take away the sense of occasion. It was clear there was a new audience who wanted more of this Irish cricket team.

A few days later in Belfast, Will Porterfield received the World Cricket League Championship trophy, after Ireland completed back-to-back victories over Scotland to take their points tally to 24 out of a possible 28; Afghanistan went on to finish a distant second. Ireland played six WCL games in 2013, starting with two comfortable victories in the UAE. That left them needing three points from two games in Amstelveen. When they beat the Netherlands by 88 runs, it was expected they would finish the job two days later. The Dutch went into the last over needing 13 with two wickets left, and a run-out off the second ball should have led to an Ireland victory. But Michael Rippon hit John Mooney's last three deliveries for two, four and six to earn a tie. The Irish were initially deflated, but soon realised a point was enough. The celebrations went on long into the night.

Ireland presented two new caps before the Intercontinental Cup game against Scotland – leg-spinner Andrew McBrine, son of former all-rounder Alex, and Craig Young, a 23-year-old seamer on Sussex's books, who took four wickets in the first innings to set up another big victory. The five-day final was played at the ICC's Global Academy Ground in Dubai, rather than the main Sports City Stadium (which was hosting a series between Pakistan and Sri Lanka), and the batsmen never got to grips with the surface. Ireland were bowled out for 187, but still earned a slim first-innings lead, then batted Afghanistan out of the match with 341. It proved more than enough: with Mooney taking his maiden first-class ten-wicket haul, Ireland completed their unique treble. (It was an eventful few months for Mooney: he was dropped for three matches following an offensive tweet about the death of Margaret Thatcher, then left the Caribbean tour in early 2014 due to a stress-related illness.)

The Intercontinental Cup final was Trent Johnston's 198th and last game for Ireland. He retired, aged 39, with 273 wickets, putting him third in their all-time list, behind Dermott Monteith and Jimmy Boucher. Johnston's 2,610 runs came at a strike-rate of 86, bettered only by Dekker Curry and Stirling. He immediately accepted a dual role as coach of the Academy fast bowlers and the women's national team, where he succeeded his former team-mate Jeremy Bray. Johnston had helped the men into the 2014 World Twenty20 in Bangladesh with a Man of the Match performance in the Qualifier final, and his first task was to prepare Isobel Joyce's side for their first appearance in the women's event. That was after Ireland had held off the Netherlands by two runs to secure the third qualifying spot behind Pakistan and Sri Lanka in a rain-blighted tournament in Dublin.

The revamped and expanded inter-provincial series, played across all three formats, proved an instant success. While Leinster Lightning's experienced players ensured they hit the ground running, both Northern Knights and North West Warriors improved throughout the season, climaxing in Warriors' last-day victory against Lightning, which handed the 50-over Cup to Knights, denying the Dublin side the treble.

Winners of Irish Leagues and Cups
RSA Irish Cup Clontarf. **Leinster League** The Hills. **Leinster Senior Cup** YMCA. **Munster League** Cork County. **Munster Senior Cup** Cork County. **Northern League** Instonians and Waringstown. **Northern Challenge Cup** Waringstown. **North West League** Coleraine. **North West Senior Cup** Donemana.

Ireland v Pakistan

At Clontarf, May 23. **First one-day international: Tied** (D/L). ‡**Pakistan 266-5** (47 overs) (Mohammad Hafeez 122*, Asad Shafiq 84); **Ireland 275-5** (47 overs) (P. R. Stirling 103, K. J. O'Brien 84*). MoM: K. J. O'Brien. *Trent Johnston and Kevin O'Brien, the pair who had steered Ireland to victory over Pakistan at the 2007 World Cup, were left deflated at the end of this thrilling match. O'Brien needed to hit Saeed Ajmal's last ball for six to achieve Ireland's fifth one-day international win over a Full Member, but he could only flick through square leg for four; as the batsmen met in the middle, Johnston wondered whether O'Brien should have let it go for a leg-side wide. Everyone stood around for a few moments before the PA announcer confirmed a tie; Ireland had actually scored nine more runs from the same number of overs, but Duckworth/Lewis had set them 276 after Pakistan's innings was interrupted three times by showers. "Ireland deserved to win," said Pakistan captain Misbah-ul-Haq; O'Brien said it felt like a defeat. From 33-1 after 13 overs (with Nasir Jamshed briefly retiring hurt), Mohammad Hafeez and Asad Shafiq skilfully countered extravagant seam movement and put on 188 in 30 overs; Misbah was run out at the non-striker's end without facing a ball. Paul Stirling then cracked his second century against Pakistan, and O'Brien tore into the bowlers with 84* from 47 balls, dealing brutally with a surprising dose of long-hops from Ajmal. O'Brien's six and four in the last over meant Ajmal finished with 10-0-71-0 – his worst one-day international analysis.*

At Clontarf, May 26. **Second one-day international: Pakistan won by two wickets.** **Ireland 229-9** (50 overs) (E. C. Joyce 116*, K. J. O'Brien 38; Abdur Rehman 4-48); ‡**Pakistan 230-8** (48.4 overs) (Shoaib Malik 43, Kamran Akmal 81, Wahab Riaz 47*). MoM: Kamran Akmal. MoS: K. J. O'Brien. *One-day international debuts: J. N. K. Shannon (Ireland); Asad Ali (Pakistan). Two days before the match, Ireland switched to a greener strip in the hope of negating Pakistan's spinners; it cost them €7,000 to move the grandstands and scaffolding. It looked money well spent when Pakistan, chasing 230, nosedived to 17-4, then 133-7. But Kamran Akmal and Wahab Riaz struck the ball with frightening power, and Ireland's resistance was crushed when Riaz belted Tim Murtagh for 24 in the 47th over. Riaz was one of three chances to a Pakistan attack (Ajmal also made way for Abdur Rehman) that kept Ireland under wraps. The exception was Ed Joyce, who struck his first one-day international hundred for his country, after one for England in Australia in 2006-07.*

IRELAND v ENGLAND

One-Day International

CHRIS STOCKS

At Malahide, September 3. England won by six wickets. Toss: England. One-day international debuts: M. C. Sorensen; G. S. Ballance, M. A. Carberry.

The build-up to this match was dominated by talk of local resentment towards the ECB for sending over a weakened squad, poaching Ireland's best players, and showing insufficient support for their attempts to gain Test status by 2020. So it was perhaps inevitable that Morgan, a Dubliner captaining England in the absence of the rested Alastair Cook, would extinguish Ireland's hopes on the ground where he made his senior club debut. Malahide was a different place now, with temporary seating installed to swell the attendance close to 10,000, an Irish record. Rankin became the eighth man to play one-day internationals for two different teams, and soon squared up Stirling and induced Joyce to tread on his stumps (Rankin had also dismissed Joyce when they were on opposite sides – though the other way round – at the 2007 World Cup). Porterfield battled through dreadful form to shore up the innings with his sixth one-day international hundred, but first against a major Full Member. He and Niall O'Brien were both put down in the deep by Carberry, who also bowled an expensive over and was out cheaply on a miserable debut; on the bobbly outfield, Buttler had a difficult day, too. By the time Morgan was joined by Bopara, England had stumbled to 48 for four in the 15th over, following a three-wicket burst from Murtagh, the London Irishman. But after Murtagh bowled his ten overs off the reel, they cashed in against the slower men. Morgan ended a spell of three years without a hundred in the format, while Bopara galloped to his first, in his 90th match, from 74 balls, with a series of devastating pick-ups over midwicket. The pair put on an unbroken 226 in 28 overs, a fifth-wicket world record, surpassing 223 from India's Mohammad Azharuddin and Ajay Jadeja in Colombo in 1997.

Man of the Match: E. J. G. Morgan.

Ireland

*W. T. S. Porterfield b Rankin	112	D. T. Johnston not out	12
P. R. Stirling c Ballance b Rankin	10	M. C. Sorensen not out	24
E. C. Joyce hit wkt b Rankin	1	B 6, l-b 13, w 10, n-b 3	32
N. J. O'Brien b Tredwell	26		
†G. C. Wilson lbw b Tredwell	2	1/25 (2) 2/36 (3) (7 wkts, 50 overs)	269
K. J. O'Brien c Morgan b Bopara	23	3/95 (4) 4/121 (5)	
J. F. Mooney lbw b Rankin	27	5/161 (6) 6/224 (1) 7/229 (7) 10 overs: 40-2	

G. H. Dockrell and T. J. Murtagh did not bat.

Finn 10–1–44–0; Rankin 9–1–46–4; Bopara 7–0–41–1; Stokes 10–0–51–0; Tredwell 10–0–35–2; Wright 3–0–21–0; Carberry 1–0–12–0.

England

M. A. Carberry lbw b Johnston	10	R. S. Bopara not out	101
L. J. Wright b Murtagh	5	B 4, l-b 2, w 3	9
J. W. A. Taylor b Murtagh	25		
G. S. Ballance c Wilson b Murtagh	0	1/11 (1) 2/25 (2) (4 wkts, 43 overs)	274
*E. J. G. Morgan not out	124	3/25 (4) 4/48 (3) 10 overs: 27-3	

B. A. Stokes, †J. C. Buttler, J. C. Tredwell, S. T. Finn and W. B. Rankin did not bat.

Murtagh 10–2–33–3; Johnston 7–0–34–1; Sorensen 4–0–24–0; Dockrell 10–0–73–0; K. J. O'Brien 4–0–41–0; Stirling 5–0–36–0; Mooney 3–0–27–0.

Umpires: M. Hawthorne and R. S. A. Palliyaguruge.   Third umpire: R. P. Smith.
Referee: R. S. Mahanama.

For reports on Ireland's matches in the World Twenty20 Qualifier, see page 1201; and for the Intercontinental Cup and World Cricket League Championship, see page 1213.

CRICKET IN SCOTLAND, 2013

Colly wobbles

WILLIAM DICK

By almost any measure 2013 was an *annus horribilis* for Scottish cricket. In all formats of the game the national side underperformed to such an extent that some supporters may have wished for a return of the rains of 12 months earlier, if only to offer a little respite. In January 2014, the mood changed dramatically when Scotland qualified for the 2015 World Cup in Australia and New Zealand. But there was no escaping the grimness of what came before.

The competitive year had begun in Sharjah, previously a graveyard for the Scottish team. It proved so again, not just during Twenty20 and one-day whitewashes by Afghanistan, but also – damagingly – during a failed bid later in the year to qualify for the World Twenty20.

Peter Steindl's team were boosted for the first time in official internationals by their newly qualified contingent of county stars with a Scottish parent. However, Matt Machan, David Murphy, Rob Taylor and Iain Wardlaw were powerless against a rampant Afghan side, while the semi-retired Neil Carter did not enjoy a happy start to his international career, as Afghanistan comfortably won the two-match Twenty20 series.

They then defeated Scotland twice in the 50-over World Cricket League Championship, despite 133 off 136 balls from Kyle Coetzer in the second game – a Scottish record in a one-day international. (Coetzer went on to make the highest first-class score by a Scot, hitting 219 for Northamptonshire at Leicester in June, to surpass Douglas Jardine's 214 against Tasmania on England's 1928-29 Ashes tour.) But Afghanistan emphasised their all-round supremacy with an innings victory at Abu Dhabi, as Scotland's hopes of a second consecutive appearance in the Intercontinental Cup final began to recede.

The arrival of the British summer brought renewed hope, but little cause for celebration. There was a new captain in place for the visit of Pakistan in Edinburgh, after Coetzer replaced Gordon Drummond, who had opted to focus on trying to retain his place. However, victory against a Full Member remained elusive, as the Pakistanis forged a comfortable 96-run victory at The Grange in Edinburgh, after the venue had been restored following the storm damage that caused the cancellation of England's visit the previous summer.

It also hosted Australia A in June, for a four-day match given first-class status – but Scotland's second-class status was sadly confirmed in a 360-run defeat which would have been even more painful but for the resolve of Calum MacLeod in both innings. When the full Australian side visited Edinburgh in September, they won the one-day international by a whopping 200 runs, with openers Aaron Finch (148 in 114 balls) and Shaun Marsh (151 in 151) putting on 246.

Meanwhile, the Saltires' final season of competitive county action for the foreseeable future was equally hard to endure. Officials had announced before the YB40 campaign that caps would no longer be awarded for matches against counties – a logical move, since the Saltires team these days bears little resemblance to the one that represents Scotland on the international stage. However, given the team's imminent departure from the competition, it felt like an irrelevant gesture, and not one designed to motivate the players.

The team went through the summer without beating a county – the first time this had happened in eight seasons of participation since first entering the old National League in 2003. If there was consolation it came in the performances of players such as Calvin Burnett, Freddie Coleman, Matthew Cross and Michael Leask, who at least gained useful experience. But the sooner Cricket Scotland and the ECB sit down to correct the illogical decision to omit the Saltires, the better.

Amid the negativity came a little midsummer respite, when Kenya arrived in Aberdeen and were beaten in every format. However, Scotland's hopes of claiming one of the two automatic World Cup places granted by success at the WCL Championship were killed off by old foes Ireland, who completed a one-day double in Belfast. Scotland's one-wicket defeat in the first game was particularly galling: with Ireland needing nine off three balls, Tim Murtagh hit Rob Taylor for a six, then a four. That typified a year of ifs, buts and maybes for the Scots, whose Intercontinental Cup hopes were also brought to an end by the Irish at Dublin in September. The WCL defeat meant Scotland had to travel to New Zealand in early 2014 for the World Cup Qualifier, where they achieved their goal by reaching the final against the UAE.

In November 2013, also in the UAE, Scotland made a forlorn attempt to claim one of a generous six places on offer at the World Twenty20, scheduled for Bangladesh in March 2014. It should have been a relatively straightforward assignment, and Scotland were confident after appointing Paul Collingwood and Craig Wright to the coaching staff. Sadly, the influence of the former England and Scotland captains failed to sufficiently galvanise a team who were playing catch-up after losing their first group match to Bermuda.

When defeats by Afghanistan and Kenya followed, the Scots risked missing out on the knockout phase, before rallying with victories over Papua New Guinea, the Netherlands and Denmark. The win over the Danes, however, was tinged with controversy: an ICC miscalculation was partially to blame for Scotland's failure by just 0.000026 of a run to overhaul Nepal in the group placings. And so, instead of being handed the task of beating Hong Kong to qualify, Scotland were left needing victory against both Italy and the Netherlands. Italy were brushed aside, but the Dutch avenged their defeat of a week earlier. Steindl stood down as head coach after six years in the job, and was replaced on a temporary basis by Collingwood and Wright.

The Under-19s fared better, winning their World Cup qualifying event for the second time running, in the process completing a fifth consecutive victory over Ireland.

Arbroath and Uddingston recorded notable triumphs in the Cricket Scotland League Eastern and Western Premier Divisions respectively, with Arbroath pulling off an emphatic win in the Grand Final. The Regional Tri-Series was condensed into a two-team Pro-Series – the Highlanders and Reivers met in three formats of the game – ahead of a possible European League. A potential precursor of this saw the Scottish Pro teams take on Dutch counterparts in 50-over and Twenty20 double-headers; the Scots won both matches in the longer format, before losing the 20-over games.

Winners of Scottish Leagues and Cups
Eastern Premier Division Arbroath. **Western Premier Division** Uddingston. **Eastern First Division** Forfarshire. **Western First Division** East Kilbride. **Scottish Cup** Grange. **Murgitroyd Twenty20 Cup** Grange.

Scotland v Pakistan

At Edinburgh, May 17. **First one-day international: Pakistan won by 96 runs.** ‡Pakistan 231-7 (50 overs) (Imran Farhat 46, Misbah-ul-Haq 83*; R. M. Haq 3-83); Scotland 135 (39.4 overs) (K. J. Coetzer 32; Junaid Khan 3-19, Saeed Ajmal 3-25). *One-day international debuts:* Ehsan Adil (Pakistan); N. M. Carter (Scotland). *An 80-ball 83* from Pakistan captain Misbah-ul-Haq rescued his side from 115-5. Seven Scotland batsmen reached double figures, but none made more than opener Kyle Coetzer's 32.*

At Edinburgh, May 19. **Second one-day international: Abandoned.** *Rain meant Pakistan claimed the series 1–0.*

Scotland v Kenya

At Aberdeen, July 4. **First Twenty20 international: Scotland won by 35 runs.** ‡Scotland 113-6 (20 overs) (T. Mishra 3-25); Kenya 78 (18.5 overs) (G. Goudie 3-22). *Twenty20 international debuts:* F. R. J. Coleman, M. H. Cross, M. A. Leask (Scotland). *Mannofield Park's first Twenty20 international ended in an easy win for Scotland after Kenya collapsed. No. 7 Duncan Allan top-scored for the Kenyans with 15, while off-spinner Majid Haq returned figures of 4–0–10–1, equalling the most economical Twenty20 analysis for Scotland.*

At Aberdeen, July 5. **Second Twenty20 international: Scotland won by seven wickets.** ‡Kenya 100-8 (20 overs) (C. O. Obuya 38*; C. G. Burnett 3-18); Scotland 106-3 (18.3 overs) (C. S. MacLeod 46*). *Twenty20 international debut:* C. G. Burnett. *Scotland wrapped up the series with another facile win, secured by 46* from Calum MacLeod.*

Scotland v Australia

At Edinburgh, September 3. **One-day international: Australia won by 200 runs. Australia 362-3** (50 overs) (A. J. Finch 148, S. E. Marsh 151, S. R. Watson 37); ‡Scotland 162 (44 overs) (M. W. Machan 39; M. G. Johnson 4-36). *One-day international debuts:* H. J. W. Gardiner (Scotland); Fawad Ahmed (Australia). *Australia warmed up for their one-day series against England with a rout set up by brutal hitting from their openers. Five days after crashing 156 off 63 balls in a Twenty20 international at Southampton, Finch hammered 148 off 114 – his first century in the format, including 16 fours and seven sixes. Marsh was no slouch either, finishing with a run-a-ball 151, with 16 fours and five sixes; his first 50 had come from 87 deliveries, his next 100 from 61. Their stand of 246 was Australia's second-highest for any one-day wicket, behind 252* for the second by Watson and Ricky Ponting against England at Centurion in 2009-10. Australia's total was their fourth-highest in one-day internationals, and the most Scotland had conceded, beating Australia's own 345 here four years earlier. Scotland's reply seemed futile, especially when they slipped to 2-2, then 27-3. Johnson got into the groove for England with four wickets.*

For reports of Scotland's matches in the YB40, see page 738; their Twenty20 matches against Afghanistan in the UAE see page 1224; the World Twenty20 Qualifier see page 1201; and for the Intercontinental Cup and World Cricket League Championship, see page 1213.

CRICKET IN THE NETHERLANDS, 2013

Time to go Dutch

DAVID HARDY

In October, two months after the national team failed to achieve automatic qualification for the 2015 World Cup, the Netherlands Cricket Board (KNCB) announced the contract of head coach Peter Drinnen would not be extended. Drinnen, a Queenslander, had been in charge for nearly six years, and could reflect on a historic win over England at Lord's in the 2009 World Twenty20, qualification for the 2011 World Cup, and victories over Bangladesh in both limited-overs formats. The set-up became more professional, allowing the introduction of player contracts, year-round coaching, permanent support staff, the acquisition of high-class Dutch-qualified players such as Tom Cooper, Stephan Myburgh and Michael Swart and, latterly, the integration of home-grown youngsters into the national squad.

Anton Roux graduated from assistant coach for the two global qualifying tournaments at the turn of the year. He had coaching experience at both club and national level, and was also Academy director for Northerns in his native South Africa. His first task was accomplished when the Netherlands were one of six Associates to qualify for the World Twenty20 in Bangladesh – but only after a play-off against Scotland. The hard-hitting Ben Cooper was belatedly moved up to open, and he, Wesley Barresi and Swart helped overhaul Scotland's 147. Seamer Ahsan Malik Jamil was the tournament's leading wicket-taker, with 21.

The Netherlands touched down in New Zealand as favourites to win the World Cup Qualifier, with the coaching set-up bolstered by Amol Muzumdar, a former Ranji Trophy batsman. But they were beaten comfortably by Namibia, before Kenya chased down 266 to deny them a spot in the Super Sixes. It meant that, for the first time since 1999, the Netherlands had not qualified for a World Cup – and the failure to make the top four meant they were stripped of one-day international status too. The ICC can hardly have expected that when they granted the KNCB $1.5m through their Targeted Assistance and Performance Programme earlier in the year. "The team face a new period of at least four years outside top-flight cricket," said Jeroen Smits, who quit his role on the board. "A new Dutch side will have to be built up."

The Dutch came off worst when the ICC decided that the World Cricket League Championship series would determine the first two World Cup qualifiers, and included games which had already been played. In June 2011, they had sent an understrength team to play two one-day internationals in Scotland, lost them both, and later learned they counted towards qualification.

Still, the first two WCL matches of 2013, in Namibia, went well. Then came the visit of Ireland in July. The Netherlands put in their worst batting performance for years to be bowled out for 148 at Amstelveen. But in the second game, tailender Michael Rippon rescued a tie by swatting the last two balls for four and six. That left the Netherlands needing to win both games in Canada in August to stand a chance of automatic qualification. The drainage at King City left much to be desired, however, and the first fixture could not be completed. The Netherlands won the next emphatically, but Afghanistan sneaked the second World Cup qualifying spot ahead of both them and the UAE.

Imports still formed the backbone of the team, but born-and-bred Dutchmen began to get opportunities again. Daan van Bunge returned after prioritising his education for three years. At the other end of the spectrum, pace bowlers Vivian Kingma (aged 18), Paul van Meekeren (20) and Quirijn Gunning (22), and batsman James Gruijters (19) all made their one-day debuts in 2013. The youngest of all was 6ft 7in left-arm spinner Daniel Doram, born on the Caribbean island of Sint Maarten. Aged 15, he took five for 82 on first-class debut in the Intercontinental Cup against Ireland. After a series of seven four-day matches spread over three years, the Netherlands finished the tournament with precisely no wins.

In April, Worcestershire batsman Alexei Kervezee announced he would no longer be available, almost seven years after his international debut. Sydney-born Timm van der Gugten did not return for a second club season, but did figure in Namibia and Canada, while the Western Australian Swart, in his third season with the national team, finally turned out in the *Topklasse* (Premier League), for Dosti. Controversially, the South African Rippon – a left-arm wrist-spinner on Sussex's books – was preferred to Pieter Seelaar in the WCL matches against Ireland.

For the first time since 2006, a Full Member – South Africa – visited for a one-day international, after a training camp in Amstelveen to prepare for the Champions Trophy. A sizeable crowd witnessed them thump 120 off the last six overs. The Netherlands replied with a respectable 258, thanks to 98 from Eric Szwarczynski, who was denied a first international century by an unlucky run-out at the bowler's end.

It was the fourth and final summer of Dutch participation in England's 40-over competition. Three of the six home games in 2013 were abandoned, and one that survived the weather was practically an away match, played in Truro as part of the Cornish Cricket Festival. Of their 48 fixtures over four seasons, the Netherlands won 13, including nine in England, and three in a row in Worcestershire. They had a peculiar tendency to do better away, which was probably down to superior facilities and no club distractions. Their policy of fielding an official overseas player – not qualified to represent the Netherlands in any other competition – baffled those who would have preferred to see another young Dutch cricketer given a go.

Anticipating a gap in the calendar from 2014 onwards, the KNCB organised a limited-overs series between North Holland Hurricanes and South Holland Seafarers, plus matches against Scottish regional sides – a precursor to a regional competition which will hopefully involve Irish franchises.

The 2013 *Topklasse* produced an exciting best-of-three final. Quick, from The Hague, ran out 2–1 winners over VRA of Amstelveen, to win their first national championship since 1986. The arrival of Barresi from VRA was the catalyst Quick needed, and he responded with 678 runs. Edgar Schiferli led an efficient side featuring two sets of brothers, the Mols and the Gruijters – all four of them internationals. Tim Gruijters was named Player of the Finals, scoring 47 not out and 48 in two, and taking four for 48 with his off-spin in the other. Ben Cooper was the leading run-scorer overall, with 866 at 54, including the first double-hundred for 18 years, while Luuk van Troost of Excelsior 20 Schiedam became the seventh batsman to record 10,000 runs in the top division. The New Zealander Brett Hampton of Excelsior 20 was probably the paciest bowler around, and 21-year-old leg-spinner Vinoo Tewarie of VRA the most successful. Dosti of Amsterdam, in only their second top-flight season, won the Twenty20 competition, with Zimbabwean Charles Coventry and Pakistani Yasir Hameed making vital contributions on finals day.

The Under-19 national team had a great chance to cement a spot at their first World Cup since 2000, with the European Championship played on home soil. They started with a win over Ireland, but narrowly lost to eventual champions Scotland, then faded badly, with defeats by Jersey and Guernsey. The women lost their County Championship Division Two/Three play-off to Durham by two wickets, and their 2014 Women's World Twenty20 play-off to Ireland by two runs. It was a minor miracle that Dutch women have a competitive national team at all, with only nine senior sides playing league cricket. There was, however, encouraging growth reported in girls' cricket, despite an overall youth playing pool of under 1,000.

Netherlands v South Africa

At Amstelveen, May 31. **One-day international: South Africa won by 83 runs.** ‡**South Africa 341-3** (50 overs) (C. A. Ingram 82, J. P. Duminy 150*, F. du Plessis 62*); **Netherlands 258-9** (50 overs) (E. S. Szwarczynski 98, P. W. Borren 48; R. J. Peterson 4-67). *One-day international debut: P. A. van Meekeren (Netherlands). After two months off the international treadmill, the South Africans reunited with a cycle dash along Amsterdam's canal network. The bonding session evidently did them no harm, as J-P. Duminy and Faf du Plessis plundered 120 in the last six overs. Duminy, on his competitive comeback from an Achilles injury sustained at Brisbane five months earlier, raced from 101 to 150* in 19 balls. Eric Szwarczynski, part of the Netherlands' all-South African top three, cut and deflected beautifully before being run out backing up by a fingertip deflection from Farhaan Behardien, two short of a maiden hundred.* TIM BROOKS

For reports of the Netherlands' matches in the World Twenty20 Qualifier, see page 1201; in the Intercontinental Cup and World Cricket League Championship, see page 1213; in the YB40, see page 729; and for their Twenty20 internationals against Kenya, see page 1207.

PART FIVE

Overseas Cricket

WORLD CRICKET IN 2013

Travel sickness

Simon Wilde

It was a year in which it proved near-impossible for Test teams to win away from home, with two lop-sided Ashes contests providing the most overwhelming examples. Of the 17 series played to a finish in 2013, home sides won 12, while the other five – one of them on neutral territory – were drawn. Of the draws, three took place in Zimbabwe and Bangladesh, which in itself lent support to the idea that they too found sustenance from their own soil: **Zimbabwe's** victory over Pakistan in Harare was their first in Tests against anyone bar Bangladesh since 2001. In another drawn series, hosts New Zealand were one England wicket away in Auckland from winning 1–0.

Overall, 29 Tests (excluding those on neutral territory) were won by home teams, and only two by visitors – **Pakistan** and **Bangladesh**, both in Zimbabwe. That was an annual win–loss ratio of 14.5 to one, unmatched in Test history. It is possible that home sides made additional efforts to prepare pitches suiting

TEST MATCHES IN 2013

	Tests	Won	Lost	Drawn	% won	% lost	% drawn
South Africa	9	7	1	1	77.77	11.11	11.11
India	8	6	1	1	75.00	12.50	12.50
England	14	5	4	5	35.71	28.57	35.71
Australia	14	5	7	2	35.71	50.00	14.28
Zimbabwe	6	2	4	0	33.33	66.66	0.00
Sri Lanka	3	1	1	1	33.33	33.33	33.33
West Indies	7	2	4	1	28.57	57.14	14.28
Pakistan	7	2	5	0	28.57	71.42	0.00
New Zealand	12	2	4	6	16.66	33.33	50.00
Bangladesh	6	1	2	3	16.66	33.33	50.00
Totals	43	33	33	10	76.74	76.74	23.25

Figures do not include the First Test between Pakistan and Sri Lanka, which began on December 31, 2013, and ended in a draw on January 4, 2014.

their strengths. **England** certainly did, to assist off-spinner Graeme Swann, who took 26 wickets in five Ashes Tests at home, before finding life so tough in Australia that he retired mid-series. Perhaps the demands of touring in a never-ending schedule took a heavier toll on visitors. But it might also have been that the difficulty of winning in alien conditions was beyond the limited skills of a set of largely mediocre teams. **Australia** lost 4–0 in India and 3–0 in England, while winning every Test they played at home.

It may also have been relevant that **South Africa**, clear-cut leaders of the Test rankings and a team with an excellent touring record, spent most of the year camped at home, where they won six out of seven Tests. When they did

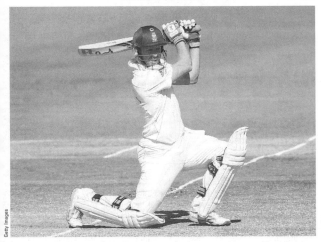

Good for glovemen: South Africa's A. B. de Villiers became the first wicketkeeper-batsman to score four Test hundreds in a calendar year.

venture abroad, for a neutral series in the UAE with Pakistan, they came away with a 1–1 draw.

One old truth still seemed to apply: Asian sides whose strength was spin lacked the fast bowlers to win outside the subcontinent, while non-Asian sides whose strength was pace generally lacked the spinners to win in Asia. (The only, striking, exception to this had been England's victory in India at the end of 2012.) But it was also striking that, even when non-Asian sides met each other, the home team's seamers generally outperformed the visitors'. Dale Steyn and Vernon Philander took 75 wickets in seven home Tests for South Africa, Stuart Broad and James Anderson 65 in seven for England, Mitchell Johnson and Ryan Harris 62 in six for Australia (including the Sydney Test in the first week of 2014), and Trent Boult and Tim Southee 55 in six for **New Zealand**. Overall, bowlers averaged 25 at home, and nearly 40 away.

There was no such disparity in one-day internationals and Twenty20s: visiting teams fared better than in recent years and, over the two formats combined, won precisely as many matches as they lost. The most notable success for an away team came when India won the ICC Champions Trophy in England, narrowly beating the hosts in a rain-curtailed final.

Concerns were expressed at the low esteem in which Test cricket was held in some quarters. **Sri Lanka** and **West Indies** scrapped two Tests in favour of a one-day triangular involving India (thereby avoiding a clash with the IPL, as well as generating more cash), while the BCCI, in a naked show of muscle-flexing, demanded a drastically shortened tour of South Africa, whose chief

MOST HOME WINS IN A CALENDAR YEAR

(combined record of all home teams; excludes matches on neutral soil)

	Played	Won	Lost	Drawn	Win–loss ratio
2013	**41**	**29**	**2**	**10**	**14.50**
2002	49	28	13	8	2.15
2001	55	27	16	12	1.68
2005	49	25	12	12	2.08
1998	45	24	10	11	2.40
2004	51	21	19	11	1.10
2006	46	21	13	12	1.61

The only other years in which the win–loss ratios for home sides exceeded four are:

	Played	Won	Lost	Drawn	Win–loss ratio
1990	26	14	2	10	7.00
1931	14	7	1	6	7.00

executive Haroon Lorgat had crossed swords with them during his time at the ICC. He had also unilaterally announced a longer itinerary. The situation was inflamed by David Becker, a former legal head at the ICC, who accused the BCCI of bullying the world governing body.

South Africa exacted modest payback by denying **India** a win in Tests or one-day internationals, but passed up a golden opportunity to create history at the Wanderers during their pursuit of what would have been the highest successful run-chase in Tests; needing only 16 more towards a target of 458 with three wickets and 19 balls left, they opted for the draw, though it's true that India had also prematurely settled for stalemate.

India did bring forward by a year an additional two-Test series against West Indies at short notice, but this appeared to be motivated by a desire to allow Sachin Tendulkar to retire in front of a home audience and against a friendly attack. South Africa's Jacques Kallis, statistically the most successful all-rounder in Tests, also retired at home, after the India series.

Australia's ultra-attacking approach played its part

It was an exceptional year for Test wicketkeeper-batsmen, who collectively averaged more (39.80) than in any previous calendar year, and for only the second time topped 5,000 runs. M. S. Dhoni of India and Mushfiqur Rahim of Bangladesh both scored double-centuries (uniquely so, in that they were also captains), while A. B. de Villiers became the first wicketkeeper-batsman to score four hundreds in the same year (and did it while batting in the top six). With 493 runs in the second Ashes series, Australia's Brad Haddin set a record for a batsman batting at No. 7 or lower, and narrowly failed to become the second, after Denis Lindsay (for South Africa against Australia in 1966-67), to accomplish the double of 500 runs and 20 dismissals in a series.

Haddin contributed to another record, as 65 sixes were struck in the Australian Ashes, comfortably surpassing the previous best of 51 (the 2005 Ashes). Australia's ultra-attacking approach played its part – they hit 40 sixes to England's 25, with Haddin leading the way on nine – but the frequency of

LEADING TEST BATSMEN IN 2013 – HOME

(500 runs, average 45.00)

	M	R	Avge	HS	100
L. R. P. L. Taylor (NZ)	6	589	98.16	217*	3
C. A. Pujara (I)	6	549	78.42	204	2
A. B. de Villiers (SA)	7	660	73.33	121	3
D. A. Warner (A)	5	576	64.00	124	2
H. M. Amla (SA)	7	505	56.11	110	1
I. R. Bell (E)	7	635	48.84	113	3

AWAY

(400 runs, average 45.00)

	M	R	Avge	HS	100
Mushfiqur Rahim (B)	4	406	58.00	200	1
Younis Khan (P)	5	493	54.77	111	2
M. J. Clarke (A)	8	667	47.64	187	2
M. J. Prior (E)	6	418	46.44	82	1

LEADING TEST BOWLERS IN 2013 – HOME

(30 wickets, average 25.00)

	Style	M	O	W	BB	Avge
M. G. Johnson (A)	LF	5	193.5	34	7-40	15.76
D. W. Steyn (SA)	RF	7	288.2	43	6-8	16.74
V. D. Philander (SA)	RFM	6	223	32	5-7	17.12
R. Ashwin (I)	OB	6	313.2	41	7-103	19.87
T. A. Boult (NZ)	LFM	6	250.5	31	6-40	20.29
S. C. J. Broad (E)	RFM	7	243.5	34	7-44	23.38

AWAY

(20 wickets, average 30.00)

	Style	M	O	W	BB	Avge
R. J. Harris (A)	RFM	4	162.1	24	7-117	19.58
Saeed Ajmal (P)	OB	5	228.2	25	7-95	25.24
S. C. J. Broad (E)	RFM	7	234.2	28	6-51	28.75

Figures do not include matches played by Pakistan in the UAE (neutral territory).

sixes in this series and during the year as a whole (334, fourth on the all-time list) lent further support to the MCC world cricket committee's argument for legislation to curb the depth of bats.

Two high-profile Ashes series brought a harsh spotlight on the four non-English and non-Australian members of the ICC's Elite Panel of umpires eligible to stand (it became five when New Zealander Billy Bowden was specially reinstated for England's tour of Australia). The officials' questionable handling of DRS in England led to an expansion in technology, with the experimental use of real-time Snicko, and the number of challenges, both sides having their quota topped up to two after 80 overs. India continued to have nothing to do with DRS.

ONE-DAY INTERNATIONALS IN 2013

(Full Member matches only)

	ODI	Won	Lost	Tied	NR	% won	% lost
India	34	22	10	0	2	**68.75**	31.25
Bangladesh	9	5	3	0	1	**62.50**	37.50
Australia	23	11	8	0	4	**57.89**	42.10
Sri Lanka	30	14	13	0	3	**51.85**	48.14
South Africa	28	13	13	1	1	**50.00**	50.00
England	20	9	10	0	1	**47.36**	52.63
Pakistan	31	14	16	1	0	**46.77**	53.22
West Indies	24	9	13	2	0	**41.66**	58.33
New Zealand	19	7	10	0	2	**41.17**	58.82
Zimbabwe	14	3	11	0	0	**21.42**	78.57
Totals	116	107	107	2	7		

The following teams also played official one-day internationals in 2013, some against Full Members (not included in the table above): Afghanistan (PW W4); Ireland (P7 W3 L2 T2); Netherlands (P5 W1 L2 T1 NR1); Kenya (P6 W2 L4); Scotland (P8 W2 L6); Canada (P4 L3 NR1). The % won and lost excludes no-results; ties are counted as half a win.

TWENTY20 INTERNATIONALS IN 2013

(Full Member matches only)

	T20I	Won	Lost	No result	% won	% lost
India	1	1	0	0	**100.00**	0.00
Sri Lanka	9	6	3	0	**66.66**	33.33
Pakistan	11	7	4	0	**63.63**	36.36
South Africa	8	5	3	0	**62.50**	37.50
West Indies	5	3	2	0	**60.00**	40.00
England	7	3	3	1	**50.00**	50.00
New Zealand	7	3	3	1	**50.00**	50.00
Bangladesh	4	1	3	0	**25.00**	75.00
Australia	6	1	5	0	**16.66**	83.33
Zimbabwe	6	1	5	0	**16.66**	83.33
Totals	32	31	31	1		

The following teams also played official Twenty20 internationals in 2013, though only Afghanistan met a Full Member (Pakistan, not included in the table above): Ireland (P2 W2); Afghanistan (P9 W5 L4); Kenya (P12 W6 L6); Netherlands (P6 W3 L3); Scotland (P8 W3 L5); Canada (P4 W1 L3). The % won and lost excludes no-results.

> **❝** The weight of runs had him picked for the last two Tests against Australia, replacing – of all people – Virender Sehwag, the original 21st-century Delhi swashbuckler."
> Five Cricketers of the Year, page 98.

RELIANCE MOBILE ICC TEAM RANKINGS

ICC TEST CHAMPIONSHIP

(As at January 20, 2014)

		Matches	Points	Rating
1	South Africa	30	3,988	133
2	India	36	4,213	117
3	Australia	39	4,314	111
4	England	44	4,713	107
5	Pakistan	29	2,890	100
6	Sri Lanka	30	2,703	90
7	West Indies	29	2,516	87
8	New Zealand	34	2,773	82
9	Zimbabwe	11	372	34
10	Bangladesh	16	285	18

ICC ONE-DAY CHAMPIONSHIP

(As at January 8, 2014)

		Matches	Points	Rating
1	India	58	6,967	120
2	Australia	42	4,808	114
3	England	42	4,671	111
4	South Africa	44	4,825	110
5	Sri Lanka	56	6,059	108
6	Pakistan	58	5,873	101
7	West Indies	48	4,300	90
8	New Zealand	38	3,259	86
9	Bangladesh	26	2,165	83
10	Zimbabwe	26	1,439	55
11	Ireland	11	423	38
12	Netherlands	7	88	13
13	Kenya	4	40	10

ICC TWENTY20 CHAMPIONSHIP

(As at December 31, 2013)

		Matches	Points	Rating
1	Sri Lanka	20	2,570	129
2	India	15	1,843	123
3	South Africa	23	2,818	123
4	Pakistan	30	3,638	121
5	West Indies	17	2,041	120
6	England	21	2,357	112
7	Australia	20	2,047	102
8	New Zealand	21	2,139	102
9	Ireland	9	783	87
10	Bangladesh	11	791	72
11	Afghanistan	13	908	70
12	Netherlands	9	508	56
13	Scotland	11	545	50
14	Zimbabwe	12	553	46
15	Kenya	15	633	42
16	Canada	6	11	2

The ratings are based on all Test series, one-day and Twenty20 internationals completed since August 1, 2010.

RELIANCE MOBILE ICC PLAYER RANKINGS

Introduced in 1987, the rankings have been backed by various sponsors, but were taken over by the ICC in January 2005. They rank cricketers on a scale up to 1,000 on their performances in Tests. The rankings take into account playing conditions, the quality of the opposition, and the result of the matches. A similar set of rankings for one-day internationals had been launched in August 1998, and Twenty20 rankings were added in October 2011.

The leading players in the Test rankings on January 20, 2014, were:

Rank	Batsmen	Points	Rank	Bowlers	Points
1	A. B. de Villiers (*South Africa*)...	912	1	V. D. Philander (*South Africa*) ...	909
2	S. Chanderpaul (*West Indies*)	876	2	D. W. Steyn (*South Africa*)......	901
3	L. R. P. L. Taylor (*New Zealand*) .	871	3	R. J. Harris (*Australia*)	866
4	H. M. Amla (*South Africa*)	868	4	H. M. R. K. B. Herath (*Sri Lanka*)	789
5	C. A. Pujara (*India*)..........	851	5	Saeed Ajmal (*Pakistan*)	787
6	Misbah-ul-Haq (*Pakistan*).......	824	6	P. M. Siddle (*Australia*)	779
7	K. C. Sangakkara (*Sri Lanka*)....	822	7	R. Ashwin (*India*)	759
8	M. J. Clarke (*Australia*)........	817	8	M. G. Johnson (*Australia*)......	743
9	G. C. Smith (*South Africa*)	785	9	P. P. Ojha (*India*)	741
10	Younis Khan (*Pakistan*)	759	10	{ T. A. Boult (*New Zealand*)	729
				{ S. C. J. Broad (*England*)........	729

The leading players in the one-day international rankings on January 8, 2014 were:

Rank	Batsmen	Points	Rank	Bowlers	Points
1	A. B. de Villiers (*South Africa*)...	872	1	Saeed Ajmal (*Pakistan*)	776
2	V. Kohli (*India*)	859	2	D. W. Steyn (*South Africa*)......	742
3	H. M. Amla (*South Africa*)	840	3	S. T. Finn (*England*)	708
4	G. J. Bailey (*Australia*)	835	4	S. P. Narine (*West Indies*)	703
5	K. C. Sangakkara (*Sri Lanka*)....	816	5	J. M. Anderson (*England*).......	696
6	M. S. Dhoni (*India*)...........	789	6	R. A. Jadeja (*India*)	692
7	T. M. Dilshan (*Sri Lanka*).......	760	7	H. M. R. K. B. Herath (*Sri Lanka*)	678
8	I. J. L. Trott (*England*)	754	8	L. L. Tsotsobe (*South Africa*)	674
9	Misbah-ul-Haq (*Pakistan*).......	735	9	M. Morkel (*South Africa*)	673
10	S. Dhawan (*India*).............	717	10	M. G. Johnson (*Australia*)......	670

The leading players in the Twenty20 international rankings on December 31, 2013 were:

Rank	Batsmen	Points	Rank	Bowlers	Points
1	A. D. Hales (*England*)...........	842	1	S. P. Narine (*West Indies*)	817
2	B. B. McCullum (*New Zealand*) ..	786	2	Saeed Ajmal (*Pakistan*).........	714
3	V. Kohli (*India*)................	749	3	Mohammad Hafeez (*Pakistan*) ...	670
4	S. R. Watson (*Australia*)........	729	4	B. A. W. Mendis (*Sri Lanka*).....	669
5	D. A. Warner (*Australia*)........	728	5	S. T. Finn (*England*)	667
6	S. K. Raina (*India*)............	712	6	J. W. Dernbach (*England*).......	664
7	M. J. Guptill (*New Zealand*)	708	7	{ L. L. Tsotsobe (*South Africa*)	659
8	Yuvraj Singh (*India*)	705		{ P. Utseya (*Zimbabwe*)	659
9	{ A. J. Finch (*Australia*)..........	702	9	K. M. D. N. Kulasekara (*S. Lanka*)	657
	{ C. H. Gayle (*West Indies*)	702	10	Shakib Al Hasan (*Bangladesh*) ...	655

In October 2008, the ICC launched a set of rankings for women cricketers, based on one-day international performances because of the paucity of Tests. The ICC said they hoped to raise the profile of the women's game by identifying where the leading players stood, and to give it further competition and context. Twenty20 rankings were added in September 2012.

The leading players in the women's one-day international rankings on December 31, 2013, were:

Rank	Batsmen	Points	Rank	Bowlers	Points
1	M. Raj (*India*)	703	1	S. R. Taylor (*West Indies*)	733
2	S. J. Taylor (*England*)	693	2	K. H. Brunt (*England*)	712
3	S. W. Bates (*New Zealand*)	685	3	J. Goswami (*India*)	655
4	S. R. Taylor (*West Indies*)	680	4	S. F. Daley (*West Indies*)	627
5	M. M. Lanning (*Australia*)	673	5	J. L. Gunn (*England*)	612
6	H. Kaur (*India*)	669	6	E. A. Perry (*Australia*)	609
7	C. M. Edwards (*England*)	657	7	A. Mohammed (*West Indies*)	604
8	J. E. Cameron (*Australia*)	652	8	H. L. Colvin (*England*)	595
9	A. E. Satterthwaite (*New Zealand*)	610	9	E. A. Osborne (*Australia*)	569
10	D. J. S. Dottin (*West Indies*)	582	10	S. Loubser (*South Africa*)	561

The leading players in the women's Twenty20 international rankings on December 31, 2013, were:

Rank	Batsmen	Points	Rank	Bowlers	Points
1	S. J. Taylor (*England*)	666	1	S. F. Daley (*West Indies*)	657
2	D. J. S. Dottin (*West Indies*)	648	2	Sadia Yousuf (*Pakistan*)	635
3	C. M. Edwards (*England*)	644	3	A. Mohammed (*West Indies*)	618
4	M. M. Lanning (*Australia*)	640	4	J. L. Hunter (*Australia*)	615
5	S. W. Bates (*New Zealand*)	626	5	D. Hazell (*England*)	613
6	S. R. Taylor (*West Indies*)	618	6	S. R. Taylor (*West Indies*)	603
7	M. Raj (*India*)	597	7	E. A. Perry (*Australia*)	594
8	J. E. Cameron (*Australia*)	582	8	E. A. Osborne (*Australia*)	591
9	C. M. A. Shillington (*Ireland*)	572		S. L. Quintyne (*West Indies*)	591
10	P. G. Raut (*India*)	567		H. L. Colvin (*England*)	591

TEST AVERAGES IN CALENDAR YEAR 2013

BATTING (300 runs, average 30.00)

	T	I	NO	R	HS	100	Avge	SR	Ct/St
L. D. Chandimal (SL)	3‡	4	2	304	116*	2	152.00	63.73	7/3
†K. C. Sangakkara (SL)	2‡	4	0	441	142	3	110.25	57.12	0
†Mominul Haque (B)	5	9	2	584	181	2	83.42	60.08	4
A. B. de Villiers (SA)	9	13	1	933	164	4	77.75	58.42	45/1
C. A. Pujara (I)	8	13	2	829	204	3	75.36	56.24	1
L. R. P. L. Taylor (NZ)	10	17	5	866	217*	3	72.16	57.23	20
R. G. Sharma (I)	4	6	1	333	177	2	66.60	62.83	4
†S. Chanderpaul (WI)	7	12	3	523	122*	2	58.11	51.32	2
H. M. Amla (SA)	8	12	1	633	118	2	57.54	54.66	2
V. Kohli (I)	8	12	1	616	119	2	56.00	54.65	7
Mushfiqur Rahim (B)	6	9	0	491	200	1	54.55	52.79	14/1
B. R. M. Taylor (Z)	5	10	1	469	171	2	52.11	48.45	4
†G. C. Smith (SA)	9	14	1	651	234	1	50.07	59.50	17
M. Vijay (I)	8	13	0	647	167	2	49.76	46.95	10
Nasir Hossain (B)	6	9	1	387	100	1	48.37	59.08	5
M. J. Clarke (A)	13	26	3	1,093	187	4	47.52	56.39	15
Misbah-ul-Haq (P)	7‡	14	2	570	100	1	47.50	41.39	2
M. S. Dhoni (I)	8	12	2	459	224	1	45.90	72.39	16/6
Younis Khan (P)	7‡	14	2	549	200*	1	45.75	42.55	7
†S. Dhawan (I)	5	7	0	319	187	1	45.57	75.95	2
D. Ramdin (WI)	7	12	3	410	107	1	45.55	57.90	12/2
Mohammad Ashraful (B)	4	8	1	318	190	1	45.42	41.89	1
F. du Plessis (SA)	9	12	1	489	137	2	44.45	43.27	5
†Tamim Iqbal (B)	4	8	0	336	95	0	42.00	48.69	1
I. R. Bell (E)	14	27	3	1,005	113	3	41.87	42.62	13
K. S. Williamson (NZ)	11	19	1	747	114	1	41.50	43.15	13
†C. J. L. Rogers (A)	9	17	0	700	116	2	41.17	44.98	8
B-J. Watling (NZ)	11	16	1	596	103	1	39.73	47.41	35
†D. A. Warner (A)	12	24	1	909	124	2	39.52	66.73	7
B. J. Haddin (A)	10	18	1	647	118	1	38.05	59.68	51/1
I. J. L. Trott (E)	11	21	0	793	121	1	37.76	49.93	12
S. P. D. Smith (A)	11	21	2	711	138*	2	37.42	45.87	10
†D. M. Bravo (WI)	6	11	1	374	218	1	37.40	47.10	3
P. G. Fulton (NZ)	10	17	0	620	136	2	36.47	37.82	9
K. P. Pietersen (E)	11	21	0	758	113	1	36.09	51.74	8
S. R. Watson (A)	12	24	1	810	176	2	35.21	60.00	7
†H. D. Rutherford (NZ)	10	17	1	558	171	1	34.87	60.91	7
J. E. Root (E)	14	27	2	862	180	2	34.48	40.64	8
†A. N. Cook (E)	14	27	0	916	130	2	33.92	42.54	18
A. N. Petersen (SA)	9	14	1	438	106	1	33.69	52.58	13
Asad Shafiq (P)	7‡	13	0	436	130	1	33.53	42.57	6
B. B. McCullum (NZ)	12	19	1	586	113	1	32.55	64.25	10
M. J. Prior (E)	13	24	5	594	110*	1	31.26	56.14	44
H. Masakadza (Z)	6	12	1	338	111*	1	30.72	39.12	4

‡ *The Pakistan v Sri Lanka Test which started on December 31 is excluded. L. D. Chandimal (0) and K. C. Sangakkara (16) batted on the first day of that match; Misbah-ul-Haq, Younis Khan and Asad Shafiq (1 ct) played but did not bat.*

BOWLING (10 wickets, average 50.00)

	Style	O	M	R	W	BB	5I	Avge	SR
M. N. Samuels (WI)	OB	40	4	117	10	4-13	0	11.70	24.00
M. G. Johnson (A)	LF	212.5	54	596	34	7-40	3	17.52	37.55
D. W. Steyn (SA)	RF	357.4	101	901	51	6-8	4	17.66	42.07
V. D. Philander (SA)	RFM	278	82	686	38	5-7	2	18.05	43.89

	Style	O	M	R	W	BB	5I	Avge	SR
R. A. Jadeja (I)	SLA	255.4	68	573	30	6-138	2	19.10	51.13
C. J. Anderson (NZ)	LFM	88	18	213	11	3-47	0	19.36	48.00
R. J. Harris (A)	RFM	304.5	78	834	38	7-117	2	21.94	48.13
Robiul Islam (B)	RFM	153	33	419	19	6-71	2	22.05	48.31
S. Shillingford (WI)	OB	261.5	47	802	36	6-49	5	22.27	43.63
R. Ashwin (I)	OB	355.2	96	923	41	7-103	4	22.51	52.00
H. M. R. K. B. Herath (SL)	SLA	178.2‡	29	475	21	7-89	2	22.61	50.95
P. P. Ojha (I)	SLA	152.3	36	416	18	5-40	2	23.11	50.83
S. W. Masakadza (Z)	RFM	121.1	27	308	13	4-32	0	23.69	55.92
Imran Tahir (SA)	LBG	78.4	18	246	10	5-32	1	24.60	47.20
Saeed Ajmal (P)	OB	346‡	65	915	37	7-95	3	24.72	56.10
T. G. Southee (NZ)	RFM	333.3	74	898	36	6-50	1	24.94	55.58
T. A. Boult (NZ)	LFM	429.5	110	1,154	46	6-40	2	25.08	56.06
S. C. J. Broad (E)	RFM	478.1	87	1,600	62	7-44	5	25.80	46.27
Mohammed Shami (I)	RFM	124.1	15	445	17	5-47	1	26.17	43.82
T. L. Chatara (Z)	RFM	148.1	34	405	15	5-61	1	27.00	59.26
M. Morkel (SA)	RF	226.5	74	521	19	3-14	0	27.42	71.63
K. M. Jarvis (Z)	RFM	121.2	24	446	16	5-54	1	27.87	45.50
P. M. Siddle (A)	RFM	472.1	129	1,269	42	5-50	2	30.21	67.45
Rahat Ali (P)	LFM	126.1‡	18	432	14	6-127	2	30.85	54.07
J. M. Anderson (E)	RFM	531.5	125	1,655	52	5-47	3	31.82	61.36
K. S. Williamson (NZ)	OB	149.2	30	454	14	4-44	0	32.42	64.00
Shakib Al Hasan (B)	SLA	122.3	28	365	11	5-103	1	33.18	66.81
T. T. Bresnan (E)	RFM	153.3	34	502	15	2-24	0	33.46	61.40
S. T. Finn (E)	RF	179.1	30	670	20	6-125	1	33.50	53.75
Junaid Khan (P)	LFM	186.1‡	42	505	15	4-67	0	33.66	74.46
N. M. Lyon (A)	OB	431.4	81	1,429	42	7-94	2	34.02	61.66
G. P. Swann (E)	OB	440	75	1,466	43	6-90	3	34.09	61.39
J. L. Pattinson (A)	RFM	170.1	40	557	16	5-96	1	34.81	63.81
J. H. Kallis (SA)	RFM	132.3	33	349	10	3-68	0	34.90	79.50
P. Utseya (Z)	OB	113.3	14	355	10	3-60	0	35.50	68.10
N. Wagner (NZ)	LFM	373	70	1,271	35	5-64	1	36.31	63.94
Sohag Gazi (B)	OB	290.3	43	807	22	6-77	1	36.68	79.22
Mohammad Irfan (P)	LFM	118.4	15	389	10	3-44	0	38.90	71.20
M. A. Starc (A)	LFM	209.3	34	677	17	3-71	0	39.82	73.94
R. J. Peterson (SA)	SLA	197.1	41	612	15	4-74	0	40.80	78.86
I. Sharma (I)	RFM	187	40	578	12	4-79	0	48.16	93.50

‡ *The Pakistan v Sri Lanka Test which started on December 31 is excluded. Saeed Ajmal (14–3–32–2), Rahat Ali (16–3–41–0), Junaid Khan (20–4–58–5) and H. M. R. K. B. Herath (5–3–5–0) bowled on the first day of that match.*

MOST DISMISSALS BY A WICKETKEEPER

Dis		T		Dis		T	
52	(51ct, 1st)	10	B. J. Haddin (A)	22	(16ct, 6st)	8	M. S. Dhoni (I)
46	(45ct, 1st)	9	A. B. de Villiers (SA)	16‡	(14ct, 2st)	4	Adnan Akmal (P)
44	(44ct)	13	M. J. Prior (E)	15	(14ct, 1st)	6	Mushfiqur Rahim (B)
35	(35ct)	11	B-J. Watling (NZ)				

‡ *The Pakistan v Sri Lanka Test which started on December 31 is excluded. Adnan Akmal made five dismissals (4ct, 1st) on the first day of that match.*

MOST CATCHES IN THE FIELD

Ct	T			Ct	T		
20	10	L. R. P. L. Taylor (NZ)		15	13	M. J. Clarke (A)	
18	14	A. N. Cook (E)		13	9	A. N. Petersen (SA)	
17	9	G. C. Smith (SA)		13	11	K. S. Williamson (NZ)	
16	7	D. J. G. Sammy (WI)		13	14	I. R. Bell (E)	

864

ONE-DAY INTERNATIONAL AVERAGES
IN CALENDAR YEAR 2013

BATTING (500 runs)

	M	I	NO	R	HS	100	50	Avge	SR	4	6
G. J. Bailey (A)	22	20	3	1,098	156	2	8	64.58	100.00	88	30
†K. C. Sangakkara (SL).....	25	23	4	1,201	169	2	10	63.21	89.56	116	14
M. S. Dhoni (I)	26	20	8	753	139*	1	5	62.75	96.04	67	24
I. J. L. Trott (E)	14	14	4	611	109*	1	4	61.10	86.05	47	1
T. M. Dilshan (SL)	25	25	6	1,160	125	3	7	61.05	81.06	126	1
Misbah-ul-Haq (P)........	34	32	7	1,373	96*	0	15	54.92	73.54	87	28
V. Kohli (I)	34	30	6	1,268	115*	4	7	52.83	97.53	137	20
R. G. Sharma (I)	28	27	4	1,196	209	2	8	52.00	80.81	119	30
A. B. de Villiers (SA)	27	26	3	1,163	128	3	7	50.56	97.07	94	21
†S. Dhawan (I)............	26	25	2	1,162	119	5	4	50.52	97.89	146	9
Mohammad Hafeez (P)	33	33	5	1,301	140*	5	4	46.46	84.37	122	25
L. R. P. L. Taylor (NZ) ...	13	13	2	510	107*	2	3	46.36	77.98	41	10
†Q. de Kock (SA)	16	16	0	741	135	4	0	46.31	86.56	80	9
S. R. Watson (A)	17	16	0	693	143	3	2	43.31	106.28	74	21
I. R. Bell (E)	16	16	1	645	113*	1	4	43.00	76.87	68	6
J. E. Root (E)............	20	19	3	626	79*	0	4	39.12	82.15	51	4
Ahmed Shehzad (P).......	21	21	0	809	124	2	5	38.52	71.91	74	7
H. M. Amla (SA)	23	22	0	838	122	2	4	38.09	84.56	85	2
†D. M. Bravo (WI)	24	24	3	788	100*	1	8	37.52	74.62	76	11
†P. J. Hughes (A).........	20	19	1	660	138*	2	2	36.66	74.57	74	4
†J-P. Duminy (SA)	21	21	3	659	150*	1	3	36.61	83.52	45	16
J. Charles (WI)..........	19	19	0	686	130	2	2	36.10	86.07	72	18
†S. K. Raina (I)	34	27	5	770	89*	0	5	35.00	84.52	66	10
†A. N. Cook (E)..........	16	16	0	560	78	0	5	35.00	75.16	68	4
†E. J. G. Morgan (E)......	21	20	4	560	124*	1	2	35.00	91.20	43	16
D. P. M. D. Jayawardene (SL)	21	19	2	557	107	1	2	32.76	81.43	59	4
A. D. Mathews (SL)	28	21	3	585	74*	0	4	32.50	80.68	41	11
†D. A. Miller (SA)........	24	24	7	544	85*	0	4	32.00	90.96	39	16
A. J. Finch (A)...........	18	17	0	514	148	1	2	30.23	92.11	65	12
F. du Plessis (SA)	21	21	1	539	62*	0	3	26.95	79.03	48	9
†Nasir Jamshed (P)	23	23	0	568	106	1	2	24.69	61.60	54	7

BOWLING (15 wickets, average 40.00)

	Style	O	M	R	W	BB	4I	Avge	SR	ER
J. M. Anderson (E)	RFM	82.5	5	351	23	5-34	1	15.26	21.60	4.23
D. W. Steyn (SA).........	RF	117	16	428	27	6-39	2	15.85	26.00	3.65
A. Mishra (I)	LBG	57.3	2	287	18	6-48	2	15.94	19.16	4.99
M. A. Starc (A)	LFM	55.1	3	276	15	5-20	2	18.40	22.06	5.00
M. J. McClenaghan (NZ)...	LFM	133.3	3	761	40	5-58	5	19.02	20.02	5.70
H. M. R. K. B. Herath (SL) .	SLA	124.5	6	509	26	4-20	1	19.57	28.80	4.07
Saeed Ajmal (P)..........	OB	306.3	15	1,268	62	5-24	3	20.45	29.66	4.13
Junaid Khan (P)	LFM	228.3	17	1,116	52	4-15	1	21.46	26.36	4.88
J. C. Tredwell (E)	OB	111.2	4	559	25	4-44	1	22.36	26.72	5.02
R. McLaren (SA)	RFM	208.3	6	1,070	45	4-19	4	23.77	27.80	5.13
Mohammad Irfan (P)......	LFM	205.2	12	923	38	4-33	1	24.28	32.42	4.49
M. Morkel (SA)	RF	136.3	10	610	25	3-34	0	24.40	32.76	4.46
M. G. Johnson (A)	LF	172.4	12	811	33	4-55	2	24.57	31.39	4.69
R. A. Jadeja (I)...........	SLA	303.3	22	1,321	52	5-36	2	25.40	35.01	4.35
I. Wardlaw (Scot)	RFM	78.3	1	409	15	4-43	1	27.26	31.40	5.21
D. J. Bravo (WI)	RFM	150.4	5	902	33	6-43	2	27.33	27.39	5.98
C. J. McKay (A)	RFM	192.4	14	946	34	4-33	2	27.82	34.00	4.91
J. O. Holder (WI).........	RFM	95.2	8	474	17	4-13	1	27.88	33.64	4.97

	Style	O	M	R	W	BB	4I	Avge	SR	ER
K. M. D. N. Kulasekara (SL)	RFM	144.5	10	703	25	5-22	2	28.12	34.76	4.85
I. Sharma (I)	RFM	176.2	14	993	35	4-40	1	28.37	30.22	5.63
K. D. Mills (NZ)	RFM	141.4	13	680	23	4-30	1	29.56	36.95	4.80
L. L. Tsotsobe (SA)	LFM	215.5	23	1,046	35	4-22	3	29.88	37.00	4.84
Mohammed Shami (I)	RFM	167.1	13	902	30	3-42	0	30.06	33.43	5.39
S. L. Malinga (SL)	RF	218.1	16	1,176	39	4-34	2	30.15	33.56	5.39
S. T. Finn (E)	RF	125.4	11	601	19	3-27	0	31.63	39.68	4.78
Shahid Afridi (P)	LBG	178.2	5	862	27	7-12	1	31.92	39.62	4.83
J. P. Faulkner (A)	LFM	140.4	5	802	25	4-48	1	32.08	33.76	5.70
K. A. J. Roach (WI)	RF	139	23	670	20	4-27	1	33.50	41.70	4.82
R. Ashwin (I)	OB	259.5	6	1,353	40	3-39	0	33.82	38.97	5.20
Bhuvneshwar Kumar (I) . . .	RFM	203	25	948	28	4-8	1	33.85	43.50	4.66
S. P. Narine (WI)	OB	204	16	899	26	4-26	2	34.57	47.07	4.40
A. D. Mathews (SL)	RFM	152.4	11	666	19	4-29	1	35.05	48.21	4.36
N. L. T. C. Perera (SL)	RFM	96.4	1	577	16	3-31	0	36.06	36.25	5.96

MOST DISMISSALS BY A WICKETKEEPER

Dis		M			Dis		M	
34	(21ct, 13st)	26	M. S. Dhoni (I)		25	(25ct)	15	Q. de Kock (SA)
32	(23ct, 9st)	18	Umar Akmal (P)		23	(19ct, 4st)	13	Kamran Akmal (P)
32	(26ct, 6st)	25	K. C. Sangakkara (SL)		22	(21ct, 1st)	14	B. R. M. Taylor (Z)
31	(30ct, 1st)	18	J. C. Buttler (E)					

When not keeping wicket, Umar Akmal made a further three catches in one match, and Q. de Kock none in one. A. B. de Villiers made 25 catches in 27 matches, but only 17 of those in his 14 matches playing as a wicketkeeper.

MOST CATCHES IN THE FIELD

Ct	M			Ct	M	
17	23	H. M. Amla (SA)		13	24	D. M. Bravo (WI)
17	34	S. K. Raina (I)		12	22	D. J. Bravo (WI)
15	19	N. L. McCullum (NZ)		12	33	Mohammad Hafeez (P)
14	21	F. du Plessis (SA)		12	34	R. A. Jadeja (I)

TWENTY20 INTERNATIONAL AVERAGES IN CALENDAR YEAR 2013

BATTING (150 runs)

	M	I	NO	R	HS	100	50	Avge	SR	4	6
A. J. Finch (A)	6	6	0	262	156	1	1	43.66	194.07	27	15
B. B. McCullum (NZ)	5	4	0	178	74	0	2	44.50	160.36	18	7
A. D. Hales (E)	7	7	2	247	94	0	2	49.40	153.41	29	8
Mohammad Shahzad (Afg) . . .	9	9	0	258	55	0	1	28.66	149.13	34	4
†M. J. Lumb (E)	7	7	1	188	53*	0	1	31.33	148.03	16	11
†H. D. Rutherford (NZ)	7	6	0	151	62	0	1	25.16	145.19	12	9
Shahid Afridi (P)	12	10	5	199	46	0	0	39.80	143.16	15	9
W. Barresi (Neth)	6	6	3	176	75*	0	2	58.66	136.43	16	2
Mohammad Hafeez (P)	12	12	3	323	86	0	3	35.88	132.92	27	11
Umar Akmal (P)	10	10	2	230	64	0	1	28.75	132.18	17	8
M. R. Swart (Neth)	5	5	1	212	89	0	1	53.00	131.67	15	4
†M. W. Machan (Scot)	6	6	2	276	67*	0	3	69.00	131.42	29	4
†D. A. Warner (A)	4	4	1	151	90*	0	2	50.33	131.30	11	6
†M. D. K. J. Perera (SL)	9	9	0	301	84	0	3	33.44	128.08	26	12
R. R. Patel (Kenya)	12	12	2	267	52	0	1	26.70	127.14	12	16

	M	I	NO	R	HS	100	50	Avge	SR	4	6
M. J. Guptill (NZ).	3	3	0	150	59	0	1	50.00	**127.11**	9	5
†J-P. Duminy (SA).	6	5	2	190	51*	0	2	63.33	**125.82**	13	5
†K. C. Sangakkara (SL).	5	5	3	183	59*	0	1	91.50	**123.64**	19	2
Ahmed Shehzad (P)	12	12	1	347	98*	0	2	31.54	**121.32**	34	12
†Q. de Kock (SA).	7	7	1	187	48*	0	0	31.16	**114.72**	28	2
T. M. Dilshan (SL).	7	7	2	219	74*	0	2	43.80	**114.65**	26	3
H. Masakadza (Z).	6	6	1	182	59	0	2	36.40	**110.97**	17	3
F. du Plessis (SA)	8	8	2	234	85	0	2	39.00	**108.83**	17	8
C. O. Obuya (Kenya)	12	12	4	293	75*	0	2	36.62	**107.32**	18	8
C. S. MacLeod (Scot).	8	8	1	151	56	0	1	21.57	**89.34**	7	4

BOWLING (7 wickets, 20 overs)

	Style	O	M	R	W	BB	4I	Avge	SR	ER
Imran Tahir (SA)	LBG	21	0	109	7	2-17	0	15.57	18.00	**5.19**
S. M. S. M. Senanayake (SL)	OB	23	0	122	10	3-14	0	12.20	13.80	**5.30**
S. P. Narine (WI)	OB	20	0	108	8	3-26	0	13.50	15.00	**5.40**
R. M. Haq (Scot)	OB	30	0	173	10	3-20	0	17.30	18.00	**5.76**
Samiullah Shenwari (Afg). .	LBG	22.4	0	133	12	5-13	1	11.08	11.33	**5.86**
H. A. Varaiya (Kenya).	SLA	35	1	210	10	2-10	0	21.00	21.00	**6.00**
Mudassar Bukhari (Neth) . .	RFM	23.1	2	144	11	3-14	0	13.09	12.63	**6.21**
L. L. Tsotsobe (SA).	LFM	26	2	163	7	2-9	0	23.28	22.28	**6.26**
Mohammad Hafeez (P)	OB	41	1	258	12	3-25	0	21.50	20.50	**6.29**
Saeed Ajmal (P).	OB	34	0	220	10	3-25	0	22.00	20.40	**6.47**
R. G. Aga (Kenya).	RFM	26.1	0	170	10	3-24	0	17.00	15.70	**6.49**
Hamid Hassan (Afg)	RFM	22	2	148	8	4-22	1	18.50	16.50	**6.72**
Hamza Hotak (Afg)	SLA	22.5	1	154	7	3-39	0	22.00	19.57	**6.74**
Sohail Tanvir (P)	LFM	36	2	250	9	2-11	0	27.77	24.00	**6.94**
S. L. Malinga (SL).	RF	31	0	218	8	3-26	0	27.25	23.25	**7.03**
Shapoor Zadran (Afg)	LFM	21	0	149	8	2-21	0	18.62	15.75	**7.09**
K. M. D. N. Kulasekara (SL)	RFM	25.3	0	182	8	2-22	0	22.75	19.12	**7.13**
W. D. Parnell (SA).	LFM	22	2	159	8	3-25	0	19.87	16.50	**7.22**
S. O. Ngoche (Kenya)	SLA	38	0	275	14	4-34	1	19.64	16.28	**7.23**
Shahid Afridi (P)	LBG	36.3	0	272	10	3-25	0	27.20	21.90	**7.45**
J. W. Dernbach (E)	RFM	24	0	195	13	3-23	0	15.00	11.07	**8.12**
J. P. Faulkner (A).	LFM	20	0	164	7	3-28	0	23.42	17.14	**8.20**
M. J. McClenaghan (NZ). . .	LFM	22.2	1	209	7	2-24	0	29.85	19.14	**9.35**

MOST DISMISSALS BY A WICKETKEEPER

Dis		M		Dis		M	
12	(8ct, 4st)	7	Q. de Kock (SA)	6	(6ct)	6	W. Barresi (Neth)
7	(4ct, 3st)	8	Mohammad Shahzad (Afg)	6	(6ct)	7	J. C. Buttler (E)
7	(4ct, 3st)	10	M. A. Ouma (Kenya)	5	(3ct, 2st)	5	K. C. Sangakkara (SL)

MOST CATCHES IN THE FIELD

Ct	M		Ct	M	
8	12	C. O. Obuya (Kenya)	5	6	A. B. de Villiers (SA)
7	12	R. R. Patel (Kenya)	5	6	L. R. P. L. Taylor (NZ)
6	11	H. A. Varaiya (Kenya)	5	7	T. M. Dilshan (SL)
5	3	J. M. Bairstow (E)	5	11	R. G. Aga (Kenya)
5	5	D. J. Bravo (WI)	5	12	Shahid Afridi (P)

INDEX OF TEST MATCHES

Seven earlier 2012-13 Test series – India v New Zealand, Australia v South Africa, Bangladesh v West Indies, India v England, Sri Lanka v New Zealand, Australia v Sri Lanka and South Africa v New Zealand – appeared in *Wisden 2013*.

THE WOMEN'S WORLD CUP, 2012-13

Alison Mitchell

1. Australia   2. West Indies   3. England   4. New Zealand

In 40 years of the women's World Cup, the traditional powerhouses of Australia, England, New Zealand and – to a lesser extent – India have rarely been challenged. But the tenth edition brought a significant shift: an emergent Sri Lanka upset two of the top nations, ensuring an early exit for hosts India, while the mercurial West Indies reached their first final. The shift did not prove seismic, however: Australia lifted the trophy for a record sixth time, adding it to the World Twenty20 they had won in Colombo four months earlier.

The tournament was memorable for a higher standard of play from a greater number of teams, several tight finishes, a record number of World Cup centuries, pitches conducive to entertaining cricket, and an audience from over 150 territories watched the ten televised matches.

But there were complications, including doubts over whether the Pakistan team could stay safely in Mumbai, the host city: Indo-Pakistani tensions had recently led to right-wing political protests, forcing Pakistani hockey players out of the Mumbai Magicians squad. And once Mumbai's male cricketers made the final of the Ranji Trophy, they declared they wanted to play it at the Wankhede Stadium, their home ground, which had been earmarked as one of the World Cup's main venues.

When the Wankhede was duly withdrawn by the BCCI on January 21, ten days before the opening match, it was regarded as a snub to the women's game. The nearby Brabourne Stadium became the central venue for all televised games, including the final. As it transpired, the smaller ground – home of the Cricket Club of India – was well suited to the tournament: dripping with history, it offered a more intimate experience for players and spectators. As for Pakistan, it was decided that an additional host city was needed. India, England, Sri Lanka and West Indies made up Group A in Mumbai, while Australia, New Zealand, Pakistan and South Africa contested Group B, roughly a thousand miles away in Cuttack. Pakistan were forced to stay in the Barabati Stadium's academy accommodation – officially for security reasons, though it was understood some hotels were reluctant to take them.

The revised schedule was confirmed only six days before the tournament began. It followed the same format as in 2008-09: the top three teams from each group of four would qualify for the Super Sixes, from which the top two would contest the final.

Once the cricket got under way, it was captivating. In the opening match, Thirush Kamini became the first Indian woman to hit a century in a World Cup (a pity there was only one half-full stand to see it). A 22-year-old left-hander from Chennai, Kamini was playing her first one-day international in three years. After a steady start, she stroked her way to a rousing 100 off 146 balls, lofting the first six of the tournament over deep midwicket, as India demolished

West Indies by 105 runs. It was to be the first of 11 centuries – almost twice as many as at any other World Cup – including two more for India and two from England captain Charlotte Edwards, who passed Belinda Clark to become the all-time leading scorer in women's one-day internationals.

On the morning of the first match, *The Times of India* had devoted almost the whole front page of their sport section to **India's** chances, together with profiles of key players. And media coverage gathered pace after Kamini's hundred. But it was not to last. A loss to England, followed by a surprise 138-run defeat by Sri Lanka, meant India did not qualify for the Super Sixes, and the wave of support receded. No more Bollywood actors or wives of IPL owners would be seen at the World Cup. A century for captain Mithali Raj and victory over arch-rivals **Pakistan** in the seventh-place play-off in Cuttack were scant consolation; the BCCI bore the brunt of media criticism for failing to support the women's game sufficiently.

Sri Lanka's win over India was their second major upset. They had arrived as the second-lowest ranked side, having failed to win a single fixture at the previous World Cup. Yet the introduction of match fees, and contracts to play

Dottin delivered
a blistering fifty
in 20 balls

for the Armed Forces had already helped them stage the biggest upset in the tournament's history: a thrilling one-wicket win off the last ball against defending champions England.

That game marked Eshani Kaushalya's coming of age. Playing in her third World Cup as a medium-pace all-rounder, she batted with a swagger and a stance reminiscent of compatriot Sanath Jayasuriya – and hit the ball almost as hard. With 86 still needed at a run a ball, she crashed 56 off 41 and took her team to the brink. Sri Lanka had never beaten England or India before and, although they possessed bowling talent as well as batting, defeat by West Indies illustrated a damaging inconsistency. Three losses followed in the Super Sixes, including one by 110 runs to **South Africa**, though they went on to beat them by 88 runs in the fifth-place play-off.

Inconsistency was also the scourge of **West Indies**, who sneaked through the group on net run-rate, yet won all three Super Six matches, including an unlikely victory over Australia, to reach their first World Cup final and consign a disgruntled England to the third-place play-off against New Zealand. All-rounder Deandra Dottin's reputation preceded her – she had made a 38-ball hundred in the World Twenty20 of 2010 – and she now delivered the fastest recorded fifty in women's international cricket: a blistering half-century in 20 deliveries to help brush aside Sri Lanka. West Indies' total of 368 for eight, a team record, was built around Stafanie Taylor's career-best 171 off 137 balls.

Australia were unbeaten until their surprise loss to West Indies in the Super Sixes. Their batting faltered at times, though it was at its best when they beat **New Zealand** in a group game. The New Zealanders had looked like the form side until they too lost to West Indies in the Super Sixes. Captain Suzie Bates was in particularly good touch, and was the tournament's leading run-scorer with 407, including 102 against Australia. **England's** highly regarded wicketkeeper-batter, Sarah Taylor, had a poor start, missing the first game

Shock and awe: Eshani Kaushalya's muscular 56 sped Sri Lanka towards their first win over England, and set the tone for a World Cup full of upsets. Keeping wicket is Amy Jones, standing in for the injured Sarah Taylor.

through injury and later racking up three successive ducks. That nearly became four: she was dropped on nought in the last Super Six match, against New Zealand, before going on to a sparkling 88 off 79 balls. But it was too little too late, as news filtered through of West Indies' win over Australia.

Australia possessed the tournament's leading wicket-taker, pace bowler Megan Schutt from Adelaide, who took 15 scalps at 16 apiece. They had to cope with the loss of star bowler Ellyse Perry in the middle of the tournament through injury: forced out of their first Super Six fixture, against England, she could not play again until the final. But it meant the door opened for another tall, blonde fast bowler. Holly Ferling, a 17-year-old Queenslander who had made her international debut a week earlier, bowled quickly, if not always accurately, with the exuberance of youth and a white ribbon holding in place her long ponytail.

Perry returned for the final, despite what was later diagnosed as a stress fracture in her left ankle. After a scare when she twice aborted her run-up, she found her rhythm to take three for 19 as Australia successfully defended their 259 for seven, the highest total in a women's World Cup final. All-rounder Lisa Sthalekar bowled a miserly spell of two for 20 and took a stunning diving catch to seal victory, before announcing her retirement from international cricket, aged 33. The captaincy of Jodie Fields was superb throughout.

Despite large TV audiences, attendances in Mumbai in particular were low. There was no World Cup branding in the streets or indeed at the three grounds. At the Brabourne, a single hoarding at the entrance gates signposted the World Cup. A few months earlier, when the women's World Twenty20 was held in Sri Lanka alongside the men's, there had been life-size cardboard cut-outs of star women players in airport arrival halls or perched on roundabouts. The ICC, running their second World Cup after taking charge of the women's international game in 2005, preferred to focus their marketing campaign online. But it did not have the desired effect.

The standard of umpiring was disappointing. There was no official from the ICC's Elite Panel; in the previous tournament, the highly respected Steve Davis had mentored the other umpires and stood in three matches, including the final. The format was also questioned, with suggestions that teams should have carried through all points gained from the group stage, instead of only those gained against other teams who had qualified for the Super Sixes. Players said privately that they would have enjoyed national anthems at the start of every match, as in 2008-09, instead of the final alone. The World Cup is the pinnacle of every player's career, and anthems would have added to the sense of occasion at a tournament where the cricket repeatedly hit the high notes.

Group A

At Mumbai (Brabourne), January 31, 2013 (day/night). **India won by 105 runs. India 284-6** (50 overs) (P. G. Raut 72, M. D. Thirush Kamini 100, J. Goswami 36, H. Kaur 36; D. J. S. Dottin 3-32); ‡**West Indies 179** (44.3 overs) (D. J. S. Dottin 39; N. Niranjana 3-52). *ODI debut:* R. Parwin (India). *PoM:* M. D. Thirush Kamini. *Thirush Kamini reached her maiden international hundred and India's first in the World Cup after sharing an opening stand of 175 with Punam Raut. They set India on course for their third-highest one-day total and best in the World Cup. Deandra Dottin lifted four sixes in her 39 from 16 balls, but West Indies had little hope once she was gone.*

At Mumbai (Brabourne), February 1, 2013. **Sri Lanka won by one wicket. England 238-8** (50 overs) (A. Brindle 31, H. C. Knight 38, J. L. Gunn 52, A. Jones 41); ‡**Sri Lanka 244-9** (50 overs) (A. C. Jayangani 62, B. Y. A. Mendis 46, H. A. S. D. Siriwardene 34, L. E. Kaushalya 56). *ODI debut:* A. Jones. *PoM:* L. E. Kaushalya. *Sri Lanka pulled off a shock win over defending champions England when, with the scores level, No. 10 Dilani Manodara Surangika hit the last ball of the match for six. It was the first of her international career. Chamari Atapattu Jayangani and Avanthika Mendis had set up the run-chase with 103, and Eshani Kaushalya – dropped on ten – struck 56 in 41 balls, including three sixes, before she was run out in the final over. Sri Lanka's 244 was then the highest World Cup total batting second. Earlier, England had recovered from 29-3 thanks to Jenny Gunn and debutant keeper Amy Jones, who added 83 for the sixth wicket.*

At Mumbai (Brabourne), February 3, 2013. **England won by 32 runs. England 272-8** (50 overs) (C. M. Edwards 109, S. J. Taylor 35, A. Brindle 37*); ‡**India 240-9** (50 overs) (H. Kaur 107*, K. V. Jain 56; K. H. Brunt 4-29). *PoM:* C. M. Edwards. *Charlotte Edwards hit her seventh one-day century for England, which took her past Belinda Clark's record of 4,844 one-day international runs. She and Sarah Taylor, returning after injury, put on 100 for the second wicket. India were 29-3 in reply before Harmanpreet Kaur, who scored her maiden hundred for India, and Karu Jain added 106 for the fourth. But Katherine Brunt saw off India's challenge.*

At Mumbai (Middle Income Group), February 3, 2013. **West Indies won by 209 runs. West Indies 368-8** (50 overs) (Kycia A. Knight 30, S. R. Taylor 171, Kyshona A. Knight 44, D. J. S. Dottin 50, M. R. Aguilleira 47*); ‡**Sri Lanka 159** (40 overs) (S. L. Quintyne 3-32). *PoM:* S. R. Taylor. *West Indies raised their highest one-day total, and the biggest by any team in the tournament, thanks to Stafanie Taylor, whose 171 in 137 balls was the third-highest score in women's one-day internationals and the best for West Indies; to Kyshona Knight, one of twin sisters in the side, who helped Taylor* *add 110 for the third wicket; and to Dottin, who hit a 20-ball fifty with four sixes. Nine West Indians bowled as Sri Lanka folded with ten overs to go. After four matches in Group A, all four teams were tied on two points apiece.*

At Mumbai (Bandra Kurla), February 5, 2013. **England won by six wickets. ‡West Indies 101** (36.4 overs) (Kyshona A. Knight 33, S. F. Daley 30*; A. Shrubsole 4-21, A. Brindle 3-0); **England 103-4** (35 overs) (D. N. Wyatt 40; D. J. S. Dottin 3-20). *PoM:* A. Shrubsole. *West Indies crumbled against the medium-pace of Anya Shrubsole, returning her best one-day figures for England, and Arran Brindle, who also took a career-best, claiming three wickets in two maiden overs. There were six ducks as nine West Indians scored ten runs between them. England cruised into the Super Sixes with 15 overs in hand, despite Taylor's first-ball dismissal.*

At Mumbai (Brabourne), February 5, 2013 (day/night). **Sri Lanka won by 138 runs. ‡Sri Lanka 282-5** (50 overs) (B. Y. A. Mendis 55, H. M. D. Rasangika 84, H. A. S. D. Siriwardene 59, L. E. Kaushalya 56*; J. Goswami 3-63); **India 144** (42.2 overs) (R. Malhotra 38). *PoM:* H. M. D. Rasangika. *Sri Lanka knocked out the home team and qualified themselves. Mendis and Deepika Rasangika got them going with 117 for the second wicket, before Kaushalya struck 56 in 31 balls, rounding off the innings with her third six. India needed 251 to qualify ahead of West Indies on net run-rate, but made little headway against tight bowling.*

Group B

At Cuttack (Barabati), February 1, 2013. **Australia won by 91 runs. ‡Australia 175** (46.1 overs) (R. L. Haynes 39, L. C. Sthalekar 32, S. J. Coyte 35*; Sadia Yousuf 3-30); **Pakistan 84** (33.2 overs) (Bismah Maroof 43; S. J. Coyte 3-20). *ODI debuts:* R. K. Chappell, H. L. Ferling. *PoM:* S. J. Coyte. *Australia looked shaky at 99-6; Lisa Sthalekar and Sarah Coyte put them back on track, then took the lead in skittling Pakistan.*

At Cuttack (Dhaneswar Rath), February 1, 2013. **New Zealand won by 151 runs. New Zealand 321-5** (50 overs) (S. W. Bates 73, S. F. M. Devine 145, S. J. McGlashan 32, N. J. Browne 40*); **‡South Africa 170** (41 overs) (S. M. Benade 37, S. Ismail 31; S. E. A. Ruck 4-31, M. J. G. Nielsen 3-34). *PoM:* S. F. M. Devine. *Sophie Devine scored 145 in 131 balls, with six sixes and 13 fours – the second-highest score for New Zealand in women's one-day internationals. She put on 128 with Suzie Bates and 102 with Nicola Browne. From 82-7, Susan Benade and Shabnim Ismail added 71 for South Africa, a World Cup record for the eighth wicket, before left-armers Sian Ruck and Morna Nielsen completed the demolition.*

At Cuttack (Dhaneswar Rath), February 3, 2013. **Australia won by three wickets. ‡South Africa 188-9** (50 overs) (T. Chetty 59, M. Kapp 61; E. A. Perry 3-35); **Australia 190-7** (45.4 overs) (R. L. Haynes 83; S. Ismail 4-41). *PoM:* R. L. Haynes. *Ellyse Perry reduced South Africa to 0-2 in the third over before Trisha Chetty and Marizanne Kapp added 122. Shabnim Ismail's pace had Australia looking uneasy again, at 34-3, but Rachael Haynes took them in sight of victory, which guaranteed qualification for the Super Sixes.*

At Cuttack (Barabati), February 3, 2013. **New Zealand won by seven wickets. ‡Pakistan 104** (41.2 overs) (R. H. Candy 5-19); **New Zealand 108-3** (29.4 overs) (S. W. Bates 65*). *PoM:* R. H. Candy. *Pakistan struggled once more, this time against Rachel Candy, reaching 23-4 in 12 overs. Bates steered New Zealand into the Super Sixes with 20 overs in hand.*

At Cuttack (Dhaneswar Rath), February 5, 2013. **Australia won by seven wickets. New Zealand 227-6** (50 overs) (S. W. Bates 102, K. T. Perkins 41, N. J. Browne 39*; M. L. Schutt 3-40); **‡Australia 228-3** (38.2 overs) (M. M. Lanning 112, J. E. Cameron 82). *PoM:* M. M. Lanning. *Australia finished on top of the group despite Suzie Bates's century; her 103-run stand with Katie Perkins could not compensate for New Zealand's poor start of 39-4. Meg Lanning scored Australia's only hundred of the tournament, and added 182 with Jess Cameron to ensure victory with nearly 12 overs to spare.*

At Cuttack (Barabati), February 5, 2013. **South Africa won by 126 runs. ‡South Africa 207-5** (50 overs) (M. Kapp 102*, D. van Niekerk 55*); **Pakistan 81** (29.4 overs) (M. Kapp 3-18). *PoM:* M. Kapp. *South Africa claimed the last place in the Super Sixes thanks to Marizanne Kapp, who scored her first international century while putting on 128* with Dane van Niekerk, then claimed three wickets with her medium-pace as Pakistan were dismissed in the eighties for the second time in three matches.*

GROUP TABLES

Group A	Played	Won	Lost	Points	Net run-rate
ENGLAND	3	2	1	4	0.64
SRI LANKA	3	2	1	4	−0.43
WEST INDIES	3	1	2	2	0.27
India.	3	1	2	2	−0.43

Group B	Played	Won	Lost	Points	Net run-rate
AUSTRALIA.	3	3	0	6	1.09
NEW ZEALAND	3	2	1	4	1.43
SOUTH AFRICA	3	1	2	2	−0.29
Pakistan	3	0	3	0	−1.98

Win = 2pts. Where teams were tied on points, their position was determined on net run-rate, calculated by subtracting runs conceded per over from runs scored per over.

Super Six

At Mumbai (Brabourne), February 8, 2013. **Australia won by two runs. Australia 147** (44.4 overs) (L. C. Sthalekar 41, S. J. Coyte 44; A. Shrubsole 3-24); ‡**England 145** (47.3 overs) (L. S. Greenway 49; H. L. Ferling 3-35). *PoM:* L. C. Sthalekar. *As in the group stage, England started the Super Sixes by losing a thriller. They had Australia in trouble at 32-5, with Shrubsole taking three in 15 balls and, despite an 82-run stand between Sthalekar and Coyte, England's target was only 148. But they slumped in turn to 39-6 and, shortly after Lydia Greenway became 17-year-old Holly Ferling's third victim, it was 114-9. The last pair, Holly Colvin and Shrubsole, put on 31, only for Colvin to edge to the keeper with three required.*

At Mumbai (Bandra Kurla), February 8, 2013. **New Zealand won by eight wickets. Sri Lanka 103** (42 overs) (M. A. D. D. Surangika 34; S. E. A. Ruck 3-16, L. M. M. Tahuhu 4-27); ‡**New Zealand 108-2** (23 overs) (F. L. Mackay 39*, S. W. Bates 37). *PoM:* L. M. M. Tahuhu. *Lea Tahuhu struck with her first ball, and both Sri Lankan openers went for ducks. New Zealand coasted home, with Sophie Devine (29*) hitting the winning six with 27 overs to go.*

At Cuttack (Barabati), February 8, 2013. **West Indies won by two wickets. ‡South Africa 230-7** (50 overs) (T. Chetty 45, M. du Preez 31, C-Z. Brits 44, D. van Niekerk 33*); **West Indies 234-8** (45.3 overs) (Kycia A. Knight 46, S. R. Taylor 75, S. A. Campbelle 33; D. van Niekerk 3-47). *PoM:* S. R. Taylor. *Solid batting by South Africa was not enough; West Indies effectively ended their interest in the tournament as Taylor, whose 75 took 78 balls, and Kycia Knight shared a second-wicket stand of 126. Despite some late wickets, the tail finished the job.*

At Mumbai (Brabourne), February 10, 2013. **Australia won by nine wickets. Sri Lanka 131** (45.2 overs) (H. M. D. Rasangika 43; E. A. Osborne 3-9); ‡**Australia 132-1** (22.2 overs) (M. M. Lanning 37, R. L. Haynes 71*). *PoM:* E. A. Osborne. *Australia's fifth win in five games booked their place in the final with a round to spare. Off-spinner Erin Osborne helped to suffocate Sri Lanka's batting with figures of 10–6–9–3, before Australia knocked off a straightforward target; Haynes ran up 71* in 61 balls.*

At Cuttack (Barabati), February 10, 2013. **England won by seven wickets. South Africa 77** (29.3 overs) (A. Shrubsole 5-17, D. N. Wyatt 3-7); ‡**England 81-3** (9.3 overs) (M. M. Lanning). *PoM:* A. Shrubsole. *England squashed South Africa in a match that lasted only 39 overs. Shrubsole claimed their first five wickets, improving her career-best for the second time in six days; her figures were also England's second-best in World Cup cricket, and South Africa's total was the lowest in this tournament. Seeking quick runs – to improve their chances of reaching the final by raising the run-rate – England lost their own top three cheaply (including Taylor for her third consecutive duck), but galloped home at 8.5 an over.*

At Mumbai (Brabourne), February 11, 2013. **West Indies won by 48 runs. West Indies 207-9** (50 overs) (S. R. Taylor 49, S. F. Daley 37, A. Mohammed 31*; M. J. G. Nielsen 3-27); ‡**New Zealand 159** (44.3 overs) (S. W. Bates 30, R. H. Priest 36; T. D. Smartt 3-39). *PoM:* A. Mohammed. *West Indies beat New Zealand for the first time in a 50-over international – having done so in the World Twenty20 five months earlier. They were 159-8 before Shanel Daley and Anisa Mohammed added 45, and the contribution from their last two wickets matched the winning margin. Tremayne Smartt's* *inswing claimed three wickets in the first ten overs and, when Mohammed held a return catch off Bates, New Zealand were 83-6. Rachel Priest restored some dignity, but was last out in the 45th over.*

At Mumbai (Middle Income Group), February 13, 2013. **West Indies won by eight runs. ‡West Indies 164** (47 overs) (D. J. S. Dottin 60; M. L. Schutt 3-50, H. L. Ferling 3-27); **Australia 156** (48.2 overs) (J. E. Cameron 39, A. J. Blackwell 45; S. F. Daley 3-22). PoM: D. J. S. Dottin. *West Indies' first victory over Australia in any women's international put them in the final; they had won all three Super Six games, finished level with Australia on eight points, and headed the table on net run-rate. But they had to fight for the win. Dottin helped them recover from 59-5 with 60 in 67 balls, but Australia looked comfortable at 130-4, needing 35 from 68 deliveries – only to lose their last six for 26. Daley ended the game with her third wicket, and was also responsible for one of three run-outs. Had Australia won, they would have faced England in the final instead – and Jodie Fields had to deal with suggestions they might have gone down a little easily, in order to avoid playing the tournament favourites. "I don't think it's ever good to have a loss," she said. "We definitely came out to win, and wanted to go through the tournament undefeated."*

At Cuttack (Barabati), February 13, 2013. **South Africa won by 110 runs. South Africa 227-8** (50 overs) (M. du Preez 37, C-Z. Brits 52, S. A. Fritz 64, D. van Niekerk 40; C. R. Seneviratne 3-44); **‡Sri Lanka 117** (36.4 overs) (A. C. Jayangani 63; D. van Niekerk 4-18). *ODI debut:* E. Theunissen. *PoM: D. van Niekerk. South Africa inflicted Sri Lanka's third Super Six defeat, seizing their last seven wickets for 13. Leg-spinner van Niekerk collected four, and Trisha Chetty equalled the South African record of five dismissals in a one-day international.*

At Mumbai (Brabourne), February 13, 2013 (day/night). **England won by 15 runs. ‡England 266-6** (50 overs) (C. M. Edwards 54, S. J. Taylor 88); **New Zealand 251-9** (50 overs) (S. W. Bates 79, A. E. Satterthwaite 103; H. L. Colvin 3-48). *PoM: S. J. Taylor. Taylor finally came good after being dropped on nought, helping England to set a challenging target. New Zealand's 251 was the highest World Cup total batting second, beating Sri Lanka's 244, made 12 days earlier. Amy Satterthwaite scored their third century of the tournament, adding 134 for the second wicket with Bates. But it was not enough to win, and the match had already lost its significance after West Indies' victory earlier in the day eliminated both teams.*

FINAL SUPER SIX TABLE

	Played	Won	Lost	Points	Net run-rate
WEST INDIES	5	4	1	8	0.94
AUSTRALIA.	5	4	1	8	0.71
England	5	3	2	6	1.00
New Zealand	5	2	3	4	0.69
South Africa.	5	1	4	2	−1.13
Sri Lanka	5	1	4	2	−2.47

Each team carried forward their results against the two fellow qualifiers from their group, then played the other three qualifiers.

Win = 2pts. Where teams were tied on points, their position was determined on net run-rate, calculated by subtracting runs conceded per over from runs scored per over.

Seventh-place Play-off

At Cuttack (Barabati), February 7, 2013. **India won by six wickets. ‡Pakistan 192-7** (50 overs) (Nain Abidi 58, Nida Dar 68*; N. Niranjana 3-35); **India 195-4** (46 overs) (M. Raj 103*). *PoM: M. Raj. Pakistan reached their highest World Cup total but left the tournament as the only winless team, as Mithali Raj's fourth one-day international hundred secured India a consolation victory.*

Fifth-place Play-off

At Cuttack (Barabati), February 15, 2013. **Sri Lanka won by 88 runs. ‡Sri Lanka 244-7** (50 overs) (A. C. Jayangani 52, H. M. D. Rasangika 43, H. A. S. D. Siriwardene 44, L. E. Kaushalya 43); **South Africa 156** (40.1 overs) (S. A. Fritz 54; H. A. S. D. Siriwardene 4-32). *PoM: H. A. S. D.*

Siriwardene. Sri Lanka rediscovered their group-stage form to take revenge for their defeat two days earlier. After they lost their openers cheaply, the rest of the batting rose to the occasion. Captain Shashikala Siriwardene followed her 44 with four wickets as South Africa lost their last five for 16.

Third-place Play-off

At Mumbai (Brabourne), February 15, 2013. **England won by four wickets. New Zealand 220-8** (50 overs) (F. L. Mackay 30, A. E. Satterthwaite 85; H. L. Colvin 3-31); ‡**England 222-6** (47 overs) (C. M. Edwards 106*, L. S. Greenway 31; L. R. Doolan 3-50). PoM: C. M. Edwards. *The finalists of the previous World Cup produced the same result in the quest for third place: a four-wicket win for England. After New Zealand captain Bates took her tournament aggregate to 407 runs, her counterpart Edwards scored her second century in a fortnight, and her eighth in all one-day internationals, equalling the record of Karen Rolton (Australia) and former England team-mate Claire Taylor. She also became the first woman to reach 5,000 one-day international runs.*

FINAL

AUSTRALIA v WEST INDIES

At Mumbai (Brabourne), February 17, 2013 (day/night). Australia won by 114 runs. Toss: Australia.
    After some wobbly batting earlier in the tournament, Australia came together at the right time as Jodie Fields led them to a historic sixth World Cup. They became only the second team of either gender to hold the World Cup, World Twenty20 and Ashes simultaneously (England's women had achieved this in 2009). West Indies had not appeared in a global final before, and perhaps the occasion unnerved them: their fielding was well below their previous standards. Played under lights, the match took on a pattern familiar from the Brabourne's group games, with a demanding total by the team batting first. Australia's 259 for seven was the highest in a women's final, and Jess Cameron's 75 off 76 balls earned the match award. The other key factor was the return of experienced fast bowler Ellyse Perry after an ankle injury. Clearly handicapped – she pulled out of her run-up twice before managing to bowl her first delivery, and later needed surgery for a stress fracture – she nevertheless struck in each of her first three overs. Fields used her bowlers judiciously to stifle the opposition; all-rounder Lisa Sthalekar's parsimonious off-spin claimed two for 20, one of them the threatening Deandra Dottin, which effectively sealed victory. West Indies' fight was ended in the 44th over by a one-handed diving catch from Sthalekar, who afterwards announced her retirement.
    Player of the Match: J. E. Cameron. *Player of the Tournament:* S. W. Bates (New Zealand).

Australia Women

M. M. Lanning c Kyshona A. Knight b Taylor .	31	E. A. Osborne c Quintyne b Mohammed . . 7
R. L. Haynes c Kycia A. Knight b Quintyne	52	E. A. Perry not out. 25
J. E. Cameron c Kyshona A. Knight b Daley	75	
A. J. Blackwell c Aguilleira b Smartt	3	L-b 3, w 4, n-b 4 11
L. C. Sthalekar c Campbell b Quintyne . . .	12	
S. J. Coyte c Daley b Quintyne	7	1/52 (1) 2/116 (2) (7 wkts, 50 overs) 259
*†J. M. Fields not out.	36	3/126 (4) 4/181 (3)
		5/187 (5) 6/190 (6) 7/209 (8) 10 overs: 52-1

J. L. Hunter and M. L. Schutt did not bat.

Daley 10-0-43-1; Smartt 5-0-43-1; Taylor 9-1-44-1; Quintyne 10-1-27-3; Mohammed 10-0-61-1; Kyshona A. Knight 3-0-23-0; Campbell 3-0-15-0.

West Indies Women

Kycia A. Knight lbw b Perry	17	A. Mohammed c Schutt b Osborne	14
N. Y. McLean lbw b Perry	13	T. D. Smartt c Sthalekar b Hunter	0
S. R. Taylor c and b Perry	5		
Kyshona A. Knight not out	21	B 1, l-b 8, w 6	15
*†M. R. Aguilleira b Sthalekar	23		
D. J. S. Dottin b Sthalekar	22	1/32 (1) 2/38 (3) 3/41 (2) (43.1 overs) 145	
S. A. Campbelle c Lanning b Schutt	11	4/88 (5) 5/109 (6) 6/109 (7)	
S. F. Daley c and b Schutt	2	7/114 (9) 8/114 (8) 9/141 (10)	
S. L. Quintyne c Blackwell b Osborne	2	10/145 (11) 10 overs: 32-1	

Kyshona A. Knight, when 6, retired hurt at 57-3 and resumed at 114-8.

Schutt 10–2–38–2; Hunter 4.1–0–18–1; Sthalekar 10–3–20–2; Perry 10–3–19–3; Osborne 7–2–26–2; Coyte 2–0–15–0.

Umpires: S. George and V. A. Kulkarni.   Third umpire: R. S. A. Palliyaguruge.
Referee: D. T. Jukes.

WOMEN'S WORLD CUP WINNERS

1973	*ENGLAND‡ (279-3) beat Australia (187-9) by 92 runs at Birmingham.
1977-78	*AUSTRALIA‡ (100-2) beat England (96-8) by eight wickets at Hyderabad.
1981-82	AUSTRALIA (152-7) beat England‡ (151-5) by three wickets at Christchurch.
1988-89	AUSTRALIA (129-2) beat England‡ (127-7) by eight wickets at Melbourne.
1993	ENGLAND (195-5) beat New Zealand‡ (128) by 67 runs at Lord's.
1997-98	AUSTRALIA (165-5) beat New Zealand‡ (164) by five wickets at Calcutta.
2000-01	NEW ZEALAND‡ (184) beat Australia (180) by four runs at Lincoln.
2004-05	AUSTRALIA‡ (215-4) beat India (117) by 98 runs at Centurion.
2008-09	ENGLAND (167-6) beat New Zealand‡ (166) by four wickets at North Sydney.
2012-13	AUSTRALIA‡ (259-7) beat West Indies (145) by 114 runs at Mumbai.

* *The first two Women's World Cups were played solely as a round-robin league, but in both the last scheduled match was between England and Australia, and decided the title.*

AUSTRALIAN CRICKET, 2013

Raised from the dead

DANIEL BRETTIG

Lazarus Rising, the title of former Australian prime minister – and self-confessed cricket tragic – John Howard's autobiography, would make an appropriate tagline for any book written about the nation's fortunes in 2013. So divergent were the highs and lows that a Hollywood studio would have rejected the option to film the tale on the grounds that it was simply too far-fetched.

Having fallen to pieces in India, then bottomed out in England, Australia renewed themselves wondrously at home, regaining the Ashes with a team unchanged across five Tests – a source of enormous joy and pride, and the pinnacle of so many careers, from captain Michael Clarke to young batsman Steve Smith. Their deservedly raucous celebrations, epitomised by the dancing

AUSTRALIA IN 2013

	Played	Won	Lost	Drawn/No result
Tests	14	5	7	2
One-day internationals	24	12	8	4
Twenty20 internationals	6	1	5	–

DECEMBER JANUARY	3 Tests, 5 ODIs and 2 T20Is (h) v Sri Lanka	(see *Wisden 2013*, page 919)
FEBRUARY	5 ODIs and 1 T20I (h) v West Indies	(page 882)
MARCH	4 Tests (a) v India	(page 919)
APRIL		
MAY		
JUNE	Champions Trophy (in England)	(page 301)
JULY AUGUST	5 Tests, 5 ODIs and 2 T20Is (a) v England	(page 325)
SEPTEMBER	1 ODI (a) v Scotland	(page 849)
OCTOBER NOVEMBER	7 ODIs and 1 T20I (a) v India	(page 934)
DECEMBER JANUARY FEBRUARY	5 Tests, 5 ODIs and 3 T20Is (h) v England	(page 373)

For a review of Australian domestic cricket from the 2012-13 season, see page 892.

feet and hungover grin of the 36-year-old Chris Rogers, rivalled those of England in 2005.

For a governing body under mounting pressure as the home summer approached, it was cause for relief. On the day the urn was regained in Perth, Cricket Australia chief executive James Sutherland departed from the innate conservatism of his accountancy background to buy drinks for the entire CA office in Melbourne. When a 5–0 sweep was completed breathlessly and ruthlessly in Sydney three weeks later, Sutherland and team performance manager Pat Howard were spotted in a corner of the dressing-room, sharing drinks and smiles with the players.

Those two had worn sterner expressions on a Bristol morning in late June, when they announced that Mickey Arthur, their joint-choice as coach in 2011, had been sacked halfway through his three-year term. His replacement was former Test batsman and Queensland coach Darren Lehmann, who had been serving as a batting consultant on the Australia A-tour that preceded the first of the back-to-back Ashes bouts.

A good and personable man with a fine record in South Africa, Arthur had nonetheless presided over the breakdown of the team's on-field cohesion during the horrendous 4–0 loss in India, and their off-field discipline, both there and in England. With Clarke and team manager Gavin Dovey, he handed out suspensions to four players for failing to follow instructions ahead of the Mohali Test. This overreaction said as much about the leadership's inability to connect with, and control, the players, as it did about any waywardness from the four involved – Shane Watson, Mitchell Johnson, Usman Khawaja and James Pattinson.

Watson's dislike for the insular, cliquey and intense direction the team had taken under the Arthur–Clarke axis was well known, and his was not the only voice of dissent. David Warner's behaviour had spiralled into dangerous territory. Though he evaded censure in India, he would soon be fined for tweeting abuse at two senior Australian cricket journalists while at the IPL. Any contrition dissipated rapidly and, following the team's Champions Trophy defeat by England, Warner threw a punch at Joe Root in a Birmingham bar.

Having warned Arthur and others for "letting things get to that point" after the Mohali suspensions, Sutherland and Howard acted swiftly. Warner was in effect suspended from the first two Tests in England, before Lehmann was offered the coaching job in the same few hours in which Arthur was relieved of it, taking control on the official first day of the Ashes tour. He quickly established a brand of authority that was at once relaxed and demanding, lending to the squad what national selector John Inverarity called an "energising lightness".

Such a vibe was desperately needed after India. Sorely lacking the experience of the retired Ricky Ponting and Mike Hussey, or even assistant coaches with relevant knowledge of playing on the subcontinent, Clarke's men had been atomised on pitches prepared to home specifications. Save for Clarke and the obstinate Ed Cowan, Australia's batting was poor, while their hard-working bowlers struggled for impact.

Their best hope had seemed to lie with the off-breaks of Nathan Lyon, but muddled selection meant he was dropped after the First Test and replaced by

Quite a turnaround: Brad Haddin, Michael Clarke and Mitchell Johnson, three giants of the 2013-14
Ashes, enjoy a smile before the Fifth Test at Sydney.

the ineffectual Xavier Doherty. Lyon returned to claim nine wickets in the
final match, at Delhi, but by then it was too late. Clarke had gone home to
nurse a relapse of his chronic back condition, leaving Watson in uneasy
command of a team he had been barred from representing in the previous
match; he later quit as vice-captain, having suggested he was considering his
future in the game. The man who would replace him, Brad Haddin, flew in for
one match because of injury to Matthew Wade, and summed up the scene:
"That wasn't the Australian cricket team I knew."

By the time they departed for England, CA had secured the game's financial
future for years to come, inking in a new broadcast rights deal with the Nine
and Ten networks that put both international and Twenty20 Big Bash League
cricket on free-to-air television for five years at a combined price of $590m.
Sutherland took credit for the windfall, though much of the heavy lifting had
been done by CA's lead negotiator Stephanie Beltrame and legal chief
Dean Kino.

Many mused that the deal was a rich one, considering performances on the
field. The Champions Trophy did little to dispel that notion. The timid opening
loss to England in Birmingham was that of a team scared of their own shadows,
before a washout against New Zealand and another poor defeat, by Sri Lanka,
completed a dreadful campaign. Lehmann had much work to do, and reasoned
it could not all be accomplished in England – a notion Arthur had previously
discussed with Clarke on the premise that the Ashes could be won at home, so
long as ground was gained on the road.

Batting frailty was the common denominator as the first two Tests were lost,
even if the margin at Trent Bridge was narrowed to a thrilling 14 runs by the
lower-order interventions of Ashton Agar and Haddin. The 19-year-old Agar's

98 on debut was a joyous moment, but his star was a shooting one: his undeveloped left-arm spin did not hold up to repeated scrutiny. Lyon, meanwhile, had again been discarded harshly, but was recalled for Manchester, where Australia took their first steps back after the hiding at Lord's.

Gradually the core of the team was established. Rogers, chosen late on in a career that had seemed destined to end unfulfilled, formed an effective opening combination with Warner, now back from exile. Watson moved down to No. 3, and bowled important bridging overs, while Clarke overcame a personal aversion to No. 4; Smith and Haddin settled in to the middle order. Ryan Harris delivered pace bowling of his usual high class, and was delighted to find his body failing him less frequently. Peter Siddle proved the most wholehearted of seam-bowling supports.

Rain intervened at Old Trafford and The Oval to scupper hopes of Australian victories, either side of one more fatal batting collapse, at Chester-le-Street. But valuable confidence had been gained. It was demonstrated in the limited-overs fixtures that followed the Tests, as Lehmann oversaw a team now playing with aggression and freedom. Added to their number was Johnson, who had regained his own sense of purpose via the advice of Dennis Lillee and a handful of swift spells in the IPL. He had England's batsmen hopping around, most notably Jonathan Trott, while the Australians secured a series win. Lehmann and Inverarity took note.

When the home summer opened up, a new schedule was in place, with the domestic limited-overs tournament now at the start, ahead of a block of six Sheffield Shield matches. They were played on pitches far less amenable to seam bowlers than in recent seasons, allowing batsmen to gather form shaken by results-orientated grassy strips. A limited-overs tour of India added momentum to the Australian team's train, as George Bailey won his Test place via a string of high scores, and Johnson stung Haddin's gloves on pitches that had no right to offer such speed.

And so, despite a few untimely revelations in the autobiographies of Hussey and Ponting, it was a settled and focused team that gathered in Brisbane. Early nerves were evident in some poor first-day batting, then in Johnson's wayward opening spell. But from the moment the irrepressible Harris coaxed an outside edge from Cook, and Johnson worried out Trott, the Australians took on the predatory posture of the great sides that had preceded them. When Clarke's expletive to James Anderson on the final evening was inadvertently broadcast on the stump mike, the Australian public expressed delight that even their clean-cut captain had found a gruffer voice.

Brisbane's shattering success begat another mismatch in Adelaide, then another in Perth. Johnson was at the centre of it all, rivalling Jeff Thomson's 1974-75 reign of terror, and finishing the series with 37 wickets at under 14 each. But he had plenty of help. In the words of Haddin, Australia's players had learned to thrive by a simple philosophy. "Do your job and create the environment that allows you to enjoy the success you and your team-mates have," he said. That they had managed to reach such a state of grace after the travails of earlier months still beggared belief.

AUSTRALIA v WEST INDIES, 2012-13

Andrew Wu

One-day internationals (5): Australia 5, West Indies 0
Twenty20 international (1): Australia 0, West Indies 1

There was a time when West Indies drew full houses in Australia, with legions of fans expecting a thumping contest between the world's two best sides. Now, it seemed Channel 9 were yet to wake up to the changed reality, trailing this series with snapshots of Viv Richards and Curtly Ambrose. Sadly, however, the five-match one-day encounter was a predictable let-down, as West Indies took their run of one-day defeats by Australia in this country to 17. Unsurprisingly, the punters stayed away.

The teams had shared one-day honours in the Caribbean a year earlier. But this time West Indies were no match for Australia, who completed a whitewash, despite injuries to key players and the potentially distracting prospect of a far bigger prize – the Border–Gavaskar Trophy – around the corner. By the time the solitary 20-over international came around, many of Australia's Test squad were already in India, leaving a barely recognisable side to take on the Twenty20 world champions at Brisbane. Cricket Australia chief executive James Sutherland's desire for a separate Twenty20 side had come to pass.

The gulf between the sides had been so vast during the one-day matches that David Warner's absence with a fractured thumb mattered little; nor did the fact that Michael Clarke and Shane Watson featured in only two games together. Watson still topped the run charts, from only three innings, ahead of George Bailey and Kieron Pollard, who made an unbeaten 109 in the fourth game, at Sydney. David Hussey had been dropped in advance and, when injuries began to bite, the selectors turned instead to Adam Voges, who at the age of 33 responded with his first century for Australia.

But it was Australia's deep bowling stocks which made the difference. The call-up of 22-year-old James Faulkner to fill the all-rounder's role meant they fielded three left-arm quicks in the first three games. The top five wicket-takers were all Australian, led by Mitchell Starc. His late swing caused problems, especially for Chris Gayle, who mustered 18 in four innings, and Ramnaresh Sarwan, who made his first appearance for West Indies since June 2011, but was dropped after three games.

West Indies' previous assignment had been on spinning tracks in Bangladesh in late 2012, and they were dealt no favours by Cricket Australia, who made them play first up in Perth – the quickest wicket in the country. That game did not last three hours, even with the 15-minute break for change of innings, after West Indies capitulated for 70. They grew more competitive as the tour wore on, but could not play well enough for long enough, and were left to celebrate only snippets of individual skill – most notably Johnson Charles's maiden hundred in all cricket, and the economy of spinner Sunil Narine.

WEST INDIES TOURING PARTY

*D. J. G. Sammy, T. L. Best, D. J. Bravo, D. M. Bravo, J. Charles, N. Deonarine, C. H. Gayle, J. O. Holder, S. P. Narine, K. A. Pollard, K. O. A. Powell, K. A. J. Roach, A. D. Russell, R. R. Sarwan, D. C. Thomas. *Coach:* O. D. Gibson.

At Canberra, January 29, 2013 (day/night). **Prime Minister's XI won by 23 runs. ‡Prime Minister's XI 333-6** (50 overs) (U. T. Khawaja 69, J. R. Dean 51, A. J. Doolan 87); **West Indians 310** (49 overs) (K. O. A. Powell 92 retired hurt, R. R. Sarwan 63, A. D. Russell 54; J. P. Faulkner 4-54). *MoM:* J. P. Faulkner. *Weeks after stepping down from international cricket, Ricky Ponting captained the Prime Minister's XI – but was one of only two batsmen to fail. Andre Russell pulled up in his fourth over with a knee problem, though was fit enough to blaze 54 from 24 balls before succumbing to James Faulkner, who the previous day had been called up to Australia's squad. Kieran Powell retired hurt with cramp on 172-1, eight runs away from a century, which possibly cost the West Indians victory.*

AUSTRALIA v WEST INDIES

First One-Day International

At Perth, February 1, 2013 (day/night). Australia won by nine wickets. Toss: West Indies. One-day international debuts: J. P. Faulkner; J. O. Holder.

Quite simply, Sammy pulled the wrong rein by deciding to bat first. In recent seasons Perth had developed a reputation as a batsman's graveyard, particularly when a favourable breeze accompanied a lively pitch. Australia duly packed their line-up with pace, including three left-arm quicks for the first time in any format, and Starc was the spectacular beneficiary of a stiff north-easterly, which helped him swing the ball back into the right-handers at will in a spell of four for one in eight balls; he finished with a one-day best five for 20. Few had imagined there would be a lower score during

LOWEST ONE-DAY INTERNATIONAL TOTALS IN AUSTRALIA

63	India v Australia at Sydney	1980-81
69	South Africa v Australia at Sydney	1993-94
70	Australia v New Zealand at Adelaide	1985-86
70	**West Indies v Australia at Perth**	**2012-13**
71	Pakistan v West Indies at Brisbane	1992-93
74	Pakistan v England at Adelaide	1991-92
74	Bangladesh v Australia at Darwin	2008-09
74	**Australia v Sri Lanka at Brisbane**	**2012-13**

the home summer than Australia's 74 against Sri Lanka at Brisbane in January, but West Indies obliged with their third-lowest one-day international total, after 54 at Cape Town in 2003-04, and 61 at Chittagong in 2011-12. Clarke kicked the dying dog by promoting Maxwell, whose haywire 35-ball assault ended the contest after a total of just 199 deliveries.

Man of the Match: M. A. Starc.

West Indies

C. H. Gayle c Finch b McKay	4	S. P. Narine c Wade b McKay		0
K. O. A. Powell c Clarke b Starc	11	K. A. J. Roach not out		1
R. R. Sarwan b Starc	0			
D. M. Bravo c Clarke b Faulkner	11	B 8, l-b 3, w 6		17
D. J. Bravo c Hughes b Starc	0			
K. A. Pollard b Starc	0	1/14 (1) 2/18 (2) 3/19 (3)	(23.5 overs)	70
†D. C. Thomas c Clarke b Faulkner	3	4/19 (5) 5/19 (6) 6/28 (7)		
*D. J. G. Sammy c Bailey b McKay	16	7/39 (4) 8/65 (8) 9/68 (10)		
J. O. Holder b Starc	7	10/70 (9)	10 overs: 26-5	

McKay 7–3–10–3; Starc 6.5–2–20–5; Faulkner 5–1–14–2; Johnson 5–0–15–0.

Australia

G. J. Maxwell not out	51
A. J. Finch c Thomas b Holder	10
U. T. Khawaja not out	8
W 2	2

1/39 (2)   (1 wkt, 9.2 overs)   71

P. J. Hughes, *M. J. Clarke, G. J. Bailey, †M. S. Wade, J. P. Faulkner, M. G. Johnson, M. A. Starc and C. J. McKay did not bat.

Roach 2–0–29–0; Holder 4.2–0–18–1; Narine 3–0–24–0.

Umpires: Asad Rauf and P. R. Reiffel.   Third umpire: N. J. Llong.

AUSTRALIA v WEST INDIES

Second One-Day International

At Perth, February 3, 2013 (day/night). Australia won by 54 runs. Toss: West Indies.
Twice West Indies had their foot on Australia's throat, only to twice let them wriggle free. Sammy learned from the previous fiasco by inserting Australia, who quickly slipped to 98 for six amid an athletic fielding display. But West Indies could find no way past Bailey, who overcame a scratchy start to add 100 with Faulkner, his fellow Launcestonian, and register his maiden international century – 125 off 110 balls, including 30 off his final six as he laid waste to Dwayne Bravo. Starc then collected his second consecutive five-wicket haul, carving through the top order with late movement. Powell and Bravo distilled West Indies' equation to a manageable 108 at just under five an over, but Bravo's tickle behind, giving Maxwell his first one-day international wicket, triggered a collapse. Thomas was given out first ball on review, when third umpire Asad Rauf overlooked the absence of a Hot Spot mark and trusted instead the sound detected on the stump mike. Maxwell started his day with a first-ball duck, had to stomach four sixes by No. 10 Narine from the first four balls of an over, but finished with four wickets and a $US1m contract from the IPL auction in Chennai.
Man of the Match: G. J. Bailey.

Australia

A. J. Finch c D. M. Bravo b Holder	11	J. P. Faulkner c Powell b Sammy	39
U. T. Khawaja c Powell b Roach	3	M. G. Johnson not out	16
P. J. Hughes c D. M. Bravo b Sammy	21	L-b 10, w 9	19
*M. J. Clarke b D. J. Bravo	16		
G. J. Bailey not out	125	1/16 (2) 2/25 (1) (7 wkts, 50 overs) 266	
†M. S. Wade c Sammy b Narine	16	3/56 (3) 4/56 (4)	
G. J. Maxwell b Sammy	0	5/93 (6) 6/98 (7) 7/198 (8) 10 overs: 39-2	

M. A. Starc and C. J. McKay did not bat.

Roach 10–0–51–1; Holder 10–1–56–1; Sammy 10–0–48–3; D. J. Bravo 10–0–67–1; Narine 10–0–34–1.

West Indies

C. H. Gayle lbw b Starc	4	S. P. Narine st Wade b Maxwell	24
K. O. A. Powell lbw b Starc	83	K. A. J. Roach not out	0
R. R. Sarwan lbw b Starc	0		
D. M. Bravo lbw b Starc	14	L-b 13, w 11	24
D. J. Bravo c Wade b Maxwell	45		
K. A. Pollard c Finch b Maxwell	1	1/10 (1) 2/10 (3) 3/33 (4) (38.1 overs) 212	
†D. C. Thomas c Wade b Starc	0	4/159 (5) 5/166 (2) 6/166 (7)	
*D. J. G. Sammy c Faulkner b Maxwell	24	7/168 (6) 8/179 (8)	
J. O. Holder run out	9	9/209 (10) 10/212 (9) 10 overs: 35-3	

McKay 6–0–32–0; Starc 8–1–32–5; Faulkner 7–0–40–0; Johnson 9–0–32–0; Maxwell 8.1–1–63–4.

Umpires: N. J. Llong and P. R. Reiffel.   Third umpire: Asad Rauf.

AUSTRALIA v WEST INDIES

Third One-Day International

At Canberra, February 6, 2013 (day/night). Australia won by 39 runs. Toss: Australia.

The returning Watson could not have hoped for a better start to life as a specialist batsman. Having decided to shelve his bowling temporarily after breaking down with a calf injury in the Boxing Day Test, he reaped instant dividend with his first one-day international century for almost two years, finishing with 122 from 111 balls. West Indies' attempt to keep the series alive as they set off in pursuit of 330 was unsettled by a side strain to Gayle in the field, which forced him to come in at No. 5; Sarwan was relegated lower still. The Bravo brothers' third-wicket stand of 114 set the scene for Gayle, but he played round a length ball from Faulkner, whose hollered send-off earned him a fine. Lusty late hitting by Russell, returning in style after sitting out the Perth games with a knee injury, gave West Indies a glimmer, but Faulkner was nerveless at the death. This was Australia's first international match in the capital, which celebrated its centenary the following month.

Man of the Match: S. R. Watson.

Australia

S. R. Watson c Pollard b Roach	122	J. P. Faulkner b D. J. Bravo	2
A. J. Finch c Thomas b Sammy	38	M. G. Johnson not out	8
P. J. Hughes c Thomas b Sammy	86	B 1, w 3, n-b 2	6
*M. J. Clarke c and b Pollard	15		
G. J. Bailey c Pollard b Narine	44	1/89 (2) 2/201 (1) (7 wkts, 50 overs)	329
G. J. Maxwell c Pollard b Narine	4	3/242 (4) 4/284 (3)	
†M. S. Wade not out	4	5/299 (6) 6/317 (5) 7/321 (8) 10 overs: 59-0	

M. A. Starc and C. J. McKay did not bat.

Roach 9–1–72–1; Russell 5–0–41–0; Sammy 8–0–49–2; D. J. Bravo 7–0–39–1; Narine 10–0–55–2; Gayle 5–0–36–0; Pollard 6–0–36–1.

West Indies

K. O. A. Powell c Wade b Maxwell	47	S. P. Narine b Faulkner	1
†D. C. Thomas c Hughes b McKay	19	K. A. J. Roach not out	1
D. M. Bravo b Faulkner	86		
D. J. Bravo b Starc	51	L-b 4, w 6, n-b 1	11
C. H. Gayle b Faulkner	2		
K. A. Pollard run out	9	1/54 (2) 2/81 (1) (47.3 overs)	290
A. D. Russell c Wade b McKay	43	3/195 (4) 4/214 (5) 5/215 (3)	
R. R. Sarwan b Johnson	12	6/234 (6) 7/264 (8) 8/281 (7)	
*D. J. G. Sammy b Faulkner	8	9/289 (10) 10/290 (9) 10 overs: 55-1	

McKay 10–1–62–2; Starc 7–0–50–1; Johnson 9–1–59–1; Faulkner 8.3–1–48–4; Maxwell 10–0–44–1; Clarke 3–0–23–0.

Umpires: Asad Rauf and S. D. Fry.   Third umpire: N. J. Llong.

AUSTRALIA v WEST INDIES

Fourth One-Day International

At Sydney, February 8, 2013 (day/night). Australia won by five wickets. Toss: West Indies.

With the series already won, Mitchell Starc was given the last two games off to rest his ankle – only for another left-armer, Johnson, to dismantle West Indies. At 55 for six, a repeat of the Perth debacle was on the cards, but Pollard's return to form at least spared that embarrassment. Though renowned more for hefty hitting, he knuckled down to make 109 from 136 balls, his third century in the format. But West Indies' score was never defendable once Watson got in, especially after he was badly dropped behind by Thomas on 32. Watson was able to neutralise the threat of Narine, who came on in the mandatory powerplay and troubled all the batsmen in a teasing ten-over spell. But otherwise the West Indian bowling lacked bite, and once Watson had put on 53 with Finch and 62 with Hughes, the result took on a grim inevitability. Clarke felt discomfort in his troublesome hamstring while helping knock off the runs, and withdrew from the next match.

Man of the Match: K. A. Pollard.

West Indies

K. O. A. Powell c Maxwell b Johnson	9		S. P. Narine c Wade b McKay............	23
J. Charles b Johnson	0		T. L. Best run out	1
D. M. Bravo c Finch b Johnson..........	4			
D. J. Bravo lbw b Maxwell	3		B 1, l-b 1, w 9	11
K. A. Pollard not out	109			
N. Deonarine c Finch b Cutting..........	10		1/5 (2) 2/17 (1) 3/17 (3) (49.4 overs)	220
†D. C. Thomas c Finch b Cutting	7		4/22 (4) 5/45 (6) 6/55 (7)	
*D. J. G. Sammy c Clarke b Cutting	25		7/98 (8) 8/133 (9) 9/197 (10)	
A. D. Russell c Maxwell b Faulkner	18		10/220 (11) 10 overs: 20-3	

McKay 10–2–41–1; Johnson 10–1–36–3; Maxwell 10–0–34–1; Cutting 10–1–45–3; Faulkner 9.4–1–62–1.

Australia

S. R. Watson c Thomas b Best	76		G. J. Maxwell not out	1
A. J. Finch lbw b Narine	25		L-b 8, w 8, n-b 2	18
P. J. Hughes c D. J. Bravo b Narine	23			
*M. J. Clarke c Thomas b Best	37		1/53 (2) 2/115 (3) (5 wkts, 44.5 overs)	221
A. C. Voges c Sammy b Russell	28		3/145 (1) 4/198 (5)	
†M. S. Wade not out	13		5/220 (4) 10 overs: 53-1	

J. P. Faulkner, M. G. Johnson, B. C. J. Cutting and C. J. McKay did not bat.

Best 9.5–0–38–2; Russell 6–0–40–1; Sammy 2–0–16–0; Narine 10–1–34–2; D. J. Bravo 4–0–25–0; Deonarine 8–0–38–0; Pollard 5–0–22–0.

Umpires: S. D. Fry and N. J. Llong.   Third umpire: Asad Rauf.

AUSTRALIA v WEST INDIES

Fifth One-Day International

At Melbourne, February 10, 2013 (day/night). Australia won by 17 runs. Toss: West Indies.

Opportunities had been scarce for Adam Voges in the six years since he first played for Australia, but now he took his chance, ensuring a whitewash with a maiden international hundred. Now aged 33, Voges had written off his own chances, but a hamstring injury to George Bailey had opened the door unexpectedly in the previous game at Sydney. There, he made only 28; now, he cashed in with an unbeaten 112 from 106 deliveries. Best had claimed Watson first ball and Finch with his tenth, but West Indies again failed to pull the trigger, allowing Voges to add 111 for the fifth wicket with Haddin, then an unbroken 81 with the increasingly impressive Faulkner in the last 8.3 overs to tip the game Australia's way. Fate appeared to be with Charles, who was only seven years old when West Indies last beat Australia in a one-day international there, in 1996-97. He was dropped twice, and escaped two marginal reviews to bring up his first hundred in any form of elite cricket. But Pollard's dismissal, when 41 were needed from four overs, proved decisive.

Man of the Match: A. C. Voges.   *Man of the Series:* M. A. Starc.

Australia

*S. R. Watson c Best...............	0	J. P. Faulkner not out...............	31	
A. J. Finch c Narine b Best.........	1	B 1, l-b 9, w 7, n-b 1........	18	
P. J. Hughes c Pollard b D. J. Bravo......	29			
S. E. Marsh c Thomas b D. J. Bravo......	40	1/0 (1) 2/2 (2) (5 wkts, 50 overs)	274	
A. C. Voges not out.................	112	3/63 (3) 4/82 (4)		
†B. J. Haddin c Powell b Roach..........	43	5/193 (6) 10 overs: 23-2		

M. G. Johnson, B. C. J. Cutting, C. J. McKay and X. J. Doherty did not bat.

Best 10–1–71–2; Sammy 10–1–37–0; Roach 10–0–52–1; Narine 10–1–27–0; D. J. Bravo 8–0–62–2; Pollard 2–0–15–0.

West Indies

J. Charles c Cutting b McKay...........	100	K. A. J. Roach not out...............	2	
K. O. A. Powell c Finch b Johnson.......	2	T. L. Best c sub (N. M. Coulter-Nile)		
D. M. Bravo c Faulkner b Doherty.......	33	b McKay.	0	
D. J. Bravo b Johnson................	13	B 1, l-b 6, w 9................	16	
K. A. Pollard c Finch b Faulkner........	45			
N. Deonarine c Haddin b Cutting........	4	1/7 (2) 2/113 (3) (49.5 overs)	257	
†D. C. Thomas run out................	19	3/129 (4) 4/182 (1) 5/186 (6)		
*D. J. G. Sammy c Haddin b McKay.......	23	6/228 (7) 7/234 (5) 8/246 (9)		
S. P. Narine b Johnson................	0	9/257 (8) 10/257 (11) 10 overs: 41-1		

McKay 9.5–0–52–3; Johnson 10–1–50–3; Cutting 10–0–53–1; Faulkner 10–0–47–1; Doherty 9–0–46–1; Finch 1–0–2–0.

Umpires: Asad Rauf and P. R. Reiffel.   Third umpire: N. J. Llong.
Series referee: R. S. Madugalle.

AUSTRALIA v WEST INDIES

Twenty20 International

At Brisbane, February 13, 2013 (floodlit). West Indies won by 27 runs. Toss: West Indies. Twenty20 international debuts: N. M. Coulter-Nile, J. R. Hazlewood, B. J. Rohrer; T. L. Best.

West Indies capitalised on a clash in the international schedule to beat Australia on their own turf for the first time in 16 years. The only survivor from their last victory, in February 1997 – when Courtney Walsh's side beat Mark Taylor's in the Perth Test – was Paul Reiffel, then an Australian seamer and now standing as an umpire. As Bailey led a barely recognisable side on to the Gabba, another Australian XI were in the midst of a two-day match in Chennai, preparing for the Test series against India. Those players would probably have made little difference against a bevy of West Indian hitters bursting with Big Bash pedigree. Gayle flopped again, but Charles and the rest battered Australia's all-pace attack. The chase was cruelled by two run-outs in four balls, both involving Voges soon after he had brought up his fifty, and Australia lacked the firepower to fight back.

Man of the Match: K. A. Pollard.

West Indies

		B	4	6
C. H. Gayle c 9 b 11	8	7	0	1
J. Charles b 9	57	35	7	1
D. M. Bravo run out	32	27	3	0
K. A. Pollard c 2 b 7	26	17	2	1
D. J. Bravo b 7	13	13	0	0
A. D. Russell not out	23	11	3	0
*D. J. G. Sammy c 2 b 7	20	7	1	2
N. Deonarine not out	6	3	1	0
L-b 4, w 2	6			

6 overs: 43-1   (20 overs) 191-6

1/11 2/99 3/106 4/139 5/141 6/172

†D. C. Thomas, S. P. Narine and T. L. Best did not bat.

McKay 4–0–44–0; Hazlewood 4–0–36–1; Faulkner 4–0–28–3; Coulter-Nile 4–0–36–1; Cutting 4–0–43–0.

Australia

		B	4	6
A. J. Finch b 7	4	6	0	0
S. E. Marsh run out	21	19	0	1
A. C. Voges run out	51	33	2	2
*G. J. Bailey c 8 b 10	15	11	2	0
B. J. Rohrer c 8 b 4	16	14	0	1
†B. J. Haddin c 6 b 4	22	11	1	2
J. P. Faulkner c 7 b 4	7	6	0	0
B. C. J. Cutting st 9 b 10	0	1	0	0
N. M. Coulter-Nile not out	16	11	0	2
C. J. McKay not out	6	8	0	0
B 1, l-b 2, w 3	6			

6 overs: 51-1   (20 overs) 164-8

1/5 2/79 3/82 4/96 5/121 6/139 7/139 8/141

J. R. Hazlewood did not bat.

Best 3–0–19–0; Sammy 3–0–30–1; Narine 4–0–19–2; Russell 1–0–9–0; Deonarine 3–0–37–0; D. J. Bravo 2–0–17–0; Pollard 4–0–30–3.

Umpires: P. R. Reiffel and J. D. Ward.   Third umpire: S. D. Fry.
Referee: R. S. Madugalle.

ENGLAND LIONS IN AUSTRALIA, 2012-13

One-day matches (5): Australia A 4, England Lions 0

In March 2013, India regained the Border–Gavaskar Trophy with a 4–0 whitewash, plunging Australian cricket into its most serious bout of introspection since the mid-1980s. Yet events back home suggested all was not necessarily lost. Australia's A side had just completed their own 4–0 shellacking of England Lions – though in one-day cricket – and might have won all five had rain not killed off the series finale in Sydney. Not only that, but the Lions lost all three warm-up games to Victoria, failing in the second to defend 335 against what amounted to the state's development XI.

When Australia A clinched the series, the national broadcaster ABC could not resist sticking the boot in, chuckling that the trip had "begun to resemble the tour from hell". Critics had already been given plenty of ammunition: two days earlier, Ben Stokes and Matt Coles were sent home for persistent late-night drinking. That came only 14 months after Stokes, the 21-year-old Durham all-rounder, had been arrested and cautioned for obstructing a policeman in an alcohol-related incident in Newcastle. The pair, room-mates on tour, continued to breach curfews even after a written warning from the management. England team director Andy Flower, who came to watch two games en route to the Test series in New Zealand, was in town when the decision was made.

Flower and Ashley Giles, England's limited-overs coach, were taking notes on potential participants over the next two winters, which would involve two one-day international series in Australia and the 2015 World Cup. But barely anyone put their hand up. James Taylor, out of England favour since an unconvincing Test debut against South Africa in 2012, regained the Lions captaincy after Joe Root was called up to the senior one-day party, and responded with two seventies at Hobart – but on both occasions the others collapsed around him. Taylor's 331 tour runs were not enough for him to be selected in England's Performance Squad for the 2013 home summer.

Varun Chopra scored two hundreds, while the Zimbabwe-born Gary Ballance – now England-qualified – might have helped win the fourth match had he not hooked a bumper into his jaw when he had 73. David Parsons, the Lions head coach, was also encouraged by 18-year-old Craig Overton, who made the trip after only one season in county cricket with Somerset, and was the sole frontline seamer to go at less than five an over. Like Overton, the Essex wicketkeeper-batsman Ben Foakes was promoted a year after graduating from the England Under-19s; he made his List A debut on this tour.

Many of these Lions, reared on a diet of 40-over domestic cricket, admitted they found it tough adapting to match conditions which reflected the regulation changes recently introduced in one-day internationals: a new ball at each end, two bouncers permitted an over, tighter restrictions on fielders outside the circle, and the abolition of the bowling powerplay. The Australian batsmen, especially captain Aaron Finch – who scored 80, 0, 57 and 109 – came out punching early on, and the tourists were reduced to taking pace off the ball on slow pitches in Melbourne and Hobart.

Above all, the trip was a timely guard against hubris heading into the most intensive series of England–Australia encounters in history. For all the problems in Australian cricket, they still possessed batsmen capable of giving the ball a mighty clout, and seemingly bottomless pits of fast bowlers ready to knock English heads off.

ENGLAND LIONS TOURING PARTY

*J. W. A. Taylor (Nottinghamshire), G. S. Ballance (Yorkshire), S. G. Borthwick (Durham), V. Chopra (Warwickshire), R. Clarke (Warwickshire), M. T. Coles (Kent), B. T. Foakes (Essex), A. D. Hales (Nottinghamshire), S. C. Kerrigan (Lancashire), S. C. Meaker (Surrey), C. Overton (Somerset), T. S. Roland-Jones (Middlesex), B. A. Stokes (Durham), R. J. W. Topley (Essex), J. M. Vince (Hampshire), C. J. C. Wright (Warwickshire).

J. A. R. Harris (Middlesex) and J. E. Root (Yorkshire) were originally selected – Root as captain – but were called into the full England squad for the one-day international series in New Zealand in February. They were replaced by Clarke and Overton. D. R. Briggs (Hampshire) withdrew after he sprained an ankle on England's tour of India in January. Hales and Meaker joined the squad after the warm-up matches. Coles and Stokes were sent home from the tour in Hobart, after persistently breaking the team curfew.

Coach: D. Parsons. *Manager:* G. A. M. Jackson. *Batting coaches:* G. P. Thorpe, M. R. Ramprakash. *Fast bowling coach:* K. J. Shine. *Spin bowling coach:* P. M. Such. *Fielding coach:* C. G. Taylor. *Wicketkeeping coach:* B. N. French. *Physiotherapist:* S. McAllister. *Strength and conditioning:* P. Atkinson. *Team analyst:* L. T. Sanders. *Media relations manager:* A. Phillips.

At Melbourne (St Kilda), February 7, 2013. **Victoria won by eight wickets. England Lions 225-8** (50 overs) (G. S. Ballance 86); ‡**Victoria 227-2** (36.1 overs) (R. J. Quiney 122, P. S. P. Handscomb 67*). *Rob Quiney hit 122 from 104 balls, and put on 125 for the second wicket with Peter Handscomb. Lions wicketkeeper Ben Foakes made a duck on List A debut, while leg-spinner Fawad Ahmed, a 31-year-old Pakistani asylum seeker hoping to obtain Australian citizenship, bowled with control in a spell of 10–1–30–2 in his first match for Victoria.*

At Melbourne (St Kilda), February 11, 2013. **Victoria XI won by four wickets. England Lions 335-4** (50 overs) (V. Chopra 115, J. W. A. Taylor 102, B. T. Foakes 53); ‡**Victoria XI 336-6** (49.4 overs) (M. P. Stoinis 57, R. G. L. Carters 127, A. R. Keath 60). *Each side chose from 12 players. The Lions could scarcely have considered the prospect of defeat against a virtual Victoria development side, including six who had never played a first-class or List A game. And it was all going swimmingly when Varun Chopra (115 from 123 balls) and James Taylor (102 retired out from 114) were adding 181 for the second wicket. But openers Marcus Stoinis and Dean Russ (34) responded steadily, and Ryan Carters accelerated neatly to 127. Victoria needed 11 off seven deliveries, at which point Chris Wright (10–0–78–0) bowled a no-ball which Carters struck for six.*

At Melbourne, February 13, 2013. **Victoria won by eight wickets. England Lions 173** (48.4 overs) (G. S. Ballance 57; S. M. Boland 4-29); ‡**Victoria 174-2** (37.3 overs) (R. J. Quiney 76). *Victoria brought back several first-team players for this match at the MCG, and routed the tentative tourists. Despite Gary Ballance's second fifty, the Lions never got going.*

50-over series

At Hobart, February 16, 2013 (day/night). **Australia A won by seven wickets. ‡England Lions 259-6** (50 overs) (V. Chopra 105, B. T. Foakes 56); **Australia A 260-3** (49.1 overs) (S. E. Marsh 100 retired hurt, A. J. Finch 80). *Chopra, grassed on nought by wicketkeeper Tim Paine, exploited the reprieve to make a century that stood out for its handsome square-drives. But with Chopra's wicket, five overs from the end, went the Lions' fluency: they hit only one more boundary. Shaun Marsh and Aaron Finch took toll of an out-of-sorts attack in an opening stand of 172 in 33.3 overs; the greatest threat to Australia A was Marsh himself, who poleaxed Finch with a stinging* *straight-drive. Later, turning for the run that would have brought up his hundred, Marsh ruptured a hamstring tendon and collapsed in a heap. He hobbled the single he needed off the next ball he faced, before retiring hurt.*

At Hobart, February 18, 2013. **Australia A won by 122 runs. Australia A 315-7** (50 overs) (J. A. Burns 114, C. J. Ferguson 74; R. Clarke 4-55); ‡**England Lions 193** (41.3 overs) (J. W. A. Taylor 79). *Stuart Meaker, a late arrival on the tour, began the match with a wide, then had Finch caught at slip. But the first delivery proved more prophetic than the second: the Lions bowlers would ship 28 in wides. Joe Burns's composed hundred – part of a lengthy alliance with Callum Ferguson – alerted him to Leicestershire, who soon signed him as an overseas player. After James Taylor was stumped off Finch's left-arm medium-pace in the 36th over, the Lions shed their last six wickets for 23.*

At Hobart, February 22, 2013. **Australia A won by 113 runs. Australia A 256-6** (50 overs) (A. J. Finch 57, C. J. Ferguson 65); ‡**England Lions 143** (37 overs) (J. W. A. Taylor 78*). *The Lions lost the series at the earliest opportunity, two days after Ben Stokes and Matt Coles were booted off the tour. Slow left-armer Simon Kerrigan (10–0–27–2) provided control in the middle overs, and Taylor rebuilt the reply after two early wickets. But the demise of Ballance triggered an unfathomable collapse of eight for 49.*

At Sydney, February 25, 2013. **Australia A won by 45 runs. ‡Australia A 285-8** (50 overs) (A. J. Finch 109, A. C. Voges 81); **England Lions 240** (47 overs) (G. S. Ballance 73 retired hurt). *Adam Voges, fresh from winning back his place in Australia's senior one-day side, helped administer another blow to the Lions' resolve, while Finch continued his triumphant series as captain with a hundred. The Lions needed 86 off the last ten overs, but came to a shuddering halt when Ballance top-edged an Alister McDermott bouncer under his grille, causing him to retire hurt.*

At Sydney, March 1, 2013 (day/night). **Australia A v England Lions. Abandoned.**

DOMESTIC CRICKET IN AUSTRALIA, 2012-13

PETER ENGLISH

For the first time in the Australian first-class tournament's 111 seasons, every team won the same number of matches. With four victories apiece, the six states finished the qualifying stages of the Sheffield Shield separated by just four points, after the top three and bottom three swapped places in the last round. The upshot was that the eventual finalists were the same as the previous year, though this time Tasmania hosted Queensland.

That meant **Tasmania** needed only a draw to win the Shield and prevent Queensland from completing a clean sweep of trophies – and the result was a tame stalemate. The Tasmanian batsmen often seemed becalmed, like yachts on the Derwent River. But once they had run up 419 it was mostly plain sailing, with Queensland finishing well short of a target of 446. Victory was the perfect leaving gift for coach Tim Coyle, who had decided to go after eight seasons in charge – in which Tasmania had won their first three first-class titles. It was also the first time Ricky Ponting had lifted the trophy in 20 years of intermittent domestic service, thanks to his midsummer Test retirement. In challenging conditions for batsmen across the country, he led the run-list with 911 at 75, and was named Shield Player of the Year. Mark Cosgrove provided hefty support with 784 runs, while Luke Butterworth delivered 45 wickets, and James Faulkner, a left-arm swing bowler, earned an Ashes trip with 39.

Coached by Darren Lehmann, **Queensland** had already won the one-day Ryobi Cup in a thrilling final with Victoria at the MCG, where Ryan Harris stole two wickets in the final over to see them home by two runs. A few weeks earlier, their alter egos, the Brisbane Heat, had taken the Big Bash League Twenty20. It attracted smaller crowds and television ratings than the previous edition, despite an increased presence over Christmas – and a rash of cringes involving Shane Warne, who at 43 was a faded force. Captaining the Melbourne Stars, he was suspended for a match and fined $A4,500 after an ugly altercation with West Indies' Marlon Samuels, playing for the Melbourne Renegades. Samuels eventually responded to Warne's barbs and ball-throwing by flinging his bat over his tormentor's head. Later, Warne was fined a further $A5,000 for installing Faulkner as captain to dodge a potential ban for slow over-rates. In July 2013, he announced his retirement from all forms of the game.

Following their heart-breaking one-day final defeat, **Victoria** led the Shield table with a game to play but faded to fourth. Their highlight was 742 runs, including three centuries, from Chris Rogers; Aaron Finch scored 504 in one-day cricket and David Hussey 355. Fawad Ahmed, a Pakistani leg-spinner who had sought asylum in Australia in 2010, took 16 wickets in three Shield games, and was discussed as an Australian Test hope.

It was a tumultuous season for **New South Wales**, with a complete changeover at the top. Coach Anthony Stuart was sacked before Christmas; Steve O'Keefe, captain in Michael Clarke's absence, later resigned to focus on his left-arm spin; and chief executive David Gilbert walked away after 11 years, soon followed by chairman Harry Harinath. They missed the Shield final by a single point, deducted for a slow over-rate.

There was upheaval, too, in **Western Australia** in the early summer, when Marcus North resigned as captain and Lachlan Stevens as coach. Justin Langer returned to take the coaching job. Despite a late resurgence, Western Australia finished fifth in the Shield and last in the one-day competition.

South Australia again relied on imports, though the home-grown Chadd Sayers, shaping the ball away, was the Shield's leading wicket-taker with 48. Second entering the last round, they still finished bottom for the fourth year running. At least that avoided the embarrassment of staging the final at the Glenelg club instead of Adelaide Oval, which was being dug up to prepare for the arrival of two Australian rules football teams as the ground's co-tenants.

FIRST-CLASS AVERAGES, 2012-13

BATTING (400 runs)

	M	I	NO	R	HS	100	Avge	Ct/St
M. J. Clarke (*New South Wales/Australia*)....	9	16	3	1,065	259*	3	81.92	12
H. M. Amla (*South Africa*)	4	7	0	430	196	2	61.42	0
R. T. Ponting (*Tasmania/Australia*)........	12	21	4	943	200*	3	55.47	16
B. J. Haddin (*New South Wales*)	7	11	2	468	114	2	52.00	19/3
†M. E. K. Hussey (*Western Aus. & Australia*) ..	12	22	4	930	115*	3	51.66	23
A. J. Doolan (*Tasmania/Australia A*)........	11	19	2	876	161*	2	51.52	7
†P. J. Hughes (*South Aus., Aus. A & Aus.*).....	10	19	1	912	158	2	50.66	8
†C. J. L. Rogers (*Victoria*)	10	17	2	742	131	3	49.46	5
†M. S. Wade (*Victoria/Australia*)	9	14	4	478	102*	1	47.80	36/1
†D. A. Warner (*New South Wales & Aus.*).....	7	12	0	519	119	1	43.25	4
C. J. Ferguson (*South Australia*)	9	17	1	639	164	1	39.93	5
†U. T. Khawaja (*Queensland*)................	6	11	0	438	138	1	39.81	3
†M. J. Cosgrove (*Tasmania*).................	11	20	0	784	104	1	39.20	7
C. L. White (*Victoria*)....................	9	15	1	510	144	1	36.42	13
†N. J. Maddinson (*New South Wales*)........	8	16	1	532	154	1	35.46	5
J. P. Faulkner (*Tasmania*).................	10	16	3	444	89	0	34.15	5
J. A. Burns (*Queensland*).................	10	19	1	587	120	2	32.61	7
J. R. Hopes (*Queensland*).................	8	15	0	473	88	0	31.53	5
†E. J. M. Cowan (*Tasmania/Australia*).......	10	17	0	514	136	1	30.23	7
†C. D. Hartley (*Queensland*)...............	11	20	2	510	103*	1	28.33	51/1
†R. J. Quiney (*Vic., Aus. A & Australia*)	10	18	3	400	85	0	26.66	11
T. P. Ludeman (*South Australia*)	10	19	1	479	85	0	26.61	45/2
†S. M. Whiteman (*Western Australia*)	8	16	0	422	96	0	26.37	14/2
P. M. Nevill (*New South Wales*)	10	18	2	421	65*	0	26.31	19
†M. S. Harris (*Western Australia*)..........	10	20	0	510	114	1	25.50	4
†T. M. Head (*South Australia*)	10	19	1	441	95*	0	24.50	1
†S. O. Henry (*New South Wales*)	10	19	1	408	81*	0	22.66	3

BOWLING (20 wickets)

	Style	O	M	R	W	BB	5I	Avge
G. D. Putland (*South Australia*)	LFM	153.1	46	393	22	7-64	3	17.86
C. J. Sayers (*South Australia*)..........	RM	353	106	889	48	6-49	3	18.52
B. C. J. Cutting (*Queensland*)...........	RFM	142.2	28	414	22	4-25	0	18.81
J. M. Bird (*Tasmania/Australia*).........	RFM	236.5	53	733	38	6-25	1	19.28
J. P. Faulkner (*Tasmania*)..............	LFM	282.4	68	793	39	5-23	2	20.33
L. R. Butterworth (*Tasmania*)...........	RM	376.4	122	936	45	6-49	4	20.80
J. L. Pattinson (*Victoria/Australia*)	RFM	210	43	650	30	6-32	1	21.66
J. M. Mennie (*South Australia*)...........	RM	234	49	727	33	6-43	1	22.03
S. N. J. O'Keefe (*New South Wales*)......	SLA	239	60	533	24	4-47	0	22.20
J. R. Hopes (*Queensland*)...............	RM	335	105	728	32	5-27	1	22.75
C. J. Gannon (*Queensland*)..............	RFM	274.1	78	729	31	6-53	1	23.51
L. W. Feldman (*Queensland*)............	RFM	192	35	609	25	4-33	0	24.36
M. G. Hogan (*Western Australia*)........	RFM	300.5	91	750	30	5-40	1	25.00
E. P. Gulbis (*Tasmania*)................	RFM	157.4	25	555	22	5-104	1	25.22
M. G. Johnson (*Western Aus. & Australia*) ..	LF	240.4	39	828	32	4-63	0	25.87
M. A. Starc (*New South Wales/Australia*) ..	LFM	168.4	24	650	25	6-154	2	26.00
B. W. Hilfenhaus (*Tasmania/Australia*) ..	RFM	346.2	95	877	33	4-33	0	26.57
T. A. Copeland (*New South Wales*)	RFM	315	96	806	30	4-56	0	26.86
P. M. Siddle (*Victoria/Australia*).........	RFM	317.4	76	951	35	5-54	1	27.17
D. E. Bollinger (*New South Wales*)	LFM	253.2	60	765	28	4-31	0	27.32
J. W. Hastings (*Victoria, Aus. A & Aus.*) ..	RFM	275	62	847	29	5-30	2	29.20
J. R. Hazelwood (*New South Wales*)	RFM	225	48	703	24	3-35	0	29.29
N. M. Coulter-Nile (*West. Aus. & Aus. A*) .	RFM	249.5	61	792	26	6-84	1	30.46
N. M. Lyon (*South Australia & Australia*).	OB	408.5	97	1293	26	3-41	0	49.73

SHEFFIELD SHIELD, 2012-13

	Played	Won	Lost	Drawn	1st-inns points	Points	Quotient
Tasmania	10	4	3	3	6	30	1.375
Queensland	10	4	5	1	6	30	0.989
New South Wales	10	4	2	4	6	29*	1.153
Victoria	10	4	4	2	4	28	0.945
Western Australia	10	4	5	1	4	28	0.820
South Australia	10	4	5	1	2	26	0.853

Final: Tasmania drew with Queensland but won the Sheffield Shield by virtue of heading the table.
* 1pt deducted for slow over-rate.

Outright win = 6pts; lead on first-innings in a drawn or lost game = 2pts. Teams tied on points were separated on quotient (runs per wicket scored divided by runs per wicket conceded).

At Perth, September 18–20, 2012. **New South Wales won by eight wickets. Western Australia 217 and 248**; ‡**New South Wales 358 and 108-2.** *New South Wales 6pts. For the first time, Sheffield Shield cricket was played in September; the previous earliest date was October 8 in 2010, but this season began even earlier because of the Champions League and an early start to the South African tour. Test captain Michael Clarke led New South Wales for the first time in the Shield.*

At Sydney (Bankstown Oval), September 26–29, 2012. **Drawn.** ‡**New South Wales 442** (B. J. Haddin 114, M. C. Henriques 161*) **and 198-6 dec**; **Tasmania 298-8 dec and 262-7.** *New South Wales 2pts. New South Wales recovered from losing their top three with seven runs on the board as Brad Haddin and Moises Henriques, with a maiden century, put on 168 for the sixth wicket.*

At Perth, September 30–October 2, 2012. **Victoria won by ten wickets. Western Australia 175 and 200** (J. W. Hastings 5-30); ‡**Victoria 375** (A. B. McDonald 101) **and 4-0.** *Victoria 6pts. James Pattinson bowled Liam Davis with the game's first delivery, and Chris Rogers struck the winning runs off the first of Victoria's second innings. Andrew McDonald hit an 87-ball century, and John Hastings took seven wickets in his first first-class match since December 2010 after shoulder surgery.*

At Brisbane, October 4, 2012. **Queensland won by 191 runs. Queensland 398** (B. C. J. Cutting 109; G. D. Putland 5-100) **and 248-8 dec** (C. D. Hartley 103*); ‡**South Australia 184** (J. R. Hopes 5-27) **and 271.** *Queensland 6pts. Ben Cutting, at No. 8, hit a maiden hundred in 78 balls before lunch on the second day, and added 122 for the eighth wicket with Cameron Boyce. Two former New South Wales batsmen thrived on debut for their new states: Usman Khawaja hit 88 for Queensland, and Phil Hughes 95 and 83 for South Australia.*

At Adelaide, October 9–12, 2012. **Tasmania won by an innings and 30 runs.** ‡**Tasmania 403-3 dec** (M. J. Cosgrove 104, A. J. Doolan 149); **South Australia 224** (L. R. Butterworth 6-49) **and 149.** *Tasmania 6pts. Alex Doolan scored a career-best 149, adding 166 for Tasmania's second wicket with Mark Cosgrove and 141 for the third with Ricky Ponting, who hit seven sixes in 85*. In reply, Tim Ludeman (85) and Chadd Sayers (38*) put on 107 for the ninth wicket after South Australia had stumbled to 111-8. Luke Butterworth took ten in a match for the first time.*

At Brisbane, October 10–12, 2012. **Victoria won by ten wickets. Queensland 149 and 125** (J. L. Pattinson 6-32); ‡**Victoria 227 and 48-0.** *Victoria 6pts. Victoria completed their second successive ten-wicket away win.*

At Adelaide, October 23–26, 2012. **Drawn.** ‡**South Australia 402-9 dec** (C. J. Ferguson 164) **and 225**; **Queensland 406-9 dec** (W. J. Townsend 129, J. A. Burns 116) **and 129-6.** *Queensland 2pts. Callum Ferguson's 164 was a career-best, and he added 162 for South Australia's sixth wicket with Ludeman. Wade Townsend and Joe Burns put on 189 for Queensland's fourth wicket.*

At Melbourne, October 23–26, 2012. **Drawn. Tasmania 439-5 dec** (R. T. Ponting 162*) **and 165-2**; ‡**Victoria 320.** *Tasmania 2pts. Ponting and Doolan shared two third-wicket century stands for Tasmania – 151 and 123*.*

At Hobart, November 1–3, 2012. **South Australia won by 15 runs. South Australia 112** (J. P. Faulkner 5-23) **and 237**; ‡**Tasmania 138 and 196.** *South Australia 6pts, Tasmania 2pts. South Australia won a Shield game for the first time since November 2010, at the 20th attempt (after 14 defeats and five draws). In a low-scoring match on a recently relaid surface, Tasmania were 148-8 chasing 212; Butterworth and Ben Hilfenhaus added 46 for the ninth wicket but could not deny*

South Australia their long-awaited victory. Substitute Steve Cazzulino was allowed to bat in Tasmania's second innings as a full replacement for Ponting, nursing an injury ahead of the Tests.

At Melbourne, November 1–3, 2012. **Victoria won by five wickets. Western Australia 248 and 138; ‡Victoria 219 and 171-5.** *Victoria 6pts, Western Australia 2pts. Mike Hussey led Western Australia after Marcus North resigned, but they still went down to their third straight defeat.*

At Brisbane (Allan Border Field), November 2–4, 2012. **Queensland won by six wickets. New South Wales 184 and 175; ‡Queensland 256 and 106-4.** *Queensland 6pts. Clarke made his third and last Shield appearance of the season, but managed only 36 runs. His vice-captain and New South Wales team-mate Shane Watson went to hospital for scans on a painful left calf muscle and did not play again until the final Test against South Africa four weeks later.*

At Hobart, November 9–11, 2012. **Queensland won by an innings and 123 runs. Tasmania 95 and 142** (C. J. Gannon 6-53); **‡Queensland 360** (U. T. Khawaja 138). *Queensland 6pts. The first day was wiped out after a tornado warning, but on the second Tasmania were blown away in 25.1 overs. Queensland reached 319-8 by the close and wrapped up an innings win in five sessions. Their wicketkeeper Chris Hartley held eight catches in the match.*

At Perth, November 12–15, 2012. **Western Australia won by 110 runs. ‡Western Australia 400-9 dec** (M. S. Harris 114) **and 191; South Australia 237 and 244.** *Western Australia 6pts. After three defeats, Western Australia won at last, thanks to solid first-innings batting led by Marcus Harris.*

At Sydney, November 13–16, 2012. **Drawn. ‡New South Wales 293** (B. J. Haddin 108*) **and 194-3; Victoria 330** (C. J. L. Rogers 125). *Victoria 2pts, New South Wales –1pt. Victorian captain Cameron White held four catches in the field on the opening day. New South Wales were fined one point for a slow over-rate, which would eventually cost them a place in the final.*

At Melbourne, November 23–26, 2012. **South Australia won by nine wickets. Victoria 346** (G. D. Putland 7-64) **and 132** (G. D. Putland 5-28); **‡South Australia 443** (P. J. Hughes 158; J. W. Hastings 5-66) **and 36-1.** *South Australia 6pts. South Australia secured their first Shield victory at the MCG for 14 years, thanks to left-arm seamer Gary Putland, whose first-innings 7-64 (including three top-order wickets in his tenth over) and match return of 12-92 were both the best of the season. Hughes and Ferguson (73) put on 189 for South Australia's third wicket.*

At Hobart, November 25–27, 2012. **Tasmania won by an innings and 118 runs. ‡Western Australia 67** (J. M. Bird 6-25) **and 263** (L. R. Butterworth 5-50); **Tasmania 448.** *Tasmania 6pts. Now coached by Justin Langer, Western Australia collapsed for the season's lowest total. Tasmania's Jackson Bird returned a career-best, and George Bailey passed 5,000 Shield runs.*

At Canberra, November 27–30, 2012. **New South Wales won by three wickets. ‡Queensland 243 and 173; New South Wales 319-8 dec and 98-7.** *New South Wales 6pts. Doug Bollinger struck twice in the first three balls of the match, and Queensland never quite recovered – but victory was not enough to save the job of New South Wales coach Anthony Stuart. Queensland and Victoria led the table at the midsummer break, with three wins and 20 points apiece.*

At Sydney (Blacktown Olympic Park Oval), January 24–27, 2013. **Drawn. Western Australia 242 and 219-8; ‡New South Wales 344.** *New South Wales 2pts. Rain permitted only ten overs on the last day, frustrating New South Wales, whose captain, Steve O'Keefe, took four in each innings.*

At Adelaide, January 24–27, 2013. **South Australia won by one wicket. ‡Victoria 319** (C. J. L. Rogers 131; C. J. Sayers 6-49) **and 136** (J. M. Mennie 6-43); **South Australia 267** (P. J. Hughes 120) **and 191-9.** *South Australia 6pts, Victoria 2pts. Opener Sam Raphael (27*), who had retired hurt, resumed at 163-7 and helped South Australia scrape a third victory after 19 winless games.*

At Brisbane, February 4–7, 2013. **Western Australia won by 99 runs. Western Australia 111 and 496; ‡Queensland 168 and 340** (G. D. Moller 120; N. M. Coulter-Nile 6-84). *Western Australia 6pts, Queensland 2pts. The first 23 wickets in this match put on 341, before the next 17 added 774 as Western Australia's middle order and tail fought back, and Queensland's Greg Moller scored a maiden century. But Nathan Coulter-Nile's career-best bowling won the day.*

At Hobart, February 6–9, 2013. **Drawn. ‡Tasmania 425-6 dec** (R. T. Ponting 200*, J. J. Krejza 118*) **and 245** (C. P. Tremain 5-57); **New South Wales 500** (N. J. Maddinson 154, T. A. Copeland 106; L. R. Butterworth 5-83) **and 123-8.** *New South Wales 2pts. A high-scoring match featured the tournament's only double-hundred and double-century stand. Now retired from Test cricket, Ponting scored the ninth 200 of his career. He added 293, a Tasmanian seventh-wicket record, with Jason Krejza, who made a maiden Shield hundred. In reply, career-bests from Nic Maddinson and Trent*

Copeland, who put on 188 for the sixth wicket, helped New South Wales run up the season's first 500. Set 171 in 25 overs, they initially went for it, before hanging on for the draw with eight down.

At Melbourne, February 18–21, 2013. **Victoria won by eight wickets.** ‡Queensland 322 (P. J. Forrest 119) **and 249** (Fawad Ahmed 5-83); **Victoria 536-9 dec** (C. J. L. Rogers 101, M. W. Hill 144, C. L. White 144; N. M. Hauritz 5-135) **and 36-2.** *Victoria 6pts. Pakistani leg-spinner Fawad Ahmed took seven wickets on his competition debut. Victoria scored 536-9, the tournament's highest total. Michael Hill, with a maiden Shield hundred, put on 146 for the second wicket with Chris Rogers, who scored his 30th in Shield cricket, and 186 for the fourth with Cameron White.*

At Adelaide, February 19–21, 2013. **South Australia won by four wickets.** ‡New South Wales 157 (C. J. Sayers 5-54) **and 173; South Australia 240 and 94-6.** *South Australia 6pts. Sayers and Joe Mennie took eight wickets apiece, and wicketkeeper Ludeman caught nine in the match to help South Australia to their fourth win and second place.*

At Perth, February 21–24, 2013. **Western Australia won by two wickets.** Tasmania 211 and 242; ‡Western Australia 97 (L. R. Butterworth 5-35) **and 358-8.** *Western Australia 6pts, Tasmania 2pts. For the second time in three months, Tasmania dismissed Western Australia for double figures; this time they lost. Set 357, Western Australia looked set to collapse again at 37-3, but held their nerve. Sam Whiteman (83) and Ashton Agar (71*) added 121 for the seventh wicket, and they finished an extended third day on 351-8; No. 10 Burt Cockley knocked off seven in eight balls next morning.*

At Brisbane, March 7–10, 2013. **Tasmania won by 163 runs.** Tasmania 245 and 342-6 dec; ‡Queensland 281 (J. A. Burns 120) **and 143.** *Tasmania 6pts, Queensland 2pts. Ryan Harris returned for his first first-class match since touring the West Indies in April, and managed four wickets for Queensland. But Tasmania, desperate to win, set them 307 in two sessions; Queensland lost their first four for eight, and their last six for 39, with four each for Hilfenhaus and Butterworth.*

At Adelaide, March 7–10, 2013. **Western Australia won by one wicket.** South Australia 248 (M. G. Hogan 5-40) **and 193** (A. C. Agar 5-65); ‡Western Australia 235 (J. Botha 5-59) **and 211-9.** *Western Australia 6pts, South Australia 2pts. Western Australia pulled off a third straight win, despite being 143-9 in pursuit of 207; last man Michael Hogan scored 47* and put on 68* with No. 8 Agar.*

At Melbourne, March 7–9, 2013. **New South Wales won by six wickets.** ‡Victoria 128 (G. S. Sandhu 5-31) **and 289; New South Wales 268 and 150-4.** *New South Wales 6pts. Victoria hung on to first place despite suffering a three-day home defeat.*

At Sydney, March 14–16, 2013. **New South Wales won by eight wickets.** South Australia 182 and 127; ‡New South Wales 219 (C. J. Sayers 5-53) **and 91-2.** *New South Wales 6pts. New South Wales briefly headed the table. Sayers finished as the Shield's leading wicket-taker with 48.*

At Hobart, March 14–17, 2013. **Tasmania won by 111 runs.** Tasmania 369-6 dec (R. T. Ponting 104) **and 325-7 dec** (J. C. Silk 127); ‡Victoria 358 (D. J. Hussey 112; E. P. Gulbis 5-104) **and 225** (J. P. Faulkner 5-56). *Tasmania 6pts. Tasmania declared twice and leapfrogged leaders Victoria to reach a third successive final, thanks to Ponting's third hundred of the tournament and the 80th in his first-class career, and to Jordan Silk, who scored a maiden century in his second match.*

At Perth, March 14–17, 2013. **Queensland won by 120 runs.** Queensland 164 and 336-9 dec; ‡Western Australia 228 (R. J. Harris 6-58) **and 152.** *Queensland 6pts, Western Australia 2pts. After a first-day washout, 15 wickets fell on the second, and Queensland trailed on first innings. But a ninth-wicket stand of 86 between Michael Neser (77) and Harris (54*), enabled them to set a target of 273, and only Mike Hussey managed 30 as Queensland surged past them into the final.*

FINAL

TASMANIA v QUEENSLAND

At Hobart, March 22–26, 2013. Drawn. Tasmania won the Sheffield Shield by virtue of leading the qualifying table. Toss: Tasmania.

The drama of the last round, when all six teams were still fighting to reach the final, evaporated as Tasmania, needing only a draw to claim the Shield, settled for avoiding defeat. The openers crawled to three figures after tea; next morning, 20-year-old Silk plodded on to 108 from 358 balls, his second century in his third first-class match. Butterworth finally lifted the pace with 86, taking Tasmania past 400 with help from Faulkner in a stand of 125. Hilfenhaus bowled Moller with his first delivery, and third-day rain added to Queensland's difficulties, with Gulbis and Faulkner ensuring a 194-run deficit. But their thoughts raced from despair to hope as Harris, back to his best after another injury-hit summer, reduced Tasmania to 15 for five with a burst of four wickets in four overs before lunch on the fourth day. Faulkner, with a career-best 89, and wicketkeeper Paine firmly dispelled the panic, negotiating a variable pitch to add 161. The eventual target was 446, but a poor start left Queensland batting out time. To add to their gloom, seam bowler Gannon was reported for a suspect action, later ruled illegal.

Man of the Match: J. P. Faulkner. *Attendance:* 10,845.

Close of play: first day, Tasmania 176-2 (Silk 82, Ponting 20); second day, Queensland 12-1 (Pomersbach 4, Forrest 8); third day, Queensland 185-7 (Hopes 23, Hauritz 0); fourth day, Tasmania 240-7 (Faulkner 83, Butterworth 14).

Tasmania

J. C. Silk c Pomersbach b Neser	108	– (2) b Harris	1
M. J. Cosgrove b Neser	58	– (1) b Hopes	4
A. J. Doolan c Forrest b Harris	6	– lbw b Gannon	26
R. T. Ponting lbw b Hopes	35	– lbw b Harris	1
*G. J. Bailey lbw b Gannon	42	– b Harris	0
J. W. Wells c Hartley b Harris	5	– b Harris	1
†T. D. Paine lbw b Harris	0	– c Burns b Hopes	87
J. P. Faulkner b Hopes	46	– c Hartley b Neser	89
L. R. Butterworth c Hartley b Hopes	86	– c Moller b Neser	17
E. P. Gulbis not out	15	– not out	1
B. W. Hilfenhaus lbw b Hopes	0	– c Hartley b Gannon	0
B 6, l-b 6, n-b 6	18	B 8, l-b 11, w 1, n-b 4	24

1/133 (2) 2/147 (3) 3/199 (4)   (173.4 overs) 419   1/5 (2) 2/5 (1)   (96.5 overs) 251
4/240 (1) 5/253 (6) 6/253 (7)   3/6 (4) 4/6 (5)
7/269 (5) 8/394 (8) 9/411 (9) 10/419 (11)   5/15 (6) 6/56 (3) 7/217 (7)
8/249 (8) 9/250 (9) 10/251 (11)

Harris 40–12–107–3; Hopes 40.4–17–71–4; Gannon 32–5–88–1; Hauritz 35–13–70–0; Neser 26–4–71–2. *Second innings*—Harris 14–7–32–4; Hopes 24–3–76–2; Neser 21–6–43–2; Gannon 20.5–5–35–2; Hauritz 14–1–40–0; Reardon 3–1–6–0.

Queensland

G. D. Moller b Hilfenhaus	0	– b Faulkner	13
L. A. Pomersbach b Butterworth	17	– b Hilfenhaus	4
P. J. Forrest lbw b Gulbis	56	– b Gulbis	8
N. J. Reardon c Paine b Gulbis	13	– lbw b Hilfenhaus	51
J. A. Burns b Paine b Faulkner	6	– b Butterworth	32
†C. D. Hartley run out	36	– not out	23
*J. R. Hopes b Faulkner	36	– lbw b Butterworth	10
M. G. Neser c Paine b Gulbis	12	– not out	18
N. M. Hauritz c and b Gulbis	16		
R. J. Harris lbw b Faulkner	0		
C. J. Gannon not out	11		
B 8, l-b 11, n-b 3	22	B 16, l-b 4, n-b 4	24

1/0 (1) 2/46 (2) 3/70 (4)   (87.2 overs) 225   1/15 (2)   (6 wkts, 87 overs) 183
4/81 (5) 5/128 (3) 6/163 (6)   2/26 (1) 3/32 (3)
7/185 (8) 8/207 (9) 9/210 (10) 10/225 (7)   4/95 (5) 5/140 (4) 6/156 (7)

Hilfenhaus 19–5–43–1; Butterworth 19–7–48–1; Gulbis 21–4–62–4; Faulkner 22.2–3–40–3; Cosgrove 6–0–13–0. *Second innings*—Hilfenhaus 22–6–58–2; Butterworth 20–9–30–2; Faulkner 14–5–20–1; Gulbis 18–5–42–1; Wells 12–7–12–0; Cosgrove 1–0–1–0.

Umpires: S. D. Fry and J. D. Ward.   Third umpire: M. D. Martell.
Referee: R. W. Stratford.

CHAMPIONS

Sheffield Shield

1892-93	Victoria	1934-35	Victoria	1979-80	Victoria
1893-94	South Australia	1935-36	South Australia	1980-81	Western Australia
1894-95	Victoria	1936-37	Victoria	1981-82	South Australia
1895-96	New South Wales	1937-38	New South Wales	1982-83	New South Wales*
1896-97	New South Wales	1938-39	South Australia	1983-84	Western Australia
1897-98	Victoria	1939-40	New South Wales	1984-85	New South Wales
1898-99	Victoria	1940–46	No competition	1985-86	New South Wales
1899-1900	New South Wales	1946-47	Victoria	1986-87	Western Australia
1900-01	Victoria	1947-48	Western Australia	1987-88	Western Australia
1901-02	New South Wales	1948-49	New South Wales	1988-89	Western Australia
1902-03	New South Wales	1949-50	New South Wales	1989-90	New South Wales
1903-04	New South Wales	1950-51	Victoria	1990-91	Victoria
1904-05	New South Wales	1951-52	New South Wales	1991-92	Western Australia
1905-06	New South Wales	1952-53	South Australia	1992-93	New South Wales
1906-07	New South Wales	1953-54	New South Wales	1993-94	New South Wales
1907-08	Victoria	1954-55	New South Wales	1994-95	Queensland
1908-09	New South Wales	1955-56	New South Wales	1995-96	South Australia
1909-10	South Australia	1956-57	New South Wales	1996-97	Queensland*
1910-11	New South Wales	1957-58	New South Wales	1997-98	Western Australia
1911-12	New South Wales	1958-59	New South Wales	1998-99	Western Australia*
1912-13	South Australia	1959-60	New South Wales		
1913-14	New South Wales	1960-61	New South Wales	*Pura Milk Cup*	
1914-15	Victoria	1961-62	New South Wales	1999-2000	Queensland
1915-19	No competition	1962-63	Victoria		
1919-20	New South Wales	1963-64	South Australia	*Pura Cup*	
1920-21	New South Wales	1964-65	New South Wales	2000-01	Queensland
1921-22	Victoria	1965-66	New South Wales	2001-02	Queensland
1922-23	New South Wales	1966-67	Victoria	2002-03	New South Wales*
1923-24	Victoria	1967-68	Western Australia	2003-04	Victoria
1924-25	Victoria	1968-69	South Australia	2004-05	New South Wales*
1925-26	New South Wales	1969-70	Victoria	2005-06	Queensland
1926-27	South Australia	1970-71	South Australia	2006-07	Tasmania
1927-28	Victoria	1971-72	Western Australia	2007-08	New South Wales
1928-29	New South Wales	1972-73	Western Australia		
1929-30	Victoria	1973-74	Victoria	*Sheffield Shield*	
1930-31	Victoria	1974-75	Western Australia	2008-09	Victoria
1931-32	New South Wales	1975-76	South Australia	2009-10	Victoria
1932-33	New South Wales	1976-77	Western Australia	2010-11	Tasmania
1933-34	Victoria	1977-78	Western Australia	2011-12	Queensland
		1978-79	Victoria	2012-13	Tasmania

New South Wales have won the title 45 times, Victoria 28, Western Australia 15, South Australia 13, Queensland 7, Tasmania 3.

* *Second in table but won final. Finals were introduced in 1982-83.*

RYOBI CUP, 2012-13

50-over league plus final

	Played	Won	Lost	No result	Bonus points	Points	Net run-rate
Victoria	8	5	3	0	3	23	0.70
Queensland	8	4	3	1	1	19	−0.63
South Australia	8	4	4	0	2	18	0.26
New South Wales	8	4	4	0	1	17	−0.33
Tasmania	8	3	4	1	1	15	−0.02
Western Australia	8	3	5	0	2	14	−0.02

Win = 4pts; 1 bonus pt awarded for achieving win with a run-rate 1.25 times that of the opposition.
Net run-rate was calculated by subtracting runs conceded per over from runs scored per over.

Final

At Melbourne, February 27, 2013. **Queensland won by two runs** (D/L). Queensland 146-9 (32 overs); ‡**Victoria 144** (31.4 overs). *MoM:* R. J. Harris. *Attendance:* 1,140. *Rain interrupted Queensland's innings and reduced the match to 32 overs a side; Victoria's target remained 147. Jason Floros rescued Queensland from 81-6 with 47 in 32 balls, including 16 in the final over. But Victoria struggled just as much and finally capitulated to Ryan Harris, who took 4-26, including the last two wickets in the final over, when they needed only three runs from four deliveries.*

KFC T20 BIG BASH LEAGUE, 2012-13

20-over league plus semi-finals and final

	Played	Won	Lost	Points	Net run-rate
Melbourne Renegades	8	7	1	14	0.79
Perth Scorchers	8	5	3	10	1.32
Melbourne Stars	8	5	3	10	0.24
Brisbane Heat	8	4	4	8	0.46
Adelaide Strikers	8	4	4	8	−0.16
Hobart Hurricanes	8	4	4	8	−0.56
Sydney Sixers	8	3	5	6	−0.38
Sydney Thunder	8	0	8	0	−1.36

Teams tied on points were separated on net run-rate (calculated by subtracting runs conceded per over from runs scored per over).

Semi-finals

At Melbourne (Docklands), January 15, 2013 (floodlit). **Brisbane Heat won by 15 runs.** ‡**Brisbane Heat 183-3** (20 overs) (L. A. Pomersbach 112*); **Melbourne Renegades 168-9** (20 overs). *MoM:* L. A. Pomersbach. *Attendance:* 16,285. *Luke Pomersbach hit 112*, his maiden Twenty20 century, in 70 balls.*

At Perth, January 16, 2013 (floodlit). **Perth Scorchers won by eight wickets** (D/L). **Melbourne Stars 183-2** (18 overs); ‡**Perth Scorchers 142-2** (13 overs). *MoM:* S. E. Marsh. *Attendance:* 17,903. *After two rainbreaks Perth Scorchers' revised target was 139 in 13 overs; Shaun Marsh's 68 in 40 balls put them on course. Shane Warne was fined A$5,000 after appointing James Faulkner as the nominal captain, though he himself was clearly in charge in the field, a ploy intended to protect Warne from being banned for slow over-rates if the Melbourne Stars reached the final.*

Final

At Perth, January 19, 2013 (floodlit). **Brisbane Heat won by 34 runs.** ‡**Brisbane Heat 167-5** (20 overs); **Perth Scorchers 133-9** (20 overs). *MoM:* M. C. Henriques. *Attendance:* 18,517. *Joe Burns (43 in 27 balls) and Daniel Christian (37 in 21) dominated Brisbane's innings; Adam Voges's 49 in 32 deliveries could not regain the initiative for Perth.*

BANGLADESH CRICKET, 2013

Too many tears, not enough Tests

UTPAL SHUVRO

There had been the odd unsubstantiated rumour, but the poison of match-fixing had largely stayed away from Bangladesh cricket. That all changed in 2013, as the former national captain Mohammad Ashraful – one of the country's favourite sporting sons, and recently re-established in the Test team after scoring 190 in Sri Lanka – admitted he had been involved in some murky business. His testimony dragged several others into the scandal, too.

The Bangladesh Cricket Board had beefed up the security arrangements for the second edition of their Twenty20 Premier League, after a few whispers about the first, in 2012. Two officials were deployed from the ICC's Anti-Corruption and Security Unit and, while investigating the molehill of two matches, they discovered – with the help of Ashraful's confession – a mountain. Bangladesh's leading daily newspaper, *Prothom Alo*, said he had confessed to involvement in fixing not only BPL matches, but also internationals. Three

BANGLADESH IN 2013

	Played	Won	Lost	Drawn/No result
Tests	6	1	2	3
One-day internationals	9	5	3	1
Twenty20 internationals	4	1	3	–

JANUARY		
FEBRUARY		
MARCH	2 Tests, 3 ODIs and 1 T20I (a) v Sri Lanka	(page 1116)
APRIL MAY	2 Tests, 3 ODIs and 2 T20Is (a) v Zimbabwe	(page 1181)
JUNE		
JULY		
AUGUST		
SEPTEMBER		
OCTOBER NOVEMBER	2 Tests, 3 ODIs and 1 T20I (h) v New Zealand	(page 903)
DECEMBER		

For a review of Bangladesh domestic cricket from the 2012-13 season, see page 910.

other prominent players were also implicated – the paper claimed Ashraful had fingered them for initiating him into corruption in 2004, and also provided information on their involvement in fixing in other matches.

A tribunal was set up, and the judgment process creaked into action. The ICC did not comment on the international aspects but, during a press conference with the BCB chief in August, their chief executive, Dave Richardson, accused nine people of being involved in match-fixing in the BPL. They were not named for legal reasons, but Kent's Darren Stevens later confirmed he was one, and had been charged with not reporting a corrupt approach.

All this detracted from what happened on the field where, for once, Bangladesh had a reasonable time of it. Six Tests produced one win and only two defeats – a fine return in comparison to previous years. Bangladesh held their own in three draws, one against Sri Lanka at Galle in March, then twice at home against New Zealand in October. In April, they shared the series in Zimbabwe.

For the second year running, they achieved a new record total: 638 at Galle eclipsed the 556 at Mirpur against West Indies in November 2012, and meant that, for the first time in 25 Tests, Bangladesh had not lost after conceding a total of more than 500. Mushfiqur Rahim made his country's first Test double-century, after Ashraful just missed out; their stand of 267 was

Lifting the lid: Mohammad Ashraful confesses to spot-fixing.

Bangladesh's highest for any wicket. And after they were finally separated, Nasir Hossain also reached three figures, to give Bangladesh three centuries in an innings for the first time. Overall, it was a big step forward: Sri Lanka had won all the previous 12 Tests between the sides (normal service was resumed at Colombo).

Not long after these heroics, Bangladesh actually did win a Test – their first for nearly four years – although success in Harare only squared the series, after Zimbabwe's thumping victory in the First Test.

In a year generally flooded with one-day internationals, Bangladesh played only nine, not helped by missing the cut for the Champions Trophy. But the results column wasn't too bad – they won five, including a 3–0 victory over New Zealand, which repeated the clean sweep from their previous home series against them three years earlier. Bangladesh also drew the one-day series in Sri Lanka – no mean feat for any visiting team. The New Zealanders had arrived in October with revenge on their minds, though they were too polite to say so. The local media were less sensitive, and soon reminded the tourists of that 4–0 whitewash in 2010-11. Yet even the most diehard Bangladesh fans were not really expecting a repeat.

It proved that, at home at least, Bangladesh were no pushovers. In the last one-dayer against New Zealand, at Fatullah, they successfully chased 308, having only once before overhauled a target of more than 300, four years earlier in Zimbabwe. Tamim Iqbal had hammered 154 then – but he was injured now. Also absent was Shakib Al Hasan, who had dengue fever. To win without their biggest names suggested Bangladesh were no longer reliant on a couple of stars.

This had already been evident in the Tests against New Zealand, where two youngsters stood out. Mominul Haque, who made his Test debut at Galle (where he scored 55), hit hundreds in both Tests and broke the national record for most runs in a two-match series. But even the diminutive Mominul was outshone by the off-spinning all-rounder Sohag Gazi, who in the First Test uniquely scored a century and took a hat-trick.

A regular theme crops up at the end of every Test series involving Bangladesh. Their captain – currently Mushfiqur, although he did make a short-lived attempt to resign during 2013 after a one-day defeat in Zimbabwe – will be asked why his side have not performed very well. With a look of regret, he will reply: "How can we play well in Tests when we play so few? Whatever lessons the players learn in one series, they forget by the time the next one comes around." And then he will issue a plea for more Test cricket.

But the repeated requests have not yet borne fruit. The number of Tests Bangladesh are scheduled to play actually goes down every time the Future Tours Programme is rejigged – and it remains to be seen what effect the controversial new plans to reorganise the ICC may have. Individual countries have always been free to negotiate additional series outside the FTP – but the BCB haven't managed any yet. Indeed, they find it a struggle to play the ones supposedly set down in stone in the first place. From February 2009 to the end of 2013, Bangladesh played only 22 Tests, which included one drought of 14 months, and another of 11. Poor performances have put off potential opponents, which in turn has meant less chance of improvement. It's a vicious circle.

The administration of cricket in Bangladesh underwent a big change in 2013, to satisfy the ICC directives about political interference. Nazmul Hassan became the BCB's first elected president: previous office-bearers had all been appointed by the government. Still, the enduring image of the year was the sight of Mohammad Ashraful, sobbing openly after admitting his misdeeds, and asking for forgiveness.

BANGLADESH v NEW ZEALAND, 2013-14

Utpal Shuvro

Test matches (2): Bangladesh 0, New Zealand 0
One-day internationals (3): Bangladesh 3, New Zealand 0
Twenty20 international (1): Bangladesh 0, New Zealand 1

"Banglawash" was the portmanteau of choice from the moment New Zealand arrived. On their previous visit, three years earlier, they had lost the one-day series 4–0. In between, the term had crept into the Bangladeshi cricketing lexicon – and the local media were not about to let the New Zealanders forget it. Some of them brushed aside mention of that series with a smile; Ross Taylor deadpanned that he couldn't remember it at all. But captain Brendon McCullum didn't try to conceal the wound. "It was a damaging tour," he said. "It hurt a lot of peoples' careers, and hurt our country as well."

New Zealand, while experimenting a little before the World Twenty20 in Bangladesh in early 2014, prepared extensively for this tour in an attempt to lay Banglawash to rest. Ten of the squad had been on a recent A-tour to India and Sri Lanka, while the rest joined them at a training camp in Sri Lanka before departure. And New Zealand's one-day record over the previous 12 months had been encouraging, with series victories in South Africa and England. So when they lost all three 50-over games, it was McCullum's standing which suffered most. To say he had a dismal time was an understatement: he failed to pass 22 in five innings in all formats, before a back problem flared up during the one-day series and he had to fly home. He later quit wicketkeeping altogether. His departure meant New Zealand went through four keepers in six matches. It was worse for Kane Williamson, who was their leading scorer in the Tests, but then fractured a finger in the first one-day international and was ruled out of this tour and the next to Sri Lanka, where he had been scheduled to captain while McCullum rested.

Bangladesh proved once again that they were hard to beat at home. Their one-day series win was achieved without talismanic all-rounder Shakib Al Hasan, hero of the 2010-11 series, who was diagnosed with dengue fever on the eve of the first match. But drawing the Test series was arguably just as worthy an achievement. In the previous nine Tests between the countries, New Zealand had won eight, five by an innings, with the single draw down to rain rather than any fight from Bangladesh.

This time, they did not wilt. In the First Test at Chittagong, New Zealand ran up a large total, but Bangladesh stretched out their resistance so far that No. 8 Sohag Gazi scored a maiden Test century – and later added a hat-trick. The batsmen then responded with unusual composure when McCullum challenged them to bat out the last session and a half. Bangladesh's bowling looked toothless in the Second Test, but they were steered to safety by 22-year-old Mominul Haque, who belied his frail figure by becoming only the second Bangladeshi – after Tamim Iqbal, at Lord's and Manchester in 2010 –

Dhaka delirium: Bangladesh captain Mushfiqur Rahim celebrates after Tim Southee is bowled, sealing another home series win against New Zealand.

to score hundreds in back-to-back Tests. His total of 276 runs was the most for Bangladesh in a two-match series.

Twenty20, however, continued to dumbfound Bangladesh. "To be honest, we still can't understand this format," admitted their captain Mushfiqur Rahim, after New Zealand inflicted their seventh defeat in eight. Bangladesh had played fewer Twenty20 internationals than any Full Member aside from Zimbabwe, and the suspicion remained that their players simply didn't have enough high-level Twenty20 experience to compete with the strongest countries. It was a headache, only four months before they would have to pre-qualify against the Associates for the World Twenty20 proper, to be held on their own soil.

NEW ZEALAND TOURING PARTY

*B. B. McCullum (T/50), C. J. Anderson (T/50/20), T. A. Boult (T), D. A. J. Bracewell (T), D. G. Brownlie (T), A. P. Devcich (50/20), G. D. Elliott (50/20), P. G. Fulton (T), M. R. Gillespie (T), T. W. M. Latham (T/50/20), B. P. Martin (T), M. J. McClenaghan (50/20), N. L. McCullum (50/20), K. D. Mills (50/20), A. F. Milne (50/20), C. Munro (50/20), J. D. S. Neesham (50/20), L. Ronchi (50/20), H. D. Rutherford (T/50/20), I. S. Sodhi (T), T. G. Southee (T), L. R. P. L. Taylor (T/50/20), N. Wagner (T), B-J. Watling (T), K. S. Williamson (T/50). *Coach:* M. J. Hesson.

Williamson, originally selected in all three formats, fractured his thumb in the first one-day international, and was withdrawn from the rest of the tour. B. B. McCullum flew back after the second one-dayer with back pain, and was replaced by Ronchi in both limited-overs squads. Mills took over as captain.

At Chittagong (M. A. Aziz), October 4–6, 2013 (not first-class). **Bangladesh Cricket Board XI v New Zealanders. Abandoned.**

BANGLADESH v NEW ZEALAND

First Test Match

At Chittagong, October 9–13, 2013. Drawn. Toss: New Zealand. Test debuts: Marshall Ayub; C. J. Anderson, I. S. Sodhi.

This otherwise humdrum match will be remembered for the achievements of Sohag Gazi. For all the great all-round performances in Test history, it took until the 2,097th game, and a 22-year-old Bangladeshi picked as a specialist off-spinner, for a player to score a century and take a hat-trick in the same match; remarkably Gazi was also the most recent player to achieve the feat in first-class cricket (see page 912).

Gazi's hat-trick – only the second in Tests for Bangladesh, after Alok Kapali's against Pakistan at Peshawar in August 2003 – was a pleasant diversion as the game plodded to a draw on a last-day pitch lacking turn or carry. Operating with the second new ball, he had the debutant Corey Anderson lbw with an arm-ball, before Watling edged his first delivery behind: it struck Mushfiqur Rahim in the chest, and fell into his gloves. The third arrived with a beautiful doosra, which took Bracewell's edge, hit Mushfiqur's right leg and popped up in the air for Shakib Al Hasan to lunge forward from leg slip and take a stunning one-handed catch. Gazi, who now had six wickets in the innings, had no idea that he had just written a new chapter in Test history.

But it was Gazi's maiden Test century which had done most to help Bangladesh avoid defeat against New Zealand for only the second time in ten matches. When he came out at No. 8 on the third evening, after Mominul Haque and Mushfiqur Rahim had fallen within six balls, Bangladesh were trailing by 168. That they were able to pass 500, and claim a first-innings lead over New Zealand for the first time, was largely down to the 105 put on by Gazi and Robiul Islam for the ninth wicket.

New Zealand's tail had proved just as hard to dislodge. Watling had barely got off the mark when he was caught at gully off a Rubel Hossain no-ball, and capitalised by making his second Test century, in a stand of 127 with last man Boult. (Only Brian Hastings and Richard Collinge, who added 151 against Pakistan at Auckland in 1972-73, had put on more for New Zealand's tenth wicket.) Williamson, fleet-footed and unafraid to leave the crease, had earlier eased to his third Test hundred in the subcontinent.

Bangladesh's first innings began dismally: Boult launched it with a wide, but then lured Tamim Iqbal into nicking a drive for his first golden duck in first-class cricket; Anamul Haque followed soon after. Enter Mominul, playing only his fourth Test. His boyish frame hardly looked cut out for modern international cricket, but he launched a blistering counter-attack by rollicking to 50 in 36 deliveries, with almost all of them in front of square as New Zealand bowled too full. His first Test hundred followed next morning, from only 98 balls. At under 5ft 4in, Mominul was among the very shortest Test centurions, along with his captain Mushfiqur. Unlike some of their predecessors in the Bangladesh team, Mominul and Mushfiqur then got down to the hard work of saving the follow-on.

When Bangladesh got there, it was telling that there were no wild celebrations in the crowd, as in years gone by. Mominul was eventually lbw to his 274th ball, of which he had hit 27 for four – the most by a Bangladeshi in a Test innings. Gazi enjoyed enough support to cut and thrash his way to a hundred, and a couple of the Bangladesh fielders were seen yawning when they emerged for New Zealand's second innings. The tourists still had pretensions of victory, but those were harmed when rain cut short the fourth day, and they delayed their charge until after Gazi's hat-trick, which nudged McCullum to declare with a lead of 255, and 48 overs remaining. Bangladesh saw them out with ease.

Man of the Match: Sohag Gazi.

Close of play: first day, New Zealand 280-5 (Martin 0); second day, Bangladesh 103-2 (Marshall Ayub 21, Mominul Haque 77); third day, Bangladesh 380-7 (Sohag Gazi 28, Abdur Razzak 1); fourth day, New Zealand 117-1 (Fulton 44, Williamson 28).

New Zealand

P. G. Fulton c Mominul Haque b Nasir Hossain . . .	73	– lbw b Sohag Gazi	. . .	59
H. D. Rutherford c Abdur Razzak b Sohag Gazi . . .	34	– lbw b Nasir Hossain	. . .	32
K. S. Williamson lbw b Shakib Al Hasan	114	– c Anamul Haque b Sohag Gazi	. . .	74
L. R. P. L. Taylor c sub (Naeem Islam)				
b Abdur Razzak.	28	– not out	. . .	54
*B. B. McCullum lbw b Abdur Razzak	21	– b Sohag Gazi	. . .	22
B. P. Martin c Mushfiqur Rahim b Rubel Hossain .	1			
C. J. Anderson c Nasir Hossain b Abdur Razzak. . .	1	– (6) lbw b Sohag Gazi	. . .	8
†B-J. Watling st Mushfiqur Rahim b Mominul Haque	103	– (7) c Mushfiqur Rahim b Sohag Gazi	.	0
D. A. J. Bracewell b Sohag Gazi	29	– (8) c Shakib Al Hasan b Sohag Gazi .		0
I. S. Sodhi lbw b Shakib Al Hasan.	1	– (9) not out	. . .	22
T. A. Boult not out.	52			
B 4, l-b 6, n-b 2	12	B 11, l-b 4, n-b 1		16

1/57 (2) 2/183 (1) 3/244 (4) (157.1 overs) 469 | 1/48 (2) (7 wkts dec, 90 overs) 287
4/276 (3) 5/280 (5) 6/282 (6) 2/149 (1) 3/200 (3)
7/282 (7) 8/339 (9) 9/342 (10) 10/469 (8) 4/250 (5) 5/260 (6) 6/260 (7) 7/260 (8)

Robiul Islam 13–3–23–0; Rubel Hossain 20–2–77–1; Abdur Razzak 55–10–147–3; Sohag Gazi 32–6–79–2; Shakib Al Hasan 24–5–89–2; Marshall Ayub 2–0–15–0; Nasir Hossain 5–1–19–1; Mominul Haque 6.1–0–10–1. *Second innings*—Abdur Razzak 32–5–116–0; Rubel Hossain 6–0–21–0; Sohag Gazi 26–4–77–6; Shakib Al Hasan 9–1–19–0; Nasir Hossain 9–4–20–1; Robiul Islam 4–1–9–0; Mominul Haque 4–0–10–0.

Bangladesh

Tamim Iqbal c Williamson b Boult	0	– c Williamson b Martin		46
Anamul Haque lbw b Bracewell	3	– c Anderson b Martin		18
Marshall Ayub c Watling b Anderson	25	– lbw b Sodhi		31
Mominul Haque lbw b Anderson	181	– not out		22
Shakib Al Hasan c Watling b Williamson	19	– not out		50
*†Mushfiqur Rahim c Taylor b Bracewell	67			
Nasir Hossain c Williamson b Sodhi	46			
Sohag Gazi not out.	101			
Abdur Razzak lbw b Boult.	7			
Robiul Islam c Taylor b Bracewell	33			
Rubel Hossain c Taylor b Sodhi.	4			
B 5, l-b 8, w 1, n-b 1	15	B 2, n-b 4		6

1/1 (1) 2/8 (2) 3/134 (3) (148.5 overs) 501 | 1/39 (2) (3 wkts, 48.2 overs) 173
4/180 (5) 5/301 (4) 6/301 (6) 2/99 (1) 3/101 (3)
7/371 (7) 8/387 (9) 9/492 (10) 10/501 (11)

Boult 24–9–50–2; Bracewell 25–2–96–3; Martin 27–3–113–0; Sodhi 28.5–3–112–2; Anderson 17–7–34–2; Williamson 27–4–83–1. *Second innings*—Boult 4–1–9–0; Bracewell 5–0–14–0; Anderson 2–2–0–0; Williamson 10–3–24–0; Martin 16–4–62–2; Sodhi 10.2–1–57–1; Taylor 1–0–5–0.

Umpires: B. N. J. Oxenford and S. Ravi. Third umpire: Enamul Haque.

BANGLADESH v NEW ZEALAND

Second Test Match

At Mirpur, October 21–25, 2013. Drawn. Toss: Bangladesh. Test debut: Al-Amin Hossain.
   The series was on the line heading into the final day, with Bangladesh 114 ahead and seven wickets in hand. A draw was the likeliest outcome, but the fifth day of Tests in Asia have been known to spring the odd surprise. New Zealand said they were confident of chasing anything. But incessant rain meant not a single ball was bowled; even the post-match presentation had to take place indoors. Bangladesh emerged the happier, given their

history of vulnerability in the second innings. They began it 155 behind but, for once, didn't buckle.

New Zealand brought in Wagner as a fourth seamer in place of left-arm spinner Bruce Martin, who had looked ordinary at Chittagong. It meant they fielded three left-arm seamers (the others were Boult and Anderson) in a Test for the first time; leg-spinner Ish Sodhi completed an unorthodox attack. The change worked: Wagner, who had toured Bangladesh with a South African academy team in 2007-08, bowled with heart, and bagged his first five-wicket haul for his adopted country.

Bangladesh had bargained for more than 282 after winning the toss. Reasonably placed at the end of the first day, they lost their last five for 36 next morning, as their old inability to bat time resurfaced: other than Tamim Iqbal, no one stayed longer than 80 minutes. Tamim himself was dropped on five and ten, both times off Bracewell behind the wicket. But his luck ran out on 95 when, after a game of cat-and-mouse with Williamson in the gully, he was cramped up by Wagner, and Williamson took a superb diving catch.

Tamim is known for his flamboyance, and often castigated when it verges on the reckless. But in the second innings he ground it out according to the team's needs. Wagner reduced Bangladesh to 55 for two with a day and a half remaining, and the New Zealanders smelled victory. Tamim stood firm, and found an ally in the in-form Mominul, who helped add 157, a Bangladesh record for the third wicket. Once again it took a superb catch, one-handed by Taylor above his head at slip, to oust Tamim, on 70 from 218 balls – his slowest 50-plus score. Two near-misses extended his century drought to 23 innings since his *annus mirabilis* in England in 2010. But Tamim did stick around long enough to watch Mominul complete back-to-back hundreds, thus emulating his own feat. With Mominul on 99, McCullum packed the off side, asking his bowlers to tempt the young left-hander outside off stump, and even got in his ear. No matter: 12 balls later, he bashed Wagner over his head for four.

New Zealand's commanding position had been built on an unflashy 140-run stand between Williamson and Anderson for the fifth wicket. Williamson had retired hurt on 27 when he was struck on the grille by Rubel Hossain, drawing blood, but he returned a few overs later at the fall of McCullum's wicket, and crossed 50 for the third innings in a row. Anderson, meanwhile, never went long without a boundary, and achieved his maiden Test hundred in his debut series. Shakib Al Hasan, who had been a shadow of himself at Chittagong after a long injury lay-off, came into his own with his tenth five-wicket haul in Tests – but his figures betrayed the limpness of his team-mates.

Man of the Match: Mominul Haque.   *Man of the Series:* Mominul Haque.

Close of play: first day, Bangladesh 228-5 (Mushfiqur Rahim 14); second day, New Zealand 107-3 (Taylor 37, Williamson 28); third day, New Zealand 419-8 (Watling 59, Sodhi 55); fourth day, Bangladesh 269-3 (Mominul Haque 126, Shakib Al Hasan 32).

Bangladesh

Tamim Iqbal c Williamson b Wagner	95	– c Taylor b Williamson	70
Anamul Haque c Williamson b Boult	7	– c Fulton b Wagner	22
Marshall Ayub b Wagner	41	– c Taylor b Wagner	9
Mominul Haque c Watling b Anderson	47	– not out	126
Shakib Al Hasan lbw b Sodhi	20	– not out	32
*†Mushfiqur Rahim c Fulton b Wagner	18		
Nasir Hossain c Taylor b Sodhi	19		
Sohag Gazi c Williamson b Wagner	14		
Abdur Razzak b Sodhi	13		
Rubel Hossain c Watling b Wagner	4		
Al-Amin Hossain not out	0		
B 2, l-b 1, w 1	4	B 8, l-b 1, n-b 1	10

1/23 (2) 2/90 (3) 3/166 (4)   (74.5 overs) 282   1/39 (2)   (3 wkts, 89 overs) 269
4/208 (1) 5/228 (5) 6/246 (6)   2/55 (3) 3/212 (1)
7/252 (7) 8/266 (8) 9/274 (10) 10/282 (9)

Boult 16–2–55–1; Bracewell 14–1–57–0; Wagner 19–5–64–5; Sodhi 18.5–3–59–3; Williamson 4–0–30–0; Anderson 3–0–14–1. *Second innings*—Boult 16–2–62–0; Bracewell 14–2–47–0; Wagner 18–4–52–2; Sodhi 14–2–37–0; Anderson 9–2–18–0; Williamson 18–4–44–1.

New Zealand

P. G. Fulton lbw b Shakib Al Hasan	14
H. D. Rutherford c Mominul Haque	
b Shakib Al Hasan .	13
K. S. Williamson c Tamim Iqbal	
b Abdur Razzak .	62
L. R. P. L. Taylor c Nasir Hossain	
b Shakib Al Hasan .	53
*B. B. McCullum c Rubel Hossain	
b Shakib Al Hasan .	11
C. J. Anderson c Sohag Gazi	
b Al-Amin Hossain .	116

†B-J. Watling not out	70
D. A. J. Bracewell c Mushfiqur Rahim	
b Shakib Al Hasan .	17
N. Wagner c Marshall Ayub b Nasir Hossain	8
I. S. Sodhi run out	58
T. A. Boult lbw b Abdur Razzak	4
B 4, l-b 4, w 2, n-b 1	11

1/31 (2) 2/32 (1) 3/101 (5) (140 overs) 437
4/127 (4) 5/267 (3) 6/287 (6)
7/318 (8) 8/335 (9) 9/428 (10) 10/437 (11)

Williamson, when 27, retired hurt at 76-2 and resumed at 101-3.

Al-Amin Hossain 16–3–58–1; Sohag Gazi 34–8–77–0; Shakib Al Hasan 43–13–103–5; Abdur Razzak 23–1–96–2; Rubel Hossain 18–1–81–0; Nasir Hossain 3–1–7–1; Mominul Haque 3–0–7–0.

Umpires: R. K. Illingworth and B. N. J. Oxenford.　　Third umpire: Sharfuddoula.
Series referee: J. Srinath.

At Mirpur, October 29, 2013 (day/night). **First one-day international: Bangladesh won by 43 runs** (D/L). **Bangladesh 265** (49.5 overs) (Mushfiqur Rahim 90, Naeem Islam 84; T. G. Southee 3-34, J. D. S. Neesham 4-42); ‡**New Zealand 162** (29.5 overs) (G. D. Elliott 71, C. J. Anderson 46; Rubel Hossain 6-26). *MoM:* Rubel Hossain. *One-day international debut:* A. P. Devcich (New Zealand). *Rubel Hossain, whose four wickets here had sealed Bangladesh's clean sweep three years earlier, again delivered the telling blows. When rain halted New Zealand at 82-3 after 20 overs, they were set a revised 206 off 33. That seemed possible while Grant Elliott was thriving in an enforced promotion to No. 3 – Kane Williamson had broken a finger in the field – and especially when Corey Anderson whacked three quick sixes. But Rubel foxed Anderson with a slower ball, Brendon McCullum sliced the next delivery to backward point, and Mushfiqur Rahim came on when James Neesham gloved a half-tracker – completing the third one-day hat-trick for Bangladesh. Rubel finished with 5.5–0–26–6 – the joint-best figures for Bangladesh, with Mashrafe bin Mortaza. Bangladesh lost three wickets in the first seven overs, and five in the last six, but were boosted by a fourth-wicket stand of 154 between the free-flowing Mushfiqur – after spending 16 balls on nought – Naeem Islam, a late replacement when Shakib Al Hasan went down with dengue fever.*

At Mirpur, October 31, 2013 (day/night). **Second one-day international: Bangladesh won by 40 runs.** ‡**Bangladesh 265** (49 overs) (Tamim Iqbal 58, Mominul Haque 51, Mushfiqur Rahim 31; J. D. S. Neesham 4-53, C. J. Anderson 4-40); **New Zealand 207** (46.4 overs) (L. R. P. L. Taylor 45, C. J. Anderson 37; Mashrafe bin Mortaza 3-43, Sohag Gazi 3-34). *MoM:* Sohag Gazi. *One-day international debut:* Shamsur Rahman (Bangladesh). *Bangladesh completed only their fourth one-day series win over a top-eight nation, and their second over New Zealand. It was the Bangladeshi bowlers who did the job, after their batsmen failed to reach 250. Tamim Iqbal's 58 proved the lone half-century of the match, and his unusual restraint forewarned the New Zealanders about the slowness of the wicket. Mushfiqur Rahim's ploy of using pace and spin with the two new balls worked nicely, with Mashrafe bin Mortaza producing two excellent spells. Anton Devcich and Elliott fell in consecutive deliveries as New Zealand lurched to 45-3, and Sohag Gazi tempted Ross Taylor to hole out.*

At Fatullah, November 3, 2013. **Third one-day international: Bangladesh won by four wickets.** **New Zealand 307-5** (50 overs) (A. P. Devcich 46, T. W. M. Latham 43, L. R. P. L. Taylor 107*, C. Munro 85); ‡**Bangladesh 309-6** (49.2 overs) (Shamsur Rahman 96, Mominul Haque 32, Naeem Islam 63, Nasir Hossain 44*). *MoM:* Shamsur Rahman. *MoS:* Mushfiqur Rahim (Bangladesh). *International cricket returned to a redeveloped Fatullah after seven years: such was the demand that 30 people were injured in clashes with police after failing to secure tickets. New Zealand, who had trained over at Mirpur, possibly misjudged a strong total, but they prospered with the bat all the* *same. Brendon McCullum had flown home with a sore back, and Luke Ronchi flown in to become their third wicketkeeper of the series (Tom Latham had taken the gloves in the second ODI), leaving Taylor as the only batsman with more than 50 caps. Dropped on 12 by Rubel Hossain off his own bowling, Taylor went on to his eighth century in the format. A partnership of 130 in 23 overs with Chris Munro, who reverse-pulled Abdur Razzak for six, preceded an onslaught of 73 runs in the last five, with Taylor hitting three consecutive sixes off Sohag Gazi. Just once before, at Bulawayo in 2009, had Bangladesh successfully chased more than 300, and the architect of that one, Tamim Iqbal, was out ill. But Ziaur Rahman pinched a quick 22 in his stead. And though Shamsur Rahman edged behind for 96 in his second ODI, Nasir Hossain played the role of finisher to perfection – earning a hug from Mushfiqur Rahim's delirious father as he ran on to the field.*

At Mirpur, November 6, 2013. **Twenty20 international: New Zealand won by 15 runs. ‡New Zealand 204-5** (20 overs) (A. P. Devcich 59, C. Munro 73*); **Bangladesh 189-9** (20 overs) (Mushfiqur Rahim 50, Mahmudullah 34; T. G. Southee 3-38). *MoM:* C. Munro. *Twenty20 international debuts:* Al-Amin Hossain (Bangladesh); A. P. Devcich (New Zealand). *The switch to Twenty20 allowed New Zealand to close their nightmarish tour on a winning note. Devcich, from New Zealand's sizeable Croatian population, led the charge after being dropped by fellow debutant Al-Amin Hossain at short fine leg, and a brutal onslaught by the unorthodox Munro, who slammed 73 off 39 balls, including four sixes in eight deliveries off the spinners, meant the hosts conceded their record total. After losing three wickets in the first ten balls, Bangladesh hit out frantically, which proved inadequate – and left them with much to ponder before hosting the 2014 World Twenty20.*

DOMESTIC CRICKET IN BANGLADESH, 2012-13

UTPAL SHUVRO

Bangladeshi domestic cricket had a welcome vibrancy in 2012-13, thanks to the introduction of an additional franchise-based first-class tournament: the Bangladesh Cricket League. The standards of the existing National Cricket League, contested by divisions, had been diluted as their numbers rose to eight the previous season. A plan to turn the divisions into franchises was dropped, and four zonal teams were created: Central (drawing on Dhaka and Dhaka Metropolis), North (Rajshahi and Rangpur), South (Khulna and Barisal), and East (Sylhet and Chittagong).

The intensity of the new competition, a single league leading to a final, was a few notches higher, and the teams took a more professional approach. The final was Bangladesh's maiden first-class day/night match, played with a pink ball in front of a large crowd at the Mirpur stadium. Five days were scheduled, but **Central Zone**, who had headed the qualifying league, defeated **North Zone** inside four.

There were some notable performances: in the opening round Ziaur Rahman of South Zone hit 15 sixes, one short of the world record, during an astonishing 152 not out in 118 balls. A few days later, Central Zone's Marshall Ayub and Mehrab Hossain threatened to break the fifth-wicket world record partnership: their stand of 494 against East Zone fell only 26 short, but was an all-wicket national record.

To accommodate the new competition, the NCL's format was streamlined. After three seasons in which a round-robin league had been followed by a Super Four and a final, the title was decided on the basis of a single league, staged before the BCL began. **Khulna** ended Rajshahi's run of four consecutive titles, and became champions for the third time, winning all but one match. Their only defeat came against Dhaka in their penultimate game, which made the final round a three-horse race, with Dhaka and Rajshahi having a chance to overtake them. Khulna clinched it in dramatic fashion: Rajshahi appeared to be cruising when their openers put on 102 in pursuit of 187, but inexplicably lost six for seven and were bundled out for 153. Dhaka officials alleged foul play, but were overruled; they had to be content with runners-up, a huge improvement on the previous season, when they failed to win a single match, just as Barisal did this term.

Marshall Ayub of Dhaka Metropolis and Central Zone was the highest scorer in both first-class tournaments, with a record 1,069 runs in all, earning a Test debut in October 2013. The dashing left-hander Tamim Iqbal played only twice for Chittagong because of international commitments, but scored centuries in three successive first-class innings, a Bangladeshi first. Barisal's Sohag Gazi was only the 12th player to score a century and take a hat-trick in the same first-class match – and a year later, against New Zealand, the first to do it in a Test. That made him the second player, after Mike Procter, to achieve the feat twice. Bangladesh's endless production line of left-arm spinners supplied the top five NCL wicket-takers, and the top three in all first-class cricket, headed by Mosharraf Hossain (Dhaka and Central Zone) with 59, and Abdur Razzak (Khulna and South Zone) with 54, including nine for 84 against Chittagong, the best first-class return by a Bangladeshi.

A match-fixing scandal marred the second Bangladesh Premier League. **Dhaka Gladiators**, who retained the title, were at the centre of the storm: the owners, chief executive, bowling coach and several players – including former Test captain Mohammad Ashraful, the first to confess – were accused of fixing-related crimes by the ICC's anti-corruption unit, and faced trial by the BCB's own anti-corruption tribunal.

There was no top-level 50-over tournament in 2012-13: the club-based Dhaka Premier League was given List A status but postponed to September 2013 because of international tours, player strikes and the BPL investigations. An extra Twenty20 competition was staged as part of the Eighth Bangladesh Games, a multi-sport quadrennial tournament which had been dropped after 2002; it reappeared in April 2013, and **Rajshahi** won the final against Rangpur.

FIRST-CLASS AVERAGES, 2012-13

BATTING (500 runs)

	M	I	NO	R	HS	100	Avge	Ct/St
*Tamim Iqbal (*Chittagong/Bangladesh*)	4	7	1	625	192	3	104.16	0
Marshall Ayub (*Dhaka Met./Central Zone*) .	11	17	2	1,069	289	4	71.26	15
†Mehrab Hossain (*Dhaka Metropolis/C Zone*)	11	19	3	936	218	4	58.50	4
Nasir Hossain (*Rangpur/Bang./North Zone*)	8	15	0	819	131	1	54.60	6
†Faisal Hossain (*Chittagong/East Zone*)	10	14	1	674	123*	2	51.84	6
Naeem Islam (*Rangpur/Bang./North Zone*) .	8	15	1	698	137*	3	49.85	1
Jahurul Islam (*Rajshahi/North Zone*)	8	14	2	595	118	1	49.58	12/1
Anamul Haque (*Khulna/South Zone*)	7	14	2	577	127*	1	48.08	8/3
Dhiman Ghosh (*Rangpur/East Zone*)	9	14	2	506	159	2	42.16	11/1
Maisuqur Rahman (*Rajshahi*)	8	16	1	628	102	1	41.86	14
Farhad Reza (*Rajshahi/North Zone*)	11	18	4	560	100*	1	40.00	11
Tushar Imran (*Khulna/South Zone*)	10	19	1	678	156	1	37.66	7
Mithun Ali (*Khulna/South Zone*)	9	17	0	634	120	1	37.29	19/2
Ziaur Rahman (*Khulna/South Zone*).......	9	17	1	594	152*	1	37.12	7
Alok Kapali (*Sylhet/East Zone*)	10	15	1	508	133	1	36.28	7
Shamsur Rahman (*Dhaka Met./C Zone*)....	11	19	3	575	107*	1	35.93	14
Nafis Iqbal (*Chittagong/East Zone*)	10	16	0	537	83	0	33.56	4
†Imrul Kayes (*Khulna/South Zone*)	10	20	1	620	104	1	32.63	12
†Soumya Sarkar (*Khulna/South Zone*)	10	20	1	559	96	0	29.42	11

BOWLING (25 wickets)

	Style	O	M	R	W	BB	5I	Avge
Murad Khan (*Khulna/South Zone*)......	SLA	150.2	27	513	27	6-47	2	19.00
Abdur Razzak (*Khulna/South Zone*)....	SLA	390.3	92	1039	54	9-84	4	19.24
Mosharraf Hossain (*Dhaka/Central Zone*)	SLA	420.2	85	1191	59	7-55	4	20.18
Yasin Arafat (*Chittagong/East Zone*).....	OB	205.3	33	568	28	5-25	1	20.28
Farhad Reza (*Rajshahi/North Zone*)	RFM	199.2	58	570	28	4-18	0	20.35
Sajidul Islam (*Rangpur/North Zone*)	LFM	183.4	39	588	27	4-27	0	21.77
Sanjamul Islam (*Rajshahi/North Zone*) ..	SLA	185.2	28	655	28	8-73	2	23.39
Mohammad Ashraful (*Dhaka Met./CZ*)..	LBG/OB	193	37	682	28	5-41	1	24.35
Saqlain Sajib (*Rajshahi/North Zone*) ...	SLA	326	65	1004	41	6-74	1	24.48
Robiul Islam (*Khulna/South Zone*).......	RFM	166	20	718	29	5-17	1	24.75
Shahadat Hossain (*Dhaka/Bang./C Zone*)	RFM	221.5	29	770	31	5-51	1	24.83
Enamul Haque (*Sylhet/East Zone*)	SLA	370.5	63	1161	46	7-54	6	25.23
Sohag Gazi (*Barisal/Bang./South Zone*) .	OB	385.5	60	1214	42	7-79	4	28.90

WALTON NATIONAL CRICKET LEAGUE, 2012-13

	P	W	L	D	1st-inns pts	Inns/ 10W	Bonus points Batting	Bowling	Pts	Runs per wkt
Khulna	7	6	1	0	0	1	3	0	40	31.21
Dhaka	7	5	1	1	0	2	3	0	38	28.07
Dhaka Metropolis	7	3	2	2	4	0	1	3	28	32.21
Rajshahi	7	3	3	1	2	1	1	2	26	27.79
Sylhet	7	2	3	2	4	1	1	2	22	23.75
Chittagong	7	2	2	3	2	1	3	0	21	31.79
Rangpur	7	1	4	2	2	1	3	0	14	27.56
Barisal..............	7	0	6	1	2	0	0	0	3	19.60

Outright win = 6pts; draw = 1pt; first-innings lead in a drawn match = 2pts; no decision on first innings = 2pts. An extra point was available for winning by an innings or ten wickets. First-innings bonus points were awarded as follows, as long as both first innings were completed: one batting point for scoring 350 or more; one bowling point for dismissing the opposing team for 175 or fewer.

At Bogra, October 20–23, 2012. **Drawn.** ‡Chittagong 411 (Tamim Iqbal 192, Mominul Haque 120) **and** 163-1 (Tamim Iqbal 113*); **Dhaka Metropolis 632-7 dec** (Marshall Ayub 209, Mehrab Hossain 122, Tasamul Haque 135*). *Chittagong 2pts, Dhaka Metropolis 4pts. In his first NCL game for five years, Tamim Iqbal scored twin hundreds: a career-best 192, adding 276 for Chittagong's third wicket with Mominul Haque, followed by 113* in 104 balls. In between, Marshall Ayub completed a maiden double-hundred and put on 311 for Dhaka Metropolis's fourth wicket with Mehrab Hossain; 632-7 was the second-highest total in any NCL match.*

At Mirpur, October 20–22, 2012. **Dhaka won by 127 runs. Dhaka 116 and 322** (Sanjamul Islam 5-129); ‡**Rajshahi 178 and 133.** *Dhaka 6pts, Rajshahi 1pt. Rajshahi and Bangladesh captain Mushfiqur Rahim and team-mate Saqlain Sajib collided going for a catch on the opening day; Mushfiqur did not bat until the second innings, and Saqlain missed the rest of the match.*

At Khulna, October 20–23, 2012. **Khulna won by 52 runs. Khulna 314 and 220** (Sohag Gazi 7-79); ‡**Barisal 278** (Sohag Gazi 119; Taposh Ghosh 5-59) **and 204** (Abdur Razzak 6-72). *Khulna 6pts. Sohag Gazi scored 119 in 93 balls, then claimed a career-best 7-79, including a hat-trick, to finish Khulna's second innings – and still finished on the losing side.*

At Rangpur, October 20–23, 2012. **Drawn.** ‡**Rangpur 295** (Naeem Islam 137*; Enamul Haque 5-101) **and 258-6; Sylhet 323.** *Rangpur 1pt, Sylhet 3pts.*

At Savar, November 2–5, 2012. **Drawn.** ‡**Chittagong 367** (Tamim Iqbal 183; Enamul Haque 6-98); **Sylhet 188-8.** *Chittagong 3pts, Sylhet 3pts. Tamim scored his third century in three innings – 183 in 187 balls, with 13 fours and 12 sixes, out of 279-6. It was his final appearance of the tournament.*

At Mirpur, November 2–5, 2012. **Drawn. Dhaka Metropolis 205** (Shahadat Hossain 5-51) **and 128-6;** ‡**Dhaka 165.** *Dhaka 1pt, Dhaka Metropolis 4pts.*

At Khulna, November 2–5, 2012. **Khulna won by five wickets.** ‡**Rangpur 388** (Naeem Islam 127; Abdur Razzak 5-103) **and 92** (Soumya Sarkar 5-34); **Khulna 249** (Alauddin Babu 6-56) **and 234-5** (Anamul Haque 104*). *Khulna 6pts, Rangpur 1pt. Rangpur led by 139 on first innings, thanks largely to No. 10 Ariful Haque, who hit 75*, including seven sixes, but collapsed for 92 second time round to leave a target of 232; Anamul Haque cracked six sixes while steering Khulna home.*

At Rajshahi, November 2–5, 2012. **Drawn.** ‡**Rajshahi 466-3** (Mizanur Rahman 148, Junaid Siddique 181) **v Barisal.** *Rajshahi 3pts, Barisal 3pts. Mizanur Rahman and Junaid Siddique put on 267 for Rajshahi's first wicket.*

At Chittagong (M. A. Aziz), November 9–11, 2012. **Dhaka Metropolis won by seven wickets. Barisal 242 and 138;** ‡**Dhaka Metropolis 241 and 145-3.** *Dhaka Metropolis 6pts.*

At Bogra, November 9–12, 2012. **Khulna won by 299 runs. Khulna 416 and 343-5 dec** (Anamul Haque 127*); ‡**Chittagong 307** (Abdur Razzak 9-84) **and 153** (Nizamuddin 5-51). *Khulna 7pts. Khulna owed their first-innings lead to Ziaur Rahman (77 in 70 balls, including seven sixes) and Dolar Mahmud (70), who added 129 for the ninth wicket. Abdur Razzak's 9-84 was the best innings return in Bangladeshi cricket; he took 13-112 in all.*

At Rangpur, November 9–12, 2012. **Rajshahi won by 224 runs. Rajshahi 232** (Maisuqur Rahman 102) **and 297-9 dec** (Farhad Reza 100*); ‡**Rangpur 171 and 134.** *Rajshahi 7pts.*

At Sylhet, November 9–12, 2012. **Sylhet won by ten wickets. Dhaka 84** (Tapash Baisya 6-37) **and 307** (Enamul Haque 5-57); ‡**Sylhet 390** (Rajin Saleh 132, Alok Kapali 133) **and 6-0.** *Sylhet 9pts. Dhaka lost two wickets in the first over of the match, then their last eight for 33 to register their second-lowest first-class total; Sylhet took a first-innings lead of 306 thanks to a 240-run stand for the fourth wicket between Rajin Saleh and Alok Kapali.*

At Barisal, November 16–19, 2012. **Sylhet won by 165 runs.** ‡**Sylhet 206 and 239; Barisal 131** (Enamul Haque 7-54) **and 149** (Enamul Haque 6-61). *Sylhet 7pts. Enamul Haque took 13-115 to help Sylhet into second place behind Khulna.*

At Savar, November 16–19, 2012. **Chittagong won by an innings and 113 runs. Rajshahi 239** (Jahurul Islam 118) **and 158** (Mohammad Younus 5-62); ‡**Chittagong 510** (Mahbubul Karim 154, Mominul Haque 114, Faisal Hossain 111; Farhad Hossain 6-143). *Chittagong 8pts.*

At Bogra, November 16–19, 2012. **Dhaka won by seven wickets.** ‡**Rangpur 283 and 153; Dhaka 355** (Suhrawadi Shuvo 5-101) **and 82-3.** *Dhaka 7pts.*

At Sylhet, November 16–19, 2012. **Khulna won by 188 runs. Khulna 355** (Mithun Ali 120) **and 361-9 dec;** ‡**Dhaka Metropolis 320** (Abdur Razzak 7-122) **and 208** (Murad Khan 6-47). *Khulna 7pts. Abdur Razzak took 10-215, his second successive haul of ten or more, to extend Khulna's winning run. His fellow slow left-armer Murad Khan collected six in 8.1 overs as Dhaka Metropolis folded on the last day.*

At Rajshahi, November 23–26, 2012. **Rangpur won by an innings and 40 runs. Barisal 245 and 229;** ‡**Rangpur 514** (Dhiman Ghosh 159, Alauddin Babu 110). *Rangpur 8pts. Rangpur wicketkeeper Liton Das made five catches and a stumping in Barisal's first innings, and ten dismissals in the match. After Rangpur collapsed to 48-5, their last five wickets added 144, 99, 103, 114 and 6 – a total of 466.*

At Chittagong (M. A. Aziz), November 23–25, 2012. **Dhaka won by an innings and 69 runs.** ‡**Chittagong 206 and 194** (Mosharraf Hossain 5-49); **Dhaka 401** (Nadif Chowdhury 114). *Dhaka 9pts. Dhaka took second place.*

At Mirpur, November 23–26, 2012. **Rajshahi won by 76 runs. Rajshahi 256 and 275;** ‡**Dhaka Metropolis 129 and 326** (Asif Ahmed 148). *Rajshahi 7pts.*

At Rangpur, November 23–25, 2012. **Khulna won by ten wickets.** ‡**Sylhet 244** (Imtiaz Hossain 108) **and 130** (Murad Khan 6-64); **Khulna 367** (Tushar Imran 156) **and 8-0.** *Khulna 8pts. This was Khulna's fifth successive win.*

At Sylhet, December 1–4, 2012. **Chittagong won by eight wickets. Barisal 204** (Yasin Arafat 5-25) **and 163** (Noor Hossain 5-29); ‡**Chittagong 296** (Faisal Hossain 123*; Kamrul Islam 5-65) **and 72-2.** *Chittagong 6pts. Off-spinner Yasin Arafat had first-innings figures of 23.4–11–25–5, including a hat-trick to finish off Barisal.*

At Rajshahi, December 1–4, 2012. **Dhaka won by five wickets. Khulna 171** (Mosharraf Hossain 7-55) **and 268** (Imrul Kayes 104); ‡**Dhaka 229 and 216-5.** *Dhaka 7pts. Dhaka inflicted Khulna's only defeat, and went into the final round just four points behind them.*

At Bogra, December 1–3, 2012. **Dhaka Metropolis won by nine wickets.** ‡**Rangpur 129** (Talha Jubair 8-35) **and 266; Dhaka Metropolis 253 and 147-1** (Shamsur Rahman 107*). *Dhaka Metropolis 7pts. Talha Jubair reduced Rangpur to 41-8, but was denied the chance to take all ten by a new tournament rule restricting seamers to 15 overs a day. He finished the match with 11-103. Shamsur Rahman hit 107* in 87 balls, with 11 fours and seven sixes.*

At Savar, December 1–4, 2012. **Rajshahi won by ten wickets. Sylhet 218 and 202** (Taijul Islam 5-74); ‡**Rajshahi 390** (Sabbir Rahman 136; Enamul Haque 6-120) **and 31-0.** *Rajshahi 8pts. Defending champions Rajshahi kept the title in sight with a win that put them only eight points behind leaders Khulna.*

At Rajshahi, December 7–10, 2012. **Dhaka won by an innings and 105 runs. Barisal 256 and 113** (Mosharraf Hossain 5-50); ‡**Dhaka 474** (Raqibul Hasan 160). *Dhaka 8pts. Dhaka closed the gap with Khulna to two points, but had to settle for runners-up. Raqibul Hasan and Mohammad Sharif (54) ensured they would need to bat only once, putting on 123 for their ninth wicket.*

At Sylhet, December 7–10, 2012. **Drawn. Chittagong 350 and 187-6;** ‡**Rangpur 487** (Liton Das 157, Tanveer Haider 107; Noor Hossain 6-146). *Chittagong 2pts, Rangpur 4pts.*

At Rangpur, December 7–10, 2012. **Dhaka Metropolis won by nine wickets. Dhaka Metropolis 345** (Marshall Ayub 116, Mehrab Hossain 110) **and 78-1;** ‡**Sylhet 155** (Mohammad Ashraful 5-41) **and 265** (Sharifullah 5-63). *Dhaka Metropolis 7pts. Marshall Ayub and Mehrab Hossain added 209 for Dhaka Metropolis's fifth wicket, and Sylhet were made to follow on.*

At Bogra, December 7–9, 2012. **Khulna won by 33 runs. Khulna 228 and 180;** ‡**Rajshahi 222 and 153.** *Khulna 6pts. Khulna won the title with a day to spare, despite a scare when Rajshahi reached 102-0 chasing 187. But all ten wickets fell for 51 in 20 overs, with seamers Robiul Islam and Nizamuddin claiming four each.*

NATIONAL CRICKET LEAGUE WINNERS

†1999-2000	Chittagong	2003-04	Dhaka	2008-09	Rajshahi
2000-01	Biman Bangladesh	2004-05	Dhaka	2009-10	Rajshahi
	Airlines	2005-06	Rajshahi	2010-11	Rajshahi
2001-02	Dhaka	2006-07	Dhaka	2011-12	Rajshahi
2002-03	Khulna	2007-08	Khulna	2012-13	Khulna

†   *The National Cricket League was not first-class in 1999-2000.*

Rajshahi have won the title 5 times, Dhaka 4 times, Khulna 3 times, Biman Bangladesh Airlines and Chittagong 1.

BANGLADESH CRICKET LEAGUE, 2012-13

				1st-inns	Bonus points		
	Played	Won	Lost	Drawn	points	Batting	Bowling	Points
Central Zone..........	3	0	0	3	6	3	2	14
North Zone.............	3	1	0	2	2	2	1	13
South Zone.............	3	1	1	1	0	1	2	10
East Zone..............	3	0	1	2	4	2	1	9

Outright win = 6pts; draw = 1pt; first-innings lead in a drawn match = 2pts; no decision on first innings = 2pts. An extra point was available for winning by an innings or ten wickets. First-innings bonus points were awarded as follows: one batting point for scoring 300 or more in the first 100 overs; one bowling point for dismissing the opposing team.

At Mirpur, December 27–30, 2012. **Drawn. South Zone 343** (Ziaur Rahman 152*; Mosharraf Hossain 5-52) **and 216**; ‡**Central Zone 433-9 dec** (Marshall Ayub 125) **and 93-6** (Robiul Islam 5-17). *Central Zone 5pts, South Zone 2pts. Ziaur Rahman reached a maiden hundred in 88 balls, then rushed on to 152* in 118, with seven fours and 15 sixes, one short of the record of 16 shared by Andrew Symonds, Graham Napier and Jesse Ryder. South Zone's last two wickets added 151, of which Ziaur's partners contributed 15. Central Zone lost four wickets in the opening over of their second innings – 2W0WWnbW from Robiul – but held out for the draw and first-innings points.*

At Bogra, December 27–30, 2012. **Drawn. North Zone 499-6 dec; ‡East Zone 419-8** (Dhiman Ghosh 107*). *North Zone 4pts, East Zone 4pts. Fog prevented the completion of East's first innings.*

At Mirpur, January 2–5, 2013. **South Zone won by 37 runs. South Zone 248 and 248** (Nabil Samad 6-81); ‡**East Zone 232** (Sohag Gazi 6-66) **and 227** (Sohag Gazi 5-73). *South Zone 7pts, East Zone 1pt. South Zone claimed the first outright win of the new tournament, thanks to Sohag Gazi's 11-139.*

At Bogra, January 2–5, 2013. **Drawn. ‡North Zone 361 and 397-6** (Nasir Hossain 131); **Central Zone 436-9 dec** (Mohammad Ashraful 133, Mehrab Hossain 131). *North Zone 2pts, Central Zone 5pts. Mohammad Ashraful and Mehrab added 228 for Central Zone's fifth wicket. Nasir Hossain hit 131 in 112 balls in North Zone's second innings, when all 11 Central players bowled.*

At Bogra, January 8–11, 2013. **Drawn. Central Zone 655-7 dec** (Marshall Ayub 289, Mehrab Hossain 218); ‡**East Zone 396-8**. *Central Zone 4pts, East Zone 4pts. Marshall Ayub reached his second double-hundred of the season, batting for 564 minutes and 367 balls, with 30 fours and four sixes; his 289 was the second-highest innings in Bangladesh. Mehrab completed a maiden double. They followed their earlier stands of 311 and 209 for Dhaka Metropolis by adding 494, the second-highest fifth-wicket stand in all first-class cricket and an all-wicket national record. The total of 655-7 was the third-highest in Bangladesh. Central Zone headed the qualifying table.*

At Mirpur, January 8–11, 2013. **North Zone won by 170 runs. North Zone 291 and 362-7 dec;** ‡**South Zone 205** (Saqlain Sajib 6-74) **and 278**. *North Zone 7pts, South Zone 1pt. North Zone overtook South to claim a place in the final. They were 125-8 on the opening day before Sanjamul Islam (73) and Sajidul Islam (76) put on 127; on the last day another ninth-wicket pair, Sohag Gazi (85) and Shafaq Al Zabir, delayed North's victory with a stand of 100.*

Final

At Mirpur, February 22–25, 2013 (day/night). **Central Zone won by 31 runs. Central Zone 277** (Raqibul Hasan 125) **and 247** (Sanjamul Islam 8-73); ‡**North Zone 274 and 219.** *Central Zone won the inaugural Bangladesh Cricket League. Raqibul Hasan helped them double an unpromising start of 135-5, and Mohammad Ashraful grabbed a hat-trick just as North Zone were poised to take first-innings lead. Sanjamul Islam's left-arm spin collected 11-144, and he helped Jahurul Islam (81) add 106 from 71-5, but Jahurul was last out with over a day to spare.*

BANGLADESH PREMIER LEAGUE, 2012-13

20-over league plus knockout

	Played	Won	Lost	Points	Net run-rate
Dhaka Gladiators	12	9	3	18	0.92
Sylhet Royals	12	9	3	18	0.08
Chittagong Kings	12	6	6	12	1.17
Duronto Rajshahi	12	5	7	10	−0.55
Rangpur Riders	12	5	7	10	−0.50
Barisal Burners	12	5	7	10	−0.04
Khulna Royal Bengals	12	3	9	6	−1.06

Preliminary finals

1st v 2nd: Dhaka Gladiators beat Sylhet Royals by four runs. **3rd v 4th:** Chittagong Kings beat Duronto Rajshahi by four wickets. **Final play-off:** Chittagong Kings beat Sylhet Royals by three wickets.

Final

At Mirpur, February 19, 2013 (floodlit). **Dhaka Gladiators won by 43 runs. Dhaka Gladiators 172-9** (20 overs); ‡**Chittagong Kings 129** (16.5 overs). *Dhaka retained their title in the second BPL. Mosharraf Hossain won the match award for a burst of 3-26 that reduced Chittagong to 65-5; he was one of nine individuals later charged with match-fixing in this tournament.*

EIGHTH BANGLADESH GAMES CRICKET, 2012-13

20-over knockout

Semi-finals

At Bogra, April 25. **Rajshahi won by eight wickets.** ‡**Khulna 97** (17.5 overs); **Rajshahi 99-2** (12.5 overs). *Khulna collapsed from 50-1, giving Rajshahi an easy win.*

At Bogra, April 25. **Rangpur won by 42 runs** (D/L). ‡**Rangpur 173-5** (20 overs); **Dhaka Metropolis 85-6** (14.2 overs). *When play stopped, Dhaka Metropolis's retrospective target was 128.*

Third-place play-off

At Bogra, April 27. **Dhaka Metropolis won by 75 runs. Dhaka Metropolis 171-7** (20 overs); ‡**Khulna 96** (18.2 overs).

Final

At Bogra, April 27. **Rajshahi won by five wickets.** ‡**Rangpur 150-7** (20 overs); **Rajshahi 154-5** (19 overs). *Delwar Hussain reduced Rangpur to 34-3, and Sabbir Rahman led the run-chase with 64*, including five sixes.*

INDIAN CRICKET, 2013

In Sachin's shadow

A N A N D   V A S U

It was a fine year for the Indian team and, though only eight Tests were played, all six at home were won. Australia were whitewashed 4–0 on pitches that turned, bounced variably and were designed to thwart the seamers. The surfaces frustrated Australia's batsmen and bowlers, and allowed Ravindra Jadeja, written off by many as a humble one-day spinner, to scalp the twinkle-toed Australian captain Michael Clarke five times out of six. Defeat in a two-match series in South Africa at the end of the year did not reflect how close India came to sharing the honours.

Jadeja was also India's most effective bowler as they won the Champions Trophy outright for the first time, beating England in a shortened final at Edgbaston to leave them in possession of both major one-day international titles. India spent much of the year on top of the ICC's 50-over rankings,

INDIA IN 2013

	Played	Won	Lost	Drawn/No result
Tests	8	6	1	1
One-day internationals	34	22	10	2
Twenty20 internationals	1	1	–	–

DECEMBER	3 ODIs and 2 T20Is (h) v Pakistan	(see *Wisden 2013*, page 986)
JANUARY	5 ODIs (h) v England	(see *Wisden 2013*, page 408)
FEBRUARY — MARCH	4 Tests (h) v Australia	(page 919)
APRIL		
MAY		
JUNE	Champions Trophy (in England)	(page 301)
	Triangular ODI tournament (a) (in West Indies) v Sri Lanka and West Indies	(page 1155)
JULY	5 ODIs (a) v Zimbabwe	(page 1187)
AUGUST		
SEPTEMBER		
OCTOBER	7 ODIs and 1 T20I (h) v Australia	(page 934)
NOVEMBER	2 Tests and 3 ODIs (h) v West Indies	(page 943)
DECEMBER	2 Tests and 3 ODIs (a) v South Africa	(page 1079)

For a review of Indian domestic cricket from the 2012-13 season, see page 978.

boosted by five hundreds from the flamboyant newcomer Shikhar Dhawan, who formed a vibrant opening partnership with Rohit Sharma, and four from Virat Kohli. They had won six bilateral one-day series in a row, until Quinton de Kock halted them with centuries in all three matches in South Africa.

If 2013 included the blossoming of Jadeja, Dhawan and Bengali seamer Mohammed Shami, everything was in danger of being obscured by Sachin Tendulkar's farewell. Tendulkar had made his Test debut in 1989, when he should have been sitting in a classroom in Shardashram Vidya Mandir School, wondering how Dilip Vengsarkar was getting on against Pakistan. Instead he was showing his elders how to play quick bowling, even while wearing Waqar Younis bouncers on the teeth.

According to the ICC's Future Tours Programme, Tendulkar's 200th Test was scheduled for Newlands in January 2014. However, when Tendulkar told the BCCI he was calling it a day, there was no way they would allow the story to end in faraway Africa. With all credible opposition otherwise occupied, the BCCI invited Darren Sammy's West Indians to play a two-match series, squeezed in before the South Africa tour, which at one point looked as if it might not take place at all. It would culminate in Tendulkar finishing at home, at the Wankhede Stadium in Mumbai. At the venue where he was once a ballboy at a World Cup match in 1987, Tendulkar would give his superstitious mother, Rajni, a chance to watch her son in action for the first time.

West Indies were no match for India, losing the First Test in Kolkata on the third day, and surrendering even sooner in the Second (Sharma made hundreds in both his first two Tests). At least Tendulkar went out in style, reeling off several trademark shots in his 74 at Mumbai, as if for old time's sake.

When he eventually took the microphone, Tendulkar – a reluctant and usually uninspiring speaker – wrenched a tear from every Indian eye. "All my friends, settle down, let me talk," he said, as the crowd went ballistic. "I will get more and more emotional. My life, between 22 yards for 24 years – it is hard to believe that wonderful journey has come to an end." He thanked everyone who had contributed to his career, without missing a beat or looking at the list in his hand. "You are the best partnership I've had in my life," he told his wife Anjali, who failed to hide her tears behind oversized sunglasses. To his daughter Sara and son Arjun, he said: "For 16 years, I have not spent enough time with you, but the next 16 years, or even beyond, is for you."

There were no thoughts of how long it had been since Tendulkar last scored a Test hundred (January 2011). Instead, a nation rose to their feet, and wept like they never might again for a cricketer. Once the emotion subsided, however, attention refocused on all that had gone wrong in other spheres.

The sixth edition of the IPL could easily have been an advertisement for global Twenty20 leagues, with Rajasthan Royals, the cheapest team in the event, cast as unlikely poster boys for success. But then, on May 16, three of their players – Sreesanth, Ankeet Chavan and Ajit Chandila – were detained by police on suspicion of spot-fixing. They would eventually get bail, but not before being banned from all cricket by the BCCI.

The Delhi and Mumbai police investigations that ended in their arrest also exposed suspicious telephone conversations between Gurunath Meiyappan, a prominent member of the management team of Chennai Super Kings – the franchise owned by India Cements, which belonged to his father-in-law, BCCI president N. Srinivasan – and Vindoo Dara Singh, a small-time Bollywood actor with connections to bookies.

The storm threatened to overrun the BCCI, as they agonised whether it was proper for Srinivasan to stay in office when Meiyappan was being investigated. The ensuing furore took in the resignations of Sanjay Jagdale, BCCI secretary, and Ajay Shirke, the treasurer, but stopped short of revolt. Srinivasan stepped aside temporarily from the presidency, and a working committee called upon Bengal's Jagmohan Dalmiya – a former BCCI and ICC chief, once expelled by the board over corruption allegations, though later exonerated – to take over the day-to-day functions of the post while the IPL probe was carried out. I. S. Bindra, the Punjab Cricket Association president, claimed he was the only board member to ask for Srinivasan's resignation; it was clear there was no real internal opposition to the boss man of cricket.

Up in smoke: Sreesanth was banned for spot-fixing in the IPL.

Support for Srinivasan was underlined in September, when BCCI members voted 29–0 to expel Lalit Modi, the former IPL supremo now in exile, from participating in their affairs. Modi, a strident critic of Srinivasan, might have been a rallying force in mustering credible opposition, even by proxy from London. But the fact that he could not generate a single vote showed how strong Srinivasan's grip remained. Modi's later attempt to win back his old post as Rajasthan Cricket Association chairman was held up in the Supreme Court.

In December, Star TV added Indian team sponsorship up to April 2017 to their exclusive broadcasting rights and title sponsorship for international and domestic competitions (excluding the IPL). The end of Sahara's involvement, after 12 years, came as no surprise once their IPL franchise, Pune Warriors, had been terminated by the BCCI in October, due to non-payment of bank guarantees. The change was also a factor in the cancellation of Cape Town's New Year Test: by ensuring the tour was over by December 30, India avoided a messy mid-series switch of shirt sponsors.

To the rest of the world, in a year when the IPL was tarnished by the worst corruption allegations in its history, these machinations were less than edifying. Yet, Indian cricket's nadir was soon forgotten, as the story turned to Tendulkar's long kiss goodbye. Even in his leaving, he was Indian cricket's saviour.

INDIA v AUSTRALIA, 2012-13

Brydon Coverdale

Test matches (4): India 4, Australia 0

Clean sweeps involving Australia were once a thing of regularity. Glenn McGrath could predict a whitewash at the start of each Ashes series in the belief that one day he would be proved right. As late as 2011-12, the Australians crushed India 4–0 in a home series that was as one-sided as a Möbius strip. But the boot on the other foot? Even in a country where Australia had won only one series since 1969-70? For more than two decades, their fans had greeted that prospect as they would the colonisation of the moon: possible in theory, but not something for this generation to worry about.

All that changed over five weeks in India, where M. S. Dhoni's men were methodical and merciless in racking up a 4–0 triumph. The retirements of Ricky Ponting and Mike Hussey in the months before the series had left a yawning hole in Australia's middle order – and Michael Clarke in charge of one of their least-fancied squads ever to have visited the subcontinent. True, it was an evolving group of players. But adaptation is the key to evolution and, at almost every level – not least on the slow, dry, turning pitches – Australia failed to adapt.

Inevitably, perhaps, on-field failures were accompanied by off-field dysfunction, the like of which Australia had rarely seen. Four players, including vice-captain Shane Watson, were suspended for the Third Test in Mohali after neglecting to complete a task set for them by coach Mickey Arthur. The severity of the punishment was the subject of incandescent debate, especially as Watson flew back to Australia on the same day for the birth of his first child, calling the penalty "extremely harsh" and saying he would use his time at home to consider his future.

India, meanwhile, chastised by their loss to England before Christmas, went from triumph to triumph, and for the first time won four Tests in a series. It was a cathartic result given their 4–0 defeat in Australia 14 months earlier – even if two such stark scorelines suggested neither team could be considered the equal of South Africa or England until they could perform in unfamiliar conditions. As if to underline the point, spinners Ravichandran Ashwin – revitalised after his struggles against the English – and Ravindra Jadeja took 53 of the 78 wickets that fell to India's bowlers.

While Murali Vijay and Cheteshwar Pujara calmly gathered big scores, the batting of Dhoni and Shikhar Dhawan, by contrast, wreaked havoc. Dhoni's double-century in the First Test felt like a blow – or a series of blows – from which Australia never recovered. And the emergence of Dhawan, who at Mohali converted the fastest recorded hundred by a Test debutant into a memorable 187, turned the one potential downer for India – the axing of the established opening pair of Gautam Gambhir and Virender Sehwag – into another reason for excitement. Gambhir, after three years without a Test hundred, was dropped before the series, and Sehwag – who resorted to batting in glasses – failed at Chennai and Hyderabad, where India's batsmen otherwise handled Australia's modest spin attack with ease. Their patient batting was exemplified by Vijay and Pujara, comfortably the two leading run-scorers in the series. The serene Vijay was the only man to make two centuries, even if he was overshadowed on both occasions – by Pujara's double-hundred at Hyderabad, where the pair added 370 for the second wicket, and by Dhawan at Mohali.

Australia's batsmen failed to find any sort of balance between defence and attack. With the exceptions of Clarke and, briefly, Steve Smith, their footwork against India's spinners came as naturally as cursing in Hindi. They managed 29 scores above 20, but only one hundred – from Clarke, on the first day of the series – to India's six; and their largest partnership was 151. Seldom has the batting unit performed so poorly: Watson, David Warner, Phillip Hughes and Matthew Wade all averaged under 25. Fear of the turning ball was personified by Hughes, who until his sixth innings appeared to have no scoring plan against the slow bowlers at all: his only options seemed to be defence or dismissal. After nudging a few runs on day one in Chennai, he endured a drought of 58 scoreless deliveries against spin across three Tests; meanwhile, Ashwin and Jadeja dismissed him four times.

MOST WICKETS IN A SERIES FOR INDIA

W		T	Avge		
35	B. S. Chandrasekhar. . . .	5	18.91	v England (h)	1972-73
34	V. Mankad	5	16.79	v England (h)	1951-52
34	S. P. Gupte	5	19.67	v New Zealand (h)	1955-56
32	Harbhajan Singh.	3	17.03	v Australia (h)	2000-01
32	Kapil Dev	6	17.68	v Pakistan (h)	1979-80
31	B. S. Bedi	5	23.87	v Australia (a).	1977-78
29	Kapil Dev	6	18.51	v West Indies (h)	1983-84
29	**R. Ashwin**	**4**	**20.10**	**v Australia (h). . . . .**	**2012-13**
28	Kapil Dev	6	22.32	v Australia (h)	1979-80
28	B. S. Chandrasekhar. . . .	5	25.14	v Australia (a).	1977-78

The bite and bounce achieved by Ashwin made him a constant threat, and his tally of 29 wickets was the best by an Indian in any Test series since Harbhajan Singh took 32 in three matches during the epic 2000-01 encounter between these teams. Jadeja's steady left-arm spin collected 24 victims, including the priceless wicket of a startled Clarke in five innings out of six.

By comparison Nathan Lyon, Xavier Doherty and Glenn Maxwell were toothless. Lyon entered and exited the series as Australia's first-choice spinner, but lacked the Indians' subtle variations in length and flight. Despite that, the selectors erred by dropping him in Hyderabad for Doherty – a one-day specialist who, not surprisingly, proved tidy but unpenetrative. The confusion was exemplified by Maxwell: drafted in for the Second Test, dropped for the Third, recalled for the Fourth. The fast bowlers, especially James Pattinson and Peter Siddle, were tireless and solid, but did not generally have enough runs to defend.

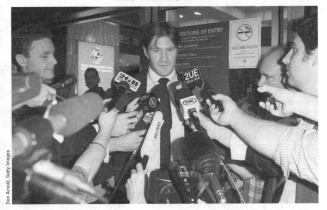

Don Arnold, Getty Images

Into the storm: Shane Watson popped home to Sydney for the birth of his son, having already been axed for the Third Test for disciplinary reasons.

Watson, without a Test century since October 2010, was especially disappointing. One of just four men in the squad with Test experience in India, he had opted to play as a batsman only, in an effort to avoid exacerbating the calf and hamstring problems which had blighted his two most recent home summers. Yet he survived only 239 deliveries in six innings for 99 runs; Lyon, usually at No. 11, faced 244.

But in the absence of Hussey and Ponting, Australia lacked leadership as much as batsmanship. That became acutely obvious when Clarke, Arthur and team manager Gavin Dovey announced three days before the Third Test that Watson, Pattinson, Mitchell Johnson and Usman Khawaja would not be considered for selection. After their Hyderabad humiliation, the players had been asked by Arthur for three ideas to improve their own performance and the team's. The four ignored the task, which was taken as a sign they were not hurting enough. The management stressed that standards had slipped throughout the tour among the whole squad: players had turned up late to meetings, failed tests relating to body fat, and worn the wrong uniforms. They decided an example had to be made.

The decision was extreme but sound. Who, many wondered at the time, would risk taking liberties with Arthur and Clarke after such a stand? Arthur, by his own admission, had "put his neck on the line" – a phrase which took on an unexpected turn when he was sacked in late June, two weeks before the first Ashes Test. Yet it was troubling that discipline had been allowed to slide – and telling that Watson, second in command, was one of the offenders. Pat Howard, Australia's team performance manager, said he thought Watson acted in the best interests of the team "sometimes"; the caveat felt damning. And the final irony came when Clarke missed the Fourth Test at Delhi because of his injured back, at which point the captaincy passed to, yes, Watson – now back from Sydney following the birth of his son. While Clarke went home, which did little to encourage notions of a unified group, Watson's introduction to Test leadership was a three-day defeat; a few weeks later, he quit the vice-captaincy to focus on his batting.

Australia had won all four tosses – and batted first each time – but it was not much help. They were whitewashed for only the fourth time in a series of three or more Tests, following 1982-83 (when they lost 3–0 in Pakistan), 1969-70 (when Bill Lawry led an exhausted squad to South Africa and went down 4–0), and 1886 (when they lost 3–0 in England).

India, meanwhile, could put their defeat by England behind them, and settle into a long absence from Test cricket, with none scheduled for another eight months. That hiatus meant questions could be put aside about the immediate future of Sachin Tendulkar, who began the series with a sparkling 81 at Chennai before falling away. Dhoni could be feted after becoming India's most successful Test captain, having passed Sourav Ganguly's record of 21 victories, at Hyderabad. And India's fans could soak up the joy of their first 4–0 whitewash. Their mirror-image defeat in Australia felt like another world.

AUSTRALIAN TOURING PARTY

*M. J. Clarke, J. M. Bird, E. J. M. Cowan, X. J. Doherty, M. C. Henriques, P. J. Hughes, M. G. Johnson, U. T. Khawaja, N. M. Lyon, G. J. Maxwell, J. L. Pattinson, P. M. Siddle, S. P. D. Smith, M. A. Starc, M. S. Wade, D. A. Warner, S. R. Watson. *Coach:* J. M. Arthur.

A. C. Agar was added to the squad for the warm-up matches. Clarke, Doherty, Hughes, Johnson, Starc, Warner and Watson arrived for the second practice game, having been involved in Australia's one-day series against West Indies. Bird flew home during the First Test; scans later revealed a stress fracture of his back. B. J. Haddin was added to the squad when Wade sprained an ankle playing basketball between the Second and Third Tests. Watson went home for the birth of his child but returned for the Fourth Test, while Clarke and Starc departed with back and ankle injuries respectively.

TEST MATCH AVERAGES

INDIA – BATTING AND FIELDING

	T	I	NO	R	HS	100	50	Avge	Ct/St
C. A. Pujara	4	7	2	419	204	1	2	83.80	1
M. S. Dhoni	4	6	2	326	224	1	0	81.50	9/5
M. Vijay	4	7	0	430	167	2	1	61.42	2
V. Kohli	4	6	1	284	107	1	1	56.80	5
S. R. Tendulkar	4	7	1	192	81	0	1	32.00	1
Bhuvneshwar Kumar . . .	4	4	1	80	38	0	0	26.66	2
†R. A. Jadeja	4	5	1	85	43	0	0	21.25	1
V. Sehwag	2	3	0	27	19	0	0	9.00	6
R. Ashwin	4	4	0	20	12	0	0	5.00	1
I. Sharma	4	4	2	6	4*	0	0	3.00	1

Played in two Tests: Harbhajan Singh 11, 0; †P. P. Ojha 1, 0. Played in one Test: †S. Dhawan 187; A. M. Rahane 7, 1 (1 ct).

BOWLING

	Style	O	M	R	W	BB	5I	Avge
R. A. Jadeja	SLA	193.2	53	419	24	5-58	1	17.45
R. Ashwin	OB	241.2	74	583	29	7-103	4	20.10
P. P. Ojha.............	SLA	86.1	19	238	7	2-19	0	34.00
I. Sharma	RFM	97	23	265	7	3-72	0	37.85
Bhuvneshwar Kumar ...	RFM	64	9	239	6	3-31	0	39.83
Harbhajan Singh.......	OB	84	17	204	5	2-52	0	40.80

Also bowled: S. R. Tendulkar (RM/OB/LBG) 2–0–2–0.

AUSTRALIA – BATTING AND FIELDING

	T	I	NO	R	HS	100	50	Avge	Ct/St
M. J. Clarke	3	6	0	286	130	1	1	47.66	2
S. P. D. Smith........	2	4	0	161	92	0	1	40.25	1
†M. A. Starc...........	2	4	0	145	99	0	1	36.25	1
†E. J. M. Cowan......	4	8	0	265	86	0	1	33.12	4
M. C. Henriques.......	3	6	1	156	81*	0	2	31.20	1
†D. A. Warner	4	8	0	195	71	0	2	24.37	0
†X. J. Doherty	2	4	3	24	18*	0	0	24.00	2
†M. S. Wade..........	3	6	0	113	62	0	1	18.83	4/1
†P. J. Hughes	4	8	0	147	69	0	1	18.37	2
N. M. Lyon..........	3	6	3	54	18	0	0	18.00	1
P. M. Siddle	4	8	0	139	51	0	2	17.37	0
†J. L. Pattinson.........	3	6	2	68	30	0	0	17.00	0
S. R. Watson	3	6	0	99	28	0	0	16.50	1
G. J. Maxwell.........	2	4	0	39	13	0	0	9.75	2

Played in one Test: B. J. Haddin 21, 30 (4 ct, 1 st); †M. G. Johnson 3, 0.

BOWLING

	Style	O	M	R	W	BB	5I	Avge
G. J. Maxwell.........	OB	41	2	193	7	4-127	0	27.57
J. L. Pattinson.........	RFM	79	19	250	9	5-96	1	27.77
P. M. Siddle	RFM	110.4	27	305	9	5-71	1	33.88
N. M. Lyon..........	OB	127.1	9	560	15	7-94	1	37.33
X. J. Doherty	SLA	77.1	25	242	4	3-131	0	60.50

Also bowled: M. J. Clarke (SLA) 8–2–25–0; M. C. Henriques (RFM) 53–12–155–2; M. G. Johnson (LF) 19–3–60–0; S. P. D. Smith (LBG) 10–0–63–1; M. A. Starc (LFM) 58.3–9–200–2; D. A. Warner (LBG) 4–0–33–0.

At Chennai (Guru Nanak), February 12–13, 2013 (not first-class). **Drawn. ‡Australians 241** (E. J. M. Cowan 58; Parvez Rasool 7-45) **and 15-0**; **Indian Board President's XI 230** (A. T. Rayudu 87; N. M. Lyon 3-69, M. C. Henriques 4-12). *Seven of Australia's squad had yet to arrive in India, so Matthew Wade captained a bowler-heavy side including Ashton Agar, a 19-year-old left-arm spinner from Western Australia drafted in for experience. The tourists lost their last eight wickets for 74, chiefly to off-spinner Parvez Rasool.*

At Chennai (Guru Nanak), February 16–18, 2013. **Drawn. ‡India A 451** (G. Gambhir 112, R. G. Sharma 77, M. K. Tiwary 129; X. J. Doherty 3-108, A. C. Agar 3-107); **Australians 235** (S. R. Watson 84; R. V. Dhruve 5-51, J. S. Saxena 4-61) **and 195-3** (S. R. Watson 60, E. J. M. Cowan 53). *This match suggested Australia could be in for a rough ride. In the first innings, their spinners – Agar, Nathan Lyon and Xavier Doherty – took eight for 328; India A's slow bowlers Rakesh Dhruve and Jalaj Saxena managed nine for 112. Gautam Gambhir scored his first first-class hundred for more than three years, but had already been dropped from India's Test squad. Shane Watson and Ed Cowan shared century opening stands in both innings, but in between their team-mates struggled against the turning ball, and were made to follow on.*

INDIA v AUSTRALIA

First Test Match

At Chennai, February 22–26, 2013. India won by eight wickets. Toss: Australia. Test debuts: Bhuvneshwar Kumar; M. C. Henriques.

There was no mistaking the scenario on the third morning when long, tightly formed queues assembled outside the M. A. Chidambaram Stadium. Tendulkar had gone to stumps the previous evening within sight of a hundred, and his devotees arrived anticipating a spot of idolatry. They got it – though not because of Tendulkar, who added only ten to his overnight 71. By the close, he had been all but forgotten, as far as that is possible in India: a double-century from Dhoni had eclipsed everything else.

Dhoni came to the crease with the match evenly poised, if not slightly in Australia's favour, and proceeded to savage their attack in a way few have managed. He sprinted to 200 from 231 deliveries, annihilated Lyon, one of eight men playing their first Test in India, and comprehensively broke Australian spirits. It was an innings that defined the series: the solid cricket Australia had played on the first two days vanished, never to return.

They had entered the game cautiously optimistic, following India's 2–1 defeat at home by England only two months earlier. Seamer Bhuvneshwar Kumar made his debut, while India surprisingly dropped slow left-armer Pragyan Ojha, their leading wicket-taker against England, preferring instead the off-breaks of Harbhajan Singh, who earned his 100th Test appearance against his favourite opponents. With Ashwin and Jadeja, Harbhajan formed part of a three-man spin attack which shared all 20 wickets – testimony to the bowlers' skill and the ineptitude of Australia's batsmen against the turning ball.

Australia opted for pace, which was their strength, leaving Lyon as the sole specialist spinner. Mike Hussey, who had retired after the home summer, was absent for the first time since making his debut in November 2005, and they were a bowler down because of Watson's decision to play solely as a batsman. His replacement as all-rounder was debutant Moises Henriques, the second Portuguese-born Test cricketer, after South Africa's Dick Westcott, who had died in January, aged 85. But with Wade at No. 6, the batting line-up looked as thin as any Australia had fielded since the mid-1980s.

HIGHEST TEST SCORE BY A WICKETKEEPER

232*	A. Flower	Zimbabwe v India at Nagpur	2000-01
230	K. C. Sangakkara	Sri Lanka v Pakistan at Lahore	2001-02
224	**M. S. Dhoni**	**India v Australia at Chennai**	**2012-13**
210*	Taslim Arif	Pakistan v Australia at Faisalabad	1979-80
209	Imtiaz Ahmed	Pakistan v New Zealand at Lahore	1955-56
204*	A. C. Gilchrist	Australia v South Africa at Johannesburg	2001-02
201*	D. S. B. P. Kuruppu	Sri Lanka v New Zealand at Colombo (CCC)	1986-87
200	**Mushfiqur Rahim**	**Bangladesh v Sri Lanka at Galle**	**2012-13**

Clarke chose to bat, and Dhoni set the tone for the series by introducing spin after only 22 minutes. Three overs into the second session, Ashwin had dismissed the top four: Warner, Hughes and Watson, more at home against fast bowling on bouncy surfaces, were too tentative, while Cowan – uncharacteristically – was too aggressive, stumped as he hustled injudiciously down the pitch. It was left to Clarke to master the environment. On a surface that looked like one of Roland Garros's clay courts, he ignored tennis wisdom and embarked instead on cricket's equivalent of serve-and-volley, light on his feet as he advanced to the spinners. He had luck, too, benefiting from India's opposition to the Decision Review System when he inside-edged a catch to short leg on 39, only for umpire Dharmasena to turn down Ashwin's appeal. Clarke was assisted in a stand of 151 for the sixth wicket by the impressive Henriques, who was lbw sweeping for 68, part of a career-best seven wicket haul for Ashwin.

Clarke pushed on to 130 before he was caught at long-off on the second morning, and chastised himself as he walked off, certain a bigger hundred had been there for the taking. Still, Australia's 380 looked competitive – even more so when Pattinson breached 93mph and had India 12 for two, bowling both Vijay and Sehwag. But Clarke was too cautious with his young fast bowler, who was returning from a side injury, and India moved to 182 for three at stumps – by which time Pattinson, who also removed Pujara and was comfortably the pick of the attack, had bowled only six overs.

Pattinson and Siddle applied pressure during a fascinating first hour on day three, and Lyon reaped the reward when he bowled Tendulkar for 81 with a beauty that drifted away before turning back sharply to defeat the drive and leave India 196 for four. The game was

---

MOST RUNS CONCEDED IN A TEST INNINGS IN INDIA

53.3–2–240–3	H. M. R. K. B. Herath	Sri Lanka v India at Mumbai (Brabourne) . . .	2009-10
43.5–1–215–8	J. J. Krejza	Australia v India at Nagpur.	2008-09
47–1–215–3	**N. M. Lyon**	**Australia v India at Chennai**	**2012-13**
53.1–6–203–3	P. L. Harris	South Africa v India at Chennai	2007-08
58–6–203–1	A. Mishra	India v Sri Lanka at Ahmedabad.	2009-10
75–16–202–3	V. Mankad	India v West Indies at Bombay (Brabourne) .	1948-49
84–19–202–6	Haseeb Ahsan	Pakistan v India at Madras	1960-61
57–5–200–4	D. L. Vettori	New Zealand v India at Ahmedabad.	1999-2000

---

in the balance – and then came Dhoni, who muscled the Australians all round the ground. Kohli made a finely constructed 107, but his contribution of 53 to a stand of 128 with his captain reflected his role as second fiddle. For his part, Dhoni sustained a Twenty20-style innings for all but six hours.

Australia's fast bowlers had no answers, but it was Lyon, initially extracting some bite from the pitch, who suffered most: Dhoni hit him for 104 from 85 deliveries, used his wrists to force the ball into gaps, and finished with 224 from 265, the highest Test score by an Indian wicketkeeper – surpassing Budhi Kunderan's 192, made a couple of miles away at the Nehru Stadium against England in 1963-64. His stand of 140 for the ninth wicket with Kumar allowed India to reach 572; seven of their nine highest totals against Australia had now come since the turn of the millennium.

India's three spinners all posed different questions on an unpredictable surface: Hughes received a snorter from Jadeja which ripped to slip off his glove, while Clarke – who survived two near-adjacent lbw appeals, also from Jadeja – was eventually hit in front by one from Ashwin which barely got up. The only sustained resistance came from Henriques, who stretched the game into the last day and finished unbeaten on 81, the fifth Australian to score twin half-centuries on debut. Ashwin's five wickets gave him 12 in the match, and Tendulkar hurried India towards victory by hitting his first two balls, from Lyon, for six. But it was to Dhoni that the game belonged.

Man of the Match: M. S. Dhoni.

Close of play: first day, Australia 316-7 (Clarke 103, Siddle 1); second day, India 182-3 (Tendulkar 71, Kohli 50); third day, India 515-8 (Dhoni 206, Bhuvneshwar Kumar 16); fourth day, Australia 232-9 (Henriques 75, Lyon 8).

" New Zealand spirits were suppressed by Prior, carving through the off side like a chef mutilating the Sunday roast with a chainsaw."
New Zealand v England, 2012-13, Second Test, page 273

Australia

E. J. M. Cowan st Dhoni b Ashwin	29	– lbw b Ashwin	32
D. A. Warner lbw b Ashwin	59	– (3) lbw b Harbhajan Singh	23
P. J. Hughes b Ashwin	6	– (4) c Sehwag b Jadeja	0
S. R. Watson lbw b Ashwin	28	– (2) c Sehwag b Ashwin	17
*M. J. Clarke c Bhuvneshwar Kumar b Jadeja	130	– lbw b Ashwin	31
†M. S. Wade lbw b Ashwin	12	– b Harbhajan Singh	8
M. C. Henriques lbw b Ashwin	68	– not out	81
M. A. Starc b Jadeja	3	– (10) c Tendulkar b Ashwin	8
P. M. Siddle c Sehwag b Harbhajan Singh	19	– (8) b Jadeja	2
J. L. Pattinson not out	15	– (9) c Sehwag b Ashwin	11
N. M. Lyon c Kohli b Ashwin	3	– c Vijay b Jadeja	11
B 1, l-b 7	8	B 15, l-b 2	17

1/64 (1) 2/72 (3) 3/126 (4)   (133 overs) 380   1/34 (2) 2/64 (1)   (93 overs) 241
4/131 (5) 5/153 (6) 6/304 (7)   3/65 (4) 4/101 (3)
7/307 (8) 8/361 (5) 9/364 (9) 10/380 (11)   5/121 (6) 6/131 (5) 7/137 (8)
                                                   8/161 (9) 9/175 (10) 10/241 (11)

Bhuvneshwar Kumar 13–1–52–0; Sharma 17–3–59–0; Harbhajan Singh 25–2–87–1; Ashwin 42–12–103–7; Jadeja 36–10–71–2. *Second innings*—Ashwin 32–6–95–5; Harbhajan Singh 27–6–55–2; Jadeja 31–8–72–3; Sharma 3–1–2–0.

India

M. Vijay b Pattinson	10	– c Henriques b Pattinson	6
V. Sehwag b Pattinson	2	– c Clarke b Lyon	19
C. A. Pujara b Pattinson	44	– not out	8
S. R. Tendulkar b Lyon	81	– not out	13
V. Kohli c Starc b Lyon	107		
*†M. S. Dhoni c Wade b Pattinson	224		
R. A. Jadeja b Pattinson	16		
R. Ashwin b Lyon	3		
Harbhajan Singh b Henriques	11		
Bhuvneshwar Kumar c Clarke b Siddle	38		
I. Sharma not out	4		
B 14, l-b 14, w 4	32	B 4	4

1/11 (1) 2/12 (2) 3/105 (3)   (154.3 overs) 572   1/16 (1)   (2 wkts, 11.3 overs) 50
4/196 (4) 5/324 (5) 6/365 (7)   2/36 (2)
7/372 (8) 8/406 (9) 9/546 (6) 10/572 (10)

Starc 25–3–75–0; Pattinson 30–6–96–5; Siddle 24.3–5–66–1; Lyon 47–1–215–3; Henriques 17–4–48–1; Clarke 8–2–25–0; Warner 3–0–19–0. *Second innings*—Pattinson 3–1–13–1; Lyon 5.3–0–29–1; Siddle 3–2–4–0.

Umpires: H. D. P. K. Dharmasena and M. Erasmus. Third umpire: V. A. Kulkarni.
Referee: B. C. Broad.

INDIA v AUSTRALIA

Second Test Match

At Hyderabad (Uppal), March 2–5, 2013. India won by an innings and 135 runs. Toss: Australia. Test debut: G. J. Maxwell.

Australia's tenth-heaviest defeat could be summed up by a single statistic: two Indians scored more in one partnership than 11 Australians managed in the entire game. While a stand of 370 between Vijay and Pujara served as a prototype for batting in India, Australia could not have been more dispirited after totalling 368 across two innings. It took only ten sessions for India to move into a 2–0 lead.

India were unchanged from the First Test, while Australia chose two spinners, neither of whom was Nathan Lyon. Their first-choice slow bowler for 18 months, Lyon was dropped amid claims from coach Mickey Arthur that he had technical issues after leaking 244 runs at Chennai. Mitchell Starc was also left out, so in came slow left-armer Xavier Doherty for a rare Test outing, and debutant Glenn Maxwell, a batting all-rounder who bowled off-spin. The whole thing reeked of a selectorial fudge.

Australia batted first on a pitch that had a few cracks but did not resemble Chennai's clay-like appearance. Bhuvneshwar Kumar, wicketless on debut, was a greater threat here, and his accurate, skiddy seamers produced three wickets in the first session. Ashwin accounted for the hapless Hughes, and it was not until Clarke and Wade – who had fractured a cheekbone during throwdowns the day before the game – that Australia produced a partnership of substance. Their stand of 145 for the fifth wicket showed the conditions could be mastered with patience and common sense. But Wade's fortitude deserted him on 62: the ball after surviving a stumping chance, he thrashed Harbhajan Singh to backward point.

The Australians lost wickets in clumps: four for 63 at the top, five for 28 at the bottom. Jadeja and Harbhajan ran through the middle order, and Clarke threw his wicket away on 91 trying for late runs. Despite being Australia's best batsman over the last two years, he had insisted on staying at No. 5. But his experience here, where he ran out of partners, later persuaded him that he would have to move up the order.

The innings ended not with a wicket but a declaration: on 237 for nine, Clarke called in the last pair, hoping his bowlers could winkle a breakthrough in the three overs before stumps. Excluding rain-affected matches, it was the lowest total on which a captain had declared in the first innings of a Test, and the first time it had been done on an opening day since Pakistan's Intikhab Alam tried something similar at Lord's in 1974. But Clarke's boldness was not rewarded with a late strike.

WORTH THE PUNT?

Captains who declared in the first innings of a Test, and went on to lose:

Captain	Total		
Imtiaz Ahmed	387-9	Pakistan v England at Lahore (lost by five wickets)	1961-62
G. S. Sobers	526-7	West Indies v England at Port-of-Spain (seven wickets). . . .	1967-68
B. S. Bedi	306-6	India v West Indies at Kingston (ten wickets).	1975-76
K. J. Hughes	401-9	Australia v England at Leeds (18 runs)	1981
W. J. Cronje	248-8	South Africa v England at Centurion (two wickets)	1999-2000
H. H. Streak	422-9	Zimbabwe v India at Delhi (seven wickets).	2000-01
B. C. Lara	395-9	West Indies v England at Manchester (seven wickets)	2004
G. C. Smith	451-9	South Africa v Australia at Sydney (eight wickets).	2005-06
A. Flintoff	551-6	England v Australia at Adelaide (six wickets).	2006-07
D. J. G. Sammy	449-9	West Indies v Australia at Bridgetown (three wickets)	2011-12
M. J. Clarke	**237-9**	**Australia v India at Hyderabad (an innings and 135 runs)**	**2012-13**

The second morning began with a minute's silence for the victims of terrorist bombings in Hyderabad the day before the series began: 17 people had been killed and more than 100 injured.

Once the cricket got under way, Sehwag was caught behind for six, his ninth successive Test innings without a fifty; he would soon be dropped for the rest of the series. His dismissal also marked the starting point of one of India's greatest partnerships. Whereas Australia's batting had been as fluent as a bad jazz improvisation, Vijay and Pujara raised the tempo like master composers guiding their audience to a climax. They began with 37 in 22 overs; added 106 between lunch and tea as they became more comfortable with the conditions; then opened out with 151 before stumps as Australia wilted.

Their coda was another 76 on the third morning, before Maxwell had Vijay caught at leg slip for 167. Pujara hooked a catch to fine leg soon afterwards for 204, but together they had shared India's fourth-highest Test partnership. Their alliance lasted seven and a quarter hours, fell only six short of the 376 added by Rahul Dravid and V. V. S. Laxman against Australia during the follow-on at Kolkata in 2000-01, and left India 150 ahead with eight wickets still to come.

Clarke described shot selection as "horrible"

In the event, the Australians did well to dismiss them for 503. Maxwell took four wickets and Doherty three, but it could not disguise the fact that, when it mattered, neither posed any real threat. Doherty bowled too full and spun it too little; Maxwell imparted some turn, but lacked guile against the two right-handers, and was easily worked through – and over – leg. The only Australian spinner whose standing was enhanced during this Test was the absent Lyon.

Australia began the second innings trailing by 266, but had at least been shown how to bat. And for a time it appeared Cowan and Warner, who put on 56, had taken notice. But from there it all fell apart. The Australians had discussed the importance of playing straight and avoiding cross-bat shots, but Warner was bowled around his legs trying to sweep Ashwin, and Hughes – continuing his awful record against spin – fell immediately in exactly the same manner. From 75 for two, they lost eight for 56 and, three minutes after the fourth day's scheduled lunch break, the match was over. Only Cowan, with 44 from 150 balls, showed any resolve. Clarke, who had become the first captain in history to lose a Test by an innings after declaring in the first, described Australia's shot selection as "horrible" – and it was impossible to disagree.

As India celebrated, the Australians set up a makeshift net on the pitch, desperate for their batsmen to gain as much exposure as possible to the conditions. Little did they know that their problems in the week ahead would instead emerge off the field.

Man of the Match: C. A. Pujara.

Close of play: first day, India 5-0 (Vijay 0, Sehwag 4); second day, India 311-1 (Vijay 129, Pujara 162); third day, Australia 74-2 (Cowan 26, Watson 9).

Australia

D. A. Warner b Bhuvneshwar Kumar	6	– (2) b Ashwin ... 26
E. J. M. Cowan lbw b Bhuvneshwar Kumar	4	– (1) c Sehwag b Jadeja ... 44
P. J. Hughes c Dhoni b Ashwin	19	– b Ashwin ... 0
S. R. Watson lbw b Bhuvneshwar Kumar	23	– c Dhoni b Sharma ... 9
*M. J. Clarke b Jadeja	91	– b Jadeja ... 16
†M. S. Wade c Bhuvneshwar Kumar b Harbhajan Singh	62	– c Sehwag b Ashwin ... 10
M. C. Henriques b Jadeja	5	– run out ... 0
G. J. Maxwell c Dhoni b Jadeja	13	– lbw b Ashwin ... 8
P. M. Siddle lbw b Harbhajan Singh	0	– c Kohli b Jadeja ... 4
J. L. Pattinson not out	1	– lbw b Ashwin ... 0
X. J. Doherty not out	0	– not out ... 1
B 10, l-b 3	13	B 7, l-b 6 ... 13

1/10 (1) 2/15 (2) (9 wkts dec, 85 overs) 237   1/56 (2) 2/56 (3) (67 overs) 131
3/57 (4) 4/63 (3) 5/208 (6)   3/75 (4) 4/108 (5)
6/217 (7) 7/233 (8) 8/236 (9) 9/236 (5)   5/111 (1) 6/111 (7) 7/123 (8)
    8/130 (9) 9/130 (6) 10/131 (10)

Bhuvneshwar Kumar 15–2–53–3; Sharma 17–5–45–0; Ashwin 15–6–41–1; Harbhajan Singh 22–2–52–2; Jadeja 16–4–33–3. *Second innings*—Bhuvneshwar Kumar 6–4–7–0; Ashwin 28–12–63–5; Harbhajan Singh 10–7–10–0; Jadeja 18–8–33–3; Sharma 5–2–5–1.

India

M. Vijay c Cowan b Maxwell	167	Bhuvneshwar Kumar st Wade b Doherty . . 10
V. Sehwag c Wade b Siddle	6	I. Sharma not out	2
C. A. Pujara c Doherty b Pattinson	204	
S. R. Tendulkar c Wade b Pattinson	7	B 1, l-b 13, w 4 18
V. Kohli c Cowan b Maxwell	34	
*†M. S. Dhoni c Doherty b Maxwell	44	1/17 (2) 2/387 (1) (154.1 overs) 503
R. A. Jadeja c and b Maxwell	10	3/393 (3) 4/404 (4)
R. Ashwin c Hughes b Doherty	1	5/460 (6) 6/484 (7) 7/485 (8)
Harbhajan Singh c Maxwell b Doherty	0	8/489 (9) 9/491 (5) 10/503 (10)

Pattinson 29–11–80–2; Siddle 31–6–92–1; Henriques 21–7–45–0; Doherty 46.1–15–131–3; Maxwell 26–2–127–4; Warner 1–0–14–0.

Umpires: H. D. P. K. Dharmasena and M. Erasmus.   Third umpire: S. Ravi.
Referee: B. C. Broad.

INDIA v AUSTRALIA

Third Test Match

At Mohali, March 14–18, 2013. India won by six wickets. Toss: Australia. Test debut: S. Dhawan.

India regained the Border–Gavaskar Trophy after Australia were impaired by their own hands, then impaled by Shikhar Dhawan, who scored the fastest recorded Test century on debut. After the hefty loss in Hyderabad, Australia's coach Mickey Arthur had asked every player to assess where they and the team could improve. Four of them – vice-captain Shane Watson, James Pattinson, Mitchell Johnson and Usman Khawaja – failed to respond and, in an unprecedented move, were suspended for this Test.

That contributed to a number of changes, which – depending on your perspective – either underlined the resolve of the management's decision, or reflected the increasingly chaotic nature of Australia's tour. Steve Smith, Starc and Lyon (suddenly deemed worthy of inclusion once more after being dropped at Hyderabad) came in for Watson, Pattinson and Glenn Maxwell (ditched after only one game); Haddin, meanwhile, was flown in to replace Matthew Wade, who had sprained his ankle playing basketball on a day off. India also made changes, replacing the out-of-form Virender Sehwag, a veteran of 104 Tests, with Dhawan, and bringing back Ojha for Harbhajan Singh, whose five wickets in the series had cost over 40 each.

The first day was lost to persistent rain and, when the toss eventually took place on the second morning, Clarke again called correctly. Cowan and Warner gave Australia their strongest start in any Test in India with a stand of 139 but, not for the first time, wickets fell in clusters. When Warner, on 71, edged Jadeja into his pad and the catch bobbed up to Dhoni, it was the first of three for 12 runs. Clarke's move up to No. 3 failed: advancing to Jadeja, he was beautifully beaten by flight and turn, and stumped for a golden duck. Hughes, meanwhile, made an agonising two in 39 minutes. Cowan knew his role was crease occupation, and survived almost five hours for 86 before he was caught at slip off Ashwin. Smith's skill against spin had earned him a place on this tour, and his footwork was impeccable – until he was dragged fractionally out of his crease by Ojha. He would not be the only man out in the nineties.

Starc, down at No. 9, offered Smith staunch support, then became the senior partner alongside Lyon. He was helped by some oddly defensive fields from Dhoni, who at times pushed six men back to the boundary to gift him singles in an attempt to get at Lyon. But Lyon was untroubled, and their stand ended only when Starc reached 99 and Dhoni brought the field in. To his dismay, Starc edged a drive off Sharma.

Australia's 408 seemed competitive enough – until Dhawan and Vijay embarked on India's reply. If the Australians thought Dhoni's double-century at Chennai had been hard

STUMPED FIRST BALL IN A TEST

W. Barnes st A. H. Jarvis b F. R. Spofforth	England v Australia at Sydney	1884-85
F. E. Woolley st W. A. Oldfield b C. V. Grimmett	England v Australia at Nottingham	1930
Q. McMillan st W. A. Oldfield b H. Ironmonger	South Africa v Australia at Melbourne	1931-32
N. Gordon st L. E. G. Ames b T. W. J. Goddard	South Africa v England at Johannesburg	1938-39
C. N. McCarthy st R. A. Saggers b C. L. McCool	South Africa v Australia at Cape Town	1949-50
F. S. Trueman st A. T. W. Grout b R. Benaud	England v Australia at Sydney	1958-59
R. T. Ponting st S. S. Dighe b Harbhajan Singh	Australia v India at Chennai	2000-01
Mashrafe bin Mortaza st A. Flower b D. A. Marillier	Bangladesh v Zimbabwe at Chittagong	2001-02
G. J. Batty st K. C. Sangakkara b M. Muralitharan	England v Sri Lanka at Colombo (SSC)	2003-04
M. Muralitharan st A. C. Gilchrist b S. C. G. MacGill	Sri Lanka v Australia at Galle	2003-04
M. J. Clarke st M. S. Dhoni b R. A. Jadeja	**Australia v India at Mohali**	**2012-13**

to shackle, they must have felt utterly helpless against Dhawan. At least Dhoni had given them hope by hitting a few in the air; Dhawan achieved the preposterous feat of scoring an 85-ball hundred without once going over the top. Equally remarkable was his capacity to pinpoint small gaps, and he was phenomenally strong on the cover-drive, square-drive and cut: two-thirds of his runs came through the off side. He was just as classy against the spinners, whether advancing, sweeping, reverse-sweeping, or on the drive. It was a ruthless, risk-free innings – and it completely overshadowed the diligence of Vijay.

Between lunch and tea on day three, India amassed 153, of which Dhawan made 106; by stumps, they were 283 for nought, and he was well past Gundappa Viswanath's national record for the highest score on Test debut (137 against Australia at Kanpur in 1969-70). Dhawan added only two on the fourth morning before the stand ended at 289 – India's third-highest for the first wicket – but Vijay continued to frustrate the Australians. He scored his second consecutive century, and was undone only when the second new ball was belatedly taken after 101 overs, and Starc hooped the first delivery to trap him for 153. Dhoni fell in similar fashion three balls later and, after a 61-run eighth-wicket stand between Kohli and Bhuvneshwar Kumar, the last three fell for seven. In an innings in which the other five Australian bowlers managed five for 410, Siddle's five for 71 was not far short of heroic.

Australia began the second innings 91 behind, but Hughes – who would probably have been axed for this Test had Khawaja done his homework – was the only batsman who threatened. Kumar accounted for the rest of the top order cheaply, and Clarke, who had been on and off the field during India's innings for treatment on his back, dropped down to No. 6; he was clearly hampered in making 18. Hughes showed a new-found intent against the spinners, and was unluckily given out lbw on 69 to a ball from Ashwin that was drifting down leg.

The last two wickets added 80, but Australia were all out for 223, leaving India 133 to win in a little over a session. Top-order wickets tied them down, and Clarke could

HIGHEST STRIKE-RATE IN A TEST HUNDRED ON DEBUT

SR		*Score (balls)*		
107.47	S. Dhawan	**187 (174)**	India v Australia at Mohali	**2012-13**
100.00	D. R. Smith	105* (105)	West Indies v South Africa at Cape Town	2003-04
98.43	M. J. Prior	126* (128)	England v West Indies at Lord's	2007
91.86	Abul Hasan	113 (123)	Bangladesh v West Indies at Khulna	2012-13
84.74	A. B. Williams	100 (118)	West Indies v Australia at Georgetown	1977-78
83.54	R. S. Kaluwitharana	132* (158)	Sri Lanka v Australia at Colombo (SSC)	1992-93
80.62	Umar Akmal	129 (160)	Pakistan v New Zealand at Dunedin	2009-10
78.80	**H. D. Rutherford**	**171 (217)**	**New Zealand v England at Dunedin**	**2012-13**
75.36	A. B. Barath	104 (138)	West Indies v Australia at Brisbane	2009-10

Balls faced are not available for many early Tests.

have decelerated proceedings, but instead rattled through 21 overs before the final hour, giving India an extra nine for their chase. His logic was that only an Australian victory could keep the series alive; a draw would be of no consolation. The Australians duly collected four wickets and, with Dhawan unable to bat after injuring his hand in the field, India were in effect five down. But despite some late tension – they needed 17 off four overs as stumps approached – Dhoni sealed things with 15 balls to spare by hitting three consecutive fours off Starc. All that remained for a one-sided series were the last rites.

Man of the Match: S. Dhawan.

Close of play: first day, no play; second day, Australia 273-7 (Smith 58, Starc 20); third day, India 283-0 (Vijay 83, Dhawan 185); fourth day, Australia 75-3 (Hughes 53, Lyon 4).

Australia

E. J. M. Cowan c Kohli b Ashwin	86	– (2) lbw b Bhuvneshwar Kumar	8
D. A. Warner c Dhoni b Jadeja	71	– (1) c Dhoni b Bhuvneshwar Kumar	2
*M. J. Clarke st Dhoni b Jadeja	0	– (6) c Pujara b Jadeja	18
P. J. Hughes c Dhoni b Ojha	2	– (3) lbw b Ashwin	69
S. P. D. Smith st Dhoni b Ojha	92	– (4) b Bhuvneshwar Kumar	5
†B. J. Haddin b Sharma	21	– (7) lbw b Ashwin	30
M. C. Henriques b Sharma	0	– (8) c and b Jadeja	2
P. M. Siddle lbw b Jadeja	0	– (9) b Ojha	13
M. A. Starc c Dhoni b Sharma	99	– (10) c Ashwin b Jadeja	35
N. M. Lyon not out	9	– (5) c Dhoni b Ojha	18
X. J. Doherty lbw b Ashwin	5	– not out	18
B 8, l-b 12, n-b 3	23	L-b 3, w 1, n-b 1	5

1/139 (2) 2/139 (3) 3/151 (4) (141.5 overs) 408
4/198 (1) 5/244 (6) 6/244 (7)
7/251 (8) 8/348 (5) 9/399 (9) 10/408 (11)

1/2 (1) 2/35 (2) (89.2 overs) 223
3/55 (4) 4/89 (5)
5/119 (6) 6/123 (3) 7/126 (8)
8/143 (9) 9/179 (7) 10/223 (10)

Bhuvneshwar Kumar 9–0–44–0; Sharma 30–8–72–3; Ashwin 43.5–9–97–2; Ojha 28–5–98–2; Jadeja 31–7–77–3. *Second innings*—Bhuvneshwar Kumar 10–1–31–3; Sharma 9–1–34–0; Ashwin 31–9–72–2; Jadeja 16.2–6–35–3; Ojha 21–6–46–2; Tendulkar 2–0–2–0.

India

M. Vijay lbw b Starc	153	– st Haddin b Doherty	26
S. Dhawan c Cowan b Lyon	187		
C. A. Pujara lbw b Siddle	1	– (2) lbw b Lyon	28
S. R. Tendulkar c Cowan b Smith	37	– run out	21
V. Kohli not out	67	– (3) c Hughes b Siddle	34
*†M. S. Dhoni lbw b Starc	4	– (5) not out	18
R. A. Jadeja lbw b Haddin b Siddle	8	– (6) not out	8
R. Ashwin c Haddin b Siddle	4		
Bhuvneshwar Kumar c Haddin b Henriques	18		
I. Sharma c Haddin b Siddle	0		
P. P. Ojha b Siddle	1		
B 5, l-b 13, n-b 1	19	W 1	1

1/289 (2) 2/292 (3) 3/384 (4) (132.1 overs) 499
4/412 (1) 5/416 (6) 6/427 (7)
7/431 (8) 8/492 (9) 9/493 (10) 10/499 (11)

1/42 (1) (4 wkts, 33.3 overs) 136
2/70 (2) 3/103 (3)
4/116 (4)

Starc 23–5–74–2; Siddle 29.1–9–71–5; Henriques 15–1–62–1; Lyon 31–4–124–1; Doherty 24–8–87–0; Smith 10–0–63–1. *Second innings*—Starc 10.3–1–51–0; Siddle 11–2–34–1; Lyon 5–0–27–1; Doherty 7–2–24–1.

Umpires: Aleem Dar and R. A. Kettleborough.   Third umpire: S. Asnani.
Referee: R. S. Madugalle.

INDIA v AUSTRALIA

Fourth Test Match

At Delhi, March 22–24. India won by six wickets. India won by six wickets. Toss: Australia. Test debut: A. M. Rahane.

India completed their first 4–0 clean sweep with a one-sided victory inside three days. Yet again, Australia's batsmen struggled on a challenging pitch, although this time they were at least in touch on first innings; it was their collapse for 164 on the third day that cost them. Spin did most of the damage for both teams: Ashwin and Jadeja collected seven wickets each, and Lyon nine.

At the toss, Australia were represented by their 44th Test captain. Michael Clarke had been declared unfit after struggling with a back injury during the Third Test, and Watson – who had been suspended as part of the homework saga, before flying home for the birth of his child, and dashing back in time for this Test – was named as the stand-in. Wade, who missed Mohali because of an ankle injury, was fit again and replaced Brad Haddin. And, in the latest round of Australian musical chairs, Maxwell, Johnson and Pattinson came in for Moises Henriques, Mitchell Starc and Xavier Doherty.

India's only change was the forced omission of Shikhar Dhawan, who had hurt his hand in Mohali and was replaced by debutant Ajinkya Rahane, batting at No. 5 as the opening roles were entrusted to Vijay and Pujara. But India's batsmen had to wait as, for the fourth time in the series, Australia won the toss and took first use of a pitch showing significant cracks and offering early movement for the fast bowlers.

Still, Cowan and Hughes displayed some grit in a 67-run partnership after Warner had thrown away his wicket with a loose slash at Sharma in the second over. A far more probing over from the same bowler eventually accounted for Hughes. Struck on the helmet by a delivery that rose sharply off a length, Hughes – plainly rattled – grew tentative. Three balls later, he went neither forward nor back, and played on.

A lunchtime score of 94 for two was a reasonable start but, yet again, Australia's innings deteriorated quickly. Cowan was bowled around his legs trying to sweep Ashwin – the same fate that had befallen Warner and Hughes in Hyderabad – to start a slump of five for 30, all to the spin of Ashwin and Jadeja, in 21 painful overs. It was left to Siddle to lead a recovery during fifty stands with Smith and Pattinson. But, after reaching his first half-century in Test cricket, Siddle became the fifth victim for Ashwin, who had troubled the Australians with his bounce, bite, and variations: the carrom ball that bowled Johnson, who offered no shot, was masterly.

Their total lead of 262 was modest, but the bowlers prevented India from gaining a significant lead, despite an opening stand of 108 between Pujara and Vijay. For the first time in the series, none of India's batsmen managed to capitalise on a first-innings start. This was largely because Lyon – also for the first time in the series – came round the wicket for an extended spell, and turned lbw into a serious threat to India's right-handers. He also altered his length: earlier in the tour, he had erred on the full side, but here he dropped a fraction shorter, just enough to prevent easy drives. His battle with Tendulkar was especially gripping. After a number of close lbw shouts – with no recourse to the DRS in India – Lyon finally had him plumb on 32. Australia grew more vocal than at any time in the series. Lyon finished with a career-best seven for 94, including the final two wickets in successive balls early on the third day; astonishingly, it would also prove to be the game's last.

Australia sprang a surprise by sending in Maxwell to open with Warner, hoping his Twenty20-style hitting would allow them to build a quick lead. The plan failed when both men fell for eight to Jadeja, with the dismissal of Warner, the sledger-in-chief, prompting a raucous send-off. Watson, meanwhile, showed a poor appreciation of the variable bounce when he wound up for a big pull and bottom-edged an Ojha delivery that kept low on to his stumps. Jadeja picked up five for 58, and Australia avoided total capitulation only thanks to Siddle, who became the first No. 9 to score two half-centuries in a Test – this one from 44 balls. No other Australian batsman reached fifty in either innings.

Set 155 for victory, India lost Vijay early to Maxwell, who became the first Australian since Percy Hornibrook in 1928-29 to open the batting and bowling in the same Test. And, as Lyon shared the new ball, it was only the third time Australia had opened with two spinners. It mattered not a jot: Pujara and Kohli steered India to within 32 of their target, and Pujara was still there on 82 when Dhoni crunched the winning boundary.

Man of the Match: R. A. Jadeja. *Man of the Series:* R. Ashwin.

Close of play: first day, Australia 231-8 (Siddle 47, Pattinson 11); second day, India 266-8 (Bhuvneshwar Kumar 10).

Australia

E. J. M. Cowan b Ashwin	38	– (3) lbw b Jadeja	24
D. A. Warner c Kohli b Sharma	0	– (1) lbw b Jadeja	8
P. J. Hughes b Sharma	45	– (4) lbw b Ashwin	6
*S. R. Watson st Dhoni b Jadeja	17	– (5) b Ojha	5
S. P. D. Smith c Rahane b Ashwin	46	– (6) b Jadeja	18
†M. S. Wade c Vijay b Ashwin	2	– (7) c Dhoni b Ojha	19
G. J. Maxwell c Sharma b Jadeja	10	– (2) b Jadeja	8
M. G. Johnson b Ashwin	3	– b Jadeja	0
P. M. Siddle b Ashwin	51	– st Dhoni b Ashwin	50
J. L. Pattinson c Kohli b Ojha	30	– b Sharma	11
N. M. Lyon not out	8	– not out	5
B 5, l-b 7	12	B 8, l-b 2	10

1/4 (2) 2/71 (3) 3/106 (1)   (112.1 overs) 262   1/15 (2) 2/20 (1)   (46.3 overs) 164
4/115 (4) 5/117 (6) 6/129 (7)   3/41 (4) 4/51 (5)
7/136 (8) 8/189 (5) 9/243 (9) 10/262 (10)   5/53 (3) 6/94 (6) 7/94 (8)
8/122 (7) 9/157 (10) 10/164 (9)

Bhuvneshwar Kumar 9–1–43–0; Sharma 14–3–35–2; Ashwin 34–18–57–5; Ojha 26.1–6–75–1; Jadeja 29–8–40–2. *Second innings*—Bhuvneshwar Kumar 2–0–9–0; Ashwin 15.3–2–55–2; Jadeja 16–2–58–5; Ojha 11–2–19–2; Sharma 2–0–13–1.

India

M. Vijay c Wade b Siddle	57	– b Maxwell	11
C. A. Pujara b Lyon	52	– not out	82
V. Kohli lbw b Lyon	1	– lbw b Lyon	41
S. R. Tendulkar lbw b Lyon	32	– lbw b Lyon	1
A. M. Rahane c Smith b Lyon	7	– c Lyon b Maxwell	1
*†M. S. Dhoni c Watson b Pattinson	24	– not out	12
R. A. Jadeja lbw b Maxwell	43		
R. Ashwin lbw b Lyon	12		
Bhuvneshwar Kumar not out	14		
I. Sharma b Lyon	0		
P. P. Ojha lbw b Lyon	0		
B 12, l-b 18	30	B 9, l-b 1	10

1/108 (2) 2/114 (3) 3/148 (1)   (70.2 overs) 272   1/19 (1)   (4 wkts, 31.2 overs) 158
4/165 (5) 5/180 (4) 6/210 (6)   2/123 (3) 3/127 (4)
7/254 (7) 8/266 (8) 9/272 (10) 10/272 (11)   4/128 (5)

Johnson 17–3–44–0; Pattinson 14–1–54–1; Siddle 12–3–38–1; Lyon 23.2–4–94–7; Maxwell 4–0–12–1. *Second innings*—Lyon 15.2–0–71–2; Maxwell 11–0–54–2; Johnson 2–0–16–0; Pattinson 3–0–7–0.

Umpires: Aleem Dar and R. A. Kettleborough.   Third umpire: S. Ravi.
Referee: R. S. Madugalle.

INDIA v AUSTRALIA, 2013-14

Shamya Dasgupta

Twenty20 international (1): India 1, Australia 0
One-day internationals (7): India 3, Australia 2

This tour crept up on everyone. With Australian thoughts preoccupied by the Ashes Part II, and all the hype in India centring on the upcoming Tendulkar Tests against West Indies, a seven-match one-day series seemed like an intrusion. And when it turned into one of the most run-laden encounters of all time, there were serious questions to be asked about its usefulness to both sides ahead of their respective Test series – and about the overwhelming dominance of bat over ball.

Australia had an excuse: they were fielding players who mostly weren't part of their Ashes plans, and Michael Clarke's recurring back problem meant he didn't travel either. With Darren Lehmann staying at home too, Australia were captained and coached by two stand-ins – George Bailey and Steve Rixon. India's personnel, however, tend to overlap in the three formats, and the truth was that, while one-day run-fests boost the coffers, behind-the-scenes preparation for Test cricket does not. And one-dayers in India, with pitches like graveyards for bowlers, offer run-fests in Technicolor.

The solitary Twenty20 international in Rajkot established the pattern, with India overhauling Australia's 201 for seven in the final over. Still, few could have guessed just how worse it would get for the bowlers. After two games scheduled for eastern India were ruined by Cyclone Phailin, the lowest total in the five completed matches was India's 232 in the opener at Gahunje. Overall, 11 completed innings (India's reply at Ranchi was interrupted after only 25 deliveries) brought an aggregate of 3,569 runs for 73 wickets – which meant an average total of 324. At Jaipur, Australia racked up 359; India chased it down in 43.3 overs. At Nagpur, India got past Australia's 350. And in the deciding match, Rohit Sharma became the third double-centurion in one-day internationals, and the third Indian, as they ran up 383 for six. Even that was under threat for a while. The overall run-rate of 6.64 was the highest for any one-day series.

M. S. Dhoni joked that bowling machines might have been a better bet than human beings, and questioned the new regulations that allowed only four fielders outside the 30-yard circle in non-powerplay overs. But those rules hadn't made for such scores in England during the Champions Trophy. The main factor, it stood to reason, was the pitches.

Mitchell Johnson was, despite bouts of waywardness, the only Australian bowler to leave with his reputation enhanced, after scaring the Indians with his 150kph bolts aimed at the throat. The spin pair of Ravichandran Ashwin and Ravindra Jadeja – the only two frontline Indian bowlers to make it through the series – managed economy-rates of under six, as did Bhuvneshwar Kumar, although he bowled most of his 43 overs at the start with a swinging new ball.

BLOW-BY-BLOW: THE SERIES IN RECORDS

MOST RUNS SCORED IN BOUNDARIES IN AN ODI

	4	6		
504	87	26	South Africa v Australia at Johannesburg	2005-06
464	80	24	India v Sri Lanka at Rajkot........................	2009-10
464	**59**	**38**	**India v Australia at Bangalore**	**2013-14**
438	**75**	**23**	**India v Australia at Jaipur**........................	**2013-14**
434	62	31	New Zealand v India at Christchurch......................	2008-09
400	79	14	India v West Indies at Indore	2011-12
394	**79**	**13**	**India v Australia at Nagpur**........................	**2013-14**
390	72	17	Australia v South Africa at Basseterre, St Kitts	2006-07

MOST SIXES IN A BILATERAL SERIES

6	M		
107	**6**	**India v Australia**	**2013-14**
62	5	West Indies v New Zealand.........................	2012
61	7	India v Australia	2007-08
60	5	New Zealand v India	2008-09
59	5	South Africa v Australia	2005-06
55	5	West Indies v Australia	2011-12

MOST INDIVIDUAL RUNS IN A BILATERAL SERIES

		I	100	Avge	SR		
491	**R. G. Sharma (I)**	**6**	**2**	**122.75**	**108.62**	**India v Australia**	**2013-14**
478	**G. J. Bailey (A)**	**6**	**1**	**95.60**	**116.01**	**India v Australia**	**2013-14**
467	H. Masakadza (Z)	5	2	116.75	97.29	Zimbabwe v Kenya.............	2009-10
455	C. H. Gayle (WI)	7	3	65.00	94.98	India v West Indies	2002-03
454	K. P. Pietersen (E)	6	3	151.33	105.58	South Africa v England..........	2004-05
451	Salman Butt (P)	5	2	90.20	97.19	Pakistan v Bangladesh	2007-08

The previous best for India is S. R. Tendulkar's 374 (from seven innings) in England in 2007;
for Australia, A. Symonds's 365 (six innings) in India in 2007-08.

MOST RUNS BY A PAIR IN A BILATERAL SERIES

			Highest		
		I	p'ship		
590	Imran Farhat/Yasir Hameed (P)	5	197	Pakistan v New Zealand ..	2003-04
533	**S. Dhawan/R. G. Sharma (I)**	**6**	**178**	**India v Australia**.......	**2013-14**
472	S. C. Ganguly/S. R. Tendulkar (I)	7	150	England v India	2007
406	S. T. Jayasuriya/W. U. Tharanga (SL)	5	286	England v Sri Lanka.....	2006
406	B. B. McCullum/J. D. Ryder (NZ)	5	165*	New Zealand v England ..	2007-08

All were opening partnerships.

FASTEST ONE-DAY HUNDREDS AGAINST AUSTRALIA

Balls			
52	**V. Kohli (I)**	**100* at Jaipur**.............................	**2013-14**
61	**V. Kohli (I)**	**115* at Nagpur**.............................	**2013-14**
67	C. D. McMillan (NZ)	117 at Hamilton	2006-07
69	K. A. Pollard (WI)	102 at Gros Islet, St Lucia	2011-12
71	J. D. P. Oram (NZ)	101* at Perth	2006-07
79	H. H. Gibbs (SA)	175 at Johannesburg........................	2005-06

Ishant Sharma was the other bowler who hogged attention – for returning two for 189 from 24 overs, which cost him his place. The final straw came when James Faulkner hit him for 30 in an over to secure an astonishing Australian victory in Mohali.

So dominant were India's top three – with Virat Kohli reaching three figures in 52 balls at Jaipur and 61 at Nagpur – that their middle order barely got a hit. When they did, their returns were underwhelming: Suresh Raina managed 100 runs in four innings, Yuvraj Singh 19 in four, and Jadeja 13 in three. Dhoni was needed more than ever. A rejuvenated Yuvraj had, however, already won the Twenty20 international with a blistering unbeaten 77 in 35 balls.

Through all the leather-chasing, the teams somehow managed to identify personnel for the Test arena. Rohit Sharma's 491 runs were a record for a bilateral one-day series, while Mohammed Shami emerged as a fiery option with the new ball. Bailey also broke the old record, with 478 runs – making a compelling, if not watertight, case to fill Australia's No. 6 Test spot. And Australia saw enough in Johnson's performance to pull him out early for the Ashes; they soon regretted not doing the same for Shane Watson, who aggravated a hamstring in the last game.

AUSTRALIAN TOURING PARTY

*G. J. Bailey (50/20), N. M. Coulter-Nile (50/20), X. J. Doherty (50/20), J. P. Faulkner (50/20), C. J. Ferguson (50), A. J. Finch (50/20), B. J. Haddin (50/20), M. C. Henriques (50/20), P. J. Hughes (50/20), M. G. Johnson (50/20), C. J. McKay (50/20), N. J. Maddinson (20), G. J. Maxwell (50/20), A. C. Voges (50/20), S. R. Watson (50/20). *Coach:* S. J. Rixon.

M. J. Clarke was originally selected as captain, but withdrew before the tour to rest his back. He was replaced by Ferguson in the one-day squad, and Maddinson for the Twenty20. Johnson returned home before the last game to prepare for the Ashes.

INDIA v AUSTRALIA

Twenty20 International

At Rajkot, October 10, 2013 (floodlit). India won by six wickets. Toss: India. Twenty20 international debut: N. J. Maddinson.

Yuvraj Singh, looking ten years younger for a summer's intensive training in France, marked his latest comeback with a rumbustious innings to haul India up to their second-highest run-chase in Twenty20. Their initial response had been steady rather than spectacular, and they required nearly 12 an over from the last nine when Yuvraj was joined by Dhoni. But Rajkot, one of the highest-scoring grounds in the world, is no place to be a bowler, and Yuvraj hit 13 of his 35 balls to the boundary, with a freedom of movement not seen since being diagnosed with cancer in early 2012. Australia's batsmen had shown no mercy to Ashwin: Finch and his 21-year-old opening partner Nic Maddinson deposited his first over for 17, and Maxwell launched three sixes in his second. But the prospect of an unreachable target subsided after Finch knocked a low full toss straight back to Vinay Kumar. Australia made only 27 from their last 21 balls – small fry in the circumstances.

Man of the Match: Yuvraj Singh.

Australia

	B	4	6
A. J. Finch *c and b 10*	89	52	14	1
N. J. Maddinson *b 9*	34	16	6	1
S. R. Watson *lbw b 10*	6	5	1	0
*G. J. Bailey *c 7 b 10*	0	3	0	0
G. J. Maxwell *c 11 b 7*	27	13	0	4
†B. J. Haddin *c 6 b 9*	5	3	1	0
M. C. Henriques *c 5 b 9*	12	12	1	0
N. M. Coulter-Nile *not out*	12	11	1	0
J. P. Faulkner *not out*	10	5	0	1
W 6	6			

6 overs: 74-1   (20 overs)   201-7

1/56 2/84 3/84 4/124 5/146 6/174 7/180

C. J. McKay and X. J. Doherty did not bat.

Bhuvneshwar Kumar 4–0–35–3; Vinay Kumar 4–0–26–3; Ashwin 2–0–41–0; I. Sharma 4–0–52–0; Jadeja 4–0–23–1; Kohli 2–0–24–0.

India

	B	4	6
R. G. Sharma *c 6 b 10*	8	8	0	1
S. Dhawan *st 5 b 11*	32	19	5	0
S. K. Raina *c 3 b 8*	19	13	2	1
V. Kohli *c 9 b 10*	29	22	2	1
Yuvraj Singh *not out*	77	35	8	5
*†M. S. Dhoni *not out*	24	21	2	0
L-b 4, w 9	13			

6 overs: 53-2   (19.4 overs)   202-4

1/12 2/50 3/80 4/100

R. A. Jadeja, R. Ashwin, Bhuvneshwar Kumar, R. Vinay Kumar and I. Sharma did not bat.

Watson 3.4–0–29–0; McKay 4–0–50–2; Faulkner 4–0–36–0; Coulter-Nile 4–0–44–1; Henriques 1–0–15–0; Doherty 3–0–24–1.

Umpires: A. K. Chowdhury and C. Shamshuddin.   Third umpire: V. A. Kulkarni.
Referee: R. S. Mahanama.

INDIA v AUSTRALIA

First One-Day International

At Gahunje, October 13, 2013 (day/night). Australia won by 72 runs. Toss: Australia.

Australia's openers provided another excellent start. But the real impetus was injected by Bailey and Maxwell, who hit three sixes in an entertaining 23-ball stay. The tail crashed 38 from the last three overs, and only Bhuvneshwar Kumar's early control and an economic spell from Jadeja kept Australia to 304. All Australia's frontline bowlers were tight, and Johnson was monstrously fast with the new ball. Kohli and Raina, granted the promotion he had craved to No. 4, managed to keep India in the game with a 71-run stand for the third wicket but, after they were separated, India went down with surprising ease. It took some tactical ingenuity to dislodge Kohli, India's chaser extraordinaire: set up by three shortish balls, he tried to hook Watson's next delivery, a fuller one, across the line – and was struck in front. Hughes kept wicket for 23 overs after the dismissal of Dhawan: Faulkner's celebratory high-five caught Haddin in the eye, and he left for treatment one ball later.

Man of the Match: G. J. Bailey.

Australia

P. J. Hughes *c Raina b Jadeja*	47
A. J. Finch *c Kohli b Yuvraj Singh*	72
S. R. Watson *c Jadeja b Yuvraj Singh*	2
*G. J. Bailey *c Raina b Ashwin*	85
A. C. Voges *run out*	7
G. J. Maxwell *c R. G. Sharma* *b Vinay Kumar*	31
†B. J. Haddin *lbw b Ashwin*	10

J. P. Faulkner *c Vinay Kumar b I. Sharma* .	27
M. G. Johnson *not out*	9
C. J. McKay *not out*	11
L-b 3	3

X. J. Doherty did not bat.

1/110 (1) 2/113 (3)   (8 wkts, 50 overs) 304
3/146 (2) 4/172 (5) 5/214 (6)
6/231 (7) 7/264 (4) 8/293 (8)   10 overs: 50-0

Bhuvneshwar Kumar 7–2–41–0; Vinay Kumar 9–1–68–1; I. Sharma 7–0–56–1; Ashwin 10–0–55–2; Jadeja 10–0–35–1; Kohli 1–0–12–0; Yuvraj Singh 6–0–34–2.

India

S. Dhawan c Haddin b Faulkner	7	R. Vinay Kumar b Voges	11
R. G. Sharma c Hughes b Watson	42	I. Sharma not out	1
V. Kohli lbw b Watson	61		
S. K. Raina c Doherty b Faulkner	39	B 2, l-b 4, w 5	11
Yuvraj Singh c Hughes b Johnson	7		
*†M. S. Dhoni b McKay	19	1/26 (1) 2/66 (2) 3/137 (4) (49.4 overs) 232	
R. A. Jadeja c Bailey b Faulkner	11	4/147 (5) 5/166 (3) 6/192 (7)	
R. Ashwin c Watson b McKay	5	7/196 (6) 8/200 (8) 9/230 (10)	
Bhuvneshwar Kumar b Voges b Finch	18	10/232 (9)	10 overs: 43-1

Johnson 10–0–38–1; McKay 10–0–36–2; Faulkner 8–0–47–3; Doherty 10–1–54–0; Watson 8–0–31–2; Voges 3–0–18–1; Finch 0.4–0–2–1.

Umpires: R. A. Kettleborough and V. A. Kulkarni.   Third umpire: C. Shamshuddin.
Referee: R. S. Mahanama.

INDIA v AUSTRALIA

Second One-Day International

At Jaipur, October 16, 2013 (day/night). India won by nine wickets. Toss: Australia.
   When Australia reached 95 for one after 20 overs, it seemed all the talk of Jaipur as a batting paradise had been overblown. But in the 73.3 overs that followed, the two sides plundered 626 runs and rewrote countless records. All of Australia's top five made half-centuries, the first time any side had managed this in a one-day international – with Watson, Bailey and Maxwell especially brutal. India's seamers dropped too short, and Jadeja proved unusually costly. But if the Australian innings was entertaining, the fare dished out by India's top three belonged in the blockbuster category. Rohit Sharma batted from start to finish, ending a sequence of 57 innings without a hundred – enough to hush at least some of his critics. Dhawan was put down on 18, when a steepling catch popped out of Haddin's gloves, and he traded punch for punch with Sharma during an opening stand of 176 in 26 overs. Then came Kohli, who walked in with 184 still needed, hit four of his first 17 deliveries for six, and leapt to a 52-ball century – the fastest for India. It was his 16th one-day hundred, his tenth in a successful run-chase, and it allowed the Indians to knock off a 300-plus target against Australia for the first time.
   Man of the Match: R. G. Sharma.

Australia

A. J. Finch run out	50	†B. J. Haddin not out	1
P. J. Hughes c Dhoni b Ashwin	83		
S. R. Watson c I. Sharma b Vinay Kumar	59	L-b 5, w 5	10
*G. J. Bailey not out	92		
G. J. Maxwell run out	53	1/74 (1) 2/182 (3) (5 wkts, 50 overs) 359	
A. C. Voges c Bhuvneshwar Kumar b Vinay Kumar	11	3/212 (2) 4/308 (5) 5/347 (6)	10 overs: 46-0

J. P. Faulkner, M. G. Johnson, C. J. McKay and X. J. Doherty did not bat.

Bhuvneshwar Kumar 10–0–54–0; I. Sharma 9–1–70–0; Vinay Kumar 9–0–73–2; Jadeja 10–0–72–0; Ashwin 8–0–50–1; Yuvraj Singh 4–0–35–0.

India

R. G. Sharma not out		141
S. Dhawan c Haddin b Faulkner		95
V. Kohli not out		100
L-b 5, w 21		26

1/176 (2)   (1 wkt, 43.3 overs) 362
10 overs: 69-0

S. K. Raina, Yuvraj Singh, *†M. S. Dhoni, R. A. Jadeja, R. Ashwin, Bhuvneshwar Kumar, R. Vinay Kumar and I. Sharma did not bat.

Johnson 9–1–57–0; McKay 7–0–64–0; Watson 5–0–47–0; Doherty 10–0–70–0; Maxwell 5.3–0–48–0; Faulkner 7–0–60–1.

Umpires: R. A. Kettleborough and V. A. Kulkarni.   Third umpire: C. Shamshuddin.
Referee: R. S. Mahanama.

INDIA v AUSTRALIA

Third One-Day International

At Mohali, October 19, 2013 (day/night). Australia won by four wickets. Toss: Australia.

If there has been a bigger disintegration in one-day cricket, history failed to record it. Australia needed 44 off 18 deliveries, when Ishant Sharma served up an over of length balls and half-trackers, crunched for 30 by Faulkner, who – accompanied by Voges – could then take it easy in Ashwin's next. With nine needed from the last over, bowled by Vinay Kumar, Dhoni placed all four of his fielders permitted outside the circle on the leg side, but a full toss meant Faulkner was able to clear them all, finishing with 64 not out from 29 balls and a gleeful punch of the air. Earlier, Dhoni's knack of resurrecting an innings was sorely needed by India after Kohli proved the only specialist batsman able to cope with Johnson's searing pace and bounce. Dhoni had hurt his knee before even facing a ball, but shrugged off the pain to strike all five of his side's sixes in an undefeated 139 from 121 deliveries, the first one-day century for India at Mohali. After Bailey put down a skyer with 12 balls to go, Dhoni pillaged another 34, with Faulkner bearing the brunt of it. A few hours later, he took his revenge.

Man of the Match: J. P. Faulkner.

India

R. G. Sharma c Finch b Watson	11	R. Vinay Kumar run out		0
S. Dhawan c Haddin b McKay	8	I. Sharma not out		0
V. Kohli c Haddin b Maxwell	68			
S. K. Raina c Watson b Johnson	17	L-b 13, w 7		20
Yuvraj Singh c Haddin b Johnson	0			
*†M. S. Dhoni not out	139	1/14 (2) 2/37 (1) (9 wkts, 50 overs)	303
R. A. Jadeja c Haddin b Johnson	2	3/76 (4) 4/76 (5)	
R. Ashwin c Haddin b Johnson	28	5/148 (3) 6/154 (7) 7/230 (8)	
Bhuvneshwar Kumar c Bailey b Faulkner	10	8/267 (9) 9/299 (10) 10 overs: 60-2	

Johnson 10–1–46–4; McKay 10–0–49–1; Watson 8–0–74–1; Faulkner 10–0–65–1; Doherty 10–0–45–0; Voges 1–0–3–0; Maxwell 1–0–8–1.

Australia

P. J. Hughes c Dhoni b Vinay Kumar	22	J. P. Faulkner not out		64
A. J. Finch lbw b I. Sharma	38			
S. R. Watson lbw b Jadeja	11	L-b 14, w 9		23
*G. J. Bailey lbw b Vinay Kumar	43			
A. C. Voges not out	76	1/68 (1) 2/82 (2) (6 wkts, 49.3 overs)	304
G. J. Maxwell run out	3	3/88 (4) 4/171 (4)	
†B. J. Haddin c Jadeja b Bhuvneshwar Kumar	24	5/174 (6) 6/213 (7) 10 overs: 64-0	

M. G. Johnson, C. J. McKay and X. J. Doherty did not bat.

Bhuvneshwar Kumar 10–1–50–1; Vinay Kumar 8.3–0–50–2; I. Sharma 8–1–63–1; Jadeja 10–0–31–1; Yuvraj Singh 3–0–20–0; Ashwin 9–0–58–0; Kohli 1–0–18–0.

Umpires: R. A. Kettleborough and C. Shamshuddin.   Third umpire: A. K. Chowdhury.
Referee: R. S. Mahanama.

INDIA v AUSTRALIA

Fourth One-Day International

At Ranchi, October 23, 2013 (day/night). No result. Toss: India.

Dhoni, winning the toss for the first time in the series, and on his home ground, said he fielded first because of a forecast promising unseasonal rain. The first shower arrived in the eighth over, though it did not prevent Australia from completing a full innings. India's decision to shake up their seam attack paid off as Mohammed Shami found pace and inward movement to bowl Finch and Watson, plus surprising bounce to have Hughes caught behind. Bailey nicked Shami first ball, but Kohli put down the chance at slip – one of five drops by India – and he took full advantage in a restorative partnership of 153 with the predictably gung-ho Maxwell, whose 92 contained five sixes. Even so, Australia's 295 for eight were their lowest total of the series, and it would have been entirely in keeping with the prevailing trend had India bettered it. They didn't get the chance, as heavy rain caused a halt in the fifth over of their reply.

Australia

A. J. Finch b Mohammed Shami	5	M. G. Johnson st Dhoni b Ashwin	25
P. J. Hughes c Dhoni b Mohammed Shami	11	C. J. McKay not out	7
S. R. Watson b Mohammed Shami	14	L-b 7, w 3	10
*G. J. Bailey c Sharma b Vinay Kumar	98		
A. C. Voges lbw b Ashwin	7	1/5 (1) 2/24 (2) (8 wkts, 50 overs)	295
G. J. Maxwell lbw b Vinay Kumar	92	3/32 (3) 4/71 (5)	
†B. J. Haddin b Jadeja	3	5/224 (4) 6/232 (7)	
J. P. Faulkner not out	23	7/238 (6) 8/281 (9) 10 overs: 40-3	

X. J. Doherty did not bat.

Unadkat 6–0–31–0; Mohammed Shami 8–1–42–3; Vinay Kumar 8–0–52–2; Ashwin 9–0–57–2; Jadeja 10–0–56–1; Yuvraj Singh 1–0–12–0; Raina 8–0–38–0.

India

R. G. Sharma not out	9
S. Dhawan not out	14
B 4	4
(no wkt, 4.1 overs)	27

V. Kohli, S. K. Raina, Yuvraj Singh, *†M. S. Dhoni, R. A. Jadeja, R. Ashwin, R. Vinay Kumar, Mohammed Shami and J. D. Unadkat did not bat.

Johnson 2.1–0–10–0; McKay 2–0–13–0.

Umpires: R. A. Kettleborough and V. A. Kulkarni.   Third umpire: A. K. Chowdhury.
Referee: R. S. Mahanama.

INDIA v AUSTRALIA

Fifth One-Day International

At Cuttack, October 26, 2013 (day/night). Abandoned.

Cyclone Phailin hit eastern India on October 11, causing more than half a million people to be evacuated from their homes. The BCCI chose to stick with the venue, but there was never any chance of play on a waterlogged field.

INDIA v AUSTRALIA

Sixth One-Day International

At Nagpur, October 30, 2013 (day/night). India won by six wickets. Toss: India.

India had never chased down 350 before this series, but now pulled off the feat for the second time in a fortnight to level things at 2–2. The same three batsmen did the job – again with barely a slog in sight. Dhoni surprisingly chose to field and, after the openers fell cheaply, Watson and Bailey found the spinners tough going. Yet the conditions were so stacked in the batsmen's favour that a rush of 261 from the last 28 overs came as no real surprise. Having reached 85 three times already in the series without making three figures, Bailey surged to 156 in 114 balls – the second-highest one-day score by an Australian captain, after Ricky Ponting's 164 in the famous Johannesburg match in 2005-06. Jadeja cost himself two wickets, overstepping before Watson and Voges both spooned up catches. Mohammed Shami was also no-balled because Raina, fielding at silly mid-on, had his left foot on the wicket at the point of delivery. But Australia faltered too, and Dhawan was dropped again, this time on 19 as Maxwell put down a comfortable chance at point. The miss cost Australia dear, as he and Rohit Sharma piled up 178. Kohli made 40 of a 56-run stand with Dhawan – who suffered from cramp as he neared his hundred – before becoming the first batsman to achieve five consecutive fifties on two separate occasions. Dhoni instructed Kohli to hold back an outright assault until Johnson had finished his allocation and, as if made to order, the pair pummelled the required 35 off the last three overs. For only the second time in one-day internationals, four batsmen made hundreds in the same game, following Ijaz Ahmed, Yousuf Youhana, Adam Gilchrist and Ponting in a match between Pakistan and Australia at Lahore in 1998-99.

Man of the Match: V. Kohli.

Australia

P. J. Hughes c Kohli b Bhuvneshwar Kumar	13	M. G. Johnson c Dhawan b Jadeja		0
A. J. Finch b Ashwin	20	†B. J. Haddin not out		0
S. R. Watson b Mohammed Shami	102	W 3, n-b 3		6
*G. J. Bailey c Kohli b Jadeja	156			
G. J. Maxwell c Bhuvneshwar Kumar		1/30 (1) 2/45 (2)	(6 wkts, 50 overs)	350
b Ashwin	9	3/213 (3) 4/224 (5)		
A. C. Voges not out	44	5/344 (4) 6/346 (7)	10 overs: 44-1	

J. P. Faulkner, C. J. McKay and X. J. Doherty did not bat.

Bhuvneshwar Kumar 8–0–42–1; Mohammed Shami 8–1–66–1; Jadeja 10–0–68–2; Ashwin 10–0–64–2; Mishra 10–0–78–0; Kohli 2–0–15–0; Raina 2–0–17–0.

India

R. G. Sharma c Faulkner b Finch	79	*†M. S. Dhoni not out		25
S. Dhawan b Faulkner	100	L-b 8, w 7, n-b 1		16
V. Kohli not out	115			
S. K. Raina c Haddin b Johnson	16	1/178 (1) 2/234 (2)	(4 wkts, 49.3 overs)	351
Yuvraj Singh b Johnson	0	3/290 (4) 4/290 (5)	10 overs: 56-0	

R. A. Jadeja, R. Ashwin, Bhuvneshwar Kumar, A. Mishra and Mohammed Shami did not bat.

Johnson 10–0–72–2; McKay 7–0–47–0; Faulkner 9.3–0–73–1; Doherty 6–0–40–0; Watson 6–0–51–0; Maxwell 7–0–40–0; Finch 4–0–20–1.

Umpires: N. J. Llong and S. Ravi.   Third umpire: V. A. Kulkarni.
Referee: A. J. Pycroft.

❝ IPL6 proved greed can rarely be sated – and the cloud of corruption obscured the cricket.”
The Indian Premier League, 2012-13, page 956

INDIA v AUSTRALIA

Seventh One-Day International

At Bangalore, November 2, 2013 (day/night). India won by 57 runs. Toss: Australia.

Somehow the schedulers got their wish: a seven-match series that headed into the last game all-square. Batting first was not the preferred option – by now it was impossible to know what represented a good score – but with little moisture around, Rohit Sharma and Dhawan racked up their third century stand of the series. Sharma ran out his partner for a duck, but he made amends against a knackered attack who may have wished they had joined Mitchell Johnson back home for some R&R; Watson strained a hamstring 19 days before the Ashes. Australia missed the last opportunity to keep the score down to something respectable when substitute Moises Henriques parried the ball over the square-leg boundary for the eighth of Sharma's 16 sixes, which broke Watson's one-day international record of 15, against Bangladesh at Mirpur in 2010-11. He and Dhoni butchered 100 from the final five overs – even though both were out in the last. Sharma finished on 209 from 158 balls, the third double-hundred in the format, after Sachin Tendulkar and Virender Sehwag. Australia slumped to 138 for six in the 23rd over, but still gave India a scare. Maxwell had started the show by hitting his first ball for six and reaching 50 in 18, though the chase truly took off after Faulkner brought out the big shots in a partnership of 115 for the ninth wicket with McKay. Vinay Kumar became the first bowler to concede 100 or more and finish on the winning side; the 19 sixes hit by each side were a record, both for an innings and a match. Things got heated when Watson, forced down to No. 8 and facing his first ball, drove towards Dhawan at extra cover, who unkindly mimicked his hobble. Watson sought him out for choice words when he took a single next ball. Jadeja was fined 10% of his match fee for giving Watson an abusive send-off.

Man of the Match: R. G. Sharma. *Man of the Series:* R. G. Sharma.

India

R. G. Sharma c sub (M. C. Henriques)		R. A. Jadeja not out	0
b McKay	209		
S. Dhawan lbw b Doherty	60	L-b 5, w 7	12
V. Kohli run out	0		
S. K. Raina lbw b Doherty	28	1/112 (2) 2/113 (3)	(6 wkts, 50 overs) 383
Yuvraj Singh c Haddin b Faulkner	12	3/185 (4) 4/207 (5)	
*†M. S. Dhoni run out	62	5/374 (1) 6/383 (6)	10 overs: 64-0

R. Ashwin, Bhuvneshwar Kumar, R. Vinay Kumar and Mohammed Shami did not bat.

McKay 10–0–89–1; Coulter-Nile 10–0–80–0; Faulkner 10–0–75–1; Watson 5–0–26–0; Doherty 10–0–74–2; Maxwell 4–0–32–0; Finch 1–0–2–0.

Australia

A. J. Finch lbw b Mohammed Shami	5	N. M. Coulter-Nile c Kohli b Jadeja	3
P. J. Hughes c Yuvraj Singh b Ashwin	23	C. J. McKay b Jadeja	18
†B. J. Haddin b Ashwin	40	X. J. Doherty not out	0
*G. J. Bailey run out	4	L-b 1, w 2, n-b 1	4
A. C. Voges b Mohammed Shami	4		
G. J. Maxwell c Jadeja b Vinay Kumar	60	1/7 (1) 2/64 (2) 3/70 (4)	(45.1 overs) 326
J. P. Faulkner c Dhawan		4/74 (3) 5/132 (5) 6/138 (6)	
b Mohammed Shami	116	7/205 (8) 8/211 (9) 9/326 (10)	
S. R. Watson c Mohammed Shami b Jadeja	49	10/326 (7)	10 overs: 46-1

Bhuvneshwar Kumar 8–1–47–0; Mohammed Shami 8.1–0–52–3; Vinay Kumar 9–0–102–1; Ashwin 10–0–51–2; Jadeja 10–0–73–3.

Umpires: N. J. Llong and S. Ravi. Third umpire: A. K. Chowdhury.
Referee: A. J. Pycroft.

INDIA v WEST INDIES, 2013-14

Nagraj Gollapudi

Test matches (2): India 2, West Indies 0
One-day internationals (3): India 2, West Indies 1

This was not so much a series as a pilgrimage – and all in honour of one man. In fact, the series was not even supposed to be happening: according to the schedule, West Indies had not been due to arrive in India until October 2014. That they were asked to advance their travels by 12 months was primarily because the BCCI wanted to give Sachin Tendulkar a fond farewell in his 200th Test.

The preamble was far from smooth. The Indian selectors had been growing restless and, keeping in mind future overseas assignments, were desperate to test out new batsmen. Not-so-young pretenders such as Rohit Sharma and Ajinkya Rahane had been kicking their heels for too long. But, as usual, all eyes were on Tendulkar. In the 21 Tests after January 2011, when he had last scored a century, his average had been 31. He still could muster fifties every now and then, but his reflexes were in terminal decline, and bowlers were breaching his defences. News leaked out that chairman of selectors Sandeep Patil had told BCCI president N. Srinivasan that Tendulkar's time was up; Patil called the reports "nonsense". But Tendulkar understood it was over. He conveyed that message to the BCCI, and two Tests against West Indies were quickly put in place. So the expectation – enticing to many – that Tendulkar's career would end at the turn of the year in South Africa, against the world's No. 1 Test side, was scotched. To South Africa's understandable annoyance, the BCCI promptly halved India's tour there, in part to find room for Tendulkar's home jamboree.

And so the circus moved from Lahli in northern India, venue of Tendulkar's final Ranji Trophy appearance, to Kolkata in the east, before arriving on the west coast in Mumbai, his home city. His reputation had been constructed using bricks of purity. He was a man who would grow to become best batsman, captain, senior statesman, mentor and inspiration. Thousands of devotees turned up at the three venues to pay homage.

He did not disappoint them. In the dusty village of Lahli, on a ground surrounded by rice and cane fields, Tendulkar came out to bat for Mumbai in a tricky run-chase against Haryana. On a green pitch, in swinging conditions, against nagging medium-pacers, he slowed the pace of the game, steadily transferring the advantage towards Mumbai. He finished undefeated on 79.

That innings boded well for the Tests. However, Tendulkar was sawn off in Kolkata by a doubtful lbw decision. It was his only innings of the game, which was over by the third evening – catching the local authorities off guard. The Bengal chief minister had to cancel all her appointments and rush to the ground to felicitate Tendulkar. There were plans for 199kg of rose petals to be showered across the stadium's expanse to symbolise his 199th Test, and for

Putting out the bunting: Jagmohan Kanojia, a kitemaker from Amritsar, bids farewell.

65,000 Tendulkar face masks to be distributed among the crowd – but time ran out. The Cricket Association of Bengal had invited Brian Lara, his one equal as a batsman in the 1990s, to be part of the celebrations. But Lara was reportedly stranded in mid-air when the match finished.

Mistakes were made, too. M. S. Dhoni pointed out that Tendulkar's first name has been misspelt as "Sachine" above his portrait – painted by the Bengali artist Jogen Chowdhury – which hung from the High Court End. On the first day, the electronic scoreboard referred to his wife as "Mr Anjali Tendulkar" for nearly half an hour before the error was corrected. The men responsible were given a fearsome rebuke by a CAB official.

In Mumbai, Tendulkar finally regained his footing. He walked out after two wickets fell in an over to Shane Shillingford's off-breaks, returned unbeaten on 38 at the end of the first day, and next morning briefly dazzled a full house, crossing 50 with an exquisite straight-drive, one of his signature strokes. Such fluency and command led all to assume that a valedictory hundred was a given. The stands were swelling as the countdown began. But just after the first drinks break, Tendulkar tried to cut Narsingh Deonarine's off-spin, and Darren Sammy clung on at slip. A momentary hush wrapped around the ground like a cold blanket. For one last time India's show-stopper walked back, head bowed, eyes full of tears.

West Indies had arrived in reasonable nick, having won their last three Test series 2–0, admittedly against New Zealand, Bangladesh and Zimbabwe. But they had not played a Test since March, and they had little more planned than a team-building exercise in Miami ahead of their tour of New Zealand when they got the call from their impoverished board. Suddenly, they were upping sticks for India. Compelled to play cheerleaders at Tendulkar's carnival, West Indies merrily donned the pom-poms – rather too merrily, for some tastes.

They could not keep either Test alive even for three days, occupying just 234.3 overs across four innings, and mustering two individual half-centuries. Their batsmen averaged 18 (their fourth-lowest in a series) and their bowlers 48. Shillingford was the only player to hold his own, and joined Charlie

LONGEST TEST CAREERS

Years	Days	T		
30	315	58	W. Rhodes (England)......................	1899 to 1929-30
26	356	22	D. B. Close (England)	1949 to 1976
25	13	64	F. E. Woolley (England)	1909 to 1934
24	10	22	G. A. Headley (West Indies)	1929-30 to 1953-54
24	**1**	**200**	**S. R. Tendulkar (India)**	**1989-90 to 2013-14**
23	40	7	A. J. Traicos (South Africa/Zimbabwe).........	1969-70 to 1992-93
22	233	61	J. B. Hobbs (England)	1907-08 to 1930
22	120	15	G. Gunn (England)........................	1907-08 to 1929-30
22	32	58	S. E. Gregory (Australia)..................	1890 to 1912
21	336	22	F. R. Brown (England).....................	1931 to 1953
21	313	45	A. W. Nourse (South Africa)................	1902-03 to 1924

"Terror" Turner, Tom Richardson and Alec Bedser as bowlers to have taken five successive five-wicket hauls in Tests. But so easily did West Indies collapse that he bowled in only two innings. Their former captain Clive Lloyd declared: "They are drunk on Twenty20 cricket."

Worse was to follow, when Shillingford and Marlon Samuels were reported for suspect actions by English umpires Richard Kettleborough and Nigel Llong at Mumbai. Both men were sent to Perth for testing, but Shillingford failed to convince the ICC that his stock off-break met the requirements, and was suspended from bowling for the second time in his international career; Samuels was barred from bowling his quicker delivery. Some questioned the West Indies Cricket Board's failure to hire a specialist spin-bowling coach.

India's biggest gains were Rohit Sharma and Mohammed Shami, debutants and match-winners at Kolkata: Sharma with a big century, Shami a nine-wicket haul. The most telling images of the series were of Shami uprooting the stumps to signal the end of both matches. His coaches told of how, as a youngster, he would wait for training to finish so he could take the old red balls home to polish them and cultivate reverse swing, a skill he had refined with Wasim Akram at Kolkata Knight Riders. He consistently hit 85mph, darting the ball in or out after pitching, so the batsmen did not know whether to look for the shine or pay attention to the seam. Shami's match figures of nine for 118 in the First Test were the best by an Indian seamer on debut.

Yet the most profound moment of all followed Tendulkar's final dismissal. After observing a mournful silence, then a standing ovation, the crowd did not flood out of the ground – as had been the custom in India whenever his wicket fell. Instead, they stayed to appreciate the calmness of Cheteshwar Pujara, the daring of Virat Kohli, the wristiness of Sharma and the pace of Shami. Deep down, Tendulkar would have been proud: it was he who had taught the youngsters to dream big. The India of the 1990s, which had relied on him, was a chapter from the previous millennium. All these young men, most of them toddlers when he first wore the India cap, had grown into match-winners. On the eve of the series, Dhoni said he and his troops would do their bit, which implicitly suggested Tendulkar would have to do his bit too. Both parties honoured their word.

So how did I do, sir?

This is an edited extract from Sachin Tendulkar's speech to the crowd after his final Test in Mumbai.

Ajit, my brother, now what do I talk about him? I don't know. We have lived this dream together. He was the one who sacrificed his career for my cricket. He spotted the spark in me. And it all started from the age of 11 when he took me to [Ramakant] Achrekar sir, my coach, and from there on my life changed. You will find this hard to believe but even last night he [Achrekar] called to discuss my dismissal, knowing that there was a remote chance of batting again. But just the habit we have developed, the rapport we have developed has continued and it will continue. Maybe when I'm not playing cricket we will still be discussing technique.

Various things we agreed upon about my technique, and so many technical things which I didn't agree with him. We have had arguments and disagreements, but when I look back at all these things in my life, I would have been a lesser cricketer.

I was extremely delighted to see him up in the stands. Normally he sits in front of the television and watches all the games that I play. When I was 11, 12, those were the days when I used to hop back on his scooter and play a couple of practice matches a day. The first half I would be batting at Shivaji Park, the second half at some other match in Azad Maidan. He would take me all over Mumbai to make sure I got match practice.

On a lighter note, in the last 29 years, sir has never ever said "well played" to me because he thought I would get complacent and I would stop working hard. Maybe now he can push his luck and wish me well done on my career, because there are no more matches, sir, in my life. I will be witnessing cricket, and cricket will always stay in my heart, but you have had an immense contribution in my life, so thank you very much.

A day later, Achrekar called Tendulkar to say "well done" on receiving the Bharat Ratna, India's highest civilian honour.

WEST INDIES TOURING PARTY

*D. J. G. Sammy (T/50), T. L. Best (T/50), D. J. Bravo (50), D. M. Bravo (T/50), S. Chanderpaul (T), J. Charles (50), S. S. Cottrell (T), N. Deonarine (T/50), K. A. Edwards (T), C. H. Gayle (T/50), J. O. Holder (50), S. P. Narine (50), V. Permaul (T/50), K. O. A. Powell (T/50), D. Ramdin (T/50), R. Rampaul (50), K. A. J. Roach (T), M. N. Samuels (T/50), S. Shillingford (T), L. M. P. Simmons (50), C. A. K. Walton (T). *Coach:* O. D. Gibson.

Roach went home with a shoulder injury before the Second Test, and was replaced by S. T. Gabriel. Gayle tore a hamstring in the first one-day international, and returned home. D. J. Bravo captained in the one-day series.

At Kolkata (Jadavpur University), October 31–November 2, 2013. Drawn. ‡West Indians 466 (K. O. A. Powell 64, D. M. Bravo 61, S. Chanderpaul 112, N. Deonarine 94; R. P. Singh 3-86, Imtiaz

Ahmed 5-117) **and 199-5** (C. H. Gayle 58, M. N. Samuels 58; P. P. Chawla 4-72); **Uttar Pradesh 372-9 dec** (Parvinder Singh 112; S. S. Cottrell 3-65, V. Permaul 3-124). *Storms around India's east coast had written off the one-day international between India and Australia at Cuttack on October 26, and the Odisha Cricket Association had to relinquish hosting the West Indians' tour opener too. The fixture was moved 400km north-east to a university ground in eastern Kolkata, which had never hosted a first-class match before – and was not much closer to the northern state of Uttar Pradesh, which provided the home team. Play started late on all three days because of a damp outfield, and was curtailed further by bad light on the first two. The outfield was still quick, though, and helped the West Indians' top six all pass 50 against a side featuring former Test bowlers R. P. Singh and Piyush Chawla. However, their own attack – missing Kemar Roach (shoulder) and Shane Shillingford (stiff neck) – were also easy to score off.*

INDIA v WEST INDIES

First Test Match

At Kolkata, November 6–8, 2013. India won by an innings and 51 runs. Toss: West Indies. Test debuts: Mohammed Shami, R. G. Sharma; S. S. Cottrell.

At 83 for five on the second morning, India were in a spot of bother. Shillingford, the tall off-spinner, had found turn and bounce on a relaid pitch to grab four wickets. Eden Gardens was not even half full, and Sachin Tendulkar was already back in the dressing-room. This was not how it was meant to be. Tendulkar had spent 41 minutes compiling ten, then failed to read Shillingford's doosra. The ball hit him on his right thigh as he pushed forward down the wrong line, losing his balance in the process. After some contemplation umpire Nigel Llong raised his finger. It looked messy, and replays also suggested it looked high. Sections of the crowd berated Llong; others mocked India for opposing DRS. Tendulkar walked off without much fuss, though he did gesture to team-mates back in the dressing-room that he felt the ball would have gone over the stumps.

The morning haze had not yet lifted. Here was a perfect opportunity for West Indies to keep the Indians down. But it came as little surprise that they let the chance slip. Rohit Sharma, making his Test debut after 144 matches in the shorter formats (including a record 111 one-day internationals), and Ashwin combined to raise 280 in 72 overs – Test cricket's third-highest stand for the seventh wicket, and India's second-highest for any wicket against West Indies (Sunil Gavaskar and Dilip Vengsarkar put on an unbroken 344 on this ground against Alvin Kallicharran's Packer-reduced side in 1978-79). The partnership thoroughly punctured the Caribbean spirit.

In February 2010, Sharma had been minutes away from a maiden Test, against South Africa in his home town of Nagpur, when he turned his ankle playing football in the warm-up. Now, following a one-day double-hundred five days earlier against Australia, he finally had another opportunity. He walked in at the fall of Tendulkar's wicket, and straightaway slipped into the driver's seat – monitoring the bowling, manoeuvring the score, and wristily manipulating the field. His eventual 177 was ten short of Dhawan's record for the highest score by an Indian on Test debut earlier in the year, but Sharma did surpass Doug Walters's 155, against England at Brisbane in 1965-66, as the highest from a debutant No. 6.

Many of his team-mates had not paid Shillingford due respect. Indeed, when Vijay walked past a straight one to be stumped, Shillingford became the second-fastest West Indian spinner to 50 Test wickets, in 11 matches, behind Alf Valentine and level with Sonny Ramadhin. Sharma, though, played him well off the back foot, and swept expertly. With Ashwin, whose only previous Test century had come at Mumbai against the same opponents two years earlier, Sharma accelerated on the third morning to give India a lead of 219.

Endurance was called for from the West Indians. But twice they threw away a good start. In the first innings – after Sammy called "heads", and a special commemorative coin landed with Tendulkar's smile facing up – they were decently perched at 138 for two, only

HARD AND FAST

Best match figures by Indian seamers in home Tests:

13-132 (5-46, 8-86)	J. Srinath	v Pakistan at Calcutta	1998-99
11-146 (4-90, 7-56)	Kapil Dev	v Pakistan at Madras	1979-80
10-135 (1-52, 9-83)	Kapil Dev	v West Indies at Ahmedabad	1983-84
9-118 (4-71, 5-47)	**Mohammed Shami**	**v West Indies at Kolkata**	**2013-14**
9-121 (5-58, 4-63)	Kapil Dev	v Pakistan at Delhi	1979-80
9-141 (4-81, 5-60)	J. Srinath	v Zimbabwe at Delhi	2000-01
9-171 (5-76, 4-95)	L. Balaji	v Pakistan at Mohali	2004-05

The best figures for any India bowler are N. D. Hirwani's 16-136 v West Indies at Madras in 1987-88.

for eight to fall for 96 as the pacy local boy Mohammed Shami started to make the old ball swerve. Tendulkar even picked up his 201st international wicket (and 46th in Tests), when Shillingford played down the wrong line.

Second time round, West Indies should have corrected some of their mistakes. But from 101 for one just before tea on the third day, they lost nine wickets in 24 overs. Shami was the main reason for the incredible submission. He had forced his way into the Test side after fiery one-day spells against Australia, and in the continued absence of Zaheer Khan, who was seeking to rebuild his reputation and fitness. Somewhat incongruously, Shami was presented with his Test cap by Ishant Sharma, another seamer he had usurped. It did not take long to realise he was a skilful manipulator of the old ball: six of his nine victims were embarrassed to see their stumps rattled, and on some occasions uprooted.

Before the match, Sammy was loud and proud about the experience in West Indies' batting department. Yet Gayle was twice an easy scalp for Bhuvneshwar Kumar. Darren Bravo, the highest scorer on West Indies' last trip here, was committing childish mistakes: first running himself out, then cutting loosely to point. And Chanderpaul couldn't hold up India by himself. As for Ramdin and Sammy, it was hard to make a case for them as Test Nos 6 and 7. Only Samuels could count himself unlucky: he was beaten by probably the ball of the match in the first innings, a swinging indipper from Shami; then given lbw in the second, when there was again enough doubt for Llong to have turned down the appeal.

Man of the Match: R. G. Sharma.

Close of play: first day, India 37-0 (Dhawan 21, Vijay 16); second day, India 354-6 (Sharma 127, Ashwin 92).

West Indies

C. H. Gayle c Vijay b Bhuvneshwar Kumar	18	– c Kohli b Bhuvneshwar Kumar	33
K. O. A. Powell c Bhuvneshwar Kumar b Mohammed Shami	28	– lbw b Ashwin	36
D. M. Bravo run out	23	– c Sharma b Ashwin	37
M. N. Samuels b Mohammed Shami	65	– lbw b Mohammed Shami	4
S. Chanderpaul b Ashwin	36	– not out	31
†D. Ramdin b Mohammed Shami	4	– c Vijay b Mohammed Shami	1
*D. J. G. Sammy c Bhuvneshwar b Ojha	16	– b Mohammed Shami	8
S. Shillingford lbw b Tendulkar	5	– b Mohammed Shami	0
V. Permaul c and b Ashwin	14	– run out	0
T. L. Best not out	14	– c Ojha b Ashwin	3
S. S. Cottrell b Mohammed Shami	0	– b Mohammed Shami	5
B 4, l-b 7	11	L-b 10	10

1/34 (1) 2/47 (2) 3/138 (4)   (78 overs) 234
4/138 (3) 5/143 (6) 6/172 (7)
7/192 (8) 8/211 (9) 9/233 (5) 10/234 (11)

1/33 (1) 2/101 (2)   (54.1 overs) 168
3/110 (4) 4/120 (3)
5/125 (6) 6/152 (7) 7/152 (8)
8/152 (9) 9/159 (10) 10/168 (11)

Bhuvneshwar Kumar 14–6–33–1; Mohammed Shami 17–2–71–4; Ashwin 21–9–52–2; Ojha 24–6–62–1; Tendulkar 2–1–5–1. *Second innings*—Bhuvneshwar Kumar 6–1–20–1; Mohammed Shami 13.1–0–47–5; Ashwin 19–2–46–3; Ojha 13–3–27–0; Tendulkar 3–0–18–0.

India

S. Dhawan b Shillingford	23	Bhuvneshwar Kumar c Gayle b Shillingford 12
M. Vijay st Ramdin b Shillingford	26	Mohammed Shami st Ramdin b Permaul 1
C. A. Pujara c Ramdin b Cottrell	17	P. P. Ojha not out 2
S. R. Tendulkar lbw b Shillingford	10	B 4, l-b 8, w 1, n-b 3 16
V. Kohli c Powell b Shillingford	3	
R. G. Sharma lbw b Permaul	177	1/42 (1) 2/57 (2) 3/79 (3) (129.4 overs) 453
*†M. S. Dhoni c Ramdin b Best	42	4/82 (4) 5/83 (5) 6/156 (7)
R. Ashwin b Shillingford	124	7/436 (6) 8/444 (8) 9/451 (9) 10/453 (10)

Best 17–0–71–1; Cottrell 18–3–72–1; Shillingford 55–9–167–6; Permaul 23.4–2–67–2; Sammy 12–1–52–0; Samuels 4–0–12–0.

Umpires: R. A. Kettleborough and N. J. Llong.   Third umpire: V. A. Kulkarni.

INDIA v WEST INDIES

Second Test Match

At Mumbai (Wankhede Stadium), November 14–16, 2013. India won by an innings and 126 runs. Toss: India.

It was never going to be a tearless farewell. As soon as Tendulkar walked out to bat in his 200th Test – a world record – with 20 overs of the first day remaining, anxiety set in. His every move was watched, noted, and interpreted as his innings spilled over into the second day. It was the story of his career – and it was about to come to an end.

Pujara, who batted with Tendulkar throughout his two and a half hours in the middle, later told of how distracted he became by the extreme reaction of the near-full house, and of his admiration at how composed his partner remained. Pujara and Tendulkar had come in after the fall of openers Dhawan and Vijay within three balls, both offering catches off Shillingford. And although Pujara walked out at No. 3, it was Tendulkar who faced a ball first – after he had threaded his way through a guard of honour formed by Pujara, the West Indians and, a touch controversially perhaps, the two umpires. Early in Tendulkar's innings, it wasn't entirely clear whether the crowd wanted him to be on or off strike, such was the nervous tension every time the bowler ran in. Luckily for them, Tendulkar did not appear to succumb to any emotion until he walked back unbeaten on 38 at the close, and allowed himself a wave of the bat to the crowd and his loved ones.

The second day marked precisely 24 years since Tendulkar's Test debut at Karachi. Hearts were in mouths when, on 48, he tried to upper-cut Best, but missed by some

Thank you and goodnight

LAWRENCE BOOTH

As Sachin Tendulkar walked out to bat shortly after 3.30pm on the opening day of the Second Test, he was greeted by a guard of honour and, somewhere out there, a billion salutes. One of the Wankhede's giant screens helpfully advised: "Don't even blink!!" Mumbai likes a superfluous instruction (signs above the city's roads forbid horn-honking). After all, spectators did not seem inclined to rise from their seats in disgust and ask for their money back. And so no one blinked, which may explain why many appeared to have tears in their eyes. After 24 years of imagined intimacy with cricket's least knowable star, this was it.

The mood was hard to reconcile with Test cricket. The best of the genre encompasses grudgingly relinquished ebb and hard-fought flow, plus the unspoken conviction that all 22 players would rather be nowhere else. Yet the basic premise of cricket as a team game felt under threat. The scoreboard told you it was India v West Indies. Everything else told you it was a pageant.

Conflicting emotions filled the sticky air. The crowd wanted to see Tendulkar, but they knew one ball would be enough – and West Indies, already bundled out for 182, were unlikely to make India bat again. There was nothing for it but to follow a well-worn template. They went berserk.

Tendulkar's first run was – Homer nodding – a leg-side smear off Shane Shillingford. Soon, he cut a long hop for four, then eased four more past mid-off. Shannon Gabriel was driven through extra cover. When Marlon Samuels was glanced to fine leg, Tendulkar's mother, Rajni, appeared on a giant screen, staring down impassively – or was it nervously? – as if from Mount Olympus. This was her first Test match. Who, frankly, was going to dare claim her son's wicket?

Tendulkar reached stumps on 38, and stumbled on the pavilion steps as he made his way up to the dressing-room – a touching moment of humanity. Next morning, the crowds gathered. "I consider myself the most fortunate person in the world because I have seen God in a new avatar," declared a text message on the tireless screen. "I will tell this for life. I was here today," read a banner. Another lamented: "Cricket is retiring with this match."

As for the *mis*match, few cared. This was a full-scale celebration now, with Tino Best ramping up his role as court jester, apparently having promised his son the birthday present of Tendulkar's wicket. When it came – though not to Best – it was as if the parents had arrived home and spoiled their teenage son's party by switching on the lights. Narsingh Deonarine was the pooper, finding turn and bounce as Tendulkar steered an off-break to slip.

There are reckoned to be no fairytale endings, and "c Sammy b Deonarine" seemed to confirm as much; India did not bat again. But Tendulkar did address the crowd once the match was over. Again, no one blinked. The occasion may have been manufactured. The emotions were gratifyingly real.

distance. He once said he never batted while harbouring negative thoughts. And so, next ball, he hit *that* straight-drive: the inimitable punch played with minimal movement or flourish.

As he passed 70, anxiety levels started to spike once more. Two years ago, against the same opponents on the same ground, he had walked back in disbelief as he fell six runs short of what would have been his 100th international hundred. Sammy, the man who had

FEWEST TESTS TO 100 WICKETS

T	Years	Days		
16	9	243	G. A. Lohmann (England)	1886 to 1895-96
17	8	7	C. T. B. Turner (Australia)	1886-87 to 1894-95
17	10	79	S. F. Barnes (England)	1901-02 to 1911-12
17	5	327	C. V. Grimmett (Australia)	1924-25 to 1930-31
18	**2**	**8**	**R. Ashwin (India)**	**2011-12 to 2013-14**
19	8	91	C. Blythe (England)	1901-02 to 1909-10
19	3	262	A. L. Valentine (West Indies)	1950 to 1953-54
19	2	142	A. M. E. Roberts (West Indies)	1973-74 to 1976
19	2	9	I. T. Botham (England)	1977 to 1979
19	2	208	Saeed Ajmal (Pakistan)	2009 to 2011-12
19	**2**	**41**	**V. D. Philander (South Africa)**	**2011-12 to 2013-14**

The fastest bowler to 100 wickets by time is Kapil Dev (India), who took 1 year 107 days (25 Tests).

caught him superbly back then, was standing at slip now. The players had taken drinks after the first hour. The ground was filling up fast. There was a lot of movement in the stands. Tendulkar tried to cut hard and fine against the off-spinner Deonarine, and Sammy picked up a smart catch with both hands in front of his face. It took a few seconds for the crowd to react. Then they stood as one and gave a rousing ovation.

The rest of the match – before and after Tendulkar – followed the same pattern as Kolkata. In their first innings, West Indies' impetuosity bordered on criminal. The wicket of Darren Bravo, who had flailed against Bhuvneshwar Kumar but come through it, sparked a collapse of nine for 96 to the spinners. Sammy, who had spent much of his captaincy talking about batsmen taking responsibility, heaved across the line second ball and spooned a leading edge. There was even the rare sight of an Indian pace bowler – Mohammed Shami – operating with four slips and a gully. The Indians used these pliant opponents to enhance their Test records: Ashwin became the fastest bowler to 100 wickets since Clarrie Grimmett, and Dhoni the seventh keeper to 250 dismissals, while Ojha drew level with Ian Botham on three five-wicket hauls at the Wankhede (and passed him in the second innings).

Soon after Tendulkar's dismissal, Pujara had a lucky escape on 76, when third umpire Vineet Kulkarni somehow ruled Powell had not got his fingers under a catch at short leg; Pujara took advantage to press on to his fifth hundred in 15 Tests. Rohit Sharma, meanwhile, was busy transforming his reputation, and joined a small group (Lawrence Rowe, Alvin Kallicharran, Sourav Ganguly and Yasir Hameed) to score centuries in their first two Test innings.

The best part of it came from 46 onwards, when Sharma was joined by last man Shami, and delivered a masterclass in how to bat with the tail: ten overs into their partnership, Shami had been exposed to only nine balls, and made none of their 44 runs. Thirty-nine came after Sharma, on 85, holed out to deep midwicket, but was reprieved because replays showed Shillingford had overstepped.

On a pitch taking turn and bounce, West Indies remained hapless against the spinners, and lost the match before lunch on the third day. Chanderpaul, who through all the Tendulkar idolatry had become the first West Indian to play 150 Tests, was cast in the familiar role of firefighter – and eventually overwhelmed by the flames. One last bauble eluded Tendulkar: Dhoni brought him on to bowl at eight wickets down in the hope that he could finish off the match. Ramdin and Shillingford survived Tendulkar's 12 balls, but barely much longer. At only 210.2 overs, it was India's second-shortest completed home Test in terms of balls bowled, following their 2004-05 victory against Australia, also on this ground. But the story was already over.

Man of the Match: P. P. Ojha. *Man of the Series:* R. G. Sharma.
Close of play: first day, India 157-2 (Pujara 34, Tendulkar 38); second day, West Indies 43-3 (Gayle 6).

West Indies

C. H. Gayle c Sharma b Mohammed Shami	11	– c Dhoni b Ojha 35
K. O. A. Powell c Dhawan b Ojha	48	– c Mohammed Shami b Ashwin 9
D. M. Bravo c Dhoni b Ashwin	29	– (4) c Vijay b Ashwin 11
M. N. Samuels c Vijay b Ojha	19	– (5) st Dhoni b Ojha. 11
S. Chanderpaul c Ashwin b Bhuvneshwar Kumar. .	25	– (6) lbw b Ashwin 41
N. Deonarine c Vijay b Ashwin	21	– (7) c and b Ojha 0
†D. Ramdin not out	12	– (8) not out. 53
*D. J. G. Sammy c Sharma b Ashwin	0	– (9) lbw b Ojha 1
S. Shillingford lbw b Ojha	0	– (10) lbw b Ashwin 8
T. L. Best c Dhoni b Ojha	0	– (3) lbw b Ojha 9
S. T. Gabriel c Dhoni b Ojha	1	– b Mohammed Shami 0
B 8, l-b 8	16	B 4, l-b 5 9

1/25 (1) 2/86 (3) 3/97 (2)	(55.2 overs) 182	1/15 (2) 2/28 (3)	(47 overs) 187
4/140 (4) 5/148 (5) 6/162 (6)		3/43 (4) 4/74 (5)	
7/162 (8) 8/162 (9) 9/172 (10) 10/182 (11)		5/87 (1) 6/89 (7) 7/157 (6)	
		8/162 (9) 9/185 (10) 10/187 (11)	

Bhuvneshwar Kumar 17–2–45–1; Mohammed Shami 12–2–36–1; Ashwin 15–4–53–3; Ojha 11.2–2–40–5. *Second innings*—Bhuvneshwar Kumar 3–0–4–0; Mohammed Shami 7–0–28–1; Ashwin 17–4–89–4; Ojha 18–6–49–5; Tendulkar 2–0–8–0.

India

M. Vijay c Sammy b Shillingford	43	P. P. Ojha run out	0
S. Dhawan c Chanderpaul b Shillingford . .	33	Mohammed Shami c Best b Deonarine. . . .	11
C. A. Pujara c and b Shillingford	113		
S. R. Tendulkar c Sammy b Deonarine. . . .	74		
V. Kohli c Sammy b Shillingford	57	B 8, l-b 2, w 2, n-b 3	15
R. G. Sharma not out.	111		
*†M. S. Dhoni c Sammy b Best.	4	1/77 (2) 2/77 (1)	(108 overs) 495
R. Ashwin c and b Gabriel	30	3/221 (4) 4/315 (5)	
Bhuvneshwar Kumar c Sammy		5/354 (3) 6/365 (7) 7/409 (8)	
b Shillingford .	4	8/414 (9) 9/415 (10) 10/495 (11)	

Sammy 9–1–41–0; Gabriel 16–0–85–1; Shillingford 43–6–179–5; Best 18–0–93–1; Samuels 11–0–42–0; Deonarine 11–0–45–2.

Umpires: R. A. Kettleborough and N. J. Llong.   Third umpire: V. A. Kulkarni.
Series referee: A. J. Pycroft.

INDIA v WEST INDIES

First One-Day International

At Kochi, November 21, 2013 (day/night). India won by six wickets. Toss: West Indies.

Gayle chanced a risky single to the second ball of the match, was run out by the bowler Bhuvneshwar Kumar's swivel and throw, and dived for his ground so violently that he tore a hamstring and was stretchered out of this series and the next, in New Zealand. For West Indies, it was a sign of things to come. His opening partner, Charles, offered a leading edge to Jadeja after a jaunty 42, and Dhoni, having noted West Indies' ineptitude against spin in the Tests, needed no further encouragement to introduce it at both ends; India's three main slow bowlers accounted for eight wickets. Kochi's sluggish, two-paced pitch was far removed from the featherbeds Australia had recently played on – Samuels and Darren Bravo were both aghast at being castled by shooters – but West Indies' total was still unlikely to test a confident Indian batting unit which had regularly breached 300 the previous month against better bowling. Sure enough, Sharma and Kohli fast-tracked victory with a dominant stand of 133. Kohli raced to 5,000 one-day international runs in his 114th innings, placing him alongside Viv Richards as the joint-fastest to the milestone.

Man of the Match: V. Kohli.

West Indies

C. H. Gayle run out	0	J. O. Holder not out	16
†J. Charles c and b Jadeja	42	S. P. Narine c and b Ashwin	0
M. N. Samuels b Raina	24	R. Rampaul c Dhawan b Ashwin	1
D. M. Bravo b Mohammed Shami	59	L-b 1, w 6	7
L. M. P. Simmons lbw b Raina	29		
N. Deonarine b Raina	4	1/0 (1) 2/65 (2) 3/77 (3) (48.5 overs) 211
*D. J. Bravo st Dhoni b Jadeja	24	4/142 (5) 5/152 (6) 6/183 (4)
D. J. G. Sammy c Bhuvneshwar Kumar		7/187 (7) 8/204 (8) 9/206 (10)
b Jadeja	5	10/211 (11) 10 overs: 63-1

Bhuvneshwar Kumar 5–0–26–0; Unadkat 6–0–39–0; Mohammed Shami 6–0–28–1; Jadeja 10–0–37–3; Raina 10–1–34–3; Ashwin 9.5–0–42–2; Sharma 2–0–4–0.

India

R. G. Sharma c Simmons b Rampaul	72	*†M. S. Dhoni not out	13
S. Dhawan c Charles b Holder	5	B 5, w 15	20
V. Kohli c Narine b Holder	86		
Yuvraj Singh not out	16	1/17 (2) 2/150 (1) (4 wkts, 35.2 overs) 212
S. K. Raina c Holder b Narine	0	3/192 (3) 4/194 (5) 10 overs: 57-1

R. A. Jadeja, R. Ashwin, Bhuvneshwar Kumar, Mohammed Shami and J. D. Unadkat did not bat.

Rampaul 8–0–39–1; Holder 8–0–48–2; Sammy 2–0–14–0; Narine 10–1–57–1; Deonarine 2–0–15–0; Simmons 3–0–14–0; D. J. Bravo 2.2–0–20–0.

Umpires: V. A. Kulkarni and R. J. Tucker.   Third umpire: A. K. Chowdhury.

INDIA v WEST INDIES

Second One-Day International

At Visakhapatnam, November 24, 2013 (day/night). West Indies won by two wickets. Toss: West Indies.

During the Tests, Sammy had undermined his position by getting out to shots that were either careless or clueless. But at Vizag, free of leadership duties, he found his feet on a dewy surface, inspiring West Indies to a series-squaring win even while most of his team-mates slipped up. Kohli had earlier hauled India back from a middle-order stumble, but he hooked to a diving long leg on 99 – just failing to become the first player to record five one-day international hundreds two years running. Dhoni's customary late assault brought up his 50th half-century (excluding those he turned into three figures) in one-day internationals. As night fell, the conditions turned in West Indies' favour, with the ball changed three times because of dew. Only once before had four West Indians scored fifties in the format. But, barring Sammy, they lacked resolve: Darren Bravo was dropped three times in four deliveries, and Powell, knowing a relatively dry replacement ball had just been taken, was stumped on the charge. For Jadeja to concede just 44 in these damp conditions was no mean feat; he picked up Simmons late on to become the first man to 50 one-day international wickets in the calendar year, pipping Pakistan's Saeed Ajmal, in Cape Town, by an hour or so. Wild slogging from Holder and Narine only added to the pressure, but Sammy stayed resilient, and hit the winning run with three balls to spare. It was West Indies' fourth-highest successful run-chase, and the first time they had reached a 280-plus target since 2004.

Man of the Match: D. J. G. Sammy.

India

R. G. Sharma c Sammy b Rampaul	12	R. Ashwin c Charles b Holder	19	
S. Dhawan lbw b Permaul	35	Bhuvneshwar Kumar not out	1	
V. Kohli c Holder b Rampaul	99	L-b 1, w 9	10	
Yuvraj Singh c Samuels b Sammy	28			
S. K. Raina c D. J. Bravo b Rampaul	23	1/21 (1) 2/69 (2)	(7 wkts, 50 overs) 288	
*†M. S. Dhoni not out	51	3/138 (4) 4/203 (5)		
R. A. Jadeja b Rampaul	10	5/209 (3) 6/240 (7) 7/287 (8)	10 overs: 48-1	

Mohammed Shami and M. Sharma did not bat.

Rampaul 10–0–60–4; Holder 10–0–63–1; D. J. Bravo 8–0–54–0; Permaul 10–0–55–1; Narine 10–2–39–0; Sammy 1–0–11–1; Simmons 1–0–5–0.

West Indies

†J. Charles c and b Bhuvneshwar Kumar	12	S. P. Narine c sub (A. T. Rayudu)		
K. O. A. Powell st Dhoni b Ashwin	59	b Mohammed Shami	0	
M. N. Samuels c Dhoni b M. Sharma	8	V. Permaul not out	0	
D. M. Bravo c Dhoni b Ashwin	50	L-b 7, w 3	10	
L. M. P. Simmons lbw b Jadeja	62			
*D. J. Bravo c Dhawan		1/14 (1) 2/23 (3)	(8 wkts, 49.3 overs) 289	
b Bhuvneshwar Kumar	18	3/123 (4) 4/147 (2)		
D. J. G. Sammy not out	63	5/185 (6) 6/267 (5)		
J. O. Holder c Dhoni b Mohammed Shami	7	7/285 (8) 8/285 (9)	10 overs: 60-2	

R. Rampaul did not bat.

Bhuvneshwar Kumar 9–1–56–2; M. Sharma 6.3–0–48–1; Mohammed Shami 7–0–55–2; Ashwin 10–1–37–2; Raina 7–0–42–0; Jadeja 10–1–44–1.

Umpires: V. A. Kulkarni and R. J. Tucker.   Third umpire: A. K. Chowdhury.

INDIA v WEST INDIES

Third One-Day International

At Kanpur, November 27, 2013. India won by five wickets. Toss: India.

After a dewy evening in Vizag came a hazy morning in Kanpur, but West Indies seemed to have adapted well to the 9am start as Powell and Samuels stitched together a century partnership. As in the previous match, however, they lost their way, giving up two wickets in the powerplay; Darren Bravo's third consecutive fifty and Sammy's late thrust were not quite enough to stretch India. Rampaul induced Kohli into an edge behind, thus ensuring his 100th one-day international wicket was the most sought-after in the world game. But from 61 for two, Dhawan cracked the fifth one-day century of both his career and 2013, twirled his moustache, raised both hands and set up an easy win. Yuvraj Singh, in desperate need of runs to retain his place, rode in Dhawan's slipstream to score his first half-century in 11 one-day innings. It was India's ninth successful run-chase in ten attempts, and sealed their sixth consecutive one-day series victory (equalling their best sequence, between August 2008 and September 2009).

Man of the Match: S. Dhawan.   *Man of the Series:* V. Kohli.

West Indies

†J. Charles b Bhuvneshwar Kumar	11	D. J. G. Sammy not out	37	
K. O. A. Powell c Dhawan b Ashwin	70	L-b 2, w 3, n-b 1	6	
M. N. Samuels b Ashwin	71			
D. M. Bravo not out	51	1/20 (1) 2/137 (2)	(5 wkts, 50 overs) 263	
L. M. P. Simmons c Dhoni b Jadeja	13	3/168 (3) 4/187 (5)		
*D. J. Bravo c Ashwin b Mohammed Shami	4	5/196 (6)	10 overs: 39-1	

J. O. Holder, S. P. Narine, V. Permaul and R. Rampaul did not bat.

Bhuvneshwar Kumar 8–0–42–1; M. Sharma 7–0–47–0; Mohammed Shami 10–1–49–1; Ashwin 10–0–45–2; Raina 5–0–29–0; Jadeja 10–0–49–1.

India

R. G. Sharma c D. J. Bravo b Rampaul....	4	R. A. Jadeja not out...................	2
S. Dhawan c and b D. J. Bravo..........	119	L-b 5, w 4, n-b 1	10
V. Kohli c Charles b Rampaul...........	19		
Yuvraj Singh c D. J. Bravo b Narine.....	55	1/29 (1) 2/61 (3)	(5 wkts, 46.1 overs) 266
S. K. Raina c Charles b D. J. Bravo	34	3/190 (4) 4/218 (2)	
*†M. S. Dhoni not out	23	5/255 (5)	10 overs: 63-2

R. Ashwin, Bhuvneshwar Kumar, Mohammed Shami and M. Sharma did not bat.

Rampaul 10–1–55–2; Holder 6–0–47–0; D. J. Bravo 10–0–57–2; Narine 10–1–32–1; Sammy 3–0–22–0; Simmons 3–0–17–0; Permaul 4.1–0–31–0.

Umpires: A. K. Chowdhury and R. J. Tucker.   Third umpire: V. A. Kulkarni.
Series referee: D. C. Boon.

THE INDIAN PREMIER LEAGUE, 2012-13

Review by Nagraj Gollapudi

On the evening of May 15, a team of Delhi police officers visited the Wankhede Stadium, where Mumbai Indians were hosting Rajasthan Royals. They were there to see Ankeet Chavan, the Rajasthan left-arm spinner; more specifically, they were there to see whether he would fiddle with his wristband – a signal, they believed, to bookies – and deliver on his word to give at least 13 runs away in his second over. An up-and-coming Ranji Trophy player for Mumbai, Chavan had conceded just two off his first. Now, after making the sign, he leaked 15, including 14 off the first three balls.

In the small hours, the police picked him up. Also arrested were two other Rajasthan bowlers: Sreesanth, the former India seamer, and Ajit Chandila, a little-known off-spinner from Haryana in his second IPL season. Later that day, Delhi police commissioner Neeraj Kumar revealed that, following a tip-off in April, a police cell had been keeping tabs on the trio and tapping their phones; that the Mumbai underworld were probably involved; and that a group of bookies were in constant touch with the cricketers.

The hooded faces of the three players paraded in front of the Delhi court would become the indelible image of the sixth edition of the IPL. It seemed to confirm the fears raised by the ICC's Anti-Corruption and Security Unit, who had long believed the IPL was vulnerable to shady dealings. Yet N. Srinivasan, president of the BCCI, rebutted the allegations, preferring to label the trio "dirty cricketers" while insisting the IPL as a whole was clean. Soon, though, he too was being dragged closer to a whirlpool of corruption and scandal.

As the IPL entered its final week, the Mumbai Crime Branch arrested Gurunath Meiyappan, Srinivasan's son-in-law, for allegedly betting on the IPL. Shortly before his arrest, Meiyappan had removed the words "Team Principal Chennai Super Kings" from his Twitter account. Srinivasan's India Cements company – the CSK owners – issued a press release claiming Meiyappan was "only one of the Members (Honorary) of the Management Team of Chennai Super Kings". Srinivasan called Meiyappan "an enthusiast", even though many pages on the franchise's website had listed him as a team owner. They were quickly taken down and, as public criticism mounted, Srinivasan declared: "I cannot be bulldozed, and I will not allow the press or the others to railroad me. I have done nothing wrong."

It was one of Indian cricket's darkest hours. The country had striven to cleanse itself of the match-fixing muck uncovered in 2000, and the BCCI believed their players were above board, since they were well paid. Yet IPL6 proved greed can rarely be sated – and the cloud of corruption obscured the cricket. On June 2, a week after the final, Srinivasan stepped aside temporarily as board president, paving the way for an astonishing return to power for Jagmohan Dalmiya, who had been forced out of the job in December 2006 amid claims he had misappropriated funds intended for the 1996 World Cup – charges that were quickly overturned. Now, Dalmiya – optimistically pledging to "clean up cricket in a limited time frame" – was appointed interim president while the board probed Meiyappan's alleged misdemeanour and the role of Raj Kundra, co-owner of Rajasthan Royals, who Delhi police claimed had confessed to placing bets on IPL matches. In late July came the news that the two-man panel, comprising a pair of retired judges, had found "no evidence of wrongdoing" against either India Cements or Kundra. The Bombay High Court, however, ruled the appointment of the panel "illegal and unconstitutional", which summed up the confusion. The credibility of both the tournament and Indian cricket as a whole had taken a huge blow.

Even the news of Sachin Tendulkar's retirement from the IPL failed to create the expected high-decibel response. He made his decision public just minutes after **Mumbai Indians** had defeated **Chennai Super Kings** to claim their first title, saying he had waited six years for the moment; some viewed it as a belated return on a heavy investment, though Tendulkar's own contribution of one half-century in 14 innings, and a tournament average of 22, felt distinctly pricey. Mumbai had placed former India coach John Wright in charge, and splashed $400,000 on Ricky Ponting. In the end, they triumphed without both Tendulkar, who missed the final with a wrist injury, and Ponting, who began the tournament as captain, only to drop himself after six games.

But nothing could drown out the noise generated by Chris Gayle during **Royal Challengers Bangalore's** match against Pune Warriors. Indisputably the world's best Twenty20 batsman, Gayle hammered an unbeaten 175,

---

FASTEST HUNDRED IN TWENTY20

Balls

30	C. H. Gayle (175* from 66 balls)......	Bangalore v Pune at Bangalore...	**2012-13**
34	A. Symonds (112 from 43)............	Kent v Middlesex at Maidstone....	2004
35	L. P. van der Westhuizen (145 from 50)..	Namibia v Kenya at Windhoek....	2011-12
37	Y. K. Pathan (100 from 37)...........	Rajasthan v Mumbai at Mumbai...	2009-10
37	S. B. Styris (100* from 37)...........	Sussex v Gloucestershire at Hove...	2012
38	D. A. Miller (101* from 38)...........	Punjab v Bangalore at Mohali....	**2012-13**
39	C. J. Simmons (102 from 41).........	Perth v Adelaide at Perth........	**2013-14**
40	Ahmed Shehzad (113* from 49).......	Barisal v Rajshahi at Mirpur.......	2011-12

---

prompting Pune coach Allan Donald to concede that some of his players had been scared. He took 30 balls to reach three figures, the fastest century in the format, and in all hit 17 sixes, another record; Bangalore posted 263, yet another.

After apparently exhausting their superlatives, the media were forced to dig deep once more when the South African David Miller blasted a 38-ball hundred for **Kings XI Punjab** against Bangalore. Both lightning centuries had come from teams playing at home, a trend in IPL6: the win–loss ratio at home was more than double the average of the five previous seasons. Mumbai and **Rajasthan Royals** won all eight home matches, while Bangalore and **Sunrisers Hyderabad** (who had replaced the bankrupt Deccan Chargers) lost only once each.

Bangalore, Hyderabad, Chennai and Rajasthan were the most consistent sides, probably because they had more than one match-winner. By contrast,

Kolkata Knight Riders – the defending champions – **Delhi Daredevils** and **Pune Warriors** all failed to pull together, lacked leadership, and were slow to adapt. Delhi fell like a skydiver with a faulty parachute: flying high at the top of the table a year earlier, they plummeted to earth, with just three wins from 16 games. In October, Pune were disbanded for non-payment of fees.

Some teams suffered from the failings of big-name batsmen. Three Sri Lankans – Kumar Sangakkara (Hyderabad), Mahela Jayawardene (Delhi) and Angelo Mathews (Pune) – between them managed only 623 runs in 34 innings. Australians Adam Gilchrist, David Hussey (both Punjab), and Ponting (Mumbai) totalled 581 in 29, and the fading Indian superstars Virender Sehwag (295 in 13 for Delhi) and Yuvraj Singh (238 in 13 for Pune) were similarly listless.

By way of balance, several inexperienced Indian players made an encouraging impression. Chennai seamer Mohit Sharma took 20 wickets, while 18-year-old Sanju Samson, Rajasthan's wicketkeeper-batsman, showed a cool temperament to hit 206 runs, including some important late-order knocks, and hold 13 catches. Sharma, a medium-pacer from Haryana, was thrown the new ball by M. S. Dhoni, and responded well, claiming 15 of his wickets in the powerplay overs, and later played for India.

And yet, amid the allegations of corruption, did the cricket mean anything? Sreesanth, who spent 27 days in judicial custody, was accosted by a 12-year-old fan, who asked him why he had spot-fixed. Denying he had done anything wrong, Sreesanth signed his autograph, and asked the youngster to pray for him. Neeraj Kumar, the Delhi police commissioner, said he had stopped watching the IPL because he felt cheated. That rang out like a clarion call to IPL7: to restore faith – both among India's fans and the cricketing world.

IPL STATISTICS

Leading run-scorers

	M	I	NO	Runs	HS	50	Avge	SR	4	6
†M. E. K. Hussey (*Chennai*)	17	17	3	733	95	6	52.35	129.50	81	17
†C. H. Gayle (*Bangalore*)	16	16	4	708	175*	4	59.00	156.29	57	51
V. Kohli (*Bangalore*)	16	16	2	634	99	4	45.28	138.73	64	22
†S. K. Raina (*Chennai*)	18	17	4	548	100*	4	42.15	150.13	50	18
S. R. Watson (*Rajasthan*)	16	16	2	543	101	2	38.78	142.89	59	22
R. G. Sharma (*Mumbai*)	19	19	5	538	79*	4	38.42	131.54	35	28
K. D. Karthik (*Mumbai*)	19	19	1	510	86	2	28.33	124.08	54	14
A. M. Rahane (*Rajasthan*)	18	18	4	488	68*	4	34.85	106.55	42	11
R. Dravid (*Rajasthan*)	18	17	1	471	65	4	29.43	110.82	64	5
M. S. Dhoni (*Chennai*)	18	16	5	461	67*	4	41.90	162.89	32	25
A. J. Finch (*Pune*)	14	14	0	456	67	4	32.57	135.71	54	16
R. V. Uthappa (*Pune*)	16	16	0	434	75	2	27.12	116.98	42	12
K. A. Pollard (*Mumbai*)	18	18	8	420	66*	3	42.00	149.46	27	29
D. A. Miller (*Punjab*)	12	12	5	418	101*	3	59.71	164.56	28	24
D. R. Smith (*Mumbai*)	13	13	0	418	68	4	32.15	122.58	40	19
†D. A. Warner (*Delhi*)	16	16	3	410	77	4	31.53	126.93	41	14
†G. Gambhir (*Kolkata*)	16	16	0	406	60	4	25.37	118.36	51	5

There were four centuries (two fewer than in 2011-12): 175* by C. H. Gayle (Bangalore v Pune); 101* by D. A. Miller (Punjab v Bangalore); 101 by S. R. Watson (Rajasthan v Chennai); and 100* by S. K. Raina (Chennai v Punjab).

Leading wicket-takers

	Style	O	M	R	W	BB	4I	Avge	ER	SR
D. J. Bravo (*Chennai*)	RFM	62.3	0	497	32	4-42	1	15.53	7.95	11.71
J. P. Faulkner (*Rajasthan*)	LFM	63.1	2	427	28	5-16	2	15.25	6.75	13.53
Harbhajan Singh (*Mumbai*)	OB	70.0	0	456	24	3-14	0	19.00	6.51	17.50
M. G. Johnson (*Mumbai*).	LF	64.0	0	459	24	3-27	0	19.12	7.17	16.00
R. Vinay Kumar (*Bangalore*)	RFM	60.1	0	493	23	3-18	0	21.43	8.19	15.69
S. P. Narine (*Kolkata*)	OB	64.0	1	350	22	4-13	2	15.90	5.46	17.45
A. Mishra (*Hyderabad*)	LBG	62.0	1	394	21	4-19	1	18.76	6.35	17.71
M. M. Sharma (*Chennai*).	RFM	50.4	0	326	20	3-10	0	16.30	6.43	15.20
S. L. Malinga (*Mumbai*)	RF	65.2	0	468	20	3-39	0	23.40	7.16	19.60
D. W. Steyn (*Hyderabad*)	RF	67.5	3	384	19	3-11	0	20.21	5.66	21.42
K. Cooper (*Rajasthan*).	RFM	54.0	0	449	19	3-15	0	23.63	8.31	17.05
N. L. T. C. Perera (*Hyderabad*)...	RFM	59.4	0	478	19	3-20	0	25.15	8.01	18.84
P. P. Ojha (*Mumbai*)	SLA	52.2	0	381	16	3-11	0	23.81	7.28	19.62
J. H. Kallis (*Kolkata*).	RFM	53.0	1	394	16	3-13	0	24.62	7.43	19.87
A. B. Dinda (*Pune*)	RFM	49.0	0	465	16	3-31	0	29.06	9.48	18.37
U. T. Yadav (*Delhi*).	RFM	57.5	0	508	16	4-24	1	31.75	8.78	21.68

J. P. Faulkner took a five-for on two occasions (5-16 and 5-20, both Rajasthan v Hyderabad). The only other bowler to take five in an innings was J. D. Unadkat (5-25, Bangalore v Delhi).

Leading wicketkeepers

Dismissals	M			Dismissals	M	
17 (15 ct, 2 st)	18	M. S. Dhoni (*Chennai*)		12 (12 ct)	13	A. C. Gilchrist (*Punjab*)
14 (12 ct, 2 st)	19	K. D. Karthik (*Mumbai*)		11 (9 ct, 2 st)	12	K. B. A. Karthik (*Bangalore*)

Most catches

Ct	M			Ct	M	
14	18	D. J. Bravo (*Chennai*)		10	17	M. E. K. Hussey (*Chennai*)
12	18	K. A. Pollard (*Mumbai*)		10	18	A. M. Rahane (*Rajasthan*)
10	10	M. K. Tiwary (*Kolkata*)		10	18	S. K. Raina (*Chennai*)
10	13	C. L. White (*Hyderabad*)				

INDIAN PREMIER LEAGUE, 2012-13

20-over league plus knockout

	Played	Won	Lost	Points	Net run-rate
CHENNAI SUPER KINGS	16	11	5	22	0.53
MUMBAI INDIANS	16	11	5	22	0.44
RAJASTHAN ROYALS	16	10	6	20	0.32
SUNRISERS HYDERABAD...............	16	10	6	20	0.00
Royal Challengers Bangalore	16	9	7	18	0.45
Kings XI Punjab	16	8	8	16	0.22
Kolkata Knight Riders	16	6	10	12	−0.09
Pune Warriors	16	4	12	8	−1.00
Delhi Daredevils	16	3	13	6	−0.84

At Kolkata, April 3, 2013. **Kolkata Knight Riders won by six wickets. Delhi Daredevils 128** (20 overs) (D. P. M. D. Jayawardene 66; S. P. Narine 4-13); ‡**Kolkata Knight Riders 129-4** (18.4 overs) (G. Gambhir 41). *MoM:* S. P. Narine. *With the first ball of the new IPL season, Kolkata's Brett Lee uprooted Unmukt Chand's off stump. Mahela Jayawardene gained support from David Warner (21), but nine Delhi batsman failed to reach double figures, as Sunil Narine carried over his form from IPL5.*

At Bangalore, April 4, 2013. **Royal Challengers Bangalore won by two runs. Royal Challengers Bangalore 156-5** (20 overs) (C. H. Gayle 92*; J. J. Bumrah 3-32); ‡**Mumbai Indians 154-5**

(20 overs) (K. D. Karthik 60; R. Vinay Kumar 3-27). MoM: C. H. Gayle. *Chris Gayle slammed 11 fours and five sixes from 58 balls, including one of each from Munaf Patel's last two deliveries of the innings. That flourish proved crucial: Mumbai required ten from six, but Vinay Kumar followed up two wickets with a last-ball yorker that Kieron Pollard could only squeeze for a single when four were needed. Jasprit Bumrah, a 19-year-old medium-pacer from Gujarat, took three wickets in his first IPL match.*

At Hyderabad (Uppal), April 5, 2013. **Sunrisers Hyderabad won by 22 runs. Sunrisers Hyderabad 126-6** (20 overs) (N. L. T. C. Perera 30); ‡**Pune Warriors 104** (18.5 overs) (D. W. Steyn 3-11, A. Mishra 3-19). MoM: A. Mishra. *Sunrisers Hyderabad made a winning IPL debut. Their $675,000 Sri Lankan all-rounder Tissara Perera stood out on a sluggish pitch: he thrashed 30 to revive a tentative innings, then took the first Pune two wickets and ran out Mitchell Marsh. Pune lost their core to Amit Mishra, and their last three in four balls to Dale Steyn.*

At Delhi, April 6, 2013. **Rajasthan Royals won by five runs.** ‡**Rajasthan Royals 165-7** (20 overs) (R. Dravid 65, S. T. R. Binny 40; U. T. Yadav 4-24); **Delhi Daredevils 160-6** (20 overs) (D. A. Warner 77; K. Cooper 3-30). MoM: R. Dravid. *The match swung Rajasthan's way when acting-captain Brad Hodge ran out Warner from extra cover with Delhi needing 13 off ten balls with seven wickets in hand. Requiring nine off the final over, they could manage only three as Kevon Cooper produced six yorkers. Rahul Dravid had held Rajasthan's innings together with 65 from 51 balls.*

At Chennai, April 6, 2013. **Mumbai Indians won by nine runs.** ‡**Mumbai Indians 148-6** (20 overs) (K. D. Karthik 57*); **Chennai Super Kings 139-9** (20 overs) (M. S. Dhoni 51; M. M. Patel 3-29). MoM: K. A. Pollard. *The crucial moment came when Pollard acrobatically caught M. S. Dhoni on the midwicket boundary. Had it gone over the rope, Chennai would have needed six from five balls. Pollard had earlier smashed five sixes off 38 deliveries to revive Mumbai.*

At Gahunje, April 7, 2013. **Kings XI Punjab won by eight wickets.** ‡**Pune Warriors 99-9** (20 overs); **Kings XI Punjab 100-2** (12.2 overs) (Mandeep Singh 31, M. Vohra 43*). MoM: M. Vohra. *Punjab began with a win: good fielding – especially Mandeep Singh's run-out of Marlon Samuels from deep midwicket – helped reduce Pune to 38-5 after ten overs. They eventually limped to 99-9, and Punjab won with 46 balls to spare as Manan Vohra, aged 19, batted responsibly on IPL debut.*

At Hyderabad (Uppal), April 7, 2013. **Sunrisers Hyderabad won after an eliminator over, following a tie.** ‡**Royal Challengers Bangalore 130-8** (20 overs) (V. Kohli 46, M. C. Henriques 44; I. Sharma 3-27); **Sunrisers Hyderabad 130-7** (20 overs) (G. H. Vihari 44*). MoM: G. H. Vihari. *For the second match running, Bangalore's Vinay Kumar bowled a tight 20th over. He conceded six to take the game to a tiebreaker, but then leaked 20 in the eliminator, which began with a no-ball and included two sixes by Cameron White. Gayle and Virat Kohli managed only 15 off Steyn in reply. Otherwise, the game belonged to 19-year-old Hanuma Vihari, whose first ball in the IPL tempted Gayle to nick behind. Vihari then led Hyderabad's run-chase, but failed to connect with the last delivery.*

At Jaipur, April 8, 2013. **Rajasthan Royals won by 19 runs. Rajasthan Royals 144-6** (20 overs) (A. M. Rahane 36, B. J. Hodge 46*); ‡**Kolkata Knight Riders 125** (19 overs) (E. J. G. Morgan 51; K. Cooper 3-15, S. K. Trivedi 3-23). MoM: S. K. Trivedi. *Kolkata slipped to 56-6 after 11 overs, rendering Eoin Morgan's 38-ball 51 an exercise in futility. Morgan had earlier caught Watson at extra cover when his bat handle broke, and play was held up after 13 overs because of a haze created by insect repellent at a bug-laden Sawai Mansingh Stadium.*

At Bangalore, April 9, 2013. **Royal Challengers Bangalore won by seven wickets.** ‡**Sunrisers Hyderabad 161-6** (20 overs) (C. L. White 52, N. L. T. C. Perera 40; R. P. Singh 3-27); **Royal Challengers Bangalore 162-3** (17.4 overs) (V. Kohli 93*). MoM: V. Kohli. *White and Perera, who added 80 from 44 balls, gave oomph to Hyderabad's sluggish start. But Kohli eclipsed both with 93* from 47 as Bangalore coasted home.*

At Mumbai (Wankhede), April 9, 2013. **Mumbai Indians won by 44 runs.** ‡**Mumbai Indians 209-5** (20 overs) (K. D. Karthik 86, R. G. Sharma 74*); **Delhi Daredevils 165-9** (20 overs) (D. A. Warner 61, M. C. Juneja 49). MoM: K. D. Karthik. *Mumbai fans feared the worst when Ricky Ponting was out in the opening over – caught at mid-off in a wicket maiden from Irfan Pathan – and Sachin Tendulkar run out in the next. But Dinesh Karthik (86 from 48 balls) and Rohit Sharma piled on 133 in 13 overs, and the eventual total proved well beyond Delhi once Warner sliced Mitchell Johnson to deep point for a 37-ball 61.*

At Mohali, April 10, 2013. **Chennai Super Kings won by ten wickets. Kings XI Punjab 138** (19.5 overs) (D. J. Hussey 41, Gurkeerat Singh 31; D. J. Bravo 3-27); ‡**Chennai Super Kings 139-0** (17.2 overs) (M. Vijay 50*, M. E. K. Hussey 86*). *MoM:* M. E. K. Hussey. *Punjab's last seven fell for 32; towards the end, Dhoni kept wicket with only his left glove to allow him a better aim at the stumps. Mike Hussey, on 22, survived a lucky run-out reprieve from the third umpire, allowing him to take his average against Punjab to 209.*

At Bangalore, April 11, 2013. **Royal Challengers Bangalore won by eight wickets. Kolkata Knight Riders 154-8** (20 overs) (G. Gambhir 59; R. P. Singh 3-27); ‡**Royal Challengers Bangalore 158-2** (17.3 overs) (C. H. Gayle 85*, V. Kohli 35). *MoM:* C. H. Gayle. *Gayle butchered nine sixes in 50 balls as Bangalore romped home with 15 deliveries to spare. Kolkata captain Gautam Gambhir top-scored for his side, but had to be separated from Indian team-mate Kohli after appearing to make a comment following Kohli's dismissal.*

At Gahunje, April 11, 2013. **Pune Warriors won by seven wickets. ‡Rajasthan Royals 145-5** (20 overs) (A. M. Rahane 30, R. S. Dravid 54); **Pune Warriors 148-3** (18.4 overs) (R. V. Uthappa 32, A. J. Finch 64). *MoM:* A. J. Finch. *Pune made sure a run of 11 successive defeats did not extend to a dirty dozen. Rajasthan looked to have a solid base at 80-1 after 11 overs, but Rahul Sharma's leg-spin (4–0–16–2) proved hard to get away. Aaron Finch then hit 64 from 53 balls.*

At Delhi, April 12, 2013. **Sunrisers Hyderabad won by three wickets. ‡Delhi Daredevils 114-8** (20 overs) (K. M. Jadhav 30*); **Sunrisers Hyderabad 115-7** (19.2 overs). *MoM:* A. Mishra. *Wickets fell regularly in a low-scoring game: Steyn had figures of 4–11–11–2, and later hit the winning runs as Hyderabad inflicted Delhi's fourth defeat out of four. Towards the end Mishra (whose leg-breaks had brought him 1-15 from four overs) was hit on the back by a throw at the stumps: Delhi appealed unsuccessfully for obstructing the field, but Mishra survived as he had not changed his line.*

At Mumbai (Wankhede), April 13, 2013. **Mumbai Indians won by 41 runs. ‡Mumbai Indians 183-3** (20 overs) (S. R. Tendulkar 44, K. D. Karthik 41, R. G. Sharma 62*); **Pune Warriors 142-8** (20 overs) (M. R. Marsh 38; M. G. Johnson 3-33). *MoM:* R. G. Sharma. *In his fourth game of IPL6, Tendulkar found his feet, stroking Ashok Dinda for four consecutive boundaries. But the real fireworks came from Sharma, who blazed 47 from his last 15 balls, as Dinda emerged with 4–0–63–0, then the joint-worst bowling figures in IPL history. The contest was over at 13-3, after Johnson seared his first and ninth balls through the defences of Finch and Robin Uthappa.*

At Chennai, April 13, 2013. **Chennai Super Kings won by four wickets. Royal Challengers Bangalore 165-6** (20 overs) (V. Kohli 58, A. B. de Villiers 64; C. H. Morris 3-40); ‡**Chennai Super Kings 166-6** (19.5 overs) (S. K. Raina 30, S. Badrinath 34, M. S. Dhoni 33, R. A. Jadeja 38*; R. Rampaul 3-31). *MoM:* R. A. Jadeja. *With Chennai needing two off the last ball, Ravindra Jadeja was caught at third man – only for a call of no-ball to snuff out Bangalore's celebrations: R. P. Singh had overstepped by a foot, and the batsmen completed what became the winning single. Earlier, A. B. de Villiers's 64 off 32 balls had underpinned Bangalore.*

At Kolkata, April 14, 2013. **Kolkata Knight Riders won by 48 runs. ‡Kolkata Knight Riders 180-4** (20 overs) (G. Gambhir 53, J. H. Kallis 41, E. J. G. Morgan 47); **Sunrisers Hyderabad 132-7** (20 overs) (C. L. White 34, N. L. T. C. Perera 36; J. H. Kallis 3-13). *MoM:* G. Gambhir. *Increasingly swift contributions from the Kolkata batsmen – Morgan faced 21 balls for his 47 – fired Kolkata to 180. Jacques Kallis derailed Hyderabad's reply with 3-13 from four overs.*

At Jaipur, April 14, 2013. **Rajasthan Royals won by six wickets. Kings XI Punjab 124** (18.5 overs) (D. J. Hussey 41); ‡**Rajasthan Royals 126-4** (19.2 overs) (S. R. Watson 32, A. M. Rahane 34*). *MoM:* J. P. Faulkner. *Rajasthan stumbled in pursuit of a modest target when smart catches by Gilchrist off Praveen Kumar accounted for Rahul Dravid and Stuart Binny. But opener Ajinkya Rahane kept calm and carried on, helped by 18-year-old debutant wicketkeeper Sanju Samson, who added 27* to three catches and a run-out.*

At Chennai, April 15, 2013. **Pune Warriors won by 24 runs. ‡Pune Warriors 159-5** (20 overs) (A. J. Finch 67, S. P. D. Smith 39*); **Chennai Super Kings 135-8** (20 overs) (S. Badrinath 34). *MoM:* S. P. D. Smith. *Finch struck seven fours in the powerplay, before Steve Smith rattled off three late sixes – the last an outrageous switch hit that landed beyond third man. Smith was in Pune's side only because the Tamil Nadu state government requested that Sri Lankans Angelo Mathews and Ajantha Mendis should not play on security grounds.*

At Mohali, April 16, 2013. **Kings XI Punjab won by four runs. Kings XI Punjab 157-9** (20 overs) (Mandeep Singh 41, M. S. Gony 42; J. H. Kallis 3-24, S. P. Narine 3-33); ‡**Kolkata Knight Riders**

153-9 (20 overs) (G. Gambhir 60, E. J. G. Morgan 47; Azhar Mahmood 3-21). *MoM:* M. S. Gony. *Manpreet Gony twice rescued Punjab. First he made 42 off 18 balls to lift them from 109-7. Then, with Gambhir and Morgan seemingly in charge, he embarked on a spell of three overs for seven, including the wicket of Gambhir, for a 39-ball 60. From 106-2, Kolkata declined sharply, and could manage only six of the 11 they needed from the final over, bowled by Praveen Kumar.*

At Bangalore, April 16, 2013. **Royal Challengers Bangalore won after an eliminator over, following a tie. Delhi Daredevils 152-5** (20 overs); **‡Royal Challengers Bangalore 152-7** (20 overs) (V. Kohli 65, A. B. de Villiers 39). *MoM:* V. Kohli. *Bangalore made a meal of a victory that, with 24 needed from 25 balls and eight wickets in hand, should have been a doddle. But they imploded on a sluggish pitch, and were saved from defeat by Ravi Rampaul, who smashed a last-over six and scrambled a bye off the final ball to prompt a super over. De Villiers walloped two sixes off Umesh Yadav, setting Delhi 16; Rampaul then conceded 11, as Bangalore put their choke behind them.*

At Gahunje, April 17, 2013. **Sunrisers Hyderabad won by 11 runs. Sunrisers Hyderabad 119-8** (20 overs) (B. B. Samantray 37, A. Mishra 30; Bhuvneshwar Kumar 3-18); **‡Pune Warriors 108** (19 overs) (N. L. T. C. Perera 3-20, A. Mishra 4-19). *MoM:* A. Mishra. *When Pune reached 101-4 in the 17th over the game looked finished – but Mishra had other ideas. After two wickets fell at the other end, he dismissed Mathews with the second ball of the 19th, then polished the match off with his third IPL hat-trick, pinning Bhuvneshwar Kumar in front with a googly, before bowling Sharma and Dinda; the over went 1W1WW.*

At Jaipur, April 17, 2013. **Rajasthan Royals won by 87 runs. ‡Rajasthan Royals 179-3** (20 overs) (S. R. Watson 31, A. M. Rahane 68*, D. H. Yagnik 34); **Mumbai Indians 92** (18.2 overs) (K. D. Karthik 30; J. P. Faulkner 3-16). *MoM:* A. M. Rahane. *Rajasthan decided against picking Sreesanth on fitness grounds, and off-spinner Ajit Chandila opened the bowling instead. He removed Tendulkar, top-edging a sweep, and Ponting, via a return catch, in his first two overs, as Mumbai crashed to their heaviest IPL defeat. Rajasthan opener Rahane then played a pragmatic hand.*

At Delhi, April 18, 2013. **Chennai Super Kings won by 86 runs. ‡Chennai Super Kings 169-4** (20 overs) (M. E. K. Hussey 65*, S. K. Raina 30, M. S. Dhoni 44); **Delhi Daredevils 83** (17.3 overs) (K. M. Jadhav 31; M. Sharma 3-10). *MoM:* M. E. K. Hussey. *Delhi slumped to their eighth straight defeat dating back to IPL5 – their worst sequence – after slipping to their lowest total.*

At Hyderabad (Uppal), April 19, 2013. **Sunrisers Hyderabad won by five wickets. ‡Kings XI Punjab 123-9** (20 overs); **Sunrisers Hyderabad 127-5** (18.5 overs) (G. H. Vihari 46). *MoM:* G. H. Vihari. *Unfancied Hyderabad went top of the table after snatching a low-scoring contest on a pitch taking spin. With 18 needed from two overs, Perera smote Azhar Mahmood for three sixes in five (legitimate) deliveries. Punjab had foundered after reaching 88-3 from 14 overs, and at one stage wickets fell to four successive balls.*

At Kolkata, April 20, 2013. **Chennai Super Kings won by four wickets. ‡Kolkata Knight Riders 119-9** (20 overs) (R. A. Jadeja 3-20); **Chennai Super Kings 124-6** (19.1 overs) (M. E. K. Hussey 40, R. A. Jadeja 36*). *MoM:* R. A. Jadeja. *After their openers put on 46, Kolkata lost their way – with Kallis run out by Badrinath's direct hit from backward point without facing a ball. Hussey anchored Chennai's sedate reply, before departing at 89-6 in the 17th over. But Jadeja spanked 36* from 13 balls, winning the match with his third six, off Yusuf Pathan, who had just dropped him at backward square leg.*

At Bangalore, April 20, 2013. **Royal Challengers Bangalore won by seven wickets. Rajasthan Royals 117** (19.4 overs) (R. Dravid 35, S. T. R. Binny 33; R. P. Singh 3-13, R. Vinay Kumar 3-18); **‡Royal Challengers Bangalore 123-3** (17.5 overs) (C. H. Gayle 49*). *MoM:* R. Vinay Kumar. *On the day he resigned Australia's vice-captaincy, Shane Watson – after declining to bowl on their tour of India – took wickets in his first two overs of 2013, though Rajasthan were already heading for defeat. Vinay Kumar and R. P. Singh had earlier cut through Rajasthan's middle order.*

At Delhi, April 21, 2013. **Delhi Daredevils won by nine wickets. ‡Mumbai Indians 161-4** (20 overs) (S. R. Tendulkar 54, R. G. Sharma 73); **Delhi Daredevils 165-1** (17 overs) (D. P. M. D. Jayawardene 59, V. Sehwag 95*). *MoM:* V. Sehwag. *Delhi won their first game of the season, at the seventh attempt, after Sehwag (57 balls) and Jayawardene began with 151 in 15.5 overs. Mumbai's total on a slow track had been based around Sharma's powerful 73 from 43 deliveries.*

At Mohali, April 21, 2013. **Kings XI Punjab won by seven wickets. Pune Warriors 185-4** (20 overs) (R. V. Uthappa 37, A. J. Finch 64, Yuvraj Singh 34, L. J. Wright 34); **‡Kings XI Punjab 186-3** (19.5 overs) (Mandeep Singh 77*, D. A. Miller 80*). *MoM:* D. A. Miller. *Punjab needed 16* *off the last over, bowled by Luke Wright. Singles came from the first two balls, heaping pressure on David Miller, who responded with six, two and six to see them home with a delivery to spare. Wright had earlier given Pune quite a send-off: he hit his first six balls for four, and fell in the last over for a ten-ball 34.*

At Chennai, April 22, 2013. **Chennai Super Kings won by five wickets. ‡Rajasthan Royals 185-4** (20 overs) (S. R. Watson 101, S. T. R. Binny 36*); **Chennai Super Kings 186-5** (19.5 overs) (M. E. K. Hussey 88, S. K. Raina 51; J. P. Faulkner 3-20). *MoM: M. E. K. Hussey. Hussey biffed 88 from 51 balls – and put on 90 in ten overs with Raina – to negate Watson's 101 from 61 balls, which included six sixes. Watson's misery was compounded when Dwayne Bravo hit the winning six off his penultimate ball.*

At Delhi, April 23, 2013. **Kings XI Punjab won by five wickets. Delhi Daredevils 120-7** (20 overs) (D. A. Warner 40; H. S. Bansal 3-24); **‡Kings XI Punjab 121-5** (17 overs) (D. A. Miller 34*). *MoM: H. S. Bansal. Punjab cakewalked a low-key game with three overs to spare after Delhi failed to establish any momentum on another slow track at the Feroz Shah Kotla. David Hussey's off-breaks returned 4–0–14–0 – indicative of the nature of the pitch.*

At Bangalore, April 23, 2013. **Royal Challengers Bangalore won by 130 runs. Royal Challengers Bangalore 263-5** (20 overs) (C. H. Gayle 175*, T. M. Dilshan 33, A. B. de Villiers 31); **‡Pune Warriors 133-9** (20 overs) (S. P. D. Smith 41). *MoM: C. H. Gayle. Gayle shattered records and bowlers' confidence with an unbeaten 175 from 66 balls – one of the most phenomenal exhibitions of hitting seen in the professional game. Among the Twenty20 records he reset were: fastest hundred*

GAYLE v PUNE'S BOWLERS

	Balls	Runs	4	6	Dots	SR
A. J. Finch (LM)	5	28	1	4	0	560.00
A. G. Murtaza (SLA)	10	43	3	5	2	430.00
M. R. Marsh (RM)	12	37	1	5	4	308.33
I. C. Pandey (RM)	9	22	5	0	2	244.44
A. B. Dinda (RFM)	10	18	0	2	2	180.00
Bhuvneshwar Kumar (RFM)	7	11	2	0	2	157.14
L. J. Wright (RFM)	13	16	1	1	6	123.07

175 NOT OUT – BALL BY BALL

• • 1 // 4 4 • 4 4 • 4 // 1 // 6 6 4 • 6 6 [50 from 17 balls]

// // 4 6 1 6 • // 6 6 4 6 6 // • 1 6 [102 from 30 balls] 1 // •

1 1 • // 1 1 // • • 6 1 wd • // 1 • 1 6 // 4 1 // 4 6 wd 6

6 [153 from 53 balls] // 1 1 // • 1 // 4 1 4 1 // 1 wd • // 6 1 1

(at 30 balls, it was four quicker than Andrew Symonds for Kent v Middlesex in 2004); highest individual score (17 more than Brendon McCullum made for Kolkata v Bangalore on this ground in the first IPL match, in 2007-08); most sixes in an innings (17 was one more than Graham Napier struck for Essex v Sussex in 2008), and most runs in boundaries (154 surpassed Napier by 18). With de Villiers smacking 31 off eight balls, Bangalore made the highest Twenty20 total (263 was three more than Sri Lanka made against Kenya in the inaugural World Twenty20, in 2007-08), and the most team sixes in an innings (21 beat the 18 hit by Namibia against Scotland in 2011-12). Gayle had a customary careful start, nudging only a single from three balls as he sized up the pitch. It was a good one: only one of his 30 boundaries qualified as a mis-hit, when he thick-edged Ali Murtaza through third man. Dinda also beat him outside off stump with a yorker, but three balls later Gayle hoisted a six to reach his hundred. Pune's bowlers persisted with a full length, allowing Gayle to hit through the line; Pandey, Finch, Marsh and Murtaza all went for 20 or more in an over. Pune's improbable target became close to impossible when Uthappa fell second ball. With 136 required off the last over, Kohli threw Gayle the ball; he removed two of the bowlers he had just tormented.

CORRUPTION AT THE IPL

Notes on a scandal

May 14   Mumbai police arrest Ramesh Vyas, an alleged bookmaker, leading to a trail of other bookies in Delhi.

May 16   Delhi police arrest three Rajasthan Royals bowlers – Sreesanth, Ajit Chandila and Ankeet Chavan – on suspicion of fulfilling promises to bookies, in return for sums of $36,000 to $109,000. The BCCI suspend the players pending an inquiry. Eleven bookies are also arrested, including Amit Singh, a former Rajasthan player released by the franchise the previous year. Police pinpoint three Rajasthan matches: v Pune Warriors on May 5, Kings XI Punjab on May 9, and Mumbai Indians on May 15.

May 17   Sreesanth's lawyer maintains he is "totally innocent". Kent R-O Systems, a water purifying company, are the first team sponsor to withdraw adverts featuring him. Rajiv Shukla, the IPL chairman, says the "strongest possible action will be taken against the guilty".

May 18   Police seize the belongings of Sreesanth and Jiju Janardhan, a suspected middleman who had been posing as his agent, from a Mumbai hotel.

May 19   After an emergency meeting of their working committee, the BCCI appoint their first anti-corruption head, Ravi Sawani, to lead an inquiry into the allegations.

May 20   Rajasthan file a police complaint against the three players, and suspend their contracts. The BCCI assign additional anti-corruption officers to the four remaining teams in IPL 2013. India's union law minister, Kapil Sibal, says fixing in sport should become a criminal offence.

May 22   Delhi police commissioner Neeraj Kumar says the BCCI "should maintain a better vigil" of corruption in the IPL.

May 23   The Pakistani umpire Asad Rauf is withdrawn from the Champions Trophy, after it emerged he was under investigation for corruption; he had flown out of the country a few days earlier.

May 24   Mumbai police arrest Gurunath Meiyappan, a leading Chennai Super Kings official and son-in-law of BCCI president N. Srinivasan, on charges of cheating, forgery and fraud.

May 25   Srinivasan maintains Meiyappan will be dealt with "objectively and fairly" by the BCCI.

May 26   The BCCI suspend Meiyappan from involvement in cricket pending the outcome of investigations. Srinivasan is booed at the presentation ceremony after the IPL final in Kolkata.

May 28   The IPL governing council appoint a three-member commission – comprising BCCI secretary Sanjay Jagdale and two former high court judges – to look into allegations of corruption against Meiyappan and India Cements, and Raj Kundra, co-owner of Rajasthan Royals.

May 29   Shukla warns Srinivasan to "stay away" from the commission's inquiry. India's sports ministry calls for Srinivasan to resign. In Lahore, Rauf denies any involvement in corruption.

May 31   Jagdale and BCCI treasurer Ajay Shirke resign; Jagdale also steps down from the commission. Srinivasan denies knowledge of an alleged warning from the ICC about Meiyappan before IPL 2013. Rajasthan bowler Siddarth Trivedi appears at a Delhi district court. He tells reporters he had rejected multiple fixing approaches from bookies.

Jun 1	Shukla resigns as IPL chairman.
Jun 2	Two members of the IPL governing council confess they were unaware how and when the three-member commission was set up. Srinivasan steps aside as president until the commission complete their investigation, but continues to represent the board at ICC level. He is replaced on day-to-day matters by Jagmohan Dalmiya, a former BCCI president and now head of the Cricket Association of Bengal.
Jun 6	Kundra admits betting on IPL matches, some involving Rajasthan, through Umesh Goenka, his partner in the steel industry. Dalmiya appoints Sanjay Patel as BCCI secretary, but declines to restore a third member to the investigating commission.
Jun 10	The BCCI suspend Kundra pending investigations, and announce a 12-point "operation clean-up" of the IPL to take effect before the 2014 competition.
Jul 6	Harmeet Singh, a 20-year-old Rajasthan spinner, is questioned by Sawani amid reports he met with Jitender Singh, a bookie recently arrested in connection with the spot-fixing probe.
Jul 28	The judges' report finds "no evidence of wrongdoing" by Kundra or India Cements.
Jul 30	Delhi police charge 39 people – including Sreesanth, Chandila and Chavan – for offences under the Indian Penal Code and local organised-crime laws. Bombay High Court rules that the BCCI's two-member commission was constituted illegally, as they did not replace Jagdale with a member of the Code of Behaviour committee.
Aug 3	Chavan says he is "shocked" at the allegations against him, and denies being approached by fixers.
Sep 13	The BCCI's disciplinary committee ban Sreesanth and Chavan for life. Amit Singh receives a five-year ban, while Trivedi is suspended for a year from BCCI-organised cricket for failing to report an approach. In their only departure from Sawani's recommendations, Harmeet is let off due to a lack of evidence. A decision is deferred on Chandila.
Sep 16	Sreesanth claims his confession was forced from him by police under duress.
Sep 21	Mumbai police charge Meiyappan with cheating, forgery and criminal conspiracy, and also with betting against his own team – but not with any fixing offences. Rauf is named as a "wanted accused" for leaving India before he could be questioned.
Sep 27	The Supreme Court of India clear Srinivasan to contest BCCI elections, but warn he cannot take charge as president while hearings are ongoing.
Sep 29	Srinivasan, the only candidate, is re-elected president at the BCCI's AGM.
Oct 1	In his autobiography, Mike Hussey, the Chennai batsman, claims Srinivasan "gave control of the team to his son-in-law Mr Gurunath. He ran the team along with Kepler Wessels, who was coach". Hussey later backtracks.
Oct 8	The Supreme Court of India clear Srinivasan to resume his duties as president, as long as he stays clear of IPL matters.
Oct 9	Supreme Court appoint a new three-member commission, headed by Justice Mukul Mudgal, to investigate the allegations of spot-fixing and betting.
Feb 10, 2014	Mudgal's commission finds Meiyappan guilty of betting and passing on information, and rules he was the "face of Chennai Super Kings". Their report requests further investigations against Kundra.

Research by James Coyne

At Kolkata, April 24, 2013. **Mumbai Indians won by five wickets. ‡Kolkata Knight Riders 159-6** (20 overs) (J. H. Kallis 37, M. K. Tiwary 33, E. J. G. Morgan 31); **Mumbai Indians 162-5** (19.5 overs) (D. R. Smith 62, R. G. Sharma 34, K. A. Pollard 33; S. P. Narine 3-17). *MoM:* D. R. Smith. *Harbhajan Singh began the match by haemorrhaging 26 runs in the first over, but made up for it in the last by smashing his first ball for six. Narine – who picked up 3-17, including Dwayne Smith for a curate's-egg 62 – had been the main concern for Mumbai, who won off the penultimate ball.*

At Chennai, April 25, 2013. **Chennai Super Kings won by five wickets. ‡Sunrisers Hyderabad 159-6** (20 overs) (S. Dhawan 63*, A. Ashish Reddy 36*); **Chennai Super Kings 160-5** (19.4 overs) (M. E. K. Hussey 45, M. S. Dhoni 67*; A. Mishra 3-26). *MoM:* M. S. Dhoni. *Shikhar Dhawan stroked ten fours on his Hyderabad debut, despite briefly retiring after being hit in the groin. Late fireworks from Ashish Reddy at No. 8 ensured a handy total. Chennai started slowly and, after three wickets for the prolific Mishra and a maiden from another leg-spinner, Karan Sharma (4–1–8–0), needed 46 from four overs. Steyn was unusually expensive (4–0–45–1), and Dhoni supervised Chennai's fourth straight victory with 67* from 37 balls.*

At Kolkata, April 26, 2013. **Kolkata Knight Riders won by six wickets. ‡Kings XI Punjab 149-6** (20 overs) (M. Vohra 31); **Kolkata Knight Riders 150-4** (18.2 overs) (M. Bisla 51*, J. H. Kallis 37, E. J. G. Morgan 42; Azhar Mahmood 3-35). *MoM:* J. H. Kallis. *Kallis shrugged off a knee injury to claim 2-14 from four overs, then hit 37. The over after Kallis was out, Morgan wound up for a sweep at Piyush Chawla. He missed, the ball brushed leg stump, but the bail stayed in the groove; Morgan went on to strike four sixes.*

At Jaipur, April 27, 2013. **Rajasthan Royals won by eight wickets. ‡Sunrisers Hyderabad 144-9** (20 overs) (D. J. G. Sammy 60; J. P. Faulkner 5-20); **Rajasthan Royals 146-2** (17.5 overs) (R. Dravid 36, S. R. Watson 98*). *MoM:* J. P. Faulkner. *Watson's brutal 53-ball 98* sped Rajasthan home with 13 balls to spare after left-arm seamer James Faulkner had picked up the first five-for of IPL6. He helped reduce Hyderabad to 29-6, before Darren Sammy hit back, celebrating his half-century by sucking on a pink dummy in honour of his new baby daughter.*

At Mumbai (Wankhede), April 27, 2013. **Mumbai Indians won by 58 runs. ‡Mumbai Indians 194-7** (20 overs) (D. R. Smith 50, K. D. Karthik 43, K. A. Pollard 34); **Royal Challengers Bangalore 136-7** (20 overs) (D. S. Kulkarni 3-19). *MoM:* D. R. Smith. *Gayle returned to earth after his unbeaten 175, caught for 18 off a thick edge that almost carried over the midwicket boundary, sparking a Gangnam-style celebration from the bowler, Harbhajan Singh. Bangalore's chase never fully recovered. Dhawal Kulkarni's medium-pace accounted for three top-order wickets. Earlier, Dwayne Smith was the backbone of the Mumbai innings.*

At Chennai, April 28, 2013. **Chennai Super Kings won by 14 runs. Chennai Super Kings 200-3** (20 overs) (W. P. Saha 39, M. E. K. Hussey 95, S. K. Raina 44); **‡Kolkata Knight Riders 186-4** (20 overs) (M. Bisla 92, E. J. G. Morgan 32*). *MoM:* M. E. K. Hussey. *Hussey again dominated the Chennai innings, this time clattering 95 from 59 balls. Kolkata's reply began in bizarre style: Dirk Nannes sent down a wide that flew to the boundary, followed by a front-foot no-ball; the free-hit delivery then ricocheted off the stumps for four byes, making the score 10-0 before a legal delivery had been bowled. Despite that, and Manvinder Bisla's 92 from 61 balls, Kolkata couldn't prevent Chennai's fifth successive victory, which put them top of the table.*

At Raipur, April 28, 2013. **Delhi Daredevils won by 15 runs. Delhi Daredevils 164-5** (20 overs) (D. A. Warner 51*; A. B. Dinda 3-31); **‡Pune Warriors 149-4** (20 overs) (R. V. Uthappa 37, A. J. Finch 37, Yuvraj Singh 31). *MoM:* D. A. Warner. *Raipur is roughly 200km closer to Pune than Delhi, but an overwhelmingly pro-Daredevils "home" crowd got the result they wanted on the city's IPL debut, thanks to 51* from 25 balls by Warner.*

At Jaipur, April 29, 2013. **Rajasthan Royals won by four wickets. Royal Challengers Bangalore 171-6** (20 overs) (C. H. Gayle 34, V. Kohli 32; S. R. Watson 3-22); **‡Rajasthan Royals 173-6** (19.5 overs) (S. V. Samson 63, S. R. Watson 41, B. J. Hodge 32). *MoM:* S. V. Samson. *Samson was the star in only his second IPL game, hitting 63 off 41 deliveries. A late stumble meant Rajasthan completed victory with just one ball to spare, highlighting the value of Watson's economic seamers.*

At Mumbai (Wankhede), April 29, 2013. **Mumbai Indians won by four runs. ‡Mumbai Indians 174-3** (20 overs) (D. R. Smith 33, R. G. Sharma 79*); **Kings XI Punjab 170** (20 overs) (D. J. Hussey 34, D. A. Miller 56; Harbhajan Singh 3-14). *MoM:* R. G. Sharma. *Punjab, their last pair at the crease, needed 26 from two overs. Nine came from the 19th, then Praveen Kumar, aided by a series of full tosses from Kulkarni, took it to the last ball: five to win; four would trigger a super over. Instead Kumar picked out point, though the tension continued as the umpires checked the* *ball – another full toss – for height; they decided it was legitimate. Sharma had given the Mumbai innings a rousing conclusion by smashing 79* from 39 deliveries and outscoring Pollard, who later held a breathtaking one-handed catch on the boundary.*

At Gahunje, April 30, 2013. **Chennai Super Kings won by 37 runs.** ‡**Chennai Super Kings 164-3** (20 overs) (S. K. Raina 63*, S. Badrinath 34, M. S. Dhoni 45*); **Pune Warriors 127-9** (20 overs) (S. P. D. Smith 35; M. Sharma 3-21). *MoM:* M. S. Dhoni. *Hussey failed for once, but Raina ensured a serviceable total for table-toppers Chennai. Then Mohit Sharma took three wickets in seven balls to reduce Pune to 43-4; there was no way back.*

At Hyderabad (Uppal), May 1, 2013. **Sunrisers Hyderabad won by seven wickets.** ‡**Mumbai Indians 129-4** (20 overs) (D. R. Smith 38, A. T. Rayudu 34*); **Sunrisers Hyderabad 130-3** (18 overs) (S. Dhawan 73*). *MoM:* I. Sharma (Mumbai Indians). *Tendulkar had the better of an early bout with Steyn, before Ishant Sharma (4–1–15–2) bowled him, and ensured Mumbai rarely got out of third gear. Dhawan broke free in the 12th over to make 73* from 55 balls.*

At Raipur, May 1, 2013. **Delhi Daredevils won by seven wickets.** ‡**Kolkata Knight Riders 136-7** (20 overs); **Delhi Daredevils 137-3** (17.5 overs) (U. Chand 37, D. A. Warner 66*). *MoM:* D. A. Warner. *Warner settled the matter with three sixes in a 42-ball 66, after Kolkata's batsmen had been kept quiet by Irfan Pathan (4–0–16–1) and seamer Sumit Narwal (4 –1–23–1).*

At Chennai, May 2, 2013. **Chennai Super Kings won by 15 runs.** ‡**Chennai Super Kings 186-4** (20 overs) (M. E. K. Hussey 35, S. K. Raina 100*); **Kings XI Punjab 171-6** (20 overs) (S. E. Marsh 73, D. A. Miller 51*; D. J. Bravo 3-34). *MoM:* S. K. Raina. *Raina's first IPL hundred, reached from his 53rd ball, was at the heart of Chennai's daunting total. Punjab began slowly, but Marsh and Miller put on 95 in 51 deliveries to bring the task down to 19 from the last over. Three wickets for Bravo secured a seventh successive win for Chennai.*

At Gahunje, May 2, 2013. **Royal Challengers Bangalore won by 17 runs.** ‡**Royal Challengers Bangalore 187-3** (20 overs) (S. S. Tiwary 52, A. B. de Villiers 50*); **Pune Warriors 170-9** (20 overs) (R. V. Uthappa 75, A. D. Mathews 32; R. Vinay Kumar 3-31). *MoM:* A. B. de Villiers. *Pune, propping up the table, conceded a big total that had been boosted by de Villiers's innovative 50* from 23 balls. Uthappa blasted five sixes in his 75 from 45 deliveries, but couldn't prevent Bangalore's first away win of the season.*

At Kolkata, May 3, 2013. **Kolkata Knight Riders won by eight wickets.** ‡**Rajasthan Royals 132-6** (20 overs) (S. R. Watson 35, S. V. Samson 40); **Kolkata Knight Riders 133-2** (17.2 overs) (J. H. Kallis 33*, Y. K. Pathan 50*). *MoM:* Y. K. Pathan. *Rahul Dravid's attempt to unsettle Kolkata by sending in Faulkner at No. 3, and himself at No. 8 – his lowest spot in a professional match – backfired when they made only seven between them.*

At Hyderabad (Uppal), May 4, 2013. **Sunrisers Hyderabad won by six wickets.** ‡**Delhi Daredevils 80** (19.1 overs); **Sunrisers Hyderabad 81-4** (13.5 overs). *MoM:* D. J. G. Sammy. *Hyderabad made it five wins in a row after Delhi were bundled out for what was then the lowest score of the tournament. Only four of their batsmen reached double figures – none higher than Chand's 17 – as the last eight fell for 30.*

At Mumbai (Wankhede), May 5, 2013. **Mumbai Indians won by 60 runs.** ‡**Mumbai Indians 139-5** (20 overs) (R. G. Sharma 39*; R. A. Jadeja 3-29); **Chennai Super Kings 79** (15.2 overs) (M. G. Johnson 3-27, P. P. Ojha 3-11). *MoM:* M. G. Johnson. *Between innings, Chennai looked on course for an unprecedented eighth consecutive IPL win after limiting Mumbai to 139. And it quickly seemed luck was a close ally: from the fourth, fifth and sixth ball of their reply, Pollard, at point, dropped Hussey. But Johnson, the unlucky bowler, made up for lost time with three wickets in the third over. By the 16th, Chennai were shot down for 79, their lowest IPL total – and the lowest of IPL6.*

At Jaipur, May 5, 2013. **Rajasthan Royals won by five wickets.** ‡**Pune Warriors 178-4** (20 overs) (R. V. Uthappa 54, A. J. Finch 45, M. R. Marsh 35*); **Rajasthan Royals 182-5** (19.5 overs) (R. Dravid 58, A. M. Rahane 67, S. T. R. Binny 32*; W. D. Parnell 3-27). *MoM:* A. M. Rahane. *An opening stand of 98 in 12 overs between Dravid and Rahane helped preserve Rajasthan's unbeaten home record. The match later featured in the investigations into spot-fixing, following the arrests of Sreesanth and two other Rajasthan players. The police alleged opening bowler Ajit Chandila agreed to concede 14 runs in his second over (he did, and was taken off, but reportedly ran into trouble with the bookies after forgetting to make the prearranged signal that the fix was on).*

At Mohali, May 6, 2013. **Kings XI Punjab won by six wickets. Royal Challengers Bangalore 190-3** (20 overs) (C. A. Pujara 51, C. H. Gayle 61, A. B. de Villiers 38*); ‡**Kings XI Punjab 194-4**

(18 overs) (D. A. Miller 101*). *MoM:* D. A. Miller. *"If it's in the V, it's in the tree; if it's in the arc, it's out of the park" – Bangalore's bowlers offered Miller plenty of both, enough for him to apply his father's mantra with a phenomenal century, at 38 balls the sixth-fastest in Twenty20, and third only to Gayle (30) and Yusuf Pathan (37) in IPL matches. Miller completed victory and his hundred with his seventh six. Kohli spilled him on 42, and Miller responded by taking Vinay Kumar for 14 off the next three balls, and for 26 next over. Rajagopal Sathish contributed just 27 to their partnership of 130, as 99 flowed from the final five overs. That made the hundred partnership between Gayle (61 from 33 balls) and Pujara (with a maiden Twenty20 fifty from 45) seem sedate.*

At Jaipur, May 7, 2013. **Rajasthan Royals won by nine wickets.** ‡**Delhi Daredevils 154-4** (20 overs) (D. P. M. D. Jayawardene 34, B. J. Rohrer 64*); **Rajasthan Royals 155-1** (17.5 overs) (R. Dravid 53, A. M. Rahane 63*). *MoM:* A. M. Rahane. *Rajasthan moved into second place with their seventh straight home win – and Delhi's ninth loss in 12 – after Dravid and Rahane made light of a tricky target with 108 in 13.4 overs. Rajasthan included leg-spinner Pravin Tambe (4–0–30–0), making his senior debut aged 41.*

At Mumbai (Wankhede), May 7, 2013. **Mumbai Indians won by 65 runs.** ‡**Mumbai Indians 170-6** (20 overs) (D. R. Smith 47, S. R. Tendulkar 48, K. D. Karthik 34*); **Kolkata Knight Riders 105** (18.2 overs) (Harbhajan Singh 3-27). *MoM:* S. R. Tendulkar. *A floodlight failure stopped Tendulkar in his tracks when he had 29 from 17 balls, including five successive fours off Ryan McLaren (whose four overs cost 60). It hardly bothered Mumbai, who moved second after Kolkata botched the chase.*

At Hyderabad (Uppal), May 8, 2013. **Chennai Super Kings won by 77 runs. Chennai Super Kings 223-3** (20 overs) (M. E. K. Hussey 67, S. K. Raina 99*; N. L. T. C. Perera 3-45); ‡**Sunrisers Hyderabad 146-8** (20 overs) (P. A. Patel 44, K. V. Sharma 39*). *MoM:* S. K. Raina. *Raina clouted three sixes and 11 fours from 52 balls, and became the first to be stranded on 99* in the IPL (two days later Kohli became the first to be out for 99). Ishant Sharma's four wicketless overs cost 66, the most expensive analysis in the IPL. Hyderabad lost at home for the first time.*

At Mohali, May 9, 2013. **Rajasthan Royals won by eight wickets. Kings XI Punjab 145-6** (20 overs) (A. C. Gilchrist 42, S. E. Marsh 77; K. Cooper 3-23); ‡**Rajasthan Royals 147-2** (19 overs) (A. M. Rahane 59*, S. R. Watson 31, S. V. Samson 47*). *MoM:* K. Cooper. *Canny bowling at the death by Cooper and Faulkner undid the fine work of Gilchrist – captaining Punjab after leaving himself out for three games – and Marsh, who put on 102 for the second wicket. Samson sparkled in a late stand of 76 with Rahane. The two overs bowled for 18 by Sreesanth at the start of the match soon came under the scanner in the spot-fixing scandal. It was later claimed he was supposed to have conceded 14 from his second over. He leaked only 13 but, in a phone conversation with a bookmaker taped by Delhi police, Sreesanth complained that a deliberate no-ball had been missed by the umpire: "What's my fault if the umpire didn't notice?"*

At Gahunje, May 9, 2013. **Kolkata Knight Riders won by 46 runs.** ‡**Kolkata Knight Riders 152-6** (20 overs) (G. Gambhir 50, R. N. ten Doeschate 31; Bhuvneshwar Kumar 3-25); **Pune Warriors 106** (19.3 overs) (R. V. Uthappa 31, A. D. Mathews 40; L. Balaji 3-19). *MoM:* G. Gambhir. *Nine Pune batsmen fell in single figures en route to their 11th defeat; Mathews' four sixes were in vain. Kolkata had themselves stumbled to 97-5 in the 16th over, but Ryan ten Doeschate (21 balls) supplied late zip. For the first time of his career, seamer Bhuvneshwar Kumar had a batsman stumped (Bisla) when Mahesh Rawat stood up to him.*

At Delhi, May 10, 2013. **Royal Challengers Bangalore won by four runs. Royal Challengers Bangalore 183-4** (20 overs) (V. Kohli 99, A. B. de Villiers 32*); ‡**Delhi Daredevils 179-7** (20 overs) (U. Chand 41, B. J. Rohrer 32; J. D. Unadkat 5-25). *MoM:* J. D. Unadkat. *Kohli enjoyed two lives – caught off a no-ball from his first delivery, then dropped on 14 – though he was run out at the end of the innings attempting a second that would have brought a century from 58 balls. He was especially severe on Yadav, whose last two overs disappeared for 47, giving him figures of 4–0–65–0, the second-most expensive in IPL history. Delhi kept in touch with the rate, despite five wickets for Jaydev Unadkat.*

At Gahunje, May 11, 2013. **Mumbai Indians won by five wickets.** ‡**Pune Warriors 112-8** (20 overs) (Yuvraj Singh 33); **Mumbai Indians 116-5** (18.5 overs) (R. G. Sharma 37). *MoM:* M. G. Johnson. *Johnson (4–0–8–2), Abu Nechim and Lasith Malinga (both 2-27) made regular inroads as Pune were restricted to 112. Despite the first-ball loss of Dwayne Smith, Mumbai were unworried and unhurried, inflicting Pune's 12th defeat out of 14 and going second in the table.*

At Mohali, May 11, 2013. **Sunrisers Hyderabad won by 30 runs. Sunrisers Hyderabad 150-7** (20 overs) (P. A. Patel 61, N. L. T. C. Perera 29*; S. Sharma 3-21); ‡**Kings XI Punjab 120-9**

(20 overs) (L. A. Pomersbach 33*; D. J. G. Sammy 4-22). *MoM:* P. A. Patel. *Both teams were guilty of shoddy fielding and strokeplay – but ultimately it was Luke Pomersbach's pedestrian 33* from 40 balls that cost Punjab. With green patches at either end, Hyderabad targeted line and length as if in a first-class match. Parthiv Patel survived a fine spell from Sandeep Sharma, then profited from a Gilchrist miss and off-key death bowling to hit his first IPL fifty for three years.*

At Ranchi, May 12, 2013. **Kolkata Knight Riders won by five wickets. Royal Challengers Bangalore 115-9** (20 overs) (C. H. Gayle 33; S. P. Narine 4-22); ‡**Kolkata Knight Riders 116-5** (19.2 overs) (J. H. Kallis 41). *MoM:* J. H. Kallis. *The first IPL game to be staged at Ranchi – birthplace of M. S. Dhoni, though his Chennai team weren't involved here – brought a routine victory for Kolkata, the nominal home side. Narine masterminded Bangalore's collapse from 70-2: the stumping of Gayle was the first of eight wickets for 35.*

At Jaipur, May 12, 2013. **Rajasthan Royals won by five wickets. Chennai Super Kings 141-4** (20 overs) (M. E. K. Hussey 40, M. Vijay 55); ‡**Rajasthan Royals 144-5** (17.1 overs) (S. R. Watson 70, S. T. R. Binny 41*). *MoM:* S. R. Watson. *On a seaming pitch, Chennai failed to build on a foundation of 83-0 in the 12th over – yet when Rajasthan were floundering at 45-4 in the tenth, a total of 141 looked plenty. Then Watson, who faced 34 balls, and Binny (23) cut loose.*

At Mumbai (Wankhede), May 13, 2013. **Mumbai Indians won by seven wickets.** ‡**Sunrisers Hyderabad 178-3** (20 overs) (S. Dhawan 59, G. H. Vihari 41, C. L. White 43*); **Mumbai Indians 184-3** (19.3 overs) (S. R. Tendulkar 38*, K. D. Karthik 30, K. A. Pollard 66*). *MoM:* K. A. Pollard. *At 99-3 in the 14th over, Mumbai looked in trouble, but Pollard smashed 66* from 27 balls to put them top of the table. Pollard hit six sixes in seven balls from Perera (whose third over cost 29) and Mishra; and when Perera returned for the last over, Pollard smashed him for two more. Earlier, Tendulkar retired after injuring his left wrist; he played no further part in the tournament.*

At Bangalore, May 14, 2013. **Kings XI Punjab won by seven wickets. Royal Challengers Bangalore 174-5** (20 overs) (C. H. Gayle 77, V. Kohli 57; P. Awana 3-39); ‡**Kings XI Punjab 176-3** (18.1 overs) (A. C. Gilchrist 85*, Azhar Mahmood 61). *MoM:* A. C. Gilchrist. *A one-off switch to lime-green kits – in support of the environmental charity Go Green! – did little for Bangalore's attack, who endured a stand of 118 between Gilchrist and Azhar Mahmood. Gilchrist said he "scratched around like a chook" at the start, and was lucky to survive being plumb to Muralitharan's doosra and to receive the match award ahead of Mahmood. Gayle mislaid his timing at first, and escaped a convincing lbw shout from Parvinder Awana, but managed to club six sixes as he and Kohli put on 136.*

At Chennai, May 14, 2013. **Chennai Super Kings won by 33 runs.** ‡**Chennai Super Kings 168-4** (20 overs) (M. Vijay 31, M. S. Dhoni 58*); **Delhi Daredevils 135-9** (20 overs) (D. A. Warner 44; J. A. Morkel 3-32). *MoM:* M. S. Dhoni. *Dhoni's muscularity took Chennai two points clear at the top. After scoring 17 off his first 19 deliveries, he smashed 41 off the next 16. Delhi lost Sehwag second ball and, from 63-5 in the tenth over, there was no way back.*

At Ranchi, May 15, 2013. **Pune Warriors won by seven runs. Pune Warriors 170-4** (20 overs) (A. J. Finch 48, M. K. Pandey 66, Yuvraj Singh 30); ‡**Kolkata Knight Riders 163-7** (20 overs) (Y. K. Pathan 72, R. N. ten Doeschate 42). *MoM:* M. K. Pandey. *Yusuf Pathan was threatening to steer Kolkata to victory when, in the 18th over, he blocked a yorker from Wayne Parnell and set off for a single. The ball rolled up the pitch, where Parnell and Pathan collided; in the melee, Pathan kicked the ball, sparking an appeal for obstructing the field – an appeal eventually upheld by the third umpire, who ruled Pathan's footwork deliberate. Without him, Kolkata's assault tailed away. By contrast, Manish Pandey helped Pune crash 72 from the last six overs; the result ended their run of nine defeats – and ensured Kolkata could not retain their trophy.*

At Mumbai (Wankhede), May 15, 2013. **Mumbai Indians won by 14 runs. Mumbai Indians 166-8** (20 overs) (A. P. Tare 59); ‡**Rajasthan Royals 152-7** (20 overs) (S. T. R. Binny 37*, B. J. Hodge 39). *MoM:* A. P. Tare. *Aditya Tare, replacing the injured Tendulkar and playing his first IPL match for three years, hit 59 from 37 balls as leaders Mumbai made just enough, and replaced Chennai at the top. Rajasthan were always up against it after slipping to 28-4 in the sixth. This match was later implicated in the spot-fixing scandal: police alleged Rajasthan's Ankeet Chavan agreed to concede 13 or more runs in his second over; after Glenn Maxwell hit the first and third balls for six, it cost 15.*

At Dharmasala, May 16, 2013. **Kings XI Punjab won by seven runs. Kings XI Punjab 171-4** (20 overs) (A. C. Gilchrist 42, S. E. Marsh 45, D. A. Miller 44*); ‡**Delhi Daredevils 164-7** (20 overs) (D. P. M. D. Jayawardene 39, V. Sehwag 30, B. J. Rohrer 49; S. Sharma 3-23). *MoM:* D. A. Miller.

Sandeep Sharma caused havoc with early swing, removing Irfan Pathan and Warner with successive balls. Ben Rohrer's 49 from 29 deliveries came too late to deny Punjab.

At Hyderabad (Uppal), May 17, 2013. **Sunrisers Hyderabad won by 23 runs.** ‡**Sunrisers Hyderabad 136-9** (20 overs) (B. B. Samantray 55; J. P. Faulkner 5-16); **Rajasthan Royals 113-9** (20 overs). *MoM:* A. Mishra. *With both sides vying for the play-offs, Mishra returned figures of 4–0–8–2, the joint-most-economical four-over spell of IPL6, to damage Rajasthan's hopes. Earlier, Faulkner surpassed his 5-20 against these opponents with 5-16 – the two best analyses of the tournament. Rajasthan might have won had they bothered to appeal for a run-out when Biplab Samantray had made eight of his eventual 55.*

At Dharmasala, May 18, 2013. **Kings XI Punjab won by 50 runs. Kings XI Punjab 183-8** (20 overs) (Azhar Mahmood 80, S. E. Marsh 63; S. L. Malinga 3-39); ‡**Mumbai Indians 133** (19.1 overs). *MoM:* Azhar Mahmood. *Nothing hung on this match: Mumbai were certain of finishing in the top two, while Punjab were out. Thanks to a stand of 148 in 14.2 overs between Azhar Mahmood and Marsh, Punjab recovered from 6-2 to set a stiff target. Four Mumbaikar batsmen reached 22, but none managed 27. With an impossible 51 needed from the 20th over, and one wicket remaining, Gilchrist – in his 80th and final IPL match – removed his gloves and immediately dismissed Harbhajan with his little-seen off-breaks. Gilchrist's first senior wicket marked the final moment of a career comprising 648 games and stretching back more than 20 years.*

At Bangalore, May 18, 2013. **Royal Challengers Bangalore won by 24 runs.** Reduced to eight overs a side. **Royal Challengers Bangalore 106-2** (8 overs) (V. Kohli 56*); ‡**Chennai Super Kings 82-6** (8 overs) (M. Vijay 32; Z. Khan 4-17). *MoM:* V. Kohli. *Bangalore pulled off the victory they needed to keep their slim play-off hopes alive, in a shortened match which started at 11pm after heavy rain. Chennai remained top.*

At Gahunje, May 19, 2013. **Pune Warriors won by 38 runs.** ‡**Pune Warriors 172-5** (20 overs) (A. J. Finch 52, A. D. Mathews 30*, L. J. Wright 44); **Delhi Daredevils 134-9** (20 overs) (C. M. Gautam 30; A. G. Murtaza 3-15, A. D. Mathews 3-14). *MoM:* L. J. Wright. *Mathews took three wickets in six balls to consign Delhi to their 13th defeat – and last place.*

At Hyderabad (Uppal), May 19, 2013. **Sunrisers Hyderabad won by five wickets.** ‡**Kolkata Knight Riders 130-7** (20 overs) (Y. K. Pathan 49*); **Sunrisers Hyderabad 132-5** (18.5 overs) (P. A. Patel 47, S. Dhawan 42; Iqbal Abdulla 3-29). *MoM:* P. A. Patel. *Successive sixes from Sammy eased Hyderabadi nerves and secured the final play-off place after five wickets had fallen for 23 in pursuit of a modest 130; a Kolkata win would have seen Bangalore qualify instead. Patel and Dhawan began the chase with 89 in 11.3 overs, before the wobble briefly unsettled the home crowd.*

First qualifying final

At Delhi, May 21, 2013. **Chennai Super Kings won by 48 runs.** ‡**Chennai Super Kings 192-1** (20 overs) (M. E. K. Hussey 86*, S. K. Raina 82*); **Mumbai Indians 144** (18.4 overs) (D. R. Smith 68; R. A. Jadeja 3-31, D. J. Bravo 3-9). *MoM:* M. E. K. Hussey. *Chennai breezed past Mumbai to reach the final for the fifth time in six tournaments. Hussey hit 86* from 58 balls, and Raina 82* from 42 as they added 140* in 12.4 overs; the last ten brought 123. Dwayne Smith then set off at an even more furious pace, rocketing to 68 from 27 balls before Jadeja dismissed him to make it 87-2. His Mumbai team-mates collapsed in a heap, though – the last six wickets fell for just 17.*

Elimination final

At Delhi, May 22, 2013. **Rajasthan Royals won by four wickets.** ‡**Sunrisers Hyderabad 132-7** (20 overs) (S. Dhawan 33, C. L. White 31); **Rajasthan Royals 135-6** (19.2 overs) (B. J. Hodge 54*). *MoM:* B. J. Hodge. *In the battle between third and fourth, Rajasthan looked out of contention at 57-5. But they had the experienced Brad Hodge at No. 7; he was joined by Faulkner, his fellow Australian, at 102-6, and together they hauled their side over the line and into the second qualifying final. Rajasthan started the last over needing ten, but Hodge promptly launched Sammy over the ropes for the fourth and fifth sixes of his 29-ball onslaught.*

Second qualifying final

At Kolkata, May 24, 2013. **Mumbai Indians won by four wickets.** ‡**Rajasthan Royals 165-6** (20 overs) (R. Dravid 43, D. H. Yagnik 31*; Harbhajan Singh 3-23); **Mumbai Indians 169-6** (19.5 overs) (D. R. Smith 62, A. P. Tare 35). MoM: Harbhajan Singh. *Before the game, Rajasthan captain Dravid said his cash-strapped franchise did not wish to invest in bowling and fielding coaches – and it was a poor display in the field that cost them. Mumbai needed 15 from nine balls when Ambati Rayudu mis-hit a sweep, and Hodge dropped the chance galloping in from square leg. Watson castled Rayudu next over, but Mumbai stuttered over the line. Malinga, enduring his worst IPL season yet, had given Rajasthan a boost with an unpredictable final over costing 18, including three wides and three pinpoint yorkers.*

FINAL

CHENNAI SUPER KINGS v MUMBAI INDIANS

At Kolkata, May 26, 2013. Mumbai Indians won by 23 runs. Toss: Mumbai Indians.

Mumbai won their first IPL title thanks to Pollard's power and some intelligent new-ball bowling from Malinga and Johnson. Set a gettable 149, Chennai slipped to three for three after ten deliveries and, by the time Dhoni walked out in the seventh over, they were already five down. Five overs later, it was 58 for eight, and Dhoni's 45-ball 63 did little more than delay the inevitable – though many felt he should have entered the fray earlier than No. 7. Mumbai had been in trouble themselves, at 16 for three, but Rayudu added 36 with Karthik and 48 with Pollard, who then cut loose as wickets fell around him. In all, he launched seven fours and three sixes, including the last two balls of the innings, off Bravo. Chennai stumbled immediately, and Mumbai never ceded control.

Man of the Match: K. A. Pollard.   *Man of the Tournament:* S. R. Watson.

Mumbai Indians

		B	4	6
D. R. Smith *lbw b 11*	4	4	1	0
A. P. Tare *b 8*	0	1	0	0
†K. D. Karthik *b 9*	21	26	3	0
*R. G. Sharma *c and b 8*	2	5	0	0
A. T. Rayudu *b 5*	37	36	4	0
K. A. Pollard *not out*	60	32	7	3
Harbhajan Singh *c 1 b 5*	14	8	3	0
R. Dhawan *run out*	3	3	0	0
M. G. Johnson *c 7 b 5*	1	2	0	0
S. L. Malinga *c 7 b 5*	0	2	0	0
P. P. Ojha *not out*	1	1	0	0
L-b 2, w 3	5			

6 overs: 34-3   (20 overs) 148-9

1/4 2/8 3/16 4/52 5/100 6/125 7/133 8/135 9/135

12th man: A. R. Patel.

Sharma 4–0–26–1; Morkel 3–0–12–2; Morris 4–0–25–1; Ashwin 3–0–22–0; Jadeja 2–0–19–0; Bravo 4–0–42–4.

Chennai Super Kings

		B	4	6
M. E. K. Hussey *b 10*	1	2	0	0
M. Vijay *c 4 b 9*	18	20	2	0
S. K. Raina *c 1 b 10*	0	1	0	0
S. Badrinath *c 3 b 9*	0	3	0	0
D. J. Bravo *c 9 b 8*	15	16	3	0
R. A. Jadeja *c 6 b 7*	0	2	0	0
*†M. S. Dhoni *not out*	63	45	3	5
J. A. Morkel *b 11*	10	10	0	1
C. H. Morris *c 3 b 7*	0	1	0	0
R. Ashwin *c 12 b 6*	9	18	0	0
M. Sharma *not out*	0	2	0	0
L-b 2, w 7	9			

6 overs: 35-4   (20 overs) 125-9

1/2 2/2 3/3 4/35 5/36 6/39 7/57 8/58 9/99

Malinga 4–0–22–2; Johnson 4–0–19–2; Ojha 4–0–28–1; Dhawan 1–0–6–1; Harbhajan Singh 3–0–14–2; Pollard 4–0–34–1.

Umpires: H. D. P. K. Dharmasena and S. J. A. Taufel. Third umpire: C. Shamshuddin.
Referee: R. S. Madugalle.

CHAMPIONS LEAGUE TWENTY20, 2013-14

R. KAUSHIK

The fifth edition of the Champions League, played across five venues in India, caught fire like no other. Perhaps it was because there were four IPL franchises in the tournament proper; perhaps because it marked the last time Sachin Tendulkar and Rahul Dravid would play competitive Twenty20 cricket. Whatever the reason, it was lapped up by the fans, and there was a popular winner in Mumbai Indians, the defending IPL champions, who became the first to win the Champions League twice. Led from the front by Rohit Sharma, they flirted with elimination before the semis, but in the knockouts there was simply no stopping them.

Mumbai's opponents in the Delhi final were Rajasthan Royals, a team in the spotlight for all the wrong reasons during IPL6. Despite three players – Sreesanth, Ajit Chandila and Ankeet Chavan – serving bans handed down by the BCCI for their roles in the spot-fixing scandal, Rajasthan imposed themselves on this competition. They went unbeaten at the Sawai Mansingh Stadium in Jaipur (where they had won all eight matches in IPL6), and were marshalled astutely by Dravid, who made up for a lack of runs with outstanding leadership. He was lucky to have the tournament's most consistent batsman: Ajinkya Rahane hit four successive fifties, ending with 288 runs. The Man of the Tournament was Mumbai opener Dwayne Smith.

The cricket was high quality, especially once the four-team qualification preamble was over. Otago Volts, New Zealand's champions, progressed to the main tournament (along with Sunrisers Hyderabad), and did exceptionally well until they were let down by one poor performance. For the second time in five years, there were no English teams, but Trinidad & Tobago again showed they could compete with the best, even though three key players – Dwayne Bravo, Kieron Pollard and Kevon Cooper – ended up representing their IPL franchises. Displaying flair and substance, T&T became the only non-IPL team to make the last four. For once, Chennai Super Kings struggled to live up to their reputation for winning when it counts. Twice they suffered extraordinary batting collapses, fatally so against Rajasthan in the first semi-final. Their strong start to the tournament counted for nothing.

Neil Broom hit a brutal hundred for Otago, and Quinton de Kock did so for Highveld Lions, against Otago, a few days later. De Kock, though, finished on the losing side in a remarkable tussle, which was tied at the end of both the game itself and the one-over eliminator; Lions eventually lost to Otago, who had hit one more boundary. The talk of the tournament, however, was Rajasthan's Pravin Tambe, an unknown 41-year-old leg-spinner from Mumbai who pushed the ball through briskly. Without a first-class appearance at the time, he finished as the leading wicket-taker, with 12 at 6.50 each; he also had an economy-rate of 4.10. His spunk and spirit reflected the combativeness of Rajasthan, who consistently punched above their weight.

The early stages of the Champions League suffered their share of controversy. The qualifying games were initially scheduled for Hyderabad, but the local cricket association pulled out, citing security concerns, and they were shifted to Mohali. However, when Pakistani champions Faisalabad Wolves, granted visas only after the intervention of the prime minister, landed in India, they discovered those visas did not cover their hotel in Chandigarh. They had to spend the night in the clubhouse at the stadium in Mohali, around 6km away, before the bureaucracy was sorted and they were able to check in. The palaver cannot have helped, but in truth they had just two quality players – Misbah-ul-Haq and Saeed Ajmal – and they won only once, against Sri Lanka's Kandurata Maroons, who lost all three games. The Australian clubs, Brisbane Heat and Perth Scorchers, also depleted by losing key players to the wealthier IPL sides, had been given automatic entry into the main tournament; despite their names, there was little fervency to their play.

QUALIFYING TOURNAMENT

At Mohali, September 17, 2013 (floodlit). **Otago Volts won by eight wickets. ‡Faisalabad Wolves 139-8** (20 overs) (Misbah-ul-Haq 46); **Otago Volts 142-2** (17.5 overs) (B. B. McCullum 83*, D. C. de Boorder 30*). *MoM:* B. B. McCullum. *Brendon McCullum's aggressive batting – 83* from 65 balls – complemented a potent four-pronged pace attack as Otago began with a convincing win. For Faisalabad, Misbah-ul-Haq alone put up any resistance.*

At Mohali, September 17, 2013 (floodlit). **Sunrisers Hyderabad won by eight wickets. Kandurata Maroons 168-3** (20 overs) (K. C. Sangakkara 61*, H. D. R. L. Thirimanne 54); **‡Sunrisers Hyderabad 174-2** (18.3 overs) (P. A. Patel 52, S. Dhawan 71, N. L. T. C. Perera 32*). *MoM:* S. Dhawan. *Shikhar Dhawan's exceptional strokeplay stood out in a match which left-handers provided all five scores of 30 or more. Kumar Sangakkara and Lahiru Thirimanne made fifties for the Sri Lankan champions, but Dhawan and Parthiv Patel gave Hyderabad the perfect start, putting on 121 in 14 overs.*

At Mohali, September 18, 2013 (floodlit). **Otago Volts won by six wickets. Kandurata Maroons 154-9** (20 overs) (W. U. Tharanga 76; I. G. Butler 3-21); **‡Otago Volts 157-4** (18 overs) (R. N. ten Doeschate 64, J. D. S. Neesham 32*; L. H. D. Dilhara 3-20). *MoM:* R. N. ten Doeschate. *Ryan ten Doeschate was the star of Otago's commanding win. Just a few hours after touching down from England, he took 2-9 in two overs, helping keep Kandurata within bounds from a promising 99-2 in the 13th. Then he smashed Kaushal Lokuarachchi for three consecutive sixes on his way to 64 off 32 balls.*

At Mohali, September 18, 2013 (floodlit). **Sunrisers Hyderabad won by seven wickets. Faisalabad Wolves 127-5** (20 overs) (Ammar Mahmood 31, Misbah-ul-Haq 56*); **‡Sunrisers Hyderabad 131-3** (17.3 overs) (S. Dhawan 59). *MoM:* A. Mishra. *With two preliminary matches to go, another powerful Hyderabad display determined the qualifiers: they and Otago would progress. Misbah again ploughed a lone furrow, though Ammar Mahmood did his best to jog alongside with an unhurried 31. Dhawan's more urgent 59 ensured a comfortable win.*

At Mohali, September 20, 2013 (floodlit). **Faisalabad Wolves won by ten runs. Faisalabad Wolves 146-6** (20 overs) (Misbah-ul-Haq 93*; L. H. D. Dilhara 3-21); **‡Kandurata Maroons 136-7** (20 overs) (K. C. Sangakkara 44; Ehsan Adil 3-26). *MoM:* Misbah-ul-Haq. *Misbah finally had something to show for his consistency when Faisalabad gained a consolation victory in a battle of the eliminated teams. He hammered a 60-ball 93* – all but 30 of the runs from the bat while he was at the crease. Despite possessing nine Sri Lanka internationals, Kandurata fell short.*

At Mohali, September 20, 2013 (floodlit). **Otago Volts won by five wickets. Sunrisers Hyderabad 143-5** (20 overs) (J. P. Duminy 57*); **‡Otago Volts 144-5** (16.2 overs) (B. B. McCullum 67*). *MoM:* N. L. McCullum. *Brendon McCullum set himself up for the challenges ahead with more stunning ball-striking, as Otago finished the qualifying stage with three straight wins. Apart from J-P. Duminy's intelligent 57*, Hyderabad struggled for fluency, before McCullum's pyrotechnics sped Otago home. Earlier, his brother Nathan had stifled Hyderabad with 2-23.*

OTAGO VOLTS 12pts, SUNRISERS HYDERABAD 8pts, Faisalabad Wolves 4pts, Kandurata Maroons 0pts.

Group A

At Jaipur, September 21, 2013 (floodlit). **Rajasthan Royals won by seven wickets. Mumbai Indians 142-7** (20 overs) (R. G. Sharma 44, K. A. Pollard 42; V. Malik 3-24); ‡**Rajasthan Royals 148-3** (19.4 overs) (A. M. Rahane 33, S. V. Samson 54). *MoM:* V. Malik. *Vikramjeet Malik, a medium-pacer from Himachal Pradesh, emerged an unlikely hero as Rajasthan made the most of home advantage to defeat the IPL champions. Malik struck two early blows, then returned to dismiss the dangerous Kieron Pollard as Mumbai made only 142-7. A rapid, if scratchy, half-century from 18-year-old wicketkeeper Sanju Samson helped Rajasthan pace their response.*

At Ahmedabad, September 23, 2013 (floodlit). **Perth Scorchers v ‡Lions. Abandoned.** *This game and the next – a scheduled double-header – were washed out by torrential rain.*

At Ahmedabad, September 23, 2013 (floodlit). **Mumbai Indians v Otago Volts. Abandoned.**

At Jaipur, September 25, 2013 (floodlit). **Otago Volts won by 62 runs. Otago Volts 242-4** (20 overs) (N. T. Broom 117*, D. C. de Boorder 45, R. N. ten Doeschate 66); ‡**Perth Scorchers 180-6** (20 overs) (A. C. Voges 36, H. W. R. Cartwright 68*; I. G. Butler 3-47). *MoM:* N. T. Broom. *An outstanding 56-ball 117* by Neil Broom propelled Otago to the highest total of the tournament. At 82-3 after 11 overs, they looked set for a run-of-the-mill score, but Broom and ten Doeschate (66 from 26) ransacked 122 from 41 balls. Perth recovered from 11-3, but never threatened their mountainous target.*

At Jaipur, September 25, 2013 (floodlit). **Rajasthan Royals won by 30 runs. Rajasthan Royals 183-5** (20 overs) (R. S. Dravid 31, S. R. Watson 33, S. T. R. Binny 38, B. J. Hodge 46*); ‡**Lions 153-9** (20 overs) (A. N. Petersen 40; P. V. Tambe 4-15). *MoM:* P. V. Tambe. *Rajasthan's heavyweight middle order amassed 114 from the last ten overs to power them to 183. At 88-3 after 11, Lions were on track, but then Pravin Tambe, a fortnight short of his 42nd birthday, cut out any escape route, taking 4-15 with his speedy leg-breaks.*

At Jaipur, September 27, 2013 (floodlit). **Mumbai Indians won by seven wickets. Lions 140-5** (20 overs) (A. N. Petersen 35*, D. Pretorius 31*); ‡**Mumbai Indians 141-3** (18.3 overs) (D. R. Smith 63*, K. A. Pollard 31*). *MoM:* D. R. Smith. *A meaty 63* from Dwayne Smith ensured the Mumbai bowlers' steady line was not wasted. A late flourish from Alviro Petersen and Dwaine Pretorius had steered Lions to 140-5 but, with Smith in awesome touch and Pollard raising the tempo, Mumbai cantered to their first win of the tournament. This game was scheduled for Ahmedabad, but switched to Jaipur because of heavy rains.*

At Jaipur, September 29, 2013 (floodlit). **Otago Volts won after the eliminator over was tied, having hit more boundaries. Lions 167-4** (20 overs) (Q. de Kock 109*); ‡**Otago Volts 167-7** (20 overs) (H. D. Rutherford 32, D. C. de Boorder 32, J. D. S. Neesham 52*). *MoM:* J. D. S. Neesham. *With these teams inseparable in both 20-over and one-over contests, Otago eventually prevailed by dint of having hit one more boundary – 21 to Lions' 20 – to maintain their unbeaten run. Quinton de Kock's 109* from 63 deliveries seemed to have given Lions the edge, but Neesham, who came in with 71 needed from 43 balls, walloped 52 from 25 to tie the game at the end of regulation play. Neesham was busy in the super overs, too, batting with Brendon McCullum – they struck 13 off Sohail Tanvir – and then taking the ball. De Kock despatched him for a four and a six from the first two deliveries, reducing the requirement to one ball, then took a single from the third. But Jean Symes picked out a fielder from the fourth, and poor running saw Lions squander their promising position.*

At Jaipur, September 29, 2013 (floodlit). **Rajasthan Royals won by nine wickets. Perth Scorchers 120** (20 overs) (K. Cooper 4-18); ‡**Rajasthan Royals 121-1** (16.3 overs) (A. M. Rahane 62*, S. V. Samson 50*). *MoM:* K. Cooper. *Rajasthan raced to a third consecutive victory and into the semi-finals. Kevon Cooper's change of pace flummoxed Perth, who crashed to 120 all out. Rajasthan lost Rahul Dravid for a four-ball duck, but Ajinkya Rahane and Samson had no problems completing the formalities.*

At Jaipur, October 1, 2013 (floodlit). **Rajasthan Royals won by four wickets. Otago Volts 139-7** (20 overs) (J. D. S. Neesham 32; R. A. Shukla 3-22); ‡**Rajasthan Royals 142-6** (19.1 overs) (A. M. Rahane 52, B. J. Hodge 52*; J. D. S. Neesham 3-22). *MoM:* R. A. Shukla. *Invincible at home, Rajasthan made sure their semi would also be at their Jaipur stronghold after seeing off Otago, another of the tournament's form sides. Three wickets in the fourth over, by little-known medium-pacer Rahul Shukla, rocked Otago, who scrambled from 21-4 to 139-7. The nerveless Brad Hodge helped Rajasthan overcome a mid-innings stutter.*

At Delhi, October 2, 2013 (floodlit). **Mumbai Indians won by six wickets. Perth Scorchers 149-6** (20 overs) (A. C. Agar 35, S. M. Whiteman 51*; N. M. Coulter-Nile 3-19); ‡**Mumbai Indians 152-4** (13.2 overs) (D. R. Smith 48, R. G. Sharma 51*). *MoM:* R. G. Sharma. *Staring elimination in the face, Mumbai were relieved to win the toss. Rohit Sharma leapt at the chance to bowl and, once Mumbai – spurred on by Nathan Coulter-Nile – had restricted Perth to 149, they knew their task: win inside 14.2 overs, and they were in the semis, at Otago's expense. Their charge was spearheaded by Sharma, who hammered 51* from 24 balls; they roared home with an over to spare.*

Group B

At Ranchi, September 22, 2013 (floodlit). **Trinidad & Tobago won by 25 runs. Trinidad & Tobago 135-9** (20 overs) (D. Ramdin 48; A. C. McDermott 4-37); ‡**Brisbane Heat 110** (18.4 overs) (J. A. Burns 45; R. Rampaul 4-14). *MoM:* D. Ramdin. *In a mediocre contest on a sluggish surface, Denesh Ramdin – one of only two players to reach 20 – and Ravi Rampaul were the heroes for T&T. Ramdin's enterprising 48 took them to 135-9, which proved well beyond Brisbane: Rampaul, cramping the batsmen for room, did the early damage, while Sunil Narine tied the middle order in knots.*

At Ranchi, September 22, 2013 (floodlit). **Chennai Super Kings won by four wickets. Titans 185-5** (20 overs) (H. Davids 52, A. B. de Villiers 77); ‡**Chennai Super Kings 187-6** (18.5 overs) (M. E. K. Hussey 47, S. K. Raina 47, D. J. Bravo 38; R. R. Richards 3-29). *MoM:* S. K. Raina. *Henry Davids made a measured half-century and A. B. de Villiers a spectacular one, from 36 balls, as Titans amassed 185-5. That should have tested even the formidable Chennai batting, but Mike Hussey and Suresh Raina sped merrily along, before Dwayne Bravo applied the finishing touches. Although Titans were handicapped by the dew, they should not have gifted Chennai 12 wide deliveries, which conceded 24 extras.*

At Mohali, September 24, 2013 (floodlit). **Titans won by four runs. Titans 123** (18.5 overs) (H. Davids 39, H. G. Kuhn 31; M. G. Gale 4-10); ‡**Brisbane Heat 119** (20 overs) (J. R. Hopes 37; M. de Lange 3-13). *MoM:* M. de Lange. *Two meltdowns, one in each innings, created a fascinating encounter. Titans reached 107-4 in the 15th over, then lost six for 16; seamer Matthew Gale, nephew of England bowling coach David Saker, picked up 4-10 on Twenty20 debut. Against an accurate Titans attack, Brisbane struggled to keep up with the rate, and wickets tumbled in a frenzied finish.*

At Mohali, September 24, 2013 (floodlit). **Sunrisers Hyderabad won by four wickets. Trinidad & Tobago 160-8** (20 overs) (D. M. Bravo 66); ‡**Sunrisers Hyderabad 164-6** (19.3 overs) (N. L. T. C. Perera 57*; S. P. Narine 4-9). *MoM:* N. L. T. C. Perera. *T&T conspired to lose a tight game, despite Darren Bravo's sublime 66 and Narine's extraordinary 4–1–9–4. Hyderabad needed 66 from six overs – and got them with three deliveries to spare, thanks to Tissara Perera's 32-ball 57*.*

At Ranchi, September 26, 2013 (floodlit). **Chennai Super Kings won by 12 runs. Chennai Super Kings 202-4** (20 overs) (S. K. Raina 84, M. S. Dhoni 63*); ‡**Sunrisers Hyderabad 190-7** (20 overs) (P. A. Patel 37, S. Dhawan 48, D. J. G. Sammy 50). *MoM:* S. K. Raina. *M. S. Dhoni, in his home town, was at his scintillating best, conjuring 63* from just 19 deliveries to sweep Chennai past 200. He pillaged 32 runs from one Perera over which, with two wides, cost 34. Perera ended with 0-60, the most expensive three-over analysis in Twenty20 cricket. By comparison, Suresh Raina's 57-ball 84 was a model of restraint. Hyderabad made a decent fist of their reply – Darren Sammy contributing a 25-ball 50 – but fell short.*

At Ranchi, September 28, 2013 (floodlit). **Titans won by eight wickets. Sunrisers Hyderabad 145-7** (20 overs) (S. Dhawan 37; D. Wiese 3-17); ‡**Titans 147-2** (16.3 overs) (J. A. Rudolph 49*, H. Davids 64). *MoM:* H. Davids. *Hyderabad squandered an excellent start, all but playing themselves out of the tournament. Openers Parthiv Patel and Shikhar Dhawan put on 62 in 6.3 overs, but poor strokes down the order left them on a lame 145-7. Titans hardly needed to break sweat after their own opening stand of 112, by Jacques Rudolph and Henry Davids.*

At Ranchi, September 28, 2013 (floodlit). **Chennai Super Kings won by eight wickets. Brisbane Heat 137-7** (20 overs) (C. D. Hartley 35, B. C. J. Cutting 42*); ‡**Chennai Super Kings 140-2** (15.5 overs) (M. E. K. Hussey 57*, M. Vijay 42). *MoM:* M. E. K. Hussey. *A facile win made Chennai the first to nail a semi-final berth. Guileful spin was at the heart of their performance: Ravichandran Ashwin had figures of 4–1–10–1 and, all told, 11 overs of slow bowling brought 4-37. Brisbane's 137-7 proved little obstacle.*

At Ahmedabad, September 30, 2013 (floodlit). **Trinidad & Tobago won by six runs** (D/L). **Trinidad & Tobago 188-6** (20 overs) (E. Lewis 70, D. M. Bravo 63; M. de Lange 3-38); ‡**Titans 153-6** (17 overs) (H. Davids 42, J. A. Rudolph 31). *MoM:* E. Lewis. *A. B. de Villiers seemed about to launch an attack when the heavens opened, handing T&T a six-run Duckworth/Lewis victory. They had ridden on half-centuries by Evin Lewis and Darren Bravo to make 188-6; Titans had reached 153-6 in 17 overs, with de Villiers on 23 from 13 balls, when play ended.*

At Ahmedabad, September 30, 2013 (floodlit). **Brisbane Heat v Sunrisers Hyderabad. Abandoned.** *Brisbane, already eliminated, were joined by Hyderabad when the second match of the double-header was washed out.*

At Delhi, October 2, 2013. **Trinidad & Tobago won by eight wickets. Chennai Super Kings 118** (19.4 overs) (S. K. Raina 38; R. R. Emrit 3-21); ‡**Trinidad & Tobago 119-2** (15.1 overs) (L. M. P. Simmons 63, E. Lewis 38). *MoM:* L. M. P. Simmons. *T&T completed the semi-final line-up, flummoxing Chennai – guaranteed a place in the last four and unbeaten until now – on a slow pitch. Once Chennai were dismissed for 118, T&T knew a win inside 17.4 overs would see them finish above their opponents. Lendl Simmons motored to 63 from 41 as they made it with ease.*

FINAL GROUP TABLES

Group A

	P	W	L	No result	Points	Net run-rate
RAJASTHAN ROYALS	4	4	0	0	16	0.96
MUMBAI INDIANS	4	2	1	1	10	1.06
Otago Volts	4	2	1	1	10	0.86
Lions	4	0	3	1	2	–0.72
Perth Scorchers	4	0	3	1	2	–2.85

Group B

	P	W	L	No result	Points	Net run-rate
TRINIDAD & TOBAGO	4	3	1	0	12	0.81
CHENNAI SUPER KINGS	4	3	1	0	12	0.27
Titans	4	2	2	0	8	0.22
Sunrisers Hyderabad	4	1	2	1	6	–0.62
Brisbane Heat	4	0	3	1	2	–1.02

Where two or more teams finished with an equal number of points, the positions were decided by (a) most wins (b) net run-rate.

Semi-finals

At Jaipur, October 4, 2013 (floodlit). **Rajasthan Royals won by 14 runs. Rajasthan Royals 159-8** (20 overs) (A. M. Rahane 70, S. R. Watson 32; D. J. Bravo 3-26); ‡**Chennai Super Kings 145-8** (20 overs) (R. Ashwin 46; P. V. Tambe 3-10). *MoM:* P. V. Tambe. *Rajasthan's unbeaten home run, stretching back almost 17 months to IPL5, now stood at 13. Ajinkya Rahane's classy 70 hauled them to 159-8, which felt vulnerable against Chennai's accomplished batting line-up. But there was another tale in the telling: leg-spinner Pravin Tambe, after spending decades in the shadows, showed immense control to claim figures of 4–0–10–3, and leave Chennai reeling at 72-7. Ravichandran Ashwin and Chris Morris (26*) more than doubled the score in seven overs, but the rate was always just out of their grasp.*

At Delhi, October 5, 2013 (floodlit). **Mumbai Indians won by six wickets. Trinidad and Tobago 153-5** (20 overs) (E. Lewis 62, K. Y. G. Ottley 41*); ‡**Mumbai Indians 157-4** (19.1 overs) (D. R. Smith 59, S. R. Tendulkar 35, K. D. Karthik 33*; S. P. Narine 3-17). *MoM:* D. R. Smith. *Mumbai swatted T&T aside to make it an all-Indian final, after following a disciplined bowling display with a composed, clinical run-chase. Evin Lewis provided the backbone of T&T's 153-5, a score that seemed competitive only until Dwayne Smith unfurled a frenzy of boundaries, and Sachin Tendulkar found some form – including his 50,000th run in senior cricket. Dinesh Karthik maintained the pace, and Mumbai won comfortably.*

FINAL

MUMBAI INDIANS v RAJASTHAN ROYALS

At Delhi, October 6 (floodlit). Mumbai Indians won by 33 runs. Toss: Rajasthan Royals.

For two grandees of Indian cricket, this was a farewell appearance to the Twenty20 stage. It brought delight for Tendulkar and despair for Dravid (who had demoted himself to No. 8), though neither played a major role in the drama. All Mumbai's top seven reached 15, and an inability to forge a meaningful partnership – their highest was 42 – caused no concern: the acceleration late in the innings happened just the same, and 83 came from the last 30 balls. Rajasthan were well set at 117-1 in the 12th over but, once the Rahane–Samson century stand was broken, the game was up. Harbhajan Singh struck three times in the 17th to reduce the innings to tatters. The last seven wickets clattered for 14 runs in 17 balls as Mumbai added the Champions League to the IPL trophy they had won in May.

Man of the Match: Harbhajan Singh.   *Man of the Tournament:* D. R. Smith.

Mumbai Indians

		B	4	6
D. R. Smith *b 11*	44	39	5	1
S. R. Tendulkar *b 4*	15	13	3	0
A. T. Rayudu *b 11*	29	24	4	0
*R. G. Sharma *c 9 b 10*	33	14	3	2
K. A. Pollard *b 9*	15	10	1	1
G. J. Maxwell *run out*	37	14	4	2
†K. D. Karthik *not out*	15	5	0	2
Harbhajan Singh *not out*	7	2	0	1
L-b 2, w 4, n-b 1	7			

6 overs: 46-1   (20 overs) 202-6

1/35 2/77 3/104 4/140 5/152 6/193

N. M. Coulter-Nile, R. Dhawan and P. P. Ojha did not bat.

Faulkner 4–0–46–1; Watson 3–0–30–1; Shukla 4–0–49–1; Cooper 4–0–40–0; Tambe 4–0–19–2; Binny 1–0–16–0.

Rajasthan Royals

		B	4	6
M. D. K. J. Perera *run out*	8	4	2	0
A. M. Rahane *c 1 b 8*	65	47	5	2
S. V. Samson *c 8 b 11*	60	33	4	4
S. R. Watson *c 5 b 8*	8	8	0	1
S. T. R. Binny *b 8*	10	8	0	1
†D. H. Yagnik *c 7 b 5*	6	5	1	0
K. Cooper *st 7 b 8*	4	2	1	0
*R. Dravid *b 9*	1	2	0	0
J. P. Faulkner *c 1 b 5*	2	4	0	0
R. A. Shukla *c 1 b 5*	0	1	0	0
P. V. Tambe *not out*	0	0	0	0
L-b 3, w 1, n-b 1	5			

6 overs: 71-1   (18.5 overs) 169

1/8 2/117 3/137 4/155 5/155 6/159 7/163 8/169 9/169

Maxwell 1–0–10–0; Dhawan 3–0–34–0; Harbhajan Singh 4–0–32–4; Coulter-Nile 3–0–33–1; Ojha 4–0–26–1; Pollard 3.5–0–31–3.

Umpires: H. D. P. K. Dharmasena and R. J. Tucker.   Third umpire: C. Shamshuddin.
Referee: R. S. Madugalle.

CHAMPIONS LEAGUE FINALS

2009-10   NEW SOUTH WALES BLUES beat Trinidad & Tobago‡ by 41 runs at Hyderabad.
2010-11   CHENNAI SUPER KINGS beat Warriors‡ by eight wickets at Johannesburg.
2011-12   MUMBAI INDIANS‡ beat Royal Challengers Bangalore by 31 runs at Chennai.
2012-13   SYDNEY SIXERS‡ beat Lions by ten wickets at Johannesburg.
2013-14   MUMBAI INDIANS beat Rajasthan Royals‡ by 33 runs at Delhi.

DOMESTIC CRICKET IN INDIA, 2012-13

R. Mohan

Away from the spotlights on international cricket and the IPL, which was plunged into a new crisis by the arrest of a number of players for spot-fixing, the domestic programme made peaceful progress. A reshuffle led to more first-class cricket, with the Ranji Trophy expanded from 88 games to 115. To suit the climate, longer matches were played in the earlier, less cruel months, and limited-overs in the end-of-season heat. The Ranji format changed, with two Elite and two Plate groups replaced by three qualifying groups of nine teams each, guaranteeing a minimum of eight matches before the knockouts. Two of the groups, drawn from the previous Elite plus teams who would have been promoted, supplied three quarter-finalists each, while the third, drawn from the Plate sides, provided two. All knockout games, and not just the final, were allotted five days, and the points for outright victory rose from five to six. It did little to encourage positive play: 60% of Ranji matches were drawn, exactly the same as in 2011-12.

Mumbai claimed their 40th Ranji title, despite winning only two of their 11 matches (Punjab and Uttar Pradesh won four each). They needed less than three of the final's five days to bag an innings victory over the inexperienced **Saurashtra** – who missed their two best players, Cheteshwar Pujara and Ravi Jadeja, required by the one-day squad against England, while Mumbai could field Sachin Tendulkar and Wasim Jaffer. Saurashtra's batsmen found a seaming pitch away from their placid home environment too hot to handle, and collapsed for 81 on the third morning.

Mumbai proceeded straight to the Irani Cup match between the Ranji champions and Rest of India, now moved to the end of the first-class programme, though it was staged twice in this transitional season. A high-scoring draw included centuries from Tendulkar and Jaffer, but the Rest's first-innings lead was enough to maintain their hold on the trophy they had won against previous champions Rajasthan a few months earlier.

In another change, the Duleep Trophy was held before the Ranji tournament. Yuvraj Singh, who had just made an emotional comeback in the World Twenty20 after cancer, ensured a brief Test recall with a semi-final double-hundred for North Zone, but **East Zone** – first-time winners in 2011-12 – retained the title in a rain-affected final with **Central**. A fortuitous bowling change, when part-time leg-spinner Anustup Majumdar came on so that slow left-armer Iresh Saxena could swap ends, brought four crucial wickets, instrumental in East squeezing out a first-innings lead. A Duleep experiment with Kookaburra balls was dropped, with the nationally used SG brand preferred.

The season ended with a flurry of limited-overs tournaments: **Delhi** became the national one-day champions, winning the Vijay Hazare final against Assam, while **West Zone** won the Deodhar Trophy, and **Gujarat** the Twenty20 Syed Mushtaq Ali Trophy. In the final of the only one-day tournament played in the early season, the Challenger Trophy, **India B** beat India A – thanks to 155 from Murali Vijay, following Shikhar Dhawan's 152 for A, and Pujara's 158 for B, when the same sides met a few days before.

It was a high-scoring season, with five first-class triple-centuries equalling the record for a national season, set in England in 2006. Three of them – two for Jadeja and one for Pujara – were for Saurashtra. Having scored another a year earlier, Jadeja joined an elite group of batsmen to have made three triple-hundreds: W. G. Grace, Bill Ponsford, Don Bradman, Wally Hammond, Graeme Hick, Brian Lara and Mike Hussey. The leading Ranji run-scorer was Jiwanjot Singh of Punjab, who made 995, including five centuries, in his debut season; he was one of six batsmen with 1,000 first-class runs. Pujara was well ahead of the field with 1,585, including double-hundreds against England and Australia. Meanwhile Jaffer, the leading scorer in Ranji history, completed a record 32nd century in the competition. Only Jadeja and Madhya Pradesh seamer Ishwar Pandey managed 50 first-class wickets; the Ranji statistics told an unexpected story, with pace bowlers taking twice as many as spinners.

FIRST-CLASS AVERAGES, 2012-13

BATTING (700 runs, average 50.00)

	M	I	NO	R	HS	100	Avge	Ct/St
C. M. Gautam (*S Zone/Karnataka/India A*) .	11	17	7	1,007	264*	3	100.70	38/5
C. A. Pujara (*Rest/W Zone/Ind/Saurashtra*)	13	23	6	1,585	352	5	93.23	5
†A. N. Cook (*England*)	6	11	2	780	190	4	86.66	4
Wasim Jaffer (*Mumbai*)	8	13	1	1,016	171	4	84.66	11
P. Dogra (*North Zone/Himachal Pradesh*) . .	10	16	4	960	210	5	80.00	12
A. A. Muzumdar (*Andhra*).	8	12	1	868	180	5	78.90	4
R. Paliwal (*Services*)	10	13	3	784	167	4	78.40	4
†R. A. Jadeja (*Saurashtra/India*).	10	14	2	891	331	2	74.25	5
A. T. Rayudu (*India A/Baroda/Rest*)	9	15	3	873	156*	2	72.75	9
V. A. Jagadeesh (*Kerala*)	8	14	2	871	199*	4	72.58	16
Yashpal Singh (*Services*)	10	15	4	790	250*	2	71.81	9
†A. M. Nayar (*West Zone/Mumbai/India A*) .	14	21	7	977	132	3	69.78	4
†P. A. Patel (*West Zone/Gujarat*)	9	14	0	946	162	3	67.57	17/6
M. Manhas (*Delhi*).	8	12	1	742	161*	2	67.45	2
M. C. Juneja (*Gujarat*)	8	13	1	796	159	3	66.33	5
M. K. Tiwary (*India A/Bengal/Rest*)	8	13	2	727	191	2	66.09	11
†S. Dhawan (*North Zone/Delhi/Rest/India*) .	11	18	2	1,020	187	5	63.75	11
Jiwanjot Singh (*Punjab/India A*).	11	18	2	1,019	213	5	63.68	13
J. S. Saxena (*C Zone/M Pradesh/India A*) . .	11	17	4	821	142	2	63.15	5
R. G. Sharma (*Punjab*).	8	13	0	790	203	3	60.76	5
H. H. Khadiwale (*Maharashtra*)	8	13	0	762	168	2	58.61	5
S. P. Jackson (*Saurashtra*)	9	16	3	756	118*	3	58.15	5
†H. N. Shah (*Mumbai*).	10	15	1	773	156	3	55.21	12
M. Vijay (*Rest/India A/Tamil Nadu/India*) .	12	20	0	1,024	266	4	51.20	10

BOWLING (30 wickets)

	Style	O	M	R	W	BB	5I	Avge
B. C. Mohanty (*East Zone/Odisha*)	RFM	326.5	114	633	35	5-24	1	18.08
Parvez Rasool (*Jammu and Kashmir*) . . .	OB	230.4	58	597	33	7-41	3	18.09
A. Rajpoot (*Uttar Pradesh*)	RM	198.4	48	583	31	6-68	3	18.80
S. Sharma (*Punjab*).	RFM	296.1	70	796	41	7-25	3	19.41
R. A. Jadeja (*Saurashtra/India*).	SLA	478	145	1,038	51	6-71	2	20.35
S. Narwal (*Delhi*)	RM	262.2	72	663	32	5-35	1	20.71
S. Yadav (*Services*)	RM	401.3	106	942	43	7-71	2	21.90
V. Malik (*Himachal Pradesh*)	RM	311.5	88	793	36	5-36	3	22.02
I. C. Pandey (*C Zone/M Pradesh/Rest*). .	RFM	393.4	102	1,154	52	6-54	5	22.19
M. Sharma (*Haryana*).	RFM	285.1	65	860	37	5-47	3	23.24
S. Kaul (*Punjab*)	RM	338	64	1,047	44	6-63	2	23.79
R. V. Dhruve (*Gujarat/India A*).	SLA	370	103	1,028	42	8-31	4	24.47
A. Rajan (*Madhya Pradesh*)	RFM	266.1	64	809	33	7-77	1	24.51
Imtiaz Ahmed (*Uttar Pradesh*).	RFM	285	66	942	37	5-29	3	25.45
A. G. Konwar (*Assam*)	OB	278.5	61	799	31	6-67	2	25.77
R. Dhawan (*N Zone/Himachal Pradesh*) .	RM	402.4	100	1,057	41	6-63	2	25.78
S. Nadeem (*Jharkhand*)	SLA	412.3	100	1,091	42	6-54	2	25.97
D. S. Kulkarni (*Mumbai/India A*)	RM	330.1	106	866	33	5-32	2	26.24
Bhuvneshwar Kumar (*Ind A/UP/CZ/Ind*)	RFM	323.1	75	953	36	5-34	2	26.47
S. Nazar (*Services*)	RM	322.1	65	925	34	6-50	3	27.20
A. Mishra (*North Zone/Haryana*)	LBG	292.4	45	989	34	5-97	1	29.08
R. Ashwin (*Tamil Nadu/India*)	OB	478.1	122	1,320	43	7-103	4	30.69
A. A. Chavan (*Mumbai*)	SLA	348	57	1,131	36	9-23	1	31.41
K. R. Makwana (*West Zone/Saurashtra*) .	OB	351	65	1,078	34	6-102	3	31.70
P. P. Ojha (*Rest/Hyderabad/India*)	SLA	527.1	119	1,477	40	5-45	2	36.92

IRANI CUP, 2012-13

Ranji Trophy Champions (Rajasthan) v Rest of India

At Bangalore (Chinnaswamy), September 21–24, 2012. **Rest of India won by an innings and 79 runs. Rajasthan 253** (R. D. Bist 117*; U. T. Yadav 5-55) **and 275; ‡Rest of India 607-7 dec** (M. Vijay 266). *Murali Vijay's third and highest double-century was an Irani Cup record, passing Pravin Amre's 246 in 1990-91. He batted for 618 minutes and hit 36 fours and six sixes in 394 balls, sharing stands of 173, 153 and 141 for the Rest's first three wickets with Ajinkya Rahane (81), Cheteshwar Pujara (78) and Subramaniam Badrinath (55) against a severely weakened Rajasthan.*

Ranji Trophy Champions (Mumbai) v Rest of India

At Mumbai (Wankhede), February 6–10, 2013. **Drawn.** Rest of India won the Irani Cup by virtue of their first-innings lead. **Rest of India 526** (M. Vijay 116, S. K. Raina 134) **and 389-5 dec** (A. T. Rayudu 156*); ‡**Mumbai 409** (S. R. Tendulkar 140*) **and 160-4** (Wasim Jaffer 101*). *Uniquely there was a second Irani Cup match, as the board shifted the competition to the end of the first-class domestic programme. Both games featured a century from Vijay, who built an opening stand of 144 with Shikhar Dhawan (63). Later, Suresh Raina and Abhimanyu Mithun put on 153 for the Rest's seventh wicket. An unbeaten century from Sachin Tendulkar, which equalled Sunil Gavaskar's total of 81 hundreds and took him past 25,000 first-class runs, was not enough to deny the Rest a first-innings lead which gave them their eighth successive Irani Cup. Wasim Jaffer finished with his fourth century in five first-class matches.*

DULEEP TROPHY, 2012-13

Quarter-final

At Chennai (Chidambaram), October 6–9, 2012. **Drawn.** North Zone qualified for the semi-finals by virtue of their first-innings lead. ‡**North Zone 484** (S. Dhawan 101; K. R. Makwana 5-140) **and 208-7 dec** (K. R. Makwana 5-80); **West Zone 164 and 69-2.** *Forceful batting by Shikhar Dhawan and Paras Dogra (77), and seven first-innings wickets from Ishant Sharma and Amit Mishra, ensured that North Zone progressed.*

Semi-finals

At Hyderabad (Uppal), October 14–17, 2012. **Drawn.** Central Zone qualified for the final by virtue of their first-innings lead. ‡**North Zone 451** (S. Dhawan 121, Yuvraj Singh 208) **and 187-4 dec; Central Zone 469** (Bhuvneshwar Kumar 128) **and 39-1.** *In his first first-class match for 11 months because of cancer treatment, Yuvraj Singh batted for 333 minutes and 241 balls, and hit 33 fours and three sixes in his third double-century, adding 160 for North Zone's third wicket with Dhawan. In reply, Bhuvneshwar Kumar hit a maiden hundred, from No. 8, and claimed the decisive first-innings lead for Central Zone in a last-wicket stand of 127 with Rituraj Singh (39*).*

At Visakhapatnam (Rajasekhara Reddy), October 14–17, 2012. **Drawn.** East Zone qualified for the final by virtue of their first-innings lead. ‡**South Zone 244 and 85-8** (A. B. Dinda 7-26). **East Zone 267** (S. S. Tiwary 145) **and 215;** *Saurabh Tiwary and Basant Mohanty (58) rescued East Zone's first innings from 66-6 on a damp pitch in a stand of 153. On the final day, South Zone collapsed to 42-8, the first seven falling to Ashok Dinda, but the ninth-wicket pair held on for 11 overs to save the game – to no effect, as the draw meant East Zone advanced.*

Final

At Chennai (Chidambaram), October 21–25, 2012. **Drawn.** East Zone won the Duleep Trophy by virtue of their first-innings lead. **East Zone 232** (I. R. Jaggi 100*; I. Saxena 5-62) **and 8-0;** ‡**Central Zone 189** (I. Saxena 5-58). *In a final severely affected by rain, Ishank Jaggi's century and the spin of Iresh Saxena and Anustup Majumdar meant East Zone retained the Duleep Trophy.*

RANJI TROPHY, 2012-13

Group A	Played	Won	Lost	Drawn	1st-inns points	Bonus points	Points	Quotient
Punjab	8	4	2	2	6	2	32	1.276
Saurashtra	8	2	1	5	11	0	23	1.198
Mumbai	8	1	0	7	17	0	23	1.423
Gujarat.	8	2	0	6	10	0	22	0.922
Railways	8	2	0	6	8	1	21	0.962
Madhya Pradesh	8	2	2	4	8	0	20	1.035
Bengal	8	1	4	3	7	0	13	0.805
Rajasthan	8	0	3	5	11	0	11	0.741
Hyderabad	8	0	2	6	10	0	10	0.800

Group B	Played	Won	Lost	Drawn	1st-inns points	Bonus points	Points	Quotient
Uttar Pradesh.	8	4	0	4	8	1	33	1.365
Baroda	8	2	1	5	9	1	22	1.019
Karnataka	8	2	1	5	9	0	21	1.081
Delhi	8	2	3	3	7	1	20	1.251
Vidarbha	8	2	0	6	8	0	20	0.840
Odisha*	8	2	4	2	4	0	16	0.825
Tamil Nadu	8	1	1	6	8	0	14	0.947
Haryana	8	1	3	4	8	0	14	0.790
Maharashtra.	8	0	3	5	11	0	11	0.930

Group C	Played	Won	Lost	Drawn	1st-inns points	Bonus points	Points	Quotient
Services.	8	2	1	5	13	1	26	1.198
Jharkhand	8	3	2	3	5	1	24	1.068
Andhra	8	1	0	7	17	1	24	1.089
Assam	8	2	2	4	8	1	21	0.893
Kerala	8	2	1	5	5	2	19	1.082
Goa	8	0	0	8	16	0	16	1.119
Jammu and Kashmir	8	2	3	3	3	0	15	0.772
Himachal Pradesh	8	0	1	7	15	0	15	1.284
Tripura.	8	1	3	4	4	0	10	0.691

* The eastern state of Orissa officially changed its name to Odisha in 2011.

Outright win = 6ts; lead on first innings in a drawn match = 3pts; deficit on first innings in a drawn match = 1pt; no decision on first innings = 1pt each; win by an innings or ten wickets = 1 bonus pt. Teams tied on points were ranked on most wins, and then on quotient (runs scored per wicket divided by runs conceded per wicket).

Group A

At Kolkata (Eden Gardens), November 2–5, 2012. **Drawn. Bengal** 258 (Pankaj Singh 5-50) **and** 232-9 dec; ‡**Rajasthan** 161 and 181-3. *Bengal 3pts, Rajasthan 1pt.*

At Indore (Holkar), November 2–5, 2012. **Drawn. Gujarat** 355 (P. A. Patel 162; A. Rajan 7-77) **and 301-6 dec**; ‡**Madhya Pradesh** 250 and 258-7. *Madhya Pradesh 1pt, Gujarat 3pts.*

At Mumbai (Wankhede), November 2–5, 2012. **Drawn. Mumbai** 570 (A. M. Rahane 129, S. R. Tendulkar 137, A. M. Nayar 107*) **and 230-5**; ‡**Railways** 426. *Mumbai 3pts, Railways 1pt. Ajinkya Rahane and Sachin Tendulkar, whose 79th century was his first for Mumbai since January 2009, added 200 for the fourth wicket.*

At Mohali, November 2–5, 2012. **Punjab won by an innings and 68 runs. Hyderabad** 258 and 239 (S. Kaul 5-53); ‡**Punjab 565-6 dec** (Jiwanjot Singh 213, K. Goel 129). *Punjab 7pts. Jiwanjot Singh, who turned 22 the day after this match, scored 213 on first-class debut, batting for 496* *minutes and 368 balls, with 33 fours; he and Karan Goel put on 288 for Punjab's first wicket. Their team-mate Harbhajan Singh later took his 700th first-class wicket.*

At Surat, November 9–12, 2012. **Drawn. Gujarat 600-9 dec** (M. C. Juneja 159, R. H. Bhatt 160*); ‡**Saurashtra 716-3** (S. D. Jogiyani 282, R. A. Jadeja 303*). *Gujarat 1pt, Saurashtra 3pts. Manprit Juneja and Rujul Bhatt added 239 for Gujarat's sixth wicket, but Saurashtra claimed first-innings points, thanks to a stand of 539 between Sagar Jogiyani and Ravi Jadeja, the second-highest for the third wicket in all first-class cricket, and the highest outside Tests. Jogiyani, who conceded no byes in Gujarat's total of 600, reached a maiden double-hundred; he batted for 651 minutes and 493 balls, with 35 fours and two sixes, but was outscored by Jadeja's third double and second triple, which lasted 561 minutes and 400 balls, with 37 fours and four sixes. It was the second season running in which Jadeja had passed 300 in his opening first-class innings. Saurashtra's total was their biggest – until the quarter-finals.*

At Hyderabad (Uppal), November 9–12, 2012. **Drawn. ‡Hyderabad 341** (V. V. S. Laxman 120) **and 8-0; Madhya Pradesh 431-8 dec** (D. Bundela 142, J. S. Saxena 142). *Hyderabad 1pt, Madhya Pradesh 3pts. Devendra Bundela and Jalaj Saxena put on 204 for Madhya Pradesh's sixth wicket.*

At Mohali, November 9–12, 2012. **Punjab won by an innings and 27 runs. Bengal 326 and 226** (M. S. Gony 5-41); ‡**Punjab 579-7 dec** (Jiwanjot Singh 158, M. Sidana 115, U. Kaul 165*). *Punjab 7pts. Jiwanjot followed his double-hundred on debut with 158 here; he added 224 for Punjab's second wicket with Mayank Sidana to help set up their second innings win.*

At Jaipur (K. L. Saini), November 9–12, 2012. **Drawn. Rajasthan 478** (V. A. Saxena 114, H. H. Kanitkar 119); ‡**Mumbai 579** (H. N. Shah 140, A. M. Nayar 105*). *Rajasthan 1pt, Mumbai 3pts. Vineet Saxena and Hrishikesh Kanitkar, who passed 10,000 first-class runs during his third successive century against Mumbai, put on 220 for Rajasthan's second wicket.*

At Kolkata (Eden Gardens), November 17–20, 2012. **Drawn. Gujarat 260 and 272-8** (R. H. Bhatt 102*); ‡**Bengal 526-7 dec** (M. K. Tiwary 191, L. R. Shukla 113*). *Bengal 3pts, Gujarat 1pt. Gujarat recovered from 18-5 on the last day; Bhatt and Dhruve (83) added 149 for their eighth wicket.*

At Hyderabad (Uppal), November 17–20, 2012. **Drawn. ‡Saurashtra 260** (A. Ashish Reddy 6-56) **and 270-6 dec; Hyderabad 186** (R. A. Jadeja 6-71) **and 232-6.** *Hyderabad 1pt, Saurashtra 3pts. Ashish Reddy took 6-56 on first-class debut.*

At Bhubaneswar, November 17–20, 2012. **Drawn. Railways 205 and 353-5 dec** (A. G. Paunikar 166); ‡**Punjab 314** (U. Kaul 100) **and 59-2.** *Railways 1pt, Punjab 3pts.*

At Jaipur (K. L. Saini), November 17–20, 2012. **Drawn. Madhya Pradesh 256 and 466-6 dec** (N. V. Ojha 111); ‡**Rajasthan 379** (R. R. Parida 108; I. C. Pandey 6-92) **and 88-4.** *Rajasthan 3pts, Madhya Pradesh 1pt.*

At Hyderabad (Uppal), November 24–27, 2012. **Drawn. ‡Mumbai 443** (H. N. Shah 156, R. G. Sharma 112); **Hyderabad 699** (P. Akshath Reddy 196, G. H. Vihari 191, B. P. Sandeep 117). *Hyderabad 3pts, Mumbai 1pt. Hiken Shah and Rohit Sharma put on 213 for Mumbai's third wicket, but 21-year-old acting-captain Akshath Reddy and 19-year-old Hanuma Vihari countered with 386 for Hyderabad's second before falling in successive overs.*

At Indore (Holkar), November 24–27, 2012. **Madhya Pradesh won by 138 runs. Madhya Pradesh 342** (Mohammed Shami 7-79) **and 233;** ‡**Bengal 299** (A. A. Jhunjhunwala 107; I. C. Pandey 5-87) **and 138** (I. C. Pandey 5-58). *Madhya Pradesh 6pts. Mohammed Shami's career-best 7-79 concluded with a hat-trick to end Madhya Pradesh's first innings.*

At Mohali, November 24–26, 2012. **Punjab won by eight wickets. Saurashtra 90** (S. Sharma 7-25) **and 233** (S. Kaul 6-63); ‡**Punjab 205** (S. K. Trivedi 5-64) **and 120-2.** *Punjab 6pts. On the opening day, Saurashtra lost their last nine wickets for 17, as Sandeep Sharma collected a career-best 11–3–25–7.*

At Bhubaneswar, November 24–27, 2012. **Drawn. Gujarat 117** (S. B. Bangar 5-12) **and 551-8 dec** (M. C. Juneja 153*, R. B. Kalaria 100); ‡**Railways 308.** *Railways 3pts, Gujarat 1pt. Juneja added 131 with Dhruve (76) and 159 with Rush Kalaria for Gujarat's seventh and eighth wickets.*

At Valsad, December 1–4, 2012. **Drawn. Gujarat 566** (S. K. Patel 114, P. A. Patel 111, M. C. Juneja 106); ‡**Hyderabad 375 and 124-2.** *Gujarat 3pts, Hyderabad 1pt.*

At Mumbai (Brabourne), December 1–4, 2012. **Drawn. Mumbai 297** (L. R. Shukla 5-38) **and 294-5 dec** (H. N. Shah 118); ‡**Bengal 201 and 198-7** (A. M. Nayar 6-13). *Mumbai 3pts, Bengal 1pt. Wasim*

Jaffer scored 80 in his first match of the season after a Haj pilgrimage to Mecca, and Hiken Shah made his third hundred in successive games. Arindam Das carried his bat for 98* through Bengal's first innings, and Abhishek Nayar had figures of 19–12–13–6 in their second.

At Mohali, December 1–4, 2012. **Punjab won by nine wickets. Rajasthan 222 and 196** (S. Sharma 5-57); **‡Punjab 215** (Pankaj Singh 5-45) **and 206-1** (Jiwanjot Singh 110*). *Punjab 6pts. Punjab's fourth win in five matches.*

At Rajkot (Khandheri), December 1–4, 2012. **Drawn. ‡Saurashtra 576-9 dec** (R. A. Jadeja 331, K. R. Makwana 100*; H. R. Rathod 5-98); **Railways 335** (K. R. Makwana 6-102) **and 27-0.** *Saurashtra 3pts, Railways 1pt. Jadeja scored his second triple-hundred in three weeks and six innings – and his third altogether, all coming in 11 innings since November 2011 (he made no smaller centuries in this time). He was the first Indian to complete three triples. Jadeja batted for 707 minutes and 501 balls, hit 29 fours and seven sixes, and broke his own record for Saurashtra's highest score. Kamlesh Makwana, who reached a maiden century, helped him add 292 for the seventh wicket, and they later removed nine Railways batsmen between them.*

At Ahmedabad (Motera), December 8–11, 2012. **Gujarat won by eight wickets. ‡Rajasthan 294** (H. H. Kanitkar 100*; R. V. Dhruve 6-65) **and 119** (R. V. Dhruve 8-31); **Gujarat 312 and 105-2.** *Gujarat 6pts. Left-arm spinner Dhruve improved his career-best in both innings to finish with 14-96.*

At Mumbai (Wankhede), December 8–11, 2012. **Drawn. Punjab 580** (Mandeep Singh 211) **and 59** (A. A. Chavan 9-23); **‡Mumbai 485** (R. G. Sharma 203; M. S. Gony 5-87) **and 61-2.** *Mumbai 1pt, Punjab 3pts. Mandeep Singh completed a maiden double-century, and Rohit Sharma replied with his fourth. After the first two innings totalled 1,065, Punjab caved in for 59, their second-lowest total, as 19 wickets fell on the final day; only Goel reached double figures as left-arm spinner Ankeet Chavan claimed a career-best 11.5–2–23–9 (and 12-165 in all), but there was no time for Mumbai to pursue 155. First-innings points guaranteed Punjab's entry to the quarter-finals.*

At Bhubaneswar, December 8–11, 2012. **Drawn. Madhya Pradesh 377** (Rameez Khan 128); **‡Railways 214** (I. C. Pandey 6-61) **and 251-8** (M. Rawat 106). *Railways 1pt, Madhya Pradesh 3pts.*

At Rajkot (Khandheri), December 8–11, 2012. **Saurashtra won by 270 runs. ‡Saurashtra 209** (I. Saxena 5-17) **and 333-8 dec** (S. P. Jackson 118*; I. Saxena 6-133); **Bengal 112 and 160.** *Saurashtra 6pts.*

At Kolkata (Eden Gardens), December 15–17, 2012. **Bengal won by four wickets. Hyderabad 115 and 181** (Mohammed Shami 6-71); **‡Bengal 116** (Anwar Ahmed 5-44, A. Ashish Reddy 5-51) **and 183-6.** *Bengal 6pts.*

At Gwalior, December 15–18, 2012. **Madhya Pradesh won by eight wickets. Madhya Pradesh 323** (D. Bundela 108; S. Sharma 5-92) **and 193-2** (D. Bundela 100*); **‡Punjab 148 and 364** (Jiwanjot Singh 103, Yuvraj Singh 131). *Madhya Pradesh 6pts. Bundela scored a century in each innings to inflict the group leaders' first defeat.*

At Bhubaneswar, December 15–18, 2012. **Railways won by an innings and 12 runs. ‡Railways 405** (S. S. Shukla 109); **Rajasthan 135** (K. Anureet Singh 5-40) **and 258** (K. V. Sharma 8-97). *Railways 7pts. Leg-spinner Karan Sharma wrapped up Railways' innings win with a career-best.*

At Rajkot (Khandheri), December 15–18, 2012. **Drawn. ‡Mumbai 606-5 dec** (A. P. Tare 222, R. G. Sharma 166) **and 169-5 dec; Saurashtra 300** (A. V. Vasavada 111*). *Saurashtra 1pt, Mumbai 3pts. Aditya Tare converted a maiden hundred into a double, batting for 623 minutes and 417 balls, and hitting 31 fours and a six. He and Rohit Sharma put on 278 for Mumbai's third wicket.*

At Valsad, December 22–25, 2012. **Gujarat won by 37 runs. Gujarat 266 and 232; ‡Punjab 268 and 193** (R. V. Dhruve 5-76). *Gujarat 6pts.*

At Hyderabad (Uppal), December 22–25, 2012. **Drawn. ‡Hyderabad 337 and 196-8 dec; Railways 213** (A. J. Shinde 5-78) **and 280-7.** *Hyderabad 3pts, Railways 1pt.*

At Indore (Holkar), December 22–25, 2012. **Mumbai won by seven runs. Mumbai 304** (K. R. Pawar 111*; I. C. Pandey 6-54) **and 250-5 dec; ‡Madhya Pradesh 244 and 303** (J. S. Saxena 128; Zaheer Khan 5-79). *Mumbai 6pts. Kaustubh Pawar carried his bat through Mumbai's first innings. Later, they set Madhya Pradesh a target of 311; the last pair, Amarjeet Singh and Ishwar Pandey, came together at 267-9 and took them within eight runs of victory before succumbing. It was Mumbai's only outright win before the final.*

At Jaipur (K. L. Saini), December 22–25, 2012. **Drawn. Rajasthan 299** (A. L. Menaria 103) **and 234-9 dec;** ‡**Saurashtra 228** (Pankaj Singh 5-61) **and 217-5.** *Rajasthan 3pts, Saurashtra 1pt.*

At Kolkata (Jadavpur), December 29, 2012–January 1, 2013. **Railways won by 122 runs. Railways 214 and 314-9 dec;** ‡**Bengal 157 and 249.** *Railways 6pts.*

At Mumbai (Dr D. Y. Patil), December 29, 2012–January 1, 2013. **Drawn. Gujarat 244** (P. A. Patel 101) **and 337;** ‡**Mumbai 447** (Wasim Jaffer 171) **and 65-1.** *Mumbai 3pts, Gujarat 1pt. Jaffer, who scored his 30th Ranji hundred, and Hiken Shah (82) added 213 for Mumbai's third wicket, helping them reach the quarter-finals at the last gasp. Jaffer subsequently left the game after his father suffered a heart attack.*

At Jaipur (K. L. Saini), December 29, 2012–January 1, 2013. **Drawn. Rajasthan 384** (A. Ashish Reddy 5-67) **and 329-9 dec** (V. A. Saxena 146*); ‡**Hyderabad 349 and 38-0.** *Rajasthan 3pts, Hyderabad 1pt.*

At Rajkot (Khandheri), December 29, 2012–January 1, 2013. **Saurashtra won by 227 runs.** ‡**Saurashtra 242 and 303-4 dec** (C. A. Pujara 203*); **Madhya Pradesh 135 and 183** (D. A. Jadeja 6-51). *Saurashtra 6pts. Saurashtra reached the quarter-finals, thanks largely to Cheteshwar Pujara's fifth double-hundred (and second of the season, following 206* against England); he took 303 minutes and 221 balls, hit 30 fours and a six, and scored 67% of Saurashtra's total. Dharmendrasinh Jadeja took 6-51 on debut (and 9-102 in the match).*

Group B

At Vadodara (Moti Bagh), November 2–5, 2012. **Drawn.** ‡**Baroda 406** (A. A. Waghmode 129, I. K. Pathan 121; S. T. R. Binny 5-65) **and 249; Karnataka 284** (Gagandeep Singh 5-49) **and 102-1.** *Baroda 3pts, Karnataka 1pt. Aditya Waghmode and Irfan Pathan, who both scored career-bests, pulled Baroda round from 88-4 by adding 239.*

At Rohtak, November 2–4, 2012. **Vidarbha won by eight wickets. Haryana 55** (U. T. Yadav 5-18) **and 183;** ‡**Vidarbha 205 and 37-2.** *Vidarbha 6pts. Only one batsman reached double figures as Haryana collapsed for 55, their lowest first-class total.*

At Cuttack (Barabati), November 2–5, 2012. **Drawn. Tamil Nadu 67-3 v** ‡**Odisha.** *Odisha 1pt, Tamil Nadu 1pt.*

At Ghaziabad, November 2–5, 2012. **Uttar Pradesh won by six wickets. Delhi 235** (Imtiaz Ahmed 5-59) **and 322** (V. Sehwag 107); ‡**Uttar Pradesh 403** (M. B. Dagar 116) **and 158-4.** *Uttar Pradesh 6pts.*

At Vadodara (Moti Bagh), November 9–12, 2012. **Drawn. Vidarbha 264** (H. K. Badani 111*) **and 218-4;** ‡**Baroda 514-7 dec** (A. R. Chauhan 118, R. K. Solanki 120). *Baroda 3pts, Vidarbha 1pt.*

At Delhi (Feroz Shah Kotla), November 9–12, 2012. **Delhi won by ten wickets.** ‡**Odisha 143 and 269** (P. Suyal 5-93); **Delhi 331** (M. Manhas 161*) **and 82-0.** *Delhi 7pts.*

At Gahunje, November 9–12, 2012. **Drawn.** ‡**Maharashtra 764-6 dec** (K. M. Jadhav 327, R. H. Motwani 147); **Uttar Pradesh 669-7** (T. M. Srivastava 179, M. B. Dagar 126, P. P. Chawla 156). *Maharashtra 1pt, Uttar Pradesh 1pt. All five centuries in this match achieved career-bests. Kedar Jadhav converted his maiden double-hundred into a triple; he faced just 312 balls in 524 minutes, and hit 54 fours and two sixes, adding 231 for Maharashtra's fourth wicket with Ankit Bawne (78), and 314 for the fifth with Rohit Motwani, setting up the highest total of this tournament. Tanmay Srivastava and Mukul Dagar opened Uttar Pradesh's reply with a stand of 248, and Piyush Chawla hit 18 fours and eight sixes in 140 balls, which helped to set up their team's biggest score. Earlier, Chawla had conceded 233 in 51 overs of leg-spin – though he did have Jadhav stumped.*

At Chennai (Chidambaram), November 9–12, 2012. **Drawn.** ‡**Tamil Nadu 538-4 dec** (R. N. B. Apparajith 112, K. D. Karthik 154*); **Karnataka 562-6** (G. Satish 200*, C. M. Gautam 130*). *Tamil Nadu 1pt, Karnataka 3pts. All six Tamil Nadu batsmen reached 50, and Dinesh Karthik and Ramaswamy Prasanna (74*) added 200* for the fifth wicket. But Ganesh Satish, with a maiden double-century, and Muralidharan Gautam put on 204* for Karnataka's sixth before Gautam dislocated his shoulder celebrating his century; he briefly retired hurt, but steered them to first-innings points on his return.*

At Delhi (Feroz Shah Kotla), November 17–20, 2012. **Drawn. Baroda 561** (A. R. Chauhan 113, A. T. Rayudu 131); ‡**Delhi 505-6** (M. Manhas 106, R. Bhatia 133*). *Delhi 1pt, Baroda 1pt. Abhimanyu Chauhan and Ambati Rayudu shared a fourth-wicket stand of 213.*

At Rohtak, November 17–20, 2012. **Odisha won by four wickets. Haryana 66** (B. C. Mohanty 5-24) **and 300;** ‡**Odisha 219** (M. Sharma 5-49) **and 152-6.** *Odisha 6pts. For the second time in successive Ranji matches, both at Rohtak, Haryana were put in and collapsed for under 70 on the first day. Odisha completed their first win for four years.*

At Chennai (Chidambaram), November 17–20, 2012. **Tamil Nadu won by 104 runs.** ‡**Tamil Nadu 276 and 149; Maharashtra 233 and 88.** *Tamil Nadu 6pts.*

At Meerut (Bhamashah), November 17–20, 2012. **Drawn. Uttar Pradesh 283** (M. Kaif 122; H. S. Sharath 5-67) **and 343-5 dec** (Parvinder Singh 143*); ‡**Karnataka 181** (Bhuvneshwar Kumar 5-36) **and 274-8.** *Uttar Pradesh 3pts, Karnataka 1pt. Bhuvneshwar Kumar (91) and Parvinder Singh rescued Uttar Pradesh's second innings from 88-4 by adding 230.*

At Delhi (Feroz Shah Kotla), November 24–27, 2012. **Drawn. Delhi 555-4 dec** (U. Chand 138, S. Dhawan 104, M. Sharma 175, V. Rawal 100*); ‡**Tamil Nadu 226 and 220-2** (K. B. Arun Karthik 121*). *Delhi 3pts, Tamil Nadu 1pt. Four of Delhi's top five scored centuries. Unmukt Chand and Shikhar Dhawan opened with 205, and Mohit Sharma and debutant Vaibhav Rawal added 221 for the fourth wicket.*

At Rohtak, November 24–27, 2012. **Baroda won by one wicket.** ‡**Haryana 295** (R. Dalal 104; U. B. Patel 5-83) **and 160; Baroda 324** (S. P. Wakaskar 100; A. Mishra 5-97) **and 133-9** (M. Sharma 5-50). *Baroda 6pts. Baroda were 108-9 chasing 132, but Nos 10 and 11 Utkarsh Patel and Bhargav Bhatt, with 14* apiece, inflicted a third successive defeat on Haryana.*

At Bangalore (Chinnaswamy), November 24–27, 2012. **Odisha won by 65 runs. Odisha 202 and 255** (R. Vinay Kumar 7-58); ‡**Karnataka 213 and 179.** *Odisha 6pts. Odisha had waited four years for a win, and now two came along at once – this a week after the first.*

At Nagpur (VCA Ground), November 24–27, 2012. **Drawn.** ‡**Maharashtra 282** (V. S. Awate 126; S. B. Wagh 5-23) **and 261-7 dec** (V. S. Awate 112); **Vidarbha 266 and 103-1.** *Vidarbha 1pt, Maharashtra 3pts. Virag Awate scored a century in each innings on first-class debut. Shrikant Wagh had figures of 27.1–17–23–5.*

At Rohtak, December 1–4, 2012. **Haryana won by 83 runs.** ‡**Haryana 307** (P. Awana 5-71) **and 209** (S. Narwal 5-35); **Delhi 224 and 209.** *Haryana 6pts. After losing their first three matches of the season, Haryana secured their first Ranji victory over Delhi.*

At Sambalpur, December 1–4, 2012. **Drawn. Maharashtra 315 and 333-5;** ‡**Odisha 441** (N. J. Behera 111, B. B. Samantray 107). *Odisha 3pts, Maharashtra 1pt.*

At Kanpur (Modi), December 1–3, 2012. **Uttar Pradesh won by ten wickets. Baroda 254 and 114** (Bhuvneshwar Kumar 5-34); ‡**Uttar Pradesh 361** (A. N. Alam 106) **and 8-0.** *Uttar Pradesh 7pts.*

At Nagpur (VCA Ground), December 1–4, 2012. **Drawn. Tamil Nadu 443-8 dec** (S. Badrinath 192); ‡**Vidarbha 566-8** (F. Y. Fazal 143). *Vidarbha 3pts, Tamil Nadu 1pt.*

At Vadodara (Moti Bagh), December 8–10, 2012. **Baroda won by ten wickets. Odisha 181** (B. A. Bhatt 6-73) **and 123;** ‡**Baroda 301** (D. R. Behera 5-77) **and 4-0.** *Baroda 7pts.*

At Bangalore (Chinnaswamy), December 8–11, 2012. **Karnataka won by 159 runs.** ‡**Karnataka 192** (P. Awana 5-81) **and 475-9 dec; Delhi 258 and 250.** *Karnataka 6pts.*

At Gahunje, December 8–11, 2012. **Drawn.** ‡**Haryana 257 and 255-7; Maharashtra 540-8 dec** (S. D. Atitkar 190, K. M. Jadhav 109). *Maharashtra 3pts, Haryana 1pt.*

At Nagpur (VCA Ground), December 8–11, 2012. **Drawn.** ‡**Uttar Pradesh 548-8 dec** (M. B. Dagar 116, A. N. Alam 100) **and 175-3** (S. K. Raina 105*); **Vidarbha 308.** *Vidarbha 1pt, Uttar Pradesh 3pts.*

At Vadodara (Moti Bagh), December 15–18, 2012. **Drawn. Baroda 208** (V. Y. Mahesh 5-26) **and 260;** ‡**Tamil Nadu 230 and 108-2.** *Baroda 1pt, Tamil Nadu 3pts.*

At Delhi (Roshanara), December 15–18, 2012. **Delhi won by seven wickets. Maharashtra 196 and 266;** ‡**Delhi 193** (S. M. Fallah 5-67) **and 273-3** (S. Dhawan 116*). *Delhi 6pts.*

At Mysore, December 15–18, 2012. **Drawn. Karnataka 619-8 dec** (K. L. Rahul 157, C. M. Gautam 257) **and 81-3;** ‡**Vidarbha 447** (A. V. Ubarhande 137). *Karnataka 3pts, Vidarbha 1pt. Gautam reached a maiden double-hundred, lasting 576 minutes and 394 balls, and hitting 20 fours; he put on 272 for Karnataka's third wicket with Lokesh Rahul. Amol Ubarhande and Shalabh Shrivastava (97) responded with 228 for Vidarbha's third wicket.*

At Lucknow, December 15–18, 2012. **Drawn. Uttar Pradesh 227** (M. Sharma 5-47) **and 348** (E. R. Dwivedi 121); ‡**Haryana 276** (A. Rajpoot 6-68) **and 106-3.** *Uttar Pradesh 1pt, Haryana 3pts.*

At Hubli, December 22–25, 2012. **Drawn. Haryana 587-9 dec** (A. Mishra 202*, J. Yadav 211); ‡**Karnataka 272** (K. R. Kapoor 106; H. V. Patel 5-79) **and 332-2** (R. V. Uthappa 137, K. R. Kapoor 100*). *Karnataka 1pt, Haryana 3pts. This was the first first-class match at the D. R. Bendre Karnataka SCA Stadium, built on the site of an old toilet block. Haryana were 168-7 before Amit Mishra and Jayant Yadav piled up 392, the second-highest eighth-wicket stand in all first-class cricket; neither had previously scored a century, but both went on to doubles. Kunal Kapoor scored the first and – as Karnataka followed on – second hundreds of his career.*

At Gahunje, December 22–25, 2012. **Drawn. Baroda 362** (A. A. Waghmode 113, K. H. Devdhar 104) **and 231-1** (S. P. Wakaskar 100*, A. R. Chauhan 109*); ‡**Maharashtra 449-8 dec** (H. H. Khadiwale 168). *Maharashtra 3pts, Baroda 1pt. In Baroda's second innings, Saurabh Wakaskar and Abhimanyu Chauhan put on 217* for the second wicket.*

At Cuttack (Dhaneswar Rath), December 22–24, 2012. **Vidarbha won by 106 runs. Vidarbha 206 and 140** (A. G. Mangaraj 5-19); ‡**Odisha 121 and 119** (A. G. Jungade 5-44). *Vidarbha 6pts.*

At Chennai (Chemplast), December 22–25, 2012. **Uttar Pradesh won by 195 runs.** ‡**Uttar Pradesh 392** (A. G. Murtaza 106) **and 207;** **Tamil Nadu 179** (A. G. Murtaza 7-80) **and 225.** *Uttar Pradesh 6pts. Ali Murtaza added 10-142 to his century as Uttar Pradesh's third win put them in the quarter-finals. Baba Apparajith held five catches in the field in Uttar Pradesh's first innings, and six in all.*

At Gahunje, December 29, 2012–January 1, 2013. **Karnataka won by eight wickets. Karnataka 572-9 dec** (C. M. Gautam 264*, S. T. R. Binny 168) **and 92-2;** ‡**Maharashtra 99** (A. Mithun 6-36) **and 561** (H. H. Khadiwale 136, A. R. Bawne 155*). *Karnataka 6pts. Karnataka won with eight balls to spare to rise from sixth place to third, and join Uttar Pradesh and Baroda in the quarter-finals. Gautam hit his second double-hundred in a fortnight; he was unbeaten for 642 minutes and 464 balls, with 32 fours and a six, and shared a stand of 340 with Stuart Binny for Karnataka's fifth wicket. Mithun and Binny then shot out Maharashtra for 99 – the last nine fell for 31 – a deficit of 473, though they passed 500 following on.*

At Cuttack (Barabati), December 29–31, 2012. **Uttar Pradesh won by 43 runs. Uttar Pradesh 160** (D. R. Behera 6-37) **and 111;** ‡**Odisha 127** (Imtiaz Ahmed 5-45) **and 101** (Imtiaz Ahmed 5-29). *Uttar Pradesh 6pts. Uttar Pradesh's fourth match saw 15 wickets fall on the first day and 19 on the second.*

At Chennai (Guru Nanak), December 29, 2012–January 1, 2013. **Drawn.** ‡**Tamil Nadu 571-6 dec** (K. D. Karthik 187, V. Shankar 100*); **Haryana 180-3.** *Tamil Nadu 1pt, Haryana 1pt. Leg-spinner Yuzvendra Chahal conceded 235 in 57 overs in Tamil Nadu's innings, but wicketkeeper Nitin Saini allowed no byes.*

At Nagpur (VCA Ground), December 29, 2012–January 1, 2013. **Drawn.** ‡**Delhi 523-9 dec** (V. Rawal 104); **Vidarbha 257 and 216-7.** *Vidarbha 1pt, Delhi 3pts.*

Group C

At Anantapur, November 2–5, 2012. **Drawn. Services 297 and 59-2;** ‡**Andhra 251.** *Andhra 1pt, Services 3pts.*

At Guwahati (Nehru), November 2–5, 2012. **Assam won by ten wickets.** ‡**Assam 450** (D. S. Jadhav 243; T. K. Chanda 5-74) **and 62-0;** **Tripura 145 and 366** (A. Ratra 124). *Assam 7pts. Dheeraj Jadhav's fifth double-century lasted 635 minutes and 462 balls, and included 30 fours and a six; he added 213 with Syed Mohammad (89) for Assam's sixth wicket.*

At Amtar, November 2–5, 2012. **Drawn.** ‡**Kerala 229** (S. V. Samson 127*) **and 256-6** (P. Rohan Prem 100*); **Himachal Pradesh 536-6 dec** (P. Dogra 121, Amit Kumar 101, R. Dhawan 102*). *Himachal Pradesh 3pts, Kerala 1pt. This was the first match at the Atal Bihari Vajpayee Stadium.*

At Jammu (Gandhi), November 2–4, 2012. **Jharkhand won by an innings and 31 runs. ‡Jammu and Kashmir 195 and 151** (S. Nadeem 6-54); **Jharkhand 377.** *Jharkhand 7pts.*

At Anantapur, November 9–12, 2012. **Drawn. ‡Tripura 260** (S. Abbas Ali 103) **and 170-4; Andhra 436-8 dec** (D. B. Prasanth Kumar 119, H. H. Watekar 116). *Andhra 3pts, Tripura 1pt. Prasanth Kumar and Hemal Watekar opened with 227.*

At Porvorim, November 9–12, 2012. **Drawn. ‡Jammu and Kashmir 338** (Parvez Rasool 171) **and 95-6; Goa 406-6 dec** (S. A. Asnodkar 103). *Goa 3pts, Jammu and Kashmir 1pt.*

At Amtar, November 9–12, 2012. **Drawn. Services 312 and 314-4** (S. M. Swain 118*); **‡Himachal Pradesh 544-6 dec** (P. Dogra 210). *Himachal Pradesh 3pts, Services 1pt. Paras Dogra completed his second double-hundred and added 210 for Himachal Pradesh's fourth wicket with Amit Kumar (91).*

At Jamshedpur, November 9–12, 2012. **Assam won by 53 runs. Assam 179 and 207; ‡Jharkhand 174** (A. G. Konwar 6-67) **and 159** (J. Syed Mohammad 5-52). *Assam 6pts.*

At Amtar, November 17–20, 2012. **Drawn. Andhra 372** (B. A. Sumanth 102, A. A. Muzumdar 101; V. Malik 5-74) **and 282-7 dec** (A. A. Muzumdar 104; R. Dhawan 5-77); **‡Himachal Pradesh 265** (P. Dogra 122; P. D. Vijaykumar 6-80) **and 108-4.** *Himachal Pradesh 1pt, Andhra 3pts. Amol Muzumdar scored twin centuries to briefly overtake Wasim Jaffer as the leading Ranji run-scorer, while in reply Dogra scored his third hundred in three innings. Himachal Pradesh's 21-year-old wicketkeeper Aatish Bhalaik held nine catches in the match.*

At Jamshedpur, November 17–20, 2012. **Drawn. ‡Jharkhand 360; Goa 208** (S. Nadeem 5-64) **and 292-8** (S. Gupta 6-93). *Jharkhand 3pts, Goa 1pt.*

At Perintalmanna, November 17–20, 2012. **Drawn. ‡Kerala 264** (A. G. Konwar 5-53) **and 294-5 dec** (A. M. Hegde 129, V. A. Jagadeesh 127); **Assam 286 and 201-6** (K. R. Sreejith 5-75). *Kerala 1pt, Assam 3pts. Abhishek Hegde and V. A. Jagadeesh added 228 for the second wicket in Kerala's second innings.*

At Agartala, November 17–20, 2012. **Drawn. ‡Services 563-4 dec** (A. H. Gupta 147, Yashpal Singh 250*, R. Paliwal 104*) **and 7-0; Tripura 484** (S. Abbas Ali 121, A. A. Dey 107; S. Nazar 6-108). *Tripura 1pt, Services 3pts. Yashpal Singh's fifth and highest double-century occupied 528 minutes and 361 balls, with 31 fours and five sixes, and beat his own record of 240 for Services. He added 291 with Anshul Gupta for the fourth wicket, and 206* with Rajat Paliwal for the fifth; both reached maiden hundreds. Tripura racked up their highest total in reply.*

At Jammu (Gandhi), November 24–26, 2012. **Andhra won by an innings and 15 runs. Jammu and Kashmir 153** (K. S. Sahabuddin 5-53) **and 222; ‡Andhra 390** (A. G. Pradeep 136; R. Punia 5-63). *Andhra 7pts. Andhra completed an innings win after being reduced to 8-3.*

At Ranchi (Heavy Engineering), November 24–27, 2012. **Drawn. ‡Jharkhand 236** (S. S. Tiwary 102; R. Dhawan 6-63) **and 244-2** (A. R. Verma 117); **Himachal Pradesh 442-7 dec** (P. Chopra 101, R. Dhawan 128). *Jharkhand 1pt, Himachal Pradesh 3pts.*

At Perintalmanna, November 24–27, 2012. **Drawn. ‡Goa 512-8 dec** (S. K. Kamat 107, R. D. Asnodkar 100*); **Kerala 297 and 120-4.** *Kerala 1pt, Goa 3pts.*

At Delhi (Palam), November 24–26, 2012. **Services won by ten wickets. Assam 182 and 170** (S. Nazar 6-50); **‡Services 326** (R. Paliwal 167) **and 27-0.** *Services 7pts.*

At Visakhapatnam (Rajasekhara Reddy), December 1–4, 2012. **Drawn. Andhra 393** (D. Sivakumar 106*; S. S. Bandekar 5-107) **and 193-6 dec; ‡Goa 328** (R. U. Shukla 121; D. Sivakumar 6-45) **and 14-0.** *Andhra 3pts, Goa 1pt.*

At Guwahati (Nehru), December 1–4, 2012. **Jammu and Kashmir won by 235 runs. Jammu and Kashmir 323** (A. K. Das 6-87) **and 318-5 dec** (I. Dev Singh 118, Parvez Rasool 120*); **‡Assam 165** (Parvez Rasool 7-41) **and 241** (Tarjinder Singh 105). *Jammu and Kashmir 6pts. This was Jammu and Kashmir's first win for three years.*

At Amtar, December 1–4, 2012. **Tripura won by 169 runs. Tripura 441** (S. S. Roy 111) **and 177** (V. Malik 5-36); **‡Himachal Pradesh 260 and 189** (P. Dogra 105*). *Tripura 6pts.*

At Delhi (Palam), December 1–4, 2012. **Drawn. Kerala 314** (V. A. Jagadeesh 199*) **and 193-3 dec** (A. M. Hegde 107); **‡Services 335** (S. Chatarjee 107) **and 85-0.** *Services 3pts, Kerala 1pt. Jagadeesh* *carried his bat through Kerala's first innings, but was stranded one short of a maiden double-century.*

At Guwahati (Nehru), December 8–11, 2012. **Drawn. Assam 354; ‡Himachal Pradesh 316-5** (R. Dhawan 114*). *Assam 1pt, Himachal Pradesh 1pt.*

At Porvorim, December 8–11, 2012. **Drawn. ‡Services 473** (S. Chatarjee 103, Yashpal Singh 166*) **and 99-2; Goa 381.** *Goa 1pt, Services 3pts.*

At Perintalmanna, December 8–10, 2012. **Jammu and Kashmir won by 74 runs. ‡Jammu and Kashmir 215** (I. Dev Singh 117*; C. P. Shahid 8-51) **and 151** (P. Prasanth 5-16); **Kerala 163 and 129** (Parvez Rasool 5-43, M. Gupta 5-26). *Jammu and Kashmir 6pts. Slow left-armer Payarambath Shahid claimed a career-best 8-51 on the first day as Ian Dev Singh carried his bat. Jammu and Kashmir won a second match in a season for the first time since 2000-01.*

At Agartala, December 8–9, 2012. **Jharkhand won by seven wickets. Tripura 106** (A. R. Yadav 6-38) **and 86** (S. S. Rao 5-36); **‡Jharkhand 139** (T. K. Chanda 6-44) **and 55-3.** *Jharkhand 6pts. Jharkhand won inside two days.*

At Porvorim, December 15–18, 2012. **Drawn. ‡Himachal Pradesh 338 and 237-4** (P. Dogra 119*); **Goa 347** (Rahul Singh 5-71). *Goa 3pts, Himachal Pradesh 1pt.*

At Dhanbad, December 15–18, 2012. **Drawn. Jharkhand 257** (S. S. Tiwary 119) **and 295-9 dec** (S. M. Basha 6-74); **‡Andhra 410** (A. A. Muzumdar 180) **and 32-4.** *Jharkhand 1pt, Andhra 3pts.*

At Delhi (Palam), December 15–18, 2012. **Services won by five wickets. ‡Jammu and Kashmir 85 and 269** (Nishan Singh 5-73); **Services 221** (R. Paliwal 120; R. Punia 5-71) **and 134-5.** *Services 6pts.*

At Agartala, December 15–18, 2012. **Kerala won by an innings and 77 runs. Kerala 400** (P. Rohan Prem 170); **‡Tripura 127** (U. Manukrishnan 6-37) **and 196** (S. Sandeep Warrier 5-46). *Kerala 7pts.*

At Guwahati (Nehru), December 22–25, 2012. **Drawn. Andhra 249** (A. A. Muzumdar 108*) **and 229-7; ‡Assam 394-5 dec** (Tarjinder Singh 103*). *Assam 3pts, Andhra 1pt.*

At Jammu (Gandhi), December 22–25, 2012. **Drawn. Jammu and Kashmir 175** (V. Malik 5-41) **and 248; ‡Himachal Pradesh 189** (R. Punia 6-50) **and 189-2.** *Jammu and Kashmir 1pt, Himachal Pradesh 3pts.*

At Perintalmanna, December 22–24, 2012. **Kerala won by an innings and 35 runs. Jharkhand 120 and 170** (S. Sandeep Warrier 6-44); **‡Kerala 325** (V. A. Jagadeesh 138, R. M. Fernandez 111). *Kerala 7pts. Both teams lost an opener in their first over, but Jagadeesh and Robert Fernandez paved the way for Kerala's victory in a second-wicket stand of 230.*

At Agartala, December 22–25, 2012. **Drawn. Tripura 278; ‡Goa 116-6.** *Tripura 1pt, Goa 1pt.*

At Cuddapah, December 29, 2012–January 1, 2013. **Drawn. Andhra 329** (A. A. Muzumdar 146) **and 191** (C. P. Shahid 5-52); **‡Kerala 312** (V. A. Jagadeesh 117, S. V. Samson 122) **and 192-4.** *Andhra 3pts, Kerala 1pt. Muzumdar became the first player to score 9,000 Ranji runs during his fifth hundred of the season.*

At Porvorim, December 29, 2012–January 1, 2013. **Drawn. Goa 381** (A. S. Desai 105; A. K. Das 5-83) **and 241-4; ‡Assam 366.** *Goa 3pts, Assam 1pt.*

At Jammu (Gandhi), December 29, 2012–January 1, 2013. **Drawn. Tripura 355-8 dec** (A. Ratra 103*; Parvez Rasool 6-91); **‡Jammu and Kashmir 47-1.** *Jammu and Kashmir 1pt, Tripura 1pt.*

At Delhi (Palam), December 29, 2012–January 1, 2013. **Jharkhand won by five wickets. Services 185** (A. R. Yadav 5-30) **and 152** (A. R. Yadav 6-43); **‡Jharkhand 120** (S. Yadav 6-43) **and 219-5.** *Jharkhand 6pts. Jharkhand joined Services in the quarter-finals.*

Quarter-finals

At Jamshedpur, January 6–10, 2013. **Drawn.** Punjab qualified for the semi-finals by virtue of their first-innings lead. **‡Jharkhand 401** (R. K. Nemat 100, I. R. Jaggi 132) **and 33-0; Punjab 699-3 dec** (Jiwanjot Singh 131, T. Kohli 300*, U. Kaul 113*). *On the final day Taruwar Kohli, in only his second game since December 2009, advanced from a maiden double-century to the fifth and last triple of this tournament (a few hours after Pujara, below). He faced 609 balls in 823 minutes, and* *struck 34 fours and two sixes, adding 156 with Jiwanjot (whose century was the fifth of his debut season), 204 with Mandeep Singh (96), and 264* with Uday Kaul for Punjab's second, third and fourth wickets.*

At Mumbai (Wankhede), January 6–10, 2013. **Drawn.** Mumbai qualified for the semi-finals by virtue of their first-innings lead. ‡**Mumbai 645-9 dec** (Wasim Jaffer 150, S. R. Tendulkar 108, A. M. Nayar 132) **and 295-6 dec** (K. R. Pawar 115); **Baroda 271 and 137-3.** *Tendulkar scored his 80th first-class hundred, and put on 234 for Mumbai's third wicket with Jaffer, who reached 9,000 Ranji runs. Wakaskar and Waghmode shared opening stands of 102 and 101 for Baroda.*

At Rajkot (Saurashtra University), January 6–10, 2013. **Drawn.** Saurashtra qualified for the semi-finals by virtue of their first-innings lead. ‡**Saurashtra 469** (A. V. Vasavada 152*) **and 718-9** (C. A. Pujara 352, S. P. Jackson 117); **Karnataka 396** (M. K. Pandey 177). *This was the first match at the Saurashtra University Ground (the main Rajkot stadium was required for a one-day international against England) and featured 1,583 runs in all. After taking the first-innings lead, Saurashtra set out to make sure Karnataka could not win. Pujara moved from his sixth double-hundred to his second triple, and then the highest innings in the world since Stephen Cook's 390 for Lions v Warriors in October 2009; he batted 548 minutes and 427 balls, hitting 49 fours and a six, and put on 343 for Saurashtra's fourth wicket with Sheldon Jackson. Pujara's score was his third double of the season, and he was to add a fourth, against Australia. It was also the third triple-century for Saurashtra in two months; both that and the total of 718-9 were team records. They scored 463-3 on the fourth day.*

At Indore (Holkar), January 6–8, 2013. **Services won by five wickets. Uttar Pradesh 134** (S. Nazar 5-51) **and 241** (S. Yadav 7-71); ‡**Services 263** (R. Paliwal 112; A. Rajpoot 5-61) **and 116-5** (A. Rajpoot 5-36). *The only outright result of the quarter-finals arrived inside three days. Services almost doubled Uttar Pradesh's first innings, then won 54-5 chasing 113 when their captain, Soumik Chatarjee, who had to be carried to the team bus after injuring his knee on the opening day, arrived at the crease; he saw them through by hopping and limping to 34* in 46 balls.*

Semi-finals

At Rajkot (Khandheri), January 16–20, 2013. **Saurashtra won by 229 runs.** ‡**Saurashtra 477** (S. P. Jackson 107) **and 170; Punjab 299 and 119** (V. H. Joshi 5-43). *Despite missing their star batsmen Jadeja and Pujara, Saurashtra reached their first final since the 1930s, when they played as Nawanagar. Off-spinner Vishal Joshi took 9-102 in the match, and Punjab lost their last eight wickets in 15 overs on the last day.*

At Delhi (Palam), January 16–21, 2013. **Drawn.** Mumbai qualified for the final by virtue of their first-innings lead. ‡**Mumbai 454-8 dec** (A. P. Tare 120, A. B. Agarkar 145); **Services 240** (D. S. Kulkarni 5-33). *Only 100 people came to watch Tendulkar bat on the opening day. Tare and Ajit Agarkar, with a career-best 145, added 246 after Mumbai were 169-6. But with hail and rain wiping out the third and fourth, the match went into a sixth day – available if the first-innings lead was not decided in five – at which point Services collapsed.*

Final

At Mumbai (Wankhede), January 26–28, 2013. **Mumbai won by an innings and 125 runs. Saurashtra 148 and 82** (D. S. Kulkarni 5-32); ‡**Mumbai 355** (Wasim Jaffer 132). *Jaffer passed 16,000 first-class runs during his 47th century. It was also his 32nd in Ranji cricket, beating Ajay Sharma's record, and enabled him to overtake Muzumdar again as the leading Ranji run-scorer. On the third day, Saurashtra collapsed to 11-5 and then 34-7; their tail restored some dignity, but they lost with two days to spare, giving Mumbai their 40th Ranji title. The match displaced the Women's World Cup from the Wankhede Stadium.*

RANJI TROPHY WINNERS

1934-35	Bombay	1938-39	Bengal	1942-43	Baroda
1935-36	Bombay	1939-40	Maharashtra	1943-44	Western India
1936-37	Nawanagar	1940-41	Maharashtra	1944-45	Bombay
1937-38	Hyderabad	1941-42	Bombay	1945-46	Holkar

1946-47	Baroda	1969-70	Bombay	1992-93	Punjab
1947-48	Holkar	1970-71	Bombay	1993-94	Bombay
1948-49	Bombay	1971-72	Bombay	1994-95	Bombay
1949-50	Baroda	1972-73	Bombay	1995-96	Karnataka
1950-51	Holkar	1973-74	Karnataka	1996-97	Mumbai
1951-52	Bombay	1974-75	Bombay	1997-98	Karnataka
1952-53	Holkar	1975-76	Bombay	1998-99	Karnataka
1953-54	Bombay	1976-77	Bombay	1999-2000	Mumbai
1954-55	Madras	1977-78	Karnataka	2000-01	Baroda
1955-56	Bombay	1978-79	Delhi	2001-02	Railways
1956-57	Bombay	1979-80	Delhi	2002-03	Mumbai
1957-58	Baroda	1980-81	Bombay	2003-04	Mumbai
1958-59	Bombay	1981-82	Delhi	2004-05	Railways
1959-60	Bombay	1982-83	Karnataka	2005-06	Uttar Pradesh
1960-61	Bombay	1983-84	Bombay	2006-07	Mumbai
1961-62	Bombay	1984-85	Bombay	2007-08	Delhi
1962-63	Bombay	1985-86	Delhi	2008-09	Mumbai
1963-64	Bombay	1986-87	Hyderabad	2009-10	Mumbai
1964-65	Bombay	1987-88	Tamil Nadu	2010-11	Rajasthan
1965-66	Bombay	1988-89	Delhi	2011-12	Rajasthan
1966-67	Bombay	1989-90	Bengal	2012-13	Mumbai
1967-68	Bombay	1990-91	Haryana		
1968-69	Bombay	1991-92	Delhi		

Bombay/Mumbai have won the Ranji Trophy 40 times, Delhi 7, Karnataka 6, Baroda 5, Holkar 4, Bengal, Hyderabad, Madras/Tamil Nadu, Maharashtra, Railways and Rajasthan 2, Haryana, Nawanagar, Punjab, Uttar Pradesh and Western India 1.

N. K. P. SALVE CHALLENGER TROPHY, 2012-13

50-over mini-league plus final

Final

At Rajkot (Khandheri), October 2, 2012 (day/night). **India B won by 139 runs. ‡India B 356-3** (50 overs) (M. Vijay 155); **India A 217** (42.1 overs). *Murali Vijay hit a one-day-best 155 in 121 balls, with 18 fours and five sixes, and added a match-winning 192 with Cheteshwar Pujara (79) for India B's second wicket.*

VIJAY HAZARE TROPHY, 2012-13

Five 50-over zonal leagues plus knockout

Semi-finals

At Visakhapatnam (Rajasekhara Reddy), March 2, 2013. **Assam won by five wickets. Kerala 197** (48.5 overs); **‡Assam 200-5** (46 overs). *Kerala lost their last four wickets for three runs in 14 balls, whereas Assam fought back from 28-3.*

At Visakhapatnam (Port Trust), March 2, 2013. **Delhi won by six wickets. Bengal 156** (40.1 overs); **‡Delhi 160-4** (34.3 overs). *Only two batsmen reached double figures for Bengal, and Delhi cruised home with more than 15 overs to spare.*

Final

At Visakhapatnam (Rajasekhara Reddy), March 3, 2013. **Delhi won by 75 runs. Delhi 290-9** (50 overs) (U. Chand 116); **‡Assam 215** (44.2 overs). *Nineteen-year-old Unmukt Chand, with a maiden one-day hundred, and Jagrit Anand (48) helped secure the trophy with 115 for Delhi's third wicket.*

DEODHAR TROPHY, 2012-13

50-over knockout

Quarter-final

At Guwahati (Nehru), March 10, 2013. **South Zone won by 11 runs.** ‡**South Zone 284-5** (50 overs) (R. N. B. Apparajith 121); **East Zone 273-7** (50 overs). *Eighteen-year-old Baba Apparajith scored 121, his maiden one-day hundred, in 129 balls.*

Semi-finals

At Guwahati (Nehru), March 11, 2013. **North Zone won by eight wickets** (VJD method). **Central Zone 190** (41.5 overs); ‡**North Zone 160-2** (29.5 overs). *Central Zone's innings was reduced by rain to 45 overs, and North Zone's target revised to 160 in 33. Yuvraj Singh hit 77 in 70 balls, and added 129* for North Zone's third wicket with Unmukt Chand (56*).*

At Guwahati (Nehru), March 12, 2013. **West Zone won by five wickets. South Zone 258-8** (50 overs); ‡**West Zone 259-5** (41.1 overs). *Vijay Zol led West Zone's run-chase with 75 in 88 balls.*

Final

At Guwahati (Nehru), March 13, 2013. **West Zone won by five wickets. North Zone 289-8** (50 overs); ‡**West Zone 293-5** (48.2 overs). *The same finalists met for the fourth year running; following two victories for North Zone, West Zone retained the title they had won in 2011-12. Chand (88) and Yuvraj (67) shared another big stand, 120 for North Zone's third wicket, but Ambati Rayudu (78*) and Kedar Jadhav (57) swung the match with 87 for West Zone's fifth.*

SYED MUSHTAQ ALI TROPHY, 2012-13

Five 20-over zonal leagues, two super leagues plus final

Final

At Indore (Holkar), March 31, 2013. **Gujarat won by six wickets.** ‡**Punjab 122-8** (20 overs); **Gujarat 128-4** (17.5 overs). *Punjab struggled to fight back from 20-4 in the sixth over, a crisis caused largely by Jasprit Bumrah (3-14).*

NEW ZEALAND CRICKET, 2013

Twelve topsy-turvy months

ANDREW ALDERSON

James Bond and Ernst Stavro Blofeld. Han Solo and Darth Vader. The New
Zealand cricket team and the New Zealand cricket team. No other international
side played hero and villain quite like them during 2013, oscillating between
compelling victories, frustrating draws and ignominious defeats.

Test trouncings by South Africa, in the wake of Ross Taylor's sacking as
captain the previous year, were countered by a victorious recovery in the one-
day internationals. Test improvements in a drawn home series against England
were tempered by dire batting collapses at Lord's and Headingley. A
subsequent one-day series triumph in England was diluted by a rain-affected
Champions Trophy exit at the group stage. Drawing the Test series and losing
the one-dayers in Bangladesh provided little cheer, nor did a limited-overs

NEW ZEALAND IN 2013

	Played	Won	Lost	Drawn/No result
Tests	12	2	4	6
One-day internationals	19	7	10	2
Twenty20 internationals	7	3	3	1

DECEMBER JANUARY	2 Tests, 3 ODIs and 3 T20Is (a) v South Africa	(see *Wisden 2013*, page 1075)
FEBRUARY MARCH	3 Tests, 3 ODIs and 3 T20Is (h) v England	(page 255)
APRIL		
MAY	2 Tests, 3 ODIs and 2 T20Is (a) v England	(page 279)
JUNE	Champions Trophy (in England)	(page 301)
JULY		
AUGUST		
SEPTEMBER		
OCTOBER	2 Tests, 3 ODIs and 1 T20I (a) v Bangladesh	(page 903)
NOVEMBER	3 ODIs and 2 T20Is (a) v Sri Lanka	(page 1131)
DECEMBER JANUARY	3 Tests, 5 ODIs and 2 T20Is (h) v West Indies	(page 995)

For a review of New Zealand domestic cricket from the 2012-13 season, see page 1009.

series – again disrupted by rain – in Sri Lanka. But things began to look up at the end of the year, when West Indies were dismantled 2–0, New Zealand's first win in a three-Test series for eight years. Consistency remained elusive.

The nadir came early – at Cape Town on January 2. A team suffering from Taylor's self-imposed absence, and also missing Jesse Ryder, Tim Southee and Daniel Vettori, was torpedoed for 45 by South Africa's fast bowlers, after Brendon McCullum had chosen to bat in his first Test as captain. The gilded lettering was apparently still on the ball at the end of the 19.2-over innings, and fans bellowed "What have you done today?" as the team trudged to their bus. New Zealand had made two lower totals in Tests, but this was their shortest innings; even the record low of 26, against England at Auckland in 1954-55, lasted 27 overs.

However, it wouldn't feel like an annual summary of New Zealand cricket without a couple of other nominees for the "worst moment" Oscar. Both involved lawyers. In April, McCullum announced his intention to launch defamation proceedings against the for-  mer Test opener John Parker, over a leaked document examining the way Taylor was removed as captain. McCullum believed it impugned his integrity as a professional sportsman. He was prepared to pay for the case, and did not seek damages. Mike Hesson, the coach, also left the issue with his lawyers. Parker apologised to them both, and issued a retraction.

Then, in December, the *New Zealand Herald* revealed that three former internationals – later reported to be Chris Cairns, Daryl Tuffey and Lou Vincent – were part of an ICC investigation into match-fixing. Cairns and Tuffey denied the allegations, and at the start of the year the investigation was ongoing.

On the field, three men in particular starred in Tests. After he returned against England, Taylor made 866 runs

Fighting spirit: Jesse Ryder scores a century on his first-class comeback seven months after spending 56 hours in a coma.

– five short of the most by a New Zealander in a calendar year, set by John Reid in 1965 – and averaged 72. He made centuries in all three Tests against West Indies. Trent Boult took 46 wickets, including ten for 80 as West Indies were beaten by an innings at Wellington, while Southee claimed 36, including ten in vain at Lord's. Both averaged around 25. They may have lacked frightening speed but – mentored by Shane Bond – worked intelligently, seizing on weaknesses.

Taylor's career average of 47.51 by the end of 2013 was the highest by any New Zealander with more than ten Tests, and he joined Nathan Astle with 11 hundreds, behind only John Wright (12) and Martin Crowe (17).

Martin Guptill and Mitchell McClenaghan dominated the limited-overs formats. Guptill showed his prowess with consecutive 50-overs centuries against England, including New Zealand's highest score, 189 not out, at Southampton. He averaged 50 in both one-dayers and Twenty20s. And when McCullum gave left-armer McClenaghan free licence with the new ball, he obliged with 40 wickets at 19 in one-day internationals – 17 more than Kyle Mills – and also topped the Twenty20 charts.

Other issues simmered. Jesse Ryder was the embodiment of mercurial. An attack outside a Christchurch pub in March had left him in intensive care, and a medically induced coma. He returned to health, was slapped with a six-month suspension for taking a banned stimulant, joined Otago… and scored three first-class hundreds and two half-centuries, before returning to the national one-day team.

Daniel Vettori opted to reject a central contract, and underwent surgery on an Achilles tendon in June in a bid to prolong his career. The focus moved to his successors: leg-spinner Ish Sodhi looked the part, but his 11 wickets in five Tests cost more than 50 apiece. Nathan McCullum and Kane Williamson padded out the spin quota in one-day internationals. Chris Martin retired, aged 38, after more than 12 years' service. In 71 Tests, he took 233 wickets – third on New Zealand's all-time list – although he was just as well loved for his almost complete lack of batting ability. Martin never appeared to be affected by the trappings of fame, and soon became a default choice for journalists seeking insightful analysis delivered with a common touch.

The board's director of cricket, John Buchanan, left in July because of "family circumstances", while the contract of selection manager Kim Littlejohn – another Australian – was not renewed in September; the former Test opener Bruce Edgar took his place.

New Zealand Cricket agreed a new constitution, and a revamped eight-strong board, now chaired by Otago businessman Stuart Heal, was elected. Three former players – Sir Richard Hadlee, Geoff Allott and Martin Snedden – were among the newcomers.

Administrators had to prepare for the 2015 World Cup. The New Zealand part of the operation, led by Therese Walsh, outlined a "patriotism over profit" vision, which revealed an even split of pool matches with Australia (21 out of 42), a quarter-final in Wellington, and a semi in Auckland. Cricket Australia will receive twice as much revenue from ticket sales, but Walsh said the objective was to take as much cricket to as many destinations as possible, to enhance the goodwill that had been fostered during the 1992 tournament. With Christchurch's Lancaster Park still out of action because of earthquake damage, Hagley Oval was approved for construction after submissions to the Environment Court, and will host the World Cup's opening match.

NEW ZEALAND v WEST INDIES, 2013-14

Andrew McGlashan

Test matches (3): New Zealand 2, West Indies 0
One-day internationals (5): New Zealand 2, West Indies 2
Twenty20 internationals (2): New Zealand 2, West Indies 0

This was a low-key tour which had to compete for airtime with the Ashes across the Tasman, and India's visit to South Africa. Neither side began in particularly good shape: West Indies had just been thrashed in India, while New Zealand had not long returned from trips to Bangladesh and Sri Lanka which brought little success. But New Zealand felt much better after thumping victories in two of the three Tests here – although the one-day internationals were shared, much to the annoyance of their captain, Brendon McCullum.

Only two of the West Indian Test squad – Shivnarine Chanderpaul and Denesh Ramdin – had played in that format in New Zealand before, and it showed. The others were not helped by a chaotic build-up: having a single warm-up game was not unusual, but only half the Test squad had arrived for this one, as the rest were still involved in the one-day series in India. The "West Indian XI" had to be filled up by local players – one of whom, Aaron Redmond, did so well that he played against his erstwhile team-mates in the First Test the following week.

The others did eventually show up, but some were still jetlagged when the First Test started in Dunedin. West Indies spent the first half of the match sleepwalking, and had to follow on after conceding a deficit of 396 – so it was a minor miracle that they escaped with a draw, thanks to Darren Bravo's maiden double-century and a spot of rain.

Their comeback raised hopes of an exciting series – but West Indies collapsed badly in both, failing to come to terms with New Zealand's pace-bowling strength. Tim Southee and Trent Boult shared 38 wickets in the series, and McCullum hailed them as close to world-class. Boult was particularly eye-catching at Wellington, where he troubled the batsmen with a deceptively sharp bouncer as well as artful swing, and finished with ten for 80.

New Zealand's Test year had been pockmarked with some horrendous batting lows – 45 at Cape Town, 68 at Lord's – but at home they were more secure. Ross Taylor stood above everyone, and joined Mark Burgess as the only New Zealander to make hundreds in three consecutive Tests; Taylor's came in the space of three weeks, while Burgess's had taken three years, between 1969 and 1972. Taylor's final tally of 495 runs was second only to Andrew Jones's 513 (against Sri Lanka at home in 1990-91) for New Zealand in a three-Test series. It was the ideal end to a year that had begun with his withdrawal from the side after being sacked as captain.

Contributions elsewhere were less prolific, although Kane Williamson's elegance stood out when he returned from a broken thumb, and McCullum plundered his first hundred in three years – although he continued to divide opinion, in terms of both where he batted and his leadership. This first Test-series victory as captain was a relief, as it backed up his claims about the strides the team were making at home.

For West Indies there was precious little to cheer from the Tests, other than Bravo's defiance. Their fast bowling was threadbare: Kemar Roach and Fidel Edwards were both absent injured, while Ravi Rampaul was not selected because of doubts about his fitness. By the Third Test they were playing two frontline spinners. Shane Shillingford began the series as the No. 1 slow bowler, but ended it suspended for a second time after his action was deemed illegal, and flying home. The news came on the eve of the final Test, and left both captain Darren Sammy and coach Ottis Gibson biting their lips.

He wasn't the last player to depart. Marlon Samuels, one of the disappointments of the Test series, flew home for surgery on a wrist injury (he, too, had been banned, from bowling his quicker ball). During the one-day series Darren Bravo left early for undisclosed family reasons, Sammy went lame, and Rampaul broke a finger. There was briefly a worry that West Indies might not be able to muster 11 fit men. That they shared the 50-over series was no mean feat – especially after Corey Anderson's world-record 36-ball hundred at Queenstown on New Year's Day had threatened to overwhelm them.

WEST INDIAN TOURING PARTY

*D. J. G. Sammy (T/50/20), S. Badree (20), T. L. Best (T/50/20), K. C. Brathwaite (T), D. J. Bravo (50/20), D. M. Bravo (T), S. Chanderpaul (T), J. Charles (50/20), S. S. Cottrell (T), N. Deonarine (T/50/20), K. A. Edwards (T/50), A. D. S. Fletcher (20), S. T. Gabriel (T), J. O. Holder (50/20), N. O. Miller (50/20), S. P. Narine (T/50/20), V. Permaul (T), K. O. A. Powell (T/50/20), D. Ramdin (T/50/20), R. Rampaul (50/20), A. D. Russell (50/20), M. N. Samuels (T), S. Shillingford (T), L. M. P. Simmons (50/20), C. A. K. Walton (T/50/20). *Coach:* O. D. Gibson.

C. H. Gayle was originally selected, but failed to recover from a leg injury sustained on the tour of India, and was replaced by Brathwaite. D. J. Bravo captained in the one-day internationals, and in the Twenty20 matches too after Sammy injured a hamstring. Russell, chosen only for the Twenty20 squad, played in the final one-day international as well. Samuels was originally selected for the limited-overs matches, but injured his wrist and was replaced by Walton. D. M. Bravo returned home for personal reasons after the first one-day international, but was not replaced.

TEST MATCH AVERAGES

NEW ZEALAND – BATTING AND FIELDING

	T	I	NO	R	HS	100	50	Avge	Ct
L. R. P. L. Taylor	3	5	3	495	217*	3	0	247.50	7
K. S. Williamson	2	3	0	159	58	0	2	53.00	4
B. B. McCullum	3	4	0	171	113	1	0	42.75	1
B-J. Watling	3	3	0	126	65	0	1	42.00	13
†H. D. Rutherford	3	5	1	151	62	0	1	37.75	1
†C. J. Anderson	3	4	1	97	39	0	0	32.33	2
I. S. Sodhi	3	3	0	71	35	0	0	23.66	1
†N. Wagner	3	3	0	59	37	0	0	19.66	0
P. G. Fulton	3	5	0	91	61	0	1	18.20	4
T. G. Southee	3	3	0	41	21	0	0	13.66	3

Played in three Tests: T. A. Boult 38*, 1* (1 ct). Played in one Test: A. J. Redmond 20, 6.

BOWLING

	Style	O	M	R	W	BB	5I	Avge
T. A. Boult	LFM	116.5	29	308	20	6-40	1	15.40
T. G. Southee	RFM	108.5	17	326	18	4-52	0	18.11
C. J. Anderson	LFM	57	7	147	8	3-47	0	18.37
N. Wagner	LFM	95	13	364	8	3-112	0	45.50
I. S. Sodhi	LBG	84.3	10	301	5	2-63	0	60.20

Also bowled: A. J. Redmond (LBG) 5–1–18–0; K. S. Williamson (OB) 10–1–38–0.

WEST INDIES – BATTING AND FIELDING

	T	I	NO	R	HS	100	50	Avge	Ct
†D. M. Bravo	2	4	0	262	218	1	0	65.50	2
†S. Chanderpaul	3	6	2	256	122*	1	1	64.00	0
D. Ramdin	3	6	1	192	107	1	0	38.40	7
D. J. G. Sammy	3	6	1	134	80	0	1	26.80	6
K. A. Edwards	3	6	0	156	59	0	2	26.00	4
M. N. Samuels	3	6	0	117	60	0	1	19.50	2
†N. Deonarine	3	6	0	116	52	0	1	19.33	4
†K. O. A. Powell	3	6	0	104	36	0	0	17.33	1
T. L. Best	3	6	0	49	25	0	0	8.16	1
S. Shillingford	2	4	0	25	15	0	0	6.25	1
S. T. Gabriel	2	4	1	0	0*	0	0	0.00	1

Played in one Test: K. C. Brathwaite 45, 7; †S. P. Narine 2, 0*; V. Permaul 20, 0.

BOWLING

	Style	O	M	R	W	BB	5I	Avge
S. P. Narine	OB	58.3	23	130	6	6-91	1	21.66
D. J. G. Sammy	RM	80.1	18	261	7	2-69	0	37.28
S. Shillingford	OB	89	16	256	6	4-26	0	42.66
N. Deonarine	OB	44.4	2	137	3	2-76	0	45.66
T. L. Best	RF	84.1	11	369	8	4-110	0	46.12

Also bowled: S. T. Gabriel (RFM) 58–10–250–2; V. Permaul (OB) 42–7–132–2.

At Lincoln, November 27–29, 2013. **Drawn. ‡New Zealand XI 227-8 dec** (H. D. Rutherford 61) **and 168-3 dec** (P. G. Fulton 53, H. D. Rutherford 72); **West Indians 230-6 dec** (A. J. Redmond 67, S. Chanderpaul 89; M. D. Craig 4-78) **and 121-2** (C. A. K. Walton 61*). *As several of the West Indian squad were still in India – the final international of their hastily arranged tour there was on November 27 – their side for this first-class match included six New Zealanders, one of whom, Aaron Redmond, pressed his case for a Test recall the following week with a polished 67. Peter Fulton and Hamish Rutherford put on 142 in the second innings before both retired out.*

NEW ZEALAND v WEST INDIES

First Test Match

At Dunedin (University Oval), December 3–7, 2013. Drawn. Toss: West Indies.

Eight months after being denied by England's last-wicket pair at Auckland, New Zealand again left with a draw when victory had appeared certain. This time weather played a part, curtailing their unconvincing run-chase five minutes before tea on the final day. However, West Indies showed incredible resolve after following on midway through the match. Having spent more than eight hours in the field watching Taylor compile his maiden double-hundred, Darren Bravo spent nine and a half making one of his own: his 218 was the second-highest score by a West Indian in New Zealand, behind Seymour Nurse's 258 at Christchurch in 1968-69.

When play was finally abandoned at 6.10, with New Zealand 33 short of victory and six wickets in hand, McCullum's expression was as drawn as the match itself. Exactly a year on from his appointment as captain following the sacking of Taylor, he was still awaiting his first victory. McCullum did score his first Test hundred for three years on the opening day, but that didn't make the result any less galling.

Sammy had bowled first on a well-grassed pitch, but West Indies were woeful with the new ball, allowing Rutherford – with his first Test fifty since his 171 on debut against England earlier in the year – and Fulton to canter to 95. The platform was not wasted, although Best came within inches of nabbing Taylor when he gloved over slip on two. Taylor and McCullum joined forces in a free-wheeling fourth-wicket partnership eventually worth 195 in 43 overs. There was a regular supply of loose balls, but it was a hugely significant performance by two players under such scrutiny: McCullum said he had "never played under so much media and public pressure". Taylor, without a hundred since his final match as captain in Colombo more than a year earlier, had also been in need of a big innings. As he resisted his trademark slog-sweep, and rarely hit in the air, he exuded self-denial.

McCullum was first to three figures, from 101 balls, then Taylor reached his, in 150; the new captain's celebrations were more exuberant than his predecessor's. McCullum finally fell early on the second day, but West Indies were hampered when Sammy strained a glute muscle in his 24th over and could not bowl again in the match. Taylor was dropped at short leg when 131, but largely went about his business as he pleased to get to 200 from 295 balls. It was his country's 17th Test double-century, and the first since McCullum's 225 in India in November 2010. New Zealand reached 600 for the fourth time in Tests – and for the fourth time they would be denied victory.

West Indies' reply began predictably badly against probing new-ball spells from Boult and Southee. Both openers were gone within ten overs and, on the third day of a series which would prove full of flat-footed wafts, there were regular catches for the cordon. As so often, only Chanderpaul showed the ability to resist, rattling up 76 off 87 balls, but Boult eventually trapped him too, lbw offering no stroke. McCullum was soon enforcing the follow-on, a no-brainer with a lead of 396, although it did risk a long spell in the field.

Wickets proved harder to come by second time round, but New Zealand chipped away efficiently at first. When Samuels and Chanderpaul departed early on the fourth morning, leaving West Indies 185 for four and still more than 200 adrift, bags were being packed and airline schedules checked.

But Bravo was going nowhere. His overseas record was already formidable: all his previous five Test hundreds had come away from home, and he finished this match averaging 57 overseas, against just under 30 in the Caribbean. Still, this was a display few believed possible from any West Indian apart from Chanderpaul. Bravo had some luck. On 44 he fended a bouncer from Wagner to first slip, and New Zealand reviewed the original not-out decision. Replays appeared to show a touch on the glove, but the third umpire, Ian Gould, thought otherwise. Then, when Bravo had 82, Wagner spilled a return catch. At the time these appeared to be no more than annoyances for New Zealand.

But over by over, hour by hour, session by session, Bravo ploughed on. His 200 came up late on the fourth day, from 390 balls. References to his famous cousin were never far away, not least from Sammy: "Even the great Lara would have been proud of that innings." Bravo and Sammy added 90 for the seventh wicket to take West Indies into the lead, but Bravo was finally defeated by a grubber from Boult early on the final morning, after 572 minutes, 416 balls and 31 fours. Sammy was left to edge the advantage into three figures as the sky began to fill in.

New Zealand needed only 112, but began like a team unused to winning. Shillingford, handed the new ball thanks to Sammy's injury and Gabriel's profligacy, preyed on their nerves. When McCullum skied a slog-sweep it was 44 for four, and there were whispers of a comeback bordering on Kolkata 2000-01. Taylor and Anderson kept calm, but the early wickets had curbed their attacking instincts. This would prove crucial: when the rain came, it wouldn't stop. After so much hard work, New Zealand were left cursing the win that got away.

Man of the Match: L. R. P. L. Taylor.

Close of play: first day, New Zealand 367-3 (Taylor 103, McCullum 109); second day, West Indies 67-2 (Bravo 37, Samuels 14); third day, West Indies 168-2 (Bravo 72, Samuels 17); fourth day, West Indies 443-6 (Bravo 210, Sammy 44).

New Zealand

P. G. Fulton c Edwards b Sammy	61	– c Ramdin b Shillingford	3
H. D. Rutherford c Deonarine b Shillingford	62	– b Gabriel b Shillingford	20
A. J. Redmond c Samuels b Best	20	– c Deonarine b Shillingford	6
L. R. P. L. Taylor not out	217	– not out	16
*B. B. McCullum b Sammy	113	– c Ramdin b Shillingford	9
C. J. Anderson c Ramdin b Best	0	– not out	20
†B-J. Watling c Edwards b Best	41		
T. G. Southee c Bravo b Deonarine	2		
I. S. Sodhi c and b Deonarine	35		
N. Wagner run out	37		
B 10, l-b 10, n-b 1	21	B 1, l-b 3, w 1	5

1/95 (2) 2/117 (3) (9 wkts dec, 153.1 overs) 609
3/185 (1) 4/380 (5) 5/385 (6)
6/469 (7) 7/472 (8) 8/548 (9) 9/609 (10)

1/3 (1) 2/15 (3) (4 wkts, 30 overs) 79
3/31 (2) 4/44 (5)

T. A. Boult did not bat.

Best 34.1–5–148–3; Gabriel 27.5–4–148–0; Sammy 23.1–4–79–2; Shillingford 46–7–138–1; Deonarine 22–0–76–2. *Second innings*—Best 8–1–26–0; Shillingford 15–5–26–4; Gabriel 5–1–16–0; Deonarine 2–0–7–0.

West Indies

K. A. Edwards c Fulton b Boult	0	– lbw b Sodhi	59
K. O. A. Powell c Watling b Southee	7	– c Southee b Boult	14
D. M. Bravo c McCullum b Southee	40	– b Boult	218
M. N. Samuels c Taylor b Southee	14	– c and b Southee	23
S. Chanderpaul lbw b Boult	76	– lbw b Wagner	1
N. Deonarine c Taylor b Southee	15	– c Watling b Anderson	52
†D. Ramdin c Watling b Boult	12	– b Sodhi	24
*D. J. G. Sammy not out	27	– c Sodhi b Southee	80
S. Shillingford b Sodhi	9	– c Taylor b Wagner	15
T. L. Best run out	0	– c Taylor b Wagner	3
S. T. Gabriel lbw b Sodhi	0	– not out	0
L-b 11, w 1, n-b 1	13	B 4, l-b 7, w 5, n-b 2	18

1/4 (1) 2/24 (2) 3/70 (3) (62.1 overs) 213
4/73 (4) 5/106 (6) 6/174 (7)
7/183 (5) 8/202 (9) 9/205 (10) 10/213 (11)

1/18 (2) 2/135 (1) (162.1 overs) 507
3/178 (4) 4/185 (5)
5/307 (6) 6/363 (7) 7/453 (3)
8/491 (9) 9/507 (10) 10/507 (8)

Boult 18–5–40–3; Southee 16–1–52–4; Wagner 13–2–47–0; Sodhi 15.1–2–63–2. *Second innings*—Southee 29.1–4–101–2; Boult 35–11–81–2; Wagner 30–3–112–3; Anderson 14–2–29–1; Sodhi 49–7–155–2; Redmond 5–1–18–0.

Umpires: N. J. Llong and P. R. Reiffel. Third umpire: I. J. Gould.

NEW ZEALAND v WEST INDIES

Second Test Match

At Wellington (Basin Reserve), December 11–13, 2013. New Zealand won by an innings and 73 runs. Toss: West Indies.

After the frustration of Dunedin, New Zealand secured their first Test victory of 2013, and their first on home soil in nine attempts, overpowering a West Indian side which produced dire cricket from start to finish. Sixteen wickets fell on the third day, with Boult bagging a career-best ten for 80 – the second-best match figures for New Zealand against West Indies, after Richard Hadlee's 11 for 102 at Dunedin in 1979-80.

Boult bowled with skill and pace – as he had done for much of the year – but the batting was feeble. For the first time, West Indies' last four batsmen were dismissed for ducks in the first innings, then in the second all ten wickets clattered for 101 after a useful start. The positive vibes felt after Dunedin evaporated.

West Indies had again wasted favourable bowling conditions after Sammy won the toss. Even the New Zealanders said they had never seen so much grass on a Basin Reserve pitch, and the first ball suggested life wouldn't be easy: Fulton was given lbw to Best, but was saved when DRS showed an inside edge. Both openers still fell cheaply, but Taylor was dropped at third slip by Edwards before he had scored. That would have left New Zealand 26 for three – but they recovered, and from then on it was barely a contest.

The West Indian pacemen – especially Best, who appeared to lose the confidence of his captain – could not find any consistency. Taylor skipped to his second hundred of the series, his tenth in Tests, and was offered two more lives after passing three figures. He eventually carved to deep point shortly before the close, suffering from exhaustion. Still, a first-day total of 307 for six was well above par.

If anything, West Indies were even worse on the second morning, when the opening session – delayed by rain – brought 134 runs in 25 overs. Watling marshalled the lower order, who more than held their own. A last-wicket stand of 58 in 8.1 overs left the visitors ragged; the low point came when Best palmed a catch over the midwicket boundary with Boult on three, much to the frustration of Ottis Gibson, the coach, who was standing behind him.

New Zealand's bowlers immediately pitched the ball further up, which provided boundary opportunities, but also the threat of edges. West Indies had no problem scoring freely, but could not form substantial partnerships. Anderson's bustling left-arm seamers removed Bravo and Edwards, then Deonarine's departure to Boult on the third morning – via a juggling slip catch – opened the floodgates. The last six wickets crumbled for 18.

Boult claimed five of them in the space of 15 deliveries for a Test-best six for 40. When the last wicket fell, the New Zealand think-tank had a huddle in the middle to discuss the follow-on: McCullum enforced it, despite the experience of the previous week, and admitted it had not been a straightforward decision. He may have been nervous as Edwards and Powell added 74, but after lunch his bowlers began to make inroads. Southee was particularly impressive during a nine-over burst that brought him three for 19, while Wagner produced his best spell of the series to date. Boult had bowled only two overs with the new ball, but returned to run through the lower order once again, although his most stunning contribution was a breathtaking catch at backward point to intercept Ramdin's cut.

Sammy completed a pair, the first by a Test captain in nine years – it was a bad Friday the 13th for him – and his forlorn signal for DRS summed up West Indies' haplessness. For McCullum there was relief, and a chance to remind themselves of the words to the team song "Black and White" as they gathered on the pitch a couple of hours after victory was sealed.

Man of the Match: T. A. Boult.

Close of play: first day, New Zealand 307-6 (Watling 8, Southee 9); second day, West Indies 158-4 (Samuels 50, Deonarine 11).

New Zealand

P. G. Fulton c Ramdin b Sammy	6	N. Wagner c Sammy b Best	0
H. D. Rutherford c Ramdin b Best	11	T. A. Boult not out	38
K. S. Williamson c Sammy b Best	45		
L. R. P. L. Taylor c Shillingford b Gabriel	129	B 16, l-b 6, n-b 2	24
*B. B. McCullum c Edwards b Deonarine	37		
C. J. Anderson c Powell b Shillingford	38	1/14 (1) 2/24 (2) (115.1 overs)	441
†B-J. Watling b Gabriel	65	3/112 (3) 4/189 (5)	
T. G. Southee c Bravo b Sammy	21	5/257 (6) 6/296 (4) 7/334 (8)	
I. S. Sodhi c Ramdin b Best	27	8/383 (9) 9/383 (10) 10/441 (7)	

Best 21–1–110–4; Gabriel 25.1–5–86–2; Sammy 25–3–92–2; Shillingford 28–4–92–1; Deonarine 16–2–39–1.

West Indies

K. A. Edwards c Rutherford b Anderson	55	– c Williamson b Southee	35
K. O. A. Powell lbw b Southee	21	– b Southee	36
D. M. Bravo c Fulton b Anderson	4	– c Watling b Wagner	0
M. N. Samuels c Watling b Boult	60	– c Anderson b Southee	12
S. Chanderpaul c Anderson b Boult	6	– not out	31
N. Deonarine c Taylor b Boult	22	– b Boult	12
†D. Ramdin not out	12	– c Boult b Anderson	19
*D. J. G. Sammy b Boult	0	– lbw b Boult	0
S. Shillingford b Boult	0	– c Taylor b Wagner	1
T. L. Best b Boult	0	– c Fulton b Boult	21
S. T. Gabriel b Southee	0	– b Boult	0
L-b 8, w 1, n-b 4	13	L-b 6, w 1, n-b 1	8

1/46 (2) 2/67 (3) 3/103 (1)	(49.5 overs) 193	1/74 (2) 2/75 (3)	(54.5 overs) 175
4/119 (5) 5/175 (4) 6/182 (4)		3/85 (1) 4/94 (4)	
7/182 (8) 8/188 (9) 9/188 (10) 10/193 (11)		5/117 (6) 6/146 (7) 7/147 (8)	
		8/148 (9) 9/175 (10) 10/175 (11)	

Boult 15–5–40–6; Southee 15.5–2–58–2; Wagner 7–1–37–0; Anderson 7–1–20–2; Sodhi 3–1–18–0; Williamson 2–0–12–0. *Second innings*—Boult 12.5–2–40–4; Southee 11–2–24–3; Wagner 17–2–67–2; Anderson 11–1–29–1; Williamson 3–1–9–0.

Umpires: I. J. Gould and P. R. Reiffel.   Third umpire: N. J. Llong.

NEW ZEALAND v WEST INDIES

Third Test Match

At Hamilton, December 19–22, 2013. New Zealand won by eight wickets. Toss: New Zealand.

When New Zealand were dismissed on the third afternoon for 349, a deficit of 18 on a pitch offering considerable help for Sunil Narine on his return to Test cricket, the match was on a knife-edge. But 31 overs later the series had been decided, after another inept batting performance from West Indies. This time they were shot out for 103 – so quickly, in fact, that New Zealand were batting again before the close. The seamers, led by the increasingly dynamic duo of Southee and Boult, dismantled West Indies once more, but they were given a considerable helping hand. "We keep hearing the same song," said a dejected Sammy. It was New Zealand's first series victory over anyone other than Bangladesh or Zimbabwe for eight years, since beating West Indies at home in 2005-06.

Michael Bradley, AFP/Getty Images

Drive in the park: Ross Taylor has to work a little harder for his third hundred of the series.

For two and a half days this match had produced the most compelling cricket of the series. The pattern at the toss continued: for the tenth Test in succession in New Zealand, the captain winning it had bowled first. But this was a much drier surface than normal, and there was significant spin in the first session. Though relieved the result had gone his way, McCullum later admitted he had made the wrong call.

Yet when West Indies slid to 86 for five it did not seem to matter. They were missing Bravo, ruled out on the morning of the game after being hit on the arm in the nets by Sammy. But his replacement, Kraigg Brathwaite – in his first innings of the tour after arriving late because of visa problems – showed real application before steering Southee to gully to trigger the loss of four for nine.

The innings was revived by Chanderpaul and Ramdin, who added 200 in 50 overs of counter-attack. Ramdin was the main aggressor, particularly strong through the off side, although he was given a life on 57 at midwicket by Williamson as he slog-swept Sodhi's leg-spin. Ramdin's fourth Test hundred came up with a slash over the slips, before he jabbed a full delivery to the keeper off Anderson, who continued to excel in his fourth-seamer role. On the second morning Chanderpaul proceeded calmly to his 29th century, in the process overtaking Allan Border's 11,174 runs to become the sixth-highest scorer in Test cricket. He chiselled out 60 for the last two wickets with Permaul and Best.

West Indies soon applied pressure with the ball, especially through Narine, who had been recalled in place of the suspended Shane Shillingford. He struck in his first over, having Fulton brilliantly held at leg slip by Sammy – the first of his three sharp catches – and tilted the match in his side's favour with the scalps of Williamson and McCullum.

But Taylor stood in their way again, though even he struggled against Narine's variations. Once past fifty, however, another century felt inevitable – and he eventually became only the second New Zealander to score hundreds in three successive Tests. Still, after Taylor carved to third man, Narine mopped up the last three wickets to leave New Zealand vulnerable. Or so it appeared.

Brathwaite's ugly swipe across the line of an inswinger set the tone for West Indies' second innings, and by Boult's fifth over he had removed the top three. This time, New Zealand's catching was outstanding, particularly Williamson's fine effort to remove Chanderpaul in the gully: the ball was behind him when he grasped it, full stretch to his right. Southee then burst through to take the last three in five balls, the second of which (Permaul lbw) was his 100th Test wicket.

On the fourth morning the chase was a formality once Narine had been unable to create any early panic. Williamson punched nine fours in a classy half-century, and Taylor's brief stay lifted him to 495 runs in the series.

Man of the Match: L. R. P. L. Taylor.

Close of play: first day, West Indies 289-6 (Chanderpaul 94, Sammy 0); second day, New Zealand 156-3 (Taylor 56, McCullum 11); third day, New Zealand 6-0 (Fulton 4, Rutherford 0).

West Indies

K. C. Brathwaite c Williamson b Southee	45	– b Boult	7
K. O. A. Powell c Watling b Wagner	26	– (3) c Southee b Boult	0
K. A. Edwards c Watling b Southee	6	– (2) c Watling b Boult	1
M. N. Samuels c Williamson b Anderson	0	– c Watling b Anderson	8
S. Chanderpaul not out	122	– c Williamson b Wagner	20
N. Deonarine lbw b Anderson	2	– c Taylor b Wagner	13
†D. Ramdin c Watling b Anderson	107	– lbw b Boult	18
*D. J. G. Sammy c Watling b Southee	3	– c Watling b Southee	24
S. P. Narine b Boult	2	– not out	0
V. Permaul c Fulton b Southee	20	– lbw b Southee	0
T. L. Best c Watling b Sodhi	25	– lbw b Southee	0
B 2, l-b 6, w 1	9	L-b 12	12
	367		103

1/41 (2) 2/77 (1) 3/78 (3) (116.2 overs) 367
4/82 (4) 5/86 (6) 6/286 (7)
7/296 (8) 8/307 (9) 9/332 (10) 10/367 (11)

1/12 (1) 2/12 (3) (31.5 overs) 103
3/13 (2) 4/40 (4)
5/46 (5) 6/75 (6) 7/91 (7)
8/103 (8) 9/103 (10) 10/103 (11)

Boult 26–2–84–1; Southee 28–3–79–4; Wagner 21–4–67–1; Anderson 19–3–47–3; Williamson 5–0–17–0; Sodhi 17.2–0–65–1. *Second innings*—Boult 10–4–23–4; Southee 8.5–5–12–3; Anderson 6–0–22–1; Wagner 7–1–34–2.

New Zealand

P. G. Fulton c Sammy b Narine	11	– c and b Sammy	10
H. D. Rutherford c and b Sammy	10	– not out	48
K. S. Williamson lbw b Narine	58	– b Permaul	56
L. R. P. L. Taylor c Samuels b Best	131	– not out	2
*B. B. McCullum c Sammy b Narine	12		
C. J. Anderson c Deonarine b Permaul	39		
†B-J. Watling c Ramdin b Sammy	20		
T. G. Southee lbw b Narine	18		
I. S. Sodhi b Narine	9		
N. Wagner c Edwards b Narine	22		
T. A. Boult not out	1		
B 6, l-b 8, n-b 4	18	B 7, n-b 1	8
	349		124

1/18 (2) 2/43 (1) 3/138 (3) (117.3 overs) 349
4/174 (5) 5/224 (6) 6/269 (7)
7/306 (4) 8/317 (8) 9/332 (9) 10/349 (10)

1/33 (1) (2 wkts, 40.4 overs) 124
2/116 (3)

Best 14–1–63–1; Sammy 23–8–69–2; Permaul 35–6–103–1; Narine 42.3–17–91–6; Deonarine 3–0–9–0. *Second innings*—Best 7–3–22–0; Narine 16–6–39–0; Sammy 9–3–21–1; Permaul 7–1–29–1; Deonarine 1.4–0–6–0.

Umpires: I. J. Gould and N. J. Llong. Third umpire: P. R. Reiffel.
Series referee: R. S. Mahanama.

NEW ZEALAND v WEST INDIES

First One-Day International

At Auckland, December 26, 2013 (day/night). West Indies won by two wickets. Toss: West Indies.

A match low on batting quality was swung West Indies' way by Sammy's 43 off 27 balls; he almost angrily carried them across the line with a series of vicious blows as team-mates departed regularly. They needed 61 when Sammy arrived at six down, and were still 36 short when Ramdin became McClenaghan's fifth victim. But Holder helped reduce the target to ten before he was caught down the leg side, and Sammy was not going to hang around to see what the last two batsmen could offer: he heaved a six and swatted a four in McClenaghan's last over to seal victory with more than 22 overs to spare. New Zealand had lost their top four for single figures after being put in. That included Jesse Ryder, who drove to point for a five-ball duck on his return to international cricket after a gap of nearly two years, the last ten months of which had included life-threatening injuries from an assault, and a ban for taking a prohibited substance. The only meaningful contributions came from the McCullum brothers, though Brendon was far from impressed at his lbw decision, upheld on referral, believing he was so far down the pitch as to make DRS unreliable.

Man of the Match: D. J. G. Sammy.

New Zealand

M. J. Guptill lbw b Rampaul	2	K. D. Mills c Sammy b D. J. Bravo	3
J. D. Ryder c D. M. Bravo b Rampaul	0	M. J. McClenaghan not out	3
K. S. Williamson c Ramdin b Holder	8		
L. R. P. L. Taylor run out	3	L-b 6, w 3	9
*B. B. McCullum lbw b D. J. Bravo	51		
C. J. Anderson c Simmons b D. J. Bravo	13	1/2 (2) 2/3 (1) 3/10 (4) (42.1 overs) 156	
†L. Ronchi c Charles b Narine	7	4/32 (3) 5/57 (6) 6/66 (7)	
J. D. S. Neesham c D. M. Bravo b D. J. Bravo	10	7/93 (8) 8/104 (5) 9/112 (10)	
N. L. McCullum c D. M. Bravo b Holder	47	10/156 (9) 10 overs: 20-3	

Holder 7.1–1–21–2; Rampaul 9–0–27–2; Sammy 6–0–30–0; Narine 10–2–28–1; D. J. Bravo 10–0–44–4.

West Indies

J. Charles b McClenaghan	9	D. J. G. Sammy not out	43
K. O. A. Powell b McClenaghan	4	J. O. Holder c Ronchi b Neesham	10
D. M. Bravo c Williamson b McClenaghan	14	S. P. Narine not out	0
L. M. P. Simmons c Taylor b Mills	34	L-b 8, w 14, n-b 1	23
*D. J. Bravo lbw b McClenaghan	12		
N. Deonarine b Mills	6	1/5 (2) 2/19 (1) (8 wkts, 27.3 overs) 157	
†D. Ramdin c B. B. McCullum		3/32 (4) 4/60 (5) 5/94 (4)	
b McClenaghan	2	6/96 (6) 7/121 (7) 8/147 (9) 10 overs: 47-3	

R. Rampaul did not bat.

Mills 8–1–37–2; McClenaghan 9.3–0–58–5; Neesham 6–0–35–1; Anderson 4–0–19–0.

Umpires: G. A. V. Baxter and R. E. J. Martinesz.   Third umpire: I. J. Gould.

NEW ZEALAND v WEST INDIES

Second One-Day International

At Napier, December 29, 2013 (day/night). Abandoned.

The match was called off at 5.20 because of a wet outfield. The drainage problems raised concerns about the World Cup matches scheduled for McLean Park in 2015.

NEW ZEALAND v WEST INDIES
Third One-Day International

At Queenstown, January 1, 2014. New Zealand won by 159 runs. Toss: West Indies.

This game was minutes away from another washout, but the weather cleared around the Remarkables mountain range just in time to allow a feat that matched the stunning location. The New Year was welcomed in by a new world record, as Corey Anderson blasted the fastest century in international cricket, a 36-ball display of fireworks that edged Shahid Afridi's 17-year-old mark by one delivery. In October 1996, Afridi had batted for Pakistan at No. 3 against Sri Lanka in Nairobi – but Anderson was at No. 5, and – in a contest reduced to 21 overs per side – arrived at the crease as late as the eighth over. It was scarcely believable, despite the small boundaries and ragged bowling, when he reached his hundred with his 12th six in an over from Miller costing 27 – the most expensive of an innings in which 13 overs leaked double figures. In all, Anderson faced 47 balls, and hit 14 sixes en route equalling the fastest List A hundred, by Graham Rose for Somerset against Devon at Torquay in 1990. But it wasn't the innings' only hundred: Ryder's 46-ball century (the sixth-fastest in one-day internationals) had to settle for second billing. He had 41 when Anderson joined him, but reached three figures an over later during a stand of 191 from 75 deliveries. Once West Indies lost three quick wickets, New Zealand's only concern was completing 20 overs before the rain returned.

Man of the Match: C. J. Anderson.

New Zealand

M. J. Guptill c Ramdin b Holder	1	†L. Ronchi not out	3
J. D. Ryder c Miller b Holder	104	W 2	2
*B. B. McCullum c Simmons b Narine	33		
L. R. P. L. Taylor c Powell b Miller	9	1/5 (1) 2/56 (3) (4 wkts, 21 overs)	283
C. J. Anderson not out	131	3/84 (4) 4/275 (2)	
		4 overs: 48-1	

J. D. S. Neesham, N. L. McCullum, K. D. Mills, A. F. Milne and M. J. McClenaghan did not bat.

Narine 4–0–50–1; Holder 4–0–48–2; Rampaul 3–0–64–0; Miller 4–0–44–1; Bravo 4–0–48–0; Simmons 2–0–29–0.

West Indies

J. Charles c Neesham b Mills	0	†D. Ramdin not out	1
L. M. P. Simmons c Milne b McClenaghan	13	L-b 5, w 2	7
C. A. K. Walton c Milne b Ryder	17		
K. O. A. Powell c Neesham b McClenaghan	1	1/0 (1) 2/17 (2) (5 wkts, 21 overs)	124
*D. J. Bravo not out	56	3/19 (4) 4/56 (3)	
N. Deonarine c Milne b Neesham	29	5/112 (6)	
		4 overs: 19-3	

N. O. Miller, J. O. Holder, S. P. Narine and R. Rampaul did not bat.

Mills 2–0–11–1; McClenaghan 2–0–7–2; N. L. McCullum 5–0–27–0; Ryder 4–0–13–1; Neesham 4–0–21–1; Guptill 2–0–13–0; Milne 2–0–27–0.

Umpires: C. B. Gaffaney and R. E. J. Martinesz. Third umpire: I. J. Gould.

NEW ZEALAND v WEST INDIES
Fourth One-Day International

At Nelson, January 4, 2014. New Zealand won by 58 runs (D/L). Toss: New Zealand.

New Zealand took the series lead with a solid all-round performance in the first one-day international at the Saxton Oval. Guptill struggled at times for fluency, but anchored the innings with 81 from 119 balls, his first significant contribution after four single-figure scores since returning from injury. West Indies did not help themselves by dropping Ryder twice (one a sitter to Ramdin) in the first ten overs, both off the luckless Holder, who later had a third chance spilled when Brendon McCullum was reprieved first ball at deep square. Taylor provided some middle-order impetus, before New Zealand's total assumed daunting proportions when both West Indian openers fell for ducks. Edwards and Simmons made a decent fist of rebuilding, but were never on top of the asking-rate, or the D/L par score as rain threatened. As at Queenstown, New Zealand hustled through some overs of spin to reach 20. And when Simmons picked out deep midwicket, the game was up, well before the weather closed in.

Man of the Match: M. J. Guptill.

New Zealand

M. J. Guptill c Bravo b Holder	81	N. L. McCullum not out		9
J. D. Ryder c Ramdin b Bravo	47			
K. S. Williamson c Ramdin b Best	47	L-b 5, w 6, n-b 1		12
L. R. P. L. Taylor run out	49			
*B. B. McCullum c Bravo b Narine	14	1/56 (2) 2/144 (3)	(6 wkts, 50 overs)	285
C. J. Anderson not out	17	3/203 (1) 4/232 (5)		
†L. Ronchi b Bravo	9	5/253 (4) 6/267 (7)	10 overs: 38-0	

K. D. Mills, T. G. Southee and M. J. McClenaghan did not bat.

Holder 10–2–58–1; Best 9–0–70–1; Bravo 7–0–35–2; Miller 10–0–47–0; Narine 10–0–47–1; Deonarine 4–0–23–0.

West Indies

C. A. K. Walton run out	0	†D. Ramdin not out		17
J. Charles c Southee b McClenaghan	0	L-b 3, w 1		4
K. A. Edwards run out	24			
L. M. P. Simmons c Guptill b Williamson	43	1/0 (1) 2/2 (2)	(5 wkts, 33.4 overs)	134
*D. J. Bravo not out	43	3/62 (3) 4/83 (4)		
N. Deonarine c Mills b N. L. McCullum	3	5/92 (6)	10 overs: 40-2	

N. O. Miller, J. O. Holder, S. P. Narine and T. L. Best did not bat.

Southee 5–1–21–0; McClenaghan 6.4–1–30–1; Mills 2–0–10–0; Anderson 2–0–10–0; N. L. McCullum 10–0–30–1; Williamson 8–0–30–1.

Umpires: B. F. Bowden and I. J. Gould.   Third umpire: R. E. J. Martinesz.

NEW ZEALAND v WEST INDIES

Fifth One-Day International

At Hamilton, January 8, 2014 (day/night). West Indies by 203 runs. Toss: New Zealand.

Against the odds, West Indies secured an overwhelming victory to square the series after amassing their highest one-day total, surpassing 360 for four against Sri Lanka at Karachi during the 1987 World Cup. Edwards made his maiden one-day century, and Bravo only the second of his 154-match career; they added 211, West Indies' third-highest partnership for any wicket, to build on the rapid start provided by Powell. He zoomed to 73 from 44 balls, with a dozen fours and two sixes – one of which was caught one-handed in the crowd, earning spectator Michael Morton $NZ100,000 as part of a sponsor's competition. Edwards favoured the leg side, where he struck three of his four sixes, while Bravo was a delight to watch when driving straight or through extra cover. In all, the last ten overs produced 117 runs. The contest was effectively settled when New Zealand lost their top five inside 15 overs; slow left-armer Miller, taking advantage of players throwing the bat, helped himself to four wickets.

Man of the Match: D. J. Bravo.

West Indies

K. O. A. Powell lbw b N. L. McCullum	73	A. D. Russell not out		6
J. Charles run out	31	L-b 4, w 11		15
K. A. Edwards not out	123			
L. M. P. Simmons c Williamson b Anderson	9	1/95 (1) 2/116 (2)	(4 wkts, 50 overs)	363
*D. J. Bravo c N. L. McCullum b Williamson	106	3/143 (4) 4/354 (5)	10 overs: 83-0	

C. A. K. Walton, †D. Ramdin, N. O. Miller, J. O. Holder and S. P. Narine did not bat.

Southee 10–0–64–0; McClenaghan 8–0–64–0; N. L. McCullum 10–0–64–1; Anderson 10–1–77–1; Mills 8–0–60–0; Williamson 4–0–30–1.

New Zealand

M. J. Guptill b Bravo	6		T. G. Southee c Bravo b Miller		9
J. D. Ryder c Simmons b Holder	17		M. J. McClenaghan not out		0
K. S. Williamson lbw b Holder	16				
L. R. P. L. Taylor c Ramdin b Miller	9		L-b 6, w 3		9
*B. B. McCullum c Charles b Miller	6				
C. J. Anderson c Bravo b Russell	29		1/21 (1) 2/37 (2) 3/45 (3)	(29.5 overs)	160
†L. Ronchi hit wkt b Miller	15		4/50 (4) 5/65 (5) 6/94 (6)		
N. L. McCullum c Ramdin b Russell	18		7/123 (8) 8/125 (7) 9/151 (10)		
K. D. Mills run out	26		10/160 (9)	10 overs: 47-3	

Holder 5–0–35–2; Bravo 5–0–12–1; Miller 10–1–45–4; Narine 5.5–0–31–0; Russell 4–0–31–2.

Umpires: C. B. Gaffaney and R. E. J. Martinesz.   Third umpire: I. J. Gould.

Series referee: B. C. Broad.

NEW ZEALAND v WEST INDIES

First Twenty20 International

At Auckland, January 11, 2014 (floodlit). New Zealand won by 81 runs. Toss: New Zealand. Twenty20 international debuts: K. O. A. Powell, C. A. K. Walton.

Brendon McCullum took out his frustration of seeing the one-day series slip away with an unbeaten 60 to set up a resounding victory. But it was Ronchi who played the decisive hand with 48 – in their stand of 85 in seven overs – after New Zealand had threatened to lose their way when Best struck twice in four balls during the 13th. Much to the crowd's disappointment he claimed Anderson second ball, caught at deep square, but the last three overs of the innings brought 46 runs to sway the match back towards New Zealand. West Indies never got going in the chase, losing Simmons in the second over when he edged the rapid Milne, who touched 95mph. Nathan McCullum made it a good day for the family with four wickets, all to catches in the deep by Guptill and Ryder.

Man of the Match: L. Ronchi.

New Zealand		B	4	6		West Indies		B	4	6
M. J. Guptill c 1 b 11	25	16	3	1		J. Charles c 7 b 8	16	14	3	0
J. D. Ryder c 1 b 8	22	14	3	0		L. M. P. Simmons c 7 b 11	0	4	0	0
*B. B. McCullum not out	60	45	2	4		†A. D. S. Fletcher c 2 b 9	23	25	0	1
L. R. P. L. Taylor c 5 b 8	5	7	0	0		K. O. A. Powell c 1 b 9	12	14	1	0
C. Munro c 3 b 11	22	12	1	2		*D. J. Bravo c 2 b 9	10	11	1	0
C. J. Anderson c 4 b 11	0	2	0	0		A. D. Russell c 1 b 9	0	2	0	0
†L. Ronchi not out	48	25	3	4		C. A. K. Walton c 5 b 8	9	8	0	1
B 5, w 1, n-b 1	7					N. O. Miller not out	15	18	1	0
						S. P. Narine c 11 b 8	0	2	0	0
6 overs: 55-1	(20 overs) 189-5					S. Badree not out	14	22	1	0
						L-b 2, w 7	9			

1/38 2/56 3/66 4/103 5/104

J. D. S. Neesham, N. L. McCullum, T. G. Southee and A. F. Milne did not bat.

6 overs: 39-2   (20 overs) 108-8

1/11 2/31 3/53 4/59 5/64 6/75 7/77 8/77

T. L. Best did not bat.

Badree 4–0–25–0; Best 4–0–40–3; Narine 4–0–46–0; Miller 3–0–26–2; Bravo 4–0–24–0; Russell 1–0–23–0.

Southee 4–0–36–0; Milne 4–0–15–1; Neesham 4–0–16–3; N. L. McCullum 4–0–24–4; Anderson 4–0–15–0.

Umpires: C. B. Gaffaney and D. J. Walker.   Third umpire: G. A. V. Baxter.

NEW ZEALAND v WEST INDIES

Second Twenty20 International

At Wellington (Westpac Stadium), January 15, 2014 (floodlit). New Zealand won by four wickets.
Toss: West Indies. Twenty20 international debut: J. O. Holder.

When New Zealand stumbled to 79 for five in the 11th over, it looked as if West Indies would add
a share of the Twenty20 series to their 50-over draw the previous week. However, Ronchi played his
second crucial innings in five days, reaching his first half-century for New Zealand (he previously
made one for Australia, in a one-day international in St Kitts in 2008), and sharing the defining stand
of 68 in seven overs with Taylor. West Indies' spirit was sapped in the 15th over, bowled by Bravo,
which cost 17 and brought the requirement down to 37 off 30 balls. Ronchi's fifty arrived, from only
25 deliveries, with a thunderous straight-drive – and, although Taylor fell to Narine, Neesham
finished the series with two fours and a six in four balls from Best. Earlier West Indies, whose side
included five players who had kept wicket at international level, were floundering at 67 for four
before Ramdin's maiden Twenty20 fifty lifted them to a competitive total.

Man of the Match: L. Ronchi.

West Indies		*B*	*4*	*6*
L. M. P. Simmons *c 8 b 11*	29	19	5	1
J. Charles *c 1 b 10*	7	12	1	0
A. D. S. Fletcher *run out*	40	36	3	1
*D. J. Bravo *b 9*	12	12	0	1
C. A. K. Walton *c 7 b 10*	0	3	0	0
†D. Ramdin *not out*	55	31	3	3
A. D. Russell *not out*	10	7	1	0
L-b 2, w 4	6			

6 overs: 37-2　　　(20 overs) 159-5

1/22 2/37 3/66 4/67 5/137

N. O. Miller, J. O. Holder, S. P. Narine and
T. L. Best did not bat.

McClenaghan 4–0–29–1; Milne 4–0–22–2;
Neesham 4–0–39–0; Anderson 4–0–50–0;
N. L. McCullum 4–0–17–1.

New Zealand		*B*	*4*	*6*
M. J. Guptill *c 6 b 9*	1	4	0	0
J. D. Ryder *c 1 b 9*	23	9	2	2
*B. B. McCullum *lbw b 10*	17	11	2	1
L. R. P. L. Taylor *c 5 b 10*	39	41	3	0
C. Munro *c 8 b 7*	5	6	0	0
C. J. Anderson *c 2 b 7*	6	9	1	0
†L. Ronchi *not out*	51	28	4	2
J. D. S. Neesham *not out*	14	6	2	1
L-b 3, w 4	7			

6 overs: 53-3　　　(19 overs) 163-6

1/8 2/36 3/49 4/69 5/79 6/147

N. L. McCullum, A. F. Milne and M. J.
McClenaghan did not bat.

Holder 3–0–34–2; Best 3–0–37–0; Bravo
3–0–31–0; Narine 4–0–18–2; Miller
3–0–24–0; Russell 3–0–16–2.

Umpires: G. A. V. Baxter and C. B. Gaffaney.　　Third umpire: D. J. Walker.
Series referee: B. C. Broad.

DOMESTIC CRICKET IN NEW ZEALAND, 2012-13

MARK GEENTY

Few first-class teams span two major islands and require a winding five-hour drive between their two main venues. But **Central Districts** survived a draining season shuttling around the Napier, New Plymouth and Nelson triangle to take the Plunket Shield, ending a seven-year drought in the first-class competition.

Their campaign began at home base in Napier with a demoralising defeat by Wellington, whose one-man wrecking-ball Jesse Ryder turned the contest with innings of 117 and 174. But after that opening hiccup Central set the pace, winning their next three games under new captain Kieran Noema-Barnett. They lost only once more, again to Wellington, won another three on the trot, and finally, across Cook Strait in Nelson, clung on to draw their final game, just holding off a late charge from Otago.

Four Central batsmen were among the top 13 Plunket run-scorers: South African-born Carl Cachopa, Jeet Raval, Jamie How and Mathew Sinclair all passed 600. Their all-time leading scorer, Sinclair, ended his 17-year career on a high. His 13,717 runs included 36 centuries, one of them a memorable 214 on Test debut against West Indies in 1999-2000. Coach Alan Hunt also departed, and was replaced by a surprise choice, South African Heinrich Malan.

Otago finished 11 points adrift of their first first-class title in 25 years. A fourth consecutive victory, in their last game, would have made them champions, but their ambitions were shattered by Wellington's giant-killers. Aaron Redmond was the leading Plunket scorer with 941 at 55. A tight-knit unit under coach Vaughn Johnson, Otago deservedly won the Twenty20 HRV Cup; after an opening defeat, they embarked on a ten-match winning streak, culminating with victory over Wellington in the final. That booked a spot in the Champions League, where they were pipped to the semi-finals on net run-rate. Dutch import Ryan ten Doeschate was the second-highest HRV run-scorer, with 401 at a strike-rate of 154, while left-arm spinner Nick Beard and young seamer Jacob Duffy were the most successful bowlers, with 15 wickets apiece.

In a rare year with no trophies, **Northern Districts** did have the joint-leading Plunket wicket-taker: 34-year-old seamer Brent Arnel claimed 45, as did Mark Gillespie, whom Arnel joined at Wellington for 2013-14, hired as bowling coach while continuing to play. Meanwhile Northern's coach, Grant Bradburn, left to take charge of New Zealand A, and was succeeded by former Auckland batsman James Pamment.

Wellington won only three first-class games – all against the leading contenders – but reached the Twenty20 final thanks to some magnificent ball-striking from Ryder, who provided the story of the season, on and off the field. He had not played for New Zealand since February 2012, taking time off to address personal issues. But for Wellington he was carefree and unstoppable. He plundered 723 first-class runs at 51, and blasted 584 in the Twenty20 competition at a strike-rate of 174. But word spread that he was drinking again, having sworn off alcohol for several months. After Wellington's last one-day game, he was involved in an altercation in a Christchurch bar which led to an assault and an induced coma. Two men were charged. Ryder missed opportunities at the IPL and Caribbean Premier League as he recovered. Meanwhile, a drugs test taken a few days earlier revealed a banned substance contained in fat-burning pills. A retrospective six-month suspension was issued in August, but it ended just in time for the 2013-14 season, when Ryder made a new start with Otago, after ten years with Wellington, and regained his place in New Zealand's one-day team.

In the 50-over Ford Trophy final, **Auckland** beat **Canterbury** by three wickets, chasing a paltry 140. Their fast bowler Chris Martin took 14 wickets at 22, his last hurrah before announcing his retirement. He was New Zealand's third-highest wicket-taker in Tests, with 233 wickets from 71. Victory continued Auckland's impressive limited-overs run, and gave their coach, Zimbabwean Paul Strang, a fitting send-off.

FIRST-CLASS AVERAGES, 2012-13

BATTING (500 runs)

	M	I	NO	R	HS	100	Avge	Ct/St
†C. Munro (*Auckland*)	4	6	1	623	269*	3	124.60	1
L. Ronchi (*Wellington*).................	9	15	2	807	135	4	62.07	37/2
P. G. Fulton (*Canterbury/New Zealand*)....	12	23	2	1,249	136	5	59.47	13
A. J. Redmond (*Otago*)	10	19	2	941	152	3	55.35	5
D. J. Mitchell (*Northern Districts*).........	9	15	2	709	136	1	54.53	7
†C. J. Anderson (*Northern Districts/NZ XI*) ..	7	14	1	674	167	1	51.84	5
†J. D. Ryder (*Wellington*).................	8	15	1	723	174	3	51.64	10
C. Cachopa (*Auckland*)	9	16	0	795	166	3	49.68	6
†D. R. Flynn (*Northern Districts*)	7	13	0	622	182	3	47.84	7
†H. D. Rutherford (*NZA/Otago/New Zealand*)	13	23	0	1,077	171	2	46.82	11
M. H. W. Papps (*Wellington*).............	10	20	2	810	206*	2	45.00	8
†J. A. Raval (*Central Districts*)	10	19	2	750	121	1	44.11	17
J. A. H. Marshall (*Northern Districts*)	10	19	3	690	156*	1	43.12	6
C. Cachopa (*Central Districts & NZ XI*) ...	11	20	1	813	179*	3	42.78	3
G. J. Hopkins (*Auckland*)	10	17	2	633	122*	2	42.20	33/1
J. M. How (*Central Districts*).............	10	19	2	706	124	1	41.52	11
N. T. Broom (*New Zealand A/Otago/NZ XI*)	13	23	4	782	146*	3	41.15	8
†S. R. Wells (*New Zealand A/Otago*)	10	14	1	529	81	0	40.69	2
D. G. Brownlie (*NZ A/Canterbury/NZ*)	16	28	2	1,057	135*	4	40.65	16
M. S. Sinclair (*Central Districts*)	10	18	2	646	143	2	40.37	16
S. C. Kuggeleijn (*Wellington*)	8	14	1	517	142*	1	39.76	5
†T. W. M. Latham (*NZ A/Canterbury/NZ XI*)	11	20	2	668	132	1	37.11	22
†L. J. Woodcock (*New Zealand A/Wellington*)	10	19	2	604	76	0	35.52	2
†M. G. Bracewell (*Otago*)	10	18	1	586	190	1	34.47	10
†J. M. Brodie (*Wellington*)................	9	18	1	533	86	0	31.35	4
†J. A. F. Yovich (*Northern Districts*)........	10	19	0	584	128	2	30.73	5

BOWLING (15 wickets)

	Style	O	M	R	W	BB	5I	Avge
R. J. McCone (*Canterbury*)	LM	231	42	719	37	5-56	1	19.43
B. M. Wheeler (*Central Districts*)	LM	109.5	20	338	17	5-91	1	19.88
I. G. Butler (*Otago*)	RFM	292	61	980	39	6-65	2	25.12
M. B. McEwan (*Canterbury*).........	RFM	143.4	26	504	20	5-20	1	25.20
D. A. J. Bracewell (*Central Districts*) ..	RFM	191.3	33	589	23	7-35	1	25.60
B. J. Arnel (*NZ A/Northern Districts*) ..	RFM	420.5	98	1,341	52	5-55	2	25.78
G. W. Aldridge (*Northern Districts*) ...	RFM	140.2	30	493	19	5-45	1	25.94
K. D. Mills (*Auckland*)...............	RFM	140.5	36	459	17	5-38	2	27.00
S. R. Wells (*New Zealand A/Otago*) ...	RM	194.5	40	642	23	4-74	0	27.91
N. Wagner (*NZ A/Otago/New Zealand*)	LFM	455.5	101	1,454	51	5-54	1	28.50
T. G. Southee (*N. Districts/N. Zealand*)	RFM	213	49	630	22	5-52	2	28.63
M. D. Bates (*Auckland*)	LM	199.3	37	665	22	4-44	0	30.22
M. R. Gillespie (*Wellington/NZ XI*)....	RFM	403	68	1,611	50	6-83	2	32.22
A. Y. Patel (*Central Districts*)	SLA	176.3	40	485	15	6-57	1	32.33
J. D. S. Neesham (*Otago/NZ XI*)......	RFM	239.4	63	784	24	4-73	0	32.66
A. R. Lamb (*Central Districts*)........	RFM	216.3	42	705	21	5-49	1	33.57
A. W. Mathieson (*Central Districts*) ...	RM	189.2	26	768	21	5-39	1	36.57
B. P. Martin (*Auckland/New Zealand*) .	SLA	579.1	141	1,686	41	5-45	1	41.12
T. S. Nethula (*NZ A/Central Districts*)	LBG	285.1	30	1,098	26	6-55	1	42.23
C. S. Martin (*Auckland*)	RFM	200.2	30	725	17	3-26	0	42.64
S. C. Kuggeleijn (*Wellington*)	RFM	196.2	23	964	22	5-72	1	43.81
M. D. Craig (*Otago*).................	OB	223.5	44	667	15	5-120	1	44.46
I. S. Sodhi (*Northern Districts*)	LBG	219.5	25	896	20	5-128	1	44.80
T. G. Johnston (*Canterbury*)	OB	265.3	54	846	17	5-105	1	49.76
J. S. Patel (*Wellington/New Zealand XI*)	OB	248.4	57	864	17	5-80	1	50.82

PLUNKET SHIELD, 2012-13

	Played	Won	Lost	Drawn	Bonus points Batting	Bowling	Points	Net avge runs per wkt
Central Districts.....	10	6	2	2	21	39	132	7.20
Otago.............	10	5	2	3	24	38	122	7.70
Northern Districts ...	10	4	3	3	13	39	100	3.58
Wellington.........	10	3	5	2	22	31	89	−8.64
Canterbury.........	10	3	5	2	13	39	88	−3.83
Auckland..........	10	2	6	2	13	32	69	−6.41

Outright win = 12pts. Bonus points were awarded as follows for the first 110 overs of each team's first innings: one batting point for the first 250 runs and then for 300, 350 and 400; one bowling point for the third wicket taken and then for the fifth, seventh and ninth. Net average runs per wicket is calculated by subtracting average runs conceded per wicket from average runs scored per wicket.

At Rangiora, October 27–30, 2012. **Otago won by eight wickets.** ‡Canterbury 297 and 352 (D. G. Brownlie 113; M. D. Craig 5-120); **Otago 383** (A. J. Redmond 133; T. G. Johnston 5-105) **and 267-2** (A. J. Redmond 123). *Otago 19pts, Canterbury 5pts. Todd Astle (78) and debutant Ben McCord (47) added 108 for the ninth wicket of Canterbury's second innings, but Aaron Redmond's second century of the match helped Otago to a winning start.*

At Napier (Nelson Park), October 28–31, 2012. **Wellington won by five wickets. Central Districts 383-8 dec** (C. Cachopa 105, M. S. Sinclair 143) **and 298-7 dec;** ‡Wellington 340 (J. D. Ryder 117*) **and 343-5** (J. D. Ryder 174). *Wellington 16pts, Central Districts 6pts. Carl Cachopa and Mathew Sinclair put on 224 for Canterbury's third wicket, and two declarations left Wellington a target of 342; Jesse Ryder got them on their way with 174 in 136 balls, his second century of the match.*

At Napier (Nelson Park), November 4–7, 2012. **Central Districts won by four wickets. Central Districts 430-9 dec** (C. Cachopa 179*) **and 149-6;** ‡Auckland 210 and 365 (C. Munro 103). *Central Districts 19pts, Auckland 3pts. Carl Cachopa scored his fifth hundred in six matches.*

At Hamilton, November 4–7, 2012. **Drawn. Northern Districts 204 and 533-6 dec** (D. R. Flynn 182, C. J. Anderson 167); ‡Otago 298 (J. D. S. Neesham 124; B. J. Arnel 5-74) **and 353-8** (N. T. Broom 146*). *Northern Districts 4pts, Otago 5pts. Derek de Boorder held six catches in Northern's first innings and nine in all. Daniel Flynn and Corey Anderson, with a maiden century, added 283 for the fourth wicket. Neil Broom and Mark Craig (93) saved Otago from 191-7, putting on 149.*

At Auckland (Eden Park Outer Oval), November 10–12, 2012. **Auckland won by ten wickets. Northern Districts 208** (J. A. F. Yovich 106) **and 196;** ‡Auckland 392 (B. P. Martin 114) **and 14-0.** *Auckland 19pts, Northern Districts 3pts. Bruce Martin turned the match Auckland's way with seven wickets and a maiden century; he added 168 for the seventh wicket with Craig Cachopa (82).*

At Dunedin (University Oval), November 12–15, 2012. **Drawn.** ‡Canterbury 254 (P. G. Fulton 102) **and 252-9 dec** (P. G. Fulton 108); *Otago* 272 and 203-7. *Otago 5pts, Canterbury 5pts. Peter Fulton scored twin hundreds. Team-mate Will Williams was out handled the ball on debut, unaware of the law as he tried to protect his stumps; it was the first case in New Zealand since 1991-92.*

At Gisborne, November 17–20, 2012. **Central Districts won by eight wickets.** Northern Districts 183 and 252; ‡Central Districts 341 and 95-2. *Central Districts 18pts, Northern Districts 4pts.*

At Rangiora, November 19–22, 2012. **Canterbury won by six wickets.** Wellington 239 (A. M. Ellis 6-58) **and 364-5 dec** (M. H. W. Papps 206*); ‡Canterbury 301-8 dec (D. G. Brownlie 133) **and 303-4** (P. G. Fulton 104). *Canterbury 18pts, Wellington 3pts. Nos 10 and 11, Andy McKay (33) and Mark Gillespie (77), almost doubled Wellington's first-innings total with a last-wicket stand of 113, while Michael Papps, with a maiden double-hundred, and Josh Brodie (74) opened their second innings with 211. But Fulton's 80-ball 104, his third century in four innings, won the game.*

At Auckland (Eden Park Outer Oval), November 26–29, 2012. **Drawn. Wellington 380** (L. Ronchi 127) **and 145-2;** ‡Auckland 658-9 dec (C. Munro 269*, C. Cachopa 166). *Auckland 8pts, Wellington 5pts. Auckland were 174-5 before Colin Munro, with a maiden double-hundred, and Craig Cachopa, with a first century (two days after his brother Carl's sixth for Central), added 377, the sixth-highest sixth-wicket stand in first-class cricket. Munro batted for 443 minutes and 252 balls, hitting 27 fours and 14 sixes; his 269* was the season's highest score, 658-9 the biggest total.*

At Napier (Nelson Park), November 26–29, 2012. **Central Districts won by ten wickets. Central Districts 476** (C. Cachopa 123, T. S. Nethula 108) **and 21-0; ‡Otago 257** (A. F. Milne 5-47) **and 239** (A. W. Mathieson 5-39). *Central Districts 20pts, Otago 4pts. Central's third successive win gave them a 30-point lead over second-placed Otago.*

At Auckland (Eden Park Outer Oval), December 2–4, 2012. **Otago won by three wickets. Auckland 196** (I. G. Butler 5-57) **and 274** (C. Munro 118); **‡Otago 253** (D. J. Bartlett 5-53) **and 223-7.** *Otago 17pts, Auckland 4pts.*

At Hamilton, December 2–5, 2012. **Drawn. Northern Districts 200 and 410-5 dec** (J. A. F. Yovich 128); **‡Canterbury 186** (G. W. Aldridge 5-45) **and 112-2.** *Northern Districts 4pts, Canterbury 4pts.*

At Wellington (Karori Park), December 10–13, 2012. **Wellington won by seven wickets. Central Districts 260** (W. A. Young 121) **and 389; ‡Wellington 403** (M. H. W. Papps 117, J. D. Ryder 162) **and 248-3** (S. C. Kuggeleijn 142*). *In their first innings, Central completed the double over table-leaders Central. In their second innings, Papps put on 256 for the third wicket with Ryder; in their second, a match-clinching 214* for the fourth with Scott Kuggeleijn.*

At Auckland (Eden Park Outer Oval), December 16–19, 2012. **Auckland won by seven wickets. ‡Canterbury 405-9 dec** (G. M. Andrew 180*; K. D. Mills 5-109) **and 120** (K. D. Mills 5-38, B. P. Martin 5-45); **Auckland 307** (G. J. Hopkins 122*; R. J. McCone 5-56) **and 219-3.** *Auckland 17pts, Canterbury 7pts. Worcestershire's Gareth Andrew hit a maiden hundred from No. 8, with 21 fours and seven sixes in all. But Gareth Hopkins and Kyle Mills (70) put on 145 for Auckland's eighth wicket, and Mills's ten wickets set up their victory.*

At Dunedin (University Oval), December 17–20, 2012. **Drawn. ‡Otago 427** (R. N. ten Doeschate 118) **and 227-4 dec; Central Districts 449** (M. S. Sinclair 142). *Otago 7pts, Central Districts 6pts.*

At Wellington (Karori Park), December 17–20, 2012. **Northern Districts won by six wickets. ‡Northern Districts 403-8 dec** (T. G. Southee 156) **and 196-4** (K. S. Williamson 121*); **Wellington 206** (L. Ronchi 113; T. G. Southee 5-69) **and 390** (L. Ronchi 108; I. S. Sodhi 5-128). *Northern Districts 20pts, Wellington 3pts. Northern were 161-6 before Tim Southee and Daryl Mitchell (43) added 166. Southee's 156, a maiden century, took 130 balls, with 18 fours and six sixes. Luke Ronchi, who held six catches in that innings, arrived at 37-6 to score 113 in 94 balls, with 13 fours and six sixes; following on, he was the fourth batsman of the season to complete twin hundreds.*

At Napier (McLean Park), January 24–27, 2013. **Central Districts won by 81 runs. ‡Central Districts 303-8 dec and 320; Canterbury 292 and 250** (A. Y. Patel 6-57). *Central Districts 18pts, Canterbury 4pts.*

At Hamilton, January 24–26, 2013. **Northern Districts won by an innings and 90 runs. Auckland 240** (D. N. Hakaraia 141*; A. Verma 7-82) **and 284** (C. Cachopa 115); **‡Northern Districts 614-7 dec** (D. R. Flynn 166, B. S. Wilson 139, J. A. H. Marshall 102). *Northern Districts 20pts, Auckland 1pt. Hawaii-born debutant Dusan Hakaraia hit 141* when no one else passed 23, as Anurag Verma claimed 7-82 in his second match. Flynn and Brad Wilson put on 301 for Northern's second wicket.*

At Dunedin (University Oval), January 24–26, 2013. **Otago won by an innings and 240 runs. Wellington 254** (B. E. Soper 5-76) **and 157** (J. K. Fuller 6-24); **‡Otago 651-9 dec** (M. G. Bracewell 190, N. T. Broom 134). *Otago 20pts, Wellington 3pts. First-time centurion Michael Bracewell and Broom put on 291 for Otago's third wicket; their highest total, 651-9, led to their biggest win.*

At Auckland (Eden Park Outer Oval), January 30–February 2, 2013. **Central Districts won by 191 runs. Central Districts 233 and 457-7 dec** (J. M. How 124); **‡Auckland 348** (C. Cachopa 145; B. J. Small 5-61) **and 151** (T. S. Nethula 6-55). *Central Districts 16pts, Auckland 6pts. Craig Cachopa's third century contained 16 fours and seven sixes.*

At Queenstown, January 31–February 2, 2013. **Otago won by eight wickets. Northern Districts 217** (I. G. Butler 6-65) **and 227; ‡Otago 319** (H. D. Rutherford 162) **and 126-2.** *Otago 18pts, Northern Districts 4pts.*

At Wellington (Basin Reserve), January 31–February 3, 2013. **Canterbury won by 20 runs. ‡Canterbury 329-9 dec and 410-7 dec** (G. H. Worker 107); **Wellington 356** (S. J. Murdoch 102) **and 363.** *Canterbury 18pts, Wellington 7pts. Wellington went down to a third consecutive defeat, despite the efforts of Gillespie, who came in at 280-7 chasing 384 and was last out for 63.*

At Christchurch (Hagley Oval), February 7–9, 2013. **Northern Districts won by six wickets. ‡Canterbury 172** (B. J. Arnel 5-55) **and 149; Northern Districts 108** (M. B. McEwan 5-20) **and 217-4.** *Northern Districts 16pts, Canterbury 4pts.*

At Wellington (Basin Reserve), February 7–10, 2013. **Drawn. Auckland 346** (M. R. Gillespie 5-66) **and 345** (G. J. Hopkins 121; M. R. Gillespie 6-83); **‡Wellington 426** (L. Ronchi 135) **and 199-8.** *Wellington 8pts, Auckland 6pts. Ronchi – playing as a full substitute after being released from international duties – completed his fourth hundred of the season.*

At Rangiora, February 14–17, 2013. **Central Districts won by four wickets. Canterbury 252** (D. A. J. Bracewell 7-35) **and 255** (D. G. Brownlie 135*; A. R. Lamb 5-49); **‡Central Districts 249 and 259-6.** *Central Districts 16pts, Canterbury 4pts. Doug Bracewell's career-best 7-37, the best return of the season, helped Central to a third consecutive win.*

At Whangarei, February 14–17, 2013. **Northern Districts won by five wickets. Wellington 423** (H. K. P. Boam 102) **and 234** (T. G. Southee 5-52); **‡Northern Districts 510** (D. R. Flynn 102, D. J. Mitchell 136; S. C. Kuggeleijn 5-72) **and 148-5.** *Northern Districts 20pts, Wellington 7pts. Southee took nine wickets on his comeback following two months out after rupturing thumb ligaments.*

At Dunedin (University Oval), February 14–17, 2013. **Otago won by ten wickets. ‡Auckland 221** (N. Wagner 5-54) **and 351; Otago 569-8 dec** (N. B. Beard 188, N. T. Broom 103) **and 4-0.** *Otago 20pts, Auckland 1pt. Nightwatchman Nick Beard reached a maiden hundred and added 239 with Broom for Otago's fourth wicket; their third successive win cut Central's lead to nine points.*

At Christchurch (Hagley Oval), February 20–22, 2013. **Canterbury won by nine wickets. Auckland 173** (S. L. Stewart 5-42) **and 170; ‡Canterbury 302 and 43-1.** *Canterbury 18pts, Auckland 4pts.*

At Nelson (Saxton Oval), February 20–23, 2013. **Drawn. Northern Districts 267 and 435-9 dec** (J. A. H. Marshall 156*; B. M. Wheeler 5-91); **‡Central Districts 418** (J. A. Raval 121) **and 116-2.** *Central Districts 8pts, Northern Districts 5pts. Jeet Raval and Jamie How (93) put on 215 for Central's first wicket; Otago's defeat meant a draw was enough to win Central the Plunket Shield.*

At Wellington (Basin Reserve), February 20–23, 2013. **Wellington won by 54 runs. Wellington 255 and 322; ‡Otago 378** (A. J. Redmond 152; J. S. Patel 5-80) **and 145.** *Wellington 17pts, Otago 7pts. Otago faltered on the last day, chasing 200 for their first first-class title since 1987-88.*

CHAMPIONS

Plunket Shield					
1921-22	Auckland	1950-51	Otago	*Shell Trophy*	
1922-23	Canterbury	1951-52	Canterbury	1975-76	Canterbury
1923-24	Wellington	1952-53	Otago	1976-77	Otago
1924-25	Otago	1953-54	Central Districts	1977-78	Auckland
1925-26	Wellington	1954-55	Wellington	1978-79	Otago
1926-27	Auckland	1955-56	Canterbury	1979-80	Northern Districts
1927-28	Wellington	1956-57	Wellington	1980-81	Auckland
1928-29	Auckland	1957-58	Otago	1981-82	Wellington
1929-30	Wellington	1958-59	Auckland	1982-83	Wellington
1930-31	Canterbury	1959-60	Canterbury	1983-84	Canterbury
1931-32	Wellington	1960-61	Wellington	1984-85	Wellington
1932-33	Otago	1961-62	Wellington	1985-86	Otago
1933-34	Auckland	1962-63	Northern Districts	1986-87	Central Districts
1934-35	Canterbury	1963-64	Auckland	1987-88	Otago
1935-36	Wellington	1964-65	Canterbury	1988-89	Auckland
1936-37	Auckland	1965-66	Wellington	1989-90	Wellington
1937-38	Auckland	1966-67	Central Districts	1990-91	Auckland
1938-39	Auckland	1967-68	Central Districts	1991-92	{ Central Districts
1939-40	Auckland	1968-69	Auckland		{ Northern Districts
1945-46	Canterbury	1969-70	Otago	1992-93	Northern Districts
1946-47	Auckland	1970-71	Central Districts	1993-94	Canterbury
1947-48	Otago	1971-72	Otago	1994-95	Auckland
1948-49	Canterbury	1972-73	Wellington	1995-96	Auckland
1949-50	Wellington	1973-74	Wellington	1996-97	Canterbury
		1974-75	Otago	1997-98	Canterbury

1998-99	Central Districts	2004-05	Auckland	*Plunket Shield*	
1999-2000	Northern Districts	2005-06	Central Districts	2009-10	Northern Districts
2000-01	Wellington	2006-07	Northern Districts	2010-11	Canterbury
		2007-08	Canterbury	2011-12	Northern Districts
State Championship		2008-09	Auckland	2012-13	Central Districts
2001-02	Auckland				
2002-03	Auckland				
2003-04	Wellington				

Auckland have won the title outright 22 times, Wellington 20, Canterbury 16, Otago 13, Central Districts 8, Northern Districts 7. Central Districts and Northern Districts also shared the title once.

THE FORD TROPHY, 2012-13

50-over league plus knockout

	Played	Won	Lost	No result	Bonus points	Points	Net run-rate
Auckland	8	5	2	1	1	23	0.62
Canterbury	8	4	3	1	4	22	0.77
Wellington	8	4	3	1	2	20	0.89
Northern Districts	8	4	3	1	2	20	−0.00
Otago	8	2	5	1	0	10	−0.69
Central Districts	8	2	5	1	0	10	−1.43

Preliminary finals

1st v 2nd: Auckland beat Canterbury by 128 runs. **3rd v 4th:** Wellington beat Northern Districts by eight wickets. **Final play-off:** Canterbury beat Wellington by 61 runs.

Final

At Auckland (Eden Park Outer Oval), March 31, 2013. **Auckland won by three wickets. Canterbury 139** (34.5 overs); ‡**Auckland 143-7** (25.1 overs). *Needing 140, Auckland slid to 131-7 when Ryan McCone took three in successive overs, but Gareth Hopkins saw them home with 34*.*

HRV CUP, 2012-13

	Played	Won	Lost	Points	Net run-rate
Otago	10	9	1	36	1.01
Wellington	10	6	4	24	0.41
Auckland	10	5	5	20	0.12
Northern Districts	10	5	5	20	−0.13
Canterbury	10	3	7	12	−0.42
Central Districts	10	2	8	8	−1.02

Play-off

At Wellington (Basin Reserve), January 18, 2013. **Wellington won by 23 runs.** ‡**Wellington 182-4** (20 overs); **Auckland 159-8** (20 overs). *Jesse Ryder hit 46 in 17 balls out of 49-1 for Wellington.*

Final

At Dunedin (University Oval), January 20, 2013. **Otago won by four wickets.** ‡**Wellington 143-9** (20 overs) (J. K. Fuller 4-24); **Otago 145-6** (18.3 overs). *Wellington slumped to 54-6 in seven overs, despite 30 in 15 balls from Ryder, before Otago claimed the cup with their tenth straight win.*

PAKISTAN CRICKET, 2013

Dynamite drama on the dance floor

OSMAN SAMIUDDIN

Hold your breath now. A one-day series win in India; whitewashed in Tests in South Africa; a tie with Ireland; a one-day series win in the West Indies; wiped out at the Champions Trophy; a one-day and a Test defeat by Zimbabwe; a drawn Test series against South Africa; a one-day caning by South Africa; a historic one-day triumph in South Africa; and, against Sri Lanka, a record-breaking sunset Test chase of 302. That, condensed, is Pakistan's year and a bit. Is there anything to be gained, or any sanity to be retained, from trying to assess their performance?

Those polarised results reflect the tempo, though not the personality, of the man who charted their course. In the arrhythmic style of Misbah-ul-Haq's

PAKISTAN IN 2013

	Played	Won	Lost	Drawn/No result
Tests	7	2	4	1
One-day internationals	34	16	16	2
Twenty20 internationals	12	8	4	–

Results exclude the Pakistan v Sri Lanka Test beginning on December 31, 2013.

For a review of Pakistan domestic cricket from the 2012-13 season, see page 1047.

Change of pace: whether hitting sixes against South Africa or blocking v Sri Lanka, Misbah-ul-Haq was the face of Pakistan in 2013.

batting – long barren deserts of dot balls relieved by oases of verdant boundaries – is captured the essence of Pakistan's work: silly, apocalyptic defeats, and grand, life-affirming triumphs. Yet Misbah always acted with his team's best interests at heart. And his record was a thing of wonder.

From January 2013 until the end of the series against Sri Lanka in the UAE a year later, he made 934 Test runs at an average of 58 (he was 100 clear of the next man, Younis Khan, who in turn scored 337 more than third-placed Asad Shafiq). In one-day internationals Misbah was even more prolific, racking up 1,373 at almost 55 during the calendar year. In 15 out of 32 innings, he made a half-century. Again, only one team-mate came close: Mohammad Hafeez made 1,301 runs, miles ahead of Ahmed Shehzad (809) in third. Misbah, who will be 40 in May, was there when matches were won, and he was invariably the last bastion when they were being lost. In times of crisis, he guided the younger, shakier men around him. He simply could not have done more, and yet he still couldn't change the intrinsic nature of Pakistan cricket.

Perhaps that isn't such a bad thing. In difficult times for Pakistan, it is possible to see this very capriciousness as a source of reassurance: their magnetic instability on the field almost represents a form of stability in itself. When they conjure victory in matches no one expects them to win – such as the Abu Dhabi Test against South Africa – it is impossible not to be overwhelmed, to fall in love. When they collapse in a heap and lose, as they did against Zimbabwe, the emotions are just as strong. The eternal sense of doom and disaster makes for dynamite drama.

It is an important point, because in 2013 the jibes about a drab Misbah draining or misplacing the true, colourful (and, frankly, over-mythologised) soul of Pakistan were particularly barbed. And they were wrong: it was patently clear that Pakistan's soul still belonged more to the dance floor than the library.

Of course, they did not build on the gains of 2011 and 2012, when they showed such mettle to recover from a truly traumatic five years. And the whitewash in South Africa was especially depressing, made all the more grim by its inevitability. Pakistan were as fragile as ever away from home in tough conditions. But were they ever really going to build? They don't do transition: Pakistan simply turn up, ready to amaze or appal.

One of the reasons for the lack of progress since their 3–0 win over England in the UAE in early 2012 had been apparent at the time. Their schedule is so uneven it is impossible to thread anything together. After that series, an ageing side did not play another Test for almost five months. In 2013, following the matches in South Africa in February – themselves coming after a hiatus of seven months – they didn't play another for more than six. Those long gaps have hurt them, and 24 international matches against the same opponents (South Africa) in ten months meant it was hard to get a rounded picture – though playing one of the strongest sides in world cricket should at least make them battle-hardened. The problem shows no signs of going away: once the Sri Lankan series ended in January this year, Pakistan's next scheduled Test was against Australia in October.

Proceedings off the field did not help, but when did they ever? The latest board shenanigans, largely played out in the courts, were even more complex than usual. Zaka Ashraf was ousted as PCB chairman, then replaced by Najam Sethi, who in turn made way for the return of Ashraf in January 2014. A month later, Sethi was back, at the behest of the patron, now the prime minister Nawaz Sharif. Indeed the switching of the board patron from a theoretically apolitical president to an intrinsically partisan prime minister – by the courts – felt as though it could have deeper ramifications.

It was hard to think of anything less helpful than long-term instability for a board who have been unable to stage international cricket at home for five years, or play a Test series against India anywhere for more than six. So it is a relief that the financial implications of this exile and India-isolation have been less severe than some predicted.

Indeed, gate revenues in the UAE for one-day and Twenty20 internationals have held up, and the sponsorship from UAE-based companies is greater than could have been raised for matches inside Pakistan. On the downside, there is no long-term broadcast deal in place, and the board have in the last two years become increasingly dependent on money from the ICC. The crunch cannot be put off indefinitely.

It is in this light that the large-scale revamp of international cricket led by India, England and Australia, the three richest boards, should be seen. Pakistan objected vigorously at first, but eventually accepted that in the new scheme of things lay the promise – no more – of a resumption of ties with India and the resulting incomes. The other side of the coin is that whatever small say they may have had on the running of the game will be compromised further. So much in Pakistan cricket is polarised.

PAKISTAN v SOUTH AFRICA IN THE UAE, 2013-14

OSMAN SAMIUDDIN

Test matches (2): Pakistan 1, South Africa 1
One-day internationals (5): Pakistan 1, South Africa 4
Twenty20 internationals (2): Pakistan 0, South Africa 2

"Bilateralism doesn't brook multilateral defiances." These were words uttered during this series by Najam Sethi, head of the Pakistan Cricket Board. Sitting next to him at the press conference was Haroon Lorgat, his counterpart at Cricket South Africa, who had just been told by his employers that he was forbidden to deal with matters India. Sethi is better-known in Pakistan as a political journalist, editor, TV anchor, one-time publisher and a liberal crusader of sorts. His sentence was well-constructed and statesmanlike, and it came in response to an intriguing question. He and Lorgat had just signed off on a quickie limited-overs series in South Africa, to start five days after this one. Was it, asked the reporter, an act of defiance against the BCCI?

No shadow stretches over cricket with as sharp a definition as that of the BCCI. A tussle between Pakistan and South Africa in the United Arab Emirates was engrossing in its own right, but minds were elsewhere, and the question crashed through the prevailing politeness. Both sides were in the BCCI's bad books. South Africa needed to fill a hole in their calendar, which existed because the BCCI had cut short the original itinerary for India's visit after this series – itself partly the result of their displeasure at Lorgat's appointment as CSA chief executive. Pakistan, meanwhile, needed to play as much as possible, wherever they could, to gain exposure – but also to make some money. India–Pakistan matches were on hold, and the cost to the PCB was high: 80% of their last broadcast deal had been based on two series against India.

Sethi's response may have sounded more meaningful than it really was, but it did reflect the role of realpolitik in the world game. The add-on series solidified another point: the PCB and CSA are, historically, steady allies. Pakistan's schedule is generally haphazard, even more so after the Lahore terror attacks on Sri Lanka in March 2009 which ruled out the country as a venue. Tours are modified or cancelled at short notice; others hurriedly snuck in at even shorter notice. There are periods of terrible crunch, but also yawning gaps. Commitments with South Africa, however, remain as regular as can be. Every three or four years since 2002-03, Pakistan have gone to South Africa in the (northern) winter, and the following autumn South Africa have returned the favour. Other than a series with Sri Lanka, it is the only near-certainty in Pakistan's programme. And the PCB have never forgotten that the South Africans played on in Pakistan in October 2007, after a suicide-bomb attempt on Benazir Bhutto's life.

On the field there were enough reasons for engagement. Pakistan's win in the First Test at Abu Dhabi was surprising, but it also had the familiarity of a home victory: they played precisely as conditions demanded. It was one thread in a heavier, more complex tapestry of home and exile. This was the ninth tour Pakistan had hosted in the UAE since the real start of their security troubles at home, from late 2008. In that time, concerns about the financial implications of playing in the Gulf have been acute. But the near-full-houses in the limited-overs matches (and a wonderful Eid Al-Adha holiday crowd through the Abu Dhabi Test) confirmed the calculations of the PCB's bean counters: it costs more to host a series in the Middle East, but the revenues are far greater than they could ever be in Pakistan.

Apart from the First Test and a few ropey moments in the one-day internationals, South Africa looked every bit the world's best travellers, and their rebound victory in Dubai – ensuring their 12th consecutive overseas Test series without defeat – was particularly impressive. So impressive, in fact, that it took the sting out of Faf du Plessis being caught and punished for tampering with the ball using the zip on his trouser pocket. Before du Plessis pleaded guilty, A. B. de Villiers had the gall to insist "we are not a team that scratches the ball". Had this been a not-so-friendly opponent, in a less sterile atmosphere than Dubai, the incident might have caused a diplomatic row.

Gary Kirsten, South Africa's former head coach, was flown in to mentor the batsmen in the four days between the second and third one-day internationals, after some of the problems they had encountered on their tour of Sri Lanka in July resurfaced. Kirsten's arrival had the desired tonic, as South Africa posted 259, 266 and 268 in the next three games, and won 4–1. The result meant South Africa had won all six bilateral one-day series against Pakistan since the relationship was consummated in 2002-03.

SOUTH AFRICA TOURING PARTY

*G. C. Smith (T/50), H. M. Amla (T/50/20), H. Davids (20), Q. de Kock (50/20), A. B. de Villiers (T/50/20), J-P. Duminy (T/50/20), F. du Plessis (T/50/20), D. Elgar (T), Imran Tahir (T/50/20), J. H. Kallis (T), R. K. Kleinveldt (T), R. McLaren (50/20), D. A. Miller (50/20), M. Morkel (T/50/20), W. D. Parnell (50/20), A. N. Petersen (T), R. J. Peterson (T/50), A. M. Phangiso (20), V. D. Philander (T/50), D. W. Steyn (T/50/20), T. L. Tsolekile (T), L. L. Tsotsobe (50/20), D. Wiese (20). *Coach:* R. C. Domingo.

Amla went home after the First Test for the birth of his first child, and was replaced in the one-day squad by C. A. Ingram, until he returned for the third match. Smith returned home after the second one-day international for treatment on post-concussion syndrome related to a blow on the head during the Second Test. Davids replaced him in the squad for the remainder of the one-dayers. De Villiers captained in the 50-over series, du Plessis in the Twenty20s.

At Sharjah, October 8–10, 2013 (not first-class). **Drawn. South Africans 354-8 dec** (A. N. Petersen 58, H. M. Amla 50, J. H. Kallis 70, A. B. de Villiers 58) **and 109-3**; ‡**Pakistan A 311-6 dec** (Shan Masood 50, Ahmed Shehzad 66, Azhar Ali 54). *Each side chose from 13 players. Graeme Smith, in his first innings after five months out nursing his ankle, was the only one of South Africa's top seven to fail on a pitch unhelpful for seam or spin. Temperatures reached 37˚C on the second day, when many of the South Africans took the field wearing ice vests and other cooling accessories. Shan Masood and Ahmed Shehzad both made fifties, but Masood would win the battle to form Pakistan's opening pair with Khurram Manzoor in the First Test.*

PAKISTAN v SOUTH AFRICA

First Test Match

At Abu Dhabi, October 14–17, 2013. Pakistan won by seven wickets. Toss: South Africa. Test debuts: Shan Masood, Zulfiqar Babar.

South Africa should have known. Given where Pakistan were coming from, both on and off the field, the tourists should have twigged that no force on earth could bring them victory in this Test. A month earlier, Pakistan had failed to chase 264 against Zimbabwe at Harare, and lost by 24 runs. In the summer months running into this tour, a judicial coup had hamstrung Pakistan's administration even more than usual. Then, on the eve of this series, Saeed Ajmal chose to question why the team needed a foreign coach.

In fact, when Misbah-ul-Haq walked out for the toss with a full and ready XI waiting to take the field, it was a minor victory in itself. So complicated had the PCB's latest wrangle become that the Islamabad High Court had stopped Najam Sethi, an interim chairman appointed to replace one who had been elected through a dubious process, from taking any day-to-day decisions. Sethi was prevented from appointing a chief selector, which theoretically meant Pakistan could not actually choose a side. On the second day of the match, on the verge of missing a court deadline which had demanded the PCB hold fair elections to elect a new, permanent chairman, Pakistan's prime minister Nawaz Sharif dissolved the executive and officially turned it into what it had been for so long anyway: an ad hoc board. It was given a sexier acronym, though: Sethi was now heading an IMC (Interim Management Committee).

Pakistan were in a complete mess. So of course they won this Test and, despite a late wobble, won it convincingly. One of their broadest platforms was their sixth different opening pair in seven Tests, after Mohammad Hafeez was dropped following 12 innings

---

BIRTHDAY BOYS

Test cricketers who made their debut on their birthday:

B. B. Cooper (33)	Australia v England at Melbourne......................	1876-77
F. G. J. Ford (28)	England v Australia at Sydney	1894-95
F. W. Tate (35)	England v Australia at Manchester	1902
A. E. R. Gilligan (28)	England v South Africa at Johannesburg................	1922-23
B. J. Sealey (34)	West Indies v England at The Oval.....................	1933
J. Iddon (33)	England v West Indies at Bridgetown, Barbados	1934-35
D. G. Phadkar (22)	India v Australia at Sydney	1947-48
S. B. Joshi (27)	India v England at Birmingham.........................	1996
R. D. Jacobs (31)	West Indies v South Africa at Johannesburg.............	1998-99
R. L. Powell (21)	West Indies v New Zealand at Hamilton.................	1999-2000
S. Chattergoon (27)	West Indies v Sri Lanka at Port-of-Spain, Trinidad.	2007-08
Shan Masood (24)	**Pakistan v South Africa at Abu Dhabi.**................	**2013-14**

Cooper's birthday debut came on Test cricket's birthday.

---

without a fifty. Shan Masood made his debut on his 24th birthday – the third Test player born in nearby Kuwait, after Shakeel Ahmed and Tanvir Ahmed – and he and Khurram Manzoor put on 135 on the second day, Pakistan's first century opening stand for 21 months.

That partnership ate healthily into South Africa's inadequate first innings. They had been undone on the opening day by a smart attack, full of bowlers who knew precisely what to do on a deceptive surface. It is always good to bat at the Sheikh Zayed Stadium, but if the right length can be found early by faster bowlers, rewards can be had. Junaid Khan and Mohammad Irfan, forgoing the natural length his height seemed to demand, went fuller and cashed in – even if Irfan was fortunate to escape several no-balls missed by umpire Paul Reiffel.

What pickings they left, the spinners mopped up; slow left-armer Zulfiqar Babar, Pakistan's fourth-oldest debutant at nearly 35, was especially good. They were helped by a careless moment from de Villiers, who dragged his back foot out of the crease while holding the pose on a forward thrust designed to deter the umpire from giving him lbw; Younis Khan threw the ball in from slip to run him out. Amla stood out, playing the spinners with unerring assurance off the back foot to score his 20th Test hundred.

One reason why Manzoor and Masood added as many – and both gave chances early – was that Steyn, Philander (playing his first Test in Asia) and Morkel did not hit those fuller lengths or attack the stumps enough. Pakistan knew patience was key, and went about building their lead gradually by picking off the spin of Peterson and Duminy.

Manzoor fell early on the third day, for a punchy maiden hundred and the highest score for Pakistan against South Africa – beating Azhar Mahmood's 136 at Johannesburg in 1997-98. For once, that left Misbah with a healthy situation in which to bat. Thus unburdened, he played one of his most fluent Test innings. When he reached three figures in the afternoon – at a more advanced age (39 years, 141 days) than any centurion since Graham Gooch in 1994 – he celebrated it with unusually expressive but understandable vigour: this was a first international century in two and a half years for a man whose bloody-minded batting is often the butt of ridicule. It secured a lead of 193, which, on a surface now assisting spin, was more than enough.

The South Africans struggled a second time, none more so than Kallis, who was worked out – rather than over – by Junaid twice in the match. De Villiers made up for his first-innings aberration with an accomplished 90, but Pakistan's attack was a potent collective: none of the four bowlers ended with fewer than four wickets, none more than Saeed Ajmal's six. Whenever Misbah turned to one of them, it seemed to bring a wicket.

Steyn and Philander finally figured out the right lengths in the second innings, and gave Pakistan an almighty scare by leaving them seven for three, chasing just 40. That recalibration would prove critical in the following Test, but here it ended with Misbah first stabilising the innings, then launching Peterson into the sightscreen to seal a notable win. It brought to an end South Africa's 15-match unbeaten run, a sequence unsurpassed in their Test history.

Man of the Match: Khurram Manzoor.

Close of play: first day, South Africa 245-8 (Amla 118, Steyn 13); second day, Pakistan 263-3 (Khurram Manzoor 131, Misbah-ul-Haq 44); third day, South Africa 72-4 (de Villiers 11, Steyn 0).

South Africa

A. N. Petersen c Shan Masood b Mohammad Irfan	3	– (2) c Adnan Akmal b Mohammad Irfan.	17
*G. C. Smith c Adnan Akmal b Mohammad Irfan . .	15	– (1) st Adnan Akmal b Saeed Ajmal . .	32
H. M. Amla c Younis Khan b Mohammad Irfan . . .	118	– c Adnan Akmal b Zulfiqar Babar. . . .	10
J. H. Kallis c Adnan Akmal b Junaid Khan	5	– lbw b Junaid Khan	0
†A. B. de Villiers run out.	19	– c Shan Masood b Junaid Khan	90
J-P. Duminy c Asad Shafiq b Zulfiqar Babar.	57	– (7) lbw b Junaid Khan	0
F. du Plessis c Asad Shafiq b Zulfiqar Babar.	1	– (8) c and b Saeed Ajmal.	9
R. J. Peterson b Zulfiqar Babar	5	– (9) not out.	47
V. D. Philander lbw b Saeed Ajmal	3	– (10) c Adnan Akmal b Saeed Ajmal . .	10
D. W. Steyn st Adnan Akmal b Saeed Ajmal	15	– (6) b Zulfiqar Babar.	7
M. Morkel not out	2	– c and b Saeed Ajmal	0
B 1, l-b 4, n-b 1	6	B 4, l-b 4, n-b 2	10

1/6 (1) 2/19 (2) 3/43 (4)   (93.1 overs) 249
4/104 (5) 5/199 (6) 6/205 (7)
7/217 (8) 8/222 (9) 9/245 (3) 10/249 (10)

1/38 (2) 2/57 (1)   (82.4 overs) 232
3/58 (4) 4/72 (3)
5/104 (6) 6/109 (7) 7/133 (8)
8/190 (5) 9/232 (10) 10/232 (11)

Mohammad Irfan 18.2–4–44–3; Junaid Khan 18.4–2–52–1; Zulfiqar Babar 27–2–89–3; Saeed Ajmal 29.1–6–59–2. *Second innings*—Mohammad Irfan 13–1–42–1; Junaid Khan 18–1–57–3; Saeed Ajmal 32.4–7–74–4; Zulfiqar Babar 19–6–51–2.

Pakistan

Khurram Manzoor c Kallis b Philander	146	– c de Villiers b Philander	4
Shan Masood lbw b Duminy	75	– c de Villiers b Philander	0
Azhar Ali c de Villiers b Philander	11	– c Kallis b Steyn	3
Younis Khan c Petersen b Morkel	1	– not out	9
*Misbah-ul-Haq lbw b Steyn	100	– not out	28
Asad Shafiq c Petersen b Duminy	54		
†Adnan Akmal b Steyn	32		
Saeed Ajmal c de Villiers b Philander	13		
Zulfiqar Babar run out	2		
Junaid Khan c Morkel b Steyn	3		
Mohammad Irfan not out	0		
L-b 4, n-b 1	5	L-b 1	1

1/135 (2) 2/173 (3) 3/178 (4) (138.4 overs) 442   1/4 (2) (3 wkts, 13.5 overs) 45
4/290 (1) 5/372 (6) 6/394 (5)   2/7 (3) 3/7 (1)
7/423 (8) 8/429 (9) 9/437 (10) 10/442 (7)

Steyn 28.4–5–88–3; Philander 26–5–84–3; Morkel 23–5–35–1; Kallis 13–2–44–0; Peterson 27–2–111–0; Duminy 19–1–68–2; du Plessis 2–0–8–0. *Second innings*—Steyn 5–3–7–1; Philander 5–1–11–2; Morkel 2–0–12–0; Peterson 1.5–0–14–0.

Umpires: P. R. Reiffel and R. J. Tucker. Third umpire: I. J. Gould.

PAKISTAN v SOUTH AFRICA

Second Test Match

At Dubai, October 23–26, 2013. South Africa won by an innings and 92 runs. Toss: Pakistan.

South Africa won this Test comprehensively but – this is not often said – Pakistan could, if they so wished, look down on their opponents from a high-ish moral pedestal. For all the past controversies in which Pakistan had been the perpetrators, this might even have counted as a small victory. But their response to the opposition being caught red-handed in the cookie jar was thankfully free of righteous indignation.

Just after tea on the third afternoon, Pakistan were 62 for three, still 356 runs from making South Africa bat again. Hopes of a series victory over the world's No. 1 side had gone, and only pride remained at stake. Then, at the start of the 31st over, the umpires called Smith over for a chat. Not long after, reserve umpire Shozab Raza came out with a box of balls; a replacement was picked, and Ian Gould signalled five penalty runs. It was the first time since the Oval Test in August 2006, when Darrell Hair penalised Pakistan and triggered an almighty spat, that an international team had been fingered for ball-tampering. It was also the first incident under new ICC rules that enhanced the umpires' power to act.

However, this was not an on-field investigation, but a sting operation, carried out by a broadcaster. Prompted by an eagle-eyed commentator to keep an eye on South Africa, Ten Sports captured du Plessis vigorously rubbing the ball against the zip of his right trouser pocket. The images were first shown to third umpire Paul Reiffel, who immediately alerted his on-field partners, before the world tuned in.

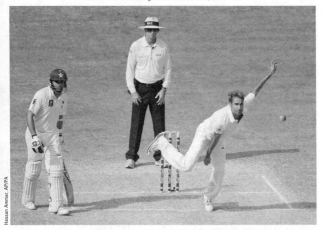

Cricket's ultimate globaliser? Imran Tahir runs through his native Pakistan to maintain South Africa's formidable sequence in overseas Test series. Azhar Ali and Rod Tucker look on.

It was about as conclusive as evidence of tampering might get, but match referee David Boon fined du Plessis only 50% of his match fee, with no further sanction. He seemed to buy into the South African defence that, while the ball may have been tampered with – and it was reversing – the tampering was not deliberate, or as part of a prolonged process. A second player, Philander, was caught by the cameras apparently scratching the ball with his finger, though Boon chose to ignore this image. The irony that it happened against Pakistan was not lost on anyone, nor was the justifiable Pakistani fury at du Plessis getting away so lightly: Shahid Afridi had been banned for two games for the ball-biting incident of January 2010. It later emerged that the ICC had previously given international sides until 2015 to phase out all kit with zips on.

The incident sparked a brief and predictable storm, and diverted attention away from a dominant performance by South Africa that confirmed their status as the best side in the world. At a time when assured home performances are offset by limp away results, this 1–1 scoreline maintained South Africa's remarkable record of not having lost a Test series abroad since 2006, in Sri Lanka. Smith was the foundation of it all. His fourth double-hundred as captain, in only his third Test innings since returning from a lengthy lay-off including ankle surgery, was ground out from that unmatched granite which had seen him through more than a decade in charge of a deeply complex country. A blow to the helmet by Mohammad Irfan was later shown to have caused him concussion, yet Smith soldiered on to make another 96 runs.

It certainly helped that Imran Tahir bowled Pakistan out for just 99 on the first day, after Misbah-ul-Haq had chosen to bat. The last time Pakistan had been bowled out for 99 was in their previous Test in Dubai, against England in 2011-12. They went on to win that game, but this time they couldn't recover, and lost a Test in the UAE for the first time in ten matches since going into exile. The broader story of Tahir's maiden Test five-for was more compelling than his actual bowling. In his previous Test, at Adelaide a year earlier, he had been mauled to the tune of 37–1–260–0. Yet here he ran through the country he left behind, unfurling exuberant celebrations for every wicket (and much public love for his South African wife, Sumayya, watching from the stands). In truth, it was an ordinary spell. Pakistan were abysmal and clueless, true to their history of enhancing the reputations of out-of-form bowlers.

South Africa were missing their only centurion from Abu Dhabi, Hashim Amla, who had flown home for the birth of his first child. But Smith and de Villiers took advantage of their side's enviable position in a national-record fifth-wicket stand of 338. That too was built on Pakistani largesse: they used up both reviews inside the first five overs, then Adnan Akmal spilled de Villiers first ball off Irfan, which would have left South Africa 134 for five. From there, who knows where the game might have gone. Most likely, South Africa would have found a way through.

Pakistan ended up trailing by 418 on first innings – their third-highest deficit in Tests, after two matches against West Indies in 1957-58. But, after an initial wobble that included Khurram Manzoor's pair, they put up stiffer resistance second time round. Asad Shafiq enhanced his growing reputation with a fourth Test hundred, adding 197 with Misbah. But, on the 62nd anniversary of Pakistan's maiden Test victory, this was a reassertion of many of their traditional frailties.

Man of the Match: G. C. Smith.   *Man of the Series:* A. B. de Villiers.

Close of play: first day, South Africa 128-3 (Smith 67, Steyn 3); second day, South Africa 460-4 (Smith 227, de Villiers 157); third day, Pakistan 132-4 (Misbah-ul-Haq 42, Asad Shafiq 28).

Pakistan

Khurram Manzoor c du Plessis b Steyn	0	– (2) c Kallis b Philander	0
Shan Masood b Imran Tahir	21	– (1) lbw b Steyn	0
Azhar Ali lbw b Morkel	19	– lbw b Duminy	19
Younis Khan c de Villiers b Steyn	10	– b Imran Tahir	36
*Misbah-ul-Haq lbw b Imran Tahir	2	– c Kallis b Elgar	88
Asad Shafiq b Imran Tahir	10	– st de Villiers b Duminy	130
†Adnan Akmal b Imran Tahir	0	– lbw b Imran Tahir	5
Saeed Ajmal run out	0	– lbw b Imran Tahir	9
Zulfiqar Babar not out	25	– absent hurt	
Mohammad Irfan b Imran Tahir	0	– (9) b Duminy	14
Junaid Khan b Steyn	4	– (10) not out	2
B 5, l-b 3	8	B 10, l-b 5, w 1, n-b 2, p 5	23

1/0 (1) 2/38 (3) 3/52 (2)   (36.4 overs) 99
4/60 (4) 5/60 (5) 6/60 (7)
7/64 (8) 8/76 (6) 9/76 (10) 10/99 (11)

1/0 (1) 2/2 (2)   (135.1 overs) 326
3/48 (3) 4/70 (4)
5/267 (5) 6/278 (7) 7/301 (8)
8/323 (9) 9/326 (6)

Steyn 13.4–2–38–3; Philander 5–2–9–0; Morkel 5–1–12–1; Imran Tahir 13–3–32–5. *Second innings*—Steyn 22–9–48–1; Philander 19–7–34–1; Morkel 22–7–47–0; Imran Tahir 42–14–98–3; Kallis 7–3–9–0; Duminy 21.1–3–67–3; Elgar 2–0–3–1.

South Africa

A. N. Petersen lbw b Zulfiqar Babar	26	
*G. C. Smith c Younis Khan b Saeed Ajmal	234	
D. Elgar c Azhar Ali b Saeed Ajmal	23	
J. H. Kallis lbw b Saeed Ajmal	7	
D. W. Steyn b Mohammad Irfan	7	
†A. B. de Villiers c Adnan Akmal		
b Mohammad Irfan	164	
J-P. Duminy b Mohammad Irfan	7	
F. du Plessis not out	17	
V. D. Philander b Saeed Ajmal	8
M. Morkel c Younis Khan b Saeed Ajmal	7
Imran Tahir c Misbah-ul-Haq b Saeed Ajmal	2
B 5, l-b 8, w 2	15

1/37 (1) 2/91 (3)   (163.1 overs) 517
3/119 (4) 4/134 (5) 5/472 (6)
6/478 (2) 7/486 (7) 8/505 (9)
9/515 (10) 10/517 (11)

Mohammad Irfan 34.3–5–102–3; Junaid Khan 31.3–2–105–0; Saeed Ajmal 55.5–8–151–6; Zulfiqar Babar 36.2–2–124–1; Azhar Ali 5–0–22–0.

Umpires: I. J. Gould and R. J. Tucker.   Third umpire: P. R. Reiffel.
Series referee: D. C. Boon.

PAKISTAN v SOUTH AFRICA

First One-Day International

At Sharjah, October 30, 2013 (day/night). South Africa won by one run. Toss: South Africa.

It took one match for Pakistan to reaffirm their reputation for flakiness in one-day run-chases. After de Villiers established the pattern for the series by choosing to bat on a sluggish pitch, South Africa crumbled to 86 for six in the face of some outstanding bowling from Saeed Ajmal and Shahid Afridi. Parnell looked out his depth against them but, with help from Miller and Tsotsobe, he managed to drag South Africa up to the lowest end of a defendable total. Even then, as Pakistan calmly picked their way to 107 for two, then 165 for four, it looked at least 50 short. But with Umar Amin out the previous ball and 19 still needed, Umar Akmal got into a terrible tangle against Imran Tahir, and South Africa were presented with the tiniest opening. They barnstormed through it, with Tahir – recalled only because of illness to Robin Peterson – the delirious leader of the charge. He took two wickets in his next over, when Afridi top-edged a long-hop to deep midwicket, and Wahab Riaz was lbw to a googly. With the ask whittled down to two from 22 balls, Ajmal made the fatal mistake of exposing last man Mohammad Irfan to Morne Morkel. He had his off stump trimmed almost immediately, and Pakistan had lost their last six wickets for 17 runs inside six overs.

Man of the Match: W. D. Parnell.

South Africa

C. A. Ingram c Umar Akmal	
b Mohammad Irfan .	0
G. C. Smith st Umar Akmal b Saeed Ajmal	20
J-P. Duminy c Umar Amin b Sohail Tanvir	20
F. du Plessis lbw b Saeed Ajmal	12
*†A. B. de Villiers c and b Saeed Ajmal	4
D. A. Miller c and b Shahid Afridi	37
R. McLaren c and b Shahid Afridi	8
W. D. Parnell c Ahmed Shehzad	
b Saeed Ajmal .	56

M. Morkel lbw b Shahid Afridi	4
L. L. Tsotsobe not out	16
Imran Tahir c Wahab Riaz b Sohail Tanvir	1
L-b 1, w 4	5
	—
	(49.5 overs) 183

1/0 (1) 2/38 (3) 3/48 (2)   (49.5 overs) 183
4/54 (4) 5/63 (5) 6/86 (7)
7/125 (6) 8/129 (9) 9/181 (8)
10/183 (11)   10 overs: 38-2

Mohammad Irfan 10–1–35–1; Sohail Tanvir 9.5–1–33–2; Saeed Ajmal 10–2–30–4; Wahab Riaz 6–0–24–0; Mohammad Hafeez 5–0–23–0; Shahid Afridi 9–1–37–3.

Pakistan

Nasir Jamshed c Miller b Morkel	0
Ahmed Shehzad c Smith b Parnell	58
Mohammad Hafeez c de Villiers b Parnell .	28
*Misbah-ul-Haq c du Plessis b Parnell	31
Umar Amin c de Villiers b Tsotsobe	20
†Umar Akmal lbw b Imran Tahir	18
Shahid Afridi c Miller b Imran Tahir	9
Sohail Tanvir c de Villiers b Tsotsobe	2
Wahab Riaz lbw b Imran Tahir	0

Saeed Ajmal not out	1
Mohammad Irfan b Morkel	2
L-b 4, w 9	13
	—
	(46.3 overs) 182

1/4 (1) 2/75 (3) 3/107 (2)   (46.3 overs) 182
4/135 (4) 5/165 (5) 6/165 (6)
7/174 (8) 8/176 (7) 9/177 (9)
10/182 (11)   10 overs: 16-1

Morkel 9.3–3–23–2; Tsotsobe 10–3–28–2; Parnell 8–1–41–3; Imran Tahir 10–1–45–3; McLaren 8–0–34–0; Duminy 1–0–7–0.

Umpires: R. K. Illingworth and Shozab Raza.   Third umpire: S. J. Davis.

PAKISTAN v SOUTH AFRICA

Second One-Day International

At Dubai, November 1, 2013 (day/night). Pakistan won by 66 runs. Toss: Pakistan.

Morkel, McLaren and Imran Tahir did well to confine Pakistan to an innings of fits and starts, after South Africa had lost an important toss. But the surface was bound to turn more as the day wore on, and South Africa were reminded of their recent struggles in Sri Lanka. Ingram's run of three successive ducks would have been four had it not been for the donation of four overthrows from Shahid Afridi. Smith and Duminy rebuilt without too much alarm, but it did not take long for the spinners to pull the rug from beneath them: they swept up six for 66 from 23.4 overs. McLaren and Parnell fought as hard as they could, but another top-order failure had left them with too steep a mountain to climb.

Man of the Match: Shahid Afridi.

Pakistan

Nasir Jamshed c Tsotsobe b Morkel	1	Saeed Ajmal lbw b McLaren	0
Ahmed Shehzad c and b Imran Tahir	58	Mohammad Irfan not out	0
Mohammad Hafeez b McLaren	26		
*Misbah-ul-Haq c Miller b McLaren	25	L-b 4, w 9, n-b 1	14
Umar Amin c de Villiers b McLaren	14		
†Umar Akmal c Ingram b Morkel	18	1/4 (1) 2/52 (3) 3/112 (4) (49.4 overs) 209	
Shahid Afridi c Smith b Morkel	26	4/117 (2) 5/148 (6) 6/148 (5)	
Sohail Tanvir run out	9	7/170 (8) 8/198 (7) 9/200 (10)	
Wahab Riaz c du Plessis b Parnell	18	10/209 (9) 10 overs: 40-1	

Morkel 10–0–38–3; Tsotsobe 8–1–39–0; Parnell 7.4–0–49–1; Imran Tahir 10–1–28–1; McLaren 10–0–34–4; Duminy 4–0–17–0.

South Africa

G. C. Smith b Saeed Ajmal	14	M. Morkel b Mohammad Irfan	5
C. A. Ingram b Sohail Tanvir	4	L. L. Tsotsobe lbw b Saeed Ajmal	4
J-P. Duminy c Mohammad Hafeez b Mohammad Irfan	25	Imran Tahir st Umar Akmal b Shahid Afridi	3
*†A. B. de Villiers c Umar Akmal b Shahid Afridi	10	L-b 1, w 3, n-b 1	5
F. du Plessis lbw b Shahid Afridi	12		
D. A. Miller lbw b Mohammad Hafeez	11	1/7 (2) 2/43 (1) 3/49 (3) (40.4 overs) 143	
R. McLaren not out	29	4/66 (5) 5/73 (4) 6/83 (6)	
W. D. Parnell c Umar Akmal b Mohammad Irfan	21	7/118 (8) 8/126 (9) 9/131 (10)	
		10/143 (11) 10 overs: 37-1	

Mohammad Irfan 10–0–53–3; Sohail Tanvir 5–0–15–1; Mohammad Hafeez 10–1–25–1; Saeed Ajmal 8–1–15–2; Shahid Afridi 5.4–0–26–3; Wahab Riaz 2–0–8–0.

Umpires: S. J. Davis and Shozab Raza.   Third umpire: R. K. Illingworth.

PAKISTAN v SOUTH AFRICA

Third One-Day International

At Abu Dhabi, November 6, 2013 (day/night). South Africa won by 68 runs. Toss: South Africa.

South Africa had been without Amla (back home for his child's birth) and Steyn (rested) for the first two one-day internationals, so were not overly despondent to arrive in Abu Dhabi all-square – and with Gary Kirsten back in their stable as a batting consultant. In the case of Steyn the impact was immediate. He picked up just one wicket, but it took only a few balls for him to change the mood of Pakistan's chase. Ahmed Shehzad, teeming with confidence, was aiming for his fourth consecutive one-day international fifty. But Steyn, held back to first change, dismissed him with his seventh ball, and Pakistan's hopes were swiftly punctured. Tsotsobe followed up with 21 consecutive dot balls, and the rest of the batting combusted. South Africa's total had been built on organic virtues, with the top five rejigged following the axing of Ingram, Smith's return home with problems related to his blow to the head in the Second Test, and the recall of Amla and de Kock as openers. De Kock reported back from his Sri Lanka experience tighter outside off stump (though he found keeping wicket tough in these conditions), while du Plessis thrived upon his promotion to No. 3. But the engine-room was a 70-run stand between Duminy and de Villiers, low on boundaries but high on hard running and endeavour.

Man of the Match: F. du Plessis.

South Africa

H. M. Amla b Mohammad Irfan		10
†Q. de Kock st Umar Akmal b Shahid Afridi		40
F. du Plessis st Umar Akmal b Shahid Afridi		55
J-P. Duminy c Misbah-ul-Haq		
b Sohail Tanvir		64
*A. B. de Villiers c Mohammad Hafeez		
b Saeed Ajmal		34
D. A. Miller b Saeed Ajmal		34
R. McLaren lbw b Mohammad Irfan		13

D. W. Steyn c Ahmed Shehzad		
b Mohammad Irfan		2
M. Morkel not out		0
L. L. Tsotsobe not out		0
B 1, l-b 1, w 5		7

1/20 (1) 2/97 (2) (8 wkts, 50 overs) 259
3/112 (3) 4/182 (5) 5/243 (6)
6/245 (4) 7/248 (8) 8/258 (7) 10 overs: 47-1

Imran Tahir did not bat.

Mohammad Irfan 10–0–46–3; Sohail Tanvir 8–0–47–1; Mohammad Hafeez 6–0–45–0; Saeed Ajmal 10–1–38–2; Wahab Riaz 6–0–40–0; Shahid Afridi 10–0–41–2.

Pakistan

Mohammad Hafeez c du Plessis b Morkel		15
Ahmed Shehzad c Amla b Steyn		32
Umar Amin c de Kock b Tsotsobe		13
*Misbah-ul-Haq lbw b Imran Tahir		19
Asad Shafiq c du Plessis b Imran Tahir		11
†Umar Akmal c and b Imran Tahir		7
Shahid Afridi lbw b McLaren		6
Sohail Tanvir c Amla b McLaren		31
Wahab Riaz c de Kock b Morkel		33

Saeed Ajmal lbw b Imran Tahir		1
Mohammad Irfan not out		4
B 5, l-b 2, w 12		19

1/50 (2) 2/52 (1) 3/86 (3) (44.3 overs) 191
4/89 (4) 5/106 (6) 6/114 (5)
7/116 (7) 8/177 (9) 9/182 (10)
10/191 (8) 10 overs: 52-2

Morkel 9–1–35–2; Tsotsobe 10–2–34–1; Steyn 8–0–31–1; Imran Tahir 10–1–53–4; McLaren 7.3–0–31–2.

Umpires: Ahsan Raza and R. K. Illingworth. Third umpire: S. J. Davis.

PAKISTAN v SOUTH AFRICA

Fourth One-Day International

At Abu Dhabi, November 8, 2013 (day/night). South Africa won by 28 runs. Toss: South Africa. One-day international debut: Sohaib Maqsood.

After Steyn's return two days earlier, de Villiers had spoken of the game-changing intensity his premier fast bowler brought to the side. As he ripped through Pakistan's middle and lower order, changing this match in two spells, Steyn backed up his captain's assertion with career-best figures that secured South Africa an unexpected but merited series victory with a game to play. His second spell claimed the assured debutant Sohaib Maqsood after a sprightly fifty, and three more wickets in the 47th over killed off Pakistan's spirited chase. Steyn's performance rewarded another skilful batting performance, in which South Africa never let slip the start provided by de Kock and Amla. Put down on two by Mohammad Hafeez at slip, de Kock dropped anchor in his ninth one-day international, batting until the 43rd over for his maiden century for his country.

Man of the Match: D. W. Steyn.

South Africa

†Q. de Kock c Misbah-ul-Haq b Junaid Khan		112
H. M. Amla b Mohammad Hafeez		46
F. du Plessis c Saeed Ajmal		
b Mohammad Irfan		10
*A. B. de Villiers c Mohammad Hafeez		
b Junaid Khan		30
D. A. Miller lbw b Mohammad Hafeez		5

J-P. Duminy not out		25
R. McLaren not out		28
B 1, l-b 9		10

1/87 (2) 2/129 (3) (5 wkts, 50 overs) 266
3/198 (4) 4/210 (1)
5/214 (5) 10 overs: 45-0

D. W. Steyn, M. Morkel, L. L. Tsotsobe and Imran Tahir did not bat.

Mohammad Irfan 8–0–51–1; Sohail Tanvir 6–0–38–0; Junaid Khan 9–0–42–2; Saeed Ajmal 10–0–53–0; Shahid Afridi 8–0–38–0; Mohammad Hafeez 9–0–34–2.

Pakistan

Ahmed Shehzad run out	43	Mohammad Irfan not out	2
Mohammad Hafeez b Imran Tahir	33	Junaid Khan b McLaren	4
Sohaib Maqsood c de Villiers b Steyn	56		
Asad Shafiq c Morkel b Tsotsobe	1	L-b 1, w 7	8
*Misbah-ul-Haq c de Villiers b Steyn	65		
Sohail Tanvir c Amla b Steyn	1	1/74 (1) 2/85 (2) 3/86 (4) (49.2 overs) 238	
†Umar Akmal c Morkel b Steyn	22	4/174 (3) 5/180 (6) 6/228 (7)	
Shahid Afridi run out	3	7/230 (5) 8/231 (9) 9/232 (8)	
Saeed Ajmal b Steyn	0	10/238 (11) 10 overs: 31-0	

Steyn 10–1–25–5; Tsotsobe 10–0–49–1; Morkel 10–0–44–0; McLaren 9.2–0–59–1; Imran Tahir 8–0–51–1; Duminy 2–0–9–0.

Umpires: Ahsan Raza and S. J. Davis.   Third umpire: R. K. Illingworth.

PAKISTAN v SOUTH AFRICA

Fifth One-Day International

At Sharjah, November 11, 2013 (day/night). South Africa won by 117 runs. Toss: South Africa.

An outstanding hundred from de Villiers rounded off South Africa's comprehensive series win. His innings came in two distinct parts: his half-century took 70 balls, but the moment he got there, with a big six, de Villiers raced through the gears. His next 65 would come off only 32 deliveries, a reminder of his frightening range and tempo. He went past 6,000 one-day international runs in 147 innings, second only to Viv Richards (141). South Africa plundered 114 off the last ten overs, as McLaren made yet another handy contribution to punish Junaid Khan's sloppiness at the death. South Africa rested Dale Steyn and Morne Morkel, giving Philander only his second one-day cap since 2008, but with Pakistan's batsmen misfiring so much, and the toss proving so crucial throughout the series, it made little difference. Only Sohaib Maqsood, with a second successive fifty, looked remotely comfortable or even interested as the seamers helped themselves.

Man of the Match: A. B. de Villiers.   *Man of the Series:* R. McLaren.

South Africa

H. M. Amla lbw b Mohammad Irfan	3	R. J. Peterson b Junaid Khan	2
†Q. de Kock lbw b Saeed Ajmal	34	W. D. Parnell not out	8
F. du Plessis c Sohail Tanvir b Junaid Khan	46		
J-P. Duminy c Ahmed Shehzad		B 4, l-b 5, w 7	16
b Mohammad Hafeez	2		
*A. B. de Villiers not out	115	1/4 (1) 2/54 (2) (7 wkts, 50 overs) 268	
D. A. Miller c and b Saeed Ajmal	15	3/62 (4) 4/124 (3)	
R. McLaren c Junaid Khan b Saeed Ajmal	27	5/150 (6) 6/233 (7) 7/240 (8) 10 overs: 45-1	

V. D. Philander and L. L. Tsotsobe did not bat.

Mohammad Irfan 10–0–52–1; Sohail Tanvir 8–0–58–0; Saeed Ajmal 10–0–45–3; Mohammad Hafeez 3–0–10–1; Shahid Afridi 10–0–37–0; Junaid Khan 9–0–57–2.

Pakistan

Mohammad Hafeez b Philander		6
Ahmed Shehzad c Philander b Tsotsobe		2
Sohaib Maqsood c Philander b Duminy		53
Umar Amin lbw b Philander		5
*Misbah-ul-Haq c Miller b McLaren		18
†Umar Akmal lbw b Duminy		30
Shahid Afridi c and b Parnell		9
Sohail Tanvir c de Kock b McLaren		15
Saeed Ajmal lbw b Parnell		1
Mohammad Irfan c Amla b Parnell		0
Junaid Khan not out		1
W 11		11

1/8 (2) 2/8 (1) 3/17 (4) (35.3 overs) 151
4/56 (5) 5/110 (6) 6/128 (7)
7/130 (3) 8/131 (9) 9/131 (10)
10/151 (8) 10 overs: 27-3

Philander 8–2–23–2; Tsotsobe 7–0–28–1; McLaren 4.3–1–21–2; Peterson 5–0–29–0; Parnell 7–1–36–3; Duminy 4–1–14–2.

Umpires: Ahsan Raza and R. K. Illingworth.   Third umpire: S. J. Davis.
Series referee: R. S. Madugalle.

PAKISTAN v SOUTH AFRICA

First Twenty20 International

At Dubai, November 13, 2013 (floodlit). South Africa won by nine wickets. Toss: Pakistan.

This was the first of seven 20-over internationals for each side leading into the 2014 World Twenty20. But two overs into the scheduled 40 – with Pakistan slipping to four for three – the match was done and dusted. Their captain, Mohammad Hafeez, fell once more to Steyn, who even afforded himself a laugh at his victim's expense: it was the 12th time in 18 innings across all formats that he had dismissed him. Others chipped in: Tsotsobe bowled two maidens, and 18 dot balls in all, while Imran Tahir continued to torment his former countrymen. Umar Akmal saved Pakistan from total obliteration, but his 49 still could not quite take them into triple figures. South Africa didn't need to tear into their target and, to rub it in, Sohaib Maqsood missed the chance to catch Amla first ball. De Kock and du Plessis both carried over their good one-day form to take South Africa home with more than five overs to spare.

Man of the Match: D. W. Steyn.

Pakistan	B	4	6
Ahmed Shehzad c 1 b 10	0	5	0	0
Sohaib Maqsood c 2 b 9	4	4	1	0
Shahid Afridi c 7 b 10	10	13	1	0
*Mohammad Hafeez c 2 b 9	0	2	0	0
Shoaib Malik st 2 b 11	12	23	0	0
†Umar Akmal run out	49	41	4	1
Abdul Razzaq c 6 b 7	10	16	1	0
Sohail Tanvir st 2 b 11	0	3	0	0
Abdur Rehman not out	7	12	0	0
Saeed Ajmal b 9	0	1	0	0
L-b 1, w 5	6			

6 overs: 18-3 (20 overs) 98-9

1/0 2/4 3/4 4/21 5/41 6/70 7/72 8/98 9/98

Mohammad Irfan did not bat.

Tsotsobe 4–2–9–2; Steyn 4–0–15–3; McLaren 4–0–29–1; Parnell 4–0–27–0; Imran Tahir 4–0–17–2.

South Africa	B	4	6
H. M. Amla b 8	13	9	2	0
†Q. de Kock not out	48	38	3	2
*F. du Plessis not out	37	40	4	1
L-b 1	1			

6 overs: 39-1 (14.3 overs) 99-1

1/16

J-P. Duminy, A. B. de Villiers, D. A. Miller, R. McLaren, W. D. Parnell, D. W. Steyn, L. L. Tsotsobe and Imran Tahir did not bat.

Mohammad Hafeez 3–0–24–0; Mohammad Irfan 2–0–7–0; Sohail Tanvir 2–0–21–1; Saeed Ajmal 4–0–12–0; Shahid Afridi 2.3–0–16–0; Abdur Rehman 1–0–18–0.

Umpires: Ahsan Raza and Shozab Raza.   Third umpire: Zameer Haider.

PAKISTAN v SOUTH AFRICA

Second Twenty20 International

At Dubai, November 15, 2013 (floodlit). South Africa won by six runs. Toss: South Africa.

Fittingly, Pakistan ended things with one final batting blowout. Chasing 151, they were handily placed at 101 for three midway through the 14th over. Umar Akmal was looking sensible, Sohaib Maqsood a great find, and a share of the series seemed likely. Five overs later, they were 139 for nine, down and out in a heap of thoughtless, panic-stricken strokeplay. The beneficiaries were, by now, predictable: it is unlikely Steyn, Parnell and Imran Tahir had ever picked up wickets quite so easily at this level. There was also a welcome return to form for Amla, whose sparkling 48 set the pace and took advantage of a hip injury to Mohammad Irfan, who had finally broken down, in his 118th over of the tour. Pakistan's travails were summed up by Abdul Razzaq, who went for 14 in his first international over for more than a year, then tried to leave his first ball, from Tahir – a googly that bowled him. South Africa moved to second in the Twenty20 international rankings, behind India by one hundredth of a decimal point.

Man of the Match: F. du Plessis.   *Man of the Series:* F. du Plessis.

South Africa

		B	4	6
†Q. de Kock *c 12 b 10*	30	19	6	0
H. M. Amla *c 4 b 10*	48	41	3	2
*F. du Plessis *not out*	58	48	1	3
A. B. de Villiers *c 1 b 9*	5	6	1	0
D. A. Miller *lbw b 10*	4	4	0	0
H. Davids *b 9*	0	2	0	0
L-b 2, w 3	5			

6 overs: 44-1   (20 overs)   150-5

1/37 2/115 3/137 4/147 5/150

R. McLaren, W. D. Parnell, D. W. Steyn, L. L. Tsotsobe and Imran Tahir did not bat.

Mohammad Irfan 1.4–0–12–0; Abdul Razzaq 1–0–14–0; Shoaib Malik 1.2–0–12–0; Sohail Tanvir 4–0–21–0; Saeed Ajmal 4–0–25–3; Mohammad Hafeez 4–0–21–0; Shahid Afridi 4–0–43–0.

Pakistan

		B	4	6
Nasir Jamshed *c 2 b 6*	19	20	3	0
Ahmed Shehzad *c 7 b 8*	21	14	3	0
*Mohammad Hafeez *lbw b 8*	0	1	0	0
Shoaib Malik *b 11*	15	18	1	0
Sohaib Maqsood *c 1 b 8*	37	26	2	1
†Umar Akmal *c 11 b 7*	11	12	1	0
Abdul Razzaq *b 11*	0	1	0	0
Shahid Afridi *c 3 b 9*	14	10	0	1
Sohail Tanvir *b 9*	6	5	1	0
Saeed Ajmal *not out*	7	10	0	0
Mohammad Irfan *not out*	2	4	0	0
B 2, l-b 2, w 7, n-b 1	12			

6 overs: 44-2   (20 overs)   144-9

1/39 2/39 3/46 4/101 5/112 6/112 7/112 8/121 9/139

Shoaib Malik, when 13, retired hurt at 75-3 and resumed at 101-4.

12th man: Umar Amin.

Steyn 4–1–20–2; Tsotsobe 3–0–30–0; McLaren 4–0–38–1; Parnell 4–0–25–3; Davids 1–0–6–1; Imran Tahir 4–0–21–2.

Umpires: Ahsan Raza and Zameer Haider.   Third umpire: Shozab Raza.
Series referee: R. S. Madugalle.

PAKISTAN v SRI LANKA IN THE UAE, 2013-14

Qamar Ahmed

Twenty20 internationals (2): Pakistan 1, Sri Lanka 1
One-day internationals (5): Pakistan 3, Sri Lanka 2
Test matches (3): Pakistan 1, Sri Lanka 1

Angelo Mathews was a whisker away from leading Sri Lanka to their most significant overseas series victory for 14 years – but, at the crunch, they snapped. Of the eight leading Test nations, Sri Lanka had been perhaps the most nervous travellers: excluding formalities in Bangladesh and Zimbabwe, they had not won abroad since a 2–1 victory in Pakistan in 1999-2000, when Muttiah Muralitharan was at the peak of his powers. And had Sri Lanka not been so passive on the last three days of this series, they would surely have become only the second visiting team to win in the UAE, after Steve Waugh's all-conquering Australians in 2002-03 (though the first of those three Tests was played in Colombo).

That prospect seemed fanciful when Sri Lanka – who had arranged no red-ball warm-up match – collapsed on the opening day of the First Test at Abu Dhabi. But Mathews stirred his side into action by batting throughout the fourth to score his second Test century, long enough to save the game. Sri Lanka's unfancied seam attack then put in a superb stint at Dubai which, along with Mahela Jayawardene's elusive 32nd Test century, catapulted them to a surprise nine-wicket win.

All that was required to knock the stuffing out of Pakistan were a few emphatic strokes on the fourth evening at Sharjah. But Sri Lanka's incessant blocks and leaves invited Pakistan to go for broke, and Mathews lapsed into the worst sort of negative tactics adopted by captains who are protecting a target in the last session of a match. If anything, his spread leg-side fields – in both innings – helped Pakistan pull off a sensational chase of 302 in 57.3 overs. The recalled Azhar Ali played the innings of his life and, as the light grew painfully thin, Misbah-ul-Haq hit the winning run with nine balls to spare. "This was my best victory," he said. It was the fastest 300-plus run-chase in Test history, surpassing the 1984 West Indians at Lord's, and provided a triumphant farewell for coach Dav Whatmore, who decided to quit for family reasons after two years in charge. It was also the end of a two-year term for Sri Lanka coach Graham Ford, who headed for Surrey.

A 1–1 draw meant Pakistan remained unbeaten in all five Test series in the UAE since being forced to relocate following the terrorist attack on buses carrying the Sri Lankan team and match officials in Lahore in 2009. But there was no doubt where they would rather have been. The day before the opening Twenty20 international – and in the wake of Jonathan Trott's withdrawal from England's Ashes tour with a stress-related illness – Misbah reiterated his concerns about Pakistan's nomadic existence. "Being away from our families is taking its toll," he said. "You come back from a tour and hardly get time to

HIGHEST FOURTH-INNINGS TEST AVERAGE

		I	NO	R	HS	100	50
73.40	D. G. Bradman (Australia)	15	5	734	173*	3	4
66.55	**Misbah-ul-Haq (Pakistan)**	**18**	**9**	**599**	**79***	**0**	**7**
58.76	G. Boycott (England)	34	13	1,234	128*	3	7
58.25	S. M. Gavaskar (India)	33	9	1,398	221	4	8
57.58	J. B. Hobbs (England)	23	6	979	126*	2	6
55.50	**Younis Khan (Pakistan)**	**30**	**10**	**1,110**	**131***	**4**	**5**
55.31	**G. C. Smith (South Africa/World)**	**39**	**10**	**1,604**	**154***	**4**	**9**
54.40	Javed Miandad (Pakistan)	22	7	816	103*	2	5
53.66	H. Sutcliffe (England)	15	3	644	135	3	1
53.50	K. R. Stackpole (Australia)	19	5	749	136	1	6
53.19	C. G. Greenidge (West Indies)	38	12	1,383	214*	3	6
52.41	M. E. K. Hussey (Australia)	17	5	629	121	1	2
51.38	**L. R. P. L. Taylor (New Zealand)**	**16**	**3**	**668**	**107**	**1**	**5**
50.41	R. T. Ponting (Australia)	43	14	1,462	156	4	6

Minimum 15 innings.

settle, then you are off again." There were complaints too, after the Test defeat in Dubai, that Misbah was not getting the turning pitches he wanted, although wet weather around the Gulf was certainly a factor. The surfaces were sometimes so bland that Rangana Herath and Saeed Ajmal, two experienced spinners who had both enjoyed success in the UAE, were made to look ordinary.

Both boards were feeling the financial pinch, so it was no surprise that seven limited-overs matches preceded the Tests. Some of the best players were missing: Herath and Jayawardene sat out for personal reasons, while injury had caught up with Pakistan's towering spearhead Mohammad Irfan. Yet the cricket turned out to be some of the most compelling these countries had played for years. Three centuries by Mohammad Hafeez – who went on to lose his Test place – all led to Pakistan wins.

This was the third full series between these two old allies since October 2011, but the first to feature DRS. Pakistan never got their heads around it, failing in 20 reviews out of 21. During the Tests and the fifth one-day international, the ICC trialled their Officiating Replay System, designed to smooth out the more cumbersome aspects of DRS. If implemented, it would give third umpires the power to control the TV replays available to them, rather than wait for the broadcasters.

SRI LANKA TOURING PARTY

*A. D. Mathews (T/50/20), L. D. Chandimal (T/50/20), T. M. Dilshan (50/20), R. M. S. Eranga (T), A. N. P. R. Fernando (T), M. V. T. Fernando (T), H. M. R. K. B. Herath (T), D. P. M. D. Jayawardene (T), H. A. P. W. Jayawardene (T), F. D. M. Karunaratne (T/50), K. M. D. N. Kulasekara (T/50/20), R. A. S. Lakmal (T/50/20), S. L. Malinga (50/20), B. A. W. Mendis (50/20), M. D. K. Perera (T), M. D. K. J. Perera (T/50/20), N. L. T. C. Perera (50/20), S. Prasanna (50/20), S. M. A. Priyanjan (50), R. L. B. Rambukwella (20), K. C. Sangakkara (T/50/20), S. M. S. M. Senanayake (T/50/20), J. K. Silva (T), H. D. R. L. Thirimanne (T/50/20), K. D. K. Vithanage (50/20). Coach: G. X. Ford.

Chandimal captained in the Twenty20 matches. Herath was originally selected in the one-day squad, but withdrew for personal reasons; Mendis stayed on after the Twenty20 matches to replace him. Kulasekara (torn hamstring) and Thirimanne (twisted ankle) flew home after the First Test; Thirimanne was replaced by M. D. K. J. Perera.

TEST MATCH AVERAGES

PAKISTAN – BATTING AND FIELDING

	T	I	NO	R	HS	100	50	Avge	Ct
Misbah-ul-Haq	3	5	1	364	135	1	3	91.00	0
Younis Khan	3	6	1	285	136	1	1	57.00	3
Ahmed Shehzad	3	6	0	273	147	1	1	45.50	2
Mohammad Hafeez	2	4	1	113	80*	0	1	37.66	2
Bilawal Bhatti	2	3	1	70	32	0	0	35.00	0
Sarfraz Ahmed	2	4	0	134	74	0	1	33.50	2
Khurram Manzoor	3	6	0	181	73	0	2	30.16	3
Asad Shafiq	3	5	1	61	23	0	0	15.25	3
Junaid Khan	3	4	2	24	16	0	0	12.00	2
Saeed Ajmal	3	4	1	29	21	0	0	9.66	0
Rahat Ali	2	3	0	8	8	0	0	2.66	2

Played in one Test: †Abdur Rehman 2 (1 ct); Adnan Akmal 6 (5 ct, 1 st); Azhar Ali 8, 103 (4 ct); Mohammad Talha 2.

BOWLING

	Style	O	M	R	W	BB	5I	Avge
Mohammad Talha	RFM	55	5	164	6	3-65	0	27.33
Junaid Khan	LFM	154	27	402	14	5-58	1	28.71
Abdur Rehman	SLA	83	24	157	5	4-56	0	31.40
Saeed Ajmal	OB	195	52	421	10	3-53	0	42.10
Bilawal Bhatti	RFM	73	12	291	6	3-65	0	48.50

Also bowled: Azhar Ali (LBG) 3–0–11–0; Mohammad Hafeez (OB) 23–5–56–1; Rahat Ali (LFM) 101.3–19–293–2.

SRI LANKA – BATTING AND FIELDING

	T	I	NO	R	HS	100	50	Avge	Ct
A. D. Mathews	3	5	1	412	157*	1	2	103.00	1
J. K. Silva	3	6	0	307	95	0	3	51.16	4
D. P. M. D. Jayawardene	3	5	0	227	129	1	0	45.40	0
H. A. P. W. Jayawardene	3	5	1	161	63*	0	1	40.25	18
†F. D. M. Karunaratne	3	6	1	198	62*	0	1	39.60	3
†K. C. Sangakkara	3	6	1	166	55	0	2	33.20	2
L. D. Chandimal	3	5	0	125	89	0	1	25.00	2
R. M. S. Eranga	3	4	1	56	25*	0	0	18.66	0
†H. M. R. K. B. Herath	3	4	0	6	6	0	0	1.50	0
R. A. S. Lakmal	3	4	4	16	10*	0	0	–	0

Played in one Test: A. N. P. R. Fernando 3; M. D. K. Perera 95, 8; S. M. S. M. Senanayake 5 (1 ct).

BOWLING

	Style	O	M	R	W	BB	5I	Avge
A. N. P. R. Fernando	RFM	37	5	112	5	3-62	0	22.40
R. M. S. Eranga	RFM	130.3	24	345	12	4-60	0	28.75
R. A. S. Lakmal	RFM	130.3	24	405	12	4-78	0	33.75
H. M. R. K. B. Herath	SLA	172.1	38	513	14	5-125	1	36.64

Also bowled: A. D. Mathews (RFM) 38–5–124–2; M. D. K. Perera (OB) 17–1–71–1; K. C. Sangakkara (OB) 1–0–7–0; S. M. S. M. Senanayake (OB) 23–2–96–0.

For a report of Pakistan's Twenty20 international against Afghanistan in Sharjah, see page 1224.

PAKISTAN v SRI LANKA

First Twenty20 International

At Dubai, December 11, 2013 (floodlit). Pakistan won by three wickets. Toss: Pakistan. Twenty20 international debut: Usman Khan.

Shahid Afridi cast aside sketchy form to see Pakistan over the line. Entering with 50 needed off 35 balls, he first rotated the strike, then opened up with a pair of sixes off Kulasekara in the 16th over to light up the chase. A typically mean penultimate over from Malinga took it down to the last, but Afridi paddle-swept Kulasekara's first ball into the stands at long leg to secure victory. He became the first man to combine 1,000 runs and 50 wickets in Twenty20 internationals. Mohammad Hafeez's hunch that evening dew would hamper the side fielding second proved spot on, as Sri Lanka – despite a stupendous groping catch at short cover by Thirimanne, who plucked the ball one-handed when it had gone past his head – made several slip-ups. Pakistan, aside from one wild Bilawal Bhatti over punished by Mathews, had clamped down on every Sri Lankan surge. Chandimal did not make the most of his promotion to No. 3 in Mahela Jayawardene's absence, and Sangakkara mistimed to cover, giving Saeed Ajmal his 400th international wicket. The match began with a moment's silence for Nelson Mandela.

Man of the Match: Shahid Afridi.

Sri Lanka

		B	4	6
T. M. Dilshan *c 2 b 9*	7	8	1	0
M. D. K. J. Perera *lbw b 10*	15	16	0	1
*L. D. Chandimal *lbw b 7*	22	22	3	0
†K. C. Sangakkara *c 7 b 10*	21	22	1	0
A. D. Mathews *c 1 b 9*	50	34	5	1
H. D. R. L. Thirimanne *not out*	23	16	1	1
N. L. T. C. Perera *not out*	2	2	0	0
W 5	5			

6 overs: 41-2   (20 overs)   145-5

1/9 2/41 3/59 4/84 5/142

K. M. D. N. Kulasekara, S. M. S. M. Senanayake, S. L. Malinga and B. A. W. Mendis did not bat.

Mohammad Hafeez 4–0–24–0; Sohail Tanvir 4–0–34–2; Usman Khan 1–0–9–0; Bilawal Bhatti 3–0–23–0; Saeed Ajmal 4–0–35–2; Shahid Afridi 4–0–20–1.

Pakistan

		B	4	6
Sharjeel Khan *c 1 b 7*	34	31	3	0
Ahmed Shehzad *c 6 b 9*	4	9	0	0
*Mohammad Hafeez *lbw b 11*	32	27	2	1
†Umar Akmal *run out*	5	3	1	0
Sohaib Maqsood *lbw b 10*	13	9	1	1
Umar Amin *c 3 b 10*	8	9	1	0
Shahid Afridi *not out*	39	20	2	3
Bilawal Bhatti *c 7 b 10*	10	8	1	0
Sohail Tanvir *not out*	0	0	0	0
N-b 1	1			

6 overs: 36-1   (19.1 overs)   146-7

1/12 2/69 3/76 4/76 5/96 6/117 7/139

Saeed Ajmal and Usman Khan did not bat.

Malinga 4–0–26–3; Kulasekara 3.1–0–30–0; Senanayake 3–0–14–1; Mendis 4–0–29–1; Mathews 2–0–20–0; N. L. T. C. Perera 3–0–27–1.

Umpires: Ahsan Raza and Shozab Raza.   Third umpire: Zameer Haider.

PAKISTAN v SRI LANKA

Second Twenty20 International

At Dubai, December 13, 2013 (floodlit). Sri Lanka won by 24 runs. Toss: Pakistan. Twenty20 international debut: S. Prasanna.

Sri Lanka cut loose from the start to slam 211 for three – the highest Twenty20 total against Pakistan – which was enough to square the series and secure their No. 1 ranking going into 2014. Their hyper-aggressive openers racked up 100 inside 12 overs: Kushal Perera was the more violent, whipping a six from outside off stump over midwicket, while Dilshan's unorthodox placement forced Mohammad Hafeez into constant tinkering. Pakistan's fielding let them down: Perera should have been run out following a mix-up in the first over, but the throw came in too wide for Umar Akmal, and Hafeez was furious with youngsters Sharjeel Khan and Umar Amin, who twice collided trying to stop runs off his bowling. Pakistan's experimental side were undaunted by attempting the highest run-chase in the format, despite a slippery ball. Sharjeel batted with brutal efficiency for his maiden international fifty, and Shahid Afridi whacked 28 before Sangakkara, having overrun the swirling ball, corrected himself and took a stunning one-handed catch. But Pakistan's longest innings turned out to be Sohail Tanvir's late flurry, which produced a Twenty20-international record 63 with Saeed Ajmal for the ninth wicket.

Man of the Match: M. D. K. J. Perera. *Man of the Series:* Shahid Afridi.

Sri Lanka

		B	4	6
M. D. K. J. Perera *run out*.		84	59	5	4
T. M. Dilshan *c 7 b 10*		48	33	8	0
S. Prasanna *c 11 b 10*		21	8	2	2
†K. C. Sangakkara *not out*		44	21	4	2
L-b 12, w 12, n-b 1		14			

6 overs: 52-0   (20 overs)   211-3

1/100 2/133 3/211

*L. D. Chandimal, A. D. Mathews, H. D. R. L. Thirimanne, N. L. T. C. Perera, K. M. D. N. Kulasekara, S. M. S. M. Senanayake and S. L. Malinga did not bat.

12th man: K. D. K. Vithanage.

Usman Khan 4–0–52–0; Sohail Tanvir 4–0–31–0; Bilawal Bhatti 2–0–32–0; Saeed Ajmal 4–0–25–2; Mohammad Hafeez 4–0–45–0; Shahid Afridi 2–0–25–0.

Pakistan

		B	4	6
Ahmed Shehzad *c 12 b 10*		8	10	1	0
Sharjeel Khan *b 3*		50	25	5	3
*Mohammad Hafeez *c 4 b 9*		7	7	1	0
Sohaib Maqsood *c 5 b 8*		15	16	2	0
†Umar Akmal *b 3*		0	1	0	0
Shahid Afridi *c 4 b 8*		28	13	2	2
Umar Amin *c 5 b 10*		0	2	0	0
Bilawal Bhatti *st 4 b 10*		0	1	0	0
Sohail Tanvir *c 3 b 11*		41	26	5	1
Saeed Ajmal *lbw b 9*		20	15	1	1
Usman Khan *not out*		2	3	0	0
B 1, l-b 2, w 10, n-b 3		16			

6 overs: 40-2   (19.2 overs)   187

1/18 2/27 3/62 4/83 5/84 6/85 7/85 8/121 9/184

Malinga 4–0–30–1; Kulasekara 3.2–0–23–2; Senanayake 4–0–27–3; Mathews 1–0–10–0; Dilshan 1–0–13–0; Prasanna 3–0–45–2; N. L. T. C. Perera 3–0–36–2.

Umpires: Ahsan Raza and Zameer Haider.   Third umpire: Shozab Raza.
Series referee: D. C. Boon.

PAKISTAN v SRI LANKA

First One-Day International

At Sharjah, December 18, 2013 (day/night). Pakistan won by 11 runs. Toss: Pakistan. One-day international debut: Sharjeel Khan.

Pakistan's victory looked a done deal when Sri Lanka slumped to 221 for seven in the 42nd over. But a few hearty blows from Prasanna and Senanayake sent nerves jangling, and Pakistan lapsed into all kinds of errors. The eighth-wicket partnership realised 87 off 45 balls, and it was not until Senanayake toe-ended to cover in the penultimate over – twelfth man Anwar Ali took the catch at the second attempt – that Sri Lanka's challenge fizzled out. Mohammad Hafeez, without a fifty in the home and away series against South Africa, made a patient seventh one-day century, augmented by breezy innings from Sharjeel Khan, who shrugged off a blow to the shoulder from Malinga to make fifty on his one-day international debut, and his childhood friend Sohaib Maqsood. Lakmal, preferred to Nuwan Kulasekara, was savaged late on by Shahid Afridi in a 12-ball 34. Despite their victory, Pakistan ran into problems with DRS: Ahmed Shehzad took more than the permitted 15 seconds to tell the umpires he wanted to review his dismissal; Afridi later pestered his sceptical team-mates into trying one out on Chandimal, and received an ear-bashing when the technology showed the ball sliding down leg.

Man of the Match: Mohammad Hafeez.

Pakistan

Sharjeel Khan c Senanayake b Prasanna . . .	61
Ahmed Shehzad lbw b Lakmal	11
Mohammad Hafeez c Chandimal b Lakmal	122
Sohaib Maqsood run out	73
Shahid Afridi b N. L. T. C. Perera.	34
†Umar Akmal not out	9

Bilawal Bhatti not out	1
L-b 4, w 7	11
1/35 (2) 2/118 (1) (5 wkts, 50 overs)	322
3/258 (4) 4/301 (5)	
5/320 (3) 10 overs: 47-1	

*Misbah-ul-Haq, Sohail Tanvir, Saeed Ajmal and Junaid Khan did not bat.

Lakmal 10–0–73–2; Malinga 10–1–59–0; Senanayake 9–1–46–0; N. L. T. C. Perera 6–0–53–1; Mathews 5–0–29–0; Prasanna 8–0–39–1; Dilshan 2–0–19–0.

Sri Lanka

M. D. K. J. Perera lbw b Mohammad Hafeez	64
T. M. Dilshan c Mohammad Hafeez	
b Junaid Khan .	30
†K. C. Sangakkara c Umar Akmal	
b Shahid Afridi .	23
L. D. Chandimal run out	46
H. D. R. L. Thirimanne c Sohaib Maqsood	
b Shahid Afridi .	10
*A. D. Mathews c Sohail Tanvir	
b Junaid Khan .	31
N. L. T. C. Perera c Misbah-ul-Haq	
b Bilawal Bhatti .	6

S. Prasanna c Sharjeel Khan b Junaid Khan	42
S. M. S. M. Senanayake c sub (Anwar Ali)	
b Sohail Tanvir .	42
S. L. Malinga run out	0
R. A. S. Lakmal not out.	1
B 8, l-b 4, w 4	16
1/66 (2) 2/113 (1) (49.4 overs)	311
3/127 (3) 4/141 (5) 5/214 (4)	
6/216 (6) 7/221 (7) 8/308 (9)	
9/310 (10) 10/311 (8) 10 overs: 52-0	

Mohammad Hafeez 10–0–52–1; Sohail Tanvir 10–0–69–1; Junaid Khan 5.4–0–44–3; Saeed Ajmal 10–0–48–0; Shahid Afridi 7–0–30–2; Bilawal Bhatti 7–0–56–1.

Umpires: J. D. Cloete and Shozab Raza.   Third umpire: R. K. Illingworth.
Referee: D. C. Boon.

PAKISTAN v SRI LANKA

Second One-Day International

At Dubai, December 20, 2013 (day/night). Sri Lanka won by two wickets. Toss: Sri Lanka.

Sri Lanka's batting depth served them well as they soared past the second-highest score at Dubai with two balls to spare. Dilshan was at fault for Kushal Perera's run-out, and soon came a cropper himself when he grounded his bat in a wet patch centimetres from the line, and the handle slipped out of his grasp. Sangakkara and Chandimal withstood the threat of Junaid Khan, and gradually restored calm in a stand of 94. Mathews hit only one four in his first 42 – adopting Javed Miandad's old tactic of deliberate slow running to provoke overthrows – but his second boundary, off Junaid in the penultimate over, was the killer blow. Mathews did fall soon after, but Karunaratne, a Test opener, emerged at No. 9 to help knock off the winning runs. Mathews' approach recalled the earlier patient hundred from Ahmed Shehzad; only seven boundaries were scored in the first half of Pakistan's innings. Misbah-ul-Haq sped things up a little with his customary late fifty. But he was later fined 20% of his match fee, and his team-mates 10%, for a slow over-rate.

Man of the Match: A. D. Mathews.

Pakistan

Sharjeel Khan lbw b Malinga	7
Ahmed Shehzad lbw b Kulasekara	124
Mohammad Hafeez run out.	32
Sohaib Maqsood c Chandimal b Prasanna . .	18
*Misbah-ul-Haq not out.	59

Shahid Afridi not out.	30
L-b 3, w 10, n-b 1	14
1/8 (1) 2/84 (3) (4 wkts, 50 overs)	284
3/128 (4) 4/233 (2) 10 overs: 43-1	

†Umar Akmal, Bilawal Bhatti, Sohail Tanvir, Saeed Ajmal and Junaid Khan did not bat.

Kulasekara 10–0–56–1; Malinga 10–0–78–1; N. L. T. C. Perera 2.4–0–19–0; Mathews 3.4–0–17–0; Prasanna 10–0–45–1; Senanayake 10–0–42–0; Karunaratne 1.4–0–11–0; Dilshan 2–0–13–0.

Sri Lanka

M. D. K. J. Perera run out	16		S. Prasanna b Junaid Khan	6
T. M. Dilshan run out	40		F. D. M. Karunaratne not out	16
†K. C. Sangakkara b Saeed Ajmal	58		S. M. S. M. Senanayake not out	6
L. D. Chandimal b Junaid Khan	44		L-b 9, w 6, n-b 2	17
N. L. T. C. Perera b Junaid Khan	5			
*A. D. Mathews c Ahmed Shehzad			1/49 (1) 2/65 (2) (8 wkts, 49.4 overs) 287	
b Shahid Afridi .	47		3/159 (3) 4/168 (4)	
K. M. D. N. Kulasekara b Umar Akmal			5/173 (5) 6/230 (7)	
b Shahid Afridi .	32		7/237 (8) 8/281 (6) 10 overs: 50-1	

S. L. Malinga did not bat.

Mohammad Hafeez 8–0–39–0; Sohail Tanvir 9–0–58–0; Saeed Ajmal 10–0–44–1; Bilawal Bhatti 7–2–39–0; Junaid Khan 10–0–52–3; Shahid Afridi 5.4–0–46–2.

Umpires: Ahsan Raza and R. K. Illingworth.   Third umpire: J. D. Cloete.
Referee: D. C. Boon.

PAKISTAN v SRI LANKA

Third One-Day International

At Sharjah, December 22, 2013 (day/night). Pakistan won by 113 runs. Toss: Sri Lanka.

Mohammad Hafeez hit a career-best 140 not out to clear the path for the highest total at Sharjah in almost 20 years. It set up Pakistan's 78th win there in one-day internationals – equalling Australia's ground record at the SCG (though Australia pulled clear again when they beat England there four weeks later). Sri Lanka's task would have been a great deal easier had Malinga not dropped a sitter at long-on to reprieve Hafeez on 26; even his unexpected direct hit to run out Ahmed Shehzad, halting the second-wicket stand at 160, could not fully atone. After that, Sri Lanka's misdirected stream of yorkers were punished by Misbah-ul-Haq and Umar Akmal. Umar Gul made a spectacular return after nine months out with knee problems, removing Kushal Perera and Karunaratne in the fourth over, and thereafter Sri Lanka's resistance was limited to Dilshan's punchy fifty. Shehzad was docked 50% of his match fee for grabbing Dilshan's bat and pushing him on the shoulder. Kulasekara was Saeed Ajmal's 102nd international wicket of 2013, breaking Saqlain Mushtaq's Pakistan record for most in a calendar year, set in 1997.

Man of the Match: Mohammad Hafeez.

Pakistan

Sharjeel Khan b Kulasekara	2		Shahid Afridi b Malinga	2
Ahmed Shehzad run out	81		†Umar Akmal not out	23
Mohammad Hafeez not out	140		L-b 10, w 7	17
Sohaib Maqsood c Senanayake				
b N. L. T. C. Perera .	21		1/2 (1) 2/162 (2) (5 wkts, 50 overs) 326	
*Misbah-ul-Haq c Karunaratne			3/200 (4) 4/275 (5)	
b N. L. T. C. Perera .	40		5/281 (6) 10 overs: 37-1	

Bilawal Bhatti, Umar Gul, Saeed Ajmal and Junaid Khan did not bat.

Kulasekara 10–1–67–1; Malinga 10–0–58–1; Senanayake 10–0–58–0; N. L. T. C. Perera 8–0–58–2; Prasanna 8–0–46–0; Mathews 4–0–29–0.

Sri Lanka

M. D. K. J. Perera c Ahmed Shehzad	
b Umar Gul .	7
T. M. Dilshan b Shahid Afridi	59
F. D. M. Karunaratne c Umar Akmal	
b Umar Gul .	0
†K. C. Sangakkara c Sohaib Maqsood	
b Junaid Khan .	14
L. D. Chandimal c Sohaib Maqsood	
b Mohammad Hafeez .	36
*A. D. Mathews c Umar Akmal	
b Saeed Ajmal .	44
K. M. D. N. Kulasekara c Umar Akmal	
b Saeed Ajmal .	1

S. Prasanna c Saeed Ajmal	
b Mohammad Hafeez .	22
N. L. T. C. Perera c Shahid Afridi	
b Junaid Khan .	2
S. M. S. M. Senanayake not out	4
S. L. Malinga b Umar Gul	19
L-b 2, w 3	5
1/17 (1) 2/17 (3) (44.4 overs) 213
3/44 (4) 4/103 (2) 5/132 (5)
6/136 (7) 7/163 (8) 8/187 (9)
9/192 (6) 10/213 (11) 10 overs: 46-3

Junaid Khan 9–0–40–2; Umar Gul 5.4–0–19–3; Shahid Afridi 9–0–41–1; Bilawal Bhatti 6–0–39–0; Saeed Ajmal 10–1–37–2; Mohammad Hafeez 5–0–35–2.

Umpires: J. D. Cloete and Shozab Raza. Third umpire: R. K. Illingworth.
Referee: D. C. Boon.

PAKISTAN v SRI LANKA

Fourth One-Day International

At Abu Dhabi, December 25, 2013 (day/night). Pakistan won by eight wickets. Toss: Sri Lanka. One-day international debuts: S. M. A. Priyanjan, K. D. K. Vithanage.

A third century of the series from Mohammad Hafeez – matching the achievement of seven others, including Pakistan's Zaheer Abbas in 1982-83, and South Africa's Quinton de Kock a few weeks earlier – carried his side to a series victory on Christmas Day. Hafeez lapped up Sri Lanka's persistent use of the short ball, racing to 50 off 38 deliveries, and his ninth hundred in the format. After Sri Lanka batted first, Umar Gul could not believe how his rank long-hop to Kushal Perera ended up in cover's hands, but there was genuine craft in the way he set up Dilshan and Chandimal to make it 36 for three. Debutant Ashan Priyanjan gave the innings direction in a classy fifty marked by fast hands and back-foot class. But he and Sangakkara had not quite completed the repair job when Sangakkara sacrificed his wicket in a mix-up. Junaid Khan and Saeed Ajmal dampened token resistance put up by Mathews and another debutant, Kithuruwan Vithanage.

Man of the Match: Mohammad Hafeez.

Sri Lanka

M. D. K. J. Perera c Misbah-ul-Haq	
b Umar Gul .	8
T. M. Dilshan b Umar Gul	8
†K. C. Sangakkara run out	51
L. D. Chandimal c Misbah-ul-Haq	
b Umar Gul .	5
S. M. A. Priyanjan b Junaid Khan	74
*A. D. Mathews lbw b Saeed Ajmal	38
K. M. D. N. Kulasekara c and b Saeed Ajmal	1
K. D. K. Vithanage c Sohaib Maqsood	
b Junaid Khan .	27

S. M. S. M. Senanayake b Saeed Ajmal . . .	0
R. A. S. Lakmal not out	2
S. L. Malinga c Umar Akmal b Saeed Ajmal	0
L-b 1, w 9, n-b 1	11
1/15 (1) 2/22 (2) (48.5 overs) 225
3/36 (4) 4/125 (3) 5/165 (5)
6/170 (7) 7/210 (6) 8/210 (9)
9/225 (8) 10/225 (11) 10 overs: 50-3

Junaid Khan 9–0–42–2; Umar Gul 7–1–37–3; Shahid Afridi 7–0–37–0; Bilawal Bhatti 7–1–23–0; Saeed Ajmal 9.5–1–39–4; Mohammad Hafeez 9–0–46–0.

Pakistan

Sharjeel Khan b Mathews	13	
Ahmed Shehzad c Senanayake b Lakmal . .	44	
Mohammad Hafeez not out	113	
Sohaib Maqsood not out	46	
B 4, l-b 1, w 5	10	

1/31 (1)   (2 wkts, 41.1 overs) 226
2/115 (2)   10 overs: 57-1

*Misbah-ul-Haq, Shahid Afridi, †Umar Akmal, Bilawal Bhatti, Umar Gul, Saeed Ajmal and Junaid Khan did not bat.

Kulasekara 4–0–28–0; Malinga 7–0–40–0; Lakmal 9–0–49–1; Mathews 6–0–15–1; Senanayake 10–0–49–0; Vithanage 1–0–10–0; Dilshan 3.1–0–25–0; Priyanjan 1–0–5–0.

Umpires: Ahsan Raza and R. K. Illingworth.   Third umpire: J. D. Cloete.
Referee: J. Srinath.

PAKISTAN v SRI LANKA

Fifth One-Day International

At Abu Dhabi, December 27, 2013 (day/night). Sri Lanka won by two wickets. Toss: Pakistan.

Chandimal and Mendis overcame high pressure to sneak a consolation win from the depths of 195 for eight. Three wickets had gone down in 12 balls, bringing Ajantha Mendis to the crease for the first time on tour. Saeed Ajmal won an lbw verdict against him first ball but, as Mendis began to walk off, Chandimal persuaded him to review: the majority of the ball had pitched outside leg stump. Chandimal pulled his first four in the next over to end a sequence of 19 innings without a fifty, and Mendis was put down by Sohaib Maqsood at cover off Ajmal. The mistake probably cost Pakistan

MOST INTERNATIONAL WICKETS IN A CALENDAR YEAR

W	M			W	M		
136	45	M. Muralitharan (SL)	2001	111	50	**Saeed Ajmal (P)**	**2013**
128	40	M. Muralitharan (SL)	2006	109	31	M. Muralitharan (SL)	2000
120	39	S. K. Warne (A)	1994	107	27	A. A. Donald (SA)	1998
119	41	G. D. McGrath (A)	1999	105	28	D. K. Lillee (A)	1981
113	47	M. G. Johnson (A)	2009	105	28	J. Garner (WI)	1984
111	39	G. P. Swann (E)	2010				

the match: both batsmen swung Umar Gul for six in the penultimate over. Sri Lanka dawdled a little over their target, after Kushal Perera swung four sixes in the opening powerplay, part of a 75-run stand with Dilshan, who became the sixth Sri Lankan to 8,000 runs in one-day internationals. Earlier, Sri Lanka put in their best bowling performance of the tour. Mohammad Hafeez's tilt at an unprecedented fourth hundred in a series was scotched by one that kept low from Mathews, but his 41 was enough to make him the format's second-highest run-scorer in 2013, with 1,301. The only man ahead of him was Misbah-ul-Haq, who – having abandoned the reverse sweep – propped up the innings with his 15th half-century of the year, but then fell to Malinga. Anwar Ali did his best filling in for Shahid Afridi (absent for personal reasons) at No. 7, but Pakistan lacked a true finisher.

Man of the Match: L. D. Chandimal.   *Man of the Series:* Mohammad Hafeez.

Pakistan

Sharjeel Khan c and b Malinga	18	Saeed Ajmal lbw b Lakmal	8
Ahmed Shehzad c Priyanjan b Lakmal	17	Junaid Khan lbw b Lakmal	0
Mohammad Hafeez b Mathews	41		
Sohaib Maqsood c Dilshan b Malinga	7	L-b 10, w 10	20
*Misbah-ul-Haq c Sangakkara b Malinga	51		
†Umar Akmal c Dilshan b Mendis	20	1/30 (2) 2/54 (1) (49.3 overs)	232
Anwar Ali not out	41	3/70 (4) 4/128 (3) 5/169 (5)	
Abdur Rehman lbw b Malinga	1	6/173 (6) 7/176 (8) 8/194 (9)	
Umar Gul run out	8	9/232 (10) 10/232 (11) 10 overs: 43-1	

Mathews 10–1–26–1; Lakmal 7.3–0–42–3; Senanayake 10–1–44–0; Malinga 10–0–57–4; Mendis 10–1–42–1; Dilshan 2–0–11–0.

Sri Lanka

M. D. K. J. Perera lbw b Mohammad Hafeez	47	S. L. Malinga b Saeed Ajmal	0
T. M. Dilshan c Saeed Ajmal b Junaid Khan	45	B. A. W. Mendis not out	19
†K. C. Sangakkara b Junaid Khan	22		
L. D. Chandimal not out	64	L-b 7, w 5	12
S. M. A. Priyanjan c Umar Akmal b Umar Gul	1	1/75 (1) 2/113 (2) (8 wkts, 49.4 overs)	235
*A. D. Mathews c Umar Akmal b Anwar Ali	8	3/129 (3) 4/137 (5)	
K. D. K. Vithanage b Saeed Ajmal	14	5/166 (6) 6/189 (7)	
S. M. S. M. Senanayake c Mohammad Hafeez b Junaid Khan	3	7/194 (8) 8/195 (9) 10 overs: 68-0	

R. A. S. Lakmal did not bat.

Umar Gul 7.5–0–44–1; Anwar Ali 5.4–0–36–1; Mohammad Hafeez 9–0–36–1; Junaid Khan 7.1–0–31–3; Saeed Ajmal 10–0–43–2; Abdur Rehman 10–0–38–0.

Umpires: J. D. Cloete and Shozab Raza.   Third umpire: R. K. Illingworth.
Referee: J. Srinath.

PAKISTAN v SRI LANKA

First Test Match

At Abu Dhabi, December 31, 2013–January 4, 2014. Drawn. Toss: Pakistan. Test debuts: Ahmed Shehzad, Bilawal Bhatti; S. M. S. M. Senanayake.

Sri Lanka showed great resilience to bat through the fourth day and escape with a draw. Bilawal Bhatti, a fiery fast bowler on Test debut, had removed the big beasts Sangakkara and Mahela Jayawardene on the third evening and, by the close, Sri Lanka were four wickets down and leading by only seven. The game could easily have been over with a day to spare. But, 24 hours later, it was Pakistan who were under the pump: they had lost wicketkeeper Adnan Akmal to a broken finger, and Sri Lanka had lost only one wicket all day. When Pakistan finally emerged for the run-chase on the fifth morning, they cut their losses and batted out time.

Both sides named six players with fewer than 15 Test caps; Sri Lanka made four changes from their last Test, eight months earlier in Colombo. Kaushal Silva was brought back as a specialist opener in place of the retired Tillekeratne Dilshan; four wicketkeepers in the side did little for Sri Lanka's fill-in bowling. The first to be exposed, though, was their batting, as Misbah-ul-Haq put them in on a green but placid surface. They lost only one wicket in the first session, but seven in a disastrous passage after lunch. Jayawardene, who missed the limited-overs leg to attend the birth of his child, nicked a rising beauty from Bhatti, only to be saved on replay when it emerged the bowler had overstepped; next ball, Bhatti fired in a legitimate yorker, and Jayawardene edged that one too. Junaid Khan led the line to pick up his fourth Test five-for – all against Sri Lanka. Mathews, sensing the way things were heading after Sangakkara drove loosely to point, figured that boundaries were the only way to salvage the innings, and managed to scrape together 61 for the ninth wicket with Eranga.

From the uncertainty of 83 for three before lunch on New Year's Day (this was the first Test to span two calendar years since 1984-85), Younis Khan and Misbah batted with authority in a four-hour stand of 218. Younis eventually chopped on to the second new ball, but not before he had equalled Javed Miandad's mark of 23 Test centuries for Pakistan. Misbah was having few problems carrying his form into 2014, and made the most of Sri Lanka's sloppiness: Jayawardene should have caught him darting behind the keeper from slip on 69, and Lakmal lacked the confidence to review an lbw shout seven runs later. Misbah was last out as Sri Lanka swept up the final six wickets next morning; the last seven had fallen for 82.

Silva and Sangakkara, in a stand of 99, began to claw Sri Lanka back into the match. Then, soon after the last drinks break of the evening, Younis took a smart low catch to remove Sangakkara and, first ball, Jayawardene was squared up, edging Bhatti for the third delivery in a row. Silva followed to the final ball of the day; the downside was that Akmal fractured his left index finger taking the catch, so Younis stood behind the stumps for the rest of the innings.

For a team that had too often relied on Sangakkara and Jayawardene, the 138 now put on by Chandimal and Mathews felt significant. Sri Lanka calmly added 234 in the day's 86.5 overs, of which their captain contributed 116. Those two, plus Prasanna Jayawardene, tamed Saeed Ajmal, a master in these conditions, to the extent that he bowled an unprecedented 49 overs without a wicket. Mathews' show of defiance pulled Sri Lanka out of danger, and allowed him to declare 25 minutes before lunch, with the lead past 300.

Pakistan, however, had no intention of going 1–0 down in a three-match series. Mohammad Hafeez made the most of his limited-overs form to score his first Test fifty since July 2012 – without quite staving off the critics who felt him unsuited to No. 3. In normal circumstances, Herath might have proved a handful, but the pitch refused to break up.

Man of the Match: A. D. Mathews.

Close of play: first day, Pakistan 46-1 (Ahmed Shehzad 25); second day, Pakistan 327-4 (Misbah-ul-Haq 105, Asad Shafiq 12); third day, Sri Lanka 186-4 (Chandimal 24); fourth day, Sri Lanka 420-5 (Mathews 116, H. A. P. W. Jayawardene 48).

Sri Lanka

F. D. M. Karunaratne c Asad Shafiq b Junaid Khan	38	– b Junaid Khan	24
J. K. Silva c Mohammad Hafeez b Bilawal Bhatti	20	– c Adnan Akmal b Junaid Khan	81
K. C. Sangakkara c Ahmed Shehzad b Junaid Khan	16	– c Younis Khan b Bilawal Bhatti	55
D. P. M. D. Jayawardene c Adnan Akmal b Bilawal Bhatti	5	– c Asad Shafiq b Bilawal Bhatti	0
L. D. Chandimal c Mohammad Hafeez b Bilawal Bhatti	0	– c Rahat Ali b Junaid Khan	89
*A. D. Mathews st Adnan Akmal b Saeed Ajmal	91	– not out	157
†H. A. P. W. Jayawardene c Adnan Akmal b Junaid Khan	5	– not out	63
S. M. S. M. Senanayake c Adnan Akmal b Junaid Khan	5		
H. M. R. K. B. Herath b Junaid Khan	0		
R. M. S. Eranga c Adnan Akmal b Saeed Ajmal	14		
R. A. S. Lakmal not out	1		
B 4, l-b 4, n-b 1	9	B 4, l-b 7	11

1/57 (1) 2/67 (2) 3/76 (4) (65 overs) 204
4/76 (5) 5/82 (3) 6/104 (7)
7/124 (8) 8/124 (9) 9/185 (10) 10/204 (6)

1/47 (1) (5 wkts dec, 168.3 overs) 480
2/146 (3) 3/150 (4)
4/186 (2) 5/324 (5)

Junaid Khan 20–4–58–5; Rahat Ali 16–3–41–0; Bilawal Bhatti 15–1–65–3; Saeed Ajmal 14–3–32–2. *Second innings*—Junaid Khan 36–3–93–3; Rahat Ali 38.3–9–92–0; Bilawal Bhatti 36–8–146–2; Saeed Ajmal 49–10–115–0; Mohammad Hafeez 9–1–23–0.

Pakistan

Khurram Manzoor run out	21	– c H. A. P. W. Jayawardene b Lakmal 8
Ahmed Shehzad c Karunaratne b Eranga	38	– lbw b Herath 55
Mohammad Hafeez c Silva b Lakmal	11	– not out 80
Younis Khan b Eranga	136	– not out 13
*Misbah-ul-Haq c Sangakkara b Herath	135	
Asad Shafiq c Silva b Lakmal	13	
†Adnan Akmal c Senanayake b Eranga	6	
Bilawal Bhatti c H. A. P. W. Jayawardene b Mathews	14	
Saeed Ajmal lbw b Herath	0	
Rahat Ali b Herath	0	
Junaid Khan not out	4	
L-b 2, w 1, n-b 2	5	L-b 1, n-b 1 2

1/46 (1) 2/59 (3) 3/83 (2)   (129.1 overs) 383   1/24 (1)   (2 wkts, 52 overs) 158
4/301 (4) 5/329 (6) 6/342 (7)   2/125 (2)
7/369 (8) 8/378 (9) 9/378 (10) 10/383 (5)

Lakmal 33–9–99–2; Mathews 13–1–43–1; Eranga 30–6–80–3; Herath 35.1–9–93–3; Senanayake 18–2–66–0. *Second innings*—Lakmal 13–1–43–1; Eranga 11–0–38–0; Herath 21–8–37–1; Mathews 2–0–9–0; Senanayake 5–0–30–0.

Umpires: R. A. Kettleborough and B. N. J. Oxenford.   Third umpire: S. Ravi.

PAKISTAN v SRI LANKA

Second Test Match

At Dubai, January 8–12, 2014. Sri Lanka won by nine wickets. Toss: Sri Lanka.

Pakistan paid a heavy price for their inept batting on the opening day. With the match bookended by unsettled weather in the Gulf, they were taken aback by an unusually grassy and responsive surface, and could not adapt their leaden-footed strokeplay. The upshot was their second Test defeat of the winter at Dubai, and the feeling that their dominion in this part of the world was loosening a little. It was a landmark win for Sri Lanka – just their second victory overseas in 19 attempts.

Mathews' decision to bowl was unprecedented at this venue, but not a complete surprise given Pakistan's collapses for 99 in their previous two Tests here, against England and South Africa. Those were two countries with serious fast-bowling pedigree; Mathews cannot have expected his own trio of seamers, all in their mid-twenties and with intermittent Test careers, to have proved so potent. But Lakmal and Eranga kept it tight, and the recalled Nuwan Pradeep conjured up the odd beauty, making the ball move late to bemuse Ahmed Shehzad and Mohammad Hafeez. Khurram Manzoor was a shining exception, but Herath – summoned unusually late in the piece – mopped up the tail. Pakistan lost their last eight wickets for 58, and a total of 165 compelled their bowlers to chase the game.

When Mahela Jayawardene walked out to bat at 88 for three, one position lower than usual following a miserable First Test, Sri Lanka had yet to exert their will. That soon changed. Jayawardene, his right hand strapped after he split the webbing while dropping a catch on the first day, battled his way back to form. He again edged his first ball from Bilawal Bhatti, but this time it skimmed the turf and ran away for four. The seam movement that unsettled Pakistan's batsmen on the first day was nowhere to be seen, and Jayawardene and Silva were able to carry Sri Lanka into the lead without much fuss.

Silva fell five short of a maiden hundred, before Mathews was put down on five by Sarfraz Ahmed (replacing the injured Adnan Akmal), who stuck out his right glove when he should have gone with both hands; the pair put on a further 80 before Mathews edged Rahat Ali again, and Sarfraz clung on. Jayawardene, after a wait of 18 innings stretching back to April 2012 against England in Colombo, reached his 32nd Test hundred with successive late cuts off Bhatti, and moved ahead of Steve Waugh into eighth in the all-time run-scorers list.

Pakistan, responding to a deficit of 223, were as good as buried when they careered to 19 for three. Misbah-ul-Haq joined Younis Khan with another rescue mission to carry out and, helped by a ball change in the 13th over that seemed to reduce the swing, they set about dulling Sri Lanka's edge. Misbah lost Younis to a frustrated cut on 77, then reviewed his own dismissal on 78 (Pakistan's only successful use of DRS in the series). Misbah had just taken Pakistan into the lead, and was within three runs of hundreds in back-to-back Tests, when Herath turned one past his forward prod to hit off stump. Sarfraz, with his first international fifty, fought hard to a premature close, when heavy rain swept through the desert. With no part-time bowlers in a side stocked with wicketkeepers, Sangakkara even turned his arm over, for only the fourth time in his long Test career.

Rain continued to fall during the night, but the floodlights ensured play began on time on the final morning. Sarfraz could add only four to his overnight score, and Pakistan were dismissed 75 minutes into the day. Strikingly, it was Lakmal and Eranga who did the mopping up; only six times before had as many as 15 wickets gone down to Sri Lankan seamers in a Test. Silva chipped in with his second fifty of the match to help guide Sri Lanka to their small target of 137, and an unexpected series lead.

Man of the Match: D. P. M. D. Jayawardene.

Close of play: first day, Sri Lanka 57-1 (Silva 12, Sangakkara 12); second day, Sri Lanka 318-4 (D. P. M. D. Jayawardene 106, Mathews 42); third day, Pakistan 132-3 (Younis Khan 62, Misbah-ul-Haq 53); fourth day, Pakistan 330-7 (Sarfraz Ahmed 70, Saeed Ajmal 7).

Pakistan

Khurram Manzoor c H. A. P. W. Jayawardene b Lakmal	73	– c H. A. P. W. Jayawardene b Fernando	6
Ahmed Shehzad lbw b Fernando	3	– c H. A. P. W. Jayawardene b Herath	9
Mohammad Hafeez b Fernando	21	– c H. A. P. W. Jayawardene b Fernando	1
Younis Khan c H. A. P. W. Jayawardene b Eranga	13	– c H. A. P. W. Jayawardene b Lakmal	77
*Misbah-ul-Haq c H. A. P. W. Jayawardene b Eranga	1	– b Herath	97
Asad Shafiq c Silva b Lakmal	6	– c Karunaratne b Eranga	23
†Sarfraz Ahmed c H. A. P. W. Jayawardene b Fernando	7	– b Lakmal	74
Bilawal Bhatti not out	24	– b Eranga	32
Saeed Ajmal c Silva b Herath	8	– b Lakmal	21
Rahat Ali lbw b Herath	0	– c H. A. P. W. Jayawardene b Lakmal	8
Junaid Khan lbw b Herath	2	– not out	2
L-b 7	7	B 1, l-b 8	9

1/28 (2) 2/78 (3) 3/107 (4) (63.5 overs) 165   1/11 (2) 2/12 (3) (137.3 overs) 359
4/109 (5) 5/118 (1) 6/127 (6)   3/19 (1) 4/148 (4)
7/129 (7) 8/151 (9) 9/151 (10) 10/165 (11)   5/200 (6) 6/245 (5) 7/312 (8)
8/334 (7) 9/354 (10) 10/359 (9)

Lakmal 21–6–45–2; Eranga 14–4–25–2; Fernando 18–2–62–3; Herath 10.5–3–26–3. *Second innings*—Lakmal 28.3–4–78–4; Fernando 19–3–50–2; Herath 48–10–132–2; Eranga 36–9–74–2; Mathews 5–1–9–0; Sangakkara 1–0–7–0.

Sri Lanka

F. D. M. Karunaratne lbw b Junaid Khan	32	– not out	62
J. K. Silva lbw b Mohammad Hafeez	95	– lbw b Saeed Ajmal	58
K. C. Sangakkara lbw b Rahat Ali	26	– not out	9
L. D. Chandimal c Rahat Ali b Junaid Khan	12		
D. P. M. D. Jayawardene b Saeed Ajmal	129		
*A. D. Mathews c Sarfraz Ahmed b Rahat Ali	42		
†H. A. P. W. Jayawardene b Junaid Khan	9		
H. M. R. K. B. Herath run out	6		
R. M. S. Eranga b Bilawal Bhatti	14		
R. A. S. Lakmal not out	10		
A. N. P. R. Fernando lbw b Saeed Ajmal	3		
B 1, l-b 7, w 1, n-b 1	10	B 3, l-b 4, n-b 1	8

1/40 (1) 2/75 (3) 3/88 (4) (134 overs) 388   1/124 (2) (1 wkt, 46.2 overs) 137
4/227 (2) 5/320 (6) 6/341 (7)
7/348 (8) 8/365 (5) 9/377 (9) 10/388 (11)

Junaid Khan 36–7–102–3; Rahat Ali 36–6–131–2; Saeed Ajmal 34–11–56–2; Bilawal Bhatti 22–3–80–1; Mohammad Hafeez 6–1–11–1. *Second innings*—Mohammad Hafeez 8–3–22–0; Junaid Khan 10–2–34–0; Rahat Ali 11–1–29–0; Saeed Ajmal 17.2–5–45–1.

Umpires: B. N. J. Oxenford and S. Ravi.   Third umpire: R. A. Kettleborough.

PAKISTAN v SRI LANKA

Third Test Match

At Sharjah, January 16–20, 2014. Pakistan won by five wickets. Toss: Sri Lanka. Test debut: M. D. K. Perera.

The first four and half days contained some of the dreariest cricket imaginable; the last session and a half was stuff from the firmament. Pakistan had to score 302 in 59 overs to preserve their unbeaten home Test series record, stretching back to 2007-08. That they managed it exposed the unnecessarily soporific cricket earlier in the match – mostly by Sri Lanka. The run-rate of 5.25 in Pakistan's second innings, ending in an astonishing victory, was the quickest of any 300-plus chase in Test history. Pakistan had famously lost to England in the gloom at Karachi in 2000-01, despite captain Moin Khan's constant appeals against the light; now, it was their turn to be grateful for some firm umpiring.

Sri Lanka took almost 102 overs to score 214 in their second innings, which finished in the extended period before lunch on the last day. Mathews, astonishingly, blamed his batsmen for being too impatient. "We didn't need to give them a sniff," he said. "I thought we should have been a bit more cautious because we'd already won the series. All we needed was to bat for another hour." It was like subcontinental cricket beamed from the early 1980s. The truth was that, after Mathews' brilliant series with the bat, it was his 99-ball crawl to 14 on the fourth evening that had given Pakistan their sniff.

Pakistan's only way to save the series was to go for it, and they benefited from the clarity. By tea, they had lost three wickets, and still required 195 from 35 overs – but their aggression had already sent Mathews on the defensive. Misbah's decision to promote Sarfraz Ahmed ahead of him worked a treat. Sarfraz showed how to counter Herath, bowling over the wicket outside leg stump, by taking guard in line with the markings for leg-side wides, and either sweeping, or lofting through the unguarded off side. Azhar Ali, recalled at No. 3 in place of Mohammad Hafeez, accumulated all around the wicket. By the time Sarfraz gloved down the leg side for 48 from 46 balls, Pakistan needed a less

HIGHEST RUN-RATE IN THE FOURTH INNINGS OF A TEST

Run-rate		Overs		
5.77	England (205-2)	35.3	beat South Africa at The Oval............	1994
5.51	England (204-6)†	37.0	drew with Zimbabwe at Bulawayo........	1996-97
5.25	**Pakistan (302-5)**	**57.3**	**beat Sri Lanka at Sharjah**	**2013-14**
5.19	West Indies (344-1)	66.1	beat England at Lord's	1984
5.15	**England (206-5)‡**	**40.0**	**drew with Australia at The Oval**	**2013**
5.10	Australia (212-4)	41.3	beat New Zealand at Hamilton	1999-2000

Minimum target of 200.

† *Scores tied.* ‡ *England were 21 runs short of victory when bad light stopped play.*

intimidating 116 off 22 overs. When Misbah came on strike, Mathews set all nine fielders back on the ropes; Azhar and Misbah simply milked the ones and twos. Not once did Mathews turn to the debutant off-spinner, Dilruwan Perera.

In the last half hour, Sri Lanka began resorting to delaying tactics, but the umpires did not fall for it. Eranga received lengthy treatment after colliding with Misbah, and Richard Kettleborough ordered the physio to stay away when Lakmal tumbled in the field. The light was fading badly, but the umpires refused to look at their meters. Azhar scored a stupendous 103 off 137 balls, before sprinting off to ensure no time was lost. In the next over, with nine deliveries left, Misbah tapped a single to complete one of Pakistan's most famous victories.

After winning the toss on a slow, flat pitch, and with no need or desire to force the issue, Sri Lanka had taken almost two days to amass 428. Pakistan at last felt confident to play Abdur Rehman as a second spinner, with Bilawal Bhatti home with a hamstring injury. Rehman's inclusion had a beneficial effect on Saeed Ajmal who – after 16.5 more joyless overs – chipped in with the wickets of Mahela Jayawardene and Chandimal in three balls. Pakistan's close catching was shaky, and they had no luck with DRS. Then again, they used it poorly: Mathews twice escaped being lbw to Rehman on the umpire's call. While Pakistan fumed, Mathews and Perera stuck to the script, adding 112 at barely two an over. Mathews was out in the nineties for the fourth time, and Perera caught on the hook for 95, making him only the second debutant to be out in the nineties from No. 8 or lower, after Ashton Agar at Trent Bridge the previous July. A few moments later, Mathews called time.

Pakistan had a lot of catching up to do. They began steadily, as their openers built a century partnership. Ahmed Shehzad upped the tempo and reached his maiden Test hundred on the third evening – with the ball starting to reverse, Mathews resorted to a seven–two leg-side field. With the help of some quicksilver keeping from Prasanna Jayawardene, Herath was able to prey on Pakistan's impatience to pick up the series' only five-wicket haul.

Sri Lanka claimed a lead of 87, so it was a surprise just how tentative they were in building on it. Mahela Jayawardene resolved to leave everything outside off, and it was a rare six off Ajmal that took him past 11,000 Test runs. Mathews followed his lead before becoming the sixth wicket in the game for Mohammad Talha, who had replaced Rahat Ali. In the last session, Sri Lanka added just 45 in 33 overs. Prasanna Jayawardene injected some welcome direction next morning, but the run-rate had returned to a dribble by the time Rehman removed Perera and Herath in consecutive balls. Herath went on to become the first man in Test history to bag a king pair and concede 100 runs in an innings. But the statistics were soon giving way to a memorable finish.

Man of the Match: Azhar Ali. *Man of the Series:* A. D. Mathews.

Close of play: first day, Sri Lanka 220-5 (Mathews 24, H. A. P. W. Jayawardene 28); second day, Pakistan 19-0 (Khurram Manzoor 14, Ahmed Shehzad 5); third day, Pakistan 291-6 (Misbah-ul-Haq 36); fourth day, Sri Lanka 133-5 (Mathews 14, H. A. P. W. Jayawardene 6).

Sri Lanka

F. D. M. Karunaratne c Younis Khan b Abdur Rehman .	34	– b Mohammad Talha 8
J. K. Silva c Sarfraz Ahmed b Mohammad Talha . .	17	– b Abdur Rehman 36
K. C. Sangakkara c Khurram Manzoor b Junaid Khan .	52	– c Khurram Manzoor b Abdur Rehman 8
D. P. M. D. Jayawardene c Azhar Ali b Saeed Ajmal	47	– c Azhar Ali b Saeed Ajmal 46
L. D. Chandimal c Asad Shafiq b Saeed Ajmal	11	– b Mohammad Talha 13
*A. D. Mathews c Ahmed Shehzad b Junaid Khan . .	91	– c Khurram Manzoor b Mohammad Talha . 31
†H. A. P. W. Jayawardene c Junaid Khan b Mohammad Talha .	35	– c Azhar Ali b Saeed Ajmal 49
M. D. K. Perera c Junaid Khan b Mohammad Talha	95	– c Azhar Ali b Abdur Rehman 8
H. M. R. K. B. Herath lbw b Junaid Khan	0	– c Younis Khan b Abdur Rehman 0
R. M. S. Eranga not out	25	– c Abdur Rehman b Saeed Ajmal 3
R. A. S. Lakmal not out	3	– not out 2
B 5, l-b 11, n-b 2	18	B 2, l-b 4, w 2, n-b 2 10

1/31 (2) 2/65 (1) (9 wkts dec, 172 overs) 428
3/125 (3) 4/159 (4) 5/166 (5)
6/239 (7) 7/351 (6) 8/351 (9) 9/423 (8)

1/13 (1) 2/37 (3) (101.4 overs) 214
3/66 (2) 4/89 (5)
5/127 (4) 6/189 (6) 7/203 (8)
8/203 (9) 9/209 (7) 10/214 (10)

Junaid Khan 32–5–81–3; Mohammad Talha 32–3–99–3; Saeed Ajmal 55–16–120–2; Abdur Rehman 50–14–101–1; Azhar Ali 3–0–11–0. *Second innings*—Junaid Khan 20–6–34–0; Mohammad Talha 23–2–65–3; Abdur Rehman 33–10–56–4; Saeed Ajmal 25.4–7–53–3.

Pakistan

Khurram Manzoor c H. A. P. W. Jayawardene b Eranga .	52	– c H. A. P. W. Jayawardene b Lakmal 21
Ahmed Shehzad b Herath	147	– c Karunaratne b Lakmal 21
Azhar Ali c Mathews b Perera	8	– c H. A. P. W. Jayawardene b Lakmal 103
Younis Khan c H. A. P. W. Jayawardene b Herath .	17	– c Sangakkara b Mathews 29
*Misbah-ul-Haq c Chandimal b Herath	63	– (6) not out 68
Asad Shafiq lbw b Eranga	18	– (7) not out 1
†Sarfraz Ahmed c H. A. P. W. Jayawardene b Herath	5	– (5) c H. A. P. W. Jayawardene b Eranga . 48
Abdur Rehman c H. A. P. W. Jayawardene b Eranga	2	
Mohammad Talha lbw b Eranga	2	
Saeed Ajmal not out	0	
Junaid Khan c Chandimal b Herath	16	
B 3, l-b 6, w 1, n-b 1	11	B 6, l-b 1, w 3, n-b 1 11

1/114 (1) 2/149 (3) 3/189 (4) (109.1 overs) 341
4/245 (2) 5/274 (6) 6/291 (7)
7/294 (8) 8/300 (9) 9/325 (5) 10/341 (11)

1/35 (2) (5 wkts, 57.3 overs) 302
2/48 (1) 3/97 (4)
4/186 (5) 5/295 (3)

Herath 38.1–8–125–5; Lakmal 23–4–61–0; Perera 17–1–71–1; Eranga 24–5–60–4; Mathews 7–3–15–0. *Second innings*—Lakmal 12–0–79–3; Eranga 15.3–0–68–1; Herath 19–0–100–0; Mathews 11–0–48–1.

Umpires: R. A. Kettleborough and S. Ravi. Third umpire: B. N. J. Oxenford.
Series referee: J. Srinath.

This was the 400th Test covered by the Pakistani reporter Qamar Ahmed. He has attended almost one fifth of all Tests ever played.

DOMESTIC CRICKET IN PAKISTAN, 2012-13

ABID ALI KAZI

While international teams – barring Afghanistan – shunned Pakistan for a fourth successive season because of security doubts, the principal interest at home was another shake-up of the domestic format. The Pakistan Cricket Board have repeatedly changed their policy on whether the regional teams and the departmental sides should compete in separate tournaments, or share one. After five seasons in which 22 sides of both types played together in the Quaid-e-Azam Trophy, they were divided again.

The thinking was that teams pitched against each other should be of similar strength, so the President's Trophy (effectively a restoration of the Patron's Trophy) was introduced for the departmental sides, which are stronger, because better paid. A revamped Quaid-e-Azam competition was reserved once more for the regional teams, who were allowed to recruit five departmental players each, though only four could play at a time. The Pentangular Trophy was dropped again after seven seasons. The PCB also insisted on the use of Kookaburra balls, preferred in most international cricket, rather than locally manufactured products.

The President's Trophy opened the season with a round-robin league for ten teams, including many of the leading international players. **Sui Northern Gas** and **Habib Bank**, who both won six of their nine league games, contested the final (which was staged six weeks later, in January, following a Twenty20 tournament), and were led respectively by Pakistan captain Misbah-ul-Haq and Younis Khan, one of his predecessors. Mohammad Hafeez played a key role in Sui Northern's victory with his off-spin, although Umar Gul took a hat-trick for Habib Bank. Sui Northern added a second trophy when they won the one-day President's Cup in April. An 11th team, Pakistan Television, were promoted from the non-first-class Patron's Trophy to join the two departmental competitions in 2013-14.

The 55th Quaid-e-Azam Trophy, held in early 2013, was radically revised. In the first phase, 14 regional teams played in two round-robin leagues, with the top four from each group progressing to the Super Eights, also divided into two pools, while there was another league for the Bottom Six. The top teams in each of the second-phase pools contested a final. **Karachi Blues** were easy leaders in both the qualifying group and the Super Eight, and in the final beat **Sialkot** by nine wickets. A magnificent 178 from Akbar-ur-Rehman, and fine bowling from Anwar Ali and Tariq Haroon, helped them to the 20th title won by a Karachi outfit since the Quaid-e-Azam Trophy began in 1953-54. The Bottom Six final was won by **Faisalabad**.

The regional teams' 50-over trophy – the Faysal Bank One-Day Cup – was shared by **Karachi Zebras** and **Lahore Lions** when the final was rained off. But Lahore Lions had already won the Faysal Bank T20 Cup in December, when the all-round performance of captain Mohammad Hafeez helped them defeat Faisalabad Wolves in the final. The top eight teams from that competition later competed for the Faysal Bank Super Eight T20 Cup in March, when **Faisalabad Wolves** – also led by Misbah – had their revenge, ending Lahore Lions' run of 11 Twenty20 wins in the semi-final, then beating defending champions **Sialkot Stallions** to enter the qualifying stage of the Champions League.

Nine batsmen crossed the 1,000-run mark in first-class cricket, headed by Umar Amin of Port Qasim Authority and Rawalpindi, who hit 1,321 runs from 15 matches. Fellow left-hander Haris Sohail played only five games, all for ZTBL, but scored four hundreds to top the batting averages with 673 runs at 134. Left-arm spinner Zulfiqar Babar of WAPDA and Multan was the leading wicket-taker, claiming 93 at 17 apiece, while ten more bowlers passed 50. Sohaib Maqsood of WAPDA and Multan fell only 56 short of 1,000 List A runs in his 13 matches, while Ahmed Shehzad played a major role in Lahore Lions' successful Twenty20 run, with 511. Bilawal Bhatti of Sui Northern and Sialkot took 23 one-day wickets, as did Asad Ali of Faisalabad in Twenty20 games.

FIRST-CLASS AVERAGES, 2012-13

BATTING (600 runs, average 35.00)

	M	I	NO	R	HS	100	Avge	Ct/St
†Haris Sohail (*ZTBL*)	5	9	4	673	152	4	134.60	2
Akbar-ur-Rehman (*Karachi Blues*)	10	16	5	986	225	3	89.63	9
Shoaib Malik (*PIA/Sialkot*)	7	12	2	692	152	2	69.20	5
†Imran Farhat (*Habib Bank/Lahore Ravi*)	10	17	0	1,171	308	3	68.88	3
Adnan Akmal (*Sui Northern/Lahore Ravi*)	9	13	3	668	149*	2	66.80	17
Kamran Hussain (*Habib Bank/Bahawalpur*)	11	19	6	846	139	2	65.07	1
Imran Butt (*Lahore Shalimar*)	9	14	2	740	126	2	61.66	9
Rizwan Anwar (*Hyderabad*)	9	16	2	818	157	5	58.42	11
Umar Akmal (*Sui N/Lahore Shalimar*)	9	15	1	765	119	2	54.64	7
†Fakhar Zaman (*Karachi Blues*)	7	13	1	635	101	1	52.91	5
†Fawad Alam (*National Bank/Karachi Whites*)	16	25	3	1,069	153*	4	48.59	7
Majid Jahangir (*Sialkot*)	10	17	3	679	112*	3	48.50	4
†Ali Waqas (*Sui Northern/Faisalabad*)	15	27	5	1,065	105*	2	48.40	20
†Umar Amin (*Port Qasim A/Rawalpindi*)	15	29	0	1,321	281	2	45.55	7
Mohammad Rizwan (*Sui N/Peshawar*)	16	25	4	948	154*	2	45.14	55/5
Sohaib Maqsood (*WAPDA/Multan*)	16	24	1	1,020	116	3	44.34	13
Umar Waheed (*Rawalpindi*)	9	17	2	640	183	1	42.66	6
†Saeed Anwar (*KRL/Multan*)	13	19	1	767	100*	1	42.61	2
Shoaib Ahmed (*KRL/Rawalpindi*)	14	23	3	847	177	3	42.35	4
†Shan Masood (*Habib Bank/Islamabad*)	17	29	2	1,123	199	1	41.59	11
†Naved Yasin (*KRL/Multan*)	14	20	1	766	141	3	40.31	8
Abid Ali (*United Bank/Lahore Ravi*)	16	29	1	1,083	202*	5	38.67	15
†Ali Asad (*United Bank/Quetta*)	16	29	4	934	210*	2	37.36	7
†Mohtashim Ali (*State Bank/Karachi Whites*)	14	24	3	772	121	2	36.76	8
Khurram Manzoor (*Port Qasim A/Kar. Blues*)	18	33	4	1,065	162	2	36.72	16
†Sharjeel Khan (*ZTBL/Hyderabad*)	17	32	2	1,052	141	3	35.06	11

BOWLING (35 wickets)

	Style	O	M	R	W	BB	5I	Avge
Hammad Azam (*Nat. Bank/Rawalpindi*)	RM	175.5	43	512	36	7-46	1	14.22
Sohail Tanvir (*ZTBL/Rawalpindi*)	LFM	227.3	53	689	42	7-61	3	16.40
Junaid Khan (*WAPDA*)	LFM	218.5	39	688	41	6-79	2	16.78
Zulfiqar Babar (*WAPDA/Multan*)	SLA	621.4	145	1,585	93	7-67	8	17.04
Samiullah Khan (*Sui N/Faisalabad*)	LFM	474.1	114	1,391	80	7-52	7	17.38
Ali Khan (*KRL/Sialkot*)	RFM	192.4	39	644	36	5-11	1	17.88
Aizaz Cheema (*PIA/Lahore Shalimar*)	RFM	542.2	133	1,618	89	6-62	3	18.17
Azam Hussain (*Port QA/Karachi Blues*)	SLA	466.1	108	1,242	66	7-99	5	18.81
Ehsan Adil (*Habib Bank/Faisalabad*)	RFM	336.2	65	1,118	59	6-58	3	18.94
Wahab Riaz (*Nat. Bank/Lahore Shal.*)	LFM	325.5	65	1,009	52	9-59	3	19.40
Asad Ali (*Sui Northern/Faisalabad*)	RFM	357.2	58	1,202	61	7-42	5	19.70
Tanvir Ahmed (*Port QA/Karachi Blues*)	RFM	266.1	40	1,003	49	7-41	3	20.46
Imran Khan (*National Bank/Peshawar*)	RFM	376.1	77	1,232	57	6-40	3	21.61
Atif Maqbool (*Karachi Whites*)	OB	397.1	65	1,235	55	7-59	7	22.45
Rahat Ali (*KRL/Multan*)	LFM	353.2	75	1,021	45	5-44	1	22.68
Adnan Rasool (*State Bank/Lahore Ravi*)	OB	606.3	140	1,440	61	5-50	5	23.60
Kashif Bhatti (*United Bank*)	SLA	271.2	60	888	37	5-55	3	24.00
Najaf Shah (*PIA/Quetta*)	LFM	385.1	100	1,052	43	5-38	4	24.46
Mohammad Khalil (*ZTBL/Lahore Ravi*)	LM	340.5	58	1,184	48	5-44	3	24.66
Yasir Shah (*Sui Northern/Abbottabad*)	LBG	337	66	1,051	41	6-20	3	25.63
Anwar Ali (*PIA/Karachi Blues*)	RFM	438.4	85	1,411	54	5-61	4	26.12
Ahmed Jamal (*Port QA/Abbottabad*)	RFM	317.3	56	1,032	37	6-80	2	27.89
Nayyer Abbas (*KRL/Sialkot*)	SLA	357.4	68	980	35	5-75	1	28.00
Saad Altaf (*State Bank/Rawalpindi*)	LFM	356.1	80	1,143	38	6-71	2	30.07
Rehan Riaz (*ZTBL/Hyderabad*)	RFM	364.4	57	1,246	36	5-60	1	34.61

PRESIDENT'S TROPHY, 2012-13

	Played	Won	Lost	Drawn	1st-inns points	Points	Net run-rate
Sui Northern Gas	9	6	0	3	21	57	0.07
Habib Bank	9	6	1	2	15	51	0.21
KRL	9	4	3	2	15	39	0.27
PIA	9	4	2	3	9	33	−0.04
ZTBL	9	4	4	1	9	33	0.20
WAPDA	9	3	3	3	15	33	−0.10
National Bank	9	3	4	2	9	27	0.26
State Bank	9	2	4	3	6	18	0.03
Port Qasim Authority	9	2	5	2	3	15	−0.12
United Bank	9	0	8	1	3	3	−0.75

KRL = Khan Research Laboratories; PIA = Pakistan International Airlines; ZTBL = Zarai Taraqiati Bank Limited (formerly ADBP); WAPDA = Water and Power Development Authority.

Final: Sui Northern Gas beat Habib Bank by 75 runs.

Outright win = 6pts; lead on first innings in a won or drawn game = 3pts. Net run-rate is calculated by subtracting runs conceded per over from runs scored per over.

At Lahore (Gaddafi), October 3–6, 2012. **Habib Bank won by five wickets. National Bank 329** (Fawad Alam 113) **and 184; ‡Habib Bank 318 and 198-5.** *Habib Bank 6pts.*

At Sialkot (Jinnah), October 3–6, 2012. **KRL won by an innings and 117 runs. KRL 496** (Naved Yasin 100, Shoaib Ahmed 152); **‡ZTBL 194 and 185** (Nayyer Abbas 5-75). *KRL 9pts. In his second first-class match, Shoaib Ahmed added 137 with Naved Yasin for KRL's fifth wicket and 152 with Nayyer Abbas (62) for the seventh.*

At Karachi (National), October 3–6, 2012. **Drawn. PIA 321** (Faisal Iqbal 100) **and 261-4 dec; ‡State Bank 338** (Usman Arshad 113) **and 92-2.** *State Bank 3pts.*

At Karachi (NBP), October 3–6, 2012. **Drawn. United Bank 323 and 225-8 dec** (Azam Hussain 5-63); **‡Port Qasim Authority 237** (Kashif Bhatti 5-55) **and 232-6** (Kashif Bhatti 5-105). *United Bank 3pts. Port Qasim Authority made their first-class debut.*

At Faisalabad (Iqbal), October 3–6, 2012. **Sui Northern Gas won by three wickets. WAPDA 200 and 180; ‡Sui Northern Gas 266** (Zulfiqar Babar 5-56) **and 115-7.** *Sui Northern Gas 9pts.*

At Lahore (Gaddafi), October 9–12, 2012. **Habib Bank won by 184 runs. Habib Bank 288** (Junaid Khan 6-79) **and 282; ‡WAPDA 235 and 151** (Ehsan Adil 5-39). *Habib Bank 9pts.*

At Faisalabad (Iqbal), October 9–12, 2012. **Sui Northern Gas won by 219 runs. Sui Northern Gas 291 and 195-4 dec; ‡KRL 183** (Samiullah Khan 6-48) **and 84** (Yasir Shah 6-30). *Sui Northern Gas 9pts.*

At Sialkot (Jinnah), October 9–12, 2012. **ZTBL won by 84 runs. ‡ZTBL 372** (Sharjeel Khan 121) **and 239-8 dec; National Bank 222 and 305** (Fawad Alam 112*). *ZTBL 9pts.*

At Karachi (National), October 9–12, 2012. **State Bank won by six wickets. ‡Port Qasim Authority 218 and 160; State Bank 180 and 202-4.** *State Bank 6pts.*

At Karachi (UBL), October 9–12, 2012. **PIA won by 69 runs. PIA 214 and 222** (Kashif Bhatti 5-75); **‡United Bank 125 and 242.** *PIA 9pts.*

At Lahore (Gaddafi), October 15–18, 2012. **Habib Bank won by nine wickets. ZTBL 106** (Ehsan Adil 5-41) **and 168; ‡Habib Bank 249** (Saeed Ajmal 6-64) **and 28-1.** *Habib Bank 9pts.*

At Faisalabad (Iqbal), October 15–18, 2012. **Drawn. KRL 331-9 dec** (Zulfiqar Babar 6-108); **‡WAPDA 162.** *KRL 3pts.*

At Sialkot (Jinnah), October 15–18, 2012. **Drawn. Sui Northern Gas 195** (Uzair-ul-Haq 6-58) **and 252-9** (Imran Khan 6-68); **‡National Bank 343.** *National Bank 3pts.*

At Karachi (National), October 15–18, 2012. **PIA won by 113 runs. PIA 334** (Mohammad Sami 7-61) **and 171; ‡Port Qasim Authority 278** (Najaf Shah 5-63) **and 114** (Najaf Shah 5-44). *PIA 9pts.*

At Karachi (UBL), October 15–18, 2012. **State Bank won by four wickets. United Bank 252** (Adnan Rasool 5-50) **and 218; ‡State Bank 369** (Adnan Raees 115) **and 105-6.** *State Bank 9pts.*

At Faisalabad (Iqbal), October 21–24, 2012. **Habib Bank won by 129 runs. ‡Habib Bank 327** (Younis Khan 101) **and 148-5 dec; State Bank 198 and 148.** *Habib Bank 9pts. State Bank lost their last five first-innings wickets for 12 as opening batsman Ahmed Shehzad's leg-breaks earned a career-best 2.5–0–7–4. Habib Bank had now won their first four matches of the season.*

At Lahore (Gaddafi), October 21–24, 2012. **Drawn. National Bank 323** (Qaiser Abbas 106) **and 428** (Amin-ur-Rehman 137; Anwar Ali 5-115); **‡PIA 341** (Shoaib Khan 121*) **and 10-1.** *PIA 3pts.*

At Sialkot (Jinnah), October 21–24, 2012. **Sui Northern Gas won by 32 runs. Sui Northern Gas 266 and 225** (Azam Hussain 6-50); **‡Port Qasim Authority 244 and 215.** *Sui Northern Gas 9pts.*

At Rawalpindi (KRL), October 21–24, 2012. **KRL won by four wickets. United Bank 319** (Abid Ali 130) **and 143; ‡KRL 290** (Mohammad Irshad 5-94) **and 176-6.** *KRL 6pts.*

At Sargodha, October 21–24, 2012. **Drawn. WAPDA 294** (Sohaib Maqsood 110; Abdul Razzaq 5-58) **and 259** (Saeed Ajmal 6-56); **‡ZTBL 283** (Haris Sohail 115*) **and 158-5.** *WAPDA 3pts.*

At Sialkot (Jinnah), November 2–5, 2012. **PIA won by six wickets. ‡Habib Bank 200 and 147** (Najaf Shah 5-38); **PIA 172** (Fahad Masood 6-33) **and 176-4.** *PIA 6pts.*

At Faisalabad (Iqbal), November 2–5, 2012. **Drawn. ‡KRL 311 and 183-5 dec; State Bank 188 and 207-4.** *KRL 3pts.*

At Lahore (Gaddafi), November 2–4, 2012. **National Bank won by two wickets. ‡Port Qasim Authority 150** (Imran Khan 6-40) **and 177** (Umaid Asif 5-55); **National Bank 117** (Tanvir Ahmed 7-41) **and 211-8** (Tanvir Ahmed 5-100). *National Bank 6pts. Tanvir Ahmed's 12-141 was the best match return of this tournament but not enough to earn Port Qasim Authority's maiden first-class win; he reduced National Bank's chase to 122-6, but Qaiser Abbas (52*) steered them home.*

At Rawalpindi (Cricket), November 2–5, 2012. **Sui Northern Gas won by 186 runs. Sui Northern Gas 250** (Misbah-ul-Haq 110; Abdul Razzaq 6-74) **and 256-2 dec** (Azhar Ali 129*); **‡ZTBL 99** (Samiullah Khan 6-31) **and 221** (Haris Sohail 117*). *Sui Northern Gas 9pts.*

At Sargodha, November 2–4, 2012. **WAPDA won by an innings and 109 runs. United Bank 121 and 91; ‡WAPDA 321.** *WAPDA 9pts.*

At Rawalpindi (KRL), November 8–11, 2012. **Habib Bank won by 65 runs. Habib Bank 161 and 399-8 dec** (Imran Farhat 102); **‡KRL 253** (Ehsan Adil 6-58) **and 242** (Abdul Ameer 7-66). *Habib Bank 6pts. Imran Farhat passed 10,000 runs, and KRL wicketkeeper Zulfiqar Jan 500 dismissals.*

At Lahore (Gaddafi), November 8–10, 2012. **National Bank won by an innings and 31 runs. National Bank 304** (Saad Altaf 5-75); **‡State Bank 136** (Wahab Riaz 7-29) **and 137.** *National Bank 9pts. Wahab Riaz's career-best 7-29 was the best innings return of this tournament.*

At Islamabad (Diamond), November 8–11, 2012. **PIA won by four wickets. ZTBL 212** (Haris Sohail 120) **and 131; ‡PIA 152** (Mohammad Khalil 5-62) **and 192-6.** *PIA 6pts. Haris Sohail scored his fourth century in successive matches since February. PIA's Faisal Iqbal passed 10,000 runs.*

At Faisalabad (Iqbal), November 8–11, 2012. **Port Qasim Authority won by 17 runs. ‡Port Qasim Authority 215** (Junaid Khan 5-68) **and 173** (Zulfiqar Babar 5-40); **WAPDA 271 and 100.** *Port Qasim Authority 6pts. Port Qasim Authority's first first-class win, in their sixth match, came when Azam Hussain (4-41) and Tanvir Ahmed (4-12) wrecked WAPDA's pursuit of 118.*

At Rawalpindi (Cricket), November 8–10, 2012. **Sui Northern Gas won by an innings and 216 runs. United Bank 165 and 74** (Asad Ali 7-42); **‡Sui Northern Gas 455-5 dec** (Mohammad Hafeez 193, Misbah-ul-Haq 109). *Sui Northern Gas 9pts. Mohammad Hafeez, who batted for seven and a half hours, added 196 with Ali Waqas (95) for Sui Northern's third wicket, and 218 with Misbah-ul-Haq for the fourth. United Bank were bowled out in double figures for the second time in a week, with Asad Ali taking 7-42 in eight overs.*

At Rawalpindi (Cricket), November 14–17, 2012. **Habib Bank won by 251 runs. Habib Bank 193** (Rumman Raees 5-70) **and 376-8 dec** (Younis Khan 133); **‡United Bank 141 and 177** (Umar Gul 5-42). *Habib Bank 9pts.*

At Rawalpindi (KRL), November 14–17, 2012. **Port Qasim Authority won by six wickets. KRL 289 and 136; ‡Port Qasim Authority 344** (Khurram Manzoor 152) **and 83-4.** *Port Qasim Authority 9pts.*

At Faisalabad (Iqbal), November 14–16, 2012. **WAPDA won by an innings and nine runs. National Bank 164 and 113; ‡WAPDA 286.** *WAPDA 9pts.*

At Lahore (Gaddafi), November 14–17, 2012. **Sui Northern Gas won by 143 runs. Sui Northern Gas 234** (Ali Waqas 105; Anwar Ali 5-66) **and 145-5 dec; ‡PIA 101** (Asad Ali 5-39) ,**and 135** (Samiullah Khan 5-36). *Sui Northern Gas 9pts. Sui Northern completed their fourth successive victory to qualify for the final with two rounds to spare.*

At Islamabad (Diamond), November 14–17, 2012. **ZTBL won by four wickets. State Bank 298** (Sohail Tanvir 7-61) **and 140** (Mohammad Khalil 5-48); **‡ZTBL 239** (Saad Altaf 6-71) **and 200-6.** *ZTBL 6pts. Sohail Tanvir took 11-86.*

At Islamabad (Diamond), November 20–23, 2012. **Drawn. ‡Sui Northern Gas 232 and 199; Habib Bank 293 and 73-5.** *Habib Bank 3pts. First-innings points saw Habib Bank into the final.*

At Rawalpindi (KRL), November 20–23, 2012. **KRL won by seven wickets. ‡PIA 268 and 194; KRL 343** (Shoaib Ahmed 177) **and 123-3.** *KRL 9pts.*

At Rawalpindi (Cricket), November 20–22, 2012. **National Bank won by an innings and 49 runs. United Bank 101** (Imran Khan 5-38) **and 167** (Wahab Riaz 5-62); **‡National Bank 317-9 dec** (Nasir Jamshed 123). *National Bank 9pts.*

At Islamabad (Marghzar), November 20–22, 2012. **ZTBL won by nine wickets. Port Qasim Authority 148 and 257** (Sohail Tanvir 5-94); **‡ZTBL 365** (Azam Hussain 7-99) **and 41-1.** *ZTBL 9pts. Tanvir Ahmed of ZTBL passed 500 first-class wickets.*

At Faisalabad (Iqbal), November 20–23, 2012. **WAPDA won by four runs. ‡WAPDA 202 and 118** (Adnan Rasool 5-60); **State Bank 156 and 160** (Zulfiqar Babar 7-74). *WAPDA 9pts. Needing 165, State Bank were 127-9 at the close of the third day; last pair Adnan Rees (46) and Mohammad Naved (1*) added 33 next morning, until Adnan was stumped five runs short of victory.*

At Islamabad (Diamond), November 26–29, 2012. **Drawn. Port Qasim Authority 675-6 dec** (Khalid Latif 128, Umar Amin 281); **‡Habib Bank 198-2.** *Port Qasim captain Khalid Latif retired ill on 0, but returned to add 337 for the fourth wicket with Umar Amin, who scored a maiden double-century, batting for 596 minutes and 397 balls, and hitting 34 fours and two sixes.*

At Rawalpindi (KRL), November 26–28, 2012. **KRL won by ten wickets. National Bank 124** (Ali Khan 5-11) **and 151; ‡KRL 239 and 39-0.** *KRL 9pts.*

At Mirpur, November 26–29, 2012. **Drawn. WAPDA 240** (Saad Nasim 101*; Anwar Ali 5-83) **and 209; ‡PIA 94** (Zulfiqar Babar 5-17) **and 291-5** (Shoaib Khan 120, Faisal Iqbal 128*). *WAPDA 3pts. After a first-innings collapse in which PIA lost their last seven for 11, they were 39-4 pursuing 356 before Shoaib Khan and Faisal Iqbal added 251. This match was moved from Sialkot because of a dispute between the Pakistan Cricket Board and the government of Punjab province.*

At Islamabad (National), November 26–29, 2012. **Drawn. Sui Northern Gas 310** (Mohammad Rizwan 136) **and 149-2; ‡State Bank 117.** *Sui Northern Gas 3pts. This match was moved from Faisalabad because of the dispute between the PCB and the Punjab government.*

At Islamabad (Marghzar), November 26–29, 2012. **ZTBL won by an innings and 256 runs. ZTBL 643-6 dec** (Sharjeel Khan 141, Haris Sohail 152, Imran Nazir 185); **‡United Bank 179 and 208.** *ZTBL 9pts. Imran Nazir added 190 with Haris Sohail for ZTBL's fifth wicket and 158 with Zohaib Khan (55*) for the sixth; three bowlers conceded 145 runs or more. United Bank went down to their eighth successive defeat; four of the last five had been by an innings, the other by 251 runs.*

Final

At Karachi (National), January 14–18, 2013. **Sui Northern Gas won by 75 runs. Sui Northern Gas 283** (Fahad Masood 5-67) **and 182** (Umar Gul 6-67); **‡Habib Bank 137 and 253.** *Test all-rounder Mohammad Hafeez restricted Habib Bank's first innings with figures of 13.4–8–16–4 to ensure a 146-run lead. Umar Gul took a hat-trick in Sui Northern's second innings, but a target of 329 defeated Habib Bank as Hafeez picked up another three wickets.*

WINNERS

Ayub Trophy				*PCB Patron's Trophy*	
1960-61	Railways-Quetta	1977-78	Habib Bank	1995-96	ADBP
1961-62	Karachi	1978-79	National Bank	1996-97	United Bank
1962-63	Karachi	†1979-80	IDBP	1997-98	Habib Bank
1964-65	Karachi	†1980-81	Rawalpindi	1998-99	Habib Bank
1965-66	Karachi Blues	†1981-82	Allied Bank	†1999-2000	Lahore City Blues
1967-68	Karachi Blues	†1982-83	PACO	2000-01	Pakistan Customs
1969-70	PIA	1983-84	Karachi Blues	2001-02	National Bank
		1984-85	Karachi Whites	2002-03	No competition
BCCP Trophy		1985-86	Karachi Whites	2003-04	ZTBL
1970-71	PIA	1986-87	National Bank	2004-05 {	Habib Bank
1971-72	PIA	1987-88	Habib Bank		PIA
		1988-89	Karachi	2005-06	National Bank
BCCP Patron's Trophy		1989-90	Karachi Whites	2006-07	Habib Bank
1972-73	Karachi Blues	1990-91	ADBP		
1973-74	Railways	1991-92	Habib Bank	*President's Trophy*	
1974-75	National Bank	1992-93	Habib Bank	2012-13	Sui Northern Gas
1975-76	National Bank	1993-94	ADBP		
1976-77	Habib Bank	1994-95	Allied Bank		

† *The competition has not been contested in all seasons, and was not first-class between 1979-80 and 1982-83, when it served as a qualifier for the Quaid-e-Azam Trophy, or in 1999-2000.*

QUAID-E-AZAM TROPHY, 2012-13

PRELIMINARY GROUPS

Group One	P	W	L	D	Pts	Group Two	P	W	L	D	Pts
Karachi Blues	6	3	0	3	36	Rawalpindi	6	3	1	2	30
Islamabad	6	2	2	2	18	Lahore Shalimar	6	3	1	2	30
Lahore Ravi	6	1	0	5	12	Karachi Whites	6	2	1	3	24
Sialkot	6	1	1	4	12	Hyderabad	6	2	2	2	18
Quetta	6	1	2	3	9	Abbottabad	6	1	2	3	15
Multan	6	0	1	5	9	Bahawalpur	6	0	1	5	3
Peshawar	6	0	2	4	3	Faisalabad	6	0	3	3	0

SUPER EIGHT

Group A	P	W	L	D	Pts	Group B	P	W	L	D	Pts
Sialkot	3	1	0	2	15	Karachi Blues	3	3	0	0	27
Rawalpindi	3	1	1	1	12	Lahore Shalimar	3	1	1	1	12
Islamabad	3	0	0	3	9	Hyderabad	3	0	1	2	0
Karachi Whites	3	0	1	2	0	Lahore Ravi	3	0	2	1	0

Final: Karachi Blues beat Sialkot by nine wickets.

BOTTOM SIX

Group A	P	W	L	D	Pts	Group B	P	W	L	D	Pts
Faisalabad	2	1	0	1	12	Bahawalpur	2	0	0	2	6
Multan	2	0	0	2	3	Peshawar	2	0	0	2	0
Abbottabad	2	0	1	1	0	Quetta	2	0	0	2	0

Final: Faisalabad beat Bahwalpur by 122 runs.

Outright win = 6pts; lead on first innings in a won or drawn game = 3pts. Teams tied on points were ranked on most wins, then fewest losses, then on net run-rate.

Group One

At Islamabad (Diamond), December 28–31, 2012. **Islamabad won by 71 runs. Islamabad forfeited first innings and 209;** ‡**Multan forfeited first innings and 138** (Shehzad Azam 5-21). *Islamabad 6pts. The first two days were lost to fog and rain.*

At Karachi (NBP), December 28–31, 2012. **Drawn. Karachi Blues 502-9 dec** (Khurram Manzoor 162, Faisal Iqbal 117) **and 14-1 dec;** ‡**Quetta 242** (Azam Hussain 5-50) **and 127-3.** *Karachi Blues 3pts.*

At Gujrat, December 28–31, 2012. **Drawn. Sialkot forfeited first innings and 117-1 dec;** ‡**Lahore Ravi forfeited first innings and 28-1.** *The first three days were washed out.*

At Islamabad (Diamond), January 2–5, 2013. **Drawn.** ‡**Lahore Ravi 216 and 178-8; Islamabad 352** (Umair Khan 113). *Islamabad 3pts.*

At Karachi (National), January 2–3, 2013. **Karachi Blues won by ten wickets. Peshawar 166 and 95** (Tanvir Ahmed 5-47, Tabish Khan 5-48); ‡**Karachi Blues 252** (Waqar Ahmed 5-56) **and 10-0.** *Karachi Blues 9pts. Karachi Blues won inside two days.*

At Multan (Cricket), January 3–6, 2013. **Drawn. Quetta 210;** ‡**Multan 77-3.**

At Karachi (NBP), January 7–9, 2013. **Karachi Blues won by ten wickets.** ‡**Karachi Blues 354 and 22-0; Sialkot 124 and 249.** *Karachi Blues 9pts.*

At Lahore (LCCA), January 8–11, 2013. **Lahore Ravi won by an innings and 72 runs. Lahore Ravi 414-4 dec** (Abid Ali 202*); ‡**Quetta 236** (Qaiser Abbas 117; Adnan Rasool 5-67) **and 106** (Mohammad Khalil 5-44). *Lahore Ravi 9pts. Abid Ali batted 512 minutes and 386 balls for a maiden double-century, hit 30 fours, and added 208 with Adnan Akmal (86) for Lahore Ravi's third wicket. Off-spinner Adnan Rasool had second-innings figures of 28.3–17–22–4.*

At Multan (Cricket), January 8–11, 2013. **Drawn. Peshawar 194** (Shahbaz Hussain 5-40) **and 294-5** (Israrullah 127); ‡**Multan 340** (Naved Yasin 141, Ahsan Nazir 105*; Sajjad Ahmed 6-62). *Multan 3pts. Israrullah and Mohammad Rizwan (89) added 214 for Peshawar's second wicket.*

At Lahore (Gaddafi), January 13–16, 2013. **Sialkot won by nine wickets. Islamabad 193 and 217;** ‡**Sialkot 202** (Iftikhar Anjum 5-62) **and 212-1** (Majid Jahangir 112*). *Sialkot 9pts.*

At Lahore (LCCA), January 13–16, 2013. **Drawn. Multan 309** (Sohaib Maqsood 107; Adnan Rasool 5-91) **and 252-5 dec;** ‡**Lahore Ravi 248** (Rahat Ali 5-44) **and 219-5** (Ikhlaq Butt 105). *Multan 3pts.*

At Peshawar (Arbab Niaz), January 14–16, 2013. **Quetta won by an innings and 171 runs. Quetta 483-8 dec** (Ali Asad 210*, Taimur Ali 120); ‡**Peshawar 117** (Gohar Faiz 5-39) **and 195** (Arun Lal 5-69). *Quetta 9pts. Ali Asad, who batted throughout Quetta's 140 overs for a maiden double-hundred, and Taimur Ali added 222 for the third wicket.*

At Multan (Cricket), January 19–22, 2013. **Drawn. Karachi Blues 410** (Mohammad Waqas 150; Zulfiqar Babar 6-149) **and 203-4;** ‡**Multan 363.** *Karachi Blues 3pts.*

At Peshawar (Arbab Niaz), January 19–22, 2013. **Drawn.** ‡**Peshawar 346** (Mohammad Rizwan 154*) **and 209-5 dec; Sialkot 269 and 32-0.** *Peshawar 3pts.*

At Islamabad (Diamond), January 20–23, 2013. **Islamabad won by nine wickets.** ‡**Quetta 263 and 122** (Nasrullah Khan 5-27); **Islamabad 134** (Gohar Faiz 8-50) **and 252-1** (Raheel Majeed 124*). *Islamabad 6pts. Raheel Majeed and Shan Masood (96) shared an opening stand of 207. Wicketkeeper Naeem Anjum held six catches in Quetta's second innings and eight in the match.*

At Lahore (Gaddafi), January 25–28, 2013. **Drawn.** ‡**Lahore Ravi 261** (Imran Farhat 127) **and 305** (Adnan Akmal 108*); **Karachi Blues 481** (Akbar-ur-Rehman 225; Adnan Rasool 5-133) **and 69-5.** *Karachi Blues 3pts. Akbar-ur-Rehman scored a maiden double-hundred, batting for 477 minutes and 353 balls, and hitting 22 fours and two sixes.*

At Lahore (LCCA), January 25–28, 2013. **Drawn.** ‡**Sialkot 232** (Najaf Shah 5-62) **and 262; Quetta 225 and 193-3.** *Sialkot 3pts.*

At Peshawar (Arbab Niaz), January 26–29, 2013. **Drawn.** ‡**Peshawar 103** (Iftikhar Anjum 5-28) **and 439-9 dec** (Israrullah 155); **Islamabad 179 and 221-5.** *Islamabad 3pts.*

At Islamabad (Diamond), January 31–February 2, 2013. **Karachi Blues won by an innings and 33 runs.** Islamabad 197 (Azam Hussain 6-53) **and 115;** ‡**Karachi Blues 345.** *Karachi Blues 9pts.*

At Lahore (LCCA), January 31–February 3, 2013. **Drawn. Lahore Ravi 512-6 dec** (Imran Farhat 308); ‡**Peshawar 209 and 59-3.** *Lahore Ravi 3pts. Imran Farhat converted his sixth double-hundred into the first triple for any first-class Lahore team; he batted for 603 minutes and 429 balls, hitting 50 fours and passing 1,000 runs in the season.*

At Multan (Cricket), January 31–February 3, 2013. **Drawn.** Sialkot 189 (Majid Jahangir 105; Zulfiqar Babar 7-67) **and 100-2;** ‡**Multan 428** (Sohaib Maqsood 116, Naved Yasin 109). *Multan 3pts.*

Group Two

At Faisalabad (Iqbal), December 28–31, 2012. **Drawn.** Bahawalpur 181 (Naseer Akram 5-45); ‡**Faisalabad 120-4.**

At Hyderabad (Niaz), December 28–31, 2012. **Drawn.** Abbottabad 228 (Zahid Mahmood 5-58) **and 275;** ‡**Hyderabad 170 and 225-4** (Rizwan Ahmed 100*). *Abbottabad 3pts.*

At Karachi (National), December 28–30, 2012. **Lahore Shalimar won by ten wickets.** ‡**Karachi Whites 170** (Aizaz Cheema 6-62) **and 142; Lahore Shalimar 254** (Mohammad Sami 5-77) **and 59-0.** *Lahore Shalimar 9pts.*

At Hyderabad (Niaz), January 2–5, 2013. **Rawalpindi won by six wickets.** ‡**Hyderabad 177** (Sadaf Hussain 5-25) **and 320; Rawalpindi 302 and 199-4.** *Rawalpindi 9pts.*

At Karachi (NBP), January 2–4, 2013. **Karachi Whites won by an innings and 145 runs.** ‡**Abbottabad 146** (Atif Maqbool 6-60) **and 168** (Atif Maqbool 7-59); **Karachi Whites 459-3 dec** (Khalid Latif 155, Mohtashim Ali 103). *Karachi Whites 9pts. Off-spinner Atif Maqbool improved his career-best twice on his way to 13-119, the best match return of the season. Khalid Latif and Mohtashim Ali added 233 for Karachi Whites' second wicket.*

At Lahore (LCCA), January 3–6, 2013. **Drawn.** Bahawalpur 65-1 v ‡Lahore Shalimar.

At Karachi (National), January 7–9, 2013. **Karachi Whites won by three wickets.** Rawalpindi 153 (Atif Maqbool 5-62) **and 199;** ‡**Karachi Whites 185** (Sadaf Hussain 6-52) **and 171-7.** *Karachi Whites 9pts.*

At Rawalpindi (Cricket), January 8–11, 2013. **Drawn.** Bahawalpur 216 (Ahmed Jamal 6-80) **and 296** (Ahmed Jamal 5-96); ‡**Abbottabad 337** (Yasir Hameed 103) **and 70-2.** *Abbottabad 3pts. Ahmed Jamal took 11-176.*

At Lahore (Gaddafi), January 8–11, 2013. **Drawn.** Faisalabad 265 (Aizaz Cheema 5-64) **and 47-0;** ‡**Lahore Shalimar 458** (Umar Akmal 157). *Lahore Shalimar 3pts.*

At Mirpur, January 13–16, 2013. **Rawalpindi won by two wickets.** Faisalabad 226 **and 130;** ‡**Rawalpindi 132 and 225-8** (Waqas Maqsood 6-93). *Rawalpindi 6pts. Umar Waheed (99*) saw Rawalpindi to a narrow victory after they trailed by 94 on first innings and slid to 46-4 chasing 225.*

At Hyderabad (Niaz), January 13–16, 2013. **Drawn.** ‡**Hyderabad 305** (Rizwan Ahmed 105; Atif Maqbool 5-97) **and 277-6** (Rizwan Ahmed 104); **Karachi Whites 496-8 dec** (Mohtashim Ali 121, Fawad Alam 153*). *Karachi Whites 3pts. Rizwan Ahmed scored a century in each innings. Fawad Alam and Mohammad Sami (77) added 167 for Karachi Whites' eighth wicket.*

At Swabi, January 14–17, 2013. **Lahore Shalimar won by 222 runs.** Lahore Shalimar 199 **and 385-4 dec** (Imran Butt 124, Fahad-ul-Haq 121); ‡**Abbottabad 104 and 258** (Mohammad Irfan 5-96). *Lahore Shalimar 9pts. Imran Butt and Fahad-ul-Haq added 236 for Lahore's second wicket.*

At Swabi, January 19–20, 2013. **Abbottabad won by eight wickets.** Faisalabad 92 (Yasir Shah 6-20) **and 152** (Yasir Shah 6-49); ‡**Abbottabad 135** (Waqas Maqsood 7-40) **and 114-2.** *Abbottabad 9pts. Abbottabad won inside two days, thanks to leg-spinner Yasir Shah's 12-69.*

At Hyderabad (Niaz), January 19–22, 2013. **Hyderabad won by an innings and 146 runs.** Hyderabad 513-9 dec (Rizwan Ahmed 157, Aqeel Anjum 104); ‡**Bahawalpur 194 and 173** (Nasir Awais 6-62). *Hyderabad 9pts. Rizwan Ahmed, who scored his third century in successive innings and his sixth in seven matches, added 212 for Hyderabad's fourth wicket with Aqeel Anjum.*

At Mirpur, January 19–22, 2013. **Rawalpindi won by 24 runs. Rawalpindi 157 and 198** (Zia-ul-Haq 5-84); ‡**Lahore Shalimar 116 and 215.** *Rawalpindi 9pts.*

At Swabi, January 25–28, 2013. **Drawn. Rawalpindi 498-9 dec** (Umar Waheed 183) **and 289-8 dec** (Aziz-ur-Rehman 5-56); ‡**Abbottabad 146 and 110-5.** *Rawalpindi 3pts.*

At Multan (Cricket), January 25–28, 2013. **Drawn.** ‡**Bahawalpur 362** (Kamran Hussain 139; Atif Maqbool 5-113) **and 245-8 dec** (Kamran Hussain 118*); **Karachi Whites 351** (Owais Rehmani 146*) **and 65-2.** *Bahawalpur 3pts. Kamran Hussain hit twin centuries to help Bahawalpur secure their first points of the season.*

At Mirpur, January 25–28, 2013. **Hyderabad won by 87 runs. Hyderabad 254** (Asad Ali 5-54) **and 142** (Asad Ali 6-53); ‡**Faisalabad 187 and 122.** *Hyderabad 9pts. Asad Ali took 11-107, only to finish on the losing side as Faisalabad suffered their third successive defeat.*

At Mirpur, January 31–February 3, 2013. **Drawn. Karachi Whites 297** (Asad Ali 7-97) **and 207** (Khalid Latif 113; Samiullah Khan 6-40); ‡**Faisalabad 148** (Atif Maqbool 5-55) **and 213-6.** *Karachi Whites 3pts.*

At Lahore (Gaddafi), January 31–February 2, 2013. **Lahore Shalimar won by an innings and 25 runs. Hyderabad 103** (Aizaz Cheema 5-33) **and 218;** ‡**Lahore Shalimar 346-9 dec** (Usman Salahuddin 101*; Rehan Riaz 5-60). *Lahore Shalimar 9pts.*

At Rawalpindi (Cricket), January 31–February 3, 2013. **Drawn.** ‡**Rawalpindi 404-7 dec** (Umar Amin 129) **and 137-3; Bahawalpur 316** (Usman Tariq 102). *Rawalpindi 3pts.*

SUPER EIGHT

Group A

At Rawalpindi (Cricket), February 6–9, 2013. **Drawn. Rawalpindi 362** (Babar Naeem 101, Shoaib Ahmed 147; Iftikhar Anjum 5-73) **and 187-4; Islamabad 196.** *Rawalpindi 3pts.*

At Islamabad (Diamond), February 7–10, 2013. **Drawn. Sialkot 254** (Atif Maqbool 6-119) **and 184-3** (Majid Jahangir 101*); ‡**Karachi Whites 238.** *Sialkot 3pts.*

At Islamabad (Diamond), February 12–15, 2013. **Drawn. Islamabad 303** (Raheel Majeed 115; Faisal Rasheed 5-71); ‡**Sialkot 377-8** (Shoaib Malik 114, Zeeshan Mushtaq 133*). *Sialkot 3pts. Raheel Majeed and Ali Sarfraz (97) added 221 for Islamabad's second wicket.*

At Rawalpindi (Cricket), February 12–13, 2013. **Rawalpindi won by an innings and 23 runs. Karachi Whites 69** (Sohail Tanvir 5-20) **and 200** (Hammad Azam 7-46); ‡**Rawalpindi 292** (Abdul Ameer 8-98). *Rawalpindi 9pts. Rawalpindi rolled over Karachi Whites for 69 on the first day and wrapped up the match on the second, despite Abdul Ameer's career-best 8-98.*

At Islamabad (Diamond), February 18–21, 2013. **Drawn.** ‡**Islamabad 414** (Shan Masood 199); **Karachi Whites 209 and 325-5** (Khalid Latif 123, Fawad Alam 127). *Islamabad 3pts. Shan Masood, who had begun this tournament with 99 against Multan, finished it with a career-best 199. In the follow-on, Khalid Latif and Fawad Alam added 242 for Karachi Whites' third wicket.*

At Rawalpindi (Cricket), February 18–20, 2013. **Sialkot won by an innings and 60 runs. Rawalpindi 294 and 209** (Shoaib Malik 5-64); ‡**Sialkot 563-7 dec** (Mohammad Ayub 160, Shoaib Malik 152). *Sialkot 9pts. Mohammad Ayub and Shoaib Malik (who also took eight wickets in the match) added 225 for Sialkot's fourth wicket to help them leapfrog Rawalpindi into the final.*

Group B

At Lahore (LCCA), February 6–9, 2013. **Lahore Shalimar won by ten wickets.** ‡**Lahore Ravi 153** (Wahab Riaz 9-59) **and 255; Lahore Shalimar 322 and 87-0.** *Lahore Shalimar 9pts. Wahab Riaz's career-best 9-59, including a hat-trick, was the season's best return. He finished with 12-120.*

At Mirpur, February 7–10, 2013. **Karachi Blues won by 114 runs. Karachi Blues 205** (Lal Kumar 5-49) **and 329** (Akbar-ur-Rehman 161); ‡**Hyderabad 141 and 279** (Sharjeel Khan 101). *Karachi Blues 9pts.*

At Islamabad (National), February 12–15, 2013. **Drawn. Hyderabad 584** (Azeem Ghumman 107, Rizwan Ahmed 105, Lal Kumar 109; Mohammad Irshad 5-144); ‡**Lahore Ravi 353-5** (Sami Aslam 144, Adnan Akmal 149*). *Rizwan Ahmed scored his fifth century of the tournament. Lahore Ravi were 64-4 before Sami Aslam and Adnan Akmal added 277 for the fifth wicket.*

At Lahore (LCCA), February 12–14, 2013. **Karachi Blues won by seven wickets. Lahore Shalimar 137** (Zohaib Shera 7-42) **and 299;** ‡**Karachi Blues 255** (Fakhar Zaman 101) **and 182-3.** *Karachi Blues 9pts. Karachi Blues wicketkeeper Javed Mansoor held four catches in each innings; five of them were off Zohaib Shera, who took a career-best 7-42 in nine overs on the first day.*

At Lahore (Gaddafi), February 18–20, 2013. **Karachi Blues won by eight wickets. Lahore Ravi 175 and 209** (Anwar Ali 5-61); ‡**Karachi Blues 265** (Mohammad Irshad 5-81) **and 121-2.** *Karachi Blues 9pts. Karachi Blues reduced Lahore Ravi to 70-7 on the first day, and sailed into the final with their fourth successive win.*

At Lahore (LCCA), February 18–21, 2013. **Drawn. Lahore Shalimar 473-7 dec** (Imran Butt 126, Umar Akmal 119) **and 309-4 dec;** ‡**Hyderabad 258 and 28-0.** *Lahore Shalimar 3pts.*

Final

At Lahore (Gaddafi), February 24–28, 2013. **Karachi Blues won by nine wickets. Sialkot 229 and 248** (Tariq Haroon 5-74); ‡**Karachi Blues 428** (Akbar-ur-Rehman 178) **and 51-1.** *Karachi Blues secured the trophy and Rs1.5m with their fifth successive victory, having dominated the game from winning the toss to knocking off a target of 50 inside eight overs. Akbar-ur-Rehman, who batted nearly seven hours for his 178, ended the tournament with 986 runs.*

QUAID-E-AZAM TROPHY WINNERS

1953-54	Bahawalpur	1977-78	Habib Bank	1996-97	Lahore City
1954-55	Karachi	1978-79	National Bank	1997-98	Karachi Blues
1956-57	Punjab	1979-80	PIA	1998-99	Peshawar
1957-58	Bahawalpur	1980-81	United Bank	1999-2000	PIA
1958-59	Karachi	1981-82	National Bank	2000-01	Lahore City Blues
1959-60	Karachi	1982-83	United Bank	2001-02	Karachi Whites
1961-62	Karachi Blues	1983-84	National Bank	2002-03	PIA
1962-63	Karachi A	1984-85	United Bank	2003-04	Faisalabad
1963-64	Karachi Blues	1985-86	Karachi	2004-05	Peshawar
1964-65	Karachi Blues	1986-87	National Bank	2005-06	Sialkot
1966-67	Karachi	1987-88	PIA	2006-07	Karachi Urban
1968-69	Lahore	1988-89	ADBP	2007-08	Sui Northern Gas
1969-70	PIA	1989-90	PIA	2008-09	Sialkot
1970-71	Karachi Blues	1990-91	Karachi Whites	2009-10	Karachi Blues
1972-73	Railways	1991-92	Karachi Whites	2010-11	Habib Bank
1973-74	Railways	1992-93	Karachi Whites	2011-12	PIA
1974-75	Punjab A	1993-94	Lahore City	2012-13	Karachi Blues
1975-76	National Bank	1994-95	Karachi Blues		
1976-77	United Bank	1995-96	Karachi Blues		

The competition has been contested sometimes by regional teams, sometimes by departments, and sometimes by a mixture of the two. Karachi teams have won the Quaid-e-Azam Trophy 20 times, PIA 7, National Bank 5, Lahore teams and United Bank 4, Bahawalpur, Habib Bank, Peshawar, Punjab, Railways and Sialkot 2, ADBP, Faisalabad and Sui Northern Gas 1.

SIX BOTTOM TEAMS

Group A

At Swabi, February 6–9, 2013. **Drawn. Abbottabad 131** (Saeed Anwar 5-14); ‡**Multan 220-4** (Saeed Anwar 100*). *Multan 3pts. Saeed Anwar (not the Test player) claimed a career-best 14–8–14–5 with his left-arm spin; his unbeaten century then took him past 10,000 first-class runs.*

At Mirpur, February 12–15, 2013. **Faisalabad won by eight wickets. Faisalabad 453** (Khurram Shehzad 136) **and 60-2;** ‡**Abbottabad 203** (Samiullah Khan 5-47) **and 306** (Rameez Ahmed 131). *Faisalabad 9pts. Mohammad Shahid (96) and Khurram Shehzad added 214 for their fourth wicket.*

At Multan (Cricket), February 18–21, 2013. **Drawn.** ‡**Faisalabad 256** (Ali Waqas 105*; Zulfiqar Babar 6-77) **and 198; Multan 250** (Samiullah Khan 7-52) **and 45-3.** *Faisalabad 3pts. Slow left-armer Zulfiqar Babar ended the season with 93 wickets.*

Group B

At Peshawar (Arbab Niaz), February 6–9, 2013. **Drawn. Peshawar forfeited first innings and 322-7 dec** (Nawaz Ahmed 111); ‡**Quetta forfeited first innings and 261-8** (Ali Asad 100). *Most of the first two days were lost to rain, and a double forfeit of innings could not produce a result.*

At Multan (Cricket), February 12–15, 2013. **Drawn. Bahawalpur 268** (Kamran Hussain 123) **and 275-8 dec;** ‡**Quetta 159** (Bilal Khilji 5-23) **and 241-6.** *Bahawalpur 3pts. Kamran Hussain hit his third century in successive innings.*

At Mirpur, February 18–21, 2013. **Drawn.** ‡**Bahawalpur 292** (Afaq Ahmed 6-46) **and 376** (Sajjad Ahmed 5-62); **Peshawar 172** (Kamran Hussain 5-44) **and 149-4.** *Bahawalpur 3pts. Peshawar wicketkeeper Mohammad Rizwan made nine dismissals in the match.*

Bottom Six Final

At Multan (Cricket), February 24–28, 2013. **Faisalabad won by 122 runs. Faisalabad 273** (Imranullah Aslam 5-83) **and 390** (Khurram Shehzad 117); ‡**Bahawalpur 279** (Bilal Khilji 131; Samiullah Khan 5-73) **and 262.** *Both teams recovered in their first innings – Faisalabad from 97-5, Bahawalpur from 4-3 – and it was Bahawalpur who claimed a narrow lead. But Khurram Shehzad helped Faisalabad leave a target of 385, which proved too much.*

FAYSAL BANK ONE-DAY CUP, 2012-13

Two 50-over leagues plus knockout

Semi-finals

At Rawalpindi (Cricket), March 20, 2013. **Lahore Lions won by 46 runs** (D/L). **Lahore Lions 232** (44 overs); ‡**Sialkot Stallions 192** (42.5 overs). *Rain interrupted Lahore's innings and reduced the match to 44 overs a side; Sialkot's target was revised to 239.*

At Rawalpindi (Cricket), March 21, 2013. **Karachi Zebras won by 81 runs. Karachi Zebras 239** (49.3 overs); ‡**Karachi Dolphins 158** (43.1 overs).

Final

At Rawalpindi (Cricket), March 23, 2013 (day/night). **No result.** ‡**Lahore Lions 37-1** (8.5 overs) **v Karachi Zebras.** *The teams shared the cup when the match was washed out.*

PRESIDENT'S CUP ONE-DAY TOURNAMENT, 2012-13

Two 50-over leagues plus knockout

Semi-finals

At Karachi (National), April 16, 2013. **Sui Northern Gas won by eight wickets. Habib Bank 111** (35.1 overs); ‡**Sui Northern Gas 113-2** (23.5 overs).

At Karachi (National), April 18, 2013. **WAPDA won by 119 runs. WAPDA 330-5** (50 overs) (Rafatullah Mohmand 115); ‡**National Bank 211** (40.2 overs). *Rafatullah Mohmand scored his third consecutive century in this tournament.*

Final

At Karachi (National), April 19, 2013. **Sui Northern Gas won by 32 runs. Sui Northern Gas 283-8** (50 overs); ‡**WAPDA 251-9** (50 overs). *Misbah-ul-Haq led Sui Northern to their second trophy of the year – and his third, following Faisalabad Wolves' victory in the Super Eight Twenty20 Cup.*

FAYSAL BANK T20 CUP, 2012-13

Two 20-over leagues plus knockout

Semi-finals

At Lahore (Gaddafi), December 8, 2012. **Lahore Lions won by 51 runs. Lahore Lions 211-5** (20 overs) (Ahmed Shehzad 107); ‡**Bahawalpur Stags 160** (19.2 overs). *Ahmed Shehzad hit 107 in 57 balls. His team-mate Abdul Razzaq, out first ball, had his revenge when he struck with the first two legitimate deliveries of Bahawalpur's reply – interspersed with three wides.*

At Lahore (Gaddafi), December 8, 2012 (floodlit). **Faisalabad Wolves won by five wickets.** ‡**Multan Tigers 120-7** (20 overs); **Faisalabad Wolves 122-5** (19 overs).

Final

At Lahore (Gaddafi), December 9, 2012. **Lahore Lions won by 33 runs.** ‡**Lahore Lions 154-7** (20 overs); **Faisalabad Wolves 121-8** (20 overs). *Mohammad Hafeez helped Lahore to victory with a run-a-ball 22 plus 4-11.*

FAYSAL BANK SUPER EIGHT T20 CUP, 2012-13

Two 20-over leagues plus knockout

Semi-finals

At Lahore (Gaddafi), March 30, 2013 (floodlit). **Faisalabad Wolves won by two runs.** ‡**Faisalabad Wolves 125-8** (20 overs); **Lahore Lions 123** (20 overs). *Needing four runs from the last five balls, Lahore lost three wickets, in their first Twenty20 defeat of the season after 11 successive wins.*

At Lahore (Gaddafi), March 30, 2013 (floodlit). **Sialkot Stallions won by three runs.** ‡**Sialkot Stallions 139-8** (20 overs); **Rawalpindi Rams 136** (20 overs). *Rawalpindi needed eight from the last over but lost three wickets.*

Final

At Lahore (Gaddafi), March 31, 2013 (floodlit). **Faisalabad Wolves won by 36 runs.** ‡**Faisalabad Wolves 158-3** (20 overs); **Sialkot Stallions 122** (19.1 overs). *Misbah-ul-Haq led Faisalabad to victory over defending champions Sialkot to earn a place in the Champions League qualifier.*

SOUTH AFRICAN CRICKET, 2013

On top of the Test world

COLIN BRYDEN

South Africa's Test team enjoyed another dominant year, winning seven of their nine matches – four by an innings – to remain unchallenged at the top of the ICC rankings. Graeme Smith's side were now unconquered in 14 series since being beaten at home by Australia in 2008-09. They did, however, lose a Test for the first time since December 2011, when they were defeated by Pakistan in Abu Dhabi in October, ending a national-record 15-match unbeaten streak. But they quickly atoned for that lapse by squaring the series with an innings win in Dubai.

The biggest disappointment for followers of the Test team was that a series against India, second in the rankings, was reduced to two matches – without the traditional New Year Test in Cape Town. Many saw this as vindictive behaviour by the Indian board, retaliation for the appointment by their South

SOUTH AFRICA IN 2013

	Played	Won	Lost	Drawn/No result
Tests	9	7	1	1
One-day internationals	29	14	13	2
Twenty20 internationals	8	5	3	–

DECEMBER / JANUARY	2 Tests, 3 ODIs and 3 T20Is (h) v New Zealand	(see *Wisden 2013*, page 1075)
FEBRUARY / MARCH	3 Tests, 5 ODIs and 3 T20Is (h) v Pakistan	(page 1063)
APRIL		
MAY	1 ODI (a) v Netherlands	(page 852)
JUNE	Champions Trophy (in England)	(page 301)
JULY / AUGUST	5 ODIs and 3 T20Is (a) v Sri Lanka	(page 1123)
SEPTEMBER		
OCTOBER	2 Tests, 5 ODIs and 2 T20Is (a) (in UAE) v Pakistan	(page 1018)
NOVEMBER	3 ODIs and 2 T20Is (h) v Pakistan	(page 1079)
DECEMBER	2 Tests and 3 ODIs (h) v India	(page 1084)

For a review of South African domestic cricket from the 2012-13 season, see page 1100.

African counterparts of Haroon Lorgat as chief executive. During his tenure as CEO of the ICC, Lorgat had apparently upset the Indians, who felt he was trying to diminish their influence – though precisely what he did was never spelled out.

South Africa did well to draw the First Test against India at Johannesburg, ending within touching distance of a record fourth-innings run-chase. It was perhaps a sign of heightened expectations that, after one of the most gripping days in recent memory, Smith was booed because his team had quite reasonably settled for a draw once Faf du Plessis, who made a heroic century, was dismissed. He was seventh out, leaving South Africa needing 16 from 19 balls to reach a target of 458, but the batsmen to come were an injured Morne Morkel and Imran Tahir, a genuine No. 11. As if making light of that drama, South Africa won the Second Test at Durban by ten wickets, though they had to work hard to gain the ascendancy.

The ingredients for success were similar to those that had taken them to the top of the rankings in 2012. A settled batting order churned out consistently high totals – Smith, A. B. de Villiers and Hashim Amla all averaged more than 50 – while Dale Steyn and Vernon Philander spearheaded an attack that was seldom tamed. Steyn's 51 wickets cost just under 18; Philander's 38 a fraction over. Morkel, the third member of the fast-bowling battery, took only 19, but posed a constant threat. They could be devastating. After dismissing Australia for 47 at Newlands in November 2011, they shot out New Zealand there for 45 in January 2013, with Philander taking for seven, and Pakistan for 49 at the Wanderers in February, when Steyn claimed six for eight.

South Africa used only 15 players in Tests, with change caused primarily by injury or, in the case of Amla, unavailability because of the birth of a child. The only first-choice players dropped were the spinners: Robin Peterson was replaced by Imran Tahir for two matches, though Peterson was back for the final Test against India.

There will have to be at least one major change in 2014, however, following the retirement from Test cricket of Jacques Kallis, South Africa's all-round colossus. It had been a disappointing year, with just 194 runs in 11 innings, when he announced on Christmas Day that the Boxing Day Test against India in Durban would be his last. Aged 38, he managed one final outstanding performance, grinding out a crucial century. But he said afterwards he felt he was losing his edge. He will remain available for one-day cricket, and hoped to play in the 2015 World Cup.

Kallis finished his 166-Test career with 13,289 runs, 292 wickets and 200 catches. That made him the third-highest run-scorer, 29th-highest wicket-taker and second-most prolific outfielder in the game's history. No one who has retired with 10,000 or more runs has a higher batting average (55.37), while his 45 centuries have been exceeded only by Sachin Tendulkar. Kallis was a fixture at No. 4 for a decade and a half.

The most obvious successor for his slot was de Villiers, who had an outstanding year, scoring 933 Test runs at 77, with four centuries and five fifties. Although it would require moving only one place up the order, it would

Handover: Gary Kirsten (*right*) and his successor as South Africa coach, Russell Domingo.

reignite the debate about whether de Villiers, as a senior batsman, should keep wicket. Smith was adamant that de Villiers was already an all-rounder.

While his role as a bowler diminished, Kallis remained a useful back-up to the frontline seamers, as he showed when taking three for 68 from 20 overs in the First Test against India after Morkel was injured. He also left a significant gap in the slip cordon.

South Africa will hope Kallis's departure is as straightforward as the transition from one coach to another. In August, Russell Domingo quietly took over from his former boss, Gary Kirsten. Domingo, who never played a first-class match, is the first non-white to be in charge of the national team. Kirsten, meanwhile, accepted a post as head coach of Delhi Daredevils.

The limited-overs teams remained works in progress. The one-day side, captained by de Villiers, lost at home to New Zealand and Pakistan, and away to Sri Lanka, while they were unconvincing in reaching the Champions Trophy semi-finals, where they were outplayed by hosts England. There were signs of improvement towards the end of the year, however, especially when Steyn, Morkel and Philander were included.

De Villiers was the outstanding one-day batsman, hitting 1,163 runs at over 50, with a strike-rate of 97. Quinton de Kock, a precocious left-handed opener, took over as wicketkeeper and hit four centuries – three in succession against India – before his 21st birthday. Ryan McLaren shone as a seam-bowling all-rounder, and was the leading wicket-taker, with 45 at 23. The Twenty20 team, captained by du Plessis, won five and lost three.

The long-running saga over the disgraced former chief executive of Cricket South Africa, Gerald Majola, came to an end in August when the Labour Court rejected his challenge to the legitimacy of the Nicholson Enquiry, whose findings precipitated his suspension in 2012. The subsequent appointment of Lorgat was logical in terms of his business and cricket experience, but led to a near-total breakdown of relations with India, and a major tour was reduced to a bare-bones programme of two Tests and three one-day internationals. No high-ranking Indian officials flew to South Africa. A hastily arranged tour by Pakistan, their second of the year, filled in some of the gaps. In all, South Africa and Pakistan played each other 24 times during the year.

Rumblings continued over the lack of a black African player in the Test side. Thami Tsolekile remained the reserve wicketkeeper, but did not add to the three caps he won in 2004-05. He turned 33 in October, and his chances of being selected for anything other than political reasons appeared to be diminishing, especially with de Kock coming to the fore. CSA made much of their commitment to transformation, yet the only black Africans to represent South Africa in 2013 were left-arm seamer Lonwabo Tsotsobe, a regular in the limited-overs sides, and left-arm spinner Aaron Phangiso, who played infrequently. It is not an easy process.

SOUTH AFRICA v PAKISTAN, 2012-13

Neil Manthorp

Test matches (3): South Africa 3, Pakistan 0
Twenty20 internationals (2): South Africa 0, Pakistan 1
One-day internationals (5): South Africa 3, Pakistan 2

New Zealand had played their part perfectly as an appetising, though insubstantial, starter to the South African season. Could Pakistan provide a more challenging main course? The answer was a deflating no. The cricket was mainly gristly and ultimately disappointing, with little to linger on the palate. It's true that a beleaguered Cricket South Africa emerged from two years of political infighting at board level, and excelled themselves in promoting Graeme Smith's 100th Test as captain – including one in charge of the World XI – with a series of eye-catching and appropriately chosen celebrations before the First Test at the Wanderers. But, while Pakistan may have been determined not to just make up the numbers, there was a distinct feeling in the build-up to the series of distant cousins at a family gathering.

South Africa were relieved that the controversy surrounding the non-selection of wicketkeeper Thami Tsolekile faded in the afterglow of A. B. de Villiers's record-equalling haul of 11 dismissals at Johannesburg. De Villiers had been Mark Boucher's designated understudy on the tour of England seven months earlier, and was such a success that coach Gary Kirsten asked him to carry on for the Australian tour at the end of the year. Tsolekile was named as de Villiers's deputy in England, with an "understanding" provided by selection convenor Andrew Hudson that he would assume the main role for the home season against New Zealand and Pakistan.

But de Villiers enjoyed the combined roles of middle-order fulcrum and keeper far more than he had expected, and expressed his willingness to carry on. "I want to become the best wicketkeeper-batsman in the world," he said. It was something Kirsten was only too happy to hear. There were many critics, however, who felt the need for a black African player was more important than seven batsmen.

Those more interested in results had no complaints. The series whitewash was just the third achieved by South Africa in a series of three Tests or more, following the Ali Bacher-led 4–0 defeat of Australia in 1969-70, and Hansie Cronje's 5–0 drubbing of a weak and disjointed West Indian team in 1998-99. Smith was immense as a leader and a personality, spurning opportunities to win enormously in favour of winning quickly. "Winning in three days is like scoring 700," he explained. But every bit as impressive were his senior players, none more than de Villiers and Dale Steyn, whose 11 for 60 at the Wanderers was a career-best and a record fifth ten-wicket haul for South Africa. De Villiers made a mountain of runs and kept immaculately.

Pakistan were roundly criticised by former players for their inadequacies against the swinging ball – and, as usual, for their inability to cope with

Shaun Roy, Getty Images

Next please! Dale Steyn's mastery over the Pakistani batsmen was close to absolute. Younis Khan is ushered off at Cape Town.

extreme pace and bounce. But they couldn't be faulted for their attitude or effort. Their own pace-bowling attack was one of the most inexperienced they had fielded, especially when Umar Gul was omitted for the Third Test, leaving Ehsan Adil, Rahat Ali and Mohammad Irfan with a grand total of two caps.

Irfan was the highlight for the tourists. South Africans were obsessed by his enormous height – usually given as 7ft 1in, which would make him the tallest Test player of all time – and the home batsmen took to having throwdowns from colleagues perched on cooler boxes. It was a distraction from his talent, however. Not only did Irfan swing the ball, he did so consistently, at around 87mph. He enjoyed no luck whatsoever in the two Tests he did play – but needed none in the one-day series, in which he made the greatest contribution in the two matches Pakistan won.

But they failed to take any of the Tests into a fifth day, and they lost the one-day series, too. It's hard to imagine that their victory in what turned out to be the solitary Twenty20 match was much consolation. The South Africans, meanwhile, stretched their lead at the top of the ICC Test rankings – and seemed to unearth another fast-bowling talent when the 25-year-old Kyle

Abbott blew Pakistan away at Centurion. The questions about *whether* they were a great team had universally given way to *how* great they were.

PAKISTAN TOURING PARTY

*Misbah-ul-Haq (T/50), Abdur Rehman (T/50), Ahmed Shehzad (20), Asad Ali (20), Asad Shafiq (T/50), Azhar Ali (T), Ehsan Adil (T), Faisal Iqbal (T), Haris Sohail (T), Imran Farhat (T/50), Junaid Khan (T/50/20), Kamran Akmal (50/20), Mohammad Hafeez (T/50/20), Mohammad Irfan (T/50/20), Nasir Jamshed (T/50/20), Rahat Ali (T), Saeed Ajmal (T/50/20), Sarfraz Ahmed (T), Shahid Afridi (50/20), Shoaib Malik (50/20), Tanvir Ahmed (T), Taufeeq Umar (T), Umar Akmal (50/20), Umar Amin (20), Umar Gul (T/50/20), Wahab Riaz (50/20), Younis Khan (T/50), Zulfiqar Babar (20). *Coach:* D. F. Whatmore.

Rahat Ali and Tanvir Ahmed were late additions to the Test squad. Taufeeq Umar injured his leg and returned home before the First Test, and was replaced by Imran Farhat. Haris Sohail returned home after the First Test with an ankle injury, and was not replaced. Sohail Tanvir, who was appearing in domestic cricket in South Africa, was added to the ODI squad as cover, but did not play. Mohammad Hafeez captained in the Twenty20 internationals.

TEST MATCH AVERAGES

SOUTH AFRICA – BATTING AND FIELDING

	T	I	NO	R	HS	100	50	Avge	Ct
A. B. de Villiers	3	5	1	352	121	2	1	88.00	17
H. M. Amla	3	5	1	286	92	0	3	71.50	0
†R. J. Peterson	3	4	1	113	84	0	1	37.66	1
V. D. Philander	3	3	0	97	74	0	1	32.33	2
F. du Plessis	3	4	0	113	41	0	0	28.25	2
D. W. Steyn	3	3	2	27	12*	0	0	27.00	0
†G. C. Smith	3	5	0	129	52	0	1	25.80	8
†D. Elgar	3	4	1	68	27	0	0	22.66	4
J. H. Kallis	2	4	0	80	50	0	1	20.00	1
A. N. Petersen	3	5	0	75	27	0	0	15.00	4

Played in two Tests: †M. Morkel 0, 8*. Played in one Test: K. J. Abbott 13; R. K. Kleinveldt 0 (1 ct).

BOWLING

	Style	O	M	R	W	BB	5I	Avge
K. J. Abbott	RFM	28.4	11	68	9	7-29	1	7.55
D. W. Steyn	RF	115.2	38	258	20	6-8	2	12.90
V. D. Philander	RFM	101	30	237	15	5-59	1	15.80
J. H. Kallis	RFM	46.2	11	106	3	2-11	0	35.33
R. J. Peterson	SLA	73.2	13	229	6	3-73	0	38.16
M. Morkel	RF	54.4	16	167	4	2-59	0	41.75

Also bowled: D. Elgar (SLA) 2–0–14–0; R. K. Kleinveldt (RFM) 25–3–82–2.

PAKISTAN – BATTING AND FIELDING

	T	I	NO	R	HS	100	50	Avge	Ct
Asad Shafiq	3	6	0	199	111	1	1	33.16	3
Younis Khan	3	6	0	184	111	1	0	30.66	3
Misbah-ul-Haq	3	6	0	135	64	0	1	22.50	0
Azhar Ali	3	6	0	133	65	0	1	22.16	2
Sarfraz Ahmed	3	6	0	83	40	0	0	13.83	8
Saeed Ajmal	3	6	1	68	31	0	0	13.60	1
†Nasir Jamshed	2	4	0	51	46	0	0	12.75	1
Rahat Ali	2	4	2	25	22	0	0	12.50	0
Mohammad Hafeez	3	6	0	43	18	0	0	7.16	3
Umar Gul	2	4	0	23	23	0	0	5.75	2
Mohammad Irfan	2	4	1	14	6*	0	0	4.66	0

Played in one Test: Ehsan Adil 9, 12; †Imran Farhat 30, 43; Junaid Khan 8*, 9; Tanvir Ahmed 44, 10*.

BOWLING

	Style	O	M	R	W	BB	5I	Avge
Mohammad Hafeez	OB	28.3	3	107	5	4-16	0	21.40
Saeed Ajmal	OB	130.1	22	365	11	6-96	1	33.18
Rahat Ali	LFM	52.2	2	227	6	6-127	1	37.83
Umar Gul	RFM	61	9	234	5	2-56	0	46.80
Mohammad Irfan	LFM	52.5	5	201	3	3-86	0	67.00

Also bowled: Azhar Ali (LBG) 2–0–13–0; Ehsan Adil (RFM) 12.1–2–54–2; Junaid Khan (LFM) 31–9–96–2; Tanvir Ahmed (RFM) 15–4–60–1; Younis Khan (RM/LBG) 11–1–44–2.

At East London, January 25–28, 2013. **Drawn.** ‡**Pakistanis 329** (Mohammad Hafeez 55, Nasir Jamshed 68, Sarfraz Ahmed 93; K. J. Abbott 3-82, S. R. Harmer 5-88) **and 250-9 dec** (Mohammad Hafeez 83, Nasir Jamshed 51, Misbah-ul-Haq 55; K. J. Abbott 4-26); **South African Invitation XI 257** (V. B. van Jaarsveld 92, D. J. Vilas 62*; Junaid Khan 3-76, Saeed Ajmal 3-66) **and 190-5** (J. L. Ontong 51*). *After an opening partnership of 105, the Pakistanis declined to 145-6 in the first innings, before wicketkeeper Sarfraz Ahmed and Umar Gul (49) put on 81. Warriors off-spinner Simon Harmer finished with five wickets. After another century opening stand between Mohammad Hafeez and Nasir Jamshed, the Invitation XI were left to score 323, but a draw was agreed after 50 overs.*

SOUTH AFRICA v PAKISTAN

First Test Match

At Johannesburg, February 1–4, 2013. South Africa won by 211 runs. Toss: South Africa. Test debuts: Nasir Jamshed, Rahat Ali.

Readers in years to come may wonder how Pakistan could possibly have been dismissed for 49 in an age of video analysis and ultra-professionalism. The unexpected answer is that they fought their backsides off on the second morning during a session of fast bowling so intense and unrelenting that it was hard to imagine it had ever been surpassed. It says much about Steyn's quality that Morkel produced one of his most accurate and probing spells for South Africa, yet finished wicketless.

Steyn claimed the first three with his trademark late awayswing at extreme pace. The uncharitable, unforgiving and possibly inexperienced suggested that Mohammad Hafeez and Younis Khan had played away from their bodies at wide deliveries – but they were not wide when they left the bowler's hand, and they were certainly not of a pace which afforded the batsmen much time to think. Nasir Jamshed, a left-hander playing his first Test after 33 limited-overs internationals, had no chance against one which swung from off stump and would have hit the top of leg.

Smith jumped at the chance to introduce Kallis into the attack in helpful, swinging conditions, and he swiftly accounted for Azhar Ali with a snorting bouncer worthy of a man 20 years younger; in his next over, Kallis had Misbah-ul-Haq caught behind after Hot Spot seemed to confirm the faintest of edges. It was inconceivable that Philander would miss out, and he duly located another couple of edges shortly before lunch, into which the tourists crawled at 40 for seven. Just 25 balls after the break the cull was completed by Steyn, who ended with a Victorian-era analysis of six for eight.

That Pakistan's crash to 49 all out took almost 30 overs said much about their approach. Azhar's 13 – the top score of the innings – lasted 46 balls, every one of them an individual battle, while Misbah's 12 occupied 45. They certainly did not give it away. Still, it followed South Africa's demolition of Australia for 47 in November 2011, and New Zealand for 45 in January 2013, both at Cape Town. This was no fluke.

Conditions had been similar on the first day here, and there were times when it seemed South Africa, who had chosen to bat, might be dismissed for around 150. The top seven fought their hardest, with some fortune, and although Kallis's 78-ball 50 stood out for its passive aggression, twenties from openers Smith and Petersen were no less valuable – they were not separated until the 19th over, after more than an hour and a half. Supporters accustomed to high scores and centuries were unmoved by the eventual total of 253 but, in truth, it was at least 50 above par.

In fact, it turned out to be enough for a lead of 204, but Smith was never tempted to enforce the follow-on, partly because he suspected Pakistan's spirit would flatten far more quickly than the pitch. And he was right. Umar Gul was out of sorts leading a raw three-man pace attack, with Junaid Khan in only his ninth Test and Rahat Ali, another left-armer, in his first.

Smith's bullish half-century made it clear that his intention was to win quickly, not boost his own statistics. By the close of play on the second day, South Africa were already 411 ahead. Amla and de Villiers slammed the lid on the game with an unbroken fourth-wicket stand of 176 which was brutal and elegant in equal measure. Both caressed at first, but de Villiers exploded on the third morning with a flurry of mouth-opening boundaries to reach his 15th Test century.

Most onlookers assumed Smith would allow Amla to reach his own hundred, and declare after lunch with a lead in excess of 500. But he surprised everyone by pulling out over an hour before the interval, with Amla untroubled on 74 and the overall advantage 479. Well, not quite everyone was surprised: "Graeme told us exactly what the plan was, and that was to win on day three," explained de Villiers. "It was just luck that I was able to get to a hundred. Neither of us even thought about it and Hash was unfazed."

Smith's three-day plan was well on course when Pakistan slipped to 82 for four ten overs before tea, but was undone by a stubborn fifth-wicket stand of 127 between Misbah and Asad Shafiq, which spanned 53 overs. They were not parted until the eighth over of the fourth morning, when the second new ball was just three overs old, and the tail was duly sent on its way. Despite ticking off a South African record fifth ten-wicket haul, Steyn refused to relinquish his end, eventually sending down an 11-over spell and finishing with match figures of 11 for 60. Five more catches for de Villiers – to go with six from the first innings – gave him a share of the Test record established here by England's Jack Russell 17 years earlier.

Man of the Match: D. W. Steyn.

Close of play: first day, Pakistan 6-0 (Mohammad Hafeez 6, Nasir Jamshed 0); second day, South Africa 207-3 (Amla 50, de Villiers 63); third day, Pakistan 183-4 (Misbah-ul-Haq 44, Asad Shafiq 53).

South Africa

*G. C. Smith c Sarfraz Ahmed b Umar Gul........	24	– (2) c Sarfraz Ahmed b Umar Gul.... 52
A. N. Petersen c Mohammad Hafeez b Junaid Khan	20	– (1) c Mohammad Hafeez b Umar Gul 27
H. M. Amla c Azhar Ali b Younis Khan	37	– not out 74
J. H. Kallis c Asad Shafiq b Umar Gul.........	50	– c Asad Shafiq b Saeed Ajmal....... 7
†A. B. de Villiers c Sarfraz Ahmed b Mohammad Hafeez.	31	– not out 103
F. du Plessis b Junaid Khan	41	
D. Elgar c Sarfraz Ahmed b Mohammad Hafeez....	27	
R. J. Peterson b Mohammad Hafeez	0	
V. D. Philander run out	1	
D. W. Steyn not out	12	
M. Morkel b Mohammad Hafeez...............	0	
B 4, l-b 4, w 1, n-b 1	10	L-b 4, w 3, n-b 5.......... 12

1/46 (2) 2/46 (1) 3/125 (4)   (85.2 overs) 253   1/82 (1)   (3 wkts dec, 62 overs) 275
4/135 (3) 5/199 (5) 6/232 (6)   2/87 (2) 3/99 (4)
7/239 (8) 8/240 (7) 9/243 (9) 10/253 (11)

Umar Gul 19–2–56–2; Junaid Khan 18–8–33–2; Rahat Ali 14–0–56–0; Saeed Ajmal 23–4–68–0; Younis Khan 4–0–16–1; Mohammad Hafeez 7.2–1–16–4. *Second innings*—Umar Gul 14–2–58–2; Junaid Khan 13–1–63–0; Rahat Ali 11–1–44–0; Mohammad Hafeez 5–0–32–0; Saeed Ajmal 18–1–74–1; Younis Khan 1–1–0–0.

Pakistan

Mohammad Hafeez c de Villiers b Steyn........	6	– c de Villiers b Philander........... 2
Nasir Jamshed lbw b Steyn	2	– c Peterson b Steyn 46
Azhar Ali c de Villiers b Kallis	13	– lbw b Kallis 18
Younis Khan c Smith b Steyn	0	– c de Villiers b Morkel 15
*Misbah-ul-Haq c de Villiers b Kallis............	12	– c de Villiers b Steyn 64
Asad Shafiq c de Villiers b Philander	1	– c Kallis b Steyn 56
†Sarfraz Ahmed c de Villiers b Steyn	2	– b Philander..................... 6
Umar Gul c Smith b Philander................	0	– c de Villiers b Steyn............. 23
Saeed Ajmal c de Villiers b Steyn	1	– c de Villiers b Morkel 11
Junaid Khan not out..........................	8	– lbw b Steyn 9
Rahat Ali c du Plessis b Steyn	0	– not out 3
L-b 3, w 1......................	4	B 4, l-b 4, w 3, n-b 4 15

1/9 (1) 2/12 (2) 3/12 (4)   (29.1 overs) 49   1/7 (1) 2/64 (2)   (100.4 overs) 268
4/36 (3) 5/37 (5) 6/39 (6)   3/70 (4) 4/82 (4)
7/39 (8) 8/40 (9) 9/41 (7) 10/49 (11)   5/209 (6) 6/210 (5) 7/218 (7)
                                             8/240 (9) 9/261 (8) 10/268 (10)

Philander 9–5–16–2; Steyn 8.1–6–8–6; Morkel 6–3–11–0; Kallis 6–2–11–2. *Second innings*—Steyn 28.4–10–52–5; Philander 22–3–60–2; Morkel 25–7–89–2; Kallis 15–5–35–1; Peterson 10–3–24–0.

Umpires: B. F. Bowden and B. N. J. Oxenford.   Third umpire: S. J. Davis.

At Rondebosch, February 10–11, 2013 (not first-class). **Pakistanis won by ten wickets, but continued to bat. ‡Emerging Cape Cobras 156** (Mohammad Irfan 4-20, Abdur Rehman 3-31) **and 78** (Mohammad Irfan 3-20); **Pakistanis 176-6 dec** (J. P. Bothma 3-24) **and 126-1** (Younis Khan 74*). *The home side chose from 12 players and the Pakistanis 14. The tourists needed 59 to win, and reached their target without losing a wicket, before batting on for more practice.*

SOUTH AFRICA v PAKISTAN

Second Test Match

At Cape Town, February 14–17, 2013. South Africa won by four wickets. Toss: South Africa. Test debut: Mohammad Irfan.

Two recent Tests at Newlands, against Australia in November 2011 and New Zealand the previous month, had been three-day affairs – financial disasters for the Western Province Union. Specific instructions may not have been delivered to head groundsman Evan Flint, but his duty this time round was made clear. There was barely a blade of grass, never mind the green stuff which had made those previous Tests so exciting, if brief. In fact, the pitch for Cape Town's 50th Test match was dry and bare enough for Smith to express his concern before play started: "It certainly brings their spinners into the game more than we would have expected." It was prophetic stuff, and Saeed Ajmal did all he could to square the series with ten wickets in the match – but South Africa continued to find a way to respond to what Smith called the "big moments".

After the usual new-ball outburst had reduced Pakistan to 33 for four, Younis Khan and Asad Shafiq hit back with a gritty stand of 219. Philander broke the partnership – both men would fall for 111 – then claimed three more victims. But 70 were added for the final two wickets on the back of an old-fashioned tailender's crash-bang from Tanvir Ahmed.

Pakistan's total felt about par, but it was looking considerably better than that when Ajmal ripped through South Africa's top order to reduce them to 109 for five. He took his sixth wicket with the score at 164, but his chances of all ten were scuppered when the pacy left-armer Mohammad Irfan dismissed de Villiers for 61.

With only three wickets left and still 128 behind, South Africa were up against it. They were rescued by Peterson, primarily a left-arm spinner but also an underrated batsman who had enjoyed few chances to excel in an on–off international career. His 84 – only his second score above 34 in 11 Tests spread over ten years – and important contributions from the three seamers restricted Pakistan's lead to 12. Batting conditions had started deteriorating by the second day, leaving no doubt about the importance of South Africa's recovery.

The uneven bounce now made Steyn a nightmare, though a hamstring strain spared Pakistan the hostility of Morkel. But Philander was like a cat in a canary cage, pouncing with every delivery and licking his lips at the discomfort. Match figures of nine for 99 were consistent with the jet-propelled start to his Test career, but such numbers do not happen by accident: his skill was matched by his control, and the batsmen rarely, if ever, felt secure.

Pakistan slipped to 45 for three, but were dragged back by a stand of 69, with Azhar Ali fighting an admirable rearguard and Misbah-ul-Haq striking three sixes in a brave attempt to counter-attack. But in the ninth over of the fourth morning Misbah made what he admitted was "a big mistake", top-edging a sweep off Peterson to short fine leg. Before this rush of blood, his team were leading by 126 with seven wickets in hand: the general wisdom was that even South Africa's celebrated batting line-up would struggle to chase much more than 200. But Misbah's wicket was the first of seven to fall for 55, with Peterson an excellent foil for the seamers.

In the run-chase, Amla defied Ajmal until 150 of the required 182 had been scored – and that, in effect, was that. Two further wickets went down after Amla fell for a classy 58, which made the eventual margin of victory look tighter than it really was. This was no consolation to Pakistan, although they had provided South Africa with the first genuine test of their home summer. But it was a significant source of satisfaction for Smith and coach Gary Kirsten that they had shown they could win tough, having displayed their ability to win easy.

Man of the Match: R. J. Peterson.

Close of play: first day, Pakistan 253-5 (Asad Shafiq 111, Sarfraz Ahmed 0); second day, South Africa 139-5 (de Villiers 24, Elgar 11); third day, Pakistan 100-3 (Azhar Ali 45, Misbah-ul-Haq 36).

Pakistan

Mohammad Hafeez c Smith b Steyn	17 –	lbw b Steyn 0
Nasir Jamshed c de Villiers b Philander	3 –	lbw b Philander 0
Azhar Ali c de Villiers b Morkel	4 –	c de Villiers b Philander 65
Younis Khan c de Villiers b Philander	111 –	b Steyn 14
*Misbah-ul-Haq c Elgar b Morkel	0 –	c Smith b Peterson 44
Asad Shafiq c Smith b Philander	111 –	b Philander 19
†Sarfraz Ahmed c Petersen b Philander	13 –	b Peterson 5
Tanvir Ahmed c Philander b Peterson	44 –	not out 10
Umar Gul lbw b Philander	0 –	c Petersen b Philander 0
Saeed Ajmal not out	21 –	b Peterson 4
Mohammad Irfan b Peterson	6 –	c Petersen b Steyn 2
L-b 5, n-b 3	8	L-b 2, w 4 6

1/10 (2) 2/21 (1) 3/33 (3) (116.2 overs) 338   1/0 (1) 2/7 (2) (75.3 overs) 169
4/33 (5) 5/252 (4) 6/259 (6)   3/45 (4) 4/114 (5)
7/266 (7) 8/268 (9) 9/332 (8) 10/338 (11)   5/147 (6) 6/152 (7) 7/152 (3)
                                                  8/152 (9) 9/158 (10) 10/169 (11)

Steyn 25–7–55–1; Philander 26–10–59–5; Morkel 20.3–6–59–2; Kallis 19.3–2–52–0; Peterson 23.2–0–94–2; Elgar 2–0–14–0. *Second innings*—Steyn 18.3–5–38–3; Philander 19–6–40–4; Morkel 3.1–0–8–0; Peterson 29–8–73–3; Kallis 5.5–2–8–0.

South Africa

*G. C. Smith lbw b Saeed Ajmal	19 –	(2) lbw b Saeed Ajmal 29
A. N. Petersen c Azhar Ali b Saeed Ajmal	17 –	(1) lbw b Umar Gul 1
H. M. Amla c Younis Khan b Saeed Ajmal	25 –	b Saeed Ajmal 58
F. du Plessis c Younis Khan b Saeed Ajmal	28 –	(6) lbw b Saeed Ajmal 15
J. H. Kallis lbw b Saeed Ajmal	2 –	(4) lbw b Saeed Ajmal 21
†A. B. de Villiers c Umar Gul b Mohammad Irfan	61 –	(5) c Sarfraz Ahmed b Tanvir Ahmed 36
D. Elgar c Younis Khan b Saeed Ajmal	23 –	not out 11
R. J. Peterson c Umar Gul b Mohammad Hafeez	84 –	not out 1
V. D. Philander c Nasir Jamshed b Mohammad Irfan	22	
D. W. Steyn c Sarfraz Ahmed b Mohammad Irfan	10	
M. Morkel not out	8	
B 12, l-b 8, n-b 7	27	B 5, n-b 5 10

1/36 (1) 2/50 (2) 3/84 (3) (102.1 overs) 326   1/10 (1) (6 wkts, 43.1 overs) 182
4/102 (5) 5/109 (4) 6/164 (7)   2/63 (2) 3/88 (4)
7/210 (6) 8/277 (9) 9/303 (10) 10/326 (8)   4/150 (3) 5/168 (5) 6/180 (6)

Umar Gul 20–5–74–0; Tanvir Ahmed 21–1–86–3; Mohammad Irfan 21–4–26–0; Saeed Ajmal 42–9–96–6; Mohammad Hafeez 9.1–1–24–1. *Second innings*—Mohammad Irfan 10–1–35–0; Umar Gul 8–0–46–1; Saeed Ajmal 18.1–2–51–4; Mohammad Hafeez 2–1–11–0; Tanvir Ahmed 5–0–34–1.

Umpires: S. J. Davis and B. N. J. Oxenford. Third umpire: B. F. Bowden.

SOUTH AFRICA v PAKISTAN

Third Test Match

At Centurion, February 22–24, 2013. South Africa won by an innings and 18 runs. Toss: South Africa. Test debuts: K. J. Abbott; Ehsan Adil.

It was business as usual after the tension of Cape Town. South Africa dominated from start to finish, with stunning batting from two superstars and a seven-wicket haul from a debutant which answered any doubts about their fast-bowling depth. Amla and de Villiers were at their exhilarating best, while Kyle Abbott was "surprised but thrilled" to be added to the squad three days before the match following the injury to Morne Morkel. Towards the end of the final practice session, however, Jacques Kallis was treated for a thigh strain,

APPA

Breeding monsters: Kyle Abbott, the latest fast bowler off the South African production line, feasted on uncertain Pakistan batting, this time having Imran Farhat caught behind.

and Abbott was placed on standby. "I never thought for a moment I'd actually play," he said. "Jacques is such a pro I just assumed he'd recover."

And when play began, Smith was out cheaply, providing the 19-year-old Ehsan Adil with a wicket from his third ball in Tests. But Amla was in glorious touch from the off, happy on this occasion to make use of the air as well as the grass. He cruised into the nineties, and seemed assured of a 20th Test century until a fine delivery from left-armer Rahat Ali produced an outside edge.

De Villiers was more circumspect but, when given a scoring opportunity, no less ruthless. He was even the junior partner in a seventh-wicket stand of 129 with Philander, whose Test-best 74 reminded those dazzled by the bright lights of his bowling record that he started professional life as a No. 6 batsman. Rahat was too loose to apply consistent pressure, but his pace never dropped, and he delivered enough dangerous deliveries to be good value for his six wickets.

When Pakistan batted, Abbott had Mohammad Hafeez caught in the gully with his sixth delivery, and never looked back. A remorseless off-stump line, movement away from the right-hander, and a sharp, well-directed bouncer were all he needed to earn five more catches in the cordon, plus an lbw to remove Younis Khan, last out for an obdurate 33. Only Lance Klusener had returned better figures on debut for South Africa than Abbott's seven for 29.

The follow-on may have become unfashionable but, armed with a lead of 253, Smith sensed another quick victory. The signs looked ominous for Pakistan when Steyn bowled a tentative Hafeez off the inside edge first ball, and they finished the second day contemplating another defeat. Next morning, Steyn had Younis caught at first slip, then ran out Azhar Ali with an athletic gather at fine leg and throw of astonishing power. Abbott had hopes of ten wickets in the match when Imran Farhat, batting in the middle order with a bruised finger, edged to the keeper. But it was Kleinveldt who nipped in with

BEST BOWLING ON TEST DEBUT FOR SOUTH AFRICA

8-64	L. Klusener	v India at Calcutta	1996-97
7-29	**K. J. Abbott**	**v Pakistan at Centurion**	**2012-13**
7-63	A. E. Hall	v England at Cape Town	1922-23
7-81	M. de Lange	v Sri Lanka at Durban	2011-12
7-95	W. H. Ashley	v England at Cape Town	1888-89
6-38	P. M. Pollock	v New Zealand at Durban	1961-62
6-43	C. N. McCarthy	v England at Durban	1948-49
6-99	A. J. Bell	v England at Lord's	1929
6-128	S. F. Burke	v New Zealand at Cape Town	1961-62
6-152	G. M. Parker	v England at Birmingham	1924

the wickets of Misbah-ul-Haq and Asad Shafiq in quick succession to leave the innings broken-backed at 114 for six a dozen overs after lunch.

Sarfraz Ahmed and Saeed Ajmal formed an unlikely alliance, which lasted past the tea interval and contained some carefree hitting – although the fun was more that of a wake than a celebration. Eventually Steyn ended it when Ajmal was trapped in front, then Sarfraz top-edged to third man. Ehsan Adil chipped Abbott to mid-on to give him a ninth wicket, but Peterson claimed the last one. That left Abbott with nine for 68 – debut match figures bettered for his country only by Alf Hall in 1922-23 and Syd Burke in 1961-62 – and the rest of the world now wondering exactly when South Africa's procession of fast bowlers was going to dry up.

Man of the Match: K. J. Abbott. *Man of the Series:* A. B. de Villiers.

Close of play: first day, South Africa 334-6 (de Villiers 98, Philander 45); second day, Pakistan 14-1 (Azhar Ali 5, Younis Khan 8).

South Africa

*G. C. Smith c Younis Khan b Ehsan Adil	5
A. N. Petersen lbw b Rahat Ali	10
H. M. Amla c Sarfraz Ahmed b Rahat Ali	92
F. du Plessis c Sarfraz Ahmed b Ehsan Adil	29
†A. B. de Villiers c Asad Shafiq b Rahat Ali	121
D. Elgar lbw b Rahat Ali	7
R. J. Peterson run out	28
V. D. Philander c Mohammad Hafeez b Younis Khan	74
K. J. Abbott b Rahat Ali	13
R. K. Kleinveldt c Saeed Ajmal b Rahat Ali	0
D. W. Steyn not out	5
B 1, l-b 6, w 6, n-b 12	25
	409

1/13 (2) 2/38 (1) (103.2 overs) 409
3/107 (4) 4/186 (3)
5/196 (6) 6/248 (7) 7/377 (8)
8/394 (5) 9/402 (10) 10/409 (9)

Mohammad Irfan 21.5–3–80–0; Rahat Ali 27.2–1–127–6; Ehsan Adil 12.1–2–54–2; Saeed Ajmal 29–6–76–0; Younis Khan 6–0–28–1; Mohammad Hafeez 5–0–24–0; Azhar Ali 2–0–13–0.

Pakistan

Mohammad Hafeez c Elgar b Abbott	18	– b Steyn	0
Imran Farhat lbw b Philander	30	– (4) c de Villiers b Abbott	43
Azhar Ali b Philander	6	– (2) run out	27
Younis Khan lbw b Abbott	33	– (3) c Smith b Steyn	11
*Misbah-ul-Haq c Petersen b Abbott	10	– c de Villiers b Kleinveldt	5
Asad Shafiq lbw b Steyn	6	– c Philander b Kleinveldt	6
†Sarfraz Ahmed c Smith b Abbott	17	– c Elgar b Steyn	40
Saeed Ajmal c Smith b Abbott	0	– lbw b Steyn	31
Ehsan Adil c du Plessis b Abbott	9	– c Kleinveldt b Abbott	12
Mohammad Irfan c Elgar b Abbott	0	– (11) not out	6
Rahat Ali not out	0	– (10) lbw b Peterson	22
L-b 17, w 8, n-b 2	27	B 9, l-b 10, w 11, n-b 2	32
	156		235

1/46 (2) 2/56 (1) 3/56 (3) (46.4 overs) 156
4/75 (5) 5/95 (6) 6/132 (7)
7/132 (8) 8/149 (9) 9/149 (10) 10/156 (4)

1/0 (1) 2/39 (3) (78 overs) 235
3/93 (2) 4/107 (4)
5/107 (5) 6/114 (6) 7/183 (8)
8/202 (7) 9/202 (9) 10/235 (10)

Steyn 12–5–25–1; Philander 10–2–30–2; Kleinveldt 12–1–49–0; Abbott 11.4–4–29–7; Peterson 1–0–6–0. *Second innings*—Steyn 23–5–80–4; Philander 15–4–32–0; Abbott 17–7–39–2; Kleinveldt 13–2–33–2; Peterson 10–2–32–1.

Umpires: B. F. Bowden and S. J. Davis. Third umpire: B. N. J. Oxenford.
Series referee: J. J. Crowe.

SOUTH AFRICA v PAKISTAN

First Twenty20 International

At Durban, March 1, 2013 (floodlit). Abandoned.
Continuous rain led to the match being called off at 6.30pm.

SOUTH AFRICA v PAKISTAN

Second Twenty20 International

At Centurion, March 3, 2013. Pakistan won by 95 runs. Toss: Pakistan. Twenty20 international debut: K. J. Abbott.
The Durban washout meant the Twenty20 leg of the tour became a one-game shootout. Still, the overwhelming nature of Pakistan's victory here made their celebrations after lifting the series trophy less incongruous: victory by 95 runs in a 20-over game was just about worth two wins. Mohammad Hafeez dominated the innings, thanks to some wildly erratic bowling and his ability to hammer it. Four overs of spin from Peterson and Ontong cost 58. If Hafeez ate well on South Africa's inadequacy, Umar Gul positively feasted on it. The batting was wretched, but Gul was inspired, taking five for six from 14 balls. He really was that good – and the batsmen that bad.
Man of the Match: Mohammad Hafeez.

Pakistan

		B	4	6
Nasir Jamshed *c 5 b 11*	13	13	2	0
Ahmed Shehzad *run out*	46	25	6	2
*Mohammad Hafeez *hit wkt b 9*	86	51	9	4
Umar Akmal *c 3 b 4*	11	6	1	0
Shoaib Malik *c 7 b 9*	7	5	1	0
Shahid Afridi *not out*	19	13	3	0
†Kamran Akmal *c 8 b 4*	1	3	0	0
Umar Gul *c 6 b 10*	1	4	0	0
Saeed Ajmal *not out*	0	0	0	0
L-b 6, w 5	11			

6 overs: 52-1   (20 overs) 195-7

1/29 2/112 3/155 4/170 5/171 6/174 7/190

Junaid Khan and Mohammad Irfan did not bat.

Abbott 4–0–41–1; Tsotsobe 4–0–28–1; Kleinveldt 4–0–27–2; Morris 4–0–35–2; Peterson 2–0–26–0; Ontong 2–0–32–0.

South Africa

		B	4	6
†A. B. de Villiers *b 11*	36	22	4	2
H. Davids *c 9 b 10*	7	6	1	0
*F. du Plessis *c 7 b 8*	6	4	0	0
C. H. Morris *c 9 b 8*	0	1	0	0
J. L. Ontong *lbw b 8*	0	1	0	0
F. Behardien *c 2 b 8*	0	1	0	0
D. A. Miller *c 2 b 3*	9	15	0	0
R. J. Peterson *c 6 b 3*	13	14	1	0
R. K. Kleinveldt *c 4 b 3*	22	7	1	3
K. J. Abbott *c 7 b 8*	2	2	0	0
L. L. Tsotsobe *not out*	0	1	0	0
L-b 1, w 4	5			

6 overs: 53-5   (12.2 overs) 100

1/20 2/50 3/50 4/51 5/53 6/53 7/67 8/98 9/98

Mohammad Irfan 3–0–27–1; Junaid Khan 2–0–22–1; Umar Gul 2.2–0–6–5; Mohammad Hafeez 3–0–25–3; Saeed Ajmal 2–0–19–0.

Umpires: J. D. Cloete and S. George. Third umpire: A. T. Holdstock.
Referee: J. J. Crowe.

At Kimberley, March 6, 2013 (day/night). **Pakistanis won by one wicket. ‡South African Invitation XI 266-8** (50 overs) (Q. de Kock 65); **Pakistanis 270-9** (49.4 overs) (G. C. Viljoen 3-29, Imran Tahir 3-49). *The Pakistanis were in trouble at 154-6 in the 30th over, but Shahid Afridi (29), Abdur Rehman (35*) and Umar Gul (30) dragged them towards their target, and the win was sealed when Rehman steered a four past short third man in the final over.*

SOUTH AFRICA v PAKISTAN

First One-Day International

At Bloemfontein, March 10, 2013. South Africa won by 125 runs. Toss: Pakistan. One-day international debut: K. J. Abbott.

After being put in on a surface posing little threat, South Africa's batsmen were as meticulous as forensic auditors for all but the final few overs. Smith guardedly defended, while Amla and de Villiers scored at a run a ball – which, for them, seemed pedestrian. Ingram's chanceless century – his third, in only his 19th one-day international – also finished at an even pace, and was an excellent riposte to questions about his temperament. Yet all the while it seemed there could be more. That promise finally materialised in three dreadful overs of long-hops from Shahid Afridi costing 29, and some clever guesswork by Behardien, who launched a series of premeditated swings at Umar Gul. He made clean contact with most of them during his 14-ball 34, ensuring a total above 300. Pakistan attempted a similar approach for much of their reply, but their patience was not rewarded: wickets fell regularly to Kleinveldt's swing, and McLaren's seam movement and well-camouflaged changes of pace. Afridi walloped 34 from 16 balls in an all-too-brief show of defiance, but the result was rarely in doubt.

Man of the Match: C. A. Ingram.

South Africa

G. C. Smith c Kamran Akmal b Saeed Ajmal	30	F. du Plessis c Umar Gul b Junaid Khan	26
H. M. Amla c Shoaib Malik		F. Behardien not out	34
b Mohammad Hafeez	43	B 1, l-b 5, w 6	12
*†A. B. de Villiers c Younis Khan			
b Saeed Ajmal	65	1/72 (1) 2/83 (2) (4 wkts, 50 overs)	315
C. A. Ingram not out	105	3/203 (3) 4/265 (5) 10 overs: 50-0	

R. McLaren, R. J. Peterson, R. K. Kleinveldt, K. J. Abbott and L. L. Tsotsobe did not bat.

Junaid Khan 9–0–59–1; Umar Gul 10–1–68–0; Mohammad Hafeez 10–0–48–1; Saeed Ajmal 10–0–53–2; Shahid Afridi 8–0–60–0; Shoaib Malik 3–0–21–0.

Pakistan

Mohammad Hafeez run out	25	Saeed Ajmal lbw b Kleinveldt	0
Nasir Jamshed c Smith b Kleinveldt	25	Junaid Khan not out	0
Younis Khan c de Villiers b Abbott	30		
Asad Shafiq c Abbott b McLaren	5	L-b 6, w 4	10
*Misbah-ul-Haq c de Villiers b McLaren	38		
Shoaib Malik c McLaren b Tsotsobe	19	1/42 (2) 2/52 (1) (36.2 overs)	190
†Kamran Akmal c Smith b McLaren	2	3/65 (4) 4/114 (3) 5/135 (5)	
Shahid Afridi c Behardien b Kleinveldt	34	6/148 (7) 7/165 (6) 8/178 (9)	
Umar Gul c and b Kleinveldt	2	9/178 (10) 10/190 (8) 10 overs: 47-1	

Tsotsobe 9–0–52–1; Abbott 6–0–35–1; Kleinveldt 5.2–2–22–4; Peterson 8–0–47–0; McLaren 7–0–19–3; Behardien 1–0–9–0.

Umpires: J. D. Cloete and H. D. P. K. Dharmasena. Third umpire: B. F. Bowden.

SOUTH AFRICA v PAKISTAN

Second One-Day International

At Centurion, March 15, 2013 (day/night). Pakistan won by six wickets (D/L). Toss: South Africa.

Mohammad Irfan's threat had grown throughout the tour, and now he claimed a match-winning four wickets as South Africa slipped to 62 for five. Behardien was combative, reaching 50 from 60 balls, and briefly threatened something respectable with the help of McLaren and Peterson, until he pulled a long-hop to deep midwicket. A lengthy rainbreak towards the end of South Africa's innings meant Pakistan's target became 192 from 44 overs – and the game dragged on until midnight. Mohammad Hafeez and Younis Khan weathered the early storm created by Steyn and the other seamers, but at 115 for four the match was in the balance. Misbah-ul-Haq blocked stubbornly in between lashing three fours and three sixes, while Shoaib Malik batted with unusual freedom and variety during an unbroken stand of 77.

Man of the Match: Mohammad Irfan.

South Africa

H. M. Amla c Kamran Akmal b Mohammad Irfan .	17	R. J. Peterson c Nasir Jamshed b Saeed Ajmal .	44
G. C. Smith c Kamran Akmal b Junaid Khan	10	K. J. Abbott c Shahid Afridi b Saeed Ajmal	5
C. A. Ingram c Kamran Akmal b Mohammad Irfan .	0	D. W. Steyn b Junaid Khan	0
*A. B. de Villiers c Younis Khan b Mohammad Irfan .	4	L. L. Tsotsobe not out	0
F. du Plessis c and b Mohammad Irfan	17	L-b 10, w 9	19
F. Behardien c Shoaib Malik b Mohammad Hafeez .	58		
R. McLaren lbw b Mohammad Hafeez	17		

1/26 (1) 2/26 (3) 3/35 (4) (43.2 overs) 191
4/43 (2) 5/62 (5) 6/106 (7)
7/173 (6) 8/179 (9) 9/191 (10)
10/191 (8)   10 overs: 52-4

Mohammad Irfan 7–0–33–4; Junaid Khan 6–0–29–2; Saeed Ajmal 8.2–0–23–2; Umar Gul 5–0–37–0; Shahid Afridi 8–0–24–0; Mohammad Hafeez 9–0–35–2.

Pakistan

Nasir Jamshed c Smith b McLaren	10	Shoaib Malik not out	35
Mohammad Hafeez c Abbott b Steyn	31	L-b 3, w 6	9
†Kamran Akmal b Peterson	18		
Younis Khan c Amla b Peterson	32	1/29 (1) 2/63 (2) (4 wkts, 39.2 overs) 192
*Misbah-ul-Haq not out	57	3/69 (3) 4/115 (4) 9 overs: 37-1

Shahid Afridi, Umar Gul, Saeed Ajmal, Junaid Khan and Mohammad Irfan did not bat.

Steyn 9–1–29–1; Tsotsobe 6–1–37–0; Abbott 8.2–0–31–0; McLaren 8–0–40–1; Peterson 8–0–52–2.

Umpires: B. F. Bowden and A. T. Holdstock. Third umpire: H. D. P. K. Dharmasena.

SOUTH AFRICA v PAKISTAN

Third One-Day International

At Johannesburg, March 17, 2013. South Africa won by 34 runs. Toss: Pakistan.

A record fourth-wicket partnership between Amla and de Villiers provided entertainment of the highest quality for a huge crowd, and appeared to have put South Africa on course for a massive victory – until Shahid Afridi rolled back the years with an innings of eye-watering brutality. Mohammad Irfan's early brace brought the world's two highest-ranked batsmen together in the 14th over, and by the time they were finally parted in the 45th they had beaten by a single run the unbroken stand of 237 by Rahul Dravid and Sachin Tendulkar for India against Kenya at Bristol during the 1999 World Cup. Much has been made of Amla's silkiness, but several of his square-drives flashed to the boundary in a blur. De Villiers's repertoire of ambidextrous trick shots was on full display even before he reached his century, and the back-foot extra-cover drive for six off Mohammad Hafeez's off-spin was the pick. Wahab Riaz conceded 93 runs, a Pakistan record in one-day internationals. Hafeez started well in reply, though at 132 for five the match looked over. But Afridi's bat-speed was as memorable as his violence and unorthodoxy. One of his seven sixes landed on the roof of the five-storey Centenary Stand, then disappeared on to the Wanderers golf course, the first time anybody could recall such a blow. An innings of 88 from 48 balls was certainly too late, but it seemed inappropriate to call it too little.

Men of the Match: H. M. Amla and A. B. de Villiers.

South Africa

G. C. Smith b Mohammad Irfan	3	F. Behardien not out	6
H. M. Amla c Misbah-ul-Haq b Wahab Riaz	122	R. McLaren not out	0
C. A. Ingram c Kamran Akmal b Mohammad Irfan	17	L-b 8, w 13, n-b 1	22
*†A. B. de Villiers c Shoaib Malik b Saeed Ajmal	128	1/4 (1) 2/42 (3) (5 wkts, 50 overs) 343	
F. du Plessis c Younis Khan b Wahab Riaz	45	3/280 (2) 4/301 (4)	
		5/342 (5) 10 overs: 26-1	

R. J. Peterson, R. K. Kleinveldt, D. W. Steyn and L. L. Tsotsobe did not bat.

Mohammad Irfan 7–1–34–2; Junaid Khan 10–2–42–0; Wahab Riaz 10–0–93–2; Shahid Afridi 7–0–55–0; Mohammad Hafeez 6–0–49–0; Saeed Ajmal 10–0–62–1.

Pakistan

Nasir Jamshed c Amla b Tsotsobe	10	Junaid Khan c and b Steyn	9
Mohammad Hafeez c Steyn b Peterson	57	Mohammad Irfan not out	0
†Kamran Akmal c de Villiers b McLaren	30		
Younis Khan b Peterson	19	L-b 3, w 7, n-b 1	11
*Misbah-ul-Haq c de Villiers b McLaren	28		
Shoaib Malik c Kleinveldt b Tsotsobe	4	1/15 (1) 2/97 (3) (48.1 overs) 309	
Shahid Afridi c McLaren b Tsotsobe	88	3/111 (2) 4/123 (4) 5/132 (6)	
Wahab Riaz b Kleinveldt	45	6/203 (5) 7/244 (7) 8/282 (9)	
Saeed Ajmal c Kleinveldt b McLaren	8	9/304 (10) 10/309 (8) 10 overs: 54-1	

Steyn 10–1–48–1; Tsotsobe 10–0–74–3; Kleinveldt 9.1–1–77–1; Peterson 10–0–51–2; McLaren 9–0–56–3.

Umpires: B. F. Bowden and S. George.   Third umpire: H. D. P. K. Dharmasena.

SOUTH AFRICA v PAKISTAN

Fourth One-Day International

At Durban, March 21, 2013. Pakistan won by three wickets. Toss: South Africa.

Mohammad Hafeez became the fourth man given out in a one-day international for obstructing the field – and the first under regulations introduced in 2011 that punish altering the course of a run. TV umpire Billy Bowden was absolutely correct, despite the controversy his decision aroused in the second over of Pakistan's reply. Hafeez later claimed he had "not looked behind" when the ball was thrown by keeper de Villiers towards the stumps. Television replays were hardly needed to confirm the evidence of the naked eye: Hafeez had altered the line of his run by two yards in order to protect the stumps. But from 33 for three, Pakistan were boosted by a stand of 153 between Imran Farhat, whose obduracy – his half-century required 97 balls – was perfect for the circumstances, and the aggressive Misbah-ul-Haq. Despite a couple of late scares, Pakistan squared the series with eight balls to spare. Earlier, Mohammad Irfan made early inroads for the third game in a row, this time dramatically removing Amla and Ingram with the first two balls of the match. De Villiers found an ally in Miller, who eventually fell to Saeed Ajmal's quicker ball to end a fifth-wicket stand of 115. The omission of Nasir Jamshed meant that, for the first time, Pakistan fielded nine players aged 30 or over – one short of the record, by Bermuda against the Netherlands at Potchefstroom in November 2006.

Man of the Match: Misbah-ul-Haq.

South Africa

H. M. Amla c Kamran Akmal b Mohammad Irfan	0	R. J. Peterson not out	25
G. C. Smith b Junaid Khan	12	R. K. Kleinveldt b Mohammad Irfan	18
C. A. Ingram b Mohammad Irfan	0	D. W. Steyn b Junaid Khan	9
*†A. B. de Villiers c Kamran Akmal b Saeed Ajmal	75	L. L. Tsotsobe not out	5
F. Behardien c Kamran Akmal b Junaid Khan	1	L-b 2, w 9	11
D. A. Miller lbw b Saeed Ajmal	67		
R. McLaren c Mohammad Irfan b Saeed Ajmal	19	1/0 (1) 2/0 (3) (9 wkts, 50 overs) 234	

1/0 (1) 2/0 (3) (9 wkts, 50 overs) 234
3/34 (2) 4/38 (5)
5/153 (6) 6/170 (4) 7/177 (7)
8/207 (9) 9/221 (10)   10 overs: 38-4

Mohammad Irfan 9–0–46–3; Junaid Khan 9–2–45–3; Mohammad Hafeez 10–0–40–0; Wahab Riaz 4–0–16–0; Saeed Ajmal 10–0–42–3; Shahid Afridi 8–0–43–0.

Pakistan

Imran Farhat c Behardien b Steyn	93	Wahab Riaz run out	0
Mohammad Hafeez obstructing the field	0	Saeed Ajmal not out	5
†Kamran Akmal c Miller b Tsotsobe	11	B 1, l-b 4, w 13	18
Younis Khan b Kleinveldt	6		
*Misbah-ul-Haq c Behardien b Peterson	80	1/2 (2) 2/18 (3) (7 wkts, 48.4 overs) 236	
Shahid Afridi c de Villiers b Peterson	4	3/33 (4) 4/186 (5)	
Shoaib Malik not out	19	5/191 (6) 6/226 (1) 7/227 (8) 10 overs: 29-2	

Junaid Khan and Mohammad Irfan did not bat.

Steyn 10–3–26–1; Tsotsobe 9.4–1–51–1; Kleinveldt 10–0–51–1; Peterson 10–0–46–2; McLaren 8–0–40–0; Ingram 1–0–17–0.

Umpires: H. D. P. K. Dharmasena and S. George.   Third umpire: B. F. Bowden.

SOUTH AFRICA v PAKISTAN

Fifth One-Day International

At Benoni, March 24, 2013. South Africa won by six wickets. Toss: Pakistan.

One of South Africa's most dilapidated first-class grounds was an odd choice of venue for what became the decider, and the contest was equally disappointing. After Steyn took his 100th wicket in one-day internationals, Kamran Akmal's selectively aggressive 48 repaired the early damage; then the middle order ensured a platform for what promised to be a competitive target on a two-paced pitch. But Shahid Afridi slogged his third ball straight to deep square leg, opening the door for McLaren and Morkel to reduce Pakistan to 189 for nine – though Junaid Khan's cheerful swinging at least pushed the total beyond 200. The surface slowed during the chase, persuading Amla to dig in. His 65-ball vigil ended when he changed tactics and top-edged a hook, and at 83 for three Pakistan sniffed an upset. But de Villiers continued his astonishing form, and his unbeaten 95 took his series tally to 367 at an average of 91. As in the Tests, he won the series award.

Man of the Match: A. B. de Villiers.   *Man of the Series:* A. B. de Villiers.

Pakistan

Imran Farhat c de Villiers b Tsotsobe	13	Junaid Khan b Morkel	25
Mohammad Hafeez c Ingram b Steyn	5	Mohammad Irfan not out	4
†Kamran Akmal c McLaren b Peterson	48		
Younis Khan c Amla b Behardien	29	L-b 4, w 11, n-b 1	16
*Misbah-ul-Haq c de Villiers b McLaren	24		
Shoaib Malik c Behardien b McLaren	28	1/11 (1) 2/31 (1) 3/97 (3) (49.1 overs) 205	
Shahid Afridi c Ingram b McLaren	0	4/104 (4) 5/151 (6) 6/151 (7)	
Wahab Riaz run out	12	7/161 (5) 8/162 (9) 9/189 (8)	
Saeed Ajmal b Morkel	1	10/205 (10) 10 overs: 31-2	

Steyn 10–0–33–1; Tsotsobe 10–2–42–1; Morkel 9.1–0–33–2; McLaren 10–0–32–3; Peterson 7–1–51–1; Behardien 3–0–10–1.

South Africa

H. M. Amla c Shoaib Malik		D. A. Miller not out	20
b Mohammad Irfan	22		
Q. de Kock b Junaid Khan	3	B 6, l-b 5, w 7	18
C. A. Ingram b Mohammad Hafeez	15		
*†A. B. de Villiers not out	95	1/12 (2) 2/34 (3) (4 wkts, 44 overs)	208
F. Behardien c Saeed Ajmal		3/83 (1) 4/170 (5)	
b Mohammad Irfan	35	10 overs: 33-1	

R. McLaren, R. J. Peterson, D. W. Steyn, M. Morkel and L. L. Tsotsobe did not bat.

Mohammad Irfan 10–1–38–2; Junaid Khan 7–1–30–1; Mohammad Hafeez 4–0–23–1; Wahab Riaz 7–0–44–0; Saeed Ajmal 10–1–34–0; Shahid Afridi 6–0–28–0.

Umpires: B. F. Bowden and J. D. Cloete.   Third umpire: H. D. P. K. Dharmasena.
Series referee: A. J. Pycroft.

SOUTH AFRICA v PAKISTAN, 2013-14

NEIL MANTHORP

Twenty20 internationals (2): South Africa 1, Pakistan 1
One-day internationals (3): South Africa 1, Pakistan 2

Barely a week before it started, this most hastily organised mini-tour was still in doubt. Cricket South Africa were desperate to fill some of the empty spaces in their international schedule following the BCCI's decision to cut short India's visit, and Pakistan just happened to be the only major team with a fortnight to spare.

The sides had just been playing each other in the United Arab Emirates, and had also met in a full series in South Africa six months earlier. But this was no deterrent, and CSA's chief executive, Haroon Lorgat, negotiated the 12-day visit – only to have the rug pulled from under his feet with days to go, when Najam Sethi, the PCB's acting-president, was told he did not have the authority to agree the tour. That ruling was then itself reversed, and what was widely regarded as an exercise in futility was finally able to begin.

The tour did not enable CSA to make up any of the estimated $20m the BCCI's decision had cost them; in fact, it actually cost them *more* money. The objective, however, was to appease their sponsors, by providing – as closely as possible – the number of days of international exposure stipulated by their contracts. It was all rather bewildering for the players, but familiarity on the field had led to friendship rather than contempt, and there were jokes about seeing each other "in a couple of days" by the time the last match was played in Dubai, on November 15 – less than a week before the first Twenty20 international in Johannesburg.

The last-minute fixtures were modestly attended by locals still stunned by the Indian tour debacle, but they were strongly contested and entertaining, a credit to both teams. And when Misbah-ul-Haq raised the fresh-out-of-the-box one-day series trophy, there could be absolutely no mistaking how much it meant to be the first Pakistan captain to prevail in a bilateral series in South Africa. Misbah hailed his side's success as "an important victory for all future Pakistan teams". To further cheer Pakistan, seamers Anwar Ali and Bilawal Bhatti made promising debuts.

In the circumstances, the administrators and players did well to organise and contest five matches at such short notice. But that was the problem: the circumstances were created by selfish and spiteful administration and, for South Africans at least, the taste never left the palate.

PAKISTAN TOURING PARTY

*Misbah-ul-Haq, Abdul Razzaq, Abdur Rehman, Ahmed Shehzad, Anwar Ali, Asad Shafiq, Bilawal Bhatti, Junaid Khan, Mohammad Hafeez, Nasir Jamshed, Saeed Ajmal, Shahid Afridi, Shoaib Malik, Sohaib Maqsood, Sohail Tanvir, Umar Akmal, Umar Amin. *Coach:* D. F. Whatmore.

Mohammad Hafeez captained in the Twenty20 internationals. Abdul Razzaq (hamstring) and Shoaib Malik (finger) were injured before the first match and returned home, but were not replaced.

SOUTH AFRICA v PAKISTAN

First Twenty20 International

At Johannesburg, November 20, 2013 (floodlit). South Africa won by four runs (D/L). Toss: Pakistan. Twenty20 international debut: Bilawal Bhatti.

When a downpour ended the match Pakistan were comfortably placed, needing 94 from 65 balls with eight wickets left on a hard, true pitch and a fast outfield – but they narrowly lost out on Duckworth/Lewis. Du Plessis, South Africa's Twenty20 captain, admitted his side had been "a bit fortunate". De Kock and Amla had given them a flying start, but the spinners applied the brakes. Shahid Afridi whipped through four overs for 14, and only some late hitting from Miller took the total past 150.

Man of the Match: Q. de Kock.

South Africa		B	4	6
†Q. de Kock *c 8 b 3*	43	33	8	0
H. M. Amla *b 3*	31	20	6	0
*F. du Plessis *c 5 b 10*	22	22	1	0
H. Davids *b 7*	3	5	0	0
J-P. Duminy *c 3 b 9*	11	16	1	0
D. A. Miller *not out*	19	11	2	1
W. D. Parnell *run out*	6	6	0	0
D. W. Steyn *c 12 b 10*	1	3	0	0
M. Morkel *not out*	8	5	2	0
B 4, l-b 2, w 2, n-b 1	9			
6 overs: 60-0 (20 overs)	153-7			

1/72 2/81 3/87 4/110 5/116 6/134 7/140

L. L. Tsotsobe and Imran Tahir did not bat.

Anwar Ali 2–0–22–0; Sohail Tanvir 3–0–27–0; Junaid Khan 3–0–24–2; Mohammad Hafeez 4–0–25–2; Bilawal Bhatti 4–0–35–1; Shahid Afridi 4–0–14–1.

Pakistan		B	4	6
Ahmed Shehzad *b 10*	9	9	2	0
Nasir Jamshed *c and b 5*	18	25	3	0
*Mohammad Hafeez *not out*	13	15	1	0
†Umar Akmal *not out*	7	6	1	0
L-b 7, w 6	13			
6 overs: 40-1 (9.1 overs)	60-2			

1/18 2/50

Sohaib Maqsood, Umar Amin, Shahid Afridi, Sohail Tanvir, Bilawal Bhatti, Junaid Khan and Anwar Ali did not bat.

12th man: Abdur Rehman.

Tsotsobe 4–0–19–1; Steyn 2–0–13–0; Morkel 1–0–10–0; Duminy 1.1–0–3–1; Imran Tahir 1–0–8–0.

Umpires: J. D. Cloete and S. George.   Third umpire: K. H. Hurter.

SOUTH AFRICA v PAKISTAN

Second Twenty20 International

At Cape Town, November 22, 2013 (floodlit). Pakistan won by six runs. Toss: Pakistan.

Two overs in Pakistan's innings decided this match: first Phangiso, the left-arm spinner, was carted for three straight sixes in his third over, which cost 21, before Morkel was walloped for 22 in his third. Mohammad Hafeez and Umar Akmal were equally adept at driving down the ground and slashing square of the wicket, but there was nothing indiscriminate about their attacks: in just 55 balls they piled on 102. South Africa batted rather too calmly in reply: instead of creating a platform for an assault, they slipped behind the asking-rate. When Amla finally fell, after a serene innings, 60 were still required from 27 balls – and Pakistan squared the series, despite the strong-arming of Duminy and Miller.

Man of the Match: Mohammad Hafeez.   *Man of the Series:* Mohammad Hafeez.

Pakistan

	B	4	6
Nasir Jamshed *st 2 b 11*	19	19	3	0
Ahmed Shehzad *c 1 b 8*	9	11	0	1
*Mohammad Hafeez *c 4 b 9*	63	41	5	3
†Umar Akmal *c 5 b 9*	64	37	5	4
Shahid Afridi *not out*	13	14	2	0
Sohaib Maqsood *not out*	0	0	0	0
L-b 2, w 4, n-b 2	8			

6 overs: 30-1   (20 overs) 176-4

1/25 2/44 3/146 4/172

Umar Amin, Sohail Tanvir, Bilawal Bhatti, Saeed Ajmal and Junaid Khan did not bat.

Morkel 4–0–37–0; Steyn 4–0–29–2; Parnell 4–1–37–1; Wiese 3–0–24–0; Phangiso 3–0–33–1; Duminy 2–0–14–0.

South Africa

	B	4	6
H. M. Amla *c 9 b 10*	48	40	5	0
†Q. de Kock *c 1 b 5*	26	24	4	0
*F. du Plessis *c 3 b 5*	6	10	0	0
A. B. de Villiers *b 5*	13	8	2	0
J-P. Duminy *not out*	47	26	3	2
D. A. Miller *not out*	22	13	1	1
L-b 4, w 3, n-b 1	8			

6 overs: 53-0   (20 overs) 170-4

1/58 2/70 3/87 4/117

D. Wiese, W. D. Parnell, D. W. Steyn, M. Morkel and A. M. Phangiso did not bat.

Mohammad Hafeez 3–0–26–0; Sohail Tanvir 3–0–34–0; Junaid Khan 2–0–29–0; Saeed Ajmal 4–0–30–1; Bilawal Bhatti 4–0–19–0; Shahid Afridi 4–0–28–3.

Umpires: J. D. Cloete and S. George.   Third umpire: K. H. Hurter.
Series referee: A. J. Pycroft.

SOUTH AFRICA v PAKISTAN

First One-Day International

At Cape Town, November 24, 2013. Pakistan won by 23 runs. Toss: Pakistan. One-day international debuts: Anwar Ali, Bilawal Bhatti.

A slow, dry pitch, which became progressively more difficult for the batsmen, made for an absorbing, low-scoring game. Against some disciplined bowling, Pakistan inched to 218, which looked totally inadequate – until South Africa batted. Kallis made 50, in his first one-day international for 21 months, but they slid to 123 for six in the 30th over, and never threatened after that, despite another handy innings from Duminy. Pakistan's two debutants, the brisk seamers Anwar Ali and Bilawal Bhatti, shared five wickets; the floppy-haired Anwar lifted the match award. Earlier they had rescued their side from an even worse position – 131 for seven – by putting on 74 in less than 12 overs. Anwar presented an impeccably resolute bat, while Bhatti tore into the seamers, hitting three fours and three straight sixes. All in all, the two newcomers made a mockery of their captain Misbah-ul-Haq's pre-tour lament about Pakistan's lack of quality all-rounders.

Man of the Match: Anwar Ali.

Pakistan

Nasir Jamshed c Kallis b Steyn	24
Ahmed Shehzad c de Kock b Kallis	35
Mohammad Hafeez c Amla b Steyn	5
Sohaib Maqsood c Imran Tahir b Kallis ...	22
*Misbah-ul-Haq c de Kock b Morkel	13
†Umar Akmal c de Kock b Philander	0
Shahid Afridi b Steyn	26
Bilawal Bhatti lbw b Morkel............	39
Anwar Ali not out	43

Saeed Ajmal c Duminy b Morkel	3
Junaid Khan not out...................	0
B 2, l-b 1, w 5	8

1/49 (1) 2/58 (3)   (9 wkts, 50 overs) 218
3/73 (2) 4/97 (5)
5/98 (6) 6/124 (4) 7/131 (7)
8/205 (8) 9/213 (10)   10 overs: 31-0

Steyn 10–2–33–3; Philander 10–0–37–1; Morkel 10–0–39–3; Duminy 5–0–23–0; Imran Tahir 7–1–30–0; Kallis 8–0–53–2.

South Africa

G. C. Smith st Umar Akmal			
b Mohammad Hafeez .	12	D. W. Steyn b Bilawal Bhatti	15
H. M. Amla b Junaid Khan	3	M. Morkel b Bilawal Bhatti.	17
†Q. de Kock b Bilawal Bhatti	19	Imran Tahir not out	0
J. H. Kallis b Anwar Ali	50		
*A. B. de Villiers b Shahid Afridi	10	W 2	2
J-P. Duminy c Umar Akmal b Saeed Ajmal	49		
D. A. Miller c Umar Akmal b Anwar Ali . .	4	1/12 (2) 2/20 (1) 3/62 (3) (48.1 overs) 195
V. D. Philander c Sohaib Maqsood		4/79 (5) 5/115 (4) 6/123 (7)	
b Saeed Ajmal .	14	7/155 (8) 8/168 (6) 9/192 (9)	
		10/195 (10) 10 overs: 52-2	

Junaid Khan 8–0–38–1; Anwar Ali 6–0–24–2; Mohammad Hafeez 10–0–34–1; Bilawal Bhatti 7.1–0–37–3; Saeed Ajmal 10–0–28–2; Shahid Afridi 7–0–34–1.

Umpires: J. D. Cloete and C. B. Gaffaney.   Third umpire: B. N. J. Oxenford.

SOUTH AFRICA v PAKISTAN

Second One-Day International

At Port Elizabeth, November 27, 2013. Pakistan won by one run. Toss: South Africa.
South Africa added a new chapter to their history of choking to hand Pakistan the series. With two overs remaining, they needed 11 to win with six wickets in hand, one of which was Amla, who had purred into the nineties – but somehow they contrived to lose by a single run. They had struggled in the first half of their chase of 263, in a match reduced by rain to 45 overs, but de Villiers produced a riveting display of power and ingenuity. Only 36 were needed from 38 deliveries when he paddle-swept a low full toss to deep backward square leg after sprinting to 74 from 45 balls. Still, the game seemed won. But Saeed Ajmal conceded just two runs from the penultimate over: Duminy swung and missed, and Amla also did so twice, before holing out to deep square off the last ball. Junaid Khan then defended nine runs in the final over, helped by a tremendous low catch at deep midwicket by the substitute Umar Amin to remove Duminy. Earlier, Ahmed Shehzad had produced a perfectly paced century – his third in one-day internationals. But Pakistan were restricted by a classic display of fast bowling from Steyn, whose career-best one-day figures included four men caught in the cordon. Anwar Ali was given out obstructing the field – the fifth instance in one-day internationals, but the fourth from Pakistan – after changing direction while running. The umpires viewed this as a deliberate attempt to get in the way of wicketkeeper de Kock's throw, which hit Anwar on the shoulder as he attempted a bye.
Man of the Match: Ahmed Shehzad.

Pakistan

Nasir Jamshed b Steyn.	2	Saeed Ajmal c Kallis b Steyn	0
Ahmed Shehzad run out	102	Junaid Khan not out.	1
Mohammad Hafeez c de Kock b Steyn	8		
Sohaib Maqsood c Amla b McLaren	42	L-b 1, w 13	14
*Misbah-ul-Haq c de Kock b Imran Tahir . .	12		
†Umar Akmal c de Kock b Steyn	42	1/2 (1) 2/22 (3) 3/146 (4) (45 overs) 262
Shahid Afridi c de Villiers b Steyn	11	4/176 (5) 5/180 (2) 6/214 (7)	
Bilawal Bhatti c de Kock b Steyn	21	7/241 (8) 8/261 (9) 9/261 (6)	
Anwar Ali obstructing the field	7	10/262 (10) 9 overs: 39-2

Steyn 9–0–39–6; Tsotsobe 9–0–47–0; McLaren 9–0–71–1; Kallis 8–0–49–1; Imran Tahir 8–0–33–1; Duminy 2–0–22–0.

South Africa

H. M. Amla c Mohammad Hafeez		D. A. Miller not out	2
b Saeed Ajmal	98	R. McLaren not out	0
G. C. Smith c Umar Akmal b Junaid Khan	1		
†Q. de Kock c Misbah-ul-Haq b Shahid Afridi	47		
J. H. Kallis c Saeed Ajmal b Shahid Afridi	6	B 1, l-b 12, w 5	18
*A. B. de Villiers c Shahid Afridi			
b Junaid Khan	74	1/9 (2) 2/96 (3) (6 wkts, 45 overs)	261
J-P. Duminy c sub (Umar Amin)		3/117 (4) 4/227 (5)	
b Junaid Khan	15	5/254 (1) 6/255 (6) 9 overs: 26-1	

D. W. Steyn, L. L. Tsotsobe and Imran Tahir did not bat.

Junaid Khan 9–0–42–3; Anwar Ali 7–1–39–0; Saeed Ajmal 8–0–46–1; Mohammad Hafeez 8–0–44–0; Bilawal Bhatti 4–0–39–0; Shahid Afridi 9–0–38–2.

Umpires: S. George and B. N. J. Oxenford.   Third umpire: C. B. Gaffaney.

SOUTH AFRICA v PAKISTAN

Third One-Day International

At Centurion, November 30, 2013. South Africa won by four wickets. Toss: South Africa. One-day international debut: H. Davids.

Vernon Philander's return to the 50-over side – he had played only one match, 22 months previously, since August 2008 – produced three early wickets, as Pakistan collapsed to 97 for seven. They might have been rolled for 120, but for a determined display from Misbah-ul-Haq, who was still there at the end after facing 107 deliveries. The only support of note came from Abdur Rehman, who made 22 in an hour during an eighth-wicket stand of 51. Still, 179 looked inadequate, and South Africa made no mistake this time, steaming home with 68 balls to spare, despite another fine spell from Saeed Anwar, which slowed things down in the middle.

Man of the Match: V. D. Philander.   *Man of the Series:* Saeed Ajmal.

Pakistan

Umar Amin c Amla b McLaren	25	Sohail Tanvir c Parnell b Tsotsobe	6
Ahmed Shehzad c Amla b Philander	0	Saeed Ajmal c de Villiers b Parnell	0
Asad Shafiq c de Kock b Tsotsobe	1		
Sohaib Maqsood c and b McLaren	25	L-b 1, w 13	14
*Misbah-ul-Haq not out	79		
†Umar Akmal c de Kock b Philander	5	1/2 (2) 2/7 (3) 3/48 (1) (46.5 overs)	179
Bilawal Bhatti c Amla b Imran Tahir	1	4/67 (4) 5/85 (6) 6/96 (7)	
Anwar Ali c de Kock b Philander	1	7/97 (8) 8/148 (9) 9/164 (10)	
Abdur Rehman c Amla b Imran Tahir	22	10/179 (11) 10 overs: 43-2	

Philander 10–3–26–3; Tsotsobe 10–2–38–2; McLaren 8–1–28–2; Parnell 8.5–0–30–1; Imran Tahir 10–0–56–2.

South Africa

†Q. de Kock c Saeed Ajmal b Bilawal Bhatti	15	R. McLaren b Saeed Ajmal	17
H. M. Amla run out	41	W. D. Parnell not out	7
H. Davids st Umar Akmal b Saeed Ajmal	7	L-b 4, n-b 2	6
J-P. Duminy c Umar Akmal			
b Abdur Rehman	16	1/39 (1) 2/49 (3) (6 wkts, 38.4 overs)	181
*A. B. de Villiers not out	48	3/75 (2) 4/84 (4)	
D. A. Miller c Umar Akmal b Sohail Tanvir	24	5/124 (6) 6/164 (7) 10 overs: 49-1	

V. D. Philander, L. L. Tsotsobe and Imran Tahir did not bat.

Sohail Tanvir 7.4–0–42–1; Anwar Ali 2–0–15–0; Bilawal Bhatti 8–1–35–1; Saeed Ajmal 10–1–34–2; Abdur Rehman 9–0–40–1; Sohaib Maqsood 2–0–11–0.

Umpires: C. B. Gaffaney and S. George.   Third umpire: B. N. J. Oxenford.
Series referee: B. C. Broad.

SOUTH AFRICA v INDIA, 2013-14

TELFORD VICE

One-day internationals (3): South Africa 2, India 0
Test matches (2): South Africa 1, India 0

For months before the Indians arrived in South Africa, there was doubt over whether they would come at all. And if they did, how many matches would they actually play? For months afterwards, conversations centred on Jacques Kallis's shock decision to retire from Tests. And, all the while, Sachin Tendulkar's long goodbye was hogging the limelight.

The teams, despite being governed by events off the field, played memorable cricket. But before we get to the sport, we need to wade through the politics. In February 2013, the BCCI told Cricket South Africa of their unhappiness at the prospect of having to deal again with Haroon Lorgat, a man they thought they had seen the last of in 2012, when his tenure as ICC chief executive had ended. Now, as the frontrunner to be CSA's next chief executive, Lorgat loomed large in the BCCI's future.

In danger if that happened was the two boards' cosy relationship, which in 2009 had led to the IPL going on an African safari, bringing millions of dollars with it. Even CSA's own risk assessment warned that appointing Lorgat would be reckless. So it was problematic that he was easily the best and most qualified of the 200-plus applicants.

Lorgat's appointment was announced on July 20. The BCCI complained that the tour itinerary as released by CSA – three Tests, seven one-day internationals and two Twenty20s – had not been agreed. After much bowing and scraping by CSA, the parties settled on two Tests and three one-dayers. South African cricket lost some £11.5m in revenue.

On October 5, David Becker, the ICC's head of legal throughout Lorgat's tenure and subsequently a legal adviser to CSA, released a statement that made damning allegations against both the ICC and BCCI president N. Srinivasan. "The ICC board have real and grave governance issues," Becker wrote. "There is one man who makes decisions at board level, and they are certainly not in the interests of world cricket. Directors' duties, conflicts of interest and matters of ethical compliance are routinely ignored. It's not only hugely concerning for the game: it's contrary to the regulatory framework within which ICC operates, and hence it's illegal."

In attempting to stop publication of the statement, Lorgat made offers to journalists that they considered improper. Those journalists then found themselves removed from CSA's mailing lists without notice, and ignored when they asked questions. Lorgat's conduct concerning Becker's statement was the subject of an ICC investigation. In a joint statement, CSA and the BCCI said Lorgat would not have "involvement in any aspect of CSA's relationship with the BCCI, including, but not limited to, the upcoming tour". The statement continued: "All parties have agreed that no further

Do I get another go? Rohit Sharma is knocked over first ball by a fired-up Dale Steyn at Durban.

media comment will be made until [the ICC investigation] has been concluded."

Within days, Lorgat had been interviewed by an Indian newspaper and a South African radio station. When the tour started, he was often seen in the president's suites – where 12 places had been reserved for Indian board members, who never made the trip to South Africa. Somehow, the tour had been saved, but in a truncated state and – to South African fury – without a New Year Test in Cape Town, which is where the locals had assumed Tendulkar would play his 200th Test.

What did India's captain M. S. Dhoni think of the set-to between the suits? "We can arrange a match for the administrators and let them go at it," he said. What to do if India's players became the targets of missile-throwing crowds? "We'll pick it up and give it back," Dhoni said. "Whenever we have been here we have had a fantastic reception, and I don't think that will change."

Happily, he was right. But spectators at the Wanderers Test came close to throwing things at Vernon Philander and Dale Steyn when, with three wickets standing, they declined to chase the 16 runs South Africa required off the last 19 balls to reach what would have been a world-record 458.

At Kingsmead, Kallis scored a century in his last Test, as South Africa – whose batsmen and fast bowlers had already bullied their way to victory in the one-day games – swept to a series win. For a few days, sport mattered more than politics.

INDIA TOURING PARTY

*M. S. Dhoni (T/50), R. Ashwin (T/50), Bhuvneshwar Kumar (T/50), S. Dhawan (T/50), R. A. Jadeja (T/50), V. Kohli (T/50), A. Mishra (50), Mohammed Shami (T/50), P. P. Ojha (T), C. A. Pujara (T), A. M. Rahane (50), S. K. Raina (50), A. T. Rayudu (T/50), W. P. Saha (T), I. Sharma (T/50), M. Sharma (50), R. G. Sharma (T/50), M. Vijay (T), U. T. Yadav (T/50), Yuvraj Singh (50), Zaheer Khan (T). *Coach:* D. A. G. Fletcher.

SOUTH AFRICA v INDIA

First One-Day International

At Johannesburg, December 5, 2013 (day/night). South Africa won by 141 runs. Toss: India.

Quinton de Kock's 135, the highest one-day score by a South African against India, all but blew the tourists off the park. His opening stand of 152 with Amla was the team's first century partnership for the first wicket in 68 games. It helped South Africa to 358 for four, their second-highest total against India, after 365 for two at Ahmedabad in February 2010. The rest of the job was done first in a stand of 105 off 46 balls between de Villiers and Duminy, then by McLaren and Steyn, who shared six wickets. India slipped to 65 for four in reply, but Dhoni was dropped on 18, and made the most of the reprieve by staying until the 41st over, when Steyn bowled him for 65; Kohli, dropped on two, was the only other Indian batsman to pass 30. Without a warm-up match to prepare for the series, India were plainly out of touch, and went down to their second-heaviest defeat by South Africa in the format. South Africa, still under the cloud of their first one-day series loss to Pakistan – at home, no less – needed an emphatic performance. This was it.

Man of the Match: Q. de Kock.

South Africa

H. M. Amla b Mohammed Shami	65	D. A. Miller not out		5
†Q. de Kock c and b Kohli	135	L-b 2, w 4, n-b 1		7
J. H. Kallis c Jadeja b Mohammed Shami	10			
*A. B. de Villiers b Mohammed Shami	77	1/152 (1) 2/172 (3)	(4 wkts, 50 overs)	358
J-P. Duminy not out	59	3/247 (2) 4/352 (4)	10 overs: 53-0	

R. McLaren, W. D. Parnell, D. W. Steyn, M. Morkel and L. L. Tsotsobe did not bat.

M. Sharma 10–0–82–0; Bhuvneshwar Kumar 9–0–68–0; Mohammed Shami 10–1–68–3; Ashwin 10–0–58–0; Jadeja 8–0–58–0; Raina 1–0–7–0; Kohli 2–0–15–1.

India

R. G. Sharma run out	18	M. Sharma not out		0
S. Dhawan c de Kock b Morkel	12	Mohammed Shami c and b Steyn		0
V. Kohli c Kallis b McLaren	31			
Yuvraj Singh b McLaren	0	B 4, l-b 1, w 24		29
S. K. Raina run out	14			
*†M. S. Dhoni b Steyn	65	1/14 (2) 2/60 (3) 3/60 (4)	(41 overs)	217
R. A. Jadeja b Kallis	29	4/65 (1) 5/108 (5) 6/158 (7)		
R. Ashwin c de Kock b McLaren	19	7/183 (8) 8/190 (9) 9/217 (6)		
Bhuvneshwar Kumar c Kallis b Steyn	0	10/217 (11)	10 overs: 36-1	

Steyn 8–3–25–3; Tsotsobe 9–0–52–0; Morkel 8–1–29–1; McLaren 8–0–49–3; Parnell 5–0–37–0; Kallis 3–0–20–1.

Umpires: A. T. Holdstock and R. K. Illingworth.   Third umpire: J. D. Cloete.

> **❝**Cook was a dark cloud and a spit of rain away from looking a darned fool.❞
> England v New Zealand, 2013, page 291

SOUTH AFRICA v INDIA

Second One-Day International

At Durban, December 8, 2013. South Africa won by 134 runs. Toss: India.

South Africa wrapped up the series, as de Kock delivered another commanding display to make 106, this time showing the patience of a man far older than his 20 years. He hit just nine fours, a stark contrast to the 18 – as well as three sixes – that had punctuated his hundred at the Wanderers three days earlier. At the other end throughout de Kock's innings stood Amla. On 59, he became the fastest batsman to 4,000 one-day international runs (needing 81 innings, seven fewer than Viv Richards). Their partnership of 194 set South Africa on their way to 280 for six in 49 overs after rain lopped one off. In another batting disaster, India were bowled out for 146 with nearly 14 overs to spare. Only Raina and Jadeja made it past 20. Rahane, brought in for the unfit Yuvraj Singh, was unlucky to be given out caught behind: as the ball passed the bat, with Rahane aiming a full-blooded cut, the umpire was deceived by the sound of his necklace clattering against the grille of his helmet. Steyn's aggression was again too hot for the Indians to handle, but Tsotsobe's cold precision was even more dangerous, bringing him four for 25.

Man of the Match: Q. de Kock.

South Africa

†Q. de Kock c R. G. Sharma b Ashwin	106	V. D. Philander not out		14
H. M. Amla c Dhoni b Mohammed Shami	100			
*A. B. de Villiers st Dhoni b Jadeja	3	B 1, l-b 2, w 6		9
J-P. Duminy run out	26			
D. A. Miller lbw b Mohammed Shami	0	1/194 (1) 2/199 (3)	(6 wkts, 49 overs)	280
J. H. Kallis b Mohammed Shami	10	3/233 (2) 4/234 (5)		
R. McLaren not out	12	5/249 (4) 6/255 (6)	10 overs: 58-0	

D. W. Steyn, M. Morkel and L. L. Tsotsobe did not bat.

Yadav 6–0–45–0; Mohammed Shami 8–0–48–3; I. Sharma 7–0–38–0; Ashwin 9–0–48–1; Raina 6–0–32–0; Kohli 3–0–17–0; Jadeja 10–0–49–1.

India

R. G. Sharma c Amla b Tsotsobe	19	U. T. Yadav b Steyn		1
S. Dhawan c Duminy b Steyn	0	I. Sharma not out		0
V. Kohli c de Kock b Tsotsobe	0			
A. M. Rahane c de Kock b Morkel	8	B 4, l-b 1, w 8, n-b 1		14
S. K. Raina c Miller b Morkel	36			
*†M. S. Dhoni c de Kock b Philander	19	1/10 (2) 2/16 (3) 3/29 (1)	(35.1 overs)	146
R. A. Jadeja c de Villiers b Tsotsobe	26	4/34 (4) 5/74 (6) 6/95 (5)		
R. Ashwin c de Kock b Steyn	15	7/133 (8) 8/145 (7) 9/146 (10)		
Mohammed Shami b Tsotsobe	8	10/146 (9)	10 overs: 35-4	

Steyn 7–1–17–3; Tsotsobe 7.1–0–25–4; Morkel 6–0–34–2; Philander 6–1–20–1; Duminy 5–0–20–0; McLaren 4–0–25–0.

Umpires: S. George and R. K. Illingworth.   Third umpire: A. T. Holdstock.

SOUTH AFRICA v INDIA

Third One-Day International

At Centurion, December 11, 2013 (day/night). No result. Toss: South Africa.

De Kock joined Zaheer Abbas, Saeed Anwar, Herschelle Gibbs and A. B. de Villiers as the only players to have scored centuries in three successive one-day internationals. He was also the second, after Ireland's Paul Stirling, to score four hundreds before his 21st birthday (which he celebrated six days later). This time, he prospered despite South Africa's early collapse to 28 for three. He and de

MOST RUNS IN A THREE-MATCH ONE-DAY SERIES

		HS	100	50	SR		
342	Q. de Kock (SA)	135	3	0	95.26	SA v I	**2013-14**
330	M. J. Guptill (NZ)	189*	2	0	105.09	E v NZ	**2013**
310	B. R. M. Taylor (Z)	128*	2	1	106.89	Z v NZ	2011-12
294	S. R. Watson (A)	185*	1	1	175.00	B v A	2010-11
289	G. A. Gooch (E)	117*	2	1	64.79	E v A	1985
276	I. V. A. Richards (WI)	189*	1	1	111.74	E v WI	1984

Villiers took on the responsibility of righting the innings in a stand of 171, a South African fourth-wicket record against India. The partnership endured into the 38th over, when de Kock went for 101, while de Villiers stayed until the 44th for his 109. He and Miller ramped up the scoring-rate in a stand of 53 at more than nine an over, with Miller hitting his unbeaten 56 off 34 balls. Ishant Sharma alone countered de Kock, claiming four wickets, but it all came to nought during the supper break, when a thunderstorm drowned out any prospect of further play. Sharma brightened a dismal evening by telling reporters de Kock had been "lucky" to score his three centuries.

Man of the Series: Q. de Kock.

South Africa

H. M. Amla c Yuvraj Singh b Mohammed Shami	13	
†Q. de Kock b I. Sharma	101	
H. Davids c Raina b I. Sharma	1	
J-P. Duminy c Raina b I. Sharma	0	
*A. B. de Villiers lbw b Yadav	109	
D. A. Miller not out	56	
R. McLaren c Yadav b I. Sharma	6	
W. D. Parnell c R. G. Sharma b Mohammed Shami	9	

V. D. Philander b Mohammed Shami 0
L. L. Tsotsobe not out 1

L-b 2, w 3 5

1/22 (1) 2/28 (3)   (8 wkts, 50 overs) 301
3/28 (4) 4/199 (2)
5/252 (5) 6/269 (7)
7/291 (8) 8/298 (9)   10 overs: 38-3

Imran Tahir did not bat.

I. Sharma 10-1-40-4; Yadav 9-0-57-1; Mohammed Shami 10-0-69-3; Ashwin 9-0-63-0; Jadeja 6-0-32-0; Raina 3-0-16-0; Kohli 3-0-22-0.

India

R. G. Sharma, S. Dhawan, V. Kohli, Yuvraj Singh, S. K. Raina, *†M. S. Dhoni, R. A. Jadeja, R. Ashwin, Mohammed Shami, U. T. Yadav and I. Sharma.

Umpires: J. D. Cloete and R. K. Illingworth.   Third umpire: S. George.
Series referee: A. J. Pycroft.

At Benoni, December 13–14, 2013 (not first-class). **South African Invitation XI v Indians. Abandoned.** *India's only warm-up match was brought forward by a day to avoid clashing with Nelson Mandela's funeral on December 15. But the city of Benoni had received 800mm of rain – usually a year's worth – in the three weeks leading up to the match, and no play was possible.*

SOUTH AFRICA v INDIA

First Test Match

At Johannesburg, December 18–22, 2013. Drawn. Toss: India.

An astonishing match had the tamest of endings as both teams shied away from victory. When du Plessis was run out, South Africa needed 16 runs off 19 balls. India needed three wickets. South Africa had been asked to chase a world-record 458; India had the chance to stave off that ignominy, and to set up a first series victory in South Africa. Instead, everyone unscrewed their courage from its sticking place.

Philander and Steyn blocked three of those last 19 deliveries, left three others, and declined three singles off three more. Zaheer Khan and Mohammed Shami bowled five harmless short deliveries, and three more balls wide of the stumps, and never to a field set with more than two fielders in catching positions. The players were booed off by a gouty crowd, who were still in dark voice when Smith returned for his television interview.

As if they knew they had blundered but couldn't bring themselves to admit it, both teams tried to blame the other for the diabolical draw. "India were ahead of the game; they would be very disappointed that they didn't win it," Smith said. "I'd be surprised if M. S. [Dhoni] didn't feel his bowlers should have won that game." Smith also wondered why India "didn't have four slips, a short leg and a gully" in the final overs. Undeterred, Kohli insisted: "We were pretty shocked. Vernon Philander was hitting the ball well and we know Dale Steyn can bat."

Kohli had been the focus ahead of the match, India's first Test since Sachin Tendulkar's retirement. What would he make of his opportunity? By the first evening, he had a new career-best score, of 119 – and the world had its answer. Poised and purposeful, Kohli did not offer a chance in an innings of calm courage against hostile bowling, which had begun at 24 for two. His most serious error was to change his mind about a single too late for Pujara to scramble back to safety, so ending a third-wicket stand of 89.

CLOSEST DRAWS BY RUNS REMAINING

Runs		Total	Overs		
1	England	204-6	37	v Zimbabwe at Bulawayo	1996-97
1	India	242-9	64	v West Indies at Mumbai (Wankhede)	2011-12
6	India	355-8	107	v West Indies at Bombay (Brabourne)	1948-49
6	England	228-9	91	v West Indies at Lord's	1963
8	Australia.......	238-8	80†	v England at Melbourne	1974-75
8	**South Africa ...**	**450-7**	**136**	**v India at Johannesburg**	**2013-14**
9	India	429-8	150.5	v England at The Oval................	1979
10	New Zealand ...	274-6	57	v Australia at Brisbane.................	2001-02

† *Eight-ball overs.*

The pitch did not give the players nearly as much as it took. It demanded the full focus of all who bowled and batted, hence India's neither-here-nor-there 255 for five at stumps. But South Africa had made "this team finds a way" part of their mantra, and did exactly that on the second morning: after waiting nine overs for the breakthrough, they took the last five wickets for 16 in 25 balls. Philander, who had been moaning publicly about toothache since the previous midnight, vented his mood on the batsmen in a fine recitation of swerve and verve.

But the bowlers remained on top and, by the close on the second day, South Africa had crashed to 213 for six. With bizarre symmetry, they also lost five for 16, three wickets tumbling at 130. Amla had left an inswinger from Ishant Sharma and was bowled, and with his next delivery Sharma inflicted on Kallis only the second first-ball duck of his career, by trapping him in front. Smith shone out of the gloom with a defiant 68 before being dismissed by Zaheer Khan for the 14th time in 26 matches across all formats. Zaheer had poleaxed Smith with a blow to the knee early in his innings, and Smith was also dropped at first slip on 19, before surviving another screamer through the cordon. By the time he was removed, lbw to a delivery more likely to have hit leg slip than leg stump, he had bucked the trend of the innings for more than three hours.

Philander now replicated the spirit he had shown with the ball, scoring 59 before becoming one of Zaheer's four victims. But South Africa lost their last four wickets for 18 on the third morning, to concede a deficit of 36. By stumps, India had built their lead to 320, by scoring 175 in 38 overs in the third session. Pujara and Kohli had put them in complete control.

To make matters worse for South Africa, Morkel had left the field with a badly twisted ankle. Meanwhile, Amla kept wicket for the first time in Tests, when de Villiers was called on to bowl for the first time since 2006. Closer to normality was a record for Philander who, in his 19th Test, became the fastest South African to 100 wickets.

Next day, Pujara and Kohli took their partnership to 222, before Kallis had Pujara caught behind for 153 by de Villiers, now restored to the keeper's role. Kohli failed by four runs to become the first Indian No. 4 to score a century in each innings of a Test, when he edged a cut off Duminy, and Rohit Sharma was Kallis's 292nd and final Test victim. India were dismissed after lunch, a touch carelessly perhaps, and by the close South Africa had whittled their target down to 320.

They had eight wickets in hand at the start of the fifth day, but quickly lost Petersen for his overnight score of 76. Midway through the morning session, Kallis was given out lbw by Rod Tucker to make Zaheer the fourth Indian, after Kapil Dev, Anil Kumble and Harbhajan Singh, to take 300 Test wickets. Kallis, though, had clearly edged the ball, and walked off screaming blue murder.

At 197 for four, South Africa teetered on the edge. But they regrouped in a stand of 205 between du Plessis and de Villiers. India began to panic, and Dhoni – in his 50th Test as captain, breaking Sourav Ganguly's Indian record – tried everything. He even brought himself on to bowl: this was the first Test in which both wicketkeepers enjoyed a trundle. De Villiers chopped on to Sharma for 103 and, with 16 needed, Rahane ran out a sprawling – and by now exhausted – du Plessis from mid-off for 134. With only the injured Morkel and the rabbit Imran Tahir still to come, Philander and Steyn had to make a decision. Then the fun started. Steyn's last-ball six, hit with angry eyes, suggested he did not appreciate the crowd's jeers. The Second Test at Durban could not come soon enough.

Man of the Match: V. Kohli.

Close of play: first day, India 255-5 (Rahane 43, Dhoni 17); second day, South Africa 213-6 (du Plessis 17, Philander 48); third day, India 284-2 (Pujara 135, Kohli 77); fourth day, South Africa 138-2 (Petersen 76, du Plessis 10).

India

M. Vijay c de Villiers b Morkel	6	– (2) c de Villiers b Kallis	39
S. Dhawan c Imran Tahir b Steyn	13	– (1) c Kallis b Philander	15
C. A. Pujara run out	25	– c de Villiers b Kallis	153
V. Kohli c Duminy b Kallis	119	– c de Villiers b Duminy	96
R. G. Sharma c de Villiers b Philander	14	– b Kallis	6
A. M. Rahane c de Villiers b Philander	47	– c Smith b Duminy	15
*†M. S. Dhoni c de Villiers b Morkel	19	– c sub (D. Elgar) b Philander	29
R. Ashwin not out	11	– c du Plessis b Philander	7
Zaheer Khan lbw b Philander	0	– not out	29
I. Sharma b Philander	0	– lbw b Imran Tahir	4
Mohammed Shami b Morkel	0	– b Imran Tahir	4
B 4, l-b 6, w 14, n-b 2	26	B 9, l-b 7, w 8	24

1/17 (2) 2/24 (1) 3/113 (3)   (103 overs) 280
4/151 (5) 5/219 (4) 6/264 (7)
7/264 (6) 8/264 (9) 9/278 (10) 10/280 (11)

1/23 (1) 2/93 (2)   (120.4 overs) 421
3/315 (3) 4/325 (5)
5/327 (4) 6/358 (7) 7/369 (8)
8/384 (7) 9/405 (10) 10/421 (11)

Steyn 26–7–61–1; Philander 27–6–61–4; Morkel 23–12–34–3; Kallis 14–4–37–1; Imran Tahir 8–0–47–0; Duminy 5–0–30–0. *Second innings*—Steyn 30–5–104–0; Philander 28–10–68–3; Morkel 2–1–4–0; Kallis 20–5–68–3; Imran Tahir 15.4–1–69–2; de Villiers 1–0–5–0; Duminy 24–0–87–2.

South Africa

*G. C. Smith lbw b Zaheer Khan	68	– (2) run out 44
A. N. Petersen lbw b I. Sharma	21	– (1) b Mohammed Shami 76
H. M. Amla b I. Sharma	36	– b Mohammed Shami 4
J. H. Kallis lbw b I. Sharma	0	– (5) lbw b Zaheer Khan 34
†A. B. de Villiers lbw b Mohammed Shami	13	– (6) b I. Sharma 103
J-P. Duminy c Vijay b Mohammed Shami	2	– (7) b Mohammed Shami 5
F. du Plessis c Dhoni b Zaheer Khan	20	– (4) run out 134
V. D. Philander c Ashwin b Zaheer Khan	59	– not out 25
D. W. Steyn c R. G. Sharma b I. Sharma	10	– not out 6
M. Morkel b Zaheer Khan	7	
Imran Tahir not out	0	
L-b 4, w 1, n-b 3	8	B 2, l-b 7, w 8, n-b 2 19

1/37 (2) 2/130 (3) 3/130 (4)   (75.3 overs) 244
4/130 (1) 5/145 (6) 6/146 (5)
7/226 (8) 8/237 (9) 9/239 (7) 10/244 (10)

1/108 (2)   (7 wkts, 136 overs) 450
2/118 (3) 3/143 (1)
4/197 (5) 5/402 (6) 6/407 (7) 7/442 (4)

Zaheer Khan 26.3–6–88–4; Mohammed Shami 18–3–48–2; I. Sharma 25–5–79–4; Ashwin 6–0–25–0. *Second innings*—Zaheer Khan 34–1–135–1; I. Sharma 29–4–91–1; Mohammed Shami 28–5–107–3; Ashwin 36–5–83–0; Vijay 1–0–3–0; Dhoni 2–0–4–0; Kohli 6–0–18–0.

Umpires: S. J. Davis and R. J. Tucker.   Third umpire: S. George.

SOUTH AFRICA v INDIA

Second Test Match

At Durban, December 26–30, 2013. South Africa won by ten wickets. Toss: India.

South Africans were given the most unwanted Christmas present when, with the nation sitting down to lunch with all the trimmings, Kallis announced that his 166th Test would be his last. A South African team without him had been unthinkable for 18 years. The future was as dark as a dead braai fire, even if he did leave with another hundred and one last Test victory, securing a brief but eventful 1–0 triumph.

It was darker still when bad light limited the first day's play to 61 overs, in which India reached 181 for one. The lone bright spot for the hosts was Morkel, who had supposedly been ruled out for seven to ten days when he twisted an ankle at Johannesburg, but was now making what Smith called a "miracle" recovery. To Morkel went South Africa's only success of the first day – Dhawan taken at third slip straight after drinks. Then Vijay and Pujara made themselves at home on a pitch that would not have seemed out of place in Chennai or Bangalore, and which helped explain why South Africa had lost their four previous Tests at Kingsmead.

Rain put paid to the second morning, but South Africa quickly made up for lost time, taking the nine remaining wickets in 50 overs for 153. Having gone 69 Test overs without a wicket, and been relieved by Philander of the No. 1 Test ranking he had held since 2009, Steyn found furious intensity and no little swing to claim six for 100. His first victim was Pujara, caught behind for 70 to end the second-wicket partnership at 157. He followed that by removing Vijay on 97, gloving a leg-side catch to de Villiers. Still, at 320 for five, India remained in control, only for the last five to fall for 14, leaving Rahane high and dry. The collapse included Kallis's 200th Test catch; he was only the second to reach that mark, after Rahul Dravid.

By the close, Smith and Petersen had chipped 82 runs off the arrears, only for three quick wickets on the third morning to swing the game India's way once more. Enter Kallis,

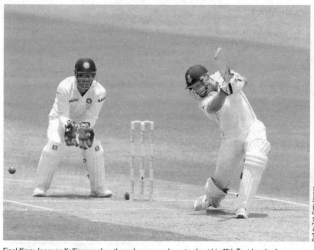

Duff du Toit, Getty Images

Final fling: Jacques Kallis crunches through cover as he sets about his 45th Test hundred.

who was greeted by an Indian guard of honour, waited 16 balls to get off the mark, and reached the close ominously unbeaten on 78. This was no ceremonial last hurrah – South Africa needed their rock to do what he did best. Stands of 127 with de Villiers and 58 with Duminy turned the innings around. Kallis's best friend, Mark Boucher, had arrived by now to join in the grand occasion. He looked forward to getting his mate back full-time: "We can sit around a fire for four hours and not say a word to each other except: 'Your round.'" Kallis's agent, Dave Rundle, had interrupted his trip to New York to be there. There was only one polite way to oblige.

An hour into the fourth day, Kallis dabbed Jadeja to midwicket for a single to bring up his 45th Test century, his seventh against India (he had more against only England and West Indies – eight each), and his fifth at Kingsmead. He inched, by a single, past the Test tally of Rahul Dravid – at the ground as a commentator – and into third place on the all-time list, on 13,289. Only Ricky Ponting and Sachin Tendulkar remained out of reach.

Three balls later, Kallis went for 115, top-edging a sweep off Jadeja to Dhoni, who refused to accept the new ball until the seam split on the old one after 146 overs (regulations necessitate a new ball if the old one has to be changed after 110 overs). That was a factor in Jadeja's haul of six for 138, but he wouldn't have made the most of his opportunity had he not found biting turn.

A stand of 110 between du Plessis and Peterson – who somehow survived an lbw shout from Mohammed Shami on 31, but later played an outrageous switch hit for six off Rohit Sharma – helped South Africa reach 500 before they were dismissed with a lead of 166. By the close, India were 68 for two, and fighting for their lives.

South Africa strengthened their grip on the last morning. Steyn had Kohli caught behind with the first ball of the day, though it came off his sleeve; he then bowled Pujara with one that turned into a beauty after deviating off a crack. Peterson chipped in: Dhoni and Jadeja both carelessly offered catches, before Zaheer Khan was undone by a previously unseen carrom ball, suggested moments earlier by wicketkeeper de Villiers (had DRS been in use,

HIGHEST TEST AVERAGE AT NO. 4

		T	I	NO	R	HS	100	50
61.86	J. H. Kallis (South Africa)	111	170	24	9,033	224	35	36
59.12	G. S. Chappell (Australia)	54	86	13	4,316	247*	15	19
54.40	S. R. Tendulkar (India)	179	275	27	13,492	248*	44	58
54.10	Javed Miandad (Pakistan).	104	140	12	6,925	280*	19	31
53.59	D. C. S. Compton (England)	57	86	7	4,234	278	13	20
52.90	Inzamam-ul-Haq (Pakistan)	68	98	6	4,867	329	15	21
51.79	D. P. M. D. Jayawardene (Sri Lanka).	116	181	12	8,754	374	28	30
51.25	B. C. Lara (West Indies/World)	91	148	1	7,535	277	24	31
49.39	M. D. Crowe (New Zealand)	67	106	9	4,841	299	16	16
48.43	K. P. Pietersen (England).	90	139	5	6,490	227	19	27

Minimum 4,000 runs.

it would have spared Zaheer: the ball was comfortably sliding down leg). Steyn and Philander cleaned up, but not before Rahane had once more got stuck in. He deserved a century, and the six he hit off Philander – over point, one foot off the ground – was worth at least a dozen. Alas, he went for 96.

When Ishant Sharma mimed a giraffe in the headlights and fended a bouncer off his sternum to de Villiers, Steyn joined Richard Hadlee in taking 350 wickets in 69 Tests, three more than Muttiah Muralitharan. Steyn got there in nine years and 14 days. South Africa needed 58 to win; Smith and Petersen obliged.

Then it was time for Kallis's Test-match goodbye, which started with a lap of honour and a pause to down a beer proffered from beyond the boundary. At the press conference, he managed to list three former girlfriends among his acknowledgments, said he had "lost a little hair, gained a little hair" (he had transplants in 2010), and described his Test career as "one big, fun experience". For once, the most telling words came from a reporter: "Jacques, what the hell are we going to write about now?"

Man of the Match: D. W. Steyn.   *Man of the Series:* A. B. de Villiers.

Close of play: first day, India 181-1 (Vijay 91, Pujara 58); second day, South Africa 82-0 (Smith 35, Petersen 46); third day, South Africa 299-5 (Kallis 78, Steyn 0); fourth day, India 68-2 (Pujara 32, Kohli 11).

India

S. Dhawan c Petersen b Morkel.	29	– c du Plessis b Peterson	19
M. Vijay c de Villiers b Steyn	97	– c Smith b Philander	6
C. A. Pujara c de Villiers b Steyn	70	– b Steyn	32
V. Kohli c de Villiers b Morkel	46	– c de Villiers b Steyn.	11
R. G. Sharma b Steyn.	0	– lbw b Philander	25
A. M. Rahane not out.	51	– b Philander	96
*†M. S. Dhoni c Smith b Steyn	24	– c Petersen b Peterson	15
R. A. Jadeja c Kallis b Duminy	0	– c Morkel b Peterson	8
Zaheer Khan c de Villiers b Steyn	0	– lbw b Peterson	3
I. Sharma c de Villiers b Steyn.	4	– c de Villiers b Steyn.	1
Mohammed Shami c Smith b Morkel	1	– not out	1
L-b 7, w 4, n-b 1.	12	B 4, w 2.	6

1/41 (1) 2/198 (3) 3/199 (2)   (111.3 overs) 334   1/8 (2) 2/53 (1)   (86 overs) 223
4/199 (5) 5/265 (4) 6/320 (7)   3/68 (4) 4/71 (3)
7/321 (8) 8/322 (9) 9/330 (10) 10/334 (11)   5/104 (5) 6/146 (7) 7/154 (8)
8/189 (9) 9/206 (10) 10/223 (6)

Steyn 30–9–100–6; Philander 21–6–56–0; Morkel 23.3–6–50–3; Kallis 11–1–36–0; Peterson 22–2–75–0; Duminy 4–0–10–1. *Second innings*—Steyn 21–8–47–3; Philander 16–4–43–3; Morkel 16–6–34–0; Peterson 24–3–74–4; Duminy 8–2–20–0; du Plessis 1–0–1–0.

South Africa

*G. C. Smith c Dhawan b Jadeja	47	– (2) not out		27
A. N. Petersen c Vijay b Jadeja	62	– (1) not out		31
H. M. Amla b Mohammed Shami	3			
J. H. Kallis c Dhoni b Jadeja	115			
†A. B. de Villiers c Kohli b Jadeja	74			
J-P. Duminy lbw b Jadeja	28			
D. W. Steyn c Dhoni b Zaheer Khan	44			
F. du Plessis run out	43			
R. J. Peterson c Vijay b Zaheer Khan	61			
V. D. Philander not out	0			
M. Morkel c and b Jadeja	0			
B 3, l-b 15, w 2, n-b 3	23	W 1		1

1/103 (1) 2/113 (3) 3/113 (2)   (155.2 overs) 500   (no wkt, 11.4 overs) 59
4/240 (5) 5/298 (6) 6/384 (4)
7/387 (7) 8/497 (9) 9/500 (8) 10/500 (11)

Zaheer Khan 28–4–97–2; Mohammed Shami 27–2–104–1; I. Sharma 31–7–114–0; Jadeja
58.2–15–138–6; R. G. Sharma 11–1–29–0. *Second innings*—Mohammed Shami 2–1–4–0; I. Sharma
5–1–29–0; Jadeja 4–0–16–0; R. G. Sharma 0.4–0–10–0.

Umpires: S. J. Davis and R. J. Tucker.   Third umpire: A. T. Holdstock.
Series referee: A. J. Pycroft.

ENGLAND UNDER-19 IN SOUTH AFRICA, 2012-13

Under-19 Test matches (2): South Africa 1, England 1
Under-19 one-day internationals (5): South Africa 5, England 0

After South Africa had somehow won the Second Test at Paarl, despite plummeting to eight for four in the first innings and 25 for four in the second, their captain Diego Rosier admitted: "England dominated us for six of the eight days." The heist left the tourists deeply frustrated: at Under-19 level, Test series wins abroad are a rare old bird, mainly because the youthful visitors are still unfamiliar with conditions. It was 16 years since England had last won an overseas series at this level – in Pakistan, under what *Wisden* called the "mature captaincy" of Andrew Flintoff.

Northamptonshire seamer Olly Stone did not suffer by comparison. Thrust into the leadership when Shiv Thakor broke a finger in the opening tour match, Stone wasted little time suggesting he was made of granite. During catching practice on the second morning of the First Test at Cape Town, he took a painful blow to the ring finger of his right hand, badly dislocating it. He was taken to hospital and his finger was reset under anaesthetic. Stone might have been expected to sit out at least the rest of the day, but he was back at Newlands that afternoon, pleading with the medical staff to let him lead the attack. They relented, and Stone brought himself on to bowl almost immediately, striking twice in his third over, and inspiring England to their first Test victory overseas since 2002-03.

"In this game, there are a lot of players content to hide in the corner of the dressing-room when things start to go wrong," said Tim Boon, the England player development head coach. "Not Stoney. His response to that injury spoke volumes. Moments like that have such a profound effect on a young team."

Seventeen wickets in two Tests at 9.88 were astonishing statistics, and Boon said that Stone's awayswing – quick, accurate and carrying nicely on South African pitches – came up to the standard of an experienced first-class cricketer. But the purpose of development tours is not to flog young players into the ground and, when Stone needed a breather in the Second Test, South Africa cashed in against the other bowlers. By the end of the tour, Stone was suffering from dehydration too – but Boon concluded he had never seen a more accomplished 19-year-old.

Thakor's misfortune was felt personally by Boon, who had watched his development since the age of nine at Leicestershire, and left him out of the 2012 Under-19 World Cup squad when his progress threatened to stall. His absence weakened the bowling attack, but England decided against calling up three eligible seamers – Reece Topley, Craig Overton and Tom Helm – and sent them instead to the England Performance Programme's fast bowling camp in Potchefstroom. As it happened, the Second Test, at Paarl, was played on a turning wicket, and South Africa's spinners comfortably outbowled their opponents.

South Africa, featuring several of the squad that had narrowly lost the World Cup semi-final to Australia, built some formidable totals as they administered a 5–0 whitewash in the one-day series. It was clear that England's batsmen (all eligible for the next Under-19 World Cup, in the United Arab Emirates in 2014) needed to be savvier at rotating the strike; too often, they fell behind the required run-rate. The management hoped some of these traditional weaknesses could be ironed out on a limited-overs tour of the UAE later in the year, when they would play Pakistan.

ENGLAND UNDER-19 TOURING PARTY

*S. J. Thakor (Leicestershire), T. Barber (Hampshire), E. Barnard (Worcestershire), B. M. Duckett (Northamptonshire), H. Z. Finch (Sussex), R. Gibson (Yorkshire), G. T. Griffiths (Lancashire), M. A. H. Hammond (Gloucestershire), C. F. Jackson (Sussex), J. Shaw (Yorkshire), T. W. Shrewsbury (Gloucestershire), D. P. Sibley (Surrey), O. P. Stone (Northamptonshire), J. A. Tattersall (Yorkshire), K. S. Velani (Essex).

Thakor broke a finger in the opening warm-up match, and flew home. He was replaced in the one-day squad by J. Overton (Somerset) and T. Alsop (Hampshire). Stone captained in the Test matches, Duckett in the one-day series.

Coach: T. J. Boon. *Manager:* J. Abrahams. *Batting coach:* W. I. Jefferson. *Bowling coach:* C. E. W. Silverwood. *Strength and conditioning:* S. Bradley. *Team analyst:* S. Seligman. *Psychologist:* J. Bell. *Welfare:* R. Symes.

At Rondebosch, January 23–24, 2013. **Western Cape Invitation XI won by seven wickets.** ‡**England Under-19 XI 132-7 dec** (H. Z. Finch 52) **and 182-5 dec** (D. P. Sibley 54); **Western Cape Invitation XI 117** (M. A. H. Hammond 3-26) **and 201-3** (H. van der Berg 86*). *Western Cape Invitation XI chose from 12 players and England from 15. Seventeen wickets fell on the opening day, when England claimed a narrow first-innings lead, but lost captain Shiv Thakor, who broke a finger attempting a slip catch. England declared a second time to set Western Cape 198 in half a day, which Hayes van der Berg achieved in the nick of time.*

SOUTH AFRICA v ENGLAND

First Under-19 Test

At Cape Town, January 27–30, 2013. England won by 107 runs. Toss: South Africa.

Sometimes, Test matches can be won and lost on treatment tables. Five days after injury had ended Shiv Thakor's tour, his replacement as England captain, Olly Stone, horribly dislocated the ring finger of his bowling hand during catching practice on the second morning. A little pushing and shoving was required at hospital, and he was back on the park just before tea. South Africa were going along nicely until tea, finger strapped, brought himself on as fifth change. With the second delivery after tea, he ripped one past Murray Coetzee's airy on-drive; Vassilli Orros poked the next ball to second slip. Stone finished the innings with four wickets, helping his team to a lead of 119 – the prelude to the first Test win abroad by an England Under-19 side for ten years. South Africa were not helped by having to bat a man short in each innings, after opening bowler Craig Kirsten broke down with a stress fracture in his back on the first morning. England were 19 for three when he left the field, but wriggled off the hook as moisture lifted from the surface and the bowlers began to tire. Kishen Velani and Callum Jackson ran hard, before 17-year-old Ed Barnard, missed on one, scored a freewheeling century from 158 balls. England could afford to lose their last seven wickets for 41 in the second innings, and still set South Africa 271 in 123 overs. Stone took his rightful place with the new ball, and Harry Finch swung it both ways in a rush of three for three before stumps, as England closed in.

Man of the Match: E. Barnard.

Close of play: first day, England Under-19 277-7 (Barnard 107, Hammond 17); second day, England Under-19 24-0 (Tattersall 9, Sibley 10); third day, South Africa Under-19 66-4 (Gous 30, Moore 0).

England Under-19

J. A. Tattersall c Fortuin b Williams	2	– c Williams b Faasen	11
D. P. Sibley c Rosier b Kirsten	0	– c Bedingham b Moore	62
H. Z. Finch lbw b Williams	9	– c Fortuin b Pillay	14
B. M. Duckett c Fortuin b Moore	13	– c Fortuin b Moore	8
K. S. Velani b Williams	49	– c and b Pillay	7
†C. F. Jackson b Williams	43	– c Fortuin b Pillay	0
E. Barnard b Faasen	114	– c Fortuin b Williams	17
*O. P. Stone b Pillay	29	– (11) b Faasen	1
M. A. H. Hammond c Fortuin b Moore	39	– (8) c Gous b Moore	1
G. T. Griffiths lbw b Faasen	4	– not out	12
J. Shaw not out	2	– (9) lbw b Faasen	7
B 1, l-b 4, w 2, n-b 2	9	B 1, l-b 8, w 2	11

1/2 (2) 2/6 (1) 3/14 (3) 4/48 (4)   (119.1 overs) 313
5/89 (5) 6/152 (6) 7/212 (8)
8/302 (7) 9/306 (10) 10/313 (9)

1/34 (1) 2/65 (3)   (75.1 overs) 151
3/93 (4) 4/110 (5)
5/110 (6) 6/112 (2) 7/115 (8)
8/130 (9) 9/150 (7) 10/151 (11)

Williams 29–3–71–4; Kirsten 4–1–12–1; Moore 28.1–7–83–2; Pillay 24.5–5–60–1; Faasen 21–5–52–2; Orros 12–4–29–0; Rosier 1–0–1–0. *Second innings*—Williams 17–8–29–1; Moore 15–3–27–3; Faasen 26.1–6–61–3; Pillay 16–3–23–3; Orros 1–0–2–0.

South Africa Under-19

M. G. Coetzee b Stone	50	– c Duckett b Finch	7
A. G. S. Gous c Jackson b Finch	14	– b Griffiths	83
S. Pillay c Jackson b Finch	4	– lbw b Finch	4
*D. S. Rosier lbw b Hammond	26	– lbw b Finch	3
D. G. Bedingham c Hammond b Stone	21	– c Duckett b Hammond	12
V. L. Orros c Finch b Stone	0	– (7) b Shaw	6
†C. Fortuin c Duckett b Shaw	15	– (8) c Barnard b Griffiths	20
M. J. Faasen c Jackson b Stone	9	– (9) c Jackson b Stone	9
V. P. Moore not out	6	– (6) lbw b Stone	5
L. B. Williams c Finch b Hammond	19	– not out	0
C. M. Kirsten absent hurt		– absent hurt	
B 6, l-b 2, n-b 22	30	B 4, l-b 2, w 2, n-b 6	14

1/40 (2) 2/49 (3) 3/109 (4)   (62 overs) 194
4/120 (1) 5/120 (6) 6/155 (5)
7/165 (7) 8/165 (8) 9/194 (10)

1/19 (1) 2/29 (3)   (67.4 overs) 163
3/34 (4) 4/65 (5)
5/75 (6) 6/82 (7) 7/152 (2)
8/163 (9) 9/163 (8)

Shaw 11–1–53–1; Griffiths 11–3–17–0; Finch 10–1–35–2; Hammond 11–2–25–2; Velani 5–2–14–0; Barnard 2–0–2–0; Stone 11–1–40–4; Sibley 1–1–0–0. *Second innings*—Stone 19–3–49–2; Griffiths 15.4–3–34–2; Finch 8–3–11–3; Shaw 10–3–28–1; Hammond 12–5–30–1; Sibley 3–0–5–0.

Umpires: M. W. Brown and A. Paleker.

SOUTH AFRICA v ENGLAND

Second Under-19 Test

At Paarl, February 3–6, 2013. South Africa won by 67 runs. Toss: South Africa.

If Stone had ever wondered why fast bowlers often end up bearing the haggard look of an Angus Fraser, he was left in no doubt now. Stone was more than eligible for membership of the knackered bowlers' union after a monumental effort with the new ball earned him 11 for 79 – England's best match figures in youth Tests, beating Richard Pearson's 11 for 212 against Australia at Old Trafford in 1991 – yet he could not prevent defeat. After his first two spells in each innings, his figures had stood at 11–7–12–4 and 10–6–6–4, but so spectacularly did South Africa cash in against the change bowlers that they were able to square the series easily. They would have been eight for five inside an hour had the first of three drops been taken. First Vassilli Orros, then the two Test debutants Jan Frylinck and Kagiso Rabada – in a breezy last-wicket stand of 79 – burrowed South Africa out of trouble. England's middle order squandered the friendliest batting conditions of the match, and required Dominic Sibley, put down on 36 and 37, to hold the innings together for almost seven hours, becoming only the second player – after Paul Persaud of West Indies, against Australia at Kingston in 1990-91 – to carry his bat in a youth Test. Stone soon had South Africa writhing on 25 for four. But they did not strike again until Stone returned two hours later, by which time David Bedingham had begun to demoralise the attack. England were given more than a day to attempt 318, on a pitch now taking turn, and came within four overs of seeing out the draw that would have clinched the series. But South Africa were woken from their somnolence by a rollicking from coach Ray Jennings, and Barnard and Stone fell quickly after the second new ball was taken, exposing the tail to Rabada's pace.

Man of the Match: D. G. Bedingham. *Man of the Series:* O. P. Stone.

Close of play: first day, England Under-19 52-3 (Sibley 14, Duckett 0); second day, South Africa Under-19 17-2 (Pillay 7, Rosier 6); third day, England Under-19 31-0 (Tattersall 10, Sibley 10).

South Africa Under-19

M. G. Coetzee b Stone	2	– b Stone 0
A. G. S. Gous c Duckett b Griffiths	0	– b Stone 2
S. Pillay c Finch b Stone	2	– c Duckett b Stone 63
*D. S. Rosier run out	22	– lbw b Stone 6
D. G. Bedingham lbw b Stone	0	– (6) c Finch b Shaw 131
†C. Fortuin c Sibley b Stone	22	– (7) c Finch b Stone 27
V. L. Orros c Duckett b Tattersall	69	– (8) not out 50
V. P. Moore c Duckett b Stone	27	– (5) b Stone 1
M. J. Faasen lbw b Tattersall	1	
J. N. Frylinck not out	33	– (9) c Tattersall b Finch 31
K. Rabada b Barnard	46	
L-b 2, n-b 2	4	B 2, l-b 2, w 1, n-b 4 9

1/2 (1) 2/4 (2) 3/6 (3) 4/8 (5)   (75.5 overs) 228   1/0 (1)   (8 wkts dec, 100 overs) 320
5/47 (4) 6/54 (6) 7/145 (7)   2/5 (2) 3/19 (4)
8/147 (8) 9/149 (9) 10/228 (11)   4/25 (5) 5/119 (3) 6/201 (7)
                                                         7/264 (6) 8/320 (9)

Stone 21–11–31–5; Griffiths 13–4–32–1; Shaw 9–3–17–0; Hammond 10–0–42–0; Barnard 5.5–0–25–1; Sibley 1–0–1–0; Tattersall 11–1–58–2. *Second innings*—Stone 23–9–48–6; Griffiths 16–6–35–0; Shaw 18–2–50–1; Hammond 18–2–64–0; Finch 11–1–52–1; Velani 3–0–13–0; Sibley 2–0–7–0; Tattersall 6–1–29–0; Barnard 3–0–18–0.

England Under-19

J. A. Tattersall b Rabada	2	– c Fortuin b Pillay 63
D. P. Sibley not out	112	– c Bedingham b Moore 23
H. Z. Finch c Bedingham b Frylinck	1	– c Faasen b Rosier 46
K. S. Velani c Rosier b Pillay	25	– c Frylinck b Moore 15
†B. M. Duckett c Fortuin b Pillay	29	– lbw b Rosier 0
C. F. Jackson lbw b Faasen	18	– c Fortuin b Orros 13
E. Barnard lbw b Orros	11	– lbw b Faasen 28
M. A. H. Hammond c Gous b Orros	6	– c Rosier b Faasen 26
J. Shaw c Pillay b Orros	0	– (10) not out 3
G. T. Griffiths lbw b Faasen	5	– (11) c Rosier b Rabada 0
*O. P. Stone lbw b Faasen	7	– (9) c Fortuin b Rabada 0
B 6, l-b 5, w 1, n-b 3	15	B 15, l-b 4, w 9, n-b 5 33

1/6 (1) 2/7 (3) 3/48 (4) 4/109 (5)   (104.4 overs) 231   1/63 (2) 2/143 (3)   (104.2 overs) 250
5/150 (6) 6/191 (7) 7/207 (8)   3/166 (4) 4/167 (5)
8/207 (9) 9/215 (10) 10/231 (11)   5/180 (1) 6/191 (6) 7/240 (7)
                                                         8/242 (9) 9/250 (8) 10/250 (11)

Frylinck 9–3–30–1; Rabada 16–1–34–1; Pillay 13–5–10–2; Moore 14–2–48–0; Faasen 35.4–9–59–3; Orros 17–1–39–3. *Second innings*—Rabada 21.2–3–43–2; Frylinck 5–1–9–0; Faasen 24–9–48–2; Orros 16–1–44–1; Moore 10–1–24–2; Rosier 25–6–58–2; Pillay 3–0–5–1.

Umpires: M. W. Brown and B. P. Jele.
Series referee: D. Govindjee.

At Franschhoek, February 10, 2013. **Western Cape Invitation XI v England Under-19 XI. Abandoned.**

50-over series

At Paarl, February 13, 2013. **South Africa Under-19 won by seven wickets. England Under-19 221-9** (50 overs) (B. M. Duckett 51); ‡**South Africa Under-19 223-3** (46 overs) (C. Fortuin 75). *MoM:* C. Fortuin. *England were kept grounded by the bustling Lizaad Williams, whose six-over opening spell included three wickets and 30 dot balls. Ben Duckett, captain for the one-day series, improved matters with a steady fifty, but went down with cramp 13 overs into the reply, and was forced to hand wicketkeeping duties to Tom Alsop. By that stage, Clyde Fortuin – who led partnerships of 74, 71 and 36 – was well on the way to securing South Africa's victory.*

At Rondebosch, February 15, 2013. **South Africa Under-19 won by 12 runs. South Africa Under-19 241-9** (50 overs) (M. G. Coetzee 58); ‡**England Under-19 229-9** (50 overs). *MoM:* M. G. Coetzee. *England gambled on taking early wickets, but were frustrated by opener Murray Coetzee's 58 from 90 balls. They then scored too slowly until Jamie Overton struck 48 from 46, but his threat was ended by Corbin Bosch, son of the late Test bowler Tertius.*

At Paarl, February 16, 2013. **South Africa Under-19 won by ten runs. South Africa Under-19 270-8** (50 overs) (G. Oldfield 82); ‡**England Under-19 260-9** (50 overs) (J. A. Tattersall 83, J. Shaw 52). *MoM:* G. Oldfield. *England were undone by Greg Oldfield, who was keen to Dilscoop the quicker bowlers, and Bosch, whose powerful 23 from eight deliveries ended only when he slipped trying to regain his ground; they helped South Africa plunder 97 from their last ten overs on a plumb pitch. Jonathan Tattersall (83 from 76 balls) and Josh Shaw (52 from 46) injected some Yorkshire gusto to the last third of England's innings, but the top order had been too easily smothered.*

At Stellenbosch, February 19, 2013. **South Africa Under-19 won by six wickets** (D/L). ‡**England Under-19 205-8** (49 overs) (C. F. Jackson 62, K. S. Velani 78; N. Sigwili 4-34); **South Africa Under-19 157-4** (37.4 overs) (C. Fortuin 62). *MoM:* N. Sigwili. *Callum Jackson and Kishen Velani put on 133 in 32 overs for the second wicket, but then Nqazabini Sigwili, a whippy 17-year-old left-armer from the Eastern Cape, derailed England with four wickets in five overs at the death. Rain and bad light upset England's rhythm, and cut 11 overs from South Africa's reply; when play resumed, their requirement was adjusted to 33 from a further five, which they achieved with eight balls in hand. Overton pulled a muscle while batting, and bowled a maiden before limping off.*

At Cape Town, February 21, 2013. **South Africa Under-19 won by nine wickets. England Under-19 210-8** (50 overs) (D. P. Sibley 84, E. Barnard 53); ‡**South Africa Under-19 211-1** (33.3 overs) (C. Fortuin 99, M. G. Coetzee 103*). *MoM:* M. G. Coetzee. *MoS:* C. Fortuin. *England had competed gamely against a stronger side until now – but this was a pummelling. Alsop and Velani were bounced out in the first four balls by Kagiso Rabada, and though Dominic Sibley and Ed Barnard responded with a stand of 136, England's last 15 overs produced just one boundary – an edge past the wicketkeeper. South Africa's openers feasted on anything short as they crashed 199 inside 31 overs, before Fortuin pulled to midwicket on 99. Shortly afterwards, Coetzee became the only batsman to score a century in the series, then hit the winning runs to secure the whitewash.*

DOMESTIC CRICKET IN SOUTH AFRICA, 2012-13

Colin Bryden

The two most successful domestic teams in 2012-13 were managed by coaches representing the new order in South Africa, both in their first season in charge.

Paul Adams, the unorthodox spin bowler who in 1995-96 became South Africa's youngest Test cricketer – and only their second non-white player – steered the Cape Cobras to the Sunfoil Series (previously SuperSport) four-day title. Geoffrey Toyana, meanwhile, one of the first black Africans to play first-class cricket after the unification of the South African game in 1991, guided the underachieving Lions to the lucrative Ram Slam Twenty20 Challenge title, plus second place in the four-day competition. The Cobras and the Lions shared the Momentum One-Day Cup, after two attempts to play the final were foiled by rain.

Adams was credited with creating a more relaxed atmosphere in the **Cape Cobras** camp, working with captain Justin Ontong. In the frequent absence of Test seamers Vernon Philander and Rory Kleinveldt, 33-year-old Johann Louw led the attack with distinction, taking 45 wickets at 17. He was backed up by another old hand, Justin Kemp, and 22-year-old Beuran Hendricks. South Africa Under-19 fast bowler Lizaad Williams showed promise. The left-hander Stiaan van Zyl was the mainstay of the batting, topping the tournament averages with 673 runs at 61, while openers Alistair Gray and Andrew Puttick had solid seasons.

Former Test batsman Neil McKenzie hailed Toyana's "excellent man-management" of the **Lions**. "He was honest and he gave responsibility to the players," said McKenzie – at the age of 37 the leading run-scorer in the Sunfoil Series, with 776 at 51. Sound batting and a balanced attack were hallmarks of their season. The precocious Quinton de Kock – who turned 20 in December – Temba Bavuma and Stephen Cook also passed 500 runs, and Cook led the side in nine matches; the appointed captain, Alviro Petersen, was injured in the opening game, then stepped down because of national calls, though he took charge for the successful Twenty20 campaign. In Chris Morris and G. C. Viljoen, the Lions – based in Johannesburg – had two of the country's most promising fast bowlers, while leg-spinner Imran Tahir put the disappointment of a poor Australian tour behind him with 37 first-class wickets at 22.

The Durban-based **Dolphins** finished third in the Sunfoil Series, largely thanks to the fast-medium bowling of Kyle Abbott, the competition's leading wicket-taker with 49 at 15. They failed to contend in limited-overs cricket. In the Eastern Cape, the **Warriors** unearthed an exciting talent in Aya Gqamane, a slightly built fast bowler who headed the four-day averages with 31 wickets at 14. The Warriors finished second on the Twenty20 log but missed out on the final, beaten by third-placed Titans in a play-off. The medium-fast Andrew Birch was outstanding in all three competitions.

The **Knights** had a frustrating season. Three first-class and three one-day matches were rained off – only one of them at their Bloemfontein headquarters. Their thin resources were stretched by injuries, notably to captain Morne van Wyk, who missed all but one game, and national calls for Dean Elgar and Ryan McLaren. The **Titans**, normally one of the strongest franchises, made a dismal defence of their four-day title, losing eight and winning none. Their bowling lacked penetration, and no batsman recorded a first-class century, though they had six in the one-day cup, where they finished third. The Titans redeemed their season in financial terms by reaching the Twenty20 final, and thus a place in the 2013 Champions League.

In the amateur provincial competitions, **Gauteng** took the first-class title, **Border** the 50-over final and **Free State** the Twenty20 league. The outstanding performance came from 20-year-old seamer Marcello Piedt of **South Western Districts**, who took seven for six on first-class debut and 59 wickets in all, a record for a South African's first season.

FIRST-CLASS AVERAGES, 2012-13

BATTING (650 runs, average 30.00)

	M	I	NO	R	HS	100	Avge	Ct/St
P. J. van Biljon (*Free State*)........	9	17	5	715	145*	1	59.58	7
†S. van Zyl (*Cape Cobras/SA Inv. XI*)	10	14	1	725	148	2	55.76	4
H. E. van der Dussen (*North West*) ..	12	19	0	1,034	166	4	54.42	7
S. A. Engelbrecht (*W. Province*)	10	16	1	789	214*	2	52.60	2
N. D. McKenzie (*Lions*)...........	10	19	4	776	125*	2	51.73	7
†D. A. Hendricks (*Lions/Gauteng*)...	14	23	3	943	176*	1	47.15	18/1
R. C. C. Canning (*Boland*).........	13	21	3	848	121*	4	47.11	30
†R. R. Rossouw (*Knights/Free State*) .	9	17	1	751	118	2	46.93	15
C. G. Williams (*Namibia*)	9	17	2	687	122*	3	45.80	6
G. L. van Buuren (*Titans/Northerns*)	13	20	1	848	142	3	44.63	5
†S. J. Erwee (*KwaZulu-Natal Inland*) .	12	22	3	783	90*	0	41.21	6
R. S. Second (*Knights/Free State*) ..	18	34	3	1,275	210	5	41.12	58/2
G. N. Addicott (*SW Districts*)	13	22	2	816	145	1	40.80	5
R. D. McMillan (*SW Districts*)	12	21	0	848	125	1	40.38	16
†D. P. Conway (*Gauteng*)	13	20	0	782	142	2	39.10	8
†V. B. van Jaarsveld (*Dol./SA Inv. XI*)	10	17	0	659	160	2	38.76	14
†N. Hendrie (*KwaZulu-Natal Inland*) .	12	22	2	772	115	1	38.60	9
D. J. Jacobs (*Warriors/SA Inv. XI*) ..	10	20	3	650	104	2	38.23	9
S. Burger (*Gauteng*)..............	13	20	2	686	88	0	38.11	20
A. K. Kruger (*Griqualand West*)	12	21	2	722	92	0	38.00	7
W. R. Landsdale (*Griqualand West*) .	13	22	1	769	203*	2	36.61	23
P. J. Malan (*Titans/Northerns*)	15	26	1	910	191	2	36.40	6
S. von Berg (*Titans/Northerns*)	15	25	5	721	100*	1	36.05	7
†A. Jacobs (*Warriors/E. Province*)...	13	22	2	688	105	1	34.40	11
†M. C. Kleinveldt (*Western Province*)	13	22	2	680	84	0	34.00	6
M. L. Price (*Warriors/E. Province*) .	13	25	3	670	106	2	30.45	4
†P. Botha (*Knights/Free State*)......	16	26	3	694	102*	1	30.17	21

BOWLING (35 wickets, average 25.00)

	Style	O	M	R	W	BB	5I	Avge
K. J. Abbott (*Dolphins/SA Inv. XI/SA*).....	RFM	328.3	88	929	65	8-45	4	14.29
A. C. R. Birch (*Warriors*)	RFM	239.1	57	643	40	8-30	1	16.07
M. N. Piedt (*South Western Districts*)	RFM	307.4	73	999	59	7-6	4	16.93
B. J. Pelser (*Lions/North West*)............	RM	237.5	75	598	35	5-38	1	17.08
B. E. Hendricks (*Cobras/WP/SA Inv. XI*).....	LFM	307.5	64	1,026	60	6-26	4	17.10
A. Gqamane (*Warriors/Border*)	RFM	174.1	23	634	37	7-24	3	17.13
S. W. Liebisch (*Titans/Easterns*)	RFM	276.1	94	697	39	5-32	1	17.87
G. J-P. Kruger (*Lions/North West*)	RFM	259.3	54	778	43	6-55	3	18.09
S. Khan (*Gauteng*).....................	RFM	235	53	711	39	5-33	1	18.23
J. Louw (*Cape Cobras/Boland*)	RFM	305	77	901	49	7-42	3	18.38
G. I. Hume (*Gauteng*)	RFM	241.1	64	768	41	5-27	3	18.73
C. Viljoen (*Namibia*)...................	RM	302.4	63	867	41	6-43	2	21.14
W. E. Bell (*Eastern Province*).............	RFM	280	77	945	44	7-56	2	21.47
P. J. N. Jeftha (*Boland*)	RFM	207.5	36	752	35	5-70	1	21.48
G. A. Vries (*Free State*).................	RFM	299.3	86	805	37	5-26	1	21.75
Imran Tahir (*Lions*)	LBG	254.3	39	827	37	7-64	3	22.35
C. H. Raubenheimer (*Boland*)	LBG	393.2	59	1,242	55	7-71	5	22.58
E. Leie (*Gauteng/Lions*)	LBG	392.5	65	1,280	56	5-41	3	22.85
L. Klazinga (*Namibia*)...................	RFM	232.5	41	853	37	5-52	3	23.05
D. Klein (*Lions/North West*).............	LFM	317.5	54	1,122	47	5-1	2	23.87
G. R. Rabie (*Warriors/SW Districts*).......	RFM	429	104	1,244	52	5-47	3	23.92

Note: Averages include CSA Provincial Three-Day Challenge matches played in Namibia.

SUNFOIL SERIES, 2012-13

	Played	Won	Lost	Drawn	Bonus points Batting	Bowling	Points
Cape Cobras.	10	6	2	1†	31.32	35	131.32
Lions	10	5	2	3	30.74	36	116.74
Dolphins.	10	4	3	2†	29.56	31	105.56
Warriors.	10	4	4	1†	19.00	36	100.00
Knights.	10	2	2	3‡	29.16	24	88.16
Titans	10	0	8	2	22.68	30	49.68*

† *Plus one match abandoned.*　　‡ *Plus three matches abandoned.*　　* *3pts deducted for over-rate.*

Outright win = 10pts; abandoned = 5pts. Bonus points awarded for the first 100 overs of each team's first innings. One batting point was awarded for the first 150 runs and 0.02 of a point for every subsequent run. One bowling point was awarded for the third wicket taken and for every subsequent two.

At Kimberley, September 20–23, 2012. **Drawn.** ‡**Knights 455** (R. T. Bailey 220, M. N. van Wyk 133; N. E. Mbhalati 6-98) **and 246** (N. E. Mbhalati 5-50); **Titans 300** (R. McLaren 5-57, Q. Friend 5-77) **and 159-4**. *Knights 9.68pts, Titans 7pts. Ryan Bailey's maiden double-hundred remained the highest score of the season. He added 259 for Knights' fifth wicket with Morne van Wyk. Ethy Mbhalati took 11-148.*

At Potchefstroom, September 20–23, 2012. **Cape Cobras won by ten wickets.** ‡**Cape Cobras 543** (A. G. Puttick 194; Imran Tahir 5-176) **and 7-0**; **Lions 210 and 339** (Q. de Kock 194; D. L. Piedt 5-113). *Cape Cobras 18.54pts, Lions 2.2pts. Openers on both sides – Andrew Puttick and Quinton de Kock – made 194; de Kock's came as Lions followed on, and took him past 1,000 first-class runs in his 21st innings, the joint-third-fastest by a South African. Lions captain Alviro Petersen could not bat in either innings after breaking his left hand in the field, and was out for three weeks. Imran Tahir's figures in Cobras' first innings were 47–1–176–5.*

At Paarl, September 27–30, 2012. **Cape Cobras v Knights. Abandoned.** *Cape Cobras 5pts, Knights 5pts.*

At Johannesburg, September 27–30, 2012. **Lions won by 53 runs. Lions 265 and 238;** ‡**Dolphins 263 and 187** (C. H. Morris 8-44). *Lions 17.3pts, Dolphins 7.26pts. Chris Morris took 12-101, including 8-44, a Lions record, to end Dolphins' pursuit of 241; from 160-4 on the final morning they lost six for 27.*

At Port Elizabeth, September 27–30, 2012. **Warriors won by 161 runs. Warriors 276 and 353-5 dec** (M. L. Price 105, D. J. Jacobs 103); ‡**Titans 216** (B. D. Walters 5-57) **and 252** (G. R. Rabie 5-61). *Warriors 17.52pts, Titans 6.32pts. Michael Price and Davey Jacobs opened with 201 in Warriors' second innings to set up their first win in nine months, against the defending champions.*

At East London, October 4–7, 2012. **Drawn.** ‡**Dolphins 296 and 220; Warriors 154** (K. J. Abbott 6-64) **and 205-7.** *Warriors 5.08pts, Dolphins 7.92pts. Bad light spoiled Dolphins' victory hopes.*

At Paarl, October 11–14, 2012. **Cape Cobras won by 18 runs.** ‡**Cape Cobras 262 and 297-8 dec** (A. J. A. Gray 125); **Warriors 266 and 275** (D. J. Jacobs 104). *Cape Cobras 17.24pts, Warriors 7.32pts. Warriors lost their last six wickets for 30 after threatening a target of 294.*

At Pietermaritzburg, October 11–14, 2012. **Dolphins v Knights. Abandoned.** *Dolphins 5pts, Knights 5pts.*

At Pietermaritzburg, October 18–21, 2012. **Drawn.** ‡**Dolphins 310** (R. K. Kleinveldt 5-54); **Cape Cobras 66-0.** *Dolphins 3.82pts, Cape Cobras 3pts. Weather permitted only 87.2 overs.*

At East London, October 21–24, 2012. **Warriors v Knights. Abandoned.** *Warriors 5pts, Knights 5pts. Knights were washed out for the third successive match, all away from home.*

At Cape Town, December 20–22, 2012. **Cape Cobras won by ten wickets. Titans 192** (J. M. Kemp 5-45) **and 301** (J. Louw 5-89); ‡**Cape Cobras 476-8 dec** (A. G. Puttick 126) **and 21-0**. *Cape Cobras 18.98pts, Titans 2.84pts. Titans' first five wickets raised 47; Cobras' first five 402.*

At Bloemfontein, December 20–23, 2012. **Knights won by eight wickets. Dolphins 221 and 391;** ‡**Knights 498** (J. J. van der Wath 154) **and 118-2**. *Knights 19.38pts, Dolphins 5.42pts. Shadley van*

Schalkwyk (80) and Malusi Siboto (41*) put on 104 for Knights' last wicket in their first innings, ensuring a decisive lead.

At Johannesburg, December 20–22, 2012. **Warriors won by ten wickets. ‡Lions 315 and 59** (A. Gqamane 7-24); **Warriors 235 and 140-0.** *Warriors 16.7pts, Lions 8.3pts. Lions' 59 was the lowest total of the tournament; Aya Gqamane finished with 11-70 on Warriors debut. Christiaan Jonker hit 68 in 63 balls, with five sixes and five fours, in Warriors' first innings.*

At Durban, December 27–29, 2012. **Dolphins won by an innings and 247 runs. Dolphins 548-6 dec** (V. B. van Jaarsveld 160, C. Chetty 101*); **‡Titans 167 and 134** (K. J. Abbott 5-40). *Dolphins 18.66pts, Titans 2.34pts. Dolphins' 548-6 was the competition's highest total, and their Nos 2 to 7 all reached 50; Cody Chetty hit 101* in 114 balls. Titans keeper Heino Kuhn conceded no byes. It was the second-biggest innings win in SuperSport/Sunfoil Series history – after Dolphins' innings-and-325-run defeat by the same opponents ten months earlier.*

At Potchefstroom, December 27–30, 2012. **Drawn. Lions 348** (J. J. van der Wath 5-63) **and 313-8 dec** (T. Bavuma 132); **‡Knights 293-9 dec** (G. J-P. Kruger 6-77) **and 187-3.** *Lions 8.96pts, Knights 7.86pts. Imran Tahir of Lions was later banned for one match for abusive language.*

At East London, December 27–28, 2012. **Cape Cobras won by an innings and 50 runs. Warriors 107** (B. E. Hendricks 5-34) **and 84** (J. Louw 7-42); **‡Cape Cobras 241** (B. D. Walters 6-64). *Cape Cobras 16.82pts, Warriors 4pts. Johann Louw took a career-best 7-42 in 8.3 overs, including four in nine balls, as Warriors collapsed for the second time in a two-day defeat.*

At Durban, January 3–6, 2013. **Lions won by 252 runs. Lions 248 and 322-4 dec** (N. D. McKenzie 125*); **‡Dolphins 155** (Imran Tahir 5-42) **and 163** (Imran Tahir 7-64). *Lions 16.96pts, Dolphins 5.1pts. Imran Tahir took 12-106, a record fourth return of ten or more in all SuperSport/Sunfoil matches, to bring about Lions' biggest win by runs.*

At Centurion, January 3–5, 2013. **Warriors won by ten wickets. ‡Titans 222 and 204** (A. Gqamane 6-40); **Warriors 413** (A. Jacobs 105) **and 14-0.** *Warriors 18.76pts, Titans 5.44pts. A ninth-wicket stand of 129 between Simon Harmer (66*) and Gqamane, who followed 86 in 89 balls with six wickets, gave Warriors an impregnable advantage.*

At Cape Town, January 10–12, 2013. **Lions won by eight wickets. Cape Cobras 224** (Z. de Bruyn 5-39) **and 169; ‡Lions 270 and 125-2.** *Lions 17.4pts, Cape Cobras 6.48pts. The umpires changed the ball during Lions' run-chase, suspecting Cobras had tampered with it, though captain Justin Ontong was later cleared. De Kock, invited by the umpires to pick a replacement, chose a much older ball, leading to an altercation in which he pushed fielder Alistair Gray; de Kock was later banned for one match. Earlier, while keeping wicket, he had held four catches in each innings.*

At Benoni, January 10–13, 2013. **Knights won by ten wickets. ‡Titans 335 and 181** (D. du Preez 5-53); **Knights 475** (R. S. Second 210, D. du Preez 118) **and 42-0.** *Knights 17.1pts, Titans 7.6pts. The only two double-hundreds in this tournament came for Knights v Titans: following Bailey in Kimberley in September, Rudi Second scored his second double and added 253 for the eighth wicket with Dillon du Preez. It was Titans' fifth successive defeat.*

At Cape Town, January 17–19, 2013. **Dolphins won by 15 runs. Dolphins 174** (B. E. Hendricks 5-47) **and 214; ‡Cape Cobras 206 and 167** (K. J. Abbott 8-45). *Dolphins 15.48pts, Cape Cobras 6.12pts. Needing 182 in the fourth innings, Cobras were bowled out by Kyle Abbott's career-best 8-45; in all, he took 12-96. After Cobras had led the table from the start of the season, their second defeat in a row cut their lead to a fraction of a point.*

At Bloemfontein, January 17–19, 2013. **Warriors won by ten wickets. ‡Knights 268** (R. R. Rossouw 100) **and 106** (A. C. R. Birch 8-30); **Warriors 281 and 94-0.** *Warriors 17.62pts, Knights 7.36pts. Rilee Rossouw hit 100 in 108 balls. Andrew Birch's career-best 8-30 was the best return of the tournament, and the second-best in all SuperSport/Sunfoil matches, and helped Warriors complete their third ten-wicket win of the season.*

At Johannesburg, January 17–20, 2013. **Drawn. Lions 303; ‡Titans 120 and 137-7.** *Lions 8.06pts, Titans 4pts. Rain and bad light saved Titans from a sixth defeat.*

At Benoni, January 24–26, 2013. **Lions won by six wickets. ‡Titans 195 and 187** (G. C. Viljoen 6-24); **Lions 202 and 184-4.** *Lions 16.04pts, Titans 5.9pts. Lions overtook Cobras at the top of the table with two rounds to go.*

At Durban, January 31–February 2, 2013. **Dolphins won by nine wickets. Warriors 92** (M. Shezi 5-28) **and 198**; ‡**Dolphins 245 and 47-1**. *Dolphins 16.9pts, Warriors 4pts. Warriors were bowled out in double figures for the second time in six innings, with five catches for keeper Daryn Smit.*

At Kimberley, January 31–February 3, 2013. **Drawn.** ‡**Knights 348 and 257**; **Lions 219 and 108-2**. *Knights 8.96pts, Lions 6.38pts. Lions trailed Cobras by ten points after a rain-affected draw.*

At Benoni, January 31–February 2, 2013. **Cape Cobras won by nine wickets. Titans 194 and 195**; ‡**Cape Cobras 373** (S. van Zyl 123) **and 20-1**. *Cape Cobras 19.08pts, Titans 5.88pts. Cobras regained first place with their second three-day win over Titans.*

At Bloemfontein, February 7–9, 2013. **Cape Cobras won by ten wickets. Knights 191 and 227** (J. Louw 5-70); ‡**Cape Cobras 416-6 dec** (R. E. Levi 121, S. van Zyl 148, J. L. Ontong 109) **and 4-0**. *Cape Cobras 20.06pts, Knights 2.82pts. Cobras' third ten-wicket win of the season made sure of the title. Stiaan van Zyl and Ontong added 200 for their third wicket to set up a 225-run lead, which Knights barely cleared.*

At Centurion, February 7–9, 2013. **Dolphins won by 393 runs.** ‡**Dolphins 456** (V. B. van Jaarsveld 101) **and 224-5 dec**; **Titans 218 and 69** (K. A. Maharaj 5-11). *Dolphins 20pts, Titans 5.36pts. On the opening day Vaughn van Jaarsveld hit 101 in 110 balls. Slow left-armer Keshav Maharaj clinched victory, bowling out Titans for 69 on the third day, with figures of 5-11. It was the largest victory by runs in the tournament's history, and ensured that defending champions Titans finished with eight defeats and no wins.*

At Port Elizabeth, February 7–10, 2013. **Lions won by 125 runs.** ‡**Lions 157 and 367** (A. N. Petersen 119, N. D. McKenzie 104); **Warriors 135 and 264**. *Lions 15.14pts, Warriors 4pts. Warriors keeper Adrian McLaren held five catches in Lions' first innings and four in their second, when Alviro Petersen and Neil McKenzie, who scored a record 25th SuperSport/Sunfoil century, put on 222 for the third wicket. But it was too late for Lions to claim more than second place.*

CHAMPIONS

Currie Cup			
1889-90	Transvaal	1950-51	Transvaal
1890-91	Kimberley	1951-52	Natal
1892-93	Western Province	1952-53	Western Province
1893-94	Western Province	1954-55	Natal
1894-95	Transvaal	1955-56	Western Province
1896-97	Western Province	1958-59	Transvaal
1897-98	Western Province	1959-60	Natal
1902-03	Transvaal	1960-61	Natal
1903-04	Transvaal	1962-63	Natal
1904-05	Transvaal	1963-64	Natal
1906-07	Transvaal	1965-66	Natal
1908-09	Western Province		Transvaal
1910-11	Natal	1966-67	Natal
1912-13	Natal	1967-68	Natal
1920-21	Western Province	1968-69	Transvaal
1921-22	Transvaal	1969-70	Transvaal
	Natal		Western Province
	Western Province	1970-71	Transvaal
1923-24	Transvaal	1971-72	Transvaal
1925-26	Transvaal	1972-73	Transvaal
1926-27	Transvaal	1973-74	Natal
1929-30	Transvaal	1974-75	Western Province
1931-32	Western Province	1975-76	Natal
1933-34	Natal	1976-77	Natal
1934-35	Transvaal	1977-78	Western Province
1936-37	Natal	1978-79	Transvaal
1937-38	Natal	1979-80	Transvaal
	Transvaal	1980-81	Natal
1946-47	Natal	1981-82	Western Province
1947-48	Natal	1982-83	Transvaal
		1983-84	Transvaal

1984-85	Transvaal	
1985-86	Western Province	
1986-87	Transvaal	
1987-88	Transvaal	
1988-89	Eastern Province	
1989-90	{ Eastern Province	
	Western Province	
Castle Cup		
1990-91	Western Province	
1991-92	Eastern Province	
1992-93	Orange Free State	
1993-94	Orange Free State	
1994-95	Natal	
1995-96	Western Province	
SuperSport Series		
1996-97	Natal	
1997-98	Free State	

1998-99	Western Province	
1999-2000	Gauteng	
2000-01	Western Province	
2001-02	KwaZulu-Natal	
2002-03	Easterns	
2003-04	Western Province	
2004-05	{ Dolphins	
	Eagles	
2005-06	{ Dolphins	
	Titans	
2006-07	Titans	
2007-08	Eagles	
2008-09	Titans	
2009-10	Cape Cobras	
2010-11	Cape Cobras	
2011-12	Titans	
Sunfoil Series		
2012-13	Cape Cobras	

Transvaal/Gauteng have won the title outright 25 times, Natal/KwaZulu-Natal 21, Western Province 18, Cape Cobras, Orange Free State/Free State and Titans 3, Eastern Province 2, Eagles, Easterns and Kimberley 1. The title has been shared seven times as follows: Transvaal 4, Natal and Western Province 3, Dolphins 2, Eagles, Eastern Province and Titans 1.

From 1971-72 to 1990-91, the non-white South African Cricket Board of Control (later the South African Cricket Board) organised its own three-day tournaments. These are now recognised as first-class (see *Wisden 2006*, pages 79–80). A list of winners appears in *Wisden 2007*, page 1346.

CSA PROVINCIAL THREE-DAY CHALLENGE, 2012-13

	Played	Won	Lost	Drawn	Bonus points Batting	Bonus points Bowling	Points
Gauteng	13	7	1	5	50.22	52	172.22
North West	13	6	0	7	49.04	49	158.04
Boland	13	5	4	3†	38.86	47	141.86
South Western Districts	13	6	3	4	32.94	46	138.94
Free State	13	5	2	6	37.00	50	137.00
Northerns	13	5	2	6	33.60	43	126.60
Western Province	13	4	4	3	37.36	46	122.36*
Easterns	13	4	4	5	32.26	50	120.26§
Eastern Province	13	3	6	4	34.92	46	110.92
Border	13	3	4	5†	25.62	51	112.62
Griqualand West	13	2	5	6	27.64	49	96.64
KwaZulu-Natal	13	3	4	6	26.88	41	95.88§
KwaZulu-Natal Inland	13	2	5	6	34.34	39	93.34
Namibia	13	0	9	4	26.22	41	67.22

† *Plus one match tied.* * *1pt deducted for slow over-rate.* § *2pts deducted for slow over-rate.*

Outright win = 10pts; tied = 6pts. Bonus points awarded for the first 100 overs of each team's first innings. One batting point was awarded for the first 150 runs and 0.02 of a point for every subsequent run. One bowling point was awarded for the third wicket taken and for every subsequent two.

At Paarl, October 4–6, 2012. **Drawn. Boland 332** (T. W. R. Cloete 121; M. Shezi 6-73); ‡**KwaZulu-Natal 266-9**. *Boland 8.64pts, KwaZulu-Natal 7.32pts.*

At Port Elizabeth (Union), October 4–6, 2012. **Eastern Province won by ten wickets. KwaZulu-Natal Inland 189 and 285**; ‡**Eastern Province 461-7 dec** (M. B. A. Smith 155) **and 18-0**. *Eastern Province 20.48pts, KwaZulu-Natal Inland 3.78pts.*

At Kimberley, October 4–6, 2012. **Drawn. North West 448-8 dec** (H. E. van der Dussen 166, B. J. Pelser 136) **and 206-4 dec**; ‡**Griqualand West 355-8 dec** (W. R. Landsdale 140). *Griqualand West 6.1pts, North West 7.62pts. Rassie van der Dussen and Brett Pelser added 239 for North West's fourth wicket.*

At Cape Town, October 4–6, 2012. **Drawn. Border 156** (T. Muller 5-71) **and 214-8**; ‡**Western Province 352** (M. Q. Adams 147). *Western Province 9.04pts, Border 5.12pts.*

At East London, October 11–13, 2012. **Tied. Border 210 and 210** (C. H. Raubenheimer 6-86); ‡**Boland 219** (G. V. J. Koopman 5-36) **and 201** (D. L. Brown 6-32). *Border 12.2pts, Boland 12.38pts. This was only the fifth first-class tie in South Africa, and the first for 27 years.*

At Bloemfontein (OFS University), October 11–13, 2012. **Drawn. Free State 115** (G. I. Hume 5-27) **and 319**; ‡**Gauteng 208** (D. Olivier 5-68) **and 165-5**. *Free State 4pts, Gauteng 6.16pts.*

At Windhoek (United), October 11–13, 2012. **Easterns won by four wickets. Namibia 326-9 dec** (C. G. Williams 108, N. R. P. Scholtz 114*) **and 60**; ‡**Easterns 217** (L. Klazinga 5-72) **and 170-6** (L. Klazinga 5-65). *Easterns 16.34pts, Namibia 8.52pts. Shaun Liebisch had figures of 7.1-6-1-4 in Namibia's collapse for 60.*

At Rondebosch, October 11–13, 2012. **Western Province won by ten wickets.** ‡**KwaZulu-Natal Inland 239 and 161** (B. E. Hendricks 6-26); **Western Province 373-6 dec and 30-0.** *Western Province 18.4pts, KwaZulu-Natal Inland 4.78pts. This was the first first-class match in Rondebosch, and was staged at the Wally Wilson Oval.*

At Chatsworth, October 18–20, 2012. **Drawn.** ‡**Eastern Province 150 and 66-2**; **KwaZulu-Natal 123** (S. S. N. Nqweni 7-48). *KwaZulu-Natal 4pts, Eastern Province 5pts.*

At Potchefstroom, October 18–20, 2012. **Drawn. Free State 394 and 179-5 dec**; ‡**North West 146 and 320-9** (N. J. van den Bergh 118*, D. R. Deeb 106). *North West 3pts, Free State 8.68pts. North West's second innings slumped to 88-7 before Nos 8 and 9 Nicky van den Bergh and Dale Deeb added 212, enabling them to hang on for a draw, still 107 behind with one wicket left.*

At Pretoria, October 18–20, 2012. **Drawn.** ‡**Northerns 327-9 dec** (S. von Berg 100*) **and 58-2**; **Griqualand West 198** (S. von Berg 6-57). *Northerns 8.54pts, Griqualand West 5.96pts.*

At Oudtshoorn, October 18–19, 2012. **South Western Districts won by an innings and 54 runs. Western Province 141 and 34** (M. N. Piedt 7-6); ‡**South Western Districts 229** (T. Muller 6-54). *South Western Districts 16.58pts, Western Province 3pts. Marcello Piedt, aged 20, had figures of 10–5–6–7, the best on first-class debut in South Africa for 52 years, to wrap up the match in two days. Western Province's highest score in a total of 34 was 18 by No. 10 Beuran Hendricks, which rescued them from 15-9.*

At Port Elizabeth, October 25–27, 2012. **Boland won by four wickets. Eastern Province 118 and 234**; ‡**Boland 162 and 194-6**. *Boland 15.24pts, Eastern Province 4pts.*

At Benoni, October 25–27, 2012. **Drawn. Free State 179** (S. W. Liebisch 5-32) **and 233-7 dec**; ‡**Easterns 188 and 70-3**. *Easterns 5.76pts, Free State 5.58pts.*

At Chatsworth, October 25–27, 2012. **Drawn. KwaZulu-Natal 170** (A. Gqamane 5-26) v ‡**Border.** *KwaZulu-Natal 1.4pts, Border 4pts.*

At Windhoek (United), October 25–27, 2012. **Drawn. Griqualand West 190 and 401-9 dec**; ‡**Namibia 241 and 249-9**. *Namibia 6.82pts, Griqualand West 5.8pts.*

At Paarl, November 1–3, 2012. **Boland won by an innings and 92 runs. Boland 403** (K. D. Petersen 187); ‡**South Western Districts 172 and 139** (O. J. Erasmus 5-21). *Boland 19.5pts, South Western Districts 4.44pts.*

At Johannesburg (Sir Lionel Phillips Park), November 1–3, 2012. **Drawn.** ‡**Gauteng 269** (S. von Berg 6-64) **and 300-5 dec** (O. A. Ramela 142, D. P. Conway 110); **Northerns 302 and 90-1**. *Gauteng 7.38pts, Northerns 8.04pts. This was the first first-class match at this ground.*

At Potchefstroom, November 1–3, 2012. **North West won by eight wickets. Easterns 175 and 183**; ‡**North West 291 and 69-2**. *North West 17.82pts, Easterns 3.5pts.*

At Cape Town, November 1–3, 2012. **Eastern Province won by ten wickets. Western Province 138** (S. S. N. Nqweni 6-44) **and 282**; ‡**Eastern Province 386-9 dec** (M. L. Price 106) **and 35-0**. *Eastern Province 19.14pts, Western Province 3pts.*

At Bloemfontein, November 8–10, 2012. **Drawn. Free State 302** (P. J. van Biljon 145*) **and 235-2 dec**; ‡**Northerns 159** (D. Olivier 5-43) **and 245-6**. *Free State 8.04pts, Northerns 5.18pts.*

At Pietermaritzburg, November 8–10, 2012. **Drawn. South Western Districts 232**; ‡**KwaZulu-Natal Inland 151-1**. *KwaZulu-Natal Inland 5.02pts, South Western Districts 2.64pts.*

At Potchefstroom, November 8–10, 2012. **Drawn.** ‡**North West 296 and 245-9**; **Gauteng 314**. *North West 7.92pts, Gauteng 8.28pts.*

At Benoni, November 15–17, 2012. **Drawn.** ‡**Easterns 325** (G. I. Hume 5-52) **and 150-9 dec**; **Gauteng 198-9 dec and 210-7** (C. J. August 5-51). *Easterns 8.5pts, Gauteng 5.96pts.*

At Bloemfontein (OFS University), November 15–17, 2012. **Free State won by 52 runs. Free State 238** (L. Klazinga 5-52) **and 201-6 dec**; ‡**Namibia 147** (G. A. Vries 5-26) **and 240**. *Free State 16.76pts, Namibia 4pts.*

At Pretoria, November 15–17, 2012. **North West won by an innings and 189 runs. North West 432-8 dec** (H. E. van der Dussen 141, K. M. Vardhan 131); ‡**Northerns 78 and 165**. *North West 18.62pts, Northerns 1pt. Van der Dussen and Kyllin Vardhan added 270 for North West's third wicket, more than Northerns' combined total of 243 in two innings; they followed on 354 behind.*

At Oudtshoorn, November 15–17, 2012. **Drawn.** ‡**Eastern Province 360 and 126-8**; **South Western Districts 129** (W. E. Bell 7-56) **and 411** (K. R. Smuts 5-92). *South Western Districts 4pts, Eastern Province 9.2pts.*

At East London, November 22–24, 2012. **KwaZulu-Natal Inland won by seven wickets. KwaZulu-Natal Inland 305 and 196-3**; ‡**Border 113 and 387-7 dec** (V. Makhaphela 165*). *KwaZulu-Natal Inland 18.1pts, Border 4pts.*

At Kimberley, November 22–23, 2012. **Easterns won by an innings and 122 runs. Griqualand West 124 and 159** (J. C. Fourie 5-17); ‡**Easterns 405-9 dec** (G. M. Thomson 139). *Easterns 20.1pts, Griqualand West 4pts.*

At Chatsworth, November 22–24, 2012. **Drawn. KwaZulu-Natal 240** (B. E. Hendricks 6-63) **and 105-1**; ‡**Western Province 235-6 dec**. *KwaZulu-Natal 2.8pts, Western Province 6.7pts.*

At Centurion, November 22–24, 2012. **Drawn.** ‡**Northerns 409-7 dec** (P. J. Malan 108, G. L. van Buuren 142); **Namibia 259-7**. *Northerns 7.32pts, Namibia 5.18pts. Pieter Malan and Graeme van Buuren added 232 for Northerns' third wicket.*

At Pietermaritzburg, November 29–December 1, 2012. **Drawn.** ‡**KwaZulu-Natal Inland 286-5 v KwaZulu-Natal.** *KwaZulu-Natal Inland 3.72pts, KwaZulu-Natal 2pts.*

At Paarl, December 13–15, 2012. **Western Province won by an innings and 104 runs.** ‡**Western Province 365** (C. H. Raubenheimer 5-103); **Boland 143 and 118**. *Western Province 18.28pts, Boland 3pts.*

At Port Elizabeth, December 13–15, 2012. **Border won by five wickets.** ‡**Eastern Province 349 and 148**; **Border 231 and 270-5** (B. L. Bennett 138*). *Border 16.62pts, Eastern Province 8.98pts.*

At Johannesburg (Alan Lawson Oval), December 13–15, 2012. **Drawn. Namibia 264** (C. G. Williams 122*) **and 136-8**; ‡**Gauteng 232** (C. Viljoen 5-50). *Gauteng 6.64pts, Namibia 7.28pts. The Old Edwardians A ground had been renamed after club chairman Alan Lawson.*

At Kimberley, December 13–15, 2012. **Free State won by five wickets. Griqualand West 152 and 258**; ‡**Free State 299** (R. R. Rossouw 118; J. Coetzee 5-44) **and 114-5**. *Free State 17.98pts, Griqualand West 5.04pts. Dillon du Preez took a hat-trick to end Griquas' second innings. Rossouw hit 118 in 109 balls.*

At Oudtshoorn, December 20–22, 2012. **South Western Districts won by an innings and one run.** ‡**KwaZulu-Natal 227** (K. A. Maharaj 103) **and 203** (M. N. Piedt 6-53); **South Western Districts 431-7 dec** (A. P. McLaren 212*). *South Western Districts 17.3pts, KwaZulu-Natal 4.54pts. McLaren scored a maiden double-century, including nine sixes and 17 fours.*

At Alice, December 27–28, 2012. **South Western Districts won by an innings and 80 runs.** ‡**South Western Districts 327** (P. A. Stuurman 101, B. I. Louw 101); **Border 66** (M. N. Piedt 7-24) **and 181**. *South Western Districts 18.54pts, Border 4pts. This was the first first-class match in Alice, and was staged at Fort Hare University. South Western Districts slumped to 48-5, but fought back, with Pieter Stuurman and Brendon Louw scoring centuries down the order, before Piedt bowled Border* *out for 66. He finished with seven in an innings for the second time in his first six first-class games, and nine in a match for the third.*

At Benoni (Northerns), January 3–4, 2013. **Northerns won by four wickets. Easterns 97 and 138** (J. P. de Villiers 5-56); **‡Northerns 99 and 137-6**. *Northerns 14pts, Easterns 4pts. This was the first first-class match at the Northerns club in Benoni, rather than Willowmoore Park; 25 wickets fell on the opening day. Only one man (Easterns' Jean-Pierre Kok, with 64) reached 40.*

At Johannesburg, January 3–5, 2013. **Gauteng won by two wickets. Gauteng 353** (S. Masondo 103) **and 174-8; ‡Griqualand West 146 and 380** (W. R. Landsdale 203*). *Gauteng 19.04pts, Griqualand West 4pts. Gihan Cloete held seven catches in Gauteng's first innings and ten in the match. Wesley Landsdale scored a maiden double-hundred in 214 balls, with nine sixes and 23 fours.*

At Pietermaritzburg, January 3–5, 2013. **Drawn. Boland 222** (R. C. C. Canning 113) **and 342-6 dec** (R. C. C. Canning 106*); **‡KwaZulu-Natal Inland 320** (B. Moses 119) **and 194-6**. *KwaZulu-Natal Inland 8.4pts, Boland 6.44pts.*

At Windhoek (Wanderers), January 3–5, 2013. **Drawn. ‡North West 345-7 dec** (W. A. Deacon 113*) **and 243-7 dec** (D. Pretorius 100*); **Namibia 276 and 98-2**. *Namibia 6.52pts, North West 8.46pts.*

At Benoni, January 17–19, 2013. **Drawn. Boland 291; ‡Easterns 242-9**. *Easterns 6.84pts, Boland 7.82pts.*

At Durban, January 17–19, 2013. **Drawn. KwaZulu-Natal 91 and 190-6; ‡Griqualand West 195**. *KwaZulu-Natal 4pts, Griqualand West 5.9pts.*

At Pietermaritzburg, January 17–19, 2013. **Gauteng won by nine wickets. Gauteng 365-4 dec** (J. Symes 170*) **and 11-1; ‡KwaZulu-Natal Inland 175 and 200** (R. Das Neves 5-33). *Gauteng 19.3pts, KwaZulu-Natal Inland 2.5pts.*

At Centurion, January 17–19, 2013. **Drawn. Western Province 458-5 dec** (S. A. Engelbrecht 175, B. G. Barnes 142); **‡Northerns 45-2**. *Northerns 1pt, Western Province 6.64pts. Sybrand Engelbrecht and Bradley Barnes added 289 for Western Province's fourth wicket, but only 10.1 overs were possible after the opening day.*

At Paarl, January 24–26, 2013. **Boland won by 82 runs. ‡Boland 208 and 226; Namibia 173 and 179** (C. H. Raubenheimer 6-69). *Boland 16.16pts, Namibia 5.46pts.*

At Port Elizabeth, January 24–26, 2013. **Drawn. ‡Eastern Province 291 and 175-8 dec; North West 213** (S. Gidana 6-37) **and 124-6**. *Eastern Province 7.16pts, North West 5.26pts.*

At Bloemfontein (OFS University), January 24–26, 2013. **Free State won by eight wickets. Western Province 330** (S. P. Gomes 129) **and 118; ‡Free State 271 and 179-2** (R. S. Second 100*). *Free State 17.42pts, Western Province 8.34pts.*

At Chatsworth, January 24–26, 2013. **KwaZulu-Natal won by an innings and 35 runs. ‡KwaZulu-Natal 356-9 dec** (K. Zondo 126); **Easterns 166 and 155** (B. M. Scullard 7-26). *KwaZulu-Natal 18.22pts, Easterns 4.32pts.*

At Pretoria, January 24–26, 2013. **Northerns won by eight wickets. ‡Border 203 and 183; Northerns 315 and 72-2**. *Northerns 18.3pts, Border 6.06pts.*

At East London, January 31–February 2, 2013. **Border won by six wickets. Easterns 182 and 130; ‡Border 224** (I. Manack 5-78) **and 92-4**. *Border 16.48pts, Easterns 5.64pts.*

At Port Elizabeth (Union), January 31–February 2, 2013. **Griqualand West won by ten wickets. ‡Eastern Province 263 and 126; Griqualand West 381 and 9-0**. *Griqualand West 19.22pts, Eastern Province 6.26pts.*

At Windhoek (Wanderers), January 31–February 1, 2013. **KwaZulu-Natal Inland won by nine wickets. Namibia 128** (R. Pretorius 7-36) **and 182** (R. Pretorius 5-40); **‡KwaZulu-Natal Inland 177 and 134-1**. *KwaZulu-Natal Inland 15.54pts, Namibia 4pts. Ruhan Pretorius took 12-76.*

At Pretoria, January 31–February 2, 2013. **KwaZulu-Natal won by 208 runs. ‡KwaZulu-Natal 291** (K. A. Maharaj 114*) **and 208-3 dec** (M. Ramsaroop 104*); **Northerns 181 and 110** (K. A. Maharaj 5-12). *KwaZulu-Natal 17.82pts, Northerns 5.62pts. Maharaj scored a career-best 114*, followed by figures of 15–8–9–1 in Northerns' first innings and 6.5–2–12–5 in their second.*

At Oudtshoorn, January 31–February 2, 2013. **South Western Districts won by 59 runs. South Western Districts 339** (R. D. McMillan 125, G. N. Addicott 145) **and 138; ‡Gauteng 176 and 242**. *South Western Districts 18.78pts, Gauteng 5.52pts. Glen Addicott hit ten sixes and ten fours.*

At Pietermaritzburg, February 7–9, 2013. **Drawn. ‡KwaZulu-Natal Inland 396-9 dec** (N. Hendrie 115) **and 165-6 dec** (V. L. Orros 5-45); **Free State 296-7 dec** (P. Botha 102*) **and 30-2**. *KwaZulu-Natal Inland 7.1pts, Free State 5.92pts.*

At Windhoek (Wanderers), February 7–9, 2013. **Eastern Province won by 96 runs. Eastern Province 217 and 216-5 dec; ‡Namibia 129 and 208** (W. E. Bell 5-69). *Eastern Province 16.34pts, Namibia 4pts.*

At Potchefstroom, February 7–9, 2013. **Drawn. North West 461-9 dec** (H. E. van der Dussen 119, D. Pretorius 177; P. Fojela 6-78); **‡South Western Districts 200 and 387-3** (C. Jonker 102*). *North West 10.9pts, South Western Districts 5pts. Van der Dussen and Dwaine Pretorius – who hit all but 21 of his runs in boundaries – added 264 for North West's sixth wicket.*

At Bloemfontein, February 14–16, 2013. **Free State won by three wickets. ‡KwaZulu-Natal 299** (A. M. Amla 118*) **and 207-8 dec; Free State 193 and 315-7** (R. S. Second 110). *Free State 15.86pts, KwaZulu-Natal 7.98pts. Free State's first innings collapsed to 84-9, before their last two batsmen, Corne Dry (74*) and Gino Vries (31), added 109.*

At Johannesburg, February 14–16, 2013. **Gauteng won by an innings and 56 runs. Border 120 and 194** (G. I. Hume 5-29); **‡Gauteng 370**. *Gauteng 19.4pts, Border 4pts.*

At Benoni, February 21–23, 2013. **Easterns won by nine wickets. ‡South Western Districts 224 and 205; Easterns 217** (G. R. Rabie 5-47) **and 213-1** (T. M. Bodibe 114*). *Easterns 16.34pts, South Western Districts 6.48pts.*

At Bloemfontein (OFS University), February 21–23, 2013. **Free State won by an innings and 39 runs. ‡Eastern Province 154** (C. A. Dry 5-25) **and 252; Free State 445** (M. N. Erlank 141, R. S. Second 132). *Free State 18.12pts, Eastern Province 2.08pts. Michael Erlank and Second added 267 for Free State's second wicket, with Second passing 1,000 first-class runs in the season.*

At Johannesburg, February 21–23, 2013. **Gauteng won by 126 runs. Gauteng 379 and 177-6 dec; ‡Western Province 198 and 232** (S. Khan 5-33). *Gauteng 19.58pts, Western Province 5.96pts.*

At Kimberley, February 21–23, 2013. **Boland won by 120 runs. Boland 321 and 283-8 dec** (R. C. C. Canning 105; L. Rodolo 5-51); **‡Griqualand West 217 and 267** (P. J. N. Jeftha 5-70). *Boland 18.42pts, Griqualand West 6.34pts.*

At Chatsworth, February 21–23, 2013. **North West won by an innings and four runs. ‡KwaZulu-Natal 121 and 172** (B. J. Pelser 5-38); **North West 297**. *North West 17.94pts, KwaZulu-Natal 4pts.*

At Pietermaritzburg, February 21–23, 2013. **Northerns won by 103 runs. ‡Northerns 310 and 230-9 dec; KwaZulu-Natal Inland 186** (R. R. Richards 5-56) **and 251** (S. von Berg 7-108). *Northerns 18.2pts, KwaZulu-Natal Inland 5.72pts.*

At Windhoek (Wanderers), February 28–March 2, 2013. **Border won by an innings and 119 runs. ‡Namibia 182 and 127; Border 428-6 dec** (B. C. de Wett 201). *Border 20.26pts, Namibia 3.64pts. Burton de Wett scored a maiden double-hundred and added 206 for Border's third wicket with Somila Seyibokwe.*

At Potchefstroom, February 28–March 1, 2013. **North West won by an innings and 69 runs. ‡Boland 84** (D. Klein 5-21) **and 113** (G. J-P. Kruger 5-40); **North West 266** (H. E. van der Dussen 128; C. H. Raubenheimer 7-71). *North West 17.32pts, Boland 4pts.*

At Oudtshoorn, February 28–March 2, 2013. **Drawn. Northerns 292 and 272-8 dec; ‡South Western Districts 280** (W. Lategan 119; S. von Berg 6-79) **and 108-8**. *South Western Districts 7.6pts, Northerns 7.84pts. In Northerns' second innings, Shaun von Berg (84*) and Juan-Pierre de Villiers (88*) put on 154* for the ninth wicket.*

At Rondebosch, February 28–March 2, 2013. **Western Province won by 92 runs. ‡Western Province 174** (A. R. Swanepoel 5-48) **and 196** (G. N. Nieuwoudt 5-35); **Griqualand West 112** (G. F. Linde 6-41) **and 166**. *Western Province 15.48pts, Griqualand West 4pts.*

At Paarl, March 7–9, 2013. **Northerns won by four wickets. Boland 343-6 dec** (R. C. C. Canning 121*) **and forfeited second innings; ‡Northerns forfeited first innings and 346-6** (G. L. van

Buuren 140, H. Klaasen 116*). *Northerns 12pts, Boland 4.86pts. Both teams forfeited an innings after the second day was washed out. Van Buuren and Heinrich Klaasen, with a maiden hundred, added 208 for Northerns' sixth wicket to take them within 18 runs of victory.*

At East London, March 7–9, 2013. **Drawn. Border 234 and 263-8 dec**; ‡**Griqualand West 213** (Y. Pangabantu 5-46) **and 176-5**. *Border 6.68pts, Griqualand West 6.26pts.*

At Port Elizabeth, March 7–9, 2013. **Drawn.** ‡**Easterns 286** (L. C. Ngoepe 134) **and 234-9 dec**; **Eastern Province 214** (D. Stanley 5-28) **and 123-2**. *Eastern Province 6.28pts, Easterns 7.72pts.*

At Oudtshoorn, March 7–9, 2013. **South Western Districts won by 189 runs.** ‡**South Western Districts 319-9 dec** (W. Lategan 112) **and 214-7 dec**; **Free State 146 and 198** (M. N. Piedt 5-57). *South Western Districts 18.38pts, Free State 4pts.*

At Bloemfontein, March 14–16, 2013. **Drawn. Free State 432-7 dec** (R. S. Second 179, L. van Wyk 147) **and 217-4 dec** (J. van Wyk 109); ‡**Border 304 and 103-2**. *Free State 10.64pts, Border 7.08pts. Second his fifth century of the season and added 274 for Free State's fifth wicket with Lenert van Wyk; Jandre van Wyk made 109 at a run a ball in their second innings.*

At Johannesburg (Lenasia), March 14–16, 2013. **Gauteng won by ten wickets.** ‡**Eastern Province 137 and 216** (E. Leie 5-80); **Gauteng 348** (D. P. Conway 142) **and 9-0**. *Gauteng 18.96pts, Eastern Province 4pts.*

At Chatsworth, March 14–15, 2013. **KwaZulu-Natal won by an innings and 114 runs. Namibia 110 and 191** (K. G. Buckthorp 5-61); ‡**KwaZulu-Natal 415-3 dec** (M. Ramsaroop 111, M. G. Alexander 164, J. D. Vandiar 100*). *KwaZulu-Natal 18.8pts.*

At Potchefstroom, March 14–15, 2013. **North West won by an innings and 76 runs. North West 289-9 dec**; ‡**KwaZulu-Natal Inland 26** (D. Klein 5-1) **and 187**. *North West 17.78pts, KwaZulu-Natal Inland 4pts. KwaZulu-Natal Inland's 26 was the lowest total of the season. Left-armer Dieter Klein had figures of 3.4–2–1–5.*

At Rondebosch, March 14–16, 2013. **Easterns won by four wickets.** ‡**Western Province 199 and 135**; **Easterns 162 and 173-6**. *Easterns 15.24pts, Western Province 5.98pts.*

At Paarl, March 21–22, 2013. **Boland won by an innings and 81 runs.** ‡**Free State 58 and 175** (C. H. Raubenheimer 5-72); **Boland 314** (U-K. J. Birkenstock 112). *Boland 18.28pts, Free State 4pts. Free State elected to bat, but collapsed inside two hours and lost inside two days.*

At Johannesburg, March 21–23, 2013. **Gauteng won by an innings and 125 runs.** ‡**KwaZulu-Natal 142 and 149** (E. Leie 5-41); **Gauteng 416-8 dec** (D. A. Hendricks 176*). *Gauteng 19.84pts, KwaZulu-Natal 3pts.*

At Kimberley, March 21–23, 2013. **Drawn. KwaZulu-Natal Inland 232** (D. D. Carolus 7-66) **and 319-7 dec** (M. M. Hulett 117*); ‡**Griqualand West 288 and 139-3**. *Griqualand West 7.76pts, KwaZulu-Natal Inland 6.64pts.*

At Pretoria, March 21–23, 2013. **Northerns won by an innings and 108 runs.** ‡**Eastern Province 132** (C. J. D. de Villiers 5-30) **and 214**; **Northerns 454** (P. J. Malan 191, G. L. van Buuren 138). *Northerns 19.56pts, Eastern Province 2pts. Malan and van Buuren added 242 for Northerns' third wicket, their second double-century stand of the season.*

At Oudtshoorn, March 21–23, 2013. **South Western Districts won by 32 runs. South Western Districts 160 and 218** (C. Viljoen 6-43); ‡**Namibia 221** (R. A. H. Pitchers 114) **and 125**. *South Western Districts 15.2pts, Namibia 6.42pts.*

At Cape Town, March 21–23, 2013. **North West won by seven wickets. Western Province 146 and 192**; ‡**North West 197 and 142-3**. *North West 15.94pts, Western Province 4pts. North West's van der Dussen ended the tournament with 1,034 runs at 54.*

At Paarl, April 4–6, 2013. **Gauteng won by five wickets. Boland 256 and 224** (E. Leie 5-72); ‡**Gauteng 208** (L. B. Williams 5-40) **and 275-5**. *Gauteng 16.16pts, Boland 7.12pts.*

At East London, April 4–6, 2013. **Drawn.** ‡**North West 373-9 dec** (F. J. L. Botha 144) **and 190-3 dec**; **Border 206** (G. J-P. Kruger 6-55) **and 314-8** (B. L. Bennett 107; D. R. Deeb 5-97). *Border 6.12pts, North West 9.46pts.*

MOST WICKETS IN DEBUT SEASON IN SOUTH AFRICA

	Season	M	Runs	Wkts	Avge	BB
M. N. Piedt (South Western Districts)	**2012-13**	**13**	**999**	**59**	**16.93**	**7-6**
P. Anker (Boland)	1981-82	7	731	50	14.62	6-83
T. Shamsi (Gauteng/Lions)	2009-10	11	1,082	50	21.64	6-89
S. von Berg (Northerns/Titans)	2009-10	12	1,144	49	23.34	6-34
P. R. Adams (W. Prov/South Africa A/South Africa)	1995-96	8	1,065	43	24.76	6-101
B. L. Whatmore (KwaZulu-Natal).	2010-11	11	860	42	20.47	7-42
R. H. Kaschula (Rhodesia)	1970-71	7	608	41	14.82	5-13
D. P. Conyngham (Natal)	1921-22	6	581	40	14.52	5-20
M. de Lange (Easterns/Titans).	2010-11	10	952	40	23.80	6-36

Research: Andrew Samson

At Benoni, April 4–6, 2013. **Drawn.** KwaZulu-Natal Inland 386-7 dec (K. Nipper 101*) **and 168-5 dec**; ‡**Easterns 248-8 dec** (S. Mjekula 6-37) **and 294-7**. *Easterns 5.96pts, KwaZulu-Natal Inland 8.04pts.*

At Kimberley, April 4–6, 2013. **Griqualand West won by 192 runs.** Griqualand West 213 (G. R. Rabie 5-53) **and 241-6 dec** (G. L. Cloete 107*); ‡**South Western Districts 108** (A. K. Kruger 5-19) **and 154**. *Griqualand West 16.26pts, South Western Districts 4pts. Piedt's four wickets for South Western Districts took him to 59, a record for a South African debut season, and the most in this domestic season.*

At Windhoek (Wanderers), April 4–6, 2013. **Western Province won by ten wickets.** ‡**Namibia 304** (C. G. Williams 100) **and 176**; **Western Province 473-9 dec** (S. A. Engelbrecht 214*) **and 8-0**. *Western Province 17.54pts, Namibia 5.38pts. Engelbrecht scored a maiden double-hundred, the highest score of this tournament.*

MOMENTUM ONE-DAY CUP, 2012-13

50-over league plus knockout

	Played	Won	Lost	No result	Bonus points	Points	Net run-rate
Lions	10	5	2	3	4	30	1.92
Cape Cobras.........	10	6	3	1	3	29	0.74
Titans	10	5	5	0	1	21	–0.62
Knights.............	10	3	4	3	2	20	–0.77
Dolphins............	10	3	4	3	1	18*	–0.11
Warriors............	10	2	6	2	1	11§	–0.61

* 1pt deducted.   § 2pts deducted.

Play-off

At Cape Town, December 9, 2012. **Cape Cobras won by three wickets.** Titans 241-9 (50 overs) (A. B. de Villiers 107; D. W. Steyn 5-45); ‡**Cape Cobras 245-7** (46.3 overs). *MoM: D. W. Steyn. Dale Steyn topped and tailed Titans, while A. B. de Villiers hit 109 in 123 balls. Yaseen Vallie and Justin Ontong added 109 for Cobras' fifth wicket after Dane Vilas was out obstructing the field.*

Final

At Johannesburg, December 14, 2012 (day/night). **No result. Cape Cobras 64-4** (16.2 overs) **v** ‡**Lions.** *Hardus Viljoen took all four wickets to fall before a thunderstorm ended play.*

At Johannesburg, December 15, 2012 (day/night). **No result. Lions 241-7** (50 overs); ‡**Cape Cobras 69-2** (11 overs). *The teams shared the trophy after another thunderstorm halted the second attempt.*

RAM SLAM T20 CHALLENGE, 2012-13

	Played	Won	Lost	Abandoned	Bonus points	Points	Net run-rate
Lions	10	7	3	0	2	30	0.69
Warriors.	10	6	3	1	1	27	0.20
Titans.	10	6	3	1	0	26	0.14
Knights	10	5	5	0	1	21	−0.05
Dolphins	10	2	6	2	0	12	−0.78
Cape Cobras	10	2	8	0	0	8	−0.38

Play-off

At East London, April 3, 2013 (floodlit). **Titans won by four wickets.** Warriors 127-9 (20 overs) (A. C. Thomas 5-24); ‡Titans **130-6** (19.5 overs). *MoM:* F. Behardien and A. C. Thomas. *Alfonso Thomas claimed three in Warriors' final over and Farhaan Behardien hit 41 in 26 balls.*

Final

At Johannesburg, April 7, 2013. **Lions won by 30 runs.** ‡Lions **155-5** (20 overs); Titans **125** (18.1 overs). *MoM:* Q. de Kock and A. M. Phangiso. *This was only Lions' second trophy, following the Pro20 title in 2006-07. De Kock's 44 in 31 balls took him to 524, a tournament record.*

CSA PROVINCIAL ONE-DAY CHALLENGE, 2012-13

50-over league plus final

Coastal	P	W	L	NR	BP	Pts	NRR		**Inland**	P	W	L	NR	BP	Pts	NRR
Border	6	4	0	2	1	21	1.03		Free State	6	5	1	0	2	22	0.54
Boland	6	4	2	0	1	17	−0.04		North West	6	5	1	0	1	21	0.46
W. Province	6	2	2	2	0	12	−0.19		Gauteng	6	3	3	0	2	14	0.26
KwaZulu-Natal . .	6	2	2	2	0	12	−0.14		Namibia	6	3	3	0	2	14	−0.11
SW Districts	6	2	3	1	1	11	−0.93		Northerns	6	2	4	0	1	9	−1.10
KZN Inland	6	2	4	0	2	10	0.36		Easterns	6	1	4	1	1	7	−0.07
E. Province	6	1	4	1	1	7	−0.14		Griqualand W.	6	1	4	1	1	7	−0.13

Final

At Bloemfontein, January 12, 2013. **Border won by three wickets.** ‡Free State **207** (48.5 overs); **Border 208-7** (45.3 overs). *Bevan Bennett established Border's run-chase with 65 in 78 balls.*

CSA PROVINCIAL T20, 2012-13

20-over league

	P	W	L	T	NR	Bonus points	Points	NRR
Free State	7	7	0	0	0	4	32	1.85
Gauteng	7	5	1	0	1	3	25	1.02
Griqualand West.	7	4	2	1	0	1	20	0.00
KwaZulu-Natal.	7	4	2	1	0	0	19	−0.14
Eastern Province.	7	4	3	0	0	2	18	0.14
Northerns	7	3	3	0	1	1	15	−0.24
Border	7	3	4	0	0	2	14	0.06
Namibia	7	3	4	0	0	2	14	0.02
South Western Districts	7	3	3	0	1	0	14	−0.38
Western Province	7	2	3	1	1	1	14	−0.07
Easterns	7	1	4	1	1	1	10	−0.36
KwaZulu-Natal Inland	7	2	5	0	0	1	9	−0.86
North West	7	2	5	0	0	0	8	−0.71
Boland	7	1	5	0	1	0	6	−0.30

SRI LANKA CRICKET, 2013

Crying out for more

Sa'adi Thawfeeq

The Sri Lankan board endured one of their worst years – and there has been some stiff competition. Two Tests against West Indies and three against South Africa were cancelled to accommodate one-day and Twenty20 internationals, which were expected to rake in revenue for a governing body up to their neck in debt. From a purely financial point of view, the move had merit. But the decisions felt sacrilegious: not long ago Sri Lanka were clamouring for Test cricket.

There was more bad news when, because of financial constraints, Zimbabwe cancelled a tour scheduled to include two Tests. So instead of playing ten Tests in 2013, Sri Lanka ended up with only three, two of them against Bangladesh

SRI LANKA IN 2013

	Played	Won	Lost	Drawn/ No result
Tests	3	–	1	2
One-day internationals	30	14	13	3
Twenty20 internationals	9	6	3	–

Results exclude the Pakistan v Sri Lanka Test beginning on December 31, 2013.

DECEMBER JANUARY	3 Tests, 5 ODIs and 2 T20Is (a) v Australia	(see *Wisden 2013*, page 919)
FEBRUARY		
MARCH	2 Tests, 3 ODIs and 1 T20I (h) v Bangladesh	(page 1116)
APRIL		
MAY		
JUNE	Champions Trophy (in England)	(page 301)
JULY	Triangular ODI tournament (in West Indies) v India and West Indies	(page 1155)
AUGUST	5 ODIs and 3 T20Is (h) v South Africa	(page 1123)
SEPTEMBER		
OCTOBER		
NOVEMBER	3 ODIs and 2 T20Is (h) v New Zealand	(page 1131)
DECEMBER JANUARY	3 Tests, 5 ODIs and 2 T20Is (a) (in UAE) v Pakistan	(page 1031)

For a review of Sri Lankan domestic cricket from the 2012-13 season, see page 1135.

(though a fourth, against Pakistan in Abu Dhabi, began on December 31). It was the lowest by any country for the calendar year, three fewer than even Bangladesh and Zimbabwe. By contrast, only India and Pakistan played more one-day internationals than Sri Lanka's 30, and – among the Full Members – only Pakistan more than their nine Twenty20 matches.

The most damning decision taken by Sri Lanka Cricket was the cancellation of the South Africa Tests to make way for the Sri Lanka Premier League, which never happened: the eight franchises refused to pay their tournament fee, and failed to produce bank guarantees for player payments. The board claimed they had called off the SLPL to safeguard both their own integrity and the tournament's. The players were left high and dry, with no Tests between the visit of Bangladesh in March and the trip to the UAE in December.

The absence of any Tests against the top-ranked South Africans was galling. The last time South Africa had lost a Test series away from home had been in Sri Lanka, in 2006 – and their 4–1 loss in the one-day internationals this time suggested the Sri Lankans had missed a golden opportunity to exploit their weakness against spin in the Test arena.

The result against South Africa proved the high point of the year. Rain-affected home one-day series with Bangladesh and New Zealand were drawn and, in between, the disappointment of a Champions Trophy semi-final exit to India after the exhilaration of a superb run-chase against England

The young ones: twentysomethings Angelo Mathews and Dinesh Chandimal were tasked with plotting Sri Lanka's course.

at The Oval was followed by a one-wicket defeat by India in the final of a 50-over triangular in the Caribbean. Sri Lanka then lost 3–2 to Pakistan in the UAE, a result that prefigured the trauma of sacrificing the chance of a rare away Test win in January 2014, when Pakistan squared the series by chasing down more than 300 on the final afternoon.

During the series with Bangladesh, Kumar Sangakkara made three successive hundreds, taking his Test tally to 34 – one ahead of Mahela Jayawardene's national record of 33. Left-arm spinner Rangana Herath's 25 Test wickets, meanwhile, were 16 ahead of the next best, seamer Shaminda Eranga.

But the paucity of five-day matches led to a delay in the development of players such as Dinesh Chandimal and Lahiru Thirimanne, supposed successors to Jayawardene and Sangakkara. Instead, these two youngsters were left to carve out an international career playing one-day and Twenty20 cricket in batting positions unsuited to their styles. Outgoing coach Graham Ford, who joined Surrey after the series in the UAE, said: "They are not really the 50-over-finishing type of batsmen. They are batsmen who get in the engine-room and set up the innings."

Two of Sri Lanka's most experienced batsmen retired from the game. Thilan Samaraweera, dropped for the visit of Bangladesh, quit international cricket, saying he would not wait another nine months for his next Test, and threw in his lot with Worcestershire. Later in the year, Tillekeratne Dilshan retired from Tests, but said he would continue to play in the limited-overs formats until the 2015 World Cup. At one-day level, Sri Lanka were at least boosted by the emergence of Kushal Perera. A hard-hitting left-handed opener, he has already been compared to Sanath Jayasuriya, the former national captain.

Prior to the Bangladesh series a pay dispute took place between SLC and their 23 contracted cricketers, which was eventually sorted out by Jayasuriya, now an MP. He succeeded Ashantha de Mel as chairman of selectors following the decision by the Minister of Sports, Mahindananada Aluthgamage, to revamp the selection panel. Jayasuriya was joined by former cricketers Hashan Tillekeratne, Pramodya Wickremasinghe, Chaminda Mendis and Eric Upashantha.

Sri Lankan legislation now allows office-bearers elected to a sporting body a term of two years, so Jayantha Dharmadasa and Nishantha Ranatunga continued for another 12 months as president and secretary. But intrigue is never far from the surface in Sri Lankan cricket, and K. Mathivanan quit as a vice-president in September, five months after winning the elections for the presidency. He reportedly claimed there was "a mafia in operation which is running cricket". He later cited personal reasons. It was well known there was no love lost between him and Ranatunga, who had ended his eight-year reign as president of Colombo Colts CC.

There was also controversy surrounding Mathivanan's replacement as vice-president, when Asanga Seneviratne, the losing candidate at the previous election, was chosen. Seneviratne, head of the country's rugby union body, had caused a stir with comments that rugby would supplant cricket in Sri Lanka within a decade. The scope for a conflict of interest was clear.

But it was the manner in which he was picked for the post that really raised a public outcry. There were allegations that Aluthgamage had been involved, only a year after the former ICC chief executive Haroon Lorgat's review into Sri Lankan cricket's governance had recommended the end of political interference. The board had promised to heed Lorgat's advice.

SLC did manage to clear the SLR960m (£4.5m) still outstanding to their creditors, and reduced the loan from the Bank of Ceylon from \$US18.43m to \$10.5m. The debts had been incurred while building or renovating stadiums in Hambantota, Pallekele and Colombo ahead of the 2011 World Cup. SLC agreed to repay the loan by the end of 2015, when they should have received money from ICC events.

SRI LANKA v BANGLADESH, 2012-13

Andrew Fernando

Test matches (2): Sri Lanka 1, Bangladesh 0
One-day internationals (3): Sri Lanka 1, Bangladesh 1
Twenty20 international (1): Sri Lanka 1, Bangladesh 0

Bangladesh's tour of Sri Lanka brought together two teams at different stages of their development, and some unexpected results showed how much closer they had grown. The series marked a fresh beginning for Sri Lanka, with new captains – Angelo Mathews had succeeded Mahela Jayawardene, while Dinesh Chandimal took over for the Twenty20 game – and a squad swimming with youthful talent. But Bangladesh's steady improvement ensured the fresh start was less triumphant than the Sri Lankans had hoped for.

The tour was preceded by a whirlwind off-field conflict that threatened to deprive it of meaning. As Bangladesh prepared for a warm-up match in Matara, Sri Lanka Cricket suspended 23 top players, including both captains, after they refused to sign new contracts because of a clause removing their right to a quarter of SLC's earnings from ICC events. A settlement was reached a day later, after a meeting organised by chief selector Sanath Jayasuriya. But the episode turned public opinion against the players, who were perceived as pampered and arrogant; Sri Lanka's modest returns were readily seen in that unflattering light.

Bangladesh's achievements – to draw a Test and win a one-day international in Sri Lanka for the first time – were all the more impressive given the absence of all-round talisman Shakib Al Hasan and limited-overs spearhead Mashrafe bin Mortaza, both injured. Opening batsman Tamim Iqbal did come, but missed those two matches: he was ruled out of the First Test with a sore wrist, then departed after fracturing a thumb – and hitting a hundred – in the first one-dayer.

Instead, the supporting cast made the best of the limelight, and were led superbly by captain Mushfiqur Rahim, who hit Bangladesh's first Test double-hundred, at Galle, after Mohammad Ashraful had fallen just short. This was the latest comeback of Ashraful's career since his century as a teenage debutant; he had been recalled, after four vexingly lean years, only after Shahriar Nafees cut his hand while shaving his bat with a sharp blade. Three 21-year-olds also displayed their promise. Off-spinner Sohag Gazi was Bangladesh's best bowler in the Tests, in his second international series, and batsman Nasir Hossain not only showed a sound defence and steady temperament while making a hundred in Galle, but provided rapid finishes under pressure in two one-day innings. Left-hander Mominul Haque was less eye-catching in the shorter formats, but two fluent Test fifties, including one in his debut innings, made plain his potential.

Sri Lanka's selectors had approached the tour with the intention of blooding young talent to prepare for the departure of Jayawardene (who

Shaking things up: at Galle, Mohammad Ashraful, unbeaten on 189 at the end of the third day, is congratulated by Sri Lankan captain Angelo Mathews and by his own, Mushfiqur Rahim, who went on to make Bangladesh's first double-century.

sat out this series with a broken finger), Tillekeratne Dilshan, Kumar Sangakkara and Rangana Herath, who were all over 35 by its end. That plan met with mixed success. Wicketkeeper-batsman Chandimal, suddenly saddled with the 20-over captaincy five months after he had been unable to get a game at the World Twenty20, was the best of the new generation, hitting two Test hundreds and keeping wicket immaculately in place of the discarded Prasanna Jayawardene; Lahiru Thirimanne looked increasingly at ease.

But for all the talk of new faces, it was old-timers who shone most brightly. Sangakkara and Dilshan were unstoppable, each hitting three hundreds and two fifties in five games (they were rested for the Twenty20 match). And Herath proved again that he was Sri Lanka's most valuable Test asset. He bowled the side to only their fifth Test victory in the post-Muralitharan era; and for the fourth time, Herath had been a match-winner.

BANGLADESHI TOURING PARTY

Mushfiqur Rahim (T/50/20), Abdur Razzak (T/50/20), Abul Hasan (T/50/20), Anamul Haque (T/50/20), Elias Sunny (T), Jahurul Islam (T/50/20), Mahmudullah (T/50/20), Marshall Ayub (T), Mohammad Ashraful (T/50/20), Mominul Haque (T/50/20), Mosharraf Hossain (50/20), Nasir Hossain (T/50/20), Robiul Islam (T), Rubel Hossain (T/50/20), Shahadat Hossain (T/50/20), Shamsur Rahman (50/20), Sohag Gazi (T/50/20), Tamim Iqbal (T/50). Coach: S. J. Jurgensen.

Enamul Haque, jun., Naeem Islam and Shahriar Nafees were originally selected for the Test squad but withdrew with injuries (hamstring, quadriceps and hand, respectively); they were replaced by Elias Sunny, Marshall Ayub and Mohammad Ashraful. Abdur Razzak joined the tour before the Second Test. Nazmul Hossain was selected for the ODI squad but injured his left knee in training, and Tamim Iqbal left the tour after fracturing his thumb in the first one-day game; he was replaced by Shamsur Rahman. Anamul Haque left after the ODIs to sit a school exam.

At Matara, March 3–5, 2013. **Drawn. ‡Sri Lanka Development Emerging Team 410** (K. D. K. Vithanage 168*, S. M. A. Priyanjan 83; Sohag Gazi 5-104, Elias Sunny 3-74); **Bangladeshis 479** (Mohammad Ashraful 102, Mominul Haque 99, Mahmudullah 56, Mushfiqur Rahim 81, Sohag Gazi 82*; W. A. A. M. Silva 3-7). *Off-spinner Sohag Gazi sent down 30 overs for his five wickets on the opening day, when Abul Hasan had to go off after bowling six overs, suffering from sunstroke and dehydration. Kithuruwan Vithanage earned his Test debut with a career-best 168* in 165 balls. Rain permitted only six overs next day, but on the last Mohammad Ashraful and Mominul Haque ensured their Test recall, putting on 178 for Bangladesh's third wicket. Sohag Gazi had the final word after he and Mushfiqur Rahim ran up 112 for the seventh wicket in just 12 overs.*

SRI LANKA v BANGLADESH

First Test Match

At Galle, March 8–12, 2013. Drawn. Toss: Sri Lanka. Test debuts: K. D. K. Vithanage; Anamul Haque, Mominul Haque.

Galle routinely hosts the first Test of a series, and tends to reprise a familiar plot: a hundred for Mahela Jayawardene, a heavy haul for Sri Lanka's ace spinner, and a win that seats the home side comfortably for the next match. But not this time – and, on an uncharacteristically placid pitch, Bangladesh emerged the happier.

Not only was it their first Test draw against Sri Lanka, after 12 straight defeats, only one of which had lasted into the fifth day. But Bangladesh also reached 600 for the first time in a Test innings, and recorded their two highest individual scores – including their first double-century – as well as an all-wicket record partnership of 267. By the end, the fact that they had conceded 570 inside the first five sessions had been all but forgotten.

The meat in Bangladesh's historic reply was supplied by Mohammad Ashraful and Mushfiqur Rahim, who on the third day put together only their country's second double-hundred stand. For a while, it was Ashraful who seemed poised to score that 200, having passed his own national record and eschewed the flashy strokeplay that had defined his promising early years but which, in more recent times, had often caused his downfall. He was parked on 189 at stumps, but rushed at Herath early next day and was caught at slip. Still, his first international century for four years launched a fruitful tour.

Instead, it was Mushfiqur who was to celebrate the milestone no compatriot had achieved, getting there shortly after lunch on the fourth day. It was an innings full of calculation and prudence, and he scored heavily square of the wicket on both sides, employing the cut and square-drive to good effect against the fast bowlers, who grew wayward during their long stint in the field. With the pitch lacking any pace, and the bounce steadily getting lower, the pull was another of Mushfiqur's favourites. He did not offer a chance until Kulasekara trapped him with the next ball he faced after reaching 200.

But Bangladesh were not done, and Nasir Hossain pushed on past their previous-highest total – 556 against West Indies at Mirpur four months earlier – to complete a maiden Test hundred. It was the first time Bangladesh had compiled three in one innings. And it was the longest they had batted, a full 196 overs by the time they were bowled out at tea on the fourth day.

The exceptional batting conditions had been designed to give the inexperienced members of Sri Lanka's top order a gentle ride. And, after Mathews had won the toss, Thirimanne and Chandimal reached maiden hundreds, before Sangakkara equalled Jayawardene's national record of 31 Test centuries, in his first innings since breaking his hand at Melbourne in December. Sri Lanka declared at 570 for four, little expecting that they would concede a deficit of 68.

HIGHEST SCORES FOR BANGLADESH

200	Mushfiqur Rahim	v Sri Lanka at Galle	**2012-13**
190	Mohammad Ashraful	v Sri Lanka at Galle	**2012-13**
158*	Mohammad Ashraful	v India at Chittagong (M. A. Aziz)	2004-05
151	Tamim Iqbal	v India at Mirpur	2009-10
145	Aminul Islam	v India at Dhaka (*Bangladesh's first Test*)	2000-01
144	Shakib Al Hasan	v Pakistan at Mirpur	2011-12
138	Shahriar Nafees	v Australia at Fatullah	2005-06
136	Mohammad Ashraful	v Sri Lanka at Chittagong (CDS)	2005-06

After Bangladesh's enormous response, hundreds for Dilshan and Sangakkara made it plain the pitch was no worse for batting on the fifth day; it was the first time Sangakkara had scored two in a Test. The eventual total of eight centuries equalled the world record, set by West Indies and South Africa at St John's in 2004-05. Debutant Kithuruwan Vithanage finally had a chance to bat on the last afternoon, and made a rapid 59, before Mathews declared with a lead of 267. Sri Lanka could remove only one Bangladesh batsman in the 22 overs that remained – which more or less summed up the match.

Man of the Match: Mushfiqur Rahim.

Close of play: first day, Sri Lanka 361-3 (Thirimanne 74, Mathews 25); second day, Bangladesh 135-2 (Mohammad Ashraful 65, Mominul Haque 35); third day, Bangladesh 438-4 (Mohammad Ashraful 189, Mushfiqur Rahim 152); fourth day, Sri Lanka 116-1 (Dilshan 63, Sangakkara 49).

Sri Lanka

F. D. M. Karunaratne lbw b Sohag Gazi	41	– c Abul Hasan b Shahadat Hossain . . .	3
T. M. Dilshan c Mominul Haque b Sohag Gazi . . .	54	– c Abul Hasan b Mahmudullah	126
K. C. Sangakkara c Jahurul Islam b Sohag Gazi	142	– c Jahurul Islam b Mahmudullah	105
H. D. R. L. Thirimanne not out	155	– (6) not out	2
*A. D. Mathews c and b Abul Hasan	27	– not out	38
†L. D. Chandimal not out	116		
K. D. K. Vithanage (did not bat)		– (4) b Mahmudullah	59
B 8, l-b 17, w 3, n-b 7	35	N-b 2	2

1/114 (2) 2/181 (1)   (4 wkts dec, 135 overs) 570   1/17 (1)   (4 wkts dec, 83 overs) 335
3/305 (3) 4/367 (5)   2/230 (3) 3/249 (2)
                                                                   4/320 (4)

K. M. D. N. Kulasekara, H. M. R. K. B. Herath, R. M. S. Eranga and B. A. W. Mendis did not bat.

In the first innings Karunaratne, when 15, retired hurt at 46-0 and resumed at 114-1.

Shahadat Hossain 21–2–95–0; Abul Hasan 27–4–112–1; Sohag Gazi 50–6–164–3; Elias Sunny 20–0–89–0; Mohammad Ashraful 4–0–23–0; Mahmudullah 11–1–45–0; Mominul Haque 2–0–17–0. *Second innings*—Shahadat Hossain 9–1–33–1; Abul Hasan 10–0–45–0; Sohag Gazi 15–1–58–0; Elias Sunny 20–0–76–0; Mominul Haque 5–0–25–0; Mohammad Ashraful 1–0–10–0; Mahmudullah 20–1–70–3; Nasir Hossain 3–0–18–0.

Bangladesh

Jahurul Islam c Chandimal b Eranga	20	– not out		41
Anamul Haque b Mendis	13	– b Eranga		1
Mohammad Ashraful c Mathews b Herath	190	– not out		22
Mominul Haque c Mathews b Kulasekara	55			
Mahmudullah st Chandimal b Herath	0			
*†Mushfiqur Rahim lbw b Kulasekara	200			
Nasir Hossain c Karunaratne b Dilshan	100			
Sohag Gazi c Vithanage b Mendis	21			
Abul Hasan not out	16			
Elias Sunny c Chandimal b Dilshan	0			
Shahadat Hossain b Eranga	13			
B 2, l-b 1, n-b 7	10	B 4, l-b 1, n-b 1		6

1/23 (1) 2/65 (2) 3/170 (4)   (196 overs) 638   1/2 (2)   (1 wkt, 22 overs) 70
4/177 (5) 5/444 (3) 6/550 (6)
7/581 (8) 8/618 (7) 9/618 (10) 10/638 (11)

Kulasekara 27–3–94–2; Eranga 34–4–122–2; Herath 62–11–161–2; Mendis 36–3–152–2; Mathews 9–2–18–0; Dilshan 26–5–75–2; Thirimanne 2–0–13–0. *Second innings*—Kulasekara 4–1–6–0; Eranga 3–1–10–1; Herath 4–0–15–0; Mendis 7–1–23–0; Dilshan 4–0–11–0.

Umpires: R. K. Illingworth and N. J. Llong.   Third umpire: T. H. Wijewardene.

SRI LANKA v BANGLADESH

Second Test Match

At Colombo (RPS), March 16–19, 2013. Sri Lanka won by seven wickets. Toss: Sri Lanka.

Sri Lanka salvaged a victory to emerge from the series with their reputation merely bruised rather than broken. Both teams, perhaps dazed by the run-fest in Galle, misread the pitch and played only one specialist spinner. And it fell to slow left-armer Herath to deliver a Sri Lankan win again: he did so on his 35th birthday, collecting the last four of his 12 for 157 on the fourth morning, before his team-mates surged to their target at nearly four an over.

After Galle, where Herath had managed only two wickets in 66 overs, Sri Lanka may have worried that the Bangladeshis, who are rumoured to possess a slow left-armer in every family, had become immune to bowling of his type. They need not have been concerned. The batsmen may have been familiar with the style, but at the Premadasa they could not contend with Herath's class. He undid Bangladesh with guile, intuition and persistence.

Sri Lanka had sent Bangladesh in on a pitch tinged with green and offering help to bowlers of every persuasion. Their seamers removed the openers, but it was not until Herath began his work that they achieved the upper hand. He claimed five wickets on the first day, most memorably that of Mushfiqur Rahim, who was nailed to the crease by a slew of full, quick deliveries, before being beaten by a shorter one that turned across him and clipped off stump. Mominul Haque had shown his pedigree with 55 on debut in the previous Test, and here he was the only batsman to breach 50.

Even so, Sri Lanka's batsmen instantly threatened to hand over the advantage as they stumbled to 69 for four on the second morning. But Sangakkara, who hit his third Test hundred in ten days, and Chandimal lifted them out of the mire by adding 195. Sangakkara was typically unruffled – his 33rd Test century took him to seventh on the all-time list – though Chandimal began nervously, particularly against Sohag Gazi's off-spin, before piecing his defence together and flourishing. Once Sangakkara perished, however, the last four wickets added only 30 – and Mushfiqur completed his fifth catch of the innings, a Bangladesh Test record – so that Sri Lanka's eventual lead was a not-quite-decisive 106.

Tamim Iqbal and Jahurul Islam came within 15 runs of swallowing that deficit. But their stand was to be Bangladesh's biggest of the match, and batsmen continued to fall to Herath before they could launch any sustained resistance. At times, Mathews's use of his bowlers was perplexing but, even in strangely short spells, Herath was effective, and he received keen support from Eranga. Herath reeled in a career-best seven, culminating in his 200th Test wicket, and Sri Lanka's target was just 160. Opener Karunaratne capped another unconvincing Test by departing for 16, but Dilshan progressed to a brisk 57, while Sangakkara's dismissal for 55 reduced his series average to 110.

Man of the Match: H. M. R. K. B. Herath. *Man of the Series:* K. C. Sangakkara.

Close of play: first day, Sri Lanka 18-1 (Karunaratne 12, Sangakkara 3); second day, Sri Lanka 294-6 (Sangakkara 127, Kulasekara 2); third day, Bangladesh 158-4 (Mominul Haque 36, Mushfiqur Rahim 7).

Bangladesh

Tamim Iqbal lbw b Kulasekara	10	– b Eranga	59
Jahurul Islam c Chandimal b Eranga	33	– st Chandimal b Herath	48
Mohammad Ashraful run out	16	– b Herath	4
Mominul Haque c Chandimal b Herath	64	– c Karunaratne b Herath	37
Mahmudullah c Mathews b Herath	8	– b Herath	0
*†Mushfiqur Rahim b Herath	7	– c Mathews b Herath	40
Nasir Hossain lbw b Herath	48	– b Herath	0
Sohag Gazi st Chandimal b Herath	32	– c Lakmal b Herath	26
Abul Hasan c Karunaratne b Kulasekara	4	– not out	25
Rubel Hossain c Herath b Kulasekara	0	– b Dilshan	7
Robiul Islam not out	1	– b Eranga	10
L-b 8, w 7, n-b 2	17	B 1, l-b 4, n-b 4	9

1/16 (1) 2/51 (3) 3/100 (2)   (83.3 overs) 240
4/128 (5) 5/152 (6) 6/163 (4)
7/222 (8) 8/232 (9) 9/232 (10) 10/240 (7)

1/91 (1) 2/96 (3)   (100.4 overs) 265
3/143 (2) 4/143 (5)
5/160 (4) 6/171 (7) 7/202 (8)
8/228 (6) 9/239 (10) 10/265 (11)

Kulasekara 18-3-54-3; Lakmal 16-4-44-0; Mathews 3-1-7-0; Eranga 14-2-40-1; Herath 28.3-6-68-5; Dilshan 4-0-19-0. *Second innings*—Kulasekara 12-0-36-0; Lakmal 9-1-26-0; Herath 36-9-89-7; Dilshan 25-4-62-1; Eranga 15.4-3-39-2; Mathews 3-2-8-0.

Sri Lanka

F. D. M. Karunaratne c Mushfiqur Rahim b Abul Hasan	17	– lbw b Robiul Islam	16
T. M. Dilshan c Mushfiqur Rahim b Robiul Islam	0	– b Robiul Islam	57
K. C. Sangakkara c Mushfiqur Rahim b Abul Hasan	139	– b Sohag Gazi	55
H. D. R. L. Thirimanne c Mushfiqur Rahim b Robiul Islam	0	– not out	13
*A. D. Mathews c Mahmudullah b Sohag Gazi	16	– not out	13
†L. D. Chandimal b Rubel Hossain	102		
K. D. K. Vithanage c Mominul Haque b Rubel Hossain	12		
K. M. D. N. Kulasekara c Mushfiqur Rahim b Sohag Gazi	22		
H. M. R. K. B. Herath b Sohag Gazi	3		
R. M. S. Eranga c Mohammad Ashraful b Mahmudullah	15		
R. A. S. Lakmal not out	0		
B 2, l-b 2, w 6, n-b 10	20	B 2, l-b 1, n-b 3	6

1/7 (2) 2/39 (1) 3/43 (4)   (111.3 overs) 346
4/69 (5) 5/264 (6) 6/280 (7)
7/316 (3) 8/323 (9) 9/346 (8) 10/346 (10)

1/31 (1)   (3 wkts, 41.4 overs) 160
2/125 (2) 3/135 (3)

Robiul Islam 15–1–52–2; Sohag Gazi 39–4–111–3; Abul Hasan 23–4–80–2; Rubel Hossain 17–5–45–2; Mahmudullah 11.3–1–37–1; Mominul Haque 2–0–6–0; Mohammad Ashraful 2–0–9–0; Nasir Hossain 2–0–2–0. *Second innings*—Robiul Islam 11–0–42–2; Abul Hasan 4–0–21–0; Sohag Gazi 13–1–47–1; Rubel Hossain 3–0–16–0; Nasir Hossain 4–0–11–0; Mahmudullah 3–0–12–0; Mohammad Ashraful 3.4–0–8–0.

Umpires: R. K. Illingworth and N. J. Llong.   Third umpire: R. S. A. Palliyaguruge.
Series referee: D. C. Boon.

At Hambantota, March 23, 2013 (day/night). **First one-day international: Sri Lanka won by eight wickets** (D/L). **Bangladesh 259-8** (50 overs) (Tamim Iqbal 112, Nasir Hossain 73*); ‡**Sri Lanka 238-2** (35.4 overs) (M. D. K. J. Perera 42, T. M. Dilshan 113*, K. C. Sangakkara 63). *ODI debut: Ziaur Rahman. MoM: T. M. Dilshan. A breakneck start launched Sri Lanka towards a target of 238 in 41 overs, after malfunctioning floodlights caused a 99-minute delay. Kushal Perera partnered Tillekeratne Dilshan in even more brutal mood: together, against wayward bowling, they hit 83 in the eight-over-powerplay. Perera fell in sight of his fifty, but Dilshan progressed to an unbeaten 113 in 108 balls, trumping Tamim Iqbal's century, which set up what had looked like a competitive total.*

At Hambantota, March 25, 2013 (day/night). **Second one-day international: No result. Sri Lanka 33-0** (5 overs) v ‡**Bangladesh.** *Perera and Dilshan briefly exploited more poor bowling, particularly from Rubel Hossain, but the covers came on at the end of the fifth over and were never removed.*

At Pallekele, March 28, 2013 (day/night). **Third one-day international: Sri Lanka won by three wickets** (D/L). ‡**Sri Lanka 302-9** (50 overs) (M. D. K. J. Perera 56, T. M. Dilshan 125, K. C. Sangakkara 48; Abdur Razzak 5-62); **Bangladesh 184-7** (26 overs) (Anamul Haque 40, Nasir Hossain 33*). *MoM: T. M. Dilshan. MoS: T. M. Dilshan. It was Bangladesh's turn to triumph in a shortened chase, and they embellished an already encouraging tour by squaring the one-day series. Sri Lanka breached 300 on the back of another Dilshan hundred, despite five wickets for Abdur Razzak, but a confident start from Anamul Haque and Mohammad Ashraful (29) ensured that Duckworth/Lewis favoured Bangladesh when rain interrupted play at 78-1 in the 14th over. Upon resumption, their revised target was 183 in 27 – a further 105 from 13.2. Nasir Hossain marshalled the middle order wonderfully, with a personal strike-rate of 122. It was Bangladesh's fourth win over Sri Lanka in all internationals, and their first away from home.*

At Pallekele, March 31, 2013. **Twenty20 international: Sri Lanka won by 17 runs. Sri Lanka 198-5** (20 overs) (M. D. K. J. Perera 64, A. D. Mathews 30*, B. M. A. J. Mendis 37); ‡**Bangladesh 181-7** (20 overs) (Mohammad Ashraful 43, Mushfiqur Rahim 39, Mahmudullah 31). *T20I debuts: A. K. Perera; Shamsur Rahman. MoM: M. D. K. J. Perera. With four senior players rested, Jeewan Mendis was the only Sri Lankan as old as 30 – but the youngsters set up a comfortable victory. Kushal Perera scored a blistering maiden international fifty, launching five fours and four sixes, and routinely planting his front foot outside off stump to crash bowlers through midwicket. Sri Lanka's middle-order all-rounders followed up with their own flurry of boundaries. Mohammad Ashraful began Bangladesh's reply briskly, and hit Tissara Perera for 16 in three deliveries before, in the same over, he was given lbw to a ball which hit him outside leg. After his demise, Bangladesh simply had too much to do.*

SRI LANKA v SOUTH AFRICA, 2013

Rex Clementine

One-day internationals (5): Sri Lanka 4, South Africa 1
Twenty20 internationals (3): Sri Lanka 1, South Africa 2

South Africa arrived for their first tour of Sri Lanka in seven years to find the home board under fire – and themselves at the centre of the fuss. Back in October 2012, Cricket South Africa had acceded to a request by their Sri Lankan counterparts to postpone the three scheduled Tests from this tour until mid-2015, in order to free up space for the Sri Lanka Premier League and the national team's participation in a triangular series in the Caribbean. But when the SLPL was cancelled with weeks to go, Sri Lanka Cricket were berated for their priorities.

CSA said they had agreed to defer the Tests so their players could have more time to recover from the Champions Trophy in England in June. Kumar Sangakkara, however, felt it was a missed opportunity for Sri Lanka to improve their lowly position of No. 7, even against the world's best Test side. "The South Africans don't like these conditions much," he said. His captain, Angelo Mathews, said he was "bitterly disappointed", while former skipper Arjuna Ranatunga called the cancellation "a crime". The blame, though, belonged with the Sri Lankans.

Sangakkara's hunch seemed prescient when South Africa collapsed to a 4–1 defeat in the one-day series – their worst result since losing 4–0 in England in 2008. There was some mitigation. J-P. Duminy and Robin Peterson were the only squad members who had previously played a one-day international in Sri Lanka. Graeme Smith had just undergone ankle surgery, while Dale Steyn and Jacques Kallis were rested. And it showed, as the South Africans struggled with the heat, humidity and slow pitches.

Hashim Amla did tour, but missed the first one-dayer with a stiff neck, couldn't bat in the second after he injured his groin, and was forced out of the third. The opening positions rotated between Colin Ingram, Alviro Petersen, Peterson, Quinton de Kock and Amla, but none could muster a stand above 35. South Africa's two left-arm spinners, Peterson and Aaron Phangiso, were swatted away with ease by mainly left-handed batsmen. By the end, South Africa's record against Sri Lanka away stood at two wins from 15 completed matches.

Sangakkara savaged the bowling, racking up 372 runs – the most by a Sri Lankan in a bilateral series. Ajantha Mendis, omitted until the third match, took ten cheap wickets, exploiting South African uncertainty against quality spin. Mathews also sat out the first two games as he served a suspension for his team's slow over-rate in the tri-series final earlier in the month. He inherited a 2–0 lead from Dinesh Chandimal, who at 23 years and 244 days was younger than Ranatunga had been when he first captained Sri Lanka.

South Africa shook up their bowling attack for the Twenty20 series, and won it, although Sri Lanka's successful run-chase in the final game allowed them to hold on to their No. 1 ranking. Faf du Plessis and A. B. de Villiers both endured torrid tours with the bat, but du Plessis's captaincy in the Twenty20s, where he took over from de Villiers, brought a new energy to the side – and many believed he emerged the stronger leader.

SOUTH AFRICAN TOURING PARTY

*A. B. de Villiers (50/20), H. M. Amla (50), F. Behardien (50/20), H. Davids (20), Q. de Kock (50/20), J-P. Duminy (50/20), F. du Plessis (50/20), Imran Tahir (20), C. A. Ingram (50), R. K. Kleinveldt (50/20), R. McLaren (50/20), D. A. Miller (50/20), M. Morkel (50/20), C. H. Morris (50/20), W. D. Parnell (20), A. N. Petersen (50), R. J. Peterson (50), A. M. Phangiso (50/20), L. L. Tsotsobe (50/20), D. Wiese (20). *Coach:* R. C. Domingo.
    Du Plessis captained in the Twenty20 series.

At Colombo (Colts), July 17, 2013. **South Africans won by 73 runs.** ‡**South Africans 271-6** (50 overs) (J-P. Duminy 92); **Sri Lanka Cricket Board President's XI 198** (44.5 overs) (C. H. Morris 3-27, R. J. Peterson 3-37). *Morne Morkel was forced off after his third over due to tightness in his left thigh, but new-ball partner Chris Morris took up the slack. J-P. Duminy showed his aptitude in Sri Lankan conditions until he was bowled trying to shovel Dammika Prasad to leg.*

SRI LANKA v SOUTH AFRICA

First One-Day International

At Colombo (RPS), July 20, 2013 (day/night). Sri Lanka won by 180 runs. Toss: South Africa.
    This was South Africa's first one-day international in Sri Lanka for nine years – and it showed. They gambled on bowling first, but had their spirits and skills sapped by the imperious Sangakkara in Colombo's unforgiving heat and humidity. He paddle-swept and scooped his way to the highest one-day score by a Sri Lankan at home, with 131 of his 169 made on the leg side. Morkel and Morris helped the hosts' cause by conceding eight wides in the first two overs and, when McLaren finally bowled Sangakkara on 135, he was denied the wicket because too many fielders had slipped outside the circle. Sangakkara accounted for exactly 100 of a 123-run partnership with Thirimanne, as Sri Lanka soared to their record score against South Africa. Malinga then seared an inswinging yorker through Ingram first ball, and South Africa floundered through 32 overs before collapsing to their second-heaviest defeat by runs. It was an easy initiation for Chandimal, the youngest man to captain Sri Lanka in the format.
    Man of the Match: K. C. Sangakkara.

Sri Lanka

W. U. Tharanga b Morkel	43	*L. D. Chandimal not out	1
T. M. Dilshan b Morris	10		
†K. C. Sangakkara c Duminy b Phangiso	169	B 1, l-b 5, w 15, n-b 1	22
D. P. M. D. Jayawardene c Ingram b Morkel	42		
H. D. R. L. Thirimanne c Peterson b McLaren	17	1/23 (2) 2/93 (1) (5 wkts, 50 overs)	320
N. L. T. C. Perera not out	16	3/167 (4) 4/290 (5)	
		5/303 (3) 10 overs: 50-1	

J. Mubarak, H. M. R. K. B. Herath, R. M. S. Eranga and S. L. Malinga did not bat.

Morkel 10-2-34-2; Morris 9-0-80-1; McLaren 10-0-69-1; Peterson 5-0-30-0; Duminy 7-0-51-0; Phangiso 9-0-50-1.

South Africa

C. A. Ingram b Malinga	0		M. Morkel c Thirimanne b Herath	0
A. N. Petersen c Sangakkara b Perera	29		A. M. Phangiso st Sangakkara b Herath	0
J-P. Duminy c Sangakkara b Eranga	15			
*†A. B. de Villiers b Herath	23		B 4, l-b 7, w 2	13
F. du Plessis c Chandimal b Perera	4			
D. A. Miller b Dilshan	14		1/0 (1) 2/29 (3) 3/73 (4) (31.5 overs)	140
R. J. Peterson c Tharanga b Perera	29		4/75 (2) 5/82 (5) 6/103 (6)	
R. McLaren c Perera b Dilshan	4		7/119 (8) 8/138 (7) 9/138 (10)	
C. H. Morris not out	9		10/140 (11) 10 overs: 63-2	

Malinga 4–1–21–1; Eranga 5–0–27–1; Perera 7–0–31–3; Herath 8.5–1–25–3; Dilshan 5–0–11–2; Mubarak 2–0–14–0.

Umpires: R. A. Kettleborough and R. E. J. Martinesz. Third umpire: R. J. Tucker.

SRI LANKA v SOUTH AFRICA

Second One-Day International

At Colombo (RPS), July 23, 2013 (day/night). Sri Lanka won by 17 runs (D/L). Toss: Sri Lanka.

After their demolition in the first game, South Africa were relieved when Amla recovered from a stiff neck in time to play. But he slipped and hurt his groin trying to reel the ball in at fine leg, which left him unable to bat. Sri Lanka's innings was a staccato affair, not least because of the 20 wides donated by South Africa, who had now conceded 35 across the first two games. Heavy rain arrived four balls before the change of innings, leaving South Africa to chase 176 in 29 overs. With Amla indisposed, Robin Peterson was handed the job of facing Malinga first up – making him the first spinner to open the bowling and batting for South Africa in one-day internationals. He managed to keep out one solitary ball, but the second cleaned him up. South Africa stuttered after Dilshan persuaded his sceptical team-mates to review an lbw appeal against de Villiers, and they were well behind the required rate when another downpour ended the game after 21 overs.

Man of the Match: L. D. Chandimal.

Sri Lanka

W. U. Tharanga c Peterson b Morkel	3		H. M. R. K. B. Herath run out	13
T. M. Dilshan c de Villiers b Morkel	43		R. M. S. Eranga not out	7
†K. C. Sangakkara c Petersen b Phangiso	37		S. L. Malinga not out	0
D. P. M. D. Jayawardene b Peterson	17		L-b 6, w 20, n-b 2	28
H. D. R. L. Thirimanne lbw b McLaren	13			
*L. D. Chandimal c du Plessis b Morkel	43		1/7 (1) 2/66 (3) (9 wkts, 49.2 overs)	223
J. Mubarak c and b Duminy	8		3/106 (4) 4/120 (2)	
N. L. T. C. Perera c sub (C. A. Ingram)			5/143 (5) 6/167 (7) 7/192 (8)	
b Morris	11		8/205 (6) 9/220 (9) 10 overs: 38-1	

Peterson 10–0–39–1; Morkel 10–0–34–3; Morris 7–0–38–1; McLaren 9.2–0–45–1; Phangiso 10–0–52–1; Duminy 3–0–9–1.

South Africa

A. N. Petersen lbw b Herath	24		R. McLaren not out	14
R. J. Peterson b Malinga	3		L-b 2, w 4	6
J-P. Duminy c Sangakkara b Perera	15			
*†A. B. de Villiers lbw b Dilshan	12		1/7 (2) 2/39 (3) (5 wkts, 21 overs)	104
F. du Plessis c Sangakkara b Herath	8		3/55 (1) 4/67 (4)	
D. A. Miller not out	22		5/69 (5) 6 overs: 39-1	

H. M. Amla, C. H. Morris, M. Morkel and A. M. Phangiso did not bat.

Malinga 3–0–17–1; Eranga 4–0–21–0; Perera 4–0–23–1; Herath 4–0–16–2; Dilshan 5–0–20–1; Mubarak 1–0–5–0.

Umpires: R. S. A. Palliyaguruge and R. R. Wimalasiri.   Third umpire: R. A. Kettleborough.

SRI LANKA v SOUTH AFRICA

Third One-Day International

At Pallekele, July 26, 2013 (day/night). South Africa won by 56 runs. Toss: South Africa. One-day international debut: A. K. Perera.

South Africa had lost their last 11 one-day internationals away to Sri Lanka, and had not looked like halting that sequence on this trip. But of all Sri Lanka's international venues, Pallekele tends to do most for the seamers, and the South Africans' had more menace. In fact, bowling held sway throughout – except for three astonishing overs. The first two came with South Africa 185 for seven after 48, at which point Miller tore into Tissara Perera and Malinga to salvage a competitive score; in all, 38 runs accrued, including four sixes. Tsotsobe, finally deemed fit to play, found movement to knock over Sri Lanka's top three, and they had limped into the 33rd over on 94 for seven. Then came the game's third remarkable over, as Perera thrashed Peterson for five sixes between square leg and long-on. The over, which also included a wide and a four, eventually cost 35, one short of the world record: South Africa's Herschelle Gibbs had hit Dutch leg-spinner Daan van Bunge for six sixes during the 2007 World Cup. Perera also enjoyed a huge let-off on 61, when Tsotsobe let a gentle lob slip through his hands at short fine leg. South Africa could breathe easily only when Perera finally holed out off Behardien, whose selection ahead of Aaron Phangiso proved the right call.

Man of the Match: D. A. Miller.

South Africa

A. N. Petersen c Sangakkara b Malinga	8	R. J. Peterson b Mendis	3
†Q. de Kock c Sangakkara b N. L. T. C. Perera	20	R. McLaren not out	14
J-P. Duminy b N. L. T. C. Perera	23	L-b 3, w 2	5
*A. B. de Villiers c Sangakkara b Mendis	47		
F. du Plessis run out	16	1/14 (1) 2/50 (2) (7 wkts, 50 overs) 223	
F. Behardien b Mendis	2	3/53 (3) 4/95 (5)	
D. A. Miller not out	85	5/100 (6) 6/148 (4) 7/154 (8) 10 overs: 33-1	

M. Morkel and L. L. Tsotsobe did not bat.

Malinga 10–0–57–1; Mathews 5–1–17–0; Dilshan 10–0–39–0; N. L. T. C. Perera 8–0–51–2; Mendis 10–0–35–3; Herath 7–1–21–0.

Sri Lanka

W. U. Tharanga c Petersen b Tsotsobe	5	S. L. Malinga b Behardien	0
T. M. Dilshan c de Villiers b Tsotsobe	6	B. A. W. Mendis c Tsotsobe b Duminy	0
†K. C. Sangakkara c Duminy b Tsotsobe	0		
D. P. M. D. Jayawardene b Peterson	24	B 1, l-b 4, w 6	11
L. D. Chandimal c de Kock b McLaren	29		
*A. D. Mathews c de Villiers b Tsotsobe	14	1/14 (2) 2/14 (3) 3/16 (1) (43.2 overs) 167	
A. K. Perera c de Villiers b Behardien	1	4/71 (4) 5/78 (5) 6/81 (7)	
N. L. T. C. Perera c du Plessis b Behardien	65	7/93 (6) 8/165 (8) 9/166 (10)	
H. M. R. K. B. Herath not out	12	10/167 (11) 10 overs: 24-3	

Morkel 8–1–29–0; Tsotsobe 7–2–22–4; McLaren 6–1–18–1; Peterson 7–0–51–1; Duminy 9.2–1–23–1; Behardien 6–0–19–3.

Umpires: R. A. Kettleborough and R. E. J. Martinesz.   Third umpire: R. J. Tucker.

SRI LANKA v SOUTH AFRICA

Fourth One-Day International

At Pallekele, July 28, 2013 (day/night). Sri Lanka won by eight wickets. Toss: South Africa.

Sri Lanka came back strongly from their loss two days earlier to pull off the highest successful run-chase at Pallekele, and clinch the series with a game to spare. South Africa were sturdier for the presence of Amla, who made 77 in his first innings of the series, but he and Duminy erred in taking the batting powerplay after only 15 overs, and managed just 22 from it against the spinners. The innings declined rapidly after Dilshan dismissed Amla and de Villiers in consecutive overs, and Duminy missed out on a century when he was reduced to swiping alongside the tail. Jayawardene was restored to open in place of the misfiring Tharanga, and helped Dilshan see off the threat of two new balls. South Africa's best chance to get Sangakkara early passed when de Villiers declined to review an adjacent lbw shout from Duminy, and he wrapped up the series in a stand of 184 with Dilshan – Sri Lanka's best for any wicket against South Africa. Dilshan completed a hundred short on thrills, his 17th in one-day internationals and fifth in ten innings on this ground; Sangakkara missed his own 17th when he top-edged to mid-off. Tsotsobe, included in the touring party only on the condition he sort out his fitness and attitude, twice let the ball go through him at fine leg.

Man of the Match: T. M. Dilshan.

South Africa

H. M. Amla lbw b Dilshan	77		M. Morkel lbw b Mendis		0
†Q. de Kock b Malinga	8		L. L. Tsotsobe not out		3
J-P. Duminy b Mendis	97				
*A. B. de Villiers c Sangakkara b Dilshan	4		B 4		4
F. du Plessis st Sangakkara b Herath	23				
D. A. Miller b Mendis	1		1/17 (2) 2/118 (1)	(48.4 overs)	238
F. Behardien c Thirimanne b Mendis	0		3/126 (4) 4/172 (5) 5/173 (6)		
R. J. Peterson c Sangakkara b Malinga	13		6/173 (7) 7/191 (8) 8/203 (9)		
R. K. Kleinveldt c Dilshan b Malinga	8		9/205 (10) 10/238 (3)	10 overs: 54-1	

Malinga 9–0–52–3; Mathews 7–1–31–0; Mendis 9.4–0–51–4; Perera 3–0–22–0; Herath 10–0–38–1; Dilshan 10–0–40–2.

Sri Lanka

T. M. Dilshan not out	115
D. P. M. D. Jayawardene c Amla b Tsotsobe	12
†K. C. Sangakkara c Kleinveldt b Morkel	91
H. D. R. L. Thirimanne not out	1
L-b 2, w 17, n-b 1	20

1/45 (2)	(2 wkts, 44 overs)	239
2/229 (3)	10 overs: 45-1	

W. U. Tharanga, L. D. Chandimal, *A. D. Mathews, N. L. T. C. Perera, H. M. R. K. B. Herath, S. L. Malinga and B. A. W. Mendis did not bat.

Morkel 10–1–62–1; Tsotsobe 7–0–48–1; Kleinveldt 8–0–33–0; Peterson 8–0–46–0; Duminy 10–1–34–0; Behardien 1–0–14–0.

Umpires: R. S. A. Palliyaguruge and R. J. Tucker. Third umpire: R. A. Kettleborough.

SRI LANKA v SOUTH AFRICA

Fifth One-Day International

At Colombo (RPS), July 31, 2013 (day/night). Sri Lanka won by 128 runs. Toss: Sri Lanka.

Sri Lanka recalled four fringe players for this dead rubber, but South Africa's fate remained much the same. Dilshan was one run from back-to-back hundreds, only to linger for four deliveries before missing McLaren's slower ball. But Sangakkara, at his innovative best, raced them to a near-unassailable score with an unbeaten 75 that tipped his career average to the brink of 40. Morkel's figures were the most expensive of his one-day international career. Sri Lanka's replacements for Herath and Malinga worked a treat: Senanayake, brought on for the sixth over, foxed de Kock and Amla out of the hand, and Lakmal snapped up two in an over. De Villiers fought alone with a run-a-ball fifty, his only half-century of the series, but his leadership lacked verve. It was a view apparently shared by national selector Shafiek Abrahams, who declared on television minutes after the match that he believed du Plessis was the superior leader.

Man of the Match: T. M. Dilshan. *Man of the Series:* K. C. Sangakkara.

Sri Lanka

T. M. Dilshan b McLaren	99	N. L. T. C. Perera not out	17
M. D. K. J. Perera c de Kock b Morkel	9		
H. D. R. L. Thirimanne c Duminy		L-b 8, w 8	16
b Phangiso	68		—
†K. C. Sangakkara not out	75	1/13 (2) 2/176 (3) (4 wkts, 50 overs)	307
*A. D. Mathews c Miller b Tsotsobe	23	3/212 (1) 4/257 (5) 10 overs: 39-1	

L. D. Chandimal, A. K. Perera, S. M. S. M. Senanayake, R. A. S. Lakmal and B. A. W. Mendis did not bat.

Morkel 10–0–78–1; Tsotsobe 10–2–52–1; McLaren 10–0–47–1; Behardien 4–0–28–0; Duminy 7–0–46–0; Phangiso 9–0–48–1.

South Africa

†Q. de Kock b Senanayake	27	M. Morkel b Mendis	0
H. M. Amla lbw b Senanayake	18	A. M. Phangiso not out	18
J-P. Duminy lbw b Dilshan	15	L. L. Tsotsobe b Lakmal	1
F. du Plessis c Sangakkara		L-b 2, w 11	13
b N. L. T. C. Perera	6		—
*A. B. de Villiers c Mathews b Mendis	51	1/35 (2) 2/60 (2) 3/61 (3) (43.5 overs)	179
F. Behardien c Mathews b Lakmal	1	4/69 (4) 5/85 (6) 6/85 (7)	
D. A. Miller c Sangakkara b Lakmal	0	7/137 (5) 8/137 (9) 9/171 (8)	
R. McLaren c Mathews b Mendis	29	10/179 (11) 10 overs: 60-2	

Lakmal 5.5–0–22–3; Mathews 4–0–32–0; Senanayake 10–2–29–2; Dilshan 10–0–41–1; N. L. T. C. Perera 5–1–17–1; Mendis 9–2–36–3.

Umpires: R. A. Kettleborough and R. R. Wimalasiri.   Third umpire: R. E. J. Martinesz.
Series referee: A. J. Pycroft.

SRI LANKA v SOUTH AFRICA

First Twenty20 International

At Colombo (RPS), August 2, 2013 (floodlit). South Africa won by 12 runs. Toss: South Africa. Twenty20 international debuts: Imran Tahir, D. Wiese.

Sri Lanka ought to have managed 70 from their last ten overs, with Sangakkara one of their seven wickets in hand, but instead they popped up a series of catches to the grateful South Africans. "There was nothing in the pitch that warranted scores that low," said Chandimal, forced to stomach his first defeat as captain. The rot really set in when Mathews prodded back to Duminy, then Jeewan Mendis tamely swept the next ball to square leg. Sri Lanka needed 21 off the last 12 balls, but Parnell – left out of the one-day series – doused that prospect with a double-wicket maiden. Duminy had given South Africa's innings much-needed direction after Senanayake bamboozled the young openers, and du Plessis, who shaped to leg, changed his mind, and was bowled trying belatedly to defend.

Man of the Match: J-P. Duminy.

South Africa

		B	4	6
H. Davids *lbw b 9*	1	8	0	0
†Q. de Kock *lbw b 9*	5	7	1	0
*F. du Plessis *b 9*	8	11	1	0
J-P. Duminy *c 2 b 11*	51	52	3	1
A. B. de Villiers *c 1 b 5*	15	16	2	0
D. A. Miller *c 2 b 10*	25	24	0	1
D. Wiese *not out*	3	2	0	0
W. D. Parnell *not out*	0	0	0	0
L-b 5, w 2	7			

6 overs: 23-3   (20 overs)   115-6

1/6 2/12 3/23 4/50 5/106 6/113

M. Morkel, Imran Tahir and L. L. Tsotsobe did not bat.

Malinga 4–0–25–1; Senanayake 4–0–14–3; Mathews 3–0–15–0; Dilshan 3–0–15–0; N. L. T. C. Perera 1–0–11–0; B. A. W. Mendis 4–0–32–1.

Sri Lanka

		B	4	6
M. D. K. J. Perera *c 7 b 9*	11	14	2	0
T. M. Dilshan *c 5 b 4*	9	19	0	0
*L. D. Chandimal *c 2 b 11*	8	9	2	0
†K. C. Sangakkara *not out*	59	53	9	0
A. D. Mathews *c and b 4*	4	7	0	0
B. M. A. J. Mendis *c 10 b 4*	0	1	0	0
H. D. R. L. Thirimanne *c 5 b 10*	5	9	0	0
N. L. T. C. Perera *c 3 b 9*	0	3	0	0
S. M. S. M. Senanayake *c 2 b 8*	0	4	0	0
S. L. Malinga *c 3 b 8*	0	2	0	0
B. A. W. Mendis *not out*	0	0	0	0
L-b 1, w 5, n-b 1	7			

6 overs: 29-2   (20 overs)   103-9

1/15 2/25 3/44 4/72 5/72 6/90 7/91 8/95 9/95

Tsotsobe 3–0–11–1; Morkel 4–0–28–2; Parnell 3–1–8–2; Imran Tahir 4–0–22–1; Duminy 4–0–18–3; Wiese 1–0–8–0; Davids 1–0–7–0.

Umpires: R. E. J. Martinesz and R. R. Wimalasiri.   Third umpire: R. S. A. Palliyaguruge.

SRI LANKA v SOUTH AFRICA

Second Twenty20 International

At Hambantota, August 4, 2013 (floodlit). South Africa won by 22 runs. Toss: South Africa.

Most teams struggle with the strong winds at Hambantota, but South Africa appeared to learn from their visit here during the previous year's World Twenty20. Sri Lanka still had them under control until Miller struck two of the game's four sixes in a typically jaunty finish. After Kushal Perera was given lbw to an Imran Tahir googly that pitched outside leg stump (there was no recourse to DRS), the equation again boiled down to Sangakkara versus South Africa. But he picked out extra cover with 56 needed. Sri Lanka's series defeat brought into question the rotation policy adopted for their big three – Jayawardene had been left out of the first match, Dilshan for this must-win game, and Sangakkara's turn would come – and also the performances of their next generation of batsmen.

Man of the Match: D. A. Miller.

South Africa

		B	4	6
H. Davids *b 8*	7	10	0	0
†Q. de Kock *st 4 b 9*	19	23	3	0
*F. du Plessis *b 10*	12	15	0	1
J-P. Duminy *c 6 b 9*	30	23	3	0
A. B. de Villiers *run out*	15	14	1	0
D. A. Miller *c 3 b 8*	36	21	1	2
D. Wiese *not out*	7	8	0	0
W. D. Parnell *not out*	10	6	1	0
L-b 2, w 7	9			

6 overs: 30-1   (20 overs)   145-6

1/11 2/44 3/48 4/86 5/105 6/132

M. Morkel, Imran Tahir and L. L. Tsotsobe did not bat.

Kulasekara 4–0–22–2; Malinga 4–0–32–1; Senanayake 4–0–18–2; Mathews 4–0–32–0; Mendis 4–0–39–0.

Sri Lanka

		B	4	6
M. D. K. J. Perera *lbw b 10*	21	22	3	0
D. P. M. D. Jayawardene *c 2 b 11*	6	5	1	0
*L. D. Chandimal *c 2 b 11*	2	7	0	0
†K. C. Sangakkara *c 7 b 9*	39	35	4	0
H. D. R. L. Thirimanne *b 8*	18	18	1	0
A. D. Mathews *c 5 b 7*	1	3	0	0
N. L. T. C. Perera *not out*	22	20	2	0
K. M. D. N. Kulasekara *c 2 b 9*	10	9	0	1
S. M. S. M. Senanayake *not out*	1	1	0	0
L-b 1, w 2	3			

6 overs: 42-2   (20 overs)   123-7

1/8 2/27 3/48 4/85 5/88 6/90 7/112

S. L. Malinga and B. A. W. Mendis did not bat.

Tsotsobe 4–0–17–2; Morkel 4–0–34–2; Parnell 4–0–25–1; Wiese 4–0–25–1; Imran Tahir 4–0–21–1.

Umpires: R. E. J. Martinesz and R. S. A. Palliyaguruge.   Third umpire: R. R. Wimalasiri.

SRI LANKA v SOUTH AFRICA

Third Twenty20 International

At Hambantota, August 6, 2013 (floodlit). Sri Lanka won by six wickets. Toss: South Africa.

South Africa saved their best batting performance for last, leaving Sri Lanka on the cusp of a series whitewash and the loss of their No. 1 ranking in Twenty20 internationals. But Dilshan gave the run-chase a shot in the arm: leaping on Tsotsobe, he pulled his fourth ball for six, followed by two Dilscoops for four. Sri Lanka lost momentum after the fall of Jayawardene, but Tissara Perera took Parnell for 20 in the 18th over, before Dilshan slog-swept Morkel for six next ball to win the game. Du Plessis finally came good with the bat against an attack lacking the injured Malinga, though he was lucky to survive Mendis twice – first an lbw appeal on 24, then on 56 when Thirimanne put down an easy chance at midwicket. Duminy was more assured, and cemented his status as South Africa's most accomplished batsman on the tour.

Man of the Match: T. M. Dilshan. *Man of the Series:* J-P. Duminy.

South Africa		B	4	6
H. Davids *lbw b 8*	0	1	0	0
†Q. de Kock *lbw b 10*	16	19	3	0
*F. du Plessis *b 11*	85	65	10	3
J-P. Duminy *not out*	51	34	3	2
A. B. de Villiers *not out*	1	1	0	0
L-b 1, w 9	10			

6 overs: 35-1   (20 overs) 163-3

1/0 2/45 3/157

D. A. Miller, D. Wiese, W. D. Parnell, M. Morkel, Imran Tahir and L. L. Tsotsobe did not bat.

Kulasekara 4–0–37–1; Lakmal 4–0–29–1; Senanayake 4–0–20–0; N. L. T. C. Perera 1–0–10–0; Mendis 4–0–31–1; Mathews 1–0–14–0; Dilshan 2–0–21–0.

Sri Lanka		B	4	6
T. M. Dilshan *not out*	74	51	9	2
D. P. M. D. Jayawardene *c 5 b 8*	33	16	7	0
M. D. K. J. Perera *c 8 b 7*	1	4	0	0
*†L. D. Chandimal *st 2 b 10*	14	18	1	0
A. D. Mathews *b 7*	14	10	2	0
N. L. T. C. Perera *not out*	25	11	3	1
L-b 1, w 1, n-b 1	3			

6 overs: 67-1   (18.1 overs) 164-4

1/67 2/71 3/100 4/123

H. D. R. L. Thirimanne, K. M. D. N. Kulasekara, S. M. S. M. Senanayake, B. A. W. Mendis and R. A. S. Lakmal did not bat.

Tsotsobe 4–0–49–0; Morkel 3.1–0–33–0; Parnell 3–0–37–1; Imran Tahir 4–0–20–1; Wiese 4–0–24–2.

Umpires: R. E. J. Martinesz and R. S. A. Palliyaguruge. Third umpire: R. R. Wimalasiri.
Series referee: A. J. Pycroft.

SRI LANKA v NEW ZEALAND, 2013-14

Sa'adi Thawfeeq

One-day internationals (3): Sri Lanka 1, New Zealand 1
Twenty20 internationals (2): Sri Lanka 1, New Zealand 0

Sri Lanka gave New Zealand a hearty welcome for their short tour, as circumstances had conspired to deprive the hosts of much international competition in 2013. First a two-Test series in the West Indies was replaced by a one-day triangular tournament, then South Africa's visit was shorn of its Test matches to accommodate the Sri Lanka Premier League – which never actually took place. Finally, a scheduled tour of Zimbabwe was cancelled.

There was some disappointment that New Zealand did not send their strongest side. Brendon McCullum and Ross Taylor were rested, while Kane Williamson, the stand-in captain, had broken his thumb in Bangladesh. Kyle Mills took charge instead. The weather posed further problems: the first four matches were all affected, with the first Twenty20 international completely washed out. The one-day series was shared, but Sri Lanka claimed a convincing win in the second Twenty20 after the rain relented.

Sri Lanka had planned to include some new faces, with Twenty20 and 50-over World Cups on the horizon. But the main contributors were familiar names: Tillekeratne Dilshan passed 50 in each of his four innings, while Kumar Sangakkara batted with his customary panache. The only fresh blood was the young off-spinner Ramith Rambukwella, the son of Sri Lanka's Minister for Media and Information.

After a one-day whitewash in Bangladesh, New Zealand were relieved to share the 50-over series, which they did thanks to a remarkable blitz from Nathan McCullum. Needing 17 from the last four balls to win the second game at Hambantota, he pummelled Rangana Herath for six, four, six and six. McCullum also bowled well throughout, while Mills welcomed the contribution of wicketkeeper Luke Ronchi, whose three useful innings helped atone for an underwhelming start to his New Zealand career in England earlier in the year.

NEW ZEALAND TOURING PARTY

*K. D. Mills, C. J. Anderson, A. P. Devcich, G. D. Elliott, A. M. Ellis, T. W. M. Latham, M. J. McClenaghan, N. L. McCullum, A. F. Milne, C. Munro, J. D. S. Neesham, R. J. Nicol, L. Ronchi, H. D. Rutherford. *Coach:* M. J. Hesson.

K. S. Williamson was originally named as captain, but broke his thumb during the preceding tour of Bangladesh, and was replaced in the squad by Nicol; Mills took over as captain. I. G. Butler was originally selected, but pulled out with a back injury and was replaced by Ellis. Anderson suffered a rib injury in the second one-day international, and was replaced by N. T. Broom.

SRI LANKA v NEW ZEALAND

First One-Day International

At Hambantota, November 10, 2013 (day/night). No result. Toss: New Zealand.

A stand of 137 in 26 overs between Dilshan and Sangakkara put Sri Lanka back on course after Karunaratne had fallen to the first ball of the match. Mathews later spanked an unbeaten 74 from 64 balls to set up a challenging total. Rain was always forecast – it was one reason Mills decided to bowl first – and it swept in for good early in New Zealand's innings, during which Malinga also took a wicket in the first over.

Sri Lanka

F. D. M. Karunaratne lbw b Mills	0		S. M. S. M. Senanayake b McClenaghan	14
T. M. Dilshan c Ronchi b Anderson	81		H. M. R. K. B. Herath not out	0
†K. C. Sangakkara c McCullum b Devcich	79			
D. P. M. D. Jayawardene c Nicol b Devcich	1		L-b 7, w 8, n-b 1	16
*A. D. Mathews not out	74			
H. D. R. L. Thirimanne c and b McCullum	2		1/0 (1) 2/137 (3) (9 wkts, 50 overs)	288
L. D. Chandimal b McClenaghan	9		3/139 (4) 4/197 (2)	
K. M. D. N. Kulasekara c McCullum b Mills	12		5/216 (6) 6/240 (7) 7/267 (8)	
S. L. Malinga b Mills	0		8/268 (9) 9/283 (6) 10 overs: 54-1	

Mills 9–0–49–3; McClenaghan 8–0–74–2; Milne 8–0–41–0; Devcich 10–1–33–2; McCullum 9–0–38–1; Anderson 4–0–32–1; Nicol 2–0–14–0.

New Zealand

A. P. Devcich b Malinga	0	
T. W. M. Latham not out	4	
R. J. Nicol not out	1	
L-b 2, w 6	8	
1/7 (1) (1 wkt, 4.2 overs)	13	

G. D. Elliott, C. Munro, †L. Ronchi, C. J. Anderson, N. L. McCullum, *K. D. Mills, A. F. Milne and M. J. McClenaghan did not bat.

Malinga 2.2–0–8–1; Kulasekara 2–1–3–0.

Umpires: B. N. J. Oxenford and R. S. A. Palliyaguruge.   Third umpire: R. R. Wimalasiri.

SRI LANKA v NEW ZEALAND

Second One-Day International

At Hambantota, November 12, 2013 (day/night). New Zealand won by four wickets (D/L). Toss: Sri Lanka.

An astonishing last-over assault from Nathan McCullum took New Zealand to a victory that scarcely seemed possible when they slipped to 34 for three – or indeed when they entered the last over needing 20. Neesham took a two and a single off Herath, leaving McCullum on strike with 17 required from four deliveries. He smashed a six and a four over extra cover, then tied the scores on Duckworth/Lewis with another huge six over long-off. Finally, with a flourish reminiscent of his resting brother Brendon, McCullum drilled the last ball over long-on for six more, to finish with 32 from just nine deliveries. Sri Lanka had appeared in charge ever since rain curtailed their innings before halfway, and New Zealand's revised target mushroomed to 198 from 23 overs. Latham, who made 86 from 68 balls, regained some ground in a stand of 93 with Ronchi, but they both fell in the 21st to Kulasekara, who had also taken two wickets in his first over. It looked done and dusted – but then came McCullum.

Man of the Match: T. W. M. Latham.

Sri Lanka

F. D. M. Karunaratne c Neesham b Mills	..	4
T. M. Dilshan not out	....	55
†K. C. Sangakkara not out	....	71
B 1, l-b 2, w 4, n-b 1	....	8

1/12 (1)   (1 wkt, 23 overs) 138
                    10 overs: 51-1

D. P. M. D. Jayawardene, *A. D. Mathews, H. D. R. L. Thirimanne, L. D. Chandimal, K. M. D. N. Kulasekara, S. M. S. M. Senanayake, H. M. R. K. B. Herath and S. L. Malinga did not bat.

Mills 5–2–16–1; Milne 3–0–20–0; Neesham 3–0–25–0; McCullum 4–0–23–0; Devcich 5–0–31–0; Nicol 2–0–12–0; Ellis 1–0–8–0.

New Zealand

T. W. M. Latham c Senanayake			J. D. S. Neesham not out	....	5
	b Kulasekara	86	N. L. McCullum not out	....	32
A. P. Devcich c Sangakkara b Kulasekara	.	1	L-b 5, w 3	....	8
R. J. Nicol c Sangakkara b Kulasekara	..	0			
G. D. Elliott st Sangakkara b Senanayake	..	7	1/8 (2) 2/8 (3)	(6 wkts, 23 overs)	203
C. Munro c Thirimanne b Senanayake	....	15	3/34 (4) 4/68 (5)		
†L. Ronchi c Dilshan b Kulasekara	....	49	5/161 (6) 6/165 (1)	5 overs: 27-2	

*K. D. Mills, A. F. Milne and A. M. Ellis did not bat.

Malinga 5–0–42–0; Kulasekara 5–0–34–4; Mathews 5–0–35–0; Senanayake 4–0–31–2; Dilshan 1–0–13–0; Herath 3–0–43–0.

Umpires: B. N. J. Oxenford and R. S. A. Palliyaguruge.   Third umpire: R. R. Wimalasiri.

SRI LANKA v NEW ZEALAND

Third One-Day International

At Dambulla, November 16, 2013. Sri Lanka won by 36 runs (D/L). Toss: New Zealand.

Another rain-affected match, and another New Zealand fightback – but the weather had the final say, as bad light closed in with the tourists still needing 90 from eight overs to overhaul their revised target of 216 from 33. It would have been a tall order, but Neesham and McCullum had already doubled the score from the depths of 63 for six. In a game originally shortened to 43 overs, then trimmed to 33 by another downpour, Sri Lanka had started well, with an opening stand of 91 in 86 balls between Jayawardene and Dilshan, who hit his third successive half-century. When New Zealand batted, Herath – the last-over fall guy four nights previously – claimed three victims, and the innings could not be recovered.

Man of the Match: S. M. S. M. Senanayake.   *Man of the Series:* T. M. Dilshan.

Sri Lanka

D. P. M. D. Jayawardene c Ronchi			K. M. D. N. Kulasekara c Mills b Neesham		14
	b McCullum	46	S. M. S. M. Senanayake not out	....	21
T. M. Dilshan c Ronchi b McClenaghan	...	53	H. M. R. K. B. Herath not out	....	17
†K. C. Sangakkara b McCullum	....	0	B 1, l-b 3, w 9, n-b 1	....	14
H. D. R. L. Thirimanne c Latham b Mills	..	23			
*A. D. Mathews c Ronchi b McClenaghan	..	0	1/91 (1) 2/91 (3)	(8 wkts, 33 overs)	211
L. D. Chandimal lbw b Neesham	....	15	3/110 (2) 4/110 (5) 5/144 (4)		
N. L. T. C. Perera c Latham b Ellis	....	8	6/146 (6) 7/165 (7) 8/184 (8)	9 overs: 56-0	

S. L. Malinga did not bat.

Mills 6–1–35–1; McClenaghan 7–0–34–2; Ellis 6–0–51–1; Devcich 3–0–17–0; Nicol 2–0–17–0; McCullum 4–0–13–2; Neesham 5–0–26–2.

New Zealand

T. W. M. Latham lbw b Senanayake	9	N. L. McCullum not out	35
A. P. Devcich c Herath b Kulasekara	5		
R. J. Nicol st Sangakkara b Herath	1	L-b 1, w 6	7
G. D. Elliott b Herath	3		
C. Munro b Senanayake	1	1/12 (2) 2/17 (1) (6 wkts, 25 overs) 126	
†L. Ronchi c Senanayake b Herath	23	3/21 (4) 4/22 (5)	
J. D. S. Neesham not out	42	5/26 (3) 6/63 (6) 7 overs: 17-2	

*K. D. Mills, A. M. Ellis and M. J. McClenaghan did not bat.

Senanayake 5–1–14–2; Kulasekara 4–1–20–1; Mathews 1–0–4–0; Herath 6–0–25–3; Dilshan 6–0–31–0; Malinga 3–0–31–0.

Umpires: B. N. J. Oxenford and R. S. A. Palliyaguruge.   Third umpire: R. R. Wimalasiri.
Series referee: B. C. Broad.

SRI LANKA v NEW ZEALAND

First Twenty20 International

At Pallekele, November 19, 2013 (floodlit). Abandoned.

SRI LANKA v NEW ZEALAND

Second Twenty20 International

At Pallekele, November 21, 2013 (floodlit). Sri Lanka won by eight wickets. Toss: Sri Lanka. Twenty20 international debut: R. L. B. Rambukwella.

The monsoon finally allowed an uninterrupted match, and Sri Lanka showed why they were top of the Twenty20 rankings. New Zealand dipped to 93 for five in the 15th over, as Chandimal thoughtfully managed a varied attack which included the 22-year-old off-spinner Ramith Rambukwella. Ronchi and McCullum added 45 in 4.5 overs to ensure a reasonable total – but, despite the early loss of Jayawardene, Sri Lanka rarely looked troubled.

Man of the Match: M. D. K. J. Perera.

New Zealand

		B	*4*	*6*
H. D. Rutherford c 4 b 9	3	4	0	0
A. P. Devcich c 9 b 11	30	23	4	1
N. T. Broom c 11 b 5	6	6	0	0
T. W. M. Latham c 2 b 8	20	24	1	0
C. Munro c 9 b 7	17	19	2	0
†L. Ronchi not out	34	25	3	1
N. L. McCullum run out	26	16	3	0
R. J. Nicol lbw b 10	2	2	0	0
A. M. Ellis not out	2	1	0	0
L-b 2	2			

6 overs: 42-2   (20 overs) 142-7

1/3 2/14 3/49 4/62 5/93 6/138 7/140

*K. D. Mills and M. J. McClenaghan did not bat.

Malinga 4–0–33–1; Kulasekara 4–0–31–1; Mathews 2–0–17–1; Rambukwella 4–0–19–1; Mendis 3–0–20–1; Dilshan 1–0–7–0; N. L. T. C. Perera 2–0–13–1.

Sri Lanka

		B	*4*	*6*
D. P. M. D. Jayawardene lbw b 11	3	4	0	0
T. M. Dilshan not out	59	49	8	0
M. D. K. J. Perera c and b 8	57	37	6	2
†K. C. Sangakkara not out	20	17	1	0
L-b 3, w 1	4			

6 overs: 54-1   (17.5 overs) 143-2

1/8 2/104

A. D. Mathews, *L. D. Chandimal, N. L. T. C. Perera, R. L. B. Rambukwella, K. M. D. N. Kulasekara, S. L. Malinga and B. A. W. Mendis did not bat.

Mills 3–0–26–0; McClenaghan 4–0–34–1; McCullum 3.5–0–34–0; Ellis 2–0–15–0; Devcich 3–0–13–0; Nicol 2–0–18–1.

Umpires: R. S. A. Palliyaguruge and R. R. Wimalasiri.   Third umpire: T. H. Wijewardene.
Referee: B. C. Broad.

DOMESTIC CRICKET IN SRI LANKA, 2012-13

SA'ADI THAWFEEQ

In a season that saw a clutch of batting records and the emergence of several exciting young players, **Sinhalese** regained their status as Sri Lanka's most successful club with their seventh first-class title.

For one season only, the Premier League was contested by 20 teams in two groups of ten, whose winners met in a final; in 2013-14, Sri Lanka Cricket planned to reduce the first-class tournament to 14 sides, with the other six relegated to a non-first-class league, the first step in a three-year plan to raise standards by cutting the number of teams.

As it happened, the top two in each group met in the final qualifying round, effectively creating two semi-finals. In Group A, **Moors** pulled ahead of **Panadura** in a thrilling seven-run win, thanks to slow left-armer Malinda Pushpakumara, the season's leading wicket-taker with 68. In Group B, Sinhalese and **Tamil Union** began the final round with seven wins apiece. Sinhalese qualified after a drawn run-fest in which they accumulated the highest total in domestic first-class history – 787 for eight, against a Tamil Union attack including three Test bowlers. The Sinhalese captain, Thilina Kandamby, contributed a monumental 340 not out, also a domestic record.

Wicketkeeper-batsman Kaushal Silva handed Sinhalese the title after starring in the final against Moors with innings of 171 and 88. That made him the only batsman to top 1,000 runs in the season; his outstanding form brought him five centuries and an average just below 90. Denied a regular place in the national team by Test keeper Prasanna Jayawardene and, in one-day matches, Kumar Sangakkara, he appeared to have earned a chance as a middle-order batsman after the international retirement of Thilan Samaraweera – a long-time bulwark of the Test line-up, who scored three hundreds for Sinhalese, but decided to quit after being left out of the Tests against Bangladesh.

Apart from Silva, three batsmen reached 800 runs: Madawa Warnapura of Bloomfield, Air Force's 20-year-old Yashodha Lanka, and former Test batsman Upul Tharanga. But of the thrilling young talents bursting on to the scene, none was as devastating as 22-year-old left-hander Kushal Perera, who tore into the bowling from the start. His most pleasingly destructive performance was an innings of 336 – a domestic record until overtaken by Kandamby – for defending champions Colts against Saracens, hammering 14 sixes and 29 fours off 275 balls. A fortnight earlier, he had hit 203 off 192 deliveries against Burgher. Perera averaged 115 in five first-class matches before resuming one-day international duties.

Although batsmen prospered on vastly improved pitches that encouraged strokeplay, it was worrying that the leading 14 wicket-takers in the Premier League were spinners (the top three – Pushpakumara, Panadura's Gayan Sirisoma and Dinuka Hettiarachchi of Colombo – were all slow left-armers). Most clubs continued to ignore SLC's demands for pitches suiting fast bowlers; in some games, spinners even took the new ball. This bias towards slow bowling has resulted in a paucity of quality pace in Test cricket, despite the appointment of Sri Lanka's most successful fast bowler, Chaminda Vaas, as an assistant coach to the national team.

Sinhalese missed a double when they lost the Premier limited-overs final to **Ragama**, who claimed only their second title, after the Twenty20 Cup in 2006-07. **Wayamba's** powerful batting crushed Kandurata & Uva in the Interprovincial 50-over final.

When the second season of the Sri Lankan Premier League did not materialise, after the franchises failed to pay bank guarantees demanded to ensure that the players would be paid, SLC set up a Super Fours Twenty20 tournament in August 2013 to provide a national representative for the Champions League in India; it was won by **Kandurata Maroons**.

In the women's tournament, **Navy** won all their seven games to emerge as champions.

FIRST-CLASS AVERAGES, 2012-13

BATTING (550 runs, average 40.00)

	M	I	NO	R	HS	100	Avge	Ct/St
†M. D. K. J. Perera (*Colts*)................	5	6	0	695	336	2	115.83	13/2
J. K. Silva (*Sinhalese*)	10	13	1	1,073	180	5	89.41	20/5
†K. D. K. Vithanage (*Tamil Union/SL/SL Dev*)	8	9	2	583	168*	2	83.28	5
A. D. Mathews (*Colts/Sri Lanka*)	6	10	2	606	155	1	75.75	8
T. T. Samaraweera (*Sinhalese/Sri Lanka*)...	6	9	1	564	134	3	70.50	5
†S. H. T. Kandamby (*Sinhalese*)	10	12	2	682	340*	1	68.20	5
†W. U. Tharanga (*Nondescripts*)	9	14	2	800	205*	3	66.66	2
M. S. Warnapura (*Bloomfield*)	9	15	2	804	200*	3	61.84	7
†D. S. N. F. G. Jayasuriya (*Moors/SL Dev*)...	9	15	1	823	195	2	58.78	5
A. R. S. Silva (*Colts*)	8	13	3	557	154*	2	55.70	14
A. K. Perera (*Nondescripts/SL Dev*)	7	12	2	553	120	2	55.30	9
†F. D. M. Karunaratne (*Sinhalese/Sri Lanka*).	11	18	3	823	137	4	54.86	16/1
L. J. P. Gunaratne (*Moors*)...............	10	17	3	761	199*	2	54.35	8
†N. T. Paranavitana (*Sinhalese/Sri Lanka*) ...	11	18	4	759	132*	2	54.21	13
A. K. K. Y. Lanka (*Air Force*)...........	9	15	0	802	171	3	53.46	7
†R. P. Thattil (*Burgher*)	9	15	4	584	145*	1	53.09	5
†W. W. A. G. Maneshan (*Ports Authority*) ...	9	13	1	596	234	1	49.66	17/3
†R. J. M. G. M. Rupasinghe (*Colombo*)......	9	16	2	664	131	1	47.42	13
†M. D. U. S. Jayasundera (*Ragama/SL Dev*) ..	9	15	1	660	222	1	47.14	8
S. M. A. Priyanjan (*Ports Authority/SL Dev*)	9	13	0	586	235	1	45.07	19
L. P. C. Silva (*Panadura*)................	9	15	1	631	104	2	45.07	21

BOWLING (35 wickets)

	Style	O	M	R	W	BB	5I	Avge
P. H. T. Kaushal (*Nondescripts*).......	OB	192.4	28	760	50	7-69	6	15.20
R. M. G. K. Sirisoma (*Panadura*)......	SLA	260	36	886	58	6-66	5	15.27
S. M. S. M. Senanayake (*Sinhalese*)....	OB	281.5	65	800	49	6-41	6	16.32
M. D. K. Perera (*Panadura*)..........	OB	270.4	33	961	56	6-91	5	17.16
P. A. S. S. Jeewantha (*Badureliya*).....	RFM	187.5	25	651	37	8-53	2	17.59
H. M. R. K. B. Herath (*Tamil Union/SL*)	SLA	353.3	67	864	46	7-89	6	18.78
B. A. W. Mendis (*Army/Sri Lanka*)....	OB/LBG	269.4	24	1,029	51	7-67	4	20.17
P. M. Pushpakumara (*Moors*)..........	SLA	403.2	50	1,428	68	7-56	7	21.00
D. Hettiarachchi (*Colombo*)	SLA	388.2	56	1,361	58	7-57	5	23.46
S. Weerakoon (*Colts*)	SLA	303.3	60	1,101	46	6-136	4	23.93
H. M. C. M. Bandara (*Ragama*).......	LBG	237.2	27	912	38	7-70	3	24.00
S. Randiv (*Bloomfield/Sri Lanka*)......	OB	372.5	50	1,385	55	7-61	3	25.18
B. M. D. K. Mendis (*Navy/SL Dev*)....	LBG	340.4	28	1,361	52	7-76	5	26.17
S. Prasanna (*Army*).................	LBG	262.2	16	1,100	42	6-34	4	26.19
T. M. U. S. Karunaratne (*Chilaw Mar.*).	OB	294.1	41	1,076	39	7-119	2	27.58
D. H. A. Isanka (*Air Force*)	SLA	268.1	19	1,143	38	6-96	2	30.07

PREMIER LEAGUE, 2012-13

Group A	P	W	L	D	Pts	Group B	P	W	L	D	Pts
Moors SC...........	9	7	2	0	123.490	Sinhalese SC......	9	7	0	2	144.365
Panadura SC	9	6	2	1	119.855	Tamil Union C&AC	9	7	0	2	129.955
Army SC	9	5	0	4	117.355	Nondescripts CC...	9	6	0	3	120.870
Bloomfield C&AC...	9	5	2	2	117.015	Ports Authority CC .	9	3	3	3	98.750
Colts CC	9	4	2	3	101.680	Colombo CC	9	4	3	2	92.770
Ragama CC	9	4	2	3	91.530	Chilaw Marians CC	9	4	4	1	56.325
Air Force SC	9	1	4	4	63.115	Badureliya SC.....	9	1	2	6	54.630
Burgher RC	9	1	4	4	53.755	Navy SC..........	9	1	6	2	53.215
Lankan CC.........	9	0	7	2	36.385	Galle CC..........	9	2	6	1	49.190
Saracens SC........	9	0	7	2	28.300	Kurunegala Y. CC .	9	1	7	1	39.545

Final: Sinhalese beat Moors by six wickets.

Burgher, Lankan, Saracens, Navy, Galle and Kurunegala were relegated to a non-first-class tier.

Outright win = 12pts; win by an innings = 2pts extra; lead on first innings in a drawn game = 8pts. Bonus points were awarded as follows: 0.1pt for each wicket taken and 0.005pt for each run scored, up to 400 runs per innings.

Group A

At Panagoda, February 1–2, 2013. **Army won by an innings and 16 runs.** Air Force 130 (S. Prasanna 5-35) **and** 174 (B. A. W. Mendis 6-47); ‡**Army 320** (D. H. A. Isanka 6-96). *Army 17.6pts, Air Force 2.52pts. Air Force collapsed in two days as Ajantha Mendis took 9-86 in the match.*

At Colombo (Bloomfield), February 1–3, 2013. **Bloomfield won by 171 runs. Bloomfield 236 and 301-8 dec;** ‡**Burgher 184** (A. N. P. R. Fernando 5-71) **and** 182. *Bloomfield 16.685pts, Burgher 3.63pts. Bloomfield's Nadeera Nawela held six catches in the field.*

At Colombo (Colts), February 1–3, 2013. **Colts won by 130 runs. Colts 143 and 282;** ‡**Ragama 165 and** 130. *Colts 16.125pts, Ragama 3.475pts.*

At Colombo (Bloomfield), February 1–3, 2013. **Moors won by an innings and 77 runs. Moors 547-9 dec** (S. I. de Saram 129, L. H. D. Dilhara 151); ‡**Saracens 241** (P. M. Pushpakumara 5-74) **and** 229 (P. M. Pushpakumara 5-93). *Moors 18pts, Saracens 3.25pts.*

At Panadura, February 1–3, 2013. **Panadura won by 229 runs.** ‡**Panadura 331 and 224-4 dec** (L. P. C. Silva 100*); **Lankan 180** (M. D. K. Perera 5-69) **and** 146. *Panadura 16.775pts, Lankan 3.03pts.*

At Colombo (Bloomfield), February 8–10, 2013. **Drawn.** ‡**Bloomfield 307** (M. S. Warnapura 125, K. P. N. M. Karunanayake 103) **and 208-8 dec;** Air Force 232 (S. Randiv 7-61) **and** 233-6. *Bloomfield 12.175pts, Air Force 4.125pts.*

At Colombo (Burgher), February 8–10, 2013. **Drawn.** Saracens 377 (I. R. Weerasinghe 127, L. Abeyratne 131) **and 200-4** (L. Abeyratne 142*); ‡**Burgher 410-7 dec** (D. W. A. N. D. Vitharana 158, M. L. Cooray 107*). *Burgher 11.4pts, Saracens 3.585pts.*

At Colombo (Colts), February 8–9, 2013. **Colts won by ten wickets. Lankan 163** (S. Weerakoon 5-49) **and** 119 (H. I. A. Jayaratne 7-37); ‡**Colts 263 and 20-0.** *Colts 15.415pts, Lankan 2.41pts. Ishan Jayaratne's second-innings 7.5–2–37–7 helped Colts to win in two days.*

At Colombo (RPS), February 8–10, 2013. **Ragama won by nine wickets. Moors 195** (T. A. M. Siriwardene 5-37) **and** 138 (A. M. L. Perera 5-16); ‡**Ragama 253** (M. G. Vandort 102) **and 85-1.** *Ragama 15.69pts, Moors 2.765pts.*

At Panadura, February 8–9, 2013. **Army won by 52 runs.** ‡**Army 172 and** 135 (R. M. G. K. Sirisoma 6-66); **Panadura 121** (S. Prasanna 6-45) **and 134** (B. A. W. Mendis 5-42). *Army 15.535pts, Panadura 3.275pts. Army won in two days again. Their attack bowled 65.3 overs in the match, all but six balls from spinners.*

At Colombo (Air Force), February 15–17, 2013. **Air Force won by an innings and 82 runs.** Saracens 172 (D. M. A. D. Karunaratne 5-54) **and** 169 (D. M. A. D. Karunaratne 5-33); ‡**Air Force 423-8 dec** (G. S. K. de Silva 127, A. K. K. Y. Lanka 139). *Air Force 18pts, Saracens 2.505pts. Yashodha Lanka hit 139 in 116 balls, with ten fours and ten sixes.*

At Panagoda, February 15–17, 2013. **Army won by an innings and 24 runs.** ‡**Lankan 200** (B. A. W. Mendis 7-67) **and** 107 (S. Prasanna 6-36); **Army 331.** *Army 17.655pts, Lankan 2.535pts.*

At Colombo (Burgher), February 15–17, 2013. **Drawn. Burgher 367** (H. M. C. M. Bandara 6-90) **and 238-6;** ‡**Ragama 556-8 dec** (M. D. U. S. Jayasundera 222, G. I. Daniel 172). *Burgher 3.825pts, Ragama 11.6pts. Udara Jayasundera scored a maiden double-hundred and shared an opening partnership of 333 with Ian Daniel, who also made a career-best.*

At Colombo (Colts), February 15–17, 2013. **Moors won by six wickets. Colts 149** (L. H. D. Dilhara 5-45) **and** 261 (P. C. de Silva 5-75); ‡**Moors 103** (S. Weerakoon 5-17) **and 313-4** (M. I. Ghouse

112*, L. J. P. Gunaratne 155*). *Moors 16.08pts, Colts 3.45pts. Moors were 53-4 chasing 308 before Isham Ghouse and Janaka Gunaratne, who hit 11 sixes, shared a match-winning stand of 260*.*

At Panadura, February 15–17, 2013. **Panadura won by 101 runs. ‡Panadura 214** (Imran Khan 5-67) **and 285-5 dec** (L. P. C. Silva 104); **Bloomfield 131 and 267** (M. D. K. Perera 6-105). *Panadura 16.495pts, Bloomfield 3.49pts.*

At Colombo (Air Force), February 22–24, 2013. **Ragama won by an innings and 27 runs. ‡Air Force 355** (H. M. C. M. Bandara 6-107) **and 209** (T. A. M. Siriwardene 5-48); **Ragama 591-9 dec** (M. G. Vandort 251). *Ragama 18pts, Air Force 3.72pts. Michael Vandort's 251, his third and highest double-century, included 23 fours and 11 sixes.*

At Panagoda, February 22–24, 2013. **Drawn. Colts 387** (A. D. Mathews 155) **and 69-1**; **‡Army 151 and 469** (H. H. R. Kavinga 125, D. A. S. Gunaratne 118; S. Weerakoon 5-167). *Army 3.855pts, Colts 12.28pts. New Test captain Angelo Mathews hit his first hundred since September 2011.*

At Colombo (Bloomfield), February 22–24, 2013. **Bloomfield won by 92 runs. ‡Bloomfield 278 and 183**; **Lankan 210 and 159** (S. Randiv 6-69). *Bloomfield 16.305pts, Lankan 3.845pts.*

At Colombo (Burgher), February 22–24, 2013. **Moors won by an innings and 233 runs. Moors 519-8 dec** (D. S. N. F. G. Jayasuriya 123, P. C. de Silva 113); **‡Burgher 225** (P. M. Pushpakumara 7-70) **and 61** (P. M. Pushpakumara 5-24). *Moors 18pts, Burgher 2.23pts. Slow left-armer Malinda Pushpakumara had 12-94 after bowling out Burgher in the 25th over of their follow-on.*

At Panadura, February 22–24, 2013. **Panadura won by an innings and 75 runs. Panadura 470** (H. R. M. C. Gunasekera 123); **‡Saracens 174** (M. D. K. Perera 5-30) **and 221** (I. R. Weerasinghe 109). *Panadura 18pts, Saracens 2.975pts. Malith Gunasekera came in at 235-6, and his maiden century helped the last four wickets to double Panadura's total.*

At Colombo (Bloomfield), March 1–3, 2013. **Drawn. Bloomfield 443-8 dec** (M. S. Warnapura 200*); **‡Army 222** (S. K. C. Randunu 6-77) **and 279-6** (B. A. W. Mendis 101). *Bloomfield 11.6pts, Army 3.305pts. Madawa Warnapura hit a maiden double-hundred, adding 229 for the fourth wicket with Daminda Ranaweera (90). Test spinner Ajantha Mendis hit his first century, in 70 balls.*

At Colombo (Colts), March 1–3, 2013. **Colts won by an innings and 39 runs. ‡Burgher 285 and 278** (M. D. H. D. Gunathilleke 107); **Colts 602-7 dec** (M. D. K. J. Perera 203, A. R. S. Silva 154*). *Colts 18pts, Burgher 3.515pts. Kushal Perera reached his first double-century, batting for 192 balls and hitting 14 fours and ten sixes; he added 249 for the fourth wicket with Roshen Silva.*

At Katunayake, March 1–3, 2013. **Drawn. ‡Lankan 301 and 276-5 dec** (G. P. Smith 127*); **Saracens 258** (S. S. M. Perera 5-56) **and 223-6**. *Lankan 12.485pts, Saracens 3.905pts. In Lankan's second innings, Leicestershire's Greg Smith and Deshan Dias (89) put on 209 for the third wicket.*

At Colombo (Moors), March 1–3, 2013. **Moors won by nine wickets. Moors 519** (L. J. P. Gunaratne 199*; P. W. B. Sandaruwan 5-113) **and 35-1**; **‡Air Force 136** (L. H. D. Dilhara 6-30) **and 417** (K. A. Kumara 121). *Moors 16.175pts, Air Force 3.78pts. Gunaratne, who hit 15 fours and 11 sixes, and Rajitha Wickramarachchi (99) added 224 for Moors' seventh wicket.*

At Colombo (CCC), March 4–6, 2013. **Panadura won by 161 runs. Panadura 315** (H. R. M. C. Gunasekera 120) **and 249-6 dec** (M. M. D. R. Cooray 110*; T. A. M. Siriwardene 5-62); **‡Ragama 204 and 199**. *Panadura 16.82pts, Ragama 3.615pts.*

At Colombo (Air Force), March 8–10, 2013. **Drawn. ‡Colts 464** (K. G. N. Randika 158; S. T. R. Jayawardene 5-145) **and 290-5**; **Air Force 432** (A. K. K. Y. Lanka 171; K. G. N. Randika 5-81). *Air Force 3.5pts, Colts 12.45pts. Lanka hit 171 in 144 balls, with 17 fours and nine sixes.*

At Colombo (Bloomfield), March 8–10, 2013. **Bloomfield won by 154 runs. ‡Bloomfield 314-8 dec** (M. S. Warnapura 102) **and 218-4 dec** (E. M. D. Y. Munaweera 112); **Saracens 255** (E. M. D. Y. Munaweera 5-47) **and 123** (S. K. C. Randunu 5-46). *Bloomfield 16.66pts, Saracens 3.09pts. Dilshan Munaweera made 112 in 78 deliveries.*

At Colombo (Burgher), March 8–10, 2013. **Panadura won by seven wickets. ‡Burgher 223 and 215** (M. D. K. Perera 6-91); **Panadura 320** (W. A. H. N. Wickramasinghe 5-74) **and 124-3**. *Panadura 16.22pts, Burgher 3.49pts.*

At Colombo (Moors), March 8–10, 2013. **Moors won by nine wickets. Lankan 190 and 160** (D. S. N. F. G. Jayasuriya 5-50); **‡Moors 232 and 119-1**. *Moors 15.755pts, Lankan 2.85pts.*

At Katunayake, March 8–10, 2013. **Drawn. Army 401** (H. H. M. de Zoysa 128*) **and 202-8 dec**; ‡**Ragama 281** (S. Prasanna 5-94) **and 101-5**. *Ragama 3.71pts, Army 12.51pts.*

At Colombo (Air Force), March 15–17, 2013. **Panadura won by 245 runs. Panadura 309 and 303-7 dec**; ‡**Air Force 173** (R. M. G. K. Sirisoma 5-72) **and 194** (R. M. G. K. Sirisoma 5-64). *Panadura 17.06pts, Air Force 3.535pts. Panadura's fifth successive victory.*

At Panagoda, March 15–17, 2013. **Army won by 153 runs.** ‡**Army 365** (H. H. M. de Zoysa 142) **and 158** (P. M. Pushpakumara 5-60); **Moors 259** (D. S. N. F. G. Jayasuriya 153) **and 111** (D. K. R. C. Jayatissa 6-41). *Army 16.615pts, Moors 3.85pts.*

At Colombo (Bloomfield), March 15–17, 2013. **Bloomfield won by an innings and 41 runs.** ‡**Bloomfield 366**; **Ragama 172** (S. A. D. U. Indrasiri 5-41) **and 153** (S. A. D. U. Indrasiri 5-23). *Bloomfield 17.83pts, Ragama 2.625pts.*

At Colombo (Colts), March 15–17, 2013. **Colts won by an innings and 287 runs. Colts 611-8 dec** (M. D. K. J. Perera 336); ‡**Saracens 184 and 140** (H. I. A. Jayaratne 5-53). *Colts 18pts, Saracens 2.42pts. Colts passed 600 for the second time in three matches. Kushal Perera led the way again, with 336, then the tournament record, in 275 balls, with 29 fours and 14 sixes; his last three innings had brought him 636 runs. He outscored both Saracens' innings single-handed, and added 224 for the third wicket with Nisal Randika (93).*

At Katunayake, March 15–17, 2013. **Burgher won by an innings and 13 runs.** ‡**Lankan 197 and 134**; **Burgher 344** (D. R. F. Weerasinghe 6-62). *Burgher 17.72pts, Lankan 2.655pts.*

At Colombo (Burgher), March 22–24, 2013. **Drawn.** ‡**Army 350 and 266-9 dec** (T. D. T. Soysa 107; S. Madanayake 5-74); **Burgher 328** (R. P. Thattil 145*) **and 100-2**. *Burgher 4.04pts, Army 12.28pts.*

At Katunayake, March 22–24, 2013. **Drawn. Lankan 228 and 214**; ‡**Air Force 321** (A. K. K. Y. Lanka 113; D. R. F. Weerasinghe 7-99) **and 6-0**. *Lankan 3.21pts, Air Force 11.635pts.*

At Colombo (Moors), March 22–24, 2013. **Moors won by 149 runs.** ‡**Moors 231 and 372** (D. S. N. F. G. Jayasuriya 195; S. Randiv 5-160); **Bloomfield 100** (P. M. Pushpakumara 5-55) **and 354** (E. M. D. Y. Munaweera 104). *Moors 17.015pts, Bloomfield 4.27pts.*

At Panadura, March 22–24, 2013. **Drawn.** ‡**Colts 277 and 268-8 dec** (A. R. S. Silva 102*; M. D. K. Perera 5-83); **Panadura 319** (S. Weerakoon 6-136). *Panadura 11.395pts, Colts 3.725pts.*

At Colombo (Bloomfield), March 22–24, 2013. **Ragama won by five wickets.** ‡**Saracens 302 and 125** (T. A. M. Siriwardene 5-37); **Ragama 279** (R. S. S. S. de Zoysa 107) **and 150-5**. *Ragama 16.145pts, Saracens 3.635pts.*

At Colombo (Air Force), March 30–April 1, 2013. **Drawn. Air Force 244** (T. Nadeera 105*) **and 316** (B. M. R. N. B. Ratnayake 121; W. A. H. N. Wickramasinghe 8-76); ‡**Burgher 215** (D. H. A. Isanka 5-90) **and 166-5**. *Air Force 12.3pts, Burgher 3.905pts. The original match was stopped in the seventh over when the umpires ruled the pitch unsafe. A new game started at 4pm on a different pitch, under the supervision of the SLC tournament committee. The eight points for first-innings lead meant that Air Force stayed up and Burgher were relegated, despite their leg-spinner Hasitha Wickramasinghe's career-best 8-76 (which gave him 11-121 in his fifth first-class match).*

At Panagoda, March 30–April 1, 2013. **Army won by an innings and two runs.** ‡**Saracens 155** (B. A. W. Mendis 5-50) **and 252**; **Army 409-9 dec** (T. D. T. Soysa 118). *Army 18pts, Saracens 2.935pts.*

At Colombo (Bloomfield), March 30–April 1, 2013. **Bloomfield won by an innings and 163 runs.** ‡**Colts 99** (M. V. T. Fernando 5-35) **and 168**; **Bloomfield 430-9 dec** (S. Randiv 103*; A. Dananjaya 7-139). *Bloomfield 18pts, Colts 2.235pts.*

At Katunayake, March 30–April 1, 2013. **Ragama won by 201 runs. Ragama 366** (D. M. de Silva 121; M. A. Aponso 5-54) **and 168-7 dec**; ‡**Lankan 134 and 199** (H. M. C. M. Bandara 7-70). *Ragama 16.67pts, Lankan 3.365pts.*

At Colombo (Moors), March 30–April 1, 2013. **Moors won by seven runs. Moors 240** (R. M. G. K. Sirisoma 5-41) **and 130** (R. M. G. K. Sirisoma 5-27); ‡**Panadura 120** (P. M. Pushpakumara 7-56) **and 243**. *Moors 15.85pts, Panadura 3.815pts. This match, a straight contest for a place in the final, began with Panadura 8.4 points ahead of Moors at the top of the group. But their first innings was* *wrecked by Pushpakumara, who later completed his third return of ten or more wickets in his ninth match of the season. Panadura's last-wicket pair – Gayan Sirisoma and Sujeewa de Silva – joined forces at 220-9 chasing 251 and added 23 together, only to perish eight runs short of victory.*

Group B

At Galle, February 1–3, 2013. **Badureliya won by an innings and 81 runs.** ‡Badureliya 407; Galle 170 (A. A. S. Silva 5-45) **and** 156 (P. A. S. S. Jeewantha 5-13). *Badureliya 18pts, Galle 2.63pts.*

At Welisara, February 1–3, 2013. **Colombo won by five wickets.** ‡Navy 198 (D. Hettiarachchi 7-57) **and** 174 (M. A. Liyanapathiranage 5-57); **Colombo** 257 **and** 117-5. *Colombo 15.87pts, Navy 3.36pts.*

At Colombo (NCC), February 1–2, 2013. **Nondescripts won by an innings and 255 runs. Kurunegala Youth** 60 (S. C. D. Boralessa 6-13) **and** 245 (P. H. T. Kaushal 5-65); ‡**Nondescripts 560-7 dec** (D. P. D. N. Dickwella 146, A. K. Perera 120, C. K. B. Kulasekara 103). *Nondescripts 18pts, Kurunegala Youth 2.225pts. Nondescripts bowled out Kurunegala for 60 – the lowest total of the season – took a 500-run first-innings lead, and wrapped up the match in two days. Schoolboy of the Year Niroshan Dickwella, aged 19, followed three one-day centuries with 146 on first-class debut, before Angelo Perera and Kosala Kulasekara, who hit 103 in 69 balls, added 221 for the fifth wicket. Another 19-year-old debutant, off-spinner Tharindu Kaushal, took seven wickets in all.*

At Colombo (SSC), February 1–3, 2013. **Sinhalese won by ten wickets.** ‡Chilaw Marians 142 **and** 377 (G. T. H. N. D. Kavinda 109; S. M. S. M. Senanayake 6-127); **Sinhalese 450-9 dec** (J. K. Silva 141, T. T. Samaraweera 134; T. M. U. S. Karunaratne 7-119) **and** 71-0. *Sinhalese 16.355pts, Chilaw Marians 3.495pts.*

At Colombo (PSO), February 1–3, 2013. **Tamil Union won by eight wickets. Tamil Union** 353 (K. D. K. Vithanage 122) **and** 93-2; ‡**Ports Authority** 136 (R. M. S. Eranga 6-21) **and** 306. *Tamil Union 16.23pts, Ports Authority 3.41pts.*

At Colombo (CCC), February 8–10, 2013. **Tamil Union won by eight wickets. Tamil Union 423-7 dec** (B. M. A. J. Mendis 206*) **and** 128-2; ‡**Colombo** 263 **and** 287 (R. A. S. Lakmal 5-63). *Tamil Union 16.64pts, Colombo 3.65pts. Jeewan Mendis gave Tamil Union a decisive advantage, batting for 234 balls in all in his second double-century.*

At Kurunegala, February 8–10, 2013. **Ports Authority won by an innings and 37 runs. Kurunegala Youth 171 and** 315 (D. M. G. S. Dissanayake 5-65); ‡**Ports Authority 523-8 dec** (S. M. A. Priyanjan 235). *Ports Authority 18pts, Kurunegala Youth 3.23pts. Ashan Priyanjan converted his maiden hundred into a double; in all, he scored 235 in only 162 balls, with 26 fours and 11 sixes.*

At Welisara, February 8–10, 2013. **Galle won by 140 runs. Galle** 111 (W. M. N. K. Weerakkody 5-10) **and 309-8 dec** (I. S. S. Samarasooriya 107); ‡**Navy 114 and** 166 (J. U. Chaturanga 6-58). *Galle 16.1pts, Navy 3.2pts. Left-armer Nishantha Weerakkody's full figures were 10–7–10–5.*

At Colombo (NCC), February 8–10, 2013. **Nondescripts won by 289 runs. Nondescripts 405-6 dec** (W. U. Tharanga 205*) **and 236-3 dec** (A. K. Perera 100*); ‡**Chilaw Marians** 256 (P. H. T. Kaushal 7-69) **and** 96 (P. H. T. Kaushal 5-22). *Nondescripts 17.18pts, Chilaw Marians 2.66pts. Upul Tharanga batted throughout the first innings for his second double-hundred. Kaushal's 12-91, in his second first-class game, remained the best match return of the competition.*

At Colombo (SSC), February 8–10, 2013. **Sinhalese won by six wickets. Badureliya** 227 **and** 115; ‡**Sinhalese 102** (P. A. S. S. Jeewantha 8-53) **and 241-4** (F. D. M. Karunaratne 109*). *Sinhalese 15.715pts, Badureliya 3.11pts. Saliya Saman Jeewantha took a hat-trick in his opening over of the match, on his way to a career-best 8-53, the best figures of the tournament; he helped Badureliya take a 125-run first-innings lead, but still finished on the losing side.*

At Maggona, February 15–17, 2013. **Drawn. Navy** 358 (T. R. Rasanga 144) **and** 1-0; ‡**Badureliya** 151 (S. Chamika 5-39) **and 365-9 dec** (D. P. W. Diminguwa 107). *Badureliya 3.58pts, Navy 11.695pts.*

At Colombo (Moors), February 15–17, 2013. **Drawn. Chilaw Marians** 140 **and** 264; ‡**Ports Authority 356-6 dec** (M. Pushpakumara 122*) **and** 18-1. *Chilaw Marians 2.72pts, Ports Authority 11.87pts.*

At Galle, February 15–17, 2013. **Tamil Union won by eight wickets. Galle 137** (R. A. S. Lakmal 5-21) **and 131** (H. M. R. K. B. Herath 5-20); ‡**Tamil Union 226 and 43-2**. *Tamil Union 15.345pts, Galle 2.54pts.*

At Kurunegala, February 15–17, 2013. **Colombo won by eight wickets. Kurunegala Youth 213** (M. A. Liyanapathiranage 5-59) **and 258-9 dec** (D. Hettiarachchi 6-105); ‡**Colombo 220 and 257-2** (K. R. P. Silva 106*). *Colombo 16.285pts, Kurunegala Youth 3.555pts.*

At Colombo (SSC), February 15–17, 2013. **Drawn. Sinhalese 511-7 dec** (F. D. M. Karunaratne 116, T. T. Samaraweera 111) **and 232-9 dec**; ‡**Nondescripts 232 and 44-3**. *Sinhalese 12.46pts, Nondescripts 2.98pts.*

At Galle, February 22–24, 2013. **Galle won by 104 runs. Galle 235 and 226-6 dec**; ‡**Kurunegala Youth 130** (K. P. Gajasinghe 5-29) **and 227**. *Galle 16.305pts, Kurunegala Youth 3.385pts.*

At Colombo (Colts), February 22–24, 2013. **Nondescripts won by 101 runs. Nondescripts 287** (N. C. Komasaru 6-77) **and 178-7 dec**; ‡**Ports Authority 120** (P. H. T. Kaushal 5-30) **and 244**. *Nondescripts 16.325pts, Ports Authority 3.52pts.*

At Colombo (SSC), February 22–24, 2013. **Sinhalese won by an innings and 42 runs. Navy 163** (S. M. S. M. Senanayake 5-51) **and 296**; ‡**Sinhalese 501-7 dec** (J. K. Silva 109, T. T. Samaraweera 118*). *Sinhalese 18pts, Navy 2.995pts. Thilan Samaraweera scored his third hundred in four matches before twisting his knee. He still hoped to play in the forthcoming Tests with Bangladesh, but announced his international retirement when left out; his next game was for Worcestershire in April.*

At Colombo (PSO), February 22–24, 2013. **Tamil Union won by seven wickets. Badureliya 310** (D. P. W. Dimunguwa 111) **and 153**; ‡**Tamil Union 250 and 214-3** (M. L. Udawatte 124*). *Tamil Union 16.32pts, Badureliya 3.615pts. Another 19-year-old, Pabasara Waduge Dimunguwa, scored his second hundred in consecutive innings – in his fourth first-class match – but could not prevent Tamil Union's fourth straight win.*

At Colombo (CCC), February 23–25, 2013. **Colombo won by 199 runs. Colombo 373** (S. S. Pathirana 5-110) **and 224** (S. S. Pathirana 6-96); ‡**Chilaw Marians 287 and 111** (D. Hettiarachchi 5-55). *Colombo 16.985pts, Chilaw Marians 3.99pts.*

At Maggona, March 1–3, 2013. **Drawn.** ‡**Badureliya 271 and 204-4 dec**; **Kurunegala Youth 206 and 162-4** (D. M. Sarathchandra 100*). *Badureliya 11.775pts, Kurunegala Youth 3.24pts.*

At Colombo (CCC), March 1–3, 2013. **Nondescripts won by seven wickets.** ‡**Colombo 267** (P. H. T. Kaushal 5-72) **and 219** (P. H. T. Kaushal 5-93); **Nondescripts 357** (D. Hettiarachchi 6-146) **and 130-3**. *Nondescripts 16.435pts, Colombo 3.73pts.*

At Galle, March 1–3, 2013. **Drawn.** ‡**Chilaw Marians 290 and 217-2 dec**; **Galle 152 and 271-9**. *Galle 3.315pts, Chilaw Marians 12.435pts.*

At Welisara, March 1–3, 2013. **Tamil Union won by 98 runs.** ‡**Tamil Union 428-8 dec** (S. C. Serasinghe 159, D. H. A. P. Tharanga 101*) **and 298-5 dec** (T. M. Dilshan 155); **Navy 319** (D. V. B. Hasaranga 109) **and 309** (K. Y. Kumara 111*). *Tamil Union 17.49pts, Navy 4.44pts. Tillekeratne Dilshan hit 155 in just 88 balls, with 17 fours and six sixes.*

At Colombo (NCC), March 1–3, 2013. **Sinhalese won by an innings and 137 runs.** ‡**Sinhalese 548-8 dec** (M. D. Gunathilleke 152); **Ports Authority 220** (S. M. S. M. Senanayake 5-62) **and 191** (S. M. S. M. Senanayake 5-41, J. M. U. B. Jayasena 5-57). *Sinhalese 18pts, Ports Authority 2.855pts. Sinhalese reached 500 for the third match running.*

At Colombo (CCC), March 8–10, 2013. **Sinhalese won by 266 runs.** ‡**Sinhalese 354-8 dec and 241-5 dec** (N. T. Paranavitana 105*); **Colombo 226** (R. J. M. G. M. Rupasinghe 131; S. M. S. M. Senanayake 6-83) **and 103** (H. U. K. Madushanka 7-35). *Sinhalese 16.975pts, Colombo 2.945pts. Seamer Kasun Madushanka's full career-best figures were 8.4–4–35–7.*

At Colombo (Colts), March 8–10, 2013. **Ports Authority won by an innings and 123 runs. Ports Authority 400-7 dec** (I. Udana 103*); ‡**Galle 122** (N. C. Komasaru 5-42) **and 155** (N. C. Komasaru 5-55). *Ports Authority 18pts, Galle 2.085pts.*

At Welisara, March 8–10, 2013. **Drawn. Chilaw Marians 354 and 174-8 dec**; ‡**Navy 218** (N. G. R. P. Jayasuriya 5-72, H. G. Kumara 5-52) **and 233-7**. *Navy 4.055pts, Chilaw Marians 12.34pts.*

At Colombo (NCC), March 8–10, 2013. **Drawn. Nondescripts 275** (D. P. D. N. Dickwella 111) **and 212-3 dec** (W. U. Tharanga 120*); ‡**Badureliya 195** (M. F. Maharoof 5-46) **and 178-7**. *Nondescripts 12.135pts, Badureliya 3.165pts.*

At Colombo (PSO), March 8–10, 2013. **Tamil Union won by an innings and 88 runs. Tamil Union 466-4 dec** (M. L. R. Buddika 203*, B. M. A. J. Mendis 100*); ‡**Kurunegala Youth 200** (B. M. A. J. Mendis 5-53) **and 178**. *Tamil Union 18pts, Kurunegala Youth 2.29pts. Rumesh Buddika scored a maiden double-century; Jeewan Mendis, who helped him add 179, followed up with eight wickets.*

At Colombo (NCC), March 15–17, 2013. **Drawn.** ‡**Badureliya 233 and 270**; **Ports Authority 413** (D. M. G. S. Dissanayake 140) **and 57-3**. *Badureliya 3.815pts, Ports Authority 12.285pts. In a match for tailenders, No. 8 Shanuka Dissayanake and Chaminda Bandara (22*) put on 144 for the ninth wicket of Ports Authority's first innings. Mapa Bandara and Jeewantha, who came together at 105-7 in Badureliya's second, still 75 behind, scored 91 each and added 165 for the eighth.*

At Colombo (CCC), March 15–17, 2013. **Colombo won by an innings and 56 runs.** ‡**Colombo 367** (W. M. G. Ramyakumara 104); **Galle 188 and 123** (D. Hettiarachchi 7-58). *Colombo 17.835pts, Galle 2.555pts.*

At Kurunegala, March 15–17, 2013. **Sinhalese won by an innings and 70 runs.** ‡**Kurunegala Youth 164** (S. M. S. M. Senanayake 6-41) **and 178**; **Sinhalese 412-8 dec** (J. K. Silva 148). *Sinhalese 18pts, Kurunegala Youth 2.51pts.*

At Welisara, March 15–17, 2013. **Nondescripts won by five wickets.** ‡**Navy 180 and 278** (D. Thissakuttige 100*; S. C. D. Boralessa 7-96); **Nondescripts 354** (M. F. Maharoof 116; B. M. D. K. Mendis 5-117) **and 105-5** (B. M. D. K. Mendis 5-42). *Nondescripts 16.295pts, Navy 3.79pts.*

At Colombo (PSO), March 15–16, 2013. **Tamil Union won by four wickets.** ‡**Chilaw Marians 209** (B. M. A. J. Mendis 5-53) **and 155** (T. M. N. Sampath 5-45); **Tamil Union 156** (S. S. Pathirana 5-63) **and 209-6**. *Tamil Union 15.825pts, Chilaw Marians 3.42pts. Tamil Union completed their seventh win in seven games, and did it in two days.*

At Maggona, March 22–24, 2013. **Drawn. Badureliya 324** (G. K. D. B. Gunaratne 5-81) **and 43-2**; ‡**Colombo 422** (W. M. G. Ramyakumara 120*). *Badureliya 2.835pts, Colombo 11.2pts.*

At Colombo (RPS), March 22–24, 2013. **Kurunegala Youth won by seven wickets. Chilaw Marians 227 and 120** (T. P. Gamage 5-24); ‡**Kurunegala Youth 195** (N. G. R. P. Jayasuriya 5-59) **and 153-3**. *Kurunegala Youth 15.74pts, Chilaw Marians 3.035pts.*

At Colombo (Colts), March 22–24, 2013. **Ports Authority won by 144 runs. Ports Authority 375-9 dec** (M. Pushpakumara 119; B. M. D. K. Mendis 6-129) **and 227-5 dec**; ‡**Navy 197 and 261**. *Ports Authority 17.01pts, Navy 3.69pts.*

At Colombo (NCC), March 22–24, 2013. **Drawn.** ‡**Nondescripts 280** (R. A. S. Lakmal 6-68) **and 279-7 dec** (J. Mubarak 112*); **Tamil Union 314 and 93-2**. *Nondescripts 3.995pts, Tamil Union 11.735pts.*

At Colombo (SSC), March 25–26, 2013. **Sinhalese won by an innings and 18 runs. Galle 169 and 185**; ‡**Sinhalese 372-4 dec** (F. D. M. Karunaratne 137, N. T. Paranavitana 132*). *Sinhalese 17.86pts, Galle 2.17pts. Dimuth Karunaratne and Tharanga Paranavitana added 247 for Sinhalese's second wicket, more than Galle managed in either innings as they succumbed in two days; their last man, Ushan Manohara, registered his fifth duck in six innings. It was Sinhalese's fifth successive win.*

At Maggona, March 30–April 1, 2013. **Drawn.** ‡**Badureliya 265** (T. M. U. S. Karunaratne 5-47) **and 322** (A. A. S. Silva 109); **Chilaw Marians 293 and 153-8** (A. A. S. Silva 6-37). *Badureliya 4.735pts, Chilaw Marians 12.23pts. Chilaw Marians wicketkeeper Rukshan Shehan made nine dismissals in the match, five caught and four stumped.*

At Colombo (CCC), March 30–April 1, 2013. **Drawn.** ‡**Colombo 404** (K. H. R. K. Fernando 129*; K. M. C. Bandara 5-78) **and 254-8**; **Ports Authority 490** (W. W. A. G. Maneshan 234). *Colombo 4.27pts, Ports Authority 11.8pts. Colombo captain and slow left-armer Dinuka Hettiarachchi took his 800th first-class wicket. Gayan Maneshan hit a maiden double-century.*

At Kurunegala, March 30–April 1, 2013. **Navy won by six wickets.** ‡**Navy 369** (L. A. C. Ruwansiri 122) **and 29-4**; **Kurunegala Youth 212** (B. M. D. K. Mendis 5-86) **and 182** (B. M. D. K. Mendis 7-76). *Navy 15.99pts, Kurunegala Youth 3.37pts. Leg-spinner Dulanjana Mendis took 12-162, giving him 29 wickets in his last three games. But Navy were relegated after failing to dismiss Kurunegala for 156 second time round and gain the extra two points for an innings win.*

At Colombo (NCC), March 30–31, 2013. **Nondescripts won by an innings and 87 runs. Galle 111 and 107**; ‡**Nondescripts 305-4 dec** (W. U. Tharanga 134). *Nondescripts 17.525pts, Galle 1.49pts. Niroshan Dickwella (86) and Tharanga opened with 224; Galle lost in two days again.*

At Colombo (PSO), March 30–April 1, 2013. **Drawn.** ‡**Sinhalese 787-8 dec** (F. D. M. Karunaratne 115, J. K. Silva 180, S. H. T. Kandamby 340*); **Tamil Union 314**. *Tamil Union 2.37pts, Sinhalese 11pts. As in Group A, this settled a place in the final; Sinhalese began 5.78pts ahead. Their 787-8 was the second-highest total in Sri Lankan first-class cricket, after the Test team's 952-6 v India in 1997-98. The only Sri Lankan score higher than Thilina Kandamby's 340* – his second of 200-plus, including 40 fours and eight sixes in 367 balls – was Mahela Jayawardene's 374 v South Africa in 2006. Dimuth Karunaratne and Kaushal Silva added 209 for the third wicket, Silva and Kandamby 195 for the fourth, and Kandamby and Upul Jayasena (88) 226 for the seventh.*

Final

At Colombo (SSC), April 5–8, 2013. **Sinhalese won by six wickets.** ‡**Moors 262 and 323** (S. I. de Saram 101); **Sinhalese 324** (J. K. Silva 171) **and 262-4**. *Moors fell away from 108-0, but Sinhalese fought back from 59-4 thanks to Kaushal Silva's fifth hundred of the tournament and third in successive innings; stands of 102 with Dammika Prasad (47) and 54 with Kasun Madushanka (5) for the last two wickets gave them a lead of 62. Indika de Saram kept Moors in it, adding 167 for their seventh wicket with Dilhara Lokuhettige (78), but Silva led the way again in the last-day pursuit of 262: his 88 took him past 1,000 first-class runs for the season and ensured Sinhalese's first championship for five years. Moors' Malinda Pushpakumara finished with 68 wickets.*

CHAMPIONS

Lakspray Trophy	1994-95 {	Bloomfield C&AC	2002-03	Moors SC
1988-89 { Nondescripts CC		Sinhalese SC	2003-04	Bloomfield C&AC
Sinhalese SC	1995-96	Colombo CC	2004-05	Colts CC
1989-90 Sinhalese SC	1996-97	Bloomfield C&AC	2005-06	Sinhalese SC
	1997-98	Sinhalese SC	2006-07	Colombo CC
			2007-08	Sinhalese SC
P. Saravanamuttu Trophy	*Premier League*		2008-09	Colts CC
1990-91 Sinhalese SC	1998-99	Bloomfield C&AC	2009-10	Chilaw Marians
1991-92 Colts CC	1999-2000	Colts CC	2010-11	Bloomfield C & AC
1992-93 Sinhalese SC	2000-01	Nondescripts CC	2011-12	Colts CC
1993-94 Nondescripts CC	2001-02	Colts CC	2012-13	Sinhalese SC

Sinhalese have won the title outright 7 times, Colts 6, Bloomfield 4, Colombo and Nondescripts 2, Moors 1. Sinhalese have shared it twice, Bloomfield, Chilaw Marians and Nondescripts once each.

PREMIER LIMITED-OVERS TOURNAMENT, 2012-13

Two 50-over leagues plus knockout

Semi-finals

At Colombo (SSC), January 8, 2013. **Sinhalese won by seven wickets. Nondescripts 222-9** (50 overs) (M. D. Gunathilleke 5-28); ‡**Sinhalese 223-3** (42.2 overs) (J. K. Silva 103*). *Dhanushka Gunathilleke took five wickets for the first time before Kaushal Silva struck 103* in 113 balls.*

At Colombo (SSC), January 9, 2013. **Ragama won by 93 runs.** Reduced to 49 overs a side. **Ragama 206-9** (49 overs); ‡**Colts 113** (32.1 overs). *Only Shihan Kamileen (39*) passed 12 for Colts.*

Final

At Colombo (SSC), January 12, 2013. **Ragama won by four wickets. Sinhalese 218** (43.2 overs); ‡**Ragama 224-6** (43.4 overs). *Kaushalya Weeraratne saw Ragama home with 61* in 41 balls. It was only their second major title, after winning the Twenty20 Cup in 2006-07.*

INTERPROVINCIAL LIMITED-OVERS TOURNAMENT, 2012-13

50-over league plus knockout

	Played	Won	Lost	Bonus points	Points	Net run-rate
Kandurata & Uva..............	4	3	1	2	14	0.92
Wayamba....................	4	3	1	1	13	0.44
Ruhuna.....................	4	2	2	1	9	0.27
Nagenahira & Uthura	4	2	2	1	9	−0.74
Basnahira...................	4	0	4	0	0	−0.68

Semi-finals

At Colombo (SSC), January 27, 2013. **Kandurata & Uva won by four wickets. Nagenahira & Uthura 310-4** (50 overs); ‡**Kandurata & Uva 312-6** (50 overs) (S. H. T. Kandamby 113*). *Thilina Kandamby steered Kandurata & Uva to a last-ball victory with 113* in 87 deliveries.*

At Colombo (PSO), January 28, 2013. **Wayamba won by seven wickets.** ‡**Ruhuna 161** (39 overs); **Wayamba 162-3** (19.5 overs). *Wayamba needed only 58.5 of the scheduled 100 overs to win.*

Final

At Colombo (NCC), January 30, 2013. **Wayamba won by 133 runs. Wayamba 348-4** (50 overs) (D. P. D. N. Dickwella 104, M. F. Maharoof 112); ‡**Kandurata & Uva 215** (38.4 overs) (A. N. P. R. Fernando 5-46). *Seven weeks after his debut, 19-year-old Niroshan Dickwella scored his third List A century. Farveez Maharoof put on 157 with him and 121 with Jehan Mubarak (77) to set up victory.*

SRI LANKA CRICKET PRESIDENT'S TROPHY, 2013

50-over league plus final

	Played	Won	Lost	Bonus points	Points	Net run-rate
The Rest.....................	4	3	1	1	13	−0.27
Sri Lanka Cricket Combined XI ...	4	2	2	1	9	0.53
Sri Lanka A	4	1	3	1	5	−0.16

Final

At Pallekele, May 20, 2013 (day/night). **The Rest won by 76 runs.** ‡**The Rest 205** (48.5 overs); **Sri Lanka Cricket Combined XI 129** (32.5 overs). *The Rest were 151-8 before Thilina Kandamby and Suranga Lakmal added 49. Dilruwan Perera and Rangana Herath took three SLC wickets each.*

SRI LANKA CRICKET SUPER FOURS TWENTY20, 2013

20-over league plus final

	Played	Won	Lost	Points	Net run-rate
Basnahira Greens	3	2	1	4	0.36
Kandurata Maroons	3	2	1	4	0.15
Ruhuna Reds	3	1	2	2	−0.01
Uthura Yellows	3	1	2	2	−0.48

Final

At Colombo (RPS), August 17, 2013. **Kandurata Maroons won by seven wickets.** ‡**Basnahira Greens 109-7** (20 overs); **Kandurata Maroons 113-3** (17 overs). *MoM:* K. M. D. N. Kulasekara (Kandurata). *MoS:* C. K. B. Kulasekara (Basnahira). *Kandurata secured a place in the Champions League qualifiers. They were the only team to win batting second in this seven-match tournament, after Nuwan Kulasekara pinned back Basnahira with 3-19.*

WEST INDIES CRICKET, 2013

Heading south – again

TONY COZIER

Perhaps it was triggered by the spirit of the season, but the Christmas message from Whycliffe "Dave" Cameron, the new president of the West Indies Cricket Board, carried more than a touch of fantasy. Cameron, a 42-year-old Jamaican businessman, was elected at the board's AGM in March, narrowly ousting Julian Hunte (whose vice-president he had been for six years) after an intense and often bitter campaign. The year had been challenging for West Indies cricket, Cameron conceded, but he felt there had been "some significant successes" and "marked strides on the field and off it as well".

Hunte's report the previous year had been similarly upbeat. After all, 2012 had brought four consecutive Test victories, triumph in the World Twenty20, new deals with an Indian TV production company, and the sale of the regional

WEST INDIES IN 2013

	Played	Won	Lost	Drawn/No result
Tests	7	2	4	1
One-day internationals	24	9	13	2
Twenty20 internationals	5	3	2	–

JANUARY		
FEBRUARY	5 ODIs and 1 T20I (a) v Australia	(page 882)
MARCH	2 Tests, 3 ODIs and 2 T20Is (h) v Zimbabwe	(page 1149)
APRIL		
MAY		
JUNE	Champions Trophy (in England)	(page 301)
	Triangular ODI tournament (h) v India and Sri Lanka	(page 1155)
JULY	5 ODIs and 2 T20Is (h) v Pakistan	(page 1163)
AUGUST		
SEPTEMBER		
OCTOBER		
NOVEMBER	2 Tests and 3 ODIs (a) v India	(page 943)
DECEMBER	2 Tests, 5 ODIs and 2 T20Is (a) v New Zealand	(page 995)
JANUARY		

For a review of West Indian domestic cricket from the 2012-13 season, see page 1171.

Twenty20 tournament to an international wealth-management corporation. Hunte had been able to boast that the game in the Caribbean was "better positioned for the rest of the decade on many fronts". A year on, though, the situation had reverted to its more familiar guise of despair.

Just as Cameron was making his optimistic pronouncement, West Indies' Test captain Darren Sammy was gloomily observing that "we cannot continue like this", after four devastating defeats in five Tests in India and New Zealand. He admitted some careers, including his own, were on the line. Nor was head coach Ottis Gibson safe, after more than three frustrating years in the post.

The new director of cricket, Richard Pybus, who had been appointed on November 1, was immediately facing a tricky task, made even more daunting by the board's choice of an Englishman ahead of several West Indian candidates. Pybus may have coached Pakistan, and forged a solid reputation with provincial teams in South Africa, but he was virtually unknown in the Caribbean.

Cameron's "marked strides" were mainly off the field, and financial. And even they had their drawbacks. The inclusion of India in a triangular one-day series in July did bring welcome funds into the board's coffers, thanks to Indian TV coverage, attendant sponsors and ground-perimeter advertisers; the downside was that two Tests against Sri Lanka, long part of the ICC's Future Tours Programme, were scrapped to accommodate it. Two more Tests scheduled for Pakistan's subsequent visit were also jettisoned; instead seven limited-overs matches were squeezed into a hectic fortnight before the start of the much-hyped Caribbean Premier League, which had originally been contracted for 20 years to Verus International for $US1m dollars annually. It meant more money for the board; the hitch was that the major sponsors would be Digicel, the Irish mobile-phone company who were already the title sponsors of West Indies cricket – this was downgraded to team sponsorship, so they could concentrate on the new venture.

On the field, highlights were scarce. The durable Shivnarine Chanderpaul's consistent but increasingly lonely efforts to shore up the fragile batting continued through his 150th Test (he was the first West Indian to reach the mark). And the women's advance to their World Cup final in Sri Lanka, followed by victories over New Zealand in a one-day series, and England in the final of a triangular Twenty20 tournament at home in October, showed they now belonged among the top few nations.

The CPL, efficiently but expensively organised, was boosted by a dozen high-profile overseas players and the involvement of Hollywood stars Mark Wahlberg and Gerard Butler. It proved a very Caribbean mixture of cricket and carnival. Matches between six franchise teams with unfamiliar names – including the champions, Jamaica Tallawahs (patois for tough), St Lucia Zouks (creole music) and Antigua Hawksbills (local turtles) – filled stands everywhere.

Otherwise, a slew of dismal results did not support Cameron's Yuletide cheer. Overall in 2013, West Indies endured as difficult a period as any during their long decline from the heights of the 1980s. Even on their own grounds, they were also-rans, with India and Sri Lanka contesting the tri-nations final. Then it was Pakistan's turn to inflict further damage. Only a clean sweep of all

Driving ahead: Deandra Dottin was the most feared member of the West Indies women's side who reached the World Cup final for the first time.

seven internationals – including two Tests – against the callow Zimbabwean tourists in March offered any relief.

Away from home, West Indies lost all five one-day internationals in Australia in February, and were eliminated at the group stage of the Champions Trophy in England, if on the Duckworth/Lewis method. In the Tests in India in November, belatedly agreed by a willing West Indian board to engineer an emotional home farewell for Sachin Tendulkar, and in New Zealand a few weeks later, they were not so much beaten as humiliated.

Such a depressing record was compounded by injuries which repeatedly struck down key players, and by the suspension (for the second time) of the year's leading wicket-taker, off-spinner Shane Shillingford: his elbow-flex exceeded the permitted 15 degrees. For similar reasons, Marlon Samuels was banned from bowling his quicker ball.

The premature exit of Darren Bravo from New Zealand for undisclosed personal reasons prompted uneasy speculation, after his elder brother Dwayne – who had replaced Sammy as the 50-over captain in June – questioned the unity of the team. Darren's match-saving 218 in the First Test in New Zealand had confirmed that he was the likely linchpin of the batting, once Chanderpaul – who turns 40 in August – retires.

Clive Lloyd, the captain of the iconic teams of the 1980s, said after the defeats in India that the West Indians "looked drunk" on an overdose of Twenty20. Nor were they dealt any favours by their unsatisfactory preparation for two tough series, or by the board's shambolic organisation. Immediately before their departure for India, a leisurely week-long "bonding" camp, without so much as a net session, was held in Florida, hardly a bastion of the game. According to Cameron, the aim was to "create a culture of unity, winning and overall success". None followed.

Seemingly unaware of the inevitable clash overlapping tours would cause, the board accepted the final one-day international in India on the day set for the start of their lone warm-up game in New Zealand. Six local players had to be hastily recruited to make up the "West Indian XI", along with the five authentic West Indians who were not required in India.

With only six days between that match in India and the First Test in New Zealand, the remaining players were flown west to Dubai before turning around for the flight south. After a journey lasting 30 hours, they arrived in Dunedin two days before the start of the Test. Chris Gayle, eliminated by a hamstring damaged in India, was not among them. Kraigg Brathwaite, the slim 21-year-old Barbadian opener, was named in his stead. He waited two weeks for the board to obtain his visa, by which time the Test was lost. In the end, he played only the final Test, and was part of a second-innings collapse and another heavy defeat.

Such disarray was not new. It simply bore out Sammy's observation that "we cannot continue like this". But there was no indication they could do anything else.

WEST INDIES v ZIMBABWE, 2012-13

TONY COZIER

One-day internationals (3): West Indies 3, Zimbabwe 0
Twenty20 internationals (2): West Indies 2, Zimbabwe 0
Test matches (2): West Indies 2, Zimbabwe 0

West Indies have rarely, if ever, had it so easy. Although they had beaten New Zealand 2–0 at home the previous summer, and won both Tests in Bangladesh in November, there were times during both those series when they were under pressure. But in extending their victorious streak to six Tests, a sequence they had last achieved in 1988 against rather stiffer opposition in England and Australia under the captaincy of Viv Richards, they encountered negligible resistance from Zimbabwe. Building on a dominance established in the limited-overs matches, West Indies finished off both Tests inside eight sessions.

However, this was not really a sign of the long hoped for revival. Instead, it revealed the damage caused to Zimbabwe by their six-year, self-imposed exile from Test cricket and the scarcity of opposition: since a similarly ill-fated trip to New Zealand more than a year before, their only official international cricket had been two games at the World Twenty20 in Sri Lanka. At the end of this tour, captain Brendan Taylor said: "It's been massively disappointing. We have been taught a proper lesson."

The Zimbabweans were also handicapped by the decision of their cash-strapped board not to allow batting coach Grant Flower, bowling coach Heath Streak or trainer Lorraine Chivandire to accompany the team. Head coach Alan Butcher, the former Surrey and England batsman on his last assignment, said the trio had been "a big part of our preparations"; Taylor described the move as "steps in the wrong direction".

On the field, Zimbabwe were ill-equipped to deal with unsatisfactory pitches that were over-helpful to spin. Shane Shillingford and his accomplice Marlon Samuels had a ball, sharing 29 wickets in the Tests. Shillingford claimed 19, a West Indian record for a two-match series, and his performance vindicated his selection ahead of the more celebrated white-ball man of mystery, Sunil Narine: in the circumstances, Shillingford's sharper turn and greater bounce provided a more aggressive option. The two off-spinners operated almost exclusively with fielders clustered around crease-bound batsmen: Kieran Powell and skipper Darren Sammy snared 13 close catches between them. Fast bowling was virtually redundant, although Shannon Gabriel – tall, strong and hostile – was always a threat.

The 50 made by opener Tino Mawoyo at Bridgetown was Zimbabwe's highest individual score in the Tests, while 211 in the same innings was their highest total. The top-order trio of Taylor, Vusi Sibanda and Hamilton Masakadza, who had been expected to carry the batting, all struggled. Zimbabwe did have their moments: the controlled swing of the lively Kyle Jarvis helped reduce West Indies to 151 for six in the First Test, and 114 for three in the Second. But with their spinners ineffective, Zimbabwe could not sustain the pressure. At Bridgetown, they were denied by Sammy and Denesh Ramdin; and in Dominica, Chris Gayle hit a century after eight Test innings without a fifty, while Shivnarine Chanderpaul scored his third hundred in four Tests.

In the one-dayers, Zimbabwe's best effort was 273 for eight in the second match, but even that was overhauled with seven wickets to spare. Sammy was given a rest during the 50-over series, along with Gayle, who asked to be excused. Dwayne Bravo stood in as captain – and the appointment became permanent shortly afterwards.

ZIMBABWEAN TOURING PARTY

*B. R. M. Taylor (T/50/20), R. W. Chakabva (T/50/20), T. L. Chatara (T/50/20), C. J. Chibhabha (50/20), A. G. Cremer (T), C. R. Ervine (T/50/20), K. M. Jarvis (T/50/20), T. Maruma (T), H. Masakadza (T/50/20), T. M. K. Mawoyo (T/50/20), K. O. Meth (T/50/20), C. B. Mpofu (T/50/20), N. Mushangwe (50/20), T. C. Mutombodzi (50/20), R. W. Price (T), V. Sibanda (T/50/20), P. Utseya (T/50/20), M. N. Waller (T/50/20), S. C. Williams (T). *Coach:* A. R. Butcher.

At St Andrew's, Grenada, February 20, 2013. **Zimbabweans won by 76 runs. ‡Zimbabweans 346-7** (50 overs) (V. Sibanda 147, H. Masakadza 56); **University of West Indies Vice-Chancellor's XI 270** (48.4 overs) (R. R. Sarwan 90; M. N. Waller 3-8). *The Zimbabweans chose from 13 players. Vusi Sibanda faced 114 balls before retiring out; he put on 110 with Tino Mawoyo (30) and 100 with Hamilton Masakadza. Kyle Jarvis dismissed both Vice-Chancellor's XI openers for ducks, and Ramnaresh Sarwan's 72-ball innings proved in vain.*

At St George's, Grenada, February 22, 2013. **First one-day international: West Indies won by 156 runs. West Indies 337-4** (50 overs) (J. Charles 130, K. O. A. Powell 79, D. M. Bravo 100*); **‡Zimbabwe 181-9** (50 overs) (C. R. Ervine 41, M. N. Waller 51; S. P. Narine 3-28). *MoM:* J. Charles. *Twelve days earlier, Johnson Charles had hit his maiden century in senior cricket, in a one-day international against Australia at Melbourne. Now he added another, and his partnerships of 168 with Kieran Powell and 80 with Darren Bravo set up a commanding total. Bravo's own hundred, his first in the format, was completed off the last ball of the innings, his 71st. Zimbabwe lost four early wickets – two to Sunil Narine, including Masakadza to Kemar Roach's flying catch at long-on – and never recovered. Grenada's first international match for nearly four years came three days after the New National Party's return to office with a sweep of all 15 seats in parliamentary elections – cause for a public holiday and a celebratory post-match rally at the stadium.*

At St George's, Grenada, February 24, 2013. **Second one-day international: West Indies won by seven wickets. ‡Zimbabwe 273-8** (50 overs) (V. Sibanda 51, H. Masakadza 60, C. R. Ervine 80; D. J. Bravo 6-43); **West Indies 274-3** (49 overs) (K. O. A. Powell 57, R. R. Sarwan 120*, N. Deonarine 42, K. A. Pollard 41*). *MoM:* D. J. Bravo. *ODI debut:* T. L. Chatara (Zimbabwe). *Zimbabwe's total – their third-highest against West Indies in ODIs – was founded on a fourth-wicket partnership of 110 between Masakadza and Craig Ervine. Both were among stand-in captain Dwayne Bravo's six wickets, his one-day best. Powell and Sarwan, promoted to open instead of Charles, who had strained a hamstring, laid the foundation for West Indies, putting on 111. Had umpire Peter Nero called for a TV replay to confirm a clear-cut run-out when Sarwan had 53, West Indies might have found their task more demanding. And while they needed Pollard's 41 off 20 balls to seal the issue with an over to spare, Sarwan was still there at the end, having completed his fifth ODI hundred.*

At St George's, Grenada, February 26, 2013. **Third one-day international: West Indies won by five wickets. ‡Zimbabwe 211-9** (50 overs) (V. Sibanda 41, B. R. M. Taylor 39, C. J. Chibhabha 48*; V. Permaul 3-40); **West Indies 215-5** (46.2 overs) (K. O. A. Powell 42, D. M. Bravo 72*). *MoM:* D. M. Bravo. *MoS:* D. M. Bravo. *ODI debut:* T. C. Mutombodzi (Zimbabwe). *West Indies completed a clean sweep in the 50-over series with 22 balls to spare after some weak batting from*

Zimbabwe, who were without the fever-struck Craig Ervine. Darren Bravo compiled 72 from 103 balls in the chase which, allied to his unbeaten hundred in the first match, gave him an average of 172 and the Man of the Series award. Natsai Mushangwe and debutant Tinotenda Mutombodzi provided the rare sight of leg-spinners wheeling away at both ends, and conceded 66 from their combined 20 overs. Mutombodzi dismissed Sarwan with his third ball in international cricket, and later added Powell.

At North Sound, Antigua, March 2, 2013. **First Twenty20 international: West Indies won by eight wickets.** ‡Zimbabwe **130-8** (20 overs) (C. R. Ervine 34, M. N. Waller 49; T. L. Best 3-18); **West Indies 131-2** (16.1 overs) (L. M. P. Simmons 63*, D. J. Bravo 38*). MoM: L. M. P. Simmons. *T20I debuts*: N. Mushangwe, T. C. Mutombodzi (Zimbabwe). *The loss of their three most experienced batsmen in the first five overs – among them Masakadza to Kieron Pollard's leaping one-handed catch at point off a searing cut – put Zimbabwe under early pressure. An enterprising run-a-ball stand of 60 between Ervine and Waller provided temporary relief, but when Waller departed the innings quickly subsided. Johnson Charles's five consecutive fours in Jarvis's second over immediately put their inadequate total in perspective. Christopher Mpofu dismissed Charles and Darren Bravo in successive overs, but Lendl Simmons – who hit six sixes and a solitary four – and Dwayne Bravo completed the job with 23 balls to spare.*

At North Sound, Antigua, March 3, 2013. **Second Twenty20 international: West Indies won by 41 runs.** ‡West Indies **158-7** (20 overs) (L. M. P. Simmons 41, K. A. Pollard 45*); **Zimbabwe 117-6** (20 overs) (H. Masakadza 53*; S. Badree 3-17). MoM: S. Badree. MoS: L. M. P. Simmons. *T20I debut*: S. T. Gabriel (West Indies). *West Indies completed a whitewash of the white-ball matches. Pollard's power-hitting set up a testing total, then the bowlers again exploited Zimbabwe's frail batting. Earlier, West Indies had been restricted to 64 from the first ten overs – but 94 came in the second half, and 59 from the last five. Pollard smacked two sixes and two fours in the 18th over, from Tendai Chatara, which cost 23 in all. Zimbabwe's cause was lost once Samuel Badree's flat, skidding leg-spin accounted for the first three wickets.*

At Black Rock, Barbados, March 7–9, 2013 (not first-class). **Drawn. Zimbabweans 255-8 dec** (H. Masakadza 112, M. N. Waller 64) **and 209-7** (V. Sibanda 80); **Sagicor High Performance Centre 230** (M. N. Samuels 55, K. A. Hope 62; A. G. Cremer 7-79). *Both sides chose from 13 players. Zimbabwe owed much to Masakadza, who batted for almost six hours, and Waller, who helped him put on 74 for the sixth wicket. The home side struggled against the in-form Graeme Cremer, who had taken a career-best 8-61 with his leg-breaks in a domestic match the previous week, before flying to the Caribbean for the Test leg of the tour.*

WEST INDIES v ZIMBABWE

First Test Match

At Bridgetown, Barbados, March 12–14, 2013. West Indies won by nine wickets. Toss: Zimbabwe. Test debut: T. L. Chatara.

This was only Zimbabwe's fifth Test since returning from exile in August 2011, and their first since losing to New Zealand by an innings and 301 runs at Napier almost 14 months previously. As in the preceding limited-overs matches, the effect of such inactivity was obvious. Twice they were in promising positions: they reached 100 for two on the opening day, and later removed West Indies' top six for 151. But Zimbabwe could not exploit either situation. Their last six first-innings wickets tumbled for 76, while West Indies emerged from their own batting troubles thanks to a vigorous partnership of 106 between Ramdin and Sammy.

The inviting look of a bare, beige surface had persuaded Taylor to bat first. Roach broke through Sibanda's on-drive to hit leg stump, and Samuels's left hand fastened on to

Masakadza's thick edge inches from the grass at gully. Mawoyo and Taylor progressed confidently into the afternoon but, once Mawoyo became the first of Shillingford's bat–pad victims after an attractive 50, the innings subsided. Gabriel beat Taylor for pace, then Shillingford combined with fellow off-spinner Samuels to scatter the Zimbabweans.

Jarvis, swinging the ball at a decent pace, cheered them up before the close, despatching Powell and nightwatchman Roach, first ball, to what was in fact the seventh delivery of the seventh over. West Indies faltered again next day, losing four wickets to leave the contest evenly balanced. Jarvis had both Bravo and Chanderpaul caught behind, while fast bowler Tendai Chatara – a late replacement for the injured Christopher Mpofu – claimed a distinguished first Test scalp when Gayle stabbed a lifter to slip. After enthralling the 1,500 spectators with the stylish strokeplay that characterised his *annus mirabilis* of 2012, Samuels played a lazy drive at Masakadza's medium-pace shortly before lunch.

But West Indies regained control through Sammy's calculated aggression, with Ramdin in support – though they were helped by Taylor's prolonged trust in the leg-spin of Cremer. Sammy lashed four sixes in five overs off him and, when he eventually played on to Masakadza, had faced only 69 balls for his 73. Ramdin was more sedate, before he was ninth out after three hours at the crease.

Trailing by 96, Zimbabwe were undone by off-spin for a second time. Shillingford, preferred to Sunil Narine for his first Test since the previous May in England, gained bounce from his height, and purchase from the pitch for match figures of nine for 107. Five were pouched by the ever-present close catchers on the leg side. Samuels's four wickets in the first innings, starting with one from his first ball, were his best return in international cricket; he wasn't required in the second.

Zimbabwe's spirit was undermined as the top three fell in the last seven overs of the second day. Mawoyo edged Gabriel to slip, then Shillingford removed Masakadza with his first delivery and Sibanda with his tenth. Next morning he added four more, and Gabriel completed the rout. The only resistance came from the left-hander Ervine. The umpires allowed West Indies to bat for three overs into the designated lunch break to knock off the dozen runs required for victory. But they couldn't manage it after Powell was out cheaply for the second time, and had to wait until after their meal for the three still needed.

Man of the Match: S. Shillingford.
Close of play: first day, West Indies 18-2 (Gayle 11, Bravo 0); second day, Zimbabwe 41-3 (Price 7, Taylor 0).

Zimbabwe

T. M. K. Mawoyo c Powell b Shillingford		50	– c Sammy b Gabriel		9
V. Sibanda b Roach		12	– c and b Shillingford		15
H. Masakadza c Samuels b Roach		17	– c Sammy b Shillingford		1
*B. R. M. Taylor b Gabriel		26	– (5) c Powell b Shillingford		6
C. R. Ervine b Samuels		29	– (6) not out		23
M. N. Waller lbw b Shillingford		9	– (7) c Powell b Shillingford		5
†R. W. Chakabva c Powell b Shillingford		15	– (8) b Shillingford		6
A. G. Cremer c Bravo b Samuels		25	– (9) c Ramdin b Shillingford		14
R. W. Price not out		12	– (4) b Roach		7
K. M. Jarvis c Powell b Samuels		0	– c Ramdin b Gabriel		9
T. L. Chatara c Roach b Samuels		2	– b Gabriel		0
B 4, l-b 10		14	B 8, l-b 2, w 1, n-b 1		12

1/17 (2) 2/59 (3) 3/100 (1)   (76.4 overs) 211
4/110 (4) 5/135 (6) 6/158 (5)
7/196 (8) 8/196 (7) 9/197 (10) 10/211 (11)

1/25 (1) 2/26 (3)   (41.4 overs) 107
3/39 (2) 4/47 (5)
5/47 (4) 6/58 (7) 7/77 (8)
8/97 (9) 9/107 (10) 10/107 (11)

Roach 13–3–31–2; Best 12–3–33–0; Gabriel 14–5–45–1; Sammy 9–5–17–0; Shillingford 22–4–58–3; Samuels 6.4–1–13–4. *Second innings*—Roach 10–7–12–1; Best 8–2–26–0; Gabriel 7.4–3–10–3; Shillingford 16–4–49–6.

West Indies

C. H. Gayle c Taylor b Chatara	40	– not out	4
K. O. A. Powell lbw b Jarvis	5	– c Cremer b Chatara	6
K. A. J. Roach lbw b Jarvis	0		
D. M. Bravo c Chakabva b Jarvis	11	– (3) not out	1
M. N. Samuels c Chakabva b Masakadza	51		
S. Chanderpaul c Chakabva b Jarvis	26		
†D. Ramdin c Sibanda b Chatara	62		
*D. J. G. Sammy b Masakadza	73		
S. Shillingford c Jarvis b Price	1		
T. L. Best c Cremer b Jarvis	24		
S. T. Gabriel not out	0		
B 9, l-b 3, w 1, n-b 1	14	B 1	1

1/8 (2) 2/8 (3) 3/43 (4) 4/81 (1)   (84.2 overs) 307   1/8 (2)   (1 wkt, 5 overs) 12
5/144 (5) 6/151 (6) 7/257 (8)
8/268 (9) 9/301 (7) 10/307 (10)

Jarvis 17.2–4–54–5; Chatara 19–6–66–2; Cremer 20–0–103–0; Masakadza 10–2–25–2; Price 18–2–47–1. *Second innings*—Jarvis 3–1–10–0; Chatara 2–1–1–1.

Umpires: R. E. J. Martinesz and B. N. J. Oxenford.   Third umpire: A. L. Hill.

WEST INDIES v ZIMBABWE

Second Test Match

At Roseau, Dominica, March 20–22, 2013. West Indies won by an innings and 65 runs. Toss: West Indies. Test debut: S. C. Williams.

Zimbabwe's batting was as fragile as it had been in Barbados. Again, they failed to carry the contest beyond tea on the third day, depriving Dominica's keen supporters of play at the weekend as West Indies won the Clive Lloyd Trophy 2–0. But there was some good news for the locals: Shane Shillingford, the Dominican off-spinner playing his second Test at Windsor Park, repeated his performance against Australia the previous April with another ten wickets in the match. Defeat had somewhat devalued his performance in that game; this time it was the limitations of outclassed opposition which subdued the celebrations.

Exploiting a surface that encouraged turn and bounce, Shillingford and Samuels (who took three cheap wickets in each innings) were even more of a handful than in the First Test. Gabriel triggered the initial crash, but after that pace was virtually redundant. West Indies then built a commanding lead of 206: Gayle's 15th Test hundred was followed by Chanderpaul's 28th (though his first against Zimbabwe), and another significant contribution from Ramdin. Sammy declared before the start on the third day, after which the end was only a matter of time – and there was not much of it.

In the first innings Ervine had resisted for 73 balls and Sean Williams – a 26-year-old left-hander finally making his Test debut after playing the most recent of his 47 one-day internationals – for 88. But still no one passed 35 in either innings. Sibanda did reach 30 twice and hinted at more, but his penchant for choosing the wrong shot was again his undoing. He began with a volley of boundaries – six in all, three off successive balls from Roach – but then drove Gabriel's low full toss straight to mid-on.

Once more, Shillingford's impact was immediate: his sixth ball was a doosra that cleaned up Masakadza. He had to wait until his seventh over before claiming another, when Taylor's botched reverse sweep dropped the ball on to the stumps via various parts of his body. Ervine and Williams battled through 17 overs, but a collapse never seemed far away – and it duly followed after Samuels accounted for both, and the last six tumbled for 34.

Jarvis's opening burst again removed Powell and Bravo, for his first Test duck in his 41st innings (among West Indians, only Clive Lloyd, Basil Butcher and Garry Sobers had waited longer for their first). And they were tottering briefly at 114 for three when

Chatara's outswinging yorker bemused Samuels first ball next morning. But Gayle and Chanderpaul took them into the lead, then Chanderpaul and Ramdin extended it with a partnership of 173. Gayle initially batted with unusual care, after a run of 17 consecutive international innings in all formats without a fifty. But he moved to a half-century with six and four off Utseya, and later launched three more sixes in four deliveries to reach 99; a single followed next ball. Attempting a fifth six, however, he hoisted a catch to long-off: it was a first Test wicket for Utseya, almost nine years after his only previous cap.

Zimbabwe were again stalled by Ramdin, who made 86, before providing Cremer with his first wicket of the series in his 49th over, courtesy of an unchallenged lbw. Chanderpaul, not satisfied with 284 balls at the crease, was more reluctant to leave when Williams came up with a grass-high catch at cover.

The visitors made another promising start in their second innings, this time from Sibanda and Masakadza, opening instead of Mawoyo, who was ill. But once Best and Sammy each claimed their only wickets of the series, the innings disintegrated against Shillingford and Samuels, who ended an unequal contest by dismissing Jarvis and Chatara with successive balls. Shillingford's 19 wickets were a West Indian record for a two-Test series, beating Courtney Walsh's 16 in New Zealand in 1994-95.

Man of the Match: S. Shillingford.   *Man of the Series:* S. Shillingford.

Close of play: first day, West Indies 114-2 (Gayle 61, Samuels 26); second day, West Indies 381-8 (Shillingford 4, Best 11).

Zimbabwe

T. M. K. Mawoyo b Gabriel	8	– (7) c Sammy b Shillingford	0
V. Sibanda c Roach b Gabriel	32	– (1) lbw b Sammy	35
H. Masakadza b Shillingford	14	– (2) c Ramdin b Best	17
*†B. R. M. Taylor b Shillingford	33	– (3) c Powell b Shillingford	7
C. R. Ervine lbw b Samuels	18	– (4) c Gayle b Shillingford	8
S. C. Williams c Powell b Samuels	31	– (5) c Chanderpaul b Shillingford	6
M. N. Waller c Best b Shillingford	9	– (6) c Sammy b Samuels	20
A. G. Cremer c Powell b Samuels	0	– c Samuels b Shillingford	20
P. Utseya lbw b Shillingford	9	– not out	10
K. M. Jarvis not out	1	– c Sammy b Samuels	1
T. L. Chatara lbw b Shillingford	4	– c Gabriel b Samuels	0
B 10, l-b 4, w 1, n-b 1	16	B 8, l-b 9	17
	175		**141**

1/42 (1) 2/43 (2) 3/64 (3)   (60.5 overs) 175
4/105 (4) 5/141 (5) 6/158 (7)
7/158 (8) 8/161 (6) 9/171 (9) 10/175 (11)

1/37 (2) 2/64 (3)   (42.2 overs) 141
3/64 (1) 4/73 (5)
5/92 (4) 6/96 (7) 7/114 (6)
8/138 (8) 9/141 (10) 10/141 (11)

Roach 7–0–30–0; Best 10–0–32–0; Gabriel 8–6–10–2; Sammy 5–1–15–0; Shillingford 21.5–4–59–5; Samuels 9–3–15–3. *Second innings*—Best 7–2–11–1; Roach 3–0–12–0; Gabriel 3–0–19–0; Shillingford 15–4–34–5; Sammy 5–1–13–1; Samuels 9.2–0–35–3.

West Indies

C. H. Gayle c Jarvis b Utseya	101	K. A. J. Roach b Utseya	0
K. O. A. Powell b Jarvis	24	T. L. Best not out	11
D. M. Bravo c Taylor b Jarvis	0	B 4, l-b 7, w 1	12
M. N. Samuels b Chatara	26		
S. Chanderpaul c Williams b Utseya	108	1/35 (2) (8 wkts dec, 117 overs) 381
†D. Ramdin lbw b Cremer	86	2/35 (3) 3/114 (4)
*D. J. G. Sammy c Masakadza b Cremer	9	4/181 (1) 5/354 (6) 6/366 (7)
S. Shillingford not out	4	7/370 (5) 8/370 (9)

S. T. Gabriel did not bat.

Jarvis 21–3–82–2; Chatara 22–2–69–1; Masakadza 17–6–48–0; Cremer 34–6–102–2; Utseya 22–6–60–3; Williams 1–0–9–0.

Umpires: A. L. Hill and R. E. J. Martinesz.   Third umpire: B. N. J. Oxenford.
Series referee: J. J. Crowe.

CELKON MOBILE CUP, 2013

TONY COZIER

1. India   2. Sri Lanka   3. West Indies

The ICC's Future Tours Programme had suggested that, in April and May 2013, West Indies would host two Tests, three one-day internationals and two Twenty20 games against Sri Lanka. But that clashed with the closing stages of the IPL, which would have ruled out several leading players on both sides. Instead, a three-way one-day series, also involving India, was arranged for a few weeks later. To make it work, the three teams travelled from London to Jamaica immediately after the Champions Trophy.

That, in any case, was the official rationale. As ever with India, it was not difficult to read between the lines. The competition was sponsored by a Hyderabadi mobile-phone business, and a host of other Indian products and services – household names in the subcontinent, but unheard of in the Caribbean – filled the perimeter advertising boards at the two venues, Sabina Park in Jamaica and Queen's Park Oval in Trinidad.

They were there because live coverage of the matches was being beamed back to India by Ten Sports, the Dubai-based Indian production company which had won the rights to international cricket from the West Indies Cricket Board a year earlier.

> It was payback for their roasting in Jamaica

To cement the Indian theme, their captain M. S. Dhoni raised yet another one-day trophy after powering six, four and six off successive balls in the last over to clinch a tense one-wicket victory in a low-scoring final against Sri Lanka. India had started with two defeats in Jamaica, as the exertion of going all the way in the Champions Trophy appeared to take its toll. They also lost Dhoni to a hamstring injury, which kept him out until the final. But by the time they arrived in Trinidad, India seemed refreshed.

They trounced the inconsistent West Indians to avenge a narrow defeat in the first match, then booked a place in the final by routing Sri Lanka for 96 in the decisive qualifier; it was payback for their roasting in Jamaica, where Upul Tharanga made an unbeaten 174 and shared an opening partnership of 213 with Mahela Jayawardene. There were also hundreds by Chris Gayle for West Indies and Virat Kohli, India's stand-in captain. But the most consistent batsmen on sluggish pitches that suited the finger-spinners were the ever-dependable Kumar Sangakkara for Sri Lanka and India's Rohit Sharma, who seemed to be fulfilling his potential at long last after being moved up to open earlier in the year.

India also prospered thanks to the seam and swing of Bhuvneshwar Kumar, eight months into his international career, which brought him the series award after ten wickets at 9.70 and an economy-rate of 3.34; for Sri Lanka, Angelo Mathews grew in confidence as captain. But for West Indies, the only benefits were financial.

NATIONAL SQUADS

West Indies *D. J. Bravo, T. L. Best, D. M. Bravo, J. Charles, C. H. Gayle, S. P. Narine, K. A. Pollard, R. Rampaul, R. Rampaul, K. A. J. Roach, D. J. G. Sammy, M. N. Samuels, L. M. P. Simmons, D. S. Smith. *Coach:* O. D. Gibson.

Rampaul sprained his ankle in the first game, and was replaced by J. O. Holder for the matches in Trinidad. Pollard took over as captain when D. J. Bravo was first injured (groin) and then suspended for the team's slow over-rate.

India *M. S. Dhoni, R. Ashwin, Bhuvneshwar Kumar, S. Dhawan, R. A. Jadeja, K. D. Karthik, V. Kohli, A. Mishra, S. K. Raina, Shami Ahmed, I. Sharma, R. G. Sharma, M. Vijay, R. Vinay Kumar, U. T. Yadav. *Coach:* D. A. G. Fletcher.

I. K. Pathan was originally selected, but withdrew with a hamstring injury and was replaced by Shami Ahmed. Dhoni tweaked his own hamstring in the first match, and A. T. Rayudu joined the team as cover. Kohli took over as captain, but Dhoni returned for the final.

Sri Lanka *A. D. Mathews, L. D. Chandimal, L. H. D. Dilhara, R. M. S. Eranga, H. M. R. K. B. Herath, D. P. M. D. Jayawardene, K. M. D. N. Kulasekara, S. L. Malinga, B. A. W. Mendis, B. M. A. J. Mendis, M. D. K. J. Perera, K. C. Sangakkara, S. M. S. M. Senanayake, W. U. Tharanga, H. D. R. L. Thirimanne. *Coach:* G. X. Ford.

Kulasekara was injured in Sri Lanka's third match, and replaced by R. A. S. Lakmal.

WEST INDIES v SRI LANKA

At Kingston, Jamaica, June 28, 2013. West Indies won by six wickets. Toss: West Indies. West Indies 5pts.

Gayle's 21st hundred in one-day internationals put an emphatic end to a rare slump since his century against New Zealand a year earlier, also on his home ground. He had gone 14 matches without reaching 40, but here he was back in more familiar mode from the start, eventually clubbing seven sixes and nine fours from 100 balls. Charles was little more than a bystander in an opening partnership of 115 in 20.2 overs that helped West Indies on their way to a bonus point. By the time Gayle top-edged to square leg, victory was virtually assured. Sri Lanka, sent in, had collapsed after reaching 104 for two in the 22nd over. Narine set them back by despatching Jayawardene in his first over and Sangakkara in his third, then he and Rampaul returned to share five more. The last seven wickets tumbled for 68, and it should have been worse: Gayle dropped a straightforward slip catch off Roach when Mathews, who finished unbeaten with 55, had made only seven.

Man of the Match: C. H. Gayle.

Sri Lanka

W. U. Tharanga c Ramdin b D. J. Bravo	25	S. L. Malinga lbw b Narine	8
D. P. M. D. Jayawardene c Ramdin b Narine	52	B. A. W. Mendis c Charles b D. J. Bravo	2
†K. C. Sangakkara c Pollard b Narine	17		
L. D. Chandimal c D. J. Bravo b Samuels	21	B 5, l-b 2, w 4	11
*A. D. Mathews not out	55		
H. D. R. L. Thirimanne c Charles b Rampaul	6	1/62 (1) 2/85 (2) (48.3 overs)	208
K. M. D. N. Kulasekara c Pollard b Rampaul	2	3/104 (3) 4/140 (4) 5/151 (6)	
B. M. A. J. Mendis c Samuels b Narine	5	6/159 (7) 7/176 (8) 8/190 (9)	
H. M. R. K. B. Herath c Sammy b Rampaul	4	9/205 (10) 10/208 (11) 10 overs: 50-0	

Roach 7–1–41–0; Rampaul 10–0–38–3; Sammy 10–0–34–0; D. J. Bravo 7.3–0–37–2; Narine 10–0–40–4; Samuels 4–1–11–1.

West Indies

C. H. Gayle c Chandimal b B. A. W. Mendis	109	*D. J. Bravo not out	8
J. Charles c Jayawardene b Herath	29	B 4, l-b 7, w 10	21
D. M. Bravo run out	27		
M. N. Samuels not out	15	1/115 (2) (4 wkts, 37.5 overs)	209
K. A. Pollard lbw b Kulasekara	0	2/181 (1) 3/190 (3) 4/193 (5) 10 overs: 48-0	

†D. Ramdin, D. J. G. Sammy, K. A. J. Roach, S. P. Narine and R. Rampaul did not bat.

Malinga 7–0–34–0; Kulasekara 8–1–39–1; B. A. W. Mendis 10–0–53–1; Mathews 5–0–28–0; Herath 6–0–37–1; B. M. A. J. Mendis 1.5–1–7–0.

Umpires: I. J. Gould and J. S. Wilson.   Third umpire: N. Duguid.
Referee: J. J. Crowe.

WEST INDIES v INDIA

At Kingston, Jamaica, June 30, 2013. West Indies won by one wicket. Toss: West Indies. West Indies 4pts.

Just as in West Indies' lone victory in the Champions Trophy shortly before – by two wickets over Pakistan – steady nerves from the lower order were required to creep past the target. Roach hit the winning run, as he had at The Oval, after spending three overs with last man Best carefully compiling the ten needed to defeat India in their first match since their Champions Trophy triumph. Roach's initial impact had come in an opening spell of 6–2–13–1 on a helpful pitch; Sammy backed him up with 5–3–11–1. The batsmen played more freely as conditions improved, before Rohit Sharma's careless drive ended his diligent 89-ball 60. Dhoni was handicapped by a hamstring torn while sprinting a single; he was unable to take the field later. West Indies were wobbling at 26 for three in the fifth over, before Charles and Darren Bravo steadied them with a stand of 116. A further decline followed Bravo's dismissal; then, just as Charles seemed likely to go all the way, he drove Yadav to mid-off after a typically robust 97, leaving the fast bowlers to seal the deal. It meant victory for Pollard in his first match as captain, in place of Dwayne Bravo, who had a groin strain.

Man of the Match: J. Charles.

India

R. G. Sharma c Charles b Sammy	60	R. Ashwin not out		5
S. Dhawan c and b Roach	11	Bhuvneshwar Kumar not out		11
V. Kohli c Gayle b Sammy	11	B 5, l-b 6, w 9, n-b 2		22
K. D. Karthik c and b Samuels	23			
S. K. Raina c Ramdin b Roach	44	1/25 (2) 2/39 (3)	(7 wkts, 50 overs)	229
*†M. S. Dhoni b Best	27	3/98 (4) 4/124 (1)		
R. A. Jadeja b Best	15	5/182 (5) 6/197 (6) 7/212 (7)	10 overs: 39-2	

I. Sharma and U. T. Yadav did not bat.

Roach 10–2–41–2; Best 10–0–52–2; Sammy 10–3–41–2; Pollard 1–0–8–0; Narine 10–0–56–0; Samuels 9–1–20–1.

West Indies

C. H. Gayle c Raina b Yadav	11	S. P. Narine c Dhawan b Raina		5
J. Charles c I. Sharma b Yadav	97	T. L. Best not out		3
D. S. Smith lbw b Yadav	0			
M. N. Samuels b Bhuvneshwar Kumar	1	L-b 2, w 5		7
D. M. Bravo c Dhawan b Ashwin	55			
*K. A. Pollard c Karthik b I. Sharma	4	1/13 (1) 2/25 (3)	(9 wkts, 47.4 overs)	230
†D. Ramdin b Ashwin	4	3/26 (4) 4/142 (5)		
D. J. G. Sammy c Ashwin b I. Sharma	29	5/155 (6) 6/161 (7) 7/197 (8)		
K. A. J. Roach not out	14	8/211 (2) 9/220 (10)	10 overs: 44-3	

Bhuvneshwar Kumar 7–1–36–1; Yadav 9.4–2–43–3; Jadeja 10–1–50–0; I. Sharma 9–0–51–2; Ashwin 10–0–44–2; Raina 2–1–4–1.

Umpires: I. J. Gould and P. J. Nero.   Third umpire: J. S. Wilson.
Referee: J. J. Crowe.

INDIA v SRI LANKA

At Kingston, Jamaica, July 2, 2013. Sri Lanka won by 161 runs. Toss: India. Sri Lanka 5pts.

India's second setback in three days spawned several overwhelming statistics; stand-in captain Kohli, in charge for the first time, described it as "a reality check". Sri Lanka's largest opening partnership (and second-highest for any wicket) against India – 213 between Tharanga and

Jayawardene – set up India's heaviest one-day defeat in terms of runs after choosing to bowl. Tharanga had been recalled for the tour only after an injury to Tillekeratne Dilshan, but eclipsed his previous-best with an unbeaten 174 from 159 balls; it was his 13th one-day century, and the highest score in any one-day international at Sabina Park. Jayawardene's 16th hundred, meanwhile, was his first in two years and 50 innings. No team had previously lost only one wicket in a full quota of overs. India were ragged in the field. None of the frontline bowlers went for less than a run a ball, and two chances to separate the openers were missed: Vijay dropped Jayawardene at short third man when he had 25, and Yadav put down Tharanga on 91 at deep point. Their batting was not much better, and a frantic approach led to regular wickets.

Man of the Match: W. U. Tharanga.

Sri Lanka

W. U. Tharanga not out		174
D. P. M. D. Jayawardene c Yadav		
	b Ashwin	107
*A. D. Mathews not out		44
B 1, l-b 6, w 16		23

1/213 (2)　　　　　　　　(1 wkt, 50 overs) 348
　　　　　　　　　　　　　　　10 overs: 47-0

M. D. K. J. Perera, †K. C. Sangakkara, L. D. Chandimal, H. D. R. L. Thirimanne, K. M. D. N. Kulasekara, S. M. S. M. Senanayake, H. M. R. K. B. Herath and S. L. Malinga did not bat.

Shami Ahmed 10–0–68–0; Yadav 8–0–64–0; I. Sharma 9–0–68–0; Jadeja 9–0–55–0; Ashwin 10–0–67–1; Kohli 2–0–9–0; Raina 2–0–10–0.

India

R. G. Sharma c Mathews b Kulasekara	5		I. Sharma c Sangakkara b Herath	2
S. Dhawan c Tharanga b Herath	24		U. T. Yadav b Malinga	0
M. Vijay b Malinga	30			
*V. Kohli c Malinga b Mathews	2		L-b 4, w 12	16
†K. D. Karthik st Sangakkara b Herath	22			
S. K. Raina run out	33		1/12 (1) 2/52 (2)	(44.5 overs) 187
R. A. Jadeja not out	49		3/57 (4) 4/65 (3) 5/118 (5)	
R. Ashwin c Malinga b Senanayake	4		6/142 (6) 7/153 (8) 8/153 (9)	
Shami Ahmed b Senanayake	0		9/166 (10) 10/187 (11)	10 overs: 28-1

Kulasekara 9–0–37–1; Mathews 8–2–23–1; Senanayake 10–0–46–2; Herath 10–0–37–3; Malinga 7.5–0–40–2.

Umpires: I. J. Gould and J. S. Wilson.　Third umpire: P. J. Nero.
Referee: J. J. Crowe.

WEST INDIES v INDIA

At Port-of-Spain, Trinidad, July 5, 2013. India won by 102 runs (D/L). Toss: West Indies. India 5pts.
　Stung by their defeats in Kingston, India dominated from start to finish to earn a crucial bonus point. Rohit Sharma and Dhawan set the stage for a formidable total, putting on 123 in 23 overs. Once Dhawan fell – shortly after blitzing Narine for two sixes and a four off successive balls – Kohli took charge with a classy 102 from 83 deliveries, his 14th one-day hundred. He and Ashwin rounded off an innings that was faltering at 221 for six in the 42nd over by piling on 90 from the last 50 balls. Oddly, West Indies' two most economical bowlers, Sammy and Samuels, each bowled only eight of their possible ten overs, while the last three, from skipper Bravo and Roach, went for 38. Rain interrupted West Indies' response at 44 for two after nine overs, and a revised target of 274 from 39 was always well beyond them.

Man of the Match: V. Kohli.

India

R. G. Sharma c Ramdin b Best	46	R. Ashwin not out		25
S. Dhawan c D. M. Bravo b Roach	69			
*V. Kohli c Sammy b D. J. Bravo	102	B 4, l-b 7, w 13		24
S. K. Raina c Sammy b Samuels	10			
†K. D. Karthik c Ramdin b Best	6	1/123 (2) 2/141 (1)	(7 wkts, 50 overs)	311
M. Vijay c Charles b Pollard	27	3/156 (4) 4/168 (5)		
R. A. Jadeja run out	2	5/210 (6) 6/221 (7) 7/311 (3)	10 overs: 39-0	

Bhuvneshwar Kumar, I. Sharma and U. T. Yadav did not bat.

Sammy 8–1–28–0; Roach 10–2–69–1; Best 10–0–51–2; D. J. Bravo 7–0–57–1; Narine 5–1–35–0; Samuels 8–0–39–1; Pollard 2–0–21–1.

West Indies

C. H. Gayle c Karthik		D. J. G. Sammy lbw b Yadav		12
b Bhuvneshwar Kumar	10	K. A. J. Roach b Jadeja		34
J. Charles c Raina b I. Sharma	45	S. P. Narine c I. Sharma b Jadeja		21
D. M. Bravo c Ashwin		T. L. Best not out		0
b Bhuvneshwar Kumar	1	B 1, l-b 10, w 8		19
M. N. Samuels c Karthik b I. Sharma	6			
K. A. Pollard c Ashwin		1/14 (1) 2/25 (3) 3/64 (4)	(34 overs)	171
b Bhuvneshwar Kumar	0	4/65 (5) 5/69 (2) 6/91 (7)		
*D. J. Bravo lbw b Yadav	14	7/108 (6) 8/113 (8)		
†D. Ramdin c Bhuvneshwar Kumar b Yadav	9	9/171 (10) 10/171 (9)	10 overs: 56-2	

Bhuvneshwar Kumar 8–1–29–3; Yadav 8–1–32–3; I. Sharma 7–1–30–2; Jadeja 7–1–44–2; Ashwin 4–0–25–0.

Umpires: N. J. Llong and P. J. Nero. Third umpire: N. Duguid.
Referee: J. J. Crowe.

WEST INDIES v SRI LANKA

At Port-of-Spain, Trinidad, July 7–8, 2013. Sri Lanka won by 39 runs (D/L). Toss: West Indies. Sri Lanka 4pts.

Sangakkara required all his experience to cope with some testing seam bowling from Roach and Holder after Sri Lanka were sent in on a damp, treacherous pitch. He battled through 33 balls for 11 before rain ended play on the first day, with Sri Lanka 60 for three after 19 overs. When play resumed on the reserve day, Sangakkara mounted a masterclass as conditions improved, reaching 50 off 76 deliveries, but adding 40 off his next 19. The last ten of the adjusted 41 overs yielded 105. Mathews maintained the momentum as the West Indian bowlers became increasingly indisciplined, spraying 24 wides in all directions. At 31 for four in the ninth over, West Indies' cause appeared hopeless until Simmons (recalled in place of Dwayne Bravo, suspended for his team's dilatory over-rate in the previous match) and Darren Bravo put on 123 in 24 overs. As rain threatened with the total still short of the Duckworth/Lewis par, Simmons was out aiming for his fifth six. Pollard and Sammy, the likeliest hitters, went cheaply, Bravo followed for 70 from 84 balls, and it was left to Roach and Best to deny Sri Lanka the bonus point that would have guaranteed them a place in the final.

Man of the Match: K. C. Sangakkara.
Close of play: first day, Sri Lanka 60-3 (19 overs) (Sangakkara 11, Thirimanne 13).

Sri Lanka

W. U. Tharanga c Bravo b Holder	7	K. M. D. N. Kulasekara c Bravo b Holder		14
D. P. M. D. Jayawardene c Smith b Roach	7	S. M. S. M. Senanayake c Bravo b Pollard		7
†K. C. Sangakkara not out	90	L-b 4, w 24, n-b 3		31
L. D. Chandimal b Roach	2			
H. D. R. L. Thirimanne b Samuels	23	1/19 (1) 2/19 (2)	(8 wkts, 41 overs)	219
*A. D. Mathews c Smith b Roach	30	3/29 (4) 4/93 (5) 5/139 (6)		
B. M. A. J. Mendis c Charles b Roach	8	6/147 (7) 7/201 (8) 8/219 (9)	10 overs: 37-3	

R. M. S. Eranga and S. L. Malinga did not bat.

Roach 8–2–27–4; Holder 8–0–50–2; Sammy 9–2–24–0; Best 6–0–42–0; Samuels 7–0–48–1; Pollard 3–0–24–1.

West Indies

C. H. Gayle c Eranga b Mathews	14
†J. Charles c and b Eranga	14
D. S. Smith lbw b Mathews	0
M. N. Samuels c Jayawardene b Eranga	0
D. M. Bravo c Mendis b Mathews	70
L. M. P. Simmons c Thirimanne b Eranga	67
*K. A. Pollard c Sangakkara b Malinga	0
D. J. G. Sammy c and b Malinga	3
K. A. J. Roach not out	8

J. O. Holder b Mathews	0
T. L. Best not out	5
W 9	9
	—
(9 wkts, 41 overs)	190

1/25 (1) 2/29 (2)   (9 wkts, 41 overs) 190
3/29 (4) 4/31 (3)
5/154 (6) 6/154 (7) 7/172 (8)
8/176 (5) 9/177 (10)   8 overs: 30-3

Kulasekara 1.5–0–8–0; Eranga 8–0–46–3; Thirimanne 4.1–0–16–0; Mathews 8–1–29–4; Senanayake 9–0–41–0; Malinga 8–2–42–2; Mendis 2–0–8–0.

Umpires: N. J. Llong and J. S. Wilson.   Third umpire: P. J. Nero.
Referee: J. J. Crowe.

INDIA v SRI LANKA

At Port-of-Spain, Trinidad, July 9, 2013. India won by 81 runs (D/L). Toss: Sri Lanka. India 5pts.
Another weather-affected match and another pitch that offered all things to all bowlers rendered batting a struggle. India's toil seemed to justify Mathews's decision to bowl first. Rohit Sharma had fought his way to 48 from 83 balls when rain ended the innings after 29 overs; Kohli had needed 52 deliveries for 31. In his 400th one-day international, Jayawardene became the first outfielder to take 200 catches when he held Dhawan at slip. In such conditions Sri Lanka's target, reset to 178 from 26 overs after a break of four and a half hours, was palpably beyond them. So too was the 167 that would have eliminated India on net run-rate and made West Indies their opponents in the final. If anything, conditions became even more difficult for batting. Within his first five overs, Bhuvneshwar Kumar struck four times, including Jayawardene and Sangakkara, who fell first ball to a harsh lbw decision; only Chandimal, with 26 from 58 balls, survived more than 22 deliveries as Sri Lanka succumbed for 96, the lowest total by a Test nation in a one-day international in the Caribbean.
Man of the Match: Bhuvneshwar Kumar.

India

R. G. Sharma not out	48
S. Dhawan c Jayawardene b Mathews	15
*V. Kohli lbw b Herath	31
†K. D. Karthik b Herath	12
S. K. Raina not out	4
B 1, l-b 3, w 3, n-b 2	9

1/27 (2) 2/76 (3)   (3 wkts, 29 overs) 119
3/111 (4)   10 overs: 37-1

M. Vijay, R. A. Jadeja, R. Ashwin, Bhuvneshwar Kumar, I. Sharma and U. T. Yadav did not bat.

Eranga 6–0–27–0; Dilhara 8–0–40–0; Mathews 5–1–5–1; Malinga 3–1–7–0; Herath 6–0–32–2; Mendis 1–0–4–0.

Sri Lanka

W. U. Tharanga c Raina b Bhuvneshwar Kumar.	6	
D. P. M. D. Jayawardene c Vijay b Bhuvneshwar Kumar.	11	
†K. C. Sangakkara lbw b Bhuvneshwar Kumar.	0	
L. D. Chandimal st Karthik b Jadeja	26	
H. D. R. L. Thirimanne c Kohli b Bhuvneshwar Kumar.	0	
*A. D. Mathews c Karthik b Jadeja.	10	
B. M. A. J. Mendis b Ashwin	13	

L. H. D. Dilhara c Karthik b I. Sharma	6
H. M. R. K. B. Herath c Vijay b I. Sharma	4
R. M. S. Eranga not out	2
S. L. Malinga c Jadeja b Yadav	7
L-b 6, w 5	11

1/14 (1) 2/14 (3) 3/27 (2)   (24.4 overs) 96
4/31 (5) 5/56 (6) 6/63 (4)
7/78 (7) 8/84 (9) 9/87 (8)
10/96 (11)   5 overs: 18-2

Bhuvneshwar Kumar 6–1–8–4; Yadav 4.4–0–28–1; I. Sharma 4–0–17–2; Jadeja 5–0–17–2; Ashwin 5–0–20–1.

Umpires: N. J. Llong and P. J. Nero. Third umpire: J. S. Wilson.
Referee: J. J. Crowe.

QUALIFYING TABLE

	Played	Won	Lost	Bonus points	Points	Net run-rate
INDIA	4	2	2	2	10	0.05
SRI LANKA	4	2	2	1	9	0.34
West Indies	4	2	2	1	9	−0.38

Win = 4pts. One bonus point awarded for victory with a run-rate 1.25 times that of the opposition. Net run-rate is calculated by subtracting runs conceded per over from runs scored per over.

FINAL

INDIA v SRI LANKA

At Port-of-Spain, Trinidad, July 11, 2013. India won by one wicket. Toss: India.

Dhoni's customary composure, on his return from injury, clinched another trophy for India with two balls remaining and a panicky No. 11 at the other end. Deliberately shunning singles to keep the strike away from Ishant Sharma, Dhoni saw off four Sri Lankan bowlers before, with 15 required from the final over, he belted Eranga for a six into the upper boxes of the stand at long-off, a four to extra cover, and a six over point. Dhoni's first piece of bravado had been to defy the earlier prognosis that the hamstring injury he picked up in the first match would end his tournament. His initial decision to bowl first appeared questionable as Sangakkara and Thirimanne compiled 122 for the third wicket, and looked even worse when Sangakkara stroked Sharma for four, four and six off successive deliveries in the 38th over. But the dismissal in quick succession of Thirimanne and Sangakkara sparked a collapse: Sri Lanka's last eight wickets clattered for 30, mainly to the spin of Jadeja and Ashwin. Sri Lanka's varied bowling then kept India in check throughout, although they got through their overs so slowly that Mathews was banned for two one-dayers. Herath bowled his ten overs off the reel for just 20, and took four key wickets, two of them with successive balls in his last over, a double-wicket maiden. But for Dhoni, it would have been enough.

Man of the Match: M. S. Dhoni.   *Man of the Series:* Bhuvneshwar Kumar.

Sri Lanka

W. U. Tharanga c Dhoni b Bhuvneshwar Kumar.	11	
D. P. M. D. Jayawardene c Ashwin b Bhuvneshwar Kumar.	22	
†K. C. Sangakkara c Vinay Kumar b Ashwin	71	
H. D. R. L. Thirimanne c Bhuvneshwar Kumar b I. Sharma.	46	
*A. D. Mathews c Vinay Kumar b I. Sharma	10	
M. D. K. J. Perera st Dhoni b Ashwin	2	
L. D. Chandimal c Ashwin b Jadeja	5	
H. M. R. K. B. Herath st Dhoni b Jadeja	5	

R. M. S. Eranga not out 5
S. L. Malinga c Bhuvneshwar Kumar b Jadeja . 0
R. A. S. Lakmal st Dhoni b Jadeja 1
B 4, l-b 6, w 13 23
                                                    ——
1/27 (1) 2/49 (2)   (48.5 overs) 201
3/171 (4) 4/174 (3) 5/176 (6)
6/183 (7) 7/193 (5) 8/196 (8)
9/196 (10) 10/201 (11)   10 overs: 29-1

Bhuvneshwar Kumar 8–4–24–2; Vinay Kumar 6–1–15–0; I. Sharma 8–1–45–2; Kohli 3–0–17–0; Raina 6–0–25–0; Ashwin 10–0–42–2; Jadeja 7.5–1–23–4.

India

R. G. Sharma b Herath	58	
S. Dhawan c Sangakkara b Eranga	16	
V. Kohli c Sangakkara b Eranga	2	
K. D. Karthik c Jayawardene b Herath	23	
S. K. Raina c Sangakkara b Lakmal	32	
*†M. S. Dhoni not out	45	
R. A. Jadeja lbw b Herath	5	
R. Ashwin lbw b Herath	0	
Bhuvneshwar Kumar lbw b Malinga	0	

R. Vinay Kumar c sub (S. M. S. M. Senanayake) b Mathews . 5
I. Sharma not out 2
B 2, l-b 2, w 11 15
                                                    ——
1/23 (2) 2/27 (3)   (9 wkts, 49.4 overs) 203
3/77 (4) 4/139 (1)
5/145 (5) 6/152 (7) 7/152 (8)
8/167 (9) 9/182 (10)   10 overs: 25-1

Eranga 9.4–2–50–2; Lakmal 10–1–33–1; Mathews 10–1–38–1; Malinga 10–1–58–1; Herath 10–2–20–4.

Umpires: N. J. Llong and P. J. Nero. Third umpire: J. S. Wilson.
Referee: D. C. Boon.

WEST INDIES v PAKISTAN, 2013

Tony Cozier

One-day internationals (5): West Indies 1, Pakistan 3
Twenty20 internationals (2): West Indies 0, Pakistan 2

Pakistan were not amused when their proposed series of two Tests, five one-day internationals and two Twenty20s – long ago inked in on the ICC's Future Tours Programme – was pared down so West Indies could squeeze in both a 50-over triangular tournament with India and Sri Lanka, and the inaugural Caribbean Premier League. Since Pakistan were unable to reschedule the tour for August, the two Tests disappeared, providing more evidence of the lip service paid to Test cricket by national boards, and the FTP's growing insignificance. The Pakistanis could do no more than shrug their shoulders.

As it turned out, their 3–1 triumph in the one-day series, and wins in both Twenty20 internationals against the world champions, dispelled much of the discontent that had followed their joyless performances in South Africa and at the Champions Trophy. For West Indies, the inconsistency that had dogged them throughout the year meant they slid to No. 8 in the 50-over rankings, where they had languished during the darkest days of their decline.

The fortunes of the two captains were a microcosm of the cricket. Back home at least, much of the blame for Pakistan's downturn had been heaped on Misbah-ul-Haq, whose tactical and technical methods were said to be ill-suited to the modern limited-overs game. But he rubbished the theory with four decisive half-centuries and the series award. He was again deemed too slow for the Twenty20 side, but the St Lucia Zouks franchise snapped him up for the CPL, which began two days after the tour finished.

The aim of installing Dwayne Bravo as West Indies one-day captain for the Champions Trophy and beyond was to "freshen the leadership", according to chief selector Clyde Butts. The intention had yet to be realised. Bravo's decision to bowl the closing overs himself proved costly – he conceded 18, 22 and 19 off his last two in West Indies' three defeats. His unbeaten 43 and two late wickets did help their solitary win, but he acknowledged difficulties in coming to terms with the role.

Five months' non-stop cricket appeared to have irritated West Indies. There were open grouses from Bravo about the Duckworth/Lewis adjustment in the rain-affected fourth one-day international, and from Bravo and head coach Ottis Gibson about umpiring decisions in the fifth.

Two out-of-form power-hitters, previously seen as essential in 50-over cricket, were dropped: Chris Gayle to No. 5 in the order, and Kieron Pollard to the substitutes' bench after successive scores of 0, 4, 0, 0, 3, 30 and 0. Marlon Samuels was West Indies' leading run-scorer with 243, including the only hundred on either side, though at the tardy overall strike-rate of 55. Gayle, feared assassin of bowling the world over, could muster a strike-rate of just 58, and a top score of 30.

West Indies needed to win the last one-day international to square the series, and slack boundary fielding by Sunil Narine and Samuels prompted a livid reaction from spectators and some team-mates; Narine's response was a dismissive hand gesture. Even before play, former West Indies fast bowler Ian Bishop commented on television that he detected a lack of cohesion within the team.

Pakistan, themselves so often undermined by internal politics, appeared far more settled under a calm, unruffled captain. But it was Shahid Afridi, a habitual loose cannon, who lit the fuse. In his first match since being left out of the Champions Trophy squad, he smashed 76, then took seven for 12, the second-best figures in one-day international history. Umar Akmal, often just as erratic, was a key batsman in the closing overs.

In the UK, the *Mail on Sunday* reported that the series was being investigated by the ICC's Anti-Corruption and Security Unit for "suspicious betting patterns" related to "unusually slow run-rates during certain overs, followed by bursts of high scoring". The report paid specific reference to the third one-day international, which finished in a tie, and the fifth, which Pakistan won off the penultimate ball. The Pakistan Cricket Board maintained they had "zero tolerance" of corruption, and expected the ICC to make a statement on the matter; none was immediately forthcoming.

PAKISTAN TOURING PARTY

*Misbah-ul-Haq (50), Abdur Rehman (50), Ahmed Shehzad (50/20), Asad Ali (50/20), Asad Shafiq (50), Hammad Azam (20), Haris Sohail (50/20), Junaid Khan (50/20), Mohammad Hafeez (50/20), Mohammad Irfan (50/20), Mohammad Rizwan (50), Nasir Jamshed (50/20), Saeed Ajmal (50/20), Shahid Afridi (50/20), Sohail Tanvir (20), Umar Akmal (50/20), Umar Amin (50/20), Wahab Riaz (50/20), Zulfiqar Babar (20). *Coach:* D. F. Whatmore.

Hafeez captained in the Twenty20 matches.

At Georgetown (Bourda), Guyana, July 11, 2013. **Pakistanis won by seven runs. Pakistanis 246-9** (50 overs) (Ahmed Shehzad 68; V. Permaul 3-27, D. Bishoo 3-39); ‡**Guyana 239** (49.4 overs) (N. Deonarine 55; Mohammad Irfan 3-27, Saeed Ajmal 5-37). *Each team chose from 14 players. The Pakistanis were given a tough workout at Guyana's old Test ground, on a pitch that played to the strengths of home spinners Veerasammy Permaul and Devendra Bishoo. After Mohammad Irfan removed the openers cheaply, Saeed Ajmal kept Guyana in check.*

WEST INDIES v PAKISTAN

First One-Day International

At Providence, Guyana, July 14, 2013. Pakistan won by 126 runs. Toss: West Indies.

Shahid Afridi, restored to Pakistan's one-day side for the umpteenth time, delivered one of his most electrifying all-round performances. He entered at 47 for five in the 21st over, after Pakistan's top order had caved in to Holder's seam movement in an opening spell of 8–4–8–4, with the first three all dismissed leaving the ball. Afridi, though, belted his third delivery, from Roach, over long-off for the first of his five sixes, and hit the spinners out of the attack on a pitch well-suited to them. Gayle missed a stiff chance at slip to stop him on 20 and, by the time Afridi failed to pick Pollard's slower one, he had plundered 76 from 55 balls. At the other end, Misbah-ul-Haq ground out 52 from 121. Mohammad Irfan then picked up the first two wickets, and Gayle ran himself out in his 250th one-day international; Samuels and Simmons were desperately clinging on by the time Misbah threw Afridi the ball. After going wicketless in his last six one-dayers, he now gobbled up seven for 12 in nine overs – the second-best figures in all one-day internationals, behind Chaminda Vaas's eight for 19 for Sri Lanka against Zimbabwe in Colombo in 2001-02. Afridi was now the only man to combine a fifty and five wickets on three separate occasions, and out on his own with 7,000 runs and 350 wickets. West Indies were bowled out for under 100 for just the second time at home. It was no sort of show for the Guyanese, staging their first international fixture for two years following a prolonged conflict between the country's government and cricket board.

Man of the Match: Shahid Afridi.

Pakistan

Nasir Jamshed lbw b Holder	6	Asad Ali b D. J. Bravo	11
Ahmed Shehzad b Holder	5	Mohammad Irfan not out	4
Mohammad Hafeez b Holder	1		
*Misbah-ul-Haq c Charles b D. J. Bravo	52	B 1, l-b 4, w 23	28
Asad Shafiq c Charles b Holder	0		
†Umar Akmal c D. J. Bravo b Roach	19	1/15 (2) 2/18 (3) (9 wkts, 50 overs) 224	
Shahid Afridi c Sammy b Pollard	76	3/21 (1) 4/23 (5)	
Wahab Riaz c Holder b Roach	7	5/47 (6) 6/167 (7) 7/183 (8)	
Saeed Ajmal not out	15	8/200 (4) 9/220 (10) 10 overs: 24-4	

Roach 10–0–38–2; Holder 10–4–13–4; Sammy 8–2–35–0; D. J. Bravo 10–3–52–2; Narine 3–0–32–0; Samuels 3–0–24–0; Pollard 6–0–25–1.

West Indies

C. H. Gayle run out	1	D. J. G. Sammy not out	21
†J. Charles b Mohammad Irfan	0	K. A. J. Roach c and b Shahid Afridi	1
D. M. Bravo c Umar Akmal b Mohammad Irfan	5	S. P. Narine c Nasir Jamshed b Shahid Afridi	14
		J. O. Holder lbw b Shahid Afridi	0
M. N. Samuels lbw b Shahid Afridi	25	B 1, l-b 6, w 11	18
L. M. P. Simmons st Umar Akmal b Shahid Afridi	10	1/1 (2) 2/7 (3) 3/7 (1) (41 overs) 98	
*D. J. Bravo lbw b Shahid Afridi	0	4/41 (5) 5/41 (6) 6/50 (7) 7/51 (4)	
K. A. Pollard c Wahab Riaz b Shahid Afridi	3	8/55 (9) 9/98 (10) 10/98 (11) 10 overs: 20-3	

Mohammad Irfan 7–2–17–2; Asad Ali 5–0–13–0; Wahab Riaz 5–1–8–0; Saeed Ajmal 7–0–25–0; Mohammad Hafeez 8–1–16–0; Shahid Afridi 9–3–12–7.

Umpires: P. R. Reiffel and J. S. Wilson.   Third umpire: N. J. Llong.

WEST INDIES v PAKISTAN

Second One-Day International

At Providence, Guyana, July 16, 2013. West Indies won by 37 runs. Toss: Pakistan.

West Indies levelled the series in slightly unconvincing fashion. Suffocated again by Shahid Afridi on another spinning pitch, they managed only 18 for the loss of two wickets – slipping to 155 for five – in the powerplay, a sticky period during which chewing gum had to be scrubbed off the ball with a wet towel. But Pollard helped Dwayne Bravo raise 70 from 58 deliveries towards the end. Pakistan were grounded by Roach's opening burst of four maidens in six overs, and Narine took four for 26 after his mauling in the previous match at the hands of Afridi, who was now among his victims. Nasir Jamshed was dropped on nought off his 21st ball, and missed four more times; Umar Akmal's 50 off 46 was considerably more cultured, but he could not shield the lower order from Narine. The 38 extras conceded by Pakistan almost matched their margin of defeat.

Man of the Match: S. P. Narine.

West Indies

C. H. Gayle c Umar Akmal	
b Mohammad Irfan.	1
†J. Charles st Umar Akmal b Shahid Afridi .	31
D. M. Bravo b Saeed Ajmal	54
M. N. Samuels b Saeed Ajmal.	21
L. M. P. Simmons c Umar Akmal	
b Shahid Afridi	10
*D. J. Bravo not out.	43
K. A. Pollard b Asad Ali	30

J. O. Holder did not bat.

D. J. G. Sammy run out.	3
K. A. J. Roach run out.	0
S. P. Narine not out.	1
B 5, l-b 11, w 21, n-b 1	38
	—
(8 wkts, 50 overs)	232

1/2 (1) 2/81 (2)   (8 wkts, 50 overs) 232
3/123 (3) 4/137 (4)
5/150 (5) 6/220 (7)
7/226 (8) 8/226 (9)   10 overs: 49-1

Mohammad Irfan 10–0–38–1; Asad Ali 6–1–35–1; Saeed Ajmal 10–0–45–2; Mohammad Hafeez 7–0–32–0; Wahab Riaz 7–0–37–0; Shahid Afridi 10–0–29–2.

Pakistan

Nasir Jamshed c Roach b Pollard	54
Ahmed Shehzad c Charles b Roach.	19
Mohammad Hafeez c Simmons b Narine ..	20
*Misbah-ul-Haq b Sammy.	17
Asad Shafiq c Holder b Samuels.	10
†Umar Akmal c Samuels b D. J. Bravo.	50
Shahid Afridi st Charles b Narine	5
Wahab Riaz b Narine	3
Saeed Ajmal c Sammy b Narine	1

Asad Ali c Pollard b D. J. Bravo	2
Mohammad Irfan not out.	0
L-b 3, w 11	14

1/37 (2) 2/64 (3)   (47.5 overs) 195
3/103 (4) 4/122 (5) 5/137 (1)
6/151 (7) 7/162 (8) 8/164 (9)
9/195 (6) 10/195 (10)   10 overs: 33-0

Roach 6–4–14–1; Holder 7–2–30–0; Narine 10–1–26–4; Sammy 10–0–46–1; Samuels 7–0–32–1; Pollard 6–0–35–1; D. J. Bravo 1.5–0–9–2.

Umpires: N. J. Llong and P. J. Nero.   Third umpire: P. R. Reiffel.

WEST INDIES v PAKISTAN

Third One-Day International

At Gros Islet, St Lucia, July 19, 2013. Tied. Toss: West Indies. One-day international debut: Haris Sohail.

With the game in the balance, West Indies lost four wickets in 11 balls, which left them needing 39 from three overs with only Nos 9, 10 and 11 to call upon. Narine reasoned he had nothing to lose, and belted his first ball, from Saeed Ajmal, for a straight six, followed by two fours, before being bowled by the fifth. Holder and Roach reduced the equation to 15 off the last, entrusted to Wahab Riaz. They took singles off the first two deliveries but, with the off-side boundaries strangely unprotected – to coach Dav Whatmore's evident fury – Holder threaded the third to the extra-cover rope and blasted the fifth over it. Pakistan, after a lengthy conference, kept the same field for the last ball. Holder thick-edged it to third man, but wicketkeeper Umar Akmal was unable to gather Junaid Khan's return cleanly, which allowed the batsmen to scramble two runs for a tie – the third between these countries in one-day internationals. Pakistan had lost their nerve again, but were unlucky to have had a run shaved off their score when umpire Joel Wilson signalled one short; replays indicated Akmal had grounded his bat perfectly well. After Misbah-ul-Haq's steady acceleration, Akmal and Wahab had given Pakistan's innings further polish. West Indies were stalled by early wickets, then Samuels's painstaking 46 off 106 balls. Though Simmons quickened the pace, the required run-rate was nearly 11 an over when he was brilliantly taken at midwicket by Ahmed Shehzad.

Men of the Match: Misbah-ul-Haq and L. M. P. Simmons.

Pakistan

Ahmed Shehzad c Roach b Holder	17	Wahab Riaz not out	19
Nasir Jamshed c Roach b Sammy	20		
Mohammad Hafeez c Sammy b D. J. Bravo	14	L-b 6, w 11	17
*Misbah-ul-Haq b D. J. Bravo	75		
Haris Sohail c Pollard b Roach	26	1/39 (1) 2/39 (2) (6 wkts, 50 overs) 229	
†Umar Akmal not out	40	3/92 (3) 4/152 (5)	
Shahid Afridi c Narine b Holder	1	5/174 (4) 6/177 (7) 10 overs: 29-0	

Saeed Ajmal, Junaid Khan and Mohammad Irfan did not bat.

Roach 10–1–35–1; Holder 10–0–40–2; Sammy 10–0–30–1; Narine 9–0–55–0; D. J. Bravo 7–0–50–2; Samuels 3–1–4–0; Pollard 1–0–9–0.

West Indies

C. H. Gayle b Junaid Khan	8	D. J. G. Sammy c Mohammad Hafeez	
†J. Charles c Umar Akmal b Mohammad Irfan	6	b Junaid Khan	10
D. M. Bravo c Mohammad Hafeez		K. A. J. Roach not out	6
b Wahab Riaz	17	S. P. Narine b Saeed Ajmal	14
M. N. Samuels c Umar Akmal		J. O. Holder not out	19
b Mohammad Irfan	46	B 1, l-b 2, w 12	15
L. M. P. Simmons c Ahmed Shehzad			
b Saeed Ajmal	75	1/13 (2) 2/16 (1) (9 wkts, 50 overs) 229	
*D. J. Bravo b Saeed Ajmal	13	3/50 (3) 4/141 (4) 5/178 (5) 6/179 (6)	
K. A. Pollard b Junaid Khan	0	7/184 (7) 8/191 (8) 9/205 (10) 10 overs: 32-2	

Mohammad Irfan 10–0–34–2; Junaid Khan 10–1–54–3; Wahab Riaz 10–1–63–1; Mohammad Hafeez 6–0–16–0; Shahid Afridi 4–0–23–0; Saeed Ajmal 10–1–36–3.

Umpires: P. R. Reiffel and J. S. Wilson. Third umpire: S. J. Davis.

WEST INDIES v PAKISTAN

Fourth One-Day International

At Gros Islet, St Lucia, July 21, 2013. Pakistan won by six wickets (D/L). Toss: Pakistan.

Dwayne Bravo's grumpy reaction when presented with the Duckworth/Lewis tables following a lengthy stoppage for rain seemed to rub off on his team when they came back out to field. Pakistan were 68 for two off 17 overs, requiring a further 121 off 14. The reduction – the game had already begun as 49 overs a side – meant that one bowler was now permitted seven overs and the rest six; Bravo was unhappy that his opening bowlers had only three left between them. Even so, Pakistan's new goal was hardly straightforward; Misbah-ul-Haq's energetic partnerships of 72 from 55 balls with Mohammad Hafeez, and 45 off 28 with Umar Akmal, just made it seem so. Misbah overtook Wasim Akram as the player to have hit most one-day international runs without making a hundred. Akmal took three consecutive fours off Bravo to finish the debate with time to spare. West Indies ought to have had more confidence after building the highest total of the series on the back of Samuels's 106 from 104 balls, his fifth one-day international hundred.

Man of the Match: M. N. Samuels.

MOST ONE-DAY INTERNATIONAL RUNS WITHOUT A HUNDRED

Runs		I	HS	50s
4,384	**Misbah-ul-Haq (Pakistan)**	**128**	**96***	**35**
3,717	Wasim Akram (Pakistan)	280	86	6
3,266	Moin Khan (Pakistan)	183	72*	12
2,998	**E. Chigumbura (Zimbabwe/Africa XI)**	**141**	**79**	**15**
2,943	H. H. Streak (Zimbabwe/Africa XI)	159	79*	13
2,784	A. H. Jones (New Zealand)	87	93	25
2,705	G. J. Whittall (Zimbabwe)	142	83	11
2,653	Mudassar Nazar (Pakistan)	115	95	16

West Indies

D. S. Smith c Umar Akmal	
b Mohammad Irfan . 8	
†J. Charles lbw b Junaid Khan 32	
D. M. Bravo c Saeed Ajmal b Wahab Riaz . 9	
M. N. Samuels not out 106	
C. H. Gayle c sub (Umar Amin)	
b Shahid Afridi . 30	
L. M. P. Simmons b Saeed Ajmal 46	

D. J. G. Sammy b Mohammad Irfan 7	
*D. J. Bravo run out 6	
K. A. J. Roach not out 0	
L-b 6, w 9, n-b 2 17	
1/20 (1) 2/50 (3) (7 wkts, 49 overs) 261	
3/63 (2) 4/120 (5)	
5/215 (6) 6/239 (7) 7/253 (8) 10 overs: 36-1	

S. P. Narine and J. O. Holder did not bat.

Mohammad Irfan 10–1–60–2; Mohammad Hafeez 8–1–30–0; Junaid Khan 9–2–39–1; Wahab Riaz 6–0–42–1; Shahid Afridi 6–0–41–1; Saeed Ajmal 10–0–43–1.

Pakistan

Nasir Jamshed run out 22	
Ahmed Shehzad lbw b Holder 14	
Mohammad Hafeez c D. M. Bravo b Roach 59	
*Misbah-ul-Haq not out 53	
Shahid Afridi c Simmons b D. J. Bravo . . . 7	

†Umar Akmal not out 29	
L-b 1, w 3, n-b 1 5	
1/20 (2) 2/60 (1) (4 wkts, 30 overs) 189	
3/132 (4) 4/144 (5) 10 overs: 47-1	

Haris Sohail, Wahab Riaz, Saeed Ajmal, Junaid Khan and Mohammad Irfan did not bat.

Holder 5–0–41–1; Roach 6–1–33–1; Narine 7–0–29–0; Sammy 3–0–10–0; D. J. Bravo 6–0–49–1; Samuels 3–0–26–0.

Umpires: S. J. Davis and P. J. Nero.   Third umpire: P. R. Reiffel.

WEST INDIES v PAKISTAN

Fifth One-Day International

At Gros Islet, St Lucia, July 24, 2013. Pakistan won by four wickets. Toss: Pakistan.

    Pakistan completed a 3–1 series triumph when Saeed Ajmal hared a single off the penultimate ball, and Pollard's throw from close mid-on missed the stumps. West Indies were left aggrieved by a crucial call when Pakistan were still 53 away: they were convinced Misbah-ul-Haq had gloved Best down the leg side, but Paul Reiffel turned down the appeal, and third umpire Steve Davis – with Hot Spot not part of the DRS in this series – backed up his on-field colleague. Davis had, though, earlier given Darren Bravo out on the basis of sound from the stump microphone. Misbah overcame the hostile Best, then helped make 80 off the last ten overs with Umar Akmal and Shahid Afridi before he popped a full toss to midwicket with the scores level and four balls remaining. Earlier, Mohammad Irfan had removed Charles and Samuels after their restorative stand of 54 in 13 overs, and Junaid Khan returned to account for Gayle, down at No. 5 for the second game in succession; his one six on to the roof at long-on was the only time he approached his best.

    Man of the Match: Misbah-ul-Haq.   *Man of the Series:* Misbah-ul-Haq.

West Indies

†J. Charles c Haris Sohail b Mohammad Irfan 43	
D. S. Smith c Mohammad Hafeez	
b Junaid Khan . 7	
D. M. Bravo c Umar Akmal b Junaid Khan 9	
M. N. Samuels c Shahid Afridi	
b Mohammad Irfan . 45	
C. H. Gayle c Umar Akmal b Junaid Khan . 21	
L. M. P. Simmons c Mohammad Hafeez	
b Saeed Ajmal . 25	

*D. J. Bravo c Haris Sohail b Saeed Ajmal . . 48	
D. J. G. Sammy not out 29	
S. P. Narine not out 0	
L-b 6, w 9 15	
1/26 (2) 2/44 (3) (7 wkts, 50 overs) 242	
3/98 (1) 4/131 (5)	
5/159 (4) 6/170 (6) 7/223 (7) 10 overs: 37-1	

J. O. Holder and T. L. Best did not bat.

Mohammad Hafeez 6–2–22–0; Mohammad Irfan 10–1–34–2; Junaid Khan 10–1–48–3; Asad Ali 9–1–45–0; Shahid Afridi 5–0–30–0; Saeed Ajmal 10–2–57–2.

Pakistan

Nasir Jamshed run out	23	Saeed Ajmal not out 1
Ahmed Shehzad c D. J. Bravo b Best	64	
Mohammad Hafeez c Simmons b Sammy	11	L-b 5, w 9 14
*Misbah-ul-Haq c D. J. Bravo b Holder	63	
Haris Sohail c Simmons b Best	17	1/51 (1) 2/64 (3) (6 wkts, 49.5 overs) 243
†Umar Akmal c sub (K. A. J. Roach) b Best	37	3/123 (2) 4/160 (5)
Shahid Afridi not out	13	5/226 (6) 6/242 (4) 10 overs: 47-0

Junaid Khan, Asad Ali and Mohammad Irfan did not bat.

Holder 9.5–0–47–1; Best 10–2–48–3; Sammy 10–0–35–1; Narine 10–0–42–0; Samuels 5–0–25–0; D. J. Bravo 5–0–41–0.

Umpires: P. R. Reiffel and J. S. Wilson. Third umpire: S. J. Davis.
Series referee: D. C. Boon.

WEST INDIES v PAKISTAN

First Twenty20 International

At Arnos Vale, St Vincent, July 27, 2013. Pakistan won by two wickets. Toss: West Indies. Twenty20 international debuts: Umar Amin, Zulfiqar Babar.

At 34 years 218 days, left-arm spinner Zulfiqar Babar marked his maiden international appearance by hitting the top of Simmons's off stump with his fourth ball, then adding Samuels and Bravo. When Pakistan needed six off the last over, Zulfiqar punched Samuels's first ball to the cover boundary and, with the scores tied on the last, hoisted a low full toss over long-off. Earlier, Pollard had not shared the West Indian top-order's problems against spin and, helped by Sammy – who remained spectator in this format – took 54 from the last four overs. Their hitting was matched by Umar Amin, who helped bring 61 from the Pakistan powerplay, and Shahid Afridi's 46, which earned him the match award. "I should give it to Zulfiqar," he said afterwards. It was West Indies' first defeat in ten Twenty20 matches.

Man of the Match: Shahid Afridi.

West Indies

		B	4	6
†J. Charles b 3	1	2	0	0
C. H. Gayle lbw b 3	5	6	1	0
M. N. Samuels c and b 8	25	22	4	1
L. M. P. Simmons b 8	6	5	0	1
D. J. Bravo c 9 b 8	25	35	2	0
K. A. Pollard not out	49	36	4	2
*D. J. G. Sammy c 6 b 11	30	14	2	3
S. P. Narine run out	0	0	0	0
B 2, l-b 3, w 6	11			

6 overs: 41-3   (20 overs) 152-7

1/2 2/13 3/33 4/42 5/98 6/151 7/152

T. L. Best, S. Badree and S. T. Gabriel did not bat.

Mohammad Hafeez 2–0–4–2; Mohammad Irfan 3–0–39–1; Zulfiqar Babar 4–0–23–3; Saeed Ajmal 4–0–23–0; Shahid Afridi 4–0–24–0; Junaid Khan 3–0–34–0.

Pakistan

		B	4	6
Nasir Jamshed c 4 b 11	6	4	0	1
Ahmed Shehzad c 6 b 10	3	6	0	0
*Mohammad Hafeez c 11 b 8	13	7	3	0
Umar Amin st 1 b 3	47	34	9	0
†Umar Akmal run out	9	9	1	0
Hammad Azam c 6 b 11	10	15	0	0
Shahid Afridi c 5 b 11	46	27	4	2
Zulfiqar Babar not out	13	17	1	1
Saeed Ajmal run out	0	1	0	0
Junaid Khan not out	0	0	0	0
L-b 2, w 9	11			

6 overs: 61-3   (20 overs) 158-8

1/7 2/10 3/45 4/77 5/86 6/116 7/145 8/152

Mohammad Irfan did not bat.

Gabriel 4–0–44–3; Badree 3–0–27–1; Narine 4–0–24–1; Best 4–0–24–0; Samuels 4–0–33–1; Sammy 4–0–4–0.

Umpires: G. O. Brathwaite and P. J. Nero. Third umpire: J. S. Wilson.

WEST INDIES v PAKISTAN

Second Twenty20 International

At Arnos Vale, St Vincent, July 28, 2013. Pakistan won by 11 runs. Toss: Pakistan. Twenty20 international debuts: Asad Ali, Haris Sohail.

Pakistan defended their middling score against opponents who looked a pale shadow of the team who had become World Twenty20 champions ten months earlier. Ahmed Shehzad and Umar Akmal received scant support at the top and tail of Pakistan's innings, but managed to monopolise the strike. The exodus from the packed stands began when West Indies limped to 17 for four after eight overs, with Gayle recording his fifth consecutive single-figure score in Twenty20 internationals – leaving him stranded on 999 runs – and Charles and Samuels cramped by Sohail Tanvir's angle of delivery. Narine, promoted to No. 6, and Pollard raised unrealistic hopes, but Best's couple of sixes at the end could not camouflage a substandard performance.

Man of the Match: Umar Akmal. *Man of the Series:* Zulfiqar Babar.

Pakistan

		B	4	6
Ahmed Shehzad *c 4 b 7*	44	46	4	2
*Mohammad Hafeez *c 4 b 11*	10	7	1	0
Umar Amin *c and b 8*	7	6	1	0
Haris Sohail *c and b 11*	1	4	0	0
†Umar Akmal *not out*	46	36	3	1
Shahid Afridi *c 3 b 6*	6	10	0	0
Hammad Azam *st 1 b 6*	1	2	0	0
Sohail Tanvir *c 5 b 6*	0	3	0	0
Zulfiqar Babar *not out*	11	6	1	0
B 2, l-b 4, w 3	9			

6 overs: 39-1   (20 overs) 135-7

1/24 2/39 3/42 4/78 5/96 6/109 7/109

Saeed Ajmal and Asad Ali did not bat.

Sammy 4–0–20–1; Badree 4–0–16–2; Narine 4–0–26–3; Best 2–0–16–0; Bravo 4–0–35–0; Pollard 2–0–16–1.

West Indies

		B	4	6
†J. Charles *c 5 b 8*	0	9	0	0
C. H. Gayle *c 6 b 2*	1	3	0	0
M. N. Samuels *c 5 b 8*	1	4	0	0
L. M. P. Simmons *b 6*	3	16	0	0
D. J. Bravo *c 7 b 9*	35	44	2	1
S. P. Narine *c 3 b 10*	28	16	3	1
K. A. Pollard *c 4 b 9*	23	10	2	2
*D. J. G. Sammy *c 6 b 10*	1	4	0	0
C. D. Barnwell *run out*	10	5	2	0
T. L. Best *not out*	17	9	0	2
S. Badree *not out*	1	1	0	0
L-b 1, w 2, n-b 1	4			

6 overs: 13-3   (20 overs) 124-9

1/2 2/2 3/4 4/17 5/64 6/94 7/94 8/105 9/105

Mohammad Hafeez 4–0–9–1; Sohail Tanvir 4–0–20–2; Zulfiqar Babar 4–0–37–2; Shahid Afridi 3–0–29–1; Saeed Ajmal 4–0–21–2; Asad Ali 1–0–7–0.

Umpires: G. O. Brathwaite and J. S. Wilson.   Third umpire: P. J. Nero.
Series referee: D. C. Boon.

DOMESTIC CRICKET IN THE WEST INDIES, 2012-13

HAYDN GILL

Jamaica's stranglehold on the four-day championship was finally ended as Barbados claimed their 20th first-class title, but the tournament once more unearthed shortcomings in the Caribbean game. It had seemed a foregone conclusion that **Jamaica** would win the Headley–Weekes Trophy for an unprecedented sixth successive season, after they sailed through the preliminary phase with a 100% record. But they were shocked in the semi-finals – their only hiccup of the tournament – by a depleted **Trinidad & Tobago**, who had lost several top players to the IPL. The other form team of the preliminaries, **Windward Islands** – who had beaten everyone except Jamaica – also collapsed in the semis, their hopes of a maiden first-class title wrecked when they were brushed aside for 44 and 67 in a two-day defeat by the eventual champions.

Barbados came good when it mattered most. After an uncertain start, they won their last four matches, reducing Trinidad & Tobago to 19 for five on the first morning of the final, and sweeping them away just after lunch on the third day. It was a record 20th outright title for Barbados (they also shared one in 1975-76), but their first since 2006-07.

Windwards did win their third one-day trophy, the Super50. For the first time in six seasons, it was played in conjunction with the first-class competition, and followed a similar course in that its group stage was also dominated by two teams – in this case T&T and Jamaica – who both went out in the semis. T&T had enjoyed more success in converting their dominance into silverware back in January, when they completed a hat-trick of Caribbean Twenty20 titles. Of the other teams, **Guyana** and **Combined Campuses & Colleges** had to be content with appearances in the limited-overs finals, while **Leeward Islands** finished bottom in all three tournaments.

Yet again, the standard of the competition was a concern, as it duplicated some unflattering statistics from the previous season. Only one of the 24 matches was drawn; even more worrying, 13 games, including the final, ended in three days, and a couple more, one of them a semi-final, in two. Only two batsmen passed 500 runs; there were a mere 14 centuries, just two team totals of more than 400 and eight under 100.

Some positives, however, did emerge. Devon Smith was the star batsman of the domestic season: his three centuries helped him to 700 runs at 70. He was also the leading run-scorer in the Super50, and it was enough to convince the West Indies selectors to recall him, at the age of 31, for the Champions Trophy in England. The only other batsman to cross 500 runs was Barbados opener Kraigg Brathwaite.

Barbados managed to draw telling performances from two relatively inexperienced players. Miguel Cummins, who had previously played a single first-class match, was head and shoulders above all other fast bowlers, grabbing 35 wickets to land a place in the West Indies A-team; off-spinner Ashley Nurse, previously regarded as a Twenty20 specialist, seized his opportunity in the longer game to capture 45, including 14 in the semi-final.

Ahead of them, two familiar names led the wicket-takers' list. Jamaican slow left-armer Nikita Miller and Windward Islands off-spinner Shane Shillingford collected 52 scalps each (with Shillingford adding 19 against Zimbabwe), and also dominated the Super50, with 30 between them. As so often in recent years, fast bowlers hardly made an impression: of the 11 men who managed 20 first-class wickets, only Cummins and Trinidad's Rayad Emrit were not spinners.

A new Twenty20 tournament, the Caribbean Premier League, was introduced in July 2013. It was contested by six franchise teams, who could top up a quota of local players and Under-23s with West Indians from other territories as well as international stars – some Barbadians were shocked to see a Trinidadian, Kieron Pollard, lead their franchise. The tournament was regarded as an overwhelming success, attracting capacity crowds as it toured the six venues (the previous regional Twenty20 competition visited only two). It was won by **Jamaica Tallawahs**, who qualified for the 2014-15 Champions League.

FIRST-CLASS AVERAGES, 2012-13

BATTING (225 runs, average 20.00)

	M	I	NO	R	HS	100	Avge	Ct/St
†D. S. Smith (*Windward Islands*)	7	14	4	700	150*	3	70.00	15
†S. Chanderpaul (*Guyana/West Indies*)	3	4	0	250	108	2	62.50	3
K. C. Brathwaite (*Barbados*)	8	12	2	577	165	2	57.70	7
C. A. K. Walton (*Campuses & Colleges*)	6	12	1	409	101*	1	37.18	11/1
L. M. P. Simmons (*Trinidad & Tobago*)	7	13	0	473	140	1	36.38	6
C. S. Baugh (*Jamaica*)	7	14	3	395	99	0	35.90	16/1
†L. R. Johnson (*Guyana*)	6	12	0	430	87	0	35.83	7
K. A. Edwards (*Barbados*)	8	11	0	379	120	2	34.45	8
†J. L. Carter (*Barbados*)	8	11	0	367	116	1	33.36	10
J. N. Hamilton (*Leeward Islands*)	5	10	0	297	106	1	29.70	12
T. A. Willett (*Leeward Islands*)	5	10	1	266	58	0	29.55	1
J. Blackwood (*Jamaica*)	5	10	0	285	81	0	28.50	3
S. C. Joseph (*Leeward Islands*)	6	12	0	333	68	0	27.75	9
D. Ramdin (*Trinidad & Tobago/WI*)	8	13	0	347	86	0	26.69	15/1
†A. B. Fudadin (*Guyana*)	6	12	1	289	87	0	26.27	4
I. Khan (*Trinidad & Tobago*)	7	12	3	234	50*	0	26.00	9
†R. A. Reifer (*Campuses & Colleges*)	6	12	0	305	85	0	25.41	3
S. A. Jacobs (*Guyana*)	5	10	0	245	75	0	24.50	6
R. H. Boucher (*Barbados*)	8	12	1	268	81	0	24.36	7
†A. T. Alleyne (*Campuses & Colleges*)	6	12	0	286	84	0	23.83	4
T. Theophile (*Windward Islands*)	7	14	1	308	91	0	23.69	7
A. B. Barath (*Trinidad & Tobago*)	7	14	1	299	71	0	23.00	3
K. A. M. Corbin (*Campuses & Colleges*)	6	12	0	263	62	0	21.91	12
S. E. Thomas (*Campuses & Colleges*)	6	12	0	245	35	0	20.41	4

BOWLING (12 wickets)

	Style	O	M	R	W	BB	5I	Avge
N. O. Miller (*Jamaica*)	SLA	244.1	80	419	52	7-13	6	8.05
S. Shillingford (*Windward Islands/WI*)	OB	356.4	88	839	71	8-82	7	11.81
L. A. S. Sebastien (*Windward Islands*)	OB	97.3	33	205	16	5-30	1	12.81
A. R. Nurse (*Barbados*)	OB	219.1	52	622	45	7-10	3	13.82
S. J. Benn (*Barbados*)	SLA	145.5	35	377	27	6-43	2	13.96
M. L. Cummins (*Barbados*)	RF	145	27	517	35	7-45	3	14.77
C. J. Jordan (*Barbados*)	RFM	73	13	243	16	7-43	1	15.18
D. E. Bernard (*Jamaica*)	RFM	102.1	23	251	16	6-39	1	15.68
M. K. A. Richards (*Trinidad & Tobago*)	RFM	87.3	15	279	17	5-46	1	16.41
V. Permaul (*Guyana*)	SLA	224.2	63	538	30	5-73	1	17.93
O. V. Brown (*Jamaica*)	LBG	135.1	34	346	19	5-31	1	18.21
S. S. Cottrell (*Jamaica*)	LFM	115.5	29	328	17	5-43	1	19.29
A. P. Richardson (*Jamaica*)	RFM	103	22	316	16	3-30	0	19.75
D. E. Johnson (*Windward Islands*)	LF	100	22	278	14	3-21	0	19.85
I. Khan (*Trinidad & Tobago*)	SLA	127	22	398	20	5-28	1	19.90
R. R. Emrit (*Trinidad & Tobago*)	RFM	162	39	439	20	6-35	1	21.95
S. A. Jacobs (*Guyana*)	SLA	151.2	25	385	17	4-61	0	22.64
A. M. A. Dewar (*Campuses & Colleges*)	LBG	172.1	23	561	20	7-116	1	28.05
G. C. Tonge (*Leeward Islands*)	RFM	112.4	32	350	12	3-55	0	29.16
S. T. Gabriel (*Trinidad & Tobago/WI*)	RFM	162.4	34	568	19	3-10	0	29.89
R. R. Beaton (*Guyana*)	RFM	152	31	487	16	4-52	0	30.43
R. A. Austin (*Campuses & Colleges*)	OB	218.5	34	616	20	6-48	1	30.80
N. T. Pascal (*Windward Islands*)	RF	103.4	13	407	13	5-81	1	31.30
D. Bishoo (*Guyana*)	LBG	228.4	50	629	20	5-67	1	31.45

Does not include tour by Sri Lanka A in June 2013.

HEADLEY–WEEKES TROPHY, 2012-13

	Played	Won	Lost	Drawn	1st-inns points	Points
Jamaica	6	6	0	0	0	72
Windward Islands	6	5	1	0	0	60
Barbados	6	4	2	0	0	48
Trinidad & Tobago	6	3	3	0	0	36
Guyana	6	1	4	1	3	18
Combined Campuses & Colleges	6	1	5	0	0	12
Leeward Islands	6	0	5	1	4	7

Semi-finals: Trinidad & Tobago beat Jamaica by three wickets; Barbados beat Windward Islands by an innings and 101 runs.

Final: Barbados beat Trinidad & Tobago by an innings and 22 runs.

Win = 12pts; draw = 3pts; first-innings lead in a drawn match = 3pts; first-innings lead in a lost match = 4pts.

At Bridgetown (Kensington Oval), Barbados, February 9–11, 2013. **Jamaica won by 63 runs. ‡Jamaica 165** (M. L. Cummins 5-58) **and 188; Barbados 162** (N. O. Miller 5-33) **and 128** (N. O. Miller 5-34). *Jamaica 12pts.*

At North Sound, Antigua, February 9–12, 2013. **Drawn. Leeward Islands 182 and 322** (J. N. Hamilton 106; V. Permaul 5-73); **‡Guyana 279 and 173-6**. *Leeward Islands 3pts, Guyana 6pts. This was the only draw of the competition. Leewards wicketkeeper Jahmar Hamilton's maiden century followed six first-innings catches; his victims included Guyanese opener Tagenarine Chanderpaul, 16-year-old son of Shivnarine, on his first-class debut.*

At Gros Islet, St Lucia, February 9–12, 2013. **Windward Islands won by seven wickets. Combined Campuses & Colleges 309 and 284** (N. T. Pascal 5-81); **‡Windward Islands 409** (D. S. Smith 139) **and 187-3** (D. S. Smith 106*). *Windward Islands 12pts. Devon Smith scored two hundreds; the first helped Windwards reach 409, which would remain the biggest total of this tournament.*

At Bridgetown (Kensington Oval), Barbados, February 15–18, 2013. **Barbados won by 93 runs. Barbados 367** (K. A. Edwards 120) **and 235-7 dec; ‡Guyana 225 and 284**. *Barbados 12pts. Kirk Edwards and Jonathan Carter (85) added 164 for Barbados's fourth wicket, until Carter was caught behind by Derwin Christian, who made seven dismissals in the match.*

At Arnos Vale, St Vincent, February 15–17, 2013. **Windward Islands won by ten wickets. Trinidad & Tobago 179 and 86; ‡Windward Islands 260** (R. Rampaul 5-65) **and 6-0**. *Windward Islands 12pts. Windwards' Devon Smith fell for 99, just missing his third century in successive innings; he also held seven catches in the field – a match record in this competition.*

At Bridgetown (Three Ws Oval), Barbados, February 27–March 1, 2013. **Barbados won by an innings and 185 runs. ‡Combined Campuses & Colleges 109** (C. J. Jordan 7-43) **and 78; Barbados 372** (K. A. Edwards 109; A. M. A. Dewar 7-116). *Barbados 12pts. Barbados's first wicket raised 204, of which 16 came before Rashidi Boucher retired hurt, and another 188 once Kraigg Brathwaite (90) joined Kirk Edwards. Chris Jordan (who had recently completed a move from Surrey to Sussex) and leg-spinner Akeem Dewar both took seven in an innings for the first time.*

At Basseterre, St Kitts, February 27–March 2, 2013. **Trinidad & Tobago won by 120 runs. ‡Trinidad & Tobago 279 and 249; Leeward Islands 194 and 214**. *Trinidad & Tobago 12pts. Trinidad & Tobago recovered from 98-5 in their first innings, and 90-6 in their second.*

At Arnos Vale, St Vincent, February 27–March 1, 2013. **Windward Islands won by four wickets. Guyana 151 and 211** (S. Shillingford 7-63); **‡Windward Islands 276** (D. Bishoo 5-67) **and 90-6**. *Windward Islands 12pts. Shane Shillingford's 11-103 set up Windwards' third straight victory.*

At Bridgetown (Three Ws Oval), Barbados, March 6–9, 2013. **Combined Campuses & Colleges won by 152 runs. Combined Campuses & Colleges 180 and 367-6 dec** (C. A. K. Walton 101*); **‡Leeward Islands 243 and 152** (R. A. Austin 6-48). *Combined Campuses & Colleges 12pts, Leeward Islands 4pts.*

At Port-of-Spain, Trinidad, March 6–9, 2013. **Trinidad & Tobago won by 45 runs. Trinidad & Tobago 319 and 251-2 dec**; ‡**Guyana 195** (S. P. Narine 6-38) **and 330** (S. Chanderpaul 108). *Trinidad & Tobago 12pts. Shivnarine Chanderpaul, playing alongside his son Tagenarine for the first time at this level, scored his 65th first-class century. They were only the second West Indian father and son to appear in the same first-class team, following Lebrun and Learie Constantine for Trinidad v Barbados in the 1922-23 Inter-Colonial final. Tagenarine made 42 and 29.*

At St George's (Queen's Park New), Grenada, March 6–8, 2013. **Jamaica won by 91 runs.** ‡**Jamaica 207 and 97; Windward Islands 130** (O. V. Brown 5-31) **and 83** (N. O. Miller 7-30). *Jamaica 12pts. In only their second game of the tournament, Jamaica rallied from 66-6 to inflict on table leaders Windwards' their only defeat of the preliminary rounds.*

At Bridgetown (Kensington Oval), Barbados, March 23–25, 2013. **Windward Islands won by 216 runs.** ‡**Windward Islands 184 and 301-4 dec** (D. S. Smith 150*); **Barbados 64 and 205** (S. Shillingford 8-82). *Windward Islands 12pts. Shillingford's 12-102 took him past 50 wickets for the season. His second-innings 8-32 was the best return of this tournament; five of them were caught in the field by Garey Mathurin, who held seven in the match, equalling the competition record of Devon Smith. Smith scored his third century of the season and put on 170 for Windwards' first wicket with Tyrone Theophile (91).*

At Kingston, Jamaica, March 23–25, 2013. **Jamaica won by 170 runs. Jamaica 209 and 225**; ‡**Leeward Islands 108** (N. O. Miller 7-13) **and 156**. *Jamaica 12pts. In Jamaica's second innings Nos 10 and 11, Odean Brown (59) and Sheldon Cottrell (48*), almost doubled the total by adding 109. Slow left-armer Nikita Miller (11-47) had taken 30 wickets in his first three games; his first-innings figures were 20.2–13–13–7. It was the fifth time he had taken ten or more in a match, a record in the regional competition.*

At Port-of-Spain, Trinidad, March 23–25, 2013. **Trinidad & Tobago won by ten wickets. Trinidad & Tobago 406-9 dec** (J. N. Mohammed 138) **and 13-0**; ‡**Combined Campuses & Colleges 188** (R. R. Emrit 6-35) **and 228**. *Trinidad & Tobago 12pts.*

At Providence, Guyana, March 30–April 2, 2013. **Guyana won by 46 runs. Guyana 231 and 175**; ‡**Combined Campuses & Colleges 167 and 193**. *Guyana 12pts.*

At Kingston, Jamaica, March 30–April 1, 2013. **Jamaica won by 93 runs. Jamaica 147** (K. Kantasingh 5-35) **and 259** (I. Khan 5-28); ‡**Trinidad & Tobago 121** (S. S. Cottrell 5-43) **and 192**. *Jamaica 12pts. Jamaica's fourth straight victory took them top of the table.*

At Basseterre, St Kitts, March 30–April 2, 2013. **Barbados won by an innings and 31 runs.** ‡**Leeward Islands 201** (A. R. Nurse 6-89) **and 149** (S. J. Benn 6-43); **Barbados 381-6 dec** (K. C. Brathwaite 165, K. A. Stoute 114). *Barbados 12pts. Brathwaite batted almost nine hours for a career-best 165, while he and Kevin Stoute added 230 for the fifth wicket – the highest individual score and only double-century partnership of this tournament. Off-spinner Ashley Nurse took 10-136 in all, his first return of ten in a match.*

At Providence, Guyana, April 10–12, 2013. **Jamaica won by 214 runs.** ‡**Jamaica 208 and 257-8 dec**; **Guyana 96 and 155**. *Jamaica 12pts. Jamaica were 12-4 in their first innings, but recovered; Guyana were 10-5, and did not.*

At North Sound, Antigua, April 10–12, 2013. **Windward Islands won by nine wickets. Leeward Islands 129** (S. Shillingford 7-45) **and 158** (L. A. S. Sebastien 5-30); ‡**Windward Islands 268 and 23-1**. *Windward Islands 12pts. Shillingford took 10-90 – his third successive match haul of ten or more, starting with the Second Test against Zimbabwe, and his fifth in all regional domestic cricket, equalling Nikita Miller's record. Leewards went down to their fifth successive loss.*

At Port-of-Spain, Trinidad, April 10–11, 2013. **Barbados won by ten wickets. Trinidad & Tobago 109** (M. L. Cummins 7-45) **and 129** (S. J. Benn 5-49); ‡**Barbados 194 and 45-0**. *Barbados 12pts. In two days, Trinidad & Tobago went down to their second ten-wicket defeat of the season.*

At Kingston, Jamaica, April 25–27, 2013. **Jamaica won by five wickets. ‡Combined Campuses & Colleges 150 and 152** (N. O. Miller 6-33); **Jamaica 238** (D. C. Sealy 5-58) **and 66-5**. *Jamaica 12pts. Jamaica ended the qualifying rounds with a clean sweep of their six matches, and their 15th successive win since April 2011, a competition record.*

Semi-finals

At Kingston, Jamaica, May 2–5, 2013. **Trinidad & Tobago won by three wickets. ‡Jamaica 246** (M. K. A. Richards 5-46) **and 102**; **Trinidad & Tobago 170** (N. O. Miller 5-41) **and 179-7** (D. E. Bernard 6-39). *Jamaica's first stumble cost them a sixth consecutive title – although Cottrell (44) shared his second last-wicket century stand in six weeks, adding 103 with Carlton Baugh (88*) in the first innings, and David Bernard reduced Trinidad & Tobago's chase to 73-6 before Miller took his 52nd wicket of the season. It was still not enough to avert Jamaica's first defeat in 26 first-class matches since February 2010. It was also their third defeat in a semi-final/play-off in 2012-13.*

At St George's (Queen's Park New), Grenada, May 2–3, 2013. **Barbados won by an innings and 101 runs. ‡Barbados 212** (J. L. Carter 116; S. Shillingford 6-81); **Windward Islands 44** (A. R. Nurse 7-10) **and 67** (A. R. Nurse 7-30). *In a match where only six other players reached double figures, and the next-highest score was 27, Carter's maiden hundred outscored both Windwards' innings combined. Nurse collected 14-40, his second return of ten or more in three matches, including 10.1–4–10–7 as Windwards folded for 44, the third-lowest total in the competition's history. Shillingford took five or more in an innings for the seventh time in seven first-class games to end his season with 52 in this tournament and 71 in all; his team-mate Devon Smith finished with 700 runs.*

Final

At Bridgetown (Kensington Oval), Barbados, May 9–11, 2013. **Barbados won by an innings and 22 runs. Trinidad & Tobago 110** (M. L. Cummins 5-30) **and 237** (L. M. P. Simmons 140); **‡Barbados 369** (K. C. Brathwaite 122). *Barbados's fourth innings win of the season secured the title. Miguel Cummins reduced Trinidad to 19-5 in the tenth over of the match, before Brathwaite batted seven hours in reply. Lendl Simmons hit a consolation century in 53 balls, finishing with 12 fours and eight sixes in all, but Barbados completed a straightforward victory with a day to spare.*

REGIONAL CHAMPIONS

Shell Shield		1983-84	Barbados	*Busta Cup*	
1965-66	Barbados	1984-85	Trinidad & Tobago	1998-99	Barbados
1966-67	Barbados	1985-86	Barbados	1999-2000	Jamaica
1967-68	No competition	1986-87	Guyana	2000-01	Barbados
1968-69	Jamaica			2001-02	Jamaica
1969-70	Trinidad	*Red Stripe Cup*			
1970-71	Trinidad	1987-88	Jamaica	*Carib Beer Cup*	
1971-72	Barbados	1988-89	Jamaica	2002-03	Barbados
1972-73	Guyana	1989-90	Leeward Islands	2003-04	Barbados
1973-74	Barbados	1990-91	Barbados	2004-05	Jamaica
1974-75	Guyana	1991-92	Jamaica	2005-06	Trinidad & Tobago
1975-76	{ Trinidad	1992-93	Guyana	2006-07	Barbados
	{ Barbados	1993-94	Leeward Islands	2007-08	Jamaica
1976-77	Barbados	1994-95	Barbados		
1977-78	Barbados	1995-96	Leeward Islands	*Headley–Weekes Trophy*	
1978-79	Barbados	1996-97	Barbados	2008-09	Jamaica
1979-80	Barbados			2009-10	Jamaica
1980-81	Combined Islands	*President's Cup*		2010-11	Jamaica
1981-82	Barbados	1997-98	{ Leeward Islands	2011-12	Jamaica
1982-83	Guyana		{ Guyana	2012-13	Barbados

Barbados have won the title outright 20 times, Jamaica 12, Guyana 5, Trinidad/Trinidad & Tobago 4, Leeward Islands 3, Combined Islands 1. Barbados, Guyana, Leeward Islands and Trinidad have also shared the title.

REGIONAL SUPER50, 2012-13

50-over league plus knockout

	Played	Won	Lost	Bonus points	Points	Net run-rate
Trinidad & Tobago.	6	6	0	1	25	0.77
Jamaica.	6	5	1	3	23	0.77
Windward Islands.	6	3	3	0	12	−0.41
Combined Campuses & Colleges. . . .	6	2	4	2	10	−0.05
Barbados.	6	2	4	2	10	−0.01
Guyana.	6	2	4	0	8	−0.34
Leeward Islands	6	1	5	0	4	−0.65

Semi-finals

At Bridgetown (Kensington Oval), Barbados, April 18, 2013 (day/night). **Combined Campuses & Colleges won by 140 runs.** ‡**Combined Campuses & Colleges 232-7** (50 overs); **Trinidad & Tobago 92** (31.2 overs). *MoM:* A. T. Alleyne (CC&C). *Keswick Williams reduced Trinidad to 19-3, and the whole team could not match Anthony Alleyne's 99 in 139 balls.*

At Bridgetown (Kensington Oval), Barbados, April 19, 2013 (day/night). **Windward Islands won by five wickets.** ‡**Jamaica 242-8** (50 overs); **Windward Islands 244-5** (49 overs). *MoM:* A. D. S. Fletcher (Windwards). *Brenton Parchment and Nkruma Bonner put on 166 for Jamaica's second wicket, but Devon Smith responded with 59 in 44 balls, and Andre Fletcher with 68 in 81.*

Final

At Bridgetown (Kensington Oval), Barbados, April 21, 2013 (day/night). **Windward Islands won by nine wickets** (D/L). **Combined Campuses & Colleges 174** (49.2 overs); ‡**Windward Islands 134-1** (22.2 overs). *MoM:* K. K. Peters and D. S. Smith (Windwards). *Kenroy Peters reduced Campuses & Colleges to 21-3 in the eighth over. After a rain-break, Windwards were set 134 in 29 overs; Devon Smith saw them home with 67* in 70 balls.*

CARIBBEAN T20, 2012-13

20-over league plus knockout

	Played	Won	Lost	No result	Points	Net run-rate
Trinidad & Tobago.	6	5	0	1	21	2.69
Jamaica.	6	4	1	1	17	−0.09
Guyana.	6	4	2	0	16	−0.29
Windward Islands.	6	3	3	0	12	0.20
Barbados.	6	2	4	0	8	0.18
Combined Campuses & Colleges.	6	1	5	0	4	−0.66
Leeward Islands	6	1	5	0	4	−1.59

Play-off

At Gros Islet, St Lucia, January 19, 2013 (floodlit). **Guyana won by six wickets. Jamaica 183-6** (20 overs) (C. H. Gayle 122*); ‡**Guyana 187-4** (18.4 overs). *MoM:* C. D. Barnwell (Guyana). *Chris Gayle hit 122* in 61 balls, with 12 sixes, but finished on the losing side after Christopher Barnwell fought back with 88 in 49.*

Final

At Gros Islet, St Lucia, January 20, 2013 (floodlit). **Trinidad & Tobago won by nine wickets. Guyana 116-6** (20 overs); ‡**Trinidad & Tobago 120-1** (12.3 overs). *MoM:* S. T. Gabriel (T&T). *MoS:* D. M. Bravo (T&T). *Trinidad & Tobago won a third successive title after Shannon Gabriel* *pinned Guyana back with 4–0–16–2, and Lendl Simmons steered them home with 52 in 37 balls. They advanced to the 2013-14 Champions League as the final winners of this regional Twenty20 competition, which was to be superseded by the franchise-based Caribbean Premier League.*

LIMACOL CARIBBEAN PREMIER LEAGUE, 2013

20-over league plus knockout

	Played	Won	Lost	Points	Net run-rate
Guyana Amazon Warriors	7	5	2	10	0.62
Jamaica Tallawahs	7	5	2	10	0.16
Barbados Tridents	7	4	3	8	1.06
Trinidad & Tobago Red Steel	7	3	4	6	−0.64
Antigua Hawksbills	7	2	5	4	−0.15
St Lucia Zouks	7	2	5	4	−1.19

Semi-finals

At Port-of-Spain, Trinidad, August 22, 2013 (floodlit). **Guyana Amazon Warriors won by seven wickets. Trinidad & Tobago Red Steel 103** (19.3 overs); ‡**Guyana Amazon Warriors 107-3** (16.2 overs). *MoM:* T. M. Dilshan (Guyana). *Tillekeratne Dilshan took two key Trinidad wickets as they collapsed to 32-5 and followed up with 39 in 29 balls.*

At Port-of-Spain, Trinidad, August 23, 2013 (floodlit). **Jamaica Tallawahs won by seven wickets. Barbados Tridents 148-6** (20 overs); ‡**Jamaica Tallawahs 152-3** (18.3 overs). *MoM:* K. C. Sangakkara (Jamaica). *Raymon Reifer and Shoaib Malik shared the first century stand of the CPL, 102 for Barbados's third wicket. Kumar Sangakkara anchored Jamaica's chase with 50* in 38 balls – while Andre Russell arrived at the end to smash 29 in six, with four sixes.*

Final

At Port-of-Spain, Trinidad, August 24, 2013 (floodlit). **Jamaica Tallawahs won by seven wickets. Guyana Amazon Warriors 128-5** (20 overs); ‡**Jamaica Tallawahs 129-3** (17.3 overs). *MoM:* C. H. Gayle (Jamaica). *MoS:* K. Santokie (Guyana). *Two overs in Jamaica's innings turned the match; captain Chris Gayle (47*) and Russell (33*) hit 20 off Christopher Barnwell in the 13th, and Krishmar Santokie, the tournament's leading bowler with 16 wickets, conceded another 20 in the 17th, when he bowled five wides. Jamaica's victory in the inaugural CPL earned them a place in the 2014-15 Champions League.*

ZIMBABWE CRICKET, 2013

On the brink?

MEHLULI SIBANDA

In 2013, the horror of Zimbabwe Cricket's financial situation came home to roost. It had long been known the board were sitting on huge debts, although the true extent – said to have reached around $US20m – was shielded from the public. By the end of the year, ZC had reportedly asked the ICC for an additional loan of $3m. First, though, the ICC demanded to see an audit of the $1.5m issued through their Targeted Assistance and Performance Programme in October 2012.

After two years in the post, Alan Butcher stepped down as coach in March following the tour of the West Indies, where he had to make do without bowling coach Heath Streak, batting coach Grant Flower and trainer Lorraine Chivandire – all told to stay at home because ZC could not afford to send them. The trip turned out to be catastrophic for Zimbabwe, who lost all seven internationals heavily. Butcher's assistant, Stephen Mangongo, stood in as interim coach for the home Test leg in April against Bangladesh where he got

ZIMBABWE IN 2013

	Played	Won	Lost	Drawn/No result
Tests	6	2	4	–
One-day internationals	14	3	11	–
Twenty20 internationals	6	1	5	–

JANUARY		
FEBRUARY }	2 Tests, 3 ODIs and 2 T20Is (a) v West Indies	(page 1149)
MARCH		
APRIL }	2 Tests, 3 ODIs and 2 T20Is (h) v Bangladesh	(page 1181)
MAY		
JUNE		
JULY }	5 ODIs (h) v India	(page 1187)
AUGUST		
SEPTEMBER }	2 Tests, 3 ODIs and 2 T20Is (h) v Pakistan	(page 1189)
OCTOBER		
NOVEMBER		
DECEMBER		

For a review of Zimbabwean domestic cricket from the 2012-13 season, see page 1196.

Jekesai Njikizana, AFP/Getty Images

No quick fix: the visit of Virat Kohli's star-studded India was no financial panacea; Kyle Jarvis (*right*) was playing his last series for Zimbabwe before joining Lancashire.

into trouble for pushing Natsai Mushangwe, who he claimed had failed to pass on a message to a team-mate on the field; he later apologised. Andy Waller, a veteran of three World Cups, then took up the role full-time. Streak's contract was not renewed.

Waller inherited a side shorn of several key players. Charles Coventry had taken up a gig in the Netherlands, while Craig Ervine, the most successful limited-overs batsman on the West Indies tour, turned down a winter contract with ZC for a summer contract in Northern Ireland; he did not appear for the rest of the year. The squad briefly considered boycotting some of the Bangladesh matches as a show of solidarity to non-centrally contracted players who had to make do on a small daily allowance.

ZC had long been pining for a visit from India. To maximise television and sponsorship revenues, they wanted a full tour, but the BCCI would agree only to a five-match one-day series. M. S. Dhoni sat it out, while Virat Kohli led India to a predictable whitewash; Kyle Jarvis, one of Zimbabwe's most promising fast bowlers, played what could be his last game for them, before taking up a Kolpak deal with Lancashire.

Tours were coming too fast for ZC to handle. Pakistan, themselves desperate for cricket, were the third Asian side to visit inside four months, and committed to matches in all three formats. The build-up was again disrupted by a strike over unpaid allowances: this time, with the help of the South African Cricketers' Association, the Zimbabweans formed a players' union to help them present a united front against their board. Again, the impasse was ended before any matches were affected.

It came as a surprise when Zimbabwe proved the equal of Pakistan. In the First Test at Harare, Zimbabwe sailed into a first-innings lead, and it was not until Younis Khan mastered the bowling with a double-century that their resistance faded. As discontent rumbled on in the home camp, ZC switched the Second Test, long since scheduled for Bulawayo, to Harare. Officially, the Queens Sports Club groundstaff were not ready to host a five-day match, but no one believed that. It clearly had more to do with avoiding the cost of ferrying everyone from one city to another.

The decision, while met with anger by marginalised cricket lovers in Bulawayo, paid off handsomely when Zimbabwe recorded a remarkable victory. Two of their young fast bowlers, Brian Vitori and Tendai Chatara, each took five-fors to dismantle Pakistan for fewer than 240 in both innings. It was Zimbabwe's first win over an established Full Member since beating India in 2000-01 – and reinstated them in the ICC Test rankings for the first time since their voluntary withdrawal in 2006, into ninth above Bangladesh.

The euphoria did not last. A proposed tour by Sri Lanka in October fell through because of ZC's parlous position, as did a potentially ground-breaking visit in January 2014 by Afghanistan, who had been prepared to pay their own way for the sake of competing in a first full series against a Test nation. The cancellation left Zimbabwe facing no international cricket until March 2014, when they would have to get past the Associates in a preliminary round of the World Twenty20 in Bangladesh.

ZC did send the Under-19 team to a quadrangular one-day tournament in India, where they lost all their matches by big margins. Meanwhile, Zimbabwe's women, the weakest of the Full Members, were beaten by Thailand in the World Twenty20 Qualifier. One of the players, Sharyce Saili, disappeared during the tournament in Dublin.

To accommodate the Sri Lanka tour that never happened, ZC postponed the start of the 2013-14 domestic franchise season (which traditionally runs from September to April) until November 9. But as they struggled to find sponsors for their three competitions, the delay dragged on. To stay fit, some of the players headed for Bangladesh to play in the Dhaka Premier Division. The season finally got under way on December 7 – minus sponsorship – and within a week players from Mountaineers and Mashonaland Eagles had boycotted a Pro50 match over unpaid salaries. Two Logan Cup games suffered the same fate, and the season did not restart in the New Year as planned. By mid-January, nationally contracted players had gone without pay since November, and their franchise colleagues had received nothing since September. It was all sadly typical.

ZIMBABWE v BANGLADESH, 2012-13

Tristan Holme

Test matches (2): Zimbabwe 1, Bangladesh 1
One-day internationals (3): Zimbabwe 2, Bangladesh 1
Twenty20 internationals (2): Zimbabwe 1, Bangladesh 1

In a low-key tour inevitably overshadowed by the Indian Premier League, Test cricket's two weakest teams provided no evidence they would be catching up with the rest of the pack any time soon – or even stealing a march on each other. While Bangladesh often gave the impression of being uninterested, Zimbabwe's obvious enthusiasm was compromised by a lack of support from their board. The result was a series of matches too often decided by the dubious tie-breaker of which side had performed less badly: a case of the resistible force versus the movable object.

Zimbabwe's preparations were hampered by a two-day strike by players who were not on central contracts. Offered $US100 per week by Zimbabwe Cricket to get them through the winter months – plus a $2 daily bus fare – the fringe players took a stand until ZC came up with something closer to a liveable wage. Even then, Craig Ervine opted instead for a gig with Lisburn CC in Northern Ireland.

Deep in debt (informed estimates put the figure at close to $20m), ZC were attempting to cut corners at every opportunity while they awaited the hoped-for cash influx from hosting India in July: Heath Streak's contract as bowling coach was not renewed at the end of March, and groundstaff found their salaries reduced. The austerity measures were immediately obvious to anyone watching the series on television, with the board opting for SuperSport's cheapest package – one which the broadcaster generally provided for domestic matches in South Africa. There were only nine cameras in the ground, compared to the usual 24 for international cricket, and no Decision Review System. To limit travel costs, both Tests were played at Harare, and all the shorter games at Bulawayo.

Bangladesh, fresh from an encouraging tour of Sri Lanka, arrived as favourites, but their decision not to play a warm-up match was called into question when Zimbabwe won the First Test comprehensively. Cue much wailing and gnashing of teeth back home.

Matters were put into perspective three days later when, on the eve of the Second Test, an eight-storey factory just outside Dhaka collapsed, killing more than a thousand people. Bangladesh wore black armbands the next day, and dedicated their victory to the victims.

Although the series ended 1–1, the quality of the cricket hardly left the neutral pining for a decider. Only Brendan Taylor, who became the third Zimbabwean to make hundreds in both innings of a Test, and Robiul Islam, who carried the Bangladesh attack with 15 wickets, came away with their reputations enhanced.

Zimbabwe benefited from bowling first in all three one-day internationals, with 9am starts providing early assistance for the seamers. But Taylor's fortune at the toss was less decisive than the tendency of the Bangladesh top order to throw away their wickets. Their series defeat led Mushfiqur Rahim to announce he would resign the captaincy, though it was clear he had made an emotional and hasty decision without consulting his peers. By the end of the Twenty20s, he had realised his folly, and sought talks with the BCB to restore his position.

BANGLADESH TOURING PARTY

Mushfiqur Rahim (T/50/20), Abdur Razzak (50/20), Enamul Haque, jun. (T), Jahurul Islam (T/50/20), Mahmudullah (T/50/20), Mohammad Ashraful (T/50/20), Mominul Haque (T/50/20), Nasir Hossain (T/50/20), Robiul Islam (T/50/20), Rubel Hossain (T), Sajidul Islam (T/50/20), Shafiul Islam (T/50/20), Shahadat Hossain (T), Shahriar Nafees (T), Shakib Al Hasan (T/50/20), Shamsur Rahman (50/20), Sohag Gazi (T/50/20), Tamim Iqbal (T/50/20), Ziaur Rahman (T/50/20). Coach: S. J. Jurgensen.

Shafiul Islam and Ziaur Rahman were called up for the Second Test as cover for Rubel Hossain (shoulder) and Shahadat Hossain (knee). Rubel was withdrawn from the limited-overs matches after contracting chickenpox.

ZIMBABWE v BANGLADESH

First Test Match

At Harare, April 17–20, 2013. Zimbabwe won by 335 runs. Toss: Bangladesh. Test debuts: T. Maruma, K. O. Meth, R. Mutumbami.

In a match otherwise devoid of excellence, one man stood above the rest. As many around him – Bangladesh's batsmen in particular – plumbed new depths of haplessness, Brendan Taylor calmly went about scaling the peaks with two innings of authority.

In the first of them, Taylor marked his country's 33rd independence day with the highest score by a Zimbabwe captain, passing Andy Flower's 156 against Pakistan on this ground in 1994-95. Then, once the Bangladesh reply had fallen 37 runs short of his 171, Taylor went about constructing a second century, to become the first Zimbabwean outside the Flower family to score two in the same Test. And he was the first to achieve the feat in a winning cause – Zimbabwe's tenth in Tests, and the sixth against these opponents.

Bangladesh had decided to bowl first on Harare Sports Club's greenest pitch for some time, yet by fielding just two seamers they lacked the resources to take advantage. Robiul Islam worked hard to make up for the shortfall, bowling 57 overs for his nine wickets in the match, yet Taylor outlasted him each time in what became a key battle. Bangladesh would have preferred it had Shakib Al Hasan not been needed to bowl on his comeback from a shin injury, but in desperation they briefly turned to his left-arm spin too.

It might have been different had Shahriar Nafees held a tough chance in the first innings, running in from long-off when Taylor had 35. Zimbabwe were 94 for three at the time, with Taylor and Waller building cautiously; they added a further 98. Taylor went on to his century shortly before stumps, and upped the rate on the second day, with Cremer offering useful company in a stand of 106. Zimbabwe's 389 was probably worth an extra 30 – the square boundaries were enormous and the outfield was slow – though their total looked a touch slim when Bangladesh reached stumps on 95 for one from 25 overs.

But the match took its decisive turn next morning, when Bangladesh rolled over in the most submissive fashion, reaching 102 for one before losing nine for 32 – including the last five without addition, only the fourth such sequence in Test history, and the first not by New Zealand.

Despite a lead of 255, Taylor played safe by not enforcing the follow-on, a decision which almost backfired when Robiul's opening spell brought him four for 15. Taylor withstood the blitz, however, and – proving a little application was all that was required in seam-friendly conditions – found enough support from Cremer, once more, and debutant Keegan Meth to bring up his second century early on the fourth morning.

Set an implausible 483, the demoralised Bangladeshis lasted less than four hours in their second innings. Jarvis did the early damage, and Cremer took four for four to wrap up the tail. "I thought we had the technique to cope with their pace bowling," said captain Mushfiqur Rahim, "but there were just too many soft dismissals in the middle, particularly from our experienced players."

Man of the Match: B. R. M. Taylor.

Close of play: first day, Zimbabwe 217-4 (Taylor 105, Chigumbura 6); second day, Bangladesh 95-1 (Jahurul Islam 38, Mohammad Ashraful 23); third day, Zimbabwe 187-7 (Taylor 81, Meth 13).

Zimbabwe

T. Maruma lbw b Robiul Islam	10	– lbw b Robiul Islam	10
V. Sibanda b Robiul Islam	5	– b Robiul Islam	4
H. Masakadza c Mahmudullah b Enamul Haque	25	– c and b Robiul Islam	0
*B. R. M. Taylor c Mushfiqur Rahim b Enamul Haque	171	– not out	102
M. N. Waller b Rubel Hossain	55	– c Nasir Hossain b Robiul Islam	4
E. Chigumbura c and b Rubel Hossain	12	– c Jahurul Islam b Robiul Islam	27
†R. Mutumbami c Mushfiqur Rahim b Robiul Islam	0	– lbw b Robiul Islam	0
A. G. Cremer c Mahmudullah b Sohag Gazi	42	– run out	43
K. O. Meth c Nasir Hossain b Enamul Haque	21	– not out	31
S. W. Masakadza c Jahurul Islam b Sohag Gazi	21		
K. M. Jarvis not out	3		
B 1, l-b 5, w 2, n-b 5	13	L-b 2, w 2, n-b 2	6

1/10 (2) 2/22 (1) 3/65 (3)   (152.3 overs) 389   1/7 (2)   (7 wkts dec, 64 overs) 227
4/192 (5) 5/223 (6) 6/238 (7)   2/9 (3) 3/16 (1)
7/344 (8) 8/344 (4) 9/381 (9) 10/389 (10)   4/27 (5) 5/84 (6) 6/84 (7) 7/163 (8)

Robiul Islam 38–11–84–3; Rubel Hossain 30–6–87–2; Nasir Hossain 5–2–3–0; Enamul Haque 47–5–133–3; Sohag Gazi 22.3–1–55–2; Mahmudullah 3–0–7–0; Shakib Al Hasan 7–3–14–0. *Second innings*—Robiul Islam 19–1–71–6; Rubel Hossain 10–0–44–0; Shakib Al Hasan 9–2–22–0; Enamul Haque 13–2–45–0; Sohag Gazi 9–0–24–0; Mahmudullah 4–2–19–0.

Bangladesh

Jahurul Islam lbw b Meth	43	– c Mutumbami b S. W. Masakadza	22
Shahriar Nafees c Maruma b Jarvis	29	– b Jarvis	11
Mohammad Ashraful c Waller b S. W. Masakadza	38	– run out	40
Mahmudullah b Meth	3	– c sub (S. C. Williams) b Jarvis	21
Shakib Al Hasan c Sibanda b S. W. Masakadza	5	– c Sibanda b Jarvis	4
*†Mushfiqur Rahim lbw b S. W. Masakadza	3	– c Taylor b Chigumbura	3
Nasir Hossain c Mutumbami b Jarvis	7	– b Cremer	23
Sohag Gazi c Waller b S. W. Masakadza	0	– st Mutumbami b Cremer	4
Enamul Haque, jun. b Jarvis	0	– not out	6
Rubel Hossain b Jarvis	0	– c S. W. Masakadza b Cremer	4
Robiul Islam not out	0	– c Jarvis b Cremer	0
B 4, l-b 1, w 1	6	B 8, n-b 1	9

1/53 (2) 2/102 (1) 3/112 (4)   (54.1 overs) 134   1/21 (2) 2/41 (1)   (49.2 overs) 147
4/123 (5) 5/124 (6) 6/134 (6)   3/77 (4) 4/81 (5)
7/134 (7) 8/134 (9) 9/134 (10) 10/134 (8)   5/85 (6) 6/132 (3) 7/136 (7)
                                                     8/139 (8) 9/147 (10) 10/147 (11)

Jarvis 16–8–40–4; Meth 20–6–41–2; S. W. Masakadza 14.1–4–32–4; Chigumbura 3–0–16–0; Cremer 1–1–0–0. *Second innings*—Jarvis 17–1–75–3; Meth 12–5–16–0; S. W. Masakadza 10–4–26–1; Chigumbura 5–0–18–1; Cremer 5.2–1–4–4.

Umpires: B. F. Bowden and A. L. Hill.   Third umpire: T. J. Matibiri.

ZIMBABWE v BANGLADESH

Second Test Match

At Harare, April 25–29, 2013. Bangladesh won by 143 runs. Toss: Zimbabwe. Test debut: Ziaur Rahman.

If the First Test was decided by the skill of one player, the Second boiled down to all-round incompetence – with Bangladesh marginally less guilty than Zimbabwe. Catches went down as if in a club match and, when the fielders failed to oblige, batsmen contrived to get themselves out. The bowling was rarely threatening or consistent; it didn't need to be.

Taylor bowled first on winning the toss, a plan formed in the days leading up to the match. But the pitch lacked the zest of the one used in the First Test, and Zimbabwe's bowlers were punished. They did not exactly help themselves in the field, either: on the first day alone, they missed four run-out chances and three catches – two by Cremer.

Bangladesh also had their moments. They gift-wrapped their first five wickets, but still closed the day on 300 for six – thanks largely to Shakib Al Hasan and Mushfiqur Rahim, who provided some much-needed sanity in a stand of 123. "Aside from the captain, we all gave our wickets away," admitted Tamim Iqbal. "Mine was a disgraceful dismissal – a rush of blood to the head." Tamim could have been run out in both the first over of the Test and the first after lunch, before he actually was, panicking one run short of fifty. His assessment extended to many others, even if no one else was quite so honest in public.

After Nasir Hossain extended the total on the second morning, Zimbabwe's batsmen travelled their own train of shame, although Robiul Islam deserved credit for his tireless display. Where Zimbabwe's quicks had lacked the mental capacity to employ a more patient length on a benign pitch, Robiul was relentless and strong, becoming the first Bangladesh seamer to take five consecutive five-wicket hauls.

Bangladesh devised a crafty plan to Taylor, their nemesis in the First Test – a barrage of short stuff from Robiul, with a fine third man stationed to discourage his favourite ramp shot. Attempting to force the pace against the off-spin of Sohag Gazi, Taylor eventually holed out to deep midwicket.

A counter-attacking Test-best 86 from Chigumbura waylaid Zimbabwean concerns about the follow-on, and they suddenly found themselves back in the game for an hour either side of tea on day three, courtesy of some wobbly Bangladesh batting and – in the absence of the DRS – questionable umpiring. Tamim was fined 10% of his match fee for showing dissent after Tony Hill gave him out caught behind to a ball which missed the edge. The Masakadza brothers did an admirable job filling in for Meth, who could not bowl because of a knee problem. But once the trio of Shakib, Mushfiqur and Nasir had performed a second rescue act, the game was up.

Zimbabwe needed at least two serious contributions if they were going to challenge a target of 401 in four and a half sessions, but received just one, as Hamilton Masakadza achieved his third Test hundred. Bangladesh's victory was their first in Zimbabwe in seven attempts, their first in 18 Tests since beating a badly weakened West Indies four years earlier, and only their fourth overall out of 79. It was not hard to see why.

Man of the Match: Mushfiqur Rahim.   *Man of the Series:* Robiul Islam.

Close of play: first day, Bangladesh 300-6 (Nasir Hossain 37, Ziaur Rahman 8); second day, Zimbabwe 158-4 (Waller 30, Chigumbura 45); third day, Bangladesh 163-5 (Mushfiqur Rahim 50, Nasir Hossain 6); fourth day, Zimbabwe 138-4 (H. Masakadza 46, S. W. Masakadza 7).

Bangladesh

Tamim Iqbal run out	49	– c Mutumbami b S. W. Masakadza	7
Jahurul Islam c Waller b Meth	24	– c Mutumbami b S. W. Masakadza	2
Mohammad Ashraful c Cremer b S. W. Masakadza	4	– lbw b Jarvis	4
Mominul Haque c S. W. Masakadza b Chigumbura	23	– c H. Masakadza b S. W. Masakadza	29
Shakib Al Hasan c Mutumbami b Chigumbura	81	– c Mutumbami b H. Masakadza	59
*†Mushfiqur Rahim lbw b Jarvis	60	– c Sibanda b H. Masakadza	93
Nasir Hossain b Cremer	77	– not out	67
Ziaur Rahman lbw b Meth	14	– st Mutumbami b Cremer	0
Sohag Gazi c Chigumbura b Cremer	21	– c Sibanda b H. Masakadza	11
Sajidul Islam c Mutumbami b Chigumbura	0	– c Mutumbami b S. W. Masakadza	4
Robiul Islam not out	24	– not out	4
B 2, l-b 7, w 1, n-b 4	14	L-b 5, w 2, n-b 4	11

1/44 (2) 2/58 (3) 3/102 (1)   (113.2 overs) 391   1/7 (1)   (9 wkts dec, 88 overs) 291
4/125 (4) 5/248 (5) 6/280 (6)   2/12 (2) 3/18 (3)
7/313 (8) 8/364 (9) 9/367 (7) 10/391 (10)   4/65 (4) 5/149 (5) 6/233 (6)
                                             7/234 (8) 8/255 (9) 9/279 (10)

Jarvis 25–4–105–1; Meth 22–7–41–2; S. W. Masakadza 17–2–52–1; Chigumbura 24.2–7–75–3; Cremer 25–3–109–2. *Second innings*—Jarvis 22–3–80–1; S. W. Masakadza 24–5–58–4; Cremer 17–1–70–1; Chigumbura 14–0–54–0; H. Masakadza 11–1–24–3.

Zimbabwe

V. Sibanda c Mushfiqur Rahim b Robiul Islam	10	– c Sohag Gazi b Shakib Al Hasan	32
R. W. Chakabva c Mushfiqur Rahim b Robiul Islam	12	– b Shakib Al Hasan	22
H. Masakadza b Shakib Al Hasan	14	– not out	111
*B. R. M. Taylor c Shakib Al Hasan b Sohag Gazi	36	– lbw b Ziaur Rahman	10
M. N. Waller c Shakib Al Hasan b Sohag Gazi	32	– b Ziaur Rahman	15
E. Chigumbura b Robiul Islam	86	– (7) c Robiul Islam b Sohag Gazi	2
†R. Mutumbami lbw b Robiul Islam	42	– (8) b Ziaur Rahman	12
A. G. Cremer not out	11	– (9) c Nasir Hossain b Ziaur Rahman	3
K. O. Meth c Mushfiqur Rahim b Sohag Gazi	16	– (10) lbw b Robiul Islam	4
S. W. Masakadza c Mushfiqur Rahim b Robiul Islam	5	– (6) lbw b Mohammad Ashraful	24
K. M. Jarvis b Sohag Gazi	0	– lbw b Shakib Al Hasan	7
B 5, l-b 11, w 1, n-b 1	18	B 4, l-b 7, n-b 4	15

1/23 (2) 2/26 (1) 3/45 (3)   (96 overs) 282   1/36 (2) 2/66 (1)   (95.3 overs) 257
4/97 (4) 5/163 (5) 6/248 (7)   3/96 (4) 4/118 (5)
7/257 (6) 8/274 (9) 9/281 (10) 10/282 (11)   5/164 (6) 6/169 (7) 7/200 (8)
                                            8/214 (9) 9/219 (10) 10/257 (11)

Robiul Islam 33–11–85–5; Sajidul Islam 16–5–48–0; Ziaur Rahman 7–3–8–0; Shakib Al Hasan 19–4–66–1; Sohag Gazi 19–1–59–4; Mohammad Ashraful 2–2–0–0. *Second innings*—Robiul Islam 20–5–53–1; Sajidul Islam 3–1–9–0; Shakib Al Hasan 11.3–0–52–3; Sohag Gazi 31–11–56–1; Ziaur Rahman 23–8–63–4; Mohammad Ashraful 7–1–13–1.

Umpires: I. J. Gould and A. L. Hill. Third umpire: O. Chirombe.
Series referee: B. C. Broad.

At Bulawayo, May 3, 2013. **First one-day international: Bangladesh won by 121 runs.** **Bangladesh 269-8** (50 overs) (Mominul Haque 38, Nasir Hossain 68, Mahmudullah 36, Extras 36; S. W. Masakadza 4-51); ‡**Zimbabwe 148** (32.1 overs) (H. Masakadza 38, B. R. M. Taylor 33, S. W. Masakadza 33; Ziaur Rahman 5-30). *MoM:* Ziaur Rahman. *ODI debuts:* Sikandar Raza (Zimbabwe); Robiul Islam (Bangladesh). *Bangladesh registered their heaviest victory over Zimbabwe in terms of runs, and improved their record in Bulawayo to seven wins out of nine. They were grateful to Nasir Hossain for digging them out of a hole at 94-4, and then to the Zimbabwean batsmen for playing across the line: eight were either bowled or lbw. Abdur Razzak took the key wicket of Taylor, which precipitated a collapse from 78-2, with Ziaur Rahman finding a hint of reverse-swing to claim five of* *the last six. Shafiul Islam became the first international bowler to be no-balled for disturbing the non-striker's stumps in his delivery stride, under the new Law triggered by Steven Finn's crooked knee. However, Shafiul did not merely clip the stump: he uprooted it entirely.*

At Bulawayo, May 5, 2013. **Second one-day international: Zimbabwe won by six wickets. Bangladesh 252-9** (50 overs) (Shakib Al Hasan 34, Nasir Hossain 36, Mahmudullah 31, Abdur Razzak 53*; E. Chigumbura 3-39); ‡**Zimbabwe 253-4** (47.5 overs) (V. Sibanda 49, B. R. M. Taylor 37, S. C. Williams 78*, M. N. Waller 39*). *MoM:* S. C. Williams. *Sean Williams produced a career-best innings of skill and composure to end Zimbabwe's seven-match losing streak in the format. Their bowlers had exploited the early-morning start, but four catches went down – one of which allowed Razzak to rescue the innings from 185-7 in the 44th over with a 21-ball maiden List A fifty, Bangladesh's equal-fastest in one-day internationals. But the Bangladeshi attack lacked energy, and Williams guided Zimbabwe home. Shakib Al Hasan was docked 75% of his match fee for slamming his bat against his pad after being given lbw to a ball he felt he nicked.*

At Bulawayo, May 8, 2013. **Third one-day international: Zimbabwe won by seven wickets. Bangladesh 247-9** (50 overs) (Tamim Iqbal 32, Mushfiqur Rahim 32, Nasir Hossain 63, Mahmudullah 75*); ‡**Zimbabwe 251-3** (47.1 overs) (V. Sibanda 103*, H. Masakadza 41, Sikandar Raza 37, S. C. Williams 55*). *MoM:* V. Sibanda. *MoS:* V. Sibanda. *Zimbabwe recorded their first series triumph of any kind since their opponents' last visit in 2011, prompting an emotional Mushfiqur Rahim to announce his resignation as Bangladesh captain. Brian Vitori marked his return to one-day colours after 15 months by removing Mohammad Ashraful and Jahurul Islam with consecutive balls in his second over, but Nasir and Mahmudullah responded with feisty half-centuries. Sibanda's second one-day international hundred secured Zimbabwe's 2–1 victory.*

At Bulawayo, May 11, 2013. **First Twenty20 international: Zimbabwe won by six runs.** ‡**Zimbabwe 168-5** (20 overs) (H. Masakadza 59, B. R. M. Taylor 40); **Bangladesh 162-8** (20 overs) (Shamsur Rahman 53, Shakib Al Hasan 65; T. Panyangara 3-32). *MoM:* H. Masakadza. *T20I debuts:* T. Panyangara, Sikandar Raza (Zimbabwe); Sajidul Islam (Bangladesh). *The first Twenty20 international staged at Queens Sports Club drew Zimbabwe's best crowd for years, and they were kept on the edge of their camper chairs by a thriller. Hamilton Masakadza anchored the innings as Taylor and Waller laid on the clean hitting, yet Zimbabwe looked out of it when Shamsur Rahman and Shakib put on 118 for the second wicket. Prosper Utseya dismissed both in the 15th over, however, and Bangladesh choked, losing Nasir and Mahmudullah to run-outs in the next. They required ten off the last, but Tinashe Panyangara allowed just three, and took two wickets.*

At Bulawayo, May 12, 2013. **Second Twenty20 international: Bangladesh won by 34 runs.** ‡**Bangladesh 168-7** (20 overs) (Tamim Iqbal 43, Shakib Al Hasan 40); **Zimbabwe 134-9** (20 overs) (V. Sibanda 32, Sikandar Raza 31; Shakib Al Hasan 4-21). *MoM:* Shakib Al Hasan. *MoS:* Shakib Al Hasan. *T20I debut:* Robiul Islam (Bangladesh). *Bangladesh's tour ended with their most ardent fan, the tiger-suited Shoaib Ali, on the dance stage roaring "Shabaaash!" His side were always in control after making 99 in the first ten overs, though Taylor should have held Tamim Iqbal on five; he survived to add 82 with Shakib. Zimbabwe's chase fired only briefly, with Mushfiqur rotating his bowlers well, then admitting regret at his earlier decision to resign the captaincy.*

ZIMBABWE v INDIA, 2013

Liam Brickhill

One-day internationals (5): Zimbabwe 0, India 5

India's five-match one-day tour was supposed to provide an audition for fringe players ahead of sterner challenges at home to Australia and away to South Africa. But Zimbabwe, who had played practically no cricket since Bangladesh's visit in May ten weeks earlier, offered precious little resistance in a series played out against the backdrop of the corruption scandal in India. Wisely, the Indian selectors arranged for ten of the touring party to stay on in South Africa with the A side. It was hard, though, to escape the feeling that the tour amounted to crumbs sent from the master's table to keep an old ally alive.

India romped to a whitewash, their first away from home, and several players did advance their cause – even taking the weak opposition into account. Virat Kohli enjoyed an easy apprenticeship in his first full series as captain in the absence of the resting M. S. Dhoni, while batsman Ambati Rayudu, and seamers Jaydev Unadkat and Mohit Sharma, all caught the eye. Leg-spinner Amit Mishra, who had not played for India for two years, perplexed Zimbabwe's hapless batsmen with his googly. He took six for 48 in the last game to finish with 18 wickets – a record for a five-match one-day series.

For Zimbabwe, the only bright spot was Elton Chigumbura's rejuvenated batting. Brendan Taylor, normally their most dependable batsman, scraped together just 35 runs – including three ducks – and was as culpable as anyone for the mistakes in the field. Andy Waller, in his first full series as coach, thought the batsmen were too keen on bashing over the top, when a little skilful improvisation was called for. After the rout had been completed, he sent the players to the away dressing-room to glean as much as they could from the Indians.

Performances, though, were not the crux of the matter. Far more important was the money raised via the sale of TV rights and sponsorship, which according to local reports amounted to between $US6m and $8m. A visit by the world's most lucrative side allowed Zimbabwe Cricket to turn in a rare profit. Had the BCCI decided not to send a team, as seemed possible in May, other tours would also have been put in jeopardy. In any case, ZC chairman Peter Chingoka said the revenue was "just a drop in the ocean" when set against the financial bailout the board were said to need.

INDIAN TOURING PARTY

*V. Kohli, S. Dhawan, R. A. Jadeja, K. D. Karthik, A. Mishra, Parvez Rasool, C. A. Pujara, A. M. Rahane, S. K. Raina, A. T. Rayudu, Shami Ahmed, M. Sharma, R. G. Sharma, J. D. Unadkat, R. Vinay Kumar. *Coach:* D. A. G. Fletcher.

At Harare, July 24, 2013. **First one-day international: India won by six wickets. Zimbabwe 228-7** (50 overs) (V. Sibanda 34, Sikandar Raza 82, E. Chigumbura 43*; A. Mishra 3-43); ‡**India 230-4** (44.5 overs) (V. Kohli 115, A. T. Rayudu 63*). *MoM:* V. Kohli. *ODI debuts:* A. T. Rayudu, J. D. Unadkat (India). *India won the toss for a 9am start, and their seamers zipped the ball around in the* *first hour. Zimbabwe's openers battled gamely, but their stand ended at 72 when Amit Mishra set the tone for the series by foxing Vusi Sibanda with a googly. Sikandar Raza, dropped at slip by Virat Kohli on 28, pressed on to a maiden international fifty, and eventually fell in the desperate crash for runs. India cruised past the target in benign afternoon conditions: Kohli hit his 15th ODI hundred in his 106th innings, comfortably the quickest, beating Saeed Anwar's 143. He was assisted by the calm debutant Ambati Rayudu in a 159-run stand. The umpires began the match wearing crimson shirts, but switched to sky blue for India's innings to stand out from the Zimbabwe fielders.*

At Harare, July 26, 2013. **Second one-day international: India won by 58 runs. India 294-8** (50 overs) (S. Dhawan 116, K. D. Karthik 69); ‡**Zimbabwe 236-9** (50 overs) (V. Sibanda 55, H. Masakadza 34, E. Chigumbura 46, P. Utseya 52*; J. D. Unadkat 4-41). *MoM:* S. Dhawan. *Zimbabwe twice found themselves on top, but lacked the mettle to ram home the advantage. Brian Vitori struck with his first ball of the series, tempting Rohit Sharma to chase a wide one, and India were wobbling at 65-4 in the 17th over. But Shikhar Dhawan got a raft of let-offs: he was caught behind from a Kyle Jarvis no-ball on three, then dropped on 14 and 70. He punished anything loose and, alongside the secure Dinesh Karthik, blasted India to an unassailable score with his third ODI century in six weeks. Sibanda cheerily took on the short stuff, but his dismissal at 109-2 triggered a Zimbabwe collapse of five for 24.*

At Harare, July 28, 2013. **Third one-day international: India won by seven wickets. Zimbabwe 183** (46 overs) (H. Masakadza 38, S. C. Williams 45; A. Mishra 4-47); ‡**India 145-1** (30.5 overs) (S. Dhawan 35, V. Kohli 68*, A. T. Rayudu 33). *MoM:* A. Mishra. *ODI debut:* M. T. Chinouya (Zimbabwe). *India waltzed to a series victory as Zimbabwe were dismantled by swing, seam and Mishra's variations. As with Kohli in the previous match, Brendan Taylor stood his ground when a catch was claimed off him; as with Kohli, TV replays sided with the fielder. The loudest cheer came when No. 9 Tendai Chatara scored his first runs in his seventh one-day international via four overthrows. Rohit Sharma departed early once more, feathering an edge off debutant seamer Mike Chinouya, but Kohli ended the match with a flurry of boundaries. Zimbabwe's decision to leave out Ray Price for the third time on his home ground prompted him to retire from international cricket.*

At Bulawayo, August 1, 2013. **Fourth one-day international: India won by nine wickets. Zimbabwe 144** (42.4 overs) (M. N. Waller 35, E. Chigumbura 50*; A. Mishra 3-25); ‡**India 145-1** (30.5 overs) (R. G. Sharma 64*, S. K. Raina 65*). *MoM:* M. Sharma (India). *ODI debuts:* C. A. Pujara, M. Sharma (India). *It was hoped Zimbabwe might find batting easier in Bulawayo but, after Taylor lost his third toss his demoralised batsmen were shot out for 144. Mohit Sharma, 24, with just six domestic List A matches to his name, enjoyed an impeccable first day out as he found Raza's edge in his opening spell, and returned to snap a stubborn 80-run stand between Malcolm Waller and Elton Chigumbura, who had again been left high and dry. Cheteshwar Pujara made only 13 in his first limited-overs innings for India, but Rohit Sharma and Suresh Raina (sent in ahead of Kohli) helped themselves to fifties.*

At Bulawayo, August 3, 2013. **Fifth one-day international: India won by seven wickets. Zimbabwe 163** (39.5 overs) (H. Masakadza 32, S. C. Williams 51; A. Mishra 6-48); ‡**India 167-3** (34 overs) (S. Dhawan 41, A. M. Rahane 50, R. A. Jadeja 48*). *MoM:* A. Mishra. *Zimbabwe made four changes, but the final match followed a familiar pattern. They lost early wickets, floundered against a now unstoppable Mishra – whose 6-48 were the fifth-best figures for India in one-day internationals – then offered the tourists little more than batting practice. Jarvis, perhaps slighted at being left out of the previous two games, bowled with pace and direction, and took 2-18. It would be his final international game before retiring and joining Lancashire as a Kolpak. Taylor's miserable series concluded with a third duck, a dropped catch, and a fluffed chance to run out Ajinkya Rahane. He survived to compile a neat fifty, and Ravindra Jadeja sealed the whitewash with a six.*

ZIMBABWE v PAKISTAN, 2013-14

Neil Manthorp

Twenty20 internationals (2): Zimbabwe 0, Pakistan 2
One-day internationals (3): Zimbabwe 1, Pakistan 2
Test matches (2): Zimbabwe 1, Pakistan 1

Like many things in Zimbabwe, not least life itself, this tour did not unfold as predicted. The shorter the format, supposedly, the greater chance of the home side causing an upset. Yet Zimbabwe were hammered in the two Twenty20s, won the first one-day international, and were easily at their most dangerous in the Tests, dominating much of – but losing – the First, before prevailing in an emotional nailbiter in the Second. Pakistan had arrived with several important questions, and left with them unanswered, unless one was: "Are Misbah-ul-Haq, Younis Khan and Saeed Ajmal still our best players?"

From a financial point of view, Zimbabwe Cricket – close to $US20m in debt – could not afford to host the tour; from a cricketing perspective, they could not afford *not* to. The players had trained for weeks under the relentless drive of hardman coach Andy Waller, and were desperate to test themselves. If Zimbabwe were to follow the ICC's directive and become more competitive, they needed to play more regularly against Full Members, so the tour went ahead – with all expenses spared.

Well, as many expenses as possible – including the players' wages, which led to the threat of strike action a week before Pakistan landed. The Zimbabweans briefly boycotted training, and formed a union – long-overdue, some argued – to demand that match fees and outstanding salaries be paid. While every effort was made to ensure the Pakistanis remained as comfortable as possible – and they never publicly complained about the water and power cuts in their hotel – the Zimbabweans were getting by without daily allowances and with basic, but adequate, meals. Luxuries such as new practice balls weren't even considered; it was hard enough finding balls for the actual matches. And austerity meant that the Second Test was moved from Bulawayo to the Harare Sports Club: all seven matches across three formats were played at the same venue – a first in international cricket.

Even when the threat of a strike subsided, Zimbabwe's complications did not. Brendan Taylor, the captain, withdrew on the morning of the opening Test after an exhausting night at his wife's side for the birth of their son; Hamilton Masakadza assumed leadership responsibilities, and his decision-making was near-faultless. Taylor's absence was compounded by the late withdrawal of Sean Williams, probably Zimbabwe's best player of spin, who said he "wasn't in the right space" to play a Test until he received his dues. Kyle Jarvis, their quickest bowler, had already announced his retirement from international cricket in order to pursue a Kolpak career with Lancashire.

Misbah, meanwhile, was outstanding both as leader and batsman. He made light of the occasional fickleness of some of his players, and displayed an equanimity of spirit through good times and bad that would be the envy of many a captain. Yet, with two defeats chalked up against his name, even some usually restrained voices in Pakistan cricket were calling for his three-year spell in charge to end.

PAKISTAN TOURING PARTY

*Misbah-ul-Haq (T/50), Abdur Rehman (T/50), Adnan Akmal (T), Ahmed Shehzad (50/20), Anwar Ali (50/20), Asad Ali (50/20), Asad Shafiq (T/50), Azhar Ali (T), Ehsan Adil (T), Faisal Iqbal (T), Haris Sohail (50/20), Junaid Khan (T/50/20), Khurram Manzoor (T), Mohammad Hafeez (T/50/20), Mohammad Irfan (50/20), Nasir Jamshed (50/20), Rahat Ali (T), Saeed Ajmal (T/50/20), Sarfraz Ahmed (50/20), Shahid Afridi (50/20), Shan Masood (20), Sohaib Maqsood (20), Sohail Tanvir (20), Umar Amin (50/20), Wahab Riaz (T), Younis Khan (T), Zulfiqar Babar (20).

Mohammad Hafeez captained in the Twenty20 matches. Umar Akmal was initially selected for the limited-overs games, but was withdrawn when he suffered a seizure on a flight during the Caribbean Premier League; he was replaced by Sarfraz Ahmed. Imran Farhat was initially selected for the Tests, but withdrew citing personal reasons; he was replaced by Shan Masood.

At Harare, August 23, 2013. **First Twenty20 international: Pakistan won by 25 runs. Pakistan 161-5** (20 overs) (Ahmed Shehzad 70); ‡**Zimbabwe 136-5** (20 overs) (V. Sibanda 31, B. R. M. Taylor 32*); Shahid Afridi 3-25). *MoM:* Ahmed Shehzad. *Twenty20 international debut: Sohaib Maqsood (Pakistan). Ahmed Shehzad's 70 from 50 balls hardly set the contest ablaze, but it was far too good for Zimbabwe. Prosper Utseya's off-spin was treated with a respect bordering on reverence – he got through four overs for 15 by the 12th over – but debutant Sohaib Maqsood (26) and Shahid Afridi (23*) whacked quick runs after a modest start. Sohail Tanvir and Mohammad Irfan were too savvy for Zimbabwe's top order, with opener Vusi Sibanda's struggle to 31 from 42 balls contributing to the oddly embarrassing situation of Brendan Taylor finishing on 32* at No. 3; Elton Chigumbura's belated entrance, just 17 balls from the end, summed it up.*

At Harare, August 24, 2013. **Second Twenty20 international: Pakistan won by 19 runs. Pakistan 179-1** (20 overs) (Ahmed Shehzad 98*, Mohammad Hafeez 54*); ‡**Zimbabwe 160-6** (20 overs) (H. Masakadza 41, E. Chigumbura 35*; Mohammad Hafeez 3-30). *MoM:* Ahmed Shehzad. *MoS:* Ahmed Shehzad. *The second game was a repeat of the first, only with the numbers inflated. Shehzad again top-scored, but with greater dynamism through the leg side. He needed to hit three from the final ball, his 64th, to become Pakistan's first Twenty20 international centurion – he had already broken Misbah-ul-Haq's national record of 87*, against Bangladesh at Karachi in 2007-08 – but could manage only a single to deep midwicket. Zulfiqar Babar (2-21) and Mohammad Hafeez both started with maidens, as Sibanda (23 off 33) once more acted as a dead weight rather than an anchor. Chigumbura's feisty 35* made the run-chase look closer than it actually was.*

ZIMBABWE v PAKISTAN

First One-Day International

At Harare, August 27, 2013. Zimbabwe won by seven wickets. Toss: Pakistan.

No venue in world cricket is more bowl-first than the Harare Sports Club in winter. For two decades of one-day internationals, Zimbabwean captains have referred to it as a "win toss, win match" ground. And so, in Harare's 100th one-dayer, Misbah-ul-Haq chose to bat first. It came as no surprise to see the Pakistan openers, who took 14 overs to put on 50, frequently playing and missing in the seaming early-morning conditions. Even the experienced pair of Mohammad Hafeez and Misbah, who made a fourth consecutive half-century in the format, felt the need to proceed with caution through the middle overs, and the final total was around 30 short of a strong one. The African sun finally radiated warmth after lunch, and the pitch sleepily basked in it. Masakadza took part in stands of 107 and 69 for the first two wickets, and it was evidently Zimbabwe's day by the time Williams cut Junaid Khan on to his leg stump without the bails coming off; the ball ran away for four. Taylor and Williams steered their side home, and it must have required great restraint for the Zimbabwe captain not to thank his opposite number for his contribution to their victory at the toss. It was Zimbabwe's first win against Pakistan in all cricket for 15 years.

Man of the Match: H. Masakadza.

Pakistan

Nasir Jamshed c Taylor b Chatara	27
Ahmed Shehzad st Taylor b Utseya	24
Mohammad Hafeez c Maruma b Chatara	70
*Misbah-ul-Haq not out	83
Umar Amin run out	1
Shahid Afridi c Taylor b Vitori	11
Haris Sohail c Utseya b Vitori	2

†Sarfraz Ahmed run out	7
Saeed Ajmal not out	3
L-b 7, w 9	16

1/56 (2) 2/80 (1)   (7 wkts, 50 overs) 244
3/179 (3) 4/184 (5)
5/198 (6) 6/202 (7) 7/223 (8)   10 overs: 41-0

Junaid Khan and Mohammad Irfan did not bat.

Panyangara 10–2–38–0; Vitori 10–0–42–2; Chatara 10–2–32–2; Utseya 10–0–60–1; Chigumbura 2–0–11–0; Waller 2–0–19–0; Williams 4–0–18–0; Masakadza 2–0–17–0.

Zimbabwe

H. Masakadza c Misbah-ul-Haq b Saeed Ajmal	85
V. Sibanda lbw b Saeed Ajmal	54
*†B. R. M. Taylor not out	43
T. Maruma c Ahmed Shehzad b Junaid Khan	18

S. C. Williams not out	39
B 1, l-b 3, w 3	7

1/107 (2) 2/176 (1)   (3 wkts, 48.2 overs) 246
3/201 (4)   10 overs: 48-0

M. N. Waller, E. Chigumbura, P. Utseya, T. Panyangara, T. L. Chatara and B. V. Vitori did not bat.

Mohammad Irfan 9.2–1–45–0; Junaid Khan 9–0–55–1; Saeed Ajmal 10–0–44–2; Mohammad Hafeez 10–0–40–0; Shahid Afridi 9–0–51–0; Umar Amin 1–0–7–0.

Umpires: R. K. Illingworth and R. B. Tiffin.   Third umpire: O. Chirombe.
Referee: J. J. Crowe.

At Harare, August 29, 2013. **Second one-day international: Pakistan won by 90 runs. Pakistan 299-4** (50 overs) (Nasir Jamshed 32, Mohammad Hafeez 136*, Umar Amin 59, Shahid Afridi 39*); ‡**Zimbabwe 209** (42.4 overs) (B. R. M. Taylor 79, S. C. Williams 37, M. N. Waller 40; Junaid Khan 4-15). *MoM:* Mohammad Hafeez. *Having been taught a painful lesson about the Zimbabwean winter two days earlier, Pakistan – this time put in to bat – waited as long as possible for the sun to flatten the pitch, and then flogged an eye-watering 99 from the final nine overs. Misbah fell in single figures for only the second time in his last 20 one-day internationals, but Hafeez paced his hundred perfectly: 50 from 65 balls, 100 from 111, then 36 from his final 19. Shahid Afridi delighted a small but enthusiastic group of Pakistan supporters with three trademark baseball hits for six, one of which landed in the HSC rugby ground next door, well over 100 metres away. Zimbabwe attempted a similar strategy, but Junaid Khan (7–2–15–4) was hostile, accurate and almost unhittable.*

At Harare, August 31, 2013. **Third one-day international: Pakistan won by 108 runs. Pakistan 260-6** (50 overs) (Nasir Jamshed 38, Ahmed Shehzad 54, Misbah-ul-Haq 67, Umar Amin 33; T. L. Chatara 3-48); ‡**Zimbabwe 152** (40 overs) (M. N. Waller 48). *MoM:* Misbah-ul-Haq. *MoS:* Mohammad Hafeez (Pakistan). *Zimbabwe's hopes of pulling off their first one-day series triumph over a major nation since January 2001 – when they won in New Zealand – ended in anticlimax. They failed miserably to cope with another late onslaught from Pakistan's batsmen, or with the beguiling spin of Saeed Ajmal and Abdur Rehman, who between them claimed four for 38 from 15 overs. Umar Amin and Sarfraz Ahmed (27) showed clean-striking finesse after studious work from the openers and more careful graft from Misbah, as a potentially average total was again turned into a good one. Batting was less straightforward on a drier pitch than those used for the previous two games, but Zimbabwe's effort was feeble nonetheless – and made worse by two run-outs from Misbah to remove Taylor and Williams. Pakistan threw an unusual monkey off their backs: it was the first time since 2002, in Australia, that they had won the deciding match of a bilateral one-day series.*

ZIMBABWE v PAKISTAN

First Test Match

At Harare, September 3–7, 2013. Pakistan won by 221 runs. Toss: Zimbabwe. Test debut: Sikandar Raza.

It is hardly unprecedented for a team to dominate the first three and a half days of a Test before losing, but for Zimbabwe the scenario was genuinely surprising and hard to stomach. Pakistan required monumental performances from two veterans, Younis Khan and Saeed Ajmal, to wrench control from a team whose collective strength was built on stubborn determination and discipline, rather than flair – or indeed anything approaching an X-factor.

Ajmal was a virtual certainty to prosper, and without his haul of 11 for 118 – his second-best in Tests – a Pakistan victory would have been impossible. Even Younis, who had seen just about everything in 14 years playing for the world's most protean team, wouldn't have forecast arriving at the crease in such a predicament, and then having to work so hard for his runs. Only after nine hours of studious graft was he able to cut loose and fly, handsomely, to his fourth Test double-hundred (Javed Miandad alone had made more for Pakistan). It allowed the spinners to wrap up the match just before lunch on the fifth day.

Zimbabwe's seam trio of Tendai Chatara, Tinashe Panyangara and Shingi Masakadza lacked genuine pace, but their accuracy and patience were unprecedented in the side's post-2004 era. Azhar Ali spent almost four and a half hours compiling 78, but his colleagues were either impatient or careless; Misbah-ul-Haq and Asad Shafiq paid the price for attacking Utseya's underrated off-spin. At 182 for eight, Pakistan were in horrible trouble on a good pitch, before Ajmal cannily nudged and whacked the total to semi-respectability.

> **Ajmal was a virtual certainty to prosper**

The Zimbabweans' hopes of a decisive lead were undone, almost inevitably, by Ajmal, who dismissed all three half-centurions among his collection of seven for 95; their number included Sikandar Raza, a 27-year-old whose family had emigrated from Sialkot to Harare, and who made his debut when Brendan Taylor withdrew to be with his wife and new baby boy. Ajmal's doosra was, at times, far too good, and earned him four wickets. Nevertheless, Zimbabwe's lead of 78 appeared sufficient when Pakistan crashed to 23 for three. Misbah's rescue attempt ended on 52, with a soft drive to cover. And when Asad Shafiq was bowled by a Chatara off-cutter, with Pakistan five down and leading by just 91, they required something out of the ordinary. Younis, however, was just getting started.

Adnan Akmal made light of the situation by reverse-sweeping with joyous freedom. His stand of 118 with Younis, who was missed by close catchers on 83 and 117, changed the game. Akmal was run out in a ridiculous mix-up but, once the lead passed 250, Younis sensed safety and unclipped the shackles. Even so, an unbroken tenth-wicket stand of 88 exceeded expectations: last man Rahat Ali, preferred in the Test squad to Mohammad Irfan, clubbed three sixes, and Misbah was able to give Younis a few extra overs to strive for 200. He got there with a mountainous six, over midwicket off Utseya – his third, to go with 15 fours in 404 balls. The eventual target of 342 was far beyond Zimbabwe.

When Mawoyo played back to Ajmal's doosra with what became the last ball of the fourth day, the gloom of predictable defeat hung heavily. Junaid Khan was excellent next morning, and Pakistan's spinners wasted little time wrapping up a win which had seemed unlikely when Younis was battening down the hatches on the third evening.

Man of the Match: Younis Khan.

Close of play: first day, Pakistan 249-9 (Saeed Ajmal 49); second day, Zimbabwe 281-7 (Chigumbura 40, S. W. Masakadza 2); third day, Pakistan 168-4 (Younis Khan 76, Asad Shafiq 15); fourth day, Zimbabwe 13-1 (Sibanda 5).

Pakistan

Khurram Manzoor lbw b Panyangara	11	– lbw b Panyangara	5
Mohammad Hafeez c Sibanda b Chatara	5	– c Mawoyo b Chatara	16
Azhar Ali c Sibanda b S. W. Masakadza	78	– lbw b Panyangara	0
Younis Khan b Panyangara	3	– not out	200
*Misbah-ul-Haq c Sibanda b Utseya	53	– c Sibanda b S. W. Masakadza	52
Asad Shafiq c Mawoyo b Utseya	4	– b Chatara	15
†Adnan Akmal b Chatara	18	– run out	64
Abdur Rehman lbw b S. W. Masakadza	7	– lbw b Utseya	9
Saeed Ajmal b Chatara	49	– lbw b Utseya	1
Junaid Khan c Mutumbami b Panyangara	17	– b Utseya	8
Rahat Ali not out	0	– not out	35
L-b 3, w 1	4	B 11, l-b 1, w 2	14

1/13 (2) 2/21 (1) 3/27 (4) (90.1 overs) 249
4/120 (5) 5/132 (6) 6/157 (7)
7/173 (8) 8/182 (3) 9/249 (10) 10/249 (9)

1/17 (1) (9 wkts dec, 149.3 overs) 419
2/21 (3) 3/23 (2)
4/139 (5) 5/169 (6) 6/287 (7)
7/309 (8) 8/313 (9) 9/331 (10)

Chatara 22.1–6–64–3; Panyangara 20–2–71–3; S. W. Masakadza 22–8–40–2; Chigumbura 2–0–15–0; Utseya 23–1–55–2; H. Masakadza 1–0–1–0. *Second innings*—Chatara 33–7–99–2; Panyangara 30–14–42–2; Utseya 37.3–5–137–3; S. W. Masakadza 34–4–100–1; H. Masakadza 15–5–29–0.

Zimbabwe

T. M. K. Mawoyo c Adnan Akmal b Junaid Khan	13	– lbw b Saeed Ajmal	2
V. Sibanda c Adnan Akmal b Junaid Khan	31	– lbw b Junaid Khan	6
*H. Masakadza b Saeed Ajmal	19	– c Azhar Ali b Junaid Khan	1
Sikandar Raza c Misbah-ul-Haq b Saeed Ajmal	60	– c Azhar Ali b Abdur Rehman	24
M. N. Waller c Mohammad Hafeez b Saeed Ajmal	70	– c Rahat Ali b Abdur Rehman	17
E. Chigumbura c Azhar Ali b Saeed Ajmal	69	– c Mohammad Hafeez b Abdur Rehman	28
†R. Mutumbami lbw b Saeed Ajmal	13	– not out	16
P. Utseya b Rahat Ali	16	– b Saeed Ajmal	0
S. W. Masakadza lbw b Saeed Ajmal	14	– b Saeed Ajmal	0
T. Panyangara not out	4	– lbw b Abdur Rehman	6
T. L. Chatara c Younis Khan b Saeed Ajmal	0	– lbw b Saeed Ajmal	13
B 5, l-b 11, w 2	18	B 1, l-b 5, n-b 1	7

1/25 (1) 2/68 (2) 3/68 (3) (103.3 overs) 327
4/195 (5) 5/212 (4) 6/235 (7)
7/278 (8) 8/310 (9) 9/327 (6) 10/327 (11)

1/13 (1) 2/14 (3) (46.4 overs) 120
3/19 (2) 4/49 (5)
5/58 (4) 6/89 (6) 7/90 (8)
8/90 (9) 9/101 (10) 10/120 (11)

Junaid Khan 25–8–71–2; Rahat Ali 23–3–70–1; Abdur Rehman 19–5–56–0; Saeed Ajmal 32.3–4–95–7; Younis Khan 4–1–19–0. *Second innings*—Junaid Khan 10–3–20–2; Rahat Ali 7–1–35–0; Saeed Ajmal 16.4–5–23–4; Abdur Rehman 13–5–36–4.

Umpires: S. J. Davis and R. E. J. Martinesz. Third umpire: T. J. Matibiri.

ZIMBABWE v PAKISTAN

Second Test Match

At Harare, September 10–14, 2013. Zimbabwe won by 24 runs. Toss: Zimbabwe.

This was more than just a series-levelling victory for Zimbabwe. It was only their fifth win in 82 matches against the eight leading Test nations – though their third over Pakistan – and their biggest act of giant-killing since beating India on this ground in 2001, three years before the exodus of many experienced white players. They were rewarded by leapfrogging Bangladesh in the ICC Test rankings, while Pakistan slipped from fourth to sixth.

Heading into the last day it was too close to call the winner: Pakistan needed 106, Zimbabwe five wickets. Misbah-ul-Haq, who resumed on 26, held the key. The Zimbabweans told each other that, if he was there at the end, they would probably lose. Yet they were proved gloriously wrong: stranded not out for the umpteenth time, the Pakistan captain watched in dismay after he turned down Rahat Ali's quest for a single off the last ball of an over and the No. 11 was run out by a gaggle of exultant fielders.

The 22-year-old Chatara emerged as the hero, capturing three wickets on a dramatic final day, when Pakistan's incoming batsmen struggled to get to grips with an underprepared pitch. Bulawayo had been scheduled to host the match until, six days before the start, it was shifted to Harare to save around $US50,000 on travel costs and expenses. There was no pace in the strip, and cracks were widening on a length by the third morning. Misbah, though, blamed his batsmen. "We were playing shots and drives which were not there for the first three days because the ball was stopping," he said. "It was all in the batsman's mind."

Taylor, returning to lead Zimbabwe, had snapped up the chance to bat first. The pitch behaved itself initially, as Taylor and Hamilton Masakadza repelled Junaid Khan's most threatening spell of the Tests with a century stand. Gutsy work from the tail, who strung together 107 for the last four wickets, would also prove vital. In the afternoon session, a stray chicken wandered on to the field and had to be chased off by a security guard.

ZIMBABWE'S TEST VICTORIES

Opposition	Margin	Venue	
Pakistan	innings and 64 runs	Harare	1994-95
India	61 runs	Harare	1998-99
Pakistan	seven wickets	Peshawar	1998-99
Bangladesh	innings and 32 runs	Bulawayo	2000-01
Bangladesh	eight wickets	Harare	2000-01
India	four wickets	Harare	2001
Bangladesh	eight wickets	Chittagong (M. A. Aziz)	2001-02
Bangladesh	183 runs	Harare	2003-04
Bangladesh	130 runs	Harare	2011
Bangladesh	335 runs	Harare	2012-13
Pakistan	**24 runs**	**Harare**	**2013-14**

Younis Khan, who became the fourth Pakistani – after Javed Miandad, Inzamam-ul-Haq and Mohammad Yousuf – to pass 7,000 Test runs, had to work hard alongside his captain to earn a position of 163 for three by stumps on the second day. But after they had added only 19 in 12 overs next morning, Misbah lunged desperately at Vitori's second delivery with the new ball and edged to slip. Younis, trying to pick up the pace after lunch, gave a leading edge, and Abdur Rehman was lbw next ball. It turned into a bona fide batting collapse: Pakistan lost their last six for 19. Much of the pain was caused by the left-armer Vitori who, after 19 injury-hit months out of the Test side, swung the ball from both over and round the wicket, and gave the tail nothing.

As in the First Test, Zimbabwe had taken the lead on first innings, of the kind just about big enough to make up for a fitful performance in the second. By now, the ball was regularly staying low: Pakistan's bowlers did little more than keep it tight and aim at the cracks. After the early loss of Utseya, promoted to open when Sibanda fell ill, Mawoyo and Masakadza survived on their wits to add a vital 104 for the second wicket, with Junaid unable to make the harder ball dance to his tune.

Pakistan have seldom thrived on the pressure-cooker environment of a run-chase: they had not knocked off anything over 200 since Inzamam did it three times in 2003-04. They set out on the fourth afternoon in pursuit of 264, determined to play aggressively against an inexperienced attack: of the first 100 runs, 84 came in boundaries. Khurram Manzoor was the most ruthless, hitting 11 fours in his second half-century of the match. But

Mohammad Hafeez paid the price for walking out of his crease to the pace bowlers and provided a leading edge for mid-on. Chatara cleaned up Azhar Ali with a beauty that held its line, and Younis stepped too far across his stumps trying to whip Vitori, and was bowled behind his legs. Misbah was as defiant as ever, but not even he could pull this off by himself.

Man of the Match: T. L. Chatara. *Man of the Series:* Younis Khan.

Close of play: first day, Zimbabwe 237-8 (Utseya 14, Chatara 0); second day, Pakistan 163-3 (Younis Khan 52, Misbah-ul-Haq 27); third day, Zimbabwe 121-4 (Taylor 0); fourth day, Pakistan 158-5 (Misbah-ul-Haq 26, Adnan Akmal 17).

Zimbabwe

T. M. K. Mawoyo c Adnan Akmal b Junaid Khan .	0	– lbw b Abdur Rehman............ 58
V. Sibanda b Rahat Ali	14	– (6) c Adnan Akmal b Rahat Ali..... 10
H. Masakadza c Mohammad Hafeez b Saeed Ajmal	75	– lbw b Rahat Ali 44
*B. R. M. Taylor lbw b Abdur Rehman...........	51	– (5) c Azhar Ali b Rahat Ali 27
M. N. Waller c Adnan Akmal b Junaid Khan	23	– (7) c Khurram Manzoor
		b Saeed Ajmal . 3
E. Chigumbura b Abdur Rehman..............	15	– (8) c Adnan Akmal b Junaid Khan... 3
†R. Mutumbami c Adnan Akmal b Junaid Khan....	8	– (9) c Abdur Rehman b Saeed Ajmal . 29
P. Utseya c Rahat Ali b Junaid Khan...........	22	– (2) c Asad Shafiq b Rahat Ali 5
T. Panyangara b Rahat Ali................	24	– (4) c Azhar Ali b Abdur Rehman.... 0
T. L. Chatara lbw b Abdur Rehman............	21	– c Adnan Akmal b Rahat Ali........ 1
B. V. Vitori not out	19	– not out 0
B 7, l-b 14, w 1...................	22	B 3, l-b 11, w 5........... 19

1/0 (1) 2/31 (2) 3/141 (3) (109.5 overs) 294
4/172 (5) 5/176 (4) 6/187 (7)
7/203 (6) 8/234 (9) 9/248 (8) 10/294 (10)

1/13 (2) 2/117 (1) (89.5 overs) 199
3/121 (3) 4/121 (4)
5/136 (6) 6/149 (7) 7/156 (8)
8/177 (5) 9/199 (9) 10/199 (10)

Junaid Khan 33–11–67–4; Rahat Ali 19.7–7–48–2; Younis Khan 3–0–7–0; Saeed Ajmal 27–6–92–1; Abdur Rehman 23.5–6–47–3; Mohammad Hafeez 4–0–12–0. *Second innings*—Junaid Khan 19–6–37–1; Rahat Ali 24.5–5–52–5; Saeed Ajmal 22–7–56–2; Abdur Rehman 24–5–40–2.

Pakistan

Khurram Manzoor run out	51	– c Waller b Utseya............... 54
Mohammad Hafeez c Masakadza b Vitori........	22	– c Vitori b Chatara............... 16
Azhar Ali lbw b Panyangara	7	– b Chatara 0
Younis Khan c Mawoyo b Panyangara	77	– b Vitori...................... 29
*Misbah-ul-Haq c Masakadza b Vitori	33	– not out 79
Asad Shafiq b Chatara	10	– c Mutumbami b Utseya........... 14
†Adnan Akmal c Taylor b Vitori	6	– lbw b Chatara.................. 20
Abdur Rehman lbw b Panyangara	0	– c Mutumbami b Panyangara 16
Saeed Ajmal c Mutumbami b Vitori	7	– lbw b Chatara 2
Junaid Khan b Vitori	3	– c Waller b Chatara 1
Rahat Ali not out	1	– run out 1
B 4, l-b 6, w 2, n-b 1	13	L-b 2, w 4, n-b 1........... 7

1/29 (2) 2/62 (3) 3/96 (1) (104.5 overs) 230
4/182 (5) 5/211 (6) 6/212 (4)
7/212 (8) 8/224 (7) 9/229 (9) 10/230 (10)

1/30 (2) 2/46 (3) (81 overs) 239
3/90 (1) 4/100 (4)
5/133 (6) 6/163 (7) 7/197 (8)
8/214 (9) 9/238 (10) 10/239 (11)

Panyangara 22–9–43–3; Vitori 26.5–8–61–5; Chatara 27–10–45–1; Masakadza 12–5–24–0; Utseya 12–0–41–0; Chigumbura 5–2–6–0. *Second innings*—Panyangara 16–3–43–1; Vitori 22–5–69–1; Chatara 23–2–61–5; Utseya 19–2–62–2; Masakadza 1–0–2–0.

Umpires: S. J. Davis and R. E. J. Martinesz. Third umpire: O. Chirombe.
Series referee: J. Srinath.

DOMESTIC CRICKET IN ZIMBABWE, 2012-13

John Ward

Matabeleland Tuskers won their third successive Logan Cup, though in most countries the circumstances would have caused a furore. The five franchise teams set out believing the points system was unchanged from 2011-12: six for a win, one for first-innings lead, none for a draw. As a consequence, pitches were generally prepared to assist bowlers, and some poor batting against pace meant there were no draws before February 1. But that match – between Matabeleland and Mashonaland – triggered the award of three points to each team, a detail which turned out to have been in the small print of the handbook circulated to the franchises. Suddenly pitches became flatter as tactics adjusted.

Matabeleland had started with a bang, winning their first four games. Then they tailed off, drawing twice, while Mountaineers won three of their last four. A washed-out fixture between Matabeleland and Southern Rocks was rescheduled for early March, when Southern Rocks won a poor match between two depleted teams. Under (what now felt like) the new points system, Matabeleland had already secured the title, with 41 points to Mountaineers' 39; under the old system, it would have been 35 to 36, so Mountaineers would have been champions – though Matabeleland would probably have shown more resolution against Southern Rocks had the Logan Cup still been at stake.

Given Zimbabwe Cricket's recent focus on outright results, it was suspected that the change had been a clerical error which was too late to undo by the time it was queried. To their credit, Mountaineers accepted the situation. They had only themselves to blame for not putting the title beyond doubt, having unaccountably collapsed for 26 when set 64 by Southern Rocks.

The programme was restructured. Previously, teams had played a four-day and a 50-over match in the same week, with a day's rest in between, and there was a single ten-day Twenty20 tournament in Harare. Instead, the season was split into blocks of limited-overs and four-day cricket. Twenty20 matches were staged the morning after each 50-over game, enabling teams to save on accommodation by travelling home that day. The new format won approval, although the Sunday 20-over games might have attracted larger crowds had they taken place in the afternoon. Mashonaland Eagles beat Matabeleland by five runs in the Pro50 final, but were pipped by Mountaineers in the T20.

For the second season running **Matabeleland Tuskers**, coached by Heath Streak, were unbeaten until their last Logan Cup match; they also improved considerably in the limited-overs formats. A powerful batting line-up included six men averaging over 40, and a strong pace attack was led by Glenn Querl and Keegan Meth. Querl, whose action remained controversial, scored a monumental 188 not out as a nightwatchman.

Mountaineers, making the most of a small population's limited resources, had a good all-round season, apart from the diabolical collapse against Southern Rocks. Tino Mawoyo looked like a possible future national captain. **Mid-West Rhinos** were handicapped by a long tail, and leg-spinner Graeme Cremer was injured for half the season, though Ed Rainsford, the Logan Cup's leading wicket-taker, and Mike Chinouya made a formidable new-ball pairing.

Dave Houghton took on the coaching of **Southern Rocks** after three dismal seasons without a first-class victory. Some overdue luck helped them secure three wins, sometimes involving farcical declaration bowling, but the improvement in morale was clear. Opening bowlers Tinashe Panyangara and Tawanda Mupariwa combined well, and Richmond Mutumbami was the Logan Cup's leading run-scorer. The once powerful **Mashonaland Eagles**, coached by Stephen Mangongo after Kevin Curran died in October, did well in one-day cricket, but their first-class season was a disaster. The batting was fragile and, when Kyle Jarvis was unavailable, the bowling lacked penetration. By the end, the mood was at rock bottom and fighting spirit almost non-existent.

FIRST-CLASS AVERAGES, 2012-13

BATTING (350 runs, average 35.00)

	M	I	NO	R	HS	100	Avge	Ct/St
B. M. Shafayat (*Matabeleland Tuskers*)	3	5	0	437	152	2	87.40	12
R. G. Querl (*Matabeleland Tuskers*)	7	11	6	413	188*	1	82.60	4
B. R. M. Taylor (*Mid West Rhinos & Zimbabwe*)	6	11	1	813	171	5	81.30	8
†S. M. Ervine (*Matabeleland Tuskers*)	4	7	2	361	153*	1	72.20	9
M. L. Pettini (*Mountaineers*).	8	16	5	600	104*	2	54.54	9
†S. C. Williams (*Matabeleland Tuskers*)	7	11	0	564	118	1	51.27	7
H. Masakadza (*Mountaineers & Zimbabwe*). . .	6	12	2	495	178	2	49.50	7
T. Maruma (*Mountaineers & Zimbabwe*)	9	14	2	538	105*	1	44.83	6
C. K. Coventry (*Matabeleland Tuskers*)	5	9	1	358	106*	1	44.75	14
M. N. Waller (*Mid West Rhinos & Zimbabwe*) . .	8	14	1	579	208*	1	44.53	5
R. Mutumbami (*Southern Rocks & Zimbabwe*) .	10	18	0	751	150	2	41.72	24/2
C. J. Chibhabha (*Mashonaland Eagles*)	6	12	1	447	104	2	40.63	3
G. A. Lamb (*Mountaineers*)	8	13	0	476	157	2	36.61	6
K. T. Kasuza (*Mountaineers*)	8	14	3	385	75*	0	35.00	7

BOWLING (20 wickets)

	Style	O	M	R	W	BB	5I	Avge
E. C. Rainsford (*Mid West Rhinos*)	RFM	228.1	63	586	38	8-42	1	15.42
R. G. Querl (*Matabeleland Tuskers*)	RFM	274.3	77	615	37	5-24	3	16.62
T. Mupariwa (*Southern Rocks*)	RFM	172.2	50	448	26	6-17	2	17.23
K. O. Meth (*Matabeleland Tuskers & Zim.*) . .	RFM	197.5	68	473	26	6-41	3	18.19
M. T. Chinouya (*Mid West Rhinos*)	RFM	154.2	24	477	24	5-30	3	19.87
A. G. Cremer (*Mid West Rhinos & Zim.*)	LBG	227.1	42	722	35	8-61	3	20.62
S. W. Masakadza (*Mountaineers & Zim.*)	RFM	354.4	99	1,056	47	4-21	0	22.46
N. Mushangwe (*Mountaineers*)	LBG	135.3	13	566	25	4-11	0	22.64
T. Panyangara (*Southern Rocks*)	RFM	205	52	529	23	4-4	0	23.00
K. M. Jarvis (*Mashonaland Eagles & Zim.*) . .	RFM	152.1	30	551	23	7-35	1	23.95
D. T. Tiripano (*Mountaineers*).	RFM	264.2	52	822	27	4-49	0	30.44

Includes tour by Bangladesh in April 2013.

LOGAN CUP, 2012-13

	Played	Won	Lost	Drawn	1st-inns points	Points
Matabeleland Tuskers	8	5	1	2	5	41
Mountaineers.	8	5	2	1	6	39
Mid West Rhinos	8	4	4	0	4	28
Southern Rocks.	8	3	4	1	4	25
Mashonaland Eagles	8	0	6	2	1	7

Win = 6pts; draw = 3pts; lead on first innings = 1pt.

At Harare (Sports Club), October 30–November 2, 2012. **Southern Rocks won by 141 runs.** ‡**Southern Rocks 459-8 dec** (R. Mutumbami 141, P. I. Burgoyne 102*) **and forfeited second innings; Mashonaland Eagles 159-1 dec** (C. J. Chibhabha 102*) **and 159**. *Southern Rocks 7pts. Peter Burgoyne, on Derbyshire's books, scored 102* on first-class debut and added 153 for Southern Rocks' fifth wicket with Richmond Mutumbani. After third-day rain, Mashonaland were fed 74 in 3.3 overs before a forfeited innings set up a target of 301; they never threatened it.*

At Bulawayo (Queens), October 30–November 2, 2012. **Matabeleland Tuskers won by five wickets.** ‡**Mountaineers 264** (R. G. Querl 5-56) **and 357-7 dec** (H. Masakadza 178); **Matabeleland Tuskers 317-8 dec and 307-5**. *Matabeleland Tuskers 7pts. Hamilton Masakadza scored his 17th century in his 100th first-class match to help Mountaineers set a target of 305, which Matabeleland reached five overs into the final hour.*

At Mutare, November 6–9, 2012. **Mountaineers won by six wickets. ‡Mashonaland Eagles 343 and 270** (C. T. Mutombodzi 100); **Mountaineers 377** (T. M. K. Mawoyo 130; I. M. Chinyoka 5-66) **and 237-4** (M. L. Pettini 104*). *Mountaineers 7pts. Essex batsman Mark Pettini steered Mountaineers to victory from 13-3.*

At Masvingo, November 6–8, 2012. **Mid West Rhinos won by an innings and 92 runs. Southern Rocks 149** (M. T. Chinouya 5-30) **and 157** (M. T. Chinouya 5-46); **‡Mid West Rhinos 398-9 dec** (J. C. Mickleburgh 112, B. R. M. Taylor 132). *Mid West Rhinos 7pts. A second Essex player, Jaik Mickleburgh, put on 187 with Brendan Taylor for Mid West Rhinos' third wicket to set up a resounding win after Mike Chinouya took 10-76.*

At Harare (Sports Club), November 13–16, 2012. **Mid West Rhinos won by 323 runs. Mid West Rhinos 265 and 433-7 dec** (M. A. Vermeulen 146); **‡Mashonaland Eagles 245** (M. T. Chinouya 5-61) **and 130.** *Mid West Rhinos 7pts. A century from Mark Vermeulen, at his fifth franchise/ province, set up Mid West Rhinos' biggest victory by runs and Mashonaland's heaviest defeat.*

At Bulawayo (Queens), November 13–16, 2012. **Matabeleland Tuskers won by ten wickets. ‡Southern Rocks 152** (C. B. Mpofu 6-21) **and 292; Matabeleland Tuskers 380** (R. G. Querl 188*) **and 67-0.** *Matabeleland Tuskers 7pts. Nightwatchman Glenn Querl, whose career-best was 26*, romped to 188* in 222 balls, easily surpassing Southern Rocks' first-innings total single-handed, and followed up with 4-31 in a convincing win.*

At Bulawayo (Queens), November 20–23, 2012. **Matabeleland Tuskers won by 312 runs. Matabeleland Tuskers 143** (K. M. Jarvis 7-35) **and 518-8 dec** (M. M. Ali 101, S. M. Ervine 153*); **‡Mashonaland Eagles 245** (K. O. Meth 5-46) **and 104** (K. O. Meth 5-42). *Matabeleland Tuskers 6pts, Mashonaland Eagles 1pt. Matabeleland's 518-8 was the biggest total of the season. Opener Terry Duffin (96) put on 152 for the second wicket with Worcestershire's Moeen Ali and 114 for the fourth with Sean Ervine; despite trailing by 102 on first innings, Matabeleland completed their largest win by runs.*

At Mutare, November 20–22, 2012. **Mountaineers won by eight wickets. ‡Mid West Rhinos 151 and 247** (B. R. M. Taylor 133); **Mountaineers 299** (M. L. Pettini 100; E. C. Rainsford 8-42) **and 100-2.** *Mountaineers 7pts. Ed Rainsford's career-best 8-42 was the best return of the season, but neither he nor Taylor – who, like Pettini, scored his second century of the tournament – could prevent defeat.*

At Kwekwe, November 27–30, 2012. **Matabeleland Tuskers won by three wickets. ‡Mid West Rhinos 65** (R. G. Querl 5-24) **and 491** (B. R. M. Taylor 140, M. N. Waller 208*); **Matabeleland Tuskers 216 and 346-7** (S. C. Williams 118, C. K. Coventry 106*). *Matabeleland Tuskers 7pts. Mid West Rhinos managed only 65 in their first innings, and were 31-3 in their second, before Taylor and Malcolm Waller, with a maiden double-century and the only one in this tournament, put on 257. For the second time in a month, Matabeleland were set more than 300 to win; from 4-3, they surged to 346-7, the highest winning fourth-innings total in the Logan Cup, and their fourth successive victory, thanks largely to Sean Williams and Charles Coventry, who added 186 for the sixth wicket.*

At Masvingo, November 27–29, 2012. **Southern Rocks won by 37 runs. Southern Rocks 164 and 58; ‡Mountaineers 159 and 26** (T. Mupariwa 6-17). *Southern Rocks 7pts. Southern Rocks collapsed for 58, the season's lowest total – until the next day. Left with an apparently straightforward target of 64, Mountaineers were all out for 26, the second-lowest total in Zimbabwean first-class cricket, with nearly two days to spare. Timycen Maruma's seven was the highest score as Tinashe Panyangara (8–5–4–4) and Tawanda Mupariwa (7.3–1–17–6) bowled unchanged.*

At Kwekwe, January 22–24, 2013. **Mid West Rhinos won by nine wickets. Mashonaland Eagles 166 and 170** (A. G. Cremer 5-64); **‡Mid West Rhinos 279 and 58-1.** *Mid West Rhinos 7pts. Mashonaland's unhappy season continued with their fifth straight defeat, early on the third afternoon.*

At Harare (Sports Club), January 29–February 1, 2013. **Drawn. Matabeleland Tuskers 268 and 269-6 dec; ‡Mashonaland Eagles 250** (K. O. Meth 6-41) **and 261-9** (C. J. Chibhabha 104). *Mashonaland Eagles 3pts, Matabeleland Tuskers 4pts. Mashonaland's final pair – keeper Regis Chakabva, who hit 80* including six sixes, and Innocent Chinyoka, who had to survive the last five balls of the match from Querl – saved them from a sixth loss in a row. The much-travelled Bilal Shafayat, keeping wicket for Matabeleland, held five catches in the first innings.*

At Kwekwe, January 29–31, 2013. **Mountaineers won by 55 runs. ‡Mountaineers 252 and 216** (A. G. Cremer 5-67); **Mid West Rhinos 183 and 230.** *Mountaineers 7pts. Mountaineers began the surge that brought them three wins in their last four matches.*

At Bulawayo (Queens), February 5–8, 2013. **Matabeleland Tuskers won by an innings and 104 runs. Matabeleland Tuskers 406-9 dec** (B. M. Shafayat 114); ‡**Mid West Rhinos 179** (R. G. Querl 5-33, N. Ncube 5-67) **and 123**. *Matabeleland Tuskers 7pts. In Matabeleland's fifth victory, keeper Shafayat followed a century with five catches in an innings, as Mid West Rhinos followed on.*

At Mutare, February 5–8, 2013. **Mountaineers won by 116 runs. ‡Mountaineers 394** (G. A. Lamb 139) **and 238-2 dec**; **Southern Rocks 333** (R. Mutumbami 150) **and 183** (T. Mufudza 5-27). *Mountaineers 7pts. As in the opening match, Southern Rocks fed their opponents runs to contrive a finish – this time 228 in 15.3 overs on the final morning. But a target of 300 proved well beyond them.*

At Mutare, February 19–22, 2013. **Drawn. ‡Mountaineers 475-7 dec** (G. A. Lamb 157, T. Maruma 105*) **and 13-0**; **Matabeleland Tuskers 298 and 312** (B. M. Shafayat 152). *Mountaineers 4pts, Matabeleland Tuskers 3pts. Mountaineers made leaders Matabeleland follow on, but Shafayat's second hundred of the season – including six sixes – helped maintain their unbeaten record and guarantee the title.*

At Masvingo, February 19–22, 2013. **Drawn. ‡Mashonaland Eagles 352 and 384-8** (T. Munyaradzi 5-45); **Southern Rocks 427**. *Southern Rocks 4pts, Mashonaland Eagles 3pts.*

At Harare (Sports Club), February 26–28, 2013. **Mountaineers won by eight wickets. Mashonaland Eagles 222 and 153**; ‡**Mountaineers 259 and 117-2**. *Mountaineers 7pts. Ray Price returned figures of 18–9–20–3 in Mountaineers' first innings. But they finished the season with their fifth victory, which left them two points short of champions Matabeleland; Mashonaland remained without a win.*

At Kwekwe, February 26–March 1, 2013. **Mid West Rhinos won by 118 runs. ‡Mid West Rhinos 415** (N. P. Mayavo 101) **and 175-5 dec**; **Southern Rocks 292** (P. I. Burgoyne 104) **and 180** (A. G. Cremer 8-61). *Mid West Rhinos 7pts. Leg-spinner Graeme Cremer was the second Mid West bowler to take eight in an innings during this tournament; his 8-61 was a career-best, and his 11-155 the best match return of the season.*

At Masvingo, March 5–7, 2013. **Southern Rocks won by six wickets. Matabeleland Tuskers 86** (T. Mupariwa 5-26) **and 199**; ‡**Southern Rocks 210 and 80-4**. *Southern Rocks 7pts. In a match postponed from January, Matabeleland suffered their only defeat of the tournament after subsiding for 86 on the opening day; Mupariwa had reduced them to 36-6 in the 15th over. Under the revised points system, however, they were too far ahead for their third successive title to be under threat.*

LOGAN CUP WINNERS

1993-94	Mashonaland Under-24	1999-2000	Mashonaland	2006-07	Easterns
1994-95	Mashonaland	2000-01	Mashonaland	2007-08	Northerns
1995-96	Matabeleland	2001-02	Mashonaland	2008-09	Easterns
1996-97	Mashonaland	2002-03	Mashonaland	2009-10	Mashonaland Eagles
1997-98	Mashonaland	2003-04	Mashonaland	2010-11	Matabeleland Tuskers
1998-99	Matabeleland	2004-05	Mashonaland	2011-12	Matabeleland Tuskers
		2005-06	*No competition*	2012-13	Matabeleland Tuskers

Mashonaland/Northerns/Mashonaland Eagles have won the title 11 times, Matabeleland/Matabeleland Tuskers five times, Easterns twice, Mashonaland Under-24 once.

PRO50 CHAMPIONSHIP, 2012-13

50-over league plus final

	Played	Won	Lost	No result	Bonus points	Points	Net run-rate
Matabeleland Tuskers.........	8	5	2	1	3	25	0.85
Mashonaland Eagles..........	8	3	2	3	1	19	–0.01
Mid West Rhinos	8	4	2	2	3	18*	1.36
Mountaineers	8	3	3	2	0	16	–0.75
Southern Rocks.	8	0	6	2	0	4	–1.65

* *5pts deducted for fielding an ineligible player.*

Final

At Bulawayo (Queens), January 19, 2013. **Mashonaland Eagles won by five runs** (D/L). **Mashonaland Eagles 222** (49.1 overs); ‡**Matabeleland Tuskers 203-8** (47.5 overs). *Mashonaland Eagles retained the title when rain ended play with Matabeleland Tuskers six short of the 209 they needed to win under Duckworth/Lewis. Prosper Utseya had boosted Mashonaland's batting with 53 in 44 balls before he was out obstructing the field. Gavin Ewing (94) and Brian Chari (47) opened with 138 in reply, but Utseya pinned them back with 3-41.*

DOMESTIC TWENTY20, 2012-13

20-over league plus final

	Played	Won	Lost	No result	Bonus points	Points	Net run-rate
Mashonaland Eagles.........	8	7	0	1	4	34	1.67
Mountaineers	8	4	3	1	2	20	0.21
Mid West Rhinos	8	3	4	1	1	10*	−0.36
Southern Rocks.............	8	1	4	3	0	10	−1.07
Matabeleland Tuskers........	8	1	5	2	0	8	−0.89

* 5pts deducted for fielding an ineligible player.

Final

At Harare (Sports Club), February 10, 2013. **Mountaineers won by seven wickets** (D/L). ‡**Mashonaland Eagles 106** (19.3 overs); **Mountaineers 103-3** (17.1 overs). *MoM:* T. Mufudza. *Off-spinner Tapiwa Mufudza took 4-14 in Mashonaland's innings, in which no one passed 22. Rain revised Mountaineers' target to 103 in 19 overs; Mark Pettini set them on their way with 40.*

ICC WORLD TWENTY20 QUALIFIER, 2013-14

REVIEW BY TIM BROOKS

1. Ireland   2. Afghanistan   3. Nepal   4. UAE   5. Netherlands   6. Hong Kong

With six places up for grabs at the 2014 World Twenty20, this was the most open, entertaining and dramatic qualifying tournament so far. It provided the best opportunity yet for emerging nations such as Nepal and Papua New Guinea to join Ireland and Afghanistan – the two strongest Associates – in a major competition. The one frustration was that, for the main event in Bangladesh, the six qualifiers would have to come through another preliminary round, against the hosts and Zimbabwe, before taking on the big guns.

The qualifier event for the previous World Twenty20, also in the UAE two seasons earlier, had contained just two wins by a lesser Associate over one of the High Performance Programme nations (Afghanistan, Canada, Ireland, Kenya, the Netherlands and Scotland). But when PNG bloodied Ireland's noses in a warm-up game, it was clear the old guard were going to be challenged. Ireland and Afghanistan secured places in Bangladesh by topping their groups, but otherwise reputation counted for little in a round full of upsets: Bermuda beat Scotland, PNG shocked Kenya and the Netherlands on consecutive days, while Nepal chased 183 against the Kenyans. Canada were awful, losing to the USA, Hong Kong, the UAE and Namibia – yet would still probably have sneaked into the play-offs had rain not helped Italy pick up a point against Ireland.

It was a vindication of the ICC's investment in the development programme that the quality of the field was higher than ever, with all the teams boasting rope-clearers and match-winners. However, three of the HPP countries – Canada, Kenya and Scotland – were frequently outgunned, and their head coaches all lost their jobs.

Nepal, the UAE and Hong Kong took advantage of their shortcomings. Nepal's qualification for their first major tournament, barely two decades after the first serious development drive by their board, was wildly celebrated by the devoted Nepalese expat following in Abu Dhabi. PNG, vastly improved by a flow of Australian coaches in recent years, came close, but failed to chase down 138 against a young Hong Kong side who fielded like tigers. That result meant half the participating nations in Bangladesh would be from Asia.

Live streaming has helped make Associate cricket more visible than ever and, with players such as Paul Stirling, Kevin O'Brien and Paras Khadka enjoying a global fan base, social media was abuzz with opinions, denouncements, and patriotism.

A pair of shimmering centuries sparked the biggest shocks: Tony Ura sped PNG to 193 for three against the Netherlands, and Hong Kong's Irfan Ahmed hammered 100 from 53 balls against the Canadian rabble. Khadka cemented his Beckham-like status in Nepal with a composed 46 that carried them to Bangladesh, while Sussex's Matt Machan was the tournament's highest

Graham Crouch, IDI/Getty Images

Rarefied air: Paras Khadka, captain and national icon, drives Nepal towards their first major
tournament with a last-ball win over Hong Kong.

run-scorer, with 364, in an otherwise depressing campaign for Scotland –
despite the presence of Paul Collingwood, a World Twenty20-winning
captain, as assistant coach.

During the mid-innings break in their last group game, the Scots were
informed by ICC officials that they needed to restrict Denmark to fewer than
121 in order to make the quarter-finals, when in fact the crucial figure was 130.
It affected Kyle Coetzer's field placings, and the Danes finished on 130 for six,
which pushed Scotland behind Nepal by 0.000026 of a run – and ultimately
into a sudden death play-off against the Netherlands, which they lost.

Seventy-two games were crammed into 16 days, yet the event confirmed
Twenty20 as a format for the worldly-wise. Kenya sprung a shock by dragging
42-year-old Steve Tikolo out of retirement, and he shone in a fading side.
Others in vintage form were Bermuda's David Hemp, 43, UAE's Khurram
Khan, 42, and Trent Johnston, who looked better than ever at 39, in his
tournament swansong for Ireland.

Group A

	Played	Won	Lost	No result	Points	Net run-rate
IRELAND	7	6	0	1	13	2.05
HONG KONG	7	5	2	0	10	0.44
UNITED ARAB EMIRATES	7	5	2	0	10	0.26
NAMIBIA	7	4	3	0	8	0.19
ITALY	7	2	4	1	5	0.45
Canada.....................	7	2	5	0	4	−0.35
Uganda.....................	7	1	5	1	3	−1.49
USA	7	1	5	1	3	−1.64

Group B

	Played	Won	Lost	No result	Points	Net run-rate
AFGHANISTAN	7	6	1	0	12	1.20
NETHERLANDS................	7	5	2	0	10	1.08
NEPAL......................	7	4	3	0	8	0.37
SCOTLAND	7	4	3	0	8	0.37
PAPUA NEW GUINEA	7	3	3	1	7	−0.05
Kenya......................	7	3	4	0	6	1.07
Bermuda....................	7	2	5	0	4	−1.25
Denmark....................	7	0	6	1	1	−3.21

Nepal were ranked above Scotland on the fifth decimal point of net run-rate.

The two group winners progressed to the semi-finals, and qualified for the main tournament in Bangladesh. The second- and third-placed teams progressed to the quarter-finals; the winners of that stage qualified for the main tournament. The fourth- and fifth-placed teams entered a qualifying play-off semi-final; the winners of that stage entered a qualifying play-off against the defeated quarter-finalists to decide the last two qualifiers for the main tournament.

Group matches

Of the 56 group games, only the seven between HPP sides had official Twenty20 international status; their scores are given below. Full scores from the group and plate matches can be found under "Cricket in the United Arab Emirates 2013-14" at cricketarchive.co.uk

Group A

At Abu Dhabi, November 16, 2013. **Ireland won by two runs. Ireland 168-5** (20 overs) (K. J. O'Brien 31, D. T. Johnston 39*); ‡**Canada 166-3** (20 overs) (R. Gunasekera 65, A. Bagai 67*). *Twenty20 international debuts:* D. Daesrath, J. O. A. Gordon (Canada). *MoM:* A. Bagai. *Alex Cusack, defending 14 off the last over against two set batsmen, held his nerve, even after Jimmy Hansra (22* from 12 balls) hit the third delivery for six. Ruvindu Gunasekera (65 from 22) and Ashish Bagai (67* from 55) had pulled Canada around after Max Sorensen struck with the first two balls of the reply.*

Group B

At Sharjah, November 15, 2013. **Netherlands won by seven wickets.** ‡**Afghanistan 90** (19.1 overs); **Netherlands 92-3** (12.5 overs) (P. W. Borren 38*). *Twenty20 international debut:* B. N. Cooper (Netherlands). *MoM:* P. W. Borren. *Mudassar Bukhari (2-7) and Paul van Meekeren (2-18) reduced Afghanistan to 14-3, and they barely crept past their lowest Twenty20 total of 80. Wesley Barresi chopped Shapoor Zadran's first ball on to his stumps, but Peter Borren hastened victory with four sixes.*

At Sharjah, November 16, 2013. **Afghanistan won by 17 runs.** ‡**Afghanistan 171-6** (20 overs) (Mohammad Shahzad 42, Mohammad Nabi 46, Samiullah Shenwari 31*; I. Wardlaw 3-40); **Scotland 154-6** (20 overs) (C. S. MacLeod 56, M. W. Machan 54). *Twenty20 international debut:* R. M. L. Taylor (Scotland). *MoM:* Dawlat Zadran (Afghanistan). *Calum MacLeod and Matt Machan added 76 at a decent lick, but they left too much to do in the last six overs, after MacLeod edged Dawlat Zadran behind. Mohammad Nabi, promoted to No. 4 following defeat by the Dutch, gave Afghanistan a boost with back-to-back sixes off Machan. Scotland had lost both their opening matches.*

At Dubai (ICC Academy), November 19, 2013. **Kenya won by 92 runs.** ‡Kenya 183-7 (20 overs) (C. O. Obuya 36, R. G. Aga 52*); **Scotland 91** (13.2 overs) (S. O. Tikolo 4-2). *MoM:* R. G. Aga. *Steve Tikolo, aged 42 and brought on with Scotland 88-5 after 11 overs, swept up three wickets in four balls, all from leading edges. Tikolo finished the match when Iain Wardlaw top-edged the second delivery of his second over, to give him figures of 1.2–0–2–4, the cheapest four-for in all Twenty20 cricket. Kenya had been teetering at 117-6 in the 14th over, until Ragheb Aga hit a 24-ball fifty.*

At Dubai (ICC Academy), November 22, 2013. **Scotland won by 15 runs. Scotland 165-4** (20 overs) (R. D. Berrington 38, M. W. Machan 67*, R. M. L. Taylor 41*); ‡**Netherlands 150-6** (20 overs) (W. Barresi 70*; R. M. Haq 3-20). *MoM:* R. M. L. Taylor. *Scotland came through a must-win game, while defeat dented the Netherlands' hopes of beating Afghanistan to top spot. The Scots were carried to a strong total by Sussex's Machan (67* off 46 balls) and Leicestershire all-rounder Rob Taylor (41* from 19), who thumped 62 off the last four overs from Bukhari and Malik Jamil. Barresi was fluent, but the rest were tied down by Majid Haq's off-spin.*

At Dubai (ICC Academy), November 23, 2013. **Netherlands won by 29 runs.** ‡**Netherlands 130-7** (20 overs) (M. R. Swart 44; T. M. Odoyo 3-17); **Kenya 101-9** (20 overs) (S. O. Ngoche 38; Mudassar Bukhari 3-14). *MoM:* Mudassar Bukhari. *A blistering burst by Bukhari and Michael Swart (4–0–8–2) had Kenya 8-5 in the sixth over, although Tikolo was unlucky to be given caught behind off his leg. The Netherlands fielded superbly, save for a dropped catch and five penalty runs when the ball hit a helmet.*

At Sharjah, November 24, 2013. **Afghanistan won by 34 runs.** ‡**Afghanistan 148-9** (20 overs) (Karim Sadiq 30, Noor Ali Zadran 50, Najibullah Zadran 33); **Kenya 114** (18.2 overs) (R. R. Patel 52; Samiullah Shenwari 5-13). *MoM:* Samiullah Shenwari. *A Kenyan victory would have salvaged a play-off place and, quite possibly, meant qualification for the Netherlands at Afghanistan's expense. Tikolo set off like a train, knocking off 31 in the first two overs of the reply, but Nabi's decision to throw leg-spinner Samiullah Shenwari the ball paid off with three wickets in his first eight deliveries. Rakep Patel resisted stoutly, but received little support. A few weeks earlier Afghanistan had qualified for their maiden World Cup; now they secured a place at their third consecutive World Twenty20.*

11th Place Play-off

At Sharjah, November 26, 2013. **Kenya won by 21 runs.** ‡**Kenya 146-7** (20 overs) (S. O. Tikolo 40, C. O. Obuya 40); **Canada 125** (19.2 overs) (A. Bagai 48; S. O. Tikolo 3-16). *MoM:* S. O. Tikolo. *The Associate landscape was changing fast: two teams who had played at the 2011 World Cup were now slipping out of the world's top 20 in the Twenty20 format. Obuya, who stood down as captain after this game, and Bagai, who retired, propped up an innings each, but three run-outs, and Tikolo's two wickets in the 18th over, put the seal on Kenya's consolation win.*

Quarter-Finals

At Abu Dhabi, November 27, 2013. **Nepal won by five wickets. Hong Kong 143-8** (20 overs) (J. K. Mukhiya 3-32); ‡**Nepal 144-5** (20 overs) (G. Malla 30, P. Khadka 46). *MoM:* P. Khadka. *This was the tournament's defining moment: Nepal, a country with only two decades' cricketing experience, reached their first major finals. Their batsmen were little more than steady in pursuit of a modest target, and had slowed dangerously by the time Gyanendra Malla holed out. At that point Nepal required 57 from 41 balls, but Paras Khadka, their adored captain, kept his cool. Hong Kong had their chance when, with Nepal needing 27 from 13, Khadka edged Irfan Ahmed, and wicketkeeper Jamie Atkinson dropped a chance to his right, hurting a finger in the process. He went off, and Khadka was run out in the next over, but Sharad Vesawkar did the rest. Nepal's players celebrated wildly with the hundreds of expats who had packed into the main stand.*

At Abu Dhabi, November 27, 2013. **United Arab Emirates won by ten runs.** ‡**United Arab Emirates 117-8** (20 overs) (Khurram Khan 32; M. A. A. Jamil 4-17); **Netherlands 107-9** (20 overs) (Nasir Aziz 3-21). *MoM:* E. H. S. N. Silva (United Arab Emirates). *After the euphoria that greeted Nepal's qualification, there were fewer Emiratis on hand to watch the UAE's amateurs reach their first major tournament since the 1996 World Cup – when Sultan Zarawani batted in a sunhat against Allan Donald. The Netherlands ought to have won after a UAE innings marked by messy shot* *selection and running. But they also proved hapless between the wickets, while slow left-armer Shadeep Silva got through 3–1–3–0 at the start. Off-spinner Nasir Aziz, reported for a suspect action on the opening day of the tournament, was all over the Dutch, claiming three wickets, a good catch in the deep, and a hand in two run-outs. His juggling reflex return catch to dismiss Ben Cooper for 20 sealed the deal.*

Qualifying Play-off Semi-Finals

At Abu Dhabi (Nursery Ground No. 1), November 27, 2013. **Papua New Guinea won by 25 runs. Papua New Guinea 145-4** (20 overs) (T. P. Ura 34, G. O. Jones 36, J. N. T. Vare 30*); ‡**Namibia 120** (18.1 overs) (C. G. Williams 42; P. Raho 3-10). *MoM:* P. Raho. *The Scholtz brothers, leg-spinner Nicolaas (2-24) and slow left-armer Bernard (2-22), kept PNG under wraps, but Geraint Jones and Jack Vare sped up towards the end. Namibia then ran into the Papuans' nagging swing bowlers Pipi Raho and Willie Gavera, who had them reeling at 16-4.*

At Abu Dhabi (Nursery Ground No. 2), November 27, 2013. **Scotland won by seven wickets.** ‡**Italy 125-8** (20 overs) (A. M. Northcote 46*); **Scotland 126-3** (17.3 overs) (R. D. Berrington 52, C. S. MacLeod 56). *MoM:* C. S. MacLeod. *Scotland removed Italy's dangerous Gareth Berg for 24 in the fourth over, and restricted his opening partner Andrew Northcote to 46*. Scotland's openers then put on 112 inside 15 overs to set up a sudden-death qualifier against the Netherlands.*

Qualifying Play-offs

At Abu Dhabi, November 28, 2013. **Hong Kong won by 29 runs.** ‡**Hong Kong 137-9** (20 overs) (Babar Hayat 48; P. Raho 3-22, W. T. Gavera 3-23); **Papua New Guinea 108** (19.1 overs) (C. J. A. Amini 30; Munir Dar 3-26). *MoM:* Babar Hayat. *Hong Kong misjudged the conditions by choosing to face PNG's swing bowlers first up, and were soon 19-4. They required Babar Hayat's 48 to turn their score into something defendable. Munir Dar, a 41-year-old left-arm spinner originally from Pakistan, helped dismantle PNG's middle order, but was reported for a suspect action for the second time in the competition. Hong Kong progressed to their first major finals.*

At Abu Dhabi, November 28, 2013. **Netherlands won by eight wickets.** ‡**Scotland 147-6** (M. W. Machan 61, M. A. Leask 58); **Netherlands 149-2** (B. N. Cooper 40, W. Barresi 75*, M. R. Swart 30*). *MoM:* W. Barresi. *In the first two World Twenty20s, these sides were the cream of the Associate crop; now they were scrambling to make the sixth qualifying place. The Netherlands sneaked in, after removing Berrington and MacLeod for ducks in the first seven balls, and not losing their heads when Michael Leask hit five sixes in the middle overs; Cooper caught him superbly, one-handed. Stephan Myburgh was bowled by Neil Carter fourth ball, but Cooper, promoted from No. 7 to open, and Barresi responded with a steadying 67-run stand, and the Dutch kept wickets in hand.*

Semi-Finals

At Abu Dhabi, November 29, 2013. **Afghanistan won by seven wickets. Nepal 90-8** (20 overs) (Samiullah Shenwari 3-19); ‡**Afghanistan 96-3** (14.2 overs) (Nawroz Mangal 48). *MoM:* Samiullah Shenwari. *With a place in Bangladesh already secured, Nepal were overwhelmed by Afghanistan's formidable attack. The Afghans were briefly worried when Avinash Karn removed the openers, and Noor Ali Zadran limped off with cramp in between. But Nawroz Mangal hustled them to their modest target.*

At Abu Dhabi, November 29, 2013 (floodlit). **Ireland won by 62 runs.** ‡**Ireland 147-8** (20 overs) (K. J. O'Brien 31, D. T. Johnston 35; A. M. Guruge 3-21); **United Arab Emirates 85** (17.4 overs) (M. C. Sorensen 4-15, T. J. Murtagh 4-24). *MoM:* M. C. Sorensen. *Ireland struggled initially, as the UAE took pace off the ball, but were resuscitated by John Mooney's partnerships of 41 with Kevin O'Brien and 55 with Trent Johnston, who thumped Nasir Aziz for 6444 at the start of the 18th over. Mooney was lucky to escape Aziz's lbw shout with the score on 68. The UAE faced the first floodlit run-chase of the tournament, and were dismantled by Sorensen's fiery opening spell, before Tim Murtagh cleaned up the tail.*

FINAL

AFGHANISTAN v IRELAND

At Abu Dhabi, November 30, 2013 (floodlit). Ireland won by 68 runs. Toss: Ireland. Twenty20 international debut: J. N. K. Shannon.

Associate cricket's two benchmark teams met in the World Twenty20 Qualifier final for the third successive time; Ireland's victory maintained recent bragging rights, and ensured they would face Zimbabwe, rather than host nation Bangladesh, in the main tournament's preliminary round in March. Porterfield, Stirling and O'Brien (who clubbed 14 off his first three balls, from Hamza Hotak) stunned the Afghans with an onslaught of 82 in the powerplay, and the in-form Johnston, shunted up the order, marked his last Twenty20 appearance for Ireland with a resourceful maiden fifty. The crispness of Stirling's strokeplay led some to press his case for the IPL. Ireland's total was the fourth-highest in Twenty20 internationals, and 42 better than the next by an Associate nation. Oozing exuberance, Afghanistan were up with the rate at first, thanks to Mohammad Shahzad's brutality. But Cusack's gentler pace claimed Mohammad Nabi and Karim Sadiq from the last two balls of the seventh over, and from there Afghanistan nosedived. Gulbadeen Naib hit hard and long, but Johnston took three wickets to end his career in green with another garland.

Man of the Match: D. T. Johnston. *Man of the Tournament:* Samiullah Shenwari.

Ireland

		B	4	6
*W. T. S. Porterfield b 11	27	14	4	1
P. R. Stirling c 4 b 11	76	43	8	4
K. J. O'Brien c 9 b 5	20	12	2	1
D. T. Johnston b 10	62	32	5	4
†G. C. Wilson b 9	2	3	0	0
J. F. Mooney c 1 b 10	12	6	2	0
M. C. Sorensen not out	6	6	1	0
J. N. K. Shannon c 6 b 11	2	3	0	0
A. R. Cusack not out	1	1	0	0
B 1, l-b 10, w 6	17			

6 overs: 82-1   (20 overs) 225-7

1/68 2/104 3/168 4/183 5/212 6/212 7/223

G. H. Dockrell and T. J. Murtagh did not bat.

Shapoor Zadran 4–0–36–2; Dawlat Zadran 4–0–52–1; Samiullah Shenwari 2–0–22–0; Hamza Hotak 4–0–39–3; Mohammad Nabi 3–0–32–0; Karim Sadiq 2–0–19–1; Mirwais Ashraf 1–0–14–0.

Afghanistan

		B	4	6
†Mohammad Shahzad c 8 b 10	38	18	8	1
Nawroz Mangal b 10	14	10	3	0
Mirwais Ashraf c 2 b 7	22	17	2	1
*Mohammad Nabi c 2 b 9	6	6	1	0
Karim Sadiq c 4 b 9	0	1	0	0
Gulbadeen Naib c 6 b 4	43	19	3	4
Samiullah Shenwari c 2 b 4	5	7	0	0
Najibullah Zadaran c 6 b 4	4	6	0	0
Dawlat Zadran b 11	8	4	0	1
Shapoor Zadran b 11	13	20	0	2
Hamza Hotak not out	2	5	0	0
W 2	2			

6 overs: 74-2   (18.5 overs) 157

1/36 2/59 3/76 4/76 5/101 6/129 7/129 8/138 9/142

Sorensen 4–0–22–1; Murtagh 2.5–0–24–2; Cusack 3–0–18–2; Dockrell 3–0–37–2; Johnston 4–1–34–3; Stirling 2–0–22–0.

Umpires: M. A. Gough and S. Ravi. Third umpire: S. J. Davis. Referee: D. Govindjee.

Final rankings

1. Ireland 2. Afghanistan 3. Nepal 4. UAE 5. Netherlands 6. Hong Kong 7. Scotland 8. Papua New Guinea 9. Italy 10. Namibia 11. Kenya 12. Canada 13. Uganda 14. Bermuda 15. USA 16. Denmark.

OTHER TWENTY20 INTERNATIONALS, 2012-13

Canada v Kenya

At Dubai (ICC Academy), March 15, 2013. **First Twenty20 international: Canada won by five wickets.** ‡**Kenya 126-9** (20 overs) (R. R. Patel 48*; H. Osinde 3-36, Junaid Siddiqui 3-10); **Canada 128-5** (18.3 overs) (H. Patel 40). *MoM: Junaid Siddiqui. Twenty20 international debut:* Hamza Tariq (Canada). *With the World Twenty20 Qualifier to be held in the UAE later in the year, Canada and Kenya arranged a pair of Twenty20 internationals between other commitments in Dubai. Kenya slipped to 45-6 in the eighth over, as seamer Henry Osinde and leg-spinner Junaid Siddiqui bowled their full quota at the start. Canada took care to keep wickets in hand.*

At Dubai (ICC Academy), March 16, 2013. **Second Twenty20 international: Kenya won by 21 runs.** ‡**Kenya 139-7** (20 overs) (R. G. Aga 31); **Canada 118** (18.5 overs) (R. Gunasekara 38; C. O. Obuya 3-17, E. A. Otieno 3-18). *MoM: C. O. Obuya. Twenty20 international debut:* I. A. Karim (Kenya). *Kenya accumulated steadily, before Rakep Patel (23 from 17 balls) and Ragheb Aga (31 from 23) accelerated at the end. Hiral Patel and Ruvindu Gunasekara put on 45 for the second wicket, but Canada's innings unravelled against spinners Hiren Varaiya (1-22) and Collins Obuya, who claimed his best Twenty20 figures since his format debut, for Warwickshire in 2003.*

Kenya v Netherlands

At Windhoek, April 19, 2013. **Twenty20 international: Kenya won by five wickets.** ‡**Netherlands 172-5** (20 overs) (S. J. Myburgh 41, M. R. Swart 89; R. G. Aga 3-24); **Kenya 176-5** (19 overs) (A. A. Obanda 47, C. O. Obuya 75*; R. R. Patel 36). *Twenty20 international debuts:* L. Oluoch (Kenya); M. J. G. Rippon (Netherlands). *Obuya crashed Kenya to their highest successful run-chase in Twenty20 (until they surpassed it two days later, against South Africa Emerging Players) with 75* from 37 balls. He was well supported by Alex Obanda and Patel. Obuya's run-out of Michael Swart (89 from 55) in the 15th over had stopped the Dutch getting out of sight.*

At Windhoek, April 20, 2013. **Twenty20 international: Kenya won by seven wickets. Netherlands 113** (18.4 overs) (S. O. Ngoche 4-34); ‡**Kenya 114-3** (12.2 overs) (R. R. Patel 46*). *Twenty20 international debut:* P. A. van Meekeren (Netherlands). *Swart again set off like a train, but was lbw to Shem Ngoche for 27 in the fourth over, and the Netherlands never recovered. Kenya came through Bukhari's fiery opening spell of 3–1–13–2, with Patel smacking Michael Rippon's left-arm chinamen for four consecutive sixes. This was the opening match of a quadrangular tournament also featuring Namibia and South Africa Emerging Players. Namibia went on to beat Kenya in the final.*

UNDER-19 TRI-SERIES IN THE UAE, 2013-14

1. Pakistan   2. England   3. UAE

England's last destination in the Under-19 World Cup cycle was a reconnaissance mission in December 2013 to the United Arab Emirates, venue of the Under-19 showpiece event in February 2014. It was the final chance for England Development Programme head selector David Graveney and the coaching staff to make on-field judgments about the intake, before whittling them down to 15. But on the eve of the trip two players, Northamptonshire wicketkeeper Ben Duckett and Essex batsman Kishen Velani, were axed for failing fitness tests at Loughborough.

The decision to discipline Duckett was a serious message from the management, after he had been entrusted with the captaincy since the South Africa tour early in the year. "I'm disappointed *in* him, not *for* him," said Northamptonshire chief executive David Smith. "At that age you should be passing these tests." Although Duckett came back into the squad for the World Cup, the selectors chose Yorkshire's Will Rhodes, one of four players given a taste of captaincy in this series, to lead England into the big event.

With or without Duckett, England had their work cut out against Pakistan, one of the World Cup favourites. Across the two one-day series in England and the UAE, Pakistan beat them eight times in a row, part of a 17-match winning streak which ended with defeat in the Under-19 Asia Cup final by India shortly after this series. Their more accomplished spinners took advantage of warm and dry conditions in the UAE, and their batsmen thrashed England 5–1 in the half-century count. Sami Aslam, their impressive captain, came into the series on the back of two first-class centuries and a List A hundred for the National Bank of Pakistan, and finished with 287 runs. Ryan Higgins, a punchy right-hander on Middlesex's books, had coped best against Pakistan's varied attack, with three fifties home and away.

The third team were the UAE, who forced their way on to the bill after qualifying for the Under-19 World Cup for the first time. They were far from outclassed, and even became the second Associate nation to beat England at Under-19 level (albeit in an unofficial youth one-day international) when they chased down 251 at Dubai's Fair Grounds.

ENGLAND UNDER-19 TOURING PARTY

E. G. Barnard (Worcestershire), K. Carver (Yorkshire), J. M. Clarke (Worcestershire), H. Z. Finch (Sussex), M. D. Fisher (Yorkshire), M. A. H. Hammond (Gloucestershire), R. F. Higgins (Middlesex), R. Jones (Lancashire), L. D. McManus (Hampshire), S. Mahmood (Lancashire), W. M. H. Rhodes (Yorkshire), R. J. Sayer (Leicestershire), J. Shaw (Yorkshire), D. P. Sibley (Surrey), J. A. Tattersall (Yorkshire), J. R. Winslade (Surrey), L. Wood (Nottinghamshire). *Coach:* T. J. Boon. *Manager:* J. Abrahams.

T. E. Barber (Hampshire) pulled out with a back injury before departure. B. M. Duckett (Northamptonshire, captain) and K. S. Velani (Essex) were originally selected, but failed fitness tests, and were replaced by Mahmood and Wood. The captaincy alternated between Barnard, McManus, Rhodes and Tattersall.

At Abu Dhabi, December 7, 2013. **Pakistan Under-19 won by 26 runs. Pakistan Under-19 253-7** (50 overs) (Sami Aslam 56, Imam-ul-Haq 60); ‡**United Arab Emirates Under-19 227-8** (50 overs)

(S. Vijayakumar 51). Pakistan 4pts. *Pakistan began with a solid if unspectacular win. Chirag Suri (35) and Shivank Vijayakumar put on 80 for UAE's first wicket, but the middle order could not push on.*

At Abu Dhabi, December 8, 2013. **England Under-19 won by 42 runs.** ‡**England Under-19 300-6** (50 overs) (E. G. Barnard 53, J. M. Clarke 81*); **United Arab Emirates Under-19 258** (49.1 overs) (C. Suri 70, Rohit Singh 58). England 4pts. *England were the only side to reach 300 in the tournament. Wicketkeeper Joe Clarke whacked 81* from 64 balls in an unbroken 108-run partnership with Rob Jones in the last ten overs. Suri and Rohit Singh put up a fight, though, adding 107, before a telling spell of leg-spin from Jonny Tattersall (3-34).*

At Abu Dhabi, December 9, 2013. **Pakistan Under-19 won by three wickets. England Under-19 168** (43 overs) (R. F. Higgins 80); ‡**Pakistan Under-19 171-7** (44.1 overs) (Saud Shakil 63). Pakistan 4pts. *England had Pakistan 113-6 after 32 overs, but let the game slip away during a fifty stand between Saud Shakil and Zafar Gohar (32). Opener Ryan Higgins scored almost half England's runs.*

At Sharjah, December 11, 2013. **Pakistan Under-19 won by eight wickets. United Arab Emirates Under-19 104** (30.3 overs) (Zafar Gohar 5-18); ‡**Pakistan Under-19 105-2** (19.5 overs) (Sami Aslam 72*). Pakistan 5pts. *Zafar Gohar's left-arm spin (10–1–18–5) proved too good for the UAE, and Sami Aslam fast-tracked victory with three sixes in a row.*

At Sharjah, December 13, 2013. **England Under-19 won by seven wickets. United Arab Emirates Under-19 94** (27.5 overs); ‡**England Under-19 97-3** (21.2 overs). England 5pts. *Seamers Jack Winslade (2-19) and Harry Finch (2-20) reduced the hosts to 25-4, before the spinners went to work.*

At Sharjah, December 15, 2013. **Pakistan Under-19 won by 47 runs. Pakistan Under-19 241-8** (50 overs) (Kamran Ghulam 53); ‡**England Under-19 194** (45.3 overs). Pakistan 4pts. *Once Winslade's run-out had broken a stand of 73 between Kamran Ghulam and Imam-ul-Haq (41), England chipped away, but none of their batsman could play the commanding innings required. No. 9 Rob Sayer did have a little fun at the end, striking three sixes in a chirpy 47.*

At Dubai (Fair Grounds Oval), December 17, 2013. **United Arab Emirates Under-19 won by three wickets.** ‡**England Under-19 250-9** (50 overs) (R. F. Higgins 75; Moaaz Qazi 4-22); **United Arab Emirates Under-19 251-7** (49.3 overs) (Rohit Singh 70). United Arab Emirates 4pts. *England rested three players, and paid the price with defeat by an Associate nation at Under-19 level for only the second time (Bangladesh beat them at the 1997-98 World Cup, two years before becoming a Full Member). Off-spinner Moaaz Qazi caused the top order problems, but Higgins underpinned the innings (his 75 contained no fours bar three sixes). The new ball, however, yielded nothing, and England's weakness in the spin department allowed Rohit Singh and Qazi to string together a fifth-wicket stand of 98. They were out in successive balls to Finch and Matthew Fisher, and UAE still needed seven with five deliveries remaining. But Shahrukh Ahmed thumped Finch for six, then scampered the winning run.*

At Dubai (ICC Academy), December 18, 2013. **Pakistan Under-19 won by 73 runs.** ‡**Pakistan Under-19 261-8** (50 overs) (Sami Aslam 129); **United Arab Emirates Under-19 188** (47 overs) (D. S. D'Souza 56). Pakistan 5pts. *UAE required an even greater scalp if they were to stand a chance of pipping England to the final, but that prospect was doused by the formidable Sami Aslam, who dominated the bowling with 129 from 150 balls. UAE were 3-2 after two overs.*

At Dubai (ICC Academy), December 20, 2013. **Pakistan Under-19 won by 90 runs.** ‡**Pakistan Under-19 229-8** (50 overs) (Hasan Raza 55); **England Under-19 139** (41.5 overs) (Kamran Ghulam 4-18). Pakistan 5pts. *Luke Wood, a Nottinghamshire left-arm seamer making his youth international debut, removed the openers in a superb opening spell, but Hasan Raza and Shayan Jahangir put on 97 for the third wicket to lead Pakistan's recovery.*

Pakistan 27pts, England 9pts, UAE 4pts.

Final

At Dubai (Sports City), December 22, 2013. **Pakistan Under-19 won by 97 runs. Pakistan Under-19 247-7** (50 overs) (Imam-ul-Haq 51, Kamran Ghulam 51); ‡**England Under-19 150** (40 overs). *For the eighth time in a row in 2013, Pakistan beat England in a youth one-day international. England won the toss, and Wood removed Sami Aslam in the first over, but they could not make the prize wicket count. Imam-ul-Haq and Kamran Ghulam dragged Pakistan back on top with responsible fifties. England were 19-2 inside the opening powerplay, and never got back on terms.*

OTHER FIRST-CLASS TOURS

SRI LANKA A IN WEST INDIES, 2013

Sri Lanka A, captained by Dimuth Karunaratne, toured West Indies in June 2013, playing two first-class matches with West Indies A, both drawn. West Indies A won a subsequent Twenty20 series 1–0 (with one no-result), and a one-day series 2–1. After the Sri Lankans had arrived home, all-rounder Ramith Rambukwella was fined half his tour fee for trying to open an aeroplane cabin door at 35,000 feet on the return flight; he insisted he had not been not drunk, but half-asleep.

At Basseterre, St Kitts, June 5–8, 2013. **Drawn. ‡Sri Lanka A 472** (M. D. U. S. Jayasundera 57, F. D. M. Karunaratne 101, K. D. K. Vithanage 62, S. M. A. Priyanjan 65, P. C. de Silva 109; S. S. Cottrell 3-93, N. O. Miller 6-141) **and 165-4** (F. D. M. Karunaratne 100*); **West Indies A 636-8 dec** (A. B. Fudadin 145, K. A. Edwards 190, L. R. Johnson 144, N. O. Miller 50*; P. H. T. Kaushal 5-238). *In a match of six centuries Dimuth Karunaratne scored two, backed up by No. 7 Chaturanga de Silva in the first innings, when Nikita Miller bowled 51 overs. In between, three West Indians responded with career-bests: Assad Fudadin and Kirk Edwards shared a second-wicket stand of 256, before Leon Johnson lashed out with four sixes.*

At Arnos Vale, St Vincent, June 12–15, 2013. **Drawn. ‡Sri Lanka A 314** (J. K. Silva 119, A. K. Perera 50; M. L. Cummins 4-74, J. L. Carter 3-51) **and 140-3** (M. D. U. S. Jayasundera 50*); **West Indies A 294** (K. C. Brathwaite 77, N. Deonarine 110; R. A. S. Lakmal 4-55, P. M. Pushpakumara 5-94). *Overcast conditions gave bowlers more of a chance, but the second day was washed out, leaving little prospect of a result.*

AUSTRALIA A IN ZIMBABWE AND SOUTH AFRICA, 2013

Australia A, captained by Aaron Finch, toured Zimbabwe and South Africa in July and August 2013, playing one first-class match against a Zimbabwe Select XI and two against South Africa A, losing the second. They also took part in a triangular one-day series with South Africa A and India A in August; they headed the table, but lost the final to India A.

At Harare (Country Club), July 18–20, 2013. **Australia A won by 80 runs. ‡Australia A 226** (M. C. Henriques 71, G. J. Maxwell 61; K. M. Jarvis 4-54, E. Chigumbura 3-42) **and 156** (A. J. Doolan 52; N. Mushangwe 3-43, E. Chigumbura 4-26); **Zimbabwe Select XI 142** (J. R. Hazlewood 3-22, Fawad Ahmed 4-54, P. J. Cummins 3-19) **and 160** (H. Masakadza 69; J. R. Hazlewood 3-32, Fawad Ahmed 4-23). *Fifteen wickets fell on the first day, and 19 on the second, before Australia A beat a full-strength Zimbabwean team on the third morning.*

At Pretoria, July 24–27, 2013. **Drawn. Australia A 474-5 dec** (A. J. Finch 51, D. A. Warner 193, G. J. Maxwell 155*) **and 254-6** (A. J. Finch 88); **‡South Africa A 614-7 dec** (D. Elgar 283, J. L. Ontong 60, T. L. Tsolekile 159; Fawad Ahmed 3-177). *David Warner, sent to southern Africa after being suspended from the Ashes tour, and Glenn Maxwell added 204 for Australia A's fifth wicket. But a sixth-wicket stand of 267 between Dean Elgar, who batted 561 minutes for his second double-hundred, and Thami Tsolekile, who also reached a career-best, helped South Africa A take a 140-run lead. Australia A batted out the final day – during which Warner and Tsolekile exchanged words before the umpires intervened.*

At Rustenburg, July 31–August 2, 2013. **South Africa A won by seven wickets. ‡Australia A 146** (N. J. Maddinson 88; M. de Lange 3-45, B. E. Hendricks 5-52) **and 277** (N. J. Maddinson 90; S. R. Harmer 8-87); **South Africa A 356** (D. Elgar 83, R. R. Rossouw 115*; Fawad Ahmed 4-80) **and 71-3**. *Left-armer Beuran Hendricks reduced Australia A to 68-7 on the opening day, and off-spinner Simon Harmer wrecked them on the third; only Nic Maddinson did much to delay South Africa A in either innings, and they wrapped up victory with a day to spare.*

INDIA A IN SOUTH AFRICA, 2013

India A, captained by Cheteshwar Pujara, toured South Africa in August 2013, playing two first-class matches against South Africa A, which they drew 1–1. They also took part in a triangular one-day series with South Africa A and Australia A in August, beating Australia A by 50 runs in the final.

At Rustenburg, August 17–20, 2013. **India A won by an innings and 13 runs.** ‡**India A 582-9 dec** (C. A. Pujara 137, R. G. Sharma 119, S. K. Raina 135; W. D. Parnell 3-93, J-P. Duminy 3-80); **South Africa A 357** (R. R. Rossouw 57, J-P. Duminy 84; I. C. Pandey 4-46, S. K. Raina 3-40) **and 212** (T. Bavuma 65; I. C. Pandey 3-25, Shami Ahmed 3-33). *India A batted for most of the first two days, running up three centuries. With Ishwar Pandey breaking several significant partnerships, they were able to enforce the follow-on on the final morning, and South Africa A could not find their way back from 15-3.*

At Pretoria, August 24–27, 2013. **South Africa A won by 121 runs.** ‡**South Africa A 341** (W. D. Parnell 91, S. R. Harmer 96; I. C. Pandey 3-67, S. Nadeem 3-99) **and 166-5 dec** (D. Elgar 62; S. Nadeem 3-56); **India A 201** (C. A. Pujara 54; B. E. Hendricks 5-36, S. R. Harmer 4-74) **and 185** (A. M. Rahane 86, W. P. Saha 77*; B. E. Hendricks 6-27, S. R. Harmer 3-79). *South Africa A recovered from 97-6 on the opening day, when Wayne Parnell and Simon Harmer added 186. Parnell complained of breathlessness after bowling two overs, was sent to hospital and took no further part, but Beuran Hendricks collected a career-best 11-63 and Harmer 7-153 to level the series. Apart from Ajinkya Rahane and Wriddhaman Saha, who came together at 125 in India A's second innings, no batsman passed five in India A's second innings. They added 160 – only three times in all first-class cricket had one partnership formed a higher proportion of a completed innings than their 86.48%.*

NEW ZEALAND A IN INDIA AND SRI LANKA, 2013-14

New Zealand A, captained by Tom Latham and Andrew Ellis, toured India and Sri Lanka in August and September 2013, playing two first-class matches in each country, all drawn until they lost the last game with Sri Lanka A. They also contested a one-day series, losing 3–0 to India A and 2–1 to Sri Lanka A.

At Visakhapatnam (Port Trust), August 28–30, 2013. **Drawn.** ‡**New Zealand A 310** (L. Ronchi 125, T. D. Astle 63; J. S. Saxena 6-106); **India A 388-7** (V. H. Zol 110, A. M. Nayar 102*; T. D. Astle 3-106). *Only three days were scheduled, and the first was lost to rain. Off-spinner Jalaj Saxena then reduced New Zealand A to 55-4, before Luke Ronchi hit back with 125 in 110 balls. The final day brought a century on debut from Vijay Zol, an 18-year-old left-hander from Maharashtra, and a hundred from India A captain Abhishek Nayar.*

At Visakhapatnam (Rajasekhara Reddy), September 2–5, 2013. **Drawn.** ‡**New Zealand A 437** (C. J. Anderson 100, A. P. Devcich 115, D. A. J. Bracewell 96; I. S. Sodhi 57; D. S. Kulkarni 3-53) **and 176-3** (T. W. M. Latham 61, C. Cachopa 76); **India A 430** (V. A. Jagadeesh 91, M. C. Juneja 193, A. M. Nayar 57; M. R. Gillespie 4-88, D. A. J. Bracewell 3-88). *New Zealand A recovered from another shaky start (43-4) thanks to 165 for the fifth wicket from Corey Anderson and Anton Devcich, who scored a maiden century, followed by 162 for the ninth from Doug Bracewell and Ish Sodhi. Manpreet Juneja narrowly missed a double-hundred, but secured near-parity on first innings; rain cut short the final day.*

At Dambulla, September 17–20, 2013. **Drawn. Sri Lanka A 252** (J. K. Silva 103; I. S. Sodhi 3-34) **and 498-7 dec** (M. D. K. J. Perera 147, K. D. K. Vithanage 70, S. M. A. Priyanjan 103, P. C. de Silva 103*; D. A. J. Bracewell 3-102); ‡**New Zealand A 299-9 dec** (C. Cachopa 104; M. D. K. Perera 6-87, P. C. de Silva 3-60). *Kaushal Silva managed a century between frequent showers over the first two days, but Carl Cachopa gave New Zealand A the lead, despite nine wickets for the spinners. When they batted again, however, Sri Lanka A charged ahead: Kushal Perera scored 147 in 139 balls, while Ashan Priyanjan and Chaturanga de Silva were almost as brisk. There was no attempt to set a target.*

At Pallekele, September 23–26, 2013. **Sri Lanka A won by 168 runs.** ‡**Sri Lanka A 555-6 dec** (F. D. M. Karunaratne 84, J. K. Silva 193, L. D. Chandimal 80, K. D. K. Vithanage 116) **and 275-4 dec** (F. D. M. Karunaratne 62, M. D. K. J. Perera 55, K. D. K. Vithanage 71*; A. P. Devcich 3-120); **New Zealand A 391** (T. W. M. Latham 77, L. Ronchi 134; A. N. P. R. Fernando 4-101, P. M. Pushpakumara 3-86) **and 271** (D. A. J. Bracewell 104*; M. D. K. Perera 3-93, P. C. de Silva 3-55, P. M. Pushpakumara 4-60). *Kaushal Silva steered Sri Lanka A towards a substantial total with his second hundred of the series. Though Ronchi scored at almost a run a ball, he lacked support, and more quick Sri Lankan runs set a target of 440. It looked over at 127-7, but New Zealand A's last three wickets added 144, with No. 9 Bracewell scoring an unbeaten maiden century; he struck eight fours and seven sixes in just 85 balls. He could only postpone Sri Lanka A's victory, however, and slow left-armer Malinda Pushpakumara completed it with his seventh wicket of the match.*

WEST INDIES A IN INDIA, 2013-14

West Indies A, captained by Kirk Edwards, toured India in September and October 2013, playing three first-class matches with India A; they drew the series 1–1. Under Kieran Powell's leadership, West Indies A had already taken a one-day series 2–1, while India A won a one-off Twenty20 game.

At Mysore, September 25–28, 2013. **West Indies A won by 162 runs. West Indies A 429** (K. C. Brathwaite 92, K. A. Edwards 91, A. B. Fudadin 86*; Parvez Rasool 5-116) **and 130-3 dec** (K. O. A. Powell 68); ‡**India A 245** (M. C. Juneja 84; V. Permaul 5-85, N. O. Miller 4-61) **and 152** (M. C. Juneja 70; N. O. Miller 5-40, V. Permaul 3-56). *West Indian spinners claimed 19 wickets and the early advantage in the series. Solid batting from Kraigg Brathwaite, Kirk Edwards and Assad Fudadin paved the way for a 184-run first-innings lead, and Edwards was able to declare overnight to set a last-day target of 315. India A scraped only 152 from 85.4 overs.*

At Shimoga, October 2–5, 2013. **Drawn. ‡West Indies A 406** (K. C. Brathwaite 82, A. B. Fudadin 63, L. R. Johnson 91, N. O. Miller 64*; B. A. Bhatt 7-113) **and 223-3** (K. C. Brathwaite 104*, N. Deonarine 93); **India A 359** (V. A. Jagadeesh 86, A. M. Nayar 89, U. Kaul 64*; M. L. Cummins 3-58). *India A included three former Test stars seeking a comeback – Gautam Gambhir, Virender Sehwag and Zaheer Khan – but they managed only 18 runs and two wickets between them. A slow, flat pitch produced stalemate, though left-arm spinner Bhargav Bhatt claimed career-best figures, and Brathwaite scored 186 in the match for once out.*

At Hubli, October 9–12, 2013. **India A won by an innings and 54 runs. West Indies A 268** (L. R. Johnson 81; D. S. Kulkarni 3-60, A. M. Nayar 4-61) **and 242** (N. Deonarine 99; Zaheer Khan 4-59); ‡**India A 564-9 dec** (G. Gambhir 123, C. A. Pujara 306*; A. R. Nurse 3-106). *India A levelled the series in an eventful game. Cheteshwar Pujara became the ninth batsman to score three first-class triple-hundreds, and only the second Indian, following his Saurashtra team-mate Ravi Jadeja 11 months earlier. He hit 33 fours in 579 minutes and 415 balls, adding 207 for the second wicket with Gambhir, despite the distractions of a swarm of bees invading the pitch and news of Sachin Tendulkar's impending retirement. Injuries forced West Indies A to use four wicketkeepers, including a substitute. For the first time in the series, the quicker bowlers played a decisive role, with Zaheer claiming four wickets as he wrapped up an innings win.*

ICC INTERCONTINENTAL CUP, 2011–13

Ireland completed a unique treble in 2013, adding their fourth Intercontinental Cup title to earlier triumphs in the World Twenty20 Qualifier and the 50-over World Cricket League. It led to renewed talk of Test status – something Cricket Ireland had been aiming for by 2020 – although the opportunity may just come more quickly, as the far-reaching ICC changes announced early in 2014 included a proposal that the leading Associate should play off against the bottom-ranked Test team. That is something this Ireland side would relish: "It would be a shame if none of the current team got to pull on a Test-match jersey for Ireland," said all-rounder Kevin O'Brien.

In many respects the WCL Championship was the bigger event of the year, as it carried the carrot of World Cup qualification for the top two. Ireland made their priorities clear when they did not enforce the follow-on in their four-day match against UAE, preferring to rest their bowlers for the upcoming one-day encounters – both of which they won, to strengthen their hold on the table. Afghanistan, Ireland's opponents in all three finals in 2013, claimed the second automatic place; the other teams had to endure a further qualification tournament, early in 2014, from which Scotland and the UAE progressed, along with Hong Kong and Papua New Guinea from the WCL's second division.

ICC INTERCONTINENTAL CUP TABLE

	Played	Won	Lost	Drawn	Abandoned	First-inns lead	Points
IRELAND	7	5	0	2	0	6	116
AFGHANISTAN	7	5	0	2	0	4	104
Scotland	7	2	2	2	1	3	66
United Arab Emirates	7	2	1	4	0	3	60
Namibia	7	3	3	1	0	3	57
Canada	7	1	4	1	1	2	43
Kenya	7	1	5	0	1	1	42
Netherlands	7	0	4	2	1	0	36

Win = 14pts. Tie = 7pts. Draw with more than ten hours lost to weather = 7pts. Draw with less than ten hours lost to weather = 3pts. First-innings lead = 6pts. Tie on first innings = 3pts. Abandoned = 10pts. Details of previous matches in this tournament appeared in Wisdens 2012 and 2013.

At Abu Dhabi, March 12–14, 2013. **Afghanistan won by an innings and five runs. Scotland 125** (Izatullah Dawlatzai 6-57, Mirwais Ashraf 3-31) **and 145** (K. J. Coetzer 57; Dawlat Zadran 4-51, Izatullah Dawlatzai 5-37); ‡**Afghanistan 275** (Rahmat Shah 67*; J. H. Davey 4-53). *Afghanistan 20pts. First-class debuts: Mohibullah Paak, Rahmat Shah (Afghanistan). MoM: Izatullah Dawlatzai. Scotland were up against it after lurching from 35-2 to 44-7; they reached three figures thanks only to a last-wicket stand of 57 between Rob Taylor of Leicestershire and Safyaan Sharif (20). Afghanistan were in front by the end of the first day, and one wicket short of victory at stumps on the second. Dawlat Zadran ended the match with the sixth delivery of the third. His new-ball partner Izatullah Dawlatzai, who modelled his action on Pakistan's Mohammad Asif, took 11 wickets, and won the match award (which was subject to local sponsorship and not presented at all games).*

At Sharjah, March 12–15, 2013. **Drawn. Ireland 589-7 dec** (W. T. S. Porterfield 82, P. R. Stirling 61, E. C. Joyce 155, N. J. O'Brien 126, G. C. Wilson 84) **and 188-3** (W. T. S. Porterfield 101*, A. R. White 52); ‡**United Arab Emirates 360** (Arshad Ali 95, Khurram Khan 115, S. P. Patil 89*; D. T. Johnston 4-62). *UAE 3pts, Ireland 9pts. MoM: E. C. Joyce. First-class debuts: Mohammad Azam,*

Mohammad Naveed, R. Mustafa, Saqib Shah (UAE). *Ireland's highest first-class total owed much to a third-wicket stand of 181 between Ed Joyce, who made his first century for them since 2005, and Niall O'Brien. The UAE replied in dogged fashion, with Arshad Ali and 42-year-old Khurram Khan putting on 187 for the second wicket in 77 overs. When they were all out an hour into the final day, Ireland decided not to enforce the follow-on, sparing their bowlers in advance of two 50-over WCL matches – crucial for 2015 World Cup qualification – later in the week. It worked, as they won both.*

At Dubai (ICC Academy), March 18–21, 2013. **Kenya won by four wickets. Canada 358** (N. R. Kumar 89, Raza-ur-Rehman 51; E. A. Otieno 3-50) **and 175** (H. Patel 93; N. N. Odhiambo 5-43); ‡**Kenya 406** (T. Mishra 57, R. R. Patel 130; R. K. Pathan 3-76, A. S. Hansra 3-77) **and 129-6** (H. Patel 4-41). *Kenya 20pts. MoM: R. R. Patel. First-class debuts:* N. Dutta, R. K. Pathan, Raza-ur-Rehman (Canada). *Only 18, but an international cricketer for three years, Nitish Kumar top-scored in Canada's solid first innings. But – after Rakep Patel's fine century helped Kenya into the lead – Kumar was out for a duck in the second. Hiral Patel made his highest first-class score (and later added his best bowling figures), but after Nehemiah Odhiambo polished off the tail, Kenya needed only 128. They made a meal of it, losing Irfan Karim first ball, and five more besides, but Tanmay Mishra held firm, and hit the winning boundary deep into the fourth day.*

At Windhoek (Wanderers), April 11–14, 2013. **Namibia won by 82 runs. Namibia 276** (S. F. Burger 71, R. van Schoor 110; T. van der Gugten 7-68, Mudassar Bukhari 3-38) **and 336** (S. J. Baard 85, C. G. Williams 65; T. van der Gugten 3-53); ‡**Netherlands 293** (M. J. G. Rippon 65, T. L. W. Cooper 83; L. Klazinga 3-62, C. Viljoen 4-76) **and 237** (T. L. W. Cooper 109; B. M. Scholtz 5-58). *Namibia 14pts, Netherlands 6pts. Namibia recovered from 53-4 thanks to a stand of 163 between Sarel Burger and Raymond van Schoor. Sydney-born seamer Timm van der Gugten took seven wickets (and ten in the match). Nine men reached double figures as the Netherlands eked out a lead, but nine Namibians matched them in their second innings to set a target of 320. It proved too much for the Dutch, despite Tom Cooper's second classy knock of the match.*

At Deventer, July 1–3, 2013. **Ireland won by 279 runs.** ‡**Ireland 332** (J. Anderson 127, J. F. Mooney 63; D. T. Doram 5-82) **and 222-8 dec** (A. R. White 62); **Netherlands 148** (T. L. W. Cooper 51; G. H. Dockrell 3-32) **and 127** (M. C. Sorensen 3-32, G. H. Dockrell 6-39). *Ireland 20pts. First-class debuts:* D. T. Doram, J. F. M. Gruijters, Q. W. M. Gunning (Netherlands). *John Anderson's maiden first-class century underpinned Ireland's useful total, although his dismissal prompted a collapse of five for 45; the 6ft 7in 15-year-old slow left-armer Daniel Doram, born in Sint Maarten in the Caribbean, finished with a five-for on first-class debut. Despite predictable resistance from Cooper, the Netherlands fell well short. A fine spell from another precocious left-arm spinner, George Dockrell (now three years into his international career, at 20), polished them off with a day to spare.*

At Aberdeen, July 7–9, 2013. **Scotland won by 152 runs.** ‡**Scotland 212** (R. D. Berrington 62, C. S. MacLeod 67; N. N. Odhiambo 3-29, J. O. Ngoche 4-58) **and 230** (E. F. Chalmers 106; J. O. Ngoche 3-62, H. A. Varaiya 5-62); **Kenya 101** (A. C. Evans 6-30, R. M. Haq 3-27) **and 189** (C. O. Obuya 91*). *Scotland 20pts. First-class debut:* C. D. Wallace (Scotland). *Scotland kept up their challenge with a comfortable victory in a low-scoring game at Mannofield Park. They were in control once seamer Alasdair Evans demolished Kenya for 101 with a career-best 6-30, five of them bowled or lbw. A maiden first-class hundred for Ewan Chalmers left a target of 342, which Kenya never threatened, despite 206 minutes of defiance from skipper Collins Obuya.*

At King City, August 1–4, 2013. **Drawn. United Arab Emirates 116** (S. P. Patil 76*; J. O. A. Gordon 6-43) **and 207-4** (Khurram Khan 121*); ‡**Canada 369-6 dec** (N. R. Kumar 103, A. S. Hansra 67, D. Daesrath 111; Amjad Javed 3-72). *Canada 9pts, UAE 3pts. First-class debuts:* Nasir Aziz (UAE). *No play was possible until late on the second day, and Canada took charge after UAE's last five wickets clattered for 14. Kumar and Damodar Daesrath combined in a fifth-wicket stand of 170, but UAE – led by Khurram Khan, whose 121* occupied 337 minutes – batted out almost the entire final day.*

At Windhoek (Wanderers), August 4–6, 2013. **Afghanistan won by ten wickets.** ‡**Namibia 190** (S. J. Baard 72; Mohammad Nabi 6-33) **and 168** (Izatullah Dawlatzai 5-23); **Afghanistan 354** (Nawroz Mangal 59, Asghar Stanikzai 127, Dawlat Zadran 50; B. M. Scholtz 5-123) **and 5-0.** *Afghanistan 20pts. First-class debut:* M. P. Delport (Namibia). *Afghanistan showed up Namibia's* *suspect batting, twice dismissing them for fewer than 200, and in between Asghar Stanikzai made a fine century. Izatullah Dawlatzai ended Namibia's second innings with a hat-trick.*

At King City, August 22–24, 2013. **Canada won by eight wickets. Netherlands 164** (E. S. Szwarczynski 57; J. O. A. Gordon 4-56, Raza-ur-Rehman 4-8) **and 336** (E. S. Szwarczynski 85, D. L. S. van Bunge 54, P. M. Seelaar 75*; J. O. A. Gordon 4-93, H. S. Baidwan 4-69); ‡**Canada 436** (R. Gunasekera 150, Salman Nazar 60, A. S. Hansra 53; V. J. Kingma 4-89) **and 68-2**. *Canada 20pts. First-class debuts: C. Pervez, Salman Nazar (Canada); V. J. Kingma, P. A. van Meekeren (Netherlands). Canada completed their only victory of the tournament, winning inside three days after opener Ruvindu Gunasekera extended his maiden first-class hundred to 150. After Eric Szwarczynski's second patient half-century of the match, Pieter Seelaar's hitting from No. 9 staved off an innings defeat, but Canada's target was a modest one.*

At Dublin (Clontarf), September 11–14, 2013. **Ireland won by an innings and 44 runs. Scotland 138** (C. A. Young 4-53, G. J. McCarter 3-13) **and 168** (S. M. Sharif 60; M. C. Sorensen 5-37); ‡**Ireland 350** (P. R. Stirling 65, J. Anderson 56; M. M. Iqbal 4-68, R. M. Haq 4-69). *Ireland 20pts. First-class debuts: A. R. McBrine, C. A. Young (Ireland); H. J. W. Gardiner (Scotland). A comprehensive victory over their old rivals ensured Ireland top spot in the table, which meant a draw against Afghanistan in the final would be enough to give them the trophy. Scotland's modest batting efforts would have been even more embarrassing had No. 9 Sharif not top-scored in both innings, with 41 and 60.*

At Sharjah, September 22–23, 2013. **United Arab Emirates won by nine wickets.** ‡**Namibia 90** (Ahmed Raza 7-37) **and 155** (E. H. S. N. Silva 3-31, Nasir Aziz 5-48); **United Arab Emirates 230** (Shaiman Anwar 81; J. J. Smit 3-33, C. Viljoen 4-32) **and 17-1**. *UAE 20pts. MoM: Ahmed Raza. First-class debuts: M. D. du Preez, C. F. Snyman (Namibia); Kamran Shazad (UAE). Namibia's fragile batting collapsed twice, first to the local-born slow left-armer Ahmed Raza, to hand the UAE a facile two-day victory. Khurram Khan's 49 left him as the tournament's leading scorer with 674; his team-mate Swapnil Patil was third with 401, behind Ireland's Andrew White (469). Medium-pacer Christi Viljoen's four wickets made him the leading wicket-taker with 39, which Dockrell of Ireland equalled in the final.*

At Dubai (ICC Academy), October 6–8, 2013. **Afghanistan won by eight wickets. Kenya 162 and 140** (Sayed Shirzad 3-17, Yamin Ahmadzai 3-17); ‡**Afghanistan 234** (Rahmat Shah 144; R. G. Aga 5-46) **and 70-2**. *Afghanistan 20pts. MoM: Rahmat Shah. First-class debuts: Fazal Niazai, Hashmatullah Sahidi, Nasim Baras, Rahmatullah Sahaq, Sayed Shirzad, Yamin Ahmadzai (Afghanistan). With qualification for the final assured, Afghanistan fielded an experimental side with six first-class debutants – and still won easily. Their batting was dominated by Rahmat Shah, whose 144 included five sixes. Kenya dipped to 36-5 in the first hour, and never really recovered.*

Final

At Dubai (ICC Academy), December 10–13, 2013. **Ireland won by 122 runs. Ireland 187** (J. Anderson 55; Dawlat Zadran 4-44, Rahmat Shah 3-36) **and 341** (E. C. Joyce 78, N. J. O'Brien 87; Mohammad Nabi 4-38); ‡**Afghanistan 182** (G. H. Dockrell 3-52, J. F. Mooney 5-45) **and 224** (Rahmat Shah 86*; J. F. Mooney 5-36, G. H. Dockrell 3-58). *MoM: J. F. Mooney. Ireland won the Intercontinental Cup for the fourth time out of six, once again pipping Afghanistan to claim their third title of the year in all formats, despite a hesitant start. They were rescued from 106-6 by a partnership of 54 between Anderson and John Mooney, whose innocent-looking medium-pacers then accounted for the first four wickets as Afghanistan struggled too. Ireland batted better second time, with Joyce and Niall O'Brien adding 110 for the third wicket, then Kevin O'Brien's 47 from 43 balls propelled them towards a lead of 346. It was more than enough: Mooney took four more wickets, to finish with ten in a match for the first time. Rahmat Shah was left high and dry after facing 246 balls. Ireland's captain William Porterfield paid tribute to the retiring Trent Johnston, 39, who was forced to watch the closing stages from the dressing-room, nursing an injury: "He has been a massive figure since a lot of this team started playing. This was the perfect send-off for Trent. He is a traditionalist of the game – he loves this format."*

ICC WORLD CRICKET LEAGUE CHAMPIONSHIP TABLE

	Played	Won	Lost	Tied	No Result	Points	Net run-rate
IRELAND	14	11	1	1	1	24	0.98
AFGHANISTAN	14	9	4	0	1	19	0.76
United Arab Emirates	14	9	5	0	0	18	0.35
Netherlands	14	8	4	1	1	18	0.62
Scotland	14	7	6	0	1	15	−0.11
Kenya	14	5	9	0	0	10	−0.46
Namibia	14	2	12	0	4	4	−1.16
Canada	14	1	11	0	2	4	−0.96

Win = 2pts. Tie/no result = 1pt. The top two teams qualified for the 2015 World Cup. Where teams were level on points, the one with more wins was placed higher. All matches had official one-day international status, except those involving Namibia and the United Arab Emirates. Details of previous matches in this tournament appeared in Wisdens 2012 *and* 2013.

At Sharjah, March 6, 2013. **Afghanistan won by seven wickets.** ‡Scotland 199-8 (50 overs) (R. D. Berrington 51; Gulbadeen Naib 4-31); **Afghanistan 203-3** (33.5 overs) (Nawroz Mangal 112*, Samiullah Shenwari 55*). MoM: Nawroz Mangal. *One-day international debuts: Mohibullah Paak, Rahmat Shah (Afghanistan); M. W. Machan, D. Murphy, I. Wardlaw (Scotland). Nawroz Mangal, recently replaced as captain, went in first and blitzed 112* from 96 balls – including 25 off a Preston Mommsen over – as Afghanistan easily overhauled Scotland's modest total. He claimed the match award (which was subject to local sponsorship and not presented in all games).*

At Sharjah, March 8, 2013. **Afghanistan won by five wickets.** Scotland 259-9 (50 overs) (K. J. Coetzer 133, J. H. Davey 64); **‡Afghanistan 261-5** (48.4 overs) (Mohammad Nabi 51). MoM: Samiullah Shenwari. *One-day international debut: R. M. L. Taylor (Scotland). A disciplined batting performance both Afghanistan home in a much closer game, notable for Kyle Coetzer's fine 133 from 136 balls; he shared a second-wicket stand of 134 with Josh Davey. Samiullah Shenwari took 3-42 with his leg-spin, and later scored 30*. Rahmat Shah's dismissal for 35 left Afghanistan wobbling at 160-4 in the 33rd over, but Mohammad Nabi biffed 51 from 44 balls to swing the match back their way. The result left both sides on 11 points, two behind leaders Ireland.*

At Dubai (ICC Academy), March 11, 2013. **Kenya won by six wickets.** ‡Canada 227-8 (50 overs) (R. Gunasekera 72, Raza-ur-Rehman 70; E. A. Otieno 4-33); **Kenya 228-4** (47.4 overs) (I. A. Karim 65). MoM: E. A. Otieno. *One-day international debut: N. Dutta, Raza-ur-Rehman (Canada). The Zimbabwe-born debutant Raza-ur-Rehman hit 70 to lift Canada to a reasonable total, but Kenya – anchored by Irfan Karim's 108-ball 65 – were always in charge.*

At Dubai (ICC Academy), March 13, 2013. **Kenya won by six wickets.** ‡Canada 253-9 (50 overs) (Rizwan Cheema 55, Raza-ur-Rehman 51); **Kenya 254-4** (48 overs) (I. A. Karim 112, C. O. Obuya 57). MoM: I. A. Karim. *One-day international debuts: R. K. Pathan (Canada). Karim again led the way as Kenya chased down a competitive total, this time making 112, his maiden hundred in his fourth ODI. Earlier, Rizwan Cheema was unusually restrained in scoring 55 from 66 balls.*

At Sharjah, March 18, 2013. **Ireland won by six wickets.** United Arab Emirates 165 (46.4 overs) (S. P. Patil 65); ‡Ireland 169-5 (42 overs) (G. C. Wilson 72*). MoM: G. C. Wilson. *A fine bowling performance, in which Alex Cusack took 3-21 and Paul Stirling 3-32, set up Ireland's win with eight overs to spare. They were in trouble at 51-4, but were rescued by Gary Wilson's 72*.*

At Sharjah, March 20, 2013. **Ireland won by six wickets.** United Arab Emirates 196 (49.4 overs) (D. T. Johnston 4-25); ‡Ireland 199-4 (47.4 overs) (W. T. S. Porterfield 77). MoM: D. T. Johnston. *Ireland strengthened their position by completing the double over the UAE. Trent Johnston took two early wickets, then returned to dismiss the UAE's leading batsmen, Swapnil Patil and Khurram Khan, in successive overs, both for 30. William Porterfield oversaw the chase with 77 from 104 balls and, after he was out at 138-4, Wilson (39*) and Kevin O'Brien (25*) calmly closed the deal.*

At Windhoek (Wanderers), April 16, 2013. **Netherlands won by 31 runs.** Netherlands 268-9 (50 overs) (W. Barresi 60); ‡Namibia 237 (48.5 overs) (C. G. Williams 116). *The Netherlands overcame a poor start – 17-2 in the fifth over – to post a total that proved too much for Namibia, despite Craig Williams's hard-working century. The Netherlands moved second in the table.*

At Windhoek (Wanderers), April 18, 2013. **Netherlands won by one wicket. Namibia 236-5** (50 overs) (R. van Schoor 93*, N. R. P. Scholtz 51*); ‡**Netherlands 240-9** (48 overs) (W. Barresi 58, D. L. S. van Bunge 60). *Raymond van Schoor – out first ball in the previous game – made 93 from 130 deliveries to supervise a competitive total. The Dutch looked secure at 150-3, but slipped to 178-7. Daan van Bunge coaxed his side level – but then got out to his 83rd ball, leaving last man Ahsan Malik Jamil to face the music. He edged the winning four off Christi Viljoen.*

At Aberdeen, June 30, 2013. **Scotland won by 12 runs. Scotland 242-4** (50 overs) (M. W. Machan 114, P. L. Mommsen 63*); ‡**Kenya 230** (49.1 overs) (M. A. Ouma 57, T. Mishra 61, R. R. Patel 50; I. Wardlaw 4-43). *One-day international debut: F. R. J. Coleman (Scotland). A maiden international century for Sussex's Matt Machan – and his fourth-wicket stand of 162 with Mommsen – propelled Scotland to 242, which looked enough when Alex Obanda and Collins Obuya both fell for ducks. But Kenya got close, with Tanmay Mishra and Rakep Patel putting on 84 for the fifth wicket, before Yorkshire's Iain Wardlaw claimed three wickets in nine balls.*

At Aberdeen, July 2–3, 2013. **Scotland won by four wickets** (D/L). **Kenya 183** (46.3 overs) (T. Mishra 59); ‡**Scotland 139-6** (33.4 overs) (K. J. Coetzer 57). *Rain shortened the first day, which ended with Scotland 22-0 from 6.2 overs, then further interruption on the reserve day meant their target was revised to 139 in 35. They wobbled from 84-1 to 117-5 after 31, but sneaked home.*

At Amstelveen, July 7, 2013. **Ireland won by 88 runs.** ‡**Ireland 236** (49.5 overs) (W. T. S. Porterfield 79, N. J. O'Brien 70); **Netherlands 148** (36 overs) (W. Barresi 55; K. J. O'Brien 4-13). *One-day international debut: M. J. G. Rippon (Netherlands). Porterfield and Niall O'Brien put on 125 for the third wicket, lifting Ireland to a total the Netherlands never threatened once Tom Cooper fell to Kevin O'Brien for 8.*

At Amstelveen, July 9, 2013. **Tied.** ‡**Ireland 268-5** (50 overs) (E. C. Joyce 96*, N. J. O'Brien 50); **Netherlands 268-9** (50 overs). *For the second match running a big third-wicket stand featuring Niall O'Brien – 113 this time, with Ed Joyce – set up an imposing Irish total. The Netherlands made a good start, reaching 135-1 in the 27th over, and were 244-5 in the 47th. But a wicket fell in that over and each of the next three, and Ireland looked to have it won when No. 9 Michael Rippon needed 11 off the last two balls, from John Mooney. But he slogged a four, then a six over long-on, to force a tie. Ireland had gone into the match knowing a win would ensure qualification for the 2015 World Cup, and were briefly distraught – before realising that one point for a tie was enough.*

At King City, August 6, 2013. **United Arab Emirates won by 46 runs. United Arab Emirates 269-4** (50 overs) (Shaiman Anwar 102*, R. Mustafa 68*); ‡**Canada 223** (46.5 overs) (R. Gunasekera 50, Usman Limbada 58; Mohammad Naveed 4-39, Nasir Aziz 4-32). *The UAE reached a big total thanks to a fifth-wicket stand of 147* in 20 overs between Shaiman Anwar and Rohan Mustafa. Canada lost regular wickets to seamer Mohammad Naveed and off-spinner Nasir Aziz.*

At King City, August 8, 2013. **United Arab Emirates won by two wickets. Canada 179-9** (50 overs) (H. Patel 53; Nasir Aziz 4-20); ‡**United Arab Emirates 183-8** (48.5 overs) (Shaiman Anwar 57; Rizwan Cheema 4-16). *MoM: Nasir Aziz. Nasir Aziz took four wickets for the second match running to set up the UAE's double, although their batsmen made heavy weather of a target of 180.*

At Windhoek (Wanderers), August 9, 2013. **Afghanistan won by 190 runs. Afghanistan 289-4** (50 overs) (Mohammad Shahzad 113, Karim Sadiq 50, Mohammad Nabi 81*); ‡**Namibia 99** (32.1 overs) (Mohammad Nabi 5-12). *Mohammad Shahzad's century, backed up by Mohammad Nabi's 81* from 45 balls, flayed the bowlers before Nabi's off-spin (8.1–2–12–5) ensured a small one for Namibia.*

At Windhoek (Wanderers), August 11, 2013. **Afghanistan won by five wickets.** ‡**Namibia 193** (46.2 overs) (R. A. H. Pieters 57, S. J. Baard 67; Hamid Hassan 4-32); **Afghanistan 199-5** (31.4 overs) (Mohammad Shahzad 62). *Namibia appeared on course for a reasonable score at 174-3 in the 38th over, but lost their last seven wickets for 19. The result was never in doubt once Mohammad Shahzad and Nawroz Mangal (41) shared an opening stand of 106 in 18 overs. Mohammad Nabi clouted 46* from 23 balls, and ended the match with his fourth six.*

At King City, August 27–28, 2013. **No result. Netherlands 143** (27.5 overs) (B. N. Cooper 74; K. Kamyuka 4-38); ‡**Canada 62-1** (10 overs). *A late start meant the match was reduced to 28 overs* *a side, but more rain curtailed the first day with Canada ten overs into their reply, and prevented any play on the reserve day.*

At King City, August 29, 2013. **Netherlands won by nine wickets. Canada 67** (24.4 overs) (T. van der Gugten 5-24, P. M. Seelaar 4-15); ‡**Netherlands 70-1** (10.4 overs) (S. J. Myburgh 52*). *MoM:* T. van der Gugten. *The Netherlands played the match under protest at the state of the ground, whose drainage was lamentable. They needn't have worried: Timm van der Gugten reduced Canada to 7-5; it was 10-6 when Mudassar Bukhari dismissed Ashish Bagai, who had been restored as Canada's captain. After some brief resistance, slow left-armer Seelaar took four wickets to complete the rout, then Stephan Myburgh rushed the Dutch to victory with almost 40 overs to spare.*

At Belfast (Stormont), September 6, 2013. **Ireland won by one wicket. ‡Scotland 223-9** (50 overs) (P. L. Mommsen 91*; G. H. Dockrell 4-24); **Ireland 225-9** (49.5 overs) (W. T. S. Porterfield 62). *One-day international debut: E. J. Richardson (Ireland). Ireland had already reached the 2015 World Cup, but now ended Scotland's chances of automatic qualification with a narrow victory which looked unlikely when they dipped to 146-7, chasing 224. But the Irish tail wagged, and after Max Sorensen was out for 31, making it 209-9 with nine balls left, it boiled down to nine off the last three deliveries: Tim Murtagh (23*) carved Rob Taylor for six over long-off and four through point.*

At Belfast (Stormont), September 8, 2013. **Ireland won by seven wickets. ‡Scotland 165** (49.3 overs); **Ireland 166-3** (33 overs) (N. J. O'Brien 65*). *One-day international debut: S. R. Thompson (Ireland). Victory ensured Ireland won the competition, and the result was in little doubt once Scotland declined to 165 all out.*

At Sharjah, September 27, 2013 (day/night). **United Arab Emirates won by 158 runs. United Arab Emirates 197** (46.1 overs) (Shaiman Anwar 54); ‡**Namibia 39** (24.4 overs). *Four men made ducks as Namibia subsided for 39. The damage was done by three slow left-armers – Shadeep Silva (3-11), Ahmed Raza (3-13) and Khurram Khan (3-2). Only opener Xander Pitchers (13) made double figures.*

At Sharjah, September 29, 2013 (day/night). **United Arab Emirates won by 135 runs. United Arab Emirates 215** (50 overs) (Shaiman Anwar 57; C. Viljoen 4-40); ‡**Namibia 80** (31.3 overs). *For the second time in three days, Namibia crumbled for less than 100. Zane Green, a 16-year-old left-hander making his List A debut, came in at No. 5 at 46-3, and was still there at the end with 9* from 45 balls. The UAE went above the Netherlands to second in the table, three points ahead of Afghanistan in the race for the second World Cup spot.*

At Sharjah, October 2, 2013. **Afghanistan won by eight wickets. ‡Kenya 89** (37.5 overs) (Hamid Hassan 4-19); **Afghanistan 95-2** (17.5 overs) (Nawroz Mangal 52*). *One-day international debuts: Hashmatullah Sahidi (Afghanistan); D. M. Gondaria (Kenya). Afghanistan needed to win both their last two matches to qualify for the World Cup, and started well by dismissing Kenya for 89. They looked set for a ten-wicket victory as the openers put on 79. Nawroz Mangal won the game with his fourth six.*

At Sharjah, October 4, 2013. **Afghanistan won by seven wickets. ‡Kenya 93** (43.3 overs); ‡**Afghanistan 96-3** (20.5 overs). *One-day international debut: Gurdeep Singh (Kenya). Afghanistan's clinical victory, achieved with 175 balls to spare after bowling Kenya out for under 100 for the second time in three days, meant they qualified for their first World Cup, in 2015, a point ahead of the UAE and the Netherlands. Kenya's debutant Gurdeep Singh, a left-hand opener who made nine from 23 balls, was only 15 years 258 days old – the second-youngest player in one-day international history, behind Hasan Raza of Pakistan (whose age is the subject of some dispute).*

ICC INTERCONTINENTAL CUP FINALS

WEST INDIES WOMEN v ENGLAND WOMEN, 2013-14

Twenty20 tri-nation series: 1. West Indies   2. England   3. New Zealand
One-day internationals (3): West Indies 0, England 2

West Indies captain Merissa Aguilleira admitted they had been "roughly treated" by England in the past, but this time they gave as good as they got. Both sides ended England's second trip to the Caribbean reasonably satisfied.

Ten years after their first home one-day series – a 6–0 humiliation by Sri Lanka – West Indies confirmed they had become serious contenders. They cruised to victory in the Twenty20 triangular, also involving a weak New Zealand side. And, to huge applause at the Kensington Oval, England's captain Charlotte Edwards called them the great success of women's cricket in recent years. Meanwhile, an England team including several young players made up for the narrow defeat they suffered on their only previous one-day series in the Caribbean, back in 2009-10. They dominated both completed matches, showing that their envied but expensive Academy system wasn't all just space-age buildings and fancy gym programmes.

England won four of their seven games. "I think this was probably one of my favourite tours," said Edwards, "purely because I was put out of my comfort zone with a young squad." Her side were missing five of the senior players who had just retained the Ashes, including injured seam bowlers Katherine Brunt and Anya Shrubsole. But their Academy-graduate replacements thrived. Seventeen-year-old Sevenoaks schoolgirl Tash Farrant was economical, while Kate Cross – daughter of the West Ham FA Cup winner David – took four wickets on what was effectively her first one-day international (rain had ended her actual debut after just three overs). However, slow left-armer Holly Colvin – comfortably England's most frugal bowler – announced after the tour that she would be unavailable while pursuing other career options. The batting was shakier: Sarah Taylor made a peerless hundred and a fifty in the one-dayers, and ended the series ranked No. 2 in the world, but otherwise the highest score was Lauren Winfield's 31. And a lack of firepower hurt in the Twenty20: England hit three sixes to West Indies' 13.

The West Indians relied on two players whom Edwards called "outstanding... real stars of the game" – the graceful all-rounder Stafanie Taylor and the hard-hitting Deandra Dottin, who launched eight of those sixes. Taylor began the one-day series top of the world rankings in both batting and bowling and went on to anchor the batting, and turn the Twenty20 final into a doodle. She scored 160 runs in the tournament, while 156 came from Dottin, a cousin of current West Indies men's coach Ottis Gibson.

The hosts' other strength in the short form was spin: on helpful pitches, their slow bowlers were instrumental in two victories. Schoolgirl leg-spinner Shaquana Quintyne later became the first woman to play in the top level of Barbados men's club cricket. It was a long way from the team who, in 2003, had foundered so badly. And it confirmed that their recent World Cup final appearance had not been a glorious freak.

ENGLAND TOURING PARTY

*C. M. Edwards (Kent), T. T. Beaumont (Kent), H. L. Colvin (Sussex), K. L. Cross (Lancashire), N. E. Farrant (Kent), K. L. S. Greenway (Kent), J. L. Gunn (Nottinghamshire), D. Hazell (Yorkshire), A. E. Jones (Warwickshire), B. A. Langston (Essex), N. R. Sciver (Surrey), S. J. Taylor (Sussex), L. Winfield (Yorkshire), D. N. Wyatt (Nottinghamshire). *Coach:* P. Shaw.

Twenty20 tri-nation series

At Bridgetown, October 14, 2013 (floodlit). **West Indies won by 23 runs.** ‡West Indies 104-6 (20 overs) (D. J. S. Dottin 52); **New Zealand 81** (19 overs) (A. E. Satterthwaite 31; A. Mohammed 5-12). *PoM:* A. Mohammed. *Off-spinner Anisa Mohammed made sure West Indies defended a modest 104, taking five wickets in two late overs as New Zealand tried in vain to accelerate. Her 5-12 made her the only woman to have taken two five-fors in T20 internationals.*

At Bridgetown, October 16, 2013 (floodlit). **England won by five wickets.** ‡New Zealand 109-6 (20 overs) (S. W. Bates 48); **England 111-5** (19.1 overs) (C. M. Edwards 42). *PoM:* T. T. Beaumont. *On a humid night under floodlights, opener Charlotte Edwards's 42 and Tammy Beaumont's 29* from 23 balls helped England home with five balls to spare. Arriving at 56-4 after 11 overs, Beaumont showed nimble foot movement and attacking intent. Earlier, the accuracy of 17-year-old Tash Farrant – still at Sevenoaks School and playing in only her third T20 international – had built pressure. Her four overs cost 12, and she was unlucky to go wicketless.*

At Bridgetown, October 18, 2013 (floodlit). **West Indies won by 11 runs.** West Indies 140-6 (20 overs) (S. R. Taylor 40, D. J. S. Dottin 32; D. Hazell 3-19); ‡England 129-8 (20 overs) (C. M. Edwards 39, L. Winfield 36; S. L. Quintyne 5-16). *PoM:* S. L. Quintyne. *West Indies' 17-year-old leg-spinner Shaquana Quintyne – the sixth bowler tried – perplexed England's top order, taking 5-16 after they had made a good start in pursuit of a challenging score. On a spinner's pitch, Quintyne came on for the tenth over, struck with her fourth ball – to make England 69-1 – and then at least once in her next three overs. She put the recent success of West Indies' spinners down to coaching from Saqlain Mushtaq. Earlier, their middle order had blasted their way to the highest total of the series. They hit seven sixes in front of a crowd of 2,500, and Stacy-Ann King's 24 at the death came in ten balls.*

At Bridgetown, October 20, 2013 (floodlit). **New Zealand won by nine runs.** ‡New Zealand 101-7 (20 overs); **West Indies 92-8** (20 overs). *PoM:* R. H. Priest. *New Zealand were cruising at 44-0 halfway through their pursuit of 102. But Juliana Nero charged leg-spinner Erin Bermingham and was stumped; Bermingham produced a ripper to Deandra Dottin next delivery, and the crash had begun. In an innings broken up by rain, no one else managed more than ten. Earlier, New Zealand reached respectability thanks to wicketkeeper Rachel Priest's 17-ball 26.*

At Bridgetown, October 22, 2013 (floodlit). **England won by 19 runs.** ‡England 125-8 (20 overs) (D. N. Wyatt 37); **New Zealand 106** (20 overs) (S. W. Bates 46; J. L. Gunn 5-18, N. R. Sciver 4-21). *PoM:* J. L. Gunn. *Natalie Sciver, a Loughborough University student who had broken into the team in the summer, took a penultimate-over hat-trick – the fourth in women's T20 internationals – as New Zealand were eliminated. Sciver had Maddie Green caught, bowled Bermingham and trapped Frances Mackay lbw. The stand-in captain Jenny Gunn also profited as New Zealand needed ten an over in the closing stages; her 5-18 had been bettered for England only by Anya Shrubsole, who took 5-11, also against New Zealand, in 2011-12. Sciver had earlier made an important 23 from 21 balls.*

At Bridgetown, October 24, 2013 (floodlit). **West Indies won after an eliminator over, following a tie.** ‡West Indies 118-7 (20 overs) (S. R. Taylor 40); **England 118-7** (20 overs) (L. S. Greenway 36; S. R. Taylor 3-15). *PoM:* S. R. Taylor. *This was an arresting dress rehearsal for the final. A gripping tied match went to a one-over decider, in which England managed only six runs. West Indies' big-hitter Dottin needed just two deliveries (one a no-ball) to smack the boundaries that brought victory. On a sluggish pitch, the match had swung back and forth. West Indies toiled before Dottin hit 26 in 12 balls, then – in a tense, floodlit reply – the key moment came in the 18th over when, after reviving the innings with a brisk 36, Lydia Greenway was run out.*

West Indies 12pts, England 8pts, New Zealand 4pts.

At Bridgetown, October 26, 2013 (floodlit). **Final: West Indies won by eight wickets.** ‡**England 115-5** (20 overs) (N. R. Sciver 36*); **West Indies 119-2** (16.5 overs) (S. R. Taylor 51*, D. J. S. Dottin 46*). *PoM:* S. R. Taylor. *These sides had proved the most successful in the short history of women's Twenty20, and their previous game had been a thriller. This, though, was not. England's top order collapsed, before Stafanie Taylor and Dottin turned an undemanding chase into a stroll, putting on 78* for the third wicket. After choosing to bat, England lost three wickets on 22.*

West Indies v England

At Port-of-Spain, October 29, 2013. **First one-day international: no result. England 5-0** (3 overs) v ‡**West Indies.** *One-day international debut:* K. L. Cross (England). *Rain reduced the match to 23 overs a side, but permitted only three in total.*

At Port-of-Spain, November 1, 2013 (day/night). **Second one-day international: England won by seven wickets.** ‡**West Indies 126** (38.1 overs) (S. L. Quintyne 42; K. L. Cross 4-51, N. R. Sciver 3-19); **England 127-3** (33.3 overs) (L. Winfield 31, S. J. Taylor 55*). *PoM:* K. L. Cross. *Kate Cross produced a destructive opening spell for England, and Holly Colvin enjoyed figures of 10–6–7–2, but both were in danger of being upstaged by a fingernail-sized silver pig. This was a replica of the one clenched throughout West Ham's win in the 1980 FA Cup final by Cross's father, David. The original was lost, but the family bought a replacement as a good-luck charm. She quickly removed West Indies' top three, including Stafanie Taylor. West Indies, never comfortable against Colvin's left-arm spin, did recover slightly from 56-6, but Sarah Taylor steered England to victory.*

At Port-of-Spain, November 3, 2013 (day/night). **Second one-day international: England won by 89 runs. England 185** (50 overs) (S. J. Taylor 100; A. Mohammed 4-26); ‡**West Indies 96** (36.4 overs) (S. L. Quintyne 36*; H. L. Colvin 4-17). *PoM:* S. J. Taylor. *England became the first side to win a one-day series here in the eight rubbers since 2002-03. On a lively pitch, the difference was Sarah Taylor, who batted masterfully to make 100 from 108 balls, eventually falling to the last delivery of the innings. None of her team-mates managed more than 18. Tash Farrant ensured the West Indies reply never got started. She bowled June Ogle with her fifth ball, though even more significant was her direct hit from cover that ran out Stafanie Taylor for a duck, perhaps the only player capable of matching her namesake's effort. West Indies sank to 24-6, before Quintyne again oversaw a minor revival.*

CRICKET IN AFGHANISTAN, 2013

Part of the furniture

SHAHID HASHMI

October 4, 2013 was a red-letter day in Afghanistan's short cricketing history, as a country torn apart by war qualified for their maiden World Cup. For Mohammad Nabi, who took on the captaincy in March – and in May had to contend with the kidnapping of his father, before he was released in August – the day was "the most memorable in my life".

Afghanistan's seven-wicket win over Kenya at their surrogate headquarters in Sharjah sparked a nationwide celebration – even in the Taliban stronghold of Kandahar, where police had warned against firing bullets in the air: jubilant fans ignored the order. Thousands of Afghans tuned in to watch the match on big screens and via the ICC's live stream. Seven weeks later, another victory over Kenya sealed Afghanistan's place at a third successive World Twenty20. A few months after the Afghanistan Cricket Board had finally been upgraded to ICC Associate Member status, it all added up to a year of acceptance.

No wonder coach Kabir Khan was ecstatic: "We have taken big strides in 2013. We achieved a double distinction this year, and World Cup qualification alone will help us promote the game in Afghanistan in a big way." In 2013, $1.1m was channelled into Afghanistan cricket through the ICC's Targeted Assistance and Performance Programme, and a further $750,000 through the annual development fund. They will be provided with an additional $1m to prepare for the World Cup, and the ACB had already signed an agreement with the Pakistan Cricket Board extending access for Afghan players, coaches and umpires to Lahore's National Academy ahead of 2015.

Afghanistan actually began the year languishing in fifth in the 50-over World Cricket League Championship, and were by no means assured of securing the second automatic qualification spot for the 2015 World Cup. Despite useful preparation matches in Pakistan, Nawroz Mangal was removed as captain after five years, and replaced by Nabi. Afghanistan won six consecutive WCL matches against Scotland, Namibia and Kenya to seal second place behind Ireland.

The gap between the two leading Associates was less obvious in Twenty20: Afghanistan bounced back from defeat by the Netherlands in the qualifying tournament to win their group – and thus progress to the main competition in Bangladesh – although Ireland beat them in the final a little too easily. Ireland's greater first-class experience also proved decisive in the Intercontinental Cup final in Dubai a couple of weeks later.

Afghanistan's only senior silverware turned out to be the Asian Cricket Council Twenty20 Cup in April, when they overcame host nation Nepal in the final. Lost among the raft of qualification matches was a 28-run victory over

India Under-23s in the ACC Emerging Teams Cup in Singapore, where spinners Nabi and Rahmat Shah shared five wickets. The tournament provided the kind of interaction with Full Member nations that Afghanistan craved. "We have just over a year to prepare for the World Cup," said Kabir, "and we badly need some cricket against top countries."

Many had been waiting for the day that Afghanistan, the second-strongest Associate, would meet Bangladesh, the second-weakest Full Member – and they were due to get their wish in the opening games of the 2014 World Twenty20 and 2015 World Cup.

During the year, some of their best players gained experience in the Bangladesh Premier League, and Nabi bludgeoned 146 from 90 balls in a Dhaka Premier Division match. It was, however, a bone of contention that Bangladesh – and others – had shown little inclination to engage Afghanistan in bilateral contests since they won one-day international status in 2009.

Pakistan, similarly exiled in the UAE, were the honourable exception: Afghanistan took them down to the last ball in a one-off Twenty20 international in Sharjah in December. Pakistan were the principal backers of Afghanistan's bid for Associate status, and also influential in securing them a place in the Asia Cup for the first time. Unfortunately, Afghanistan's offer to pay their own way on a tour of Zimbabwe in January 2014 fell flat because of the hosts' financial problems.

The ACB insisted they were doing all they could to promote the game in Afghanistan, where there are only nine turf grounds to serve a player base which had spiralled to around 280,000. "Our team have brought happiness to the faces of 30 million people back home, and the board want to build on that," said ACB chief executive Noor Muhammad. "We will start to host teams in the next couple of years." From 2014, matches in the regional competition will be played over four days rather than three, while funding from UNICEF and other bodies had helped polish the infrastructure and pay for tours. The board also signed a memorandum of understanding with the ministry of education to establish cricket on the national curriculum. Sadly, there was less sign of progress in the women's game (see *Wisden 2013*, page 1216).

> "Trust me, it will go higher and higher"

The success of Afghanistan's junior sides showed that cricket's foundations extended well beyond the first generation, who had learned the game in refugee camps. Fifteen of the Under-19 squad were on ACB national contracts, and that stability began to bear fruit. Afghanistan shocked Sri Lanka in the opening match of the Under-19 Asia Cup in the UAE, and lost by just two wickets to Pakistan in the semi-final. Pakistan beat them twice more in 50-over matches in Lahore, but Afghanistan bounced back to win the last match of the series by a scarcely believable 214 runs, with Hashmatullah Sahidi scoring a century and left-arm seamer Fareed Ahmad taking seven for 21.

"We want to take big strides every year," said Kabir. "The whole nation now loves cricket. It was once a new game, but has now become a daily routine in Afghanistan. Trust me, it will go higher and higher."

Afghanistan v Scotland

At Sharjah, March 3, 2013 (floodlit). **First Twenty20 international: Afghanistan won by 27 runs.** ‡**Afghanistan 132-7** (20 overs) (Mohammad Shahzad 55, Asghar Stanikzai 30; M. W. Machan 3-23); **Scotland 105-6** (20 overs) (M. W. Machan 42*). *MoM:* Mohammad Shahzad. *Twenty20 international debuts: Hamza Hotak (Afghanistan); N. M. Carter, M. W. Machan, D. Murphy, I. Wardlaw (Scotland). Scotland took advantage of a relaxation in ICC eligibility criteria to give international debuts to four county players with Scottish heritage. Two of them, Iain Wardlaw and Neil Carter, each struck in their first over, and Matt Machan picked up three wickets in Afghanistan's late dash. But Mohammad Shahzad's 55 from 46 balls proved enough. Afghanistan's four spinners kept the runs down and, from a long way out, Scotland were resigned to using the innings as practice for the upcoming World Cricket League Championship fixtures between the sides.*

At Sharjah, March 4, 2013 (floodlit). **Second Twenty20 international: Afghanistan won by seven wickets.** ‡**Scotland 139-7** (20 overs) (C. S. MacLeod 31, M. W. Machan 39, M. M. Iqbal 31; Hamid Hassan 4-22); **Afghanistan 140-3** (17.3 overs) (Karim Sadiq 34, Mohammad Shahzad 46). *MoM:* Mohammad Shahzad. *Hamid Hassan's pace and full length were too good for four Scotland batsmen – all bowled. Karim Sadiq and Nawroz Mangal (20), deposed as captain before this series, got Afghanistan off to a flying start, before another haywire blitz from Shahzad (46 from 25 balls), which was stopped only by a superb diving catch from Gordon Drummond.*

Afghanistan v Kenya

At Sharjah, September 30, 2013 (floodlit). **First Twenty20 international: Afghanistan won by 106 runs.** ‡**Afghanistan 162-6** (20 overs) (Mohammad Shahzad 36, Asghar Stanikzai 43, Samiullah Shenwari 39*); **Kenya 56** (18.4 overs) (Hamid Hassan 3-4). *MoM:* Hamid Hassan. *Twenty20 international debut: Hashmatullah Sahidi (Afghanistan). Kenya were carved up for 56, resetting their own record for the lowest Twenty20 international total (previously 67 at Belfast in 2008). That looked almost inevitable from the moment Hamid Hassan took three wickets in seven balls – two bowled, one lbw – to shake Kenya to 7-4. Hassan's final figures of 3–1–4–3 were the joint-second-most economical in Twenty20 internationals. Afghanistan, by contrast, sprinted along at eight an over. The scale of the defenestration prompted Kenya to recall 42-year-old Steve Tikolo for the upcoming World Twenty20 Qualifier back in the UAE.*

At Sharjah, October 11, 2013 (floodlit). **Second Twenty20 international: Kenya won by 34 runs.** ‡**Kenya 149-4** (20 overs) (C. O. Obuya 60*, N. N. Odhiambo 41); **Afghanistan 115-8** (20 overs) (Nawroz Mangal 36; E. A. Otieno 3-16). *Twenty20 international debuts: Afsar Zazai (Afghanistan); D. M. Gondaria (Kenya). Between the two Twenty20 games, Afghanistan had beaten Kenya twice in 50-over matches to qualify for the 2015 World Cup, and won an Intercontinental Cup match. That intensity disappeared as Collins Obuya and Nehemiah Odhiambo put on 87 in Kenya's first ten overs. Mangal struck three quick sixes, but Afghanistan folded meekly.*

Afghanistan v Pakistan

At Sharjah, December 8, 2013 (floodlit). **Twenty20 international: Pakistan won by six wickets.** ‡**Afghanistan 137-8** (20 overs) (Najibullah Zadaran 38; Junaid Khan 3-24); **Pakistan 138-4** (19.5 overs) (Ahmed Shehzad 35, Mohammad Hafeez 42*). *MoM:* Mohammad Hafeez. *Twenty20 international debut: Sharjeel Khan (Pakistan). Pakistan, who had already tied a one-dayer with Ireland in 2013, were made to work hard to avoid an upset in their first Twenty20 international against their neighbours. Afghanistan fought ferociously to take their defence of a middling total down to the last over, but their lack of composure cost them. With Pakistan needing four off three balls, Dawlat Zadran banged one in short to Shahid Afridi – so short that the umpires called a wide for height. Afridi and Mohammad Hafeez took singles off the next two deliveries, yet Dawlat again went for a bouncer off the last. It was signalled a no-ball, handing Pakistan the game. Najibullah Zadaran (38 from 30 deliveries) and Mirwais Ashraf (28* from 20) earlier resuscitated Afghanistan after they limped into the fifth over on 8-2.* QAMAR AHMED

For Pakistan's series against Sri Lanka in the UAE which followed this match, see page 1031.

For reports of Afghanistan's matches in the ICC Intercontinental Cup and World Cricket League Championship, see page 1213.

CRICKET IN CANADA, 2013

The road to obscurity

FARAZ SARWAT

Canadian cricket was bracing itself for the most uncertain period in recent history. Dreadful performances at both global qualifying events at the turn of the year left Canada without one-day or Twenty20 international status for the first time since 2005, and their ICC High Performance Programme funds cut by half. With only ten teams admitted to the 2019 World Cup, and their World Cricket League Championship future in flux, the chances of Canada making a return looked slim.

Following heavy defeats in their first three matches of 2013, in Trinidad, Canada flew to Dubai to take on Kenya in all three formats. Both WCL matches were lost by six wickets, the Twenty20 series was shared, and a hard-fought Intercontinental Cup game narrowly lost.

Back in the home summer, National Cricket League games were staged in Toronto. What was ostensibly a national tournament, drawing together cricketers from across the country, was in reality stocked with generous numbers from the Toronto area, precluding the chance of any unknowns being thrown into the pot. Winners and losers were unimportant: the purpose was to provide selectors with an opportunity to see the national talent pool in action. As with many of Canada's internationals, the games were streamed online by Rogers TV and Sportsnet. The highlight of the club scene was Rizwan Cheema's 207, including 20 sixes, in a 50-over Toronto & District Cricket Association Elite Division match. The innings was notable for being sandwiched between Cheema being dropped from, then recalled to, the national side (as captain).

Years of questionable selection processes finally compelled Cricket Canada to undertake the sensitive task of overhauling the panel. A 12-point job spec requested "a good communicator who is not under suspension or investigation by his/her provincial cricket organisation or any other body". An aspiring candidate was expected to have played at international or first-class level; the abandon with which Canada have awarded caps over the years meant this was not as daunting as it appeared at first blush.

The traditional midsummer visit of the USA did allow Canada to chalk up some much-needed wins. They retained the Auty Cup by virtue of a first-innings lead, and won both Twenty20 matches. It was good preparation for the impending visit of the UAE and the Netherlands. Canada had the better of a drawn Intercontinental Cup match with the UAE, who were bowled out for 116 in the first innings, thanks to a fiery six for 43 from Jeremy Gordon. But the UAE won all four limited-overs games without much fuss.

It was clear by now that Canada needed Ashish Bagai – who had not played for them since the 2011 World Cup – if they were to challenge in the global qualifiers. He was coaxed back to keep wicket against the UAE, and a few weeks later was at the helm for the visit of the Netherlands: in Bagai's first game back as captain, Canada put in their finest performance for years to claim their only win of the Intercontinental Cup cycle. Gordon led the line with eight for 149 in the match, while 22-year-old Ruvindu Gunasekera came of age with a brisk double of 150 and 44 not out.

The Netherlands played the two WCL matches under protest over conditions at King City's Maple Leaf ground. They were unhappy at the inadequate drainage – long a problem at the venue, despite the club receiving a sizeable grant in 2006 to improve facilities – with standing water preventing a prompt start. The ICC also had to cancel plans to live-stream the match due to a dispute over the position of scaffolding. The first game was abandoned because of rain, with Canada in command, but the second was a disaster: Canada were bowled out for 67, which the Dutch chased down in less than 11 overs. The Netherlands' official complaint to the ICC was met with a shrug of the shoulders by Cricket Canada.

Canada put together their best possible squad for the World Twenty20 Qualifier in the UAE, preceded by a short training camp in Sri Lanka. With six places up for grabs at the main event, they were confident of making their maiden World Twenty20 appearance, especially under a qualifying format that allowed the odd slip-up. Gunasekara and Bagai put in a brave performance against Ireland, but Canada fell short by two runs. However, that came between shambolic performances against the USA and Hong Kong. In a frantic attempt to unsettle the rampaging Hong Kong opener Irfan Ahmed, Bagai turned to eight bowlers in the first 12 overs. The UAE coach Aqib Javed told a Canadian player he had no idea how to prepare his team against them, because they kept chopping and changing.

Canada finished a miserable 12th – behind six non-HPP sides – and, on returning home, the head of coach Gus Logie was the first to roll. Then came the axing of six players for the World Cup Qualifier in the New Year, including star all-rounder Cheema and veteran seamer Henry Osinde. Bagai was again named as captain, but withdrew and retired again, aged 31, citing work commitments. Jimmy Hansra, sacked a year earlier because of poor results, was put back in charge, and Canada continued their tradition of recycling coaches by rehiring Andy Pick on a short-term basis.

A side in such disarray were never likely to challenge for the top-two finish required to reach the World Cup, but Canada were desperate to make fourth and cling on to one-day international status. But defeats by the UAE and Hong Kong meant they failed to make it out of their group. That put an end to Canada's proud run of three consecutive World Cup appearances. The most painful by-product of the funding cut will be the end of full-time player contracts.

And so, the long-feared winter for Canadian cricket is now here. When the thaw will arrive is less clear.

For reports of Canada's matches in the World Twenty20 Qualifier, see page 1201; for their Twenty20 internationals against Kenya, see page 1207; and in the Intercontinental Cup and World Cricket League Championship, see page 1213.

CRICKET IN KENYA, 2013

Hitting rock bottom

MARTIN WILLIAMSON

Following Kenya's World Cup semi-final appearance against India in 2003, there were widespread predictions that they were poised to become the 11th Test nation. But as the side did a lap of honour, one ICC official told a senior Kenyan administrator: "Enjoy this. It won't happen again."

Those words were prescient. Rather than being a launch pad to success, that match in Durban marked Kenyan cricket's zenith. Many associated with the game in the country grew to see it as a millstone. Within a fortnight the players had gone on strike, seeking greater rewards, as they would frequently in the years that followed. By the time the Champions Trophy came around 18 months later, Kenyan cricket – hamstrung by a dysfunctional and corrupt board – was an international pariah.

Years of decline and decay culminated in their failure to reach the 2015 World Cup, after another below-par performance, at the qualifying event in New Zealand early in 2014. That followed an equally poor effort in the World Twenty20 Qualifier two months earlier. Kenya, an ever-present flag-bearer for the Associates at the World Cup since 1996, not only missed the next tournament, but also lost their coveted official one-day international status.

Many blamed the lack of a viable domestic infrastructure for the decline. That 42-year-old Steve Tikolo, whose career spanned his country's rise and fall, came out of retirement after three years and topped the batting averages at both qualifying tournaments, added fuel to criticism of the development system. His remarkable dedication also highlighted a different approach to the game.

Rather than greeting the loss of status with more in-fighting, those running the game appear to have seen it as a chance to start again, the final nail in the constant harking-back to the glory days of 2003. As one long-serving Kenyan administrator put it: "That World Cup was our biggest success, but it was also our biggest nightmare. We have been papering over the cracks for a decade. What we've had now is a reality check."

Kenyan cricket finally seems to have accepted that the current structure is not producing enough players, and changes will be made in the next year at school and club level. The aim is to mount a serious bid to qualify for the 2019 World Cup. Most crucially, the professional national squad will be dismantled. Financially, it is unsustainable, and has failed to produce results or even the right attitude.

Jackie Janmohamed, who took over as chairman of Cricket Kenya at the end of 2012, endured – and survived – a tough first year. It started with an open challenge to the board, engineered by the discredited former chairman Sharad Ghai, with the staging of an unofficial Cricket Wars Twenty20 tournament.

Like her predecessor, Janmohamed struggled to attract sides to Kenya. The country's precarious political situation did not help; nor did the ICC, who declined to appoint officials for a series against Afghanistan. Zimbabwe, themselves faced with player strikes, added to her headache by cancelling an agreed series at short notice.

There was a tour of Sri Lanka, on which results were poor but player attitudes positive, and the Under-19s provided cause for hope with some good performances. The East Africa competition gave much-needed higher-quality cricket to players in and around the national side, and attracted good media interest. The board's finances remain strong, and there is a real desire to start again from the bottom up.

It is always darkest before the dawn. Dispiriting though 2013 was, there is a sense that Kenya might just be ready to start the long process of rebuilding.

For reports of Kenya's matches in the World Twenty20 Qualifier, see page 1201; for the Intercontinental Cup and World Cricket League Championship, see page 1213; for Twenty20 internationals in Scotland, see page 849; against Canada and the Netherlands, see page 1207.

CRICKET ROUND THE WORLD, 2013

COMPILED BY JAMES COYNE AND TIMOTHY ABRAHAM

ICC WORLD CRICKET LEAGUE

When 19-year-old Steven Taylor battered Nepal for 162 from 102 balls, including 12 sixes, on the opening day of World Cricket League Division Three in April, the USA seemed set to stroll into the 2015 World Cup Qualifier. Nepal fell 95 runs short of their 366 for six – and that relatively small margin would prove crucial in the final reckoning. But Taylor managed only nine against host nation Bermuda in the last round as the USA slipped to a surprise five-wicket defeat against a team they had routinely despatched. At the same time, Nepal pummelled Italy with 35 overs to spare – giving their run-rate a huge shot in the arm – to pip the Americans into second place. The outcome had far-reaching implications in Associate cricket: it meant Uganda and Nepal, two nations with a sizeable indigenous player base, progressed to the World Cup Qualifier, while the USA and Bermuda missed out. Each had appeared at a major ICC tournament over the previous decade, yet had little to show for it but squandered largesse.

Argentina's slide continued with their fifth consecutive relegation, which eliminated them from the WCL altogether. They did at least end a 25-match WCL losing streak by beating Bahrain in the opening match of Division Six in Jersey, before last pair Agustin Casime and Hernan Fennell sneaked them home in the final over against Kuwait. But Argentina finished fourth out of six – and the ICC's Development Committee had already decided to relegate the bottom three to the regions, following their decision to scrap Divisions Seven and Eight in the next WCL cycle, to begin in 2014. Argentina's lifeline is a new regional qualifying stage to decide the last five places in the WCL.

CHINA

The Olympic Games have been at the forefront of the national sporting psyche ever since China ended their two-decade boycott at Los Angeles '84. To cater for this obsession, almost every academic institution has an astroturf athletics track encircling a football pitch. Not the ideal setting for a game of cricket, you might think, but it is the most feasible way to introduce the game to Chinese schoolchildren. For all the talk over the past decade about developing a Chinese market for cricket, those at the sharp end are convinced that getting Twenty20 into the Olympics is what really matters. But in June, the ICC Full Member nations decided not to apply for Twenty20 to be played at the 2020 Tokyo Games – robbing themselves of a great marketing slogan, if nothing else. The Chinese Cricket Association look on with envy at the stream of government funding destined for rugby sevens, which returns to the Olympics at Rio 2016. But boardroom politics didn't stop the first generation of Chinese cricketing enthusiasts finding new ways to join long-standing expat leagues. The Shanghai Cricket Club, originally established in 1858 by British merchants, last season freed a slot in the SCC Second Division 30-over league for a Shanghai team of students aged 16 to 18. They were mostly thrashed, but the experience toughened them up for their return to national high-school competition. Up in the First Division, 23-year-old all-rounder Zhang Yufei, considered the best strokemaker in the fledgling national team, scored what was thought to be the first century by a Chinese player, for Shanghai Daredevils, on the way to their third consecutive title. Zhang's arrival in London, for a second summer playing club cricket and coaching for the Capital Kids Cricket charity, transformed the campaign of Chinatown CC in the Victoria Park Community League. Zhang was their leading scorer as they embarked on an 11-game winning streak, cleaning up both league and cup. He received tips from England's victorious Ashes-winning side at Chester-le-Street, and netted with Durham MCCU. JON NEWTON

COLOMBIA

Cricket's revival over the past few years is largely down to David Muirhead, an Englishman based in Santiago de Cali, the tropical southern city famous for its salsa dancing. Determined to provide cricketers in Colombia's sporting capital with a more reliable surface, he built a net in the garden of the restaurant owned by his long-suffering partner; unsuspecting diners must now dodge cricket balls while enjoying their *sancocho de gallina*. In 2007, Muirhead rescued decaying equipment which had been sent over in the diplomatic bag for a match five years previously between Cali and Bogota – the first Ernie Field Cup tie for 21 years – and set about securing cricket's future on the sporting calendar. Since 2011 the season has been split in two, each half culminating in a match held alternately in the two cities. While Bogotanos have the luxury of a carpeted concrete strip between two football pitches at the Bogota Sports Club, where they have played since 1961, Caleños have to play *on* a football pitch at a local school. Cali's performances have improved since Muirhead erected his net, but Bogota remain champions. Unfortunately, only a couple of players on either side are Colombians, but that may change: Cali player Tony Williams, a Guyanese mechanic, regularly attracts around 15 youngsters from some of the city's poorer barrios to weekly cricket sessions. An inaugural Coca Cup match between Peru and Colombia is planned for Bogota in October. WILL FINCH

CZECH REPUBLIC

The spirit of the Routemaster bus, now limited to a couple of tourist routes in London, lives on in Prague, as a mobile pavilion for the Czech Cricket Union. Ondrej Souček, exiled from Czechoslovakia since the 1968 Prague Spring, purchased the double-decker in 1991 following its decommission from service in Glasgow, and used it to take his family on a summer holiday jaunt through Eastern Europe during the first heady days of the post-communist era. But the bus was left to rust in Prague, before being rescued by Souček's cricket-mad son, Ben. "It wasn't in great condition," he explained. "A drug addict had stolen the bus and crashed it into a low-level bridge, blocking Prague transport for the day. The roof was cut open like a tin of sardines." When the game first appeared in the late 1990s, Czech cricketers had to make do with a Flicx pitch in Vypich public park, with occasional interruptions from stray dogs and drunken vagabonds, but two years ago they secured a picturesque ground at Vinor, on the outskirts of Prague. The CCU lacked the funds to build a traditional pavilion, but Ben, with the help of motor enthusiast and ex-British Army officer Hugo Banks, set about sourcing the parts needed to restore the bus to its former glory. "We realised it would make the perfect mobile pavilion," he said. "It could also act as a sightseeing tour bus for visiting teams, and would be great for promoting Czech cricket." The Routemaster is now fully insured and fitted with veteran Czech registration plates. But clues to its origin remain on its signs: "Clyde Tunnel" and "Renfrew Ferry". TIMOTHY ABRAHAM

ETHIOPIA

Once or twice a year, an unlikely team of Rastafarian cricketers living in the remote town of Shashamane undertake the 150-mile drive into Addis Ababa to face their great rivals and friends, the British embassy. This improbable match-up is the highlight of the Ethiopian cricketing calendar. The artists, musicians, carpenters, metal workers, cobblers, plumbers and ketchup makers pile into a small van sent for them by the embassy, and sing songs all the way into the capital and back, regardless of the result. If there is an air of abandon about their approach, there is no denying the skill on display. Some of the more elderly players do not even bother with a run-up, preferring instead to roll their arms over from a stationary position; somehow the cork ball fizzes and hurries off the pitch. But their jollity belies the struggles Rastafarians have endured as a community not officially recognised by the Ethiopian government, and whose legal status in the country is often described as "unresolved". The first major wave of Rastafarians arrived in the 1960s, mostly from Jamaica, in answer to Emperor Haile Selassie's invitation to realise their dream of repatriation to Africa. (The Lion of Judah had attended a day of India v Australia at Bombay in 1956-57.) But it has been a slippery slope ever since: most of the land Selassie donated was taken away under the Mengistu regime, along with the right to work. "We don't have Bob Marley money, man," laughs Teddy Dan, who – as Shashamane captain – spends much of his time petitioning embassies in Addis to host them for a game, and scrounging professional-grade equipment. So far, the British embassy alone have agreed to a few matches and donating a child-size set of stumps, some tennis balls and tape, and bats carved out of brittle plywood. The team are mostly Rastafarian, but there are a few Ethiopian youngsters learning the ropes as well. Dan believes the contentious and often misunderstood relationship between the Rastafarian and Ethiopian communities must be repaired – and cricket could be a way to achieve it.   R. RAJKUMAR

GERMANY

The British legacy on Heligoland, a rocky 170-hectare island in the German Bight, will forever be tainted by the "British Bang" of April 1947 – when the Royal Navy detonated almost 7,000 tonnes of explosives in order to destroy the remaining U-boat pens. It still ranks among the biggest non-nuclear blasts in history, and is not remembered with fondness by the exiled *Helgoländer*, who had to rebuild everything from scratch when they were allowed to resettle from 1952. It is tempting to wonder if the Navy would have been more cautious had there been a cricket club on the island. But, surprisingly, no cricket seems to have been played on the "Gibraltar of the North" during the 83 years of British occupation, which ended in 1890 when the government traded it for Zanzibar, much to Queen Victoria's displeasure. It was not until late 2012 that Mark Richardson, head of the flourishing cricket section at THCC Rot-Gelb in Hamburg, came up with the idea of launching a sister club on Heligoland, now a popular duty-free day trip three hours' ferry ride from the mouth of the River Elbe. Heligoland Pilgrims CC were inducted as the newest – and most isolated – member of the Deutscher Cricket Bund, and made their debut against THCC Rot-Gelb in the inaugural Atlantik Cup tie last July, on an artificial football pitch belonging to VfL Fosite, the island's sports club. The Pilgrims, backed by sponsorship from Erdinger beer, now have more than 30 members of all ages and backgrounds, and plan to enter German youth tournaments and invite more touring sides. Heligoland's speciality, *Knieper* (crab) sandwiches, are served at tea. The crab is also the club's mascot, and has inspired their team song "Jeepers Kniepers" – sung to the tune of Louis Armstrong's "Jeepers Creepers".   JAMES COYNE

HUNGARY

An entire squad of native Hungarian cricketers, the Danube Benders, toured England for the first time – led by a woman. Claudia Balogh, 22, was among the first Hungarians to fall in love with the game, after an English teacher, Andy Grieve, introduced cricket to Comenius Bilingual Grammar School, in her home city of Székesfehérvár, in 2006. She now commands respect in Hungary's domestic scene as an all-rounder for Budapest Falcons, primarily a Pakistani and Afghan club, and has been the driving force behind the women's team, who made their international debut in Jersey last summer. "The bounce is much truer on turf surfaces than back home," says Balogh. "But the best thing was being able to jump and slide around in the field. You could tell from the green on our trousers who'd given their all." Benders' trump card was opening batsman Erno Tekauer, a strapping water polo player, who thumped the first half-century by a Hungarian in England during the opening game, against Broadclyst Nomads, then steered Benders to a win over Exeter side Mount Radford.   JAMES COYNE

IRAN

Rolling down their sleeves

MONIR HABIBI

I have been a runner, a football goalkeeper, and played volleyball and basketball too. I was first introduced to cricket at university in Tehran ten years ago. For the first time in my life, I was able to play sport on a grassy field without being physically hurt (at least until I got hit by a bouncer). I learned to apply skills from other games, developed my medium-pace, and took the new ball for my club in the Iranian Women's Championship. Soon, I was selected for the national team. But I was about to get married, and didn't have the time to commit. So I gave up playing, and concentrated my efforts on umpiring and coaching Iran's next generation of female cricketers.

Unfortunately, the old Iran Baseball–Cricket Federation was so incompetent that, in 2011 – eight years after Iran became an ICC Affiliate Member – cricket was being played in only five out of 31 provinces. Iranian cricket owes a great deal to Saeed Behrozi, the general secretary of the reformed Iran Cricket Association, for keeping the game afloat. The international sanctions imposed on Iran since 2006 – because of the uranium enrichment programme – mean the government are not able to provide us with any funding. The Asian Cricket Council used to send coaches and equipment but, following the crackdown on foreign investment, they no longer can.

We are keen to prepare two new grounds in Tehran, but we can't bring in the ACC's expert curators to help. Still, I was determined cricket would survive, so I volunteered for the ICA. I now hold free training courses for women and girls, and managed the national team to the ACC Women's Championship in Thailand in January 2013, where we beat Qatar, Kuwait and Singapore. The game is now played in 20 provinces, from Kurdistan in the far north-west to the thriving Baluchistan region bordering Pakistan.

I am often asked why so many Iranian women play cricket. The answer is: because it is a game which values fairness, and it is important to us, as Muslims, that like our opponents, we are able to wear long-sleeved shirts and trousers, which allows us to participate in international competitions on equal terms. We are sometimes criticised by religious conservatives for playing in view of men but, given that we meet the Muslim dress code, they have no argument.

Monir Habibi is international affairs spokesperson for the ICA. In February 2013 she was named Volunteer of the Year at the ICC Development Awards.

ITALY

Across Italy, South Asian immigrants play street matches with a tape-ball – sometimes for money. For these men, often living away from their families on low incomes, it is a source of joy, but also has the potential to turn nasty, and every year there are killings and injuries related to quarrels. Tragically, a female Italian doctor was run down and killed while coming to the aid of a stricken Indian immigrant in Bergamo last September, due to a cricket feud. Such dreadful events make the story told by *Italian Cricket Club: il gioco dei nuovi Italiani* ("the game of the new Italians") all the more important. This book, co-written by three journalists from *Corriere della Sera*, *Secolo XIX* and *La Stampa*, is an Italian-language history of the game in the peninsula, and its publication in October led to an unprecedented level of coverage for cricket in the national press. And after all, even in our beloved football, Italy have never been European champions in both genders. In July, the men held off Freddie Klokker to beat Denmark by 18 runs in the ICC European Championship final, played under floodlights at Hove's County Ground. Then, in Bologna, Italy's women were emphatic winners of an unofficial Twenty20 tournament, involving the best European teams not involved in the World Twenty20 Qualifier. The single biggest triumph of the last two years has been the quadrupling of female cricketers. Olimpia Postioma, from Treviso, won their first women's championship, under the stewardship of a former professional softball player. The Federazione Cricket Italiana has introduced incentives for clubs to establish a women's section, and set a target of 1,000 female cricketers by 2020 – with the ultimate goal a place in the Women's World Cup.

SIMONE GAMBINO

JAPAN

The Royal Navy officers who were rowed ashore to play the first cricket match in Japan, against the Yokohama Shore team in 1863, had to be guarded by Royal Marines to defend them from attacks by *rōnins*. Tensions were high in the foreign settlement following the assassination of British merchant Charles Richardson by Satsuma samurai the previous autumn, and an order for foreigners to leave Japan by June 25, or face death, was issued in the name of shogun Tokugawa Iemochi. As the date approached, Yokohama's local population fled the town, but the British residents were reluctant to leave without compensation. Even with the presence of the Royal Marines ringed around the ground, many of the players carried weapons on to the field. "It was a most novel sensation for the [Navy] wicketkeeper, as he carried his revolver backwards and forwards and placed it behind the stumps," wrote James Campbell Fraser, an Old Harrovian and captain of the Shore team. "It is, I suppose, the only match on record in which the players had to be armed," mused the future Arctic explorer Lt Albert Hastings Markham, who was on the Navy XI. The match passed off without a shot being fired, but a few weeks later some of the Navy players were involved in the bombardment of Kagoshima, in a bid to extract blood money for Richardson's killing.

There was more amity in the air on December 1, 2013, when the Royal Navy crew of HMS *Daring* played a 150-year anniversary rematch against the Shore team at the Yokohama Country & Athletic Club, Japan's oldest sporting club. This time, the Navy were driven by coach from Harumi Pier in Tokyo. There were marines in tow once more – in the form of the Royal Marines marching band, who opened the event with the Japanese and British national anthems. But this game came under threat too. HMS *Daring* had been expecting a leisurely cruise up to Japan from Singaporean waters, but when Typhoon Haiyan devastated the eastern Philippines in early November, she was redirected to carry out disaster relief operations. The crew were first on the scene in several of the islands, where many survivors had lost everything. HMS *Daring* was eventually relieved by HMS *Illustrious*, and sailed north for the cricket. They were unable to repeat the Navy's 1863 victory, though, going down by 90 runs in a Twenty20 game against a Shore team made up of players from YC&AC, the Japanese national side and the British embassy.

The match brought down the curtain on Japanese cricket's memorable sesquicentennial year. In April and May, the men's and women's national teams toured England and Scotland, playing on consecutive days against MCC on the Lord's Nursery Ground, with the men attracting a crowd of 1,300. Many UK-based Japanese families came to watch, prompting the Japan Cricket Association to stage hourly tutorials to explain the differences from baseball. Around £5,000 was raised from the tour in aid of Cricket for Smiles, the JCA's disaster relief initiative in the Tohoku region (see below). The players also visited the Scottish Parliament at Holyrood, which passed a commendation for the JCA's half-Scottish chief executive, Naoki Alex Miyaji, for his work in co-ordinating disaster relief through sport. One of the tourists was Makoto Taniyama, 17, who learned leg-spin by watching Shane Warne on YouTube, and has even found success on Japan's unforgiving artificial wickets. Taniyama is the youngest player to represent Japan, and was the only Asian among the Pacific Islanders chosen for the East Asia–Pacific Select XI in a Rising Stars tournament in Brisbane last year. MIKE GALBRAITH

Cricket near the Fukushima exclusion zone

It was almost certainly the first cricket match opened by four men dressed in samurai costume blowing conch shells. The event pitted the British embassy against a Select XI from Tohoku, the region devastated in March 2011 by an earthquake and subsequent tsunami that wrecked the Fukushima nuclear plant; the venue was the Kita-Niida baseball ground in Minamisoma City, close to the 20km nuclear exclusion zone. "We're not playing down the problems that exist at the Fukushima plant or for the people having to deal with the situation," said the UK ambassador Tim Hitchens. "But the reason we wanted to come here is that people in places like this are being forgotten." Science and safety remain complex issues, and the clean-up operation continues to suffer setbacks: days before the match in September, the Japanese government had pledged £300m to construct an ice wall to contain leaks of highly radioactive water. "Of course we worry and it's natural people outside Fukushima should worry," said Japan national team player Yoshitaka Uehara, a Minamisoma native who opened the batting for Tohoku. "But events such as this will help spread the word that not all of Fukushima is unsafe."

ROB GILHOOLY

MYANMAR

The expat-dominated league in Yangon (formerly Rangoon) had to be suspended in 2013 following the wave of anti-Muslim violence that plagued Myanmar. Many of the players were of Pakistani and Bangladeshi descent, and their safety might have been compromised. In December 2012, the best native Burmese players were sent to the Asian Cricket Council Trophy Challenge, but Myanmar were predictably outgunned by Middle Eastern states able to draw on subcontinental expats. "Our boys trained for four to five hours each day, with no sleep and not enough food," said U Hla Oo, national team supervisor. "But I worry it's not enough." Myanmar have yet to win a match at senior international level, and the Myanmar Cricket Federation are under constant financial pressure as they strive to promote the sport among the indigenous, overwhelmingly Buddhist, population. Cricket dates back to when the British took Rangoon in 1824, and even Thibaw, the last king of Burma, fell under its spell. According to F. S. Ashley-Cooper in *Cricket Highways and Byways*, he "batted fairly well, but refused to do his fair share of fielding, and was in the habit of using very injurious language to anyone who bowled him". Sadly, the British never did expand the game beyond narrow confines, and it almost died out under the socialist regime that followed independence. But since gaining ICC Membership in 2006, the MCF have been able to channel funds into developing a dedicated ground and turf wicket at Saw Pong. The quasi-civilian government that took power in 2011 have been more receptive to cricket. Last October, the MCF welcomed Craigengower CC of Hong Kong – believed to be the first overseas side to visit the country since colonial days – and a Myanmar XI beat them in a Twenty20 match. But hopes that the 27th Southeast Asian Games, hosted in the new capital Naypyidaw in December 2013, might include a cricket tournament at Saw Pong came to nought. TONY YOO

NAMIBIA

Cricket Namibia have been under the spotlight since they were accused of racism two years ago by Carlos Kambaekwa, a journalist from the national daily newspaper *New Era*. While Kambaekwa's precise allegations were never fully investigated, many were questioning the pace of transformation more than two decades after independence from

South Africa. In 2013, only one black African, opening batsman Pikky Ya France, played for the national team, while the 20-year-old Groenewald twins Shalako and Zhivago (both "coloured", in southern African terminology) have been on the fringes. The game remains dominated by Afrikaners, despite whites forming only 7% of Namibia's 2.1m population. There was further unease when CN tried and failed to select two South Africans, both qualified for Namibia, for the 2012 Under-19 World Cup. Under pressure from main sponsors MTC Namibia – a mobile phone company – CN announced a transformation charter aimed at involving non-whites at all levels of play and administration, including racial quotas (which have never been followed through). A year later, MTC declared they were unsatisfied at the level of progress, and would not be renewing their sponsorship. CN denied racism, stressing that transformation was a gradual process in a country where the black population prefers football, and said they had always found it hard to recruit non-whites to roles in the association. CN chief executive Graham McMillan – brother of former South Africa all-rounder Brian – pointed towards the development programmes in the coastal towns of Walvis Bay, Swakopmund and other previously untapped regions as proof that they were serious about opening up the game for all Namibians.

JESSE JACKSON KAURAISA

NAURU

In September 2012, as part of their "Pacific Solution", the Australian government began deporting male asylum seekers to the island of Nauru (the world's tiniest republic) where they were housed at a processing centre until their claims for refugee status were determined. The first wave of detainees slept on camp beds in cramped army tents that reached temperatures close to 50°C, and were liable to flood in the monsoon. Mental and physical illness, self-harm and suicide attempts became commonplace – and the UN Refugee Agency criticised the conditions. It was hoped that a cricket league might provide some kind of escape from detainees' anxieties and the monotony of camp life. A Tamil team had already thrashed the Australian Defence Forces in an impromptu game, so there was an appetite for more. An experimental tournament inside the camp grounds, with sides divided by boat number, and army personnel umpiring at square leg, ended when a ball jumped off a rock and struck a batsman on the nose, sending him to the infirmary. It persuaded us to approach the Department of Immigration to allow us to run future games outside the compound: our application was accepted. The only suitable area was the island's Aussie Rules football oval – a rubbish-strewn bowl covered in dust from the phosphate refinery that loomed behind the ground, and propped up Nauru's economy. Thirty men were transported there for each Twenty20 game, supervised by three security guards who often fell asleep in deckchairs. The players organised themselves into four Tamil sides, one Sinhalese, and one Pakistani. They swept the pitch with leaves, and set up boundary markers with whatever debris they could find. Tennis balls were wrapped in sky-blue electrical tape for extra weight. The disaster of a blue ball was foreseeable – and it often crashed into the full water containers we used as stumps. Lbws were usually met with dissent, but at least the men weren't talking about their traumas and grievances. In one game, a Pakistani Hazara opening the batting for one of the Tamil teams hit five sixes in an over. Scorecards and oddities such as this were posted on the camp noticeboard. A community grew in the camp: Tamils were learning the names of Pakistanis; Sinhalese were thanking Tamils for a great game – moments of happiness embedded in so much sadness.   MARK ISAACS

Mark Isaacs is a writer and a case manager for asylum seekers in Sydney, and spent nine months working for the Salvation Army on Nauru. This is an edited extract from his upcoming book, The Undesirables.

Having a gander: geese patrol the outfield at Piotrowice Nyskie country house, near Poland's border with the Czech Republic.

POLAND

Absent from the Central European scene until 2013 was country-house cricket: cream teas, the lowing of cows, and the fruitless search for balls lost in the hedge. My wife, Anna, and I are rescuing a crumbling Renaissance pile, formerly the property of the Prince-Bishop of Wroclaw. It is in a village in the middle of nowhere, a few kilometres from the Czech border, with the Sudeten Mountains in sight. English stately homes nearly all have a cricket pitch (don't they?), and I felt Piotrowice Nyskie should have one too. The Piotrowice Nyskie International Rugby Festival, after three editions, had achieved cult status – why not indulge another love? An unlikely plot was hatched with the assistance of some European cricket enthusiasts, who were en route to Cluj to donate a plastic Flicx pitch in celebration of Romania's admission to the ICC. As Warsaw beat off opposition from Prague and Krakow to win the Sixes tournament, the Flicx proved a godsend, as my grass wasn't quite the batsman's paradise I'd hoped for. In 2014, however, I promise the best turf pitch in Poland; as it may be the only one, I expect to succeed. We hope the Piotrowice Nyskie ostler, footman and gardeners will play, rather than look on with puzzlement. And while the cows kept a respectful distance, the meddlesome geese will be discouraged from the outfield. Anyone who scores a direct hit on a goose will get to take it home, plucked and trussed – a prize offered in 2013, but won by nobody.   JIM PARTON

RUSSIA

Glasnost and perestroika arrived three decades late to Russian cricket – but now the sport is opening up and restructuring to accommodate the indigenous population. Cricket in Russia has always been the preserve of expats, from the games played by the British in Tsarist St Petersburg, to the collapse of the Soviet Union and the South Asian-dominated Moscow league that followed. Matches in the capital became so competitive in the 2000s that some players were paid well enough to make a living. However, a drive to develop more native Russian cricketers – part of the successful bid to win ICC Affiliate Membership in 2012 – resulted in the formation of a breakaway organisation. The Board of Control for Cricket in Russia continue to run a largely expat league at the picturesque tree-lined Moscow State University baseball stadium. On the other side is the United Cricket League, overseen by Cricket Russia – the ICC-approved body from which the national team are drawn. Their president Ashwani Chopra says he realised his board had to embrace the native population when he turned out for the national team at an invitational tournament in Macedonia in 2010. "Frankly, wearing a Russian shirt in a team without a single native Russian player, with everyone talking Hindi, made me uncomfortable and embarrassed," he said.

The UCL is now shorn of some of the best players in Moscow, but their efforts to attract more natives flowered with the involvement of Sergey Kurchenko, a former coach of the Russian baseball team, who managed to lure some of his old charges on to the cricket field. While batting and bowling are still being mastered, the accuracy and speed of their throwing arms would not look out of place in professional cricket. Moscow now has around 30 Russian men playing the game, just about enough to scrape together a women's team, and over 100 native boys and girls enrolled in its academy. Russia's sheer size presents its own issues, with ad hoc cricket popping up in cities across the country. "It's just a matter of time before an email from someone in Vladivostok about cricket drops in my inbox," says Chopra, only half-joking.

Another potential recruit is Russian chess grandmaster Peter Svidler, a frequent visitor to Tests in England, who bemused the chess world a few years ago by entering a middle-ranking tournament in Gibraltar just so he could have a net at The Rock's cricket ground. He has promised to help promote the game in Russia when he retires from the chess circuit.

Chopra offered to host an ICC tournament in Moscow, but that looks a slim prospect after ICC Europe scrapped the lower levels of their Twenty20 competition. So for the time being Alexander Bogatyrev, Egor Sarubhukov and the Kochnov brothers, Vasily and Grigory, have to live out their dreams of playing at the World Cup on their PlayStations and XBoxes. Cricket Russia had the foresight to sell the licensing rights of the Russian players to the Australian makers of *Don Bradman Cricket 14* – which at least allows their virtual profiles to lock horns with Michael Clarke and Stuart Broad. TIMOTHY ABRAHAM

THAILAND

Barely a decade after the first curious Thai woman picked up a bat, the national team shocked the world by beating the Netherlands, Canada and Zimbabwe at last summer's Women's World Twenty20 Qualifier to win the Shield competition. With a better run-rate in the group stage, Thailand would have been playing off for a place in the tournament finals in Bangladesh. The entire team are Thais, as are almost all the country's female cricketers. Much of the national team work in the Cricket Association of Thailand offices, and remain involved throughout the year as qualified coaches, umpires and scorers. In late 2013, the captain Somnarin Tippoch and opening bowler Nattaya Boochatham were drafted in as overseas players in Sri Lankan women's domestic cricket. CAT are striving to make the men's teams similarly sustainable: one intrepid development officer even ventured to Pattani in southern Thailand – under martial law because of a decade-long insurgency by Malay separatists – and returned with some budding cricketers. There are also projects to engage children from the Karen, Akha and Hmong hill tribes from remote villages of northern Thailand, many of them stateless and sent to the city by families unable to support them. A number were recently enrolled in CAT's centre of excellence with access to superb facilities at Chiang Mai, thanks to funds raised by the famous Sixes tournament. Wicketkeeper-batsman Bunchuai Sombatraska, probably the most talented of the intake, made his debut for Thailand Under-19s last May and, in a league match, scored the first century by a hill-tribe boy. RICHARD LOCKWOOD

USA

Darren Beazley's arrival from Australia in February 2013 as the USA Cricket Association's new chief executive was intended to pave the road to professionalism. By the end of the year, though, political chicanery and ham-fisted administrative practices were still firmly entrenched. The national side, resting several first-team players, peaked in March with an 8–0 record in ICC Americas Division One on home soil, with Steven Taylor scoring the first two Twenty20 centuries by an American player. However, the scale of the success duped the selectors into leaving out two veterans, Aditya Thyagarajan and Usman Shuja, for the more important assignment of World Cricket League Division Three, after they had booked time off work. USA failed to finish in the top two, and missed out on the 2015 World Cup Qualifier.

Despite such setbacks, coach Robin Singh's power continued to grow. Andy Pick, the former England Under-19 coach, was hired in August as USACA's High Performance Officer on secondment from ICC Americas, but lasted just two months before resigning over a selection dispute. Pick was flabbergasted when seamer Imran Awan, not chosen for the training camp ahead of the World Twenty20 Qualifier, paid his own way to Florida and impressed Singh sufficiently to force his way into the squad. "It became obvious that certain people are not ready for change and structure, and are determined to maintain control, even if it holds back cricket in the USA," wrote Pick in a leaked resignation letter. "I was not prepared to sacrifice my personal and professional reputation working for these people." Steve Massiah, expected to captain the side to the tournament, pulled out late, citing work commitments; USACA sources suggested a selection dispute was to blame. USA slumped to last place in their group, and by the end of the tournament Timroy Allen had become their seventh captain in a year.

Beazley managed to secure a few sponsorships, but they were small fry compared with the task of reforming USACA's governance structure. He had the ICC's support, not least in seeking to reduce the powers of the Gladstone Dainty-controlled board and place it in the hands of independent directors, and spent the summer campaigning across the country to convince officials to approve the measures at USACA's AGM. But in the week leading up to the AGM in November, Dainty – now in his tenth year as president – appointed Mascelles Bailey as general secretary, a position vacant since Kenwyn Williams's social-media meltdown cost him his position a year earlier. A USACA press release praised Bailey's "impressive administration credentials" as president of the New York Metropolitan & District Cricket Association, while omitting the fact that his league was one of 32 disenfranchised by the board ahead of the 2012 USACA elections, ostensibly for non-compliance with governance demands. Rather than holding a vote on the proposed reforms at the AGM, any changes to governance were postponed until summer 2014 – assuming they happen at all.

While USACA had not held a national tournament since 2011, the rebel American Cricket Federation staged their second annual Twenty20 national championship in October. They also appointed their first chief executive: the well-respected Baltimore native Jamie Harrison, co-founder and president of the US Youth Cricket Association. Harrison was pleasantly surprised when USYCA were wired $8,100 from the ICC – only to be asked to return it because the money was actually a grant intended for USACA. The ACF grow in confidence with each folly to befall American cricket, but it may be a few years before they can mount a serious challenge to replace USACA as the country's official cricket body.   Peter Della Penna

UZBEKISTAN

Last September, two Pakistani brothers, Zeeshan and Irfan Karimi, aged 13 and 11, organised Uzbekistan's first cricket league. Four teams, made up of pupils at the Ulugbek International School in Tashkent, played after classes on the school's *maidon*. Batsmen paid for ambitious strokes with their wicket if any shot landed on the school roof, or 1,000 *soms* (27p) for a new tennis ball if one was lost. Each team fielded Uzbek boys keen for a first taste of the game they had seen in Bollywood movies, but their international class-mates dominated the matches. It was thought to be the most meaningful cricket in Uzbekistan for at least a decade: employees at an Indo-Uzbek pharmaceutical company used to play regularly at the Chilonzor Stadium, including an annual fixture against the British embassy. The weekly match award was a meal for two at Ragu's Indian restaurant. But many expats left during the global recession. The Karimis may meet stronger opposition in 2014, thanks to a new arrival across the city: Jarrod Dale, an Australian teacher at Tashkent International School, and a former club-mate of Bruce Reid and Marcus North in Perth grade cricket, plans to teach the game to his pupils, as well as to older Uzbeks.   JONATHAN CAMPION

VATICAN CITY

Of all the eye-catching declarations in Pope Francis's first year, few caused such consternation in parts of the Catholic world as the Vatican's decision to embrace cricket. In the Anglophone press at least, the formation of St Peter's Cricket Club was met with an inevitable avalanche of puns. "He always wears whites, he's fast approaching a century, and was even known in his youth to bowl the odd maiden over," chuckled the *Daily Mail*. "But Pope Francis's latest initiative could still leave some Vatican insiders stumped." And how about this for a clever stroke, from *Vatican Radio*: "Perhaps the popular expression 'the Vatican thinks in centuries' will suddenly take on a whole new meaning as St Peter's batsmen stride out to play." There was an immediate clamour for a Church of England v Vatican fixture, and Canterbury needed little arm-twisting to accept Rome's challenge to play at Lord's in September 2014; feelers have been put out to television and radio companies about broadcasting the event. Officials in both churches were talking of an annual fixture, staged alternately in Rome and England. The assumption that the Anglican Church will assert the dominance expected of a Test nation might be a little hasty: there are many skilled and experienced cricketers in Rome, of all ages and backgrounds. For over 40 years, Alfonso Jayarajah, a Sri Lankan émigré, has been fostering cricket in Italy. He was co-founder of Capannelle CC, whose ground, in the middle of a hippodrome, has already hosted a series of games between students from the Mater Ecclesiae College and the Pontifical Urbaniana University. Added to the mix are 300 priests and seminarians living in Rome originating from cricket-playing nations. They will form six teams in an internal St Peter's cup competition, with the best going on to be selected for the Vatican team. There is real desire to push this initiative through, not least in the Pontifical Council of Culture, which views cricket as an exciting avenue for interfaith and ecumenical relations, especially in Asia. In future years, St Peter's will invite teams from overseas Hindu and Muslim educational establishments to Rome. Naturally, the Vatican will play in white, with the gold and white colours of the Papacy and the crossed-keys emblem of St Peter on their caps, shirts and blazers. There will also be a women's team, drawn from nuns and female students living in Rome. Yes – the nuns will wear veils in the field, and discard them for helmets at the crease!   JOHN MCCARTHY

John McCarthy is the Australian ambassador to the Holy See.

> **❝** By the time he returned to Canterbury from active service in North Africa, he had become a batsman – a result, he explained, of the pitches he encountered in Egypt."
> Obituaries, page 214.

ICC GLOBAL TOURNAMENTS

WORLD CRICKET LEAGUE, 2013

Competition	Date	Winner	Runner-up	Others (in finishing order)
WCL Division Three	Apr	Nepal	Uganda	USA, Bermuda, Oman, Italy
WCL Division Six	Jul	Jersey	Nigeria	Vanuatu, Argentina, Bahrain, Kuwait
WCL Division Seven	Apr	Nigeria	Vanuatu	Botswana, Fiji, Ghana, Germany

REGIONAL ONE-DAY TOURNAMENTS

Competition	Date	Winner	Runner-up	Others (in finishing order)
ACC Emerging Teams Cup	Aug	India U23	Pakistan U23	Sri Lanka U23/UAE, Afghanistan, Bangladesh U23, Nepal, Singapore

TWENTY20 REGIONAL TOURNAMENTS

Competition	Date	Winner	Runner-up	Others (in finishing order)
Africa Division One	Feb	Kenya	Uganda	Tanzania, Botswana, Nigeria
Americas Division One	Mar	USA	Bermuda	Suriname, Bahamas, Cayman Islands
Americas Division Two	Feb	Bahamas	Panama	Belize, Argentina, Turks & Caicos Islands
ACC Twenty20 Cup	Mar	Afghanistan	Nepal	UAE, Hong Kong, Kuwait, Malaysia, Oman, Maldives, Singapore, Bahrain
East Asia–Pacific Championship	Feb	PNG	Vanuatu	Fiji, Samoa, Japan, Cook Islands, Indonesia
European Championship	Jul	Italy	Denmark	Jersey, Guernsey, France, Austria, Germany, Norway, Isle of Man, Gibraltar, Sweden, Belgium

WOMEN'S TOURNAMENTS

Competition	Date	Winner	Runner-up	Others (in finishing order)
ICC Women's World Twenty20 Qualifier	Jul	Sri Lanka/ Pakistan	–	Ireland, Netherlands, Thailand, Zimbabwe, Canada, Japan
Africa Women's World Twenty20 Qualifier	Dec 2012	S. Africa A	Zimbabwe	Tanzania, Uganda, Namibia, Kenya
ACC Women's Championship	Jan	Thailand	China	Nepal, Hong Kong, Bhutan, Iran, Malaysia, Qatar, Singapore, UAE

PART SIX

Records and Registers

FEATURES OF 2013

This section now covers the calendar year. Some of the features listed occurred in matches reported in *Wisden 2013* and some will be reported in *Wisden 2015*; these items are indicated by [W13] or [W15].

Double-Hundreds (90)

	Mins	Balls	4	6		
352	548	427	49	1	‡C. A. Pujara	Saurashtra v Karnataka at Rajkot.
340*		367	40	8	S. H. T. Kandamby. . .	Sinhalese v Tamil Union at Colombo.
336		275	29	14	‡M. D. K. J. Perera . . .	Colts v Saracens at Colombo.
313*	423	312	41	3	S. S. Agarwal	Oxford U. v Cambridge U. at Cambridge.
308	603	429	50	0	Imran Farhat	Lahore Ravi v Peshawar at Lahore.
306*	579	415	33	0	‡C. A. Pujara.	India A v West Indies A at Hubli.
300*	823	609	34	2	T. Kohli	Punjab v Jharkhand at Jamshedpur.
289	564	367	30	4	Marshall Ayub	Central Zone v East Zone at Bogra.
275*	555	436	38	1	A. Z. Lees	Yorkshire v Derbyshire at Chesterfield.
273	590	461	35	0	R. Dewan	Haryana v Orissa at Bhubaneswar.[W15]
272	535	404	25	4	A. W. Gale	Yorkshire v Nottinghamshire at Scarborough.
270*	544	415	40	3	C. F. Hughes	Derbyshire v Yorkshire at Leeds.
269	741	461	33	0	‡C. A. Pujara.	Saurashtra v Tamil Nadu at Chennai.[W15]
268	561	430	29	4	D. Elgar	South Africa A v Australia A at Pretoria.
262	595	396	32	2	H. H. Khadiwale	Maharashtra v Goa at Gahunje.[W15]
256*	363	211	42	0	Faizan Riaz	Islamabad v Quetta at Islamabad.[W15]
256	249	224	29	12	S. R. Patel	Nottinghamshire v Durham MCCU at Nottingham.
255*	353	279	36	3	D. J. Sales	Northamptonshire v Gloucestershire at Northampton.
251		334	23	11	M. G. Vandort	Ragama v Air Force at Colombo.
250	493	367	26	2	M. M. Ali	Worcestershire v Glamorgan at Worcester.
248	643	448	28	0	S. Badrinath	Tamil Nadu v Madhya Pradesh at Indore.[W15]
243	508	434	28	1	J. C. Mickleburgh	Essex v Leicestershire at Chelmsford.
242	599	536	24	2	D. P. Sibley	Surrey v Yorkshire at The Oval.
241*	606	423	21	3	T. W. M. Latham	Canterbury v Wellington at Wellington.[W15]
241	496	434	39	1	A. G. Puttick	Cape Cobras v Warriors at Port Elizabeth.[W15]
240	570	411	27	1	R. W. Chakabva	Mashonaland Eagles v Mid West Rhinos at Harare.[W15]
240	701	437	20	1	A. Mukund	Tamil Nadu v Saurashtra at Chennai.
239*	633	496	30	1	S. D. Choudhary	Madhya Pradesh v Railways at Indore.[W15]
238	395	299	26	12	S. S. Tiwary	Jharkhand v Mumbai at Mumbai.[W15]
236	465	336	24	0	J. E. Root	Yorkshire v Derbyshire at Leeds.
235*	457	322	31	0	A. C. Voges	Western Australia v Queensland at Perth.[W15]
235		162	26	11	S. M. A. Priyanjan . . .	Ports Authority v Kurunegala Youth at Kurunegala.
234		392	22	0	W. W. A. G. Maneshan	Ports Authority v Colombo at Colombo.
234	627	388	16	0	G. C. Smith	South Africa v Pakistan (Second Test) at Dubai.
228*	569	428	20	0	V. Chopra	Warwickshire v Middlesex at Uxbridge.
225*	471	379	26	3	K. D. Petersen	Boland v North West at Paarl.[W15]
225	375	271	22	3	Aamer Yamin	Multan v Quetta at Multan.[W15]
225	477	353	22	2	Akbar-ur-Rehman	Karachi Blues v Lahore Ravi at Lahore.
224	365	265	24	6	M. S. Dhoni	India v Australia (First Test) at Chennai.
222	360	269	32	3	Israrullah	Peshawar v Lahore Ravi at Peshawar.[W15]
222		298	22	5	M. D. U. S. Jayasundera	Ragama v Burgher at Colombo.
221*	387	291	28	1	M. J. Lumb	Nottinghamshire v Derbyshire at Nottingham.
221	473	383	32	0	R. I. Keogh	Northamptonshire v Hampshire at Southampton.
219*	520	382	29	0	‡J. H. K. Adams.	Hampshire v Worcestershire at Southampton.
219	503	402	36	1	K. J. Coetzer	Northamptonshire v Leicestershire at Leicester.
218	575	444	35	1	‡J. H. K. Adams.	Hampshire v Northamptonshire at Southampton.
218	572	416	31	0	D. M. Bravo	West Indies v New Zealand (First Test) at Dunedin.
218	498	388	27	2	Mehrab Hossain	Central Zone v East Zone at Bogra.
217*	491	319	23	0	L. R. P. L. Taylor	New Zealand v West Indies (First Test) at Dunedin.
215*	416	307	22	1	S. D. Robson	Middlesex v Warwickshire at Birmingham.
215*	469	335	27	0	P. J. van Biljon	Free State v SW Districts at Bloemfontein.[W15]

	Mins	Balls	4	6		
214*		291	12	2	S. A. Engelbrecht	Western Province v Namibia at Windhoek.
214	431	307	20	2	C. J. L. Rogers	Middlesex v Surrey at Lord's.
213	399	303	13	5	M. K. Pandey	South Zone v West Zone at Chennai.[W15]
212	493	351	17	1	‡R. N. B. Apparajith	South Zone v West Zone at Chennai.[W15]
212	533	400	18	3	Y. V. Takawale	Tripura v Hyderabad at Hyderabad.[W15]
211	430	347	25	2	A. P. R. Gidman	Gloucestershire v Kent at Cheltenham.
211	488	345	21	5	N. V. Ojha	Madhya Pradesh v Services at Delhi.[W15]
211	478	337	23	5	S. V. Samson	Kerala v Assam at Guwahati.[W15]
210*	589	418	24	0	Ali Asad	Quetta v Peshawar at Peshawar.
210	610	432	21	1	R. S. Second	Knights v Titans at Benoni.
209*	500	345	26	1	P. Dogra	Himachal Pradesh v Goa at Dharamsala.[W15]
208*	514	380	24	2	A. N. Ghosh	Railways v Baroda at Vadodara.[W15]
208	526	412	26	1	L. W. P. Wells	Sussex v Surrey at The Oval.
206*		234	21	3	B. M. A. J. Mendis	Tamil Union v Colombo at Colombo.
205*	450	295	32	0	‡Abid Ali	United Bank v Habib Bank at Islamabad.[W15]
205*	295	218	21	3	D. I. Stevens	Kent v Lancashire at Canterbury.
205*		266	17	3	W. U. Tharanga	Nondescripts v Chilaw Marians at Colombo.
205	433	321	26	0	A. V. Vasavada	Saurashtra v Uttar Pradesh at Rajkot.[W15]
204*	317	239	24	3	E. C. Joyce	Sussex v Nottinghamshire at Nottingham.
204*	501	358	21	0	J. W. A. Taylor	Nottinghamshire v Sussex at Nottingham.
204	533	393	26	0	P. J. Hughes	South Australia v Western Australia at Adelaide.[W15]
204	394	267	29	1	K. M. Jadhav	Maharashtra v Hyderabad at Hyderabad.[W15]
204	450	341	30	1	‡C. A. Pujara	India v Australia (Second Test) at Hyderabad.
203*		274	13	1	M. L. R. Buddika	Tamil Union v Kurunegala Youth at Colombo.
203*	313	214	23	9	W. R. Landsdale	Griqualand West v Gauteng at Johannesburg.
203	578	395	19	1	‡R. N. B. Apparajith	Tamil Nadu v Services at Delhi.[W15]
203		192	14	10	‡M. D. K. J. Perera	Colts v Burgher at Colombo.
202*	512	386	30	0	‡Abid Ali	Lahore Ravi v Quetta at Lahore.
202	443	297	26	2	Usman Arshad	State Bank v KRL at Rawalpindi.[W15]
201*	531	378	24	3	G. H. Vihari	Hyderabad v Goa at Porvorim.[W15]
201		216	16	6	B. C. de Wett	Border v Namibia at Windhoek.
201	514	381	26	2	Sunny Singh	Haryana v Gujarat at Ahmedabad.[W15]
200*	448	349	27	1	R. T. Ponting	Tasmania v New South Wales at Hobart.
200*		358	20	0	M. S. Warnapura	Bloomfield v Army at Colombo.
200*	614	404	15	3	Younis Khan	Pakistan v Zimbabwe (First Test) at Harare.
200*	453	324	19	1	V. H. Zol	Maharashtra v Tripura at Gahunje.[W15]
200	377	217	25	0	Jiwanjot Singh	Punjab v Vidarbha at Mohali.[W15]
200	486	322	26	1	S. M. Katich	Lancashire v Northamptonshire at Northampton.
200	437	321	22	1	Mushfiqur Rahim	Bangladesh v Sri Lanka (First Test) at Galle.

‡ *Pujara scored four double-hundreds (including two triples), while Abid Ali, Adams, Apparajith and Perera each scored two.*

Hundred on First-Class Debut

114	Adeel Basit	Bahawalpur v Rawalpindi at Multan.[W15]
146	D. P. D. N. Dickwella . . .	Nondescripts v Kurunegala Youth at Colombo.
116	Fahim Ashraf	Faisalabad v Multan at Faisalabad.[W15]
141*	D. N. Hakaraia	Auckland v Northern Districts at Hamilton.
133	Mohammad Ali	Abbottabad v Sialkot at Abbottabad.[W15]
110	V. H. Zol	India A v New Zealand A at Visakhapatnam.

> ❝
> Few enjoyed themselves more than Hedley Verity, who took seven Sussex wickets for nine to win the game. The same day, Germany invaded Poland. Verity never played first-class cricket again.❞
> Cricket Books, 2013, page 133.

Three Hundreds in Successive Innings

N. B. Behera (Orissa)	158	v Delhi at Sambalpur.[W15]
	130 and 127*	v Mumbai at Mumbai.[W15]
	106	v Gujarat at Ahmedabad.[W15]
A. W. Gale (Yorkshire)	272	v Nottinghamshire at Scarborough.
	103	v Middlesex at Lord's.
	148	v Surrey at Leeds.
Kamran Hussain (Bahawalpur). . . .	139 and 118*	v Karachi Whites at Multan.
	123	v Quetta at Multan.
A. U. Rashid (Yorkshire)	180	v Somerset at Leeds.
	110*	v Warwickshire at Birmingham.
	103*	v Somerset at Taunton.
Rizwan Ahmed (Hyderabad)	105 and 104	v Karachi Whites at Hyderabad.
	157	v Bahawalpur at Hyderabad.
J. E. Root (Yorkshire).	182	v Durham at Chester-le-Street.
	236	v Derbyshire at Leeds.
	179	England Lions v New Zealanders at Leicester.
K. C. Sangakkara (Sri Lanka).	142 and 105	v Bangladesh (First Test) at Galle.
	139	v Bangladesh (Second Test) at Colombo.
R. G. Sharma (India).	119	India A v South Africa A at Rustenburg.
	177	v West Indies (First Test) at Kolkata.
	111*	v West Indies (Second Test) at Mumbai.
J. K. Silva (Sinhalese).	148	v Kurunegala Youth at Kurunegala.
	180	v Tamil Union at Colombo.
	171	v Moors at Colombo.

Hundred in Each Innings of a Match

L. Abeyratne	131	124*	Saracens v Burgher at Colombo.
M. M. Ali	104	109	Worcestershire v Lancashire at Worcester.
G. S. Ballance	148	108*	Yorkshire v Surrey at The Oval.
N. B. Behera	130	127*	Orissa v Mumbai at Mumbai.[W15]
R. C. C. Canning	113	106*	Boland v KwaZulu-Natal Inland at Pietermaritzburg.
E. J. H. Eckersley	106	119	Leicestershire v Worcestershire at Leicester.
P. G. Fulton	136	110	New Zealand v England (Third Test) at Auckland.
Imad Wasim	110	110*	Islamabad v Lahore Shalimar at Islamabad.[W15]
Kamran Hussain	139	118*	Bahawalpur v Karachi Whites at Multan.
F. D. M. Karunaratne .	101	100*	Sri Lanka A v West Indies A at Basseterre.
D. A. Miller	109	104	Dolphins v Lions at Potchefstroom.[W15]
K. D. Petersen	134	110	Boland v Free State at Bloemfontein.[W15]
A. G. Prince	134	108	Lancashire v Kent at Canterbury.
Rehan Afridi	139*	115	Abbottabad v Karachi Blues at Karachi.[W15]
Rizwan Ahmed	105	104	Hyderabad v Karachi Whites at Hyderabad.
K. C. Sangakkara	142	105	Sri Lanka v Bangladesh (First Test) at Galle.
D. S. Smith.	139	106*	Windward Islands v Comb. Campuses & Colls at Gros Islet.
Y. V. Takawale	125	109*	Tripura v Maharashtra at Gahunje.[W15]
B. R. M. Taylor	171	102*	Zimbabwe v Bangladesh (First Test) at Harare.
B. R. M. Taylor	102	150*	Mid West Rhinos v Mashonaland Eagles at Harare.[W15]
Umar Siddiq	143	119*	Lahore Shalimar v Quetta at Lahore.[W15]

Carrying Bat through Completed Innings

Abid Ali.	205*	United Bank (386) v Habib Bank at Islamabad.[W15]
J. H. K. Adams	138*	Hampshire (274) v Gloucestershire at Bristol.
K. C. Brathwaite	91*	Barbados (205) v Windward Islands at Bridgetown.
C. F. Hughes	270*	Derbyshire (475) v Yorkshire at Leeds.
T. Nadeera.	105*	Air Force (244) v Burgher at Colombo.
M. H. W. Papps.	183*	Wellington (459) v Canterbury at Rangiora.[W15]
V. A. Saxena	119*	Rajasthan (244) v Bengal at Jaipur.[W15]
Shabih Haider	88*	Hyderabad (222) v Lahore Shalimar at Hyderabad.[W15]

Hundred before Lunch

R. J. Hamilton-Brown	126*	Sussex v Yorkshire at Hove (4th day).
C. D. Nash	21* to 167*	Sussex v Yorkshire at Hove (4th day).
S. R. Watson	102*	Worcestershire v Australians at Worcester (1st day).

Hamilton-Brown and Nash were facing declaration bowling.

Most Sixes in an Innings

14	M. D. K. J. Perera (336)	Colts v Saracens at Colombo.
12	S. R. Patel (256)	Nottinghamshire v Durham MCCU at Nottingham.
12	S. S. Tiwary (238)	Jharkhand v Mumbai at Mumbai.[W15]
11	L. J. P. Gunaratne (155*)	Moors v Colts at Colombo.
11	L. J. P. Gunaratne (199*)	Moors v Air Force at Colombo.
11	S. M. A. Priyanjan (235)	Ports Authority v Kurunegala Youth at Kurunegala.
11	M. G. Vandort (251)	Ragama v Air Force at Colombo.
10	G. N. Addicott (145)	South Western Districts v Gauteng at Oudtshoorn.
10	A. B. T. Lakshitha (87)	Bloomfield v Saracens at Colombo.
10	A. K. K. Y. Lanka (139)	Air Force v Saracens at Colombo.
10	M. D. K. J. Perera (203)	Colts v Burgher at Colombo.

Most Runs in Boundaries

	4	6		
208	40	8	S. H. T. Kandamby (340*)	Sinhalese v Tamil Union at Colombo.
202	49	1	C. A. Pujara (352)	Saurashtra v Karnataka at Rajkot.
200	50	0	Imran Farhat (308)	Lahore Ravi v Peshawar at Lahore.
200	29	14	M. D. K. J. Perera (336)	Colts v Saracens at Colombo.

Longest Innings

Mins		
823	T. Kohli (300*)	Punjab v Jharkhand at Jamshedpur.
741	C. A. Pujara (269)	Saurashtra v Tamil Nadu at Chennai.[W15]
701	A. Mukund (240)	Tamil Nadu v Saurashtra at Chennai.[W15]
658	S. U. Shrivastava (193)	Vidarbha v Karnataka at Nagpur.[W15]
643	S. Badrinath (248)	Tamil Nadu v Madhya Pradesh at Indore.[W15]
633	S. D. Choudhary (239*)	Madhya Pradesh v Railways at Indore.[W15]
627	G. C. Smith (234)	South Africa v Pakistan (Second Test) at Dubai.
614	Younis Khan (200*)	Pakistan v Zimbabwe (First Test) at Harare.
610	R. S. Second (210)	Knights v Titans at Benoni.
607	D. B. Prasanth Kumar (199)	Andhra v Himachal Pradesh at Cuddapah.[W15]
606	T. W. M. Latham (241*)	Canterbury v Wellington at Wellington.[W15]
603	Imran Farhat (308)	Lahore Ravi v Peshawar at Lahore.

First-Wicket Partnership of 100 in Each Innings

102	101	S. P. Wakaskar/A. A. Waghmode, Baroda v Mumbai at Mumbai.
105	142	Mohammad Hafeez/Nasir Jamshed, Pakistanis v S. African Invitation XI at E. London.
116	104	S. R. Watson/E. J. M. Cowan, Australians v India A at Chennai.
106	110*	C. J. L. Rogers/S. D. Robson, Middlesex v Nottinghamshire at Nottingham.
101	127	Yasir Hameed/Sharjeel Khan, ZTBL v State Bank at Rawalpindi.[W15]
131	193	L. A. Pomersbach/J. A. Burns, Queensland v Victoria at Brisbane.[W15]

Highest Wicket Partnerships

First Wicket

333   M. D. U. S. Jayasundera/G. I. Daniel, Ragama v Burgher at Colombo.
318   A. N. Cook/M. A. Carberry, England XI v Australia A at Hobart.
289   M. Vijay/S. Dhawan, India v Australia (Third Test) at Mohali.
283   Asif Zakir/Fazal Subhan, Karachi Whites v Lahore Shalimar at Lahore.^{W15}
259   C. J. L. Rogers/S. D. Robson, Middlesex v Surrey at Lord's.
253   M. Klinger/P. J. Hughes, South Australia v Western Australia at Adelaide.^{W15}

Second Wicket

370   M. Vijay/C. A. Pujara, India v Australia (Second Test) at Hyderabad.
311   A. Z. Lees/P. A. Jaques, Yorkshire v Derbyshire at Chesterfield.
308   V. Chopra/W. T. S. Porterfield, Warwickshire v MCC at Abu Dhabi.
307   J. S. Saxena/N. V. Ojha, Madhya Pradesh v Saurashtra at Indore.^{W15}
301   D. R. Flynn/B. S. Wilson, Northern Districts v Auckland at Hamilton.
270   Jiwanjot Singh/U. Kaul, Punjab v Vidarbha at Mohali.^{W15}
267   M. N. Erlank/R. S. Second, Free State v Eastern Province at Bloemfontein.
264   P. A. Jaques/K. S. Williamson, Yorkshire v Durham at Scarborough.
260   A. P. Tare/A. M. Rahane, Mumbai v Vidarbha at Mumbai.^{W15}
258   C. F. Hughes/W. L. Madsen, Derbyshire v Yorkshire at Leeds.
256   A. B. Fudadin/K. A. Edwards, West Indies A v Sri Lanka A at Basseterre.
250   P. Akshath Reddy/D. B. Ravi Teja, Hyderabad v Tripura at Hyderabad.^{W15}

Third Wicket

311   R. Dewan/S. Rana, Haryana v Orissa at Bhubaneswar.^{W15}
291   M. G. Bracewell/N. T. Broom, Otago v Wellington at Dunedin.
282   T. Kohli/Mandeep Singh, Punjab v Orissa at Mohali.^{W15}
278   S. C. Cook/N. D. McKenzie, Lions v Warriors at Potchefstroom.^{W15}
275   M. H. Yardy/M. W. Machan, Sussex v Somerset at Taunton.
267   C. D. J. Dent/A. P. R. Gidman, Gloucestershire v Kent at Cheltenham.
267   Israrullah/Mohammad Idrees, Peshawar v Lahore Ravi at Peshawar.^{W15}
265   W. L. Madsen/S. Chanderpaul, Derbyshire v Surrey at Derby.
250* L. A. Dawson/J. M. Vince, Hampshire v Leicestershire at Leicester.

Fourth Wicket

353   C. A. Pujara/J. N. Shah, Saurashtra v Tamil Nadu at Chennai.^{W15}
343   C. A. Pujara/S. P. Jackson, Saurashtra v Karnataka at Rajkot.
325   Sami Aslam/Kamran Akmal, National Bank v State Bank at Sialkot.^{W15}
310   P. J. van Biljon/A. J. Pienaar, Free State v South Western Districts at Bloemfontein.^{W15}
289   S. A. Engelbrecht/G. B. Barnes, Western Province v Northerns at Centurion.
280   D. M. Housego/H. J. H. Marshall, Gloucestershire v Essex at Chelmsford.
269   A. Javid/L. J. Evans, Warwickshire v Somerset at Birmingham.
264* T. Kohli/U. Kaul, Punjab v Jharkhand at Jamshedpur.
260* C. D. Nash/R. J. Hamilton-Brown, Sussex v Yorkshire at Hove.

Fifth Wicket

494† Marshall Ayub/Mehrab Hossain, Central Zone v East Zone at Bogra.
338   G. C. Smith/A. B. de Villiers, South Africa v Pakistan (Second Test) at Dubai.
317   A. N. Ghosh/M. Rawat, Railways v Uttar Pradesh at Lucknow.^{W15}
297   A. W. Gale/G. S. Ballance, Yorkshire v Nottinghamshire at Scarborough.
277   Sami Aslam/Adnan Akmal, Lahore Ravi v Hyderabad at Islamabad.
274   R. S. Second/L. van Wyk, Free State v Border at Bloemfontein.
270   J. C. Mickleburgh/B. T. Foakes, Essex v Leicestershire at Chelmsford.
268   Umar Siddiq/Agha Salman, Lahore Shalimar v Quetta at Lahore.^{W15}
267   Mohammad Ashraful/Mushfiqur Rahim, Bangladesh v Sri Lanka (First Test) at Galle.
260* M. I. Ghouse/L. J. P. Gunaratne, Moors v Colts at Colombo.
256   B. H. Merai/Y. Venugopal Rao, Gujarat v Haryana at Ahmedabad.^{W15}

Sixth Wicket

267	D. Elgar/T. L. Tsolekile, South Africa A v Australia A at Pretoria.	
264	H. E. van der Dussen/D. Pretorius, North West v South Western Districts at Potchefstroom.	
218	P. D. Trego/C. F. K. van Wyk, Central Districts v Auckland at Napier.[W15]	
208	G. L. van Buuren/H. Klaasen, Northerns v Boland at Paarl.	
200	M. J. Clarke/B. J. Haddin, Australia v England (Second Test) at Adelaide.	
200	S. Chanderpaul/D. Ramdin, West Indies v New Zealand (Third Test) at Hamilton.	

Seventh Wicket

294	Sarfraz Ahmed/Tahir Khan, PIA v ZTBL at Rawalpindi.[W15]
293*	R. T. Ponting/J. J. Krejza, Tasmania v New South Wales at Hobart.
280	R. G. Sharma/R. Ashwin, India v West Indies (First Test) at Kolkata.
246	A. P. Tare/A. B. Agarkar, Mumbai v Services at Delhi.
226	S. H. T. Kandamby/J. M. U. B. Jayasena, Sinhalese v Tamil Union at Colombo.
224	L. J. P. Gunaratne/R. S. Wickramarachchi, Moors v Air Force at Colombo.
218	K. K. Jennings/M. J. Richardson, Durham v Sussex at Hove.
211	A. Javid/K. H. D. Barker, Warwickshire v Surrey at Guildford.
207	Aftab Alam/Jamal Anwar, Habib Bank v United Bank at Islamabad.[W15]
200	J. W. A. Taylor/A. Shahzad, Nottinghamshire v Sussex at Nottingham.

Eighth Wicket

253	R. S. Second/D. du Preez, Knights v Titans at Benoni.
219	H. Klaasen/J. P. de Villiers, Northerns v Boland at Pretoria.[W15]
195	Ali Khan/Nayyer Abbas, KRL v State Bank at Rawalpindi.[W15]
191	A. J. Wheater/M. T. Coles, Hampshire v Lancashire at Southport.
177	P. P. Chawla/A. Mishra, Uttar Pradesh v Tamil Nadu at Meerut.[W15]
174	Aamer Yamin/Haziq Habibullah, Multan v Quetta at Multan.[W15]
165	Fawad Alam/Mohammad Sami, Karachi Whites v Hyderabad at Hyderabad.
165	M. R. D. G. Mapa Bandara/P. A. S. S. Jeewantha, Badureliya v Ports Authority at Colombo.
158*	R. E. van der Merwe/S. von Berg, Titans v Cape Cobras at Benoni.
156	G. S. Ballance/R. J. Sidebottom, Yorkshire v Leeds/Bradford MCCU at Leeds.
151	R. M. Fernandez/P. Prasanth, Kerala v Hyderabad at Hyderabad.[W15]

Ninth Wicket

166	C. R. Woakes/M. A. Chambers, Warwickshire v Derbyshire at Derby.
166	Faheem Ahmed/Khurram Shahzad, Karachi Whites v Multan at Karachi.[W15]
165	Rehan Afridi/Umair Khan, Abbottabad v Karachi Blues at Karachi.[W15]
162	D. A. J. Bracewell/I. S. Sodhi, New Zealand A v India A at Visakhapatnam.[W15]
154*	S. von Berg/J. P. de Villiers, Northerns v South Western Districts at Oudtshoorn.
154	S. S. Tiwary/S. S. Rao, Jharkhand v Mumbai at Mumbai.[W15]
152	N. Gangta/V. Malik, Himachal Pradesh v Andhra at Cuddapah.[W15]

Tenth Wicket

163	P. J. Hughes/A. C. Agar, Australia v England (First Test) at Nottingham.
127	B. J. Watling/T. A. Boult, New Zealand v Bangladesh (First Test) at Chittagong.
117	S. P. Crook/T. A. Copeland, Northamptonshire v Essex at Northampton.
114	G. Chapple/S. C. Kerrigan, Lancashire v Hampshire at Southport.
109	C. A. Dry/G. A. Vries, Free State v KwaZulu-Natal at Bloemfontein.
109	O. V. Brown/S. S. Cottrell, Jamaica v Leeward Islands at Kingston.
103	C. S. Baugh/S. S. Cottrell, Jamaica v Trinidad & Tobago at Kingston.

† *National record.*

Most Wickets in an Innings

9-59	Wahab Riaz	Lahore Shalimar v Lahore Ravi at Lahore.
9-69	Imran Khan	ZTBL v United Bank at Islamabad.[W15]
8-20	S. J. Magoffin	Sussex v Somerset at Horsham.
8-30	A. C. R. Birch	Warriors v Knights at Bloemfontein.
8-31	R. Pretorius	KwaZulu-Natal Inland v North West at Pietermaritzburg.[W15]
8-37	A. Richardson	Worcestershire v Gloucestershire at Worcester.

8-42	Imran Ali................	Sui Northern Gas v Port Qasim Authority at Rawalpindi.[W15]
8-45	K. J. Abbott..............	Dolphins v Cape Cobras at Cape Town.
8-46	O. P. Rayner	Middlesex v Surrey at The Oval.
8-48	R. L. Mali...............	Railways v Baroda at Vadodara.[W15]
8-50	Gohar Faiz	Quetta v Islamabad at Islamabad.
8-50	Sadaf Hussain	KRL v National Bank at Faisalabad.[W15]
8-53	P. A. S. S. Jeewantha	Badureliya v Sinhalese at Colombo.
8-61	A. G. Cremer.............	Mid West Rhinos v Southern Rocks at Kwekwe.
8-73	Sanjamul Islam	North Zone v Central Zone at Mirpur.
8-76	W. A. H. N. Wickramasinghe	Burgher v Air Force at Colombo.
8-81	Imad Wasim	Islamabad v Multan at Karachi.[W15]
8-82	S. Shillingford..........	Windward Islands v Barbados at Bridgetown.
8-84	I. C. Pandey.............	Madhya Pradesh v Railways at Indore.[W15]
8-87	S. R. Harmer.............	South Africa A v Australia A at Rustenburg.
8-96	C. T. Tremlett	Surrey v Durham at Chester-le-Street.
8-98	Abdul Ameer	Karachi Whites v Rawalpindi at Rawalpindi.
8-120	Zulfiqar Babar...........	WAPDA v PIA at Faisalabad.[W15]

Most Wickets in a Match

15-118	O. P. Rayner	Middlesex v Surrey at The Oval.
15-201	Zulfiqar Babar..........	WAPDA v PIA at Faisalabad.[W15]
14-40	A. R. Nurse.............	Barbados v Windward Islands at St George's.
13-97	Imran Ali...............	Sui Northern Gas v Port Qasim Authority at Rawalpindi.[W15]
13-107	J. Coetzee	Griqualand West v Boland at Paarl.[W15]
13-119	Atif Maqbool	Karachi Whites v Abbottabad at Karachi.
13-124	J. S. Saxena............	Madhya Pradesh v Baroda at Vadodara.[W15]
12-31	S. J. Magoffin	Sussex v Somerset at Horsham.
12-63	A. Richardson...........	Worcestershire v Kent at Canterbury.
12-69	Yasir Shah..............	Abbottabad v Faisalabad at Swabi.
12-76	R. Pretorius............	KwaZulu-Natal Inland v Namibia at Windhoek.
12-91	P. H. T. Kaushal	Nondescripts v Chilaw Marians at Colombo.
12-94	P. M. Pushpakumara......	Moors v Burgher at Colombo.
12-96	K. J. Abbott.............	Dolphins v Cape Cobras at Cape Town.
12-102	Imad Wasim	Islamabad v Multan at Karachi.[W15]
12-102	S. Shillingford..........	Windward Islands v Barbados at Bridgetown.
12-106	Imran Tahir	Lions v Dolphins at Durban.
12-107	A. Richardson...........	Worcestershire v Gloucestershire at Worcester.
12-120	Wahab Riaz	Lahore Shalimar v Lahore Ravi at Lahore.
12-157	H. M. R. K. B. Herath.....	Sri Lanka v Bangladesh (Second Test) at Colombo.
12-162	B. M. D. K. Mendis	Navy v Kurunegala Youth at Kurunegala.
12-198	R. Ashwin..............	India v Australia (First Test) at Chennai.
12-252	S. C. Kerrigan...........	Lancashire v Glamorgan at Manchester.

Outstanding Innings Analyses

10.1–4–10–7	A. R. Nurse........	Barbados v Windward Islands at St George's.
8.1–6–8–6	D. W. Steyn	South Africa v Pakistan (First Test) at Johannesburg.
3.4–2–1–5	D. Klein	North West v KwaZulu-Natal Inland at Potchefstroom.
3–3–0–4	J. L. Carter	Barbados v Jamaica at Bridgetown.

Hat-Tricks (13)

R. V. Dhruve	Gujarat v Vidarbha at Nagpur.[W15]
J. K. Fuller.....................	Gloucestershire v Worcestershire at Cheltenham.
J. O. A. Gordon	Canada v United Arab Emirates at King City.
H. F. Gurney....................	Nottinghamshire v Sussex at Hove.
Izatullah Dawlatzai..............	Afghanistan v Namibia at Windhoek.

P. A. S. S. Jeewantha	Badureliya v Sinhalese at Colombo.	
L. M. G. Masekela	Free State v KwaZulu-Natal at Chatsworth.[W15]	
Mohammad Ashraful	Central Zone v North Zone at Mirpur.	
A. Richardson	Worcestershire v Leicestershire at Leicester.	
T. S. Roland-Jones	Middlesex v Derbyshire at Lord's.	
Sohag Gazi	Bangladesh v New Zealand (First Test) at Chittagong.	
Umar Gul	Habib Bank v Sui Northern Gas at Karachi.	
Wahab Riaz	Lahore Shalimar v Lahore Ravi at Lahore.	

Most Balls Bowled in an Innings

498	83–21–193–2	S. Nadeem	Jharkhand v Punjab at Jamshedpur.
450	75–29–143–3	A. J. Shinde	Hyderabad v Assam at Guwahati.[W15]

Match Double (100 runs and 10 wickets)

W. R. S. Gidman .   143; 6-15, 4-28   Gloucestershire v Leicestershire at Bristol.

Most Wicketkeeping Dismissals in an Innings

7 (7ct)	G. L. Cloete	Griqualand West v Gauteng at Johannesburg.
7 (7ct)	O. B. Cox	Worcestershire v Oxford MCCU at Oxford.
6 (6ct)	J. M. Bairstow	Yorkshire v Middlesex at Leeds.
6 (5ct, 1st)	B. G. Barnes	Western Province v North West at Cape Town.
6 (6ct)	B. G. Barnes	Western Province v Gauteng at Cape Town.[W15]
6 (6ct)	M. D. Bates.	Hampshire v Northamptonshire at Southampton.
6 (6ct)	A. B. de Villiers	South Africa v Pakistan (First Test) at Johannesburg.
6 (6ct)	J. N. Hamilton	Leeward Islands v Guyana at North Sound.
6 (6ct)	Jamal Anwar.	Habib Bank v KRL at Rawalpindi.[W15]
6 (5ct, 1st)	H. Klaasen	Northerns v Eastern Province at Pretoria.
6 (6ct)	S. Masondo.	Gauteng v Griqualand West at Johannesburg.
6 (6ct)	P. Mustard	Durham v Surrey at Chester-le-Street.
6 (6ct)	Naeem Anjum	Islamabad v Quetta at Islamabad.
6 (6ct)	M. J. Prior.	Sussex v Warwickshire at Hove.
6 (6ct)	C. M. W. Read	Nottinghamshire v Yorkshire at Nottingham.
6 (6ct)	K. N. Saikia	Assam v Himachal Pradesh at Dharamsala.[W15]
6 (6ct)	J. A. Simpson	Middlesex v Yorkshire at Leeds.
6 (5ct, 1st)	K. Srikar Bharat	Andhra v Assam at Anantapur.[W15]
6 (5ct, 1st)	K. Srikar Bharat	Andhra v Goa at Porvorim.[W15]
6 (5ct, 1st)	N. Surendran.	Kerala v Goa at Porvorim.[W15]
6 (6ct)	Talha Qureshi.	Rawalpindi v Sialkot at Sialkot.[W15]
6 (6ct)	N. J. van den Bergh . .	North West v Boland at Potchefstroom.
6 (5ct, 1st)	N. J. van den Bergh . .	North West v South Western Districts at Oudtshoorn.[W15]
6 (6ct)	L. R. Walters	Eastern Province v Northerns at Port Elizabeth.[W15]

Most Wicketkeeping Dismissals in a Match

11 (11ct)	A. B. de Villiers	South Africa v Pakistan (First Test) at Johannesburg.
10 (7ct, 3st)	Anop Santosh	PIA v Pakistan Television at Islamabad.[W15]
10 (10ct)	G. L. Cloete	Griqualand West v Gauteng at Johannesburg.
10 (9ct, 1st)	T. D. Paine	Tasmania v Western Australia at Hobart.[W15]
10 (10ct)	S. A. Westaway	Oxford University v Cambridge University at Cambridge.
9 (9ct)	B. C. Brown	Sussex v Somerset at Taunton.
9 (9ct)	O. B. Cox	Worcestershire v Oxford MCCU at Oxford.
9 (8ct, 1st)	Jamal Anwar.	Habib Bank v KRL at Rawalpindi.[W15]
9 (9ct)	Javed Mansoor	Karachi Blues v Bahawalpur at Karachi.[W15]
9 (9ct)	U. Kaul	Punjab v Haryana at Rohtak.[W15]
9 (9ct)	T. P. Ludeman	South Australia v New South Wales at Adelaide.
9 (9ct)	A. P. McLaren	Warriors v Lions at Port Elizabeth.
9 (8ct, 1st)	Mohammad Rizwan . .	Peshawar v Bahawalpur at Mirpur.

9 (9ct)	D. Murphy	Northamptonshire v Glamorgan at Northampton.
9 (5ct, 4st)	M. A. R. Shehan	Chilaw Marians v Badureliya at Maggona.
9 (7ct, 2st)	N. Surendran.	Kerala v Goa at Porvorim.[W15]
9 (9ct)	N. J. van den Bergh . .	North West v Boland at Potchefstroom.

Most Catches in an Innings in the Field

5	G. E. Mathurin	Windward Islands v Barbados at Bridgetown.
5	D. J. G. Sammy	West Indies v India (Second Test) at Mumbai.
5	M. E. Trescothick.	Somerset v Middlesex at Lord's.

Most Catches in a Match in the Field

7	G. E. Mathurin	Windward Islands v Barbados at Bridgetown.
7	D. S. Smith.	Windward Islands v Trinidad & Tobago at Arnos Vale.
6	N. M. N. P. Nawela	Bloomfield v Burgher at Colombo.
6	M. H. W. Papps	Wellington v Otago at Invercargill.[W15]
6	Taimur Ali	Quetta v Bahawalpur at Multan.

No Byes Conceded in Total of 500 or More

Amir Khan	Uttar Pradesh v Railways (518-9 dec) at Lucknow.[W15]
D. P. D. N. Dickwella. . .	Sri Lanka Cricket Development XI v SL Board XI (575) at Colombo.[W15]
J. S. Foster	Essex v Northamptonshire (531) at Colchester.
Jamal Anwar.	Rawalpindi v Sialkot (563-7 dec) at Rawalpindi.
Kamran Akmal	National Bank v State Bank (526) at Sialkot.[W15]
K. D. Karthik	Tamil Nadu v Uttar Pradesh (500-9 dec) at Meerut.[W15]
U. Kaul	Punjab v Karnataka (505-9 dec) at Hubli.[W15]
Mohammad Rizwan	Peshawar v Lahore Ravi (512-6 dec) at Lahore.
M. Mosehle.	Titans v Warriors (502-5 dec) at Port Elizabeth.[W15]
M. J. Prior.	England v Australia (527-7 dec) (Third Test) at Manchester.
K. A. Vaz	Goa v Maharashtra (635) at Gahunje.[W15]
K. A. Vaz	Goa v Hyderabad (514-6 dec) at Porvorim.[W15]

Highest Innings Totals

787-8 dec	Sinhalese v Tamil Union at Colombo.
718-9	Saurashtra v Karnataka at Rajkot.
699-3 dec	Punjab v Jharkhand at Jamshedpur.
677-7 dec	Yorkshire v Derbyshire at Leeds.
655-7 dec	Central Zone v East Zone at Bogra.
651-9 dec	Otago v Wellington at Dunedin.
650-8 dec	Tripura v Hyderabad at Hyderabad.[W15]
645-9 dec	Mumbai v Baroda at Mumbai.
638	Bangladesh v Sri Lanka (First Test) at Galle.
636-8 dec	West Indies A v Sri Lanka A at Basseterre.
635	Maharashtra v Goa at Gahunje.[W15]
634-5 dec	Surrey v Yorkshire at The Oval.
632-7 dec	Saurashtra v Uttar Pradesh at Rajkot.[W15]
631-9 dec	Warwickshire v Surrey at Guildford.
626-4 dec	Haryana v Orissa at Bhubaneswar.[W15]
619-8 dec	Madhya Pradesh v Saurashtra at Indore.[W15]
617-5 dec	Yorkshire v Derbyshire at Chesterfield.
616-9 dec	Maharashtra v Hyderabad at Hyderabad.[W15]
614-7 dec	Northern Districts v Auckland at Hamilton.
614-7 dec	South Africa A v Australia A at Pretoria.
611-8 dec	Colts v Saracens at Colombo.
609-9 dec	New Zealand v West Indies (First Test) at Dunedin.
602-7 dec	Colts v Burgher at Colombo.

601-8 dec   South Western Districts v Northerns at Pretoria.[W15]
601   South Australia v Western Australia at Adelaide.[W15]
600-9 dec   South Zone v West Zone at Chennai.[W15]

Lowest Innings Totals

20   Essex v Lancashire at Chelmsford.
26   KwaZulu-Natal Inland v North West at Potchefstroom.
31   Services v Baroda at Vadodara.[W15]
39   Bahawalpur v Sialkot at Bahawalpur.[W15]
44   Windward Islands v Barbados at St George's.
45   New Zealand v South Africa (First Test) at Cape Town.
45   Quetta v Karachi Whites at Karachi.[W15]
48   Griqualand West v Eastern Province at Kimberley.[W15]
49   Pakistan v South Africa (First Test) at Johannesburg.
51   Karachi Blues v Rawalpindi at Rawalpindi.[W15]
53†   State Bank v National Bank at Sialkot.[W15]
58   Free State v Boland at Paarl.
58   Free State v Western Province at Rondebosch.[W15]
60   Kurunegala Youth v Nondescripts at Colombo.
60   Derbyshire v Middlesex at Lord's.
60   Madhya Pradesh v Baroda at Vadodara.[W15]
61   Burgher v Moors at Colombo.
62   Northamptonshire v Lancashire at Manchester.
63   Kent v Worcestershire at Canterbury.
63   Derbyshire v Durham at Derby.
63   Lahore Ravi v Karachi Blues at Karachi.[W15]
64   Barbados v Windward Islands at Bridgetown.
64   Pakistan Television v United Bank at Islamabad.[W15]
65   Quetta v Karachi Whites at Karachi.[W15]
65   Port Qasim Authority v Habib Bank at Sialkot.[W15]
67   Windward Islands v Barbados at St George's.
68   New Zealand v England (First Test) at Lord's.
69   Titans v Dolphins at Centurion.
69   Karachi Whites v Rawalpindi at Rawalpindi.
69   Multan v Lahore Shalimar at Lahore.[W15]
69   Pakistan Television v WAPDA at Lahore.[W15]
71   KRL v Port Qasim Authority at Lahore.[W15]
72   Lions v Knights at Kimberley.[W15]
72   Services v Saurashtra at Rajkot.[W15]
74   Punjab v Delhi at Delhi.[W15]

†   *One batsman absent hurt.*

Highest Fourth-Innings Totals

459   Wellington v Canterbury at Rangiora (set 470).[W15]
450-7 South Africa v India (First Test) at Johannesburg (set 458).
427-9 Warwickshire v Somerset at Taunton (set 515).
418-8 Kent v Lancashire at Canterbury (set 418).
411-8 Kent v Gloucestershire at Cheltenham (set 411).
409-4 Auckland v Northern Districts at Auckland (set 409).[W15]

Match Aggregate of 1,500 Runs

1,613 for 19   Sri Lanka (570-4 dec and 335-4 dec) v Bangladesh (638 and 70-1) (First Test) at Galle.
1,599 for 19   Gloucestershire (562-5 dec and 237-1 dec) v Kent (389-5 dec and 411-8) at Cheltenham.

1,583 for 29   Saurashtra (469 and 718-9) v Karnataka (396) at Rajkot.
1,521 for 17   Northern Districts (461-4 dec and 299-5 dec) v Auckland (352-4 dec and 409-4) at Auckland.[W15]

Four Individual Hundreds in an Innings

North Zone (591-8 dec) v East Zone at Kochi.[W15]

Eight Individual Hundreds in a Match

Sri Lanka v Bangladesh (First Test) at Galle.

Six Individual Fifties in an Innings

Hyderabad (584) v Lahore Ravi at Islamabad.
Western Australia Cricket Association Chairman's XI (451-5 dec) v England XI at Perth.
Titans (491-7 dec) v Cape Cobras at Benoni.[W15]
Australia (570-9 dec) v England (Second Test) at Adelaide.

Large Margin of Victory

Nottinghamshire (396-3 dec and 408-9 dec) beat Durham MCCU (142 and 121) at Nottingham by 541 runs.

Eleven Bowlers in an Innings

Central Zone v North Zone (397-6) at Bogra.
Northerns v South Western Districts (601-8 dec) at Pretoria.[W15]
North West v Boland (449-4 dec) at Paarl.[W15]

Most Extras in an Innings

b	l-b	w	n-b	pen	
70	44	9	5	7	5	Rajasthan (438) v Tamil Nadu at Chennai.[W15]
56	19	19	5	8	5	Hampshire (545) v Northamptonshire at Southampton.
53	5	16	0	32		Gloucestershire (410-9 dec) v Hampshire at Southampton.
52	29	7	7	9		Bloomfield (366) v Ragama at Colombo.
51	7	16	16	12		Middlesex (353) v Nottinghamshire at Nottingham.
51	8	9	1	33		Hampshire (456) v Essex at Southampton.
50	23	25	0	2		Lancashire (448-7 dec) v Worcestershire at Manchester.
50	10	10	10	20		Derbyshire (298) v Durham at Derby.
50	24	12	4	10		Andhra (431) v Kerala at Thalassery.[W15]

Career Aggregate Milestones

25,000 runs	S. R. Tendulkar.
20,000 runs	S. M. Katich, C. J. L. Rogers.
15,000 runs	I. R. Bell, A. N. Cook, P. A. Jaques, A. G. Prince, T. T. Samaraweera, K. C. Sangakkara.
10,000 runs	M. A. Carberry, J. S. Foster, A. J. Hall, J. C. Hildreth, N. T. Paranavitana, Saeed Anwar, Yasir Hameed.
500 wickets	H. M. C. M. Bandara, G. J. Batty, Iftikhar Anjum, Mohammad Sami, Sarfraz Ahmed, D. W. Steyn.

RECORDS

Compiled by Philip Bailey

This section covers
- first-class records to December 31, 2013 (page 1260).
- List A one-day records to December 31, 2013 (page 1290).
- List A Twenty20 records to December 31, 2013 (page 1293).
- Test records to January 20, 2014, the end of the Pakistan v Sri Lanka series (page 1295).
- Test records series by series (page 1332).
- one-day international records to January 8, 2014 (page 1373).
- World Cup finals (page 1382).
- Twenty20 international records to December 31, 2013 (page 1383).
- miscellaneous other records to December 31, 2013 (page 1387).
- women's Test records to January 13, 2014, and women's one-day international and Twenty20 international records to December 31, 2013 (page 1391).

The sequence
- Test series records begin with those involving England, arranged in the order their opponents entered Test cricket (Australia, South Africa, West Indies, New Zealand, India, Pakistan, Sri Lanka, Zimbabwe, Bangladesh). Next come all remaining series involving Australia, then South Africa – and so on until Zimbabwe v Bangladesh records appear on page 1370.

Notes
- Unless otherwise stated, all records apply only to first-class cricket. This is considered to have started in 1815, after the Napoleonic War.
- mid-year seasons taking place outside England are given simply as 2002, 2003, etc.
- (E), (A), (SA), (WI), (NZ), (I), (P), (SL), (Z) or (B) indicates the nationality of a player or the country in which a record was made.
- in career records, dates in italic indicate seasons embracing two different years (i.e. non-English seasons). In these cases, only the first year is given, e.g. *2008* for 2008-09.

See also
- up-to-date records on www.wisdenrecords.com.
- Features of 2013 (page 1242).

CONTENTS

FIRST-CLASS RECORDS

BATTING RECORDS

TEAM RECORDS

LIST A ONE-DAY RECORDS

LIST A TWENTY20 RECORDS

TEST RECORDS

BATTING RECORDS

BOWLING RECORDS

ALL-ROUND RECORDS

WICKETKEEPING RECORDS

FIELDING RECORDS

TEAM RECORDS

PLAYERS

UMPIRES

TEST SERIES

ONE-DAY INTERNATIONAL RECORDS

TWENTY20 INTERNATIONAL RECORDS

MISCELLANEOUS RECORDS

WOMEN'S TEST AND OTHER INTERNATIONAL RECORDS

NOTES ON RECORDS

Corey, what a scorcher!

ROB SMYTH

Records are intrinsically vulnerable. And, in this age of fearless power hitting, few must feel as imperilled as retired batsmen. In 2013, Australia's Aaron Finch made the highest score in Twenty20 internationals with an innings of 156 against England at Southampton, while New Zealand's Corey Anderson needed only 36 balls to whack the fastest one-day international hundred, against West Indies at Queenstown, beating Shahid Afridi's record, set in October 1996, by one delivery.

Even Test bowlers were not safe: George Bailey equalled Brian Lara's record for most runs in a Test over, walloping James Anderson for 28 at Perth. During the English Ashes, Ashton Agar charmed the world while adding 163 with Phillip Hughes, Test cricket's highest tenth-wicket partnership. Another unlikely success story was Bangladesh's Sohag Gazi, who became the first person to score a hundred and take a hat-trick in the same Test.

Many of the overall Test and one-day international records – matches, runs, hundreds – will belong to Sachin Tendulkar for the foreseeable future, though in 2014 Shivnarine Chanderpaul may at least overtake Lara as West Indies' highest Test run-getter. James Anderson could pass Ian Botham as England's leading Test wicket-taker: he needs a further 41. Adam Gilchrist's record of 100 Test sixes is under threat from Chris Gayle, who began 2014 with 90. Jacques Kallis retired with 97, a surprising second in the table.

The world of Twenty20, where records are less established, offers the greatest scope for change. Brendon McCullum was set to become the first to score 2,000 runs in Twenty20 internationals, while the Pakistan trio of Saeed Ajmal, Umar Gul and Shahid Afridi were in a race to become the first to 100 wickets – a reflection, in part, of Pakistani's predilection for the format (they have played more Twenty20 international matches than anyone). As it turned out, McCullum broke a Test record first, though one that came too late for inclusion in this section: against India at Wellington in February, he became the first New Zealander to score a triple-century.

The following players have served or are serving bans after being found guilty of some form of corruption, or have admitted to some form of on-field corruption: Amit Singh (I), Ata-ur-Rehman (P), M. Azharuddin (I), A. Bali (I), A. A. Chavan (I), W. J. Cronje (SA), Danish Kaneria (P), H. H. Gibbs (SA), A. Jadeja (I), M. D. Mishra (I), Mohammad Aamer (P), Mohammad Ashraful (B), Mohammad Asif (P), M. O. Odumbe (Kenya), M. Prabhakar (I), Salim Malik (P), Salman Butt (P), M. N. Samuels (WI), Shariful Haque (B), Ajay Sharma (I), S. Sreesanth (I), S. J. Srivastava (I), T. P. Sudhindra (I), S. K. Trivedi (I), M. S. Westfield (E), H. S. Williams (SA), A. R. Yadav (I).

FIRST-CLASS RECORDS

Note: Throughout this section, bold type denotes performances in the calendar year 2013 or, in career figures, players who appeared in first-class cricket in that year.

BATTING RECORDS

HIGHEST INDIVIDUAL INNINGS

In all first-class cricket, there have been **194** individual scores of 300 or more. The highest are:

501*	B. C. Lara	Warwickshire v Durham at Birmingham	1994
499	Hanif Mohammad	Karachi v Bahawalpur at Karachi	1958-59
452*	D. G. Bradman	NSW v Queensland at Sydney	1929-30
443*	B. B. Nimbalkar	Maharashtra v Kathiawar at Poona	1948-49
437	W. H. Ponsford	Victoria v Queensland at Melbourne	1927-28
429	W. H. Ponsford	Victoria v Tasmania at Melbourne	1922-23
428	Aftab Baloch	Sind v Baluchistan at Karachi	1973-74
424	A. C. MacLaren	Lancashire v Somerset at Taunton	1895
405*	G. A. Hick	Worcestershire v Somerset at Taunton	1988
400*	B. C. Lara	West Indies v England at St John's	2003-04
394	Naved Latif	Sargodha v Gujranwala at Gujranwala	2000-01
390	S. C. Cook	Lions v Warriors at East London	2009-10
385	B. Sutcliffe	Otago v Canterbury at Christchurch	1952-53
383	C. W. Gregory	NSW v Queensland at Brisbane	1906-07
380	M. L. Hayden	Australia v Zimbabwe at Perth	2003-04
377	S. V. Manjrekar	Bombay v Hyderabad at Bombay	1990-91
375	B. C. Lara	West Indies v England at St John's	1993-94
374	D. P. M. D. Jayawardene	Sri Lanka v South Africa at Colombo	2006
369	D. G. Bradman	South Australia v Tasmania at Adelaide	1935-36
366	N. H. Fairbrother	Lancashire v Surrey at The Oval	1990
366	M. V. Sridhar	Hyderabad v Andhra at Secunderabad	1993-94
365*	C. Hill	South Australia v NSW at Adelaide	1900-01
365*	G. S. Sobers	West Indies v Pakistan at Kingston	1957-58
364	L. Hutton	England v Australia at The Oval	1938
359*	V. M. Merchant	Bombay v Maharashtra at Bombay	1943-44
359	R. B. Simpson	NSW v Queensland at Brisbane	1963-64
357*	R. Abel	Surrey v Somerset at The Oval	1899
357	D. G. Bradman	South Australia v Victoria at Melbourne	1935-36
356	B. A. Richards	South Australia v Western Australia at Perth	1970-71
355*	G. R. Marsh	Western Australia v South Australia at Perth	1989-90
355	B. Sutcliffe	Otago v Auckland at Dunedin	1949-50
353	V. V. S. Laxman	Hyderabad v Karnataka at Bangalore	1999-2000
352	W. H. Ponsford	Victoria v NSW at Melbourne	1926-27
352	**C. A. Pujara**	**Saurashtra v Karnataka at Rajkot**	**2012-13**
350	Rashid Israr	Habib Bank v National Bank at Lahore	1976-77

A fuller list can be found in *Wisdens* up to 2011.

DOUBLE-HUNDRED ON DEBUT

227	T. Marsden	Sheffield & Leicester v Nottingham at Sheffield	1826
207	N. F. Callaway†	New South Wales v Queensland at Sydney	1914-15
240	W. F. E. Marx	Transvaal v Griqualand West at Johannesburg	1920-21
200*	A. Maynard	Trinidad v MCC at Port-of-Spain	1934-35
232*	S. J. E. Loxton	Victoria v Queensland at Melbourne	1946-47
215*	G. H. G. Doggart	Cambridge University v Lancashire at Cambridge	1948
202	J. Hallebone	Victoria v Tasmania at Melbourne	1951-52
230	G. R. Viswanath	Mysore v Andhra at Vijayawada	1967-68

260	A. A. Muzumdar	Bombay v Haryana at Faridabad.................	1993-94
209*	A. Pandey	Madhya Pradesh v Uttar Pradesh at Bhilai.........	1995-96
210*	D. J. Sales	Northamptonshire v Worcestershire at Kidderminster	1996
200*	M. J. Powell	Glamorgan v Oxford University at Oxford..........	1997
201*	M. C. Juneja	Gujarat v Tamil Nadu at Ahmedabad..............	2011-12
213	Jiwanjot Singh	Punjab v Hyderabad at Mohali...................	2012-13

† *In his only first-class innings. He was killed in action in France in 1917.*

TWO SEPARATE HUNDREDS ON DEBUT

148	and 111	A. R. Morris	New South Wales v Queensland at Sydney.....	1940-41
152	and 102*	N. J. Contractor	Gujarat v Baroda at Baroda.................	1952-53
132*	and 110	Aamer Malik	Lahore A v Railways at Lahore..............	1979-80
130	and 100*	Noor Ali	Afghanistan v Zimbabwe XI at Mutare.......	2009
158	and 103*	K. H. T. Indika	Police v Seeduwa Raddoluwa at Colombo......	2010-11
126	and 112	V. S. Awate	Maharashtra v Vidarbha at Nagpur...........	2012-13

TWO DOUBLE-HUNDREDS IN A MATCH

| A. E. Fagg.......... | 244 | 202* | Kent v Essex at Colchester............... | 1938 |

TRIPLE-HUNDRED AND HUNDRED IN A MATCH

| G. A. Gooch......... | 333 | 123 | England v India at Lord's............... | 1990 |

DOUBLE-HUNDRED AND HUNDRED IN A MATCH

In addition to Fagg and Gooch, there have been **57** further instances of a batsman scoring a double-hundred and a hundred in the same first-class match. The most recent are:

S. A. Newman........	117	219	Surrey v Glamorgan at The Oval..........	2005
P. A. Jaques..........	240	117	Australia A v India A at Cairns...........	2006
C. J. L. Rogers........	128	222*	Northamptonshire v Somerset at Taunton....	2006
M. W. Goodwin......	119	205*	Sussex v Surrey at Hove.................	2007
Younis Khan.........	106	202*	Yorkshire v Hampshire at Southampton.....	2007
V. Sibanda..........	209	116*	Zimbabwe XI v Kenya at Kwekwe.........	2009-10
S. M. Ervine.........	208	160	Southern Rocks v MW Rhinos at Masvingo..	2009-10
C. J. L. Rogers........	200	140*	Derbyshire v Surrey at The Oval..........	2010
M. R. Ramprakash	223	103*	Surrey v Middlesex at The Oval...........	2010

Notes: Zaheer Abbas achieved the feat four times, for Gloucestershire between 1976 and 1981, and was not out in all eight innings. M. R. Hallam did it twice for Leicestershire, in 1959 and 1961; N. R. Taylor twice for Kent, in 1990 and 1991; G. A. Gooch for England in 1990 (see above) and Essex in 1994; M. W. Goodwin twice for Sussex, in 2001 and 2007; and C. J. L. Rogers for Northamptonshire in 2006 and for Derbyshire in 2010.

TWO SEPARATE HUNDREDS IN A MATCH MOST TIMES

R. T. Ponting..........	**8**	J. B. Hobbs............	6	M. L. Hayden..........	5
Zaheer Abbas..........	8	G. M. Turner...........	6	G. A. Hick............	5
W. R. Hammond	7	C. B. Fry..............	5		
M. R. Ramprakash......	7	G. A. Gooch............	5		

Notes: W. Lambert scored 107 and 157 for Sussex v Epsom at Lord's in 1817, and it was not until W. G. Grace made 130 and 102* for South of the Thames v North of the Thames at Canterbury in 1868 that the feat was repeated.

FIVE HUNDREDS OR MORE IN SUCCESSION

D. G. Bradman (1938-39)	6	B. C. Lara (1993-94/1994)	5
C. B. Fry (1901)	6	P. A. Patel (2007/2007-08)	5
M. J. Procter (1970-71)	6	E. D. Weekes (1955-56)	5
M. E. K. Hussey (2003)	5		

Notes: Bradman also scored four hundreds in succession twice, in 1931-32 and 1948/1948-49; W. R. Hammond did it in 1936-37 and 1945/1946, and H. Sutcliffe in 1931 and 1939.

T. W. Hayward (Surrey v Nottinghamshire and Leicestershire), D. W. Hookes (South Australia v Queensland and New South Wales) and V. Sibanda (Zimbabwe XI v Kenya and Mid West v Southern Rocks) are the only players to score two hundreds in each of two successive matches. Hayward scored his in six days, June 4-9, 1906.

The most fifties in consecutive innings is ten – by E. Tyldesley in 1926, by D. G. Bradman in the 1947-48 and 1948 seasons and by R. S. Kaluwitharana in 1994-95.

MOST HUNDREDS IN A SEASON

D. C. S. Compton (1947)	18	T. W. Hayward (1906)	13
J. B. Hobbs (1925)	16	E. H. Hendren (1923)	13
W. R. Hammond (1938)	15	E. H. Hendren (1927)	13
H. Sutcliffe (1932)	14	E. H. Hendren (1928)	13
G. Boycott (1971)	13	C. P. Mead (1928)	13
D. G. Bradman (1938)	13	H. Sutcliffe (1928)	13
C. B. Fry (1901)	13	H. Sutcliffe (1931)	13
W. R. Hammond (1933)	13		
W. R. Hammond (1937)	13		

Since 1969 (excluding G. Boycott – above)

G. A. Gooch (1990)	12	M. R. Ramprakash (1995)	10
S. J. Cook (1991)	11	M. R. Ramprakash (2007)	10
Zaheer Abbas (1976)	11	G. M. Turner (1970)	10
G. A. Hick (1988)	10	Zaheer Abbas (1981)	10
H. Morris (1990)	10		

Notes: The most achieved outside England is nine by V. Sibanda in Zimbabwe (2009-10), followed by eight by D. G. Bradman in Australia (1947-48), D. C. S. Compton (1948-49), R. N. Harvey and A. R. Morris (both 1949-50) all three in South Africa, M. D. Crowe in New Zealand (1986-87), Asif Mujtaba in Pakistan (1995-96), V. V. S. Laxman in India (1999-2000) and M. G. Bevan in Australia (2004-05).

The most double-hundreds in a season is six by D. G. Bradman (1930), five by K. S. Ranjitsinhji (1900) and E. D. Weekes (1950), and four by Arun Lal (1986-87), C. B. Fry (1901), W. R. Hammond (1933 and 1934), E. H. Hendren (1929-30), V. M. Merchant (1944-45), **C. A. Pujara (2012-13)** and G. M. Turner (1971-72).

MOST DOUBLE-HUNDREDS IN A CAREER

D. G. Bradman	37	C. P. Mead	13	R. Dravid	10
W. R. Hammond	36	W. H. Ponsford	13	M. W. Gatting	10
E. H. Hendren	22	J. T. Tyldesley	13	S. M. Gavaskar	10
M. R. Ramprakash	17	P. Holmes	13	J. Hardstaff, jun	10
H. Sutcliffe	17	Javed Miandad	12	V. S. Hazare	10
C. B. Fry	16	J. L. Langer	12	B. J. Hodge	10
G. A. Hick	16	R. B. Simpson	12	I. V. A. Richards	10
J. B. Hobbs	16	J. W. Hearne	11	A. Shrewsbury	10
C. G. Greenidge	14	L. Hutton	11	R. T. Simpson	10
K. S. Ranjitsinhji	14	D. S. Lehmann	11	G. M. Turner	10
G. A. Gooch	13	V. M. Merchant	11	**Younis Khan**	**10**
W. G. Grace	13	A. Sandham	11	Zaheer Abbas	10
B. C. Lara	13	G. Boycott	10		

MOST HUNDREDS IN A CAREER

(100 or more)

		Total	Total Inns	100th Season	100th 100 Inns	400+	300+	200+
1	J. B. Hobbs..........	197	1,315	1923	821	0	1	16
2	E. H. Hendren	170	1,300	1928-29	740	0	1	22
3	W. R. Hammond	167	1,005	1935	680	0	4	36
4	C. P. Mead	153	1,340	1927	892	0	0	13
5	G. Boycott	151	1,014	1977	645	0	0	10
6	H. Sutcliffe	149	1,088	1932	700	0	1	17
7	F. E. Woolley........	145	1,532	1929	1,031	0	1	9
8	G. A. Hick	136	871	1998	574	1	3	16
9	L. Hutton	129	814	1951	619	0	1	11
10	G. A. Gooch	128	990	1992-93	820	0	1	13
11	W. G. Grace	126	1,493	1895	1,113	0	3	13
12	D. C. S. Compton.....	123	839	1952	552	0	1	9
13	T. W. Graveney	122	1,223	1964	940	0	0	7
14	D. G. Bradman	117	338	1947-48	295	1	6	37
15 {	I. V. A. Richards	114	796	1988-89	658	0	1	10
	M. R. Ramprakash	114	764	2008	676	0	1	17
17	Zaheer Abbas........	108	768	1982-83	658	0	0	10
18 {	A. Sandham	107	1,000	1935	871	0	1	11
	M. C. Cowdrey.......	107	1,130	1973	1,035	0	1	3
20	T. W. Hayward	104	1,138	1913	1,076	0	1	8
21 {	G. M. Turner	103	792	1982	779	0	1	10
	J. H. Edrich	103	979	1977	945	0	1	4
23 {	L. E. G. Ames	102	951	1950	916	0	0	9
	E. Tyldesley	102	961	1934	919	0	0	7
	D. L. Amiss	102	1,139	1986	1,081	0	0	3

Notes: In the above table, 200+, 300+ and 400+ include all scores above those figures.

G. A. Gooch's record includes his century in South Africa in 1981-82, which is no longer accepted by the ICC. Zaheer Abbas and G. Boycott scored their 100th hundreds in Test matches.

Other Current Players

The following who played in 2013 have scored 30 or more hundreds.

R. T. Ponting	82	M. E. Trescothick	51	K. C. Sangakkara.......	44
S. R. Tendulkar	81	Wasim Jaffer	51	M. J. Clarke...........	43
M. W. Goodwin.......	71	N. D. McKenzie	50	D. J. Hussey...........	43
S. Chanderpaul	69	K. P. Pietersen	49	T. T. Samaraweera......	43
C. J. L. Rogers	64	D. P. M. D. Jayawardene	48	Younis Khan	43
J. H. Kallis..........	62	J. A. Rudolph..........	46	P. A. Jaques...........	42
M. E. K. Hussey	61	I. R. Bell	45	H. M. Amla	41
S. M. Katich..........	58	A. N. Cook	45		
R. W. T. Key	51	O. A. Shah............	45		

MOST RUNS IN A SEASON

	Season	I	NO	R	HS	100	Avge
D. C. S. Compton......	1947	50	8	3,816	246	18	90.85
W. J. Edrich	1947	52	8	3,539	267*	12	80.43
T. W. Hayward........	1906	61	8	3,518	219	13	66.37
L. Hutton	1949	56	6	3,429	269*	12	68.58
F. E. Woolley	1928	59	4	3,352	198	12	60.94

	Season	I	NO	R	HS	100	Avge
H. Sutcliffe............	1932	52	7	3,336	313	14	74.13
W. R. Hammond	1933	54	5	3,323	264	13	67.81
E. H. Hendren.........	1928	54	7	3,311	209*	13	70.44
R. Abel..............	1901	68	8	3,309	247	7	55.15

Notes: 3,000 in a season has been surpassed on 19 other occasions (a full list can be found in *Wisden* 1999 and earlier editions). W. R. Hammond, E. H. Hendren and H. Sutcliffe are the only players to achieve the feat three times. K. S. Ranjitsinhji was the first batsman to reach 3,000 in a season, with 3,159 in 1899. M. J. K. Smith (3,245 in 1959) and W. E. Alley (3,019 in 1961) are the only players except those listed above to have reached 3,000 since World War II.

W. G. Grace scored 2,739 runs in 1871 – the first batsman to reach 2,000 runs in a season. He made ten hundreds including two double-hundreds, with an average of 78.25 in all first-class matches.

The highest aggregate in a season since the reduction of County Championship matches in 1969 is 2,755 by S. J. Cook (42 innings) in 1991, and the last batsman to achieve 2,000 was M. R. Ramprakash (2,026 in 2007).

2,000 RUNS IN A SEASON MOST TIMES

J. B. Hobbs............ 17	F. E. Woolley.......... 13	C. P. Mead 11
E. H. Hendren......... 15	W. R. Hammond 12	T. W. Hayward........ 10
H. Sutcliffe........... 15	J. G. Langridge........ 11	

Note: Since the reduction of County Championship matches in 1969, G. A. Gooch is the only batsman to have reached 2,000 runs in a season five times.

1,000 RUNS IN A SEASON MOST TIMES

Includes overseas tours and seasons

W. G. Grace........... 28	A. Jones.............. 23	G. Gunn.............. 20
F. E. Woolley 28	T. W. Graveney........ 22	T. W. Hayward 20
M. C. Cowdrey........ 27	W. R. Hammond 22	G. A. Hick 20
C. P. Mead............ 27	D. Denton 21	James Langridge 20
G. Boycott............ 26	J. H. Edrich 21	J. M. Parks........... 20
J. B. Hobbs 26	G. A. Gooch 21	M. R. Ramprakash...... 20
E. H. Hendren 25	W. Rhodes............ 21	A. Sandham.......... 20
D. L. Amiss 24	D. B. Close 20	M. J. K. Smith 20
W. G. Quaife 24	K. W. R. Fletcher 20	C. Washbrook 20
H. Sutcliffe 24	M. W. Gatting 20	

Notes: F. E. Woolley reached 1,000 runs in 28 consecutive seasons (1907–1938), C. P. Mead in 27 (1906–1936).

Outside England, 1,000 runs in a season has been reached most times by D. G. Bradman (in 12 seasons in Australia).

Three batsmen have scored 1,000 runs in a season in each of four different countries: G. S. Sobers in West Indies, England, India and Australia; M. C. Cowdrey and G. Boycott in England, South Africa, West Indies and Australia.

HIGHEST AGGREGATES OUTSIDE ENGLAND

	Season	I	NO	R	HS	100	Avge
In Australia							
D. G. Bradman............	1928-29	24	6	1,690	340*	7	93.88
In South Africa							
J. R. Reid................	1961-62	30	2	1,915	203	7	68.39
In West Indies							
E. H. Hendren	1929-30	18	5	1,765	254*	6	135.76
In New Zealand							
M. D. Crowe	1986-87	21	3	1,676	175*	8	93.11

	Season	I	NO	R	HS	100	Avge
In India							
C. G. Borde	1964-65	28	3	1,604	168	6	64.16
In Pakistan							
Saadat Ali	1983-84	27	1	1,649	208	4	63.42
In Sri Lanka							
R. P. Arnold.	1995-96	24	3	1,475	217*	5	70.23
In Zimbabwe							
V. Sibanda	2009-10	26	4	1,612	215	9	73.27
In Bangladesh							
Marshall Ayub	**2012-13**	**17**	**2**	**1,069**	**289**	**4**	**71.26**

Note: In more than one country, the following aggregates of over 2,000 runs have been recorded:

M. Amarnath (P/I/WI)	1982-83	34	6	2,234	207	9	79.78
J. R. Reid (SA/A/NZ)	1961-62	40	2	2,188	203	7	57.57
S. M. Gavaskar (I/P)	1978-79	30	6	2,121	205	10	88.37
R. B. Simpson (I/P/A/WI) . . .	1964-65	34	4	2,063	201	8	68.76
M. H. Richardson (Z/SA/NZ) .	2000-01	34	3	2,030	306	4	65.48

LEADING BATSMEN IN AN ENGLISH SEASON

(Qualification: 8 completed innings)

Season	Leading scorer	Runs	Avge	Top of averages	Runs	Avge
1946	D. C. S. Compton	2,403	61.61	W. R. Hammond	1,783	84.90
1947	D. C. S. Compton	3,816	90.85	D. C. S. Compton	3,816	90.85
1948	L. Hutton	2,654	64.73	D. G. Bradman	2,428	89.92
1949	L. Hutton	3,429	68.58	J. Hardstaff	2,251	72.61
1950	R. T. Simpson	2,576	62.82	E. D. Weekes	2,310	79.65
1951	J. D. Robertson	2,917	56.09	P. B. H. May	2,339	68.79
1952	L. Hutton	2,567	61.11	D. S. Sheppard	2,262	64.62
1953	W. J. Edrich	2,557	47.35	R. N. Harvey	2,040	65.80
1954	D. Kenyon	2,636	51.68	D. C. S. Compton	1,524	58.61
1955	D. J. Insole	2,427	42.57	D. J. McGlew	1,871	58.46
1956	T. W. Graveney	2,397	49.93	K. Mackay	1,103	52.52
1957	T. W. Graveney	2,361	49.18	P. B. H. May	2,347	61.76
1958	P. B. H. May	2,231	63.74	P. B. H. May	2,231	63.74
1959	M. J. K. Smith	3,245	57.94	V. L. Manjrekar	755	68.63
1960	M. J. K. Smith	2,551	45.55	R. Subba Row	1,503	55.66
1961	W. E. Alley	3,019	56.96	W. M. Lawry	2,019	61.18
1962	J. H. Edrich	2,482	51.70	R. T. Simpson	867	54.18
1963	J. B. Bolus	2,190	41.32	G. S. Sobers	1,333	47.60
1964	T. W. Graveney	2,385	54.20	K. F. Barrington	1,872	62.40
1965	J. H. Edrich	2,319	62.67	M. C. Cowdrey	2,093	63.42
1966	A. R. Lewis	2,198	41.47	G. S. Sobers	1,349	61.31
1967	C. A. Milton	2,089	46.42	K. F. Barrington	2,059	68.63
1968	B. A. Richards	2,395	47.90	G. Boycott	1,487	64.65
1969	J. H. Edrich	2,238	69.93	J. H. Edrich	2,238	69.93
1970	G. M. Turner	2,379	61.00	G. S. Sobers	1,742	75.73
1971	G. Boycott	2,503	100.12	G. Boycott	2,503	100.12
1972	Majid Khan	2,074	61.00	G. Boycott	1,230	72.35
1973	G. M. Turner	2,416	67.11	G. M. Turner	2,416	67.11
1974	R. T. Virgin	1,936	56.94	C. H. Lloyd	1,458	63.39
1975	G. Boycott	1,915	73.65	R. B. Kanhai	1,073	82.53
1976	Zaheer Abbas	2,554	75.11	Zaheer Abbas	2,554	75.11
1977	I. V. A. Richards	2,161	65.48	G. Boycott	1,701	68.04

Season	Leading scorer	Runs	Avge	Top of averages	Runs	Avge
1978	D. L. Amiss.........	2,030	53.42	C. E. B. Rice..........	1,871	66.82
1979	K. C. Wessels	1,800	52.94	G. Boycott	1,538	102.53
1980	P. N. Kirsten	1,895	63.16	A. J. Lamb	1,797	66.55
1981	Zaheer Abbas	2,306	88.69	Zaheer Abbas	2,306	88.69
1982	A. I. Kallicharran ...	2,120	66.25	G. M. Turner.........	1,171	90.07
1983	K. S. McEwan	2,176	64.00	I. V. A. Richards.....	1,204	75.25
1984	G. A. Gooch	2,559	67.34	C. G. Greenidge	1,069	82.23
1985	G. A. Gooch	2,208	71.22	I. V. A. Richards.....	1,836	76.50
1986	C. G. Greenidge	2,035	67.83	C. G. Greenidge	2,035	67.83
1987	G. A. Hick	1,879	52.19	M. D. Crowe........	1,627	67.79
1988	G. A. Hick	2,713	77.51	R. A. Harper........	622	77.75
1989	S. J. Cook	2,241	60.56	D. M. Jones.........	1,510	88.82
1990	G. A. Gooch	2,746	101.70	G. A. Gooch	2,746	101.70
1991	S. J. Cook	2,755	81.02	C. L. Hooper........	1,501	93.81
1992	{ P. D. Bowler	2,044	65.93	Salim Malik	1,184	78.93
	M. A. Roseberry ...	2,044	56.77			
1993	G. A. Gooch	2,023	63.21	D. C. Boon	1,437	75.63
1994	B. C. Lara	2,066	89.82	J. D. Carr	1,543	90.76
1995	M. R. Ramprakash ...	2,258	77.86	M. R. Ramprakash	2,258	77.86
1996	G. A. Gooch	1,944	67.03	S. C. Ganguly	762	95.25
1997	S. P. James	1,775	68.26	G. A. Hick	1,524	69.27
1998	J. P. Crawley	1,851	74.04	J. P. Crawley	1,851	74.04
1999	S. G. Law	1,833	73.32	S. G. Law	1,833	73.32
2000	D. S. Lehmann	1,477	67.13	M. G. Bevan	1,124	74.93
2001	M. E. K. Hussey	2,055	79.03	D. R. Martyn........	942	104.66
2002	I. J. Ward..........	1,759	62.82	R. Dravid	773	96.62
2003	S. G. Law	1,820	91.00	S. G. Law	1,820	91.00
2004	R. W. T. Key........	1,896	79.00	R. W. T. Key........	1,896	79.00
2005	O. A. Shah.........	1,728	66.46	M. E. K. Hussey	1,074	76.71
2006	M. R. Ramprakash ...	2,278	103.54	M. R. Ramprakash	2,278	103.54
2007	M. R. Ramprakash ...	2,026	101.30	M. R. Ramprakash	2,026	101.30
2008	S. C. Moore........	1,451	55.80	T. Frost............	1,003	83.58
2009	M. E. Trescothick ...	1,817	75.70	M. R. Ramprakash	1,350	90.00
2010	M. R. Ramprakash ...	1,595	61.34	J. C. Hildreth	1,440	65.45
2011	M. E. Trescothick ...	1,673	79.66	I. R. Bell	1,091	90.91
2012	N. R. D. Compton	1,494	99.60	N. R. D. Compton.....	1,494	99.60
2013	**C. J. L. Rogers......**	**1,536**	**51.20**	**S. M. Katich......**	**1,097**	**73.13**

Notes: The highest average recorded in an English season was 115.66 (2,429 runs, 26 innings) by D. G. Bradman in 1938.

In 1953, W. A. Johnston averaged 102.00 from 17 innings, 16 not out.

MOST RUNS

Dates in italics denote the first half of an overseas season; i.e. *1945* denotes the 1945-46 season.

		Career	R	I	NO	HS	100	Avge
1	J. B. Hobbs.........	1905–1934	61,237	1,315	106	316*	197	50.65
2	F. E. Woolley.......	1906–1938	58,969	1,532	85	305*	145	40.75
3	E. H. Hendren......	1907–1938	57,611	1,300	166	301*	170	50.80
4	C. P. Mead	1905–1936	55,061	1,340	185	280*	153	47.67
5	W. G. Grace	1865–1908	54,896	1,493	105	344	126	39.55
6	W. R. Hammond	1920–1951	50,551	1,005	104	336*	167	56.10
7	H. Sutcliffe........	1919–1945	50,138	1,088	123	313	149	51.95
8	G. Boycott	1962–1986	48,426	1,014	162	261*	151	56.83
9	T. W. Graveney	1948–*1971*	47,793	1,223	159	258	122	44.91
10	G. A. Gooch	1973–2000	44,846	990	75	333	128	49.01
11	T. W. Hayward......	1893–1914	43,551	1,138	96	315*	104	41.79
12	D. L. Amiss	1960–1987	43,423	1,139	126	262*	102	42.86
13	M. C. Cowdrey......	1950–1976	42,719	1,130	134	307	107	42.89

		Career	R	I	NO	HS	100	Avge
14	A. Sandham	1911–1937	41,284	1,000	79	325	107	44.82
15	G. A. Hick	1983–2008	41,112	871	84	405*	136	52.23
16	L. Hutton	1934–1960	40,140	814	91	364	129	55.51
17	M. J. K. Smith	1951–1975	39,832	1,091	139	204	69	41.84
18	W. Rhodes	1898–1930	39,802	1,528	237	267*	58	30.83
19	J. H. Edrich	1956–1978	39,790	979	104	310*	103	45.47
20	R. E. S. Wyatt	1923–1957	39,405	1,141	157	232	85	40.04
21	D. C. S. Compton	1936–1964	38,942	839	88	300	123	51.85
22	E. Tyldesley	1909–1936	38,874	961	106	256*	102	45.46
23	J. T. Tyldesley	1895–1923	37,897	994	62	295*	86	40.66
24	K. W. R. Fletcher	1962–1988	37,665	1,167	170	228*	63	37.77
25	C. G. Greenidge	1970–1992	37,354	889	75	273*	92	45.88
26	J. W. Hearne	1909–1936	37,252	1,025	116	285*	96	40.98
27	L. E. G. Ames	1926–1951	37,248	951	95	295	102	43.51
28	D. Kenyon	1946–1967	37,002	1,159	59	259	74	33.63
29	W. J. Edrich	1934–1958	36,965	964	92	267*	86	42.39
30	J. M. Parks	1949–1976	36,673	1,227	172	205*	51	34.76
31	M. W. Gatting	1975–1998	36,549	861	123	258	94	49.52
32	D. Denton	1894–1920	36,479	1,163	70	221	69	33.37
33	G. H. Hirst	1891–1929	36,323	1,215	151	341	60	34.13
34	I. V. A. Richards	1971–1993	36,212	796	63	322	114	49.40
35	A. Jones	1957–1983	36,049	1,168	72	204*	56	32.89
36	W. G. Quaife	1894–1928	36,012	1,203	185	255*	72	35.37
37	R. E. Marshall	1945–1972	35,725	1,053	59	228*	68	35.94
38	M. R. Ramprakash . . .	1987–2012	35,659	764	93	301*	114	53.14
39	G. Gunn	1902–1932	35,208	1,061	82	220	62	35.96

Note: Some works of reference provide career figures which differ from those in this list, owing to the exclusion or inclusion of matches recognised or not recognised as first-class by *Wisden.* A fuller list can be found in *Wisdens* up to 2011.

Current Players with 20,000 Runs

	Career	R	I	NO	HS	100	Avge
S. R. Tendulkar	1988–2013	25,396	490	51	248*	81	57.84
R. T. Ponting	1992–2013	24,150	494	62	257	82	55.90
M. W. Goodwin	1994–2013	23,376	539	46	344*	71	47.41
S. Chanderpaul	1991–2013	23,321	516	96	303*	69	55.52
M. E. K. Hussey	1994–2012	22,783	486	49	331*	61	52.13
C. J. L. Rogers	1998–2013	21,128	456	32	319	64	49.83
M. E. Trescothick	1993–2013	21,064	534	30	284	51	41.79
S. M. Katich	1996–2013	20,926	448	52	306	58	52.84

HIGHEST CAREER AVERAGE

(Qualification: 10,000 runs)

Avge		Career	I	NO	R	HS	100
95.14	D. G. Bradman	1927–1948	338	43	28,067	452*	117
71.22	V. M. Merchant	1929–1951	229	43	13,248	359*	44
67.46	Ajay Sharma	1984–2000	166	16	10,120	259*	38
65.18	W. H. Ponsford	1920–1934	235	23	13,819	437	47
64.99	W. M. Woodfull	1921–1934	245	39	13,388	284	49
58.24	A. L. Hassett	1932–1953	322	32	16,890	232	59
58.19	V. S. Hazare	1934–1966	365	45	18,621	316*	60
57.84	**S. R. Tendulkar**	**1988–2013**	**490**	**51**	**25,396**	**248***	**81**
57.83	D. S. Lehmann	1987–2007	479	33	25,795	339	82
57.32	M. G. Bevan	1989–2006	400	66	19,147	216	68
57.22	A. F. Kippax	1918–1935	256	33	12,762	315*	43
56.83	G. Boycott	1962–1986	1,014	162	48,426	261*	151

Avge		Career	I	NO	R	HS	100
56.55	C. L. Walcott	*1941–1963*	238	29	11,820	314*	40
56.37	K. S. Ranjitsinhji	1893–1920	500	62	24,692	285*	72
56.22	R. B. Simpson	*1952–1977*	436	62	21,029	359	60
56.10	W. R. Hammond	1920–1951	1,005	104	50,551	336*	167
56.02	M. D. Crowe	*1979–1995*	412	62	19,608	299	71
55.90	**R. T. Ponting**	***1992–2013***	**494**	**62**	**24,150**	**257**	**82**
55.52	**S. Chanderpaul**	***1991–2013***	**516**	**96**	**23,321**	**303***	**69**
55.51	L. Hutton	1934–1960	814	91	40,140	364	129
55.34	E. D. Weekes	*1944–1964*	241	24	12,010	304*	36
55.33	R. Dravid	*1990–2011*	497	67	23,794	270	68
55.11	S. V. Manjrekar	*1984–1997*	217	31	10,252	377	31
54.87	G. S. Sobers	*1952–1974*	609	93	28,315	365*	86
54.74	B. A. Richards	*1964–1982*	576	58	28,358	356	80
54.67	R. G. Pollock	*1960–1986*	437	54	20,940	274	64
54.24	F. M. M. Worrell	*1941–1964*	326	49	15,025	308*	39
54.10	**J. H. Kallis**	***1993–2013***	**421**	**57**	**19,695**	**224**	**62**
54.05	A. Flower	1986–2006	372	69	16,379	271*	49

Note: G. A. Headley (*1927–1954*) scored 9,921 runs, average 69.86.

FASTEST FIFTIES

Minutes

11	C. I. J. Smith (66)	Middlesex v Gloucestershire at Bristol	1938
13	Khalid Mahmood (56)	Gujranwala v Sargodha at Gujranwala	2000-01
14	S. J. Pegler (50)	South Africans v Tasmania at Launceston	1910-11
14	F. T. Mann (53)	Middlesex v Nottinghamshire at Lord's	1921
14	H. B. Cameron (56)	Transvaal v Orange Free State at Johannesburg	1934-35
14	C. I. J. Smith (52)	Middlesex v Kent at Maidstone	1935

Note: The number of balls taken to achieve fifties was rarely recorded until recently. C. I. J. Smith's two fifties (above) may have taken only 12 balls each. Khalid Mahmood reached his fifty in 15 balls.

Fifties scored in contrived circumstances and with the bowlers' compliance are excluded from the above list, including the fastest of them all, in 8 minutes (13 balls) by C. C. Inman, Leicestershire v Nottinghamshire at Nottingham, 1965, and 10 minutes by G. Chapple, Lancashire v Glamorgan at Manchester, 1993.

FASTEST HUNDREDS

Minutes

35	P. G. H. Fender (113*)	Surrey v Northamptonshire at Northampton	1920
40	G. L. Jessop (101)	Gloucestershire v Yorkshire at Harrogate	1897
40	Ahsan-ul-Haq (100*)	Muslims v Sikhs at Lahore	1923-24
42	G. L. Jessop (191)	Gentlemen of South v Players of South at Hastings	1907
43	A. H. Hornby (106)	Lancashire v Somerset at Manchester	1905
43	D. W. Hookes (107)	South Australia v Victoria at Adelaide	1982-83
44	R. N. S. Hobbs (100)	Essex v Australians at Chelmsford	1975

Notes: The fastest recorded authentic hundred in terms of balls received was scored off 34 balls by D. W. Hookes (above). Research of the scorebook has shown that P. G. H. Fender scored his hundred from between 40 and 46 balls. He contributed 113 to an unfinished sixth-wicket partnership of 171 in 42 minutes with H. A. Peach.

E. B. Alletson (Nottinghamshire) scored 189 out of 227 runs in 90 minutes against Sussex at Hove in 1911. It has been estimated that his last 139 runs took 37 minutes.

Hundreds scored in contrived circumstances and with the bowlers' compliance are excluded, including the fastest of them all, in 21 minutes (27 balls) by G. Chapple, Lancashire v Glamorgan at Manchester, 1993, 24 minutes (27 balls) by M. L. Pettini, Essex v Leicestershire at Leicester, 2006, and 26 minutes (36 balls) by T. M. Moody, Warwickshire v Glamorgan at Swansea, 1990.

FASTEST DOUBLE-HUNDREDS

Minutes

113	R. J. Shastri (200*)	Bombay v Baroda at Bombay	1984-85
120	G. L. Jessop (286)	Gloucestershire v Sussex at Hove	1903
120	C. H. Lloyd (201*)	West Indians v Glamorgan at Swansea	1976
130	G. L. Jessop (234)	Gloucestershire v Somerset at Bristol	1905
131	V. T. Trumper (293)	Australians v Canterbury at Christchurch	1913-14

FASTEST TRIPLE-HUNDREDS

Minutes

181	D. C. S. Compton (300)	MCC v North Eastern Transvaal at Benoni	1948-49
205	F. E. Woolley (305*)	MCC v Tasmania at Hobart	1911-12
205	C. G. Macartney (345)	Australians v Nottinghamshire at Nottingham......	1921
213	D. G. Bradman (369)	South Australia v Tasmania at Adelaide	1935-36

MOST RUNS IN A DAY BY ONE BATSMAN

390*	B. C. Lara	Warwickshire v Durham at Birmingham	1994
345	C. G. Macartney	Australians v Nottinghamshire at Nottingham......	1921
334	W. H. Ponsford	Victoria v New South Wales at Melbourne	1926-27
333	K. S. Duleepsinhji	Sussex v Northamptonshire at Hove	1930
331*	J. D. Robertson	Middlesex v Worcestershire at Worcester	1949
325*	B. A. Richards	South Australia v Western Australia at Perth.......	1970-71

Note: These scores do not necessarily represent the complete innings. See page 1260.

There have been another **14** instances of a batsman scoring 300 runs in a day, most recently 319 by R. R. Rossouw, Eagles v Titans at Centurion in 2009-10 (see *Wisden* 2003, pages 278–279, for full list).

LONGEST INNINGS

Hrs	Mins			
16	55	R. Nayyar (271)	Himachal Pradesh v Jammu and Kashmir at Chamba	1999-2000
16	10	Hanif Mohammad (337)	Pakistan v West Indies at Bridgetown.....	1957-58
		Hanif believes he batted 16 hours 39 minutes.		
15	7	V. A. Saxena (257)	Rajasthan v Tamil Nadu at Chennai	2011-12
14	38	G. Kirsten (275)	South Africa v England at Durban	1999-2000
13	58	S. C. Cook (390)	Lions v Warriors at East London	2009-10
13	**43**	**T. Kohli (300*)**	**Punjab v Jharkhand at Jamshedpur**....	**2012-13**
13	41	S. S. Shukla (178*)	Uttar Pradesh v Tamil Nadu at Nagpur....	2008-09
13	32	A. Chopra (301*)	Rajasthan v Maharashtra at Nasik........	2010-11
13	19	S. T. Jayasuriya (340)	Sri Lanka v India at Colombo...........	1997-98
13	17	L. Hutton (364)	England v Australia at The Oval.........	1938
13	16	S. H. Kotak (168*)	Saurashtra v Mumbai at Mumbai	2007-08
13	10	H. M. Amla (311*)	South Africa v England at The Oval......	2012
13	5	Bhupinder Singh, jun. (297)	Punjab v Delhi at Delhi................	1994-95
13	0	Naved Latif (394)	Sargodha v Gujranwala................	2000-01

1,000 RUNS IN MAY

	Runs	Avge
W. G. Grace, May 9 to May 30, 1895 (22 days)	1,016	112.88
Grace was 46 years old.		
W. R. Hammond, May 7 to May 31, 1927 (25 days)	1,042	74.42
Hammond scored his 1,000th run on May 28, thus equalling		
Grace's record of 22 days.		
C. Hallows, May 5 to May 31, 1928 (27 days)	1,000	125.00

1,000 RUNS IN APRIL AND MAY

	Runs	Avge
T. W. Hayward, April 16 to May 31, 1900	1,074	97.63
D. G. Bradman, April 30 to May 31, 1930	1,001	143.00
On April 30 Bradman was 75 not out.		
D. G. Bradman, April 30 to May 31, 1938	1,056	150.85
Bradman scored 258 on April 30, and his 1,000th run on May 27.		
W. J. Edrich, April 30 to May 31, 1938	1,010	84.16
Edrich was 21 not out on April 30. All his runs were scored at Lord's.		
G. M. Turner, April 24 to May 31, 1973	1,018	78.30
G. A. Hick, April 17 to May 29, 1988	1,019	101.90
Hick scored a record 410 runs in April, and his 1,000th run on May 28.		

MOST RUNS SCORED OFF AN OVER

(All instances refer to six-ball overs)

36	G. S. Sobers	off M. A. Nash, Nottinghamshire v Glamorgan at Swansea (six sixes)	1968
36	R. J. Shastri	off Tilak Raj, Bombay v Baroda at Bombay (six sixes)	1984-85
34	E. B. Alletson	off E. H. Killick, Nottinghamshire v Sussex at Hove (46604446; including two no-balls)	1911
34	F. C. Hayes	off M. A. Nash, Lancashire v Glamorgan at Swansea (646666)	1977
34†	A. Flintoff	off A. J. Tudor, Lancashire v Surrey at Manchester (64444660; including two no-balls)	1998
34	C. M. Spearman	off S. J. P. Moreton, Gloucestershire v Oxford UCCE at Oxford (666646) *Moreton's first over in first-class cricket.*	2005
32	I. T. Botham	off I. R. Snook, England XI v Central Districts at Palmerston North (466466)	1983-84
32	P. W. G. Parker	off A. I. Kallicharran, Sussex v Warwickshire at Birmingham (466664)	1982
32	I. R. Redpath	off N. Rosendorff, Australians v Orange Free State at Bloemfontein (666644)	1969-70
32	C. C. Smart	off G. Hill, Glamorgan v Hampshire at Cardiff (664664)	1935
32	Khalid Mahmood	off Naved Latif, Gujranwala v Sargodha at Gujranwala (666662)	2000-01

† *Altogether 38 runs were scored off this over, the two no-balls counting for two extra runs each under ECB regulations.*

Notes: The following instances have been excluded because of the bowlers' compliance: 34 – M. P. Maynard off S. A. Marsh, Glamorgan v Kent at Swansea, 1992; 34 – G. Chapple off P. A. Cottey, Lancashire v Glamorgan at Manchester, 1993; 34 – F. B. Touzel off F. J. J. Viljoen, Western Province B v Griqualand West at Kimberley, 1993-94. Chapple scored a further 32 off Cottey's next over.

There were 35 runs off an over received by A. T. Reinholds off H. T. Davis, Auckland v Wellington at Auckland 1995-96, but this included 16 extras and only 19 off the bat.

In a match against KwaZulu-Natal at Stellenbosch in 2006-07, W. E. September (Boland) conceded 34 in an over: 27 to M. Bekker, six to K. Smit, plus one no-ball.

In a match against Canterbury at Christchurch in 1989-90, R. H. Vance (Wellington) deliberately conceded 77 runs in an over of full tosses which contained 17 no-balls and, owing to the umpire's understandable miscalculation, only five legitimate deliveries.

The greatest number of runs scored off an eight-ball over is 34 (40446664) by R. M. Edwards off M. C. Carew, Governor-General's XI v West Indians at Auckland, 1968-69.

MOST SIXES IN AN INNINGS

16	A. Symonds (254*)	Gloucestershire v Glamorgan at Abergavenny	1995
16	G. R. Napier (196)	Essex v Surrey at Croydon	2011
16	J. D. Ryder (175)	New Zealanders v Australia A at Brisbane	2011-12
15	J. R. Reid (296)	Wellington v Northern Districts at Wellington	1962-63
15	Ziaur Rahman (152*)	South Zone v Central Zone at Mirpur	2012-13

14	Shakti Singh (128)	Himachal Pradesh v Haryana at Dharmsala	1990-91
14	D. J. Hussey (275)	Nottinghamshire v Essex at Nottingham	2007
14	C. H. Gayle (165)	Jamaica v Windward Islands at Kingston	2011-12
14	C. Munro (269*)	Auckland v Wellington at Auckland	2012-13
14	**M. D. K. J. Perera (336)**	**Colts v Saracens at Colombo**	**2012-13**
13	Majid Khan (147*)	Pakistanis v Glamorgan at Swansea	1967
13	C. G. Greenidge (273*)	D. H. Robins' XI v Pakistanis at Eastbourne	1974
13	C. G. Greenidge (259)	Hampshire v Sussex at Southampton	1975
13	G. W. Humpage (254)	Warwickshire v Lancashire at Southport	1982
13	R. J. Shastri (200*)	Bombay v Baroda at Bombay	1984-85

Notes: F. B. Touzel (128*) hit 13 sixes for Western Province B v Griqualand West in contrived circumstances at Kimberley in 1993-94.

There have been **15** instances of 12 sixes in an innings.

MOST SIXES IN A MATCH

20	A. Symonds (254*, 76)	Gloucestershire v Glamorgan at Abergavenny	1995
17	W. J. Stewart (155, 125)	Warwickshire v Lancashire at Blackpool	1959

MOST SIXES IN A SEASON

80	I. T. Botham	1985	49	I. V. A. Richards	1985
66	A. W. Wellard	1935	48	A. W. Carr	1925
57	A. W. Wellard	1936	48	J. H. Edrich	1965
57	A. W. Wellard	1938	48	A. Symonds	1995
51	A. W. Wellard	1933			

MOST BOUNDARIES IN AN INNINGS

	4s/6s			
72	62/10	B. C. Lara (501*)	Warwickshire v Durham at Birmingham	1994
68	68/–	P. A. Perrin (343*)	Essex v Derbyshire at Chesterfield	1904
65	64/1	A. C. MacLaren (424)	Lancashire v Somerset at Taunton	1895
64	64/–	Hanif Mohammad (499)	Karachi v Bahawalpur at Karachi	1958-59
57	52/5	J. H. Edrich (310*)	England v New Zealand at Leeds	1965
57	52/5	Naved Latif (394)	Sargodha v Gujranwala at Gujranwala	2000-01
56	54/2	K. M. Jadhav (327)	Maharashtra v Uttar Pradesh at Gahunje	2012-13
55	55/–	C. W. Gregory (383)	NSW v Queensland at Brisbane	1906-07
55	53/2	G. R. Marsh (355*)	W. Australia v S. Australia at Perth	1989-90
55	51/3†	S. V. Manjrekar (377)	Bombay v Hyderabad at Bombay	1990-91
55	52/3	D. S. Lehmann (339)	Yorkshire v Durham at Leeds	2006
55	54/1	D. K. H. Mitchell (298)	Worcestershire v Somerset at Taunton	2009
55	54/1	S. C. Cook (390)	Lions v Warriors at East London	2009-10
55	47/8	R. R. Rossouw (319)	Eagles v Titans at Centurion	2009-10
54	53/1	G. H. Hirst (341)	Yorkshire v Leicestershire at Leicester	1905
53	53/–	A. W. Nourse (304*)	Natal v Transvaal at Johannesburg	1919-20
53	45/8	K. R. Rutherford (317)	NZ v D. B. Close's XI at Scarborough	1986
53	51/2	V. V. S. Laxman (353)	Hyderabad v Karnataka at Bangalore	1999-2000
53	52/1	M. W. Goodwin (335*)	Sussex v Leicestershire at Hove	2003
52	47/5	N. H. Fairbrother (366)	Lancashire v Surrey at The Oval	1990
52	50/2	C. J. L. Rogers (319)	Northamptonshire v Glos at Northampton	2006
51	51/–	W. G. Grace (344)	MCC v Kent at Canterbury	1876
51	47/4	C. G. Macartney (345)	Australians v Notts at Nottingham	1921
51	50/1	B. B. Nimbalkar (443*)	Maharashtra v Kathiawar at Poona	1948-49
51	49/2	G. A. Hick (315*)	Worcestershire v Durham at Worcester	2002
51	50/1	Salman Butt (290)	Punjab v Federal Areas at Lahore	2007-08
51	44/7	Sunny Singh (312)	Haryana v Madhya Pradesh at Indore	2009-10
50	47/–‡	A. Ducat (306*)	Surrey v Oxford U. at The Oval	1919
50	46/4	D. G. Bradman (369)	South Australia v Tasmania at Adelaide	1935-36
50	35/15	J. R. Reid (296)	Wellington v N. Districts at Wellington	1962-63

	4s/6s			
50	42/8	I. V. A. Richards (322)	Somerset v Warwickshire at Taunton.....	1985
50	50/–	Shoaib Khan (300*)	Peshawar v Quetta at Peshawar.........	2003-04
50	**49/1**	**C. A. Pujara (352)**	**Saurashtra v Karnataka at Rajkot....**	**2012-13**
50	**50/–**	**Imran Farhat (308)**	**Lahore Ravi v Peshawar at Lahore....**	**2012-13**

† _Plus one five._   ‡ _Plus three fives._

PARTNERSHIPS OVER 500

624	for 3rd	K. C. Sangakkara (287)/D. P. M. D. Jayawardene (374), Sri Lanka v South Africa at Colombo...	2006
580	for 2nd	Rafatullah Mohmand (302*)/Aamer Sajjad (289), WAPDA v Sui Southern Gas at Sheikhupura..	2009-10
577	for 4th	V. S. Hazare (288)/Gul Mahomed (319), Baroda v Holkar at Baroda.....	1946-47
576	for 2nd	S. T. Jayasuriya (340)/R. S. Mahanama (225), Sri Lanka v India at Colombo...	1997-98
574*	for 4th	F. M. M. Worrell (255*)/C. L. Walcott (314*), Barbados v Trinidad at Port-of-Spain...	1945-46
561	for 1st	Waheed Mirza (324)/Mansoor Akhtar (224*), Karachi Whites v Quetta at Karachi...	1976-77
555	for 1st	P. Holmes (224*)/H. Sutcliffe (313), Yorkshire v Essex at Leyton.......	1932
554	for 1st	J. T. Brown (300)/J. Tunnicliffe (243), Yorks v Derbys at Chesterfield...	1898
539	for 3rd	S. D. Jogiyani (282)/R. A. Jadeja (303*), Saurashtra v Gujarat at Surat...	2012-13
523	for 3rd	M. A. Carberry (300*)/N. D. McKenzie (237), Hampshire v Yorkshire at Southampton...	2011
520*	for 5th	C. A. Pujara (302*)/R. A. Jadeja (232*), Saurashtra v Orissa at Rajkot...	2008-09
502*	for 4th	F. M. M. Worrell (308*)/J. D. C. Goddard (218*), Barbados v Trinidad at Bridgetown..	1943-44

HIGHEST PARTNERSHIPS FOR EACH WICKET

First Wicket

561	Waheed Mirza/Mansoor Akhtar, Karachi Whites v Quetta at Karachi.........	1976-77
555	P. Holmes/H. Sutcliffe, Yorkshire v Essex at Leyton...................	1932
554	J. T. Brown/J. Tunnicliffe, Yorkshire v Derbyshire at Chesterfield..........	1898
490	E. H. Bowley/J. G. Langridge, Sussex v Middlesex at Hove................	1933
464	R. Sehgal/R. Lamba, Delhi v Himachal Pradesh at Delhi.................	1994-95

Second Wicket

580	Rafatullah Mohmand/Aamer Sajjad, WAPDA v Sui S. Gas at Sheikhupura....	2009-10
576	S. T. Jayasuriya/R. S. Mahanama, Sri Lanka v India at Colombo............	1997-98
480	D. Elgar/R. R. Rossouw, Eagles v Titans at Centurion....................	2009-10
475	Zahir Alam/L. S. Rajput, Assam v Tripura at Gauhati....................	1991-92
465*	J. A. Jameson/R. B. Kanhai, Warwicks v Gloucestershire at Birmingham......	1974

Third Wicket

624	K. C. Sangakkara/D. P. M. D. Jayawardene, Sri Lanka v SA at Colombo......	2006
539	S. D. Jogiyani/R. A. Jadeja, Saurashtra v Gujarat at Surat.................	2012-13
523	M. A. Carberry/N. D. McKenzie, Hampshire v Yorks at Southampton........	2011
467	A. H. Jones/M. D. Crowe, New Zealand v Sri Lanka at Wellington..........	1990-91
459	C. J. L. Rogers/M. J. North, Western Australia v Victoria at Perth...........	2006-07

Fourth Wicket

577	V. S. Hazare/Gul Mahomed, Baroda v Holkar at Baroda.	1946-47
574*	C. L. Walcott/F. M. M. Worrell, Barbados v Trinidad at Port-of-Spain.	1945-46
502*	F. M. M. Worrell/J. D. C. Goddard, Barbados v Trinidad at Bridgetown	1943-44
470	A. I. Kallicharran/G. W. Humpage, Warwicks v Lancs at Southport.	1982
462*	D. W. Hookes/W. B. Phillips, South Australia v Tasmania at Adelaide	1986-87

Fifth Wicket

520*	C. A. Pujara/R. A. Jadeja, Saurashtra v Orissa at Rajkot	2008-09
494	**Marshall Ayub/Mehrab Hossain, Central Zone v East Zone at Bogra**	**2012-13**
479	Misbah-ul-Haq/Usman Arshad, Sui N. Gas v Lahore Shalimar at Lahore	2009-10
464*	M. E. Waugh/S. R. Waugh, New South Wales v Western Australia at Perth.	1990-91
420	Mohammad Ashraful/Marshall Ayub, Dhaka v Chittagong at Chittagong.	2006-07

Sixth Wicket

487*	G. A. Headley/C. C. Passailaigue, Jamaica v Lord Tennyson's XI at Kingston.	1931-32
428	W. W. Armstrong/M. A. Noble, Australians v Sussex at Hove	1902
417	W. P. Saha/L. R. Shukla, Bengal v Assam at Kolkata	2010-11
411	R. M. Poore/E. G. Wynyard, Hampshire v Somerset at Taunton	1899
379	S. L. Stewart/C. F. K. van Wyk, Canterbury v C. Dists at New Plymouth	2009-10

Seventh Wicket

460	Bhupinder Singh, jun./P. Dharmani, Punjab v Delhi at Delhi	1994-95
347	D. St E. Atkinson/C. C. Depeiza, West Indies v Australia at Bridgetown	1954-55
344	K. S. Ranjitsinhji/W. Newham, Sussex v Essex at Leyton	1902
340	K. J. Key/H. Philipson, Oxford University v Middlesex at Chiswick Park	1887
336	F. C. W. Newman/C. R. N. Maxwell, Sir J. Cahn's XI v Leics at Nottingham	1935

Eighth Wicket

433	A. Sims and V. T. Trumper, A. Sims' Aust. XI v Canterbury at Christchurch.	1913-14
392	A. Mishra/J. Yadav, Haryana v Karnataka at Hubli	2012-13
332	I. J. L. Trott/S. C. J. Broad, England v Pakistan at Lord's	2010
313	Wasim Akram/Saqlain Mushtaq, Pakistan v Zimbabwe at Sheikhupura	1996-97
292	R. Peel/Lord Hawke, Yorkshire v Warwickshire at Birmingham.	1896

Ninth Wicket

283	A. Warren/J. Chapman, Derbyshire v Warwickshire at Blackwell.	1910
268	J. B. Commins/N. Boje, South Africa A v Mashonaland at Harare	1994-95
261	W. L. Madsen/T. Poynton, Derbyshire v Northants at Northampton	2012
251	J. W. H. T. Douglas/S. N. Hare, Essex v Derbyshire at Leyton	1921
249*†	A. S. Srivastava/K. Seth, Madhya Pradesh v Vidarbha at Indore	2000-01

† *276 unbeaten runs were scored for this wicket in two separate partnerships; after Srivastava retired hurt, Seth and N. D. Hirwani added 27.*

Tenth Wicket

307	A. F. Kippax/J. E. H. Hooker, New South Wales v Victoria at Melbourne	1928-29
249	C. T. Sarwate/S. N. Banerjee, Indians v Surrey at The Oval	1946
239	Aqeel Arshad/Ali Raza, Lahore Whites v Hyderabad at Lahore	2004-05
235	F. E. Woolley/A. Fielder, Kent v Worcestershire at Stourbridge	1909
233	Ajay Sharma/Maninder Singh, Delhi v Bombay at Bombay	1991-92

Note: There have been only 11 last-wicket stands of 200 or more.

UNUSUAL DISMISSALS

Handled the Ball

There have been **57** instances in first-class cricket. The most recent are:

S. R. Waugh	Australia v India at Chennai...........................	2000-01
M. P. Vaughan	England v India at Bangalore...........................	2001-02
Tushar Imran	Bangladesh A v Jamaica at Spanish Town.................	2001-02
Al Sahariar	Dhaka v Chittagong at Dhaka...........................	2003-04
Junaid Zia	Rawalpindi v Lahore at Lahore.........................	2003-04
D. J. Watson	Dolphins v Eagles at Bloemfontein.....................	2004-05
M. Zondeki	Cape Cobras v Eagles at Bloemfontein..................	2006-07
L. N. Mosena	Free State v Limpopo at Bloemfontein..................	2006-07
W. S. A. Williams	Canterbury v Otago at Dunedin........................	2012-13

Obstructing the Field

There have been **23** instances in first-class cricket. T. Straw of Worcestershire was given out for obstruction v Warwickshire in both 1899 and 1901. The most recent are:

R. C. Rupasinghe	Rio v Kurunegala Youth at Colombo....................	2001-02
K. N. S. Fernando	Lankan v Army at Welisara............................	2006-07
H. R. Jadhav	Baroda v Uttar Pradesh at Baroda......................	2006-07
Riaz Kail	Abbottabad v Quetta at Abbottabad.....................	2009-10
M. R. Ramprakash	Surrey v Gloucestershire at Cheltenham	2011
Z. E. Surkari	Canada v Afghanistan at King City	2011

Hit the Ball Twice

There have been **21** instances in first-class cricket. The last occurrence in England involved J. H. King of Leicestershire v Surrey at The Oval in 1906. The most recent are:

Aziz Malik	Lahore Division v Faisalabad at Sialkot................	1984-85
Javed Mohammad	Multan v Karachi Whites at Sahiwal....................	1986-87
Shahid Pervez	Jammu and Kashmir v Punjab at Srinagar...............	1986-87
Ali Naqvi	PNSC v National Bank at Faisalabad....................	1998-99
A. George	Tamil Nadu v Maharashtra at Pune.....................	1998-99
Maqsood Raza	Lahore Division v PNSC at Sheikhupura.................	1999-2000
D. Mahajan	Jammu and Kashmir v Bihar at Jammu	2005-06

Timed Out

There have been **four** instances in first-class cricket:

A. Jordaan	Eastern Province v Transvaal at Port Elizabeth (SACB match)....	1987-88
H. Yadav	Tripura v Orissa at Cuttack...........................	1997-98
V. C. Drakes	Border v Free State at East London	2002-03
A. J. Harris	Nottinghamshire v Durham UCCE at Nottingham...........	2003

BOWLING RECORDS

TEN WICKETS IN AN INNINGS

In the history of first-class cricket, there have been **80** instances of a bowler taking all ten wickets in an innings:

	O	M	R		
E. Hinkly (Kent).............				v England at Lord's............	1848
*J. Wisden (North)............				v South at Lord's..............	1850
V. E. Walker (England)	43	17	74	v Surrey at The Oval............	1859
V. E. Walker (Middlesex).......	44.2	5	104	v Lancashire at Manchester	1865

	O	M	R		
G. Wootton (All England)	31.3	9	54	v Yorkshire at Sheffield	1865
W. Hickton (Lancashire)	36.2	19	46	v Hampshire at Manchester	1870
S. E. Butler (Oxford)	24.1	11	38	v Cambridge at Lord's	1871
James Lillywhite (South)	60.2	22	129	v North at Canterbury	1872
A. Shaw (MCC)	36.2	8	73	v North at Lord's	1874
E. Barratt (Players)	29	11	43	v Australians at The Oval	1878
G. Giffen (Australian XI)	26	10	66	v The Rest at Sydney	1883-84
W. G. Grace (MCC)	36.2	17	49	v Oxford University at Oxford	1886
G. Burton (Middlesex)	52.3	25	59	v Surrey at The Oval	1888
†A. E. Moss (Canterbury)	21.3	10	28	v Wellington at Christchurch	1889-90
S. M. J. Woods (Cambridge U.)	31	6	69	v Thornton's XI at Cambridge	1890
T. Richardson (Surrey)	15.3	3	45	v Essex at The Oval	1894
H. Pickett (Essex)	27	11	32	v Leicestershire at Leyton	1895
E. J. Tyler (Somerset)	34.3	15	49	v Surrey at Taunton	1895
W. P. Howell (Australians)	23.2	14	28	v Surrey at The Oval	1899
C. H. G. Bland (Sussex)	25.2	10	48	v Kent at Tonbridge	1899
J. Briggs (Lancashire)	28.5	7	55	v Worcestershire at Manchester	1900
A. E. Trott (Middlesex)	14.2	5	42	v Somerset at Taunton	1900
A. Fielder (Players)	24.5	1	90	v Gentlemen at Lord's	1906
E. G. Dennett (Gloucestershire)	19.4	7	40	v Essex at Bristol	1906
A. E. E. Vogler (E. Province)	12	2	26	v Griqualand W. at Johannesburg	1906-07
C. Blythe (Kent)	16	7	30	v Northants at Northampton	1907
J. B. King (Philadelphia)	18.1	7	53	v Ireland at Haverford‡	1909
A. Drake (Yorkshire)	8.5	0	35	v Somerset at Weston-s-Mare	1914
W. Bestwick (Derbyshire)	19	2	40	v Glamorgan at Cardiff	1921
A. A. Mailey (Australians)	28.4	5	66	v Gloucestershire at Cheltenham	1921
C. W. L. Parker (Glos.)	40.3	13	79	v Somerset at Bristol	1921
T. Rushby (Surrey)	17.5	4	43	v Somerset at Taunton	1921
J. C. White (Somerset)	42.2	11	76	v Worcestershire at Worcester	1921
G. C. Collins (Kent)	19.3	4	65	v Nottinghamshire at Dover	1922
H. Howell (Warwickshire)	25.1	5	51	v Yorkshire at Birmingham	1923
A. S. Kennedy (Players)	22.4	10	37	v Gentlemen at The Oval	1927
G. O. B. Allen (Middlesex)	25.3	10	40	v Lancashire at Lord's	1929
A. P. Freeman (Kent)	42	9	131	v Lancashire at Maidstone	1929
G. Geary (Leicestershire)	16.2	8	18	v Glamorgan at Pontypridd	1929
C. V. Grimmett (Australians)	22.3	8	37	v Yorkshire at Sheffield	1930
A. P. Freeman (Kent)	30.4	8	53	v Essex at Southend	1930
H. Verity (Yorkshire)	18.4	6	36	v Warwickshire at Leeds	1931
A. P. Freeman (Kent)	36.1	9	79	v Lancashire at Manchester	1931
V. W. C. Jupp (Northants)	39	6	127	v Kent at Tunbridge Wells	1932
H. Verity (Yorkshire)	19.4	16	10	v Nottinghamshire at Leeds	1932
T. W. Wall (South Australia)	12.4	2	36	v New South Wales at Sydney	1932-33
T. B. Mitchell (Derbyshire)	19.1	4	64	v Leicestershire at Leicester	1935
J. Mercer (Glamorgan)	26	10	51	v Worcestershire at Worcester	1936
T. W. J. Goddard (Glos.)	28.4	4	113	v Worcestershire at Cheltenham	1937
T. F. Smailes (Yorkshire)	17.1	5	47	v Derbyshire at Sheffield	1939
E. A. Watts (Surrey)	24.1	8	67	v Warwickshire at Birmingham	1939
*W. E. Hollies (Warwickshire)	20.4	4	49	v Notts at Birmingham	1946
J. M. Sims (East)	18.4	2	90	v West at Kingston	1948
T. E. Bailey (Essex)	39.4	9	90	v Lancashire at Clacton	1949
J. K. Graveney (Glos.)	18.4	2	66	v Derbyshire at Chesterfield	1949
R. Berry (Lancashire)	36.2	9	102	v Worcestershire at Blackpool	1953
S. P. Gupte (President's XI)	24.2	7	78	v Combined XI at Bombay	1954-55
J. C. Laker (Surrey)	46	18	88	v Australians at The Oval	1956
J. C. Laker (England)	51.2	23	53	v Australia at Manchester	1956
G. A. R. Lock (Surrey)	29.1	18	54	v Kent at Blackheath	1956
K. Smales (Nottinghamshire)	41.3	20	66	v Gloucestershire at Stroud	1956
P. M. Chatterjee (Bengal)	19	11	20	v Assam at Jorhat	1956-57
J. D. Bannister (Warwickshire)	23.3	11	41	v Comb. Services at Birmingham§	1959
A. J. G. Pearson (Cambridge U.)	30.3	8	78	v Leics at Loughborough	1961

	O	M	R		
N. I. Thomson (Sussex)	34.2	19	49	v Warwickshire at Worthing	1964
P. J. Allan (Queensland)	15.6	3	61	v Victoria at Melbourne	1965-66
I. J. Brayshaw (W. Australia)	17.6	4	44	v Victoria at Perth	1967-68
Shahid Mahmood (Karachi Whites)	25	5	58	v Khairpur at Karachi	1969-70
E. E. Hemmings (International XI)	49.3	14	175	v West Indies XI at Kingston . . .	1982-83
P. Sunderam (Rajasthan)	22	5	78	v Vidarbha at Jodhpur	1985-86
S. T. Jefferies (W. Province)	22.5	7	59	v Orange Free State at Cape Town .	1987-88
Imran Adil (Bahawalpur)	22.5	3	92	v Faisalabad at Faisalabad	1989-90
G. P. Wickremasinghe (Sinhalese)	19.2	5	41	v Kalutara at Colombo	1991-92
R. L. Johnson (Middlesex)	18.5	6	45	v Derbyshire at Derby	1994
Naeem Akhtar (Rawalpindi B) . .	21.3	10	28	v Peshawar at Peshawar	1995-96
A. Kumble (India)	26.3	9	74	v Pakistan at Delhi	1998-99
D. S. Mohanty (East Zone)	19	5	46	v South Zone at Agartala	2000-01
O. D. Gibson (Durham)	17.3	1	47	v Hampshire at Chester-le-Street . .	2007
M. W. Olivier (Warriors)	26.3	4	65	v Eagles at Bloemfontein	2007-08
Zulfiqar Babar (Multan)	39.4	3	143	v Islamabad at Multan	2009-10

Note: In addition, the following instances were achieved in 12-a-side matches:

	O	M	R		
E. M. Grace (MCC)	32.2	7	69	v Gents of Kent at Canterbury . . .	1862
W. G. Grace (MCC)	46.1	15	92	v Kent at Canterbury	1873
†D. C. S. Hinds (A. B. St Hill's XII) .	19.1	6	36	v Trinidad at Port-of-Spain	1900-01

* J. Wisden and W. E. Hollies achieved the feat without the direct assistance of a fielder. Wisden's ten were all bowled; Hollies bowled seven and had three lbw.
† On debut in first-class cricket. ‡ Pennsylvania. § Mitchells & Butlers Ground.

OUTSTANDING BOWLING ANALYSES

	O	M	R	W		
H. Verity (Yorkshire)	19.4	16	10	10	v Nottinghamshire at Leeds . . .	1932
G. Elliott (Victoria)	19	17	2	9	v Tasmania at Launceston	1857-58
Ahad Khan (Railways)	6.3	4	7	9	v Dera Ismail Khan at Lahore . . .	1964-65
J. C. Laker (England)	14	12	2	8	v The Rest at Bradford	1950
D. Shackleton (Hampshire)	11.1	7	4	8	v Somerset at Weston-s-Mare . .	1955
E. Peate (Yorkshire)	16	11	5	8	v Surrey at Holbeck	1883
K. M. Dabengwa (Westerns) . .	4.4	3	1	7	v Northerns at Harare	2006-07
F. R. Spofforth (Australians) . .	8.3	6	3	7	v England XI at Birmingham .	1884
W. A. Henderson (NE Transvaal)	9.3	7	4	7	v OFS at Bloemfontein	1937-38
Rajinder Goel (Haryana)	7	4	4	7	v Jammu and Kashmir at Chandigarh	1977-78
N. W. Bracken (NSW)	7	5	4	7	v South Australia at Sydney . . .	2004-05
V. I. Smith (South Africans) . .	4.5	3	1	6	v Derbyshire at Derby	1947
S. Cosstick (Victoria)	21.1	20	1	6	v Tasmania at Melbourne	1868-69
Israr Ali (Bahawalpur)	11	10	1	6	v Dacca U. at Bahawalpur	1957-58
A. D. Pougher (MCC)	3	3	0	5	v Australians at Lord's	1896
G. R. Cox (Sussex)	6	6	0	5	v Somerset at Weston-s-Mare .	1921
R. K. Tyldesley (Lancashire) . . .	5	5	0	5	v Leicestershire at Manchester	1924
P. T. Mills (Gloucestershire) . . .	6.4	6	0	5	v Somerset at Bristol	1928

MOST WICKETS IN A MATCH

19-90	J. C. Laker	England v Australia at Manchester	1956
17-48†	C. Blythe	Kent v Northamptonshire at Northampton	1907
17-50	C. T. B. Turner	Australians v England XI at Hastings	1888
17-54	W. P. Howell	Australians v Western Province at Cape Town	1902-03
17-56	C. W. L. Parker	Gloucestershire v Essex at Gloucester	1925
17-67	A. P. Freeman	Kent v Sussex at Hove	1922

17-89	W. G. Grace	Gloucestershire v Nottinghamshire at Cheltenham ...	1877
17-89	F. C. L. Matthews	Nottinghamshire v Northants at Nottingham	1923
17-91	H. Dean	Lancashire v Yorkshire at Liverpool	1913
17-91†	H. Verity	Yorkshire v Essex at Leyton	1933
17-92	A. P. Freeman	Kent v Warwickshire at Folkestone	1932
17-103	W. Mycroft	Derbyshire v Hampshire at Southampton	1876
17-106	G. R. Cox	Sussex v Warwickshire at Horsham...............	1926
17-106†	T. W. J. Goddard	Gloucestershire v Kent at Bristol	1939
17-119	W. Mead	Essex v Hampshire at Southampton..............	1895
17-137	W. Brearley	Lancashire v Somerset at Manchester	1905
17-137	J. M. Davison	Canada v USA at Fort Lauderdale	2004
17-159	S. F. Barnes	England v South Africa at Johannesburg...........	1913-14
17-201	G. Giffen	South Australia v Victoria at Adelaide	1885-86
17-212	J. C. Clay	Glamorgan v Worcestershire at Swansea...........	1937

† *Achieved in a single day.*

Note: H. Arkwright took 18-96 for MCC v Gentlemen of Kent in a 12-a-side match at Canterbury in 1861.

There have been **58** instances of a bowler taking 16 wickets in an 11-a-side match, the most recent being 16-100 by J. U. Chaturanga for Singha v Antonians at Gampaha, 2010-11.

FOUR WICKETS WITH CONSECUTIVE BALLS

There have been **39** instances in first-class cricket. R. J. Crisp achieved the feat twice, for Western Province in 1931-32 and 1933-34. A. E. Trott took four in four balls and another hat-trick in the same innings for Middlesex v Somerset in 1907, his benefit match. Occurrences since 2000:

G. P. Butcher	Surrey v Derbyshire at The Oval	2000
Fazl-e-Akbar	PIA v Habib Bank at Lahore	2001-02
C. M. Willoughby	Cape Cobras v Dolphins at Durban	2005-06
Tabish Khan	Karachi Whites v ZTBL at Karachi	2009-10
Kamran Hussain	Habib Bank v Lahore Shalimar at Lahore	2009-10
N. Wagner	Otago v Wellington at Queenstown	2010-11
Khalid Usman	Abbottabad v Karachi Blues at Karachi.................	2011-12

Notes: In their match with England at The Oval in 1863, Surrey lost four wickets in the course of a four-ball over from G. Bennett.

Sussex lost five wickets in the course of the final (six-ball) over of their match with Surrey at Eastbourne in 1972. P. I. Pocock, who had taken three wickets in his previous over, captured four more, taking in all seven wickets with 11 balls, a feat unique in first-class matches. (The eighth wicket fell to a run-out.)

K. D. James took four in four balls for Hampshire against Indians at Southampton in 1996 and then scored a century, a unique double.

HAT-TRICKS

Double Hat-Trick

Besides Trott's performance, which is mentioned in the preceding section, the following instances are recorded of players having performed the hat-trick twice in the same match, Rao doing so in the same innings.

A. Shaw	Nottinghamshire v Gloucestershire at Nottingham	1884
T. J. Matthews	Australia v South Africa at Manchester	1912
C. W. L. Parker	Gloucestershire v Middlesex at Bristol	1924
R. O. Jenkins	Worcestershire v Surrey at Worcester	1949
J. S. Rao	Services v Northern Punjab at Amritsar.....................	1963-64
Amin Lakhani	Combined XI v Indians at Multan	1978-79

Five Wickets in Six Balls

W. H. Copson	Derbyshire v Warwickshire at Derby	1937
W. A. Henderson	N.E. Transvaal v Orange Free State at Bloemfontein	1937-38
P. I. Pocock	Surrey v Sussex at Eastbourne	1972
Yasir Arafat	Rawalpindi v Faisalabad at Rawalpindi	2004-05
N. Wagner	Otago v Wellington at Queenstown	2010-11

Yasir Arafat's five wickets were spread across two innings and interrupted only by a no-ball. Wagner was the first to take five wickets in a single over.

Most Hat-Tricks

D. V. P. Wright	7	R. G. Barlow	4	T. G. Matthews	4
T. W. J. Goddard	6	Fazl-e-Akbar	4	M. J. Procter	4
C. W. L. Parker	6	A. P. Freeman	4	T. Richardson	4
S. Haigh	5	J. T. Hearne	4	F. R. Spofforth	4
V. W. C. Jupp	5	J. C. Laker	4	F. S. Trueman	4
A. E. G. Rhodes	5	G. A. R. Lock	4		
F. A. Tarrant	5	G. G. Macaulay	4		

Hat-Trick on Debut

There have been **18** instances in first-class cricket. Occurrences since the Second World War:

J. C. Treanor	New South Wales v Queensland at Brisbane	1954-55
V. B. Ranjane	Maharashtra v Saurashtra at Poona	1956-57
Arshad Khan	Dacca University v East Pakistan B at Dacca	1957-58
N. Fredrick	Ceylon v Madras at Colombo	1963-64
J. S. Rao	Services v Jammu and Kashmir at Delhi	1963-64
Mehboodullah	Uttar Pradesh v Madhya Pradesh at Lucknow	1971-72
R. O. Estwick	Barbados v Guyana at Bridgetown	1982-83
S. A. Ankola	Maharashtra v Gujarat at Poona	1988-89
J. Srinath	Karnataka v Hyderabad at Secunderabad	1989-90
S. P. Mukherjee	Bengal v Hyderabad at Secunderabad	1989-90
S. M. Harwood	Victoria v Tasmania at Melbourne	2002-03
P. Connell	Ireland v Netherlands at Rotterdam	2008
A. Mithun	Karnataka v Uttar Pradesh at Meerut	2009-10
Zohaib Shera	Karachi Whites v National Bank at Karachi	2009-10

Notes: R. R. Phillips (Border) took a hat-trick in his first over in first-class cricket (v Eastern Province at Port Elizabeth, 1939-40) having previously played in four matches without bowling.

    J. S. Rao took two more hat-tricks in his next match.

250 WICKETS IN A SEASON

	Season	O	M	R	W	Avge
A. P. Freeman	1928	1,976.1	423	5,489	304	18.05
A. P. Freeman	1933	2,039	651	4,549	298	15.26
T. Richardson	1895‡	1,690.1	463	4,170	290	14.37
C. T. B. Turner	1888†	2,427.2	1,127	3,307	283	11.68
A. P. Freeman	1931	1,618	360	4,307	276	15.60
A. P. Freeman	1930	1,914.3	472	4,632	275	16.84
T. Richardson	1897‡	1,603.4	495	3,945	273	14.45
A. P. Freeman	1929	1,670.5	381	4,879	267	18.27
W. Rhodes	1900	1,553	455	3,606	261	13.81
J. T. Hearne	1896‡	2,003.1	818	3,670	257	14.28
A. P. Freeman	1932	1,565.5	404	4,149	253	16.39
W. Rhodes	1901	1,565	505	3,797	251	15.12

† *Indicates 4-ball overs.*   ‡ *5-ball overs.*

Notes: In four consecutive seasons (1928-31), A. P. Freeman took 1,122 wickets, and in eight consecutive seasons (1928-35), 2,090 wickets. In each of these eight seasons he took over 200 wickets.

T. Richardson took 1,005 wickets in four consecutive seasons (1894-97).

The earliest date by which any bowler has taken 100 wickets in an English season is June 12, achieved by J. T. Hearne in 1896 and C. W. L. Parker in 1931, when A. P. Freeman did it on June 13.

100 WICKETS IN A SEASON MOST TIMES

(Includes overseas tours and seasons)

W. Rhodes 23	C. W. L. Parker 16	G. H. Hirst 15
D. Shackleton 20	R. T. D. Perks 16	A. S. Kennedy 15
A. P. Freeman 17	F. J. Titmus 16	
T. W. J. Goddard 16	J. T. Hearne 15	

Notes: D. Shackleton reached 100 wickets in 20 successive seasons – 1949 to 1968.

Since the reduction of County Championship matches in 1969, D. L. Underwood (five times) and J. K. Lever (four times) are the only bowlers to have reached 100 wickets in a season more than twice. The highest aggregate in a season since 1969 is 134 by M. D. Marshall in 1982.

The most instances of 200 wickets in a season is eight by A. P. Freeman, who did it in eight successive seasons – 1928 to 1935 – including 304 in 1928. C. W. L. Parker did it five times, T. W. J. Goddard four times, and J. T. Hearne, G. A. Lohmann, W. Rhodes, T. Richardson, M. W. Tate and H. Verity three times each.

The last bowler to reach 200 wickets in a season was G. A. R. Lock (212 in 1957).

100 WICKETS IN A SEASON OUTSIDE ENGLAND

W		Season	Country	R	Avge
116	M. W. Tate	1926-27	India/Ceylon	1,599	13.78
113	Kabir Khan	1998-99	Pakistan	1,706	15.09
107	Ijaz Faqih	1985-86	Pakistan	1,719	16.06
106	C. T. B. Turner	1887-88	Australia	1,441	13.59
106	R. Benaud	1957-58	South Africa	2,056	19.39
105	Murtaza Hussain	1995-96	Pakistan	1,882	17.92
104	S. F. Barnes	1913-14	South Africa	1,117	10.74
104	Sajjad Akbar	1989-90	Pakistan	2,328	22.38
103	Abdul Qadir	1982-83	Pakistan	2,367	22.98

LEADING BOWLERS IN AN ENGLISH SEASON

(Qualification: 10 wickets in 10 innings)

Season	Leading wicket-taker	Wkts	Avge	Top of averages	Wkts	Avge
1946	W. E. Hollies	184	15.60	A. Booth.	111	11.61
1947	T. W. J. Goddard	238	17.30	J. C. Clay	65	16.44
1948	J. E. Walsh	174	19.56	J. C. Clay	41	14.17
1949	R. O. Jenkins	183	21.19	T. W. J. Goddard	160	19.18
1950	R. Tattersall	193	13.59	R. Tattersall	193	13.59
1951	R. Appleyard	200	14.14	R. Appleyard	200	14.14
1952	J. H. Wardle	177	19.54	F. S. Trueman.	61	13.78
1953	B. Dooland.	172	16.58	C. J. Knott	38	13.71
1954	B. Dooland.	196	15.48	J. B. Statham	92	14.13
1955	G. A. R. Lock.	216	14.49	R. Appleyard	85	13.01
1956	D. J. Shepherd	177	15.36	G. A. R. Lock.	155	12.46
1957	G. A. R. Lock.	212	12.02	G. A. R. Lock.	212	12.02

Season	Leading wicket-taker	Wkts	Avge	Top of averages	Wkts	Avge
1958	G. A. R. Lock	170	12.08	H. L. Jackson	143	10.99
1959	D. Shackleton	148	21.55	J. B. Statham	139	15.01
1960	F. S. Trueman	175	13.98	J. B. Statham	135	12.31
1961	J. A. Flavell	171	17.79	J. A. Flavell	171	17.79
1962	D. Shackleton	172	20.15	C. Cook	58	17.13
1963	D. Shackleton	146	16.75	C. C. Griffith	119	12.83
1964	D. Shackleton	142	20.40	J. A. Standen	64	13.00
1965	D. Shackleton	144	16.08	H. J. Rhodes	119	11.04
1966	D. L. Underwood	157	13.80	D. L. Underwood	157	13.80
1967	T. W. Cartwright	147	15.52	D. L. Underwood	136	12.39
1968	R. Illingworth	131	14.36	O. S. Wheatley	82	12.95
1969	R. M. H. Cottam	109	21.04	A. Ward	69	14.82
1970	D. J. Shepherd	106	19.16	Majid Khan	11	18.81
1971	L. R. Gibbs	131	18.89	G. G. Arnold	83	17.12
1972	{ T. W. Cartwright	98	18.64	I. M. Chappell	10	10.60
	{ B. Stead	98	20.38			
1973	B. S. Bedi	105	17.94	T. W. Cartwright	89	15.84
1974	A. M. E. Roberts	119	13.62	A. M. E. Roberts	119	13.62
1975	P. G. Lee	112	18.45	A. M. E. Roberts	57	15.80
1976	G. A. Cope	93	24.13	M. A. Holding	55	14.38
1977	M. J. Procter	109	18.04	R. A. Woolmer	19	15.21
1978	D. L. Underwood	110	14.49	D. L. Underwood	110	14.49
1979	{ D. L. Underwood	106	14.85	J. Garner	55	13.83
	{ J. K. Lever	106	17.30			
1980	R. D. Jackman	121	15.40	J. Garner	49	13.93
1981	R. J. Hadlee	105	14.89	R. J. Hadlee	105	14.89
1982	M. D. Marshall	134	15.73	R. J. Hadlee	61	14.57
1983	{ J. K. Lever	106	16.28	Imran Khan	12	7.16
	{ D. L. Underwood	106	19.28			
1984	R. J. Hadlee	117	14.05	R. J. Hadlee	117	14.05
1985	N. V. Radford	101	24.68	R. M. Ellison	65	17.20
1986	C. A. Walsh	118	18.17	M. D. Marshall	100	15.08
1987	N. V. Radford	109	20.81	R. J. Hadlee	97	12.64
1988	F. D. Stephenson	125	18.31	M. D. Marshall	42	13.16
1989	{ D. R. Pringle	94	18.64	T. M. Alderman	70	15.64
	{ S. L. Watkin	94	25.09			
1990	N. A. Foster	94	26.61	I. R. Bishop	59	19.05
1991	Waqar Younis	113	14.65	Waqar Younis	113	14.65
1992	C. A. Walsh	92	15.96	C. A. Walsh	92	15.96
1993	S. L. Watkin	92	22.80	Wasim Akram	59	19.27
1994	M. M. Patel	90	22.86	C. E. L. Ambrose	77	14.45
1995	A. Kumble	105	20.40	A. A. Donald	89	16.07
1996	C. A. Walsh	85	16.84	C. E. L. Ambrose	43	16.67
1997	A. M. Smith	83	17.63	A. A. Donald	60	15.63
1998	C. A. Walsh	106	17.31	V. J. Wells	36	14.27
1999	A. Sheriyar	92	24.70	Saqlain Mushtaq	58	11.37
2000	G. D. McGrath	80	13.21	C. A. Walsh	40	11.42
2001	R. J. Kirtley	75	23.32	G. D. McGrath	40	15.60
2002	{ M. J. Saggers	83	21.51	C. P. Schofield	18	18.38
	{ K. J. Dean	83	23.50			
2003	Mushtaq Ahmed	103	24.65	Shoaib Akhtar	34	17.05
2004	Mushtaq Ahmed	84	27.59	D. S. Lehmann	15	17.40
2005	S. K. Warne	87	22.50	M. Muralitharan	36	15.00
2006	Mushtaq Ahmed	102	19.91	Naved-ul-Hasan	35	16.71
2007	Mushtaq Ahmed	90	25.66	Harbhajan Singh	37	18.54
2008	J. A. Tomlinson	67	24.76	M. Davies	41	14.63
2009	Danish Kaneria	75	23.69	G. Onions	69	19.95
2010	A. R. Adams	68	22.17	J. K. H. Naik	35	17.68
2011	D. D. Masters	93	18.13	T. T. Bresnan	29	17.68
2012	G. Onions	72	14.73	G. Onions	72	14.73
2013	**G. Onions**	**73**	**18.92**	**T. A. Copeland**	**45**	**18.26**

2,000 WICKETS

Dates in italics denote the first half of an overseas season; i.e. *1970* denotes the 1970-71 season.

		Career	W	R	Avge
1	W. Rhodes	1898–1930	4,187	69,993	16.71
2	A. P. Freeman	1914–1936	3,776	69,577	18.42
3	C. W. L. Parker	1903–1935	3,278	63,817	19.46
4	J. T. Hearne	1888–1923	3,061	54,352	17.75
5	T. W. J. Goddard	1922–1952	2,979	59,116	19.84
6	W. G. Grace	1865–1908	2,876	51,545	17.92
7	A. S. Kennedy	1907–1936	2,874	61,034	21.23
8	D. Shackleton	1948–1969	2,857	53,303	18.65
9	G. A. R. Lock	1946–*1970*	2,844	54,709	19.23
10	F. J. Titmus	1949–1982	2,830	63,313	22.37
11	M. W. Tate	1912–1937	2,784	50,571	18.16
12	G. H. Hirst	1891–1929	2,739	51,282	18.72
13	C. Blythe	1899–1914	2,506	42,136	16.81
14	D. L. Underwood	1963–1987	2,465	49,993	20.28
15	W. E. Astill	1906–1939	2,431	57,783	23.76
16	J. C. White	1909–1937	2,356	43,759	18.57
17	W. E. Hollies	1932–1957	2,323	48,656	20.94
18	F. S. Trueman	1949–1969	2,304	42,154	18.29
19	J. B. Statham	1950–1968	2,260	36,999	16.37
20	R. T. D. Perks	1930–1955	2,233	53,770	24.07
21	J. Briggs	1879–1900	2,221	35,431	15.95
22	D. J. Shepherd	1950–1972	2,218	47,302	21.32
23	E. G. Dennett	1903–1926	2,147	42,571	19.82
24	T. Richardson	1892–1905	2,104	38,794	18.43
25	T. E. Bailey	1945–1967	2,082	48,170	23.13
26	R. Illingworth	1951–1983	2,072	42,023	20.28
27	N. Gifford	1960–1988	2,068	48,731	23.56
	F. E. Woolley	1906–1938	2,068	41,066	19.85
29	G. Geary	1912–1938	2,063	41,339	20.03
30	D. V. P. Wright	1932–1957	2,056	49,307	23.98
31	J. A. Newman	1906–1930	2,032	51,111	25.15
32	†A. Shaw	1864–1897	2,027	24,580	12.12
33	S. Haigh	1895–1913	2,012	32,091	15.94

† *The figures for A. Shaw exclude one wicket for which no analysis is available.*

Note: Some works of reference provide career figures which differ from those in this list, owing to the exclusion or inclusion of matches recognised or not recognised as first-class by *Wisden*. A fuller list can be found in *Wisdens* up to 2011.

Current Players with 750 Wickets

	Career	W	R	Avge
G. Chapple	1992–2013	936	24,410	26.07
C. W. Henderson	*1990*–2013	905	27,841	30.76
J. Lewis	1995–2013	832	21,757	26.15
H. M. R. K. B. Herath	*1996*–2013	825	20,470	24.81
D. Hettiarachchi	*1994*–2012	802	18,163	22.64
M. J. Hoggard	1996–2013	786	21,739	27.65
Yasir Arafat	*1997*–2013	767	18,480	24.09

An expanded and regularly updated online version of the Records can be found at www.wisdenrecords.com

ALL-ROUND RECORDS

REMARKABLE ALL-ROUND MATCHES

V. E. Walker	20*	108	10-74	4-17	England v Surrey at The Oval	1859
W. G. Grace	104		2-60	10-49	MCC v Oxford University at Oxford .	1886
G. Giffen	271		9-96	7-70	South Australia v Victoria at Adelaide	1891-92
B. J. T. Bosanquet	103	100*	3-75	8-53	Middlesex v Sussex at Lord's	1905
G. H. Hirst	111	117*	6-70	5-45	Yorkshire v Somerset at Bath	1906
F. D. Stephenson	111	117	4-105	7-117	Notts v Yorkshire at Nottingham.	1988

Note: E. M. Grace, for MCC v Gentlemen of Kent in a 12-a-side match at Canterbury in 1862, scored 192* and took 5-77 and 10-69.

HUNDRED AND HAT-TRICK

G. Giffen, Australians v Lancashire at Manchester	1884
W. E. Roller, Surrey v Sussex at The Oval. *Unique instance of 200 and hat-trick*	1885
W. B. Burns, Worcestershire v Gloucestershire at Worcester	1913
V. W. C. Jupp, Sussex v Essex at Colchester	1921
R. E. S. Wyatt, MCC v Ceylonese at Colombo	1926-27
L. N. Constantine, West Indians v Northamptonshire at Northampton	1928
D. E. Davies, Glamorgan v Leicestershire at Leicester	1937
V. M. Merchant, Dr C. R. Pereira's XI v Sir Homi Mehta's XI at Bombay	1946-47
M. J. Procter, Gloucestershire v Essex at Westcliff-on-Sea.	1972
M. J. Procter, Gloucestershire v Leicestershire at Bristol	1979
K. D. James, Hampshire v Indians at Southampton. *Unique instance of 100 and four wickets in four balls*	1996
J. E. C. Franklin, Gloucestershire v Derbyshire at Cheltenham.	2009
Sohag Gazi, Barisal v Khulna at Khulna	2012-13
Sohag Gazi, Bangladesh v New Zealand at Chittagong	**2013-14**

THE DOUBLE

The double was traditionally regarded as 1,000 runs and 100 wickets in an English season. The feat became exceptionally rare after the reduction of County Championship matches in 1969.

Remarkable Seasons

	Season	R	W			Season	R	W
G. H. Hirst	1906	2,385	208		J. H. Parks	1937	3,003	101

1,000 Runs and 100 Wickets

W. Rhodes	16	W. G. Grace	8	F. J. Titmus	8
G. H. Hirst	14	M. S. Nichols	8	F. E. Woolley	7
V. W. C. Jupp	10	A. E. Relf	8	G. E. Tribe	7
W. E. Astill	9	F. A. Tarrant	8		
T. E. Bailey	8	M. W. Tate	8†		

† *M. W. Tate also scored 1,193 runs and took 116 wickets on the 1926-27 MCC tour of India and Ceylon.*

Note: R. J. Hadlee (1984) and F. D. Stephenson (1988) are the only players to perform the feat since the reduction of County Championship matches in 1969. A complete list of those performing the feat before then may be found on page 202 of the 1982 *Wisden*. T. E. Bailey (1959) was the last player to achieve 2,000 runs and 100 wickets in a season; M. W. Tate (1925) the last to reach 1,000 runs and 200 wickets. Full lists may be found in *Wisdens* up to 2003.

Wicketkeeper's Double

The only wicketkeepers to achieve 1,000 runs and 100 dismissals in a season were L. E. G. Ames (1928, 1929 and 1932, when he scored 2,482 runs) and J. T. Murray (1957).

WICKETKEEPING RECORDS

MOST DISMISSALS IN AN INNINGS

9 (8ct, 1st)	Tahir Rashid	Habib Bank v PACO at Gujranwala	1992-93
9 (7ct, 2st)	W. R. James*	Matabeleland v Mashonaland CD at Bulawayo	1995-96
8 (all ct)	A. T. W. Grout	Queensland v Western Australia at Brisbane	1959-60
8 (all ct)†	D. E. East	Essex v Somerset at Taunton	1985
8 (all ct)	S. A. Marsh‡	Kent v Middlesex at Lord's	1991
8 (6ct, 2st)	T. J. Zoehrer	Australians v Surrey at The Oval	1993
8 (7ct, 1st)	D. S. Berry	Victoria v South Australia at Melbourne	1996-97
8 (7ct, 1st)	Y. S. S. Mendis	Bloomfield v Kurunegala Youth at Colombo	2000-01
8 (7ct, 1st)	S. Nath§	Assam v Tripura at Guwahati	2001-02
8 (all ct)	J. N. Batty¶	Surrey v Kent at The Oval	2004
8 (all ct)	Golam Mabud	Sylhet v Dhaka at Dhaka	2005-06
8 (all ct)	A. Z. M. Dyili	Eastern Province v Free State at Port Elizabeth	2009-10
8 (all ct)	D. C. de Boorder	Otago v Wellington at Wellington	2009-10
8 (all ct)	R. S. Second	Free State v North West at Bloemfontein	2011-12
8 (all ct)	T. L. Tsolekile	South Africa A v Sri Lanka A at Durban	2012

There have been **91** further instances of seven dismissals in an innings. R. W. Taylor achieved the feat three times, and G. J. Hopkins, Kamran Akmal, S. A. Marsh, K. J. Piper, Shahin Hossain and Wasim Bari twice. One of Marsh's two instances was of eight dismissals (see above). A fuller list can be found in *Wisdens* before 2004.

* W. R. James also scored 99 and 99 not out.   *† The first eight wickets to fall.*
‡ S. A. Marsh also scored 108 not out.   *§ On his only first-class appearance.*
¶ J. N. Batty also scored 129.

WICKETKEEPERS' HAT-TRICKS

W. H. Brain, Gloucestershire v Somerset at Cheltenham, 1893 – three stumpings off successive balls from C. L. Townsend.

G. O. Dawkes, Derbyshire v Worcestershire at Kidderminster, 1958 – three catches off successive balls from H. L. Jackson.

R. C. Russell, Gloucestershire v Surrey at The Oval, 1986 – three catches off successive balls from C. A. Walsh and D. V. Lawrence (2).

MOST DISMISSALS IN A MATCH

14 (11ct, 3st)	I. Khaleel	Hyderabad v Assam at Guwahati	2011-12
13 (11ct, 2st)	W. R. James*	Matabeleland v Mashonaland CD at Bulawayo	1995-96
12 (8ct, 4st)	E. Pooley	Surrey v Sussex at The Oval	1868
12 (9ct, 3st)	D. Tallon	Queensland v New South Wales at Sydney	1938-39
12 (9ct, 3st)	H. B. Taber	New South Wales v South Australia at Adelaide	1968-69
12 (all ct)	P. D. McGlashan	Northern Districts v Central Districts at Whangarei	2009-10
12 (11ct, 1st)	T. L. Tsolekile	Lions v Dolphins at Johannesburg	2010-11
12 (all ct)	Kashif Mahmood	Lahore Shalimar v Abbottabad at Abbottabad	2010-11
12 (all ct)	R. S. Second	Free State v North West at Bloemfontein	2011-12

* W. R. James also scored 99 and 99 not out.

100 DISMISSALS IN A SEASON

128 (79ct, 49st)	L. E. G. Ames	1929	104 (82ct, 22st)	J. T. Murray......	1957
122 (70ct, 52st)	L. E. G. Ames	1928	102 (69ct, 33st)	F. H. Huish	1913
110 (63ct, 47st)	H. Yarnold.......	1949	102 (95ct, 7st)	J. T. Murray......	1960
107 (77ct, 30st)	G. Duckworth	1928	101 (62ct, 39st)	F. H. Huish	1911
107 (96ct, 11st)	J. G. Binks.......	1960	101 (85ct, 16st)	R. Booth	1960
104 (40ct, 64st)	L. E. G. Ames	1932	100 (91ct, 9st)	R. Booth	1964

Notes: L. E. G. Ames achieved the two highest stumping totals in a season: 64 in 1932, and 52 in 1928.

1,000 DISMISSALS

Dates in italics denote the first half of an overseas season; i.e. *1914* denotes the 1914-15 season.

			Career	M	Ct	St
1	R. W. Taylor	1,649	1960–1988	639	1,473	176
2	J. T. Murray	1,527	1952–1975	635	1,270	257
3	H. Strudwick	1,497	1902–1927	675	1,242	255
4	A. P. E. Knott.............	1,344	1964–1985	511	1,211	133
5	R. C. Russell	1,320	1981–2004	465	1,192	128
6	F. H. Huish...............	1,310	1895–1914	497	933	377
7	B. Taylor	1,294	1949–1973	572	1,083	211
8	S. J. Rhodes..............	1,263	1981–2004	440	1,139	124
9	D. Hunter	1,253	1888–1909	548	906	347
10	H. R. Butt................	1,228	1890–1912	550	953	275
11	J. H. Board...............	1,207	1891–*1914*	525	852	355
12	H. Elliott.................	1,206	1920–1947	532	904	302
13	J. M. Parks	1,181	1949–1976	739	1,088	93
14	R. Booth	1,126	1951–1970	468	948	178
15	L. E. G. Ames	1,121	1926–1951	593	703	418†
16	D. L. Bairstow	1,099	1970–1990	459	961	138
17	G. Duckworth.............	1,096	1923–1947	504	753	343
18	H. W. Stephenson	1,082	1948–1964	462	748	334
19	J. G. Binks...............	1,071	1955–1975	502	895	176
20	T. G. Evans	1,066	1939–1969	465	816	250
21	A. Long	1,046	1960–1980	452	922	124
22	G. O. Dawkes.............	1,043	1937–1961	482	895	148
23	R. W. Tolchard............	1,037	1965–1983	483	912	125
24	W. L. Cornford............	1,017	1921–1947	496	675	342

† *Record.*

Current Players with 500 Dismissals

		Career	M	Ct	St
910	C. M. W. Read.....................	*1997*–2013	290	863	47
711	Kamran Akmal	*1997*–*2013*	188	656	55
676	J. S. Foster......................	2000–2013	223	624	52
673	J. N. Batty	1994–2013	221	605	68
652	M. J. Prior	2001–*2013*	242	611	41
616	G. O. Jones	2001–2013	190	580	36
610	H. A. P. W. Jayawardene.............	*1997*–*2013*	227	503	107
592	M. A. Wallace	1999–2013	216	543	49
588	B. J. Haddin......................	*1999*–*2013*	167	551	37
571	P. Mustard.......................	2002–2013	165	553	18
524	Zulfiqar Jan	*1999*–*2013*	143	499	25

Note: Some of these figures include catches taken in the field.

FIELDING RECORDS

excluding wicketkeepers

MOST CATCHES IN AN INNINGS

7	M. J. Stewart	Surrey v Northamptonshire at Northampton	1957
7	A. S. Brown	Gloucestershire v Nottinghamshire at Nottingham	1966
7	R. Clarke	Warwickshire v Lancashire at Liverpool.	2011

MOST CATCHES IN A MATCH

10	W. R. Hammond†	Gloucestershire v Surrey at Cheltenham	1928
9	R. Clarke	Warwickshire v Lancashire at Liverpool.	2011
8	W. B. Burns	Worcestershire v Yorkshire at Bradford	1907
8	F. G. Travers	Europeans v Parsees at Bombay	1923-24
8	A. H. Bakewell	Northamptonshire v Essex at Leyton.	1928
8	W. R. Hammond	Gloucestershire v Worcestershire at Cheltenham	1932
8	K. J. Grieves	Lancashire v Sussex at Manchester.	1951
8	C. A. Milton	Gloucestershire v Sussex at Hove	1952
8	G. A. R. Lock	Surrey v Warwickshire at The Oval	1957
8	J. M. Prodger	Kent v Gloucestershire at Cheltenham	1961
8	P. M. Walker	Glamorgan v Derbyshire at Swansea.	1970
8	Masood Anwar	Rawalpindi v Lahore Division at Rawalpindi	1983-84
8	M. C. J. Ball	Gloucestershire v Yorkshire at Cheltenham	1994
8	J. D. Carr	Middlesex v Warwickshire at Birmingham.	1995
8	G. A. Hick	Worcestershire v Essex at Chelmsford	2005

† *Hammond also scored a hundred in each innings.*

MOST CATCHES IN A SEASON

78	W. R. Hammond	1928		69	P. M. Walker.	1960
77	M. J. Stewart	1957		66	J. Tunnicliffe.	1895
73	P. M. Walker	1961		65	W. R. Hammond	1925
71	P. J. Sharpe	1962		65	P. M. Walker.	1959
70	J. Tunnicliffe.	1901		65	D. W. Richardson	1961
69	J. G. Langridge	1955				

Note: The most catches by a fielder since the reduction of County Championship matches in 1969 is 59 by G. R. J. Roope in 1971.

750 CATCHES

Dates in italics denote the first half of an overseas season; i.e. *1970* denotes the 1970-71 season.

		Career	*M*			*Career*	*M*
1,018	F. E. Woolley	1906–1938	979	784	J. G. Langridge . . .	1928–1955	574
887	W. G. Grace	1865–1908	879	764	W. Rhodes	1898–1930	1,107
830	G. A. R. Lock	1946–*1970*	654	758	C. A. Milton	1948–1974	620
819	W. R. Hammond .	1920–1951	634	754	E. H. Hendren	1907–1938	833
813	D. B. Close	1949–1986	786				

Note: The most catches by a current player is 426 by M. E. Trescothick (1993–2013).

TEAM RECORDS

HIGHEST INNINGS TOTALS

1,107	Victoria v New South Wales at Melbourne	1926-27
1,059	Victoria v Tasmania at Melbourne	1922-23
952-6 dec	Sri Lanka v India at Colombo...............................	1997-98
951-7 dec	Sind v Baluchistan at Karachi..............................	1973-74
944-6 dec	Hyderabad v Andhra at Secunderabad	1993-94
918	New South Wales v South Australia at Sydney	1900-01
912-8 dec	Holkar v Mysore at Indore	1945-46
912-6 dec†	Tamil Nadu v Goa at Panjim	1988-89
910-6 dec	Railways v Dera Ismail Khan at Lahore......................	1964-65
903-7 dec	England v Australia at The Oval............................	1938
900-6 dec	Queensland v Victoria at Brisbane	2005-06
887	Yorkshire v Warwickshire at Birmingham....................	1896
868†	North Zone v West Zone at Bhilai	1987-88
863	Lancashire v Surrey at The Oval	1990
855-6 dec†	Bombay v Hyderabad at Bombay............................	1990-91
850-7 dec	Somerset v Middlesex at Taunton	2007

† *Tamil Nadu's total of 912-6 dec included 52 penalty runs from their opponents' failure to meet the required bowling rate. North Zone's total of 868 included 68, and Bombay's total of 855-6 dec included 48.*

Note: The highest total in a team's second innings is 770 by New South Wales v South Australia at Adelaide in 1920-21.

HIGHEST FOURTH-INNINGS TOTALS

654-5	England v South Africa at Durban	1938-39
	After being set 696 to win. The match was left drawn on the tenth day.	
604	Maharashtra (*set 959 to win*) v Bombay at Poona.....................	1948-49
576-8	Trinidad (*set 672 to win*) v Barbados at Port-of-Spain	1945-46
572	New South Wales (*set 593 to win*) v South Australia at Sydney............	1907-08
541-7	West Zone (*won*) v South Zone at Hyderabad	2009-10
529-9	Combined XI (*set 579 to win*) v South Africans at Perth	1963-64
518	Victoria (*set 753 to win*) v Queensland at Brisbane	1926-27
513-9	Central Province (*won*) v Southern Province at Kandy.................	2003-04
507-7	Cambridge University (*won*) v MCC and Ground at Lord's..............	1896
506-6	South Australia (*won*) v Queensland at Adelaide	1991-92
503-4	South Zone (*won*) v England A at Gurgaon	2003-04
502-6	Middlesex (*won*) v Nottinghamshire at Nottingham...................	1925
502-8	Players (*won*) v Gentlemen at Lord's	1900
500-7	South African Universities (*won*) v Western Province at Stellenbosch	1978-79

MOST RUNS IN A DAY (ONE SIDE)

721	Australians (721) v Essex at Southend (1st day)........................	1948
651	West Indians (651-2) v Leicestershire at Leicester (1st day)	1950
649	New South Wales (649-7) v Otago at Dunedin (2nd day)	1923-24
645	Surrey (645-4) v Hampshire at The Oval (1st day).....................	1909
644	Oxford U. (644-8) v H. D. G. Leveson Gower's XI at Eastbourne (1st day) ...	1921
640	Lancashire (640-8) v Sussex at Hove (1st day)........................	1937
636	Free Foresters (636-7) v Cambridge University at Cambridge (1st day)	1938
625	Gloucestershire (625-6) v Worcestershire at Dudley (2nd day)	1934

MOST RUNS IN A DAY (BOTH SIDES)

(excluding the above)

685	North (169-8 and 255-7), South (261-8 dec) at Blackpool (2nd day).........	1961
666	Surrey (607-4), Northamptonshire (59-2) at Northampton (2nd day).........	1920
665	Rest of South Africa (339), Transvaal (326) at Johannesburg (1st day).......	1911-12
663	Middlesex (503-4), Leicestershire (160-2) at Leicester (2nd day)	1947
661	Border (201), Griqualand West (460) at Kimberley (1st day)...............	1920-21
649	Hampshire (570-8), Somerset (79-3) at Taunton (2nd day)	1901

HIGHEST AGGREGATES IN A MATCH

Runs	Wkts		
2,376	37	Maharashtra v Bombay at Poona	1948-49
2,078	40	Bombay v Holkar at Bombay	1944-45
1,981	35	South Africa v England at Durban	1938-39
1,945	18	Canterbury v Wellington at Christchurch....................	1994-95
1,929	39	New South Wales v South Australia at Sydney	1925-26
1,911	34	New South Wales v Victoria at Sydney	1908-09
1,905	40	Otago v Wellington at Dunedin	1923-24

In Britain

Runs	Wkts		
1,815	28	Somerset v Surrey at Taunton............................	2002
1,808	20	Sussex v Essex at Hove.................................	1993
1,795	34	Somerset v Northamptonshire at Taunton....................	2001
1,723	31	England v Australia at Leeds	1948
1,706	23	Hampshire v Warwickshire at Southampton..................	1997

LOWEST INNINGS TOTALS

12†	Oxford University v MCC and Ground at Oxford	1877
12	Northamptonshire v Gloucestershire at Gloucester......................	1907
13	Auckland v Canterbury at Auckland................................	1877-78
13	Nottinghamshire v Yorkshire at Nottingham	1901
14	Surrey v Essex at Chelmsford....................................	1983
15	MCC v Surrey at Lord's..	1839
15†	Victoria v MCC at Melbourne....................................	1903-04
15†	Northamptonshire v Yorkshire at Northampton	1908
15	Hampshire v Warwickshire at Birmingham	1922
	Following on, Hampshire scored 521 and won by 155 runs.	
16	MCC and Ground v Surrey at Lord's...............................	1872
16	Derbyshire v Nottinghamshire at Nottingham..........................	1879
16	Surrey v Nottinghamshire at The Oval	1880
16	Warwickshire v Kent at Tonbridge	1913
16	Trinidad v Barbados at Bridgetown	1942-43
16	Border v Natal at East London (first innings)	1959-60
17	Gentlemen of Kent v Gentlemen of England at Lord's...................	1850
17	Gloucestershire v Australians at Cheltenham	1896
18	The Bs v England at Lord's......................................	1831
18†	Kent v Sussex at Gravesend	1867
18	Tasmania v Victoria at Melbourne	1868-69
18†	Australians v MCC and Ground at Lord's............................	1896
18	Border v Natal at East London (second innings).......................	1959-60
18†	Durham MCCU v Durham at Chester-le-Street	2012
19	Sussex v Surrey at Godalming	1830

19†	Sussex v Nottinghamshire at Hove	1873
19	MCC and Ground v Australians at Lord's	1878
19	Wellington v Nelson at Nelson	1885-86
19	Matabeleland v Mashonaland at Harare	2000-01

† _One man absent._

Note: At Lord's in 1810, The Bs, with one man absent, were dismissed by England for 6.

LOWEST TOTALS IN A MATCH

34	(16 and 18) Border v Natal at East London	1959-60
42	(27 and 15) Northamptonshire v Yorkshire at Northampton	1908

Note: Northamptonshire batted one man short in each innings.

LOWEST AGGREGATE IN A COMPLETED MATCH

Runs	Wkts		
85	11†	Quetta v Rawalpindi at Islamabad	2008-09
105	31	MCC v Australians at Lord's	1878

† _Both teams forfeited their first innings._

Note: The lowest aggregate in a match in which the losing team was bowled out twice since 1900 is 157 for 22 wickets, Surrey v Worcestershire at The Oval, 1954.

LARGEST VICTORIES

Largest Innings Victories

Inns and 851 runs	Railways (910-6 dec) v Dera Ismail Khan at Lahore	1964-65
Inns and 666 runs	Victoria (1,059) v Tasmania at Melbourne	1922-23
Inns and 656 runs	Victoria (1,107) v New South Wales at Melbourne	1926-27
Inns and 605 runs	New South Wales (918) v South Australia at Sydney	1900-01
Inns and 579 runs	England (903-7 dec) v Australia at The Oval	1938
Inns and 575 runs	Sind (951-7 dec) v Baluchistan at Karachi	1973-74
Inns and 527 runs	New South Wales (713) v South Australia at Adelaide	1908-09
Inns and 517 runs	Australians (675) v Nottinghamshire at Nottingham	1921

Largest Victories by Runs Margin

685 runs	New South Wales (235 and 761-8 dec) v Queensland at Sydney	1929-30
675 runs	England (521 and 342-8 dec) v Australia at Brisbane	1928-29
638 runs	New South Wales (304 and 770) v South Australia at Adelaide	1920-21
609 runs	Muslim Commercial Bank (575 and 282-0 dec) v WAPDA at Lahore	1977-78
585 runs	Sargodha (336 and 416) v Lahore Municipal Corporation at Faisalabad	1978-79
573 runs	Sinhalese (395-7 dec and 350-2 dec) v Sebastianites at Colombo	1990-91
571 runs	Victoria (304 and 649) v South Australia at Adelaide	1926-27
562 runs	Australia (701 and 327) v England at The Oval	1934
556 runs	Nondescripts (397-8 dec and 313-6 dec) v Matara at Colombo	1998-99
552 runs	South Zone (443 and 504-7 dec) v Central Zone at Hyderabad	2010-11

Victory Without Losing a Wicket

Lancashire (166-0 dec and 66-0) beat Leicestershire by ten wickets at Manchester		1956
Karachi A (277-0 dec) beat Sind A by an innings and 77 runs at Karachi		1957-58

Railways (236-0 dec and 16-0) beat Jammu and Kashmir by ten wickets at Srinagar 1960-61
Karnataka (451-0 dec) beat Kerala by an innings and 186 runs at Chikmagalur......... 1977-78

Notes: There have been **29** wins by an innings and 400 runs or more, the most recent being an innings and 415 runs by Islamabad v Quetta at Islamabad in 2008-09.

There have been **21** wins by 500 runs or more, the most recent being **541 runs by Nottinghamshire v Durham MCCU at Durham in 2013**.

There have been **32** wins by a team losing only one wicket, the most recent being by Rawalpindi v Quetta at Islamabad in 2008-09.

TIED MATCHES

Since 1948, a tie has been recognised only when the scores are level with all the wickets down in the fourth innings. There have been **34** instances since then, including two Tests (see Test record section); Sussex have featured in five of those, Essex and Kent in four each.

The most recent instances are:

Somerset v West Indies A at Taunton...	†2002
Warwickshire v Essex at Birmingham...	2003
Worcestershire v Zimbabweans at Worcester	2003
Habib Bank v WAPDA at Lahore	2011-12
Border v Boland at East London	2012-13

† *Somerset (453) made the highest total to tie a first-class match.*

MATCHES COMPLETED ON FIRST DAY

(Since 1946)

Derbyshire v Somerset at Chesterfield, June 11................................	1947
Lancashire v Sussex at Manchester, July 12	1950
Surrey v Warwickshire at The Oval, May 16	1953
Somerset v Lancashire at Bath, June 6 (H. F. T. Buse's benefit).................	1953
Kent v Worcestershire at Tunbridge Wells, June 15	1960
Griqualand West v Easterns at Kimberley, March 10	2010-11

SHORTEST COMPLETED MATCHES

Balls

121	Quetta (forfeit and 41) v Rawalpindi (forfeit and 44-1) at Islamabad	2008-09
350	Somerset (35 and 44) v Middlesex (86) at Lord's	1899
352	Victoria (82 and 57) v Tasmania (104 and 37-7) at Launceston	1850-51
372	Victoria (80 and 50) v Tasmania (97 and 35-2) at Launceston	1853-54
419*	England XI (82 and 26) v Australians (76 and 33-6) at Aston.................	1884
425	Derbyshire (180-0 dec and forfeit) v Northamptonshire (forfeit and 181-2) at Northampton	1992
432	Victoria (78 and 67) v Tasmania (51 and 25) at Hobart	1857-58
435	Northamptonshire (4-0 dec and 86) v Yorkshire (4-0 dec and 88-5) at Bradford ..	1931
442*	Wellington (31 and 48) v Nelson (73 and 7-1) at Nelson	1887-88
445	Glamorgan (272-1 dec and forfeit) v Lancashire (forfeit and 51) at Liverpool	1997
450	Bengal Governor's XI (33 and 59) v Maharaja of Cooch-Behar's XI (138) at Calcutta	1917-18

* *Match completed on first day.*

An expanded and regularly updated online version of the Records can be found at www.wisdenrecords.com

LIST A ONE-DAY RECORDS

List A is a concept intended to provide an approximate equivalent in one-day cricket of first-class status. It was introduced by the Association of Cricket Statisticians and Historians and is now recognised by the ICC, with a separate category for Twenty20 cricket. Further details are available at stats.acscricket.com/ListA/Description.html. List A games comprise:

(a) One-day internationals.
(b) Other international matches (e.g. A-team internationals).
(c) Premier domestic one-day tournaments in Test-playing countries.
(d) Official tourist matches against the main first-class teams (e.g. counties, states, provinces and national Board XIs).

The following matches are excluded:

(a) Matches originally scheduled as less than 40 overs per side (e.g. Twenty20 games).
(b) World Cup warm-up games.
(c) Tourist matches against teams outside the major domestic competitions (e.g. universities).
(d) Festival games and pre-season friendlies.

Notes: This section covers one-day cricket to December 31, 2013. Bold type denotes performances in the calendar year 2013 or, in career figures, players who appeared in List A cricket in that year.

BATTING RECORDS

HIGHEST INDIVIDUAL INNINGS

268	A. D. Brown	Surrey v Glamorgan at The Oval......................	2002
248	**S. Dhawan**	**India A v South Africa A at Pretoria**.................	**2013**
222*	R. G. Pollock	Eastern Province v Border at East London..............	1974-75
222	**J. M. How**	**Central Districts v Northern Districts at Hamilton......**	**2012-13**
219	V. Sehwag	India v West Indies at Indore......................	2011-12
209	**R. G. Sharma**	**India v Australia at Bangalore**......................	**2013-14**
207	Mohammad Ali	Pakistan Customs v DHA at Sialkot..................	2004-05
206	A. I. Kallicharran	Warwickshire v Oxfordshire at Birmingham...........	1984
204*	Khalid Latif	Karachi Dolphins v Quetta Bears at Karachi..........	2008-09
203	A. D. Brown	Surrey v Hampshire at Guildford....................	1997
202*	A. Barrow	Natal v SA African XI at Durban....................	1975-76
201*	R. S. Bopara	Essex v Leicestershire at Leicester..................	2008
201	V. J. Wells	Leicestershire v Berkshire at Leicester	1996
200*	S. R. Tendulkar	India v South Africa at Gwalior.....................	2009-10

MOST RUNS

	Career	M	I	NO	R	HS	100	Avge
G. A. Gooch.........	1973–1997	614	601	48	22,211	198*	44	40.16
G. A. Hick	1983–2008	651	630	96	22,059	172*	40	41.30
S. R. Tendulkar	1989–2011	551	538	55	21,999	200*	60	45.54
I. V. A. Richards	1973–1993	500	466	61	16,995	189*	26	41.96
R. T. Ponting........	*1992–2013*	**456**	**445**	**53**	**16,363**	**164**	**34**	**41.74**
C. G. Greenidge......	1970–1992	440	436	33	16,349	186*	33	40.56
K. C. Sangakkara....	*1997–2013*	**461**	**434**	**47**	**15,990**	**169**	**25**	**41.31**
S. T. Jayasuriya	1989–2011	557	542	25	16,128	189	31	31.19
A. J. Lamb	1972–1995	484	463	63	15,658	132*	19	39.14
D. L. Haynes	1976–1996	419	416	44	15,651	152*	28	42.07
S. C. Ganguly........	1989–2011	437	421	43	15,622	183	31	41.32
K. J. Barnett	1979–2005	527	500	54	15,564	136	17	34.89
R. Dravid	1992–2011	449	416	55	15,271	153	21	42.30
M. G. Bevan.........	1989–2006	427	385	124	15,103	157*	13	57.86

HIGHEST PARTNERSHIP FOR EACH WICKET

326*	for 1st	Ghulam Ali and Sohail Jaffer, PIA v ADBP at Sialkot	2000-01
331	for 2nd	S. R. Tendulkar and R. Dravid, India v New Zealand at Hyderabad...	1999-2000
309*	for 3rd	T. S. Curtis and T. M. Moody, Worcestershire v Surrey at The Oval ..	1994
276	**for 4th**	**Mominul Haque and A. R. S. Silva, Prime Doleshwar v Abahani**	**2013-14**
		at Bogra	
267*	for 5th	Minhazul Abedin and Khaled Mahmud, Bangladeshis v Bahawalpur	
		at Karachi..	1997-98
226	for 6th	N. J. Llong and M. V. Fleming, Kent v Cheshire at Bowdon	1999
203*	for 7th	S. H. T. Kandamby and H. M. R. K. B. Herath, Sri Lanka A v South	
		Africa A at Benoni..	2008-09
203	for 8th	Shahid Iqbal and Haaris Ayaz, Karachi Whites v Hyderabad at Karachi	1998-99
155	for 9th	C. M. W. Read and A. J. Harris, Notts v Durham at Nottingham	2006
106*	for 10th	I. V. A. Richards and M. A. Holding, West Indies v England at	
		Manchester..	1984

BOWLING RECORDS

BEST BOWLING ANALYSES

8-15	R. L. Sanghvi	Delhi v Himachal Pradesh at Una	1997-98
8-19	W. P. U. J. C. Vaas	Sri Lanka v Zimbabwe at Colombo	2001-02
8-20*	D. T. Kottehewa	Nondescripts v Ragama at Colombo	2007-08
8-21	M. A. Holding	Derbyshire v Sussex at Hove..........................	1988
8-26	K. D. Boyce	Essex v Lancashire at Manchester	1971
8-30	G. D. R. Eranga	Burgher v Army at Colombo..........................	2007-08
8-31	D. L. Underwood	Kent v Scotland at Edinburgh	1987
8-43	S. W. Tait	South Australia v Tasmania at Adelaide	2003-04
8-52	K. A. Stoute	West Indies A v Lancashire at Manchester	2010
8-66	S. R. G. Francis	Somerset v Derbyshire at Derby	2004

* Including two hat-tricks.

MOST WICKETS

	Career	M	B	R	W	BB	4I	Avge
Wasim Akram........	1984–2003	594	29,719	19,303	881	5-10	46	21.91
A. A. Donald........	1985–2003	458	22,856	14,942	684	6-15	38	21.84
M. Muralitharan.....	1991–2010	453	23,734	15,270	682	7-30	29	22.39
Waqar Younis.......	1988–2003	412	19,841	15,098	675	7-36	44	22.36
J. K. Lever	1968–1990	481	23,208	13,278	674	5-8	34	19.70
J. E. Emburey	1975–2000	536	26,399	16,811	647	5-23	26	25.98
I. T. Botham	1973–1993	470	22,899	15,264	612	5-27	18	24.94

WICKETKEEPING AND FIELDING RECORDS

MOST DISMISSALS IN AN INNINGS

8	(all ct)	D. J. S. Taylor	Somerset v Combined Universities at Taunton ...	1982
8	(5ct, 3st)	S. J. Palframan	Boland v Easterns at Paarl	1997-98
8	(all ct)	D. J. Pipe	Worcestershire v Hertfordshire at Hertford	2001
7	(6ct, 1st)	R. W. Taylor	Derbyshire v Lancashire at Manchester	1975
7	(4ct, 3st)	Rizwan Umar	Sargodha v Bahawalpur at Sargodha	1991-92
7	(all ct)	A. J. Stewart	Surrey v Glamorgan at Swansea................	1994
7	(all ct)	I. Mitchell	Border v Western Province at East London	1998-99
7	(6ct, 1st)	M. K. P. B. Kularatne	Galle v Colts at Colombo	2001-02
7	(5ct, 2st)	T. R. Ambrose	Warwickshire v Middlesex at Birmingham	2009
7	(3ct, 4st)	W. A. S. Niroshan	Chilaw Marians v Saracens at Katunayake.......	2009-10
7	(all ct)	M. Rawat	Railways v Madhya Pradesh at Nagpur	2011-12
7	**(all ct)**	**H. C. Madushan**	**Badureliya v Colombo at Colombo**	**2013-14**

MOST CATCHES IN AN INNINGS IN THE FIELD

5	V. J. Marks	Combined Universities v Kent at Oxford	1976
5	J. M. Rice	Hampshire v Warwickshire at Southampton	1978
5	A. J. Kourie	Transvaal v Western Province at Johannesburg	1979-80
5	J. N. Rhodes	South Africa v West Indies at Bombay	1993-94
5	J. W. Wilson	Otago v Auckland at Dunedin	1993-94
5	K. C. Jackson	Boland v Natal at Durban	1995-96
5	Mohammad Ramzan	PNSC v PIA at Karachi	1998-99
5	Amit Sharma	Punjab v Jammu and Kashmir at Ludhiana	1999-2000
5	B. E. Young	South Australia v Tasmania at Launceston	2001-02
5	Hasnain Raza	Bahawalpur v Pakistan Customs at Karachi	2002-03
5	D. J. Sales	Northamptonshire v Essex at Northampton	2007
5	L. N. Mosena	Free State v North West at Bloemfontein	2007-08

TEAM RECORDS

HIGHEST INNINGS TOTALS

496-4	(50 overs)	Surrey v Gloucestershire at The Oval	2007
443-9	(50 overs)	Sri Lanka v Netherlands at Amstelveen	2006
438-5	(50 overs)	Surrey v Glamorgan at The Oval	2002
438-9	(49.5 overs)	South Africa v Australia at Johannesburg	2005-06
434-4	(50 overs)	Australia v South Africa at Johannesburg	2005-06
433-3	**(50 overs)**	**India A v South Africa A at Pretoria**	**2013**
429	(49.5 overs)	Glamorgan v Surrey at The Oval	2002
424-5	(50 overs)	Buckinghamshire v Suffolk at Dinton	2002
418-5	(50 overs)	South Africa v Zimbabwe at Potchefstroom	2006-07
418-5	(50 overs)	India v West Indies at Indore	2011-12
417-6	**(50 overs)**	**Central Districts v Northern Districts at Hamilton**	**2012-13**
414-7	(50 overs)	India v Sri Lanka at Rajkot	2009-10
413-4	(60 overs)	Somerset v Devon at Torquay	1990
413-5	(50 overs)	India v Bermuda at Port-of-Spain	2006-07
412-4	(50 overs)	United Arab Emirates v Argentina at Windhoek	2007-08
412-6	(50 overs)	Madhya Pradesh v Railways at Indore	2009-10
411-6	(50 overs)	Yorkshire v Devon at Exmouth	2004
411-8	(50 overs)	Sri Lanka v India at Rajkot	2009-10
410-5	(50 overs)	Canterbury v Otago at Timaru	2009-10
409-6	(50 overs)	Trinidad & Tobago v North Windward Islands at Kingston	2001-02
408-4	(50 overs)	KRL v Sialkot at Sialkot	2002-03
406-5	(60 overs)	Leicestershire v Berkshire at Leicester	1996
405-4	(50 overs)	Queensland v Western Australia at Brisbane	2003-04

LOWEST INNINGS TOTALS

18	(14.3 overs)	West Indies Under-19 v Barbados at Blairmont	2007-08
19	(10.5 overs)	Saracens v Colts at Colombo	2012-13
23	(19.4 overs)	Middlesex v Yorkshire at Leeds	1974
30	(20.4 overs)	Chittagong v Sylhet at Dhaka	2002-03
31	(13.5 overs)	Border v South Western Districts at East London	2007-08
34	(21.1 overs)	Saurashtra v Mumbai at Mumbai	1999-2000
35	(18 overs)	Zimbabwe v Sri Lanka at Harare	2003-04
35	**(20.2 overs)**	**Cricket Coaching School v Abahani at Fatullah**	**2013-14**
36	(25.4 overs)	Leicestershire v Sussex at Leicester	1973
36	(18.4 overs)	Canada v Sri Lanka at Paarl	2002-03
38	(15.4 overs)	Zimbabwe v Sri Lanka at Colombo	2001-02
39	(26.4 overs)	Ireland v Sussex at Hove	1985
39	(15.2 overs)	Cape Cobras v Eagles at Paarl *(one man absent)*	2008-09
39	**(24.4 overs)**	**Namibia v United Arab Emirates at Sharjah**	**2013-14**

LIST A TWENTY20 RECORDS

Notes: This section covers Twenty20 cricket to December 31, 2013. Bold type denotes performances in the calendar year 2013 or, in career figures, players who appeared in Twenty20 cricket in that year.

BATTING RECORDS

HIGHEST INDIVIDUAL INNINGS

175*	C. H. Gayle	**RC Bangalore v Pune Warriors at Bangalore**	**2012-13**
158*	B. B. McCullum	Kolkata Knight Riders v RC Bangalore at Bangalore	2007-08
156	**A. J. Finch**	**Australia v England at Southampton**	**2013**
152*	G. R. Napier	Essex v Sussex at Chelmsford	2008
145	L. P. van der Westhuizen	Namibia v Kenya at Windhoek	2011-12
141*	C. L. White	Somerset v Worcestershire at Worcester	2006
135*	D. A. Warner	New South Wales v Chennai Super Kings at Chennai	2011-12
130	**Tamim Iqbal**	**UCB BCB XI v Mohammedan at Mirpur**	**2013-14**

MOST RUNS

	Career	M	I	NO	R	HS	100	Avge
C. H. Gayle	2005–*2013*	156	153	22	5,762	175*	11	43.90
B. J. Hodge	2003–*2013*	203	193	38	5,706	106	2	36.81
D. J. Hussey	2004–*2013*	223	214	41	5,422	100*	1	31.34
O. A. Shah	2003–*2013*	194	184	44	4,817	84	0	34.40
B. B. McCullum	2004–*2013*	170	167	17	4,815	158*	5	32.10
D. A. Warner	2006–*2013*	160	159	14	4,557	135*	5	31.42
S. K. Raina	2006–*2013*	158	150	24	4,294	101	2	34.07
K. A. Pollard	2006–*2013*	217	192	54	4,166	89*	0	30.18
R. G. Sharma	2006–*2013*	165	154	30	4,023	109*	2	32.44
R. N. ten Doeschate	2003–*2013*	193	173	35	3,988	121*	2	28.89
C. L. White	2004–*2013*	175	166	37	3,910	141*	2	30.31
H. H. Gibbs	2003–*2013*	171	167	13	3,895	101*	1	25.29
D. P. M. D. Jayawardene	2004–*2013*	164	159	23	3,893	110*	2	28.62
S. E. Marsh	2005–*2013*	110	108	14	3,833	115	2	40.77
L. R. P. L. Taylor	2005–*2013*	168	157	31	3,772	111*	1	29.93
K. C. Sangakkara	2004–*2013*	146	141	15	3,747	94	0	29.73
G. Gambhir	2006–*2012*	143	140	15	3,743	93	0	29.94
Azhar Mahmood	2003–*2013*	191	176	36	3,649	106*	2	26.06
Shoaib Malik	2004–*2013*	144	133	41	3,626	88*	0	39.41
L. J. Wright	2004–*2013*	172	153	15	3,617	117	2	26.21
S. B. Styris	2004–*2013*	177	163	27	3,616	106*	2	26.58

HIGHEST PARTNERSHIP FOR EACH WICKET

201	for 1st	P. J. Ingram and J. M. How, C. Dist. v Wellington at New Plymouth		2011-12
206	for 2nd	A. C. Gilchrist and S. E. Marsh, KXI Punjab v RC Bangalore at Dharmasala		2010-11
162	for 3rd	Abdul Razzaq and Nasir Jamshed, Lahore Lions v Quetta Bears at Lahore		2009
202*	**for 4th**	**M. C. Juneja and A. Malik, Gujarat v Kerala at Indore**		**2012-13**
149	for 5th	Y. V. Takawale and S. V. Bahutule, Maharashtra v Gujarat at Mumbai		2006-07
122*	for 6th	A. T. Rayudu and K. A. Pollard, Mumbai Ind. v RC Bang. at Bangalore		2011-12
99*	for 7th	A. Thyagarajan and O. M. Baker, USA v Ireland at Abu Dhabi		2009-10
120	for 8th	Azhar Mahmood and I. Udana, Wayamba v Uva at Colombo		2012
64	for 9th	K. Magage and H. S. M. Zoysa, Burgher v Panadura at Colombo		2011-12
59	for 10th	H. H. Streak and J. E. Anyon, Warwickshire v Worcs at Birmingham		2005

BOWLING RECORDS

BEST BOWLING ANALYSES

6-5	A. V. Suppiah	Somerset v Glamorgan at Cardiff.....................	2011
6-6	**Shakib Al Hasan**	**Barbados v Trinidad & Tobago at Bridgetown.........**	**2013**
6-7	S. L. Malinga	Melbourne Stars v Perth Scorchers at Perth	2012-13
6-8	B. A. W. Mendis	Sri Lanka v Zimbabwe at Hambantota.................	2012-13
6-14	Sohail Tanvir	Rajasthan Royals v Chennai Superstars at Jaipur.........	2007-08
6-15	S. R. Abeywardene	Panadura v Air Force at Colombo	2005-06

MOST WICKETS

	Career	M	B	R	W	BB	4I	Avge
A. C. Thomas	2003–2013	196	4,003	4,900	232	5-24	4	21.12
S. L. Malinga	2004–2013	168	3,659	4,059	227	6-7	9	17.88
Azhar Mahmood .	2003–2013	191	3,983	5,017	218	5-24	3	23.01
D. P. Nannes	2007–2013	183	3,962	4,778	216	5-40	7	22.12
Yasir Arafat	2005–2013	167	3,403	4,474	211	4-5	7	21.20
J. A. Morkel	2003–2013	243	4,055	5,236	201	4-25	3	26.04
D. J. Bravo	2005–2013	183	3,291	4,381	184	4-23	3	23.80
M. Muralitharan .	2005–2013	154	3,507	3,729	171	4-16	3	21.80
Saeed Ajmal	2004–2013	121	2,681	2,817	167	4-14	6	16.86
Shahid Afridi ...	2004–2013	141	3,043	3,323	166	5-20	5	20.01
K. A. Pollard....	2006–2013	217	2,785	3,664	164	4-15	3	22.34
Sohail Tanvir	2004–2013	146	3,007	3,624	160	6-14	4	22.65
Umar Gul	2004–2013	111	2,368	2,868	158	5-6	10	18.15
Naved-ul-Hasan ..	2004–2013	122	2,525	3,032	152	5-17	3	19.94
D. W. Steyn......	2004–2013	134	3,000	3,203	151	4-9	1	21.21

WICKETKEEPING AND FIELDING RECORDS

MOST DISMISSALS IN AN INNINGS

7 (all ct)   E. F. M. U. Fernando Lankan v Moors at Colombo.................... 2005-06

MOST CATCHES IN AN INNINGS IN THE FIELD

5	Manzoor Ilahi	Jammu and Kashmir v Delhi at Delhi..................	2010-11
5	J. M. Vince	Hampshire v Leeward Islands at North Sound	2010-11

TEAM RECORDS

HIGHEST INNINGS TOTALS

263-5	**(20 overs)**	**RC Bangalore v Pune Warriors at Bangalore.............**	**2012-13**
260-6	(20 overs)	Sri Lanka v Kenya at Johannesburg.......................	2007-08
254-3	(20 overs)	Gloucestershire v Middlesex at Uxbridge	2011
250-3	(20 overs)	Somerset v Gloucestershire at Taunton	2006

LOWEST INNINGS TOTALS

30	(11.1 overs)	Tripura v Jharkhand at Dhanbad............................	2009-10
44	(12.5 overs)	Leeward Islands v Trinidad & Tobago at North Sound	2011-12
45	**(8.4 overs)**	**Mohammedan v Prime Bank at Sylhet....................**	**2013-14**
47	(14.3 overs)	Titans v Eagles at Centurion..............................	2003-04
47	(12.5 overs)	Northamptonshire v Durham at Chester-le-Street	2011

TEST RECORDS

Notes: This section covers all Tests up to January 20, 2014.

Throughout this section, bold type denotes performances since January 1, 2013, or, in career figures, players who have appeared in Test cricket since that date.

BATTING RECORDS

HIGHEST INDIVIDUAL INNINGS

400*	B. C. Lara	West Indies v England at St John's	2003-04
380	M. L. Hayden.	Australia v Zimbabwe at Perth.	2003-04
375	B. C. Lara	West Indies v England at St John's	1993-94
374	D. P. M. D. Jayawardene . .	Sri Lanka v South Africa at Colombo (SSC)	2006
365*	G. S. Sobers.	West Indies v Pakistan at Kingston	1957-58
364	L. Hutton	England v Australia at The Oval	1938
340	S. T. Jayasuriya	Sri Lanka v India at Colombo (RPS)	1997-98
337	Hanif Mohammad	Pakistan v West Indies at Bridgetown	1957-58
336*	W. R. Hammond	England v New Zealand at Auckland.	1932-33
334*	M. A. Taylor	Australia v Pakistan at Peshawar	1998-99
334	D. G. Bradman.	Australia v England at Leeds.	1930
333	G. A. Gooch.	England v India at Lord's.	1990
333	C. H. Gayle	West Indies v Sri Lanka at Galle	2010-11
329*	M. J. Clarke	Australia v India at Sydney	2011-12
329	Inzamam-ul-Haq	Pakistan v New Zealand at Lahore.	2002
325	A. Sandham.	England v West Indies at Kingston	1929-30
319	V. Sehwag	India v South Africa at Chennai.	2007-08
317	C. H. Gayle	West Indies v South Africa at St John's.	2004-05
313	Younis Khan	Pakistan v Sri Lanka at Karachi.	2008-09
311*	H. M. Amla	South Africa v England at The Oval	2012
311	R. B. Simpson	Australia v England at Manchester	1964
310*	J. H. Edrich	England v New Zealand at Leeds.	1965
309	V. Sehwag	India v Pakistan at Multan	2003-04
307	R. M. Cowper	Australia v England at Melbourne	1965-66
304	D. G. Bradman.	Australia v England at Leeds.	1934
302	L. G. Rowe	West Indies v England at Bridgetown	1973-74

Note: There have been **57** further instances of 250 or more runs in a Test innings.

The highest innings for the countries not mentioned above are:

299	M. D. Crowe	New Zealand v Sri Lanka at Wellington	1990-91
266	D. L. Houghton	Zimbabwe v Sri Lanka at Bulawayo	1994-95
200	**Mushfiqur Rahim**	**Bangladesh v Sri Lanka at Galle**.	**2012-13**

HUNDRED ON TEST DEBUT

C. Bannerman (165*)	Australia v England at Melbourne	1876-77
W. G. Grace (152)	England v Australia at The Oval	1880
H. Graham (107)	Australia v England at Lord's.	1893
†K. S. Ranjitsinhji (154*)	England v Australia at Manchester.	1896
†P. F. Warner (132*)	England v South Africa at Johannesburg	1898-99
†R. A. Duff (104)	Australia v England at Melbourne	1901-02
§R. E. Foster (287)	England v Australia at Sydney	1903-04
G. Gunn (119)	England v Australia at Sydney	1907-08
†R. J. Hartigan (116)	Australia v England at Adelaide.	1907-08
†H. L. Collins (104).	Australia v England at Sydney	1920-21
W. H. Ponsford (110).	Australia v England at Sydney	1924-25
A. A. Jackson (164)	Australia v England at Adelaide.	1928-29
†G. A. Headley (176).	West Indies v England at Bridgetown	1929-30
J. E. Mills (117)	New Zealand v England at Wellington	1929-30

Nawab of Pataudi sen. (102)	England v Australia at Sydney	1932-33
B. H. Valentine (136)	England v India at Bombay	1933-34
†L. Amarnath (118)	India v England at Bombay	1933-34
†P. A. Gibb (106)	England v South Africa at Johannesburg	1938-39
S. C. Griffith (140)	England v West Indies at Port-of-Spain	1947-48
A. G. Ganteaume (112)	West Indies v England at Port-of-Spain	1947-48
†J. W. Burke (101*)	Australia v England at Adelaide	1950-51
P. B. H. May (138)	England v South Africa at Leeds	1951
R. H. Shodhan (110)	India v Pakistan at Calcutta	1952-53
B. H. Pairaudeau (115)	West Indies v India at Port-of-Spain	1952-53
†O. G. Smith (104)	West Indies v Australia at Kingston	1954-55
A. G. Kripal Singh (100*)	India v New Zealand at Hyderabad	1955-56
C. C. Hunte (142)	West Indies v Pakistan at Bridgetown	1957-58
C. A. Milton (104*)	England v New Zealand at Leeds	1958
†A. A. Baig (112)	India v England at Manchester	1959
Hanumant Singh (105)	India v England at Delhi	1963-64
Khalid Ibadulla (166)	Pakistan v Australia at Karachi	1964-65
B. R. Taylor (105)	New Zealand v India at Calcutta	1964-65
K. D. Walters (155)	Australia v England at Brisbane	1965-66
J. H. Hampshire (107)	England v West Indies at Lord's	1969
†G. R. Viswanath (137)	India v Australia at Kanpur	1969-70
G. S. Chappell (108)	Australia v England at Perth	1970-71
‡§L. G. Rowe (214, 100*)	West Indies v New Zealand at Kingston	1971-72
A. I. Kallicharran (100*)	West Indies v New Zealand at Georgetown	1971-72
R. E. Redmond (107)	New Zealand v Pakistan at Auckland	1972-73
†F. C. Hayes (106*)	England v West Indies at The Oval	1973
†C. G. Greenidge (107)	West Indies v India at Bangalore	1974-75
†L. Baichan (105*)	West Indies v Pakistan at Lahore	1974-75
G. J. Cosier (109)	Australia v West Indies at Melbourne	1975-76
S. Amarnath (124)	India v New Zealand at Auckland	1975-76
Javed Miandad (163)	Pakistan v New Zealand at Lahore	1976-77
†A. B. Williams (100)	West Indies v Australia at Georgetown	1977-78
†D. M. Wellham (103)	Australia v England at The Oval	1981
†Salim Malik (100*)	Pakistan v Sri Lanka at Karachi	1981-82
K. C. Wessels (162)	Australia v England at Brisbane	1982-83
W. B. Phillips (159)	Australia v Pakistan at Perth	1983-84
¶M. Azharuddin (110)	India v England at Calcutta	1984-85
D. S. B. P. Kuruppu (201*)	Sri Lanka v New Zealand at Colombo (CCC)	1986-87
†M. J. Greatbatch (107*)	New Zealand v England at Auckland	1987-88
M. E. Waugh (138)	Australia v England at Adelaide	1990-91
A. C. Hudson (163)	South Africa v West Indies at Bridgetown	1991-92
R. S. Kaluwitharana (132*)	Sri Lanka v Australia at Colombo (SSC)	1992-93
D. L. Houghton (121)	Zimbabwe v India at Harare	1992-93
P. K. Amre (103)	India v South Africa at Durban	1992-93
†G. P. Thorpe (114*)	England v Australia at Nottingham	1993
G. S. Blewett (102*)	Australia v England at Adelaide	1994-95
S. C. Ganguly (131)	India v England at Lord's	1996
†Mohammad Wasim (109*)	Pakistan v New Zealand at Lahore	1996-97
Ali Naqvi (115)	Pakistan v South Africa at Rawalpindi	1997-98
Azhar Mahmood (128*)	Pakistan v South Africa at Rawalpindi	1997-98
M. S. Sinclair (214)	New Zealand v West Indies at Wellington	1999-2000
†Younis Khan (107)	Pakistan v Sri Lanka at Rawalpindi	1999-2000
Aminul Islam (145)	Bangladesh v India at Dhaka	2000-01
†H. Masakadza (119)	Zimbabwe v West Indies at Harare	2001
T. T. Samaraweera (103*)	Sri Lanka v India at Colombo (SSC)	2001
Taufeeq Umar (104)	Pakistan v Bangladesh at Multan	2001-02
†Mohammad Ashraful (114)	Bangladesh v Sri Lanka at Colombo (SSC)	2001-02
V. Sehwag (105)	India v South Africa at Bloemfontein	2001-02
L. Vincent (104)	New Zealand v Australia at Perth	2001-02
S. B. Styris (107)	New Zealand v West Indies at St George's	2002
J. A. Rudolph (222*)	South Africa v Bangladesh at Chittagong	2003

‡Yasir Hameed (170, 105)......	Pakistan v Bangladesh at Karachi	2003
†D. R. Smith (105*)............	West Indies v South Africa at Cape Town	2003-04
A. J. Strauss (112)	England v New Zealand at Lord's	2004
M. J. Clarke (151)	Australia v India at Bangalore	2004-05
†A. N. Cook (104*)............	England v India at Nagpur	2005-06
M. J. Prior (126*).............	England v West Indies at Lord's	2007
M. J. North (117).............	Australia v South Africa at Johannesburg	2008-09
†Fawad Alam (168)............	Pakistan v Sri Lanka at Colombo (PSS)........	2009
†I. J. L. Trott (119)	England v Australia at The Oval	2009
Umar Akmal (129)............	Pakistan v New Zealand at Dunedin	2009-10
†A. B. Barath (104)............	West Indies v Australia at Brisbane	2009-10
A. N. Petersen (100)	South Africa v India at Kolkata	2009-10
S. K. Raina (120).............	India v Sri Lanka at Colombo (SSC)	2010
K. S. Williamson (131)	New Zealand v India at Ahmedabad	2010-11
†K. A. Edwards (110)	West Indies v India at Roseau	2011
S. E. Marsh (141).............	Australia v Sri Lanka at Pallekele	2011-12
Abul Hasan (113).............	Bangladesh v West Indies at Khulna	2012-13
†F. du Plessis (110*)...........	South Africa v Australia at Adelaide	2012-13
H. D. Rutherford (171)	**New Zealand v England at Dunedin**	**2012-13**
S. Dhawan (187)...........	**India v Australia at Mohali**	**2012-13**
R. G. Sharma (177)	**India v West Indies at Kolkata**	**2013-14**

† *In his second innings of the match.*

‡ *L. G. Rowe and Yasir Hameed are the only batsmen to score a hundred in each innings on debut.*

§ *R. E. Foster (287, 19) and L. G. Rowe (214, 100*) are the only batsmen to score 300 runs in their debut Tests.*

¶ *M. Azharuddin is the only batsman to score hundreds in each of his first three Tests.*

Notes: L. Amarnath and S. Amarnath were father and son.

Ali Naqvi and Azhar Mahmood achieved the feat in the same innings.

Only Bannerman, Houghton and Aminul Islam scored hundreds in their country's first Test.

TRIPLE-HUNDRED AND HUNDRED IN A TEST

G. A. Gooch (England) .... 333 and 123 v India at Lord's 1990

DOUBLE-HUNDRED AND HUNDRED IN A TEST

K. D. Walters (Australia)........	242 and 103 v West Indies at Sydney...........	1968-69
S. M. Gavaskar (India)..........	124 and 220 v West Indies at Port-of-Spain	1970-71
†L. G. Rowe (West Indies)	214 and 100* v New Zealand at Kingston	1971-72
G. S. Chappell (Australia)	247* and 133 v New Zealand at Wellington.......	1973-74
B. C. Lara (West Indies)	221 and 130 v Sri Lanka at Colombo (SSC)......	2001-02

† *On Test debut.*

TWO SEPARATE HUNDREDS IN A TEST

S. M. Gavaskar (I)	3	P. A. de Silva (SL)......	2‡	J. H. Kallis (SA)........	2
R. T. Ponting (A)	3	R. Dravid (I)...........	2	H. Sutcliffe (E).........	2
A. R. Border (A)	2†	M. L. Hayden (A).......	2	C. L. Walcott (WI)......	2§
G. S. Chappell (A)	2	G. A. Headley (WI)	2		

† *A. R. Border scored 150* and 153 against Pakistan in 1979-80 to become the first to score 150 in each innings of a Test match.*

‡ *P. A. de Silva scored 138* and 103* against Pakistan in 1996-97 to become the first to score two not-out hundreds in a Test match.*

§ *C. L. Walcott scored twin hundreds twice in one series, against Australia in 1954-55.*

Notes: A further 48 batsmen have scored two separate hundreds in a Test once. L. G. Rowe and Yasir Hameed both achieved the feat on Test debut.

MOST DOUBLE-HUNDREDS

D. G. Bradman (A)	12	M. S. Atapattu (SL)	6	**V. Sehwag (I)**	**6**
B. C. Lara (WI)	9	Javed Miandad (P)	6	**S. R. Tendulkar (I)**	**6**
K. C. Sangakkara (SL)	**8**	**D. P. M. D. Jayawardene (SL)**	**6**	R. Dravid (I)	5
W. R. Hammond (E)	7	R. T. Ponting (A)	6	**G. C. Smith (SA)**	**5**

Note: M. J. Clarke (Australia) scored four double-hundreds in the calendar year 2012.

MOST HUNDREDS

S. R. Tendulkar (I)	**51**	**M. J. Clarke (A)**	**26**	M. C. Cowdrey (E)	22
J. H. Kallis (SA)	**45**	G. S. Sobers (WI)	26	W. R. Hammond (E)	22
R. T. Ponting (A)	41	**A. N. Cook (E)**	**25**	D. C. Boon (A)	21
R. Dravid (I)	36	Inzamam-ul-Haq (P)	25	R. N. Harvey (A)	21
S. M. Gavaskar (I)	34	G. S. Chappell (A)	24	G. Kirsten (SA)	21
B. C. Lara (WI)	34	Mohammad Yousuf (P)	24	A. J. Strauss (E)	21
K. C. Sangakkara (SL)	**33**	I. V. A. Richards (WI)	24	**H. M. Amla (SA)**	**20**
D. P. M. D. Jayawardene (SL)	**32**	Javed Miandad (P)	23	K. F. Barrington (E)	20
S. R. Waugh (A)	32	J. L. Langer (A)	23	**I. R. Bell (E)**	**20**
M. L. Hayden (A)	30	**K. P. Pietersen (E)**	**23**	P. A. de Silva (SL)	20
D. G. Bradman (A)	29	**V. Sehwag (I)**	**23**	G. A. Gooch (E)	20
S. Chanderpaul	**29**	**Younis Khan (P)**	**23**	M. E. Waugh (A)	20
A. R. Border (A)	27	M. Azharuddin (I)	22		
G. C. Smith (SA)	**27**	G. Boycott (E)	22		

Note: The most hundreds for New Zealand is 17 by M. D. Crowe, the most for Zimbabwe is 12 by A. Flower, and the most for Bangladesh is **6** by **Mohammad Ashraful**.

MOST HUNDREDS AGAINST ONE TEAM

D. G. Bradman	19	Australia v England	**S. R. Tendulkar**	**11**	**India v Australia**
S. M. Gavaskar	13	India v West Indies	G. S. Sobers	10	West Indies v England
J. B. Hobbs	12	England v Australia	S. R. Waugh	10	Australia v England

MOST DUCKS

	0s	Inns		0s	Inns
C. A. Walsh (WI)	43	185	B. S. Chandrasekhar (I)	23	80
C. S. Martin (NZ)	**36**	**104**	M. S. Atapattu (SL)	22	156
G. D. McGrath (A)	35	138	S. R. Waugh (A)	22	260
S. K. Warne (A)	34	199	S. J. Harmison (E)	21	86
M. Muralitharan (SL)	33	164	M. Ntini (SA)	21	116
Zaheer Khan (I)	**29**	**124**	Waqar Younis (P)	21	120
M. Dillon (WI)	26	68	**M. S. Panesar (E)**	**20**	**68**
C. E. L. Ambrose (WI)	26	145	B. S. Bedi (I)	20	101
Danish Kaneria (P)	25	84	D. L. Vettori (NZ/World)	20	173
D. K. Morrison (NZ)	24	71	M. A. Atherton (E)	20	212

An expanded and regularly updated online version of the Records can be found at
www.wisdenrecords.com

CARRYING BAT THROUGH TEST INNINGS

(Figures in brackets show team's total)

A. B. Tancred	26*	(47)	South Africa v England at Cape Town		1888-89
J. E. Barrett	67*	(176)†	Australia v England at Lord's		1890
R. Abel	132*	(307)	England v Australia at Sydney		1891-92
P. F. Warner	132*	(237)†	England v South Africa at Johannesburg		1898-99
W. W. Armstrong	159*	(309)	Australia v South Africa at Johannesburg		1902-03
J. W. Zulch	43*	(103)	South Africa v England at Cape Town		1909-10
W. Bardsley	193*	(383)	Australia v England at Lord's		1926
W. M. Woodfull	30*	(66)§	Australia v England at Brisbane		1928-29
W. M. Woodfull	73*	(193)‡	Australia v England at Adelaide		1932-33
W. A. Brown	206*	(422)	Australia v England at Lord's		1938
L. Hutton	202*	(344)	England v West Indies at The Oval		1950
L. Hutton	156*	(272)	England v Australia at Adelaide		1950-51
Nazar Mohammad¶	124*	(331)	Pakistan v India at Lucknow		1952-53
F. M. M. Worrell	191*	(372)	West Indies v England at Nottingham		1957
T. L. Goddard	56*	(99)	South Africa v Australia at Cape Town		1957-58
D. J. McGlew	127*	(292)	South Africa v New Zealand at Durban		1961-62
C. C. Hunte	60*	(131)	West Indies v Australia at Port-of-Spain		1964-65
G. M. Turner	43*	(131)	New Zealand v England at Lord's		1969
W. M. Lawry	49*	(107)	Australia v India at Delhi		1969-70
W. M. Lawry	60*	(116)‡	Australia v England at Sydney		1970-71
G. M. Turner	223*	(386)	New Zealand v West Indies at Kingston		1971-72
I. R. Redpath	159*	(346)	Australia v New Zealand at Auckland		1973-74
G. Boycott	99*	(215)	England v Australia at Perth		1979-80
S. M. Gavaskar	127*	(286)	India v Pakistan at Faisalabad		1982-83
Mudassar Nazar¶	152*	(323)	Pakistan v India at Lahore		1982-83
S. Wettimuny	63*	(144)	Sri Lanka v New Zealand at Christchurch		1982-83
D. C. Boon	58*	(103)	Australia v New Zealand at Auckland		1985-86
D. L. Haynes	88*	(211)	West Indies v Pakistan at Karachi		1986-87
G. A. Gooch	154*	(252)	England v West Indies at Leeds		1991
D. L. Haynes	75*	(176)	West Indies v England at The Oval		1991
A. J. Stewart	69*	(175)	England v Pakistan at Lord's		1992
D. L. Haynes	143*	(382)	West Indies v Pakistan at Port-of-Spain		1992-93
M. H. Dekker	68*	(187)	Zimbabwe v Pakistan at Rawalpindi		1993-94
M. A. Atherton	94*	(228)	England v New Zealand at Christchurch		1996-97
G. Kirsten	100*	(239)	South Africa v Pakistan at Faisalabad		1997-98
M. A. Taylor	169*	(350)	Australia v South Africa at Adelaide		1997-98
G. W. Flower	156*	(321)	Zimbabwe v Pakistan at Bulawayo		1997-98
Saeed Anwar	188*	(316)	Pakistan v India at Calcutta		1998-99
M. S. Atapattu	216*	(428)	Sri Lanka v Zimbabwe at Bulawayo		1999-2000
R. P. Arnold	104*	(231)	Sri Lanka v Zimbabwe at Harare		1999-2000
Javed Omar	85*	(168)†‡	Bangladesh v Zimbabwe at Bulawayo		2000-01
V. Sehwag	201*	(329)	India v Sri Lanka at Galle		2008
S. M. Katich	131*	(268)	Australia v New Zealand at Brisbane		2008-09
C. H. Gayle	165*	(317)	West Indies v Australia at Adelaide		2009-10
Imran Farhat	117*	(223)	Pakistan v New Zealand at Napier		2009-10
R. Dravid	146*	(300)	India v England at The Oval		2011
T. M. K. Mawoyo	163*	(412)	Zimbabwe v Pakistan at Bulawayo		2011-12
D. A. Warner	123*	(233)	Australia v New Zealand at Hobart		2011-12

† *On debut.*   ‡*One man absent.*   § *Two men absent.*   ¶ *Father and son.*

Notes: G. M. Turner (223*) holds the record for the highest score by a player carrying his bat through a Test innings. He is also the youngest player to do so, being 22 years 63 days old when he first achieved the feat (1969).

D. L. Haynes, who is alone in achieving this feat on three occasions, also opened the batting and was last man out in each innings for West Indies v New Zealand at Dunedin, 1979-80.

750 RUNS IN A SERIES

	T	I	NO	R	HS	100	Avge		
D. G. Bradman	5	7	0	974	334	4	139.14	A v E	1930
W. R. Hammond...	5	9	1	905	251	4	113.12	E v A	1928-29
M. A. Taylor......	6	11	1	839	219	2	83.90	A v E	1989
R. N. Harvey......	5	9	0	834	205	4	92.66	A v SA	1952-53
I. V. A. Richards...	4	7	0	829	291	3	118.42	WI v E	1976
C. L. Walcott	5	10	0	827	155	5	82.70	WI v A	1954-55
G. S. Sobers	5	8	2	824	365*	3	137.33	WI v P	1957-58
D. G. Bradman	5	9	0	810	270	3	90.00	A v E	1936-37
D. G. Bradman	5	5	1	806	299*	4	201.50	A v SA	1931-32
B. C. Lara	5	8	0	798	375	2	99.75	WI v E	1993-94
E. D. Weekes	5	7	0	779	194	4	111.28	WI v I	1948-49
†S. M. Gavaskar...	4	8	3	774	220	4	154.80	I v WI	1970-71
A. N. Cook	5	7	1	766	235*	3	127.66	E v A	2010-11
B. C. Lara	6	10	1	765	179	3	85.00	WI v E	1995
Mudassar Nazar ...	6	8	2	761	231	4	126.83	P v I	1982-83
D. G. Bradman	5	8	0	758	304	2	94.75	A v E	1934
D. C. S. Compton .	5	8	0	753	208	4	94.12	E v SA	1947
‡G. A. Gooch	3	6	0	752	333	3	125.33	E v I	1990

† *Gavaskar's aggregate was achieved in his first Test series.*

‡ *G. A. Gooch is alone in scoring 1,000 runs in Test cricket during an English season with 1,058 runs in 11 innings against New Zealand and India in 1990.*

MOST RUNS IN A CALENDAR YEAR

	T	I	NO	R	HS	100	Avge	Year
Mohammad Yousuf (P)......	11	19	1	1,788	202	9	99.33	2006
I. V. A. Richards (WI).......	11	19	0	1,710	291	7	90.00	1976
G. C. Smith (SA)..........	15	25	2	1,656	232	6	72.00	2008
M. J. Clarke (A)...........	11	18	3	1,595	329*	5	106.33	2012
S. R. Tendulkar (I).	14	23	3	1,562	214	7	78.10	2010
S. M. Gavaskar (I).........	18	27	1	1,555	221	5	59.80	1979
R. T. Ponting (A)..........	15	28	5	1,544	207	6	67.13	2005
R. T. Ponting (A)..........	11	18	3	1,503	257	6	100.20	2003

Notes: M. Amarnath reached 1,000 runs in 1983 on May 3, in his ninth Test of the year.

The only batsman to score 1,000 runs in a year before World War II was C. Hill of Australia: 1,060 in 1902.

M. L. Hayden (Australia) scored 1,000 runs in each year from 2001 to 2005.

MOST RUNS

		T	I	NO	R	HS	100	Avge
1	S. R. Tendulkar (India)........	200	329	33	15,921	248*	51	53.78
2	R. T. Ponting (Australia)........	168	287	29	13,378	257	41	51.85
3	J. H. Kallis (South Africa/World)	166	280	40	13,289	224	45	55.37
4	R. Dravid (India/World) ..	164	286	32	13,288	270	36	52.31
5	B. C. Lara (West Indies/World) ..	131	232	6	11,953	400*	34	52.88
6	S. Chanderpaul (West Indies) ..	153	261	45	11,219	203*	29	51.93
7	A. R. Border (Australia)	156	265	44	11,174	205	27	50.56
8	D. P. M. D. Jayawardene (SL) ..	141	237	14	11,033	374	32	49.47
9	S. R. Waugh (Australia)........	168	260	46	10,927	200	32	51.06
10	K. C. Sangakkara (Sri Lanka) ..	120	206	17	10,652	287	33	56.35
11	S. M. Gavaskar (India)	125	214	16	10,122	236*	34	51.12
12	G. C. Smith (South Africa/Wld).	114	199	13	9,220	277	27	49.56
13	G. A. Gooch (England).........	118	215	6	8,900	333	20	42.58
14	Javed Miandad (Pakistan).......	124	189	21	8,832	280*	23	52.57
15	Inzamam-ul-Haq (Pakistan/World)	120	200	22	8,830	329	25	49.60

		T	I	NO	R	HS	100	Avge
16	V. V. S. Laxman (India)	134	225	34	8,781	281	17	45.97
17	M. L. Hayden (Australia)	103	184	14	8,625	380	30	50.73
18	**V. Sehwag (India/World)**	**104**	**180**	**6**	**8,586**	**319**	**23**	**49.34**
19	I. V. A. Richards (West Indies)	121	182	12	8,540	291	24	50.23
20	A. J. Stewart (England)	133	235	21	8,463	190	15	39.54
21	D. I. Gower (England)	117	204	18	8,231	215	18	44.25
22	**K. P. Pietersen (England)**	**104**	**181**	**8**	**8,181**	**227**	**23**	**47.28**
23	G. Boycott (England)	108	193	23	8,114	246*	22	47.72
24	**A. N. Cook (England)**	**102**	**183**	**10**	**8,047**	**294**	**25**	**46.51**
25	G. S. Sobers (West Indies)	93	160	21	8,032	365*	26	57.78
26	M. E. Waugh (Australia)	128	209	17	8,029	153*	20	41.81
27	**M. J. Clarke (Australia)**	**102**	**174**	**18**	**8,019**	**329***	**26**	**51.40**
28	M. A. Atherton (England)	115	212	7	7,728	185*	16	37.69
29	J. L. Langer (Australia)	105	182	12	7,696	250	23	45.27
30	M. C. Cowdrey (England)	114	188	15	7,624	182	22	44.06
31	C. G. Greenidge (West Indies)	108	185	16	7,558	226	19	44.72
32	Mohammad Yousuf (Pakistan)	90	156	12	7,530	223	24	52.29
33	M. A. Taylor (Australia)	104	186	13	7,525	334*	19	43.49
34	C. H. Lloyd (West Indies)	110	175	14	7,515	242*	19	46.67
35	D. L. Haynes (West Indies)	116	202	25	7,487	184	18	42.29
36	D. C. Boon (Australia)	107	190	20	7,422	200	21	43.65
37	**Younis Khan (Pakistan)**	**89**	**158**	**14**	**7,399**	**313**	**23**	**51.38**
38	G. Kirsten (South Africa)	101	176	15	7,289	275	21	45.27
39	W. R. Hammond (England)	85	140	16	7,249	336*	22	58.45
40	S. C. Ganguly (India)	113	188	17	7,212	239	16	42.17
41	S. P. Fleming (New Zealand)	111	189	10	7,172	274*	9	40.06
42	G. S. Chappell (Australia)	87	151	19	7,110	247*	24	53.86
43	A. J. Strauss (England)	100	178	6	7,037	177	21	40.91
44	D. G. Bradman (Australia)	52	80	10	6,996	334	29	99.94
45	S. T. Jayasuriya (Sri Lanka)	110	188	14	6,973	340	14	40.07
46	L. Hutton (England)	79	138	15	6,971	364	19	56.67
47	**C. H. Gayle (West Indies)**	**99**	**174**	**9**	**6,933**	**333**	**15**	**42.01**
48	D. B. Vengsarkar (India)	116	185	22	6,868	166	17	42.13
49	**A. B. de Villiers (South Africa)**	**89**	**148**	**16**	**6,827**	**278***	**18**	**51.71**
50	K. F. Barrington (England)	82	131	15	6,806	256	20	58.67

MOST RUNS FOR EACH COUNTRY

ENGLAND

G. A. Gooch	8,900	D. I. Gower	8,231	G. Boycott	8,114
A. J. Stewart	8,463	**K. P. Pietersen**	**8,181**	**A. N. Cook**	**8,047**

AUSTRALIA

R. T. Ponting	13,378	S. R. Waugh	10,927	M. E. Waugh	8,029
A. R. Border	11,174	M. L. Hayden	8,625	**M. J. Clarke**	**8,019**

SOUTH AFRICA

J. H. Kallis	**13,206**	G. Kirsten	7,289	H. H. Gibbs	6,167
G. C. Smith	**9,208**	**A. B. de Villiers**	**6,827**	**H. M. Amla**	**5,956**

† *J. H. Kallis also scored 44 and 39* and G. C. Smith 12 and 0 for the World XI v Australia (2005-06 Super Series Test).*

WEST INDIES

B. C. Lara 11,912	I. V. A. Richards 8,540	C. G. Greenidge 7,558
S. Chanderpaul **11,219**	G. S. Sobers 8,032	C. H. Lloyd 7,515

† B. C. Lara also scored 5 and 36 for the World XI v Australia (2005-06 Super Series Test).

NEW ZEALAND

S. P. Fleming 7,172	J. G. Wright 5,334	**B. B. McCullum** **4,684**
M. D. Crowe 5,444	N. J. Astle 4,702	D. L. Vettori 4,508

† D. L. Vettori also scored 8* and 0 for the World XI v Australia (2005-06 Super Series Test).

INDIA

S. R. Tendulkar **15,921**	S. M. Gavaskar 10,122	**V. Sehwag** **8,503**
R. Dravid 13,265	V. V. S. Laxman 8,781	S. C. Ganguly 7,212

† R. Dravid also scored 0 and 23 and V. Sehwag 76 and 7 for the World XI v Australia (2005-06 Super Series Test).

PAKISTAN

Javed Miandad 8,832	Mohammad Yousuf . . 7,530	Salim Malik 5,768
Inzamam-ul-Haq 8,829	**Younis Khan** **7,399**	Zaheer Abbas 5,062

† Inzamam-ul-Haq also scored 1 and 0 for the World XI v Australia (2005-06 Super Series Test).

SRI LANKA

D. P. M. D. Jayawardene 11,033	S. T. Jayasuriya 6,973	M. S. Atapattu 5,502
K. C. Sangakkara . . . **10,652**	P. A. de Silva 6,361	T. T. Samaraweera . . . 5,462

ZIMBABWE

A. Flower 4,794	A. D. R. Campbell . . . 2,858	H. H. Streak 1,990
G. W. Flower 3,457	G. J. Whittall 2,207	S. V. Carlisle 1,615

BANGLADESH

Habibul Bashar 3,026	**Tamim Iqbal** **2,221**	Mushfiqur Rahim 2,078
Mohammad Ashraful 2,737	**Shakib Al Hasan** **2,105**	Javed Omar 1,720

CAREER AVERAGE OVER 50

(Qualification: 20 innings)

Avge		T	I	NO	R	HS	100
99.94	D. G. Bradman (A)	52	80	10	6,996	334	29
66.25	**C. A. Pujara (I)**	17	28	4	**1,590**	**206***	**6**
60.97	R. G. Pollock (SA)	23	41	4	2,256	274	7
60.83	G. A. Headley (WI)	22	40	4	2,190	270*	10
60.73	H. Sutcliffe (E)	54	84	9	4,555	194	16
59.23	E. Paynter (E)	20	31	5	1,540	243	4

Avge		T	I	NO	R	HS	100
58.67	K. F. Barrington (E)	82	131	15	6,806	256	20
58.61	E. D. Weekes (WI)	48	81	5	4,455	207	15
58.45	W. R. Hammond (E)	85	140	16	7,249	336*	22
57.78	G. S. Sobers (WI)	93	160	21	8,032	365*	26
56.94	J. B. Hobbs (E)	61	102	7	5,410	211	15
56.68	C. L. Walcott (WI)	44	74	7	3,798	220	15
56.67	L. Hutton (E)	79	138	15	6,971	364	19
56.35	**K. C. Sangakkara (SL)**	**120**	**206**	**17**	**10,652**	**287**	**33**
55.37	J. H. Kallis (SA/World)	166	280	40	13,289	224	45
55.00	E. Tyldesley (E)	14	20	2	990	122	3
54.20	C. A. Davis (WI)	15	29	5	1,301	183	4
54.20	V. G. Kambli (I)	17	21	1	1,084	227	4
53.86	G. S. Chappell (A)	87	151	19	7,110	247*	24
53.81	A. D. Nourse (SA)	34	62	7	2,960	231	9
53.78	**S. R. Tendulkar (I)**	**200**	**329**	**33**	**15,921**	**248***	**51**
52.88	B. C. Lara (WI/World)	131	232	6	11,953	400*	34
52.57	Javed Miandad (P)	124	189	21	8,832	280*	23
52.31	R. Dravid (I/World)	164	286	32	13,288	270	36
52.29	Mohammad Yousuf (P)	90	156	12	7,530	223	24
51.93	**S. Chanderpaul (WI)**	**153**	**261**	**45**	**11,219**	**203***	**29**
51.85	R. T. Ponting (A)	168	287	29	13,378	257	41
51.71	**A. B. de Villiers (SA)**.	**89**	**148**	**16**	**6,827**	**278***	**18**
51.62	J. Ryder (A)	20	32	5	1,394	201*	3
51.54	A. Flower (Z)	63	112	19	4,794	232*	12
51.52	**M. E. K. Hussey (A)**	**79**	**137**	**16**	**6,235**	**195**	**19**
51.40	**M. J. Clarke (A)**	**102**	**174**	**18**	**8,019**	**329***	**26**
51.38	**Younis Khan (P)**	**89**	**158**	**14**	**7,399**	**313**	**23**
51.34	**H. M. Amla (SA)**	**73**	**126**	**10**	**5,956**	**311***	**20**
51.12	S. M. Gavaskar (I)	125	214	16	10,122	236*	34
51.06	S. R. Waugh (A)	168	260	46	10,927	200	32
50.73	M. L. Hayden (A)	103	184	14	8,625	380	30
50.56	A. R. Border (A)	156	265	44	11,174	205	27
50.23	I. V. A. Richards (WI)	121	182	12	8,540	291	24
50.06	D. C. S. Compton (E)	78	131	15	5,807	278	17

Note: S. G. Barnes (A) scored 1,072 runs at 63.05 from 19 innings.

BEST CAREER STRIKE-RATES

(Runs per 100 balls. Qualification: 1,000 runs)

SR		T	I	NO	R	100	Avge
86.97	Shahid Afridi (P)	27	48	1	1,716	5	36.51
82.22	**V. Sehwag (I)**	**104**	**180**	**6**	**8,586**	**23**	**49.34**
81.98	A. C. Gilchrist (A)	96	137	20	5,570	17	47.60
76.49	**G. P. Swann (E)**	**60**	**76**	**14**	**1,370**	**0**	**22.09**
70.29	**D. A. Warner (A)**	**27**	**50**	**3**	**1,924**	**5**	**40.93**
70.28	M. Muralitharan (SL)	133	164	56	1,261	0	11.67
67.88	**D. J. G. Sammy (WI)**	**38**	**63**	**2**	**1,323**	**1**	**21.68**
65.98	Umar Akmal (P)	16	30	2	1,003	1	35.82
65.54	**T. M. Dilshan (SL)**	**87**	**145**	**11**	**5,492**	**16**	**40.98**
65.13*	S. T. Jayasuriya (SL)	110	188	14	6,973	14	40.07
65.09	**Harbhajan Singh (I)**	**101**	**142**	**22**	**2,202**	**2**	**18.35**

* The above figures are complete except for Jayasuriya, who played one innings for which the balls faced are not recorded. Comprehensive data on balls faced has been available only in recent decades, and its introduction varied from country to country. Among earlier players for whom partial data is available, Kapil Dev (India) had a strike-rate of 80.91 and I. V. A. Richards (West Indies) 70.19 in those innings which were fully recorded.

HIGHEST PERCENTAGE OF TEAM'S RUNS OVER TEST CAREER

(Qualification: 20 Tests)

	Tests	Runs	Team Runs	% of Team Runs
D. G. Bradman (Australia)	52	6,996	28,810	24.28
G. A. Headley (West Indies)	22	2,190	10,239	21.38
B. C. Lara (West Indies)	131	11,953	63,328	18.87
L. Hutton (England)	79	6,971	38,440	18.13
J. B. Hobbs (England)	61	5,410	30,211	17.90
A. D. Nourse (South Africa)	34	2,960	16,659	17.76
E. D. Weekes (West Indies)	48	4,455	25,667	17.35
B. Mitchell (South Africa)	42	3,471	20,175	17.20
H. Sutcliffe (England)	54	4,555	26,604	17.12
B. Sutcliffe (New Zealand)	42	2,727	16,158	16.87

The percentage shows the proportion of a team's runs scored by that player in all Tests in which he played, including team runs in innings in which he did not bat.

FASTEST FIFTIES

Minutes			
27	Mohammad Ashraful	Bangladesh v India at Mirpur	2007
28	J. T. Brown	England v Australia at Melbourne	1894-95
29	S. A. Durani	India v England at Kanpur	1963-64
30	E. A. V. Williams	West Indies v England at Bridgetown	1947-48
30	B. R. Taylor	New Zealand v West Indies at Auckland	1968-69

The fastest fifties in terms of balls received (where recorded) are:

Balls			
24	J. H. Kallis	South Africa v Zimbabwe at Cape Town	2004-05
26	Shahid Afridi	Pakistan v India at Bangalore	2004-05
26	Mohammad Ashraful	Bangladesh v India at Mirpur	2007
27	Yousuf Youhana	Pakistan v South Africa at Cape Town	2002-03
28	E. A. V. Williams	West Indies v England at Bridgetown	1947-48
28	I. T. Botham	England v India at Delhi	1981-82
29	B. Yardley	Australia v West Indies at Bridgetown	1977-78
29	T. G. Southee	New Zealand v England at Napier	2007-08
30	Kapil Dev	India v Pakistan at Karachi	1982-83
30	T. M. Dilshan	Sri Lanka v New Zealand at Galle	2009

FASTEST HUNDREDS

Minutes			
70	J. M. Gregory	Australia v South Africa at Johannesburg	1921-22
75	G. L. Jessop	England v Australia at The Oval	1902
78	R. Benaud	Australia v West Indies at Kingston	1954-55
80	J. H. Sinclair	South Africa v Australia at Cape Town	1902-03
81	I. V. A. Richards	West Indies v England at St John's	1985-86
86	B. R. Taylor	New Zealand v West Indies at Auckland	1968-69

The fastest hundreds in terms of balls received (where recorded) are:

Balls

56	I. V. A. Richards	West Indies v England at St John's	1985-86
57	A. C. Gilchrist	Australia v England at Perth	2006-07
67	J. M. Gregory	Australia v South Africa at Johannesburg	1921-22
69	S. Chanderpaul	West Indies v Australia at Georgetown	2002-03
69	D. A. Warner	Australia v India at Perth	2011-12
70	C. H. Gayle	West Indies v Australia at Perth	2009-10
71	R. C. Fredericks	West Indies v Australia at Perth	1975-76
74	Majid Khan	Pakistan v New Zealand at Karachi	1976-77
74	Kapil Dev	India v Sri Lanka at Kanpur	1986-87
74	M. Azharuddin	India v South Africa at Calcutta	1996-97
75	A. B. de Villiers	South Africa v India at Centurion	2010-11
76	G. L. Jessop	England v Australia at The Oval	1902

FASTEST DOUBLE-HUNDREDS

Minutes

214	D. G. Bradman	Australia v England at Leeds	1930
217	N. J. Astle	New Zealand v England at Christchurch	2001-02
223	S. J. McCabe	Australia v England at Nottingham	1938
226	V. T. Trumper	Australia v South Africa at Adelaide	1910-11
234	D. G. Bradman	Australia v England at Lord's	1930
240	W. R. Hammond	England v New Zealand at Auckland	1932-33
241	S. E. Gregory	Australia v England at Sydney	1894-95
245	D. C. S. Compton	England v Pakistan at Nottingham	1954

The fastest double-hundreds in terms of balls received (where recorded) are:

Balls

153	N. J. Astle	New Zealand v England at Christchurch	2001-02
168	V. Sehwag	India v Sri Lanka at Mumbai (Brabourne)	2009-10
182	V. Sehwag	India v Pakistan at Lahore	2005-06
194	V. Sehwag	India v South Africa at Chennai	2007-08
211	H. H. Gibbs	South Africa v Pakistan at Cape Town	2002-03
212	A. C. Gilchrist	Australia v South Africa at Johannesburg	2001-02
220	I. T. Botham	England v India at The Oval	1982
221	C. H. Gayle	West Indies v Sri Lanka at Galle	2010-11
222	V. Sehwag	India v Pakistan at Multan	2003-04
226	M. J. Clarke	Australia v South Africa at Adelaide	2012-13
227	V. Sehwag	India v Sri Lanka at Galle	2008
229	P. A. de Silva	Sri Lanka v Bangladesh at Colombo (PSS)	2002

FASTEST TRIPLE-HUNDREDS

Minutes

288	W. R. Hammond	England v New Zealand at Auckland	1932-33
336	D. G. Bradman	Australia v England at Leeds	1930

The fastest triple-hundred in terms of balls received (where recorded) is:

Balls

278	V. Sehwag	India v South Africa at Chennai	2007-08

An expanded and regularly updated online version of the Records can be found at
www.wisdenrecords.com

MOST RUNS SCORED OFF AN OVER

28	B. C. Lara (466444)	off R. J. Peterson	WI v SA at Johannesburg . .	2003-04
28	**G. J. Bailey (462466)**	**off J. M. Anderson**	**A v E at Perth**	**2013-14**
27	Shahid Afridi (666621)	off Harbhajan Singh	P v I at Lahore	2005-06
26	C. D. McMillan (444464)	off Younis Khan	NZ v P at Hamilton	2000-01
26	B. C. Lara (406664)	off Danish Kaneria	WI v P at Multan	2006-07
26	M. G. Johnson (446066)	off P. L. Harris	A v SA at Johannesburg . . .	2009-10

MOST RUNS IN A DAY

309	D. G. Bradman	Australia v England at Leeds	1930
295	W. R. Hammond	England v New Zealand at Auckland	1932-33
284	V. Sehwag	India v Sri Lanka at Mumbai	2009-10
273	D. C. S. Compton	England v Pakistan at Nottingham	1954
271	D. G. Bradman	Australia v England at Leeds	1934

MOST SIXES IN A CAREER

A. C. Gilchrist (A)	100		A. Flintoff (E/World)	82
J. H. Kallis (SA/World)	**97**		M. L. Hayden (A)	82
V. Sehwag (I/World)	**91**		**K. P. Pietersen (E)**	**81**
C. H. Gayle (WI)	**90**		**M. S. Dhoni (I)**	**75**
B. C. Lara (WI)	88		R. T. Ponting (A)	73
C. L. Cairns (NZ)	87		C. H. Lloyd (WI)	70
I. V. A. Richards (WI)	84			

SLOWEST INDIVIDUAL BATTING

0	in 101 minutes	G. I. Allott, New Zealand v South Africa at Auckland	1998-99
4*	in 110 minutes	Abdul Razzaq, Pakistan v Australia at Melbourne	2004-05
6	**in 137 minutes**	**S. C. J. Broad, England v New Zealand at Auckland.**	**2012-13**
9*	in 184 minutes	Arshad Khan, Pakistan v Sri Lanka at Colombo (SSC)	2000
18	in 194 minutes	W. R. Playle, New Zealand v England at Leeds	1958
19*	in 217 minutes	M. D. Crowe, New Zealand v Sri Lanka at Colombo (SSC). . . .	1983-84
25	in 242 minutes	D. K. Morrison, New Zealand v Pakistan at Faisalabad	1990-91
28*	in 250 minutes	J. W. Burke, Australia v England at Brisbane	1958-59
29*	in 277 minutes	R. C. Russell, England v South Africa at Johannesburg	1995-96
35	in 332 minutes	C. J. Tavaré, England v India at Madras	1981-82
43	in 340 minutes	Javed Omar, Bangladesh v Zimbabwe at Dhaka	2004-05
55	in 348 minutes	J. G. Wright, New Zealand v England at Wellington	1977-78
60	in 390 minutes	D. N. Sardesai, India v West Indies at Bridgetown	1961-62
62	in 408 minutes	Ramiz Raja, Pakistan v West Indies at Karachi	1986-87
68	in 458 minutes	T. E. Bailey, England v Australia at Brisbane	1958-59
86	in 474 minutes	Shoaib Mohammad, Pakistan v West Indies at Karachi	1990-91
99	in 505 minutes	M. L. Jaisimha, India v Pakistan at Kanpur	1960-61
104	in 529 minutes	S. V. Manjrekar, India v Zimbabwe at Harare	1992-93
105	in 575 minutes	D. J. McGlew, South Africa v Australia at Durban	1957-58
114	in 591 minutes	Mudassar Nazar, Pakistan v England at Lahore	1977-78
120*	in 609 minutes	J. J. Crowe, New Zealand v Sri Lanka at Colombo (CCC)	1986-87
136*	in 675 minutes	S. Chanderpaul, West Indies v India at St John's	2001-02
163	in 720 minutes	Shoaib Mohammad, Pakistan v New Zealand at Wellington . . .	1988-89
201*	in 777 minutes	D. S. B. P. Kuruppu, Sri Lanka v NZ at Colombo (CCC).	1986-87
275	in 878 minutes	G. Kirsten, South Africa v England at Durban	1999-2000
337	in 970 minutes	Hanif Mohammad, Pakistan v West Indies at Bridgetown	1957-58

SLOWEST HUNDREDS

557 minutes	Mudassar Nazar, Pakistan v England at Lahore.....................	1977-78
545 minutes	D. J. McGlew, South Africa v Australia at Durban.................	1957-58
535 minutes	A. P. Gurusinha, Sri Lanka v Zimbabwe at Harare	1994-95
516 minutes	J. J. Crowe, New Zealand v Sri Lanka at Colombo (CCC)	1986-87
500 minutes	S. V. Manjrekar, India v Zimbabwe at Harare	1992-93
488 minutes	P. E. Richardson, England v South Africa at Johannesburg...........	1956-57

Notes: The slowest hundred for any Test in England is 458 minutes (329 balls) by K. W. R. Fletcher, England v Pakistan, The Oval, 1974.

The slowest double-hundred in a Test was scored in 777 minutes (548 balls) by D. S. B. P. Kuruppu for Sri Lanka v New Zealand at Colombo (CCC), 1986-87, on his debut.

PARTNERSHIPS OVER 400

624	for 3rd	K. C. Sangakkara (287)/D. P. M. D. Jayawardene (374)..................	SL v SA	Colombo (SSC)	2006
576	for 2nd	S. T. Jayasuriya (340)/R. S. Mahanama (225)	SL v I	Colombo (RPS)	1997-98
467	for 3rd	A. H. Jones (186)/M. D. Crowe (299)......	NZ v SL	Wellington	1990-91
451	for 2nd	W. H. Ponsford (266)/D. G. Bradman (244) .	A v E	The Oval	1934
451	for 3rd	Mudassar Nazar (231)/Javed Miandad (280*)	P v I	Hyderabad	1982-83
446	for 2nd	C. C. Hunte (260)/G. S. Sobers (365*)	WI v P	Kingston	1957-58
438	for 2nd	M. S. Atapattu (249)/K. C. Sangakkara (270)	SL v Z	Bulawayo	2003-04
437	for 4th	D. P. M. D. Jayawardene (240)/T. T. Samaraweera (231)	SL v P	Karachi	2008-09
429*	for 3rd	J. A. Rudolph (222*)/H. H. Dippenaar (177*)	SA v B	Chittagong	2003
415	for 1st	N. D. McKenzie (226)/G. C. Smith (232) ...	SA v B	Chittagong	2007-08
413	for 1st	V. Mankad (231)/Pankaj Roy (173)........	I v NZ	Madras	1955-56
411	for 4th	P. B. H. May (285*)/M. C. Cowdrey (154)..	E v WI	Birmingham	1957
410	for 1st	V. Sehwag (254)/R. Dravid (128*)	I v P	Lahore	2005-06
405	for 5th	S. G. Barnes (234)/D. G. Bradman (234).....	A v E	Sydney	1946-47

Notes: 415 runs were added for the third wicket for India v England at Madras in 1981-82 by D. B. Vengsarkar (retired hurt), G. R. Viswanath and Yashpal Sharma. 408 runs were added for the first wicket for India v Bangladesh at Mirpur in 2007 by K. D. Karthik (retired hurt), Wasim Jaffer (retired hurt), R. Dravid and S. R. Tendulkar.

HIGHEST PARTNERSHIPS FOR EACH WICKET

First Wicket

415	N. D. McKenzie (226)/G. C. Smith (232).........	SA v B	Chittagong	2007-08
413	V. Mankad (231)/Pankaj Roy (173)	I v NZ	Madras	1955-56
410	V. Sehwag (254)/R. Dravid (128*)	I v P	Lahore	2005-06
387	G. M. Turner (259)/T. W. Jarvis (182)	NZ v WI	Georgetown	1971-72
382	W. M. Lawry (210)/R. B. Simpson (201).........	A v WI	Bridgetown	1964-65

Second Wicket

576	S. T. Jayasuriya (340)/R. S. Mahanama (225)	SL v I	Colombo (RPS)	1997-98
451	W. H. Ponsford (266)/D. G. Bradman (244).......	A v E	The Oval	1934
446	C. C. Hunte (260)/G. S. Sobers (365*)...........	WI v P	Kingston	1957-58
438	M. S. Atapattu (249)/K. C. Sangakkara (270)......	SL v Z	Bulawayo	2003-04
382	L. Hutton (364)/M. Leyland (187)	E v A	The Oval	1938

Third Wicket

624	K. C. Sangakkara (287)/			
	D. P. M. D. Jayawardene (374).	SL v SA	Colombo (SSC)	2006
467	A. H. Jones (186)/M. D. Crowe (299).	NZ v SL	Wellington	1990-91
451	Mudassar Nazar (231)/Javed Miandad (280*)	P v I	Hyderabad	1982-83
429*	J. A. Rudolph (222*)/H. H. Dippenaar (177*)	SA v B	Chittagong	2003
397	Qasim Omar (206)/Javed Miandad (203*)	P v SL	Faisalabad	1985-86

Fourth Wicket

437	D. P. M. D. Jayawardene (240)/			
	T. T. Samaraweera (231).	SL v P	Karachi	2008-09
411	P. B. H. May (285*)/M. C. Cowdrey (154)	E v WI	Birmingham	1957
399	G. S. Sobers (226)/F. M. M. Worrell (197*).	WI v E	Bridgetown	1959-60
388	W. H. Ponsford (181)/D. G. Bradman (304).	A v E	Leeds	1934
386	R. T. Ponting (221)/M. J. Clarke (210).	A v I	Adelaide	2011-12

Fifth Wicket

405	S. G. Barnes (234)/D. G. Bradman (234)	A v E	Sydney	1946-47
385	S. R. Waugh (160)/G. S. Blewett (214)	A v SA	Johannesburg	1996-97
376	V. V. S. Laxman (281)/R. Dravid (180)	I v A	Kolkata	2000-01
338	**G. C. Smith (234)/A. B. de Villiers (164)**	**SA v P**	**Dubai**	**2013-14**
334*	M. J. Clarke (329*)/M. E. K. Hussey (150*)	A v I	Sydney	2011-12

Sixth Wicket

351	D. P. M. D. Jayawardene (275)/			
	H. A. P. W. Jayawardene (154*).	SL v I	Ahmedabad	2009-10
346	J. H. Fingleton (136)/D. G. Bradman (270)	A v E	Melbourne	1936-37
339	M. J. Guptill (189)/B. B. McCullum (185).	NZ v B	Hamilton	2009-10
317	D. R. Martyn (133)/A. C. Gilchrist (204*)	A v SA	Johannesburg	2001-02
307	M. E. K. Hussey (195)/B. J. Haddin (136)	A v E	Brisbane	2010-11

Seventh Wicket

347	D. St E. Atkinson (219)/C. C. Depeiza (122)	WI v A	Bridgetown	1954-55
308	Waqar Hassan (189)/Imtiaz Ahmed (209)	P v NZ	Lahore	1955-56
280	**R. G. Sharma (177)/R. Ashwin (124)**.	**I v WI**	**Kolkata**	**2013-14**
259*	V. V. S. Laxman (143*)/M. S. Dhoni (132*)	I v SA	Kolkata	2009-10
248	Yousuf Youhana (203)/Saqlain Mushtaq (101*)	P v NZ	Christchurch	2000-01

Eighth Wicket

332	I. J. L. Trott (184)/S. C. J. Broad (169).	E v P	Lord's	2010
313	Wasim Akram (257*)/Saqlain Mushtaq (79)	P v Z	Sheikhupura	1996-97
256	S. P. Fleming (262)/J. E. C. Franklin (122*)	NZ v SA	Cape Town	2005-06
253	N. J. Astle (156*)/A. C. Parore (110)	NZ v A	Perth	2001-02
246	L. E. G. Ames (137)/G. O. B. Allen (122)	E v NZ	Lord's	1931

Ninth Wicket

195	M. V. Boucher (78)/P. L. Symcox (108).	SA v P	Johannesburg	1997-98
190	Asif Iqbal (146)/Intikhab Alam (51).	P v E	The Oval	1967
184	Mahmudullah (76)/Abul Hasan (113).	B v WI	Khulna	2012-13
180	J-P. Duminy (166)/D. W. Steyn (76)	SA v A	Melbourne	2008-09
163*	M. C. Cowdrey (128*)/A. C. Smith (69*)	E v NZ	Wellington	1962-63

Tenth Wicket

163	**P. J. Hughes (81*)/A. C. Agar (98)**	**A v E**	**Nottingham**	**2013**
151	B. F. Hastings (110)/R. O. Collinge (68*)	NZ v P	Auckland	1972-73
151	Azhar Mahmood (128*)/Mushtaq Ahmed (59)	P v SA	Rawalpindi	1997-98
143	D. Ramdin (107*)/T. L. Best (95).	WI v E	Birmingham	2012
133	Wasim Raja (71)/Wasim Bari (60*)	P v WI	Bridgetown	1976-77
133	S. R. Tendulkar (248*)/Zaheer Khan (75)	I v B	Dhaka	2004-05

HIGHEST PARTNERSHIPS FOR EACH COUNTRY

ENGLAND

359	for 1st	L. Hutton (158)/C. Washbrook (195)	v SA	Johannesburg	1948-49
382	for 2nd	L. Hutton (364)/M. Leyland (187)	v A	The Oval	1938
370	for 3rd	W. J. Edrich (189)/D. C. S. Compton (208) . . .	v SA	Lord's	1947
411	for 4th	P. B. H. May (285*)/M. C. Cowdrey (154) . . .	v WI	Birmingham	1957
254	for 5th	K. W. R. Fletcher (113)/A. W. Greig (148) . . .	v I	Bombay	1972-73
281	for 6th	G. P. Thorpe (200*)/A. Flintoff (137)	v NZ	Christchurch	2001-02
197	for 7th	M. J. K. Smith (96)/J. M. Parks (101*).	v WI	Port-of-Spain	1959-60
332	for 8th	I. J. L. Trott (184)/S. C. J. Broad (169).	v P	Lord's	2010
163*	for 9th	M. C. Cowdrey (128*)/A. C. Smith (69*) . . .	v NZ	Wellington	1962-63
130	for 10th	R. E. Foster (287)/W. Rhodes (40*)	v A	Sydney	1903-04

AUSTRALIA

382	for 1st	W. M. Lawry (210)/R. B. Simpson (201)	v WI	Bridgetown	1964-65
451	for 2nd	W. H. Ponsford (266)/D. G. Bradman (244). . .	v E	The Oval	1934
315	for 3rd	R. T. Ponting (206)/D. S. Lehmann (160)	v WI	Port-of-Spain	2002-03
388	for 4th	W. H. Ponsford (181)/D. G. Bradman (304). . .	v E	Leeds	1934
405	for 5th	S. G. Barnes (234)/D. G. Bradman (234)	v E	Sydney	1946-47
346	for 6th	J. H. Fingleton (136)/D. G. Bradman (270) . . .	v E	Melbourne	1936-37
217	for 7th	K. D. Walters (250)/G. J. Gilmour (101)	v NZ	Christchurch	1976-77
243	for 8th	R. J. Hartigan (116)/C. Hill (160).	v E	Adelaide	1907-08
154	for 9th	S. E. Gregory (201)/J. McC. Blackham (74) . .	v E	Sydney	1894-95
163	**for 10th**	**P. J. Hughes (81*)/A. C. Agar (98)**	**v E**	**Nottingham**	**2013**

SOUTH AFRICA

415	for 1st	N. D. McKenzie (226)/G. C. Smith (232).	v B	Chittagong	2007-08
315*	for 2nd	H. H. Gibbs (211*)/J. H. Kallis (148*).	v NZ	Christchurch	1998-99
429*	for 3rd	J. A. Rudolph (222*)/H. H. Dippenaar (177*) .	v B	Chittagong	2003
249	for 4th	J. H. Kallis (177)/G. Kirsten (137)	v WI	Durban	2003-04
338	**for 5th**	**G. C. Smith (234)/A. B. de Villiers (164)**	**v P**	**Dubai**	**2013-14**
271	for 6th	A. G. Prince (162*)/M. V. Boucher (117)	v B	Centurion	2008-09
246	for 7th	D. J. McGlew (255*)/A. R. A. Murray (109) . .	v NZ	Wellington	1952-53
150	for 8th	N. D. McKenzie (103)/S. M. Pollock (111) . . .	v SL	Centurion	2000-01
		G. Kirsten (130)/M. Zondeki (59).	v E	Leeds	2003
195	for 9th	M. V. Boucher (78)/P. L. Symcox (108)	v P	Johannesburg	1997-98
107*	for 10th	A. B. de Villiers (278*)/M. Morkel (35*).	v P	Abu Dhabi	2010-11

WEST INDIES

298	for 1st	C. G. Greenidge (149)/D. L. Haynes (167).... v E	St John's	1989-90
446	for 2nd	C. C. Hunte (260)/G. S. Sobers (365*)..... v P	Kingston	1957-58
338	for 3rd	E. D. Weekes (206)/F. M. M. Worrell (167).. v E	Port-of-Spain	1953-54
399	for 4th	G. S. Sobers (226)/F. M. M. Worrell (197*)... v E	Bridgetown	1959-60
322	for 5th†	B. C. Lara (213)/J. C. Adams (94) .... v A	Kingston	1998-99
282*	for 6th	B. C. Lara (400*)/R. D. Jacobs (107*) ...... v E	St John's	2003-04
347	for 7th	D. St E. Atkinson (219)/C. C. Depeiza (122).. v A	Bridgetown	1954-55
148	for 8th	J. C. Adams (101*)/F. A. Rose (69) .... v Z	Kingston	1999-2000
161	for 9th	C. H. Lloyd (161*)/A. M. E. Roberts (68) .... v I	Calcutta	1983-84
143	for 10th	D. Ramdin (107*)/T. L. Best (95)........... v E	Birmingham	2012

† 344 runs were added between the fall of the 4th and 5th wickets: P. T. Collins retired hurt when he and Lara had added 22 runs.

NEW ZEALAND

387	for 1st	G. M. Turner (259)/T. W. Jarvis (182)....... v WI	Georgetown	1971-72
241	for 2nd	J. G. Wright (116)/A. H. Jones (143) .... v E	Wellington	1991-92
467	for 3rd	A. H. Jones (186)/M. D. Crowe (299) .... v SL	Wellington	1990-91
271	for 4th	L. R. P. L. Taylor (151)/J. D. Ryder (201) ... v I	Napier	2008-09
222	for 5th	N. J. Astle (141)/C. D. McMillan (142) ...... v Z	Wellington	2000-01
339	for 6th	M. J. Guptill (189)/B. B. McCullum (185)..... v B	Hamilton	2009-10
225	for 7th	C. L. Cairns (158)/J. D. P. Oram (90)........ v SA	Auckland	2003-04
256	for 8th	S. P. Fleming (262)/J. E. C. Franklin (122*) .. v SA	Cape Town	2005-06
136	for 9th	I. D. S. Smith (173)/M. C. Snedden (22) ..... v I	Auckland	1989-90
151	for 10th	B. F. Hastings (110)/R. O. Collinge (68*) .... v P	Auckland	1972-73

INDIA

413	for 1st	V. Mankad (231)/Pankaj Roy (173) .... v NZ	Madras	1955-56
370	**for 2nd**	**M. Vijay (167)/C. A. Pujara (204)** .... **v A**	**Hyderabad**	**2012-13**
336	for 3rd†	V. Sehwag (309)/S. R. Tendulkar (194*) ...... v P	Multan	2003-04
353	for 4th	S. R. Tendulkar (241*)/V. V. S. Laxman (178) .. v A	Sydney	2003-04
376	for 5th	V. V. S. Laxman (281)/R. Dravid (180)....... v A	Kolkata	2000-01
298*	for 6th	D. B. Vengsarkar (164*)/R. J. Shastri (121*).. v A	Bombay	1986-87
280	**for 7th**	**R. G. Sharma (177/R. Ashwin (124)**....... **v WI**	**Kolkata**	**2013-14**
161	for 8th	A. Kumble (88)/M. Azharuddin (109) .... v SA	Calcutta	1996-97
149	for 9th	P. G. Joshi (52*)/R. B. Desai (85) .... v P	Bombay	1960-61
133	for 10th	S. R. Tendulkar (248*)/Zaheer Khan (75) .... v B	Dhaka	2004-05

†415 runs were scored for India's 3rd wicket v England at Madras in 1981-82, in two partnerships: D. B. Vengsarkar and G. R. Viswanath put on 99 before Vengsarkar retired hurt, then Viswanath and Yashpal Sharma added a further 316.

PAKISTAN

298	for 1st	Aamir Sohail (160)/Ijaz Ahmed, sen. (151) ... v WI	Karachi	1997-98
291	for 2nd	Zaheer Abbas (274)/Mushtaq Mohammad (100) v E	Birmingham	1971
451	for 3rd	Mudassar Nazar (231)/Javed Miandad (280*) . v I	Hyderabad	1982-83
350	for 4th	Mushtaq Mohammad (201)/Asif Iqbal (175) .. v NZ	Dunedin	1972-73
281	for 5th	Javed Miandad (163)/Asif Iqbal (166) .... v NZ	Lahore	1976-77
269	for 6th	Mohammad Yousuf (223)/Kamran Akmal (154) v E	Lahore	2005-06
308	for 7th	Waqar Hassan (189)/Imtiaz Ahmed (209) .... v NZ	Lahore	1955-56
313	for 8th	Wasim Akram (257*)/Saqlain Mushtaq (79) .. v Z	Sheikhupura	1996-97
190	for 9th	Asif Iqbal (146)/Intikhab Alam (51)......... v E	The Oval	1967
151	for 10th	Azhar Mahmood (128*)/Mushtaq Ahmed (59) v SA	Rawalpindi	1997-98

SRI LANKA

335	for 1st	M. S. Atapattu (207*)/S. T. Jayasuriya (188)..	v P	Kandy	2000
576	for 2nd	S. T. Jayasuriya (340)/R. S. Mahanama (225) .	v I	Colombo (RPS)	1997-98
624	for 3rd	K. C. Sangakkara (287)/ D. P. M. D. Jayawardene (374)...........	v SA	Colombo (SSC)	2006
437	for 4th	D. P. M. D. Jayawardene (240)/ T. T. Samaraweera (231)	v P	Karachi	2008-09
280	for 5th	T. T. Samaraweera (138)/T. M. Dilshan (168).	v B	Colombo (PSS)	2005-06
351	for 6th	D. P. M. D. Jayawardene (275)/ H. A. P. W. Jayawardene (154*)	v I	Ahmedabad	2009-10
223*	for 7th	H. A. P. W. Jayawardene (120*)/ W. P. U. J. C. Vaas (100*)	v B	Colombo (SSC)	2007
170	for 8th	D. P. M. D. Jayawardene (237)/ W. P. U. J. C. Vaas (69)	v SA	Galle	2004
118	for 9th	T. T. Samaraweera (83)/B. A. W. Mendis (78) .	v I	Colombo (PSS)	2010
79	for 10th	W. P. U. J. C. Vaas (68*)/M. Muralitharan (43)	v A	Kandy	2003-04

ZIMBABWE

164	for 1st	D. D. Ebrahim (71)/A. D. R. Campbell (103) .	v WI	Bulawayo	2001
135	for 2nd	M. H. Dekker (68*)/A. D. R. Campbell (75) ..	v P	Rawalpindi	1993-94
194	for 3rd	A. D. R. Campbell (99)/D. L. Houghton (142).	v SL	Harare	1994-95
269	for 4th	G. W. Flower (201*)/A. Flower (156)	v P	Harare	1994-95
277*	for 5th	M. W. Goodwin (166*)/A. Flower (100*)	v P	Bulawayo	1997-98
165	for 6th	D. L. Houghton (121)/A. Flower (59)........	v I	Harare	1992-93
154	for 7th	H. H. Streak (83*)/A. M. Blignaut (92)	v WI	Harare	2001
168	for 8th	H. H. Streak (127*)/A. M. Blignaut (91)	v WI	Harare	2003-04
87	for 9th	P. A. Strang (106*)/B. C. Strang (42)........	v P	Sheikhupura	1996-97
97*	for 10th	A. Flower (183*)/H. K. Olonga (11)	v I	Delhi	2000-01

BANGLADESH

185	for 1st	Tamim Iqbal (103)/Imrul Kayes (75)	v E	Lord's	2010
200	for 2nd	Tamim Iqbal (151)/Junaid Siddique (55)	v I	Mirpur	2009-10
157	**for 3rd**	**Tamim Iqbal (70)/Mominul Haque (126*) ..**	**v NZ**	**Mirpur**	**2013-14**
167	for 4th	Naeem Islam (108)/Shakib Al Hasan (89)	v WI	Mirpur	2012-13
267	**for 5th**	**Mohammad Ashraful (190)/ Mushfiqur Rahim (200)**	**v SL**	**Galle**	**2012-13**
191	for 6th	Mohammad Ashraful (129*)/ Mushfiqur Rahim (80).	v SL	Colombo (PSS)	2007
145	for 7th	Shakib Al Hasan (87)/Mahmudullah (115) ...	v NZ	Hamilton	2009-10
113	for 8th	Mushfiqur Rahim (79)/Naeem Islam (38).....	v E	Chittagong	2009-10
184	for 9th	Mahmudullah (76)/Abul Hasan (113)	v WI	Khulna	2012-13
69	for 10th	Mohammad Rafique (65)/Shahadat Hossain (3*)	v A	Chittagong	2005-06

UNUSUAL DISMISSALS

Handled the Ball

W. R. Endean	South Africa v England at Cape Town	1956-57
A. M. J. Hilditch	Australia v Pakistan at Perth................................	1978-79
Mohsin Khan	Pakistan v Australia at Karachi..............................	1982-83
D. L. Haynes	West Indies v India at Bombay..............................	1983-84
G. A. Gooch	England v Australia at Manchester...........................	1993
S. R. Waugh	Australia v India at Chennai	2000-01
M. P. Vaughan	England v India at Bangalore	2001-02

Obstructing the Field

L. Hutton   England v South Africa at The Oval......................... 1951

Note: There have been no cases of Hit the Ball Twice or Timed Out in Test cricket.

BOWLING RECORDS

MOST WICKETS IN AN INNINGS

10-53	J. C. Laker.............	England v Australia at Manchester...............	1956
10-74	A. Kumble.............	India v Pakistan at Delhi......................	1998-99
9-28	G. A. Lohmann........	England v South Africa at Johannesburg.........	1895-96
9-37	J. C. Laker.............	England v Australia at Manchester...............	1956
9-51	M. Muralitharan........	Sri Lanka v Zimbabwe at Kandy...............	2001-02
9-52	R. J. Hadlee............	New Zealand v Australia at Brisbane............	1985-86
9-56	Abdul Qadir...........	Pakistan v England at Lahore...................	1987-88
9-57	D. E. Malcolm..........	England v South Africa at The Oval.............	1994
9-65	M. Muralitharan........	Sri Lanka v England at The Oval...............	1998
9-69	J. M. Patel...........	India v Australia at Kanpur....................	1959-60
9-83	Kapil Dev.............	India v West Indies at Ahmedabad..............	1983-84
9-86	Sarfraz Nawaz.........	Pakistan v Australia at Melbourne..............	1978-79
9-95	J. M. Noreiga..........	West Indies v India at Port-of-Spain...........	1970-71
9-102	S. P. Gupte............	India v West Indies at Kanpur.................	1958-59
9-103	S. F. Barnes...........	England v South Africa at Johannesburg........	1913-14
9-113	H. J. Tayfield..........	South Africa v England at Johannesburg........	1956-57
9-121	A. A. Mailey...........	Australia v England at Melbourne..............	1920-21

Note: There have been **71** instances of eight wickets in a Test innings.

The best bowling figures for the countries not mentioned above are:

8-109	P. A. Strang...........	Zimbabwe v New Zealand at Bulawayo..........	2000-01
7-36	Shakib Al Hasan.......	Bangladesh v New Zealand at Chittagong........	2008-09

OUTSTANDING BOWLING ANALYSES

	O	M	R	W		
J. C. Laker (E)	51.2	23	53	10	v Australia at Manchester.........	1956
A. Kumble (I)	26.3	9	74	10	v Pakistan at Delhi...............	1998-99
G. A. Lohmann (E)	14.2	6	28	9	v South Africa at Johannesburg....	1895-96
J. C. Laker (E)	16.4	4	37	9	v Australia at Manchester.........	1956
G. A. Lohmann (E)	9.4	5	7	8	v South Africa at Port Elizabeth	1895-96
J. Briggs (E)	14.2	5	11	8	v South Africa at Cape Town......	1888-89
S. J. Harmison (E)	12.3	8	12	7	v West Indies at Kingston........	2003-04
J. Briggs (E)	19.1	11	17	7	v South Africa at Cape Town......	1888-89
M. A. Noble (A)	7.4	2	17	7	v England at Melbourne..........	1901-02
W. Rhodes (E)	11	3	17	7	v Australia at Birmingham........	1902
J. J. C. Lawson (WI)	6.5	4	3	6	v Bangladesh at Dhaka..........	2002-03
A. E. R. Gilligan (E)	6.3	4	7	6	v South Africa at Birmingham.....	1924
D. W. Steyn (SA)	**8.1**	**6**	**8**	**6**	**v Pakistan at Johannesburg......**	**2012-13**
M. J. Clarke (A)	6.2	0	9	6	v India at Mumbai...............	2004-05
S. Haigh (E)	11.4	6	11	6	v South Africa at Cape Town......	1898-99
Shoaib Akhtar (P)	8.2	4	11	6	v New Zealand at Lahore.........	2002
D. L. Underwood (E)	11.6	7	12	6	v New Zealand at Christchurch.....	1970-71
S. L. V. Raju (I)	17.5	13	12	6	v Sri Lanka at Chandigarh........	1990-91
H. J. Tayfield (SA)	14	7	13	6	v New Zealand at Johannesburg....	1953-54
C. T. B. Turner (A)	18	11	15	6	v England at Sydney.............	1886-87
M. H. N. Walker (A)	16	8	15	6	v Pakistan at Sydney.............	1972-73
E. R. H. Toshack (A)	2.3	1	2	5	v India at Brisbane..............	1947-48

WICKET WITH FIRST BALL IN TEST CRICKET

Batsman dismissed

T. P. Horan	W. W. Read	A v E	Sydney	1882-83
A. Coningham	A. C. MacLaren	A v E	Melbourne	1894-95
W. M. Bradley	F. Laver	E v A	Manchester	1899
E. G. Arnold	V. T. Trumper	E v A	Sydney	1903-04
A. E. E. Vogler	E. G. Hayes	SA v E	Johannesburg	1905-06
J. N. Crawford	A. E. E. Vogler	E v SA	Johannesburg	1905-06
G. G. Macaulay	G. A. L. Hearne	E v SA	Cape Town	1922-23
M. W. Tate	M. J. Susskind	E v SA	Birmingham	1924
M. Henderson	E. W. Dawson	NZ v E	Christchurch	1929-30
H. D. Smith	E. Paynter	NZ v E	Christchurch	1932-33
T. F. Johnson	W. W. Keeton	WI v E	The Oval	1939
R. Howorth	D. V. Dyer	E v SA	The Oval	1947
Intikhab Alam	C. C. McDonald	P v A	Karachi	1959-60
R. K. Illingworth	P. V. Simmons	E v WI	Nottingham	1991
N. M. Kulkarni	M. S. Atapattu	I v SL	Colombo (RPS)	1997-98
M. K. G. C. P. Lakshitha	Mohammad Ashraful	SL v B	Colombo (SSC)	2002
N. M. Lyon	K. C. Sangakkara	A v SL	Galle	2011-12
R. M. S. Eranga	S. R. Watson	SL v A	Colombo (SSC)	2011-12

HAT-TRICKS

F. R. Spofforth	Australia v England at Melbourne	1878-79
W. Bates	England v Australia at Melbourne	1882-83
J. Briggs	England v Australia at Sydney	1891-92
G. A. Lohmann	England v South Africa at Port Elizabeth	1895-96
J. T. Hearne	England v Australia at Leeds	1899
H. Trumble	Australia v England at Melbourne	1901-02
H. Trumble	Australia v England at Melbourne	1903-04
T. J. Matthews† T. J. Matthews†	Australia v South Africa at Manchester	1912
M. J. C. Allom‡	England v New Zealand at Christchurch	1929-30
T. W. J. Goddard	England v South Africa at Johannesburg	1938-39
P. J. Loader	England v West Indies at Leeds	1957
L. F. Kline	Australia v South Africa at Cape Town	1957-58
W. W. Hall	West Indies v Pakistan at Lahore	1958-59
G. M. Griffin	South Africa v England at Lord's	1960
L. R. Gibbs	West Indies v Australia at Adelaide	1960-61
P. J. Petherick‡	New Zealand v Pakistan at Lahore	1976-77
C. A. Walsh§	West Indies v Australia at Brisbane	1988-89
M. G. Hughes§	Australia v West Indies at Perth	1988-89
D. W. Fleming‡	Australia v Pakistan at Rawalpindi	1994-95
S. K. Warne	Australia v England at Melbourne	1994-95
D. G. Cork	England v West Indies at Manchester	1995
D. Gough	England v Australia at Sydney	1998-99
Wasim Akram¶	Pakistan v Sri Lanka at Lahore	1998-99
Wasim Akram¶	Pakistan v Sri Lanka at Dhaka	1998-99
D. N. T. Zoysa‖	Sri Lanka v Zimbabwe at Harare	1999-2000
Abdul Razzaq	Pakistan v Sri Lanka at Galle	2000
G. D. McGrath	Australia v West Indies at Perth	2000-01
Harbhajan Singh	India v Australia at Kolkata	2000-01
Mohammad Sami	Pakistan v Sri Lanka at Lahore	2001-02
J. J. C. Lawson§	West Indies v Australia at Bridgetown	2002-03
Alok Kapali	Bangladesh v Pakistan at Peshawar	2003
A. M. Blignaut	Zimbabwe v Bangladesh at Harare	2003-04
M. J. Hoggard	England v West Indies at Bridgetown	2003-04
J. E. C. Franklin	New Zealand v Bangladesh at Dhaka	2004-05
I. K. Pathan‖	India v Pakistan at Karachi	2005-06

R. J. Sidebottom	England v New Zealand at Hamilton	2007-08
P. M. Siddle	Australia v England at Brisbane	2010-11
S. C. J. Broad	England v India at Nottingham	2011
Sohag Gazi#	**Bangladesh v New Zealand**	**2013-14**

† T. J. Matthews did the hat-trick in each innings of the same match.
‡ On Test debut.
§ Not all in the same innings.
¶ Wasim Akram did the hat-trick in successive matches.
‖ D. N. T. Zoysa did the hat-trick in the match's second over; I. K. Pathan in the match's first over.
Sohag Gazi also scored 101 not out.

FOUR WICKETS IN FIVE BALLS

M. J. C. Allom	England v New Zealand at Christchurch	1929-30
	On debut, in his eighth over: WOWWW	
C. M. Old	England v Pakistan at Birmingham	1978
	Sequence interrupted by a no-ball: WW0WW	
Wasim Akram	Pakistan v West Indies at Lahore (*WW0WW*)	1990-91

MOST WICKETS IN A TEST

19-90	J. C. Laker	England v Australia at Manchester	1956
17-159	S. F. Barnes	England v South Africa at Johannesburg	1913-14
16-136†	N. D. Hirwani	India v West Indies at Madras	1987-88
16-137†	R. A. L. Massie	Australia v England at Lord's	1972
16-220	M. Muralitharan	Sri Lanka v England at The Oval	1998
15-28	J. Briggs	England v South Africa at Cape Town	1888-89
15-45	G. A. Lohmann	England v South Africa at Port Elizabeth	1895-96
15-99	C. Blythe	England v South Africa at Leeds	1907
15-104	H. Verity	England v Australia at Lord's	1934
15-123	R. J. Hadlee	New Zealand v Australia at Brisbane	1985-86
15-124	W. Rhodes	England v Australia at Melbourne	1903-04
15-217	Harbhajan Singh	India v Australia at Chennai	2000-01

† On Test debut.

Note: There have been **ten** further instances of 14 wickets in a Test match.

The best bowling figures for the countries not mentioned above are:

14-116	Imran Khan	Pakistan v Sri Lanka at Lahore	1981-82
14-149	M. A. Holding	West Indies v England at The Oval	1976
13-132	M. Ntini	South Africa v West Indies at Port-of-Spain	2004-05
12-200	Enamul Haque, jun.	Bangladesh v Zimbabwe at Dhaka	2004-05
11-255	A. G. Huckle	Zimbabwe v New Zealand at Bulawayo	1997-98

MOST BALLS BOWLED IN A TEST

S. Ramadhin (West Indies) sent down 774 balls in 129 overs against England at Birmingham, 1957. It was the most delivered by any bowler in a Test, beating H. Verity's 766 for England against South Africa at Durban, 1938-39. In this match Ramadhin also bowled the most balls (588) in a Test or first-class innings, since equalled by Arshad Ayub, Hyderabad v Madhya Pradesh at Secunderabad, 1991-92.

MOST WICKETS IN A SERIES

	T	R	W	Avge		
S. F. Barnes	4	536	49	10.93	England v South Africa	1913-14
J. C. Laker	5	442	46	9.60	England v Australia	1956
C. V. Grimmett	5	642	44	14.59	Australia v South Africa	1935-36
T. M. Alderman	6	893	42	21.26	Australia v England	1981
R. M. Hogg	6	527	41	12.85	Australia v England	1978-79
T. M. Alderman	6	712	41	17.36	Australia v England	1989
Imran Khan	6	558	40	13.95	Pakistan v India	1982-83
S. K. Warne	5	797	40	19.92	Australia v England	2005

Notes: The most for South Africa is 37 by H. J. Tayfield against England in 1956-57, for West Indies 35 by M. D. Marshall against England in 1988, for India 35 by B. S. Chandrasekhar against England in 1972-73 (all in five Tests), for New Zealand 33 by R. J. Hadlee against Australia in 1985-86, for Sri Lanka 30 by M. Muralitharan against Zimbabwe in 2001-02, for Zimbabwe 22 by H. H. Streak against Pakistan in 1994-95 (all in three Tests), and for Bangladesh 18 by Enamul Haque, jun. against Zimbabwe in 2004-05 (two Tests).

75 WICKETS IN A CALENDAR YEAR

	T	R	W	Avge	5I	10M	Year
S. K. Warne (Australia)	15	2,114	96	22.02	6	2	2005
M. Muralitharan (Sri Lanka)	11	1,521	90	16.89	9	5	2006
D. K. Lillee (Australia)	13	1,781	85	20.95	5	2	1981
A. A. Donald (South Africa)	14	1,571	80	19.63	7	–	1998
M. Muralitharan (Sri Lanka)	12	1,699	80	21.23	7	4	2001
J. Garner (West Indies)	15	1,604	77	20.83	4	–	1984
Kapil Dev (India)	18	1,739	75	23.18	5	1	1983
M. Muralitharan (Sri Lanka)	10	1,463	75	19.50	7	3	2000

MOST WICKETS

		T	Balls	R	W	Avge	5I	10M
1	M. Muralitharan (SL/World)	133	44,039	18,180	800	22.72	67	22
2	S. K. Warne (Australia)	145	40,704	17,995	708	25.41	37	10
3	A. Kumble (India)	132	40,850	18,355	619	29.65	35	8
4	G. D. McGrath (Australia)	124	29,248	12,186	563	21.64	29	3
5	C. A. Walsh (West Indies)	132	30,019	12,688	519	24.44	22	3
6	Kapil Dev (India)	131	27,740	12,867	434	29.64	23	2
7	R. J. Hadlee (New Zealand)	86	21,918	9,611	431	22.29	36	9
8	S. M. Pollock (South Africa)	108	24,353	9,733	421	23.11	16	1
9	Wasim Akram (Pakistan)	104	22,627	9,779	414	23.62	25	5
10	**Harbhajan Singh (India)**	**101**	**28,293**	**13,372**	**413**	**32.27**	**25**	**5**
11	C. E. L. Ambrose (WI)	98	22,103	8,501	405	20.99	22	3
12	M. Ntini (South Africa)	101	20,834	11,242	390	28.82	18	4
13	I. T. Botham (England)	102	21,815	10,878	383	28.40	27	4
14	M. D. Marshall (West Indies)	81	17,584	7,876	376	20.94	22	4
15	Waqar Younis (Pakistan)	87	16,224	8,788	373	23.56	22	5
16	Imran Khan (Pakistan)	88	19,458	8,258	362	22.81	23	6
17	D. L. Vettori (NZ/World)	112	28,670	12,392	360	34.42	20	3
18	D. K. Lillee (Australia)	70	18,467	8,493	355	23.92	23	7
18	W. P. U. J. C. Vaas (SL)	111	23,438	10,501	355	29.58	12	2
20	**D. W. Steyn (South Africa)**	**69**	**14,724**	**8,016**	**350**	**22.90**	**22**	**5**
21	**J. M. Anderson (England)**	**92**	**20,350**	**10,522**	**343**	**30.67**	**15**	**2**
22	A. A. Donald (South Africa)	72	15,519	7,344	330	22.25	20	3
23	R. G. D. Willis (England)	90	17,357	8,190	325	25.20	16	–
24	B. Lee (Australia)	76	16,531	9,554	310	30.81	10	–
25	L. R. Gibbs (West Indies)	79	27,115	8,989	309	29.09	18	2

		T	Balls	R	W	Avge	5I	10M
26	F. S. Trueman (England) ...	67	15,178	6,625	307	21.57	17	3
27	**Zaheer Khan (India)**	**90**	**18,143**	**9,865**	**302**	**32.66**	**10**	**1**
28	D. L. Underwood (England)	86	21,862	7,674	297	25.83	17	6
29	**J. H. Kallis (SA/World)** ...	**166**	**20,232**	**9,535**	**292**	**32.65**	**5**	**–**
30	C. J. McDermott (Australia)	71	16,586	8,332	291	28.63	14	2
31	B. S. Bedi (India)	67	21,364	7,637	266	28.71	14	1
32	Danish Kaneria (Pakistan) ..	61	17,697	9,082	261	34.79	15	2
33 {	J. Garner (West Indies)	58	13,169	5,433	259	20.97	7	–
	J. N. Gillespie (Australia) ..	71	14,234	6,770	259	26.13	8	–
35	**G. P. Swann (England)** ...	**60**	**15,349**	**7,642**	**255**	**29.96**	**17**	**3**
36	J. B. Statham (England)	70	16,056	6,261	252	24.84	9	1

MOST WICKETS FOR EACH COUNTRY

ENGLAND

I. T. Botham 383	R. G. D. Willis 325	D. L. Underwood 297
J. M. Anderson **343**	F. S. Trueman 307	**G. P. Swann** **255**

AUSTRALIA

S. K. Warne 708	D. K. Lillee 355	C. J. McDermott 291
G. D. McGrath 563	B. Lee 310	J. N. Gillespie 259

SOUTH AFRICA

S. M. Pollock 421	**D. W. Steyn** **350**	**J. H. Kallis** **291**
M. Ntini 390	A. A. Donald 330	**M. Morkel** **183**

† *J. H. Kallis also took 0-35 and 1-3 for the World XI v Australia (2005-06 Super Series Test).*

WEST INDIES

C. A. Walsh 519	M. D. Marshall 376	J. Garner 259
C. E. L. Ambrose 405	L. R. Gibbs 309	M. A. Holding 249

NEW ZEALAND

R. J. Hadlee 431	**C. S. Martin** **233**	D. K. Morrison 160
D. L. Vettori 359	C. L. Cairns 218	B. L. Cairns 130

† *D. L. Vettori also took 1-73 and 0-38 for the World XI v Australia (2005-06 Super Series Test).*

INDIA

A. Kumble 619	**Harbhajan Singh** **413**	B. S. Bedi 266
Kapil Dev 434	**Zaheer Khan** **302**	B. S. Chandrasekhar 242

PAKISTAN

Wasim Akram 414	Imran Khan 362	Abdul Qadir 236
Waqar Younis 373	Danish Kaneria 261	Saqlain Mushtaq 208

SRI LANKA

M. Muralitharan	795	**H. M. R. K. B. Herath**	**214**	C. R. D. Fernando	100
W. P. U. J. C. Vaas	355	S. L. Malinga	101	S. T. Jayasuriya	98

† *M. Muralitharan also took 2-102 and 3-55 for the World XI v Australia (2005-06 Super Series Test).*

ZIMBABWE

H. H. Streak	216	P. A. Strang	70	B. C. Strang	56
R. W. Price	**80**	H. K. Olonga	68	A. M. Blignaut	53

BANGLADESH

Shakib Al Hasan	**113**	Mashrafe bin Mortaza	78	**Enamul Haque, jun.**	**44**
Mohammad Rafique	100	**Shahadat Hossain**	**70**	Tapash Baisya	36

BEST CAREER AVERAGES

(Qualification: 75 wickets)

Avge		T	W	Avge		T	W
10.75	G. A. Lohmann (E)	18	112	18.56	F. H. Tyson (E)	17	76
16.43	S. F. Barnes (E)	27	189	18.63	C. Blythe (E)	19	100
16.53	C. T. B. Turner (A)	17	101	20.39	J. H. Wardle (E)	28	102
16.98	R. Peel (E)	20	101	20.53	A. K. Davidson (A)	44	186
17.75	J. Briggs (E)	33	118	20.94	M. D. Marshall (WI)	81	376
18.00	**V. D. Philander (SA)**	**20**	**105**	20.97	J. Garner (WI)	58	259
18.41	F. R. Spofforth (A)	18	94	20.99	C. E. L. Ambrose (WI)	98	405

BEST CAREER STRIKE-RATES

(Balls per wicket. Qualification: 75 wickets)

SR		T	W	SR		T	W
34.19	G. A. Lohmann (E)	18	112	45.46	C. Blythe (E)	19	100
38.75	S. E. Bond (NZ)	18	87	45.74	Shoaib Akhtar (P)	46	178
39.62	**V. D. Philander (SA)**	**20**	**105**	**46.05**	**R. J. Harris (A)**	**21**	**93**
41.65	S. F. Barnes (E)	27	189	46.76	M. D. Marshall (WI)	81	376
42.06	**D. W. Steyn (SA)**	**69**	**350**	47.02	A. A. Donald (SA)	72	330
43.49	Waqar Younis (P)	87	373	**48.31**	**S. T. Finn (E)**	**23**	**90**
44.52	F. R. Spofforth (A)	18	94	48.78	Mohammad Asif (P)	23	106
45.12	J. V. Saunders (A)	14	79	49.32	C. E. H. Croft (WI)	27	125
45.18	J. Briggs (E)	33	118	49.43	F. S. Trueman (E)	67	307
45.42	F. H. Tyson (E)	17	76				

An expanded and regularly updated online version of the Records can be found at
www.wisdenrecords.com

BEST CAREER ECONOMY-RATES

(Runs per six balls. Qualification: 75 wickets)

ER		T	W	ER		T	W
1.64	T. L. Goddard (SA)	41	123	1.94	H. J. Tayfield (SA)	37	170
1.67	R. G. Nadkarni (I)	41	88	1.95	A. L. Valentine (WI)	36	139
1.88	H. Verity (E)	40	144	1.95	F. J. Titmus (E)	53	153
1.88	G. A. Lohmann (E)	18	112	1.97	S. Ramadhin (WI)	43	158
1.89	J. H. Wardle (E)	28	102	1.97	R. Peel (E)	20	101
1.91	R. Illingworth (E)	61	122	1.97	A. K. Davidson (A)	44	186
1.93	C. T. B. Turner (A)	17	101	1.98	L. R. Gibbs (WI)	79	309
1.94	M. W. Tate (E)	39	155				
1.94	W. J. O'Reilly (A)	27	144				

HIGHEST PERCENTAGE OF TEAM'S WICKETS OVER TEST CAREER

(Qualification: 20 Tests)

	Tests	Wkts	Team Wkts	% of Team Wkts
M. Muralitharan (Sri Lanka/World)............	133	800	2,070	38.64
S. F. Barnes (England).....................	27	189	494	38.25
R. J. Hadlee (New Zealand).................	86	431	1,255	34.34
C. V. Grimmett (Australia)	37	216	636	33.96
Fazal Mahmood (Pakistan)	34	139	410	33.90
W. J. O'Reilly (Australia)	27	144	446	32.28
S. P. Gupte (India)........................	36	149	470	31.70
Saeed Ajmal (Pakistan)	**33**	**169**	**543**	**31.12**
Mohammad Rafique (Bangladesh)............	33	100	328	30.48
A. V. Bedser (England)	51	236	777	30.37

Note: Excluding the Super Series Test, Muralitharan took 795 out of 2,050 wickets in his 132 Tests for Sri Lanka, a percentage of 38.78.

The percentage shows the proportion of a team's wickets taken by that player in all Tests in which he played, including team wickets in innings in which he did not bowl.

ALL-ROUND RECORDS

HUNDRED AND FIVE WICKETS IN AN INNINGS

England

A. W. Greig	148	6-164	v West Indies	Bridgetown	1973-74
I. T. Botham	103	5-73	v New Zealand	Christchurch	1977-78
I. T. Botham	108	8-34	v Pakistan........	Lord's	1978
I. T. Botham	114	6-58, 7-48	v India	Bombay........	1979-80
I. T. Botham	149*	6-95	v Australia	Leeds..........	1981
I. T. Botham	138	5-59	v New Zealand....	Wellington	1983-84

Australia

C. Kelleway	114	5-33	v South Africa	Manchester	1912
J. M. Gregory	100	7-69	v England........	Melbourne.....	1920-21
K. R. Miller	109	6-107	v West Indies	Kingston	1954-55
R. Benaud	100	5-84	v South Africa	Johannesburg ...	1957-58

South Africa					
J. H. Sinclair	106	6-26	v England........	Cape Town.....	1898-99
G. A. Faulkner	123	5-120	v England........	Johannesburg...	1909-10
J. H. Kallis	110	5-90	v West Indies.....	Cape Town.....	1998-99
J. H. Kallis	139*	5-21	v Bangladesh.....	Potchefstroom...	2002-03
West Indies					
D. St E. Atkinson	219	5-56	v Australia.......	Bridgetown.....	1954-55
O. G. Smith	100	5-90	v India..........	Delhi..........	1958-59
G. S. Sobers	104	5-63	v India..........	Kingston.......	1961-62
G. S. Sobers	174	5-41	v England........	Leeds..........	1966
New Zealand					
B. R. Taylor†	105	5-86	v India..........	Calcutta........	1964-65
India					
V. Mankad	184	5-196	v England........	Lord's.........	1952
P. R. Umrigar	172*	5-107	v West Indies.....	Port-of-Spain....	1961-62
R. Ashwin	103	5-156	v West Indies.....	Mumbai........	2011-12
Pakistan					
Mushtaq Mohammad	201	5-49	v New Zealand....	Dunedin........	1972-73
Mushtaq Mohammad	121	5-28	v West Indies.....	Port-of-Spain....	1976-77
Imran Khan	117	6-98, 5-82	v India..........	Faisalabad......	1982-83
Wasim Akram	123	5-100	v Australia.......	Adelaide.......	1989-90
Zimbabwe					
P. A. Strang	106*	5-212	v Pakistan........	Sheikhupura....	1996-97
Bangladesh					
Shakib Al Hasan	144	6-82	v Pakistan........	Mirpur........	2011-12
Sohag Gazi	**101***	**6-77‡**	**v New Zealand ...**	**Chittagong.....**	**2013-14**

† *On debut.*   ‡ *Including a hat-trick; Sohag Gazi is the only player to score a hundred and take a hat-trick in the same Test.*

HUNDRED AND FIVE DISMISSALS IN AN INNINGS

D. T. Lindsay	182	6ct	SA v A.............	Johannesburg........	1966-67
I. D. S. Smith	113*	4ct, 1st	NZ v E.............	Auckland...........	1983-84
S. A. R. Silva	111	5ct	SL v I.............	Colombo (PSS)......	1985-86
A. C. Gilchrist	133	4ct, 1st	A v E.............	Sydney.............	2002-03
M. J. Prior	118	5ct	E v A.............	Sydney.............	2010-11
A. B. de Villiers	**103***	**6ct and 5ct**	**SA v P ....**	**Johannesburg........**	**2012-13**
M. J. Prior	**110***	**5 ct**	**E v NZ............**	**Auckland ....**	**2012-13**

100 RUNS AND TEN WICKETS IN A TEST

A. K. Davidson	44 80	5-135 6-87 }	A v WI.............	Brisbane..........	1960-61
I. T. Botham	114	6-58 7-48 }	E v I.............	Bombay..........	1979-80
Imran Khan	117	6-98 5-82 }	P v I.............	Faisalabad.........	1982-83

Note: Wicketkeeper A. B. de Villiers scored 103* and held 11 catches for South Africa against Pakistan at Johannesburg in 2012-13.

2,000 RUNS AND 200 WICKETS

	Tests	Runs	Wkts	Tests for 1,000/100 Double
R. Benaud (Australia)	63	2,201	248	32
†I. T. Botham (England)	102	5,200	383	21
S. C. J. Broad (England)	**67**	**2,010**	**238**	**35**
C. L. Cairns (New Zealand)	62	3,320	218	33
A. Flintoff (England/World)	79	3,845	226	43
R. J. Hadlee (New Zealand)	86	3,124	431	28
Harbhajan Singh (India)	**101**	**2,202**	**413**	**93**
Imran Khan (Pakistan)	88	3,807	362	30
†**J. H. Kallis (South Africa/World)**	**166**	**13,289**	**292**	**53**
Kapil Dev (India)	131	5,248	434	25
A. Kumble (India)	132	2,506	619	56
S. M. Pollock (South Africa)	108	3,781	421	26
†G. S. Sobers (West Indies)	93	8,032	235	48
W. P. U. J. C. Vaas (Sri Lanka)	111	3,089	355	47
D. L. Vettori (New Zealand/World)	112	4,516	360	47
†S. K. Warne (Australia)	145	3,154	708	58
Wasim Akram (Pakistan)	104	2,898	414	45

Note: H. H. Streak scored 1,990 runs and took 216 wickets in 65 Tests for Zimbabwe.

† *J. H. Kallis has also taken 200 catches, S. K. Warne 125, I. T. Botham 120 and G. S. Sobers 109. These four and C. L. Hooper (5,762 runs, 114 wickets and 115 catches for West Indies) are the only players to have achieved the treble of 1,000 runs, 100 wickets and 100 catches in Test cricket.*

WICKETKEEPING RECORDS

MOST DISMISSALS IN AN INNINGS

7 (all ct)	Wasim Bari	Pakistan v New Zealand at Auckland	1978-79
7 (all ct)	R. W. Taylor	England v India at Bombay	1979-80
7 (all ct)	I. D. S. Smith	New Zealand v Sri Lanka at Hamilton	1990-91
7 (all ct)	R. D. Jacobs	West Indies v Australia at Melbourne	2000-01

Notes: The first instance of seven wicketkeeping dismissals in a Test innings was a joint effort for Pakistan v West Indies at Kingston in 1976-77. Majid Khan made four catches, deputising for the injured wicketkeeper Wasim Bari, who made three more catches on his return.

There have been **24** instances of players making six dismissals in a Test innings, the most recent being **A. B. de Villiers (all ct) for South Africa v Pakistan at Johannesburg, 2012-13.**

MOST STUMPINGS IN AN INNINGS

5	K. S. More	India v West Indies at Madras	1987-88

An expanded and regularly updated online version of the Records can be found at www.wisdenrecords.com

MOST DISMISSALS IN A TEST

11 (all ct)	R. C. Russell	England v South Africa at Johannesburg ...	1995-96
11 (all ct)	**A. B. de Villiers**	**South Africa v Pakistan at Johannesburg**.	**2012-13**
10 (all ct)	R. W. Taylor	England v India at Bombay	1979-80
10 (all ct)	A. C. Gilchrist	Australia v New Zealand at Hamilton	1999-2000
9 (8ct, 1st)	G. R. A. Langley	Australia v England at Lord's	1956
9 (all ct)	D. A. Murray	West Indies v Australia at Melbourne	1981-82
9 (all ct)	R. W. Marsh	Australia v England at Brisbane	1982-83
9 (all ct)	S. A. R. Silva	Sri Lanka v India at Colombo (SSC)	1985-86
9 (8ct, 1st)	S. A. R. Silva	Sri Lanka v India at Colombo (PSS)	1985-86
9 (all ct)	D. J. Richardson	South Africa v India at Port Elizabeth	1992-93
9 (all ct)	Rashid Latif	Pakistan v New Zealand at Auckland	1993-94
9 (all ct)	I. A. Healy	Australia v England at Brisbane	1994-95
9 (all ct)	C. O. Browne	West Indies v England at Nottingham	1995
9 (7ct, 2st)	R. C. Russell	England v South Africa at Port Elizabeth	1995-96
9 (8ct, 1st)	M. V. Boucher	South Africa v Pakistan at Port Elizabeth ...	1997-98
9 (8ct, 1st)	R. D. Jacobs	West Indies v Australia at Melbourne	2000-01
9 (all ct)	Kamran Akmal	Pakistan v West Indies at Kingston	2004-05
9 (all ct)	G. O. Jones	England v Bangladesh at Chester-le-Street. .	2005
9 (8ct, 1st)	A. C. Gilchrist	Australia v England at Sydney	2006-07
9 (8ct, 1st)	B. B. McCullum	New Zealand v Pakistan at Napier	2009-10
9 (all ct)	B. J. Haddin	Australia v Pakistan at Sydney	2009-10
9 (all ct)	M. V. Boucher	South Africa v India at Durban	2010-11
9 (all ct)	**H. A. P. W. Jayawardene**	**Sri Lanka v Pakistan at Dubai**	**2013-14**

Notes: S. A. R. Silva made 18 dismissals in two successive Tests.

The most stumpings in a match is 6 by K. S. More for India v West Indies at Madras in 1987-88.

J. J. Kelly (8ct) for Australia v England in 1901-02 and L. E. G. Ames (6ct, 2st) for England v West Indies in 1933 were the only keepers to make eight dismissals in a Test before World War II.

MOST DISMISSALS IN A SERIES

(Played in 5 Tests unless otherwise stated)

29 (all ct)	**B. J. Haddin**	**Australia v England**	**2013**
28 (all ct)	R. W. Marsh	Australia v England	1982-83
27 (25ct, 2st)	R. C. Russell	England v South Africa	1995-96
27 (25ct, 2st)	I. A. Healy	Australia v England (6 Tests)	1997
26 (23ct, 3st)	J. H. B. Waite	South Africa v New Zealand	1961-62
26 (all ct)	R. W. Marsh	Australia v West Indies (6 Tests)	1975-76
26 (21ct, 5st)	I. A. Healy	Australia v England (6 Tests)	1993
26 (25ct, 1st)	M. V. Boucher	South Africa v England	1998
26 (24ct, 2st)	A. C. Gilchrist	Australia v England	2001
26 (24ct, 2st)	A. C. Gilchrist	Australia v England	2006-07
25 (23ct, 2st)	I. A. Healy	Australia v England	1994-95
25 (23ct, 2st)	A. C. Gilchrist	Australia v England	2002-03
25 (all ct)	A. C. Gilchrist	Australia v India	2007-08

Notes: S. A. R. Silva made 22 dismissals (21ct, 1st) in three Tests for Sri Lanka v India in 1985-86.

H. Strudwick, with 21 (15ct, 6st) for England v South Africa in 1913-14, was the only wicketkeeper to make as many as 20 dismissals in a series before World War II.

200 DISMISSALS

			T	Ct	St
1	M. V. Boucher (South Africa/World)	555	147	532	23
2	A. C. Gilchrist (Australia)	416	96	379	37
3	I. A. Healy (Australia)	395	119	366	29
4	R. W. Marsh (Australia)	355	96	343	12
5	P. J. L. Dujon (West Indies)	270	79	265	5
6	A. P. E. Knott (England)	269	95	250	19
7	**M. S. Dhoni (India)**	**256**	**81**	**219**	**37**
8	A. J. Stewart (England)	241	82	227	14
9	**M. J. Prior (England)**	**230**	**75**	**217**	**13**
10	Wasim Bari (Pakistan)	228	81	201	27
11	**B. J. Haddin (Australia)**	**220**	**54**	**215**	**5**
12	R. D. Jacobs (West Indies)	219	65	207	12
	T. G. Evans (England)	219	91	173	46
14	Kamran Akmal (Pakistan)	206	53	184	22
15	A. C. Parore (New Zealand)	201	67	194	7

Notes: The record for P. J. L. Dujon excludes two catches taken in two Tests when not keeping wicket; A. J. Stewart's record likewise excludes 36 catches taken in 51 Tests and A. C. Parore's three in 11 Tests.

Excluding the Super Series Test, M. V. Boucher made 553 dismissals (530ct, 23st in 146 Tests) for South Africa, a national record.

W. A. Oldfield made 52 stumpings, a Test record, in 54 Tests for Australia; he also took 78 catches.

The most dismissals by a wicketkeeper playing for the countries not mentioned above are:

		T	Ct	St
K. C. Sangakkara (Sri Lanka)	151	48	131	20
A. Flower (Zimbabwe)	151	55	142	9
Khaled Mashud (Bangladesh)	87	44	78	9

Note: K. C. Sangakkara's record excludes 40 catches taken in 72 matches when not keeping wicket but includes two catches taken as wicketkeeper in a match where he took over when the designated keeper was injured; A. Flower's record excludes nine catches in eight Tests when not keeping wicket.

FIELDING RECORDS

(Excluding wicketkeepers)

MOST CATCHES IN AN INNINGS

5	V. Y. Richardson	Australia v South Africa at Durban	1935-36
5	Yajurvindra Singh	India v England at Bangalore	1976-77
5	M. Azharuddin	India v Pakistan at Karachi	1989-90
5	K. Srikkanth	India v Australia at Perth	1991-92
5	S. P. Fleming	New Zealand v Zimbabwe at Harare	1997-98
5	G. C. Smith	South Africa v Australia at Perth	2012-13
5	**D. J. G. Sammy**	**West Indies v India at Mumbai**	**2013-14**

MOST CATCHES IN A TEST

7	G. S. Chappell	Australia v England at Perth	1974-75
7	Yajurvindra Singh	India v England at Bangalore	1976-77
7	H. P. Tillekeratne	Sri Lanka v New Zealand at Colombo (SSC)	1992-93
7	S. P. Fleming	New Zealand v Zimbabwe at Harare	1997-98
7	M. L. Hayden	Australia v Sri Lanka at Galle	2003-04

Note: There have been **27** instances of players taking six catches in a Test, the most recent being G. C. Smith for South Africa v Australia at Perth, 2012-13.

MOST CATCHES IN A SERIES

(Played in 5 Tests unless otherwise stated)

15	J. M. Gregory	Australia v England		1920-21
14	G. S. Chappell	Australia v England (6 Tests)		1974-75
13	R. B. Simpson	Australia v South Africa		1957-58
13	R. B. Simpson	Australia v West Indies		1960-61
13	B. C. Lara	West Indies v England (6 Tests)		1997-98
13	R. Dravid	India v Australia (4 Tests)		2004-05
13	B. C. Lara	West Indies v India (4 Tests)		2005-06

100 CATCHES

Ct	T		Ct	T	
210	164†	R. Dravid (India/World)	120	102	I. T. Botham (England)
200	**166†**	**J. H. Kallis (SA/World)**	120	114	M. C. Cowdrey (England)
196	168	R. T. Ponting (Australia)	**119**	**102**	**M. J. Clarke (Australia)**
194	**141**	**D. P. M. D. Jayawardene (SL)**	115	102	C. L. Hooper (West Indies)
181	128	M. E. Waugh (Australia)	**115**	**200**	**S. R. Tendulkar (India)**
171	111	S. P. Fleming (New Zealand)	112	168	S. R. Waugh (Australia)
164	**114†**	**G. C. Smith (SA/World)**	110	62	R. B. Simpson (Australia)
164	131†	B. C. Lara (West Indies/World)	110	85	W. R. Hammond (England)
157	104	M. A. Taylor (Australia)	109	93	G. S. Sobers (West Indies)
156	156	A. R. Border (Australia)	108	125	S. M. Gavaskar (India)
135	134	V. V. S. Laxman (India)	105	75	I. M. Chappell (Australia)
128	103	M. L. Hayden (Australia)	105	99	M. Azharuddin (India)
125	145	S. K. Warne (Australia)	105	100	G. P. Thorpe (England)
122	87	G. S. Chappell (Australia)	103	118	G. A. Gooch (England)
122	121	I. V. A. Richards (West Indies)			
121	100	A. J. Strauss (England)			

† *Excluding the Super Series Test, Dravid has made 209 catches in 163 Tests for India, Kallis 196 in 165 Tests for South Africa, and Lara 164 in 130 Tests for West Indies, all national records. G. C. Smith has made 161 catches in 113 Tests for South Africa.*

Note: The most catches in the field for other countries are Pakistan **98** in 89 Tests (**Younis Khan**); Zimbabwe 60 in 60 Tests (A. D. R. Campbell); Bangladesh **25** in 61 Tests (**Mohammad Ashraful**).

TEAM RECORDS

HIGHEST INNINGS TOTALS

952-6 dec	Sri Lanka v India at Colombo (RPS)	1997-98
903-7 dec	England v Australia at The Oval	1938
849	England v West Indies at Kingston	1929-30
790-3 dec	West Indies v Pakistan at Kingston	1957-58
765-6 dec	Pakistan v Sri Lanka at Karachi	2008-09
760-7 dec	Sri Lanka v India at Ahmedabad	2009-10
758-8 dec	Australia v West Indies at Kingston	1954-55
756-5 dec	Sri Lanka v South Africa at Colombo (SSC)	2006
751-5 dec	West Indies v England at St John's	2003-04
749-9 dec	West Indies v England at Bridgetown	2008-09
747	West Indies v South Africa at St John's	2004-05
735-6 dec	Australia v Zimbabwe at Perth	2003-04
729-6 dec	Australia v England at Lord's	1930
726-9 dec	India v Sri Lanka at Mumbai (BS)	2009-10
713-3 dec	Sri Lanka v Zimbabwe at Bulawayo	2003-04
710-7 dec	England v India at Birmingham	2011

708	Pakistan v England at The Oval	1987
707	India v Sri Lanka at Colombo (SSC)	2010
705-7 dec	India v Australia at Sydney	2003-04
701	Australia v England at The Oval	1934

The highest innings for the countries not mentioned above are:

682-6 dec	South Africa v England at Lord's	2003
671-4	New Zealand v Sri Lanka at Wellington	1990-91
638	**Bangladesh v Sri Lanka at Galle**	**2012-13**
563-9 dec	Zimbabwe v West Indies at Harare	2001

HIGHEST FOURTH-INNINGS TOTALS

To win

418-7	West Indies (needing 418) v Australia at St John's	2002-03
414-4	South Africa (needing 414) v Australia at Perth	2008-09
406-4	India (needing 403) v West Indies at Port-of-Spain	1975-76
404-3	Australia (needing 404) v England at Leeds	1948
387-4	India (needing 387) v England at Chennai	2008-09
369-6	Australia (needing 369) v Pakistan at Hobart	1999-2000
362-7	Australia (needing 359) v West Indies at Georgetown	1977-78
352-9	Sri Lanka (needing 352) v South Africa at Colombo (PSS)	2006
348-5	West Indies (needing 345) v New Zealand at Auckland	1968-69
344-1	West Indies (needing 342) v England at Lord's	1984

To tie

| 347 | India v Australia at Madras | 1986-87 |

To draw

654-5	England (needing 696 to win) v South Africa at Durban	1938-39
450-7	**South Africa (needing 458 to win) v India at Johannesburg**	**2013-14**
429-8	India (needing 438 to win) v England at The Oval	1979
423-7	South Africa (needing 451 to win) v England at The Oval	1947
408-5	West Indies (needing 836 to win) v England at Kingston	1929-30

To lose

451	New Zealand (lost by 98 runs) v England at Christchurch	2001-02
445	India (lost by 47 runs) v Australia at Adelaide	1977-78
440	New Zealand (lost by 38 runs) v England at Nottingham	1973
431	New Zealand (lost by 121 runs) v England at Napier	2007-08
417	England (lost by 45 runs) v Australia at Melbourne	1976-77
413	Bangladesh (lost by 107 runs) v Sri Lanka at Mirpur	2008-09
411	England (lost by 193 runs) v Australia at Sydney	1924-25
410	Sri Lanka (lost by 96 runs) v Australia at Hobart	2007-08
406	Australia (lost by 115 runs) v England at Lord's	2009
402	Australia (lost by 103 runs) v England at Manchester	1981

MOST RUNS IN A DAY (BOTH SIDES)

588	England (398-6), India (190-0) at Manchester (2nd day)	1936
522	England (503-2), South Africa (19-0) at Lord's (2nd day)	1924
509	Sri Lanka (509-9) v Bangladesh at Colombo (PSS) (2nd day)	2002
508	England (221-2), South Africa (287-6) at The Oval (3rd day)	1935

MOST RUNS IN A DAY (ONE SIDE)

509	Sri Lanka (509-9) v Bangladesh at Colombo (PSS) (2nd day)	2002
503	England (503-2) v South Africa at Lord's (2nd day)	1924
494	Australia (494-6) v South Africa at Sydney (1st day)	1910-11
482	Australia (482-5) v South Africa at Adelaide (1st day)	2012-13
475	Australia (475-2) v England at The Oval (1st day)	1934
471	England (471-8) v India at The Oval (1st day)	1936
458	Australia (458-3) v England at Leeds (1st day)	1930
455	Australia (455-1) v England at Leeds (2nd day)	1934
452	New Zealand (452-9 dec) v Zimbabwe at Harare (1st day)	2005-06
450	Australia (450) v South Africa at Johannesburg (1st day)	1921-22

MOST WICKETS IN A DAY

27	England (18-3 to 53 all out and 62) v Australia (60) at Lord's (2nd day).	1888
25	Australia (112 and 48-5) v England (61) at Melbourne (1st day)	1901-02

HIGHEST AGGREGATES IN A TEST

Runs	Wkts			Days played
1,981	35	South Africa v England at Durban	1938-39	10†
1,815	34	West Indies v England at Kingston.	1929-30	9‡
1,764	39	Australia v West Indies at Adelaide	1968-69	5
1,753	40	Australia v England at Adelaide	1920-21	6
1,747	25	Australia v India at Sydney.	2003-04	5
1,723	31	England v Australia at Leeds	1948	5
1,702	28	Pakistan v India at Faisalabad.	2005-06	5

† *No play on one day.*   ‡ *No play on two days.*

LOWEST INNINGS TOTALS

26	New Zealand v England at Auckland	1954-55
30	South Africa v England at Port Elizabeth	1895-96
30	South Africa v England at Birmingham	1924
35	South Africa v England at Cape Town	1898-99
36	Australia v England at Birmingham	1902
36	South Africa v Australia at Melbourne	1931-32
42	Australia v England at Sydney	1887-88
42	New Zealand v Australia at Wellington	1945-46
42†	India v England at Lord's	1974
43	South Africa v England at Cape Town	1888-89
44	Australia v England at The Oval	1896
45	England v Australia at Sydney	1886-87
45	South Africa v Australia at Melbourne	1931-32
45	**New Zealand v South Africa at Cape Town**	**2012-13**
46	England v West Indies at Port-of-Spain	1993-94
47	South Africa v England at Cape Town	1888-89
47	New Zealand v England at Lord's.	1958
47	West Indies v England at Kingston	2003-04
47	Australia v South Africa at Cape Town.	2011-12
49	**Pakistan v South Africa at Johannesburg**.	**2012-13**

The lowest innings for the countries not mentioned above are:

51	Zimbabwe v New Zealand at Napier.	2011-12
62	Bangladesh v Sri Lanka at Colombo (PSS).	2007
71	Sri Lanka v Pakistan at Kandy	1994-95

FEWEST RUNS IN A FULL DAY'S PLAY

95	Australia (80), Pakistan (15-2) at Karachi (1st day, $5^{1}/_{2}$ hrs)	1956-57
104	Pakistan (0-0 to 104-5) v Australia at Karachi (4th day, $5^{1}/_{2}$ hrs).............	1959-60
106	England (92-2 to 198) v Australia at Brisbane (4th day, 5 hrs)...........	1958-59
	England were dismissed five minutes before the close of play, leaving no time for Australia to start their second innings.	
111	S. Africa (48-2 to 130-6 dec), India (29-1) at Cape Town (5th day, $5^{1}/_{2}$ hrs) ...	1992-93
112	Australia (138-6 to 187), Pakistan (63-1) at Karachi (4th day, $5^{1}/_{2}$ hrs) ...	1956-57
115	Australia (116-7 to 165 and 66-5 after following on) v Pakistan at Karachi (4th day, $5^{1}/_{2}$ hrs)	1988-89
117	India (117-5) v Australia at Madras (1st day, $5^{1}/_{2}$ hrs)	1956-57
117	New Zealand (6-0 to 123-4) v Sri Lanka at Colombo (SSC) (5th day, $5^{3}/_{4}$ hrs).	1983-84

In England

151	England (175-2 to 289), New Zealand (37-7) at Lord's (3rd day, 6 hrs)	1978
158	England (211-2 to 369-9) v South Africa at Manchester (5th day, 6 hrs)......	1998
159	Pakistan (208-4 to 350), England (17-1) at Leeds (3rd day, 6 hrs)...........	1971

LOWEST AGGREGATES IN A COMPLETED TEST

Runs	Wkts			Days played
234	29	Australia v South Africa at Melbourne	1931-32	3†
291	40	England v Australia at Lord's	1888	2
295	28	New Zealand v Australia at Wellington	1945-46	2
309	29	West Indies v England at Bridgetown.............	1934-35	3
323	30	England v Australia at Manchester	1888	2

† *No play on one day.*

LARGEST VICTORIES

Largest Innings Victories

Inns & 579 runs	England (903-7 dec) v Australia (201 & 123†) at The Oval	1938
Inns & 360 runs	Australia (652-7 dec) v South Africa (159 & 133) at Johannesburg ..	2001-02
Inns & 336 runs	West Indies (614-5 dec) v India (124 & 154) at Calcutta..........	1958-59
Inns & 332 runs	Australia (645) v England (141 & 172) at Brisbane...............	1946-47
Inns & 324 runs	Pakistan (643) v New Zealand (73 & 246) at Lahore..............	2002
Inns & 322 runs	West Indies (660-5 dec) v New Zealand (216 & 122) at Wellington..	1994-95
Inns & 310 runs	West Indies (536) v Bangladesh (139 & 87) at Dhaka.............	2002-03
Inns & 301 runs	New Zealand (495-7 dec) v Zimbabwe (51 & 143) at Napier	2011-12

† *Two men absent in both Australian innings.*

Largest Victories by Runs Margin

675 runs	England (521 & 342-8 dec) v Australia (122 & 66†) at Brisbane...........	1928-29
562 runs	Australia (701 & 327) v England (321 & 145‡) at The Oval	1934
530 runs	Australia (328 & 578) v South Africa (205 & 171§) at Melbourne	1910-11
491 runs	Australia (381 & 361-5 dec) v Pakistan (179 & 72) at Perth..............	2004-05
465 runs	Sri Lanka (384 and 447-6 dec) v Bangladesh (208 and 158) at Chittagong ...	2008-09
425 runs	West Indies (211 & 411-5 dec) v England (71 & 126) at Manchester	1976
409 runs	Australia (350 & 460-7 dec) v England (215 & 186) at Lord's.............	1948
408 runs	West Indies (328 & 448) v Australia (203 & 165) at Adelaide.............	1979-80

† *One man absent in Australia's first innings; two men absent in their second.*
‡ *Two men absent in England's first innings; one man absent in their second.*
§ *One man absent in South Africa's second innings.*

TIED TESTS

West Indies (453 & 284) v Australia (505 & 232) at Brisbane 1960-61
Australia (574-7 dec & 170-5 dec) v India (397 & 347) at Madras. 1986-87

MOST CONSECUTIVE TEST VICTORIES

16	Australia	1999-2000–2000-01		9	South Africa	2001-02–2003
16	Australia	2005-06–2007-08		8	Australia	1920-21–1921
11	West Indies	1983-84–1984-85		8	England.	2004–2004-05
9	Sri Lanka.	2001–2001-02				

MOST CONSECUTIVE TESTS WITHOUT VICTORY

44	New Zealand	1929-30–1955-56		23	New Zealand	1962-63–1967-68
34	Bangladesh.	2000-01–2004-05		22	Pakistan	1958-59–1964-65
31	India	1981-82–1984-85		21	Sri Lanka	1985-86–1992-93
28	South Africa	1935–1949-50		20	West Indies.	1968-69–1972-73
24	India	1932–1951-52		20	West Indies.	2004-05–2007
24	Bangladesh.	2004-05–2008-09				

WHITEWASHES

Teams winning every game in a series of four Tests or more:

Five-Test Series

Australia beat England	1920-21	West Indies beat England	1985-86
Australia beat South Africa.	1931-32	South Africa beat West Indies	1998-99
England beat India	1959	Australia beat West Indies	2000-01
West Indies beat India.	1961-62	Australia beat England	2006-07
West Indies beat England	1984	**Australia beat England**.	**2013-14**

Four-Test Series

Australia beat India.	1967-68	England beat India	2011
South Africa beat Australia.	1969-70	Australia beat India.	2011-12
England beat West Indies	2004	**India beat Australia**	**2012-13**

Note: The winning team in each instance was at home, except for West Indies in England, 1984.

PLAYERS

YOUNGEST TEST PLAYERS

Years	Days			
15	124	Mushtaq Mohammad	Pakistan v West Indies at Lahore	1958-59
16	189	Aqib Javed	Pakistan v New Zealand at Wellington.	1988-89
16	205	S. R. Tendulkar.	India v Pakistan at Karachi	1989-90

The above table should be treated with caution. All birthdates for Bangladesh and Pakistan (after Partition) must be regarded as questionable because of deficiencies in record-keeping. Hasan Raza was claimed to be 14 years 227 days old when he played for Pakistan against Zimbabwe at Faisalabad in 1996-97; this age was rejected by the Pakistan Cricket Board, although no alternative has been offered. Suggestions that Enamul Haque jun. was 16 years 230 days old when he played for Bangladesh against England in Dhaka in 2003-04 have been discounted by well-informed local observers, who believe he was 18.

The youngest Test players for countries not mentioned above are:

17	122	J. E. D. Sealy.	West Indies v England at Bridgetown	1929-30
17	128	Mohammad Sharif	Bangladesh v Zimbabwe at Bulawayo	2000-01
17	189	C. D. U. S. Weerasinghe .	Sri Lanka v India at Colombo (PSS).	1985-86
17	239	I. D. Craig.	Australia v South Africa at Melbourne.	1952-53
17	352	H. Masakadza	Zimbabwe v West Indies at Harare.	2001
18	10	D. L. Vettori	New Zealand v England at Wellington.	1996-97
18	149	D. B. Close	England v New Zealand at Manchester	1949
18	340	P. R. Adams	South Africa v England at Port Elizabeth.	1995-96

OLDEST PLAYERS ON TEST DEBUT

Years	Days			
49	119	J. Southerton.	England v Australia at Melbourne	1876-77
47	284	Miran Bux.	Pakistan v India at Lahore	1954-55
46	253	D. D. Blackie	Australia v England at Sydney	1928-29
46	237	H. Ironmonger.	Australia v England at Brisbane.	1928-29
42	242	N. Betancourt	West Indies v England at Port-of-Spain .	1929-30
41	337	E. R. Wilson	England v Australia at Sydney	1920-21
41	27	R. J. D. Jamshedji	India v England at Bombay	1933-34
40	345	C. A. Wiles	West Indies v England at Manchester.	1933
40	295	O. Henry	South Africa v India at Durban.	1992-93
40	216	S. P. Kinneir	England v Australia at Sydney	1911-12
40	110	H. W. Lee	England v South Africa at Johannesburg	1930-31
40	56	G. W. A. Chubb	South Africa v England at Nottingham.	1951
40	37	C. Ramaswami	India v England at Manchester	1936

Note: The oldest Test player on debut for New Zealand was H. M. McGirr, 38 years 101 days, v England at Auckland, 1929-30; for Sri Lanka, D. S. de Silva, 39 years 251 days, v England at Colombo (PSS), 1981-82; for Zimbabwe, A. C. Waller, 37 years 84 days, v England at Bulawayo, 1996-97; for Bangladesh, Enamul Haque, sen. 35 years 58 days, v Zimbabwe at Harare, 2000-01. A. J. Traicos was 45 years 154 days old when he made his debut for Zimbabwe (v India at Harare, 1992-93) having played three Tests for South Africa in 1969-70.

OLDEST TEST PLAYERS

(Age on final day of their last Test match)

Years	Days			
52	165	W. Rhodes	England v West Indies at Kingston.	1929-30
50	327	H. Ironmonger.	Australia v England at Sydney	1932-33
50	320	W. G. Grace	England v Australia at Nottingham.	1899
50	303	G. Gunn	England v West Indies at Kingston.	1929-30
49	139	J. Southerton.	England v Australia at Melbourne	1876-77
47	302	Miran Bux.	Pakistan v India at Peshawar	1954-55
47	249	J. B. Hobbs.	England v Australia at The Oval.	1930
47	87	F. E. Woolley	England v Australia at The Oval.	1934
46	309	D. D. Blackie	Australia v England at Adelaide.	1928-29
46	206	A. W. Nourse.	South Africa v England at The Oval.	1924
46	202	H. Strudwick.	England v Australia at The Oval.	1926

Years	Days			
46	41	E. H. Hendren	England v West Indies at Kingston	1934-35
45	304	A. J. Traicos	Zimbabwe v India at Delhi	1992-93
45	245	G. O. B. Allen	England v West Indies at Kingston	1947-48
45	215	P. Holmes	England v India at Lord's	1932
45	140	D. B. Close	England v West Indies at Manchester	1976

MOST TEST APPEARANCES

200	**S. R. Tendulkar (India)**		133	A. J. Stewart (England)
168	R. T. Ponting (Australia)		132	A. Kumble (India)
168	S. R. Waugh (Australia)		132	C. A. Walsh (West Indies)
166	**J. H. Kallis (South Africa/World)**		131	Kapil Dev (India)
164	R. Dravid (India/World)		131	B. C. Lara (West Indies/World)
156	A. R. Border (Australia)		128	M. E. Waugh (Australia)
153	**S. Chanderpaul (West Indies)**		125	S. M. Gavaskar (India)
147	M. V. Boucher (South Africa/World)		124	Javed Miandad (Pakistan)
145	S. K. Warne (Australia)		124	G. D. McGrath (Australia)
141	**D. P. M. D. Jayawardene (Sri Lanka)**		121	I. V. A. Richards (West Indies)
134	V. V. S. Laxman (India)		120	Inzamam-ul-Haq (Pakistan/World)
133	M. Muralitharan (Sri Lanka/World)		**120**	**K. C. Sangakkara (Sri Lanka)**

Note: Excluding the Super Series Test, **J. H. Kallis** has made **165** appearances for South Africa, a national record. The most appearances for New Zealand is 111 by S. P. Fleming; for Zimbabwe, 67 by G. W. Flower; and for Bangladesh **61** by **Mohammad Ashraful**.

MOST CONSECUTIVE TEST APPEARANCES FOR A COUNTRY

153	A. R. Border (Australia)	March 1979 to March 1994
107	M. E. Waugh (Australia)	June 1993 to October 2002
106	S. M. Gavaskar (India)	January 1975 to February 1987
100	**A. N. Cook (England)**	**May 2006 to January 2014**
96†	A. C. Gilchrist (Australia)	November 1999 to January 2008
93	R. Dravid (India)	June 1996 to December 2005
93	D. P. M. D. Jayawardene (Sri Lanka)	November 2002 to January 2013
89†	**A. B. de Villiers (South Africa)**	**December 2004 to December 2013**
87	G. R. Viswanath (India)	March 1971 to February 1983
86	M. L. Hayden (Australia)	March 2000 to January 2008
85	G. S. Sobers (West Indies)	April 1955 to April 1972
84	S. R. Tendulkar (India)	November 1989 to June 2001
82†	**B. B. McCullum (New Zealand)**	**March 2004 to December 2013**
79†	**M. E. K. Hussey (Australia)**	**November 2005 to January 2013**
75	M. V. Boucher (South Africa)	February 1998 to August 2004
73	R. T. Ponting (Australia)	November 2004 to December 2010
72	S. P. Fleming (New Zealand)	July 1999 to March 2008
72	D. L. Haynes (West Indies)	December 1979 to June 1988
71	I. M. Chappell (Australia)	January 1966 to February 1976

The most consecutive Test appearances for the countries not mentioned above are:

56	A. D. R. Campbell (Zimbabwe)	October 1992 to September 2001
53	Javed Miandad (Pakistan)	December 1977 to January 1984
38	Mohammad Ashraful (Bangladesh)	February 2004 to February 2010

† *Complete Test career.*

Bold type denotes sequence which was still in progress after January 1, 2014.

MOST TESTS AS CAPTAIN

	P	W	L	D		P	W	L	D
G. C. Smith (SA/World)	106	52	27†	27	M. A. Taylor (A)	50	26	13	11
A. R. Border (A)	93	32	22	38*	A. J. Strauss (E)	50	24	11	15
S. P. Fleming (NZ)	80	28	27	25	S. C. Ganguly (I)	49	21	13	15
R. T. Ponting (A)	77	48	16	13	G. S. Chappell (A)	48	21	13	14
C. H. Lloyd (WI)	74	36	12	26	Imran Khan (P)	48	14	8	26
S. R. Waugh (A)	57	41	9	7	M. Azharuddin (I)	47	14	14	19
A. Ranatunga (SL)	56	12	19	25	B. C. Lara (WI)	47	10	26	11
M. A. Atherton (E)	54	13	21	20	S. M. Gavaskar (I)	47	9	8	30
W. J. Cronje (SA)	53	27	11	15	N. Hussain (E)	45	17	15	13
M. P. Vaughan (E)	51	26	11	14	P. B. H. May (E)	41	20	10	11
M. S. Dhoni (I)	**51**	**26**	**13**	**12**	Nawab of Pataudi jun. (I)	40	9	19	12
I. V. A. Richards (WI)	50	27	8	15					

* *One match tied.*
† *Includes defeat as World XI captain in Super Series Test against Australia.*

Most Tests as captain of other countries:

	P	W	L	D
A. D. R. Campbell (Z)	21	2	12	7
Habibul Bashar (B)	18	1	13	4

Notes: A. R. Border captained Australia in 93 consecutive Tests.

W. W. Armstrong (Australia) captained his country in the most Tests without being defeated: ten matches with eight wins and two draws.

Mohammad Ashraful (Bangladesh) captained his country in the most Tests without ever winning: 12 defeats and one draw.

UMPIRES

MOST TESTS

		First Test	Last Test
128	S. A. Bucknor (West Indies)	1988-89	2008-09
108	R. E. Koertzen (South Africa)	1992-93	2010
95	D. J. Harper (Australia)	1998-99	2011
92	D. R. Shepherd (England)	1985	2004-05
87	**Aleem Dar (Pakistan)**	**2003-04**	**2013-14**
78	D. B. Hair (Australia)	1991-92	2008
76	**B. F. Bowden (New Zealand)**	**1999-2000**	**2013-14**
74	S. J. A. Taufel (Australia)	2000-01	2012
73	S. Venkataraghavan (India)	1992-93	2003-04
66	H. D. Bird (England)	1973	1996

An expanded and regularly updated online version of the Records can be found at www.wisdenrecords.com

SUMMARY OF TESTS

To January 20, 2014

	Opponents	Tests	E	A	SA	WI	NZ	I	P	SL	Z	B	Wld	Tied	Drawn
							Won by								
England	Australia	**336**	105	138	–	–	–	–	–	–	–	–	–	–	93
	South Africa	**141**	56	–	31	–	–	–	–	–	–	–	–	–	54
	West Indies	**148**	45	–	–	53	–	–	–	–	–	–	–	–	50
	New Zealand	**99**	47	–	–	–	8	–	–	–	–	–	–	–	44
	India	**107**	40	–	–	–	–	20	–	–	–	–	–	–	47
	Pakistan	**74**	22	–	–	–	–	–	16	–	–	–	–	–	36
	Sri Lanka	**26**	10	–	–	–	–	–	–	7	–	–	–	–	9
	Zimbabwe	**6**	3	–	–	–	–	–	–	–	0	–	–	–	3
	Bangladesh	**8**	8	–	–	–	–	–	–	–	–	0	–	–	0
Australia	South Africa	**88**	–	48	20	–	–	–	–	–	–	–	–	–	20
	West Indies	**111**	–	54	–	32	–	–	–	–	–	–	–	1	24
	New Zealand	**52**	–	27	–	–	8	–	–	–	–	–	–	–	17
	India	**86**	–	38	–	–	–	24	–	–	–	–	–	1	23
	Pakistan	**57**	–	28	–	–	–	–	12	–	–	–	–	–	17
	Sri Lanka	**26**	–	17	–	–	–	–	–	1	–	–	–	–	8
	Zimbabwe	**3**	–	3	–	–	–	–	–	–	0	–	–	–	0
	Bangladesh	**4**	–	4	–	–	–	–	–	–	–	0	–	–	0
	ICC World XI	**1**	–	1	–	–	–	–	–	–	–	–	0	–	0
South Africa	West Indies	**25**	–	–	16	3	–	–	–	–	–	–	–	–	6
	New Zealand	**40**	–	–	23	–	4	–	–	–	–	–	–	–	13
	India	**29**	–	–	13	–	–	7	–	–	–	–	–	–	9
	Pakistan	**23**	–	–	12	–	–	–	4	–	–	–	–	–	7
	Sri Lanka	**20**	–	–	10	–	–	–	–	5	–	–	–	–	5
	Zimbabwe	**7**	–	–	6	–	–	–	–	–	0	–	–	–	1
	Bangladesh	**8**	–	–	8	–	–	–	–	–	–	0	–	–	0
West Indies	New Zealand	**42**	–	–	–	12	11	–	–	–	–	–	–	–	19
	India	**90**	–	–	–	30	–	16	–	–	–	–	–	–	44
	Pakistan	**46**	–	–	–	15	–	–	16	–	–	–	–	–	15
	Sri Lanka	**15**	–	–	–	3	–	–	–	6	–	–	–	–	6
	Zimbabwe	**8**	–	–	–	6	–	–	–	–	0	–	–	–	2
	Bangladesh	**10**	–	–	–	6	–	–	–	–	–	2	–	–	2
New Zealand	India	**52**	–	–	–	–	9	18	–	–	–	–	–	–	25
	Pakistan	**50**	–	–	–	–	7	–	23	–	–	–	–	–	20
	Sri Lanka	**28**	–	–	–	–	10	–	–	8	–	–	–	–	10
	Zimbabwe	**15**	–	–	–	–	9	–	–	–	0	–	–	–	6
	Bangladesh	**11**	–	–	–	–	8	–	–	–	–	0	–	–	3
India	Pakistan	**59**	–	–	–	–	–	9	12	–	–	–	–	–	38
	Sri Lanka	**35**	–	–	–	–	–	14	–	6	–	–	–	–	15
	Zimbabwe	**11**	–	–	–	–	–	7	–	–	2	–	–	–	2
	Bangladesh	**7**	–	–	–	–	–	6	–	–	–	0	–	–	1
Pakistan	Sri Lanka	**46**	–	–	–	–	–	–	17	11	–	–	–	–	18
	Zimbabwe	**17**	–	–	–	–	–	–	10	–	3	–	–	–	4
	Bangladesh	**8**	–	–	–	–	–	–	8	–	–	0	–	–	0
Sri Lanka	Zimbabwe	**15**	–	–	–	–	–	–	–	10	0	–	–	–	5
	Bangladesh	**14**	–	–	–	–	–	–	–	13	–	0	–	–	1
Zimbabwe	Bangladesh	**11**	–	–	–	–	–	–	–	–	6	2	–	–	3
		2,115	336	358	139	160	74	121	118	67	11	4	0	2	725

	Tests	Won	Lost	Drawn	Tied	% Won	Toss Won
England	945	336	273	336	–	35.55	455
Australia	764†	358†	202	202	2	46.85	389
South Africa	381	139	127	115	–	36.48	185
West Indies	495	160	166	168	1	32.32	256
New Zealand	389	74	158	157	–	19.02	197
India	476	121	150	204	1	25.42	239
Pakistan	380	118	107	155	–	31.05	177
Sri Lanka	225	67	81	77	–	29.77	122
Zimbabwe	93	11	56	26	–	11.82	54
Bangladesh	81	4	67	10	–	4.93	41
ICC World XI	1	0	1	0	–	0.00	0

† *Includes Super Series Test between Australia and ICC World XI.*

ENGLAND v AUSTRALIA

		Captains					
Season	England		Australia	T	E	A	D
1876-77	James Lillywhite		D. W. Gregory	2	1	1	0
1878-79	Lord Harris		D. W. Gregory	1	0	1	0
1880	Lord Harris		W. L. Murdoch	1	1	0	0
1881-82	A. Shaw		W. L. Murdoch	4	0	2	2
1882	A. N. Hornby		W. L. Murdoch	1	0	1	0

THE ASHES

		Captains						
Season	England		Australia	T	E	A	D	Held by
1882-83	Hon. Ivo Bligh		W. L. Murdoch	4*	2	2	0	E
1884	Lord Harris[1]		W. L. Murdoch	3	1	0	2	E
1884-85	A. Shrewsbury		T. P. Horan[2]	5	3	2	0	E
1886	A. G. Steel		H. J. H. Scott	3	3	0	0	E
1886-87	A. Shrewsbury		P. S. McDonnell	2	2	0	0	E
1887-88	W. W. Read		P. S. McDonnell	1	1	0	0	E
1888	W. G. Grace[3]		P. S. McDonnell	3	2	1	0	E
1890†	W. G. Grace		W. L. Murdoch	2	2	0	0	E
1891-92	W. G. Grace		J. McC. Blackham	3	1	2	0	A
1893	W. G. Grace[4]		J. McC. Blackham	3	1	0	2	E
1894-95	A. E. Stoddart		G. Giffen[5]	5	3	2	0	E
1896	W. G. Grace		G. H. S. Trott	3	2	1	0	E
1897-98	A. E. Stoddart[6]		G. H. S. Trott	5	1	4	0	A
1899	A. C. MacLaren[7]		J. Darling	5	0	1	4	A
1901-02	A. C. MacLaren		J. Darling[8]	5	1	4	0	A
1902	A. C. MacLaren		J. Darling	5	1	2	2	A
1903-04	P. F. Warner		M. A. Noble	5	3	2	0	E
1905	Hon. F. S. Jackson		J. Darling	5	2	0	3	E
1907-08	A. O. Jones[9]		M. A. Noble	5	1	4	0	A
1909	A. C. MacLaren		M. A. Noble	5	1	2	2	A
1911-12	J. W. H. T. Douglas		C. Hill	5	4	1	0	E
1912	C. B. Fry		S. E. Gregory	3	1	0	2	E
1920-21	J. W. H. T. Douglas		W. W. Armstrong	5	0	5	0	A
1921	Hon. L. H. Tennyson[10]		W. W. Armstrong	5	0	3	2	A
1924-25	A. E. R. Gilligan		H. L. Collins	5	1	4	0	A
1926	A. W. Carr[11]		H. L. Collins[12]	5	1	0	4	E
1928-29	A. P. F. Chapman[13]		J. Ryder	5	4	1	0	E
1930	A. P. F. Chapman[14]		W. M. Woodfull	5	1	2	2	A
1932-33	D. R. Jardine		W. M. Woodfull	5	4	1	0	E
1934	R. E. S. Wyatt[15]		W. M. Woodfull	5	1	2	2	A
1936-37	G. O. B. Allen		D. G. Bradman	5	2	3	0	A
1938†	W. R. Hammond		D. G. Bradman	4	1	1	2	A
1946-47	W. R. Hammond[16]		D. G. Bradman	5	0	3	2	A
1948	N. W. D. Yardley		D. G. Bradman	5	0	4	1	A
1950-51	F. R. Brown		A. L. Hassett	5	1	4	0	A
1953	L. Hutton		A. L. Hassett	5	1	0	4	E
1954-55	L. Hutton		I. W. Johnson[17]	5	3	1	1	E
1956	P. B. H. May		I. W. Johnson	5	2	1	2	E
1958-59	P. B. H. May		R. Benaud	5	0	4	1	A
1961	P. B. H. May[18]		R. Benaud[19]	5	1	2	2	A
1962-63	E. R. Dexter		R. Benaud	5	1	1	3	A
1964	E. R. Dexter		R. B. Simpson	5	0	1	4	A
1965-66	M. J. K. Smith		R. B. Simpson[20]	5	1	1	3	A
1968	M. C. Cowdrey[21]		W. M. Lawry[22]	5	1	1	3	A
1970-71†	R. Illingworth		W. M. Lawry[23]	6	2	0	4	E
1972	R. Illingworth		I. M. Chappell	5	2	2	1	E

	Captains						
Season	*England*	*Australia*	*T*	*E*	*A*	*D*	*Held by*
1974-75	M. H. Denness[24]	I. M. Chappell	6	1	4	1	A
1975	A. W. Greig[25]	I. M. Chappell	4	0	1	3	A
1976-77‡	A. W. Greig	G. S. Chappell	1	0	1	0	—
1977	J. M. Brearley	G. S. Chappell	5	3	0	2	E
1978-79	J. M. Brearley	G. N. Yallop	6	5	1	0	E
1979-80‡	J. M. Brearley	G. S. Chappell	3	0	3	0	—
1980‡	I. T. Botham	G. S. Chappell	1	0	0	1	—
1981	J. M. Brearley[26]	K. J. Hughes	6	3	1	2	E
1982-83	R. G. D. Willis	G. S. Chappell	5	1	2	2	A
1985	D. I. Gower	A. R. Border	6	3	1	2	E
1986-87	M. W. Gatting	A. R. Border	5	2	1	2	E
1987-88‡	M. W. Gatting	A. R. Border	1	0	0	1	—
1989	D. I. Gower	A. R. Border	6	0	4	2	A
1990-91	G. A. Gooch[27]	A. R. Border	5	0	3	2	A
1993	G. A. Gooch[28]	A. R. Border	6	1	4	1	A
1994-95	M. A. Atherton	M. A. Taylor	5	1	3	1	A
1997	M. A. Atherton	M. A. Taylor	6	2	3	1	A
1998-99	A. J. Stewart	M. A. Taylor	5	1	3	1	A
2001	N. Hussain[29]	S. R. Waugh[30]	5	1	4	0	A
2002-03	N. Hussain	S. R. Waugh	5	1	4	0	A
2005	M. P. Vaughan	R. T. Ponting	5	2	1	2	E
2006-07	A. Flintoff	R. T. Ponting	5	0	5	0	A
2009	A. J. Strauss	R. T. Ponting	5	2	1	2	E
2010-11	A. J. Strauss	R. T. Ponting[31]	5	3	1	1	E
2013	**A. N. Cook**	**M. J. Clarke**	**5**	**3**	**0**	**2**	**E**
2013-14	**A. N. Cook**	**M. J. Clarke**	**5**	**0**	**5**	**0**	**A**
	In Australia		**175**	**57**	**91**	**27**	
	In England		**161**	**48**	**47**	**66**	
	Totals		**336**	**105**	**138**	**93**	

* *The Ashes were awarded in 1882-83 after a series of three matches which England won 2–1. A fourth match was played and this was won by Australia.*
† *The matches at Manchester in 1890 and 1938 and at Melbourne (Third Test) in 1970-71 were abandoned without a ball being bowled and are excluded.*
‡ *The Ashes were not at stake in these series.*

Notes: The following deputised for the official touring captain or were appointed by the home authority for only a minor proportion of the series:

[1]A. N. Hornby (First). [2]W. L. Murdoch (First), H. H. Massie (Third), J. McC. Blackham (Fourth). [3]A. G. Steel (First). [4]A. E. Stoddart (First). [5]J. McC. Blackham (First). [6]A. C. MacLaren (First, Second and Fifth). [7]W. G. Grace (First). [8]H. Trumble (Fourth and Fifth). [9]F. L. Fane (First, Second and Third). [10]J. W. H. T. Douglas (First and Second). [11]A. P. F. Chapman (Fifth). [12]W. Bardsley (Third and Fourth). [13]J. C. White (Fifth). [14]R. E. S. Wyatt (Fifth). [15]C. F. Walters (First). [16]N. W. D. Yardley (Fifth). [17]A. R. Morris (Second). [18]M. C. Cowdrey (First and Second). [19]R. N. Harvey (Second). [20]B. C. Booth (First and Third). [21]T. W. Graveney (Fourth). [22]B. N. Jarman (Fourth) [23]I. M. Chappell (Seventh). [24]J. H. Edrich (Fourth). [25]M. H. Denness (First). [26]I. T. Botham (First and Second). [27]A. J. Lamb (First). [28]M. A. Atherton (Fifth and Sixth). [29]M. A. Atherton (Second and Third). [30]A. C. Gilchrist (Fourth). [31]M. J. Clarke (Fifth).

HIGHEST INNINGS TOTALS

For England in England: 903-7 dec at The Oval	1938
in Australia: 644 at Sydney	2010-11
For Australia in England: 729-6 dec at Lord's	1930
in Australia: 659-8 dec at Sydney	1946-47

LOWEST INNINGS TOTALS

For England in England: 52 at The Oval 1948
        in Australia: 45 at Sydney 1886-87

For Australia in England: 36 at Birmingham 1902
        in Australia: 42 at Sydney 1887-88

DOUBLE-HUNDREDS

For England (13)

364	L. Hutton at The Oval	1938	227	K. P. Pietersen at Adelaide	2010-11
287	R. E. Foster at Sydney	1903-04	216*	E. Paynter at Nottingham	1938
256	K. F. Barrington at Manchester .	1964	215	D. I. Gower at Birmingham	1985
251	W. R. Hammond at Sydney	1928-29	207	N. Hussain at Birmingham	1997
240	W. R. Hammond at Lord's	1938	206	P. D. Collingwood at Adelaide . .	2006-07
235*	A. N. Cook at Brisbane	2010-11	200	W. R. Hammond at Melbourne .	1928-29
231*	W. R. Hammond at Sydney	1936-37			

For Australia (23)

334	D. G. Bradman at Leeds	1930	232	S. J. McCabe at Nottingham	1938
311	R. B. Simpson at Manchester . . .	1964	225	R. B. Simpson at Adelaide	1965-66
307	R. M. Cowper at Melbourne	1965-66	219	M. A. Taylor at Nottingham	1989
304	D. G. Bradman at Leeds	1934	212	D. G. Bradman at Adelaide	1936-37
270	D. G. Bradman at Melbourne . . .	1936-37	211	W. L. Murdoch at The Oval	1884
266	W. H. Ponsford at The Oval	1934	207	K. R. Stackpole at Brisbane	1970-71
254	D. G. Bradman at Lord's	1930	206*	W. A. Brown at Lord's	1938
250	J. L. Langer at Melbourne	2002-03	206	A. R. Morris at Adelaide	1950-51
244	D. G. Bradman at The Oval	1934	201*	J. Ryder at Adelaide	1924-25
234	S. G. Barnes at Sydney	1946-47	201	S. E. Gregory at Sydney	1894-95
234	D. G. Bradman at Sydney	1946-47	200*	A. R. Border at Leeds	1993
232	D. G. Bradman at The Oval	1930			

INDIVIDUAL HUNDREDS

For England (237)

12: J. B. Hobbs.

9: D. I. Gower, W. R. Hammond.

8: H. Sutcliffe.

7: G. Boycott, J. H. Edrich, M. Leyland.

5: K. F. Barrington, D. C. S. Compton, M. C. Cowdrey, L. Hutton, F. S. Jackson, A. C. MacLaren.

4: I. R. Bell, I. T. Botham, B. C. Broad, A. N. Cook, M. W. Gatting, G. A. Gooch, **K. P. Pietersen**, A. J. Strauss, M. P. Vaughan.

3: M. A. Butcher, E. H. Hendren, P. B. H. May, D. W. Randall, A. C. Russell, A. Shrewsbury, G. P. Thorpe, I. J. L. Trott, J. T. Tyldesley, R. A. Woolmer.

2: C. J. Barnett, L. C. Braund, E. R. Dexter, B. L. D'Oliveira, W. J. Edrich, W. G. Grace, G. Gunn, T. W. Hayward, N. Hussain, A. P. E. Knott, B. W. Luckhurst, K. S. Ranjitsinhji, R. T. Robinson, Rev. D. S. Sheppard, R. A. Smith, A. G. Steel, A. E. Stoddart, R. Subba Row, C. Washbrook, F. E. Woolley.

1: R. Abel, L. E. G. Ames, M. A. Atherton, R. W. Barber, W. Barnes, J. Briggs, J. T. Brown, A. P. F. Chapman, P. D. Collingwood, M. H. Denness, K. S. Duleepsinhji, K. W. R. Fletcher, A. Flintoff, R. E. Foster, C. B. Fry, T. W. Graveney, A. W. Greig, W. Gunn, J. Hardstaff, jun., J. W. Hearne, K. L. Hutchings, G. L. Jessop, A. J. Lamb, J. W. H. Makepeace, C. P. Mead, Nawab of Pataudi, sen., E. Paynter, M. J. Prior, M. R. Ramprakash, W. W. Read, W. Rhodes, C. J. Richards, P. E. Richardson, **J. E. Root**, R. C. Russell, J. Sharp, R. T. Simpson, A. J. Stewart, **B. A. Stokes**, G. Ulyett, A. Ward, W. Watson.

For Australia (301)

19: D. G. Bradman.

10: S. R. Waugh.

9: G. S. Chappell.

8: A. R. Border, A. R. Morris, R. T. Ponting.

7: D. C. Boon, **M. J. Clarke**, W. M. Lawry, M. J. Slater.

6: R. N. Harvey, M. A. Taylor, V. T. Trumper, M. E. Waugh, W. M. Woodfull.

5: M. L. Hayden, J. L. Langer, C. G. Macartney, W. H. Ponsford.

4: W. W. Armstrong, P. J. Burge, I. M. Chappell, S. E. Gregory, A. L. Hassett, C. Hill, M. E. K. Hussey, S. J. McCabe, K. D. Walters.

3: W. Bardsley, G. S. Blewett, W. A. Brown, H. L. Collins, J. Darling, A. C. Gilchrist, **B. J. Haddin**, K. J. Hughes, D. M. Jones, P. S. McDonnell, K. R. Miller, **C. J. L. Rogers**, **S. P. D. Smith**, K. R. Stackpole, G. M. Wood, G. N. Yallop.

2: S. G. Barnes, B. C. Booth, R. A. Duff, R. Edwards, M. T. G. Elliott, J. H. Fingleton, H. Graham, I. A. Healy, F. A. Iredale, R. B. McCosker, C. C. McDonald, G. R. Marsh, D. R. Martyn, W. L. Murdoch, M. J. North, N. C. O'Neill, C. E. Pellew, I. R. Redpath, J. Ryder, R. B. Simpson, **D. A. Warner**, **S. R. Watson**.

1: C. L. Badcock, C. Bannerman, G. J. Bonnor, J. W. Burke, R. M. Cowper, J. Dyson, G. Giffen, J. M. Gregory, R. J. Hartigan, H. L. Hendry, A. M. J. Hilditch, T. P. Horan, A. A. Jackson, S. M. Katich, C. Kelleway, A. F. Kippax, R. R. Lindwall, J. J. Lyons, C. L. McCool, C. E. McLeod, R. W. Marsh, G. R. J. Matthews, M. A. Noble, V. S. Ransford, A. J. Richardson, V. Y. Richardson, G. M. Ritchie, H. J. H. Scott, A. Symonds, J. M. Taylor, G. H. S. Trott, D. M. Wellham, K. C. Wessels.

RECORD PARTNERSHIPS FOR EACH WICKET

For England

323 for 1st	J. B. Hobbs and W. Rhodes at Melbourne..........................	1911-12
382 for 2nd†	L. Hutton and M. Leyland at The Oval	1938
262 for 3rd	W. R. Hammond and D. R. Jardine at Adelaide....................	1928-29
310 for 4th	P. D. Collingwood and K. P. Pietersen at Adelaide................	2006-07
206 for 5th	E. Paynter and D. C. S. Compton at Nottingham	1938
215 for 6th {	L. Hutton and J. Hardstaff jun. at The Oval	1938
	G. Boycott and A. P. E. Knott at Nottingham	1977
143 for 7th	F. E. Woolley and J. Vine at Leeds.............................	1911-12
124 for 8th	E. H. Hendren and H. Larwood at Brisbane	1928-29
151 for 9th	W. H. Scotton and W. W. Read at The Oval......................	1884
130 for 10th†	R. E. Foster and W. Rhodes at Sydney	1903-04

For Australia

329 for 1st	G. R. Marsh and M. A. Taylor at Nottingham.....................	1989
451 for 2nd†	W. H. Ponsford and D. G. Bradman at The Oval	1934
276 for 3rd	D. G. Bradman and A. L. Hassett at Brisbane.....................	1946-47
388 for 4th†	W. H. Ponsford and D. G. Bradman at Leeds	1934
405 for 5th‡	S. G. Barnes and D. G. Bradman at Sydney	1946-47
346 for 6th†	J. H. Fingleton and D. G. Bradman at Melbourne..................	1936-37
165 for 7th	C. Hill and H. Trumble at Melbourne	1897-98
243 for 8th†	R. J. Hartigan and C. Hill at Adelaide...........................	1907-08
154 for 9th†	S. E. Gregory and J. McC. Blackham at Sydney...................	1894-95
163 for 10th‡	**P. J. Hughes and A. C. Agar at Nottingham ....**	**2013**

† Record partnership against all countries.   ‡ World record.

MOST RUNS IN A SERIES

England in England	732 (average 81.33)	D. I. Gower	1985
England in Australia............	905 (average 113.12)	W. R. Hammond	1928-29
Australia in England	974 (average 139.14)	D. G. Bradman	1930
Australia in Australia	810 (average 90.00)	D. G. Bradman	1936-37

TEN WICKETS OR MORE IN A MATCH

For England (40)

10-158 (5-85, 5-73)	**J. M. Anderson, Nottingham**	**2013**
13-163 (6-42, 7-121)	S. F. Barnes, Melbourne	1901-02
14-102 (7-28, 7-74)	W. Bates, Melbourne	1882-83
10-105 (5-46, 5-59)	A. V. Bedser, Melbourne	1950-51
14-99 (7-55, 7-44)	A. V. Bedser, Nottingham	1953
11-102 (6-44, 5-58)	C. Blythe, Birmingham	1909
11-176 (6-78, 5-98)	I. T. Botham, Perth	1979-80
10-253 (6-125, 4-128)	I. T. Botham, The Oval	1981
11-74 (5-29, 6-45)	J. Briggs, Lord's	1886
12-136 (6-49, 6-87)	J. Briggs, Adelaide	1891-92
10-148 (5-34, 5-114)	J. Briggs, The Oval	1893
11-121 (5-71, 6-50)	**S. C. J. Broad, Chester-le-Street**	**2013**
10-215 (3-121, 7-94)	A. R. Caddick, Sydney	2002-03
10-104 (6-77, 4-27)†	R. M. Ellison, Birmingham	1985
10-179 (5-102, 5-77)†	K. Farnes, Nottingham	1934
10-60 (6-41, 4-19)	J. T. Hearne, The Oval	1896
11-113 (5-58, 6-55)	J. C. Laker, Leeds	1956
19-90 (9-37, 10-53)	J. C. Laker, Manchester	1956
10-124 (5-96, 5-28)	H. Larwood, Sydney	1932-33
11-76 (6-48, 5-28)	W. H. Lockwood, Manchester	1902
12-104 (7-36, 5-68)	G. A. Lohmann, The Oval	1886
10-87 (8-35, 2-52)	G. A. Lohmann, Sydney	1886-87
10-142 (6-58, 2-84)	G. A. Lohmann, Sydney	1891-92
12-102 (6-50, 6-52)†	F. Martin, The Oval	1890
11-68 (7-31, 4-37)	R. Peel, Manchester	1888
15-124 (7-56, 8-68)	W. Rhodes, Melbourne	1903-04
10-156 (5-49, 5-107)†	T. Richardson, Manchester	1893
11-173 (6-39, 5-134)	T. Richardson, Lord's	1896
13-244 (7-168, 6-76)	T. Richardson, Manchester	1896
10-204 (8-94, 2-110)	T. Richardson, Sydney	1897-98
11-228 (6-130, 5-98)†	M. W. Tate, Sydney	1924-25
11-88 (5-58, 6-30)	F. S. Trueman, Leeds	1961
11-93 (7-66, 4-27)	P. C. R. Tufnell, The Oval	1997
10-130 (4-45, 6-85)	F. H. Tyson, Sydney	1954-55
10-82 (4-37, 6-45)	D. L. Underwood, Leeds	1972
11-215 (7-113, 4-102)	D. L. Underwood, Adelaide	1974-75
15-104 (7-61, 8-43)	H. Verity, Lord's	1934
10-57 (6-41, 4-16)	W. Voce, Brisbane	1936-37
13-256 (5-130, 8-126)	J. C. White, Adelaide	1928-29
10-49 (5-29, 5-20)	F. E. Woolley, The Oval	1912

For Australia (43)

10-151 (5-107, 5-44)	T. M. Alderman, Leeds	1989
10-239 (4-129, 6-110)	L. O'B. Fleetwood-Smith, Adelaide	1936-37
10-160 (4-88, 6-72)	G. Giffen, Sydney	1891-92
11-82 (5-45, 6-37)†	C. V. Grimmett, Sydney	1924-25
10-201 (5-107, 5-94)	C. V. Grimmett, Nottingham	1930
10-122 (5-65, 5-57)	R. M. Hogg, Perth	1978-79
10-66 (5-30, 5-36)	R. M. Hogg, Melbourne	1978-79
12-175 (5-85, 7-90)†	H. V. Hordern, Sydney	1911-12
10-161 (5-95, 5-66)	H. V. Hordern, Sydney	1911-12
10-164 (7-88, 3-76)	E. Jones, Lord's	1899
11-134 (6-47, 5-87)	G. F. Lawson, Brisbane	1982-83
10-181 (5-58, 5-123)	D. K. Lillee, The Oval	1972
11-165 (6-26, 5-139)	D. K. Lillee, Melbourne	1976-77
11-138 (6-60, 5-78)	D. K. Lillee, Melbourne	1979-80
11-159 (7-89, 4-70)	D. K. Lillee, The Oval	1981

11-85 (7-58, 4-27)	C. G. Macartney, Leeds	1909
11-157 (8-97, 3-60)	C. J. McDermott, Perth	1990-91
12-107 (5-57, 7-50)	S. C. G. MacGill, Sydney	1998-99
10-302 (5-160, 5-142)	A. A. Mailey, Adelaide	1920-21
13-236 (4-115, 9-121)	A. A. Mailey, Melbourne	1920-21
16-137 (8-84, 8-53)†	R. A. L. Massie, Lord's	1972
10-152 (5-72, 5-80)	K. R. Miller, Lord's	1956
13-77 (7-17, 6-60)	M. A. Noble, Melbourne	1901-02
11-103 (5-51, 6-52)	M. A. Noble, Sheffield	1902
10-129 (5-63, 5-66)	W. J. O'Reilly, Melbourne	1932-33
11-129 (4-75, 7-54)	W. J. O'Reilly, Nottingham	1934
10-122 (5-66, 5-56)	W. J. O'Reilly, Leeds	1938
11-165 (7-68, 4-97)	G. E. Palmer, Sydney	1881-82
10-126 (7-65, 3-61)	G. E. Palmer, Melbourne	1882-83
13-148 (6-97, 7-51)	B. A. Reid, Melbourne	1990-91
13-110 (6-48, 7-62)	F. R. Spofforth, Melbourne	1878-79
14-90 (7-46, 7-44)	F. R. Spofforth, The Oval	1882
11-117 (4-73, 7-44)	F. R. Spofforth, Sydney	1882-83
10-144 (4-54, 6-90)	F. R. Spofforth, Sydney	1884-85
12-89 (6-59, 6-30)	H. Trumble, The Oval	1896
10-128 (4-75, 6-53)	H. Trumble, Manchester	1902
12-173 (8-65, 4-108)	H. Trumble, The Oval	1902
12-87 (5-44, 7-43)	C. T. B. Turner, Sydney	1887-88
10-63 (5-27, 5-36)	C. T. B. Turner, Lord's	1888
11-110 (3-39, 8-71)	S. K. Warne, Brisbane	1994-95
11-229 (7-165, 4-64)	S. K. Warne, The Oval	2001
10-162 (4-116, 6-46)	S. K. Warne, Birmingham	2005
12-246 (6-122, 6-124)	S. K. Warne, The Oval	2005

† *On first appearance in England–Australia Tests.*

Note: A. V. Bedser, J. Briggs, J. C. Laker, T. Richardson in 1896, R. M. Hogg, A. A. Mailey, H. Trumble and C. T. B. Turner took ten wickets or more in successive Tests. J. Briggs was omitted, however, from the England team for the first Test match in 1893.

MOST WICKETS IN A SERIES

England in England	46 (average 9.60)	J. C. Laker	1956
England in Australia	38 (average 23.18)	M. W. Tate	1924-25
Australia in England	42 (average 21.26)	T. M. Alderman (6 Tests)	1981
Australia in Australia	41 (average 12.85)	R. M. Hogg (6 Tests)	1978-79

WICKETKEEPING – MOST DISMISSALS

	M	Ct	St	Total
†R. W. Marsh (Australia)	42	141	7	148
I. A. Healy (Australia)	33	123	12	135
A. P. E. Knott (England)	34	97	8	105
A. C. Gilchrist (Australia)	20	89	7	96
†W. A. Oldfield (Australia)	38	59	31	90
A. A. Lilley (England)	32	65	19	84
A. J. Stewart (England)	26	76	2	78
A. T. W. Grout (Australia)	22	69	7	76
T. G. Evans (England)	31	64	12	76
B. J. Haddin (Australia)	19	74	1	75

† *The number of catches by R. W. Marsh (141) and stumpings by W. A. Oldfield (31) are respective records in England–Australia Tests.*

Note: Stewart held a further six catches in seven matches when not keeping wicket.

SCORERS OF OVER 2,000 RUNS

	T	I	NO	R	HS	100s	Avge
D. G. Bradman (Australia) .	37	63	7	5,028	334	19	89.78
J. B. Hobbs (England)	41	71	4	3,636	187	12	54.26
A. R. Border (Australia) . . .	47	82	19	3,548	200*	8	56.31
D. I. Gower (England).	42	77	4	3,269	215	9	44.78
S. R. Waugh (Australia) . . .	46	73	18	3,200	177*	10	58.18
G. Boycott (England).	38	71	9	2,945	191	7	47.50
W. R. Hammond (England).	33	58	3	2,852	251	9	51.85
H. Sutcliffe (England)	27	46	5	2,741	194	8	66.85
C. Hill (Australia)	41	76	1	2,660	188	4	35.46
J. H. Edrich (England).	32	57	3	2,644	175	7	48.96
G. A. Gooch (England)	42	79	0	2,632	196	4	33.31
G. S. Chappell (Australia) . .	35	65	8	2,619	144	9	45.94
M. A. Taylor (Australia) . . .	33	61	2	2,496	219	6	42.30
R. T. Ponting (Australia) . . .	35	58	2	2,476	196	8	44.21
M. C. Cowdrey (England) . .	43	75	4	2,433	113	5	34.26
L. Hutton (England).	27	49	6	2,428	364	5	56.46
R. N. Harvey (Australia) . . .	37	68	5	2,416	167	6	38.34
V. T. Trumper (Australia) . .	40	74	5	2,263	185*	6	32.79
D. C. Boon (Australia).	31	57	8	2,237	184*	7	45.65
W. M. Lawry (Australia) . . .	29	51	5	2,233	166	7	48.54
M. E. Waugh (Australia) . . .	29	51	7	2,204	140	6	50.09
S. E. Gregory (Australia). . .	52	92	7	2,193	201	4	25.80
W. W. Armstrong (Aus.) . . .	42	71	9	2,172	158	4	35.03
K. P. Pietersen (England) .	**27**	**50**	**2**	**2,158**	**227**	**4**	**44.95**
I. M. Chappell (Australia) . .	30	56	4	2,138	192	4	41.11
K. F. Barrington (England) .	23	39	6	2,111	256	5	63.96
M. J. Clarke (Australia) . .	**30**	**53**	**6**	**2,109**	**187**	**7**	**44.87**
A. R. Morris (Australia). . . .	24	43	2	2,080	206	8	50.73

BOWLERS WITH 100 WICKETS

	T	Balls	R	W	5W/i	10W/m	Avge
S. K. Warne (Australia)	36	10,757	4,535	195	11	4	23.25
D. K. Lillee (Australia).	29	8,516	3,507	167	11	4	21.00
G. D. McGrath (Australia)	30	7,280	3,286	157	10	0	20.92
I. T. Botham (England)	36	8,479	4,093	148	9	2	27.65
H. Trumble (Australia).	31	7,895	2,945	141	9	3	20.88
R. G. D. Willis (England).	35	7,294	3,346	128	7	0	26.14
M. A. Noble (Australia)	39	6,895	2,860	115	9	2	24.86
R. R. Lindwall (Australia)	29	6,728	2,559	114	6	0	22.44
W. Rhodes (England).	41	5,790	2,616	109	6	1	24.00
S. F. Barnes (England)	20	5,749	2,288	106	12	1	21.58
C. V. Grimmett (Australia).	22	9,224	3,439	106	11	2	32.44
D. L. Underwood (England).	29	8,000	2,770	105	4	2	26.38
A. V. Bedser (England)	21	7,065	2,859	104	7	2	27.49
G. Giffen (Australia)	31	6,391	2,791	103	7	1	27.09
W. J. O'Reilly (Australia)	19	7,864	2,587	102	8	3	25.36
C. T. B. Turner (Australia).	17	5,179	1,670	101	11	2	16.53
R. Peel (England)	20	5,216	1,715	101	5	1	16.98
T. M. Alderman (Australia)	17	4,717	2,117	100	11	1	21.17
J. R. Thomson (Australia)	21	4,951	2,418	100	5	0	24.18

RESULTS ON EACH GROUND

In England

	Matches	England wins	Australia wins	Drawn
The Oval.	36	16	6	14
Manchester.	29	7	7	15†
Lord's.	35	7	14	14
Nottingham	21	5	7	9
Leeds	24	7	9	8
Birmingham	13	5	3	5
Sheffield	1	0	1	0
Cardiff	1	0	0	1
Chester-le-Street.	1	1	0	0

† *Excludes two matches abandoned without a ball bowled.*

In Australia

	Matches	England wins	Australia wins	Drawn
Melbourne	55	20	28	7†
Sydney	55	22	26	7
Adelaide	31	9	17	5
Brisbane				
Exhibition Ground	1	1	0	0
Woolloongabba	20	4	11	5
Perth	13	1	9	3

† *Excludes one match abandoned without a ball bowled.*

ENGLAND v SOUTH AFRICA

	Captains		T	E	SA	D
Season	England	South Africa	T	E	SA	D
1888-89	C. A. Smith[1]	O. R. Dunell[2]	2	2	0	0
1891-92	W. W. Read	W. H. Milton	1	1	0	0
1895-96	Lord Hawke[3]	E. A. Halliwell[4]	3	3	0	0
1898-99	Lord Hawke	M. Bisset	2	2	0	0
1905-06	P. F. Warner	P. W. Sherwell	5	1	4	0
1907	R. E. Foster	P. W. Sherwell	3	1	0	2
1909-10	H. D. G. Leveson Gower[5]	S. J. Snooke	5	2	3	0
1912	C. B. Fry	F. Mitchell[6]	3	3	0	0
1913-14	J. W. H. T. Douglas	H. W. Taylor	5	4	0	1
1922-23	F. T. Mann	H. W. Taylor	5	2	1	2
1924	A. E. R. Gilligan[7]	H. W. Taylor	5	3	0	2
1927-28	R. T. Stanyforth[8]	H. G. Deane	5	2	2	1
1929	J. C. White[9]	H. G. Deane	5	2	0	3
1930-31	A. P. F. Chapman	H. G. Deane[10]	5	0	1	4
1935	R. E. S. Wyatt	H. F. Wade	5	0	1	4
1938-39	W. R. Hammond	A. Melville	5	1	0	4
1947	N. W. D. Yardley	A. Melville	5	3	0	2
1948-49	F. G. Mann	A. D. Nourse	5	2	0	3
1951	F. R. Brown	A. D. Nourse	5	3	1	1
1955	P. B. H. May	J. E. Cheetham[11]	5	3	2	0
1956-57	P. B. H. May	C. B. van Ryneveld[12]	5	2	2	1
1960	M. C. Cowdrey	D. J. McGlew	5	3	0	2
1964-65	M. J. K. Smith	T. L. Goddard	5	1	0	4
1965	M. J. K. Smith	P. L. van der Merwe	3	0	1	2
1994	M. A. Atherton	K. C. Wessels	3	1	1	1

Captains

Season	England	South Africa	T	E	SA	D
1995-96	M. A. Atherton	W. J. Cronje	5	0	1	4
1998	A. J. Stewart	W. J. Cronje	5	2	1	2
1999-2000	N. Hussain	W. J. Cronje	5	1	2	2
2003	M. P. Vaughan[13]	G. C. Smith	5	2	2	1

THE BASIL D'OLIVEIRA TROPHY

Captains

Season	England	South Africa	T	E	SA	D	Held by
2004-05	M. P. Vaughan	G. C. Smith	5	2	1	2	E
2008	M. P. Vaughan[14]	G. C. Smith	4	1	2	1	SA
2009-10	A. J. Strauss	G. C. Smith	4	1	1	2	SA
2012	A. J. Strauss	G. C. Smith	3	0	2	1	SA
	In South Africa		77	29	18	30	
	In England		64	27	13	24	
	Totals		141	56	31	54	

Notes: *The following deputised for the official touring captain or were appointed by the home authority for only a minor proportion of the series:*

[1]M. P. Bowden (Second). [2]W. H. Milton (Second). [3]Sir T. C. O'Brien (First). [4]A. R. Richards (Third). [5]F. L. Fane (Fourth and Fifth). [6]L. J. Tancred (Second and Third). [7]J. W. H. T. Douglas (Fourth). [8]G. T. S. Stevens (Fifth). [9]A. W. Carr (Fourth and Fifth). [10]E. P. Nupen (First), H. B. Cameron (Fourth and Fifth). [11]D. J. McGlew (Third and Fourth). [12]D. J. McGlew (Second). [13]N. Hussain (First). [14]K. P. Pietersen (Fourth).

SERIES RECORDS

Highest score	E	243	E. Paynter at Durban	1938-39
	SA	311*	H. M. Amla at The Oval	2012
Best bowling	E	9-28	G. A. Lohmann at Johannesburg	1895-96
	SA	9-113	H. J. Tayfield at Johannesburg	1956-57
Highest total	E	654-5	at Durban	1938-39
	SA	682-6 dec	at Lord's	2003
Lowest total	E	76	at Leeds	1907
	SA {	30	at Port Elizabeth	1895-96
		30	at Birmingham	1924

ENGLAND v WEST INDIES

Captains

Season	England	West Indies	T	E	WI	D
1928	A. P. F. Chapman	R. K. Nunes	3	3	0	0
1929-30	Hon. F. S. G. Calthorpe	E. L. G. Hoad[1]	4	1	1	2
1933	D. R. Jardine[2]	G. C. Grant	3	2	0	1
1934-35	R. E. S. Wyatt	G. C. Grant	4	1	2	1
1939	W. R. Hammond	R. S. Grant	3	1	0	2
1947-48	G. O. B. Allen[3]	J. D. C. Goddard[4]	4	0	2	2
1950	N. W. D. Yardley[5]	J. D. C. Goddard	4	1	3	0
1953-54	L. Hutton	J. B. Stollmeyer	5	2	2	1
1957	P. B. H. May	J. D. C. Goddard	5	3	0	2
1959-60	P. B. H. May[6]	F. C. M. Alexander	5	1	0	4

THE WISDEN TROPHY

Season	England	Captains West Indies	T	E	WI	D	Held by
1963	E. R. Dexter	F. M. M. Worrell	5	1	3	1	WI
1966	M. C. Cowdrey[7]	G. S. Sobers	5	1	3	1	WI
1967-68	M. C. Cowdrey	G. S. Sobers	5	1	0	4	E
1969	R. Illingworth	G. S. Sobers	3	2	0	1	E
1973	R. Illingworth	R. B. Kanhai	3	0	2	1	WI
1973-74	M. H. Denness	R. B. Kanhai	5	1	1	3	WI
1976	A. W. Greig	C. H. Lloyd	5	0	3	2	WI
1980	I. T. Botham	C. H. Lloyd[8]	5	0	1	4	WI
1980-81†	I. T. Botham	C. H. Lloyd	4	0	2	2	WI
1984	D. I. Gower	C. H. Lloyd	5	0	5	0	WI
1985-86	D. I. Gower	I. V. A. Richards	5	0	5	0	WI
1988	J. E. Emburey[9]	I. V. A. Richards	5	0	4	1	WI
1989-90‡	G. A. Gooch[10]	I. V. A. Richards[11]	4	1	2	1	WI
1991	G. A. Gooch	I. V. A. Richards	5	2	2	1	WI
1993-94	M. A. Atherton	R. B. Richardson[12]	5	1	3	1	WI
1995	M. A. Atherton	R. B. Richardson	6	2	2	2	WI
1997-98§	M. A. Atherton	B. C. Lara	6	1	3	2	WI
2000	N. Hussain[13]	J. C. Adams	5	3	1	1	E
2003-04	M. P. Vaughan	B. C. Lara	4	3	0	1	E
2004	M. P. Vaughan	B. C. Lara	4	4	0	0	E
2007	M. P. Vaughan[14]	R. R. Sarwan[15]	4	3	0	1	E
2008-09§	A. J. Strauss	C. H. Gayle	5	0	1	4	WI
2009	A. J. Strauss	C. H. Gayle	2	2	0	0	E
2012	A. J. Strauss	D. J. G. Sammy	3	2	0	1	E
	In England		83	32	29	22	
	In West Indies		65	13	24	28	
	Totals		148	45	53	50	

† *The Second Test, at Georgetown, was cancelled owing to political pressure and is excluded.*
‡ *The Second Test, at Georgetown, was abandoned without a ball being bowled and is excluded.*
§ *The First Test at Kingston in 1997-98 and the Second Test at North Sound in 2008-09 were called off on their opening days because of unfit pitches and are shown as draws.*

Notes: The following deputised for the official touring captain or were appointed by the home authority for only a minor proportion of the series:

[1]N. Betancourt (Second), M. P. Fernandes (Third), R. K. Nunes (Fourth). [2]R. E. S. Wyatt (Third). [3]K. Cranston (First). [4]G. A. Headley (First), G. E. Gomez (Second). [5]F. R. Brown (Fourth). [6]M. C. Cowdrey (Fourth and Fifth). [7]M. J. K. Smith (First), D. B. Close (Fifth). [8]I. V. A. Richards (Fifth). [9]M. W. Gatting (First), C. S. Cowdrey (Fourth), G. A. Gooch (Fifth). [10]A. J. Lamb (Fourth and Fifth). [11]D. L. Haynes (Third). [12]C. A. Walsh (Fifth). [13]A. J. Stewart (Second). [14]A. J. Strauss (First). [15]D. Ganga (Third and Fourth).

SERIES RECORDS

Highest score	E	325	A. Sandham at Kingston	1929-30
	WI	400*	B. C. Lara at St John's	2003-04
Best bowling	E	8-53	A. R. C. Fraser at Port-of-Spain	1997-98
	WI	8-45	C. E. L. Ambrose at Bridgetown	1989-90
Highest total	E	849	at Kingston	1929-30
	WI	751-5 dec	at St John's	2003-04
Lowest total	E	46	at Port-of-Spain	1993-94
	WI	47	at Kingston	2003-04

ENGLAND v NEW ZEALAND

		Captains				
Season	*England*	*New Zealand*	*T*	*E*	*NZ*	*D*
1929-30	A. H. H. Gilligan	T. C. Lowry	4	1	0	3
1931	D. R. Jardine	T. C. Lowry	3	1	0	2
1932-33	D. R. Jardine[1]	M. L. Page	2	0	0	2
1937	R. W. V. Robins	M. L. Page	3	1	0	2
1946-47	W. R. Hammond	W. A. Hadlee	1	0	0	1
1949	F. G. Mann[2]	W. A. Hadlee	4	0	0	4
1950-51	F. R. Brown	W. A. Hadlee	2	1	0	1
1954-55	L. Hutton	G. O. Rabone	2	2	0	0
1958	P. B. H. May	J. R. Reid	5	4	0	1
1958-59	P. B. H. May	J. R. Reid	2	1	0	1
1962-63	E. R. Dexter	J. R. Reid	3	3	0	0
1965	M. J. K. Smith	J. R. Reid	3	3	0	0
1965-66	M. J. K. Smith	B. W. Sinclair[3]	3	0	0	3
1969	R. Illingworth	G. T. Dowling	3	2	0	1
1970-71	R. Illingworth	G. T. Dowling	2	1	0	1
1973	R. Illingworth	B. E. Congdon	3	2	0	1
1974-75	M. H. Denness	B. E. Congdon	2	1	0	1
1977-78	G. Boycott	M. G. Burgess	3	1	1	1
1978	J. M. Brearley	M. G. Burgess	3	3	0	0
1983	R. G. D. Willis	G. P. Howarth	4	3	1	0
1983-84	R. G. D. Willis	G. P. Howarth	3	0	1	2
1986	M. W. Gatting	J. V. Coney	3	0	1	2
1987-88	M. W. Gatting	J. J. Crowe[4]	3	0	0	3
1990	G. A. Gooch	J. G. Wright	3	1	0	2
1991-92	G. A. Gooch	M. D. Crowe	3	2	0	1
1994	M. A. Atherton	K. R. Rutherford	3	1	0	2
1996-97	M. A. Atherton	L. K. Germon[5]	3	2	0	1
1999	N. Hussain[6]	S. P. Fleming	4	1	2	1
2001-02	N. Hussain	S. P. Fleming	3	1	1	1
2004	M. P. Vaughan[7]	S. P. Fleming	3	3	0	0
2007-08	M. P. Vaughan	D. L. Vettori	3	2	1	0
2008	M. P. Vaughan	D. L. Vettori	3	2	0	1
2012-13	**A. N. Cook**	**B. B. McCullum**	**3**	**0**	**0**	**3**
2013	**A. N. Cook**	**B. B. McCullum**	**2**	**2**	**0**	**0**
	In New Zealand		47	18	4	25
	In England		52	29	4	19
	Totals		**99**	**47**	**8**	**44**

Notes: The following deputised for the official touring captain or were appointed by the home authority for only a minor proportion of the series:

[1]R. E. S. Wyatt (Second). [2]F. R. Brown (Third and Fourth). [3]M. E. Chapple (First). [4]J. G. Wright (Third). [5]S. P. Fleming (Third). [6]M. A. Butcher (Third). [7]M. E. Trescothick (First).

SERIES RECORDS

Highest score	E	336*	W. R. Hammond at Auckland...............	1932-33
	NZ	222	N. J. Astle at Christchurch	2001-02
Best bowling	E	7-32	D. L. Underwood at Lord's................	1969
	NZ	7-74	B. L. Cairns at Leeds.....................	1983
Highest total	E	593-6 dec	at Auckland............................	1974-75
	NZ	551-9 dec	at Lord's	1973
Lowest total	E	64	at Wellington...........................	1977-78
	NZ	26	at Auckland............................	1954-55

ENGLAND v INDIA

Captains

Season	England	India	T	E	I	D
1932	D. R. Jardine	C. K. Nayudu	1	1	0	0
1933-34	D. R. Jardine	C. K. Nayudu	3	2	0	1
1936	G. O. B. Allen	Maharaj of Vizianagram	3	2	0	1
1946	W. R. Hammond	Nawab of Pataudi sen.	3	1	0	2
1951-52	N. D. Howard[1]	V. S. Hazare	5	1	1	3
1952	L. Hutton	V. S. Hazare	4	3	0	1
1959	P. B. H. May[2]	D. K. Gaekwad[3]	5	5	0	0
1961-62	E. R. Dexter	N. J. Contractor	5	0	2	3
1963-64	M. J. K. Smith	Nawab of Pataudi jun.	5	0	0	5
1967	D. B. Close	Nawab of Pataudi jun.	3	3	0	0
1971	R. Illingworth	A. L. Wadekar	3	0	1	2
1972-73	A. R. Lewis	A. L. Wadekar	5	1	2	2
1974	M. H. Denness	A. L. Wadekar	3	3	0	0
1976-77	A. W. Greig	B. S. Bedi	5	3	1	1
1979	J. M. Brearley	S. Venkataraghavan	4	1	0	3
1979-80	J. M. Brearley	G. R. Viswanath	1	1	0	0
1981-82	K. W. R. Fletcher	S. M. Gavaskar	6	0	1	5
1982	R. G. D. Willis	S. M. Gavaskar	3	1	0	2
1984-85	D. I. Gower	S. M. Gavaskar	5	2	1	2
1986	M. W. Gatting[4]	Kapil Dev	3	0	2	1
1990	G. A. Gooch	M. Azharuddin	3	1	0	2
1992-93	G. A. Gooch[5]	M. Azharuddin	3	0	3	0
1996	M. A. Atherton	M. Azharuddin	3	1	0	2
2001-02	N. Hussain	S. C. Ganguly	3	0	1	2
2002	N. Hussain	S. C. Ganguly	4	1	1	2
2005-06	A. Flintoff	R. Dravid	3	1	1	1
2007	M. P. Vaughan	R. Dravid	3	0	1	2
2008-09	K. P. Pietersen	M. S. Dhoni	2	0	1	1
2011	A. J. Strauss	M. S. Dhoni	4	4	0	0
2012-13	A. N. Cook	M. S. Dhoni	4	2	1	1
	In England		52	27	5	20
	In India..................................		55	13	15	27
	Totals		107	40	20	47

* *Since 1951-52, series in India have been for the De Mello Trophy. Since 2007, series in England have been for the Pataudi Trophy.*

Notes: The 1932 Indian touring team was captained by the Maharaj of Porbandar but he did not play in the Test match.

The following deputised for the official touring captain or were appointed by the home authority for only a minor proportion of the series:
[1]D. B. Carr (Fifth). [2]M. C. Cowdrey (Fourth and Fifth). [3]Pankaj Roy (Second). [4]D. I. Gower (First). [5]A. J. Stewart (Second).

SERIES RECORDS

Highest score	E	333	G. A. Gooch at Lord's	1990
	I	224	V. G. Kambli at Bombay....................	1992-93
Best bowling	E	8-31	F. S. Trueman at Manchester................	1952
	I	8-55	V. Mankad at Madras	1951-52
Highest total	E	710-7 dec	at Birmingham............................	2011
	I	664	at The Oval	2007
Lowest total	E	101	at The Oval	1971
	I	42	at Lord's.................................	1974

ENGLAND v PAKISTAN

Captains

Season	England	Pakistan	T	E	P	D
1954	L. Hutton[1]	A. H. Kardar	4	1	1	2
1961-62	E. R. Dexter	Imtiaz Ahmed	3	1	0	2
1962	E. R. Dexter[2]	Javed Burki	5	4	0	1
1967	D. B. Close	Hanif Mohammad	3	2	0	1
1968-69	M. C. Cowdrey	Saeed Ahmed	3	0	0	3
1971	R. Illingworth	Intikhab Alam	3	1	0	2
1972-73	A. R. Lewis	Majid Khan	3	0	0	3
1974	M. H. Denness	Intikhab Alam	3	0	0	3
1977-78	J. M. Brearley[3]	Wasim Bari	3	0	0	3
1978	J. M. Brearley	Wasim Bari	3	2	0	1
1982	R. G. D. Willis[4]	Imran Khan	3	2	1	0
1983-84	R. G. D. Willis[5]	Zaheer Abbas	3	0	1	2
1987	M. W. Gatting	Imran Khan	5	0	1	4
1987-88	M. W. Gatting	Javed Miandad	3	0	1	2
1992	G. A. Gooch	Javed Miandad	5	1	2	2
1996	M. A. Atherton	Wasim Akram	3	0	2	1
2000-01	N. Hussain	Moin Khan	3	1	0	2
2001	N. Hussain[6]	Waqar Younis	2	1	1	0
2005-06	M. P. Vaughan[7]	Inzamam-ul-Haq	3	0	2	1
2006†	A. J. Strauss	Inzamam-ul-Haq	4	3	0	1
2010	A. J. Strauss	Salman Butt	4	3	1	0
2011-12*U*	A. J. Strauss	Misbah-ul-Haq	3	0	3	0
	In England		47	20	9	18
	In Pakistan		24	2	4	18
	In United Arab Emirates		3	0	3	0
	Totals		74	22	16	36

† *In 2008, the ICC changed the result of the forfeited Oval Test of 2006 from an England win to a draw, in contravention of the Laws of Cricket, only to rescind their decision in January 2009.*

U Played in United Arab Emirates.

Notes: The following deputised for the official touring captain or were appointed by the home authority for only a minor proportion of the series:
[1]D. S. Sheppard (Second and Third). [2]M. C. Cowdrey (Third). [3]G. Boycott (Third). [4]D. I. Gower (Second). [5]D. I. Gower (Second and Third). [6]A. J. Stewart (Second). [7]M. E. Trescothick (First).

SERIES RECORDS

Highest score	E	278	D. C. S. Compton at Nottingham.	1954
	P	274	Zaheer Abbas at Birmingham	1971
Best bowling	E	8-34	I. T. Botham at Lord's	1978
	P	9-56	Abdul Qadir at Lahore.	1987-88
Highest total	E	558-6 dec	at Nottingham	1954
	P	708	at The Oval	1987
Lowest total	E	72	at Abu Dhabi	2011-12
	P	72	at Birmingham.	2010

An expanded and regularly updated online version of the Records can be found at www.wisdenrecords.com

ENGLAND v SRI LANKA

		Captains				
Season	*England*	*Sri Lanka*	*T*	*E*	*SL*	*D*
1981-82	K. W. R. Fletcher	B. Warnapura	1	1	0	0
1984	D. I. Gower	L. R. D. Mendis	1	0	0	1
1988	G. A. Gooch	R. S. Madugalle	1	1	0	0
1991	G. A. Gooch	P. A. de Silva	1	1	0	0
1992-93	A. J. Stewart	A. Ranatunga	1	0	1	0
1998	A. J. Stewart	A. Ranatunga	1	0	1	0
2000-01	N. Hussain	S. T. Jayasuriya	3	2	1	0
2002	N. Hussain	S. T. Jayasuriya	3	2	0	1
2003-04	M. P. Vaughan	H. P. Tillekeratne	3	0	1	2
2006	A. Flintoff	D. P. M. D. Jayawardene	3	1	1	1
2007-08	M. P. Vaughan	D. P. M. D. Jayawardene	3	0	1	2
2011	A. J. Strauss	T. M. Dilshan[1]	3	1	0	2
2011-12	A. J. Strauss	D. P. M. D. Jayawardene	2	1	1	0
	In England		13	6	2	5
	In Sri Lanka		13	4	5	4
	Totals		26	10	7	9

Note: The following deputised for the official touring captain for only a minor proportion of the series:

[1]K. C. Sangakkara (Third).

SERIES RECORDS

Highest score	E	203	I. J. L. Trott at Cardiff	2011
	SL	213*	D. P. M. D. Jayawardene at Galle	2007-08
Best bowling	E	7-70	P. A. J. DeFreitas at Lord's	1991
	SL	9-65	M. Muralitharan at The Oval	1998
Highest total	E	551-6 dec	at Lord's................................	2006
	SL	628-8 dec	at Colombo (SSC)	2003-04
Lowest total	E	81	at Galle...................................	2007-08
	SL	81	at Colombo (SSC)	2000-01

ENGLAND v ZIMBABWE

		Captains				
Season	*England*	*Zimbabwe*	*T*	*E*	*Z*	*D*
1996-97	M. A. Atherton	A. D. R. Campbell	2	0	0	2
2000	N. Hussain	A. Flower	2	1	0	1
2003	N. Hussain	H. H. Streak	2	2	0	0
	In England		4	3	0	1
	In Zimbabwe		2	0	0	2
	Totals		6	3	0	3

SERIES RECORDS

Highest score	E	137	M. A. Butcher at Lord's	2003
	Z	148*	M. W. Goodwin at Nottingham.................	2000
Best bowling	E	6-33	R. L. Johnson at Chester-le-Street.............	2003
	Z	6-87	H. H. Streak at Lord's.......................	2000
Highest total	E	472	at Lord's	2003
	Z	376	at Bulawayo.............................	1996-97
Lowest total	E	147	at Nottingham	2000
	Z	83	at Lord's	2000

ENGLAND v BANGLADESH

	Captains					
Season	England	Bangladesh	T	E	B	D
2003-04	M. P. Vaughan	Khaled Mahmud	2	2	0	0
2005	M. P. Vaughan	Habibul Bashar	2	2	0	0
2009-10	A. N. Cook	Shakib Al Hasan	2	2	0	0
2010	A. J. Strauss	Shakib Al Hasan	2	2	0	0
	In England		4	4	0	0
	In Bangladesh.....................		4	4	0	0
	Totals		8	8	0	0

SERIES RECORDS

Highest score	E	226	I. J. L. Trott at Lord's	2010
	B	108	Tamim Iqbal at Manchester.................	2010
Best bowling	E	5-35	S. J. Harmison at Dhaka	2003-04
	B	5-98	Shahadat Hossain at Lord's.................	2010
Highest total	E	599-6 dec	at Chittagong	2009-10
	B	419	at Mirpur	2009-10
Lowest total	E	295	at Dhaka...............................	2003-04
	B	104	at Chester-le-Street	2005

AUSTRALIA v SOUTH AFRICA

	Captains					
Season	Australia	South Africa	T	A	SA	D
1902-03S	J. Darling	H. M. Taberer[1]	3	2	0	1
1910-11A	C. Hill	P. W. Sherwell	5	4	1	0
1912E	S. E. Gregory	F. Mitchell[2]	3	2	0	1
1921-22S	H. L. Collins	H. W. Taylor	3	1	0	2
1931-32A	W. M. Woodfull	H. B. Cameron	5	5	0	0
1935-36S	V. Y. Richardson	H. F. Wade	5	4	0	1
1949-50S	A. L. Hassett	A. D. Nourse	5	4	0	1
1952-53A	A. L. Hassett	J. E. Cheetham	5	2	2	1
1957-58S	I. D. Craig	C. B. van Ryneveld[3]	5	3	0	2
1963-64A	R. B. Simpson[4]	T. L. Goddard	5	1	1	3
1966-67S	R. B. Simpson	P. L. van der Merwe	5	1	3	1
1969-70S	W. M. Lawry	A. Bacher	4	0	4	0
1993-94A	A. R. Border	K. C. Wessels[5]	3	1	1	1
1993-94S	A. R. Border	K. C. Wessels	3	1	1	1
1996-97S	M. A. Taylor	W. J. Cronje	3	2	1	0
1997-98A	M. A. Taylor	W. J. Cronje	3	1	0	2
2001-02A	S. R. Waugh	S. M. Pollock	3	3	0	0
2001-02S	S. R. Waugh	M. V. Boucher	3	2	1	0
2005-06A	R. T. Ponting	G. C. Smith	3	2	0	1
2005-06S	R. T. Ponting	G. C. Smith[6]	3	3	0	0
2008-09A	R. T. Ponting	G. C. Smith	3	1	2	0
2008-09S	R. T. Ponting	G. C. Smith[7]	3	2	1	0
2011-12S	M. J. Clarke	G. C. Smith	2	1	1	0
2012-13A	M. J. Clarke	G. C. Smith	3	0	1	2
	In South Africa......................		47	26	12	9
	In Australia.........................		38	20	8	10
	In England		3	2	0	1
	Totals		88	48	20	20

S Played in South Africa.   A Played in Australia.   E Played in England.

Notes: The following deputised for the official touring captain or were appointed by the home authority for only a minor proportion of the series:

[1]J. H. Anderson (Second), E. A. Halliwell (Third). [2]L. J. Tancred (Third). [3]D. J. McGlew (First). [4]R. Benaud (First). [5]W. J. Cronje (Third). [6]J. H. Kallis (Third). [7]J. H. Kallis (Third).

SERIES RECORDS

Highest score	A	299*	D. G. Bradman at Adelaide	1931-32
	SA	274	R. G. Pollock at Durban.	1969-70
Best bowling	A	8-61	M. G. Johnson at Perth	2008-09
	SA	7-23	H. J. Tayfield at Durban.	1949-50
Highest total	A	652-7 dec	at Johannesburg	2001-02
	SA	651	at Cape Town.	2008-09
Lowest total	A	47	at Cape Town.	2011-12
	SA	36	at Melbourne	1931-32

AUSTRALIA v WEST INDIES

		Captains					
Season	Australia	West Indies	T	A	WI	T	D
1930-31A	W. M. Woodfull	G. C. Grant	5	4	1	0	0
1951-52A	A. L. Hassett[1]	J. D. C. Goddard[2]	5	4	1	0	0
1954-55W	I. W. Johnson	D. St E. Atkinson[3]	5	3	0	0	2

THE FRANK WORRELL TROPHY

		Captains						
Season	Australia	West Indies	T	A	WI	T	D	Held by
1960-61A	R. Benaud	F. M. M. Worrell	5	2	1	1	1	A
1964-65W	R. B. Simpson	G. S. Sobers	5	1	2	0	2	WI
1968-69A	W. M. Lawry	G. S. Sobers	5	3	1	0	1	A
1972-73W	I. M. Chappell	R. B. Kanhai	5	2	0	0	3	A
1975-76A	G. S. Chappell	C. H. Lloyd	6	5	1	0	0	A
1977-78W	R. B. Simpson	A. I. Kallicharran[4]	5	1	3	0	1	WI
1979-80A	G. S. Chappell	C. H. Lloyd[5]	3	0	2	0	1	WI
1981-82A	G. S. Chappell	C. H. Lloyd	3	1	1	0	1	WI
1983-84W	K. J. Hughes	C. H. Lloyd[6]	5	0	3	0	2	WI
1984-85A	A. R. Border[7]	C. H. Lloyd	5	1	3	0	1	WI
1988-89A	A. R. Border	I. V. A. Richards	5	1	3	0	1	WI
1990-91W	A. R. Border	I. V. A. Richards	5	1	2	0	2	WI
1992-93A	A. R. Border	R. B. Richardson	5	1	2	0	2	WI
1994-95W	M. A. Taylor	R. B. Richardson	4	2	1	0	1	A
1996-97A	M. A. Taylor	C. A. Walsh	5	3	2	0	0	A
1998-99W	S. R. Waugh	B. C. Lara	4	2	2	0	0	A
2000-01A	S. R. Waugh[8]	J. C. Adams	5	5	0	0	0	A
2002-03W	S. R. Waugh	B. C. Lara	4	3	1	0	0	A
2005-06A	R. T. Ponting	S. Chanderpaul	3	3	0	0	0	A
2007-08W	R. T. Ponting	R. R. Sarwan[9]	3	2	0	0	1	A
2009-10A	R. T. Ponting	C. H. Gayle	3	2	0	0	1	A
2011-12W	M. J. Clarke	D. J. G. Sammy	3	2	0	0	1	A
	In Australia		63	35	18	1	9	
	In West Indies		48	19	14	0	15	
	Totals		111	54	32	1	24	

A Played in Australia.   W Played in West Indies.

Notes: The following deputised for the official touring captain or were appointed by the home authority for only a minor proportion of the series:
[1]A. R. Morris (Third). [2]J. B. Stollmeyer (Fifth). [3]J. B. Stollmeyer (Second and Third). [4]C. H. Lloyd (First and Second). [5]D. L. Murray (First). [6]I. V. A. Richards (Second). [7]K. J. Hughes (First and Second). [8]A. C. Gilchrist (Third). [9]C. H. Gayle (Third).

SERIES RECORDS

Highest score	A	242	K. D. Walters at Sydney	1968-69
	WI	277	B. C. Lara at Sydney	1992-93
Best bowling	A	8-71	G. D. McKenzie at Melbourne	1968-69
	WI	7-25	C. E. L. Ambrose at Perth	1992-93
Highest total	A	758-8 dec	at Kingston	1954-55
	WI	616	at Adelaide...........................	1968-69
Lowest total	A	76	at Perth..............................	1984-85
	WI	51	at Port-of-Spain	1998-99

AUSTRALIA v NEW ZEALAND

	Captains					
Season	Australia	New Zealand	T	A	NZ	D
1945-46N	W. A. Brown	W. A. Hadlee	1	1	0	0
1973-74A	I. M. Chappell	B. E. Congdon	3	2	0	1
1973-74N	I. M. Chappell	B. E. Congdon	3	1	1	1
1976-77N	G. S. Chappell	G. M. Turner	2	1	0	1
1980-81A	G. S. Chappell	G. P. Howarth[1]	3	2	0	1
1981-82N	G. S. Chappell	G. P. Howarth	3	1	1	1

TRANS-TASMAN TROPHY

	Captains						
Season	Australia	New Zealand	T	A	NZ	D	Held by
1985-86A	A. R. Border	J. V. Coney	3	1	2	0	NZ
1985-86N	A. R. Border	J. V. Coney	3	0	1	2	NZ
1987-88A	A. R. Border	J. J. Crowe	3	1	0	2	A
1989-90A	A. R. Border	J. G. Wright	1	0	0	1	A
1989-90N	A. R. Border	J. G. Wright	1	0	1	0	NZ
1992-93N	A. R. Border	M. D. Crowe	3	1	1	1	NZ
1993-94A	A. R. Border	M. D. Crowe[2]	3	2	0	1	A
1997-98A	M. A. Taylor	S. P. Fleming	3	2	0	1	A
1999-2000N	S. R. Waugh	S. P. Fleming	3	3	0	0	A
2001-02A	S. R. Waugh	S. P. Fleming	3	0	0	3	A
2004-05A	R. T. Ponting	S. P. Fleming	2	2	0	0	A
2004-05N	R. T. Ponting	S. P. Fleming	3	2	0	1	A
2008-09A	R. T. Ponting	D. L. Vettori	2	2	0	0	A
2009-10N	R. T. Ponting	D. L. Vettori	2	2	0	0	A
2011-12A	M. J. Clarke	L. R. P. L. Taylor	2	1	1	0	A
	In Australia......................		28	15	3	10	
	In New Zealand		24	12	5	7	
	Totals		52	27	8	17	

A Played in Australia. N Played in New Zealand.

Notes: The following deputised for the official touring captain: [1]M. G. Burgess (Second). [2]K. R. Rutherford (Second and Third).

SERIES RECORDS

Highest score	A	250	K. D. Walters at Christchurch...............		1976-77
	NZ	188	M. D. Crowe at Brisbane..................		1985-86
Best bowling	A	6-31	S. K. Warne at Hobart....................		1993-94
	NZ	9-52	R. J. Hadlee at Brisbane		1985-86
Highest total	A	607-6 dec	at Brisbane		1993-94
	NZ	553-7 dec	at Brisbane		1985-86
Lowest total	A	103	at Auckland...........................		1985-86
	NZ	42	at Wellington..........................		1945-46

AUSTRALIA v INDIA

	Captains						
Season	*Australia*	*India*	*T*	*A*	*I*	*T*	*D*
1947-48A	D. G. Bradman	L. Amarnath	5	4	0	0	1
1956-57I	I. W. Johnson[1]	P. R. Umrigar	3	2	0	0	1
1959-60I	R. Benaud	G. S. Ramchand	5	2	1	0	2
1964-65I	R. B. Simpson	Nawab of Pataudi jun.	3	1	1	0	1
1967-68A	R. B. Simpson[2]	Nawab of Pataudi jun.[3]	4	4	0	0	0
1969-70I	W. M. Lawry	Nawab of Pataudi jun.	5	3	1	0	1
1977-78A	R. B. Simpson	B. S. Bedi	5	3	2	0	0
1979-80I	K. J. Hughes	S. M. Gavaskar	6	0	2	0	4
1980-81A	G. S. Chappell	S. M. Gavaskar	3	1	1	0	1
1985-86A	A. R. Border	Kapil Dev	3	0	0	0	3
1986-87I	A. R. Border	Kapil Dev	3	0	0	1	2
1991-92A	A. R. Border	M. Azharuddin	5	4	0	0	1

THE BORDER–GAVASKAR TROPHY

	Captains							
Season	*Australia*	*India*	*T*	*A*	*I*	*T*	*D*	*Held by*
1996-97I	M. A. Taylor	S. R. Tendulkar	1	0	1	0	0	I
1997-98I	M. A. Taylor	M. Azharuddin	3	1	2	0	0	I
1999-2000A	S. R. Waugh	S. R. Tendulkar	3	3	0	0	0	A
2000-01I	S. R. Waugh	S. C. Ganguly	3	1	2	0	0	I
2003-04A	S. R. Waugh	S. C. Ganguly	4	1	1	0	2	I
2004-05I	R. T. Ponting[4]	S. C. Ganguly[5]	4	2	1	0	1	A
2007-08A	R. T. Ponting	A. Kumble	4	2	1	0	1	A
2008-09I	R. T. Ponting	A. Kumble[6]	4	0	2	0	2	I
2010-11I	R. T. Ponting	M. S. Dhoni	2	0	2	0	0	I
2011-12A	M. J. Clarke	M. S. Dhoni[7]	4	4	0	0	0	A
2012-13I	**M. J. Clarke[8]**	**M. S. Dhoni**	**4**	**0**	**4**	**0**	**0**	**I**
	In Australia....................		40	26	5	0	9	
	In India		**46**	**12**	**19**	**1**	**14**	
	Totals........................		86	38	24	1	23	

A Played in Australia. I Played in India.

Notes: The following deputised for the official touring captain or were appointed by the home authority for only a minor proportion of the series:

[1]R. R. Lindwall (Second). [2]W. M. Lawry (Third and Fourth). [3]C. G. Borde (First). [4]A. C. Gilchrist (First, Second and Third). [5]R. Dravid (Third and Fourth). [6]M. S. Dhoni (Second and Fourth). [7]V. Sehwag (Fourth). [8]S. R. Watson (Fourth).

SERIES RECORDS

Highest score	A	329*	M. J. Clarke at Sydney....................	2011-12
	I	281	V. V. S. Laxman at Kolkata................	2000-01
Best bowling	A	8-215	J. J. Krejza at Nagpur....................	2008-09
	I	9-69	J. M. Patel at Kanpur....................	1959-60
Highest total	A	674	at Adelaide............................	1947-48
	I	705-7 dec	at Sydney.............................	2003-04
Lowest total	A	83	at Melbourne..........................	1980-81
	I	58	at Brisbane...........................	1947-48

AUSTRALIA v PAKISTAN

	Captains					
Season	*Australia*	*Pakistan*	*T*	*A*	*P*	*D*
1956-57P	I. W. Johnson	A. H. Kardar	1	0	1	0
1959-60P	R. Benaud	Fazal Mahmood[1]	3	2	0	1
1964-65P	R. B. Simpson	Hanif Mohammad	1	0	0	1
1964-65A	R. B. Simpson	Hanif Mohammad	1	0	0	1
1972-73A	I. M. Chappell	Intikhab Alam	3	3	0	0
1976-77A	G. S. Chappell	Mushtaq Mohammad	3	1	1	1
1978-79A	G. N. Yallop[2]	Mushtaq Mohammad	2	1	1	0
1979-80P	G. S. Chappell	Javed Miandad	3	0	1	2
1981-82A	G. S. Chappell	Javed Miandad	3	2	1	0
1982-83P	K. J. Hughes	Imran Khan	3	0	3	0
1983-84A	K. J. Hughes	Imran Khan[3]	5	2	0	3
1988-89P	A. R. Border	Javed Miandad	3	0	1	2
1989-90A	A. R. Border	Imran Khan	3	1	0	2
1994-95P	M. A. Taylor	Salim Malik	3	0	1	2
1995-96A	M. A. Taylor	Wasim Akram	3	2	1	0
1998-99P	M. A. Taylor	Aamir Sohail	3	1	0	2
1999-2000A	S. R. Waugh	Wasim Akram	3	3	0	0
2002-03S/U	S. R. Waugh	Waqar Younis	3	3	0	0
2004-05A	R. T. Ponting	Inzamam-ul-Haq[4]	3	3	0	0
2009-10A	R. T. Ponting	Mohammad Yousuf	3	3	0	0
2010E	R. T. Ponting	Shahid Afridi[5]	2	1	1	0
	In Pakistan		20	3	7	10
	In Australia.........................		32	21	4	7
	In Sri Lanka		1	1	0	0
	In United Arab Emirates		2	2	0	0
	In England		2	1	1	0
	Totals		57	28	12	17

P Played in Pakistan.   A Played in Australia.
S/U First Test played in Sri Lanka, Second and Third Tests in United Arab Emirates.   E Played in England.

Notes: The following deputised for the official touring captain or were appointed by the home authority for only a minor proportion of the series:
[1]Imtiaz Ahmed (Second). [2]K. J. Hughes (Second). [3]Zaheer Abbas (First, Second and Third).
[4]Yousuf Youhana *later known as Mohammad Yousuf* (Second and Third). [5]Salman Butt (Second).

SERIES RECORDS

Highest score	A	334*	M. A. Taylor at Peshawar	1998-99
	P	237	Salim Malik at Rawalpindi	1994-95
Best bowling	A	8-24	G. D. McGrath at Perth	2004-05
	P	9-86	Sarfraz Nawaz at Melbourne...................	1978-79
Highest total	A	617	at Faisalabad	1979-80
	P	624	at Adelaide..................................	1983-84
Lowest total	A	80	at Karachi	1956-57
	P	53	at Sharjah...................................	2002-03

AUSTRALIA v SRI LANKA

	Captains					
Season	*Australia*	*Sri Lanka*	*T*	*A*	*SL*	*D*
1982-83S	G. S. Chappell	L. R. D. Mendis	1	1	0	0
1987-88A	A. R. Border	R. S. Madugalle	1	1	0	0
1989-90A	A. R. Border	A. Ranatunga	2	1	0	1
1992-93S	A. R. Border	A. Ranatunga	3	1	0	2
1995-96A	M. A. Taylor	A. Ranatunga[1]	3	3	0	0
1999-2000S	S. R. Waugh	S. T. Jayasuriya	3	0	1	2
2003-04S	R. T. Ponting	H. P. Tillekeratne	3	3	0	0
2004A	R. T. Ponting[2]	M. S. Atapattu	2	1	0	1

THE WARNE–MURALITHARAN TROPHY

	Captains						
Season	*Australia*	*Sri Lanka*	*T*	*A*	*SL*	*D*	*Held by*
2007-08A	R. T. Ponting	D. P. M. D. Jayawardene	2	2	0	0	A
2011-12S	M. J. Clarke	T. M. Dilshan	3	1	0	2	A
2012-13A	**M. J. Clarke**	**D. P. M. D. Jayawardene**	**3**	**3**	**0**	**0**	**A**
	In Australia		13	11	0	2	
	In Sri Lanka		13	6	1	6	
	Totals............................		**26**	**17**	**1**	**8**	

A Played in Australia. S Played in Sri Lanka.

Note: The following deputised for the official touring captain or was appointed by the home authority for only a minor proportion of the series:
[1]P. A. de Silva (Third). [2]A. C. Gilchrist (First).

SERIES RECORDS

Highest score	A	219	M. J. Slater at Perth	1995-96
	SL	192	K. C. Sangakkara at Hobart	2007-08
Best bowling	A	7-39	M. S. Kasprowicz at Darwin	2004
	SL	7-157	H. M. R. K. B. Herath at Colombo (SSC)	2011-12
Highest total	A	617-5 dec	at Perth.................................	1995-96
	SL	547-8 dec	at Colombo (SSC)	1992-93
Lowest total	A	120	at Kandy................................	2003-04
	SL	97	at Darwin	2004

AUSTRALIA v ZIMBABWE

		Captains				
Season	*Australia*	*Zimbabwe*	*T*	*A*	*Z*	*D*
1999-2000Z	S. R. Waugh	A. D. R. Campbell	1	1	0	0
2003-04A	S. R. Waugh	H. H. Streak	2	2	0	0
	In Australia....................		2	2	0	0
	In Zimbabwe		1	1	0	0
	Totals		3	3	0	0

A Played in Australia.   Z Played in Zimbabwe.

SERIES RECORDS

Highest score	A	380	M. L. Hayden at Perth...................	2003-04
	Z	118	S. V. Carlisle at Sydney.................	2003-04
Best bowling	A	6-65	S. M. Katich at Sydney	2003-04
	Z	6-121	R. W. Price at Sydney	2003-04
Highest total	A	735-6 dec	at Perth..............................	2003-04
	Z	321	at Perth..............................	2003-04
Lowest total	A	403	at Sydney............................	2003-04
	Z	194	at Harare	1999-2000

AUSTRALIA v BANGLADESH

		Captains				
Season	*Australia*	*Bangladesh*	*T*	*A*	*B*	*D*
2003A	S. R. Waugh	Khaled Mahmud	2	2	0	0
2005-06B	R. T. Ponting	Habibul Bashar	2	2	0	0
	In Australia....................		2	2	0	0
	In Bangladesh..................		2	2	0	0
	Totals		4	4	0	0

A Played in Australia.   B Played in Bangladesh.

SERIES RECORDS

Highest score	A	201*	J. N. Gillespie at Chittagong	2005-06
	B	138	Shahriar Nafees at Fatullah	2005-06
Best bowling	A	8-108	S. C. G. MacGill at Fatullah	2005-06
	B	5-62	Mohammad Rafique at Fatullah..............	2005-06
Highest total	A	581-4 dec	at Chittagong	2005-06
	B	427	at Fatullah	2005-06
Lowest total	A	269	at Fatullah	2005-06
	B	97	at Darwin..............................	2003

AUSTRALIA v ICC WORLD XI

Season	*Australia*	*ICC World XI*	*T*	*A*	*ICC*	*D*
2005-06A	R. T. Ponting	G. C. Smith	1	1	0	0

A Played in Australia.

SERIES RECORDS

Highest score	A	111	M. L. Hayden at Sydney	2005-06
	Wld	76	V. Sehwag at Sydney	2005-06
Best bowling	A	5-43	S. C. G. MacGill at Sydney	2005-06
	Wld	4-59	A. Flintoff at Sydney	2005-06
Highest total	A	345	at Sydney	2005-06
	Wld	190	at Sydney	2005-06
Lowest total	A	199	at Sydney	2005-06
	Wld	144	at Sydney	2005-06

SOUTH AFRICA v WEST INDIES

		Captains					
Season	*South Africa*		*West Indies*	*T*	*SA*	*WI*	*D*
1991-92N	K. C. Wessels		R. B. Richardson	1	0	1	0
1998-99S	W. J. Cronje		B. C. Lara	5	5	0	0

SIR VIVIAN RICHARDS TROPHY

		Captains						
Season	*South Africa*		*West Indies*	*T*	*SA*	*WI*	*D*	*Held by*
2000-01W	S. M. Pollock		C. L. Hooper	5	2	1	2	SA
2003-04S	G. C. Smith		B. C. Lara	4	3	0	1	SA
2004-05W	G. C. Smith		S. Chanderpaul	4	2	0	2	SA
2007-08 S	G. C. Smith		C. H. Gayle[1]	3	2	1	0	SA
2010W	G. C. Smith		C. H. Gayle	3	2	0	1	SA
	In South Africa			12	10	1	1	
	In West Indies			13	6	2	5	
	Totals			25	16	3	6	

S Played in South Africa. W Played in West Indies.

Note: The following deputised for the official touring captain:
[1]D. J. Bravo (Third).

SERIES RECORDS

Highest score	SA	192	H. H. Gibbs at Centurion.	2003-04
	WI	317	C. H. Gayle at St John's	2004-05
Best bowling	SA	7-37	M. Ntini at Port-of-Spain.	2004-05
	WI	7-84	F. A. Rose at Durban.	1998-99
Highest total	SA	658-9 dec	at Durban.	2003-04
	WI	747	at St John's	2004-05
Lowest total	SA	141	at Kingston	2000-01
	WI	102	at Port-of-Spain	2010

SOUTH AFRICA v NEW ZEALAND

		Captains					
Season	*South Africa*		*New Zealand*	*T*	*SA*	*NZ*	*D*
1931-32N	H. B. Cameron		M. L. Page	2	2	0	0
1952-53N	J. E. Cheetham		W. M. Wallace	2	1	0	1
1953-54S	J. E. Cheetham		G. O. Rabone[1]	5	4	0	1

Season	South Africa	Captains	New Zealand	T	SA	NZ	D
1961-62S	D. J. McGlew		J. R. Reid	5	2	2	1
1963-64N	T. L. Goddard		J. R. Reid	3	0	0	3
1994-95S	W. J. Cronje		K. R. Rutherford	3	2	1	0
1994-95N	W. J. Cronje		K. R. Rutherford	1	1	0	0
1998-99N	W. J. Cronje		D. J. Nash	3	1	0	2
2000-01S	S. M. Pollock		S. P. Fleming	3	2	0	1
2003-04N	G. C. Smith		S. P. Fleming	3	1	1	1
2005-06S	G. C. Smith		S. P. Fleming	3	2	0	1
2007-08S	G. C. Smith		D. L. Vettori	2	2	0	0
2011-12N	G. C. Smith		L. R. P. L. Taylor	3	1	0	2
2012-13S	**G. C. Smith**		**B. B. McCullum**	**2**	**2**	**0**	**0**
	In New Zealand			17	7	1	9
	In South Africa			**23**	**16**	**3**	**4**
	Totals			40	23	4	13

N Played in New Zealand.   S Played in South Africa.

Note: The following deputised for the official touring captain: [1]B. Sutcliffe (Fourth and Fifth).

SERIES RECORDS

Highest score	SA	275*	D. J. Cullinan at Auckland	1998-99
	NZ	262	S. P. Fleming at Cape Town	2005-06
Best bowling	SA	8-53	G. B. Lawrence at Johannesburg	1961-62
	NZ	6-60	J. R. Reid at Dunedin	1963-64
Highest total	SA	621-5 dec	at Auckland	1998-99
	NZ	595	at Auckland	2003-04
Lowest total	SA	148	at Johannesburg	1953-54
	NZ	**45**	**at Cape Town**	**2012-13**

SOUTH AFRICA v INDIA

Season	South Africa	Captains	India	T	SA	I	D
1992-93S	K. C. Wessels		M. Azharuddin	4	1	0	3
1996-97I	W. J. Cronje		S. R. Tendulkar	3	1	2	0
1996-97S	W. J. Cronje		S. R. Tendulkar	3	2	0	1
1999-2000I	W. J. Cronje		S. R. Tendulkar	2	2	0	0
2001-02S†	S. M. Pollock		S. C. Ganguly	2	1	0	1
2004-05I	G. C. Smith		S. C. Ganguly	2	0	1	1
2006-07S	G. C. Smith		R. Dravid	3	2	1	0
2007-08S	G. C. Smith		A. Kumble[1]	3	1	1	1
2009-10I	G. C. Smith		M. S. Dhoni	2	1	1	0
2010-11S	G. C. Smith		M. S. Dhoni	3	1	1	1
2013-14S	**G. C. Smith**		**M. S. Dhoni**	**2**	**1**	**0**	**1**
	In South Africa			17	8	2	7
	In India			12	5	5	2
	Totals			29	13	7	9

S Played in South Africa.   I Played in India.

† *The Third Test at Centurion was stripped of its official status by the ICC after a disciplinary dispute and is excluded.*

Note: The following was appointed by the home authority for only a minor proportion of the series: [1]M. S. Dhoni (Third).

SERIES RECORDS

Highest score	SA	253*	H. M. Amla at Nagpur.....................	2009-10
	I	319	V. Sehwag at Chennai.....................	2007-08
Best bowling	SA	8-64	L. Klusener at Calcutta	1996-97
	I	7-87	Harbhajan Singh at Kolkata...............	2004-05
Highest total	SA	620-4 dec	at Centurion............................	2010-11
	I	643-6 dec	at Kolkata	2009-10
Lowest total	SA	84	at Johannesburg.........................	2006-07
	I	66	at Durban...............................	1996-97

SOUTH AFRICA v PAKISTAN

Season	South Africa	Captains Pakistan	T	SA	P	D
1994-95*S*	W. J. Cronje	Salim Malik	1	1	0	0
1997-98*P*	W. J. Cronje	Saeed Anwar	3	1	0	2
1997-98*S*	W. J. Cronje[1]	Rashid Latif[2]	3	1	1	1
2002-03*S*	S. M. Pollock	Waqar Younis	2	2	0	0
2003-04*P*	G. C. Smith	Inzamam-ul-Haq[3]	2	0	1	1
2006-07*S*	G. C. Smith	Inzamam-ul-Haq	3	2	1	0
2007-08*P*	G. C. Smith	Shoaib Malik	2	1	0	1
2010-11*U*	G. C. Smith	Misbah-ul-Haq	2	0	0	2
2012-13*S*	**G. C. Smith**	**Misbah-ul-Haq**	**3**	**3**	**0**	**0**
2013-14*U*	**G. C. Smith**	**Misbah-ul-Haq**	**2**	**1**	**1**	**0**
	In South Africa...................		**12**	**9**	**2**	**1**
	In Pakistan		7	2	1	4
	In United Arab Emirates...........		**4**	**1**	**1**	**2**
	Totals...........................		**23**	**12**	**4**	**7**

S Played in South Africa. P Played in Pakistan. U Played in United Arab Emirates.

Notes: The following deputised for the official touring captain or were appointed by the home authority for only a minor proportion of the series:

[1]G. Kirsten (First). [2]Aamir Sohail (First and Second). [3]Yousuf Youhana *later known as Mohammad Yousuf* (First).

SERIES RECORDS

Highest score	SA	278*	A. B. de Villiers at Abu Dhabi	2010-11
	P	**146**	**Khurram Manzoor at Abu Dhabi**	**2013-14**
Best bowling	SA	**7-29**	**K. J. Abbott at Centurion**................	**2012-13**
	P	6-78	Mushtaq Ahmed at Durban.................	1997-98
		6-78	Waqar Younis at Port Elizabeth	1997-98
Highest total	SA	620-7 dec	at Cape Town	2002-03
	P	456	at Rawalpindi	1997-98
Lowest total	SA	124	at Port Elizabeth	2006-07
	P	**49**	**at Johannesburg**	**2012-13**

An expanded and regularly updated online version of the Records can be found at www.wisdenrecords.com

SOUTH AFRICA v SRI LANKA

		Captains					
Season	*South Africa*		*Sri Lanka*	*T*	*SA*	*SL*	*D*
1993-94*SL*	K. C. Wessels		A. Ranatunga	3	1	0	2
1997-98*SA*	W. J. Cronje		A. Ranatunga	2	2	0	0
2000*SL*	S. M. Pollock		S. T. Jayasuriya	3	1	1	1
2000-01*SA*	S. M. Pollock		S. T. Jayasuriya	3	2	0	1
2002-03*SA*	S. M. Pollock		S. T. Jayasuriya[1]	2	2	0	0
2004*SL*	G. C. Smith		M. S. Atapattu	2	0	1	1
2006*SL*	A. G. Prince		D. P. M. D. Jayawardene	2	0	2	0
2011-12*SA*	G. C. Smith		T. M. Dilshan	3	2	1	0
	In South Africa.............................			10	8	1	1
	In Sri Lanka...............................			10	2	4	4
	Totals.................................			20	10	5	5

SA Played in South Africa.   SL Played in Sri Lanka.

Note: The following deputised for the official captain:
  [1]M. S. Atapattu (Second).

SERIES RECORDS

Highest score	SA	224	J. H. Kallis at Cape Town..................	2011-12
	SL	374	D. P. M. D. Jayawardene at Colombo (SSC)...	2006
Best bowling	SA	7-81	M. de Lange at Durban....................	2011-12
	SL	7-84	M. Muralitharan at Galle..................	2000
Highest total	SA	580-4 dec	at Cape Town...........................	2011-12
	SL	756-5 dec	at Colombo (SSC).......................	2006
Lowest total	SA	168	at Durban..............................	2011-12
	SL	95	at Cape Town...........................	2000-01

SOUTH AFRICA v ZIMBABWE

		Captains					
Season	*South Africa*		*Zimbabwe*	*T*	*SA*	*Z*	*D*
1995-96*Z*	W. J. Cronje		A. Flower	1	1	0	0
1999-2000*S*	W. J. Cronje		A. D. R. Campbell	1	1	0	0
1999-2000*Z*	W. J. Cronje		A. Flower	1	1	0	0
2001-02*Z*	S. M. Pollock		H. H. Streak	2	1	0	1
2004-05*S*	G. C. Smith		T. Taibu	2	2	0	0
	In Zimbabwe.....................			4	3	0	1
	In South Africa...................			3	3	0	0
	Totals..........................			7	6	0	1

S Played in South Africa.   Z Played in Zimbabwe.

SERIES RECORDS

Highest score	SA	220	G. Kirsten at Harare.....................	2001-02
	Z	199*	A. Flower at Harare......................	2001-02
Best bowling	SA	8-71	A. A. Donald at Harare...................	1995-96
	Z	5-101	B. C. Strang at Harare...................	1995-96
Highest total	SA	600-3 dec	at Harare..............................	2001-02
	Z	419-9 dec	at Bulawayo...........................	2001-02
Lowest total	SA	346	at Harare..............................	1995-96
	Z	54	at Cape Town...........................	2004-05

SOUTH AFRICA v BANGLADESH

		Captains				
Season	*South Africa*	*Bangladesh*	*T*	*SA*	*B*	*D*
2002-03*S*	S. M. Pollock[1]	Khaled Mashud	2	2	0	0
2003*B*	G. C. Smith	Khaled Mahmud	2	2	0	0
2007-08*B*	G. C. Smith	Mohammad Ashraful	2	2	0	0
2008-09*S*	G. C. Smith	Mohammad Ashraful	2	2	0	0
	In South Africa....................		4	4	0	0
	In Bangladesh.....................		4	4	0	0
	Totals		8	8	0	0

S Played in South Africa.   B Played in Bangladesh.

Note: The following deputised for the official captain:
[1]M. V. Boucher (First).

SERIES RECORDS

Highest score	SA	232	G. C. Smith at Chittagong	2007-08
	B	75	Habibul Bashar at Chittagong	2003
Best bowling	SA	5-19	M. Ntini at East London	2002-03
	B	6-27	Shahadat Hossain at Mirpur................	2007-08
Highest total	SA	583-7 dec	at Chittagong	2007-08
	B	259	at Chittagong	2007-08
Lowest total	SA	170	at Mirpur	2007-08
	B	102	at Dhaka................................	2003

WEST INDIES v NEW ZEALAND

		Captains				
Season	*West Indies*	*New Zealand*	*T*	*WI*	*NZ*	*D*
1951-52*N*	J. D. C. Goddard	B. Sutcliffe	2	1	0	1
1955-56*N*	D. St E. Atkinson	J. R. Reid[1]	4	3	1	0
1968-69*N*	G. S. Sobers	G. T. Dowling	3	1	1	1
1971-72*W*	G. S. Sobers	G. T. Dowling[2]	5	0	0	5
1979-80*N*	C. H. Lloyd	G. P. Howarth	3	0	1	2
1984-85*W*	I. V. A. Richards	G. P. Howarth	4	2	0	2
1986-87*N*	I. V. A. Richards	J. V. Coney	3	1	1	1
1994-95*N*	C. A. Walsh	K. R. Rutherford	2	1	0	1
1995-96*W*	C. A. Walsh	L. K. Germon	2	1	0	1
1999-2000*N*	B. C. Lara	S. P. Fleming	2	0	2	0
2002*W*	C. L. Hooper	S. P. Fleming	2	0	1	1
2005-06*N*	S. Chanderpaul	S. P. Fleming	3	0	2	1
2008-09*N*	C. H. Gayle	D. L. Vettori	2	0	0	2
2012*W*	D. J. G. Sammy	L. R. P. L. Taylor	2	2	0	0
2013-14*N*	**D. J. G. Sammy**	**B. B. McCullum**	**3**	**0**	**2**	**1**
	In New Zealand..................		27	7	10	10
	In West Indies...................		15	5	1	9
	Totals		**42**	**12**	**11**	**19**

N Played in New Zealand.   W Played in West Indies.

Notes: The following deputised for the official touring captain or were appointed by the home authority for only a minor proportion of the series:
[1]H. B. Cave (First). [2]B. E. Congdon (Third, Fourth and Fifth).

SERIES RECORDS

Highest score	WI	258	S. M. Nurse at Christchurch	1968-69
	NZ	259	G. M. Turner at Georgetown	1971-72
Best bowling	WI	7-37	C. A. Walsh at Wellington	1994-95
	NZ	7-27	C. L. Cairns at Hamilton	1999-2000
Highest total	WI	660-5 dec	at Wellington	1994-95
	NZ	**609-9 dec**	**at Dunedin (University)**	**2013-14**
Lowest total	WI	77	at Auckland	1955-56
	NZ	74	at Dunedin	1955-56

WEST INDIES v INDIA

		Captains				
Season	*West Indies*	*India*	*T*	*WI*	*I*	*D*
1948-49*I*	J. D. C. Goddard	L. Amarnath	5	1	0	4
1952-53*W*	J. B. Stollmeyer	V. S. Hazare	5	1	0	4
1958-59*I*	F. C. M. Alexander	Ghulam Ahmed[1]	5	3	0	2
1961-62*W*	F. M. M. Worrell	N. J. Contractor[2]	5	5	0	0
1966-67*I*	G. S. Sobers	Nawab of Pataudi jun.	3	2	0	1
1970-71*W*	G. S. Sobers	A. L. Wadekar	5	0	1	4
1974-75*I*	C. H. Lloyd	Nawab of Pataudi jun.[3]	5	3	2	0
1975-76*W*	C. H. Lloyd	B. S. Bedi	4	2	1	1
1978-79*I*	A. I. Kallicharran	S. M. Gavaskar	6	0	1	5
1982-83*W*	C. H. Lloyd	Kapil Dev	5	2	0	3
1983-84*I*	C. H. Lloyd	Kapil Dev	6	3	0	3
1987-88*I*	I. V. A. Richards	D. B. Vengsarkar[4]	4	1	1	2
1988-89*W*	I. V. A. Richards	D. B. Vengsarkar	4	3	0	1
1994-95*I*	C. A. Walsh	M. Azharuddin	3	1	1	1
1996-97*W*	C. A. Walsh[5]	S. R. Tendulkar	5	1	0	4
2001-02*W*	C. L. Hooper	S. C. Ganguly	5	2	1	2
2002-03*I*	C. L. Hooper	S. C. Ganguly	3	0	2	1
2005-06*W*	B. C. Lara	R. Dravid	4	0	1	3
2011*W*	D. J. G. Sammy	M. S. Dhoni	3	0	1	2
2011-12*I*	D. J. G. Sammy	M. S. Dhoni	3	0	2	1
2013-14*I*	**D. J. G. Sammy**	**M. S. Dhoni**	**2**	**0**	**2**	**0**
	In India		45	14	11	20
	In West Indies		45	16	5	24
	Totals		**90**	**30**	**16**	**44**

I Played in India.   W Played in West Indies.

Notes: The following deputised for the official touring captain or were appointed by the home authority for only a minor proportion of the series:

[1]P. R. Umrigar (First), V. Mankad (Fourth), H. R. Adhikari (Fifth). [2]Nawab of Pataudi jun. (Third, Fourth and Fifth). [3]S. Venkataraghavan (Second). [4]R. J. Shastri (Fourth). [5]B. C. Lara (Third).

SERIES RECORDS

Highest score	WI	256	R. B. Kanhai at Calcutta	1958-59
	I	236*	S. M. Gavaskar at Madras	1983-84
Best bowling	WI	9-95	J. M. Noreiga at Port-of-Spain	1970-71
	I	9-83	Kapil Dev at Ahmedabad	1983-84
Highest total	WI	644-8 dec	at Delhi	1958-59
	I	644-7 dec	at Kanpur	1978-79
Lowest total	WI	103	at Kingston	2005-06
	I	75	at Delhi	1987-88

WEST INDIES v PAKISTAN

	Captains					
Season	*West Indies*	*Pakistan*	*T*	*WI*	*P*	*D*
1957-58*W*	F. C. M. Alexander	A. H. Kardar	5	3	1	1
1958-59*P*	F. C. M. Alexander	Fazal Mahmood	3	1	2	0
1974-75*P*	C. H. Lloyd	Intikhab Alam	2	0	0	2
1976-77*W*	C. H. Lloyd	Mushtaq Mohammad	5	2	1	2
1980-81*P*	C. H. Lloyd	Javed Miandad	4	1	0	3
1986-87*P*	I. V. A. Richards	Imran Khan	3	1	1	1
1987-88*W*	I. V. A. Richards[1]	Imran Khan	3	1	1	1
1990-91*P*	D. L. Haynes	Imran Khan	3	1	1	1
1992-93*W*	R. B. Richardson	Wasim Akram	3	2	0	1
1997-98*P*	C. A. Walsh	Wasim Akram	3	0	3	0
1999-2000*W*	J. C. Adams	Moin Khan	3	1	0	2
2001-02*U*	C. L. Hooper	Waqar Younis	2	0	2	0
2004-05*W*	S. Chanderpaul	Inzamam-ul-Haq[2]	2	1	1	0
2006-07*P*	B. C. Lara	Inzamam-ul-Haq	3	0	2	1
2010-11*W*	D. J. G. Sammy	Misbah-ul-Haq	2	1	1	0
	In West Indies		23	11	5	7
	In Pakistan		21	4	9	8
	In United Arab Emirates		2	0	2	0
	Totals		46	15	16	15

P Played in Pakistan. W Played in West Indies. U Played in United Arab Emirates.

Note: The following were appointed by the home authority or deputised for the official touring captain for a minor proportion of the series:
[1]C. G. Greenidge (First). [2]Younis Khan (First).

SERIES RECORDS

Highest score	WI	365*	G. S. Sobers at Kingston	1957-58
	P	337	Hanif Mohammad at Bridgetown	1957-58
Best bowling	WI	8-29	C. E. H. Croft at Port-of-Spain	1976-77
	P	7-80	Imran Khan at Georgetown	1987-88
Highest total	WI	790-3 dec	at Kingston	1957-58
	P	657-8 dec	at Bridgetown	1957-58
Lowest total	WI	53	at Faisalabad	1986-87
	P	77	at Lahore	1986-87

WEST INDIES v SRI LANKA

	Captains					
Season	*West Indies*	*Sri Lanka*	*T*	*WI*	*SL*	*D*
1993-94*S*	R. B. Richardson	A. Ranatunga	1	0	0	1
1996-97*W*	C. A. Walsh	A. Ranatunga	2	1	0	1
2001-02*S*	C. L. Hooper	S. T. Jayasuriya	3	0	3	0
2003*W*	B. C. Lara	H. P. Tillekeratne	2	1	0	1
2005*S*	S. Chanderpaul	M. S. Atapattu	2	0	2	0
2007-08*W*	C. H. Gayle	D. P. M. D. Jayawardene	2	1	1	0
2010-11*S*	D. J. G. Sammy	K. C. Sangakkara	3	0	0	3
	In West Indies		6	3	1	2
	In Sri Lanka		9	0	5	4
	Totals		15	3	6	6

W Played in West Indies. S Played in Sri Lanka.

SERIES RECORDS

Highest score	WI	333	C. H. Gayle at Galle	2010-11
	SL	204*	H. P. Tillekeratne at Colombo (SSC)	2001-02
Best bowling	WI	7-57	C. D. Collymore at Kingston...............	2003
	SL	8-46	M. Muralitharan at Kandy.................	2005
Highest total	WI	580-9 dec	at Galle	2010-11
	SL	627-9 dec	at Colombo (SSC).......................	2001-02
Lowest total	WI	113	at Colombo (SSC)	2005
	SL	150	at Kandy	2005

WEST INDIES v ZIMBABWE

		Captains					
Season	West Indies		Zimbabwe	T	WI	Z	D
1999-2000W	J. C. Adams		A. Flower	2	2	0	0

THE CLIVE LLOYD TROPHY

		Captains						
Season	West Indies		Zimbabwe	T	WI	Z	D	Held by
2001Z	C. L. Hooper		H. H. Streak	2	1	0	1	WI
2003-04Z	B. C. Lara		H. H. Streak	2	1	0	1	WI
2012-13W	**D. J. G. Sammy**		**B. R. M. Taylor**	**2**	**2**	**0**	**0**	**WI**
	In West Indies...................			4	4	0	0	
	In Zimbabwe			4	2	0	2	
	Totals...........................			8	6	0	2	

W Played in West Indies.   Z Played in Zimbabwe.

SERIES RECORDS

Highest score	WI	191	B. C. Lara at Bulawayo.................	2003-04
	Z	127*	H. H. Streak at Harare	2003-04
Best bowling	WI	**6-49**	S. Shillingford at Bridgetown...........	**2012-13**
	Z	6-73	R. W. Price at Harare....................	2003-04
Highest total	WI	559-6 dec	at Bulawayo...........................	2001
	Z	563-9 dec	at Harare	2001
Lowest total	WI	128	at Bulawayo...........................	2003-04
	Z	63	at Port-of-Spain	1999-2000

WEST INDIES v BANGLADESH

		Captains					
Season	West Indies		Bangladesh	T	WI	B	D
2002-03B	R. D. Jacobs		Khaled Mashud	2	2	0	0
2003-04W	B. C. Lara		Habibul Bashar	2	1	0	1
2009W	F. L. Reifer		Mashrafe bin Mortaza[1]	2	0	2	0
2011-12B	D. J. G. Sammy		Mushfiqur Rahim	2	1	0	1
2012-13B	D. J. G. Sammy		Mushfiqur Rahim	2	2	0	0
	In West Indies			4	1	2	1
	In Bangladesh....................			6	5	0	1
	Totals............................			10	6	2	2

B Played in Bangladesh.   W Played in West Indies.

Note: The following deputised for the official touring captain for a minor proportion of the series:
[1]Shakib Al Hasan (Second).

SERIES RECORDS

Highest score	WI	261*	R. R. Sarwan at Kingston	2003-04
	B	128	Tamim Iqbal at St Vincent................	2009
Best bowling	WI	6-3	J. J. C. Lawson at Dhaka....................	2002-03
	B	6-74	Sohag Gazi at Mirpur	2012-13
Highest total	WI	648-9 dec	at Khulna...............................	2012-13
	B	556	at Mirpur	2012-13
Lowest total	WI	181	at St Vincent	2009
	B	87	at Dhaka................................	2002-03

NEW ZEALAND v INDIA

Season	New Zealand	*Captains* India	T	NZ	I	D
1955-56*I*	H. B. Cave	P. R. Umrigar[1]	5	0	2	3
1964-65*I*	J. R. Reid	Nawab of Pataudi jun.	4	0	1	3
1967-68*N*	G. T. Dowling[2]	Nawab of Pataudi jun.	4	1	3	0
1969-70*I*	G. T. Dowling	Nawab of Pataudi jun.	3	1	1	1
1975-76*N*	G. M. Turner	B. S. Bedi[3]	3	1	1	1
1976-77*I*	G. M. Turner	B. S. Bedi	3	0	2	1
1980-81*N*	G. P. Howarth	S. M. Gavaskar	3	1	0	2
1988-89*I*	J. G. Wright	D. B. Vengsarkar	3	1	2	0
1989-90*N*	J. G. Wright	M. Azharuddin	3	1	0	2
1993-94*N*	K. R. Rutherford	M. Azharuddin	1	0	0	1
1995-96*I*	L. K. Germon	M. Azharuddin	3	0	1	2
1998-99*N*†	S. P. Fleming	M. Azharuddin	2	1	0	1
1999-2000*I*	S. P. Fleming	S. R. Tendulkar	3	0	1	2
2002-03*N*	S. P. Fleming	S. C. Ganguly	2	2	0	0
2003-04*I*	S. P. Fleming	S. C. Ganguly[4]	2	0	0	2
2008-09*N*	D. L. Vettori	M. S. Dhoni[5]	3	0	1	2
2010-11*I*	D. L. Vettori	M. S. Dhoni	3	0	1	2
2012-13*I*	L. R. P. L. Taylor	M. S. Dhoni	2	0	2	0
	In India........................		31	2	13	16
	In New Zealand		21	7	5	9
	Totals		52	9	18	25

I Played in India.   N Played in New Zealand.

† *The First Test at Dunedin was abandoned without a ball being bowled and is excluded.*

Notes: The following deputised for the official touring captain or were appointed by the home authority for a minor proportion of the series:
[1]Ghulam Ahmed (First). [2]B. W. Sinclair (First). [3]S. M. Gavaskar (First). [4]R. Dravid (Second). [5]V. Sehwag (Second).

SERIES RECORDS

Highest score	NZ	239	G. T. Dowling at Christchurch	1967-68
	I	231	V. Mankad at Madras	1955-56
Best bowling	NZ	7-23	R. J. Hadlee at Wellington	1975-76
	I	8-72	S. Venkataraghavan at Delhi.............	1964-65
Highest total	NZ	630-6 dec	at Mohali...............................	2003-04
	I	583-7 dec	at Ahmedabad	1999-2000
Lowest total	NZ	94	at Hamilton	2002-03
	I	81	at Wellington........................	1975-76

NEW ZEALAND v PAKISTAN

	Captains					
Season	*New Zealand*	*Pakistan*	*T*	*NZ*	*P*	*D*
1955-56P	H. B. Cave	A. H. Kardar	3	0	2	1
1964-65N	J. R. Reid	Hanif Mohammad	3	0	0	3
1964-65P	J. R. Reid	Hanif Mohammad	3	0	2	1
1969-70P	G. T. Dowling	Intikhab Alam	3	1	0	2
1972-73N	B. E. Congdon	Intikhab Alam	3	0	1	2
1976-77P	G. M. Turner[1]	Mushtaq Mohammad	3	0	2	1
1978-79N	M. G. Burgess	Mushtaq Mohammad	3	0	1	2
1984-85P	J. V. Coney	Zaheer Abbas	3	0	2	1
1984-85N	G. P. Howarth	Javed Miandad	3	2	0	1
1988-89N†	J. G. Wright	Imran Khan	2	0	0	2
1990-91P	M. D. Crowe	Javed Miandad	3	0	3	0
1992-93N	K. R. Rutherford	Javed Miandad	1	0	1	0
1993-94N	K. R. Rutherford	Salim Malik	3	1	2	0
1995-96N	L. K. Germon	Wasim Akram	1	0	1	0
1996-97P	L. K. Germon	Saeed Anwar	2	1	1	0
2000-01N	S. P. Fleming	Moin Khan[2]	3	1	1	1
2002P‡	S. P. Fleming	Waqar Younis	1	0	1	0
2003-04N	S. P. Fleming	Inzamam-ul-Haq	2	0	1	1
2009-10N	D. L. Vettori	Mohammad Yousuf	3	1	1	1
2010-11N	D. L. Vettori	Misbah-ul-Haq	2	0	1	1
	In Pakistan		21	2	13	6
	In New Zealand		29	5	10	14
	Totals		50	7	23	20

N Played in New Zealand.   P Played in Pakistan.

† *The First Test at Dunedin was abandoned without a ball being bowled and is excluded.*
‡ *The Second Test at Karachi was cancelled owing to civil disturbances.*

Note: The following were appointed by the home authority for only a minor proportion of the series or deputised for the official touring captain:
[1]J. M. Parker (Third). [2]Inzamam-ul-Haq (Third).

SERIES RECORDS

Highest score	NZ	204*	M. S. Sinclair at Christchurch..................	2000-01
	P	329	Inzamam-ul-Haq at Lahore....................	2002
Best bowling	NZ	7-52	C. Pringle at Faisalabad.....................	1990-91
	P	7-52	Intikhab Alam at Dunedin....................	1972-73
Highest total	NZ	563	at Hamilton	2003-04
	P	643	at Lahore	2002
Lowest total	NZ	70	at Dacca..................................	1955-56
	P	102	at Faisalabad	1990-91

NEW ZEALAND v SRI LANKA

	Captains					
Season	*New Zealand*	*Sri Lanka*	*T*	*NZ*	*SL*	*D*
1982-83N	G. P. Howarth	D. S. de Silva	2	2	0	0
1983-84S	G. P. Howarth	L. R. D. Mendis	3	2	0	1
1986-87St	J. J. Crowe	L. R. D. Mendis	1	0	0	1
1990-91N	M. D. Crowe[1]	A. Ranatunga	3	0	0	3
1992-93S	M. D. Crowe	A. Ranatunga	2	0	1	1
1994-95N	K. R. Rutherford	A. Ranatunga	2	0	1	1

1996-97*N*	S. P. Fleming	A. Ranatunga	2	2	0	0
1997-98*S*	S. P. Fleming	A. Ranatunga	3	1	2	0
2003*S*	S. P. Fleming	H. P. Tillekeratne	2	0	0	2
2004-05*N*	S. P. Fleming	M. S. Atapattu	2	1	0	1
2006-07*N*	S. P. Fleming	D. P. M. D. Jayawardene	2	1	1	0
2009*S*	D. L. Vettori	K. C. Sangakkara	2	0	2	0
2012-13*S*	L. R. P. L. Taylor	D. P. M. D. Jayawardene	2	1	1	0
	In New Zealand		13	6	2	5
	In Sri Lanka		15	4	6	5
	Totals		28	10	8	10

N Played in New Zealand.   S Played in Sri Lanka.

† *The Second and Third Tests were cancelled owing to civil disturbances.*

Note: The following was appointed by the home authority for only a minor proportion of the series:
[1]I. D. S. Smith (Third).

SERIES RECORDS

Highest score	NZ	299	M. D. Crowe at Wellington	1990-91
	SL	267	P. A. de Silva at Wellington	1990-91
Best bowling	NZ	7-130	D. L. Vettori at Wellington	2006-07
	SL	6-43	H. M. R. K. B. Herath at Galle	2012-13
Highest total	NZ	671-4	at Wellington	1990-91
	SL	498	at Napier	2004-05
Lowest total	NZ	102	at Colombo (SSC)	1992-93
	SL	93	at Wellington	1982-83

NEW ZEALAND v ZIMBABWE

		Captains				
Season	*New Zealand*	*Zimbabwe*	*T*	*NZ*	*Z*	*D*
1992-93*Z*	M. D. Crowe	D. L. Houghton	2	1	0	1
1995-96*N*	L. K. Germon	A. Flower	2	0	0	2
1997-98*Z*	S. P. Fleming	A. D. R. Campbell	2	0	0	2
1997-98*N*	S. P. Fleming	A. D. R. Campbell	2	2	0	0
2000-01*Z*	S. P. Fleming	H. H. Streak	2	2	0	0
2000-01*N*	S. P. Fleming	H. H. Streak	1	0	0	1
2005-06*Z*	S. P. Fleming	T. Taibu	2	2	0	0
2011-12*Z*	L. R. P. L. Taylor	B. R. M. Taylor	1	1	0	0
2011-12*N*	L. R. P. L. Taylor	B. R. M. Taylor	1	1	0	0
	In New Zealand		6	3	0	3
	In Zimbabwe		9	6	0	3
	Totals		15	9	0	6

N Played in New Zealand.   Z Played in Zimbabwe.

SERIES RECORDS

Highest score	NZ	157	M. J. Horne at Auckland	1997-98
	Z	203*	G. J. Whittall at Bulawayo	1997-98
Best bowling	NZ	6-26	C. S. Martin at Napier	2011-12
	Z	8-109	P. A. Strang at Bulawayo	2000-01
Highest total	NZ	495-7 dec	at Napier	2011-12
	Z	461	at Bulawayo	1997-98
Lowest total	NZ	207	at Harare	1997-98
	Z	51	at Napier	2011-12

NEW ZEALAND v BANGLADESH

Season	New Zealand	Captains	Bangladesh	T	NZ	B	D
2001-02N	S. P. Fleming		Khaled Mashud	2	2	0	0
2004-05B	S. P. Fleming		Khaled Mashud	2	2	0	0
2007-08N	D. L. Vettori		Mohammad Ashraful	2	2	0	0
2008-09B	D. L. Vettori		Mohammad Ashraful	2	1	0	1
2009-10N	D. L. Vettori		Shakib Al Hasan	1	1	0	0
2013-14B	**B. B. McCullum**		**Mushfiqur Rahim**	**2**	**0**	**0**	**2**
	In New Zealand			5	5	0	0
	In Bangladesh			**6**	**3**	**0**	**3**
	Totals			11	8	0	3

B Played in Bangladesh.   N Played in New Zealand.

SERIES RECORDS

Highest score	NZ	202	S. P. Fleming at Chittagong	2004-05
	B	**181**	**Mominul Haque at Chittagong**	**2013-14**
Best bowling	NZ	7-53	C. L. Cairns at Hamilton	2001-02
	B	7-36	Shakib Al Hasan at Chittagong	2008-09
Highest total	NZ	553-7 dec	at Hamilton	2009-10
	B	**501**	**at Chittagong**	**2013-14**
Lowest total	NZ	171	at Chittagong	2008-09
	B	108	at Hamilton	2001-02

INDIA v PAKISTAN

Season	India	Captains	Pakistan	T	I	P	D
1952-53I	L. Amarnath		A. H. Kardar	5	2	1	2
1954-55P	V. Mankad		A. H. Kardar	5	0	0	5
1960-61I	N. J. Contractor		Fazal Mahmood	5	0	0	5
1978-79P	B. S. Bedi		Mushtaq Mohammad	3	0	2	1
1979-80I	S. M. Gavaskar[1]		Asif Iqbal	6	2	0	4
1982-83P	S. M. Gavaskar		Imran Khan	6	0	3	3
1983-84I	Kapil Dev		Zaheer Abbas	3	0	0	3
1984-85P	S. M. Gavaskar		Zaheer Abbas	2	0	0	2
1986-87I	Kapil Dev		Imran Khan	5	0	1	4
1989-90P	K. Srikkanth		Imran Khan	4	0	0	4
1998-99I	M. Azharuddin		Wasim Akram	2	1	1	0
1998-99I†	M. Azharuddin		Wasim Akram	1	0	1	0
2003-04P	S. C. Ganguly[2]		Inzamam-ul-Haq	3	2	1	0
2004-05I	S. C. Ganguly		Inzamam-ul-Haq	3	1	1	1
2005-06P	R. Dravid		Inzamam-ul-Haq[3]	3	0	1	2
2007-08I	A. Kumble		Shoaib Malik[4]	3	1	0	2
	In India			33	7	5	21
	In Pakistan			26	2	7	17
	Totals			59	9	12	38

I Played in India.   P Played in Pakistan.

† This Test was part of the Asian Test Championship and was not counted as part of the preceding bilateral series.

Note: The following were appointed by the home authority for only a minor proportion of the series or deputised for the official touring captain:
¹G. R. Viswanath (Sixth). ²R. Dravid (First and Second). ³Younis Khan (Third). ⁴Younis Khan (Second and Third).

SERIES RECORDS

Highest score	I	309	V. Sehwag at Multan......................	2003-04
	P	280*	Javed Miandad at Hyderabad	1982-83
Best bowling	I	10-74	A. Kumble at Delhi	1998-99
	P	8-60	Imran Khan at Karachi	1982-83
Highest total	I	675-5 dec	at Multan	2003-04
	P	699-5	at Lahore	1989-90
Lowest total	I	106	at Lucknow	1952-53
	P	116	at Bangalore............................	1986-87

INDIA v SRI LANKA

		Captains				
Season	*India*	*Sri Lanka*	*T*	*I*	*SL*	*D*
1982-83*I*	S. M. Gavaskar	B. Warnapura	1	0	0	1
1985-86*S*	Kapil Dev	L. R. D. Mendis	3	0	1	2
1986-87*I*	Kapil Dev	L. R. D. Mendis	3	2	0	1
1990-91*I*	M. Azharuddin	A. Ranatunga	1	1	0	0
1993-94*S*	M. Azharuddin	A. Ranatunga	3	1	0	2
1993-94*I*	M. Azharuddin	A. Ranatunga	3	3	0	0
1997-98*S*	S. R. Tendulkar	A. Ranatunga	2	0	0	2
1997-98*I*	S. R. Tendulkar	A. Ranatunga	3	0	0	3
1998-99*S*†	M. Azharuddin	A. Ranatunga	1	0	0	1
2001*S*	S. C. Ganguly	S. T. Jayasuriya	3	1	2	0
2005-06*I*	R. Dravid¹	M. S. Atapattu	3	2	0	1
2008*S*	A. Kumble	D. P. M. D. Jayawardene	3	1	2	0
2009-10*I*	M. S. Dhoni	K. C. Sangakkara	3	2	0	1
2010*S*	M. S. Dhoni	K. C. Sangakkara	3	1	1	1
	In India................................		17	10	0	7
	In Sri Lanka		18	4	6	8
	Totals.................................		35	14	6	15

I Played in India. S Played in Sri Lanka.

† *This Test was part of the Asian Test Championship.*

Note: The following was appointed by the home authority for only a minor proportion of the series:
¹V. Sehwag (Third).

SERIES RECORDS

Highest score	I	293	V. Sehwag at Mumbai (BS)...............	2009-10
	SL	340	S. T. Jayasuriya at Colombo (RPS)..........	1997-98
Best bowling	I	7-51	Maninder Singh at Nagpur	1986-87
	SL	8-87	M. Muralitharan at Colombo (SSC)	2001
Highest total	I	726-9 dec	at Mumbai (BS).........................	2009-10
	SL	952-6 dec	at Colombo (RPS)	1997-98
Lowest total	I	138	at Colombo (SSC)	2008
	SL	82	at Chandigarh...........................	1990-91

INDIA v ZIMBABWE

Season	India	Captains	Zimbabwe	T	I	Z	D
1992-93Z	M. Azharuddin		D. L. Houghton	1	0	0	1
1992-93I	M. Azharuddin		D. L. Houghton	1	1	0	0
1998-99Z	M. Azharuddin		A. D. R. Campbell	1	0	1	0
2000-01I	S. C. Ganguly		H. H. Streak	2	1	0	1
2001Z	S. C. Ganguly		H. H. Streak	2	1	1	0
2001-02I	S. C. Ganguly		S. V. Carlisle	2	2	0	0
2005-06Z	S. C. Ganguly		T. Taibu	2	2	0	0
	In India			5	4	0	1
	In Zimbabwe			6	3	2	1
	Totals			11	7	2	2

I Played in India.   Z Played in Zimbabwe.

SERIES RECORDS

Highest score	I	227	V. G. Kambli at Delhi	1992-93
	Z	232*	A. Flower at Nagpur	2000-01
Best bowling	I	7-59	I. K. Pathan at Harare	2005-06
	Z	6-73	H. H. Streak at Harare	2005-06
Highest total	I	609-6 dec	at Nagpur	2000-01
	Z	503-6	at Nagpur	2000-01
Lowest total	I	173	at Harare	1998-99
	Z	146	at Delhi	2001-02

INDIA v BANGLADESH

Season	India	Captains	Bangladesh	T	I	B	D
2000-01B	S. C. Ganguly		Naimur Rahman	1	1	0	0
2004-05B	S. C. Ganguly		Habibul Bashar	2	2	0	0
2007B	R. Dravid		Habibul Bashar	2	1	0	1
2009-10B	M. S. Dhoni[1]		Shakib Al Hasan	2	2	0	0
	In Bangladesh			7	6	0	1

B Played in Bangladesh.

Note: The following deputised for the official touring captain for a minor proportion of the series:
   [1]V. Sehwag (First).

SERIES RECORDS

Highest score	I	248*	S. R. Tendulkar at Dhaka	2004-05
	B	158*	Mohammad Ashraful at Chittagong	2004-05
Best bowling	I	7-87	Zaheer Khan at Mirpur	2009-10
	B	6-132	Naimur Rahman at Dhaka	2000-01
Highest total	I	610-3 dec	at Mirpur	2007
	B	400	at Dhaka	2000-01
Lowest total	I	243	at Chittagong	2009-10
	B	91	at Dhaka	2000-01

PAKISTAN v SRI LANKA

Captains

Season	Pakistan	Sri Lanka	T	P	SL	D
1981-82*P*	Javed Miandad	B. Warnapura[1]	3	2	0	1
1985-86*P*	Javed Miandad	L. R. D. Mendis	3	2	0	1
1985-86*S*	Imran Khan	L. R. D. Mendis	3	1	1	1
1991-92*P*	Imran Khan	P. A. de Silva	3	1	0	2
1994-95*S*†	Salim Malik	A. Ranatunga	2	2	0	0
1995-96*P*	Ramiz Raja	A. Ranatunga	3	1	2	0
1996-97*S*	Ramiz Raja	A. Ranatunga	2	0	0	2
1998-99*P*‡	Wasim Akram	H. P. Tillekeratne	1	0	0	1
1998-99*B*‡	Wasim Akram	P. A. de Silva	1	1	0	0
1999-2000*P*	Saeed Anwar[2]	S. T. Jayasuriya	3	1	2	0
2000*S*	Moin Khan	S. T. Jayasuriya	3	2	0	1
2001-02*P*‡	Waqar Younis	S. T. Jayasuriya	1	0	1	0
2004-05*P*	Inzamam-ul-Haq	M. S. Atapattu	2	1	1	0
2005-06*S*	Inzamam-ul-Haq	D. P. M. D. Jayawardene	2	1	0	1
2008-09*P*§	Younis Khan	D. P. M. D. Jayawardene	2	0	0	2
2009*S*	Younis Khan	K. C. Sangakkara	3	0	2	1
2011-12*U*	Misbah-ul-Haq	T. M. Dilshan	3	1	0	2
2012*S*	Misbah-ul-Haq[3]	D. P. M. D. Jayawardene	3	0	1	2
2013-14*U*	**Misbah-ul-Haq**	**A. D. Mathews**	**3**	**1**	**1**	**1**
	In Pakistan		21	8	6	7
	In Sri Lanka		18	6	4	8
	In Bangladesh.		1	1	0	0
	In United Arab Emirates		**6**	**2**	**1**	**3**
	Totals		**46**	**17**	**11**	**18**

P Played in Pakistan.   S Played in Sri Lanka.   B Played in Bangladesh.
U Played in United Arab Emirates.

† *One Test was cancelled owing to the threat of civil disturbances following a general election.*
‡ *These Tests were part of the Asian Test Championship.*
§ *The Second Test ended after a terrorist attack on the Sri Lankan team bus on the third day.*

Note: The following deputised for the official touring captain or were appointed by the home authority for only a minor proportion of the series:
[1]L. R. D. Mendis (Second). [2]Moin Khan (Third). [3]Mohammad Hafeez (First).

SERIES RECORDS

Highest score	*P*	313	Younis Khan at Karachi	2008-09
	SL	253	S. T. Jayasuriya at Faisalabad	2004-05
Best bowling	*P*	8-58	Imran Khan at Lahore	1981-82
	SL	8-83	J. R. Ratnayeke at Sialkot	1985-86
Highest total	*P*	765-6 dec	at Karachi.	2008-09
	SL	644-7 dec	at Karachi.	2008-09
Lowest total	*P*	90	at Colombo (PSS)	2009
	SL	71	at Kandy.	1994-95

PAKISTAN v ZIMBABWE

Captains

Season	Pakistan	Zimbabwe	T	P	Z	D
1993-94*P*	Wasim Akram[1]	A. Flower	3	2	0	1
1994-95*Z*	Salim Malik	A. Flower	3	2	1	0
1996-97*P*	Wasim Akram	A. D. R. Campbell	2	1	0	1

		Captains				
Season	*Pakistan*	*Zimbabwe*	*T*	*P*	*Z*	*D*
1997-98Z	Rashid Latif	A. D. R. Campbell	2	1	0	1
1998-99P†	Aamir Sohail²	A. D. R. Campbell	2	0	1	1
2002-03Z	Waqar Younis	A. D. R. Campbell	2	2	0	0
2011-12Z	Misbah-ul-Haq	B. R. M. Taylor	1	1	0	0
2013-14Z	**Misbah-ul-Haq**	**B. R. M. Taylor³**	**2**	**1**	**1**	**0**
	In Pakistan		7	3	1	3
	In Zimbabwe..................		**10**	**7**	**2**	**1**
	Totals............................		17	10	3	4

P Played in Pakistan.   Z Played in Zimbabwe.

† *The Third Test at Faisalabad was abandoned without a ball being bowled and is excluded.*

Notes: The following were appointed by the home authority for only a minor proportion of the series:
¹Waqar Younis (First). ²Moin Khan (Second). ³H. Masakadza (First).

SERIES RECORDS

Highest score	*P*	257*	Wasim Akram at Sheikhupura	1996-97
	Z	201*	G. W. Flower at Harare	1994-95
Best bowling	*P*	7-66	Saqlain Mushtaq at Bulawayo..............	2002-03
	Z	6-90	H. H. Streak at Harare	1994-95
Highest total	*P*	553	at Sheikhupura..........................	1996-97
	Z	544-4 dec	at Harare	1994-95
Lowest total	*P*	103	at Peshawar	1998-99
	Z	**120**	**at Harare**	**2013-14**

PAKISTAN v BANGLADESH

		Captains				
Season	*Pakistan*	*Bangladesh*	*T*	*P*	*B*	*D*
2001-02P†	Waqar Younis	Naimur Rahman	1	1	0	0
2001-02B	Waqar Younis	Khaled Mashud	2	2	0	0
2003-04P	Rashid Latif	Khaled Mahmud	3	3	0	0
2011-12B	Misbah-ul-Haq	Mushfiqur Rahim	2	2	0	0
	In Pakistan		4	4	0	0
	In Bangladesh...................		4	4	0	0
	Totals		8	8	0	0

P Played in Pakistan.   B Played in Bangladesh.

† *This Test was part of the Asian Test Championship.*

SERIES RECORDS

Highest score	*P*	204*	Yousuf Youhana at Chittagong	2001-02
	B	144	Shakib Al Hasan at Mirpur	2011-12
Best bowling	*P*	7-77	Danish Kaneria at Dhaka..................	2001-02
	B	6-82	Shakib Al Hasan at Mirpur	2011-12
Highest total	*P*	594-5 dec	at Chittagong	2011-12
	B	361	at Peshawar	2003-04
Lowest total	*P*	175	at Multan	2003-04
	B	96	at Peshawar	2003-04

SRI LANKA v ZIMBABWE

Captains

Season	Sri Lanka	Zimbabwe	T	SL	Z	D
1994-95Z	A. Ranatunga	A. Flower	3	0	0	3
1996-97S	A. Ranatunga	A. D. R. Campbell	2	2	0	0
1997-98S	A. Ranatunga	A. D. R. Campbell	2	2	0	0
1999-2000Z	S. T. Jayasuriya	A. Flower	3	1	0	2
2001-02S	S. T. Jayasuriya	S. V. Carlisle	3	3	0	0
2003-04Z	M. S. Atapattu	T. Taibu	2	2	0	0
	In Sri Lanka		7	7	0	0
	In Zimbabwe		8	3	0	5
	Totals		15	10	0	5

S Played in Sri Lanka.   Z Played in Zimbabwe.

SERIES RECORDS

Highest score	SL	270	K. C. Sangakkara at Bulawayo	2003-04
	Z	266	D. L. Houghton at Bulawayo.	1994-95
Best bowling	SL	9-51	M. Muralitharan at Kandy	2001-02
	Z	5-106	P. A. Strang at Colombo (RPS)	1996-97
Highest total	SL	713-3 dec	at Bulawayo.	2003-04
	Z	462-9 dec	at Bulawayo.	1994-95
Lowest total	SL	218	at Bulawayo.	1994-95
	Z	79	at Galle.	2001-02

SRI LANKA v BANGLADESH

Captains

Season	Sri Lanka	Bangladesh	T	SL	B	D
2001-02S†	S. T. Jayasuriya	Naimur Rahman	1	1	0	0
2002S	S. T. Jayasuriya	Khaled Mashud	2	2	0	0
2005-06S	M. S. Atapattu	Habibul Bashar	2	2	0	0
2005-06B	D. P. M. D. Jayawardene	Habibul Bashar	2	2	0	0
2007S	D. P. M. D. Jayawardene	Mohammad Ashraful	3	3	0	0
2008-09B	D. P. M. D. Jayawardene	Mohammad Ashraful	2	2	0	0
2012-13S	**A. D. Mathews**	**Mushfiqur Rahim**	**2**	**1**	**0**	**1**
	In Sri Lanka		**10**	**9**	**0**	**1**
	In Bangladesh		4	4	0	0
	Totals		**14**	**13**	**0**	**1**

S Played in Sri Lanka.   B Played in Bangladesh.

† This Test was part of the Asian Test Championship.

SERIES RECORDS

Highest score	SL	222*	K. C. Sangakkara at Kandy	2007
	B	**200**	**Mushfiqur Rahim at Galle**	**2012-13**
Best bowling	SL	7-89	H. M. R. K. B. Herath at Colombo (RPS) . . .	**2012-13**
	B	5-70	Shakib Al Hasan at Mirpur	2008-09
Highest total	SL	577-6 dec	at Colombo (SSC)	2007
	B	**638**	**at Galle**	**2012-13**
Lowest total	SL	293	at Mirpur	2008-09
	B	62	at Colombo (PSS)	2007

ZIMBABWE v BANGLADESH

Captains

Season	Zimbabwe	Bangladesh	T	Z	B	D
2000-01Z	H. H. Streak	Naimur Rahman	2	2	0	0
2001-02B	B. A. Murphy¹	Naimur Rahman	2	1	0	1
2003-04Z	H. H. Streak	Habibul Bashar	2	1	0	1
2004-05B	T. Taibu	Habibul Bashar	2	0	1	1
2011-12Z	B. R. M. Taylor	Shakib Al Hasan	1	1	0	0
2012-13Z	**B. R. M. Taylor**	**Mushfiqur Rahim**	**2**	**1**	**1**	**0**
	In Zimbabwe.		7	5	1	1
	In Bangladesh.		4	1	1	2
	Totals.		11	6	2	3

Z Played in Zimbabwe. B Played in Bangladesh.

Note: The following deputised for the official touring captain:

¹S. V. Carlisle (Second).

SERIES RECORDS

Highest score	Z	**171**	B. R. M. Taylor at Harare	**2012-13**
	B	121	Nafis Iqbal at Dhaka	2004-05
Best bowling	Z	**6-59**	D. T. Hondo at Dhaka	2004-05
	B	7-95	Enamul Haque, jun. at Dhaka	2004-05
Highest total	Z	**542-7 dec**	at Chittagong	2001-02
	B	488	at Chittagong	2004-05
Lowest total	Z	**154**	at Chittagong	2004-05
	B	107	at Dhaka.	2001-02

TEST GROUNDS

in chronological order

	City and Ground	First Test Match		Tests
1	**Melbourne, Melbourne Cricket Ground**	**March 15, 1877**	A v E	106
2	**London, Kennington Oval**	**September 6, 1880**	E v A	96
3	**Sydney, Sydney Cricket Ground (No. 1)**	**February 17, 1882**	A v E	102
4	**Manchester, Old Trafford**	**July 11, 1884**	E v A	75
5	**London, Lord's**	**July 21, 1884**	E v A	127
6	**Adelaide, Adelaide Oval**	**December 12, 1884**	A v E	72
7	**Port Elizabeth, St George's Park**	**March 12, 1889**	SA v E	24
8	**Cape Town, Newlands**	**March 25, 1889**	SA v E	50
9	Johannesburg, Old Wanderers	March 2, 1896	SA v E	22
	Now the site of Johannesburg Railway Station.			
10	**Nottingham, Trent Bridge**	**June 1, 1899**	E v A	59
11	**Leeds, Headingley**	**June 29, 1899**	E v A	72
12	Birmingham, Edgbaston	May 29, 1902	E v A	47
13	Sheffield, Bramall Lane	July 3, 1902	E v A	1
	Sheffield United Football Club have built a stand over the cricket pitch.			
14	Durban, Lord's	January 21, 1910	SA v E	4
	Ground destroyed and built on.			
15	**Durban, Kingsmead**	**January 18, 1923**	SA v E	40
16	Brisbane, Exhibition Ground	November 30, 1928	A v E	2
	No longer used for cricket.			
17	Christchurch, Lancaster Park	January 10, 1930	NZ v E	40
	Ground also known under sponsors' names.			
18	**Bridgetown, Kensington Oval**	**January 11, 1930**	WI v E	49
19	**Wellington, Basin Reserve**	**January 24, 1930**	NZ v E	55

	City and Ground	First Test Match		Tests
20	Port-of-Spain, Queen's Park Oval	February 1, 1930	WI v E	58
21	**Auckland, Eden Park**	**February 14, 1930**	**NZ v E**	**48**
22	Georgetown, Bourda	February 21, 1930	WI v E	30
23	Kingston, Sabina Park	April 3, 1930	WI v E	46
24	**Brisbane, Woolloongabba**	**November 27, 1931**	**A v SA**	**56**
25	Bombay, Gymkhana Ground	December 15, 1933	I v E	1
	No longer used for first-class cricket.			
26	**Calcutta (*now Kolkata*), Eden Gardens**	**January 5, 1934**	**I v E**	**39**
27	**Madras (*now Chennai*),**	**February 10, 1934**	**I v E**	**31**
	Chepauk (Chidambaram Stadium)			
28	**Delhi, Feroz Shah Kotla**	**November 10, 1948**	**I v WI**	**32**
29	Bombay (*now Mumbai*), Brabourne Stadium	December 9, 1948	I v WI	18
	Rarely used for first-class cricket.			
30	Johannesburg, Ellis Park	December 27, 1948	SA v E	6
	Mainly a football and rugby stadium, no longer used for cricket.			
31	Kanpur, Green Park (Modi Stadium)	January 12, 1952	I v E	21
32	Lucknow, University Ground	October 25, 1952	I v P	1
	Ground destroyed, now partly under a river bed.			
33	Dacca (*now Dhaka*),	January 1, 1955	P v I	17
	Dacca (*now Bangabandhu*) Stadium			
	Originally in East Pakistan, now Bangladesh, no longer used for cricket.			
34	Bahawalpur, Dring (*now Bahawal*) Stadium	January 15, 1955	P v I	1
	Still used for first-class cricket.			
35	Lahore, Lawrence Gardens (Bagh-e-Jinnah)	January 29, 1955	P v I	3
	Still used for club and occasional first-class matches.			
36	Peshawar, Services Ground	February 13, 1955	P v I	1
	Superseded by new stadium.			
37	Karachi, National Stadium	February 26, 1955	P v I	41
38	Dunedin, Carisbrook	March 11, 1955	NZ v E	10
39	Hyderabad, Fateh Maidan (Lal Bahadur Stadium)	November 19, 1955	I v NZ	3
40	Madras, Corporation Stadium	January 6, 1956	I v NZ	9
	Superseded by rebuilt Chepauk Stadium.			
41	**Johannesburg, Wanderers**	**December 24, 1956**	**SA v E**	**35**
42	Lahore, Gaddafi Stadium	November 21, 1959	P v A	40
43	Rawalpindi, Pindi Club Ground	March 27, 1965	P v NZ	1
	Superseded by new stadium.			
44	Nagpur, Vidarbha C.A. Ground	October 3, 1969	I v NZ	9
	Superseded by new stadium.			
45	**Perth, Western Australian C.A. Ground**	**December 11, 1970**	**A v E**	**41**
46	Hyderabad, Niaz Stadium	March 16, 1973	P v E	5
47	Bangalore, Karnataka State C.A. Ground	November 22, 1974	I v WI	20
	(Chinnaswamy Stadium)			
48	**Bombay (*now Mumbai*), Wankhede Stadium**	**January 23, 1975**	**I v WI**	**24**
49	Faisalabad, Iqbal Stadium	October 16, 1978	P v I	24
50	Napier, McLean Park	February 16, 1979	NZ v P	10
51	Multan, Ibn-e-Qasim Bagh Stadium	December 30, 1980	P v WI	1
	Superseded by new stadium.			
52	St John's (Antigua), Recreation Ground	March 27, 1981	WI v E	22
53	Colombo, P. Saravanamuttu (Sara) Stadium	February 17, 1982	SL v E	17
54	Kandy, Asgiriya Stadium	April 22, 1983	SL v A	21
55	Jullundur, Burlton Park	September 24, 1983	I v P	1
56	Ahmedabad, Sardar Patel (Gujarat) Stadium	November 12, 1983	I v WI	12
57	Colombo, Sinhalese Sports Club Ground	March 16, 1984	SL v NZ	36
58	Colombo, Colombo Cricket Club Ground	March 24, 1984	SL v NZ	3
59	Sialkot, Jinnah Stadium	October 27, 1985	P v SL	4
60	Cuttack, Barabati Stadium	January 4, 1987	I v SL	2
61	Jaipur, Sawai Mansingh Stadium	February 21, 1987	I v P	1
62	Hobart, Bellerive Oval	December 16, 1989	A v SL	11
63	Chandigarh, Sector 16 Stadium	November 23, 1990	I v SL	1
	Superseded by Mohali ground.			

	City and Ground	First Test Match		Tests
64	**Hamilton, Seddon Park**	**February 22, 1991**	**NZ v SL**	**20**
	Ground also known under various sponsors' names.			
65	Gujranwala, Municipal Stadium	December 20, 1991	P v SL	1
66	**Colombo, R. Premadasa (Khettarama) Stadium**	**August 28, 1992**	**SL v A**	**8**
67	Moratuwa, Tyronne Fernando Stadium	September 8, 1992	SL v A	4
68	**Harare, Harare Sports Club**	**October 18, 1992**	**Z v I**	**31**
69	Bulawayo, Bulawayo Athletic Club	November 1, 1992	Z v NZ	1
	Superseded by Queens Sports Club ground.			
70	Karachi, Defence Stadium	December 1, 1993	P v Z	1
71	Rawalpindi, Rawalpindi Cricket Stadium	December 9, 1993	P v Z	8
72	Lucknow, K. D. Singh "Babu" Stadium	January 18, 1994	I v SL	1
73	Bulawayo, Queens Sports Club	October 20, 1994	Z v SL	19
74	**Mohali, Punjab Cricket Association Stadium**	**December 10, 1994**	**I v WI**	**11**
75	Peshawar, Arbab Niaz Stadium	September 8, 1995	P v SL	6
76	**Centurion (*formerly Verwoerdburg*), Centurion Park**	**November 16, 1995**	**SA v E**	**18**
77	Sheikhupura, Municipal Stadium	October 17, 1996	P v Z	2
78	St Vincent, Arnos Vale	June 20, 1997	WI v SL	2
79	**Galle, International Stadium**	**June 3, 1998**	**SL v NZ**	**22**
80	Bloemfontein, Springbok Park	October 29, 1999	SA v Z	4
	Ground also known under various sponsors' names.			
81	Multan, Multan Cricket Stadium	August 29, 2001	P v B	5
82	Chittagong, Chittagong Stadium	November 15, 2001	B v Z	8
	Ground also known as M. A. Aziz Stadium.			
83	**Sharjah, Sharjah Cricket Association Stadium**	**January 31, 2002**	**P v WI**	**6**
84	St George's, Grenada, Queen's Park New Stadium	June 28, 2002	WI v NZ	2
85	East London, Buffalo Park	October 18, 2002	SA v B	1
86	Potchefstroom, North West Cricket Stadium	October 25, 2002	SA v B	1
	Ground now known under sponsor's name.			
87	**Chester-le-Street, Riverside Ground**	**June 5, 2003**	**E v Z**	**5**
	Ground also known under sponsor's name.			
88	Gros Islet, St Lucia, Beausejour Stadium	June 20, 2003	WI v SL	3
89	Darwin, Marrara Cricket Ground	July 18, 2003	A v B	2
90	Cairns, Cazaly's Football Park	July 25, 2003	A v B	2
	Ground also known under sponsor's name.			
91	**Chittagong, Chittagong Divisional Stadium**	**February 28, 2006**	**B v SL**	**11**
	Also known as Bir Shrestha Shahid Ruhul Amin Stadium and Zohur Ahmed Chowdhury Stadium.			
92	Bogra, Shaheed Chandu Stadium	March 8, 2006	B v SL	1
93	Fatullah, Narayanganj Osmani Stadium	April 9, 2006	B v A	1
94	Basseterre, St Kitts, Warner Park	June 22, 2006	WI v I	3
95	**Mirpur (Dhaka), Shere Bangla National Stadium**	**May 25, 2007**	**B v I**	**10**
96	**Dunedin, University Oval**	**January 4, 2008**	**NZ v B**	**6**
97	Providence Stadium, Guyana	March 22, 2008	WI v SL	2
98	North Sound, Antigua, Sir Vivian Richards Stadium	May 30, 2008	WI v A	3
99	Nagpur, Vidarbha C. A. Stadium, Jamtha	November 6, 2008	I v A	4
100	Cardiff, Sophia Gardens	July 8, 2009	E v A	2
	Ground now known under sponsor's name.			
101	**Hyderabad, Rajiv Gandhi International Stadium**	**November 12, 2010**	**I v NZ**	**3**
102	**Dubai, Dubai Sports City Stadium**	**November 12, 2010**	**P v SA**	**6**
103	**Abu Dhabi, Sheikh Zayed Stadium**	**November 20, 2010**	**P v SA**	**5**
104	Pallekele, Muttiah Muralitharan Stadium	December 1, 2010	SL v WI	3
105	Southampton, Rose Bowl	June 16, 2011	E v SL	1
106	**Roseau, Dominica, Windsor Park**	**July 6, 2011**	**WI v I**	**3**
107	Khulna, Khulna Division Stadium	November 21, 2012	B v WI	1
	Ground also known as Bir Shrestha Shahid Flight Lieutenant Motiur Rahman Stadium and Shaikh Abu Naser Stadium.			

Bold type denotes grounds used for Test cricket since January 1, 2013.

ONE-DAY INTERNATIONAL RECORDS

Matches in this section do not have first-class status.

Note: Throughout this section, bold type denotes performances since January 1, 2013, or, in career figures, players who have appeared in one-day internationals since that date.

SUMMARY OF ONE-DAY INTERNATIONALS

1970-71 to January 8, 2014

	Opponents	Matches	Won by														
			E	A	SA	WI	NZ	I	P	SL	Z	B	Ass	Asia	Wld	Afr	Tied	NR
England	Australia	122	48	69	–	–	–	–	–	–	–	–	–	–	–	–	2	3
	South Africa	51	22	–	25	–	–	–	–	–	–	–	–	–	–	–	1	3
	West Indies	85	40	–	–	41	–	–	–	–	–	–	–	–	–	–	–	4
	New Zealand	77	33	–	–	–	38	–	–	–	–	–	–	–	–	–	2	4
	India	87	35	–	–	–	–	47	–	–	–	–	–	–	–	–	2	3
	Pakistan	72	42	–	–	–	–	–	28	–	–	–	–	–	–	–	–	2
	Sri Lanka	51	26	–	–	–	–	–	–	25	–	–	–	–	–	–	–	–
	Zimbabwe	30	21	–	–	–	–	–	–	–	8	–	–	–	–	–	–	1
	Bangladesh	15	13	–	–	–	–	–	–	–	–	2	–	–	–	–	–	–
	Associates	18	16	–	–	–	–	–	–	–	–	–	1	–	–	–	–	1
Australia	South Africa	80	–	41	36	–	–	–	–	–	–	–	–	–	–	–	3	–
	West Indies	135	–	70	–	59	–	–	–	–	–	–	–	–	–	–	3	3
	New Zealand	125	–	85	–	–	34	–	–	–	–	–	–	–	–	–	–	6
	India	115	–	66	–	–	–	40	–	–	–	–	–	–	–	–	–	9
	Pakistan	89	–	54	–	–	–	–	31	–	–	–	–	–	–	–	1	3
	Sri Lanka	90	–	55	–	–	–	–	–	31	–	–	–	–	–	–	–	4
	Zimbabwe	28	–	26	–	–	–	–	–	–	1	–	–	–	–	–	–	1
	Bangladesh	19	–	18	–	–	–	–	–	–	–	1	–	–	–	–	–	–
	Associates	19	–	18	–	–	–	–	–	–	–	–	0	–	–	–	–	1
	ICC World XI	3	–	3	–	–	–	–	–	–	–	–	–	–	0	–	–	–
South Africa	West Indies	52	–	–	38	12	–	–	–	–	–	–	–	–	–	–	1	1
	New Zealand	58	–	–	34	–	20	–	–	–	–	–	–	–	–	–	–	4
	India	70	–	–	42	–	–	25	–	–	–	–	–	–	–	–	–	3
	Pakistan	71	–	–	47	–	–	–	23	–	–	–	–	–	–	–	–	1
	Sri Lanka	56	–	–	26	–	–	–	–	28	–	–	–	–	–	–	1	1
	Zimbabwe	32	–	–	29	–	–	–	–	–	2	–	–	–	–	–	–	1
	Bangladesh	14	–	–	13	–	–	–	–	–	–	1	–	–	–	–	–	–
	Associates	20	–	–	20	–	–	–	–	–	–	–	0	–	–	–	–	–
West Indies	New Zealand	60	–	–	–	30	23	–	–	–	–	–	–	–	–	–	–	7
	India	112	–	–	–	59	–	50	–	–	–	–	–	–	–	–	1	2
	Pakistan	126	–	–	–	68	–	–	55	–	–	–	–	–	–	–	3	–
	Sri Lanka	51	–	–	–	27	–	–	–	21	–	–	–	–	–	–	–	3
	Zimbabwe	44	–	–	–	34	–	–	–	–	9	–	–	–	–	–	–	1
	Bangladesh	25	–	–	–	16	–	–	–	–	–	7	–	–	–	–	–	2
	Associates	19	–	–	–	17	–	–	–	–	–	–	1	–	–	–	–	1
New Zealand	India	88	–	–	–	–	37	46	–	–	–	–	–	–	–	–	–	5
	Pakistan	89	–	–	–	–	35	–	51	–	–	–	–	–	–	–	1	2
	Sri Lanka	82	–	–	–	–	37	–	–	38	–	–	–	–	–	–	1	6
	Zimbabwe	35	–	–	–	–	25	–	–	–	8	–	–	–	–	–	1	1
	Bangladesh	24	–	–	–	–	16	–	–	–	–	8	–	–	–	–	–	–
	Associates	13	–	–	–	–	13	–	–	–	–	–	0	–	–	–	–	–
India	Pakistan	125	–	–	–	–	–	50	71	–	–	–	–	–	–	–	–	4
	Sri Lanka	143	–	–	–	–	–	78	–	53	–	–	–	–	–	–	1	11
	Zimbabwe	56	–	–	–	–	–	44	–	–	10	–	–	–	–	–	2	–
	Bangladesh	24	–	–	–	–	–	21	–	–	–	3	–	–	–	–	–	–
	Associates	24	–	–	–	–	–	22	–	–	–	–	2	–	–	–	–	–
Pakistan	Sri Lanka	137	–	–	–	–	–	–	80	52	–	–	–	–	–	–	1	4
	Zimbabwe	47	–	–	–	–	–	–	42	–	3	–	–	–	–	–	1	1
	Bangladesh	31	–	–	–	–	–	–	30	–	–	1	–	–	–	–	1	–
	Associates	25	–	–	–	–	–	–	23	–	–	–	1	–	–	–	1	–
Sri Lanka	Zimbabwe	47	–	–	–	–	–	–	–	39	7	–	–	–	–	–	–	1
	Bangladesh	33	–	–	–	–	–	–	–	28	–	4	–	–	–	–	–	1
	Associates	16	–	–	–	–	–	–	–	15	–	–	1	–	–	–	–	–
Zimbabwe	Bangladesh	59	–	–	–	–	–	–	–	–	28	31	–	–	–	–	–	–
	Associates	43	–	–	–	–	–	–	–	–	34	–	6	–	–	–	1	2

	Opponents	Matches						Won by									
			E	A	SA	WI	NZ	I	P	SL	Z	B	Ass	Asia	Wld	Afr	Tied	NR
Bangladesh	Associates	**32**	–	–	–	–	–	–	–	–	–	22	10	–	–	–	–	–
Associates	Associates	**152**	–	–	–	–	–	–	–	–	–	–	145	–	–	–	1	6
Asian CC XI	ICC World XI	**1**	–	–	–	–	–	–	–	–	–	–	–	0	1	–	–	–
	African XI	**6**	–	–	–	–	–	–	–	–	–	–	–	4	–	1	–	1
		3,453	296	505	310	363	278	423	434	330	110	80	167	4	1	1	31	120

Note: Associate and Affiliate Members of ICC who have played one-day internationals are Afghanistan, Bermuda, Canada, East Africa, Hong Kong, Ireland, Kenya, Namibia, Netherlands, Scotland, United Arab Emirates and USA. Sri Lanka, Zimbabwe and Bangladesh played one-day internationals before gaining Test status; these are not included among the Associate results.

RESULTS SUMMARY OF ONE-DAY INTERNATIONALS

1970-71 to January 8, 2014 (3,453 matches)

	Matches	Won	Lost	Tied	No Result	% Won (excl. NR)
Australia	825	505	281	9	30	64.08
South Africa	504	310	174	6	14	63.87
Pakistan.	812	434	353	8	17	55.09
West Indies	709	363	314	8	24	53.57
India	844	423	378	6	37	52.78
England.	608	296	284	7	21	51.02
Sri Lanka	706	330	341	4	31	49.18
New Zealand	651	278	333	5	35	45.53
Bangladesh	276	80	193	–	3	29.30
Zimbabwe.	421	110	297	5	9	27.30
Asian Cricket Council XI	7	4	2	–	1	66.66
Afghanistan.	27	16	11	–	–	59.25
Ireland.	81	37	37	3	4	50.00
Netherlands.	74	27	43	1	3	38.73
Scotland	63	21	39	–	3	35.00
Kenya	152	41	106	–	5	27.89
ICC World XI	4	1	3	–	–	25.00
Canada	75	17	56	–	2	23.28
Bermuda	35	7	28	–	–	20.00
African XI	6	1	4	–	1	20.00
United Arab Emirates	11	1	10	–	–	9.09
USA	2	–	2	–	–	0.00
East Africa	3	–	3	–	–	0.00
Hong Kong	4	–	4	–	–	0.00
Namibia.	6	–	6	–	–	0.00

Note: Matches abandoned without a ball bowled are not included except (from 2004) where the toss took place, in accordance with an ICC ruling. Such matches, like those called off after play began, are now counted as official internationals in their own right, even when replayed on another day. In the percentages of matches won, ties are counted as half a win.

BATTING RECORDS

HIGHEST INDIVIDUAL INNINGS

219	V. Sehwag	India v West Indies at Indore	2011-12
209	**R. G. Sharma**	**India v Australia at Bangalore**	**2013-14**
200*	S. R. Tendulkar	India v South Africa at Gwalior	2009-10
194*	C. K. Coventry	Zimbabwe v Bangladesh at Bulawayo	2009
194	Saeed Anwar	Pakistan v India at Chennai	1997-97
189*	I. V. A. Richards	West Indies v England at Manchester	1984

189*	M. J. Guptill	**New Zealand v England at Southampton**	**2013**
189	S. T. Jayasuriya	Sri Lanka v India at Sharjah	2000-01
188*	G. Kirsten	South Africa v UAE at Rawalpindi	1995-96
186*	S. R. Tendulkar	India v New Zealand at Hyderabad	1999-2000
185*	S. R. Watson	Australia v Bangladesh at Mirpur	2010-11
183*	M. S. Dhoni	India v Sri Lanka at Jaipur	2005-06
183	S. C. Ganguly	India v Sri Lanka at Taunton	1999
183	V. Kohli	India v Pakistan at Mirpur	2011-12
181*	M. L. Hayden	Australia v New Zealand at Hamilton	2006-07
181	I. V. A. Richards	West Indies v Sri Lanka at Karachi	1987-88
178*	H. Masakadza	Zimbabwe v Kenya at Harare	2009-10
177	P. R. Stirling	Ireland v Canada at Toronto	2010
175*	Kapil Dev	India v Zimbabwe at Tunbridge Wells	1983
175	H. H. Gibbs	South Africa v Australia at Johannesburg	2005-06
175	S. R. Tendulkar	India v Australia at Hyderabad	2009-10
175	V. Sehwag	India v Bangladesh at Mirpur	2010-11

Note: The highest individual scores for other Test countries are:

167*	R. A. Smith	England v Australia at Birmingham	1993
154	Tamim Iqbal	Bangladesh v Zimbabwe at Bulawayo	2009

MOST HUNDREDS

S. R. Tendulkar (I).	49	A. C. Gilchrist (A/World). .	16	P. A. de Silva (SL).	11
R. T. Ponting (A/World). . .	30	**D. P. M. D. Jayawardene**		**G. Gambhir (I)**.	**11**
S. T. Jayasuriya (SL/Asia). .	28	**(SL/Asia)**	**16**	C. G. Greenidge (WI) . . .	11
S. C. Ganguly (I/Asia). . .	22	**K. C. Sangakkara (SL/**		I. V. A. Richards (WI). . .	11
C. H. Gayle (WI/World)	**21**	**World/Asia)**	**16**	M. L. Hayden (A/World)	10
H. H. Gibbs (SA).	21	Mohammad Yousuf (P/As)	15	Ijaz Ahmed, sen. (P)	10
Saeed Anwar (P)	20	**V. Sehwag (I/Wld/Asia)** .	**15**	Inzamam-ul-Haq (P/Asia)	10
B. C. Lara (WI/World) . . .	19	G. Kirsten (SA)	13	**G. C. Smith (SA/Af)**. . . .	**10**
M. E. Waugh (A)	18	**W. U. Tharanga (SL)**	**13**	
T. M. Dilshan (SL).	**17**	Yuvraj Singh (I/Asia) . . .	13	*Most hundreds for other*
D. L. Haynes (WI)	17	**H. M. Amla (SA)**	**12**	*countries:*
J. H. Kallis (SA/Wld/Af). .	**17**	R. Dravid (I/World/Asia) .	12	A. D. R. Campbell (Z). . .	7
V. Kohli (I)	**17**	M. E. Trescothick (E) . . .	12	**Shakib Al Hasan (B)** . . .	**5**
N. J. Astle (NZ)	16	M. S. Atapattu (SL)	11	
A. B. de Villiers (SA) . . .	**16**	S. Chanderpaul (WI)	11	

Note: Ponting's total includes one for the World XI, the only hundred for a combined team.

MOST RUNS

		M	I	NO	R	HS	100	Avge
1	S. R. Tendulkar (India)	463	452	41	18,426	200*	49	44.83
2	R. T. Ponting (Australia/World)	375	365	39	13,704	164	30	42.03
3	S. T. Jayasuriya (Sri Lanka/Asia)	445	433	18	13,430	189	28	32.36
4	**K. C. Sangakkara (SL/Asia/World)**. . . .	**362**	**339**	**37**	**12,116**	**169**	**16**	**40.11**
5	Inzamam-ul-Haq (Pakistan/Asia)	378	350	53	11,739	137*	10	39.52
6	**J. H. Kallis (S. Africa/World/Africa)**. .	**325**	**311**	**53**	**11,574**	**139**	**17**	**44.86**
7	**D. P. M. D. Jayawardene (SL/Asia)**. . . .	**407**	**380**	**38**	**11,401**	**144**	**16**	**33.33**
8	S. C. Ganguly (India/Asia)	311	300	23	11,363	183	22	41.02
9	R. Dravid (India/World/Asia)	344	318	40	10,889	153	12	39.16
10	B. C. Lara (West Indies/World)	299	289	32	10,405	169	19	40.48
11	Mohammad Yousuf (Pakistan/Asia)	288	273	40	9,720	141*	15	41.71
12	A. C. Gilchrist (Australia/World)	287	279	11	9,619	172	16	35.89
13	M. Azharuddin (India).	334	308	54	9,378	153*	7	36.92
14	P. A. de Silva (Sri Lanka)	308	296	30	9,284	145	11	34.90
15	Saeed Anwar (Pakistan)	247	244	19	8,824	194	20	39.21
16	S. Chanderpaul (West Indies)	268	251	40	8,778	150	11	41.60
17	**C. H. Gayle (West Indies)**	**255**	**250**	**40**	**8,743**	**153***	**21**	**37.52**

		M	I	NO	R	HS	100	Avge
18	D. L. Haynes (West Indies)..........	238	237	28	8,648	152*	17	41.37
19	M. S. Atapattu (Sri Lanka).........	268	259	32	8,529	132*	11	37.57
20	M. E. Waugh (Australia)............	244	236	20	8,500	173	18	39.35
21	**Yuvraj Singh (India/Asia)........**	**293**	**268**	**39**	**8,329**	**139**	**13**	**36.37**
22	**V. Sehwag (India/Asia/World)......**	**251**	**245**	**9**	**8,273**	**219**	**15**	**35.05**
23	H. H. Gibbs (South Africa)........	248	240	16	8,094	175	21	36.13
24	S. P. Fleming (New Zealand/World).....	280	269	21	8,037	134*	8	32.40
25	**T. M. Dilshan (SL).................**	**275**	**250**	**39**	**8,014**	**160***	**17**	**37.98**

Notes: The leading aggregates for players who have appeared for other Test countries are:

	M	I	NO	R	HS	100	Avge
A. Flower (Zimbabwe)................	213	208	16	6,786	145	4	35.34
P. D. Collingwood (England)........	197	181	37	5,092	120*	5	35.36
Tamim Iqbal (Bangladesh)	**124**	**124**	**1**	**3,702**	**154**	**4**	**30.09**

Excluding runs scored for combined teams, the record aggregate for Australia is 13,589 in 374 matches by R. T. Ponting; for Sri Lanka, 13,364 in 441 matches by S. T. Jayasuriya; for Pakistan, 11,701 in 375 matches by Inzamam-ul-Haq; for South Africa, **11,545** in 320 matches by **J. H. Kallis**; for West Indies, 10,348 in 295 matches by B. C. Lara; and for New Zealand, 8,007 in 279 matches by S. P. Fleming.

BEST CAREER STRIKE-RATES BY BATSMEN

(Runs per 100 balls. Qualification: 700 runs)

SR		Position	M	I	R	Avge
115.11	**Shahid Afridi (P/World/Asia)** ...	2/7	373	345	7,516	23.34
113.60	Y. K. Pathan (India)	7	57	41	810	27.00
111.53	**Rizwan Cheema (Canada)**	2/6	33	32	764	24.64
105.22	B. L. Cairns (NZ)	9/8	78	65	987	16.72
104.33	**V. Sehwag (I/World/Asia).......**	1/2	251	245	8,273	35.05
104.17	J. M. Davison (Canada)...........	1/2	32	32	799	26.63
101.31	**D. J. G. Sammy (WI)...........**	7/8	107	88	1,461	23.95
100.25	J. A. Morkel (SA)	7/8	58	43	782	23.69
99.43	I. D. S. Smith (NZ)	8	98	77	1,055	17.29
96.94	A. C. Gilchrist (A/World)........	1/2	287	279	9,619	35.89
96.89	**D. A. Miller (SA)..............**	6	40	37	811	31.19
96.66	R. L. Powell (WI)...............	6	109	100	2,085	24.82
96.16	Kapil Dev (I)..................	7/6	225	198	3,783	23.79

Note: Position means a batsman's most usual position in the batting order.

FASTEST ONE-DAY INTERNATIONAL FIFTIES

Balls

Balls			
17	S. T. Jayasuriya	Sri Lanka v Pakistan at Singapore	1995-96
18	S. P. O'Donnell	Australia v Sri Lanka at Sharjah....................	1989-90
18	Shahid Afridi	Pakistan v Sri Lanka at Nairobi	1996-97
18	Shahid Afridi........	Pakistan v Netherlands at Colombo (SSC)............	2002
18	**G. J. Maxwell.......**	**Australia v India at Bangalore**	**2013-14**
19	M. V. Boucher.......	South Africa v Kenya at Cape Town	2001-02
19	J. M. Kemp	South Africa v Zimbabwe at Durban	2004-05
19	B. B. McCullum	New Zealand v Bangladesh at Queenstown	2007-08
19	D. J. Hussey........	Australia v West Indies at Basseterre...............	2008

FASTEST ONE-DAY INTERNATIONAL HUNDREDS

Balls

36	**C. J. Anderson**	**New Zealand v West Indies at Queenstown**	**2013-14**
37	Shahid Afridi	Pakistan v Sri Lanka at Nairobi	1996-97
44	M. V. Boucher	South Africa v Zimbabwe at Potchefstroom	2006-07
45	B. C. Lara	West Indies v Bangladesh at Dhaka	1999-2000
45	Shahid Afridi	Pakistan v India at Kanpur	2004-05
46	**J. D. Ryder**	**New Zealand v West Indies at Queenstown**	**2013-14**
48	S. T. Jayasuriya	Sri Lanka v Pakistan at Singapore	1995-96

HIGHEST PARTNERSHIP FOR EACH WICKET

286	for 1st	W. U. Tharanga and S. T. Jayasuriya	SL v E	Leeds	2006
331	for 2nd	S. R. Tendulkar and R. Dravid	I v NZ	Hyderabad	1999-2000
238	**for 3rd**	**H. M. Amla and A. B. de Villiers**	**SA v P**	**Johannesburg**	**2012-13**
275*	for 4th	M. Azharuddin and A. Jadeja	I v Z	Cuttack	1997-98
226*	**for 5th**	**E. J. G. Morgan and R. S. Bopara**	**E v Ire**	**Dublin**	**2013**
218	for 6th	D. P. M. D. Jayawardene and M. S. Dhoni	As v Af	Chennai	2007
130	for 7th	A. Flower and H. H. Streak	Z v E	Harare	2001-02
138*	for 8th	J. M. Kemp and A. J. Hall	SA v I	Cape Town	2006-07
132	for 9th	A. D. Mathews and S. L. Malinga	SL v A	Melbourne	2010-11
106*	for 10th	I. V. A. Richards and M. A. Holding	WI v E	Manchester	1984

BOWLING RECORDS

BEST BOWLING ANALYSES

8-19	W. P. U. J. C. Vaas	Sri Lanka v Zimbabwe at Colombo (SSC)	2001-02
7-12	**Shahid Afridi**	**Pakistan v West Indies at Providence**	**2013**
7-15	G. D. McGrath	Australia v Namibia at Potchefstroom	2002-03
7-20	A. J. Bichel	Australia v England at Port Elizabeth	2002-03
7-30	M. Muralitharan	Sri Lanka v India at Sharjah	2000-01
7-36	Waqar Younis	Pakistan v England at Leeds	2001
7-37	Aqib Javed	Pakistan v India at Sharjah	1991-92
7-51	W. W. Davis	West Indies v Australia at Leeds	1983

Note: The best analyses for other countries are:

6-12	A. Kumble	India v West Indies at Calcutta	1993-94
6-19	S. E. Bond	New Zealand v India at Bulawayo	2005-06
6-19	H. K. Olonga	Zimbabwe v England at Cape Town	1999-2000
6-22	M. Ntini	South Africa v Australia at Cape Town	2005-06
6-26	Mashrafe bin Mortaza	Bangladesh v Kenya at Nairobi	2006
6-26	**Rubel Hossain**	**Bangladesh v New Zealand at Mirpur**	**2013-14**
6-31	P. D. Collingwood	England v Bangladesh at Nottingham	2005

HAT-TRICKS

Jalal-ud-Din	Pakistan v Australia at Hyderabad	1982-83
B. A. Reid	Australia v New Zealand at Sydney	1985-86
Chetan Sharma	India v New Zealand at Nagpur	1987-88
Wasim Akram	Pakistan v West Indies at Sharjah	1989-90
Wasim Akram	Pakistan v Australia at Sharjah	1989-90
Kapil Dev	India v Sri Lanka at Calcutta	1990-91
Aqib Javed	Pakistan v India at Sharjah	1991-92
D. K. Morrison	New Zealand v India at Napier	1993-94
Waqar Younis	Pakistan v New Zealand at East London	1994-95
Saqlain Mushtaq‡	Pakistan v Zimbabwe at Peshawar	1996-97
E. A. Brandes	Zimbabwe v England at Harare	1996-97
A. M. Stuart	Australia v Pakistan at Melbourne	1996-97
Saqlain Mushtaq	Pakistan v Zimbabwe at The Oval	1999
W. P. U. J. C. Vaas	Sri Lanka v Zimbabwe at Colombo (SSC)	2001-02
Mohammad Sami	Pakistan v West Indies at Sharjah	2001-02

W. P. U. J. C. Vaas§	Sri Lanka v Bangladesh at Pietermaritzburg	2002-03
B. Lee	Australia v Kenya at Durban	2002-03
J. M. Anderson	England v Pakistan at The Oval	2003
S. J. Harmison	England v India at Nottingham	2004
C. K. Langeveldt	South Africa v West Indies at Bridgetown	2004-05
Shahadat Hossain	Bangladesh v Zimbabwe at Harare	2006
J. E. Taylor	West Indies v Australia at Mumbai	2006-07
S. E. Bond	New Zealand v Australia at Hobart	2006-07
S. L. Malinga†	Sri Lanka v South Africa at Providence	2006-07
A. Flintoff	England v West Indies at Gros Islet, St Lucia	2008-09
M. F. Maharoof	Sri Lanka v India at Dambulla	2010
Abdur Razzak	Bangladesh v Zimbabwe at Mirpur	2010-11
K. A. J. Roach	West Indies v Netherlands at Delhi	2010-11
S. L. Malinga	Sri Lanka v Kenya at Colombo (RPS)	2010-11
S. L. Malinga	Sri Lanka v Australia at Colombo (RPS)	2011-12
D. T. Christian	Australia v Sri Lanka at Melbourne	2011-12
N. L. T. C. Perera	Sri Lanka v Pakistan at Colombo (RPS)	2012
C. J. McKay	**Australia v England at Cardiff**	**2013**
Rubel Hossain	**Bangladesh v New Zealand at Mirpur**	**2013-14**

† *Four wickets in four balls.*   ‡ *Four wickets in five balls.*   § *The first three balls of the match*

MOST WICKETS

		M	Balls	R	W	BB	4I	Avge
1	M. Muralitharan (SL/World/Asia)	350	18,811	12,326	534	7-30	25	23.08
2	Wasim Akram (Pakistan)	356	18,186	11,812	502	5-15	23	23.52
3	Waqar Younis (Pakistan)	262	12,698	9,919	416	7-36	27	23.84
4	W. P. U. J. C. Vaas (SL/Asia)	322	15,775	11,014	400	8-19	13	27.53
5	S. M. Pollock (SA/World/Africa)	303	15,712	9,631	393	6-35	17	24.50
6	G. D. McGrath (Australia/World)	250	12,970	8,391	381	7-15	16	22.02
7	B. Lee (Australia)	221	11,185	8,877	380	5-22	23	23.36
8	**Shahid Afridi (Pakistan/World/Asia)**	**373**	**16,346**	**12,592**	**375**	**7-12**	**13**	**33.57**
9	A. Kumble (India/Asia)	271	14,496	10,412	337	6-12	10	30.89
10	S. T. Jayasuriya (Sri Lanka/Asia)	445	14,874	11,871	323	6-29	12	36.75
11	J. Srinath (India)	229	11,935	8,847	315	5-23	10	28.08
12	S. K. Warne (Australia/World)	194	10,642	7,541	293	5-33	13	25.73
13	Saqlain Mushtaq (Pakistan)	169	8,770	6,275	288	5-20	17	21.78
	A. B. Agarkar (India)	191	9,848	8,021	288	6-42	12	27.85
15	**D. L. Vettori (New Zealand/World)**	**275**	**13,029**	**8,946**	**284**	**5-7**	**9**	**31.50**
16	Zaheer Khan (India/Asia)	200	10,097	8,301	282	5-42	8	29.43
17	**J. H. Kallis (S. Africa/World/Africa)**	**325**	**10,750**	**8,680**	**273**	**5-30**	**4**	**31.79**
18	A. A. Donald (South Africa)	164	8,561	5,926	272	6-23	13	21.78
19	Abdul Razzaq (Pakistan/Asia)	265	10,941	8,564	269	6-35	11	31.83
20	M. Ntini (South Africa/World)	173	8,687	6,559	266	6-22	12	24.65
21	Harbhajan Singh (India/Asia)	229	12,059	8,651	259	5-31	5	33.40
22	Kapil Dev (India)	225	11,202	6,945	253	5-43	4	27.45
23	Shoaib Akhtar (Pakistan/Wld/Asia)	163	7,764	6,168	247	6-16	10	24.97
24	**J. M. Anderson (England)**	**174**	**8,609**	**7,132**	**245**	**5-23**	**12**	**29.11**
25	**S. L. Malinga (Sri Lanka)**	**160**	**7,694**	**6,608**	**242**	**6-38**	**13**	**27.30**
26	H. H. Streak (Zimbabwe)	189	9,468	7,129	239	5-32	8	29.82
27	D. Gough (England/World)	159	8,470	6,209	235	5-44	12	26.42
28	**K. D. Mills (New Zealand)**	**162**	**7,803**	**6,157**	**231**	**5-25**	**9**	**26.65**
29	C. A. Walsh (West Indies)	205	10,822	6,918	227	5-1	7	30.47
30	C. E. L. Ambrose (West Indies)	176	9,353	5,429	225	5-17	10	24.12

Notes: The leading aggregates for players who have appeared for other countries are:

Abdur Razzak (Bangladesh)	**147**	**7,641**	**5,728**	**204**	**5-29**	**9**	**28.07**

Excluding wickets taken for combined teams, the record for Sri Lanka is 523 in 343 matches by M. Muralitharan; for South Africa, 387 in 294 matches by S. M. Pollock; for Australia, 380 in 249 matches by G. D. McGrath; for India, 334 in 269 matches by A. Kumble; for New Zealand, **276** in 271 matches by **D. L. Vettori**; and for Zimbabwe, 237 in 187 matches by H. H. Streak.

BEST CAREER STRIKE-RATES BY BOWLERS

(Balls per wicket. Qualification: 1,500 balls)

SR		M	W
27.10	**Junaid Khan (P)**	**42**	**73**
27.22	S. W. Tait (A)......................	35	62
28.68	**B. A. W. Mendis (SL)**	**66**	**110**
28.72	R. N. ten Doeschate (Netherlands)	33	55
29.11	**N. L. T. C. Perera (SL)**	**67**	**85**
29.21	S. E. Bond (NZ)	82	147
29.38	G. I. Allott (NZ)	31	52
29.43	B. Lee (A)........................	221	380
29.54	**M. Morkel (SA/Africa)**	**73**	**124**
29.55	**A. R. Cusack (Ireland)**	**50**	**52**
29.58	L. S. Pascoe (A)	29	53

BEST CAREER ECONOMY-RATES

(Runs conceded per six balls. Qualification: 50 wickets)

ER		M	W
3.09	J. Garner (WI).....................	98	146
3.28	R. G. D. Willis (E)	64	80
3.30	R. J. Hadlee (NZ)	115	158
3.32	M. A. Holding (WI)	102	142
3.40	A. M. E. Roberts (WI)	56	87
3.48	C. E. L. Ambrose (WI)	176	225

WICKETKEEPING AND FIELDING RECORDS

MOST DISMISSALS IN AN INNINGS

6 (all ct)	A. C. Gilchrist.......	Australia v South Africa at Cape Town	1999-2000
6 (all ct)	A. J. Stewart	England v Zimbabwe at Manchester..........	2000
6 (5ct, 1st)	R. D. Jacobs	West Indies v Sri Lanka at Colombo (RPS)	2001-02
6 (5ct, 1st)	A. C. Gilchrist.......	Australia v England at Sydney	2002-03
6 (all ct)	A. C. Gilchrist.......	Australia v Namibia at Potchefstroom.........	2002-03
6 (all ct)	A. C. Gilchrist.......	Australia v Sri Lanka at Colombo (RPS)	2003-04
6 (all ct)	M. V. Boucher.......	South Africa v Pakistan at Cape Town	2006-07
6 (5ct, 1st)	M. S. Dhoni.........	India v England at Leeds....................	2007
6 (all ct)	A. C. Gilchrist.......	Australia v India at Vadodara	2007-08
6 (5ct, 1st)	A. C. Gilchrist.......	Australia v India at Sydney.................	2007-08
6 (all ct)	M. J. Prior	England v South Africa at Nottingham........	2008
6 (all ct)	**J. C. Buttler ....**	**England v South Africa at The Oval ....**	**2013**

MOST DISMISSALS

			M	Ct	St
1	472	A. C. Gilchrist (Australia/World)......................	282	417	55
2	424	M. V. Boucher (South Africa/Africa)....................	294	402	22
	424	**K. C. Sangakkara (Sri Lanka/World/Asia)**	**318**	**338**	**86**
4	**299**	**M. S. Dhoni (India/Asia)**	**238**	**220**	**79**
5	287	Moin Khan (Pakistan)	219	214	73
6	**242**	**B. B. McCullum (New Zealand)**	**185**	**227**	**15**
7	234	I. A. Healy (Australia)..............................	168	195	39
8	220	Rashid Latif (Pakistan)..............................	166	182	38
9	206	R. S. Kaluwitharana (Sri Lanka)	186	131	75
10	204	P. J. L. Dujon (West Indies)	169	183	21
11	189	R. D. Jacobs (West Indies)...........................	147	160	29

			M	Ct	St
12	187	**Kamran Akmal (Pakistan)**................	**154**	**156**	**31**
13	{165	D. J. Richardson (South Africa)............	122	148	17
	165	A. Flower (Zimbabwe)......................	186	133	32
15	163	A. J. Stewart (England)	138	148	15
16	154	N. R. Mongia (India)	140	110	44
17	151	**B. J. Haddin (Australia)**................	**93**	**142**	**9**

Notes: The leading aggregate for Bangladesh is:

126	Khaled Mashud (Bangladesh)	126	91	35

Excluding dismissals for combined teams, the most for Australia is 470 (416ct, 54st) in 281 matches by A. C. Gilchrist; for South Africa, 415 (394ct, 21st) in 289 matches by M. V. Boucher; for Sri Lanka, **415** (332ct, 83st) in 311 matches by **K. C. Sangakkara**; and for India, **293** (217ct, 76st) in 235 matches by **M. S. Dhoni**.

M. V. Boucher's list excludes 1 catch taken in 1 one-day international when not keeping wicket; K. C. Sangakkara's record excludes 19 in 44; B. B. McCullum's excludes 19 in 39; R. S. Kaluwitharana's 1 in 3; A. Flower's 8 in 27; A. J. Stewart's 11 in 32. A. C. Gilchrist played five one-day internationals without keeping wicket and B. J. Haddin nine, but neither made any catches in those games. R. Dravid (India) made 210 dismissals (196ct, 14st) in 344 one-day internationals but only 86 (72ct, 14st) in 74 as wicketkeeper (including one where he took over during the match).

MOST CATCHES IN AN INNINGS IN THE FIELD

5	J. N. Rhodes...............	South Africa v West Indies at Bombay...........	1993-94

Note: There have been **27** instances of four catches in an innings.

MOST CATCHES

Ct	M		Ct	M	
201	407	D. P. M. D. Jayawardene (SL/Asia)	109	213	R. S. Mahanama (Sri Lanka)
160	375	R. T. Ponting (Australia/World)	108	197	P. D. Collingwood (England)
156	334	M. Azharuddin (India)	108	244	M. E. Waugh (Australia)
140	463	S. R. Tendulkar (India)	108	248	H. H. Gibbs (South Africa)
133	280	S. P. Fleming (New Zealand/World)	**108**	**255**	**C. H. Gayle (West Indies)**
130	350	M. Muralitharan (SL/World/Asia)	108	303	S. M. Pollock (SA/Wld/Africa)
129	325	J. H. Kallis (SA/World/Africa)	105	185	M. E. K. Hussey (Australia)
127	273	A. R. Border (Australia)	**105**	**197**	**G. C. Smith (South Africa)**
126	250	Younis Khan (Pakistan)	105	245	J. N. Rhodes (South Africa)
124	271	R. Dravid (India/World/Asia)	100	187	I. V. A. Richards (West Indies)
123	445	S. T. Jayasuriya (Sri Lanka/Asia)	100	311	S. C. Ganguly (India/Asia)
120	227	C. L. Hooper (West Indies)			
120	299	B. C. Lara (West Indies/World)			*Most catches for other countries:*
119	373	Shahid Afridi (Pak/World/Asia)	Ct	M	
113	378	Inzamam-ul-Haq (Pakistan/Asia)	86	221	G. W. Flower (Zimbabwe)
111	325	S. R. Waugh (Australia)	**41**	**131**	**Mashrafe bin Mortaza (Bang)**

Notes: Excluding catches taken for combined teams, the record aggregate for Sri Lanka is **196** in 401 matches by **D. P. M. D. Jayawardene**; for Australia, 158 in 374 by R. T. Ponting; for New Zealand, 132 in 279 by S. P. Fleming; and for South Africa, **129** in 320 by **J. H. Kallis**.

R. Dravid's record excludes 72 catches and 14 stumpings made in 74 one-day internationals as wicketkeeper (including one where he took over during the match); Younis Khan's excludes 5 in 3.

TEAM RECORDS

HIGHEST INNINGS TOTALS

443-9	(50 overs)	Sri Lanka v Netherlands at Amstelveen	2006
438-9	(49.5 overs)	South Africa v Australia at Johannesburg............	2005-06
434-4	(50 overs)	Australia v South Africa at Johannesburg............	2005-06
418-5	(50 overs)	South Africa v Zimbabwe at Potchefstroom	2006-07
418-5	(50 overs)	India v West Indies at Indore.......................	2011-12
414-7	(50 overs)	India v Sri Lanka at Rajkot	2009-10

413-5	(50 overs)	India v Bermuda at Port-of-Spain	2006-07
411-8	(50 overs)	Sri Lanka v India at Rajkot	2009-10
402-2	(50 overs)	New Zealand v Ireland at Aberdeen	2008
401-3	(50 overs)	India v South Africa at Gwalior	2009-10

Note: The highest totals by other countries are:

391-4	(50 overs)	England v Bangladesh at Nottingham	2005
385-7	(50 overs)	Pakistan v Bangladesh at Dambulla	2010
363-4	**(50 overs)**	**West Indies v New Zealand at Hamilton**	**2013-14**
351-7	(50 overs)	Zimbabwe v Kenya at Mombasa	2008-09
320-8	(50 overs)	Bangladesh v Zimbabwe at Bulawayo	2009

HIGHEST TOTALS BATTING SECOND

438-9	(49.5 overs)	South Africa v Australia at Johannesburg (*Won by 1 wicket*) . .	2005-06
411-8	(50 overs)	Sri Lanka v India at Rajkot (*Lost by 3 runs*)	2009-10
362-1	**(43.3 overs)**	**India v Australia at Jaipur** (*Won by 9 wickets*)	**2013-14**
351-4	**(49.3 overs)**	**India v Australia at Nagpur** (*Won by 6 wickets*)	**2013-14**
350-9	(49.3 overs)	New Zealand v Australia at Hamilton (*Won by 1 wicket*) . .	2006-07
347	(49.4 overs)	India v Australia at Hyderabad (*Lost by 3 runs*)	2009-10
344-8	(50 overs)	Pakistan v India at Karachi (*Lost by 5 runs*)	2003-04
340-5	(48.4 overs)	New Zealand v Australia at Auckland (*Won by 5 wickets*)	2006-07
340-7	(50 overs)	New Zealand v England at Napier (*Tied*)	2007-08

HIGHEST MATCH AGGREGATES

872-13	(99.5 overs)	South Africa v Australia at Johannesburg	2005-06
825-15	(100 overs)	India v Sri Lanka at Rajkot	2009-10
726-14	(95.1 overs)	New Zealand v India at Christchurch	2008-09
721-6	**(93.3 overs)**	**India v Australia at Jaipur**	**2013-14**

LOWEST INNINGS TOTALS

35	(18 overs)	Zimbabwe v Sri Lanka at Harare	2003-04
36	(18.4 overs)	Canada v Sri Lanka at Paarl	2002-03
38	(15.4 overs)	Zimbabwe v Sri Lanka at Colombo (SSC)	2001-02
43	(19.5 overs)	Pakistan v West Indies at Cape Town	1992-93
43	(20.1 overs)	Sri Lanka v South Africa at Paarl	2011-12
44	(24.5 overs)	Zimbabwe v Bangladesh at Chittagong	2009-10
45	(40.3 overs)	Canada v England at Manchester	1979
45	(14 overs)	Namibia v Australia at Potchefstroom	2002-03

The lowest totals by other Test-playing countries are:

54	(26.3 overs)	India v Sri Lanka at Sharjah	2000-01
54	(23.2 overs)	West Indies v South Africa at Cape Town	2003-04
58	(18.5 overs)	Bangladesh v West Indies at Mirpur	2010-11
64	(35.5 overs)	New Zealand v Pakistan at Sharjah	1985-86
69	(28 overs)	South Africa v Australia at Sydney	1993-94
70	(25.2 overs)	Australia v England at Birmingham	1977
70	(26.3 overs)	Australia v New Zealand at Adelaide	1985-86
86	(32.4 overs)	England v Australia at Manchester	2001

LARGEST VICTORIES

290 runs	New Zealand (402-2 in 50 overs) v Ireland (112 in 28.4 ov) at Aberdeen	2008
272 runs	South Africa (399-6 in 50 overs) v Zimbabwe (127 in 29 overs) at Benoni	2010-11
258 runs	South Africa (301-8 in 50 overs) v Sri Lanka (43 in 20.1 overs) at Paarl	2011-12
257 runs	India (413-5 in 50 overs) v Bermuda (156 in 43.1 overs) at Port-of-Spain	2006-07
256 runs	Australia (301-6 in 50 overs) v Namibia (45 in 14 overs) at Potchefstroom . . .	2002-03
256 runs	India (374-4 in 50 overs) v Hong Kong (118 in 36.5 overs) at Karachi	2008

There have been **45** instances of victory by ten wickets.

TIED MATCHES

There have been **31** tied one-day internationals. Australia have tied nine matches; Bangladesh are the only Test-playing country never to have tied. The most recent ties are:

India (338 in 49.5 overs) v England (338-8 in 50 overs) at Bangalore   2010-11
India (280-5 in 50 overs) v England (270-8 in 48.5 overs) at Lord's (D/L)   2011
Australia (220 in 49.5 overs) v West Indies (220 in 49.4 overs) at St Vincent   2011-12
Sri Lanka (236-9 in 50 overs) v India (236-9 in 50 overs) at Adelaide   2011-12
South Africa (230-6 in 31 overs) v West Indies (190-6 in 26.1 overs) at Cardiff (D/L) .   **2013**
Ireland (268-5 in 50 overs) v Netherlands (268-9 in 50 overs) at Amsteleven **2013**
Pakistan (229-6 in 50 overs) v West Indies (229-9 in 50 overs) at Gros Islet **2013**
Pakistan (266-5 in 47 overs) v Ireland (275-5 in 47 overs) at Dublin (D/L) **2013**

OTHER RECORDS

MOST APPEARANCES

463	S. R. Tendulkar (I)	344	R. Dravid (I/World/Asia)
445	S. T. Jayasuriya (SL/Asia)	334	M. Azharuddin (I)
407	**D. P. M. D. Jayawardene (SL/Asia)**	**325**	**J. H. Kallis (SA/World/Africa)**
378	Inzamam-ul-Haq (P/Asia)	325	S. R. Waugh (A)
375	R. T. Ponting (A/World)	322	W. P. U. J. C. Vaas (SL/Asia)
373	**Shahid Afridi (P/World/Asia)**	311	S. C. Ganguly (I/Asia)
362	**K. C. Sangakkara (SL/World/Asia)**	308	P. A. de Silva (SL)
356	Wasim Akram (P)	303	S. M. Pollock (SA/World/Africa)
350	M. Muralitharan (SL/World/Asia)		

Notes: The most appearances for other countries are 295 by B. C. Lara (WI), 279 by S. P. Fleming (NZ), 221 by G. W. Flower (Z), 197 by P. D. Collingwood (E), and **177** by **Mohammad Ashraful** (B). Excluding appearances for combined teams, the record for Sri Lanka is 441 appearances by S. T. Jayasuriya; for Pakistan, 375 by Inzamam-ul-Haq; for Australia, 374 by R. T. Ponting; and for South Africa, **320** by **J. H. Kallis**.

MOST MATCHES AS CAPTAIN

	P	W	L	T	NR		P	W	L	T	NR
R. T. Ponting (A/World)	230	165	51	2	12	S. C. Ganguly (I/Asia) .	147	76	66	0	5
S. P. Fleming (NZ)	218	98	106	1	13	Imran Khan (P).	139	75	59	1	4
A. Ranatunga (SL)	193	89	95	1	8	W. J. Cronje (SA)	138	99	35	1	3
A. R. Border (A)	178	107	67	1	3	**D. P. M. D.**	138	99	35	1	3
M. Azharuddin (I)	174	90	76	2	6	**Jayawardene (SL/As)** .	**129**	**71**	**49**	**1**	**8**
M. S. Dhoni (I)	**154**	**88**	**53**	**3**	**10**	B. C. Lara (WI)	125	59	59	1	7
G. C. Smith (SA/Af) . .	150	92	51	1	6						

WORLD CUP FINALS

1975	WEST INDIES (291-8) beat Australia (274) by 17 runs	Lord's
1979	WEST INDIES (286-9) beat England (194) by 92 runs	Lord's
1983	INDIA (183) beat West Indies (140) by 43 runs	Lord's
1987	AUSTRALIA (253-5) beat England (246-8) by seven runs	Calcutta
1992	PAKISTAN (249-6) beat England (227) by 22 runs	Melbourne
1996	SRI LANKA (245-3) beat Australia (241-7) by seven wickets	Lahore
1999	AUSTRALIA (133-2) beat Pakistan (132) by eight wickets	Lord's
2003	AUSTRALIA (359-2) beat India (234) by 125 runs	Johannesburg
2007	AUSTRALIA (281-4) beat Sri Lanka (215-8) by 53 runs (D/L method)	Bridgetown
2011	INDIA (277-4) beat Sri Lanka (274-6) by six wickets	Mumbai

TWENTY20 INTERNATIONAL RECORDS

Matches in this section do not have first-class status.

Note: Throughout this section, bold type denotes performances in the calendar year 2013 or, in career figures, players who appeared in Twenty20 internationals in that year.

RESULTS SUMMARY OF TWENTY20 INTERNATIONALS

2004-05 to December 31, 2013 (351 matches)

	Matches	Won	Lost	No Result	% Won (excl. NR)
South Africa	63	39	23	1	62.90
Pakistan.	78	48*	30*	0	61.53
Sri Lanka	58	35*	22	1	61.40
India	46	26*	19	1	57.77
England.	62	31	27	4	53.44
West Indies.	51	25†	25*	1	50.00
Australia	64	31	32†	1	49.20
New Zealand.	69	32†	35‡	2	47.76
Bangladesh	31	9	22	0	29.03
Zimbabwe	28	5*	23	0	17.85
Ireland.	32	17	12	3	58.62
Netherlands.	22	12	9	1	57.14
Afghanistan.	22	11	11	0	50.00
Kenya	29	10	19	0	34.48
Scotland	25	8	16	1	33.33
Canada	19	4	15*	0	21.05
Bermuda	3	0	3	0	0.00

* *Includes one game settled by a tie-break.*   † *Includes two settled by a tie-break.*
‡ *Includes three settled by a tie-break. Ties were decided by bowling contests or one-over eliminators.*

Note: Matches abandoned without a ball bowled are not included except where the toss took place, when they are shown as no result.

BATTING RECORDS

HUNDREDS

156	**A. J. Finch**	**Australia v England at Southampton**	**2013**
123	B. B. McCullum	New Zealand v Bangladesh at Pallekele.	2012-13
117*	R. E. Levi	South Africa v New Zealand at Hamilton.	2011-12
117	C. H. Gayle	West Indies v South Africa at Johannesburg	2007-08
116*	B. B. McCullum	New Zealand v Australia at Christchurch.	2009-10
104*	T. M. Dilshan	Sri Lanka v Australia at Pallekele.	2011-12
101*	M. J. Guptill	New Zealand v South Africa at East London	2012-13
101	S. K. Raina	India v South Africa at Gros Islet, St Lucia	2010
100	D. P. M. D. Jayawardene	Sri Lanka v Zimbabwe at Providence.	2010
100	R. D. Berrington	Scotland v Bangladesh at Voorburg	2012

MOST RUNS

		M	I	NO	R	HS	100	Avge
1	**B. B. McCullum (New Zealand)**	62	61	8	1,882	123	2	**35.50**
2	**D. P. M. D. Jayawardene (Sri Lanka)** . .	49	49	7	1,335	100	1	31.78
3	**T. M. Dilshan (Sri Lanka)**.	53	52	5	1,317	104*	1	30.62
4	**K. C. Sangakkara (Sri Lanka)**	48	46	8	1,263	78	0	33.23

		M	I	NO	R	HS	100	Avge
5	D. A. Warner (Australia)	46	46	2	1,260	90*	0	28.63
6	Mohammad Hafeez (Pakistan)	54	52	3	1,250	86	0	25.51
7	K. P. Pietersen (England)	37	36	5	1,176	79	0	37.93
8	M. J. Guptill (New Zealand)	41	39	6	1,168	101*	1	35.39
9	J-P. Duminy (South Africa)	48	44	12	1,142	96*	0	35.68
10	Umar Akmal (Pakistan)	52	49	9	1,093	64	0	27.32
11	Shahid Afridi (Pakistan)	70	65	10	1,044	54*	0	18.98
12	S. R. Watson (Australia)	39	38	3	1,030	81	0	29.42

HIGHEST PARTNERSHIP FOR EACH WICKET

170	for 1st	G. C. Smith and L. L. Bosman	SA v E	Centurion	2009-10
166	for 2nd	D. P. M. D. Jayawardene and K. C. Sangakkara	SL v WI	Bridgetown	2010
137	for 3rd	M. J. Guptill and K. S. Williamson	NZ v Z	Auckland	2011-12
112	for 4th	K. P. Pietersen and E. J. G. Morgan	E v P	Dubai	2009-10
119*	for 5th	Shoaib Malik and Misbah-ul-Haq	P v A	Johannesburg	2007-08
101*	for 6th	M. E. K. Hussey and C. L. White	A v SL	Bridgetown	2010
91	for 7th	P. D. Collingwood and M. H. Yardy	E v WI	The Oval	2007
64*	for 8th	W. D. Parnell and J. Theron	SA v A	Johannesburg	2011-12
63	**for 9th**	**Sohail Tanvir and Saeed Ajmal**	**P v SL**	**Dubai**	**2013-14**
31*	for 10th	Wahab Riaz and Shoaib Akhtar	P v NZ	Auckland	2010-11

BOWLING RECORDS

BEST BOWLING ANALYSES

6-8	B. A. W. Mendis	Sri Lanka v Zimbabwe at Hambantota	2012-13
6-16	B. A. W. Mendis	Sri Lanka v Australia at Pallekele	2011-12
5-6	Umar Gul	Pakistan v New Zealand at The Oval	2009
5-6	**Umar Gul**	**Pakistan v South Africa at Centurion**	**2012-13**
5-13	Elias Sunny	Bangladesh v Ireland at Belfast	2012
5-13	**Samiullah Shenwari**	**Afghanistan v Kenya at Sharjah**	**2013-14**
5-18	T. G. Southee	New Zealand v Pakistan at Auckland	2010-11
5-19	R. McLaren	South Africa v West Indies at North Sound	2010
5-20	N. N. Odhiambo	Kenya v Scotland at Nairobi	2009-10
5-26	D. J. G. Sammy	West Indies v Zimbabwe at Port-of-Spain	2009-10
5-31	S. L. Malinga	Sri Lanka v England at Pallekele	2012-13

HAT-TRICKS

B. Lee	Australia v Bangladesh at Cape Town	2007-08
J. D. P. Oram	New Zealand v Sri Lanka at Colombo	2009
T. G. Southee	New Zealand v Pakistan at Auckland	2010-11

MOST WICKETS

		M	B	R	W	BB	4I	Avge
1	Saeed Ajmal (Pakistan)	59	1,320	1,379	81	4-19	4	17.02
2	Umar Gul (Pakistan)	52	1,050	1,217	74	5-6	6	16.44
3	Shahid Afridi (Pakistan)	70	1,520	1,643	73	4-11	3	22.50
4	B. A. W. Mendis (Sri Lanka)	34	774	794	60	6-8	5	13.23
5	S. C. J. Broad (England)	48	1,023	1,279	57	4-24	1	22.43
6	S. L. Malinga (Sri Lanka)	48	1,008	1,243	56	5-31	1	22.19
7	G. P. Swann (England)	39	810	859	51	3-13	0	16.84
8	D. W. Steyn (South Africa)	33	702	726	46	4-9	1	15.78
9	Mohammad Hafeez (Pakistan)	54	914	1,008	44	4-10	1	22.90
10	M. Morkel (South Africa)	36	766	904	43	4-17	2	21.02
10	N. L. McCullum (New Zealand)	49	823	954	43	4-16	1	22.18

WICKETKEEPING AND FIELDING RECORDS

MOST DISMISSALS IN AN INNINGS

4 (all ct)	A. C. Gilchrist	Australia v Zimbabwe at Cape Town	2007-08
4 (all ct)	M. J. Prior	England v South Africa at Cape Town	2007-08
4 (all ct)	A. C. Gilchrist	Australia v New Zealand at Perth	2007-08
4 (all st)	Kamran Akmal	Pakistan v Netherlands at Lord's	2009
4 (3ct, 1st)	N. J. O'Brien	Ireland v Sri Lanka at Lord's	2009
4 (2ct, 2st)	A. B. de Villiers	South Africa v West Indies at North Sound	2010
4 (all ct)	M. S. Dhoni	India v Afghanistan at Gros Islet	2010
4 (3ct, 1st)	G. C. Wilson	Ireland v Kenya at Dubai	2011-12
4 (all ct)	A. B. de Villiers	South Africa v Zimbabwe at Hambantota	2012-13
4 (all ct)	M. S. Dhoni	India v Pakistan at Colombo (RPS)	2012-13
4 (all ct)	**W. Barresi**	**Netherlands v Kenya at Dubai**	**2013-14**
4 (2ct, 2st)	**Q. de Kock**	**South Africa v Pakistan at Dubai**	**2013-14**

MOST DISMISSALS

			M	Ct	St
1	54	Kamran Akmal (Pakistan)	49	24	30
2	42	K. C. Sangakkara (Sri Lanka)	48	23	19
3	34	D. Ramdin (West Indies)	35	26	8
4	32	B. B. McCullum (New Zealand)	42	24	8
5	30	M. S. Dhoni (India)	43	22	8

Note: B. B. McCullum's record excludes ten catches taken in 20 Twenty20 internationals when not keeping wicket. Kamran Akmal played one Twenty20 international in which he did not keep wicket and did not take a catch.

MOST CATCHES IN AN INNINGS IN THE FIELD

4	D. J. G. Sammy	West Indies v Ireland at Providence	2010

MOST CATCHES

Ct	M		Ct	M	
36	53	L. R. P. L. Taylor (New Zealand)	27	46	D. A. Warner (Australia)
27	29	A. B. de Villiers (South Africa)	25	55	Shoaib Malik (Pakistan)

Note: A. B. de Villiers's record excludes 26 dismissals (20ct, 6st) in 22 Twenty20 internationals when keeping wicket.

TEAM RECORDS

HIGHEST INNINGS TOTALS

260-6	(20 overs)	Sri Lanka v Kenya at Johannesburg	2007-08
248-6	**(20 overs)**	**Australia v England at Southampton**	**2013**
241-6	(20 overs)	South Africa v England at Centurion	2009-10
225-7	**(20 overs)**	**Ireland v Afghanistan at Abu Dhabi**	**2013-14**
221-5	(20 overs)	Australia v England at Sydney	2006-07
219-4	(20 overs)	South Africa v India at Johannesburg	2011-12
218-4	(20 overs)	India v England at Durban	2007-08
215-5	(20 overs)	Sri Lanka v India at Nagpur	2009-10
214-4	(20 overs)	Australia v New Zealand at Christchurch	2009-10
214-5	(20 overs)	Australia v New Zealand at Auckland	2004-05
214-6	(20 overs)	New Zealand v Australia at Christchurch	2009-10
214-7	**(20 overs)**	**England v New Zealand at Auckland**	**2012-13**

LOWEST INNINGS TOTALS

56	(18.4 overs)	**Kenya v Afghanistan at Sharjah**	**2013-14**
67	(17.2 overs)	Kenya v Ireland at Belfast	2008
68	(16.4 overs)	Ireland v West Indies at Providence......................	2010
70	(20 overs)	Bermuda v Canada at Belfast............................	2008
71	(19 overs)	Kenya v Ireland at Dubai	2011-12
73	(16.5 overs)	Kenya v New Zealand at Durban	2007-08
74	(17.3 overs)	India v Australia at Melbourne..........................	2007-08
74	(19.1 overs)	Pakistan v Australia at Dubai...........................	2012
75	(19.2 overs)	Canada v Zimbabwe at King City	2007-08

OTHER RECORDS

MOST APPEARANCES

70	**Shahid Afridi (Pakistan)**	**53**	**L. R. P. L. Taylor (New Zealand)**
62	**B. B. McCullum (New Zealand)**	**52**	**Umar Akmal (Pakistan)**
59	**Saeed Ajmal (Pakistan)**	**52**	**Umar Gul (Pakistan)**
55	**Shoaib Malik (Pakistan)**	**51**	**A. B. de Villiers (South Africa)**
54	**Mohammad Hafeez (Pakistan)**	**50**	**Kamran Akmal (Pakistan)**
53	**T. M. Dilshan (Sri Lanka)**		

WORLD TWENTY20 FINALS

2007-08	INDIA (157-5) beat Pakistan (152) by five runs...................	Johannesburg
2009	PAKISTAN (139-2) beat Sri Lanka (138-6) by eight wickets	Lord's
2010	ENGLAND (148-3) beat Australia (147-6) by seven wickets	Bridgetown
2012-13	WEST INDIES (137-6) beat Sri Lanka (101) by 36 runs.............	Colombo (RPS)

An expanded and regularly updated online version of the Records can be found at www.wisdenrecords.com

MISCELLANEOUS RECORDS

LARGE ATTENDANCES

Test Series

943,000	Australia v England (5 Tests)	1936-37

In England
549,650	England v Australia (5 Tests)	1953

Test Matches

†‡465,000	India v Pakistan, Calcutta	1998-99
350,534	Australia v England, Melbourne (Third Test)	1936-37

Note: Attendance at India v England at Calcutta in 1981-82 may have exceeded 350,000.

In England
158,000+	England v Australia, Leeds	1948
140,111	England v India, Lord's...................................	2011
137,915	England v Australia, Lord's................................	1953

Test Match Day

‡100,000	India v Pakistan, Calcutta (first four days).................	1998-99
91,112	**Australia v England, Melbourne (Fourth Test, first day)**	**2013-14**
90,800	Australia v West Indies, Melbourne (Fifth Test, second day).....	1960-61
89,155	Australia v England, Melbourne (Fourth Test, first day).........	2006-07

Other First-Class Matches in England

93,000	England v Australia, Lord's (Fourth Victory Match, 3 days)	1945
80,000+	Surrey v Yorkshire, The Oval (3 days)	1906
78,792	Yorkshire v Lancashire, Leeds (3 days).......................	1904
76,617	Lancashire v Yorkshire, Manchester (3 days)	1926

One-Day Internationals

‡100,000	India v South Africa, Calcutta.............................	1993-94
‡100,000	India v West Indies, Calcutta..............................	1993-94
‡100,000	India v West Indies, Calcutta..............................	1994-95
‡100,000	India v Sri Lanka, Calcutta (World Cup semi-final)	1995-96
‡100,000	India v Australia, Kolkata	2003-04
‡90,000	India v Pakistan, Calcutta	1986-87
‡90,000	India v South Africa, Calcutta.............................	1991-92
87,182	England v Pakistan, Melbourne (World Cup final)	1991-92
86,133	Australia v West Indies, Melbourne	1983-84

Twenty20 International

84,041	Australia v India, Melbourne..............................	2007-08

† *Estimated.*
‡ *No official attendance figures were issued for these games, but capacity at Calcutta (now Kolkata) is believed to have reached 100,000 following rebuilding in 1993.*

LORD'S CRICKET GROUND

Lord's and the Marylebone Cricket Club were founded in London in 1787. The Club has enjoyed an uninterrupted career since that date, but there have been three grounds known as Lord's. The first (1787–1810) was situated where Dorset Square now is; the second (1809–13), at North Bank, had to be abandoned owing to the cutting of the Regent's Canal; and the third, opened in 1814, is the present one at St John's Wood. It was not until 1866 that the freehold of Lord's was secured by MCC. The present pavilion was erected in 1890 at a cost of £21,000.

MINOR CRICKET

HIGHEST INDIVIDUAL SCORES

628*	A. E. J. Collins, Clark's House v North Town at Clifton College.	
	A junior house match. His innings of 6 hours 50 minutes was spread over four	
	afternoons	1899
566	C. J. Eady, Break-o'-Day v Wellington at Hobart	1901-02
546	**P. P. Shaw, Rizvi Springfield School v St Francis D'Assisi School at Mumbai**	**2013-14**
515	D. R. Havewalla, B. B. and C. I. Railways v St Xavier's at Bombay	1933-34
506*	J. C. Sharp, Melbourne GS v Geelong College at Melbourne	1914-15
502*	Chaman Lal, Mehandra Coll., Patiala v Government Coll., Rupar at Patiala	1956-57
498	Arman Jaffer, Rizvi Springfield School v IES Raja Shivaji School at Mumbai. . .	2010-11
485	A. E. Stoddart, Hampstead v Stoics at Hampstead.	1886
475*	Mohammad Iqbal, Muslim Model HS v Islamia HS, Sialkot at Lahore.	1958-59
473	**Arman Jaffer, Rizvi Springfield School v IES VN Sule School at Mumbai** . .	**2012-13**
466*	G. T. S. Stevens, Beta v Lambda (University College School house match) at	
	Neasden. *Stevens scored his 466 and took 14 wickets on one day*	1919
461*	Ali Zorain Khan, Nagpur Cricket Academy v Reshimbagh Gymkhana at Nagpur	2010-11
459	J. A. Prout, Wesley College v Geelong College at Geelong	1908-09
451*	V. H. Mol, Maharashtra Under-19 v Assam Under-19 at Nasik	2011-12

Note: The highest score in a Minor County match is 323* by F. E. Lacey for Hampshire v Norfolk at Southampton in 1887; the highest in the Minor Counties Championship is 282 by E. Garnett for Berkshire v Wiltshire at Reading in 1908.

HIGHEST PARTNERSHIPS

721* for 1st	B. Manoj Kumar and M. S. Tumbi, St Peter's High School v St Philip's High School at Secunderabad.	2006-07
664* for 3rd	V. G. Kambli and S. R. Tendulkar, Sharadashram Vidyamandir School v St Xavier's High School at Bombay.	1987-88

Notes: Manoj Kumar and Tumbi scored 721 in 40 overs in an Under-13 inter-school match; they hit 103 fours between them, but no sixes. Their opponents were all out for 21 in seven overs.

Kambli was 16 years old, Tendulkar 14. Tendulkar made his Test debut 21 months later.

MOST WICKETS WITH CONSECUTIVE BALLS

There are **two** recorded instances of a bowler taking nine wickets with consecutive balls. Both came in school games: Paul Hugo, for Smithfield School v Aliwal North at Smithfield, South Africa, in 1930-31, and Stephen Fleming (not the future Test captain), for Marlborough College A v Bohally School at Blenheim, New Zealand, in 1967-68. There are five further verified instances of eight wickets in eight balls, the most recent by Mike Walters for the Royal Army Educational Corps v Joint Air Transport Establishment at Beaconsfield in 1979.

TEN WICKETS FOR NO RUNS

There are **24** recorded instances of a bowler taking all ten wickets in an innings for no runs, the most recent by David Morton, for Bayside Muddies v Ranatungas in Brisbane in 1998-99. The previous instance was also in Australia, by the schoolgirl Emma Liddell, for Metropolitan East v West at Penrith (Sydney) in 1995-96. When Jennings Tune did it, for the Yorkshire club Cliffe v Eastrington at Cliffe in 1923, all ten of his victims were bowled.

NOUGHT ALL OUT

In minor matches, this is more common than might be imagined. The historian Peter Wynne-Thomas says the first recorded example was in Norfolk, where an Eleven of Fakenham, Walsingham and Hempton were dismissed for nought by an Eleven of Licham, Dunham and Brisley in July 1815.

MOST DISMISSALS IN AN INNINGS

The only recorded instance of a wicketkeeper being involved in all ten dismissals in an innings was by Welihinda Badalge Bennett, for Mahinda College against Richmond College in Ceylon (now Sri Lanka) in 1952-53. His feat comprised six catches and four stumpings. There are three other known instances of nine dismissals in the same innings, one of which – by H. W. P. Middleton for Priory v Mitre in a Repton School house match in 1930 – included eight stumpings. Young Rangers' innings against Bohran Gymkhana in Karachi in 1969-70 included nine run-outs.

The widespread nature – and differing levels of supervision – of minor cricket matches mean that record claims have to be treated with caution. Additions and corrections to the above records for minor cricket will only be considered for inclusion in Wisden *if they are corroborated by independent evidence of the achievement.*

Research: Steven Lynch

RECORD HIT

The Rev. W. Fellows, while at practice on the Christ Church ground at Oxford in 1856, drove a ball bowled by Charles Rogers 175 yards from hit to pitch.

BIGGEST HIT AT LORD'S

The only known instance of a batsman hitting a ball over the present pavilion at Lord's occurred when A. E. Trott, appearing for MCC against Australians on July 31, August 1, 2, 1899, drove M. A. Noble so far and high that the ball struck a chimney pot and fell behind the building.

THROWING THE CRICKET BALL

140 yards 2 feet, Robert Percival, on the Durham Sands racecourse, Co. Durham.		c1882
140 yards 9 inches, Ross Mackenzie, at Toronto		1872
140 yards, "King Billy" the Aborigine, at Clermont, Queensland		1872

Note: Extensive research by David Rayvern Allen has shown that these traditional records are probably authentic, if not necessarily wholly accurate. Modern competitions have failed to produce similar distances although Ian Pont, the Essex all-rounder who also played baseball, was reported to have thrown 138 yards in Cape Town in 1981. There have been speculative reports attributing throws of 150 yards or more to figures as diverse as the South African Test player Colin Bland, the Latvian javelin thrower Janis Lusis, who won a gold medal for the Soviet Union in the 1968 Olympics, and the British sprinter Charley Ransome. The definitive record is still awaited.

COUNTY CHAMPIONSHIP

MOST APPEARANCES

762	W. Rhodes	Yorkshire	1898–1930
707	F. E. Woolley	Kent	1906–1938
668	C. P. Mead	Hampshire	1906–1936
617	N. Gifford	Worcestershire (484), Warwickshire (133)	1960–1988
611	W. G. Quaife	Warwickshire	1895–1928
601	G. H. Hirst	Yorkshire	1891–1921

MOST CONSECUTIVE APPEARANCES

423	K. G. Suttle	Sussex	1954–1969
412	J. G. Binks	Yorkshire	1955–1969

Notes: J. Vine made 417 consecutive appearances for Sussex in all first-class matches (399 of them in the Championship) between July 1900 and September 1914.

J. G. Binks did not miss a Championship match for Yorkshire between making his debut in June 1955 and retiring at the end of the 1969 season.

UMPIRES

MOST COUNTY CHAMPIONSHIP APPEARANCES

570	T. W. Spencer	1950–1980	517	H. G. Baldwin	1932–1962
531	F. Chester	1922–1955	511	A. G. T. Whitehead	1970–2005
523	D. J. Constant	1969–2006			

MOST SEASONS ON ENGLISH FIRST-CLASS LIST

38	D. J. Constant	1969–2006	27	B. Dudleston	1984–2010
36	A. G. T. Whitehead	1970–2005	27	J. W. Holder	1983–2009
31	K. E. Palmer	1972–2002	27	J. Moss	1899–1929
31	T. W. Spencer	1950–1980	26	W. A. J. West	1896–1925
30	R. Julian	1972–2001	25	H. G. Baldwin	1932–1962
30	P. B. Wight	1966–1995	25	A. Jepson	1960–1984
29	H. D. Bird	1970–1998	25	J. G. Langridge	1956–1980
28	F. Chester	1922–1955	25	B. J. Meyer	1973–1997
28	B. Leadbeater	1981–2008	25	D. R. Shepherd	1981–2005
28	R. Palmer	1980–2007			

An expanded and regularly updated online version of the Records can be found at www.wisdenrecords.com

WOMEN'S TEST RECORDS

Amended to January 13, 2014

Note: Throughout this section, bold type denotes performances since January 1, 2013, or, in career figures, players who have appeared in women's Tests since that date.

BATTING RECORDS

HIGHEST INDIVIDUAL INNINGS

242	Kiran Baluch	Pakistan v West Indies at Karachi	2003-04
214	M. Raj	India v England at Taunton	2002
209*	K. L. Rolton	Australia v England at Leeds	2001
204	K. E. Flavell	New Zealand v England at Scarborough	1996
204	M. A. J. Goszko	Australia v England at Shenley	2001
200	J. Broadbent	Australia v England at Guildford	1998

1,000 RUNS IN A CAREER

R	T		R	T	
1,935	27	J. A. Brittin (England)	1,110	13	S. Agarwal (India)
1,621	**21**	**C. M. Edwards (England)**	1,078	12	E. Bakewell (England)
1,594	22	R. Heyhoe-Flint (England)	1,030	15	S. C. Taylor (England)
1,301	19	D. A. Hockley (New Zealand)	1,007	14	M. E. Maclagan (England)
1,164	18	C. A. Hodges (England)	1,002	14	K. L. Rolton (Australia)

BOWLING RECORDS

BEST BOWLING ANALYSES

8-53	N. David	India v England at Jamshedpur	1995-96
7-6	M. B. Duggan	England v Australia at Melbourne	1957-58
7-7	E. R. Wilson	Australia v England at Melbourne	1957-58
7-10	M. E. Maclagan	England v Australia at Brisbane	1934-35
7-18	A. Palmer	Australia v England at Brisbane	1934-35
7-24	L. Johnston	Australia v New Zealand at Melbourne	1971-72
7-34	G. E. McConway	England v India at Worcester	1986
7-41	J. A. Burley	New Zealand v England at The Oval	1966
7-51	L. C. Pearson	England v Australia at Sydney	2002-03
7-59	Shaiza Khan	Pakistan v West Indies at Karachi	2003-04
7-61	E. Bakewell	England v West Indies at Birmingham	1979

MOST WICKETS IN A MATCH

13-226	Shaiza Khan	Pakistan v West Indies at Karachi	2003-04

50 WICKETS IN A CAREER

W	T		W	T	
77	17	M. B. Duggan (England)	60	19	S. Kulkarni (India)
68	11	E. R. Wilson (Australia)	57	16	R. H. Thompson (Australia)
63	20	D. F. Edulji (India)	55	15	J. Lord (New Zealand)
60	13	C. L. Fitzpatrick (Australia)	50	12	E. Bakewell (England)
60	14	M. E. Maclagan (England)			

WICKETKEEPING RECORDS

SIX DISMISSALS IN AN INNINGS

8 (6ct, 2st) L. Nye . . . . England v New Zealand at New Plymouth 1991-92
6 (2ct, 4st) B. A. Brentnall . . . . New Zealand v South Africa at Johannesburg 1971-72

25 DISMISSALS IN A CAREER

		T	Ct	St
58	C. Matthews (Australia)	20	46	12
43	J. Smit (England)	21	39	4
36	S. A. Hodges (England)	11	19	17
28	B. A. Brentnall (New Zealand)	10	16	12

TEAM RECORDS

HIGHEST INNINGS TOTALS

569-6 dec	Australia v England at Guildford	1998
525	Australia v India at Ahmedabad	1983-84
517-8	New Zealand v England at Scarborough	1996
503-5 dec	England v New Zealand at Christchurch	1934-35

LOWEST INNINGS TOTALS

35	England v Australia at Melbourne	1957-58
38	Australia v England at Melbourne	1957-58
44	New Zealand v England at Christchurch	1934-35
47	Australia v England at Brisbane	1934-35
50	Netherlands v South Africa at Rotterdam	2007

WOMEN'S ONE-DAY INTERNATIONAL RECORDS

Amended to December 31, 2013

Note: Throughout this section, bold type denotes performances in the calendar year 2013 or, in career figures, players who appeared in women's one-day internationals in that year.

BATTING RECORDS

HIGHEST INDIVIDUAL INNINGS

229*	B. J. Clark	Australia v Denmark at Mumbai	1997-98
173*	C. M. Edwards	England v Ireland at Pune	1997-98
171	**S. R. Taylor**	**West Indies v Sri Lanka at Mumbai**	**2012-13**
168	S. W. Bates	New Zealand v Pakistan at Sydney	2008-09
156*	L. M. Keightley	Australia v Pakistan at Melbourne	1996-97
156*	S. C. Taylor	England v India at Lord's	2006
154*	K. L. Rolton	Australia v Sri Lanka at Christchurch	2000-01
153*	J. Logtenberg	South Africa v Netherlands at Deventer	2007
151	K. L. Rolton	Australia v Ireland at Dublin	2005

MOST RUNS IN A CAREER

R	M		R	M	
5,357	**175**	**C. M. Edwards (England)**	**4,622**	**145**	**M. Raj (India)**
4,844	118	B. J. Clark (Australia)	4,101	126	S. C. Taylor (England)
4,814	141	K. L. Rolton (Australia)	4,064	118	D. A. Hockley (New Zealand)

BOWLING RECORDS

BEST BOWLING ANALYSES

7-4	Sajjida Shah	Pakistan v Japan at Amsterdam	2003
7-8	J. M. Chamberlain	England v Denmark at Haarlem	1991
7-14	A. Mohammed	West Indies v Pakistan at Mirpur	2011-12
7-24	S. Nitschke	Australia v England at Kidderminster	2005
6-10	J. Lord	New Zealand v India at Auckland	1981-82
6-10	M. Maben	India v Sri Lanka at Kandy	2003-04
6-10	S. Ismail	South Africa v Netherlands at Savar	2011-12

MOST WICKETS IN A CAREER

W	M		W	M	
180	109	C. L. Fitzpatrick (Australia)	**106**	**115**	**J. L. Gunn (England)**
154	**130**	**J. Goswami (India)**	102	105	C. E. Taylor (England)
146	125	L. C. Sthalekar (Australia)	101	83	I. T. Guha (England)
141	97	N. David (India)	100	78	N. Al Khader (India)

WICKETKEEPING RECORDS

MOST DISMISSALS IN AN INNINGS

6 (4ct, 2st)	S. L. Illingworth	New Zealand v Australia at Beckenham	1993
6 (1ct, 5st)	V. Kalpana	India v Denmark at Slough	1993
6 (2ct, 4st)	Batool Fatima	Pakistan v West Indies at Karachi	2003-04
6 (4ct, 2st)	Batool Fatima	Pakistan v Sri Lanka at Colombo	2010-11

MOST DISMISSALS IN A CAREER

		M	Ct	St
133	R. J. Rolls (New Zealand)	104	90	43
114	J. Smit (England)	109	69	45
100	J. C. Price (Australia)	84	70	30
100	**S. J. Taylor (England)**	**85**	**67**	**33**

† *Price's total includes one catch taken in the field after giving up the gloves in mid-game, and S. J. Taylor's two in eight matches while not keeping wicket.*

TEAM RECORDS

HIGHEST INNINGS TOTALS

455-5	New Zealand v Pakistan at Christchurch	1996-97
412-3	Australia v Denmark at Mumbai	1997-98
397-4	Australia v Pakistan at Melbourne	1996-97
376-2	England v Pakistan at Vijayawada	1997-98
375-5	Netherlands v Japan at Schiedam	2003
373-7	New Zealand v Pakistan at Sydney	2008-09
368-8	**West Indies v Sri Lanka at Mumbai**	**2012-13**

LOWEST INNINGS TOTALS

22	Netherlands v West Indies at Deventer	2008
23	Pakistan v Australia at Melbourne	1996-97
24	Scotland v England at Reading	2001
26	India v New Zealand as St Saviour	2002
27	Pakistan v Australia at Hyderabad (India)	1997-98
28	Japan v Pakistan at Amsterdam	2003
29	Netherlands v Australia at Perth	1988-89

WOMEN'S WORLD CUP WINNERS

1973	England	1993	England	2008-09	England
1977-78	Australia	1997-98	Australia	**2012-13**	**Australia**
1981-82	Australia	2000-01	New Zealand		
1988-89	Australia	2004-05	Australia		

WOMEN'S TWENTY20 INTERNATIONAL RECORDS

Amended to December 31, 2013

Note: Throughout this section, bold type denotes performances in the calendar year 2013 or, in career figures, players who appeared in women's Twenty20 internationals in that year.

BATTING RECORDS

HIGHEST INDIVIDUAL INNINGS

116*	S. A. Fritz	South Africa v Netherlands at Potchefstroom	2010-11
112*	D. J. S. Dottin	West Indies v South Africa at Basseterre	2010
96*	K. L. Rolton	Australia v England at Taunton	2005
90	S. R. Taylor	West Indies v Ireland at Dublin	2008
90	A. J. Healy	Australia v India at Visakhapatnam	2011-12

MOST RUNS IN A CAREER

R	M		R	M	
1,789	69	C. M. Edwards (England)	1,202	54	S. W. Bates (New Zealand)
1,425	55	S. J. Taylor (England)	1,120	61	D. J. S. Dottin (West Indies)
1,321	49	S. R. Taylor (West Indies)	998	62	L. S. Greenway (England)

BOWLING RECORDS

BEST BOWLING ANALYSES

6-17	A. E. Satterthwaite	New Zealand v England at Taunton	2007
5-10	A. Mohammed	West Indies v South Africa at Cape Town	2009-10
5-11	J. Goswami	India v Australia at Visakhapatnam	2011-12
5-11	A. Shrubsole	England v New Zealand at Wellington	2011-12
5-12	**A. Mohammed**	**West Indies v New Zealand at Bridgetown**	**2013-14**
5-15	**S. F. Daley**	**West Indies v Sri Lanka at Colombo (RPS)**	**2012-13**

MOST WICKETS IN A CAREER

W	M		W	M	
71	54	A. Mohammed (West Indies)	53	45	D. Hazell (England)
63	50	H. L. Colvin (England)	53	49	S. R. Taylor (West Indies)
61	54	S. F. Daley (West Indies)	51	55	L. A. Marsh (England)
60	54	L. C. Sthalekar (Australia)			

WICKETKEEPING RECORDS

MOST DISMISSALS IN AN INNINGS

5 (1ct, 4st)	Kycia A. Knight.....	West Indies v Sri Lanka at Colombo (RPS)	2012-13
5 (1ct, 4st)	Batool Fatima.......	Pakistan v Ireland at Dublin.................	2013
5 (1ct, 4st)	Batool Fatima.......	Pakistan v Ireland at Dublin (semi-final)	2013

MOST DISMISSALS IN A CAREER

		M	Ct	St
48	S. J. Taylor (England)	55	16	32
46	*J. L. Gunn (England)	71	46	
40	J. M. Fields (Australia)	37	25	15
39	Batool Fatima (Pakistan)	32	8	31
38	R. H. Priest (New Zealand)	35	20	18
35†	M. R. Aguilleira (West Indies)......	52	16	19

* *Catches made by non-wicketkeeper in the field.*

† *Aguilleira's total includes two catches in ten matches while not keeping wicket. Taylor's and Priest's totals both include one match in the field where they made no catches.*

TEAM RECORDS

HIGHEST INNINGS TOTALS

205-1	South Africa v Netherlands at Potchefstroom	2010-11
191-4	West Indies v Netherlands at Potchefstroom	2010-11
186-7	New Zealand v South Africa at Taunton	2007
184-4	West Indies v Ireland at Dublin	2008
180-5	England v South Africa at Taunton	2007
180-5	New Zealand v West Indies at Gros Islet, St Lucia	2010

LOWEST INNINGS TOTALS

57	Sri Lanka v Bangladesh at Guanggong	2012-13
60	Pakistan v England at Taunton	2009
62	India v Australia at Billericay	2011
62	Bangladesh v Sri Lanka at Guanggong	2012-13
63	Pakistan v India at Guanggong	2012-13
65	Pakistan v West Indies at St Andrew's, Grenada.....................	2011-12
65	**Ireland v Pakistan at Dublin**.....................................	**2013**

WOMEN'S WORLD TWENTY20 WINNERS

2009	England	2010	Australia	2012-13	Australia

BIRTHS AND DEATHS

TEST CRICKETERS

Full list from 1876-77 to January 20, 2014

In the Test career column, dates in italics indicate seasons embracing two different years (i.e. non-English seasons). In these cases, only the first year is given, e.g. *1876-77* for 1876-77. Some non-English series taking place outside the host country's normal season are dated by a single year.

The Test career figures are complete up to January 20, 2014; the one-day international totals are complete up to January 8, 2014; and the Twenty20 international totals up to December 31, 2013. Career figures are for one national team only; those players who have appeared for more than one Test team are listed on page 1477, and for more than one one-day international team on page 1479.

The forename by which a player is known is underlined if it is not his first name.

Family relationships are indicated by superscript numbers; where the relationship is not immediately apparent from a shared name, see the notes at the end of this section. (CY 1889) signifies that the player was a Wisden Cricketer of the Year in the 1889 Almanack. The 5/10 column indicates instances of a player taking five wickets in a Test innings and ten wickets in a match. O/T signifies number of one-day and Twenty20 internationals played.

¹ Father and son(s).   ² Brothers.   ³ Grandfather, father and son.   ⁴ Grandfather and grandson.   ⁵ Great-grandfather and grandson.   ⁵ Great-grandfather and great-grandson.

† Excludes matches for another Test team.   ‡ Excludes matches for another ODI or T20I team.

ENGLAND (661 players)

	Born	Died	Tests	Test Career	Runs	HS	100s	Avge	Wkts	BB	Avge	5/10	Ct/St	O/T
Abel Robert (CY 1890)	30.11.1857	10.12.1936	13	1888–1902	744	132*	2	37.20	–	–	–	–/–	13	
Absolom Charles Alfred	7.6.1846	30.7.1889	1	1878	58	52	0	29.00	–	–	–	–/–	0	
Adams Christopher John (CY 2004)	6.5.1970		5	1999	104	31	0	13.00	1	1-42	59.00	0/0	6	5
Afzaal Usman	9.6.1977		3	2001	83	54	0	16.60	1	1-49	49.00	0/0	0	
Agnew Jonathan Philip (CY 1988)	4.4.1960		3	1984–1985	10	5	0	10.00	4	2-51	93.25	0/0	0	3
Ali Kabir	24.11.1980		1	2003	10	9	0	5.00	5	3-80	27.20	0/0	0	14
Allen David Arthur	29.10.1935		39	1959–1966	918	88	0	25.50	122	5-30	30.97	4/0	10	
Allen Sir George Oswald Browning ("Gubby")	31.7.1902	29.11.1989	25	1930–1947	750	122	1	24.19	81	7-80	29.37	5/1	20	
Allom Maurice James Carrick	23.3.1906	8.4.1995	5	1929–1930	14	8*	0	14.00	14	5-38	18.92	1/0	0	
Allott Paul John Walter	14.9.1956		13	1981–1985	213	52*	0	14.20	26	6-61	41.69	1/0	4	13
Ambrose Timothy Raymond	1.12.1982		11	2007–2008	447	102	1	29.80	–	–	–	–/–	31	5/1
Ames Leslie Ethelbert George CBE (CY 1929)	3.12.1905	27.2.1990	47	1929–1938	2,434	149	8	40.56	–	–	–	–/–	74/23	
Amiss Dennis Leslie MBE (CY 1975)	7.4.1943		50	1966–1977	3,612	262*	11	46.30	–	–	–	–/–	24	18

	Born	Died	Tests	Test Career	Runs	HS	100s	Avge	Wkts	BB	5/10	Avge	Ct/St	O/I
Anderson James Michael (CY 2009)	30.7.1982		92	2003–2013	828	34	0	10.35	343	7-43	15/2	30.67	55	174/19
Andrew Keith Vincent	15.12.1929	27.12.2010	2	1954–1963	29	15	0	9.66	–	–	–	–	1	
Appleyard Robert MBE (CY 1952)	27.6.1924		9	1954–1956	51	19*	0	17.00	31	5-51	1/0	17.87	4	
Archer Alfred German	6.12.1871	15.7.1935	1	1898	31	24*	0	31.00	–	–	–	–	0	
Armitage Thomas	25.4.1848	21.9.1922	2	1876	33	21	0	11.00	0	0-15	0/0	–	0	
Arnold Edward George	7.11.1876	25.10.1942	10	1903–1907	160	40	0	13.33	31	5-37	1/0	25.41	8	
Arnold Geoffrey Graham (CY 1972)	3.9.1944		34	1967–1975	421	59	0	12.02	115	6-45	6/0	28.29	9	14
Arnold John	30.11.1907	4.4.1984	1	1931	34	34	0	17.00	–	–	–	–	0	
Astill William Ewart (CY 1933)	1.3.1888	10.2.1948	9	1927–1929	190	40	0	12.66	25	4-58	0/0	34.24	7	
Atherton Michael Andrew OBE (CY 1991)	23.3.1968		115	1989–2001	7,728	185*	16	37.69	2	1-20	0/0	151.00	83	54
Athey Charles William Jeffrey	27.9.1957		23	1980–1988	919	123	0	22.97	–	–	–	–	13	31
Attewell William (CY 1892)	12.6.1861	11.6.1927	10	1884–1891	150	43*	0	16.66	28	4-42	0/0	22.35	9	
Bailey Robert John	28.10.1963		4	1988–1989	119	43	0	14.87	–	–	–	–	0	4
Bailey Trevor Edward CBE (CY 1950)	3.12.1923	10.2.2011	61	1949–1958	2,290	134*	1	29.74	132	7-34	5/1	29.21	32	21
Bairstow David Leslie	1.9.1951	5.1.1998	4	1979–1980	125	59	0	20.83	–	–	–	–	12/1	21
Bairstow Jonathan Marc	26.9.1989		14	2012–2013	593	95	0	26.95	–	–	–	–	16	7/18
Bakewell Alfred Harry (CY 1934)	2.11.1908	23.1.1983	6	1931–1935	409	107	1	45.44	0	0-8	0/0	–	3	
Balderstone John Christopher	16.11.1940	6.3.2000	2	1976	39	35	0	9.75	1	1-80	0/0	80.00	1	
Ballance Gary Simon	22.11.1989		1	2013	25	18	0	12.50	–	–	–	–	0	1
Barber Robert William (CY 1967)	26.9.1935		28	1960–1968	1,495	185	1	35.59	42	4-132	0/0	43.00	21	
Barber Wilfred	18.4.1901	10.9.1968	2	1935	83	44	0	20.75	1	1-0	0/0	0.00	1	
Barlow Graham Derek	26.3.1950		3	1976–1977	17	7*	0	4.25	–	–	–	–	0	6
Barlow Richard Gorton	28.5.1851	31.7.1919	17	1881–1886	591	62	0	22.73	34	7-40	3/0	22.55	14	
Barnes Sydney Francis (CY 1910)	19.4.1873	26.12.1967	27	1901–1913	242	38*	0	8.06	189	9-103	24/7	16.43	12	
Barnes William (CY 1890)	27.5.1852	24.3.1899	21	1880–1890	725	134	1	23.38	51	6-28	3/0	15.54	19	
Barnett Charles John (CY 1937)	3.7.1910	28.5.1993	20	1933–1948	1,098	129	2	35.41	0	0-1	0/0	–	14	
Barnett Kim John (CY 1989)	17.7.1960		4	1988–1989	207	80	0	29.57	0	0-32	0/0	–	2	1
Barratt Fred	12.4.1894	29.1.1947	5	1929–1930	28	23	0	9.33	5	1-8	0/0	47.00	2	
Barrington Kenneth Frank (CY 1960)	24.11.1930	14.3.1981	82	1955–1968	6,806	256	20	58.67	29	3-4	0/0	44.82	58	
Barton Victor Alexander	6.10.1867	23.3.1906	1	1891	23	23	0	23.00	–	–	–	–	0	
Bates Willie	19.11.1855	8.1.1900	15	1881–1886	656	64	0	27.33	50	7-28	4/1	16.42	9	
Batty Gareth Jon	13.10.1977		7	2003–2005	144	38	0	20.57	11	3-55	0/0	66.63	4	10/1
Bean George	7.3.1864	16.3.1923	3	1891	92	50	0	18.40	–	–	–	–	4	
Bedser Sir Alec Victor CBE (CY 1947)	4.7.1918	4.4.2010	51	1946–1955	714	79	0	12.75	236	7-44	15/5	24.89	26	
Bell Ian Ronald MBE (CY 2008)	11.4.1982		98	2004–2013	6,722	235	20	45.41	1	1-33	0/0	76.00	78	135/7
Benjamin Joseph Emmanuel	2.2.1961		1	1994	0	0	0	0.00	4	4-42	0/0	20.00	0	2

	Born	Died	Tests	Test Career	Runs	HS	100s	Avge	Wkts	BB	5/10	Avge	Ct/St	O/T
Benson Mark Richard	6.7.1958		1	1986	51	30	0	25.50	–	–	–/–	–	0	1
Berry Robert	29.1.1926	2.12.2006	2	1950	6	4*	0	3.00	9	5-63	1/0	25.33	0	
Bicknell Martin Paul (CY 2001)	14.1.1969		4	1993–2003	45	15	0	6.42	14	4-84	1/0	38.78	2	7
Binks James Graham (CY 1969)	5.10.1935		2	1963	91	55	0	22.75	–	–	–/–	–	8	
Bird Morice Carlos	25.3.1888	9.12.1933	10	1909–1913	280	61	0	18.66	8	3-11	0/0	15.00	5	
Birkenshaw Jack MBE	13.11.1940		5	1972–1973	148	64	0	21.14	13	5-57	1/0	36.07	3	
Blackwell Ian David	10.6.1978		1	2005	4	4	0	4.00	0	0-28	0/0	–	0	34
Blakey Richard John	15.1.1967		2	1992	7	6	0	1.75	–	–	–/–	–	2	3
Bligh *Hon.* Ivo Francis Walter	13.3.1859	10.4.1927	4	1882	62	19	0	10.33	–	–	–/–	–	7	
Blythe Colin (CY 1904)	30.5.1879	8.11.1917	19	1901–1909	183	27	0	9.63	100	8-59	9/4	18.63	6	
Board John Henry	23.2.1867	15.4.1924	6	1898–1905	108	29	0	10.80	–	–	–/–	–	8/3	
Bolus John Brian	31.1.1934		7	1963–1963	496	88	0	41.33	0	0-16	0/0	–	2	
Booth Major William (CY 1914)	10.12.1886	1.7.1916	2	1913	46	32	0	23.00	7	4-49	0/0	18.57	0	
Bopara Ravinder Singh	4.5.1985		13	2007–2012	575	143	3	31.94	7	1-39	0/0	290.00	6	94/26
Borthwick Scott George	19.4.1990		1	2013	5	4	0	2.50	4	3-33	0/0	20.50	2	2/1
Bosanquet Bernard James Tindal (CY 1905)	13.10.1877	12.10.1936	7	1903–1905	147	27	0	13.36	25	8-107	2/0	24.16	9	
Botham Sir Ian Terence OBE (CY 1978)	24.11.1955		102	1977–1992	5,200	208	14	33.54	383	8-34	27/4	28.40	120	116
Bowden Montague Parker	1.11.1865	19.2.1892	2	1888	25	25	0	12.50	–	–	–/–	–	1	
Bowes William Eric (CY 1932)	25.7.1908	4.9.1987	15	1932–1946	28	10*	0	4.66	68	6-33	6/0	22.33	2	
Bowley Edward Henry (CY 1930)	6.6.1890	9.7.1974	5	1929–1929	252	109	1	36.00	0	0-7	0/0	–	2	
Boycott Geoffrey OBE (CY 1965)	21.10.1940		108	1964–1981	8,114	246*	22	47.72	7	3-47	0/0	54.57	33	36
Bradley Walter Morris	2.1.1875	19.6.1944	2	1899	23	23*	0	23.00	6	5-67	1/0	38.83	0	
Braund Leonard Charles (CY 1902)	18.10.1875	23.12.1955	23	1901–1907	987	104	3	25.97	47	8-81	3/0	38.51	39	
Brearley John Michael OBE (CY 1977)	28.4.1942		39	1976–1981	1,442	91	0	22.88	–	–	–/–	–	52	25
Brearley Walter (CY 1909)	11.3.1876	30.1.1937	4	1905–1912	21	11*	0	7.00	17	5-110	2/0	21.11	0	
Brennan Donald Vincent	10.2.1920	9.1.1985	2	1951	16	16	0	8.00	–	–	–/–	–	0/1	
Bresnan Timothy Thomas (CY 2012)	28.2.1985		23	2009–2013	575	91*	0	26.13	72	5-48	1/0	32.73	8	76/25
Briggs John (CY 1889)	3.10.1862	11.1.1902	33	1884–1899	815	121	0	18.11	118	8-11	9/4	17.75	12	
Broad Brian Christopher	29.9.1957		25	1984–1989	1,661	162	6	39.54	0	0-4	0/0	–	10	34
Broad Stuart Christopher John (CY 2010)	24.6.1986		67	2007–2013	2,010	169	1	24.21	238	7-44	11/2	30.31	20	102/48
Brockwell William (CY 1895)	21.11.1865	30.6.1935	7	1893–1899	202	49	0	16.83	5	3-33	0/0	61.80	6	
Bromley-Davenport Hugh Richard	18.8.1870	23.5.1954	4	1895–1898	128	84	0	21.33	4	2-46	0/0	24.50	1	
Brookes Dennis (CY 1957)	29.10.1915	9.3.2006	1	1947	17	10	0	8.50	–	–	–/–	–	0	
Brown Alan	17.10.1935		2	1961	3	3*	0	–	3	3-27	0/0	50.00	1	
Brown David John	30.1.1942		26	1965–1969	342	44*	0	11.79	79	5-42	2/0	28.31	7	
Brown Frederick Richard MBE (CY 1933)	16.12.1910	24.7.1991	22	1931–1953	734	79	0	25.31	45	5-49	1/0	31.06	22	

Name	Born	Died	Tests	Test Career	Runs	HS	100s	Avge	Wkts	BB	5/10	Avge	Ct/St	O/T
Brown George	6.10.1887	3.12.1964	7	1921–1922	299	84	1	29.90	–	–	–/–	–	9/3	–
Brown John Thomas (CY 1895)	20.8.1869	4.11.1904	8	1894–1899	470	140	1	36.15	0	0-22	0/0	–	7	–
Brown Simon John Emmerson	29.6.1969	–	1	1996	11	10*	0	11.00	2	1-60	0/0	69.00	1	–
Buckenham Claude Percival	16.1.1876	23.2.1937	4	1909	43	17	0	6.14	21	5-115	1/0	28.23	2	–
Butcher Alan Raymond (CY 1991)	7.1.1954	–	1	1979	34	20	0	17.00	0	0-9	0/0	–	0	–
[1] Butcher Mark Alan	23.8.1972	–	71	1997–2004	4,288	173*	8	34.58	15	4-42	0/0	36.06	61	1
Butcher Roland Orlando	14.10.1953	–	3	1980	71	32	0	14.20	–	–	–/–	–	3	3
Butler Harold James	12.3.1913	17.7.1991	2	1947–1947	15	15*	0	7.50	12	4-34	0/0	17.91	1	–
Butt Henry Rigden	27.12.1865	21.12.1928	3	1895	22	13	0	7.33	–	–	–/–	–	1/1	–
Caddick Andrew Richard (CY 2001)	21.11.1968	–	62	1993–2002	861	49*	0	10.37	234	7-46	13/1	29.91	21	54
Calthorpe *Hon.* Frederick Somerset Gough.	27.5.1892	19.11.1935	4	1929	129	49	0	18.42	1	1-38	0/0	91.00	3	–
Capel David John	6.2.1963	–	15	1987–1989	374	98	0	15.58	21	3-88	0/0	50.66	6	23
Carberry Michael Alexander	29.9.1980	–	6	2009–2013	345	60	0	28.75	–	–	–/–	–	7	5
Carr Arthur William (CY 1923)	21.5.1893	7.2.1963	11	1922–1929	237	63	0	19.75	–	–	–/–	–	3	–
Carr Donald Bryce OBE (CY 1960)	28.12.1926	–	2	1951	135	76	0	33.75	2	2-84	0/0	70.00	3	–
Carr Douglas Ward (CY 1910)	17.3.1872	23.3.1950	1	1909	0	0	0	0.00	7	5-146	1/0	40.28	0	–
Cartwright Thomas William MBE	22.7.1935	30.4.2007	5	1964–1965	26	9	0	5.20	15	6-94	1/0	36.26	2	–
Chapman Arthur Percy Frank (CY 1919)	3.9.1900	16.9.1961	26	1924–1930	925	121	1	28.90	–	0-10	0/0	–	32	–
Charlwood Henry Rupert James	19.12.1846	6.6.1888	2	1876	63	36	0	15.75	–	–	–/–	–	0	–
Chatterton William	27.12.1861	19.3.1913	1	1891	48	48	0	48.00	–	–	–/–	–	0	–
Childs John Henry (CY 1987)	15.8.1951	–	2	1988	2	2*	0	–	3	1-13	0/0	61.00	0	–
Christopherson Stanley	11.11.1861	6.4.1949	1	1884	17	17	0	17.00	1	1-52	0/0	69.00	0	–
Clark Edward Winchester	9.8.1902	28.4.1982	8	1929–1934	36	10	0	9.00	32	5-98	1/0	28.09	0	–
Clarke Rikki	29.9.1981	–	2	2003	96	55	0	32.00	4	2-7	0/0	15.00	1	20
Clay John Charles	18.3.1898	11.8.1973	1	1935	–	–	–	–	0	0-30	0/0	–	–	–
Close Dennis Brian CBE (CY 1964)	24.2.1931	–	22	1949–1976	887	70	0	25.34	18	4-35	0/0	29.55	24	3
Coldwell Leonard John	10.1.1933	6.8.1996	7	1962–1964	9	6*	0	4.50	22	6-85	1/0	27.72	1	–
Collingwood Paul Denis MBE (CY 2007)	26.5.1976	–	68	2003–2010	4,259	206	10	40.56	17	3-23	0/0	59.88	96	197/35
*Compton Denis Charles Scott CBE (CY 1939).	23.5.1918	23.4.1997	78	1937–1956	5,807	278	17	50.06	25	5-70	1/0	56.40	49	–
[4] Compton Nicholas Richard Denis (CY 2013)	26.6.1983	–	9	2012–2013	479	117	2	31.93	–	–	–/–	–	4	–
Cook Alastair Nathan MBE (CY 2012)	25.12.1984	–	102	2005–2013	8,047	294	25	46.51	0	0-1	0/0	–	96	72/4
Cook Cecil ("Sam")	23.8.1921	5.9.1996	1	1947	4	4	0	2.00	0	0-127	0/0	–	0	–
Cook Geoffrey	9.10.1951	–	7	1981–1982	203	66	0	15.61	0	0-4	0/0	–	9	6
Cook Nicholas Grant Billson	17.6.1956	–	15	1983–1989	179	31	0	13.33	52	6-65	4/1	32.48	5	3
Cope Geoffrey Alan	23.2.1947	–	3	1977	40	22	0	13.33	8	3-102	0/0	34.62	1	2
Copson William Henry (CY 1937).	27.4.1908	13.9.1971	3	1939–1947	6	6	0	6.00	15	5-85	1/0	19.80	1	–

Name	Born	Died	Tests	Test Career	Runs	HS	100s	Avge	Wkts	BB	5/10	Avge	Ct/St	O/T
Cork Dominic Gerald (CY 1996)	7.8.1971		37	1995–2002	864	59	0	18.00	131	7-43	5/0	29.81	18	32
Cornford Walter Latter	25.12.1900	6.2.1964	4	1929	36	18	0	9.00	–	–	–/–	–	5/3	
Cottam Robert Michael Henry	16.10.1944		4	1968–1972	27	13	0	6.75	14	4-50	–/–	23.35	2	
Coventry *Hon.* Charles John	26.2.1867	2.6.1929	2	1888	13	12	0	13.00	–	–	–/–	–	0	
Cowans Norman George	17.4.1961		19	1982–1985	175	36	0	7.95	51	6-77	2/0	39.27	9	23
Cowdrey Christopher Stuart	20.10.1957		6	1984–1988	101	38	0	14.42	4	2-65	0/0	77.25	5	3
Cowdrey *Lord* [Michael Colin] CBE (CY 1956)	24.12.1932	4.12.2000	114	1954–1974	7,624	182	22	44.06	–	0-1	0/0	–	120	1
Coxon Alexander	18.1.1916	22.1.2006	1	1948	19	19	0	9.50	3	2-90	0/0	57.33	0	
Cranston James	9.1.1859	10.12.1904	1	1890	31	16	0	15.50	–	–	–/–	–	1	
Cranston Kenneth	20.10.1917	8.1.2007	8	1947–1948	209	45	0	14.92	18	4-12	0/0	25.61	1	
Crapp John Frederick	14.10.1912	13.2.1981	7	1948–1948	319	56	0	29.00	–	–	–/–	–	7	
Crawford John Neville (CY 1907)	1.12.1886	2.5.1963	12	1905–1907	469	74	0	22.33	39	5-48	3/0	29.48	13	
Crawley John Paul	21.9.1971		37	1994–2002	1,800	156*	4	34.61	–	–	–/–	–	29	13
Croft Robert Damien Bale MBE	25.5.1970		21	1996–2001	421	37*	0	16.19	49	5-95	1/0	37.24	10	50
Curtis Timothy Stephen	15.1.1960		5	1988–1989	140	41	0	15.55	0	0-7	0/0	–	3	
Cuttell Willis Robert (CY 1898)	13.9.1863	9.12.1929	2	1898	65	21	0	16.25	6	3-17	0/0	12.16	2	
Dawson Edward William	13.2.1904	4.6.1979	5	1927–1929	175	55	0	19.44	–	–	–/–	–	0	
Dawson Richard Kevin James	4.8.1980		7	2001–2002	114	19*	0	11.40	11	4-134	0/0	61.54	3	
Dean Harry	13.8.1884	12.3.1957	3	1912	10	8	0	5.00	11	4-19	0/0	13.90	2	
DeFreitas Phillip Anthony Jason (CY 1992)	18.2.1966		44	1986–1995	934	88	0	14.82	140	7-70	4/0	33.57	14	103
Denness Michael Henry OBE (CY 1975)	1.12.1940		28	1969–1975	1,667	188	4	39.69	–	–	–/–	–	28	12
Denton David (CY 1906)	4.7.1874	16.2.1950	11	1905–1909	424	104	1	20.19	–	–	–/–	–	8	
Dewes John Gordon	11.10.1926		5	1948–1950	121	67	0	12.10	–	–	–/–	–	0	
Dexter Edward Ralph CBE (CY 1961)	15.5.1935		62	1958–1968	4,502	205	9	47.89	66	4-10	0/0	34.93	29	
Dilley Graham Roy	18.5.1959	5.10.2011	41	1979–1989	521	56	0	13.35	138	6-38	6/0	29.76	10	36
Dipper Alfred Ernest	9.11.1885	7.11.1945	1	1921	51	40	0	25.50	–	–	–/–	–	0	
Doggart George Hubert Graham OBE	18.7.1925		2	1950	76	29	0	19.00	–	–	–/–	–	3	
D'Oliveira Basil Lewis CBE (CY 1967)	4.10.1931	18.11.2011	44	1966–1972	2,484	158	5	40.06	47	3-46	0/0	39.55	29	4
Dollery Horace Edgar ("Tom") (CY 1952)	14.10.1914	20.1.1987	4	1947–1950	72	37	0	10.28	–	–	–/–	–	1	
Dolphin Arthur	24.12.1885	23.10.1942	1	1920	1	1	0	0.50	–	–	–/–	–	1	
Douglas John William Henry Tyler (CY 1915)	3.9.1882	19.12.1930	23	1911–1924	962	119	1	29.15	45	5-46	1/0	33.02	9	28
Downton Paul Rupert	4.4.1957		30	1980–1988	785	74	0	19.62	–	–	–/–	–	70/5	
Druce Norman Frank (CY 1898)	1.1.1875	27.10.1954	5	1897	252	64	0	28.00	–	–	–/–	–	5	
Ducat Andrew (CY 1920)	16.2.1886	23.7.1942	1	1921	5	3	0	2.50	–	–	–/–	–	1	
Duckworth George (CY 1929)	9.5.1901	5.1.1966	24	1924–1936	234	39*	0	14.62	–	–	–/–	–	45/15	
Duleepsinhji Kumar Shri (CY 1930)	13.6.1905	5.12.1959	12	1929–1931	995	173	3	58.52	–	–	–/–	–	10	

	Born	Died	Tests	Test Career	Runs	HS	100s	Avge	Wkts	BB	5/10	Avge	Ct/St	O/T
Durston Frederick John	11.7.1893	8.4.1965	1	1921	8	6*	0	8.00	5	4-102	0/0	27.20	0	64
Ealham Mark Alan	27.8.1969		8	1996–1998	210	53*	0	21.00	17	4-21	0/0	28.70	4	29
Edmonds Philippe-Henri	8.3.1951		51	1975–1987	875	64	0	17.50	125	7-66	2/0	34.18	42	7
Edrich John Hugh MBE (CY 1966)	21.6.1937		77	1963–1976	5,138	310*	12	43.54	0	0-6	0/0	–	43	
Edrich William John (CY 1940)	26.3.1916	24.4.1986	39	1938–1954	2,440	219	6	40.00	41	4-68	0/0	41.29	39	
Elliott Harry	2.11.1891	2.2.1976	4	1927–1933	61	37*	0	15.25				–	8/3	
Ellison Richard Mark (CY 1986)	21.9.1959		11	1984–1986	202	41	0	13.46	35	6-77	3/1	29.94	2	14
Emburey John Ernest (CY 1984)	20.8.1952		64	1978–1995	1,713	75	0	22.53	147	7-78	6/0	38.40	34	61
Emmett George Malcolm	2.12.1912	18.12.1976	1	1948	10	10	0	5.00			–	–	0	
Emmett Thomas	3.9.1841	29.6.1904	7	1876–1881	160	48	0	13.33	9	7-68	1/0	31.55	9	
Evans Alfred John	1.5.1889	18.9.1960	1	1921	18	14	0	9.00			–	–	0	
Evans Thomas Godfrey CBE (CY 1951)	18.8.1920	3.5.1999	91	1946–1959	2,439	104	2	20.49			–	–	173/46	
Fagg Arthur Edward	18.6.1915	13.9.1977	5	1936–1939	150	39	0	18.75	0		–	–	5	
Fairbrother Neil Harvey	9.9.1963		10	1987–1992	219	83	0	15.64	0	0-9	0/0	–	4	75
Fane Frederick Luther	27.4.1875	27.11.1960	14	1905–1909	682	143	0	26.23			–	–	6	
Farnes Kenneth (CY 1939)	8.7.1911	20.10.1941	15	1934–1938	58	20	0	4.83	60	6-96	3/1	28.65	1	
Farrimond William	23.5.1903	15.11.1979	4	1930–1935	116	35	0	16.57			–	–	5/2	
Fender Percy George Herbert (CY 1915)	22.8.1892	15.6.1985	13	1920–1929	380	60	0	19.00	29	5-90	2/0	40.86	14	
Ferris John James	21.5.1867	17.11.1900	1†	1891	16	16	0	16.00	13	7-37	2/1	7.00	0	
Fielder Arthur (CY 1907)	19.7.1877	30.8.1949	6	1903–1907	78	20	0	11.14	26	6-82	1/0	27.34	4	
Finn Steven George	4.4.1989		23	2009–2013	169	56	0	11.26	90	6-125	4/0	29.40	6	39/18
Fishlock Laurence Barnard (CY 1947)	2.1.1907	25.6.1986	4	1936–1946	47	19*	0	11.75			–	–	1	
Flavell John Alfred (CY 1965)	15.5.1929	25.2.2004	4	1961–1964	31	14	0	7.75	7	2-65	0/0	52.42	0	
Fletcher Keith William Robert OBE (CY 1974)	20.5.1944		59	1968–1981	3,272	216	7	39.90	2	1-6	0/0	96.50	54	24
Flintoff Andrew MBE (CY 2004)	6.12.1977		78§	1998–2009	3,795	167	5	31.89	219	5-58	3/0	33.34	52	138/7
Flowers Wilfred	7.12.1856	1.11.1926	8	1884–1893	254	56	0	18.14	14	5-46	1/0	21.14	2	
Ford Francis Gilbertson Justice	14.12.1866	7.2.1940	5	1894	168	48	0	18.66	1	1-47	0/0	129.00	5	
Foster Frank Rowbotham (CY 1912)	31.1.1889	3.5.1958	11	1911–1912	330	71	0	23.57	45	6-91	4/0	20.57	11	
Foster James Savin	15.4.1980		7	2001–2002	226	48	0	25.11			–	–	17/1	11/5
Foster Neil Alan (CY 1989)	6.5.1962		29	1983–1993	446	39	0	11.73	88	8-107	5/1	32.85	7	48
Foster Reginald Erskine ("Tip")(CY 1900)	16.4.1878	13.5.1914	8	1903–1907	602	287	1	46.30			–	–	13	
Fothergill Arnold James	26.8.1854	1.8.1932	2	1888	33	32	0	16.50	8	4-19	0/0	11.25	1	
Fowler Graeme	20.4.1957		21	1982–1984	1,307	201	3	35.32	0	0-0	0/0	–	10	26
Fraser Angus Robert Charles MBE (CY 1996)	8.8.1965		46	1989–1998	388	32	0	7.46	177	8-53	13/2	27.32	9	42
Freeman Alfred Percy ("Tich")(CY 1923)	17.5.1888	28.1.1965	12	1924–1929	154	50*	0	14.00	66	7-71	5/3	25.86	4	

§ *Flintoff's figures exclude 50 runs and seven wickets for the ICC World XI v Australia in the Super Series Test in 2005-06.*

	Born	Died	Tests	Test Career	Runs	HS	100s	Avge	Wkts	BB	5/10	Avge	Ct/St	O/T
French Bruce Nicholas	13.8.1959		16	1986–1987	308	59	0	18.11	–	–	–/–	–	38/1	13
Fry Charles Burgess (CY 1895)	25.4.1872	7.9.1956	26	1895–1912	1,223	144	2	32.18	0	0-3	0/0	–	17	
Gallian Jason Edward Riche	25.6.1971		3	1995–1995	74	28	0	12.33	0	0-6	0/0	–	3/1	
Gatting Michael William OBE (CY 1984)	6.6.1957		79	1977–1994	4,409	207	10	35.55	4	1-14	0/0	79.25	59	92
Gay Leslie Hewitt	24.3.1871	1.11.1949	1	1894	37	33	0	18.50					3/1	
Geary George (CY 1927)	9.7.1893	6.3.1981	14	1924–1934	249	66	0	15.56	46	7-70	4/1	29.41	13	
Gibb Paul Antony	11.7.1913	7.12.1977	8	1938–1946	581	120	2	44.69					3/1	
Giddins Edward Simon Hunter	20.7.1971		4	1999–2000	10	7	0	2.50	12	5-15	1/0	20.00	0	
Gifford Norman MBE (CY 1975)	30.3.1940		15	1964–1973	179	25*	0	16.27	33	5-55	1/0	31.09	8	
Giles Ashley Fraser MBE (CY 2005)	19.3.1973		54	1998–2006	1,421	59	0	20.89	143	5-57	5/0	40.60	33	2
²Gilligan Alfred Herbert Harold	29.6.1896	5.5.1978	4	1929	71	32	0	17.75					0	
²Gilligan Arthur Edward Robert (CY 1924)	23.12.1894	5.9.1976	11	1922–1924	209	39*	0	16.07	36	6-7	2/1	29.05	3	62
Gimblett Harold (CY 1953)	19.10.1914	30.3.1978	3	1936–1939	129	67*	0	32.25					1	
Gladwin Clifford	3.4.1916	9.4.1988	8	1947–1949	170	51*	0	28.33	15	3-21	0/0	38.06	4	
Goddard Thomas William John (CY 1938)	1.10.1900	22.5.1966	8	1930–1939	13	8	0	6.50	22	6-29	1/0	26.72	3	
Gooch Graham Alan OBE (CY 1980)	23.7.1953		118	1975–1994	8,900	333	20	42.58	23	3-39	0/0	46.47	103	125
Gough Darren (CY 1999)	18.9.1970		58	1994–2003	855	65	0	12.57	229	6-42	9/0	28.39	13	158‡/2
Gover Alfred Richard MBE (CY 1937)	29.2.1908	7.10.2001	4	1936–1946	2	2*	0	–	8	3-85	0/0	44.87	1	
Gower David Ivon OBE (CY 1979)	1.4.1957		117	1978–1992	8,231	215	18	44.25	1	1-1	0/0	20.00	74	114
²Grace Edward Mills	28.11.1841	20.5.1911	1	1880	36	36	0	18.00					1	
²Grace George Frederick	13.12.1850	22.9.1880	1	1880	0	0	0	0.00					2	
²Grace William Gilbert (CY 1896)	18.7.1848	23.10.1915	22	1880–1899	1,098	170	2	32.29	9	2-12	0/0	26.22	39	
Graveney Thomas William OBE (CY 1953)	16.6.1927		79	1951–1969	4,882	258	11	44.38	1	1-34	0/0	167.00	80	
Greenhough Thomas	9.11.1931	15.9.2009	4	1959–1960	4	2	0	1.33	16	5-35	1/0	22.31	4	
Greenwood Andrew	20.8.1847	12.2.1889	2	1876	77	49	0	19.25					2	
²Greig Anthony William (CY 1975)	6.10.1946	29.12.2012	58	1972–1977	3,599	148	8	40.43	141	8-86	6/2	32.20	87	22
²Greig Ian Alexander	8.12.1955		2	1982	26	14	0	6.50	4	4-53	0/0	28.50	2	
Grieve Basil Arthur Firebrace	28.5.1864	19.11.1917	2	1888	40	14*	0	40.00					0	
Griffith Stewart Cathie CBE ("Billy")	16.6.1914	7.4.1993	3	1947–1948	157	140	1	31.40					5	
Gunn George (CY 1914)	13.6.1879	29.6.1958	15	1907–1929	1,120	122*	2	40.00	0	0-8	0/0	–	15	
²Gunn John Richmond (CY 1904)	19.7.1876	21.8.1963	6	1901–1905	85	24	0	10.62	18	5-76	1/0	21.50	3	
²Gunn William (CY 1890)	4.12.1858	29.1.1921	11	1886–1899	392	102*	1	21.77					5	
Habib Aftab	7.2.1972		2	1999	26	19	0	8.66					3	
Haig Nigel Esmé	12.12.1887	27.10.1966	5	1921–1929	126	47	0	14.00	13	3-73	0/0	34.46	4	
Haigh Schofield (CY 1901)	19.3.1871	27.2.1921	11	1898–1912	113	25	0	7.53	24	6-11	1/0	25.91	8	
Hallows Charles (CY 1928)	4.4.1895	10.11.1972	2	1921–1928	42	26	0	42.00					–	

	Born	Died	Tests	Test Career	Runs	HS	100s	Avge	Wkts	BB	5/10	Avge	Ct/St	O/T
Hamilton Gavin Mark	16.9.1974		1	1999	0	0	0	0.00	0	0-63	0/0		0	0‡
Hammond Walter Reginald (CY 1928)	19.6.1903	1.7.1965	85	1927-1946	7,249	336*	22	58.45	83	5-36	2/0	37.80	110	3
Hampshire John Harry	10.2.1941		8	1969-1975	403	107	1	26.86			-/-		9	
Hardinge Harold Thomas William ("Wally") (CY 1915)	25.2.1886	8.5.1965	1	1921	30	25	0	15.00					0	
¹Hardstaff Joseph, sen	9.11.1882	2.4.1947	5	1907	311	72	0	31.10					0	
¹Hardstaff Joseph, jun (CY 1938)	3.7.1911	1.1.1990	23	1935-1948	1,636	205*	4	46.74			-/-		9	58/2
Harmison Stephen James MBE (CY 2005)	23.10.1978		62§	2002-2009	742	49*	0	12.16	222	7-12	8/1	31.94	7	
Harris Lord [George Robert Canning]	3.2.1851	24.3.1932	4	1878-1884	145	52	0	29.00	0	0-14	0/0		2	
Hartley John Cabourn	15.11.1874	8.3.1963	2	1905	15	9	0	3.75	1	1-62	0/0	115.00	2	
Hawke Lord [Martin Bladen] (CY 1909)	16.8.1860	10.10.1938	5	1895-1898	55	30	0	7.85					2	
Hayes Ernest George (CY 1907)	6.11.1876	2.12.1953	5	1905-1912	86	35	0	10.75	1	1-28	0/0	52.00	3	
Hayes Frank Charles	6.12.1946		9	1973-1976	244	106*	1	15.25			-/-		7	6
Hayward Thomas Walter (CY 1895)	29.3.1871	19.7.1939	35	1895-1909	1,999	137	3	34.46	14	4-22	0/0	36.71	19	
³Headley Dean Warren	27.1.1970		15	1997-1999	186	31	0	8.45	60	6-60	1/0	27.85	7	13
²Hearne Alec (CY 1894)	22.7.1863	16.5.1952	1	1891	9	9	0	9.00	1		0/0	9.00	1	
²Hearne Frank	23.11.1858	14.7.1949	2†	1888	47	27	0	23.50			-/-		1	
¹˒²Hearne George Gibbons	7.7.1856	13.2.1932	1	1891	0	0	0	0.00					0	
Hearne John Thomas (CY 1892)	3.5.1867	17.4.1944	12	1891-1899	126	40	0	9.00	49	6-41	4/1	22.08	4	
Hearne John William (CY 1912)	11.2.1891	13.9.1965	24	1911-1926	806	114	1	26.00	30	5-49	1/0	48.73	13	
Hegg Warren Kevin	23.2.1968		2	1998	30	15	0	7.50					8	
Hemmings Edward Ernest	20.2.1949		16	1982-1990	383	95	0	22.52	43	6-58	1/0	42.44	5	33
Hendren Elias Henry ("Patsy") (CY 1920)	5.2.1889	4.10.1962	51	1920-1934	3,525	205*	7	47.63	1	1-27	0/0	31.00	33	
Hendrick Michael (CY 1978)	22.10.1948		30	1974-1981	128	15	0	6.40	87	4-28	0/0	25.83	25	22
Heseltine Christopher	26.11.1869	13.6.1944	2	1895	18	18	0	9.00	5	5-38	1/0	16.80	3	
Hick Graeme Ashley MBE (CY 1987)	23.5.1966		65	1991-2000	3,383	178	6	31.32	23	4-126	0/0	56.78	90	120
Higgs Kenneth (CY 1968)	14.1.1937		15	1965-1968	185	63	0	11.56	71	6-91	2/0	20.74	4	
Hill Allen	14.11.1843	28.8.1910	2	1876	101	49	0	50.50	7	4-27	0/0	18.57	1	
Hill Arthur James Ledger	26.7.1871	6.9.1950	3	1895	251	124	1	62.75	4	4-8	0/0	2.00	1	
Hilton Malcolm Jameson (CY 1957)	2.8.1928	8.7.1990	4	1950-1951	37	15	0	7.40	14	5-61	1/0	34.07	1	
Hirst George Herbert (CY 1901)	7.9.1871	10.5.1954	24	1897-1909	790	85	0	22.57	59	5-48	3/0	30.00	18	
Hitch John William (CY 1914)	7.5.1886	7.7.1965	7	1911-1921	103	51*	0	14.71	7	2-31	0/0	46.42	4	
Hobbs Sir John Berry (CY 1909)	16.12.1882	21.12.1963	61	1907-1930	5,410	211	15	56.94	1	1-19	0/0	165.00	17	
Hobbs Robin Nicholas Stuart	8.5.1942		7	1967-1971	34	15*	0	6.80	12	3-25	0/0	40.08	8	
Hoggard Matthew James MBE (CY 2006)	31.12.1976		67	2000-2007	473	38	0	7.27	248	7-61	7/1	30.50	24	26

§ Harmison's figures exclude one run and four wickets for the ICC World XI v Australia in the Super Series Test in 2005-06.

Name	Born	Died	Tests	Test Career	Runs	HS	100s	Avge	Wkts	BB	5/10	Avge	Ct/St	O/T
Hollies William Eric (CY 1955)	5.6.1912	16.4.1981	13	1934–1950	37	18*	0	5.28	44	7-50	5/0	30.27	2	35
²Hollioake Adam John (CY 2003)	5.9.1971		4	1997–1997	65	45	0	10.83	2	2-31	0/0	33.50	4	20
²Hollioake Benjamin Caine	11.11.1977	23.3.2002	2	1997–1998	44	28	0	11.00	4	2-105	0/0	49.75	2	
Holmes Errol Reginald Thorold (CY 1936)	21.8.1905	16.8.1960	5	1934–1935	114	85*	0	16.28	2	1-10	0/0	38.00	4	
Holmes Percy (CY 1920)	25.11.1886	3.9.1971	7	1921–1932	357	88	0	27.46	–	–	–/–	–	3	
Hone Leland	30.1.1853	31.12.1896	1	1878	13	7	0	6.50	–	–	–/–	–	2	
Hopwood John Leonard	30.10.1903	15.6.1985	2	1934	12	8	0	6.00	0	0-16	0/0	–	0	
Hornby Albert Neilson ("Monkey")	10.2.1847	17.12.1925	3	1878–1884	21	9	0	3.50	1	1-0	0/0	0.00	0	
Horton Martin John	21.4.1934	3.4.2011	2	1959	60	58	0	30.00	2	2-24	0/0	29.50	2	
Howard Nigel David	18.5.1925	31.5.1979	4	1951	86	23	0	17.20	–	–	–/–	–	4	
Howell Henry	29.11.1890	9.7.1932	5	1920–1924	15	5	0	7.50	7	4-115	0/0	79.85	0	
Howorth Richard	26.4.1909	2.4.1980	5	1947–1947	145	45*	0	18.12	19	6-124	1/0	33.42	2	
Humphries Joseph	19.5.1876	7.5.1946	3	1907	44	16	0	8.80	–	–	–/–	–	7	
Hunter Joseph	3.8.1855	4.1.1891	5	1884	93	39*	0	18.60	–	–	–/–	–	8/3	
Hussain Nasser OBE (CY 2003)	28.3.1968		96	1989–2004	5,764	207	14	37.18	0	0-15	0/0	–	67	88
Hutchings Kenneth Lotherington (CY 1907)	7.12.1882	3.9.1916	7	1907–1909	341	126	1	28.41	1	1-5	0/0	81.00	9	
¹Hutton Sir Leonard (CY 1938)	23.6.1916	6.9.1990	79	1937–1954	6,971	364	19	56.67	3	1-2	0/0	77.33	57	
¹Hutton Richard Anthony	6.9.1942		5	1971	219	81	0	36.50	9	3-72	0/0	28.55	9	
Iddon John	8.1.1902	17.4.1946	5	1934–1935	170	73	0	28.33	0	0-3	0/0	–	3	4
Igglesden Alan Paul	8.10.1964		3	1989–1993	6	3*	0	3.00	6	2-91	0/0	54.83	1	
Ikin John Thomas	7.3.1918	15.9.1984	18	1946–1955	606	60	0	20.89	3	1-38	0/0	118.00	31	
Illingworth Raymond CBE (CY 1960)	8.6.1932		61	1958–1973	1,836	113	2	23.24	122	6-29	3/0	31.20	45	3
Illingworth Richard Keith	23.8.1963		9	1991–1995	128	28	0	18.28	19	4-96	0/0	32.36	5	25
Ilott Mark Christopher	27.8.1970		5	1993–1995	28	15	0	7.00	12	3-48	0/0	45.16	0	
Insole Douglas John CBE (CY 1956)	18.4.1926		9	1950–1957	408	110*	1	27.20	–	–	–/–	–	8	31
Irani Ronald Charles	26.10.1971		3	1996–1999	86	41	0	17.20	3	1-22	0/0	37.33	2	15
Jackman Robin David (CY 1981)	13.8.1945		4	1980–1982	42	17	0	7.00	14	4-110	0/0	31.78	0	
Jackson Sir Francis Stanley (CY 1894)	21.11.1870	9.3.1947	20	1893–1905	1,415	144*	5	48.79	24	5-52	1/0	33.29	10	31
Jackson Herbert Leslie (CY 1959)	5.4.1921	25.4.2007	2	1949–1961	15	8	0	15.00	7	2-26	0/0	22.14	1	15
James Stephen Peter	7.9.1967		2	1998	71	36	0	17.75	–	–	–/–	–	0	
Jameson John Alexander	30.6.1941		4	1971–1973	214	82	0	26.75	1	1-17	0/0	17.00	3	
Jardine Douglas Robert (CY 1928)	23.10.1900	18.6.1958	22	1928–1933	1,296	127	1	48.00	0	0-10	0/0	–	26	3
Jarvis Paul William	29.6.1965		9	1987–1992	132	29*	0	10.15	21	4-107	0/0	45.95	2	
Jenkins Roland Oliver (CY 1950)	24.11.1918	22.7.1995	9	1948–1952	198	39	0	18.00	32	5-116	1/0	34.31	4	16
Jessop Gilbert Laird (CY 1898)	19.5.1874	11.5.1955	18	1899–1912	569	104	1	21.88	10	4-68	0/0	35.40	11	
Johnson Richard Leonard	29.12.1974		3	2003–2003	59	26	0	14.75	16	6-33	2/0	17.18	0	10

	Born	Died	Test Career	Tests	Runs	HS	100s	Avge	Wkts	BB	5/10	Avge	Ct/St	O/T
Jones Arthur Owen	16.8.1872	21.12.1914	1899–1909	12	291	34	0	13.85	3	3-73	0/0	44.33	15	—
Jones Geraint Owen MBE	14.7.1976		2003–2006	34	1,172	100	1	23.91	—	—	—/—	—	128/5	49/2
Jones Ivor Jeffrey	10.12.1941		1963–1967	15	38	16	0	4.75	44	6-118	3/0	40.20	4	—
Jones Simon Philip MBE (CY 2006)	25.12.1978		2002–2005	18	205	44	0	15.76	59	6-53	3/0	28.23	4	8
Jupp Henry	19.11.1841	8.4.1889	1876	2	68	63	0	17.00	—	—	—/—	—	2	—
Jupp Vallance William Crisp (CY 1928)	27.3.1891	9.7.1960	1921–1928	8	208	38	0	17.33	28	4-37	0/0	22.00	5	—
Keeton William Walter (CY 1940)	30.4.1905	10.10.1980	1934–1939	2	57	25	0	14.25	—	—	—/—	—	—	—
Kennedy Alexander Stuart (CY 1933)	24.1.1891	15.11.1959	1922	5	93	41*	0	15.50	31	5-76	2/0	19.32	5	—
Kenyon Donald	15.5.1924	12.11.1996	1951–1955	8	192	87	0	12.80	—	—	—/—	—	5	—
Kerrigan Simon Christopher	10.5.1989		2013	1	1	1*	0	—	0	0-53	0/0	—	—	—
Key Robert William Trevor (CY 2005)	12.5.1979		2002–2004	15	775	221	1	31.00	—	—	—/—	—	11	5/1
Khan Amjad	14.10.1980		2008	1	—	—	—	—	1	1-111	0/0	122.00	—	0/1
Killick *Rev.* Edgar Thomas	9.5.1907	18.5.1953	1929	2	81	31	0	20.25	—	—	—/—	—	2	—
Kilner Roy (CY 1924)	17.10.1890	5.4.1928	1924–1926	9	233	74	0	33.28	24	4-51	0/0	30.58	6	—
King John Herbert	16.4.1871	18.11.1946	1909	1	64	60	0	32.00	1	1-99	0/0	99.00	0	—
Kinneir Septimus Paul (CY 1912)	13.5.1871	16.10.1928	1911	1	52	30	0	26.00	—	—	—/—	—	0	—
Kirtley Robert James	10.1.1975		2003–2003	4	32	12	0	5.33	19	6-34	1/0	29.52	3	11/1
Knight Albert Ernest (CY 1904)	8.10.1872	25.4.1946	1903	3	81	70*	0	16.20	—	—	—/—	—	—	—
Knight Barry Rolfe	18.2.1938		1961–1969	29	812	127	2	26.19	70	4-38	0/0	31.75	14	—
Knight Donald John (CY 1915)	12.5.1894	5.1.1960	1921	2	54	38	0	13.50	—	—	—/—	—	—	—
Knight Nicholas Verity	28.11.1969		1995–2001	17	719	113	1	23.96	—	—	—/—	—	26	100
Knott Alan Philip Eric (CY 1970)	9.4.1946		1967–1981	95	4,389	135	5	32.75	—	—	—/—	—	250/19	20
Knox Neville Alexander (CY 1907)	10.10.1884	3.3.1935	1907	2	24	8*	0	8.00	3	2-39	0/0	35.00	0	—
Laker James Charles (CY 1952)	9.2.1922	23.4.1986	1947–1958	46	676	63	0	14.08	193	10-53	9/3	21.24	12	—
Lamb Allan Joseph (CY 1981)	20.6.1954		1982–1992	79	4,656	142	14	36.09	1	1-6	0/0	23.00	75	122
Langridge James (CY 1932)	10.7.1906	10.9.1966	1933–1946	8	242	70	0	26.88	19	7-56	2/0	21.73	6	—
Larkins Wayne	22.11.1953		1979–1990	13	493	64	0	20.54	—	—	—/—	—	8	25
Larter John David Frederick	24.4.1940		1962–1965	10	16	10	0	3.20	37	5-57	2/0	25.43	5	—
Larwood Harold MBE (CY 1927)	14.11.1904	22.7.1995	1926–1932	21	485	98	0	19.40	78	6-32	4/1	28.35	15	—
Lathwell Mark Nicholas	26.12.1971		1993	2	78	33	0	19.50	—	—	—/—	—	0	—
Lawrence David Valentine ("Syd")	28.1.1964		1988–1991	5	60	34	0	10.00	18	5-106	1/0	37.55	0	1
Leadbeater Edric	15.8.1927	17.4.2011	1951	2	40	38	0	20.00	2	1-38	0/0	109.00	3	—
Lee Harry William	26.10.1890	21.4.1981	1930	1	19	18	0	9.50	—	—	—/—	—	0	—
Lees Walter Scott (CY 1906)	25.12.1875	10.9.1924	1905	5	66	25*	0	11.00	26	6-78	2/0	17.96	2	—
Legge Geoffrey Bevington	26.1.1903	21.11.1940	1927–1929	5	299	196	1	49.83	0	0-34	0/0	—	1	—
Leslie Charles Frederick Henry	8.12.1861	12.2.1921	1882	4	106	54	0	15.14	4	3-31	0/0	11.00	1	—

Name	Born	Died	Tests	Test Career	Runs	HS	100s	Avge	Wkts	BB	5/10	Avge	Ct/St	O/T
Lever John Kenneth MBE (CY 1979)	24.2.1949		21	1976–1986	306	53	0	11.76	73	7-46	3/1	26.72	11	22
Lever Peter	17.9.1940		17	1970–1975	350	88*	0	21.87	41	6-38	2/0	36.80	11	10
Leveson Gower Sir Henry Dudley Gresham	8.5.1873	1.2.1954	3	1909	95	31	0	23.75	–	–	–	–	1	
Levett William Howard Vincent ("Hopper")	25.1.1908	1.12.1995	1	1933	7	5	0	7.00	–	–	–/–	–	3	
Lewis Anthony Robert CBE	6.7.1938		9	1972–1973	457	125	1	32.64	–	–	–/–	–	0	
Lewis Clairmonte Christopher	14.2.1968		32	1990–1996	1,105	117	1	23.02	93	6-111	3/0	37.52	25	53
Lewis Jonathan	26.8.1975		1	2006	27	20	0	13.50	3	3-68	0/0	40.66	0	
Leyland Maurice (CY 1929)	20.7.1900	1.1.1967	41	1928–1938	2,764	187	9	46.06	6	3-91	0/0	97.50	13	13/2
Lilley Arthur Frederick Augustus ("Dick") (CY 1897)	28.11.1866	17.11.1929	35	1896–1909	903	84	0	20.52	1	1-23	0/0	23.00	70/22	
Lillywhite James	23.2.1842	25.10.1929	2	1876	16	10	0	8.00	8	4-70	0/0	15.75	1	
Lloyd David	18.3.1947		9	1974–1974	552	214*	1	42.46	0	0-4	0/0	–	11	8
Lloyd Timothy Andrew	5.11.1956		1	1984	10	10*	0	–	–	–	–/–	–	0	3
Loader Peter James (CY 1958)	25.10.1929	15.3.2011	13	1954–1958	76	17	0	5.84	39	6-36	1/0	22.51	2	
Lock Graham Anthony Richard (CY 1954)	5.7.1929	30.3.1995	49	1952–1967	742	89	0	13.74	174	7-35	9/3	25.58	59	
Lockwood William Henry (CY 1899)	25.3.1868	26.4.1932	12	1893–1902	231	52*	0	17.76	43	7-71	5/1	20.53	4	
Lohmann George Alfred (CY 1889)	2.6.1865	1.12.1901	18	1886–1896	213	62*	0	8.87	112	9-28	9/5	10.75	28	
Lowson Frank Anderson	1.7.1925	8.9.1984	7	1951–1955	245	68	0	18.84	–	–	–/–	–	5	
Lucas Alfred Perry	20.2.1857	12.10.1923	5	1878–1884	157	55	0	19.62	0	0-23	0/0	–	1	
Luckhurst Brian William (CY 1971)	5.2.1939	1.3.2005	21	1970–1974	1,298	131	4	36.05	1	1-9	0/0	32.00	14	3
Lyttelton Hon. Alfred	7.2.1857	5.7.1913	4	1880–1884	94	31	0	15.66	4	4-19	0/0	4.75	2	
Macaulay George Gibson (CY 1924)	7.12.1897	13.12.1940	8	1922–1933	112	76	0	18.66	24	5-64	1/0	27.58	5	
MacBryan John Crawford William (CY 1925)	22.7.1892	14.7.1983	1	1924	–	–	–	–	–	–	–/–	–	0	
McCague Martin John	24.5.1969		3	1993–1994	21	11	0	4.20	6	4-121	0/0	65.00	1	
McConnon James Edward	21.6.1922	26.1.2003	2	1954	18	11	0	9.00	4	3-19	0/0	18.50	4	
McGahey Charles Percy (CY 1902)	12.2.1871	10.1.1935	2	1901	38	18	0	9.50	0	–	–/–	–	3	
McGrath Anthony	6.10.1975		4	2003	201	81	0	40.20	4	3-16	0/0	14.00	3	14
MacGregor Gregor (CY 1891)	31.8.1869	20.8.1919	8	1890–1893	96	31	0	12.00	–	–	–/–	–	14/3	
McIntyre Arthur John William (CY 1958)	14.5.1918	26.12.2009	3	1950–1955	19	7	0	3.16	–	–	–/–	–	8	
MacKinnon Francis Alexander	9.4.1848	27.2.1947	1	1878	5	5	0	2.50	–	–	–/–	–	0	
MacLaren Archibald Campbell (CY 1895)	1.12.1871	17.11.1944	35	1894–1909	1,931	140	5	33.87	–	–	–/–	–	29	
McMaster Joseph Emile Patrick	16.3.1861	7.6.1929	1	1888	0	0	0	0.00	0	–	–/–	–	0	
Maddy Darren Lee	23.5.1974		3	1999–1999	46	24	0	11.50	0	0-40	0/0	–	4	8/4
Mahmood Sajid Iqbal	21.12.1981		8	2006–2006	81	34	0	8.10	20	4-22	0/0	38.10	0	26/4
Makepeace Joseph William Henry	22.8.1881	19.12.1952	4	1920	279	117	1	34.87	–	–	–/–	–	0	
Malcolm Devon Eugene (CY 1995)	22.2.1963		40	1989–1997	236	29	0	6.05	128	9-57	5/2	37.09	7	10

	Born	Died	Tests	Test Career	Runs	HS	100s	Avge	Wkts	BB	5/10	Avge	Ct/St	O/T
Mallender Neil Alan	13.8.1961		2	1992	8	4	0	2.66	10	5-50	1/0	21.50	0	
[1]Mann Francis George CBE	6.9.1917	8.8.2001	7	1948–1949	376	136*	1	37.60					3	
[1]Mann Francis Thomas	3.3.1888	6.10.1964	5	1922	281	84	0	35.12					4	
Marks Victor James	25.6.1955		6	1982–1983	249	83	0	27.66	11	3-78	0/0	44.00	0	34
Marriott Charles Stowell ("Father")	14.9.1895	13.10.1966	1	1933	0	0	0	0.00	11	6-59	2/1	8.72	0	
Martin Frederick (CY 1892)	12.10.1861	13.12.1921	2	1890–1891	14	13	0	7.00	14	6-50	2/1	10.07	2	
Martin John William	16.2.1917	4.1.1987	1	1947	26	26	0	13.00	1	1-111	0/0	129.00		
Martin Peter James	15.11.1968		8	1995–1997	115	29	0	8.84	17	4-60	0/0	34.11	6	20
Mason John Richard (CY 1898)	26.3.1874	15.10.1958	5	1897	129	32	0	12.90	2	1-8	0/0	74.50	3	
Matthews Austin David George	3.5.1904	29.7.1977	1	1937	2	2*	0	–	2	1-13	0/0	32.50	0	
May Peter Barker Howard CBE (CY 1952)	31.12.1929	27.12.1994	66	1951–1961	4,537	285*	13	46.77					42	
Maynard Matthew Peter (CY 1998)	21.3.1966		4	1988–1993	87	35	0	10.87					3	14
Mead Charles Philip (CY 1912)	9.3.1887	26.3.1958	17	1911–1928	1,185	182*	4	49.37					4	
Mead Walter (CY 1904)	1.4.1868	18.3.1954	4	1899	7	7	0	3.50	1	1-91	0/0	91.00	1	
Midwinter William Evans	19.6.1851	3.12.1890	4†	1881	95	36	0	13.57	10	4-81	1/0	27.20	5	
Milburn Colin ("Ollie") (CY 1967)	23.10.1941	28.2.1990	9	1966–1968	654	139	2	46.71					7	
Miller Audley Montague	19.10.1869	26.6.1959	1	1895	24	20*	0	–					0	
Miller Geoffrey OBE	8.9.1952		34	1976–1984	1,213	98*	0	25.80	60	5-44	1/0	30.98	17	25
Milligan Frank William	19.3.1870	31.3.1900	2	1898	58	38	0	14.50		0-0				
Millman Geoffrey	2.10.1934	6.4.2005	6	1961–1962	60	32*	0	12.00					13/2	
Milton Clement Arthur (CY 1959)	10.3.1928	25.4.2007	6	1958–1959	204	104*	1	25.50		0-12			5	
Mitchell Arthur	13.9.1902	25.12.1976	6	1933–1936	298	72	0	29.80		0-4			9	
Mitchell Frank (CY 1902)	13.8.1872	11.10.1935	2†	1898	88	41	0	22.00					2	
Mitchell Thomas Bignall	4.9.1902	27.1.1996	5	1932–1935	20	5	0	5.00	8	2-49	0/0	62.25		
Mitchell-Innes Norman Stewart ("Mandy")	7.9.1914	28.12.2006	1	1935	5	5	0	5.00						
Mold Arthur Webb (CY 1892)	27.5.1863	29.4.1921	3	1893	0	0*	0	0.00	7	3-44	0/0	33.42		
Moon Leonard James	9.2.1878	23.11.1916	1	1905	182	36	0	22.75					4	
Morgan Eoin Joseph Gerard (CY 2011)	10.9.1986		16	2010–2011	700	130	2	30.43					11	84†/38
Morley Frederick	16.12.1850	28.9.1884	4	1880–1882	6	2*	0	1.50	16	5-56	1/0	18.50	4	
Morris Hugh	5.10.1963		3	1991	115	44	0	19.16					3	
Morris John Edward	1.4.1964		3	1990	71	32	0	23.66					3	8
Mortimore John Brian	14.5.1933	13.2.2014	9	1958–1964	243	73*	0	24.30	13	3-36	0/0	56.38	3	
Moss Alan Edward	14.11.1930		9	1953–1960	61	26	0	10.16	21	4-35	0/0	29.80	1	
Moxon Martyn Douglas (CY 1993)	4.5.1960		10	1986–1989	455	99	0	28.43		0-3			10	8
Mullally Alan David	12.7.1969		19	1996–2001	127	24	0	5.52	58	5-105	1/0	31.24	6	50
Munton Timothy Alan (CY 1995)	30.7.1965		2	1992	25	25*	0	25.00	4	2-22	0/0	50.00	0	

Name	Born	Died	Tests	Test Career	Runs	HS	100s	Avge	Wkts	BB	5/10	Avge	Ct/St	O/T
Murdoch William Lloyd MBE (CY 1967)	18.10.1854	18.2.1911	1†	1891	12	12	0	12.00	–	–	–/–	–	0/1	
Murray John Thomas MBE	1.4.1935	–	21	1961–1967	506	112	1	22.00	–	–	–/–	–	52/3	
Newham William	12.12.1860	26.6.1944	1	1887	26	17	0	13.00	–	–	–/–	–	0	
Newport Philip John	11.10.1962		3	1988–1990	110	40*	0	27.50	10	4-87	0/0	41.70	1	
Nichols Morris Stanley (CY 1934)	6.10.1900	26.1.1961	14	1929–1939	355	78*	0	29.58	41	6-35	2/0	28.09	11	
Oakman Alan Stanley Myles	20.4.1930		2	1956	14	14	0	7.00	0	0-21	0/0	–	7	
O'Brien Sir Timothy Carew	5.11.1861	9.12.1948	5	1884–1895	59	20	0	7.37	–	–	–/–	–	4	
O'Connor Jack	6.11.1897	22.2.1977	4	1929–1930	153	51	0	21.85	1	1-31	0/0	72.00	2	
Old Christopher Middleton (CY 1979)	22.12.1948		46	1972–1981	845	65	0	14.82	143	7-50	4/0	28.11	22	32
Oldfield Norman	5.5.1911	19.4.1996	1	1939	99	80	0	49.50	–	–	–/–	–	0	
Onions Graham (CY 2010)	9.9.1982		9	2009–2012	30	17*	0	10.00	32	5-38	1/0	29.90	0	4
Ormond James	20.8.1977		2	2001–2007	38	18	0	12.66	2	1-70	0/0	92.50	0	
Padgett Douglas Ernest Vernon	20.7.1934		2	1960	51	31	0	12.75	0	0-8	0/0	–	0	
Paine George Alfred Edward (CY 1935)	11.6.1908	30.3.1978	4	1934	97	49	0	16.16	17	5-168	1/0	27.47	5	
Palairet Lionel Charles Hamilton (CY 1893)	27.5.1870	27.3.1933	2	1902	49	20	0	12.25	–	–	–/–	–	2	
Palmer Charles Henry CBE	15.5.1919	31.3.2005	1	1953	22	22	0	11.00	0	0-15	0/0	–	0	
Palmer Kenneth Ernest MBE	22.4.1937		1	1964	10	10	0	10.00	1	1-113	0/0	189.00	0	
Panesar Mudhsuden Singh ("Monty")(CY2007)	25.4.1982		50	2005–2013	220	26	0	4.88	167	6-37	12/2	34.71	10	26/1
Parfitt Peter Howard (CY 1963)	8.12.1936		37	1961–1972	1,882	131*	7	40.91	12	2-5	0/0	47.83	42	
Parker Charles Warrington Leonard (CY 1923)	14.10.1882	11.7.1959	1	1921	3	3*	0	–	2	2-32	0/0	16.00	0	
Parker Paul William Giles	15.1.1956		1	1981	13	13	0	6.50	–	–	–/–	–	0	
Parkhouse William Gilbert Anthony	12.10.1925		7	1950–1959	373	78	0	28.69	–	–	–/–	–	3	
Parkin Cecil Harry (CY 1924)	18.2.1886	15.6.1943	10	1920–1924	160	36	0	12.30	32	5-38	2/0	35.25	3	
Parks James Horace (CY 1938)	12.5.1903	21.11.1980	1	1937	29	22	0	14.50	3	2-26	0/0	12.00	0	
Parks James Michael (CY 1968)	21.10.1931		46	1954–1967	1,962	108*	2	32.16	1	1-43	0/0	51.00	103/11	
Patandi Iftikhar Ali Khan, Nawab of (CY 1932)	16.3.1910	5.1.1952	3†	1932–1934	144	102	1	28.80	–	–	–/–	–	0	
Patel Minal Mahesh	7.7.1970		2	1996	45	27	0	22.50	1	1-101	0/0	180.00	2	
Patel Samit Rohit	30.11.1984		5	2011–2012	109	33	0	15.57	4	2-27	0/0	64.25	2	36/18
Pattinson Darren John	2.8.1979		1	2008	21	13	0	10.50	2	2-95	0/0	48.00	0	
Paynter Edward (CY 1938)	5.11.1901	5.2.1979	20	1931–1939	1,540	243	4	59.23	–	–	–/–	–	7	
Peate Edmund	2.3.1855	11.3.1900	9	1881–1886	70	13	0	11.66	31	6-85	2/0	22.03	2	
Peebles Ian Alexander Ross (CY 1931)	20.1.1908	27.2.1980	13	1927–1931	98	26	0	10.88	45	6-63	3/0	30.91	5	
Peel Robert (CY 1889)	12.2.1857	12.8.1941	20	1884–1896	427	83	0	14.72	101	7-31	5/1	16.98	17	
Penn Frank	7.3.1851	26.12.1916	1	1880	50	27*	0	50.00	0	0-2	0/0	–	0	
Perks Reginald Thomas David	4.10.1911	22.11.1977	2	1938–1939	3	2*	0	–	11	5-100	0/2	32.27	1	
Philipson Hylton	8.6.1866	4.12.1935	5	1891–1894	63	30	0	9.00	–	–	–/–	–	8/3	

	Born	Died	Tests	Test Career	Runs	HS	100s	Avge	Wkts	BB	5/10	Avge	Ct/St	O/T
Pietersen Kevin Peter MBE (CY 2006)	27.6.1980		104	2005–2013	8,181	227	23	47.28	10	3-52	0/0	88.60	62	1344/37
Pigott Anthony Charles Shackleton	4.6.1958		1	1983	12	8*	0	12.00	2	2-75	0/0	37.50	0	
Pilling Richard (CY 1891)	11.8.1855	28.3.1891	8	1881–1888	91	23	0	7.58	–	–	–/–	–	10/4	
Place Winston	7.12.1914	25.1.2002	3	1947	144	107	1	28.80	–	–	–/–	–	3	29/1
Plunkett Liam Edward	6.4.1985		9	2005–2007	126	44*	0	11.45	23	3-17	0/0	39.82	3	1
Pocock Patrick Ian	24.9.1946		25	1967–1984	206	33	0	6.24	67	6-79	3/0	44.41	15	
Pollard Richard	19.6.1912	16.12.1985	4	1946–1948	13	10*	0	13.00	15	5-24	1/0	25.20	3	
Poole Cyril John	13.3.1921	11.2.1996	3	1951	161	69*	0	40.25	–	0-9	0/0	–	1	
Pope George Henry	27.1.1911	29.10.1993	1	1947	8	8*	0	–	1	1-49	0/0	85.00	0	
Pougher Arthur Dick	19.4.1865	20.5.1926	1	1891	17	17	0	17.00	3	3-26	0/0	8.66	2	
Price John Sidney Ernest	22.7.1937		15	1963–1972	66	32	0	7.33	40	5-73	0/0	35.02	7	
Price Wilfred Frederick Frank	25.4.1902	13.1.1969	1	1938	6	6	0	3.00	–	–	–/–	–	2	
Prideaux Roger Malcolm	31.7.1939		3	1968–1968	102	64	0	20.40	0	0-0	0/0	–	0	
Pringle Derek Raymond	18.9.1958		30	1982–1992	695	63	0	15.10	70	5-95	3/0	35.97	10	44
Prior Matthew James (CY 2010)	26.2.1982		75	2007–2013	3,920	131*	7	40.83	–	1-1	–/–	–	217/13	68/10
Pullar Geoffrey (CY 1960)	1.8.1935		28	1959–1962	1,974	175	4	43.86	1	1-1	0/0	37.00	2	
Quaife William George (CY 1902)	17.3.1872	13.10.1951	7	1899–1901	228	68	0	19.00	0	0-6	0/0	–	4	
Radford Neal Victor (CY 1986)	7.6.1957		3	1986–1987	21	12*	0	7.00	4	2-131	0/0	87.75	0	6
Radley Clive Thornton MBE (CY 1979)	13.5.1944		8	1977–1978	481	158	2	48.10	–	–	–/–	–	4	4
Ramprakash Mark Ravin MBE (CY 2007)	5.9.1969		52	1991–2001	2,350	154	2	27.32	4	1-2	0/0	119.25	39	18
Randall Derek Williams (CY 1980)	24.2.1951		47	1976–1984	2,470	174	7	33.37	0	0-1	0/0	–	31	49
Ranjitsinhji Kumar Shri (CY 1897)	10.9.1872	2.4.1933	15	1896–1902	989	175	2	44.95	1	1-23	0/0	39.00	13	
Rankin William Boyd	5.7.1984		1	2013	13	13	0	6.50	1	1-47	0/0	81.00	0	5/2‡
Read Christopher Mark Wells (CY 2011)	10.8.1978		15	1999–2006	360	55	0	18.94	–	–	–/–	–	48/6	36/1
Read Holcombe Douglas ("Hopper")	28.1.1910	5.1.2000	1	1935	–	–	–	–	6	4-136	0/0	33.33	0	
Read John Maurice (CY 1890)	9.2.1859	17.2.1929	17	1882–1893	461	57	0	17.07	0	0-27	0/0	–	8	
Read Walter William (CY 1893)	23.11.1855	6.1.1907	18	1882–1893	720	117	1	27.69	0	0-4	0/0	–	16	
Reeve Dermot Alexander OBE (CY 1996)	2.4.1963		3	1991	124	59	0	24.80	2	1-4	0/0	30.00	1	29
Relf Albert Edward (CY 1914)	26.6.1874	26.3.1937	13	1903–1913	416	63	0	23.11	25	5-85	1/0	24.96	14	
Rhodes Harold James	22.7.1936		2	1959	0	0*	0	–	9	4-50	0/0	27.11	4	
Rhodes Steven John (CY 1995)	17.6.1964		11	1994–1994	294	65*	0	24.50	–	–	–/–	–	46/3	9
Rhodes Wilfred (CY 1899)	29.10.1877	8.7.1973	58	1899–1929	2,325	179	2	30.19	127	8-68	6/1	26.96	60	
Richards Clifton James ("Jack")	10.8.1958		8	1986–1988	285	133	1	21.92	–	–	–/–	–	20/1	22
Reeve Derek Walter ("Dick")	3.11.1934		1	1957	33	33	0	33.00	–	–	–/–	–	1	
²Richardson Peter Edward (CY 1957)	4.7.1931		34	1956–1963	2,061	126	5	37.47	3	2-10	0/0	16.00	6	
²Richardson Thomas (CY 1897)	11.8.1870	2.7.1912	14	1893–1897	177	25*	0	11.06	88	8-94	11/4	25.22	5	

Name	Born	Died	Tests	Test Career	Runs	HS	100s	Avge	Wkts	BB	5/10	Avge	Ct/St	O/T
Richmond Thomas Leonard	23.6.1890	29.12.1957	1	1921	6	4	0	3.00	2	2-69	0/0	43.00	3	
Ridgway Frederick	10.8.1923		5	1951	49	24	0	8.16	7	4-83	0/0	54.14	3	
Robertson John David Benbow (CY 1948)	22.2.1917	12.10.1996	11	1947-1951	881	133	2	46.36	2	2-17	0/0	29.00	6	
Robins Robert Walter Vivian (CY 1930)	3.6.1906	12.12.1968	19	1929-1937	612	108	1	26.60	64	6-32	1/0	27.46	12	
Robinson Robert Timothy (CY 1986)	21.11.1958		29	1984-1989	1,601	175	4	36.38	0	0-0	0/0		8	26
Roope Graham Richard James	12.7.1946		21	1972-1978	860	77	0	30.71	0	0-2	0/0		35	8
Root Charles Frederick	16.4.1890	20.1.1954	3	1926					8	4-84	0/0	24.25		
Root Joseph Edward (CY 2014)	30.12.1990		15	2012-2013	955	180	2	36.73	3	2-9	0/0	56.33	8	20/4
Rose Brian Charles (CY 1980)	4.6.1950		9	1977-1980	358	70	0	25.57	0				2	2
Royle Vernon Peter Fanshawe Archer	29.11.1854	21.5.1929	1	1878	21	18	0	10.50	0	0-6	0/0		0	
Rumsey Frederick Edward	4.12.1935		5	1964-1965	30	21*	0	15.00	17	4-25	0/0	27.11	0	
Russell Albert Charles ("Jack") (CY 1923)	7.10.1887	23.3.1961	10	1920-1922	910	140	5	56.87					8	
Russell Robert Charles ("Jack") (CY 1990)	15.8.1963		54	1988-1997	1,897	128*	2	27.10	0				153/12	40
Russell William Eric	3.7.1936		10	1961-1967	362	70	0	21.29	0	0-19	0/0		4	
Saggers Martin John	23.5.1972		3	2003-2004	1	1	0	0.33	11	2-29	0/0	35.28	4	
Salisbury Ian David Kenneth (CY 1993)	21.11.1970		15	1992-2000	368	50	0	16.72	20	4-163	0/0	76.95	5	4
Sandham Andrew (CY 1923)	6.7.1890	20.4.1982	14	1921-1929	879	325	2	38.21	0				4	
Schofield Christopher Paul	6.10.1978		2	2000	67	57	0	22.33	1	0-73	0/0	26.00	0	0/4
Schultz Sandford Spence	29.8.1857	18.12.1937	1	1878	20	20	0	20.00	0				4	
Scotton William Henry	15.11.1856	9.7.1893	15	1881-1886	510	90	0	22.17	0	1-16	0/0		4	
Selby John	1.7.1849	11.3.1894	6	1876-1881	256	70	0	23.27	0	0-20	0/0		1	
Selvey Michael Walter William	25.4.1948		3	1976-1976	15	5*	0	7.50	6	4-41	0/0	57.16	2	
Shackleton Derek (CY 1959)	12.8.1924	28.9.2007	7	1950-1963	113	42	0	18.83	18	4-72	0/0	42.66	2	
Shah Owais Alam	22.10.1978		6	2005-2008	269	88	0	26.90	0	0-12	0/0		4	71/17
Shahzad Ajmal	27.7.1985		1	2010	5	5	0	5.00	4	3-45	0/0	15.75	2	11/3
Sharp John	15.2.1878	28.1.1938	3	1909	188	105	1	47.00	3	3-67	0/0	37.00	2	
Sharpe John William (CY 1892)	9.12.1866	19.6.1936	3	1890-1891	44	26	0	22.00	11	6-84	1/0	27.72	2	
Sharpe Philip John (CY 1963)	27.12.1936		12	1963-1969	786	111	1	46.23	0				17	
Shaw Alfred	29.8.1842	16.1.1907	7	1876-1881	111	40	0	10.09	12	5-38	1/0	23.75	4	
Sheppard Rt Rev. Lord [David Stuart] (CY 1953)	6.3.1929	5.3.2005	22	1950-1962	1,172	119	3	37.80	0				12	
Sherwin Mordecai (CY 1891)	26.2.1851	3.7.1910	3	1886-1888	30	21*	0	15.00	0				5/2	
Shrewsbury Arthur (CY 1890)	11.4.1856	19.5.1903	23	1881-1893	1,277	164	3	35.47	0	0-2	0/0		29	
Shuter John	9.2.1855	5.7.1920	1	1888	28	28	0	28.00	0				0	
Shuttleworth Kenneth	13.11.1944		5	1970-1971	46	21	0	7.66	12	5-47	1/0	35.58	1	
Sidebottom Arnold	1.4.1954		1	1985	2	2	0	2.00	1	1-65	0/0	65.00	0	
Sidebottom Ryan Jay (CY 2008)	15.1.1978		22	2001-2009	313	31	0	15.65	79	7-47	5/1	28.24	5	25/18

	Born	Died	Tests	Test Career	Runs	HS	100s	Avge	Wkts	BB	5/10	Avge	Ct/St	O/T
Silverwood Christopher Eric Wilfred	5.3.1975		6	1996–2002	29	10	0	7.25	11	5-91	1/0	40.36	2	7
Simpson Reginald Thomas (CY 1950)	27.2.1920	24.11.2013	27	1948–1954	1,401	156*	4	33.35	–	2-4	0/0	11.00	5	
Simpson-Hayward George Hayward Thomas	7.6.1875	2.10.1936	5	1909	105	29*	0	15.00	23	6-43	2/0	18.26	1	
Sims James Morton	13.5.1903	27.4.1973	4	1935–1936	16	12	0	4.00	11	5-73	1/0	43.63	6	
Sinfield Reginald Albert	24.12.1900	17.3.1988	1	1938	6	6	0	6.00	2	1-51	0/0	61.50	0	
Slack Wilfred Norris	12.12.1954	15.1.1989	3	1985–1986	81	52	0	13.50	–				3	2
Smailes Thomas Francis	27.3.1910	1.12.1970	1	1946	25	25	0	25.00	3	3-44	0/0	20.66	0	
Small Gladstone Cleophas	18.10.1961		17	1986–1990	263	59	0	15.47	55	5-48	2/0	34.01	9	53
Smith Alan Christopher CBE	25.10.1936		6	1962	118	69*	0	29.50	–				20	
Smith Andrew Michael	1.10.1967		1	1997	4	4*	0	4.00	0	0-89	0/0	–	0	
Smith Cedric Ivan James (CY 1935)	25.8.1906	8.2.1979	5	1934–1937	102	27	0	10.20	15	5-16	1/0	26.20	1	
Smith Sir Charles Aubrey	21.7.1863	20.12.1948	1	1888	3	3	0	3.00	7	5-19	1/0	8.71	0	
[2]Smith Christopher Lyall (CY 1984)	15.10.1958		8	1983–1986	392	91	0	30.15	3	2-31	0/0	13.00	5	4
Smith David Mark	9.1.1956		2	1985	80	47	0	20.00	–				1	2
Smith David Robert	5.10.1934		5	1961	38	34	0	9.50	6	2-60	0/0	59.83	2	
Smith Denis (CY 1935)	24.1.1907	12.9.1979	5	1935	128	57	0	32.00	1	1-12	0/0	97.00	1	
Smith Donald Victor	14.6.1923		3	1957	25	16*	0	8.33	–				0	
Smith Edward Thomas	19.7.1977		3	2003	87	64	0	17.40	–				5	
Smith Ernest James ("Tiger")	6.2.1886	31.8.1979	11	1911–1913	113	22	0	8.69	–				17/3	
Smith Harry	21.5.1891	12.11.1937	1	1928	7	7	0	7.00	–				2	
Smith Michael John Knight OBE (CY 1960)	30.6.1933		50	1958–1972	2,278	121	3	31.63	1	1-10	0/0	128.00	53	
[2]Smith Robin Arnold (CY 1990)	13.9.1963		62	1988–1995	4,236	175	9	43.67	0	0-6	0/0	–	39	71
Smith Thomas Peter Bromley (CY 1947)	30.10.1908	4.8.1967	4	1946–1946	33	24	0	6.60	3	2-172	0/0	106.33	1	
Smithson Gerald Arthur	1.11.1926	6.9.1970	2	1947	70	35	0	23.33	–				1	
Snow John Augustine (CY 1973)	13.10.1941		49	1965–1976	772	73	0	13.54	202	7-40	8/1	26.66	16	9
Southerton James	16.11.1827	16.6.1880	2	1876	7	6	0	3.50	7	4-46	0/0	15.28	2	
Spooner Reginald Herbert (CY 1905)	21.10.1880	2.10.1961	10	1905–1912	481	119	0	32.06	–				2	
Spooner Richard Thompson	30.12.1919	20.12.1997	7	1951–1955	354	92	0	27.23	–				10/2	
Stanyforth Ronald Thomas	30.5.1892	20.2.1964	4	1927	13	6*	0	2.60	–				7/2	
Staples Samuel James (CY 1929)	18.9.1892	4.6.1950	3	1927	65	39	0	13.00	15	3-50	0/0	29.00	0	
Statham John Brian CBE (CY 1955)	17.6.1930	10.6.2000	70	1950–1965	675	38	0	11.44	252	7-39	9/1	24.84	28	
Steel Allan Gibson	24.9.1858	15.6.1914	13	1880–1888	600	148	2	35.29	29	3-27	0/0	20.86	5	
Steel David Stanley OBE (CY 1976)	29.9.1941		8	1975–1980	673	106	1	42.06	2	1-1	0/0	19.50	7	1
Stephenson John Patrick	14.3.1965		1	1989	36	25	0	18.00	–				0	
Stevens Greville Thomas Scott (CY 1918)	7.1.1901	19.9.1970	10	1922–1929	263	69	0	15.47	20	5-90	2/1	32.40	9	
Stevenson Graham Barry	16.12.1955	21.1.2014	2	1979–1980	28	27*	0	28.00	5	3-111	0/0	36.60	0	4

	Born	Died	Tests	Test Career	Runs	HS	100s	Avge	Wkts	BB	Avge	5/10	Ct/St	O/T
[1]Stewart Alec James OBE (CY 1993)	8.4.1963		133	1989–2003	8,463	190	15	39.54	0	0-5	–	0/0	263/14	170
[1]Stewart Michael James OBE (CY 1958)	16.9.1932		8	1962–1963	385	87	0	35.00	–	–	–	–/–	6	–
Stoddart Andrew Ernest (CY 1893)	11.3.1863	3.4.1915	16	1887–1897	996	173	2	35.57	2	1-10	47.00	–/–	6	–
Stokes Benjamin Andrew	4.6.1991		4	2013	279	120	1	34.87	15	6-99	32.80	1/0	1	10/4
Storer William (CY 1899)	25.1.1867	28.2.1912	6	1897–1899	215	51	0	19.54	2	1-24	54.00	–/–	11	–
Strauss Andrew John OBE (CY 2005)	2.3.1977		100	2004–2012	7,037	177	21	40.91	–	–	–	–/–	121	127/4
Street George Benjamin	6.12.1889	24.4.1924	1	1922	11	7*	0	11.00	–	–	–	–/–	0/1	–
Strudwick Herbert (CY 1912)	28.11.1880	14.2.1970	28	1909–1926	230	24	0	7.93	–	–	–	–/–	61/12	–
[2]Studd Charles Thomas	2.12.1860	16.7.1931	5	1882–1882	160	48	0	20.00	3	2-35	32.66	0/0	5	–
[2]Studd George Brown	20.10.1859	13.2.1945	5	1882	31	9	0	4.42	–	–	–	–/–	8	–
Subba Row Raman CBE (CY 1961)	29.1.1932		13	1958–1961	984	137	3	46.85	0	0-2	–	0/0	5	–
Such Peter Mark	12.6.1964		11	1993–1999	67	14*	0	6.09	37	6-67	33.56	2/0	4	–
Sugg Frank Howe (CY 1890)	11.1.1862	29.5.1933	2	1888	55	31	0	27.50	–	–	–	–/–		–
Sutcliffe Herbert (CY 1920)	24.11.1894	22.1.1978	54	1924–1935	4,555	194	16	60.73	–	–	–	–/–	23	–
Swann Graeme Peter (CY 2010)	24.3.1979		60	2008–2013	1,370	85	0	22.09	255	6-65	29.96	17/3	54	79/39
Swetman Roy	25.10.1933		11	1958–1959	254	65	0	16.93	–	–	–	–/–	24/2	–
[1]Tate Frederick William	24.7.1867	24.2.1943	2	1902	9	5*	0	9.00	2	2-7	25.50	0/0	2	–
[1]Tate Maurice William (CY 1924)	30.5.1895	18.5.1956	39	1924–1935	1,198	100*	1	25.48	155	6-42	26.16	7/1	11	–
Tattersall Roy	17.8.1922	9.12.2011	16	1950–1954	50	10*	0	5.00	58	7-52	26.08	4/1	8	–
Tavaré Christopher James	27.10.1954		31	1980–1989	1,755	149	2	32.50	0	0-0	–	0/0	20	–
Taylor James William Arthur	6.1.1990		2	2012	48	34	0	16.00	–	–	–	–/–	2	29
Taylor Jonathan Paul	8.8.1964		2	1992–1994	34	17*	0	17.00	3	1-18	44.50	0/0	0	–
Taylor Kenneth	21.8.1935		3	1959–1964	57	24	0	11.40	0	0-6	–	0/0	1	–
Taylor Leslie Brian	25.7.1941		2	1985	1	1*	0	1.00	4	2-34	52.00	0/0	2	–
Taylor Robert William MBE (CY 1977)	17.7.1941		57	1970–1983	1,156	97	0	16.28	–	–	–	–/–	167/7	27
Tennyson *Lord* Lionel Hallam (CY 1914)	7.11.1889	6.6.1951	9	1913–1921	345	74*	0	31.36	0	0-1	–	0/0	6	–
Terry Vivian Paul	14.1.1959		2	1984	16	8	0	5.33	–	–	–	–/–	8	–
Thomas John Gregory	12.8.1960		5	1985–1986	83	31*	0	13.83	10	4-70	50.40	0/0		3
Thompson George Joseph (CY 1906)	27.10.1877	3.3.1943	6	1909–1910	273	63	0	30.33	23	4-50	27.73	0/0	5	–
Thomson Norman Ian	23.11.1929		5	1964	69	39	0	23.00	9	2-55	63.11	0/0	3	–
Thorpe Graham Paul MBE (CY 1998)	1.8.1969		100	1993–2005	6,744	200*	16	44.66	0	0-0	–	0/0	105	82
Titmus Frederick John MBE (CY 1963)	24.11.1932	23.3.2011	53	1955–1974	1,449	84*	0	22.29	153	7-79	32.22	7/0	35	2
Tolchard Roger William	15.6.1946		4	1976	129	67	0	25.80	–	–	–	–/–		1
[1]Townsend Charles Lucas (CY 1899)	7.11.1876	17.10.1958	2	1899	51	38	0	17.00	3	3-50	25.00	0/0		–
Townsend David Charles Humphery	20.4.1912	27.1.1997	3	1934	77	36	0	12.83	0	0-9	–	0/0	1	–
[1]Townsend Leslie Fletcher (CY 1934)	8.6.1903	17.2.1993	4	1929–1933	97	40	0	16.16	6	2-22	34.16	0/0	2	–

	Born	Died	Tests	Test Career	Runs	HS	100s	Avge	Wkts	BB	5/10	Avge	Ct/St	OTT
Tredwell James Cullum	27.2.1982		1	2009	37	37	0	37.00	6	4-82	0/0	30.16	1	24/7
⁴Tremlett Christopher Timothy	2.9.1981		12	2007–2013	113	25*	0	10.27	53	6-48	2/0	27.00	4	15/1
⁴Tremlett Maurice Fletcher	5.7.1923	30.7.1984	3	1947	20	18*	0	6.66	4	2-98	0/0	56.50	0	
Trescothick Marcus Edward MBE (CY 2005)	25.12.1975		76	2000–2006	5,825	219	14	43.79	1	1-34	0/0	155.00	95	123/3
²Trott Albert Edwin (CY 1899)	6.2.1873	30.7.1914	2†	1898	23	16	0	5.75	17	5-49	1/0	11.64	0	
²Trott Ian Jonathan Leonard (CY 2011)	22.4.1981		49	2009–2013	3,763	226	9	46.45	5	1-5	0/0	79.60	29	68/7
Trueman Frederick Sewards OBE (CY 1953)	6.2.1931	1.7.2006	67	1952–1965	981	39*	0	13.81	307	8-31	17/3	21.57	64	
Tudor Alex Jeremy	23.10.1977		10	1998–2002	229	99*	0	19.08	28	5-44	1/0	34.39	3	
Tufnell Neville Charsley	13.6.1887	3.8.1951	1	1909	14	14	0	14.00					0/1	3
Tufnell Philip Clive Roderick	29.4.1966		42	1990–2001	153	22*	0	5.10	121	7-47	5/2	37.68	12	20
Turnbull Maurice Joseph Lawson (CY 1931)	16.3.1906	5.8.1944	9	1929–1936	224	61	0	20.36					1	
²Tyldesley [George] Ernest (CY 1920)	5.2.1889	5.5.1962	14	1921–1928	990	122	3	55.00	0	0-2	0/0	–	2	
²Tyldesley John Thomas (CY 1902)	22.11.1873	27.11.1930	31	1898–1909	1,661	138	4	30.75					16	
Tyldesley Richard Knowles (CY 1925)	11.3.1897	17.9.1943	7	1924–1930	47	29	0	7.83	19	3-50	0/0	32.57	1	
Tylecote Edward Ferdinando Sutton	23.6.1849	15.3.1938	6	1882–1886	152	66	0	19.00			–/–	–	5/5	
Tyler Edwin James	13.10.1864	25.1.1917	1	1895	0	0	0	0.00	4	3-49	0/0	16.25	0	
Tyson Frank Holmes (CY 1956)	6.6.1930		17	1954–1958	230	37*	0	10.95	76	7-27	4/1	18.56	4	
Udal Shaun David	18.3.1969		4	2005	109	33*	0	18.16	8	4-14	0/0	43.00	1	11
Ulyett George	21.10.1851	18.6.1898	25	1876–1890	949	149	1	24.33	50	7-36	1/0	20.40	19	
Underwood Derek Leslie MBE (CY 1969)	8.6.1945	6.6.1984	86	1966–1981	937	45*	0	11.56	297	8-51	17/6	25.83	44	26
Valentine Bryan Herbert	17.1.1908	2.2.1983	7	1933–1938	454	136	2	64.85					2	
Vaughan Michael Paul OBE (CY 2003)	29.10.1974		82	1999–2008	5,719	197	18	41.44	6	2-71	0/0	93.50	44	862/6
Verity Hedley (CY 1932)	18.5.1905	31.7.1943	40	1931–1939	669	66*	0	20.90	144	8-43	5/2	24.37	30	
Vernon George Frederick	20.6.1856	10.8.1902	1	1882	14	11*	0	14.00					0	
Vine Joseph (CY 1906)	15.5.1875	25.4.1946	2	1911	46	36	0	46.00					0	
Voce William (CY 1933)	8.8.1909	6.6.1984	27	1929–1946	308	66	0	13.39	98	7-70	3/2	27.88	15	
Waddington Abraham	4.2.1893	28.10.1959	2	1920	16	7	0	4.00	1	1-35	0/0	119.00	1	
Wainwright Edward (CY 1894)	8.4.1865	28.10.1919	5	1893–1897	132	49	0	14.66	0	0-11	0/0	–	2	
Walker Peter Michael	17.2.1936		3	1960	128	52	0	32.00	0	0-8	0/0	–	5	
Walters Cyril Frederick (CY 1934)	28.8.1905	23.12.1992	11	1933–1934	784	102	1	52.26					6	
Ward Alan	10.8.1947		5	1969–1976	40	21	0	8.00	14	4-61	0/0	32.35	3	
Ward Albert (CY 1890)	21.11.1865	6.1.1939	7	1893–1894	487	117	1	37.46					1	
Ward Ian James	30.9.1972		5	2001	129	39	0	16.12					1	
Wardle John Henry (CY 1954)	8.1.1923	23.7.1985	28	1947–1957	653	66	0	19.78	102	7-36	5/1	20.39	12	
Warner Sir Pelham Francis (CY 1904)	2.10.1873	30.11.1963	15	1898–1912	622	132*	1	23.92					3	
Warr John James	16.7.1927		2	1950	4	4	0	1.00	1	1-76	0/0	281.00	0	

	Born	Died	Tests	Test Career	Runs	HS	100s	Avge	Wkts	BB	5/10	Avge	Ct/St	O/T
Warren Arnold	2.4.1875	3.9.1951	1	1905	7	7	0	7.00	6	5-57	1/0	18.83	1	—
Washbrook Cyril CBE (CY 1947)	6.12.1914	27.4.1999	37	1937–1956	2,569	195	6	42.81	—	—	—	—	12	4
Watkins Steven Llewellyn (CY 1994)	15.9.1964		3	1991–1992	25	13	0	5.00	11	1-25	0/0	33.00	1	
Watkins Albert John ("Allan")	21.4.1922	3.8.2011	15	1948–1952	810	137*	2	40.50	11	4-65	0/0	27.72	17	
Watkinson Michael	1.8.1961		4	1995–1995	167	82*	0	33.40	10	3-20	0/0	50.36		1
Watson Willie (CY 1954)	7.3.1920	23.4.2004	23	1951–1958	879	116	2	25.85	—	3-64	—/—	34.80	8	
Webbe Alexander Josiah	16.1.1855	19.2.1941	1	1878	4	4	0	2.00	—	—	—/—	—	2	
Wellard Arthur William (CY 1936)	8.4.1902	31.12.1980	2	1937–1938	47	38	0	11.75	7	4-81	0/0	33.85	2	
Wells Alan Peter	2.10.1961		1	1995	3	3*	0	3.00	—	—	—/—	—	0	1
Wharton Alan	30.4.1923	26.8.1993	1	1949	20	13	0	10.00	—	—	—/—	—	1	
Whitaker John James (CY 1987)	5.5.1962		1	1986	11	11	0	11.00	—	—	—/—	—	1	2
White Craig	16.12.1969		30	1994–2002	1,052	121	1	24.46	59	5-32	3/0	37.62	14	51
White David William ("Butch")	14.12.1935	1.8.2008	2	1961	0	0	0	0.00	4	3-65	0/0	29.75	0	
White John Cornish (CY 1929)	19.2.1891	2.5.1961	15	1921–1930	239	29	0	18.38	49	8-126	3/1	32.26	6	
Whysall William Wilfrid (CY 1925)	31.10.1887	11.11.1930	4	1924–1930	209	76	0	29.85	0	0-9	0/0	—	7	
Wilkinson Leonard Litton	5.11.1916	3.9.2002	3	1938	3	2	0	3.00	7	2-12	0/0	38.71	1	
Willey Peter	6.12.1949		26	1976–1986	1,184	102*	2	26.90	7	2-73	0/0	65.14	3	26
Williams Neil FitzGerald	2.7.1962	27.3.2006	1	1990	38	38	0	38.00	2	2-148	0/0	74.00	0	
[2]Willis Robert George Dylan MBE (CY 1978)	30.5.1949		90	1970–1984	840	28*	0	11.50	325	8-43	16/0	25.20	39	64
[2]Wilson Clement Eustace Macro	15.5.1875	8.2.1944	2	1898	42	18	0	14.00	—	—	—/—	—	1	
Wilson Donald	7.8.1937	21.7.2012	6	1963–1970	75	42	0	12.50	11	2-17	0/0	42.36	6	
Wilson Evelyn Rockley	25.3.1879	21.7.1957	1	1920	10	5	0	5.00	3	2-28	0/0	12.00	0	
Woakes Christopher Roger	2.3.1989		1	2013	42	25	0	42.00	1	1-96	0/0	96.00	1	13/4
Wood Arthur (CY 1939)	25.8.1898	1.4.1973	4	1938–1939	80	53	0	20.00	—	—	—/—	—	10/1	
Wood Barry	26.12.1942		12	1972–1978	454	90	0	21.61	0	0-2	0/0	—	6	13
Wood George Edward Charles	22.8.1893	18.3.1971	3	1924	7	6	0	3.50	—	—	—/—	—	5/1	
Wood Henry (CY 1891)	14.12.1853	30.4.1919	4	1888–1891	204	134*	1	68.00	—	—	—/—	—	2/1	
Wood Reginald	7.3.1860	6.1.1915	1	1886	6	6	0	3.00	—	—	—/—	—	0	
Woods Samuel Moses James (CY 1889)	13.4.1867	30.4.1931	3	1895	122	53	0	30.50	5	3-28	0/0	25.80	4	
Woolley Frank Edward (CY 1911)	27.5.1887	18.10.1978	64	1909–1934	3,283	154	5	36.07	83	7-76	4/1	33.91	64	
Woolmer Robert Andrew (CY 1976)	14.5.1948	18.3.2007	19	1975–1981	1,059	149	3	33.09	4	1-8	0/0	74.75	10	6
Worthington Thomas Stanley (CY 1937)	21.8.1905	31.8.1973	9	1929–1936	321	128	1	29.18	8	2-19	0/0	39.50	8	
Wright Charles William	27.5.1863	10.1.1936	3	1895	125	71	0	31.25	—	—	—/—	—	0	
Wright Douglas Vivian Parson (CY 1940)	21.8.1914	13.11.1998	34	1938–1950	289	45	0	11.11	108	7-105	6/1	39.11	10	
Wyatt Robert Elliott Storey (CY 1930)	2.5.1901	20.4.1995	40	1927–1936	1,839	149	2	31.70	18	3-4	0/0	35.66	16	
Wynyard Edward George	1.4.1861	30.10.1936	3	1896–1905	72	30	0	12.00	0	0-2	0/0	—	0	

	Born	Died	Tests	Test Career	Runs	HS	100s	Avge	Wkts	BB	5/10	Avge	Ct/St	O/T
Yardley Norman Walter Dransfield (CY 1948)	19.3.1915	3.10.1989	20	1938–1950	812	99	0	25.37	21	3-67	0/0	33.66	14	
Young Harding Isaac ("Sailor")	5.2.1876	12.12.1964	2	1899	43	43	0	21.50	12	4-30	0/0	21.83	1	65
Young John Albert	14.10.1912	5.2.1993	8	1947–1949	28	10*	0	5.60	17	3-65	0/0	44.52	5	
Young Richard Alfred	16.9.1885	1.7.1968	2	1907	27	13	0	6.75	–	–	–/–	–	6	

AUSTRALIA (436 players)

	Born	Died	Tests	Test Career	Runs	HS	100s	Avge	Wkts	BB	5/10	Avge	Ct/St	O/T
a'Beckett Edward Lambert	11.8.1907	2.6.1989	4	1928–1931	143	41	0	20.42	3	1-41	0/0	105.66	4	
Agar Ashton Charles	14.10.1993		2	2013	130	98	0	32.50	2	2-82	0/0	124.00	1	
Alderman Terence Michael (CY 1982)	12.6.1956		41	1981–1990	203	26*	0	6.54	170	6-47	14/1	27.15	27	65
Alexander George	22.4.1851	6.11.1930	2	1880–1884	52	33	0	13.00	2	2-69	0/0	46.50	2	
Alexander Harry Houston	9.6.1905	15.4.1993	1	1932	17	17*	0	17.00	1	1-129	0/0	154.00	0	
Allan Francis Erskine	2.12.1849	9.2.1917	1	1878	5	5	0	5.00	4	2-30	0/0	20.00	2	
Allan Peter John	31.12.1935		1	1965	–	–	–	–	2	2-58	0/0	41.50	0	
Allen Reginald Charles	2.7.1858	2.5.1952	1	1886	44	30	0	22.00	–	–	–/–	–	0	
Andrews Thomas James Edwin	26.8.1890	28.1.1970	16	1921–1926	592	94	0	26.90	1	1-23	0/0	116.00	12	3
[2] Angel Jo	22.4.1968		4	1992–1994	35	11	0	5.83	10	3-54	0/0	46.30	1	
[2] Archer Kenneth Alan	17.1.1928		5	1950–1951	234	48	0	26.00	–	–	–/–	–	0	
[2] Archer Ronald Graham	25.10.1933	27.5.2007	19	1952–1956	713	128	0	24.58	48	5-53	1/0	27.45	20	
Armstrong Warwick Windridge (CY 1903)	22.5.1879	13.7.1947	50	1901–1921	2,863	159*	6	38.68	87	6-35	3/0	33.59	44	
Badcock Clayvel Lindsay ("Jack")	10.4.1914	13.12.1982	7	1936–1938	160	118	1	14.54	–	–	–/–	–	3	
Bailey George John	7.9.1982		5	2013	183	53	0	26.14	–	–	–/–	–	10	35/19
[2] Bannerman Alexander Chalmers	21.3.1854	19.9.1924	28	1878–1893	1,108	94	0	23.08	4	3-111	0/0	40.75	21	
[2] Bannerman Charles	23.7.1851	20.8.1930	3	1876–1878	239	165*	1	59.75	–	–	–/–	–	0	
Bardsley Warren (CY 1910)	6.12.1882	20.1.1954	41	1909–1926	2,469	193*	6	40.47	–	–	–/–	–	12	
Barnes Sidney George	5.6.1916	16.12.1973	13	1938–1948	1,072	234	3	63.05	4	2-25	0/0	54.50	14	
Barnett Benjamin Arthur	23.3.1908	29.6.1979	4	1938	195	57	0	27.85	–	–	–/–	–	3/2	
Barrett John Edward	15.10.1866	6.2.1916	2	1890	80	67*	0	26.66	–	–	–/–	–	0	
Beard Graeme Robert	19.8.1950		3	1979	114	49	0	22.80	1	1-26	0/0	109.00	0	
Beer Michael Anthony	9.6.1984		2	2010–2011	6	2*	0	3.00	1	2-56	0/0	59.33	1	2
[2] Benaud John	11.5.1944		3	1972	223	142	1	44.60	2	2-12	0/0	6.00	0	
[2] Benaud Richard OBE (CY 1962)	6.10.1930		63	1951–1963	2,201	122	3	24.45	248	7-72	16/1	27.03	65	
Bennett Murray John	6.10.1956		3	1984–1985	71	23	0	23.66	6	3-79	0/0	54.16	5	8
Bevan Michael Gwyl	8.5.1970		18	1994–1997	785	91	0	29.07	29	6-82	1/1	24.24	8	232

	Born	Died	Tests	Test Career	Runs	HS	100s	Avge	Wkts	BB	5/10	Avge	Ct/St	O/T
Bichel Andrew John	27.8.1970		19	1996–2003	355	71	0	16.90	58	5-60	1/0	32.24	16	67
Bird Jackson Munro	11.12.1986		3	2012–2013	7	6*	0	7.00	13	4-41	0/0	23.30	1	
Blackham John McCarthy (CY 1891)	11.5.1854	28.12.1932	35	1876–1894	800	74	0	15.68					37/24	
Blackie Donald Dearnes	5.4.1882	18.4.1955	3	1928	24	11*	0	8.00	14	6-94	1/0	31.71	2	
Blewett Gregory Scott	28.10.1971		46	1994–1999	2,552	214	4	34.02	14	2-9	0/0	51.42	45	32
Bollinger Douglas Erwin	24.7.1981		12	2008–2010	54	21	0	7.71	50	5-28	2/0	25.92	2	39/2
Bonnor George John	25.2.1855	27.6.1912	17	1880–1888	512	128	1	17.06					16	
Boon David Clarence MBE (CY 1994)	29.12.1960		107	1984–1995	7,422	200	21	43.65	0	0-0	0/0	–	99	181
Booth Brian Charles MBE	19.10.1933		29	1961–1965	1,773	169	5	42.21	3	2-33	0/0	48.66	17	
Border Allan Robert (CY 1982)	27.7.1955		156	1978–1993	11,174	205	27	50.56	39	7-46	2/1	39.10	156	273
Boyle Henry Frederick	10.12.1847	21.11.1907	12	1878–1884	153	36*	0	12.75	32	6-42	1/0	20.03	10	
Bracken Nathan Wade	12.9.1977		5	2003–2005	70	37	0	17.50	22	4-48	0/0	42.08	2	116/19
Bradman Sir Donald George AC (CY 1931)	27.8.1908	25.2.2001	52	1928–1948	6,996	334	29	99.94	2	1-8	0/0	36.00	32	
Bright Raymond James	13.7.1954		25	1977–1986	445	33	0	14.35	53	7-87	4/1	41.13	13	11
Bromley Ernest Harvey	2.9.1912	1.2.1967	2	1932–1934	38	26	0	9.50	0	0-19	0/0	–	2	
Brown William Alfred (CY 1939)	31.7.1912	16.3.2008	22	1934–1948	1,592	206*	4	46.82					14	
Bruce William	22.5.1864	3.8.1925	14	1884–1894	702	80	0	29.25	12	3-88	–/–	36.66	12	
Burge Peter John Parnell (CY 1965)	17.5.1932	5.10.2001	42	1954–1965	2,290	181	4	38.16					23	
Burke James Wallace (CY 1957)	12.6.1930	2.2.1979	24	1950–1958	1,280	189	3	34.59	8	4-37	0/0	28.75	18	
Burn Edwin James Kenneth (K. E.)	17.9.1862	20.7.1956	2	1890	41	19	0	10.25					0	
Burton Frederick John	2.11.1865	25.8.1929	2	1886–1887	4	2*	0	2.00					1/1	
Callaway Sydney Thomas	6.2.1868	25.11.1923	3	1891–1894	87	41	0	17.40	6	5-37	1/0	23.66	0	
Callen Ian Wayne	2.5.1955		1	1977	26	22*	0	–	6	3-83	0/0	31.83	1	5
Campbell Gregory Dale	10.3.1964		4	1989–1989	10	6	0	2.50	13	3-79	0/0	38.69	1	12
Carkeek William ("Barlow")	17.10.1878	20.2.1937	6	1912	16	6*	0	5.33					6	
Carlson Phillip Henry	8.8.1951		2	1978	23	21	0	5.75	2	2-41	0/0	49.50	2	4
Carter Hanson	15.3.1878	8.6.1948	28	1907–1921	873	72	0	22.97					44/21	
Casson Beau	7.12.1982		1	2007	10	10	0	10.00	3	3-86	0/0	43.00	2	
[2,4] Chappell Gregory Stephen MBE (CY 1973)	7.8.1948		87	1970–1983	7,110	247*	24	53.86	47	5-61	1/0	40.70	122	74
[2,4] Chappell Ian Michael (CY 1976)	26.9.1943		75	1964–1979	5,345	196	14	42.42	20	2-21	0/0	65.80	105	16
[2,4] Chappell Trevor Martin	21.10.1952		3	1981	79	27	0	15.80					2	20
Charlton Percie Chater	9.4.1867	30.9.1954	2	1890	29	11	0	7.25	3	3-18	0/0	8.00	0	
Chipperfield Arthur Gordon	17.11.1905	29.7.1987	14	1934–1938	552	109	1	32.47	5	3-91	0/0	87.40	15	
Clark Stuart Rupert	28.9.1975		24	2005–2009	248	39	0	13.05	94	5-32	2/0	23.86	4	39/9
Clark Wayne Maxwell	19.9.1953		10	1977–1978	98	33	0	5.76	44	4-46	0/0	28.75	6	2

Name	Born	Died	Tests	Test Career	Runs	HS	100s	Avge	Wkts	BB	5/10	Avge	Ct/St	O/T
Clarke Michael John (CY 2010)	2.4.1981		105	2004–2013	8,019	329*	26	51.40	30	6-9	2/0	37.63	119	232/34
Colley David John	15.3.1947		3	1972	84	54	0	21.00	6	3-83	0/0	52.00	1	1
Collins Herbert Leslie	21.1.1888	28.5.1959	19	1920–1926	1,352	203	4	45.06	4	2-47	0/0	63.00	13	–
Coningham Arthur	14.7.1863	13.6.1939	1	1894	13	10	0	6.50	2	2-17	0/0	38.00	–	–
Connolly Alan Norman	29.6.1939		29	1963–1970	260	37	0	10.40	102	6-47	4/0	29.22	17	1
Cook Simon Hewitt	29.1.1972		2	1997	3	3*	0	–	7	5-39	1/0	20.28	0	–
Cooper Bransby Beauchamp	15.3.1844	7.8.1914	1	1876	18	15	0	9.00	–	–	–/–	–	2	–
Cooper William Henry	11.9.1849	5.4.1939	2	1881–1884	13	7	0	6.50	9	6-120	1/0	25.11	2	–
Copeland Trent Aaron	14.3.1986		3	2011	39	23*	0	13.00	6	2-24	0/0	37.83	1	–
Corling Grahame Edward	13.7.1941		5	1964	5	3	0	1.66	12	4-60	0/0	37.25	2	–
Cosier Gary John	25.4.1953		18	1975–1978	897	168	2	28.93	5	2-26	0/0	68.20	14	9
Cottam John Thomas	5.9.1867	30.1.1897	1	1886	4	3	0	2.00	–	–	–/–	–	1	–
Cotter Albert ("Tibby")	3.12.1883	31.10.1917	21	1903–1911	457	45	0	13.05	89	7-148	7/0	28.64	8	–
Coulthard George	1.8.1856	22.10.1883	1	1881	6	6*	0	–	–	–	–/–	–	0	–
Cowan Edward James McKenzie	16.6.1982		18	2011–2013	1,001	136	1	31.28	–	–	–/–	–	24	5
Cowper Robert Maskew	5.10.1940		27	1964–1968	2,061	307	5	46.84	36	4-48	0/0	31.63	21	–
Craig Ian David	12.6.1935		11	1952–1957	358	53	0	19.88	–	–	–/–	–	2	–
Crawford William Patrick Anthony	3.8.1933	21.1.2009	4	1956–1957	53	34	0	17.66	7	3-28	0/0	15.28	1	–
Cullen Daniel James	10.4.1984		1	2006	–	–	–	–	1	1-25	0/0	54.00	0	–
Cummins Patrick James	8.5.1993		1	2011	15	13*	0	15.00	7	6-79	1/0	16.71	1	5/11
Dale Adam Craig	30.12.1968		2	1997–1998	6	5	0	2.00	6	3-71	0/0	31.16	0	30
Darling Joseph (CY 1900)	21.11.1870	2.1.1946	34	1894–1905	1,657	178	3	28.56	–	–	–/–	–	27	–
Darling Leonard Stuart	14.8.1909	24.6.1992	12	1932–1936	474	85	0	27.88	0	0-3	0/0	–	8	–
Darling Warrick Maxwell	1.5.1957		14	1977–1979	697	91	0	26.80	–	–	–/–	–	5	18
Davidson Alan Keith MBE (CY 1962)	14.6.1929		44	1953–1962	1,328	80	0	24.59	186	7-93	14/2	20.53	42	–
Davis Ian Charles	25.6.1953		15	1973–1977	692	105	1	26.61	0	–	–/–	–	9	3
Davis Simon Peter	8.11.1959		1	1985	0	0	0	0.00	0	0-70	0/0	–	0	39
De Courcey James Harry	18.4.1927	20.6.2000	3	1953	81	41	0	16.20	–	–	–/–	–	3	–
Dell Anthony Ross	6.8.1947		2	1970–1973	6	3*	0	–	6	3-65	0/0	26.66	0	–
Dodemaide Anthony Ian Christopher	5.10.1963		10	1987–1992	202	50	0	22.44	34	6-58	1/0	28.02	6	24
Doherty Xavier John	22.12.1982		4	2010–2012	51	18*	0	12.75	7	3-131	0/0	78.28	2	51/11
Donnan Henry	12.11.1864	13.8.1956	5	1891–1896	75	15	0	8.33	–	0-22	0/0	–	2	–
Dooland Bruce (CY 1955)	1.11.1923	8.9.1980	3	1946–1947	76	29	0	19.00	9	4-69	0/0	46.55	3	–
Duff Reginald Alexander	17.8.1878	13.12.1911	22	1901–1905	1,317	146	2	35.59	4	2-43	0/0	21.25	14	–
Duncan John Ross Frederick	25.3.1944		1	1970	3	3	0	3.00	0	0-30	0/0	–	0	–

§ Clarke's figures include 44 runs and one catch for Australia v the ICC World XI in the Super Series Test in 2005-06.

Name	Born	Died	Tests	Test Career	Runs	HS	100s	Avge	Wkts	BB	5/10	Avge	Ct/St	O/T
Dyer Gregory Charles	16.3.1959		6	1986-1987	131	60	0	21.83	–	–	–/–	–	22/2	23
Dymock Geoffrey	21.7.1945		21	1973-1979	236	31*	0	9.44	78	7-67	5/1	27.12	–	15
Dyson John	11.6.1954		30	1977-1984	1,359	127*	2	26.64	–	–	–/–	–	10	29
Eady Charles John	29.10.1870	20.12.1945	2	1896-1901	20	10*	0	6.66	7	3-30	0/0	16.00	2	
Eastwood Kenneth Humphrey	23.11.1935		1	1970	5	5	0	2.50	1	1-21	0/0	21.00	0	
Ebeling Hans Irvine	1.1.1905	12.1.1980	1	1934	43	41	0	21.50	3	3-74	0/0	29.66	0	
Edwards John Dunlop	12.6.1860	31.7.1911	3	1888	48	26	0	9.60	–	–	–/–	–	1	
Edwards Ross	1.12.1942		20	1972-1975	1,171	170*	2	40.37	0	0-20	–/–	–	7	9
Edwards Walter John	23.12.1949		3	1974	68	30	0	11.33	0	0-0	–/–	–	7	1
Elliott Matthew Thomas Gray (CY 1998)	28.9.1971		21	1996-2004	1,172	199	3	33.48	0	0-0	–/–	–	14	1
Emery Philip Allen	25.6.1964		1	1994	8	8*	0	–	–	–	–/–	–	5/1	
Emery Sidney Hand	15.10.1885	7.1.1967	4	1912	6	5	0	3.00	5	2-46	0/0	49.80	2	
Evans Edwin	26.3.1849	2.7.1921	6	1881-1886	82	33	0	10.25	7	3-64	0/0	47.42	5	
Fairfax Alan George	16.6.1906	17.5.1955	10	1928-1930	410	65	0	51.25	21	4-31	0/0	30.71	15	
Faulkner James Peter	29.4.1990		1	2013	45	23	0	22.50	6	4-51	0/0	16.33	–	19/6
Favell Leslie Ernest MBE	6.10.1929	14.6.1987	19	1954-1960	757	101	1	27.03	–	–	–/–	–	9	
Ferris John James (CY 1889)	21.5.1867	17.11.1900	8†	1886-1890	98	20*	0	8.16	48	5-26	4/0	14.25	4	
Fingleton John Henry Webb OBE	28.4.1908	22.11.1981	18	1931-1938	1,189	136	5	42.46	–	–	–/–	–	13	
Fleetwood-Smith Leslie O'Brien ("Chuck")	30.3.1908	16.3.1971	10	1935-1938	54	16*	0	9.00	42	6-110	2/1	37.38	9	
Fleming Damien William	24.4.1970		20	1994-2000	305	71*	0	19.06	75	5-30	2/0	25.89	9	88
Francis Bruce Colin	18.2.1948		3	1972	52	27	0	10.40	–	–	–/–	–	1	
Freeman Eric Walter	13.7.1944		11	1967-1969	345	76	0	19.16	34	4-52	0/0	33.17	5	
Freer Frederick Alfred William	4.12.1915	2.11.1998	1	1946	28	28*	0	–	3	2-49	0/0	24.66	5	
Gannon John Bryant ("Sam")	8.2.1947		3	1977	3	3*	0	3.00	11	4-77	0/0	32.81	3	
Garrett Thomas William	26.7.1858	6.8.1943	19	1876-1887	339	51*	0	12.55	36	6-78	2/0	26.94	7	
Gaunt Ronald Arthur	26.2.1934	30.3.2012	3	1957-1963	6	3	0	3.00	7	3-53	0/0	44.28	1	
Gehrs Donald Raeburn Algernon	29.11.1880	25.6.1953	6	1903-1910	221	67	0	20.09	0	0-4	0/0	–	6	
George Peter Robert	16.10.1986		1	2010	2	2	0	1.00	2	2-48	0/0	38.50	0	
[2]Giffen George (CY 1894)	27.3.1859	29.11.1927	31	1881-1896	1,238	161	1	23.35	103	7-117	7/1	27.09	24	
[2]Giffen Walter Frank	20.9.1861	28.6.1949	3	1886-1891	11	3	0	1.83	–	–	–/–	–	1	
Gilbert David Robert	29.12.1960		9	1985-1986	57	15	0	7.12	16	3-48	0/0	52.68	1	14
Gilchrist Adam Craig (CY 2002)	14.11.1971		96§	1999-2007	5,570	204*	17	47.60	–	–	–/–	–	379/37	286/13
Gillespie Jason Neil (CY 2002)	19.4.1975		71	1996-2005	1,218	201*	1	18.73	259	7-37	8/0	26.13	27	97/1
Gilmour Gary John	26.6.1951		15	1973-1976	483	101	1	23.00	54	6-85	3/0	26.03	8	5
Gleeson John William	14.3.1938		29	1967-1972	395	45	0	10.39	93	5-61	3/0	36.20	17	

§ Gilchrist's figures include 95 runs, five catches and two stumpings for Australia v the ICC World XI in the Super Series Test in 2005-06.

	Born	Died	Tests	Test Career	Runs	HS	100s	Avge	Wkts	BB	5/10	Avge	Ct/St	O/T
Graham Henry	22.11.1870	7.2.1911	6	1893–1896	301	107	2	30.10	0	0-9	–/–	–	3	1
² Gregory David William	15.4.1845	4.8.1919	3	1876–1878	60	43	0	20.00	0	0-9	–/–	–	0	–
¹.² Gregory Edward James	29.5.1839	22.4.1899	1	1876	11	11	0	5.50	0	0-9	–/–	–	1	21/3
¹.² Gregory Jack Morrison (CY 1922)	14.8.1895	7.8.1973	24	1920–1928	1,146	119	2	36.96	85	7-69	4/0	31.15	37	–
Gregory Ross Gerald	28.2.1916	10.6.1942	2	1936	153	80	0	51.00	0	0-14	0/0	–	1	–
¹ Gregory Sydney Edward (CY 1897)	14.4.1870	31.7.1929	58	1890–1912	2,282	201	4	24.53	0	0-4	0/0	–	25	–
Grimmett Clarence Victor (CY 1931)	25.12.1891	2.5.1980	37	1924–1935	557	50	0	13.92	216	7-40	21/7	24.21	17	–
Groube Thomas Underwood	2.9.1857	5.8.1927	1	1880	11	11	0	5.50	–	–	–/–	–	0	–
Grout Arthur Theodore Wallace	30.3.1927	9.11.1968	51	1957–1965	890	74	0	15.08	–	–	–/–	–	163/24	–
Guest Colin Ernest John	7.10.1937		1	1962	11	11	0	11.00	0	0-8	0/0	–	0	–
Haddin Bradley James	23.10.1977		54	2007–2013	3,006	169	4	36.65	–	–	–/–	–	215/5	102/27
Hamence Ronald Arthur	25.11.1915	24.3.2010	3	1946–1947	81	30*	0	27.00	–	–	–/–	–	1	–
Hammond Jeffrey Roy	19.4.1950		5	1972	28	19	0	9.33	15	4-38	0/0	32.53	2	1
Harris Ryan James (CY 2014)	11.10.1979		21	2009–2013	428	68*	0	19.45	93	7-117	5/0	21.56	10	21/3
Harry John	1.8.1857	27.10.1919	1	1894	8	6	0	4.00	0	0-7	0/0	–	1	–
Hartigan Roger Joseph	12.12.1879	7.6.1958	2	1907	170	116	1	42.50	0	0-7	0/0	–	2	–
Hartkopf Albert Ernst Victor	28.12.1889	20.5.1968	1	1924	80	80	0	40.00	1	1-120	0/0	134.00	0	–
² Harvey Mervyn Roye	29.4.1918	18.3.1995	1	1946	43	31	0	21.50	–	–	–/–	–	0	–
² Harvey Robert Neil MBE (CY 1954)	8.10.1928		79	1947–1962	6,149	205	21	48.41	3	1-8	0/0	40.00	64	–
Hassett Arthur Lindsay MBE (CY 1949)	28.8.1913	16.6.1993	43	1938–1953	3,073	198*	10	46.56	0	0-1	0/0	–	30	–
Hastings John Wayne	4.11.1985		1	2012	32	32	0	26.00	1	1-51	0/0	153.00	1	11/3
Hauritz Nathan Michael	18.10.1981		17	2004–2010	426	75	0	25.05	63	5-53	2/0	34.98	3	58/3
Hawke Neil James Napier	27.6.1939	25.12.2000	27	1962–1968	365	45*	0	16.59	91	7-105	6/1	29.41	9	–
Hayden Matthew Lawrence (CY 2003)	29.10.1971		103§	1993–2008	8,625	380	30	50.73	0	0-7	0/0	–	128	160§/9
Hazlitt Gervys Rignold	4.9.1888	30.10.1915	9	1907–1912	89	34*	0	11.12	23	7-25	1/0	27.08	4	–
Healy Ian Andrew (CY 1994)	30.4.1964		119	1988–1999	4,356	161*	4	27.39	–	–	–/–	–	366/29	168
Hendry Hunter Scott Thomas Laurie ("Stork")	24.5.1895	16.12.1988	11	1921–1928	335	112	1	20.93	16	3-36	0/0	40.00	10	–
Henriques Moises Constantino	1.2.1987		3	2012	156	81*	0	31.20	2	1-48	0/0	77.50	1	5/2
Hibbert Paul Anthony	23.7.1952	27.11.2008	1	1977	15	13	0	7.50	–	–	–/–	–	1	–
Higgs James Donald	11.7.1950		22	1977–1980	111	16	0	5.55	66	7-143	2/0	31.16	3	–
Hilditch Andrew Mark Jefferson	20.5.1956		18	1978–1985	1,073	119	2	31.55	–	–	–/–	–	13	8
Hilfenhaus Benjamin William	15.3.1983		27	2008–2012	355	56*	0	13.65	99	5-75	2/0	28.50	7	25/7
Hill Clement (CY 1900)	18.3.1877	5.9.1945	49	1896–1911	3,412	191	7	39.21	0	0-0	–/–	–	33	–
Hill John Charles	25.6.1923	11.8.1974	3	1953–1954	21	8*	0	7.00	8	3-35	0/0	34.12	2	–
Hoare Desmond Edward	19.10.1934		1	1960	35	35	0	17.50	2	2-68	0/0	78.00	2	–

§ *Hayden's figures include 188 runs and three catches for Australia v the ICC World XI in the Super Series Test in 2005-06.*

Name	Born	Died	Tests	Test Career	Runs	HS	100s	Avge	Wkts	BB	5/10	Avge	Ct/St	O/T
Hodge Bradley John	29.12.1974		6	2005–2013	503	203*	1	55.88	0	0-8	0/0	–	9	25/8
Hodges John Robart	11.8.1855	d unknown	2	1876	10	8	0	3.33	6	2-7	0/0	14.00		
Hogan Tom George	23.9.1956		7	1982–1983	205	42*	0	18.63	15	5-66	1/0	47.06	2	16
Hogg George Bradley	6.2.1971		7	1996–2007	186	79	0	26.57	17	2-40	0/0	54.88	1	123/12
Hogg Rodney Malcolm	5.3.1951		38	1978–1984	439	52	0	9.75	123	6-74	6/2	28.47	7	71
Hohns Trevor Victor	23.1.1954		7	1988–1989	136	40	0	22.66	17	3-59	0/0	34.11	3	
Hole Graeme Blake	6.1.1931	14.2.1990	18	1950–1954	789	66	0	25.45	3	1-9	0/0	42.00	21	
Holland Robert George	19.01.1946		11	1984–1985	35	10	0	3.18	34	6-54	3/2	39.76	5	2
Hookes David William	3.5.1955	19.1.2004	23	1976–1985	1,306	143*	1	34.36	1	1-4	0/0	41.00	12	39
Hopkins Albert John Young	3.5.1874	25.4.1931	20	1901–1909	509	43	0	16.41	26	4-81	0/0	26.76	11	
Horan Thomas Patrick	8.3.1854	16.4.1916	15	1876–1884	471	124	1	18.84	11	6-40	1/0	13.00	6	
Hordern Herbert Vivian MBE	10.2.1883	17.6.1938	7	1910–1911	254	50	0	23.09	46	7-90	5/2	23.36	6	
Hornibrook Percival Mitchell	27.7.1899	25.8.1976	6	1928–1930	60	26	0	10.00	17	7-92	1/0	39.05	7	
Howell William Peter	29.12.1869	14.7.1940	18	1897–1903	158	35	0	7.52	49	5-81	1/0	28.71	12	
Hughes Kimberley John (CY 1981)	26.1.1954		70	1977–1984	4,415	213	9	37.41	0	0-0	0/0	–	50	97
Hughes Mervyn Gregory (CY 1994)	23.11.1961		53	1985–1993	1,032	72*	0	16.64	212	8-87	7/1	28.38	23	33
Hughes Phillip Joel	30.11.1988		26	2008–2013	1,535	160	3	32.65	0	0-0	0/0	–	15	20
Hunt William Alfred	26.8.1908	30.12.1983	1	1931	3	1*	0	0.00	0	0-14	0/0	–		
Hurst Alan George	15.7.1950		12	1973–1979	102	26	0	6.00	43	5-28	2/0	27.90	3	8
Hurwood Alexander	17.6.1902	26.9.1982	2	1930	5	5	0	2.50	1	4-22	0/0	15.45	2	
Hussey Michael Edward Killeen	27.5.1975		79	2005–2012	6,235	195	19	51.52	7	1-0	0/0	43.71	85	185/38
Inverarity Robert John	31.1.1944		6	1968–1972	174	56	0	17.40	4	3-26	0/0	23.25	4	
Iredale Francis Adams	19.6.1867	15.4.1926	14	1894–1899	807	140	2	36.68	0	0-3	0/0	–	16	
Ironmonger Herbert	7.4.1882	31.5.1971	14	1928–1932	42	12	0	2.62	74	7-23	4/2	17.97	3	
Iverson John Brian	27.7.1915	24.10.1973	5	1950	3	1*	0	0.75	21	6-27	1/0	15.23	2	
Jackson Archibald Alexander	5.9.1909	16.2.1933	8	1928–1930	474	164	1	47.40	–	–	–	–	7	
Jaques Philip Anthony	3.5.1979		11	2005–2007	902	150	3	47.47	–	–	–	–	7	6
Jarman Barrington Noel	17.2.1936		19	1959–1968	400	78	0	14.81	–	–	–	–	50/4	
Jarvis Arthur Harwood	19.10.1860	15.11.1933	11	1884–1894	303	82	0	16.83	–	–	–	–	9/9	
Jenner Terrence James	8.9.1944	24.5.2011	9	1970–1975	208	74	0	23.11	24	5-90	1/0	31.20	5	
Jennings Claude Burrows	5.6.1884	20.6.1950	6	1912	107	32	0	17.83	–	–	–	–	5	
Johnson Ian William Geddes CBE	8.12.1917	9.10.1998	45	1945–1956	1,000	77	0	18.51	109	7-44	3/0	29.19	30	
Johnson Leonard Joseph	18.3.1919	20.4.1977	1	1947	25	25*	0	–	6	3-8	0/0	12.33	2	
Johnson Mitchell Guy	2.11.1981		56	2007–2013	1,571	123*	1	22.44	242	8-61	10/2	28.33	21	134/30
Johnston William Arras (CY 1949)	26.2.1922	25.5.2007	40	1947–1954	273	29	0	11.37	160	6-44	7/0	23.91	16	
Jones Dean Mervyn (CY 1990)	24.3.1961		52	1983–1992	3,631	216	11	46.55	11	1-5	0/0	64.00	34	164

	Born	Died	Tests	Test Career	Runs	HS	100s	Avge	Wkts	BB	5/10	Avge	Ct/St	O/T
Jones Ernest	30.9.1869	23.11.1943	19	1894–1902	126	20	0	5.04	64	7-88	3/1	29.01	21	
Jones Samuel Percy	1.8.1861	14.7.1951	12	1881–1887	428	87	0	21.40	6	4-47	0/0	18.66	12	
Joslin Leslie Ronald	13.12.1947		1	1967	9	7	0	4.50					0	
Julian Brendon Paul	10.8.1970		7	1993–1995	128	56*	0	16.00	15	4-36	0/0	39.93	4	25
Kasprowicz Michael Scott	10.2.1972		38	1996–2005	445	25	0	10.59	113	7-36	4/0	32.88	16	43/2
Katich Simon Mathew	21.8.1975		56§	2001–2010	4,188	157	10	45.03	21	6-65	1/0	30.23	39	45/3
Kelleway Charles	25.4.1886	16.11.1944	26	1910–1928	1,422	147	3	37.42	52	5-33	1/0	32.36	24	
Kelly James Joseph (CY 1903)	10.5.1867	14.8.1938	36	1896–1905	664	46*	0	17.02					43/20	
Kelly Thomas Joseph Dart	3.5.1844	20.7.1893	2	1876–1878	64	35	0	21.33					1	
Kendall Thomas Kingston	24.8.1851	17.8.1924	2	1876	39	17*	0	13.00	14	7-55	1/0	15.35	2	
Kent Martin Francis	23.11.1953		3	1981	171	54	0	28.50					6	5
Kerr Robert Byers	16.6.1961		2	1985	31	17	0	7.75					5	4
Khawaja Usman Tariq	18.12.1986		9	2010–2013	377	65	0	25.13	0	0-2	0/0		13	3
Kippax Alan Falconer	25.5.1897	5.9.1972	22	1924–1934	1,192	146	2	36.12					13	
Kline Lindsay Francis	29.9.1934		13	1957–1960	58	15*	0	8.28	34	7-75	1/1	22.82	9	
Krejza Jason John	14.11.1983		2	2008	71	32	0	23.66	13	8-215	1/1	43.23	4	8
Laird Bruce Malcolm	21.11.1950		21	1979–1982	1,341	92	0	35.28					16	23
Langer Justin Lee (CY 2001)	21.11.1970		105§	1992–2006	7,696	250	23	45.27	0	0-3	0/0		73	8
Langley Gilbert Roche Andrews (CY 1957)	14.9.1919	14.5.2001	26	1951–1956	374	53	0	14.96	0	0-3	0/0		83/15	
Laughlin Trevor John	30.1.1951		3	1977–1978	87	35	0	17.40	6	5-101	1/0	43.66	3	6
Laver Frank Jonas	7.12.1869	24.9.1919	15	1899–1909	196	45	0	11.52	37	8-31	2/0	26.05	8	
Law Stuart Grant (CY 1998)	18.10.1968		1	1995	54	54*	0		0	0-9	0/0		1	54
Lawry William Morris MBE (CY 1962)	11.2.1937		67	1961–1970	5,234	210	13	47.15					30	1
Lawson Geoffrey Francis	7.12.1957		46	1980–1989	894	74	0	15.96	180	8-112	11/2	30.56	10	79
Lee Brett (CY 2006)	8.11.1976		76§	1999–2008	1,451	64	0	20.15	310	5-30	10/0	30.81	23	221/25
Lee Philip Keith	15.9.1904	9.8.1980	2	1931–1932	57	42	0	19.00	4	4-111	0/0	42.40	1	
Lehmann Darren Scott (CY 2001)	5.2.1970		27	1997–2004	1,798	177	5	44.95	15	3-42	0/0	27.46	23	117
Lillee Dennis Keith MBE (CY 1973)	18.7.1949		70	1970–1983	905	73*	0	13.71	355	7-83	23/7	23.92	23	63
Lindwall Raymond Russell MBE (CY 1949)	3.10.1921	23.6.1996	61	1945–1959	1,502	118	2	21.15	228	7-38	12/0	23.03	26	
Love Hampden Stanley Bray	10.8.1895	22.7.1969	1	1932	8	5	0	4.00					3	
Love Martin Lloyd	30.3.1974		5	2002–2003	233	100*	1	46.60					7	
Loxton Samuel John Everett OBE	29.3.1921	3.12.2011	12	1947–1950	554	101	1	36.93	8	3-55	0/0	43.62	7	
Lyon Nathan Michael	20.11.1987		30	2011–2013	304	40*	0	16.88	104	7-94	4/0	32.52	12	2
Lyons John James	21.5.1863	21.7.1927	14	1886–1897	731	134	1	27.07	6	5-30	1/0	24.83	3	

§ Katich's figures include two runs and one catch, Langer's figures 22 runs and one catch, and Lee's four runs, two wickets and one catch for Australia v the ICC World XI in the Super Series Test in 2005-06.

Name	Born	Died	Tests	Test Career	Runs	HS	100s	Avge	Wkts	BB	5/10	Avge	Ct/St	O/T
McAlister Peter Alexander	11.7.1869	10.5.1938	8	1903–1909	252	41		16.80	–	–	–/–	–	10	
Macartney Charles George (CY 1922)	27.6.1886	9.9.1958	35	1907–1926	2,131	170	7	41.78	45	7-58	2/1	27.55	17	
McCabe Stanley Joseph (CY 1935)	16.7.1910	25.8.1968	39	1930–1938	2,748	232	6	48.21	36	4-13	0/0	42.86	41	
McCool Colin Leslie	9.12.1916	5.4.1986	14	1945–1949	459	104*	1	35.30	36	5-41	3/0	26.61	14	
McCormick Ernest Leslie	16.5.1906	28.6.1991	12	1935–1938	54	17*		6.00	36	4-101	0/0	29.97	8	
McCosker Richard Bede (CY 1976)	11.12.1946		25	1974–1979	1,622	127	4	39.56	–	–	–/–	–	21	14
McDermott Craig John (CY 1986)	14.4.1965		71	1984–1995	940	42*	0	12.20	291	8-97	14/2	28.63	19	138
McDonald Andrew Barry	15.6.1981		4	2008	107	68	0	21.40	9	3-25	0/0	33.33	2	
McDonald Colin Campbell	17.11.1928		47	1951–1961	3,107	170	5	39.32	–	0-3	0/0	–	14	
McDonald Edgar Arthur (CY 1922)	6.1.1891	22.7.1937	11	1920–1921	116	36	0	16.57	43	5-32	2/0	33.27	3	
McDonnell Percy Stanislaus	13.11.1858	24.9.1896	19	1880–1888	955	147	3	28.93	–	0-11	0/0	–	6	
McGain Bryce Edward	25.3.1972		1	2008	2	2	0	1.00	0	0-149	0/0	–	0	
MacGill Stuart Charles Glyndwr.	25.2.1971		44§	1997–2007	349	43	0	9.69	208	8-108	12/2	29.02	16	3
McGrath Glenn Donald (CY 1998)	9.2.1970		124§	1993–2006	641	61	0	7.36	563	8-24	29/3	21.64	38	249§/2
McIlwraith John.	7.9.1857	5.7.1938	1	1886	9	7	0	4.50	–	–	–/–	–	1	
McIntyre Peter Edward.	27.4.1966		2	1994–1996	22	16	0	7.33	5	3-103	0/0	38.80	0	
McKay Clinton James.	22.2.1983		1	2009	10	10	0	10.00	1	1-56	0/0	101.00	1	56/6
Mackay Kenneth Donald MBE	24.10.1925	13.6.1982	37	1956–1962	1,507	89	0	33.48	50	6-42	2/0	34.42	16	
McKenzie Graham Douglas (CY 1965)	24.6.1941		60	1961–1970	945	76	0	12.27	246	8-71	16/3	29.78	34	1
McKibbin Thomas Robert	10.12.1870	15.12.1939	5	1894–1897	88	28*	0	14.66	17	3-35	0/0	29.17	4	
McLaren John William	22.12.1886	17.11.1921	1	1911	0	0*	0	–	1	1-23	0/0	70.00	0	
Maclean John Alexander	27.4.1946		4	1978	79	33*	0	11.28	–	–	–/–	–	18	2
[2] McLeod Charles Edward	24.10.1869	26.11.1918	17	1894–1905	573	112	1	23.87	33	5-65	2/0	40.15	9	
[2] McLeod Robert William	19.1.1868	14.6.1907	6	1891–1893	146	31	0	13.27	12	5-53	1/0	31.83	3	
McShane Patrick George	18.4.1858	11.12.1903	3	1884–1887	26	12*	0	5.20	1	1-39	0/0	48.00	2	
Maddocks Leonard Victor	24.5.1926		7	1954–1956	177	69	0	17.70	–	–	–/–	–	19/1	
Maguire John Norman.	15.9.1956		3	1983	28	15*	0	7.00	10	4-57	0/0	32.30	2	23
Mailey Arthur Alfred.	3.1.1886	31.12.1967	21	1920–1926	222	46*	0	11.10	99	9-121	6/2	33.91	14	
Mallett Ashley Alexander	13.7.1945		38	1968–1980	430	43*	0	11.62	132	8-59	6/1	29.84	30	9
Malone Michael Francis	9.10.1950		1	1977	46	46	0	46.00	6	5-63	1/0	12.83	2	10
Mann Anthony Longford	8.11.1945		4	1977	189	105	1	23.62	4	3-12	0/0	79.00	2	4
Manou Graham Allan	23.4.1979		1	2009	21	13*	0	21.00	–	–	–/–	–	3	
Marr Alfred Percy	28.3.1862	15.3.1940	1	1884	5	5	0	2.50	–	–	–/–	–	–	
[1] Marsh Geoffrey Robert	31.12.1958		50	1985–1991	2,854	138	4	33.18	0	0-3	0/0	–	38	117
[1] Marsh Rodney William MBE (CY 1982)	4.11.1947		96	1970–1983	3,633	132	3	26.51	0	0-3	0/0	–	343/12	92

§ MacGill's figures include no runs and nine wickets and McGrath's two runs and three wickets for Australia v the ICC World XI in the Super Series Test in 2005-06.

Name	Born	Died	Tests	Test Career	Runs	HS	100s	Avge	Wks	BB	5/10	Avge	Cl/St	O/T
[1]Marsh Shaun Edward	9.7.1983		7	2011	301	141	1	27.36					4	41/13
Martin John Wesley	28.1.1931	16.7.1992	8	1960–1966	214	55	0	17.83	17	3-56	0/0	48.94	5	
Martyn Damien Richard (CY 2002)	21.10.1971		67	1992–2006	4,406	165	13	46.37	2	1-0	0/0	84.00	36	208/4
Massie Hugh Hamon	11.4.1854	12.10.1938	9	1881–1884	249	55	0	15.56					5	
Massie Robert Arnold Lockyer (CY 1973)	14.4.1947		9	1972–1972	78	42	0	11.14	31	8-53	2/1	20.87	1	3
Matthews Christopher Darrell	22.9.1962		3	1986–1986	54	32	0	10.80	6	3-95	0/0	52.16		59
Matthews Gregory Richard John	15.12.1959		33	1983–1992	1,849	130	4	41.08	61	5-103	2/1	48.22	17	
Matthews Thomas James	3.4.1884	14.10.1943	8	1911–1912	153	53	0	17.00	16	4-29	0/0	26.18	7	
Maxwell Glenn James	14.10.1988		2	2012	39	13	0	9.75				27.57	2	19/12
May Timothy Brian Alexander	26.1.1962		24	1987–1994	225	42*	0	14.06	75	5-9	3/0	34.74	6	47
Mayne Edgar Richard	2.7.1882	26.10.1961	4	1912–1921	64	25*	0	21.33	0	0-1	0/0	–	2	
Mayne Lawrence Charles	23.1.1942		6	1964–1969	76	13	0	9.50	19	4-43	0/0	33.05	6	
Meckiff Ian	6.1.1935		18	1957–1963	154	45*	0	11.84	45	6-38	2/0	31.62	9	
Meuleman Kenneth Douglas	5.9.1923	10.9.2004	1	1945	0	0	0	0.00						
Midwinter William Evans	19.6.1851	3.12.1890	8†	1876–1886	174	37	0	13.38	14	5-78	1/0	23.78	1	
Miller Colin Reid	6.2.1964		18	1998–2000	174	43	0	8.28	69	5-32	3/1	26.15	5	
Miller Keith Ross MBE (CY 1954)	28.11.1919	11.10.2004	55	1945–1956	2,958	147	7	36.97	170	7-60	7/1	22.97	38	
Minnett Roy Baldwin	13.6.1888	21.10.1955	9	1911–1912	391	90	0	26.06	11	4-34	0/0	26.36	0	
Misson Francis Michael	19.11.1938		5	1960–1961	38	25*	0	19.00	16	4-58	0/0	38.50	6	
Moody Thomas Masson (CY 2000)	2.10.1965		8	1989–1992	456	106	2	32.57	2	1-17	0/0	73.50	9	76
Moroney John	24.7.1917	1.7.1999	1	1951–1951	383	118	2	34.81						
Morris Arthur Robert MBE (CY 1949)	19.1.1922		46	1946–1954	3,533	206	12	46.48	2	1-5	0/0	25.00	15	
Morris Samuel	22.6.1855	20.9.1931	1	1884	14	10*	0	14.00					1	
Moses Henry	13.2.1858	7.12.1938	6	1886–1894	198	33	0	19.80						
[1]Moss Jeffrey Kenneth	29.6.1947		1	1978	60	38*	0	60.00						1
Moule William Henry	31.1.1858	24.8.1939	1	1880	40	34	0	20.00	3	3-23	0/0	7.66	1	
Muller Scott Andrew	11.7.1971		2	1999	6	6*	0	–	7	3-68	0/0	36.85	2	
Murdoch William Lloyd	18.10.1854	18.2.1911	18†	1876–1890	896	211	2	32.00					14	
Musgrove Henry Alfred	27.11.1858	2.11.1931	1	1884	13	9	0	6.50					0	
Nagel Lisle Ernest	6.3.1905	23.11.1971	1	1932	21	21*	0	21.00	2	2-110	0/0	55.00	0	
Nash Laurence John	2.5.1910	24.7.1986	2	1931–1936	30	17	0	15.00	10	4-18	0/0	12.60	6	
Nicholson Matthew James	2.10.1974		1	1998	14	9	0	7.00	4	3-56	0/0	28.75	1	
Nitschke Homesdale Carl ("Jack")	14.4.1905	29.9.1982	1	1931	53	47	0	26.50					3	
Noble Montague Alfred (CY 1900)	28.1.1873	22.6.1940	42	1897–1909	1,997	133	1	30.25	121	7-17	9/2	25.00	26	
Noblet Geffery	14.9.1916	16.8.2006	3	1949–1952	22	13*	0	7.33	7	3-21	0/0	26.14	1	
North Marcus James	28.7.1979		21	2008–2010	1,171	128	5	35.48	14	6-55	1/0	42.21	17	2/1

	Born	Died	Tests	Test Career	Runs	HS	100s	Avge	Wkts	BB	5/10	Avge	Ct/St	O/T
Nothling Otto Ernest	1.8.1900	26.9.1965	1	1928	52	44	0	26.00	0	0-12	–/–	–	0	
O'Brien Leo Patrick Joseph	2.7.1907	13.3.1997	5	1932–1936	211	61	0	26.37	–	–		–	3	
O'Connor John Denis Alphonsus	9.9.1875	23.8.1941	4	1907–1909	86	20	0	12.28	13	5-40	1/0	26.15	3	87
O'Donnell Simon Patrick	26.1.1963		6	1985–1985	206	48	0	29.42	6	3-37	0/0	84.00	4	
Ogilvie Alan David	3.6.1951		5	1977	178	47	0	17.80	–	–	–/–	–	5	
O'Keeffe Kerry James	25.11.1949		24	1970–1977	644	85	0	25.76	53	5-101	1/0	38.07	15	2
Oldfield William Albert Stanley MBE (CY 1927)	9.9.1894	10.8.1976	54	1920–1936	1,427	65*	0	22.65	–	–	–/–	–	78/52	
O'Neill Norman Clifford Louis (CY 1962)	19.2.1937	3.3.2008	42	1958–1964	2,779	181	6	45.55	17	4-41	0/0	39.23	21	
O'Reilly William Joseph OBE (CY 1935)	20.12.1905	6.10.1992	27	1931–1945	410	56*	0	12.81	144	7-54	11/3	22.59	7	
Oxenham Ronald Keven	28.7.1891	16.8.1939	7	1928–1931	151	48	0	15.10	14	4-39	0/0	37.28	4	26/5
Paine Timothy David	8.12.1984		4	2010–2010	287	92	0	35.87	–	–	–/–	–	16/1	
Palmer George Eugene	22.2.1859	22.8.1910	17	1880–1886	296	48	0	14.09	78	7-65	6/2	21.51	13	
Park Roy Lindsay	30.7.1892	23.1.1947	1	1920	0	0	0	0.00	0	0-9	0/0	–	0	
Pascoe Leonard Stephen	13.2.1950		14	1977–1981	106	30*	0	10.60	64	5-59	1/0	26.06	5	29
2 Pattinson James Lee	3.5.1990		12	2011–2013	331	42	0	30.09	47	5-27	3/0	26.42	2	11/4
Pellew Clarence Everard ("Nip")	21.9.1893	9.5.1981	10	1920–1921	484	116	2	37.23	0	0-3	0/0	–	4	
Phillips Wayne Bentley	1.3.1958		27	1983–1985	1,485	159	2	32.28	–	–	–/–	–	52	48
Phillips Wayne Norman	7.11.1962		1	1991	22	14	0	11.00	–	–	–/–	–	–	
Philpott Peter Ian	21.11.1934		8	1964–1965	93	22	0	10.33	26	5-90	1/0	38.46	5	
Ponsford William Harold MBE (CY 1935)	19.10.1900	6.4.1991	29	1924–1934	2,122	266	7	48.22	–	–	–/–	–	21	
Ponting Ricky Thomas (CY 2006)	19.12.1974		168§	1995–2012	13,378	257	41	51.85	5	1-0	0/0	55.20	196	374§/17
Pope Roland James	18.2.1864	27.7.1952	1	1884	3	3	0	1.50	–	–	–/–	–	1	
Quiney Robert John	20.8.1982		2	2012	9	9	0	3.00	0	0-3	0/0	–	0	
Rackemann Carl Gray	3.6.1960		12	1982–1990	53	15*	0	5.30	39	6-86	3/1	29.15	5	52
Ransford Vernon Seymour (CY 1910)	20.3.1885	19.3.1958	20	1907–1911	1,211	143*	1	37.84	1	1-9	0/0	28.00	10	
Redpath Ian Ritchie MBE	11.5.1941		66	1963–1975	4,737	171	8	43.45	0	0-0	0/0	–	83	5
Reedman John Cole	9.10.1865	25.3.1924	1	1894	21	17	0	10.50	1	1-12	0/0	24.00	1	
Reid Bruce Anthony	14.3.1963		27	1985–1992	93	13	0	4.65	113	7-51	5/2	24.63	5	61
Reiffel Paul Ronald	19.4.1966		35	1991–1997	955	79*	0	26.52	104	6-71	5/0	26.96	15	92
Renneberg David Alexander	23.9.1942		8	1966–1967	22	9	0	3.66	23	5-39	2/0	36.08	2	
4 Richardson Arthur John	24.7.1888	23.12.1973	9	1924–1926	403	100	1	31.00	12	2-20	0/0	43.41	4	
4 Richardson Victor York OBE	7.9.1894	30.10.1969	19	1924–1935	706	138	1	23.53	–	–	–/–	–	24	
Rigg Keith Edward	21.5.1906	28.2.1995	8	1930–1936	401	127	1	33.41	–	–	–/–	–	5	
Ring Douglas Thomas	14.10.1918	23.6.2003	13	1947–1953	426	67	0	22.42	35	6-72	2/0	37.28	5	
Ritchie Gregory Michael	23.1.1960		30	1982–1986	1,690	146	3	35.20	0	0-10	0/0	–	14	44

§ *Ponting's figures include 100 runs and one catch for Australia v the ICC World XI in the Super Series Test in 2005–06.*

	Born	Died	Tests	Test Career	Runs	HS	100s	Avge	Wkts	BB	5/10	Avge	Ct/St	O/T
Rixon Stephen John	25.2.1954		13	1977–1984	394	54	0	18.76	13	4-72	–/–	39.61	42/5	6
Robertson Gavin Ron	28.5.1966		4	1997–1998	140	57	0	20.00	13	0-24	0/0		1	13
Robertson William Roderick	6.10.1861	24.6.1938	1	1884	2	2	0	1.00	–	–	–	–	0	
Robinson Richard Daryl	8.6.1946		3	1977	100	34	0	16.66	–	–	–/–	–	4	2
Robinson Rayford Harold	26.3.1914	10.8.1965	1	1936	5	3	0	2.50	–	–	–/–	–	1	
Rogers Christopher John Llewellyn (CY 2014)	31.8.1977		11	2007–2013	849	119	3	40.42	–	–	–/–	–	9	
Rorke Gordon Frederick	27.6.1938		4	1958–1959	9	7	0	4.50	10	3-23	0/0	20.30	–	
Rutherford John Walter	25.9.1929		1	1956	30	30	0	30.00	1	1-11	0/0	15.00	–	
Ryder John	8.8.1889	3.4.1977	20	1920–1928	1,394	201*	3	51.62	17	2-20	0/0	43.70	17	
Saggers Ronald Arthur	15.5.1917	17.3.1987	6	1948–1949	30	14	0	10.00	–	–	–	–	16/8	
Saunders John Victor	21.3.1876	21.12.1927	14	1901–1907	39	11*	0	2.29	79	7-34	6/0	22.73	5	
Scott Henry James Herbert	26.12.1858	23.9.1910	8	1884–1886	359	102	1	27.61	0	0-9	0/0	–	8	17/2
Sellers Reginald Hugh Durning	20.8.1940		1	1964	0	0	0	0.00	0	0-17	0/0	–	–	
Serjeant Craig Stanton	1.11.1951		12	1977–1977	522	124	1	23.72	–	–	–/–	–	13	3
5 Sheahan Andrew Paul	30.9.1946		31	1967–1973	1,594	127	2	33.91	–	–	–/–	–	17	3
Shepherd Barry Kenneth	23.4.1937	17.9.2001	9	1962–1964	502	96	0	41.83	0	0-3	0/0	–	2	
Siddle Peter Matthew	25.11.1984		51	2008–2013	910	51	0	14.21	183	6-54	8/0	28.68	16	17/2
Sievers Morris William	13.4.1912	10.5.1968	3	1936	67	25*	0	13.40	9	5-21	1/0	17.88	4	
Simpson Robert Baddeley (CY 1965)	3.2.1936		62	1957–1977	4,869	311	10	46.81	71	5-57	2/0	42.26	110	2
Sincock David John	1.2.1942		3	1964–1965	80	29	0	26.66	8	3-67	0/0	51.25	2	
Slater Keith Nichol	12.3.1936		1	1958	1	1*	0		2	2-40	0/0	50.50	0	
Slater Michael Jonathon	21.2.1970		74	1993–2001	5,312	219	14	42.83	1	1-4	0/0	10.00	33	42
Sleep Peter Raymond	4.5.1957		14	1978–1989	483	90	0	24.15	31	5-72	1/0	45.06	4	
Slight James	20.10.1855	9.12.1930	1	1880	11	11	0	5.50	–	–	–/–	–	0	
Smith David Bertram Miller	14.9.1884	29.7.1963	2	1912	30	24*	0	15.00	–	–	–	–	0	
Smith Steven Barry	18.10.1961		3	1983	41	12	0	8.20	–	–	–/–	–	0	28
Smith Steven Peter Devereux	2.6.1989		17	2010–2013	1,092	138*	3	36.40	9	3-18	0/0	49.66	14	33/20
Spofforth Frederick Robert	9.9.1853	4.6.1926	18	1876–1886	217	50	0	9.43	94	7-44	7/4	18.41	11	
Stackpole Keith Raymond MBE (CY 1973)	10.7.1940		43	1965–1973	2,807	207	7	37.42	15	2-33	0/0	66.73	47	6
Stare Mitchell Aaron	13.11.1990		12	2011–2013	431	99	0	30.78	41	6-154	2/0	33.60	4	19/10
Stevens Gavin Byron	29.2.1932		4	1959	112	28	0	16.00	–	–	–/–	–	2	
Symonds Andrew	9.6.1975		26	2003–2008	1,462	162*	2	40.61	24	3-50	0/0	37.33	22	198/14
Taber Hedley Brian	29.4.1940		16	1966–1969	353	48	0	16.04	–	–	–/–	–	56/4	
Tait Shaun William	22.2.1983		3	2005–2007	20	8	0	6.66	5	3-97	0/0	60.40	0	35/19
Tallon Donald (CY 1949)	17.2.1916	7.9.1984	21	1945–1953	394	92	0	17.13	–	–	–/–	–	50/8	
Taylor John Morris	10.10.1895	12.5.1971	20	1920–1926	997	108	1	35.60	1	1-25	0/0	45.00	11	

	Born	Died	Tests	Test Career	Runs	HS	100s	Avge	Wkts	BB	Avge	5/10	Ct/St	O/T
Taylor Mark Anthony (CY 1990)	27.10.1964		104	1988–1998	7,525	334*	19	43.49	1	1-11	26.00	0/0	157	113
Taylor Peter Laurence	22.8.1956		13	1986–1991	431	87	0	26.93	27	6-78	39.55	1/0	10	83
Thomas Grahame	21.3.1938		8	1964–1965	325	61	0	29.54					3	
Thoms George Ronald	22.3.1927	29.8.2003	1	1951	44	28	0	22.00					0	
Thomson Alan Lloyd ('Froggy')	2.12.1945		4	1970	22	12*	0	22.00	12	3-79	54.50	0/0	0	1
Thomson Jeffrey Robert	16.8.1950		51	1972–1985	679	49	0	12.81	200	6-46	28.00	8/0	20	50
Thomson Nathaniel Frampton Davis	29.5.1839	2.9.1896	2	1876	67	41	0	16.75	1	1-14	31.00	0/0	3	
Thurlow Hugh Motley ("Pud")		3.12.1975	1	1931	0	0	0	0.00	0	0-33		0/0		
Toohey Peter Michael	20.4.1954		15	1977–1979	893	122	1	31.89	0	0-4		0/0	9	5
Toshack Ernest Raymond Herbert	8.12.1914	11.5.2003	12	1945–1948	73	20*	0	14.60	47	6-29	21.04	4/1	4	
Travers Joseph Patrick Francis	10.1.1871	15.9.1942	1	1901	10	9	0	5.00	1	1-14	14.00	0/0	1	
Tribe George Edward (CY 1955)	4.10.1920	5.4.2009	3	1946	35	25*	0	17.50	2	2-48	165.00	0/0	0	
[2] Trott Albert Edwin (CY 1899)	6.2.1873	30.7.1914	3†	1894	205	85*	1	102.50	9	8-43	21.33	1/0	4	
[2] Trott George Henry Stevens (CY 1894)	5.8.1866	10.11.1917	24	1888–1897	921	143	1	21.92	29	4-71	35.13	0/0	21	
[2] Trumble Hugh (CY 1897)	12.5.1867	14.8.1938	32	1890–1903	851	70	0	19.79	141	8-65	21.78	9/3	45	
[2] Trumble John William	16.9.1863	17.8.1944	7	1884–1886	243	59	0	20.25	10	3-29	22.20	0/0	3	
[2] Trumper Victor Thomas (CY 1903)	2.11.1877	28.6.1915	48	1899–1911	3,163	214*	8	39.04	8	3-60	39.62	0/0	31	
Turner Alan	23.7.1950		14	1975–1976	768	136	0	29.53					15	6
[2] Turner Charles Thomas Biass (CY 1889)	16.11.1862	1.1.1944	17	1886–1894	323	29	0	11.53	101	7-43	16.53	11/2	8	
Veivers Thomas Robert	6.4.1937		21	1963–1966	813	88	0	31.26	33	4-68	41.66	0/0	7	
Veletta Michael Robert John	30.10.1963		8	1987–1989	207	39	0	18.81					12	
Wade Matthew Scott	26.12.1987		12	2011–2012	623	106	2	34.61	0	0-0		0/0	33/3	40/19
Waite Mervyn George	7.1.1911	16.12.1985	2	1938	11	8	0	3.66	1	1-150	190.00	0/0	1	
Walker Maxwell Henry Norman	12.9.1948		34	1972–1977	586	78*	0	19.53	138	8-143	27.47	6/0	12	17
Wall Thomas Welbourn ("Tim")	13.5.1904	26.3.1981	18	1928–1934	121	20	0	6.36	56	5-14	35.89	3/0	11	
Walters Francis Henry	9.2.1860	1.6.1922	1	1884	12	7	0	6.00					2	
Walters Kevin Douglas MBE	21.12.1945		74	1965–1980	5,357	250	15	48.26	49	5-66	29.08	1/0	43	28
Ward Francis Anthony	23.2.1906	25.3.1974	4	1936–1938	36	18	0	6.00	11	6-102	52.18	1/0	1	
Warne Shane Keith (CY 1994)	13.9.1969		145§	1991–2006	3,154	99	0	17.32	708	8-71	25.41	37/10	125	193‡
Warner David Andrew	27.10.1986		27	2011–2013	1,924	180	5	40.93	4	2-45	51.25	0/0	22	39/46
Watkins John Russell	16.4.1943		1	1972	39	36	0	39.00	0	0-21		0/0	1	
Watson Graeme Donald	8.3.1945		5	1966–1972	97	50	0	10.77	6	2-67	42.33	0/0	9	
Watson Shane Robert	17.6.1981		51§	2004–2013	3,343	176	4	36.33	68	6-33	31.83	3/0	33	171/39
Watson William James	31.1.1931		4	1954	106	30	0	17.66	0	0-5		0/0	2	
[2] Waugh Mark Edward (CY 1991)	2.6.1965		128	1990–2002	8,029	153*	20	41.81	59	5-40	41.16	1/0	181	244

§ Warne's figures include 12 runs and six wickets and Watson's 34 runs and no wicket for Australia v the ICC World XI in the Super Series Test in 2005-06.

	Born	Died	Test Career	Tests	Runs	HS	100s	Avge	Wkts	BB	5/10	Avge	Ct/St	O/T
²Waugh Stephen Rodger (CY 1989)	2.6.1965		1985-2003	168	10,927	200	32	51.06	92	5-28	3/0	37.44	112	325
Wellham Dirk Macdonald	13.3.1959		1981-1986	6	257	103	1	23.36	0			–	5	17
Wessels Kepler Christoffel (CY 1995)	14.9.1957		1982-1985	24†	1,761	179	4	42.95	0	0-2	0/0	–	18	54‡
Whatmore Davenell Frederick	16.3.1954		1978-1979	7	293	77	1	22.53	0	0-11	0/0	–	13	
White Cameron Leon	18.8.1983		2008	4	146	46	0	29.20	5	2-71	0/0	68.40	1	87/38
Whitney Michael Roy	24.2.1959		1981-1992	12	68	13	0	6.18	39	7-27	2/1	33.97	2	38
Whitty William James	15.8.1886	30.1.1974	1909-1912	14	161	39*	0	13.41	65	6-17	3/0	21.12	4	
Wiener Julien Mark	1.5.1955		1979	6	281	93	0	25.54	0	0-19	0/0	–	4	7
Williams Brad Andrew	20.11.1974		2003	4	23	10*	0	7.66	9	4-53	0/0	45.11	4	25
Wilson John William	20.8.1921	13.10.1985	1956	1					1	1-25	0/0	64.00	0	
Wilson Paul	12.1.1972		1997	1	0	0*	0	–	0	0-50	0/0	–	0	11
Wood Graeme Malcolm	6.11.1956		1977-1988	59	3,374	172	9	31.83	0			–	41	83
Woodcock Ashley James	27.2.1947		1973	1	27	27	0	27.00						1
Woodfull William Maldon OBE (CY 1927)	22.8.1897	11.8.1965	1926-1934	35	2,300	161	7	46.00					7	
Woods Samuel Moses James (CY 1889)	13.4.1867	30.4.1931	1888	3†	32	18	0	5.33	5	2-35	0/0	24.20	1	
Woolley Roger Douglas	16.9.1954		1982-1983	2	21	13	0	10.50					7	4
Worrall John	20.6.1860	17.11.1937	1884-1899	11	478	76	0	25.15	1	1-97	0/0	127.00	13	
Wright Kevin John	27.12.1953		1978-1979	10	219	55*	0	16.84					31/4	5
Yallop Graham Neil	7.10.1952		1975-1984	39	2,756	268	8	41.13	1	1-21	0/0	116.00	23	30
Yardley Bruce	5.9.1947		1977-1982	33	978	74	0	19.56	126	7-98	6/1	31.63	31	7
Young Shaun	13.6.1970		1997	1	4	4*	0	4.00	0	0-5	0/0	–	0	
Zoehrer Timothy Joseph	25.9.1961		1985-1986	10	246	52*	0	20.50					18/1	22

SOUTH AFRICA (316 players)

	Born	Died	Test Career	Tests	Runs	HS	100s	Avge	Wkts	BB	5/10	Avge	Ct/St	O/T
Abbott Kyle John	18.6.1987		2012	1	13	13	0	13.00	9	7-29	1/0	7.55	0	2/1
Ackerman Hylton Deon	14.2.1973		1997	4	161	57	0	20.12					1	
Adams Paul Regan	20.1.1977		1995-2003	45	360	35	0	9.00	134	7-128	4/1	32.87	29	24
Adcock Neil Amwin Treharne (CY 1961)	8.3.1931		1953-1961	26	146	24	0	5.40	104	6-43	5/0	21.10	4	
Amla Hashim Mahomed (CY 2013)	31.3.1983		2004-2013	73	5,956	311*	20	51.34	0	0-4	0/0	–	58	85/19
Anderson James Henry	26.4.1874	11.3.1926	1902	1	43	32	0	21.50					1	
Ashley William Hare	10.2.1862	14.7.1930	1888	1					7	7-95	1/0	13.57	0	
Bacher Adam Marc	29.10.1973		1996-1999	19	833	96	0	26.03	0	0-4	0/0	–	11	13
Bacher Aron ("Ali")	24.5.1942		1965-1969	12	679	73	0	32.33					10	

	Born	Died	Tests	Test Career	Runs	HS	100s	Avge	Wkts	BB	5/10	Avge	Ct/St	O/T
Balaskas Xenophon Constantine	15.10.1910	12.5.1994	9	1930–1938	174	122*	1	14.50	22	5-49	0/0	36.63	5	
Barlow Edgar John	12.8.1940	30.12.2005	30	1961–1969	2,516	201	6	45.74	40	5-85	1/0	34.05	35	
Baumgartner Harold Vane	17.11.1883	8.4.1938	1	1913	19	16	0	9.50	2	2-99	0/0	49.50	1	
Beaumont Rolland	4.2.1884	25.5.1958	5	1912–1913	70	31	0	7.77	0	0-0	0/0	–	1	
Begbie Denis Warburton	12.12.1914	10.3.2009	5	1948–1949	138	48	0	19.71	1	1-38	0/0	130.00	2	
Bell Alexander John	15.4.1906	1.8.1985	16	1929–1935	69	26*	0	6.27	48	6-99	4/0	32.64	6	
Bisset Sir Murray	14.4.1876	24.10.1931	3	1898–1909	103	35	0	25.75	–	–	–/–	–	2/1	
Bisset George Finlay	5.11.1905	14.11.1965	4	1927	38	23	0	19.00	25	7-29	2/0	18.76	0	
Blanckenberg James Manuel	31.12.1892	d unknown	18	1913–1924	455	59	0	19.78	60	6-76	4/0	30.28	9	
Bland Kenneth Colin (CY 1966)	5.4.1938		21	1961–1966	1,669	144*	3	49.08	2	2-16	0/0	62.50	10	
Bock Ernest George	17.9.1908	5.9.1961	3	1935	11	9*	0		0	0-42	0/0	–	0	113†/1
Boje Nico	20.3.1973		43	1999–2006	1,312	85	0	25.23	100	5-62	3/0	42.65	18	
Bond Gerald Edward	5.4.1909	27.8.1965	3	1938	0	0	0	0.00	0	0-16	0/0	–	0	
Bosch Tertius	14.3.1966	14.2.2000	1	1991	5	5*	0		3	2-61	0/0	34.66	0	2
Botha Johan	2.5.1982		5	2005–2010	83	25	0	20.75	17	4-56	0/0	33.70	3	76†/40
Botten James Thomas ("Jackie")	21.6.1938	14.5.2006	3	1965	65	33	0	10.83	8	2-56	0/0	42.12	1	
Boucher Mark Verdon (CY 2009)	3.12.1976		146§	1997–2011	5,498	125	5	30.54	1	1-6	0/0	6.00	530/23	290§/25
Brann William Henry	4.4.1899	22.9.1953	3	1922	71	50	0	14.20	0	–	–/–	–	2	
Briscoe Arthur Wellesley ("Dooley")	6.2.1911	22.4.1941	2	1935–1938	33	16	0	11.00	0	–	–/–	–		
Bromfield Harry Dudley	26.6.1932		9	1961–1965	59	21	0	11.80	17	5-88	1/0	35.23	13	
Brown Lennox Sidney	24.11.1910	1.9.1983	2	1931	17	8	0	5.66	3	1-30	0/0	63.00	0	
Burger Christopher George de Villiers	12.7.1935		2	1957	62	37*	0	20.66	0	–	–/–	–	0	
Burke Sydney Frank	11.3.1934		2	1961–1964	42	20	0	14.00	11	6-128	2/1	23.36	0	
Buys Isaac Daniel	4.2.1895	d unknown	1	1922	4	4*	0	4.00	0	0-20	–/–	–	0	
Cameron Horace Brakenridge ("Jock") (CY 1936)	5.7.1905	2.11.1935	26	1927–1935	1,239	90	0	30.21	–	–	–/–	–	39/12	
Campbell Thomas	9.2.1882	5.10.1924	5	1909–1912	90	48	0	15.00	–	–	–/–	–	7/1	
Carlstein Peter Rudolph	28.10.1938		8	1957–1963	190	42	0	14.61	–	–	–/–	–	3	
Carter Claude Pagdett	23.4.1881	8.11.1952	10	1912–1924	181	45	0	18.10	28	6-50	2/0	24.78	2	
Catterall Robert Hector (CY 1925)	10.7.1900	3.11.1961	24	1922–1924	1,555	120	3	37.92	7	3-15	0/0	23.14	12	
Chapman Horace William	30.6.1890	1.12.1941	2	1913–1921	39	17	0	13.00	1	1-51	0/0	104.00	–	
Cheetham John Erskine	26.5.1920	21.8.1980	24	1948–1955	883	89	0	23.86	0	–	0/0	–	13	
Chevalier Grahame Anton	9.3.1937		1	1969	0	0*	0	0.00	5	3-68	0/0	20.00	0	
Christy James Alexander Joseph	12.12.1904	1.2.1971	10	1929–1931	618	103	1	34.33	2	2-15	0/0	46.00	1	
Chubb Geoffrey Walter Ashton	12.4.1911	28.8.1982	5	1951	63	15*	0	10.50	21	6-51	2/0	27.47	0	

§ Boucher's figures exclude 17 runs and two catches for the ICC World XI v Australia in the Super Series Test in 2005-06.

Name	Born	Died	Tests	Test Career	Runs	HS	100s	Avge	Wkts	BB	5/10	Avge	Ct/St	OIT
Cochran John Alexander Kennedy	15.7.1909	15.6.1987	1	1930	4	4	0	4.00	–	0-47	0/0	–	0	0
Coen Stanley Keppel ("Shunter")	14.10.1902	29.1.1967	2	1927	101	41*	0	50.50	–	0-7	0/0	–	1	–
Connaille John McIllwaine Moore ("Mick")	21.2.1883	28.7.1956	12	1909–1927	355	47	0	16.90	–	–	–/–	–	1	1
Commins John Brian	19.2.1965		3	1994	125	45	0	25.00	–	–	–/–	–	2	–
Conyngham Dalton Parry	10.5.1897	7.7.1979	1	1922	6	3*	0	–	2	1-40	0/0	51.50	0	–
Cook Frederick James	1870	30.11.1915	1	1895	7	7	0	3.50	–	–	–/–	–	0	–
Cook Stephen James (CY 1990)	31.7.1953		3	1992–1993	107	43	0	17.83	–	–	–/–	–	1	4
Cooper Alfred Henry Cecil	2.9.1893	18.7.1963	1	1913	6	6	0	3.00	–	–	–/–	–	–	–
Cox Joseph Lovell	28.6.1886	4.7.1971	3	1913	17	12*	0	3.40	4	2-74	0/0	61.25	1	–
Cripps Godfrey	19.10.1865	27.7.1943	1	1891	21	18	0	10.50	0	0-23	0/0	–	0	–
Crisp Robert James	28.5.1911	2.3.1994	9	1935–1935	123	35	0	10.25	20	5-99	1/0	37.35	3	–
Cronje Wessel Johannes ("Hansie")	25.9.1969	1.6.2002	68	1991–1999	3,714	135	6	36.41	43	3-14	0/0	29.95	33	188
Cullinan Daryll John	4.3.1967		70	1992–2000	4,554	275*	14	44.21	2	1-10	0/0	35.50	67	138
Curnow Sydney Harry	16.12.1907	28.7.1986	7	1930–1931	168	47	0	12.00	–	–	–/–	–	5	–
Dalton Eric Londesbrough	2.12.1906	3.6.1981	15	1929–1938	698	117	2	31.72	12	4-59	0/0	40.83	5	–
Davies Eric Quail	26.8.1909	11.11.1976	5	1935–1938	9	3	0	1.80	7	4-75	0/0	68.71	0	–
Dawson Alan Charles	27.11.1969		2	2003	10	10	0	10.00	5	2-20	0/0	23.40	0	19
Dawson Oswald Charles	1.9.1919	22.12.2008	9	1947–1948	293	55	0	20.92	10	2-57	0/0	57.80	10	–
Deane Hubert Gouvaine ("Nummy")	21.7.1895	21.10.1939	17	1924–1930	628	93	0	25.12	3	2-32	0/0	30.66	8	–
de Bruyn Zander	5.7.1975		3	2004	155	83	0	38.75	3	2-35	0/0	30.77	1	1/2
de Lange Marchant	13.10.1990		2	2011	9	9	0	4.50	9	7-81	1/0	–	1	–
de Villiers Abraham Benjamin	17.2.1984		89	2004–2013	6,827	278*	18	51.71	2	2-49	0/0	52.00	161/3	154‡/51
de Villiers Petrus Stephanus ("Fanie")	13.10.1964		18	1993–1997	359	67*	0	18.89	85	6-23	5/2	24.27	11	83
de Wet Friedel	26.6.1980		2	2009	20	20	0	10.00	6	4-55	0/0	31.00	–	–
Dippenaar Hendrik Human ("Boeta")	14.6.1977		38	1999–2006	1,718	177*	3	30.14	–	0-1	0/0	–	27	101‡/1
Dixon Cecil Donovan	12.2.1891	9.9.1969	1	1913	0	0	0	0.00	3	2-62	0/0	–	1	–
Donald Allan Anthony (CY 1992)	20.10.1966		72	1991–2001	652	37	0	10.68	330	8-71	20/3	22.25	18	164
Dower Robert Reid	4.6.1876	15.9.1964	1	1898	9	9	0	4.50	–	–	–/–	–	2	–
Draper Ronald George	24.12.1926		2	1949	25	15	0	8.33	–	–	–/–	–	2	–
Duckworth Christopher Anthony Russell	22.3.1933		2	1956	28	13	0	7.00	–	–	–/–	–	3	–
Dumbrill Richard	19.11.1938		5	1965–1966	153	36	0	15.30	9	4-30	0/0	37.33	3	–
Duminy Jacobus Petrus	16.12.1897	31.1.1980	3	1927–1929	30	12	0	5.00	1	1-17	0/0	39.00	1	–
Duminy Jean-Paul	14.4.1984		21	2008–2013	888	166	2	32.88	20	3-67	0/0	39.60	15	115/48
Dunell Owen Robert	15.7.1856	21.10.1929	1	1888	42	26*	0	14.00	0	–	–/–	–	–	–
Du Plessis Francois	13.7.1984		11	2012–2013	782	137	3	60.15	0	0-1	0/0	–	7	47/15
Du Preez John Harcourt	14.11.1942		2	1966	0	0	0	0.00	0	2-22	0/0	17.00	2	–

	Born	Died	Tests	Test Career	Runs	HS	100s	Avge	Wkts	BB	5/10	Avge	Ct/St	O/T
Du Toit Jacobus Francois	2.4.1869	10.7.1909	1	1891	2	2*	0	–	1	1-47	0/0	47.00	1	–
Dyer Dennis Victor	2.5.1914	16.6.1990	3	1947	96	62	0	16.00	–	–	–/–	–	0	6
Eksteen Clive Edward	2.12.1966		7	1993–1999	91	22	0	10.11	8	3-12	0/0	61.75	5	5
Elgar Dean	11.6.1987		7	2012–2013	215	103*	1	30.71	1	1-3	0/0	21.00	6	
Elgie Michael Kelsey ("Kim")	6.3.1933		3	1961	75	56	0	12.50	0	0-18	0/0	–	4	
Elworthy Steven	23.2.1965		4	1998–2002	72	48	0	18.00	13	4-66	0/0	34.15	1	39
Endean William Russell	31.5.1924	28.6.2003	28	1951–1957	1,630	162*	3	33.95	–	–	–/–	–	41	
Farrer William Stephen ("Buster")	8.12.1936		6	1961–1963	221	40	0	27.62	–	–	–/–	–	2	
Faulkner George Aubrey	17.12.1881	10.9.1930	25	1905–1924	1,754	204	4	40.79	82	7-84	4/0	26.58	20	
Fellows-Smith Jonathan Payn	3.2.1932	28.9.2013	4	1960	166	35	0	27.66	0	0-13	0/0	–	2	
Fichardt Charles Gustav	20.3.1870	30.5.1923	2	1891–1895	15	10	0	3.75	–	–	–/–	–	2	
Finlason Charles Edward	19.2.1860	31.7.1917	1	1888	6	6	0	3.00	0	0-7	0/0	–	0	
Floquet Claude Eugene	3.11.1884	22.11.1963	1	1909	12	11*	0	12.00	0	0-24	0/0	–	0	
Francis Howard Henry	26.5.1868	7.1.1936	2	1898	39	29	0	9.75	–	–	–/–	–	1	
Francois Cyril Matthew	20.6.1897	26.5.1944	5	1922	252	72	0	31.50	6	3-23	0/0	37.50	5	
Frank Charles Newton	27.11.1891	25.12.1961	3	1921	236	152	1	39.33	–	–	–/–	–	0	
Frank William Hughes Bowker	23.11.1872	16.2.1945	1	1895	7	5	0	3.50	1	1-52	0/0	52.00	0	
Fuller Edward Russell Henry	2.8.1931	19.7.2008	7	1952–1957	64	17	0	8.00	22	5-66	1/0	30.36	3	
Fullerton George Murray	8.12.1922	19.11.2002	7	1947–1951	325	88	0	25.00	–	–	–/–	–	10/2	
Funston Kenneth James	3.12.1925	15.4.2005	18	1952–1957	824	92	0	25.75	–	–	–/–	–	7	
Gamsy Dennis	17.2.1940		2	1969	39	30*	0	19.50	–	–	–/–	–	5	
Gibbs Herschelle Herman	23.2.1974		90	1996–2007	6,167	228	14	41.95	0	0-4	0/0	–	94	248/23
Gleeson Robert Anthony	6.12.1873	27.9.1919	1	1895	4	3	0	2.00	–	–	–/–	–	2	
Glover George Keyworth	13.5.1870	15.11.1938	1	1895	21	18*	0	21.00	1	1-28	0/0	28.00	0	
Goddard Trevor Leslie	1.8.1931		41	1955–1969	2,516	112	1	34.46	123	6-53	5/0	26.22	48	
Gordon Norman	6.8.1911		5	1938	8	7*	0	2.00	20	5-103	2/0	40.35	1	
Graham Robert	16.9.1877	21.4.1946	2	1898	6	4	0	1.50	3	2-22	0/0	42.33	2	
Grieveson Ronald Eustace	24.8.1909	24.7.1998	2	1938	114	75	0	57.00	–	–	–/–	–	7/3	
Griffin Geoffrey Merton	12.6.1939	16.11.2006	2	1960	25	14	0	6.25	8	4-87	0/0	24.00	0	
Hall Alfred Ewart	23.11.1896	1.1.1964	7	1922–1930	11	5	0	1.83	40	7-63	3/1	22.15	4	
Hall Andrew James	31.7.1975		21	2001–2006	760	163	1	26.20	45	3-1	0/0	35.93	16	88/2
Hall Glen Gordon	24.5.1938	26.6.1987	1	1964	0	0	0	0.00	1	1-94	0/0	94.00	0	
Halliwell Ernest Austin (CY 1905)	7.9.1864	2.10.1919	8	1891–1902	188	57	0	12.53	–	–	–/–	–	10/2	
Halse Clive Gray	28.2.1935	27.4.1991	3	1963	30	19*	0	25.00	6	3-50	0/0	43.33	1	
² Hands Philip Albert Myburgh	18.3.1890	27.4.1951	7	1913–1924	300	83	0	25.00	0	0-1	0/0	–	3	
³ Hands Reginald Harry Myburgh	26.7.1888	20.4.1918	1	1913	7	7	0	3.50	–	–	–/–	–	0	

Name	Born	Died	Tests	Test Career	Runs	HS	100s	Avge	Wkts	BB	5/10	Avge	Ct/St	OIT
Hanley Martin Andrew	10.11.1918	2.6.2000	1	1948	0	0	0	0.00	1	1-57	0/0	88.00	0	3
Harris Paul Lee	2.11.1978		37	2006–2010	460	46	0	20.00	103	6-127	3/0	37.87	16	
Harris Terence Anthony	27.8.1916	7.3.1993	3	1947–1948	100	60	0	25.00					1	
Hartigan Gerald Patrick Desmond	30.12.1884	7.1.1955	5	1912–1913	114	51	0	11.40	1	1-72	0/0	141.00	0	
Harvey Robert Lyon	14.9.1911	20.7.2000	2	1935	51	28	0	12.75					0	
Hathorn Christopher Mailand Howard	7.4.1878	17.5.1920	12	1902–1910	325	102	1	17.10					5	
Hayward Mornantau ("Nantie")	6.3.1977		16	1999–2004	66	14	0	7.33	54	5-56	1/0	29.79	4	21
¹,² Hearne Frank	23.11.1858	14.7.1949	4†	1891–1895	121	30	0	15.12	2	2-40	0/0	20.00	2	
¹ Hearne George Alfred Lawrence	27.3.1888	13.11.1978	3	1922–1924	59	28	0	11.80					3	
Heine Peter Samuel	28.6.1928	4.2.2005	14	1955–1961	209	31	0	9.95	58	6-58	4/0	25.08	8	4
Henderson Claude William	14.6.1972		7	2001–2002	65	30	0	9.28	22	4-116	0/0	42.18	2	3
Henry Omar	23.1.1952		3	1992	53	34	0	17.66	3	2-56	0/0	63.00	2	
Hime Charles Frederick William	24.10.1869	6.12.1940	1	1895	8	8	0	4.00	1	1-20	0/0	31.00	0	
Hudson Andrew Charles	17.3.1965		35	1991–1997	2,007	163	4	33.45					36	89
Hutchinson Philip	25.1.1862	30.9.1925	2	1888	14	11	0	3.50					3	
Imran Tahir	27.3.1979		13	2011–2013	90	29*	0	11.25	36	5-32	1/0	43.08	5	136
Ironside David Ernest James	2.5.1925	21.8.2005	3	1953	37	73	0	18.50	15	5-51	1/0	18.33	1	
Irvine Brian Lee	9.3.1944		4	1969	353	102	1	50.42					2	
Jack Steven Douglas	4.8.1970		2	1994	7	7	0	3.50	8	4-69	0/0	24.50	0	2
Johnson Clement Lecky	31.3.1871	31.5.1908	1	1895	10	7	0	5.00	0	0-57	0/0		1	
Kallis Jacques Henry (CY 2013)	16.10.1975		165§	1995–2013	13,206	224	45	55.25	291	6-54	5/0	32.63	196	320‡/25
Keith Headley James	25.10.1927	17.11.1997	8	1952–1956	318	73	0	21.20	0	0-19	0/0		9	
Kemp Justin Miles	2.10.1977		5	2000–2005	80	55	0	13.33	9	3-33	0/0	24.66	3	79‡/8
Kempis Gustav Adolph	4.8.1865	19.5.1890	1	1888	0	0*	0	0.00	4	3-53	0/0	19.00	1	
² Khan Imran	27.4.1984		1	2008	20	20	0	20.00					1	
² Kirsten Gary (CY 2004)	23.11.1967		101	1993–2003	7,289	275	21	45.27	2	1-0	0/0	71.00	83	185
² Kirsten Peter Noel	14.5.1955		12	1991–1994	626	104	1	31.30	0	0-5	0/0		2	40
Kleinveldt Rory Keith	15.3.1983		4	2012	27	17*	0	9.00	10	3-65	0/0	42.20	2	106
Klusener Lance (CY 2000)	4.9.1971		49	1996–2004	1,906	174*	4	32.86	80	8-64	1/0	37.91	34	171
Kotze Johannes Jacobus ("Kodgee")	7.8.1879	7.7.1931	3	1902–1907	2	2	0	0.40	6	3-64	0/0	40.50	3	
Kuiper Adrian Paul	24.8.1959		1	1991	34	34	0	17.00					1	25
Kuys Frederick	21.3.1870	12.9.1953	1	1898	26	26	0	13.00	2	2-31	0/0	15.50	0	
Lance Herbert Roy ("Tiger")	6.6.1940	10.11.2010	13	1961–1969	591	70	0	28.14	12	3-30	0/0	39.91	7	
Langeveldt Charl Kenneth	17.12.1974		6	2004–2005	16	17*	0	8.00	16	5-46	1/0	37.06	2	72/9
Langton Arthur Chudleigh Beaumont ("Chud")	2.3.1912	27.11.1942	15	1935–1938	298	73*	0	15.68	40	5-58	2/0	45.67	8	

§ *Kallis's figures exclude 83 runs, one wicket and four catches for the ICC World XI v Australia in the Super Series Test in 2005-06.*

Name	Born	Died	Tests	Test Career	Runs	HS	100s	Avge	Wkts	BB	Avge	5/10	Ct/St	O/T
Lawrence Godfrey Bernard	31.3.1932	22.9.1963	5	1961	141	43	0	17.62	28	8-53	18.28	2/0	2	
le Roux Frederick Louis	5.2.1882	30.1.1976	1	1913	1	1	0	0.50	0	0-5	–	0/0	0	
Lewis Percy Tyson	2.10.1884		1	1913	0	0	0	0.00	–	–	–	–	0	
[1]Liebenberg Gerhardus Frederick Johannes	7.4.1972		5	1997–1998	104	45	0	13.00	–	–	–	–	5	4
[1]Lindsay Denis Thomson	4.9.1939	30.11.2005	19	1963–1969	1,130	182	3	37.66	–	–	–	–	57/2	
[1]Lindsay John Dixon	8.9.1908	31.8.1990	3	1947	21	9*	0	7.00	–	–	–	–	4/1	
Lindsay Nevil Vernon	30.7.1886	2.2.1976	1	1921	35	29	0	17.50	0	0-20	–	0/0	1	
Ling William Victor Stone	3.10.1891	26.9.1960	6	1921–1922	168	38	0	16.80	–	–	–	–	1	
Llewellyn Charles Bennett (CY 1911)	26.9.1876	7.6.1964	15	1895–1912	544	90	0	20.14	48	6-92	29.60	4/1	7	
Lundie Eric Balfour	15.3.1888	12.9.1917	1	1913	1	1	0	1.00	4	4-101	26.75	0/0	0	
Macaulay Michael John	19.4.1939		1	1964	33	21	0	16.50	2	1-10	36.50	0/0	0	
McCarthy Cuan Neil	24.3.1929	14.8.2000	15	1948–1951	28	5	0	3.11	36	6-43	41.94	2/0	6	
McClew Derrick John ("Jackie") (CY 1956)	11.3.1929	9.6.1998	34	1951–1967	2,440	255*	7	42.06	0	0-7	–	0/0	18	
McKenzie Neil Douglas (CY 2009)	24.11.1975		58	2000–2008	3,253	226	5	37.39	0	0-1	–	0/0	54	64/2
McKinnon Atholl Henry	20.8.1932	2.12.1983	8	1960–1966	107	33*	0	17.83	26	4-128	35.57	0/0	1	
McLaren Ryan	9.2.1983		1	2009	33	33*	0	–	1	1-30	43.00	0/0	0	40/10
McLean Roy Alastair (CY 1961)	9.7.1930	26.8.2007	40	1951–1964	2,120	142	5	30.28	0	0-1	–	0/0	23	
McMillan Brian Mervin	22.12.1963		38	1992–1998	1,968	113	0	39.36	75	4-65	33.82	2/0	49	78
McMillan Quintin	23.6.1904	3.7.1948	13	1929–1931	306	50*	0	18.00	36	5-66	34.52	1/0	8	
Mann Norman Bertram Fleetwood ("Tufty")	28.12.1920	31.7.1952	19	1947–1951	400	52	0	13.33	58	6-59	33.10	0/0	3	
Mansell Percy Neville Frank MBE	16.3.1920	9.5.1995	13	1951–1955	355	90	0	17.75	11	3-58	66.90	0/0	15	
Markham Lawrence Anderson	12.9.1924	5.8.2000	1	1948	20	20	0	20.00	4	1-34	72.00	0/0	0	
Marx Waldemar Frederick Eric	4.7.1895	2.6.1974	3	1921	125	36	0	20.83	4	3-85	36.00	0/0	0	
Matthews Craig Russell	15.2.1965		18	1992–1995	348	62*	0	18.31	52	5-42	28.88	2/0	14	56
Meintjes Douglas James	9.6.1890	17.7.1979	2	1922	43	21	0	14.33	6	3-38	19.16	0/0	3	
Melle Michael George	3.6.1930	28.12.2003	7	1949–1952	68	17	0	8.50	26	6-71	32.73	2/0	4	
Melville Alan (CY 1948)	19.5.1910	18.4.1983	11	1938–1948	894	189	4	52.58	–	–	–	–	8	
Middleton James	30.9.1865	23.12.1913	6	1895–1902	52	22	0	7.42	24	5-51	18.41	2/0	1	
Mills Charles Henry	26.11.1867	26.7.1948	1	1891	25	21	0	12.50	2	2-83	41.50	0/0	1	
Milton Sir William Henry	3.12.1854	6.3.1930	3	1888–1891	68	21	0	11.33	2	1-5	24.00	0/0	2	
Mitchell Bruce (CY 1936)	8.1.1909	1.7.1995	42	1929–1948	3,471	189*	8	48.88	27	5-87	51.11	1/0	56	
Mitchell Frank (CY 1902)	13.8.1872	11.10.1935	3†	1912	28	12	0	4.66	–	–	–	–	0	
[2]Morkel Denijs Paul Beck	25.11.1906	6.10.1980	16	1927–1931	663	88	0	24.55	18	4-93	45.61	0/0	13	
[2]Morkel Johannes Albertus	10.6.1981		1	2008	58	58	0	58.00	1	1-44	132.00	0/0	0	
[2]Morkel Morne	6.10.1984		53	2006–2013	673	40	0	12.94	183	6-23	29.91	6/0	14	56/42 70/36
Murray Anton Ronald Andrew	30.4.1922	17.4.1995	10	1952–1953	289	109	1	22.23	18	4-169	39.44	4/0	3	

Name	Born	Died	Tests	Test Career	Runs	HS	100s	Avge	Wkts	BB	5/10	Avge	Ct/St	O/T
Nel Andre	15.7.1977		36	2001–2008	337	34	0	9.91	123	6-32	3/1	31.86	16	79/2
Nel John Desmond	10.7.1928		6	1949–1957	150	38	0	13.63					1	
Newberry Claude	1889	1.8.1916	4	1913	62	16	0	7.75	11	4-72	0/0	24.36	3	
Newson Edward Serrurier OBE	2.12.1910	24.4.1988	3	1930–1938	30	16	0	7.50	4	2-58	0/0	66.25	3	
Ngam Mfuneko	29.1.1979		3	2000	0	0*	0	—	11	3-26	0/0	17.18	1	
Nicholson Frank	17.9.1909	30.7.1982	4	1935	76	29	0	10.85					3	
Nicholson John Fairless William	19.7.1899	13.12.1935	1	1927	179	78	0	35.80	0	0-5	0/0		0	
Norton Norman Ogilvie	11.5.1881	27.6.1968	1	1909	9	7	0	4.50	4	4-47	0/0	11.75	0	
[1] Nourse Arthur Dudley (CY 1948)	12.11.1910	14.8.1981	34	1935–1951	2,960	231	9	53.81	0	0-0	0/0		12	
[2] Nourse Arthur William ("Dave")	25.11.1879	8.7.1948	45	1902–1924	2,234	111	1	29.78	41	4-25	0/0	37.87	43	
Ntini Makhaya	6.7.1977		101	1997–2009	699	32*	0	9.84	390	7-37	18/4	28.82	25	172½/10
Nupen Eiulf Peter ("Buster")	1.1.1902	29.1.1977	17	1921–1935	348	69	0	14.50	50	6-46	5/1	35.76	9	
Ochse Arthur Edward	11.3.1870	11.4.1918	2	1888	16	8	0	4.00					0	
Ochse Arthur Lennox	11.10.1899	5.5.1949	7	1927–1929	11	4*	0	3.66	10	4-79	0/0	36.20	1	
O'Linn Sidney	5.5.1927		7	1960–1961	297	98	0	27.00					4	
Ontong Justin Lee	4.1.1980		2	2001–2004	57	32	0	19.00	1	1-79	0/0	133.00	1	27½/12
Owen-Smith Harold Geoffrey ("Tuppy") (CY 1930)	18.2.1909	28.2.1990	5	1929	252	129	1	42.00	0	0-3	0/0		4	
Palm Archibald William	8.6.1901	17.8.1966	2	1927	15	13	0	7.50						
Parker George Macdonald	27.5.1899	1.5.1969	1	1924	3	2*	0	1.50	8	6-152	1/0	34.12	0	
Parkin Durant Clifford	20.2.1873	20.3.1936	1	1891	6	6	0	3.00	3	3-82	0/0	27.33		
Parnell Wayne Dillon	30.7.1989		3	2009	34	22	0	17.00	5	2-17	0/0	45.40	1	33/24
Partridge Joseph Titus	9.12.1932	6.6.1988	11	1963–1964	73	13*	0	10.42	44	7-91	3/0	31.20	6	
Pearse Charles Ormerod Cato	10.10.1884	7.5.1953	2	1910	55	31	0	9.16	3	3-56	0/0	35.33	1	
Pegler Sidney James	28.7.1888	10.9.1972	16	1902–1924	356	35*	0	15.47	47	7-65	2/0	33.44	5	
Petersen Alviro Nathan	25.11.1980		28	2009–2013	1,825	182	5	38.82	1	1-2	0/0	62.00	23	21/2
Peterson Robin John	4.8.1979		14	2003–2013	433	84	0	28.86	35	5-33	1/0	36.57	8	77/20
Philander Vernon Darryl	24.6.1985		20	2011–2013	469	74	0	23.45	105	6-44	9/2	18.00	5	13/7
Pithey Anthony John	17.7.1933	17.11.2006	17	1956–1964	819	154	1	31.50	0	0-5	0/0		6	
[2] Pithey David Bartlett	4.10.1936		8	1963–1966	138	55	0	12.54	12	6-58	1/0	48.08	3	
Plimsoll Jack Bruce	27.10.1917	11.11.1999	1	1947	16	8*	0	16.00	3	3-128	0/0	47.66		
[1,2] Pollock Peter Maclean (CY 1966)	30.6.1941		28	1961–1969	607	75*	0	21.67	116	6-38	9/1	24.18	9	
[2] Pollock Robert Graeme (CY 1966)	27.2.1944		23	1963–1969	2,256	274	7	60.97	4	2-50	0/0	51.00	17	
[1,2] Pollock Shaun Maclean (CY 2003)	16.7.1973		108	1995–2007	3,781	111	2	32.31	421	7-87	16/1	23.11	72	294½/12
Poore Robert Montagu (CY 1900)	20.3.1866	14.7.1938	3	1895	76	20	0	12.66	1	1-4	0/0	4.00	3	
Pothecary James Edward	6.12.1933		3	1960	26	12	0	6.50	9	4-58	0/0	39.33	2	

	Born	Died	Tests	Test Career	Runs	HS	100s	Avge	Wkts	BB	5/10	Avge	Ct/St	O/T
Powell Albert William	18.7.1873	11.9.1948	1	1898	16	11	0	8.00	1	1-10	0/0	10.00	2	
Pretorius Dewald	6.12.1977		4	2001–2003	22	9	0	7.33	6	4-115	0/0	71.66	2	
Prince Ashwell Gavin	28.5.1977		66	2001–2011	3,665	162*	11	41.64	1	1-2	0/0	47.00	47	49½/1
Prince Charles Frederick Henry	11.9.1874	2.2.1949	1	1898	6	5	0	3.00	—	—	-/-	—	0	
Pringle Meyrick Wayne	22.6.1966		4	1991–1995	67	33	0	16.75	5	2-62	0/0	54.00	2	17
Procter Michael John (CY 1970)	15.9.1946		7	1966–1969	226	48	0	25.11	41	6-73	1/0	15.02	4	
Promnitz Henry Louis Ernest	23.2.1904	7.9.1983	2	1927	14	5	0	3.50	8	5-58	1/0	20.12	2	
Quinn Neville Anthony	21.2.1908	5.8.1934	12	1929–1931	90	28	0	6.00	35	6-92	1/0	32.71	1	
Reid Norman	26.12.1890	6.6.1947	1	1921	17	11	0	8.50	2	2-63	0/0	31.50	0	
Rhodes Jonathan Neil (CY 1999)	27.7.1969		52	1992–2000	2,532	117	3	35.66	0	0-0	0/0	—	34	245
Richards Alfred Renfrew	14.12.1867	9.1.1904	1	1895	6	6	0	3.00	—	—	-/-	—	0	
² Richards Barry Anderson (CY 1969)	21.7.1945		4	1969	508	140	2	72.57	1	1-12	0/0	26.00	3	
² Richards William Henry Matthews	26.3.1862	4.1.1903	1	1888	4	4	0	2.00	—	—	-/-	—	0	
Richardson David John	16.9.1959		42	1991–1997	1,359	109	0	24.26	—	—	-/-	—	150/2	122
Robertson John Benjamin	5.6.1906	5.7.1985	3	1935	51	17	0	10.20	6	3-143	0/0	53.50	2	
Rose-Innes Albert	16.2.1868	22.11.1946	2	1888	14	13	0	3.50	5	5-43	1/0	17.80	2	
Routledge Thomas Walter	18.4.1867	9.5.1927	4	1891–1895	72	24	0	9.00	—	—	-/-	—	2	
² Rowan Athol Matthew Burchell	7.2.1921	22.2.1998	15	1947–1951	290	41	0	17.05	54	5-68	4/0	38.59	7	
² Rowan Eric Alfred Burchell (CY 1952)	20.7.1909	30.4.1993	26	1935–1951	1,965	236	3	43.66	0	0-0	0/0	—	14	
Rowe George Alexander	15.6.1874	8.1.1950	5	1895–1902	26	13*	0	4.33	15	5-115	1/0	30.40	1	
Rudolph Jacobus Andries	4.5.1981		48	2003–2012	2,622	222*	6	35.43	4	1-1	0/0	108.00	29	43½/1
Rushmere Mark Weir	7.1.1965		1	1991	6	3	0	3.00	—	—	-/-	—	0	4
Samuelson Sivert Vause	21.11.1883	18.11.1958	1	1909	22	15	0	11.00	0	0-64	0/0	—	0	
Schultz Brett Nolan	26.8.1970		9	1992–1997	9	6	0	1.50	37	5-48	2/0	20.24	2	1
Schwarz Reginald Oscar (CY 1908)	4.5.1875	18.11.1918	20	1905–1912	374	61	0	13.85	55	6-47	2/0	25.76	18	
Seccull Arthur William	14.9.1868	20.7.1945	1	1895	23	17*	0	23.00	2	2-37	0/0	18.50	1	
Seymour Michael Arthur ("Kelly")	5.6.1936		7	1963–1969	84	36	0	12.00	9	3-80	0/0	65.33	3	
Shalders William Alfred	12.2.1880	18.3.1917	12	1898–1907	355	42	0	16.13	1	1-6	0/0	6.00	3	
Shepstone George Harold	9.4.1876	3.7.1940	2	1895–1898	38	21	0	9.50	0	0-8	0/0	—	2	
Sherwell Percy William	17.8.1880	17.4.1948	13	1905–1910	427	115	1	23.72	—	—	-/-	—	20/16	
Siedle Ivan Julian ("Jack")	11.1.1903	24.8.1982	18	1927–1935	977	141	1	28.73	1	1-7	0/0	7.00	7	
Sinclair James Hugh	16.10.1876	23.2.1913	25	1895–1910	1,069	106	3	23.23	63	6-26	1/0	31.68	9	
Smith Charles James Edward	25.12.1872	27.3.1947	3	1902	106	45	0	21.20	—	—	-/-	—	2	
Smith Frederick William	31.3.1861	17.4.1914	1	1888–1895	45	12	0	9.00	—	—	-/-	—	1	
§ Smith Graeme Craig (CY 2004)	1.2.1981		117	2001–2013	9,208	277	27	50.04	8	2-145	0/0	110.62	161	196½/33

§ G. C. Smith's figures exclude 12 runs and three catches for the ICC World XI v Australia in the Super Series Test in 2005-06.

	Born	Died	Tests	Test Career	Runs	HS	100s	Avge	Wkts	BB	5/10	Avge	Ct/St	O/T
Smith Vivian Ian	23.2.1925		9	1947–1957	39	11*	0	3.90	12	4-143	0/0	64.08	3	–
Snell Richard Peter	12.9.1968		5	1991–1994	95	48	0	13.57	19	4-74	0/0	28.31	1	42
[2]**Snooke** Sibley John ("Tip")	1.2.1881	14.8.1966	26	1905–1922	1,008	103	1	22.40	35	8-70	1/1	20.05	24	–
[2]**Snooke** Stanley de la Courtte	11.11.1878	6.4.1959	1	1907	0	0	0	0.00	–	–	–/–	–	2	–
Solomon William Rodger Thomson	23.4.1872	13.7.1964	1	1898	4	2	0	2.00	–	–	–/–	–	1	–
Stewart Robert Burnard	3.9.1856	12.9.1913	1	1888	13	9	0	6.50	–	–	–/–	–	2	–
Steyn Dale Willem (CY 2013)	27.6.1983		69	2004–2013	955	76	0	14.25	350	7-51	22/5	22.90	18	77‡/33
Steyn Philippus Jeremia Rudolf	30.6.1967		3	1994	127	46	0	21.16	–	–	–/–	–	3	1
Stricker Louis Anthony	26.5.1884	5.2.1960	13	1909–1912	344	48	0	14.33	1	1-36	0/0	105.00	3	–
Strydom Pieter Coenraad	10.6.1969		2	1999	35	30	0	11.66	0	0-27	0/0	–	1	10
Susskind Manfred Fred	8.6.1891	9.7.1957	5	1924	268	65	0	33.50	–	–	–/–	–	1	–
Symcox Patrick Leonard	14.4.1960		20	1993–1998	741	108	1	28.50	37	4-69	0/0	43.32	5	80
Taberer Henry Melville	7.10.1870	5.6.1932	1	1902	2	2	0	2.00	1	1-25	0/0	48.00		–
[2]**Tancred** Augustus Bernard	20.8.1865	23.11.1911	2	1888	87	29	0	29.00	–	–	–/–	–	2	–
[2]**Tancred** Louis Joseph	7.10.1876	28.7.1934	14	1902–1913	530	97	0	21.20	–	–	–/–	–	3	–
[2]**Tancred** Vincent Maximillian	7.7.1875	3.6.1904	1	1898	25	18	0	12.50	–	–	–/–	–	1	–
[2]**Tapscott** George Lancelot ("Dusty")	7.11.1889	13.12.1940	1	1913	5	4	0	2.50	–	–	–/–	–		–
[2]**Tapscott** Lionel Eric ("Doodles")	18.3.1894	7.7.1934	2	1922	58	50*	0	29.00	0	0-2	0/0	–	1	–
Tayfield Hugh Joseph (CY 1956)	30.1.1929	24.2.1994	37	1949–1960	862	75	0	16.90	170	9-113	14/2	25.91	26	–
[2]**Taylor** Alistair Innes ("Scotch")	25.7.1925	7.2.2004	2	1956	18	12	0	9.00	–	–	–/–	–	0	–
[2]**Taylor** Daniel	9.1.1887	24.1.1957	2	1913	85	36	0	21.25	–	–	–/–	–	3	–
[2]**Taylor** Herbert Wilfred (CY 1925)	5.5.1889	8.2.1973	42	1912–1931	2,936	176	7	40.77	5	3-15	0/0	31.20	19	–
[2]**Terbrugge** David John	31.1.1977		7	1998–2003	16	4*	0	5.33	20	5-46	1/0	25.85	4	4
Theunissen Nicolaas Hendrik Christiaan de Jong	4.5.1867	9.11.1929	1	1888	2	2*	0	2.00	1	0-51	0/0	–		–
Thornton George	24.12.1867	31.1.1939	1	1902	1	1*	0	–	1	1-20	0/0	20.00		–
Tomlinson Denis Stanley	4.9.1910	11.7.1993	1	1935	9	9	0	9.00	4	0-38	0/0	–		0‡
Traicos Athanasios John	17.5.1947		3†	1969	8	5*	0	4.00	4	2-70	0/0	51.75	4	–
Trimborn Patrick Henry Joseph	18.5.1940		4	1966–1969	13	11*	0	6.50	11	3-12	0/0	23.36	7	–
Tsolekile Thami Lungisa	9.10.1980		3	2004	47	22	0	9.40	–	–	–/–	–	6	–
Tsotsobe Lonwabo Lennox	7.3.1984		5	2010–2010	19	8*	0	6.33	9	3-43	0/0	49.77	4	61/18
[1]**Tuckett** Lindsay	6.2.1919		9	1947–1948	131	40*	0	11.90	19	5-68	2/0	51.57	9	–
[1]**Tuckett** Lindsay Richard ("Len")	19.4.1885	8.4.1963	1	1913	0	0*	0	0.00	–	–	–/–	–	2	–
Twentyman-Jones Percy Sydney	13.9.1876	8.3.1954	1	1902	0	0	0	0.00	–	–	–/–	–	0	–
van der Bijl Pieter Gerhard Vintcent	21.10.1907	16.2.1973	5	1938	460	125	1	51.11	–	–	–/–	–	1	–
van der Merwe Edward Alexander	9.11.1903	26.2.1971	2	1929–1935	27	19	0	9.00	–	–	–/–	–	3	–
van der Merwe Peter Laurence	14.3.1937	23.1.2013	15	1963–1966	533	76	0	25.38	1	1-6	0/0	22.00	11	–

	Born	Died	Tests	Test Career	Runs	HS	100s	Avge	Wkts	BB	5/10	Avge	Ct/St	O/T
van Jaarsveld Martin	18.6.1974		9	2002–2004	397	73	0	30.53	0	0-28	0/0	–	11	11
van Ryneveld Clive Berrange	19.3.1928		19	1951–1957	724	83	0	26.81	17	4-67	0/0	39.47	14	
Varnals George Derek	24.7.1935		3	1964	97	23	0	16.16	0	0-2	0/0	–	0	
Viljoen Kenneth George	14.5.1910	21.1.1974	27	1930–1948	1,365	124	2	28.43	0	0-10	0/0	–	5	
Vincent Cyril Leverton	16.2.1902	24.8.1968	25	1927–1935	526	60	0	20.23	84	6-51	3/0	31.32	27	
Vintcent Charles Henry	2.9.1866	28.9.1943	3	1888–1891	26	9	0	4.33	4	3-88	0/0	48.25	1	
Vogler Albert Edward Ernest (CY 1908)	28.11.1876	9.8.1946	15	1905–1910	340	65	0	17.00	64	7-94	5/1	22.73	20	
²Wade Herbert Frederick	14.9.1905	23.11.1980	10	1935–1935	327	40*	0	20.43	–	–	–/–	–	4	
²Wade Walter Wareham ("Billy")	18.6.1914	31.5.2003	11	1938–1949	511	125	1	28.38	–	–	–/–	–	15/2	
Waite John Henry Bickford	19.1.1930	22.6.2011	50	1951–1964	2,405	134	4	30.44	–	–	–/–	–	124/17	
Walter Kenneth Alexander	5.11.1939	13.9.2003	2	1961	11	10	0	3.66	6	4-63	0/0	32.83	3	
Ward Thomas Alfred	2.8.1887	16.2.1936	23	1912–1924	459	64	0	13.90	–	–	–/–	–	19/13	
Watkins John Cecil	10.4.1923		15	1949–1956	612	92	0	23.53	29	4-22	0/0	28.13	12	
Wesley Colin	5.9.1937		3	1960	49	35	0	9.80	–	–	–/–	–	1	
Wessels Kepler Christoffel (CY 1995)	14.9.1957		16†	1991–1994	1,027	118	2	38.03	–	–	–/–	–	12	55‡
Westcott Richard John	19.9.1927	16.1.2013	5	1953–1957	166	62	0	18.44	0	0-22	0/0	–	1	
White Gordon Charles	5.2.1882	17.10.1918	17	1905–1912	872	147	2	30.06	9	4-47	0/0	33.44	10	
Willoughby Charl Myles	3.12.1974		2	2003	–	–	–	–	1	1-47	0/0	125.00	0	3
Willoughby Joseph Thomas	7.11.1874	11.3.1952	2	1895	8	5	0	2.00	6	2-37	0/0	26.50	0	
Wimble Clarence Skelton	22.4.1861	28.1.1930	1	1891	0	0	0	0.00	–	–	–/–	–	0	
Winslow Paul Lyndhurst	21.5.1929	24.5.2011	5	1949–1955	186	108	1	20.66	–	–	–/–	–	1	
Wynne Owen Edgar	1.6.1919	13.7.1975	6	1948–1949	219	50	0	18.25	–	–	–/–	–	3	
Zondeki Monde	25.7.1982		6	2003–2008	82	59	0	16.40	19	6-39	1/0	25.26	1	11‡/1
Zulch Johan Wilhelm	2.1.1886	19.5.1924	16	1909–1921	983	150	2	32.76	0	0-2	0/0	–	4	

WEST INDIES (297 players)

	Born	Died	Tests	Test Career	Runs	HS	100s	Avge	Wkts	BB	5/10	Avge	Ct/St	O/T
Achong Ellis Edgar	16.2.1904	30.8.1986	6	1929–1934	81	22	0	8.10	8	2-64	0/0	47.25	6	127
Adams James Clive	9.1.1968		54	1991–2000	3,012	208*	6	41.26	27	5-17	1/0	49.48	48	
Alexander Franz Copeland Murray ("Gerry")	2.11.1928	16.4.2011	25	1957–1960	961	108	1	30.03	–	–	–/–	–	85/5	
Ali Imtiaz	28.7.1954		1	1975	1	1*	0	–	2	2-37	0/0	44.50	0	
Ali Inshan	25.9.1949	24.6.1995	12	1970–1976	172	25	0	10.75	34	5-59	1/0	47.67	7	
Allan David Walter	5.11.1937		5	1961–1966	75	40*	0	12.50	–	–	–/–	–	15/3	
Allen Ian Basil Alston	6.10.1965		2	1991	5	4*	0	–	5	2-69	0/0	36.00	1	

	Born	Died	Test Career	Tests	Runs	HS	100s	Avge	Wkts	BB	5/10	Avge	Ct/St	O/T
Ambrose Curtly Elconn Lynwall (CY 1992)	21.9.1963		1987–2000	98	1,439	53	0	12.40	405	8-45	22/3	20.99	18	176
Arthurton Keith Lloyd Thomas	21.2.1965		1988–1995	33	1,382	157*	2	30.71	1	1-17	0/0	183.00	22	105
Asgarali Nyron Sultan	28.12.1920	5.11.2006	1957	2	62	29	0	15.50					0	
²**Atkinson Denis St Eval**	9.8.1926	9.11.2001	1948–1957	22	922	219	1	31.79	47	7-53	3/0	35.04	11	–
²**Atkinson Eric St Eval**	6.11.1927	29.5.1998	1957–1958	8	126	37	0	15.75	25	5-42	1/0	23.56	2	
Austin Richard Arkwright	5.9.1954		1977	2	22	20	0	11.00	0	0-5	0/0	–	2	1
Austin Ryan Anthony	15.11.1981		2009	2	39	19	0	9.75	3	1-29	0/0	51.66	0	
Bacchus Sheik Faoud Ahamul Fasiel	31.1.1954		1977–1981	19	782	250	1	26.06	0	0-3	0/0	–	17	29
Baichan Leonard	12.5.1946		1974–1975	3	184	105*	1	46.00					2	
Baker Lionel Siome	6.9.1984		2008–2009	4	23	17	0	11.50	5	2-39	0/0	79.00	1	10/3
Banks Omari Ahmed Clemente	17.7.1982		2002–2005	10	318	50*	0	26.50	28	4-87	0/0	48.82	6	5
Baptiste Eldine Ashworth Elderfield	12.3.1960		1983–1989	10	233	87*	0	23.30	16	3-31	0/0	35.18	2	43
Barath Adrian Boris	14.4.1990		2009–2012	15	657	104	1	23.46	0	0-3	0/0	–	13	14/2
Barrett Arthur George	4.4.1944		1970–1974	6	40	19	0	6.66	13	3-43	0/0	46.38	0	
Barrow Ivanhoe Mordecai	16.1.1911	2.4.1979	1929–1939	11	276	105	1	16.23					17/5	
Bartlett Edward Lawson	10.3.1906	21.12.1976	1928–1930	5	131	84	0	18.71					2	
Baugh Carlton Seymour	23.6.1982		2002–2011	21	610	68	0	17.94					43/5	47/3
Benjamin Kenneth Charlie Griffith	8.4.1967		1991–1997	26	222	43*	0	7.92	92	6-66	4/1	30.27	2	26
Benjamin Winston Keithroy Matthew	31.12.1964		1987–1994	21	470	85	0	18.80	61	4-46	0/0	27.01	12	85
Benn Sulieman Jamaal	22.7.1981		2007–2010	17	381	42	0	15.87	51	6-81	3/0	41.41	7	25/17
Bernard David Eddison	19.7.1981		2002–2009	3	202	69	0	40.40	4	2-30	0/0	46.25	0	20/1
Bess Brandon Jeremy	13.12.1987		2010	1	11	11*	0	11.00	1	1-65	0/0	92.00	0	
Best Carlisle Alonza	14.5.1959		1985–1990	8	342	164	1	28.50	0	0-2	0/0	–	6	24
Best Tino la Bertram	26.8.1981		2002–2013	25	401	95	0	12.53	57	6-40	2/0	40.19	6	26/4
Betancourt Nelson	4.6.1887	12.10.1947	1929	1	52	39	0	26.00					–	
Binns Alfred Phillip	24.7.1929	16.1.1998	1952–1955	5	64	27	0	9.14					14/3	
Birkett Lionel Sydney	14.4.1905		1930	4	136	64	0	17.00	1	1-16	0/0	71.00	4	
Bishoo Devendra	6.11.1985		2010–2011	11	143	26	0	13.00	40	5-90	1/0	39.55	8	13/4
Bishop Ian Raphael	24.10.1967		1988–1997	43	632	48	0	12.15	161	6-40	6/0	24.27	4	84
Black Marlon Ian	7.6.1975		2000–2001	6	21	6	0	2.62	12	4-83	0/0	49.75	5	
Boyce Keith David (CY 1974)	11.10.1943	11.10.1996	1970–1975	21	657	95*	0	24.33	60	6-77	2/1	30.01	8	
Bradshaw Ian David Russell	9.7.1974		2005	5	96	33	0	13.71	9	3-73	0/0	60.00	3	62/1
Brathwaite Kraigg Clairmonte	1.12.1992		2010–2013	10	415	68	0	21.84	1	1-43	0/0	50.00	5	
²**Bravo Dwayne John**	7.10.1983		2004–2010	40	2,200	113	3	31.42	86	6-55	0/0	39.83	41	154/37
²**Bravo Darren Michael**	6.2.1989		2010–2013	27	2,011	218	5	44.68	0	–			19	69/10
Breese Gareth Rohan	9.1.1976		2002	1	5	5	0	2.50	2	2-108	0/0	67.50	1	

	Born	Died	Tests	Test Career	Runs	HS	100s	Avge	Wkts	BB	5/10	Avge	Ct/St	O/T
Browne Courtney Oswald	7.12.1970		20	1994–2004	387	68	0	16.12	–	–	–/–	–	79/2	46
Browne Cyril Rutherford	8.10.1890	12.1.1964	4	1928–1929	176	70*	0	25.14	6	2-72	0/0	48.00	7	
Butcher Basil Fitzherbert (CY 1970)	3.9.1933	1.9.2009	44	1958–1969	3,104	209*	7	43.11	5	5-34	0/0	18.00	15	
Butler Lennox Stephen	9.2.1929		1	1954	16	16	0	16.00	2	2-151	0/0	75.50	0	
Butts Clyde Godfrey	8.7.1957		7	1984–1987	108	38	0	15.42	10	4-73	0/0	59.50	2	
Bynoe Michael Robin	23.2.1941		4	1958–1966	111	48	0	18.50	1	1-5	0/0	5.00	4	
Camacho George Stephen	15.10.1945		11	1967–1970	640	87	0	29.09	–	0-12	0/0	–	4	
² **Cameron** Francis James	22.6.1923	10.6.1994	5	1948	151	75*	0	25.16	3	2-74	0/0	92.66	4	
Cameron John Hemsley	8.4.1914	13.2.2000	2	1939	6	5	0	2.00	3	3-66	0/0	29.33	0	
Campbell Sherwin Legay	1.11.1970		52	1994–2001	2,882	208	4	32.38	–	–	–/–	–	47	90
Carew George McDonald	4.6.1910	9.12.1974	4	1934–1948	170	107	1	28.33	–	0-2	0/0	–	1	
Carew Michael Conrad ("Joey")	15.9.1937	8.1.2011	19	1963–1971	1,127	109	1	34.15	8	1-11	0/0	54.62	13	
Challenor George	28.6.1888	30.7.1947	3	1928	101	46	0	16.83	–	–	–/–	–	0	
Chanderpaul Shivnarine (CY 2008)	16.8.1974		153	1993–2013	11,219	203*	29	51.93	9	1-2	0/0	98.11	64	268/22
Chang Herbert Samuel	27.7.1952		1	1978	8	6	0	4.00	–	–	–/–	–	0	
Chattergoon Sewnarine	3.4.1981		4	2007–2008	127	46	0	18.14	–	–	–/–	–	4	18
² **Christiani** Cyril Marcel	28.10.1913	4.4.1938	4	1934	98	32*	0	19.60	–	–	–/–	–	6/1	
² **Christiani** Robert Julian	19.7.1920	4.1.2005	22	1947–1953	896	107	1	26.35	3	3-52	0/0	36.00	19/2	
Clarke Carlos Bertram OBE	7.4.1918	14.10.1993	3	1939	3	2	0	1.00	6	3-59	0/0	43.50	0	
Clarke Sylvester Theophilus	11.12.1954	4.12.1999	11	1977–1981	172	35*	0	15.63	42	5-126	1/0	27.85	2	10
Collins Pedro Tyrone	12.8.1976		32	1998–2005	235	24	0	5.87	106	6-53	3/0	34.63	7	30
Constantine Lord [Learie Nicholas] MBE (CY 1940)	21.9.1901	1.7.1971	18	1928–1939	635	90	0	19.24	58	5-75	2/0	30.10	28	84
Cottrell Sheldon Shane	19.8.1989		1	2013	5	5	0	2.50	1	1-72	0/0	72.00	0	
Croft Colin Everton Hunte	15.3.1953		27	1976–1981	158	33	0	10.53	125	8-29	3/0	23.30	8	19
Cuffy Cameron Eustace	8.2.1970		15	1994–2002	58	15	0	4.14	43	4-82	0/0	33.83	5	41
Cummins Anderson Cleophas	7.5.1966		5	1992–1994	98	50	0	19.60	8	4-54	0/0	42.75	1	63
Da Costa Oscar Constantine	11.9.1907	1.10.1936	5	1929–1934	153	39	0	19.12	3	1-14	0/0	58.33	5	
Daniel Wayne Wendell	16.1.1956		10	1975–1983	46	11	0	6.57	36	5-39	1/0	25.27	4	18
Davis Bryan Allan	2.5.1940		4	1964	245	68	0	30.62	–	–	–/–	–	2	
² **Davis** Charles Allan	1.1.1944		15	1968–1972	1,301	183	4	54.20	2	1-27	0/0	165.00	4	
Davis Winston Walter	18.9.1958		15	1982–1987	202	77	0	15.53	45	4-19	0/0	32.71	10	35
De Caires Francis Ignatius	12.5.1909	2.2.1959	3	1929	232	80	0	38.66	0	0-9	0/0	–	1	
Deonarine Narsingh	16.8.1983		18	2004–2013	725	82	0	25.89	24	4-37	0/0	29.70	16	29/8
Depeiza Cyril Clairmonte	10.10.1928	10.11.1995	5	1954–1955	187	122	1	31.16	0	0-3	0/0	–	7/4	

	Born	Died	Tests	Test Career	Runs	HS	100s	Avge	Wkts	BB	5/10	Avge	Ct/St	O/T
Dewdney David Thomas	23.10.1933		9	1954–1957	17	5*	0	2.42	21	5-21	1/0	38.42	0	
Dhanraj Rajindra	6.2.1969		4	1994–1995	17	9	0	4.25	8	2-49	0/0	74.37	1	6
Dillon Mervyn	5.6.1974		38	1996–2003	549	43	0	8.44	131	5-71	2/0	33.57	16	108
Dowe Uton George	29.3.1949		4	1970–1972	8	5*	0	8.00	12	4-69	0/0	44.50	3	
Dowlin Travis Montague	24.2.1977		6	2009–2010	343	95	0	31.18	–	0-3	0/0	–	5	11/2
Drakes Vasbert Conniel	5.8.1969		12	2002–2003	386	67	0	21.44	33	5-93	1/0	41.27	2	34
Dujon Peter Jeffrey Leroy (CY 1989)	28.5.1956		81	1981–1991	3,322	139	5	31.94	–	–	–/–	–	267/5	169
[2]Edwards Fidel Henderson	6.2.1982		55	2003–2012	394	30	0	6.56	165	7-87	12/0	37.87	10	50/20
Edwards Kirk Anton	3.11.1984		12	2011–2013	821	121	2	35.69	–	0-19	0/0	–	11	11
Edwards Richard Martin	3.6.1940		5	1968	65	22	0	9.28	18	5-84	1/0	34.77	11	
Ferguson Wilfred	14.12.1917	23.2.1961	8	1947–1953	200	75	0	28.57	34	6-92	3/1	34.26	11	
Fernandes Maurius Pacheco	12.8.1897	8.5.1981	2	1928–1929	49	22	0	12.25	–	–	–/–	–		
Findlay Thaddeus Michael MBE	19.10.1943		10	1969–1972	212	44*	0	16.30	–	–	–/–	–	19/2	
Foster Maurice Linton Churchill	9.5.1943		14	1969–1977	580	125	1	30.52	9	2-41	0/0	66.66	3	2
Francis George Nathaniel	11.12.1897	12.1.1942	10	1928–1933	81	19*	0	5.78	23	4-40	0/0	33.17	7	
Frederick Michael Campbell	6.5.1927		1	1953	30	30	0	15.00	–	–	–/–	–	0	
Fredericks Roy Clifton (CY 1974)	11.11.1942	5.9.2000	59	1968–1976	4,334	169	8	42.49	7	1-12	0/0	78.28	62	12
Fudadin Assad Badyr	1.8.1985		3	2012	122	55	0	30.50	–	0-11	0/0	–	4	
Fuller Richard Livingston	30.1.1913	3.5.1987	1	1934	1	1	0	1.00	0	0-2	0/0	–	0	
Furlonge Hammond Allan	19.6.1934		3	1954–1955	99	64	0	19.80	–	–	–/–	–		
Gabriel Shannon Terry	28.4.1988		6	2012–2013	14	13	0	2.00	13	3-10	0/0	38.84	3	
Ganga Daren	14.1.1979		48	1998–2007	2,160	135	3	25.71	1	1-20	0/0	106.00	30	35/1
Ganteaume Andrew Gordon	22.1.1921		1	1947	112	112	0	112.00	–	–	–/–	–		
Garner Joel MBE (CY 1980)	16.12.1952		58	1976–1986	672	60	0	12.44	259	6-56	7/0	20.97	42	98
Garrick Leon Vivian	11.11.1976		2	2000	27	27	0	13.50	–	–	–/–	–	1	3
Gaskin Berkeley Bertram McGarrell	21.3.1908	2.5.1979	2	1947	10	10	0	5.66	2	1-15	0/0	79.00	2	
Gayle Christopher Henry	21.9.1979		99	1999–2013	6,933	333	15	42.01	72	5-34	2/0	42.00	90	252/34
Gibbs Glendon Lionel	27.12.1925	21.2.1979	1	1954	12	12	0	6.00	–	0-2	0/0	–		
Gibbs Lancelot Richard (CY 1972)	29.9.1934		79	1957–1975	488	25	0	6.97	309	8-38	18/2	29.09	52	3
Gibson Otis Delroy (CY 2008)	16.3.1969		2	1995–1998	93	37	0	23.25	3	2-81	0/0	91.66	4	15
Gilchrist Roy	28.6.1934	18.7.2001	13	1957–1958	60	12	0	5.45	57	6-55	2/0	26.68	4	
Gladstone George	14.1.1901	19.5.1978	1	1930	12	12*	0	–	1	1-139	0/0	189.00		
[2]Goddard John Douglas Claude OBE	21.4.1919	26.8.1987	27	1947–1957	859	83*	0	30.67	33	5-31	1/0	31.81	22	
Gomes Hilary Angelo ("Larry") (CY 1985)	13.7.1953		60	1976–1986	3,171	143	9	39.63	15	2-20	0/0	62.00	18	83
Gomez Gerald Ethridge	10.10.1919	6.8.1996	29	1939–1953	1,243	101	1	30.31	58	7-55	1/1	27.41	18	
[2]Grant George Copeland ("Jackie")	9.5.1907	26.10.1978	12	1930–1934	413	71*	0	25.81	0	0-1	0/0	–	10	

Name	Born	Died	Tests	Test Career	Runs	HS	100s	Avge	Wkts	BB	5/10	Avge	Ct/St	O/T
²Grant Rolph Stewart	15.12.1909	18.10.1977	7	1934–1939	220	77	0	22.00	11	3-68	0/0	32.09	13	
Gray Anthony Hollis	23.5.1963		5	1986	48	12*	0	8.00	22	4-39	0/0	17.13	6	25
Greenidge Alvin Ethelbert	20.8.1956		6	1977–1978	222	69	0	22.20	0	—	—/—	—	5	1
Greenidge Cuthbert Gordon MBE (CY 1977)	1.5.1951		108	1974–1990	7,558	226	19	44.72	0	0-0	0/0	—	96	128
Greenidge Geoffrey Alan	26.5.1948		5	1971–1972	209	50	0	29.85	0	0-2	0/0	—	3	
Grell Mervyn George	18.12.1899	11.1.1976	1	1929	34	21	0	17.00	0	0-7	0/0	—		
Griffith Adrian Frank Gordon	19.11.1971		14	1996–2000	638	114	1	24.53	—	—	—/—	—	5	9
Griffith Charles Christopher (CY 1964)	14.12.1938		28	1959–1968	530	54	0	16.56	94	6-36	5/0	28.54	16	
Griffith Herman Clarence	1.12.1893	18.3.1980	13	1928–1933	91	18	0	5.05	44	6-103	2/0	28.25	4	
Guillen Simpson Clairmonte ("Sam")	24.9.1924	2.3.2013	5†	1951	104	54	0	26.00	0	—	—/—	—	9/2	
Hall Sir Wesley Winfield	12.9.1937		48	1958–1968	818	50*	0	15.73	192	7-69	9/1	26.38	11	
Harper Roger Andrew	17.3.1963		25	1983–1993	535	74	0	18.44	46	6-57	1/0	28.06	36	105
Haynes Desmond Leo (CY 1991)	15.2.1956		116	1977–1993	7,487	184	18	42.29	1	1-2	0/0	8.00	65	238
³Headley George Alphonso MBE (CY 1934)	30.5.1909	30.11.1983	22	1929–1953	2,190	270*	10	60.83	0	0-0	0/0	—	14	
³Headley Ronald George Alphonso	29.6.1939		2	1973	62	42	0	15.50	—	—	—/—	—	2	1
Hendriks John Leslie	21.12.1933		20	1961–1969	447	64	0	18.62	—	—	—/—	—	42/5	
Hinds Ryan O'Neal	17.2.1981		15	2001–2009	505	42	0	21.04	13	2-45	0/0	66.92	7	14
Hinds Wavell Wayne	7.9.1976		45	1999–2005	2,608	213	5	33.01	16	3-79	0/0	36.87	32	119/5
Hoad Edward Lisle Goldsworthy	29.1.1896	5.3.1986	4	1928–1933	98	36	0	12.25	—	—	—/—	—		
Holder Roland Irwin Christopher	22.12.1967		11	1996–1998	380	91	0	25.33	—	—	—/—	—	9	37
Holder Vanburn Alonzo	10.10.1945		40	1969–1978	682	42	0	14.20	109	6-28	3/0	33.27	16	12
Holding Michael Anthony (CY 1977)	16.2.1954		60	1975–1987	910	73	0	13.78	249	8-92	13/2	23.68	22	102
Holford David Anthony Jerome	16.4.1940		24	1966–1976	768	105*	1	22.58	51	5-23	1/0	39.39	18	
Holt John Kenneth Constantine	12.8.1923	3.6.1997	17	1953–1958	1,066	166	2	36.75	—	1-20	0/0	20.00	8	
Hooper Carl Llewellyn	15.12.1966		102	1987–2002	5,762	233	13	36.46	114	5-26	4/0	49.42	115	227
Howard Anthony Bourne	27.8.1946		1	1971			0		2	2-140	0/0	70.00	0	
Hunte Sir Conrad Cleophas (CY 1964)	9.5.1932	3.12.1999	44	1957–1966	3,245	260	8	45.06	2	1-17	0/0	55.00	16	
Hunte Errol Ashton Clairmonte	3.10.1905	26.6.1967	3	1929	166	58	0	33.20	—	—	—/—	—	5	
Hylton Leslie George	29.3.1905	17.5.1955	6	1934–1939	70	19	0	11.66	16	4-27	0/0	26.12		
Jacobs Ridley Detamore	26.11.1967		65	1998–2004	2,577	118	3	28.31	—	—	—/—	—	207/12	147
Jaggernauth Amit Sheldon	16.11.1983		1	2007	0	0*	0	0.00		1-74	0/0	96.00	0	
Johnson Hophnie Hobah Hines	13.7.1910	24.6.1987	3	1947–1950	38	22	0	9.50	13	5-41	2/1	18.30	0	
Johnson Tyrell Fabian	10.1.1917	5.4.1985	1	1939	9	9*	0	9.00	3	2-53	0/0	43.00	1	
Jones Charles Ernest Llewellyn	3.11.1902	10.12.1959	4	1929–1934	63	19	0	9.00	0	0-2	0/0	—	3	
Jones Prior Erskine Waverley	6.6.1917	21.11.1991	9	1947–1951	47	10*	0	5.22	25	5-85	1/0	30.04	4	
Joseph David Rolston Emmanuel	15.11.1969		4	1998	141	50	0	20.14	—	—	—/—	—	10	

Name	Born	Died	Tests	Test Career	Runs	HS	100s	Avge	Wks	BB	5/10	Avge	Ct/St	O/T
Joseph Sylvester Cleofoster	5.9.1978		5	2004–2007	147	45	0	14.70	0	0-8	0/0	–	3	13
Julien Bernard Denis	13.3.1949		24	1973–1976	866	121	1	30.92	50	5-57	1/0	37.36	14	12
Jumadeen Raphick Rasif	12.4.1948		12	1971–1978	84	56	0	21.00	44	4-72	0/0	39.34	4	–
Kallicharran Alvin Isaac (CY 1983)	21.3.1949		66	1971–1980	4,399	187	12	44.43	4	2-16	0/0	39.50	51	31
Kanhai Rohan Bholalall (CY 1964)	26.12.1935		79	1957–1973	6,227	256	15	47.53	0	0-1	0/0	–	50	7
Kentish Esmond Seymour Maurice	21.11.1916	10.6.2011	2	1947–1953	1	1*	0	1.00	8	5-49	1/0	22.25	–	–
King Collis Llewellyn	13.6.1951		9	1976–1980	418	100*	1	32.15	3	1-30	0/0	94.00	5	18
King Frank McDonald	14.12.1926	23.12.1990	14	1952–1955	116	21	0	8.28	29	5-74	1/0	39.96	5	–
King Lester Anthony	27.2.1939	9.7.1998	2	1961–1967	41	20	0	10.25	9	5-46	1/0	17.11	2	–
King Reon Dane	6.10.1975		19	1998–2004	66	12*	0	3.47	53	5-51	1/0	32.69	8	50
Lambert Clayton Benjamin	10.2.1962		5	1991–1998	284	104	0	31.55	1	1-4	0/0	5.00	2	11
Lara Brian Charles (CY 1995) §	2.5.1969		131	1990–2006	11,912	400*	34	53.17	0	0-0	0/0	–	164	295
Lashley Patrick Douglas ("Peter")	11.2.1937		4	1960–1966	159	49	0	22.71	1	1-1	0/0	1.00	4	–
Lawson Jermaine Jay Charles	13.1.1982	2003	13	2002–2005	52	14	0	3.46	51	7-78	2/0	29.64	3	13
Legall Ralph Archibald	1.12.1925		4	1952	50	23	0	10.00	–	–	–/–	–	8/1	–
Lewis Desmond Michael	21.12.1946		3	1970	259	88	1	86.33	–	–	–/–	–	0	–
Lewis Rawl Nicholas	5.9.1974		5	1997–2007	89	40	0	8.90	4	2-42	0/0	114.00	8	28/1
Lloyd Clive Hubert (CY 1971)	31.8.1944		110	1966–1984	7,515	242*	19	46.67	10	2-13	0/0	62.20	90	87
Logie Augustine Lawrence	28.9.1960		52	1982–1991	2,470	130	2	35.79	0	0-0	0/0	–	57	158
McGarrell Neil Christopher	12.7.1972		4	2000–2001	61	33	0	15.25	17	4-23	0/0	26.64	2	17
McLean Nixon Alexei McNamara	20.7.1973		19	1997–2000	368	46	0	12.26	44	3-53	0/0	42.56	5	45
McMorris Easton Dudley Ashton St John	4.4.1935		13	1957–1966	564	125	1	26.85	0	0-12	0/0	–	5	–
McWatt Clifford Aubrey	1.2.1922	20.7.1997	6	1953–1954	202	54	0	28.85	1	1-16	0/0	16.00	9/1	–
Madray Ivan Samuel	2.7.1934	23.4.2009	2	1957	3	2	0	1.00	0	0-12	0/0	–	2	–
Marshall Malcolm Denzil (CY 1983)	18.4.1958	4.11.1999	81	1978–1991	1,810	92	0	18.85	376	7-22	22/4	20.94	25	136
[2] Marshall Norman Edgar	27.2.1924	11.8.2007	4	1954	8	8	0	4.00	2	1-22	0/0	31.00	–	–
[2] Marshall Roy Edwin (CY 1959)	25.4.1930	27.10.1992	4	1951	143	30	0	20.42	0	0-3	0/0	–	0	–
Marshall Xavier Melbourne	27.3.1986		7	2005–2008	243	85	0	20.25	0	0-0	0/0	–	1	24/6
Martin Frank Reginald	12.10.1893	23.11.1967	9	1928–1930	486	123*	1	28.58	8	3-91	0/0	77.37	7	–
Martindale Emmanuel Alfred	25.11.1909	17.3.1972	10	1933–1939	58	22	0	5.27	37	5-22	3/0	21.72	5	–
Mattis Everton Hugh	11.4.1957		4	1980	145	71	0	29.00	0	0-4	0/0	–	3	2
Mendonca Ivor Leon	13.7.1934		2	1961	81	78	0	40.50	–	–	–/–	–	8/2	–
Merry Cyril Arthur	20.1.1911	19.4.1964	2	1933	34	13	0	8.50	–	–	–/–	–	1	–
Miller Nikita O'Neil	16.5.1982		1	2009	5	5	0	2.50	0	0-27	0/0	–	0	42/7
Miller Roy	24.12.1924		1	1952	23	23	0	23.00	0	0-28	0/0	–	0	–

§ *Lara's figures exclude 41 runs for the ICC World XI v Australia in the Super Series Test in 2005-06.*

	Born	Died	Tests	Test Career	Runs	HS	100s	Avge	Wks	BB	5/10	Avge	Ct/St	O/T
Mohammed Dave	8.10.1979		5	2003–2006	225	52	0	32.14	13	3-98	0/0	51.38	1	7
Moodie George Horatio	26.11.1915	8.6.2002	1	1934	5	5	0	–	3	3-23	0/0	13.33	0	–
Morton Runako Shakur	22.7.1978	4.3.2012	15	2005–2007	573	70*	0	22.03	0	0-4	0/0	–	20	56/7
Moseley Ezra Alphonsa	5.1.1958		2	1989	35	26	0	8.75	6	2-70	0/0	43.50	1	9
Murray David Anthony	29.5.1950		19	1977–1981	601	84	0	21.46	–	–	–/–	–	57/5	10
Murray Deryck Lance	20.5.1943		62	1963–1980	1,993	91	0	22.90	–	–	–/–	–	181/8	26
Murray Junior Randalph	20.1.1968		33	1992–2001	918	101*	1	22.39	–	–	–/–	–	99/3	55
Nagamootoo Mahendra Veeren	9.10.1975		5	2000–2002	185	68	0	26.42	12	3-119	0/0	53.08	2	24
Nanan Rangy	29.5.1953		1	1980	16	8	0	8.00	4	2-37	0/0	22.75	2	–
Narine Sunil Philip	26.5.1988		6	2012–2013	40	22*	0	8.00	21	6-91	2/0	40.52	2	46/18
Nash Brendan Paul	14.12.1977		21	2008–2011	1,103	114	2	33.42	2	1-21	0/0	123.50	6	9
Neblett James Montague	13.11.1901	28.3.1959	1	1934	16	11*	0	16.00	1	1-44	0/0	75.00	0	–
Noreiga Jack Mollinson	15.4.1936	8.8.2003	4	1970	11	9	0	3.66	17	9-95	2/0	29.00	–	–
Nunes Robert Karl	7.6.1894	23.7.1958	4	1928–1929	245	92	0	30.62	–	–	–/–	–	2	–
Nurse Seymour MacDonald (CY 1967)	10.11.1933		29	1959–1968	2,523	258	6	47.60	0	0-0	0/0	–	21	–
Padmore Albert Leroy	17.12.1946		2	1975–1976	8	8*	0	8.00	1	1-36	0/0	135.00	0	–
Pagon Donovan Jomo	13.9.1982		2	2004	37	35	0	12.33	–	–	–/–	–	0	–
Pairaudeau Bruce Hamilton	14.4.1931		13	1952–1957	454	115	1	21.61	0	0-3	0/0	–	6	–
Parchment Brenton Anthony	24.6.1982		2	2007	55	20	0	13.75	–	–	–/–	–	–	7/1
Parry Derick Recaldo	22.12.1954		12	1977–1979	381	65	0	22.41	23	5-15	1/0	40.69	4	6
Pascal Nelon Troy	25.4.1987		1	2010–2010	12	10	0	6.00	0	0-27	0/0	–	1	1
Passailaigue Charles Clarence	4.8.1901	7.1.1972	1	1929	46	44	0	46.00	0	0-15	0/0	–	3	–
Patterson Balfour Patrick	15.9.1961		28	1985–1992	145	21*	0	6.59	93	5-24	5/0	30.90	5	59
Payne Thelston Rodney O'Neale	13.2.1957		1	1985	5	5	0	5.00	–	–	–/–	–	5	7
Permaul Veerasammy	11.8.1989		4	2012–2013	57	20	0	9.50	12	3-32	0/0	37.66	1	6
Perry Nehemiah Odolphus	16.6.1968		4	1998–1999	74	26	0	12.33	10	5-70	1/0	44.60	2	21
Phillip Norbert	12.6.1948		9	1977–1978	297	47	0	29.70	28	4-48	0/0	37.17	5	–
Phillips Omar Jamel	12.10.1986		1	2009	160	94	0	40.00	–	–	–/–	–	1	–
Pierre Lancelot Richard	5.6.1921	14.4.1989	1	1947	13	9	0	4.33	0	0-9	0/0	–	0	–
Powell Daren Brentlyle	15.4.1978		37	2002–2008	407	36*	0	7.82	85	5-25	1/0	47.85	8	55/5
Powell Kieran Omar Akeem	6.3.1990		20	2011–2013	1,044	134	3	28.21	–	–	–/–	–	18	24
Powell Ricardo Lloyd	16.12.1978		2	1999–2003	53	30	0	17.66	0	0-13	0/0	–	1	109
Rae Allan Fitzroy	30.9.1922	27.2.2005	15	1948–1952	1,016	109	4	46.18	–	–	–/–	–	10	–
Ragoonath Suruj	22.3.1968		2	1998	13	9	0	4.33	–	–	–/–	–	0	–
Ramadhin Sonny (CY 1951)	1.5.1929		43	1950–1960	361	44	0	8.20	158	7-49	10/1	28.98	9	–
Ramdass Ryan Rakesh	3.7.1983		1	2005	26	23	0	13.00	–	–	–/–	–	2	1

Name	Born	Died	Tests	Test Career	Runs	HS	100s	Avge	Wks	BB	5/10	Avge	Ct/St	OT
Ramdin Denesh	13.3.1985		56	2005–2013	2,235	166	4	27.25			–/–		156/5	105/35
Ramnarine Dinanath	4.6.1975		12	1997–2001	106	35*	0	6.23	45	5-78	1/0	30.73	8	4
Rampaul Ravindranath	15.10.1984		18	2009–2012	335	40*	0	14.56	49	4-48	0/0	34.79	3	82/19
Reifer Floyd Lamonte	23.7.1972		6	1996–2009	111	29	0	9.25			–/–		6	8/1
Richards Dale Maurice	16.7.1976		3	2009–2010	125	69	0	20.83			–/–		3	8/1
Richards Sir Isaac Vivian Alexander (CY 1977)	7.3.1952		121	1974–1991	8,540	291	24	50.23	32	2-17	0/0	61.37	122	187
Richardson Richard Benjamin (CY 1992)	12.1.1962		86	1983–1995	5,949	194	16	44.39	0	0-0			90	224
Rickards Kenneth Roy	22.8.1923	21.8.1995	2	1947–1951	104	67	0	34.66					5	
Roach Clifford Archibald	13.3.1904	16.4.1988	16	1928–1934	952	209	2	30.70	2	1-18	0/0	51.50	8	
Roach Kemar Andre Jamal	30.6.1988		23	2009–2012	291	41	0	9.70	85	6-48	5/1	27.71	9	61/11
Roberts Alphonso Theodore	18.9.1937	24.7.1996	1	1955	28	28	0	14.00			–/–		0	
Roberts Anderson Montgomery Everton CBE (CY 1975)	29.1.1951		47	1973–1983	762	68	0	14.94	202	7-54	11/2	25.61	9	56
Roberts Lincoln Abraham	4.9.1974		1	1998	0	0	0	0.00			–/–		0	
Rodriguez William Vicente	25.6.1934		5	1961–1967	96	50	0	13.71	7	3-51	0/0	53.42	4	
Rose Franklyn Albert	1.2.1972		19	1996–2000	344	69	0	13.23	53	7-84	2/0	30.88	3	27
Rowe Lawrence George	8.1.1949		30	1971–1979	2,047	302	7	43.55	0	0-1	0/0		17	11
Russell Andre Dwayne	29.4.1988		1	2010	2	2	0	2.00	1	1-73	0/0	104.00	0	35/15
[2]St Hill Edwin Lloyd	9.3.1904	21.5.1957	2	1929	18	12	0	4.50	3	2-110	0/0	73.66	0	
[2]St Hill Wilton H	6.7.1893	d unknown	3	1928–1929	117	38	0	19.50	0	0-9	0/0		0	
Sammy Darren Julius Garvey	20.12.1983		38	2007–2013	1,323	106	1	21.68	84	7-66	4/0	35.79	65	107/42
[2]Samuels Marlon Nathaniel (CY 2013)	5.1.1981		51	2000–2013	2,983	260	5	35.51	34	4-13	0/0	52.14	23	157/25
[2]Samuels Robert George	13.3.1971		6	1995–1996	372	125	1	37.20					8	8
Sanford Adam	12.7.1975		11	2001–2003	72	18*	0	4.80	30	4-132	0/0	43.86	4	
Sarwan Ramnaresh Ronnie	23.6.1980		87	1999–2011	5,842	291	15	40.01	23	4-37	0/0	50.56	53	181/18
Scarlett Reginald Osmond	15.8.1934		3	1959	54	29*	0	18.00	2	1-46	0/0	104.50	0	
[1]Scott Alfred Homer Patrick	29.7.1934	15.6.1961	1	1952	5	5	0	5.00	0	0-52	0/0		0	
[1]Scott Oscar Charles ("Tommy")	14.8.1892	12.9.1963	8	1928–1930	171	35	0	17.10	22	5-266	1/0	42.04	0	
Sealey Benjamin James	12.8.1899	3.1.1982	1	1933	41	29	0	20.50	1	1-10	0/0	10.00	0	
Sealy James Edward Derrick	11.9.1912		11	1929–1939	478	92	0	28.11	3	2-7	0/0	31.33	6/1	
Shepherd John Neil (CY 1979)	9.11.1943		5	1969–1970	77	32	0	9.62	19	5-104	1/0	25.21	2	
Shillingford Grayson Cleophas	25.9.1944		7	1969–1971	57	25	0	8.14	15	3-63	0/0	35.80	1	
Shillingford Irvine Theodore	18.4.1944	23.12.2009	4	1976–1977	218	120	1	31.14			–/–		7	2
Shillingford Shane	22.2.1983		14	2010–2013	159	31*	0	8.36	65	6-49	6/2	32.32	6	
Shivnarine Sewdatt	13.5.1952		8	1977–1978	379	63	0	29.15	1	1-13	0/0	167.00	6	1
Simmons Lendl Mark Platter	25.11.1985		8	2008–2011	278	49	0	17.37	1	1-60	0/0	147.00	5	55/18

	Born	Died	Tests	Test Career	Runs	HS	100s	Avge	Wkts	BB	5/10	Avge	Ct/St	O/T
Simmons Philip Verant (CY 1997)	18.4.1963		26	1987–1997	1,002	110	1	22.26	4	2-34	0/0	64.25	26	143
Singh Charran Kamkaran	27.11.1935		2	1959	11	11	0	3.66	5	2-28	0/0	33.20	2	
Small Joseph A.	3.11.1892	26.4.1958	3	1928–1929	79	52	0	13.16	3	2-67	0/0	61.33	3	
Small Milton Aster	12.2.1964		2	1983–1984	3	3*	0	–	4	3-40	0/0	38.25	2	2
Smith Cameron Wilberforce	29.7.1933		5	1960–1961	222	55	0	24.66	–	–	–/–	–	4/1	
Smith Devon Sheldon	21.10.1981		33	2002–2011	1,384	108	1	24.71	–	0-3	0/0	–	28	47/6
Smith Dwayne Romel	12.4.1983		10	2003–2005	320	105*	1	24.61	7	3-71	0/0	49.14	9	87/17
Smith O'Neil Gordon ("Collie") (CY 1958)	5.5.1933	9.9.1959	26	1954–1958	1,331	168	4	31.69	48	5-90	1/0	33.85	9	
Sobers Sir Garfield St Aubrun (CY 1964)	28.7.1936		93	1953–1973	8,032	365*	26	57.78	235	6-73	6/0	34.03	109	1
Solomon Joseph Stanislaus	26.8.1930		27	1958–1964	1,326	100*	1	34.00	4	1-20	0/0	67.00	13	
Stayers Sven Conrad ("Charlie")	9.6.1937		4	1961	58	35*	0	19.33	9	3-65	0/0	40.44	2	
[2]Stollmeyer Jeffrey Baxter	11.3.1921	6.1.2005	32	1939–1954	2,159	160	4	42.33	13	3-32	0/0	39.00	20	
[2]Stollmeyer Victor Humphrey	24.1.1916	21.9.1999	1	1939	96	96	0	96.00	–	–	–/–	–	0	
Stuart Colin Ellsworth Laurie	28.9.1973		6	2000–2001	24	12*	0	3.42	20	3-33	0/0	31.40	2	5
Taylor Jaswick Ossie	3.1.1932	13.11.1999	3	1957–1958	4	4*	0	2.00	10	5-109	1/0	27.30	2	
Taylor Jerome Everton	22.6.1984		29	2003–2009	629	106	0	15.72	82	5-11	3/0	35.64	5	66/17
Thompson Patterson Ian Chesterfield	26.9.1971		2	1995–1996	17	10*	0	8.50	5	2-58	0/0	43.00	0	2
Tonge Gavin Courtney	13.2.1983		2	2009	25	23*	0	25.00	1	1-28	0/0	113.00	0	5/1
Trim John	25.1.1915	12.11.1960	4	1947–1951	21	12	0	5.25	18	5-34	1/0	16.16	2	
Valentine Alfred Louis (CY 1951)	28.4.1930	11.5.2004	36	1950–1961	141	14	0	4.70	139	8-104	8/2	30.32	13	
Valentine Vincent Adolphus	4.4.1908	6.7.1972	2	1933	35	19*	0	11.66	1	1-55	0/0	104.00	0	
Walcott Sir Clyde Leopold (CY 1958)	17.1.1926	27.2.1984	44	1947–1959	3,798	220	15	56.68	11	3-50	0/0	37.09	53/11	
Walcott Leslie Arthur	18.1.1894		1	1929	40	24	0	40.00	1	1-17	0/0	32.00	0	
Wallace Philo Alphonso	2.8.1970		7	1997–1998	279	92	0	21.46	–	–	–/–	–	9	33
Walsh Courtney Andrew (CY 1987)	30.10.1962		132	1984–2000	936	30*	0	7.54	519	7-37	22/3	24.44	29	205
Walton Chadwick Antonio Kirkpatrick	3.7.1985		2	2009	13	10	0	3.25	–	–	–/–	–	10	5
Washington Dwight Marlon	5.3.1983		1	2004	7	7*	0	–	0	0-20	0/0	–	3	
Watson Chester Donald	1.7.1938		7	1959–1961	12	5	0	2.40	19	4-62	0/0	38.10	1	
[1]Weekes Sir Everton de Courcy (CY 1951)	26.2.1925		48	1947–1957	4,455	207	15	58.61	1	1-8	0/0	77.00	49	
Weekes Kenneth Hunnell	24.1.1912	9.2.1998	2	1939	173	137	1	57.66	–	–	–/–	–	0	
White Anthony Wilbur	20.11.1938		2	1964	71	57*	0	23.66	3	2-34	0/0	50.66	1	
Wight Claude Vibart	28.7.1902	4.10.1969	2	1928–1929	67	23	0	22.33	0	0-6	0/0	–	0	
Wight George Leslie	28.5.1929	4.1.2004	1	1952	21	21	0	21.00	–	–	–/–	–	0	
Wiles Charles Archibald	11.8.1892	4.11.1957	1	1933	2	2	0	1.00	–	–	–/–	–	0	
Willett Elquemedo Tonito	1.5.1953		5	1972–1974	74	26	0	14.80	11	3-33	0/0	43.81	0	
Williams Alvadon Basil	21.11.1949		7	1977–1978	469	111	2	39.08	–	–	–/–	–	5	

Name	Born	Died	Tests	Test Career	Runs	HS	100s	Avge	Wkts	BB	5/10	Avge	Ct/St	O/T
Williams David	4.11.1963		11	1991–1997	242	65	0	13.44			–/–		40/2	36
Williams Ernest Albert Vivian ("Foffie")	10.4.1914	13.4.1997	4	1939–1947	113	72	0	18.83	9	3-51	0/0	26.77	2	
Williams Stuart Clayton	12.8.1969		31	1993–2001	1,183	128	1	24.14	0	0-19	0/0		27	57
Wishart Kenneth Leslie	28.11.1908	18.10.1972	1	1934	52		0	26.00			–/–		0	
Worrell *Sir* Frank Mortimer Maglinne (CY 1951)	1.8.1924	13.3.1967	51	1947–1963	3,860	261	9	49.48	69	7-70	2/0	38.72	43	

NEW ZEALAND (262 players)

Name	Born	Died	Tests	Test Career	Runs	HS	100s	Avge	Wkts	BB	5/10	Avge	Ct/St	O/T
Adams Andre Ryan	17.7.1975		1	2001	18	11	0	9.00	6	3-44	0/0	17.50	1	42/4
Alabaster John Chaloner	11.7.1930		21	1955–1971	272	34	0	9.71	49	4-46	0/0	38.02	1	
Allcott Cyril Francis Walter	7.10.1896	19.11.1973	6	1929–1931	113	33	0	22.60	6	2-102	0/0	90.16	3	
Allott Geoffrey Ian	24.12.1971		10	1995–1999	27	8*	0	3.37	19	4-74	0/0	58.47	2	31
Anderson Corey James	13.12.1990		5	2013	222	116	1	37.00	11	3-47	0/0	19.36	1	9/6
Anderson Robert Wickham	2.10.1948		9	1976–1978	423	92	0	23.50			–/–		1	2
Anderson William McDougall	8.10.1919	21.12.1979	1	1945	5	4	0	2.50			–/–		1	
Andrews Bryan	4.4.1945		2	1973	22	17	0	22.00	2	2-40	0/0	77.00		
Arnel Brent John	3.1.1979		6	2009–2011	45	8*	0	5.62	9	4-95	0/0	62.88	3	
Astle Nathan John	15.9.1971		81	1995–2006	4,702	222	11	37.02	51	3-27	0/0	42.01	70	223/4
Astle Todd Duncan	24.9.1986		1	2012	38	35	0	19.00	1	1-56	0/0	97.00	0	7
Badcock Frederick Theodore ("Ted")	9.8.1897	19.9.1982	7	1929–1932	137	64	0	19.57	16	4-80	0/0	38.12	1	
Barber Richard Trevor	3.6.1925		1	1955	17	12	0	8.50			–/–		1	
Bartlett Gary Alex	3.2.1941		10	1961–1967	263	40	0	15.47	24	6-38	1/0	33.00	8	
Barton Paul Thomas	9.10.1935		7	1961–1962	285	109	1	20.35			–/–		4	
Beard Donald Derek	14.11.1920	15.7.1982	4	1951–1955	101	31	0	20.20	9	3-22	0/0	33.55	2	
Beck John Edward Francis	1.8.1934	23.4.2000	8	1953–1955	394	99	0	26.26			–/–			
Bell Matthew David	25.2.1977		18	1998–2007	729	107	2	24.30			–/–		19	
Bell William	5.9.1931	23.7.2002	2	1953	21	21*	0		2	1-54	0/0	117.50	0	
Bennett Hamish Kyle	22.2.1987		1	2010	4	4	0	4.00		0-47	0/0		0	12
Bilby Grahame Paul	7.5.1941		2	1965	55	28	0	13.75			–/–		3	
Blain Tony Elston	17.2.1962		11	1986–1993	456	78	0	26.82			–/–		19/2	38
Blair Robert William	23.6.1932		19	1952–1963	189	64*	0	6.75	43	4-85	0/0	35.23	5	
Blunt Roger Charles (CY 1928)	3.11.1900	22.6.1966	9	1929–1931	330	96	0	27.50	12	3-17	0/0	39.33	5	
Bolton Bruce Alfred	31.5.1935		2	1958	59	33	0	19.66			–/–			
Bond Shane Edward	7.6.1975		18	2001–2009	168	41*	0	12.92	87	6-51	5/1	22.09	8	82/20

	Born	Died	Tests	Test Career	Runs	HS	100s	Avge	Wkts	BB	Avge	5/10	Ct/St	O/T
Boock Stephen Lewis	20.9.1951		30	1977–1988	207	37	0	6.27	74	7-87	34.64	4/0	14	14
Boult Trent Alexander	22.7.1989		20	2011–2013	254	52*	0	19.53	72	6-40	26.54	3/1	6	8/3
[1,2]Bracewell Brendon Paul	14.9.1959		6	1978–1984	24	8	0	2.40	14	3-110	41.78	0/0	1	1
Bracewell Douglas Alexander John	28.9.1990		18	2011–2013	337	43	0	10.87	50	6-40	36.26	2/0	5	7/13
[2]Bracewell John Garry	15.4.1958		41	1980–1990	1,001	110	1	20.42	102	6-32	35.81	4/1	31	53
[1]Bradburn Grant Eric	26.5.1966	25.9.2008	7	1990–2000	105	30*	0	13.12	6	3-134	76.66	0/0	6	11
[1]Bradburn Wynne Pennell	24.11.1938		2	1963	62	32	0	15.50	–	–	–	–/–	2	
Brown Vaughan Raymond	3.11.1959		2	1985	51	36*	0	25.50	1	1-17	176.00	0/0	3	
Brownlie Dean Graham	30.7.1984		14	2011–2013	711	109	0	29.62	1	1-13	52.00	0/0	17	3/4
Burgess Mark Gordon	17.7.1944		50	1967–1984	2,684	119*	5	31.20	6	3-23	35.33	0/0	34	3
Burke Cecil	27.3.1914	4.8.1997	1	1945	4	3	0	2.00	2	2-30	15.00	0/0	0	
Burtt Thomas Browning	22.1.1915	24.5.1988	10	1946–1952	252	42	0	21.00	33	6-162	35.45	3/0	2	
Butler Ian Gareth	24.11.1981		8	2001–2004	76	26	0	9.50	24	6-46	36.83	1/0	4	26/19
Butterfield Leonard Arthur	29.8.1913	5.7.1999	1	1945	0	0	0	0.00	–	0-24	–	0/0	1	
[1]Cairns Bernard Lance	10.10.1949		43	1973–1985	928	64	0	16.28	130	7-74	32.91	6/1	30	78
Cairns Christopher Lance (CY 2000)	13.6.1970		62	1989–2004	3,320	158	5	33.53	218	7-27	29.40	13/1	14	215/2
Cameron Francis James MBE	1.6.1932		19	1961–1965	116	27*	0	11.60	62	5-34	29.82	3/0	8	
Cave Henry Butler	10.10.1922	15.9.1989	19	1949–1958	229	22*	0	8.80	34	4-21	43.14	0/0	10	
Chapple Murray Ernest	25.7.1930	31.7.1985	14	1952–1965	497	76	0	19.11	1	1-84	84.00	0/0	7	
Chatfield Ewen John MBE	3.7.1950		43	1974–1988	180	21*	0	8.57	123	6-73	32.17	3/1	10	114
Cleverley Donald Charles	23.12.1909	16.2.2004	2	1931–1945	19	10*	0	19.00	–	0-51	–	0/0	4	
Collinge Richard Owen	2.4.1946		35	1964–1978	533	68*	0	14.40	116	6-63	29.25	3/0	10	15
Colquhoun Ian Alexander	8.6.1924	26.2.2005	2	1954	1	1*	0	0.50	–	–	–	–/–	4/1	
Coney Jeremy Vernon MBE (CY 1984)	21.6.1952		52	1973–1986	2,668	174*	3	37.57	27	3-28	35.77	0/0	64	88
Congdon Bevan Ernest OBE (CY 1974)	11.2.1938		61	1964–1978	3,448	176	7	32.22	59	5-65	36.50	1/0	44	11
Cowie John OBE	30.3.1912	3.6.1994	9	1937–1949	90	45	0	10.00	45	6-40	21.53	4/1	3	
Cresswell George Fenwick	22.3.1915	10.1.1966	3	1949–1951	14	12*	0	7.00	13	6-168	22.46	1/0	0	
Cromb Ian Burns	25.6.1905	6.3.1984	5	1931–1937	123	51*	0	20.50	8	3-113	55.25	0/0	1	
Crowe Jeffrey John	14.9.1958		39	1982–1989	1,601	128	3	26.24	–	0-0	–	0/0	41	75
[2]Crowe Martin David MBE (CY 1985)	22.9.1962		77	1981–1995	5,444	299	17	45.36	14	2-25	48.28	0/0	71	143
Cumming Craig Derek	31.8.1975		11	2004–2007	441	74	0	25.94	–	–	–	–/–	3	13
Cunis Robert Smith	15.1.1941		20	1963–1972	295	51	0	12.82	51	6-76	37.00	1/0	1	
D'Arcy John William	23.4.1936	9.8.2008	5	1958	136	33	0	13.60	–	–	–	–/–	5	
Davis Heath Te-Ihi-O-Te-Rangi	30.11.1971		5	1994–1997	20	8*	0	6.66	17	5-63	29.35	1/0	4	11
de Groen Richard Paul	5.8.1962		5	1993–1994	45	26	0	7.50	11	3-40	45.90	0/0	0	12
Dempster Charles Stewart (CY 1932)	15.11.1903	14.2.1974	10	1929–1932	723	136	2	65.72	0	0-10	–	0/0	2	

	Born	Died	Tests	Test Career	Runs	HS	100s	Avge	Wkts	BB	5/10	Avge	Ct/St	O/T
Dempster Eric William MBE	25.1.1925	15.8.2011	5	1952–1953	106	47	–	17.66	2	1-24	0/0	109.50	1	–
Dick Arthur Edward	10.10.1936		17	1961–1965	370	50*	–	14.23	–	–	–/–	–	47/4	–
Dickinson George Ritchie	11.3.1903	17.3.1978	3	1929–1931	31	11	–	6.20	8	3-66	0/0	30.62	3	–
Donnelly Martin Paterson (*CY 1948*)	17.10.1917	22.10.1999	7	1937–1949	582	206	1	52.90	0	0-20	0/0	–	7	–
Doull Simon Blair	6.8.1969		32	1992–1999	570	46	–	14.61	98	7-65	6/0	29.30	16	42
Dowling Graham Thorne OBE	4.3.1937		39	1961–1971	2,306	239	3	31.16	1	1-19	0/0	19.00	23	–
Drum Christopher James	10.7.1974		5	2000–2001	10	4	–	3.33	16	3-36	0/0	30.12	2	5
Dunning John Angus	6.2.1903	24.6.1971	4	1932–1937	38	19	–	7.60	5	2-35	0/0	98.60	2	–
Edgar Bruce Adrian	23.11.1956		39	1978–1986	1,958	161	3	30.59	0	0-3	0/0	–	14	64
Edwards Graham Neil ("Jock")	27.5.1955		8	1976–1980	377	55	–	25.13	–	–	–/–	–	7	6
Elliott Grant David	21.3.1979		5	2007–2009	86	25	–	10.75	4	2-8	0/0	35.00	2	51/3
Emery Raymond William George	28.3.1915	18.12.1982	2	1951	46	28	–	11.50	2	2-52	0/0	26.00	0	–
Fisher Frederick Eric	28.7.1924	19.6.1996	1	1952	23	14	–	11.50	1	1-78	0/0	78.00	0	–
Fleming Stephen Paul	1.4.1973		111	1993–2007	7,172	274*	9	40.06	–	–	–/–	–	171	279‡/5
Flynn Daniel Raymond	16.4.1985		24	2008–2012	1,038	95	–	25.95	0	0-0	0/0	–	10	20/5
Foley Henry	28.1.1906	16.10.1948	1	1929	4	2	–	2.00	–	–	–/–	–	0	–
Franklin James Edward Charles	7.11.1980		31	2000–2012	808	122*	1	20.71	82	6-119	3/0	33.97	12	110/38
Franklin Trevor John	15.3.1962		21	1983–1990	828	101	1	23.00	–	–	–/–	–	8	3
Freeman Douglas Linford	8.9.1914	31.5.1994	2	1932	2		–	1.00	1	1-91	0/0	169.00	0	–
Fulton Peter Gordon	1.2.1979		20	2005–2013	934	136	2	29.18	–	–	–/–	–	21	49/12
Gallichan Norman	3.6.1906	25.3.1969	1	1937	32	30	–	16.00	3	3-99	0/0	37.66	0	–
Gedye Sidney Graham	2.5.1929		4	1963–1964	193	55	–	24.12	–	–	–/–	–	2	–
Germon Lee Kenneth	4.11.1968		12	1995–1996	382	55	–	21.22	–	–	–/–	–	27/2	37
Gillespie Mark Raymond	17.10.1979		5	2007–2011	76	27	–	10.85	22	6-113	3/0	28.68	1	32/11
Gillespie Stuart Ross	2.3.1957		1	1985	28	28	–	28.00	1	1-79	0/0	79.00	0	19
Gray Evan John	18.11.1954		10	1983–1988	248	50	–	15.50	17	3-73	0/0	52.11	6	10
Greatbatch Mark John	11.12.1963		41	1987–1996	2,021	146*	3	30.62	0	0-0	0/0	–	27	84
Guillen Simpson Clairmonte ("Sam")	24.9.1924	2.3.2013	3†	1955	98	41	–	16.33	–	–	–/–	–	4/1	–
Guptill Martin James	30.9.1986		31	2008–2013	1,718	189	2	29.62	5	3-37	0/0	51.60	33	79/41
Guy John William	29.8.1934		12	1955–1961	440	102	1	20.95	–	–	–/–	–	3	–
[1,2] **Hadlee** Dayle Robert	6.1.1948		26	1969–1977	530	56	–	14.32	71	4-30	0/0	33.64	8	11
[1,2] **Hadlee** Sir Richard John (*CY 1982*)	3.7.1951		86	1972–1990	3,124	151*	2	27.16	431	9-52	36/9	22.29	39	115
[1,2] **Hadlee** Walter Arnold CBE	4.6.1915	29.9.2006	11	1937–1950	543	116	1	30.16	–	–	–/–	–	6	–
Harford Noel Sherwin	30.8.1930	30.3.1981	8	1955–1958	229	93	–	15.26	–	–	–/–	–	0	–
Harford Roy Ivan	30.5.1936		3	1967	7	6	–	2.33	–	–	–/–	–	11	–
[1] **Harris** Chris Zinzan	20.11.1969		23	1992–2002	777	71	–	20.44	16	2-16	0/0	73.12	14	250

Name	Born	Died	Tests	Test Career	Runs	HS	100s	Avge	Wkts	BB	5/10	Avge	Ct/St	OIT
[1] Harris Parke Gerald Zinzan	18.7.1927	1.12.1991	9	1955–1964	378	101	1	22.23	0	0-14	0/0	–	6	
Harris Roger Meredith	27.7.1933		2	1958	31	13	0	10.33				–	0	
[2] Hart Matthew Norman	16.5.1972		14	1993–1995	353	45	0	17.65	29	5-77	1/0	49.58	9	13
[2] Hart Robert Garry	2.12.1974		11	2002–2003	260	57*	0	16.25	–	–	–/–	–	29/1	2
Hartland Blair Robert	22.10.1966		9	1991–1994	303	52	0	16.83				–	5	16
Haslam Mark James	26.9.1972		4	1992–1995	4	3	0	4.00	2	1-33	0/0	122.50	5	1
Hastings Brian Frederick	23.3.1940		31	1968–1975	1,510	117*	4	30.20	0	0-3	0/0	–	23	11
Hayes John Arthur	11.11.1927	25.12.2007	15	1950–1958	73	19	0	4.86	30	4-36	0/0	40.56	3	
Henderson Matthew	2.8.1895	17.6.1970	1	1929	8	6	0	8.00	2	2-38	0/0	32.00	1	
Hopkins Gareth James	24.11.1976		2	2008–2010	71	15	0	11.83	–	–	–/–	–	9	25/10
[2] Horne Matthew Jeffery	5.12.1970		35	1996–2003	1,788	157	0	28.38	0	0-4	0/0	–	17	50
[2] Horne Philip Andrew	21.1.1960		4	1986–1990	71	27	0	10.14				–	3	4
Hough Kenneth William	24.10.1928	20.9.2009	2	1958	62	31*	0	62.00	6	3-79	0/0	29.16	18	
How Jamie Michael	19.5.1981		19	2005–2008	772	92	0	22.70	0	0-0	0/0	–	29	41/5
[2] Howarth Geoffrey Philip OBE	29.3.1951		47	1974–1984	2,531	147	6	32.44	3	1-13	0/0	90.33	33	70
[2] Howarth Hedley John	25.12.1943	7.11.2008	30	1969–1976	291	61	0	12.12	86	5-34	2/0	36.95	33	9
Ingram Peter John	25.10.1978		2	2009	61	42	0	15.25	–	–	–/–	–	0	8/3
James Kenneth Cecil	12.3.1904	21.8.1976	11	1929–1932	52	14	0	4.72				–	11/5	
Jarvis Terrence Wayne	29.7.1944		13	1964–1972	625	182	1	29.76	0	0-0	0/0	–	3	
Jones Andrew Howard	9.5.1959		39	1986–1994	2,922	186	7	44.27	1	1-40	0/0	194.00	25	87
Jones Richard Andrew	22.10.1973		4	2003	23	16	0	11.50	0	0-0	0/0	–	2	5
Kennedy Robert John	3.6.1972		4	1995	28	22	0	7.00	6	3-28	0/0	63.33	2	7
Kerr John Lambert	28.12.1910	27.5.2007	7	1931–1937	212	59	0	19.27	–	–	–/–	–	4	
Kuggeleijn Christopher Mary	10.5.1956		2	1988	7	7	0	1.75	1	1-50	0/0	67.00	1	16
Larsen Gavin Rolf	27.9.1962		8	1994–1995	127	26*	0	14.11	24	3-57	0/0	28.70	5	121
Latham Rodney Terry	12.6.1961		4	1991–1992	219	119	1	31.28	0	0-6	0/0	–	3	33
Lees Warren Kenneth MBE	19.3.1952		21	1976–1983	778	152	1	23.57	0	0-4	0/0	–	52/7	31
Leggat Ian Bruce	7.6.1930		1	1953	0	0	0	0.00	0	0-6	0/0	–	2	
Leggat John Gordon	27.5.1926	9.3.1973	9	1951–1955	351	61	0	21.93				–	0	
Lissette Allen Fisher	6.11.1919	24.1.1973	2	1955	2	1*	0	1.00	3	2-73	0/0	41.33	1	
Loveridge Greg Riaka	15.1.1975		1	1995	4	4*	0	–	0	0-0	0/0	–	–	
Lowry Thomas Coleman	17.2.1898	20.7.1976	7	1929–1931	223	80	0	27.87	0	0-0	0/0	–	8	
McCullum Brendon Barrie	27.9.1981		82	2003–2013	4,684	225	7	35.21	0	0-18	0/0	–	183/11	224/62
McEwan Paul Ernest	19.12.1953		4	1979–1984	96	40*	0	16.00	0	0-6	0/0	–	5	17
MacGibbon Anthony Roy	28.8.1924	6.4.2010	26	1950–1958	814	66	0	19.85	70	5-64	1/0	30.85	13	
McGirr Herbert Mendelson	5.11.1891	14.4.1964	2	1929	51	51	0	51.00	1	1-65	0/0	115.00	0	

Name	Born	Died	Tests	Test Career	Runs	HS	100s	Avge	Wkts	BB	5/10	Avge	Ct/St	O/T
McGregor Spencer Noel	18.12.1931	21.11.2007	25	1954–1964	892	111	1	19.82	–	–	–/–	–	9	
McIntosh Timothy Gavin	4.12.1979		17	2008–2010	854	136	2	27.54	–	–	–/–	–	10	
McKay Andrew John	17.4.1980		1	2010	25	25	0	25.00	1	1-120	0/0	120.00	0	19/2
McLeod Edwin George	14.10.1900	14.9.1989	1	1929	18	16	0	18.00	0	0-5	0/0	–	0	
McMahon Trevor George	8.11.1929		5	1955	7	4*	0	2.33	–	–	–/–	–	7/1	
McMillan Craig Douglas	13.9.1976		55	1997–2004	3,116	142	6	38.46	28	3-48	0/0	44.89	22	197/8
McRae Donald Alexander Noel	25.12.1912	10.8.1986	1	1945	8	8	0	4.00	0	0-44	0/0	–	1	
² Marshall Hamish John Hamilton	15.2.1979		13	2000–2005	652	160	1	38.35	0	0-4	0/0	–	5	66/3
³ Marshall James Andrew Hamilton	15.2.1979		7	2004–2008	218	52	0	19.81	–	–	–/–	–	1	10/3
Martin Bruce Philip	25.4.1980		5	2012–2013	74	41	0	14.80	12	4-43	0/0	53.83	0	
Martin Christopher Stewart	10.12.1974		71	2000–2012	123	12*	0	2.36	233	6-26	10/1	33.81	14	206/3
Mason Michael James	27.8.1974		1	2003	3	3	0	1.50	0	0-32	0/0	–	0	26/3
Matheson Alexander Malcolm	27.2.1906	31.12.1985	2	1929–1931	7	7	0	7.00	2	2-7	0/0	68.00	2	
Meale Trevor	11.11.1928	21.5.2010	2	1958	21	10	0	5.25	–	–	–/–	–	2	
Merritt William Edward	18.8.1908	9.6.1977	6	1929–1931	73	19	0	10.42	12	4-104	0/0	51.41	2	
Meuli Edgar Milton	20.2.1926	15.4.2007	1	1952	38	23	0	19.00	–	–	–/–	–	0	
Milburn Barry Douglas	24.11.1943		3	1968	8	4*	0	8.00	–	–	–/–	–	6/2	
Miller Lawrence Somerville Martin	31.3.1923	17.12.1996	13	1952–1958	346	47	0	13.84	0	0-1	0/0	–	1	
Mills John Ernest	3.9.1905	11.12.1972	7	1929–1932	241	117	1	26.77	–	–	–/–	–	1	
Mills Kyle David	15.3.1979		19	2004–2008	289	57	0	11.56	44	4-16	0/0	33.02	4	162/37
Moir Alexander McKenzie	17.7.1919	17.6.2000	17	1950–1958	327	41*	0	14.86	28	6-155	2/0	50.64	2	
Moloney Denis Andrew Robert ("Sonny")	11.8.1910	15.7.1942	3	1937	156	64	0	26.00	0	0-9	0/0	–	3	
Mooney Francis Leonard Hugh	26.5.1921	8.3.2004	14	1949–1953	343	46	0	17.15	–	–	–/–	–	22/8	
Morgan Ross Winston	12.2.1941		20	1964–1971	734	97	0	22.24	5	1-16	0/0	121.80	12	
Morrison Bruce Donald	17.12.1933		1	1962	10	10	0	5.00	2	2-129	0/0	64.50	1	
Morrison Daniel Kyle	3.2.1966		48	1987–1996	379	42	0	8.42	160	7-89	10/0	34.68	14	96
Morrison John Francis MacLean	27.8.1947		17	1973–1981	656	117	1	22.62	2	2-52	0/0	35.50	9	18
Motz Richard Charles (CY 1966)	12.1.1940	29.4.2007	32	1961–1969	612	60	0	11.54	100	6-63	5/0	31.48	9	
Munro Colin	11.3.1987		1	2013	15	15	0	7.50	2	2-40	0/0	20.00	0	7/10
Murray Bruce Alexander Grenfell	18.9.1940		13	1967–1970	598	90	0	23.92	1	1-0	0/0	0.00	21	
Murray Darrin James	4.9.1967		8	1994	303	52	0	20.20	–	–	–/–	–	6	1
Nash Dion Joseph	20.11.1971		32	1992–2001	729	89*	0	23.51	93	6-27	3/1	28.48	13	81
Newman Sir Jack	3.7.1902	23.9.1996	3	1931–1932	33	19	0	8.25	2	2-76	0/0	127.00	0	
Nicol Robert James	28.5.1983		2	2011	28	19	0	7.00	0	0-0	0/0	–	2	22/21
O'Brien Iain Edward	10.7.1976		22	2004–2009	219	31	0	7.55	73	6-75	1/0	33.27	7	104
O'Connor Shayne Barry	15.11.1973		19	1997–2001	103	20	0	5.72	53	5-51	1/0	32.52	6	38

	Born	Died	Tests	Test Career	Runs	HS	100s	Avge	Wkts	BB	5/10	Avge	Ct/St	O/T
Oram Jacob David Philip	28.7.1978		33	2002–2009	1,780	133	5	36.32	60	4-41	0/0	33.05	15	160/36
O'Sullivan David Robert	16.11.1944		11	1972–1976	158	23*	0	9.29	18	5-148	1/0	67.83	2	3
Overton Guy William Fitzroy	8.6.1919	7.9.1993	3	1953	8	3*	0	1.60	9	3-65	0/0	28.66	1	
Owens Michael Barry	11.11.1969		8	1992–1994	16	8*	0	2.66	17	4-99	0/0	34.41	3	1
Page Milford Laurenson ("Curly")	8.5.1902	13.2.1987	14	1929–1937	492	104	1	24.60	5	2-21	0/0	46.20	6	
Papps Michael Hugh William	2.7.1979		8	2003–2007	246	86	0	16.40	–	–	–/–	–	11	6
²Parker John Morton	21.2.1951		36	1972–1980	1,498	121	3	24.55	1	1-24	0/0	24.00	30	24
Parker Norman Murray	28.8.1948		3	1976	89	40	0	14.83	–	–	–/–	–	2	30
Parore Adam Craig	23.1.1971		78	1990–2001	2,865	110	2	26.28	–	–	–/–	–	197/7	179
Patel Dipak Narshibhai	25.10.1958		37	1986–1996	1,200	99	1	20.68	75	6-50	3/0	42.05	15	75
Patel Jeetan Shashi	7.5.1980		19	2005–2012	276	27*	0	12.00	52	5-110	1/0	48.46	12	39/11
Petherick Peter James	25.9.1942		6	1976	34	13	0	4.85	16	3-90	0/0	42.81	4	
Petrie Eric Charlton	22.5.1927	14.8.2004	14	1955–1965	258	55	0	12.90	–	–	–/–	–	25	
Playle William Rodger	1.12.1938		8	1958–1962	151	65	0	10.06	–	–	–/–	–	4	
Pocock Blair Andrew	18.6.1971		15	1993–1997	665	85	1	22.93	0	0-10	0/0	–	5	
Pollard Victor	7.9.1945		32	1964–1973	1,266	116	2	24.34	40	3-3	0/0	46.32	19	3
Poore Matt Beresford	1.6.1930		14	1952–1955	355	45	0	15.43	9	2-28	0/0	40.77	1	
Priest Mark Wellings	12.8.1961		3	1990–1997	56	26	0	14.00	3	2-42	0/0	52.66	0	18
Pringle Christopher	26.1.1968		14	1990–1994	175	30	0	10.29	30	7-52	1/1	46.30	7	64
Puna Narotam ("Tom")	28.10.1929	7.6.1996	3	1965	31	18*	0	15.50	4	2-40	0/0	60.00	1	
Rabone Geoffrey Osborne	6.11.1921	19.1.2006	12	1949–1954	562	107	1	31.22	16	6-68	1/0	39.68	1	
¹Redmond Aaron James	23.9.1979		8	2008–2013	325	83	0	21.66	6	2-47	0/0	26.66	5	67
Redmond Rodney Ernest	29.12.1944		1	1972	163	107	1	81.50	–	–	–/–	–	5	2
Reid John Fulton	3.3.1956		19	1978–1985	1,296	180	6	46.28	0	0-0	0/0	–	9	25
Reid John Richard OBE (CY 1959)	3.6.1928		58	1949–1965	3,428	142	6	33.28	85	6-60	1/0	33.35	43/1	
Richardson Mark Hunter	11.6.1971		38	2000–2004	2,776	145	4	44.77	1	1-16	0/0	21.00	26	
Roberts Albert William	20.8.1909	13.5.1978	5	1929–1937	248	66*	0	27.55	7	4-101	0/0	29.85	4	4
Roberts Andrew Duncan Glenn	6.5.1947	26.10.1989	7	1975–1976	254	84*	0	23.09	4	1-12	0/0	45.50	4	
Robertson Gary Keith	15.7.1960		1	1985	12	12	0	12.00	1	1-91	0/0	91.00	1	10
Rowe Charles Gordon	30.6.1915	9.6.1995	1	1945	0	0	0	0.00	–	–	–/–	–	1	
³Rutherford Hamish Duncan	27.4.1989		10	2012–2013	558	171	3	34.87	1	1-38	0/0	161.00	7	4/7
Rutherford Kenneth Robert	26.10.1965		56	1984–1994	2,465	107*	3	27.08	5	2-7	0/0	56.00	32	121
Ryder Jesse Daniel	6.8.1984		18	2008–2011	1,269	201	3	40.93	5	1-74	0/0	74.00	12	43/20
Scott Roy Hamilton	6.3.1917	5.8.2005	1	1946	18	18	0	18.00	1	0-5	0/0	–	0	
Scott Verdun John	31.7.1916	2.8.1980	10	1945–1951	458	84	1	28.62	0	0-9	–/–	–	7	
Sewell David Graham	20.10.1977		1	1997	1	1*	0	–	0	–	–	–	0	

	Born	Died	Tests	Test Career	Runs	HS	100s	Avge	Wkts	BB	5/10	Avge	Ct/St	O/T
Shrimpton Michael John Froud	23.6.1940		10	1962–1973	265	46	0	13.94	5	3-35	0/0	31.60	8	
Sinclair Barry Whitley	23.10.1936		21	1962–1967	1,148	138	3	29.43	2	2-32	0/0	16.00	8	
Sinclair Ian McKay	1.6.1933		2	1955	25	18*	0	8.33	1	1-79	0/0	120.00	2	
Sinclair Mathew Stuart	9.11.1975		33	1999–2009	1,635	214	3	32.05	0	0-1	0/0	–	31	54/2
Smith Frank Brunton	13.3.1912	6.7.1997	4	1946–1951	237	96	0	47.40	–	–	–	–	1	
Smith Horace Dennis	8.1.1913	25.1.1986	1	1932	4	4	0	4.00	1	1-113	0/0	113.00	0	
Smith Ian David Stockley MBE	28.2.1957		63	1980–1991	1,815	173	2	25.56	0	0-5	0/0	–	168/8	98
Snedden Colin Alexander	7.1.1918	23.4.1982	1	1946	–	–	–	–	0	0-46	0/0	–	0	
Snedden Martin Colin	23.11.1918		25	1980–1990	327	33*	0	14.86	58	5-68	1/0	37.91	7	93
Sodhi Inderbir Singh ("Ish")	31.10.1992		5	2013	152	58	0	30.40	11	3-59	0/0	51.45	1	
Southee Timothy Grant	11.12.1988		29	2007–2013	770	77*	0	18.78	101	7-64	4/1	31.44	17	74/32
Sparling John Trevor	24.7.1938		11	1958–1963	229	50	0	12.72	5	1-9	0/0	65.40	4	
Spearman Craig Murray	4.7.1972		19	1995–2000	922	112	1	26.34	–	–	–	–	21	51
Stead Gary Raymond	9.1.1972		5	1998–1999	278	78	0	34.75	0	0-1	0/0	–	1	
Stirling Derek Alexander	5.10.1961		6	1984–1986	108	26	0	15.42	13	4-88	0/0	46.23	2	6
Styris Scott Bernard	7.11.1966		29	2002–2007	1,586	170	5	36.04	20	3-28	0/0	50.75	23	188/31
Su'a Murphy Logo	7.11.1966		13	1991–1994	165	44	0	12.69	36	5-73	2/0	38.25	8	12
Sutcliffe Bert MBE (CY 1950)	17.11.1923	20.4.2001	42	1946–1965	2,727	230*	5	40.10	5	2-38	0/0	86.00	20	
Taylor Bruce Richard	12.7.1943		30	1964–1973	898	124	2	20.40	111	7-74	4/0	26.60	2	2
Taylor Donald Dougald	2.3.1923	5.12.1980	3	1946–1955	159	77	0	31.80	–	–	–	–	2	
Taylor Luteru Ross Poutoa Lote	8.3.1984		53	2007–2013	4,134	217*	11	47.51	2	2-4	0/0	24.00	88	132/53
Thomson Keith	26.2.1941		2	1967	94	69	0	31.33	1	1-9	0/0	9.00	0	
Thomson Shane Alexander	27.1.1969		19	1989–1995	958	120*	1	30.90	19	3-63	0/0	50.15	24	56
Tindill Eric William Thomas	18.12.1910	1.8.2010	5	1937–1946	73	37*	0	9.12	–	–	–	–	6/1	
Troup Gary Bertram	3.10.1952		15	1976–1985	55	13*	0	4.58	39	6-95	1/1	37.28	2	22
Truscott Peter Bennetts	14.8.1941		1	1964	29	26	0	14.50	–	–	–	–	1	
Tuffey Daryl Raymond	11.6.1978		26	1999–2009	427	80*	0	16.42	77	6-54	2/0	31.75	15	94/3
Turner Glenn Maitland (CY 1971)	26.5.1947		41	1968–1982	2,991	259	7	44.64	0	0-5	0/0	–	42	41
Twose Roger Graham	17.4.1968		16	1995–1999	628	94	0	25.12	3	2-36	0/0	43.33	5	87
Vance Robert Howard	31.3.1955		4	1987–1989	207	68	0	29.57	–	–	–	–	8	8
Van Wyk Cornelius Francois Kruger	7.2.1980		9	2011–2012	341	71	0	21.31	–	–	–	–	23/1	
Vaughan Justin Thomas Caldwell	30.8.1967		6	1992–1996	201	44	0	18.27	11	4-27	0/0	40.90	4	18
Vettori Daniel Luca	27.1.1979		113§	1996–2012	4,508	140	6	30.25	359	7-87	20/3	34.20	58	271‡/33
Vincent Lou	11.11.1978		23	2001–2007	1,332	224	3	34.15	0	0-2	0/0	–	19	102/9
Vivian Graham Ellery	28.2.1946		5	1964–1971	110	43	0	18.33	1	1-14	0/0	107.00	3	1

§ *Vettori's figures exclude eight runs and one wicket for the ICC World XI v Australia in the Super Series Test in 2005-06.*

	Born	Died	Tests	Test Career	Runs	HS	100s	Avge	Wkts	BB	5/10	Avge	Ct/St	O/T
1 Vivian Henry Gifford	4.11.1912	12.8.1983	7	1931–1937	421	100	1	42.10	17	4-58	0/0	37.23	4	13
Wadsworth Kenneth John	30.11.1946	19.8.1976	33	1969–1975	1,010	80	0	21.48	–	–	–/–	–	92/4	
Wagner Neil	13.3.1986		12	2012–2013	173	37	0	13.30	39	5-64	1/0	37.94	4	
Walker Brooke Graeme Keith	25.3.1977		5	2000–2002	118	27*	0	19.66	5	2-92	0/0	79.80	0	11
Wallace Walter Mervyn	19.12.1916	21.3.2008	13	1937–1952	439	66	0	20.90	–	0-5	–/–	–	5	
Walmsley Kerry Peter	23.8.1973		3	1994–2000	13	5	0	2.60	9	3-70	0/0	43.44	0	2
Ward John Thomas	11.3.1937		8	1963–1967	75	35*	0	12.50	–	–	–/–	–	16/1	
Watling Bradley-John	9.7.1985		19	2009–2013	956	103	2	35.40	–	–	–/–	–	49	22/3
Watson William	31.8.1965		15	1986–1993	60	11	0	5.00	40	6-78	1/0	34.67	4	61
Watt Leslie	17.9.1924		1	1954	2	2	0	1.00	–	–	–/–	–	0	
Webb Murray George	22.6.1947		3	1970–1973	12	12	0	6.00	4	2-114	0/0	117.75	0	
Webb Peter Neil	14.7.1957		2	1979	11	5	0	3.66	–	–	–/–	–	2	5
Weir Gordon Lindsay	2.6.1908	31.10.2003	11	1929–1937	416	74*	0	29.71	7	3-38	0/0	29.85	3	
White David John	26.6.1961		2	1990	31	18	0	7.75	–	0-5	–/–	–	0	3
Whitelaw Paul Erskine	10.2.1910	28.8.1988	2	1932	64	30	0	32.00	–	–	–/–	–	1	
Williamson Kane Stuart	8.8.1990		29	2010–2013	1,794	135	4	35.88	22	4-44	0/0	39.90	27	49/13
Wiseman Paul John	4.5.1970		25	1997–2004	366	36	0	14.07	61	5-82	2/0	47.59	11	15
Wright John Geoffrey MBE	5.7.1954		82	1977–1992	5,334	185	12	37.82	0	0-1	0/0	–	38	149
Young Bryan Andrew	3.11.1964		35	1993–1998	2,034	267*	2	31.78	–	–	–/–	–	54	74
Young Reece Alan	15.9.1979		5	2010–2011	169	57	0	24.14	–	–	–/–	–	8	
Yuile Bryan William	29.10.1941		17	1962–1969	481	64	0	17.81	34	4-43	0/0	35.67	12	

INDIA (280 players)

	Born	Died	Tests	Test Career	Runs	HS	100s	Avge	Wkts	BB	5/10	Avge	Ct/St	O/T
Aaron Varun Raymond	29.10.1989		1	2011	6	6	0	6.00	3	3-106	0/0	43.00	0	4
Abid Ali Syed	9.9.1941		29	1967–1974	1,018	81	0	20.36	47	6-55	1/0	42.12	32	5
Adhikari Hemchandra Ramachandra	31.7.1919	25.10.2003	21	1947–1958	872	114*	1	31.14	3	3-68	0/0	27.33	8	
Agarkar Ajit Bhalchandra	4.12.1977		26	1998–2005	571	109*	1	16.79	58	6-41	1/0	37.32	6	191/4
2 Amar Singh Ladha	4.12.1910	21.5.1940	7	1932–1936	292	51	0	22.46	28	7-86	2/0	30.64	3	
1-2 Amarnath Mohinder (CY 1984)	24.9.1950		69	1969–1987	4,378	138	11	42.50	32	4-63	0/0	55.68	47	85
1-2 Amarnath Nanik ("Lala")	11.9.1911	5.8.2000	24	1933–1952	878	118	1	24.38	45	5-96	2/0	32.91	13	
1-2 Amarnath Surinder	30.12.1948		10	1975–1978	550	124	1	30.55	–	1-5	–/–	–	4	3
Amir Elahi	1.9.1908	28.12.1980	1†	1947	17	13	0	8.50	–	–	–/–	–	0	
Amre Pravin Kalyan	14.8.1968		11	1992–1993	425	103	1	42.50	–	–	–/–	–	9	37

	Born	Died	Tests	Test Career	Runs	HS	100s	Avge	Wkts	BB	5/10	Avge	Ct/St	OIT
Ankola Salil Ashok	1.3.1968		1	1989	6	6	0	6.00	2	1-35	0/0	64.00	0	20
2 Apte Arvindrao Laxmanrao	24.10.1934		1	1959	15	8	0	7.50					0	
2 Apte Madhavrao Laxmanrao	5.10.1932		7	1952	542	163*	1	49.27					2	
Arshad Ayub	2.8.1958		13	1987–1989	257	57	0	17.13	41	5-50	3/0	35.07	2	32
Arun Bharati	14.12.1962		2	1986	4	2*	0	4.00	4	3-76	0/0	29.00	2	4
Arun Lal	1.8.1955		16	1982–1988	729	93	0	26.03	0	0-0			13	13
Ashwin Ravichandran	17.9.1986		19	2011–2013	788	124	2	39.40	104	7-103	9/2	28.50	6	70/19
Azad Kirtivardhan	2.1.1959		7	1980–1983	135	24	0	11.25	3	2-84	0/0	124.33	3	25
Azharuddin Mohammad (CY 1991)	8.2.1963		99	1984–1999	6,215	199	22	45.03	0	0-4	0/0		105	334
Badani Hemang Kamal	14.11.1976		4	2001	94	38	0	15.66	0	0-17	0/0		6	40
Badrinath Subramaniam	30.8.1980		2	2009	63	56	0	21.00					2	7/1
Bahutule Sairaj Vasant	6.1.1973		2	2000–2001	39	21*	0	13.00	3	1-32	0/–	67.66	1	8
Baig Abbas Ali	19.3.1939		10	1959–1966	428	112	1	23.77	0	0-2	0/0	–	6	
Balaji Lakshmipathy	27.9.1981		8	2003–2004	51	31	0	5.66	27	5-76	1/0	37.18	1	30/5
Banerjee Sarobindu Nath ("Shute")	3.10.1911	14.10.1980	1	1948	13	8	0	6.50	5	4-54	0/0	25.40	0	
Banerjee Subroto Tara	13.2.1969		1	1991	3	3	0	3.00	3	3-47	0/0	15.66	0	6
Banerjee Sudangsu Abinash	1.11.1917	14.9.1992	1	1948	0	0	0	0.00	5	4-120	0/0	36.20	0	
Bangar Sanjay Bapusaheb	11.10.1972		12	2001–2002	470	100*	1	29.37	7	2-23	0/0	49.00	4	15
Baqa Jilani Mohammad	20.7.1911	2.7.1941	1	1936	16	12	0	16.00	0	0-55	0/0	–	0	
Bedi Bishan Singh	25.9.1946		67	1966–1979	656	50*	0	8.98	266	7-98	14/1	28.71	26	10
Bhandari Prakash	27.11.1935		3	1954–1956	77	39	0	19.25	0	0-12	0/0	–	1	
Bharadwaj Raghvendrarao Vijay	15.8.1975		3	1999	28	22	0	9.33	1	1-26	0/0	107.00	3	10
Bhat Adwai Raghuram	16.4.1958		2	1983	6	6	0	3.00	4	2-65	0/0	37.75	0	
Bhuvneshwar Kumar	5.2.1990		6	2012–2013	96	38	0	19.20	9	3-31	0/0	37.88	4	26/3
Binny Roger Michael Humphrey	19.7.1955		27	1979–1986	830	83*	0	23.05	47	6-56	2/0	32.63	11	72
Borde Chandrakant Gulabrao	21.7.1934		55	1958–1969	3,061	177*	5	35.59	52	5-88	1/0	46.48	37	
Chandrasekhar Bhagwat Subramanya (CY 1972)	17.5.1945		58	1963–1979	167	22	0	4.07	242	8-79	16/2	29.74	25	1
Chauhan Chetandra Pratap Singh	21.7.1947		40	1969–1980	2,084	97	0	31.57	2	1-4	0/0	53.00	38	7
Chauhan Rajesh Kumar	19.12.1966		21	1992–1997	98	23	0	7.00	47	4-48	0/0	39.51	12	35
Chawla Piyush Pramod	24.12.1988		3	2005–2012	6	4	0	2.00	7	4-69	0/0	38.57	1	25/7
Chopra Aakash	19.9.1977		10	2003–2004	437	60	0	23.00					15	
Chopra Nikhil	26.12.1973		1	1999	7	4	0	3.50	0	0-78	0/0	–	0	39
Chowdhury Nirode Ranjan	23.5.1923	14.12.1979	2	1948–1951	3	3*	0	3.00	1	1-130	0/0	205.00	0	
Colah Sorabji Hormasji Munchersha	22.9.1902	11.9.1950	2	1932–1933	69	31	0	17.25					2	
Contractor Nariman Jamshedji	7.3.1934		31	1955–1961	1,611	108	1	31.58	1	1-9	0/0	80.00	18	

	Born	Died	Tests	Test Career	Runs	HS	100s	Avge	Wkts	BB	5/10	Avge	Ct/St	O/T
Dahiya Vijay	10.5.1973		2	2000	2	2*	0	–	–	–	–/–	–	6	1
Dani Hemchandra Tukaram	24.5.1933	19.12.1999	1	1952	–	–	–	–	1	1-9	0/0	19.00	1	–
Das Shiv Sunder	5.11.1977		23	2000–2001	1,326	110	2	34.89	1	0-7	0/0	–	34	4
Dasgupta Deep	7.6.1977		8	2001	344	100	1	28.66	–	–	–/–	–	13	5
Desai Ramakant Bhikaji	20.6.1939	27.4.1998	28	1958–1967	418	85	0	13.48	74	6-56	2/0	37.31	9	–
Dhawan Shikhar (CY 2014)	5.12.1985		5	2012–2013	319	187	1	45.57	–	–	–/–	–	2	31/2
Dhoni Mahendra Singh	7.7.1981		81	2005–2013	4,342	224	6	38.76	0	0-1	0/0	–	219/37	255/43
Dighe Sameer Sudhakar	8.10.1968		6	2000–2001	141	47	0	15.66	–	–	–/–	–	12/2	23
Dilawar Hussain	19.3.1907	26.8.1967	3	1933–1936	254	59	0	42.33	–	–	–/–	–	6/1	–
Divecha Ramesh Vithaldas	18.10.1927	11.2.2003	5	1951–1952	60	26	0	12.00	11	3-102	0/0	32.81	5	–
Doshi Dilip Rasiklal	22.12.1947		33	1979–1983	129	20	0	4.60	114	6-102	6/0	30.71	10	15
Dravid Rahul (CY 2000)	11.1.1973		163§	1996–2011	13,265	270	36	52.63	–	1-18	0/0	39.00	209	340‡/11
Durani Salim Aziz	11.12.1934		29	1959–1972	1,202	104	1	25.04	75	6-73	3/1	35.42	14	–
Engineer Farokh Maneksha	25.2.1938		46	1961–1974	2,611	121	2	31.08	–	–	–/–	–	66/16	5
Gadkari Chandrasekhar Vaman	3.2.1928	11.11.1998	6	1952–1954	129	50*	0	21.50	0	0-8	0/0	–	6	–
Gaekwad Anshuman Dattajirao	23.9.1952		40	1974–1984	1,985	201	2	30.07	2	1-4	0/0	93.50	15	15
Gaekwad Dattajirao Krishnarao	27.10.1928	2.1.2003	11	1952–1960	350	52	0	18.42	0	0-4	0/0	–	5	–
Gaekwad Hiralal Ghasulal	29.8.1923		1	1952	22	14	0	11.00	0	0-47	0/0	–	–	–
Gambhir Gautam	14.10.1981		54	2004–2012	4,021	206	9	44.18	0	0-4	0/0	–	38	147/37
Gandhi Devang Jayant	6.9.1971		4	1999	204	88	0	34.00	–	–	–/–	–	3	–
Gandotra Ashok	24.11.1948		2	1969	54	18	0	13.50	–	–	–/–	–	1	–
Ganesh Doddanarasaiah	30.6.1973		4	1996	25	8	0	6.25	5	2-28	0/0	57.40	0	1
Ganguly Sourav Chandidas	8.7.1972		113	1996–2008	7,212	239	16	42.17	32	3-28	0/0	52.53	71	308‡
Gavaskar Sunil Manohar (CY 1980)	10.7.1949		125	1970–1986	10,122	236*	34	51.12	1	1-34	0/0	206.00	108	108
Ghavri Karsan Devjibhai	28.2.1951		39	1974–1980	913	86	0	21.23	109	5-33	4/0	33.54	16	19
Ghorpade Jayasinghrao Mansinghrao	2.10.1930	29.3.1978	8	1952–1959	229	41	0	15.26	0	0-17	0/0	–	4	–
Ghulam Ahmed	4.7.1922	28.10.1998	22	1948–1958	192	50	0	8.72	68	7-49	4/1	30.17	11	–
Gopalan Morappakam Joysam	6.6.1909	21.12.2003	1	1933	18	11*	0	18.00	1	1-39	0/0	39.00	3	–
Gopinath Coimbatarao Doraikannu	1.3.1930		8	1951–1959	242	50*	0	22.00	1	1-11	0/0	11.00	2	–
Guard Ghulam Mustafa	12.12.1925	13.3.1978	2	1958–1959	11	7	0	5.50	3	2-69	0/0	60.66	2	–
Guha Subrata	31.1.1946	5.11.2003	4	1967–1969	17	6	0	3.40	3	2-55	0/0	103.66	2	–
Gul Mahomed	15.10.1921	8.5.1992	8†	1946–1952	166	34	0	11.06	2	2-21	0/0	12.00	3	–
²Gupte Balkrishna Pandharinath	30.8.1934	5.7.2005	3	1960–1964	28	17*	0	28.00	3	1-54	0/0	116.33	2	–
²Gupte Subhashchandra Pandharinath ("Fergie")	11.12.1929	31.5.2002	36	1951–1961	183	21	0	6.31	149	9-102	12/1	29.55	14	–
Gursharan Singh	8.3.1963		1	1989	18	18	0	18.00	–	–	–/–	–	2	–

§ Dravid's figures exclude 23 runs and one catch for the ICC World XI v Australia in the Super Series Test in 2005-06.

	Born	Died	Tests	Test Career	Runs	HS	100s	Avge	Wkts	BB	Avge	5/10	Ct/St	O/T
Hafeez Abdul (see Kardar)														
Hanumant Singh	29.3.1939	29.11.2006	14	1963-1969	686	105	2	31.18	0	0-5	—	0/0	11	
Harbhajan Singh	3.7.1980		101	1997-2012	2,202	115	2	18.35	413	8-84	32.37	25/5	42	227‡/25
Hardikar Manohar Shankar	8.2.1936	4.2.1995	2	1958	56	32*	0	18.66	4	1-9	55.00	0/0	3	
Harvinder Singh	23.12.1977		3	1997-2001	6	6	0	2.00	4	2-62	46.25	0/0	0	16
Hazare Vijay Samuel	11.3.1915	18.12.2004	30	1946-1952	2,192	164*	7	47.65	20	4-29	61.00	0/0	11	
Hindlekar Dattaram Dharmaji	1.1.1909	30.3.1949	4	1936-1946	71	26	0	14.20	—	—	—	-/-	3	
Hirwani Narendra Deepchand	18.10.1968		17	1987-1996	54	17	0	5.40	66	8-61	30.10	4/1	5	18
Ibrahim Khanmohammad Cassumbhoy	26.1.1919	12.11.2007	4	1948	169	85	1	21.12	—	—	—	-/-	5	
Indrajitsinhji Kumar Shri	15.6.1937	12.3.2011	4	1964-1969	51	23	0	8.50	—	—	—	-/-	6/3	
Irani Jamshed Khudadad	18.8.1923	25.2.1982	2	1947	3	2*	0	3.00	—	—	—	-/-	2/1	
Jadeja Ajaysinhji	1.2.1971		15	1992-1999	576	96	0	26.18	—	—	—	-/-	5	196
Jadeja Ravindrasinh Anirudhsinh	6.12.1988		6	2012-2013	105	43	0	15.00	33	6-138	20.90	2/0	2	92/15
[3] Jahangir Khan Mohammad	1.2.1910	23.7.1988	4	1932-1936	39	13	0	5.57	4	4-60	63.75	0/0	4	
Jai Laxmidas Purshottamdas	1.4.1902	29.1.1968	1	1933	19	19	0	9.50	—	—	—	-/-	0	
Jaisimha Motganhalli Laxmanarsu	3.3.1939	6.7.1999	39	1959-1970	2,056	129	3	30.68	9	2-54	92.11	0/0	17	
Jamshedji Rustomji Jamshedji Dorabji	18.11.1892	5.4.1976	1	1933	5	4*	0	5.00	3	3-137	45.66	0/0	2	
Jayantilal Kenia	13.1.1948		1	1970	5	5	0	—	—	—	—	-/-	0	
Johnson David Jude	16.10.1971		2	1996	8	5	0	4.00	3	2-52	47.66	0/0	0	
Joshi Padmanabh Govind	27.10.1926	8.1.1987	12	1951-1960	207	52*	0	10.89	—	—	—	-/-	18/9	
Joshi Sunil Bandacharya	6.6.1969		15	1996-2000	352	92	0	20.70	41	5-142	35.85	1/0	7	69
Kaif Mohammad	1.12.1980		13	1996-2005	624	148*	1	32.84	—	—	—	-/-	14	125
Kambli Vinod Ganpat	18.1.1972		17	1992-1995	1,084	227	4	54.20	0	0-4	—	0/0	7	104
[1] Kanitkar Hrishikesh Hemant	14.11.1974		2	1999	74	45	0	18.50	—	—	—	-/-	0	34
Kanitkar Hemant Shamsunder	8.12.1942		2	1974	111	65	0	27.75	—	—	—	-/-	0	
Kapil Dev (CY 1983)	6.1.1959		131	1978-1993	5,248	163	8	31.05	434	9-83	29.64	23/2	64	225
Kapoor Aashish Rakesh	25.3.1971		4	1994-1996	97	42	0	19.40	6	2-19	42.50	0/0	2	17
Kardar Abdul Hafeez	17.1.1925	21.4.1996	3†	1946	80	43	0	16.00	—	—	—	-/-	1	
Karim Syed Saba	14.11.1967		1	2000	15	15	0	—	—	—	—	-/-		34
Karthik Krishankumar Dinesh	1.6.1985		23	2004-2009	1,000	129	1	27.77	—	—	—	-/-	51/5	67/9
[1] Kartik Murali	11.9.1976		8	1999-2004	88	43	0	9.77	24	4-44	34.16	0/0	2	37/1
Kenny Ramnath Baburao	29.9.1930	21.11.1985	5	1958-1959	245	62	0	27.22	—	—	—	-/-	1	
Kirmani Syed Mujtaba Hussein	29.12.1949		88	1975-1985	2,759	102	2	27.04	—	—	—	-/-	160/38	49
Kishenchand Gogumal	14.4.1925	16.4.1997	5	1947-1952	89	44	0	8.90	1	1-9	13.00	0/0	1	
Kohli Virat	5.11.1988		22	2011-2013	1,507	119	5	44.32	0	0-3	—	0/0	25	125/21
[2] Kripal Singh Amritsar Govindsingh	6.8.1933	22.7.1987	14	1955-1964	422	100*	1	28.13	10	3-43	58.40	0/0	4	

	Born	Died	Tests	Test Career	Runs	HS	100s	Avge	Wkts	BB	5/10	Avge	Ct/St	0/T
Krishnamurthy Pochiah	12.7.1947	28.1.1999	5	1970	33	20	0	5.50	–	–	–	–	7/1	1
Kulkarni Nilesh Moreshwar	3.4.1973		3	1997–2000	5	4	0	5.00	2	1-70	0/0	166.00	1	10
Kulkarni Rajiv Ramesh	25.9.1962		3	1986	2	2	0	1.00	5	3-85	0/0	45.40	1	10
Kulkarni Umesh Narayan	7.3.1942		4	1967	13	7	0	4.33	5	2-37	0/0	47.60	0	
Kumar Praveen	2.10.1986		6	2011	149	40	0	14.90	27	5-106	1/0	25.81	2	68/10
Kumar Vaman Viswanath	22.6.1935		2	1960–1961	6	6	0	3.00	7	5-64	1/0	28.85	2	
Kumble Anil (CY 1996)	17.10.1970		132	1990–2008	2,506	110*	1	17.77	619	10-74	35/8	29.65	60	269‡
Kunderan Budhisagar Krishnappa	2.10.1939	23.6.2006	18	1959–1967	981	192	2	32.70	–	0-13	0/0	–	23/7	
Kuruvilla Abey	8.8.1968		10	1996–1997	66	35*	0	6.60	25	5-68	1/0	35.68	0	25
Lall Singh	16.12.1909	19.11.1985	1	1932	44	29	0	22.00	–	–	–/–	–	1	
Lamba Raman	2.1.1960	22.2.1998	4	1986–1987	102	53	0	20.40	–	–	–/–	–	5	32
Laxman Vangipurappu Venkata Sai (CY 2002)	1.11.1974		134	1996–2011	8,781	281	17	45.97	2	1-2	0/0	63.00	135	86
Madan Lal	20.3.1951		39	1974–1986	1,042	74	0	22.65	71	5-23	4/0	40.08	15	67
Maka Ebrahim Suleman	5.3.1922	7.9.1994	2	1952	2	2*	0	–	–	–	–/–	–	2/1	
Malhotra Ashok Omprakash	26.1.1957		7	1981–1984	226	72*	0	25.11	–	0-0	0/0	–	2	20
Maninder Singh	13.6.1965		35	1982–1992	99	15	0	3.80	88	7-27	3/2	37.36	9	59
Manjrekar Sanjay Vijay	12.7.1965		37	1987–1996	2,043	218	4	37.14	–	0-4	0/0	–	25/1	74
Manjrekar Vijay Laxman	26.9.1931	18.10.1983	55	1951–1964	3,208	189*	7	39.12	1	1-16	0/0	44.00	19/2	
Mankad Ashok Vinoo	12.10.1946	1.8.2008	22	1969–1977	991	97	0	25.41	0	0-0	0/0	–	12	
Mankad Mulvantrai Himmatlal ("Vinoo") (CY 1947)	12.4.1917	21.8.1978	44	1946–1958	2,109	231	5	31.47	162	8-52	8/2	32.32	33	1
Mantri Madhav Krishnaji	1.9.1921		4	1951–1954	67	39	0	9.57					8/1	
Meherhomji Khershedji Rustomji	9.8.1911	10.2.1982	1	1936	0	0*	0	0.00					0	
Mehra Vijay Laxman	12.3.1938	25.8.2006	8	1955–1963	329	62	0	25.30	0	0-1	0/0	–	7	
Merchant Vijay Madhavji (CY 1937)	12.10.1911	27.10.1987	10	1933–1951	859	154	3	47.72	0	0-17	0/0	–	7	
Mhambrey Paras Laxmikant	20.6.1972		2	1996	58	28	0	29.00	2	1-43	0/0	74.00	1	3
Milkha Singh Amritsar Govindsingh	31.12.1941		4	1959–1961	92	35	0	15.33	0	0-2	0/0	–	2	
Mishra Amit	24.11.1982		13	2008–2011	392	84	0	23.05	43	5-71	0/0	43.30	6	21/1
Mithun Abhimanyu	25.10.1989		4	2010–2011	120	46	0	24.00	9	4-105	0/0	50.66	0	5
Modi Rustomji Sheryar	11.11.1924	17.5.1996	10	1946–1952	736	112	1	46.00	0	0-14	0/0	–	3	
Mohammed Shami	3.9.1990		4	2013	18	11	0	3.60	17	5-47	1/0	26.17	1	20
Mohanty Debasis Sarbeswar	20.7.1976		2	1997	0	0*	0	–	4	4-78	0/0	59.75	0	45
Mongia Nayan Ramlal	19.12.1969		44	1993–2000	1,442	152	1	24.03	–	–	–/–	–	99/8	140
More Kiran Shankar	4.9.1962		49	1986–1993	1,285	73	0	25.70	0	0-12	0/0	–	110/20	94
Muddiah Venatappa Musandra	8.6.1929	1.10.2009	2	1959–1960	11	11	0	5.50	3	2-40	0/0	44.66	0	
Mukund Abhinav	6.1.1990		5	2011	211	62	0	21.10	0	0-14	0/0	–	5	

	Born	*Died*	*Tests*	*Test Career*	*Runs*	*HS*	*100s*	*Avge*	*Wkts*	*BB*	*Avge*	*5/10*	*Ct/St*	*O/T*
Mushtaq Ali Syed	17.12.1914	18.6.2005	11	1933–1951	612	112	2	32.21	3	1-45	67.33	0/0	7	
Nadkarni Rameshchandra Gangaram ("Bapu")	4.4.1933		41	1955–1967	1,414	122*	1	25.70	88	6-43	29.07	4/1	22	
Naik Sudhir Sakharam	21.2.1945		3	1974–1974	141	77	0	23.50		–	–	–/–	0	
Naoomal Jeoomal	17.4.1904	28.7.1980	3	1932–1933	108	43	0	27.00	2	1-4	34.00	0/0	0	2
Narasimha Rao Modireddy Venkateshwar	11.8.1954		4	1978–1979	46	20*	0	9.20	3	2-46	75.66	0/0	8	
Navle Janaradan Gyanoba	7.12.1902	7.9.1979	2	1932–1933	42	13	0	10.50		–	–	–/–	1	
Nayak Surendra Vithal	20.10.1954		2	1982	19	11	0	9.50	1	1-16	132.00	0/0	1	
[2]Nayudu Cottari Kanakaiya (*CY 1933*)	31.10.1895	14.11.1967	7	1932–1936	350	81	0	25.00	9	3-40	42.88	0/0	4	4
[2]Nayudu Cottari Subhanna	18.4.1914	22.11.2002	11	1933–1951	147	36	0	9.18	2	1-19	179.50	0/0	3	
[2]Nazir Ali Syed	8.6.1906	18.2.1975	2	1932–1933	30	13	0	7.50	4	4-83	20.75	0/0	0	
Nehra Ashish	29.4.1979		17	1999–2004	77	19	0	5.50	44	4-72	42.40	0/0	5	117‡/8
Nissar Mohammad	1.8.1910	11.3.1963	6	1932–1936	55	14	0	6.87	25	5-90	28.28	3/0	1	
Nyalchand Sukhlal Shah	14.9.1915	3.1.1997	1	1952	7	6*	0	7.00	3	3-97	32.33	0/0	0	
Ojha Pragyan Prayish	5.9.1986		24	2009–2013	89	18*	0	8.90	113	6-47	30.26	7/1	10	18/6
Pai Ajit Manohar	28.4.1945		1	1969	10	9	0	5.00	2	2-29	15.50	0/0	0	
Palia Phiroze Edulji	5.9.1910	9.9.1981	2	1932–1936	29	16	0	9.66	0	0-2	–	0/0	0	
Pandit Chandrakant Sitaram	30.9.1961		5	1986–1991	171	39	0	24.42		–	–	–/–	14/2	36
Parkar Ghulam Ahmed	25.10.1955		2	1982	7	6	0	3.50		–	–	–/–	0	10
Parkar Ramnath Dhondu	31.10.1946	11.8.1999	2	1972	80	35	0	20.00		–	–	–/–	3	
Parsana Dhiraj Devshibhai	2.12.1947		2	1978	1	1	0	0.50	1	1-32	50.00	0/0	0	
Patankar Chandrakant Trimbak	24.11.1930		1	1955	14	13	0	14.00		–	–	–/–	3/1	
[1]Pataudi Iftikhar Ali Khan, Nawab of (*CY 1932*)	16.3.1910	5.1.1952	3†	1946	55	22	0	11.00		–	–	–/–	0	
[1]Pataudi Mansur Ali Khan, Nawab of (*CY 1968*)	5.1.1941	22.9.2011	46	1961–1975	2,793	203*	6	34.91	1	1-10	88.00	0/0	27	10
Patel Brijesh Pursuram	24.11.1952		21	1974–1977	972	115*	1	29.45		–	–	–/–	17	
Patel Jasubhai Motibhai	26.11.1924	12.12.1992	7	1954–1959	25	12	0	2.77	29	9-69	21.96	2/1	2	
Patel Munaf Musa	12.7.1983		13	2005–2011	60	15*	0	7.50	35	4-25	38.54	0/0	6	70/3
Patel Parthiv Ajay	9.3.1985		20	2002–2008	683	69	0	29.69		–	–	–/–	41/8	38/2
Patel Rashid	1.6.1964		1	1988	0		0	0.00	1	0-14	–	0/0	1	1
Pathan Irfan Khan	27.10.1984		29	2003–2007	1,105	102	1	31.57	100	7-59	32.26	7/2	8	120/24
Patiala Maharajah of (Yadavendra Singh)	17.1.1913	17.6.1974	1	1933	84	60	0	42.00		–	–	–/–	2	
Patil Sadashiv Raoji	10.10.1933		1	1955	14	14*	0	14.00	2	1-15	25.50	0/0	0	
Patil Sandeep Madhusudan	18.8.1956		29	1979–1984	1,588	174	4	36.93	9	2-28	26.66	0/0	12	45
Phadkar Dattatraya Gajanan	12.12.1925	17.3.1985	31	1947–1958	1,229	123	1	32.34	62	7-159	36.85	3/0	21	
Powar Ramesh Rajaram	20.5.1978		2	2007	13	7	0	6.50	6	3-33	19.66	0/0	0	31
Prabhakar Manoj	15.4.1963		39	1984–1995	1,600	120	1	32.65	96	6-132	37.30	3/0	20	130
Prasad Bapu Krishnarao Venkatesh	5.8.1969		33	1996–2001	203	30*	0	7.51	96	6-33	35.00	7/1	6	161

	Born	Died	Tests	Test Career	Runs	HS	100s	Avge	Wkts	BB	5/10	Avge	Ct/St	O/T
Prasad Mamava Sri Kanth	24.4.1975	—	6	1999	106	19	0	11.77	—	—	-/-	—	15	17
Prasanna Erapalli Anatharao Srinivas	22.5.1940	—	49	1961–1978	735	37	0	11.48	189	8-76	10/2	30.38	18	—
Pujara Cheteshwar Arvind	25.1.1988	—	17	2010–2013	1,590	206*	4	66.25	0	—	-/-	—	10	2
Punjabi Pananmal Hotchand	20.9.1921	—	5	1954	164	33	0	16.40	—	—	-/-	—	5	—
Rahane Ajinkya Madhukar	6.6.1988	—	3	2012–2013	217	96	0	43.40	—	—	-/-	—	5	18/7
Rai Singh Kanwar	24.2.1922	—	1	1947	26	24	0	13.00	—	—	-/-	—	1	—
Raina Suresh Kumar	27.11.1986	—	17	2010–2012	768	120	1	28.44	13	2-1	0/0	40.92	22	186/37
Rajinder Pal	18.11.1937	—	1	1963	6	3*	0	6.00	—	0-3	-/-	—	0	—
Rajindernath Vijay	7.1.1928	22.11.1989	1	1952	—	—	—	—	—	—	-/-	—	0/4	—
Rajput Lalchand Sitaram	18.12.1961	—	2	1985	105	61	0	26.25	—	—	-/-	—	1	4
Raju Sagi Lakshmi Venkatapathy	9.7.1969	—	28	1989–2000	240	31	0	10.00	93	6-12	5/1	30.72	6	53
Raman Woorkeri Venkat	23.5.1965	—	11	1987–1996	448	96	0	24.88	2	1-7	0/0	64.50	6	27
Ramaswami Cotar	16.6.1896	1.1.1990	1	1936	170	60	0	56.66	0	—	-/-	—	20	—
Ramchand Gulabrai Sipahimalani	26.7.1927	8.9.2003	33	1952–1959	1,180	109	2	24.58	41	6-49	1/0	46.31	20	—
Ramesh Sadagoppan	16.10.1975	—	19	1998–2001	1,367	143	3	37.97	0	0-5	0/0	—	18	24
[2]Ramji Ladha	10.2.1900	20.12.1948	1	1933	1	1	0	0.50	0	0-64	0/0	—	0	—
Rangachari Commandur Rajagopalachari	14.4.1916	9.10.1993	4	1947–1948	8	8*	0	2.66	9	5-107	1/0	54.77	0	—
Rangnekar Khanderao Moreshwar	27.6.1917	11.10.1984	3	1947	33	18	0	5.50	—	—	-/-	—	0	—
Ranjane Vasant Baburao	22.7.1937	22.12.2011	7	1958–1964	40	16	0	6.66	19	4-72	0/0	34.15	1	—
Rathore Vikram	26.3.1969	—	6	1996–1996	131	44	0	13.10	0	—	-/-	—	12	7
Ratra Ajay	13.12.1981	—	6	2001–2002	163	115*	1	18.11	0	0-1	0/0	—	11/2	12
Razdan Vivek	25.8.1969	—	2	1989	6	6*	0	6.00	5	5-79	1/0	28.20	0	3
Reddy Bharath	12.11.1954	—	4	1979	38	21	0	9.50	—	—	-/-	—	9/2	3
Rege Madhusudan Ramachandra	18.3.1924	16.12.2013	1	1948	15	15	0	7.50	—	—	-/-	—	0	—
Roy Ambar	5.6.1945	19.9.1997	4	1969	91	48	0	13.00	1	1-6	0/0	66.00	0	—
[1]Roy Pankaj	31.5.1928	4.2.2001	43	1951–1960	2,442	173	5	32.56	1	—	-/-	—	16	—
[3]Roy Pranab	10.2.1957	—	2	1981	71	60*	0	35.50	—	—	-/-	—	1	—
Saha Wriddhaman Prasanta	24.10.1984	—	2	2009–2011	74	36	0	18.50	—	—	-/-	—	2	3
Sandhu Balwinder Singh	3.8.1956	—	8	1982–1983	214	71	0	30.57	10	3-87	0/0	55.70	1	22
Sanghvi Rahul Laxman	3.9.1974	—	1	2000	2	2	0	1.00	2	2-67	0/0	39.00	0	10
Sarandeep Singh	21.10.1979	—	3	2000–2001	43	39*	0	43.00	10	4-136	0/0	34.00	1	5
Sardesai Dilip Narayan	8.8.1940	2.7.2007	30	1961–1972	2,001	212	5	39.23	0	0-3	-/-	—	4	—
Sarwate Chandrasekhar Trimbak	22.7.1920	23.12.2003	9	1946–1951	208	37	0	13.00	3	1-16	0/0	124.66	0	—
Saxena Ramesh Chandra	20.7.1944	16.8.2011	1	1967	25	16	0	12.50	0	0-11	0/0	—	0	—
Sehwag Virender	20.10.1978	—	103§	2001–2012	8,503	319	23	49.43	40	5-104	1/0	47.35	90	241‡/19

§ Sehwag's figures exclude 83 runs and one catch for the ICC World XI v Australia in the Super Series Test in 2005-06.

	Born	Died	Tests	Test Career	Runs	HS	100s	Avge	Wkts	BB	5/10	Avge	Ct/St	O/T
Sekhar Thirumalai Ananthanpillai	28.3.1956		2	1982	0	0*	0	—	0	0-43	0/0	—	—	4
Sen Probir Kumar ("Khokhan")	31.5.1926	27.1.1970	14	1947–1952	165	25	0	11.78	0	—	—/—	—	20/11	
Sen Gupta Apoorva Kumar	3.8.1939		1	1958	9	8	0	4.50	0	—	—/—	—	0	
Sharma Ajay Kumar	3.4.1964		1	1987	53	30	0	26.50	0	0-9	0/0	—	0	31
Sharma Chetan	3.1.1966		23	1984–1988	396	54	0	22.00	61	6-58	4/1	35.45	7	65
Sharma Gopal	3.8.1960		5	1984–1990	11	10*	0	3.66	10	4-88	0/0	41.80	2	11
Sharma Ishant	2.9.1988		53	2007–2013	459	31*	0	9.18	149	6-55	3/1	38.81	12	70/14
Sharma Parthasarathy Harishchandra	5.1.1948	20.10.2010	5	1974–1976	187	54	0	18.70	0	0-2	0/0	—	4	2
Sharma Rohit Gurunath	30.4.1987		4	2013	333	177	2	66.60	0	0-10	0/0	—	1	114/36
Sharma Sanjeev Kumar	25.8.1965		2	1988–1990	56	38	0	28.00	6	3-37	0/0	41.16	—	23
Shastri Ravishankar Jayadritha	27.5.1962		80	1980–1992	3,830	206	11	35.79	151	5-75	2/0	40.96	36	150
Shinde Sadashiv Ganpatrao	18.8.1923	22.6.1955	7	1946–1952	85	14	0	14.16	12	6-91	1/0	59.75	0	
Shodhan Roshan Harshadlal ("Deepak")	18.10.1928		3	1952	181	110	1	60.33	0	0-1	0/0	—	0	
Shukla Rakesh Chandra	4.2.1948		1	1982			—	—	2	2-82	0/0	76.00	1	
Siddiqui Iqbal Rashid	26.12.1974		1	2001	29	24	0	29.00	1	1-32	0/0	48.00	0	
Sidhu Navjot Singh	20.10.1963		51	1983–1998	3,202	201	9	42.13	0	0-9	0/0	—	9	136
Singh Rabindra Ramanarayan ("Robin")	14.9.1963		1	1998	27	15	0	13.50	0	0-16	0/0	—	5	136
Singh Robin	1.1.1970		1	1998	0	0	0	0.00	0	2-74	0/0	58.66	1	
Singh Rudra Pratap	6.12.1985		14	2005–2011	116	30	0	7.25	40	5-59	1/0	42.05	6	58/10
Singh Vikram Rajvir	17.9.1984		5	2005–2007	47	29	0	11.75	8	3-48	0/0	53.37	1	2
Sivaramakrishnan Laxman	31.12.1965		9	1982–1985	130	25	0	16.25	26	6-64	3/1	44.03	9	16
Sohoni Sriranga Wasudev	5.3.1918	19.5.1993	4	1946–1951	83	29*	0	16.60	2	1-16	0/0	101.00	2	
Solkar Eknath Dhondu	18.3.1948	26.6.2005	27	1969–1976	1,068	102	1	25.42	18	3-28	0/0	59.44	53	7
Sood Man Mohan	6.7.1939		1	1959	3	3	0	1.50	0	—	—/—	—	0	
Sreesanth Shanthakumaran	6.2.1983		27	2005–2011	281	35	0	10.40	87	5-40	3/0	37.59	8	53/10
Srikkanth Krishnamachari	21.12.1959		43	1981–1991	2,062	123	2	29.88	0	0-1	0/0	—	40	146
Srinath Javagal	31.8.1969		67	1991–2002	1,009	76	0	14.21	236	8-86	10/1	30.49	22	229
Srinivasan Thirumalai Echambadi	26.10.1950	6.12.2010	1	1980	48	29	0	24.00		—/—		—	9	2
Subramanya Venkataraman	16.7.1936		9	1964–1967	263	75	0	18.78	3	2-32	0/0	67.00	9	
Sunderam Gundibali Rama	29.3.1930	20.6.2010	2	1955	3	3*	0	—	3	2-46	0/0	55.33	0	
Surendranath	4.1.1937	5.5.2012	11	1958–1960	136	27	0	10.46	26	5-75	2/0	40.50	4	
Surti Rusi Framroze	25.5.1936	13.1.2013	26	1960–1969	1,263	99	0	28.70	42	5-74	1/0	46.71	26	
Swamy Venkatraman Narayan	23.5.1924	1.5.1983	1	1955			—	—	0	0-15	0/0	—	0	
Tamhane Narendra Shankar	4.8.1931	19.3.2002	21	1954–1960	225	54*	0	10.22	—	—/—		—	35/16	
Tarapore Keki Khurshedji	17.12.1910	15.6.1986	1	1948	2		0	2.00	0	0-72	0/0	—	0	
Tendulkar Sachin Ramesh (CY 1997)	24.4.1973		200	1989–2013	15,921	248*	51	53.78	46	3-10	0/0	54.17	115	463/1

	Born	Died	Tests	Test Career	Runs	HS	100s	Avge	Wkts	BB	5/10	Avge	Ct/St	O/T
Umrigar Pahlanji Ratanji ("Polly")	28.3.1926	7.11.2006	59	1948–1961	3,631	223	12	42.22	35	6-74	2/0	42.08	33	7
Unadkat Jaydev Dipakbhai	18.10.1991		1		0	2*	0	2.00	0	0-101	0/0	–	0	7
Vengsarkar Dilip Balwant (CY 1987)	6.4.1956		116	1975–1991	6,868	166	17	42.13	0	0-3	0/0	–	78	129
Venkataraghavan Srinivasaraghavan	21.4.1945		57	1964–1983	748	64	0	11.68	156	8-72	3/1	36.11	44	15
Venkataramana Margashayam	24.4.1966		1	1988	0	0*	0	–	1	1-10	0/0	58.00	1	1
Vijay Murali.	1.4.1984		20	2008–2013	1,256	167	3	38.06	0	0-3	0/0	–	20	147
Vinay Kumar Ranganath.	12.2.1984		1	2011	11	6	0	5.50	1	1-73	0/0	73.00	0	31/9
Viswanath Gundappa Rangnath	12.2.1949		91	1969–1982	6,080	222	14	41.93	1	1-11	0/0	46.00	63	25
Viswanath Sadanand.	29.11.1962		3	1985	31	20	0	6.20	–	–	–/–	–	11	22
Vizianagram Maharajkumar of (Sir Vijaya Anand).	28.12.1905	2.12.1965	3	1936	33	19*	0	8.25	0	0-0	–/–	–	1	
Wadekar Ajit Laxman.	1.4.1941		37	1966–1974	2,113	143	1	31.07	0	0-0	0/0	–	46	2
Wasim Jaffer.	16.2.1978		31	1999–2007	1,944	212	5	34.10	2	2-18	0/0	9.00	27	2
Wassan Atul Satish.	23.3.1968		4	1989–1990	94	53	0	16.92	10	4-108	0/0	50.40		9
[1,2] Wazir Ali Syed.	15.9.1903	17.6.1950	7	1932–1936	237	42	0	16.92	0	0-0	0/0	–		
Yadav Nandlal Shivlal.	26.1.1957		35	1979–1986	403	43	0	14.39	102	5-76	3/0	35.09	10	7
Yadav Umeshkumar Tilak.	25.10.1987		9	2011–2012	36	21	0	6.00	32	5-93	1/0	32.50	2	28/1
Yadav Vijay.	14.3.1967		1	1992	30	30	0	30.00	–	–	–/–	–	1/2	19
Yajurvindra Singh.	1.8.1952		4	1976–1979	109	43*	0	18.16	0	0-2	0/0	–	11	
Yashpal Sharma.	11.8.1954		37	1979–1983	1,606	140	2	33.45	1	1-6	0/0	17.00	16	42
[1] Yograj Singh	25.3.1958		1	1980	10	6	0	5.00	1	1-63	0/0	63.00	0	6
[1] Yohannan Tinu	18.2.1979		3	2001–2002	13	8*	0	–	5	2-56	0/0	51.20	1	3
[1] Yuvraj Singh (CY 2008)	12.12.1981		40	2003–2012	1,900	169	3	33.92	9	2-9	0/0	60.77	31	290‡/34
Zaheer Khan (CY 2008)	7.10.1978		90	2003–2013	1,178	75	0	11.78	302	7-87	10/1	32.66	19	194‡/17

PAKISTAN (218 players)

	Born	Died	Tests	Test Career	Runs	HS	100s	Avge	Wkts	BB	5/10	Avge	Ct/St	O/T
Aamer Malik	3.1.1963		14	1987–1994	565	117	2	35.31	1	1-0	0/0	89.00	15/1	24
Aamer Nazir	2.1.1971		6	1992–1995	31	11	0	6.20	20	5-46	1/0	29.85	2	9
Aamir Sohail	14.9.1966		47	1992–1999	2,823	205	5	35.28	25	4-54	0/0	41.96	36	156
Abdul Kadir	10.5.1944		4	1964	272	95	0	34.00	–	–	–/–	–	0/1	
Abdul Qadir	15.9.1955	12.3.2002	67	1977–1990	1,029	61	0	15.59	236	9-56	15/5	32.80	15	104
Abdul Razzaq	2.12.1979		46	1999–2006	1,946	134	3	28.61	100	5-35	1/0	36.94	15	261‡/32
Abdur Rauf	9.12.1978		3	2009–2009	52	31	0	8.66	6	2-59	0/0	46.33	0	4/1

Name	Born	Died	Tests	Test Career	Runs	HS	100s	Avge	Wkts	BB	5/10	Avge	Ct/St	O/T
Abdur Rehman	1.3.1980		20	2007–2013	323	60	0	13.45	95	6-25	2/0	27.75	8	30/8
²Adnan Akmal	13.3.1985		21	2010–2013	591	64	0	24.62	–	–	–/–	–	66/11	5
Afaq Hussain	31.12.1939	25.2.2002	2	1961–1964	66	35*	0	48.50	1	1-40	0/0	106.00	2	
Aftab Baloch	1.4.1953		2	1969–1974	97	60*	0	22.75	0	0-2	0/0	–	1	
Aftab Gul	31.3.1946		6	1968–1971	182	33	0	–	0	0-4	0/0	–	3	
Agha Saadat Ali	21.6.1929	25.10.1995	1	1955	8	8*	0	7.50	–	–	–/–	–	3	
Agha Zahid	7.1.1953		1	1974	15	14	0	7.50	–			–	–	
Ahmed Shehzad	23.11.1991		3	2013	273	147	1	45.50	–			–	2	40/22
Aizaz Cheema	5.9.1979		7	2011–2012	1	1*	0	–	20	4-24	0/0	31.90	1	14/5
Akram Raza	22.11.1964		9	1989–1994	153	32	0	15.30	13	3-46	0/0	56.30	8	49
Ali Hussain Rizvi	6.1.1974		1	1997	–	–	–	–	2	2-72	0/0	36.00	–	
Ali Naqvi	19.3.1977		5	1997	242	115	1	30.25	0	0-11	0/0	–	1	
Alim-ud-Din	15.12.1930	12.7.2012	25	1954–1962	1,091	109	2	25.37	1	1-17	0/0	75.00	8	
Amir Elahi	1.9.1908	28.12.1980	5†	1952	65	47	0	10.83	7	4-134	0/0	35.42	–	
Anil Dalpat	20.9.1963		9	1983–1984	167	52	0	15.18	–	–	–/–	–	22/3	15
Anwar Hussain	16.7.1920	9.10.2002	4	1952	42	17	0	7.00	1	1-25	0/0	29.00	0	
Anwar Khan	24.12.1955		1	1978	15	12	0	15.00	0	0-12	0/0	–	0	
Aqib Javed	5.8.1972		22	1988–1998	101	28*	0	5.05	54	5-84	1/0	34.70	3	163
Arif Butt	17.5.1944	10.7.2007	3	1964	59	20	0	11.80	14	6-89	1/0	20.57	0	
Arshad Khan	22.3.1971		9	1997–2004	31	9*	0	5.16	32	5-38	1/0	30.00	5	58
Asad Shafiq	28.1.1986		26	2010–2013	1,391	130	4	36.60	–	–	–/–	–	22	46/10
Ashfaq Ahmed	6.6.1973		1	1993	1	1*	0	1.00	2	2-31	0/0	26.50	0	3
Ashraf Ali	22.4.1958		8	1981–1987	229	65	0	45.80	–	–	–/–	–	17/5	16
Asif Iqbal (CY 1968)	6.6.1943		58	1964–1979	3,575	175	11	38.85	53	5-48	2/0	28.33	36	10
Asif Masood	23.1.1946		16	1968–1976	93	30*	0	10.33	38	5-111	1/0	41.26	5	7
Asif Mujtaba	4.11.1967		25	1986–1996	928	65*	0	24.42	4	1-0	0/0	75.75	19	66
Asim Kamal	31.5.1976		12	2003–2005	717	99	0	37.73	–	–	–/–	–	10	
Ata-ur-Rehman	28.3.1975		13	1992–1996	76	19	0	8.44	31	4-50	0/0	34.54	2	30
Atif Rauf	3.3.1964		1	1993	25	16	0	12.50	–	–	–/–	–	0	
Atiq-uz-Zaman	20.7.1975		1	1999	26	25	0	13.00	–	–	–/–	–	5	3
Azam Khan	1.3.1969		1	1996	14	14	0	14.00	–	–	–/–	–	0	6
Azeem Hafeez	29.7.1963		18	1983–1984	134	24	0	8.37	63	6-46	4/0	34.98	1	15
Azhar Ali	19.2.1985		32	2010–2013	2,192	157	5	39.14	1	1-4	0/0	100.00	27	14
Azhar Khan	7.9.1955		1	1979	14	14	0	14.00	1	1-1	0/0	2.00	1	
Azhar Mahmood	28.2.1975		21	1997–2001	900	136	3	30.00	39	4-50	0/0	35.94	14	143
²Azmat Rana	3.11.1951		1	1979	49	49	0	49.00	–	–	–/–	–	0	2

	Born	Died	Tests	Test Career	Runs	HS	100s	Avge	Wkts	BB	Avge	5/10	Ct/St	O/T
Basit Ali	13.12.1970		19	1992–1995	858	103	1	26.81	0	0-6	–	0/0	6	50
[3] Baizid Khan	25.3.1981		1	2004	32	23	0	16.00	0	–	–	–/–	2	5
Bilawal Bhatti	17.9.1991		2	2013	70	29	0	35.00	6	3-65	48.50	0/0	2	7/5
Danish Kaneria	16.12.1980		61	2000–2010	360	29	0	7.05	261	7-77	34.79	15/2	18	18
D'Souza Antao	17.1.1939		6	1958–1962	76	23*	0	38.00	17	5-112	43.82	1/0	3	
Ehsan Adil	15.3.1993		1	2012	21	12	0	10.50	2	2-54	27.00	0/0	0	2
Ehtesham-ud-Din	4.9.1950		5	1979–1982	2	2	0	1.00	16	5-47	23.43	1/0	2	
Faisal Iqbal	30.12.1981		26	2000–2009	1,124	139	1	26.76	0	0-7	–	0/0	22	18
Farhan Adil	25.9.1977		1	2003	33	25	0	16.50	–	–	–	–/–	0	
Farooq Hamid	3.3.1945		1	1964	3	3	0	1.50	1	1-82	107.00	0/0	0	
Farrukh Zaman	2.4.1956		1	1976	–	–	–	–	0	0-7	–	–/–	0	
Fawad Alam	8.10.1985		3	2009–2009	250	168	1	41.66	–	–	–	–/–	3	27/24
Fazal Mahmood (CY 1955)	18.2.1927	30.5.2005	34	1952–1962	620	60	0	14.09	139	7-42	24.70	13/4	11	
Fazl-e-Akbar	20.10.1980		5	1997–2003	52	25	0	13.00	11	3-85	46.45	0/0	2	2
Ghazali Mohammad Ebrahim Zainuddin	15.6.1924	26.4.2003	2	1954	32	18	0	8.00	0	0-18	–	0/0	1	
Ghulam Abbas	1.5.1947		1	1967	12	12	0	6.00	–	–	–	–/–	0	
Gul Mahomed	15.10.1921	8.5.1992	1†	1956	39	27*	0	39.00	–	–	–	–/–	0	
[1,2] Hanif Mohammad (CY 1968)	21.12.1934		55	1952–1969	3,915	337	12	43.98	1	1-1	95.00	0/0	40	
Haroon Rashid	25.3.1953		23	1976–1982	1,217	153	3	34.77	0	0-3	–	0/0	16	12
Hasan Raza	11.3.1982		7	1996–2005	235	68	0	26.11	0	0-1	–	0/0	5	16
Haseeb Ahsan	15.7.1939	8.3.2013	12	1957–1961	61	14	0	6.77	27	6-202	49.25	2/0	1	
[2] Humayun Farhat	11.3.1982		1	2005	54	28	0	27.00	–	–	–	–/–	3	5
Ibadulla Khalid ("Billy")	20.12.1935		4	1964–1967	253	166	1	31.62	1	1-42	99.00	0/0	3	
Iftikhar Anjum	1.12.1980		1	2007	9	9*	0	–	0	0-8	–	0/0	0	62/2
Ijaz Ahmed, sen.	20.9.1968		60	1986–2000	3,315	211	12	37.67	2	1-9	38.50	0/0	45	250
Ijaz Ahmed, jun.	2.2.1969		2	1995	29	16	0	9.66	0	0-1	–	0/0	3	2
Ijaz Butt	10.3.1938		8	1958–1962	279	58	0	19.92	–	–	–	–/–	5	
Ijaz Faqih	24.3.1956		5	1980–1987	183	105	1	26.14	4	1-38	74.75	0/0	3	27
[2] Imran Farhat	20.5.1982		40	2000–2012	2,400	128	3	32.00	3	2-69	94.66	0/0	40	58/7
[2] Imran Khan (CY 1983)	25.11.1952		88	1971–1991	3,807	136	6	37.69	362	8-58	22.81	23/6	28	175
Imran Nazir	16.12.1981		8	1998–2002	427	131	2	32.84	0	–	–	–/–	4	79/25
Imtiaz Ahmed	5.1.1928		41	1952–1962	2,079	209	3	29.28	0	0-0	–	0/0	77/16	
Intikhab Alam	28.12.1941		47	1959–1976	1,493	138	0	22.28	125	7-52	35.95	5/2	20	4
Inzamam-ul-Haq	3.3.1970		119§	1992–2007	8,829	329	25	50.16	0	0-8	–	0/0	81	375/11
Iqbal Qasim	6.8.1953		50	1976–1988	549	56	0	13.07	171	7-49	28.11	8/2	42	15

§ *Inzamam-ul-Haq's figures exclude one run for the ICC World XI v Australia in the Super Series Test in 2005-06.*

	Born	Died	Tests	Test Career	Runs	HS	100s	Avge	Wkts	BB	Avge	5/10	Ct/St	O/T
Irfan Fazil	2.11.1981		1	1999	4	3	0	4.00	2	1-30	32.50	0/0	2	1
Israr Ali	1.5.1927		4	1952–1959	33	10	0	4.71	6	2-29	27.50	0/0	1	
Jalal-ud-Din	12.6.1959		6	1982–1985	3	2*	0	3.00	11	3-77	48.81	0/0	0	8
Javed Akhtar	21.11.1940		1	1962	4	2*	0	4.00	0	0-52	–	0/0	0	
Javed Burki	8.5.1938		25	1960–1969	1,341	140	3	30.47	0	0-2	–	0/0	7	
Javed Miandad (CY 1982)	12.6.1957		124	1976–1993	8,832	280*	23	52.57	17	3-74	–	0/0	93/1	233
Junaid Khan	24.12.1989		16	2011–2013	98	17	0	7.00	56	5-38	29.07	4/0	3	42/8
Kabir Khan	12.4.1974		4	1994	24	10	0	8.00	9	3-26	41.11	0/0	1	10
² Kamran Akmal	13.1.1982		53	2002–2010	2,648	158*	6	30.79				–/–	184/22	154/50
Kardar Abdul Hafeez	17.1.1925	21.4.1996	23†	1952–1957	847	93	0	24.91	21	3-35	45.42	0/0	15	
Khalid Hassan	14.7.1937	3.12.2013	1	1954	17	10	0	17.00	2	2-116	58.00	0/0	0	
³ Khalid Wazir	27.4.1936		2	1954	14	9*	0	7.00				–/–	0	
Khan Mohammad	1.1.1928	4.7.2009	13	1952–1957	100	26*	0	10.00	54	6-21	23.92	4/0	4	
Khurram Manzoor	10.6.1986		14	2008–2013	778	146	1	31.12				–/–	7	
Liaqat Ali	21.5.1955		5	1974–1978	28	12	0	7.00	6	3-80	59.83	0/0	1	7
Mahmood Hussain	2.4.1932	25.12.1991	27	1952–1962	336	35	0	10.18	68	6-67	38.64	2/0	5	3
³ Majid Jahangir Khan (CY 1970)	28.9.1946		63	1964–1982	3,931	167	8	38.92	27	4-45	53.92	0/0	70	23
Mansoor Akhtar	25.12.1957		19	1980–1989	655	111	1	25.19				–/–	9	41
² Manzoor Elahi	15.4.1963		6	1984–1994	123	52	0	15.37	7	2-38	27.71	0/0	7	54
Maqsood Ahmed	26.3.1925	4.1.1999	16	1952–1955	507	99	0	19.50	3	2-12	63.66	0/0	13	
Masood Anwar	12.12.1967		1	1990	39	37	0	19.50	3	2-59	34.00	0/0	0	
Mathias Wallis	4.2.1955	1.9.1994	21	1955–1962	783	77	0	23.72	0	0-20	–	0/0	22	
Miran Bux	20.4.1907	8.2.1991	2	1954	1	1*	0	1.00	2	2-82	57.50	0/0	0	
Misbah-ul-Haq	28.5.1974		46	2001–2013	3,218	161*	5	48.75				–/–	37	141/39
Mohammad Aamer	13.4.1992		14	2009–2010	278	30*	0	12.63	51	6-84	29.09	3/0	1	15/18
Mohammad Akram	10.9.1974		9	1995–2000	24	10*	0	2.66	17	5-138	50.52	1/0	4	23
Mohammad Asif	20.12.1982		23	2004–2010	141	29	0	5.64	106	6-41	24.36	7/1	3	35/11
Mohammad Aslam Khokhar	5.1.1920	22.1.2011	1	1954	34	18	0	17.00				–/–	0	
Mohammad Ayub	13.9.1974		1	2012	47	25	0	23.50				–/–	1	
Mohammad Farooq	8.4.1938		7	1960–1964	85	47	0	17.00	21	4-70	32.47	0/0	1	
Mohammad Hafeez	17.10.1980		36	2003–2013	2,174	196	5	33.96	35	4-16	34.00	0/0	26	141/54
Mohammad Hussain	8.10.1976		2	1996–1998	18	17	0	6.00	3	2-66	29.00	0/0	1	14
Mohammad Ilyas	19.3.1946		10	1964–1968	441	126	1	23.21	1	0-1	–	0/0	6	
Mohammad Irfan	6.6.1982		4	2012–2013	28	14	0	5.60	10	3-44	38.90	0/0	0	27/7
Mohammad Khalil	11.11.1982		2	2004	9	5	0	3.00	0	0-38	–	0/0	0	3
Mohammad Munaf	2.11.1935		4	1959–1961	63	19	0	12.60	11	4-42	31.00	0/0	0	

Name	Born	Died	Tests	Test Career	Runs	HS	100s	Avge	Wkts	BB	Avge	5/10	Ct/St	O/T
Mohammad Nazir	8.3.1946		14	1969–1983	144	29*	0	18.00	34	7-99	33.05	3/0	4	4
Mohammad Ramzan	25.12.1970		1	1997	36	29	0	18.00					1	
Mohammad Salman	7.8.1981		2	2010	25	13	0	6.25					7/2	7/1
Mohammad Sami	24.2.1981		36	2000–2012	487	49	0	11.59	85	5-36	52.74	2/0	7	85/5
Mohammad Talha	15.10.1988		2	2008–2013	2	2	0	2.00	7	3-65	36.00	0/0		
Mohammad Wasim	8.8.1977		18	1996–2000	783	192	2	30.11					22/2	25
Mohammad Yousuf (formerly Yousuf Youhana) (CY 2007)	27.8.1974		90	1997–2010	7,530	223	24	52.29	0	0-3			65	281‡/3
Mohammad Zahid	2.8.1976		5	1996–2002	7	6*	0	1.40	15	7-66	33.46	1/1	4	11
Mohsin Kamal	16.6.1963		9	1983–1994	37	13*	0	9.25	24	4-116	34.25	0/0	4	19
Mohsin Khan	15.3.1955		48	1977–1986	2,709	200	7	37.10	0	0-0			34	75
[1] Moin Khan	23.9.1971		69	1990–2004	2,741	137	4	28.55					128/20	219
Mudassar Nazar	6.4.1956		76	1976–1988	4,114	231	10	38.09	66	6-32	38.36	1/0	48	122
Mufasir-ul-Haq	16.8.1944	27.7.1983	1	1964	8	8*	0		3	2-50	28.00	0/0	1	
Munir Malik	10.7.1934	30.11.2012	3	1959–1962	7	4*	0	2.33	9	5-128	29.77	1/0		
Mushtaq Ahmed (CY 1997)	28.6.1970		52	1989–2003	656	59	0	11.71	185	7-56	32.97	10/3	23	144
[2] Mushtaq Mohammad (CY 1963)	22.11.1943		57	1958–1978	3,643	201	10	39.17	79	5-28	29.22	3/0	42	10
Nadeem Abbasi	15.4.1964		3	1989	46	36	0	23.00					6	
Nadeem Ghauri	12.10.1962		1	1989	0	0	0	0.00	0	0-20			0	6
Nadeem Khan	10.12.1969		2	1992–1998	34	25	0	17.00	2	2-147	115.00	0/0	2	2
Nasim-ul-Ghani	14.5.1941		29	1957–1972	747	101	1	16.60	52	6-67	37.67	2/0	11	1
Nasir Jamshed	6.12.1989		2	2012	51	46	0	12.75					1	43/18
Naushad Ali	1.10.1943		6	1964	156	39	0	14.18					9	
Naved Anjum	27.7.1963		2	1989–1990	44	22	0	14.66	4	2-57	40.50	0/0	0	13
Naved Ashraf	4.9.1974		2	1998–1999	64	32	0	21.33					0	
Naved Latif	21.2.1976		1	2001	20	20	0	10.00					0	11
Naved-ul-Hasan	28.2.1978		9	2004–2006	239	42*	0	19.91	18	3-30	58.00	0/0	7	74/4
[1] Nazar Mohammad	5.3.1921	12.7.1996	5	1952	277	124*	1	39.57	0	0-4			3	
Niaz Ahmed	11.11.1945	12.4.2000	2	1967–1968	17	16*	0		3	2-72	31.33	0/0	0	
[2] Pervez Sajjad	30.8.1942		19	1964–1972	123	24	0	13.66	59	7-74	23.89	3/0	9	
Qaiser Abbas	7.5.1982		2	2000	2	2	0	2.00	0	0-35			0	
Qasim Omar	9.2.1957		26	1983–1986	1,502	210	3	36.63	0	0-0			15	31
Rahat Ali	12.9.1988		6	2012–2013	70	35*	0	11.66	16	6-127	45.31	2/0	4	1
[2] Ramiz Raja	14.8.1962		57	1983–1996	2,833	122	2	31.83					34	198
Rashid Khan	15.12.1959		4	1981–1984	155	59	0	51.66	8	3-129	45.00	0/0	2	29
Rashid Latif	14.10.1968		37	1992–2003	1,381	150	1	28.77	0	0-10			119/11	166

	Born	Died	Tests	Test Career	Runs	HS	100s	Avge	Wkts	BB	5/10	Avge	Ct/St	O/T
Rehman Sheikh Fazalur	11.6.1935		1	1957	10	8	0	5.00					1	
Riaz Afridi	21.1.1985		1	2004	9	9	0	9.00	2	1-43	0/0	43.50	0	
Rizwan-uz-Zaman	4.9.1961		11	1981–1988	345	60	0	19.16		3-26	0/0	11.50	4	3
Sadiq Mohammad	3.5.1945		41	1969–1980	2,579	166	5	35.81	0	0-0	0/0		28	19
[2] Saeed Ahmed	1.10.1937		41	1957–1972	2,991	172	5	40.41	22	4-64	0/0	36.45	13	
Saeed Ajmal	14.10.1977		33	2009–2013	428	50	0	11.26	169	7-55	9/4	27.46		105/59
Saeed Anwar (CY 1997)	6.9.1968		55	1990–2001	4,052	188*	11	45.52	0	0-0	0/0		18	247
Salah-ud-Din	14.2.1947		5	1964–1969	117	34*	0	19.50	7	2-36	0/0	26.71	3	
Saleem Jaffer	19.11.1962		14	1986–1991	42	10*	0	5.25	36	5-40	1/0	31.63	3	39
Salim Altaf	19.4.1944		21	1967–1978	276	53*	0	14.52	46	4-11	0/0	37.17		6
Salim Elahi	21.11.1976		13	1995–2002	436	72	0	18.95			–/–		10/1	48
[2] Salim Malik (CY 1988)	16.4.1963		103	1981–1998	5,768	237	15	43.69	5	1-3	0/0	82.80	65	283
Salim Yousuf	7.12.1959		32	1981–1990	1,055	91*	0	27.05			–/–		91/13	86
Salman Butt	7.10.1984		33	2003–2010	1,889	122	3	30.46	1	1-36	0/0	106.00	12	78/24
Saqlain Mushtaq (CY 2000)	29.12.1976		49	1995–2003	927	101*	1	14.48	208	8-164	13/3	29.83	15	169
Sarfraz Ahmed	22.5.1987		6	2009–2013	223	74	0	18.58			–/–		14	26/4
Sarfraz Nawaz	1.12.1948		55	1968–1983	1,045	90	0	17.71	177	9-86	4/1	32.75	26	45
Shabbir Ahmed	21.4.1976		10	2003–2005	88	24*	0	8.80	51	5-48	2/0	23.03	3	32/1
Shadab Kabir	12.11.1977		5	1996–2001	148	55	0	21.14					11	
Shafiq Ahmed	28.3.1949		6	1974–1980	99	27*	0	11.00	0	0-1	0/0		5	3
Shafqat Rana	10.8.1943		5	1964–1969	221	95	0	31.57	1	1-2	0/0	9.00	10	3
Shahid Afridi	1.3.1980		27	1998–2010	1,716	156	5	36.51	48	5-52	1/0	35.60		368±70
Shahid Israr		29.4.2013	1	1976	7	7*	0	–			–/–			
Shahid Mahboob	25.8.1962		1	1989			–	–	2	2-131	0/0	65.50		10
Shahid Mahmood	17.3.1939		1	1962	25	16	0	12.50	0	0-23	0/0			
Shahid Nazir	4.12.1977		15	1996–2006	194	40	0	12.12	36	5-53	1/0	35.33	5	17
Shahid Saeed	6.1.1966		1	1989	12	12	0	12.00	0	0-7	0/0		0	10
Shakeel Ahmed, sen.	12.2.1966		1	1998	1	1	0	1.00	4	4-91	0/0	34.75		
Shakeel Ahmed, jun.	12.11.1971		3	1992–1994	74	33	0	14.80			–/–		4	2
Shan Masood	14.10.1989		2	2013	96	75	0	24.00			–/–			
Sharpe Duncan Albert	3.8.1937		3	1959	134	56	0	22.33			–/–		2	
Shoaib Akhtar	13.8.1975		46	1997–2007	544	47	0	10.07	178	6-11	12/2	25.69	12	158±15
Shoaib Malik	1.2.1982		32	2001–2010	1,606	148*	1	33.45	21	4-42	0/0	61.47	16	216/55
[1] Shoaib Mohammad	8.1.1961		45	1983–1995	2,705	203*	7	44.34	5	2-8	0/0	34.00	22	63
Shuja-ud-Din Butt	10.4.1930	7.2.2006	19	1954–1961	395	47	0	15.19	20	3-18	0/0	40.05	8	
Sikander Bakht	25.8.1957		26	1976–1982	146	22*	0	6.34	67	8-69	3/1	36.00	7	27

	Born	Died	Tests	Test Career	Runs	HS	100s	Avge	Wkts	BB	5/10	Avge	Ct/St	O/T
Sohail Khan	6.3.1984		2	2008–2011	11	11	0	11.00	5	1-62	0/0	245.00	0	5/3
Sohail Tanvir	12.12.1984		2	2007	17	13	0	5.66	5	3-83	0/0	63.20	2	58/38
Tahir Naqqash	6.6.1959		15	1981–1984	300	57	0	21.42	34	5-40	2/0	41.11	3	40
Talat Ali Malik	29.5.1950		10	1972–1978	370	61	0	23.12	0	0-1	0/0	–	4	–
Tanvir Ahmed	20.12.1978		5	2010–2012	170	57	0	34.00	17	6-120	1/0	26.64	1	2/1
Taslim Arif	1.5.1954	13.3.2008	6	1979–1980	501	210*	1	62.62	0	1-28	0/0	28.00	6/3	2
Taufeeq Umar	20.6.1981		43	2001–2012	2,943	236	7	38.72	0	0-0	0/0	–	47	22
Tauseef Ahmed	10.5.1958		34	1979–1993	318	35*	0	17.66	93	6-45	3/0	31.72	9	70
²Umar Akmal	26.5.1990		16	2009–2011	1,003	129	1	35.82	0	–	–/–	–	12	89/52
Umar Amin	16.10.1989		4	2010	99	33	0	12.37	3	1-7	0/0	21.00	1	14/9
Umar Gul	14.4.1984		47	2003–2012	577	65*	0	9.94	163	6-135	4/0	34.06	11	119/52
Wahab Riaz	28.6.1985		7	2010–2010	57	27	0	9.50	17	5-63	1/0	34.11	1	39/6
Wajahatullah Wasti	11.11.1974		6	1998–1999	329	133	2	36.55	0	0-0	0/0	–	7	15
²Waqar Hassan	12.9.1932		21	1952–1959	1,071	189	1	31.50	0	0-10	0/0	–	10	–
Waqar Younis (CY 1992)	16.11.1971		87	1989–2002	1,010	45	0	10.20	373	7-76	22/5	23.56	18	262
Wasim Akram (CY 1993)	3.6.1966		104	1984–2001	2,898	257*	3	22.64	414	7-119	25/5	23.62	44	356
Wasim Bari	23.3.1948		81	1967–1983	1,366	85	0	15.88	0	0-2	0/0	–	201/27	51
²Wasim Raja	3.7.1952	23.8.2006	57	1972–1984	2,821	125	4	36.16	51	4-50	0/0	35.80	20	54
Wazir Mohammad	22.12.1929		20	1952–1959	801	189	2	27.62	0	0-0	0/0	–	5	–
Yasir Ali	15.10.1985		1	2003	1	1*	0	–	2	1-12	0/0	27.50	0	11/13
Yasir Arafat	28.2.1982		3	2007–2008	94	50*	0	47.00	9	5-161	1/0	48.66	0	56
Yasir Hameed	28.2.1978		25	2003–2006	1,491	170	2	32.41	0	0-0	0/0	–	20	2
²Younas Ahmed	20.10.1947		4	1969–1986	177	62	0	29.50	0	0-6	0/0	–	0	–
Younis Khan	29.11.1977		89	1999–2013	7,399	313	23	51.38	9	2-23	0/0	54.55	98	253/25
Yousuf Youhana (see Mohammad Yousuf)														
Zaheer Abbas (CY 1972)	24.7.1947		78	1969–1985	5,062	274	12	44.79	3	2-21	0/0	44.00	34	62
Zahid Fazal	10.11.1973		9	1990–1995	288	78	0	18.00	–	–	–/–	–	5	19
²Zahoor Elahi	1.3.1971		2	1996	30	22	0	10.00	–	–	–/–	–	1	14
Zakir Khan	3.4.1963	3.10.2008	2	1985–1989	9	9*	0	–	5	3-80	0/0	51.80	1	17
Zulfiqar Ahmed	22.11.1926		9	1952–1956	200	63*	0	33.33	20	6-42	2/1	18.30	5	–
Zulfiqar Babar	10.12.1978		2	2013	27	25*	0	27.00	6	3-89	0/0	44.00	0	0/4
Zulqarnain	25.5.1962		3	1985	24	13	0	6.00	–	–	–/–	–	8/2	16
Zulqarnain Haider	23.4.1986		1	2010	88	88	0	44.00	–	–	–/–	–	2	4/3

SRI LANKA (126 players)

Name	Born	Died	Tests	Test Career	Runs	HS	100s	Avge	Wkts	BB	5/10	Avge	Ct/St	O/T
Ahangama Franklyn Saliya	14.9.1959		3	1985	54	34	0	18.00	18	5-52	1/0	19.33	1	1
Amalean Kaushik Naginda	7.4.1965		2	1985–1987	9	7*	0	9.00	7	4-97	0/0	22.28	1	8
Amerasinghe Amerasinghe Mudalige Jayantha Gamini	2.2.1954		2	1983	18	15*	0	9.00	3	2-73	0/0	50.00		
Amerasinghe Merenna Koralage Don Ishara	5.3.1978		1	2007	0	0*	0		1	1-62	0/0	105.00	0	8
Anurasiri Sangarange Don.	25.2.1966		18	1985–1997	91	24	0	5.35	41	4-71	0/0	37.75	4	45
Arnold Russel Premakumaran	25.10.1973		44	1996–2004	1,821	123	3	28.01	11	1-9	0/0	54.36	51	180/1
Atapattu Marvan Samson	22.11.1970		90	1990–2007	5,502	249	16	39.02					58	268/2
Bandara Herath Mudiyanselage Charitha Malinga	31.12.1979		8	1997–2005	124	43	0	15.50	16	3-84	0/0	39.56	4	31/4
Bandaratilleke Mapa Rallage Chandima Niroshan	16.5.1975		7	1997–2001	93	25	0	11.62	23	5-36	1/0	30.34	7	3
Chandana Umagiliya Durage Upul.	7.5.1972		16	1998–2004	616	92	0	26.78	37	6-179	1/0	41.48	3	147
Chandimal Lokuge Dinesh	18.11.1989		10	2011–2013	708	116*	2	47.20					12/4	74/21
Dassanayake Pubudu Bathiya	11.7.1970		11	1993–1994	196	36	0	13.06					19/5	16
de Alwis Ronald Guy	15.2.1959	12.1.2013	11	1982–1987	152	28	0	8.00					21/2	31
de Mel Ashantha Lakdasa Francis	9.5.1959		17	1981–1986	326	34	0	14.17	59	6-109	3/0	36.94	9	57
de Saram Samantha Indika	2.9.1973		4	1999	117	39	0	23.40					1	15/1
de Silva Ashley Matthew	3.12.1963		3	1992–1993	10	9	0	3.33					4/1	4
de Silva Dandeniyage Somachandra	11.6.1942		12	1981–1984	406	61	0	21.36	37	5-59	1/0	36.40	5	41
de Silva Ellawalakankanange Asoka Ranjit	28.3.1956		10	1985–1990	185	50	0	15.41	8	2-67	0/0	129.00	4	28
de Silva Ginigalgodage Ramba Ajit.	12.12.1952		4	1981–1982	41	14	0	8.20	7	2-38	0/0	55.00	0	6
de Silva Karunakalage Sajeewa Chanaka	11.1.1971		8	1996–1998	65	27	0	9.28	29	5-85	1/0	55.56	5	38
de Silva Pinnaduwage Aravinda (CY 1996).	17.10.1965		93	1984–2002	6,361	267	20	42.97	29	3-30	0/0	41.65	43	308
de Silva Sanjeewa Kumara Lanka	29.7.1975		3	1997	36	20*	0	12.00					1	11
de Silva Weddikkara Ruwan Sujeewa	7.10.1979		3	2002–2007	10	5*	0	10.00	11	4-35	0/0	19.00	1	
Dharmasena Handunnettige Deepthi Priyantha Kumar	24.4.1971		31	1993–2003	868	62*	0	19.72	69	6-72	3/0	42.31	14	141
Dias Roy Luke.	18.10.1952		20	1981–1986	1,285	109	3	36.71		0-17	0/0		6	58
Dilshan Tillekeratne Mudiyanselage	14.10.1976		87	1999–2012	5,492	193	16	40.98	39	4-10	0/0	43.87	88	275/53
Dunusinghe Chamara Iroshan.	19.10.1970		5	1994–1995	160	91	0	16.00					13/2	1
Eranga Ranaweera Mudiyanselage Shaminda	23.6.1986		10	2011–2013	105	25*	0	11.66	33	4-60	0/0	34.12	3	13/3
Fernando Aththachchi Nuwan Pradeep Roshan	19.10.1986		5	2011–2013	31	17*	0	5.16	8	3-62	0/0	73.12	0	2
Fernando Congenige Randhi Dilhara	19.7.1979		40	2000–2012	249	39*	0	8.30	100	5-42	3/0	37.84	10	146/17

	Born	Died	Tests	Test Career	Runs	HS	100s	Avge	Wkts	BB	5/10	Avge	Ct/St	O/T
Fernando Ellekunjge Rufus Nemesion Susil . . .	19.12.1955		5	1982–1983	112	46	0	11.20	4	3-63	0/0	27.00	0	7
Fernando Kandage Hasantha Ruwan Kumara . .	14.10.1979		2	2002	38	24	0	9.50			-/-		1	7
Fernando Kandana Arachchige Dinusha Manoj . .	10.8.1979		2	2003	56	51*	0	28.00	1	1-29	0/0	107.00		1
Fernando Thudellage Charitha Buddhika	22.8.1980		9	2001–2002	132	45	0	26.40	18	4-27	0/0	44.00	4	17
Gallage Indika Sanjeewa	22.11.1975		1	1999	3	3	0	3.00	0	0-24	0/0			3
Goonatillake Hettiaarachige Mahes	16.8.1952		5	1981–1982	177	56	0	22.12			-/-		10/3	6
Gunasekera Yohan	8.11.1957		2	1982	48	23	0	12.00			-/-		6	3
Gunawardene Dihan Avishka	26.5.1977		6	1998–2005	181	43	0	16.45			-/-		2	61
Guneratne Roshan Punyajith Wijesinghe . .	26.1.1962	21.7.2005	1	1982	0	0*	0		0	0-84	0/0		0	
Gurusinha Asanka Pradeep	16.9.1966		41	1985–1996	2,452	143	7	38.92	20	4-66	0/0	34.05	33	147
Hathurusinghe Upul Chandika	13.9.1968		26	1990–1998	1,274	83	0	29.62	17	2-7	0/0	46.41	7	35
Herath Herath Mudiyanselage Rangana Keerthi Bandara . .	19.3.1978		50	1999–2013	713	80*	0	12.96	214	7-89	17/3	29.98	11	55/6
Hettiarachchi Dinuka	15.7.1976		1	2000	0	0*	0	0.00	2	2-36	0/0	20.50		2
Jayasekera Rohan Stanley Amarasiriwardene . .	7.12.1957		1	1981	2	2	0	1.00			-/-			2
Jayasuriya Sanath Teran (CY 1997)	30.6.1969		110	1990–2007	6,973	340	14	40.07	98	5-34	2/0	34.34	78	441/31
Jayawardene Denagamage Proboth Mahela de Silva (CY 2007)	27.5.1977		141	1997–2013	11,033	374	32	49.47	6	2-32	0/0	49.50	194	402/49
Jayawardene Hewasandatchige Asiri Prasanna Wishvanath	9.10.1979		55	2000–2013	2,061	154*	4	31.22			-/-		115/32	6
Jeganathan Sridharan	11.7.1951	14.5.1996	6	1982	19	8	0	4.75	0	0-12	0/0		0	5
John Vinothen Bede	27.5.1960		6	1982–1984	53	27*	0	10.60	28	5-60	2/0	21.92	2	45
Jurangpathy Baba Roshan	25.6.1967		4	1985–1986	1	1	0	0.25	1	1-69	0/0	93.00	2	
Kalaviñgoda Shantha	23.12.1977		1	2004	8	7	0	4.00			-/-		2	86
Kalpage Ruwan Senani	19.2.1970		11	1993–1998	294	63	0	18.37	12	2-27	0/0	64.50	10	
Kaluhalamulla H. K. S. R. (see Randiv, Suraj)														
Kaluperuma Lalith Wasantha Silva	25.6.1949		2	1981	12	11*	0	4.00			-/-		2	4
Kaluperuma Sanath Mohan Silva	22.10.1961		4	1983–1987	88	23	0	11.00	0	0-24	0/0		6	2
Kaluwitharana Romesh Shantha	24.11.1969		49	1992–2004	1,933	132*	3	26.12	2	2-17	0/0	62.00	93/26	189
Kapugedera Chamara Kantha	24.2.1987		8	2006–2009	418	96	0	34.83			-/-		8	92/21
Karunaratne Frank Dimuth Madushanka . .	28.4.1988		9	2012–2013	475	85	0	29.68	0	0-9	0/0		6	6
Kulasekara Chamith Kosala Bandara . .	15.7.1985		1	2011	22	15	0	11.00	1	1-65	0/0	80.00		4
Kulasekara Kulasekara Mudiyanselage Dinesh Nuwan	22.7.1982		20	2004–2012	381	64	0	15.24	46	4-21	0/0	35.78	8	146/32
Kuruppu Don Sardha Brendon Priyantha . .	5.1.1962		4	1986–1991	320	201*	1	53.33			-/-		8	54
Kuruppuarachchi Ajith Kosala	1.11.1964		2	1985–1986	0	0*	0		8	5-44	1/0	18.62		

	Born	Died	Tests	Test Career	Runs	HS	100s	Avge	Wkts	BB	5/10	Avge	Ct/St	O/T
Labrooy Graeme Fredrick	7.6.1964		9	1986–1990	158	70*	0	14.36	27	5-133	1/0	44.22	3	44
Lakmal Ranasinghe Arachchige Suranga	10.3.1987		17	2010–2013	93	18	0	7.75	32	4-78	0/0	53.75	3	20/3
Lakshitha Materba Kanatha Gamage Chamila Premanath	4.1.1979													7
Liyanage Dulip Kapila	6.6.1972		2	1992–2001	42	40	0	14.00	5	2-33	0/0	31.60	1	16
Lokuarachchi Kaushal Samaraweera	20.5.1982		4	2002–2002	69	23	0	7.66	17	4-56	0/0	39.17	0	21/2
Madugalle Ranjan Senerath	22.4.1959		21	1981–1988	1,029	103	1	29.40		–	–	–	9	63
Madurasinghe Madurasinghe Arachchige Wijayasiri Ranjith	30.1.1961		3	1988–1992	24	11	0	4.80	3	3-60	0/0	57.33	0	12
Mahanama Roshan Sirwardene	31.5.1966		52	1985–1997	2,576	225	4	29.27	0	0-3	0/0	–	56	213
Maharoof Mohamed Farveez	7.9.1984		22	2003–2011	556	72	0	18.53	25	4-52	0/0	65.24	7	104/7
Malinga Separamadu Lasith	28.8.1983		30	2004–2010	275	64	0	11.45	101	5-50	3/0	33.15	7	160/48
Mathews Angelo Davis	2.6.1987		36	2009–2013	2,174	157*	2	45.29	13	2-60	0/0	71.69	20	113/45
Mendis Balapuwaduge Ajantha Winslo	11.3.1985		17	2008–2012	164	78	0	14.90	64	6-117	3/1	34.20	2	66/34
Mendis Louis Rohan Duleep	25.8.1952		24	1981–1988	1,329	124	4	31.64	–	–	–	–	9	79
Mirando Magina Thilan Thushara	1.3.1981		10	2003–2010	94	15*	0	8.54	28	5-83	1/0	37.14	3	38/6
Mubarak Jehan	10.11.1981		13	2002–2007	254	48	0	15.87	0	0-1	0/0	–	13	40/16
Muralitharan Muttiah (CY 1999)	17.4.1972		132§	1992–2010	1,259	67	0	11.87	795	9-51	67/22	22.67	70	343/12
Nawaz Mohamed Naveed	20.9.1973		1	2002	18	12*	0	6.00	–	–	–/–	–	0	3
Nissanka Ratnayake Arachchige Prabath	25.10.1982		4	2003	99	95	0	99.00	10	5-64	1/0	36.60	0	23
Paranavitana Nishad Tharanga	15.4.1982		32	2008–2012	1,792	111	2	32.58	1	1-26	0/0	86.00	27	20
Perera Anhettige Suresh Asanka	16.2.1978		3	1998–2001	77	43*	0	25.66	1	1-104	0/0	180.00	1	4/3
Perera Mahawaduge Dilruwan Kamalaneth	22.7.1982		1	2013	103	95	0	51.50	1	1-71	0/0	71.00	0	
Perera Narangoda Liyanaarachchilage Tissara Chirantha	3.4.1989		6	2011–2012	203	75	0	20.30	17	4-63	0/0	59.36	1	67/30
Perera Panagodage Don Ruchira Laksiri	6.4.1977		8	1998–2002	33	11*	0	11.00	17	3-40	0/0	38.88	2	19/2
Prasad Kariyawasam Tirana Gamage Dammika	30.5.1983		12	2008–2012	275	47	0	18.00	22	3-82	0/0	59.00	5	12/1
Prasanna Seekkuge	27.6.1985		1	2011	5	5	0	5.00	0	0-80	0/0	–	0	12/1
Pushpakumara Karuppiahyage Ravindra	21.7.1975		23	1994–2001	166	44	0	8.73	58	7-116	4/0	38.65	10	31
Ramanayake Champaka Priyadarshana Hewage	8.11.1965		18	1987–1993	143	34*	0	9.53	44	5-82	1/0	42.72	6	62
Ranyakumara Wijekoon Mudiyanselage Gayan	21.12.1976		2	2005	38	14	0	12.66	2	2-49	0/0	33.00	0	0/3
Ranasinghe Anura Nandana	13.10.1956	9.11.1998	2	1981–1982	88	77	0	22.00	2	1-23	0/0	69.00	0	9
[2] Ranatunga Arjuna (CY 1999)	1.12.1963		93	1981–2000	5,105	135*	4	35.69	16	2-17	0/0	65.00	47	269
[2] Ranatunga Dammika	12.10.1962		2	1989	87	45	0	29.00	–	–	–/–	–	0	4

§ *Muralitharan's figures exclude two runs, five wickets and two catches for the ICC World XI v Australia in the Super Series Test in 2005-06.*

Name	Born	Died	Tests	Test Career	Runs	HS	100s	Avge	Wkts	BB	5/10	Avge	Ct/St	O/T
[2]Ranatunga Sanjeeva	25.4.1969		9	1994–1996	531	118	2	33.18			–/–		2	13
Randiv Suraj (Hewa Kaluhalamulage Suraj Randiv Kaluhalamulla; formerly M. M. M. Suraj)	30.1.1985		12	2010–2012	147	39	0	9.18	43	5-82	1/0	37.51	1	28/7
Ratnayake Rumesh Joseph	2.1.1964		23	1982–1991	433	56	0	14.43	73	6-66	5/0	35.10	9	70
Ratnayeke Joseph Ravindran	2.5.1960		22	1981–1989	807	93	0	25.21	56	8-83	4/0	35.21	1	78
Samarasekera Maitipage Athula Rohitha	5.8.1961		4	1988–1991	118	57	0	16.85	3	2-38	0/0	34.66	1	39
Samaraweera Dulip Prasanna	12.2.1972		7	1993–1994	211	42	0	15.07			–/–		3	5
[2]Samaraweera Thilan Thusara	22.9.1976		81	2001–2012	5,462	231	14	48.76	15	4-49	0/0	45.93	45	53
Sangakkara Kumar Chokshanada (CY 2012)	27.10.1977		120	2000–2013	10,652	287	33	56.35	0	0-4	0/0		171/20	355‡/48
Senanayake Charith Panduka	19.12.1962		3	1990	97	64	0	19.40	0	0-30	0/0		2	7
Senanayake Senanayake Mudiyanselage Sachithra Madhushanka	9.2.1985		1	2013	5	5	0	5.00			–/–			21/8
Silva Jayan Kaushal	27.5.1986		7	2011–2013	391	95	0	32.58			–/–			
Silva Kelaniyage Jayantha	2.6.1973		6	1995–1997	6	6*	0	2.00	20	4-16	0/0	32.35		1
Silva Lindamullage Prageeth Chamara	14.12.1979		11	2006–2007	537	152*	1	33.56	2	1-57	0/0	65.00	7	75/16
Silva Sampathawaduge Amal Rohitha	12.12.1960		9	1982–1988	353	111	1	25.21			–/–		33/1	20
Taranga Warushavithana Upul	2.2.1985		15	2005–2007	713	165	2	28.52			–/–		11	170‡/10
Thirimanne Hettige Don Rumesh Lahiru	8.9.1989		10	2011–2012	526	155*	2	32.87	0	0-7	0/0		4	56/18
Tillekeratne Hashan Prasantha	14.7.1967		83	1989–2003	4,545	204*	11	42.87	0	0-0	0/0		122/2	200
Upashantha Kalutarage Eric Amila	10.6.1972		2	1998–2002	10	6	0	3.33	4	2-41	0/0	50.00		12
Vaas Warnakulasurya Patabendige Ushantha Joseph Chaminda	27.1.1974		111	1994–2009	3,089	100*	1	24.32	355	7-71	12/2	29.58	31	321‡/6
Vandort Michael Graydon	19.11.1980		20	2001–2008	1,144	140	1	36.90			–/–		6	1
Vithanage Kasun Disi Kithuruwan	26.2.1991		2	2012	71	59	0	35.50			–/–		1	2
Warnapura Bandula	1.3.1953		4	1981–1982	96	38	0	12.00	0	0-1	0/0		2	12
Warnapura Basnayake Shalith Malinda	26.5.1979		14	2007–2009	821	120	1	35.69	0	0-40	0/0		14	3
Warnaweera Kahakatchchi Patabandige Jayananda	23.11.1960		10	1985–1994	39	20	0	4.33	32	4-25	0/0	31.90	0	6
Weerasinghe Colombage Don Udesh Sanjeewa	1.3.1968		1	1985	3	3	0	3.00	0	0-8	0/0		0	
Welagedara Uda Walawwe Mahim Bandaralage Chanaka Asanka	20.3.1981		21	2007–2012	191	48	0	8.30	54	5-52	2/0	40.48	4	10/2
[3]Wettimuny Mithra de Silva	11.6.1951		2	1982	28	17	0	7.00			–/–		2	1
[2]Wettimuny Sidath (CY 1985)	12.8.1956		23	1981–1986	1,221	190	2	29.07			–/–		10	35
Wickremasinghe Anguppulige Gamini Dayantha	27.12.1965		3	1989–1992	17	13*	0	8.50			–/–		9/1	4

	Born	Died	Tests	Test Career	Runs	HS	100s	Avge	Wkts	BB	5/10	Avge	Ct/St	O/T
Wickremasinghe Gallage Pramodya	14.8.1971		40	1991–2000	555	51	0	9.40	85	6-60	3/0	41.87	18	134
Wijegunawardene Kapila Indaka Weerakkody	23.11.1964		2	1991–1991	14	6*	0	4.66	6	4-51	0/0	21.00	0	26
Wijesuriya Roger Gerard Christopher Ediriweera	18.2.1960		4	1981–1985	22	8	0	4.40	1	1-68	0/0	294.00	1	8
Wijetunge Piyal Kashyapa	6.8.1971		1	1993	10	10	0	5.00	2	1-58	0/0	59.00	0	
Zoysa Demuni Nuwan Tharanga	13.5.1978		30	1996–2004	288	28*	0	8.47	64	5-20	1/0	33.70	4	9

ZIMBABWE (90 players)

	Born	Died	Tests	Test Career	Runs	HS	100s	Avge	Wkts	BB	5/10	Avge	Ct/St	O/T
Arnott Kevin John	8.3.1961		4	1992	302	101*	1	43.14	–	–	–/–	–	4	13
Blignaut Arnoldus Mauritius ("Andy")	1.8.1978		19	2000–2005	886	92	0	26.84	53	5-73	3/0	37.05	13	54/1
Brain David Hayden	4.10.1964		9	1992–1994	115	28	0	10.45	30	5-42	1/0	30.50	1	23
Brandes Eddo André	5.3.1963		10	1992–1999	121	39	0	10.08	26	3-45	0/0	36.57	4	59
Brent Gary Bazil	13.1.1976		4	1999–2001	35	25	0	5.83	7	3-21	0/0	44.85	1	70/3
Briant Gavin Aubrey	11.4.1969		1	1992	17	16	0	8.50	–	–	–/–	–	0	5
Bruk-Jackson Glen Keith	25.4.1969		2	1993	39	31	0	9.75	–	–	–	–	1	
Burmester Mark Greville	24.1.1968		3	1992	54	30*	0	27.00	3	3-78	0/0	75.66	1	8
Butchart Iain Peter	9.5.1960		1	1994	23	15	0	11.50	0	0-11	0/0	–		20
Campbell Alistair Douglas Ross	23.9.1972		60	1992–2002	2,858	103	2	27.21	0	0-1	0/0	–	60	188
Carlisle Stuart Vance	10.5.1972		37	1994–2005	1,615	118	2	26.91	–	–	–/–	–	34	111
Chakabva Regis Wiririrai	20.9.1987		4	2011–2012	163	63	0	20.37	–	–	–	–	5	17/2
Chatara Tendai Larry	28.2.1991		4	2012–2013	41	21	0	5.12	15	5-61	1/0	27.00	1	11/4
Chigumbura Elton	14.3.1986		11	2003–2013	434	86	0	20.66	16	5-54	1/0	48.68	3	150/24
Coventry Charles Kevin	8.3.1983		2	2005	88	37	0	22.00	–	–	–/–	–	3	37/9
Cremer Alexander Graeme	19.9.1986		11	2004–2012	216	43	0	10.80	24	4-4	0/0	45.62	6	43/9
Crocker Gary John	16.5.1962		3	1992	69	33	0	23.00	2	2-65	0/0	72.33	0	6
Dabengwa Keith Mbusi	17.8.1980		3	2005	90	35	0	15.00	5	3-127	0/0	49.80	1	37/8
Dekker Mark Hamilton	5.12.1969		14	1993–1996	333	68*	0	15.85	0	0-5	0/0	–	12	23
Duffin Terrence	20.3.1982		2	2005	80	56	0	20.00	–	–	–/–	–		23
Ebrahim Dion Digby	7.8.1980		29	2000–2005	1,226	94	0	22.70	–	–	–/–	–	16	82
[2] Ervine Craig Richard	19.8.1985		4	2011–2012	174	49	0	29.00	–	–	–/–	–	3	25/7
[2] Ervine Sean Michael	6.12.1982		5	2003–2003	261	86	0	32.62	9	4-146	0/0	43.11	7	42
Evans Craig Neil	29.11.1969		3	1996–2003	52	22	0	8.66	0	0-8	0/0	–	1	53
Ewing Gavin Mackie	21.1.1981		3	2003–2005	108	71	0	18.00	2	1-27	0/0	130.00	1	7

	Born	Died	Tests	Test Career	Runs	HS	100s	Avge	Wkts	BB	5/10	Avge	Ct/St	O/T
Ferreira Neil Robert	3.6.1979		1	2005	21	16	0	10.50	0	0-0	-/-	-	-	
[2] Flower Andrew OBE (CY 2002)	28.4.1968		63	1992–2002	4,794	232*	12	51.54	0	0-0	00	-	151/9	213
Flower Grant William	20.12.1970		67	1992–2003	3,457	201*	6	29.54	25	4-41	00	61.48	43	221
Friend Travis John	7.1.1981		13	2001–2003	447	81	0	29.80	25	5-31	1/0	43.60	2	51
Goodwin Murray William	11.12.1972		19	1997–2000	1,414	166*	3	42.84	0	0-3	00	-	10	71
Gripper Trevor Raymond	28.12.1975		20	1999–2003	809	112	1	21.86	6	2-91	00	84.83	14	8
Hondo Douglas Tafadzwa	7.7.1979		9	2001–2004	83	19	0	9.22	21	6-59	1/0	36.85	5	56
Houghton David Laud	23.6.1957		22	1992–1997	1,464	266	4	43.05	0	0-0	00	-	17	63
Huckle Adam George	21.9.1971		8	1997–1998	74	28*	0	6.72	25	6-109	2/1	34.88	3	19
James Wayne Robert	27.8.1965		4	1993–1994	61	33	0	15.25	0	0-0	-/-	-	16	11
Jarvis Kyle Malcolm	16.2.1989		8	2011–2012	58	25*	0	7.25	30	5-54	2/0	31.73	3	24/9
[1] Jarvis Malcolm Peter	6.12.1955		5	1992–1994	4	2*	0	2.00	11	3-30	00	35.72	2	12
Johnson Neil Clarkson	24.1.1970		13	1998–2000	532	107	1	24.18	15	4-77	00	39.60	12	48
Lamb Gregory Arthur	4.3.1980		1	2011	46	39	0	23.00	3	3-120	00	47.00	2	15/5
Lock Alan Charles Ingram	10.9.1962		1	1995	8	8*	0	8.00	5	3-68	00	21.00	0	8
Madondo Trevor Nyasha	22.11.1976	11.6.2001	3	1997–2000	90	74*	0	30.00	0	0-0	-/-	-	1	13
Mahwire Ngonidzashe Blessing	31.7.1982		10	2002–2005	147	50*	0	13.36	18	4-92	00	50.83	1	23
Maregwede Alester	5.8.1981		2	2003	74	28	0	18.50	0	0-0	-/-	-	2	11
Marillier Douglas Anthony	24.4.1978		5	2000–2001	185	73	0	30.83	11	4-57	00	29.27	1	48
Maruma Timycen	19.4.1988		1	2012	20	10	0	10.00	0	0-0	-/-	-	2	11/6
Masakadza Hamilton	9.8.1983		25	2001–2013	1,292	119	3	26.91	10	3-24	00	27.00	12	129/28
[2] Masakadza Shingirai Winston	4.9.1986		4	2011–2013	88	24	0	14.66	14	4-32	00	29.28	2	12/7
Matambanadzo Everton Zvikomborero	13.4.1976		3	1996–1999	17	7	0	4.25	4	2-62	00	62.50	0	7
Matsikenyeri Stuart	3.5.1983		8	2003–2004	351	57	0	23.40	2	1-58	00	172.50	7	112/10
Mawoyo Tinotenda Mbiri Kanayi	8.1.1986		15	2011–2013	454	163*	1	30.26		-	-/-	-	6	4
Mbangwa Mpumelelo ("Pommie")	26.6.1976		15	1996–2000	34	8	0	2.00	32	3-23	00	31.43	0	29
Meth Keegan Orry	8.2.1988		2	2012	72	31*	0	24.00	4	2-41	00	24.50	2	11/2
Mpofu Christopher Bobby	27.11.1985		9	2004–2011	27	8	0	2.45	20	4-92	00	44.45	0	64/13
Mupariwa Tawanda	16.4.1985		1	2003	15	14	0	15.00	0	0-136	00	-	0	35/4
Murphy Brian Andrew	1.12.1976		11	1999–2001	123	30	0	10.25	18	3-32	00	61.83	11	31
Mutendera David Travolta	25.1.1979		2	2000	10	10	0	5.00		-	-/-	-	4	9
Mutizwa Forster	24.8.1985		4	2011	24	18	0	12.00		-	-/-	-	0	
Mutumbami Richmond	11.6.1989		7	2012–2013	131	42	0	18.71		-	-/-	-	12/2	17/3
Mwayenga Waddington	20.6.1984		1	2005	15	14*	0	15.00	1	1-79	00	79.00	0	3
Ncube Njabulo	14.10.1989		1	2011	17	14	0	8.50	1	1-80	00	121.00	1	1
Nkala Mluleki Luke	1.4.1981		10	2000–2004	187	47	0	14.38	11	3-82	00	66.09	4	50/1

	Born	Died	Tests	Test Career	Runs	HS	100s	Avge	Wkts	BB	5/10	Avge	Ct/St	O/T
Olonga Henry Khaaba	3.7.1976		30	1994–2002	184	24	0	5.41	68	5-70	2/0	38.52	10	50
Panyangara Tinashe	21.10.1985		5	2003–2013	162	40*	0	23.14	17	3-28	0/0	28.52	1	29/3
Peall Stephen Guy	2.9.1969		4	1993–1994	60	30	0	15.00	4	2-89	0/0	75.75	1	21
Price Raymond William	12.6.1976		22	1999–2012	261	36	0	8.70	80	6-73	5/1	36.06	4	102/16
Pycroft Andrew John	6.6.1956		3	1992	152	60	0	30.40			–/–		2	20
Ranchod Ujesh	17.5.1969		1	1992	8	7	0	4.00	1	1-45		45.00	0	3
[2] Rennie Gavin James	12.1.1976		23	1997–2001	1,023	93	0	22.73	1	1-40	0/0	84.00	13	40
[2] Rennie John Alexander	29.7.1970		4	1993–1997	62	22	0	12.40	3	2-22	0/0	97.66	1	44
Rogers Barney Guy	20.8.1982		4	2004	90	29	0	11.25	0	0-17		–	1	15
Shah Ali Hassimshah	7.8.1959		3	1992–1996	122	62	0	24.40	1	1-46	0/0	125.00	–	28
Sibanda Vusimuzi	10.10.1983		12	2003–2013	526	93	0	21.91	–	–	–/–	–	13	109½/13
Sikandar Raza	24.4.1986		1	2013	84	60	0	42.00			–/–		0	8/2
[2] Strang Bryan Colin	9.6.1972		26	1994–2001	465	53	0	12.91	56	5-101	1/0	39.33	11	49
[2] Strang Paul Andrew	28.7.1970		24	1994–2001	839	106*	1	27.06	70	8-109	4/1	36.02	15	95
Streak Heath Hilton	16.3.1974		65	1993–2005	1,990	127*	1	22.35	216	6-73	7/0	28.14	17	187‡
Taibu Tatenda	14.5.1983		28	2001–2011	1,546	153	1	30.31	1	1-27	0/0	27.00	57/5	149±/23
Taylor Brendan Ross Murray	6.2.1986		19	2003–2013	1,260	171	4	35.00	0	0-6	0/0	–	18	146/23
Traicos Athanasios John	17.5.1947		4†	1992	11	5	0	2.75	14	5-86	1/0	40.14	4	27
Useya Prosper	26.3.1985		4	2003–2013	107	45	0	15.28	10	3-60	0/0	41.00	2	151/26
Vermeulen Mark Andrew	2.3.1979		8	2002–2003	414	118	1	25.87	0	0-5	0/0	–	6	43
Viljoen Dirk Peter	11.3.1977		2	1997–2000	57	38	0	14.25	1	1-14	0/0	65.00	1	53
Vitori Brian Vitalis	22.2.1990		4	2011–2013	52	19*	0	10.40	12	5-61	1/0	38.66	2	13/6
[1] Waller Andrew Christopher	25.9.1959		2	1996	69	50	0	23.00			–/–		1	39
Waller Malcolm Noel	28.9.1984		8	2011–2013	386	72*	0	25.73	0	0-8	0/0	–	6	38/11
Watambwa Brighton Tonderai	9.6.1977		6	2000–2001	11	4*	0	3.66	14	4-64	0/0	35.00	0	63
Whittall Andrew Richard	28.3.1973		10	1996–1999	114	17	0	7.60	7	3-73	0/0	105.14	8	147
Whittall Guy James	5.9.1972		46	1993–2002	2,207	203*	4	29.42	51	4-18	0/0	40.94	19	147
Williams Sean Colin	26.9.1986		1	2012	37	31	0	18.50	0	0-9	–/–	–	1	58/5
Wishart Craig Brian	9.1.1974		27	1995–2005	1,098	114	1	22.40					15	90

BANGLADESH (70 players)

	Born	Died	Tests	Test Career	Runs	HS	100s	Avge	Wkts	BB	5/10	Avge	Ct/St	O/T
Abdur Razzak	15.6.1982		11	2005–2013	234	43	0	16.71	23	3-93	0/0	67.13	4	147/28
Abul Hasan	5.8.1992		3	2012	165	113	1	82.50	3	2-80	0/0	123.66	3	3/4
Aftab Ahmed	10.11.1985		16	2004–2009	582	82*	0	20.78	5	2-31	0/0	47.40	7	85/11
Akram Khan	1.11.1968		8	2000–2003	259	44	0	18.18	–	–	–	–	3	44
Al-Amin Hossain	1.1.1990		1	2013	0	0*	0	–	1	1-58	0/0	58.00		0/1
Al Sahariar	23.4.1978		15	2000–2003	683	71	0	22.76	–	–	–	–	10	29
Alamgir Kabir	10.1.1981		3	2002–2003	8	4	0	2.00	0	0-39	0/0	–	0	
Alok Kapali	1.1.1984		17	2002–2005	584	85	0	17.69	6	3-3	0/0	118.16	5	69/7
Aminul Islam	2.2.1968		13	2000–2002	530	145	1	21.20	1	1-66	0/0	149.00	5	39
Anamul Haque	16.12.1992		3	2012–2013	64	22	0	10.66	–	–	–	–	1	9/1
Anwar Hossain Monir	31.12.1981		3	2003–2005	22	13	0	7.33	0	0-95	0/0	–	0	1
Anwar Hossain Piju	10.12.1983		1	2002	14	12	0	7.00	–	–	–	–	0	1
Bikash Ranjan Das	14.7.1982		1	2000	2	2	0	1.00	1	1-64	0/0	72.00	0	
Ehsanul Haque	1.12.1979		1	2002	7	5	0	3.50	0	0-18	0/0	–	0	1
Elias Sunny	2.8.1986		4	2011–2012	38	20*	0	7.60	12	6-94	1/0	43.16	1	6
Enamul Haque, sen.	27.2.1966		10	2000–2003	180	24*	0	12.00	18	4-136	0/0	57.05	1	4/7
Enamul Haque, jun.	5.12.1986		15	2003–2012	59	13	0	5.90	44	7-95	3/1	40.61	3	29
Fahim Muntasir	1.11.1980		3	2001–2002	52	33	0	8.66	5	3-131	0/0	68.40	0	10
Faisal Hossain	26.10.1978		1	2003	7	5	0	3.50	–	–	–	–	0	3
Habibul Bashar	17.8.1972		50	2000–2007	3,026	113	3	30.87	–	–	–	–	22	111
Hannan Sarkar	1.12.1982		17	2002–2004	662	76	0	20.06	–	–	–	–	20	20
Hasibul Hossain	3.6.1977		5	2000–2001	97	31	0	10.77	6	2-125	0/0	95.16	2	32
Imrul Kayes	2.2.1987		16	2008–2011	549	75	0	17.15	–	–	–	–	16	48/4
Jahurul Islam	12.12.1986		7	2009–2012	347	48	0	26.69	–	–	–	–	7	14/3
Javed Omar Belim	25.11.1976		40	2000–2007	1,720	119	1	22.05	0	0-12	0/0	–	11	59
Junaid Siddique	30.10.1987		19	2007–2012	969	106	1	26.18	0	0-2	0/0	–	11	54/7
Khaled Mahmud	26.7.1971		12	2001–2003	266	45	0	12.09	13	4-37	0/0	64.00	2	77
Khaled Mashud	8.2.1976		44	2000–2007	1,409	103*	1	19.04	–	–	–	–	78/9	126
Mahbubul Alam	1.12.1983		4	2008	5	2	0	1.25	5	2-62	0/0	62.80	0	5
Mahmudullah	4.2.1986		17	2009–2012	865	115	1	27.90	28	5-51	1/0	45.07	15	94/25
Manjural Islam	7.11.1979		17	2000–2004	81	21	0	3.68	28	6-81	1/0	57.32	4	34
Manjural Islam Rana	4.5.1984	16.3.2007	6	2003–2004	257	69	0	25.70	5	3-84	0/0	80.20	4	25
Marshall Ayub	5.12.1988		2	2013	106	41	0	26.50	0	0-15	0/0	–	1	

	Born	Died	Tests	Test Career	Runs	HS	100s	Avge	Wkts	BB	5/10	Avge	Ct/St	O/T
Mashrafe bin Mortaza	5.10.1983		36	2001–2009	797	79	0	12.85	78	4-60	0/0	41.52	9	129/21
Mehrab Hossain, sen.	22.9.1978		9	2000–2003	241	71	0	13.38	–	–	0/0	–	6	18
Mehrab Hossain, jun.	8.7.1987		7	2007–2008	243	83	0	20.25	4	2-29	0/0	70.25	2	18/2
Mohammad Ashraful	9.9.1984		61	2001–2012	2,737	190	6	24.00	21	2-42	0/0	60.52	25	175/23
Mohammad Rafique	5.9.1970		33	2000–2007	1,059	111	1	18.57	100	6-77	7/0	40.76	7	123‡/51
Mohammad Salim	15.10.1981		2	2003	49	26	0	16.33	–	–	–/–	–	3/1	1
Mohammad Sharif	12.12.1983		10	2000–2007	122	24*	0	7.17	14	4-98	0/0	79.00	5	9
Mominul Haque	29.9.1991		5	2012–2013	584	181	2	83.42	1	1-10	0/0	75.00	4	12/4
Mushfiqur Rahim	1.9.1988		36	2005–2013	2,078	200	2	32.46	–	–	–/–	–	60/10	122/30
Mushfiqur Rahman	1.1.1980		10	2000–2004	232	46*	0	13.64	13	4-65	0/0	63.30	6	28
Naeem Islam	31.12.1986		8	2008–2012	416	108	1	32.00	1	1-11	0/0	303.00	2	56/10
2Nafis Iqbal	31.1.1985		11	2004–2005	518	121	1	23.54	–	–	–/–	–	2	16
Naimur Rahman	19.9.1974		8	2000–2002	210	48	0	15.00	12	6-132	1/0	59.83	4	29
Nasir Hossain	30.11.1991		12	2011–2013	859	100	1	45.21	6	3-52	0/0	52.16	7	28/15
Nazimuddin	1.10.1985		3	2011–2012	125	78	0	20.83	–	–	–/–	–	1	11/7
Nazmul Hossain	5.10.1987		2	2004–2011	16	8*	0	8.00	5	2-61	0/0	38.80	0	38/4
Rafiqul Islam	7.11.1977		1	2002	7	6	0	3.50	–	–	–/–	–	1	4
Rajin Saleh	20.11.1983		24	2003–2008	1,141	89	0	25.93	2	1-9	0/0	134.00	15	43
Raqibul Hasan	8.10.1987		9	2008–2011	336	65	0	19.76	–	–	0/0	–	9	55/5
Robiul Islam	20.10.1986		7	2010–2013	93	33	0	13.28	23	6-71	2/0	33.82	4	3/1
Rubel Hossain	1.1.1990		18	2009–2013	122	17	0	7.17	26	5-166	1/0	78.00	8	43/7
Sajidul Islam	18.1.1988		3	2007–2012	18	6	0	3.00	5	2-71	0/0	77.33	0	0/1
Sanwar Hossain	5.8.1973		9	2001–2003	345	49	0	19.16	3	2-128	0/0	62.00	1	27
Shafiul Islam	6.10.1989		6	2009–2011	149	53	0	13.54	8	3-86	0/0	71.12	1	49/11
Shahadat Hossain	7.8.1986		35	2005–2012	489	40	0	10.18	70	6-27	4/0	51.90	8	51/6
Shahriar Hossain	1.6.1976		3	2000–2003	99	48	0	19.80	–	–	–/–	–	0/1	20
Shahriar Nafees	1.5.1985		24	2005–2012	1,267	138	1	26.39	–	–	–/–	–	19	75/1
Shakib Al Hasan	24.3.1987		32	2007–2013	2,105	144	2	36.92	113	7-36	10/0	32.62	14	129/26
Sohag Gazi	5.8.1991		8	2012–2013	260	101*	1	21.66	34	6-74	2/0	35.32	4	11/5
Suhrawadi Shuvo	21.11.1988		1	2011	15	15	0	7.50	4	3-73	0/0	36.50	0	17/1
Syed Rasel	3.7.1984		6	2005–2007	37	19	0	4.62	12	4-129	0/0	47.75	0	52/8
Talha Jubair	10.12.1985		7	2002–2004	52	31	0	6.50	14	3-135	0/0	55.07	1	6
2Tamim Iqbal (CY 2011)	20.3.1989		30	2007–2013	2,221	151	4	38.29	0	0-1	0/0	–	9	124/26
Tapash Baisya	25.12.1982		21	2003–2005	384	66	0	11.29	36	4-72	0/0	59.36	6	56
Tareq Aziz	4.9.1983		3	2003–2004	22	10*	0	11.00	1	1-76	0/0	261.00	1	10
Tushar Imran	10.12.1983		5	2002–2007	89	28	0	8.90	–	–	0/0	–	6	41
Ziaur Rahman	2.12.1986		1	2012	14	14	0	7.00	4	4-63	0/0	17.75	0	7/11

Notes

In one Test, A. and G. G. Hearne played for England; their brother, F. Hearne, for South Africa.

The Waughs and New Zealand's Marshalls are the only instance of Test-playing twins.

Adnan Akmal: brother of Kamran and Umar Akmal.

Amarsingh, L.: brother of L. Ramji.

Azmat Rana: brother of Shafqat Rana.

Bazid Khan (Pakistan): son of Majid Khan (Pakistan) and grandson of M. Jahangir Khan (India).

Bravo, D. J. and D. M.: half-brothers.

Chappell, G. S., I. M. and T. M.: grandsons of V. Y. Richardson.

Collins, P. T.: half-brother of F. H. Edwards.

Cooper, W. H.: great-grandfather of A. P. Sheahan.

Edwards, F. H.: half-brother of P. T. Collins.

Hanif Mohammad: brother of Mushtaq, Sadiq and Wazir Mohammad; father of Shoaib Mohammad.

Headley, D. W. (England): son of R. G. A. and grandson of G. A. Headley (both West Indies).

Hearne, F. (England and South Africa): father of G. A. L. Hearne (South Africa).

Jahangir Khan, M. (India): father of Majid Khan and grandfather of Bazid Khan (both Pakistan).

Kamran Akmal: brother of Adnan and Umar Akmal.

Khalid Wazir (Pakistan): son of S. Wazir Ali (India).

Kirsten, G. and P. N.: half-brothers.

Majid Khan (Pakistan): son of M. Jahangir Khan (India) and father of Bazid Khan (Pakistan).

Manzoor Elahi: brother of Salim and Zahoor Elahi.

Moin Khan: brother of Nadeem Khan.

Mudassar Nazar: son of Nazar Mohammad.

Murray, D. A.: son of E. D. Weekes.

Mushtaq Mohammad: brother of Hanif, Sadiq and Wazir Mohammad.

Nadeem Khan: brother of Moin Khan.

Nafis Iqbal: brother of Tamim Iqbal.

Nazar Mohammad: father of Mudassar Nazar.

Nazir Ali, S.: brother of S. Wazir Ali.

Pattinson, D. J. (England): brother of J. L. Pattinson (Australia).

Pervez Sajjad: brother of Waqar Hassan.

Ramiz Raja: brother of Wasim Raja.

Ramji, L.: brother of L. Amarsingh.

Richardson, V. Y.: grandfather of G. S., I. M. and T. M. Chappell.

Sadiq Mohammad: brother of Hanif, Mushtaq and Wazir Mohammad.

Saeed Ahmed: brother of Younis Ahmed.

Salim Elahi: brother of Manzoor and Zahoor Elahi.

Shafqat Rana: brother of Azmat Rana.

Sheahan, A. P.: great-grandson of W. H. Cooper.

Shoaib Mohammad: son of Hanif Mohammad.

Tamim Iqbal: brother of Nafis Iqbal.

Umar Akmal: brother of Adnan and Kamran Akmal.

Waqar Hassan: brother of Pervez Sajjad.

Wasim Raja: brother of Ramiz Raja.

Wazir Ali, S. (India): brother of S. Nazir Ali (India) and father of Khalid Wazir (Pakistan).

Wazir Mohammad: brother of Hanif, Mushtaq and Sadiq Mohammad.

Weekes, E. D.: father of D. A. Murray.

Yograj Singh: father of Yuvraj Singh.

Younis Ahmed: brother of Saeed Ahmed.

Yuvraj Singh: son of Yograj Singh.

Zahoor Elahi: brother of Manzoor and Salim Elahi.

Note: Teams are listed only where relatives played for different sides.

PLAYERS APPEARING FOR MORE THAN ONE TEST TEAM

Fourteen cricketers have appeared for two countries in Test matches, namely:

Amir Elahi (India 1, Pakistan 5)
J. J. Ferris (Australia 8, England 1)
S. C. Guillen (West Indies 5, New Zealand 3)
Gul Mahomed (India 8, Pakistan 1)
F. Hearne (England 2, South Africa 4)
A. H. Kardar (India 3, Pakistan 23)
W. E. Midwinter (England 4, Australia 8)

F. Mitchell (England 2, South Africa 3)
W. L. Murdoch (Australia 18, England 1)
Nawab of Pataudi, sen. (England 3, India 3)
A. J. Traicos (South Africa 3, Zimbabwe 4)
A. E. Trott (Australia 3, England 2)
K. C. Wessels (Australia 24, South Africa 16)
S. M. J. Woods (Australia 3, England 3)

Wessels also played 54 one-day internationals for Australia and 55 for South Africa.

The following players appeared for the ICC World XI against Australia in the Super Series Test in 2005-06: M. V. Boucher, R. Dravid, A. Flintoff, S. J. Harmison, Inzamam-ul-Haq, J. H. Kallis, B. C. Lara, M. Muralitharan, V. Sehwag, G. C. Smith, D. L. Vettori.

Note: In 1970, England played five first-class matches against the Rest of the World after the cancellation of South Africa's tour. Players were awarded England caps, but the matches are no longer considered to have Test status. Alan Jones (born 4.11.1938) made his only appearance for England in this series, scoring 5 and 0; he did not bowl and took no catches.

ONE-DAY AND TWENTY20 INTERNATIONAL CRICKETERS

The following players had appeared for Test-playing countries in one-day internationals by January 8, 2014, or in Twenty20 internationals by December 31, 2013, but had not represented their countries in Test matches by January 20, 2014. (Numbers in brackets signify number of one-day internationals for each player: where a second number appears, e.g. (5/1), it signifies the number of Twenty20 internationals for that player.)

By January 8, 2014, K. A. Pollard was the most experienced international player never to have appeared in Test cricket, with 85 one-day internationals and 37 Twenty20 internationals. R. G. Sharma held the record for most international appearances before making his Test debut, with 108 one-day internationals and 36 Twenty20 internationals.

England

M. W. Alleyne (10), I. D. Austin (9), D. R. Briggs (1/6), A. D. Brown (16), D. R. Brown (9), J. C. Buttler (19/25), G. Chapple (1), J. W. M. Dalrymple (27/3), S. M. Davies (8/5), J. L. Denly (9/5), J. W. Dernbach (24/25), M. V. Fleming (11), P. J. Franks (1), I. J. Gould (18), A. P. Grayson (2), A. D. Hales (0/21), G. W. Humpage (3), T. E. Jesty (10), C. J. Jordan (1), E. C. Joyce (17/2), C. Kieswetter (46/25), G. D. Lloyd (6), A. G. R. Loudon (1), J. O. Love (3), M. B. Loye (7), M. J. Lumb (0/18), M. A. Lynch (3), A. D. Mascarenhas (20/14), S. C. Meaker (2/2), P. Mustard (10/2), P. A. Nixon (19/1), A. U. Rashid (5/5), M. J. Smith (5), N. M. K. Smith (7), J. N. Snape (10/1), V. S. Solanki (51/3), J. O. Troughton (6), C. M. Wells (2), V. J. Wells (9), A. G. Wharf (13), L. J. Wright (48/46), M. H. Yardy (28/14).

Note: D. R. Brown also played 16 one-day internationals for Scotland, and E. C. Joyce 22 one-day internationals and 11 Twenty20 internationals for Ireland.

Australia

T. R. Birt (0/4), G. A. Bishop (2), R. J. Campbell (2), D. T. Christian (17/11), M. J. Cosgrove (3), N. M. Coulter-Nile (2/3), B. J. Cutting (3/2), M. J. Di Venuto (9), B. R. Dorey (4), Fawad Ahmed (3/2), C. J. Ferguson (30/3), A. J. Finch (18/9), P. J. Forrest (15), B. Geeves (2/1), S. F. Graf (11), I. J. Harvey (73), S. M. Harwood (1/3), J. R. Hazlewood (2/2), J. R. Hopes (84/12), D. J. Hussey (69/39), B. Laughlin (5/3), S. Lee (45), M. L. Lewis (7/2), R. J. McCurdy (11), K. H. MacLeay (16), N. J. Maddinson (1), J. P. Maher (26), M. R. Marsh (4/3), D. P. Nannes (1/15), A. A. Noffke (1/2), S. N. J. O'Keefe (0/7), L. A. Pomersbach (0/1), G. D. Porter (2), K. W. Richardson (1), B. J. Rohrer (0/1), L. Ronchi (4/3), J. D. Siddons (1), A. M. Stuart (3), G. S. Trimble (1), A. C. Voges (31/7), B. E. Young (6), A. K. Zesers (2).

Note: D. P. Nannes also played two Twenty20 internationals for the Netherlands, and L. Ronchi 14 one-day internationals and two Twenty20 internationals for New Zealand.

South Africa
Y. A. Abdulla (0/2), S. Abrahams (1), F. Behardien (11/10), D. M. Benkenstein (23), G. H. Bodi (2/1), L. E. Bosman (13/14), R. E. Bryson (7), D. J. Callaghan (29), D. N. Crookes (32), H. Davids (2/9), Q. de Kock (16/10), T. Henderson (0/1), C. A. Ingram (31/9), J. C. Kent (2), L. J. Koen (5), G. J-P. Kruger (3/1), H. G. Kuhn (0/5), R. E. Levi (0/13), J. Louw (3/2), D. A. Miller (40/19), C. H. Morris (5/2), P. V. Mpitsang (2), S. J. Palframan (7), A. M. Phangiso (5/3), N. Pothas (3), A. G. Puttick (1), C. E. B. Rice (3), M. J. R. Rindel (22), D. B. Rundle (2), T. G. Shaw (9), E. O. Simons (23), E. L. R. Stewart (6), R. Telemachus (37/3), J. Theron (4/9), A. C. Thomas (0/1), T. Tshabalala (4), R. E. van der Merwe (13/13), J. J. van der Wath (10/8), V. B. van Jaarsveld (2/3), M. N. van Wyk (13/3), C. J. P. G. van Zyl (2), D. J. Vilas (0/1), D. Wiese (0/4), H. S. Williams (7), M. Yachad (1).

West Indies
H. A. G. Anthony (3), S. Badree (0/10), C. D. Barnwell (0/6), M. C. Bascombe (0/1), N. E. Bonner (0/2), C. R. Brathwaite (1/1), D. Brown (3), B. St A. Browne (4), P. A. Browne (5), H. R. Bryan (15), D. C. Butler (5/1), J. Charles (30/18), D. O. Christian (0/2), R. T. Crandon (1), R. R. Emrit (2), S. E. Findlay (9/2), A. D. S. Fletcher (15/16), R. S. Gabriel (11), R. C. Haynes (8), J. O. Holder (15), R. O. Hurley (9), D. P. Hyatt (9/5), K. C. B. Jeremy (6), L. R. Johnson (3), A. Martin (9/1), G. E. Mathurin (0/3), J. N. Mohammed (1), A. R. Nurse (0/2), W. K. D. Perkins (0/1), K. A. Pollard (85/37), M. R. Pydanna (3), A. C. L. Richards (1/1), K. Santokie (0/2), K. F. Semple (7), D. C. Thomas (21/3), C. M. Tuckett (1), L. R. Williams (15).

New Zealand
G. W. Aldridge (2/1), M. D. Bailey (1), M. D. Bates (2/3), B. R. Blair (14), N. T. Broom (22/10), C. E. Bulfin (4), T. K. Canning (4), P. G. Coman (3), C. de Grandhomme (1/4), A. P. Devcich (6/2), B. J. Diamanti (1/1), M. W. Douglas (6), A. M. Ellis (15/5), B. G. Hadlee (2), L. J. Hamilton (2), R. T. Hart (1), R. L. Hayes (1), R. M. Hira (0/15), P. A. Hitchcock (14/1), L. G. Howell (12), T. W. M. Latham (13/7), M. J. McClenaghan (18/10), N. L. McCullum (62/49), P. D. McGlashan (4/11), B. J. McKechnie (14), E. B. McSweeney (16), J. P. Millmow (5), A. F. Milne (6/4), J. D. S. Neesham (9/3), T. S. Nethula (5), C. J. Nevin (37), A. J. Penn (5), R. G. Petrie (12), R. B. Reid (9), S. J. Roberts (2), L. Ronchi (14/2), S. L. Stewart (4), L. W. Stott (1), G. P. Sulzberger (3), A. R. Tait (5), E. P. Thompson (1/1), M. D. J. Walker (3), R. J. Webb (3), J. W. Wilson (6), W. A. Wisneski (3), L. J. Woodcock (4/3).
  Note: L. Ronchi also played four one-day internationals and three Twenty20 internationals for Australia.

India
P. Awana (0/2), A. C. Bedade (13), A. Bhandari (2), Bhupinder Singh, sen. (2), G. Bose (1), V. B. Chandrasekhar (7), U. Chatterjee (3), N. A. David (4), P. Dharmani (1), A. B. Dinda (13/9), R. S. Gavaskar (11), R. S. Ghai (6), M. S. Gony (2), Joginder Sharma (4/4), A. V. Kale (1), S. C. Khanna (10), G. K. Khoda (2), A. R. Khurasiya (12), T. Kumaran (8), J. J. Martin (10), D. Mongia (57/1), S. P. Mukherjee (3), A. M. Nayar (3), N. V. Ojha (1/2), G. K. Pandey (2), Pankaj Singh (1), J. V. Paranjpe (4), A. K. Patel (3), Y. K. Pathan (57/22), Randhir Singh (2), S. S. Raul (2), A. T. Rayudu (4), A. M. Salvi (4), M. Sharma (5), R. Sharma (4/2), L. R. Shukla (3), R. P. Singh (2), R. S. Sodhi (18), S. Somasunder (2), S. Sriram (8), Sudhakar Rao (1), M. K. Tiwary (8/3), S. S. Tiwary (3), S. Tyagi (2), R. V. Uthappa (38/11), P. S. Vaidya (4), Y. Venugopal Rao (16), Jai P. Yadav (12).

Pakistan
Aamer Hameed (2), Aamer Hanif (5), Akhtar Sarfraz (4), Anwar Ali (4/4), Arshad Pervez (2), Asad Ali (4/2), Asif Mahmood (2), Awais Zia (0/3), Faisal Athar (1), Ghulam Ali (3), Haafiz Shahid (3), Hammad Azam (8/5), Haris Sohail (4/1), Hasan Jamil (5), Imran Abbas (2), Iqbal Sikandar (4), Irfan Bhatti (1), Javed Qadir (1), Junaid Zia (4), Kamran Hussain (2), Kashif Raza (1), Khalid Latif (5/7), Mahmood Hamid (1), Mansoor Amjad (1/1), Mansoor Rana (2), Manzoor Akhtar (7), Maqsood Rana (1), Masood Iqbal (2), Moin-ul-Atiq (5), Mujahid Jamshed (4), Naeem Ahmed (1), Naeem Ashraf (2), Najaf Shah (1), Naseer Malik (3), Naumanullah (1), Parvez Mir (3), Rameez Raja (0/2), Raza Hasan (0/7), Rizwan Ahmed (1), Saadat Ali (8), Saeed Azad (4), Sajid Ali (13), Sajjad Akbar (2), Salim Pervez (1), Samiullah Khan (2), Shahid Anwar (1), Shahzaib Hasan (3/10), Shakeel Ansar (0/2), Shakil Khan (1), Sharjeel Khan (5/3), Shoaib Khan (0/1), Sohaib Maqsood (10/9), Sohail Fazal (2), Tanvir Mehdi (1), Usman Khan (0/2), Usman Salahuddin (2), Wasim Haider (3), Zafar Iqbal (8), Zahid Ahmed (2).

Sri Lanka

J. W. H. D. Boteju (2), A. Dananjaya (1/5), D. L. S. de Silva (2), G. N. de Silva (4), L. H. D. Dilhara (9/2), E. R. Fernando (3), T. L. Fernando (1), U. N. K. Fernando (2), J. C. Gamage (4), W. C. A. Ganegama (4), F. R. M. Goonatilleke (1), P. W. Gunaratne (23), A. A. W. Gunawardene (1), P. D. Heyn (2), W. S. Jayantha (17), P. S. Jayaprakashdaran (1), C. U. Jayasinghe (0/5), S. A. Jayasinghe (2), S. H. T. Kandamby (38/5), S. H. U. Karnain (19), H. G. J. M. Kulatunga (0/2), B. M. A. J. Mendis (39/16), C. Mendis (1), A. M. N. Munasinghe (5), E. M. D. Y. Munaweera (0/4), H. G. D. Nayanakantha (3), A. R. M. Opatha (5), S. P. Pasqual (2), A. K. Perera (2/1), K. G. Perera (1), M. D. K. J. Perera (19/9), H. S. M. Pieris (3), S. M. A. Priyanjan (2), M. Pushpakumara (3/1), R. L. B. Rambukwella (0/1), S. K. Ranasinghe (4), N. Ranatunga (2), N. L. K. Ratnayake (2), R. J. M. G. M. Rupasinghe (0/2), A. P. B. Tennekoon (4), M. H. Tissera (3), I. Udana (2/6), M. L. Udawatte (9/5), D. M. Vonhagt (1), A. P. Weerakkody (1), S. Weerakoon (2), K. Weeraratne (15/5), S. R. de S. Wettimuny (3), R. P. A. H. Wickremaratne (3).

Zimbabwe

R. D. Brown (7), C. J. Chibhabha (63/17), M. T. Chinouya (2), K. M. Curran (11), S. G. Davies (4), K. G. Duers (6), E. A. Essop-Adam (1), D. A. G. Fletcher (6), T. N. Garwe (1), J. G. Heron (6), R. S. Higgins (11), V. R. Hogg (3), A. J. Ireland (26/1), T. Kamungozi (4), F. Kasteni (3), A. J. Mackay (3), G. C. Martin (5), M. A. Meman (1), T. V. Mufambisi (6), N. Mushangwe (5/3), C. T. Mutombodzi (3/3), I. A. Nicolson (2), G. A. Paterson (10), G. E. Peckover (3), E. C. Rainsford (39/2), P. W. E. Rawson (10), H. P. Rinke (18), R. W. Sims (3), G. M. Strydom (12), C. Zhuwao (1/5).

Bangladesh

Ahmed Kamal (1), Alam Talukdar (2), Aminul Islam, jun. (1), Anisur Rahman (2), Ather Ali Khan (19), Azhar Hussain (2), Dhiman Ghosh (14/1), Dolar Mahmud (7), Farhad Reza (34/8), Faruq Ahmed (7), Gazi Ashraf (2), Ghulam Faruq (5), Ghulam Nausher (9), Hafizur Rahman (2), Harunur Rashid (1), Jahangir Alam (3), Jahangir Badshah (5), Jamaluddin Ahmed (1), Mafizur Rahman (4), Mahbubur Rahman (1), Mazharul Haque (1), Minhazul Abedin (27), Moniruzzaman (2), Morshed Ali Khan (1), Mosharraf Hossain (2), Nadif Chowdhury (0/3), Nasir Ahmed (7), Nazmus Sadat (0/1), Neeyamur Rashid (2), Nurul Abedin (4), Rafiqul Alam (2), Raqibul Hasan, sen. (2), Saiful Islam (7), Sajjad Ahmed (2), Samiur Rahman (2), Shafiuddin Ahmed (11), Shahidur Rahman (2), Shamsur Rahman (2/4), Shariful Haq (1), Sheikh Salahuddin (6), Shuvagata Hom (4), Wahidul Gani (1), Zahid Razzak (3), Zakir Hassan (2).

PLAYERS APPEARING FOR MORE THAN ONE ONE-DAY/TWENTY20 INTERNATIONAL TEAM

The following players have played one-day internationals for the **African XI** in addition to their national side:

N. Boje (2), L. E. Bosman (1), J. Botha (2), M. V. Boucher (5), E. Chigumbura (3), A. B. de Villiers (5), H. H. Dippenaar (6), J. H. Kallis (3), J. M. Kemp (6), J. A. Morkel (2), M. Morkel (3), T. M. Odoyo (5), P. J. Ongondo (2), J. L. Ontong (1), S. M. Pollock (6), A. G. Prince (3), J. A. Rudolph (2), V. Sibanda (2), G. C. Smith (1), D. W. Steyn (2), H. H. Streak (2), T. Taibu (1), S. O. Tikolo (4), M. Zondeki (2). (Odoyo, Ongondo and Tikolo played for Kenya, who do not have Test status.)

The following players have played one-day internationals for the **Asian Cricket Council XI** in addition to their national side:

Abdul Razzaq (4), M. S. Dhoni (3), R. Dravid (1), C. R. D. Fernando (1), S. C. Ganguly (3), Harbhajan Singh (2), Inzamam-ul-Haq (3), S. T. Jayasuriya (4), D. P. M. D. Jayawardene (5), A. Kumble (2), Mashrafe bin Mortaza (2), Mohammad Ashraful (2), Mohammad Asif (3), Mohammad Rafique (2), Mohammad Yousuf (7), M. Muralitharan (4), A. Nehra (3), K. C. Sangakkara (4), V. Sehwag (3), Shahid Afridi (2), Shoaib Akhtar (3), W. U. Tharanga (1), W. P. U. J. C. Vaas (1), Yuvraj Singh (3), Zaheer Khan (6).

The following players have played one-day internationals for the **ICC World XI** in addition to their national side:

C. L. Cairns (1), R. Dravid (3), S. P. Fleming (1), A. Flintoff (3), C. H. Gayle (3), A. C. Gilchrist (1), D. Gough (1), M. L. Hayden (1), J. H. Kallis (3), B. C. Lara (4), G. D. McGrath (1), M. Muralitharan (3), M. Ntini (1), K. P. Pietersen (2), S. M. Pollock (3), R. T. Ponting (3), K. C. Sangakkara (3), V. Sehwag (3), Shahid Afridi (2), Shoaib Akhtar (2), D. L. Vettori (4), S. K. Warne (1).

K. C. Wessels appeared for both Australia and South Africa. D. R. Brown appeared for both England and Scotland. C. B. Lambert appeared for both West Indies and USA. E. C. Joyce, E. J. G. Morgan and W. B. Rankin appeared for both Ireland and England. A. C. Cummins appeared for both West Indies and Canada.

G. M. Hamilton played Test cricket for England and one-day internationals for Scotland. D. P. Nannes played one-day and Twenty20 internationals for Australia and Twenty20 internationals for the Netherlands. W. B. Rankin played one-day and Twenty20 internationals for Ireland and all three formats for England. L. Ronchi played one-day and Twenty20 internationals for both Australia and New Zealand.

ELITE TEST UMPIRES

The following umpires were on the ICC's elite panel in February 2014. The figures for Tests, one-day internationals and Twenty20 internationals and the Test Career dates refer to matches in which they have officiated as on-field umpires (excluding abandoned games). The totals of Tests are complete up to January 20, 2014, the totals of one-day internationals up to January 8, 2014, and the Twenty20 internationals up to December 31, 2013.

	Country	Born	Tests	Test Career	ODIs	T20Is
Aleem Dar	P	6.6.1968	87	*2003–2013*	159	26
Davis Stephen James	A	9.4.1952	50	*1997–2013*	122	20
Dharmasena Handunnettige Deepthi Priyantha <u>Kumar</u>	SL	24.4.1971	21	*2010–2013*	50	11
Erasmus Marais	SA	27.2.1964	23	*2009–2013*	48	15
Gould Ian James	E	19.8.1957	37	*2008–2013*	88	20
Illingworth Richard Keith	E	23.8.1963	5	*2012–2013*	28	9
Kettleborough Richard Allan	E	15.3.1973	18	*2010–2013*	40	9
Llong Nigel James	E	11.2.1969	22	*2007–2013*	72	17
Oxenford Bruce Nicholas James	A	5.3.1960	17	*2010–2013*	51	12
Reiffel Paul Ronald	A	19.4.1966	7	*2012–2013*	33	9
Tucker Rodney James	A	28.8.1964	29	*2009–2013*	38	14

Note: Asad Rauf, B. F. Bowden and A. L. Hill left the panel in 2013, though Bowden stood in one Test during the 2013–14 Ashes series because of a shortage of umpires who were not from England or Australia. Their figures were as follows:

	Country	Born	Tests	Test Career	ODIs	T20Is
Asad Rauf	P	12.5.1956	49	*2004–2012*	98	23
Bowden Brent Fraser ("Billy")	NZ	11.4.1963	76	*1999–2013*	182	19
Hill Anthony Lloyd	NZ	26.6.1951	40	*2001–2013*	96	17

BIRTHS AND DEATHS

OTHER CRICKETING NOTABLES

The following list shows the births and deaths of cricketers, and people associated with cricket, who have *not* played in men's Test matches.

Criteria for inclusion The following are included: all non-Test players who have either (1) scored 20,000 runs in first-class cricket, or (2) taken 1,500 first-class wickets, or (3) achieved 750 dismissals, or (4) reached both 15,000 runs and 750 wickets. It also includes (5) the leading players who flourished before the start of Test cricket, (6) *Wisden* Cricketers of the Year who did not play Test cricket, and (7) all others deemed of sufficient merit or interest for inclusion, either because of their playing skill, their present position, their contribution to the game in whatever capacity, or their fame in other walks of life.

Names Where players were normally known by a name other than their first, this is underlined.

Teams Where only one team is listed, this is normally the one for which the player made most first-class appearances. Additional teams are listed only if the player appeared for them in more than 20 first-class matches or if they are especially relevant to their career. School and university teams are not given unless especially relevant (e.g. for the schoolboys chosen as wartime Cricketers of the Year in the 1918 and 1919 *Wisdens*).

	Teams	Born	Died
Adams Percy Webster	Cheltenham College; *CY 1919*	5.9.1900	28.9.1962
Aird Ronald MC Hampshire; sec. MCC 1953–62, pres. MCC 1968–69		4.5.1902	16.8.1986
Aislabie Benjamin	Surrey, secretary of MCC 1822–42	14.1.1774	2.6.1842
Alcock Charles William	Secretary of Surrey 1872–1907	2.12.1842	26.2.1907
Editor, Cricket magazine, 1882–1907. Captain of Wanderers and England football teams.			
Alley William Edward	NSW, Somerset; Test umpire; *CY 1962*	3.2.1919	26.11.2004
Alleyne Mark Wayne	Gloucestershire; *CY 2001*	23.5.1968	
Altham Harry Surtees CBE Surrey, Hants; historian; pres. MCC 1959–60		30.11.1888	11.3.1965
Coach at Winchester for 30 years.			
Arlott Leslie Thomas John OBE	Broadcaster and writer	25.2.1914	14.12.1991
Arthur John Michael	Griq. W., OFS; South Africa coach 2005–10;	17.5.1968	
	Australia coach 2011–2013		
Ashdown William Henry	Kent	27.12.1898	15.9.1979
The only player to appear in English first-class cricket before and after the two world wars.			
Ashley-Cooper Frederick Samuel	Historian	22.3.1877	31.1.1932
Ashton Sir Hubert KBE MC Cam. U., Essex; pres. MCC 1960–61; *CY 1922*		13.2.1898	17.6.1979
Austin Sir Harold Bruce Gardiner	Barbados	15.7.1877	27.7.1943
Austin Ian David	Lancashire; *CY 1999*	30.5.1966	
Bailey Jack Arthur	Essex; secretary of MCC 1974–87	22.6.1930	
Bainbridge Philip	Gloucestershire, Durham; *CY 1986*	16.4.1958	
Bannister John David	Warwickshire; writer and broadcaster	23.8.1930	
Barker Gordon	Essex	6.7.1931	10.2.2006
Bartlett Hugh Tryon	Sussex; *CY 1939*	7.10.1914	26.6.1988
Beauclerk Rev. Lord Frederick	Middlesex, Surrey, MCC	8.5.1773	22.4.1850
Beldam George William	Middlesex; photographer	1.5.1868	23.11.1937
Beldham William ("Silver Billy")	Hambledon, Surrey	5.2.1766	26.2.1862
Beloff Michael Jacob QC Head of ICC Code of Conduct Commission		18.4.1942	
Benkenstein Dale Martin	KwaZulu-Natal, Durham; *CY 2009*	9.6.1974	
Berry Anthony Scyld Ivens	Editor of *Wisden* 2008–11	28.4.1954	
Berry Leslie George	Leicestershire	28.4.1906	5.2.1985
Bird Harold Dennis ("Dickie") OBE Yorkshire, Leics; umpire in 66 Tests		19.4.1933	
Blofeld Henry Calthorpe OBE	Cambridge Univ; broadcaster	23.9.1939	
Bond John David	Lancashire; *CY 1971*	6.5.1932	
Booth Roy	Yorkshire, Worcestershire	1.10.1926	
Bowley Frederick Lloyd	Worcestershire	9.11.1873	31.5.1943
Bradshaw Keith Tasmania; secretary/chief executive MCC 2006–11		2.10.1963	
Brewer Derek Michael	Secretary/chief executive MCC 2012–	2.4.1958	

	Teams	Born	Died
Briers Nigel Edwin	Leicestershire; *CY 1993*	15.1.1955	
Brookes Wilfrid H.	Editor of *Wisden* 1936–39	5.12.1894	28.5.1955
Bryan John Lindsay	Kent; *CY 1922*	26.5.1896	23.4.1985
Bucknor Stephen Anthony	Umpire in a record 128 Tests	31.5.1946	
Bull Frederick George	Essex; *CY 1898*	2.4.1875	16.9.1910
Buller John Sydney MBE	Worcestershire; Test umpire	23.8.1909	7.8.1970
Burnup Cuthbert James	Kent; *CY 1903*	21.11.1875	5.4.1960
Caine Charles Stewart	Editor of *Wisden* 1926–33	28.10.1861	15.4.1933
Calder Harry Lawton	Cranleigh School; *CY 1918*	24.1.1901	15.9.1995
Cardus *Sir* John Frederick Neville	Writer	3.4.1888	27.2.1975
Chapple Glen	Lancashire; *CY 2012*	23.1.1974	
Chester Frank	Worcestershire; Test umpire	20.1.1895	8.4.1957
Stood in 48 Tests between 1924 and 1955, a record that lasted until 1992.			
Clark David Graham	Kent; president of MCC 1977–78	27.1.1919	8.10.2013
Clarke Charles Giles CBE	Chairman of ECB, 2007–	29.5.1953	
Clarke William	Nottinghamshire	24.12.1798	25.8.1856
Founded the All-England XI, Trent Bridge ground.			
Collier David Gordon	Chief executive of ECB, 2005–	22.4.1955	
Collins Arthur Edward Jeune	Clifton College	18.8.1885	11.11.1914
Made the highest score in any cricket, 628* in a house match in 1899.			
Conan Doyle *Dr Sir* Arthur Ignatius	MCC	22.5.1859	7.7.1930
Creator of Sherlock Holmes; his only victim in first-class cricket was W. G. Grace.			
Connor Clare Joanne OBE	England Women; administrator	1.9.1976	
Constant David John	Kent, Leics; first-class umpire 1969–2006	9.11.1941	
Cook Thomas Edwin Reed	Sussex	5.1.1901	15.1.1950
Cox George, jun.	Sussex	23.8.1911	30.3.1985
Cox George, sen.	Sussex	29.11.1873	24.3.1949
Cozier Winston Anthony Lloyd	Broadcaster and writer	10.7.1940	
Dalmiya Jagmohan	President of ICC 1997–2000	30.5.1940	
Davies Emrys	Glamorgan; Test umpire	27.6.1904	10.11.1975
Davison Brian Fettes	Rhodesia, Leics, Tasmania, Gloucestershire	21.12.1946	
Dawkes George Owen	Leicestershire, Derbyshire	19.7.1920	10.8.2006
Day Arthur Percival	Kent; *CY 1910*	10.4.1885	22.1.1969
de Lisle Timothy John March Phillipps	Editor of *Wisden* 2003	25.6.1962	
Dennett Edward George	Gloucestershire	27.4.1880	14.9.1937
Di Venuto Michael James	Tasmania, Derbys, Durham	12.12.1973	
Domingo Russell Craig	South Africa coach 2013–	30.8.1974	
Eagar Edward Patrick	Photographer	9.3.1944	
Edwards Charlotte Marie MBE	England Women; *CY 2014*	17.12.1979	
Ehsan Mani	President of ICC 2003–06	23.3.1945	
Engel Matthew Lewis	Editor of *Wisden* 1993–2000, 2004–07	11.6.1951	
"Felix" (Nicholas Wanostrocht)	Kent, Surrey, All-England	4.10.1804	3.9.1876
Batsman, artist, author (Felix on the Bat) and inventor of the Catapulta bowling machine.			
Ferguson William Henry BEM	Scorer	6.6.1880	22.9.1957
Scorer and baggage-master for five Test teams on 43 tours over 52 years and "never lost a bag".			
Findlay William	Oxford U., Lancs; sec. MCC 1926–36	22.6.1880	19.6.1953
Firth John D'Ewes Evelyn	Winchester College; *CY 1918*	21.2.1900	21.9.1957
Fletcher Duncan Andrew Gwynne OBE	Zimbabwe; England coach 1999–2007; India coach 2011–	27.9.1948	
Ford Graham Xavier	Natal B; South Africa coach 1999–2002; Sri Lanka coach 2012–2014	16.11.1960	
Foster Henry Knollys	Worcestershire; *CY 1911*	30.10.1873	23.6.1950
Frindall William Howard MBE	Statistician	3.3.1939	30.1.2009
Frith David Edward John	Writer	16.3.1937	
Gibbons Harold Harry Haywood	Worcestershire	8.10.1904	16.2.1973
Gibson Clement Herbert	Eton College; *CY 1918*	23.8.1900	31.12.1976
Gibson Norman Alan Stanley	Writer	28.5.1923	10.4.1997
Gore Adrian Clements	Eton College; *CY 1919*	14.5.1900	7.6.1990
Grace *Mrs* Martha	Mother and cricketing mentor of WG	18.7.1812	25.7.1884
Grace William Gilbert, jun.	Gloucestershire; son of WG	6.7.1874	2.3.1905

	Teams	Born	Died
Graveney David Anthony	Gloucestershire, Somerset, Durham	2.1.1953	
Chairman of England selectors 1997–2008.			
Gray James Roy	Hampshire	19.5.1926	
Gray Malcolm Alexander	President of ICC 2000–03	30.5.1940	
Green David Michael	Lancashire, Gloucestershire; *CY 1969*	10.11.1939	
Grieves Kenneth James	New South Wales, Lancashire	27.8.1925	3.1.1992
Griffith Mike Grenville	Sussex, Camb. Univ; president MCC 2012–13	25.11.1943	
Haigh Gideon Clifford Jeffrey Davidson	Writer	29.12.1965	
Hall Louis	Yorkshire; *CY 1890*	1.11.1852	19.11.1915
Hallam Albert William	Lancashire, Nottinghamshire; *CY 1908*	12.11.1869	24.7.1940
Hallam Maurice Raymond	Leicestershire	10.9.1931	1.1.2000
Hallows James	Lancashire; *CY 1905*	14.11.1873	20.5.1910
Hartley Alfred	Lancashire; *CY 1911*	11.4.1879	9.10.1918
Harvey Ian Joseph	Victoria, Gloucestershire; *CY 2004*	10.4.1972	
Hedges Lionel Paget	Tonbridge School, Kent, Glos; *CY 1919*	13.7.1900	12.1.1933
Henderson Robert	Surrey; *CY 1890*	30.3.1865	28.1.1931
Hesson Michael James	New Zealand coach 2012–	30.10.1974	
Hewett Herbert Tremenheere	Somerset; *CY 1893*	25.5.1864	4.3.1921
Heyhoe Flint *Baroness* [Rachael] OBE	England Women	11.6.1939	
Hodson Richard <u>Phillip</u>	Cambridge Univ; president MCC 2011–12	26.4.1951	
Horton Henry	Hampshire	18.4.1923	2.11.1998
Howard Cecil <u>Geoffrey</u>	Middlesex; administrator	14.2.1909	8.11.2002
Hughes David Paul	Lancashire; *CY 1988*	13.5.1947	
Huish Frederick Henry	Kent	15.11.1869	16.3.1957
Humpage Geoffrey William	Warwickshire; *CY 1985*	24.4.1954	
Hunter David	Yorkshire	23.2.1860	11.1.1927
Hutchinson James Metcalf	Derbyshire	29.11.1896	7.11.2000
Believed to be the longest-lived first-class cricketer, at 103 years 344 days.			
Ingleby-Mackenzie Alexander <u>Colin</u> David OBE	Hants; president of MCC 1996–98	15.9.1933	9.3.2006
Iremonger James	Nottinghamshire; *CY 1903*	5.3.1876	25.3.1956
Isaac Alan Raymond	Chair NZC 2008–10; president ICC 2012–	20.1.1952	
Jackson Victor Edward	NSW, Leicestershire	25.10.1916	30.1.1965
James Cyril Lionel Robert ("Nello")	Writer	4.1.1901	31.5.1989
Jesty Trevor Edward	Hants, Griq W., Surrey, Lancs; umpire; *CY 1983*	2.6.1948	
Johnson Paul	Nottinghamshire	24.4.1965	
Johnston Brian Alexander CBE, MC	Broadcaster	24.6.1912	5.1.1994
Jones Alan MBE	Glamorgan; *CY 1978*	4.11.1938	
Played once for England v Rest of the World, 1970, regarded at the time as a Test match.			
Jurgensen Shane John	W. Aus, Tas, Qld; Bangladesh coach 2013–	28.4.1976	
Kilburn James Maurice	Writer	8.7.1909	28.8.1993
King John Barton	Philadelphia	19.10.1873	17.10.1965
"Beyond question the greatest all-round cricketer produced by America" – Wisden.			
Knight Roger David Verdon CBE	Surrey, Glos, Sussex; secretary of MCC 1994–2005	6.9.1946	
Knight W. H.	Editor of *Wisden* 1864–79	29.11.1812	16.8.1879
Koertzen Rudolf Eric	Umpire in 108 Tests	26.3.1949	
Lacey *Sir* Francis Eden	Hants; secretary of MCC 1898–1926	19.10.1859	26.5.1946
Lamb Timothy Michael	Middlesex, Northamptonshire; chief executive of ECB 1997–2004	24.3.1953	
Langridge John George MBE	Sussex; Test umpire; *CY 1950*	10.2.1910	27.6.1999
Lee Peter Granville	Northamptonshire, Lancashire; *CY 1976*	27.8.1945	
Lillywhite Frederick William	Sussex	13.6.1792	21.8.1854
Long Arnold	Surrey, Sussex	18.12.1940	
Lord Thomas	Middlesex; founder of Lord's Cricket Ground	23.11.1775	13.1.1832
Lorgat Haroon	Chief executive of ICC 2008–2012	26.5.1960	
Lyon Beverley Hamilton	Gloucestershire; *CY 1931*	19.1.1902	22.6.1970
McEwan Kenneth Scott	Eastern Province, Essex; *CY 1978*	16.7.1952	
McGilvray Alan David MBE	NSW; broadcaster	6.12.1909	17.7.1996
MacLaurin *Lord* [Ian Charter]	Chairman of ECB 1997–2002	30.3.1937	

	Teams	Born	Died
Marlar Robin Geoffrey	Sussex; writer	2.1.1931	
Marshal Alan	Surrey; *CY 1909*	12.6.1883	23.7.1915
Martin-Jenkins Christopher Dennis Alexander MBE	Writer; broadcaster; president of MCC 2010–11	20.1.1945	1.1.2013
Mendis Gehan Dixon	Sussex, Lancashire	20.4.1955	
Mercer John	Sussex, Glamorgan; coach and scorer; *CY 1927*	22.4.1893	31.8.1987
Meyer Rollo John Oliver OBE	Somerset	15.3.1905	9.3.1991
Modi Lalit Kumar	Chairman, Indian Premier League 2008–10	29.11.1963	
Moles Andrew James	Warwickshire, NZ coach 2008–09	12.2.1961	
Moores Peter	Sussex; England coach 2007–09	18.12.1962	
Morgan Derek Clifton	Derbyshire	26.2.1929	
Morgan Frederick David OBE	Chair ECB 2003–07, pres. ICC 2008–10	6.10.1937	
Mynn Alfred	Kent, All-England	19.1.1807	1.11.1861
Neale Phillip Anthony	Worcestershire; England manager; *CY 1989*	5.6.1954	
Newman John Alfred	Hampshire	12.11.1884	21.12.1973
Newstead John Thomas	Yorkshire; *CY 1909*	8.9.1877	25.3.1952
Nicholas Mark Charles Jefford	Hampshire; broadcaster	29.9.1957	
Nicholls Ronald Bernard	Gloucestershire	4.12.1933	21.7.1994
Nixon Paul Andrew	Leicestershire, Kent	21.10.1970	
Nyren John	Hampshire	15.12.1764	28.6.1837
Author of The Young Cricketer's Tutor, *1833.*			
Nyren Richard	Hampshire	1734	25.4.1797
Proprietor Bat & Ball Inn, Broadhalfpenny Down.			
Ontong Rodney Craig	Border, Glamorgan, N. Transvaal	9.9.1955	
Ormrod Joseph Alan	Worcestershire, Lancashire	22.12.1942	
Pardon Charles Frederick	Editor of *Wisden* 1887–90	28.3.1850	18.4.1890
Pardon Sydney Herbert	Editor of *Wisden* 1891–1925	23.9.1855	20.11.1925
Parks Henry William	Sussex	18.7.1906	7.5.1984
Parr George	Nottinghamshire, All-England	22.5.1826	23.6.1891
Captain and manager of the All-England XI.			
Partridge Norman Ernest	Malvern College, Warwickshire; *CY 1919*	10.8.1900	10.3.1982
Pawar Sharadchandra Govindrao	Pres. BCCI 2005–08, ICC 2010–12	12.12.1940	
Payton Wilfred Richard Daniel	Nottinghamshire	13.2.1882	2.5.1943
Pearce Thomas Neill	Essex; administrator	3.11.1905	10.4.1994
Pearson Frederick	Worcestershire	23.9.1880	10.11.1963
Perrin Percival Albert ("Peter")	Essex; *CY 1905*	26.5.1876	20.11.1945
Pilch Fuller	Norfolk, Kent	17.3.1804	1.5.1870
"The best batsman that has ever yet appeared" – Arthur Haygarth, 1862.			
Preston Hubert	Editor of *Wisden* 1944–51	16.12.1868	6.8.1960
Preston Norman MBE	Editor of *Wisden* 1952–80	18.3.1903	6.3.1980
Rait Kerr Colonel Rowan Scrope	Europeans; sec. MCC 1936–52	13.4.1891	2.4.1961
Reeves William	Essex; Test umpire	22.1.1875	22.3.1944
Rice Clive Edward Butler	Transvaal, Nottinghamshire; *CY 1981*	23.7.1949	
Richardson Alan	Warwicks, Middx, Worcs; *CY 2012*	6.5.1975	
Robertson-Glasgow Raymond Charles	Somerset; writer	15.7.1901	4.3.1965
Robins Derrick Harold	Warwickshire; tour promoter	27.6.1914	3.5.2004
Robinson Mark Andrew	Northants, Yorkshire, Sussex, coach	23.11.1966	
Roebuck Peter Michael	Somerset; writer; *CY 1988*	6.3.1956	12.11.2011
Rotherham Gerard Alexander	Rugby School, Warwickshire; *CY 1918*	28.5.1899	31.1.1985
Sainsbury Peter James	Hampshire; *CY 1974*	13.6.1934	
Scott Stanley Winckworth	Middlesex; *CY 1893*	24.3.1854	8.12.1933
Sellers Arthur Brian MBE	Yorkshire; *CY 1940*	5.3.1907	20.2.1981
Seymour James	Kent	25.10.1879	30.9.1930
Shepherd David Robert MBE	Gloucestershire; umpire in 92 Tests	27.12.1940	27.10.2009
Shepherd Donald John	Glamorgan; *CY 1970*	12.8.1927	
Silk Dennis Raoul Whitehall CBE	Somerset; president of MCC 1992–94, chairman of TCCB 1994–96	8.10.1931	
Simmons Jack MBE	Lancashire, Tasmania; *CY 1985*	28.3.1941	
Skelding Alexander	Leicestershire; umpire	5.9.1886	17.4.1960
First-class umpire 1931–58, when he was 72.			

	Teams	Born	Died
Smith Sydney Gordon	Northamptonshire; *CY 1915*	15.1.1881	25.10.1963
Smith William Charles ("Razor")	Surrey; *CY 1911*	4.10.1877	15.7.1946
Southerton Sydney James	Editor of *Wisden* 1934–35	7.7.1874	12.3.1935
Speed Malcolm Walter	Chief executive of ICC 2001–08	14.9.1948	
Spencer Thomas William OBE	Kent; Test umpire	22.3.1914	1.11.1995
Srinivasan Narayanaswami	Pres. BCCI 2011–; ICC chairman-elect	3.1.1945	
Stephenson Franklyn Dacosta	Nottinghamshire, Sussex; *CY 1989*	8.4.1959	
Stephenson Harold William	Somerset	18.7.1920	23.4.2008
Stephenson Heathfield Harman	Surrey, All-England	3.5.1832	17.12.1896
Captained first English team to Australia, 1861-62; umpired first Test in England, 1880.			
Stephenson *Lt.-Col.* John Robin CBE	Secretary of MCC 1987–93	25.2.1931	2.6.2003
Studd *Sir* John Edward <u>Kynaston</u>	Middlesex	26.7.1858	14.1.1944
Lord Mayor of London 1928–29; president of MCC 1930.			
Surridge Walter <u>Stuart</u>	Surrey; *CY 1953*	3.9.1917	13.4.1992
Sutherland James Alexander	Victoria; CEO Cricket Australia 2001–	14.7.1965	
Suttle Kenneth George	Sussex	25.8.1928	25.3.2005
Swanton Ernest William ("Jim") CBE	Middlesex; writer	11.2.1907	22.1.2000
Tarrant Francis Alfred	Victoria, Middlesex; *CY 1908*	11.12.1880	29.1.1951
Taylor Brian	Essex; *CY 1972*	19.6.1932	
Taylor Samantha <u>Claire</u> MBE	England Women; *CY 2009*	25.9.1975	
Taylor Tom Launcelot	Yorkshire; *CY 1901*	25.5.1878	16.3.1960
Thornton Charles Inglis ("Buns")	Middlesex	20.3.1850	10.12.1929
Timms John Edward	Northamptonshire	3.11.1906	18.5.1980
Todd Leslie John	Kent	19.6.1907	20.8.1967
Tunnicliffe John	Yorkshire; *CY 1901*	26.8.1866	11.7.1948
Turner Francis <u>Michael</u> MBE	Leicestershire; administrator	8.8.1934	
Turner Robert Julian	Somerset	25.11.1967	
Ufton Derek Gilbert	Kent	31.5.1928	
van der Bijl Vintcent Adriaan Pieter	Natal, Middx, Transvaal; *CY 1981*	19.3.1948	
Virgin Roy Thomas	Somerset, Northamptonshire; *CY 1971*	26.8.1939	
Ward William	Hampshire	24.7.1787	30.6.1849
Scorer of the first recorded double-century: 278 for MCC v Norfolk, 1820.			
Wass Thomas George	Nottinghamshire; *CY 1908*	26.12.1873	27.10.1953
Watson Frank	Lancashire	17.9.1898	1.2.1976
Webber Roy	Statistician	23.7.1914	14.11.1962
Weigall Gerald John Villiers	Kent; coach	19.10.1870	17.5.1944
West George H.	Editor of *Wisden* 1880–86	1851	6.10.1896
Wheatley Oswald Stephen CBE	Warwickshire, Glamorgan; *CY 1969*	28.5.1935	
Whitaker Edgar <u>Haddon</u> OBE	Editor of *Wisden* 1940–43	30.8.1908	5.1.1982
Wight Peter Bernard	Somerset; umpire	25.6.1930	
Wilson John <u>Victor</u>	Yorkshire; *CY 1961*	17.1.1921	5.6.2008
Wisden John	Sussex	5.9.1826	5.4.1884
"The Little Wonder"; founder of Wisden Cricketers' Almanack, *1864.*			
Wood Cecil John Burditt	Leicestershire	21.11.1875	5.6.1960
Woodcock John Charles OBE	Writer; editor of *Wisden* 1981–86	7.8.1926	
Wooller Wilfred	Glamorgan	20.11.1912	10.3.1997
Wright Graeme Alexander	Editor of *Wisden* 1987–92, 2001–02	23.4.1943	
Wright Levi George	Derbyshire; *CY 1906*	15.1.1862	11.1.1953
Young Douglas <u>Martin</u>	Worcestershire, Gloucestershire	15.4.1924	18.6.1993

REGISTER OF CURRENT PLAYERS

The qualifications for inclusion are as follows:

1. All players who appeared in Tests, one-day internationals or Twenty20 internationals for a Test-playing country in the calendar year 2013.
2. All players who appeared in the County Championship, the Sheffield Shield, the Sunfoil Series, the West Indian four-day regional competition for the Headley–Weekes Trophy, or the Duleep Trophy in the calendar year 2013.
3. All players who appeared in a first-class match in a Test-playing country in the calendar year 2013 who have previously played Tests, one-day international cricket or Twenty20 international cricket for a Test-playing country.
4. All players who appeared in a first-class match for a Test-playing country on tour or the A-team of a Test-playing country in the calendar year 2013.

Notes: The forename by which the player is known is underlined if it is not his first name.

Teams are those played for in domestic cricket in the calendar year 2013, or the last domestic team for which that player appeared.

Countries are those for which players are qualified.

The country of birth is given if it is not the one for which a player is qualified. It is also given to differentiate between West Indian nations, and where it is essential for clarity.

* *Denotes Test player.*

	Team	Country	Born	Birthplace
***Aaron** Varun Raymond	Jharkhand	I	29.10.1989	*Jamshedpur*
***Abbott** Kyle John	Dolphins	SA	18.6.1987	*Empangeni*
Abbott Sean Anthony	New South Wales	A	29.2.1992	*Windsor*
***Abdul Razzaq**	ZTBL	P	2.12.1979	*Lahore*
***Abdur Rauf**	Port Qasim Authority	P	9.12.1978	*Renala Khurd*
***Abdur Razzak**	Khulna	B	15.6.1982	*Khulna*
***Abdur Rehman**	Sialkot/Habib Bank	P	1.3.1980	*Sialkot*
***Abul Hasan**	Sylhet	B	5.8.1992	*Kulaura*
Ackermann Colin Niel	Eastern Province/Warriors	SA	4.4.1991	*George*
***Adams** Andre Ryan	Nottinghamshire	NZ	17.7.1975	*Auckland*
Adams James Henry Kenneth	Hampshire	E	23.9.1980	*Winchester*
Adams Moegamat Qaasim	Cobras/WP/Northerns/Titans	SA	29.4.1984	*Cape Town*
***Adnan Akmal**	Lahore Ravi/Sui Northern	P	13.3.1985	*Lahore*
***Aftab Ahmed**	Chittagong	B	10.11.1985	*Chittagong*
***Agar** Ashton Charles	Western Australia	A	14.10.1993	*Melbourne*
***Agarkar** Ajit Bhalchandra	Mumbai	I	4.12.1977	*Bombay*
Agathangelou Andrea Peter	Lancashire	SA	16.11.1989	*Rustenberg*
***Ahmed Shehzad**	Habib Bank/Lahore Ravi	P	23.11.1991	*Lahore*
***Aizaz Cheema**	Lahore Shalimar/PIA	P	5.9.1979	*Lahore*
Akshath Reddy Produturi	Hyderabad	I	11.2.1991	*Hyderabad*
***Al-Amin Hossain**	Khulna	B	1.1.1990	*Jhinaidah*
Aldridge Graeme William	Northern Districts	NZ	15.11.1977	*Christchurch*
Alexander Craig John	Dolphins/KZN/KZN Inland	SA	5.1.1987	*Cape Town*
Ali Moeen Munir	Worcestershire	E	18.6.1987	*Birmingham*
Allenby James	Glamorgan	E	12.9.1982	*Perth, Australia*
Alleyne Anthony Trevor	Comb. Campuses and Colls	WI	27.6.1993	*Barbados*
Allin Thomas William	Warwickshire	E	27.11.1987	*Barnstaple*
***Alok Kapali**	Sylhet	B	1.1.1984	*Sylhet*
***Ambrose** Timothy Raymond	Warwickshire	E	1.12.1982	*Newcastle, Aus*
***Amla** Hashim Mahomed	Surrey	SA	31.3.1983	*Durban*
***Anamul Haque**	Khulna	B	16.12.1992	*Kushtia*
Anderson Corey James	Northern Districts	NZ	13.12.1990	*Christchurch*
***Anderson** James Michael	Lancashire	E	30.7.1982	*Burnley*
Andrew Gareth Mark	Worcestershire	E	27.12.1983	*Yeovil*
Ansari Zafar Shahaan	Cambridge MCCU/Surrey	E	10.12.1991	*Ascot*
Anwar Ali	Karachi Blues/PIA	P	25.11.1987	*Karachi*
Anyon James Edward	Sussex	E	5.5.1983	*Lancaster*

	Team	Country	Born	Birthplace
Apparajith Redhills Narayanaswamy <u>Baba</u>	Tamil Nadu	I	8.7.1994	*Madras (Chennai)*
*****Arnel** Brent John	N. Districts/Wellington	NZ	3.1.1979	*Te Awamutu*
Arshad Usman	Durham	E	9.1.1993	*Bradford*
Asad Ali	Faisalabad/Sui Northern	P	14.10.1988	*Faisalabad*
*****Asad Shafiq**	Karachi W/Habib Bank	P	28.1.1986	*Karachi*
Ashar Zaidi	Sussex	P	13.7.1981	*Karachi*
Ashraf Moin Aqeeb	Yorkshire	E	5.1.1992	*Bradford*
*****Ashwin** Ravichandran	Tamil Nadu	I	17.9.1986	*Madras*
*****Asim Kamal**	Port Qasim Authority	P	31.5.1976	*Karachi*
*****Astle** Todd Duncan	Canterbury	NZ	24.9.1986	*Palmerston North*
Athanaze Justin Jason	Leeward Islands	WI	29.1.1988	*Antigua*
Atkinson James John	Warwickshire	HK	24.8.1990	*Hong Kong*
Aushik Srinivas Raju	Tamil Nadu	I	16.3.1993	*Coimbatore*
*****Austin** Ryan Anthony	Comb. Campuses and Colls	WI	15.11.1981	*Arima, Trinidad*
Awais Zia	Rawalpindi	P	1.9.1986	*Bhown*
Awana Parvinder	Delhi	I	19.7.1986	*Noida*
Azeem Rafiq	Yorkshire	E	27.2.1991	*Karachi, Pakistan*
*****Azhar Ali**	Sui Northern Gas	P	19.2.1985	*Lahore*
Azharullah	Northamptonshire	P	25.12.1983	*Burewala*
*****Badani** Hemang Kamal	Vidarbha	I	14.11.1976	*Madras*
Badree Samuel	Trinidad & Tobago	WI	8.3.1981	*Barrackpore, Trinidad*
*****Badrinath** Subramaniam	Tamil Nadu	I	30.8.1980	*Madras*
*****Bailey** George John	Tasmania/Hampshire	A	7.9.1982	*Launceston*
Bailey Ryan Tyrone	Knights/F. State/Warriors	SA	8.9.1982	*Cape Town*
*****Bairstow** Jonathan Marc	Yorkshire	E	26.9.1989	*Bradford*
Baker Lionel Sionne	Leeward Islands	WI	6.9.1984	*Montserrat*
*****Balaji** Lakshmipathy	Tamil Nadu	I	27.9.1981	*Madras*
Balcombe David John	Hampshire	E	24.12.1984	*London*
Ball Adam James	Kent	E	1.3.1993	*Greenwich*
*****Ballance** Gary Simon	Yorkshire	E	22.11.1989	*Harare, Zimbabwe*
Bancroft Cameron Timothy	Western Australia	A	19.11.1992	*Attadale*
*****Bandara** Herath Mudiyanselage Charitha <u>Malinga</u>	Ragama	SL	31.12.1979	*Kalutara*
Barath Adrian Boris	Trinidad & Tobago	WI	14.4.1990	*Chaguanas, Trinidad*
Barker Keith Hubert Douglas	Warwickshire	E	21.10.1986	*Manchester*
Barnwell Christopher Dion	Guyana	WI	6.1.1987	*McKenzie, Guyana*
Barrow Alexander William Rodgerson	Somerset	E	6.5.1992	*Bath*
Bates Michael David	Auckland	NZ	11.10.1983	*Auckland*
Bates Michael David	Hampshire	E	10.10.1990	*Frimley*
*****Batty** Gareth Jon	Surrey	E	13.10.1977	*Bradford*
Batty Jonathan Neil	Northamptonshire	E	18.4.1974	*Chesterfield*
*****Baugh** Carlton Seymour	Jamaica	WI	23.6.1982	*Kingston, Jamaica*
Bavuma Temba	Lions	SA	17.5.1990	*Cape Town*
Bawne Ankit Ramdas	Maharashtra	I	17.12.1992	*Paitha*
Beaton Ronsford Rodwick	Guyana	WI	17.9.1992	*Montserrat*
*****Beer** Michael Anthony	Western Australia	A	9.6.1984	*Malvern*
Beer William Andrew Thomas	Sussex	E	8.10.1988	*Crawley*
Behardien Farhaan	Titans	SA	9.10.1983	*Johannesburg*
Behrendorff Jason Paul	Western Australia	A	20.4.1990	*Camden*
*****Bell** Ian Ronald	Warwickshire	E	11.4.1982	*Walsgrave*
Bell-Drummond Daniel James	Kent	E	4.8.1993	*Lewisham*
Benkenstein Dale Martin	Durham	SA	9.6.1974	*Salisbury, Zimbabwe*
*****Benn** Sulieman Jamaal	Barbados	WI	22.7.1981	*Haynesville, Barbados*
*****Bennett** Hamish Kyle	Canterbury	NZ	22.2.1987	*Timaru*
Berg Gareth Kyle	Middlesex	E	18.1.1981	*Cape Town, SA*
Bernard David Eddison	Jamaica	WI	19.7.1981	*Kingston, Jamaica*
*****Best** Tino la Bertram	Barbados	WI	26.8.1981	*3rd Avenue, Barbados*

	Team	Country	Born	Birthplace
Bhatt Bhargav Ashokbhai	Baroda	I	13.5.1990	_Baroda_
*****Bhuvneshwar Kumar**	Uttar Pradesh	I	5.2.1990	_Meerut_
*****Bilawal Bhatti**	Sialkot/Sui Northern	P	17.9.1991	_Muridke_
Billings Samuel William	Kent	E	15.6.1991	_Pembury_
Binny Stuart Terence Roger	Karnataka	I	3.6.1984	_Bangalore_
Birch Andrew Charles Ross	Warriors	SA	7.6.1985	_East London_
*****Bird** Jackson Munro	Tasmania	A	11.12.1986	_Paddington_
*****Bishoo** Devendra	Guyana	WI	6.11.1985	_New Amsterdam, Guy._
Bist Robin Dinesh	Rajasthan	I	2.11.1987	_Delhi_
Blackwood Jermaine	Jamaica	WI	20.11.1991	_St Elizabeth, Jamaica_
Boatswain Quinton Hubert	Leeward Islands	WI	16.10.1990	_Montserrat_
Bodi Goolam Hussain	Lions	SA	4.1.1979	_Hathuran, India_
Bolan Nelson Amos	Leeward Islands	WI	29.11.1990	_Tortola, Brit. Virgin Is_
Boland Scott Michael	Victoria	A	11.4.1989	_Parkdale_
*****Bollinger** Douglas Erwin	New South Wales	A	24.7.1981	_Baulkham Hills_
Bonner Nkruma Eljego	Jamaica	WI	23.1.1989	_St Catherine_
*****Bopara** Ravinder Singh	Essex	E	4.5.1985	_Forest Gate_
Borrington Paul Michael	Derbyshire	E	24.5.1988	_Nottingham_
*****Borthwick** Scott George	Durham	E	19.4.1990	_Sunderland_
Bosisto William Giles	Western Australia	A	8.9.1993	_Geraldton_
Bosman Lungile Edgar (Loots)	Griqualand West	SA	14.4.1977	_Kimberley_
*****Botha** Johan	South Australia	SA	2.5.1982	_Johannesburg_
Botha Patrick	Knights/Free State	SA	23.1.1990	_Bloemfontein_
Boucher Rashidi Hasani	Barbados	WI	17.7.1990	_St Michael, Barbados_
*****Boult** Trent Alexander	Northern Districts	NZ	22.7.1989	_Rotorua_
Boyce Cameron John	Queensland	A	27.7.1989	_Charleville_
Boyce Matthew Andrew Golding	Leicestershire	E	13.8.1985	_Cheltenham_
*****Bracewell** Douglas Andrew John	Central Districts	NZ	28.9.1990	_Tauranga_
Bragg William David	Glamorgan	E	24.10.1986	_Newport_
Bramble Anthony	Guyana	WI	11.12.1990	_Berbice, Guyana_
*****Brathwaite** Kraigg Clairmonte	Barbados	WI	1.12.1992	_Belfield, Barbados_
Brathwaite Ruel Marlon Ricardo	Hampshire	WI	6.9.1985	_Bridgetown, Barbados_
*****Bravo** Darren Michael	Trinidad & Tobago	WI	6.2.1989	_Santa Cruz, Trinidad_
*****Bravo** Dwayne John	Trinidad & Tobago	WI	7.10.1983	_Santa Cruz, Trinidad_
*****Breese** Gareth Rohan	Durham	WI	9.1.1976	_Montego Bay, Jamaica_
*****Bresnan** Timothy Thomas	Yorkshire	E	28.2.1985	_Pontefract_
Briggs Danny Richard	Hampshire	E	30.4.1991	_Newport_
*****Broad** Stuart Christopher John	Nottinghamshire	E	24.6.1986	_Nottingham_
Brooks Jack Alexander	Yorkshire	E	4.6.1984	_Oxford_
Broom Neil Trevor	Otago	NZ	20.11.1983	_Christchurch_
Brown Ben Christopher	Sussex	E	23.11.1988	_Crawley_
Brown Jake Michael	South Australia	A	21.11.1985	_North Adelaide_
Brown Karl Robert	Lancashire	E	17.5.1988	_Bolton_
Brown Odean Vernon	Jamaica	WI	8.2.1982	_Westmoreland, Jamaica_
Browne Nicholas Laurence Joseph	Essex	E	24.3.1991	_Leytonstone_
*****Brownlie** Dean Graham	Canterbury	NZ	30.7.1984	_Perth, Australia_
Buchanan Brian	Jamaica	WI	1986	_Jamaica_
Buck Nathan Liam	Leicestershire	E	26.4.1991	_Leicester_
Buckley Ryan Sean	Durham	E	2.4.1994	_Darlington_
Burgoyne Peter Ian	Southern Rocks/Derbyshire	E	11.11.1993	_Nottingham_
Burns Joseph Antony	Queensland/Leicestershire	A	6.9.1989	_Herston_
Burns Rory Joseph	Surrey	E	26.8.1990	_Epsom_
Burton Shane Kelly Elliott	Leeward Islands	WI	25.5.1992	_Antigua_
*****Butler** Ian Gareth	Otago	NZ	24.11.1981	_Middlemore_
Butterworth Luke Rex	Tasmania	A	28.10.1983	_Hobart_
Buttler Joseph Charles	Somerset	E	8.9.1990	_Taunton_
Cachopa Carl	Central Districts	NZ	17.5.1986	_Bloemfontein, SA_
*****Carberry** Michael Alexander	Hampshire	E	29.9.1980	_Croydon_
Carey Alex Tyson	South Australia	A	27.8.1991	_Loxton_

	Team	Country	Born	Birthplace
Cariah Yannic	Trinidad & Tobago	WI	21.6.1992	Trinidad
Carter Andrew	Nottinghamshire	E	27.8.1988	Lincoln
Carter Jonathan Lyndon	Barbados	WI	16.11.1987	Belleplaine, Barbados
Carters Ryan Graham Leslie	New South Wales	A	25.7.1990	Canberra
Cartwright Hilton William Raymond	Western Australia	A	14.2.1992	Harare, Zimbabwe
Cessford Graeme	Worcestershire	E	4.10.1983	Hexham
*****Chakabva** Regis Wiriranai	Mashonaland Eagles	Z	20.9.1987	Harare
Chambers Maurice Anthony	Essex/Warwickshire	E	14.9.1987	Port Antonio, Jamaica
Chand Unmukt	Delhi	I	25.3.1993	Delhi
*****Chanderpaul** Shivnarine	Guyana/Derbyshire	WI	16.8.1974	Unity Village, Guyana
Chanderpaul Tagenarine	Guyana	WI	17.5.1996	Georgetown, Guyana
*****Chandimal** Lokuge Dinesh	Nondescripts	SL	18.11.1989	Balapitiya
Chandrika Rajindra	Guyana	WI	8.8.1989	Enterprise
Chapple Glen	Lancashire	E	23.1.1974	Skipton
Charles Johnson	Windward Islands	WI	14.11.1989	St Lucia
Chase Roston Lamar	Barbados	WI	22.3.1992	Kingsland, Barbados
*****Chatara** Tendai Larry	Mountaineers	Z	28.2.1991	Chimaniamani
*****Chattergoon** Sewnarine	Guyana	WI	3.3.1981	Fyrish, Guyana
Chawla Piyush Pramod	Uttar Pradesh/Somerset	I	24.12.1988	Aligarh
Chetty Cody	Dolphins/KwaZulu-Natal	SA	28.6.1991	Durban
Chibhabha Chamunorwa Justice	Mashonaland Eagles	Z	6.9.1986	Masvingo
*****Chigumbura** Elton	Mashonaland Eagles	Z	14.3.1986	Kwekwe
Chinouya Michael Tawanda	Mid West Rhinos	Z	9.6.1986	Kwekwe
Chopra Varun	Warwickshire	E	21.6.1987	Barking
Choudhry Aniket Vinod	Rajasthan	I	28.1.1990	Bikaner
Choudhry Shaaiq Hussain	Worcestershire	E	3.11.1985	Rotherham
Christian Daniel Trevor	Gloucestershire/Victoria	A	4.5.1983	Camperdown
Christian Derwin O'Neil	Guyana	WI	9.5.1983	Kilen, Guyana
Clare Jonathan Luke	Derbyshire	E	14.6.1986	Burnley
*****Clarke** Michael John	New South Wales	A	2.4.1981	Liverpool
*****Clarke** Rikki	Warwickshire	E	29.9.1981	Orsett
Claydon Mitchell Eric	Kent/Durham	E	25.11.1982	Fairfield, Australia
Cloete Gihan Love	Griqualand West/Knights	SA	4.10.1992	Springbok
Cobb Joshua James	Leicestershire	E	17.8.1990	Leicester
Cockbain Ian Andrew	Gloucestershire	E	17.2.1987	Liverpool
Cockley Burt Tom	Western Australia	A	3.4.1986	Waratah
Coetsee Werner Loubser	Knights/Griqualand West	SA	16.3.1983	Bethlehem
Coetzer Kyle James	Scotland/Northants	Scot	14.4.1984	Aberdeen
Coles Matthew Thomas	Kent/Hampshire	E	26.5.1990	Maidstone
Collingwood Paul David	Durham	E	26.5.1976	Shotley Bridge
*****Collymore** Corey Dalaneo	Middlesex	WI	21.12.1977	Boscobelle, Barbados
Compton Nicholas Richard Denis	Somerset/Worcestershire	E	26.6.1983	Durban, SA
*****Cook** Alastair Nathan	Essex	E	25.12.1984	Gloucester
Cook Stephen Craig	Lions/Gauteng	SA	29.11.1982	Johannesburg
Cooke Christopher Barry	Glamorgan	SA	30.5.1986	Johannesburg
Cooper Tom Lexley William	South Australia/Netherlands	NL	26.11.1986	Wollongong
*****Copeland** Trent Aaron	New South Wales/Northants	A	14.3.1986	Gosford
Corbin Kyle Anthony McDonald	Comb. Campuses and Colls	WI	15.5.1990	Newbury, Barbados
Cosgrove Mark James	Tasmania	A	14.6.1984	Elizabeth
Cosker Dean Andrew	Glamorgan	E	7.1.1978	Weymouth
*****Cottrell** Sheldon Shane	Jamaica	WI	19.8.1989	Jamaica
Coulter-Nile Nathan Mitchell	Western Australia	A	11.10.1987	Perth
*****Coventry** Charles Kevin	Matabeleland Tuskers	Z	8.3.1983	Kwekwe
*****Cowan** Edward James McKenzie	Tasmania/Nottinghamshire	A	16.6.1982	Paddington
Cox Oliver Benjamin	Worcestershire	E	2.2.1992	Wordsley
Craddock Thomas Richard	Essex	E	13.7.1989	Huddersfield
*****Cremer** Alexander Graeme	Mid West Rhinos	Z	19.9.1986	Harare
Croft Steven John	Lancashire	E	11.10.1984	Blackpool
Crook Steven Paul	Northamptonshire	E	28.5.1983	Modbury, Australia

	Team	Country	Born	Birthplace
Cross Gareth David	Lancashire	E	20.6.1984	*Bury*
Cruickshank Timothy Dale	New South Wales	A	19.5.1982	*Crows Nest*
Cummins Miguel Lamar	Barbados	WI	5.9.1990	*St Michael, Barbados*
*****Cummins** Patrick James	New South Wales	A	8.5.1993	*Westmead*
Cutting Benjamin Colin James	Queensland	A	30.1.1987	*Sunnybank*
*****Dabengwa** Keith Mbusi	Matabeleland Tuskers	Z	17.8.1980	*Bulawayo*
Dagar Mukul	Uttar Pradesh	I	17.12.1990	*Delhi*
Daggett Lee Martin	Northamptonshire	E	1.10.1982	*Bury*
Dala Carl Junior	Gauteng/Lions	SA	29.12.1989	*Lusaka, Zambia*
Dananjaya Akila	Colts	SL	4.10.1993	*Panadura*
Also known as Mahamarakkala Kurukulasooriya Patabendige Akila Dananjaya Perera				
Darekar Akshay Arun	Maharashtra	I	31.7.1988	*Raigad*
Das Pallavkumar Prasanta	Assam	I	17.11.1990	*Dewshipara*
Davids Henry	Titans	SA	19.1.1980	*Stellenbosch*
Davies Alexander Luke	Lancashire	E	23.8.1994	*Darwen*
Davies Mark	Kent	E	4.10.1980	*Stockton-on-Tees*
Davies Steven Michael	Surrey	E	17.6.1986	*Bromsgrove*
Davis Derone Yohann Anthony	Comb. Campuses and Colls	WI	14.10.1992	*Trinidad*
Davis Liam Murray	Western Australia	A	2.8.1984	*Perth*
Dawes Jason O'Brian	Comb. Campuses and Colls	WI	27.12.1988	*Westmoreland, Jam.*
Dawson David Graham	New South Wales	A	7.3.1982	*Weekangeria*
Dawson Liam Andrew	Hampshire	E	1.3.1990	*Swindon*
Deacon Wycliffe Andrew	North West/Lions	SA	23.6.1980	*Kroonstad*
de Boorder Derek Charles	Otago	NZ	25.10.1985	*Hastings*
*****de Bruyn** Zander	Lions/Surrey	SA	5.7.1975	*Johannesburg*
de Grandhomme Colin	Auckland	NZ	22.7.1986	*Harare*
de Kock Quinton	Lions	SA	17.12.1992	*Johannesburg*
*****de Lange** Marchant	Easterns/Titans	SA	13.10.1990	*Tzaneen*
Denly Joseph Liam	Middlesex	E	16.3.1986	*Canterbury*
Dent Christopher David James	Gloucestershire	E	20.1.1991	*Bristol*
*****Deonarine** Narsingh	Guyana	WI	16.8.1983	*Chesney Estate, Guy.*
Dernbach Jade Winston	Surrey	E	3.3.1986	*Johannesburg, SA*
*****de Saram** Samantha Indika	Moors	SL	2.9.1973	*Matara*
de Silva Pinnaduwage Chaturanga	Moors	SL	17.1.1990	*Galle*
*****de Silva** Weddikkara Ruwan				
Sujeewa	Panadura	SL	7.10.1979	*Beruwala*
Devcich Anton Paul	Northern Districts	NZ	28.9.1985	*Hamilton*
*****de Villiers** Abraham Benjamin	Titans	SA	17.2.1984	*Pretoria*
de Villiers Cornelius Johannes du				
Preez	Titans/Northerns	SA	16.3.1986	*Kroonstad*
de Villiers Juan-Pierre	Northerns/Titans	SA	5.4.1989	*Pretoria*
Dev Singh Ian	Jammu and Kashmir	I	1.3.1989	*Gandhinagar*
Dewar Akeem	Comb. Campuses and Colls	WI	30.8.1991	*Kingston, Jamaica*
*****de Wet** Friedel	North West	SA	26.6.1980	*Durban*
de Wett Burton Christopher	Border/Warriors	SA	25.12.1980	*East London*
Dexter Neil John	Middlesex	E	21.8.1984	*Johannesburg, SA*
Dhawan Rishi	Himachal Pradesh	I	19.2.1990	*Mandi*
*****Dhawan** Shikhar	Delhi	I	5.12.1985	*Delhi*
Dhiman Ghosh	Rangpur	B	23.11.1987	*Dinajpur*
*****Dhoni** Mahendra Singh	Jharkhand	I	7.7.1981	*Ranchi*
Dhruve Rakesh Vinubhai	Gujarat	I	12.5.1981	*Jamnagar*
Dilhara Loku Hettige Danushka	Moors	SL	3.7.1980	*Colombo*
Also known as Dilhara Lokuhettige				
*****Dilshan** Tillekeratne Mudiyanselage	Tamil Union	SL	14.10.1976	*Kalutara*
Dinda Ashok Bhimchandra	Bengal	I	25.3.1984	*Medinipur*
Dockrell George Henry	Ireland/Somerset	Ire	22.7.1992	*Dublin*
Dogra Paras	Himachal Pradesh	I	19.11.1984	*Palampur*
*****Doherty** Xavier John	Tasmania	A	22.11.1982	*Scottsdale*

	Team	Country	Born	Birthplace
Doolan Alexander James	Tasmania	A	29.11.1985	Launceston
Dowrich Shane Omari	Barbados	WI	30.10.1991	West Terrace
Dry Corné Adrian	Knights/Free State	SA	4.2.1993	Cape Town
Duckett Ben Matthew	Northamptonshire	E	17.10.1994	Farnborough
Duffield Ryan	Western Australia	A	20.6.1988	Darkan
*****Duffin** Terrence	Matabeleland Tuskers	Z	20.3.1982	Kwekwe
*****Duminy** Jean-Paul	Cape Cobras	SA	14.4.1984	Strandfontein
Dunk Ben Robert	Tasmania	A	11.3.1987	Innisfail
Dunn Matthew Peter	Surrey	E	5.5.1992	Egham
*****du Plessis** Francois	Titans	SA	13.7.1984	Pretoria
du Preez Dillon	Knights	SA	8.11.1981	Queenstown
Durston Wesley John	Derbyshire	E	6.10.1980	Taunton
Eckersley Edmund John	Leicestershire	E	9.8.1989	Oxford
*****Edwards** Fidel Henderson	Barbados	WI	6.2.1982	Gays, Barbados
Edwards George Alexander	Surrey	E	29.7.1992	Lambeth
*****Edwards** Kirk Anton	Barbados	WI	3.11.1984	Mile and a Quarter, B
*****Ehsan Adil**	Faisalabad/Habib Bank	P	15.3.1993	Sheikhupura
*****Elgar** Dean	Knights/Somerset	SA	11.6.1987	Welkom
*****Elias Sunny**	Dhaka Metropolis	B	2.8.1986	Dhaka
*****Elliott** Grant David	Wellington	NZ	21.3.1979	Johannesburg, SA
Ellis Andrew Malcolm	Canterbury	NZ	24.3.1982	Christchurch
Emrit Rayad Ryan	Trinidad & Tobago	WI	8.3.1981	Mount Hope, Trinidad
*****Enamul Haque**	Sylhet	B	5.12.1986	Sylhet
*****Eranga** Ranaweera Mudiyanselage Shaminda	Tamil Union	SL	23.6.1986	Chilaw
Erlank Michael Nicholas	Knights/Free State	SA	4.7.1990	Kimberley
*****Ervine** Craig Richard	Matabeleland Tuskers	Z	19.8.1985	Harare
*****Ervine** Sean Michael	Hampshire	Z	6.12.1982	Harare
Evans Alasdair Campbell	Derbyshire/Scotland	Scot	12.1.1989	Tunbridge Wells, Eng.
Evans Laurie John	Warwickshire	E	12.10.1987	Lambeth
*****Ewing** Gavin Mackie	Matabeleland Tuskers	Z	21.1.1981	Harare
Faisal Athar	Hyderabad	P	15.10.1975	Hyderabad
*****Faisal Hossain**	Chittagong	B	26.10.1978	Chittagong
*****Faisal Iqbal**	Karachi Blues/PIA	P	30.12.1981	Karachi
Farhad Reza	Rajshahi	B	16.6.1986	Rajshahi
*****Faulkner** James Peter	Tasmania	A	29.4.1990	Launceston
Fawad Ahmed	Victoria	A	10.3.1979	Marghuz, Pakistan
*****Fawad Alam**	Karachi Whites/Nat. Bank	P	8.10.1985	Karachi
Fekete Andrew Loton	Tasmania	A	18.5.1985	Melbourne
Feldman Luke William	Queensland	A	1.8.1984	Sunnybank
Fell Thomas Charles	Oxford MCCU/Worcs	E	17.10.1993	Hillingdon
Ferguson Callum James	South Australia	A	21.11.1984	North Adelaide
*****Fernando** Aththachchi Nuwan Pradeep Roshan	Bloomfield	SL	19.10.1986	Negombo
*****Fernando** Kandage Hasantha Ruwan Kumara	Colombo	SL	14.10.1979	Panadura
*****Fernando** Kandana Arachchige Dinusha Manoj	Chilaw Marians	SL	10.8.1979	Panadura
*****Fernando** Thudellage Charitha Buddhika Also known as Charitha Buddhika	Panadura	SL	22.8.1980	Panadura
Finch Aaron James	Victoria	A	17.11.1986	Colac
Finch Harry Zachariah	Sussex	E	10.2.1995	Hastings
*****Finn** Steven Thomas	Middlesex	E	4.4.1989	Watford
Fletcher Andre David Stephon	Windward Islands	WI	28.11.1987	La Tante, Grenada
Fletcher Luke Jack	Nottinghamshire	E	18.9.1988	Nottingham
*****Flynn** Daniel Raymond	Northern Districts	NZ	16.4.1985	Rotorua
Foakes Benjamin Thomas	Essex	E	15.2.1993	Colchester
Footitt Mark Harold Alan	Derbyshire	E	25.11.1985	Nottingham

	Team	Country	Born	Birthplace
Forrest Peter James	Queensland	A	15.11.1985	*Windsor, Australia*
*****Foster** James Savin	Essex	E	15.4.1980	*Whipps Cross*
Fowler Zeniffe Levar	Jamaica	WI	8.11.1987	*Jamaica*
*****Franklin** James Edward Charles	Wellington	NZ	7.11.1980	*Wellington*
Franks Paul John	Nottinghamshire	E	3.2.1979	*Mansfield*
Freckingham Oliver Henry	Leicestershire	E	12.11.1988	*Oakham*
Friend Quinton	Knights/Free State	SA	16.2.1982	*Bellville*
*****Fudadin** Assad Badyr	Guyana	WI	1.8.1985	*Rose Hall, Guyana*
Fuller James Kerr	Otago/Gloucestershire	NZ	24.1.1990	*Cape Town*
*****Fulton** Peter Gordon	Canterbury	NZ	1.2.1979	*Christchurch*
*****Gabriel** Shannon Terry	Trinidad & Tobago	WI	28.4.1988	*Trinidad*
Gabriel Xavier Peter	Windward Islands	WI	18.12.1985	*St Lucia*
Gale Andrew William	Yorkshire	E	28.11.1983	*Dewsbury*
Gale Matthew Geoffrey	Queensland	A	28.11.1983	*Box Hill*
Gamage Panagamuwa <u>Lihuru</u> Sampath	Badureliya	SL	5.4.1988	*Maradana*
*****Gambhir** Gautam	Delhi/Essex	I	14.10.1981	*Delhi*
Gannon Cameron John	Queensland	A	23.1.1989	*Baulkham Hills*
Garwe Trevor Nyasha	Southern Rocks	Z	7.1.1982	*Harare*
Gatting Joe Stephen	Sussex	E	25.11.1987	*Brighton*
Gautam Chidambaram <u>Muralidharan</u>	Karnataka	I	8.3.1986	*Bangalore*
Gautam Shiv Prakash	Jharkhand	I	29.10.1988	*Ranchi*
*****Gayle** Christopher Henry	Jamaica	WI	21.9.1979	*Kingston, Jamaica*
*****George** Peter Robert	South Australia	A	16.10.1986	*Woodville*
Gidman Alexander Peter Richard	Gloucestershire	E	22.6.1981	*High Wycombe*
Gidman William Robert Simon	Gloucestershire	E	14.2.1985	*High Wycombe*
*****Gillespie** Mark Raymond	Wellington	NZ	17.10.1979	*Wanganui*
Glover John Charles	Glamorgan	E	29.8.1989	*Cardiff*
Godleman Billy Ashley	Derbyshire	E	11.2.1989	*Camden*
Gony Manpreet Singh	Punjab	I	4.1.1984	*Roopnagar*
*****Goodwin** Murray William	Glamorgan	Z	11.12.1972	*Salisbury*
Gordon Recordo Olton	Warwickshire	E	12.10.1991	*St Elizabeth, Jamaica*
Gqamane Ayabulela	Warriors/Border	SA	31.8.1989	*King William's Town*
Gray Alistair John Alec	Cape Cobras/W. Province	SA	8.7.1982	*Johannesburg*
Gregory Lewis	Somerset	E	24.5.1992	*Plymouth*
Griffiths David Andrew	Hampshire	E	10.9.1985	*Newport, Isle of Wight*
Groenewald Timothy Duncan	Derbyshire	SA	10.1.1984	*Pietermaritzburg*
Guillen Justin Christopher	Trinidad & Tobago	WI	2.1.1986	*Port-of-Spain, Trinidad*
Gulbis Evan Peter	Tasmania	A	26.3.1986	*Carlton*
Gupta Sunny	Jharkhand	I	27.9.1988	*Jamshedpur*
*****Guptill** Martin James	Auckland	NZ	30.9.1986	*Auckland*
Gurney Harry Frederick	Nottinghamshire	E	25.10.1986	*Nottingham*
Haberfield Jake Andy	Victoria	A	18.6.1986	*Townsville*
*****Haddin** Bradley James	New South Wales	A	23.10.1977	*Cowra*
Haggett Calum John	Kent	E	30.10.1990	*Taunton*
Hales Alexander Daniel	Nottinghamshire	E	3.1.1989	*Hillingdon*
*****Hall** Andrew James	Northamptonshire	SA	31.7.1975	*Johannesburg*
Hamilton Jahmar Neville	Leeward Islands	WI	22.9.1990	*St Thomas, Anguilla*
Hamilton-Brown Rory James	Sussex	E	3.9.1987	*St John's Wood*
Hammad Azam	Rawalpindi/Nat. Bank	P	16.3.1991	*Attock*
Hammond Miles Arthur Halhead	Gloucestershire	E	11.11.1996	*Cheltenham*
Handscomb Peter Stephen Patrick	Victoria	A	26.4.1991	*Melbourne*
Hannon-Dalby Oliver James	Warwickshire	E	20.6.1989	*Halifax*
*****Harbhajan Singh**	Punjab	I	3.7.1980	*Jullundur*
Harinath Arun	Surrey	E	26.3.1987	*Sutton*
Haris Sohail	ZTBL	P	9.1.1989	*Sialkot*
Harmer Simon Ross	Warriors	SA	10.2.1989	*Pretoria*

	Team	Country	Born	Birthplace
Harmison Ben William	Kent	E	9.1.1986	*Ashington*
Harris James Alexander Russell	Middlesex	E	16.5.1990	*Morriston*
Harris Marcus Sinclair	Western Australia	A	21.7.1992	*Perth*
***Harris** Paul Lee	Titans	SA	2.11.1978	*Salisbury, Zimbabwe*
***Harris** Ryan James	Queensland	A	11.10.1979	*Nowra*
Harrison Jamie	Durham	E	19.11.1990	*Whiston*
Hartley Christopher Desmond	Queensland	A	24.5.1982	*Nambour*
***Hasan Raza**	Habib Bank	P	11.3.1982	*Karachi*
***Hastings** John Wayne	Victoria	A	4.11.1985	*Nepean*
Hatchett Lewis James	Sussex	E	21.1.1990	*Shoreham-by-Sea*
***Hauritz** Nathan Michael	Queensland	A	18.10.1981	*Wondai*
Hazlewood Josh Reginald	New South Wales	A	8.1.1991	*Tamworth*
Head Travis Michael	South Australia	A	29.12.1993	*Adelaide*
Hector Donwell Banister	Windward Islands	WI	31.10.1988	*St Vincent*
Helm Thomas George	Middlesex	E	7.5.1994	*Stoke Mandeville*
Hemraj Chanderpaul	Guyana	WI	3.9.1993	*Guyana*
***Henderson** Claude William	Leicestershire	SA	14.6.1972	*Worcester*
Hendricks Beuran Eric	Cape Cobras	SA	8.6.1990	*Cape Town*
Hendricks Dominic Andrew	Gauteng/Lions	SA	7.11.1990	*Port Elizabeth*
Hendricks Reeza Raphael	Griqualand West/Knights	SA	14.8.1989	*Kimberley*
***Henriques** Moises Consantino	New South Wales	A	1.2.1987	*Funchal, Portugal*
Henry Matthew James	Canterbury	NZ	14.12.1991	*Christchurch*
Henry Scott Oliver	New South Wales	A	14.2.1989	*Mudgee*
***Herath** Herath Mudiyanselage Rangana Keerthi Bandara	Tamil Union	SL	19.3.1978	*Kurunegala*
Herrick Jayde Matthew	Victoria	A	16.1.1985	*Melbourne*
Herring Cameron Lee	Gloucestershire	E	15.7.1994	*Abergavenny*
***Hettiarachchi** Dinuka	Colombo	SL	15.7.1976	*Colombo*
Higginbottom Matthew	Derbyshire	E	20.10.1990	*Stockport*
Hildreth James Charles	Somerset	E	9.9.1984	*Milton Keynes*
***Hilfenhaus** Benjamin William	Tasmania	A	15.3.1983	*Ulverstone*
Hill Michael William	Victoria	A	29.9.1988	*Melbourne*
Hira Roneel Magan	Canterbury	NZ	23.1.1987	*Auckland*
Hodd Andrew John	Yorkshire	E	12.1.1984	*Chichester*
Hodge Montcin Verniel	Leeward Islands	WI	29.9.1987	*Anguilla*
Hogan Michael Garry	W. Australia/Glamorgan	A	31.5.1981	*Newcastle*
Hogg Kyle William	Lancashire	E	2.7.1983	*Birmingham*
***Hoggard** Matthew James	Leicestershire	E	31.12.1976	*Leeds*
Holder Jason Omar	Barbados	WI	5.11.1991	*Rouens Village, Barb.*
Holland Jonathan Mark	Victoria	A	29.5.1987	*Sandringham*
Hope Kyle Antonio	Barbados	WI	20.11.1988	*Field Place*
Hope Shai Diego	Barbados	WI	10.11.1993	*Barbados*
Hopes James Redfern	Queensland	A	24.10.1978	*Townsville*
***Hopkins** Gareth James	Auckland	NZ	24.11.1976	*Lower Hutt*
Horton Paul James	Lancashire	E	20.9.1982	*Sydney, Australia*
Hosein Akeal Jerome	Trinidad & Tobago	WI	24.4.1993	*Trinidad*
Housego Daniel Mark	Gloucestershire	E	12.10.1988	*Windsor*
***How** Jamie Michael	Central Districts	NZ	19.5.1981	*New Plymouth*
Howell Benny Alexander Cameron	Gloucestershire	E	5.10.1988	*Bordeaux, France*
Hughes Alex Lloyd	Derbyshire	E	29.9.1991	*Wordsley*
Hughes Chesney Francis	Derbyshire	E	20.1.1991	*Anguilla*
Hughes Daniel Peter	New South Wales	A	16.2.1989	*Gooloogong*
***Hughes** Phillip Joel	South Australia	A	30.11.1988	*Macksville*
***Humayun Farhat**	Habib Bank	P	24.1.1981	*Lahore*
Hunn Matthew David	Kent	E	22.3.1994	*Colchester*
Hussain Gemaal Maqsood	Somerset	E	10.10.1983	*Waltham Forest*
Hussey David John	Victoria/Nottinghamshire	A	15.7.1977	*Morley*
***Hussey** Michael Edward Killeen	Western Australia	A	27.5.1975	*Morley*
Hutton Brett Alan	Nottinghamshire	E	6.2.1993	*Doncaster*
Hyatt Danza Pacino	Jamaica	WI	17.3.1983	*St Catherine, Jamaica*

	Team	Country	Born	Birthplace
*Iftikhar Anjum	Islamabad/ZTBL	P	1.12.1980	Khanewal
*Imran Farhat	Habib Bank/Lahore Ravi	P	20.5.1982	Lahore
*Imran Nazir	ZTBL	P	16.12.1981	Gujranwala
*Imran Tahir	Lions	SA	27.3.1979	Lahore, Pakistan
*Imrul Kayes	Khulna	B	2.2.1987	Meherpur
Imtiaz Ahmed	Uttar Pradesh	I	10.11.1985	Bhadohi
Ingram Colin Alexander	Warriors	SA	3.7.1985	Port Elizabeth
Ireland Anthony John	Leicestershire	Z	30.8.1984	Masvingo
*Irfan Fazil	Habib Bank	P	2.11.1981	Lahore
Jackson Simon	Jamaica	WI	18.5.1985	Jamaica
Jacobs Arno	Warriors/Eastern Province	SA	13.3.1977	Potchefstroom
Jacobs David Johan	Warriors	SA	4.11.1982	Klerksdorp
Jacobs Steven Anthony	Guyana	WI	13.9.1988	Georgetown, Guyana
*Jadeja Ajaysinhji	Haryana	I	1.2.1971	Jamnagar
*Jadeja Ravindrasinh Anirudhsinh	Saurashtra	I	6.12.1988	Navagam-Khed
Jagadeesh Vasudevanpillai Arundhathiamma	Kerala	I	25.5.1983	Kottarakara
*Jaggernauth Amit Shelden	Trinidad & Tobago	WI	16.11.1983	Lennard St, Trinidad
Jaggi Ishank Rajiv	Jharkhand	I	27.1.1989	Bacheli
*Jahurul Islam	Rajshahi	B	12.12.1986	Rajshahi
James Lindon Ormrick Dinsley	Windward Islands	WI	30.12.1984	South Rivers, St Vinc.
*Jaques Philip Anthony	Yorkshire	A	3.5.1979	Wollongong
*Jarvis Kyle Malcolm	C. Districts/Lancashire	Z	16.2.1989	Harare
Javid Ateeq	Warwickshire	E	15.10.1991	Birmingham
Jayaprakashdaran Pradeep Sri	Burgher	SL	13.1.1984	Colombo
Jayasundera Madurawelage Don Udara Supeksha	Ragama	SL	3.1.1991	Minuwangoda
*Jayawardene Denagamage Proboth Mahela de Silva	Sinhalese	SL	27.5.1977	Colombo
*Jayawardene Hewasandatchige Asiri Prasanna Wishvanath	Panadura	SL	9.10.1979	Colombo
Jennings Keaton Kent	Durham	SA	19.6.1992	Johannesburg
Jewell Thomas Melvin	Surrey	E	13.1.1991	Reading
Jiwanjot Singh	Punjab	I	6.11.1990	Patiala
Johnson Delorn Edison	Windward Islands	WI	15.9.1988	St Vincent
Johnson Leon Rayon	Guyana	WI	8.8.1987	Georgetown, Guyana
Johnson Michael Anthony	Worcestershire	A	11.8.1988	Perth
*Johnson Mitchell Guy	Western Australia	A	2.11.1981	Townsville
Johnson Richard Matthew	Derbyshire	E	1.9.1988	Solihull
Jones Alexander John	Glamorgan	E	10.11.1988	Bridgend
Jones Christopher Robert	Durham MCCU/Somerset	E	5.11.1990	Harold Wood
*Jones Geraint Owen	Kent	E	14.7.1976	Kundiawa, PNG
Jones Richard Alan	Worcestershire	E	6.11.1986	Stourbridge
Jonker Christiaan	Warriors/SW Districts	SA	24.9.1986	Rustenburg
Jordan Christopher James	Barbados/Sussex	E	4.10.1988	Lowlands, Barbados
Joseph Keon	Guyana	WI	25.11.1991	Guyana
Joseph Larry Nuron	Leeward Islands	WI	1.4.1985	All Saints, Antigua
*Joseph Sylvester Cleofoster	Leeward Islands	WI	5.9.1978	New Winthorpes, Ant.
Joyce Edmund Christopher	Ireland/Sussex	Ire	22.9.1978	Dublin, Ireland
*Junaid Khan	WAPDA	P	24.12.1989	Matra
*Junaid Siddique	Rajshahi	B	30.10.1987	Rajshahi
Juneja Manprit Charanjit	Gujarat	I	12.9.1990	Ahmedabad
*Kaif Mohammad	Uttar Pradesh	I	1.12.1980	Allahabad
*Kalavitigoda Shantha	Ports Authority	SL	23.12.1977	Colombo
*Kallis Jacques Henry	Cape Cobras/Nat. Bank	SA	16.10.1975	Pinelands
*Kamran Akmal	Lahore Shal./Nat. Bank	P	13.1.1982	Lahore
Kamran Hussain	Bahawalpur/Habib Bank	P	9.5.1977	Bahawalpur
Kamungozi Tafadzwa	Southern Rocks	Z	8.6.1987	Harare

	Team	Country	Born	Birthplace
Kandamby Sahan Hewa <u>Thilina</u>	Sinhalese	SL	4.6.1982	*Colombo*
***Kanitkar** Hrishikesh Hemant	Rajasthan	I	14.11.1974	*Pune*
Kantasingh Kavesh	Trinidad & Tobago	WI	30.9.1986	*Trinidad*
Kapil Aneesh	Worcestershire	E	3.8.1993	*Wolverhampton*
***Kapugedera** Chamara Kantha	Nondescripts	SL	24.2.1987	*Kandy*
***Karthik** Krishankumar <u>Dinesh</u>	Tamil Nadu	I	1.6.1985	*Madras*
***Kartik** Murali	Railways	I	11.9.1976	*Madras*
***Karunaratne** Frank <u>Dimuth</u> Madushanka	Sinhalese	SL	28.4.1988	*Colombo*
***Katich** Simon Mathew	Lancashire	A	21.8.1975	*Middle Swan*
Katwaroo Stephen	Trinidad & Tobago	WI	14.11.1993	*Trinidad*
Kaul Siddharth	Punjab	I	19.5.1990	*Kangra*
Kaul Uday	Punjab	I	2.12.1987	*Kangra*
Kaushal Paskuwal Handi <u>Tharindu</u>	Nondescripts	SL	5.3.1993	*Galle*
Keedy Gary	Surrey	E	27.11.1974	*Sandal*
***Kemp** Justin Miles	Cape Cobras	SA	2.10.1977	*Queenstown*
Keogh Robert Ian	Northamptonshire	E	21.10.1991	*Dunstable*
***Kerrigan** Simon Christopher	Lancashire	E	10.5.1989	*Preston*
Kervezee Alexei Nicolaas	Worcestershire	NL	11.9.1989	*Walvis Bay, Namibia*
***Key** Robert William Trevor	Kent	E	12.5.1979	*East Dulwich*
Khadiwale Harshad Hemantkumar	Maharashtra	I	21.10.1988	*Pune*
Khalid Latif	Karachi W/Port Qasim A	P	4.11.1985	*Karachi*
***Khan** Imraan	Dolphins/KZN/ KZN Inland	SA	27.4.1984	*Durban*
Khan Imran	Trinidad & Tobago	WI	6.12.1984	*Port-of-Spain, Trinidad*
***Khawaja** Usman Tariq	Queensland	A	18.12.1986	*Islamabad, Pakistan*
***Khurram** Manzoor	Karachi Blues/Port Qasim A	P	10.6.1986	*Karachi*
Kieswetter Craig	Somerset	E	28.11.1987	*Johannesburg, SA*
Kirby Steven Paul	Somerset	E	4.10.1977	*Ainsworth*
Klein Dieter	Lions/North West	SA	31.10.1988	*Lichtenburg*
***Kleinveldt** Rory Keith	Cape Cobras	SA	15.3.1983	*Cape Town*
Klinger Michael	South Australia/Glos	A	4.7.1980	*Kew*
***Kohli** Virat	Delhi	I	5.11.1988	*Delhi*
***Krejza** Jason John	Tasmania	A	14.1.1983	*Newtown*
Kruger Garnett John-Peter	North West	SA	5.1.1977	*Port Elizabeth*
Kuhn Heino Gunther	Titans	SA	1.4.1984	*Piet Retief*
***Kulasekara** Chamith <u>Kosala</u> Bandara	Nondescripts	SL	15.7.1985	*Mavanalle*
***Kulasekara** Kulasekara Mudiyanselage Dinesh <u>Nuwan</u>	Colts	SL	22.7.1982	*Nittambuwa*
Kulatunga Hettiarachchi Gamage <u>Jeevantha</u> Mahesh	Kurungela Youth	SL	2.11.1973	*Kurunegala*
Kulkarni Dhawal Sunil	Mumbai	I	10.12.1988	*Bombay*
***Lakmal** Ranasinghe Arachchige <u>Suranga</u>	Tamil Union	SL	10.3.1987	*Matara*
***Lamb** Gregory Arthur	Mountaineers	Z	4.3.1980	*Harare*
Lambert Tamar Lansford	Jamaica	WI	15.7.1981	*St Catherine, Jamaica*
***Langeveldt** Charl Kenneth	Cape Cobras	SA	17.12.1974	*Stellenbosch*
Latham Thomas William Maxwell	Canterbury	NZ	2.4.1992	*Christchurch*
Laughlin Ben	Tasmania	A	3.10.1982	*Box Hill*
Lawford Trent Lee	South Australia	A	18.4.1988	*Carlton*
Leach Joseph	Worcestershire	E	30.10.1990	*Stafford*
Leach Matthew <u>Jack</u>	Somerset	E	22.6.1991	*Taunton*
Leaning Jack Andrew	Yorkshire	E	18.10.1993	*Bristol*
le Clus Jacobus <u>Francois</u>	Northerns/Titans	SA	23.6.1987	*Johannesburg*
Lees Alexander Zak	Yorkshire	E	14.4.1993	*Halifax*
Leie Eddie	Gauteng/Lions	SA	16.11.1986	*Potchefstroom*
Leonard Yannick Robert	Leeward Islands	WI	12.5.1991	*Guyana*
Lesporis Keddy	Windward Islands	WI	27.12.1988	*St Lucia*
Levi Richard Ernst	Cape Cobras/W. Province	SA	14.1.1988	*Johannesburg*

	Team	Country	Born	Birthplace
Lewis Evin	Trinidad & Tobago	WI	27.12.1991	*Trinidad*
*****Lewis** Jonathan	Surrey	E	26.8.1975	*Aylesbury*
Liburd Steve Stuart Wayne	Leeward Islands	WI	26.2.1985	*Basseterre, St Kitts*
Liddle Christopher John	Sussex	E	1.2.1984	*Middlesbrough*
Liebisch Shaun Walter	Titans/Easterns	SA	25.4.1986	*Johannesburg*
Lilley Arron Mark	Lancashire	E	1.4.1991	*Tameside*
Linley Timothy Edward	Surrey	E	23.3.1982	*Leeds*
Lloyd David Liam	Glamorgan	E	15.5.1992	*St Asaph*
*****Lokuarachchi** Kaushal Samaraweera	Sinhalese	SL	20.5.1982	*Colombo*
London Adam Brian	Middlesex	E	12.10.1988	*Ashford*
Louw Brendon Ivan	SW Districts/Warriors	SA	15.11.1991	*Knysna*
Louw Johann	Cape Cobras	SA	12.4.1979	*Cape Town*
Lucas David Scott	Worcestershire	E	19.8.1978	*Nottingham*
Ludeman Timothy Paul	South Australia	A	23.6.1987	*Warrnambool*
Lumb Michael John	Nottinghamshire	E	12.2.1980	*Johannesburg, SA*
Lynn Christopher Austin	Queensland	A	10.4.1990	*Herston*
*****Lyon** Nathan Michael	South Australia/NSW	A	20.11.1987	*Young*
Lyth Adam	Yorkshire	E	25.9.1987	*Whitby*
McCarter Graeme John	Gloucestershire/Ireland	Ire	10.10.1992	*Londonderry*
McCarthy Andre McIntosh	Jamaica	WI	8.6.1987	*Kingston, Jamaica*
McClean Kevin Ramon	Comb. Campuses and Colls	WI	24.1.1988	*Castle, Barbados*
McClenaghan Mitchell John	Auckland	NZ	11.6.1986	*Hastings*
*****McCullum** Brendon Barrie	Otago	NZ	27.9.1981	*Dunedin*
McCullum Nathan Leslie	Otago/Glamorgan	NZ	1.9.1980	*Dunedin*
McDermott Alister Craig	Queensland	A	7.6.1991	*Brisbane*
McDonald Ronan Henry	Queensland	A	30.6.1992	*Brisbane*
Machan Matthew William	Scotland/Sussex	Scot	15.2.1991	*Brighton*
*****McIntosh** Timothy Gavin	Auckland	NZ	4.12.1979	*Auckland*
*****McKay** Andrew John	Wellington	NZ	17.4.1980	*Auckland*
*****McKay** Clinton James	Victoria	A	22.2.1983	*Melbourne*
McKay Peter John	Warwickshire	E	12.10.1994	*Staffordshire*
McKenzie Neil Douglas	Lions/Hampshire	SA	24.11.1975	*Johannesburg*
Mackin Simon Patrick	Western Australia	A	1.9.1992	*Wyalkatchem*
McLaren Adrian Peter	Warriors/SW Districts	SA	21.4.1980	*Kimberley*
*****McLaren** Ryan	Knights	SA	9.2.1983	*Kimberley*
Maddinson Nicolas James	New South Wales	A	21.12.1991	*Shoalhaven*
*****Maddy** Darren Lee	Warwickshire	E	23.5.1974	*Leicester*
Madsen Wayne Lee	Derbyshire	SA	2.1.1984	*Durban*
Magoffin Steven James	Sussex	A	17.12.1979	*Corinda*
Maharaj Keshav Athmanand	Dolphins/KwaZulu-Natal	SA	7.2.1990	*Durban*
*****Maharoof** Mohamed Farveez	Nondescripts	SL	7.9.1984	*Colombo*
Maher Adam John	Tasmania	A	14.11.1981	*Newcastle*
*****Mahmood** Sajid Iqbal	Essex	E	21.12.1981	*Bolton*
*****Mahmudullah**	Dhaka	B	4.2.1986	*Mymensingh*
Majumdar Anustup Prabir	Bengal	I	30.4.1984	*Chandannagore*
Makhaphela Viyusa	Warriors/Border	SA	20.12.1986	*Alice*
Malan Dawid Johannes	Middlesex	E	3.9.1987	*Roehampton*
Malan Pieter Jacobus	Titans/Northerns/W. Prov.	SA	13.8.1989	*Nelspruit*
*****Malinga** Separamadu Lasith	Nondescripts	SL	4.9.1983	*Galle*
Mandeep Singh	Punjab	I	18.12.1991	*Jalandhar*
Manjot Singh	New South Wales	A	2.10.1987	*St Leonards, Sydney*
Mansoor Amjad	Sialkot	P	25.12.1986	*Sialkot*
*****Maregwede** Alester	Southern Rocks	Z	5.8.1981	*Harare*
Marsh Mitchell Ross	Western Australia	A	20.10.1991	*Armadale*
*****Marsh** Shaun Edward	Western Australia	A	9.7.1983	*Narrogin*
*****Marshall** Ayub	Dhaka Metropolis	B	5.12.1988	*Dhaka*
*****Marshall** Hamish John Hamilton	Gloucestershire	NZ	15.2.1979	*Warkworth*

	Team	Country	Born	Birthplace
*Marshall James Andrew Hamilton	Northern Districts	NZ	15.2.1979	Warkworth
*Marshall Xavier Melbourne	Jamaica	WI	27.3.1986	St Ann, Jamaica
Martin Anthony	Leeward Islands	WI	18.11.1982	Bethesda, Antigua
*Martin Bruce Philip	Auckland	NZ	25.4.1980	Whangarei
*Martin Christopher Stewart	Auckland	NZ	10.12.1974	Christchurch
*Maruma Timycen	Mountaineers	Z	19.4.1988	Harare
*Masakadza Hamilton	Mountaineers	Z	9.8.1983	Harare
*Masakadza Shingirai Winston	Mountaineers	Z	4.9.1986	Harare
Mascarenhas Adrian <u>Dimitri</u>	Hampshire	E	30.10.1977	Chiswick
*Mashrafe bin Mortaza	Khulna	B	5.10.1983	Narail
Masters David Daniel	Essex	E	22.4.1978	Chatham
*Mathews Angelo Davis	Colts	SL	2.6.1987	Colombo
Mathurin Garey Earl	Windward Islands	WI	23.9.1983	Mon Repos, St Lucia
Matshikwe Pumelela	Lions/Gauteng	SA	19.6.1984	Johannesburg
*Matsikenyeri Stuart	Mashonaland Eagles	Z	3.5.1983	Harare
*Mawoyo Tinotenda Mbiri Kanayi	Mountaineers	Z	8.1.1986	Umtali
*Maxwell Glenn James	Victoria	A	14.10.1988	Kew
*Mbhalati Nkateko <u>Ethy</u>	Titans	SA	18.11.1981	Tzaneen
Meaker Stuart Christopher	Surrey	E	21.1.1989	Durban, SA
*Mehrab Hossain	Dhaka Metropolis	B	8.7.1987	Rajshahi
*Mendis Balapuwaduge <u>Ajantha</u> Winslo	Army	SL	11.3.1985	Moratuwa
Mendis Balapuwaduge Manukulasuriya Amith <u>Jeewan</u>	Tamil Union	SL	15.1.1983	Colombo
Mennie Joe Matthew	South Australia	A	24.12.1988	Coffs Harbour
Merchant Jamie Howinton	Jamaica	WI	13.7.1989	Jamaica
Meschede Craig Anthony Joseph	Somerset	E	21.11.1991	Johannesburg, SA
Meth Keegan Orry	Matabeleland Tuskers	Z	8.2.1988	Bulawayo
Michael Dominic Peter	Queensland	A	8.10.1987	Brisbane
Mickleburgh Jaik Charles	Mid West Rhinos/Essex	E	30.3.1990	Norwich
Middlebrook James Daniel	Northamptonshire	E	13.5.1977	Leeds
Miles Craig Neil	Gloucestershire	E	20.7.1994	Swindon
Miller Andrew Stephen	Sussex	E	27.9.1987	Preston
Miller David Andrew	KwaZulu-Natal/Dolphins	SA	10.6.1989	Pietermaritzburg
*Miller Nikita O'Neil	Jamaica	WI	16.5.1982	St Elizabeth, Jamaica
*Mills Kyle David	Auckland	NZ	15.3.1979	Auckland
Mills Tymal Solomon	Essex	E	12.8.1992	Dewsbury
Milne Adam Fraser	Central Districts	NZ	13.4.1992	Palmerston North
Milnes Thomas Patrick	Warwickshire	E	6.10.1992	Stourbridge
*Mirando Magina <u>Thilan Thushara</u>	Tamil Union	SL	1.3.1981	Balapitiya
Also known as Thilan Thushara				
*Misbah-ul-Haq	Sui Northern Gas	P	28.5.1974	Mianwali
*Mishra Amit	Haryana	I	24.11.1982	Delhi
Mitchell Daryl Joseph	Northern Districts	NZ	20.5.1991	Hamilton
Mitchell Daryl Keith Henry	Worcestershire	E	25.11.1983	Badsey
*Mithun Abhimanyu	Karnataka	I	25.10.1989	Dasarahalli
Mohamed Zaheer	Guyana	WI	10.10.1985	Georgetown, Guyana
*Mohammad Ashraful	Dhaka Metropolis	B	9.9.1984	Dhaka
*Mohammad Ayub	Sialkot/WAPDA	P	13.9.1979	Nankana Sahib
*Mohammad Hafeez	Sui Northern Gas	P	17.10.1980	Sargodha
*Mohammad Irfan	KRL	P	6.6.1982	Gaggu Mandi
*Mohammad Khalil	Lahore Ravi/ZTBL	P	11.11.1982	Lahore
*Mohammad Salman	Faisalabad/Port Qasim A	P	7.8.1981	Karachi
*Mohammad Sami	Karachi W/Port Qasim A	P	24.2.1981	Karachi
*Mohammad Sharif	Dhaka	B	12.12.1985	Narayanganj
*Mohammad Talha	Bahawalpur/Port Qasim A	P	15.10.1988	Faisalabad
Mohammed Jason Nazimuddin	Trinidad & Tobago	WI	23.9.1986	Barrackpore, Trinidad
*Mohammed Shami	Bengal	I	3.9.1990	Jonagar
*Mohanty Basantkumar Chintamani	Orissa	I	24.11.1986	Bhubaneswar
Moller Gregory David	Queensland	A	29.1.1983	Boonah

	Team	Country	Born	Birthplace
*Mominul Haque	Chittagong	B	29.9.1991	*Cox's Bazar*
Moore Stephen Colin	Lancashire	E	4.11.1980	*Johannesburg, SA*
*Morgan Eoin Joseph Gerard	Middlesex	E	10.9.1986	*Dublin, Ireland*
*Morkel Johannes Albertus	Titans	SA	10.6.1981	*Vereeniging*
*Morkel Morne	Titans	SA	6.10.1984	*Vereeniging*
Morris Christopher Henry	Lions	SA	30.4.1987	*Pretoria*
Mosehle Mangaliso	Titans/Easterns	SA	24.4.1990	*Duduza*
Mosena Lefa Nelson	Free State/Knights	SA	18.3.1987	*Bloemfontein*
Mosharraf Hossain	Dhaka	B	20.11.1981	*Dhaka*
Motwani Rohit Heero	Maharashtra	I	13.12.1990	*Pune*
*Mpofu Christopher Bobby	Matabeleland Tuskers	Z	27.11.1985	*Plumtree*
*Mubarak Jehan	Nondescripts	SL	10.1.1981	*Washington, USA*
Muirhead James Matthew	Victoria	A	30.7.1993	*Altona*
*Mukund Abhinav	Tamil Nadu	I	6.1.1990	*Madras*
Mullaney Steven John	Nottinghamshire	E	19.11.1986	*Warrington*
Munaweera Eldeniya Medagedara Dilshan Yasika	Bloomfield	SL	24.4.1989	*Colombo*
*Munro Colin	Auckland	NZ	11.3.1987	*Durban, SA*
Munting James Lindsay Gordon	South Australia	A	28.9.1986	*Devonport*
*Mupariwa Tawanda	S. Rocks/Mat. Tuskers	Z	16.4.1985	*Bulawayo*
Murphy David	Scotland/Northants	Scot	24.7.1989	*Welwyn Garden City*
Murtagh Timothy James	Ireland/Middlesex	Ire	2.8.1981	*Lambeth*
Mushangwe Natsai	Mountaineers	Z	9.2.1991	*Mhangura*
*Mushfiqur Rahim	Rajshahi	B	1.9.1988	*Bogra*
Mustard Philip	Durham	E	8.10.1982	*Sunderland*
*Mutizwa Forster	Mashonaland Eagles	Z	24.8.1985	*Harare*
Mutombodzi Confidence Tinotenda	Mashonaland Eagles	Z	21.12.1990	*Harare*
*Mutumbami Richmond	Southern Rocks	Z	11.6.1989	*Masvingo*
Nadeem Shahbaz	Jharkhand	I	12.8.1989	*Patna*
*Naeem Islam	Rangpur	B	31.12.1986	*Gaibandha*
*Nafis Iqbal	Chittagong	B	31.1.1985	*Chittagong*
Naik Jigar Kumar Hakumatrai	Leicestershire	E	10.8.1984	*Leicester*
Najaf Shah	Quetta/PIA	P	17.12.1984	*Gujarkhan*
Napier Graham Richard	Essex	E	6.1.1980	*Colchester*
*Narine Sunil Philip	Trinidad & Tobago	WI	26.5.1988	*Trinidad*
*Nash Brendan Paul	Kent	WI	14.12.1977	*Attadale, Australia*
Nash Christopher David	Sussex	E	19.5.1983	*Cuckfield*
*Nasir Hossain	Rangpur	B	30.11.1991	*Rangpur*
*Nasir Jamshed	National Bank	P	6.12.1989	*Lahore*
*Naved Latif	Faisalabad	P	21.2.1976	*Sargodha*
*Naved-ul-Hasan (*Rana Naved*)	WAPDA	P	28.2.1978	*Sheikhupura*
Nayar Abhishek Mohan	Mumbai	I	26.10.1983	*Secunderabad*
*Ncube Njabulo	Matabeleland Tuskers	Z	14.10.1989	*Bulawayo*
Neesham James Douglas Sheehan	Otago	NZ	17.9.1990	*Auckland*
*Nehra Ashish	Delhi	I	29.4.1979	*Delhi*
Nemat Rameez Khan	Jharkhand	I	14.11.1986	*Sitamarhi*
Neser Michael Gertges	Queensland	A	29.3.1990	*Pretoria*
Nethula Tarun Sai	Central Districts	NZ	8.5.1983	*Kurnool, India*
Nevill Peter Michael	New South Wales	A	13.10.1985	*Hawthorne*
Newby Oliver James	Lancashire	E	26.8.1984	*Blackburn*
Newton Robert Irving	Northamptonshire	E	18.1.1990	*Taunton*
*Nicol Robert James	Canterbury	NZ	28.5.1983	*Auckland*
*Nkala Mluleki Luke	Mid West Rhinos	Z	1.4.1981	*Bulawayo*
*North Marcus James	W. Australia/Glamorgan	A	28.7.1979	*Pakenham*
Northeast Sam Alexander	Kent	E	16.10.1989	*Ashford*
Norwell Liam Connor	Gloucestershire	E	27.12.1991	*Bournemouth*
Nurse Ashley Renaldo	Barbados	WI	22.12.1988	*Gibbons, Barbados*
O'Brien Niall John	Ireland/Leics	Ire	8.11.1981	*Dublin*
Ojha Naman Vijaykumar	Madhya Pradesh	I	20.7.1983	*Ujjain*

	Team	Country	Born	Birthplace
*Ojha Pragyan Prayish	Hyderabad	I	5.9.1986	Khurda
O'Keefe Stephen Norman John	New South Wales	A	9.12.1984	Malaysia
*Onions Graham	Durham/Derbyshire	E	9.9.1982	Gateshead
*Ontong Justin Lee	Cape Cobras	SA	4.1.1980	Paarl
O'Reilly Ethan	Lions/Gauteng	SA	27.12.1985	Port Elizabeth
Ottley Khesan Yannick Gabriel	Trinidad & Tobago	WI	7.9.1991	Trinidad
Ottley Kjorn Yohance	Trinidad & Tobago	WI	9.12.1989	Preysal, Trinidad
Overton Craig	Somerset	E	10.4.1994	Barnstaple
Overton Jamie	Somerset	E	10.4.1994	Barnstaple
Owen William Thomas	Glamorgan	E	2.9.1988	St Asaph
*Paine Timothy David	Tasmania	A	8.12.1984	Hobart
Paliwal Rajat	Services	I	24.12.1991	Sonepat
Palladino Antonio Paul	Derbyshire	E	29.6.1983	Tower Hamlets
Pandey Ishwar Chand	Madhya Pradesh	I	15.8.1989	Rewa
Pandey Manish Krishnanand	Karnataka	I	10.9.1989	Nainital
*Panesar Mudhsuden Singh (Monty)	Sussex/Essex	E	25.4.1982	Luton
Pankaj Singh	Rajasthan	I	6.5.1985	Sultanpur
*Panyangara Tinashe	Southern Rocks	Z	21.10.1985	Marondera
*Papps Michael Hugh William	Wellington	NZ	2.7.1979	Christchurch
*Paranavitana Nishad Tharanga	Sinhalese	SL	15.4.1982	Kegalle
*Parchment Brenton Anthony	Jamaica	WI	24.6.1982	St Elizabeth, Jamaica
Pardoe Matthew Graham	S. Rocks/Worcestershire	E	5.1.1991	Stourbridge
*Parnell Wayne Dillon	Warriors	SA	30.7.1989	Port Elizabeth
Parris Nekoli	Comb. Campuses and Colls	WI	6.6.1987	Lowland Park, Barb.
Parry Stephen David	Lancashire	E	12.1.1986	Manchester
Parvez Rasool	Jammu and Kashmir	I	13.2.1989	Bijbehara
*Pascal Nelon Troy	Windward Islands	WI	25.4.1987	St David's, Grenada
*Patel Jeetan Shashi	Wellington/Warwickshire	NZ	7.5.1980	Wellington
Patel Munaf Musa	Baroda	I	12.7.1983	Ikhar
*Patel Parthiv Ajay	Gujarat	I	9.3.1985	Ahmedabad
Patel Ravi Hasmukh	Middlesex	E	4.8.1991	Harrow
*Patel Samit Rohit	Nottinghamshire	E	30.11.1984	Leicester
Paterson Dane	KZN/WP/Cape Cobras	SA	4.4.1989	Cape Town
*Pathan Irfan Khan	Baroda	I	27.10.1984	Baroda
Pathan Yusuf Khan	Baroda	I	27.11.1984	Baroda
Patterson Kurtis Robert	New South Wales	A	5.4.1993	Hurstville
Patterson Steven Andrew	Yorkshire	E	3.10.1983	Hull
*Pattinson James Lee	Victoria	A	3.5.1990	Melbourne
Payne David Alan	Gloucestershire	E	15.2.1991	Poole
Pelser Brett Jonathan	Lions/North West	SA	23.4.1985	Durban
Perera Aganpodi Madura Lakmal	Ragama	SL	21.7.1985	Kalutara
Perera Angelo Kanishka	Nondescripts	SL	23.2.1990	Moratuwa
*Perera Mahawaduge Dilruwan Kamalaneth	Panadura	SL	22.7.1982	Panadura
Perera Mathurage Don Kushal Janith	Colts	SL	17.8.1990	Kalubovila
*Perera Narangoda Liyanaarachchilage Tissara Chirantha	Colts	SL	3.4.1989	Colombo
Perera Nawagamuwage Vimukthi Ramesh	Moors	SL	14.11.1989	Colombo
*Permaul Veerasammy	Guyana	WI	11.8.1989	Belvedere, Guyana
Peters Keon Kenroy	Windward Islands	WI	24.2.1982	Mesopotamia, St Vinc.
Peters Orlando	Leeward Islands	WI	10.5.1988	Antigua
Peters Sherwin Pele	Leeward Islands	WI	2.5.1990	Trinidad
Peters Stephen David	Northamptonshire	E	10.12.1978	Harold Wood
*Petersen Alviro Nathan	Lions/Somerset	SA	25.11.1980	Port Elizabeth
*Peterson Robin John	Cape Cobras	SA	4.8.1979	Port Elizabeth
Pettini Mark Lewis	Mountaineers/Essex	E	7.8.1983	Brighton

	Team	Country	Born	Birthplace
Phangiso Aaron Mpho	North West	SA	21.1.1984	*Garunkuwa*
***Philander** Vernon Darryl	Kent	SA	24.6.1985	*Bellville*
Phillips Timothy James	Essex	E	13.3.1981	*Cambridge*
Piedt Dane Lee-Roy	Cape Cobras/W. Province	SA	6.3.1990	*Cape Town*
Pienaar Abraham Jacobus (**Obus**)	Knights/Free State	SA	12.12.1989	*Bloemfontein*
Pienaar Jacobus Johannes	Northerns/Titans	SA	23.10.1985	*Klerksdorp*
***Pietersen** Kevin Peter	Surrey	E	27.6.1980	*Pietermaritzburg, SA*
Pinner Neil Douglas	Worcestershire	E	28.9.1990	*Wordsley*
Piolet Steffan Andreas	Warwickshire	E	8.8.1988	*Redhill*
Plunkett Liam Edward	Yorkshire	E	6.4.1985	*Middlesbrough*
Polius Dalton	Windward Islands	WI	12.9.1990	*St Lucia*
Pollard Kieron Adrian	Trinidad & Tobago	WI	12.5.1987	*Cacariqua, Trinidad*
Pomersbach Luke Anthony	Queensland	A	28.9.1984	*Bentley*
***Ponting** Ricky Thomas	Tasmania/Surrey	A	19.12.1974	*Launceston*
Porterfield William Thomas Stuart	Ireland/Warwickshire	Ire	6.9.1984	*Londonderry*
***Powar** Ramesh Rajaram	Rajasthan	I	20.5.1978	*Bombay*
***Powell** Kieran Omar Akeem	Leeward Islands	WI	6.3.1990	*Government Rd, Nevis*
Powell Michael John	Kent	E	3.2.1977	*Abergavenny*
Poynter Stuart William	Ireland/Warwickshire	Ire	18.10.1990	*Hammersmith, England*
Poynton Thomas	Derbyshire	E	25.11.1989	*Burton-on-Trent*
***Prasad** Kariyawasam Tirana Gamage **Dammika**	Sinhalese	SL	30.5.1983	*Ragama*
***Prasanna** Seekkuge	Army	SL	27.6.1985	*Balapitiya*
Price Michael Lynn	Warriors/E. Province	SA	6.10.1981	*Grahamstown*
***Price** Raymond William	Mashonaland Eagles	Z	12.6.1976	*Salisbury*
***Prince** Ashwell Gavin	Warriors/Lancashire	SA	28.5.1977	*Port Elizabeth*
***Prior** Matthew James	Sussex	E	26.2.1982	*Johannesburg, SA*
Priyanjan Subasinghe Mudiyanselage **Ashan**	Ports Authority	SL	14.8.1989	*Colombo*
Procter Luke Anthony	Lancashire	E	24.6.1988	*Oldham*
***Pujara** Cheteshwar Arvind	Saurashtra	I	25.1.1988	*Rajkot*
Pushpakumara Muthumudalige	Ports Authority	SL	26.9.1981	*Colombo*
Pushpakumara Paulage **Malinda**	Moors	SL	24.3.1987	*Colombo*
Putland Gary David	South Australia	A	10.2.1986	*Flinders*
Puttick Andrew George	Cape Cobras	SA	11.12.1980	*Cape Town*
Pyrah Richard Michael	Yorkshire	E	1.11.1982	*Dewsbury*
***Qaiser Abbas**	Quetta/National Bank	P	7.5.1982	*Muridke*
***Quiney** Robert John	Victoria/Essex	A	20.8.1982	*Brighton, Australia*
Rabie Gurshwin Renier	Warriors/SW Districts	SA	26.6.1983	*Oudtshoorn*
***Rahane** Ajinkya Madhukar	Mumbai	I	6.6.1988	*Ashwi Kurd*
***Rahat Ali**	Multan/KRL	P	12.9.1988	*Multan*
Rahul Kannur Lokesh	Karnataka	I	18.4.1992	*Bangalore*
***Raina** Suresh Kumar	Uttar Pradesh	I	27.11.1986	*Ghaziabad*
Rainbird Samuel Leigh	Tasmania	A	5.6.1992	*Hobart*
Raine Benjamin Alexander	Leicestershire	E	14.9.1991	*Sunderland*
Rainsford Edward Charles	Mid West Rhinos	Z	14.12.1984	*Kadoma*
***Rajin Saleh**	Sylhet	B	20.11.1983	*Sylhet*
Rambukwella Ramith Laksen Bandara	Nondescripts	SL	8.9.1991	*Kandy*
***Ramdin** Denesh	Trinidad & Tobago	WI	13.3.1985	*Mission Road, Trinidad*
Rameez Raja	Karachi Blues/State Bank	P	31.7.1987	*Karachi*
Ramela Omphile Abel	W. Province/Cape Cobras	SA	14.3.1988	*Soweto*
***Rampaul** Ravindranath	Trinidad & Tobago	WI	15.10.1984	*Preysal, Trinidad*
Ramsaran Kristopher	Comb. Campuses and Colls	WI	1.2.1992	*Trinidad*
***Ramyakumara** **Wijekoon** Mudiyanselage **Gayan** *Also known as Gayan Wijekoon*	Colombo	SL	21.12.1976	*Gampaha*
***Randiv** Suraj	Bloomfield	SL	30.1.1985	*Matara*

Also known as Hewa Kaluhalmullage Suraj Randiv Kaluhalmulla; formerly known as M. M. M. Suraj

	Team	Country	Born	Birthplace
Rangarajan Malolan	Tamil Nadu	I	22.4.1989	*Madras (Chennai)*
***Rankin** William Boyd	Warwickshire	E	5.7.1984	*Londonderry*
Raphael Samuel Joseph	South Australia	A	24.5.1987	*Bedford Park*
***Raqibul Hasan**	Dhaka	B	8.10.1987	*Jamalpur*
Rashid Adil Usman	Yorkshire	E	17.2.1988	*Bradford*
Rayner Oliver Philip	Middlesex	E	1.11.1985	*Fallingbostel, Germany*
Rayudu Ambati Thirupathi	Baroda	I	23.9.1985	*Guntur*
Raza Hasan	National Bank	P	8.7.1992	*Sialkot*
***Read** Christopher Mark Wells	Nottinghamshire	E	10.8.1978	*Paignton*
Reardon Nathan Jon	Queensland	A	8.11.1984	*Chinchilla*
Redfern Daniel James	Derbyshire	E	18.4.1990	*Shrewsbury*
***Redmond** Aaron James	Otago	NZ	23.9.1979	*Auckland*
Reece Luis Michael	Leeds-Brad MCCU/Lancs	E	4.8.1990	*Taunton*
Reed Michael Thomas	Glamorgan	E	10.9.1988	*Leicester*
Rees Gareth Peter	Glamorgan	E	8.4.1985	*Swansea*
***Reifer** Floyd Lamonte	Comb. Campuses and Colls	WI	23.7.1972	*Parish Land, Barbados*
Reifer Raymon Anton	Comb. Campuses and Colls	WI	11.5.1991	*Archer's Rd, Barbados*
***Riaz Afridi**	Peshawar	P	21.1.1985	*Peshawar*
Richards Austin Conroy Lenroy	Leeward Islands	WI	14.11.1983	*Freetown, Antigua*
Richards Marlon Kevin Alexander	Trinidad & Tobago	WI	10.1.1989	*Linden, Guyana*
Richards Rowan Ronaldo	Northerns/Titans	SA	8.7.1984	*East London*
Richardson Alan	Worcestershire	E	6.5.1975	*Newcastle-under-Lyme*
Richardson Andrew Peter	Jamaica	WI	6.9.1981	*Kingston, Jamaica*
Richardson Kane William	South Australia	A	12.2.1991	*Eudunda*
Richardson Lyndell Rashad	Leeward Islands	WI	7.5.1986	*Anguilla*
Richardson Michael John	Durham	E	4.10.1986	*Port Elizabeth, SA*
Riley Adam Edward Nicholas	Loughborough MCCU/Kent	E	23.3.1992	*Sidcup*
Rimmington Nathan John	Western Australia	A	11.11.1982	*Redcliffe*
Rizwan Ahmed	Hyderabad/Pakistan TV	P	1.10.1978	*Hyderabad*
***Roach** Kemar Andre Jamal	Barbados	WI	30.6.1988	*Checker Hall, Barb.*
***Roberts** Michael David Tudor	Hampshire	E	13.3.1989	*Oxford*
***Robiul Islam**	Khulna	B	20.10.1986	*Satkhira*
Robson Angus James	Leicestershire	A	19.2.1992	*Darlinghurst*
Robson Samuel David	Middlesex	E	1.7.1989	*Paddington, Aus*
Roderick Gareth Hugh	Gloucestershire	SA	29.8.1991	*Durban*
***Rogers** Christopher John Llewellyn	Victoria/Middlesex	A	31.8.1977	*St George*
Rogers John William	Western Australia	A	11.4.1987	*Canberra*
Rohan Prem Preambhasan	Kerala	I	13.9.1986	*Trivandrum*
Rohrer Ben James	New South Wales	A	26.3.1981	*Bankstown*
Roland-Jones Tobias Skelton	Middlesex	E	29.1.1988	*Ashford, Middlesex*
Ronchi Luke	Wellington	NZ	23.4.1981	*Dannevirke*
***Root** Joseph Edward	Yorkshire	E	30.12.1990	*Sheffield*
Rose Clive Andrew	Victoria/Tasmania	A	13.10.1989	*Dandenong*
Rosier Diego Steve	Griqualand West/Knights	SA	2.5.1994	*Kimberley*
Rossouw Riley Roscoe	Knights	SA	9.10.1989	*Bloemfontein*
Rouse Adam Paul	Hampshire	E	30.6.1992	*Harare, Zimbabwe*
Roy Jason Jonathan	Surrey	E	21.7.1990	*Durban*
***Rubel Hossain**	Khulna	B	1.1.1990	*Bagerhat*
***Rudolph** Jacobus Andries	Titans	SA	4.5.1981	*Springs*
***Rupasinghe** Rupasinghe Jayawardene Mudiyanselage				
Gihan Madushanka	Colombo	SL	5.3.1986	*Watupitiwala*
Rushworth Christopher	Durham	E	11.7.1986	*Sunderland*
***Russell** Andre Dwayne	Jamaica	WI	29.4.1988	*Jamaica*
Russell Christopher James	Worcestershire	E	16.2.1989	*Newport, Isle of Wight*
***Rutherford** Hamish Duncan	Otago/Essex	NZ	27.4.1989	*Dunedin*
***Ryder** Jesse Daniel	Wellington/Otago	NZ	6.8.1984	*Masterton*
***Saeed Ajmal**	ZTBL	P	14.10.1977	*Faisalabad*
***Saha** Wriddhaman Prasanta	Bengal	I	24.10.1984	*Siliguri*

	Team	Country	Born	Birthplace
Saini Nitin	Haryana	I	28.10.1988	*Rohtak*
***Sajidul Islam**	Rangpur	B	18.1.1988	*Rangpur*
Sales David John	Northamptonshire	E	3.12.1977	*Carshalton*
Salter Andrew Graham	Glamorgan	E	1.6.1993	*Haverfordwest*
Samantray Biplab Bipin	Orissa	I	14.9.1988	*Cuttack*
***Samaraweera** Thilan Thusara	Sinhalese/Worcs	SL	22.9.1976	*Colombo*
Samiullah Khan	Sui Northern/Faisalabad	P	4.8.1982	*Mianwali*
***Sammy** Darren Julius Garvey	Windward Islands	WI	20.12.1983	*Micoud, St Lucia*
***Samuels** Marlon Nathaniel	Jamaica	WI	5.1.1981	*Kingston, Jamaica*
Sandeep Warrier Sankarankutty	Kerala	I	4.1.1991	*Thrissur*
Sandhu Gurinder Singh	New South Wales	A	14.6.1993	*Blacktown*
Sandhu Gurjit Singh	Middlesex	E	24.3.1992	*Isleworth*
***Sangakkara** Kumar Chokshanada	Nondescripts	SL	27.10.1977	*Matale*
Sarabjit Singh	Punjab	I	10.7.1986	*Patiala*
***Sarfraz Ahmed**	Karachi Whites/PIA	P	22.5.1987	*Karachi*
***Sarwan** Ramnaresh Ronnie	Guyana/Leicestershire	WI	23.6.1980	*Wakenaam Island, Guy.*
Saunders Akeem	Leeward Islands	WI	17.6.1994	*St Kitts*
Savage Calvin Peter	Dolphins/KwaZulu-Natal	SA	4.1.1993	*Durban*
Saxena Jalaj Sahai	Madhya Pradesh	I	15.12.1986	*Indore*
Saxena Vineet Ashokkumar	Rajasthan	I	3.12.1980	*Margao*
Sayers Chadd James	South Australia	A	31.8.1987	*Adelaide*
Sayers Joseph John	Yorkshire	E	5.11.1983	*Leeds*
Scantlebury-Searles Javon Philip Ramon	Barbados	WI	21.12.1986	*Durants Village, Barb.*
Sealy Dawayne Carlo	Comb. Campuses and Colls	WI	22.9.1988	*Barbados*
Sebastien Liam Andrew Shannon	Windward Islands	WI	9.9.1984	*Roseau, Dominica*
Second Rudi Stewart	Knights/Free State	SA	17.7.1989	*Queenstown*
***Sehwag** Virender	Delhi	I	20.10.1978	*Delhi*
***Senanayake** Senanayage Mudiyanselage Sachithra Madhushanka	Sinhalese	SL	9.2.1985	*Colombo*
***Shafiul Islam**	Rajshahi	B	6.10.1989	*Bogra*
Shah Hiken Naresh	Mumbai	I	15.11.1984	*Bombay (Mumbai)*
***Shah** Owais Alam	Essex	E	22.10.1978	*Karachi, Pakistan*
***Shahadat Hossain**	Dhaka	B	7.8.1986	*Narayanganj*
***Shahid Afridi**	Habib Bank	P	1.3.1980	*Khyber Agency*
***Shahriar Nafees**	Barisal	B	1.5.1985	*Dhaka*
***Shahzad Ajmal**	Nottinghamshire	E	27.7.1985	*Huddersfield*
Shahzaib Hasan	Karachi W/Port Qasim A	P	25.12.1989	*Karachi*
Shakeel Ansar	Sialkot/ZTBL	P	11.11.1978	*Sialkot*
***Shakib Al Hasan**	Khulna	B	24.3.1987	*Magura*
Shamsur Rahman	Dhaka Metropolis	B	5.6.1988	*Comilla*
***Shan Masood**	Islamabad/Habib Bank	P	14.10.1989	*Kuwait*
Shantry Jack David	Worcestershire	E	29.1.1988	*Shrewsbury*
Sharath Hosagavikoppa Shivalingaiah	Karnataka	I	6.2.1993	*Mandya*
***Sharjeel Khan**	Hyderabad/ZTBL	P	14.8.1989	*Hyderabad*
***Sharma** Ishant	Delhi	I	2.9.1988	*Delhi*
Sharma Joginder	Haryana	I	23.10.1983	*Rohtak*
Sharma Mohit	Haryana	I	18.9.1988	*Ballabhgarh*
Sharma Rahul	Punjab	I	30.11.1986	*Jullundur*
***Sharma** Rohit Gurunath	Mumbai	I	30.4.1987	*Bansod*
Sheridan William David	Victoria	A	5.7.1987	*Chertsey, England*
Shezi Mthokozisi	Dolphins/KwaZulu-Natal	SA	9.9.1987	*Imbali*
***Shillingford** Shane	Windward Islands	WI	22.2.1983	*Dominica*
***Shoaib Malik**	Sialkot/PIA	P	1.2.1982	*Sialkot*
Shreck Charles Edward	Kent	E	6.1.1978	*Truro*
Shrewsbury Thomas Weldon	Gloucestershire	E	18.1.1995	*Southampton*
Shrivastava Shalabh Umeshchandra	Vidarbha	I	2.2.1986	*Nagpur*
Shukla Laxmi Ratan	Bengal	I	6.5.1981	*Howrah*
Shuvagata Hom	Dhaka	B	11.11.1986	*Mymensingh*

	Team	Country	Born	Birthplace
*Sibanda Vusimuzi	Mid West Rhinos	Z	10.10.1983	Highfields
Sibley Dominic Peter	Surrey	E	5.9.1995	Epsom
Siboto Malusi Paul	Knights	SA	20.8.1987	Cape Town
*Siddle Peter Matthew	Victoria	A	25.11.1984	Traralgon
*Sidebottom Ryan Jay	Yorkshire	E	15.1.1978	Huddersfield
Sidebottom Ryan Nathan	Victoria	A	14.8.1989	Shepparton
*Sikandar Raza	Mashonaland Eagles	Z	24.4.1986	Sialkot, Pakistan
Silk Jordan Christopher	Tasmania	A	13.4.1992	Penrith
*Silva Jayan Kaushal	Sinhalese	SL	27.5.1986	Colombo
*Silva Lindamlilage Prageeth Chamara	Panadura	SL	14.12.1979	Panadura
Simetu Siyabulela	W. Province/Cape Cobras	SA	22.8.1991	Cape Town
*Simmons Lendl Mark Platter	Trinidad & Tobago	WI	25.1.1985	Port-of-Spain, Trinidad
Simpson John Andrew	Middlesex	E	13.7.1988	Bury
*Sinclair Mathew Stuart	Central Districts	NZ	9.11.1975	Katherine, Australia
*Singh Rudra Pratap	Uttar Pradesh	I	6.12.1985	Rae Bareli
*Singh Vikram Rajvir	Punjab	I	17.9.1984	Chandigarh
Slater Benjamin Thomas	Derbyshire	E	26.8.1991	Chesterfield
Smit Daryn	Dolphins/KwaZulu-Natal	SA	28.1.1984	Durban
*Smith Devon Sheldon	Windward Islands	WI	21.10.1981	Hermitage, Grenada
*Smith Dwayne Romel	Barbados	WI	12.4.1983	Storey Gap, Barbados
*Smith Graeme Craig	Surrey	SA	1.2.1981	Johannesburg
Smith Greg Phillip	Lankan/Leicestershire	E	16.11.1988	Leicester
Smith Gregory Marc	Essex	SA	20.4.1983	Johannesburg
Smith Jamal	Comb. Campuses and Colls	WI	16.10.1984	Deacon Rd, Barbados
Smith Kelvin Ross	South Australia	A	5.9.1994	Adelaide
Smith Ruaidhri Alexander James	Glamorgan	Scot	5.8.1994	Glasgow
*Smith Steven Peter Devereux	New South Wales	A	2.6.1989	Sydney
Smith Thomas Christopher	Lancashire	E	26.12.1985	Liverpool
Smith Thomas Michael John	Middlesex/Gloucestershire	E	29.8.1987	Eastbourne
Smith William Rew	Durham	E	28.9.1982	Luton
Smuts Jon-Jon Trevor	Eastern Province/Warriors	SA	21.8.1988	Grahamstown
*Sodhi Inderbir Singh (Ish)	Northern Districts	NZ	31.10.1992	Ludhiana, India
*Sohag Gazi	Barisal	B	5.8.1991	Khulna
Sohaib Maqsood	Multan	P	15.4.1987	Multan
*Sohail Khan	Port Qasim Authority	P	6.3.1984	Malakand
*Sohail Tanvir	Rawalpindi/Hampshire	P	12.12.1984	Rawalpindi
Solanki Vikram Singh	Surrey	E	1.4.1976	Udaipur, India
Solozano Jeremy Len	Trinidad & Tobago	WI	5.10.1995	Arima, Trinidad
*Southee Timothy Grant	Northern Districts	NZ	11.12.1988	Whangarei
Spriegel Matthew Neil William	Northamptonshire	E	4.3.1987	Epsom
*Sreesanth Shanthakumaran	Kerala	I	6.2.1983	Kothamangalam
*Starc Mitchell Aaron	New South Wales	A	13.1.1990	Baulkham Hills
Stevens Darren Ian	Kent	E	30.4.1976	Leicester
Stevens Nicholas Gerard	Queensland	A	20.5.1994	Toowoomba
Stewart Shanan Luke	Canterbury	NZ	21.6.1982	Christchurch
*Steyn Dale Willem	Cape Cobras	SA	27.6.1983	Phalaborwa
Stirling Paul Robert	Ireland/Middlesex	Ire	3.9.1990	Belfast
Stoinis Marcus Peter	Victoria	A	16.8.1989	Perth
*Stokes Benjamin Andrew	Durham	E	4.6.1991	Christchurch, NZ
Stoneman Mark Daniel	Durham	E	26.6.1987	Newcastle-upon-Tyne
Stoute Kevin Andre	Barbados	WI	12.11.1985	Black Rock, Barbados
Subrayen Prenelan	KwaZulu-Natal/Dolphins	SA	23.9.1993	Tongaat
*Suhrawadi Shuvo	Rangpur	B	21.11.1988	Rajshahi
Suppiah Arul Vivasvan	Somerset	E	30.8.1983	Kuala Lumpur, Malay.
*Swann Graeme Peter	Nottinghamshire	E	24.3.1979	Northampton
Sykes James Stuart	Leicestershire	E	26.4.1992	Huntingdon
*Tamim Iqbal	Chittagong	B	20.3.1989	Chittagong
*Tanvir Ahmed	Karachi Blues/Port Qasim A	P	20.12.1978	Kuwait City

	Team	Country	Born	Birthplace
*Tapash Baisya	Sylhet	B	25.12.1982	*Sylhet*
Tarjinder Singh	Assam	I	22.12.1987	*Kamrup*
*Taufeeq Umar	Sui Northern Gas	P	20.6.1981	*Lahore*
Taylor Bradley Jacob	Hampshire	E	14.3.1997	*Winchester*
*Taylor Brendan Ross Murray	Mid West Rhinos	Z	6.2.1986	*Harare*
Taylor Jack Martin Robert	Gloucestershire	E	12.11.1991	*Banbury*
*Taylor James William Arthur	Nottinghamshire/Sussex	E	6.1.1990	*Nottingham*
*Taylor Luteru Ross Poutoa Lote	Central Districts	NZ	8.3.1984	*Lower Hutt*
Taylor Matthew David	Gloucestershire	E	8.7.1994	*Banbury*
Taylor Robert Meadows Liam	Scotland/Leicestershire	Scot	21.12.1989	*Northampton*
ten Doeschate Ryan Neil	Essex	NL	30.6.1980	*Port Elizabeth, SA*
*Tendulkar Sachin Ramesh	Mumbai	I	24.4.1973	*Bombay*
Terblanche Roman Kelvin	Knights/Free State	SA	10.6.1986	*Bloemfontein*
Terry Sean Paul	Hampshire	E	1.8.1991	*Southampton*
Thakor Shivsinh Jaysinh	Leicestershire	E	22.10.1993	*Leicester*
*Tharanga Warushavithana Upul	Nondescripts	SL	2.2.1985	*Balapitiya*
Theophile Tyrone	Windward Islands	WI	12.8.1989	*Dominica*
Theron Juan	Warriors	SA	24.7.1985	*Vereeniging*
*Thirimanne Hettige Don Rumesh Lahiru	Ragama	SL	8.9.1989	*Moratuwa*
Thomas Alfonso Clive	Somerset	SA	9.2.1977	*Cape Town*
Thomas Devon Cuthbert	Leeward Islands	WI	12.11.1989	*Bethesda, Antigua*
Thomas Shacoya Elrick	Comb. Campuses and Colls	WI	15.9.1988	*St Catherine, Jamaica*
Thornely Michael Alistair	Leicestershire	E	19.10.1987	*Camden*
Thorp Callum David	Durham	E	8.11.1975	*Mount Lawley, Aus*
Tietjens Carl	South Australia	A	25.3.1986	*Adelaide*
Tiwary Manoj Kumar	Bengal	I	14.11.1985	*Howrah*
Tiwary Saurabh Sunil	Jharkhand	I	30.12.1989	*Jamshedpur*
Tomlinson James Andrew	Hampshire	E	12.6.1982	*Winchester*
*Tonge Gavin Courtney	Leeward Islands	WI	13.2.1983	*St John's, Antigua*
Topley Reece James William	Essex	E	12.2.1994	*Ipswich*
Towers Luke James Charles	Western Australia	A	18.6.1988	*Subiaco*
*Tredwell James Cullum	Kent	E	27.2.1982	*Ashford*
Trego Peter David	Somerset/C. Districts	E	12.6.1981	*Weston-super-Mare*
Tremain Christopher Peter	New South Wales	A	10.8.1991	*Dubbo*
*Tremlett Christopher Timothy	Surrey	E	2.9.1981	*Southampton*
*Trescothick Marcus Edward	Somerset	E	25.12.1975	*Keynsham*
*Trott Ian Jonathan Leonard	Warwickshire	E	22.4.1981	*Cape Town, SA*
Troughton Jamie Oliver	Warwickshire	E	2.3.1979	*Camden*
*Tsolekile Thami Lungisa	Lions	SA	9.10.1980	*Cape Town*
Tsotsobe Lonwabo Lennox	Lions	SA	7.3.1984	*Port Elizabeth*
Turner Ashton James	Western Australia	A	25.1.1993	*Subiaco*
Turner Mark Leif	Derbyshire	E	23.10.1984	*Sunderland*
*Tushar Imran	Khulna	B	10.12.1983	*Kharki*
Tyagi Sudeep	Uttar Pradesh	I	19.9.1987	*Ghaziabad*
Udana Isuru	Ports Authority	SL	17.2.1988	*Balangoda*
Udawatte Mahela Lakmal	Tamil Union	SL	19.7.1986	*Colombo*
*Umar Akmal	Lahore Shal./Sui Northern	P	26.5.1990	*Lahore*
*Umar Amin	Rawalpindi/Port Qasim A	P	16.10.1989	*Rawalpindi*
*Umar Gul	Habib Bank	P	14.4.1984	*Peshawar*
*Unadkat Jaydev Dipakbhai	Saurashtra	I	18.10.1991	*Porbandar*
Usman Khan	ZTBL	P	1.5.1994	*Khyber Agency*
Usman Salahuddin	Lah. Shal./Habib Bank/KRL	P	2.12.1990	*Lahore*
Uthappa Robin Venu	Karnataka	I	11.11.1985	*Coorg*
*Utseya Prosper	Mashonaland Eagles	Z	26.3.1985	*Harare*
Vahora Murtuja Yakubbhai	Baroda	I	1.12.1985	*Navapur*
Vallie Mohammad Yaseen	Cape Cobras/W. Province	SA	30.9.1989	*Cape Town*
van Biljon Petrus Johannes	Free State/Knights	SA	15.4.1986	*Bloemfontein*

	Team	Country	Born	Birthplace
van Buuren Graeme Lourens	Northerns/Titans	SA	22.8.1990	*Pretoria*
van der Merwe Roelof Erasmus	Titans	SA	31.12.1984	*Johannesburg*
van der Wath Johannes Jacobus	Knights	SA	10.1.1978	*Newcastle*
Vandiar Jonathan David	Dolphins/KwaZulu-Natal	SA	25.4.1990	*Paarl*
***Vandort** Michael Graydon	Ragama	SL	19.1.1980	*Colombo*
van Jaarsveld Vaughn Bernard	Dolphins	SA	2.2.1985	*Johannesburg*
van Schalkwyk Shadley Claude	Free State/Knights	SA	5.8.1988	*Cape Town*
***van Wyk** Cornelius Francoius Kruger	Central Districts	NZ	7.2.1980	*Wolmaransstad, SA*
van Wyk Divan Jaco	Dolphins/KZN Inland	SA	25.2.1985	*Bloemfontein*
van Wyk Morne Nico	Dolphins	SA	20.3.1979	*Bloemfontein*
van Zyl Stiaan	Cape Cobras	SA	19.9.1987	*Cape Town*
Velani Kishen Shailesh	Essex	E	2.9.1994	*Newham*
Venugopal Rao Yalaka	Gujarat	I	26.2.1982	*Visakhapatnam*
***Vermeulen** Mark Andrew	MW Rhinos/Mash. Eagles	Z	2.3.1979	*Salisbury*
***Vettori** Daniel Luca	Northern Districts	NZ	27.1.1979	*Auckland*
***Vijay** Murali	Tamil Nadu	I	1.4.1984	*Madras*
Vilas Dane James	Cape Cobras	SA	10.6.1985	*Johannesburg*
Viljoen Gerhardus C. (Hardus)	Lions	SA	6.3.1989	*Witbank*
***Vinay Kumar** Ranganath	Karnataka	I	12.2.1984	*Davanagere*
Vince James Michael	Hampshire	E	14.3.1991	*Cuckfield*
***Vithanage** Kasun Disi Kithuruwan	Tamil Union	SL	26.2.1991	*Colombo*
***Vitori** Brian Vitalis	Mashonaland Eagles	Z	22.2.1990	*Masvingo*
Voges Adam Charles	Western Australia/Middlesex	A	4.10.1979	*Perth*
von Berg Shaun	Titans/Northerns	SA	16.9.1986	*Pretoria*
***Wade** Matthew Scott	Victoria	A	26.12.1987	*Hobart*
Wagg Graham Grant	Glamorgan	E	28.4.1983	*Rugby*
Wagh Shrikant Bhaskar	Vidarbha	I	9.10.1988	*Chikhli*
Waghmode Aditya Arvind	Baroda	I	8.11.1989	*Baroda*
***Wagner** Neil	Otago	NZ	13.3.1986	*Pretoria*
***Wahab Riaz**	Lahore Shal./Nat. Bank	P	28.6.1985	*Lahore*
Wainwright David John	Derbyshire	E	21.3.1985	*Pontefract*
Wakely Alexander George	Northamptonshire	E	3.11.1988	*Hammersmith*
Wallace Mark Alexander	Glamorgan	E	19.11.1981	*Abergavenny*
Waller Malcolm Noel	Mid West Rhinos	Z	28.9.1984	*Harare*
Walsh Hayden Rashidi	Leeward Islands	WI	23.4.1992	*St Croix, US Virgin Is*
Walters Basheeru-Deen	Warriors	SA	16.9.1986	*Port Elizabeth*
Walters Kelbert Orlando	Leeward Islands	WI	4.12.1990	*Anguilla*
Walters Stewart Jonathan	Glamorgan	E	25.6.1983	*Mornington, Australia*
***Walton** Chadwick Antonio Kirkpatrick	Comb. Campuses and Colls	WI	3.7.1985	*Jamaica*
***Warnapura** Basnayake Shalith Malinda	Colts	SL	26.5.1979	*Colombo*
***Warner** David Andrew	New South Wales	A	27.10.1986	*Paddington*
***Wasim Jaffer**	Mumbai	I	16.2.1978	*Bombay*
***Watling** Bradley-John	Northern Districts	NZ	9.7.1985	*Durban, SA*
***Watson** Shane Robert	New South Wales	A	17.6.1981	*Ipswich*
Weerakoon Sajeewa	Colts	SL	17.2.1978	*Galle*
Weeraratne Kaushalya	Ragama	SL	29.1.1981	*Gampola*
***Welegedara** Uda Walawwe Mahim Bandaralage Chanaka Asanka	Tamil Union	SL	20.3.1981	*Matale*
Wells Jonathan Wayne	Tasmania	A	13.8.1988	*Hobart*
Wells Luke William Peter	Sussex	E	29.12.1990	*Eastbourne*
Wells Thomas Joshua	Leicestershire	E	15.3.1993	*Grantham*
Wessels Mattheus Hendrik (Riki)	Nottinghamshire	E	12.11.1985	*Marogudoore, Aus.*
Westley Thomas	Essex	E	13.3.1989	*Cambridge*
Westwood Ian James	Warwickshire	E	13.7.1982	*Birmingham*
Wheater Adam Jack	N. Districts/Hampshire	E	13.2.1990	*Whipps Cross*
***White** Cameron Leon	Victoria/Northants	A	18.8.1983	*Bairnsdale*

	Team	Country	Born	Birthplace
White David John	E. Province/Warriors	SA	22.5.1991	*Port Elizabeth*
White Graeme Geoffrey	Notts/Northants	E	18.4.1987	*Milton Keynes*
White Wayne Andrew	Lancashire	E	22.4.1985	*Derby*
Whiteley Ross Andrew	Derbyshire/Worcs	E	13.9.1988	*Sheffield*
Whiteman Sam McFarlane	Western Australia	A	19.3.1992	*Doncaster, England*
Wiese David	Titans	SA	18.5.1985	*Roodepoort*
Willett Tonito Akanni	Leeward Islands	WI	6.2.1983	*Government Rd, Nevis*
Willey David Jonathan	Northamptonshire	E	28.2.1990	*Northampton*
Williams Kesrick Omari Kenal	Comb. Campuses and Colls	WI	8.1.1990	*Spring Village, St Vinc.*
Williams Lizaad Buyron	Cape Cobras/Boland	SA	1.10.1993	*Vredenburg*
Williams Robert Edward Morgan	Leicestershire	E	19.1.1987	*Pembury*
*****Williams** Sean Colin	Matabeleland Tuskers	Z	26.9.1986	*Bulawayo*
*****Williamson** Kane Stuart	Northern Districts/Yorks	NZ	8.8.1990	*Tauranga*
Wilson Gary Craig	Ireland/Surrey	Ire	5.2.1986	*Dundonald*
Wintz Paul Gordon	Guyana	WI	7.3.1986	*Cumberland Vill., Guy.*
*****Woakes** Christopher Roger	Warwickshire	E	2.3.1989	*Birmingham*
Wood Christopher Philip	Hampshire	E	27.6.1990	*Basingstoke*
Wood Mark Andrew	Durham	E	11.1.1990	*Ashington*
Woodcock Luke James	Wellington	NZ	19.3.1982	*Wellington*
Worrall Daniel James	South Australia	A	10.7.1991	*Melbourne*
Wright Ben James	Glamorgan	E	5.12.1987	*Preston*
Wright Christopher Julian Clement	Warwickshire	E	14.7.1985	*Chipping Norton*
Wright Luke James	Sussex	E	7.3.1985	*Grantham*
Wyatt Alexander Charles Frederick	Leicestershire	E	23.7.1990	*Roehampton*
*****Yadav** Umeshkumar Tilak	Vidarbha	I	25.10.1987	*Nagpur*
Yardy Michael Howard	Sussex	E	27.11.1980	*Pembury*
*****Yasir** Ali	Quetta/KRL	P	15.10.1985	*Hazro*
*****Yasir** Arafat	Rawalpindi/KRL	P	12.3.1982	*Rawalpindi*
*****Yasir** Hameed	Abbottabad/ZTBL	P	28.2.1978	*Peshawar*
Yasir Shah	Abbottabad/Sui Northern	P	2.5.1986	*Swabi*
Young Edward George Christopher	Gloucestershire	E	21.5.1989	*Chertsey*
*****Young** Reece Alan	Auckland	NZ	15.9.1979	*Auckland*
*****Younis** Khan	Habib Bank	P	29.11.1977	*Mardan*
*****Yuvraj** Singh	Punjab	I	12.12.1981	*Chandigarh*
*****Zaheer** Khan	Mumbai	I	7.10.1978	*Shrirampur*
Zampa Adam	NSW/South Australia	A	31.3.1992	*Shellharbour*
Zhuwao Cephas	Mashonaland Eagles	Z	15.12.1984	*Harare*
*****Ziaur** Rahman	Khulna	B	2.12.1986	*Khulna*
Zol Vijay Hari	Maharashtra	I	23.11.1994	*Jalna*
Zondo Khayelihle	Dolphins/KwaZulu-Natal	SA	7.3.1990	*Durban*
*****Zulfiqar** Babar	Multan/WAPDA	P	10.12.1978	*Okara*
*****Zulqarnain** Haider	Bahawalpur/ZTBL	P	3.4.1986	*Lahore*

REGISTER OF WOMEN PLAYERS

The qualifications for inclusion are as follows:

All players who appeared in an international match, or in the County Championship in England, the Women's National Cricket League in Australia, or the one-day competition in New Zealand, in the calendar year 2013 AND have 1,000 runs/50 wickets in one-day internationals, or a hundred/five in an innings in a Test, one-day international or Twenty20 international since 2010.

* Denotes Test player.

	Team	Country	Born	Birthplace
Aguilleira Merissa Ria	Trinidad & Tobago	WI	14.12.1985	*Trinidad*
*****Atkins** Caroline Mary Ghislaine	Somerset	E	13.1.1981	*Brighton*
Bates Suzannah Wilson	Otago/Western Australia	NZ	16.9.1987	*Dunedin*
Bismah Maroof	ZTBL	P	18.7.1991	*Lahore*
*****Blackwell** Alexandra Joy	New South Wales	A	31.8.1983	*Wagga Wagga*
Bolton Nicole Elizabeth	Otago/Western Australia	A	17.1.1989	*Subiaco*

	Team	Country	Born	Birthplace
*Brindle Arran (née Thompson)	Sussex	E	23.11.1981	Steeton
Brits Cri-Zelda	Gauteng	SA	20.11.1983	Rustenburg
*Browne Nicola Jane	Northern Districts/ACT	NZ	14.9.1983	Matamata
*Brunt Katherine Helen	Yorkshire	E	2.7.1985	Barnsley
*Cameron Jessica Evelyn	Victoria	A	27.6.1989	Williamstown
Campbelle Shemaine Altia	Guyana	WI	14.10.1992	Berbice, Guyana
Candy Rachel Helen	Canterbury	NZ	23.7.1986	Palmerston North
Chetty Trisha	KwaZulu-Natal	SA	26.6.1988	Durban
*Colvin Holly Louise	Sussex	E	7.9.1989	Chichester
Daley Shanel Francine	Staffordshire/Jamaica	WI	25.12.1988	Jamaica
Devine Sophie Frances Monique	Wellington	NZ	1.9.1989	Wellington
Dottin Deandra Jalisa Shakira	Barbados	WI	21.6.1991	Barbados
du Preez Mignon	Northerns	SA	13.6.1989	Pretoria
*Edwards Charlotte Marie	Kent	E	17.12.1979	Huntingdon
*Elliott Sarah Jane (née Edwards)	Victoria	A	4.1.1982	Melbourne
*Farrell Rene Michelle	Australian Capital Territory	A	13.1.1987	Kogarah
*Fields Jodie Maree (née Purves)	Queensland	A	19.6.1984	Toowoomba
Fritz Shandre Alvida	Western Province	SA	21.7.1985	Cape Town
*Goswami Jhulan	Bengal	I	25.11.1982	Kalyani
*Greenway Lydia Sophie	Kent	E	6.8.1985	Farnborough, Kent
*Guha Isa Tara	Berkshire	E	21.5.1985	High Wycombe
*Gunn Jennifer Louise	Nottinghamshire	E	9.5.1986	Nottingham
Hunter Julie Lauren	Victoria	A	15.3.1984	Box Hill
*Ismail Shabnim	Western Province	SA	5.10.1988	Cape Town
Javeria Khan	ZTBL	P	14.5.1988	Karachi
Jayangani Atapattumudiyanselage Chamari	Air Force	SL	9.2.1990	Gokarella
*Joyce Isobel Mary Helen Cecilia	Ireland	Ire	25.7.1983	Wicklow
Kapp Marizanne	Eastern Province	SA	4.1.1990	Port Elizabeth
Kaur Harmanpreet	Punjab	I	8.3.1989	Moga
*Knight Heather Clare	Berkshire	E	26.12.1990	Rochdale
*Lanning Meghann Moira	Victoria	A	25.5.1992	Singapore
*Loubser Sunette	Boland	SA	26.9.1982	Paarl
*Marsh Laura Alexandra	Kent	E	5.12.1986	Pembury
*McGlashan Sara Jade	C. Districts/Auckland	NZ	28.3.1982	Napier
Mohammed Anisa	Trinidad & Tobago	WI	7.8.1988	Trinidad
Nain Abidi	ZTBL	P	23.5.1985	Karachi
*Nero Juliana Barbara	St Vincent	WI	14.7.1979	St Vincent
*Osborne Erin Alyce	New South Wales	A	27.6.1989	Taree
*Perry Ellyse Alexandra	New South Wales	A	3.11.1990	Wahroonga
*Poulton Leah Joy	New South Wales	A	27.2.1984	Newcastle
Quintyne Shaquana Latish	Barbados	WI	3.1.1996	Barbados
*Raj Mithali	Railways	I	3.12.1982	Jodhpur
Sadia Yousuf	ZTBL	P	4.11.1989	Pakistan
Sana Mir	ZTBL	P	5.1.1986	Abbottabad
Satterthwaite Amy Ella	Canterbury	NZ	7.10.1986	Christchurch
*Seneviratne Chamani Roshini	Air Force	SL	14.11.1978	Anuradhapura
*Sharma Amita	Railways/Assam	I	12.9.1982	Delhi
Shillington Clare Mary Alice	Ireland	Ire	8.1.1981	Belfast
*Shrubsole Anya	Somerset	E	7.12.1991	Bath
Siriwardene Hettimulla Appuhamilage Shashikala Dedunu	Navy	SL	14.2.1985	Colombo
*Smit Jane	Nottinghamshire	E	24.12.1972	Ilkeston
*Sthalekar Lisa Caprini	New South Wales	A	13.8.1979	Poona, India
Sultana Gouher	Railways	I	31.3.1988	Hyderabad
*Taylor Sarah Jane	Sussex	E	20.5.1989	Whitechapel
Taylor Stefanie Roxann	Jamaica	WI	11.6.1991	Spanish Town, Jamaica
Thirush Kamini Murugesan Dickeshwashankar	Tamil Nadu	I	30.7.1990	Madras (Chennai)
van Niekerk Dane	Eastern Province	SA	14.5.1993	Pretoria

CRICKETERS OF THE YEAR, 1889–2014

1889	*Six Great Bowlers of the Year:* J. Briggs, J. J. Ferris, G. A. Lohmann, R. Peel, C. T. B. Turner, S. M. J. Woods.
1890	*Nine Great Batsmen of the Year:* R. Abel, W. Barnes, W. Gunn, L. Hall, R. Henderson, J. M. Read, A. Shrewsbury, F. H. Sugg, A. Ward.
1891	*Five Great Wicketkeepers:* J. McC. Blackham, G. MacGregor, R. Pilling, M. Sherwin, H. Wood.
1892	*Five Great Bowlers:* W. Attewell, J. T. Hearne, F. Martin, A. W. Mold, J. W. Sharpe.
1893	*Five Batsmen of the Year:* H. T. Hewett, L. C. H. Palairet, W. W. Read, S. W. Scott, A. E. Stoddart.
1894	*Five All-Round Cricketers:* G. Giffen, A. Hearne, F. S. Jackson, G. H. S. Trott, E. Wainwright.
1895	*Five Young Batsmen of the Season:* W. Brockwell, J. T. Brown, C. B. Fry, T. W. Hayward, A. C. MacLaren.
1896	W. G. Grace.
1897	*Five Cricketers of the Season:* S. E. Gregory, A. A. Lilley, K. S. Ranjitsinhji, T. Richardson, H. Trumble.
1898	*Five Cricketers of the Year:* F. G. Bull, W. R. Cuttell, N. F. Druce, G. L. Jessop, J. R. Mason.
1899	*Five Great Players of the Season:* W. H. Lockwood, W. Rhodes, W. Storer, C. L. Townsend, A. E. Trott.
1900	*Five Cricketers of the Season:* J. Darling, C. Hill, A. O. Jones, M. A. Noble, Major R. M. Poore.
1901	*Mr R. E. Foster and Four Yorkshiremen:* R. E. Foster, S. Haigh, G. H. Hirst, T. L. Taylor, J. Tunnicliffe.
1902	L. C. Braund, C. P. McGahey, F. Mitchell, W. G. Quaife, J. T. Tyldesley.
1903	W. W. Armstrong, C. J. Burnup, J. Iremonger, J. J. Kelly, V. T. Trumper.
1904	C. Blythe, J. Gunn, A. E. Knight, W. Mead, P. F. Warner.
1905	B. J. T. Bosanquet, E. A. Halliwell, J. Hallows, P. A. Perrin, R. H. Spooner.
1906	D. Denton, W. S. Lees, G. J. Thompson, J. Vine, L. G. Wright.
1907	J. N. Crawford, A. Fielder, E. G. Hayes, K. L. Hutchings, N. A. Knox.
1908	A. W. Hallam, R. O. Schwarz, F. A. Tarrant, A. E. E. Vogler, T. G. Wass.
1909	*Lord Hawke and Four Cricketers of the Year:* W. Brearley, Lord Hawke, J. B. Hobbs, A. Marshal, J. T. Newstead.
1910	W. Bardsley, S. F. Barnes, D. W. Carr, A. P. Day, V. S. Ransford.
1911	H. K. Foster, A. Hartley, C. B. Llewellyn, W. C. Smith, F. E. Woolley.
1912	*Five Members of MCC's team in Australia:* F. R. Foster, J. W. Hearne, S. P. Kinneir, C. P. Mead, H. Strudwick.
1913	*Special Portrait:* John Wisden.
1914	M. W. Booth, G. Gunn, J. W. Hitch, A. E. Relf, Hon. L. H. Tennyson.
1915	J. W. H. T. Douglas, P. G. H. Fender, H. T. W. Hardinge, D. J. Knight, S. G. Smith.
1916–17	No portraits appeared.
1918	*School Bowlers of the Year:* H. L. Calder, J. D. E. Firth, C. H. Gibson, G. A. Rotherham, G. T. S. Stevens.
1919	*Five Public School Cricketers of the Year:* P. W. Adams, A. P. F. Chapman, A. C. Gore, L. P. Hedges, N. E. Partridge.
1920	*Five Batsmen of the Year:* A. Ducat, E. H. Hendren, P. Holmes, H. Sutcliffe, E. Tyldesley.
1921	*Special Portrait:* P. F. Warner.
1922	H. Ashton, J. L. Bryan, J. M. Gregory, C. G. Macartney, E. A. McDonald.
1923	A. W. Carr, A. P. Freeman, C. W. L. Parker, A. C. Russell, A. Sandham.
1924	*Five Bowlers of the Year:* A. E. R. Gilligan, R. Kilner, G. G. Macaulay, C. H. Parkin, M. W. Tate.
1925	R. H. Catterall, J. C. W. MacBryan, H. W. Taylor, R. K. Tyldesley, W. W. Whysall.
1926	*Special Portrait:* J. B. Hobbs.
1927	G. Geary, H. Larwood, J. Mercer, W. A. Oldfield, W. M. Woodfull.
1928	R. C. Blunt, C. Hallows, W. R. Hammond, D. R. Jardine, V. W. C. Jupp.
1929	L. E. G. Ames, G. Duckworth, M. Leyland, S. J. Staples, J. C. White.
1930	E. H. Bowley, K. S. Duleepsinhji, H. G. Owen-Smith, R. W. V. Robins, R. E. S. Wyatt.
1931	D. G. Bradman, C. V. Grimmett, B. H. Lyon, I. A. R. Peebles, M. J. Turnbull.

1932	W. E. Bowes, C. S. Dempster, James Langridge, Nawab of Pataudi sen, H. Verity.
1933	W. E. Astill, F. R. Brown, A. S. Kennedy, C. K. Nayudu, W. Voce.
1934	A. H. Bakewell, G. A. Headley, M. S. Nichols, L. F. Townsend, C. F. Walters.
1935	S. J. McCabe, W. J. O'Reilly, G. A. E. Paine, W. H. Ponsford, C. I. J. Smith.
1936	H. B. Cameron, E. R. T. Holmes, B. Mitchell, D. Smith, A. W. Wellard.
1937	C. J. Barnett, W. H. Copson, A. R. Gover, V. M. Merchant, T. S. Worthington.
1938	T. W. J. Goddard, J. Hardstaff jun, L. Hutton, J. H. Parks, E. Paynter.
1939	H. T. Bartlett, W. A. Brown, D. C. S. Compton, K. Farnes, A. Wood.
1940	L. N. Constantine, W. J. Edrich, W. W. Keeton, A. B. Sellers, D. V. P. Wright.
1941–46	No portraits appeared.
1947	A. V. Bedser, L. B. Fishlock, V. (M. H.) Mankad, T. P. B. Smith, C. Washbrook.
1948	M. P. Donnelly, A. Melville, A. D. Nourse, J. D. Robertson, N. W. D. Yardley.
1949	A. L. Hassett, W. A. Johnston, R. R. Lindwall, A. R. Morris, D. Tallon.
1950	T. E. Bailey, R. O. Jenkins, John Langridge, R. T. Simpson, B. Sutcliffe.
1951	T. G. Evans, S. Ramadhin, A. L. Valentine, E. D. Weekes, F. M. M. Worrell.
1952	R. Appleyard, H. E. Dollery, J. C. Laker, P. B. H. May, E. A. B. Rowan.
1953	H. Gimblett, T. W. Graveney, D. S. Sheppard, W. S. Surridge, F. S. Trueman.
1954	R. N. Harvey, G. A. R. Lock, K. R. Miller, J. H. Wardle, W. Watson.
1955	B. Dooland, Fazal Mahmood, W. E. Hollies, J. B. Statham, G. E. Tribe.
1956	M. C. Cowdrey, D. J. Insole, D. J. McGlew, H. J. Tayfield, F. H. Tyson.
1957	D. Brookes, J. W. Burke, M. J. Hilton, G. R. A. Langley, P. E. Richardson.
1958	P. J. Loader, A. J. McIntyre, O. G. Smith, M. J. Stewart, C. L. Walcott.
1959	H. L. Jackson, R. E. Marshall, C. A. Milton, J. R. Reid, D. Shackleton.
1960	K. F. Barrington, D. B. Carr, R. Illingworth, G. Pullar, M. J. K. Smith.
1961	N. A. T. Adcock, E. R. Dexter, R. A. McLean, R. Subba Row, J. V. Wilson.
1962	W. E. Alley, R. Benaud, A. K. Davidson, W. M. Lawry, N. C. O'Neill.
1963	D. Kenyon, Mushtaq Mohammad, P. H. Parfitt, P. J. Sharpe, F. J. Titmus.
1964	D. B. Close, C. C. Griffith, C. C. Hunte, R. B. Kanhai, G. S. Sobers.
1965	G. Boycott, P. J. Burge, J. A. Flavell, G. D. McKenzie, R. B. Simpson.
1966	K. C. Bland, J. H. Edrich, R. C. Motz, P. M. Pollock, R. G. Pollock.
1967	R. W. Barber, B. L. D'Oliveira, C. Milburn, J. T. Murray, S. M. Nurse.
1968	Asif Iqbal, Hanif Mohammad, K. Higgs, J. M. Parks, Nawab of Pataudi jun.
1969	J. G. Binks, D. M. Green, B. A. Richards, D. L. Underwood, O. S. Wheatley.
1970	B. F. Butcher, A. P. E. Knott, Majid Khan, M. J. Procter, D. J. Shepherd.
1971	J. D. Bond, C. H. Lloyd, B. W. Luckhurst, G. M. Turner, R. T. Virgin.
1972	G. G. Arnold, B. S. Chandrasekhar, L. R. Gibbs, B. Taylor, Zaheer Abbas.
1973	G. S. Chappell, D. K. Lillee, R. A. L. Massie, J. A. Snow, K. R. Stackpole.
1974	K. D. Boyce, B. E. Congdon, K. W. R. Fletcher, R. C. Fredericks, P. J. Sainsbury.
1975	D. L. Amiss, M. H. Denness, N. Gifford, A. W. Greig, A. M. E. Roberts.
1976	I. M. Chappell, P. G. Lee, R. B. McCosker, D. S. Steele, R. A. Woolmer.
1977	J. M. Brearley, C. G. Greenidge, M. A. Holding, I. V. A. Richards, R. W. Taylor.
1978	I. T. Botham, M. Hendrick, A. Jones, K. S. McEwan, R. G. D. Willis.
1979	D. I. Gower, J. K. Lever, C. M. Old, C. T. Radley, J. N. Shepherd.
1980	J. Garner, S. M. Gavaskar, G. A. Gooch, D. W. Randall, B. C. Rose.
1981	K. J. Hughes, R. D. Jackman, A. J. Lamb, C. E. B. Rice, V. A. P. van der Bijl.
1982	T. M. Alderman, A. R. Border, R. J. Hadlee, Javed Miandad, R. W. Marsh.
1983	Imran Khan, T. E. Jesty, A. I. Kallicharran, Kapil Dev, M. D. Marshall.
1984	M. Amarnath, J. V. Coney, J. E. Emburey, M. W. Gatting, C. L. Smith.
1985	M. D. Crowe, H. A. Gomes, G. W. Humpage, J. Simmons, S. Wettimuny.
1986	P. Bainbridge, R. M. Ellison, C. J. McDermott, N. V. Radford, R. T. Robinson.
1987	J. H. Childs, G. A. Hick, D. B. Vengsarkar, C. A. Walsh, J. J. Whitaker.
1988	J. P. Agnew, N. A. Foster, D. P. Hughes, P. M. Roebuck, Salim Malik.
1989	K. J. Barnett, P. J. L. Dujon, P. A. Neale, F. D. Stephenson, S. R. Waugh.
1990	S. J. Cook, D. M. Jones, R. C. Russell, R. A. Smith, M. A. Taylor.
1991	M. A. Atherton, M. Azharuddin, A. R. Butcher, D. L. Haynes, M. E. Waugh.
1992	C. E. L. Ambrose, P. A. J. DeFreitas, A. A. Donald, R. B. Richardson, Waqar Younis.
1993	N. E. Briers, M. D. Moxon, I. D. K. Salisbury, A. J. Stewart, Wasim Akram.
1994	D. C. Boon, I. A. Healy, M. G. Hughes, S. K. Warne, S. L. Watkin.
1995	B. C. Lara, D. E. Malcolm, T. A. Munton, S. J. Rhodes, K. C. Wessels.
1996	D. G. Cork, P. A. de Silva, A. R. C. Fraser, A. Kumble, D. A. Reeve.
1997	S. T. Jayasuriya, Mushtaq Ahmed, Saeed Anwar, P. V. Simmons, S. R. Tendulkar.

1998	M. T. G. Elliott, S. G. Law, G. D. McGrath, M. P. Maynard, G. P. Thorpe.
1999	I. D. Austin, D. Gough, M. Muralitharan, A. Ranatunga, J. N. Rhodes.
2000	C. L. Cairns, R. Dravid, L. Klusener, T. M. Moody, Saqlain Mushtaq.

Cricketers of the Century D. G. Bradman, G. S. Sobers, J. B. Hobbs, S. K. Warne, I. V. A. Richards.

2001	M. W. Alleyne, M. P. Bicknell, A. R. Caddick, J. L. Langer, D. S. Lehmann.
2002	A. Flower, A. C. Gilchrist, J. N. Gillespie, V. V. S. Laxman, D. R. Martyn.
2003	M. L. Hayden, A. J. Hollioake, N. Hussain, S. M. Pollock, M. P. Vaughan.
2004	C. J. Adams, A. Flintoff, I. J. Harvey, G. Kirsten, G. C. Smith.
2005	A. F. Giles, S. J. Harmison, R. W. T. Key, A. J. Strauss, M. E. Trescothick.
2006	M. J. Hoggard, S. P. Jones, B. Lee, K. P. Pietersen, R. T. Ponting.
2007	P. D. Collingwood, D. P. M. D. Jayawardene, Mohammad Yousuf, M. S. Panesar, M. R. Ramprakash.
2008	I. R. Bell, S. Chanderpaul, O. D. Gibson, R. J. Sidebottom, Zaheer Khan.
2009	J. M. Anderson, D. M. Benkenstein, M. V. Boucher, N. D. McKenzie, S. C. Taylor.
2010	S. C. J. Broad, M. J. Clarke, G. Onions, M. J. Prior, G. P. Swann.
2011	E. J. G. Morgan, C. M. W. Read, Tamim Iqbal, I. J. L. Trott.
2012	T. T. Bresnan, G. Chapple, A. N. Cook, A. Richardson, K. C. Sangakkara.
2013	H. M. Amla, N. R. D. Compton, J. H. Kallis, M. N. Samuels, D. W. Steyn.
2014	S. Dhawan, C. M. Edwards, R. J. Harris, C. J. L. Rogers, J. E. Root.

From 2001 to 2003 the award was made on the basis of all cricket round the world, not just the English season. This ended in 2004 with the start of Wisden's Leading Cricketer in the World *award. Sanath Jayasuriya was chosen in 1997 for his influence on the English season, stemming from the 1996 World Cup. In 2011, only four were named after an ICC tribunal investigating the Lord's spot-fixing scandal made the selection of one of the five unsustainable.*

Members of the board: Bob Appleyard (1952), Geoff Boycott (1965), Ray Illingworth (1960) and Phil Sharpe (1963) at the unveiling in September 2013 of the display in the Headingley pavilion devoted to Yorkshire's Cricketers of the Year.

PART SEVEN

The Almanack

OFFICIAL BODIES

INTERNATIONAL CRICKET COUNCIL

The ICC are world cricket's governing body. They are responsible for managing the playing conditions and Code of Conduct for international fixtures, expanding the game and organising the major tournaments, including the World Cup and World Twenty20. Their mission statement says the ICC "will lead by promoting and protecting the game, and its unique spirit" and "optimising their commercial rights and properties for the benefit of their members".

Ten national governing bodies are currently Full Members of the ICC; full membership qualifies a nation (or geographic area) to play official Test matches. A candidate for full membership must meet a number of playing and administrative criteria, after which elevation is decided by a vote among existing Full Members. There are also currently 37 Associate Members (non-Test-playing nations or geographic areas where cricket is firmly established and organised) and 59 Affiliate Members (other countries or geographic areas where the ICC recognise that cricket is played in accordance with the Laws).

The ICC were founded in 1909 as the Imperial Cricket Conference by three Foundation Members: England, Australia and South Africa. Other countries (or geographic areas) became Full Members and thus acquired Test status as follows: India, New Zealand and West Indies in 1926, Pakistan in 1952, Sri Lanka in 1981, Zimbabwe in 1992 and Bangladesh in 2000. South Africa ceased to be a member on leaving the Commonwealth in 1961, but were re-elected as a Full Member in 1991.

In 1965, "Imperial" was replaced by "International", and countries from outside the Commonwealth were elected for the first time. The first Associate Members were Fiji and USA. Foundation Members retained a veto over all resolutions. In 1989, the renamed International Cricket Council (rather than "Conference") adopted revised rules, aimed at producing an organisation which could make a larger number of binding decisions, rather than simply make recommendations to national governing bodies. In 1993, the Council, previously administered by MCC, gained their own secretariat and chief executive. The category of Foundation Member was abolished.

In 1997, the Council became an incorporated body, with an executive board, and a president instead of a chairman. The ICC remained at Lord's, with a commercial base in Monaco, until August 2005, when after 96 years they moved to Dubai in the United Arab Emirates, which offered organisational and tax advantages.

In February 2014 the ICC board approved a new structure. From July, they would be led by a chairman again. India, Australia and England would have permanent places on both of two key committees, the Executive Committee and the Finance and Commercial Affairs Committee, with two other Full Member representatives also serving on each.

Officers

President: A. R. Isaac. *Vice-President:* A. H. M. Mustafa Kamal. *Chief Executive:* D. J. Richardson.

Chairs of Committees – Chief Executives' Committee: D. J. Richardson. *Cricket:* A. Kumble. *Audit:* A. Zaidi. *Governance Review:* W. J. Edwards. *Human Resources and Remuneration:* A. R. Isaac. *Development:* D. J. Richardson. *Code of Conduct Commission:* M. J. Beloff QC. *Women's Committee:* C. J. Connor. *Finance and Commercial Affairs:* C. G. Clarke. *Nominations Committee:* A. R. Isaac. *Medical Committee:* Dr P. R. Harcourt. *Anti-Corruption and Security Unit:* Sir Ronnie Flanagan. A new Executive Committee chaired by W. J. Edwards was to be introduced in 2014.

Executive Board: The president, vice-president and chief executive sit on the board *ex officio*. They are joined by W. O. Cameron (West Indies), P. F. Chingoka (Zimbabwe), C. G. Clarke (England), J. Dharmadasa (Sri Lanka), W. J. Edwards (Australia), I. Khwaja (Singapore), Najam Aziz Sethi (Pakistan), Nazmul Hassan (Bangladesh), C. Nenzani (South Africa), C. K. Oliver (Scotland), M. C. Snedden (New Zealand), N. Speight (Bermuda), N. Srinivasan (India).

Chief Executives' Committee: The chief executive, president and cricket committee chairman sit on the committee *ex officio.* They are joined by the chief executives of the ten Full Member boards and three Associate Member boards: D. G. Collier (England), J. A. Cribbin (Hong Kong), W. Deutrom (Ireland), F. Erasmus (Namibia), H. Lorgat (South Africa), M. Muirhead (West Indies), W. Mukondiwa (Zimbabwe), Nizam Uddin Chowdhury (Bangladesh), S. Patel (India), N. Ranatunga (Sri Lanka), Subhan Ahmad (Pakistan), J. A. Sutherland (Australia), D. J. White (New Zealand).

Cricket Committee: The chief executive and president sit on the committee *ex officio.* They are joined by A. Kumble (chairman), C. J. Connor, S. J. Davis, D. Kendix, R. S. Madugalle, K. C. Sangakkara, R. J. Shastri, L. Sivaramakrishnan, J. P. Stephenson, A. J. Strauss, M. A. Taylor, D. J. White.

General Manager – Cricket: G. J. Allardice. *General Manager – Commercial:* D. C. Jamieson. *Chief Financial Officer:* Faisal Hasnain. *Head of Legal / Company Secretary:* I. Higgins. *Head of Executive Programmes / Support Services:* J. Long. *Head of Anti-Corruption / Security Unit:* Y. P. Singh. *Media / Communications Manager:* Sami Ul Hasan. *Global Development Manager:* T. L. Anderson.

Constitution

President/Chairman: A. R. Isaac of New Zealand became president in June 2012. From July 2014, N. Srinivasan of India was to head the ICC as chairman, with A. H. M. Mustafa Kamal as president.

Chief Executive: Appointed by the Council. D. J. Richardson succeeded H. Lorgat in June 2012.

Membership

Full Members (10): Australia, Bangladesh, England, India, New Zealand, Pakistan, South Africa, Sri Lanka, West Indies and Zimbabwe.

Associate Members* (37): Afghanistan (2001), Argentina (1974), Belgium (2005), Bermuda (1966), Botswana (2005), Canada (1968), Cayman Islands (2002), Denmark (1966), Fiji (1965), France (1998), Germany (1999), Gibraltar (1969), Guernsey (2005), Hong Kong (1969), Ireland (1993), Israel (1974), Italy (1995), Japan (2005), Jersey (2007), Kenya (1981), Kuwait (2005), Malaysia (1967), Namibia (1992), Nepal (1996), Netherlands (1966), Nigeria (2002), Papua New Guinea (1973), Scotland (1994), Singapore (1974), Suriname (2002), Tanzania (2001), Thailand (2005), Uganda (1998), United Arab Emirates (1990), USA (1965), Vanuatu (1995), Zambia (2003).

Affiliate Members* (59): Austria (1992), Bahamas (1987), Bahrain (2001), Belize (1997), Bhutan (2001), Brazil (2002), Brunei (1992), Bulgaria (2008), Cameroon (2007), Chile (2002), China (2004), Cook Islands (2000), Costa Rica (2002), Croatia (2001), Cyprus (1999), Czech Republic (2000), Estonia (2008), Falkland Islands (2007), Finland (2000), Gambia (2002), Ghana (2002), Greece (1995), Hungary (2012), Indonesia (2001), Iran (2003), Isle of Man (2004), Lesotho (2001), Luxembourg (1998), Malawi (2003), Maldives (2001), Mali (2005), Malta (1998), Mexico (2004), Morocco (1999), Mozambique (2003), Myanmar (2006), Norway (2000), Oman (2000), Panama (2002), Peru (2007), Philippines (2000), Portugal (1996), Qatar (1999), Romania (2013), Russia (2012), Rwanda (2003), St Helena (2001), Samoa (2000), Saudi Arabia (2003), Seychelles (2010), Sierra Leone (2002), Slovenia (2005), South Korea (2001), Spain (1992), Swaziland (2007), Sweden (1997), Tonga (2000), Turkey (2008), Turks & Caicos Islands (2002).

* *Year of election shown in parentheses. Switzerland (1985) were removed in 2012 for failing to comply with the ICC's membership criteria, and Cuba (2002) in 2013 for failing to demonstrate a suitable administrative structure.*

Full Members: The governing body for cricket (recognised by the ICC) of a country, or countries associated for cricket purposes, or a geographical area, from which representative teams are qualified to play official Test matches.

Associate Members: The governing body for cricket (recognised by the ICC) of a country, or countries associated for cricket purposes, or a geographical area, which does not qualify as a Full Member, but where cricket is firmly established and organised.

Affiliate Members: The governing body for cricket (recognised by the ICC) of a country, or countries associated for cricket purposes, or a geographical area (which is not part of one of those already constituted as a Full or Associate Member) where the ICC recognise that cricket is played in accordance with the Laws of Cricket. Five Affiliate Member representatives have the right to attend or vote at the ICC annual conference.

Addresses

ICC: Street 69, Dubai Sports City, Sh Mohammed Bin Zayed Road, PO Box 500 070, Dubai, United Arab Emirates (+971 4382 8800; website www.icc-cricket.com; email enquiry@icc-cricket.com).

Australia: Cricket Australia, 60 Jolimont Street, Jolimont, Victoria 3002 (+61 3 9653 9999; website www.cricket.com.au; email penquiries@cricket.com.au).

Bangladesh: Bangladesh Cricket Board, Sher-e-Bangla National Cricket Stadium, Mirpur, Dhaka 1216 (+880 2 803 1001; website www.tigercricket.com; email office@bcb-cricket.com).

England: England and Wales Cricket Board (see below).

India: Board of Control for Cricket in India, Cricket Centre, 2nd Floor, Wankhede Stadium, D Road, Churchgate, Mumbai 400 020 (+91 22 2289 8800; website www.bcci.tv; email bcci@vsnl.com and cricketboard@gmail.com).

New Zealand: New Zealand Cricket, PO Box 8353, Level 3, 8 Nugent Street, Grafton, Auckland 1023 (+64 9 972 0605; website www.blackcaps.co.nz; email info@nzcricket.org.nz).

Pakistan: Pakistan Cricket Board, Gaddafi Stadium, Ferozpur Road, Lahore 54600 (+92 42 3571 7231; website www.pcb.com.pk; email mail@pcb.com.pk).

South Africa: Cricket South Africa, Wanderers Club, PO Box 55009, 21 North Street, Illovo, Northlands 2116 (+27 11 880 2810; website www.cricket.co.za; email info@cricket.co.za).

Sri Lanka: Sri Lanka Cricket, 35 Maitland Place, Colombo 07000 (+94 112 681 601; website www.srilankacricket.lk; email info@srilankacricket.lk).

West Indies: West Indies Cricket Board, PO Box 616 W, Factory Road, St John's, Antigua (+1 268 481 2450; website www.windiescricket.com; email wicb@windiescricket.com).

Zimbabwe: Zimbabwe Cricket, PO Box 2739, 28 Maiden Drive, Highlands, Harare (+263 4 788 090; website www.zimcricket.org; email info@zimcricket.org).

Associate and Affiliate Members' addresses may be found on the ICC website www.icc-cricket.com

ENGLAND AND WALES CRICKET BOARD

The England and Wales Cricket Board (ECB) became responsible for the administration of all cricket – professional and recreational – in England and Wales in 1997. They took over the functions of the Cricket Council, the Test and County Cricket Board and the National Cricket Association, which had run the game in England and Wales since 1968. In 2005, a new constitution streamlined and modernised the governance of English cricket. The Management Board of 18 directors were replaced by a Board of Directors numbering 12, with three appointed by the first-class counties and two by the county boards. In 2010, this expanded to 14, with the appointment of the ECB's first two women directors.

Officers

Chairman: C. G. Clarke. *Deputy Chairman:* C. Graves. *Chief Executive:* D. G. Collier.

Board of Directors: C. G. Clarke (*chairman*), D. G. Collier, M. V. Fleming, C. Graves, B. W. Havill, Baroness Heyhoe Flint, R. Jackson, I. N. Lovett, Lord Morris of Handsworth, A. J. Nash, J. B. Pickup, J. Stichbury, R. W. Thompson, P. G. Wright.

Chairmen of Committees – Cricket: P. G. Wright. *Commercial:* C. G. Clarke. *Recreational Assembly:* J. B. Pickup. *Audit:* I. N. Lovett. *Remuneration:* C. G. Clarke. *Discipline:* G. Elias QC.

Managing Director, England Cricket: P. R. Downton. *Managing Director, Cricket Partnerships:* M. W. Gatting. *Managing Director, Professional Game:* G. Hollins. *Finance Director:* B. W. Havill. *Managing Director of Marketing and Global Events:* S. Elworthy. *Director of Public Policy and International Relations:* P. French. *Director of Media and Communications:* C. R. Gibson. *Director of England Cricket Operations:* J. D. Carr. *Commercial Director:* J. Perera. *Head of Women's Cricket:* C. J. Connor. *Head of Information Technology:* D. Smith. *General Manager of Corporate Communications:* A. J. Walpole. *Head of Operations (First-class cricket):* A. Fordham. *Cricket Operations Manager (Non-first-class cricket):* P. Bedford. *National Selector:* J. J. Whitaker. *Other Selectors:* A. R. C. Fraser and A. F. Giles.

ECB: D. G. Collier, Lord's Ground, London NW8 8QZ (020 7432 1200; website www.ecb.co.uk).

THE MARYLEBONE CRICKET CLUB

The Marylebone Cricket Club evolved out of the White Conduit Club in 1787, when Thomas Lord laid out his first ground in Dorset Square. Their members revised the Laws in 1788 and gradually took responsibility for cricket throughout the world. However, they relinquished control of the game in the UK in 1968, and the International Cricket Council finally established their own secretariat in 1993. MCC still own Lord's and remain the guardian of the Laws. They call themselves "a private club with a public function" and aim to support cricket everywhere, especially at grassroots level and in countries where the game is least developed.

Patron: HER MAJESTY THE QUEEN

Officers

President: 2013–14 – M. W. Gatting. *Club Chairman:* O. H. J. Stocken. *Treasurer:* R. S. Leigh. *Trustees:* A. N. W. Beeson, M. G. Griffith, A. W. Wreford. *Hon. Life Vice-Presidents:* Lord Bramall, E. R. Dexter, G. H. G. Doggart, T. W. Graveney, Lord Griffiths, D. J. Insole, A. R. Lewis, Sir Oliver Popplewell, D. R. W. Silk, M. O. C. Sturt, J. J. Warr, J. C. Woodcock.

Chief Executive and Secretary: D. M. Brewer. *Deputy Secretary:* C. Maynard. *Assistant Secretaries – Cricket:* J. P. Stephenson. *Estates and Ground Development:* R. J. Ebdon. *Finance:* S. J. M. Gibb. *Legal:* H. A-M. Roper-Curzon. *Marketing and Catering:* J. D. Robinson.

MCC Committee: J. R. T. Barclay, R. Q. Cake, I. S. Duncan, A. R. C. Fraser, V. K. Griffiths, W. R. Griffiths, C. M. Gupte, P. L. O. Leaver, H. J. H. Loudon, N. E. J. Pocock, J. A. F. Vallance, K. M. Williams. The president, club chairman, treasurer and committee chairmen are also on the committee.

Chairmen of Committees – Arts and Library: D. J. C. Faber. *Cricket:* M. V. Fleming. *Estates:* C. J. Maber. *Finance:* R. S. Leigh. *Membership and General Purposes:* N. M. Peters. *World Cricket:* J. M. Brearley.

MCC: The Chief Executive and Secretary, Lord's Ground, London NW8 8QN (020 7616 8500; email reception@mcc.org.uk; website www.lords.org/mcc. Tickets 020 7432 1000; email ticketing@mcc.org.uk).

PROFESSIONAL CRICKETERS' ASSOCIATION

The Professional Cricketers' Association were formed in 1967 (as the Cricketers' Association) to be the collective voice of first-class professional players, and enhance and protect their interests. During the 1970s, they succeeded in establishing pension schemes and a minimum wage. In recent years their strong commercial operations and greater funding from the ECB have increased their services to current and past players, including education, legal, financial and benevolent help. In 2011, these services were extended to England's women cricketers for the first time.

President: D. Lloyd. *Chairman:* M. A. Wallace. *President – Benevolent Fund:* D. A. Graveney. *Non-Executive Group Chairman:* A. W. Wreford. *Non-Executive Director:* M. Wheeler. *Chief Executive:* A. J. Porter. *Assistant Chief Executive:* J. D. Ratcliffe. *Vice-president – Legal Affairs:* I. T. Smith. *Commercial Director:* J. M. Grave. *Financial Director:* P. Garrett. *Business Development Manager:* G. M. Hamilton. *Head of Events and Fundraising:* E. Lewis. *Head of Team England Commercial Partnerships:* E. M. Barnes. *Ambassador Commercial Manager:* E. Caldwell. *Member Services Executive:* A. Prosser. *National Personal Development Manager:* I. J. Thomas.

PCA: *London Office* – The Laker Stand, The Oval, Kennington, London SE11 5SS (0808 1684 655; email 903club@thepca.co.uk; website www.thepca.co.uk). *Birmingham Office* – Box 108–9, R. E. S. Wyatt Stand, Warwickshire CCC, Edgbaston, Birmingham B5 7QU.

CRIME AND PUNISHMENT

ICC Code of Conduct – Breaches and Penalties in 2012-13 to 2013-14

J. P. Faulkner   Australia v West Indies, third one-day international at Canberra.
Offensive language to batsman after dismissing him. Fined 10% of match fee by R. S. Mahanama.

R. Ashwin   India v Australia, First Test at Chennai.
Exceeded permitted number of logos on batting-pad straps. Fined 10% of match fee by B. C. Broad.

M. C. Henriques   Australia v India, First Test at Chennai.
Wore manufacturer's logo on helmet chin strap. Fined 10% of match fee by B. C. Broad.

C. A. Pujara   India v Australia, Second Test at Hyderabad.
Wore bat manufacturer's logos on helmet. Fined 10% of match fee by B. C. Broad.

Harbhajan Singh   India v Australia, Second Test at Hyderabad.
Wore lime-green laces in his boots (in contravention of the ICC's Clothing and Equipment regulations stipulating that at least 50% of the lace must be white). Fined 15% of match fee by B. C. Broad.

C. H. Morris   South Africa v Pakistan, second one-day international at Centurion.
Exceeded permitted number of logos on helmet. Reprimanded by J. J. Crowe.

Sohag Gazi   Bangladesh v Sri Lanka, First Test at Galle.
Showed dissent when given out. Fined 20% of match fee by D. C. Boon.

I. Sharma   India v Australia, Fourth Test at Delhi.
Pointed batsman towards pavilion after dismissing him. Fined 15% of match fee by R. S. Madugalle.

Tamim Iqbal   Bangladesh v Zimbabwe, Second Test at Harare.
Showed dissent when given out. Fined 10% of match fee by B. C. Broad.

Shakib Al Hasan   Bangladesh v Zimbabwe, second one-day international at Bulawayo.
Almost hit keeper while expressing dissent when given out. Fined 75% of match fee by B. C. Broad.

D. Ramdin   West Indies v Pakistan, Champions Trophy at The Oval.
Conduct contrary to the spirit of the game when he claimed a catch off Misbah-ul-Haq. Fined 100% of match fee and suspended for two one-day internationals by B. C. Broad.

D. P. M. D. Jayawardene/T. M. Dilshan   Sri Lanka v New Zealand, Champions Trophy at Cardiff.
Excessive and prolonged appealing. Reprimanded by A. J. Pycroft.

D. S. Lehmann (coach)   Australia v England, Fifth Test at The Oval.
Accused S. C. J. Broad of cheating in First Test. Fined 20% of match fee by R. S. Mahanama.

S. C. Williams   Zimbabwe v Pakistan, first Twenty20 international at Harare.
Showed dissent when given out. Reprimanded by J. J. Crowe.

Adnan Akmal   Pakistan v South Africa, First Test at Abu Dhabi.
Pushed batsman R. J. Peterson while trying to retrieve bail. Fined 50% of match fee by D. C. Boon.

R. J. Peterson   South Africa v Pakistan, First Test at Abu Dhabi.
Pushed wicketkeeper Adnan Akmal in retaliation. Fined 50% of match fee by D. C. Boon.

Tamim Iqbal   Bangladesh v New Zealand, Second Test at Mirpur.
Nudged batsman with shoulder while crossing field. Fined 50% of match fee by J. Srinath.

Saeed Ajmal   Pakistan v South Africa, Second Test at Dubai.
Repeatedly appealed to umpire after batsman dismissed. Reprimanded by D. C. Boon.

F. du Plessis   South Africa v Pakistan, Second Test at Dubai.
Tampered with the ball using trouser pocket zip. Fined 50% of match fee by D. C. Boon.

R. A. Jadeja   India v Australia, seventh one-day international at Bangalore.
Offensive language to batsman after dismissing him. Fined 10% of match fee by A. J. Pycroft.

Sohail Tanvir   Pakistan v South Africa, second Twenty20 international at Dubai.
Pointed batsman towards pavilion after dismissing him. Fined 10% of match fee by R. S. Madugalle.

D. W. Steyn   South Africa v Pakistan, second Twenty20 international at Cape Town.
Offensive language after completing second over. Fined 10% of match fee by A. J. Pycroft.

M. J. Clarke   Australia v England, First Test at Brisbane.
Obscene language towards batsman J. M. Anderson. Fined 20% of match fee by J. J. Crowe.

Ahmed Shehzad   Pakistan v Sri Lanka, third one-day international at Sharjah.
Pushed T. M. Dilshan's shoulder after argument. Fined 50% of match fee by D. C. Boon.

B. A. Stokes   England v Australia, fourth one-day international at Perth.
Obscene language after dismissing J. P. Faulkner. Fined 15% of match fee by A. J. Pycroft.

Under ICC regulations on minor over-rate offences, players are fined 10% of their match fee for every over their side fail to bowl in the allotted time, with the captain fined double that amount. There were ten such instances in this period:

B. R. M. Taylor/Zimbabwe v Bangladesh, Second Test at Harare, fined 60%/30% of match fee by B. C. Broad.

B. R. M. Taylor/Zimbabwe v Bangladesh, second one-day international at Bulawayo, fined 20%/10% of match fee by B. C. Broad.

G. J. Bailey/Australia v England, Champions Trophy at Birmingham, fined 20%/10% of match fee by J. Srinath.

D. J. Bravo/West Indies v South Africa, Champions Trophy at Cardiff, fined 20%/10% of match fee by A. J. Pycroft.

V. Kohli/India v Sri Lanka, Celkon Mobile Cup one-day international at Kingston, fined 20%/10% of match fee by J. J. Crowe.

D. J. Bravo/West Indies v India, Celkon Mobile Cup one-day international at Port-of-Spain, fined 20%/10% of match fee by J. J. Crowe. Bravo also suspended for one ODI as it was a second offence within 12 months.

A. D. Mathews/Sri Lanka v India, Celkon Mobile Cup one-day international at Port-of-Spain, Mathews suspended for two ODIs and team fined 40% of match fee by D. C. Boon.

K. D. Mills/New Zealand v Sri Lanka, third one-day international at Dambulla, fined 20%/10% of match fee by B. C. Broad.

L. D. Chandimal/Sri Lanka v New Zealand, second Twenty20 international at Pallekele, fined 20%/10% of match fee by B. C. Broad.

Misbah-ul-Haq/Pakistan v Sri Lanka, second one-day international at Dubai, fined 20%/10% of match fee by D. C. Boon.

Details of these and eight further breaches which took place in Associate Member matches may be found on the ICC website (www.icc-cricket.com).

INTERNATIONAL UMPIRES' PANELS

In 1993, the ICC formed an international umpires' panel, containing at least two officials from each Full Member. A third-country umpire from this panel stood with a home umpire, not necessarily from the panel, in every Test from February 1994 onwards. In March 2002, an elite panel was appointed: two elite umpires – both independent – were to stand in all Tests from April 2002, and at least one in every one-day international, where one home umpire was allowed. A supporting panel of international umpires was created to provide cover at peak times in the Test schedule, and to provide a second umpire in one-day internationals. The ICC also appointed specialist third umpires to give rulings from TV replays. The panels are sponsored by Emirates Airlines.

In January 2014, the following umpires were on the elite panel: Aleem Dar (Pakistan), S. J. Davis (Australia), H. D. P. K. Dharmasena (Sri Lanka), M. Erasmus (South Africa), I. J. Gould (England), R. K. Illingworth (England), R. A. Kettleborough (England), N. J. Llong (England), B. N. J. Oxenford (Australia), P. R. Reiffel (Australia) and R. J. Tucker (Australia). Illingworth and Reiffel had replaced Asad Rauf (Pakistan) and B. F. Bowden (New Zealand) in 2013, and A. L. Hill (New Zealand) stood down in January. Bowden was recalled for the 2013-14 Ashes series because of the shortage of elite umpires who were neither English nor Australian.

The international panel consisted of Ahsan Raza (Pakistan), R. J. Bailey (England), B. F. Bowden (New Zealand), O. Chirombe (Zimbabwe), J. D. Cloete (South Africa), Enamul Haque (Bangladesh), S. D. Fry (Australia), C. B. Gaffaney (New Zealand), S. George (South Africa), V. A. Kulkarni (India), R. E. J. Martinesz (Sri Lanka), P. J. Nero (West Indies), R. S. A. Palliyaguruge (Sri Lanka), S. Ravi (India), Sharfuddoula (Bangladesh), Shozab Raza (Pakistan), R. B. Tiffin (Zimbabwe) and J. S. Wilson (West Indies).

The specialist third umpires were Anisur Rahman (Bangladesh), G. A. V. Baxter (New Zealand), G. O. Brathwaite (West Indies), A. K. Chowdhury (India), N. Duguid (West Indies), M. A. Gough (England), A. T. Holdstock (South Africa), T. J. Matibiri (Zimbabwe), R. T. Robinson (England), C. Shamshuddin (India), D. J. Walker (New Zealand), J. D. Ward (Australia), R. R. Wimalasiri (Sri Lanka) and Zameer Haider (Pakistan).

There is also an Associate and Affiliate international panel, consisting of S. N. Bandekar (USA), K. Cross (New Zealand), M. Hawthorne (Ireland), A. W. Louw (Namibia), N. Morrison (Vanuatu), D. Odhiambo (Kenya), B. B. Pradhan (Nepal), S. S. Prasad (Singapore), I. N. Ramage (Scotland), R. P. Smith (Ireland) and C. Young (Cayman Islands).

ICC REFEREES' PANEL

In 1991, the ICC formed a panel of referees to enforce their Code of Conduct for Tests and one-day internationals, to impose penalties for slow over-rates, breaches of the Code and other ICC regulations, and to support the umpires in upholding the conduct of the game. In March 2002, the ICC launched an elite panel of referees, on full-time contracts, to act as their independent representatives in all international cricket. The panel is sponsored by Emirates Airlines.

At the start of 2014, the panel consisted of D. C. Boon (Australia), B. C. Broad (England), J. J. Crowe (New Zealand), R. S. Madugalle (Sri Lanka), R. S. Mahanama (Sri Lanka), A. J. Pycroft (Zimbabwe) and J. Srinath (India).

ENGLISH UMPIRES FOR 2014

First-class: R. J. Bailey, N. L. Bainton, M. R. Benson, M. J. D. Bodenham, N. G. B. Cook, N. G. C. Cowley, J. H. Evans, S. C. Gale, S. A. Garratt, M. A. Gough, I. J. Gould, P. J. Hartley, R. K. Illingworth, R. A. Kettleborough, N. J. Llong, D. J. Lloyd, J. W. Lloyds, N. A. Mallender, D. J. Millns, S. J. O'Shaughnessy, R. T. Robinson, M. J. Saggers, G. Sharp, A. G. Wharf, P. Willey. *Reserves:* P. K. Baldwin, M. Burns, I. Dawood, B. J. Debenham, R. Evans, P. R. Pollard, B. V. Taylor.

Minor Counties: J. Attridge, J. S. Beckwith, S. F. Bishopp, T. F. Boston, R. Burn, G. I. Callaway, T. F. Cox, M. P. Dobbs, J. Dye, R. G. Eagleton, M. T. Ennis, V. Fallows, K. Fergusson, A. H. Forward, P. R. Gardner, J. C. S. Glynn, D. J. Gower, R. C. Hampshire, A. Harris, A. Hicks, C. D. Jones, S. Lavis, T. Lungley, S. J. Malone, P. W. Matten, R. Medland, R. J. Newham, P. D. Nicholls, G. Parker, D. Price, C. T. Puckett, M. Qureshi, I. Royle, A. Shaikh, M. I. Southerton, P. J. Sparshott, I. Warne, R. J. Warren, M. D. Watton, C. M. Watts, N. Wheatley, A. J. Wheeler, C. M. B. Williams.

THE DUCKWORTH/LEWIS METHOD

In 1997, the ECB's one-day competitions adopted a new method to revise targets in interrupted games, devised by Frank Duckworth of the Royal Statistical Society and Tony Lewis of the University of the West of England. The method was gradually taken up by other countries and, in 1999, the ICC decided to incorporate it into the standard playing conditions for one-day internationals.

The system aims to preserve any advantage that one team has established before the interruption. It uses the idea that teams have two resources from which they make runs – an allocated number of overs, and ten wickets. It also takes into account when the interruption occurs, because of the different scoring-rates typical of different stages of an innings. Traditional run-rate calculations relied only on the overs available, and ignored wickets lost.

It uses one table with 50 rows, covering matches of up to 50 overs, and ten columns. Each figure gives the percentage of the total runs that would, on average, be scored with a certain number of overs left and wickets lost. If a match is shortened before it begins, to, say, 33 overs a side, the figure for 33 overs and ten wickets remaining would be the starting point.

If overs are lost, the table is used to calculate the percentage of runs the team would be expected to score in those missing overs. This is obtained by reading the figure for the number of overs left and wickets down when play stops and subtracting the figure for the number of overs left when it resumes. If the delay occurs between innings, and the second team's allocation of overs is reduced, then their target is obtained by calculating the appropriate percentage for the reduced number of overs with all ten wickets standing. For instance, if the second team's innings halves from 50 overs to 25, the table shows that they still have 66.5% of their resources left, so have to beat two-thirds of the first team's total, rather than half. If the first innings is complete and the second innings interrupted or prematurely terminated, the score to beat is reduced by the percentage of the innings lost.

The version known as the "Professional Edition" was introduced into one-day internationals from 2003, and subsequently into most national one-day competitions. Based on a more advanced mathematical formula (it is entirely computerised), in effect it adjusts the tables to make allowance for the different scoring-rates that emerge in matches with above-average first-innings scores. Extensive analysis of Twenty20 matches has shown that the same formula can be used for Twenty20 cricket, starting with the row for 20 overs remaining. The former version, now known as the "Standard Edition", is used where computers are not available and at lower levels of the game.

The system also covers interruptions to the first innings, multiple interruptions and innings terminated by rain. The tables are revised slightly every two years, taking account of changing scoring-rates; the average total in a 50-over international is now taken to be 245.

In the one-day international between England and India at Lord's on September 11, 2011, England's run-chase was ended by rain after 48.5 overs, when they were 270 for eight, having lost wickets to the last two deliveries. The computer-produced Duckworth/Lewis tables for that date showed that, with seven balls left and two wickets standing, England had used 96.43% of their run-scoring resources, and 3.57% remained unused. Multiplying India's 50-over total, 280, by 96.43% produced a figure of 270.004. This was rounded to 270 to give the par score (the runs needed to tie), and the score to win became par plus one – 271. Had England not lost wickets to the last two balls bowled, they would have used only 96.07% of their run-scoring resources, par would have been 269, and they would have won by one run. As they had equalled par exactly, the match was tied.

A similar system, usually known as the VJD method, is used in some domestic matches in India. It was devised by V. Jayadevan, a civil engineer from Kerala.

POWERPLAYS

In the first ten powerplay overs of an uninterrupted one-day international innings (first six in a Twenty20), only two fieldsmen may be positioned outside the area marked by two semi-circles of 30-yard (27.43 metres) radius behind each set of stumps, joined by straight lines parallel to the pitch. In ODIs, there must also be two close (and stationary) fielders in this initial period.

After the first mandatory ten-over powerplay in an uninterrupted one-day international, a further block of five overs must be claimed by the batsmen at the wicket, to be completed no later than the 40th over. During these, a maximum of three players may be stationed outside the 30-yard area. If the batting side do not take the powerplay, the umpires will enforce it at the latest possible point (i.e. the start of the 36th over). At all other times no more than four fieldsmen (five in Twenty20 internationals) are permitted outside the 30-yard area. In matches affected by the weather, the number of overs in each powerplay is reduced in proportion to the overall reduction of overs, and the restriction on when batting powerplays may be taken does not apply.

MEETINGS AND DECISIONS, 2013

ICC EXECUTIVE BOARD

The ICC Executive Board met in Dubai on January 29–31. Considering a report on the value of domestic Twenty20 leagues from the Chief Executives' Committee working group, they agreed that such leagues could add to the game as a whole and that co-existence between domestic Twenty20 leagues and the international game should be achieved through a workable and balanced calendar. It was also essential that Twenty20 leagues should be played in a corruption-free environment, which required timely and effective investigation and prosecution of all reported incidents.

The board agreed to combat the legal, financial and practical issues raised by online piracy – the illegal and unauthorised streaming of broadcast footage over the internet – and digital ambush marketing such as online trademark infringement and unauthorised mobile applications.

Under the Targeted Assistance and Performance Programme, aimed at developing more competitive teams among ICC members at all levels, New Zealand Cricket were allocated $1.8m over three years to support a programme of A-team cricket and the development of coaching and sports-science expertise.

ECB BOARD

An ECB board meeting at Lord's on January 31 announced an £18m programme of investment in first-class county cricket. The board agreed to offer up to £1m in loan finance to each of the 18 counties, subject to the approval of detailed business plans covering stadiums and facilities, customer relations, community programmes and business operations. Loan facilities were confirmed for the first 13 counties; business plans were expected from the other five later in the year. This finance would supplement the annual fee payments made to the first-class counties, which totalled £42.6m in 2012.

Following the impact of bad weather on community clubs during the UK's second-wettest year on record, the ECB also allocated £420,000 to repair the grounds worst affected by flooding, in addition to £104,000 already awarded to nine clubs and matched funding of £100,000 from Sport England.

ECB SPONSORSHIP DEAL

On February 5, the ECB announced that Yorkshire Bank would be the new title sponsor of the domestic 40-over competition. The Yorkshire Bank 40 – for the 18 first-class counties plus Scotland, the Netherlands and the Unicorns – would be one of three competitions making up the 2013 domestic season, and the only one with a final at Lord's. Most matches would take place on Sunday afternoons. Yorkshire Bank would also sponsor the ECB County Cups at Under-14, Under-15 and Under-17 levels.

The previous day, the ECB had announced that Yorkshire Tea was to be the "Official Brew of England Cricket" under a three-year deal, with Yorkshire Tea-Breaks at all Tests.

MCC WORLD CRICKET COMMITTEE

The MCC World Cricket Committee met in Auckland on February 25–26. On corruption in cricket, they commended the work of the ICC's Anti-Corruption and Security Unit, and efforts to encourage member boards to institute their own ACSUs. But they felt that, as international cricket cleaned up, corruption had been displaced to domestic matches, including Twenty20 leagues. The committee encouraged the ACSU and tournament organisers to scrutinise owners, selectors and administrators. Intelligence from Indian bookmakers and punters should be harnessed, along with information from Betfair and other legal betting outlets. In addition, software should be developed to assess probable outcomes in four key areas attracting betting – results, interval scores, specified periods of play and end-of-innings scores.

After a presentation on Hot Spot and Virtual Eye, the committee confirmed their support for DRS, which they felt protected the game's integrity by increasing the percentage of correct decisions. Arguing that cricket as a whole was worse off when technology was not used, they called for the universal application of ball-tracking, Hot Spot and (subject to satisfactory trials) Snickometer technologies.

The committee discussed the balance between bat and ball, and concluded that research was needed on the size of bats, particularly the thickness of the edges. They supported MCC's decision to declare a no-ball when the bowler breaks the wicket while delivering the ball, and also reaffirmed the legality of the switch hit. But they were worried that the ICC's ban on runners increased the risk of batsmen aggravating injuries. Believing the Law on substitute fielders was widely abused at international level, they wanted the ICC to allow substitutes only in cases of serious injury or illness.

They reaffirmed their support of a proposed World Test Championship. New Zealand Cricket's chief executive, David White, told them a two-tier Test championship would be catastrophic for nations outside the top four. He advocated a "3/3/3" model – three matches of each format on each tour. England captain Charlotte Edwards reported that the recent Women's World Cup in India had seen a rise in standards, and a great increase in TV viewers compared with the 2009 version.

The committee advocated Twenty20 cricket as the most suitable form for the Olympics, but appreciated lobbying for its inclusion would take a great deal of effort, and that there would be a short-term loss in income for the ICC. It would, however, be a potential boost for the game worldwide.

ECB DEPUTY CHAIRMAN

On March 19, Yorkshire chairman Colin Graves was elected deputy chairman of the ECB from May 2014 to 2016. He had been nominated after winning a ballot of the chairmen of the first-class counties and MCC, and was elected by the ECB's 41 Full Members (the 18 first-class counties, the 21 non-first-class county boards, the Minor Counties Cricket Association and MCC).

ANTI-CORRUPTION WORKSHOP

A two-day anti-corruption workshop, coordinated by the ICC's ACSU and attended by the heads of eight of the ten Full Member domestic anti-corruption units, was held in Dubai on March 20–21. They discussed how best to share information, address multi-jurisdictional threats, cooperate in investigations, and ensure consistent regulations and effective education systems.

ENGLAND PERFORMANCE SQUAD

On April 2, the ECB announced a 30-man England Performance Squad for the summer. The England coach would have the right to withdraw any of these players from domestic cricket. The squad consisted of 11 players already on 12-month ECB contracts running from October 2012: England Test and one-day captain Alastair Cook, Twenty20 captain Stuart Broad, James Anderson, Ian Bell, Tim Bresnan, Steven Finn, Eoin Morgan, Kevin Pietersen, Matt Prior, Graeme Swann and Jonathan Trott; ten on increment contracts (Jonny Bairstow, Ravi Bopara, Jos Buttler, Nick Compton, Jade Dernbach, Craig Kieswetter, Graham Onions, Samit Patel, Joe Root and James Tredwell); and nine others

(Danny Briggs, Alex Hales, James Harris, Michael Lumb, Stuart Meaker, Monty Panesar, Chris Tremlett, Chris Woakes and Luke Wright).

ICC EXECUTIVE BOARD

The ICC Executive Board met in Dubai on April 16–17. They received an update on anti-corruption matters, including a report on the March workshop. The board also heard presentations on umpire performance, assessment and training, and the ICC rankings.

They welcomed changes in the Pakistan Cricket Board's constitution, making the process of electing a chairman more democratic, and reducing the risk of inappropriate government interference.

Afghanistan were allocated $422,000 from the ICC's Targeted Assistance and Performance Programme, for the development of the National Cricket Academy in Kabul.

Also on April 17, ICC chief executive David Richardson welcomed the Court of Arbitration for Sport's rejection of appeals by Salman Butt and Mohammad Asif against the decisions of the independent Anti-Corruption Tribunal in February 2011, which banned both players after finding them guilty of charges relating to spot-fixing at the Lord's Test in August 2010.

MCC ANNUAL GENERAL MEETING

The 226th AGM of the Marylebone Cricket Club was held at Lord's on May 1, with president Mike Griffith in the chair. He announced that his successor, from October, would be Mike Gatting, the former Middlesex and England captain. Members were presented with the Ground Working Party's new masterplan for the development of Lord's. Expected to cost up to £200m and run from 2014 to 2027, it would include the reconstruction of the main stands, increasing capacity to 32,000, the re-siting of the Nursery Ground, a new entrance on Grove End Road, and underground car parking. Members were also notified of changes to various Laws of Cricket.

Resolutions were passed increasing members' entrance fees and annual subscriptions, and amending various rules of the club. Membership of the club on December 31, 2012, totalled 23,528, made up of 17,996 full members, 5,003 associate members, 333 honorary members, 103 senior members and 93 out-match members. There were 10,667 candidates awaiting election to full membership; 406 vacancies arose in 2012.

ECB ANNUAL GENERAL MEETING

On May 8, the ECB held their AGM at The Oval. Jane Stichbury and Baroness Heyhoe Flint were re-elected to the board as independent members, and the election of Richard Thompson (Surrey) and Andy Nash (Somerset) was confirmed.

The ECB announced a £96m investment in community cricket over the next four years to help clubs whose facilities had been damaged by bad weather in 2012.

The following day, it was announced that the supermarket Waitrose were to be the new team sponsors of England cricket for three years, succeeding Brit. The Waitrose logo would feature on all England teams' playing and training wear from May 2014.

ICC DATA PROVISION

On May 22, the ICC named Opta as their official data provider for the next two years, with exclusive access to the stadiums for all major ICC events, as well as the exclusive distribution rights for live data. Opta, the current suppliers of ECB data, would provide live detailed ball-by-ball data, squad statistics and scorecards to all ICC media platforms, official partners, third parties and global media.

ICC CRICKET COMMITTEE

The ICC Cricket Committee met at Lord's on May 28–29, chaired for the first time by former India captain Anil Kumble, who had succeeded Clive Lloyd. They reiterated their support for balance and differentiation between the three formats of the game. Noting cases where Test matches had been postponed to make room for limited-overs internationals, the committee recommended that all Full Members should be required to play a minimum number of Tests over a four-year period to maintain Test status. They also supported a Test play-off as the climax to a qualification period of bilateral matches in the Future Tours Programme, with the ICC Test rankings determining the qualifiers.

The committee reviewed recent changes to the one-day international playing conditions: the restriction of four fielders outside the circle during non-powerplay overs, the introduction of two bouncers per over, the abolition of the bowling powerplay, and the introduction of two new balls. While noting positive results (more boundaries and more wickets), they recognised concerns that using two balls could favour seam bowling at the expense of spin. The committee wanted further data on the impact of the changes before settling the playing conditions which would apply in the 2015 World Cup.

They accepted an MCC recommendation that the switch hit/reserve sweep should remain legitimate, as an exciting stroke requiring a lot of skill. The bowling side should have some leeway for wides when the switch hit was attempted.

The committee also discussed papers relating to over-rates (which had improved in Tests), progress with DRS technology, women's cricket, umpire performances, pink ball trials, illegal bowling actions and helmet safety research.

SPORT ENGLAND FUNDING

On May 30, Sport England announced a 50% increase in their Protecting Playing Fields Olympic and Paralympic Legacy Fund. Twenty-seven of the 75 awards in the latest round of funding went to grassroots cricket projects, which received sums from £18,000 to £50,000 each to fund initiatives such as square renovation, improved drainage and levelling of outfields. The funding awards were part of a wider shareout of £3.5m in grant aid from the National Lottery.

ICC ANNUAL MEETINGS

The ICC annual conference and associated meetings took place in London on June 25–29.

It was confirmed that the first World Test Championship would be staged in England and Wales 2017, and the second in India in early 2021. Between 2015 and 2023, the ICC would stage 16 further events: two World Cups, two World Twenty20s, three Women's World Cups, two Women's World Twenty20s, three Under-19 World Cups and four qualifying tournaments. Although the Champions Trophy just concluded had been highly acclaimed, ICC chief executive David Richardson said it would be replaced by a Test Championship to provide one pinnacle global event for each of the three formats over a four-year cycle. (Plans for the World Test Championship were subsequently abandoned in January 2014, and the Champions Trophy was reinstated.)

The ICC Board also approved the recommendation that Full Members should play a minimum of 16 Tests in each four-year period. To ensure that all one-day internationals played in the four years between World Cups counted towards a team's ranking, the one-day rankings period was raised from three years to four, and the Twenty20 rankings were similarly changed. The annual rankings update was moved from August 1 to May 1, felt to be a more logical break in the international season. These changes were backdated to May 2013.

After an inspection of the venues for the World Twenty20 in Bangladesh in 2014, concern was expressed about the progress of construction and improvements to facilities in Cox's Bazar and Sylhet. A final decision on venues would be taken after a further inspection in August. It was agreed to expand the Women's World Twenty20 in 2014 to a ten-team tournament, admitting the top three sides from the qualifying competition in Dublin in July.

The ICC Board supported the Chief Executives' Committee decision to make the following changes to the playing conditions, to come into effect from October 1:

(a) The third-umpire review for a no-ball when a wicket falls should extend to waist-high full tosses and bouncers above shoulder height.

(b) When the umpires believe the condition of the ball has been changed, but there is no eyewitness to identify the player responsible, they should replace the ball, giving the captain a first and final warning; after a second offence, they should award a five-run penalty, ask the batsman to choose a new ball and report the captain under the Code of Conduct.

(c) Zing wickets (with flashing LEDs in the bails and stumps) were approved for use in one-day and Twenty20 internationals, subject to an independent assessment of the technology.

The board agreed that a cricketer wishing to return to his original Associate or Affiliate Member side after playing for a Full Member should wait only two years, rather than four, to requalify.

The Chairman of the Anti-Corruption and Security Unit, Sir Ronnie Flanagan, presented his annual report in a joint session of the ICC Board and the Chief Executives' Committee. The board agreed to an enhanced set of principles, including a consistent framework for international and domestic anti-corruption rules, addressing the jurisdictional challenges and setting out principles to support mutual recognition of member board decisions and sanctions. They were also updated on the ACSU's investigations into the Bangladesh Premier League in 2013.

Afghanistan, an ICC Affiliate Member since 2001, became the 37th Associate Member, while Romania were accepted as an Affiliate. Membership remained at 106, with Cuba removed for failing to demonstrate a suitable administrative structure; the Associate status of Malawi, Iran, Tonga and Turkey was suspended.

MCC WORLD CRICKET COMMITTEE

The MCC World Cricket Committee met at Lord's on July 15–16, and agreed unanimously that DRS brought about more correct decisions on the field; it was poor implementation and use of DRS that led to controversies, rather than the system itself. The committee reiterated their desire to see the universal implementation of DRS in international cricket.

MCC would help to identify opportunities to play day/night Test cricket in the Future Tours Programme, to reinvigorate the five-day game in countries where attendance is poor, and would offer advice on best practice regarding issues such as dew, the quality of floodlights, the type of balls and sightscreens to use, hours of play and choosing grounds with easy access for workers.

They heard presentations from ICC president Alan Isaac, the ECB's senior investigator Steven Richardson, and Angus Porter, chief executive of the Professional Cricketers' Association, on the fight against corruption. The committee encouraged the creation of domestic ACSUs in all member countries, but felt the ICC should take central control, helping members to pool resources. Porter emphasised the importance of player representative bodies acting in the interests of players and the game, and reported that the PCA and the ECB's anti-corruption unit were working closely.

There were also presentations from bat-makers Jeremy Ruggles of J. S. Wright, and Andrew Kember of Salix, prompting a discussion on the balance between bat and ball, the increase in six-hitting and the weight, width and pressing techniques associated with modern bats. One suggestion was that the size of the cleft in a bat should be restricted, limiting its overall depth and power. Some members thought that increased six-hitting was entertaining, others that bowlers were getting a raw deal with mis-hit sixes; the rising percentage of Test results was cited as evidence that bowlers could still take wickets. It was decided to undertake more research, consulting a range of bat manufacturers and conducting laboratory testing on the power of modern bats of varying shapes and weights.

ECB SPONSORSHIP DEAL

On August 6, the ECB announced that NatWest would become the title sponsor of Twenty20 cricket at international, county and recreational level for four years from 2014 – the first time a single-format sponsorship of the game had been offered to one organisation. The deal covered the England men's and women's home Twenty20 international fixtures, the county Twenty20 competition, the women's county Twenty20 competition, the National Club Twenty20 competition, and junior competitions for boys and girls. In recreational cricket, NatWest retained the title sponsorship of the annual CricketForce weekend, where thousands of clubs hold volunteer events to boost investment in grounds and facilities, as well as the Outstanding Services to Cricket Awards (OSCAs) which recognise and reward the game's volunteers.

ECB APPOINTMENTS

On October 16, the ECB appointed former Kent, Middlesex and England wicketkeeper Paul Downton to succeed Hugh Morris as managing director for England cricket. He was to take over on February 1. In addition to his playing career, Downton had studied law, forged a career in the City and served on the Middlesex, MCC and ECB cricket committees.

At the same time, former Leicestershire and England batsman James Whitaker was named to succeed Geoff Miller as chairman of selectors and national selector from January 1. Whitaker had served as a selector under Miller since 2008.

MCC SPECIAL GENERAL MEETING

MCC held a Special General Meeting on October 17 to consider a resolution calling for an independent enquiry into the processes, finances and governance of ground redevelopment. The resolution (proposed by the Reform Group, which had supported the £400m Vision for Lord's redevelopment plan abandoned in 2011) was defeated, with 1,556 votes in favour and 6,191 against. This freed MCC to continue with their 15-year £200m masterplan for the Lord's ground.

ICC EXECUTIVE BOARD

The ICC Executive Board met in London on October 18–19. The board agreed that an ICC chairman would be appointed to take charge after the next annual conference – whose venue was confirmed a week later as Melbourne, in June 2014.

They reviewed a report on venues for the World Twenty20 in Bangladesh, and accepted the Bangladesh Cricket Board's request to extend the deadline for completing the stadiums to November 30. The schedule of the Under-19 World Cup, to be staged in the UAE in February 2014 with 16 sides, including six Associates/Affiliates, was approved.

The board were briefed on the ICC Chief Executives' Committee meeting in Dubai the previous month, and noted their discussions on issues including DRS and maintaining the current playing conditions for one-day internationals and bad light.

There was an update on investigations into the Bangladesh Premier League in 2013: seven individuals had been charged with fixing-related offences, and two others for failing to report corrupt approaches made to them. A more robust Anti-Corruption Code would be submitted to the board meeting in January.

Following Afghanistan's qualification for the World Cup, the board increased the assistance provided to Afghan cricket through the Targeted Assistance Performance Programme by $1.1m.

ENGLAND PLAYER CONTRACTS

On October 22, the ECB awarded 11 central contracts running for 12 months from October 1, 2013, one more than the previous year. They went to James Anderson, Ian Bell, Tim Bresnan, Stuart Broad, Alastair Cook, Steven Finn, Kevin Pietersen, Matt Prior, Joe Root, Graeme Swann and Jonathan Trott. Compared with the previous list, Joe Root had replaced Eoin Morgan.

On December 12, incremental contracts were awarded to Ravi Bopara, Jos Buttler, Alex Hales, Morgan and Luke Wright; the last three replaced Jonny Bairstow, Nick Compton, Jade Dernbach, Craig Kieswetter, Graham Onions, Samit Patel and James Tredwell. Players on incremental contracts receive a one-off ECB payment on top of their county salary, whereas centrally contracted players are paid by the ECB rather than their county. Incremental contracts can be earned by amassing 20 appearance points between October and September (five for a Test, two for a Twenty20 or one-day international). Hales and Wright had previously been awarded contracts on this basis in August. Michael Carberry earned an incremental contract later in December, and Ben Stokes in January.

On September 23, the ECB had named 16 players for the England Performance Programme, who would train at the National Cricket Performance Centre in Loughborough before spending a month in Australia. They were Moeen Ali, Danny Briggs, Jos Buttler, Varun Chopra, Ben Foakes, James Harris, Chris Jordan, Simon Kerrigan, Alex Lees, Tymal Mills, Jamie Overton, Sam Robson, Reece Topley, James Vince, David Willey, Mark Wood. (Kerrigan, Overton and Wood did not travel to Australia.)

ECB SPONSORSHIP DEALS

On November 7, the ECB announced that Royal London, the mutual life and pensions company, would become the headline sponsor of one-day cricket at international, county and recreational levels from 2014. A four-year deal covered men's and women's one-day internationals, a new 50-over men's county competition (replacing the 40-over competition sponsored by Yorkshire Bank), the National Club Championship and junior county cups for boys and girls. This meant game-wide title sponsorship for each format, with Royal London sponsoring all one-day cricket, NatWest all Twenty20 cricket, Investec Test cricket and LV= the County Championship.

Two weeks earlier, Marston's Pedigree agreed an extension of their "Official Beer of England Cricket" status until 2017.

ENGLISH SEASON SCHEDULE

On November 26, the ECB revealed the new schedule of the county season from 2014 to 2017, based on the recommendations of the Morgan Review into the domestic game and feedback from more than 25,000 county cricket fans. Two-thirds of LV= County Championship matches in 2014 were to start on a Sunday, 70% of Twenty20 group games – renamed the NatWest T20 Blast – would take place on Friday nights, and the 50-over Royal London One-Day Cup was given a slot in the school summer holidays.

MEETINGS AND DECISIONS, 2014

ICC EXECUTIVE BOARD

The ICC Executive Board met in Dubai on January 9, January 28-29, and again in Singapore on February 8, to discuss a comprehensive resolution relating to the governance, competition and financial models of the ICC. After amendments, this was put to the vote at the Singapore meeting and passed by the required majority of the board, including eight Full Members. The Pakistan Cricket Board and Sri Lanka Cricket abstained, saying they needed more time to discuss the amended resolution.

From July 2014, the ICC Board would be led by a chairman, N. Srinivasan from the BCCI. A new Executive Committee would be formed, reporting to the board; the initial chair would be Cricket Australia's Wally Edwards, while Giles Clarke from the ECB would continue to chair the Finance and Commercial Affairs Committee. These roles would be for a two-year transitional period, after which the board chair would be elected from within the board, with all Full Member directors eligible. The Executive Committee, and Finance and Commercial Affairs Committee, would each include representatives from the BCCI, CA and ECB, plus two representatives of the other Full Members elected by the board.

Full Members were offered "greater financial recognition based on the contribution they have made to the game, particularly in terms of finance, their ICC history and their on-field performances in the three formats". It was promised that none of the Full Members would be worse off than before, and all could be better off. Funds directly distributed to Associate and Affiliate Members would grow if revenue targets were achieved, and there was a commitment to support Associate/Affiliate tournaments and centralised services.

A Test Cricket Fund was proposed to help teams sustain a home programme of Test cricket up to 2023; this fund would be available to all Test-playing members except the BCCI, CA and the ECB. All Full Members were to enter contractually binding bilateral agreements on future series.

The winner of the next ICC Intercontinental Cup for Associate Members would be entitled to play off against the bottom-ranked Full Member and, if successful, obtain Test status.

The World Test Championship, scheduled to run every four years from 2017, was cancelled, and the Champions Trophy reinstated for 2017 and 2021.

Further details of the 2014 ICC Executive Board meetings will appear in Wisden 2015. *Comment on the changes in ICC governance appear on page 67.*

DATES IN CRICKET HISTORY

c. 1550   Evidence of cricket being played in Guildford, Surrey.

1610   Reference to "cricketing" between Weald & Upland and North Downs near Chevening, Kent.

1611   Randle Cotgrave's French–English dictionary translates the French word "crosse" as a cricket staff.
Two youths fined for playing cricket at Sidlesham, Sussex.

1624   Jasper Vinall becomes first man known to be killed playing cricket: hit by a bat while trying to catch the ball – at Horsted Green, Sussex.

1676   First reference to cricket being played abroad, by British residents in Aleppo, Syria.

1694   Two shillings and sixpence paid for a "wagger" (wager) about a match at Lewes.

1697   First reference to "a great match" with 11 players a side for fifty guineas, in Sussex.

1700   Cricket match announced on Clapham Common.

1709   First recorded inter-county match: Kent v Surrey.

1710   First reference to cricket at Cambridge University.

1727   Articles of Agreement written governing the conduct of matches between the teams of the Duke of Richmond and Mr Brodrick of Peperharow, Surrey.

1729   Date of earliest surviving bat, belonging to John Chitty, now in the Oval pavilion.

1730   First recorded match at the Artillery Ground, off City Road, central London, still the cricketing home of the Honourable Artillery Company.

1744   Kent beat All-England by one wicket at the Artillery Ground.
First known version of the Laws of Cricket, issued by the London Club, formalising the pitch as 22 yards long.

c. 1767   Foundation of the Hambledon Club in Hampshire, the leading club in England for the next 30 years.

1769   First recorded century, by John Minshull for Duke of Dorset's XI v Wrotham.

1771   Width of bat limited to $4^{1}/_{4}$ inches, where it has remained ever since.

1774   Lbw law devised.

1776   Earliest known scorecards, at the Vine Club, Sevenoaks, Kent.

1780   The first six-seamed cricket ball, manufactured by Dukes of Penshurst, Kent.

1787   First match at Thomas Lord's first ground, Dorset Square, Marylebone – White Conduit Club v Middlesex.
Formation of Marylebone Cricket Club by members of the White Conduit Club.

1788   First revision of the Laws of Cricket by MCC.

1794   First recorded inter-schools match: Charterhouse v Westminster.

1795   First recorded case of a dismissal "leg before wicket".

1806   First Gentlemen v Players match at Lord's.

1807   First mention of "straight-armed" (i.e. roundarm) bowling: by John Willes of Kent.

1809   Thomas Lord's second ground opened, at North Bank, St John's Wood.

1811   First recorded women's county match: Surrey v Hampshire at Ball's Pond, London.

1814   Lord's third ground opened on its present site, also in St John's Wood.

1827   First Oxford v Cambridge match, at Lord's: a draw.

1828   MCC authorise the bowler to raise his hand level with the elbow.

1833   John Nyren publishes *Young Cricketer's Tutor* and *The Cricketers of My Time*.

1836   First North v South match, for years regarded as the principal fixture of the season.

c. **1836**   Batting pads invented.

1841   General Lord Hill, commander-in-chief of the British Army, orders that a cricket ground be made an adjunct of every military barracks.

1844   First official international match: Canada v United States.

1845   First match played at The Oval.

1846   The All-England XI, organised by William Clarke, begin playing matches, often against odds, throughout the country.

1849   First Yorkshire v Lancashire match.

c. **1850**   Wicketkeeping gloves first used.

1850   John Wisden bowls all ten batsmen in an innings for North v South.

1853   First mention of a champion county: Nottinghamshire.

1858   First recorded instance of a hat being awarded to a bowler taking three wickets with consecutive balls.

1859   First touring team to leave England, captained by George Parr, draws enthusiastic crowds in the US and Canada.

1864   "Overhand bowling" authorised by MCC.
                John Wisden's *The Cricketer's Almanack* first published.

1868   Team of Australian aborigines tour England.

1873   W. G. Grace becomes the first player to record 1,000 runs and 100 wickets in a season.
                First regulations restricting county qualifications, regarded by some as the official start of the County Championship.

1877   First Test match: Australia beat England by 45 runs at Melbourne.

1880   First Test in England: a five-wicket win against Australia at The Oval.

1882   Following England's first defeat by Australia in England, an "obituary notice" to English cricket in the *Sporting Times* leads to the tradition of the Ashes.

1889   Present Lord's Pavilion begun.
                South Africa's first Test match.
                Declarations first authorised, but only on the third day, or in a one-day match.

1890   County Championship officially constituted.

1895   W. G. Grace scores 1,000 runs in May, and reaches his 100th hundred.

1899   A. E. J. Collins scores 628 not out in a junior house match at Clifton College, the highest recorded individual score in any game.
                Selectors choose England team for home Tests, instead of host club issuing invitations.

1900   Six-ball over becomes the norm, instead of five.

1909   Imperial Cricket Conference (ICC – now the International Cricket Council) set up, with England, Australia and South Africa the original members.

1910   Six runs given for any hit over the boundary, instead of only for a hit out of the ground.

1912   First and only triangular Test series played in England, involving England, Australia and South Africa.

1915   W. G. Grace dies, aged 67.

1926   Victoria score 1,107 v New South Wales at Melbourne, still a first-class record.

1928   West Indies' first Test match.
                A. P. Freeman of Kent and England becomes the only player to take more than 300 first-class wickets in a season: 304.

1930   New Zealand's first Test match.
Donald Bradman's first tour of England: he scores 974 runs in the five Ashes Tests, still a record for any Test series.

1931   Stumps made higher (28 inches not 27) and wider (nine inches not eight – this was optional until 1947).

1932   India's first Test match.
Hedley Verity of Yorkshire takes ten wickets for ten runs v Nottinghamshire, the best innings analysis in first-class cricket.

1932-33   The Bodyline tour of Australia in which England bowl at batsmen's bodies with a packed leg-side field to neutralise Bradman's scoring.

1934   Jack Hobbs retires, with 197 centuries and 61,237 runs, both records.
First women's Test: Australia v England at Brisbane.

1935   MCC condemn and outlaw Bodyline.

1947   Denis Compton (Middlesex and England) hits a record 3,816 runs in an English season.

1948   First five-day Tests in England.
Bradman concludes Test career with a second-ball duck at The Oval and a batting average of 99.94 – four runs short of 100.

1952   Pakistan's first Test match.

1953   England regain the Ashes after a 19-year gap, the longest ever.

1956   Jim Laker of England takes 19 wickets for 90 v Australia at Manchester, the best match analysis in first-class cricket.

1960   First tied Test: Australia v West Indies at Brisbane.

1963   Distinction between amateurs and professionals abolished in English cricket.
The first major one-day tournament begins in England: the Gillette Cup.

1969   Limited-over Sunday league inaugurated for first-class counties.

1970   Proposed South African tour of England cancelled; South Africa excluded from international cricket because of their government's apartheid policies.

1971   First one-day international: Australia v England at Melbourne.

1973   First women's World Cup: England are the winners.

1975   First World Cup: West Indies beat Australia in final at Lord's.

1976   First women's match at Lord's: England v Australia.

1977   Centenary Test at Melbourne, with identical result to the first match: Australia beat England by 45 runs.
Australian media tycoon Kerry Packer signs 51 of the world's leading players in defiance of the cricketing authorities.

1978   Graham Yallop of Australia is the first batsman to wear a protective helmet in a Test.

1979   Packer and official cricket agree peace deal.

1981   England beat Australia in Leeds Test, after following on with bookmakers offering odds of 500–1 against them winning.

1982   Sri Lanka's first Test match.

1991   South Africa return, with a one-day international in India.

1992   Zimbabwe's first Test match.
Durham become first county since Glamorgan in 1921 to attain first-class status.

1993   The ICC cease to be administered by MCC, becoming an independent organisation.

1994   Brian Lara becomes the first player to pass 500 in a first-class innings: 501 not out for Warwickshire v Durham.

2000 South Africa's captain Hansie Cronje banned from cricket for life after admitting receiving bribes from bookmakers in match-fixing scandal.
Bangladesh's first Test match.
County Championship split into two divisions, with promotion and relegation.
The Laws of Cricket revised and rewritten.

2001 Sir Donald Bradman dies, aged 92.

2003 Twenty20 Cup inaugurated in England.

2004 Lara is the first to score 400 in a Test innings, for West Indies against England in Antigua.

2005 England regain the Ashes after 16 years.

2006 Pakistan become first team to forfeit a Test, for refusing to resume at The Oval.
England lose the Ashes after 462 days, the shortest tenure in history.
Shane Warne becomes the first man to take 700 Test wickets.

2007 Australia complete 5–0 Ashes whitewash for the first time since 1920-21.
Australia win the World Cup for the third time running.
India beat Pakistan in the final of the inaugural World Twenty20 tournament.

2008 Indian Premier League of 20-over matches launched.
Durham win the County Championship for the first time.
Sachin Tendulkar becomes the leading scorer in Tests, passing Lara.

2009 Terrorists attack Sri Lankan team bus in Lahore.

2010 Tendulkar scores the first double-century in a one-day international, against South Africa; later in the year, he scores his 50th Test century.
Muttiah Muralitharan retires from Test cricket, after taking his 800th wicket.
Pakistan bowl three deliberate no-balls in Lord's Test against England; the ICC ban the three players responsible.

2011 England complete 3–1 Ashes win in Australia, with three innings victories.
India become the first team to win the World Cup on home soil.
England whitewash India 4–0 to go top of the ICC Test rankings for the first time.
Salman Butt, Mohammad Asif and Mohammad Aamer are given custodial sentences of between six and 30 months for their part in the Lord's spot-fix.
Virender Sehwag makes a world-record 219 in a one-day international, for India against West Indies at Indore.

2012 Tendulkar scores his 100th international century, in a one-day game against Bangladesh at Mirpur.
Hashim Amla makes 311 not out at The Oval, the first Test triple-century for South Africa, whose 2–0 series victory takes them top of the ICC rankings.
England win 2–1 in India, their first Test series victory there since 1984-85.

2013 150th edition of *Wisden Cricketers' Almanack* published.
Several players arrested on suspicion of spot-fixing in IPL.
England retain the Ashes in August – but lose them in December.
Tendulkar retires after his 200th Test match, with a record 15,921 runs.

2014 ICC agree far-reaching changes to their governance, pushed through by India, Australia and England.
Brendon McCullum makes 302, New Zealand's first Test triple-century.

ANNIVERSARIES IN 2014-15

COMPILED BY STEVEN LYNCH

2014

April 30   Ian Healy (Australia) born, 1964.
Wicketkeeper who made 395 dismissals in 119 Test appearances.

May 15   R. E. "Tip" Foster (Worcestershire) dies, 1914.
Scored 287 on Test debut, against Australia at Sydney in 1903-04; died of diabetes at 36.

June 15   A. G. Steel (Lancashire) dies, 1914.
Scorer of the first Test century at Lord's – 148 against Australia in 1884.

June 22   First match at the current Lord's ground, 1814.
MCC beat Hertfordshire by an innings and 27 runs.

July 30   Albert Trott (England and Australia) dies, 1914.
Hit a ball over the Pavilion at Lord's.

August 15   Fred Trueman is first to take 300 Test wickets, 1964.
Neil Hawke is caught by Colin Cowdrey at first slip in final Ashes Test at The Oval.

August 21   Doug Wright (Kent) born, 1914.
Energetic leg-spinner who took seven first-class hat-tricks, a record.

October 19   Harold Gimblett (Somerset) born, 1914.
Highly strung opener who hit a 63-minute century on first-class debut for Somerset in 1935.

October 27   Mark Taylor (Australia) born, 1964.
Scorer of 839 runs in 1989 Ashes, and later one of Australia's most successful captains.

November 11   A. E. J. Collins (Clifton College) killed in action, 1914.
Maker of the highest-known individual score, 628*, in a junior house match in 1899.

December 4   Railways (Pakistan) win first-class match by an innings and 851 runs, 1964.
In response to a total of 910-6, Dera Ismail Khan are bowled out for 32 and 27.

December 6   Cyril Washbrook (Lancashire) born, 1914.
Opened for England with Len Hutton; scored 34,101 first-class runs.

December 15   Ernie Toshack (Australia) born, 1914.
Versatile left-arm bowler who was a member of Don Bradman's 1948 "Invincibles".

December 17   Mushtaq Ali (India) born, 1914.
Graceful opener who scored India's first Test century in England, at Lord's in 1936.

2015

February 20   Norman Callaway (NSW) scores double-century in only first-class innings, 1915.
Aged 18, Callaway hit 207 v Queensland at Sydney; he was killed in action in France in 1917.

March 11   Vijay Hazare (India) born, 1915.
One of India's finest batsmen; scored two centuries in the 1947-48 Adelaide Test.

March 19   Norman Yardley (Yorkshire) born, 1915.
Amateur all-rounder who captained England in the 1948 Ashes.

April 4   Drewy Stoddart (Middlesex) dies, 1915.
England's captain in the Ashes of 1894-95 and 1897-98.

ONE HUNDRED AND FIFTY YEARS AGO

from Wisden Cricketers' Almanack 1865

GEORGE PARR   "His style of play has long ranked him the best batsman in England; his leg hitting is always a treat to witness, no man approaching him in this particular department of the game; his position in the field at the commencement of his career was generally long-leg and middle-wicket, he being able to throw the ball a great distance, having, in a match with a soldier at Lord's, June 16, 1846, thrown it about 109 yards, but of late years he has either taken slip or point. He has frequently been called to the Pavilion, both at Lord's and the Oval, to receive substantial rewards for his brilliant play, but in a match at Lord's, 1857, between the Two Elevens, the players honoured themselves and him by presenting Parr with a handsome watch as a mark of their delight and esteem for the grand performance of 56 and 19, both not outs."

ETON v HARROW   "On the 8th and 9th of July [1864] the Annual match between the Etonians and the Harrovians was played at Lord's. The company was far more numerous than on any previous occasion, there being about nine thousand spectators present. Owing to the admirable arrangements of the Honorary Secretary of the MCC very capital accommodation was afforded. A large stand had been erected capable of containing one thousand spectators, and it was all but filled. Two marquees stood in opposite corners of the ground, the one being appropriated to the supply of the more substantial necessaries of life, while the other was well stored with strawberries, ices and cooling beverages. Both were at times crowded with customers. About half-past four the Prince and Princess of Wales honoured the ground with their presence, and continued for some time taking a lively interest in the game. When their Royal Highnesses left, the crowd and pressure were in places so great that it was with difficulty those on foot made their way from one part of the ground to the other, though the Honorary Secretary had, with highly commendable forethought, formed a roped walk round the ground for the convenience of the pedestrians."

ONE HUNDRED YEARS AGO

from Wisden Cricketers' Almanack 1915

NOTES BY THE EDITOR [Sydney Pardon]   "Apart from the heavy toll imposed by the War, the casualty lists including many young officers who had gained their colours at the public schools, death was very busy among cricketers in 1914. To mention only the most famous names: Joseph Makinson, Canon McCormick and B. B. Cooper, died full of years, A. G. Steel and J. H. Brain were still in middle age, and three great players of our day, R. E. Foster, Albert Trott and A. O. Jones passed away prematurely. W. O. Moberly, one of the batsmen who helped the Graces to make Gloucestershire invincible in the seventies, was not exactly an old man, but he had reached the age of sixty-three."

OBITUARY   "LIEUT. ARTHUR EDWARD JEUNE COLLINS, of the Royal Engineers, who was killed in action on November 11, came suddenly into note by scoring 628 not out for Clarke's House v North Town, in a junior house match at Clifton College in June 1899, when only thirteen years old. Clarke's, who scored 836, won by an innings and 688 runs. Collins also obtained eleven wickets in the match, and in partnership with Redfern (13) put on as many as 183 for the last wicket… He was a free-hitting batsman, but his military duties prevented him from taking his cricket seriously: still he made many good scores in Army matches… His best performance at Lord's was to make 58 and 36 for R. E. v R. A.

in 1913. He was born in India in 1885, gazetted second Lieutenant in 1904 and promoted Lieutenant in 1907."

NOTTS v HAMPSHIRE, AT NOTTINGHAM, AUGUST 6, 7, 8 [1914]   "B. G. Melle started playing for Hampshire, but when the game had been a little time in progress he received orders to join his regiment. In the special circumstances Stone was allowed to take his place."

SURREY IN 1914   "For the first time since 1899 Surrey came out with the best record among the counties and so won the Championship. A brilliant season had a strange ending... on August 31, public feeling against the continuance of first-class cricket during the War having been worked up to rather a high pitch, the Surrey committee at a special meeting decided unanimously to cancel the two remaining fixtures – with Sussex at Brighton, and Leicestershire at the Oval. It was in some ways a pity that this drastic step should have been found necessary, but in acting as they did the Surrey committee took a wise course. Only two days before the decision was arrived at, Lord Roberts, in a recruiting speech, had made a pointed reference to people who went on playing cricket at such a time... Hobbs stood out by himself – pre-eminently the batsman of the year... Hobbs scored 226 against Notts, at the Oval, 215 not out against Essex, at Leyton, 202 against Yorkshire, at Lord's, and made seven other hundreds... His 100 against Yorkshire, at Bradford [was] for sheer brilliancy... his most remarkable effort. In an hour and a quarter he scored his 100 out of 152."

CRICKETER OF THE YEAR, J. W. H. T. DOUGLAS   "The position Mr Douglas now holds in the cricket world has been won by sheer hard work and perseverance. He was not by any means a youthful wonder [and]... is even more famous as a boxer than as a cricketer. Like his father before him, he was middleweight amateur champion, and in 1908 he won the Olympic middleweight championship in London. He has given up public boxing now, but the value of the experience he gained can be seen in his cricket. Having for three or four years known what it was to be thoroughly trained, he always looks fitter than any other man in the field, and nothing shakes his nerve. When the War broke out Mr Douglas joined the Bedford Regiment."

FIFTY YEARS AGO

from Wisden Cricketers' Almanack 1965

CRICKETER OF THE YEAR, G. BOYCOTT   "He is ruthlessly dedicated to the job of scoring runs, analyses his own game, and takes the trouble to learn about the others. Cricket for him is an all absorbing occupation and in Yorkshire, where they expect a one hundred per cent effort, he caused an uplift of eyebrows prior to the start of the 1964 season, when he gave up his job as a wages clerk earlier than the county authorities demanded, attended the Yorkshire Schoolboys practices in the mornings, stayed for the Colts and the senior coaching classes in the afternoon, and then left for the Headingley ground in order to join evening practices with the Leeds club. He had four sessions of net practice each day and regretted he could not get more."

NEVILLE CARDUS by John Arlott   "The Birthday Honours List of 1964 included the award of the CBE to Mr Neville Cardus for services to music and cricket. It was the first – and, some may feel, belated – official recognition of the modest man who, for almost fifty years, has written with sympathy and integrity about the two chief interests – indeed, enthusiasms – of his life. Throughout that time his work has never become jaded... by innovation and influence, he virtually created modern cricket writing. In doing so, he led thousands of people to greater enjoyment of the game. Today he may be regarded as just one of a number of imaginative cricket writers; but he appears so only to those who do not recall the immense novelty and impact of his writing when it first reached the public in the 1920s. Before then there had been much competent cricket reporting, informed, sound in judgment, pleasant in manner. But the Cardus of the years shortly after the First World War first brought to it the qualities of personalisation, literary allusion and imagery. By such methods as presenting the contest between bowler and batsman as a clash not only of skills but of characters, he created something near to a mythology of the game... He has made a contribution to cricket which no one can ever duplicate. It may be true that cricket was always an art, but no one until Neville Cardus presented it as an art with all an artist's perception. Because of him, thousands of people enjoy watching the game more than they would have done if he had not lived and written."

AUSTRALIANS IN ENGLAND, 1964 "Opinions differed considerably concerning the quality of the 24th Australian team to visit the United Kingdom, but the fact remained that R. B. Simpson and his men achieved their objective in that they won the rubber and returned home with the Ashes which their country had held since wresting them from P. B. H. May's side in 1958-59... it could be said they arrived in England with an experimental side... not over-blessed with talent. Indeed, when the party was chosen, the Australian critics almost to a man condemned it as one of the weakest ever to represent their country... That the side fared as well as they did was due mainly to Simpson. He proved a shrewd captain as well as an outstanding cricketer of all-round ability."

SINGLE WICKET COMPETITION IN 1964 "B. R. Knight, the Essex all-rounder, won the Carling Single Wicket competition at Lord's on July 30 and 31, defeating C. Milburn of Northamptonshire by one run in the final. The only difference in the laws which operated when this form of cricket – popular at the beginning of the nineteenth century – was revived at Scarborough in 1963 was that each of the sixteen competitors was allotted eight overs instead of ten. Again the sponsors awarded prizes of £250 to the winner, £100 to the runner-up, £50 each to the beaten semi-finalists and £10 each to the losers of the second round. R. Benaud (Australia) and G. S. Sobers (West Indies) both went out in the first round... The bowler, changing ends after each six-ball over, had the assistance of a first-class wicket-keeper (K. V. Andrew and J. T. Murray shared the duties) and nine fieldsmen from the MCC ground staff."

ENGLAND v AUSTRALIA, FOURTH TEST MATCH, AT OLD TRAFFORD, JULY 23, 24, 25, 27, 28 [1964] "For all the remarkable personal achievements in the match, a bad taste was left in the mouth of the cricket enthusiasts who saw Australia retain the Ashes. Simpson's strategy, with his team one up and two to play, was to make certain that Australia did not lose. Dexter, with England kept in the field until the third morning was well advanced, had no hope of winning and so a boring situation resulted in which twenty-eight and a quarter hours of play were needed to produce a decision on the first innings! Both sides were to blame for frequent periods of needlessly tiresome batting on a perfectly made, closely cut, firm pitch of placid pace which gave neither quick nor spin bowlers the slightest help. The intention to win was never once apparent after Simpson, for the first time in the series, won the toss, and only rarely were the justifiable expectations of the spectators for entertainment realised."

OBITUARY "FILLISTON, JOSEPH W., who died in hospital on October 25, 1964, aged 102, five days after being knocked down by a motor-scooter, acted as umpire to the BCC Cricket Club for many years. 'Old Joe' stood in the Old England v Lord's Taverners match at Lord's when over 100. In his younger days he played cricket with Dr W. G. Grace and he helped Gentlemen of Kent defeat the Philadelphians by six wickets at Town Malling in 1889. He also played as a professional in the Staffordshire League. He liked to tell of the occasion when he gave 'W. G.' out leg-before in a London County game at the Crystal Palace. The Doctor, he said, refused to leave the crease and, as nobody had the courage to contradict him, he continued his innings."

LEAGUE CRICKET IN 1964 "Many famous cricketers have graced the Lancashire League in past years but few have dominated it to such an extent as did C. C. Griffith, the West Indies fast bowler, in the 1964 season. Playing for Burnley the burly Barbados man broke all league and club records by capturing 144 wickets at the ridiculously low price of 5.20 per victim. This phenomenal bowling performance not only guaranteed Burnley the championship but... not until there remained only one more match to play did Burnley taste defeat."

ENGLAND v AUSTRALIA, FIFTH TEST MATCH, AT THE OVAL, AUGUST 13, 14, 15, 17, 18 [1964] "The drama of the third day came right on lunch time. Trueman, previously ineffective, suddenly bowled Redpath middle stump and had McKenzie caught at slip off successive balls. There was no time for another delivery before the interval and the crowd hurried back to their places to see whether Trueman could complete his hat-trick. He also needed one more wicket to become the only bowler to take 300 wickets in Test matches. Hawke survived the first ball, but eventually provided Trueman with his 300th victim."

WORCESTERSHIRE IN 1964 "Worcestershire came within an ace of winning the County Championship in 1962. They even went as far as drinking their champagne, only for Yorkshire to ease them off the top in the very last match. This time... after 65 years of trying and a few months before the club became 100 years old, the title was clinched with three matches to spare... almost invariably superior bowling wins Championships and this was no exception. There is no greater fillip than a successful start in the field; Worcestershire received that through the yeoman efforts of Flavell, assisted mainly by Coldwell and also by Standen, Carter and Brain. Between them, these five seam bowlers took 298 wickets in the competition and 340 altogether... Graveney enjoyed a glorious season, with an aggregate of 2,385 runs, only 12 short of the best he has known in 16 years of first-class cricket. He played five three-figure innings, the third of which made him the fifteenth cricketer to hit 100 centuries."

CRICKET IN ETHIOPIA "Perhaps the day may not be far distant when Ethiopia will be challenging England and Australia to Test matches. Until a few months ago cricket was unknown in that vast country. An Australian doctor resident there, Dr R. H. J. Hamlin, put forward the idea that it would be a good thing for morale if someone from Australia could go there and introduce the game. So W. A. Oldfield, who holds the wicket-keeping record for Tests between England and Australia with 90 victims in 38 matches, spent a month converting the natives to cricket... Before Oldfield left they played a charity match in which at the age of 66 he took part. The highlight of Bert Oldfield's visit was a twenty-minute audience with the Emperor, Haile Selassie."

Compiled by Christopher Lane

HONOURS AND AWARDS, 2013-14

In 2013-14, the following were decorated for their services to cricket:

Queen's Birthday Honours, 2013: C. Bolton (Warton CC; services to cricket and community) BEM; G. C. Crimp (services to grassroots cricket in Wales) MBE; W. A. Dodds (Sudbury groundsman; services to cricket and community) BEM; R. F. Fuggle (services to disabled cricket in Lincolnshire) MBE; L. Harrison (Blagdon CC treasurer; services to cricket and community) BEM; W. G. Khan (Warwickshire, Sussex and Derbyshire, director of Cricket Foundation and Chance to Shine; services to cricket and community) BEM; R. P. M. Oakley (services to education and cricket in Southampton) BEM; P. J. Rey (Helensburgh C&RFC; services to sport and charity) BEM; M. Talbot-Butler (services to cricket administration in Cheshire) BEM.

Queen's Birthday Honours (Australia), 2013: R. G. Lloyd (South Australia, Melbourne CC; services to cricket as player, coach and administrator) OAM; J. G. Moriarty (services to cricket and NSW Central Coast community) OAM; R. M. Richards (services to cricket and youth) OAM.

New Year's Honours, 2014: G. Miller (Derbyshire, Essex and England, later national selector; services to cricket) OBE; C. K. Oliver (chairman, Cricket Scotland; services to cricket) OBE; J. B. Pickup (chairman, ECB Recreational Assembly; voluntary services to community cricket) MBE; T. Vorzanger (chairman, Royal Brussels CC; services to the community in Belgium) BEM.

New Year's Honours (New Zealand), 2014: J. R. Reid (Wellington, Otago and New Zealand; services to cricket) CNZM.

Australia Day Honours, 2014: D. N. Kempe (women's coach, South Australia; services to community and cricket) OAM; C. C. McDonald (Victoria and Australia; services to cricket, tennis and community) OAM; F. C. O'Connor (former chairman, Cricket Australia; services to cricket governance) OAM; W. A. Pewtress (club coach, Victoria; services to cricket) OAM; G. L. Tamblyn (Victoria, later chairman, Cricket Victoria; services to cricket) OAM; D. Wells (curator, Bradman Museum; services to cricket history) OAM.

Bharat Ratna, 2014: S. R. Tendulkar became the youngest recipient of the Bharat Ratna, India's highest civilian award, and the first to be honoured for his achievements in sport.

ICC AWARDS

The ICC's tenth annual awards were announced in December 2013.

Sir Garfield Sobers Trophy (Cricketer of the Year)	**Michael Clarke (A)**
Test Player of the Year	**Michael Clarke (A)**
One-Day International Player of the Year	**Kumar Sangakkara (SL)**
Women's One-Day International Cricketer of the Year	**Suzie Bates (NZ)**
Emerging Player of the Year	**Cheteshwar Pujara (I)**
Associate/Affiliate Player of the Year	**Kevin O'Brien (Ire)**
Twenty20 International Performance of the Year	**Umar Gul (P)**
Women's Twenty20 International Cricketer of the Year	**Sarah Taylor (E)**
Umpire of the Year	**Richard Kettleborough (E)**
Spirit of Cricket Award	**Mahela Jayawardene (SL)**
People's Choice Award	**M. S. Dhoni (I)**

A panel of five also selected two World XIs from the previous 12 months:

ICC World Test team		*ICC World one-day team*	
1	*Alastair Cook (E)	1	T. M. Dilshan (SL)
2	Cheteshwar Pujara (I)	2	Shikhar Dhawan (I)
3	Hashim Amla (SA)	3	Hashim Amla (SA)
4	Michael Clarke (A)	4	Kumar Sangakkara (SL)
5	Mike Hussey (A)	5	A. B. de Villiers (SA)
6	A. B. de Villiers (SA)	6	*†M. S. Dhoni (I)
7	†M. S. Dhoni (I)	7	Ravindra Jadeja (I)
8	Graeme Swann (E)	8	Saeed Ajmal (P)
9	Dale Steyn (SA)	9	Mitchell Starc (A)
10	James Anderson (E)	10	James Anderson (E)
11	Vernon Philander (SA)	11	Lasith Malinga (SL)
12th	Ravichandran Ashwin (I)	12th	Mitchell McClenaghan (NZ)

Previous Cricketers of the Year were Rahul Dravid (2004), Andrew Flintoff and Jacques Kallis (jointly in 2005), Ricky Ponting (2006 and 2007), Shivnarine Chanderpaul (2008), Mitchell Johnson (2009), Sachin Tendulkar (2010), Jonathan Trott (2011) and Kumar Sangakkara (2012).

ICC CRICKET HALL OF FAME

The ICC Cricket Hall of Fame was launched in 2009 in association with the Federation of International Cricketers' Associations to recognise legends of the game. In the first year, 60 members were inducted: 55 from the earlier FICA Hall of Fame, plus five new players elected in October 2009 by a voting academy made up of the ICC president, 11 ICC member representatives, a FICA representative, a women's cricket representative, ten journalists, a statistician, and all living members of the Hall of Fame. New members have been elected every year since. Candidates must have retired from international cricket at least five years ago.

The members elected in 2013 were Glenn McGrath, Shane Warne and Adam Gilchrist (all Australia) and Waqar Younis (Pakistan), with Bob Simpson (Australia) and Debbie Hockley (New Zealand) added in January, bringing the total to 76.

ICC DEVELOPMENT PROGRAMME AWARDS

The ICC announced the global winners of their 2012 Development Programme Awards in February 2013.

Best Overall Cricket Development Programme	**Cricket Scotland**
Best Women's Cricket Initiative	**Royal Dutch Cricket Association**
Best Junior Participation Initiative	**Royal Dutch Cricket Association**
Best Cricket Promotion and Marketing Programme	**Maasai Cricket Warriors and Cricket Kenya**
Best "Spirit of Cricket" Initiative	**Vanuatu Cricket**
Lifetime Service Award	**Gary Fray** (Bermuda)
Volunteer of the Year	**Monir Habibi** (Iran)
Photo of the Year	**Cricket Peru**

ALLAN BORDER MEDAL

Michael Clarke won the Allan Border Medal in February 2013, for the best Australian international player of the past 12 months, for the second time running and the fourth time in all, equalling Ricky Ponting's record. He also won in 2005 and (jointly with Ponting) in 2009. Previous winners were Glenn McGrath, Steve Waugh, Matthew Hayden, Adam Gilchrist, Ponting (four times), Brett Lee and Shane Watson (twice). Clarke received 198 votes from team-mates, umpires and journalists, ahead of Mike Hussey and Watson (both 165). Clarke was also named Test Cricketer of the Year again. **Shane Watson** was Twenty20 International Cricketer of the Year for the second time running, while **Clint McKay** was One-Day International Player of the Year. **Phil Hughes** was State Player of the Year after moving from New South Wales to South Australia, and Queensland's **Joe Burns** was Bradman Young Player of the Year. **Jess Cameron** won the Belinda Clark Award for the Women's International Cricketer of the Year.

SHEFFIELD SHIELD PLAYER OF THE YEAR

The Sheffield Shield Player of the Year Award for 2012-13 was won by **Ricky Ponting** in March 2013, a week before he helped Tasmania win their third first-class title. Now retired from international cricket, he had scored 875 at 87.50 in the eight qualifying games. The award, instituted in 1975-76, is adjudicated by umpires over the season. The Ryobi One-Day Cup Player of the Year was **Aaron Finch** of Victoria. **Nathan Price** of New South Wales was named the Lord's Taverners Indigenous Cricketer of the Year, and **Nick Winter** of ACT the Toyota Futures League Player of the Year. **Bruce Oxenford** was Umpire of the Year. Western Australia's **Nicole Bolton** and Victoria's **Meg Lanning** won the Women's National Cricket League Player of the Year, and Bolton's team-mate **Jenny Wallace** the Women's Twenty20 Player of the Year. **Tasmania** earned the Benaud Spirit of Cricket Award for their fair play throughout the season; the women of **New South Wales** won the WNCL Spirit of Cricket Award.

CRICKET SOUTH AFRICA AWARDS

Hashim Amla was named South African Cricketer of the Year, Test Cricketer of the Year and Fans' Cricketer of the Year at the CSA Awards in September 2013, and also won the KFC "So Good!" award for his triple-century against England in the Oval Test of 2012. The one-day international award went to **A. B. de Villiers**, for the fifth time running, as did the Players' Player. The Twenty20 International Cricketer of the Year was **Dale Steyn**, and the Delivery of the Year went to **Jacques Kallis** for dismissing Ricky Ponting in the Second Test at Adelaide. The Women's Cricketer of the Year was **Marizanne Kapp**. **Kyle Abbott** was South Africa's Best Newcomer, and also won the Domestic Players' Player for his performances with Dolphins. The Sunfoil Series Cricketer of the Season was **Johann Louw** of Cape Cobras, and his team-mate **Richard Levi** was the Momentum One-Day Cup Cricketer. **Quinton de Kock** of Lions was Ram Slam Twenty20 Cricketer of the Season. **Roelof van der Merwe** of Titans was the SA Cricket Association's Most Valuable Player, and **Ayabulela Gqamane** of Warriors was Best Domestic Newcomer. **Lions** won the CSA Fair Play award, and their coach **Geoffrey Toyana** was Coach of the Year. **Johan Cloete** was Umpire of the Year, and **Shaun George** the Umpires' Umpire. **Chris Scott** of the Wanderers was best groundsman, and **Gauteng** were the best scorers' association for the sixth time running.

ENGLAND PLAYERS OF THE YEAR

In May 2013, **Matt Prior** became the first wicketkeeper to win the ECB Men's Cricketer of the Year Award. In the previous 12 months he had scored seven Test fifties, plus a match-saving hundred in Auckland, and made 33 dismissals. Prior's Auckland century also won him the TwelfthMan Moment of the Year award, voted for by fans. Pace bowler **Katharine Brunt** was the Women's Cricketer of the Year for the third time since 2006. She took 12 wickets in the Women's World Cup in February, and had been England's most economical bowler in the World Twenty20 four months earlier. Essex wicketkeeper-batsman **Ben Foakes** won the England Development Programme Cricketer of the Year award; he was England's leading run-scorer in the Under-19 World Cup in August 2012, and later returned to Australia with the England Lions. The England Disability Cricketer of the Year award went to **Matthew Dean**, who scored 490 runs for the England in the Twenty20 World Cup for the Blind, staged in India in December.

PROFESSIONAL CRICKETERS' ASSOCIATION AWARDS

The following awards were announced at the PCA's annual dinner in October 2013.

Reg Hayter Cup (NatWest PCA Player of the Year)	**Moeen Ali** (Worcestershire)
John Arlott Cup (NatWest PCA Young Player of the Year)	**Ben Stokes** (Durham)
ECB Special Award	**Jim Cumbes** (former Lancashire chief executive)
PCA Special Merit Award	**Tony Greig**
England FTI MVP of the Summer	**James Anderson**
Investec Test Player of the Summer	**Graeme Swann**
NatWest One-Day International Player of the Year	**Ravi Bopara**
LV= County Championship Player of the Year	**Graham Onions** (Durham)
Friends Life T20 Player of the Year	**David Willey** (Northamptonshire)
Yorkshire Bank 40 Player of the Year	**Peter Trego** (Somerset)
Sky Sports Sixes League	**Ryan ten Doeschate** (Essex)

FTI Team of the Year **Joe Root, Michael Klinger, Moeen Ali, Ian Bell, Samit Patel, Ben Stokes, Phil Mustard, Stuart Broad, Graeme Swann, Michael Hogan, James Anderson.**

CHRISTOPHER MARTIN-JENKINS SPIRIT OF CRICKET AWARDS

In 2013, MCC and the BBC introduced two Spirit of Cricket awards in memory of Christopher Martin-Jenkins, the former MCC president and *Test Match Special* commentator. The Elite Award, for the professional cricketer who made the biggest contribution to the Spirit of Cricket in the English season, went to **Wayne Madsen** of Derbyshire, who walked off, signalling that he had been caught off his glove, after being given not out in Derbyshire's first innings against Yorkshire at Chesterfield. The Youth Award, recognising the Under-16 junior cricketer or team in England and Wales who best demonstrated the Spirit of Cricket in action, went to **Alton CC Under-13 Girls**, who lent fielders to an under-strength opposition and allowed some of the opposing batsmen to bat twice in a league game, which Alton went on to lose by 20 runs. The girls were invited to the Yorkshire Bank 40 final at Lord's, where they were interviewed on *Test Match Special*. **City Academy** in Bristol were the first beneficiaries of a £2,000 prize supporting a school cricket programme; with Gloucestershire Cricket Board, they aimed to encourage pupils from underprivileged backgrounds to stay in full-time education by offering promising players six hours of extra-curricular coaching every week, plus access to other sports-related professional skills.

WALTER LAWRENCE TROPHY

The Walter Lawrence Trophy for the fastest century in 2013 was won by **Darren Stevens**, who hit a hundred in 44 balls, including ten sixes and six fours, to help Kent overhaul a Sussex total of 336 in a YB40 match at Canterbury on June 19. Stevens received £3,000 along with the trophy. This was the sixth time the competition had been extended to cover all senior cricket in England; traditionally, it was reserved for the fastest first-class hundred against authentic bowling (in 2013, Adam Rossington's 55-ball hundred for Middlesex against Cambridge MCCU on April 24). Durham MCCU's **Ivo Hobson** won the Walter Lawrence award for the highest score by an MCCU batsman: he made 129, also against Cambridge MCCU, at Fenner's on June 11. In its second year, the award for the highest score in English women's cricket went to **Heather Knight**, who scored 157 in nearly seven hours for England against Australia in the Ashes Test at Wormsley on August 13. Hobson and Knight each received a silver medallion and £500. The award for the highest score by a school batsman against MCC went to Canadian international player **Nitish Kumar**, who made 154 not out off 102 balls for Repton against MCC on May 7; he received a medallion and a Gray-Nicolls bat.

CRICKET WRITERS' CLUB AWARDS

The Young Cricketer of the Year was **Ben Stokes**, the first Durham player to receive the award. His all-round performances had helped Durham to win the County Championship, and his form in the one-day series against Australia led to his call-up for the 2013-14 Ashes tour. **Wayne Madsen**, who scored 1,221 runs as captain of Derbyshire, was the second County Player of the Year. The Peter Smith Memorial Award "for services to the presentation of cricket to the public" was made to **Jim Cumbes**, who had recently retired as Lancashire's chief executive. The Cricket Book of the Year award was given to *The Great Tamasha: Cricket, Corruption and the Turbulent Rise of Modern India* by James Astill.

SECOND XI PLAYER OF THE YEAR

The Association of Cricket Statisticians and Historians named **Nick Browne** of Essex the Les Hatton Second XI Player of the Year for 2013. Browne was the leading run-scorer in the Second XI Championship, with 838 at 69.83 in eight matches, including three centuries; he made 144 and 219, both unbeaten, in successive matches against Hampshire and Somerset. He also scored 332 at 55.33 in the one-day Second XI Trophy, and 187 and 26.71 in the Twenty20 tournament, and claimed six wickets in each competition with his leg-spin.

GROUNDSMEN OF THE YEAR

In the third season since the Old Trafford square was rotated through 90 degrees, Lancashire's **Matt Merchant** was the ECB's Groundsman of the Year for his four-day pitches; **Andy Fogarty** of Headingley was runner-up, with commendations for **Steve Birks** (Trent Bridge), **Mick Hunt** (Lord's) and **Stuart Kerrison** (Chelmsford). **Andy Ward** of Leicester won the award for the best one-day pitches, ahead of **David Measor** (Chester-le-Street), with **Simon Lee** (Taunton) and Fogarty commended. **John Dodds** had the best outground for the second year running, at Scarborough. **John Moden** at Fenner's in Cambridge prepared the best MCCU pitch, with **Will Relf** at Loughborough runner-up.

CRICKET SOCIETY AWARDS

Wetherell Award Leading First-class All-rounder	**Darren Stevens** (Kent)
Wetherell Award for Leading Schools All-rounder	**Nitish Kumar** (Repton School)
Most Promising Young Cricketer	**David Willey** (Northamptonshire)
Most Promising Young Woman Cricketer	**Natalie Sciver** (Surrey)
Sir John Hobbs Silver Jubilee Memorial Prize	**Nick Hammond** (King's School Worcester)
(for Outstanding Under-16 Schoolboy)	
A. A. Thomson Fielding Prize for Best Schoolboy Fielder	**Callum Brodrick** (Derbyshire)
Christopher Box-Grainger Memorial Trophy	**Brent Knoll School** (SE London)
(for schools promoting cricket to underprivileged children)	
Don Rowan Memorial Trophy	**The Spa School** (Southwark)
(for primary schools promoting cricket)	
Ian Jackson Award for Services to Cricket	**Mike Brearley**
The Perry-Lewis/Kershaw Trophy	**Tom Carmichael** and **Paul Fielding**
(for contribution to the Cricket Society XI)	

WOMBWELL CRICKET LOVERS' SOCIETY AWARDS

George Spofforth Cricketer of the Year	**Ian Bell** (Warwickshire/England)
Brian Sellers County Captain of the Year	**Paul Collingwood** (Durham)
C. B. Fry Young Cricketer of the Year	**Gary Ballance** (Yorkshire)
Arthur Wood Wicketkeeper of the Year	**Phil Mustard** (Durham)
Learie Constantine Fielder of the Year	**Marcus Trescothick** (Somerset)
Les Bailey Most Promising Young Yorkshire Player	**Alex Lees**
Ted Umbers Services to Yorkshire Cricket	**Brian Marsh***
J. M. Kilburn Cricket Writer of the Year	**Mick Pope**
Jack Fingleton Cricket Commentator of the Year	**Ed Smith**

* *Coach at the Wombwell winter nets for over quarter of a century.*

BRITISH SPORTS JOURNALISM AWARDS

In March 2013, *Wisden* editor **Lawrence Booth** won the SJA award for the Sports Scoop of 2012 for his *Daily Mail* report on Kevin Pietersen's text messages to the South African team. *Times* cricket correspondent **Michael Atherton** was named Specialist Correspondent of the Year again. Cricket photographer **Philip Brown** was judged to have the best Specialist Sports Portfolio, and the best Radio Sports Programme was BBC Radio's *Test Match Special*.

ECB COUNTY JOURNALISM AWARDS

The ECB announced the winners of the third annual County Cricket Journalism Awards for the coverage of domestic cricket in October. **Charlie Talbot-Smith** of the Sportsbeat press agency was named Christopher Martin-Jenkins Young Journalist of the Year, and received a £5,000 scholarship to report on an overseas cricket event, preferably involving county teams. **Scott Read** of BBC Radio Manchester and BBC Radio Lancashire was the inaugural winner of the Christopher Martin-Jenkins Young Broadcaster of the Year award and also received a £5,000 scholarship. *The Cricket Paper* was the National Newspaper of the Year, the *Derby Telegraph* was Regional Newspaper of the Year, and **ESPNcricinfo** was Online Publication of the Year again. The *Yorkshire Post* won the Special Award for Outstanding Innovation and Support of County Cricket, with special mention made of its supplements marking Yorkshire CCC's 150th anniversary.

ECB OSCAs

The ECB presented the 2013 NatWest Outstanding Service to Cricket Awards to volunteers from recreational cricket in September. The winners were:

NatWest CricketForce Award   **Nick Allcoat** (Nottinghamshire)
   Chairman of Attenborough CC who worked tirelessly to win grants and organise volunteers for the complete rebuilding of the club pavilion, including better provision for disability cricket.

Outstanding contribution to disability cricket **Stefan Pichowski**
Former player for the England Deaf Cricket team, later chairman of the England Cricket Association for the Deaf/vice-chairman of the Deaf International Cricket Council, he helped to bring the England side under the ECB's umbrella while working to develop the recreational game.

Building Partnerships Award **Azam Riyard** (Sussex)
Helped to integrate Crawley's communities and break down cultural barriers through his enthusiastic work with Crawley Eagles CC and local schools.

Young Volunteer Award (for under-25s) **Alex Havers** (Norfolk)
Dersingham CC's 15-year-old wicketkeeper-batsman, who also coaches the juniors and helped the club gain ECB Clubmark accreditation.

Officiating – umpires and scorers **Sue Drinkwater** (Gloucestershire)
A scorer in Gloucestershire for 30 years, whose training courses have been adapted by the ECB.

Behind the Scenes Award **Chris Moore** (Staffordshire)
Chairman, scorer and groundsman at Streetly CC who refinanced and revamped the club pavilion, attracted new players and developed the youth section.

Leagues and Boards Award **Peter Butter** (Sussex)
Assistant secretary of the Sussex Cricket League who has helped to manage and develop the league, including work on disciplinary matters, the handbook and the website.

Lifetime Achiever **Jack Greenwood** (Yorkshire)
Over half a century's service to Denholme CC, including 40 years as scorer, fund-raising, painting benches and emptying bins.

ACS STATISTICIAN OF THE YEAR

In March 2014, the Association of Cricket Statisticians and Historians awarded the Statistician of the Year trophy to **Andrew Samson** for his outstanding work on South African statistics, and in recent years as the BBC's *Test Match Special* scorer/statistician on overseas tours.

ECB BUSINESS OF CRICKET AWARDS

The ECB staged the BOCA awards, designed to celebrate Marketing and PR excellence across domestic and international cricket, in November. The winners were: Best Friends Life t20 Campaign – **Surrey**; Best Friends Life t20 Matchday Experience – **Northamptonshire**; Best Yorkshire Bank 40 Promotion – **Northamptonshire**; Best Promotion of a Major Match – **Durham**; Best Sponsorship Activation – **Somerset**; Best Membership Campaign or Promotion – **Somerset**; Best Community Programme – **Derbyshire**; Best Improvement in Customer Engagement – **Kent**; Best Use of Digital – **Essex**; The Innovation Award – **Nottinghamshire**; Team of the Year – **Durham**.

2014 FIXTURES

Inv Test	Investec Test match
RL ODI	Royal London one-day international
NW T20I	NatWest Twenty20 international
LV=CC D1/2	LV= County Championship Division 1/Division 2
RL ODC	Royal London One-Day Cup
NW T20	NatWest T20 Blast
Univs	First-class university match
Univs (nfc)	Non-first-class university match
◗	Day/night or floodlit game

Only the first two of each MCCU's three fixtures carry first-class status.

Sun Mar 23–Wed 26	Friendly	MCC	v Durham	Abu Dhabi ◗
Tue Apr 1–Thu 3	Univs	Cambridge MCCU	v Surrey	Cambridge
		Derbyshire	v Durham MCCU	Derby
		Glamorgan	v Cardiff MCCU	Cardiff
		Oxford MCCU	v Nottinghamshire	Oxford
		Sussex	v Loughboro MCCU	Hove
		Yorkshire	v Leeds/Brad MCCU	Leeds
Sun Apr 6–Wed 9	LV=CC D1	Nottinghamshire	v Lancashire	Nottingham
		Sussex	v Middlesex	Hove
	LV=CC D2	Hampshire	v Worcestershire	Southampton
		Leicestershire	v Derbyshire	Leicester
		Surrey	v Glamorgan	The Oval
Mon Apr 7–Wed 9	Univs	Cambridge MCCU	v Essex	Cambridge
		Durham	v Durham MCCU	Chester-le-St
		Gloucestershire	v Cardiff MCCU	Bristol
		Kent	v Loughboro MCCU	Canterbury
		Oxford MCCU	v Warwickshire	Oxford
		Somerset	v Leeds/Brad MCCU	Taunton Vale
Sun Apr 13–Wed 16	LV=CC D1	Middlesex	v Nottinghamshire	Lord's
		Northamptonshire	v Durham	Northampton
		Somerset	v Yorkshire	Taunton
		Warwickshire	v Sussex	Birmingham
	LV=CC D2	Essex	v Derbyshire	Chelmsford
		Gloucestershire	v Hampshire	Bristol
		Worcestershire	v Kent	Worcester
Sun Apr 20–Wed 23	LV=CC D1	Durham	v Somerset	Chester-le-St
		Lancashire	v Warwickshire	Manchester
		Yorkshire	v Northamptonshire	Leeds
	LV=CC D2	Derbyshire	v Hampshire	Derby
		Glamorgan	v Gloucestershire	Cardiff
		Kent	v Leicestershire	Canterbury
		Surrey	v Essex	The Oval
Sun Apr 27–Wed 30	LV=CC D1	Middlesex	v Yorkshire	Lord's
		Northamptonshire	v Lancashire	Northampton
		Nottinghamshire	v Warwickshire	Nottingham
		Sussex	v Somerset	Hove
	LV=CC D2	Gloucestershire	v Essex	Bristol
		Hampshire	v Surrey	Southampton
		Leicestershire	v Glamorgan	Leicester
		Worcestershire	v Derbyshire	Worcester

Sun May 4–Wed 7	LV=CC D1	Durham	v Yorkshire	Chester-le-St
		Lancashire	v Sussex	Manchester
		Somerset	v Nottinghamshire	Taunton
		Warwickshire	v Middlesex	Birmingham
	LV=CC D2	Essex	v Leicestershire	Chelmsford
		Glamorgan	v Worcestershire	Cardiff
		Kent	v Surrey	Canterbury
Mon May 5–Wed 7	Univs (nfc)	Durham MCCU	v Northamptonshire	Durham
		Hampshire	v Cardiff MCCU	Southampton
Tue May 6	ODI	**Ireland**	**v Sri Lanka**	**Clontarf**
Thu May 8	ODI	**Ireland**	**v Sri Lanka**	**Clontarf**
Fri May 9	ODI	**SCOTLAND**	**v ENGLAND**	**Aberdeen**
Sun May 11–Wed 14	LV=CC D1	Middlesex	v Lancashire	Lord's
		Nottinghamshire	v Northamptonshire	Nottingham
		Sussex	v Durham	Hove
		Yorkshire	v Warwickshire	Leeds
	LV=CC D2	Derbyshire	v Kent	Derby
		Hampshire	v Glamorgan	Southampton
		Surrey	v Gloucestershire	The Oval
Mon May 12–Wed 14	Univs (nfc)	Cambridge MCCU	v Worcestershire	Cambridge
Tue May 13	Tour match	Essex	v Sri Lankans	Chelmsford ⚲
Fri May 16	NW T20	Durham	v Worcestershire	Chester-le-St
		Gloucestershire	v Somerset	Bristol
		Hampshire	v Glamorgan	Southampton ⚲
		Leicestershire	v Derbyshire	Leicester
		Nottinghamshire	v Lancashire	Nottingham ⚲
		Sussex	v Surrey	Hove ⚲
		Yorkshire	v Northamptonshire	Leeds
	Tour match	Kent	v Sri Lankans	Canterbury ⚲
Sat May 17	NW T20	Lancashire	v Worcestershire	Manchester ⚲
		Middlesex	v Essex	Lord's
		Middlesex	v Sussex	Lord's
Sun May 18–Wed 21	LV=CC D1	Northamptonshire	v Middlesex	Northampton
	LV=CC D2	Gloucestershire	v Kent	Bristol
		Leicestershire	v Hampshire	Leicester
		Worcestershire	v Essex	Worcester
Sun May 18	NW T20	Somerset	v Surrey	Taunton
	Tour match (T20)	Sussex	v Sri Lankans	Hove
Mon May 19–Thu 22	LV=CC D1	Somerset	v Durham	Taunton
Mon May 19–Wed 21	Univs (nfc)	Loughboro MCCU	v Lancashire	Loughborough
Mon May 19	Friendly	MCC Women	v Rest of World Women	Lord's
Tue May 20	NW T20I	**ENGLAND**	**v SRI LANKA**	**The Oval ⚲**
Thu May 22	RL ODI	**ENGLAND**	**v SRI LANKA**	**The Oval ⚲**
Fri May 23	NW T20	Derbyshire	v Lancashire	Derby ⚲
		Essex	v Glamorgan	Chelmsford ⚲
		Gloucestershire	v Middlesex	Bristol
		Northamptonshire	v Leicestershire	Northampton ⚲
		Nottinghamshire	v Worcestershire	Nottingham
		Somerset	v Kent	Taunton
		Sussex	v Hampshire	Hove ⚲
		Warwickshire	v Yorkshire	Birmingham ⚲
	Varsity (T20)	Oxford U.	v Cambridge U.	Oxford

Sun May 25	RL ODI	**ENGLAND**	**v SRI LANKA**	**Chester-le-St**
Sun May 25–Wed 28	LV=CC D1	Nottinghamshire	v Durham	Nottingham
		Warwickshire	v Somerset	Birmingham
		Yorkshire	v Lancashire	Leeds
	LV=CC D2	Derbyshire	v Gloucestershire	Derby
		Essex	v Surrey	Chelmsford
		Glamorgan	v Leicestershire	Cardiff
		Kent	v Worcestershire	Tunbridge Wells
Sun May 25	NW T20	Middlesex	v Hampshire	Northwood
Mon May 26–Thu 29	LV=CC D1	Middlesex	v Sussex	Northwood
Wed May 28	RL ODI	**ENGLAND**	**v SRI LANKA**	**Manchester** ♀
Thu May 29	NW T20	Derbyshire	v Northamptonshire	Derby ♀
		Durham	v Lancashire	Chester-le-St
Fri May 30	NW T20	Glamorgan	v Sussex	Cardiff ♀
		Hampshire	v Essex	Southampton ♀
		Kent	v Gloucestershire	Canterbury
		Lancashire	v Warwickshire	Manchester ♀
		Nottinghamshire	v Durham	Nottingham
		Surrey	v Middlesex	The Oval ♀
		Worcestershire	v Northamptonshire	Worcester
		Yorkshire	v Derbyshire	Leeds
Sat May 31	RL ODI	**ENGLAND**	**v SRI LANKA**	**Lord's**
Sat May 31–Tue Jun 3	LV=CC D1	Northamptonshire	v Yorkshire	Northampton
Sun Jun 1–Wed 4	LV=CC D1	Durham	v Middlesex	Chester-le-St
		Lancashire	v Somerset	Manchester
		Sussex	v Nottinghamshire	Hove
	LV=CC D2	Essex	v Glamorgan	Chelmsford
		Hampshire	v Derbyshire	Southampton
		Surrey	v Worcestershire	The Oval
Sun Jun 1	NW T20	Leicestershire	v Warwickshire	Leicester
Mon Jun 2–Thu 5	LV=CC D2	Leicestershire	v Gloucestershire	Leicester
Tue Jun 3	RL ODI	**ENGLAND**	**v SRI LANKA**	**Birmingham** ♀
Thu Jun 5	NW T20	Hampshire	v Kent	Southampton ♀
Thu Jun 5–Sun 8	Tour match	Northamptonshire	v Sri Lankans	Northampton
Fri Jun 6	NW T20	Derbyshire	v Nottinghamshire	Derby ♀
		Kent	v Middlesex	Canterbury ♀
		Lancashire	v Yorkshire	Manchester ♀
		Leicestershire	v Worcestershire	Leicester
		Somerset	v Glamorgan	Taunton
		Surrey	v Essex	The Oval ♀
		Sussex	v Gloucestershire	Hove ♀
		Warwickshire	v Durham	Birmingham ♀
Sat Jun 7–Tue 10	LV=CC D2	Kent	v Essex	Canterbury
Sat Jun 7	NW T20	Worcestershire	v Durham	Worcester
Sun Jun 8–Wed 11	LV=CC D1	Somerset	v Sussex	Taunton
		Warwickshire	v Lancashire	Birmingham
		Yorkshire	v Nottinghamshire	Leeds
	LV=CC D2	Worcestershire	v Hampshire	Worcester
Sun Jun 8	NW T20	Gloucestershire	v Glamorgan	Bristol
Mon Jun 9–Thu 12	LV=CC D2	Gloucestershire	v Surrey	Bristol

Mon Jun 9–Wed 11	Univs (nfc)	Leeds/Brad MCCU	v Leicestershire	Weetwood
		Oxford MCCU	v Middlesex	Oxford
Wed Jun 11	NW T20	Kent	v Essex	Canterbury ♀
Thu Jun 12–Mon 16	1st Inv Test	**ENGLAND**	**v SRI LANKA**	Lord's
Fri Jun 13	NW T20	Derbyshire	v Worcestershire	Derby ♀
		Essex	v Gloucestershire	Chelmsford ♀
		Glamorgan	v Kent	Cardiff ♀
		Lancashire	v Leicestershire	Manchester ♀
		Northamptonshire	v Yorkshire	Northampton ♀
		Nottinghamshire	v Warwickshire	Nottingham
		Somerset	v Hampshire	Taunton
		Surrey	v Sussex	The Oval ♀
Sat Jun 14–Tue 17	LV=CC D1	Nottinghamshire	v Middlesex	Nottingham
Sun Jun 15–Wed 18	LV=CC D1	Durham	v Lancashire	Chester-le-St
		Northamptonshire	v Warwickshire	Northampton
	LV=CC D2	Derbyshire	v Surrey	Derby
		Glamorgan	v Kent	Cardiff
		Hampshire	v Essex	Southampton
		Leicestershire	v Worcestershire	Leicester
Sun Jun 15	NW T20	Sussex	v Somerset	Arundel
Mon Jun 16–Thu 19	LV=CC D1	Sussex	v Yorkshire	Arundel
Wed Jun 18	NW T20	Middlesex	v Somerset	The Oval
Thu Jun 19	NW T20	Leicestershire	v Nottinghamshire	Leicester
		Warwickshire	v Northamptonshire	Birmingham ♀
Fri Jun 20–Tue 24	2nd Inv Test	**ENGLAND**	**v SRI LANKA**	Leeds
Fri Jun 20	NW T20	Durham	v Leicestershire	Chester-le-St
		Essex	v Middlesex	Chelmsford ♀
		Glamorgan	v Surrey	Cardiff ♀
		Hampshire	v Gloucestershire	Southampton ♀
		Kent	v Sussex	Canterbury ♀
		Lancashire	v Northamptonshire	Manchester ♀
		Nottinghamshire	v Derbyshire	Nottingham
		Worcestershire	v Warwickshire	Worcester
	Varsity (o-d)	Oxford U.	v Cambridge U.	Lord's
Sat Jun 21–Tue 24	LV=CC D2	Gloucestershire	v Glamorgan	Bristol
Sun Jun 22–Wed 25	LV=CC D1	Durham	v Sussex	Chester-le-St
		Lancashire	v Northamptonshire	Manchester
		Nottinghamshire	v Somerset	Nottingham
		Warwickshire	v Yorkshire	Birmingham
	LV=CC D2	Kent	v Derbyshire	Canterbury
		Surrey	v Leicestershire	The Oval
Wed Jun 25	NW T20	Glamorgan	v Hampshire	Cardiff ♀
Thu Jun 26	NW T20	Middlesex	v Gloucestershire	Lord's ♀
Thu Jun 26–Sat 28	Tour match	Leicestershire	v Indians	Leicester
Fri Jun 27	NW T20	Derbyshire	v Warwickshire	Derby ♀
		Gloucestershire	v Kent	Bristol
		Northamptonshire	v Durham	Northampton ♀
		Somerset	v Essex	Taunton
		Surrey	v Hampshire	The Oval ♀
		Sussex	v Middlesex	Hove ♀
		Worcestershire	v Nottinghamshire	Worcester
		Yorkshire	v Lancashire	Leeds

Sat Jun 28–Tue Jul 1	LV=CC D2	Surrey	v Hampshire	The Oval
Sat Jun 28	NW T20	Nottinghamshire	v Yorkshire	Nottingham
Sun Jun 29–Wed Jul 2	LV=CC D1	Middlesex	v Northamptonshire	Lord's
		Somerset	v Lancashire	Taunton
		Warwickshire	v Nottinghamshire	Birmingham
	LV=CC D2	Essex	v Gloucestershire	Chelmsford
		Worcestershire	v Glamorgan	Worcester
Sun Jun 29	NW T20	Durham	v Derbyshire	Chester-le-St
Mon Jun 30–Thu Jul 3	Varsity	Oxford U.	v Cambridge U.	Oxford
Tue Jul 1	NW T20	Yorkshire	v Leicestershire	Leeds
Tue Jul 1–Thu 3	Tour match	Derbyshire	v Indians	Derby
Wed Jul 2	NW T20	Surrey	v Kent	The Oval 🏮
		Yorkshire	v Durham	Leeds
Thu Jul 3	NW T20	Middlesex	v Glamorgan	Richmond
		Northamptonshire	v Warwickshire	Northampton 🏮
Fri Jul 4	NW T20	Durham	v Nottinghamshire	Chester-le-St
		Essex	v Surrey	Chelmsford 🏮
		Glamorgan	v Somerset	Cardiff 🏮
		Gloucestershire	v Sussex	Bristol
		Kent	v Hampshire	Canterbury 🏮
		Leicestershire	v Northamptonshire	Leicester
		Warwickshire	v Lancashire	Birmingham 🏮
		Worcestershire	v Yorkshire	Worcester
Sat Jul 5	Friendly	MCC	v Rest of the World	Lord's
Sun Jul 6–Wed 9	LV=CC D1	Sussex	v Northamptonshire	Hove
	LV=CC D2	Glamorgan	v Surrey	Colwyn Bay
Sun Jul 6	NW T20	Derbyshire	v Leicestershire	Chesterfield
		Hampshire	v Somerset	Southampton
		Worcestershire	v Lancashire	Worcester
Mon Jul 7–Thu 10	LV=CC D1	Middlesex	v Somerset	Uxbridge
		Yorkshire	v Durham	Leeds
	LV=CC D2	Derbyshire	v Essex	Chesterfield
		Hampshire	v Gloucestershire	Southampton
		Leicestershire	v Kent	Leicester
Tue Jul 8	NW T20	Warwickshire	v Nottinghamshire	Birmingham 🏮
Wed Jul 9–Sun 13	1st Inv Test	**ENGLAND**	**v INDIA**	**Nottingham**
Fri Jul 11	NW T20	Durham	v Yorkshire	Chester-le-St
		Hampshire	v Middlesex	Southampton 🏮
		Leicestershire	v Lancashire	Leicester
		Northamptonshire	v Derbyshire	Northampton 🏮
		Somerset	v Gloucestershire	Taunton
		Surrey	v Glamorgan	The Oval 🏮
		Sussex	v Kent	Hove 🏮
		Warwickshire	v Worcestershire	Birmingham 🏮
Sat Jul 12–Tue 15	LV=CC D1	Northamptonshire	v Somerset	Northampton
Sat Jul 12	NW T20	Essex	v Kent	Colchester
Sun Jul 13–Wed 16	LV=CC D1	Durham	v Warwickshire	Chester-le-St
		Lancashire	v Nottinghamshire	Liverpool
	LV=CC D2	Essex	v Hampshire	Colchester
		Worcestershire	v Leicestershire	Worcester

Sun Jul 13	NW T20	Derbyshire	v Yorkshire	Chesterfield
Mon Jul 14–Thu 17	LV=CC D2	Gloucestershire	v Derbyshire	Cheltenham
Tue Jul 15	NW T20	Sussex	v Glamorgan	Hove ⚲
Wed Jul 16	NW T20	Surrey	v Somerset	The Oval ⚲
Thu Jul 17–Mon 21	2nd Inv Test	**ENGLAND**	**v INDIA**	**Lord's**
Fri Jul 18	NW T20	Glamorgan	v Essex	Cardiff ⚲
		Gloucestershire	v Surrey	Cheltenham
		Hampshire	v Sussex	Southampton ⚲
		Kent	v Somerset	Canterbury ⚲
		Lancashire	v Derbyshire	Manchester ⚲
		Leicestershire	v Durham	Leicester
		Northamptonshire	v Worcestershire	Northampton ⚲
		Yorkshire	v Warwickshire	Leeds
	Tour match	Unicorns	v Sri Lanka A	Gosforth
Sat Jul 19–Tue 22	LV=CC D1	Yorkshire	v Middlesex	Scarborough
Sun Jul 20–Wed 23	LV=CC D2	Derbyshire	v Glamorgan	Derby
		Surrey	v Kent	Guildford
Sun Jul 20	NW T20	Gloucestershire	v Essex	Cheltenham
		Nottinghamshire	v Leicestershire	Nottingham
	Tour match	Durham	v Sri Lanka A	Chester-le-St
Mon Jul 21–Thu 24	LV=CC D1	Sussex	v Warwickshire	Horsham
	LV=CC D2	Gloucestershire	v Worcestershire	Cheltenham
Tue Jul 22	NW T20	Essex	v Hampshire	Chelmsford ⚲
Wed Jul 23	NW T20	Northamptonshire	v Nottinghamshire	Northampton ⚲
Thu Jul 24	NW T20	Lancashire	v Durham	Manchester ⚲
		Middlesex	v Surrey	Lord's ⚲
Fri Jul 25	NW T20	Durham	v Northamptonshire	Chester-le-St
		Essex	v Sussex	Chelmsford
		Glamorgan	v Gloucestershire	Cardiff
		Kent	v Surrey	Canterbury
		Somerset	v Middlesex	Taunton
		Warwickshire	v Leicestershire	Birmingham
		Worcestershire	v Derbyshire	Worcester
		Yorkshire	v Nottinghamshire	Leeds
Sat Jul 26	RL ODC	Derbyshire	v Hampshire	Derby
		Glamorgan	v Middlesex	Cardiff
		Lancashire	v Yorkshire	Manchester ⚲
Sun Jul 27–Thu 31	3rd Inv Test	**ENGLAND**	**v INDIA**	**Southampton**
Sun Jul 27	RL ODC	Gloucestershire	v Northamptonshire	Cheltenham
		Lancashire	v Hampshire	Manchester ⚲
		Leicestershire	v Derbyshire	Leicester
		Middlesex	v Warwickshire	Lord's
		Somerset	v Durham	Taunton
		Surrey	v Glamorgan	Guildford
		Sussex	v Nottinghamshire	Horsham
		Worcestershire	v Essex	Worcester
Tue Jul 29	RL ODC	Kent	v Durham	Canterbury ⚲
		Northamptonshire	v Worcestershire	Milton Keynes
		Nottinghamshire	v Somerset	Nottingham
		Warwickshire	v Sussex	Birmingham ⚲
		Yorkshire	v Gloucestershire	Leeds

Wed Jul 30	RL ODC	Glamorgan	v Nottinghamshire	Cardiff ♟
Thu Jul 31		Durham	v Warwickshire	Chester-le-St
		Essex	v Leicestershire	Chelmsford ♟
		Gloucestershire	v Hampshire	Bristol
		Middlesex	v Surrey	Lord's
		Somerset	v Kent	Taunton
		Worcestershire	v Derbyshire	Worcester
	Tour match	Northamptonshire	v New Zealand A	Northampton
		Yorkshire	v Sri Lanka A	Leeds
Fri Aug 1	NW T20	**Quarter-final**		
Fri Aug 1–Mon 4	U19 Test	England U19	v South Africa U19	TBC
Sat Aug 2	NW T20	**Quarter-finals (2)**		
	Tour match	†Glamorgan	v Sri Lanka A	Cardiff
		†Warwickshire	v New Zealand A	Birmingham
Sun Aug 3	NW T20	**Quarter-final**		
Tue Aug 5	RL ODC	Essex	v Lancashire	Chelmsford
		Gloucestershire	v Leicestershire	Bristol
		Northamptonshire	v Yorkshire	Northampton ♟
		Surrey	v Kent	The Oval ♟
		Sussex	v Durham	Hove ♟
		Warwickshire	v Somerset	Birmingham ♟
	Tour match	Sri Lanka A	v New Zealand A	Taunton
Wed Aug 6	RL ODC	Hampshire	v Leicestershire	Southampton ♟
		Kent	v Glamorgan	Canterbury ♟
		Surrey	v Sussex	The Oval ♟
	Tour match	England Lions	v Sri Lanka A	Taunton
Thu Aug 7–Mon 11	4th Inv Test	**ENGLAND**	**v INDIA**	**Manchester**
Thu Aug 7	RL ODC	Derbyshire	v Lancashire	Derby ♟
		Middlesex	v Somerset	Lord's
		Yorkshire	v Worcestershire	Leeds
Thu Aug 7–Mon 10	U19 Test	England U19	v South Africa U19	Northampton
Fri Aug 8	RL ODC	Essex	v Gloucestershire	Chelmsford ♟
		Glamorgan	v Durham	Cardiff ♟
		Hampshire	v Northamptonshire	Southampton ♟
		Leicestershire	v Yorkshire	Leicester
		Nottinghamshire	v Kent	Nottingham ♟
		Sussex	v Middlesex	Hove ♟
	Tour match	England Lions	v New Zealand A	Bristol
Sat Aug 9	RL ODC	Worcestershire	v Lancashire	Worcester
	Tour match	Sri Lanka A	v New Zealand A	Bristol
Sun Aug 10	RL ODC	Derbyshire	v Essex	Derby
		Durham	v Middlesex	Chester-le-St
		Leicestershire	v Northamptonshire	Leicester
		Nottinghamshire	v Surrey	Nottingham
		Somerset	v Sussex	Taunton
		Warwickshire	v Kent	Rugby
Mon Aug 11	RL ODC	Hampshire	v Worcestershire	Southampton ♟
		Northamptonshire	v Derbyshire	Northampton ♟
		Yorkshire	v Essex	Scarborough
	Tour match	England Lions	v Sri Lanka A	Worcester

† *These fixtures are provisional, and may be rescheduled to Friday August 1 or Sunday August 3 if Glamorgan or Warwickshire reach the NatWest T20 Blast quarter-finals.*

Tue Aug 12	**RL ODC**	Durham	v Nottinghamshire	Chester-le-St
		Gloucestershire	v Lancashire	Bristol
		Somerset	v Glamorgan	Taunton
		Warwickshire	v Surrey	Birmingham ♥
	Tour match	England Lions	v New Zealand A	Worcester
Wed Aug 13–Sat 16	**Women's Test**	**ENGLAND W**	**v INDIA W**	**Wormsley**
Wed Aug 13	**RL ODC**	Essex	v Hampshire	Chelmsford ♥
		Kent	v Sussex	Canterbury ♥
		Worcestershire	v Gloucestershire	Worcester
		Yorkshire	v Derbyshire	Scarborough
Thu Aug 14	**RL ODC**	Durham	v Surrey	Chester-le-St
		Glamorgan	v Warwickshire	Swansea
		Lancashire	v Northamptonshire	Manchester ♥
		Leicestershire	v Worcestershire	Leicester
		Middlesex	v Nottinghamshire	Lord's ♥
	Tour match	Hampshire	v Sri Lanka A	Southampton
Fri Aug 15–Tue 19	**5th Inv Test**	**ENGLAND**	**v INDIA**	**The Oval**
Fri Aug 15–Mon 18	**LV=CC D1**	Lancashire	v Durham	Manchester
		Northamptonshire	v Nottinghamshire	Northampton
		Somerset	v Warwickshire	Taunton
		Yorkshire	v Sussex	Scarborough
	LV=CC D2	Glamorgan	v Essex	Swansea
		Kent	v Hampshire	Canterbury
		Leicestershire	v Surrey	Leicester
		Worcestershire	v Gloucestershire	Worcester
Fri Aug 15	**U19 ODI**	England U19	v South Africa U19	Birmingham
Sun Aug 17	**U19 ODI**	England U19	v South Africa U19	Nottingham
Mon Aug 18	**Tour match**	Ireland	v Sri Lanka A	TBC
	U19 ODI	England U19	v South Africa U19	Nottingham
Wed Aug 20	**RL ODC**	Kent	v Middlesex	Canterbury ♥
		Nottinghamshire	v Warwickshire	Nottingham ♥
		Surrey	v Somerset	The Oval ♥
		Sussex	v Glamorgan	Hove ♥
	Tour match	Ireland	v Sri Lanka A	TBC
	U19 ODI	England U19	v South Africa U19	Leicester
Thu Aug 21	**Women's ODI**	**ENGLAND W**	**v INDIA W**	**Scarborough**
	RL ODC	Derbyshire	v Gloucestershire	Derby ♥
		Hampshire	v Yorkshire	Southampton ♥
		Lancashire	v Leicestershire	Manchester ♥
		Northamptonshire	v Essex	Northampton ♥
Fri Aug 22	**Tour match**	Middlesex	v Indians	Lord's
	Tour match	Ireland	v Sri Lanka A	TBC
	U19 ODI	England U19	v South Africa U19	Derby ♥
Sat Aug 23	**Women's ODI**	**ENGLAND W**	**v INDIA W**	**Scarborough**
	NW T20	**Semi-finals and final**		Birmingham
Mon Aug 25	**Women's ODI**	**ENGLAND W**	**v INDIA W**	**Lord's**
	Tour match	Kent	v New Zealand A	Canterbury
	RL ODI	**ENGLAND**	**v INDIA**	**Bristol**
Tue Aug 26	**RL ODC**	**Quarter-final**		
Wed Aug 27	**RL ODI**	**ENGLAND**	**v INDIA**	**Cardiff**
Thu Aug 28	**RL ODC**	**Quarter-finals (2)**		

Fri Aug 29	**RL ODC**	**Quarter-final**	
Sat Aug 30	**RL ODI**	**ENGLAND** v **INDIA**	**Nottingham**
Sun Aug 31–Wed Sep 3	**LV=CC D1**	Durham v Nottinghamshire	Chester-le-St
		Lancashire v Yorkshire	Manchester
		Middlesex v Warwickshire	Lord's
		Somerset v Northamptonshire	Taunton
	LV=CC D2	Derbyshire v Worcestershire	Derby
		Hampshire v Leicestershire	Southampton
		Kent v Glamorgan	Canterbury
Sun Aug 31–Tue Sep 2	**Tour match**	Surrey v New Zealand A	The Oval
Mon Sep 1	**Women's T20I**	**ENGLAND W** v **S. AFRICA W**	**Chelmsford**
Tue Sep 2	**RL ODI**	**ENGLAND** v **INDIA**	**Birmingham**
Wed Sep 3	**Women's T20I**	**ENGLAND W** v **S. AFRICA W**	**Northampton**
Thu Sep 4	**RL ODC**	**Semi-final**	
Fri Sep 5	**RL ODI**	**ENGLAND** v **INDIA**	**Leeds**
Sat Sep 6	**RL ODC**	**Semi-final**	
Sun Sep 7	**NW T20I**	**ENGLAND** v **INDIA**	**Birmingham**
	Women's T20I	**ENGLAND W** v **S. AFRICA W**	**Birmingham**
	Village Cup	**Final**	Lord's
Tue Sep 9–Fri 12	**LV=CC D1**	Middlesex v Durham	Lord's
		Nottinghamshire v Yorkshire	Nottingham
		Sussex v Lancashire	Hove
		Warwickshire v Northamptonshire	Birmingham
	LV=CC D2	Essex v Kent	Chelmsford
		Glamorgan v Derbyshire	Cardiff
		Gloucestershire v Leicestershire	Bristol
		Worcestershire v Surrey	Worcester
Mon Sep 15–Thu 18	**LV=CC D1**	Durham v Northamptonshire	Chester-le-St
		Nottinghamshire v Sussex	Nottingham
		Somerset v Middlesex	Taunton
	LV=CC D2	Hampshire v Kent	Southampton
		Leicestershire v Essex	Leicester
		Surrey v Derbyshire	The Oval
Sat Sep 20	**RL ODC**	**Final**	Lord's
Tue Sep 23–Fri 26	**LV=CC D1**	Lancashire v Middlesex	Manchester
		Northamptonshire v Sussex	Northampton
		Warwickshire v Durham	Birmingham
		Yorkshire v Somerset	Leeds
	LV=CC D2	Derbyshire v Leicestershire	Derby
		Essex v Worcestershire	Chelmsford
		Glamorgan v Hampshire	Cardiff
		Kent v Gloucestershire	Canterbury

JOHN WISDEN IN LEAMINGTON

Stephen Baldwin

Leamington expanded rapidly during the early years of the 19th century, establishing a reputation as a health spa, but by the 1840s it had lost some of its lustre. It was agreed that, as part of a relaunch, top-class cricket should be established in the town, so arrangements were made for William Clarke to pay a visit with his recently formed All-England XI.

On the morning of September 21, 1848, a team made up of England's best cricketers turned the corner at Archery Villa (now The Cricketers pub) and entered the local ground, where XXII of Leamington and District awaited them. Sadly, an overnight thunderstorm ended the game with the locals 40 ahead and one second-innings wicket left. But the die had been cast.

John Wisden did not play in this match, but George Parr did, and it was he who came back later that year to supervise the levelling of the rough terrain and turn it in to a leading cricket venue. In March 1849, Wisden joined Parr in a partnership that was to administer the ground, and play a leading role in professional cricket for the next 20 years.

Lord Guernsey, the local MP, a county-standard cricketer and a future president of MCC, became Wisden's patron, and promised the new partnership his support. The prestige fixtures soon arrived. In both 1849 and 1850, after the South v North fixture was played at Lord's, the return match was held at Leamington. In these two games – now considered the ground's only first-class matches – the North, who included Wisden, Parr and Guernsey, won convincingly.

Barbara Baldwin

Leaving his mark: 129 years after his death, John Wisden is remembered in Leamington.

Also launched was Parr & Wisden's Leamington Cricket Club, which became a focus for the best players in the area. "Warwickshire" beat "Worcestershire" here, and in 1850 a team representing Leamington (including Wisden, Parr and Guernsey) beat good MCC sides home and away – the home game won by an innings. The Gentlemen of Warwickshire made the ground their base, and visitors included I Zingari and the Free Foresters. Local clubs hired it for prestigious matches.

Wisden's business sense told him it would not be sustained by cricket alone, and an advert soon offered its use for the exercise of hunting horses. In 1852, the Royal National Archery Meeting took place here. In 1858, the partners introduced the game of bowls, and the space beside it is now a national centre for the sport.

Although there is evidence of Parr and Wisden living in Leamington around 1850, the development of professional cricket – in particular the touring XIs –

JOHN WISDEN (1826-1884)
Cricketer and Almanack Publisher

A cricket ground was created near this spot in 1849 by John Wisden and his friend and fellow player, George Parr. Many important matches were played here to large crowds. Wisden lived in the town from 1848 to 1852. In 1850 he founded John Wisden & Co. probably selling sporting equipment. They gave up the lease of the ground in 1863. His obituary in his Almanack in the 1885 edition reads:

"...A quiet, unassuming and thoroughly upright man. A fast friend and generous employer. Beloved by his intimates and employees and respected by all in whom he came in contact."

Barbara Baldwin

In November 2013, a plaque commemorating Wisden's role in Leamington was unveiled by ex-England captain M. J. K. Smith. It is mounted on the former Archery Villa (now The Cricketers).

took them away, and the day-to-day operation passed to people who were based locally. However, Wisden maintained his support for the ground and club: in the week he launched the United All-England XI, he returned to resolve a dispute with Coventry about a fixture.

By the mid-1850s, Parr and Wisden were the leading professional cricketers in England. Following William Clarke's death in 1856, the Leamington partnership helped heal the rift between the two touring sides – Clarke's All-England and the breakaway United All-England XI – before setting up the Cricketers Fund Friendly Society (1857) and organising the first overseas tour, to the USA and Canada (1859).

After Wisden retired from professional cricket in 1863, he and Parr gave up their lease on the Leamington ground. However, it continued to be a focus for top-class cricket, and the meeting that gave birth to Warwickshire County Cricket Club was held in the nearby Regent Hotel. Even though he was busy holding together an increasingly factious cadre of professional cricketers, Wisden continued to take an interest in Leamington cricket, on one occasion travelling to Paris with a local team to act as umpire.

Following Parr & Wisden's side, a succession of cricket teams represented Leamington until 1899, when they were reformed into the present Leamington CC. The club field two teams in the Birmingham Premier League, two in the Cotswold Hills League, and a wide range of other sides. Part of the original ground is now two residential streets, but the remainder, these days known as Victoria Park, includes a cricket pitch and is used for many sports events.

Stephen Baldwin, a former player at Leamington CC, is currently researching the life of John Wisden.

ERRATA

Wisden 1948	Page 311	The headings "Surrey Bowling" and "Glamorgan Bowling" should be reversed.
Wisden 1972	Page 892	W. R. Hammond's Australian tour record of 1,553, which G. Boycott nearly broke, was in 1928-29 not 1938-39.
Wisden 1978	Page 807	In the Hertfordshire averages, J. W. D. Wright should be J. D. W. Wright.
Wisden 1982	Page 1196	Leonard Crawley played for Essex from 1926 to 1936; his 118 against Glamorgan and his first-ball dismissal against Worcestershire were in 1936, not 1937.
Wisden 1991	Page 1124	D. S. Berry, not C. R. Miller, should have the wicketkeeper's dagger. This was incorrectly stated to be on page 112 in Errata of *Wisden 2012*.
Wisden 2003	Page 1075	Saffron Walden's opening bowler in the National Club final was J. Sparrow, not R. Sparrow.
Wisden 2013	Page 102	Michael Holding bowled from The Oval's Vauxhall End, not the Nursery End.
	Page 212	George Chesterton flew Stirling bombers, not Sterling, during the Second World War.
	Page 215	Kevin Curran died near Mutare, not in Harare.
	Page 238	David Randall's middle name was Michael, not Aaron.
	Page 261	Tim Bresnan should appear in the list of England Players in 2012.
	Page 340	Leicestershire's match with the Australians was initially reduced to 47 overs a side.
	Pages 415–19	Twenty players appearing for more than one team lost their catches/ stumpings in the first-class averages. Their fielding figures were as follows (in order of batting average): N. R. D. Compton 9; K. P. Pietersen 2; C. Kieswetter 32/2; J. M. Bairstow 24; I. R. Bell 11; J. E. Root 13; J. W. A. Taylor 10; M. J. Prior 20/4; A. N. Petersen 10; J. A. Rudolph 4; S. R. Patel 10; Z. S. Ansari 4; W. S. Jones 5; S. C. Meaker 1; G. P. Swann 6; V. D. Philander 3; J. Leach 2; J. A. Brooks 3; S. C. Kerrigan 4; S. T. Finn 8.
	Page 420 and Page 471	T. S. Mills bowled 129.1 overs not 129.2.
	Page 489	Glamorgan's first innings v Essex lasted 65.5 overs not 66, and Mills bowled 8.5 overs not 9.
	Page 564	Middlesex's List A record total of 350-6 in 2012 was against Lancashire.
	Page 643	Abdur Rehman knocked over the Sussex tail, not Somerset's.
	Page 816	It was the first time that no batsman had scored a century for Ireland in a calendar year since 1995, not just 2005.
	Page 961	There should be a dagger before Abul Hasan's name to signify that he was the only No. 10 batsman to score a century on Test debut.
	Page 974	The NCL winners in 2008-09 were Rajshahi, and the team who scored 187-6 in the BCB Cup final were Bangladesh A.
	Page 1054	In the first Twenty20 international against Pakistan, Australia were 32-2 after six overs, not 82-2.
	Page 1238	Shoaib Ahmed's 152 came in his second first-class match, not on debut.
	Page 1314	J. M. Anderson should appear at No. 29 in the list of Most Test Wickets, with 288.
	Page 1384	The ninth-wicket record in Twenty20 internationals was 47* by G. C. Wilson and M. C. Sorensen for Ireland v Bangladesh at Belfast, 2012.
	Page 1532	S. F. Barnes took his 17 wickets against South Africa in December 1913, not 1914.

CHARITIES IN 2013

ARUNDEL CASTLE CRICKET FOUNDATION – over 300,000 disadvantaged youngsters, many with special needs, mainly from inner-city areas (and London's boroughs in particular), have received instruction and encouragement at Arundel since 1986. In 2013, more than 100 days were devoted to activities; over 5,000 young people benefited. Director of cricket: John Barclay, Arundel Park, Sussex BN18 9LH. Tel: 01903 882602; website: www.arundelcastlecricketfoundation.co.uk

THE BRIAN JOHNSTON MEMORIAL TRUST supports cricket for the blind, and aims to ease the financial worries of talented young players through scholarships. The BJMT spin-bowling programme, in support of the ECB, was launched in 2010 to provide expert coaching to all the first-class county Academies and the MCCUs. Registered Charity No. 1045946. Trust administrator: Richard Anstey, 178 Manor Drive North, Worcester Park, Surrey KT4 7RU. Email: contact@lords-taverners.org; website: www.lordstaverners.org

BRITISH ASSOCIATION FOR CRICKETERS WITH DISABILITIES was formed in 1991 to promote playing opportunities for cricketers with physical and learning difficulties. We work in close partnership with the ECB. Chairman: Bill Higginson. Tel: 01544 260315 (home/office), 07455 219526 (mobile); email: b.higgi4@yahoo.co.uk

BUNBURY CRICKET CLUB has raised more than £15m for national charities and local good causes for over 26 years, although it is not a registered charity. In 2012, the Bunbury-sponsored ESCA Under-15 festival – which has produced 64 England players, and 318 first-class cricketers – was held at Monmouth School. Founder: Dr David English CBE, 1 Highwood Cottages, Nan Clark's Lane, London NW7 4HJ; website: www.bunburycricket.com

CAPITAL KIDS CRICKET, formed in 1990, delivers cricket tuition to boys and girls in state schools throughout inner London, assists emerging clubs, organises competitions in local communities, and offers out-of-London residential festivals, frequently at Arundel Castle in Sussex. Its British Land Kids Cricket League involves 2,500 primary schoolchildren. William Greaves, 5 The Courtyard, London N1 1JZ. Tel: 020 7609 1988; website: www.capitalkidscricket.co.uk

CRICKET FOR CHANGE has used sport to change young lives since 1981, developing pioneering projects aimed at disadvantaged young people, running its Street20 version of the game with Chance to Shine's "StreetChance", and the Metropolitan Police in London. The charity's "Hit the Top" is still one of the world's largest disability sports programmes, with many Hit The Top clubs, and new projects always being delivered. Recent overseas work includes initiatives such as "Street20 Europe" in partnership with ICC Europe, along with building work in Afghanistan, Israel and the West Bank, Brazil, Jamaica, Barbados, France, Serbia, Rwanda, Uganda, Sri Lanka, India, Bangladesh and New York. Chief executive: Andy Sellins, The Cricket Centre, Plough Lane, Wallington, Surrey SM6 8JQ. Tel: 020 8669 2177; email: office@cricketforchange.org.uk; website: www.cricketforchange.org.uk

THE CRICKET FOUNDATION – Chance to Shine, the Foundation's charitable campaign to keep cricket alive in state schools, is one of the biggest sport-for-development programmes in the UK. It is now running in 9,000 schools, and over 2m children have enjoyed cricketing opportunities as a result. Chief executive: Wasim Khan MBE, Lord's Cricket Ground, London NW8 8QZ. Tel: 020 7432 1259; website: www.chancetoshine.org

THE CRICKET SOCIETY TRUST's principal aim is to support schools and organisations to encourage enjoyment of the game and to develop skills. Particular attention is given to children with special needs, through programmes arranged with the Arundel Castle Cricket Foundation and the Belvoir Castle Cricket Trust. Hon. secretary: Ken Merchant, 16 Louise Road, Rayleigh, Essex SS6 8LW. Tel: 01268 747414; website: www.cricketsocietytrust.com

THE DICKIE BIRD FOUNDATION, set up by the former umpire in 2004, helps financially disadvantaged young people aged under 18 to participate in the sport of their choice. Grants are made towards the cost of equipment and clothing. Trustee: Ted Cowley, 3 The Tower, Tower Drive, Arthington Lane, Pool-in-Wharfedale, Otley, Yorkshire LS21 1NQ. Tel: 07503 641457; website: www.thedickiebirdfoundation.co.uk

ENGLAND AND WALES CRICKET TRUST was established in 2005 to aid community participation in cricket, with a fund from which to make interest-free loans to amateur clubs. In its latest financial year it incurred costs on charitable activities of £8.6m – primarily grants to cricket charities and county boards to support their programmes. Trustee: Brian Havill, Lord's Cricket Ground, London NW8 8QZ. Tel: 020 7432 1201; email: brian.havill@ecb.co.uk

THE EVELINA LONDON CHILDREN'S HOSPITAL has become the official charity partner of Surrey CCC and The Kia Oval. Ten minutes from the ground, in Waterloo, Evelina is one of the country's leading children's hospitals, treating patients from all over the south-east of England. Partnership head: Jon Surtees, The Kia Oval, Kennington, London SE11 5SS. Tel: 020 7820 5780; website: kiaoval.com

FIELDS IN TRUST is the only national charity protecting and improving outdoor space for sport, play and recreation. Find out how to protect and improve your outdoor recreational space at www.fieldsintrust.org. Follow us on Facebook at www.facebook.com/fieldsintrust. Chief executive: Helen Griffiths, 15 Crinan Street, London N1 9SQ. Tel: 020 7427 2110; websites: www.fieldsintrust.org and www.fit-fields-toolkit.org

THE HORNSBY PROFESSIONAL CRICKETERS' FUND, established in 1928 from a bequest from the estate of J. H. J. Hornsby (Middlesex, MCC and the Gentlemen), supports former professionals and their families, both through regular financial help or one-off grants towards healthcare or similar essential needs. Secretary of trust: The Rev. Prebendary Mike Vockins OBE, Birchwood Lodge, Birchwood, Storridge, Malvern, Worcestershire WR13 5EZ. Tel: 01886 884366.

THE LEARNING FOR A BETTER WORLD (LBW) TRUST, established in 2006, provides tertiary education to disadvantaged students in the cricket-playing countries of the developing world. In 2013 it was assisting some 800 students in India, Pakistan, Nepal, Uganda, Afghanistan, Sri Lanka and South Africa, a commitment which will expand further over the course of 2014. Chairman: Darshak Mehta, GPO Box 3029, Sydney, NSW 2000, Australia; website: www.lbwtrust.com.au

THE LORD'S TAVERNERS is the official charity of recreational cricket, and the UK's leading youth cricket and disability sports charity, whose mission is "to give young people a sporting chance". This year the charity will donate over £3m to help young people of all abilities and backgrounds to participate in cricket and other sporting activities. Registered Charity No. 306054. The Lord's Taverners, 10 Buckingham Place, London SW1E 6HX. Tel: 020 7821 2828; email: contact@lordstaverners.org; website: www.lordstaverners.org

THE PCA BENEVOLENT FUND is part of the commitment of the Professional Cricketers' Association to aid current and former players and their dependants in times of hardship and upheaval, or to help them readjust to the world beyond the game. Assistant chief executive: Jason Ratcliffe, PCA, The Kia Oval, Kennington, London SE11 5SS. Tel: 07768 558050; website: www.thepca.co.uk

THE PRIMARY CLUB provides sporting and recreational facilities for the blind and partially sighted. Membership is nominally restricted to those dismissed first ball in any form of cricket; almost 10,000 belong. In total, the club has raised £3m, helped by sales of its tie, popularised by *Test Match Special*. Andrew Strauss is president of the Primary Club Juniors. Hon. secretary: Chris Larlham, PO Box 12121, Saffron Walden, Essex CB10 2ZF. Tel: 01799 586507; website: www.primaryclub.org

THE PRINCE'S TRUST CRICKET PROGRAMMES harness the power of the game to support the engagement and positive development of young people aged 14–25 who are unemployed or struggling with education. Through partnerships with the county boards and clubs, they gain cricket qualifications, complete work placements and attend coaching sessions, motivational talks, competitions and workshops. National programme manager: Rebecca Pike, The Prince's Trust, 18 Park Square East, London NW1 4LH. Tel: 020 7543 7315; website: www.princes-trust.org.uk

THE TOM MAYNARD TRUST – formed in 2012 after Tom's tragic death – covers four main areas: helping aspiring young professionals with education projects, currently across four sports; running an academy in Spain for young county cricketers on the first rung of the career ladder; providing grants for sportspeople to help with travel, kit, coaching, training and education; and helping establish a scholarship at Tom's former school. Contact: Mike Fatkin, 67a Radnor Road, Canton, Cardiff CF5 1RA; website: www.tommaynardtrust.com

YOUTH TRUSTS – most of the first-class counties operate youth trusts through which donations, legacies and the proceeds of fundraising are channelled for the development of youth cricket, and cricket in the community. Information may be obtained from the county chief executives.

CRICKET TRADE DIRECTORY

BOOKSELLERS

AARDVARK BOOKS, Flat 1, Weydale House, Weydale Avenue, Scarborough, North Yorkshire YO12 6AH. Email: pete@aardvarkcricketbooks.co.uk. Peter Taylor specialises in *Wisdens*, including rare hardbacks and early editions. Catalogues sent on request. *Wisdens* purchased. Restoration, cleaning and gilding undertaken.

ACUMEN BOOKS, Pennyfields, New Road, Bignall End, Stoke-on-Trent ST7 8QF. Tel: 01782 720753; email: wca@acumenbooks.co.uk; website: www.acumenbooks.co.uk. Everything for umpires, scorers, officials, etc. MCC Lawbooks, open-learning manuals, Tom Smith and other textbooks, Duckworth/Lewis, scorebooks, equipment, over & run counters, gauges, heavy and Hi-Vis bails, etc; import/export.

BOUNDARY BOOKS, The Haven, West Street, Childrey OX12 9UL. Tel: 01235 751021; email: mike@boundarybooks.com. Rare and second-hand books, autographs and memorabilia bought and sold. Catalogues issued. Large Oxfordshire showroom open by appointment. Unusual and scarce items always available.

CHRISTOPHER SAUNDERS, Kingston House, High Street, Newnham-on-Severn, Gloucestershire GL14 1BB. Tel: 01594 516030; email: chris@cricket-books.com; website: www.cricket-books.com. Office/bookroom open by appointment. Second-hand/antiquarian cricket books and memorabilia bought and sold. Regular catalogues issued containing selections from over 12,000 items in stock.

GRACE BOOKS AND CARDS (TED KIRWAN), Donkey Cart Cottage, Main Street, Bruntingthorpe, Lutterworth, Leics LE17 5QE. Tel: 0116 247 8417; email: ted@gracecricketana.co.uk. Second-hand and antiquarian cricket books, *Wisdens*, autographed material and cricket ephemera of all kinds. Now also modern postcards of current international cricketers.

JOHN JEFFERS, The Old Mill, Aylesbury Road, Wing, Leighton Buzzard LU7 0PG. Tel: 01296 688543; mobile: 07846 537692; e-mail: edgwarerover@live.co.uk. *Wisden* specialist. Immediate decision and top settlement for purchase of *Wisden* collections. Why wait for the next auction? Why pay the auctioneer's commission anyway?

J. W. McKENZIE, 12 Stoneleigh Park Road, Ewell, Epsom, Surrey KT19 0QT. Tel: 020 8393 7700; email: mckenziecricket@btconnect.com; website: www.mckenzie-cricket.co.uk. Specialist since 1971. Antiquarian and second-hand cricket books and memorabilia bought and sold. Regular catalogues issued. Large shop premises open regular business hours, 30 minutes from London Waterloo. Please phone before visiting.

KEN FAULKNER, 65 Brookside, Wokingham, Berkshire RG41 2ST. Tel: 0118 978 5255. Email: kfaulkner@bowmore.demon.co.uk; website: www.bowmore.demon.co.uk. Bookroom open by appointment. My stall, with a strong *Wisden* content, will be operating at the Cheltenham Cricket Festival in July 2014. We purchase *Wisden* collections which include pre-1946 editions.

MARTIN WOOD CRICKET BOOKS, 1c Wickenden Road, Sevenoaks, Kent TN13 3PJ. Tel: 01732 457205; email: martin@martinwoodcricketbooks.com; website: www.martinwoodcricketbooks.co.uk. Established 1970.

ROGER PAGE, 10 Ekari Court, Yallambie, Victoria 3085, Australia. Tel: (+61) 3 9435 6332; email: rpcricketbooks@unite.com.au; website: www.rpcricketbooks.com. Australia's only full-time dealer in new and second-hand cricket books. Distributor of overseas cricket annuals and magazines. Agent for Association of Cricket Statisticians and Cricket Memorabilia Society.

ST MARY'S BOOKS & PRINTS, 9 St Mary's Hill, Stamford, Lincolnshire PE9 2DP. Tel: 01780 763033; email: info@stmarysbooks.com; website: www.stmarysbooks.com. Dealers in *Wisdens* 1864–2012, second-hand, rare cricket books and *Vanity Fair* prints. Book-search service offered.

SPORTSPAGES, 7 Finns Business Park, Mill Lane, Farnham, Surrey GU10 5RX. Tel: 01252 851040; email: info@sportspages.com; website: www.sportspages.com. Large stock of *Wisdens*, fine sports books and memorabilia, including cricket, rugby, football and golf. Books and memorabilia also purchased, please offer.

TIM BEDDOW, 66 Oak Road, Oldbury, West Midlands B68 0BD. Tel: 0121 421 7117; mobile: 07956 456112; email: wisden1864@hotmail.com. Wanted: cash paid for football, cricket, speedway, motorsport and rugby union memorabilia, badges, books, programmes (amateur and professional), autographed items, match tickets, yearbooks and photographs – anything considered.

WILLIAM H. ROBERTS, Long Low, 27 Gernhill Avenue, Fixby, Huddersfield, West Yorkshire HD2 2HR. Tel: 01484 654463; email: william.roberts2@virgin.net; website: www.williamroberts-cricket.com. Second-hand/antiquarian cricket books, *Wisdens*, autographs and memorabilia bought and sold.

WILLOWS PUBLISHING, 17 The Willows, Stone, Staffordshire ST15 0DE. Tel: 01785 814700; email: jenkins.willows@ntlworld.com; website: www.willowsreprints.com. *Wisden* reprints 1864–1946.

WISDEN DIRECT, website: www.wisden.com. Various editions of *Wisden Cricketers' Almanack* since 2001 and other Wisden publications, all at discounted prices.

WISDENS.ORG, Tel: 07793 060706; email: wisdens@cridler.com; website: www.wisdens.org. The unofficial *Wisden* collectors' website. New look for 2014. Valuations, guide, discussion forum, all free to use. We also buy and sell *Wisdens* for our members. Email us for free advice about absolutely anything to do with collecting *Wisdens*.

WISDENWORLD.COM, Tel: 01480 819272; email: info@wisdenworld.com; website: www.wisdenworld.com. A unique and friendly service; quality *Wisdens* bought and sold at fair prices, along with free advice on the value of your collection. The UK's largest *Wisden*-only seller.

AUCTIONEERS

ANTHEMION AUCTIONS, 15 Norwich Road, Cardiff CF23 9AB. Tel: 029 2047 2444; email: anthemions@aol.com; website: www.anthemionauctions.com. Sporting memorabilia specialists with an international clientele and extensive dedicated database of buyers.

CHRISTIE'S, 8 King Street, St. James's, London SW1Y 6QT. Tel: 0207 389 2674; email: rneelands@christies.com; website: www.christies.com. Christie's were the MCC's auctioneer of choice in 1987 and again in 2010. Rare and valuable cricket books are the firm's particular specialty. For valuations of complete collections or single items, contact Rupert Neelands, a senior book specialist.

DOMINIC WINTER, Specialist Auctioneers & Valuers, Mallard House, Broadway Lane, South Cerney, Gloucestershire GL7 5UQ. Tel: 01285 860006; website: www.dominicwinter.co.uk. Check our website for forthcoming specialist sales.

GRAHAM BUDD AUCTIONS in association with Sotheby's, PO Box 47519, London N14 6XD. Tel: 020 8366 2525; website: www.grahambuddauctions.co.uk. Specialist auctioneer of sporting memorabilia.

KNIGHTS WISDEN, Norfolk. Tel: 01263 768488; email: tim@knights.co.uk; website: www.knightswisden.co.uk. Established and respected auctioneers; two specialist *Wisden* auctions and three major cricket/sporting memorabilia auctions per year. World-record *Wisden* prices achieved in 2007. *Wisden* auctions: April and September. Entries invited.

MULLOCK'S SPECIALIST AUCTIONEERS & VALUERS, The Old Shippon, Wall under Heywood, Church Stretton, Shropshire SY6 7DS. Tel: 01694 771771; email: info@mullocksauctions.co.uk; website: www.mullocksauctions.co.uk. For worldwide exposure, contact Europe's No. 1 sporting auction specialists. Regular cricket sales are held throughout the year and are fully illustrated on our website.

WISDENAUCTION.COM. Tel: 07793 060706; email: wisdenauction@cridler.com; website: www.wisdenauction.com. A specially designed auction website for buying and selling *Wisdens*. List your spares today and bid live for that missing year. No sale, no fee. Many books ending daily. Built by collectors for collectors, with the best descriptions on the internet. See advert on page 174.

CRICKET DATABASES

CSW DATABASE FOR PCs. Contact Ric Finlay, email: ricf@netspace.net.au; website: www.tastats.com.au. Men's and Women's International, IPL, Australian, NZ and English domestic. Full scorecards and over 2,000 records. Suitable for professionals and hobbyists alike.

WISDEN RECORDS: www.wisdenrecords.com. Up-to-date, in-depth cricket records from *Wisden*.

CRICKET EQUIPMENT

ALL ROUNDER CRICKET, 39 St Michaels Lane, Headingley, Leeds LS6 3BR. Tel: 0113 203 3679; email: info@allroundercricket.com; website: www.allroundercricket.com. One of the UK's leading cricket retailers, stocking all the top brands, hand-picked by ex-professionals. Open every day. Also online with next day delivery available.

BARRINGTON SPORTS, Northgame House, Haig Road, Parkgate Industrial Estate, Knutsford WA16 8DX. Tel: 01565 650269; email: customerservices@barringtonsports.com; website: www.barringtonsports.com. Barrington Sports, the cricket specialist, has been providing first-class products and advice to cricketers of all levels for over 30 years.

CHASE CRICKET, Dummer Down Farm, Basingstoke, Hampshire RG25 2AR. Tel: 01256 397499; email: info@chasecricket.co.uk; website: www.chasecricket.co.uk. Chase Cricket specialises in handmade bats and hi-tech soft goods. Established 1996. "Support British Manufacturing."

DUKE SPORTSWEAR, Unit 4, Magdalene Road, Torquay, Devon TQ1 4AF. Tel: 01803 292012; email: dukeknitwear@btconnect.com. Test-standard sweaters to order in your club colours, using the finest yarns.

FORDHAM SPORTS, 81/85 Robin Hood Way, Kingston Vale, London SW15 3PW. Tel: 020 8974 5654; email: fordham@fordhamsports.co.uk; website: fordhamsports.co.uk. Cricket, hockey and rugby equipment specialist with largest range of branded stock in London at discounted prices. Mail order available.

STUART & WILLIAMS (BOLA), 6 Brookfield Road, Cotham, Bristol BS6 5PQ. Tel: 0117 924 3569; email: info@bola.co.uk; website: www.bola.co.uk. Manufacturer of bowling machines and ball-throwing machines for all sports. Machines for professional and all recreational levels for sale to the UK and overseas.

THE CRICKET GROUND SHOP, c/o total-play Ltd, Quinton Green Park, Quinton Green, Northampton NN7 2EG. Tel: 01604 864643; email: sales@thecricketgroundshop.co.uk; website: www.thecricketgroundshop.co.uk. The one-stop, online shop for the cricket club; offering pitch covers, non-turf pitch supplies, pitchcare products, netting, batting cages and many more cricket ground essentials.

CRICKET MEMORABILIA AND COLLECTING

AUTOGRAPHS OF THE WORLD, Hunter Terrace, Fletchworth Gate, Coventry, West Midlands CV5 6SP. Tel: 02476 713172; email: sales@autographsoftheworld.com; website: www.autographsoftheworld.com. Official Memorabilia Licensees to the PCA and the ECB. For all your cricket personally signed items.

BUCKINGHAM COVERS, Warren House, Shearway Road, Folkestone, Kent CT19 4BF. Tel: 01303 278137; website: www.buckinghamcovers.com/wisden. Limited-edition *Wisden* stamp sheet – see advert on page 178.

CRICKET MEMORABILIA SOCIETY. Honorary Secretary: Steve Cashmore, 4 Stoke Park Court, Stoke Road, Bishops Cleeve, Cheltenham, Gloucestershire GL52 8US. Email: cms87@btinternet.com; website: www.cricketmemorabilia.org. For collectors worldwide: magazines, meetings, auctions, speakers, and – most of all – friendship.

DD DESIGNS, 62 St Catherine's Grove, Lincoln, Lincolnshire LN5 8NA. Tel: 01522 800298; email: denise@dd-designs.co.uk; website: www.dd-designs.co.uk. Official producers of *Wisden's* "Five Cricketers of the Year" limited-edition postcards and prints (many signed by cricketers) and other signed cricket portfolios.

WISDEN COLLECTORS' CLUB: Tel: 01480 819272; email: bill.wisden@btinternet.com; website: www.wisdencollectorsclub.co.uk. Free and completely impartial advice on *Wisdens*. We also offer *Wisdens* and other cricket books to our members, usually at no charge except postage. Quarterly newsletter, discounts on publications and a jolly good website.

CRICKET SPEAKERS

DAVE FULTON, Sky Sports Presenter/Reporter. Former Kent CCC captain. Author of *The Captains' Tales – Battle for the Ashes.* Tel: 07742 106991; email: d.fulton456@btinternet.com. One of the best cricket speakers on the circuit with engaging stories about Steve Waugh, Andrew Symonds, Muttiah Muralitharan, Shane Warne, Kevin Pietersen et al. Available to MC and/or act as auctioneer. Best in price range!

LOOK WHO'S TALKING (Ian Holroyd), PO Box 3257, Ufton, Leamington Spa CV33 9YZ. Tel: 01926 614443; mobile: 07831 602131; email: ian@look-whos-talking.co.uk; website: www.look-whos-talking.co.uk. A company specialising in providing first-class public speakers for cricket and other sporting events. Contact us to discuss the event and type of speaker. All budgets catered for.

CRICKET TOUR OPERATORS

GULLIVERS SPORTS TRAVEL, Fiddington Manor, Tewkesbury, Gloucestershire GL20 7BJ. Tel: 01684 878943; email: gullivers@gulliverstravel.co.uk; website: www.gulliverstravel.co.uk. The UK's longest-established and leading cricket tour operator offers a great choice of supporter packages for the most exciting events around the world and playing tours for schools, clubs and universities.

TRAVELBAG. Website: www.travelbag.co.uk. Worldwide tailor-made travel experts, specialise in creating bespoke holidays to Asia, Australasia, North America, the Middle East, Indian Ocean, Latin America, Caribbean and the Mediterranean. See advert on page 398.

PITCHES AND GROUND EQUIPMENT

CRICKET CARPETS DIRECT, Standards House, Meridian East, Meridian Business Park, Leicester LE19 1WZ. Tel: 08702 400 700; email: sales@cricketcarpetsdirect.co.uk; website: www.cricketcarpetsdirect.co.uk. Installation and refurbishment of artificial cricket pitches. Save money. Top-quality carpets supplied and installed direct from the manufacturer. Over 20 years' experience. Nationwide service.

HUCK NETS (UK) LTD, Gore Cross Business Park, Corbin Way, Bradpole, Bridport, Dorset DT6 3UX. Tel: 01308 425100; email: sales@huckcricket.co.uk; website: www.huckcricket.co.uk. Alongside manufacturing our unique knotless high-quality polypropylene cricket netting, we offer the complete portfolio of ground and club equipment necessary for cricket clubs of all levels.

NOTTS SPORT, Innovation House, Magna Park, Lutterworth LE17 4XH. Tel: 01455 883730; email: info@nottssport.com; website: www.nottssport.com. Celebrating 30 years as a leading supplier of ECB-approved non-turf cricket pitch systems for coaching, practice and matchplay. Also awarded the ECB NTP Code of Practice Accreditation in 2013.

PLUVIUS, King Henry VIII Farm, Myton Road, Warwick CV34 6SB. Tel: 01926 311324; email: pluviusltd@aol.com; website: www.pluvius.uk.com. Manufacturers of value-for-money pitch covers and sightscreens, currently used on Test, county, school and club grounds throughout the UK.

TILDENET, Hartcliffe Way, Bristol BS3 5RJ. Tel: 0117 966 9684; email: enquiries@tildenet.co.uk; website: www.tildenet.co.uk. Extensive range of equipment – grass germination sheets, mobile practice nets, fixed nets and frames, portable practice nets, netting and fabric, layflat and mobile rain covers, ball-stop fencing, boundary ropes, and sightscreens.

TOTAL-PLAY LTD, Quinton Green Park, Quinton Green, Northampton NN7 2EG. Tel: 01604 864575; email: info@total-play.co.uk; website: www.total-play.co.uk. Cricket-playing surface expert total-play designs, constructs and maintains non-turf and natural pitches for clubs of all levels; including its ECB-approved tp365 non-turf system.

CHRONICLE OF 2013

JANUARY

1 Broadcaster and journalist Christopher Martin-Jenkins dies, aged 67. **2 New Zealand bowled out for 45 in Cape Town Test; South Africa go on to win inside three days.** **6** Shane Warne banned for one match after clashing with Marlon Samuels during Big Bash game in Melbourne. **7** Australia complete 3–0 victory in home Test series against Sri Lanka. **14** South Africa sweep short series against New Zealand with another innings victory, at Port Elizabeth. **23** Former South African captain Peter van der Merwe dies, aged 75.

FEBRUARY

2 Pakistan bowled out for 49 in First Test at Johannesburg; South Africa later win Graeme Smith's 100th Test as captain. **9** Australian Shane Jurgensen confirmed as Bangladesh's full-time coach. **10** Australia complete 5–0 clean sweep of home one-day series against West Indies. **14** Mohammad Irfan becomes the tallest Test cricketer (7ft 1in); Pakistan go on to lose to South Africa at Cape Town. **17 Australia beat West Indies in Mumbai to win the Women's World Cup.** James Anderson becomes England's highest wicket-taker in all internationals, surpassing Ian Botham's 528. **23** Kyle Abbott takes seven for 29 on Test debut for South Africa, who complete 3–0 clean sweep over Pakistan at Centurion. **26** India, for whom captain M. S. Dhoni scores 224, win First Test against Australia at Chennai.

MARCH

5 India win Second Test against Australia by an innings. **8** New Zealand's Hamish Rutherford scores 171 on Test debut against England at Dunedin; match eventually drawn. **10** Australia suspend four players from Third Test in India after they fail to complete a required task. **11** Mushfiqur Rahim scores Bangladesh's first double-century, in high-scoring drawn First Test against Sri Lanka at Galle. **16** Indian opener Shikhar Dhawan reaches the fastest century on debut (85 balls), in Third Test against Australia at Mohali, to set up 3–0 lead. **18** Bangladesh umpire Nadir Shah banned for ten years after match-fixing inquiry. **22** Shane Shillingford takes ten wickets as West Indies win Second Test against Zimbabwe in Dominica. **24** India win Fourth Test at Delhi inside three days, to complete 4–0 whitewash of Australia. **26 England's last pair cling on in Third Test against New Zealand at Auckland; series drawn 0-0.** **27** New Zealand batsman Jesse Ryder left in coma after assault outside Christchurch bar.

APRIL

13 Two Pakistani umpires – Anis Siddiqui and former Test spinner Nadeem Ghauri – are banned for alleged corruption. **19 Former England captain Mike Denness dies, aged 72.** **20** Zimbabwe complete their biggest Test victory by runs (335), over Bangladesh at Harare, after captain Brendan Taylor scores two centuries. **23** Chris Gayle smashes Twenty20-record 175 not out in IPL match. **23** Lancashire's Jordan Clark hits six sixes in an over from Yorkshire slow left-armer Gurham Randhawa in Second XI game. **26** Pakistan leg-spinner Danish Kaneria loses appeal against ECB life ban for corruption. **29** Bangladesh square short series by winning Second Test against Zimbabwe at Harare.

MAY

1 Former national captain Andy Waller appointed coach of Zimbabwe. **4** Dwayne Bravo appointed West Indies' captain for one-day internationals; Darren Sammy remains in charge for Tests and Twenty20s. **10** Gary Kirsten announces he will step down as South Africa's coach in August; his assistant, Russell Domingo, is promoted. **16 Former India fast bowler Sreesanth, and two other Rajasthan Royals IPL players, are arrested by Delhi police for alleged spot-fixing.** **19** England win First Test at Lord's after New Zealand collapse for 68 on fourth day. **24** Gurunath Meiyappan, a Chennai Super Kings official and son-in-law of BCCI president N. Srinivasan, is arrested by Mumbai police on charges of "cheating, forgery and fraud". **25** Joe Root becomes first Yorkshire player to score his maiden Test century at Headingley; England go on to sweep short series against New Zealand. **26** Mumbai Indians defeat holders Chennai in IPL final.

JUNE

2 Martin Guptill hits 189 not out, New Zealand's highest one-day international score, against England at Southampton; NZ win series. **4** Former Bangladesh captain Mohammad Ashraful admits involvement in match-fixing in Bangladesh Premier League. **6** Champions Trophy starts; Shikhar Dhawan hits 114 as India defeat South Africa at Cardiff. **9** David Warner, later suspended, involved in altercation with Joe Root in Birmingham bar. Yorkshire's Matthew Fisher, 15, becomes the youngest county cricketer since the Second World War. **12** Mohammad Asif loses appeal against conviction for spot-fixing. **14** Essex bowled out for 20 by Lancashire in Championship match at Chelmsford. **17** Chris Adams sacked as Surrey's team director. **19** Kent's Darren Stevens slams 44-ball hundred – the fastest of the season – in YB40 game against Sussex. **23 India beat England in rain-reduced Champions Trophy final at Edgbaston.** **24** Mickey Arthur sacked as Australia's coach, three weeks before Ashes; Darren Lehmann replaces him.

JULY

2 New Zealand fast bowler Chris Martin announces his retirement after 233 Test wickets – and 123 runs. **9** Ireland qualify for 2015 World Cup. **11** Ricky Ponting scores 169 not out (his 82nd hundred) in his last first-class innings, for Surrey against Nottinghamshire at The Oval. **14 England win First Ashes Test at Trent Bridge, by 14 runs, despite Australia's No. 11 Ashton Agar making 98 on debut.** **19** John Buchanan steps down as New Zealand's director of cricket after two years. **20** Former ICC chief executive Haroon Lorgat appointed CEO of South African board. **21** England win Second Ashes Test, at Lord's, by 347 runs. **22** Shane Warne, 43, confirms retirement from all cricket.

AUGUST

5 England retain the Ashes after rain-hit Third Test at Old Trafford is drawn. **6** Surrey captain Gareth Batty banned from Twenty20 finals day after heated argument during quarter-final against Somerset. **7** England spinner Monty Panesar is fined after incident outside Brighton nightclub. **12** England win Fourth Ashes Test, at Chester-le-Street. **14** Darren Stevens confirms he is one of nine players under investigation for betting irregularities in Bangladesh Premier League. **17** Northamptonshire beat Surrey in FLt20 final, their first major trophy since 1992. **19** Panesar joins Essex after being released by Sussex. **24** Jamaica Tallawahs, captained by Chris Gayle, win inaugural Caribbean Premier League. **25** Fifth Ashes Test, at The Oval, is drawn; England win 3–0. **29** Australian opener Aaron Finch hammers 156, a Twenty20 international record, against England at Southampton. England retain the women's Ashes.

SEPTEMBER

1 India announce two-Test series against West Indies in November, designed to allow Sachin Tendulkar to play his 200th Test at home in Mumbai; India's prearranged tour of South Africa is shortened. **3** Leg-spinner Fawad Ahmed, a former asylum seeker from Pakistan, makes his international debut for Australia. **7** Pakistan, for whom Younis Khan scores 200 not out, win First Test against Zimbabwe by 221 runs, despite a first-innings deficit of 78. **11** Matthew Hoggard, who took 248 Test wickets for England, announces retirement. **14** Zimbabwe pull off a rare Test victory, by 24 runs, to square short series with Pakistan at Harare. **19 Durham clinch the County Championship, their third title in six seasons. 21** Nottinghamshire beat Glamorgan in YB40 final.

OCTOBER

4 Afghanistan qualify for 2015 World Cup. **6** Durham fast bowler Steve Harmison, who took 226 Test wickets, announces retirement. Mumbai Indians win Champions League Twenty20. **10 Sachin Tendulkar confirms he will retire after his 200th Test. 13** Sohag Gazi completes unique Test double of century and hat-trick, as the First Test between Bangladesh and New Zealand is drawn at Chittagong. **16** Former Test wicketkeeper Paul Downton named as managing director of England cricket, replacing Hugh Morris, who is returning to Glamorgan; James Whitaker succeeds Geoff Miller as national selector. **17** Pakistan win First Test against South Africa in Dubai. **25** Bangladesh and New Zealand share series after drawn Second Test at Mirpur. **26** South Africa, for whom Graeme Smith makes 234, beat Pakistan to square series in Dubai.

NOVEMBER

2 Rohit Sharma hits 16 sixes in his 209, as India win the decider at Bangalore to clinch one-day series 4–3 against Australia. **7** Insurance company Royal London becomes chief sponsor of all English one-day cricket. **8** Sharma, making his Test debut after 108 one-day internationals, scores 177 as India complete three-day victory over West Indies at Kolkata. **15 Sachin Tendulkar makes 74 in his final innings, in his 200th Test; India go on to beat West Indies at Mumbai and win series 2–0. 24** Australia crush England by 381 runs in First Ashes Test at Brisbane. Reg Simpson, England's oldest Test player, dies aged 93. **25** Jonathan Trott returns home from tour with stress-related illness. **30** Ireland beat Afghanistan in final of World Twenty20 qualifier.

DECEMBER

7 Darren Bravo's 218 helps West Indies save First Test in New Zealand; Ross Taylor earlier makes 217. **9** Australia win Second Test at Adelaide by 218 runs. **11** Quinton de Kock scores his third successive one-day international hundred to help South Africa win series against India. **13** New Zealand complete innings win over West Indies inside three days in Second Test at Wellington. **16** ICC suspend West Indies off-spinner Shane Shillingford after his action is deemed illegal. **17 Australia regain the Ashes, after winning Third Test at Perth by 150 runs. 20** Former Kent wicketkeeper Paul Farbrace appointed Sri Lanka's coach. **22** Graeme Swann announces retirement in mid-Ashes series, after 255 Test wickets. South Africa, set 458 to defeat India in First Test at Johannesburg, end on 450 for seven. New Zealand win Third Test at Hamilton to beat West Indies 2–0. **29** Jacques Kallis, who announced his retirement from Test cricket, scores his 45th century as South Africa take series against India by winning Second Test at Durban. Ashes whitewash looms for England as Australia win Fourth Test at Melbourne by eight wickets.

The following items were also reported during 2013:

GOLDCOAST.COM.AU   January 15

Coming in at 30 for four, Shane Basile was next man out on 190, having scored 126 from 27 balls. Playing for Coomera-Hope Island against Burleigh Heads in a sixth-grade match in Queensland, Basile butchered his century from 21 deliveries. He hit six sixes off his first seven balls and later six sixes in an over. Cricket Gold Coast later ordered Basile to move up a grade.

THE AGE, MELBOURNE/DAILY TELEGRAPH   January 25

Australia's deputy prime minister Wayne Swan invoked the 80-year-old Bodyline tour as he called for Australia to become a republic. In an article to mark Australia Day, he said the 1932-33 Ashes emphasised the differences between Britain and Australia. "Aussies are not a ruthless, whatever-it-takes people. Rather, we are a plain-speaking lot, who indulge in hard but fair play and expect no less from others. Ours is not a gentleman's code; it is a democratic code." Malcolm Turnbull, also a republican but a former leader of the Liberal opposition, said Pom-bashing was not an effective argument.

THE COURIER-MAIL, BRISBANE   February 5

Left-arm paceman Rhys Yorke, bowling for South Brisbane's second-grade team, took two hat-tricks on successive days: three lbws ("all plumb," he said) against Valleys, before another against Sunshine Coast in a cup tie on Sunday.

PINE RIVERS PRESS   February 6

Fast bowler Nathan Murray, 18, took five wickets in an over against the Bond XI for Pine Rivers in the Warehouse Cricket A3 North Division in Queensland. With the score 200 for one, his over produced two wickets, a dot ball, then three more wickets; all but the second victim were bowled.

SOUTH AFRICAN PRESS ASSOCIATION   February 13

Nine first-team cricketers from King Edward VII School in Johannesburg were taken to hospital after being struck by lightning as they tried to pull the covers on to the field during a downpour. One boy was seriously injured.

TIMES OF INDIA   February 15

Fourteen-year-old Armaan Jaffer scored 473 in the final of the Under-16 Harris Shield schools tournament, the highest score of a competition infamous for such innings. Jaffer, nephew of former Test batsman Wasim Jaffer, batted for 437 minutes, 359 balls and hit 16 sixes, playing for Rizvi Springfield against Sule Guruji. His uncle made 400 not out in the same event in 1992-93. "If one wants to be really harsh on the boy," said the paper's correspondent, "one could chide him for throwing his hand away when 500 was so close. An uncharacteristic cross-batted sweep resulted in a top edge which was caught by the keeper." In 2011, Armaan had scored 498 in the Under-14 Giles Shield (see *Wisden 2012,* page 1551, and November 20, below).

ABC NEWS   February 24

Sri Lankan cricketers Lasith Malinga and Muttiah Muralitharan are fronting Australian government adverts designed to discourage asylum seekers from taking boat journeys to Australia. The "Don't be sorry" campaign came after 98 Burmese asylum seekers died at sea. It is aimed at persuading Sri Lankans already in Australia to tell relatives not to risk their lives.

NDTV.COM   February 27

The scoresheet for the 664-run schoolboy partnership between Sachin Tendulkar and Vinod Kambli in 1988 has been destroyed by the Mumbai School Sports Association. "It was like any other sheet from a normal game, and a few years back, white ants ate into those sheets," said the association secretary H. S. Bhor. "The scoresheet was kept along with all the other records of games and has since been incinerated as we could not store them all. You cannot expect us to store files that are 25 years old."

BUCKS HERALD   March 1

Leslie Smith of Wendover has been stripped of his OBE after being jailed for sexual assault against a boy he coached at the town's cricket club. The removal of the honour followed a campaign by his victim, now in his forties. Smith received the award in 1994 for services to the rail industry.

CEYLON TODAY   March 4

For the second year running, the inter-school match between Ananda and Nalanda Colleges ended in violence at the Sinhalese Sports Club. After Ananda reached their target of 299, the crowd invaded the pitch and assaulted rival supporters with chairs. The outnumbered police tried to quell the riot with tear gas, but the canisters were thrown back at them.

ZEENEWS.COM   March 6

Retired fast bowler Merv Hughes advised the Australian team to grow facial hair after their humiliating Test defeats at Chennai and Hyderabad. Hughes said beards and moustaches brought out the best in players – and protected them from the sun.

MID-DAY, MUMBAI   March 11

Mazgaon Dock beat Dachser (Air Freight) by 572 runs in a 45-over Sheth Narottamdas Morarji Shipping Shield match in Mumbai. Their total of 614 for five included 120 penalty runs awarded because Dachser, later dismissed for 42, fell eight overs short of the required rate.

PRESS TRUST OF INDIA   March 13

Five Indian army privates were killed in a suicide attack on a cricket match in Bemina in disputed Kashmir. The killers entered the ground disguised as players, but had AK-47s and grenades concealed in their kit.

April 20

IRISH INDEPENDENT   April 10
Ireland's John Mooney, who hit the winning runs against England at the 2011 World Cup, was suspended after tweeting that he hoped Margaret Thatcher's death had been "slow and painful". Cricket Ireland chief executive Warren Deutrom called the comments "crass, insensitive and offensive".

BBC NEWS   April 20
Cambridgeshire's Minor Counties one-day match against Cumberland had to be moved from March to Wisbech because the March CC pitch had been devastated by crows. Club member Pat Ringham said they had caused more damage than "50 hooligans let loose with golf clubs". The crows were looking for grubs, which were abnormally plentiful; the spray had failed to work owing to an unusually cold March at March.

MID-DAY, MUMBAI   April 20/May 3
Pest-control experts have been called in to treat the Mumbai Cricket Association's collection of *Wisdens* at the Wankhede Stadium after 13,000 books in the Dr H. D. Kanga Memorial Library were revealed to be in an appalling condition. Valuable *Wisdens* from the 1880s had been "feasted on by insects"; they have now been moved to a steel cupboard. Australian cricket writer Mike Coward described the collection – said to be the largest sports library in Asia – as "sadly neglected" 23 years ago.

MID-DAY, MUMBAI   April 21
Sachin Tendulkar's waxwork at the new Madame Tussaud's museum in Sydney has been given the wrong shirt. It was dressed in an Indian shirt for the World Twenty20, in which Tendulkar never appeared.

TIMES OF INDIA   April 27

Congress Party supporters in Rajkot dug up the pitch at the Madhavrao Scindia Cricket Ground, which has hosted 12 one-day internationals, to protest against the use of water during a drought. The stadium was being prepared for an inter-municipal corporation Twenty20 tournament. "The city is facing a drinking-water crisis," said the protesters' leader Atul Rajani. "If they want to organise it, they should have organised it in some other city."

WATFORD OBSERVER   May 3

Rickmansworth CC, founded in 1787, have had their season delayed a month after badgers dug up the pitch. There were fears play would be impossible all summer, but an ECB grant helped the club re-lay 1,500 square metres of turf. Chairman Mark Raine said the ground looked as if "somebody has turned up with a mortar and tried to trash it". This damage was also blamed on the cold early spring, preventing the groundsman spraying against leatherjackets, which attract badgers.

MAIL ON SUNDAY   May 4

England batsman Joe Root – known as "The Milkybar Kid"– says readers of the 2013 edition of *The Cricketers' Who's Who* have been hoaxed: he did not audition for or "narrowly fail to land" the part in an advert. Former Yorkshire team-mate Anthony McGrath is suspected.

NOTTINGHAM POST   May 7

Nadeem Akhtar began his career as captain of Ellerslie Second XI in extraordinary fashion. His team bowled out Southwell Seconds for 22 in the South Notts League Division E, and knocked off the runs in nine balls.

BBC/THE OBSERVER   May 7/12

Former Pakistan captain Imran Khan's "Pakistan Tehreek-e-Insaf" party became the third-largest in the national parliament after the 2013 election, with 35 seats, having won none in 2008. However, overenthusiastic supporters were disappointed, after predicting "a tsunami" would sweep away the old parties. Five days before the vote, Imran had been detained in hospital with head and spinal injuries after falling off a platform at a campaign rally.

MARIECLAIRE.CO.UK   May 10

Karl Lagerfeld, creative director of the fashion house Chanel, unveiled their "Cruise 2014" collection in Singapore. This included – as well as cocktail dresses with lace, shimmering sequins and ruffles – "sporty cricket whites complete with ribbed V-neck jumpers, boyish shirts, leg pads and cricket bats".

BBC   May 10

The Second XI match between Derbyshire and Lancashire at Belper was abandoned after a series of explosions and a fire at the former Thorntons chocolate factory nearby. Police advised players to leave the field because of fears there was asbestos in the smoke.

SUNDAY INDEPENDENT, PLYMOUTH   May 19
Neil Curnow hit 17 sixes while scoring 229, the highest-ever score in the Cornish Premier Division, for St Just against Redruth. His second hundred came off 31 balls.

AFP/BBC MONITORING   May 23/August 3
Hajji Khubi, father of Afghanistan captain Mohammad Nabi, was kidnapped outside his home in Jalalabad and held captive for more than two months. He was released and no ransom paid, the provincial governor's office said. Two people were arrested, but no group claimed responsibility.

MAIL ON SUNDAY   June 2
MCC members expressed outrage at plans to organise a men's fashion event in the Lord's Pavilion, featuring a hundred male models. Although it was described as Savile Row-themed, one model said some outfits would be "relatively wacky". "Cricket has gone to the dogs," grumbled member George Burrough. "Every respected man who has played here will be looking on bewildered." An MCC spokesman said: "It's not something you could have done a decade ago; this is new. We are only just taking events to the next level."

BBC   June 4/10
Rob Pritchard scored his first runs in two years for Ingatestone and Fryerning in Essex after eight successive ducks. Pritchard, a competent middle-order batsman who formerly captained the club Second XI in the Mid-Essex League, had been renamed "Paddles" by team-mates. "We cringe when he comes into bat," said Matthew Taylor. Pritchard promised to end the sequence against Great Totham, but was hit in the face fifth ball and retired hurt. However, he returned nose bloodied and scored five not out.

INDO-ASIAN NEWS SERVICE June 7

The Indian matrimonial site, shaadi.com, said its "millions" of member profiles showed 32.8% of men wanted a bride who was interested in cricket. Only 11.4% of women wanted cricket-loving grooms.

BBC June 14

Mel Hughes, 65, was presented with a cake to mark his 1,000th appearance for West Mersea in Essex. In 35 years with the club as a wicketkeeper he has accumulated the most runs (14,545), catches (527) and stumpings (116). He says the highlight was hitting a four off England leg-spinner Robin Hobbs: "He was probably nearly as old as I am now."

LETTERS TO THE TIMES June 17/19

Sir, Watching the New Zealand fast bowler Neil Wagner during a quiet period at Lord's recently my friend and I put together the following XI made up of composer-cricketers: Adams, John and Jimmy; Arnold, Malcolm and Geoff; Barber, Samuel and Bob; Benjamin, Arthur and Winston; Bird, William and Dickie; Elgar, Sir Edward and Dean; Smyth, Dame Ethel and Richard; Sullivan, Sir Arthur and John; Wagner, Richard and Neil; Watkins, Huw and Allan; Weir, Judith and Lindsay. Our next project is a poets' XI.

Nicholas Tucker, Lewes

Sir, Nicholas Tucker proposes that a team of "poet-cricketers" be selected. The following are all first-class cricketers: Arnold, Geoff (Surrey) and Matthew; Barnes S. F. (Staffs/England) and William; Clare, John Wagner (Derbys) and John;

Hogg, Kyle (Lancs) and James; Lamb, Allan (Northants) and Charles; Morgan, Eoin (Middlesex) and Edwin; Pope, George (Derbys) and Alexander; Prior, Matthew (Sussex) and Matthew; Smith, M. J. K. (Warwicks) and Stevie; Thomas, Alfonso (Somerset) and Dylan or Edward; Wyatt, Bob (Warwicks) and Thomas.

David Day, Yorkshire

Sir, Nicholas Tucker would no doubt be interested in my 1979 dismissal at Northwood Cricket Club: Mendelssohn c Wagner b Haydn.

Martin Mendelssohn, London SW17

DAILY MAIL June 18
After 79 years, Bacton CC in Norfolk are moving to the high school in the nearby town of North Walsham and changing their name after being banned from using cricket balls during practice on the parish-council-owned field. Council clerk Elaine Pugh said the regulation was to protect the public. Treasurer Ramone Stringer said: "The move will probably pay off, because North Walsham should have a cricket club and it will attract youngsters."

TIVYSIDE ADVERTISER/THE TIMES June 18/20
A Division Six match in the Pembroke County League was abandoned after the batsmen began talking to each other in Welsh. Lamphey Second XI player and club chairman Andrew Skeels objected to the language being used by batsmen Rhydian Wyn and Dyfed Sion, who then walked off. "Thought the days of being told not to speak Welsh in a public place had gone," Sion tweeted.

BOURNEMOUTH DAILY ECHO June 26
Darren Cowley scored a century in 31 balls for Lymington against Mudeford in the New Forest President's Cup. His 159 not out included 15 sixes.

YORKSHIRE EVENING POST June 27
Nigel Martyn, 46, the former England goalkeeper, top-scored with 60 not out for Old Modernians in their Wetherby League Division One match against St Chad's, Broomfield.

DAILY MAIL June 29
Threlkeld CC in Cumbria, whose ground was wrecked by floods in 2012, decided to raise some of the £60,000 needed for repairs by posing for a calendar. However, the players opted out of the now-standard naked pictures ("Most of us are not particularly blessed when it comes to physiques," said treasurer Michael Webster) and instead posed playing cricket in improbable and extreme Lake District locations, ranging from the bottom of Derwentwater to the summit of Latrigg, on Boxing Day. Photographer Stuart Holmes said the exercise had taken ten months and been "a big adventure". (See colour section, rainstoppedplay.org, and December 5, below.)

IT GETS BORING SEEING MARK NICHOLAS NIGHT AFTER NIGHT!

BRUCE SPRINGSTEEN

DAILY TELEGRAPH June 29

Cricket broadcaster Mark Nicholas is planning to attend the Bruce Springsteen concert in the Olympic Park, London tonight – his fourth Springsteen gig in a fortnight and about the 70th in all. "Whenever Springsteen performs with his E Street Band, magic happens," Nicholas said.

KESBATH.COM July

Will Lewis, 13, hit 50 off 11 balls for King Edward's School, Bath, in an Under-13 match against Bristol Grammar School. Coach Mike Howarth said: "I'm especially pleased for Will as he is such a modest and unassuming young man, who hardly mentioned the feat to anybody at the time."

PGWODEHOUSESOCIETY.ORG.UK July

The P. G. Wodehouse Society held a brunch during the Cheltenham Cricket Festival to mark the centenary of Gloucestershire's match against Warwickshire, attended by the young Wodehouse, at which he was rather taken with the surname of one Warwickshire player: P. Jeeves.

DAILY POST, LIVERPOOL July 8

Nine-year-old Josh Griffiths from Northop, Flintshire, took five wickets in five balls, while having treatment for leukaemia. Playing for Northop Under-9s against Denbigh, he took five for one from two overs. Three days earlier, he had endured his latest bout of chemotherapy. He tries to play cricket three times a week and, during his intensive treatment in 2012 when cricket was impossible, the club messaged him continually to keep him in touch. His coach Roy Pierce said: "He loves to stay in the game all the time."

KENT ONLINE/BASINGSTOKE GAZETTE July 10

Hampshire insisted that a man who walked naked into a supermarket at 4.20am and tried to buy a bottle of vodka was not one of their players. After examining

CCTV footage, the club denied reports that the streaker was a member of their Second XI squad, who were staying at the next-door hotel in Ashford, Kent.

SUNDAY INDEPENDENT, PLYMOUTH   July 14

In a Cornish Division Two (East) match against Tideford, Andrew Brenton scored 311 for Luckett, with 278 in boundaries (53 fours and 11 sixes). Brenton put on 368 for the second wicket with Jack Sleep, and the 48-over total, 513 for five, beat the league record by 75.

THE NEWS, PORTSMOUTH/DAILY STAR   July 14

Jim Smallbone, 63, has taken two successive five-wicket hauls for Hampshire Over-60s a year after collapsing on the field, when his heart stopped for at least 20 minutes. He credited Mike Tindall, a first-aider who was keeping wicket for Sussex Over-60s, with keeping him alive until the air ambulance arrived.

DAILY TELEGRAPH   July 16

Players from Hoghton CC, Lancashire, formed a human barricade to prevent travellers parking their caravans on the pitch. When news spread that four wagons had already arrived, members headed for the ground, "drew on the spirit of the Ashes", according to chairman Neil Eccles, and kept vigil. Police were able to evict those travellers already on the ground as they were "interfering with community events".

AFP   July 16

Alby Shale, 22, from Oxfordshire claimed the record for continuous batting after 26 hours in the indoor nets at The Oval. He faced 200 bowlers, including prime minister David Cameron; Alby's late father was chairman of Cameron's constituency party. Shale was raising money to build an international-standard cricket ground in Rwanda. The rules, laid down by Guinness, allowed him a five-minute break every hour.

THELCA.CO.UK   July 17

David Hammond of Brentwood hit six sixes in an over off Leigh-on-Sea left-arm spinner John Elliott in an Essex League Twenty20 match. Hammond hit 170 out of 278 for two, with 17 sixes, off 59 balls. He has played for both Essex and Kent Second XIs.

THE ARGUS, BRIGHTON   July 20

Rupert Webb, the 91-year-old former Sussex wicketkeeper, confronted a motorist who attacked a traffic warden on the streets of Worthing. Webb saw a "well-built man" punch the warden and break his glasses. "I had a firm grip on my walking-stick and I was about to give the attacker a jolly good clout," said Webb. "Fortunately, at that moment, a police car came round the corner and the man was arrested and taken away." Webb is also known for his acting, especially his role in the film *Four Weddings and a Funeral*. Police said a 60-year-old man had been cautioned for assault.

THE CRICKET PAPER   July 31

The former West Indian all-rounder Collis King, 62, has scored his 50th century in 12 seasons with Dunnington, in the York Senior League.

THE TIMES   August 1

US soldiers who invaded Grenada in 1983 were advised by British diplomats to learn cricket, according to a document released by the British government. Britain thought the American forces were behaving insensitively, and advised that they could win local support by "mending roads, painting churches, giving children's parties and being photographed doing so. They could even have a shot at playing cricket. Let the Grenadians teach them something."

August 1

LANCASHIRE EVENING POST   August 4
Police enquiries stopped play in the Northern League match between Chorley and St Annes, after the visitors discovered that about £1,000 in cash had been stolen from their dressing-room. Police were told an elderly man using a zimmer frame had asked to use the toilets in the dressing-room block rather than hobble across the ground. "It would appear that this old man was not as feeble as he made out," said a police spokesman. St Annes had some compensation: a three-wicket win.

THISISDEVON.CO.UK   August 8
Nick Horne scored 208 off 73 balls as Topsham St James beat Cullompton in an Exeter Evening Twenty20 League match. Among his 25 sixes were two that hit cars, one that landed on a bowling green and another on the Paddington

main line, 100 yards away. The only other batsman to reach the railway at Cullompton was said to have been Viv Richards, in an exhibition match.

DAILY TELEGRAPH   August 8

Upminster CC of the Essex League, whose third and fourth teams play at a local sports college, were told it was impossible to roll the pitch there because it was too dangerous. The incident was cited by the Health and Safety Executive in a list of cases where officials wrongly cited "health and safety" to avoid doing something they appeared not to want to do. The HSE have started a "myth busters' panel" to adjudicate on such disputes.

WALES ONLINE   August 12

Plaid Cymru MP and keen cricketer Jonathan Edwards has called for Wales to have its own national cricket team in global competitions, on a par with Scotland and Ireland. "Wales, a cricketing nation with a proud and venerable tradition, finds itself conspicuous in its absence on the global stage, while countries with arguably less of a tradition and a weaker player base have graced competitions," he argued. Alan Hamer, chief executive of Glamorgan, said such a move would ruin the club and end Test cricket in Cardiff. And Peter Hybart, the chief executive of Cricket Wales, reacted: "The suggestion that Wales would find itself playing one-day internationals against India is wholly unrealistic. A Welsh team would be much more likely to be playing against countries like Papua New Guinea."

SHIELDS GAZETTE   August 14

An 81-year-old great-grandmother, Margaret Burn, has been suspended by Marsden CC in South Shields, the club she has supported for more than 60 years, after allegations of "suspected threatening behaviour towards junior members". Mrs Burn, who served the teas for many years, agreed she had told children to get off the pitch during a match, but denied swearing at them. "We have to follow protocol," said a club spokesman.

AFP   August 15

The bat used by Don Bradman to score 115 in his last innings before setting sail for England in 1948 has been auctioned for $A65,000 in Melbourne, three times its estimate. The bat was signed by Bradman and team-mates after the game in Perth between the tourists – en route to becoming the Invincibles – and Western Australia. It had been on display at the WACA for 20 years.

DAILY MAIL   August 16

Chloe Wallwork, 20, became the first female player in the 125-year history of the Bolton Association; she took four for 11 on first-team debut for Walshaw.

SOUTH WALES ARGUS   August 18

Six-year-old Harrison Parsons, from Abercarn, Monmouthshire, outscored his father when he opened the batting for Abercarn CC against a side put out by the village football team. Dad Jeremy made 15, Harrison 24. "It's a bit of a rivalry between the teams, and was a highly contested match. Obviously, I'm pleased as punch for him," said Jeremy. His mum, Beki, said: "Since he was two, all Harrison has done is play cricket. When I had cartoons on for him on the telly, he would get the remote and change it to the sports channels to see the cricket."

HUDDERSFIELD DAILY EXAMINER   August 19

Tom Smith, the opening bowler for Birchencliffe CC, re-enacted a historic cricketing feat by throwing a cricket ball over the Lockwood railway viaduct near Huddersfield. The viaduct is 129ft high and 30ft wide, but Smith estimates a height of 180ft is necessary to get sufficient carry. It is also important to consult the train timetable. Watched by an *Examiner* reporter and photographer, he succeeded at the first attempt.

WHITEHAVEN NEWS   September 5

Jim Folley, father of the former Lancashire and Derbyshire player Ian, made his first return visit to Whitehaven CC to mark the 20th anniversary of his son's tragic death. Ian Folley died in 1993, aged 30, due to complications from an anaesthetic, after being treated for what seemed a minor head injury while batting in his first season as Whitehaven's pro. Club spokesman Arthur Brown said: "We were really pleased to see Jim. Ian was a fantastic guy and will never ever be forgotten."

THE PRESS, YORK   September 5

An eight-year-old York girl, Mollie Ovenden, was named Junior Voice of Cricket after winning a competition organised by Yorkshire for Under-15s. Entrants had to submit their own commentary to a clip of Yorkshire cricket. In the final, Mollie interviewed the bowler Jack Brooks, and asked him: "What two things did Alastair Cook retain at Old Trafford?" Then she gleefully revealed: "The answer was the Ashes and my pen, because he kept it after signing my autograph book."

THE GUARDIAN   September 5

In the year his Almanack reached its 150th edition, John Wisden was honoured by a 21st-century information source when Google marked the 187th anniversary of his birth with one of its trademark doodles: a pastiche of the Eric Ravilious woodcut on *Wisden's* cover.

THE SPIN   September 10

The unit of the New York Police Department set up to spy on potential terrorists after the 9/11 outrage in 2001 compiled a list of hotspots in the city where Muslim men gathered, including cricket grounds. In a new book, *Enemies Within*, reporters Matt Apuzzo and Adam Goldman reveal that police were also advised to keep an eye on "cricket fan hangouts", such as Singh's Sporting Goods on 101st Avenue and the New Neimat Kada Restaurant on Lexington Avenue.

DAILY MAIL   September 17

The former Zimbabwean cricketer Guy Whittall spent a peaceful night while an eight-foot crocodile was hiding under his bed. It is thought to have sneaked into his room the previous night at the game lodge where Whittall is a director. He was unaware of his bedfellow until he went to the kitchen for breakfast and heard the maid screaming. "The really disconcerting thing is the fact that I was sitting on the edge of the bed that morning, barefoot and just centimetres away from the croc," he said.

GOV.UK   September 18

The Afghan National Army beat a British Army team by five wickets at Camp Shorabak, the Afghan HQ next to Cape Bastion in Helmand province. "The Afghans were helped by some wicked deflections to score fours, with the ball hitting loose rocks and evading our fielders," according to British opening batsman Major Kempley Buchan-Smith.

DAILY EXPRESS   September 21

Eileen Ash of Norwich credited her Tuesday morning yoga sessions for keeping her fit at the age of 101. Mrs Ash, who played for the England women's team (as Eileen Whelan) before and after the Second World War, gave up golf for bowls aged 98.

BURTON MAIL   September 25

The Derbyshire League have warned players about their use of social networks after a picture – described as "both pornographic and defamatory" – was posted on Twitter making fun of new Premier League champions Swarkestone.

WALES ONLINE   September 26

Adam Shantry, who played alongside the late Tom Maynard at Glamorgan, swam the English Channel for the Tom Maynard Trust, along with the former Warwickshire player Tom Mees and Mees's partner Emma Lawson. They completed the swim in relay in just under 14 hours. "I've never been so cold in my life," said Shantry.

YORKSHIRE EVENING POST   September 26

A driver, described as "elderly", smashed through a plate-glass window into Yorkshire's cricket museum at Headingley, which was hosting a party to celebrate Yorkshire director Robin Smith's birthday. The driver, a volunteer with the supporters' association, suffered minor injuries, as did a female guest.

THE ISLAND   October 17/20

The indigenous Vedda people of Sri Lanka should not play cricket, said cultural affairs minister T. B. Ekanayake, because it was detrimental to their culture, forcing them to wear shirts and trousers. Vedda linguist Uruwarige Wimalaratne replied that "Veddhas have been playing cricket for a long time in their habitats, and our teachers coached us on the finer points of the game introduced by the colonial masters, but we never wore trousers or shoes." Vedda men used to wear only loincloths, but now normally wear sarongs.

BBC   October 22

Developers have won a planning appeal against Norwich City Council and been given permission to build 75 houses on the former home of Norfolk cricket at Lakenham. The scheme includes a play area, allotments and five-a-side football pitch, but the cricket ground, used between 1827 and 2000, will be lost for ever, and the pavilion – described by the council as a "heritage asset"– demolished.

CAMDEN NEW JOURNAL   October 24

Bill Boon, 78, was given a round of applause at Netley School, the London Borough of Camden's oldest primary – 70 years late. As an eight-year-old, Boon took six wickets in a school match and was excited at the prospect of having his name read out in assembly next day. But he was hit on the shins when batting and had to take a day off sick. He had returned to the school on its 130th anniversary, and the current generation made good the omission.

DAILY MAIL   October 24

Charlie Elphicke, the Conservative MP for Dover, told people living next to the village cricket ground at St Margaret's to stop complaining about broken windows and buy stronger glass. Residents had demanded that the club erect a 30ft fence. "The cricket club has been there for a very long time," said Elphicke. "Those houses have not. They bought these houses knowing there was a cricket club."

COURIER-MAIL, BRISBANE/SUN-HERALD, SYDNEY
October 24/December 29

Richie Benaud, 83, was unable to commentate on the 2013-14 ashes series for Channel 9 after a car crash. Benaud's treasured 1963 Sunbeam Alpine hit a wall near his home in Coogee.

THE NEWS, KARACHI   October 25

Five women cricketers from Multan have been banned for six months by the Pakistan Cricket Board after they had alleged on a TV show that two male officials had demanded sexual favours in return for selection. A committee of inquiry said that three of the women had denied the original allegations, and the other two refused to present their case.

BBC   November 1

The life-size statue of umpire Dickie Bird in his home town of Barnsley has been placed on a higher plinth, five feet off the ground, to stop revellers hanging items from his raised finger. Decorations have included condoms, bras and knickers, and Bird has been spotted removing them himself. Sculptor Graham Ibbeson said it was impossible to stop such incidents: "What we are going to do is make it a little more difficult." Bird said his only concern was that someone might get hurt.

LAUREUS.COM   November 8

Ian Botham completed an eight-day, 160-mile walk across Sri Lanka, raising about £140,000 to support Laureus Foundation projects in the country. Allan Border and Muttiah Muralitharan joined him on the final day.

RADIO AUSTRALIA   November 10

A man wearing Australian one-day kit was among 60 asylum seekers who were rescued off Java as they tried to reach Australia. His origin was not revealed, but he told immigration officials he was a fast bowler. Christopher Pyne, a minister in the newly elected Liberal government, said the refugees would never set foot in Australia.

THE WEST AUSTRALIAN   November 11

A swarm of locusts failed to stop play in a junior match at Mukinbudin, in the wheatbelt 180 miles from Perth. "The oval was covered, and if a ball got hit out to the boundary it would stir them up and they would fly up, and hit the cricketers," said local farmer Jill Squire. "We told the boys to keep their mouths closed."

THE HINDU   November 20

Yet another batting record was set in the Harris Shield in Mumbai when Prithvi Shaw, 14, of Rizvi Springfield School scored 546 against St Francis, the best score recorded in India and the best anywhere in 112 years, behind only A. E. J. Collins (628*) and C. J. Eady (566) (see page 1388). Shaw hit 85 fours and five sixes off 200 balls spread over two days.

BBC   November 28

Ashes 2013, the official video game, has been withdrawn from sale after gamers branded it "shameful", "embarrassing" and "farcical". Buyers have been offered refunds. The game, released after months of delay, was still "clearly unfinished", according to one specialist writer, and did not even have an animation for catching. One enthusiast, however, said it should have stayed on sale because "it was clearly the comedy game of the year".

3NEWS.CO.NZ   November 29

Whakamana, the new museum in Dunedin devoted to cannabis, is planning a special exhibition called "Hit for Six". Timed to coincide with the Test against West Indies, it explores the connection between cricket and dope-smoking: "Cannabis and cricket just seem to go together for some reason," said curator Abe Gray. "It's hands-down the favourite sport among Kiwi stoners." New Zealand Cricket declined to comment.

DAILY TELEGRAPH   November 29

Commentator Henry Blofeld is to marry for the third time, aged 74. "Valeria," he said delightedly, "is the only girl I've met who loves what I do."

ECONOMIC TIMES   December 3

The owner of Chennai Super Kings passed his astrologer's advice on match strategy to the team's captain, M. S. Dhoni, during the 2013 IPL. The astrologer, Dr Venkatesan Karthikeyan, advised on toss and batting order, and suggested deities who should be propitiated before games. The ICC's anti-corruption unit and the police are aware of the emails. The team lost the final to Mumbai Indians.

TIMES & STAR, WORKINGTON   December 5

The extreme cricketers of Threlkeld CC (see June 29) added to their collection of crazy venues when they played a match inside the Honister slate mine under Fleetwith Pike, near Buttermere. Using spotlights, a plastic pitch, slate bails – and playing for a slate trophy – Threlkeld lost a six-over match against Caldbeck, who mastered the technique of not getting caught off the wall, instead pushing the ball down the tunnel into the gloom. Threlkeld are hoping they will get their reward by returning to their flood-damaged ground in 2014. A similar match planned a year earlier was snowed off when the players could not reach the mine.

INDEX OF UNUSUAL OCCURRENCES

INDEX OF ADVERTISEMENTS

PART TITLES